CPAG'S

Housing Benefit and

Council Tax Benefit

Legislation

D1823588

Twentieth edition

2007/2008

Twentieth edition revised by
Carolyn George, Stewart Wright and Richard Poynter
Commentary by
Lorna Findlay, LL.B (Hons) Barrister
Stewart Wright, MA, Dip. Law, Barrister
Deputy District Chairman, Social Security and Child Support Appeals Tribunal
Richard Poynter, BCL, MA(Oxon) Solicitor
District Chairman, Social Security and Child Support Appeals Tribunal
Deputy Social Security and Child Support Commissioner
Paul Stagg, LL.B (Hons) Barrister
Carolyn George, MA
Freelance writer on welfare rights

Published by Child Poverty Action Group

CPAG promotes action for the prevention and relief of poverty among children and families with children. To achieve this, CPAG aims to raise awareness of the causes, extent, nature and impact of poverty, and strategies for its eradication and prevention; bring about positive policy changes for families with children in poverty; and enable those eligible for income maintenance to have access to their full entitlement. If you are not already supporting us, please consider making a donation, or ask for details of our membership schemes and publications.

Published by Child Poverty Action Group
94 White Lion Street, London N1 9PF
020 7837 7979

Registered Company No. 1993854

Charity No. 294841

© Child Poverty Action Group 2007

A CIP record for this book is available from the British Library

ISBN: 978 1 906076 07 8

Typeset by David Lewis XML Associates Limited
Printed in Great Britain by William Clowes Limited, Beccles, Suffolk

Contents

Acknowledgements   vi
Foreword   vii
How to use this book   ix
Table of Cases   xi
Table of Social Security Commissioners' Decisions   xx
Housing Benefit Regulations: Destinations Table   xxvi
Council Tax Benefit Regulations: Destinations Table   xxxi
Table of abbreviations   xxxv

Part 1: Main primary legislation

Social Security Contributions and Benefits Act 1992 (c. 4)   **3**
Social Security Administration Act, 1992 (c. 5)   **27**
Social Security (Consequential Provisions) Act 1992 (c. 6)   **107**
Social Security Act 1998 (c. 14)   **108**
Human Rights Act 1998 (c. 42)   **118**
Child Support, Pensions and Social Security Act 2000 (c. 19)   **143**
Welfare Reform Act 2007   **177**

Part 2: Main secondary legislation – Housing benefit

Housing Benefit Regulations 2006, S.I. 2006 No. 213   **181**
Rent Officers (Housing Benefit Functions) Order 1997, S.I. 1997 No. 1984   **520**
Rent Officers (Housing Benefit Functions) (Scotland) Order 1997, S.I. 1997 No. 1995 (S. 144)   **540**
Rent Officers (Housing Benefit Functions) (Local Housing Allowance) Amendment Order 2003, S.I. 2003 No. 2398   **557**
Rent Officers (Housing Benefit Functions) (Local Housing Allowance) Amendment Order 2005, S.I. 2005 No. 236   **558**

Part 3: Main secondary legislation – Council tax benefit

Council Tax Benefit Regulations 2006, S.I. 2006 No. 215   **561**

Part 4: Main secondary legislation

Housing Benefit (Persons who have attained the qualifying age for state pension credit) Regulations 2006, S.I. 2006 No. 214   **679**
Council Tax Benefit (Persons who have attained the qualifying age for state pension credit) Regulations 2006, S.I. 2006 No. 216   **812**

Part 5: Secondary legislation – Decision making and appeals

Social Security Commissioners (Procedure) Regulations 1999, S.I. 1999 No. 1495   **899**
Social Security and Child Support (Decisions and Appeals) Regulations 1999, S.I. 1999 No. 991   **917**
Housing Benefit and Council Tax Benefit (Decisions and Appeals) Regulations 2001, S.I. 2001 No. 1002   **946**

Housing Benefit and Council Tax Benefit (Decisions and Appeals) (Transitional and Savings) Regulations 2001, S.I. 2001 No. 1264   **993**

Part 6: **Other primary legislation**

Local Government Finance Act 1992 (c. 14)   **1003**
Housing Act 1996 (c. 52)   **1014**
Welfare Reform and Pensions Act 1999 (c. 30)   **1016**
Immigration and Asylum Act 1999 (c. 33)   **1026**
Local Government Act 2000 (c. 22)   **1029**
Children (Leaving Care) Act 2000 (c. 35)   **1031**
Social Security Fraud Act 2001 (c. 11)   **1033**
State Pension Credit Act 2002 (c. 16)   **1042**
Tax Credits Act 2002 (c. 21)   **1043**
Gender Recognition Act 2004 (c. 7)   **1044**
Age-Related Payments Act 2004 (c. 10)   **1045**
Civil Partnership Act 2004 (c. 33)   **1046**

Part 7: **Other secondary legislation: Common and transitional provisions**

Social Security (Claims and Payments) Regulations 1987, S.I. 1987 No. 1968   **1051**
Social Security (Persons from Abroad) Miscellaneous Amendments Regulations 1996, S.I. 1996 No. 30   **1054**
Housing Benefit (Permitted Totals) Order 1996, S.I. 1996 No. 677   **1058**
Council Tax Benefit (Permitted Totals) Order 1996, S.I. 1996 No. 678   **1064**
Housing Benefit (Information from Landlords and Agents) Regulations 1997, S.I. 1997 No. 2436   **1065**
Social Security (Penalty Notice) Regulations 1997, S.I. 1997 No. 2813   **1069**
New Deal (Miscellaneous Provisions) Order 1998, S.I. 1998 No. 217   **1070**
Social Security (Immigration and Asylum) Consequential Amendments Regulations 2000, S.I. 2000 No. 636   **1072**
New Deal (Miscellaneous Provisions) Order 2001, S.I. 2001 No. 970   **1077**
Discretionary Financial Assistance Regulations 2001, S.I. 2001 No. 1167   **1079**
New Deal (Lone Parents) (Miscellaneous Provisions) Order 2001, S.I. 2001 No. 2915   **1085**
Social Security (Notification of Change of Circumstances) Regulations 2001, S.I. 2001 No. 3252   **1086**
Social Security (Loss of Benefit) Regulations 2001, S.I. 2001 No. 4022   **1087**
Contracting Out (Functions of Local Authorities: Income-Related Benefits) Order 2002, S.I. 2002 No. 1888   **1091**
Social Security (Habitual Residence) Amendment Regulations 2004, S.I. 2004 No. 1232   **1094**
Civil Partnership (Pensions, Social Security and Child Support) Consequential, etc Provisions Order 2005, S.I. 2005 No. 2877   **1095**
Civil Partnership Act 2005 (Relationships Arising Through Civil Partnership) Order 2005, S.I. 2005 No. 3137   **1097**
Housing Benefit and Council Tax Benefit (Consequential Provisions) Regulations 2006, S.I. 2006 No. 217   **1098**
Social Security (Persons from Abroad) Amendment Regulations 2006, S.I. 2006 No. 1026   **1134**

Rent Repayment (Supplementary Provisions) (England) Regulations 2007, S.I. 2007 No. 572   **1135**

Housing Benefit and Council Tax Benefit (War Pension Disregards) Regulations 2007, S.I. 2007 No. 1619   **1137**

Housing Benefit (Loss of Benefit) (Pilot Scheme) Regulations 2007, S.I. 2007 No. 2202   **1139**

Housing Benefit (Loss of Benefit) (Pilot Scheme) (Supplementary) Regulations 2007, S.I. 2007 No. 2474   **1144**

Social Security (Claims and Information) Regulations 2007, S.I. 2007 No. 2911   **1149**

Part 8: **Secondary Legislation Subsidy**

Income-Related Benefits (Subsidy to Authorities) Order 1998, S.I. 1998 No. 562   **1153**

Housing Benefit and Council Tax Benefit (Subsidy) Regulations 1994, S.I. 1994 No. 781   **1199**

The Discretionary Housing Payments (Grants) Order 2001, S.I. 2001 No. 2340   **1203**

Index   **1207**

Acknowledgements

We would like to acknowledge the help of all those who assisted with this publication including staff in CPAG's Citizen's Rights Office, colleagues at the Tribunals Service and staff at the DWP who all provide information on a regular basis. Special thanks to Robert Sutherland for checking the content.

Also we would like to thank Nicola Johnston who edited and managed the production of this book and Katherine Dawson for the index, and all those who sent in cases and materials. Thanks too to Richard Gillard at David Lewis XML Ltd for restructuring the tables.

Foreword

Welcome to the 20th edition of *CPAG's Annotated Housing Benefit and Council Tax Benefit Legislation.*

Since the last edition of this book the 2006 regulations have bedded down, though most of the caselaw which has arisen since the last edition has been concerned with the old HB and CTB regulations.

The April 2006 regulations were merely a consolidation measure; no substantive changes were intended to be made to the housing benefit (HB) or council tax benefit (CTB) schemes by those changes and none have been identified in the 18 months since the 2006 regulations came into effect. In essence all the 2006 regulations did was to tidy up and renumber the 1987 Housing Benefit Regulations and the 1992 Council Tax Benefit Regulations (as modified by the 2003 State Pension Credit Regulations where necessary). Accordingly, most of the previous caselaw and commentary should remain relevant, and the commentary to the 2006 regulations in this edition reflects that. The destinations table set out on ppxxvi to xxxiv) should enable readers, where necessary, to trace across the old regulation number to the new.

Of the new caselaw, perhaps the most important has been the decsions of the commissioners in *CH 402/2007* and *CH 2995/2006* which have confirmed that a right of appeal does arise against the decision to terminate HB or CTB under regulation 14 of the Housing Benefit and Council Tax Benefit (Decisions and Appeals) Regulations 2001. This is an important safeguard against what is far too often an arbitrary and unlawful exercise of this power by many local authorities. The news that the House of Lords has granted the claimant leave to appeal against the Court of Appeal's judgment in *R(RJM) v Secretary of State for Work and Pensions* [2007] EWCA Civ 614, 28 June (CA) will hopefully bring to an end the Government's less than edifying argument that the ECtHR's decsion in *Stec* is not to be followed by UK courts and tribunals.

We have taken the opportunity in this edition to rewrite parts of the commentary on decsion making and appeals in Parts 1 and 5 and the commentary on persons from abroad under regulation 10 of the HB Regulation 2006 in Part 2.

This book, of necessity, has to focus in any individual place upon the particular statutory provision being commented upon. For a more general guide to the schemes, we recommend CPAG's *Welfare Benefits and Tax Credits Handbook.*

We would like to thank all those who have taken the trouble to contact us with suggestions for improvements and notification of new developments since the last edition. We are always pleased to receive further such suggestions and information and can be contacted at the addresses below.

The legislation in this edition is up to date to 1 November 2007.

An online version of this book is now available. CPAG's *Housing Benefit and Council Tax Benefit Law Online* contains the full text linked to relevant commissioners' decisions, caselaw etc. The commentary is updated twice yearly (in line with the book) but the legislation and caselaw is updated throughout the year. For more information visit www.cpag.org.uk/onlineservices.

STEWART WRIGHT	RICHARD POYNTER	CAROLYN GEORGE
c/o Publications Department	c/o Publications Department	c/o Publications Department
CPAG	CPAG	CPAG
94 White Lion Street	94 White Lion Street	94 White Lion Street
London	London	London
N1 9PF	N1 9PF	N1 9PF

How to use this book

The book is divided into eight parts. Part 1 contains the main Acts of Parliament governing housing benefit (HB), council tax benefit (CTB), decision making and appeals and the Human Rights Act. Part 2 contains the HB regulations for those under state pension credit age and Part 3 contains the equivalent regulations relating to CTB. Part 4 contains the regulations governing entitlement to HB and CTB of those of state pension credit age. Part 5 contains the main regulations relating to decision making and appeals. Parts 6, 7 and 8 then contain all other relevant primary and secondary legislation, with the rules on subsidy in Part 8.

The text of the Acts and regulations incorporate any amendments (which are indicated by square brackets and numbered for ease of reference). Where relevant, this is supplemented by information covering such matters as the effective dates of amendments and the definition of important terms. Each part of each set of regulations commences with a 'General Note' giving an overview of its provisions, and each individual regulation has its own 'General Note' followed, where appropriate, by an 'Analysis' section which takes a closer look at the structure of the regulation and the specific wording used. A similar, though more limited approach is adopted towards the relevant provisions of the legislation.

Interpreting the legislation

No one would describe the legislation governing HB and CTB as easy to apply or interpret and local authority officers who are called upon to carry out this task of interpretation often do not have the benefit of legal training. A brief guide to how this task should be performed may, therefore, be of assistance.

Where there is a dispute about the meaning of legislation, the first step should always be a consideration of the words of the particular provision themselves. Words should normally be given their everyday, common sense meaning. If that does not provide a solution to a problem, then regard should be had to the context in which the provision appears, the problem it appears to be directed at and to the enabling provisions in the primary legislation where the wording of a Regulation is considered.

1. **Commentary and guidance**

Extensive discussion will be found in the commentary to the provisions set out in this book as to possible meanings. The analysis set out represents the authors' view of the law and while it is hoped that it is persuasive, tribunals are not bound to follow it. The same is true of other publications on social security law.

The DWP produces a *Housing Benefit and Council Tax Benefit Guidance Manual* published by HMSO and this may give some help with interpretation. It is not a binding statement of the law. However, DWP guidance (whether issued in relation to HB or other means-tested benefits for which the wording of the legislation is similar or identical) may assist in the interpretation of the legislation in any case of doubt: *R v Tower Hamlets LBC HBRB ex p Kapur* [2000] *The Times* 28 June, QBD.

CH 3853/2001 and *CH 1586/2004* express similar views as to the status of guidance.

2. **Caselaw**

Until 2 July 2001, applications for further review were determined by Housing Benefit Review Boards comprised of councillors of the local authority. Their decisions could only be challenged by way of an application for judicial review in the High Court (in England and Wales) or Outer House of the Court of Session (in Scotland). Since then, an appeal to an Appeal Tribunal on questions of fact and law and a further appeal to the Social Security Commissioner on a question of law have been available. Further appeals to the Court of Appeal (in England and Wales) or

Inner House of the Court of Session (in Scotland), and from there to the House of Lords, continue to exist.

The commentary below deals with the hierarchy of decision-making. Strictly speaking, the views expressed in a decision of a higher court are only binding if they were a necessary part of the reasoning (*ratio decidendi*). Views which are not necessary to the decision (*obiter dicta*) are not strictly binding, but will be persuasive according to how closely they are reasoned and whether the point was in dispute before the tribunal in question. Views on the equivalent legislation governing other income-related benefits should normally be treated as binding, though care must be taken to ensure that it is identical.

If two decisions of equivalent jurisdiction conflict, the approach depends on the extent to which the decision in the first case was binding on the body making the second decision. Since commissioners and the High Court are not bound by each others' decisions, a tribunal is free to follow whichever is thought to be more persuasive. If there is conflict between decisions of the Court of Appeal and the Court of Session, the tribunal should follow the decision in the jurisdiction in which it sits.

Decisions of other tribunals

Tribunals are not bound by previous decisions of tribunals or of Review Boards on different claims, even where dealing with the same subject-matter: *CH 3853/2001* paras 18-19. If fully reasoned and made on identical facts, they may be of limited persuasive value where there is no other authority available.

Decisions of the Courts

Decisions of the Court of Appeal must be preferred to those of the High Court (in Scotland, Inner House Court of Session decisions overrule those in the Outer House).

Tribunals should regard themselves as bound by the findings of judges in judicial review cases in the High Court or Outer House of the Court of Session.

Many of the most important court decisions on HB have been published in the *Housing Law Reports* (HLR) published by Sweet and Maxwell. Unfortunately, the HLR tend to publish cases a long time after they are decided. *The Times* will include summaries of the most important cases. A subscription to one of the commercial case providers such as Smith Bernal (which provides free subscriptions to the voluntary sector) or Lawtel will give access to transcripts. Older cases will have to be ordered from the shorthand writers of the time. Details can be obtained by contacting the Court Service.

Decisions of the commissioners

Tribunals are required to follow the decisions of commissioners.

Until 2002, certain decisions of commissioners which were thought by the commissioner concerned to raise points of general importance were "starred" and circulated among other commissioners. If there was a consensus that they were correct, they were "reported" and published by HMSO. Reported decisions are generally to be preferred to unreported ones: *R(I) 12/75* para 20. If questions of particular difficulty arise, the Chief Commissioner has powers to convene Tribunals of Commissioners. Their decisions take precedence over the decisions of single commissioners: *R(I) 12/75* para 20.

Commissioners will generally follow each other's decisions, but not if they take the view that they are wrongly decided: *R(I) 12/75* para 21. A commissioner is not bound by the decision of a High Court or Outer House of the Court of Session judge hearing an application for judicial review: *R(IS) 15/99* para 19.

Commissioners' decisions can be found at www.osscsc.gov.uk.

Table of cases

Abdirahman and another v Secretary of State for Work and Pensions and another [2007] EWCA Civ 657... **245, 246**

Abdulaziz v UK [1985] 7 EHRR 471 at 501, para 78, ECtHR... **139**

Adan v Hounslow LBC [2004] EWCA Civ 101, CA... **389**

Airey v Ireland [1979] 2 EHRR 305... **133**

Andersson v Sweden [1986] 46 DR 251, ECmHR... **134**

Andrew v City of Glasgow DC [1996] SLT 814 at 817H-L... **324**

Andronicou v Cyprus [1998] 25 EHRR 491, ECtHR... **133**

Aparau v Iceland Frozen Foods Ltd [2000] 1 All ER 228, CA... **166**

Attorney General's Reference No 4 of 2002 [2004] UKHL 43... **119**

B v Secretary of State for Work and Pensions[2005] EWCA Civ 929, [2005] 1 WLR 3796 (reported as *R(IS) 9/06)*... **43, 44, 420, 423, 974**

Banks v Chief Adjudication Officer [2001] 1 WLR 1411, HL... **205**

Barke v SEETEC Business Technology Centre Limited [2005] EWCA Civ 578, 16 May 2005, unreported... **936**

Barnet LBC v Abdi [2006] EWCA Civ 383... **245**

Barrass v Reeve [1981] 1 WLR 408, DC... **59, 62**

Bate v Chief Adjudication Officer [1994] *The Times*... **200**

Baumbast (Case C-413/99)... **246**

Beattie v Secretary of State for Social Security [2001] 1 WLR 1404, CA... **313**

Begum v Tower Hamlets LBC [2003] 2 WLR 238, HL... **134**

The Belgian Linguistics Case (No 2) [1967] 1 EHRR 252 at 283-4, para 9, ECtHR... **137**

Bellet v France [1995] unreported, case number A/333-B, ECtHR... **133**

Beltekian v Westminster City Council and Secretary of State for Work and Pensions [2004] EWCA Civ 1784, 8 December 2004 (reported as *R(H) 8/05*... **959, 980**

Bernini v Minister van Ouderings en Wetenschappen (case C-3/90) [1992] ECR I-1071 at 1106, para 21, ECJ... **248**

Bettray v Straatssecretaris van Justitie (Case 344/87) [1989] ECR 1621 at 1637, para 10, ECJ... **247, 248**

Birkett v James [1978] AC 297, HL... **925**

Blakiston v Cooper [1909] AC 104, HL... **297**

Bland v Chief Supplementary Benefit Officer [1983] 1 WLR 262, CA (reported as *R(SB) 12/83*... **160, 165, 167**

Botchett v Chief Adjudication Officer [1996] 2 CCLR 121, CA... **290**

Bradford MBC v Anderton [1991] RA 45, QBD... **572**

Braintree District Council v Thompson [2005] EWCA Civ 178, 7 March 2005, unreported... **167**

Brown v Bullock... **299**

Bruton v London & Quadrant Housing Trust [1999] 3 WLR 150... **218**

Burton v New Forest District Council [2004] EWCA Civ 1510, 12 November, reported as *R(H) 7/05*... **197**

Cameron v Cameron [1996] SLT 306 at 313F... **243, 244**

Cameron v Henry [1992] SLT 586, IH... **572**

Campbell and others v South Northamptonshire District Council and the Secretary of State for Work and Pensions [2004] EWCA Civ 409 *The Times*... **96, 136, 140, 224, 226**

Campbell v Secretary of State for Social Services [1983] 4 FLR 138, QBD... **21**

Carpenter v Secretary of State for Work and Pensions [2003] EWCA Civ 33 (reported as *R(IB) 6/03)*... **153, 160, 934, 935, 936**

Carson and Reynolds [2005] UKHL 37 *The Times*... **136, 137, 138, 139**

Casewell v Secretary of State for Work and Pensions... **485**

Centre Public d'Aide Sociale, Courcelles v Lebon (Case 316/87) [1987] ECR 2811 at 2839, para 27, ECJ... **246, 247, 249**

Cheshire CC v Secretary of State for the Environment [1988] JPL 30, QBD... **165**

Chief Adjudication Officer v Ahmed [1994] *The Times*... **245**

Chief Adjudication Officer v Bate [1996] 1 WLR 814... **174**

Chief Adjudication Officer v Carr [1994] 2 June, *The Times*... **217**

Chief Adjudication Officer v Combe [1998] SLT 15 at 17D-F, IH (reported as *R(IS) 8/98)*... **956**

Chief Adjudication Officer v Ellis [1995] 15 February, CA... **204**

Chief Adjudication Officer v Leeves [1999] ELR 90, CA... **336**

Chief Adjudication Officer v McKiernon [1993] 3 July, CA... **964**

Chief Adjudication Officer v Palfrey [1995] *The Times*... **328, 329**

Chief Adjudication Officer v Stafford [2000] 1 All ER 686 at 693g-694a, CA... **205**

Chief Adjudication Officer v Upton [1997] 2 CLY 4668, CA... **384**

Chief Adjudication Officer v Webber [1998] 1 WLR 625 at 633E, CA... **342**

Clayton's case [1861] 1 Mer 572... **67, 419, 428**

Clear v Smith [1981] 1 WLR 399 at 406, DC... **62**

Codner v Wiltshire Valuation and Community Charge Tribunal [1994] 34 RVR 169, QBD... **572**

Collins v Secretary of State for Work and Pensions Case C-138/02, *The Times*... **246**

Cooke v Secretary of State for Social Security [2002] 3 All ER 279... **165, 167**

Cottingham v Chief Adjudication Officer [1992] appendix to *R(P) 1/93*... **17**

Cox v London (South West) Valuation and Community Charge Tribunal [1994] 34 RVR 171, QBD... **572**

Crabtree v Fern Spinning Co Ltd [1901] 85 LT 549 at 552, DC... **60**

Crake and Butterworth v Supplementary Benefit Commission [1982] 1 All ER 498 at 505, QBD... **21, 22**

D [2004] EWCA Civ 1468... **250**

Denneland v Germany [1986] 8 EHRR 448 at 468, para 74, ECtHR... **132**

Denton v Chief Adjudication Officer [1999] ELR 86 at 87G-H... **342**

Department of Work and Pensions v Richards [2005] EWCA Crim 491, 3 March... **47**

Diatta v Land Berlin (Case 267/83) [1985] ECR 567 at 589-590, paras 8-11, ECJ... **249**

Dombo Beheer BV v Netherlands [1993] 18 EHRR 213 at 226-8, ECtHR... **132**

Donaghue v Poplar Housing Association Ltd [2002] QB 58, CA... **123, 125**

Donnelly v Secretary of State for Work and Pensions [2007] CSOH 01, 10 January 2007... **165**

Douglas v Phoenix Motors [1970] SLT 57 at 58, Sh Ct... **64**

DSS v Bavi [1996] COD 260 at 261, DC... **62**

DSS v Cooper [1994] 158 JPN 354, DC... **62**

Duggan v Chief Adjudication Officer [1988] The Times 18 December, CA... **423**

E v Secretary of State for the Home Department [2004] EWCA Civ 49... **162**

Environmental Agency v Empress Cars (Abertillery) Ltd [1999] 2 AC 22, HL... **413**

Fairbank v Lambeth Magistrates' Court [2003] HLR 62... **63, 197**

Fedje v Sweden [1994] 17 EHRR 14, para 32, ECtHR... **134**

Feldbrugge v Netherlands [1986] 8 EHRR 425 at 435, para 40, ECtHR... **132**

Foster v Chief Adjudication Officer [1992] QB 31 at 45... **17**

Foster v Chief Adjudication Officer [1993] AC 754, HL... **161, 579**

Francis v Secretary of State for Work and Pensions [2005] EWCA Civ 1303, 10 November (reported as R(IS) 6/06)... **137, 138**

Franklin v Chief Adjudication Officer [1995] *The Times*... **423**

Frost v Feltham [1981] 1 WLR 455... **12, 572**

Fryer-Kelsey v The Secretary of State for Work and Pensions [2005] EWCA Civ 511, 21 April... **167**

Gaumont British Distributors Ltd v Henry [1939] 2 KB 711 at 719, 723, DC... **60**

Gaygusuz, Szrabjer v Clarke v UK... **139**

General Legal Council ex parte Basil Whitter v Barrington Earl Frankson [2006] UKPC 42, 27 July... **985**

Geveran v Skjeveslan Trading Company Limited [2003] 1 All ER 1... **932**

Ghaidan v Godin-Mendoza [2004] UKHL 30, 3 All ER 411... **120, 121, 136, 138**

Giangregorio v Secretary of State for the Home Department [1983] Imm AR 104 at 110-1, IAT... **248**

Gillies v Secretary of State for Work and Pensions [2006] UKHL 2, *Times Law Report*... **131, 164**

Godwin v Rossendale BC [2002] *The Times*... **510**

Goodwin v Rossendale BC [2003] HLR 83, CA... **44**

Grant v Southwestern and County Properties Ltd [1975] Ch 185 at 197A-F, Ch D... **60**

Grice v Needs [1980] 1 WLR 45 at 47F-G... **57**

Guygusuz v Austria [1997] 23 EHRR 364, ECtHR... **137, 138**

Hamblett v Godfrey [1987] 1 WLR 357, CA... **297**

Hampshire County Council v Beer t/a Hammer Trout Farm,... **123**

Haringey LBC v Awaritefe [1999] 32 HLR 517... **66, 164, 396, 429, 1069**

Haringey LBC v Cotter [1996] 29 HLR 682, CA... **134, 399**

Harrison v DSS [1997] COD 220 at 220-1, DC... **63**

Herbert v Byrne [1964] 1 WLR 519 at 527, 528, 529, CA... **211**

Hinchy v Secretary of State for Work and Pensions [2005] UKHL 16... **423**

Hobbs and others v UK (Application No. 63684/00), 14 November 2006... **139**

Hochstrasser v Mayes [1959] Ch 22, CA... **297**

Hooper v Secretary of State for Work and Pensions [2007] EWCA Civ 495... **156**

Howker v Secretary of State for Work and Pensions [2003] ICR 405... **95**

Insurance Officer v McCaffrey [1985] 1 WLR 1353 at 1355H-1356C, HL... **31**

The House of Lords [1999] 1 WLR 1937, [1999] 4 All ER 677... **243**

The House of Lords [2001] 1 WLR 539... **1110**

James Miller & Partners Ltd v Whitworth Street Estates (Manchester) Ltd [1970] AC 572... **220**

Jewish Blind Society Trustees v Henning [1961] 1 WLR 24 at 30, 34, CA... **290**

Jia v Migrationsverket (Case C-1/05), 9 January 2007, unreported (ECJ)... **249**

Jones v Chief Adjudication Officer [1994] 1 WLR 62 at 71H, 72F, CA... **423**

Jones v City of Glasgow DC HBRB [1997] unreported, 4 July, CSOH... **237**

Jones v Secretary of State for Work and Pensions [2003] EWCA 964, unreported... **323**

Jones v Waveney DC [1999] 33 HLR 3, CA... **399**

Kazantzis v Chief Adjudication Officer [1999] *The Times*... **204**

Kempf v Staatssecretaris van Justitie (Case 139/85) [1986] ECR 1741 at 1751, para 15, ECJ... **247**

Kerr v Department for Social Development [2004] UKHL 23 (reported as *R 1/04 (SF)*)... **147, 148, 162, 415, 416, 929**

King v Kerrier District Council [2006] EWHC 500 (Admin), unreported, 27 February (DC)... **63**

Kingston-upon-Thames BC v Prince [1998] 31 HLR 794, CA... **221**

Kits van Heijerungen v Staatssecretaris van Justitie (Case C-125/89) [1990] ECR I-1753, ECJ... **247**

Kjeldsen Madsen v Denmark [1976] 1 EHRR 711, ECtHR... **137**

Kola and another v Secretary of State for Work and Pensions... **1121**

Koua Pourrez v CAF (Case C-206/91) [1992] ECR I-6685 at 6706, paras 10-13, ECJ... **248**

Lair v Universitat Hannover (Case 39/86) [1988] ECR 3161 at 3191, para 43, ECJ... **247**

Lambeth London BC v Kay [2006] 4 All ER 128... **218**

Lane v Esdaile [1891] AC 210, 212... **160**

Langley v Bradford MDC and Secretary of State for Work and Pensions [2004] EWCA Civ 1343, 15 October, CA, reported as *R(H) 6/05*... **135, 231**

Lawrie-Blum v Land Baden-Wurtternberg (Case 66/85) [1986] ECR 2121 at 2144, paras 17-21, ECJ... **246**

Leeds City Council v Price [2006] UKHL 10, [2006] 4 All ER 128... **119, 140**

Levin v Staatssecretaris van Justitie (Case 53/81) [1982] ECR 1035 at 1049, para 13, ECJ... **246, 247**

Lillystone v Supplementary Benefits Commission [1982] 3 FLR 52, CA... **279**

Lloyd v McMahon [1987] AC 625, HL... **942**

Locabail (UK) Ltd v Bayfield Properties Ltd [2000] QB 451 at 496F-497A, para 89, CA... **164**

Luisi v Ministero del Tesoro (Cases 286/82, 26/83) [1984] ECR 377 at 403, para 16, ECJ... **249**

M (A Minor) v Secretary of State for Social Security [2001] 1 WLR 1453... **1057**

Malcolm v Tweeddale District HBRB [1994] SLT 1212, CS(OH)... **1107, 1108, 1112, 1113, 1114**

Manorlike Ltd v Le Vitas Travel Agency and Consultancy Services Ltd [1986] 1 All ER 573 at 575e-h, 576b-d, CA... **956**

Massachusetts Board of Retirement v Murgia [1976] 438 US 285... **138**

McLeod v HBRB for Banff and Buchan District HBRB [1988] SLT 753, CS(OH)... **1108, 1112**

Michalak v Wandsworth LBC [2003] 1 WLR 617... **136**

Middleburgh v Chief Adjudication Officer (Case C-15/90) [1991] ECR I-4655 at 4682, para 13, ECJ... **248**

Miller v Secretary of State for Social Security [2002] GWD 25-861, CSIH... **163**

Mongan v Department for Social Development [2005] NICA 16, 13 April... **153, 155, 156**

Monteil v Secretary of State for the Home Department [1983] Imm AR 149 at 152, IAT... **247, 248**

Mooney v Secretary of State for Work and Pensions [2004] SLT 1141... **155, 165**

Moore v Branton [1974] 118 SJ 40, DC... **63**

Moore v Griffiths [1972] 1 WLR 1024, Ch D... **296**

Moorhouse v Dooland [1955] Ch 284, CA... **297**

Moser v Land Baden-Wurttenberg (Case 180/83) [1984] ECR 2539 at 2547, para 18, ECJ... **248**

Mullaney v Watford BC [1997] RA 225, QBD... **572**

Müller v Austria (Commission) [1975] 3 D and R 25... **141**

Mulvey v Secretary of State for Social Security [1997] SLT 753 at 756, HL... **101, 426**

Munro v UK [1986] 48 DR 154, ECmHR... **133**

Nessa v Chief Adjudication Officer [1998] 2 All ER 728 at 733d-g, 743e-f, CA... **243, 245**

Netherlands v Reed (Case 59/85) [1986] ECR 1283 at 1300, para 14, ECJ... **249**

Nimmo v Alexander Cowan & Sons Ltd [1968], 1967 SC (HL) 79... **148**

O'Connor v Chief Adjudication Officer [1999] ELR 209, CA... **344**

Osinunga v DPP [1997] 30 HLR 853 at 856, DC... **47**

Osman v UK [1998] 29 EHRR 245, ECtHR... **174**

Owen v Chief Adjudication Officer [1999] *The Independent*... **17**

Page v Chief Adjudication Officer [1991] *The Times* 4 July, CA... **423**

Parochial Church Council of the Parish of Aston Cantlow and Wilmcote with Billesley, Warwickshire v Wallbank and others,... **123**

Parry v Derbyshire Dales District Council [2006] EWHC 988 (Admin), 5 May, unreported... **572**

Perrot v Supplementary Benefit Commissioner [1980] 3 All ER 110 at 114j, 116a-e, 117b, CA... **204**

Petrovic v Austria [1998] 4 BHRC 232, ECtHR... **134, 139**

Plewa v Chief Adjudication Officer [1995] 1 AC 248, HL... **420, 422**

Plymouth CC v Gigg [1997] 30 HLR 284, CA... **429**

Poplar Housing Association Ltd v Donoghue [2002] QB 58, CA... **121, 122**

Porter v Magill [2002] 2 WLR 37 at 83D-84B, paras 102-103, HL... **164**

Presbytery of Lews v Fraser [1874] 1 R 888... **924**

Pretty v UK [2002] 35 EHRR 1, ECHR... **131**

Procureur du Roi v Royer (Case 48/75) [1976] ECR 497 at 514, para 31, ECJ... **249**

R (Alconbury Developments Ltd) v Secretary of State for the Environment, Transport and the Regions[2003] 2 AC 295, HL... **119, 133**

R (Anufrijeva) v Southwark LBC [2003] EWCA Civ 1406, CA... **126, 134**

R (Anufrijeva) v Secretary of State for the Home Department [2003] 3 WLR 353, HL... **127, 1121**

R(Balding) v Secretary of State for Work and Pensions [2007] EWHC 759, 3 April 2007, (Admin)... **426**

R (Barber) v Secretary of State for Work and Pensions [2002] 2 FLR 1181, QBD... **137**

R(Beeson) v Dorset County Council [2001] EWHC Admin 986, 30 November 2001... **323**

R (Beeson) v Dorset [2002] 6 CCLR 5, CA... **134**

R(Begum) v Social Security Commissioners [2002] EWHC 401... **165**

R (Ben-Abdelaziz) v Secretary of State for the Home Department [2001] 1 WLR 1485, CA... **131**

R (Bernard) v Enfield LBC [2002] 5 CCLR 589... **126, 127**

R (Bierman) v Secretary of State for Work and Pensions [2004] EWHC 1024 (Admin), 23 April, unreported... **345**

R(Bono) v Harlow DC HBRB [2002] 1 WLR 2475 paras 34-35, Richards J... **123**

R (Carson) v Secretary of State for Work and Pensions [2003] 3 All ER 577, CA... **136, 138**

R (Couronne) v Crawley BC and Secretary of State for Work and Pensions and Others [2006] EWHC 1514 (Admin)... **140**

R (Cumpsty) v Rent Officer [2002] EWHC 2526 (Admin)... **132, 133**

R(Douglas) v North Tyneside MBC and another [2004] 1 All ER 709... **141**

R(Greenfield) v Secretary of State for the Home Department [2005] UKHL 14, [2005] 2 All ER 240, HL... **127**

R (Heather) v The Leonard Cheshire Foundation [2001] 4 CCLR 211, Stanley Burton J... **123**

R (Hook) v The Social Security Commissioner [2007] EWHC 1705 (Admin), 3 July... **324**

R (Hooper) v Secretary of State for Work and Pensions [2003] 1 WLR 2623, CA... **83**

R(Iran) v Secretary of State for the Home Department [2005] EWCA Civ 982... **161**

R (Isle of Anglesey DC) v Secretary of State for Work and Pensions [2003] EWHC 2518 (Admin)... **93**

R (Laali) v Westminster CC HBRB [2002] HLR 179, QBD... **259**

R (Murphy) v Westminster CC [2002] HLR 447... **230, 231**

R (Naghshbandi) v Camden LBC [2001] EWHC Admin 813; [2003] HLR 280, CA... **258, 338, 1084**

R (Naghshbandi) v Camden LBC [2003] HLR 280... **213**

R (Nahar) v Social Security Commissioner [2002] 1 FLR 670... **169**

R (Nicholson) v Leeds CC HBRB [2000] unreported, 2 November, QBD... **422**

R (Painter) v Carmarthenshire CC HBRB[2002] HLR 447... **230, 231**

R (Reynolds) v Secretary of State for Work and Pensions[2002] EWHC Admin 426... **135, 452**

R(RJM) v Secretary of State for Work and Pensions [2007] EWCA Civ 614, 28 June (CA)... **vii, 140**

R(S) v Chief Constable of South Yorkshire Police [2004] 1 WLR 2196... **136, 137**

R (Sibley) v West Dorset DC [2001] EWHC Admin 365... **432, 1084**

R (Sier) v Cambridge CC HBRB [2001] EWHC Admin 160, QBD; [2001] EWCA Civ 1523, CA... **413, 414, 415, 416, 422**

R (T) v Richmond-upon-Thames LBC HBRB [2000] 33 HLR 65, QBD... **219**

R (Tucker) v Secretary of State for Social Security [2001] EWHC Admin 260... **134, 232**

R (Waite) v London Borough of Hammersmith and Fulham [2003] HLR 24... **216**

R (Wall) v Appeals Service [2003] EWHC 465 Admin... **134**

R v A (No 2) [2001] 2 AC 91, HL... **120, 121**

R v Allerdale DC HBRB ex p Doughty [2000] COD 462, QBD… **161, 445, 937, 1110, 1111**

R v Armour [1997] 2 Cr App R(S) 240, CA… **47**

R v Barrow BC ex p Catnach [1997] unreported, 3 September, QBD… **221, 239**

R v Beverley DC HBRB ex p Hare [1995] 27 HLR 637, QBD… **1107, 1109**

R v Birmingham CC HBRB ex p Ellery [1989] 21 HLR 398, QBD… **194**

R v Brent LBC HBRB ex p Connery [1989] 22 HLR 40 at 44, QBD… **44, 1108, 1109**

R v Brent LBC ex p Shah [1983] 2 AC 309 at 343H-344B, HL… **242, 244, 245**

R v Bristol CC ex p Jacobs [1999] 32 HLR 841, QBD… **257**

R v Cambridge CC ex p Thomas[1995] unreported, 10 February, QBD… **221**

R v Camden LBC HBRB ex p W [1999] 21 May, unreported, QBD… **1111**

R v Canterbury CC ex p Woodhouse [1994] unreported, 2 August, QBD… **1111, 1112, 1113**

R v Cardiff CC HBRB ex p Thomas [1991] 25 HLR 1 at 5, QBD… **936**

R v Chainey [1914] 1 KB 137 at 142, DC… **60**

R v Chesterfield BC ex p Fullwood [1993] 26 HLR 126 at 129, CA… **201, 364**

R v Coventry CC ex p Waite [1995] unreported, 7 July, QBD… **1108, 1109**

R v Coventry CC ex p Waite [1995] unreported, 7 October, QBD… **1109, 1112, 1114**

R v Department of Social Security ex p Okito [1998] COD 48 at 49, QBD… **1056, 1056**

R v Deputy Industrial Injuries Commissioner ex p Moore [1965] 1 QB 456… **162**

R v Derby CC ex p Third Wave Housing [2000] 33 HLR 61, QBD… **219**

R v Doncaster MBC ex p Nortrop [1998] unreported, 31 July, QBD… **319**

R v East Devon DC HBRB ex p Gibson [1993] 25 HLR, CA… **936, 1108, 1109, 1112, 1113, 1114**

R v East Devon DC HBRB ex p Preston [1998] 31 HLR 936, QBD… **1114**

R v Ghosh [1982] QB 1053 at 1064D-G, CA… **59**

R v Gloucestershire CC ex p Barry [1997] AC 584, HL… **1080**

R v Gloucestershire CC ex p Dadds [1996] 29 HLR 700, QBD… **237, 239**

R v Greenwich LBC ex p Dhadly [1999] 32 HLR 829… **225, 236, 237**

R v Greenwich LBC ex p Moult [1998] unreported, 19 June, CA… **228**

R v Haringey LBC ex p Ayub [1992] 25 HLR 566, QBD… **394, 405, 426, 428, 435**

R v Haringey LBC ex p Ayub [1990] 25 HLR 566, QBD… **402**

R v HMRC ex parte Wilkinson [2005] UKHL 30… **139**

R v Ipswich BC ex p Flowers [1994] unreported, 1 March, QBD… **1114**

R v Islington LBC ex p Ewing [1992] unreported, 5 February, QBD… **396**

R v Islington LBC HBRB ex p de Grey [1992] unreported 11 February, QBD… **414**

R v Kensington and Chelsea RBC ex p Abou-Jaoude [1996] unreported, 10 May, QBD… **1108, 1114**

R v Kensington and Chelsea RBC ex p Brandt [1995] 28 HLR 528, QBD… **256, 357, 426**

R v Kensington and Chelsea RBC ex p Carney [1997] COD 124 at 125, QBD… **1110, 1111**

R v Kensington and Chelsea RBC ex p Pirie [1997] unreported, 26 March, QBD… **1107, 1109, 1112**

R v Kensington and Chelsea RBC ex p Sheikh [1997] unreported, 14 January, QBD… **1110, 1112, 1113**

R v Kensington and Chelsea RBC HBRB ex p Robertson [1988] 28 RVR 84 at 85, QBD… **215**

R v Lambert [2002] 2 AC 545, para 80, HL… **121**

R v Lambeth LBC ex p Crookes [1995] 29 HLR 28 at 35, QBD… **394**

R v Lambeth LBC ex p Crookes [1998] 31 HLR 59, QBD… **397, 985**

R v Lambeth LBC HBRB ex p Harrington [1996] unreported 22 November, QBD… **937, 1112**

R v Liverpool CC ex p Johnson (No 1) [1994] unreported, 23 June, QBD… **394**

R v London Borough of Waltham Forest HBRB ex parte Iqbal [1997] EWHC Admin 810… **999**

R v Macclesfield BC HBRB ex p Temsamani [1999] unreported, February 24, QBD… **259**

R v Manchester CC ex p Harcup [1993] 26 HLR 402 at 408, QBD… **1109**

R v Manchester City Council ex parte Stennett [2002] UKHL 34… **489**

R v Middlesborough BC ex p Graville [1993] unreported, 26 March, QBD… **324**
R v Middlesborough BC ex p Holmes [1995] unreported, 15 February, QBD… **1099**
R v Milton Keynes BC HBRB ex p Macklen [1996] unreported, 30 April, QBD… **237**
R v Milton Keynes CC HBRB ex p Saxby [2000] unreported, 11 August, QBD; [2001] 33 HLR 82, CA… **256**
R v Newham LBC ex p Kaur [1997] 29 HLR 776 at 784, QBD… **395, 905**
R v Oadby and Wigston DC ex p Dickman [1995] 28 HLR 807… **1111, 1114**
R v Oldham MBC ex p G [1993] 1 FLR 645 at 662, CA… **221**
R v Passmore [2007] EWCA Crim 2053, 18 June, CA… **60**
R v Penwith DC ex p Burt [1990] 22 HLR 292 at 296, QBD… **211, 215**
R v Penwith DC ex p Menear [1991] 24 HLR 115, QBD… **251, 342, 392**
R v Poole Borough Council ex p Ross [1995] 28 HLR 351, QBD… **219, 227, 237, 239**
R v Rent Officer ex p Muldoon [1996] 1 WLR 1103, HL… **167**
R v Rugby BC HBRB ex p Harrison [1994] 28 HLR 36 at 48-9, QBD… **218, 226, 228**
R v Sandwell MBC ex p Wilkinson [1998] 31 HLR 22, QBD… **1109, 1113, 1114**
R v Secretary of State for Social Security ex p Association of Metropolitan Authoroties [1992] 25 HLR 131, QBD… **99**
R v Secretary of State for Social Security ex p B and JCWI [1997] 1 WLR 275… **1054, 1055**
R v Secretary of State for Social Security ex p Britnell [1989] *The Times*… **422**
R v Secretary of State for Social Security ex p Golding [1996] unreported, 1 July, CA… **67**
R v Secretary of State for Social Security ex p Grant [1997] unreported, 31 July, QBD… **1121**
R v Secretary of State for Social Security ex p Sarwar, Getachew, Urbanek and Urbanek [1995] 7 Admin LR 781… **246**
R v Secretary of State for Social Security ex p Sarwar [1997] 3 CMLR 647, CA… **5**
R v Secretary of State for Social Security ex p Smithson (case C-243/90) [1992] ECR I-467, ECJ… **1100**
R v Secretary of State for Social Security ex p Taylor and Chapman [1996] *The Times*… **426**
R v Secretary of State for Social Security ex p Vijeikis [1998] COD 49, QBD… **1055, 1056**
R v Secretary of State for Social Services ex p Britnell [1989] COD 487, DC… **426**
R v Secretary of State for the Environment ex p Hammersmith and Fulham LBC [1991] 1 AC 521 at 597E-H, HL… **92**
R v Secretary of State for the Home Department ex p Brind [1991] 1 AC 696 at 747G-748F, 760D-762B, HL… **120**
R v Secretary of State for the Home Department ex p Jeyeanthan [2000] 1 WLR 354… **164**
R v Secretary of State for the Home Department ex p Mehta [1975] 1 WLR 1087 at 1091F-G, CA… **905**
R v Secretary of State for the Home Department ex p Pinochet (No 2) [2000] 1 AC 129, HL… **163**
R v Secretary of State for the Home Department ex p Yennin [1995] Imm AR 93 at 96, QBD… **249**
R v Secretary of State for the Home Department ex parte Limbuela and others [2005] UKHL 66, 3 November, HL… **132**
R v Secretary of State for the Home Department, ex p Anderson [2002] UKHL 46… **119**
R v Secretary of State for Work and Pensions ex parte Hooper and others [2005] UKHL 29… **137**
R v Sedgemoor DC HBRB ex p Weadon [1986] 18 HLR 355, QBD… **197**
R v Sefton MBC ex p Cunningham [1991] 23 HLR 534 at 538, QBD… **936, 1108, 1110**
R v Sefton MBC HBRB ex p Brennan [1996] 29 HLR 735 at 741, QBD… **1112, 1114**
R v Sheffield CC HBRB ex p Smith [1994] 28 HLR 36 at 47-8, QBD… **197**
R v Slough BC ex p Green [1996] unreported, 15 November, QBD… **1112, 1114**
R v Social Security Commissioner ex parte Bibi [2000] 23 May, unreported, HC… **931**
R v Solihull MBC HBRB ex p Simpson [1993] 26 HLR 370 at 377, QBD… **936**
R v South Hams DC ex p Ash [1999] 32 HLR 405 at 409, QBD44, … **83, 415**
R v South Ribble DC HBRB ex p Hamilton [2000] 33 HLR 102, CA… **144, 198, 251, 281, 315, 342, 717**

R v South Tyneside MBC ex p Tooley [1996] COD 143 at 144, QBD... **237, 323, 937**

R v Southwark LBC ex p Bannerman [1989] 22 HLR 459 at 463, QBD... **165**

R v St Edmundsbury BC HBRB ex p Sandys [1997] 30 HLR 800; [1998] *The Times*... **111**

R v Stewart [1987] 2 All ER 363, CA... **47**

R v Stoke-on-Trent CC ex p Highgate Projects [1993] 26 HLR 551, QBD... **378**

R v Stoke-on-Trent CC ex p Highgate Projects [1996] 29 HLR 271 at 278, CA... **445**

R v Stratford-upon-Avon DC HBRB ex p White [1997] 30 HLR 178, QBD... **235, 236**

R v Stratford-upon-Avon DC HBRB ex p White [1998] 31 HLR 126... **218, 229, 230, 237, 238, 239, 406**

R v Sutton LBC ex p Partridge [1994] 28 HLR 315 at 319-320... **226, 228, 229**

R v Sutton LBC HBRB ex p Keegan [1992] 27 HLR 92 at 99-100, QBD... **219, 237, 238**

R v Swale BC HBRB ex p Marchant [1999] 1 FLR 1087, QBD; [2000] 1 FLR 246, CA... **210, 522**

R v Thanet DC ex p Warren Court Hotels Ltd [2000] 33 HLR 339, CA... **44, 396, 509**

R v Tower Hamlets LBC HBRB ex p Kapur [2000] *The Times*... **494**

R v Waltham Forest LBC ex p Holder [1996] 29 HLR 71 at 78-9... **1112, 1113, 1114**

R v Warrington BC ex p Williams [1997] 29 HLR 872 at 876, QBD... **22, 219, 222**

R v Westminster CC ex p Castelli and Tristan-Garcia [1995] 8 Admin LR 73 at 92E-F, QBD... **249**

R v Westminster CC HBRB ex p Mehanne [1999] 2 All ER 319, CA... **229, 1110, 1111**

R v Westminster CC HBRB ex p Pallas [1997] unreported, 23 September, QBD... **1111, 1113**

R v Westminster CC HBRB ex p Sier [1999] 32 HLR 655 at 662-3, QBD... **222, 237**

R v Westminster CC HBRB ex parte Mehanne [1997] EWHC Admin 1117... **999**

R v Woking BC ex p Crawley [1996] unreported, 19 June, QBD... **218**

R v Wyre BC ex p Lord [1997] unreported, 24 October, QBD... **431**

R v Aylesbury Vale DC ex p England [1996] 29 HLR 303... **384**

R v Doncaster BC ex p Boulton [1992] 25 HLR 195, QBD... **475, 476**

R v Liverpool CC ex p Griffiths [1990] 22 HLR 312, QBD... **403, 414, 417**

R v Liverpool CC ex p Johnson (No 2)... **389**

R v Manchester CC ex p Baragrove Properties Ltd [1991] 23 HLR 337, QBD... **238, 239, 407**

R v Oxford CC ex p Jack [1984] 17 HLR 419, QBD... **279, 280**

R v Penwith DC ex p Menear [1990] 24 HLR 120, QBD... **281**

R v Secretary of State for Social Services ex parte Connolly... **165**

R v Secretary of State for Social Security ex p T [1996] unreported, 1 November, QBD... **1055**

R v Secretary of State for Social Services ex p CPAG [1990] 2 QB 540 at 554C-555B, CA... **394**

R v Solihull MBC HBRB ex p Simpson [1995] 1 FLR 140 at 148E-F, CA... **235, 236, 237**

R v Supplementary Benefit Commission ex p Singer [1973] 1 WLR 713... **279, 280**

R v West Dorset DC ex p Poupard [1988] 28 RVR 40, CA... **279, 280, 301**

Raulin v Minister van Ondervijsen Wetenschappen (Case C-357/89) [1992] I-ECR 1027, ECJ... **247, 248**

re A (Minors) (Abduction: Habitual Residence) [1996] 1 WLR 25 at 33G, [1996] 1 All ER 24 at 32h-j, FD... **245**

re B (Minors) (Abduction) [1993] 1 FLR 993 at 995C-D, FD... **244**

re C (minors) (Adoption: Residence Order) [1994] Fam 1, CA... **231**

re Collins [1990] Fam 56, FD... **231**

re Forest of Dean Coal Mining Co [1879] 10 Ch D 451 at 453... **232**

re J (a minor) (Abduction: Custody Rights) [1990] 2 AC 562... **242, 243, 245**

re Prince Blucher [1931] 2 Ch D 70... **985**

re S [2002] 2 AC 291, HL... **120**

re Wyvern Developments Ltd [1974] 1 WLR 1097 at 1103D, Ch D... **222**

Ready-Mixed Concrete (South East) Ltd v Minister of Pensions and National Insurance [1968] 2 QB 497, CA... **233**

Rent Service v R(Heffernan) [2007] EWCA Civ 544, 13 June, CA... **529**

Rickards v Rickards [1990] Fam 194... **160**

Rider v Chief Adjudication Officer [1996] Times 30 January, CA... **459**

Rinner-Kuhn v FVW Spezial-Gebanderingung GmbH (Case 127/88) [1989] ECR 2743, ECJ... **247**

Robson v Secretary of State for Social Services [1982] 3 FLR 232, QBD... **22**

Ruiz-Mateos v Spain [1993] 16 EHRR 505... **132**

Rydqvist v Secretary of State for Work and Pensions [2002] *The Times*... **922**

Saker v Secretary of State for Social Security [1988] 16 January *The Times*... **416, 423, 956**

Salesi v Italy [1993] 26 EHRR 187 at 199, para 19, ECtHR... **132**

Saunders v Vautier [1841] 4 Bear 115... **324**

Secretary of State for Social Security v Walter [2002] ICR 540... **344**

Secretary of State for Work and Pensions v Bhakta [2006] EWCA Civ 65, *(R(IS) 7/06)*... **383**

Secretary of State for Work and Pensions v Chiltern DC [2003] HLR 1019, CA (reported as *R(H) 2/03)*... **389, 432, 929**

Secretary of State for Work and Pensions v Chiltern District Council [2003] EWCA Civ 508 *(R(H) 2/03)*... **155**

Secretary of State for Work and Pensions v Gillies [2003] 2004 SLT 14, reported at 2006 SC (HL) 71... **131, 164**

Secretary of State for Work and Pensions v Hourigan [2003] 1 WLR 608... **329**

Secretary of State for Work and Pensions v M [2006] UKHL 11, 8 March 2006, reported as *R(CS) 4/06*... **135, 137**

Secretary of State for Work and Pensions v Morina and Borrowdale [2007] EWCA Civ 749... **160, 167, 980, 981**

Secretary of State for Work and Pensions v Robinson [2004], 11 February, CA (reported as *R(H) 4/04)*... **366**

Secretary of State for Work and Pensions v Selby District Council and another [2006] EWCA Civ 271... **214**

Secretary of State for Work and Pensions v Wilson [2006] EWCA Civ 882, *29 June 2006*... **30**

Secretary of State for Work and Pensions v Esfandiari and others [2006] EWCA Civ 282, 23 March 2006, CA (reported as *R(IS) 11/06)*... **137**

Sengupta v Holmes [2002] *The Times*... **134**

Shah v Secretary of State for Social Security [2002] EWCA Civ 285, CA... **1028, 1057, 1075**

Shepherd v Dundee CC [2002] SLT 1427, CS(IH)... **265**

Singh v Post Office [1973] ICR 437 at 440... **970**

Smith v Chief Adjudication Officer [1994] unreported, 11 October, CA... **204**

Sodemare SA v Regione Lombardia (Case C-70/95) [1997] ECR 3395... **250**

Stevenson v Rogers [1992] SLT 558, IH... **572**

Stec and others v United Kingdom (Application Nos: 65731/01 and 65900/01), 6 July 2005, ECtHR... **vii, 135, 137, 139, 140**

Steymann v Staatssecretaris van Justitie (Case 197/87) [1988] ECR 6159... **247, 250**

Street v Mountford [1995] AC 809, HL... **13**

Swaddling v Chief Adjudication Officer (case C-90/97) [1999] 2 CMLR 679, ECJ... **243**

Sweet v Parsley [1970] AC 132, 155A... **323**

Szoma v Secretary of State for Work and Pensions [2005] UKHL 64, [2006] 1 All ER 1 (reported as *R(IS) 2/06)*... **1076**

Taylor's Central Garages (Exeter) Ltd v Roper [1951] 115 JP 445 at 449, 450, DC... **60, 63**

Thamesdown BC v Goonery [1995] 1 CLY 2600, CA... **200**

Thlimmenos v Greece [2001] 31 EHRR 411... **138**

Thomas v Chief Adjudication Officer reported as an appendix to *R(SB) 17/87*... **316**

Thrasyvoulou v Secretary of State for the Environment [1990] 2 AC 273 at 289, HL... **169**

Tolfree v Florence [1971] 1 WLR 141 at 144, DC... **63**

Trojani (Case C-456/02)... **245, 246**

Trustees of the Dennis Rye Pension Fund v Sheffield CC [1998] 1 WLR 840 at 849F-M, 850A, CA... **399**

Tsfayo v United Kingdom (application no: 60860/00) [2006], 14 November, unreported, ECtHR... **133, 147, 975, 993**

Tyrer v Smart [1979] 1 WLR 113, HL... **297**

Unger v BBDA (Case 75/63) [1964] ECR 177 at 184, ECJ... **246**

URSSAF v Hostellerie Le Manoir SARL (Case C-3/90) [1991] ECR I-5531 at 5541, para 8, ECJ... **247**

Uratemp Ventures Ltd v Collins [2001] 3 WLR 806... **22**

Van der Mussele v Belgium [1983] 6 EHRR 163, 179-180... **138**

Walsh v Rother DC [1978] 1 All ER 510 at 514a-e, HC... **66**

Ward v Kingston upon Hull CC [1993] RA 71, QBD... **572**

Warwick DC v Freeman [1994] 27 HLR 616, CA... **66, 406, 412, 415, 416, 429, 1069**

West Somerset DC v Sykes [1997] unreported 14 March, CA... **412, 413**

Westminster CC v Clarke [1992] 2 AC 288 at 299, HL... **22**

Westminster CC v Croyalgrange Ltd [1986] 1 WLR 674 at 684E, HL... **60**

White v Chief Adjudication Officer [1986] 2 All ER 905, CA (reported as an appendix to *R(S) 8/85)*... **160**

White v Chief Adjudication Officer [1993] *The Times*... **290**

Williams v Bayley [1866] LR 1 HL 200, HL... **67**

Williams v Horsham District Council [2004] EWCA Civ 39, 21 January, CA... **572**

Wilson v First County Trust Ltd (No 2) [2003] WLR 586... **131**

Wood v Secretary of State for Work and Pensions [2003] EWCA Civ 53, CA (reported as *R(DLA) 1/03)*... **148, 149, 154, 956, 963**

Wright v Howell [1947] 92 SJ 26, CA... **22**

X v Italy [1977] 11 DR 114... **141**

Yildiz v Secretary of State for Social Security [2001] *The Independent*... **1056, 1057**

YL (by her litigation friend the Official Solicitor) v Birmingham City Council and others [2007] UKHL 27, 20 June, HL... **123**

Zalewska v Department for Social Development [2007], unreported, 9 May... **250**

Table of commissioners' decisions

CA 4297/2004... **936**
CCS 7967/1995... **313**
CCS 1535/1997... **169**
CCS 565/1999... **163**
CCS 910/1999... **914**
CCS 2064/1999... **905, 906**
CCS 1664/2001... **936**
CCS 3175/2002... **905, 906**
CDLA 7980/1995... **290**
CDLA 1389/1997... **940**
CDLA 5793/1997... **936**
CDLA 1347/1999... **131, 922**
CDLA 4102/1999... **166**
CDLA 5413/1999... **132, 942**
CDLA 557/2001... **934**
CDLA 572/2001... **937**
CDLA 3224/2001... **922**
CDLA 3432/2001... **134, 914**
CDLA 3908/2001... **139**
CDLA 3965/2001... **932**
CDLA 4217/2001... **166**
CDLA 4895/2001... **950**
CDLA 4977/2001... **397, 919**
CDLA 164/2002... **939**
CDLA 1456/2002... **160, 161**
CDLA 2748/2002... **133, 163**
CDLA 2975/2002... **160, 161**
CDLA 4331/2002... **157**
CDLA 1138/2003... **930**
CDLA 1821/2003... **955**
CDLA 2462/2003... **930**
CDLA 581/2004... **939**
CDLA 1290/2004... **933**
CDLA 1685/2004... **158, 942**
CDLA 2429/2004... **934**
CDLA 4389/2004... **933**
CDLA 1465/2005... **932**
CDLA 487/2006... **908**
CF 6923/1999... **158**
CFC 25/1989... **296**
CFC 1537/1995... **274**
CG 1479/1999... **958**
CG 2122/2001... **949**
CG 3657/2001... **914**
CH 3776/2001... **510**
CH 3853/2001... **viii, 168, 234**
CH 3853/2001... **908**
CH 4065/2001... **412, 417**
CH 4943/2001... **389, 411, 432, 929**

CH 5135/2001... **384**
CH 5147/2001... **226**
CH 5217/2001... **395, 396**
CH 5221/2001... **162, 929**
CH 393/2002... **212**
CH 396/2002... **225, 234, 929**
CH 474/2002... **384**
CH 627/2002... **160**
CH 716/2002... **225, 231, 234**
CH 843/2002... **225**
CH 844/2002... **257**
CH 999/2002... **389**
CH 1076/2002... **161, 227, 228, 229**
CH 1085/2002... **163, 211, 929**
CH 1129/2002... **152, 156**
CH 1171/2002... **153, 218, 220, 225**
CH 1172/2002... **417**
CH 1175/2002... **152, 157, 357, 1080**
CH 1296/2002... **413**
CH 1325/2002... **229**
CH 1618/2002... **220**
CH 1992/2002... **1114**
CH 1993/2002... **1114**
CH 2191/2002... **384**
CH 2201/2002... **211, 213, 413**
CH 2302/2002... **147, 164, 411**
CH 2321/2002... **300, 304, 308, 317, 415, 480**
CH 2323/2002... **930**
CH 2349/2002... **164, 432**
CH 2387/2002... **297**
CH 2443/2002... **423**
CH 2521/2002... **211**
CH 2554/2002... **416, 418**
CH 2659/2002... **384, 936**
CH 2888/2002... **417**
CH 3008/2002... **226, 236**
CH 3009/2002... **152, 384, 950, 955, 964**
CH 3302/2002... **413**
CH 3376/2002... **222**
CH 3594/2002... **162, 931**
CH 3629/2002... **417**
CH 3679/2002... **162, 414, 422, 952**
CH 3776/2002... **258**
CH 4099/2002... **396**
CH 4383/2002... **417**
CH 4465/2002... **416, 417**
CH 4483/2002... **936**
CH 4546/2002... **213**

CH 4817/2002... **431**
CH 4831/2002... **930**
CH 4876/2002... **166**
CH 4922/2002... **219**
CH 4970/2002... **930, 1110, 1114**
CH 4972/2002... **320**
CH 5088/2002... **930**
CH 5125/2002... **96**
CH 5299/2002... **357**
CH 5302/2002... **234**
CH 5553/2002... **432, 500**
CH 69/2003... **415**
CH 216/2003... **396**
CH 296/2003... **197**
CH 299/2003... **937**
CH 329/2003... **292, 301**
CH 393/2003... **384**
CH 663/2003... **221, 227, 228**
CH 943/2003... **372, 414, 415**
CH 1176/2003... **417, 418**
CH 1208/2003... **219, 268**
CH 1210/2003... **168**
CH 1278/2003... **196, 197**
CH 1953/2003... **329**
CH 2214/2003... **1115**
CH 2329/2003... **227, 229, 256**
CH 2516/2003... **237**
CH 2743/2003... **196**
CH 2791/2003... **421**
CH 3110/2003... **257**
CH 3197/2003... **329**
CH 3579/2003... **908**
CH 3616/2003... **196, 234**
CH 3743/2003... **227, 228**
CH 4354/2003... **165, 411, 904**
CH 4390/2003... **389**
CH 4574/2003... **135, 216**
CH 4733/2003... **232, 233, 234**
CH 4854/2003... **227**
CH 4918/2003... **415, 416**
CH 296/2004... **160, 227, 228, 234**
CH 609/2004... **417**
CH 939/2004... **414**
CH 996/2004... **216, 384**
CH 1097/2004... **228**
CH 1237/2004... **215, 216**
CH 1326/2004... **235**
CH 1586/2004... **viii, 224, 225, 234**
CH 1762/2004... **359**
CH 1791/2004... **383**
CH 1854/2004... **214**
CH 2258/2004... **196**
CH 2517/2004... **478**
CH 2794/2004... **390, 392, 414, 416**
CH 3439/2004... **416, 934**

CH 3656/2004... **230**
CH 3817/2004... **377, 384, 952, 987**
CH 3857/2004... **214**
CH 3893/2004... **215**
CH 4234/2004... **45**
CH 257/2005... **220**
CH 318/2005... **199**
CH 704/2005... **169**
CH 1220/2005... **162**
CH 1419/2005... **238**
CH 1450/2005... **308**
CH 1561/2005... **278, 279, 372**
CH 1675/2005... **418**
CH 1786/2005... **211**
CH 2193/2005... **45**
CH 2409/2005... **416**
CH 2553/2005... **910, 938**
CH 2899/2005... **227, 228**
CH 2986/2005... **404, 511, 510**
CH 3083/2005... **414**
CH 3314/2005... **247**
CH 3402/2005... **383**
CH 3497/2005... **984**
CH 3761/2005... **414, 415**
CH 4108/2005... **405**
CH 48/2006... **363**
CH 180/2006... **404, 408**
CH 282/2006... **970**
CH 532/2006... **174, 394**
CH 533/2006... **174**
CH 542/2006... **230**
CH 687/2006... **415**
CH 858/2006... **413**
CH 1363/2006... **214**
CH 1821/2006... **405**
CH 1822/2006... **324**
CH 1911/2006... **213**
CH 2121/2006... **221**
CH 2959/2006... **218**
CH 2995/2006... **vii, 972, 973, 974, 975, 976**
CH 3282/2006... **227**
CH 3629/2006... **403**
CH 3736/2006... **368, 976**
CH 3933/2006... **13, 572**
CH 402/2007... **vii, 975, 976, 991**
CH 779/2007... **1103**
CH 1009/2007... **304**
CH 1289/2007... **1103, 1104**
CH 1384/2007... **636**
CH 3631/2007... **987**
CI 141/1987... **935**
CI 3887/1999... **940**
CI 5880/1999... **937**
CI 1021/2001... **929**

CI 3596/2001... **166**
CI 2000/2004... **907, 907**
CIB 24/1997... **931**
CIB 3013/1997... **940**
CIB 4497/1998... **935**
CIB 213/1999... **999**
CIB 5227/1999... **163**
CIB 3985/2001... **133**
CIB 4427/2002... **158**
CIB 4667/2002... **163**
CIB 4193/2003... **922**
CIB 805/2004... **915**
CIB 1009/2004... **931, 932, 934**
CIB 2058/2004... **931**
CIB 4253/2004... **919**
CIB 2949/2005... **158**
CIS 124/1990... **322**
CIS 159/1990... **423**
CIS 93/1991... **315**
CIS 195/1991... **227**
CIS 222/1991... **423**
CIS 754/1991... **221**
CIS 93/1992... **960**
CIS 395/1992... **423**
CIS 522/1992... **432**
CIS 671/1992... **23**
CIS 30/1993... **322**
CIS 77/1993... **298**
CIS 87/1993... **21, 22**
CIS 393/1993... **423**
CIS 590/1993... **297**
CIS 166/1994... **5**
CIS 368/1994... **496**
CIS 372/1994... **423**
CIS 564/1994... **250**
CIS 683/1994... **429**
CIS 10/1995... **249**
CIS 147/1995... **905**
CIS 1460/1995... **445, 446**
CIS 2326/1995... **242, 243, 244, 245**
CIS 5136/1995... **244, 245**
CIS 8111/1995... **243, 244**
CIS 11304/1995... **23**
CIS 11481/1995... **242**
CIS 11293/1996... **457, 1100**
CIS 12703/1996... **244, 245**
CIS 13498/1996... **242, 244, 245**
CIS 13986/1996... **344**
CIS 14591/1996... **245**
CIS 14850/1996... **200**
CIS 15611/1996... **460**
CIS 15927/1996... **242**
CIS 16410/1996... **242, 247**
CIS 16992/1996... **1055, 1056**
CIS 85/1997... **204**

CIS 1137/1997... **1121**
CIS 1304/1997... **245**
CIS 1586/1997... **322**
CIS 2575/1997... **329**
CIS 3283/1997... **328, 329**
CIS 3287/1997... **18**
CIS 3955/1997... **1056**
CIS 6002/1997... **163, 933, 942**
CIS 2132/1998... **936**
CIS 3418/1998... **1073**
CIS 4341/1998... **1121**
CIS 114/1999... **313**
CIS 217/1999... **958**
CIS 1077/1999... **1057**
CIS 1115/1999... **1056**
CIS 1769/1999... **940**
CIS 2428/1999... **157**
CIS 5825/1999... **431**
CIS 6088/1999... **1057**
CIS 6249/1999... **955**
CIS 6258/1999... **1056**
CIS 2292/2000... **933**
CIS 2345/2001... **935**
CIS 3508/2001... **1028**
CIS 4533/2001... **158, 159**
CIS 47/2002... **1028**
CIS 376/2002... **245**
CIS 521/2002... **483**
CIS 1277/2002... **968**
CIS 4901/2002... **930, 982**
CIS 426/2003... **1028**
CIS 1870/2003... **138**
CIS 1972/2003... **244**
CIS 4348/2003... **423**
CIS 4474/2003... **242, 244**
CIS 1344/2004... **109**
CIS 1675/2004... **964**
CIS 218/2005... **323**
CIS 1363/2005... **934**
CIS 2559/2005... **244**
CIS 3182/2005... **248**
CIS 3573/2005... **245**
CIS 3811/2005... **924**
CIS 3875/2005... **249**
CIS 624/2006... **153, 156**
CIS 1068/2006... **485**
CIS 1757 2006... **324**
CIS 2317/2006... **274**
CIS 2448/2006... **489**
CIS 2661/2006... **329**
CJSA 3979/1999... **390**
CJSA 4705/1999... **250**
CJSA 2375/2000... **157**
CJSA 322/2001... **937**
CJSA 5100/2001... **133, 161, 924**

CJSA 3702/2002... **250**
CJSA 549/2003... **308**
CJSA 1425/2004... **323**
CJSA 3832/2006... **205**
CJSA 3960/2006... **982**
CM 264/1993... **940**
CP 8001/1995... **21, 22**
CP 4479/2000... **979**
CP 5084/2001... **141**
CP 518/2003... **138, 139**
CPC 683/2007... **487**
CS 249/1989... **290**
CS 79/1990... **164**
CS 130/1992... **423**
CS 12770/1996... **423**
CS 14430/1996... **157**
CS 2647/1997... **290**
CS 1753/2000... **932**
CSB 150/1985... **21**
CSB 1006/1985... **423**
CSB 64/1986... **423**
CSB 598/1987... **322**
CSB 950/1987... **692**
CSDLA 855/1997... **164**
CSDLA 90/1998... **931**
CSDLA 71/1999... **905**
CSDLA 536/1999... **905**
CSDLA 1019/1999... **131, 164**
CSDLA 300/2000... **906**
CSDLA 336/2000... **157, 162**
CSDLA 531/2000... **935**
CSDLA 1207/2000... **903, 906**
CSDLA 2/2001... **904, 945**
CSDLA 2/2002... **157**
CSDLA 866/2002... **920, 936**
CSDLA 606/2003... **163, 928**
CSG 336/2003... **904**
CSHB 718/2002... **220, 225, 236, 415**
CSHB 405/2005... **215**
CSHB 606/2005... **222**
CSHB 873/2005... **213**
CSHC 352/2002... **384, 936, 940**
CSHC 729/2003... **932**
CSIB 848/1997... **163**
CSIB 389/1998... **157**
CSIB 588/1998... **157, 162**
CSIB 377/2003... **930**
CSIS 62/1991... **432**
CSIS 100/1993... **200**
CSIS 185/1995... **201**
CSIS 460/2002... **133**
CTC 626/2001... **297**
CU 47/1993... **162**
CU 12/1994... **905**
R 3/05 (DLA)... **153**

R(A) 1/72... **161, 936**
R(CS) 5/02... **160**
R(CS) 3/04... **949**
R(CS) 5/96... **244**
R(DLA) 2/01... **157**
R(DLA) 3/01... **149, 157**
R(DLA) 6/01... **167**
R(DLA) 4/02... **135**
R(DLA) 1/03... **154**
R(DLA) 5/04... **155**
R(DLA) 3/05... **950**
R(FC) 2/90... **204**
R(FC) 1/91... **304**
R(FC) 3/98... **174**
R(G) 1/79... **22**
R(H) 1/02... **156, 162, 396, 418**
R(H) 1/03... **161, 226, 227**
R(H) 2/03... **389, 432, 991**
R(H) 3/03... **225, 411**
R(H) 1/04... **413, 414, 415**
R(H) 2/04... **413, 415**
R(H) 3/04... **43, 44, 45, 66, 148, 150, 151, 153, 154, 155, 168, 396, 431, 991**
R(H) 5/04... **389, 431**
R(H) 6/04... **148, 411, 993**
R(H) 7/04... **155**
R(H) 8/04... **136, 137, 138, 224, 226**
R(H) 9/04... **251, 251**
R(H) 1/05... **431**
R(H) 2/05... **1112**
R(H) 3/05... **394**
R(H) 4/05... **579**
R(H) 5/05... **222, 280, 476**
R(H) 6/05... **231**
R(H) 7/05... **197, 225, 236**
R(H) 9/05... **211, 213, 214**
R(H) 10/05... **226, 236**
R(H) 1/06... **322, 323**
R(H) 2/06... **390**
R(H) 3/06... **1110**
R(H) 4/06... **214**
R(H) 5/06... **230**
R(H) 6/06... **43, 45, 155, 156, 420, 421, 991**
R(H) 7/06... **30**
R(H) 1/07... **957, 980, 985, 993**
R(H) 2/07... **1103**
R(H) 3/07... **196**
R(H) 4/07... **214, 215**
R(H) 5/07... **304**
R(H) 6/07... **234**
R(H) 7/07... **1103**
R(H) 8/07... **197**
R(H) 9/07... **366, 383**
R(I) 5/02... **949**

R(I) 1/03... **174, 910**
R(I) 2/06... **161**
R(I) 7/62... **988**
R(I) 2/83... **988**
R(I) 5/91... **905**
R(I) 2/94... **964**
R(IB) 3/03... **95**
R(IB) 6/03... **153**
R(IB) 2/04... **150, 152, 156, 397, 405, 411, 929, 955, 956, 963, 964**
R(IB) 4/04... **250**
R(IB) 6/05... **167**
R(IB) 2/07... **96**
R(IS) 1/90... **316**
R(IS) 2/90... **319**
R(IS) 5/92... **432**
R(IS) 6/92... **297, 298**
R(IS) 12/92... **315**
R(IS) 1/93... **204**
R(IS) 3/93... **281**
R(IS) 14/93... **235, 324**
R(IS) 17/93... **217, 364**
R(IS) 21/93... **319**
R(IS) 17/94... **221**
R(IS) 5/95... **204**
R(IS) 8/95... **205**
R(IS) 16/95... **336**
R(IS) 21/95... **204**
R(IS) 22/95... **204**
R(IS) 1/96... **344**
R(IS) 6/96... **242, 243, 244, 245**
R(IS) 8/96... **290**
R(IS) 12/96... **200**
R(IS) 3/97... **248**
R(IS) 11/98... **227**
R(IS) 12/98... **247**
R(IS) 15/98... **342**
R(IS) 19/98... **336**
R(IS) 22/98... **280**
R(IS) 1/99... **23**
R(IS) 5/99... **336**
R(IS) 7/99... **344**
R(IS) 8/99... **17**
R(IS) 11/99... **161, 905, 945**
R(IS) 1/00... **342**
R(IS) 6/00... **249**
R(IS) 3/01... **756**
R(IS) 6/01... **164, 987, 988**
R(IS) 10/01... **313**
R(IS) 2/02... **1057, 1075**
R(IS) 4/03... **329**
R(IS) 5/03... **424**
R(IS) 6/03... **280**
R(IS) 1/04... **132, 133**
R(IS) 2/04... **133**

R(IS) 3/04... **987**
R(IS) 5/04... **937**
R(IS) 6/04... **131, 132, 134, 989**
R(IS) 15/04... **132, 955, 956, 958, 959, 980**
R(IS) 16/04... **756, 982**
R(IS) 17/04... **928**
R(IS) 5/05... **487**
R(IS) 7/05... **423**
R(IS) 11/06... **138**
R(IS) 13/99... **204**
R(JSA) 1/02... **329**
R(JSA) 2/02... **344**
R(JSA) 3/02... **344**
R(JSA) 4/03... **205**
R(JSA) 1/07... **205**
R(M) 1/87... **905**
R(P) 1/06... **141**
R(P) 2/06... **136**
R(S) 2/63(T)... **384**
R(S) 4/82... **929**
R(S) 4/84... **290**
R(S) 8/85... **905**
R(S) 4/86... **956, 964**
R(SB) 10/81... **212, 489**
R(SB) 17/81... **21, 22**
R(SB) 13/82... **23**
R(SB) 21/82... **423**
R(SB) 2/83... **162**
R(SB) 4/83... **23**
R(SB) 20/83... **336**
R(SB) 30/83... **23**
R(SB) 41/83... **342**
R(SB) 54/83... **423**
R(SB) 13/84... **486**
R(SB) 25/84... **987**
R(SB) 27/84... **486**
R(SB) 40/84... **423**
R(SB) 1/85... **316**
R(SB) 4/85... **169**
R(SB) 8/85... **23**
R(SB) 9/85... **423**
R(SB) 18/85... **423**
R(SB) 35/85... **21**
R(SB) 38/85... **322**
R(SB) 40/85... **322**
R(SB) 21/86... **297**
R(SB) 12/87... **457, 464**
R(SB) 15/87... **423**
R(SB) 22/87... **230**
R(SB) 25/87... **336**
R(SB) 2/89... **313, 324**
R(SB) 1/90... **250**
R(SB) 5/91... **637**
R(SB) 9/91... **322**

R(SB) 12/91... **323**

R(TC) 1/05... **960, 981**

R3/05 (DLA)... **155**

Housing Benefit Regulations:
Destinations table

General

HB Regs 1987	HB Regs 2006		HB (SPC) Regs 2006	
Reg 1	1	p185	1	p682
Reg 2	2	p185	2	p683
Reg 2B	4	p201	4	p692
Reg 3	3	p199	3	p692
	New Reg 5	p202	New Reg 5	p693
Reg 4	6	p202	6	p693

Provisions affecting entitlement to housing benefit

HB Regs 1987	HB Regs 2006		HB (SPC) Regs 2006	
Reg 5	7	p206	7	p694
Reg 6	8	p217	8	p698
Reg 7	9	p223	9	p698
Reg 7A	10	p239	10	p700
Reg 7B	Sch 4 SI 2006 No 217	p1125	Sch 4 SI 2006 No 217	p1125

Payments in respect of a dwelling

HB Regs 1987	HB Regs 2006		HB (SPC) Regs 2006	
Reg 8	11	p252	11	p702
Reg 8A	Sch 10	p510	Sch 9	p801
	New reg 11A	p253	New reg 11A	p702
Reg 10	12	p253	12	p702
	New reg 12A	p259	New reg 12A	p704
Reg 11	13	p259	13	p704
Reg 11A	Sch 10	p510	Sch 9	p801
Reg 11B	Sch 10	p510	Sch 9	p801
Old reg 12	Sch 3 paras 4 and 5 SI 2006 No 217	p1125	Sch 3 paras 4 and 5 SI 2006 No 217	p1099
	New reg 13ZA	p265	New reg 13ZA	p707
	New reg 13A	p265	New reg 13A	p707
	New reg 13B	p265	New reg 13B	p707
Reg 12A	14	p265	14	p707
Reg 12B	15	p269	15	p709
Reg 12C	17	p271	17	p711
Reg 12CA	16	p269	16	p710
Reg 12D	18	p271	18	p711
			New reg 18A	p711
Reg 12E	Sch 10	p510	Sch 9	p801

Membership of a family

HB Regs 1987	HB Regs 2006		HB (SPC) Regs 2006	
Reg 13	19	p272	19	p711
Reg 14	20	p273	20	p712
Reg 15	21	p274	21	p712

Applicable amounts

HB Regs 1987	HB Regs 2006		HB&CTB (SPC) Regs 2003 substituted reg	HB (SPC) Regs 2006	
Reg 16	22	p276	Reg 16	22	p713
Reg 17	23	p277			
Reg 18	24 Now revoked	p278			

Income and capital

HB Regs 1987	HB Regs 2006		HB&CTB (SPC) Regs 2003 substituted reg	HB (SPC) Regs 2006	
Reg 19	25	p282	Reg 19	23	p714
Reg 20	26	p283	Reg 20	24	p715
Reg 21	27	p284	Reg 21	25	p715
Reg 21A	28	p285	Reg 22	26	p715
Reg 22	29	p290	Reg 23	27	p715
Reg 23	30	p292	Reg 24	28	p717
Reg 24	31	p292	Reg 25	29	p717
Reg 24A	32	p293	Reg 26	30	p720
Reg 25	33	p294	Reg 27	31	p721
Reg 28	35	p295	Reg 28	33	p724
Reg 29	36	p299	Reg 29	34	p726
Reg 30	37	p301	Reg 30	35	p727
Reg 31	38	p301	Reg 31	36	p728
Reg 32	39	p305	Reg 32	37	p729
Reg 33	40	p306	Reg 33	38	p729
Reg 34	41	p308	Reg 34	39	p730
Reg 35	42	p309	Reg 35	40	p732
Reg 37	43	p316	Reg 36	41	p732
Reg 38	44	p316	Reg 37	42	p735
Reg 39	45	p317	Reg 38	43	p735
Reg 40	46	p317	Reg 39	44	p735
Reg 41	47	p318	Reg 40	45	p736
Reg 42	48	p319	Reg 41	46	p736
Reg 43	49	p320	Reg 42	47	p736
Reg 43A	50	p325	Reg 43	48	p737
Reg 44	51	p328	Reg 44	49	p739
Reg 45	52	p330			

Students

HB Regs 1987	HB Regs 2006	
Reg 46	53	p332
Reg 47	54	p337
Reg 48	55	p338
Reg 48A	56	p339
Reg 50	57	p344
Reg 52	58	p346
Reg 53	59	p346
Reg 54	60	p349
Reg 55	61	p349
Reg 56	62	p350
Reg 57	63	p350
Reg 57A	64	p351
	New reg 64A	p354
Reg 57B	65	p354
Reg 58	66	p355
Reg 58A	67	p355
Reg 59	68	p355
Reg 60	69	p356

Amount of benefit

HB Regs 1987	HB Regs 2006		HB&CTB (SPC) Regs 2003 inserted reg	HB (SPC) Regs 2006	
Reg 61	70	p356		50	p739
Reg 62	71	p357		51	p740
				New reg 52	p740
Reg 62A	72	p357			
Reg 62ZB	73	p359		53	p740
			Reg 62B	54	p741
Reg 63	74	p361		55	p742
Reg 64	75	p365		56	p744

Claims

HB Regs 1987	HB Regs 2006		HB (SPC) Regs 2006	
Reg 71	82	p376	63	p753
Reg 72	83	p378	64	p754
	New Reg 83A	p385		
Reg 72A	84	p385	65	p756
Reg 72B	85	p386	66	p757
Reg 72BA	No provision		64(1)	p754
Reg 73	86	p387	67	p757
Reg 74	87	p390	68	p759
Reg 75	88	p390	69	p759
	New Reg 88A	p393		

Decisions on questions

HB Regs 1987	HB Regs 2006		HB (SPC) Regs 2006	
Reg 76	89	p393	70	p760
Reg 77	90	p394	71	p761

Payments

HB Regs 1987	HB Regs 2006		HB (SPC) Regs 2006	
Reg 88	91	p398	72	p761
	New reg 91A	p399	New reg 72A	p762
Reg 90	92	p400	73	p762
Reg 91	93	p402	74	p763
Reg 92	94	p403	75	p763
Reg 93	95	p404	76	p763
Reg 94	96	p407	77	p764
Reg 96	97	p409	78	p765
Reg 97	98	p410	79	p765

Overpayments

HB Regs 1987	HB Regs 2006		HB (SPC) Regs 2006	
Reg 98	99	p410	80	p765
Reg 99	100	p411	81	p765
Reg 100	101	p419	82	p766
Reg 101	102	p424	83	p767
Reg 102	103	p429	84	p768
Reg 103	104	p431	85	p769
Reg 104	105	p433	86	p769
1997/2435 106	106	p433	87	p770
1997/2435 107	107	p434	88	p770

Information

Source	HB Regs 2006		HB (SPC) Regs 2006	
SI 2002 No 1132, reg 2	108	p435	89	p771
SI 2002 No 1132, reg 3	109	p436	90	p771
	New reg 109A	p436	New reg 90A	p771
SI 2002 No 1132, reg 4	110	p436	91	p771
SI 2002 No 1132, reg 5	111	p436	92	p772
SI 2002 No 1132, reg 6	112	p437	93	p772
SI 1997 No 2436, reg 1	113	p437	94	p772
HB Regs 1987, reg 106	114	p437	95	p772
SI 1988 No 662, reg 5	115	p438	96	p773
SI 1988 No 662, reg 6	116	p439	97	p774
SI 1997 No 2436, reg 2	117	p440	98	p774
SI 1997 No 2436, reg 3	118	p440	99	p775
SI 1997 No 2436, reg 4	119	p441	100	p775
SI 1997 No 2436, reg 5	120	p443	101	p777
SI 1997 No 2436, reg 6	121	p443	102	p777
	New reg 122	p444	New reg 103	p777

Schedules

HB Regs 1987	HB Regs 2006		HB&CTB (SPC) Regs 2003	HB (SPC) Regs 2006	
Sch A1	2006/217 Sch 4	p1125		2006/217 Sch 4	p1125
Sch 1	Sch 1	p444		Sch 1	p777
Sch 1A	Sch 2	p448		Sch 2	p780
Sch 2	Sch 3	p451			
			Sch 2A	Sch 3	p782
Sch 3	Sch 4	p465			
			Sch 3A	Sch 4	p785
Sch 4	Sch 5	p472			
			Sch 4A	Sch 5	p788
Sch 5	Sch 6	p486			
			Sch 5ZA	Sch 6	p792
Sch 5A	Sch7	p499			
Sch 5B	Sch 8	p503		Sch 7	p797
Sch 6	Sch 9	p504		Sch 8	p799
	New Sch 10	p510		New Sch 9	p801
	New Sch 11	p518		New Sch 10	p810

Council Tax Benefit Regulations: Destinations table

CTB Regs 1992	CTB Regs 2006			CTB (SPC) Regs	
Reg 1	1		p564	1	p815
Reg 2	2		p564	2	p815
Reg 2B	4		p574	4	p822
Reg 3	3		p573	3	p822
	New reg 5		p574	New reg 5	p823
Reg 4	6		p574	6	p823
Reg 4A	7		p575	7	p823
	New reg 7A		p577	New reg 7A	p825
Reg 4C	8		p577	8	p825
Reg 4D	Sch 4 SI 2006 No 217		p1125	Sch 4 SI 2006 No 217	p1125

CTB Regs 1992	CTB Regs 2006			CTB (SPC) Regs	
Reg 5	9		p579	9	p827
Reg 6	10		p579	10	p828
Reg 7	11		p580	11	p828

Applicable amounts

CTB Regs 1992	CTB Regs 2006		HB&CTB (SPC) Regs 2003 substituted reg	CTB (SPC) Regs 2006	
Reg 8	12	p581	Reg 8	12	p829
Reg 9	13	p581			
Reg 10	14	p581			

Income and capital

CTB Regs 1992	CTB Regs 2006		HB&CTB (SPC) Regs 2003 substituted reg	CTB (SPC) Regs 2006	
Reg 11	15	p582		13	p829
Reg 12	16	p582		14	p830
Reg 13	17	p582	Reg 13	15	p830
Reg 13A	18	p583	Reg 14	16	p830
Reg 14	19	p586	Reg 15	17	p830
Reg 15	20	p587	Reg 16	18	p831
Reg 16	21	p587	Reg 17	19	p831
Reg 16A	22	p587	Reg 18	20	p834
Reg 17	23	p588	Reg 19	21	p834
Reg 18	24	p588	Reg 19A	22	p837
Reg 19	25	p588	Reg 20	23	p838
Reg 20	26	p589	Reg 21	24	p839
Reg 21	27	p590	Reg 23	25	p839

CTB Regs 1992	CTB Regs 2006		HB&CTB (SPC) Regs 2003 substituted reg	CTB (SPC) Regs 2006	
Reg 22	28	p591	Reg 23	26	p840
Reg 23	29	p592	Reg 24	27	p841
Reg 24	30	p593	Reg 25	28	p842
Reg 25	31	p594	Reg 26	29	p842
Reg 26	32	p595	Reg 27	30	p844
Reg 28	33	p598	Reg 28	31	p845
Reg 29	34	p598	Reg 29	32	p846
Reg 30	35	p598	Reg 30	33	p847
Reg 31	36	p598	Reg 31	34	p847
Reg 32	37	p599	Reg 32	35	p847
Reg 33	38	p599	Reg 33	36	p847
Reg 34	39	p599	Reg 34	37	p847
Reg 35	40	p601	Reg 35	38	p848
Reg 36	41	p603	Reg 36	39	p850
Reg 37	42	p603			

Students

CTB Regs 1992	CTB Regs 2006	
Reg 38	43	p604
Reg 39	44	p607
Reg 40	45	p608
Reg 42	46	p610
Reg 43	47	p611
Reg 44	48	p611
Reg 45	49	p612
Reg 46	50	p612
Reg 47	51	p612
	New reg 51A	p614
Reg 47A	52	p614
Reg 48	53	p614
Reg 48A	54	p614
Reg 49	55	p614
Reg 50	56	p615

Amount of benefit

CTB Regs 1992	CTB Regs 2006		HB&CTB (SPC) Regs 2003 inserted reg	CTB (SPC) Regs 2006	
Reg 51	57	p615		40	p851
				New reg 41	p851
Reg 52	58	p616		42	p851
Reg 53	59	p617		43	p853
Reg 53A	60	p617		No provision	
Reg 53ZB	61	p618		44	p853
			Reg 53B	45	p854
Reg 54	62	p619		46	p855
Reg 55	63	p620		47	p855

Changes of circumstances and increases for exceptional circumstances

CTB Regs 1992	CTB Regs 2006		CTB (SPC) Regs 2006	
Reg 56	64	p621	48	p856
Reg 56A	65	p621	No provision	
Reg 56B	66	p622	49	p856
Reg 59	67	p622	50	p857
Reg 59B	No provision		51	p858

Claims

CTB Regs 1992	CTB Regs 2006		CTB (SPC) Regs 2006	
Reg 61	68	p623	52	p859
Reg 62	69	p624	53	p860
	New reg 69A	p627	New reg 53A	p863
Reg 62A	70	p627	54	p863
Reg 62B	71	p628	55	p864
Reg 62BA	No provision		56	p864
Reg 63	72	p629	57	p864
Reg 64	73	p630	58	p866
Reg 65	74	p630	59	p866
	New reg 74A	p631	New reg 59A	p867

Decisions on questions

CTB Regs 1992	CTB Regs 2006		CTB (SPC) Regs 2006	
Reg 66	75	p632	60	p868
Reg 67	76	p632	61	p868

Awards or payments of benefit

CTB Regs 1992	CTB Regs 2006		CTB (SPC) Regs 2006	
Reg 77	77	p632	62	p868
Reg 78	78	p633	63	p869
Reg 79	79	p633	64	p869
Reg 81	80	p634	65	p869
Reg 82	81	p634	66	p870

Excess benefit

CTB Regs 1992	CTB Regs 2006		CTB (SPC) Regs 2006	
Reg 83	82	p635	67	p870
Reg 84	83	p635	68	p870
Reg 85	84	p636	69	p871
Reg 86	85	p636	70	p871
Reg 87	86	p636	71	p871
Reg 88	87	p637	72	p872
Reg 89	88	p637	73	p872
Reg 90	89	p638	74	p872
Reg 91	90	p638	75	p872

Information

Source	CTB Regs 2006		CTB (SPC) Regs 2006	
SI 2002 No 1132, reg 2	91	p639	76	p873
SI 2002 No 1132, reg 3	92	p639	77	p873
	New reg 92A	p639	New reg 77A	p874
SI 2002 No 1132, reg 4	93	p639	78	p874
SI 2002 No 1132, reg 5	94	p640	79	p874
SI 2002 No 1132, reg 6	95	p640	80	p874
Reg 95	96	p640	81	p875
Reg 96	97	p641	82	p876

Schedules

CTB Regs 1992	CTB Regs 2006		HB&CTB (SPC) Regs 2003	CTB (SPC) Regs 2006	
Sch A1	2006/217 Sch 4	p1125		2006/217 Sch 4	p1125
	Sch A1	p642		Sch A1	p876
Sch 1	Sch 1	p642			
			Sch 1A	Sch 1	p877
Sch 2	Sch 2	p650		Sch 6	p890
Sch 3	Sch 3	p651			
			Sch 3A	Sch 2	p880
Sch 4	Sch 4	p654			
			Sch 4A	Sch 3	p882
Sch 5	Sch 5	p662			
			Sch 5ZA	Sch 4	p885
Sch 5A	Sch 6	p669			
Sch 5B	Sch 7	p671		Sch 5	p889
Sch 6	Sch 8	p672		Sch 7	p891
	New Sch 9	p674		New Sch 8	p894

Table of abbreviations

Abbreviation	Meaning
AC	Appeal Cases Law Reports
AIT	Asylum and Immigration Tribunal
All ER	All England Reports
Art, Arts	Article, Articles
BC	Borough Council
BHRC	Butterworth's Human Rights Cases
CA	Carer's allowance
CA	Court of Appeal
CCLR	Community Care Law Reports
Ch	Chancery Division Law Reports
Ch D	Chancery Division
CIS, CH etc	Unreported Commissioner's decision (see introductory notes for an explanation)
Cm	Command Paper
CMLR	Common Market Law Reports
COD	Crown Office Digest
CSIH	Inner House of the Court of Session
CSOH	Outer House of the Court of Session
CSPSSA	Child Support, Pensions and Social Security Act 2000
CTB	Council tax benefit
CTB Regs	Council Tax Benefit Regulations 2006
CTB(SPC) Regs	Council Tax Benefit (Persons who have attained the qualifying age for state pension credit) Regulations 2006
CTB Regs 1992	Council Tax Benefit (General) Regulations 1992
CTC	Child tax credit
D&A Regs	Housing Benefit and Council Tax Benefit (Decisions and Appeals) Regulations 2001
D&A Transitional Regs	Housing Benefit and Council Tax Benefit (Decisions and Appeals) (Transitional and Savings) Regulations 2001
DC	District Council
DSS	Department of Social Security (predecessor to the DWP)
DWP	Department of Work and Pensions
ECJ	European Court of Justice
ECR	European Court Reports
ECtHR	European Court of Human Rights
ECmHR	European Commission of Human Rights
EHRR	European Human Rights Reports
EU	European Union
EWCA Civ	Court of Appeal Civil Division transcript
EWHC [number] (Admin), EWHC Admin	Administrative Court transcript
Ex p	Ex parte

Abbreviation	Meaning
FLR	Family Law Reports
GM	*Housing Benefit and Council Tax Benefit Guidance Manual* (DWP looseleaf publication, also available at www.dwp.gov.uk/advisers)
HB	Housing benefit
HB Regs	Housing Benefit Regulations 2006
HB(SPC) Regs	Housing Benefit (Persons who have attained the qualifying age for state pension credit) Regulations 2006
HB Regs 1987	Housing Benefit (General) Regulations 1987
HB&CTB (CP) Regs	Housing Benefit and Council Tax Benefit (Consequential Provisions) Regulations 2006
HBRB	Housing Benefit Review Board
HHJ	His/Her Honour Judge
HL	House of Lords
HLR	Housing Law Reports
Imm AR	Immigration Appeal Reports
IS	Income support
J, JJ	Mr/Mrs Justice, Justices
JSA (IB)	Income-based jobseeker's allowance.
LBC	London Borough Council
LGR	Local Government Reports
LJ, LJJ	Lord/Lady Justice, Lord/Lady Justices
MBC	Metropolitan Borough Council
PC	Pension credit
para, paras	Paragraph, Paragraphs
Prot	Protocol (to European Convention on Human Rights)
QB	Queen's Bench Law Reports
QBD	Queen's Bench Division of the High Court
RBC	Royal Borough Council
reg, regs	Regulation, Regulations
R(IS), R(H) etc	Reported Commissioner's decision (see the introductory notes for an explanation)
RVR	Rating and Valuation Reporter
s, ss	Section, Sections
Sch, Schs	Schedule, Schedules
SI	Statutory Instrument
SLT	Scots Law Times
SSA	Social Security Act (of relevant year)
SSAA	Social Security Administration Act 1992
SSA(F)A	Social Security Administration (Fraud) Act 1997
SSCBA	Social Security Contributions and Benefits Act 1992
SSFA	Social Security Fraud Act 2001
SPCA	State Pension Credit Act 2002
TCA	Tax Credits Act 2002

Table of Abbreviations

Abbreviation	Meaning
Tribunals Service	Tribunals Service for Social Security and Child Support Appeals
vol	Volume
WLR	Weekly Law Reports

Abbreviation	Meaning
WRPA	Welfare Reform and Pensions Act 1999
WTC	Working tax credit

Part 1

Main primary legislation

Social Security Contributions and Benefits Act 1992

(1992 c4)

ARRANGEMENT OF SECTIONS
PART VII
INCOME-RELATED BENEFITS
GENERAL

123.   Income-related benefits

HOUSING BENEFIT

130.   Housing benefit
130B.   Loss of housing benefit following eviction on certain grounds
130C.   Relevant orders for possession
130D.   Loss of housing benefit: supplementary
130E.   Couples
130F.   Information provision
130G.   Pilot schemes relating to loss of housing benefit
131.   Council tax benefit
132.   Couples
133.   Polygamous marriages

GENERAL

134.   Exclusions from benefit
135.   The applicable amount
136.   Income and capital
137.   Interpretation of Part VII and supplementary provisions

PART XIII
GENERAL
INTERPRETATION

172.   Applications of Act in relation to territorial waters
173.   Age
174.   References to Acts

SUBORDINATE LEGISLATION

175.   Regulations, orders and schemes
176.   Parliamentary control

SHORT TITLE, COMMENCEMENT AND EXTENT

177.   Short title, commencement and extent

PART VII
Income-Related Benefits
General

Income-related benefits

123.–(1) Prescribed schemes shall provide for the following benefits (in this Act referred to as ''income-related benefits'')–

(a)-(c) *[omitted]*

(d)   housing benefit; and

[¹(e) council tax benefit.]

(2)   *[omitted]*

(3)   Every authority granting housing benefit–

(a)   shall take such steps as appear to them appropriate for the purpose of securing that persons who may be entitled to housing benefit from the authority become aware that they may be entitled to it; and

(b)   shall make copies of the housing benefit scheme, with any modifications adopted by them under the Administration Act, available for public inspection at their principal office at all reasonable hours without payment.

[²(4)   [⁴ Each billing authority and in Scotland each local authority]

(a)   shall take such steps as appear to it appropriate for the purpose of securing that any person who may be entitled to council tax benefit in respect of council tax payable to the authority becomes aware that he may be entitled to it; and

(b)   shall make copies of the council tax benefit scheme, with any modifications adopted by it under the Administration Act, available for public inspection at its principal office at all reasonable hours without payment.]

Definitions
> "Administration Act" – s174.
> "billing authority" – s137.

Amendments
> 1.   Substituted by LGFA Sch 9 para 1(1) (1.4.93).
> 2.   Substituted by LGFA Sch 9 para 1(2).
> 3.   Substituted by Local Government etc. (Scotland) Act 1994 Sch 13 para 174(4) (1.4.96).
> 4.   Substituted by the Welfare Reform Act 2007 reg 40 and Sch 5 para 1(2) (3.7.07).

General Note
> This section provides the core basis in primary legislation for the HB and CTB schemes.
>
> **Subs (1)** provides for the setting up of the HB and CTB schemes as two of the income-related benefits provided for under the SSCBA.
>
> **Subs (3) and (4)** oblige the relevant authorities to publicise the availability of assistance under the HB and CTB schemes. There are two separate obligations: to take steps to increase awareness of the availability of HB and CTB to those on low incomes; and to make copies of the schemes (this presumably being a reference to the relevant legislation) available for inspection free of charge. The duties are entirely general in nature and authorities adopt various methods of discharging them, from advertising to providing advice in courts where proceedings for possession of property are being heard.
>
> It seems likely that the duties would be regarded as "target duties" in public law terms and hence not enforceable by a member of the general public, but it might be possible for a claimant to pray in aid poor publicisation of HB or CTB entitlement in her/his locality as being a factor showing "good cause" for a late claim: see p383.
>
> For the power to make modifications to the HB and CTB schemes, see ss134(8) and 139(6) SSAA on pp81 and 84.

Housing benefit

Housing benefit

130.–(1)   A person is entitled to housing benefit if–

(a)   he is liable to make payments in respect of a dwelling in Great Britain which he occupies as his home;

(b)   there is an appropriate maximum housing benefit in his case; and

(c)   either–

    (i)   he has no income or his income does not exceed the applicable amount; or

    (ii)   his income exceeds that amount, but only by so much that there is an amount remaining if the deduction for which subsection (3)(b) below provides is made.

(2)   In subsection (1) above "payments in respect of a dwelling" means such payments as may be prescribed, but the power to prescribe payments does not include power to prescribe–

[¹[⁴ (a) payments to a billing authority or to a local authority in Scotland in respect of council tax;]

(b)   mortgage payments, or, in relation to Scotland, payments under heritable securities.]

(3)   Where a person is entitled to housing benefit, then–

(a)   if he has no income or his income does not exceed the applicable amount, the amount of the housing benefit shall be the amount which is the appropriate maximum housing benefit in his case; and

(b)   if his income exceeds the applicable amount, the amount of the housing benefit shall be what remains after the deduction from the appropriate maximum housing benefit of prescribed percentages of the excess of his income over the applicable amount.

(4)   Regulations shall prescribe the manner in which the appropriate maximum housing benefit is to be determined in any case.

(5)   [³ ...]

Definitions

"dwelling" – see s137.
"Great Britain" – s172(a).
"prescribe" – s137.

Amendments

1.   Substituted by LGFA Sch 9 para 3 (1.4.93).
2.   Substituted by Local Government etc. (Scotland) Act 1994 Sch 13 para 174(4) (1.4.96).
3.   Deleted by Housing Act 1996 s227 and Sch 19 Pt IV (1.4.97).
4.   Substituted by the Welfare Reform Act 2007 reg 40 and Sch 5 para 1(3) (3.7.07).

General Note

Subs (1) and (2) set out the basic conditions of entitlement to HB. In case it were not obvious from the use of the word "and" after sub-paras (a) and (b), it was confirmed in *CIS 166/1994* that the conditions of entitlement in the comparable s124 in relation to income support are cumulative and must all be satisfied. The conditions, and the principal parts of the HB Regs specifying the detail, are as follows:

(1)   The claimant is liable to make payments in respect of a dwelling in Great Britain which s/he occupies as her/his home: sub-para (1)(a). The question of whether s/he is liable is dealt with by regs 8, 9 and 10 of both the HB and the HB(SPC) Regs and the question of occupation by reg 7. "Great Britain" includes territorial waters by virtue of s172(a), a provision unlikely to be of relevance in this context, but excludes Northern Ireland which has its own benefit scheme administered by the Northern Ireland Housing Executive. It is permissible to make regulations under s137(2)(i) to treat only a specified category of people as if they were not liable to make payments: *R v Secretary of State for Social Security ex p Sarwar* [1997] 3 CMLR 647, CA. Subs (2) prevents any regulations being made to allow council tax (dealt with by CTB) and mortgage payments or heritable securities (partially dealt with by housing costs payable as part of IS, income-based JSA or PC) to be met by the HB scheme. The "payments" for which liability can attract HB are set out in reg 12(1) of both the HB and the HB(SPC) Regs.

(2)   There is an appropriate maximum HB in her/his case: sub-para (1)(b). Maximum HB is calculated under reg 70 HB Regs (see p356) and reg 50 HB(SPC) Regs (see p739).

(3)   The claimant's income is sufficiently low: sub-para (1)(c). Income is calculated under Part 6 of both the HB and the HB(SPC) Regs. For the "applicable amount" see Part 5 and Sch 3 of those regs. Sub-para (c)(ii) is awkwardly worded. The second time the word "amount" is used, it does not refer to the applicable amount but refers to what is left of the claimant's maximum HB once the appropriate proportion of her/his income has been deducted under reg 71 HB Regs (reg 51 HB(SPC) Regs). The prescribed percentage is currently 65 per cent. Before a claimant is entitled to be paid any HB, her/his "amount" must be at least the figure fixed by reg 75 HB Regs (reg 56 HB(SPC) Regs) (currently 50 pence).

Subs (3) provides for the amount of HB payable. Where the claimant's income is less than the applicable amount, the maximum HB is payable. Where the income exceeds the applicable amount, sub-para (b) provides for a "taper" under which entitlement declines gradually rather than instantly to nil. This is designed to minimise the impact of any poverty trap. The current percentage prescribed by reg 71 HB Regs (reg 51 HB(SPC) Regs) is 65 per cent. Thus if the applicable amount is £40 a week, the claimant has income of £50 a week and maximum HB is £60 a week, the HB payable is the maximum HB minus 65 per cent of the difference between £40 and £50, namely £53.50 (£60 – £6.50) a week.

Subs (4) allows for regulations defining maximum HB: see Parts 3 and 8 HB Regs and Parts 3 and 7 HB(SPC) Regs.

[¹Loss of housing benefit following eviction on certain grounds

130B–(1)   If the following conditions are satisfied, then housing benefit is payable in the case of a person ("the former occupier") subject to subsection (4)–

    (a)   a court makes a relevant order for possession of a dwelling occupied by him as his home;

    (b)   in consequence of the order he ceases to occupy the dwelling;

    (c)   either of the conditions in subsections (2) and (3) is satisfied; and

    (d)   the conditions for entitlement to housing benefit are or become satisfied with respect to him.

(2)   The condition in this subsection is that the former occupier fails, without good cause, to comply with a warning notice served on him by a relevant local authority in England and Wales after he has ceased to occupy the dwelling.

(3)   The condition in this subsection is that–

    (a)   the former occupier was, after he ceased to occupy the dwelling, required by a relevant local authority in Scotland to take specified action with the aim mentioned in subsection (10),

    (b)   the former occupier was warned by the relevant local authority that if he failed to comply with the requirement the amount of housing benefit payable to him would be affected,

    (c)   the former occupier fails, without good cause, to comply with the requirement, and

    (d)   the relevant local authority recommends that housing benefit be payable to the former occupier subject to subsection (4).

(4)   During the restriction period or such part of it as may be prescribed, one or both of the following applies–

    (a)   the rate of the benefit is reduced in such a manner as may be prescribed;

    (b)   the benefit is payable only if the circumstances are such as may be prescribed.

(5)   The restriction period begins with the earliest date on which the conditions set out in subsections (1) to (3) are satisfied.

(6)   That period stops running if the relevant local authority considers that the restriction set out in subsection (4) should no longer apply (whether because the former occupier is taking action to improve his behaviour or for any other reason), but starts running again if–

    (a)   in England and Wales, the former occupier fails to comply with a further warning notice served on him;

    (b)   in Scotland, the condition in subsection (7) is satisfied.

(7)   The condition is that–

    (a)   the former occupier fails to comply with a further requirement such as is mentioned in paragraph (a) of subsection (3), having been warned as mentioned in paragraph (b) of that subsection, and

    (b)   the relevant local authority recommends that the restriction period starts running again.

(8)   The restriction period shall not include any period which falls more than five years after the date on which the order for possession was made.

(9)   A former occupier may not be subject to more than one restriction period in respect of one order for possession.

(10)   A relevant local authority is–

    (a)   in England and Wales, a local authority within the meaning of section 1 of the Local Government Act 2000, or

(b) in Scotland, a council constituted under section 2 of the Local Government etc. (Scotland) Act 1994,

which provides or may provide services to a former occupier with the aim of ending, or preventing repetition of, the conduct which may lead or has led to the making of a relevant order for possession.

(11) A warning notice is a notice in the prescribed form–

(a) requiring the former occupier to take specified action with the aim mentioned in subsection (10),

(b) specifying the time when, or within which, that action must be taken, and

(c) warning the former occupier that if he fails to take the action the amount of housing benefit payable to him would be affected.]

Amendment

1. Inserted by s31(1) of the WRA 2007 (1.11.07).

General Note

HB sanctions for anti-social behaviour are not a new idea. The idea was first raised in a housing Green Paper, *Quality and choice; a decent home for all*, published in 2000, but the idea was dropped in the face of widespread opposition. A Private Members Bill on a similar issue in 2002 was unsuccessful. Regrettably, the proposals resurfaced and ss130B to 130G SSCBA now provide for the reduction, or non-payment, of a former occupier's HB following eviction for anti-social behaviour in certain circumstances. If the conditions in subs (1) are satisfied, then restricted HB is payable during a restriction period. It is understood that the intention is for a local authority to attempt to engage with the former occupier with the aim of ending, or preventing repetition of, the anti-social behaviour through the provision of rehabilitation.

The rules are currently being piloted in eight local authority areas in England. By s31(3) of the Welfare Reform Act 2007, the provisions end on 31 December 2010. Further primary legislation will be needed for the provisions to operate after that date.

Analysis

Subs (1) to (3). HB is paid at a reduced rate, or is non-payable, if a claimant is entitled to HB but a "relevant order for possession" of a dwelling the claimant formerly occupied as her/his home was made and in consequence of the order, s/he ceased to occupy that home: subs (1)(a), (b) and (d). Relevant orders for possession are defined in s130C. In addition, one of the following conditions must be satisfied:

(1) In England and Wales, the former occupier must have failed, without good cause, to comply with a warning notice to improve behaviour, served on her/him by the local authority after s/he left the former home: subs (1)(c) and (2). See subs (11) for the requirements for the warning notice.

(2) In Scotland, the former occupier must have failed, without good cause, to comply with a requirement, after s/he left the former home, to take specified action, having been warned that if s/he failed to do so the amount of HB payable to her/him would be affected: subs (1)(c) and (3). In addition, the local authority must have recommended that HB be affected. Note however, that the rules do not currently apply in Scotland.

Regs 5 and 6 of the Housing Benefit (Loss of Benefit) (Pilot Scheme) (Supplementary) Regulations 2007 (see p1145) set out what is to be taken into account in determining whether a person has, or does not have, good cause, and circumstances in which a person must be regarded as having good cause.

See in addition s130E where the claimant is a member of a couple.

Subs (4) provides powers to prescribe the rate of HB and the circumstances when HB is payable. The rates and circumstances are in reg 4 of the Housing Benefit (Loss of Benefit) (Pilot Scheme) Regulations 2007 (see p1140). See also reg 6 of those regulations where s7 of the SSFA 2001 also applies.

Subs (5) to (9): The "restriction period". The restriction period starts on the date on which the all the conditions are satisfied. There can be only one restriction period in respect of any order for possession, but it can end if the local authority thinks the restriction should no longer apply, and can start running again in the circumstances set out in subs (6)(a) or (b). In any event, the restriction period must end no later than five years after the date the order for possession was made.

[¹Relevant orders for possession

130C–(1) In section 130B a relevant order for possession is, in England and Wales–

(a) an order made under section 84 of the Housing Act 1985 (secure tenancies) on Ground 2 set out in Schedule 2 to that Act;

(b)   an order made under section 7 of the Housing Act 1988 (assured tenancies) on Ground 14 set out in Schedule 2 to that Act;

(c)   an order made under section 98 of the Rent Act 1977 (protected or statutory tenancies) in the circumstances specified in Case 2 in Schedule 15 to that Act.

(2)   In that section a relevant order for possession is, in Scotland–

(a)   an order made under section 16(2) of the Housing (Scotland) Act 2001 (secure tenancies) on one of the grounds set out in paragraphs 2 and 7 in Part 1 of Schedule 2 to that Act;

(b)   an order made in accordance with section 18 of the Housing (Scotland) Act 1988 (assured tenancies) on Ground 15 in Part 2 of Schedule 5 to that Act;

(c)   an order made in accordance with section 11 of the Rent (Scotland) Act 1984 (protected or statutory tenancies) in the circumstances specified in Case 2 in Part 1 of Schedule 2 to that Act.

(3)   For the purposes of subsections (1) and (2) it does not matter whether the order is made on the grounds or in the circumstances there mentioned alone or together with other grounds or circumstances.

(4)   Subsections (5) and (6) apply if the court–

(a)   stays (in Scotland, sists) or suspends the execution of a relevant order for possession, or postpones the date of possession under it, and

(b)   imposes a condition (or conditions) on that stay, sist, suspension or postponement.

(5)   If a condition relates to the behaviour of a person or persons occupying the dwelling, section 130B(4) applies only if the order takes effect as a result of a breach of that condition.

(6)   Section 130B(4) does not apply if the condition (or, if there is more than one, each of them) relates only to matters other than the behaviour of a person or persons occupying the dwelling.]

Amendment

1.   Inserted by s31(1) of the WRA 2007 (1.11.07).

Analysis

Subs (1) and (2) list the relevant orders of possession for the purposes of s130B(1)(a). They are all orders made on grounds of nuisance or annoyance or, for example, allowing the house to be used for immoral or illegal purposes. Note that by subs (3), it does not matter if there were a so other grounds for possession.

Where the court stays (sists in Scotland), or suspends the order of possession, or postpones the possession date on a condition relating to the behaviour of the occupiers, HB can only be restricted under s130B if the condition relating to behaviour is breached and the order takes effect as a result: subs (4) to (6).

Note the requirement in reg 10 of the Housing Benefit (Loss of Benefit) (Pilot Scheme) (Supplementary) Regulations 2007 (see p1146) for the court to provide information to the Secretary of State where, in a Pilot Scheme area, it makes a relevant order for possession, suspends or stays the execution of a relevant order for possession or postpones the date for possession, varies the terms of a relevant order for possession or sets aside a relevant order for possession.

[¹Loss of housing benefit: supplementary

130D–(1)   Regulations may provide that, where housing benefit has been paid subject to the restriction set out in section 130B(4), in prescribed circumstances–

(a)   the former occupier must be paid some or all of the amount of the benefit which, by virtue of that subsection, has not been payable to him, and

(b)   such other adjustments must be made as are prescribed.

(2)   The Secretary of State may by order vary the definition of relevant order for possession by–

(a)   adding to or removing from it orders of a specified description;

(b)   specifying circumstances in which it includes orders of a specified description.

(3)   Regulations may prescribe–

(a)   matters which are, or are not, to be taken into account in determining whether a person has, or does not have, good cause for failing to take action specified in a warning notice or failing to comply with a requirement such as is mentioned in section 130B(3)(a);

(b)   circumstances in which a person is, or is not, to be regarded as having, or not having, such good cause.

(4)   Expressions used in this section and in section 130B have the meaning given in that section.]

Amendment

1.   Inserted by s31(1) of the WRA 2007 (1.11.07).

Analysis

Regs 5 and 6 of the Housing Benefit (Loss of Benefit) (Pilot Scheme) (Supplementary) Regulations 2007 (see p1145) set out what is to be taken into account in determining whether a person has, or does not have, good cause, and circumstances in which a person must be regarded as having good cause:subs (3).

[¹Couples

130E–(1)   This section applies where at any time the conditions for entitlement to housing benefit are satisfied with respect to a person who is a member of a couple.

(2)   Where paragraphs (a) and (b) of section 130B(1) are satisfied in relation to both members of the couple (whether or not in respect of the same dwelling), then for the purposes of subsection (2) or (3) of that section, the failure by one member of the couple to comply with a warning notice or with a requirement such as is mentioned in section 130B(3)(a) must be treated also as a failure by his partner to comply with it.

(3)   Where paragraph (a) of section 130B(1) is not satisfied in relation to one member of the couple, then subsection (4) of that section does not apply to his partner (even if paragraphs (a), (b) and (c) of section 130B(1) are satisfied in relation to the partner).

(4)   References to a person's partner are to the other member of the couple concerned.]

Amendment

1.   Inserted by s31(1) of the WRA 2007 (1.11.07).

Analysis

Where the HB claimant is a member of a couple (defined in s137), a reduction in HB under s130B(4) can only apply where both members of the couple have ceased to occupy a dwelling as a consequence of a relevant possession order (whether or not it is the same dwelling) and at least one of the couple has failed to comply with a warning or a requirment without good cause.

[¹Information provision

130F–(1)   The Secretary of State may by regulations require–

(a)   a court which makes a relevant order for possession, or

(b)   any other person or description of person who the Secretary of State thinks is or may be aware of the making of such an order,

to notify him of the making of the order and to provide him with such details of matters in connection with the order as may be prescribed.

(2)   The Secretary of State may provide–

(a)   information obtained under subsection (1), or

(b)   information which is relevant to the exercise by him of any function relating to housing benefit,

to a relevant local authority, or a person authorised to exercise any function of such an authority relating to services mentioned in section 130B(10), for use in the provision of such services.

(3)   The Secretary of State may by regulations require–

(a)   a relevant local authority, or

(b)   a person authorised to exercise any function of such an authority relating to services mentioned in section 130B(10),

to supply relevant information held by the authority or other person to, or to a person providing services to, the Secretary of State for use for any purpose relating to the administration of housing benefit.

(4)   The Secretary of State may by regulations require–

(a)   an authority administering housing benefit,

(b)   a person authorised to exercise any function of such an authority relating to such a benefit,

(c)   a relevant local authority, or

(d)   a person authorised to exercise any function of such an authority relating to services mentioned in section 130B(10),

to provide relevant information held by that authority or person to an authority or person mentioned in paragraph (a) or (b) for use for any purpose relating to the administration of housing benefit.

(5)   The Secretary of State may by regulations require–

(a)   an authotity administering housing benefit,

(b)   a person authorised to exercise any function of such an authority relating to such a benefit,

(c)   a relevant local authority, or

(d)   a person authorised to exercise any function of such an authority relating to services mentioned in section 130B(10),

to provide relevant information held by that authority or person to an authority or person mentioned in paragraph (c) or (d) for use in the provision of those services.

(6)   Relevant information is–

(a)   if the information is held by an authority administering housing benefit or a person authorised to exercise any function of such an authority, information which is relevant to the exercise of any function relating to housing benefit by the authority or person;

(b)   if the information is held by a relevant local authority or a person authorised to exercise any function of such an authority, information which is relevant to the exercise of any function relating to the provision of services mentioned in section 130B(10).

(7)   Information must be supplied under subsection (1), (3), (4) or (5) in such circumstances, in such manner and form, and in accordance with such requirements, as may be prescribed.

(8)   ''Relevant order for possession'' and ''relevant local authority'' have the same meaning as in section 130B.

(9)   Subsections (1) and (5) do not extend to Scotland.]

Amendment

1.   Inserted by s31(1) of the WRA 2007 (1.11.07).

Analysis

The regulations made are:

Subs (1). Reg 10 of the Housing Benefit (Loss of Benefit) (Pilot Scheme) (Supplementary) Regulations 2007 (see p1146).

Subs (2) to (5). Regs 11, 12 and 13 of the Housing Benefit (Loss of Benefit) (Pilot Scheme) (Supplementary) Regulations 2007 (see pp1147, 1147 and 1148).

[¹ **Pilot schemes relating to loss of housing benefit**

130–(1)   Regulations to which this section applies may be made so as to have effect for a prescribed period.

(2)   Any regulations which, by virtue of subsection (1), have effect for a limited period are referred to in this section as a "pilot scheme".

(3)   A pilot scheme may provide that it applies only in relation to–

(a)   one or more prescribed areas;

(b)   one or more prescribed classes of person;

(c)   persons selected by reference to prescribed criteria.

(4)   A pilot scheme may make consequential or transitional provision.

(5)   A pilot scheme ("the previous scheme") may be replaced by a further pilot scheme making the same, or similar, provision (apart from the prescribed period) to that made by the previous scheme.

(6)   A pilot scheme may be amended or revoked by regulations under this section.

(7)   This section applies to–

(a)   regulations made under any of sections 130B to 130F above;

(b)   regulations made under any other enactment, so far as they relate to, or are made for purposes which relate to, loss or restriction of housing benefit in pursuance of section 130B above.

(8)   This section does not extend to Scotland.]

Amendment
1.   Inserted by s31(1) of the WRA 2007 (1.11.07).

Analysis
The current pilot scheme areas are listed in the Schedule to the Housing Benefit (Loss of Benefit) (Pilot Scheme) Regulations 2007 (see p1143).

[¹Council tax benefit

131.–(1)   A person is entitled to council tax benefit in respect of a particular day falling after 31st March 1993 if the following are fulfilled, namely, the condition set out in subsection (3) below and either–

(a)   each of the two conditions set out in subsections (4) and (5) below; or

(b)   the condition set out in subsection (6) below.

(2)   Council tax benefit–

(a)   shall not be allowed to a person in respect of any day falling before the day on which his entitlement is to be regarded as commencing for that purpose by virtue of paragraph (l) of section 6(1) of the Administration Act; but

(b)   may be allowed to him in respect of not more than 6 days immediately following the day on which his period of entitlement would otherwise come to an end, if his entitlement is to be regarded by virtue of that paragraph as not having ended for that purpose.

(3)   The main condition for the purposes of subsection (1) above is that the person concerned–

(a)   is for the day liable to pay council tax in respect of a dwelling of which he is a resident; and

(b)   is not a prescribed person or a person of a prescribed class.

(4)   The first condition for the purposes of subsection (1)(a) above is that there is an appropriate maximum council tax benefit in the case of the person concerned.

(5)   The second condition for the purposes of subsection (1)(a) above is that–

(a)   the day falls within a week in respect of which the person concerned has no income;

(b)   the day falls within a week in respect of which his income does not exceed the applicable amount; or

(c)   neither paragraph (a) nor paragraph (b) above is fulfilled in his case but amount A exceeds amount B where–

(i)   amount A is the appropriate maximum council tax benefit in his case; and

(ii)   amount B is a prescribed percentage of the difference between his income in respect of the week in which the day falls and the applicable amount.

(6)   The condition for the purposes of subsection (1)(b) above is that–

(a)   no other resident of the dwelling is liable to pay rent to the person concerned in respect of the dwelling; and

(b)   there is an alternative maximum council tax benefit in the case of that person which is derived from the income or aggregate incomes of one or more residents to whom this subsection applies.

(7)   Subsection (6) above applies to any other resident of the dwelling who–

(a)   is not a person who, in accordance with Schedule 1 to the Local Government Finance Act 1992, falls to be disregarded for the purposes of discount; and

(b)   is not a prescribed person or a person of a prescribed class.

(8)   Subject to subsection (9) below, where a person is entitled to council tax benefit in respect of a day, the amount to which he is entitled shall be–

(a)   if subsection (5)(a) or (b) above applies, the amount which is the appropriate maximum council tax benefit in his case;

(b)   if subsection (5)(c) above applies, the amount found by deducting amount B from amount A, where ''amount A'' and ''amount B'' have the meanings given by that subsection; and

(c)   if subsection (6) above applies, the amount which is the alternative maximum council tax benefit in his case.

(9)   Where a person is entitled to council tax benefit in respect of a day, and both subsection (5) and subsection (6) above apply, the amount to which he is entitled shall be whichever is the greater of–

(a)   the amount given by paragraph (a) or, as the case may be, paragraph (b) of subsection (8) above; and

(b)   the amount given by paragraph (c) of that subsection.

(10)   Regulations shall prescribe the manner in which–

(a)   the appropriate maximum council tax benefit;

(b)   the alternative maximum council tax benefit, are to be determined in any case.

(11)   In this section 'dwelling' and 'resident' have the same meanings as in Part I or II of the Local Government Finance Act 1992.]

Amendment
1.   Substituted by LGFA Sch 9 para 2.

General Note
This section, setting out the basic conditions of entitlement to CTB, is harder to understand than s131. Note that it is supplemented by ss132 and 133 below.

Subsections (1) and (3) to (7): Conditions of entitlement
There are two types of CTB: that known as "main" CTB and the "alternative maximum" CTB, sometimes referred to as "second adult rebate". Subs (1) provides that in order to be entitled to either type of CTB, a person must always fulfil the conditions in subsection (3). Then, to qualify for main CTB, both conditions in subsections (4) and (5) must be fulflilled and for alternative maximum CTB, the conditions in subsection (6) must be fulfilled. See also the commentary to the definition of "resident" in reg 2(1) CTB Regs (on p572).

The general conditions
(1)   The claimant must be liable to pay council tax in respect of a dwelling of which s/he is a resident: subs (3)(a). Liability for council tax is defined by the LGFA and secondary legislation made thereunder. It is a subject outside the scope of this book: see CPAG's *Council Tax Handbook* or standard works on local taxation. The principal sections that define liability, s6 (in relation to England and Wales) and s75 (in Scotland) are set out in the extracts from the LGFA (see pp1003 and 1007). Residence is also defined by reference to the LGFA: subs (11). Being "resident" in relation to any chargeable dwelling means where an individual has her/his sole or main residence, which is a question of fact and degree in every case: *Frost v Feltham* [1981] 1 WLR 455. Accordingly, where a family had to occupy two flats in one building because of the number of members of the family,

and the father was liable for council tax in respect of both flats, the tribunal erred in holding the claimant not to be resident in both dwellings (and so not eligible for CTB for the second flat): *CH 3933/2006*. The tribunal had erred in law by conflating the meaning of "dwelling" with "residence". Commissioner Howell noted in *CH 3933/2006* (para 9) that if a person is a resident of a chargeable dwelling so as to be liable for council tax on it, then s/he must also meet the condition of being a resident of that dwelling to qualify for CTB. There was therefore a legal inconsistency in the local authority's case in on the one hand holding the claimant to be liable for council tax for the second flat because he was resident in it, but on the other hand denying him CTB on the basis that he was not resident in the second flat.

(2)   The claimant must not be a prescribed person or a member of a prescribed class: subs (3)(b). Three categories are currently prescribed. Persons from abroad are prescribed under reg 7 of both the CTB and CTB(SPC) Regs. Most full-time students are prescribed under reg 45 CTB Regs. Full-time students are *not* a prescribed person or class for claimants 60 or over who are not (and whose partner's are not) on IS or income-based JSA. Finally, people who are absent from home are prescribed by reg 8 of both the CTB and the CTB(SPC) Regs unless the absence is temporary as defined in those regulations.

Main CTB

The additional conditions for main CTB are:

(1)   There is an appropriate maximum CTB: subs (4). See reg 57 CTB Regs (reg 40 CTB(SPC) Regs).

(2)   The claimant's income is sufficiently low: subs (5). Income is calculated under Part 4 and applicable amounts under Part 3 of both the CTB and the CTB(SPC) Regs. If the claimant's income is lower than the applicable amount, s/he qualifies under sub-para (a) or (b). If it is higher, s/he still qualifies under sub-para (c) where the maximum CTB exceeds a figure obtained by the prescribed percentage of the difference between the income and the applicable amount. The daily prescribed percentage is currently two and six-sevenths per cent (which is 20 per cent weekly): see reg 59 CTB Regs (reg 43 CTB(SPC) Regs).

Alternative maximum CTB

The additional conditions for alternative maximum CTB are:

(1)   No other resident of the dwelling is liable to pay rent to the claimant: subs (6)(a). It is worthy of note that the phrase "liable to pay rent" is used rather than the phrase "liable to make payments in respect of the dwelling" as used, for example, in s130(1)(a). It would seem to follow from the difference in the wording that the liability must be in respect of rent in the strict sense, that is payment made under a tenancy. Thus if the person liable is not a tenant but is a licensee or some other form of occupant, because s/he either does not have exclusive possession of any part of the property or because the nature of the occupancy is inconsistent with the nature of a tenancy, the claimant is not excluded from CTB. There is a great deal of caselaw on whether an occupant is a tenant or not. See *Street v Mountford* [1995] AC 809, HL and any standard textbook on landlord and tenant law for general guidance.

(2)   There is an alternative maximum CTB in the claimant's case: subs (6)(b). See reg 62 and Sch 2 CTB Regs and reg 46 and Sch 6 CTB(SPC) Regs. This is based on the income of "second adults" residing with the claimant, not the income of the claimant. The aim of alternative maximum CTB is to deal with cases of multiple occupancy where some residents have low incomes and others have higher incomes. Subs (7) sets out the other residents to be taken into account in calculating alternative maximum CTB. Those who fall within Sch 1 LGFA are excluded, as are prescribed persons under reg 63 CTB Regs (reg 47 CTB(SPC) Regs).

Subsection (2): Period of entitlement

For the dates on which entitlement begins and ends, see Part 7 of the CTB Regs and Part 6 of the CTB(SPC) Regs.

Subsections (8) and (9): Amount of CTB

By virtue of subs (8)(a) and (c), the amount of CTB payable is normally either the maximum CTB or alternative maximum CTB. By subs (8)(b), if a claimant qualifies by virtue of subs (5)(c) (see above) the amount payable is the figure obtained by deducting the percentage of the difference between the claimant's income and applicable amount from the maximum CTB.

Under subs (9), if a claimant qualifies for both main CTB and alternative maximum CTB, s/he will be awarded the higher amount of the two obtained under the subs (8) calculations.

Subsections (10) and (11): Regulations and definitions

Maximum and alternative maximum CTB are calculated under Part 6 CTB Regs and Part 5 CTB(SPC) Regs.

Couples
132.–(1)   As regards any case where a person is a member of a [⁶ couple] throughout a particular day, regulations may make such provision as the Secretary of State sees fit as to–

(a)   the entitlement of the person to a [¹ council tax benefit] in respect of the day, and

(b)   the amount to which he is entitled.

(2)   Nothing in subsections (3) to (8) below shall prejudice the generality of subsection (1) above.

(3)   The regulations may provide that prescribed provisions shall apply instead of prescribed provisions of this Part of this Act, or that prescribed provisions of this Part of this Act shall not apply or shall apply subject to prescribed amendments or adaptations.

(4)   The regulations may provide that, for the purpose of calculating in the case of the person concerned the matters mentioned in subsection (5) below, prescribed amounts relating to the person and his partner are to be aggregated and the aggregate is to be apportioned.

(5)   The matters are income, capital, the applicable amount, and [² the appropriate maximum council tax benefit and the alternative maximum council tax benefit.]

(6)   The regulations may–

(a)   amend section 139(6) of the Administration Act so as to allow for disregarding the whole or part of any pension payable to the partner of the person concerned in determining the latter's income;

(b)   amend section 139(7) of that Act accordingly.

(7)   The regulations may contain different provision as to the following different cases–

(a)   cases where the [³ main] condition is fulfilled on the day concerned by the person concerned but not by his partner;

(b)   cases where the [⁴ main] condition is fulfilled on the day concerned by the person concerned and by his partner.

(8)   The regulations may include such supplementary, incidental or consequential provisions as appear to the Secretary of State to be necessary or expedient.

(9)   In this section–

(a)   references to a person's partner are to the other member of the couple concerned, and

[⁵ (b)   references to the main condition are references to the condition mentioned in section 131(3) above.]

Amendments

1.   Substituted by LGFA Sch 9 para 5(1) as from 1.4.93.
2.   Substituted by LGFA Sch 9 para 5(2) as from 1.4.93.
3.   Substituted by LGFA Sch 9 para 5(3) as from 1.4.93.
4.   Substituted by LGFA Sch 9 para 5(3) as from 1.4.93.
5.   Substituted by LGFA Sch 9 para 5(4) as from 1.4.93.
6.   Substituted by CPA 2004 Sch 24 para 45 as from 5.12.05.

Definitions

"couple" – see s137.
"partner" – see subs (9).

General Note

This section empowers the Secretary of State to make regulations in respect of the entitlement to CTB of a person who is a member of a couple and in respect of the amount to which s/he is entitled. This section does not apply to couples who were married under a law which permits polygamy where, at the time of the claim, there are more than two partners to the marriage (for such marriages, see s133 below). From 5 December 2005, it includes civil partners.

Subs (1) gives a broad power to the Secretary of State to make provision for couples in whatever way is thought fit. The generality of this power is confirmed by subs (2). See regs 15 and 68 CTB Regs and regs 13 and 52 CTB(SPC) Regs for the main provisions.

Subs (3) permits the making of regulations which substitute different provisions for the provisions of this Part, or which provide that certain provisions of this Part shall not apply or shall apply subject to prescribed modifications.

Subs (4) and (5) together provide that, in relation to the entitlement of a person covered by this section, when calculating that person's income, capital, applicable amount and appropriate maximum CTB and the alternative maximum CTB, regulations may be made which provide that certain amounts relating to that person and her/his partner are to be aggregated and apportioned between the two.

Subs (6) permits the making of regulations which provide that, in calculating the entitlement of a person covered by this section, s139(6) and (7) SSAA are to be amended so that war widow's pension or war disablement pension payable to that person's partner is to be wholly or partly ignored in calculating that person's income.

Subs (7). "the main condition" is defined in subs (9) as being a reference to s131(3). Regulations may be made which make different rules for the situation where one partner satisfies the "main condition" on a particular day but the other does not, as opposed to the situation where both partners satisfy the "main condition" on a particular day.

Subs (8) makes it clear that the power in subs (1) includes the power to make provisions by regulations which are supplementary, incidental or consequential to the main object of the powers "as appears necessary or expedient".

Polygamous marriages

133.–(1)   This section applies to any case where–

(a)   throughout a particular day a person (the person in question) is a husband or wife by virtue of a marriage entered into under a law which permits polygamy; and

(b)   either party to the marriage has for the time being any spouse additional to the other party.

(2)   For the purposes of section 132 above neither party to the marriage shall be taken to be a member of a couple on the day.

(3)   Regulations under this section may make such provision as the Secretary of State sees fit as to–

(a)   the entitlement of the person in question to a [¹ council tax benefit] in respect of the day, and

(b)   the amount to which he is entitled.

(4)   Without prejudice to the generality of subsection (3) above the regulations may include provision equivalent to that included under section 132 above subject to any modifications the Secretary of State sees fit.

Amendment
1.   Substitution made by LGFA Sch 9 para 6 (1.4.93).

General Note
This section makes the same provision for persons married under a law which permits polygamy as s132 does for couples. It covers persons married under such a law, where the marriage itself is at the relevant time polygamous.

Subs (1) and (2) deal with the applications of this section and rule out any overlap with s132 by stating that persons covered by subs (1) are not members of a couple.

Subs (3) gives the Secretary of State the same powers in relation to the entitlement and extent of entitlement of persons covered by this section to CTB as s132(1) does in relation to couples.

Subs (4) states that the powers in subs (3) include powers to make the same types of regulation as mentioned in s132 "subject to any modifications the Secretary of State sees fit".

General

Exclusions from benefit

134.–(1)   No person shall be entitled to an income-related benefit if his capital or a prescribed part of it exceeds the prescribed amount.

(2)   Except in prescribed circumstances the entitlement of one member of a family to any one income-related benefit excludes entitlement to that benefit for any other member for the same period.

(3)   [¹ . . .]

(4)   Where the amount of any income-related benefit would be less than a prescribed amount, it shall not be payable except in prescribed circumstances.

Amendment

1.   Deleted by LGFA Sch 9 para 7.

General Note

Subs (1) provides for a capital limit above which a claimant will not be entitled to HB or CTB. The prescribed figure is currently £16,000 for both HB and CTB: see reg 43 of both the HB and the HB(SPC) Regs and reg 33 of both the CTB and the CTB(SPC) Regs. Note that by reg 26 HB(SPC) Regs and reg 16 CTB(SPC) Regs, where a claimant or her/his partner is in receipt of the guarantee credit of PC, the whole of her/his capital (and income) is ignored, which means that for those claimants, there is effectively no capital limit.

Subs (2) provides that generally if one member of a "family" receives an income-related benefit for a period, the other members may not receive the same benefit for that period (for the meaning of "family" see p22).

Subs (4) provides for the fixing of a minimum level below which HB or CTB is not payable. See reg 75 HB Regs (reg 56 HB(SPC) Regs) which provides a minimum level of fifty pence a week for HB. No minimum payment of CTB has been prescribed.

The applicable amount

135.–(1)   The applicable amount, in relation to any income-related benefit, shall be such amount or the aggregate of such amounts as may be prescribed in relation to that benefit.

(2)   The power to prescribe applicable amounts conferred by subsection (1) above includes power to prescribe nil as an applicable amount.

(3)   [¹ . . .]

(4)   [¹ . . .]

(5)   [² . . .] the applicable amount for a severely disabled person shall include an amount in respect of his being a severely disabled person.

(6)   Regulations may specify circumstances in which persons are to be treated as being or as not being severely disabled.

Amendments

1.   Deleted by LGFA Sch 9 para 8 (1.4.93).

2.   Amended by the Tax Credits Act 2002 Sch 6 (8.4.03).

General Note

Subs (1) enables the making of regulations to quantify "applicable amounts". See Part 5 and Sch 3 of both the HB and the HB(SPC) Regs and Part 3 and Sch 1 of both the CTB and the CTB(SPC) Regs. This subsection is supplemented by paras (2), (5) and (6) which specify certain provisions that must be included in the Regs on applicable amounts.

Subs (2). Nil can be a valid applicable amount.

Subs (5). Specific provision is made for the addition of an extra amount for severely disabled claimants, by virtue of subs (6) and Sch 3 para 14 HB Regs, Sch 3 para 6 HB(SPC) Regs, Sch 1 para 14 CTB Regs and Sch 1 para 6 CTB(SPC) Regs, which define "severely disabled" for these purposes.

Income and capital

136.–(1)   Where a person claiming an income-related benefit is a member of a family, the income and capital of any member of that family shall, except in prescribed circumstances, be treated as the income and capital of that person.

(2)   Regulations may provide that capital not exceeding the amount prescribed under section 134(1) above but exceeding a prescribed lower amount shall be treated, to a prescribed extent, as if it were income of a prescribed amount.

(3)　Income and capital shall be calculated or estimated in such manner as may be prescribed.

(4)　A person's income in respect of a week shall be calculated in accordance with prescribed rules; and the rules may provide for the calculation to be made by reference to an average over a period (which need not include the week concerned).

(5)　Circumstances may be prescribed in which–

(a)　a person is treated as possessing capital or income which he does not possess;

(b)　capital or income which a person does possess is to be disregarded;

(c)　income is to be treated as capital;

(d)　capital is to be treated as income.

Definitions

"family" – s137.

"income-related benefits" – s123.

General Note

This section enables the making of regulations to quantify "income" and "capital" on the basis of which entitlement to HB and CTB are calculated.

Subs (1) deals with the aggregation of assets for members of a "family" – see reg 25 HB Regs (reg 23 HB(SPC) Regs) and reg 15 CTB Regs (reg 13 CTB(SPC) Regs).

Subs (2) enables the "tariff income rules" whereby capital between certain levels is deemed to produce income at a set level irrespective of the actual income received by the claimant. See reg 52 HB Regs, reg 29(2) HB(SPC) Regs, reg 42 CTB Regs and reg 19(2) CTB(SPC) Regs for the tariff income rules.

Subs (3) to (5) introduce wide powers as to the treatment of resources, as to which generally see Part 6 of both the HB and HB(CTB) Regs and Part 4 of both the CTB and CTB(SPC) Regs. For examples of the uses of the powers specified by subs (5), see reg 49, Part 6 and Schs 4 to 6, reg 46, and reg 41 HB Regs.

Analysis

The scope of the very wide powers conferred by s136 has been the subject of judicial comment. In *Foster v Chief Adjudication Officer* [1992] QB 31 at 45, Sir John Donaldson MR noted in passing that s136 permits the Secretary of State "to prescribe that black is white and that nothing is something and vice versa in the context of income and capital".

The wide scope of the provisions was confirmed in *Owen v Chief Adjudication Officer* [1999] *The Independent* 13 April, CA appendix to *R(IS) 8/99*. This case concerned an anomaly in the Income Support (General) Regulations 1987. The claimant became terminally ill and was signed off work by his doctor, receiving statutory and contractual sick pay. He was dismissed by his employer and was paid four weeks' sick pay in arrears on the last day of his employment. Notwithstanding the fact that the sick pay was paid in arrears, the regulations required that the sick pay be taken into account as income for the first four weeks of the claim as it was not "earnings": see regs 29(1), 29(2), 31(1) and 35(2) IS Regs. It should be noted that the position under the HB and CTB Regs is different as statutory and contractual sick pay are treated as "earnings": see reg 35(1)(i) and (j) HB Regs; reg 35(1)(h) and (k) HB(SPC) Regs; 25(1)(i) and (j) CTB Regs; and reg 25(1)(h) and (k) CTB(SPC) Regs.

The argument in *Owen* was that the effect of the regulations was not authorised by s136 and that the closing words of reg 29(2) were therefore ultra vires. It is plain that subs (4) envisages such regulations being made. However, as the Secretary of State conceded and the Court of Appeal accepted, that provision could not authorise the offending words in reg 29(2) because s136(4) did not appear in s22 of the Social Security Act 1986 as originally enacted. It was inserted as s22(8A) with effect from 29 July 1988 by the Local Government Finance Act 1988. However, the IS Regs had come into force on 11 April 1988 and so the subsection could not retrospectively revive any regulations that had been ultra vires in the absence of s22(8A): *Cottingham v Chief Adjudication Officer* [1992] appendix to *R(P) 1/93*, CA. The same would apply to much of the HB Regs 1987, which came into force between 1 April 1988 and 4 April 1988. Thus any provision which appeared in the HB Regs 1987 as they stood on 28 July 1988 and which could only be justified by subs (4) would be ultra vires. Any provision that had been the subject of insertion or amendment since that date, however, could be validly made under subs (4).

It was, however, argued for the Chief Adjudication Officer that the scheme was justified by either subs (3) or (5)(a). As far as subs (5)(a) was concerned, it was submitted for the claimant that as he did possess the income in question (though most of it had been spent on the previous month's bills), subs (5)(a) could not be applicable. The Court rejected this submission:

". . . it is a deeming provision prescribing circumstances in which a person is treated as possessing income he does not possess. He may not in fact possess income in a relevant period for a number of reasons: he may never have possessed the income at all; he may have in fact possessed the income at an earlier period, but he does not possess it at a later period. In the latter case a person may be treated as possessing income in a later period, even though it was paid in respect of an earlier period and even though he has already spent all the income that he did in fact possess at the earlier period. . . These enabling terms are framed widely enough to authorise a provision spreading or apportioning income possessed by a claimant over a stated period by treating it as possessed by the claimant in which he did not in fact possess it."

The difficulty with this approach is that it does not deal with the case where the income is still possessed in the later period. If the income is all spent (and the evidence in the case was that Mr Owen had spent most, but not all of it) then because s136(5)(a) refers to income being deemed to be possessed "which he does not possess" the Court's approach is justified. However, if the income is still possessed, it cannot be said that on any normal reading of the language, s136(5)(a) can apply because the income is possessed during the relevant period. If a regulation would be *intra vires* when applied to some claimants, but *ultra vires* when applied to others, it must be struck down. Against this, it might be argued that once income is possessed beyond the period in which it is received, it becomes part of the claimant's capital and so he does not possess it as income.

The Court of Appeal did not deal with the argument concerning s136(3), which centred around whether, if no income was received during a period but the claimant was deemed to have such income, such a scheme could be said to involve a "calculation or estimation" of income. In *CIS 3287/1997* (Appendix paras 12-13) Commissioner Goodman stated that the outcome had to bear some resemblance to the reality.

The Court also vigorously rejected a second submission for the claimant that the regulations were *ultra vires* as irrational. Although it was accepted that the scheme operated unfairly, it could not be said to be irrational so as to justify the striking-down of the regulations.

[¹Effect of attaining qualifying age for state pension credit

136A.–(1)   Subsections (2) and (3) below apply in relation to housing benefit and council tax benefit in the case of any person who has attained the qualifying age for state pension credit.

(2)   Regulations may make provision for section 134(1) or any provision of section 136 above not to have effect in relation to those benefits in the case of any such person.

(3)   In relation to those benefits, regulations may make provision for the determination of the income and capital of any such person; and any such regulations may include provision applying (with such modifications as the Secretary of State thinks fit)–

(a)   section 5 of the State Pension Credit Act 2002 (provision for treating income of spouse as income of claimant, etc), and

(b)   section 15 of that Act (determination of income and capital for purposes of state pension credit).

(4)   Regulations under subsection (3) above may also include provision–

(a)   authorising or requiring the use of any calculation or estimate of a person's income or capital made by the Secretary of State for the purposes of the State Pension Credit Act 2002; or

(b)   requiring that, if and so long as an assessed income period is in force under section 6 of that Act in respect of a person falling within subsection (1) above,–

(i)   the assessed amount of any element of his retirement provision shall be treated as the amount of that element for the purposes of housing benefit or council tax benefit; and

(ii)   his income shall be taken for those purposes not to include any element of retirement provision which it is taken not to include for the purposes of state pension credit by virtue of a determination under subsection (5) of section 7 of that Act.

(5)   In subsection (4) above "assessed amount", "element" and "retirement provision" have the same meaning as in the State Pension Credit Act 2002.

(6)　The Secretary of State may by regulations make provision for the preceding provisions of this section to apply with modifications in cases to which section 12 of the State Pension Credit Act 2002 (polygamous marriages) applies.

(7)　The provision that may be made by regulations under subsection (6) above includes any provision that may be made by regulations under section 133 above.]

Amendment

1.　Inserted by Sch 2 para 3 of the SPCA 2002 with effect from 27.01.03 (for making regulations) and 6.10.03.

General Note

s136A SSCBA gives extensive regulation-making powers in relation to the calculation of income and capital for HB and CTB purposes for those who have attained the qualifying age for state pension credit (currently aged 60). The provisions for such claimants are now in the HB(SPC) Regs and the CTB(SPC) Regs.

Interpretation of Part VII and supplementary provisions

137.–(1)　In this Part of this Act, unless the context otherwise requires–

[¹ "billing authority" has the same meaning as in Part I of the Local Government Finance Act 1992;]

"child" means a person under the age of 16;

[⁷ "couple" means–

(a)　a man and woman who are married to each other and are members of the same household

(b)　a man and woman who are not married to each other but are living together as husband and wife otherwise than in prescribed circumstances

(c)　two people of the same sex who are civil partners of each other and are members of the same household; or

(d)　two people of the same sex who are not civil partners of each other but are living together as if they were civil partners otherwise than in prescribed circumstances;]

"dwelling" means any residential accommodation, whether or not consisting of the whole or part of a building and whether or not comprising separate and self-contained premises;

"family" means–

(a)　a [⁶ couple];

(b)　a [⁶ couple] and a member of the same household for whom one of them is or both are responsible and who is a child of a person or a prescribed description;

(c)　except in prescribed circumstances, a person who is not a member of a [⁶ couple] and a member of the same household for whom that person is responsible and who is a child or a person of a prescribed description;

"industrial injuries scheme" means a scheme made under Schedule 8 to this Act or section 159 of the 1975 Act or under the Old Cases Act;

[¹⁰ "local authority" in relation to Scotland means a council constituted under section 2 of the Local Government etc. (Scotland) Act 1994;]

[⁸ . . .]

[⁵ "pensionable age" has the meaning given by the rules in paragraph 1 of Schedule 4 to the Pensions Act 1995 (c. 26);]

"prescribed" means specified in or determined in accordance with regulations;

[⁵ "the qualifying age for state pension credit" is (in accordance with section 1(2)(b) and (6) of the State Pension Credit Act 2002)–

(a)　in the case of a woman, pensionable age; or

(b)　in the case of a man, the age which is pensionable age in the case of a woman born on the same day as the man;]

[⁵ "state pension credit" means state pension credit under the State Pension Credit Act 2002;]

[8 . . .]

"war pension scheme'' means a scheme under which war pensions (as defined in section 25 of the Social Security Act 1989) are provided;

"week'', in relation to [3 council tax benefit], means a period of 7 days beginning with a Monday.

[9 (1A) For the purposes of this Part, two people of the same sex are to be regarded as living together as if they were civil partners if, but only if, they would be regarded as living together as husband and wife were they instead two people of the opposite sex.]

(2) Regulations may make provision for the purposes of this Part of this Act–

(a) as to circumstances in which a person is to be treated as being or not being in Great Britain;

(b) continuing a person's entitlement to benefit during periods of temporary absence from Great Britain;

(c) as to what is or is not to be treated as remunerative work or as employment;

(d) as to circumstances in which a person is or is not to be treated as
   (i) engaged or normally engaged in remunerative work
   (ii) [4 . . .]

(e) as to what is or is not to be treated as relevant education;

(f) as to circumstances in which a person is or is not to be treated as receiving relevant education;

(g) specifying the descriptions of pension increases under war pension schemes or industrial injuries schemes that are analogous to the benefits mentioned in section 129(2)(b)(i) to (iii) above;

(h) as to circumstances in which a person is or is not to be treated as occupying a dwelling as his home;

(i) for treating any person who is liable to make payments in respect of a dwelling as if he were not so liable;

(j) for treating any person who is not liable to make payments in respect of a dwelling as if he were so liable;

(k) for treating as included in a dwelling any land used for the purposes of the dwelling;

(l) as to circumstances in which persons are to be treated as being or not being members of the same household;

(m) as to circumstances in which one person is to be treated as responsible or not responsible for another.

Amendments

1.   Substituted by LGFA Sch 9 para 9(a) (1.4.93).
2.   Definition of "levying authority" repealed by Local Government etc. (Scotland) Act 1994 Sch 13 para 174(5) and Sch 14 (1.4.96).
3.   Substituted by LGFA Sch 9 para 9(d) (1.4.93).
4.   Deleted by Jobseekers Act 1995 Sch 2 para 35(2).
5.   Inserted by Sch 2 para 4 SPCA 2002 with effect from 2.7.02 (for making regulations) and 6.10.03.
6.   Substituted by Sch 24 para 46(2) CPA 2004 as from 5.12.05.
7.   Inserted by Sch 24 para 46(3) CPA 2004 as from 5.12.05.
8.   Omitted by Sch 24 para 46(4) CPA 2004 as from 5.12.05.
9.   Inserted by Sch 24 para 46(5) CPA 2004 as from 5.12.05.
10.   Inserted by the Welfare Reform Act 2007 reg 40 and Sch 5 para 1(4) (3.7.07).

General Note

Subs (1) and (1A) define certain terms for the purpose of this part of the Act. Subs (2) enables regulations to be made in order to implement the schemes set up under this Part of the Act.

Analysis

Subsection (1): Definitions

"billing authority". Section 1(2) of the 1992 Act interprets this to cover district councils, London borough councils, the Common Council or the Council of the Isles of Scilly.

"couple". This definition was introduced with effect from 5 December 2005 as a result of the changes brought in by the Civil Partnership Act 2004 (CPA 2004). There are four situations in which two people are treated as a "couple" for HB and CTB purposes:

(1)   The first two definitions carry forward the old definitions of "married couple" and "unmarried couple".

(2)   The third and fourth defintions, introduce the substantive changes under the CPA 2004 in respect of "same sex" couples.

Married couple: para (a). As to membership of the same household, see p23. Occasionally it may be necessary to consider the question of whether someone is actually married. If the marriage could be shown to be void, as distinct from voidable, under the relevant law of marriage in either England and Wales or in Scotland (which are markedly different), then it would be necessary to consider whether the two people in question were an unmarried couple: see below. The validity of foreign marriages can cause very difficult questions of law to arise. Note also the existence in Scotland of the doctrine of marriage by habit and repute. In cases where any of these issues arise, reference should be made to specialist textbooks on the subject. A useful short summary for advisers along with references to caselaw may be found in the discussion of bereavement benefits (where these issues arise much more frequently) in CPAG's *Welfare Benefits and Tax Credits Handbook.*

Unmarried couple: para (b). The main issue which arises here concerns the meaning of the phrase "living together as husband and wife". The phrase "living together as husband and wife" has been used widely in various means-tested and non means-tested benefits schemes and is again subject to a large body of caselaw. Differences of interpretation led the predecessor of the DWP to issue guidance about indications as to whether the test is satisfied. The first six of the principles below are the factors listed in the guidance, which is reproduced in the HB and CTB guidance: see GM C1 Annex A. They are "admirable signposts" (*Crake and Butterworth v Supplementary Benefit Commission* [1982] 1 All ER 498 at 505, QBD) but *CIS 87/1993* emphasised the need to stand back once all the evidence has been considered and look at the overall quality of the relationship.

(1)   If the couple share a household, they will be more likely to be a "living together as husband and wife". For the meaning of "household", see p23. If they are not part of the same household, it is highly unlikely that they are "living together" in this sense. However, one of the most common pitfalls in these cases is to consider issues relating to the sharing of a household and stop the inquiry there. While the sharing of a household is consistent with a relationship akin to husband and wife, the caselaw is replete with examples where it has been held that the facts are equally consistent with other types of relationship such as simple friendship or brother and sister (*CP 8001/ 1995* para 10), patient and carer (*R(SB) 35/85* para 8), and landlord and lodger (*Campbell v Secretary of State for Social Services* [1983] 4 FLR 138, QBD, though rejected on the facts of that particular case).

(2)   The more stable the relationship, the more likely they are to be "living together as husband and wife". However, again caution needs to be applied because some of the other relationships mentioned in the previous paragraph may last for a long time: *CP 8001/1995* para 12. A degree of permanency in a landlord and lodger relationship may take it over the line into cohabitation: see *Campbell* for an example. Note, however, point (7) below.

(3)   The closer the financial arrangements, the more likely that a finding of "living together as husband and wife" will be justified. However, in any case where this issue arises there will be some degree of financial connection between the parties and so it will only be a compelling factor if the financial arrangements are particularly close and involve, for example, joint bank accounts.

(4)   The presence of a sexual relationship is of importance: *R(SB) 17/81* (para 7). Authorities are instructed by GM C1 Annex A not to inquire into the presence or absence of a sexual relationship, and so claimants involved in these issues who are not involved in a sexual relationship may need to make this clear to the authorities at the outset. In *CIS 87/1993* (para 12) it was said that if there had never been a sexual relationship, strong alternative grounds will be required to permit a conclusion that the man and woman are a couple. In *CSB 150/1985* it was said that two Mormons engaged to each other and living in the same house could not be an unmarried couple. That decision probably goes too far in apparently excluding evidence of other factors, but it is an illustration of the significance of this factor. Its importance may vary according to the ages of the people in question and cultural factors, but authorities should be careful not to make assumptions.

(5)   If the couple have children "of their union", in the antiquated phrase that was used in the old supplementary benefit guidance, that will be a strong indication that they are "living together as husband and wife".

(6)   The degree of public acknowledgement of the relationship is a factor which is often underplayed and is often illuminating as to the true nature of the relationship and as to the intention of the parties,

as to which see below. If one partner uses the name of the other, that will be highly persuasive: *R(G) 1/79* (para 9).

(7)   The relevance of the intention of the parties is controversial. In *Crake and Butterworth,* Woolf J (at 504d-f) placed considerable emphasis on what the intention of the parties was, and Webster J thought that if the intention of the parties was capable of ascertainment, it was significant: see *Robson v Secretary of State for Social Services*. Subsequently, it was suggested that the intention of the parties could only be ascertained from their actions: see *R(SB) 17/81* (para 8). No doubt it is true that it would be wrong for an authority simply to accept a claimant's account of what her/his intention was without examining such a statement against the background of the objective evidence. However, it is suggested that if the objective evidence, perhaps coupled with credible evidence given by a claimant, clearly indicates an intention to adopt a different relationship, the two people will not be "living together as husband and wife": *CIS 87/1993* (para 14).

(8)   The nature of a relationship can change over time. Thus it is wrong for an authority to assume, just because it concludes that on a particular date that two people are an unmarried couple, that the relationship has always had that quality: *CP 8001/1995* (para 11).

If the result of this complex inquiry is that the couple are "living together as husband and wife", only one of them may claim HB and CTB in respect of their dwelling and their needs and resources are aggregated.

Civil partners: para (c). Two people of the same sex are treated as a "couple" if they are members of the same household (see p23) and have entered into a contract of civil partnership under the CPA 2004.

Not civil partners: para (d). Two people of the same sex are treated as a "couple" if they have not entered into a civil partnership contract, but are living together as if they were civil partners. Under subsection (1A) this last test can only be satisfied if the same sex couple would have been regarded as "living together as husband and wife" were they of the opposite sex.

Similar considerations to those set out above in the definition of couple under para (b) will be relevant to determining whether a same sex couple are living together as if they were civil partners.

As to when the new definitions of couple may start to apply to same sex couples claiming HB/CTB, see the commentary to Article 3 of SI 2005 No 2877 on p1095.

"dwelling". The House of Lords decision in *Uratemp Ventures Ltd v Collins* [2001] 3 WLR 806 sheds new light on the meaning of "dwelling". Previous authority had stated, in the context of statutory protection of residential tenants, that a room or rooms which a tenant was given a right to occupy could only be a "dwelling" if they provided for the three basic necessities of life: namely sleeping, cooking and eating. Of these, sleeping had been regarded as the most important factor: *Wright v Howell* [1947] 92 SJ 26, CA; *Westminister CC v Clarke* [1992] 2 AC 288 at 299, HL. In *Collins*, however, the House of Lords ruled that rooms were not excluded from the definition of "dwelling" simply by virtue of the fact that they did not contain cooking facilities. Lord Irvine stated (at 808D, para 3) that "dwelling . . . connotes a place where one lives, regarding and treating it as home". He said (at 808E, para 4) that it was not even necessary that the room or rooms should contain a bed if a person was sleeping there. Lord Bingham said (at 809G-H, para 12) that although premises would not normally be a "dwelling" unless the tenant sleeps there, there was no inflexible rule even as to this.

The House of Lords in *Collins* emphasised the importance of the statutory context in interpreting the word (at 808D, para 3, 809D-E, para 10, 810C, para 15, 822F-823A, para 57). The emphasis on the "residential" aspects in the definition given in s137 suggests that in the HB context it should be given a wide interpretation, because the essence of the HB scheme is to include all rent and allied payments for different types of accommodation. That this is the correct interpretation is further confirmed by the inclusive nature of the definition to include parts of a building and accommodation which is not self-contained. Many landlords of low-grade accommodation attempt to exclude it from the regime of statutory protection by, for example, providing that cooking facilities are not to be used. Even if these agreements are genuine, the absence of cooking facilities should not exclude the occupant from HB.

Besides the accommodation being residential in nature, it seems that the agreement under which the claimant occupies the home must reflect this fact. In *R v Warrington BC ex p Williams* [1997] 29 HLR 872 at 876, QBD, the claimant rented commercial premises and used them as a dwelling, in breach of the lease. He claimed that the landlord had orally agreed that he could stay overnight to act as a night watchman, and so was unable to assert the true character of the premises against the claimant. In view of that, it was contended that the premises had to be seen as having a joint residential and commercial use. This argument was rejected, as a waiver of a condition against use as a dwelling did not alter the commercial nature of the tenancy and so the premises were not a dwelling.

"family". This definition and its component parts determine the crucial question of who forms part of the assessment unit for HB and CTB purposes. These are couples (para (a)), couples with children (para (b)) and lone parents (para (c)). Broadly speaking, a couple's resources are to be treated as a whole for the purposes of the assessment of those resources (the resources of children are subject to special rules) whereas those who do not form part of the family will only be taken into account as non-dependants, if at all.

For the critical issue of membership of a "household", see below. This is of equal importance to opposite sex and same sex couples.

SSCBA s137(2)(l) permits the making of regulations to define the situations in which persons are not to be treated as sharing a household for these purposes. See reg 21 of both the HB and the HB(SPC) Regs and the CTB equivalents. Reg 20 of both the HB and the HB(SPC) Regs sets out the circumstances in which adults are to be treated as responsible for children and young persons (for the issue of the identity of persons of prescribed description for these purposes see reg 19 of both sets of regs).

Meaning of "household" in the definitions of "couple" and "family". This word is of significance in three respects in determining the question of membership of a family. First, in order for a child or young person to form part of a claimant's family, s/he must live in the same household. Note that reg 21 HB Regs deems continued residence in the household in certain circumstances, but does not itself define the circumstances in which a child forms part of the household. Secondly, the other member of a "married couple" or "civil partnership couple" will only form part of a claimant's family if s/he is living in the same household. Thirdly, the question of whether an unmarried man and woman are "living together as husband and wife" or whether a same sex couple are living together as if they were civil partners will involve consideration of, but is not determined by, the question of whether they share a household.

There is a considerable body of caselaw considering whether two people are members of the same "household". As was observed by the commissioner in *R(SB) 4/83* (para 19), the word is an ordinary English word and the question is to be resolved by the use of common sense. More than one interpretation of the facts before the authority or an appeal tribunal may therefore be permissible. However, the following principles can be established from the caselaw:

(1)   A person cannot be a member of more than one household at once: *R(SB) 8/85* (para 12). However, it is possible for a person to follow a regular pattern of moving from one household to another: see *CIS 11304/1995* (para 10), where a claimant spent about six months in each year living with his wife and the other part of the year living with another female partner.

(2)   The issue is not determined on a week-by-week basis but on the basis of the overall relationship between the parties: *R(SB) 30/83* (para 5) concerning a university student moving in and out of the accommodation, who was held to be resident with her partner during the periods of absence during term-time. Note the special rules in reg 7(6)(b) HB Regs that can apply in these circumstances.

(3)   If the two people are separately liable to pay for their accommodation, that is a good indication that they are not members of the same household: *R(SB) 13/82* (para 11).

(4)   If the two people have completely separate living arrangements, then they cannot be members of the same household: *R(SB) 4/83* (para 19).

(5)   However, even if two people share certain facilities, there must still be an element of domesticity about their arrangements. This is illustrated by *CIS 671/1992* para 4 where the claimant and his wife suffered from senile dementia and did not understand the fact that they were husband and wife. Accordingly, mere presence in the same room does not mean that the two people are sharing a household. There must be a reasonable level of independence and self-sufficiency: *R(IS) 1/99* (Appendix para 14). This will often be lacking where a person is living in communal accommodation and so it will be rare for the occupants to be sharing a single household: *CIS 671/1992* (paras 4-5).

(6)   In considering whether the element of shared living is sufficiently strong to constitute a single household, a number of factors may be relevant. These may include: whether there are independent arrangements for the storage and cooking of food, whether there are independent financial arrangements (apart from the question of separate liabilities for the accommodation discussed above), whether the two people eat separately, and the general evidence of family life within the accommodation. Ultimately, however, it remains a question of fact and it will often not be easy to demonstrate an error of law in the approach taken by an authority or appeal tribunal.

Subsection (2): Regulation-making powers

This sets out general regulation-making powers in relation to issues relating to entitlement to means-tested benefits. For regulation-making powers in relation to adjudication and administration issues, see ss5 and 6 SSAA. The principal regulations made under these powers are listed next to the letter of each paragraph below:

(a)   Reg 7(10) to (17) of both the HB and the HB(SPC) Regs and reg 8(1) to (6) of both the CTB and the CTB(SPC) Regs. No distinction is drawn between absences inside and outside the UK in the HB and CTB schemes.

(b)   See para (a).

(c)   Reg 6(1) to (4) HB, HB(CTB), CTB and CTB(SPC) Regs.

(d)   Reg 6(5) to (7) HB, HB(CTB), CTB and CTB(SPC) Regs.

(e)   Not relevant. This concept has nothing to do with the HB and CTB rules about students but is used in the comparable IS and income-based JSA exclusions for students.

(f)   See para (e).

(g)   This power has not been exercised.

(h)   See reg 7 of both the HB and HB(SPC) Regs and reg 8 of both the CTB and CTB(SPC) Regs.

(i)   See regs 7, 9, 10 and 56 HB Regs and regs 7, 9, and 10 HB(SPC) Regs.

(j)   See reg 8(1)(b) to (e) of both the HB and the HB(SPC) Regs.

(k)   See reg 2(4) of both the HB and the HB(SPC) Regs.

(l)   See reg 21 of both the HB and the HB(SPC) Regs and reg 11 of both the CTB and the CTB(SPC) Regs.

(m)   See reg 20 of both the HB and the HB(SPC) Regs and reg 10 of both the CTB and the CTB(SPC) Regs.

PART XIII
General
Interpretation

Applications of Act in relation to territorial waters
172. In this Act–

(a)   any reference to Great Britain includes a reference to the territorial waters of the United Kingdom adjacent to Great Britain;

(b)   any reference to the United Kingdom includes a reference to the territorial waters of the United Kingdom.

Age
173. For the purposes of this Act a person–

(a)   is over or under a particular age if he has or, as the case may be has not attained that age; and

(b)   is between two particular ages if he has attained the first but not the second;

and in Scotland (as in England and Wales) the time at which a person attains a particular age expressed in years is the commencement of the relevant anniversary of the date of his birth.

References to Acts
174. In this Act–

''the 1975 Act'' means the Social Security Act 1975;

''the 1986 Act'' means the Social Security Act 1986;

''the Administration Act'' means the Social Security Administration Act 1992;

''the Consequential Provisions Act'' means the Social Security (Consequential Provisions) Act 1992;

''the Northern Ireland Contributions and Benefits Act'' means the Social Security Contributions and Benefits (Northern Ireland) Act 1992;

''the Old Cases Act'' means the Industrial Injuries and Diseases (Old Cases) Act 1975; and

''the Pensions Act'' means the Social Security Pensions Act 1975.

Subordinate legislation

Regulations, orders and schemes
175.–(1) Subject to section 145(5) above, regulations and orders under this Act shall be made by the Secretary of State.

[(1A) *[omitted]*]

(2) Powers under this Act to make regulations, orders or schemes shall be exercisable by statutory instrument.

(3) Except in the case of an order under section 145(3) above and in so far as this Act otherwise provides, any power under this Act to make regulations or an order may be exercised–

(a) either in relation to all cases to which the power extends, or in relation to those cases subject to specified exceptions, or in relation to any specified cases or classes of case;

(b) so as to make, as respects the cases in relation to which it is exercised–

   (i) the full provision to which the power extends or any less provision (whether by way of exception or otherwise),

   (ii) the same provision for all cases in relation to which the power is exercised, or different provision for different cases or different classes of case or different provision as respects the same case or class of case for different purposes of this Act,

   (iii) any such provision either unconditionally or subject to any specified condition;

and where such a power is expressed to be exercisable for alternative purposes it may be exercised in relation to the same case or any or all of those purposes; and powers to make regulations or an order for the purposes of any one provision of this Act are without prejudice to powers to make regulations or an order for the purposes of any other provision.

(4) Without prejudice to any specific provision in this Act, any power conferred by this Act to make regulations or an order (other than the power conferred in section 145(3) above) includes power to make thereby such incidental, supplementary, consequential or transitional provision as appears to the Secretary of State to be expedient for the purposes of the regulations or order.

(5) Without prejudice to any specific provisions in this Act, a power conferred by any provision of this Act except–

(a) sections 30, 47(6), 57(9)(a) and 145(3) above and paragraph 3(9) of Schedule 7 to this Act;

(b) section 122(1) above in relation to the definition of ''payments by way of occupational or personal pension''; and

(c) Part XI,

to make regulations or an order includes power to provide for a person to exercise a discretion in dealing with any matter.

(6) Any power conferred by this Act to make orders or regulations relating to housing benefit or [¹ council tax benefit] shall include power to make different provisions for different areas.

(7) Any power of the Secretary of State under any provision of this Act, except the provisions mentioned in subsection (5)(a) and (b) above and Part IX, to make any regulations or order, where the power is not expressed to be exercisable with the consent of the Treasury, shall if the Treasury so direct be exercisable only in conjunction with them.

(8) Any power under any of sections 116 to 120 above to modify provisions of this Act or the Administration Act extends also to modifying so much of any other provision of this Act or that Act as re-enacts provisions of the 1975 Act which replaced provisions of the National Insurance (Industrial Injuries) Acts 1965 to 1974.

(9) A power to make regulations under any of sections 116 to 120 above shall be exercisable in relation to any enactment passed after this Act which is directed to be construed as one with this Act; but this subsection applies only so far as a contrary intention is not expressed in the enactment so passed, and is without prejudice to the generality of any such direction.

(10) Any reference in this section or section 176 below to an order or regulations under this Act includes a reference to an order or regulations made under any provision of an enactment passed after this Act and directed to be construed as one with this Act; but this subsection applies only so far as a contrary intention is not

expressed in the enactment so passed, and without prejudice to the generality of any such direction.

Amendment

1.   Substituted by para 10 Sch 9 Local Government Finance Act 1992 (1.4.93).

Parliamentary control

176.–(1)   *[omitted]*

(2)   *[omitted]*

(3)   A statutory instrument–

(a)   which contains (whether alone or with other provisions) any order, regulations or scheme made under this Act by the Secretary of State, other than an order under section 145(3) above; and

(b)   which is not subject to any requirement that a draft of the instrument shall be laid before and approved by a resolution of each House of Parliament,

shall be subject to annulment in pursuance of a resolution of either House of Parliament.

Short title, commencement and extent

Short title, commencement and extent

177.–(1)   This Act may be cited as the Social Security Contributions and Benefits Act 1992.

(2)   This Act is to be read, where appropriate, with the Administration Act and the Consequential Provisions Act.

(3)   The enactments consolidated by this Act are repealed, in consequence of the consolidation, by the Consequential Provisions Act.

(4)   Except as provided in Schedule 4 to the Consequential Provisions Act, this Act shall come into force on 1st July 1992.

(5)   The following provisions extend to Northern Ireland–

(a)   section 16 and Schedule 2;

(b)   section 116(2); and

(c)   this section.

(6)   Except as provided by this section, this Act does not extend to Northern Ireland.

Social Security Administration Act 1992
(1992 c5)

Arrangement of Sections

PART I
CLAIMS FOR AND PAYMENTS AND GENERAL ADMINISTRATION OF BENEFIT

Necessity of claim

1. Entitlement to benefit dependent on claim
2. Retrospective effect of provisions making entitlement to benefit dependent on claim

Work-focused interviews

2A. Claim or full entitlement to certain benefits conditional on work-focused interview
2C. Optional work-focused interviews

Claims and payments regulations

5. Regulations about claims for and payments of benefit

Council tax benefits

6. Regulations about council tax benefits administration
7. Relationship between council tax benefit and other benefits
7A. Sharing of functions as regards certain claims and information

PART II
ADJUDICATION
Housing benefit and council tax benefit

63. Adjudication

PART III
OVERPAYMENTS AND ADJUSTMENTS OF BENEFIT
Housing benefit

75. Overpayments of housing benefit

Council tax benefit

76. Excess benefit
77. Shortfall in benefit

PART VI
Enforcement

109A. Authorisations for investigators
109B. Power to require information
109C. Powers of entry
110A. Authorisations by local authorities
111. Delay, obstruction etc. of inspector
111A. Dishonest representations for the purpose of obtaining benefit etc.
112. False representations for obtaining benefit etc
113. Breach of regulations
115. Offences by bodies corporate
115A. Penalty as alternative to prosecution
115B. Penalty as alternative to prosecution: colluding employers etc

Legal proceedings

116. Legal proceedings
121DA Interpretation of Part VI

PART VII
PROVISION OF INFORMATION
Authorities administering housing benefit or council tax benefit
122C.   Supply of information to authorities administering benefit
122D.   Supply of information by authorities administering benefit
122E.   Supply of information between authorities administering benefit
123.   Unauthorised disclosure of information relating to particular persons
126A.   Information from landlords and agents

EXPEDITED CLAIMS FOR HOUSING AND COUNCIL TAX BENEFIT
128A.   Disclosure of information by authorities

PART VIII
ARRANGEMENTS FOR HOUSING BENEFIT AND COUNCIL TAX BENEFITS AND
RELATED SUBSIDIES
Housing benefit
134.   Arrangements for housing benefit

Council tax benefit
138.   Nature of benefits
139.   Arrangements for council tax benefit

Reports
139A.   Persons to report on administration
139B.   Powers of investigation
139C.   Reports

Directions by Secretary of State
139D.   Directions
139E.   Information about attainment of standards
139F.   Enforcement notices
139G.   Enforcement determinations
139H.   Enforcement determinations: supplementary

Subsidy
140A.   Subsidy
140B.   Calculation of amount of subsidy
140C.   Payment of subsidy
140D.   Rent rebate subsidy: accounting provisions

Supplementary provisions
140E   Financing of joint arrangements
and
140EE.
140F.   No requirement for annual orders
140G.   Interpretation: Part VIII

PART XIII
ADVISORY BODIES AND CONSULTATION
*The Social Security Advisory Committee and the Industrial Injuries Advisory
Council*
170.   Consultation with representative organisations
172.   Functions of Committee and Council in relation to regulations
173.   Cases in which consultation is not required
174.   Committee's report on regulations and Secretary of State's duties

Housing benefit and council tax benefit
176.   Consultation with representative organisations

PART XV
MISCELLANEOUS
182A.   Return of social security post
182B.   Requirement to supply information about redirection of post
187.   Certain benefit to be inalienable

PART XVI
GENERAL
Subordinate legislation
189.   Regulations and orders – general
190.   Parliamentary control of orders and regulations

Supplementary
191.   Interpretation – general
192.   Short title, commencement and extent

SCHEDULES
4.   Persons Employed in Social Security Administration or Adjudication
10.   Supplementary Benefit etc

PART I
Claims for and Payments and General Administration of Benefit
Necessity of claim

Entitlement to benefit dependent on claim

1.–(1)   Except in such cases as may be prescribed, and subject to the following provisions of this section and to section 3 below, no person shall be entitled to any benefit unless, in addition to any other conditions relating to that benefit being satisfied–

(a)   he makes a claim for it in the manner, and within the time, prescribed in relation to that benefit by regulations under this Part of this Act; or

(b)   he is treated by virtue of such regulations as making a claim for it.

[²(1A)   No person whose entitlement to any benefit depends on his making a claim shall be entitled to the benefit unless subsection (1B) below is satisfied in relation both to the person making the claim and to any other person in respect of whom he is claiming benefit.

(1B)   This subsection is satisfied in relation to a person if–

(a)   the claim is accompanied by–

(i)   a statement of the person's national insurance number and information or evidence establishing that that number has been allocated to the person; or

(ii)   information or evidence enabling the national insurance number that has been allocated to the person to be ascertained; or

(b)   the person makes an application for a national insurance number to be allocated to him which is accompanied by information or evidence enabling such a number to be so allocated.

(1C)   Regulations may make provision disapplying subsection (1A) above in the case of–

(a)   prescribed benefits;

(b)   prescribed descriptions of persons making claims; or

(c)   prescribed descriptions of persons in respect of whom benefit is claimed, or in other prescribed circumstances.]

(2)   Where under subsection (1) above a person is required to make a claim or to be treated as making a claim for a benefit in order to be entitled to it–
  (a)   if the benefit is a widow's payment, she shall not be entitled to it in respect of a death occurring more than 12 months before the date on which the claim is made or treated as made, and
  (b)   if the benefit is any other benefit except disablement benefit or reduced earnings allowance, the person shall not be entitled to it in respect of any period more than 12 months before that date,
except as provided by section 3 below.
  (3)   *[omitted]*
  (4)   In this section and section 2 below "benefit" means–
  (a)   benefit as defined in section 122 of the Contributions and Benefits Act; and
  [[1](aa) a jobseeker's allowance;] and
  (b)   any income-related benefit.
  (5)   This section (which corresponds to section 165A of the 1975 Act, as it had effect immediately before this Act came into force) applies to claims made on or after 1st October 1990 or treated by virtue of regulations under that section or this section as having been made on or after that date.
  (6)   Schedule 1 to this Act shall have effect in relation to other claims.

Definitions
  "benefit" – s1(4).
  "claim" – s191.
  "income-related benefit" – s191.
  "prescribe" – s191.

Amendments
  1.   Jobseekers Act 1995 Sch 2 para 38 (22.4.96).
  2.   Inserted by SSA(F) Act 1997, s19.

General Note
  Subs (1) sets out the general condition of entitlement to benefit that there must be a current claim. See Part 10 HB Regs, Part 9 HB(SPC) Regs, Part 8 CTB Regs and Part 7 CTB(SPC) Regs.
  Subs (1A) to (1C) provide a general requirement in relation to entitlement for all benefits, including HB and CTB. By subs (1B), it is necessary that the claimant either supplies her/his national insurance number or enough information to allow the number to be ascertained, or makes an application for a number. Note that these provisions were phased into force for HB and CTB purposes: reg 2A HB Regs 1987 and reg 2A CTB Regs 1992.
  The phrase "any other person in respect of whom he is claiming benefit" in subsection (1A) includes the claimant's partner with whom s/he lives: *Secretary of State for Work and Pensions v Wilson* [2006] EWCA Civ 882, *29 June 2006*, reported as *R(H) 7/06*.

Retrospective effect of provisions making entitlement to benefit dependent on claim

  2.–(1)   This section applies where a claim for benefit is made or treated as made at any time on or after 2nd September 1985 (the date on which section 165A or the 1975 Act (general provision as to necessity of claim for entitlement to benefit), as originally enacted, came into force) in respect of a period the whole or any part of which falls on or after that date.
  (2)   Where this section applies, any question arising as to–
  (a)   whether the claimant is or was at any time (whether before, on or after 2nd September 1985) entitled to the benefit in question, or to any other benefit on which his entitlement to that benefit depends; or
  (b)   in a case where the claimant's entitlement to the benefit depends on the entitlement of another person to a benefit, whether that other person is or was so entitled,

shall be determined as if the relevant claim enactment and any regulations made under or referred to in that enactment had also been in force, with any necessary modifications, at all times relevant for the purpose of determining the entitlement of the claimant, and, where applicable, of the other person, to the benefit or benefits in question (including the entitlement of any person to any benefit on which that entitlement depends, and so on).

(3)   In this section "the relevant claim enactment" means section 1 above as it has effect in relation to the claim referred to in subsection (1) above.

(4)   In any case where–

(a)   a claim for benefit was made or treated as made (whether before, on or after 2nd September 1985, and whether by the same claimant as the claim referred to in subsection (1) above or not), and benefit was awarded on that claim, in respect of a period falling wholly or partly before that date; but

(b)   that award would not have been made had the current requirements applied in relation to claims for benefit, whenever made, in respect of periods before that date; and

(c)   entitlement to the benefit claimed as mentioned in subsection (1) above depends on whether the claimant or some other person was previously entitled or treated as entitled to that or some other benefit,

then, in determining whether the conditions of entitlement to the benefit so claimed are satisfied, the person to whom benefit was awarded as mentioned in paragraphs (a) and (b) above shall be taken to have been entitled to the benefit so awarded, notwithstanding anything in subsection (2) above.

(5)   In subsection (4) above "the current requirements" means–

(a)   the relevant claim enactment, and any regulations made or treated as made under that enactment, or referred to in it, as in force at the time of the claim referred to in subsection (1) above, with any necessary modifications; and

(b)   subsection (1) (with the omission of the words following "at any time") and subsections (2) and (3) above.

Definitions
"benefit" – s1(4).
"claim" – s191.
"current requirements" – s2(4).
"relevant claim enactment" – s2(1).

General Note
This section was introduced by the Social Security Act 1990 to confirm that the predecessor of s1 above had retrospective effect. This means that a claimant cannot claim HB from before September 1985 on the basis that before that date a claim was not a requirement of entitlement to benefit: *Insurance Officer v McCaffrey* [1985] 1 WLR 1353 at 1355H-1356C, HL.

Work-focused interviews

Claim or full entitlement to certain benefits conditional on work-focused interview

2A.–(1)   Regulations may make provision for or in connection with–

(a)   imposing, as a condition falling to be satisfied by a person who–
   (i)   makes a claim for a benefit to which this section applies, and
   (ii)   is under the age of 60 at the time of making the claim, a requirement to take part in a work-focused interview;

(b)   imposing, at a time when–
   (i)   a person is under that age and entitled to such a benefit, and
   (ii)   any prescribed circumstances exist, a requirement to take part in such an interview as a condition of that person continuing to be entitled to

the full amount which is payable to him in respect of the benefit apart from the regulations.

(2) The benefits to which this section applies are–

(a) income support;

(b) housing benefit;

(c) council tax benefit;

(d) widow's and bereavement benefits falling within section 20(1)(e) and (ea) of the Contributions and Benefits Act (other than a bereavement payment);

(e) incapacity benefit;

(f) severe disablement allowance; and

(g) invalid care allowance.

(3) Regulations under this section may, in particular, make provision–

(a) for securing, where a person would otherwise be required to take part in interviews relating to two or more benefits–

(i) that he is only required to take part in one interview, and

(ii) that any such interview is capable of counting for the purposes of all those benefits;

(b) for determining the persons by whom interviews are to be conducted;

(c) conferring power on such persons or the designated authority to determine when and where interviews are to take place (including power in prescribed circumstances to determine that they are to take place in the homes of those being interviewed);

(d) prescribing the circumstances in which persons attending interviews are to be regarded as having or not having taken part in them;

(e) for securing that the appropriate consequences mentioned in subsection (4)(a) or (b) below ensue if a person who has been notified that he is required to take part in an interview–

(i) fails to take part in the interview, and

(ii) does not show, within the prescribed period, that he had good cause for that failure;

(f) prescribing–

(i) matters which are or are not to be taken into account in determining whether a person does or does not have good cause for any failure to comply with the regulations, or

(ii) circumstances in which a person is or is not to be regarded as having or not having good cause for any such failure.

(4) For the purposes of subsection (3)(e) above the appropriate consequences of a failure falling within that provision are–

(a) where the requirement to take part in an interview applied by virtue of subsection (1)(a) above, that as regards any relevant benefit either–

(i) the person in question is to be regarded as not having made a claim for the benefit, or

(ii) if (in the case of an interview postponed in accordance with subsection (7)) that person has already been awarded the benefit, his entitlement to the benefit is to terminate immediately;

(b) where the requirement to take part in an interview applied by virtue of subsection (1)(b) above, that the amount payable to the person in question in respect of any relevant benefit is to be reduced by the specified amount until the specified time.

(5) Regulations under this section may, in relation to any such reduction, provide–

(a) for the amount of the reduction to be calculated in the first instance by reference to such amount as may be prescribed;

(b) for the amount as so calculated to be restricted, in prescribed circumstances, to the prescribed extent;

(c)   where the person in question is entitled to two or more relevant benefits, for determining the extent, and the order, in which those benefits are to be reduced in order to give effect to the reduction required in his case.

(6)   Regulations under this section may provide that any requirement to take part in an interview that would otherwise apply to a person by virtue of such regulations–

(a)   is, in any prescribed circumstances, either not to apply or not to apply until such time as is specified;

(b)   is not to apply if the designated authority determines that an interview–

(i)   would not be of assistance to that person, or

(ii)   would not be appropriate in the circumstances;

(c)   is not to apply until such time as the designated authority determines, if that authority determines that an interview–

(i)   would not be of assistance to that person, or

(ii)   would not be appropriate in the circumstances, until that time; and the regulations may make provision for treating a person in relation to whom any such requirement does not apply, or does not apply until a particular time, as having complied with that requirement to such extent and for such purposes as are specified.

(7)   Where–

(a)   a person is required to take part in an interview by virtue of subsection (1)(a), and

(b)   the interview is postponed by or under regulations made in pursuance of subsection (6)(a) or (c), the time to which it is so postponed may be a time falling after an award of the relevant benefit to that person.

(8)   In this section–

"the designated authority" means such of the following as may be specified, namely–

(a)   the Secretary of State,

(b)   a person providing services to the Secretary of State,

(c)   a local authority,

(d)   a person providing services to, or authorised to exercise any function of, any such authority;

"interview" (in subsections (3) to (7)) means a work-focused interview;

"relevant benefit", in relation to any person required to take part in a work-focused interview, means any benefit in relation to which that requirement applied by virtue of subsection (1)(a) or (b) above;

"specified" means prescribed by or determined in accordance with regulations;

"work-focused interview", in relation to a person, means an interview conducted for such purposes connected with employment or training in the case of that person as may be specified; and the purposes which may be so specified include purposes connected with a person's existing or future employment or training prospects or needs, and (in particular) assisting or encouraging a person to enhance his employment prospects.

Commencement

11.11.99: see s89(4)(a) WRPA.

General Note

The principal innovation made by the WRPA in so far as the subject matter of this book is concerned was a greatly expanded role for local authorities as providers of benefit services. The Act sought to permit the implementation of the Single Work-Focused Gateway, or ONE as it was subsequently renamed.

The aim of the scheme was to set up a number of offices to handle claims and inquiries relating to all benefits for which a person might be eligible. At the time of writing, very few ONE offices were still in existence. The provisions are included in this book because some ONE offices were run by local authorities: see subs (8)(c). The offices also provided "work-focused interviews" (WFIs) designed to assist claimants in finding employment. As usual, the Act sets out the bare bones of the scheme with regulations putting the flesh on the bones.

Analysis

Subs (1). No claimant aged 60 or over can be required to attend a WFI, but in respect of claimants under that age, the regulations enable such a requirement both at the time of making a claim and at some time after benefit is awarded.

In the latter case, conditions may be imposed by the regulations before a WFI may be required and it appears from subs (1)(b)(ii) that if the claimant fails to comply, s/he will only lose part of her/his benefit. This appears to be confirmed by the terms of subs (4)(b) below.

Subs (2) confirms that HB and CTB are amongst the benefits which, if claimed, may trigger a requirement of a WFI, but there is not currently such a requirement.

Subs (3) contains a number of regulation-making powers, which may be summarised as follows:

(1)   Para (a) envisages that a claimant will receive only one WFI, even if s/he is claiming more than one benefit.

(2)   Paras (b) and (c) deal with the administration of interviews. The words in brackets in sub-para (c) provide for regulations to permit interviews to take place in the claimant's home. However, on its face para (c) appears to authorise a requirement that the interview be granted in the home. If that is so, there may be an issue as to whether such a requirement might infringe Art 8 of the European Convention of Human Rights as being an unjustifiable invasion of the claimant's privacy.

(3)   Para (d) is a deeming provision which permits people to be deemed to have or to have not taken part in an interview.

(4)   Paras (e) and (f) are the big stick. They provide for sanctions to be imposed under subs (4) in a case where the conditions in para (e) are fulfilled.

Subs (4) and (5) provide for the consequences of falling foul of subs (3)(e) and (f). Para (4) operates in three different ways. A person who has claimed benefit is treated as not having made a claim: para (a)(i). A person whose interview has been postponed under subs (7) has her/his entitlement to benefit terminated: para (a)(ii). It appears, however, that such termination will not be retrospective so as to create an overpayment. Finally, under para (b) a person who has the requirement applied to him during a period of entitlement to benefit does not have benefit terminated altogether, but has a deduction made from her/his benefit under subs (5).

Subs (6) and (7) contain wide powers to exempt claimants from the requirement to attend an interview, either permanently or temporarily. Where there is a temporary exemption, subs (7) permits an award of benefit to be made in the interim.

Subs (8) contains definitions. Note that local authorities are one of those who may be authorised to conduct WFIs.

Optional work-focused interviews

2C.–(1)   Regulations may make provision for conferring on local authorities functions in connection with conducting work-focused interviews in cases where such interviews are requested or consented to by persons to whom this section applies.

(2)   This section applies to [¹

(a)   persons making claims for or entitled to any of the benefits listed in section 2A(2) above or any prescribed benefit; and

(b)   partners of persons entitled to any of the benefits listed in section 2AA(2) above or any prescribed benefit;]

and it so applies regardless of whether such persons have, in accordance with regulations under section 2A [¹ or 2AA] above, already taken part in interviews conducted under such regulations.

(3)   The functions which may be conferred on a local authority by regulations under this section include functions relating to–

(a)   the obtaining and receiving of information for the purposes of work-focused interviews conducted under the regulations;

(b)   the recording and forwarding of information supplied at, or for the purposes of, such interviews;

(c)   the taking of steps to identify potential employment or training opportunities for persons taking part in such interviews.

(4)   Regulations under this section may make different provision for different areas or different authorities.

(5)   In this section "work-focused interview", in relation to a person to whom this section applies, means an interview conducted for such purposes connected with employment or training in the case of such a person as may be prescribed; and the purposes which may be so prescribed include–

(a)   purposes connected with the existing or future employment or training prospects or needs of such a person, and

(b)   (in particular) assisting or encouraging such a person to enhance his employment prospects.

Commencement

11.11.99: see s89(4)(a) WRPA.

Amendment

1.   Amended by the Employment Act 2002 Sch 7 para 11 (5.7.03).

General Note

This section authorised the pilot schemes for ONE that were run by local authorities. The Social Security (Claims and Information) Regulations 1999 SI No 3108 were made under this provision. The important point to note is the absence of any compulsion to attend an interview: see subs (1).

Claims and payments regulations

Regulations about claims for and payments of benefit

5.–(1) Regulations may provide–

(a)   for requiring a claim for a benefit to which this section applies to be made by such person, in such manner and within such time as may be prescribed;

(b)   for treating such a claim made in such circumstances as may be prescribed as having been made at such date earlier or later than that at which it is made as may be prescribed;

(c)   for permitting such a claim to be made, or treated as if made, for a period wholly or partly after the date on which it is made;

(d)   for permitting an award on such a claim to be made for such a period subject to the condition that the claimant satisfies the requirements for entitlement when benefit becomes payable under the award;

(e)   [⁴ for any such award to be revised under section 9 of the Social Security Act 1998, or superceded under section 10 of that Act, if any of those requirements are found not to have been satisfied;]

(f)   for the disallowance on any ground of a person's claim for a benefit to which this section applies to be treated as a disallowance of any further claim by that person for that benefit until the grounds of the original disallowance have ceased to exist;

(g)   for enabling one person to act for another in relation to a claim for a benefit to which this section applies and for enabling such a claim to be made and proceeded with in the name of a person who has died;

(h)   for requiring any information or evidence needed for the determination of such a claim or of any question arising in connection with such a claim to be furnished by such person as may be prescribed in accordance with the regulations;

[⁶(hh) for requiring such person as may be prescribed in accordance with the regulations to furnish any information or evidence needed for a determination whether a decision on an award of benefit to which this section applies–

(i)   should be revised under section 9 of the Social Security Act 1998 [⁷ or, as the case may be, under paragraph 3 of Schedule 7 to the Child Support, Pensions and Social Security Act 2000]; or

      (ii)   should be superseded under section 10 of that Act [⁷ or, as the case may be, under paragraph 4 of that Schedule];]

(i)   for the person to whom, time when and manner in which a benefit to which this section applies is to be paid and for the information and evidence to be furnished in connection with the payment of such a benefit;

(j)   for notice to be given of any change of circumstances affecting the continuance of entitlement to such a benefit or payment of such a benefit;

(k)   for the day on which entitlement to such a benefit is to begin or end;

(l)   for calculating the amounts of such a benefit according to a prescribed scale or otherwise adjusting them so as to avoid fractional amounts or facilitate computations;

(m)   for extinguishing the right to payment of such a benefit if payment is not obtained within such period, not being less than 12 months, as may be prescribed from the date on which the right is treated under the regulations as having arisen;

[⁸ . . .]

(p)   for the circumstances and manner in which payments of such a benefit may be made to another person on behalf of the beneficiary for any purpose, which may be to discharge, in whole or in part, an obligation of the beneficiary or any other person;

(q)   for the payment or distribution of such a benefit to or among persons claiming to be entitled on the death of any person and for dispensing with strict proof of their title;

(r)   for the making of a payment on account of such a benefit
      (i)   where no claim has been made and it is impracticable for one to be made immediately;
      (ii)   where a claim has been made and it is impracticable for the claim or an appeal, reference, review or application relating to it to be immediately determined;
      (iii)   where an award has been made but it is impracticable to pay the whole immediately.

(2)   This section applies to the following benefits–

(a)   benefits as defined in section 122 of the Contributions and Benefits Act;

[¹(aa) a jobseeker's allowance;]

(b)   income support;

[⁹ . . .]

[⁹ . . .]

(e)   housing benefit;

(f)   any social fund payments such as are mentioned in section 138(1)(a) or (2) of the Contributions and Benefits Act;

(g)   child benefit; and

(h)   Christmas bonus.

(3)   The reference in subsection (1)(h) above to information or evidence needed for the determination of a claim includes a reference to information or evidence required by a rent officer under [³ section 122 of the Housing Act 1996].

[⁸ . . .]

(5)   *[omitted]*

[² (6)   As it has effect in relation to housing benefit subsection (1)(p) above authorises provision requiring the making of payments of benefit to another person, on behalf of the beneficiary in such circumstances as may be prescribed.]

Definition

    "prescribed" – see s191.

Amendments

    1.   Inserted by Jobseekers Act 1996 Sch 2 para 39.

2.   Inserted by the Housing Act 1996, s120(1) and deemed always to have had effect by s120(2).
3.   Substituted by the Housing Act 1996 Sch 13 para 3(2).
4.   Substituted by the Social Security Act 1998 Sch 7 para 79(1)(a).
5.   Repealed by the Social Security Act 1998 Sch 7 para 79(1)(b) from 29.11.99. However, this repeal does not take effect in relation to HB and CTB: see Art 2(2)(a) and (b) of the Social Security Act 1998 (Commencement No 12 and Consequential and Transitional Provisions) Order 1999 SI No 3178.
6.   Inserted by the Social Security Act 1998 s74 .
7.   Amended by CSPSS Act 2000 Sch 7 para 21(1) (2.7.01).
8.   Repealed by the Social Security Act 1998 s86(2), Sch 8.
9.   Repealed by the Tax Credits Act 2002 Sch 6 (6.4.03).

General Note

This section enables the making of regulations in relation to the administration of claims and payments for HB and various other benefits.

Analysis

Paragraph (1)

By subs (2)(e), this subsection applies to HB. It does not apply to CTB, which is dealt with by s6 below. The list below refers to the lettered subparagraphs and which regulations, broadly speaking, are made under the powers given by the subparagraph:

(a)   See HB Regs regs 82 and 83 and HB(SPC) Regs regs 63 and 64.
(b)   See HB Regs reg 83(12) 72(14) and HB(SPC) Regs reg 64(1).
(c)   See HB Regs reg 83(10) and HB(SPC) Regs reg 64(11).
(d)   See HB Regs reg 83(10) and HB(SPC) Regs reg 64(11).
(e)   This power is not relevant to HB and CTB. See s34 of the Social Security Act 1998 for the regulation-making powers for reviews.
(f)   This power does not appear to have been exercised.
(g)   See HB Regs reg 82(2) to (6) and HB(SPC) Regs reg 63(2) to (6).
(h)   See HB Regs reg 86 and HB(SPC) Regs reg 67 and see paragraph (3) below.
(hh)   See HB Regs reg 86 and HB(SPC) Regs reg 67.
(i)   See HB Regs regs 91, 94 and 97 and HB(SPC) Regs reg 72, 75, 77 and 78.
(j)   See HB Regs regs 86 and 88 and HB(SPC) Regs 67 and 69.
(k)   See HB Regs reg 76 and HB(SPC) Regs 57.
(l)   See HB Regs reg 80(8) and HB(SPC) Regs reg 61(7).
(m)   This power does not appear to have been exercised.
(p)   See HB Regs regs 95 and 96 and HB(SPC) Regs reg 76 and 77, but note the doubt expressed in the Analysis to reg 95 HB Regs as to whether that regulation is valid. Note also subs (6) below.
(q)   See HB Regs reg 97 and HB(SPC) Regs reg 78.
(r)   See HB Regs reg 93 and HB(SPC) Regs reg 74.

Paragraph (3)

This gives power to make the provisions for a rent officer to require information: see the Rent Officers (Housing Benefit Functions) Order 1997 and the Rent Officers (Housing Benefit Functions) (Scotland) Order 1997 on pp520 and 540.

Paragraph (6)

The amendment made by the Housing Act 1996 removes any doubts about whether reg 93(1) HB Regs 1987 (now reg 95(1) HB Regs and reg 76(1) HB(SPC) Regs) was validly made under subs (1)(p), which only refers to circumstances in which payments of HB *may* be made, not circumstances when they *shall* be made to a third party. The amendment has retrospective effect.

Council tax benefits

Regulations about council tax benefits administration

6.–(1) Regulations may provide as follows as regards any [¹ council tax benefits]–

(a)   for requiring a claim for a benefit to be made by such person, in such manner and within such time as may be prescribed;

(b)   for treating a claim made in such circumstances as may be prescribed as having been made at such date earlier or later than that at which it is made as may be prescribed;

(c)   for permitting a claim to be made, or treated as if made, for a period wholly or partly after the date on which it is made;

(d)   for permitting an award on a claim to be made for such a period subject to the condition that the claimant satisfies the requirements for entitlement when benefit becomes payable, or any right to a reduction [² . . .] becomes available, under the award;

(e)   for a review of any award if those requirements are found not to have been satisfied;

(f)   for the disallowance on any ground of a person's claim for a benefit to be treated as a disallowance of any further claim by that person for that benefit until the grounds of the original disallowance have ceased to exist;

(g)   for enabling one person to act for another in relation to a claim for a benefit and for enabling such a claim to be made and proceeded with in the name of a person who has died;

(h)   for requiring any information or evidence needed for the determination of a claim or of any question arising in connection with a claim to be furnished by such person as may be prescribed in accordance with the regulations;

[⁶(hh) for requiring such person as may be prescribed in accordance with the regulations to furnish any information or evidence needed for a determination whether a decision on an award of a benefit–

    (i)   should be revised under paragraph 3 of Schedule 7 to the Child Support, Pensions and Social Security Act 2000; or

    (ii)   should be superseded under paragraph 4 of that Schedule;]

(i)   for the time when and manner in which any benefit (or part) which takes the form of a payment is to be paid, and for the information and evidence to be furnished in connection with the payment;

(j)   for the time when the right to make a reduction [² . . .] may be exercised;

(k)   for notice to be given of any change of circumstances affecting the continuance of entitlement to a benefit;

(l)   for the day on which entitlement to a benefit is to begin or end;

(m)   for calculating the amount of a benefit according to a prescribed scale or otherwise adjusting it so as to avoid fractional amounts or facilitate computation;

[⁷ . . .];

(p)   in the case of any benefit (or part) which takes the form of a payment, for payment or distribution to or among persons claiming to be entitled on the death of any person, and for dispensing with strict proof of their title;

(q)   in the case of any benefit (or part) which takes the form of a payment, for the circumstances and manner in which payment may be made to one person on behalf of another for any purpose, which may be to discharge, in whole or in part, an obligation of the person entitled to the benefit or any other person;

(r)   for making a payment on account of a benefit, or conferring a right to make a reduction [³ . . .] on account, where no claim has been made and it is impracticable for one to be made immediately;

(s)   for making a payment on account of a benefit, or conferring a right to make a reduction [³ . . .] on account, where a claim has been made but it is impracticable for the claim or an appeal, reference, review or application relating to it to be determined immediately;

(t)   for making a payment on account of a benefit, or conferring a right to make a reduction [³ . . .] on account, where an award has been made but it is impracticable to institute the benefit immediately;

(u)   generally as to administration.

(2)   Regulations under this section may include [⁴ provision in relation to council tax benefit that prescribed provisions shall apply instead of prescribed provisions of

Part I or II of the Local Government Finance Act 1992, or that prescribed provisions of either of those Parts shall not apply] or shall apply subject to prescribed amendments or adaptations.

[⁵ (3) References in subsection (2) above to either of the Parts there mentioned include references to regulations made under the Part concerned.]

[⁷ . . .]

Amendments

1.   Substituted by LGFA Sch 9 para 12(1)(a) (1.4.93).
2.   Repealed by LGFA Sch 9 para 12(1)(b) and Sch 14 (1.4.93).
3.   Repealed by LGFA Sch 9 para 12(1)(c) and Sch 14 (1.4.93).
4.   Substituted by LGFA Sch 9 para 12(2) (1.4.93).
5.   Substituted by LGFA Sch 9 para 12(3) (1.4.93).
6.   Inserted by CSPSS Act 2000 Sch 7 para 21(2) (2.7.01).
7.   Repealed by Social Security Act 1998 s86 (2), Sch 8 (2.7.01).

General Note

This section gives similar powers to make regulations in relation to CTB as are available under s5 in relation to the benefits listed in s5(2).

Analysis

Paragraph (1)

The following list gives the main regulations which are made under each lettered subparagraph:

(a)   See CTB Regs regs 68 and 69 and CTB(SPC) Regs regs 52 and 53.
(b)   See CTB Regs regs 69(14) and CTB(SPC) Regs reg 56.
(c)   See CTB Regs regs 69(12) and CTB(SPC) Regs reg 53(12).
(d)   See CTB Regs reg 69(10) and CTB(SPC) Regs reg 53(10).
(f)   This power does not appear to have been exercised.
(g)   See CTB Regs reg 68 and CTB(SPC) Regs reg 52.
(h)   See CTB Regs reg 72 and CTB(SPC) Regs reg 57.
(hh) See CTB Regs reg 72 and CTB(SPC) Regs 57.
(i)   See CTB Regs Part 10 and CTB(SPC) Regs Part 9.
(j)   This power does not appear to have been exercised.
(k)   See CTB Regs reg 74 and CTB(SPC) Regs reg 59.
(l)   See CTB Regs Part 7 and CTB(SPC) Regs Part 6.
(m)   See CTB Regs Part 6 and CTB(SPC) Regs Part 5.
(p)   See CTB Regs reg 80 and CTB(SPC) Regs reg 65.

(r), (s) and (t) These powers do not appear to have been exercised.

Paragraphs (2) and (3)

These paragraphs give powers to make regulations that alter the effect of Parts I and II of the Local Government Finance Act 1992 and regulations made thereunder.

Relationship between council tax benefit and other benefits

7.–(1) Regulations may provide for a claim for one relevant benefit to be treated, either in the alternative or in addition, as a claim for any other relevant benefit that may be prescribed.

(2)   Regulations may provide for treating a payment made or right conferred by virtue of regulations–

(a)   under section 5(1)(r) above; or
(b)   under section 6(1)(r) to (t) above,

as made or conferred on account of any relevant benefit that is subsequently awarded or paid.

(3)   For the purposes of subsections (1) and (2) above relevant benefits are–

(a)   any benefit to which section 5 above applies; and
(b)   any [¹ council tax benefit].

Definition

"prescribe" – see s191.

Amendment

1. Substitution made by para 13 of Sch 9 to the Local Government Finance Act 1992 (1.4.93).

General Note

For an example of regulations made under subs (2) see reg 93 HB Regs (payments on account). There is no equivalent in the CTB Regs. There is no power to treat a claim for HB or CTB as a claim for any other benefit, or *vice versa*. However, the Secretary of State retains a power under reg 4(1) Social Security (Claims and Payments) Regulations 1987 (SI No.1968) to treat any written claim sent to her/him as being sufficient in the circumstances. So if a claimant mistakenly claims HB instead of mortgage interest with IS or income-based JSA and the HB claim was made through the DWP by filling in form NHB1, it might be possible to ask the Secretary of State to exercise discretion to treat that as a claim for mortgage interest.

For the authority's powers to treat claims not made on the required form as valid, see reg 83(1) HB Regs, reg 64(2) HB(SPC) Regs, reg 69(1) CTB Regs and reg 53(1) CTB(SPC) Regs.

Sharing of functions as regards certain claims and information

7A.–(1)   Regulations may, for the purpose of supplementing the persons or bodies to whom claims for relevant benefits may be made, make provision–

(a)   as regards housing benefit or council tax benefit, for claims for that benefit to be made to–
    (i)   a Minister of the Crown, or
    (ii)   a person providing services to a Minister of the Crown;

(b)   as regards any other relevant benefit, for claims for that benefit to be made to–
    (i)   a local authority,
    (ii)   a person providing services to a local authority, or
    (iii)   a person authorised to exercise any function of a local authority relating to housing benefit or council tax benefit.

[² (c) as regards any relevant benefit, for claims for that benefit to be made to-
    (i)   a county council in England,
    (ii)   a person providing services to a county council in England, or
    (iii)   a person authorised to exercise any function a county council in England has under this section.]

(2) Regulations may make provision for or in connection with–

(a)   the forwarding by a relevant authority of–
    (i)   claims received by virtue of any provision authorised by subsection (1) above, and
    (ii)   information or evidence supplied in connection with making such claims (whether supplied by persons making the claims or by other persons);

(b)   the receiving and forwarding by a relevant authority of information or evidence relating to social security [¹ or work] matters supplied by, or the obtaining by a relevant authority of such information or evidence from–
    (i)   persons making, or who have made, claims for a relevant benefit, or
    (ii)   other persons in connection with such claims, including information or evidence not relating to the claims or benefit in question;

(c)   the recording by a relevant authority of information or evidence relating to social security [1 or work] matters supplied to, or obtained by, the authority and the holding by the authority of such information or evidence (whether as supplied or obtained or as recorded);

(d)   the giving of information or advice with respect to social security [1 or work] matters by a relevant authority to persons making, or who have made, claims for a relevant benefit.

[² (e) the verification by a relevant authority of information or evidence supplied to or obtained by the authority in connection with a claim for or an award of a relevant benefit.]

(3)   In paragraphs (b) [² , (d) and (e)] of subsection (2) above–

(a)   references to claims for a relevant benefit are to such claims whether made as mentioned in subsection [² (1)(a), (b) or (c)] above or not; and

(b)   references to persons who have made such claims include persons to whom awards of benefit have been made on the claims.

(4)   Regulations under this section may make different provision for different areas.

(5)   Regulations under any other enactment may make such different provision for different areas as appears to the Secretary of State expedient in connection with any exercise by regulations under this section of the power conferred by subsection (4) above.

(6)   In this section–

(a)   "benefit" includes child support or a war pension (any reference to a claim being read, in relation to child support, as a reference to an application under the Child Support Act 1991 for a maintenance assessment);

(b)   "local authority" means an authority administering housing benefit or council tax benefit;

[² (c)   "relevant authority" means–

    (i)   a Minister of the Crown,

    (ii)   a local authority;

    (iii)   a county council in England;

    (iv)   a person providing services to a person mentioned in sub-paragraphs (i) to (iii);

    (v)   a person authorised to exercise any function of a local authority relating to housing benefit or council tax benefit;

    (vi)   a person authorised to exercise any function a county council in England has under this section;]

(d)   "relevant benefit" means housing benefit, council tax benefit or any other benefit prescribed for the purposes of this section;

[¹ (e)   "social security or work matters" means matters relating to-

    (i)   social security, child support or war pensions, or

    (ii)   employment or training;]

Commencement

11.11.99: see s89(4)(a) WRPA.

Amendment

1.   Amended by the Employment Act 2002 Sch 7 para 12 (24.11.02).

2.   Amended by the Welfare Reform Act 2002 s41(2) (3.7.07).

General Note

This is another provision enabling the implementation of the ONE project (see commentary to s2A) and its successors. It gives power to make regulations enabling such offices to receive claims for all benefits, to receive, forward and supply information to offices where claims are adjudicated.

Use of social security information

7B.–(1)   A relevant authority may use for a relevant purpose any social security information which it holds.

(2)   Regulations may make provision as to the procedure to be followed by a relevant authority for the purposes of any function it has relating to the administration of a specified benefit if the authority holds social security information which–

(a)   is relevant for the purposes of anything which may or must be done by the authority in connection with a claim for or an award of the benefit, and

(b)   was used by another relevant authority in connection with a claim for or an award of a different specified benefit or was verified by that other authority in accordance with regulations under section 7A(2)(e) above.

(3)   A relevant purpose is anything which is done in relation to a claim which is made or which could be made for a specified benefit if it is done for the purpose of–
(a)   identifying persons who may be entitled to such a benefit;
(b)   encouraging or assisting a person to make such a claim;
(c)   advising a person in relation to such a claim.
(4)   Social security information means–
(a)   information relating to social security, child support or war pensions;
(b)   evidence obtained in connection with a claim for or an award of a specified benefit.
(5)   A specified benefit is a benefit which is specified in regulations for the purposes of this section.
(6)   Expressions used in this section and in section 7A have the same meaning in this section as in that section.
(7)   This section does not affect any power which exists apart from this section to use for one purpose social security information obtained in connection with another purpose.

Commencement
1.10.07: inserted by s41(1) Welfare Reform Act 2007.

PART II
Adjudication
Housing benefit and council tax benefit

Adjudication
[¹**63.** . . .]

Amendment
1.   Repealed by s86(2) and Sch 8 of the SSA 1998 (18.10.99).

General Note
This was the enabling section for most of the regulations concerned with adjudication. See now s34 SSA 1998 and Sch 7 CSPSSA.

PART III
Overpayments and Adjustments of Benefit
Housing benefit

Overpayments of housing benefit
75.–(1)   Except where regulations otherwise provide, any amount of housing benefit [¹ determined in accordance with regulations to have been] paid in excess of entitlement may be recovered [²] either by the Secretary of State or by the authority which paid the benefit.
(2)   Regulations may require such an authority to recover such an amount in such circumstances as may be prescribed.
[³ (3)   An amount recoverable under this section shall be recoverable–
(a)   except in such circumstances as may be prescribed, from the person to whom it was paid; and
(b)   where regulations so providefrom such other person (as well as, or instead of, the person to whom it was paid) as may be prescribed.]
(4)   Any amount recoverable under this section may, without prejudice to any other method of recovery, be recovered by deduction from prescribed benefits.
[⁴ (5)   Where an amount paid to a person on behalf of another person is recoverable under this section, subsections (3) and (4) above authorise its recovery from the person to whom it was paid by deduction–
(a)   from prescribed benefits to which he is entitled;

(b)   from prescribed benefits paid to him to discharge (in whole or in part) an obligation owed to him by the person on whose behalf the recoverable amount was paid; or

(c)   from prescribed benefits paid to him to discharge (in whole or in part) an obligation owed to him by any other person.

(6)   Where an amount is recovered as mentioned in paragraph (b) of subsection (5) above, the obligation specified in that paragraph shall in prescribed circumstances be taken to be discharged by the amount of the deduction; and where an amount is recovered as mentioned in paragraph (c) of that subsection, the obligation specified in that paragraph shall in all cases be taken to be so discharged.

(7)   Where any amount recoverable under this section is to be recovered otherwise than by deduction from prescribed benefits–

(a)   if the person from whom it is recoverable resides in England and Wales and the county court so orders, it is recoverable by execution issued from the county court or otherwise as if it were payable under an order of that court; and

(b)   if he resides in Scotland, it may be enforced in the same manner as an extract registered decree arbitral bearing a warrant for execution issued by the sheriff court of any sheriffdom in Scotland.]

Amendments

1.   Amended by SSA(F) Act, 1997 Sch 1 para (31.7.97).
2.   Repealed by SSA(F) Act 1997 Sch 2.
3.   Substituted by CSPSSA 2000 s71 (1.10.2001).
4.   Amended by SSA(F) Act 1997 s16.

Definition

"prescribe" – see s191.

General Note

This section provides for the scheme for recovery of overpaid HB to be provided for by Part 13 of the HB Regs and Part 12 of the HB(SPC) Regs.

As has been made clear by a Tribunal of Commissioners in *R(H) 3/04* and *R(H) 6/06* (the latter drawing on the Court of Appeal's decision in *B v Secretary of State for Work and Pensions* [2005] EWCA Civ 929, [2005] 1 WLR 3796 (reported as *R(IS) 9/06*)), recoupment of overpayments involves a two-stage process.

First, it is necessary for the local authority to decide that there has been an overpayment and that it is recoverable from someone. Secondly, there is the process of enforcing recovery. The distinction between these two parts of the process has involved considerable difficulty in ascertaining the extent to which overpayment decisions by local authorities can be the subject of challenge before an appeal tribunal.

Note that HB paid under the pre-1988 scheme may be recovered by virtue of s75 and the regulations made thereunder: Sch 10 para 4(3). Note the effect of s68 Welfare Reform and Pensions Act 1999 on the recoverability of certain payments.

Guidance has been issued to local authorities on overpayments from December 2003 in the form of the *HB/CTB Overpayments Guide* (referred to below as "OG"). The guidance is available at www.dwp.gov.uk/housingbenefit/manuals/overpay.

Analysis

Subsection (1): The right to recover overpayments

This provides the basic power to prescribe the circumstances when an overpayment is recoverable in Part 13 of the HB Regs and Part 12 of the HB(SPC) Regs. As to whether there is power to prescribe that an overpayment may be recoverable even when the payment was in accordance with the entitlement of the claimant at the time it was made, see the Analysis to reg 99 HB Regs on p411.

The minor amendment made by the SSA(F) Act now makes it plain that there can be no recovery of HB by an authority unless a valid determination has been made that there is a recoverable overpayment. See the Analysis to reg 90 HB Regs on p395 regarding the validity of decisions. Note that subs (1) has not been amended by CSPSSA to refer to it being "decided" rather than "determined" that an overpayment is recoverable. This forms the basis of the decision of the Tribunal of Commissioners in *R(H) 3/04* that a right to appeal against an overpayment decision arises under Sch 7 para 6(6) CSPSSA rather than para 6(1).

This, however, can cause its own difficulties: see the Analysis to Sch 7 paras 1 and 6 CSPSSA on pp148 and 152.

It is possible to challenge the recoverability of an overpayment by relying on defects in the notification of decisions: see the commentary to reg 90 HB Regs p395. In *Goodwin v Rossendale BC* [2003] HLR 83, CA, it was held to be permissible to challenge the recoverability of an overpayment by attacking the lawfulness of subsequent stages in the adjudication process as well as the initial decision in the context of County Court proceedings brought by the landlord to recover the withheld benefit. His claim was dismissed by both the County Court judge and the Court of Appeal. However, the Court of Appeal accepted that it was permissible for the landlord to impugn the Review Board proceedings in the claim for debt, accepting as correct a concession by the local authority to this effect: paras 33, 58.

This leaves open the possibility of landlords or claimants seeking to attack decisions up to six years old by way of claims for debt. The decision also makes it clear that prejudice must always be specifically proved by evidence, even where it might be thought to be obvious.

Subsection (2): Required to recover

Where an interim payment on account proves to be excessive and the claimant continues to be entitled to HB, the authority must reduce the continuing payments to recover the overpayment: reg 93(3) HB Regs (reg 76(3) HB(SPC) Regs).

Apart from that situation, as yet there are no circumstances where an authority is *required* by the Regs to recover an overpayment.

Discretion to recover

In all other cases, the authority has a discretion as to whether to exercise its right of recovery, though the subsidy rules provide a strong incentive.

It is now clear from the Tribunal of Commissioners' decision in *CH 4234/2004* and the Court of Appeal's decision in *B v Secretary of State for Work and Pensions* [2005] EWCA Civ 929, [2005] 1 WLR 3796 (reported as *R(IS) 9/06*), that, whatever may have been said in *R(H) 3/04*, a local authority has a general discretion as to whether to recover an overpayment of benefit which has been found to be recoverable.

Like all discretionary powers, the authority must consider the circumstances of each individual case: see OG 4.435. If an authority fails to exercise its discretion in recovering overpayments, its decision to recover an overpayment may be vulnerable to judicial review. In *Warren Court*, over 50 overpayment notices in standard form were sent out, followed a few days later by invoices demanding payment. The authority had never refrained from seeking recovery of an overpayment from the applicant company or its sister companies. Jackson J accepted, however, evidence from the council to the effect that there had been cases in which the council had refrained from recovering overpayments from other landlords in cases of claimant fraud. He therefore refused to hold that the council had acted unlawfully in deciding to recover the overpayments, though he quashed the determinations on the ground that the notifications of overpayment were defective: see the Analysis to reg 100(1) HB Regs on p412.

It is impossible to compile a list of the matters that an authority may need to consider, but they will commonly include the following: the moral culpability of the person from whom recovery is sought, the effect of recovery on her/his life, the effect of recovery on her/his family, the likelihood of the claimant losing her/his accommodation and the possible resulting financial burden on the authority, and the cost-effectiveness of recovery. It is probably also legitimate for the authority to have regard to the financial implications of non-recovery of the overpayment: see eg, *R v Brent LBC HBRB ex p Connery* [1989] 22 HLR 40 at 44, QBD. However, this, like any other factor, cannot be treated as determinative. OG 4.434 suggests that "financial or hardship grounds" will be the usual factors which are taken into account, and OG 4.436 gives terminal illness, senility or low intelligence and severe medical conditions as circumstances which might lead to non-recovery. Detailed guidance is given on financial hardship as a ground for non-recovery at OG 4.437-4.446.

In *R v South Hams DC ex p Ash* [1999] 33 HLR 412-3, QBD, Moses J quashed the Board's decision to recover an overpayment from a claimant awarded arrears of an increase in a war pension, holding that the reason why the war pension had been awarded (to compensate a claimant for injuries suffered in the service of his country) was a material factor to which the Board should have had regard in exercising its discretion. The Board should also have had regard to the fact that the delays on the part of the DSS in paying the increase had not been compensated for.

The authority may have a policy, but it must be sufficiently flexible to enable each case to be examined on its merits. If it is not, it will be vulnerable to challenge on judicial review. Policies that recovery will always be made or always be made from specified categories of claimants will be unlawful.

In *Ash*, it was also pointed out, correctly, that an authority has "power to limit recovery as well as to rule against it". If an authority feels that recovery of the full amount would not be appropriate but that the person against whom the decision has been made ought to pay something, it may require her/him to do so.

For the question of whether there is an appeal to a tribunal against a decision to recover an overpayment, see the commentary to the Schedule to the D&A Regs on p989.

Subsection (3): Recovery from whom?

See reg 101 HB Regs for the circumstances as to when there can be recovery from persons other than those to whom benefit was paid. Section 75(3) is wide enough to authorise recovery from a landlord's agent if the overpaid benefit was paid to that agent, notwithstanding that, as an agent, s/he may have accounted to her/his principal (ie, the landlord) for all or part of the sum: *CH 2193 2005*.

The approach to s75(3) was given extensive consideration by a Tribunal of Commissioners in *R(H) 6/06*. They said that s75(3)(b):

"requires that any regulation made under s75(3)(b) should specify whether a prescribed person is jointly liable with the person to whom the payment was made or is liable instead of that person. Under this construction the words in parentheses have a purpose. The construction is consistent with s75(3)(a) because, where the Secretary of State makes regulations providing that an overpayment is recoverable from a prescribed person instead of the person to whom it was made, he is, in effect, providing for additional, but defined, circumstances in which the person to whom the payment was made is not liable to repay an overpayment. The circumstances are defined by the terms in which the prescribed person is defined or by the circumstances in respect of which he is prescribed (see s189(4)). This construction is also consistent with para 6(6) of Schedule 7, which provides a right of appeal to a tribunal in terms that do not limit it to points of law, because all issues arising under regulations made under s75(3) as to from whom an overpayment is recoverable are justiciable. If the Secretary of State makes regulations having the effect that an overpayment is recoverable from a prescribed person as well as the person to whom it is made, the non-justiciable choice as to from which of them the overpayment should actually be recovered falls to be made by the local authority at the stage of enforcing the right of recovery and so is not within the scope of the right of appeal".

They therefore concluded:

"under the legislation in force from 1 October 2001 to 9 April 2006, an overpayment of housing benefit is always recoverable from any person within the scope of regulation 101(2) as well as, if different, the person to whom the overpayment was made, except where regulation 101(1) applies in which case it is recoverable only from any person within the scope of regulation 101(2). No non-justiciable issues fall within the scope of the right of appeal and so there is no longer any need to apply *R(H) 3/04* and construe that right as being limited to points of law."

So the only appealable point (apart from whether there has in fact been an overpayment and whether it is recoverable) under s73(3) and reg 101 HB Regs 1987 will be whether the person does in fact fall within reg 101. Once that point has been finally decided, *CH 4234/2004* makes it clear that no appeal right attaches to the enforcement decision of the local authority as against whom the recoverable overpayment should actually be recovered from.

Subsections (4) to (7): Methods of recovery

These subsections provide for various methods of recovery of HB. For recovery by deduction from other benefits, see HB Regs regs 102 and 105 (HB(SPC) Regs reg 83 and 86).

Subs (5), (6) and (7) were introduced by the 1997 Act. Subs (5) expands the scope for recovery by deduction from other benefits to include benefits paid on behalf of others to people from whom recovery is sought. The principal use of this new power will be directed at recovery from landlords by deduction of HB paid direct in respect of other tenants. Subs (6) makes provision for the consequences of such recovery. See the Analysis to HB Regs regs 95 and 102 on pp405 and 426.

Subs (7) allows authorities to use county court and sheriff court procedures for registration of the overpayment as a debt without having to bring an action against the person from whom recovery is sought. For convenience, further details are given in the Analysis to HB Regs reg 102 on p426.

Council tax benefit

Excess benefit

76.–(1) Regulations may make provision as to any case where a [¹ billing authority] or a [⁵ local authority in Scotland] has allowed a [¹ council tax benefit] to a person and the amount allowed exceeds the amount to which he is entitled in respect of the benefit.

(2) [² . . .] The regulations may provide that–

(a) a sum equal to the excess shall be due from the person concerned to the authority (whatever the form the benefit takes);

(b) any liability under any provision included under paragraph (a) above shall be met by such method mentioned in subsection (3) below as is prescribed as regards the case concerned, or by such combination or two or all three of the methods as is prescribed as regards the case concerned.

(3)   The methods are–

(a)   payment by the person concerned;

(b)   addition to any amount payable in respect of [³ council tax;]

(c)   deduction from prescribed benefits.

[⁴ (4)-(5) . . .]

(6)   In a case where the regulations provide that a sum or part of a sum is to be paid, and the sum or part is not paid on or before such day as may be prescribed, the regulations may provide that the sum or part shall be recoverable in a court of competent jurisdiction.

[⁴ (7)   . . .]

(8)   The regulations may provide that they are not to apply as regards any case falling within a prescribed category.

Definitions

"billing authority" – see s191.

"income-related benefit" – see s191.

"charge payer" – in subs (4), see Subs (7).

Amendments

1.   Substitutions by LGFA Sch 9 para 15(1) (1.4.93).

2.   Repealed by LGFA Sch 9 para 15(2) and Sch 14 (1.4.93).

3.   Substituted by LGFA Sch 9 para 15(3) (1.4.93).

4.   Repealed by LGFA Sch 9 para 15(4) and Sch 14 (1.4.93).

5.   Substituted by Local Government etc. (Scotland) Act 1994 Sch 13 para 175(3) (1.4.96).

General Note

This section deals with overpayments of CTB. An overpayment of CTB is termed an 'excess payment'. The rules on recoverability and recovery are very similar, but there are some differences. In particular, the Social Security Administration (Fraud) Act 1997 made no amendments to this section, so the powers of recovery are slightly more restricted.

Analysis

Subs (1). This provides the basic power to make the Part 11 CTB Regs and Part 10 CTB(SPC) Regs, which set out the scheme for excess payments of CTB. Note, however, that in contrast with s75(1) above, this subsection does not of itself provide that an amount can be recovered.

Subs (2) and (3). Firstly, by para (a), liability is imposed on the 'person concerned'. This must be a reference to the person referred to in subs (1) and so can only be a reference to the person to whom the excess benefit was allowed. So regulations to permit recovery from third parties would not be permitted, since they cannot be justified by subs (1) above.

Once the liability is imposed by para (b) sets out how the liability is to be met. It is suggested that *only* those methods prescribed by subs (3) may be used. The methods are:

(1)   Payment by the person concerned: see reg 86(2)(a) CTB Regs (reg 71(2)(a) CTB(SPC) Regs). This operates to create a debt owed to the authority, but note the way subs (6) affects the authority's right to sue for it (see below).

(2)   Addition to a council tax bill: see reg 86(2)(b) CTB Regs (reg 71(2)(b) CTB(SPC) Regs).

(3)   Deduction from prescribed benefits: see reg 86(3) CTB Regs (reg 71(3) CTB(SPC) Regs).

Subs (6). The regulations can only provide for court recovery after the person concerned has failed to pay within a prescribed time. Note that this provision only authorises the bringing of an action by the authority and does not authorise the registration of the debt as under s75(7), because the wording does not allow recovery "as if payable under an order of a county court": see the County Court Rules 1981 Ord 25 r12(1) in England and Wales, preserved by the Sch to the Civil Procedure Rules 1998, and the equivalent provision in the sheriff court in Scotland.

Subs (8). This permits the exceptions to recoverability of excess payments. See 83(2)and (3) CTB Regs (reg 68(2) and (3) CTB(SPC) Regs).

Shortfall in benefit

77.–(1)   Regulations may make provision as to any case where a [¹ billing authority] or a [² local authority in Scotland] has allowed [¹ council tax benefit] to a person and the amount allowed is less than the amount to which he is entitled in respect of the benefit.

Definition
   "billing authority" – see s191.

Amendments
   1.   Substituted by LGFA Sch 9 para 16(2) and Sch 14 (1.4.93).
   2.   Substituted by Local Government etc. (Scotland) Act 1994 Sch 13 para 175(3) (1.4.96).

General Note
   See reg 79 CTB Regs (reg 64 CTB(SPC) Regs).

Part VI
Enforcement

General Note on Part VI
   Part VI of the Act deals with specific criminal sanctions for abuse of the benefits system. The offences created apply to HB and CTB as well as benefits paid by the Secretary of State, though offences are prosecuted by the local authority: see s116.
   Part VI has been subject to amendment since 1992 by no less than 15 different statutes which must be something of a record. The result is a bloated, incoherent set of provisions; there can be few statutes with a subsection (2F) of section 109B. The description given by the former Law Lord, Lord Brightman, of Part VI as being a "drafting quagmire" (*Hansard* (HL) vol 623 col 338) may be thought to be flattering.
   This repeated amending has been a direct product of the priority given by successive governments to investigating and combating social security fraud. There have been two recent Acts of Parliament specifically directed towards this issue: the Social Security Administration (Fraud) Act 1997 and the Social Security Fraud Act 2001. The 1997 Act was rushed through Parliament in the period shortly before dissolution for the 1997 General Election amongst hysterical competition between the two major political parties as to which was 'toughest' on social security fraud. As a result, the measure had cross-party support. Besides widening the scope of the offences in s112 and introducing a new range of offences under s111A with higher penalties, the Act introduced a system of penalties which authorities may offer where prosecution is not thought economical. Part VII of the Act was also substantially recast.
   For its part, the 2001 Act significantly expanded the information-seeking powers of local authorities and introduced a new scheme of penalising claimants convicted of more than one offence of benefit fraud. It also reformulated the criminal offences.
   Despite the enacting of more serious offences under the Act, the practice has been to continue to prosecute such offences as general offences of dishonesty. In England and Wales, the relevant statute is the Theft Act 1968. A number of offences under that Act may be committed: theft under s1, obtaining property by deception under s15(1), and false accounting under s17(1). As to the last, it has been held that a HB claim form is a document created for accounting purposes: *Osinunga v DPP* [1997] 30 HLR 853 at 856, DC. In Scotland, a claimant could be prosecuted for the common law offences of theft or fraud.
   For sentencing guidelines for the more serious offences under ss111A and 112, see *R v Stewart* [1987] 2 All ER 363, CA and *R v Armour* [1997] 2 Cr App R(S) 240, CA. There has been a noticeable toughening in sentencing for social security fraud in recent years.
   Note that in confiscation order proceedings under section 71(1B) of the Criminal Justice Act 1988 no offfset can be made for *other* benefits which the defendant may have been entitled to but for her/his dishonest conduct when assessing how much is due under the confiscation order: *Department of Work and Pensions v Richards* [2005] EWCA Crim 491, 3 March. However, statutory offsets will apply when calculating in the first place the amount of overpaid HB/CTB: see reg 104 HB Regs (reg 85 HB(SPC) Regs); 89 CTB Regs (reg 74 CTB(SPC) Regs).

[¹Authorisations for investigators

   109A.–(1)   An individual who for the time being has the Secretary of State's authorisation for the purposes of this Part shall be entitled, for any one or more of the purposes mentioned in subsection (2) below, to exercise any of the powers which are conferred on an authorised officer by sections 109B and 109C below.
   (2)   Those purposes are–

(a) ascertaining in relation to any case whether a benefit is or was payable in that case in accordance with any provision of the relevant social security legislation;

(b) investigating the circumstances in which any accident, injury or disease which has given rise, or may give rise, to a claim for–

    (i) industrial injuries benefit, or

    (ii) any benefit under any provision of the relevant social security legislation, occurred or may have occurred, or was or may have been received or contracted;

(c) ascertaining whether provisions of the relevant social security legislation are being, have been or are likely to be contravened (whether by particular persons or more generally);

(d) preventing, detecting and securing evidence of the commission (whether by particular persons or more generally) of benefit offences.

(3) An individual has the Secretary of State's authorisation for the purposes of this Part if, and only if, the Secretary of State has granted him an authorisation for those purposes and he is–

(a) an official of a Government department;

(b) an individual employed by an authority administering housing benefit or council tax benefit;

(c) an individual employed by an authority or joint committee that carries out functions relating to housing benefit or council tax benefit on behalf of the authority administering that benefit; or

(d) an individual employed by a person authorised by or on behalf of any such authority or joint committee as is mentioned in paragraph (b) or (c) above to carry out functions relating to housing benefit or council tax benefit for that authority or committee.

(4) An authorisation granted for the purposes of this Part to an individual of any of the descriptions mentioned in subsection (3) above–

(a) must be contained in a certificate provided to that individual as evidence of his entitlement to exercise powers conferred by this Part;

(b) may contain provision as to the period for which the authorisation is to have effect; and

(c) may restrict the powers exercisable by virtue of the authorisation so as to prohibit their exercise except for particular purposes, in particular circumstances or in relation to particular benefits or particular provisions of the relevant social security legislation.

(5) An authorisation granted under this section may be withdrawn at any time by the Secretary of State.

(6) Where the Secretary of State grants an authorisation for the purposes of this Part to an individual employed by a local authority, or to an individual employed by a person who carries out functions relating to housing benefit or council tax benefit on behalf of a local authority–

(a) the Secretary of State and the local authority shall enter into such arrangements (if any) as they consider appropriate with respect to the carrying out of functions conferred on that individual by or in connection with the authorisation granted to him; and

(b) the Secretary of State may make to the local authority such payments (if any) as he thinks fit in respect of the carrying out by that individual of any such functions.

(7) The matters on which a person may be authorised to consider and report to the Secretary of State under section 139A below shall be taken to include the carrying out by any such individual as is mentioned in subsection (3)(b) to (d) above of any functions conferred on that individual by virtue of any grant by the Secretary of State of an authorisation for the purposes of this Part.

(8)   The powers conferred by sections 109B and 109C below shall be exercisable in relation to persons holding office under the Crown and persons in the service of the Crown, and in relation to premises owned or occupied by the Crown, as they are exercisable in relation to other persons and premises.

Commencement
1.11.00: see CSPSSA Sch 6 para 2 and 2001 SI No 1252.

General Note
The powers introduced by CSPSSA extend the powers of fraud inspectors still wider. s109A deals with authorisation of officers acting on behalf of the Secretary of State. It permits officers employed by the local authority to act both on behalf of the Secretary of State or the local authority employing her/him. Note, however, the important restrictions in subs (3) and (4). Subs (3) restricts the identity of people who can be granted a certificate to act as an inspector, and subs (4) gives power to restrict the scope of a certificate.
By subs (7) and (8), the Secretary of State may authorise inspectors to look into local authorities' administration of the HB scheme for the purposes of Pt VIII.

Power to require information
109B.–(1)   An authorised officer who has reasonable grounds for suspecting that a person–
(a)   is a person falling within subsection (2) [¹ or (2A)] below, and
(b)   has or may have possession of or access to any information about any matter that is relevant for any one or more of the purposes mentioned in section 109A(2) above,
may, by written notice, require that person to provide all such information described in the notice as is information of which he has possession, or to which he has access, and which it is reasonable for the authorised officer to require for a purpose so mentioned.
(2)   The persons who fall within this subsection are–
(a)   any person who is or has been an employer or employee within the meaning of any provision made by or under the Contributions and Benefits Act;
(b)   any person who is or has been a self-employed earner within the meaning of any such provision;
(c)   any person who by virtue of any provision made by or under that Act falls, or has fallen, to be treated for the purposes of any such provision as a person within paragraph (a) or (b) above;
(d)   any person who is carrying on, or has carried on, any business involving the supply of goods for sale to the ultimate consumers by individuals not carrying on retail businesses from retail premises;
(e)   any person who is carrying on, or has carried on, any business involving the supply of goods or services by the use of work done or services performed by persons other than employees of his;
(f)   any person who is carrying on, or has carried on, an agency or other business for the introduction or supply, to persons requiring them, of persons available to do work or to perform services;
(g)   any local authority acting in their capacity as an authority responsible for the granting of any licence;
(h)   any person who is or has been a trustee or manager of a personal or occupational pension scheme;
(i)   any person who is or has been liable to make a compensation payment or a payment to the Secretary of State under section 6 of the Social Security (Recovery of Benefits) Act 1997 (payments in respect of recoverable benefits); and
(j)   the servants and agents of any such person as is specified in any of paragraphs (a) to (i) above.
[² (2A)   The persons who fall within this subsection are–

(a)   any bank;

[⁵ (aa) the Director of National Savings;]

(b)   any person carrying on a business the whole or a significant part of which consists in the provision of credit (whether secured or unsecured) to members of the public;

[⁶ (c) any insurer;]

(d)   any credit reference agency (within the meaning given by section 145(8) of the Consumer Credit Act 1974 (c. 39));

(e)   any body the principal activity of which is to facilitate the exchange of information for the purpose of preventing or detecting fraud;

(f)   any person carrying on a business the whole or a significant part of which consists in the provision to members of the public of a service for transferring money from place to place;

(g)   any water undertaker or sewerage undertaker, any water and sewerage authority constituted under section 62 of the Local Government etc. (Scotland) Act 1994 (c. 39) or any authority which is a collecting authority for the purposes of section 79 of that Act;

[⁶ (h) any person who;

    (i)   is the holder of a licence under section 7 of the Gas Act 1986 (c. 44) to convey gas through pipes, or

    (ii)   is the holder of a licence under section 7A(1) of that Act to supply gas through pipes;]

(i)   any person who (within the meaning of the Electricity Act 1989 (c. 29)) distributes or supplies electricity;]

(j)   any person who provides a telecommunications service;

(k)   any person conducting any educational establishment or institution;

(l)   any body the principal activity of which is to provide services in connection with admissions to educational establishments or institutions;

(m)   the Student Loans Company;

(n)   any servant or agent of any person mentioned in any of the preceding paragraphs.

(2B)   Subject to the following provisions of this section, the powers conferred by this section on an authorised officer to require information from any person by virtue of his falling within subsection (2A) above shall be exercisable for the purpose only of obtaining information relating to a particular person identified (by name or description) by the officer.

(2C)   An authorised officer shall not, in exercise of those powers, require any information from any person by virtue of his falling within subsection (2A) above unless it appears to that officer that there are reasonable grounds for believing that the identified person to whom it relates is–

(a)   a person who has committed, is committing or intends to commit a benefit offence; or

(b)   a person who (within the meaning of Part 7 of the Contributions and Benefits Act) is a member of the family of a person falling within paragraph (a) above.

(2D)   Nothing in subsection (2B) or (2C) above shall prevent an authorised officer who is an official of a Government department and whose authorisation states that his authorisation applies for the purposes of this subsection from exercising the powers conferred by this section for obtaining from–

(a)   a water undertaker or any water and sewerage authority constituted under section 62 of the Local Government etc. (Scotland) Act 1994,

(b)   any person who (within the meaning the Gas Act 1986) supplies gas conveyed through pipes,

(c)   any person who (within the meaning of the Electricity Act 1989) supplies electricity conveyed by distribution systems, or

(d)   any servant or agent of a person mentioned in any of the preceding paragraphs,

any information which relates exclusively to whether and in what quantities water, gas or electricity are being or have been supplied to residential premises specified or described in the notice by which the information is required.

(2E)   The powers conferred by this section shall not be exercisable for obtaining from any person providing a telecommunications service any information other than information which (within the meaning of section 21 of the Regulation of Investigatory Powers Act 2000 (c. 23)) is communications data but not traffic data.

(2F)   Nothing in subsection (2B) or (2C) above shall prevent an authorised officer from exercising the powers conferred by this section for requiring information, from a person who provides a telecommunications service, about the identity and postal address of a person identified by the authorised officer solely by reference to a telephone number or electronic address used in connection with the provision of such a service.]

(3)   The obligation of a person to provide information in accordance with a notice under this section shall be discharged only by the provision of that information, at such reasonable time and in such form as may be specified in the notice, to the authorised officer who–

(a)   is identified by or in accordance with the terms of the notice; or

(b)   has been identified, since the giving of the notice, by a further written notice given by the authorised officer who imposed the original requirement or another authorised officer.

(4)   The power of an authorised officer under this section to require the provision of information shall include a power to require the production and delivery up and (if necessary) creation of, or of copies of or extracts from, any such documents containing the information as may be specified or described in the notice imposing the requirement.

[³ (5)   No one shall be required under this section to provide–

(a)   any information that tends to incriminate either himself or, in the case of a person who is married, his spouse; or

(b)   any information in respect of which a claim to legal professional privilege or, in Scotland, confidentiality as between client and professional legal adviser, would be successful in any proceedings;

and for the purposes of this subsection it is immaterial whether the information is in documentary form or not.]

[⁴ (6)   Provision may be made by order–

(a)   adding any person to the list of persons falling within subsection (2A) above;

(b)   removing any person from the list of persons falling within that subsection;

(c)   modifying that subsection for the purpose of taking account of any change to the name of any person for the time being falling within that subsection.

(7)   In this section–

[⁷ ''bank'' means–

(a)   a person who has permission under Part IV of the Financial Services and Markets Act 2000 to accept deposits;

(b)   an EEA firm of the kind mentioned in paragraph 5(b) of Schedule 3 to that Act which has permission under paragraph 15 of that Schedule (as a result of qualifying for authorisation under paragraph 12 of that Schedule) to accept deposits or other repayable funds from the public; or

(c)   a person who does not require permission under that Act to accept deposits, in the course of his business in the United Kingdom;]

''credit'' includes a cash loan or any form of financial accommodation, including the cashing of a cheque;

[[8]] "insurer" means–
  (a)   a person who has permission under Part IV of the Financial Services and Markets Act 2000 to effect or carry out contracts of insurance; or
  (b)   an EEA firm of the kind mentioned in paragraph 5(d) of Schedule 3 to that Act, which has permission under paragraph 15 of that Schedule (as a result of qualifying for authorisation under paragraph 12 of that Schedule) to effect or carry out contracts of insurance;]

"residential premises", in relation to a supply of water, gas or electricity, means any premises which–
  (a)   at the time of the supply were premises occupied wholly or partly for residential purposes, or
  (b)   are premises to which that supply was provided as if they were so occupied; and

"telecommunications service" has the same meaning as in the Regulation of Investigatory Powers Act 2000 (c. 23).]

[[9] (7A)   The definitions of "bank" and "insurer" in subsection (7) must be read with–
  (a)   section 22 of the Financial Services and Markets Act 2000;
  (b)   any relevant order under that section; and
  (c)   Schedule 2 to that Act.]

Commencement
1.11.00: see CSPSSA Sch 6 para 2 and 2001 SI No 1252.

Amendments
  1.   Amended by s1(2) SSFA as from 30.4.02.
  2.   Inserted by s1(2) SSFA as from 30.4.02.
  3.   Substituted by s1(3) SSFA as from 30.4.02.
  4.   Inserted by s1(4) SSFA as from 26.2.02.
  5.   Inserted by Art 2(a) of SI 2002 No 817 as from 1.4.02.
  6.   Substituted by Art 2(b) to (d) of SI 2002 No 817 as from 1.4.02.
  7.   Substituted by Art 3(a)(i) of SI 2002 No 817 as from 1.4.02.
  8.   Inserted by Art 3(a)(ii) of SI 2002 No 817 as from 1.4.02.
  9.   Inserted by Art 3(b) of SI 2002 No 817 as from 1.4.02.

General Note
The powers of an inspector to require information are expanded significantly by s109B. A written notice is required as a condition precedent to an obligation to provide information: subs (1). Subs (4) enables the information to be required in a form that suits the inspector. The only controls upon information requirements made under subs (2) are that they are limited to information to which a person has access, and that the requirement is reasonable. In the case of any dispute, the latter qualification is likely to prove vital. If, for example, an employee will be required to breach some confidence by disclosing information about a colleague, it will be unreasonable to require such steps since there are ample powers to require the employer to disgorge the same information. Similarly, if information can only be obtained following undue expense, it may be said to be unreasonable to require it to be furnished. The requirement of reasonableness qualifies the method of provision under subs (4) as well as the requirement to provide the information under subs (1). Thus, even if it would be reasonable to require a person to answer questions, it might be unreasonable to require a person to provide written answers, depending on the situation.

The breadth of the classes of people from whom information may be required under subs (2) is obvious. To take two examples, workers can be required to give information about colleagues, and charities may be required to reveal who is working for them.

The new subs (2A) to (2F) vastly expand the range of bodies from which information may be sought. There is also a new subs (6) to enable amendment of the bodies that may be required to supply information by statutory instrument, which requires an affirmative resolution under the new s190(1)(aza) SSAA.

There is some limitation in the powers under subs (2A). First, information may only be sought in relation to a specific person or a member of her/his family: subs (2B). Secondly, there must be "reasonable grounds" to suspect the commission of an offence by that person: subs (2C). Thirdly, the content of communications may not be disclosed to relevant officers but only the fact that communications are being made or the extent of the services provided: subs (2E). Subs (2D), which allows information regarding the services supplied to an address to be obtained from utility companies, cannot be utilised by local authority officers: see subs (5).

Note that a breach of a duty to provide information under s109B does not of itself constitute an offence under this section. There may, however, be an offence committed under s111 below. Note also that subs (5) preserves the privilege against self-incrimination, and has now been expanded to cover information which is confidential or covered by legal professional privilege. It is likely that the courts would have implied such a limitation in any event.

Powers of entry

109C.–(1)   An authorised officer shall be entitled, at any reasonable time and either alone or accompanied by such other persons as he thinks fit, to enter any premises which–

(a)   are liable to inspection under this section; and

(b)   are premises to which it is reasonable for him to require entry in order to exercise the powers conferred by this section.

(2)   An authorised officer who has entered any premises liable to inspection under this section may–

(a)   make such an examination of those premises, and

(b)   conduct any such inquiry there, as appears to him appropriate for any one or more of the purposes mentioned in section 109A(2) above.

(3)   An authorised officer who has entered any premises liable to inspection under this section may–

(a)   question any person whom he finds there;

(b)   require any person whom he finds there to do any one or more of the following–

(i)   to provide him with such information,

(ii)   to produce and deliver up and (if necessary) create such documents or such copies of, or extracts from, documents, as he may reasonably require for any one or more of the purposes mentioned in section 109A(2) above; and

(c)   take possession of and either remove or make his own copies of any such documents as appear to him to contain information that is relevant for any of those purposes.

(4)   The premises liable to inspection under this section are any premises (including premises consisting in the whole or a part of a dwelling house) which an authorised officer has reasonable grounds for suspecting are–

(a)   premises which are a person's place of employment;

(b)   premises from which a trade or business is being carried on or where documents relating to a trade or business are kept by the person carrying it on or by another person on his behalf;

(c)   premises from which a personal or occupational pension scheme is being administered or where documents relating to the administration of such a scheme are kept by the person administering the scheme or by another person on his behalf;

(d)   premises where a person who is the compensator in relation to any such accident, injury or disease as is referred to in section 109A(2)(b) above is to be found;

(e)   premises where a person on whose behalf any such compensator has made, may have made or may make a compensation payment is to be found.

(5)   An authorised officer applying for admission to any premises in accordance with this section shall, if required to do so, produce the certificate containing his authorisation for the purposes of this Part.

(6)   Subsection (5) of section 109B applies for the purposes of this section as it applies for the purposes of that section.]

Amendment

1.   Substituted by CSPSSA 2000 Sch 6 para 2 (2.4.01).

General Note

The powers of authorised officers to enter premises are also extended under s109C. Note, however, that there is no power to enter a person's home without consent, unless there are reasonable grounds for suspecting that the home also falls into one of the categories in subs (4). Subs (3) gives powers in relation to making inquiries on premises.

[¹Authorisations by local authorities

110A.–(1)   An individual who for the time being has the authorisation for the purposes of this Part of an authority administering housing benefit or council tax benefit ("a local authority authorisation") shall be entitled, for any one or more of the purposes mentioned in subsection (2) below, to exercise any of the powers which, subject to subsection (8) below, are conferred on an authorised officer by sections 109B and 109C above.

(2)   Those purposes are–

(a)   ascertaining in relation to any case whether housing benefit or council tax benefit is or was payable in that case;

(b)   ascertaining whether provisions of the relevant social security legislation that relate to housing benefit or council tax benefit are being, have been or are likely to be contravened (whether by particular persons or more generally);

(c)   preventing, detecting and securing evidence of the commission (whether by particular persons or more generally) of benefit offences relating to housing benefit or council tax benefit.

(3)   An individual has the authorisation for the purposes of this Part of an authority administering housing benefit or council tax benefit if, and only if, that authority have granted him an authorisation for those purposes and he is–

(a)   an individual employed by that authority;

(b)   an individual employed by another authority or joint committee that carries out functions relating to housing benefit or council tax benefit on behalf of that authority;

(c)   an individual employed by a person authorised by or on behalf of–

(i)   the authority in question,

(ii)   any such authority or joint committee as is mentioned in paragraph (b) above,

to carry out functions relating to housing benefit or council tax benefit for that authority or committee;

(d)   an official of a Government department.

(4)   Subsection (4) of section 109A above shall apply in relation to a local authority authorisation as it applies in relation to an authorisation under that section.

(5)   A local authority authorisation may be withdrawn at any time by the authority that granted it or by the Secretary of State.

(6)   The certificate or other instrument containing the grant or withdrawal by any local authority of any local authority authorisation must be issued under the hand of either–

(a)   the officer designated under section 4 of the Local Government and Housing Act 1989 as the head of the authority's paid service; or

(b)   the officer who is the authority's chief finance officer (within the meaning of section 5 of that Act).

(7)   It shall be the duty of any authority with power to grant local authority authorisations to comply with any directions of the Secretary of State as to–

(a)   whether or not such authorisations are to be granted by that authority;

(b)   the period for which authorisations granted by that authority are to have effect;

(c) the number of persons who may be granted authorisations by that authority at any one time; and

(d) the restrictions to be contained by virtue of subsection (4) above in the authorisations granted by that authority for those purposes.

(8) The powers conferred by sections 109B and 109C above shall have effect in the case of an individual who is an authorised officer by virtue of this section as if those sections had effect–

(a) with the substitution for every reference to the purposes mentioned in section 109A(2) above of a reference to the purposes mentioned in subsection (2) above; [² . . .]

(b) with the substitution for every reference to the relevant social security legislation of a reference to so much of it as relates to housing benefit or council tax benefit [³ ;and

(c) with the omission of section 109B(2D)].

(9) Nothing in this section conferring any power on an authorised officer in relation to housing benefit or council tax benefit shall require that power to be exercised only in relation to cases in which the authority administering the benefit is the authority by whom that officer's authorisation was granted.]

Amendments
1. Substituted by CSPSSA 2000 Sch 6 para 3 (2.4.01).
2. Amended by s19 of the SSFA as from 30.4.02.
3. Inserted by s1(5) of the SSFA as from 30.4.02.

General Note
Authorities are given the power to appoint inspectors under s110A. They have the same powers as those granted to the inspectors engaged by the Secretary of State. Note the certification requirements in subs (6). "Issued under the hand of" probably permits a junior officer directly under the supervision of the officers mentioned to sign the authorisation. Note also the power to issue directions in subs (7), a novel feature of the HB scheme. Local authority officers do not acquire any of the preserved powers under s109B(2D) by the back door.

[¹ **Power of local authority to require electronic access to information**

110AA.–(1) Subject to subsection (2) below, where it appears to an authority administering housing benefit or council tax benefit–

(a) that a person falling within section 109B(2A) keeps any electronic records,

(b) that the records contain or are likely, from time to time, to contain information about any matter that is relevant for any one or more of the purposes mentioned in section 110A(2) above, and

(c) that facilities exist under which electronic access to those records is being provided, or is capable of being provided, by that person to other persons, that authority may require that person to enter into arrangements under which authorised officers are allowed such access to those records.

(2) An authorised officer–

(a) shall be entitled to obtain information in accordance with arrangements entered into under subsection (1) above only if his authorisation states that his authorisation applies for the purposes of that subsection; and

(b) shall not seek to obtain any information in accordance with any such arrangements other than information which–

(i) relates to a particular person; and

(ii) could be the subject of any such requirement under section 109B above as may be imposed in exercise of the powers conferred by section 110A(8) above.

(3) The matters that may be included in the arrangements that a person is required to enter into under subsection (1) above may include–

(a) requirements as to the electronic access to records that is to be made available to authorised officers;

(b) requirements as to the keeping of records of the use that is made of the arrangements;

(c) requirements restricting the disclosure of information about the use that is made of the arrangements; and

(d) such other incidental requirements as the authority in question considers appropriate in connection with allowing access to records to authorised officers.

(4) An authorised officer who is allowed access in accordance with any arrangements entered into under subsection (1) above shall be entitled to make copies of, and to take extracts from, any records containing information which he is entitled to make the subject of a requirement such as is mentioned in subsection (2)(b) above.

(5) An authority administering housing benefit or council tax benefit shall not–

(a) require any person to enter into arrangements for allowing authorised officers to have electronic access to any records; or

(b) otherwise than in pursuance of a requirement under this section, enter into any arrangements with a person specified in section 109B(2A) above for allowing anyone acting on behalf of the authority for purposes connected with any benefit to have electronic access to any private information contained in any records,

except with the consent of the Secretary of State and subject to any conditions imposed by the Secretary of State by the provisions of the consent.

(6) A consent for the purposes of subsection (5) may be given in relation to a particular case, or in relation to any case that falls within a particular description of cases.

(7) In this section ''private information'', in relation to an authority administering housing benefit or council tax benefit, means any information held by a person who is not entitled to disclose it to that authority except in compliance with a requirement imposed by the authority in exercise of their statutory powers.]

Amendment
1. Inserted by s2(2) of the SSFA as from 30.4.02.

Commencement
1.4.02: SI 2002 No 1222.

General Note
s110AA enables a local authority to require access to electronic information. Subs (1) and (2) limit the scope of the powers to a similar extent to the powers in ss109B and 110A. By subs (3), there is power to impose requirements as to access, the keeping of records and the maintenance of confidentiality concerning the access arrangements. There is an important limitation in subs (5) to (7) which requires the Secretary of State to give consent for the use of the powers conferred by s110AA and also access agreed with those holding the information to "private information". The definition in subs (7) would cover "personal data" within the meaning of the Data Protection Act 1998 and information which was of a confidential nature so as to attract the protection of the law of breach of confidence.

A refusal to comply with a lawful request is an offence under s111(1)(ab) below.

Delay, obstruction etc of inspector

111.–(1) If a person–

(a) intentionally delays or obstructs an [² authorised officer] in the exercise of any power under this Act [¹ other than an Inland Revenue power];

[³ (ab) refuses or neglects to comply with any requirement under section 109BA or 110AA or with the requirements of any arrangements entered into in accordance with subsection (1) of that section, or]

(b) refuses or neglects to answer any question or to furnish any information or to produce any document when required to do so under this Act [¹ otherwise than in the exercise of an Inland Revenue power],

he shall be guilty of an offence and liable on summary conviction to a fine not exceeding level 3 on the standard scale.

(2) Where a person is convicted of an offence under [⁴ subsection (1)(ab) or (b)] above and the refusal or neglect is continued by him after his conviction, he shall be guilty of a further offence and liable on summary conviction to a fine not exceeding £40 for each day on which it is continued.

[¹ (3) and (4) *[omitted]*]

Amendments

1. Inserted by Transfer of Functions Act 1999 s5 and Sch 5 para 4 as from 1.4.99.
2. Amended by s1(6) of the SSFA as from 30.4.02.
3. Inserted by s2(3)(a) of the SSFA as from 30.4.02.
4. Amended by s2(3)(b) of the SSFA as from 30.4.02.

General Note

Now that local authorities have power to appoint inspectors under s110A, this offence may be committed by anyone who obstructs an inspector or who fails to provide information when required to do so.

Analysis

Subs (1). The offence can only be committed when the inspector is acting within her/his powers. It is implicit in subs (1)(b) that the defendant either refused to answer a question or suppy information or failed to do so properly. A defendant who truthfully stated that s/he could not answer the question (whether because s/he did not know the answer or because there was some privilege in the information or documents) or did not have access to the information or documents does not commit the offence. The maximum amount of a fine on level 3 is currently £1,000.

Subs (2). The fine is calculated on a daily rate between the date of conviction for the offence under subs (1) and the date of conviction under subs (2), not the date that the information is laid for the offence under subs (2): *Grice v Needs* [1980] 1 WLR 45 at 47F-G.

[⁰Dishonest representations for the purpose of obtaining benefit etc

111A.–(1) If a person dishonestly–

(a) makes a false statement or representation; [³ or]

(b) produces or furnishes, or causes or allows to be produced or furnished, any document or information which is false in a material particular;

[⁴ . . .]

[⁴ . . .]

with a view to obtaining any benefit or other payment or advantage under the [¹ relevant] social security legislation (whether for himself or for some other person), he shall be guilty of an offence.

[⁵ (1A) A person shall be guilty of an offence if–

(a) there has been a change of circumstances affecting any entitlement of his to any benefit or other payment or advantage under any provision of the relevant social security legislation;

(b) the change is not a change that is excluded by regulations from the changes that are required to be notified;

(c) he knows that the change affects an entitlement of his to such a benefit or other payment or advantage; and

(d) he dishonestly fails to give a prompt notification of that change in the prescribed manner to the prescribed person.

(1B) A person shall be guilty of an offence if–

(a) there has been a change of circumstances affecting any entitlement of another person to any benefit or other payment or advantage under any provision of the relevant social security legislation;

(b)   the change is not a change that is excluded by regulations from the changes that are required to be notified;

(c)   he knows that the change affects an entitlement of that other person to such a benefit or other payment or advantage; and

(d)   he dishonestly causes or allows that other person to fail to give a prompt notification of that change in the prescribed manner to the prescribed person.

(1C)   This subsection applies where–

(a)   there has been a change of circumstances affecting any entitlement of a person ('the claimant') to any benefit or other payment or advantage under any provision of the relevant social security legislation;

(b)   the benefit, payment or advantage is one in respect of which there is another person ('the recipient') who for the time being has a right to receive payments to which the claimant has, or (but for the arrangements under which they are payable to the recipient) would have, an entitlement; and

(c)   the change is not a change that is excluded by regulations from the changes that are required to be notified.

(1D)   In a case where subsection (1C) above applies, the recipient is guilty of an offence if–

(a)   he knows that the change affects an entitlement of the claimant to a benefit or other payment or advantage under a provision of the relevant social security legislation;

(b)   the entitlement is one in respect of which he has a right to receive payments to which the claimant has, or (but for the arrangements under which they are payable to the recipient) would have, an entitlement; and

(c)   he dishonestly fails to give a prompt notification of that change in the prescribed manner to the prescribed person.

(1E)   In a case where that subsection applies, a person other than the recipient is guilty of an offence if–

(a)   he knows that the change affects an entitlement of the claimant to a benefit or other payment or advantage under a provision of the relevant social security legislation;

(b)   the entitlement is one in respect of which the recipient has a right to receive payments to which the claimant has, or (but for the arrangements under which they are payable to the recipient) would have, an entitlement; and

(c)   he dishonestly causes or allows the recipient to fail to give a prompt notification of that change in the prescribed manner to the prescribed person.

(1F)   In any case where subsection (1C) above applies but the right of the recipient is confined to a right, by reason of his being a person to whom the claimant is required to make payments in respect of a dwelling, to receive payments of housing benefit–

(a)   a person shall not be guilty of an offence under subsection (1D) or (1E) above unless the change is one relating to one or both of the following–

(i)   the claimant's occupation of that dwelling;

(ii)   the claimant's liability to make payments in respect of that dwelling;

but

(b)   subsections (1D)(a) and (1E)(a) above shall each have effect as if after "knows" there were inserted "or could reasonably be expected to know".

(1G)   For the purposes of subsections (1A) to (1E) above a notification of a change is prompt if, and only if, it is given as soon as reasonably practicable after the change occurs.]

[²...]

(3)   A person guilty of an offence under this section shall be liable–

(a)   on summary conviction, to imprisonment for a term not exceeding six months, or to a fine not exceeding the statutory maximum, or to both; or

(b)   on conviction on indictment, to imprisonment for a term not exceeding seven years, or to a fine, or to both.

(4)   In the application of this section to Scotland, in [[6] subsections (1) to (1E)] for "dishonestly" substitute "knowingly".]

Amendments

0.   Inserted by s11 of the SSA(F) Act 1997 as from 1.7.97.
1.   Inserted by CSPSSA 2000 s67 (2.4.01).
2.   Repealed by CSPSSA 2000 s85 (2.4.01).
3.   Amended by SSFA s16(1)(a) (18.10.01 and 30.4.02).
4.   Repealed by SSFA ss16(1)(a) and 19 and Sch (18.10.01 and 30.4.02).
5.   Inserted by SSFA s16(1)(b) and (2) (29.9.01 and 18.10.01).
6.   Amended by SSFA s16(1)(c) (18.10.01).

General Note

This section, inserted by s13 Social Security Administration (Fraud) Act 1997 and extensively amended by the Social Security Fraud Act 2001, creates an offence relating to fraudulent acts to complement the existing offence in s112. At first glance, the two offences appear quite similar in their ambit, but it is clear that this offence is intended to be used in prosecuting more serious offenders. Three factors lead to this conclusion. First, dishonesty must be shown. Secondly, there is a requirement that the act or omission in question must have been done with a view to obtaining benefit (contrast the position under s112, as to which see below). Finally, the offence is triable either way and the maximum penalties are substantially heavier.

No offence may be committed under this section by virtue of any act or omission committed before the section came into force on 1 July 1997: s25(5) of the 1997 Act. There is no equivalent provision in the 2001 Act, but the common law and Art 7 of the European Convention on Human Rights will mean that the new offences cannot apply to conduct committed before 18 October 2001, when the new provisions were brought into force by SI 2001 No 3551.

Analysis

These offences can all be committed by a "person". That wording will apply to legal as well as natural persons, and so companies and other bodies with legal personality may be charged with the offence: Sch 1 Interpretation Act 1978. Note also s115 SSAA, which provides that officers or members of a body corporate can be charged individually with the offence if the body corporate committed it "with the consent or connivance of" that officer.

Subsection (1)

".... dishonestly ....". The meaning of "dishonesty" in English criminal law is well settled from its use in the Theft Act 1968. It must be shown that the defendant's actions would not have been seen as honest by ordinary people and that the defendant must have been aware of this: *R v Ghosh* [1982] QB 1053 at 1064D-G, CA.

It is suggested that the requirement of dishonesty qualifies the whole of the subparagraph that follows. In other words, it is not just necessary for the prosecution to prove that the defendant was dishonest in relation to the act or omission alleged. It must also be shown that there was a dishonest intent to procure payment of benefit. This point is illustrated by the facts in *Barrass v Reeve* [1981] 1 WLR 408, DC. The claimant falsely claimed that he was incapable of work, but asserted that his objective in doing so was to deceive his employer. If he was believed, then that would require his acquittal on a charge under s111A, as he would have been dishonest in making a false statement, but not in relation to obtaining benefit. His dishonesty would not be "with a view" to obtaining benefit. Such a defendant can, however, be prosecuted under s112.

"(a) makes a false statement or representation". Proof of an actual statement will be required, though the statement could presumably be oral or written.

"(b) produces or furnishes, or causes or allows to be produced or furnished ....". This is a very wide phrase. "Produces" means to personally hand something over. "Furnishes" has a slightly wider meaning and means that steps have been taken to ensure that the article in question has been handed over. It is questionable whether a defendant who has documents seized by an inspector "furnishes" them. A person "causes" documents or information to be given if s/he participates in the giving of the information. A person "allows" documents or information to be given if s/he passively stands by while the information is given. In the last case, care must be taken to ensure that the requisite dishonest intent is really present in relation to the omission. Mere carelessness or oversight will not suffice.

".... any document ....". This tends to be given a flexible meaning by the courts to include any means by which information is stored: *Grant v Southwestern and County Properties Ltd* [1975] Ch 185 at 197A-F, Ch D. It will therefore include things like computer discs.

".... with a view to obtaining any benefit ....". The complete offence is committed even though no benefit was actually paid as a result of the dishonesty, and so a defendant in such a case need not merely be charged with an attempt. All that is required is that the purpose (or one of the purposes) of the dishonesty was to procure payment.

".... or other payment ....". This phrase prevents any argument as to whether any payment made is a payment of benefit. For example, if a landlord conspired with an individual in the HB office to send out two cheques for each claim, it might be arguable that the extra cheque was not "benefit". However, the second cheque would certainly fall within the scope of "other payment".

Subsection (1A)

This deals with dishonest failures to disclose by a claimant. There are four requirements.

(1)   There has been a change of circumstances which has affected entitlement to benefit: para (a). Note that it is necessary that entitlement to benefit *was* affected and not merely that the change might have affected entitlement: *R v Passmore* [2007] EWCA Crim 2053, 18 June, CA. Where this is disputed, it may be necessary to adjourn criminal proceedings pending resolution of the issue through the appeals process.

(2)   The change is not exempted from a disclosure requirement: para (b). See reg 88(3) HB Regs (reg 69(3) HB(SPC) Regs) and reg 74(3) CTB Regs (reg 59(3) CTB(SPC) Regs) for the types of information which need not be disclosed.

(3)   The defendant knows that the change affects entitlement: para (c). This requirement is narrowly drawn. It is not enough that the defendant *ought* to have known that the change was relevant. That is clear from the modification made by subs (1F)(b). It must be proven by the prosecution that there was knowledge on the part of the defendant that there was a requirement to notify: *Gaumont British Distributors Ltd v Henry* [1939] 2 KB 711 at 719, 723, DC. It is suggested that there must have been knowledge at the time that the failure to notify occurred. This could lead to a number of difficult problems. First, it is suggested that where a defendant forgets about the obligation, having previously been aware of it, they do not have the requisite knowledge at that moment in time. If, of course, they subsequently remember the duty and fail to notify, then they can be charged with the offence for that period of time. Secondly, it seems doubtful whether it can be said that a genuinely ignorant person who did not read the literature given to her/him and did not make any inquiries can be said to know what s/he is required to notify, unless it can be said that there was a deliberate attempt to refrain from seeking information: *Taylor's Central Garages (Exeter) Ltd v Roper* [1951] 115 JP 445 at 449, 450, DC; *Westminister CC v Croyalgrange Ltd* [1986] 1 WLR 674 at 684E, HL. Finally, if a person forms a false view that no disclosure is required, then provided that view is genuinely held, it cannot be said that he "knows" that such disclosure is necessary.

(4)   There is a dishonest failure to disclose. See above on the meaning of "dishonesty". See reg 4 Social Security (Notification of Change of Circumstances) Regulations 2002 in Part 7 for the prescribed manner and person. The notification must be prompt, meaning as soon as reasonably practicable: subs (1G). In Scotland, the requirement "knowingly" is substituted: see subs (4).

Subsection (1B)

This deals with dishonestly allowing another person to omit disclosure. Again there are four requirements. The first three are identical to those in subs (1A)(a), (b) and (c) save that the change of circumstances and knowledge must relate to the effect on the other person's entitlement. "Causes or allows" requires that there must be some sort of implied permission given by the defendant to the person under the duty that they should not notify: *R v Chainey* [1914] 1 KB 137 at 142, DC. A person does not "allow" information to be given where they are unable to prevent it being given: *Crabtree v Fern Spinning Co Ltd* [1901] 85 LT 549 at 552, DC. So if a person knows that their partner is supplying false information or refraining from supplying information but they are threatened with violence, they do not "allow" that conduct.

Subsections (1C) to (1F)

These create similar offences relating to those in receipt of benefit who are not claimants. They must be those having a right to receive payments in place of the claimant: see subs (1C)(b). These might be:

(1)   Landlords to whom rent allowance is paid directly: see regs 95 and 96 HB Regs (reg 76 and 77 HB(SPC) Regs).

(2)   Officials appointed to look after the affairs of those unable to act, and others so appointed: see regs 82(2), (3), (5) and 94(2) HB Regs (reg 63(2), (3), (5) and 75(2) HB(SPC) Regs) and reg 68(2), (3), (5) and 78(2) CTB Regs (reg 52(2), (3), (5) and 63(2) CTB(SPC) Regs).

(3)   Other people to whom the authority has agreed to pay benefit, notwithstanding that the claimant is capable of managing their affairs: see reg 94(3) HB Regs (reg 75(3) HB(SPC) Regs).

Subs (1D) creates an offence which may be committed by such an individual where the claimant's benefit entitlement is affected and the change is not excluded from notification. Knowledge of the effect of the change and dishonesty in failing to notify must normally be proved, but subs (1F) modifies their effect in relation to landlords in receipt of HB.

First, the relevant change must relate to the claimant's occupation of the dwelling or their liability to make payments. Given that this statute creates a criminal offence, it is suggested that these exceptions must be read narrowly. They cannot, therefore, relate to matters which affect the question of whether there is a legal liability at all or whether the liability falls within reg 9(1) of the HB and the HB(SPC) Regs. They can relate only to the question of whether the claimant is physically in occupation, or the amount of the liability for rent. Secondly, the requirement of knowledge is softened by requiring only proof that the landlord ought reasonably to have known, but given the requirement of dishonesty it seems unlikely that anything short of the landlord shutting his eyes to the obvious will suffice to constitute the criminal offence.

Subs (1E) creates a similar offence to that in subs (1B), and is similarly modified by subs (1F) in relation to landlords in receipt of HB.

Subsection (3)

The "statutory maximum" on summary conviction is currently £5,000.

Subsection (4)

On the meaning of "knowingly" in Scottish criminal law, see Gordon, *Criminal Law* (1978 2nd edn), para 8-22; *The Laws of Scotland* (1995) vol. 7, para 79.

False representations for obtaining benefit etc

112.–(1)   If a person for the purpose of obtaining any benefit or other payment under the [⁴ relevant] [³ social security legislation] whether for himself or some other person, or for any other purpose connected with that legislation–

(a)   makes a statement or representation which he knows to be false; or

(b)   produces or furnishes, or knowingly causes or knowingly allows to be produced or furnished, any document or information which he knows to be false in a material particular,

he shall be guilty of an offence.

[⁶(1A)   A person shall be guilty of an offence if–

(a)   there has been a change of circumstances affecting any entitlement of his to any benefit or other payment or advantage under any provision of the relevant social security legislation;

(b)   the change is not a change that is excluded by regulations from the changes that are required to be notified;

(c)   he knows that the change affects an entitlement of his to such a benefit or other payment or advantage; and

(d)   he fails to give a prompt notification of that change in the prescribed manner to the prescribed person.]–

(1B)   A person is guilty of an offence under this section if–

(a)   there has been a change of circumstances affecting any entitlement of another person to any benefit or other payment or advantage under any provision of the relevant social security legislation;

(b)   the change is not a change that is excluded by regulations from the changes that are required to be notified;

(c)   he knows that the change affects an entitlement of that other person to such a benefit or other payment or advantage; and

(d)   he causes or allows that other person to fail to give a prompt notification of that change in the prescribed manner to the prescribed person.

(1C)   In a case where subsection (1C) of section 111A above applies, the recipient is guilty of an offence if–

(a)   he knows that the change affects an entitlement of the claimant to a benefit or other payment or advantage under a provision of the relevant social security legislation;

(b)   the entitlement is one in respect of which he has a right to receive payments to which the claimant has, or (but for the arrangements under which they are payable to the recipient) would have, an entitlement; and

    (c)   he fails to give a prompt notification of that change in the prescribed manner to the prescribed person.

    (1D)   In a case where that subsection applies, a person other than the recipient is guilty of an offence if–

    (a)   he knows that the change affects an entitlement of the claimant to a benefit or other payment or advantage under a provision of the relevant social security legislation;

    (b)   the entitlement is one in respect of which the recipient has a right to receive payments to which the claimant has, or (but for the arrangements under which they are payable to the recipient) would have, an entitlement; and

    (c)   he causes or allows the recipient to fail to give a prompt notification of that change in the prescribed manner to the prescribed person.

    (1E)   Subsection (1F) of section 111A above applies in relation to subsections (1C) and (1D) above as it applies in relation to subsections (1D) and (1E) of that section.

    (1F)   For the purposes of subsections (1A) to (1D) above a notification of a change is prompt if, and only if, it is given as soon as reasonably practicable after the change occurs.]

    (2)   A person guilty of an offence under [⁴ this section] shall be liable on summary conviction to a fine not exceeding level 5 on the standard scale, or to imprisonment for a term not exceeding 3 months, or to both.

    [⁵. . .]

Amendments

1. Amended by SSA(F) Act 1997, s14(1A).
2. Amended by SSA (F) Act 1997, s14(3).
3. Substituted by SSA(F) Act 1997, Sch 1 para 4(2).
4. Inserted by CSPSS Act, Sch 6 para 6 (2.4.01).
5. Repealed by CSPSS Act 2000, s85 and Sch 9 (2.4.01).
6. Substituted by SSFA s16(3) (29.9.01 and 18.10.01).

Definition

"benefit" – s191.

General Note

This section sets out the less serious offences that may be committed in relation to obligations of disclosure of information to an authority. s14 Social Security Administration (Fraud) Act 1997 considerably widened the scope of the offences to cover omissions as well as positive misstatements and again the offences have been reformulated by the Social Security Fraud Act 2001. Note the temporal effect of the new provisions in subs (1A) to (1F): see the commentary to s111A above. Note also the time limits for prosecutions imposed by s116 below.

Analysis

Subsection (1)

"If a person ...". See Analysis to s111A above.

"... for the purpose of obtaining benefit .... or for any other purpose connected with that legislation ...". The latter phrase means that it need not be shown that the defendant intended to obtain benefit. It suffices if the statement was made for purposes relating to benefit: *Clear v Smith* [1981] 1 WLR 399 at 406, DC (statement that no work was being done when claimant asserted that work was unremunerated); *Barrass v Reeve* [1981] 1 WLR 408, DC (statement that claimant was incapable of work allegedly only used to deceive employer); *DSS v Bavi* [1996] COD 260 at 261, DC (statement that claimant not working allegedly result of misunderstanding).

"(a) makes a statement or representation ....". An actual statement, whether written or oral, must be proved by the prosecution, though the place and date of the statement need not be proven: *DSS v Cooper* [1994] 158 JPN 354, DC.

In deciding whether a question on a claim form has been answered incorrectly, it is not necessary to analyse the question in a legalistic manner by reference to the meaning of a particular word in the HB Regs, but rather by taking a common-sense view. So where a claimant stated that he did not own property, but in fact was the registered owner of a house, it did not matter whether or not the claimant was an "owner" for the purposes of reg 2(1) HB and the HB(SPC) Regs. The fact that he had an interest in the property that made him the owner as a matter of common sense was sufficient: *Fairbank v Lambeth Magistrates' Court* [2003] HLR 62.

"... which he knows to be false ...". The defendant must know of the falsity at the time the statement or representation is made: *Moore v Branton* [1974] 118 SJ 40, DC. It does not matter that a specific statement may have been true when made, if on a change of circumstances the claimant continues to sign forms stating that there has been no such change. The latter will be the requisite false statement: *Tolfree v Florence* [1971] 1 WLR 141 at 144, DC. Showing that a defendant was negligent or failed to make inquiries into facts does not establish knowledge of the falsity of those facts: *Taylor's Central Garages (Exeter) Ltd v Roper* [1951] 115 JP 445 at 449, 450, DC.

The prosecution must prove that the defendant knew that the statement was false, but as long as the defendant knows that the statement or representation is false, s/he need not know that the falsity was material to her/his entitlement to benefit, since there is no requirement of materiality in para (a), unlike para (b): *Harrison v DSS* [1997] COD 220 at 220-1, DC.

Para (b). See the requirement of knowledge discussed in the previous paragraph and see the Analysis of s111A(1)(b) above.

Subsections (1A) to (1F)

These subsections create similar criminal offences to those in s111A(1A) to (1G), except that there is no requirement of dishonesty. Each of the sub-paras (a) to (d) under subs1A must be established to the criminal standard of proof, and therefore it is for the prosecution to prove beyond a reasonable doubt that the defendant knew that the change *would* affect his or her benefit entitlement: simply showing that the change could affect entitlement will not be sufficient: *King v Kerrier District Council* [2006] EWHC 500 (Admin), unreported, 27 February (DC).

Subsection (2)

The offence is triable only summarily – ie, in the magistrates' court or sheriff court in Scotland. A fine "not exceeding level 5 on the standard scale" is currently a maximum of £5,000.

[¹Breach of regulations

113.–(1)   Regulations and schemes under any of the [² legislation to which this section applies] may provide that any person who contravenes, or fails to comply with, any provision contained in regulations made under [² that legislation]–

(a)   in the case of a provision relating to contributions, shall be liable to a penalty;

(b)   in any other case, shall be guilty of an offence under [² any enactment contained in the legislation in question].

[²(1A)   The legislation to which this section applies is–

(a)   the relevant social security legislation; and

(b)   the enactments specified in section 121DA(1) so far as relating to contributions, statutory sick pay or statutory maternity pay.]

(2)   *[omitted]*

(3)   A person guilty of such an offence as is mentioned in subsection (1)(b) above shall be liable on summary conviction–

(a)   to a fine not exceeding level 3 on the standard scale;

(b)   in the case of an offence of continuing a contravention or failure after conviction, to a fine not exceeding £163.40 for each day on which it is so continued.

(4)   *[omitted]*]

Amendments

1.   Section replaced by section 60 of Social Security Act 1998 (4.3.99/6.4.99).

2.   Amended by Sch 6 para 7 CSPSSA (1.11.00).

General Note

The version of s113 substituted in 1999 made no changes of substance as far as HB and CTB are concerned (the changes were to be found in subs (2) and (4), which relate to offences relating to national insurance contributions). The section continues to allow regulations to provide that a failure to comply with requirements in such regulations amounts to a criminal offence under this section. Until 1997 there was no such provision in the HB or CTB schemes, but from 3 November 1997 the Social Security (Information from

Landlords and Agents) Regulations 1997 made such a provision. This is now in regs 117-121 HB Regs (regs 98-102 HB(SPC) Regs). These regulations require landlords and their agents to furnish a wide range of information to an authority on request. A failure to comply with such a demand amounts to an offence under this section. See the commentary to those Regulations.

As to the penalties, see the commentary to s111.

Offences by bodies corporate

115.–(1) Where an offence under this Act [[1], or under the Jobseeker's Act 1995] which has been committed by a body corporate is proved to have been committed with the consent or connivance of, or to be attributable to any neglect on the part of, a director, manager, secretary or other similar officer of the body corporate, or any person who was purporting to act in any such capacity, he, as well as the body corporate, shall be guilty of that offence and be liable to be proceeded against accordingly.

(2)   Where the affairs of a body corporate are managed by its members, subsection (1) above applies in relation to the acts and defaults of a member in connection with his functions of management as if he were a director of the body corporate.

Amendment

1.   Amended by the Jobseekers Act 1995 Sch 2 para 116.

General Note

This section might apply in HB or CTB cases where a body corporate which is a landlord or an employer commits an offence under ss111A or 112 in relation to HB or CTB. It confirms that any officer or manager of such a body can be personally liable to prosecution if s/he has deliberately or negligently caused or contributed to the commission of the offence.

It does not appear to be necessary for a prosecution under this section that the body corporate is also prosecuted, provided that it is guilty of the offence.

A 'body corporate' is not defined in the Act. In England and Wales, it means a body which is incorporated under royal charter, Act of Parliament or the Companies Act 1985. In Scottish law, however, it may include a partnership: *Douglas v Phoenix Motors* [1970] SLT 57 at 58, Sh Ct, where both English and Scottish law are discussed.

[[1]Penalty as alternative to prosecution

115A.–(1) This section applies where an overpayment is recoverable from a person by, or due from a person to, the Secretary of State or an authority under or by virtue of section 71, 71A, 75 or 76 above and it appears to the Secretary of State or authority that–

   (a)   the making of the overpayment was attributable to an act or omission on the part of that person; and

   (b)   there are grounds for instituting against him proceedings for an offence (under this Act or any other enactment) relating to the overpayment.

(2)   The Secretary of State or authority may give to the person a written notice–

   (a)   stating that he may be invited to agree to pay a penalty and that, if he does so in the manner specified by the Secretary of State or authority, no such proceedings will be instituted against him; and

   (b)   containing such information relating to the operation of this section as may be prescribed.

(3)   The amount of the penalty shall be 30 per cent. of the amount of the overpayment (rounded down to the nearest whole penny).

(4)   If the person agrees in the specified manner to pay the penalty–

   (a)   the amount of the penalty shall be recoverable by the same methods as those by which the overpayment is recoverable; and

   (b)   no proceedings will be instituted against him for an offence (under this Act or any other enactment) relating to the overpayment.

(5)　The person may withdraw his agreement to pay the penalty by notifying the Secretary of State or authority, in the manner specified by the Secretary of State or authority, at any time during the period of 28 days beginning with the day on which he agrees to pay it; and if he does so–

(a)　so much of the penalty as has already been recovered shall be repaid; and

(b)　subsection (4)(b) above shall not apply.

(6)　Where, after the person has agreed to pay the penalty, it is decided on a review or appeal or in accordance with regulations that the overpayment is not recoverable or due, so much of the penalty as has already been recovered shall be repaid.

(7)　Where, after the person has agreed to pay the penalty, the amount of the overpayment is revised on a review or appeal or in accordance with regulations–

(a)　so much of the penalty as has already been recovered shall be repaid; and

(b)　subsection (4)(b) above shall no longer apply by reason of the agreement; but if a new agreement is made under this section in relation to the revised overpayment, the amount already recovered by way of penalty, to the extent that it does not exceed the amount of the new penalty, may be treated as recovered under the new agreement instead of being repaid.

[²(7A)　Subject to subsection (7B) below, the Secretary of State and an authority which administers housing benefit or council tax benefit may agree that, to the extent determined by the agreement, one may carry out on the other's behalf, or may join in the carrying out of, any of the other's functions under this section.

(7B)　Subsection (7A) above shall not authorise any delegation of–

(a)　the function of the person by whom any overpayment is recoverable, or to whom it is due, of determining whether or not a notice should be given under subsection (2) above in respect of that overpayment; or

(b)　the Secretary of State's power to make regulations for the purposes of paragraph (b) of that subsection.]

(8)　In this section ''overpayment'' means–

(a)　a payment which should not have been made;

(b)　a sum which the Secretary of State should have received;

(c)　an amount of benefit paid in excess of entitlement; or

(d)　an amount equal to an excess of benefit allowed;

and the reference in subsection (1)(a) above to the making of the overpayment is to the making of the payment, the failure to receive the sum, the payment of benefit in excess of entitlement or the allowing of an excess of benefit.]

Amendments

1.　Inserted by the SSA(F) Act 1997, s15.

2.　Inserted by SSFA s14 (30.4.02).

General Note

One controversial innovation of the Social Security Administration (Fraud) Act 1997 was to enable an authority to offer a prospective defendant the option to pay a penalty rather than institute proceedings for the prosecution of that person. It may be argued that authorities might see this as a short-cut and a simple way of avoiding the expense of bringing criminal proceedings. In addition, there may be iniquity in the operation of the system if landlords are able to evade prosecution by accepting the penalty while impecunious claimants are unable to do so. Only time will tell how the provision is used.

A penalty may not be offered in relation to an offence alleged to have been committed before 18 December 1997, when the section came into force: s25(7) of the 1997 Act.

The scheme, in outline, is as follows. The authority may only offer a penalty when there are grounds for prosecuting for an offence in relation to an overpayment: subs (1). A written notice offering the penalty must be given: subs (2). If the person in question agrees to pay, they receive immunity from prosecution and must pay an additional 30 per cent on top of the overpayment: subs (3) and (4).

The person may withdraw from the agreement within 28 days: subs (5). If there is subsequently a decision that there is no recoverable overpayment, the penalty is not payable: subs (6). If the amount of the overpayment is revised, the agreement is void, but a new agreement may be made: subs (7).

Analysis

Subsection (1)

"... where an overpayment is recoverable .... or due ...". An overpayment is not recoverable unless a valid determination has been issued by the local authority: *Warwick DC v Freeman* [1994] 27 HLR 616, CA. This is made clear beyond doubt, in relation to HB, by the amendment to Administration Act s75(1) made by Sch 1 para 3 of the 1997 Act.

It is difficult to see what "or due" adds to this. It cannot be said that it renders the penalty system operable before there has been a determination, because an overpayment cannot be "due" until it is recoverable, and until the amount has been calculated, it would not be possible to determine the level of the penalty. It might be thought that it is intended to cover situations where the overpayment arose before the Bill comes into force, but there is a specific provision against retrospectivity in relation to s115A in s25(7) of the 1997 Act. Finally, it was said in committee that "the definition of overpayment in [section 115A] does not go any wider than what is already covered by the 1992 Act": Oliver Heald MP, Standing Committee E, 21 January 1997, col. 319. There is no room for saying that it applies to overpayments that have yet to be determined to be recoverable.

It is suggested that the penalty system cannot come into operation until the local authority has made its initial determination under reg 89(1) HB Regs (reg 70(1) HB(SPC) Regs) or reg 75(1) CTB Regs (reg 60(1) CTB(SPC) Regs) as appropriate. However, there is no need to wait until the review procedure is exhausted: see subs (6).

"... it appears to the Secretary of State or authority that ...". The prosecuting authority must satisfy itself that the two conditions set out in subsection (1) are met. If they do not carry out this thought process, the section has no application and so any notice served would be invalid.

"... under or by virtue of section ... 75 or 76 ...". Overpayments of HB and CTB are recoverable under ss75 and 76 respectively.

"... the making of the overpayment was attributable to an act or omission ...". The word "attributable" requires some connection between the overpayment and the actor omission, but the latter need not be the sole cause of the former: *Walsh v Rother DC* [1978] 1 All ER 510 at 514a-e, HC.

"... there are grounds for instituting proceedings for an offence". This must mean that there is at least enough evidence before the prosecuting authority to suggest that there is a *prima facie* case for the defendant to answer.

Subsection (2)

"... may give ...". The power to offer a penalty is discretionary and there can be no question of the authority being under any duty to do so.

"... if he does so in the manner specified ...". This phrase is a little vague. The notice words "the manner specified" apply to the invitation to make an agreement, rather than the payment of the penalty under that agreement. In other words, the notice is only required to state how the agreement is to be made. It does not have to set out how the penalty has to be paid.

It appears that there is no power for the Secretary of State to prescribe the means by which an agreement is reached and so this will be a matter for authorities. Needless to say, it ought to be in writing and authorities should take care that the chosen procedure leaves all parties clear as to whether the invitation has been accepted or not.

Paras (a) and (b). The notice must contain the specified information. If it does not, the notice will be invalid if the recipient has been disadvantaged thereby: *Freeman* (above), *Haringey LBC v Awaritefe* [1999] 32 HLR 517 and *R(H) 3/04*. It is suggested that in these circumstances, any agreement to pay a penalty may be unenforceable by reason of the invalidity of the notice, since the issue of a notice is the trigger for the making of the agreement. For the information that must be included in a penalty notice, see reg 2 Social Security (Penalty Notice) Regulations 1997 in part 7.

Subsection (3)

The amount of the overpayment is the amount as specified by the authority in its original determination that the overpayment is recoverable. Subs (6) deals with situations where the overpayment is later found not to be recoverable and subs (7) deals with the situation where the amount changes on review.

Subsection (4)

"... agrees in the specified manner to pay the penalty ...". The "specified manner" relates to the making of the agreement, not the payment: see subs (2). The significance of this is that if there is an agreement as to how the penalty is paid, but the person paying the penalty fails to adhere to that agreement, her/his failure does not render the agreement void and so the authority will not then be able to institute proceedings for a criminal offence.

Para (a). For the methods by which the overpayment will be recoverable, see the Analysis to reg 102 HB Regs on p426.

Para (b). In return for paying the penalty, the person in question cannot be prosecuted under any of the offences set out above or under any other legislation, including in particular the Theft Act 1968. There could still be a prosecution under the common law, which may be relevant in Scotland, where there is no equivalent of the 1968 Act. Such a prosecution would probably be regarded as an abuse of process.

Subsection (5)

This subsection gives a statutory 28-day 'cooling-off' period during which a person who has agreed to pay a penalty may withdraw from the agreement

Once that period has expired, it may still be possible to take civil proceedings to set the agreement aside if it was procured by undue influence on the part of the authority, namely the threat of prosecution: *Williams v Bayley* [1866] LR 1 HL 200, HL. It would have to be shown that the influence of the authority continued after the 28-day period (so that, for example, the paying person took no legal advice) and probably that there was some impropriety in the authority's actions. This latter requirement could be fulfilled by showing that the evidence would not have supported a criminal charge.

"... in the manner specified ...". By the Social Security (Penalty Notice) Regulations 1997 reg 2(1)(d), a penalty notice served under subs (2) must contain a statement that the person in question may withdraw "in the manner specified by ... the authority". It is highly arguable that this requires the authority to specifically state in the notice how a person may withdraw from the agreement, rather than simply state "the manner specified" in the notice.

"... so much of the penalty as has already been recovered shall be repaid ...". In many cases, the overpayment plus the penalty will not be paid as a lump sum, but will be paid in instalments. If the payer withdraws from the agreement, do the instalments which s/he has already paid count towards the overpayment or to the penalty? Assuming the sums paid have not been specifically attributed to one or the other, the rule in *Clayton's case* [1861] 1 Mer 572 probably applies, so that payments are applied to the debt that first arose in time until it is extinguished.

The question then is which debt arose first in time. If there is no challenge to the recoverability of the overpayment, then that debt will have arisen before the penalty. However, it may be that review of the question of recoverability has been sought. It cannot be said that there is a debt in relation to the overpayment until it has been established that the overpayment is recoverable. In such a case, it may be that the penalty is the first debt in time and that the instalments will have been applied to reduce that debt. In that case, the instalments will have to be repaid.

Subsection (6)

If the overpayment is found not to be recoverable, then the penalty disappears. Any payments made will have been attributable to the penalty, because there has never been any debt in relation to the overpayment. Note that the subsection does not provide that the claimant's immunity from prosecution disappears: compare subs (7)(b).

Subsection (7)

A change in the amount of the overpayment on review or appeal removes the effect of the agreement. The reason for this is probably to allow an authority, where it is subsequently discovered that the amount of an overpayment is much higher, to take the decision to prosecute after all. Payments already made towards the penalty must be repaid, but if a new agreement is concluded, then those payments may be treated as being on account of the newly assessed penalty.

Subsection (8)

This subsection gives a wide definition to "overpayment" for the purposes of s115A. The following categories of payment are included in the definition:

(a)   It might be thought that it was arguable that if there was an award of benefit pursuant to which the payments of benefit were made, it could not be said that the payment "should not have been made" because there was a legal obligation on the authority to pay that benefit until such time as the award was revised. However, a similar phrase also occurs in Sch 9A para 11 SSCBA which deals with recovery of overpaid mortgage interest paid as income support housing costs. In *R v Secretary of State for Social Security ex p Golding* [1996] unreported, 1 July, CA, the Court of Appeal held that a payment "ought not to have been made" if it was an overpayment, even though the payment was made pursuant to an award of an adjudication officer.

(b)   This has no application to HB or CTB.

(c)   This refers to payments not made pursuant to an award of benefit, such as double payments.

(d)   This refers to excess payments of CTB.

[¹ Penalty as alternative to prosecution: colluding employers etc

115B.–(1) This section applies where it appears to the Secretary of State or an authority that administers housing benefit or council tax benefit–

(a)   that there are grounds for instituting proceedings against any person ('the responsible person') for an offence (whether or not under this Act) in respect of any conduct; and

    (b)   that the conduct in respect of which there are grounds for instituting the proceedings is conduct falling within subsection (2) below.

    (2)   Conduct in respect of which there appear to be grounds for instituting proceedings falls within this subsection if–

    (a)   those proceedings would be for an offence under this Act in connection with an inquiry relating to the employment of relevant employees or of any one or more particular relevant employees; or

    (b)   it is conduct which was such as to facilitate the commission of a benefit offence by a relevant employee (whether or not such an offence was in fact committed).

    (3)   The Secretary of State or authority may give to the responsible person a written notice–

    (a)   specifying or describing the conduct in question;

    (b)   stating that he may be invited to agree to pay a penalty in respect of that conduct;

    (c)   stating that, if he does so in the manner specified by the Secretary of State or authority, no criminal proceedings will be instituted against him in respect of that conduct; and

    (d)   containing such information relating to the operation of this section as may be prescribed.

    (4)   If the recipient of a notice under subsection (3) above agrees, in the specified manner, to pay the penalty–

    (a)   the amount of the penalty shall be recoverable as a civil debt, and shall be capable of being set off against an amount of relevant benefit payable to the recipient of the notice; and

    (b)   no criminal proceedings shall be instituted against him in respect of the conduct to which the notice relates;

and section 71(10) above (recovery by execution etc.) shall apply in relation to an amount recoverable by virtue of paragraph (a) above as it applies in relation to an amount recoverable under the provisions mentioned in section 71(8) above.

    (5)   The amount of the penalty shall be–

    (a)   in a case in which the conduct in question falls within paragraph (a) of subsection (2) above but not within paragraph (b) of that subsection, £1,000;

    (b)   in a case in which that conduct falls within paragraph (b) of that subsection and the number of relevant employees by reference to whom it falls within that subsection is five or more, £5,000; and

    (c)   in any other case, the amount obtained by multiplying £1,000 by the number of relevant employees by reference to whom that conduct falls within that subsection.

    (6)   The responsible person may withdraw his agreement to pay a penalty under this section by notifying the Secretary of State or authority, in the manner specified by the Secretary of State or authority, at any time during the period of 28 days beginning with the day on which he agrees to pay it.

    (7)   Where the responsible person withdraws his agreement in accordance with subsection (6) above–

    (a)   so much of the penalty as has already been recovered shall be repaid; and

    (b)   subsection (4)(b) above shall not apply.

    (8)   For the purposes of this section an individual is a relevant employee in relation to any conduct of the responsible person if–

    (a)   that conduct was at or in relation to a time when that individual was an employee of the responsible person;

    (b)   that conduct was at or in relation to a time when that individual was an employee of a body corporate of which the responsible person is or has been a director; or

(c)   the responsible person, in engaging in that conduct, was acting or purporting to act on behalf of, in the interests of or otherwise by reason of his connection with, any person by whom that individual is or has been employed.

(9)   In this section–

''conduct'' includes acts, omissions and statements;

''director''–

(a)   in relation to a company (within the meaning of the Companies Act 1985), includes a shadow director;

(b)   in relation to any such company that is a subsidiary of another, includes any director or shadow director of the other company; and

(c)   in relation to a body corporate whose affairs are managed by its members, means a member of that body corporate;

''employee'' means any person who–

(a)   is employed under a contract of service or apprenticeship, or in an office (including an elective office), or

(b)   carries out any work under any contract under which he has undertaken to provide his work,

and ''employment'' shall be construed accordingly;

''relevant benefit'' means benefit prescribed for the purposes of section 71(8) above;

''shadow director'' means a shadow director as defined in [² section 251 of the Companies Act 2006];

''subsidiary'' means a subsidiary as defined in section 736 of the Companies Act 1985.]

Amendments

1.   Inserted by SSFA s15(1) (30.4.02).
2.   Amended by Art 10 and Sch 4 para 68 of SI 2007 No 2194 as from 1.10.07.

Commencement

1.4.02: SI 2002 No 1222.

General Note

This makes special provision for penalties to be payable by employers who collude with employees to commit benefit fraud. Penalties are to be paid into the Consolidated Fund: see subs (2). As with s115A, penalties are payable only by way of agreement and will give the person paying immunity from prosecution in relation to the conduct giving rise to the giving of the notice.

There is some doubt as to whether this provision may have effect in relation to conduct that took place prior to the commencement date of this section. There was no provision in the SSFA equivalent to s25(7) SSA(F)A which prevented penalties taking effect in relation to pre-commencement conduct. It is suggested that there is no reason in principle why a penalty could not be offered, provided it could be shown that there was evidence of an offence under the old law.

Analysis

References to subsections below are to those in the new s115B rather than in s15 of this Act.

Subsections (1) and (2): When a penalty may be offered

These subsections together impose two criteria which must be satisfied before a penalty may be offered. Any notice served under subs (3) in circumstances where they are not made out would be invalid.

(1)   There must be "grounds for instituting proceedings" against a person. As in s115A(1)(b) SSAA, "grounds" would require that there should be at least sufficient evidence for there to be a case to answer. "Person" will include both natural and legal persons, such as companies and other corporations: Sch 1 to the Interpretation Act 1978. It will not, however, include a partnership since a partnership has no legal personality. It would have to be shown that there were grounds for proceedings against an individual partner and the notice would have to relate to that partner alone.

(2)   The person is guilty of relevant conduct within subs (2). This may relate to "an inquiry relating to" the employment of a relevant employee under para (a) or conduct facilitating an offence by such an employee under para (b). Para (a) relates to offences under s111 SSAA for refusing to supply information when required to do so. Local authority officers are entitled to demand information from

employers under ss110A(1) and 109B(2)(a) SSAA. "Relating to" will probably include any information linked with the employment, even if the connection with the employment is indirect. Similarly under para (b), "facilitating" is a loose word and will probably cover conduct which makes it possible or even merely easier to commit a benefit offence as well as conduct which actively encourages or requires the commission of such offences. The employee need not have actually committed an offence; note, however, that the employer's conduct must itself be criminal or the first criterion above will not be satisfied.

Subsections (3) and (4): Making an agreement

Subs (3) and (4) are similar to s115A(2) and (4), with a few differences. First, the notice offering a penalty must specify the conduct of which complaint is made in addition to explaining that a penalty is offered and that it offers immunity from prosecution. The power to make regulations under subs (3)(d) has not yet been exercised, though it is likely that the courts will expect the Social Security (Penalty Notice) Regulations 1997 to be complied with.

Under subs (4), the penalty may be recovered as a civil debt by enforcement in the County Court or Sheriff Court. The wording of s71(10) SSAA is virtually identical to that in s75(7) SSAA. It may also be set off against any amount owing to the employer by way of "relevant benefit". By subs (9) this refers to benefits prescribed for the purposes of s71(8) SSAA. The relevant benefits include virtually all social security benefits and are listed in reg 15(2) of the Social Security (Payments on Account, Overpayments and Recovery) Regulations 1988 SI No 664.

Subsection (5): The amount of the penalty

If the conduct falls within subs (2)(a) and relates to failure to respond to an inquiry, the penalty is £1,000. If it is facilitating the commission of offences by employees, it is £1,000 multiplied by the number of employees affected, up to a limit of £5,000.

Subsections (6) and (7): Withdrawing from an agreement

These are identical to s115A(5) and (6).

Subsections (8) and (9): Definitions

"Relevant employee" is given a very wide definition by subs (8). It relates not merely to employees in law by para (a), but also employees of companies of which the responsible person is a director under para (b) (thus confirming that directors may have a personal liability for a penalty) and employees of persons on behalf of whom the responsible person was acting under para (c). The latter situation would cover a situation where an agent of the employer facilitates criminal offences.

"Director" is also given a wide definition. It may include the directors of sister companies, shadow directors or members of other bodies corporate. See the commentary to reg 9(1)(e) HB Regs on p232.

"Employee", by virtue of subs (9), includes independent contractors who provide labour under a contract. It also includes those who are apprentices or who are acting in an office.

Legal proceedings

Legal proceedings

116.–(1) Any person authorised by the Secretary of State in that behalf may conduct any proceedings [⁸ under any provision of this Act other than section 114 or under any provision of] [⁵ the Jobseekers Act 1995] before a magistrates' court although not a barrister or solicitor.

(2) Notwithstanding anything in any Act–

(a) proceedings for an offence under this Act [⁵ , or the Jobseekers Act 1995] other than an offence relating to housing benefit or [¹ council tax benefit] [⁵ , or for an offence under the Jobseekers Act 1995] may be begun at any time within the period of 3 months from the date on which evidence, sufficient in the opinion of the Secretary of State to justify a prosecution for the offence, comes to his knowledge or within a period of 12 months from the commission of the offence, whichever period last expires; and

(b) proceedings for an offence under this Act relating to housing benefit or [¹ council tax benefit] may be begun at any time within the period of 3 months from the date on which evidence, sufficient in the opinion of the appropriate authority to justify a prosecution for the offence, comes to the authority's knowledge or within a period of 12 months from the commission of the offence, whichever period last expires.

[⁴(2A) Subsection (2) above shall not be taken to impose any restriction on the time when proceedings may begun for an offence under section 111A above.]

(3)   For the purposes of subsection (2) above–

(a)   a certificate purporting to be signed by or on behalf of the Secretary of State as to the date on which such evidence as is mentioned in paragraph (a) of the subsection came to his knowledge shall be conclusive evidence of that date; and

(b)   a certificate of the appropriate authority as to the date on which such evidence as is mentioned in paragraph (b) of that subsection came to the authority's knowledge shall be conclusive evidence of that date.

(4)   In subsections (2) and (3) above "the appropriate authority" means, in relation to an offence which relates to housing benefit and concerns any dwelling–

[⁶ (a) . . .]

(b)   if it relates to a rent rebate, the authority who are the appropriate housing authority by virtue of [⁷ section 134 below]; and

(c)   if it relates to rent allowance, the authority who are the appropriate local authority by virtue of [⁷ that section].

(5)   In subsections (2) and (3) above "the appropriate authority" means, in relation to an offence relating to [² council tax benefit], such authority as is prescribed in relation to the offence.

[⁸(5A)   *[omitted]*]

(6)   [⁹ . . .]

(7)   In the application of this section to Scotland, the following provisions shall have effect in substitution for subsections (1) [⁸ to (5A)] above–

(a)   proceedings for an offence under this Act [⁵ , or the Jobseekers Act 1995] may, notwithstanding anything in [³ section 136 of the Criminal Procedure (Scotland) Act 1995], be commenced at any time within the period of 3 months from the date on which evidence, sufficient in the opinion of the Lord Advocate to justify proceedings, comes to his knowledge, or within the period of 12 months from the commission of the offence, whichever period last expires;

[¹⁰(aa) this subsection shall not be taken to impose any restriction on the time when proceedings may be commenced for an offence under section 111A above;]

(b)   for the purposes of this subsection–

(i)   a certificate purporting to be signed by or on behalf of the Lord Advocate as to the date on which such evidence as is mentioned above came to his knowledge shall be conclusive evidence of that date; and

(ii)   subsection (3) of section 331 of the said Act of 1975 (date of commencement of proceedings) shall have effect as it has effect for the purposes of that section.

Amendments

1.   Substituted by LGFA Sch 9 para 17(1) (1.4.93).
2.   Substituted by LGFA Sch 9 para 17(2) (1.4.93).
3.   Substituted by Criminal Procedure (Consequential Provisions) (Scotland) Act 1995 Sch 4 para 82 (1.4.96).
4.   Amended by SSA(F) Act 1997 Sch 1 para 5.
5.   Amended by Jobseekers Act 1995 Sch 2 para 56.
6.   Deleted by Housing Act 1996 Sch 13 para 3(3).
7.   Substituted by Housing Act 1996 Sch 13 para 3(3).
8.   Amended by Social Security (Transfer of Functions etc) Act 1999 Sch 1 para 21.
9.   Repealed bv SSA 1998 Sch 7 para 83.
10.   Inserted by SSFA s17 (30.4.02).

General Note

This section deals with the prosecution of offences under the Act. It provides that officers of the authority may conduct proceedings in person if authorised by the Secretary of State and for time limits for certain prosecutions.

Analysis

Subsection (2)(b)

This places time limits upon certain prosecutions in England and Wales. It only applies to offences "under this Act", so it does not apply to prosecutions under the Theft Act 1968 or any other statute, and nor does it apply to charges under s111A: subs (2A). It therefore applies to s112. A prosecution must be brought within two time periods, whichever ends later:

(1)   three months after the authority believes that it has sufficient evidence to justify a prosecution;

(2)   12 months after the commission of the offence.

Under the first of the two periods, a certificate by the authority stating when it believed that it had sufficient evidence is to be treated as conclusive evidence of that date: subs (3)(b). A defendant may question that date by way of judicial review.

Subsection (7)

This makes equivalent provision to subs (2)(b) in relation to proceedings brought in Scotland.

[¹Interpretation of Part VI

121DA.–(1) In this Part "the relevant social security legislation" means the provisions of any of the following, except so far as relating to contributions, [⁴ . . .] statutory sick pay or statutory maternity pay, that is to say–

(a)   the Contributions and Benefits Act;

(b)   this Act;

(c)   the Pensions Act, except Part III;

(d)   section 4 of the Social Security (Incapacity for Work) Act 1994;

(e)   the Jobseekers Act 1995;

(f)   the Social Security (Recovery of Benefits) Act 1997;

(g)   Parts I and IV of the Social Security Act 1998;

(h)   Part V of the Welfare Reform and Pensions Act 1999;

[⁵ (hh) the State Pension Credit Act 2002;]

(i)   the Social Security Pensions Act 1975;

(j)   the Social Security Act 1973;

(k)   any subordinate legislation made, or having effect as if made, under any enactment specified in paragraphs (a) to (j) above.]

[² (2)   In this Part "authorised officer" means a person acting in accordance with any authorisation for the purposes of this Part which is for the time being in force in relation to him.

(3)   For the purposes of this Part–

(a)   references to a document include references to anything in which information is recorded in electronic or any other form;

(b)   the requirement that a notice given by an authorised officer be in writing shall be taken to be satisfied in any case where the contents of the notice–

(i)   are transmitted to the recipient of the notice by electronic means; and

(ii)   are received by him in a form that is legible and capable of being recorded for future reference.

(4)   In this Part "premises" includes–

(a)   moveable structures and vehicles, vessels, aircraft and hovercraft;

(b)   installations that are offshore installations for the purposes of the Mineral Workings (Offshore Installations) Act 1971; and

(c)   places of all other descriptions whether or not occupied as land or otherwise; and references in this Part to the occupier of any premises shall be construed, in relation to premises that are not occupied as land, as references to any person for the time being present at the place in question.

(5)   In this Part–

"benefit" includes any allowance, payment, credit or loan;

[² "benefit offence" means–
  (a) any criminal offence in connection with a claim for a relevant social security benefit;
  (b) any criminal offence in connection with the receipt or payment of any amount by way of such a benefit;
  (c) any criminal offence committed for the purpose of facilitating the commission (whether or not by the same person) of a benefit offence;
  (d) any attempt or conspiracy to commit a benefit offence;] and
"compensation payment" has the same meaning as in the Social Security (Recovery of Benefits) Act 1997.
  (6) In this Part–
  (a) any reference to a person authorised to carry out any function relating to housing benefit or council tax benefit shall include a reference to a person providing services relating to the benefit directly or indirectly to an authority administering it; and
  (b) any reference to the carrying out of a function relating to such a benefit shall include a reference to the provision of any services relating to it.]
  [¹ (7) In this section [³ "relevant social security benefit" means a benefit under any provision of the relevant social security legislation; and] "subordinate legislation" has the same meaning as in the Interpretation Act 1978.]

Amendments
  1. Inserted by CSPSS Act, Sch 6 para 8 (1.11.00 and 2.4.01).
  2. Amended by SSFA s1(7) (30.4.02).
  3. Amended by SSFA s1(8) (30.4.02).
  4. Amended by the TCA 2002, Sch 6 (8.4.03).
  5. Amended by the SPCA 2002, Sch 2 para 12 (commenced October 2003).

PART VII
Provision of Information

General Note on Part VII
  The Social Security Administration (Fraud) Act 1997 significantly expanded the powers of the DWP and local authorities to share information with each other and with other government departments in an attempt to combat benefit fraud. Concern was expressed during the passage of the Act about the implications of giving such wide powers to share information and the consequences for the subjects of the information if it is inaccurate. One concern is the sharing of information with people providing services to social security authorities, who may well have other commercial interests which could benefit from the use of such information. It was said by the government during the committee stage of the Act that there were no current plans for wholesale privatisation of the social security authorities, but the wording of the Act leaves this possibility open: Alistair Burt MP, Standing Committee E, 14 January 1997, col. 174.
  If information is wrongfully disclosed, the law offers several possible avenues to prevent such abuse. First, there seems little doubt that information held by public bodies of this nature will be classified by the law as confidential information. It was said at the committee stage of the Act that all commercial organisations involved in work for social security authorities are generally required to sign agreements that information will be kept confidential: Oliver Heald MP, Standing Committee E, 12 December 1996, col. 106. It would be possible to obtain an injunction to prevent the revealing of such information by a recipient.
  Secondly, the Data Protection Act 1998, which replaces the Data Protection Act 1984 from various dates, contains restrictions in relation to material held on computer or, under the 1998 Act, "recorded as part of a relevant filing system": see the definition of "data" in s1 of the 1998 Act. By s13, there is a right to compensation for damage resulting from "any contravention by a data controller of any of the requirements" of the 1998 Act. The Government resisted attempts at the committee stage of the Fraud Act to subject the information sharing provisions to the supervision of the Data Protection Registrar, asserting that the 1984 Act and the new EU Directive on Data Protection, which the 1998 Act is intended to implement, already provided sufficient safeguards. The DWP has published a Code of Practice on the use of the information sharing provisions.
  Thirdly, there is a criminal sanction under the SSAA s123 relating to unauthorised disclosure by officials. The Act extends the scope of this offence to local authority officials: see General note to s123. Unauthorised

access is covered by the Computer Misuse Act 1990 s1(1)(b). It was said in Committee that DWP officers were authorised to use computer records only for work purposes and any personal use would therefore be an offence under the 1990 Act: Oliver Heald MP, Standing Committee E, 17 December 1996, col. 144.

Despite the concerns of many, the scope of Part VII and other similar provisions has been slowly expanded so as to provide for increased data-matching between different bodies holding information on claimants.

Authorities administering housing benefit or council tax benefit

[¹Supply of information to authorities administering benefit

122C.–(1) This section applies to information relating to social security which is held–
  (a)   by the Secretary of State or the Northern Ireland Department; or
  (b)   by a person providing services to the Secretary of State or the Northern Ireland Department in connection with the provision of those services.
  (2)   Information to which this section applies may be supplied to–
  (a)   an authority administering housing benefit or council tax benefit; or
  (b)   a person authorised to exercise any function of such an authority relating to such a benefit,
for use in the administration of such a benefit.
  (3)   But where information to which this section applies has been supplied to the Secretary of State, the Northern Ireland Department or the person providing services under section 122 or 122B above, it may only be supplied under subsection (2) above–
  (a)   for use in the prevention, detection, investigation or prosecution of offences relating to housing benefit or council tax benefit; or
  (b)   for use in checking the accuracy of information relating to housing benefit or to council tax benefit and (where appropriate) amending or supplementing such information.
  (4)   The Secretary of State or the Northern Ireland Department–
  (a)   may impose conditions on the use of information supplied under subsection (2) above; and
  (b)   may charge a reasonable fee in respect of the cost of supplying information under that subsection.
  (5)   Where information is supplied to an authority or other person under subsection (2) above, the authority or other person shall have regard to it in the exercise of any function relating to housing benefit or council tax benefit.
  (6)   Information supplied under subsection (2) above shall not be supplied by the recipient to any other person or body unless–
  (a)   it is supplied–
        (i)   by an authority to a person authorised to exercise any function of the authority relating to housing benefit or council tax benefit; or
        (ii)   by a person authorised to exercise any function of an authority relating to such a benefit to the authority;
  (b)   it is supplied for the purposes of any civil or criminal proceedings relating to the Contributions and Benefits Act, the Jobseekers Act 1995 or this Act or to any provision of Northern Ireland legislation corresponding to any of them; or
  (c)   it is supplied under section 122D or 122E below.
  (7)   This section does not limit the circumstances in which information may be supplied apart from this section (in particular by reason of section 122(4) or 122B(4) above).]

Amendment
  1.   Inserted by s3 of the SSA(F) Act 1997 as from 1.7.97.

General Note

This allows any information held by the Secretary of State or someone providing the DWP with services to be passed to an authority for use in the administration of HB and CTB. It may also be passed to a person carrying out functions on behalf of an authority. This includes, for example the now defunct London Organised Fraud Investigation Team: Oliver Heald MP, Standing Committee E, 12 December 1996, col. 107. By subs (4), restrictions can be imposed on its use and a charge may be levied.

A further restriction is imposed by subs (3) in relation to information which the DWP has itself only been supplied with under the new s122 or s122B. In such a case, the information may be disclosed for use in investigating fraud, or simply for comparison with information held by an authority. In relation to the latter, it appears at first sight that there must be some relevant information held by the local authority to be checked. However, it seems likely that "the accuracy of information" will be read as referring to the body of information held by an authority as a whole. So, where an authority has no information at all of the type which is supplied by the Secretary of State, they will be entitled to record that information under paragraph (b) as "supplementing" that body of information.

Subs (6) restricts the right of the authority to pass the information to other bodies. It must be supplied for the purposes of court proceedings under the social security legislation or pursuant to s122D or s122E.

[¹Supply of information by authorities administering benefit

122D.–(1) The Secretary of State or the Northern Ireland Department may require–

(a)   an authority administering housing benefit or council tax benefit; or

(b)   a person authorised to exercise any function of such an authority relating to such a benefit,

to supply benefit administration information held by the authority or other person to, or to a person providing services to, the Secretary of State or the Northern Ireland Department for use for any purpose relating to social security.

(2)   The Secretary of State or the Northern Ireland Department may require–

(a)   an authority administering housing benefit or council tax benefit; or

(b)   a person authorised to exercise any function of such an authority relating to such a benefit,

to supply benefit policy information held by the authority or other person to, or to a person providing services to, the Secretary of State or the Northern Ireland Department.

(3)   Information shall be supplied under subsection (1) or (2) above in such manner and form, and in accordance with such requirements, as may be [² specified in directions given by the Secretary of State or, as the case may be, the Northern Ireland Department].

(4)   In subsection (1) above ''benefit administration information'', in relation to an authority or other person, means any information which is relevant to the exercise of any function relating to housing benefit or council tax benefit by the authority or other person.

(5)   In subsection (2) above ''benefit policy information'' means any information which may be relevant to the Secretary of State or the Northern Ireland Department–

(a)   in preparing estimates of likely future expenditure on housing benefit or council tax benefit; or

(b)   in developing policy relating to housing benefit or council tax benefit.]

Amendments

1.   Inserted by s3 of the SSA(F) Act 1997 as from 1.7.97.
2.   Amended by SSFA s6 (30.4.02).

General Note

This section deals with information moving from local authority to DWP. The categories and uses of information are broader. "Benefit administration information" is that relevant to any function relating to HB and CTB held by an authority, and it may be supplied for any purpose relating to social security. "Benefit policy information" is that helping the DWP forecast likely expenditure or to develop policy. There is little information relating to the benefits that could not be disclosed under these provisions.

[¹Supply of information between authorities administering benefit

122E.–(1) This section applies to benefit administration information which is held by–

    (a)   an authority administering housing benefit or council tax benefit; or

    (b)   a person authorised to exercise any function of such an authority relating to such a benefit.

    (2)   Information to which this section applies may be supplied to another such authority or person–

    (a)   for use in the prevention, detection, investigation or prosecution of offences relating to housing benefit or council tax benefit; or

    (b)   for use in checking the accuracy of information relating to housing benefit or to council tax benefit and (where appropriate) amending or supplementing such information.

    (3)   The Secretary of State or the Northern Ireland Department may require information to which this section applies and which is of a prescribed description to be supplied in prescribed circumstances to another such authority or person for use in the administration of housing benefit or council tax benefit.

    (4)   Information shall be supplied under subsection (3) above in such manner and form, and in accordance with such requirements, as may be prescribed.

    (5)   Where information supplied under subsection (2) or (3) above has been used in amending or supplementing other information, it is lawful for it to be–

    (a)   supplied to any person or body to whom that other information could be supplied; or

    (b)   used for any purpose for which that other information could be used.

    (6)   In this section ''benefit administration information'', in relation to an authority or other person, means any information which is relevant to the exercise of any function relating to housing benefit or council tax benefit by the authority or other person.

    (7)   This section does not limit the circumstances in which information may be supplied apart from this section.]

Amendment

    1.   Inserted by s3 of the SSA(F) Act 1997 as from 1.7.97.

General Note

    Benefit administration information may be shared voluntarily by local authorities or at the direction of the Secretary of State. In the former case, subs (2) requires the information to be used for the detection of fraud or the checking of information. Information transferred by order under subs (3) can be used more generally for administration.

    The effect of subs (5) is that when information received is mixed with a body of information, it may be supplied to whoever is entitled to receive that body of information, even though the recipient would not be entitled to disclosure of the transferred information in the form in which it was received. This is to obviate the need for complex screening processes when mixed information is being passed on.

Unauthorised disclosure of information relating to particular persons

123.–(1) A person who is or has been employed in social security administration or adjudication is guilty of an offence if he discloses without lawful authority any information which he acquired in the course of his employment and which relates to a particular person.

    (2)   A person who is or has been employed in the audit of expenditure or the investigation of complaints is guilty of an offence if he discloses without lawful authority any information

    (a)   which he acquired in the course of his employment;

    (b)   which is, or is derived from, information acquired or held by or for the purposes of any of the government departments or other bodies or persons referred to in Part I of Schedule 4 to this Act or Part I of Schedule 3 to the Northern Ireland Administration Act; and

(c)   which relates to a particular person.

(3)   It is not an offence under this section–

(a)   to disclose information in the form of a summary or collection of information so framed as not to enable information relating to any particular person to be ascertained from it; or

(b)   to disclose information which has previously been disclosed to the public with lawful authority.

(4)   It is a defence for a person charged with an offence under this section to prove that at the time of the alleged offence

(a)   he believed that he was making the disclosure in question with lawful authority and had no reasonable cause to believe otherwise; or

(b)   he believed that the information in question had previously been disclosed to the public with lawful authority and had no reasonable cause to believe otherwise.

(5)   A person guilty of an offence under this section shall be liable

(a)   on conviction on indictment, to imprisonment for a term not exceeding two years or a fine or both; or

(b)   on summary conviction, to imprisonment for a term not exceeding six months or a fine not exceeding the statutory maximum or both.

(6)   For the purposes of this section the persons who are "employed in social security administration or adjudication" are

(a)   any person specified in Part I of Schedule 4 to this Act or in any corresponding enactment having effect in Northern Ireland;

(b)   any other person who carries out the administrative work of any of the government departments or other bodies or persons referred to in that Part of that Schedule or that corresponding enactment; and

(c)   any persons who provides, or is employed in the provision of, services to any of those departments, persons or bodies;

and "employment", in relation to any such person, shall be construed accordingly.

[¹(6A)   Subsection (6) above shall have effect as if any [⁵ health care professional] who, for the purposes of [⁴ section 19 of the Social Security Act 1998], is provided by any person in pursuance of a contract entered into with the Secretary of State were specified in Part I of Schedule 4 to this Act.]

(7)   For the purposes of subsections (2) and (6) above, any reference in Part I of Schedule 4 to the Act or any corresponding enactment having effect in Northern Ireland to a government department shall be construed in accordance with Part II of that Schedule or any corresponding enactment having effect in Northern Ireland, and for this purpose "government department" shall be taken to include

(a)   the Commissioners of Inland Revenue; and

(b)   the Scottish Courts Administration.

(8)   For the purposes of this section, the persons who are "employed in the audit of expenditure or the investigation of complaints" are

(a)   the Comptroller and Auditor General;

(b)   the Comptroller and Auditor General for Northern Ireland;

(c)   the Parliamentary Commissioner for Administration;

(d)   the Northern Ireland Parliamentary Commissioner for Administration;

(e)   the Health Service Commissioner for England;

(f)   the Health Service Commissioner for Wales;

(g)   the Health Service Commissioner for Scotland;

(h)   the Northern Ireland Commissioner for Complaints;

[²(ha) a member of the Local Commission for England;

(hb) a member of the Local Commission for Wales;

(hc) the Commissioner for Local Administration in Scotland;]

(i) any member of the staff of the National Audit Office or the Northern Ireland Audit Office;

(j) any other person who carries out the administrative work of either of those Offices, or who provides, or is employed in the provision of, services to either of them;

[²(ja) a member of the Audit Commission for Local Authorities and the National Health Service in England and Wales and any auditor appointed by that Commission;

(jb) a member of the Accounts Commission for Scotland and any auditor within the meaning of Part VII of the Local Government (Scotland) Act 1973;

(jc) a Northern Ireland local government auditor; and]

(k) any officer of any of the Commissioners [² or Commissions referred to in paragraphs (c) to (hc), (ja) and (jb) above and any person assisting an auditor referred to in paragraph (ja), (jb) or (jc) above;]

and ''employment'', in relation to any such person, shall be construed accordingly.

(9) For the purposes of this section a disclosure is to be regarded as made with lawful authority, if, and only if, it is made

(a) in accordance with his official duty
   (i) by a civil servant; or
   (ii) by a person employed in the audit of expenditure or the investing-action of complaints, who does not fall within subsection (8)(j) above;

(b) by any other person either
   (i) for the purposes of the function in the exercise of which he holds the information and without contravening any restriction duly imposes by the person responsible; or
   (ii) to, or in accordance with an authorisation duly given by, the person responsible;

(c) in accordance with any enactment or order or a court;

(d) for the purpose of instituting, or otherwise for the purposes of, any proceedings before a court or before any tribunal or other body or person referred to in Part I of Schedule 4 to this Act or Part I of Schedule 3 to the Northern Ireland Administration Act; or

(e) with the consent of the appropriate person;

and in this subsection ''the person responsible'' means the Secretary of State, the Lord Chancellor or any person authorised by the Secretary of State or the Lord Chancellor for the purposes of this subsection and includes a reference to ''the person responsible'' within the meaning of any corresponding enactment having effect in Northern Ireland.

(10) For the purposes of subsection (9)(e) above, ''the appropriate person'' means the person to whom the information in question relates, except that if the affairs of that person are being dealt with–

(a) under a power or attorney;

(b) by a receiver appointed under section 99 of the Mental Health Act 1983 or a controller appointed under Article 101 of the Mental Health (Northern Ireland) Order 1986;

(c) by a Scottish mental health custodian, [³ that is to say a guardian or other person entitled to act on behalf of the person under the Adults with Incapacity (Scotland) Act 2000 (asp 4)]; or

(d) by a mental health appointee, that is to say
   (i) a person directed or authorised as mentioned in sub-paragraph (a) of rule 41(1) of the Court of Protection Rules 1984 or sub-paragraph (a) of rule 38(1) of Order 109 of the Rules of the Supreme Court (Northern Ireland) 1980; or

(ii)   a receiver ad interim appointed under sub-paragraph (b) of the said rule 41(1) or a controller ad interim appointed under sub-paragraph (b) of the said rule 38(1),

the appropriate person is the attorney, receiver, controller, custodian or appointee, as the case may be, or, in a case falling within paragraph (a) above, the person to whom the information relates.

Amendments

1.   Inserted by Deregulation and Contracting Out Act 1994 (c.40) Sch 16 para 21 (3.1.95).
2.   Amended by the SSA(F) Act 1997 s4.
3.   Amended by art 3 of SI 2005 No 1790 as from 30.6.05.
4.   Amended by Sch 7 para 88 of the SSA 1998 as from 5.7.99.
5.   Substituted by the Welfare Reform Act 2007 s63 and Sch 7 para 3(3) (3.7.07).

General Note

This section makes it a criminal offence for officials involved in the administration or audit of benefits, or the investigation of complaints, to make an unauthorised disclosure of information which relates to particular people. It is applicable to local authority officers in relation to acts committed on or after 1 July 1997, when the amendments to Sch 4 naming officers as persons to whom s123 applies came into force.

[¹Information from landlords and agents

126A.–(1)   Regulations shall provide that where a claim for housing benefit in respect of a dwelling is made to an authority and the circumstances are such as are prescribed–

(a)   the authority; or

(b)   a person authorised to exercise any function of the authority relating to housing benefit,

may require any appropriate person to supply information of a prescribed description to the authority or other person.

(2)   Subject to subsection (4) below, for the purposes of subsection (1) above a person is an appropriate person in relation to a dwelling if he is–

(a)   a person to whom anyone is, or claims to be, liable to make relevant payments;

(b)   a person to whom, or at whose direction, a person within paragraph (a) above has agreed to make payments in consequence of being entitled to receive relevant payments; or

(c)   a person acting on behalf of a person within paragraph (a) or (b) above in connection with any aspect of the management of the dwelling.

(3)   In subsection (2) above "relevant payments", in relation to a dwelling, means payments in respect of the dwelling which are of a description in relation to which housing benefit may be paid.

(4)   Regulations may provide that any prescribed person, or any person of a prescribed description, is not an appropriate person for the purposes of subsection (1) above.

(5)   The descriptions of information which may be prescribed for the purposes of subsection (1) above include, in particular, any description of information relating to, or to any interest in or other connection with, dwellings and other property situated anywhere in the United Kingdom.

(6)   Information shall be supplied under subsection (1) above in such manner and form, and at such time and in accordance with such other requirements, as may be prescribed.

(7)   Information supplied to an authority or other person under subsection (1) above may be used by the authority or other person only in the exercise of any function relating to housing benefit or council tax benefit.

(8)   The provisions of sections 122D and 122E above apply in relation to any information supplied under subsection (1) above which is not benefit administration information (within the meaning of those provisions) as if it were.]

Amendment

1.　　Inserted by s11 of the SSA(F) Act 1997 as from 8.10.97.

General Note

During the passage of the Social Security Administration (Fraud) Act 1997, one of the main concerns of the Labour members in Committee was the failure of the Bill to make specific provision for the problem of fraud by landlords. The creation of a landlord register was proposed with criminal sanctions for non-compliance, and a power to refuse to pay benefit where fraud was suspected.

　　The Government's response was s11 of the Act, which inserts s126A. The section gives power to the authority to require information in circumstances to be prescribed by regulations. By subsection (5), it is made clear that the principal use of the provision will be to obtain lists of the landlord's property portfolio to enable cross-checks to be made.

　　For the information that may be required from landlords, see regs 117-121 HB Regs (regs 98-102 HB(SPC) Regs).

Analysis

　　Subsection (2)

　　This subsection sets out the categories of people from whom information may be required under s126A:

　　(a)　　Refers to the landlord or any person to whom the claimant is liable to make relevant payments. "Relevant payments" is defined in subs (3) as any payment (usually rent) which may lead to HB being paid. See reg 8 of both the HB and the HB(SPC) Regs for where a tenant may be so liable.

　　(b)　　This deals with situations where there is effectively a sub-letting arrangement. If A lets a flat to B, and B in turn takes in a lodger C after agreeing that A will receive a share of the rent in return for letting him take in C, A will be liable to provide information under s126A when C claims HB.

　　(c)　　This is a reference to agents.

　　Subsection (7)

　　This subsection makes it clear that the information supplied under s126A may only be used for purposes relating to benefits. See s123 for the consequences of a breach of this provision.

　　Subsection (8)

　　Sections 122D and 122E are inserted by s3. This subsection allows information collected under s126A to be passed to the Secretary of State or to other authorities under the powers conferred by those sections.

Information for purposes of housing benefit
　　[¹**127.** . . .]

Amendment

1.　　Repealed by the SSA(F) Act 1997.

Information for purposes of council tax benefit
　　[¹**128.** . . .]

Amendment

1.　　Repealed by the SSA(F) Act 1997.

　　　[¹ Expedited claims for housing and council tax benefit

Disclosure of information by authorities

　　128A.–(1) Regulations may make provision requiring the disclosure by one authority ("the disclosing authority") to another authority ("the receiving authority"), in prescribed circumstances, of information of a prescribed description obtained by the disclosing authority in respect of persons who have been entitled to a jobseeker's allowance or to income support.

　　(2)　　The regulations may in particular provide for–

　　(a)　　information to be disclosed–

　　　　(i)　　at the request of the receiving authority;

　　　　(ii)　　at the request of any person who falls within a prescribed category; or

　　　　(iii)　　otherwise than in response to such a request;

(b)   the period within which information is to be disclosed; and
(c)   information to be disclosed only if it has been obtained by the disclosing authority in the exercise of any of their functions in relation to housing benefit or council tax benefit.]

Amendments
1.   Inserted by Jobseekers Act 1995, s28(2) (12.12.95 for regulation-making purposes, 1.4.96 for other purposes).
2.   Whole section to be repealed by the SSA(F)A, s22 Sch 2 when brought into force.

General Note
This section was to be repealed by the Social Security Administration (Fraud) Act 1997 s22, but the repealing provision has not yet been brought into force. It is not clear whether the reference to s128A in Sch 2 was a mistake. For regulations under this section, see reg 115 HB Regs (reg 96 HB(SPC) Regs) and reg 96 CTB Regs (reg 81 CTB(SPC) Regs).

PART VIII
*Arrangements for Housing Benefit and Council Tax Benefits and Related Subsidies
Housing benefit*

Arrangements for housing benefit
134.–[¹(1) Housing benefit provided by virtue of a scheme under section 123 of the Social Security Contributions and Benefits Act 1992 (in this Part referred to as "the housing benefit scheme") shall be funded and administered by the appropriate housing authority or local authority.
(1A)   Housing benefit in respect of payments which the occupier of a dwelling is liable to make to a housing authority shall take the form of a rent rebate or, in prescribed cases, a rent allowance funded and administered by that authority.
The cases that may be so prescribed do not include any where the payment is in respect of property within the authority's Housing Revenue Account.
(1B)   In any other case housing benefit shall take the form of a rent allowance funded and administered by the local authority for the area in which the dwelling is situated or by such other local authority as is specified by an order made by the Secretary of State.]
(2)   The rebates and allowances referred to in [² subsections (1A) and (1B)] above may take any of the following forms, that is to say–
(a)   a payment or payments by the authority to the person entitled to the benefit;
(b)   a reduction in the amount of any payments which that person is liable to make to the authority by way of rent; or
(c)   such a payment or payments and such a reduction;
and in any enactment or instrument (whenever passed or made) "pay", in relation to housing benefit, includes discharge in any of those forms.
[¹ (3)]
[¹ (4)]
[¹ (5)   Authorities may–
(a)   agree that one shall discharge functions relating to housing benefit on another's behalf; or
(b)   discharge any such functions jointly or arrange for their discharge by a joint committee.
(5A)   Nothing in this section shall be read as excluding the general provisions of the Local Government Act 1972 or the Local Government (Scotland) Act 1973 from applying in relation to the housing benefit functions of a local authority.]
[¹ (6)]
[¹ (7)]
(8)   An authority may modify any part of the housing benefit scheme administered by the authority

(a)   so as to provide for disregarding, in determining a person's income (whether he is the occupier of a dwelling or any other person whose income falls to be aggregated with that of the occupier of a dwelling), the whole or part of any [4 prescribed] war disablement pension or [4 prescribed] war widow's [4] pension payable to that person;

(b)   to such extent in other respects as may be prescribed, and any such modification may be adopted by resolution of an authority.

(9)   Modifications other than such modifications as are mentioned in subsection (8)(a) above shall be so framed as to secure that, in the estimate of the authority adopting them, the total of [1 the housing benefit which will be paid by the authority in any year will not exceed the permitted total or any subsidiary limit specified by order of the Secretary of State.]

(10)   An authority who have adopted modifications may by resolution revoke or vary them.

(11)   If the housing benefit scheme includes power for an authority to exercise a discretion in awarding housing benefit, the authority shall not exercise that discretion so that the total of [1 the housing benefit paid by them during the year exceeds the permitted total or any subsidiary limit specified by order of the Secretary of State.]

[1 (12)   The Secretary of State–

(a)   shall by order specify the permitted total of housing benefit payable by any authority in any year; and

(b)   may by order specify one or more subsidiary limits on the amount of housing benefit payable by any authority in any year in respect of any matter or matters specified in the order.

The power to specify the permitted total or a subsidiary limit may be exercised by fixing an amount or by providing rules for its calculation.]

(13)   In this section ''modifications'' includes additions, omissions and amendments, and related expressions shall be construed accordingly.

[4 (14) In this section ''war widow's pension'' includes any corresponding pension payable to a widower or surviving civil partner.]

Definitions

"dwelling" – s191.
"housing authority" – *ibid.*
"modifications" – s134(13).
"war widow's pension" – s134(14)

Amendments

1.   Amended by the HA 1996 Sch 12 para 1 and partially repealed by Sch 19, Part VI (1.4.97).
2.   Amended by the Local Government Act 2003 s127(1) and Sch 7 para 35 (deemed to come into force on 1.4.97).
3.   Inserted by Art 7 of SI 2005 No 2053 as from 5.12.05.
4.   Amended by the Welfare Reform Act 2007 ss40 and 67 and Sch 5 para 3 and Sch 8 (3.7.07).

General Note

Subs (1A) and (1B) prescribe the two different forms that HB may take, depending on whether it is paid to a housing authority or to other types of landlord (eg, private or housing association). Note that under s191, "housing authority" means a local authority, a new town corporation or the Development Board for Rural Wales.

Subs (5) enables those administering the scheme to make arrangements whereby one will carry out the functions of the other (eg, where HB is payable in respect of two homes under reg 7(6)(d) of both the HB and the HB(SPC) Regs) the authority in the area the claimant has moved from may ask the authority in the new area to deal with HB in respect of both homes. The provision is particularly helpful for authorities who have housing estates outside their borough boundaries.

Subs (8)-(10) allow the authority to modify the basic HB scheme within limits. Subs (8) sets out the circumstances in which modifications may be made and how they may be adopted by the authority. Subs (10) permits the authority to revoke any modifications if its terms are complied with. Subs (9) sets a financial limit on the modifications which may be made.

Subs (11) puts a financial limit on the extent to which an authority may use its discretionary powers to award extra benefit. The financial limits in subs (9) and (11) are defined by subs (12).

Analysis

Subs (1) requires the HB scheme to be funded and administered by the appropriate "housing authority" or "local authority", both defined in s191.

Subs (1A) and (1B) specify the two types of HB: rent rebate which is generally paid to claimants who pay rent to the housing authority who administers the HB scheme, and rent allowance which is paid to those who pay rent to other landlords. This is not quite a rigid distinction, since certain prescribed housing authority tenants may receive rent allowance instead. The proviso to subs (1A) limits the cases which by Secretary of State prescription may take the form of a rent allowance so as to exclude payments of HB in relation to properties within the authority's housing revenue account (HRA). Such properties are detailed in s74 of the Local Government and Housing Act 1989 (c.42) and include all mainstream council housing provided under Part II of the Housing Act 1985 and accommodation the authority has leased from the private sector of the same purpose where it has chosen to account for it within its HRA.

An important distinction in the treatment of claims in rent rebate and rent allowance cases is that the requirement to refer to the rent officer for determinations and then to apply rent restriction rules only applies to the latter, and not to the former: see regs 13 and 14 of both the HB and the HB(SPC) Regs.

Subs (2). This clarifies the forms of "payment" envisaged by the terms "rebate" and "allowance" and is also important in relation to overpayments of benefit. See note on the HB Regs reg 99.

Subs (8). In the assessment of income for HB (and CTB) £10 of certain war pensions must be disregarded. Subs 8 allows an authority to resolve to disregard more of (or all of) prescribed war pensions as income for the purposes of its HB scheme. The prescribed pensions are in the Schedule to the Housing Benefit and Council Tax Benefit (War Pension Disregards) Regulations 2007 SI No. 1619 (in Part 7). Note that "war widow's pension" includes any corresponding pension payable to a widower or a surviving civil partner: subs (14).

The authority may change its mind by a further resolution: subs (10). For "occupier", see HB Regs reg 7 and for "income", see Section 1 of Part 6. No direct subsidy is paid in respect of extra benefit paid in accordance with this section.

Prior to the amendments made by SI 2007 No 1619 from 3 July 2007, reg 40(3) HB Regs (reg 33(13) HB(SPC) Regs) and reg 30(3) CTB Regs (reg 23(13) CTB(SPC) Regs), made under subs(8)(b),permitted a similar disregard in relation to a war widower's pension. A local authority would have to have found stringent justification for any disparity in treatment between widows and widowers if it was not to fall foul of Art 14 of the European Convention on Human Rights, and it would not be permitted a period of grace in order to carry out reforms: *R (Hooper) v Secretary of State for Work and Pensions* [2003] 1 WLR 2623, CA, affirmed on this point by the House of Lords in [2005] UKHL 29, The Times, 6 May.

A resolution will only usually have effect from the date it is expressed to take effect. Thus where a claimant had been overpaid due to a late payment of an increase in his war pension, a resolution of the council to ignore war pension as income did not have retrospective effect: *R v South Hams DC ex p Ash* [1999] 32 HLR 405 at 409, QBD.

Subs (11) forbids authorities to exceed the permitted total of expenditure by allowing discretionary increases in benefit.

Housing benefit finance
[¹**135.** . . .]

Amendment
1.   Repealed from 1 April 1997 by the HA 1996 Sch 19, Part VI.

Council tax benefit

Nature of benefits
138.–[¹(1) Regulations shall provide that where a person is entitled to council tax benefit in respect of council tax payable to a billing authority or [⁴ local authority in Scotland] the benefit shall take such of the following forms as is prescribed in the case of the person–

(a)   a payment or payments by the authority to the person;

(b)   a reduction in the amount the person is or becomes liable to pay to the authority in respect of the tax for the relevant or any subsequent financial year;

(c)   both such payment or payments and such reduction.]
[⁹ References in any enactment or instrument (whenever passed or made) to payment in relation to council tax benefit, include any of those ways of giving the benefit.]

[²(2)   . . .]

[³(3)–(4)   . . .]

(5)   For the purposes of [⁵ subsection (1)] above the relevant [⁵ financial year] is the [⁵ financial year] in which the relevant day falls; and the relevant day is the day in respect of which the person concerned is entitled to the benefit.

[⁶(6)–(8)   . . .]

(9)   Regulations under subsection (1), [⁷ . . .] above may include such supplementary, incidental or consequential provisions as appear to the Secretary of State to be necessary or expedient; and any such provisions may include provisions amending or adapting provisions of [⁸ Part I or II of the Local Government Finance Act 1992].

Definitions
"billing authority" – s191.
"prescribed" – *ibid.*

Amendments
1.	Substituted by LGFA Sch 9 para 19(1) (1.4.93).
2.	Deleted by LGFA Sch 9 para 19(1) (1.4.93).
3.	Deleted by LGFA Sch 9 para 19(3) (1.4.93).
4.	Substituted by Local Government etc. (Scotland) Act 1994 Sch 13 para 175(3)(1.4.96).
5.	Substituted by LGFA Sch 9 para 19(3) (1.4.93).
6.	Repealed by LGFA Sch 9 para 19(4) and Sch 14 (1.4.93).
7.	Repealed by LGFA Sch 9 para 19(5) and Sch 14 (1.4.93).
8.	Substituted by LGFA Sch 9 para 19(5) (1.4.93).
9.	Amended by the HA 1996 Sch 12 para 2 (1.4.97)

General Note
This prescribes the forms which CTB is to take. Subs (1) provides that it may take the form of a reduction from a claimant's council tax bill (whether for the present or the future financial year), a payment or both.

Arrangements for council tax benefit
139.–(1) Any [¹ council tax benefit] provided for by virtue of a scheme under section 123 of the Contributions and Benefits Act (in this Act referred to as a [¹ council tax] scheme) is to be administered by the appropriate authority.

[² (2)   For the purposes of this section the appropriate authority is the billing or [⁶ local authority in Scotland] which levied the council tax as regards which a person is entitled to the benefit.]

(3)   [² . . .]

(4)   [⁷ Nothing in this section shall be read as excluding the general provisions of the Local Government Act 1972 or the Local Government (Scotland) Act 1973 from applying in relation to the council tax benefit functions of a local authority.]

(6)   [³ A billing authority] or [⁶ local authority in Scotland] may modify any part of the [⁴ council tax benefit] scheme administered by the authority–

(a)   so as to provide for disregarding, in determining a person's income, the whole or part of any [¹⁰ prescribed] war disablement pension or [² prescribed] war widow's pension payable to that person or to his partner or to a person to whom he is polygamously married;

(b)   to such extent in other respects as may be prescribed, and any such modifications may be adopted by resolution of an authority.

(7)   Modifications other than such modifications as are mentioned in subsection (6)(a) above shall be so framed as to secure that, in the estimate of the authority adopting them, the total of [⁷ the amount of benefit which will be paid by them in

any year will not exceed the permitted total or any subsidiary limit specified by order of the Secretary of State.]

(8) An authority which has adopted modifications may by resolution revoke or vary them.

(9) If the [⁵ council tax benefit scheme] includes power for an authority to exercise a discretion in allowing [⁵ council tax benefit] the authority shall not exercise that discretion so that the total of [⁷ the amount of benefit paid by them in any year exceeds the permitted total or any subsidiary limit specified by order of the Secretary of State.]

(10) [⁷ The Secretary of State–

(a) shall by order specify the permitted total of council tax benefit payable by any authority in any year; and

(b) may by order specify one or more subsidiary limits on the amount of council tax benefit payable by any authority in any year in respect of any matter or matters specified in the order.

The power to specify the permitted total or a subsidiary limit may be exercised by fixing an amount or by providing rules for its calculation.]

(11) In this section–

"modifications" includes additions, omissions and amendments, and related expressions shall be construed accordingly;

"partner", in relation to a person, means the other member of the couple concerned; [¹⁰]

[¹⁰ "war widow's pension" includes any corresponding pension payable to a widower or surviving civil partner.]

Definitions
"appropriate authority" – see subs (2).
"billing authority" – s191.
"modifications" – see subs (11).
"partner" – *ibid.*
"permitted totals" – *ibid.*
"war widow's pension" – *ibid.*

Amendments
1.   Substituted by LGFA Sch 9 para 20(1) (1.4.93).
2.   Substituted by LGFA Sch 9 para 20(2) (1.4.93).
3.   Substituted by LGFA Sch 9 para 20(5) (1.4.93).
4.   Substituted by LGFA Sch 9 para 20(6) (1.4.93).
5.   Substituted by LGFA Sch 9 para 20(7) (1.4.93).
6.   Substituted by Local Government etc. (Scotland) Act 1994 Sch 13 para 175(3)(1.4.96).
7.   Amended from by the HA 1996 Sch 12 para 3 (1.4.97).
8.   Inserted by Sch 24 para 65(a) CPA 2004 as from 5.12.05.
9.   Inserted by Sch 24 para 65(b) CPA 2004 as from 5.12.05.
10. Amended by the Welfare Reform Act 2007 s40 and Sch 5 para 4 (3.7.07).

General Note
This is the CTB equivalent of s134.

[¹ Reports

Persons to report on administration

139A.–[²(1) The Secretary of State may authorise persons to consider and report to him on the administration by authorities of housing benefit and council tax benefit.

(2) The Secretary of State may ask persons authorised under subsection (1) to consider in particular–

(a) authorities' performance in the prevention and detection of fraud relating to housing benefit and council tax benefit;

(b)   authorities' compliance with the requirements of Part I of the Local Government Act 1999 (best value).

(2A)   A person may be authorised under subsection (1)–

(a)   on such terms and for such period as the Secretary of State thinks fit;

(b)   to act generally or in relation to a specified authority or authorities;

(c)   to report on administration generally or on specified matters.]

(3)   In sections 139B and 139C below–

"benefit" means housing benefit or council tax benefit; and

"authority" means an authority which is administering either of those benefits.]

Amendments

1.   Inserted by the SSA(F) Act 1997 s5.

2.   Substituted by s14(1) of the Local Government Act 1999 (1.4.00).

General Note

This section and those that follow it were introduced from 1 July 1997 by the Social Security Administration (Fraud) Act 1997 following concern at the apparent unwillingness of some authorities to tackle fraud. They give the Secretary of State extensive powers over recalcitrant authorities and, ultimately, to require an authority's HB and CTB functions to be privatised.

This section gives the Secretary of State the power to appoint inspectors to examine the prevention of fraud and generally the administration of HB and CTB. The Secretary of State may also require the Audit Commission in England and Wales and the Accounts Commissioner in Scotland to conduct studies of how authorities are administering HB and CTB: Local Government Finance Act 1982 s28AB and Local Government (Scotland) Act 1973 ss97(4E), 101A and 105A, both inserted from 1 July 1997 by ss6 and 7 of the 1997 Act.

The section has now been amended by the Local Government Act 1999 to permit reports to consider whether the local authority is complying with the 'best value' provisions in Part I of the 1999 Act.

[¹**Powers of investigation**

139B.–(1) A person authorised under section 139A(1) above–

(a)   has a right of access at all reasonable times to any document relating to the administration of benefit;

(b)   is entitled to require from any person holding or accountable for any such document such information and explanation as he thinks necessary; and

(c)   is entitled, if he thinks it necessary, to require any such person to produce any such document or to attend before him in person to give such information or explanation.

(2)   A person authorised under section 139A(1) above is entitled to require any officer or member of an authority or any person involved in the administration of benefit for an authority–

(a)   to give him such information and explanation relating to the administration of benefit as he thinks necessary; and

(b)   if he thinks it necessary, to require any such person to attend before him in person to give the information or explanation.

(3)   A person who without reasonable excuse fails to comply with a requirement under subsection (1) or (2) above is guilty of an offence and liable on summary conviction to a fine not exceeding level 3 on the standard scale.

(4)   A person authorised under section 139A(1) above may–

(a)   require any document or information which is to be given to him under subsection (1) or (2) above to be given in any form reasonably specified by him; and

(b)   take copies of any document produced to him.

(5)   In this section "document" means anything in which information of any description is recorded.]

Amendment

1.   Inserted by s5 SSA(F) Act 1997.

General Note

Extremely wide powers are given to the inspectors to look at documents, to require explanation of them under subs (1) and more generally to require information relating to benefit administration from local authority officials under subs (2). Such documents and information must be supplied in such form as the inspector requires and copies may be taken: subs (4). The definition of "document" in subs (5) will cover items such as computer data as well as paperwork.

A person who fails to comply with an inspector's requirements commits an offence, triable only by magistrates and punishable by a fine of up to level 3 (currently £1,000): subs (3).

Reports

[¹**139C.**–(1) A report about an authority by a person authorised under section 139A(1) above may include recommendations about improvements which could be made by that authority in its administration of benefit and, [² in particular–
 (a)   in the prevention and detection of fraud relating to benefit, or
 (b)   for the purposes of complying with the requirements of Part I of the Local Government Act 1999 (best value).]
 (2)   When the Secretary of State receives a report about an authority from a person authorised under section 139A(1) above, he shall send a copy to the authority.]

Amendments
1.   Inserted by s5 SSA(F) Act 1997.
2.   Substituted by s4(2) of the Local Government Act 1999 (1.4.2000).

General Note

By subs (2), the authority under investigation is entitled to receive a copy of any report made by the inspectors.

[¹ Directions by Secretary of State

Directions

139D.–(1) This section applies where–
 (a)   a copy of a report has been sent to an authority under section 139C(2) above;
 (b)   a copy of a report has been sent to an authority under section 18(3) of the Local Government Finance Act 1982 and to the Secretary of State under section 28AC(2) of that Act;
 (c)   a copy of a report relating to the administration of benefit has been sent to a local authority under section 102(2) of the Local Government (Scotland) Act 1973 and to the Secretary of State and section 103(1) of that Act has been complied with; or
 (d)   a copy of a report has been sent to an authority under section 28AB(7) of the Local Government Finance Act 1982 or section 105A(7) of the Local Government (Scotland) Act 1973.
 (2)   The Secretary of State may invite the authority to consider the report and to submit proposals for–
 (a)   improving its performance in relation to the prevention and detection of fraud relating to benefit or otherwise in relation to the administration of benefit; and
 (b)   remedying any failings identified by the report.
 (3)   After considering the report and any proposals made by the authority in response to it, the Secretary of State may give directions to the authority as to–
 (a)   standards which the authority is to attain in the prevention and detection of fraud relating to benefit or otherwise in the administration of benefit; and
 (b)   the time within which the standards are to be attained.
 (4)   When giving directions to an authority under subsection (3) above, the Secretary of State may make recommendations to the authority setting out any course

of action which he thinks it might take to attain the standards which it is directed to attain.

(5)   In this section "benefit" means housing benefit or council tax benefit.]

Amendment

1.   Inserted by s8 SSA(F)A 1997.

General Note

Section 139D is the initial stage of the four-part enforcement process by which the Secretary of State can compel improvements in the detection of fraud and administration of HB and CTB generally, where the performance of a local authority is thought to be unsatisfactory. It will follow a report by an inspector under s139C(2) or by the appropriate local government auditor: subs (1). This section and the three following it were introduced at the last moment in Committee.

The starting point in the process is for the Secretary of State to invite the authority's response to the report and suggest how it thinks matters could be improved. If the minister is not happy with the response, s/he may issue directions under subs (3) requiring improvements.

Analysis

Subs (3). Before directions are given, it is an essential part of the process for the Secretary of State to seek the authority's views under subs (2). If this step is omitted, it would seem that directions under subs (3) would be *ultra vires* as these can only be given by the Secretary of State "after considering ... any proposals made by the authority".

The Secretary of State may require an authority to reach a certain standard within a certain period of time. In determining this standard, the Secretary of State must act reasonably but has the widest discretion and it would have to be shown that the standards set are wholly irrational before they can be subject to any challenge. However, the structure of subs (3) suggests that the Secretary of State may only have regard to the contents of the report and the authority's response in considering whether to make a direction, and if so what direction to make. If, for example, a direction was made following a petition, then it seems that such a direction could be challenged on grounds of procedural impropriety.

Information about attainment of standards

[¹**139E.**–(1) Where directions have been given to an authority under section 139D(3) above, the Secretary of State may require the authority to supply to him any information which he considers may assist him in deciding–

(a)   whether the authority has attained the standards which it has been directed to attain; or

(b)   whether the authority is likely to attain those standards within the time specified in the directions.

(2)   Information shall be supplied under subsection (1) above in such manner and form as the Secretary of State may require.]

Amendment

1.   Inserted by s9 SSA(F) Act 1997.

General Note

This section is the second part of the enforcement process. It enables the Secretary of State to monitor the progress of the authority by requiring information to be supplied to her/him.

Enforcement notices

[¹**139F.**–(1) Where directions have been given to an authority under section 139D(3) above and the Secretary of State–

(a)   is not satisfied that the authority has attained the standards which it has been directed to attain; or

(b)   is not satisfied that the authority is likely to attain those standards within the time specified in the directions,

he may serve on the authority a written notice under this section.

(2)   The notice shall–

(a)   identify the directions and state why the Secretary of State is not satisfied as mentioned in paragraph (a) or (b) of subsection (1) above; and

(b)   require the authority to submit a written response to the Secretary of State within a time specified in the notice.

(3)   If any person (other than the authority) carrying out work relating to the administration of benefit may be affected by any determination which may be made under section 139G below, the authority shall–

(a)   consult that person before submitting its response; and

(b)   include in its response any relevant observations made by that person.

(4)   The authority's response shall either–

(a)   state that the authority has attained the standards, or is likely to attain them within the time specified in the directions, and justify that statement; or

(b)   state that the authority has not attained the standards, or is not likely to attain them within that time, and (if the authority wishes) give reasons why a determination under section 139G below should not be made or should not include any particular provision.

(5)   The notice may relate to any one or more matters covered by the directions.

(6)   The serving of a notice under this section relating to any directions or matter does not prevent the serving of further notices under this section relating to the same directions or matter.

(7)   In this section "benefit" means housing benefit or council tax benefit.]

Amendment

1.   Inserted by s9 SSA(F) Act 1997.

General Note

If it becomes clear to the Secretary of State that an authority is not going to attain the standards set by a direction under s139D, an enforcement notice may be served on the authority. A notice may be served before the expiry of any time limit specified in the direction: subs (1)(b). The notice must state, under subs (2)(a), the reasons for the Secretary of State's dissatisfaction.

The local authority is required to respond to the notice and state whether it has, or is going to be able to comply with the direction: subs (4). Before it does so, it must consult those involved in the administration of benefit and incorporate their views in its response.

Subs (5) and (6) loosen possible restrictions on the Secretary of State's power to issue enforcement notices. Under subs (5), a notice may relate to particular matters identified in the direction, rather than the whole direction. More than one notice may be served in relation to a direction, and subs (6) confirms that subsequent notices may deal with the same matters as previous notices.

Analysis

"... any person (other than the authority) carrying out work relating to the administration of benefit....". On a wide reading, this might include the administrative staff employed by the local authority as well as people or business organisations outside the authority carrying out functions relating to the administration of HB and CTB.

Enforcement determinations

[¹**139G.**–(1) Where, after the time specified in the notice under section 139F above has expired, the Secretary of State–

(a)   is not satisfied that the authority has attained the standards in question; or

(b)   is not satisfied that the authority is likely to attain those standards within the time specified in the directions, he may make a determination under this section.

(2)   The determination may be made whether or not the authority has responded to the notice under section 139F above.

(3)   The determination shall be designed to secure the attainment of the standards in question and–

(a)   shall include provision such as is specified in subsection (4) below; and

(b)   may also include provision such as is specified in subsection (5) below.

(4)   The provision referred to in paragraph (a) of subsection (3) above is provision that the authority must comply with specified requirements as to inviting, preparing, considering and accepting bids to carry out any work which–

(a)   falls to be carried out in pursuance of the authority's functions relating to the administration of benefit; and

(b)   is of a description specified in the determination.

(5)   The provision referred to in paragraph (b) of that subsection is provision of any one or more of the following kinds relating to the work, or any specified category of the work, to which the determination relates–

(a)   provision that it may not be carried out by the authority;

(b)   provision that it may not be carried out by any person (other than the authority) who has been carrying it out; and

(c)   provision that any contract made by the authority with any person for carrying it out shall include terms requiring a level of performance which will secure, or contribute to securing, the attainment of the standards in question.

(6)   In this section "benefit" means housing benefit or council tax benefit.]

Amendment

1.   Inserted by s9 SSA(F) Act 1997.

General Note

The final step in the procedure is an enforcement determination. By this draconian step, the Secretary of State will be able to require an authority to put its administration of HB and CTB, or any part thereof, out to tender: subs (4).

The Secretary of State may also impose further conditions under subs (5). The authority may be forbidden to carry out the work itself, a person who has been carrying out the work (see s139F above) may be excluded, and the authority may be required to specify attainment of the standards as conditions of the contract awarded. See also s139H(3).

Enforcement determinations: supplementary

[¹**139H.**–(1) The provisions included in a determination under section 139G above shall take effect from a date specified in the determination; and different dates may be specified in relation to different provisions.

(2)   The making of a determination under section 139G above in relation to any directions does not prevent the making of further determinations under that section in relation to the same directions.

(3)   The provision included in a determination by virtue of section 139G(3) above may include–

(a)   requirements that the Secretary of State be satisfied as to any specified matter; and

(b)   requirements that the Secretary of State authorise or consent to any specified matter.

(4)   The provision so included may also include provision as to the time at which any contract for the carrying out of work to which the determination relates (and which is not previously discharged) is to be taken to be frustrated by the determination.

(5)   A determination under section 139G above shall have effect in spite of any enactment under or by virtue of which an authority is required or authorised to carry out any work to which the determination relates.

(6)   A determination under section 139G above may make provision having effect, in relation to the work to which it relates, instead of any requirement which (apart from the determination) would have effect in relation to that work under or by virtue of the Local Government Act 1988.]

Amendment

1.   Inserted by s9 SSA(F) Act 1997.

General Note

This section makes a number of additional provisions in relation to enforcement determinations. By subs (1), time limits may be set for the determination to come into effect. More than one determination may be made in relation to a direction: subs (2). Subs (5) and (6) make it clear that the determination overrides any statutory provision requiring the authority to carry out the work in question and the requirements of the Local Government Act 1988 in relation to compulsory competitive tendering.

Finally, subs (3) allows the Secretary of State to control virtually any aspect of the tendering process or the work carried out pursuant to an enforcement direction.

Council tax benefit finance
[¹**140.** . . .]

Amendment

1.   Repealed by the Housing Act 1996 Sch 19.

[¹ Subsidy

Subsidy
140A.–(1) For each year the Secretary of State shall pay a subsidy to each authority administering housing benefit or council tax benefit.

(2)   He shall pay–

(a)   rent rebate subsidy to each housing authority;

(b)   rent allowance subsidy to each local authority; and

(c)   council tax benefit subsidy to each billing authority or levying authority.

(3)   In the following provisions of this Part ''subsidy'', without more, refers to subsidy of any of those descriptions.]

Amendment

1.   Inserted by Sch 12 para 4 Housing Act 1996.

General Note

ss140A to 140G deal with the subsidy arrangements in respect of HB and CTB. See Part 8 of this book for the secondary legislation on subsidy.

[¹Calculation of amount of subsidy
140B.–(1) The amount of subsidy to be paid to an authority [⁴ determined in accordance with an] order made by the Secretary of State.

(2)   Subject as follows, the amount of subsidy shall be calculated by reference to the amount of relevant benefit paid by the authority during the year.
[³]

(3)   The order may provide that the amount of subsidy in respect of any matter shall be a fixed sum or shall be nil.

[² (4)   The Secretary of State may–

(a)   pay as part of subsidy an additional amount specified by, or calculated in a manner specified by, the order; or

(b)   deduct from the amount which would otherwise be payable by way of subsidy an amount specified by, or calculated in a manner specified by, the order.

(4A)   The additional amounts which may be paid by virtue of subsection (4)(a) above include amounts in respect of–

(a)   the costs of administering the relevant benefit; or

(b)   success in preventing or detecting fraud relating to the relevant benefit or action to be taken with a view to preventing or detecting such fraud.

(5)   The Secretary of State may–

(a)   where an application is made by an authority on his invitation, pay to the authority as part of the subsidy such additional amount as he considers appropriate in respect of–

(i)   success in preventing or detecting fraud relating to the relevant benefit; or

(ii)   action to be taken with a view to preventing or detecting such fraud; or

(b)   deduct from the subsidy which would otherwise be payable to an authority such amount as he considers it unreasonable to pay by way of subsidy.

(5A)   The amounts which may be deducted by virtue of subsection (4)(b) or (5)(b) above include amounts in respect of–

(a)   a failure to comply with directions under section 139D(3) above; and

(b)   other failures in preventing or detecting fraud relating to the relevant benefit.]

Any such additional amount shall be a fixed sum specified by, or shall be calculated in the manner specified by, an order made by the Secretary of State.

(6)   In this section ''relevant benefit'' means housing benefit or council tax benefit, as the case may be.

[³ (7)]

Amendments

1.   Inserted by Sch 12 para 4 Housing Act 1996.
2.   Substituted by s10 SSA(F) Act 1997.
3.   Omitted/repealed by the Local Government Act 2003, s127(1) and Sch 7 para 36 and s127(2) and Part 1 Sch 8 (18.11.03).
4.   Amended by Sch 1 para 7 of the SSA(F) Act 1997 (1.7.97).

General Note

Subsection (3) permits any element of a subsidy calculation to be made on a fixed basis or to be nil.

The subsidy scheme gives greater powers to the Secretary of State to determine the amount of subsidy paid to relevant authorities, and in particular to reward success and punish failure regarding the prevention of fraud by giving extra subsidy or reducing it.

Analysis

Subs (5). The Secretary of State does not have to seek the approval of Parliament prior to making deductions from the amounts of subsidy under her/his powers. The analysis in *R v Secretary of State for the Environment ex p Hammersmith and Fulham LBC* [1991] 1 AC 521 at 597E-H, HL will not therefore apply and an order made by the Secretary of State can be subject to challenge on the grounds of unreasonableness. In particular, it is suggested that there can be no deduction from the subsidy unless the Secretary of State has some form of reliable evidence to justify such an approach, whether it be on the ground that the normal amount would be "unreasonable" under subs (4)(b) or that there have been failures in preventing fraud under subs (5A)(b). It was said that the power was a "last resort": Alistair Burt MP, Standing Committee E, 14 January 1997, col 243.

Subs (5A). Note that the power to reduce subsidy is not limited to the two factors mentioned, they are merely "included" in the circumstances that can justify a reduction.

[¹Payment of subsidy

140C.–(1) Subsidy shall be paid by the Secretary of State in such instalments, at such times, in such manner and subject to such conditions as to claims, records, certificates, audit or otherwise as may be provided by order of the Secretary of State.

[² (1A) Conditions under subsection (1) above may (in particular) be imposed to obtain information for the purposes of the carrying-out by the Secretary of State of any of his functions relating to subsidy.]

(2)   The order may provide that if an authority has not, within such period as may be specified in the order, complied with the conditions so specified as to claims, records, certificate, audit or otherwise, the Secretary of State may estimate the amount of subsidy payable to the authority and employ for that purpose such criteria as he considers relevant.

(3)   Where subsidy has been paid to an authority and it appears to the Secretary of State–

(a)   that subsidy has been overpaid; or

(b)   that there has been a breach of any condition specified in an order under this section, he may recover from the authority the whole or such part of the payment as he may determine.

Without prejudice to other methods of recovery, a sum recoverable under this subsection may be recovered by withholding or reducing subsidy.

(4)   An order made by the Secretary of State under this section may be made before, during or after the end of the year or years to which it relates.]

Amendments
1.   Inserted by Sch 12 para 4 Housing Act 1996.
2.   Inserted by the Local Government Act 2003 s127(1) and Sch 7 para 37 (18.11.03).

General Note
This section deals with the calculation of subsidy and recovery of payments of subsidy which have either been overpaid or where there has been a breach of any condition.

Analysis
Subs (1) and (2). The Secretary of State may require the maintenance and production of records by the authority in order to calculate its subsidy and carry out estimates in default.

Subs (3)(a) expands the powers for rectifying errors in the payment of subsidy. Hitherto, the statutory powers were restricted to adjusting the following year's subsidy to rectify the error: s137(6). Now the Secretary of State may require immediate repayment.

Subs (3)(b) appears to allow the Secretary of State a general discretion to recover part or the whole of a subsidy payment where an authority has failed to comply with requirements made under subs (1).

It is suggested, however, that this power cannot be exercised in a penal manner. Under subs (2), if it had been clear from the outset that the authority had failed to comply with the requirements, the Secretary of State would have had to estimate the amount of subsidy. Such method of estimation as was chosen would have to be rational and reasonable. It is not logical that the authority should be in a worse position if the failure only comes to light at a later stage. It is therefore suggested that subs (3)(b) does not allow the Secretary of State to recover so much of the subsidy that the authority has effectively received a lesser amount of subsidy than it would have received under an estimate carried out pursuant to subs (2).

This issue was to be considered in judicial review proceedings brought by Bridgnorth DC. That council had failed to implement a new version of reg 11 HB Regs 1987 properly, with the result that a large number of claims were determined without a proper reference from a rent officer. The Secretary of State decided to recover the full amount of subsidy paid in the relevant years, even though many of the claims must have been assessed correctly or even underpaid. This would have had dire consequences for the council. In its application for judicial review, the council argued that recovery of all the subsidy was disproportionate. During the hearing of the judicial review proceedings, the proceedings were settled with an agreed quashing of the decision to recover, the Secretary of State acknowledging flaws in the decision-making process and agreeing not to recover any of the subsidy.

Following a review of the Secretary of State's approach to this power, a new policy was set out in Circular S1/2002. The recovery of each overpayment of subsidy will depend on all the circumstances, and criteria are set out which will be taken into account. The implementation of the new policy was challenged in *R (Isle of Anglesey DC) v Secretary of State for Work and Pensions* [2003] EWHC 2518 (Admin). The applicant local authority had made similar mistakes to Bridgnorth DC in its administration, and the Secretary of State proposed to recover 20 per cent of the subsidy paid to the council in respect of the claims that had not been properly administered. Lindsay J rejected the suggestion that Sch 4 para 6 Income-Related Benefits (Subsidy to Authorities) Order 1998, which awards nil subsidy where a claim has not been referred to the Rent Officer, was *ultra vires* (para 40) and also held that the decision of the Secretary of State on the particular facts of the case could not be castigated as penal, disproportionate or irrational.

[¹Rent rebate subsidy: accounting provisions
140D.–(1) Rent rebate subsidy is payable–

(a)   in the case of a local authority in England and Wales, for the credit of a revenue account of theirs other than their Housing Revenue Account or Housing Repairs Account;

(b)   in the case of a local authority in Scotland, for the credit of their rent rebate account;

[² (c)]
(d)   in the case of a new town corporation in Scotland or Scottish Homes, for the credit of the account to which rent rebates granted by them, or it, are debited.

[² (2)]]

Amendments
1.   Inserted by Sch 12 para 4 Housing Act 1996.
2.   Omitted/repealed by the Local Government Act 2003, s127(1) and Sch 7 para 38 and s127(2) and Part 1 Sch 8 (18.11.03).

[¹ Supplementary provisions

Financing of joint arrangements

140E.–(1) Where two or more authorities make arrangements for the discharge of any of their functions relating to housing benefit or council tax benefit–
(a)   by one authority on behalf of itself and one or more other authorities; or
(b)   by a joint committee,
the Secretary of State may make such payments as he thinks fit to the authority or committee in respect of their expenses in carrying out those functions.

(2)   The provisions of sections 140B and 140C (subsidy: calculation and supplementary provisions) apply in relation to a payment under this section as in relation to a payment of subsidy.

(3)   The Secretary of State may (without prejudice to the generality of his powers in relation to the amount of subsidy) take into account the fact that an amount has been paid under this section in respect of expenses which would otherwise have been met in whole or in part by the participating authorities.]

Amendment
1.   Inserted by Sch 12 para 4 Housing Act 1996.

[¹ **140EE.**–(1) The Secretary of State may make to a local authority such payments as he thinks fit in respect of expenses incurred by the authority in connection with the carrying out of any relevant function–
(a)   by the authority,
(b)   by any person providing services to the authority, or
(c)   by any person authorised by the authority to carry out that function.

(2)   In subsection (1) "relevant function" means any function conferred by virtue of section 2A, 2C or 7A above.

(3)   The following provisions, namely–
(a)   in section 140B, subsections (1), (3), (4), (5)(b), [²] and (8), and
(b)   section 140C, apply in relation to a payment under this section as in relation to a payment of subsidy.

(4)   The Secretary of State may (without prejudice to the generality of his powers in relation to the amount of subsidy) take into account the fact that an amount has been paid under this section in respect of costs falling within section 140B(4A)(a) above.]

Commencement
11.11.99: see s89(4)(e) WRPA.

Amendments
1.   Inserted by the Welfare Reform and Pensions Act 1999, s84(1) and Sch 12 para 79.
2.   Repealed by the Local Government Act 2003, s127(2) and Part 1 sch 8 (18.11.03).

General Note
This section authorises the Secretary of State to make payments by way of subsidy to local authorities in respect of expenses incurred under the ONE scheme.

[¹No requirement for annual orders

140F.–(1) Any power under this Part to make provision by order for or in relation to a year does not require the making of a new order each year.

(2) Any order made under the power may be revoked or varied at any time, whether before, during or after the year to which it relates.]

Amendment
1. Inserted by Sch 12 para 4 Housing Act 1996.

[¹Interpretation: Part VIII

140G. In this Part, unless the context otherwise requires–

"Housing Repairs Account" means an account kept under section 77 of the Local Government and Housing Act 1989;

"Housing Revenue Account" means the account kept under section 74 of the Local Government and Housing Act 1989, and–

    (a)   references to property within that account have the same meaning as in Part VI of that Act, [²]

    [² (b)]

"rent rebate subsidy" and "rent allowance subsidy" shall be construed in accordance with section 134 above;

"year" means a financial year within the meaning of the Local Government Finance Act 1992.]

Amendments
1. Inserted by s4 Housing Act 1996.
2. Omitted/repealed by the Local Government Act 2003, s127(1) and Sch 7 para 39 and s127(2) and Part 1 Sch 8 (18.11.03).

PART XIII
Advisory Bodies and Consultation
The Social Security Advisory Committee and the Industrial Injuries Advisory Council

General Note

The Social Security Advisory Committee (SSAC) is a body of experts, working on a voluntary basis, which advises the Secretary of State as to the implications of new legislation to be enacted. It serves a valuable function of bringing potential problems with proposals to the attention of officials of the DWP and in speaking with an authoritative voice in doing so. Historically, however, the SSAC has only rarely persuaded the DWP to drop controversial proposals or modify them significantly, although there are exceptions such as the backdating restrictions which were due to replace the "good cause" test in reg 72(15) HB Regs 1987 and which were withdrawn by the DWP mainly as a result of the SSAC's carefully reasoned opposition.

The process by which regulations are dealt with by the SSAC is that the Secretary of State first sends draft proposals to it. The Committee then decides whether or not the proposed regulations should be referred to it under s173(1)(b) and, if it concludes that they should be, will consult the public if necessary and then produce a report under s174(1). When the regulations are laid, the Secretary of State is required to place a copy of the SSAC's report and the DWP's response before Parliament.

Certain categories of regulations are not required to be referred to the SSAC by virtue of s172(3) (below). The categories are set out in Sch 7 of the SSAA, which is not reproduced in this work. The categories that are relevant to HB and CTB are uprating regulations (para 3), Tribunal rules (para 9) in respect of which the Secretary of State is supposed to consult to Council on Tribunals, and consolidating regulations (para 10). In addition, s173(1) does not require the Secretary of State to refer regulations where "urgency" makes it "inexpedient" (see the commentary to s176) or the SSAC decides that it is unnecessary.

The SSAC seeks the views of the public on major regulations referred to it and details of current consultations can be found on its website: www.ssac.org.uk.

The significance of the SSAC for the purposes of advisers has now increased as a result of the decision in *Howker v Secretary of State for Work and Pensions* [2003] ICR 405 (also reported as *R(IB) 3/03*). In that decision, the Court of Appeal held that amendments to the regulations governing incapacity benefit were *ultra vires* because officials of the DWP had misled the SSAC as to the effect of the amending regulations, with the consequence that the SSAC did not ask for the amending regulations to be referred. It need not be shown that the misleading advice was given deliberately: para 37.

It is necessary to consider the significance of the advice: para 40, or to show that it was "seriously inaccurate": para 54. The correct approach to determining whether the SSAC was misled is to look at all the material placed before the SSAC by the Secretary of State as the basis for the amendment (including answers given by DWP officials to the SSAC) and consider whether the overall effect was misleading; and, if it was, whether there is a real possibility that (a) the information might have misled the SSAC as to the effect of the proposed regulation, and (b) had the SSAC been aware of the regulations true effect it would have wished to have the proposed regulation formally referred to it: *R(IB) 2/07*.

In *CH 5125/2002*, a challenge was made to the 1998 amendments to reg 7 HB Regs 1987 on the basis that the SSAC had been misled. Commissioner Jacobs rejected the challenge (paras 68-69), holding that the adverse effect of the amendments had been made clear.

The Court of Appeal in *Campbell and others v South Northamptonshire District Council and the Secretary of State for Work and Pensions* [2004] EWCA Civ 409 *The Times* 6 May, CA (reported as *R(H) 8/04*) – the appeal from *CH 5125/2002* – rejected the appeal and endorsed Commissioner Jacob's view that, as a whole, the adverse affects of the amendment regulations had been made clear to the SSAC and so they could not be said to have been misled.

The Social Security Advisory Committee

170.–(1) The Social Security Advisory Committee (in this Act referred to as "the Committee") constituted under section 9 of the Social Security Act 1980 shall continue in being by that name–

(a)   to give (whether in pursuance of a reference under this Act or otherwise) advice and assistance to the Secretary of State in connection with the discharge of his functions under the relevant enactments;

(b)   to give (whether in pursuance of a reference under this Act or otherwise) advice and assistance to the Northern Ireland Department in connection with the discharge of its functions under the relevant Northern Ireland enactments; and

(c)   to perform such other duties as may be assigned to the Committee under any enactment.

(2)   Schedule 5 to this Act shall have effect with respect to the constitution of the Committee and the other matters there mentioned.

(3)   The Secretary of State may from time to time refer to the Committee for consideration and advice such questions relating to the operation of any of the relevant enactments as he thinks fit (including questions as to the advisability of amending any of them).

(4)   The Secretary of State shall furnish the Committee with such information as the Committee may reasonably require for the proper discharge of its functions.

(5)   In this Act–

"the relevant enactments" means–

(a)   the provisions of the Contributions and Benefits Act and this Act, except as they apply to industrial injuries benefit and Old Cases payments; and

(aa) to (ab) *[omitted]*

[4 (ac) the provisions of the Social Security (Recovery of Benefits) Act 1997; and]

(ad) to (ae) *[omitted]*

[1 (af)   section 42, sections 62 to 65 and sections 68 to 70 of the Child Support, Pensions and Social Security Act 2000, and Schedule 7 to that Act.]

[2 (ag) sections 7 to 11 of the Social Security Fraud Act 2001.]

[3 (ah) the provisions of the State Pension Credit Act 2002.]

(b)   *[omitted]*

Amendments

1.   Inserted by s73 of the CSPSSA as from 1.12.00.
2.   Inserted by s12(3) of the SSFA as from 1.4.02.
3.   Inserted by Sch 2 para 12 of the SPCA as from 6.10.03.
4.   Inserted by Sch 3 para 8 of the Social Security (Recovery of Benefits Act 1997) as from 6.10.97.

Functions of Committee and Council in relation to regulations

172.–(1) Subject–

(a)   to subsection (3) below; and

(b)   to section 173 below,

where the Secretary of State proposes to make regulations under any of the relevant enactments, he shall refer the proposals, in the form of draft regulations or otherwise, to the Committee.

(2)   *[omitted]*

(3)   Subsection (1) above does not apply to the regulations specified in Part I of Schedule 7 to this Act.

(4)   *[omitted]*

(5)   *[omitted]*

Cases in which consultation is not required

173.–(1) Nothing in any enactment shall require any proposals in respect of regulations to be referred to the Committee or the Council if–

(a)   it appears to the Secretary of State that by reason of the urgency of the matter it is inexpedient so to refer them; or

(b)   the relevant advisory body have agreed that they shall not be referred.

(2)   Where by virtue only of subsection (1)(a) above the Secretary of State makes regulations without proposals in respect of them having been referred, then, unless the relevant advisory body agrees that this subsection shall not apply, he shall refer the regulations to that body as soon as practicable after making them.

(3)   Where the Secretary of State has referred proposals to the Committee or the Council, he may make the proposed regulations before the Committee have made their report or, as the case may be the Council have given their advice, only if after the reference it appears to him that by reason of the urgency of the matter it is expedient to do so.

(4)   Where by virtue of this section regulations are made before a report of the Committee has been made, the Committee shall consider them and make a report to the Secretary of State containing such recommendations with regard to the regulations as the Committee thinks appropriate; and a copy of any report made to the Secretary of State on the regulations shall be laid by him before each House of Parliament together, if the report contains recommendations, with a statement–

(a)   of the extent (if any) to which the Secretary of State proposes to give effect to the recommendations; and

(b)   in so far as he does not propose to give effect to them, of his reasons why not.

(5)   Except to the extent that this subsection is excluded by an enactment passed after 25th July 1986, nothing in any enactment shall require the reference to the Committee or the Council of any regulations contained in either–

(a)   a statutory instrument made before the end of the period of 6 months beginning with the coming into force of the enactment under which those regulations are made; or

(b)   a statutory instrument–

(i)   which states that it contains only regulations made by virtue of, or consequential upon, a specified enactment; and

(ii)   which is made before the end of the period of 6 months beginning with the coming into force of that specified enactment.

(6)   In relation to regulations required or authorised to be made by the Secretary of State in conjunction with the Treasury, any reference in this section to the Secretary of State shall be construed as a reference to the Secretary of State and the Treasury.

(7)   In this section ''regulations'' means regulations under any enactment, whenever passed.

Committee's report on regulations and Secretary of State's duties

174.–(1) The Committee shall consider any proposals referred to it by the Secretary of State under section 172 above and shall make to the Secretary of State a report containing such recommendations with regard to the subject-matter of the proposals as the Committee thinks appropriate.

(2) If after receiving a report of the Committee the Secretary of State lays before Parliament any regulations or draft regulations which comprise the whole or any part of the subject-matter of the proposals referred to the Committee, he shall lay with the regulations or draft regulations a copy of the Committee's report and a statement showing–

(a) the extent (if any) to which he has, in framing the regulations, given effect to the Committee's recommendations; and

(b) in so far as effect has not been given to them, his reasons why not.

(3) In the case of any regulations laid before Parliament at a time when Parliament is not sitting, the requirements of subsection (2) above shall be satisfied as respects either House of Parliament if a copy of the report and statement there referred to are laid before that House not later than the second day on which the House sits after the laying of the regulations.

(4) In relation to regulations required or authorised to be made by the Secretary of State in conjunction with the Treasury any reference in this section to the Secretary of State shall be construed as a reference to the Secretary of State and the Treasury.

Housing benefit and council tax benefit

Consultation with representative organisations

176.–(1) Subject to subsection (2) below, before making–

(a) regulations relating to housing benefit or [¹ council tax benefit] (other than regulations of which the effect is to increase any amount specified in regulations previously made);

[³(aa) regulations under section 69 of the Child Support, Pensions and Social Security Act 2000]

(b) an order under [² any provision of Part VIII above.]

the Secretary of State shall consult with organisations appearing to him to be representative of the authorities concerned.

(2) Nothing in subsection (1) above shall require the Secretary of State to undertake consultations if–

(a) it appears to him that by reason of the urgency of the matter it is inexpedient to do so; or

(b) the organisations have agreed that consultations should not be undertaken.

(3) Where the Secretary of State has undertaken such consultations, he may make any regulations or order to which the consultations relate without completing the consultations if it appears to him that by reason of the urgency of the matter it is expedient to do so.

Amendments
1.   Substitution made by para 23 Sch 9 Local Government Finance Act 1992 (1.4.93).
2.   Amended by the HA 1996 Sch 13 para 3(4) (1.4.97)
3.   Inserted by s69(6) CSPSSA (2.7.01).

Analysis
Subs (2)(a). The Secretary of State invoked the predecessor to para (2)(a) as the reason for not consulting with the local authority associations when the Housing Benefit (General) Amendment Regulations 1992 SI No 201 were introduced. Those regulations followed the introduction by the London Borough of Hackney of a scheme whereby council tenants with rent arrears would be liable to a higher rent rise than those who were not. The amending regulations were aimed at ensuring that HB would not be paid with regard to the rent arrears supplement: see the Analysis of reg 11(3) HB Regs on p253.

In *R v Secretary of State for Social Security ex p Association of Metropolitan Authorities* [1992] 25 HLR 131, QBD, Tucker J found that in relation to the making of the regulations the Secretary of State could not invoke the exemption (then s61(8)(a) Social Security Act 1986) by leaving a decision until the last moment and thus himself creating the emergency.

PART XV
Miscellaneous

[¹**Return of social security post**

182A.–(1) A social security authority may require–

(a) the Post Office; or

(b) any other person who conveys postal packets,

to return to the sender social security post sent by or on behalf of the authority which would otherwise be redirected.

(2) A social security authority shall make payments of such amount as the Secretary of State considers reasonable in respect of the return of social security post in compliance with a requirement imposed by the authority under subsection (1) above.

(3) In subsections (1) and (2) above "social security authority" means–

(a) the Secretary of State;

(b) the Northern Ireland Department; or

(c) any local or other authority administering housing benefit or council tax benefit (including the Northern Ireland Housing Executive).

(4) In subsections (1) and (2) above "social security post" means postal packets–

(a) the contents of which relate to any benefit, contributions or national insurance number or to any other matter relating to social security; and

(b) which are marked, in a manner approved by the Post Office or other person conveying them, with the name and address of the sender and with an indication that they are to be returned rather than redirected.

(5) In this section–

(a) "redirected", in relation to any postal packet, means delivered to an address other than that indicated by the sender on the packet; and

(b) "postal packet" has the same meaning as in the Post Office Act 1953.

(6) Any requirement imposed under subsection (1) above has effect subject to any order under–

(a) section 371 of the Insolvency Act 1986 or Article 342 of the Insolvency (Northern Ireland) Order 1989 (redirection of bankrupt's letters to trustee in bankruptcy);

(b) paragraph 10 of Schedule 1 to the Solicitors Act 1974 or paragraph 15 of Schedule 1 to the Solicitors (Northern Ireland) Order 1976 (redirection of letters following intervention by Law Society); or

(c) paragraph 10 of Schedule 5 to the Administration of Justice Act 1985 (redirection of letters following intervention by Council for Licensed Conveyancers).]

Amendment

1.   Inserted by s20 Social Security Administration (Fraud) Act 1997 (27.3.99).

General Note

A common form of social security fraud is to claim on behalf of non-existent persons at an address and then have mail to that address re-directed. Prior to the insertion of s182A, many local authorities had adopted the practice of marking envelopes containing HB giros "Do Not Redirect", but the Post Office generally disregarded such instructions, taking the view that without specific authority not to do so, it was obliged to obey directions from an addressee to redirect mail.

Subs (1) allows a "social security authority" to require return of mail which would be redirected. "Social security authority" includes a local authority: subs (3)(c). The requirement is imposed simply by indicating the requirement on the envelope: subs (4). The authority can be required by the Secretary of State to pay a fee for this service: subs (2).

Subs (6) makes the scheme subject to certain other statutory schemes requiring mail to be redirected.

[¹Requirement to supply information about redirection of post

182B.–(1) The Secretary of State or the Northern Ireland Department may require the Post Office or any other person who conveys postal packets to supply information relating to arrangements for the redirection of postal packets to, or to a person supplying services to, the Secretary of State or the Department–

  (a)   for use in the prevention, detection, investigation or prosecution of offences relating to social security; or

  (b)   for use in checking the accuracy of information relating to benefits, contributions or national insurance numbers or to any other matter relating to social security and (where appropriate) amending or supplementing such information.

  (2)   A local or other authority administering housing benefit or council tax benefit (including the Northern Ireland Housing Executive) may require the Post Office or any other person who conveys postal packets to supply information relating to arrangements for the redirection of postal packets to the authority or a person authorised to exercise any function of the authority relating to housing benefit or council tax benefit–

  (a)   for use in the prevention, detection, investigation or prosecution of offences relating to such a benefit; or

  (b)   for use in checking the accuracy of information relating to such a benefit and (where appropriate) amending or supplementing such information.

  (3)   Information shall be supplied under subsection (1) or (2) above in such manner and form, and in accordance with such requirements, as may be prescribed.

  (4)   Payments of such amount as the Secretary of State considers reasonable shall be made by a person or authority imposing a requirement under subsection (1) or (2) above in respect of the supply of information in compliance with the requirement.

  (5)   Information supplied under subsection (1) or (2) above shall not be supplied by the recipient to any other person or body unless–

  (a)   it could be supplied to that person or body under either of those subsections; or

  (b)   it is supplied for the purposes of any civil or criminal proceedings relating to the Contributions and Benefits Act, the Jobseekers Act 1995 or this Act or to any provision of Northern Ireland legislation corresponding to any of them.

  (6)   But where information supplied under subsection (1) or (2) above has been used (in accordance with paragraph (b) of the subsection concerned) in amending or supplementing other information, it is lawful for it to be–

  (a)   supplied to any person or body to whom that other information could be supplied; or

  (b)   used for any purpose for which that other information could be used.

  (7)   In subsections (1) and (2) above ''arrangements for the redirection of postal packets'' means arrangements made with the Post Office or other person conveying postal packets for the delivery of postal packets to addresses other than those indicated by senders on the packets.

  (8)   In this section ''postal packet'' has the same meaning as in the Post Office Act 1953.]

Amendment

1.   Inserted by s21 Social Security Administration (Fraud) Act 1997 (27.3.99).

General Note

This section requires the Post Office to gather information about the redirection of mail and supply it to social security authorities at their request. It is similar in form to the provisions requiring and enabling the supply of information from one authority to another: see Part VII above. A charge may be imposed for this service: subs (4).

Subs (2) is in similar form to s122C(3), discussed in the General Note to s122C. Similarly, for discussion of the wording of subs (6), see the General Note to s122E as it relates to s122E(5). Under subs (5) and (6), if the authority wishes to supply the information received to the Secretary of State or another authority, it must satisfy itself that the recipient would be entitled to receive the information under subs (1) or (2), or that it is being supplied for the purpose of civil or criminal proceedings under the social security legislation. Thus this provision could not, it appears, be used to justify the passing of information where a person is being prosecuted under the Theft Act 1968.

Certain benefit to be inalienable

187.–(1) Subject to the provisions of this Act, every assignment of or charge on–

(a)　benefit as defined in section 122 of the Contributions and Benefits Act;

[¹ (ab) state pension credit;]

(b)　any income-related benefit; or

(c)　child benefit,

and every agreement to assign or charge such benefit shall be void; and, on the bankruptcy of a beneficiary, such benefit shall not pass to any trustee or other person acting on behalf of his creditors.

(2)　In the application of subsection (1) above to Scotland–

(a)　the reference to assignment of benefit shall be read as a reference to assignation, "assign" being construed accordingly;

(b)　the reference to a beneficiary's bankruptcy shall be read as a reference to the sequestration of his estate or the appointment on his estate of a judicial factor under section 41 of the Solicitors (Scotland) Act 1980.

(3)　[. . .]

Amendment

1.　Inserted by SSPCA 2002 Sch 2 para 23 (commenced October 2003).

General Note

This provision prevents any assignment of a right to benefit by agreement or by operation of law. It does not prevent recovery of an overpayment by the Secretary of State (or, by the same token, a local authority) after the claimant has been made bankrupt: *Mulvey v Secretary of State for Social Security* [1997] SLT 753 at 756, HL.

PART XVI
General
Subordinate legislation

Regulations and orders–general

189.–(1) Subject to [⁷] any [⁵ . . .] express provision of this Act, regulations and orders under this Act shall be made by the Secretary of State.

[⁷ (2)]

(3)　Powers under this Act to make regulations or orders are exercisable by statutory instrument.

(4)　Except in the case of regulations under section [⁷] 175 above and in so far as this Act otherwise provides, any power conferred by this Act to make an Order in Council, regulations or an order may be exercised

(a)　either in relation to all cases to which the power extends, or in relation to those cases subject to specified exceptions, or in relation to any specified cases or classes of case;

(b)　so as to make, as respects the cases in relation to which it is exercised–

(i)   the full provision to which the power extends or any less provision (whether by way of exception or otherwise);

(ii)   the same provision for all cases in relation to which the power is exercised, or different provision for different cases or different classes of case or different provision as respects the same case or class of case for different purposes of this Act;

(iii)   any such provision either unconditionally or subject to any specified condition;

and where such a power is expressed to be exercisable for alternative purposes it may be exercised in relation to the same case for any or all of those purposes; and powers to make an Order in Council, regulations or an order for the purposes of any one provision of this Act are without prejudice to powers to make regulations or an order for the purposes of any other provision.

(5)   Without prejudice to any specific provision in this Act, a power conferred by this Act to make an Order in Council, regulations or an order [⁷] includes power to make thereby such incidental, supplementary, consequential or transitional provision as appears to Her Majesty, or the authority making the regulations or order, as the case may be, to be expedient for the purposes of the Order in Council, regulations or order.

(6)   Without prejudice to any specific provisions in this Act, a power conferred by any provision of this Act, except sections 14, [⁷] 130 and 175, to make an Order in Council, regulations or an order includes power to provide for a person to exercise a discretion in dealing with any matter.

(7)   Any power conferred by this Act to make orders or regulation relating to housing benefit or [¹ council tax benefit] shall include power to make different provision for different areas [² or different authorities].

[⁸ (7A) Without prejudice to the generality of any of the preceding provisions of this section, regulations under any of sections 2A to 2C and 7A above may provide for all or any of the provisions of the regulations to apply only in relation to any area or areas specified in the regulations.]

(8)   An order under section [³140B, 140C,] 150, 152, 165(4) or 169 above [⁶] above shall not be made [⁴ by the Secretary of State] without the consent of the Treasury.

(9)   Any power of the Secretary of State under any provision of this Act, except under sections 80, 154, 175 and 178, to make any regulations or order, where the power is not expressed to be exercisable with the consent of the Treasury, shall if the Treasury so direct be exercisable only in conjunction with them.

[⁷ (10)]

(11)   A power under any of sections 177 to 179 above to make provisions by regulations or Order in Council for modifications or adaptations of the Contributions and Benefits Actor this Act shall be exercisable in relation to any enactment passed after this Act which is directed to be construed as one with them, except in so far as any such enactment relates to a benefit in relation to which the power is not exercisable; but this subsection applies only so far as a contrary intention is not expressed in the enactment so passed, and is without prejudice to the generality of any such direction.

(12)   Any reference in this section or section 190 below to an Order in Council, or an order or regulations, under this Act includes a reference to an Order in Council, an order or regulations made under any provision of an enactment passed after this Act and directed to be construed as one with this Act; but this subsection applies only so far as a contrary intention is not expressed in the enactment so passed, and without prejudice to the generality of any such direction.

Amendments

1.   Substitution made by para 24 Sch 9 Local Government Finance Act 1992 (1.4.93).

2.   Amended by SSA(F)A 1997 Sch 1 para 10.
3.   Amended by HA 1996 Sch 13 para 3(5) (1.4.97)4.
4.   Amended by TCA 2002, Sch 4 para 3 (6.4.03)5,
5.   Amended by TCA 2002, Sch 6 (8.4.03).
6.   Amended by Social Security (Recovery of Benefits) Act 1997 Sch 3 para 11 (6.10.97)
7.   Amended by SSA 1998, Sch 7 para 109 (6.9.99).
8.   Inserted by WRPA 1999, Sch 12 para 83 (11.11.99).

Parliamentary control of orders and regulations

190.–(1) Subject to the provisions of this section, a statutory instrument containing (whether alone or with other provisions)–

(a)   an order under section 141, 143, [¹ 143A,] 145, 150, 152 or 162(7) above; or

[⁶(aa) the first regulations to be made under section 2A;]

[³(aza) any order containing provision adding any person to the list of persons falling within section 109B(2A) above;]

(b)   regulations under section [⁴] [⁵ 122B(1)(b) or] 154 above,

shall not be made unless a draft of the instrument has been laid before Parliament and been approved by a resolution of each House of Parliament.

(2)   Subsection (1) above does not apply to a statutory instrument by reason only that it contains regulations under section 154 above which are to be made for the purpose of consolidating regulations to be revoked in the instrument.

(3)   A statutory instrument–

(a)   which contains (whether alone or with other provisions) orders or regulations made under this Act by the Secretary of State; and

(b)   which is not subject to any requirement that a draft of the instrument be laid before and approved by a resolution of each House of Parliament,

shall be subject to annulment in pursuance of a resolution of either House of Parliament.

[² (4)   .....]

Amendments
1.   Inserted by SSA 1998 Sch 7 para 110 (8.10.98).
2.   Repealed by SSA 1998 Sch 7 para 110 (6.4.99).
3.   Inserted by SSFA s1(9) (26.2.02).
4.   Amended by the Social Security (Recovery of Benefits) Act 1997 Sch 3 para 11 (6.10.97).
5.   Amended by Sch 1 para 11 of the SSA(F) Act 1997 (1.7.97).
6.   Inserted by Sch 12 para 83 of the WRP Act 1999 (11.11.99).

Supplementary

Interpretation – general

191. In this Act, unless the context otherwise requires–

"the 1975 Act" means the Social Security Act 1975;

"the 1986 Act" means the Social Security Act 1986;

"benefit" means benefit under the Contributions and Benefits Act [¹⁶ and state pension credit];

[¹ "billing authority" has the same meaning as in Part I of the Local Government Finance Act 1992;]

"the Consequential Provisions Act" means the Social Security (Consequential Provisions) Act 1992;

[⁵ "contribution-based jobseeker's allowance" has the same meaning as in the Jobseekers Act 1995;]

"the Contributions and Benefits Act" means the Social Security Contributions and Benefits Act 1992;

[¹⁴ "council tax benefit scheme" shall be construed in accordance with section 139(1) above;]

"disablement benefit" is to be construed in accordance with section 94(2)(a) of the
  Contributions and Benefits Act;
"dwelling" means any residential accommodation, whether or not consisting of the
  whole or part of a building and whether or not comprising separate and self-
  contained premises;
[² "financial year" has the same meaning as in the Local Government Finance Act
  1992;]
"5 year general qualification" is to be construed in accordance with section 71 of the
  Courts and Legal Services Act 1990;
"housing authority" means a local authority [¹⁷ or a new town corporation] or the
  Development Board for Rural Wales;
"housing benefit scheme" is to be construed in accordance with section 134(1)
  above;
[⁶ "income-based jobseeker's allowance" has the same meaning as in the Jobseekers
  Act 1995;]
"income-related benefit" means–
  (a)   income support;
  [¹⁵ . . .]
  [¹⁵ . . .]
  (d)   housing benefit; and
  [³(e) council tax benefit;]
"industrial injuries benefit" means benefit under Part V of the Contributions and
  Benefits Act, other than under Schedule 8;
"invalidity benefit" has the meaning assigned to it by section 20(1)(c) of that Act;
"local authority" means–
  (a)   in relation to England [⁸ . . .], the council of a district or London borough,
         the Common Council of the City of London or the Council of the Isles of
         Scilly; and
  [⁸(aa) in relation to Wales, the council of a county or county borough;] and
  (b)   in relation to Scotland, [⁹ a council constituted under section 2 of the Local
         Government etc. (Scotland) Act 1994];
"medical examination" includes bacteriological and radiographical tests and similar
  investigations, and "medically examined" has a corresponding meaning;
"medical practitioner" means–
  (a)   a registered medical practitioner; or
  (b)   a person outside the United Kingdom who is not a registered medical
         practitioner, but has qualifications corresponding (in the Secretary of State's
         opinion) to those of a registered medical practitioner;
"medical treatment" means medical, surgical or rehabilitative treatment (including
  any course of diet or other regimen), and references to a person receiving
  or submitting himself to medical treatment are to be construed accordingly;
"new town corporation" means–
  (a)   in relation to England and Wales, a development corporation established
         under the New Towns Act 1981 or the Commission for the New Towns;
         and
  (b)   in relation to Scotland, a development corporation established under the
         New Towns (Scotland) Act 1968;
[¹⁸ "the Northern Ireland Department" means means the Department for Social
  Development but-
  (a)   in section 122 and sections 122B to 122E also includes the Department of
         Finance and Personnel; and
  (b)   in sections 121E, 121F, 122, 122ZA, 122C and 122D also includes the
         Department for Employment and Learning;]
"the Northern Ireland Administration Act" means the Social Security (Northern
  Ireland) Administration Act 1992;

"occupational pension scheme" has the same meaning as in section 66(1) of the
Pensions Act;

"the Old Cases Act" means the Industrial Injuries and Diseases (Old Cases) Act
1975;

"Old Cases payments" means payments under Part I of Schedule 8 to the
Contributions and Benefits Act;

[10 "pensionable age" has the meaning given by the rules in paragraph 1 of Schedule
4 to the Pensions Act 1995];

"the Pensions Act" means the[11 Pension Schemes Act 1993];

"personal pension scheme" has the meaning assigned to it by [12 section 1 of the
Pensions Act] [12 and "appropriate", in relation to such a scheme, shall be
construed in accordance with section 7(4) of that Act];

"prescribe" means prescribe by regulations [19 and "prescribed" must be construed
accordingly];

"rent rebate" and [13 . . .]"rent allowance" shall be construed in accordance with
section 134 above;

[13 . . .] "tax year" means the 12 months beginning with 6th April in any year;

[16 "state pension credit" means state pension credit under the State Pension Credit
Act 2002;]

"10 year general qualification" is to be construed in accordance with section 71 of
the Courts and Legal Services Act 1990; and

"widow's benefit" has the meaning assigned to it by section 20(1)(e) of the
Contributions and Benefits Act.

Amendments

1.	Substituted by LGFA Sch 9 para 25(a) (1.4.93).
2.	Inserted by LGFA Sch 9 para 25(b) (1.4.93).
3.	Substituted by LGFA Sch 9 para 25(c) (1.4.93).
4.	Substituted by LGFA Sch 9 para 25(d) (1.4.93).
5.	Inserted by Jobseekers Act 1995 Sch 2 para 73(3) (22.4.96).
6.	Inserted by Jobseekers Act 1995 Sch 2 para 73(4) (22.4.96).
7.	Definition of "levying authority" repealed (1.4.96) by para 175(5)(a) of Sch 13 to, and Sch 14 to, Local Government etc. (Scotland) Act 1994.
8.	Words repealed and para (aa) inserted by para 94 of Sch 16 to Local Government (Wales) Act 1994.
9.	Substituted by Local Government etc. (Scotland) Act 1994 Sch 13 para 175(5)(b)(1.4.96).
10.	Substitution made by para 14 of Sch 4 to Pensions Act 1995 (19.7.95).
11.	Substitution made by Pensions Schemes Act 1993 Sch 8 para 31(c) (7.2.94).
12.	Substitutions and additions made by Pensions Schemes Act 1993 Sch 8 para 31(d) (7.2.94).
13.	Repealed by the HA 1996 Sch 19, Part VI (1.4.97).
14.	Inserted by the HA 1996 Sch 13, s 6(a).15.
15.	Amended by the TCA 2002, Sch 6 (8.4.03)16.
16.	Amended by the SPCA 2002, Sch 2 para 24 (commenced October 2003).
17.	Amended by the Housing (Scotland) Act 2001, Sch 10 para 17 (1.04.02).
18.	Amended by the Employment Act 2002, Sch 7 para 16 (9.9.02).
19.	Amended by the Welfare Reform Act 2007 s40 and Sch 5 para 10 (3.7.07).

Short title, commencement and extent

192.–(1) This Act may be cited as the Social Security Administration Act 1992.

(2)   This Act is to be read, where appropriate, with the Contributions and
Benefits Act and the Consequential Provisions Act.

(3)   The enactments consolidated by this Act are repealed, in consequence of
the consolidation, by the Consequential Provisions Act.

(4)   Except as provided in Schedule 4 to the Consequential Provisions Act, this
Act shall come into force on 1st July 1992.

(5)   The following provisions extend to Northern Ireland–
[2 . . .]

Social Security Administration Act 1992

[¹ ...]
section 170 (with Schedule 5);
section 177 (with Schedule 8); and
this section.

Except as provided by this section, this Act does not extend to Northern Ireland.

Amendments

1.   Amended by the Social Security (Recovery of Benefits) Act 1997 Sch 3 para 12 (6.10.97).
2.   Amended by the SSA 1998 Sch 7 para 112 (29.11.99).

SCHEDULE 4
PERSONS EMPLOYED IN SOCIAL SECURITY ADMINISTRATION OR ADJUDICATION
PART I
The Specified Persons
Government departments

A civil servant in
[² (a)   the Department for Work and Pensions;]
[² ...]
(c)   the Lord Chancellor's Department.

Other public departments and offices

[*omitted*]

[¹ *Local authorities etc*

A member, officer or employee of an authority administering housing benefit or council tax benefit.
A person authorised to exercise any function of such an authority relating to such a benefit or any employee of such a person.
A person authorised under section 139A(1) of this Act to consider and report to the Secretary of State on the administration of housing benefit or council tax benefit.]

[³ A member, officer or employee of a county council in England who exercises–
(a) any function conferred on the county council by regulations made under section 7A of this Act;
(b) any function in connection with a relevant purpose within the meaning of section 7B(3) of this Act.
A person authorised to exercise any such function of such a county council or an employee of such a person.]

Adjudicating bodies

The clerk to, or other officer or member of staff of, any of the following bodies–
(a)   an appeal tribunal;
[*omitted*]

Amendments

1.   Inserted by the SSA(F) Act 1997, s4.
2.   Amended by SI 2002 No 1397, Sch para 8(4) as from 27.6.02.
3.   Inserted by the Welfare Reform Act 2002 s41(3) (3.7.07).

SCHEDULE 10
SUPPLEMENTARY BENEFIT ETC
Overpayments etc

4.–(1)   [omitted]
(2)   [omitted]
(3)   The reference to housing benefit in section 75 above includes a reference to housing benefits under Part II of the Social Security and Housing Benefits Act 1982.

Social Security (Consequential Provisions) Act 1992

(1992 c6)

Meaning of "the consolidating Acts"

    1.   In this Act–

"the consolidating Acts" means the Social Security Contributions and Benefits Act 1992 ("the Contributions and Benefits Act"), the Social Security Administration Act 1992 ("the Administration Act") and, so far as it reproduces the effect of the repealed enactments, this Act; and

"the repealed enactments" means the enactments repealed by this Act.

Continuity of the law

    2.–(1)   The substitution of the consolidating Acts for the repealed enactments does not affect the continuity of the law.

    (2)   Anything done or having effect as if done under or for the purposes of a provision of the repealed enactments has effect, if it could have been done under or for the purposes of the corresponding provision of the consolidating Acts, as if done under or for the purposes of that provision.

    (3)   Any reference, whether express or implied, in the consolidating Acts or any other enactment, instrument or document to a provision of the consolidating Acts shall, so far as the context permits, be construed as including, in relation to the times, circumstances and purposes in relation to which the corresponding provision of the repealed enactments has effect, a reference to that corresponding provision.

    (4)   Any reference, whether express or implied, in any enactment, instrument or document to a provision of the repealed enactments shall be construed, so far as is required for continuing its effects, as including a reference to the corresponding provision of the consolidating Acts.

Social Security Act 1998
(1998 c14)

General Note

The Social Security Act (SSA) 1998 made the most fundamental overhaul for well over a decade in the way benefits are administered by the DWP. It introduced a system for revision and supersession of decisions and a new structure for appeals. Its impact on HB and CTB, however, was much more modest but from 2 July 2001, new provision was made for HB and CTB decision making by CSPSSA s68 and Sch 7.

The principal provisions in the SSA 1998 relating to HB and CTB are ss34 and 35. The latter section has not been brought into force and so is not reproduced here. It relates to the suspension of benefit pending resolution of questions or court decisions. For these, now see Sch 7 para 13 CSPSSA.

Apart from s69 below, the balance of the Act as it relates to HB and CTB is concerned with regulation-making. Other provisions are reproduced below as they are concerned with the creation of the tribunal system.

PART I
General
Appeals

President of appeal tribunals

5.–(1)   The Lord Chancellor may, after consultation with the Lord Advocate, appoint a President of appeal tribunals.

(2)   A person is qualified to be appointed President if–

(a)   he has a 10 year general qualification (construed in accordance with section 71 of the Courts and Legal Services Act 1990); or

(b)   he is an advocate or solicitor in Scotland of at least 10 years' standing.

(3)   Schedule 1 to this Act shall have effect for supplementing this section.

Panel for appointment to appeal tribunals

6.–(1)   The Lord Chancellor shall constitute a panel of persons to act as members of appeal tribunals.

(2)   Subject to subsection (3) below, the panel shall be composed of [² persons appointed by the Lord Chancellor].

(3)   The panel shall include persons possessing such qualifications as may be prescribed by regulations made with the concurrence of the Lord Chancellor.

[³ (3A)   As part of the selection process for the appointment of a medical practitioner as a member of the panel, the Judicial Appointments Commission shall consult the Chief Medical Officer.]

(4)   The numbers of persons appointed to the panel, and the terms and conditions of their appointments, shall be determined by the Lord Chancellor with the consent of the Secretary of State.

(5)   A person may be removed from the panel by the Lord Chancellor on the ground of incapacity or misbehaviour[⁴ ; but the Lord Chancellor may remove such a person only with the concurrence of the appropriate senior judge].

[⁵ (5A)   The appropriate senior judge is the Lord Chief Justice of England and Wales, unless the person to be removed exercises functions wholly or mainly in Scotland, in which case it is the Lord President of the Court of Session.]

(6)   In this section "the Chief Medical Officer" means–

(a)   in relation to England, the Chief Medical Officer of the Department of Health;

(b)   in relation to Wales, the Chief Medical Officer of the Welsh Office; and

(c)   in relation to Scotland, the Chief Medical Officer of the [¹ Scottish Administration].

Amendments

1. Amended by Art 5 and Sch 3 para 4 of SI 1999 No 1042.
2. Substituted by Sch 4 para 272(2) Constitutional Reform Act 2005 as from 3.4.06.
3. Inserted by Sch 4 para 272(3) Constitutional Reform Act 2005 as from 3.4.06.
4. Inserted by Sch 4 para 272(4) Constitutional Reform Act 2005 as from 3.4.06.
5. Inserted by Sch 4 para 272(5) Constitutional Reform Act 2005 as from 3.4.06.

Constitution of appeal tribunals

7.–(1)   Subject to subsection (2) below, an appeal tribunal shall consist of one, two or three members drawn by the President from the panel constituted under section 6 above.

(2)   The member, or (as the case may be) at least one member, of an appeal tribunal must–

(a)   have a general qualification (construed in accordance with section 71 of the Courts and Legal Services Act 1990); or

(b)   be an advocate or solicitor in Scotland.

(3)   Where an appeal tribunal has more than one member–

(a)   the President shall nominate one of the members as chairman;

(b)   decisions shall be taken by a majority of votes; and

(c)   unless regulations otherwise provide, the chairman shall have any casting vote.

(4)   Where it appears to an appeal tribunal that a matter before it involves a question of fact of special difficulty, then, unless regulations otherwise provide, the tribunal may require one or more experts to provide assistance to it in dealing with the question.

(5)   In subsection (4) above "expert" means a member of the panel constituted under section 6 above who appears to the appeal tribunal concerned to have knowledge or experience which would be relevant in determining the question of fact of special difficulty.

(6)   Regulations shall make provision with respect to–

(a)   the composition of appeal tribunals;

(b)   the procedure to be followed in allocating cases among differently constituted tribunals; and

(c)   the manner in which expert assistance is to be given under subsection (4) above.

(7)   Schedule 1 to this Act shall have effect for supplementing this section.

General Note

This section provides for the constitution of appeal tribunals hearing benefit appeals under this act as well as HB and CTB appeals under Sch 7 para 6 CSPSSA. For a transitional period, it also provides for the constitution of appeal tribunals hearing tax credit appeals under s38 Tax Credits Act 2002 (see s63(2) of that Act). HB and CTB appeal tribunals consist of one or two members: see reg 22 D&A Regs.

Analysis

Subs (2) Under subs (2), at least one tribunal member (or in the case of a panel member sitting alone, that member) must be legally qualified as set out in subs (2)(a) and (b). The Chief Commissioner, His Honour Judge Hickinbottom, analyses the relevant statutory provisions in his notice of determination of an application for leave to appeal in *CIS 1344/2004*, where he concludes that it is not necessary for a solicitor to hold a valid and current practising certificate from the Law Society before s/he may sit as a legally qualified panel member. The only requirement is that the solicitor has her/his name on the solicitor's roll; and for a barrister the only requirement is that s/he has been called to the Bar and has not been disbarred.

Subs (4) and (5) allow a tribunal to require one or more experts to provide it with assistance where a matter before it involves a question of fact of special difficulty. Such assistance could take the form of a written report or oral evidence at an appeal hearing. 'Expert' is defined in subs (5). The expert is not part of the tribunal hearing the appeal in question and as such cannot take part in making the decision.

Social Security Decisions and Appeals
Appeals

14. (1)-(11)   *[omitted]*

(12)   Schedule 4 to this Act shall have effect with respect to the appointment, remuneration and tenure of office of Commissioners and other matters relating to them.

General Note

For HB and CTB appeals to the commissioner against tribunal decisions, see Sch 7 para 8 CSSSPA on p159.

Housing benefit and council tax benefit

Determination of claims and reviews

34.–(1)   Regulations shall provide that, where a person claims–

(a)   housing benefit; or

(b)   council tax benefit,

the authority to whom the claim is made shall notify the person of its determination of the claim.

(2)   Any such notification shall be given in such form as may be prescribed.

(3)   Regulations may make provision requiring authorities to whom claims for housing benefit or council tax benefit are made by, or in respect of, persons who have been entitled to a jobseeker's allowance or to income support [2 or state pension credit] to give priority, in prescribed circumstances, to those claims over other claims for any such benefit.

[1 . . .]

Amendments

1.   Repealed by CSPSSA 2000 Sch 9 Pt VII (2.7.01).

2.   Amended by SPCA 2002 Sch 2 para 41 (2.7.02 for the purpose of making regulations, 6.10.03 otherwise).

Commencement

18.10.99: Social Security Act 1998 (Commencement No 11, Savings and Consequential and Transitional Provisions) Order 1999 SI No 2860 Art 2(a).

General Note

This section replaced SSAA s63 as the basic piece of primary legislation upon which the decision-making structure for HB and CTB is based. So far as the mechanism for changing decisions is concerned, it has now in its turn been replaced by Sch 7 CSPSSA.

Analysis

Subs (1) to (3) are identical to the former subs (1), (2), (2A) and (3) SSAA s63. All regulations validly made under those provisions will be treated by virtue of s17(2)(b) of the Interpretation Act 1978 as if they had been made under these provisions. The following list gives the principal regulations made under the powers granted by each numbered paragraph of this section:

(1)   See reg 90 HB Regs, reg 71 HB(SPC) Regs, reg 76 CTB Regs and reg 61 CTB(SPC) Regs.

(2)   See Sch 9 HB Regs, Sch 8 HB(SPC) Regs, Sch 8 CTB Regs and Sch 7 CTB(SPC) Regs.

(3)   See reg 89(3) HB Regs, reg 70(3) HB(SPC) Regs, reg 75(3) CTB Regs and reg 60(3) CTB(SPC) Regs. Also note the different system for claiming HB and CTB for recipients of IS, income-based JSA and PC (see reg 83(4) HB Regs, reg 64(5) HB(SPC) Regs, reg 69(4) CTB Regs and reg 53(4) CTB(SPC) Regs).

Subs (4) and (5) formerly provided for regulations to make provision for reviews of determinations relating to HB and CTB (subs (4)) and matters arising out of the revision on review of such determinations (subs (5)). Both were repealed in July 2001, though preserved for certain purposes: to enable a Review Board to record its decision and send it out; to permit correction of accidental errors; to enable a Review Board to appear in judicial review proceedings; and to enable effect to be given to a Review Board's decision. See the D&A Transitional Regs for details of the transitional rules and the 18th edn of this book, pp104-5 for commentary on the repealed provisions.

PART III
Benefits

Validation of certain housing benefit determinations.

69.–(1) Subject to subsections (3) and (4) below, in so far as a housing benefit determination made before 18th August 1997 purported to determine that housing benefit was payable in respect of–

(a)   charges for medical care, nursing care or personal care; or

(b)   charges for general counselling or any other support services,

it shall be deemed to have been validly made if, on the assumption mentioned in subsection (2) below, it would have been so made.

(2)   The assumption is that, at all material times, such charges as are mentioned in subsection (1) above were eligible to be met by housing benefit where the claimant's right to occupy the dwelling was conditional on his payment of the charges.

(3)   Where the effect of a review carried out on or after 18th August 1997 was to revise the amount of housing benefit payable in respect of any validated charges–

(a)   the revision shall be deemed not to have been validly made in so far as it had the effect of increasing that amount; and

(b)   housing benefit shall cease to be payable in respect of those charges as from the beginning of the period for which the first payment of the revised amount of benefit was made.

(4)   Housing benefit shall not be payable in respect of any validated charges for any period falling after–

(a)   5th April 1998 where the rent is payable at intervals of a whole number of weeks; and

(b)   31st March 1998 in any other case.

(5)   In this section–

"the dwelling", in relation to a housing benefit determination, means the dwelling in respect of which the determination was made;

"housing benefit determination" means a determination under section 130 of the Contributions and Benefits Act or the corresponding provisions of the Social Security Act 1986, or a decision on a review of such a determination;

"medical care" includes treatment or counselling related to mental disorder, mental handicap, physical disablement or past or present alcohol or drug dependence;

"personal care" includes assistance at meal-times or with personal appearance or hygiene;

"validated charges" means charges in respect of which housing benefit is payable only by virtue of subsection (1) above.

General Note

This provision was made to alleviate accounting and subsidy difficulties that might otherwise have been experienced by local authorities following the confusion over whether service charges for the types of services mentioned in subs (1) were properly payable under the then HB Regs 1987 Sch 1 para 1(f)(i). It is now clear, following the decision in *R v St Edmundsbury BC HBRB ex p Sandys* [1997] 30 HLR 800; [1998] *The Times* 9 September, CA that such services should not have been met under that provision. Since the payments were unlawful, in the absence of a provision such as this some authorities might have been faced with difficulties in justifying their expenditure on these items.

Subs (1) and (2) retrospectively justify HB awards in respect of such service charges. The effect of the retrospective validation is limited by subs (3) and (4). Subs (4) makes clear that the validation only lasted until the end of the 1997 to 1998 financial year.

For an analysis of these provisions see the 15th edn of this work, pp117-118.

PART IV

Miscellaneous and Supplemental

Regulations and orders

79.–(1)   Subject to [¹ subsections (2) and (2A)] below and paragraph 6 of Schedule 4 to this Act, regulations under this Act shall be made by the Secretary of State.

(2)   Regulations with respect to proceedings before the Commissioners (whether for the determination of any matter or for leave to appeal to or from the Commissioners) shall be made by the Lord Chancellor; and where the Lord Chancellor proposes to make regulations under this Act it shall be his duty to consult the Lord Advocate with respect to the proposal.

[² (2A)   Subsection (1) has effect subject to any provision providing for regulations to be made by the Treasury or the Commissioners of Inland Revenue.]

(3)   Powers under this Act to make regulations or orders are exercisable by statutory instrument.

(4)   Any power conferred by this Act to make regulations or orders may be exercised–

(a)   either in relation to all cases to which the power extends, or in relation to those cases subject to specified exceptions, or in relation to any specified cases or classes of case;

(b)   so as to make, as respects the cases in relation to which it is exercised–

(i)   the full provision to which the power extends or any less provision (whether by way of exception or otherwise);

(ii)   the same provision for all cases in relation to which the power is exercised, or different provision for different cases or different classes of case or different provision as respects the same case or class of case for different purposes of this Act;

(iii)   any such provision either unconditionally or subject to any specified condition;

and where such a power is expressed to be exercisable for alternative purposes it may be exercised in relation to the same case for any or all of those purposes.

(5)   Powers to make regulations for the purposes of any one provision of this Act are without prejudice to powers to make regulations for the purposes of any other provision.

(6)   Without prejudice to any specific provision in this Act, a power conferred by this Act to make regulations includes power to make thereby such incidental, supplementary, consequential or transitional provision as appears to the authority making the regulations to be expedient for the purposes of those regulations.

(7)   Without prejudice to any specific provisions in this Act, a power conferred by any provision of this Act to make regulations includes power to provide for a person to exercise a discretion in dealing with any matter.

(8)   Any power conferred by this Act to make regulations relating to housing benefit or council tax benefit shall include power to make different provision for different areas or different authorities.

(9)   In this section ''Commissioner'' has the same meaning as in Chapter II of Part I.

Amendments

1.   Amended by the TCA 2002, Sch 4 para 13(2) (6.4.03).
2.   Inserted by the TCA 2002, Sch 4 para 13(3) (6.4.03).

Parliamentary control of regulations

80.–(1)   Subject to the provisions of this section, a statutory instrument containing (whether alone or with other provisions) regulations under–

(a)   section 7, 12(2) or 72 above; or

(b)   paragraph 12 of Schedule 1, paragraph 9 of Schedule 2 or paragraph 2 of Schedule 5 to this Act,

shall not be made unless a draft of the instrument has been laid before Parliament and been approved by a resolution of each House of Parliament.

(2)   A statutory instrument–

(a)   which contains (whether alone or with other provisions) regulations made under this Act by the Secretary of State[1 , the Treasury or the Commissioners of Inland Revenue]; and

(b)   which is not subject to any requirement that a draft of the instrument be laid before and approved by a resolution of each House of Parliament,

shall be subject to annulment in pursuance of a resolution of either House of Parliament.

(3)   A statutory instrument–

(a)   which contains (whether alone or with other provisions) regulations made under this Act by the Lord Chancellor; and

(b)   which is not subject to any requirement that a draft of the instrument be laid before and approved by a resolution of each House of Parliament,

shall be subject to annulment in pursuance of a resolution of either House of Parliament.

Amendment

1.   Amended by the TCA 2002, Sch 4 para 14 (6.4.03).

Interpretation: general

84.   In this Act–

''the Administration Act'' means the Social Security Administration Act 1992;

''the Child Support Act'' means the Child Support Act 1991;

''the Contributions and Benefits Act'' means the Social Security Contributions and Benefits Act 1992;

''the Jobseekers Act'' means the Jobseekers Act 1995;

''the Vaccine Damage Payments Act'' means the Vaccine Damage Payments Act 1979;

''prescribe'' means prescribe by regulations.

Short title, commencement and extent

87.–(1)   This Act may be cited as the Social Security Act 1998.

(2)   This Act, except–

(a)   sections 66, 69, 72 and 77 to 85, this section and Schedule 6 to this Act; and

(b)   subsection (1) of section 50 so far as relating to a sum which is chargeable to tax by virtue of section 313 of the Income and Corporation Taxes Act 1988, and subsections (2) to (4) of that section,

shall come into force on such day as may be appointed by order made by the Secretary of State; and different days may be appointed for different provisions and for different purposes.

(3)   An order under subsection (2) above may make such savings, or such transitional or consequential provision, as the Secretary of State considers necessary or expedient–

(a)   in preparation for or in connection with the coming into force of any provision of this Act; or

(b)   in connection with the operation of any enactment repealed or amended by a provision of this Act during any period when the repeal or amendment is not wholly in force.

SCHEDULE 1
APPEAL TRIBUNALS: SUPPLEMENTARY PROVISIONS
Tenure of office

1.–(1)   Subject to the following provisions of this paragraph, the President of appeal tribunals shall hold and vacate office in accordance with the terms of his appointment.

(2)   The President shall vacate his office on the day on which he attains the age of 70, but subject to section 26(4) to (6) of the Judicial Pensions and Retirement Act 1993 (power to authorise continuance in office up to the age of 75).

(3)   The President may be removed from office by the Lord Chancellor [¹ , with the concurrence of the Lord Chief Justice and the Lord President of the Court of Session,] on the ground of incapacity or misbehaviour.

(4)   Where the Lord Chancellor proposes to exercise a power conferred on him by sub-paragraph (3) above, it shall be his duty to consult the Lord Advocate with respect to the proposal.

Amendment

1.   Inserted by para 273 Sch 4 Constitutional Reform Act 2005 as from 3.4.06.

Remuneration etc.

2.   The Secretary of State may pay, or make such payments towards the provision of, such remuneration, pensions or allowances to or in respect of the President as he may determine.

3.   The Secretary of State may pay, or make such payments towards the provision of, such remuneration, pensions or allowances to or in respect of any person appointed under this Chapter to act as a member of an appeal tribunal, or as an expert to such a tribunal, as he may determine.

4.–(1)   The Secretary of State may pay–

(a)   to any person required to attend at any proceedings under section 12 of this Act [¹ , section 20 of the Child Support Act or paragraph 6 of Schedule 7 to the Child Support, Pensions and Social Security Act 2000]; or

(b)   to any person required under this Part (whether for the purposes of this Part or otherwise) to attend for or to submit himself to medical or other examination or treatment,

such travelling and other allowances as he may determine.

(2)   In this paragraph references to travelling and other allowances include references to compensation for loss of remunerative time but such compensation shall not be paid to any person in respect of any time during which he is in receipt of remuneration under paragraph 3 above.

Amendment

1.   Amended by the CSPSSA Sch 7 para 22 (2.7.01).

5.–(1)   Subject to sub-paragraph (2) below, the Secretary of State may pay such other expenses in connection with the work of any person or tribunal appointed or constituted under any provision of this Part as he may determine.

(2)   Expenses are not payable under sub-paragraph (1) above in connection with the work of a tribunal presided over by a Social Security Commissioner.

Officers and staff

6.   The Secretary of State may appoint such officers and staff as he thinks fit for the President and for appeal tribunals.

Functions of President

7.   The President shall ensure that appropriate steps are taken by an appeal tribunal to secure the confidentiality, in such circumstances as may be prescribed, of any prescribed material or any prescribed classes or categories of material.

8.–(1)   The President shall, after the requisite consultation, arrange such training for persons appointed to the panel constituted under section 6 above as he considers appropriate.

(2)   In sub-paragraph (1) above "the requisite consultation" means–

(a)   except in the case of medical practitioners, consultation with the Secretary of State;

(b)   in the case of such practitioners, consultation with the Chief Medical Officers of the Department of Health, the Welsh Office and the Scottish Office.

9.   The President shall supply the Secretary of State with such reports and other information with respect to the carrying out of the functions of appeal tribunals as the Secretary of State may require.

10. Each year the President shall make to the Secretary of State a written report, based on the cases coming before appeal tribunals, on the standards achieved by the Secretary of State in the making of decisions against which an appeal lies to an appeal tribunal; and the Secretary of State shall publish the report.

Clerks to appeal tribunals

11. The Secretary of State may by regulations provide–

(a) for clerks to be assigned to service appeal tribunals; and

(b) for clerks so assigned to be responsible for summoning members of the panel constituted under section 6 above to serve on such tribunals.

Delegation of certain functions of appeal tribunals

12.–(1) The Secretary of State may by regulations provide–

(a) for officers authorised by the Secretary of State to make any determinations which fall to be made by an appeal tribunal and which do not involve the determination of any appeal, application for leave to appeal or reference;

(b) for the procedure to be followed by such officers in making such determinations;

(c) for the manner in which such determinations by such officers may be called in question.

(2) A determination which would have the effect of preventing an appeal, application for leave to appeal or reference being determined by an appeal tribunal is not a determination of the appeal, application or reference for the purposes of sub-paragraph (1) above.

Certificates

13. A document bearing a certificate which–

(a) is signed by a person authorised in that behalf by the Secretary of State; and

(b) states that the document, apart from the certificate, is a record of a decision of an appeal tribunal or of an officer of the Secretary of State,

shall be conclusive evidence of the decision; and a certificate purporting to be so signed shall be deemed to be so signed unless the contrary is proved.

SCHEDULE 4
SOCIAL SECURITY COMMISSIONERS

1.–(1) Her Majesty may from time to time appoint, from among persons who have a 10 year general qualification or advocates or solicitors in Scotland of at least 10 years' standing–

(a) a Chief Social Security Commissioner; and

(b) such number of other Social Security Commissioners as Her Majesty thinks fit.

(2) If the Lord Chancellor considers that, in order to facilitate the disposal of the business of Social Security Commissioners, he should make an appointment in pursuance of this sub-paragraph, he may appoint–

(a) a person who has a 10 year general qualification; or

(b) an advocate or solicitor in Scotland of at least 10 years' standing; or

(c) a member of the bar of Northern Ireland or solicitor of the Supreme Court of Northern Ireland of at least 10 years' standing,

to be a Social Security Commissioner (but to be known as a deputy Commissioner) for such period or on such occasions as the Lord Chancellor thinks fit.

(3) In this paragraph ''10 year general qualification'' shall be construed in accordance with section 71 of the Courts and Legal Services Act 1990.

Remuneration etc.

2. The Lord Chancellor shall pay to a Commissioner such salary or other remuneration, and such expenses incurred in connection with the work of a Commissioner or any tribunal presided over by a Commissioner, as he may determine.

3.–(1) The Lord Chancellor or, in Scotland, the Secretary of State may pay to any person who attends any proceedings under section 14 of this Act [¹ or under paragraph 8 of Schedule 7 to the Child Support, Pensions and Social Security Act 2000] such travelling and other allowances as he may determine.

(2) In this paragraph the reference to travelling and other allowances includes a reference to compensation for loss of remunerative time.

Amendment

1. Amended by the CSPSSA Sch 7 para 22 (2.7.01).

Tenure of office

4.–(1) Commissioners shall vacate their offices on the day on which they attain the age of 70, but subject to section 26(4) to (6) of the Judicial Pensions and Retirement Act 1993 (power to authorise continuance in office up to the age of 75).

(2) Nothing in sub-paragraph (1) above or in section 13 or 32 of the Judicial Pensions Act 1981 (which relate to pensions for commissioners) shall apply to a person by virtue of his appointment in pursuance of paragraph 1(2) above.

5.–(1) A Commissioner may be removed from office by the Lord Chancellor on the ground of incapacity or misbehaviour.

[¹ (1A) The Lord Chancellor may remove a person under sub-paragraph (1) only with the concurrence of the appropriate senior judge.

(1B) The appropriate senior judge is the Lord Chief Justice of England and Wales, unless the person exercises functions wholly or mainly in Scotland, in which case it is the Lord President of the Court of Session.]

(2) Nothing in sub-paragraph (1) above applies to a Commissioner appointed before 23rd May 1980.

Amendment

1.   Inserted by para 272 Sch 4 Constitutional Reform Act 2005 as from 3.4.06.

Delegation of functions

6.   The Lord Chancellor may by regulations provide–

(a)   for officers authorised by the Lord Chancellor or, in Scotland, by the Secretary of State to make any determinations which fall to be made by Commissioners;

(b)   for the procedure to be followed by such officers in making such determinations;

(c)   for the manner in which such determinations by such officers may be called in question.

Certificates

7.   A document bearing a certificate which–

(a)   is signed by a person authorised in that behalf by the Secretary of State; and

(b)   states that the document, apart from the certificate, is a record of a decision of a Commissioner, shall be conclusive evidence of the decision; and a certificate purporting to be so signed shall be deemed to be so signed unless the contrary is proved.

Supplemental

8.   Where the Lord Chancellor proposes to exercise a power conferred on him by paragraph 1(2), 5(1) or 6 above, it shall be his duty to consult the Lord Advocate with respect to the proposal.

SCHEDULE 5

REGULATIONS AS TO PROCEDURE: PROVISION WHICH MAY BE MADE

General Note

These provisions authorise various regulations governing procedure before tribunals and commissioners. The following list shows which regulations are made under which paragraphs:

(1)   See reg 40 SSCS D&A Regs and reg 26 SSCP Regs.

(2)   See reg 46 SSCS D&A Regs.

(3)   No relevant exercise of this power.

(4)   See regs 31, 32, 33 and 58 SSCS D&A Regs and regs 9, 13 and 33 SSCP Regs.

(5)   See reg 43 SSCS D&A Regs.

(6)   See Part V SSCS D&A Regs as a whole.

(7)   No relevant exercise of this power.

(8)   See reg 48 SSCS D&A Regs, now revoked.

(9)   See reg 42 SSCS D&A Regs.

1.   Provision prescribing the procedure to be followed in connection with–

(a)   the making of decisions or determinations by the Secretary of State, an appeal tribunal or a Commissioner; and

(b)   the withdrawal of claims, applications, appeals or references falling to be decided or determined by the Secretary of State, an appeal tribunal or a Commissioner.

2.   Provision as to the striking out or reinstatement of proceedings.

3.   Provision as to the form which is to be used for any document, the evidence which is to be required and the circumstances in which any official record or certificate is to be sufficient or conclusive evidence.

4.   Provision as to the time within which, or the manner in which–
(a)   any evidence is to be produced; or
(b)   any application, reference or appeal is to be made.

5.   Provision for summoning persons to attend and give evidence or produce documents and for authorising the administration of oaths to witnesses.

6.   Provision with respect to the procedure to be followed on appeals to and in other proceedings before appeal tribunals.

7.   Provision for authorising an appeal tribunal consisting of two or more members to proceed with any case, with the consent of the claimant, in the absence of any member.

8.   Provision for empowering an appeal tribunal to give directions for the disposal of any purported appeal which the tribunal is satisfied that it does not have jurisdiction to entertain.

9.   Provision for the non-disclosure to a person of the particulars of any medical advice or medical evidence given or submitted for the purposes of a determination.

Human Rights Act 1998
(1998 c42)

General Note to the Act

The Human Rights Act 1998 was the result of the expressed intention of the Labour Government elected in 1997 to give domestic force to the European Convention on Human Rights and Fundamental Freedoms. Despite suggestions at the time it was passed that the British constitution and its traditions were under threat and that it would lead to judges, rather than Parliament, making the law, its actual impact has been modest in the social welfare field. Many challenges have been brought and few have succeeded. This is as true of challenges in the social security field as elsewhere. This is due to the fact that the Convention rights provide little by way of social rights, being directed principally to ensuring personal freedoms.

No attempt is made below to deal with the implications of the Convention in criminal proceedings, for which reference should be made to specialist works on criminal law.

ARRANGEMENT OF SECTIONS

Introduction

1. The Convention Rights.
2. Interpretation of Convention rights.

Legislation

3. Interpretation of legislation.
4. Declaration of incompatibility.
5. Right of Crown to intervene.

Public authorities

6. Acts of public authorities.
7. Proceedings.
8. Judicial remedies.
9. Judicial acts.

Remedial action

10. Power to take remedial action.

Other rights and proceedings

11. Safeguard for existing human rights.
13. Freedom of thought, conscience and religion.

Derogations and reservations (Omitted)

Judges of the European Court of Human Rights (Omitted)

Supplemental

20. Orders etc. under this Act.
21. Interpretation, etc.
22. Short title, commencement, application and extent.

SCHEDULES

1. The Articles.
2. Remedial Orders.

Introduction

The Convention Rights

1.–(1) In this Act "the Convention rights" means the rights and fundamental freedoms set out in–

(a)   Articles 2 to 12 and 14 of the Convention,

(b)   Articles 1 to 3 of the First Protocol, and

(c)   Articles 1 and 2 of the Sixth Protocol,

as read with Articles 16 to 18 of the Convention.

(2)   Those Articles are to have effect for the purposes of this Act subject to any designated derogation or reservation (as to which see sections 14 and 15).

(3)   The Articles are set out in Schedule 1.

(4)   The Secretary of State may by order make such amendments to this Act as he considers appropriate to reflect the effect, in relation to the United Kingdom, of a protocol.

(5)   In subsection (4) ''protocol'' means a protocol to the Convention–

(a)   which the United Kingdom has ratified; or

(b)   which the United Kingdom has signed with a view to ratification.

(6)   No amendment may be made by an order under subsection (4) so as to come into force before the protocol concerned is in force in relation to the United Kingdom.

Interpretation of Convention rights

2.–(1)   A court or tribunal determining a question which has arisen in connection with a Convention right must take into account any–

(a)   judgment, decision, declaration or advisory opinion of the European Court of Human Rights,

(b)   opinion of the Commission given in a report adopted under Article 31 of the Convention,

(c)   decision of the Commission in connection with Article 26 or 27(2) of the Convention, or

(d)   decision of the Committee of Ministers taken under Article 46 of the Convention,

whenever made or given, so far as, in the opinion of the court or tribunal, it is relevant to the proceedings in which that question has arisen.

(2)   Evidence of any judgment, decision, declaration or opinion of which account may have to be taken under this section is to be given in proceedings before any court or tribunal in such manner as may be provided by rules.

(3)   In this section ''rules'' means rules of court or, in the case of proceedings before a tribunal, rules made for the purposes of this section–

(a)   by the Lord Chancellor or the Secretary of State, in relation to any proceedings outside Scotland;

(b)   by the Secretary of State, in relation to proceedings in Scotland; or

(c)   by a Northern Ireland department, in relation to proceedings before a tribunal in Northern Ireland–

    (i)   which deals with transferred matters; and

    (ii)   for which no rules made under paragraph (a) are in force.

General Note

This section deals with the effect of decisions of the European Court of Human Rights and the European Commission on Human Rights. The key words in s2 are "must take into account". Decisions are not therefore binding. However, great respect is accorded to Strasbourg decisions by the domestic courts, and it has been held that there should be a "special reason" for a departure from the learning of the Court or Commission: *R (Alconbury Developments Ltd) v Secretary of State for the Environment, Transport and the Regions* [2003] 2 AC 295, HL. This will especially be the case if the Strasbourg decision is recent and authoritative: see *Attorney General's Reference No 4 of 2002 [2004] UKHL 43* (para 33); and *R v Secretary of State for the Home Department, ex p Anderson* [2002] UKHL 46 (paras 17-18).

However, in almost all cases where there is a conflict between Strasbourg caselaw and a decision of a superior court in the UK the inferior court or tribunal in the UK should follow the decision of the superior (UK) court: *Leeds City Council v Price* [2006] UKHL 10, [2006] 4 All ER 128 (paras 43-44).

The most widely available, and most useful set of reports is the *European Human Rights Reports* published by Sweet and Maxwell. Butterworths' *Human Rights Cases* also publish some decisions which are not available in the EHRR. Reports of decisions are also available on the internet through the HUDOC website which may be found at this address: http://hudoc.echr.coe.int/hudoc/.

Legislation

Interpretation of legislation

3.–(1) So far as it is possible to do so, primary legislation and subordinate legislation must be read and given effect in a way which is compatible with the Convention rights.

(2)   This section–

(a)   applies to primary legislation and subordinate legislation whenever enacted;

(b)   does not affect the validity, continuing operation or enforcement of any incompatible primary legislation; and

(c)   does not affect the validity, continuing operation or enforcement of any incompatible subordinate legislation if (disregarding any possibility of revocation) primary legislation prevents removal of the incompatibility.

General Note

This is the first of the four sections that deal with the impact of the Convention on domestic law and administration. It is concerned with the technique for interpreting legislation that may be incompatible with a Convention right.

Analysis

Subs (1) states the general interpretative principle. It is a direction in strong terms: legislation must be read consistently with the Convention "so far as it is possible to do so". Before the 1998 Act came into force, resort could be had to the Convention as an aid to interpretation only to resolve an ambiguity in the meaning of a provision: see eg, *R v Secretary of State for the Home Department ex p Brind* [1991] 1 AC 696 at 747G-748F, 760D-762B, HL. It is clear that s3(1) requires a much more robust approach. The leading cases on the approach required by s3(1) are *R v A (No 2)* [2001] 2 AC 91, HL, *Re S* [2002] 2 AC 291, HL and *Ghaidan v Godin-Mendoza* [2004] UKHL 30, 3 All ER 411. In *R v A (No 2)*, a challenge was made to legislation excluding cross-examination of complainants in rape trials about previous sexual history, including any previous relationship with the accused. Lord Steyn set out the general approach required by s3(1):

".... the interpretative obligation under section 3 of the 1998 Act is a strong one. It applies even if there is no ambiguity in the language in the sense of the language being capable of two different meanings. ... Section 3 places a duty on the court to strive to find a possible interpretation compatible with Convention rights. Under ordinary methods of interpretation a court may depart from the language of the statute to avoid absurd consequences: section 3 goes much further. Undoubtedly, a court must always look for a contextual and purposive interpretation: section 3 is more radical in its effect. It is a general principle of the interpretation of legal instruments that the text is the primary source of interpretation ... Section 3 qualifies this general principle because it requires a court to find an interpretation compatible with Convention rights if it is possible to do so. In the progress of the Bill through Parliament the Lord Chancellor observed that 'in 99% of the cases that will arise, there will be no need for judicial declarations of incompatibility' and the Home Secretary said 'We expect that, in almost all cases, the courts will be able to interpret the legislation compatibility with the Convention'. ... In accordance with the will of Parliament as reflected in section 3 it will sometimes be necessary to adopt an interpretation which linguistically may appear strained. The techniques to be used will not only involve the reading down of express language in a statute but also the implication of provisions. A declaration of incompatibility [under s4] is a measure of last resort. It must be avoided unless it is plainly impossible to do so." (at para 44)

Lord Hutton emphasised (at para 162) that s3(1) had to be utilised unless it was "impossible" to achieve the objective set out therein.

There are, however, limits to the exercise required by s3(1). It is limited to interpreting legislation, and does not allow judges "to act as legislators" and to override express or implied prohibitions in the legislation against adopting the proposed interpretation: *Re S* paras 37-41. The decision in *Re S* requires the court to be sure that the proposed modification is workable before it operates s3. Moreover, it is a precondition of carrying out the exercise under s3(1) that the ordinary interpretation of the legislation should conflict with a

Convention right: *R v A (No 2)* at para 37; *Poplar Housing Association Ltd v Donoghue* [2002] QB 58, CA. The modification of the ordinary meaning of the legislation should be the minimum possible to achieve compatibility with the Convention: *Donoghue*, para 75(b). It should be possible to formulate, in words, the way in which the legislation has to be read in order for a compatible interpretation to be adopted: *R v Lambert* [2002] 2 AC 545, para 80, HL.

Ghaidan emphasises that use of the interpretive tool provided by s3(1) is not dependent on finding an ambiguity in the legislation, and s3 may require the tribunal or court to depart from the unambiguous meaning the legislation would otherwise bear. Section 3 may therefore require the decision-making body to depart from the intention of Parliament which enacted the legislation. However, the duty under s3 does not extend to allowing the courts to legislate, in the sense of reading in words which Parliament did not intend or otherwise adopting a meaning which is inconsistent with the underlying thrust of the legislation in question.

Subs (2) preserves the sovereignty of Parliament. The 1998 Act is no different to any other statute. It does not enable other statutes to be disregarded, and does not affect the continuing validity of such statutes. The same applies to secondary legislation such as regulations but *only* if "primary legislation prevents the removal of the incompatibility". Thus secondary legislation which is made under the general powers in the SSCBA, SSAA and other primary legislation in this book will be struck down if it is incompatible with Convention rights, since those powers are permissive and not mandatory; they do not *require* the regulations to exist in the form that they exist.

If it is alleged, therefore, that regulations are incompatible with the Convention and they cannot be read in a way which is consistent with Convention rights under s3(1), then they will have become *ultra vires* from the time that the 1998 Act came into force.

Declaration of incompatibility

4.–(1) Subsection (2) applies in any proceedings in which a court determines whether a provision of primary legislation is compatible with a Convention right.

(2) If the court is satisfied that the provision is incompatible with a Convention right, it may make a declaration of that incompatibility.

(3) Subsection (4) applies in any proceedings in which a court determines whether a provision of subordinate legislation, made in the exercise of a power conferred by primary legislation, is compatible with a Convention right.

(4) If the court is satisfied–

(a) that the provision is incompatible with a Convention right, and

(b) that (disregarding any possibility of revocation) the primary legislation concerned prevents removal of the incompatibility,

it may make a declaration of that incompatibility.

(5) In this section "court" means–

(a) the House of Lords;

(b) the Judicial Committee of the Privy Council;

(c) the Courts-Martial Appeal Court;

(d) in Scotland, the High Court of Justiciary sitting otherwise than as a trial court or the Court of Session;

(e) in England and Wales or Northern Ireland, the High Court or the Court of Appeal.

(6) A declaration under this section ("a declaration of incompatibility")–

(a) does not affect the validity, continuing operation or enforcement of the provision in respect of which it is given; and

(b) is not binding on the parties to the proceedings in which it is made.

General Note

The second means by which the Convention rights can impact on the law is through a declaration of incompatibility. But the effect of such a declaration is limited. It does not affect the validity of the legislation and is not binding upon the parties: see subs (6). Its sole purpose is to allow the Secretary of State to make a remedial order under s10 and Sch 2.

A declaration of incompatibility may only be made by a "court" as defined in subs (5). Thus authorities, tribunals and commissioners have no power to grant such declarations. The usual mode of seeking a declaration of incompatibility will be by way of a claim for judicial review. The same could be done on appeal from a commissioner.

Right of Crown to intervene

5.–(1)   Where a court is considering whether to make a declaration of incompatibility, the Crown is entitled to notice in accordance with rules of court.

(2)   In any case to which subsection (1) applies–

(a)   a Minister of the Crown (or a person nominated by him),

(b)   a member of the Scottish Executive,

(c)   a Northern Ireland Minister,

(d)   a Northern Ireland department,

is entitled, on giving notice in accordance with rules of court, to be joined as a party to the proceedings.

(3)   Notice under subsection (2) may be given at any time during the proceedings.

(4)   A person who has been made a party to criminal proceedings (other than in Scotland) as the result of a notice under subsection (2) may, with leave, appeal to the House of Lords against any declaration of incompatibility made in the proceedings.

(5)   In subsection (4)–

"criminal proceedings" includes all proceedings before the Courts-Martial Appeal Court; and

"leave" means leave granted by the court making the declaration of incompatibility or by the House of Lords.

General Note

For guidance as to the procedure to adopt under s5, see *Poplar Housing Association Ltd v Donoghue* [2002] QB 58, CA.

Public authorities

Acts of public authorities

6.–(1)   It is unlawful for a public authority to act in a way which is incompatible with a Convention right.

(2)   Subsection (1) does not apply to an act if–

(a)   as the result of one or more provisions of primary legislation, the authority could not have acted differently; or

(b)   in the case of one or more provisions of, or made under, primary legislation which cannot be read or given effect in a way which is compatible with the Convention rights, the authority was acting so as to give effect to or enforce those provisions.

(3)   In this section "public authority" includes–

(a)   a court or tribunal, and

(b)   any person certain of whose functions are functions of a public nature,

but does not include either House of Parliament or a person exercising functions in connection with proceedings in Parliament.

(4)   In subsection (3) "Parliament" does not include the House of Lords in its judicial capacity.

(5)   In relation to a particular act, a person is not a public authority by virtue only of subsection (3)(b) if the nature of the act is private.

(6)   "An act" includes a failure to act but does not include a failure to–

(a)   introduce in, or lay before, Parliament a proposal for legislation; or

(b)   make any primary legislation or remedial order.

General Note

This section forbids public authorities, with important exceptions, from infringing Convention rights by the way in which they act on a day-to-day basis.

Analysis

Subsections (1), (2) and (6): The basic prohibition

Subs (1) sets out the basic prohibition, which is then qualified by subs (2) and (6). For enforcement of this obligation, see s7 below.

Subs (2) follows the same aim of preserving Parliament as the supreme legislative authority. Under para (a), any public body which "could not have" acted in a different way as a result of obedience to primary legislation will not act unlawfully under subs (1). However, the words "could not have" emphasise that where the public body is given a discretion as to how it acts, it may breach s6(1) by acting unlawfully.

Para (b) is more problematic. It applies both to primary legislation and secondary legislation. However, it is suggested that it will only apply to secondary legislation if its existence in the incompatible form is made compulsory by primary legislation, since otherwise the secondary legislation will be rendered *ultra vires* as a result of its incompatibility with the Convention right: see *R (Bono) v Harlow DC HBRB* [2002] 1 WLR 2475 paras 34-35, Richards J.

Subs (6) makes it clear that "act" includes omissions. It then goes on to preserve Parliamentary sovereignty by excluding from the definition a failure by a minister or Parliament to legislate. A failure to make a remedial order may also not be impugned under s6, since this would have the effect of enforcing the court's declaration of incompatibility.

Subsections (3) to (5): "Public body"

The critical question is: what is a "public body" for the purposes of s6? The definition in subs (3) does not purport to be a complete guide. Clearly, a local authority or the Secretary of State for Work and Pensions is a "public body". However, in the context of HB and CTB, it may be important to know whether contractors performing functions on behalf of a local authority or social landlords assisting in verification work (see Circulars HB/CTB A21/2001 and A43/2001 for proposals about this) are "public bodies". For the purposes of possession proceedings, similarly, it will be necessary to know whether social landlords are constrained by the obligation in s6(1).

Subs (3)(a) and (4) confirm that courts and tribunals (which includes appeal tribunals and commissioners) are public bodies and hence are bound by the prohibition in subs (1). Subs (4) confirms that the House of Lords, when acting in its judicial capacity, will be obliged to comply with the Convention just as any other court must.

Subs (3)(b) and (5) introduce the concept of a "functional" public authority; a body existing under private law but which is exercising functions of a public nature. The words "certain of whose" make it clear that the body may exercise private functions alongside its public functions without taking it outside the scope of "public body". Such a body will only be a "public body" in relation to its public acts, however, as subs (5) makes clear.

This distinction has now been illuminated by caselaw. In *Donaghue v Poplar Housing Association Ltd* [2002] QB 58, CA, a tenant sought to impugn the decision of her landlord, a housing association, to seek possession of her home. She was an assured shorthold tenant under a tenancy conferred on her pursuant to an obligation of the local authority and her tenancy had been terminated under s21 of the Housing Act 1988, which gives a landlord an absolute right to possession. She contended that this was a breach of her right to respect for her home under Art 8 of the Convention. The Court of Appeal held that the meaning of "public body" should be given "a generous interpretation" (para 58). It went on to say (para 59):

> "The purpose of s6(3)(b) is to deal with hybrid bodies which have both public and private functions. It is not to make a body, which does not have responsibilities to the public, a public body merely because it performs acts on behalf of a public body which would constitute public functions were such acts to be performed by the public body itself. An act can remain of a private nature even though it is performed because another body is under a public duty to ensure that that act is performed."

The court concluded (para 66) that the close links between the local authority and the housing association in that case meant that the association was a public body for the purposes of granting and terminating the claimant's tenancy. It went on to hold, however (paras 67-72) that there was no breach of Art 8.

The close links between the housing association and the local authority did not exist in *R (Heather) v The Leonard Cheshire Foundation* [2001] 4 CCLR 211, Stanley Burton J. In that case the claimants challenged the closure of a care home on Art 8 grounds. The judge distinguished *Donaghue* on the ground that the special ties between the local authority and the landlord in *Donaghue* did not exist here. That decision was upheld by the Court of Appeal [2002] 2 All ER 936. That approach to the phrase "public authority" in the context of private care homes has been reaffirmed, albeit by a bare majority, by the House of Lords in *YL (by her litigation friend the Official Solicitor) v Birmingham City Council and others* [2007] UKHL 27, 20 June, HL.

It is suggested, however, that a private company carrying out HB functions on behalf of the local authority will be a "public body" in carrying out such functions. Furthermore, if a social landlord assists with verification work, it will be a "public body" for those purposes. However, a social landlord will not be a "public body" in acting as a landlord, without the special features present in *Donaghue v Poplar Housing Association Ltd* or something akin to them.

See further on "public authority" *Parochial Church Council of the Parish of Aston Cantlow and Wilmcote with Billesley, Warwickshire v Wallbank and others,* [2003] UKHL 37; [2003] 3 WLR 283 and *Hampshire County Council v Beer t/a Hammer Trout Farm,* [2003] EWCA Civ 1056; [2004] 1 WLR 233.

Proceedings

7.–(1)   A person who claims that a public authority has acted (or proposes to act) in a way which is made unlawful by section 6(1) may–

(a)   bring proceedings against the authority under this Act in the appropriate court or tribunal, or

(b)   rely on the Convention right or rights concerned in any legal proceedings,

but only if he is (or would be) a victim of the unlawful act.

(2)   In subsection (1)(a) ''appropriate court or tribunal'' means such court or tribunal as may be determined in accordance with rules; and proceedings against an authority include a counterclaim or similar proceeding.

(3)   If the proceedings are brought on an application for judicial review, the applicant is to be taken to have a sufficient interest in relation to the unlawful act only if he is, or would be, a victim of that act.

(4)   If the proceedings are made by way of a petition for judicial review in Scotland, the applicant shall be taken to have title and interest to sue in relation to the unlawful act only if he is, or would be, a victim of that act.

(5)   Proceedings under subsection (1)(a) must be brought before the end of–

(a)   the period of one year beginning with the date on which the act complained of took place; or

(b)   such longer period as the court or tribunal considers equitable having regard to all the circumstances,

but that is subject to any rule imposing a stricter time limit in relation to the procedure in question.

(6)   In subsection (1)(b) ''legal proceedings'' includes–

(a)   proceedings brought by or at the instigation of a public authority; and

(b)   an appeal against the decision of a court or tribunal.

(7)   For the purposes of this section, a person is a victim of an unlawful act only if he would be a victim for the purposes of Article 34 of the Convention if proceedings were brought in the European Court of Human Rights in respect of that act.

(8)   Nothing in this Act creates a criminal offence.

(9)   In this section ''rules'' means–

(a)   in relation to proceedings before a court or tribunal outside Scotland, rules made by the Lord Chancellor or the Secretary of State for the purposes of this section or rules of court,

(b)   in relation to proceedings before a court or tribunal in Scotland, rules made by the Secretary of State for those purposes,

(c)   in relation to proceedings before a tribunal in Northern Ireland–

(i)   which deals with transferred matters; and

(ii)   for which no rules made under paragraph (a) are in force,

rules made by a Northern Ireland department for those purposes,

and includes provision made by order under section 1 of the Courts and Legal Services Act 1990.

(10)   In making rules, regard must be had to section 9.

(11)   The Minister who has power to make rules in relation to a particular tribunal may, to the extent he considers it necessary to ensure that the tribunal can provide an appropriate remedy in relation to an act (or proposed act) of a public authority which is (or would be) unlawful as a result of section 6(1), by order add to–

(a)   the relief or remedies which the tribunal may grant; or

(b)   the grounds on which it may grant any of them.

(12)   An order made under subsection (11) may contain such incidental, supplemental, consequential or transitional provision as the Minister making it considers appropriate.

(13)   ''The Minister'' includes the Northern Ireland department concerned.

General Note

This section deals with the procedure by which allegations of a breach of Convention rights can be raised for the consideration of the courts and tribunals.

Analysis

Subsections (1)(a), (2) to (5) and (7) to (13): Bringing proceedings for a breach of the Convention

Taken together, these subsections envisage the commencement of proceedings before a court or tribunal complaining of the breach of the Convention. By its terms, the right to commence proceedings under subs (1)(a) may apply even where the breach has not yet occurred, in which case an injunction (interdict in Scotland) may be sought to restrain the breach.

Subs (1)(a) and (2) restrict the right to bring proceedings to a court or tribunal that may be identified in accordance with rules as being the appropriate forum in which to proceed. By r7.11 of the Civil Procedure Rules 1998, in England and Wales proceedings may be issued in the High Court or the County Court, except where complaint is made about a judicial act in which case proceedings must be commenced in the High Court: see s9 below for complaints about judicial acts.

No rules have been made conferring a right to commence proceedings in a tribunal or before the commissioner. However, Convention rights may be relied upon in an appeal under subs (1)(b).

Subs (1)(a), (3), (4) and (7) deal with the right to bring proceedings. A person must be a "victim" for the purposes of the Convention if s/he is to have the right to commence proceedings. That will include proceedings for judicial review, where the test of standing (England and Wales) or title and interest (Scotland) is different.

Art 34 of the Convention, referred to in subs (7), does not define "victim". The following rules are a summary of the caselaw of the Court and commissioner on the subject: see eg, Starmer, *European Human Rights Law* (2000) paras 2.18-2.39.

(1) The Convention applies to persons not in the country or acts taking place outside the country if they are done on behalf of the state.
(2) A corporate body may be a victim. A governmental organisation, however, cannot bring proceedings.
(3) Those potentially affected, as well as those who have already been affected, may bring proceedings as long as the risk of a breach of the Convention is not merely theoretical.
(4) People indirectly affected, such as the family members of a claimant, or shareholders in a company that is a landlord, may be a "victim". Claims may also be brought by personal representatives on death or incapacity.

Subs (5) imposes a one-year limitation period in respect of the commencement of proceedings. That time limit is, however, subject to any stricter time limit provided for by relevant rules.

Subs (9) to (13) deal with rule-making powers.

Subsections (1)(b) and (6): Relying on a breach of the Convention in proceedings

Breaches of Convention rights may be relied upon in any proceedings. These will include appeals to a tribunal or subsequent appeals to the commissioner or beyond. If proceedings are brought, for example for possession, it will be possible to allege that the court would act in breach of the Convention by granting possession as well as that the claimant is itself acting in breach of the Convention if it is a public body. For an example of this approach, see *Donaghue v Poplar Housing Association Ltd* [2002] QB 58, CA, where the tenant alleged that the court was in breach of Art 6 for proceeding in an unfair manner and the claimant landlord was in breach of Art 8 by seeking possession.

Judicial remedies

8.–(1) In relation to any act (or proposed act) of a public authority which the court finds is (or would be) unlawful, it may grant such relief or remedy, or make such order, within its powers as it considers just and appropriate.

(2) But damages may be awarded only by a court which has power to award damages, or to order the payment of compensation, in civil proceedings.

(3) No award of damages is to be made unless, taking account of all the circumstances of the case, including–

(a) any other relief or remedy granted, or order made, in relation to the act in question (by that or any other court), and

(b) the consequences of any decision (of that or any other court) in respect of that act,

the court is satisfied that the award is necessary to afford just satisfaction to the person in whose favour it is made.

(4) In determining–

(a)   whether to award damages, or

(b)   the amount of an award,

the court must take into account the principles applied by the European Court of Human Rights in relation to the award of compensation under Article 41 of the Convention.

(5)   A public authority against which damages are awarded is to be treated–

(a)   in Scotland, for the purposes of section 3 of the Law Reform (Miscellaneous Provisions) (Scotland) Act 1940 as if the award were made in an action of damages in which the authority has been found liable in respect of loss or damage to the person to whom the award is made;

(b)   for the purposes of the Civil Liability (Contribution) Act 1978 as liable in respect of damage suffered by the person to whom the award is made.

(6)   In this section–

"court" includes a tribunal;

"damages" means damages for an unlawful act of a public authority; and

"unlawful" means unlawful under section 6(1).

General Note

This section deals with the remedies that a court or tribunal may grant when proceedings are brought under s7 against a public body.

Analysis

Subs (1) and (2) allow a court (which includes, by virtue of subs (6), a tribunal) to grant remedies for acts which are unlawful under s6. However, the key phrase here is "within its powers". There is no additional power to grant remedies conferred by s8. It follows that tribunals and commissioners have no power to award damages or costs by virtue of the 1998 Act, as confirmed by subs (2).

Subs (3) to (5) deal with awards of damages. An award of damages is only to be made if it is necessary to give "just satisfaction" to the victim. This is a phrase which originates in Art 41, and indeed subs (4) requires a court to consider the caselaw under Art 41 in deciding whether to award damages and, if so, how much.

However, it is difficult to distil any clear principles from the Strasbourg caselaw. Domestic caselaw has now illuminated the situations in which damages will be awarded for breaches of Art 8 of the Convention. In *R (Anufrijeva) v Southwark LBC* [2003] EWCA Civ 1406, CA, the Court of Appeal gave guidance on this question. The court said (para 65) that a broad-brush approach should be adopted. Where there is pecuniary loss caused by the breach, that will ordinarily be calculated and awarded (para 59). However, non-pecuniary loss causes greater difficulty, as recognised by the Court at para 60:

"Infringements can involve a variety of treatment of an individual which is objectionable in itself. The treatment may give rise to distress, anxiety, and, in extreme cases, psychiatric trauma. The primary object of the proceedings will often be to bring the adverse treatment to an end. If this is achieved is this enough to constitute 'just satisfaction' or is it necessary to award damages to compensate for the adverse treatment that has occurred? More particularly, should damages be awarded for anxiety and distress that has been occasioned by the breach? It is in relation to these questions that Strasbourg fails to give a consistent or coherent answer."

In cases of maladministration such as those being considered by the Court, the "critical message is that the remedy has to be 'just and appropriate' and 'necessary' to afford 'just satisfaction'" (para 66). In deciding whether the breach of rights required an award of damages, the Court said that the scale and manner of the breach, and the conduct of the parties, would all be relevant (paras 66-68). As far as quantum was concerned, the amounts awarded should be modest but not minimal, and comparable awards by the Local Government Ombudsman are a useful comparator (paras 75, 78). It appears that the £10,000 awarded to the claimants in *R (Bernard) v Enfield LBC* [2002] 5 CCLR 589 for leaving a severely disabled woman and her family in appalling and degrading living conditions for a considerable period of time is the very maximum award that should be made for a breach of Art 8.

The court also gave guidance as to the procedure that should be followed in relation to damages claims, having expressed its concern at the cost of the litigation before it (paras 81). Damages claims for maladministration should ordinarily proceed by way of judicial review and the claimant should be prepared to justify not using the Ombudsman or Adjudicator instead. Claims for damages should be determined on the papers by the appropriate level of judge, if necessary separately to any claim for other relief (such as an order to compel a local authority to determine a claim).

However, in *R(Greenfield) v Secretary of State for the Home Department* [2005] UKHL 14, [2005] 2 All ER 240, HL, the House of Lords, albeit in the context of a claim for damages for breach of Article 6, rejected the claimant's argument, which was predicated at least in part on the approach said to have been adopted in *R (Bernard) v Enfield* and *Anufrijeva*, that courts in England and Wales, when exercising their power to award damages under s8, should apply domestic scales of damages. In Lord Bingham's opinion one of the broader reasons why this approach should not be followed was that the Human Rights Act is not a tort statute: its objects are different and broader. As such, even in a case where a finding of violation is not judged to afford the applicant just satisfaction (and in most Article 6 violation cases the finding of breach of Article 6 should, in Lord Bingham's view, of itself provide the just satisfaction or remedy), such a finding will be an important part of the claimant's remedy. Accordingly, in Article 6 cases at least awards of damages should be modestly low.

Overall, Lord Bingham's view in *Greenfield* was that courts in the United Kingdom, although not inflexibly bound by Strasbourg awards in what may be different cases, should not aim to be significantly more or less generous than the European Court of Human Rights might be expected to be, in a case where it was willing to make an award at all.

Judicial acts

9.–(1) Proceedings under section 7(1)(a) in respect of a judicial act may be brought only–

(a) by exercising a right of appeal;

(b) on an application (in Scotland a petition) for judicial review; or

(c) in such other forum as may be prescribed by rules.

(2) That does not affect any rule of law which prevents a court from being the subject of judicial review.

(3) In proceedings under this Act in respect of a judicial act done in good faith, damages may not be awarded otherwise than to compensate a person to the extent required by Article 5(5) of the Convention.

(4) An award of damages permitted by subsection (3) is to be made against the Crown; but no award may be made unless the appropriate person, if not a party to the proceedings, is joined.

(5) In this section–

"appropriate person" means the Minister responsible for the court concerned, or a person or government department nominated by him;

"court" includes a tribunal;

"judge" includes a member of a tribunal, a justice of the peace and a clerk or other officer entitled to exercise the jurisdiction of a court;

"judicial act" means a judicial act of a court and includes an act done on the instructions, or on behalf, of a judge; and

"rules" has the same meaning as in section 7(9).

Remedial action

Power to take remedial action

10.–(1) This section applies if–

(a) a provision of legislation has been declared under section 4 to be incompatible with a Convention right and, if an appeal lies–

(i) all persons who may appeal have stated in writing that they do not intend to do so;

(ii) the time for bringing an appeal has expired and no appeal has been brought within that time; or

(iii) an appeal brought within that time has been determined or abandoned; or

(b) it appears to a Minister of the Crown or Her Majesty in Council that, having regard to a finding of the European Court of Human Rights made after the coming into force of this section in proceedings against the United Kingdom, a provision of legislation is incompatible with an obligation of the United Kingdom arising from the Convention.

(2)   If a Minister of the Crown considers that there are compelling reasons for proceeding under this section, he may by order make such amendments to the legislation as he considers necessary to remove the incompatibility.

(3)   If, in the case of subordinate legislation, a Minister of the Crown considers–

(a)   that it is necessary to amend the primary legislation under which the subordinate legislation in question was made, in order to enable the incompatibility to be removed, and

(b)   that there are compelling reasons for proceeding under this section,

he may by order make such amendments to the primary legislation as he considers necessary.

(4)   This section also applies where the provision in question is in subordinate legislation and has been quashed, or declared invalid, by reason of incompatibility with a Convention right and the Minister proposes to proceed under paragraph 2(b) of Schedule 2.

(5)   If the legislation is an Order in Council, the power conferred by subsection (2) or (3) is exercisable by Her Majesty in Council.

(6)   In this section "legislation" does not include a Measure of the Church Assembly or of the General Synod of the Church of England.

(7)   Schedule 2 makes further provision about remedial orders.

Other rights and proceedings

Safeguard for existing human rights

11.   A person's reliance on a Convention right does not restrict–

(a)   any other right or freedom conferred on him by or under any law having effect in any part of the United Kingdom; or

(b)   his right to make any claim or bring any proceedings which he could make or bring apart from sections 7 to 9.

Freedom of thought, conscience and religion

13.–(1)   If a court's determination of any question arising under this Act might affect the exercise by a religious organisation (itself or its members collectively) of the Convention right to freedom of thought, conscience and religion, it must have particular regard to the importance of that right.

(2)   In this section "court" includes a tribunal.

Supplemental

Orders etc under this Act

20.–(1)   Any power of a Minister of the Crown to make an order under this Act is exercisable by statutory instrument.

(2)   The power of the Lord Chancellor or the Secretary of State to make rules (other than rules of court) under section 2(3) or 7(9) is exercisable by statutory instrument.

(3)   Any statutory instrument made under section 14, 15 or 16(7) must be laid before Parliament.

(4)   No order may be made by the Lord Chancellor or the Secretary of State under section 1(4), 7(11) or 16(2) unless a draft of the order has been laid before, and approved by, each House of Parliament.

(5)   Any statutory instrument made under section 18(7) or Schedule 4, or to which subsection (2) applies, shall be subject to annulment in pursuance of a resolution of either House of Parliament.

(6)   The power of a Northern Ireland department to make–

(a)   rules under section 2(3)(c) or 7(9)(c), or

(b)   an order under section 7(11),

is exercisable by statutory rule for the purposes of the Statutory Rules (Northern Ireland) Order 1979.

(7)   Any rules made under section 2(3)(c) or 7(9)(c) shall be subject to negative resolution; and section 41(6) of the Interpretation Act Northern Ireland) 1954 (meaning of "subject to negative resolution") shall apply as if the power to make the rules were conferred by an Act of the Northern Ireland Assembly.

(8)   No order may be made by a Northern Ireland department under section 7(11) unless a draft of the order has been laid before, and approved by, the Northern Ireland Assembly.

Interpretation etc

21.–(1)   In this Act–

"amend" includes repeal and apply (with or without modifications);

"the appropriate Minister" means the Minister of the Crown having charge of the appropriate authorised government department (within the meaning of the Crown Proceedings Act 1947);

"the Commission" means the European Commission of Human Rights;

"the Convention" means the Convention for the Protection of Human Rights and Fundamental Freedoms, agreed by the Council of Europe at Rome on 4th November 1950 as it has effect for the time being in relation to the United Kingdom;

"declaration of incompatibility" means a declaration under section 4;

"Minister of the Crown" has the same meaning as in the Ministers of the Crown Act 1975;

"Northern Ireland Minister" includes the First Minister and the deputy First Minister in Northern Ireland;

"primary legislation" means any–

   (a)   public general Act;
   (b)   local and personal Act;
   (c)   private Act;
   (d)   Measure of the Church Assembly;
   (e)   Measure of the General Synod of the Church of England;
   (f)   Order in Council–
      (i)   made in exercise of Her Majesty's Royal Prerogative;
      (ii)   made under section 38(1)(a) of the Northern Ireland Constitution Act 1973 or the corresponding provision of the Northern Ireland Act 1998; or
      (iii) amending an Act of a kind mentioned in paragraph (a), (b) or (c);

and includes an order or other instrument made under primary legislation (otherwise than by the National Assembly for Wales, a member of the Scottish Executive, a Northern Ireland Minister or a Northern Ireland department) to the extent to which it operates to bring one or more provisions of that legislation into force or amends any primary legislation;

"the First Protocol" means the protocol to the Convention agreed at Paris on 20th March 1952;

"the Sixth Protocol" means the protocol to the Convention agreed at Strasbourg on 28th April 1983;

"the Eleventh Protocol" means the protocol to the Convention (restructuring the control machinery established by the Convention) agreed at Strasbourg on 11th May 1994;

"remedial order" means an order under section 10;

"subordinate legislation" means any–

   (a)   Order in Council other than one–
      (i)   made in exercise of Her Majesty's Royal Prerogative;

      (ii)   made under section 38(1)(a) of the Northern Ireland Constitution Act 1973 or the corresponding provision of the Northern Ireland Act 1998; or

      (iii)   amending an Act of a kind mentioned in the definition of primary legislation;

(b)   Act of the Scottish Parliament;

(c)   Act of the Parliament of Northern Ireland;

(d)   Measure of the Assembly established under section 1 of the Northern Ireland Assembly Act 1973;

(e)   Act of the Northern Ireland Assembly;

(f)   order, rules, regulations, scheme, warrant, byelaw or other instrument made under primary legislation (except to the extent to which it operates to bring one or more provisions of that legislation into force or amends any primary legislation);

(g)   order, rules, regulations, scheme, warrant, byelaw or other instrument made under legislation mentioned in paragraph (b), (c), (d) or (e) or made under an Order in Council applying only to Northern Ireland;

(h)   order, rules, regulations, scheme, warrant, byelaw or other instrument made by a member of the Scottish Executive, a Northern Ireland Minister or a Northern Ireland department in exercise of prerogative or other executive functions of Her Majesty which are exercisable by such a person on behalf of Her Majesty;

"transferred matters" has the same meaning as in the Northern Ireland Act 1998; and

"tribunal" means any tribunal in which legal proceedings may be brought.

    (2)   The references in paragraphs (b) and (c) of section 2(1) to Articles are to Articles of the Convention as they had effect immediately before the coming into force of the Eleventh Protocol.

    (3)   The reference in paragraph (d) of section 2(1) to Article 46 includes a reference to Articles 32 and 54 of the Convention as they had effect immediately before the coming into force of the Eleventh Protocol.

    (4)   The references in section 2(1) to a report or decision of the Commission or a decision of the Committee of Ministers include references to a report or decision made as provided by paragraphs 3, 4 and 6 of Article 5 of the Eleventh Protocol (transitional provisions).

    (5)   Any liability under the Army Act 1955, the Air Force Act 1955 or the Naval Discipline Act 1957 to suffer death for an offence is replaced by a liability to imprisonment for life or any less punishment authorised by those Acts; and those Acts shall accordingly have effect with the necessary modifications.

Short title, commencement, application and extent

    22.–(1)   This Act may be cited as the Human Rights Act 1998.

    (2)   Sections 18, 20 and 21(5) and this section come into force on the passing of this Act.

    (3)   The other provisions of this Act come into force on such day as the Secretary of State may by order appoint; and different days may be appointed for different purposes.

    (4)   Paragraph (b) of subsection (1) of section 7 applies to proceedings brought by or at the instigation of a public authority whenever the act in question took place; but otherwise that subsection does not apply to an act taking place before the coming into force of that section.

    (5)   This Act binds the Crown.

    (6)   This Act extends to Northern Ireland.

(7)   Section 21(5), so far as it relates to any provision contained in the Army Act 1955, the Air Force Act 1955 or the Naval Discipline Act 1957, extends to any place to which that provision extends.

Analysis

Subs (3) provides that the bulk of the 1998 Act was to come into force on the making of orders. The Human Rights Act (Commencement) Order 1998 SI No 2882 brought s19 (which allows ministers presenting legislation to Parliament to make statements about the compatibility of Bills with the Convention) into force from 24 November 1998. The remainder of the Act was brought into force by the Human Rights Act (Commencement No 2) Order 2000 SI No 1851 from 2 October 2000.

Subs (4) applies a limited retrospectivity to the Act. It is clear that where a public authority brings proceedings, a breach of Convention rights may be relied upon whenever the breach occurred. Thus a claimant who is prosecuted, or a person sued for recovery of an overpayment of HB, may rely on breaches of the Convention occurring prior to 2 October 2000 in those proceedings. 'Proceedings' means legal proceedings and so section 22(4) does not apply to supersession (or revision) decisions instigated by a Secretary of State decision-maker as s/he only exercises administrative, and not legal, functions: *CDLA 1347/1999* para 29.

Judicial review proceedings are only technically brought in the name of the Crown. The reality is that they are instituted by the claimant, and accordingly damages cannot be claimed by a person whose Convention rights were breached prior to 2 October 2000 in judicial review proceedings: *R (Ben-Abdelaziz) v Secretary of State for the Home Department* [2001] 1 WLR 1485, CA.

The strict limits on the retrospectivity of the 1998 Act have now been confirmed by the House of Lords in *Wilson v First County Trust Ltd (No 2)* [2003] WLR 586. In *Wilson (No 2)*, it was confirmed that the 1998 Act has no application to events occurring prior to 2 October 2000 and so cannot give rise to any cause of action arising before that date save in the strictly limited circumstances set out in subs (4). Neither can the interpretative obligation in s3 apply to the law governing such a case (paras 10-23). The House of Lords did not find it necessary to decide whether the Court of Appeal's approach, in which it had decided that s6(1) obliged it to act compatibly with the Convention on an appeal, was incorrect in all cases. It could not, however, be correct in *Wilson (No 2)* because the court had purported to disapply primary legislation, which was prohibited by s6(2)(a) (paras 24-25).

The latter argument is, of course, of importance where a claimant asserts on an appeal heard after 2 October 2000 that a decision at a lower level in the appellate hierarchy breaches Convention Rights. In *CSDLA 1019/1999* (paras 70-89), the Tribunal of Commissioners ruled that an alleged breach of Art 6 in the constitution of a tribunal sitting prior to 2 October 2000 could not be relied upon on appeal. The tribunal's conclusion that the inclusion of a doctor who also carried out medical assessments for the Benefits Agency breached the common law rule against bias was overturned by the Court of Session in *Secretary of State for Work and Pensions v Gillies* [2003] 2004 SLT 14, reported at 2006 SC (HL) 71 (the decision of the Court of Session was upheld by the House of Lords in *Gillies v Secretary of State for Work and Pensions* [2006] UKHL 2, *Times Law Report*, 30 January, reported as *R(DLA) 5/06*). However, if a Tribunal sitting after 2 October 2000 breaches a claimant's Convention rights, it does not matter whether the decision under appeal was made before or after that date: *Wilson (No 2)* para 21 and *R(IS) 6/04*; though if the decision under appeal was made before 2 October 2000 it cannot be challenged on the ground that it breached the claimant's Convention rights.

SCHEDULE 1
THE ARTICLES

General Note on Schedule 1

Only the Articles which might conceivably be relevant to HB and CTB entitlement are set out below and discussion is limited to that which is reasonably necessary to consider the arguments that might arise.

Article 3
Prohibition of torture
No one shall be subjected to torture or to inhuman or degrading treatment or punishment.

Analysis

A refusal of HB will not of itself give rise to any breach of Art 3. It is now established that while a state may have a positive obligation under Art 3 to prevent an individual suffering from "degrading treatment", the individual's condition must be of the requisite severity: *Pretty v UK* [2002] 35 EHRR 1, ECHR, para 52, where the ECHR said:

"As regards the types of "treatment" which fall within the scope of Article 3 of the Convention, the Court's case law refers to "ill-treatment" that attains a minimum level of severity and involves actual bodily injury or intense physical or mental suffering. Where treatment humiliates or debases an individual showing lack of respect for, or diminishing, his or her human dignity or arouses feelings of fear, anguish or inferiority capable of breaking an individual's moral and physical resistance, it may be characterised as degrading and also fall within the prohibition of Article 3. The suffering which flows from naturally occurring illness, physical or mental, may be treatment, where it is, or risks being, exacerbated by treatment, whether flowing from conditions of detention, expulsion or other measures, for which the authorities can be held responsible."

A claimant who is refused HB will ordinarily be able to avail her/himself of other forms of welfare support, whether by moving to a property where a claim for HB is unobjectionable or by other means. However, the threat of destitution may give rise to a breach of Art 3: *R v Secretary of State for the Home Department ex parte Limbuela and others* [2005] UKHL 66, 3 November, HL. So, even homelessness or destitution may be sufficient.

Article 6
Right to a fair trial

1.   In the determination of his civil rights and obligations or of any criminal charge against him, everyone is entitled to a fair and public hearing within a reasonable time by an independent and impartial tribunal established by law. Judgment shall be pronounced publicly but the press and public may be excluded from all or part of the trial in the interest of morals, public order or national security in a democratic society, where the interests of juveniles or the protection of the private life of the parties so require, or to the extent strictly necessary in the opinion of the court in special circumstances where publicity would prejudice the interests of justice.

2.   *[omitted]*
3.   *[omitted]*

Analysis

Paras 2 and 3 of this Article concern only criminal proceedings and accordingly are omitted here. A decision on recoverability of overpayments does not involve the determination of a "criminal charge": *R(IS) 1/04*. Art 6 is the cornerstone of the procedural protections envisaged by the Convention.

"... the determination of his civil rights and obligations ...". Art 6 only has application if the matter in dispute is a "civil right" or "civil obligation". It now seems to be clear that the determination of entitlements to welfare benefits is the determination of a "civil right". Early cases established this principle in relation to contributory benefits, in which a right of property was recognised (see Prot 1 Art 1 below): see eg, *Feldbrugge v Netherlands* [1986] 8 EHRR 425 at 435, para 40, ECtHR; *Denneland v Germany* [1986] 8 EHRR 448 at 468, para 74, ECtHR. The objection taken by the states in those cases was that entitlement to benefits was a public law right and not "civil" in nature. The now generally accepted view is that where legislation confers an enforceable right to a benefit, Art 6 applies to proceedings in which entitlement to that benefit is considered. This is confirmed by *Salesi v Italy* [1993] 26 EHRR 187 at 199, para 19, ECtHR, which concerned a non-contributory pension. A similar perspective was adopted by the Tribunal of Commissioners in *R(IS) 15/04* in the context of a decision not to revise. The commissioners reasoned firstly that a claimant is entitled to apply for a revision on the grounds of official error and, if that ground is made out, is entitled to have the decision revised. Accordingly, there is a 'right' to the revision. Secondly, although the 'civil right' in question is the right to the social security benefit which was the subject of the decision on the claim, seeking a revision of that decision is part of the process whereby entitlement to the benefit is determined, and therefore falls within the scope of Article 6.

The issue of whether decisions relating to HB entitlement concern "civil rights and obligations" has been settled by the decision of Pitchford J in *R (Cumpsty) v Rent Officer* [2002] EWHC 2526 (Admin), paras 76-80. The judge decided that even though the rent officer's determination did not itself decide the claimant's HB entitlement, it was such a vital and integral part of that decision that it was itself a determination of civil rights and obligations. See to similar effect the reasoning in *R(IS) 6/04*.

"... a fair and public hearing ...". In many respects, the concept of a fair hearing mirrors the rules of natural justice in domestic law. The incorporation of Art 6, however, arguably broadens and emphasises these rules and, more importantly, gives them teeth where unfairness results from the application of a statutory rule.

The first aspect of a fair hearing is equality of arms. There must be equal opportunities on the two sides to a dispute to present their cases: *Dombo Beheer BV v Netherlands* [1993] 18 EHRR 213 at 226-8, ECtHR, paras 30-40. It is inherent in this that parties must ordinarily have sight of the evidence before the tribunal: *Ruiz-Mateos v Spain* [1993] 16 EHRR 505, para 63. In *CDLA 5413/1999* paras 49-51, it was suggested that the provisions for deemed notification of an oral hearing before a tribunal (and hence, presumably the similar provisions deeming receipt of a notification of a decision, a statement of reasons and so on) could offend against this principle if they caused injustice. In *CJSA 5100/2001* the appeal to an appeal tribunal turned on a contested issue of fact, namely whether an investigating officer from the DWP had seen the claimant working, but the investigating officer failed to attend at the hearing and so could not be cross-examined by the claimant. Applying the 'equality of arms' principle, the commissioner ruled that while there was nothing the claimant could do to get the officer to attend, the Secretary of State could have secured his attendance, and the appeal tribunal then compounded this problem, and thereby erred in law, in failing to adjourn the case to enable the Secretary of State to seek the attendance of the investigating officer: see para 13. See also *CIB 3985/2001* where similar reasoning was applied to the Secretary of State's failure to make available to the tribunal relevant evidence in the form of a medical report which only he, and not the claimant held. In *CDLA 2748/2002* (para 11), the commissioner held that if there were difficulties with interpretation that hampered the presentation of a claimant's case, Art 6 might be breached if the tribunal failed to take appropriate action to remedy the situation.

Secondly, the process of hearing a case must be reasonably accessible. If a party suffers the loss of her/his case through misleading rules of procedure, then there might be a violation of Art 6: *Bellet v France* [1995] unreported, case number A/333-B, ECtHR. This could apply if an appeal is inadvertently lodged out of time and not subsequently admitted.

The availability of legal aid is a controversial topic. In *Airey v Ireland* [1979] 2 EHRR 305, the Court found a violation in a family case where a woman was attempting to divorce a violent husband. The question posed was whether a claimant could effectively represent her/himself in the particular proceedings in question without legal representation. Since then, the court has qualified the effect of *Airey*. In *Munro v UK* [1986] 48 DR 154, ECmHR, which concerned defamation proceedings, the Commission contrasted the nature of those proceedings with the intimate nature of the family proceedings in *Airey* and the serious consequences for the family. Moreover, if there is some other means of assistance available, *Andronicou v Cyprus* [1998] 25 EHRR 491, ECtHR suggests that there will be no violation of Art 6. Since the consequences of the loss of HB entitlement are fairly intimate and serious, involving the potential loss of a home, it may be arguable that the absence of Community Legal Service funding for a sufficiently complex tribunal or commissioner hearing might infringe Art 6, particularly if an application for funding under the Access to Justice Act 1999 has been refused.

The concept of a fair hearing also involves the right to a reasoned decision and a public hearing, neither of which should present particular difficulties within the present adjudication system, save that commissioners should exercise caution in refusing an oral hearing if a claimant wants one.

One issue of particular concern within the HB system remains the rent officer system.

However, the question of whether the system of determinations by a rent officer was compliant with Art 6 was decided affirmatively in *Cumpsty*. There, the claimant had been given a re-determination, had been given reasons for the rent officer's conclusion as to the local reference rent level and had entered into extensive correspondence with the rent officer. Pitchford J held that the rent officer was "independent and impartial" (paras 81-82) and that there was sufficient involvement of the claimant in the process to give him a "fair hearing" (para 91). It remains open to question whether that would be so in a case where the rent officer refused to give reasons or gave insufficient reasons to enable a meaningful dialogue to take place, particularly in the light of *Tsfayo* (see below).

"... within a reasonable time ...". *Feldbrugge*, *Denneland*, and *Salesi* (cited above) are all examples of complaints of breach of the right to a determination within a reasonable time. In each case, the delay was several years. In the context of HB, however, since a home can be lost in as little as three to four months if HB is not put into payment, and a claim is supposed to be decided within 14 days, it may be that the tolerable period of delay is considerably less. However, in *R(IS) 1/04* and *R(IS) 2/04* delays of seven months and two years respectively in having initial decisions heard on an appeal were held to have met the reasonable time criterion and so did not breach Article 6.

If the requirement of a hearing within "a reasonable time" is breached, it is not open to a tribunal to allow a claimant's appeal simply on that basis or even, in an overpayment case, to impose a permanent stay: *CSIS 460/2002* (paras 41-49).

"... by an independent and impartial tribunal ...". At the time that the 1998 Act came into force, it was thought to be self-evident that the old Review Board system contravened Art 6 because a tribunal composed of members of the local authority could not be "independent and impartial". That has at long last been confirmed by the European Court of Human Rights in *Tsfayo v United Kingdom* (application no: 60860/00) [2006], 14 November, unreported, ECtHR.

However, prior to *Tsfayo*, the courts in the UK had sought to limit this vital component of Art 6 as it is applied to decision-making by public authorities in social welfare matters. The reasoning of the UK courts rests on the decision of the House of Lords in *R (Alconbury Developments Ltd) v Secretary of State for the Environment, Transport and the Regions* [2003] 2 AC 295, HL, where it was held that although a planning inspector was not independent of the Secretary of State, Art 6 did not require a full appeal to an independent court on the facts as well as law and judicial review was a sufficient safeguard for those concerned with planning inquiries. A large part of the House of Lords' reasoning was that since planning matters raised matters of public interest as well as a dispute between individuals and the planning authority, it was right that the decisions on matters of fact should be taken by someone who was publicly accountable (such as the Secretary of State through her/his inspectors).

As a matter of principle, it is difficult to quarrel with such a conclusion. However, the same reasoning was then applied to situations where there is no general public interest in the outcome of the dispute between citizen and state beyond the question of expenditure of public funds. Thus in *Begum v Tower Hamlets LBC* [2003] 2 WLR 238, HL, it was held that no appeal on questions of fact was necessary in homelessness cases for compliance with Art 6, and in *R (Beeson) v Dorset* [2002] 6 CCLR 5, CA, a panel appointed by the local authority, controlled by judicial review, was held to be an adequate safeguard for a citizen aggrieved by a decision that he had deliberately disposed of capital in order to qualify for the provision of accommodation under s21 of the National Assistance Act 1948. The fears expressed by the courts of "over-judicialisation" of administrative procedures sit very uneasily with the existence of extensive rights of appeal on questions of fact in social security issues and the vital importance of the issues raised to the well-being of the individual. How much of *Alconbury* and *Begum* may read across to HB/CTB adjudication in a post-*Tsfayo* world but one where there is a right of appeal to an independent appeal tribunal against most decisions remains to be worked out.

In *R(IS) 6/04* (paras 36-49), the commissioner ruled that the exclusion of a right of appeal on questions relating to whether a valid claim had been made infringed Art 6. It is not a breach of Art 6 for a commissioner who has previously decided that leave to appeal against a tribunal's decision should be refused to decide whether or not to set aside the refusal of leave: see *CDLA 3432/2001* paras 2-3 and *Sengupta v Holmes* [2002] *The Times* 19 August, CA. The same will apply, therefore, to tribunal members sitting and determining whether to set aside their own decisions, unless perhaps there is some impropriety by the tribunal member alleged. Similarly, there can be no objection to a tribunal member hearing an appeal simply on the basis that the member has sat on a previous tribunal which dismissed an appeal by the same claimant: *R (Wall) v Appeals Service* [2003] EWHC 465 Admin, para 14. There must be some basis for satisfying the apparent bias test, as to which see the commentary to Sch 7 para 8 CSPSSA.

Application to appeals. While Art 6 does not require a state to provide a system of appeals from the court or tribunal which gives the initial independent determination required by Art 6, if such a system is provided then that system must also comply with the safeguards of the Article: *Fedje v Sweden* [1994] 17 EHRR 14, para 32, ECtHR.

Article 8
Right to respect for private and family life

1.   Everyone has the right to respect for his private and family life, his home and his correspondence.

2.   There shall be no interference by a public authority with the exercise of this right except such as is in accordance with the law and is necessary in a democratic society in the interests of national security, public safety or the economic well-being of the country, for the prevention of disorder or crime, for the protection of health or morals, or for the protection of the rights and freedoms of others.

Analysis

Art 8 is in far less absolute terms than Art 6. It confers a right only to "respect" for the matters set out therein. There is no absolute obligation on a state to provide welfare support of a particular kind: *Andersson v Sweden* [1986] 46 DR 251, ECmHR; *Petrovic v Austria* [1998] 4 BHRC 232, ECtHR (para 26); *R (Tucker) v Secretary of State for Social Security* [2001] EWHC Admin 260(para 22).

Art 8, however, might be of relevance to a case in which a local authority had failed to adjudicate a claim for HB and a claimant lost her/his home as a result. No claim for damages for breach of statutory duty would lie in such circumstances: *Haringey LBC v Cotter* [1996] 29 HLR 682, CA. However, it is arguable that by failing to comply with obligations created by the state for the protection of a claimant's home, the local authority breached Art 8 in such a situation and would be liable in damages. There is a distinction between a complaint that the HB Regs exclude a claimant from entitlement (as in *Tucker*) and a complaint that the claimant is entitled to benefit but the relevant authority failed to decide so quickly enough.

Guidance as to the circumstances in which maladministration of a statutory scheme could give rise to a breach of Art 8 was given in *R (Anufrijeva) v Southwark LBC* [2003] EWCA Civ 1406, CA. Although there is no positive duty to provide particular forms of welfare support, nevertheless if in failing to adjudicate an HB claim the local authority failed to show respect for the home, then Art 8 might be breached: compare *Anufrijeva* para 43, where it was said that if withholding welfare support resulted in a lack of respect for family life, Art 8 could be breached. It is suggested that by analogy, since HB is a scheme designed to protect a person's home and thereby show "respect" for it, a failure to administer the HB scheme properly may give rise to a claim under Art 8 in principle. In para 45, the court said:

"In so far as Article 8 imposes positive obligations, these are not absolute. Before inaction can amount to a lack of respect for private and family life, there must be some ground for criticising the failure to act. There must be an element of culpability. At the very least there must be knowledge that the claimant's private and family life were at risk . . . Where the domestic law of a State imposes positive obligations in relation to the provision of welfare support, breach of those positive obligations of domestic law may suffice to provide the element of culpability necessary to establish a breach of Article 8, provided that the impact on private or family life is sufficiently serious and was foreseeable."

If the word "home" is transposed for "private and family" it seems, for example, that there is no reason why a local authority which ignores repeated pleas by a claimant and her/his representatives to adjudicate a HB claim for no good reason and which is aware that possession proceedings are pending would not be in breach of Art 8. Problems caused by lack of resources may, however, be taken into account when deciding whether Art 8 is breached: para 47. In para 48, the court said:

"Newman J suggested . . . that it is likely that the acts of a public authority will have to have so far departed from the performance of its duty as to amount to a denial or contradiction of that duty before Article 8 will be infringed. We think that this puts the position somewhat too high, for in considering whether the threshold of Article 8 has been reached it is necessary to have regard both to the extent of the culpability of the failure to act and to the severity of the consequence. Clearly, where one is considering whether there has been a lack of respect for Article 8 rights, the more glaring the deficiency in the behaviour of the public authority, the easier it will be to establish the necessary want of respect. Isolated acts of even significant carelessness are unlikely to suffice."

It is also possible that Art 8 might be invoked in relation to a failure to adjudicate a claim to a discretionary housing payment (DHP). Refusal of a DHP alone could not constitute a breach of Art 8, unless perhaps the authority was refusing to administer the scheme properly.

However, it is unlikely that Art 8 can be invoked to challenge the level of HB or CTB that is payable under the statutory schemes. In *R (Reynolds) v Secretary of State for Work and Pensions* [2002] EWHC Admin 426, it was stated by Wilson J that:

". . . the broadly worded principle in Article 8 is [not] apt to a challenge to the level of a social security payment."

In the Court of Appeal Laws LJ, with whom the other members of the Court agreed, said the IS scheme did not *per se* come within the ambit of Article 8 (for the purposes of mounting an argument under Art 14). None of this reasoning was doubted by the House of Lords on a further appeal in *Reynolds*.

However, *CH 4574/2003* and Sedley LJ in *Langley v Bradford MDC and Secretary of State for Work and Pensions* [2004] EWCA Civ 1343, 15 October, CA, reported as *R(H) 6/05* both hold that the HB scheme does enage Art 8 as it is about respect for the home.

Although the judgment of the House of Lords in *Secretary of State for Work and Pensions v M* [2006] UKHL 11, 8 March 2006, reported as *R(CS) 4/06* may have laid down a narrower approach to the ambit of Art 8, given the decision of the Grand Chamber of the ECtHR in *Stec and others v United Kingdom* (Application Nos: 65731/01 and 65900/01), 6 July 2005, ECtHR in relation to Article 1 Protocol 1 (see commentary to that Article below) it may no longer be a necessary step (in any Article 14 discrimination argument at least) to argue that means-tested benefits (such as HB/CTB) come within the scope of Article 8 (as they will count as "possessions"); and so save for DHPs, there may no longer be any need to resort to the difficult arguments as to the scope of respect for private or family life or the home in order to mount an Article 14 challenge to the benefits rules. However, note the present bar to relying on *Stec* created by *Price* and *Reynolds*, referred to under Article 1 Protocol 1 below.

It is not a breach of respect for private life under Art 8 for an authority to film a claimant in public as part of an investigation of her/his entitlement to benefit, as long as the film is only used for that purpose: *R(DLA) 4/02* (para 21).

Article 9
Freedom of Thought, Conscience and Religion

1. Everyone has the right to freedom of thought, conscience and religion; this right includes freedom to change his religion or belief and freedom, either alone or in community with others and in public or private, to manifest his religion or belief, in worship, teaching, practice and observance.

2. Freedom to manifest one's religion or beliefs shall be subject only to such limitations as are prescribed by law and are necessary in a democratic society in the interests of public safety, for the protection of public order, health or morals, or for the protection of the rights and freedoms of others.

Analysis

While Art 9 does require some positive action on the part of a state to protect religious beliefs, it does not require the state to subsidise the manifestation of those beliefs. Any challenge, for example, to reg 9(1)(j) of either the HB Regs or the HB(SPC) Regs, or to reg 9(2) on the ground that it aims to exclude living arrangements such as those adopted by the Jesus Fellowship Church from entitlement to HB are unlikely to succeed on Art 9 grounds alone. However, they might form a basis for an Art 14 challenge, particularly in the light of the exhortation in s13. In *R(H) 8/04* (para 30), the commissioner indicated that the exclusion of church members from HB on the ground that they had adopted a communal lifestyle for religious reasons engaged Art 14 in conjunction with Art 9. This conclusion is to be challenged by the Secretary of State on the claimants' appeal to the Court of Appeal.

However, the question of whether Art 9 was 'engaged' on the facts was not given any clear or compelling answer by the Court of Appeal in *Campbell and others v South Northamptonshire District Council and the Secretary of State for Work and Pensions* [2004] EWCA Civ 409 *The Times* 6 May, CA (reported as *R(H) 8/04*). The only substantive judgment on this point was given by Jacobs LJ where he said that Art 14 was not engaged because there was no violation of Art 9 (or Arts 8 and 1 of Protocol 1). With respect to this, however, is the wrong test: it is enough for Art 14 to come into play (or 'be engaged') if the facts of the case come within the ambit, or engage, one of the substantive Articles of the Convention (see *The Belgian Linguistics* case below), there is no need for that substantive Article to itself have been breached. Moreover, in later parts of the judgment the judge considers (and rejects on the facts) arguments that reg 7(1)(a) HB Regs 1987 (now reg 9(1)(a) of both the HB and the HB(SPC) Regs) indirectly discriminated against members of the Jesus Fellowship in a disproportionate manner, all of which suggests that the Court of Appeal was proceeding on the footing that Art 14 could be in play. Perhaps the best explanation for this confusion lies in the Court's emphatic rejection of the claimants' argument that human rights considerations had any bearing on the factual assessment of whether the tenancy agreement was on a commercial basis (see further the notes on p226 to reg 9(1) HB Regs), so that their comments on Arts 9, 8 and 14 are, strictly speaking, *obiter.*

Article 14
Prohibition of discrimination

The enjoyment of the rights and freedoms set forth in this Convention shall be secured without discrimination on any ground such as sex, race, colour, language, religion, political or other opinion, national or social origin, association with a national minority, property, birth or other status.

Analysis

Art 14 deals with discrimination in the enjoyment of Convention rights. The issues to be considered in ascertaining whether there is a breach of Art 14 in a particular case have been put in various ways. Perhaps the most straightforward formulation is the four questions posed by Brooke LJ in *Michalak v Wandsworth LBC* [2003] 1 WLR 617 (para 20):

"(i)   Do the facts fall within the ambit of one or more of the substantive Convention provisions . . .?

(ii)   If so, was there different treatment as respects that right between the complainant on the one hand and other persons put forward for comparison ("the chosen comparators") on the other?

(iii) Were the chosen comparators in an analogous situation to the complainant's situation?

(iv)   If so, did the difference in treatment have an objective and reasonable justification: in other words, did it pursue a legitimate aim and did the differential treatment bear a reasonable relationship of proportionality to the aim sought to be achieved?"

In *R (Carson) v Secretary of State for Work and Pensions* [2003] 3 All ER 577, CA, Laws LJ suggested that questions (iii) and (iv) should be conflated into a composite question: "are the circumstances of X and Y so similar as to call (in the mind of a rational and fair-minded person) for a positive justification for the less favourable treatment of Y in comparison with X?". However, a rigid adherence to these four tests has subsequently been deprecated by the House of Lords in cases such as *R(S) v Chief Constable of South Yorkshire Police* [2004] 1 WLR 2196 (para 24), *Ghaidan v Godin-Mendoza* [2004] UKHL 30, 3 All ER 411 (para 134) and *Carson and Reynolds* [2005] UKHL 37 *The Times* 27 May (para 3). A Tribunal of Commissioner have recently adopted Lord Nicholls approach in this last case, in *R(P) 2/06*, where they quoted as correct his view that the better approach in benefits cases was:

"to keep formulation of the relevant issues in these cases as simple and non-technical as possible. Article 14 does not apply unless the alleged discrimination is in connection with a Convention right and on a ground stated in article 14. If this prerequisite is satisfied, the essential question for the court is whether the alleged discrimination, that is, the difference in treatment of which complaint is made, can withstand scrutiny. Sometime the answer to this question will be plain. There may be such an obvious, relevant difference between the claimant and those with whom he seeks to compare himself that their situations cannot be regarded as analogous. Sometimes, where the position is not so clear, a different approach is called for. Then the court's scrutiny may best be directed at considering whether the differentiation has a legitimate aim and whether the means chosen to achieve the aim is appropriate and not disproportionate in its adverse impact".

Facts "within the ambit" of a Convention right. The major limitation on Art 14 is that it does not provide a free-standing right not to be discriminated against. On the other hand, it is not necessary to show that another Convention right has been breached, otherwise Art 14 would be devoid of meaning. It must be shown that the circumstances of the discrimination fall within the ambit of one of the other rights guaranteed by the Convention: *The Belgian Linguistics Case (No 2)* [1967] 1 EHRR 252 at 283-4, para 9, ECtHR; *Guygusuz v Austria* [1997] 23 EHRR 364, ECtHR.

In *Guygusuz*, the applicant complained that he had been denied entitlement to an emergency needs benefit on the basis of his nationality. Although the denial of benefit did not itself amount to a breach of Protocol 1 Art 1 (see below), his entitlement to benefit was a "pecuniary right" within the ambit of that article. It followed that while there was no entitlement to benefit under that article, as the state had chosen to provide that benefit it had to ensure it did so without discriminating against the claimant.

In *Secretary of State for Work and Pensions v M* [2006] UKHL 11, 8 March 2006, reported as *R(CS) 4/ 06*, the House of Lords rejected the view that even the most tenuous connection between the allegedly discriminatory rule or regulation under challenge and the rights protected by the other articles of the Convention will suffice to bring the rule or regulation within the ambit of the other article of the Convention. Lord Bingham stated (para 4):

"It is not difficult, when considering any provision of the Convention, including article 8 and article 1 of the First Protocol ("IFP"), to identify the core values which the provision is intended to protect. But the further a situation is removed from one infringing those core values, the weaker the connection becomes, until a point is reached when there is no meaningful connection at all. At the inner extremity a situation may properly be said to be within the ambit or scope of the right, nebulous though those expressions necessarily are. At the outer extremity, it may not. There is no sharp line of demarcation between the two. An exercise of judgment is called for . . . I cannot accept that even a tenuous link is enough. That would be a recipe for artificiality and legalistic ingenuity of an unacceptable kind".

Even this approach is not necessarily free from difficulty where the ambit of Art 8 is concerned, because of its core focus being on *respect* for the home, family and private life: see Lord Walker in *M* at paras 83–84. However, in the case of *Secretary of State for Work and Pensions v Esfandiari and others* [2006] EWCA Civ 282, 23 March 2006, CA (reported as *R(IS) 11/06*), (concerning alleged discrimination in the social fund funeral payment rules not extending to burials outside the EU) the Court of Appeal had no difficulty in holding that those rules did come within the ambit of Art 8:

"The need for a decent funeral is a basic requirement of human dignity, whether from the point of view of the individual or from that of the family. In Strasbourg language the funeral payment is the "modality" by which the state ensures that that this need can be met, even by those families who have no adequate means of their own. By offering it, the state demonstrates its respect for this important aspect of family life".

However, given the decision of the ECtHR in *Stec* (see Art 1 of the First Protocol below), absent the current difficulties about applying *Stec* before courts and tribunals in the UK(see also under Art 1 Part 1 below), it is difficult to see the circumstances in which it would be necessary to argue that either housing benefit or council tax benefit came within the ambit of Art 8 (as they will clearly fall within the ambit of Art 1 of the First Protocol).

Differential treatment. Brooke LJ's questions (ii) and (iii) overlap to a considerable extent.

It would now seem that the the grounds of discrimination which can be impugned under Art 14 are limited to discrimination relating to some personal characteristic of the claimant: *Kjeldsen Madsen v Denmark* [1976] 1 EHRR 711, ECtHR (para 56); *R(S) v Chief Constable of South Yorkshire Police* [2004] 1 WLR 2196; *R v Secretary of State for Work and Pensions ex parte Hooper and others* [2005] UKHL 29 and *Carson and Reynolds*. However, this does not mean a personal attribute which is immutable or inherent to the claimant: see, eg, *Francis v Secretary of State for Work and Pensions* [2005] EWCA Civ 1303, 10 November (reported as R(IS) 6/06).

Besides the need to bring the discrimination of which complaint is made within the scope of some other Article, not all discrimination will result in a breach of Art 14. The state may escape censure if it is shown that the measure in question has a legitimate aim and the means adopted are proportionate to the aim: *The Belgian Linguistics Case (No 2)* (para 34).

Domestic discrimination law distinguishes between direct discrimination (discriminating against a woman because she is a woman) and indirect discrimination which, generally, involves the imposition of a requirement which fewer people of a particular group can comply with (discriminating against a woman by prohibiting pregnant people from participating in an activity). The Convention does not distinguish between direct and indirect discrimination and there has been some doubt as to whether Art 14 extends to the latter form of treatment. The Court in *Barber* doubted that it did but not all the relevant Strasbourg caselaw was cited and in *R(H) 8/04* (paras 39-52) the commissioner decided that the claimants, members of the Jesus Fellowship Church, could complain of the fact that it was impossible for them to follow their religion while complying with the requirement that their agreements should be made on a commercial basis. The view of the commissioner in *R(H) 8/04* has been followed by other commissioners in *CIS 1870/2003* and *CP 518/ 2003*. However, the Court of Appeal in *Esfandiari (R(IS) 11/06* - see above – the appeal from *CIS 1870/ 2003*), stated that indirect discrimination claims under Art 14 should be treated with some care because the caselaw is limited. In its view, in so far as a uniform test can be distilled from the caselaw, the relevant test to be satisfied (in order to call for the discrimination to be justified) would seem to be whether the effects on the particular group are "disproportionately prejudicial".

Justification. In *Guygusuz*, the state did not attempt to justify the discrimination. Since the burden of proof in relation to justification rests firmly on the state, a breach of Art 14 was therefore established and the claimant recovered compensation for the loss of the benefit: at 380-1, paras 40-4. However, there are plenty of statements demonstrating the width of discretion accorded to governments in social welfare matters, for example the following statement of Laws LJ in *Carson* (para 73):

"In the field of what may be called macro-economic policy, certainly including the distribution of public funds upon retirement pensions, the decision-making power of the elected arms of government is all but at its greatest, and the constraining role of the courts, absent a florid violation by government of established legal principles, is correspondingly modest. I conceive this approach to be wholly in line with our responsibilities under the Human Rights Act 1998."

Upholding both *Carson and Reynolds* in the House of Lords, Lord Hoffmann stated what may now have to be viewed as the classic test for assessing justification in the social security field.

"14. There is no doubt that Ms Carson is being treated differently from a pensioner who has the same contribution record but lives in the United Kingdom or a treaty country. But that is not enough to amount to discrimination. Discrimination means a failure to treat like cases alike. There is obviously no discrimination when the cases are relevantly different. Indeed, it may be a breach of article 14 not to recognise the difference: see *Thlimmenos v Greece* [2001] 31 EHRR 411. There is discrimination only if the cases are not sufficiently different to justify the difference in treatment. The Strasbourg court sometimes expresses this by saying that the two cases must be in an "analogous situation": see *Van der Mussele v Belgium* [1983] 6 EHRR 163, 179-180, para 46.

15. Whether cases are sufficiently different is partly a matter of values and partly a question of rationality. Article 14 expresses the Enlightenment value that every human being is entitled to equal respect and to be treated as an end and not a means. Characteristics such as race, caste, noble birth, membership of a political party and (here a change in values since the Enlightenment) gender, are seldom, if ever, acceptable grounds for differences in treatment. In some constitutions, the prohibition on discrimination is confined to grounds of this kind and I rather suspect that article 14 was also intended to be so limited. But the Strasbourg court has given it a wide interpretation, approaching that of the 14th Amendment, and it is therefore necessary, as in the United States, to distinguish between those grounds of discrimination which prima facie appear to offend our notions of the respect due to the individual and those which merely require some rational justification: *Massachusetts Board of Retirement v Murgia* [1976] 438 US 285.

16. There are two important consequences of making this distinction. First, discrimination in the first category cannot be justified merely on utilitarian grounds, eg that it is rational to prefer to employ men rather than women because more women than men give up employment to look after childen. That offends the notion that everyone is entitled to be treated as an individual and not a statistical unit. On the other hand, differences in treatment in the second category (eg on grounds of ability, education, wealth, occupation) usually depend upon considerations of the general public interest. Secondly, while the courts, as guardians of the right of the individual to equal respect, will carefully examine the reasons offered for any discrimination in the first category, decisions about the general public interest which underpin differences in treatment in the second category are very much a matter for the democratically elected branches of government.

17. There may be borderline cases in which it is not easy to allocate the ground of discrimination to one category or the other and, as I have observed, there are shifts in the values of society on these matters. *Ghaidan v Godin-Mendoza* [2004] UKHL 30, 3 All ER 411 recognised that discrimination on grounds of sexual orientation was now firmly in the first category. Discrimination on grounds of old age may be a contemporary example of a borderline case. But there is usually no difficulty about deciding whether one is dealing with a case in which the right to respect for the individuality of a human being is at stake or merely a question of general social policy. In the present case, the answer seems to me to be clear".

In social security cases, therefore, if the discrimination in question does not fall within Lord Hoffmann's specially prohibited first category, it may be relatively easy to justify on general public interest grounds (but note that *Francis* was successful).

In *Petrovic v Austria* [1998] 4 BHRC 232, ECtHR, the Court held that the disparity of provision by signatory states meant that a wide margin of appreciation was enjoyed in the field of social security, and that accordingly sex discrimination in relation to access to maternity allowances could not be impugned. That conclusion may be said to be surprising, given the critical view that the court has taken of discrimination on such grounds. Where the discrimination is on the ground of race or sex, the burden on the state to justify discrimination is particularly heavy: see eg, *Abdulaziz v UK* [1985] 7 EHRR 471 at 501, para 78, ECtHR. However, the decision of the House of Lords in *Carson and Reynolds* leaves open whether a different test or less weighty reasons apply where the sex or race discrimination arises in respect of general measures of economic or social strategy. The commissioner in *CP 518/2003* said that if the claim for (indirect) sex discrimination in the allocation of pension entitlement could be made out then weighty reasons would be needed to justify it. But in the final decision in *Stec* (12 April 2006) the Grand Chamber of the ECtHR set out what it described as the general approach to justification. That is, that although in general weighty reasons are required to justify discrimination based on sex (or race), a wide margin of appreciation will usually be allowed to national governments when it comes to general measures of economic or social strategy. In such cases, *Stec* seems to suggest that the legislature's policy choice should generally be respected, unless it is manifestly without reasonable foundation. A counter argument to this may be that *Stec* is not the appropriate test, or at least has to be modified, where what is in issue is not a general measure of economic or social strategy (such as pensionable age) but rather is a subsistence benefit rule, and so weighty reasons remain to be given for sex discrimination in relation to minimum safety net benefits.

Note, however, in terms of remedy, that just satisfaction may not require "levelling up" to award benefit to the discriminated party (if he or she has managed to show unjustified differential treatment) in all cases: *R v HMRC ex parte Wilkinson* [2005] UKHL 30 at paras [26] to [28] and [47] to [53], and *Hobbs and others v UK* (Application No. 63684/00), 14 November 2006.

Article 17
Prohibition of abuse of rights

Nothing in this Convention may be interpreted as implying for any State, group or person any right to engage in any activity or perform any act aimed at the destruction of any of the rights and freedoms set forth herein or at their limitation to a greater extent than is provided for in the Convention.

Article 18
Limitation on use of restrictions on rights

The restrictions permitted under this Convention to the said rights and freedoms shall not be applied for any purpose other than those for which they have been prescribed.

The First Protocol
Article 1
Protection of Property

Every natural or legal person is entitled to the peaceful enjoyment of his possessions. No one shall be deprived of his possessions except in the public interest and subject to the conditions provided for by law and by the general principles of international law.

The preceding provisions shall not, however, in any way impair the right of a State to enforce such laws as it deems necessary to control the use of property in accordance with the general interest or to secure the payment of taxes or other contributions or penalties.

Analysis

Art 1 of the First Protocol is breached if either (a) the State interferes with the peaceful enjoyment of the claimant's possessions; or (b) the claimant has been deprived of possessions by the State: or (c) the applicant's possessions have been subjected to control by the State.

By far the most important issue is whether benefits constitute 'possessions' under this article. Until recently a distinction was drawn between *contributory* and *non-contributory* benefits. For the former the view was, and remains, that all are covered by Art 1 Prt 1: see *Gaygusuz, Szrabjer v Clarke v UK* (Commission) (application nos. 27004/95 and 27011/95) 23 October 1997 and *Carson and Reynolds* (see above) (retirement pensions and contribution-based JSA both 'possessions'). For the latter, however, UK domestic courts and tribunals had ruled that non-contributory benefits (such as HB/CTB) did not count as 'possessions'. In *Carson and Reynolds* the House of Lords expressly refused to address the issue because of the pending decision in *Stec* (see below), but the Court of Appeal had held that income support, as a non-contributory benefit, was not a 'possession'. The same conclusion was reached in relation to DLA in *CDLA 3908/2001*. However, the view that non-contributory benefits cannot count as 'possessions' has now been emphatically reversed by the decision of the Grand Chamber of the European Court of Human Rights in *Stec and others v United Kingdom* (Application Nos: 65731/01 and 65900/01), 6 July 2005, ECtHR, which has ruled, decisively, that non-contributory benefits are possessions for the purposes of

Article 1 Protocol 1 of the ECHR, thus effectively overruling the contrary view of the Court of Appeal in *Reynolds*. Regrettably, however, because of the domestic law of precedent the one country where *Stec* seemingly does not currently apply is the UK, because of the House of Lord's ruling in *Leeds City Council v Price* [2006] UKHL 10, [2006] 4 All ER 128 (paras 43-44) that in almost all cases where there is a conflict between ECtHR caselaw and a decision of a superior court in the UK the inferior court or tribunal should follow the decision of the superior (UK) court. In *R (Couronne) v Crawley BC and Secretary of State for Work and Pensions and Others* [2006] EWHC 1514 (Admin), the High Court said that in the light of *Price* it was bound to follow the Court of Appeal's decision in *Campbell and others v South Northamptonshire District Council and the Secretary of State for Work and Pensions* [2004] EWCA Civ 409 *The Times* 6 May, CA (reported as *R(H) 8/04*), which itself had followed the decision of the Court of Appeal in *Reynolds*, to the effect that non-contributory benefits are not 'possessions', notwithstanding the Grand Chamber's expressly contrary view in *Stec*. Moreover, although in *R(RJM) v Secretary of State for Work and Pensions* [2007] EWCA Civ 614, 28 June (CA), the strictures of *Price* were avoided and *Stec* made applicable in a domestic context on the back of a concession preferred by the Secretary of State, the fall-out from that decision (following which the Secretary of State has said he will make no similar concessions in any other cases and that *Campbell* remains the binding authority to be applied at Court of Appeal level and below unless and until overruled by the House of Lords), indicates that it may be some time before *Stec* can be fully effective in the UK.

However, given its importance, it is worthwhile setting out the reasoning of the Grand Chamber of the ECtHR in *Stec* in full.

"It is in the interests of the coherence of the Convention as a whole that the autonomous concept of 'possessions' in Article 1 of Protocol No. 1 should be interpreted in a way which is consistent with the concept of pecuniary rights under Article 6. It is moreover important to adopt an interpretation of Article 1 of Protocol No. 1 which avoids inequalities of treatment based on distinctions which, at the present day, appear illogical or unsustainable.

The Court's approach to Article 1 of Protocol No. 1 should reflect the reality of the way in which welfare provision is currently organised within the Member States of the Council of Europe. It is clear that within those States, and within most individual States, there exists a wide range of social security benefits designed to confer entitlements which arise as of right. Benefits are funded in a large variety of ways: some are paid for by contributions to a specific fund; some depend on a claimant's contribution record; many are paid for out of general taxation on the basis of a statutorily defined status (see, with reference to the United Kingdom's system, Lord Hoffmann's comments in ex parte Carson). . . Given the variety of funding methods, and the interlocking nature of benefits under most welfare systems, it appears increasingly artificial to hold that only benefits financed by contributions to a specific fund fall within the scope of Article 1 of Protocol No. 1. Moreover, to exclude benefits paid for out of general taxation would be to disregard the fact that many claimants under this latter type of system also contribute to its financing, through the payment of tax.

In the modern, democratic State, many individuals are, for all or part of their lives, completely dependent for survival on social security and welfare benefits. Many domestic legal systems recognise that such individuals require a degree of certainty and security, and provide for benefits to be paid – subject to the fulfilment of the conditions of eligibility – as of right. Where an individual has an assertable right under domestic law to a welfare benefit, the importance of that interest should also be reflected by holding Article 1 of Protocol No. 1 to be applicable.

Finally . . . the Court considers that to hold that a right to a non-contributory benefit falls within the scope of Article 1 of Protocol No. 1 no more renders otiose the provisions of the Social Charter than to reach the same conclusion in respect of a contributory benefit. Whilst the Convention sets forth what are essentially civil and political rights, many of them have implications of a social or economic nature. The mere fact that an interpretation of the Convention may extend into the sphere of social and economic rights should not be a decisive factor against such an interpretation; there is no water-tight division separating that sphere from the field covered by the Convention (see Airey v. Ireland)".

The ECtHR then concluded:

"therefore, if any distinction can still be said to exist in the caselaw between contributory and non-contributory benefits for the purposes of the applicability of Article 1 of Protocol No. 1, there is no ground to justify the continued drawing of such a distinction.

If . . . a Contracting State has in force legislation providing for the payment as of right of a welfare benefit – whether conditional or not on the prior payment of contributions – that legislation must be regarded as generating a proprietary interest falling within the ambit of Article 1 of Protocol No. 1 for persons satisfying its requirements.

In cases, such as the present, concerning a complaint under Article 14 in conjunction with Article 1 of Protocol No. 1 that the applicant has been denied all or part of a particular benefit on a discriminatory ground covered by Article 14, the relevant test is whether, but for the condition of entitlement about which the applicant complains, he or she would have had a right, enforceable under domestic law, to receive the benefit in question. Although Protocol No. 1 does not include the right to receive a social security payment of any kind, if a State does decide to create a benefits scheme, it must do so in a manner which is compatible with Article 14".

However, Art 1 Prt 1 does not confer a general right to be paid a benefit constituting a 'possession' at a particular rate (or, put another way, no right not to be deprived of a larger amount), *unless* the reduction is of such a substantial amount that it affects 'the very substance of the right': *Müller v Austria* (Commission) [1975] 3 D and R 25. *CP 5084/2001* lists the factors to help determine whether there was deprivation in this sense. These are: (a) does the provision in question reduce a benefit previously in payment; (b) was that provision in force throughout the time when the claimant was paying relevant contributions (or, presumably post *Stec*, claiming the benefit in question or, perhaps, being liable to pay tax); (c) the closeness of the link between the benefit and payment of contributions (arguably, post *Stec*, this factor is no longer relevant, or at least should carry less weight); and (d) the amount of the reduction in benefit.

Moreover, a claimant cannot be said to have been deprived of a possession if s/he had no entitlement to the possession at all under the rules of entitlement: *X v Italy* [1977] 11 DR 114, applied by the Court of Appeal in *Carson and Reynolds* (and not argued on the further appeals to the House of Lords). Therefore, the rules limiting backdating of the retirement pension to three months before the date of claim do not mean that a person has been 'deprived' of her/his pension for the period more than three months before the date s/he claim it: *R(P) 1/06*. However, these decisions, and the approach to this particular point which they exemplify, have now to be read subject to *Stec* if an Art 14 challenge is in play (it was not in *R(P) 1/06*). Accordingly, if the backdating rules for a pension (or, indeed, any benefit) had been changed or introduced in a discriminatory manner (eg, allowing more backdating for men than women), then *Stec*, in principle, may enable an Art 1 Prt 1 and Art 14 argument to be made. *X v Italy*, *Carson and Reynolds* and *R(P) 1/06* remain good law, however, if all that is being raised is an argument under Art 1 Prt 1.

As with Art 8, even if it can be shown that there has been deprivation of a posession in the sense described above, that can nonetheless be justified by the State if it can show that the deprivation was in accordance with the 'public interest'. A 'fair balance' test is applied in answering this question, in which compensation is a key factor. Compensation need not be full.

Article 2
Right to Education

No person shall be denied the right to education. In the exercise of any functions which it assumes in relation to education and to teaching, the State shall respect the right of parents to ensure such education and teaching in conformity with their own religious and philosophical convictions.

Analysis

Prt 1 Art 2 does not require a state to establish or facilitate a certain degree of education at its expense. All it requires is the right to enjoy such education that the state provides: *The Belgian Linguistics Case (No 2)* at 280-1, para 3. Thus it will be difficult for students to argue that the severe restrictions on their entitlements to HB and CTB infringe Prt 1 Art 2: see *R(Douglas) v North Tyneside MBC and another* [2004] 1 All ER 709.

SCHEDULE 2
REMEDIAL ORDERS
Orders

1.–(1)   A remedial order may–

(a)   contain such incidental, supplemental, consequential or transitional provision as the person making it considers appropriate;

(b)   be made so as to have effect from a date earlier than that on which it is made;

(c)   make provision for the delegation of specific functions;

(d)   make different provision for different cases.

(2)   The power conferred by sub-paragraph (1)(a) includes–

(a)   power to amend primary legislation (including primary legislation other than that which contains the incompatible provision); and

(b)   power to amend or revoke subordinate legislation (including subordinate legislation other than that which contains the incompatible provision).

(3)   A remedial order may be made so as to have the same extent as the legislation which it affects.

(4)   No person is to be guilty of an offence solely as a result of the retrospective effect of a remedial order.

Procedure

2.   No remedial order may be made unless–

(a)   a draft of the order has been approved by a resolution of each House of Parliament made after the end of the period of 60 days beginning with the day on which the draft was laid; or

(b)   it is declared in the order that it appears to the person making it that, because of the urgency of the matter, it is necessary to make the order without a draft being so approved.

Orders laid in draft

3.–(1)   No draft may be laid under paragraph 2(a) unless–

(a)   the person proposing to make the order has laid before Parliament a document which contains a draft of the proposed order and the required information; and

(b)   the period of 60 days, beginning with the day on which the document required by this sub-paragraph was laid, has ended.

(2)   If representations have been made during that period, the draft laid under paragraph 2(a) must be accompanied by a statement containing–

(a)   a summary of the representations; and

(b)   if, as a result of the representations, the proposed order has been changed, details of the changes.

Urgent cases

4.–(1)   If a remedial order (''the original order'') is made without being approved in draft, the person making it must lay it before Parliament, accompanied by the required information, after it is made.

(2)   If representations have been made during the period of 60 days beginning with the day on which the original order was made, the person making it must (after the end of that period) lay before Parliament a statement containing–

(a)   a summary of the representations; and

(b)   if, as a result of the representations, he considers it appropriate to make changes to the original order, details of the changes.

(3)   If sub-paragraph (2)(b) applies, the person making the statement must–

(a)   make a further remedial order replacing the original order; and

(b)   lay the replacement order before Parliament.

(4)   If, at the end of the period of 120 days beginning with the day on which the original order was made, a resolution has not been passed by each House approving the original or replacement order, the order ceases to have effect (but without that affecting anything previously done under either order or the power to make a fresh remedial order).

Definitions

5.   In this Schedule–

''representations'' means representations about a remedial order (or proposed remedial order) made to the person making (or proposing to make) it and includes any relevant Parliamentary report or resolution; and

''required information'' means–

(a)   an explanation of the incompatibility which the order (or proposed order) seeks to remove, including particulars of the relevant declaration, finding or order; and

(b)   a statement of the reasons for proceeding under section 10 and for making an order in those terms.

Calculating periods

6.   In calculating any period for the purposes of this Schedule, no account is to be taken of any time during which–

(a)   Parliament is dissolved or prorogued; or

(b)   both Houses are adjourned for more than four days.

Child Support, Pensions and Social Security Act 2000
(2000 c19)

Arrangement of Sections
Part III
SOCIAL SECURITY
Housing benefit and council tax benefit etc.
68.　Housing benefit and council tax benefit: revisions and appeals
69.　Discretionary financial assistance with housing
70.　Grants towards cost of discretionary housing payments

Supplemental
84.　Expenses
85.　Repeals
86.　Commencement and transitional provisions
87.　Short title and extent

Schedules
7.　Housing benefit and council tax benefit: revisions and appeals

General Note

This Act made a number of important reforms to social security, child support and pensions law. For HB purposes, the most significant changes are the introduction by s69 of a new system of discretionary financial assistance to replace exceptional hardship payments under the former HB Regs 1987 reg 61(3), and the new decision-making and appeals system under s68 and Sch 7.

PART III
Social Security
Housing benefit and council tax benefit etc

Housing benefit and council tax benefit: revisions and appeals
68.　Schedule 7 (which makes provision for the revision of decisions made in connection with claims for housing benefit or council tax benefit and for appeals against such decisions) shall have effect.

Discretionary financial assistance with housing.
69.–(1)　The Secretary of State may by regulations make provision conferring a power on relevant authorities to make payments by way of financial assistance ("discretionary housing payments") to persons who–
(a)　are entitled to housing benefit or council tax benefit, or to both; and
(b)　appear to such an authority to require some further financial assistance (in addition to the benefit or benefits to which they are entitled) in order to meet housing costs.
(2)　Regulations under this section may include any of the following–
(a)　provision prescribing the circumstances in which discretionary housing payments may be made under the regulations;
(b)　provision conferring (subject to any provision made by virtue of paragraph (c) or (d) of this subsection or an order under section 70) a discretion on a relevant authority–
  (i)　as to whether or not to make discretionary housing payments in a particular case; and
  (ii)　as to the amount of the payments and the period for or in respect of which they are made;
(c)　provision imposing a limit on the amount of the discretionary housing payment that may be made in any particular case;

(d)　provision restricting the period for or in respect of which discretionary housing payments may be made;

(e)　provision about the form and manner in which claims for discretionary housing payments are to be made and about the procedure to be followed by relevant authorities in dealing with and disposing of such claims;

(f)　provision imposing conditions on persons claiming or receiving discretionary housing payments requiring them to provide a relevant authority with such information as may be prescribed;

(g)　provision entitling a relevant authority that are making or have made a discretionary housing payment, in such circumstances as may be prescribed, to cancel the making of further such payments or to recover a payment already made;

(h)　provision requiring or authorising a relevant authority to review decisions made by the authority with respect to the making, cancellation or recovery of discretionary housing payments.

(3)　Regulations under this section shall be made by statutory instrument, which shall be subject to annulment in pursuance of a resolution of either House of Parliament.

(4)　Subsections (4) to (6) of section 189 of the Social Security Administration Act 1992 (supplemental and incidental powers etc.) shall apply in relation to any power to make regulations under this section as they apply in relation to the powers to make regulations that are conferred by that Act.

(5)　Any power to make regulations under this section shall include power to make different provision for different areas or different relevant authorities.

(6)　*[omitted]*

(7)　In this section–

"prescribed" means prescribed by or determined in accordance with regulations made by the Secretary of State; and

"relevant authority" means an authority administering housing benefit or council tax benefit.

General Note

This section gives power to set up the scheme for discretionary financial assistance with housing, which takes the form of discretionary housing payments (DHPs). DHPs replaced exceptional hardship payments which were formerly available under reg 61(3) HB Regs 1987.

Analysis

Subs (1) introduces the scheme and sets out the two basic conditions for qualifying for a DHP, which are that a person is entitled to HB or CTB and that they "appear to require" further assistance with housing costs. "Entitled" in this context will almost certainly be construed as "lawfully entitled" and will hence exclude those who have obtained a decision awarding them benefit by deception: compare *R v South Ribble DC HBRB ex p Hamilton* [2000] 33 HLR 102, CA.

Subs (2) confers the usual very broad discretions as to the making of regulations upon the Secretary of State. The relevant provisions made under each paragraph are as follows:

(a)　Reg 3 DFA Regs.
(b)　Regs 2(2) and 5 DFA Regs.
(c)　Reg 4 DFA Regs.
(d)　Reg 2(3) DFA Regs.
(e)　Reg 6 DFA Regs.
(f)　Reg 7 DFA Regs.
(g)　Reg 8(2) DFA Regs.
(h)　Reg 8(1) DFA Regs.

Grants towards cost of discretionary housing payments

70.–(1)　The Secretary of State may, out of money provided by Parliament, make to a relevant authority such payments as he thinks fit in respect of–

(a)   the cost to that authority of the making of discretionary housing payments; and

(b)   the expenses involved in the administration by that authority of any scheme for the making of discretionary housing payments.

(2)   The following provisions, namely–

(a)   subsections (1), (3), (4), (5)(b) [¹] and (8) of section 140B of the Social Security Administration Act 1992 (calculation of amount of subsidy payable to authorities administering housing benefit or council tax benefit), and

(b)   section 140C of that Act (payment of subsidy),

shall apply in relation to payments under this section as they apply in relation to subsidy under section 140A of that Act.

(3)   The Secretary of State may by order make provision–

(a)   imposing a limit on the total amount of expenditure in any year that may be incurred by a relevant authority in making discretionary housing payments;

(b)   imposing subsidiary limits on the expenditure that may be incurred in any year by a relevant authority in making discretionary housing payments in the circumstances specified in the order.

(4)   An order imposing a limit by virtue of subsection (3)(a) or (b) may fix that limit either by specifying the amount of the limit or by providing for the means by which it is to be determined.

(5)   An order under this section shall be made by statutory instrument, which shall be subject to annulment in pursuance of a resolution of either House of Parliament.

(6)   Subsections (4) to (6) of section 189 of the Social Security Administration Act 1992 (supplemental and incidental powers etc.) shall apply in relation to any power to make an order under this section as they apply in relation to the powers to make an order that are conferred by that Act.

(7)   Any power to make an order under this section shall include power to make different provision for different areas or different relevant authorities.

(8)   In this section–

''discretionary housing payment'' means any payment made by virtue of regulations under section 69;

''relevant authority'' means an authority administering housing benefit or council tax benefit;

''subsidy'' has the same meaning as in sections 140A to 140G of the Social Security Administration Act 1992;

''year'' means a financial year within the meaning of the Local Government Finance Act 1992.

Amendment

1.   Repealed by the Local Government Act 2003, s127(2) and Part 1 Sch 8 (18.11.03).

General Note

This section authorises a system of subsidy by the Secretary of State for DHPs made by local authorities. Note subs (2) which applies most of the provisions in SSAA ss140B and 140C to DHP subsidy. For regulations under this section, see the Discretionary Housing Payments (Grants) Order 2001.

Supplemental

Expenses

84.   There shall be paid out of money provided by Parliament–

(a)   any expenditure incurred by the Secretary of State for or in connection with the carrying out of his functions under this Act; and

(b)   any increase attributable to this Act in the sums which are payable out of money so provided under any other Act.

Repeals

85.–(1) The enactments mentioned in Schedule 9 (which include some spent provisions) are hereby repealed to the extent specified in the third column of that Schedule.

(2) The repeals specified in that Schedule have effect subject to the commencement provisions and savings contained, or referred to, in the notes set out in that Schedule.

Commencement and transitional provisions

86.–(1) This section applies to the following provisions of this Act–

(a)   Part I (other than section 24);

(b)   Part II (other than sections 38 and 39 and paragraphs 4 to 6, 8(1), (3) and (4) and 13 of Schedule 5);

(c)   Part III;

(d)   sections 82 and 83 and Schedule 8;

(e)   Parts I to VII and IX of Schedule 9.

(2) The provisions of this Act to which this section applies shall come into force on such day as may be appointed by order made by statutory instrument; and different days may be appointed under this section for different purposes.

(3) The power to make an order under subsection (2) shall be exercisable–

(a)   except in a case falling within paragraph (b), by the Secretary of State; and

(b)   in the case of an order bringing into force any of the provisions of sections 82 and 83, Schedule 8 or Part IX of Schedule 9, by the Lord Chancellor.

(4) In the case of Part I (other than section 24) and of sections 62 to 66, the power under subsection (2) to appoint different days for different purposes includes power to appoint different days for different areas.

(5) The Secretary of State may by regulations make such transitional provision as he considers necessary or expedient in connection with the bringing into force of any of the following provisions of this Act–

(a)   sections 43 to 46 and section (1) of Part III of Schedule 9;

(b)   sections 68 to 70 and Schedule 7 and Part VII of Schedule 9.

(6) Regulations under subsection (5) shall be made by statutory instrument subject to annulment in pursuance of a resolution of either House of Parliament.

(7) Section 174(2) to (4) of the Pensions Act 1995 (supplementary provision in relation to powers to make subordinate legislation under that Act) shall apply in relation to the power to make regulations under subsection (5) as it applies to any power to make regulations under that Act.

(8) In this section ''subordinate legislation'' has the same meaning as in the Interpretation Act 1978.

Short title and extent

87.–(1) This Act may be cited as the Child Support, Pensions and Social Security Act 2000.

(2) The following provisions of this Act extend to Northern Ireland–

(a)   so much of section 46 as amends section 21(3) of the Pensions Act 1995;

(b)   sections 57 to 61 (except section 60(5));

(c)   section 73;

(d)   sections 78 to 81;

(e)   in Schedule 3, paragraphs 8 and 9, and in paragraph 11, sub-paragraph (2) (and sub-paragraph (1) so far as it relates to that sub-paragraph);

(f)   paragraph 6 of Schedule 5; and

(g)   this Part, except–

(i)   sections 82 and 83 and Schedule 8; and

(ii)   so much of this Part as gives effect to any repeal other than the repeals mentioned in subsection (3).

(3)   The repeals mentioned in subsection (2)(g) (which extend to Northern Ireland) are–

(a)   the repeals, in Part I of Schedule 9, that relate to the Tax Credits Act 1999;

(b)   the repeals, in sections (1), (6) and (11) of Part III of that Schedule, that relate to–

(i)   section 21(3) of the Pensions Act 1995;

(ii)   paragraph 49(a)(ii) of Schedule 3 to the Pensions (Northern Ireland) Order 1995; and

(iii)   section 52(5) of the Pension Schemes (Northern Ireland) Act 1993;

(c)   the repeals in Part IV of that Schedule (except so far as relating to the Courts and Legal Services Act 1990); and

(d)   the repeals in section (2) of Part VIII of that Schedule.

(4)   Subject to that, this Act does not extend to Northern Ireland.

SCHEDULE 7
HOUSING BENEFIT AND COUNCIL TAX BENEFIT: REVISIONS AND APPEALS

General Note on Sch 7

Under reg 89 HB Regs, reg 70 HB(SPC) Regs, reg 75 CTB Regs and reg 60 CTB(SPC) Regs, any matter that needs to be determined in order to decide a claim for HB or CTB falls to be determined by the relevant authority (ie, by a local government officer). Sch 7 and the D&A Regs (which are made under para 10 of Sch 7) are concerned with the circumstances in which the initial decisions of local authorites can be changed.

There are only three such mechanisms, revision under para 3, supersession under para 4, and appeal, initially to an appeal tribunal. Unless a decision can be revised, superseded or changed on appeal, then it is final (see para 11). Contrary to what some local authorities – and the suppliers of their computer software – still seem to believe, there is no power for an authority simply to "cancel" or "withdraw" an award of HB or CTB: see, eg, *CH 2302/2002*.

Except where otherwise stated below, Sch 7 came into force on 2 July 2001 (art 2(2) Child Support, Pensions and Social Security Act 2000 (Commencement No 8) Order 2001 No 1252) and replaced the previous system of HB and CTB adjudication, under which the determinations of local authorities were subject to review by (usually) a more senior officer under reg 79 HB Regs 1987 or reg 69 CTB Regs 1992, and then to a further review by a Review Board consisting of members (ie, councillors) of the authority concerned under regs 81-83 HB Regs 1987 and regs 70-72 CTB Regs 1992. That system did not comply with Art 6 of the European Convention on Human Rights (see *Tsfayo v United Kingdom* (application no: 60860/00) [2006], 14 November, unreported, ECtHR) and therefore could not remain in place after the Human Rights Act 1998 came into force.

Under Sch 7, those who are affected by a local authority decision on a claim for, or an award of, HB or CTB – and those from whom it is determined that an overpayment of HB or CTB is recoverable – have a right of appeal to an appeal tribunal and thereafter, on a point of law, to the social security commissioners and then (in England and Wales) the Court of Appeal or (in Scotland) the Inner House of the Court of Session. The effect is to align the appeal rights for HB and CTB with those for the social security benefits administered by the DWP and the Revenue. The scheme of Sch 7 thus follows that set out in Part I, Ch II SSA 1998 very closely and decision of the commissioners and courts on the comparable provisions will be of highly persuasive force in interpreting Sch 7. Care should be taken to note the differences between the two sets of legislation, however.

A system of revisions and supersessions is found in paras 3 and 4 which is identical to ss8 and 9 SSA 1998. Paras 6 and 7 govern appeals to tribunals in a similar fashion to ss12 and 13, and paras 8 and 9 deal with further appeals to the Commissioners and the courts in a similar fashion to ss14 and 15. There are also extensive powers to suspend benefit in paras 13 and 14 and an anti-test case rule in paras 16 to 18 which is not, however, being fully implemented.

The general approach to decision making in social security and, by implication, HB and CTB, was considered by the House of Lords in *Kerr v Department for Social Development [2004] UKHL 23 (reported as R 1/04 (SF))*. The House of Lords set out five propositions of general application to the field of benefits adjudication. First, the determination of claims should be an inquisitorial process rather than adversarial. Second, facts which may reasonably be supposed to be within the claimant's own knowledge are for the claimant to supply at each stage in the assessment of the claim. However, s/he must be given a reasonable opportunity to supply them. Third, the knowledge as to the information that is needed to deal with a claim lies with the DWP (and/or the HB/CTB authority) and not with the claimant: so it is for the former to ask the relevant questions and the claimant is not to be faulted if the relevant questions to show whether or not the claim is excluded are not asked. Fourth, the general rule is that it is for the party who alleges an affirmative to make good his or her allegation. Fifth, it is also a general rule that a party who desires to take advantage of an exception must bring her/himself within the provisions of the exception: exceptions (including grounds of disentitlement to benefit) are to be established by those who rely on them: *Nimmo v Alexander Cowan & Sons Ltd* [1968], 1967 SC (HL) 79, so that in *Kerr* it was for the Department of Social Development in Northern Ireland to prove on the wording of the sub-regulation that was relevant in that case that the named close relatives of Mr Kerr were not in receipt of a relevant benefit, as proof of that condition acted as a ground of disentitlement to a social fund funeral payment.

Introductory

1.–(1)   In this Schedule "relevant authority" means an authority administering housing benefit or council tax benefit.

(2)   In this Schedule "relevant decision" means any of the following–

(a)   a decision of a relevant authority on a claim for housing benefit or council tax benefit;

(b)   any decision under paragraph 4 of this Schedule which supersedes a decision falling within paragraph (a), within this paragraph or within paragraph (b) of sub-paragraph (1) of that paragraph;

but references in this Schedule to a relevant decision do not include references to a decision under paragraph 3 to revise a relevant decision.

Analysis

"Relevant decision". A "relevant decision" is a decision of a local authority that either decides a claim for HB or CTB or that supersedes such a decision (or a decision of a tribunal or commissioner) under para 4. The definition is important because it governs which decisions can be revised and superseded and which carry a right of appeal.

"Decision" in this context means what is sometimes described as an "outcome" decision – ie, that the claimant is not entitled to benefit or is so entitled at a specified weekly rate for a specified period. The decisions that an authority makes on the individual issues of fact and law that lead to a conclusion of entitlement or non-entitlement (eg, whether a claimant is liable to pay rent, the calculation of her/his applicable amount or the level of her/his income) are not outcome decisions but, rather, findings of fact or "determinations". Findings of fact and determinations cannot themselves be revised, superseded or (except, possibly, for determinations that an overpayment is recoverable – see below) appealed against. However, if there are grounds on which to change a finding of fact or determination that may lead to a revision or supersession if the result is to change the outcome. Another way of putting the point is to say that what is revised, superseded or appealed against is the relevant decision itself and not the reason(s) for that decision.

Decisions to revise an earlier decision under para 3 are not included in the definition of "relevant decision" because the effect of a revising decision is to alter the terms of the original decision but without replacing it. Any challenge (whether by way of an application for a further revision or an appeal) is therefore against the original decision as revised, rather than against the revising decision. This explains the words "whether as originally made or as revised under paragraph 3" in brackets in paras 4(1) and 6(1). By contrast, a superseding decision replaces the original decision, albeit (usually) with effect from a later date.

Because para 1(2)(a) is not limited to decisions taken by the authority under Sch 7, decisions taken by local government officers before 2 July 2001 under regs 76 or 79 HB Regs 1987 and regs 66 or 69 (which, at the time, were referred to as "determinations") are "relevant decisions" and can therefore be revised under para 3: *R(H) 6/04* (para 21). It follows that they can also be superseded under para 4. Decisions taken by review boards before 2 July 2001 under reg 83 HB Regs or reg 72 CTB Regs 1992 which, at the time, were referred to as "decisions") are treated (by reg 4(4) of the D&A Transitional Regs – see below) as having been made by an appeal tribunal under para 6. An authority may therefore supersede them in para 4(1)(b), but they cannot be revised under para 3.

Note that a determination that an overpayment is recoverable is not a "relevant decision" within the definition in sub-para (2): *R(H) 3/04* (para 34). See the commentary to para 6 below and to s75 SSAA 1992 (see p43).

Refusals to revise and supersede. To supersede a decision is to alter it (see the decision of the majority of the Court of Appeal in *Wood v Secretary of State for Work and Pensions* [2003] EWCA Civ 53, CA (reported as *R(DLA) 1/03*) paras 42-43 and 78. By the same reasoning, to revise a decision is also to alter it. It follows that where an authority reconsiders an existing decision and does not change the outcome then it is not revising or superseding it (or even, as used to be said before *Wood*, superseding it "at the same rate") but *refusing* to revise or supersede it. That is so even if the reasoning or findings of fact that led to the original decision are changed, as long as the outcome remains the same.

Is a *refusal* to revise or supersede a "relevant decsion" that gives rise to further rights of challenge?
For a refusal to revise, the answer is no. As revision changes the terms of the original decsion without replacing it, a refusal to revise leaves the orginal decsion unchanged. Note, however, that where the application for a revision is made within one month of the original decision (or within that time limit as extended under reg 5 D&A regs), the refusal will have the effect of extending time for an appeal against the original decision: see the commentary to paras 6 and regs 4 and 18(3) D&A Regs (see pp955 and 979).

For a refusal to supersede, the question is more difficult but it is suggested that the answer must be yes. In *Wood*, the Court of Appeal was considering ss10(1) and 12(1) and (9) SSA 1998. In order to avoid infriging Art 6 of the European Convention on Human Rights, the majority adopted a strained construction of the phrase "decision superseding any such decision" in s12(9) as meaning "decision taken pursuant to the power to supersede". A refusal to supersede was therefore a "decision taken pursuant to the power to supersede". A refusal to supersede was therefore a "decision ... under section ... 10" for the purposes of the right of appeal in s12(1) even though no supersession had actually taken place (*Wood* paras 51 and 78). Paras 1, 4 and 6 of Sch 7 are not in the same terms as ss10 and 12 SSA 1998 and the analogy is therefore not exact. Nevertheless, it is suggested that the same approach should be applied to HB and CTB decisions. This would involve reading the words "any decision under paragrapgh 4 of this Schedule which supersedes a decision) in para 1(2)(b) as meaning "any decision *taken pursuant to the power* under paragraph 4 ...". Given the decision of the majority in *Wood* that to "supersede" an earlier decision the superseding decision must change it, any other approach would inevitably infringe the Convention rights of the person affected. The approach is therefore required by s3(1) Human Rights Act 1998.

Decisions on claims for benefit
2. Where at any time a claim for housing benefit or council tax benefit is decided by a relevant authority–
   (a)   the claim shall not be regarded as subsisting after that time; and
   (b)   accordingly, the claimant shall not (without making a further claim) be entitled to the benefit on the basis of circumstances not obtaining at that time.

Analysis
The effect of para 2 is that a decision refusing a claim for HB or CTB (sometimes called a "nil award") cannot be superseded on grounds of a change of circumstances that occurs after the *decision* was made. If someone is correctly refused benefit and her/his circumstances change, s/he must instead make a fresh claim for benefit. For the situation if someone's circumstances change after an appeal against a decision is made, see Sch 7 para 6(9).

Sub-para (a). This confirms that the temporal effect of a claim ceases on the date that the authority makes its decision on the claim. The logical implication of the words "after that time" is that the claim does "subsist" prior to that time and so if a claimant is not entitled to benefit as at the date of claim but because of a change of circumstances becomes entitled on some later date before the authority makes its decision, the authority is obliged to award benefit from the later date. If this interpretation is correct, there may be some tension between sub-para (a) and reg 83(10) HB Regs (reg 64(11) HB(SPC) Regs) and the CB equivalents, which appears to restrict the power to make such an award to a period of 13 weeks after the date of claim. Delays of more than that period in adjudicating claims are, unfortunately, endemic in some authorities. However, it may be argued that the regulations do no more than give a power to make an advance award *after* the date of claim.

To minimise any injustice caused by sub-para (a), it is suggested that benefit may be awarded from any date between the date of claim and the date on which the decision is made, even if the latter date is more than 13 weeks after the former. If, however, the decision is made quickly but it is apparent that the claimant would have become entitled to benefit within the 13 week period specified in reg 83(10) HB Regs (64(11) HB(SPC) Regs), such an award should be made.

Sub-para (b), if interpreted literally, leads to some bizarre results. What does "circumstances not obtaining at that time" mean? It appears to require the authority to consider only the circumstances as at the date of its decision. If that was so, then a claimant entitled to benefit on the date of claim but who subsequently loses entitlement as a result of a change of circumstances could not be awarded benefit at all. Again, this would give the severe delays occurring in many authorities even more serious consequences than the delays themselves.

The wording of sub-para (b) is similar to that used in para 6(9)(b) and the decisions of Commissioners on the scope of s12(8)(b) SSA 1998 (the equivalent to para 6(9)(b) in relation to DWP benefits) will therefore assist. It is suggested that the position postulated in the previous paragraph would give rise to absurdities similar to those discussed in *R(DLA) 3/01* (see the commentary to para 6(9)(b) below). It is therefore appropriate to construe sub-para (b) as not excluding consideration of the position as at the date of claim and between the date of claim and date of the authority's initial decision. On that interpretation, it excludes consideration only of circumstances arising after the initial decision.

Two elements of the wording of sub-para (b) support that interpretation. First, the word "accordingly" links sub-para (b) to the rest of the paragraph and so focuses attention on the period after the decision is made. Secondly, "without making a further claim" again calls attention to the true focus of the sub-paragraph. The intention is that if a claim is rejected but a claimant subsequently becomes entitled, the claimant's means of securing benefit is a further claim and not an appeal against the initial refusal.

Revision of decisions

3.–(1)   Any relevant decision may be revised or further revised by the relevant authority which made the decision–

(a)   either within the prescribed period or in prescribed cases or circumstances; and

(b)   either on an application made for the purpose by a person affected by the decision or on their own initiative;

and regulations may prescribe the procedure by which a decision of a relevant authority may be so revised.

(2)   In making a decision under sub-paragraph (1), the relevant authority need not consider any issue that is not raised by the application or, as the case may be, did not cause them to act on their own initiative.

(3)   Subject to sub-paragraphs (4) and (5) and paragraph 18, a revision under this paragraph shall take effect as from the date on which the original decision took (or was to take) effect.

(4)   Regulations may provide that, in prescribed cases or circumstances, a revision under this paragraph shall take effect as from such other date as may be prescribed.

(5)   Where a decision is revised under this paragraph, for the purposes of any rule as to the time allowed for bringing an appeal, the decision shall be regarded as made on the date on which it is so revised.

(6)   Except in prescribed circumstances, an appeal against a decision of the relevant authority shall lapse if the decision is revised under this paragraph before the appeal is determined.

Definition

"relevant decision" – see Sch 7 para 1 CSPSSA 2000.

Analysis

Para 3 provides the statutory basis for a revision. The basic distinction between a revision and supersession is that the former alters the term of the original decision without replacing it and usually does not change the date from which the decision takes effect. A supersession replaces the original decision but usually only from some date subsequent to the date on which the decision was made.

Note that it is only a "relevant decision" as defined in para 1(2) that can be revised, or further revised, by the relevant authority that made the decision. This means that an authority cannot revise the decision of a tribunal or commissioner. Such a decision may only be altered by a supersession under para 4 or on appeal.

The detailed procedure in relation to revisions is to be found in regs 4, 5 and 6 D&A Regs. Only the bare outline is given here.

Note that following the decision of the Tribunal of Commissioners in *R(H) 3/04*, it may not be possible to revise a determination that an overpayment is recoverable. See the commentary to para 6 below.

Sub-para (1) introduces the power to revise. It includes a power to revise a decision more than once: "may be . . . further revised". A claimant may apply for a revision or it may be carried out by the authority of its own motion. For the mode of making an application, see regs 4(8) and (9) D&A Regs. For the "prescribed period", see reg 4(1) D&A Regs and note reg 5 giving power to extend time for an application by a claimant. For the "prescribed cases or circumstances" see regs 4(2), (3), (5), (7) and (7A)-(7F).

Sub-para (2) limits what the authority is required to consider in the course of a revision. The critical phrase here, however, is "need not" which confers a discretion: see *R(IB) 2/04*. Therefore, authorities should not shut their eyes where to do so would cause an injustice. However, claimants are best advised to raise all the points with which they disagree in their applications for revision and to provide relevant evidence and information to support the application. On an appeal against a revised decision (or against a refusal to revise) a tribunal may exercise this discretion for itself. See commentary to Sch 7 para 6(9)(a).

Sub-paras (3) and (4) state the general rule that a revision takes effect from the same date as did the original decision. Accordingly, where a claimant is seeking an increase in benefit, a revision is more advantageous than a supersession. For exceptions to the rule, see the anti test-case rule in para 18 and reg 6 D&A Regs.

Sub-para (5) is necessary because of the effect of a revision, which is to substitute the decision as revised for the original decision. This means that it is the date on which the decision was revised from which time runs for the purposes of bringing an appeal, and not the date of the original decision which would render many revised decisions appeal-proof.

Sub-para (6). If a decision is revised while there is an appeal pending against it, then the appeal lapses (ie, with the effect that the tribunal or commissioner no longer has jurisdiction to hear it) if the revised decision is *more advantageous* to the person affected than the orginal decision: see reg 17 D&A Regs on p978. If that person remains dissatisfied with the revised decision (ie, because it remains less favourable than would have been the case had the appeal been completely successful), then s/he must make a fresh appeal against the decision as revised.

Decisions superseding earlier decisions

4.–(1) Subject to sub-paragraph (4), the following, namely–

(a) any relevant decision (whether as originally made or as revised under paragraph 3), and

(b) any decision under this Schedule of an appeal tribunal or a Commissioner,

may be superseded by a decision made by the appropriate relevant authority, either on an application made for the purpose by a person affected by the decision or on their own initiative.

(2) In this paragraph "the appropriate relevant authority" means the authority which made the decision being superseded, the decision appealed against to the tribunal or, as the case may be, the decision to which the decision being appealed against to the Commissioner relates.

(3) In making a decision under sub-paragraph (1), the relevant authority need not consider any issue that is not raised by the application or, as the case may be, did not cause them to act on their own initiative.

(4) Regulations may prescribe the cases and circumstances in which, and the procedure by which, a decision may be made under this paragraph.

(5) Subject to sub-paragraph (6) and paragraph 18, a decision under this paragraph shall take effect as from the date on which it is made or, where applicable, the date on which the application was made.

(6) Regulations may provide that, in prescribed cases or circumstances, a decision under this paragraph shall take effect as from such other date as may be prescribed.

Definitions

"relevant decision" – see Sch 7 para 1 CSPSSA 2000.

Analysis

Sub-paras (1) and (4) permit a supersession of a decision of an authority, as originally made or as revised or superseded, or of a tribunal or a commissioner. Again, this may occur on the initiative of either the claimant or the authority. See reg 7 D&A Regs for the circumstances in which supersession is permitted, and note especially reg 7(6) which permits a notification of a change of circumstances to be treated as an application for a supersession. Note that, following the decision of the Tribunal of Commissioners in *R(H) 3/04*, it may not be possible to supersede a determination that an overpayment is recoverable. See the commentary to para 6 below.

Sub-para (3) is similar in terms to para 3(2) above – see the commentary to that provision.

Sub-paras (5) and (6) again state the general rule as to the effective date of a supersession decision. It will normally take effect from the date it was made or from the date on which the application for it was made. See regs 8 and 9 D&A Regs for the extensive exceptions to this general rule.

Use of experts by relevant authorities

5. Where it appears to a relevant authority that a matter in relation to which a relevant decision falls to be made by them involves a question of fact requiring special expertise, they may direct that, in dealing with that matter, they shall have the assistance of one or more persons appearing to them to have knowledge or experience which would be relevant in determining that question.

Analysis

It is unclear why this provision was thought necessary. Perhaps it was designed to prevent any allegation that a decision was invalid because the part of the decision that required expertise had been effectively delegated to the expert. It is unlikely that much use will be made of this power.

Appeal to appeal tribunal

6.–(1) Subject to sub-paragraph (2), this paragraph applies to any relevant decision (whether as originally made or as revised under paragraph 3) of a relevant authority which–

(a) is made on a claim for, or on an award of, housing benefit or council tax benefit; or

(b)   does not fall within paragraph (a) but is of a prescribed description.

(2)   This paragraph does not apply to–

(a)   any decision terminating or reducing the amount of a person's housing benefit or council tax benefit that is made in consequence of any decision made under regulations under section 2A of the Administration Act (work-focused interviews);

(b)   any decision of a relevant authority as to the application or operation of any modification of a housing benefit scheme or council tax benefit scheme under section 134(8)(a) or section 139(6)(a) of the Administration Act (disregard of war disablement and war widows' pensions);

(c)   so much of any decision of a relevant authority as adopts a decision of a rent officer under any order made by virtue of section 122 of the Housing Act 1996 (decisions of rent officers for the purposes of housing benefit);

(d)   any decision of a relevant authority as to the amount of benefit to which a person is entitled in a case in which the amount is determined by the rate of benefit provided for by law; or

(e)   any such other decision as may be prescribed.

(3)   In the case of a decision to which this paragraph applies, any person affected by the decision shall have a right to appeal to an appeal tribunal.

(4)   Nothing in sub-paragraph (3) shall confer a right of appeal in relation to–

(a)   a prescribed decision; or

(b)   a prescribed determination embodied in or necessary to a decision.

(5)   Regulations under sub-paragraph (4) shall not prescribe any decision or determination that relates to the conditions of entitlement to housing benefit or council tax benefit for which a claim has been validly made.

(6)   Where any amount of housing benefit or council tax benefit is determined to be recoverable under or by virtue of section 75 or 76 of the Administration Act (overpayments and excess benefits), any person from whom it has been determined that it is so recoverable shall have a right of appeal to an appeal tribunal.

(7)   A person with a right of appeal under this paragraph shall be given such notice of the decision in respect of which he has that right, and of that right, as may be prescribed.

(8)   Regulations may make provision as to the manner in which, and the time within which, appeals are to be brought.

(9)   In deciding an appeal under this paragraph, an appeal tribunal–

(a)   need not consider any issue that is not raised by the appeal; and

(b)   shall not take into account any circumstances not obtaining at the time when the decision appealed against was made.

Definitions

"relevant decision" – see para 1.
"relevant authority" – *ibid*.

Analysis

Appeal tribunals

This paragraph sets out the scope of the right of appeal to an appeal tribunal. The appeal tribunals system, which can be traced back to 1946 in its present form, is set up under s5 and Sch 1 SSA 1998. The Tribunals Service is an executive agency of the Department of Constitutional Affairs. It is responsible for the administration of appeals. The appeal tribunal itself is legally distinct from the Tribunals Service. It is now called the Social Security and Child Support Appeal Tribunal. The current President is His Honour Judge Robert Martin. It is his function to select the members of the appeal tribunal from an independent panel of tribunal members. The members are appointed to the panel by the Lord Chancellor under s6 SSA 1998, although they are selected for appointment by the Judicial Appointments Commission. The panel is comprised of legally, financially, medically and disability qualified members, although only the first two categories of member will sit in HB and CTB appeals and it will be rare for a financially qualified member to sit: reg 22 D&A Regs.

The basic approach to decision-making by tribunals

It cannot be overemphasised that a tribunal hearing an appeal is conducting a rehearing of the case: see *R(IB) 2/04* (paras 19-25), affirming *CH 1129/2002*. Subject to the restrictions imposed by sub-para (9), it must decide whether it agrees the decision of the local authority was right, not whether it thinks that the local authority was entitled to reach the decision that it did on the evidence before it as the High Court used to do in considering challenges to decisions of Review Boards: see *CH 1175/2002* (para 4). A tribunal has power to remit issues to a local authority for consideration by it: *CH 3009/2002* (para 25).

A tribunal is entitled to and must ensure that it has jurisdiction to hear the case before it. That means that it must ensure that the challenge made by a claimant to the decision is one which the claimant is entitled to make: see the commentary to sub-para (1) below. It also means that it must satisfy itself that the decision challenged is one which has been validly made. A failure by the local authority to comply with the requirement to notify a decision to the claimant in a proper form or to follow the rules concerning supersession and revision may render the decision of no effect: see the commentary to reg 90 and Sch 9 HB Regs.

Although (see below) a tribunal should consider every issue that is raised by the appeal, and that will include any issue that is "clearly apparent from the evidence" (per *Mongan v Department for Social Development* [2005] NICA 16, 13 April (reported as *R 3/05 (DLA)*, it does not follow that the tribunal must make a *decision* on *every* issue raised by the appeal if there is a more appropriate way of dealing with one or more issues: *CIS 624/2006*. The Tribunal of Commissioners in that appeal went on to say:

"When an appeal against an outcome decision raises one issue on which the appeal is allowed but it is necessary to deal with a further issue before another outcome decision is substituted, a tribunal may set aside the original outcome decision without substituting another outcome decision, provided it deals with the original issue raised by the appeal and substitutes a decision on that issue".

It will then be for the Respondent authority to make a fresh decision on the new issue, against which new appeal rights will arise.

The Tribunal of Commissioners gave the following guidance:

- in order to assist tribunals, the [Respondent's] submission to a tribunal should indicate whether it is considered that, if the appeal is allowed, there are any outstanding issues that need further consideration and whether the [Respondent] wishes the tribunal to deal with them;
- where a tribunal, having dealt with the issues originally raised in an appeal, is not able immediately to give an outcome decision, it must decide whether to adjourn or whether to remit the question of entitlement to the [Respondent] if [it] would be in a better position to decide the issue and to seek further information from the claimant;
- the tribunal's decision, as recorded on the decision notice issued at the conclusion of the hearing, should explicitly record what has and has not been decided and in particular, should make it absolutely clear whether the tribunal has made an outcome decision or has remitted the final decision on entitlement to the [Respondent authority].

For a more detailed discussion of the rules that must be followed by a tribunal, see the commentary to Sch 7 para 8(1) below and to the SSCS D&A Regs and D&A Regs, in particular reg 53 SSCS D&A Regs.

Sub-para (1): Decisions that can be appealed

The first question that arises under para 6 is whether the decision of which complaint is made is one in respect of which the tribunal has jurisdiction. A tribunal has no jurisdiction beyond that conferred by legislation: *R(H) 3/04* (para 32). Sub-para (1) sets out the general rule, which is subject to sub-paras (2) and (3) discussed below.

" . . . any relevant decision (whether as originally made or as revised . . .)". See the commentary to para 1 above for discussion of the scope of a "relevant decision" and in particular for the question of whether a refusal to supersede is a relevant decision. As regards refusals to revise, reg 18(3)(b) D&A Regs specifically envisages a notification that no revision is to be carried out, and allows for an appeal to be made, within one month of the notification of the refusal to revise, against the original decision; that is, the decision being sought to be revised. See, however, the commentary to reg 4 D&A Regs for the different position for revisions at "any time".

A tribunal must be careful, when determining an appeal against a decision which has been revised, to ensure that it is considering the revised decision and not the original decision, otherwise it will err in law: *CH 1171/2002* (paras 3-8).

Sub-para (1) does not confer a right of appeal against a determination that an overpayment is recoverable: *R(H) 3/04* (para 33). The right of appeal arises under sub-para (6) instead: see below.

" . . . made on a claim for, or on an award . . . ". An appeal may be brought against any decision (whether an original decision or a revised or superseded decision) "made on a claim for, or on an award of" HB or CTB. No regulations have been made under sub-para (1)(b) and so every appeal must fall within the quoted words. They are wide enough to extend to issues arising under other legislation that must be determined for the purposes of an HB claim. Therefore, an appeal may be validly made against a decision that a claimant is excluded from benefit under s115 Immigration and Asylum Act 1999 or as to her/his entitlement as a refugee under s123 of that Act.

There is an unfortunate tension between the definition of "relevant decision" in para 1(2) and these words in para 6(1). Para 1(2) defines a relevant decision only in terms of a decision on a claim or a supersession decision. The words "on an award" in para 6(1) must therefore be taken to refer to a decision superseding or refusing to supersede an earlier decision in order to avoid inconsistency between the two provisions.

For the question as to whether there is a right of appeal against a refusal to supersede, see the Analysis to para 1(2) above.

In *Carpenter v Secretary of State for Work and Pensions* [2003] EWCA Civ 33 (reported as *R(IB) 6/03*), the Court of Appeal had to consider whether a refusal by a tribunal to adjourn a hearing was of itself a "decision" which called for a statement of reasons under reg 53(4) SSCS D&A Regs. Laws LJ confirmed that a distinction had to be drawn between an "outcome" decision and a procedural "determination": para 16. Caution is required in relation to the application of this decision to determining the scope of the right of appeal in para 6. Laws LJ placed considerable reliance on s17 SSA 1998, which is in markedly different terms to Sch 7 para 11 CSPSSA. Para 6(4) does suggest a distinction between a "decision" and "determination". However, para 6(4)(b) only excludes a right of appeal in the case of a "prescribed" determination. This may suggest that a determination may amount to a "relevant decision" in certain circumstances.

The claimant's right to a fair hearing by an independent tribunal at common law and under Art 6 must always inform any decision as to the scope of appeal rights: *Wood v Secretary of State for Work and Pensions* [2003] EWCA Civ 53, CA (reported as *R(DLA) 1/03*). The tribunal's priority should at all times be to ensure that a person affected has a fair opportunity to challenge any aspect of a decision which affects her/him.

". . . of a prescribed description". No regulations have yet been made under para 6(1)(b), so if a decision is to be appealable it must fall within either para 6(1)(a) or para 6(6).

Sub-paras (2), (4) and (5): Decisions which cannot be appealed

Sub-paras (2) and (4) then set out a number of circumstances in which no appeal lies to a tribunal against a decision. These are:

(1)   A decision terminating or reducing the amount of HB or CTB after a decision relating to a work-focused interview: head (a). However the decision relating to the interview attracted its own right of appeal: see reg 15 of the Social Security (Work-Focused Interviews) Regulations 2000 in the 2003/04 edition of this book. Note that work-focused interviews were only required in certain local authority areas operating within the ONE scheme, now largely replaced by Jobcentre Plus, which does not require work-focused interviews for HB and CTB.

(2)   A decision as to whether war disablement and war widows' (or widowers') pensions should be disregarded for HB and CTB purposes: head (b). Such decisions are taken by resolution of the whole local authority. See the Analysis to s134(8) SSAA 1992.

(3)   Any element of a decision relating to HB that follows inevitably from the conclusion reached by the rent officer: head (c). This prevents any indirect challenge to a rent officer's determinations. However, a danger can arise here if neither the appellant or the local authority in the appeal address the issue of whether the alternative version of reg 13 HB Regs (or of reg 13 HB(SPC) Regs) may apply (and hence that the rent officer's determination may not be determinative of the eligible rent). In such a situation, there is a danger that the appeal may be struck out on the papers by a legally qualifed panel member. It is therefore suggested that local authorities should set out in any reg 13 submission that the alternative version of reg 13 does not apply (if that is the case) and why that is so. It is further suggested that legally qualified panel members should be astute to ask for this information from the local authority if it has not been provided before striking out any appeal under this provision.

(4)   Any element of a decision as to the rate of benefit: head (d). No-one can therefore make an appeal on the ground that the benefit they are receiving is insufficient, or that a premium is insufficient to meet a need. This would include, it would seem, any argument relying on the Human Rights Act 1998. As any such appeal would be hopeless in any event, it seems that these are included so as to designate them as "out-of-jurisdiction" appeals and hence capable of being dealt with under the summary procedure in reg 46(1) SSCS D&A Regs.

(5)   Any prescribed decision: head (e). See the Schedule to the D&A Regs and the commentary thereto. Sub-para (5) forbids the exclusion of any decision relating to whether the conditions of entitlement have been fulfilled.

Sub-paragraph (6): Appeals relating to recovery of overpayments

Sub-para (6) deals with the thorny subject of overpayment appeals. It was established by the decision of the Tribunal of Commissioners in *R(H) 3/04* (para 33) that the right to challenge decisions relating to recovery of overpayments arises under sub-para (6) and not under sub-para (1). The basis for that conclusion was that s75(1) SSAA still talks in terms of a "determination" that an overpayment is recoverable, and that word was to be distinguished from a "relevant decision" which would be appealable under sub-para (1). That distinction would appear to lead to the conclusion that an overpayment "determination" cannot be altered once made by revision or supersession, other than on appeal. Two possible answers to this are as follows. First, it might be possible to argue that the former legislation was preserved. Secondly, since Sch 7 para 11 presumably does not apply (on the approach of the Tribunal of Commissioners) to overpayment determinations, reliance might be placed on the common law rule that a statutory power can be exercised repeatedly unless the legislation provides otherwise: s12 Interpretation Act 1978, though see Wade and Forsyth, *Administrative Law* (2000 8th edn) pp235-236.

Most of the problems concerning the scope of the right of appeal under sub-para (6) have now been resolved by the Tribunal of Commissioners' decision in *R(H) 6/06*.

Challenging a decision that there has been an overpayment*.* Before a determination can be made that an overpayment is recoverable, it is a pre-condition that the decisions awarding benefit are altered: *R(H) 3/04* (para 34). Although the Tribunal of Commissioners referred only to the alteration being carried out by way of supersession, revision will be appropriate in the case of any award of benefit which is to be altered for the full period for which it was in effect.

There still seem to be some authorities who persist in asserting that a landlord has no right to challenge a decision that an overpayment has occurred but only that it is recoverable from her/him. That is plainly incorrect. The decision that an overpayment has occurred is made under s75(1) or 76(1) SSAA and hence falls within the right of appeal conferred by sub-para (6). The Tribunal of Commissioners in *R(H) 3/04* (para 50) and *R(H) 6/06* have confirmed that a landlord may assert on an appeal that no overpayment has occurred, even if the claimant has not challenged the decision or decisions altering entitlement to benefit.

Challenging recovery of the overpayment*.* One of the most troublesome questions under the new adjudication regime has been the extent to which a decision to recover an overpayment (as distinct from a determination that it is recoverable) may be appealed.

Whatever the correctness of the Court of Appeal's decision in *Secretary of State for Work and Pensions v Chiltern District Council* [2003] EWCA Civ 508 (*R(H) 2/03*) and the Tribunal of Commissioner's decision in *R(H) 3/04* in respect of the regime in place prior to October 2001 (and the correctness of the Court of Appeal's decision is strongly doubted in *R(H) 6/06*), the Tribunal of Commissioners' decision in *R(H) 6/06* holds that rights of appeal only attach to decisions going to the recoverability of an overpayment and do not attach to decisions concerning the recovery (or enforcement) of such recoverable overpayment decisions. See further the commentary to s75 SSAA 1992 above.

Challenging the method of recovery*.* A tribunal has no jurisdiction over *how* an overpayment is recovered. Methods of recovery are determined under s75(5) to (7) SSAA in a way that is outside the decision-making process as to recovery. Judicial review remains the only viable method of challenge.

This has been confirmed in *R(H) 7/04*, where the commissioner ruled that landlords had no jurisdiction to challenge the decision to recover a recoverable overpayment by way of deduction from future payments of HB made to the landlords (per s75(4) SSAA 1992 and reg 102 HB Regs 1987 – now reg 102 HB Regs and reg 83 HB(SPC) Regs), where the decision that there had been an overpayment and that it was recoverable had been issued against the tenants. In the commissioner's view, a clear distinction needs to be made in such cases between the determination that there is a recoverable overpayment from a named person, and the means by which recovery is effected. The latter may have consequences on the amount of future HB received by the landlord but that does not constitute a decision that the overpayment is recoverable from the landlord.

Sub-paragraphs (3) and (7): Persons with a right of appeal

Sub-para (3) provides that any "person affected" will generally have the right of appeal. That phrase has the same meaning as in the D&A Regs: see para 23(2) below and reg 3 D&A Regs.

Sub-para (7) requires a person affected to be given notice of appeal rights. See Sch 9 HB Regs, Sch 8 HB(SPC) Regs, Sch 8 CTB Regs and Sch 7 CTB(SPC) Regs and for the consequences of non-compliance with those provisions, see the Analysis to reg 90 HB Regs. See also reg 10 D&A Regs.

Sub-paragraph (8): Making an appeal

See regs 18, 19 and 20 D&A Regs for the procedure as to how an appeal is made.

Sub-paragraph (9): Extent of a tribunal's jurisdiction

Head (a): Issues not raised "by the appeal"*.* The "appeal" in this context must mean an issue raised in the appellant's appeal form or letter of appeal, along with any ancillary documentation (eg, in the appeal papers).

The commissioners, steeped as they are in the tradition of social security tribunals as being fully inquisitorial bodies, are likely to seek to construe head (a) narrowly. Thus if an issue is raised obliquely in the claimant's letter of appeal but the tribunal focuses upon another issue set out more clearly therein, declining to deal with the more obscure matter, it is likely that its decision will be vulnerable to challenge on the basis that it has failed to make any findings in a situation where it was obliged to do so. Tribunals ought to be ready to exercise the power to consider additional issues in order to ensure that a claimant has a fair consideration of her/his HB or CTB entitlement. For consideration as to when it will err in law in failing to do so, see the Analysis to para 8(1) under the heading "Scope of the appeal: failure to exercise inquisitorial jurisdiction".

While it is not necessary that an issue be raised by a party, even if represented by a skilled representative, the issue must be one which obviously demands attention: *Mooney v Secretary of State for Work and Pensions* [2004] SLT 1141, reported as *R(DLA) 5/04*. When an appeal tribunal should go into an issue not expressly raised by a party to the appeal was also considered by the Court of Appeal in Northern Ireland in *Mongan v Department for Social Development* [2005] NICA 16, 13 April, reported as *R3/05*

(DLA). The Court said that the words "raised by the appeal" suggest that a tribunal is not absolved of its duty to consider relevant issues simply because they have been neglected by the claimant or her/his legal representative. A tribunal will err in law if it does not consider an issue which is raised sufficiently by the available evidence, even if it has not been raised by the appellant or her/his legal representatives or the legal representative indicates that a particular point is not in issue in the appeal. A tribunal may have regard to the fact that an appellant is represented, but a poorly represented party should not be placed at a greater disadvantage than an unrepresented party. *Mongan* has been followed by the Court of Appeal of England and Wales in *Hooper v Secretary of State for Work and Pensions* [2007] EWCA Civ 495.

Note, however, that although a tribunal may not refuse to deal with an issue that is "clearly apparent from the evidence", it is not always necessary for it to deal with such an issue by making a decision about it. In *CIS 624/2006* (a decision concerning IS in which the decision maker was therefore the Secretary of State rather than a local authority) a Tribunal of Commissioners stated:

"47. ...what a tribunal must not do is ignore an issue that is clearly apparent from the evidence. However, it does not follow that the tribunal must make a decision on every issue raised by the appeal if there is a more appropriate way of dealing with one or more issues.

48. It is well established that a tribunal allowing an appeal because the decision under appeal was made without jurisdiction is entitled simply to set aside the decision without substituting another. So too may a tribunal when allowing an appeal on the ground that the original decision was not made against the correct parties and in such a case it is plainly open to the Sectretary of State to amke another decision in place of the one that has been set aside (*R(H) 6/06*). In our judgment, the same approach can be applied where an issue first arises in the course of an appeal. When an appeal against an outcome decision raises one issue on which the appeal is allowed but it is necessary to deal with a further issue before another outcome decision is substituted, a tribunal may set aside the original outcome decision without substituting anotheroutcome decision, provided it deals with the original issue raised by the appeal and substitutes a decision on that issue. The Secretary of State must then consider the new issue and decide what outcome decision to give. In that outcome decision, he must give effect to the tribunal's decision on the original issue unless, at the time he makes the outcome decision, he is satisfied that there are grounds on which to supersede the tribunal's decision so as, for instance, to take account of any changes of circumstances that have occurred since he made the decision that was the subject of the appeal to the tribunal. Because his decision is an outcome decision, the claimant will have a right of appeal against it."

A tribunal is not obliged to consider whether a valid determination has been issued or whether grounds for a revision had been established unless those points are put in issue by a person affected: *R(H) 1/02* (paras 8-9).

In *CH 1129/2002*, the commissioner carried out a detailed analysis of precisely what the effect of sub-para (9)(a) is. He concluded that an issue is "raised by the appeal" if it is raised by one of the parties (para 14). He also concluded (paras 16-18) that it did not matter at what stage of an appeal an issue was raised by a party. The tribunal remained obliged to consider such an issue, even if that meant adjourning to comply with the requirements of natural justice and give the other side a chance to meet the point.

The commissioner then went on to consider the circumstances in which a tribunal should raise an issue for itself and consider it. It is not obliged to do so under sub-para (9)(a). However, it has a discretion to do so and that discretion must be exercised judicially. The commissioner suggested (para 20) that a tribunal would err in law by refusing to consider a point raised by it if the claimant was "under a real and present danger of eviction". However, while it may be within the tribunal's discretion to refuse to consider a further point, it does not follow that it is undesirable for it to do so and it should do so in order to give a final determination of all matters that could be in dispute if possible. However, it must give a fair warning to parties that it is raising a point of its own motion. In *CH 1129/2002* itself, the local authority refused benefit under reg 6 HB Regs 1987 (now reg 8 HB Regs) but the tribunal substituted a decision under reg 7 of those regs (now reg 9 HB Regs) without making it clear to the claimant's representative that it proposed to take that course. The Commissioner held that to be a breach of natural justice (para 30).

In *R(IB) 2/04* a Tribunal of Commissioners considered the powers of an appeal tribunal to make a decision less favourable to a claimant than a supersession decision under appeal. It concluded that "need not" in the identical provision in s12(8)(a) SSA 1998 could not be read as "shall not". It said that in providing s12(8)(a), Parliament was implicitly providing that tribunals should consider whether to make a decision less favourable to the claimant than did the Secretary of State: para 90. However, there must be a conscious exercise of this discretion and an explanation of why it was exercised in the statement of reasons if requested. At para 94 of the decision, the Tribunal of Commissioners said:

"In exercising the discretion, the appeal tribunal must of course have in mind, in particular, two factors. First, it must bear in mind the need to comply with Article 6 of the Convention and the rules of natural justice. This will involve, at the very least, ensuring that the claimant has had sufficient notice of the tribunal's intention to consider superseding adversely to him to enable him properly to prepare his case. The fact that the claimant is entitled to withdraw his appeal any time before the appeal tribunal's decision may also be material to what Article 6 and the rules of natural justice demand. Second, the appeal tribunal may consider it more appropriate to leave the question whether the original decision should be superseded adversely to the claimant to be decided subsequently by the Secretary of State. This might be so if, for example, deciding that question would involve factual issues which do not overlap those raised by the appeal, or if it would necessitate an adjournment of the hearing."

Where a party has a representative, a tribunal might not investigate matters that the representative does not raise on the party's behalf. In *CSDLA 336/2000*, adhering to his views in *CSIB 389/1998* and *CSIB 588/1998*, the commissioner said that a tribunal could not be expected to enquire further into matters which emerged in evidence for the first time before it, when the claimant was represented by a "responsible representative" who chose not to and made no issue in respect of the evidence in submissions: para 15. However, no argument was made in the appeal on a point arising from the law of waiver. If the representative in an appeal to a tribunal was not fully aware of the facts and the law, this would raise the potential for a different representative, at a further appeal, to argue that the first representative was not sufficiently competent for the tribunal to assume that s/he had been aware of a relevant point, and hence the tribunal should have investigated it.

Head (b): Circumstances "not obtaining at the time when the decision . . . was made". The purpose of this provision is to oust the "down to the date of hearing" rule under which a decision maker or tribunal was required by the decision in *CS 14430/1996* (Appendix para 3) to consider the claimant's entitlement not merely at the date of claim, but also in relation to each date up until the date of the decision in question. For example, if a claimant was refused benefit on the basis that s/he was not habitually resident in the UK, then a tribunal might have found that habitual residence had not been established as at the date of claim or of the decision maker's decision but was obtained by some later date. This was a rule which, although sounding impractical in theory, when properly applied enabled tribunals to do practical justice and avoided the need for claimants to make repeated claims. The removal of the rule was typical of the bureaucratic approach of the SSA 1998 that is replicated in Sch 7. Its application to HB and CTB was never, however, fully settled: see the Analysis to reg 83 HB Regs 1987 on p388 of the 13th edition, eg if an application for a further review of a decision by a HB review board before 2 July 2001 has been treated as an appeal to an appeal tribunal under reg 3 D&A Transitional Regs.

Where an application has been made for a revision of the decision, which has been refused and the claimant has appealed against that refusal, the relevant date for the purposes of para 6(9)(b) is the date of the original decision, not the date of the refusal to revise: *CSDLA 2/2002* (para 22). The same is true of an appeal against an original decision that has been revised, but with which the appellant remains dissatisfied.

The equivalent provision relating to DWP benefits, s12(8)(b) SSA 1998, has had its scope substantially restricted by a number of Commissioners' decisions. First, "circumstances" are the facts relevant to the decision and not the *evidence* of those facts. It is therefore perfectly permissible for a tribunal to have regard to evidence which is only made available, or even evidence that only comes into existence, after the decision was made: *R(DLA) 2/01* (para 9); *R(DLA) 3/01* (paras 58-60); *CH 1175/2002* (para 6). Furthermore, circumstances arising between the date of claim and the date that the decision was made must be considered: *R(DLA) 3/01* (paras 58-60); *CIS 2428/1999* (para 20). In *CJSA 2375/2000* (para 31), this principle was extended further to include circumstances which relate to the period prior to the decision, even if those circumstances did not come to light until after the decision was made. That case related to an appeal against a disqualification from JSA. After the decision was made, a previous disqualification was overturned on appeal and so the second disqualification fell to be reduced to two weeks, even if upheld. The commissioner held that it was necessary to interpret the provision so as to avoid absurdity and this convoluted interpretation was the only way in which this could be achieved. In *CDLA 4331/2002* (para 9), Commissioner Rowland said that s12(8)(b) SSA 1998 should not be read so as to prevent changes of circumstance to be taken into account which the decision maker is entitled to anticipate because they are almost certain to occur. See reg 7(2)(a)(ii) D&A Regs which gives a local authority the power to supersede in such a situation.

The combined effect of this provision and that of Sch 7 para 2 above, along with the limits on backdating of benefit following a claim or a supersession (for these see reg 83(12) HB Regs; reg 64(1) HB(SPC) Regs; reg 69(14) CTB Regs; reg 56 CTB(SPC) Regs; and reg 8 D&A Regs) is that as a general rule, a claimant needs to consider making a fresh claim for benefit (or seeking a supersession) if circumstances change after the date of the decision being appealed. Once the appeal is determined, if the decision on the claim or supersession request (the new decision) would have been made differently by the decision maker had the result of the appeal been known, a revision of the new decision is possible. If the new decision has itself been appealed, see reg 4(1)(c) D&A Regs. If the new decision has not itself been appealed, see reg 4(7) D&A Regs.

Redetermination etc of appeals by tribunal

7.–(1)   This paragraph applies where an application is made to a person for leave under paragraph 8(7)(a) or (c) to appeal from a decision of an appeal tribunal.

(2)   If the person considers that the decision was erroneous in point of law, he may set aside the decision and refer the case either for redetermination by the tribunal or for determination by a differently constituted tribunal.

(3)   If each of the principal parties to the case expresses the view that the decision was erroneous in point of law, the person shall set aside the decision and refer the case for determination by a differently constituted tribunal.

(4)   In this paragraph and paragraph 8 "principal parties" means–

(a)   where he is the applicant for leave to appeal or the circumstances are otherwise such as may be prescribed, the Secretary of State;

(b)   the relevant authority against whose decision the appeal to the appeal tribunal was brought; and

(c)   the person affected by the decision against which the appeal to the appeal tribunal was brought or by the tribunal's decision on that appeal.

Analysis

Para 7 is equivalent, with the exception of sub-para (4), to s13 SSA 1998. It enables a shortcut to be taken where it is clear that a tribunal has gone wrong in law. The provision is only available where an application for leave to appeal to a commissioner is made under para 8(7)(a) or (c). It is *not* available if the application for leave under para 8 is one that the Chair of the tribunal has no power to consider – eg, where there is no statement of reasons for the tribunal's decision (under reg 53(4) SS&CS(DA) Regs): *CDLA 1685/2004*.

Note that the decision to set aside under paras (2) and (3) is made by a "person" to whom an application for leave is made (eg, the Chair of the tribunal), not an appeal tribunal so does not attract a right of appeal to a commissioner under para 8: *CIS 4533/2001* (para 10). However, the decision following the redetermination of the appeal by a tribunal does attract a right of appeal: see para 8(1).

Subs (2) deals with the situation where the person who is considering an application for leave to appeal takes the view that an error of law has been made. For the meaning of "erroneous in point of law" see the Analysis to para 8(1) below. In such a situation, the person may set aside the decision and remit the case for reconsideration by the same or a different tribunal. In *CIS 4533/2001*, Commissioner Rowland suggested that if an application is made for leave to appeal against a decision favourable to a claimant and the person determining that application proposes to set it aside under this provision, the claimant should be given the opportunity to make comments. A failure to give the claimant an opportunity to object to the setting aside would be in breach of the rules of natural justice.

It will usually be appropriate, and will tend to encourage confidence in the system, for a different tribunal to consider the case, except perhaps where what is required is a reconsideration of a pure point of law.

Subs (3) is a provision that is capable of causing inconvenience. If *both* parties state that the decision contains an error of law, the member is *required* to set aside the decision. In such a case, the case *must* be remitted to a differently constituted tribunal. The reasonableness of the position taken by the parties is not, on the face of it, a factor; and the parties need not even agree that the same error of law has occurred.

However, the way in which applications for leave to appeal are currently dealt with by the Tribunals Service may mean that this provision is rarely used in practice. Although under reg 58 SSCS D&A Regs, an application for leave to appeal by the local authority must be sent to every other party to the proceedings, there is no such requirement for applications made by the person affected by the decision. As such, the local authority may not be in a position to comment on an application for leave by a claimant, preventing para 7(3) taking effect. Further, there is no longer a right for a party to the proceedings to make further representations following receipt of a copy of an application for leave to appeal (reg 58(3) SSCS D&A Regs deleted by SI 2002 No 1379). It is suggested that in the rare case where the person affected thinks that the local authority may agree that a decision contains an error of law, s/he should send a copy of the application to the local authority.

If one party makes an application for leave which is then refused, and the other party then makes an application, para 7(3) will not be applicable and the question as to whether leave should be granted must be determined in the normal way: *CF 6923/1999*. If, however, both parties to the appeal have expressed the view that the decision of the tribunal is erroneous before leave has been granted or refused to either party by the tribunal, then the mandatory terms of para 7(3) mean that the decision of the tribunal must be set aside and the Commissioner can have no jurisdiction under para 8: *CIB 4427/2002* (paras 16-17). On the other hand, where one party is refused leave to appeal and renews the application for leave under para 8 of Sch 7, but at or about the same time the other party to the appeal applies for leave to appeal to the tribunal, whether para 7(3) or para 8 applies will depend upon the precise sequence of events: *CIB 2949/2005*. In that case the commissioner took the view that as the renewed application for leave to appeal had been registered with the Commissioners' Office, the commissioner became seised of the matter under para 8 of Sch 7 and para 7(3) therefore could no longer apply.

Appeal from tribunal to Commissioner

8.–(1) Subject to the provisions of this paragraph, an appeal lies to a Commissioner from any decision of an appeal tribunal under paragraph 6 or 7 on the ground that the decision of the tribunal was erroneous in point of law.

(2) An appeal lies under this paragraph at the instance of any of the following–

(a) the Secretary of State;

(b) the relevant authority against whose decision the appeal to the appeal tribunal was brought;

(c) any person affected by the decision against which the appeal to the appeal tribunal was brought or by the tribunal's decision on that appeal.

(3) If each of the principal parties to the appeal expresses the view that the decision appealed against was erroneous in point of law, the Commissioner may set aside the decision and refer the case to a tribunal with directions for its determination.

(4) Where the Commissioner holds that the decision appealed against was erroneous in point of law, he shall set it aside.

(5) Where under sub-paragraph (4) the Commissioner sets aside a decision–

(a) he shall have power, if he can do so without making fresh or further findings of fact, to give the decision which he considers the tribunal should have given;

(b) he shall also have power, if he considers it expedient, to make such findings and to give such decision as he considers appropriate in the light of them; and

(c) if he does not exercise the power in paragraph (a) or (b), he shall refer the case to a tribunal with directions for its determination.

(6) Subject to any direction of the Commissioner, a reference under sub-paragraph (3) or (5)(c) shall be to a differently constituted tribunal.

(7) No appeal lies under this paragraph without leave; and leave for the purposes of this sub-paragraph may be given–

(a) by the person who constituted, or was the chairman of, the tribunal when the decision to be appealed against was given;

(b) subject to and in accordance with regulations, by a Commissioner; or

(c) in a prescribed case, by such person not falling within paragraph (a) or (b) as may be prescribed.

(8) Regulations may make provision as to the manner in which, and the time within which, appeals are to be brought and applications made for leave to appeal.

Analysis

The Social Security Commissioners

Appointed under Sch 4 SSA 1998, the Social Security Commissioners are lawyers of at least ten years' standing who constitute a specialist appellate authority. Commissioners have had their jurisdiction gradually extended since they were first created to hear appeals in national insurance cases in 1946. They have a very high degree of expertise in social security law that few, if any, higher court judges have had the opportunity to acquire. Accordingly, their decisions have created caselaw of greater quantity and higher quality for the guidance of claimants, tribunals and authorities. Commissioners generally take a rigorous view of the requirements of a valid and lawful tribunal decision and can be expected to be more interventionist than judges of the higher courts considering applications for judicial review.

The commissioners are based principally in London and Edinburgh. The London address is currently 3rd Floor, Procession House, 55 Ludgate Hill, London EC4M 7JW. The Edinburgh office is currently George House, 126 George Street, Edinburgh EH2 4HH. Most cases are dealt with on paper but oral hearings regularly take place. Besides London and Edinburgh, the commissioners hear cases in Belfast and at the law courts in Bury, Cardiff, Doncaster and Plymouth. Exceptionally oral hearings are held in other court centres.

Video-conferenced hearings are available in some locations, but not currently for child support, HB or CTB cases.

For issues of precedent relating to commissioners' decisions, see the Introductory Notes.

Sub-paragraph (1): Right of appeal

Para (1) confers a right of appeal against any decision of an appeal tribunal made under paras 6 or 7. Note that it is the decision following the redetermination of an appeal, not the decision to set aside under para 7 that attracts a right of appeal: *CIS 4533/2001* (para 10). See the commentary to para 7.

There is only one ground for appeal: that the decision of the tribunal was erroneous in point of law.

Decisions that can be appealed. An appeal to the commissioner lies only against a "decision of an Appeal Tribunal". On the face of it, this suggests that a distinction is to be drawn between a "decision" of a tribunal ruling on the substance of an appeal and a "determination" by a legally qualified panel member on procedural matters, for example, whether an extension of time should be granted under reg 19 D&A Regs to enable a late appeal to be brought or whether a decision should be struck out under reg 46 SSCS D&A Regs.

Regard should be had to the decision of Commissioner Mesher in *R(CS) 5/02* (para 9) that all decisions of tribunals should be subject to an appeal to the commissioner, whether they are termed "decisions" or "determinations" under the legislation.

Para 8(1) grants an appeal to the commissioner "from any decision of an appeal tribunal". The word "decision" in that phrase will always encompass the tribunal's outcome decision (ie, to allow or refuse the appeal on the merits). But there is not always a right of appeal against procedural or interlocutory decisions (eg, decisions on whether to adjourn, or extend time for a late appeal, or strike out for lack of jursidiction).

The first question to ask is whether such a decision (or "determination" – it does not matter which word is used in the empowering legislation: see *R(CS) 5/02* (para 9)) is one that finally disposes of the appeal or is merely what has been described as "a determination of any matter along the way leading to a decision, including a determination of a procedural issue..." (see Laws LJ in *Carpenter v Secretary of State for Work and Pensions* [2003] EWCA Civ 33 (reported as *R(IB) 6/03*)). If not, then no appeal lies. So, for example, there can be no appeal against an adjournment or a refusal to adjourn (*Carpenter*) or a decision granting an extension of time or refusing to strike out for lack of jurisdiction (although, if such a decision is wrong in law and affects the eventual outcome of the appeal then that error will provide grounds for an appeal to the commissioner against the outcome decsion).

If an interocutory or procedural decision does finally dispose of the appeal (eg, a refusal of leave to appeal, a refusal to extend time or a decision to strike out for lack of jurisdiction), then the second question arises. This is whether the decision is inherently unappealable. In some cases, it is necessary to adopt a purposive construction of the word "decision" because to interpret that word in a way that confers a right of appeal would be to subvert the operation of other provisions that restrict or exclude that right. The leading case is the decision of the House of Lords in *Lane v Esdaile* [1891] AC 210, 212 which decided that there was no appeal to the House of Lords against a refusal by the Court of Appeal of leave to appeal to that court. It was clear that by imposing the requirement of leave, the legislature intended that there should be a check on unnecessary or frivolous appeals. To allow a right of appeal against the refusal of leave itself would be to frustrate that intention because the higher court could not decide whether the lower court should have granted leave without hearing the case.

Lane v Esdaile has been applied in the field of social security law on a number of occasions and it has been decided that there is no right of appeal to a commissioner from the following decisions:

(1)   A decision refusing leave to appeal to the Court of Appeal against a decision of the commissioner refusing leave to appeal from an appeal tribunal (*Bland v Chief Supplementary Benefit Officer* [1983] 1 WLR 262, CA (reported as *R(SB) 12/83*)).

(2)   A decision of the commissioner refusing to extend time so as to admit a late appliocation for leave to appeal (*White v Chief Adjudication Officer* [1986] 2 All ER 905, CA (reported as an appendix to *R(S) 8/85*)).

(3)   A decision refusing to extend time for appealing to an appeal tribunal under reg 36 SSCS D&A Regs. At least once the absolute 13-month time limit has expired (*Secretary of State for Work and Pensions v Morina and Borrowdale* [2007] EWCA Civ 749). It may be arguable that there is a right of appeal against a refusal to extend time within the 13-month limit: see the discussion of *Rickards v Rickards* [1990] Fam 194 at paras 35-37 and 45 of *Morina and Borrowdale* but also see *White* above.

(4)   A decision to strike out an appeal as "out of jurisdiction" under reg 46 SSCS D&A Regs (*Morina and Borrowdale*).

Whether there is a right of appeal aginst other interlocutory or procedural decisions is a matter of statutory construction in each case (see Sir Anthony Clarke MR and Arden LJ in *Morina and Borrowdale* at paras 50, and 42 and 47 respectively).

Procedural or interlocutory decisions that do not carry a right of appeal to the commissioner (or from the commissioner to the Court of Appeal) can only be challenged by judicial review.

Grounds for appeal. It cannot be over-emphasised that the tribunal is the fact-finding forum and that unless an error of law can be identified in a tribunal's decision, the commissioner will not be able to intervene, except possibly in the limited circumstances set out in category (10) below. A tribunal would not err in law simply because another tribunal or commissioner would have assessed the combined significance of the facts differently or come to a different conclusion: *CDLA 1456/2002*; *CH 627/2002*; *CH 296/2004*.

In *CDLA 2975/2002* (para 15), the commissioner emphasised the importance of clearly identifying points of law:

"Errors of law on the part of an experienced Tribunal . . . are not of course to be inferred, or imagined, simply because they reach a result on the questions of fact and degree they have to determine with which another Tribunal or professional person might possibly disagree; and appeals seeking to dispute the result on such grounds cannot of course succeed as all they are in effect doing is seeking to reargue the case again on the facts."

This illustrates the importance of claimants and authorities ensuring that they put all the points that they wish to put and call all the evidence they wish to call before the tribunal, because unless an error of law is made by the tribunal it will not be possible to remedy the situation at a later stage. See also the commentary to para 6(9)(a) above.

It is probably not possible to give an exhaustive summary of all the circumstances in which an error of law may arise. Nevertheless a number of different summaries exist, particularly in *R(A) 1/72*, *R(IS) 11/99* and the decision of the Court of Appeal in *R(Iran) v Secretary of State for the Home Department* [2005] EWCA Civ 982 (discussed by a Tribunal of Commissioners in *R(I) 2/06*). Those summaries are not inconsistent but may differ in emphasis and are inevitably influenced by the issues in the cases in which they are given. It is convenient to base this discussion on para 4 of *R(IS) 11/99*, which summaries the categories of error that can give rise to a right of appeal as follows:

(1)   A false proposition of law is evident from the tribunal's statement of reasons. This will include reliance on a provision in secondary legislation that is *ultra vires*: *Foster v Chief Adjudication Officer* [1993] AC 754, HL, though note Sch 7 para 18(4) below.

(2)   The tribunal has reached a decision that is supported by no evidence. Distinguishing between no evidence and little evidence is important in this context. A complaint in the latter category will only mean that there is an error of law if the conclusion reached is irrational: see below.

(3)   The tribunal has breached the relevancy principle, either by taking into account matters that should have been ignored, or ignoring matters that should have been taken into account. Where a tribunal is called upon to draw inferences from primary findings of fact, care must be taken to ensure that each of the factors relied upon in drawing the inference is relevant. A failure to do so will mean that the decision is erroneous in law, even if the tribunal has considered some of the relevant matters: *R v Allerdale DC HBRB ex p Doughty* [2000] COD 462, QBD. For that reason, commissioners may feel more able to interfere with a tribunal's inferences rather than its findings of primary fact: see *CH 1076/2002* for an example.

(4)   The tribunal's decision is irrational, in that no tribunal properly instructed as to the law could have reached a conclusion of fact set out in the statement of reasons. There will be many types of case heard by tribunals in which different tribunals could quite legitimately come to different conclusions. There may be no "right" answer in law: see *R(H) 1/03* (paras 24-25); *CDLA 1456/2002* (paras 9-11); and the quotation from *CDLA 2975/2002* above. It is rare for an appeal to succeed on this ground. Very often, appeals made on this ground are, on proper analysis, in fact complaining of some other error of law such as misconstruction of the relevant statutory provision. See *CDLA 1456/2002* (paras 9-13) for another particularly trenchant expression of this fundamental principle by Commissioner Howell.

(5)   The tribunal has failed to exercise its inquisitorial jurisdiction (see below).

(6)   There has been a breach of the rules of natural justice (see below).

(7)   There has been a relevant breach of the procedural rules (see below).

(8)   The tribunal has acted in breach of the claimant's rights under the European Convention on Human Rights. Since a tribunal is a "public body" under s6(3)(a) Human Rights Act 1998, by virtue of s6(1) it is obliged to act in a way which is compatible with a party's Convention rights. Domestic public law often protects the same rights as those protected by the Convention, in particular Art 6 thereof. However, the commissioners have been noticeably more enthusiastic than the courts about framing complaints of unfairness in terms of breach of Convention rights rather than trying to shoehorn them into the established grounds for complaint under domestic law set out above. See Commissioner Jacob's decision in *CJSA 5100/2001* (paras 5-9) for a vivid example. Attention should therefore be paid to caselaw under the Convention as a possible additional source of complaint, while not neglecting the more mundane approach under domestic law. See also the commentary to Art 6 on p132.

(9)   The tribunal has made a decision which it has no jurisdiction to make. This covers situations where a tribunal purports to hear appeals relating to matters over which it does not have jurisdiction under Sch 7 para 6 and the regulations made thereunder. It also covers a situation where there is no valid appeal because there is some fundamental defect in the Secretary of State's or local authority's decision making. This may arise where no proper revision or supersession has been carried out and the error cannot be corrected or where there has been a failure to give proper notification of a decision which has caused prejudice to a claimant: see the commentary to reg 90 and Sch 9 HB Regs (see pp395 and 504) for consideration of the question of when a decision is rendered invalid by virtue of a failure to revise or supersede or where there is a defective attempt at revision or supersession.

(10)   Despite what has been said above about the distinction between errors of law and fact, it is possible that errors of fact may amount to errors of law in certain circumstances. In *E v Secretary of State for the Home Department* [2004] EWCA Civ 49 (paras 63-69), the Court of Appeal held that where on appeal a fact-finding tribunal could be shown to have made a clear and indisputable error of fact and injustice was caused to an appellant as a result, an appellate tribunal (in that case, the Immigration Appeal Tribunal) could intervene. "Injustice" would only be caused, however, in a case where the parties had a "common interest" in ensuring the correct result was reached. That test was satisfied in the context of *E* (claims for asylum) and it is highly arguable that it would also be satisfied in the context of social security appeals. The implications of this potentially ground-breaking decision for the social security appeals system will have to be fully worked out by the Commissioners.

Scope of the right of appeal: failure to exercise inquisitorial jurisdiction. One of the fundamental distinctions between tribunals and courts is that the latter are generally concerned only with deciding disputes raised by the parties for their consideration. By contrast, tribunals are generally expected to be much more pro-active in identifying and resolving issues between the parties. They need not, therefore, come to a conclusion that is advocated by one of the parties to an appeal: *R v Deputy Industrial Injuries Commissioner ex p Moore* [1965] 1 QB 456 and *Kerr v Department for Social Development* [2004] UKHL 23 (reported as R 1/04 (SF)).

The question of when a tribunal's decision can be subject to appeal on this ground depends on all the circumstances of the case: *R(SB) 2/83* (paras 10-11). The caselaw is not always consistent in its approach. If a party takes a deliberate decision not to attend a hearing, then s/he cannot complain of a failure by the tribunal to take the role as advocate of her/his case; nor will s/he usually be able to complain that the tribunal acted contrary to her/his right not to self-incriminate by proceeding to decide the appeal when criminal proceedings are pending: *CH 1220/2005*.

In deciding whether there has been a failure to exercise the inquisitorial function, it is helpful now to consider whether it is an issue that is alleged to have been overlooked or whether it is relevant evidence that has not been considered. As far as issues are concerned, the tribunal now has substantially greater discretion by virtue of para 6(9)(a) to decline to consider issues which are not raised by the parties or at least by the appeal. See the Analysis to that provision. Authorities on the scope of a tribunal's duty to consider new issues for itself must be read in the light of para 6(9)(a), though it is suggested that an unreasonable exercise of the discretion conferred by para 6(9)(a) may still constitute an error of law. The scope of the duty depends on the extent to which it appears that the parties have presented the relevant material to it. Where a representative appears to be competent, the omission will have to be obvious before the tribunal will err in law in failing to consider the issue: see *CSDLA 336/2000* (para 15). See also *R(H) 1/02* (paras 8-9). Where a representative specifically declines an opportunity to have a point addressed, the tribunal will not err in law by failing to do so itself: *CSIB 588/1998* (para 13). See also the commentary to para 6 (9)(a) above.

The duty to consider or call for further evidence, on the other hand, may well be slightly wider. This is the case particularly where a claimant is unrepresented and may not be aware of the nature of the evidence that will be relevant to the determination of a question before the tribunal. It seems clear that if there is something to alert a tribunal that relevant evidence may exist that is not before it, it will err in law if it does not give the party the chance to produce that evidence: *CU 47/1993* (paras 4-11).

For a discussion on the position of representatives giving evidence, see p931.

A tribunal does not generally err in law by failing to take documents not placed before it into account: *CH 5221/2001* (para 3.1). However, if it needs to examine a document to decide what impression it would have given to the reader, it will err in law if it does not call for a copy of the document rather than assuming the form that it took: *CH 5221/2001* (para 5).

Scope of the right of appeal: breach of natural justice. The rules of natural justice, which are now bolstered by the right to a fair hearing under Art 6 of the European Convention on Human Rights, are comprised of two basic principles. First, there is the right to be heard. The most obvious breach of the right to be heard is a case where a "person affected" is not notified of the proceedings. In *CH 3679/2002*, a claimant appealed against a decision that an overpayment was recoverable from a landlord. Commissioner Fellner held that the tribunal had erred in law because the landlord had not been made a party to the appeal and notified of the hearing: para 3.

Provision for 14 days' notice of an oral hearing is made in reg 49 SSCS D&A Regs. In *CH 3594/2002*, the commissioner said that to ensure a fair hearing, this must apply to provision of the submissions and evidence as well as the notice of the time and date of the hearing. He said that was so "unless the appeal tribunal is prepared to take the time during the oral hearing itself to redress the unfairness by ensuring that all the evidence and submissions are presented orally by both parties." In the absence of one of the parties, this could mean that the tribunal will find it necessary to adjourn the hearing.

If a party does not appear at a hearing through no fault of her/his own, then the tribunal's decision may be vitiated by an error of law even if no other person can be shown to be at fault: *CIB 5227/1999* (paras 9-10). If the claimant fails to attend a hearing due to a deliberate decision, there is no breach of the right: *CCS 565/1999* (para 12). Similarly, if a claimant fails to attend through carelessness, there is no error of law.

In *CIB 4667/2002* the appellant's representative freely admitted that he had failed to attend a hearing because of a mistake about the date. The commissioner said that whether to adjourn a hearing in such circumstances is for the good sense, judgement and discretion of the tribunal. As tribunals are accustomed to dealing with unrepresented appellants and people who are not familiar with the legal process, the fact that a representative does not turn up to a hearing does not, in principle, make it wrong to proceed in her/his absence. In order to give rise to an appeal on a point of law, "what has to be shown is that the tribunal's exercise of judgement was so unreasonable as to be perverse and to have deprived the claimant of a substantive opportunity for a fair hearing of the relevant issues in his or her case."

Experienced representatives who do not seek oral hearings on behalf of their clients might not then be able to argue that a tribunal should have nevertheless held one. In *Miller v Secretary of State for Social Security* [2002] GWD 25-861, CSIH the appellant complained that she had not been allowed an oral hearing of her appeal to provide further evidence. However, the Court held that as the appellant's experienced representative had not sought an oral hearing, and had stated that s/he was relying on paragraphs in the application for leave to appeal, the commissioner could not be said to have erred in law for not allowing an oral hearing.

Note the right to apply to set aside a tribunal decision under reg 57(1)(b) SSCS D&A Regs where a party to the proceedings or the party's representative was not present at a hearing.

There is no obligation on a tribunal to adjourn a case to offer an unrepresented claimant a chance to obtain representation: *CSIB 848/1997* (para 9). However, if a claimant expresses the wish for an adjournment to be represented this ought ordinarily to be granted, particularly in a difficult case with serious consequences. Where a claimant suffers from difficulties such as illiteracy, this emphasises the need for a tribunal to decide whether it is appropriate to proceed in such circumstances: *CIS 6002/1997* (paras 9-11). See also p933.

Local authorities all too frequently fail to explain their decision making processes with sufficient clarity in written submissions to a tribunal. If the process may have an impact on the outcome of the appeal, it is essential for a tribunal to explain it to an unrepresented claimant: *CH 1085/2002* (para 20).

At a hearing, a party must be given a fair opportunity to present her/his case. The tribunal may exercise control over the presentation of the case to the extent of preventing disruption of its proceedings or the pursuit of irrelevant matters. It may also control undue length of presentation, though care must be taken to ensure that the case is not in reality more complex than it had first appeared. If insufficient time has been allocated for the hearing of the case and there is any danger that to restrict the amount of time available to a party to present its case would hamper its ability to place its full case before the tribunal, then the case should be adjourned and the clerk to the tribunal should be directed to list the case with a longer time estimate. It is unlikely that commissioners will be sympathetic to a superficial treatment of cases on the pretext of economy on the part of the Tribunals Service.

Where the Tribunals Service appoints an interpreter to be used at a hearing, a claimant is entitled to expect the questions to her/him and her/his replies to be interpreted professionally. In *CDLA 2748/2002* the commissioner did not accept that it was adequate to establish a fair hearing that the tribunal concluded it had "sufficient understanding". If the standard of interpretation appears inadequate, the tribunal should take appropriate action.

It is not part of the tribunal's judicial function to seek to bargain with an appellant or her/his representative as to which parts of the appeal the tribunal might accept if other parts are not pressed for at the hearing: *CSDLA 606/2003*. In this case the appeal tribunal's record of proceedings noted that an offer had been put to the appellant by the Chair of the tribunal just to reinstate her higher rate mobility component of DLA if she did not seek to argue for the care component, and the case was adjourned for 10 minutes for her to think about this. On reconvening the hearing the appellant, who at that point said she wished to proceed with her appeal, was then told that if she went ahead and sought to argue for the care component then she could risk losing everything, and she was told to think again about the matter. After a further short adjournment of five minutes the appellant "accepted the offer". Unsurprisingly, the commissioner concluded that this was not a fair and proper hearing. In her view, a "travesty of justice" had occurred in which the tribunal had pressurised the appellant into giving up her right to a hearing on the care component and had awarded the mobility component without any proper application of the relevant legal tests.

The second aspect of the rules of natural justice is the rule against bias. Bias may be actual or apparent. Cases where it can be shown that a tribunal member has a direct interest in the outcome will hopefully be rare but even remote connections may be held to vitiate the fairness of proceedings: *R v Secretary of State for the Home Department ex p Pinochet (No 2)* [2000] 1 AC 129, HL. Members who are, for example, councillors of the relevant local authority or who are instructed by a party in private practice should disclose their interest or prior involvement. The same would be true of a member that had expressed strong views in an academic context that impinged upon the merits of one party's position: *Locabail (UK) Ltd v Bayfield Properties Ltd* [2000] QB 451 at 496F-497A, para 89, CA. If other parties are happy to proceed in knowledge of the full facts, any breach of this rule would be taken to be waived.

In cases of apparent bias, the question is "whether the fair-minded and informed observer, having considered the facts, would conclude that there was a real possibility that the tribunal was biased": *Porter v Magill* [2002] 2 WLR 37 at 83D-84B, paras 102-103, HL. See the detailed discussion in *CSDLA 1019/ 1999* (paras 70-89) for further consideration of this test. Note also *CSDLA 855/1997* (para 8), where the fact that a member of a tribunal was the partner of an examining medical practitioner whose report was being called into question was a breach of natural justice. The decision in *CSDLA 1019/1999* was overturned by the Court of Session in *Secretary of State for Work and Pensions v Gillies* [2003] 2004 SLT 14, reported at 2006 SC (HL) 71, in which the Court emphasised that the fair-minded observer is someone who is "neither complacent nor unduly sensitive or suspicious". The House of Lords upheld the decision of the Court of Session in *Gillies v Secretary of State for Work and Pensions* [2006] UKHL 2, *Times Law Report*, 30 January, reported as *R(DLA) 5/06*).

Representatives will need to exercise caution and restraint in making allegations of apparent bias based on the way in which hearings are conducted by tribunals. The commissioners have been critical about unparticularised complaints of bias which amount to nothing more than a complaint about the tribunal doing that which is its primary function, namely to closely test a party's case by questioning before accepting it in cases where the facts are in dispute: *CH 2302/2002* (para 10); *CH 2349/2002* (paras 12-13). It is strongly recommended that any representative who feels that a tribunal member has gone beyond what is acceptable by expressing views during the hearing or by the mode or tone of her/his questioning should make careful notes of what was said either at the time or as soon as possible after the hearing. When applying for leave to appeal to the commissioner, the allegations should be fully and carefully set out in order to give the tribunal member an opportunity to respond and the notes should be annexed to the application for leave if possible. If a different tribunal member is asked to determine whether or not leave should be granted (as is now frequently the case), the tribunal member about whom complaint is made and, if relevant, the other members and the clerk to the tribunal should be asked for their comments. Following such a procedure will make it easier for the commissioner to ascertain whether there is any substance to the complaint.

Scope of the right of appeal: breach of procedure. The courts have emphasised in recent years the need to consider the extent, nature and effect of non-compliance rather than whether the procedural provision is set out in the form of a duty or discretion: *Haringey LBC v Awaritefe* [1999] 32 HLR 517; *R v Secretary of State for the Home Department ex p Jeyeanthan* [2000] 1 WLR 354. A breach of the terms of a procedural requirement will not, therefore, of itself render a decision erroneous in law. As a rule of thumb, if the claimant is or might be prejudiced by the non-compliance then that will vitiate the decision. Further discussion as to when a breach of the procedural provisions in the SSCS D&A Regs and the D&A Regs will be found in the commentary to those regulations.

For example, a common basis on which a decision of a tribunal is set aside is a failure to give adequate reasons, which is a breach of procedure because there has been a failure to comply with reg 53(4) SSCS D&A Regs. However, if the shortcoming in the statement of reasons is immaterial because the case could only have been decided adversely to the claimant, the commissioner will ordinarily substitute a decision to the same effect as that of the tribunal.

Sub-paragraphs (2), (7) and (8): Making an appeal
Sub-para (2) provides that the Secretary of State, the authority or a person affected may appeal against the tribunal's decision. For the meaning of "person affected" see para 23(2) below and p951. It should be noted, however, that the right of appeal is conferred on the local authority. Para 23(3), which deems decisions made by persons acting on behalf of the authority to be treated as decisions of the authority itself, has no application to an appeal to the commissioner. If a person purporting to appeal to the commissioner has no right to do so, then an appeal will be void: *R(IS) 6/01* (para 2).

If no point is taken as to the validity of the decision or appeal by other persons affected, then the commissioner may rely on the presumption of regularity in the absence of a clear indication on the papers that the decision or appeal may not have been validly made: *Phipson on Evidence* (2000 15th edn) paras 29-12–29-13. The presumption of regularity is a rule of evidence under which it is usually presumed that acts of officials have been lawfully and properly carried out until the contrary is proved. However, if the validity of an appeal is challenged before the commissioner, the issue must be examined: *CS 79/1990* (para 18).

If the above analysis is correct, it follows that every appeal by a local authority must be supported by a resolution of the authority, which will cause considerable inconvenience and difficulty with complying with time limits. However, s101(1) of the Local Government Act 1970 permits an authority to arrange for functions to be discharged by "a committee, a sub-committee or an officer of the authority . . .". Thus the authority may use s101(1) to delegate to an officer its power to make an appeal against an appeal tribunal decision. If there was a dispute, the terms of that delegation would have to be proved by reference to standing orders and minutes of the authority. From 25 July 2002, the local authority may utilise the Contracting Out (Functions of Local Authorities: Income-Related Benefits) Order 2002 SI No 1888 (see p1091) to confer these functions on its officers or on a contractor. However, that still requires an appeal to be authorised by the authority. A general authorisation may be given to make appeals, but such an authorisation must still exist.

Outside the scope of the 2002 Order, a delegation to a senior officer, such as the solicitor to the council, would probably justify the making of a decision by an officer in her/his department on behalf of the solicitor: *Cheshire CC v Secretary of State for the Environment* [1988] JPL 30, QBD; *R v Southwark LBC ex p Bannerman* (1989) 22 HLR 459 at 463, QBD.

In the absence of such delegation, an appeal lodged by an officer, or any appeal lodged by a contractor is probably invalid. Arden et al, *Local Government Constitutional and Administrative Law* (2000) para 3.2.8 states:

"It is . . . one thing to employ an officer, contractor or agent to execute a function, but quite another to turn the function over to him to discharge as a whole. What cannot be delegated to another, save so far as statute permits, are the essential elements of the function which determine what is to be done (which may, to an extent, overlap with the question of how it is to be done ...) or which define its exercise, ie the decision-making function itself. The distinction has been drawn between 'underlying decisions' which are non-delegable and permissible 'day-to-day detailed management decision-taking'."

It is perfectly in order for officers or contractors to prepare a report recommending an appeal for the authority to decide to make (or any committee or officer to which the authority may have delegated that decision under s101 of the 1970 Act). However, the decision to appeal must be made by the latter body, which must exercise an independent mind.

The validity of a delegation of a decision making function is judged according to "the importance of the decisions delegated in so far as they affect the rights of individuals, the extent of the powers delegated and, conversely, the extent of control preserved by the delegating authority and, conversely, the extent of control preserved by the delegating authority": Arden para 3.2.11. By these criteria, a delegation outside the scope of s101 of the 1970 Act is probably invalid.

Reg 27 SSCP Regs does not permit a commissioner to waive an irregularity of this nature, since it only applies to failures to comply with the regulations and not the primary legislation governing appeals to the commissioner. It is likely that these issues will have to be explored by the commissioners at some stage.

Sub-para (7) introduces the important filter for appeals, which is the requirement that leave to appeal must be granted. The effect of sub-para (7)(a) and reg 9(1) SSCP Regs is that an application must be made to the chairman of the tribunal who heard the case in the first instance (normally the legally qualified member). Under sub-para (7)(c) and reg 58(6) SSCS D&A Regs, however, if it is "impracticable, or it would be likely to cause undue delay", another legally qualified panel member may decide the application. If the Chair of the tribunal who heard the case in the first instance was fee-paid, the application can be determined by a salaried legally qualified panel member. In fact, the Tribunals Service generally refers such applications as a matter of routine to a salaried legally qualified member. If leave is refused, a fresh application may be made direct to a commissioner under sub-para (7)(b). A grant of leave to appeal by a commissioner which seeks to restrict the grounds of appeal does not prevent the commissioner hearing the appeal itself from permitting other grounds to be argued (whether or not they were put forward in the leave application); though if such other grounds are to be allowed then it may be necessary to adjourn the hearing of the appeal so as to enable the respondent to the appeal to properly address them: *CH 4354/2003*.

Where leave to appeal is refused by both the appeal tribunal and the commissioner the only remedy for the aggrieved party is judicial review of the commissioner's refusal of leave to appeal: *Bland v Chief Supplementary Benefit Officer* [1983] 1 WLR 262, CA (reported as R(SB) 12/83). However, *Donnelly v Secretary of State for Work and Pensions* [2007] CSOH 01, 10 January 2007, makes it plain that, if on an application for judicial review a party raises a point which was not before the commissioner on the application for leave to appeal, the point which is raised must be one which is obvious and has strong prospects of success (following *Regina (Begum) v Social Security Commissioners* [2002] EWHC 401, *Cooke v Secretary of State for Social Security* [2002] 3 All ER 279 and *Mooney v Secretary of State for Work and Pensions* [2004] SLT 1141), and there must have been no other reasons which would have justified the commissioner in refusing leave to appeal: per *R v Secretary of State for Social Services ex parte Connolly* [1986] 1 All ER 998.

Sub-para (8) see reg 58 SSCS D&A Regs (see p943) and Pt II SSCP Regs (see p904) for regulations made under sub-para (8). The relevant time limits for seeking leave are found in reg 58(1) and (5) SSCS D&A Regs and reg 9(2) and (3) SSCP Regs.

Sub-paragraphs (3) to (6): Powers of the commissioner
Sub-para (3) makes similar provision to para 7(3) above, save that it confers a power to take this course rather than requiring that it be taken. Commissioners have frequently declined to adopt the course under the comparable s14(7) SSA 1998, particularly where there is a serious issue of law which requires detailed consideration: *CDLA 4102/1999*.

In setting a decision aside under sub-para (3), the commissioner is not agreeing with either party's submission nor making a decision that there has been an error of law. A decision set aside does not, therefore, provide an authoritative statement of the law and cannot be cited in support of other appeals on similar issues: *CI 3596/2001*.

Sub-paras (4) to (6) give commissioners very broad powers as to the appropriate course where a decision is found to be erroneous in law. Sub-para (5)(a) envisages the use by the commissioner of the tribunal's findings of fact in order to reach the correct decision. The power under sub-para (5)(b) to receive further evidence, or even to re-hear the case completely, is one which is rarely exercised but has been taken in very complex cases where a final decision is required. In *CDLA 4217/2001* the commissioner dealt with the comparable provision in s14(8) SSA 1998. He said at para 8 that:

> "it is only where it is necessary for further findings to be made and it is not expedient for the Commissioner to make them himself that a case should be referred to another tribunal. The principal reason why it may be inexpedient for a Commissioner to make findings is that it may be necessary for there to be an oral hearing in order for a factual dispute between the parties to be resolved. However, where the findings on questions of primary fact made by the tribunal from whom the appeal is brought are adequate and the reasoning supporting those findings is also adequate, a Commissioner can rely on those findings as the basis for giving a final decision, even if it is necessary to draw some further conclusions from those findings."

In *CH 4876/2002* (para 18), the commissioner decided that it was permissible to remit only certain aspects of a case to a tribunal for redetermination, while upholding the previous tribunal's decision on the other aspects. It is suggested that this approach is not permissible, since sub-para (4) requires that the commissioner should set aside the first tribunal's decision before remitting the case to a second tribunal. The commissioner cited *Aparau v Iceland Frozen Foods Ltd* [2000] 1 All ER 228, CA, but the Employment Appeal Tribunal is not required to set aside an Employment Tribunal's decision before remitting it under s35(1) Employment Tribunals Act 1996, so the analogy is inapt.

Appeal from Commissioner on point of law
9.–(1) Subject to sub-paragraphs (2) and (3), an appeal on a question of law shall lie to the appropriate court from any decision of a Commissioner.

(2)   No appeal under this paragraph shall lie from a decision except–

(a)   with the leave of the Commissioner who gave the decision or, in a prescribed case, with the leave of a Commissioner selected in accordance with regulations; or

(b)   if he refuses leave, with the leave of the appropriate court.

(3)   An application for leave under this paragraph in respect of a Commissioner's decision may only be made by–

(a)   a person who, before the proceedings before the Commissioner were begun, was entitled to appeal to the Commissioner from the decision to which the Commissioner's decision relates;

(b)   any other person who was a party to the proceedings in which the decision to which the Commissioner's decision relates was given;

(c)   any other person who is authorised by regulations to apply for leave;

and regulations may make provision with respect to the manner in which, and the time within which, applications must be made to a Commissioner for leave under this paragraph, and with respect to the procedure for dealing with such applications.

(4)   On an application to a Commissioner for leave under this paragraph, it shall be the duty of the Commissioner to specify as the appropriate court–

(a)   the Court of Appeal if it appears to him that the relevant dwelling is in England or Wales; and

(b)   the Court of Session if it appears to him that the relevant dwelling is in Scotland;

except that if it appears to him, having regard to the circumstances of the case and in particular to the convenience of the persons who may be parties to the proposed appeal, that he should specify a different court mentioned in paragraph (a) or (b) as the appropriate court, it shall be his duty to specify that court as the appropriate court.

(5)   In this paragraph–

"the appropriate court", except in sub-paragraph (4), means the court specified in pursuance of that sub-paragraph;

"the relevant dwelling", in relation to any decision, means the dwelling by reference to which any claim or award of housing benefit or council tax benefit to which the decision relates was made.

Analysis

A further appeal lies from a commissioner, with permission, to either the Court of Appeal or to the Court of Session as appropriate. An appeal lies only from a decision of a commissioner and a refusal of leave to appeal against a tribunal's decision must be challenged by way of judicial review: *Bland v Chief Supplementary Benefit Officer* [1983] 1 WLR 262, CA (reported as *R(SB) 12/83*) and *Secretary of State for Work and Pensions v Morina and Borrowdale* [2007] EWCA Civ 749. See further the notes to regs 9 and 33 SSCP Regs (see pp904 and 915).

Sub-paragraphs (1), (4) and (5): The route of appeal

The right of appeal under sub-para (1) is again restricted to "a question of law", which will be interpreted as meaning the same as "point of law" in para 8(1). See the Analysis to that provision. *Braintree District Council v Thompson* [2005] EWCA Civ 178, 7 March 2005, unreported, is a reminder that judgment decisions of tribunals, where properly reasoned and based on findings of fact, should be difficult to interfere with as a matter of law.

The appeal goes to the "appropriate court" which is specified by the commissioner on granting or refusing leave to appeal. Normally, the appeal goes to the jurisdiction in which the relevant dwelling is located under sub-para (4). It will very rarely be appropriate to send the case to the other jurisdiction. There might conceivably be cases in which the person affected had moved to the other jurisdiction, or where the parties were located in the north of England. Before it could be appropriate, the Commissioner would have to be satisfied that no question arose on which there was likely to be a significant divergence between the law of Scotland and that in England and Wales.

Sub-paragraph (2): The requirement of leave

Leave to appeal must first be sought from the commissioner: see reg 33 SSCP Regs. The time limit for seeking leave is found in reg 33(1) SSCP Regs. Only if s/he refuses leave is it open to the claimant to seek leave to appeal from the appropriate Court.

For the procedure in Scotland for seeking leave in the Court of Session, see Rules of the Court of Session 1994 R41.18-41.22. In the Court of Appeal, an appeal is commenced by the filing of an appellant's notice: r52.4 Civil Procedure Rules 1998. This must be done within six weeks of the relevant Office of the Commissioners sending out the commissioner's determination as to whether leave is refused or granted: para 21.5 of Practice Direction 52.

In appeals brought under para 9 by a party other than the Secretary of State, the appellant must serve the appellant's notice on the Secretary of State in addition to the persons to be served under rule 52.4(3) Civil Procedures Rules 1998.

If a person affected requires leave to appeal from the Court of Appeal, an application for leave to appeal should be made in s6 of the appellant's notice. Where the person affected appeals, the proper respondent is the local authority rather than the commissioner. The Secretary of State for Work and Pensions does not have an automatic right to appear on an appeal if s/he has not been a party before the commissioner: see, by way of analogy, *R v Rent Officer ex p Muldoon* [1996] 1 WLR 1103, HL, but it would be wise to notify the Solicitor to the Departments of Health and Work and Pensions at New Court, 48 Carey Street, London WC2A 2LS of the intention to make an appeal, so that the Secretary of State can take any steps to be involved that are desired. In Scotland notification of the appeal is given to the Office of the Solicitor to the Advocate General for Scotland, Victoria Quay, Edinburgh EH6 6QQ.

In *Cooke v Secretary of State for Social Security* [2002] 3 All ER 279 (reported as *R(DLA) 6/01*), the Court of Appeal reconsidered the test for granting leave to appeal. An appeal to the Court of Appeal or Court of Session is, of course, the second appeal on a point of law. By s55 Access to Justice Act 1999, the right of appeal to the Court of Appeal where it is the second appellate court is restricted to cases where the appeal raises an "important point of principle or practice" or where there is "some other compelling reason" to hear the case. The appeal from a commissioner does not fall within the strict terms of s55, since the tribunal and commissioner are not courts, but a similar test is now to be applied by analogy. The Court decided that it would take "an appropriately modest view" in deference to the expertise of the commissioners. In *Fryer-Kelsey v The Secretary of State for Work and Pensions* [2005] EWCA Civ 511, 21 April (reported as *R(IB) 6/05*), the Court of Appeal emphasised that *Cooke* (which stated that a robust attitude to the prospects of success criterion ought to be adopted when the Court of Appeal was deciding whether to grant leave to appeal from a commissioner) should apply equally to the commissioners when they are engaged in the same exercise and that the error of law on the part of the commissioner must be clearly identified by the applicant in the application for leave.

Sub-paragraph (3): Who has the right to appeal?

Under sub-para (3), the people with a right of appeal are set out. First, there is any person who had a right of appeal to the commissioner: see para 8(2). Secondly, there is any other person who was a party to the tribunal proceedings. In fact, for HB and CTB purposes these are exactly the same parties as those with a right to appeal to the commissioner, since "party" means "principal party" under para 7(4): see regs 1(2) and 23(3)(b) D&A Regs. No regulations have been made under sub-para (3)(c).

Procedure

10.–(1)   Regulations may make for the purposes of this Schedule any such provision as is specified in Schedule 5 to the Social Security Act 1998, or as would be so specified if the references to the Secretary of State in paragraph 1 of that Schedule were references to a relevant authority.

(2)   Regulations prescribing the procedure to be followed in cases before a Commissioner shall provide that any hearing shall be in public except in so far as the Commissioner for special reasons otherwise directs.

(3)   It is hereby declared that the power by regulations to prescribe procedure includes power–

(a)   to make provision as to the representation of one person, at any hearing of a case, by another person whether having professional qualifications or not; and

(b)   to confer on the Secretary of State a right to be represented and heard in any proceedings before a Commissioner to which he is not already a party.

(4)   If it appears to a Commissioner that a matter before him involves a question of fact of special difficulty, he may direct that in dealing with that matter he shall have the assistance of one or more persons appearing to him to have knowledge or experience which would be relevant in determining that question.

(5)   If it appears to the Chief Commissioner (or, in the case of his inability to act, to such other of the Commissioners as he may have nominated to act for the purpose) that–

(a)   an application for leave under paragraph 8(7)(b), or

(b)   an appeal,

falling to be heard by one of the Commissioners involves a question of law of special difficulty, he may direct that the application or appeal be dealt with, not by that Commissioner alone, but by a tribunal consisting of any three or more of the Commissioners.

(6)   If the decision of such a tribunal is not unanimous, the decision of the majority shall be the decision of the tribunal; and the presiding Commissioner shall have a casting vote if the votes (including his first vote) are equally divided.

(7)   Where a direction is given under sub-paragraph (5)(a), paragraph 8(7)(b) shall have effect as if the reference to a Commissioner were a reference to such a tribunal as is mentioned in sub-paragraph (5).

(8)   Except so far as it may be applied in relation to England and Wales by regulations, Part I of the Arbitration Act 1996 shall not apply to any proceedings under this Schedule.

Analysis

Sub-paras (1) to (3) are regulation-making powers for the purposes of appeals. See Sch 5 of the 1998 Act on p116 for a list of regulations made under the powers set out therein. On public hearings, see reg 24(5) SSCP Regs on p911. The right to be represented is conferred by reg 17 and the Secretary of State has a right to appear under reg 24(6)(c).

Sub-para (4) confers a similar power to that enjoyed by authorities under para 5.

Sub-paras (5) to (7) deal with Tribunals of Commissioners that may sit where there is a particularly difficult issue to resolve. They are most often formed where there are conflicts in the caselaw between decisions of single commissioners.

Finality of decisions

11.   Subject to the provisions of this Schedule, any decision made in accordance with the preceding provisions of this Schedule shall be final.

Analysis

Para 11 covers the same ground as s17 SSA 1998, but is markedly different in scope. It confirms that a decision is final, except to the extent that it may be altered on revision, supersession or appeal. The main question arising is whether para 11 is restricted in scope to the actual decision in a case or whether it also extends to findings of fact and law embodied in such a decision. It is suggested that the first of these alternatives is correct. The language of para 11 may be contrasted with that in para 6(4), which suggests a contrast between a decision and a "determination embodied in or necessary to a decision". Thus if claim A is rejected on the basis that the claimant has notional capital because s/he sold a capital asset at an undervalue so as to obtain HB, the decision is final as far as it affects claim A (subject to challenge). However, if the claimant makes claim B eight weeks later, the authority cannot simply rely on para 11 in rejecting claim B but must, at least in theory, reconsider the question of notional capital. Commissioner Jacobs confirmed this approach in *CH 1210/2003*. He said that a decision relates only to a claim. Although it may be taken into account when deciding a later claim, it is not conclusive on claims in respect of different periods. It would also seem that, following the approach of the Tribunal of Commissioners in *R(H) 3/04*, para 11 has no application to a "determination" that an overpayment is recoverable.

The commissioners have consistently held that tribunals are not bound by previous decisions of tribunals. Two decisions of Commissioner Jacobs deal with the point. It was held in *CH 3853/2001* (paras

18-19) that a Review Board decision on a question of fact does not bind an appeal tribunal deciding the same question in relation to a different claim. The commissioner said:

"Nor was the Tribunal bound by the Board's finding that the claimant was compelled to act as he did. That was so despite the fact that it was made in respect of the same claimant, the same premises, the same circumstances and the same arguments. The Board's finding was made on a different claim dealing with a different period."

The same must therefore be true of authorities determining subsequent claims, and of appeal tribunals hearing appeals where a previous tribunal has dismissed an appeal: *CCS 1535/1997* (paras 24-27), where the commissioner suggested that the fact that tribunals exercised an inquisitorial jurisdiction meant that there could be no issue estoppel (under which a decision on a question between two parties is ordinarily binding on them in relation to future litigation) in tribunal proceedings.

If this interpretation is correct, it produces a desirable flexibility within the decision-making system. It is a common phenomenon for advisers to be consulted by claimants who have had an adverse decision on a question such as notional capital which cannot be challenged by the time that the adviser becomes involved. While any prospect of getting benefit on that claim may have been lost, it might cause serious injustice to such a claimant if s/he does not have the right to have the matter reconsidered on a fresh claim. The drawback of the interpretation is that it has the potential to cause administrative difficulties for authorities and the Tribunals Service where a claimant aggrieved by a decision adverse to her/him decides to make multiple claims at regular intervals. Authorities must adjudicate and decide each claim that is made in the correct time and manner and which satisfies the evidence requirements: reg 89 HB Regs; reg 70 HB(SPC) Regs; reg 75 CTB Regs; and reg 60 CTB(SPC) Regs. Authorities will probably simply rely on the reasoning of the first officer that determined the question under dispute and issue further decisions to identical effect. What authorities would have to be careful to avoid, in these circumstances, is ignoring any further information or evidence that may be presented on subsequent claims.

As far as repeated appeals are concerned, if there are several appeals outstanding at once, they can be listed for hearing and disposed of together: *R(SB) 4/85*. In cases where there is abuse of the appeals system, the procedure for misconceived appeals is no longer available: reg 48 SSCS D&A Regs omitted by SI 2004 No 3368 as from 21 December 2004.

It may be questionable whether the commissioners' decisions on this topic take sufficient account of the general law of issue estoppel in public law decision making. In *Thrasyvoulou v Secretary of State for the Environment* [1990] 2 AC 273 at 289, HL, Lord Bridge referred to the two maxims that there was a public interest in the finality of litigation and that no one should be vexed by litigation on the same question more than once. He said:

"In principle, they must apply equally to adjudications in the field of public law. In relation to adjudications subject to a comprehensive self-contained statutory code, the presumption, in my opinion, must be that where the statute has created a specific jurisdiction for the determination of any issue which establishes the existence of a legal right, the principle of *res judicata* applies to give finality to that determination unless an intention to exclude that principle can properly be inferred as a matter of construction of the relevant statutory powers."

The question, therefore, would be whether the fact that para 11 only makes decisions on claims final and not determinations embodied in those decisions is sufficient to exclude this general principle. *CH 704/2005* decides that issue estoppel can apply in respect of an issue decided by the county court which is also an issue arising on a HB or CTB appeal. In that case the issue was whether the claimant had a beneficial interest in a property and thus had capital in excess of £16,000. The commissioner said that issue estoppel could only apply if the parties to the appeal tribunal hearing were the same parties as in the county court and acting in the same capacity, but that was the case here as no valid distinction could be made between the local authority exercising its housing functions and its benefit functions. Nothing, in the commissioner's view, in the limited statutory estoppel created by para 11 of Sch 7, or the lack of any estoppel arising from findings of fact or determinations embodied in an appeal tribunal decisions created by s17(2) SSA 1998, meant that decisions made by *courts* in the exercise of their jurisdictions cannot create an issue estoppel for a later statutory appeal concerning the same parties.

This decision would seem also to decide that decisions of the statutory authorities (including appeal tribunals) concerning HB and CTB (and all other benefits) cannot bind later decision makers within that statutory arena, save to the limited extent set out in para 11 of Sch 7 (or s17(1) SSA 1998). What it seems to leave open is whether decisions of *other* statutory tribunals (such as an immigration appeal tribunal) can give rise to an issue estoppel: see, for example, *R (Nahar) v Social Security Commissioner* [2002] 1 FLR 670, paras 35-38 and the commentary to para 11 in the eighteenth edition of this book.

Matters arising as respects decisions
    12.   Regulations may make provision as respects matters arising–

(a)   pending any decision under this Schedule of a relevant authority, an appeal tribunal or a Commissioner which relates to–
   (i)   any claim for housing benefit or council tax benefit;
   (ii)   any person's entitlement to such a benefit or its receipt; or
(b)   out of the revision under paragraph 3, or on appeal, of any such decision.

Suspension in prescribed circumstances

13.–(1)   Regulations may provide for–
(a)   suspending, in whole or in part, any payments of housing benefit or council tax benefit;
(b)   suspending, in whole or in part, any reduction (by way of council tax benefit) in the amount that a person is or will become liable to pay in respect of council tax;
(c)   the subsequent making, or restoring, in prescribed circumstances of any or all of the payments, or reductions, so suspended.

(2)   Regulations made under sub-paragraph (1) may, in particular, make provision for any case where, in relation to a claim for housing benefit or council tax benefit–
(a)   it appears to the relevant authority that an issue arises whether the conditions for entitlement to such a benefit are or were fulfilled;
(b)   it appears to the relevant authority that an issue arises whether a decision as to an award of such a benefit should be revised (under paragraph 3) or superseded (under paragraph 4);
(c)   an appeal is pending against a decision of an appeal tribunal, a Commissioner or a court; or
(d)   it appears to the relevant authority, where an appeal is pending against the decision given by a Commissioner or a court in a different case, that if the appeal were to be determined in a particular way an issue would arise whether the award of housing benefit or council tax benefit in the case itself ought to be revised or superseded.

(3)   For the purposes of sub-paragraph (2), an appeal against a decision is pending if–
(a)   an appeal against the decision has been brought but not determined;
(b)   an application for leave to appeal against the decision has been made but not determined; or
(c)   the time within which–
   (i)   an application for leave to appeal may be made, or
   (ii)   an appeal against the decision may be brought,
has not expired and the circumstances are such as may be prescribed.

(4)   In sub-paragraph (2)(d) the reference to a different case–
(a)   includes a reference to a case involving a different relevant authority; but
(b)   does not include a reference to a case relating to a different benefit unless the different benefit is housing benefit or council tax benefit.

Analysis

See regs 11 and 12 D&A Regs on pp971 and 972. Note that the power in sub-para (3)(c) does not appear to have been exercised, so it appears that there is no power to suspend unless the authority has at least got to the stage of making an application for leave to appeal.

Note also the limited scope of the "different cases" which may trigger suspension under reg 11(2)(b)(ii) D&A Regs. Sub-para (4) provides that a case involving a different local authority may trigger a suspension, but cases involving other benefits may not give rise to suspension. Thus if a commissioner is due to give a ruling on the interpretation of a part of the IS legislation, it will not be open to the authority to impose a suspension on payment under HB claims which require consideration of an identical provision in the HB legislation.

Sub-para (4) does not, in terms, preclude suspension where a ruling is due in respect of legislation outside the area of social security. It would seem arguable that it would be legitimate for an authority to suspend payment where an authoritative ruling is due as to the meaning of a particular phrase replicated in the HB legislation. After all, the test is whether an issue would arise, not that the decision would make a difference for certain. Since "court" is not defined in the legislation, a pending appeal to the Court of Appeal from the High Court or some other statutory tribunal may well give a right to suspend payment.

Suspension for failure to furnish information etc

14.–(1)   The powers conferred by this paragraph are exercisable in relation to persons who fail to comply with information requirements.
(2)   Regulations may provide for–
(a)   suspending, in whole or in part, any payments of housing benefit or council tax benefit;
(b)   suspending, in whole or in part, any reduction (by way of council tax benefit) in the amount that a person is or will become liable to pay in respect of council tax;
(c)   the subsequent making, or restoring, in prescribed circumstances of any or all of the payments, or any right, so suspended.
(3)   In this paragraph and paragraph 15 ''information requirement'' means–

(a) in the case of housing benefit, a requirement in pursuance of regulations made by virtue of section 5(1)(hh) of the Administration Act to furnish information or evidence needed for a determination whether a decision on an award of that benefit should be revised under paragraph 3 or superseded under paragraph 4 of this Schedule; and

(b) in the case of council tax benefit, a requirement made in pursuance of regulations under section 6(1)(hh) of the Administration Act to furnish information or evidence needed for a determination whether a decision on an award of that benefit should be so revised or superseded.

Analysis

See reg 13 D&A Regs on p973. Reg 86 HB Regs, reg 67 HB(SPC) Regs, reg 72 CTB Regs and reg 57 CTB(SPC) Regs are partly made under ss5(1)(hh) and 6(1)(hh) SSAA.

Termination in cases of a failure to furnish information

15. Regulations may provide that, except in prescribed cases or circumstances–

(a) a person whose benefit has been suspended in accordance with regulations under paragraph 13 and who subsequently fails to comply with an information requirement, or

(b) a person whose benefit has been suspended in accordance with regulations under paragraph 14 for failing to comply with such a requirement,

shall cease to be entitled to the benefit from a date not earlier than the date on which payments were suspended.

Analysis

See reg 14 D&A Regs on p975.

Decisions involving issues that arise on appeal in other cases

16.–(1) This paragraph applies where–

(a) a relevant decision, or a decision under paragraph 3 about the revision of an earlier decision, falls to be made in any particular case; and

(b) an appeal is pending against the decision given in another case by a Commissioner or a court.

(2) A relevant authority need not make the decision while the appeal is pending if they consider it possible that the result of the appeal will be such that, if it were already determined, there would be no entitlement to benefit.

(3) If a relevant authority consider it possible that the result of the appeal will be such that, if it were already determined, it would affect the decision in some other way–

(a) they need not, except in such cases or circumstances as may be prescribed, make the decision while the appeal is pending;

(b) they may, in such cases or circumstances as may be prescribed, make the decision on such basis as may be prescribed.

(4) Where–

(a) a relevant authority act in accordance with sub-paragraph (3)(b), and

(b) following the making of the determination it is appropriate for their decision to be revised,

they shall then revise their decision (under paragraph 3) in accordance with that determination.

(5) For the purposes of this paragraph, an appeal against a decision is pending if–

(a) an appeal against the decision has been brought but not determined;

(b) an application for leave to appeal against the decision has been made but not determined; or

(c) the time within which–

(i) an application for leave to appeal may be made, or

(ii) an appeal against the decision may be brought,

has not expired and the circumstances are such as may be prescribed.

(6) In paragraphs (a), (b) and (c) of sub-paragraph (5), any reference to an appeal against a decision, or to an application for leave to appeal against a decision, includes a reference to–

(a) an application for judicial review of the decision under section 31 of the Supreme Court Act 1981 or for leave to apply for judicial review; or

(b) an application to the supervisory jurisdiction of the Court of Session in respect of the decision.

(7) In sub-paragraph (1)(b) the reference to another case–

(a) includes a reference to a case involving a decision made, or falling to be made, by a different relevant authority; but

(b) does not include a reference to a case relating to another benefit unless the other benefit is housing benefit or council tax benefit.

Analysis

Para 16 is concerned with situations where an appeal in another case (known as a "test case") is pending and a decision falls to be made on a claim or through a revision (known as a "look-alike case"). It enables the local authority to postpone making the decision in the look-alike case until the decision is made in the test case. See para 18 where a decision has already been made on a test case.

Sub-para (2) temporarily absolves the authority from its duty to make the decision if it is *possible* that the result of the appeal would result in nil entitlement.

Sub-paras (3) and (4) deal with cases where there would be some other effect on the decision (such as a change in the rate of benefit). See reg 15 D&A Regs on p977 for the cases in which a decision may nonetheless be made. If the decision turns out to be wrong following the decision on the pending appeal, sub-para (4) requires the decision to be revised.

Sub-paras (5) to (7) deal with the type of appeals with which the court is concerned. Sub-paras (5) and (7) are identical to paras 13(3) and (4): see the Analysis to those provisions. Sub-para (6) confirms that "appeal" includes pending applications for judicial review in these circumstances.

Appeals involving issues that arise on appeal in other cases

17.–(1)   This paragraph applies where–
  (a)   an appeal ("appeal A") in relation to a relevant decision (whether as originally made or as revised under paragraph 3) is made to an appeal tribunal, or from an appeal tribunal to a Commissioner; and
  (b)   an appeal ("appeal B") is pending against a decision given in a different case by a Commissioner or a court.

  (2)   If the relevant authority whose decision gave rise to appeal A consider it possible that the result of appeal B will be such that, if it were already determined, it would affect the determination of appeal A, they may serve notice requiring the tribunal or Commissioner–
  (a)   not to determine appeal A but to refer it to them; or
  (b)   to deal with the appeal in accordance with sub-paragraph (4).

  (3)   Where appeal A is referred to the authority under sub-paragraph (2)(a), following the determination of appeal B and in accordance with that determination, they shall if appropriate–
  (a)   in a case where appeal A has not been determined by the tribunal, revise (under paragraph 3) their decision which gave rise to that appeal; or
  (b)   in a case where appeal A has been determined by the tribunal, make a decision (under paragraph 4) superseding the tribunal's decision.

  (4)   Where appeal A is to be dealt with in accordance with this sub-paragraph, the appeal tribunal or Commissioner shall either–
  (a)   stay appeal A until appeal B is determined; or
  (b)   if the tribunal or Commissioner considers it to be in the interests of the appellant to do so, determine appeal A as if–
      (i)   appeal B had already been determined; and
      (ii)   the issues arising on appeal B had been decided in the way that was most unfavourable to the appellant.

  (5)   Where the appeal tribunal or Commissioner acts in accordance with sub-paragraph (4)(b), following the determination of appeal B the relevant authority whose decision gave rise to appeal A shall, if appropriate, make a decision (under paragraph 4) superseding the decision of the tribunal or Commissioner in accordance with that determination.

  (6)   For the purposes of this paragraph, an appeal against a decision is pending if–
  (a)   an appeal against the decision has been brought but not determined;
  (b)   an application for leave to appeal against the decision has been made but not determined; or
  (c)   the time within which–
      (i)   an application for leave to appeal may be made, or
      (ii)   an appeal against the decision may be brought,
  has not expired and the circumstances are such as may be prescribed.

  (7)   In this paragraph–
  (a)   the reference in sub-paragraph (1)(a) to an appeal to a Commissioner includes a reference to an application for leave to appeal to a Commissioner;
  (b)   the reference in sub-paragraph (1)(b) to a different case–
      (i)   includes a reference to a case involving a different relevant authority; but
      (ii)   does not include a reference to a case relating to a different benefit unless the different benefit is housing benefit or council tax benefit; and
  (c)   any reference in paragraph (a), (b) or (c) of sub-paragraph (6) to an appeal, or to an application for leave to appeal, against a decision includes a reference to–
      (i)   an application for judicial review of the decision under section 31 of the Supreme Court Act 1981 or for leave to apply for judicial review; or
      (ii)   an application to the supervisory jurisdiction of the Court of Session in respect of the decision.

  (8)   In sub-paragraph (4) "the appellant" means the person who appealed or, as the case may be, first appealed against the decision mentioned in sub-paragraph (1)(a).

(9)   Regulations may make provision supplementing the provision made by this paragraph.

Commencement

It is understood that the Government does not intend to bring para 17 into force.

Restrictions on entitlement to benefit in certain cases of error

18.–(1)   Subject to sub-paragraph (2), this paragraph applies where–
(a)   the effect of the determination, whenever made, of an appeal by virtue of this Schedule to a Commissioner or the court ("the relevant determination") is that the relevant authority's decision out of which the appeal arose was erroneous in point of law; and
(b)   after the date of the relevant determination a decision falls to be made by that relevant authority or another relevant authority in accordance with that determination (or would, apart from this paragraph, fall to be so made)–
  (i)   in relation to a claim for housing benefit or council tax benefit;
  (ii)   as to whether to revise, under paragraph 3, a decision as to a person's entitlement to such a benefit; or
  (iii)   on an application made under paragraph 4 for a decision as to a person's entitlement to such a benefit to be superseded.
(2)   This paragraph does not apply where the decision mentioned in sub-paragraph (1)(b)–
(a)   is one which, but for paragraph 16(2) or (3)(a), would have been made before the date of the relevant determination; or
(b)   is one made in pursuance of paragraph 17(3) or (5).
(3)   In so far as the decision relates to a person's entitlement to benefit in respect of a period before the date of the relevant determination, it shall be made as if the relevant authority's decision had been found by the Commissioner or court not to have been erroneous in point of law.
(4)   Sub-paragraph (1)(a) shall be read as including a case where–
(a)   the effect of the relevant determination is that part or all of a purported regulation or order is invalid; and
(b)   the error of law made by the relevant authority was to act on the basis that the purported regulation or order (or the part held to be invalid) was valid.
(5)   It is immaterial for the purposes of sub-paragraph (1)–
(a)   where such a decision as is mentioned in paragraph (b)(i) falls to be made, whether the claim was made before or after the date of the relevant determination;
(b)   where such a decision as is mentioned in paragraph (b)(ii) or (iii) falls to be made on an application under paragraph 3 or (as the case may be) 4, whether the application was made before or after that date.
(6)   In this paragraph "the court" means–
(a)   the High Court;
(b)   the Court of Appeal;
(c)   the Court of Session;
(d)   the House of Lords; or
(e)   the Court of Justice of the European Community.
(7)   For the purposes of this paragraph, any reference to entitlement to benefit includes a reference to entitlement–
(a)   to any increase in the rate of a benefit; or
(b)   to a benefit, or increase of benefit, at a particular rate.
(8)   The date of the relevant determination shall, in prescribed cases, be determined for the purposes of this paragraph in accordance with any regulations made for that purpose.
(9)   Regulations made under sub-paragraph (8) may include provision–
(a)   for a determination of a higher court to be treated as if it had been made on the date of a determination by a lower court or by a Commissioner; or
(b)   for a determination of a lower court or of a Commissioner to be treated as if it had been made on the date of a determination by a higher court.

Commencement

2.7.01, with the exception of para 18(2)(b) which has not been brought into force and it is understood that, as with para 17 to which it refers, it will not be brought into force.

Analysis

The aim of this para, known as the "anti-test case" rule, is to prevent large numbers of appellants taking advantage of a favourable ruling of a commissioner or of the court by deeming the law to have been as it had always previously been thought to be, except in relation to the successful appellant. It is an invidious and capricious concept and previous attempts by the then DSS to create a similar effect, principally in s69 SSAA (now repealed and replaced by s27 SSA 1998), caused a great deal of uncertainty and litigation.

It is suggested that para 18 may be vulnerable to challenge under Art 6 of the European Convention on Human Rights. In *Osman v UK* [1998] 29 EHRR 245, ECtHR, it was established that to create an exclusionary rule which prevented effective access to a court would infringe Art 6. As claimants caught by para 18 are effectively excluded from an effective remedy through the appeals system, it must be open to question whether para 18 complies with Art 6. Any challenge would, however, have to proceed by way of an application for a declaration of incompatibility since para 18 is primary legislation. The reasoning of the House of Lords in *Chief Adjudication Officer v Bate* [1996] 1 WLR 814 provides some support and justification for the existence of these rules.

See para 16 for the rules which allow a local authority to postpone making a decision pending a decision in a test case.

Sub-paragraphs (1), (2) and (4) to (6): Application of the rule

Sub-para (1) states the basic situation in which the rule takes effect. It deals with a decision ("decision B" – the "look-alike" case) that falls to be made after a decision of a court, as defined in sub-para (6), or a commissioner ("decision A" – the "test case"). This only applies where decision B is a decision on a claim, an application for a supersession under para 4 or as to whether to revise under para 3 (see sub-para (1)(b)). Where someone wants to challenge a decision on entitlement to HB or CTB as a result of a test case decision, the "anti-test case" rule can therefore be avoided by appealing against rather than seeking a revision or a supersession of the decision: see *CH 532/2006* and *CH 533/2006*.

Tribunal decisions are not, of course, binding and do not make the rule take effect. Decision A, termed "the relevant determination", must have been that the relevant authority's initial decision was erroneous in law. "Relevant authority" refers to the authority involved in the case before the court or commissioner, which may be different from the authority required to make decision B on which the rule bites.

The decision which was appealed to create decision A must have been "erroneous in point of law". In many cases, a point of principle is stated by a court or more often by a commissioner that was not considered by the authority at all. Thus it is entirely possible that an authority makes a decision which is overturned on the facts by the tribunal. The authority then subsequently appeals to the commissioner, who in decision A upholds the tribunal's decision on the facts and gives guidance as to the law. Unless it is clear that the commissioner finds some flaw in the *legal* approach of the council as opposed to its conclusions of fact, it would seem that the rule cannot bite in such a situation.

Another point of uncertainty concerns whether decision B is made "in accordance with that determination", that is in accordance with decision A. What happens if there is another binding decision, decision C, made prior to decision A but which the authority was bound to apply? It is very common for commissioners to issue decisions the implications of which are not realised until a further decision which achieves a greater degree of publicity. In these circumstances, it is the earliest authoritative decision which must be looked at for the purposes of deciding the relevant date: *R(FC) 3/98* (para 7); *R(I) 1/03* (the latter is a decision of a Tribunal of Commissioners).

Sub-para (2) limits some of the most unfair effects of the rule by disapplying it in cases where a suspension was imposed under para 16 so as to avoid making a decision prior to decision A. However, there may be difficulties in ascertaining whether a decision "would have been made" prior to the date of decision A. It is suggested that it should be assumed that the authority is complying with the time limit imposed by reg 89(2) HB Regs and the HB(SPC), CTB and CTB(SPC) equivalents. There is no specific time limit for the carrying out of a revision or supersession but it is suggested that they ought to be carried out as soon as all relevant information is before the authority, which may be as soon as the application is made.

Sub-para (4) contains an extraordinary and profoundly undemocratic provision. Under this sub-paragraph, where the error of law that is identified in decision A is the application of a regulation which turns out to be *ultra vires*, the authority must assume the regulation to be valid for the purposes of applying this rule. Parliament appears to have effectively approved the making of any rules, even those clearly outside the scope of the enabling powers, as having what may be substantial effects on the entitlements of claimants. In this way, regulations may have effect prior to "the relevant determination" even if made in breach of consultation procedures designed to protect claimants or even, apparently, if made in bad faith or in breach of the European Convention on Human Rights. It is the sort of legislation designed to recreate the discredited approach of the first half of the twentieth century, namely that it is the Secretary of State (and hence the local authorities acting under her/his guidance) who determines the validity of regulations rather than the courts. It is not an exaggeration to say that provisions such as sub-para (4) undermine the rule of law.

Sub-para (5) confirms that the rule bites whenever the claim or application for revision or supersession was made.

Sub-paragraphs (3) and (7): The effect of the rule

Sub-para (3) states the effect of the rule. In relation to the period prior to decision A being made (and therefore not from the date of that decision), entitlement to benefit must be determined in decision B as if the authority's decision under attack in the proceedings giving rise to decision A was correct. Thus if decision A means that there was entitlement to benefit when decision A was on an appeal from an initial refusal of benefit, no benefit will be payable prior to the date of decision A. Similarly, where more benefit is payable as a result of decision A, the rule takes effect so as to deprive the claimant in decision B of that additional benefit in relation to the period prior to decision A: sub-para (7).

Sub-paragraphs (8) and (9): Regulations

No regulations have yet been made under sub-paras (8) and (9) and it is accordingly suggested that the normal rules will apply for ascertaining when a judgment takes effect.

In England and Wales, a court judgment normally takes effect from the day on which it is made or such later date as the court may specify: r40.7 Civil Procedure Rules 1998.

In Scotland a court decree is enforceable once the successful party has been issued with an extract decree. In the Sheriff Court this is normally 14 days after the date of the decree. In the Court of Session this is normally seven days after the date of the decree. In certain types of cases these periods can be shortened.

Correction of errors and setting aside of decisions

19.–(1)   Regulations may make provision with respect to–

(a)   the correction of accidental errors in any decision or record of a decision made under or by virtue of any relevant provision; and

(b)   the setting aside of any such decision in a case where it appears just to set the decision aside on the ground that–

  (i)   a document relating to the proceedings in which the decision was given was not sent to, or was not received at an appropriate time by, a party to the proceedings or a party's representative, or was not received at an appropriate time by the body or person who gave the decision; or

  (ii)   a party to the proceedings or a party's representative was not present at a hearing related to the proceedings.

(2)   Nothing in sub-paragraph (1) shall be construed as derogating from any power to correct errors or set aside decisions which is exercisable apart from regulations made by virtue of that sub-paragraph.

(3)   In this paragraph "relevant provision" means–

(a)   any of the provisions of this Schedule;

(b)   any of the provisions of Part VII of the Social Security Contributions and Benefits Act 1992 so far as they relate to housing benefit or council tax benefit; or

(c)   any of the provisions of Part VIII of the Administration Act or of any regulations under section 2A of that Act, so far as the provisions or regulations relate to, or to arrangements for, housing benefit or council tax benefit.

Analysis

See regs 56 and 57 SSCS D&A Regs on pp940 and 940. For the significance of sub-para (2), see the Analysis to reg 57.

Regulations

20.–(1)   The power to make regulations under this Schedule shall be exercisable–

(a)   in the case of regulations with respect to proceedings before the Commissioners, by the Lord Chancellor; and

(b)   in any other case, by the Secretary of State;

and the Lord Chancellor shall consult with the Scottish Ministers before making any regulations under this Schedule that apply to Scotland.

(2)   Any power conferred by this Schedule to make regulations shall include power to make different provision for different areas or different relevant authorities.

(3)   Subsections (3) to (7) of section 79 of the Social Security Act 1998 (supplemental provision in connection with powers to make subordinate legislation under that Act) shall apply to any power to make regulations under this Schedule as they apply to any power to make regulations under that Act.

(4)   A statutory instrument containing (whether alone or with other provisions) regulations under paragraph 6(2)(e) or (4) shall not be made unless a draft of the instrument has been laid before Parliament and approved by a resolution of each House.

(5)   A statutory instrument–

(a)   which contains (whether alone or with other provisions) regulations made under this Schedule, and

(b)   which is not subject to any requirement that a draft of the instrument be laid before and approved by a resolution of each House of Parliament,

shall be subject to annulment in pursuance of a resolution of either House of Parliament.

(6)   In this paragraph the reference to regulations with respect to proceedings before the Commissioners includes a reference to regulations with respect to any such proceedings for the determination of any matter, or for leave to appeal to or from the Commissioners.

Interpretation

23.–(1)   In this Schedule–

"the Administration Act" means the Social Security Administration Act 1992;

"affected" shall be construed subject to any regulations under sub-paragraph (2);

"appeal tribunal" means an appeal tribunal constituted under Chapter I of Part I of the Social Security Act 1998;

"the Chief Commissioner" means the Chief Social Security Commissioner;

"Commissioner" means the Chief Commissioner or any other Social Security Commissioner, and includes a tribunal of three or more Commissioners constituted under paragraph 10(5);

"prescribed" means prescribed by regulations under this Schedule;

"relevant authority" has the meaning given by paragraph 1(1);

"relevant decision" has the meaning given by paragraph 1(2).

(2)   Regulations may make provision specifying the circumstances in which a person is or is not to be treated for the purposes of this Schedule as a person who is affected by any decision of a relevant authority.

(3)   For the purposes of this Schedule any decision that is made or falls to be made–

(a)   by a person authorised to carry out any function of a relevant authority relating to housing benefit or council tax benefit, or

(b)   by a person providing services relating to housing benefit or council tax benefit directly or indirectly to a relevant authority,

shall be treated as a decision of the relevant authority on whose behalf the function is carried out or, as the case may be, to whom those services are provided.

Analysis

Sub-para (3) permits delegation of decision making functions in relation to HB/CTB either to officers authorised by local authorities to carry out their functions, or to contractors. The wording "directly or indirectly" covers cases of employees of contractors or, indeed, of sub-contractors.

Welfare Reform Act 2007
2007 Chapter 5

31 Loss of housing benefit following eviction for anti-social behaviour, etc.

(1)   *[Omitted]*

(2)   *[Omitted]*

(3)   The preceding provisions of this section have no effect after 31st December 2010.

(4)   The Secretary of State may by order made by statutory instrument make such provision as he thinks necessary or expedient in consequence of the operation of subsection (3) for the purpose of securing that, with effect from 1st January 2011, housing benefit to which a person who is a former occupier (within the meaning of section 130B of the Contributions and Benefits Act) is entitled is not subject to any restriction as mentioned in subsection (4) of that section.

Commencement

14.6.07 for the purpose only of the exercise of the power to make regulations; 1.11.07 for all other purposes.

General Note

s31(1) of the WRF 2007 inserts ss130B-130G into the SSCBA 1992 and s31(2) amends s176 of that Act. By s31(3), these provisions have no effect after 31st December 2010.

Main secondary legislation
Housing benefit

Part 2

Main secondary legislation
Housing benefit

The Housing Benefit Regulations 2006
(SI 2006 No.213)

ARRANGEMENT OF REGULATIONS
PART 1
General

1. Citation and commencement
2. Interpretation
3. Definition of non-dependant
4. Cases in which section 1(1A) of the Administration Act is disapplied
5. Persons who have attained the qualifying age for state pension credit
6. Remunerative work

PART 2
Provisions affecting entitlement to housing benefit

7. Circumstances in which a person is or is not to be treated as occupying a dwelling as his home
8. Circumstances in which a person is to be treated as liable to make payments in respect of a dwelling
9. Circumstances in which a person is to be treated as not liable to make payments in respect of a dwelling
10. Persons from abroad
10A. Entilement of a rfugee to housing benefit

PART 3
Payments in respect of a dwelling

11. Eligible housing costs
11A. Cases where maximum housing benefit expires
12. Rent
13. Maximum rent
13ZA. Restrictions on rent increases
13A. Maximum rent (standard local rate)
13B. Publication of local housing allowances
14. Requirement to refer to rent officers
15. Applications to the rent officer for redeterminations
16. Application for redetermination by rent officer
17. Substitute determinations or substitute redeterminations
18. Application of provisions to substitute determinations or substitute redeterminations
18A. Amended determinations

PART 4
Membership of a family

19. Persons of prescribed description
20. Circumstances in which a person is to be treated as responsible or not responsible for another
21. Circumstances in which a person is to be treated as being or not being a member of the household

PART 5
Applicable amounts

22. Applicable amounts
23. Polygamous marriages
24. Patients

PART 6
Income and capital
SECTION 1
General

25. Calculation of income and capital of members of claimant's family and of a polygamous marriage
26. Circumstances in which income of non-dependant is to be treated as claimant's

SECTION 2
Income

27. Calculation of income on a weekly basis
28. Treatment of child care charges
29. Average weekly earnings of employed earners
30. Average weekly earnings of self-employed earners
31. Average weekly income other than earnings
32. Calculation of average weekly income from tax credits
33. Calculation of weekly income
34. Disregard of changes in tax, contributions etc

SECTION 3
Employed earners

35. Earnings of employed earners
36. Calculation of net earnings of employed earners

SECTION 4
Self-employed earners

37. Earnings of self-employed earners
38. Calculation of net profit of self-employed earners
39. Deduction of tax and contributions of self-employed earners

SECTION 5
Other income

40. Calculation of income other than earnings
41. Capital treated as income
42. Notional income

SECTION 6
Capital

43. Capital limit
44. Calculation of capital
45. Disregard of capital of child and young person
46. Income treated as capital
47. Calculation of capital in the United Kingdom
48. Calculation of capital outside the United Kingdom
49. Notional capital
50. Diminishing notional capital rule
51. Capital jointly held
52. Calculation of tariff income from capital

PART 7
Students
SECTION 1
General

53. Interpretation
54. Treatment of students

SECTION 2
Entitlement and payments in respect of a dwelling

55. Occupying a dwelling as a person's home
56. Full-time students to be treated as not liable to make payments in respect of a dwelling
57. Student's eligible housing costs
58. Student partners

SECTION 3
Income

59. Calculation of grant income
60. Calculation of covenant income where a contribution is assessed
61. Covenant income where no grant income or no contribution is assessed
62. Relationship with amounts to be disregarded under Schedule 5
63. Other amounts to be disregarded
64. Treatment of student loans
64A. Treatment of fee loans
65. Treatment of payments from access funds
66. Disregard of contribution and rent
67. Further disregard of student's income
68. Amounts treated as capital
69. Disregard of changes occurring during summer vacation

PART 8
Amount of benefit

70. Maximum housing benefit
71. Housing benefit tapers
72. Extended payments
73. Extended payments (severe disablement allowance and incapacity benefit)
74. Non-dependant deductions
75. Minimum housing benefit

PART 9
Calculation of weekly amounts and changes of circumstances

76. Date on which entitlement is to commence
77. Date on which housing benefit is to end
78. Date on which housing benefit is to end where entitlement to severe disablement allowance or incapacity benefit ceases
79. Date on which change of circumstances is to take effect
80. Calculation of weekly amounts
81. Rent free periods

PART 10
Claims

82. Who may claim
83. Time and manner in which claims are to be made
83A. Electronic claims for benefit
84. Date of claim where claim sent or delivered to a gateway office
85. Date of claim where claim sent or delivered to an office of a designated authority
86. Evidence and information
87. Amendment and withdrawal of claim
88. Duty to notify changes of circumstances
88A. Notice of changes of circumstances given electronically

PART 11
Decisions on questions
89. Decisions by a relevant authority
90. Notification of decisions

PART 12
Payments
91. Time and manner of payment
91A. Cases in which payment to a housing authority are to take the form of a rent allowance
92. Frequency of payment of a rent allowance
93. Payment on account of a rent allowance
94. Payment to be made to a person entitled
95. Circumstances in which payment is to be made to a landlord
96. Circumstances in which payment may be made to a landlord
97. Payment on death of the person entitled
98. Offsetting

PART 13
Overpayments
99. Meaning of overpayment
100. Recoverable overpayments
101. Person from whom recovery may be sought
102. Method of recovery
103. Diminution of capital
104. Sums to be deducted in calculating recoverable overpayments
105. Recovery of overpayments from prescribed benefits
106. Prescribed benefits
107. Restrictions on recovery of rent and consequent notifications

PART 14
Information
SECTION 1
Claims and information
108. Interpretation
109. Collection of information
110. Recording and holding information
111. Forwarding of information
112. Request for information

SECTION 2
Information from landlords and agents and between authorities etc.
113. Interpretation
114. Evidence and information required by rent officers
115. Information to be supplied by an authority to another authority
116. Supply of information: extended payments (severe disablement allowance and incapacity benefit)
117. Requiring information from landlords and agents
118. Circumstances for requiring information
119. Relevant information
120. Manner of supply of information
121. Criminal offence

PART 15
Pathfinder authorities
122.   Modifications in respect of pathfinder authorities

SCHEDULES
A1.   Treatment of claims for housing benefit by refugees
1.   Ineligible service charges
2.   Excluded tenancies
3.   Applicable amounts
4.   Sums to be disregarded in the calculation of earnings
5.   Sums to be disregarded in the calculation of income other than earnings
6.   Capital to be disregarded
7.   Extended payments of housing benefit
8.   Extended Payments (severe disablement allowance and incapacity benefit) of housing benefit
9.   Matters to be included in decision notice
10.   Pathfinder authorities
11.   Electronic communication

PART 1
General

General Note on Part I
  This Part defines terms commonly used in the HB Regs. Some regs also give their own specialist meaning
  to terms used in them, and this will be pointed out where necessary. In addition, some of the terms found in
  the regs are defined in s137 of the Social Security Contributions and Benefits Act 1992 (SSCBA – see p19)
  – an indication is also given where this applies.

Citation and commencement
1.–(1)   These Regulations may be cited as the Housing Benefit Regulations 2006.
  (2)   These Regulations are to be read, where appropriate, with the Consequential Provisions Regulations and, in a case where regulation 5(2) applies, with the Housing Benefit (Persons who have attained the qualifying age for state pension credit) Regulations 2006.
  (3)   Except as provided in Schedule 4 to the Consequential Provisions Regulations, these Regulations shall come into force on 6th March 2006.
  (4)   The regulations consolidated by these Regulations are revoked, in consequence of the consolidation, by the Consequential Provisions Regulations.

Interpretation
2.–(1)   In these Regulations–
"the Act" means the Social Security Contributions and Benefits Act 1992;
"the 1973 Act" means the Employment and Training Act 1973;
[¹"the 2000 Act" means the Electronic Communications Act 2000;]
"Abbeyfield Home" means an establishment run by the Abbeyfield Society including all bodies corporate or incorporate which are affiliated to that Society;
"adoption leave" means a period of absence from work on ordinary or additional adoption leave by virtue of section 75A or 75B of the Employment Rights Act 1996;
"the Administration Act" means the Social Security Administration Act 1992;
"appropriate DWP office" means an office of the Department for Work and Pensions dealing with state pension credit or an office which is normally open to the public for the receipt of claims for income support or a jobseeker's allowance;

"assessment period" means such period as is prescribed in regulations 29 to 31 over which income falls to be calculated;

"attendance allowance" means–

(a)   an attendance allowance under Part 3 of the Act;

(b)   an increase of disablement pension under section 104 or 105 of the Act;

(c)   a payment under regulations made in exercise of the power conferred by paragraph 7(2)(b) of Part 2 of Schedule 8 to the Act;

(d)   an increase of an allowance which is payable in respect of constant attendance under paragraph 4 of Part 1 of Schedule 8 to the Act;

(e)   a payment by virtue of article 14, 15, 16, 43 or 44 of the Personal Injuries (Civilians) Scheme 1983 or any analogous payment; or

(f)   any payment based on need for attendance which is paid as part of a war disablement pension;

"the benefit Acts" means the Act and the Jobseekers Act;

"benefit week" means a period of 7 consecutive days commencing upon a Monday and ending on a Sunday;

"care home" in England and Wales has the meaning assigned to it by section 3 of the Care Standards Act 2000 and in Scotland means a care home service within the meaning assigned to it by section 2(3) of the Regulation of Care (Scotland) Act 2001;

"child" means a person under the age of 16;

"child tax credit" means a child tax credit under section 8 of the Tax Credits Act;

"the Children Order" means the Children (Northern Ireland) Order 1995;

"claim" means a claim for housing benefit;

"claimant" means a person claiming housing benefit;

"close relative" means a parent, parent-in-law, son, son-in-law, daughter, daughter-in-law, step-parent, step-son, step-daughter, brother, sister, or if any of the preceding persons is one member of a couple, the other member of that couple;

"community charge benefit" means community charge benefits under Part 7 of the Act as originally enacted;

"concessionary payment" means a payment made under arrangements made by the Secretary of State with the consent of the Treasury which is charged either to the National Insurance Fund or to a Departmental Expenditure Vote to which payments of benefit under the Act or the Child Benefit Act 1975 are charged;

"the Consequential Provisions Regulations" means the Housing Benefit and Council Tax Benefit (Consequential Provisions) Regulations 2006;

"co-ownership scheme" meansa scheme under which the dwelling is let by a housing association and the tenant, or his personal representative, will, under the terms of the tenancy agreement or of the agreement under which he became a member of the association, be entitled, on his ceasing to be a member and subject to any conditions stated in either agreement, to a sum calculated by reference directly or indirectly to the value of the dwelling;

"couple" means–

(a)   a man and a woman who are married to each other and are members of the same household;

(b)   a man and a woman who are not married to each other but are living together as husband and wife;

(c)   two people of the same sex who are civil partners of each other and are members of the same household; or

(d)   two people of the same sex who are not civil partners of each other but are living together as if they were civil partners,

and for the purposes of sub-paragraph (d), two people of the same sex are to be regarded as living together as if they were civil partners if, but only if, they would be regarded as living together as husband and wife were they instead two people of the opposite sex;

"Crown tenant" means a person who occupies a dwelling under a tenancy or licence where the interest of the landlord belongs to Her Majesty in right of the Crown or to a government department or is held in trust for Her Majesty for the purposes of a government department, except (in the case of an interest belonging to Her Majesty in right of the Crown) where the interest is under the management of the Crown Estate Commissioners;

"date of claim" means the date on which the claim is made, or treated as made, for the purposes of regulation 83 (time and manner in which claims are to be made);

"the Decisions and Appeals Regulations" means the Housing Benefit and Council Tax Benefit (Decisions and Appeals) Regulations 2001;

"designated authority" means any of the following–

(a)   the Secretary of State;

(b)   a person providing services to the Secretary of State;

(c)   a local authority;

(d)   a person providing services to, or authorised to exercise any functions of, any such authority;

"designated office" means the office designated by the relevant authority for the receipt of claims to housing benefit–

(a)   by notice upon or with a form approved by it for the purpose of claiming housing benefit; or

(b)   by reference upon or with such a form to some other document available from it and sent by electronic means or otherwise on application and without charge; or

(c)   by any combination of the provisions set out in sub-paragraphs (a) and (b) above;

"disability living allowance" means a disability living allowance under section 71 of the Act;

"earnings" has the meaning prescribed in regulation 35 or, as the case may be, 37;

"the Eileen Trust" means the charitable trust of that name established on 29th March 1993 out of funds provided by the Secretary of State for the benefit of persons eligible for payment in accordance with its provisions;

[[1] "electronic communication" has the same meaning as in section 15(1) of the 2000 Act;]

"eligible rent" is to be construed in accordance with regulation 12 (rent);

"employed earner" is to be construed in accordance with section 2(1)(a) of the Act and also includes a person who is in receipt of a payment which is payable under any enactment having effect in Northern Ireland and which corresponds to statutory sick pay or statutory maternity pay;

"employment zone" means an area within Great Britain designated for the purposes of section 60 of the Welfare Reform and Pensions Act 1999 and an "employment zone programme" means a programme established for such an area or areas designed to assist claimants for a jobseeker's allowance to obtain sustainable employment;

"employment zone contractor" means a person who is undertaking the provision of facilities in respect of an employment zone programme on behalf of the Secretary of State for Work and Pensions;

"extended payment" means a payment of housing benefit pursuant to regulation 72 (extended payments);

"extended payment (severe disablement allowance and incapacity benefit)" means a payment of housing benefit pursuant to regulation 73 (extended payments (severe disablement allowance and incapacity benefit));

"family" has the meaning assigned to it by section 137(1) of the Act;

"the former Regulations" means the Housing Benefit (General) Regulations 1987;

"the Fund" means moneys made available from time to time by the Secretary of State for the benefit of persons eligible for payment in accordance with the provisions of a scheme established by him on 24th April 1992 or, in Scotland, on 10th April 1992;

"gateway office" means an appropriate DWP office or an office designated by the appropriate authority which is nominated by the Secretary of State as a gateway office and referred to in a notice upon or attached to a form approved by the appropriate authority for the purpose of claiming housing benefit;

"a guaranteed income payment" means a payment made under article 14(1)(b) or article 21(1)(a) of the Armed Forces and Reserve Forces (Compensation Scheme) Order 2005;

"hostel" means a building–

(a)   in which there is provided for persons generally or for a class of persons, domestic accommodation, otherwise than in separate and self-contained premises, and either board or facilities for the preparation of food adequate to the needs of those persons, or both; and

(b)   which is–
    (i)   managed or owned by a registered housing association; or
    (ii)   operated other than on a commercial basis and in respect of which funds are provided wholly or in part by a government department or agency or a local authority; or
    (iii)   managed by a voluntary organisation or charity and provides care, support or supervision with a view to assisting those persons to be rehabilitated or resettled within the community; and

(c) which is not–
    (i)   a care home;
    (ii)   an independent hospital; or
    (iii)   an Abbeyfield Home;

"Housing Act functions" has the same meaning as in section 136(1) of the Administration Act;

"housing association" has the meaning assigned to it by section 1(1) of the Housing Associations Act 1985;

"Immigration and Asylum Act" means the Immigration and Asylum Act 1999;

"an income-based jobseeker's allowance" and "a joint-claim jobseeker's allowance" have the same meanings as they have in the Jobseekers Act by virtue of section 1(4) of that Act;

"Income Support Regulations" means the Income Support (General) Regulations 1987;

"independent hospital" in England and Wales has the meaning assigned to it by section 2 of the Care Standards Act 2000 and in Scotland means an independent healthcare service as defined in section 2(5)(a) and (b) of the Regulation of Care (Scotland) Act 2001;

"the Independent Living Fund" means the charitable trust established out of funds provided by the Secretary of State for the purpose of providing financial assistance to those persons incapacitated by or otherwise suffering from very severe disablement who are in need of such assistance to enable them to live independently;

[5 "the Independent Living Fund (2006)" means the Trust of that name established by a deed dated 10th April 2006 and made between the Secretary of State for Work and Pensions of the one part and Margaret Rosemary Cooper, Michael Beresford Boyall and Marie Theresa Martin of the other part;]

"the Independent Living Funds" means the Independent Living Fund, [⁵ the Independent Living (Extension) Fund, the Independent Living (1993) Fund and the Independent Living Fund (2006)];

"the Independent Living (Extension) Fund" means the Trust of that name established by a deed dated 25th February 1993 and made between the Secretary of State for Social Security of the one part and Robin Glover Wendt and John Fletcher Shepherd of the other part;

"the Independent Living (1993) Fund" means the Trust of that name established by a deed dated 25th February 1993 and made between the Secretary of State for Social Security of the one part and Robin Glover Wendt and John Fletcher Shepherd of the other part;

"Intensive Activity Period for 50 plus" means the programme known by that name and provided in pursuance of arrangements made by or on behalf of the Secretary of State under section 2 of the 1973 Act, being a programme lasting for up to 52 weeks for any one individual aged 50 years or over on the day that he first joined any such programme, and consisting for that individual of any one or more of the following elements, namely employed earner's employment, assistance in pursuing self-employed earner's employment, education and training, work experience, assistance with job search, motivation and skills training;

"invalid carriage or other vehicle" means a vehicle propelled by petrol engine or by electric power supplied for use on the road and to be controlled by the occupant;

"Jobseekers Act" means the Jobseekers Act 1995;

"Jobseeker's Allowance Regulations" means the Jobseeker's Allowance Regulations 1996;

"the London Bombings Relief Charitable Fund" means the company limited by guarantee (number 5505072) and registered charity of that name established on 11th July 2005 for the purpose of (amongst other things) relieving sickness, disability or financial need of victims (including families or dependants of victims) of the terrorist attacks carried out in London on 7th July 2005;

"lone parent" means a person who has no partner and who is responsible for and a member of the same household as a child or young person;

"long tenancy" means a tenancy granted for a term of years certain exceeding twenty one years, whether or not the tenancy is, or may become, terminable before the end of that term by notice given by or to the tenant or by re-entry, forfeiture (or, in Scotland, irritancy) or otherwise and includes a lease for a term fixed by law under a grant with a covenant or obligation for perpetual renewal unless it is a lease by sub-demise from one which is not a long tenancy;

[⁷]

"the Macfarlane (Special Payments) Trust" means the trust of that name, established on 29th January 1990 partly out of funds provided by the Secretary of State, for the benefit of certain persons suffering from haemophilia;

"the Macfarlane (Special Payments) (No. 2) Trust" means the trust of that name, established on 3rd May 1991 partly out of funds provided by the Secretary of State, for the benefit of certain persons suffering from haemophilia and other beneficiaries;

"the Macfarlane Trust" means the charitable trust, established partly out of funds provided by the Secretary of State to the Haemophilia Society, for the relief of poverty or distress among those suffering from haemophilia;

"maternity leave" means a period during which a woman is absent from work because she is pregnant or has given birth to a child, and at the end of which she has a right to return to work either under the terms of her contract of employment or under Part 8 of the Employment Rights Act 1996;

"maximum rent" means the amount to which the eligible rent is restricted in a case where regulation 13 applies;

"mover" has the meaning assigned to it in paragraph 11 of Schedule 7;

"net earnings" means such earnings as are calculated in accordance with regulation 36 (calculation of net earnings of employed earners);

"net profit" means such profit as is calculated in accordance with regulation 38 (calculation of net profit of self-employed earners);

"the New Deal options" means the employment programmes specified in regulation 75(1)(a)(ii) of the Jobseeker's Allowance Regulations and the training scheme specified in regulation 75(1)(b)(ii) of those Regulations;

"non-dependant" has the meaning prescribed in regulation 3;

"non-dependant deduction" means a deduction that is to be made under regulation 74 (non-dependant deductions);

"occupational pension" means any pension or other periodical payment under an occupational pension scheme but does not include any discretionary payment out of a fund established for relieving hardship in particular cases;

"ordinary clothing or footwear" means clothing or footwear for normal daily use but does not include school uniforms or clothing or footwear used solely for sporting activities;

"owner" means–

(a) in relation to a dwelling in England and Wales, the person who, otherwise than as a mortgagee in possession, is for the time being entitled to dispose of the fee simple, whether or not with the consent of other joint owners;

(b) in relation to a dwelling in Scotland, the proprietor under udal tenure or the proprietor of the dominion utile or the tenant's or the lessee's interest in a long tenancy, a kindly tenancy, a lease registered or registerable under the Registration of Leases (Scotland) Act 1857 or the Land Registration (Scotland) Act 1979 or a tenant-at-will as defined in section 20(8) of that Act of 1979;

"partner" means–

(a) where a claimant is a member of a couple, the other member of that couple; or

(b) where a claimant is polygamously married to two or more members of his household, any such member;

"paternity leave" means a period of absence from work on leave by virtue of section 80A or 80B of the Employment Rights Act 1996;

"payment" includes part of a payment;

"pension fund holder" means with respect to a personal pension scheme or [³ an occupational pension scheme], the trustees, managers or scheme administrators, as the case may be, of the scheme [³] concerned;

"person affected" shall be construed in accordance with regulation 3 of the Decisions and Appeals Regulations;

"person on income support" means a person in receipt of income support;

"person on state pension credit" means a person in receipt of state pension credit;

[³ "personal pension scheme" means–

(a) a personal pension scheme as defined by section 1 of the Pension Schemes Act 1993;

(b) an annuity contract or trust scheme approved under section 620 or 621 of the Income and Corporation Taxes Act 1988 or a substituted contract within the meaning of section 622(3) of that Act which is treated as having become a registered pension scheme by virtue of paragraph 1(1)(f) of Schedule 36 to the Finance Act 2004;

(c) a personal pension scheme approved under Chapter 4 of Part 14 of the Income and Corporation Taxes Act 1988 which is treated as having become a registered pension scheme by virtue of paragraph 1(1)(g) of Schedule 36 to the Finance Act 2004;]

"policy of life insurance" means any instrument by which the payment of money is assured on death (except death by accident only) or the happening of any contingency dependent on human life, or any instrument evidencing a contract which is subject to payment of premiums for a term dependent on human life;

"polygamous marriage" means any marriage during the subsistence of which a party to it is married to more than one person and the ceremony of marriage took place under the law of a country which permits polygamy;

"the qualifying age for state pension credit" means (in accordance with section 1(2)(b) and (6) of the State Pension Credit Act 2002)–
(a) in the case of a woman, pensionable age; or
(b) in the case of a man, the age which is pensionable age in the case of a woman born on the same day as the man;

"qualifying person" means a person in respect of whom payment has been made from the Fund, the Eileen Trust, the Skipton Fund or the London Bombings Relief Charitable Fund;

"relative" means a close relative, grandparent, grandchild, uncle, aunt, nephew or niece;

"relevant authority" means an authority administering housing benefit;

"remunerative work" has the meaning prescribed in regulation 6 (remunerative work);

"rent" includes all those payments in respect of a dwelling specified in regulation 12(1);

"the Rent Officers Order" means the Rent Officers (Housing Benefit Functions) Order 1997 or, as the case may be, the Rent Officers (Housing Benefit Functions) (Scotland) Order 1997;

[³]

"second dwelling" has the meaning assigned to it in paragraph 11 of Schedule 7;

"self-employed earner" is to be construed in accordance with section 2(1)(b) of the Act;

"self-employment route" means assistance in pursuing self-employed earner's employment whilst participating in–
(a) an employment zone programme; or
(b) a programme provided or other arrangements made pursuant to section 2 of the 1973 Act (functions of the Secretary of State) or section 2 of the Enterprise and New Towns (Scotland) Act 1990 (functions in relation to training for employment, etc.);

"shared ownership tenancy" means–
(a) in relation to England and Wales, a [⁴ lease] granted on payment of a premium calculated by reference to a percentage of the value of the dwelling or the cost of providing it;
(b) in relation to Scotland, an agreement by virtue of which the tenant of a dwelling of which he and the landlord are joint owners is the tenant in respect of the landlord's interest in the dwelling or by virtue of which the tenant has the right to purchase the dwelling or the whole or part of the landlord's interest therein;

"single claimant" means a claimant who neither has a partner nor is a lone parent;

"the Skipton Fund" means the ex-gratia payment scheme administered by the Skipton Fund Limited, incorporated on 25th March 2004, for the benefit of certain persons suffering from hepatitis C and other persons eligible for payment in accordance with the scheme's provisions;

"sports award" means an award made by one of the Sports Councils named in section 23(2) of the National Lottery etc. Act 1993 out of sums allocated to it for distribution under that section;

[⁶ "starting rate", where it relates to the rate of tax, has the same meaning as in the Income Tax Act 2007 (see section 989 of that Act);]

"student" has the meaning prescribed in regulation 53 (interpretation);

"subsistence allowance" means an allowance which an employment zone contractor has agreed to pay to a person who is participating in an employment zone programme;

"the Tax Credits Act" means the Tax Credits Act 2002;

"tax year" means a period beginning with 6th April in one year and ending with 5th April in the next;

"training allowance" means an allowance (whether by way of periodical grants or otherwise) payable–

   (a)   out of public funds by a Government department or by or on behalf of the Secretary of State, Scottish Enterprise or Highlands and Islands Enterprise, the Learning and Skills Council for England or the National Assembly for Wales;

   (b)   to a person for his maintenance or in respect of a member of his family; and

   (c)   for the period, or part of the period, during which he is following a course of training or instruction provided by, or in pursuance of arrangements made with, that department or approved by that department in relation to him or so provided or approved by or on behalf of the Secretary of State, Scottish Enterprise or Highlands and Islands Enterprise or the National Assembly for Wales,

but it does not include an allowance paid by any Government department to or in respect of a person by reason of the fact that he is following a course of full-time education, other than under arrangements made under section 2 of the 1973 Act or is training as a teacher;

"voluntary organisation" means a body, other than a public or local authority, the activities of which are carried on otherwise than for profit;

[²]

"water charges" means–

   (a)   as respects England and Wales, any water and sewerage charges under Chapter 1 of Part 5 of the Water Industry Act 1991,

   (b)   as respects Scotland, any water and sewerage charges established by Scottish Water under a charges scheme made under section 29A of the Water Industry (Scotland) Act 2002

in so far as such charges are in respect of the dwelling which a person occupies as his home;

"working tax credit" means a working tax credit under section 10 of the Tax Credits Act;

"Working Tax Credit Regulations" means the Working Tax Credit (Entitlement and Maximum Rate) Regulations 2002;

"young individual" means a single claimant who has not attained the age of 25 years, but does not include such a claimant–

   (a)   whose landlord is a registered housing association;

   (b)   who has not attained the age of 22 years and has ceased to be the subject of a care order made pursuant to section 31(1)(a) of the Children Act 1989 which had previously been made in respect to him either–

      (i)   after he attained the age of 16 years; or

      (ii) before he attained the age of 16 years, but had continued after he attained that age;

   (c)   who has not attained the age of 22 years and was formerly provided with accommodation under section 20 of the Children Act 1989;

(d)   who has not attained the age of 22 years and has ceased to be subject to a supervision requirement by a children's hearing under section 70 of the Children (Scotland) Act 1995 (''the 1995 Act'') made in respect of him which had continued after he attained the age of 16 years, other than a case where–

　　(i)   the ground of referral was based on the sole condition as to the need for compulsory measures of care specified in section 52(1)(i) of the 1995 Act (commission of offences by child); or

　　(ii)   he was required by virtue of the supervision requirement to reside with a parent or guardian of his within the meaning of the 1995 Act, or with a friend or relative of his or of his parent or guardian;

(e)   who has not attained the age of 22 years and has ceased to be a child in relation to whom the parental rights and responsibilities were transferred to a local authority under a parental responsibilities order made in accordance with section 86 of the 1995 Act or treated as so vested in accordance with paragraph 3 of Schedule 3 to that Act, either–

　　(i)   after he attained the age of 16 years; or

　　(ii)   before he attained the age of 16 years, but had continued after he attained that age; or

(f)   who has not attained the age of 22 years and has ceased to be provided with accommodation by a local authority under section 25 of the 1995 Act where he has previously been provided with accommodation by the authority under that provision either–

　　(i)   after he attained the age of 16 years; or

　　(ii)   before he attained the age of 16 years, but had continued to be in such accommodation after he attained that age;

''young person'' has the meaning prescribed in regulation 19(1)(persons of prescribed description).

(2)   References in these Regulations to a person who is liable to make payments shall include references to a person who is treated as so liable under regulation 8 (circumstances in which a person is to be treated as liable to make payments in respect of a dwelling).

(3)   For the purposes of these Regulations, a person is on an income-based jobseeker's allowance on any day in respect of which an income-based jobseeker's allowance is payable to him and on any day–

(a)   in respect of which he satisfies the conditions for entitlement to an income-based jobseeker's allowance but where the allowance is not paid in accordance with section 19 or 20A of the Jobseekers Act (circumstances in which a jobseeker's allowance is not payable); or

(b)   which is a waiting day for the purposes of paragraph 4 of Schedule 1 to that Act and which falls immediately before a day in respect of which an income-based jobseeker's allowance is payable to him or would be payable to him but for section 19 or 20A of that Act; or

(c)   in respect of which he is a member of a joint-claim couple for the purposes of the Jobseekers Act and no joint-claim jobseeker's allowance is payable in respect of that couple as a consequence of either member of that couple being subject to sanctions for the purposes of section 20A of that Act; or

(d)   in respect of which an income-based jobseeker's allowance or a joint-claim jobseeker's allowance would be payable but for a restriction imposed pursuant to section 62 or 63 of the Child Support, Pensions and Social Security Act 2000 or sections 7, 8 or 9 of the Social Security Fraud Act 2001 (loss of benefit provisions).

(4)   For the purposes of these Regulations, the following shall be treated as included in a dwelling–

(a) subject to sub-paragraphs (b) to (d) any land (whether or not occupied by a structure) which is used for the purposes of occupying a dwelling as a home where either–

    (i) the occupier of the dwelling acquired simultaneously the right to use the land and the right to occupy the dwelling, and, in the case of a person liable to pay rent for his dwelling, he could not have occupied that dwelling without also acquiring the right to use the land; or

    (ii) the occupier of the dwelling has made or is making all reasonable efforts to terminate his liability to make payments in respect of the land;

(b) where the dwelling is a caravan or mobile home, such of the land on which it stands as is used for the purposes of the dwelling;

(c) where the dwelling is a houseboat, the land used for the purposes of mooring it;

(d) where in Scotland, the dwelling is situated on or pertains to a croft within the meaning of section 3(1) of the Crofters (Scotland) Act 1993, the croft land on which it is situated or to which it pertains.

Modifications

Some definitions are inserted by Sch 10 para 2 (see p511). These apply only to Pathfinder Authorities who are administering the pilot local housing allowance scheme, as from the date specified in relation to each authority as specified in Sch 10 Part 1.

    References to "step-parent" step-children and the various in-laws in the definition of "close relative" are modified by s246 Civil Partnership Act 2004 (see p1046) and art 3 and para 24 of the Sch to SI 2005 No 3137 (see p1097).

Definitions

"dwelling" – see s137(1) SSCBA.

Amendments

1.   Inserted by Art 2(2) of SI 2006 No 2968 as from 20.12.06.
2.   Omitted by Reg 4(a) of SI 2007 No 1619 as from 3.7.07.
3.   Amended by reg 4(2) of SI 2007 No 1749 as from 16.7.07.
4.   Amended by reg 2(2) of SI 2007 No 1356 as from 1.10.07.
5.   Amended by Art 8(2) of SI 2007 No 2538 as from 1.10.07.
6.   Inserted by reg 11(2) of SI 2007 No 2618 as from 1.10.07.
7.   Revoked by reg 2 and the Sch of SI 2007 No 2618 as from 1.10.07.

Analysis

Paragraph (1): General definitions

"assessment period". See notes on regs 29-31.

"benefit week". In general, entitlement to HB accrues on a weekly basis, and by virtue of this definition, each week of entitlement runs from Monday to Sunday.

"close relative". The term "couple" is defined later in this regulation by reference to s137 SSCBA. See also the modifications cited above.

"concessionary payment". For example, extra statutory payments made during a strike.

"co-ownership scheme". The term "housing association" is defined later in the regulation; for land to be included with a "dwelling", see reg 2(4). The same wording was used in the 1985 HB Regs. In a case based on those regs, Kennedy J held that equity sharing schemes run by housing associations under the Housing Corporation's model rules, whereby on leaving the scheme after a minimum period of 12 months a participant would receive an equity share payment based on the increased value of the premises, were "co-ownership schemes": *R v Birmingham CC HBRB ex p Ellery* [1989] 21 HLR 398, QBD.

"couple". The definition is the same as in s137 SSCBA (see p21).

"crown tenant". See s137(1) SSCBA for "dwelling". There is a separate scheme of relief for Crown tenants, but crown tenants entitled to IS, income-based JSA or PC may be able to claim help with their 'rent' under the housing costs rules for those benefits: see para 17(1)(e) Sch 3 Income Support (General) Regulations 1987, para 16(1)(e) Sch 2 Jobseeker's Allowance Regulations 1996 and para 13(1)(e) Sch II State Pension Credit Regulations 2002.

"disability living allowance". Disability living allowance (DLA) is available to people disabled before the age of 65. It is made up of two parts: a mobility component and a care component. The mobility component is payable at higher and lower rate while the care component is payable at three rates. DLA income is disregarded in full for HB/CTB (Sch 5 para 6 HB Regs, reg 29(1)(j) HB(SPC) Regs, Sch 4 para 7 CTB Regs and reg 19(1)(j) CTB(SPC) Regs) and receipt of DLA gives entitlement to certain premiums (see HB and HB(SPC) Regs Sch 3 and CTB and CTB(SPC) Regs Sch 1).

"earnings". See reg 35, which defines "earnings" for employees, and reg 37 which does so for self-employed people.

"eligible rent". See reg 12.

"employed earner". SSCBA s2(1)(a) defines this as "a person who is gainfully employed in Great Britain either under a contract of service, or in an office (including elective office) with general earnings".

"the Fund" refers to money made available by the government from a trust set up by the relevant Secretary of State for persons infected (including infected partners and children) with HIV through NHS blood transfusions or tissue transfers.

"gateway office". The Secretary of State can nominate certain offices to accept claims for different benefits. Under regs 84 and 85, these provide an alternative mode of claiming HB. For further details, see the commentary to s2A SSAA on p31. Reg 88 allows relevant information to be passed to a gateway office.

"hostel". This definition serves two purposes. First, hostels receive special treatment under the rent restrictions legislation: see reg 14(4)(a). Second, by reg 4, inhabitants of hostels are exempt from the 'NINO requirement' imposed by reg s1(1A) SSAA.

The criteria that must be fulfilled if a building is to qualify as a "hostel" are:

(1) The accommodation must be for "persons generally or for a class of persons". In this context, in connection with the second criterion, this means that there must be a degree of multiple occupancy. However, there is no need for the persons to have any particular need such as treatment for addiction, although this will be a feature of many of the dwellings that qualify.

(2) It must provide "domestic accommodation, otherwise than in separate and self-contained premises". This appears to require that the facilities required for the basic functions of life must be shared to some degree. At minimum, it is suggested, to be "separate and self-contained", units would have to have facilities for eating, sleeping, cooking and washing.

(3) There must either be board provided or facilities for the preparation of food adequate to the needs of the people accommodated, or both.

(4) The condition in sub-para (b) as to ownership or management must be fulfilled in one of three ways. First, under head (i), a building will qualify if it is owned *or* managed (but not necessarily both) by a "registered housing association". This is not defined in reg 2(1), the definition below not referring to registration. Given the origin of this definition in reg 12A(8) HB Regs 1987 (now reg 14(10) HB Regs), however, the definition there should be adopted.

Alternatively, under head (ii) a building will qualify if it is operated other than on a commercial basis. The caselaw set out in the Analysis to reg 9(1)(a) may assist, although the running of the accommodation as a whole must be examined rather than just the agreement with the individual tenant in question. It must also be funded in whole or in part by one of the relevant public bodies listed. It would appear that anything more than minimal funding would suffice, so a modest local authority grant would allow the dwelling to qualify.

Finally, under head (iii), a building will qualify if it is managed by a "voluntary organisation" (defined later in this regulation) or a charity, by which is presumably meant a registered charity. It must also provide suitable "care, support or supervision" to allow inhabitants "to be "rehabilitated or resettled" into the community. These are general words that should be given a wide meaning. They carry no pejorative implication and so the newly disabled, for example, require rehabilitation or resettlement just as do those with addictions.

(5) The building cannot be a "care home", "independent hospital" or an "Abbeyfield Home" (all defined elsewhere in this regulation).

"housing association". By s1(1) Housing Associations Act 1985, this means a "society, body of trustees or a company (a) which is established for the purposes of, or amongst whose objects and powers are included, those of providing, constructing, improving or managing, or facilitating or encouraging the construction or improvement of, housing accommodation, and (b) which does not trade for profit or whose constitution or rules prohibit the issue of capital with interest or dividend exceeding such rate as may be prescribed by the treasury, whether with or without differentiation between share and loan capital".

Pt I of the Housing Act 1996 empowers the Housing Corporation to maintain a register of some, but not all associations; this register can therefore be used to check whether a particular body counts as such an association.

"income-based jobseeker's allowance" and **"joint-claim jobseeker's allowance"**. Under the provisions of the Jobseekers Act 1995, jobseeker's allowance (JSA) is a benefit for claimants required to sign on as unemployed.

There are three routes into JSA: contribution-based; income-based; and joint-claim. Under the contribution-based JSA route, claimants who satisfy the NI contribution requirements receive a personal rate of JSA for 26 weeks (168 days) irrespective of their capital or partner's earnings. Under the income-based and joint-claim JSA routes, JSA is provided to unemployed people and dependants according to a means-test for as long as the conditions for receipt remain satisfied. Couples without responsibility for children must claim joint-claim JSA if at least one of the couple is 18 or over and was born after 28 October 1957 (known as a "joint-claim couple"). Both claimants must usually satisfy all the rules for getting JSA, unless exempt.

Income-based and joint-claim JSA are assessed on the basis of the same rules and rates as income support (IS). The rate depends, therefore, on a claimant's age, whether s/he has a partner, whether s/he qualifies for any premiums, eligible housing costs in line with IS rules, and on her/his income and capital.

For HB/CTB purposes: a person on income-based JSA or joint-claim JSA who is entitled to HB or CTB has income and capital disregarded and is automatically entitled to maximum HB/CTB; contribution-based JSA is taken fully into account as income.

"lone parent". "Partner" is defined later in this regulation. Part 4 of the Regs deals with membership of a family: "young person" is defined in reg 19; reg 20, deals with circumstances in which an adult is treated as "responsible" for a child or young person; reg 21 with those in which persons are to be treated as sharing a household. See also p22 for more on the meaning of household.

"long tenancy". A "term of years certain" means that the length of the lease may be ascertained and that it is intended to last for more than 21 years, subject to the potential terminating factors here set out. The term will be set out in the lease. "Re-entry" is a landlord's remedy for the breach of a condition in a lease which can no longer be exercised without a court order whilst someone is lawfully residing in the dwelling concerned: see the Protection from Eviction Act 1977. "Forfeiture" is a similarly restricted remedy for non-payment of rent.

A tenancy for life takes effect as a tenancy for 90 years in England and Wales by virtue of s149(6) Law of Property Act 1925, and so is a "long tenancy" for HB purposes: *CH 2743/2003* para 8 and *CH 2258/2004* para 16.

An oral agreement cannot create a long tenancy. Moreover, an agreement in writing (but not by deed) will not be enough to create a long tenancy, as ss52 and 53 Law of Property Act 1925 require leases in excess of three years to be made by deed. Accordingly, a written agreement purporting to create a long tenancy but which was not made by deed (ie, under seal), is not a "tenancy granted" for a term in excess of 21 years and is not, therefore, a long tenancy: *R(H) 3/07*.

"irritancy" is a Scots law remedy – the landlord's right to end the lease and repossess the property if certain terms of the lease are broken. "lease for a term fixed by law . . . perpetual renewal" refers to the provisions of s145 and Sch 15 Law of Property Act 1925 which convert perpetually renewable leases into leases lasting for a term of 2,000 years but such leases will not count as long tenancies if they are sub-leases and the person sub-letting does not have a long tenancy her/himself.

"lower rate". The 20 per cent lower rate of income tax is payable on the first block of earned income after personal allowances have been deducted.

"the New Deal Options". The New Deal is the Government's programme for tackling long-term unemployment and exclusion from the labour market and reducing welfare dependency. It consists of a number of different schemes to promote work amongst such groups.

The relevant parts of reg 75 JSA Regs 1996 refer to the following schemes:

(1)   The Self-Employed Employment Option, which assists claimants in pursuing self-employment for a period of up to 26 weeks.

(2)   The Voluntary Sector Option, which provides a combination of a job placement and training and support within the voluntary sector for up to six months.

(3)   The Environment Task Force Option, which provides similar experience in assisting with environmental schemes for up to six months.

(4)   The Full-Time Education and Training Option, which provides a combination of education, training, work experience and job search skills for up to one year.

The significance of this definition relates to the treatment of payments made by the Secretary of State: see Sch 5 para 13.

"non-dependant" and **"non-dependant deduction"**. Reg 74 provides that the maximum amount of HB payable to a claimant shall be reduced by fixed amounts if s/he lives with certain "non-dependants".

"owner". The definition of "owner" in reg 2(1) will also apply to cognate expressions such as "own", "owned" and "ownership" elsewhere in the HB Regs: *CH 1278/2003* para 13; *CH 3616/2003* para 7. Reg 12(2)(c) renders any payments by an "owner" ineligible for HB. The mortgagee is the lending institution which lends the person money on mortgage to buy the home. The other persons who have the right to sell or otherwise dispose of the dwelling should be listed on the title deeds or on the office copies relating to the title in the property which are held at the Land Registry. The inclusion in this definition of persons who cannot sell without consent is designed to overturn the decision in *R v Sedgemoor DC HBRB ex p Weadon* [1986] 18 HLR 355, QBD. That decision had held that a co-owner was able to get HB for rent paid to the other owners in respect of her occupation of the dwelling.

In *R(H) 8/07* the claimant was the registered proprietor of the freehold of a property. He occupied a flat in it, and paid rent to the person to whom he had granted a long lease of it. He claimed HB in respect of his liability for that rent. Commissioner Turnbull said that although, for most practical purposes, the long leaseholder, rather than the claimant, would be regarded as the "owner" of the flat, "owner" for HB purposes is defined by reference to the ability to dispose of the fee simple, and not by reference to the ability to dispose of any long leasehold interest in it which may have been granted. The claimant here had the right to dispose of the fee simple. Although the definition applies "unless the context otherwise requires", it was not possible to conclude that the context of what is now reg 12(2)(c) HB Regs requires that, where a long leasehold interest has been granted at a low rent, the person with the ability to dispose of that leasehold interest, rather than the person who is entitled to dispose of the freehold, is the owner.

In *R v Sheffield CC HBRB ex p Smith* [1994] 28 HLR 36 at 47-8, QBD, Blackburne J suggested that if a person has a joint beneficial interest giving her/him a right to a share in the proceeds of sale, it does not follow that s/he is a person "for the time being, entitled to dispose of the fee simple". If this is right, it appears from his rejection of the argument for the respondents (at 46-7) that it will probably be necessary to show that the individual claimant has a specific power to dispose of the legal title to the property.

In *Fairbank v Lambeth Magistrates' Court* [2003] HLR 62 the claimant asserted that he held a property as trustee for his father. The court ruled that it was not necessary for the claimant to come within the definition of "owner" to be guilty of the offence with which he was charged (see also p61) but went on to hold (paras 13-18) that a claimant who merely needs to consult beneficiaries under a trust of land is an "owner" for the purposes of reg 2(1). That finding was technically *obiter* but is fully reasoned and was followed by Commissioner Fellner in *R(H) 7/05* paras 35-41 and Commissioner Mesher in *CH 1278/2003* para 16.

The claimant in *R(H) 7/05* appealed against the decision of the commissioner but his appeal was rejected by the Court of Appeal in *Burton v New Forest District Council* [2004] EWCA Civ 1510, 12 November, reported as *R(H) 7/05*. The commissioner had decided that the claimant came within the definition of "owner" – and was thus disqualified from receiving HB by virtue of reg 10(2)(c) HB regs 1987 (now reg 12(2)(c) HB Regs) – because the claimant was the registered proprietor of the property (on the Land Charges Register), and so by virtue of s20(1) Land Registration Act 1925 was "entitled to dispose of the fee simple" without the consent of other joint owners, regardless of whether so selling the property would give rise to a breach of trust.

In rejecting the further appeal, the Court of Appeal held that there is no true distinction between the words "entitled to dispose of the fee simple" in reg 2(1)(a) and being "able" to dispose of the fee simple under s20(1) LRA 1925. Given this, it was quite impossible to construe the term "owner" in reg 2(1) as meaning exclusively a beneficial owner. Because his name remained on the title at the Land Registry as sole owner with title absolute, he was, as a matter of law, entitled to dispose of the fee simple at any point up until the Land Registry was rectified. But until any such rectification, the claimant was the "owner" and not entitled to any housing benefit. Moreover, in the Court of Appeal's view, nothing in the terms of reg 7 HB Regs 1987 (now reg 9 HB Regs) acted to alter this conclusion.

In *CH 1278/2003*, the commissioner commented that administrators of estates may also fall within the definition since they have a right to dispose of the fee simple: paras 18-19.

It appears that local authorities are having to deal with such unorthodox arrangements for the holding of property with increasing frequency. Rather than grapple with the complexities as to whether the claimant is an "owner", some are simply finding that the arrangements fall foul of the provisions in reg 9(1). However, it is important that authorities do not make an assumption of non-commerciality or contrivance simply on the basis of the unusual nature of the arrangement. Such arrangements for the holding of property are often the reflection of the values of religious or ethnic groups, and caution will be required to ensure that the relevant tests are met. See the Analysis to reg 9 for more details.

It is important to bear in mind that the definition of "owner" cannot apply to a person who is a leaseholder, as opposed to a freeholder, in England and Wales: *CH 296/2003* para 29. Long leaseholders are excluded from HB by virtue of reg 12(2)(a), but this principle may be of importance, for example, in limiting the effect of reg 9(1)(h): see the commentary to that provision.

"Udal tenure" is a form of land holding only found in the Orkney and Shetland Islands. The "proprietor of the dominium utile" is the person with the right to use and occupy the land and who now or in the past, is or would have been liable to pay feu duty; again, this should be apparent from the title deeds. "Long tenancy" is defined above. "Registered" leases will be registered at the Register of Sasines in Register

House, Edinburgh. "Registrable" leases, in Scotland, are those: (1) executed in probative writing; and (2) lasting for a period of more than 20 years, or for a shorter period if there is an obligation to renew the lease so that it will actually endure for a period exceeding that number of years.

"partner". Couples are defined above and by s137(1) SSCBA (see p21).

"person on income support". *R v South Ribble DC HBRB ex p Hamilton* [2000] 33 HLR 102, CA confirmed that the definition of "person on income support" must be read as a person lawfully in receipt of IS. Note that the definition of person "on an income-based jobseeker's allowance" is in reg 2(3).

"polygamous marriage". Note that this only covers marriages that are lawful where and when they occur. An authority faced with a problem as to the validity of a polygamous marriage should seek expert advice from a specialist lawyer.

"qualifying person". "The Fund", "the Eileen Trust", "the Skipton Fund" and the "London Bombings Relief Charitable Fund" are all defined elsewhere in this regulation. The significance of the term is in respect of certain income and capital disregards.

"relative". "Close relative" is defined earlier in this regulation. Note that neither definition covers half-sisters and brothers.

"self-employed earner". SSCBA s2(1)(b) defines this as "a person who is gainfully employed in Great Britain otherwise than in employed earner's employment (whether or not s/he is also employed in such employment)". For "employed earner's employment" see above.

"shared ownership tenancy". For "dwelling", see SSCBA s137(1) (p22) and reg 2(4). For "owner", see above.

"single claimant". For "partner" and "lone parent", see above.

"sports award". The piecemeal nature of the financial support provided for sportsmen and sportswomen in Great Britain by government and quangos, in comparison with that provided by governments elsewhere, had long been the subject of criticism, partly as sportsmen and women were unable to concentrate on sport because of a need to make themselves available for other work. Since 1999, awards made by the Sports Councils have been ignored for benefit purposes.

"training allowance". Under the New Deal (Miscellaneous Provisions) Order 1998 (see p1070) and the New Deal (Miscellaneous Provisions) Order 2001 (see p1077), payments to a trainee under the training options of the New Deal are to be treated as paid under s2 Employment and Training Act 1973 and therefore fall within the definition of "training allowance" for HB purposes.

"young individual". Reg 13(4) requires that where the claimant is a "young individual" as defined here and the rent officer has supplied the authority with a single room rent the maximum rent will be based on that figure.

For "registered housing association", see the commentary on "hostel" and "housing association" above.

In England and Wales a single claimant under 22 is not a "young individual" if s/he was the subject of a care order made under s31(l)(a) Children Act 1989 which was made after s/he turned 16 or made before age 16 but continued after that age. For this exemption to apply the court must have made an order putting the child in the care of a designated authority. A single claimant is also not a "young individual" in England and Wales if s/he is under 22 years and was formerly provided with accommodation under s20 Children Act 1989. This requires social services departments to provide accommodation to children (anyone aged under 18 years) in need. It also permits social services to provide accommodation to any child within their area – eg, if they consider that doing so would safeguard or promote the child's welfare.

In Scotland a single claimant under 22 is not a "young individual" if parental rights were assumed by a local authority under s86 Children (Scotland) Act 1995 or s/he was provided with accommodation by a local authority under s25 of that Act, in both cases after s/he turned 16 or before age 16 but continuing after that age. A single claimant under 22 is also not a "young individual" if s/he was subject to a supervision requirement under s70 Children (Scotland) Act 1995 ("provided that the supervision requirement was not made as a result of the child having committed an offence"). For this exemption to apply the authority should be satisfied that the child was living away from her/his normal place of residence but not with friends or relatives.

Paragraph (2)

This confirms that persons liable to make payments include those deemed to be so liable under reg 8.

Paragraph (3)

This provides that someone is considered to be on income-based JSA not only on any day in respect of which it is payable to her/him, but also in respect of the following:

(1)   Days on which the claimant is entitled to income-based (or joint-claim) JSA but is disqualified from payment under ss19 or 20A Jobseekers Act 1995 – ie, because the claimant has been "sanctioned" for example for failing to apply for a job or for losing a job through misconduct. See the commentary in the latest edition of *Social Security Legislation* Vol II for further details.

(2)   So-called "waiting days". Under the Jobseekers Act (JSA) 1995 Sch 1 para 4, a claimant is generally not entitled to JSA for the first three days of any jobseeking period ("waiting days"). If the waiting days immediately precede a day for which income-based JSA is payable (or would be payable were it not for a sanction under ss19 or 20A JSA 1995), the claimant is entitled to maximum HB and CTB for the waiting days.

(3)   Where income-based (or joint-claim) JSA would be payable but for the loss of JSA due to a breach of a community order or the operation of the provisions for loss of benefit on a repeat conviction for benefit fraud.

Paragraph (4)

This paragraph does not define the term "dwelling" exclusively: for a full definition, see p19. The paragraph merely lists certain areas of land which are to be treated as part of a dwelling. The principle application will be to include the land in capital disregarded under Sch 6 para 1. The basic aim is to avoid the payment of HB in respect of commercially used land.

Sub-para (a) requires that land must be used "for the purposes of occupying the dwelling as a home" as opposed to occupation for business or other purposes. Additionally, if the occupier obtained the use of the land and the dwelling at the same time, it must not have been possible for her/him to obtain the use of the one without the other. Otherwise, if the use of the land and the dwelling were obtained at different times, or the dwelling could have been occupied without the land, s/he must have made or be making "all reasonable efforts" to get rid of the liability for the land before it can be treated as part of the dwelling for HB purposes.

Sub-paras (b) and (c) include land under a caravan or mobile land or where a houseboat is moored in the definition of "dwelling". Note *CH 318/2005* which, although not relying on this provision, decides that a narrowboat can constitute a 'dwelling' for the purposes of the HB scheme.

Sub-para (d). The Crofters (Scotland) Act 1993 s3(1) sets out the conditions which must be complied with before land will count as a "croft". First, it must be situated in one of the former "crofting counties". These are "Argyll, Caithness, Inverness, Orkney, Ross and Cromarty, Sutherland and Zetland". Second, the land must amount to a "holding" in terms of s35 Agricultural Holdings Act 1908 – ie, it must be pastoral or agricultural land, a mixture of both, or a market garden; which is not let to the tenant in the capacity of the landlord's employee. Finally, these "holdings" must have been covered by the Landholders Acts prior to 1955 or be registered as crofts (on application to the Land Court) under s4 of the 1955 Act or constitue a croft by direction of the Secretary of State under s2(1) The Crofters (Scotland) Act 1961. "Registerable" holdings are those for which the annual rent does not exceed £50, or of which the area does not exceed 50 acres. The Landholders Acts applied to land of similar description.

Definition of non-dependant

3.–(1)   In these Regulations, "non-dependant" means any person, except someone to whom paragraph (2) applies, who normally resides with a claimant or with whom a claimant normally resides.

(2)   This paragraph applies to–

(a)   any member of the claimant's family;

(b)   if the claimant is polygamously married, any partner of his and any child or young person who is a member of his household and for whom he or one of his partners is responsible;

(c)   a child or young person who is living with the claimant but who is not a member of his household by virtue of regulation 21 (circumstances in which a person is to be treated as being or not being a member of the same household);

(d)   subject to paragraph (3), a person who jointly occupies the claimant's dwelling and is either a co-owner of that dwelling with the claimant or his partner (whether or not there are other co-owners) or is liable with the claimant or his partner to make payments in respect of his occupation of the dwelling;

(e)   subject to paragraph (3)–

   (i)   any person who is liable to make payments on a commercial basis to the claimant or the claimant's partner in respect of the occupation of the dwelling;

(ii)   any person to whom or to whose partner the claimant or the claimant's partner is liable to make payments on a commercial basis in respect of the occupation of the dwelling; or

(iii) any other member of the household of the person to whom or to whose partner the claimant or the claimant's partner is liable to make payments on a commercial basis in respect of the occupation of the dwelling;

(f)   a person who lives with the claimant in order to care for him or a partner of his and who is engaged by a charitable or voluntary organisation which makes a charge to the claimant or his partner for the services provided by that person.

(3)   Sub-paragraphs (d) and (e) of paragraph (2) shall not apply to any person who is treated as if he were not liable to make payments in respect of a dwelling under paragraph (1) of regulation 9 (circumstances in which a person is to be treated as not liable to make payments in respect of a dwelling).

(4)   For the purposes of this regulation and regulation 9 a person resides with another only if they share any accommodation except a bathroom, a lavatory or a communal area within the meaning prescribed in paragraph 8 of Schedule 1 but not if each person is separately liable to make payments in respect of his occupation of the dwelling to the landlord.

Definitions

"child" – see s137(1) SSCBA and reg 2.
"claimant" – see reg 2.
"communal area" – see para 8 of Sch 1.
"dwelling" – see s137(1) SSCBA and reg 2(4).
"partner" – see reg 2(1).

General Note

This regulation defines which of the persons who "reside" with the claimant or with whom the claimant resides are to be treated as "non-dependants" and therefore in respect of whom a claimant's maximum HB will be reduced under reg 74. Note that all payments made to a claimant by a non-dependant are disregarded under Sch 5 para 21.

Para (1) provides the general rule, subject to the exceptions listed in para (2). In particular, para (2)(e), provides that those residing with the landlord claimant on a commercial basis are not to be treated as non-dependants.

Para (4) defines the term "resides".

Analysis

Paragraphs (1) and (4): Persons Normally Residing with the Claimant

The basic rule is that a "non-dependant" is anyone with whom the claimant resides or who resides with the claimant. The addition of the latter category excludes any possibility of arguing that the claimant resides with the supposed non-dependent rather than the other way round, an argument accepted by the Court of Appeal in *Bate v Chief Adjudication Officer* [1994] *The Times* 12 December, but rejected by the House of Lords when overturning the decision of the Court of Appeal (*R(IS) 12/96*).

Note however that where a person stays in other places besides the claimant's home, it is a matter of fact and degree as to whether s/he is *normally* resident there. A person must have lived there for long enough to regard it as her/his usual home: *CIS 14850/1996* para 7. Relevant factors for deciding whether a person is a non-dependent may include: the relationship between the parties, how much time s/he spends at the claimant's address, where her/his post is sent, where s/he keeps clothes and other belongings, whether the stay or absence is temporary, and whether there is another permanent base that s/he could regard as home. However, where a person has connections with more than one home, it is possible that s/he may not be normally residing in any of them: *CSIS 100/1993*.

Para (4) restricts the circumstances in which a person is "residing with" another. There must be some shared accommodation other than a bathroom, lavatory, an area of common access such as a hall or passageway or common rooms in sheltered accommodation. A person shares a kitchen with another even though s/he is never there at the same time as the other person and even though s/he pays for the use of the kitchen: *Thamesdown BC v Goonery* [1995] *1 CLY 2600, CA*. However, if the claimant does not use the kitchen but simply has food prepared by the other person, the other person is not a non-dependent since it cannot be said that s/he is being accommodated in the kitchen: *CSIS 185/1995*. The same analysis applies, it is suggested, if a claimant has her/his own kitchen, but uses a feature of a neighbour's such as a washing machine. The neighbour is not a non-dependent because the claimant is not accommodated in the kitchen but is merely using it as a favour.

It is plain from the wording of para (4) that a person does not "reside with" another person unless there is relevant shared accommodation. However, the existence of such sharing is not determinative of the issue, and all that need be shown is that the two people "reside with" each other in normal use of that phrase

The result is that authorities considering this question must first ask whether accommodation other than those in the categories set out in para (4) is being shared. If they decide that it is, they must go on and consider the evidence in the round and decide whether, as a matter of common sense, the claimant is residing with the relevant person.

Paragraphs (2) and (3): The Exceptions

Para (2). The following categories of people are *not* non-dependants even if they fall within the definition set out above. For the meaning of "household", see p23.

(1)   A member of the claimant's family: para (2)(a). "Family" means the claimant's partner (if s/he has one) and any dependent children and qualifying young people who live with her/him and for whom s/he is responsible: s137(1) SSCBA and regs 19-21. Reg 20 deals with the situations in which an adult is to be treated as responsible for a child or young person, and reg 21, with those in which s/he may be treated as sharing a household with such a person.

(2)   Where a claimant is in a polygamous marriage, any partner and any dependent children (and qualifying young people) who live with her/him and for whom either s/he or the partner is responsible: para (2)(b). As above, see regs 19-21.

(3)   A child or young person living with the claimant, but excluded from counting as a member of the household under reg 21: para (2)(c).

(4)   A joint occupier who is also either a co-owner with the claimant or her/his partner or is liable with the claimant or his partner to make payments in respect of his occupation of the dwelling: para (2)(d). A "joint occupier" is someone who has a joint legal right to occupy the property, rather than merely someone who occupies the property along with the claimant or her/his partner: *R v Chesterfield BC ex p Fullwood* (1993) 26 HLR 126 at 129, CA. Thus it covers joint tenants and people who have signed a single license agreement. It has been argued in previous editions that it may be possible to argue that "payments in respect of his occupation of the dwelling" does not mean the same as "payments in respect of a dwelling" in reg 8(1) and could cover situations such as utility bills which are in joint names. In view of the fact that para (3) envisages that reg 9 may apply to the liability under this paragraph so as to render the person a non-dependent after all, this seems to be incorrect, and the payments must be payments of rent or similar.

(5)   Those residing with the claimant who are liable to make payments on a commercial basis to her/him or her/his partner: para (2)(e)(i). For liability to make payments, see reg 9. For whether such payments are "on a commercial basis", see the Analysis to reg 9(1)(a). Where the person is not a non-dependant, some (or all) of the payments made to the claimant can be disregarded. See in particular Sch 5 paras 22 and 42.

(6)   The landlord or other person to whom the claimant or her/his partner are liable to make payments on a commercial basis: para (2)(e)(ii).

(7)   Any member of the household of a person excluded by (6): para (2)(e)(iii).

(8)   A person employed by a charity or voluntary organisation to care for the claimant or her/his partner, where a charge is made for her/his services: para (2)(f). This applies whether or not there is assistance with the charges from a public or local authority.

Para (3). By para (3), anyone in categories (4) to (7) above may be a non-dependent if their liability to pay rent falls foul of any of the exclusions from HB in reg 9(1), eg where the liability was created to take advantage of the housing benefit scheme or the claimant is a close relative.

Cases in which section 1(1A) of the Administration Act is disapplied

4.   Section 1(1A) of the Administration Act (requirement to state national insurance number) shall not apply–

(a)   to a claim for housing benefit where the person making the claim, or in respect of whom the claim is made, is liable to make payments in respect of a dwelling which is a hostel;

(b)   to any child or young person in respect of whom housing benefit is claimed.

Definition

"hostel" – see reg 2(1).

General Note

The NINO requirement imposed by s1(1A) SSAA (see p29) is removed by para (a) in respect of inhabitants of hostels. Hopefully the excessively complex definition of "hostel", discussed in the Analysis to reg 2(1), will not detract from the effect of this provision.

Para (b) clarifies that a child or young person, who may not yet even have been assigned a national insurance number, need not provide her/his details when the head of the household claims.

Persons who have attained the qualifying age for state pension credit

5.–(1)   These Regulations apply to a person who–

(a)   has not attained the qualifying age for state pension credit; or

(b)   has attained the qualifying age for state pension credit if he, or if he has a partner, his partner, is a person on income support or on an income-based jobseeker's allowance.

(2)   Regulation 72 and Schedule 7 (extended payments) apply to a person if he, or if he has a partner, his partner, has attained the qualifying age for state pension credit.

(3)   Except as provided in paragraphs (1) and (2), these Regulations shall not apply in relation to any person if he, or if he has a partner, his partner, has attained the qualifying age for state pension credit.

Definitions

"person on an income-based jobseeker's allowance" – see reg 2(3).
"person on income support" – see reg 2(1).
"qualifying age for state pension credit" – see reg 2(1).

General Note

The HB Regs apply where neither the claimant nor her/his partner has reached the qualifying age for pension credit (PC) – currently aged 60 – or if either have reached that age, where one of them is in receipt of IS or income-based JSA. This is qualified in para (2) for the purposes of reg 72 and Sch 7. Where the claimant or her/his partner has reached the qualifying age for PC and neither are in receipt of IS or income-based JSA the HB(SPC) Regs instead apply (see p679).

Remunerative work

6.–(1)   Subject to the following provisions of this regulation, a person shall be treated for the purposes of these Regulations as engaged in remunerative work if he is engaged, or, where his hours of work fluctuate, he is engaged on average, for not less than 16 hours a week, in work for which payment is made or which is done in expectation of payment.

(2)   Subject to paragraph (3), in determining the number of hours for which a person is engaged in work where his hours of work fluctuate, regard shall be had to the average of hours worked over–

(a)   if there is a recognisable cycle of work, the period of one complete cycle (including, where the cycle involves periods in which the person does no work, those periods but disregarding any other absences);

(b)   in any other case, the period of 5 weeks immediately prior to the date of claim, or such other length of time as may, in the particular case, enable the person's weekly average hours of work to be determined more accurately.

(3)   Where, for the purposes of paragraph (2)(a), a person's recognisable cycle of work at a school, other educational establishment or other place of employment is one year and includes periods of school holidays or similar vacations during which he does not work, those periods and any other periods not forming part of such holidays or vacations during which he is not required to work shall be disregarded in establishing the average hours for which he is engaged in work.

(4)   Where no recognisable cycle has been established in respect of a person's work, regard shall be had to the number of hours or, where those hours will fluctuate, the average of the hours, which he is expected to work in a week.

(5)   A person shall be treated as engaged in remunerative work during any period for which he is absent from work referred to in paragraph (1) if the absence is either without good cause or by reason of a recognised, customary or other holiday.

(6)   A person on income support or an income-based jobseeker's allowance for more than 3 days in any benefit week shall be treated as not being in remunerative work in that week.

(7)   A person shall not be treated as engaged in remunerative work on any day on which the person is on maternity leave, paternity leave or adoption leave, or is absent from work because he is ill.

(8)   A person shall not be treated as engaged in remunerative work on any day on which he is engaged in an activity in respect of which–

(a)   a sports award has been made, or is to be made, to him; and

(b)   no other payment is made or is expected to be made to him.

Definitions

"benefit week" – see reg 2(1).

"claim" – see reg 2(1).

"maternity leave", "paternity leave" and "adoption leave" – see reg 2(1).

"payment" – see reg 2(1).

"person on an income-based jobseeker's allowance" – see reg 2(3).

"person on income support" – see reg 2(1).

"sports award" – see reg 2(1).

General Note

This regulation defines the term "remunerative work" for the purposes of these regulations. The test is of much greater significance in the context of other means-tested benefits such as IS, income-based JSA and tax credits, because it is a condition of entitlement to (or an exclusion from) those benefits. Its significance for HB arises in relation to the treatment of earned income (Sch 4 para 1), additional earnings disregards and childcare costs disregards (Sch 4 para 17 and regs 27(1)(c) and 28) and where a non-dependant is in remunerative work, to the appropriate non-dependant deduction (reg 74).

The structure is as follows: para (1) as qualified by paras (5) to (8) defines "remunerative work", and paras (2), (3) and (4) provide a mechanism for determining whether a claimant is in remunerative work where her/his hours of work fluctuate.

There were modifications to this provision between November 1999 and November 2001 for New Deal participants. See the commentary in the 14th edition for details.

Analysis

Paragraphs (1) and (5) to (8): Definition of remunerative work

By para (1), a person is in "remunerative work" if s/he is engaged for at least 16 hours per week in paid work or work done in the expectation of payment. This is qualified as follows:

(1)   If someone is absent from work "without good cause" or on a "recognised, customary or other holiday", s/he is treated as being at work for the period of absence: para (5). "Good cause" is not defined for these purposes. It is suggested that whether or not the employer has authorised the absence is not conclusive, but if the absence is authorised the claimant is likely to have good cause.

(2)   A person on IS or income-based JSA for more than three days in a benefit week (see the definition in reg 2) is not in remunerative work for that week: para (6). Note that if this applies to a non-dependant, this means that a lower (or no) non-dependant deduction is applicable (see reg 74).

(3)   A person on maternity, paternity or adoption leave or sick leave is not treated as being in remunerative work for the days that s/he absent from work: para (7). But see reg 28(2) to (4), (14) and (15) for situations when such a person *can* be treated as in remunerative work for the purpose of the childcare charge deduction from earnings.

(4)   A person is not treated as being in remunerative work in respect of any day where her/his sole remuneration is, or is expected to be, in the form of a "sports award": para (8). These are monies paid by the Sports Councils from National Lottery funds: see the definition in reg 2(1). The definition requires that the claimant "is engaged in an activity in respect of which" the sports award is payable.

A broad reading should be taken of this wording. If, for example, a person is receiving treatment for injury or is engaged in promotional activities relating to her/his sport, then it should be found to be satisfied. It is also a requirement that no other payment is made to her/him in respect of the sporting activities in respect of that day. Again, this provision might cause difficulties. For example, to what extent would a person who received private sponsorship fall foul of this provision? An amateur who received a modest amount for endorsing sportswear might find her/himself in a substantial poverty trap as a result. What does it mean that a payment "is expected to be made to him"? Expected when, and by whom? Hopefully, authorities will apply the provision in a commonsense way and in accordance with the intention of the legislation that receipt of sports awards should not prejudice entitlement to benefit.

"Engaged". The person must be "engaged" in work. Thus if s/he is engaged in other activities awaiting an opportunity to work, it is arguable that s/he is in a different situation from being engaged in work. In *CIS 85/1997* para 7, the commissioner distinguished between a claimant who waited in her flat above her shop until a customer called and the claimant in the case before him, who was a self-employed taxi-driver who would wait in the cab company's office for customers. The former claimant was not engaged in work, the latter was. This is not a particularly easy distinction to draw, but if the claimant pursues activities at her/his own home while awaiting a call from a client, it is hard to see how s/he can be said to be "engaged" in work. The commissioner's decision was upheld by the Court of Appeal in *Kazantzis v Chief Adjudication Officer* [1999] *The Times* 30 June (*R(IS) 13/99*). It was not possible to draw a dividing line between the waiting time and the time spent driving when determining entitlement to income support. The same will be true of the operation of reg 6.

"Work done in the expectation of payment". Even if the person is not receiving any payment for the work, it may be necessary to decide whether s/he is expecting payment for work, whether immediately or at some future time. There are a number of useful decisions on IS which must be seen as highly persuasive.

The work must be done in the *expectation*, not merely the hope, of payment. So there must be a realistic expectation of payment within the foreseeable future: *R(IS) 1/93* para 11. Usually, where the person in question is employed this will not present much difficulty, though two points should be noted. First, it is not necessary that the payment comes from the employer: *R(FC) 2/90* concerning receipt of religious covenants. Secondly, the payment must be received for the current work. It is not sufficient for someone to be doing voluntary work in the hope of being offered a paid job: *R(IS) 5/95* para 8.

The most difficult problems arise with self-employed people. Millett LJ gave useful guidance for such cases in *Chief Adjudication Officer v Ellis* [1995] , 15 February, CA (appendix to *R(IS) 22/95*). The guidance can be summarised as follows:

(1)   The question whether the work is paid for or done in the expectation of payment must be judged on a week by week basis at the time the work is done.

(2)   The type of work is not important. The issue to be determined is whether the work was paid for or expected to be paid for.

(3)   If the person in question was actually paid for the work done, s/he is in remunerative work. Only when it is not paid for does the question of whether the business can be expected to be profitable come in for consideration. However, insignificant sums received may be ignored, such as the £200 received in a year by the would-be music agent in *Smith v Chief Adjudication Officer* [1994] unreported, 11 October, CA.

(4)   Remuneration may take many forms. Just because a person's expenses in running a business are greater than her/his income from it does not prevent the income from being remuneration: *Perrot v Supplementary Benefit Commissioner* [1980] 3 All ER 110 at 114j, 116a-e, 117b, CA. However, in the case of retail and similar businesses, remuneration comes from the profit made from the store and not from the sale of the goods therein. Receipt of an Enterprise Allowance or similar payment does not amount to "payment" for the work: *Smith* (*R(IS) 21/95*).

(5)   Where the person in question is in a partnership, monies received by the partnership do not amount to remuneration until there is a distribution of profits. However, where the person is in business with her/his partner, the authority will be justified in viewing the partnership as a single economic unit.

(6)   If such a person draws on the funds of the business, this may be by way of wage, advance on profit or consumption of the capital of the business. Only if the nature of the drawings can be seen to represent the last of these can it be found that the person is not in remunerative work.

(7)   If the partners are not making drawings, they are in remunerative work if they expect to receive a share of the profits. This does not depend on the state of the annual accounts but on whether they have a realistic expectation that they will receive a share. But they must hope to be paid for the work they are currently doing, not that they will put themselves in a situation to be able to earn money from future work. Lord Bingham MR added (transcript at 16B) that the expectation of profit had to come from that financial year, when the accounts were finalised.

Paragraphs (2), (3) and (4): Determination of hours worked

"regard shall be had" Paras (2) and (4) appear to offer some degree of discretion to authorities in the way they determine the hours of work where these flucuate in that an authority need only pay "regard" to the hours (or average of hours) mentioned in those paras. The primary question is whether the person is working for more than 16 hours per week "on average": para (1). It is suggested that if the authority thinks that the provisions under paras (2) and (4) give an unfair or unrealistic result, it is open to it to adopt a different approach. Caution is therefore required in applying the extensive IS caselaw, for which reference should be made to the corresponding IS provisions in *Social Security Legislation Vol II*.

Paras (2) and (4). The first thing the authority must decide is whether the person has a recognisable cycle of work, despite the fact that the weekly hours fluctuate. If so, under para (2)(a), the average number of hours worked is obtained by dividing the total number of hours in the cycle by the number of weeks it lasts, ignoring weeks in which no work is done unless this is part of the cycle. For example, if someone works six days one week, five the next and then has the next week off (on a regular basis), the total hours worked over the cycle would be divided by three. If the person has a four-week cycle but is off during the last week due to sickness, the hours worked in that particular cycle would be divided by three only, not four.

If the person works casually or intermittently (eg, as a seasonal worker who works in the summer but is unemployed the rest of the year) the 'work cycle' is that part of the year in which s/he is working and would not include the period of unemployment. Commissioner Howell dealt with the similar provision for JSA in *R(JSA) 1/07* and two other appeals. The claimants worked from March to October in summer employment. During the out-of-season months they had no earnings or work at all. The decision maker said that as they had had their summer employment for more than one year in a row, they had a cycle of work of a year and as the average hours of work over this period was greater than 16 hours a week they were in "remunerative work". Commissioner Howell disagreed. He said that the recurrence of an inability to get work at all during the winter months could not turn the whole calendar year into one continuous period of the claimants being "engaged in work" so as to be able to call the whole year a "recognisable cycle of work". The real question is whether the person is "in" work at the material time. That means that there must be some sort of continuing relationship between the employee and the employer and, where a contract of employment has been terminated, a committment to resume the relationship: *CJSA 3832/2006*.

Paras (2)(b) and (4), at first sight, appear to contradict each other. The best way to resolve the difficulty is probably to follow the approach taken by the commissioner in *R(IS) 8/95* Appendix paras 10 to 12. A claimant who normally worked a full week was on a period of working one week on and one week off, although he might be called in on non-working days. The commissioner holds that para (4) addresses the situation where there is insufficient evidence of recent working hours to resolve the question of the average working hours. It is forward-looking, with reference to the number of hours (or average of hours) a person is *expected* to work. Para (2) applies where such evidence exists and shows a fluctuation. If a recognisable cycle of work has been "established", then para (2)(a) applies. If not, para (2)(b) requires consideration of the average hours worked in the period of five weeks immediately before the date of claim, unless a different period (shorter or longer) provides a more accurate average. It is therefore backward-looking. The commissioner states that the point at which the calculation moves from being made under para (4) to that under para (2)(b) depends on the circumstances.

Para (3) provides a particular method by which the average weekly number of hours worked is calculated where a person's recognisable cycle of work at a school, other educational establishment or any other place of employment, is one year and includes school holidays or similar vacations during which s/he is not required to work. In such cases, school holidays and any other periods during which s/he is not required to work must be disregarded in calculating the average weekly hours worked – ie, average weekly hours should generally be calculated by reference only to average weekly hours worked during term time.

It is not open to evade the effect of para (3) by treating the vacations as being excluded from the cycle of work on the basis that no work is being done at those times: *Chief Adjudication Officer v Stafford* [2000] 1 All ER 686 at 693g-694a, CA, upheld by a majority of three to two in *Banks v Chief Adjudication Officer* [2001] 1 WLR 1411, HL. That would mean that the "cycle" was effectively being ignored. Nevertheless, in the HB context it is suggested that the authority may adopt a different approach if it feels that the result of the calculation in para (3) is unfair. Although it is in mandatory terms, para (3) applies "for the purposes of paragraph (2)(a)" and so the authority is only required to have regard to the calculation and is not bound by it. Reference should be made to the very powerful dissenting speech of Lord Scott in the House of Lords in *Stafford* for the unfair results of reliance on the "cycle" and the differing (and fairer) result reached by a Tribunal of Commissioners in the context of JSA in *R(JSA) 4/03* in such cases.

PART 2
Provisions affecting entitlement to housing benefit

General Note on Part 2

By virtue of s130 SSCBA, a person is entitled to HB in respect of certain payments that s/he is liable to make in relation to the dwelling s/he occupies as her/his home. Reg 7 deals with the meaning of the phrase "occupies as his home". Regs 8 and 9 respectively deal with the situations in which a person is or is not to be treated as "liable" for payments on that home. Reg 10 provides that certain persons from abroad are to be treated as not being liable for payments. See reg 10A and Sch A1 in Sch 4 of SI 2006 No 217 (see pp1126 and 1127) for claims by asylum seekers recorded as refugees on or before 14 June 2007.

Circumstances in which a person is or is not to be treated as occupying a dwelling as his home

7.–(1) Subject to the following provisions of this regulation, a person shall be treated as occupying as his home the dwelling normally occupied as his home–

    (a)   by himself or, if he is a member of a family, by himself and his family; or

    (b)   if he is polygamously married, by himself, his partners and any child or young person for whom he or any partner of his is responsible and who is a member of that same household,

and shall not be treated as occupying any other dwelling as his home.

    (2)   In determining whether a dwelling is the dwelling normally occupied as a person's home for the purpose of paragraph (1) regard shall be had to any other dwelling occupied by that person or any other person referred to in paragraph (1) whether or not that dwelling is in Great Britain.

    (3)   Where a single claimant or a lone parent is a student, other than one to whom regulation 56(1) applies (circumstances in which certain students are treated as not liable to make payments in respect of a dwelling), or is on a training course and is liable to make payments (including payments of mortgage interest or, in Scotland, payments under heritable securities or, in either case, analogous payments) in respect of either (but not both) the dwelling which he occupies for the purpose of attending his course of study or, his training course, or as the case may be, the dwelling which he occupies when not attending his course, he shall be treated as occupying as his home the dwelling in respect of which he is liable to make such payments.

    (4)   Where a claimant has been required to move into temporary accommodation by reason of essential repairs being carried out to the dwelling normally occupied as his home, and is liable to make payments (including payments of mortgage interest or, in Scotland, payments under heritable securities or, in either case, analogous payments) in respect of either (but not both) the dwelling which he normally occupied as his home or the temporary accommodation, he shall be treated as occupying as his home the dwelling in respect of which he is liable to make payments.

    (5)   Where a person is required to reside in a dwelling which is a bail hostel or probation hostel approved by the Secretary of State under section 9(1) of the Criminal Justice and Court Services Act 2000, he shall not be treated as occupying that dwelling as his home.

    (6)   Where a person is liable to make payments in respect of two (but not more than two) dwellings, he shall be treated as occupying both dwellings as his home only–

    (a)   for a period not exceeding 52 weeks in the case where he has left and remains absent from the former dwelling occupied as his home through fear of violence in that dwelling or by a former member of his family and–

        (i)   it is reasonable that housing benefit should be paid in respect of both his former dwelling and his present dwelling occupied as the home; and

        (ii)   he intends to return to occupy the former dwelling as his home; or

(b)   in the case of a couple or a member of a polygamous marriage, where he or one partner is a student, other than one to whom regulation 56(1) applies (circumstances in which certain students are treated as not liable to make payments in respect of a dwelling), or is on a training course and it is unavoidable that the partners should occupy two separate dwellings and reasonable that housing benefit should be paid in respect of both dwellings; or

(c)   in the case where, because of the number of persons referred to in paragraph (1), they have been housed by a housing authority in two separate dwellings; or

(d)   in the case where a person has moved into a new dwelling occupied as the home, except where paragraph (4) applies, for a period not exceeding 4 benefit weeks [¹ from the date on which he moved] if he could not reasonably have avoided liability in respect of two dwellings; or

(e)   in the case where a person–

    (i)   is treated by virtue of paragraph (8) as occupying a dwelling as his home (''the new dwelling'') and sub-paragraph (c)(i) of that paragraph applies; and

    (ii)   he has occupied another dwelling as his home on any day within the period of 4 weeks immediately preceding the date he moved to the new dwelling,

for a period not exceeding 4 benefit weeks immediately preceding the date on which he moved.

(7)   Where–

(a)   a person has moved into a dwelling for which he is not liable to make payments (''the new dwelling''); and

(b)   immediately before that move, he was liable to make payments for the dwelling he previously occupied as his home (''the former dwelling''); and

(c)   that liability continues after he has moved into the new dwelling,

he shall be treated as occupying the former dwelling as his home for a period not exceeding 4 benefit weeks if he could not reasonably have avoided liability in respect of that former dwelling.

(8)   [² Where]–

(a)   [² a person] has moved into a dwelling and was liable to make payments in respect of that dwelling before moving in; and

[² (b)   either—

    (i) that person had claimed housing benefit before moving in and either no decision has yet been made on that claim or it has been refused but a further claim has been made or treated as made within 4 weeks of the date on which the claimant moved into the new dwelling occupied as the home; or

    (ii) that person notified the move to the new dwelling as a change of circumstances under regulation 88 (duty to notify changes of circumstances) before the move, or the move to the new dwelling was otherwise notified before the move under that regulation; and]

(c)   the delay in moving into the dwelling in respect of which there was liability to make payments before moving in was reasonable and–

    (i)   that delay was necessary in order to adapt the dwelling to meet the disablement needs of that person or any member of his family; or

    (ii)   the move was delayed pending the outcome of an application under Part 3 of the Act for a social fund payment to meet a need arising out of the move or in connection with setting up the home in the dwelling and either a member of the claimant's family is aged 5 or under or the claimant's applicable amount includes a premium under paragraph 9, 10, 11, 12, 14 or 16 of Schedule 3; or

    (iii)   the claimant became liable to make payments in respect of the dwelling while he was a patient or in residential accommodation,

[² the person shall be treated] as occupying the dwelling as his home for any period not exceeding 4 weeks immediately prior to the date on which he moved into the dwelling and in respect of which he was liable to make payments.

(9)   Where a person is treated by virtue of paragraph (8) as occupying a dwelling as his home in respect of the period before moving in, his claim for housing benefit in respect of that dwelling shall be treated as having been made on either–

(a)   in the case of a claim in respect of which a decision has not yet been made the date that claim was or was treated as made in accordance with regulation 83 (time and manner in which claims are to be made); or

(b)   in the case of a claim for housing benefit in respect of that dwelling which has been refused and a further claim was or was treated as made in accordance with Part 10 (claims) within 4 weeks of the date on which he moved into the dwelling, the date on which the claim was refused or was treated as made; or

(c)   the date from which he is treated by virtue of paragraph (8) as occupying the dwelling as his home,

whichever of those dates is the later.

(10)   Where a person to whom neither paragraph (6)(a) nor (16)(c)(x) applies–

(a)   formerly occupied a dwelling but has left and remains absent from it through fear of violence–

(i)   in the dwelling; or

(ii)   by a person who was formerly a member of the family of the person first mentioned; and

(b)   has a liability to make payments in respect of that dwelling which is unavoidable,

he shall be treated as occupying the dwelling as his home for a period not exceeding 4 benefit weeks.

(11)   This paragraph shall apply to a person who enters residential accommodation–

(a)   for the purpose of ascertaining whether the accommodation suits his needs; and

(b)   with the intention of returning to the dwelling which is normally occupied by him as his home should, in the event, the residential accommodation prove not to suit his needs; and

(c)   while the part of the dwelling which is normally occupied by him as his home is not let, or as the case may be, sublet.

(12)   A person to whom paragraph (11) applies shall be treated as if he is occupying the dwelling he normally occupies as his home for a period not exceeding, subject to an overall limit of 52 weeks on the absence from that home, 13 weeks beginning from the first day he enters a residential accommodation.

(13)   Subject to paragraph (17) a person shall be treated as occupying a dwelling as his home while he is temporarily absent therefrom for a period not exceeding 13 weeks beginning from the first day of that absence from the home only if–

(a)   he intends to return to occupy the dwelling as his home; and

(b)   the part of the dwelling normally occupied by him has not been let or, as the case may be, sub-let; and

(c)   the period of absence is unlikely to exceed 13 weeks.

(14)   This paragraph applies to a person who is–

(a)   detained in custody pending sentence upon conviction or under a sentence imposed by a court, other than a person who is detained in hospital under the provisions of the Mental Health Act 1983, or, in Scotland, under the provisions of the Mental Health (Care and Treatment) (Scotland) Act 2003 or the Criminal Procedure (Scotland) Act 1995; and

    (b)   on temporary release from such detention in accordance with Rules made under the provisions of the Prison Act 1952 or the Prisons (Scotland) Act 1989.

(15) Where paragraph (14) applies to a person, then, for any day when he is on temporary release–

    (a)   if such temporary release was immediately preceded by a period of temporary absence under paragraph (13) or (16), he shall be treated as if he continues to be absent from the dwelling, despite any occupation of the dwelling;

    (b)   for the purposes of paragraph (16)(c)(i), he shall be treated as if he remains in detention; and

    (c)   if he does not fall within sub-paragraph (a), he shall be treated as if he does not occupy his dwelling as his home despite any such occupation of the dwelling.

(16)   This paragraph shall apply to a person who is temporarily absent from the dwelling he normally occupies as his home (''absence''), if–

    (a)   he intends to return to occupy the dwelling as his home; and

    (b)   while the part of the dwelling which is normally occupied by him has not been let, or as the case may be, sublet; and

    (c)   he is–

        (i)   detained in custody on remand pending trial or, as a condition of bail, required to reside–

            (aa)   in a dwelling, other than the dwelling he occupies as his home; or

            (bb)   in premises approved under section 9 of the Criminal Justice and Court Services Act 2000,

        or, detained pending sentence upon conviction; or

        (ii)   resident in a hospital or similar institution as a patient; or

        (iii)   undergoing, or as the case may be, his partner or his dependant child is undergoing, in the United Kingdom or elsewhere, medical treatment, or medically approved convalescence, in accommodation other than residential accommodation; or

        (iv)   following, in the United Kingdom or elsewhere, a training course; or

        (v)   undertaking medically approved care of a person residing in the United Kingdom or elsewhere; or

        (vi)   undertaking the care of a child whose parent or guardian is temporarily absent from the dwelling normally occupied by that parent or guardian for the purpose of receiving medically approved care or medical treatment; or

        (vii)   a person who is, in the United Kingdom or elsewhere, receiving medically approved care provided in accommodation other than residential accommodation; or

        (viii) a student to whom paragraph (3) or (6)(b) does not apply;

        (ix)   a person who is receiving care provided in residential accommodation other than a person to whom paragraph (11) applies; or

        (x)   a person who has left the dwelling he occupies as his home through fear of violence, in that dwelling, or by a person who was formerly a member of the family of the person first mentioned, and to whom paragraph (6)(a) does not apply; and

    (d)   the period of his absence is unlikely to exceed 52 weeks or, in exceptional circumstances, is unlikely substantially to exceed that period.

(17)   A person to whom paragraph (16) applies shall be treated as occupying the dwelling he normally occupies at his home during any period of absence not exceeding 52 weeks beginning from the first day of that absence.

(18)   In this regulation–

"medically approved" means certified by a medical practitioner;

"patient" means a person who is undergoing medical or other treatment as an in-patient in any hospital or similar institution;

"residential accommodation" means accommodation which is provided in–

(a)   a care home;

(b)   an independent hospital;

(c)   an Abbeyfield Home; or

(d)   an establishment managed or provided by a body incorporated by Royal Charter or constituted by Act of Parliament other than a local social services authority;

"training course" means a course of training or instruction provided wholly or partly by or on behalf of or in pursuance of arrangements made with, or approved by or on behalf of, Scottish Enterprise, Highlands and Islands Enterprise, a government department or the Secretary of State.

Definitions

"benefit week" – see reg 2(1).
"child" – see s137 SSCBA and reg 2(1).
"claim" – see reg 2(1).
"claimant" – see reg 2(1).
"course of study" – see reg 53.
"dwelling" – see s137 SSCBA and reg 2(4).
"family" – see s137 SSCBA.
"housing authority" – see s191 SSAA.
"lone parent" – see reg 2(1).
"partner" – see reg 2(1).
"polygamous marriage" – see reg 2(1).
"single claimant" – see reg 2(1).
"student" – see regs 2(1) and 53.
"young person" – see reg 2(1).

Amendments

1.   Amended by reg 5 of SI 2006 No 3274 as from 8.1.07.
2.   Amended by reg 11(3) of SI 2007 No 2618 as from 1.10.07.

General Note

To be entitled to HB, a claimant must be liable to make payments in respect of a dwelling which s/he occupies as her/his home: s130 SSCBA (see p4). Paras (1) and (2) set out the general rule that a claimant is only usually treated as occupying one home, namely that normally occupied by her/him. The remainder of the regulation provides for various exceptions to this rule.

(1)   Paras (3) and (4) provide situations where if a claimant has two homes but only pays for one of them, s/he will be treated as occupying the one that is paid for. Broadly, para (3) applies to students and trainees who occupy one home during their courses and one during vacations, and para (4) applies to claimants who have had to move into temporary accommodation due to essential repairs.

(2)   Para (6) sets out a number of cases in which a claimant can be treated as occupying two homes and therefore receive HB for both.

(3)   Paras (7) to (10) deal with situations where a claimant can be treated as occupying a property which s/he has moved from or is about to move (or has moved) into.

(4)   Paras (11) to (17) deal with when someone can be treated as occupying a dwelling during a temporary absence.

Two provisions deal with claimants who are "students" who are not excluded from eligibility to HB under reg 56(1), or who are on "training courses": paras (3) and (6)(b). Residence in an approved bail or probation hostel is to be ignored in considering where a person's normal home is: see para (5).

The application of reg 7 is not restricted to the question of whether or not the claimant is entitled to HB. As the headnote suggests, the regulation determines the issue of whether or not a person is occupying the home. Thus where a claimant's children spent most of their time with their mother and she received child benefit in respect of them, each child was resident in the property where her/his "family" lived and so could not be treated as occupying the father's home for the purposes of the Rent Officer's assessment: *R v Swale BC HBRB ex p Marchant* [1999] 1 FLR 1087, QBD; [2000] 1 FLR 246, CA.

Analysis
Paragraphs (1) and (2): The general rule

The home in question is that "normally occupied" by the persons listed in paras (1)(a) or (b), as appropriate. There is no definition of "normally occupied". In *CH 1085/2002* para 13, the commissioner pointed out that "normally occupied" was a lower standard to "permanently occupied". He also suggested that the views of officers administering JSA or the social fund were relevant: para 14. It is suggested that this could only be the case if the issue has been specifically considered by such officers, and tribunals must not, of course, treat their views as binding.

Under para (2), the authority must take account of any other dwelling occupied by the claimant or by any of the other people listed in para (1) in order to decide which is the "normal" home. This includes dwellings outside Great Britain, but GM A3.356 warns local authorities that this provision is not intended to exclude from entitlement someone who has set up home in this country but whose family is no longer being part of her/his household and remains abroad. The GM says that the purpose of taking account of homes outside Great Britain is to avoid simultaneous payment of HB under both the Northern Irish and British schemes.

It is submitted that some factors which are relevant to the question of which home is "normally occupied" if more than one property is involved are the following:

(1) The amount of time that the claimant spends at the property, compared with other properties with which a comparison is being made under para (2): *R v Penwith DC ex p Burt* (1990) 22 HLR 292 at 296, QBD.

(2) The reason for any absence from the property, though note the possible application of paras (10) to (16) below.

(3) Where the claimant's personal belongings are kept. See on this *R(H) 9/05* below.

(4) Where the claimant is registered to vote, registers with GPs and dentists, is liable for council tax and utilities bills etc.

(5) Whether the claimant has any local ties such as memberships of clubs and associations.

Previous versions of this book have suggested another relevant factor as being where the claimant regards the centre of her/his existence and where s/he intends it should be in the future. However, *CH 1786/2005* (rightly) points out that a "centre of interests" test is not a substitute for making an overall assessment of the circumstances and evidence in each case in deciding which home is "normally occupied" by the claimant (per *CH 2521/2002*); and warns against chopping up what is essentially a single factual issue into series of individual tests for particular factors.

In *R(H) 9/05* the claimant took out a tenancy of a new flat from February 2004 but she could not move in immediately as the property needed to be adapted to met her needs as a disabled person. On 15 March 2004 the disabled adaptations had been completed and so she terminated her former tenancy and her family moved all her furniture and possessions into the new flat. However, the claimant herself was unable to move in on this date – and did not in fact move in until 9 August 2004 – because she became ill and had to be admitted to hospital. On these facts, the Deputy Commissioner decided that the claimant had normally occupied the flat as her home within reg 5(1) HB Regs 1987 (now reg 7(1) HB Regs) from the date her furniture and possessions had been moved into it, notwithstanding that the claimant herself had not begun living in the flat until some five months later. The use of the word "normally" did not speak to the length of time present in the property but was rather in place to help resolve cases where the claimant might be regarded as living in more than one property. Moreover, the claimant could be said to have "moved in" to the flat on 15 March, and so could be treated as occupying it for the four weeks beforehand: reg 7(8)(c)(i) HB Regs. Further the claimant's temporary absence from the propery (to August 2004) did not affect these conclusions because it is possible for the claimant to intend to return to occupy the flat as her home even though she had never physically lived there.

The decision in *R(H) 9/05*, although no doubt welcome on the facts, places a strained interpretation on the word "return" as used in sub-paras (13) to (17) of reg 7. *CH 2521/2002* rules that the comparable sub-paras in reg 5(1) HB Regs 1987 (now reg 7(1) HB Regs) could be used as an aid to construe the test. However, given that *R(H) 9/05* is a reported decision it must be preferred over any conflicting unreported decisions (such as, at least implicitly, *CH 2201/2002* and *CH 2521/2002*).

Evidence of a claimant having made a claim for HB and JSA in the area of another authority will be adequate evidence that a claimant is residing elsewhere, at least in the absence of contradictory evidence: *CH 2201/2002* para 10.

In *CH 2521/2002* para 10, Commissioner Fellner cautioned against over-heavy reliance on *Herbert v Byrne*, noting that it was a case under a different statutory provision. She went on to question in paras 11-12 whether a person may have two dwellings and still qualify for benefit on their usual residence under reg 5(1) HB regs 1987 (now reg 7(1) HB Regs). It is suggested that it is plain from para (2) that this is possible.

Paragraph (3): Absence due to study or training

This provides for the situation in which an eligible student or person on a training course who is a single claimant or a lone parent, occupies two dwellings, one to enable her/him to attend the course, and one which s/he uses at other times, but is only *liable* for payments in respect of one of them. Note that the payments in question can be mortgage and similar payments as well as payments of the nature that could attract HB. So if a claimant has one property on which s/he makes mortgage payments and another for which s/he pays rent, s/he does not come within the scope of this provision.

When the paragraph applies, the claimant is treated for HB purposes, as occupying the dwelling for which s/he has to pay. This is of benefit, for example, to students who pay for term-time accommodation but stay at their parents' home, at no cost to themselves, during the vacations (but see Part 7 of these Regulations). Note para (6)(b) where the claimant is liable to make payments for both homes.

Paragraph (4): Absence due to essential repairs

This ensures that claimants forced to leave their normal home due to essential repair work can claim HB provided that they make such payments as are referred to in respect of either the normal home or the temporary accommodation. If they make relevant payments on *both*, they are not covered by this paragraph, but see para (6) below.

There is no guidance on the meaning of "essential", but when this term was used in relation to the old supplementary benefit scheme in respect of grants for redecoration, a commissioner interpreted the term as covering work which was "necessary" rather than a luxury, but not necessarily "indispensable if life was to be maintained": *R(SB) 10/81*.

Commissioner Williams approved the relevance of the test propounded in *R(SB) 10/81* in *CH 393/ 2002*. He also held that it was not necessary for all the repairs to be completed in order for the deeming provision in para (4) to cease to have effect, as long as the essential repairs had been completed and the property was habitable: paras 15-16. However, consideration of the claimant's illness would be relevant in determining whether the property was habitable.

Paragraph (5): Approved hostels

This provision effectively requires a local authority to ignore enforced residence in an approved bail or probation hostel when deciding where someone's "normal home" is. Residence in the hostel must be "required" which will normally mean that it will be a condition of the person's bail. In England and Wales, documentary evidence of this may be obtained from the relevant Magistrates' or Crown Court.

Paragraph (6): HB on two homes

Para (6) allows the claimant to be treated as occupying two dwellings as her/his home, and hence to qualify for HB in respect of both of them, in the circumstances there set out.

Sub-para (a) enables people forced to leave home through fear of actual or threatened violence to receive benefit in respect of both the abandoned and the new home where this is considered reasonable. There must be an intention to return to occupy the former home. Once that intention no longer exists HB is not payable on the former home. Also see the commentary on para (10).

No violence need yet have occurred – the mere fear of violence is sufficient. GM A3.411 states that this fear of violence must be reasonably held and suggests that corroborative evidence may be obtained from the police to whom reports of violence may have been made. It is suggested that provided there is an honest fear of violence which has some basis, this would suffice. Furthermore, authorities should not fall into the trap of rejecting a claimant's assertions of fear of violence if no report is made to the police. Many victims of domestic violence find it very difficult to seek official help.

The fear of violence can come from either of two sources.

(1)   Fear of violence in the dwelling formerly occupied as a home. A "dwelling" can include some land – eg, that used for the purpose of occupying a dwelling or land on which a caravan or mobile home stands: s137 SSCBA and reg 2(4). So fear of violence in for example, the garden of the former home should suffice. Fear of attacks in the street will not suffice. However, it is suggested that abuse in the street towards a claimant living in her/his home which gives rise to a fear of being attacked in the home should be enough to qualify. Note that a fear of violence in the former home need not come from a former member of the claimant's family; attacks on the home by neighbours or racial violence can come within this heading.

(2)   Fear of violence by a former member of the claimant's family. For the meaning of family see p22. This does not have to be a fear of violence in the former home.

The period for which HB can be paid is restricted in such circumstances to 52 weeks.

Sub-para (b) deals with claims from people who are members of a couple or a polygamous relationship where one of the partners is a student who is not excluded from HB by reg 56(1) or on a training course. In this situation HB, can be paid in respect of both the term-time residence and the dwelling in which the other partner(s) live indefinitely, but the need for two homes must be "unavoidable" and payment of HB in respect of both homes must be reasonable in the circumstances of the particular claim.

The decision of the Court of Appeal in *R (Naghshbandi) v Camden LBC* [2003] HLR 280 produces a potential anomaly in the operation of sub-para (b). See the commentary to regs 12(5) and 54 for discussion of the decision. Since, following *Naghshbandi*, reg 56(1) only applies in relation to a student who is a claimant, it cannot apply in any case where the claimant is the student's partner. Thus if the claimant becomes liable for the rent on the student partner's accommodation, provided that the other conditions in sub-para (b) are met it will be possible for the claimant to claim HB on both properties even though if the student made a claim her/himself in respect of the student accommodation, it would be rejected because s/he does not fall into any of the categories in reg 56(2).

Sub-para (c) is a provision to cater for very large families. The dwellings need not be adjacent: GM A3.660. However, the housing must be provided by the local authority.

Sub-para (d) makes provision for HB claimants who move home and who could not reasonably avoid liability for payments in respect of both the old and the new home – eg, where s/he had to move quickly to take advantage of better accommodation and so had to leave a former home without being able to give notice to her/his landlord. HB can be paid in respect of both dwellings for up to four weeks from the date on which the claimant moved. See para (7) where there is no liability in respect of the new home and paras (8) and (9) where there is a delay in moving. *CH 1911/2006* emphasises that the "person" to which reg 5(5)(d) of HB Regs 1987 (now reg 7(6)(d) HB Regs) must be the HB claimant. Accordingly, subpara (d) cannot cover a situation where the partner of the claimant moves into the new dwelling to get it ready for the rest of the family to move in.

In previous editions it has been suggested that before a claimant can get HB on both the old and new homes, s/he must have actually moved – ie, HB can be paid to cover payments on the old home after a move but not on a new home before the claimant moves in. This approach was adopted in *CH 2201/2002*. The commissioner was considering a case where a claimant's move into a new housing association property from his council flat was delayed for just over three weeks from the start of the new tenancy due to his disability and a delay in obtaining a grant to cover removal expenses. The claimant sought HB on both properties for that period. The commissioner stated (para 6) that reg 5(5) HB Regs 1987 (now reg 7(6) HB Regs) had no application. But note now the decision in *R(H) 9/05* (above) and its view – albeit in a slightly different context – that a person can be said to have moved in once his or her furniture and personal possessions have been placed in the property.

In *CH 4546/2002* the claimant's partner and carer took a tenancy of a property and sub-let a part of the property to the claimant, who then moved in with them. The commissioner held that on the facts, the dual liability could have been avoided (para 29) but more importantly for general purposes, decided that subpara (d) could operate even where the new liability fell foul of reg 7(1) HB Regs 1987 (now reg 9(1) HB Regs), as the deeming of non-liability under reg 7(1) had no impact on whether there is a liability in fact in respect of the new dwelling for the purposes of subpara (d). It is not clear whether the commissioner considered *Naghshbandi* (see above). It is not mentioned in the decision and it is arguably inconsistent with the Court of Appeal's reasoning in that case.

For the position prior to the amendment of this sub-para from 8 January 2007, see *CSHB 873 2005* where the commissioner construed the pre-amendment form of (what is now) reg 7(6)(d) as allowing the four weeks of benefit on two homes to be awarded retrospectively back from the date the claimant moved into the second home. The amendment seeks to reverse that result and allow entitlement on two homes (if the liability to pay rent on the two homes exists) for four weeks from the date of the move to the second home.

Sub-para (e). Under this provision, where a person is treated as occupying a new home under para (8)(c)(i) (ie, because a move was delayed while adaptations were made to meet her/his disablement needs or those of any member of her/his family) and occupied a another dwelling within the four weeks immediately preceding the move, HB can be paid for both dwellings for up to four weeks.

Paragraph (7): Moving to a new home in respect of which there is no liability for payments

Para (7) deals with situations where a claimant has moved from a home for which s/he was liable to make payments, to a new dwelling for which there is no such liability. The latter could include, for example, prison or hospital. It allows HB to be paid for the former home for up to four weeks where liability continues after the move, so long as the claimant could not reasonably have avoided the liability – eg, where s/he had to leave a former home without being able to give notice to her/his landlord. See para (6)(d) and (e) where there *is* liability for payments for both homes.

Paragraphs (8) and (9): Delays in moving into new home

Like para (6)(d), these paragraphs deals with the situation where a claimant has moved house, but this provision does not authorise the treatment of more than one dwelling as the claimant's home; only para (6) lists the situations in which this is possible: *CH 2201/2002* para 7. Since its effect is retrospective in that it permits payment of HB for a period before the claimant moves, unless para (6) applies, it can only apply to people who were not receiving HB in respect of their former home.

Where this provision does apply, it permits payment of HB in respect of rent due up to four weeks before the claimant actually moved into the new home (where s/he was liable to pay in respect of that period). This is done by deeming the claimant to occupy the accommodation during that period, even though s/he had not in fact moved in. In addition, the following conditions must be satisfied:

(1) The provision may only take effect after the claimant moves in: para (8)(a). But note here the decision in *R(H) 9/05* (above), which holds, in effect, that this does not require personal presence by the claimant, but can be met by the claimant's furniture and possessions being 'moved in'.

(2) The claimant must either have claimed HB or have notified the authority of the move to the new dwelling before the move: para (8)(b)(i) and (ii). In the former case, the claim must either have been refused or not yet have been determined. If the claim has been refused, the claimant must make a fresh claim within four weeks of moving to the new home. At first sight, para (9) appears to relax the second condition, by allowing a claim made within four weeks of the move to be treated as if made prior to it. But on a careful reading the paragraph does not have this effect, because it only applies if the conditions in para (8)(a) to (c) are satisfied. Para (9) therefore simply governs the date on which a claim which was made prior to moving is treated as being effective.

(3) If (1) and (2) are satisfied, the delay between taking on liability for the home and moving in must have been "reasonable": para (8)(c).

(4) One or more of the conditions in para (8)(c)(i)-(iii) must be fulfilled. *CH 3857/2004* confirms the, perhaps obvious, point that the adaptations under para (8)(c)(i) have to meet the needs of the claimant which arise from or are particular to his or her disabilities (eg, handrails), rather than being works which would be necessary for an occupant regardless of disability (eg, redecorating or plastering). This is emphasised in *R(H) 4/07*, where the commissioner follows an earlier decision of his (*CH 1363/2006*) in holding that the word "adapt" entails a change to the fabric or structure of the dwelling and so will not encompass furnishing (eg, carpeting) or decorating the dwelling. In respect of para (8)(c)(ii), the relevant paragraphs refer to persons entitled to have pensioner, pensioner premium for those aged 75 or over, higher pensioner, disability, severe disability or disabled child premium included in their applicable amounts – see the paragraphs referred to for details. For the definitions of "patient" and "residential accommodation" in para (8)(c)(iii), see para (18) below. See para (6)(e) where someone is treated as occupying a dwelling under para (8)(c)(ii) and is also liable to make payments in respect of her/his former home.

Para (9) governs the date on which payment of HB for a period prior to that on which the claimant actually occupied the dwelling may be authorised subject to the four-week maximum provided in para (8). That period will commence on the later of the appropriate dates ascertained under (a) to (c). For "made or treated as made", see regs 76 and 83. Note also that reg 79(10) sets the effective date for a change of circumstances as the first day on which the person is treated as occupying the new dwelling as a home under reg 7(8).

Paragraph (10): Absence due to domestic violence

Where neither para (6)(a) nor (16)(c)(x) applies, if the claimant has left a former home through fear of relevant violence and has an unavoidable liability to make payments in respect of that former home, this provision requires the authority to treat the claimant as occupying the dwelling as a home (and therefore potentially entitled to HB) for up to four weeks. So where the claimant cannot be treated as occupying both the former and the new home (eg, because s/he is only liable for payments on the former home) or s/he is not temporarily absent from the former home (eg, because s/he does not intend to return to it), HB can be paid on the former home for the period specified. For the types of violence to which this provision applies, see the Analysis to para (6)(a) above. Unlike the circumstances covered by para (6)(a) this provision applies even where there is no liability to make payments in respect of the new dwelling and regardless of whether or not the claimant intends to return to the former home.

Paragraph (11) and (12): Absence for a trial period in residential accommodation

If a claimant enters residential accommodation as defined in para (18) on a permanent basis s/he is no longer entitled to HB on the former home.

Where a claimant enters such accommodation with the intention of returning home s/he is entitled to benefit for up to 52 weeks: para 16(c)(ix). Some people, however, go into residential accommodation on a trial basis to see if it suits them.

In these circumstances paras (11) and (12) may allow them to continue to receive HB for up to 13 weeks. The Court of Appeal's decision in *Secretary of State for Work and Pensions v Selby District Council and another* [2006] EWCA Civ 271, reported as *R(H) 4/06*, 13 February (overturning *CH 1854/2004*) holds that the language used in in sub-para (7B)(b) HB Regs 1987 (now para (11)(b) HB Regs) requires that the intention of returning to the dwelling which is normally occupied as the home must be present at the moment the person enters the residential accommodation; no more, no less. In other words, the intention to return home is to be gauged and fixed as at the date the person enters the residential accommodation.

On the other hand, the terms of sub-para (11)(c) are not confined to the present and have a temporal span which covers the whole of a person's time in residential accommodation. Accordingly, if at any time during the "trial" stay in residential accommodation the dwelling normally occupied is let, then the claimant will fall outside the parameters of (11) and lose her/his entitlement to HB. But that will not arise if all that has happened is that the claimant has given in her/his notice to quit the dwelling.

What reg 5(7C) HB Regs 1987 provided for (now reg 7(12) HB Regs), in the Court of Appeal's view, was to *treat* the claimant as if s/he was occupying the dwelling s/he normally occupied for 13 weeks, even though s/he had manifested the intention of not returning to it (or more accurately not returning to it after her/his right to exclusive possession has ended by operation of her/his notice to quit).

The Court of Appeal noted that its construction of reg 5(7B) and (7C) HB Regs 1987 was supported by the *different* language used in reg 5(8B) and (8C) HB Regs 1987 (now reg 7(16) and (17) HB Regs), which, in the court's view, by inference, shows that the intention there has to be present throughout the whole of the period of temporary absence (therefore endorsing, though not expressly, the views in *CH 3893/2004*).

In *CSHB 405/2005* the commissioner stated in para 30 that "desire" is not equivalent to "intention" in this statutory context, the former being a less certain or fixed state of mind than the latter. More controversially, perhaps, the commissioner said that in the context of reg 5 HB Regs 1987 (now reg 7 HB Regs) an intention to return to occupy the dwelling as the home must involve not only a subjective purpose to do so but also the objective fact that such a return is a realistic possibility. It is arguable that adding this gloss to the statutory words is both unnecessary and unhelpful. What has to be ascertained under reg 7 is the "intention" of the person, albeit to do a particular thing. As a matter of evidence the ability of the claimant to return and occupy the dwelling as her/his home may go to the cogency of her/his intention, and may reduce an intention to a desire to return, but this is all a matter of weight to be attached to the evidence when deciding whether the claimant has the relevant intention. If the commissioner is saying that, even if it is determined that a person has the relevant intention, the claim under reg 7 can still be defeated if it is decided that such a return is not a realistic possibility, it is suggested that the decision is wrong.

Paragraph (13) and (16) to (17): Temporary absence

These paragraphs deal with the situation in which the claimant is treated as occupying accommodation as her/his "home" notwithstanding a temporary absence from it. Claimants who are absent from their homes for a temporary period can obtain HB for up to 13 weeks, and only in the particular circumstances specified in paras (16) is HB available for 52 weeks, from the first day of absence (paras (13) and (17)).

R(H) 4/07 considered the phrase "from the first day of that absence from home". The claimant had been treated as occupying his home during an absence while in prison on remand under reg 5(8B)(c)(i) HB Regs 1987 (now reg 7(16)(c)(i) HB Regs). The issue was whether he could then be treated as occupying his home for 13 weeks from the date he was sentenced to a term of imprisonment under reg 5(8) HB Regs 1987 (now reg 7(13) HB Regs). Commissioner May refused the claimant's appeal. He said that the calculation of temporary absence was dependent upon the application of reg 5(8). For the purposes of that paragraph, "the first day of that absence from the home" was, as a matter of fact, the date the claimant had first been detained in prison.

In *Burt*, it was held that the absence must be for a continuous unbroken period (ie, without any returns). In cases where a claimant is moving backwards and forwards between two properties, authorities must consider reg 7(1) in order to decide what is the "normal" home in respect of which HB should be paid. It follows that authorities cannot "aggregate" periods of absence so as to make up the 13 or 52-week period. Consequently if the claimant, with the exception of prisoners on temporary leave under paras (14) and (15), returns to and occupies the dwelling as a home, even for a short time, the allowable period of temporary absence starts again. The DWP suggests that a stay at home lasting, for example, only a few hours may not be acceptable but one that lasts for at least 24 hours may be acceptable: GM A3.460.

To be entitled to HB during a period of absence, paras (13) and (16) require the following:

(1)   The claimant must intend to return to live in the dwelling: paras (13)(a) and (16)(a). Often, a good indicator of an intention to return will be personal belongings and furniture being left in the home: *R v Kensington and Chelsea RBC HBRB ex p Robertson* (1988) 28 RVR 84 at 85, QBD. Other factors might be where the claimant pays council tax, where s/he is registered to vote and other local connections. However, once a notice to quit has been given by a tenant in respect of the dwelling then he or she can no longer have a continuing intention to return to occupy the dwelling as his or her home: *CH 3893/2004* para 6. In such a situation the giving of the notice to quit cannot be treated simply as an expression of a future intention not to return to the dwelling upon the expiry of the tenancy, as the wording of (13)(a) and (16)(a) requires the continuance in the current benefit week of a positive intention to return to the dwelling: *CH 3893/2004* para 8. See also *CH 1237/2004* below which is to similar effect.

(2)   The part of the dwelling normally occupied by the claimant must not have been let or sublet: paras (13)(b) and (16)(b).

(3)   The period of absence must be unlikely to exceed 13 or 52 weeks as appropriate, or in the latter case, in exceptional circumstances, be unlikely to exceed substantially 52 weeks: paras (13)(c) and (16)(d). Once it becomes clear that a claimant is going to be away for more than the period allowed, HB entitlement ends. What is crucial is not whether the period does, in the event, exceed 13 or 52 weeks, but whether it is likely to do so on each successive day of the absence. This has been a source of confusion. There have been cases of claimants who took lengthy trips abroad, intending to return within 13 weeks (and usually booked on a return flight within that period) but were unable to return within the period due to unforeseen circumstances. Such claimants remain entitled to HB until it was no longer likely that they would return within the 13-week period. This is confirmed by the Deputy Commissioner in *CH 1237/2004*. The main point of that decision is to decide that the point from which the period of absence is to calculated – for the purpose of determining whether the absence is likely to exceed 52 (or 13) weeks – is the date the claimant left the house (para. 12), and not the date of claim. However, the decision goes on to say that continued entitlement has to be judged on a week by week basis, so that if at any date in the period of absence it becomes likely that the absence will exceed 52 (or 13) weeks, that is a change of circumstances allowing for a supersession of the entitlement decision from that date. The decision also emphasises that the test of likely period of absence is an objective one, to which the claimant's belief or opinion about the likely period of absence is relevant evidence but is not determinative.

The one exception to this rule concerns those claimants who may be absent for up to 52 weeks. If their period of absence is unlikely to exceed the 52-week period substantially, para (16)(d) gives the power to pay for up to 52 weeks, but no more, in "exceptional circumstances". GM A3.352 suggests that the term "unlikely to substantially exceed" relates to periods of absence of up to 15 months but it is for the individual authority to determine this subject, subject to appeal.

There is no requirement, however, that the intention to be temporarily absent from the dwelling needs to be notified in writing to the authority prior to departure: *CH 996/2004* para 17.

The categories of claimant who may be temporarily absent for up to 52 weeks and retain their HB entitlement are set out in para (16)(c). They are:

(i)   Claimants on remand pending trial or detained pending sentence, as well as those required to live in approved premises (eg, a bail hostel) or at an address away from their normal home as a condition of bail. This latter category removes the prior restriction in reg 5(8B)(c)(i) HB Regs 1987 to persons in bail hostels only. That rule had been challenged – by a claimant who was required to live away from her home as a condition of her bail – in *CH 4574/2003*. The commissioner held, however, that the restriction of the rule to bail hostel cases only, did not discriminate in a way which infringed the claimant's Article 14 Convention rights, as the difference in treatment between the two categories of person was within the margin of judgment that is allowed to the legislature when enacting social legislation: paras 63-66 applying *R (Waite) v London Borough of Hammersmith and Fulham* [2003] HLR 24. See paras (14) and (15) for additional rules where a detained or sentenced prisoner is given temporary release.

(ii)   Those resident in a hospital or similar institution as a patient as defined in para (18). Note that, unlike in the definition of "patient" in reg 28(11)(e), the medical or other treatment need not be provided free.

(iii) Those undergoing or whose partner or dependant child is undergoing medical treatment or medically approved convalescence, in the UK or elsewhere, but not in residential accommodation. "Medically approved" and "residential accommodation" are defined in para (18).

(iv)   Those undertaking a training course, as defined in para (18), in the UK or elsewhere.

(v)   Those providing medically approved care, in the UK or elsewhere, as defined in para (18).

(vi)   Those providing care for a child, defined in reg 2(1) as a person under the age of 16, whose parent or guardian is temporarily away from home receiving medical treatment or medically approved care.

(vii) Those receiving medically approved care in the UK or elsewhere but not in residential accommodation.

(viii) Students to whom para (3) or (6)(b) do not apply.

(ix)   Claimants receiving temporary care in residential accommodation but not those residing there on a trial basis. For the latter see paras (11) and (12).

(x)   Claimants in fear of violence who are not eligible for HB in the circumstances under para (6)(a) because, for example, they are staying with close relatives and are not liable to pay rent on two homes but intend to return to occupy their original homes. Where there is no intention to return home, see para (10).

Paragraphs (14) and (15): Temporary release from imprisonment

The purpose of this provision is to ensure that most people detained in custody who are temporarily released cannot claim HB for the home they are temporarily occupying. A similar provision in the HB Regs

1987 was inserted following the decision in *Chief Adjudication Officer v Carr* [1994] 2 June, *The Times*, CA which held that a prisoner on home release could claim IS.

Where para (14) applies:

(1) If the person's temporary release was immediately preceded by a period of temporary absence under paras (13) or (16), 13 or 52 weeks as the case may be, s/he is treated as still absent. If not, s/he is treated as not occupying the dwelling as a home: sub-paras (a) and (c).

(2) For the purposes of para (16)(c)(i), (temporary absence of up to 52 weeks) the person is treated as if still detained.

The provision only applies to a person "detained in custody" pending sentence or under a sentence. It does not therefore apply to someone required to reside in approved premises or some other address away from home pending sentence: *R(IS) 17/93*. In addition, it does not apply to somebody detained under the mental health legislation listed in sub-para (a). Note also that someone serving a very short sentence might still qualify under the temporary absence provision in para (13).

Circumstances in which a person is to be treated as liable to make payments in respect of a dwelling

8.–(1) Subject to regulation 9 (circumstances in which a person is to be treated as not liable to make payments in respect of a dwelling), the following persons shall be treated as if they were liable to make payments in respect of a dwelling–

(a) the person who is liable to make those payments;

(b) a person who is a partner of the person to whom sub-paragraph (a) applies;

(c) a person who has to make the payments if he is to continue to live in the home because the person liable to make them is not doing so and either–

(i) he was formerly a partner of the person who is so liable; or

(ii) he is some other person whom it is reasonable to treat as liable to make the payments;

(d) a person whose liability to make such payments is waived by his landlord as reasonable compensation in return for works actually carried out by the tenant in carrying out reasonable repairs or redecoration which the landlord would otherwise have carried out or be required to carry out but this sub-paragraph shall apply only for a maximum of 8 benefit weeks in respect of any one waiver of liability;

(e) a person who is a partner of a student to whom regulation 56(1) (circumstances in which certain students are treated as not liable to make payments in respect of a dwelling) applies.

(2) A person shall be treated as liable to make a payment in respect of a dwelling for the whole of the period in, or in respect of, which the payment is to be made notwithstanding that the liability is discharged in whole or in part either before or during that period and, where the amount which a person is liable to pay in respect of a period is varied either during or after that period, he shall, subject to regulations 79 to 81 (dates of relevant changes of circumstances, weekly amounts and housing benefit for rent free periods), be treated as liable to pay the amount as so varied during the whole of that period.

Definitions

"benefit week" – see reg 2(1).
"claimant" – see reg 2(1).
"dwelling" – see reg 2(4) and s137(1) SSCBA.
"partner" – see reg 2(1).
"payment" – see reg 2(1).

General Note

One of the basic conditions of entitlement to HB is that the claimant must be liable to make payments in respect of a dwelling: SSCBA s130(1)(a). Reg 8 deals with the circumstances in which a person is to be treated as "liable" to make payments on a dwelling that s/he occupies as her/his home. This regulation must be read subject to reg 9 – if reg 9 applies to exclude the persons listed here, they cannot be treated as liable. Cases often raise issues under both regulations. See the General Note to reg 9 for how such cases should be dealt with.

Analysis

Paragraph (1)

This paragraph sets out the categories of people who are treated as liable to make payments in respect of a dwelling. Before those categories are set out, however, the meaning of the basic terms must be clarified. **"Liable"** is not itself defined. The Oxford English Dictionary defines it as "legally bound, answerable for .... under obligation to do ....". The need for the obligation to be legal as opposed to moral was confirmed by Blackburne J in *R v Rugby BC HBRB ex p Harrison* [1994] 28 HLR 36 at 48-9, QBD. In that case, the claimants were members of a religious commune who signed a detailed agreement headed "Statement of Conditions of Residence". It was held that there was a question of law as to whether the agreement was intended to create legal relations between the claimants and the commune, and Blackburne J decided that there was such an intention (at 51). He also decided that it was not necessary to demonstrate that the landlord would probably take proceedings to recover unpaid payments, in order to demonstrate that the obligation was a legal one (at 51). The Court of Appeal approved this analysis in *R v Stratford-upon-Avon DC HBRB ex p White* [1998] 31 HLR 126 a case concerning the same commune (the Jesus Fellowship Church). The court stated that there was no reason why a relationship with a spiritual basis should not have legally enforceable aspects to it, and on a proper analysis of the commune's documents the obligation to make regular payments was a legal one.

In *R v Woking BC ex p Crawley* [1996] unreported, 19 June, QBD, Sedley J confirmed that the distinction that has to be drawn is between arrangements for living which will usually be made between friends and family (and, one might add, religious communities such as those in *Harrison* and *White*) and legally enforceable arrangements. If payment were made in the former cases, it would be "no more than subsidising a family arrangement which would in any event have resulted in the claimant sharing someone else's accommodation" (transcript at 7H-8B). The claimant had stayed with a friend who held an assured shorthold tenancy on condition that he paid half the rent. There was a clause in the tenancy prohibiting sub-letting.

There is a conflict in the approaches of Blackburne J and Sedley J as to whether the issue of whether an agreement gives rise to a legal liability is a question of law or of fact. Blackburne J indicated in *Harrison* that it was an issue of law (at 51). Sedley J, on the other hand, was unwilling to interfere with the review board's decision, even though saying it was "very harsh", indicating that he saw it as a question of fact. The general law of contract would indicate that Sedley J is right: see eg, *Chitty on Contracts* (Sweet and Maxwell, 1999, 28th edn) para 2-167. In *CH 1171/2002* para 11 it was confirmed that it was a question of fact whether or not a legal liability is created by an agreement.

What is required for there to be a legal liability? The three basic elements of a binding contract must be shown. The requirement of "consideration" (broadly, that both parties are giving up something in return for something) will not be an issue in HB cases. The second element is that there must be a settled agreement between the parties. Again, this will not usually present a problem. There is no need for the parties to reach a detailed written agreement (see under 'Evidence of Liability'). If A orally agrees to rent a room to B for £50 a week, that is all that is required to establish a settled agreement for HB purposes. If there is no specific agreement about what facilities B can use and about house rules, that does not prevent there being a binding agreement. The third element is an intention to create legal relations. Did the parties intend that their agreement should be legally enforceable? It is on this third element that cases such as *Harrison* and *Crawley* turned. In deciding whether there is such an intention, local authorities should be careful to separate their consideration of this question from the question as to whether any of the grounds in reg 9(1) applies.

Those who do not have an interest in land can nevertheless enter into a tenancy agreement with another party, with a consequent liability for rent. In *CH 2959/2006* the claimant had said that his brother (MI), to whom he paid rent, was acting as agent for the landlord. His claim for HB was refused on the basis that he was not liable to pay rent to the registered owner of the property (A) and that MI had no right to grant occupation. The tribunal upheld the decision. It said that in the absence of clear evidence that MI was the agent of A, he had no legal ability to enter into any contract with the claimant for the renting out of the property and consequently there could be no legal liability to make payments in respect of it. Deputy Commissioner Whybrow QC had sympathy with the difficult task faced by the tribunal but said that it erred in law by misdirecting itself that there could be no valid agreement creating a liability to make payments where the grantor had no power to let the property. He said (at para 22) that *Bruton v London & Quadrant Housing Trust* [1999] 3 WLR 150 and *Lambeth London BC v Kay* [2006] 4 All ER 128 (both House of Lords decisions):

> "establish that a party who does not have an interest in land such as to enable him to grant a leasehold estate or tenancy in favour of another party can nevertheless enter into a tenancy agreement with another party which is valid and effective between the parties to the agreement, albeit that the agreement will not be effective to create an interest or estate in land binding on third parties, including the registered owner of the relevant land. While *Bruton* and *Kay* were concerned with cases where the

landlord could not create an estate because he was only a licensee of the owner of the legal interest, in my judgement the principle in those cases apply equally to circumstances, as found by the tribunal in this case, where MI had no authority from the registered owner to let the premises. Thus, assuming that there was an otherwise valid agreement between MI and the claimants, such an agreement would be as binding and effective as between these parties, notwithstanding it could not confer on the claimants an interest or estate binding A. The tribunal in holding otherwise erred in law."

The identification of the source of the liability may be of difficulty in cases where claimants have been placed by local housing authorities in accommodation pursuant to their duties. In *CH 1208/2003*, the claimant argued that his HB was not subject to restriction because he had been placed in accommodation by a local authority and his obligation to pay rent was to the authority rather than the owner of the accommodation. The commissioner, reversing the decision of the tribunal, stated that the mere fact that the local authority owed a statutory duty to house the claimant did not mean that his liability for rent was to the local authority: para 17. It was necessary to analyse how the local authority had actually discharged its duty.

The mere fact that payments are made to a person does not mean that the payments are made pursuant to a legal liability to that person. It is possible that the claimant is making payments of rent to a third party for the convenience of the landlord and her/his creditor. Thus in *CH 4922/2002* paras 16-17, the mere fact that the claimant was making payments to the landlord's mortgagee did not mean that they had taken on a legal liability for those payments which was excluded from HB under s130(2)(b).

The fact that the liability must be legal can produce difficult problems with young claimants and claimants suffering from a degree of mental incapacity. These matters are discussed under separate headings below.

Evidence of liability. Evidence of liability for rent may take various forms – eg, letter from a landlord, receipts for payment, bank withdrawal slips. HB is paid not only in respect of payments under a lease but also in respect of payments referable to licence agreements and other types of arrangement: see reg 12(1). None of the agreements that attract entitlement to HB have to be in writing and so authorities should be prepared to take a broad view of the evidence required to establish liability for rent. Where the agreement is oral and the evidence is sparse, the authority should give due weight to the claimant's declaration on a claim form that they are liable to pay rent: *R v Sutton LBC HBRB ex p Keegan* [1992] 27 HLR 92 at 99-100, QBD. This cannot be carried too far, however; in *R v Derby CC ex p Third Wave Housing* [2000] 33 HLR 61, QBD, it was pointed out that although a party's stated understanding may be genuine, such a statement cannot be determinative of the legal status of an agreement.

There should be no need to produce a rent book, since a tenancy can exist without one: *R v Warrington BC ex p Williams* [1997] 29 HLR 872 at 876, QBD. In *R v Poole Borough Council ex p Ross* [1995] 28 HLR 351, QBD, the Review Board decided that the claimant was not "liable" to pay rent because "there was no tenancy agreement and no steps had been taken to recover rent". Sedley J. held (at 357-8) that neither of these findings could form a basis for the conclusion reached. As to the absence of a written agreement, it was clear from reg 10 HB Regs 1987 (now reg 12 HB Regs) that any kind of legal obligation sufficed to show that the claimant was obliged to make a relevant payment. As to the fact that the claimant's landlady had not sought to take proceedings, the short delay before the Board hearing and the fact that the landlady was aware of the HB dispute and could expect to be paid backdated benefit negated this factor.

In *Third Wave Housing*, Gibbs J provided guidance as to the requirements of a valid Review Board decision in a case where liability was in dispute. The applicant landlord (no point having been taken about the landlord's right to bring proceedings) was a voluntary organisation that arranged for foreign nationals to come to the UK to do voluntary work. They stayed in a hostel and claimed HB to pay their rent. Gibbs J stated that in considering whether the Board's decision that there was no liability for rent could be upheld, three matters had to be considered:

(1)   Was there material on which the finding could be made, whether individually or cumulatively?

(2)   Had the Board failed to take into account any evidence that was relevant to the question of liability?

(3)   Had the Board given adequate reasons or were they invalid as being sufficiently inadequate "so as not properly to indicate the basis of its findings"?

In that case, the judge concluded that the Review Board did have material before it in the form of evidence from the claimant to the effect that she had understood that she would not be pursued for rent arrears, the fact that the applicant's documentation had promised free accommodation, and the fact that the applicant had made arrangements with a sister company to meet any shortfall in HB.

A further illustration of the range of factors that may be relevant to a determination as to whether a true liability exists may be found in *R (T) v Richmond-upon-Thames LBC HBRB* [2000] 33 HLR 65, QBD. In that case, the claimant suffered from Alzheimer's disease and lived with his landlady, who acted as his carer. The Board gave three findings as reasons for its conclusion that there was no liability for rent: that the carer acted as appointee for benefit purposes, that there was a close friendship between them, and that it was unclear how much rent had been paid prior to the HB claim. The judge rejected submissions that these factors were irrelevant and that it was irrational to use them as a basis for its finding (judgment, paras 25 and 26).

In *CH 1618/2002* para 12, the commissioner suggested that it was not permissible to consider evidence as to how the parties actually implement an agreement in determining the question as to whether a legal liability was created. The decision of the House of Lords in *James Miller & Partners Ltd v Whitworth Street Estates (Manchester) Ltd* [1970] AC 572 was cited for that proposition, but *Chitty* para 12-124 points out that the decision only supports a proposition that subsequent conduct cannot be used as an aid to interpretation of the *terms* of the contract. Such conduct can be considered in determining whether in fact a legal liability was created at all. Such restrictions upon the evidence that may be considered seem to be inappropriate in the context of informal proceedings before a tribunal.

Note also the, arguably *obiter*, view in *CH 257/2005* which holds that a failure of the landlord to supply an address for service contrary to s48(1) Landlord and Tenant Act 1987 only postpones when the rent is in fact to be paid (until the address is in fact provided) but does not mean that the claimant is not liable for the rent. Regrettably, the decision gives no real guidance as to what a housing benefit authority should in fact do where there is a continuing failure by the landlord to comply with s48(1) Landlord and Tenant Act 1987 at the time of its decision on the claim. It is not immediately obvious that payment of the housing benefit in this situation could lawfully be suspended under either regs 11 or 13 of the D&A Regs.

'Sham' agreements. Particular difficulties may be created by cases in which a written agreement exists, but the local authority takes the view that it does not reflect the true intention of the parties. This was the issue in *CH 1171/2002*, where the commissioner referred to cases on general contract law as to the meaning of "sham": paras 10 and 11. *CH 1618/2002* was another such case. The commissioner stated that the first question was whether the document, on a proper interpretation and on the assumption that it was a genuine agreement, imposed a duty to pay rent: para 13. If that question was answered positively, then the issue of whether the obligation to pay rent was a sham needs to be considered:

"If as interpreted the document produced by the claimant does impose a duty to pay rent, the tribunal must consider whether the obligation to pay rent is a genuine part of the arrangement between the parties. If it is not, the term is a mere sham that was never intended to be implemented, but which was brought into existence to misrepresent the true arrangement between the parties and to conceal the truth from those dealing with them." (para 14)

The commissioner went on to give some useful guidelines as to the principles to be applied in answering this basic question:

(1)   It need not be shown that the whole document is a sham. "The sham may extend to the whole of the document or be confined to one or more of its terms": para 13. It is the term creating the liability for rent which is of importance, although the fact that other terms are intended to be genuine is probably at least some evidence that the whole document is genuine.

(2)   It is for the person alleging that a document is a sham to prove it. The local authority must therefore prove that the document is a sham: paras 15-16.

(3)   Whether a term is a sham is a question of fact: para 17.

(4)   The term is only a sham if neither party regards it as a genuine term: para 17.

(5)   If a term is genuine, the motivation behind the term is irrelevant to the question of whether there is a legal liability: para 17. So if an obligation to pay rent was only inserted to bring the claimant within the scope of the HB scheme, that does not mean that there is no liability for rent, although that may call into question whether the agreement falls foul of reg 9(1)(l).

(6)   The tribunal may take account of the way in which the contract has been implemented by the parties: para 18. However, a careful distinction must be drawn between a term which will never be implemented and one which might be implemented but has not in fact been enforced. Only the former terms are shams: para 19. Thus where a landlord does not enforce an obligation to pay rent while an appeal against a refusal of HB under reg 8 is outstanding, it does not necessarily follow that the obligation as to payment is a sham: paras 20-22.

CSHB 718/2002 considered the Scottish law on the subject of the creation of leases. Some of the points made in this decision are, however, of general application. The commissioner held (para 26) that where there is more than one agreement, each must be considered separately in deciding whether they are shams. He also said, correctly, that non-payment of rent was evidence that the agreement was a sham (para 28). However, any explanation for non-payment such as lack of resources would need to be taken into account.

Liability of the young. There is no lower age limit for claiming HB and claims by those under the age of 18 are quite common. The law in England and Wales and that in Scotland require separate explanation.

In England and Wales, the age of capacity is 18: Family Law Reform Act 1969 s1. It is not possible for a minor to hold any legal estate in land: Law of Property Act 1925 s1(6). So if a person under the age of 18 signs a tenancy agreement, the agreement is treated as an undertaking by the landlord to hold the property in trust for the tenant: Trusts of Land and Appointment of Trustees Act 1996 Sch 1 para 1(1). However, that would not mean that the minor was not liable to make payments of rent, since the minor would still be obliged to meet the consideration for the creation of the statutory trust: namely the payments set out in the agreement. This issue does not arise in the case of other types of contract for the occupation of property such as a contractual license, in which no estate in land passes. Note also that a minor may succeed to certain statutory tenancies: see eg, *Kingston-upon-Thames BC v Prince* [1998] 31 HLR 794, CA.

A minor is bound by a contract for "necessities". It seems probable that accommodation would be regarded as a necessity: *Chitty on Contracts* (Sweet and Maxwell, 1994, 27th edn) para 8-010. However, in deciding whether a minor can make a contract for the provision of accommodation, it will be necessary to bear in mind the following statement of Scott LJ in *R v Oldham MBC ex p G* [1993] 1 FLR 645 at 662, CA:

> "If a minor is to enter into a contract with the limited efficacy that the law allows, the minor must at least be old enough to understand the nature of the transaction and, if the transaction involves obligations of a continuing nature, the nature of those obligations."

In Scotland, the position is governed by the Age of Legal Capacity (Scotland) Act 1991. Any contract entered into by a person under the age of 16 is void: s1(1)(a). A contract entered into by a person aged between 16 and 18 is merely voidable: s1(1)(b). In the latter case it is suggested that the analysis above applies. Even if the contract is void, *R(IS) 17/94* points out that the claimant might be liable under the law of reparation. Reference should be made to that decision for a detailed analysis.

Liability of the mentally incapacitated. In England and Wales, a distinction must be drawn between those who are subject to the jurisdiction of the Court of Protection under the Mental Health Act 1983 and those who suffer from some lesser form of mental disability. As to the latter, the general rule is that they are bound by contracts made by them unless it is shown that the incapacitated person did not know what s/he was doing and the other party to the agreement did not know this. Even then, however, the contract is not void but only voidable at the option of the incapacitated party: *Chitty* para 8-064.

In *R v Barrow BC ex p Catnach* [1997] unreported, 3 September, QBD, a claim on behalf of some severely incapacitated claimants was made. The local authority rejected the claim on the basis that there was no liability to make payments (although reg 10(1) HB Regs 1987 (now reg 12(1) HB Regs) rather than reg 6 HB regs 1987 (now reg 8 HB Regs) was relied upon). Popplewell J held it was arguable that because the contract was only voidable and not void, that there was in fact a liability. He refused leave to move for judicial review, however, on the basis that the authority's secondary finding that the agreement fell foul of reg 7(1)(b) HB Regs 1987 (now reg 9(1)(b) HB Regs) could not be impugned. It is suggested that the argument is correct, unless the claimant's incapacity is of such a degree as to prevent her/him understanding the nature of what is being contracted for. Where the claimant is contracting for accommodation, it is unlikely that a high degree of comprehension is required: see eg, *CIS 754/1991* (an IS claimant with Down's syndrome had sufficient contractual capacity). In *CH 663/2003* paras 8-10, the commissioner confirmed that a claimant incapable of making a contract could be entitled to HB, since the contract was only voidable and the claimant could not take the benefit of the contract for the provision of accommodation without accepting the burden of paying rent. Following on from *CH 663/2003*, *CH 2121/2006* emphasises that there is no minimum level of understanding of a party to a transaction that can act to render the contract void from the outset.

Where a claimant is a patient under the Mental Health Act 1983, a receiver may be appointed by the Court of Protection to manage the claimant's affairs. It is not clear whether a patient may make a valid contract: *Chitty* para 8-073. However, by s96(1)(h) of the 1983 Act, the Court has power to make orders "for the carrying out of any contract entered into by the patient". Thus if the Court makes an order that HB should be applied for to pay a claimant's rent, it would seem that the order would operate as a statutory affirmation of the contract.

In Scotland, an agreement entered into by a person incapable of understanding the nature of her/his obligations is void and not merely voidable: *The Laws of Scotland* (1990) vol 15 para 661. The analysis in *R(IS) 17/94* would also apply in this situation however: see above.

"... to make payments in respect of a dwelling". It is not enough that some legal liability exists. The liability must have been undertaken in return for the occupation of a dwelling. In *R v Cambridge CC ex p Thomas* [1995] unreported, 10 February, QBD, a mother assisted one of her sons in raising funds to purchase a house. A declaration of trust was made in respect of the property, which included an obligation on the son to pay any rent received from lodgers to his mother. The property was registered solely in the son's name. The son lived there but the mother did not. Another son, the claimant, moved in and started to pay rent to the mother. It was held that since the mother had no legal title, she could not grant the claimant any right to reside in the property, and so the payments that he had agreed to make to her were not "payments in respect of a dwelling".

This conclusion seems rather dubious. It was not apparently in issue that the son was happy for his brother to move in, and it seems wrong to say that the claimant had no rights against the son. It is basic contract law that payments (or "consideration") made in return for goods or services need not be made to the person providing those goods and services. Payment to a third party is sufficient: see eg, *re Wyvern Developments Ltd* [1974] 1 WLR 1097 at 1103D, Ch D. Therefore it is suggested that the claimant's payments in *Thomas* were indeed made in return for his occupation of the dwelling, the son having given the claimant a right to occupy in exchange for payments to the mother. The case would have been better dealt with as a "contrived tenancy" case under reg 7(1) HB Regs 1987 (now reg 9(1) HB Regs).

The fact that payments must be made in respect of a "dwelling" confirms that if the payments are made under a business tenancy, they do not qualify. However, there may be difficulties where the tenancy is a mixed one or where there has been a change of use during the tenancy. With mixed tenancies, an apportionment must be made as to the rent payable for the business premises and for the residential premises. Only the latter payments can be eligible rent under reg 12.

A change of use during a tenancy which could result in premises becoming eligible for HB. It would depend on the actual use to which the premises were now put and some evidence of conversion to living accommodation would be required. However, there must also be some change in the nature of the payments made. In *R v Warrington BC ex p Williams* [1997] 29 HLR 872 at 876, QBD, the claimant took garage premises under a commercial lease containing a covenant forbidding use of the premises as a dwelling house. The claimant claimed that he had started to sleep on the premises as a night watchman, and therefore could claim HB in respect of the premises. The landlord's agents denied that the agreement was anything other than commercial. Hidden J held (at 875-6) that the agreement remained as a commercial one, even if the landlord was aware of the fact that the claimant was living on the premises. Accordingly, the claimant was not entitled to HB.

Who can be treated as liable? Having specified the type of liability required, para (1) then goes on to set out those people that can be treated as being liable:

(1)   The person who is liable under the agreement: sub-para (a).

(2)   The partner of a person coming under (1): sub-para (b). This does not mean that *both* the claimant and her/his partner may claim HB in respect of the home, but merely offers them a choice of claimant: see reg 82.

(3)   A person who has to meet the payments if s/he is to continue to live in the home because the person who is actually liable is not doing so: sub-para (c). Once these two factors are established, if the person now paying was formerly the partner of the person who is actually liable, the authority *must* treat the payer as liable. If the payer is not a former partner of the liable person, the authority need only treat her/him as liable if this seems "reasonable". Note in relation to this second category (that is, where consideration is being given to whether 8(1)(c)(ii) applies) the liable "person" can include a limited company and is not restricted to a natural person: *R(H) 5/05* para 33. It is not possible to deem a co-tenant to be liable for a co-tenant's share of the rent in addition to his own under this provision: *CH 3376/2002* para 37. In *CSHB 606/2005* the commissioner accepted (para 15) that it was not reasonable to treat a child of 15 as liable to make payments in place of her mother who was the tenant, where the mother was ineligible for HB under the terms of (what is now) reg 9(1)(d) HB Regs. On the facts the claim by the child was simply a device to circumvent reg 9(1)(d) and to hold otherwise would negate the effect of reg 9(1)(d).

(4)   A person given a rent-free period in return for carrying out repairs or decoration: sub-para (d). The work done must be reasonable and that which the landlord would have carried out or be required to carry out if the claimant had not. The duration of the rent-free period must be "reasonable compensation". However, even if all of these conditions are met, the claimant will only be able to retain her/his HB for up to eight benefit weeks in any one rent-free period. There is nothing to stop a person claiming for a subsequent eight week period, so works that will take longer can be split up into eight week portions. In *R v Westminster CC HBRB ex p Sier* [1999] 32 HLR 655 at 662-3, QBD (Latham J), it was pointed out that where the eight-week period pre-dated any payment for rent, the authority would have to satisfy itself that there was actually an obligation to pay rent (in the absence of the waiver) prior to the payments of rent starting. In that case there was no evidence to support the existence of any such pre-existing liability. The judge also ruled that the eight week period had to run from the beginning of any rent-free period. Thus it is not possible to select a convenient eight week period eg in order to preserve transitional protection.

(5)   Partners of students excluded from entitlement to HB by reg 56(1): subpara (e).

Paragraph (2)

This ensures that a claimant may receive HB in respect of all of the rent due for a particular period, even when payment is made wholly or partly in advance. Benefit is to be calculated on the basis of the period to which a payment *relates*, irrespective of when payment is actually *made*. Likewise, where rent is varied, HB is calculated on the basis of the period the variation affects, irrespective of when the variation is announced to, or paid by, the claimant. So, subject to regs 79-81, if rent is due on the first day of every month and the claimant's landlord informs her/him on the 15th that s/he is putting the rent up as of that month, for HB purposes the increase is treated as taking effect on the first day of the month.

Circumstances in which a person is to be treated as not liable to make payments in respect of a dwelling

9.–(1)   A person who is liable to make payments in respect of a dwelling shall be treated as if he were not so liable where–

   (a)   the tenancy or other agreement pursuant to which he occupies the dwelling is not on a commercial basis;

   (b)   his liability under the agreement is to a person who also resides in the dwelling and who is a close relative of his or of his partner;

   (c)   his liability under the agreement is–

      (i)   to his former partner and is in respect of a dwelling which he and his former partner occupied before they ceased to be partners; or

      (ii)   to his partner's former partner and is in respect of a dwelling which his partner and his partner's former partner occupied before they ceased to be partners;

   (d)   he is responsible, or his partner is responsible, for a child of the person to whom he is liable under the agreement;

   (e)   subject to paragraph (3), his liability under the agreement is to a company or a trustee of a trust of which–

      (i)   he or his partner;

      (ii)   his or his partner's close relative who resides with him; or

      (iii)   his or his partner's former partner;

is, in the case of a company, a director or an employee, or, in the case of a trust, a trustee or a beneficiary;

   (f)   his liability under the agreement is to a trustee of a trust of which his or his partner's child is a beneficiary;

   (g)   subject to paragraph (3), before the liability was created, he was a non-dependant of someone who resided, and continues to reside, in the dwelling;

   (h)   he previously owned, or his partner previously owned, the dwelling in respect of which the liability arises and less than five years have elapsed since he or, as the case may be, his partner, ceased to own the property, save that this sub-paragraph shall not apply where he satisfies the appropriate authority that he or his partner could not have continued to occupy that dwelling without relinquishing ownership;

   [¹ (ha) he or his partner–

      (i)   was a tenant under a long tenancy in respect of the dwelling; and

      (ii)   less than five years have elapsed since that tenancy ceased,

except where he satisfies the appropriate authority that he or his partner could not have continued to occupy that dwelling without relinquishing the tenancy;]

   (i)   his occupation, or his partner's occupation, of the dwelling is a condition of his or his partner's employment by the landlord;

   (j)   he is a member of, and is wholly maintained (disregarding any liability he may have to make payments in respect of the dwelling he occupies as his home) by, a religious order;

   (k)   he is in residential accommodation;

   (l)   in a case to which the preceding sub-paragraphs do not apply, the appropriate authority is satisfied that the liability was created to take advantage of the housing benefit scheme established under Part 7 of the Act.

(2)   In determining whether a tenancy or other agreement pursuant to which a person occupies a dwelling is not on a commercial basis regard shall be had inter alia to whether the terms upon which the person occupies the dwelling include terms which are not enforceable at law.

(3)   Sub-paragraphs (e) and (g) of paragraph (1) shall not apply in a case where the person satisfies the appropriate authority that the liability was not intended to be a means of taking advantage of the housing benefit scheme.

(4)　In this regulation ''residential accommodation'' means accommodation which is provided in–

(a)　a care home; or

(b)　an independent hospital.

Modifications

Reg 9 applies as modified by Sch 3 para 9(3)(a) HB&CTB(CP) Regs (see p1123) to a claimant who on 3 October 2005 was someone to whom reg 7(2) HB Regs 1987 as then in force applied.

Reg 9 applies as modified by Sch 3 para 9(5)(a) HB&CTB(CP) Regs (see p1124) to a claimant who on 3 October 2005 was someone to whom reg 7(5) HB Regs 1987 as then in force applied.

Reg 9 applies as modified by Sch 3 para 9(7)(a) HB&CTB(CP) Regs (see p1124) to a claimant who on 3 October 2005 was someone to whom reg 7(7) HB Regs 1987 as then in force applied.

Definitions

"close relative" – reg 2(1).

"dwelling" – see reg 2(4) and s137(1) SSCBA.

"partner" – reg 2(1).

"payment" – see reg 2(1).

"resides with" – see reg 3(4).

Amendment

1.　　Inserted by reg 2(3) of SI 2007 No 1356 as from 1.10.07.

General Note

Reg 9 is made under powers conferred by SSCBA s137(2)(i). In some ways it can be seen as the mirror image of reg 8. The latter treats certain classes of people who may not be legally liable to make payments in respect of their home as being so liable for the purposes of HB. By contrast, reg 9 treats certain classes of people who are (or may be) under a legal liability to make payments as not being liable, thereby disqualifying them from HB.

Para (2) specifies a particular factor of relevance to the determination of commerciality under reg 9(1)(a). Para (3) provides an escape route from sub-paras (1)(e) and (g) (but none of the others).

In *R(H) 8/04* Commissioner Jacobs rejected a submission that the Social Security Advisory Committee had been misled into deciding that regulations amending the former provision in the HB Regs 1987 need not be referred to it and that the regulations were therefore invalid. See the commentary to Pt XIII of the SSAA for more details. This conclusion was challenged on the claimants' appeal to the Court of Appeal. The Court of Appeal – in *Campbell and others v South Northamptonshire District Council and the Secretary of State for Work and Pensions* [2004] EWCA Civ 409 *The Times* 6 May, CA (reported as *R(H) 8/04*) – rejected the challenge. As a whole, the adverse affects of the amendment regulations had been made clear to the SSAC.

Reg 9(1) requires careful treatment by authorities to determine the question of whether an agreement falls foul of its provisions. Officers and tribunals may find the following systematic approach helpful:

(1)　　Consider which of the sub-paras may be applicable to the case under consideration. Examine carefully the various issues that arise under each and what must be proven and by whom.

(2)　　Ensure that the parties have had a fair opportunity to prepare cases on any new sub-paras identified by a tribunal as being potentially relevant and which have not been dealt with in the submissions of the parties. Note the discretion in Sch 7 para 6(9)(b) CSPSSA to decline to consider fresh issues, and the fact that a failure to give such an opportunity to consider the evidence will render a tribunal decision erroneous in law: see below.

(3)　　Consider all the evidence and make full findings of fact on all evidence, particularly where the evidence is in conflict.

(4)　　Examine any of sub-paras (a) to (k) that may be applicable. Decide whether, on the findings of fact, the claimant's case falls within any of them. Give full reasons why this is found to be so, ensuring that all relevant factors have been explicitly considered.

(5)　　If the case is found to fall within either of sub-paras (e) or (g), consider the question of whether the claimant has proved that the liability was not intended to take advantage of the HB scheme: sub-para (3).

(6)　　If none of the preceding sub-paras are found to be applicable, consider whether sub-para (l) applies (and see *CH 1586/2004* referred to below). Note the difference in language between sub-para (1)(l) and para (3) discussed below. Give full reasons for the conclusion on this issue. It may be prudent to consider sub-para (l) even in a case where the case is found to fall within one of the other sub-paras.

The facts of particular cases may bring a case within the meaning of more than one of the sub-paras in reg 9(1). If a tribunal forms the view that a sub-paragraph other than that relied upon by the authority in reaching its decision may be applicable, it is under a duty to warn the parties of that possibility and give them a fair opportunity to deal with the point, otherwise there will be a breach of natural justice and its decision will be set aside on appeal: *CH 396/2002* para 7. It makes no difference that there is evidence to support the tribunal's alternative ground for its decision: *CH 843/2002* para 7. The same applies to cases where the tribunal overturns an authority's decision that there is no liability but then goes on to find that reg 9 applies without warning the claimant: *R(H) 3/03* para 8. In the latter case, at para 1.3, the commissioner suggested that separate hearings could be held on the reg 8 and reg 9 issues. It is suggested that this will rarely be an appropriate course, because the issues overlap sufficiently that it makes far more sense for the tribunal to determine all issues at once. In *CSHB 718/2002* para 21, the commissioner said that it would be "sensible" to deal with all issues in one hearing and this course was also approved in *R(H) 7/05* para 3. Note also the view of Commissioner Levenson in *CH 1586/2004* that where a local authority or an appeal tribunal has decided that none of the provisions in para (1)(a) to (1)(k) applies the authority or tribunal is under a duty to consider para (1)(l): para:14. In his view, this duty arose because of the structure of reg 7(1) HB Regs 1987 (now reg 9(1) HB Regs) and because "the very fact that regulation 7(1) was raised at all put 7(1)(l) into issue". With respect, it is suggested that the commissioner is wrong on both of these points and the conclusion he then draws from them. There is nothing in the language of reg 9(1) which compels the decision maker to consider 9(1)(l) in every case where none of the sub-paras which proceed it apply. If it were otherwise, and the opening words in 9(1)(l) "in a case to which the preceding sub-paragraphs do not apply" were said to create the duty, then in order for the local authority or the appeal tribunal to be able to rely on reg 9(1)(l) it would first have to show that it had considered and rejected sub-paras (a) to (k). Moreover, it is suggested that on a reg 9(1) case the "issue" (eg, per Sch 7 para 6(9)(a) CSPSSA 2000) is not whether reg 9(1) in general is satisfied, but whether the claimant is not be be treated as liable to pay rent *because* s/he comes within one or more of the sub-paras in reg 9(1). The oddity of Commissioner Levenson's approach is arguably revealed by the use of an example. Suppose a local authority decides a case against a claimant on the basis that reg 9(1)(d) applies. No issue is taken by the authority on 9(1)(l). The claimant then appeals and produces evidence to the tribunal, which it accepts, that the landlord is not the father of her child and, moreover, she has never had any prior relationship with her landlord. In fact, it turns out that the local authority misread the name of the father on the child's birth certificate. Here, the whole, indeed sole, basis for the local authority invoking reg 9(1) has fallen away; yet on Commissioner Levenson's analysis the appeal tribunal would be under a duty to go on and consider reg 9(1)(l). It may have been on the facts in *CH 1586/2004* that the appeal tribunal wrongly failed to consider the issue of reg 7(1)(l) HB Regs 1987 (now reg 9(1)(l) HB Regs) under the discretion vested in it by Sch 7 para 6(9)(a) CSPSSA 2000, but it is a long way from that statement to say that the tribunal was under a legal duty to consider 7(1)(l).

In *CH 396/2002*, the commissioner also emphasised the need to use the correct terminology to avoid confusion of thought. He pointed out that speaking of any of the sub-paragraphs in terms of contrivance led to a danger of superimposing the test in sub-para (l) on the considerations appropriate to the other sub-paragraphs under consideration: para 11.

In the discussion below, the words "landlord", "tenant", and "tenancy" are used as convenient shorthand for the person to whom payment is made, the person making payment for the home, and the agreement under which the home is occupied, even where the use of these words is not strictly correct as a matter of law.

Analysis
Paragraph (1): Introduction
The interpretation of the various sub-paras of para (1) must be informed by the fact that reg 9(1) has the potential to work "rough justice" and that "it is appropriate to give them [the sub-paras] the narrowest interpretation that is consistent with the policy of protecting the scheme": *CH 716/2002* para 11.

When considering subparas (a) to (l), it must be borne in mind that these offer 13 entirely separate grounds on which the authority may refuse HB on the basis that someone must be treated as if not liable for rent. As will appear from the Analysis below, certain issues will be of relevance to more than one of the grounds. However, it is important for authorities and advisers alike to consider the possible application of each of the sub-paras separately, to avoid confusion.

Issues under subparas (a) to (l) may also be linked with the issue as to whether there is a genuine liability, which falls for consideration under reg 6. The issues are different, and again it is important to consider the legal requirements separately so as to avoid confusion: *CH 1171/2002* para 12.

The need for authorities and tribunals to draw a careful distinction between issues arising under reg 8 and reg 9 was vividly illustrated by *R v Greenwich LBC ex p Dhadly* [1999] 32 HLR 829. The claimant occupied a three bedroom property owned by his son, who lived in America. The local authority initially refused HB on the basis that there was no true liability to pay rent (though referring to SSCBA s130 rather than reg 6 HB Regs 1987 – now reg 8 HB Regs) and also on the basis that if there was a liability to pay rent, it fell foul of the former reg 7(1)(b) HB Regs 1987, now to be found in sub-para (l). On review, the refusal of HB was based solely on the absence of a liability. The Review Board stated that they were "not satisfied that Mr Dhadly was genuinely liable to pay rent".

Mr Dhadly applied in person for judicial review of the Board's decision. His application was refused at first instance by Collins J [1998] 31 HLR 446. The judge held that the Board was wrong to rely on reg 7 HB Regs 1987 but as it was possible to justify its decision on the basis that there was no genuine liability for rent (ie, by reliance on reg 6 HB Regs 1987 – now reg 8 HB Regs), permission to seek judicial review would be refused. However, that decision was overturned by the Court of Appeal, which granted permission and remitted the case to a High Court judge for hearing.

The substantive application was heard by Richards J [1999] 32 HLR 829. Counsel for the local authority argued that even if the Board's findings on reg 7 HB Regs 1987 could not be supported, judicial review should nevertheless be refused on the ground that the Board's findings clearly supported a conclusion that there was no liability to pay rent. Richards J rejected that submission in these terms:

"I am not persuaded that the matter can be dealt with as easily as that. The Board's decision fails to show that the Board has properly understood the legal issues and the precise legal test that it was applying at each stage of the analysis. If it was applying section 130, it has conspicuously failed to say so and has, on the contrary, purported to be applying regulation 7(1)(b). .... in circumstances where there is no mention of section 130, and the decision is expressed to be on a different basis, the court should be slow to hold that the Board did approach section 130 in the right way and that the decision can be upheld as a proper application of that provision."

Paragraphs (1)(a) and (2): Non-commercial agreements

It is to be noted that it is the agreement between the parties, and not just the payment made pursuant to that agreement, that must be assessed to ascertain whether it is made other than "on a commercial basis". The agreement, and the relationship between the parties, must be looked at as a whole: *R V Sutton LBC ex p Partridge* [1994] 28 HLR 315 at 319-320; *R v Rugby BC HBRB ex p Harrison* [1994] 28 HLR 36 at 48-9, QBD. See also *R(H) 1/03* para 16.4. In paras 21-22 of that decision, the commissioner described a finding as to commerciality as a "compound fact" which depended on the primary facts found by the tribunal. In *CH 5147/2001* para 9, the commissioner stated that "the regulation is in the most general terms, allowing decision makers to take a variety of circumstances into account." All the relevant circumstances must be taken into account, but the weight given to them is a matter for the tribunal and a challenge to the weight given to the factors will only succeed if no reasonable tribunal could have approached the case in the way that the tribunal did: *R(H) 8/04* paras 23, 29. On a further appeal, the Court of Appeal in *Campbell and others v South Northamptonshire District Council and the Secretary of State for Work and Pensions* [2004] EWCA Civ 409 *The Times* 6 May, CA (reported as *R(H) 8/04*) ruled that the weighing of the relevant circumstances is not analogous to the exercise of a discretion (as to which factors to take into account or not); everything in the evaluation is purely factual. Accordingly, there can be no scope for ruling certain relevant facts out of consideration because to take them into account would be to infringe a claimant's rights under the European Convention on Human Rights (here, Art 9, concerning freedom of religion).

In *CH 3008/2002*, the commissioner pointed out that the first step under sub-para (a) is to identify the agreement which is alleged not to have a commercial basis. Unlike sub-para (l), it may be possible for an agreement to pass in and out of the scope of sub-para (a). In that case, the reversionary interest of the landlord under an assured tenancy agreement had been transferred to the claimant's sister during the contractual term. At the end of the contractual term, a statutory tenancy came into existence by the operation of the Housing Act 1988. The commissioner remarked that he could not "understand how a tenancy that is created by law cannot be on a commercial basis" (para 11). This, at best, misleading sentence has been held to be wrong in *R(H) 10/05*, which should now be preferred to *CH 3008/2002* on this point. As Commissioner Turnbull puts it in *R(H) 10/05*:

"the . . . words [in *CH 3008/2002*] would appear to mean that a statutory tenancy cannot, at the point when it arises, be non-commercial, and that it can only become so by virtue of factors subsequently occurring (eg the sorts of events which the commissioner went on to mention). That is in my view plainly not correct. The statutory periodic tenancy arising under the 1988 Act has essentially the same terms as those of the preceding fixed term tenancy (section 5(3)(e) of the 1988 Act). Further, it arises simply by reason of the termination of the previous contractual tenancy. If that contractual tenancy was not on a commercial basis, then it is likely that the statutory one will also not be so. For example, if, by reason of the relationship between the parties, the terms of the contractual tenancy are very unusual, those terms will be carried over into the statutory tenancy. It is true that either the landlord or the tenant can under section 6 of the 1988 Act serve a notice proposing different terms, in which case in the event of dispute a rent assessment committee is to fix such terms "as might reasonably be expected to be found in an assured tenancy". A failure to use those provisions might be an additional factor pointing to non-commerciality, but the mere fact that the tenancy had arisen by force of the statute would not mean that it would be necessary to point to such a failure, or to some other matter arising subsequent to the arising of the statutory tenancy, in order to demonstrate non-commerciality".

However, if the agreement under which a claimant occupies a dwelling is *genuinely* on commercial terms then it follows that the agreement is necessarily on a commercial basis: *CH 3282/2006* (para 15).

It is for the authority to produce evidence to satisfy itself or a tribunal that the agreement is not on a commercial basis. A tribunal dealing with a reg 9(1)(a) case should "ask themselves whether the evidence has satisfied them on the balance of probability that the principal basis on which the agreement was made was a non-commercial one. If the test is not met the liability is excluded.": *Ross* at 358.

The word "commercial" is not susceptible of further elaboration and it is probably not possible to definitively state when an agreement is commercial and when it is not. An attempted formulation in *CH 2329/2003* para 7 that "the arrangement ... will be other than commercial only if it confers no benefit on the owner which is proportionate to the benefit conferred on the occupier" was rejected in *CH 3743/2003* paras 32-35. Commissioner Jacobs said in the latter case (para 34) that "rigid rules are inappropriate" when assessing whether or not an agreement was made on a commercial basis. However, in *CH 663/2003* the commissioner suggested that the term "on a commercial basis" connotes a financially justifiable relationship and also some generality as to who may take up the tenancy, which would shut out (as being 'commercial') an arrangement set up exclusively for the benefit of a particular claimant. This test would also seem to fall foul of the broader approach advocated in *CH 3743/2003*, as it seeks to elevate one relevant factor to being a decisive factor. The approach in *CH 663/2003* conflicts directly with *CH 296/2004*, where Commissioner Jacobs again emphasised that no factor is decisive in deciding commerciality and, rightly it is suggested, pointed out that accepting less than the contractual rent rather than evicting the tenant may simply be bowing to reality and does not necessarily mean that the arrangment is non-commercial. *CH 296/2004* also makes the rather pithy point that "Rackman is not the only model of a commercial landlord". What this division in the caselaw seems to reflect is the truth of the statement made above that it is not possible to definitively state when an agreement is or is not "commercial". It is suggested that the approach advocated in *CH 3743/2003* and *CH 296/2004* should be preferred. This suggestion is given added force by *CH 2899/2005*, which holds that in so far as *CH 2329/2003* and *CH 663/2003* put forward what may be described as the *only* relevant factors for determining commerciality they are inconsistent with *R(H) 1/033* and should not be followed.

The factors which may be relevant in assessing whether the agreement is on a commercial basis include the following.

The Relationship Between the Parties. Even if the parties are not "close relatives" so as to bring them within the scope of sub-para (b), the authority may take into account the relationship between them: *R v Poole Borough Council ex p Ross* [1995] 28 HLR 351, QBD. However, as Sedley J in *Ross* makes clear, there is nothing inherently non-commercial about letting to a close friend or relative, though the closer the relationship, the more critically the agreement may be examined. This point was emphasised by Commissioner Howell in *CH 4854/2003* where, following *Ross*, he stressed (para 11) that what is important is the nature of the arrangement: "the fact that the parties are friendly or related to one another cannot by itself turn a commercial arrangement or agreement into a non-commercial one". It will also be relevant to have regard to factors such as the desire to have a reliable and trustworthy tenant and someone companionable, particularly in cases involving single elderly people such as Ross: see Sedley J at 359. Such factors may explain why friends have decided not to live on their own. In *CH 1076/2002*, the claimant's adult son was the half-brother of the landlord. The commissioner stated, at para 19.1, that such a fact was of very little significance in view of the time that had elapsed since the relationship between the claimant and the landlord's father. The mere fact that the parties knew each other and could trust each other "proves nothing".

The 1997 GM A3.66iv made the point that fostering children is a commercial arrangement and so former foster children who remain in the family home when they are no longer dependent should be treated as paying rent on a commercial basis.

Now that it need not be shown that the claimant is residing with the landlord, the question arises as to whether that, of itself, can be a factor suggesting that the agreement is non-commercial. It is suggested that it is not. Anyone who has shared a property with a resident landlord will be aware how intensely commercial the relationship can sometimes be. It will be much more instructive to have regard to the personal ties, if any, between landlord and tenant. Not all cases where there is a close relationship between landlord and tenant will fall foul of sub-para (a). It depends on all the facts of the case.

In *CH 296/2004* the commissioner considered what difference, if any, the fact that the claimant's father was his landlord made to whether the tenancy was on a commercial basis. He concluded that there is nothing necessarily incompatible in a commercial arrangement being made between a parent and adult child, though the close family element in the relationship may make such a finding less likely: see *R(IS) 11/98* para 8 and *CIS 195/1991*. Moreover, care and support being provided to a disabled adult son by a parent under the tenancy, although different in quality from that which a stranger would provide, is not necessarily incompatible with the arrangement being commercial. If it were otherwise – and the provision of care and counselling by the landlord to the tenant would render such a tenancy arrangement automatically non-commercial, then there would have been no need make such service charges ineligible under Sch 1 para 1(f) HB Regs. Thirdly, the commissioner noted that the motivation for such arrangements will be different. However, even if the sole motivation for the arrangement is to ensure that the adult son or daughter is properly housed and supported, this does not necessarily mitigate against it being a commercial arrangement. Indeed, arrangements for supported independent living are a recognised part of the commercial rented sector. Fourthly, the commissioner emphasised that when considering the issue of eviction a realistic view should be taken about whether a landlord who is not a family member would have taken steps towards eviction, particularly where (as on the facts of this case) the claimant is able to pay a significant part of his rent even without housing benefit.

In *CH 1097/2004*, the Deputy Commissioner confirmed (para 15), following *CH 296/2004*, that there is nothing inherently non-commercial in a tenancy agreement between members of the same family or between a provider and recipient of personal care. Neither did the fact that the landlords would not have let a room to anyone other than the claimant (a friend of theirs) mean that the tenancy was not on a commercial basis, considering all the facts of the case (paras 18-20). The friends wanted a commercial return for the room and without that return they would ultimately want the room back. Although they only considered letting the room to the claimant to assist her in difficult times (and would not have let it to anyone else) the letting was on a commercial basis even though the motivation for it was largely non-commercial.

However, in *CH 663/2003*, the commissioner – following *R v Rugby BC HBRB ex p Harrison* [1994] 28 HLR 36 at 48-9, QBD, and what he characterised as the peculiar and personal rights of occupation in play in that case – agreed that the agreement was not on a commercial basis because, although the rent may have been a commercial rent in that it had been assessed as a 'fair rent', on the facts of the case the arrangement looked at as a whole was one which was strictly personal to, and set up for the benefit of the claimant and the claimant alone. It was not, therefore, an arrangement which would have been offered on the open market to anyone other than the claimant. "On a commercial basis" connotes a financially justifiable relationship and also some general class of person who may take the benefit of the arrangement, rather than one person for whom the arrangement is exclusively conceived. But see *CH 3743/2003* and *CH 2899/2005* above.

The Living Arrangements.

If the living arrangements are of an unusual character, this may suggest that the agreement is not commercial. In *R v Greenwich LBC ex p Moult* [1998] unreported, 19 June, CA, the claimant's agreement gave him occupation of the sole bedroom, but the rest of the accommodation was stated to be shared with the landlady. On a renewed application for leave to move for judicial review, it was observed that the fact that the owner jointly occupied the common parts but kept no part of the property for her sole use was "not something which one would expect to find in a commercial letting". In such a case, however, the authority should give due weight to any explanation given by the claimant for an unusual arrangement.

The Amount Payable. In *Partridge* 319-320, Laws J rejected a submission that "commercial" simply meant that some payment which was more than minimal was made for the accommodation. The same point was made in *Harrison* at 55, where it was said that even if the rent was broadly a market rent, the rest of the agreement might still lead to the conclusion that it was non-commercial. Profit is not necessary, provided the recompense is reasonable. GM A3.262 correctly emphasises the need not to place too much importance on this factor:

".... charging a low rent does not, on its own, make an agreement non-commercial. Many charities and voluntary bodies, and some individuals, choose to let properties at below market rents or do not want to make a profit from letting, but their tenancies may still constitute commercial arrangements if that is what the parties to the agreement intended."

Evidence of the Making and Amount of Payments Under the Agreement. If there is no such evidence, that will be a factor the authority may take into account in deciding that the agreement is not a commercial one: Moult. Such evidence may, of course, call into question the existence of any legal liability at all as well as the commerciality of the agreement. See the discussion in the commentary to reg 8 above.

A careful distinction needs, however, to be drawn between a case where there is no evidence that *any* payments have been made and cases where the landlord has been accepting less than the contractual rent. In *CH 1076/2002*, the contractual rent was £400 and had been subject to a restriction of about 25 percent by the Rent Officer. The landlord accepted the amount payable by way of HB. The only reason given by the tribunal for finding that the agreement in question was on a non-commercial basis was the fact that the landlord had declined to sue for the balance. The landlord adduced independent evidence from a letting agent who stated that it was not unusual for private landlords to accept the amount of HB payable and not enforce entitlement to the rest. The commissioner held that in the light of that evidence and his own experience to the same effect, the landlord's decision not to enforce the balance could not be castigated as a non-commercial decision: paras 18 and 19.3. It was not irrelevant to the commerciality issue, but neither was it conclusive as the tribunal had found. Furthermore, the fact that the parties had not formally varied the agreement so as to provide for the new lower agreed rent was of little significance, since "lay people do not always attach the same significance to legal form as lawyers do": para 19.2.

A very common issue arising in these cases concerns the significance of a landlord deciding not to take immediate possession proceedings but deciding to await the outcome of an appeal against a refusal of HB. Considerable caution needs to be exercised before heavy reliance is placed on this factor. HB claimants are generally impecunious, having little or no disposable income and few or no assets against which a judgment can be enforced. Local authorities argue that no commercial landlord would wait so long for rent; but the contrary argument in these circumstances is that if evicted, a tenant will have little incentive to pursue an appeal against a refusal of HB and there will be no chance, as against at least some chance, that a landlord will ever receive her/his money. A decision to await the outcome of a tribunal hearing, even if that takes a few months, will rarely demonstrate non-commerciality. A decision to wait considerably longer, perhaps a year or more if the case gets to commissioner level, would have to be examined with more care. Legal advice received or the landlord's perceptions as to the prospects of success of the appeal would be of importance in such a case. Independent evidence from letting agents as to common practice in such a situation, similar to that adduced in *CH 1076/2002*, would also be of assistance.

If payments are made to a third party instead of the landlord, it does not necessarily follow that the agreement is uncommercial (or that the true liability is to the payee: see the commentary to reg 8). In *CH 2329/2003*, the claimant and his wife moved into their daughter's house while she was abroad and paid all the outgoings on it themselves. The commissioner upheld the tribunal's conclusion that the agreement was a commercial one, saying (para 7):

" . . . .the arrangement between the owner of a property and the occupier will be other than commercial only if it confers no benefit on the owner which is proportionate to the benefit conferred on the occupier. In this case the owner clearly benefits from the arrangement because it enables her to retain the house while she is abroad and have it occupied by somebody whom she can trust to look after it and its contents."

The Parties' Views. How the parties view the agreement may be relevant, but their views as to the nature of the agreement cannot be conclusive: *Partridge* at 318.

Bad Faith. As with sub-para (l), if there is evidence of bad faith on the part of the parties, it may lead the tribunal to view their evidence with suspicion. However, the conclusion that the agreement is non-commercial would not automatically follow. In *CH 1325/2002*, the parties had created a tenancy agreement which had been misleading backdated to 1998 to attempt to justify a claim for backdating. The commissioner held that despite that conduct, the tribunal had been entitled to decide that there was a binding commercial agreement from 2001, the year in which the agreement was created (paras 12-14).

Non-Enforceable Terms: Para (2). Para (2) explicitly requires the authority to consider whether the contract includes terms that are not enforceable at law. However, it must be emphasised that it is not determinative of the question of non-commerciality, but is merely a factor to be placed in the equation. On the other hand, the fact that the Secretary of State has identified this as a factor of relevance means that it should be given considerable weight in the scales: compare *R v Westminster CC HBRB ex p Mehanne* [1999] 2 All ER 319, CA.

The presence of this factor requires careful disentanglement of the consideration of reg 8 and reg 9(1)(a). Under reg 8, the question is whether there is a legal liability to make a payment. Provided that the landlord could sue for rent under the agreement, reg 8 is satisfied, whether or not there are extraneous, non-legal terms: see *R v Stratford-upon-Avon DC HBRB ex p White* [1998] 31 HLR 126. Under reg 7(2) the issue is whether *any* of the terms are incapable of enforcement in the courts, not merely those relating to the payment of the rent.

A number of points need to be made about the effect of para (2). First, only "terms upon which the person occupies the dwelling" are relevant. It might be, for example, that one agreement contained the terms of the claimant's tenancy and also provided for details of her/his employment. Provided that the agreement did not make the occupation of the accommodation conditional on the employment (as to which see sub-para (i) below) the terms of the employment cannot be considered under para (2).

The question of whether a term agreed between the parties is enforceable at law should be considered broadly. This is only one factor in determining commerciality and so authorities should not overly concern themselves with technical issues of whether a landlord or tenant could sue for breach of a particular term. It must also be borne in mind that contractual terms can be "enforceable" in a number of ways. Thus a term cannot be said to be unenforceable simply because a party would not suffer any financial loss as a result of a breach and so could not sue the other party for damages. It may well be that an injunction (interdict in Scotland) could be obtained to prevent the other party breaking the agreement.

Once non-enforceable terms have been identified, the issue arises as to how much weight they should be given. It is suggested that the more fundamental they are to the whole agreement between the parties, the stronger their presence suggests that the agreement is non-commercial. The clear thrust of para (2) is to deal with cases like *White* where the legal liability is merely incidental to the spiritual relationship between landlord and tenant.

Paragraph (1)(b): Payments to resident landlords who are close relatives

As the categories of unacceptable relationships between landlord and tenant have been more exhaustively defined than under an older version of the rule, it is suggested that it is even more questionable whether this provision is compatible with Art 8 of the European Convention on Human Rights.

"Who Also Resides in the Dwelling". A subtle change in the wording of the provision may substantially change its effect. An older version of reg 7(1)(a)(i) HB Regs 1987 spoke of a claimant "who resides with" the landlord. That imported the definition in reg 3(4). Now, however, the reference is to a landlord "who also resides in the dwelling". This would appear to oust the definition in reg 3(4), though this may not have been intended.

The critical factor is what is meant by "the dwelling" for these purposes. Must the landlord share *all* the tenant's accommodation, or is it sufficient if common parts are shared? By SSCBA s137(1), "dwelling" is defined as follows:

"...any residential accommodation, whether or not consisting of the whole or part of a building and whether or not comprising separate and self-contained premises."

The effect of *R (Painter) v Carmarthenshire CC HBRB* [2002] HLR 447 and *R (Murphy) v Westminster CC* [2002] HLR 447 is that careful attention must be paid to the agreement between the parties and its legal effect and it is likely that most house-sharing arrangements will be construed as being an agreement to share a single dwelling, rather than an agreement to create two separate dwellings within the same building: see paras 11 and 12 of the judgment. The view stated in previous editions of this book – that if the claimant has a tenancy, rather than a licence, in the property, it is impossible to conclude that the landlord "resides in the dwelling" because that would be inconsistent with the exclusive possession that is the hallmark of a tenancy – was found in *CH 3656/2004* to constrain para (1)(b) too narrowly. Commissioner Fellner accepted that this view might apply where the claimant rented a bed-sit and shared only the common parts. It is not the case that the only circumstances which could come within para (1)(b) is where the claimant and landlord share a room; everything will depend on the facts. *CH 3656/2004* was followed in *R(H) 5/06,* where the claimant and her sister shared the living room, kitchen and common parts, and the commissioner said that the claimant and her sister were residing in the same dwelling: the test for the commissioner was whether the landlord and the claimant were sharing the majority of the accommodation in the residential unit. (The commissioner also rejected an argument that the terms of reg 7(1)(b) HB Regs 1987 (now reg 9(1)(b) HB Regs) were discriminatory and breached Art 14 of the European Convention on Human Rights.) The same commissioner put the issue somewhat differently in *CH 542/2006* where he said (para 13) that "[w]here...a person is entitled to and does share essential living accommodation such as living rooms and a kitchen, it is not in my judgment right to regard the "dwelling" in respect of which he pays rent as being only the rooms of which he has exclusive occupation". On that basis the claimant in *CH 542/2006* was caught by para 1(b) because his son, who was his landlord, also resided in the dwelling. Following *CH 3656/2004*, it was not necessary that the landlord son was entitled to occupy all the accommodation comprised in that dwelling.

However, even where there is no tenancy, there may be sufficient physical separation between the parts occupied by the "landlord" and the parts occupied by the tenant to lead to the conclusion that sub-para (b) does not bite. An example of this might be a self-contained "granny flat" where there is insufficient evidence of a tenancy but where the elderly relative is left to live her/his own life.

"Close Relative". This expression is defined in reg 2(1). GM A3.240 suggests, on the authority of *R(SB) 22/87*, that "brother" and "sister" includes half-brother and half-sister. That decision also establishes that a child, when adopted, no longer has any relation with his natural parents and other relatives. It is to be pointed out that step-brothers and step-sisters (unlike step-parents and children) do not fall within the definition, and GM A3.243-245 give useful examples of how divorce and death can affect who a person's "close relatives" are. Broadly, divorce and death sever the links with the family by marriage, so that a parent-in-law, for example, is no longer to be treated as such.

Paragraph (1)(c): Liability to former partners

This excludes agreements between former partners of both the claimant and her/his partner, if any. It is regrettable that para (3) does not apply to these agreements. One of the most common forms of financial settlement on divorce consists of partner A, formerly the main breadwinner, taking on responsibility for the mortgage, and partner B living in the property until their children become independent (the so-called *Mesher* order). The agreement will often include some kind of contribution made by B towards the mortgage payments, and in many cases where partner B later becomes unemployed, this contribution was met by HB. Now such arrangements are excluded, and it is likely to cause substantial difficulties for those in the position of such claimants.

Note the definition of "partner" in reg 2(1). There is no explicit requirement that the two relationships be consecutive and not separated in time, or that the occupation of the accommodation is continuous, provided that the accommodation remains the same. However, the phrase used in sub-para (c)(i) is "his former partner", instead of "a former partner of his" or "one of his former partners". It is arguable that the phrase used suggests a focus upon *one* individual rather than one of a group of individuals. Put shortly, in this context "former" means "last". This narrow interpretation gains some support from GM A3.266, which identifies the type of case towards which sub-para (c)(i) is directed in the following terms:

"If a couple, married or unmarried, separate and the claimant, or current partner if they have one, remains in the joint home and is charged 'rent' by the partner who left, then treat the claimant as not liable for housing costs."

That guidance supports the argument that sub-para (c)(i) only applies to a liability to the claimant's last partner. If a relationship is in the distant past, the case for regarding such a liability as necessarily abusive is much reduced. That may justify a narrow interpretation of the sub-paragraph under the principle identified in *CH 716/2002* para 11.

It would appear that the liability must be to the former partner alone. If, for example, the former partner jointly owned the property with a third party, it would appear that sub-para (c) does not apply. It would, however, apply if the liability was to joint landlords who were *both* former cohabitees of the claimant and/or her/his partner, there being nothing to exclude the usual principle that the singular includes the plural: see s6(c) of the Interpretation Act 1978.

The argument that the "dwelling" occupied by the claimant must be the same as the "dwelling" occupied when the claimant and her/his landlord were a couple and that if the claimant occupies a bedroom plus the common parts in a property while being excluded from the landlord's bedroom, sub-para (c) does not bite, was rejected in *Painter* and *Murphy* by Lightman J. Mr Painter and Mr Murphy had lived as lodgers in properties owned by their landladies before forming relationships with them and sharing their bedrooms. When the relationships broke down, they reverted to their status as lodgers. In Mr Painter's case, a deed of separation between the parties declared that he had a right to live in the property on paying rent but that the parties would respect each others' privacy. Lightman J held, as a matter of construction, that the agreement gave Mr Painter a right to occupy the whole property and so he was occupying the same dwelling as he formerly occupied (para 11). The agreement to respect each other's privacy, while it effectively amounted to an agreement not to go into each other's bedrooms, did not define rights of occupation.

The judge went on to hold (para 12) that a similar agreement would be inferred in Mr Murphy's case in the absence of any evidence as to the precise terms that had been agreed between the parties. The judge then went on to decide that even if the "dwelling" presently occupied by the two claimants was only part of the "dwelling" formerly occupied by each of them, that would suffice to trigger the exclusion because "it is only necessary that it was in fact occupied by the claimant and his former partner during the period of their relationship" (para 13).

It was further argued that sub-para (c) discriminated against the claimants as being people who had formerly been in a relationship with their landlady, whereas a lodger who had never been involved in such a relationship would not be excluded from HB. The sub-para therefore infringed the claimants' rights under Art 14 of the European Convention on Human Rights, taken in conjunction with Art 8. Lightman J rejected that argument (paras 15-21 of his judgment, discussed in the commentary to Art 14 on p136).

A further human rights challenge to sub-para (c) was raised in *R(H) 6/05*. It was argued that since claimants with a liability for rent to their former same sex partners were not be caught by the sub-paragraph (because their former partners would not have been a "partner" as then defined in reg 2(1)), the regulation discriminated against heterosexual claimants. The challenge failed and a further appeal to the Court of Appeal was also unsuccessful: *Langley v Bradford MDC and Secretary of State for Work and Pensions* [2004] EWCA Civ 1343, 15 October, CA, reported as *R(H) 6/05* (see the commentary to Art 14 on p136). Note that same sex partners *do now* come within the definition of "partner".

Paragraph (1)(d): Claimant responsible for landlord's child

A person is only "responsible" for a child if s/he falls to be treated as part of the responsible person's family for benefit purposes. See the commentary on Part 4 of the HB Regulations and in particular reg 20 (see p274). It follows that it will not be sufficient that the claimant or her/his partner spends a lot of time caring for the child.

One issue of interpretation under this sub-para is the meaning of "child of" the landlord. It must be broader than a child for whom the landlord is "responsible", because under reg 20 only one person can be "responsible" for a child. Logically, it would mean any child of which the landlord was the genetic parent. It will also apply to a child who is adopted, who will not be regarded as being the child of his genetic parents: s39(2) of the Adoption Act 1976 and *Re Collins* [1990] Fam 56, FD. The genetic parents will also cease to be regarded as parents of the child when a freeing order is made under the 1976 Act prior to adoption: *Re C (minors) (Adoption: Residence Order)* [1994] Fam 1, CA. Likewise, any child in respect of whom a parental order has been made pursuant to the Human Fertilisation and Embryology Act 1990 is regarded as being the child of those in favour of whom the parental order is made: see the Parental Orders (Human Fertilisation and Embryology) Regulations 1994 SI No 2767. However, a man who provides sperm for "licensed" treatment under the 1990 Act is not to be regarded as a father of the child: s28(6)(a). In such a case, if the woman receiving treatment has a partner, it is regarded as his child: s28(3).

Those are the statutory presumptions that can be stated with confidence. Other situations are not so clear. It is not clear whether step-children are properly to be regarded as a "child of" the step-parent. It is suggested that unless the step-parent has parental responsibility for the child, the definition does not apply. Any person in whose favour a residence order is made acquires parental responsibility for a child: s12(2) Children Act 1989. Guardians acquire parental responsibility for a child: s5(6) of the 1989 Act. In any of these cases, the child is probably to be regarded as a "child of" the guardian: s5(6) Children Act 1989.

The above discussion concerns the legislation in England and Wales. Scottish family law is to be found in different statutes.

The validity of sub-para (d) was subjected to an attack in *R (Tucker) v Secretary of State for Social Security* [2001] EWHC Admin 260; [2002] HLR 500, CA. Maurice Kay J rejected arguments of invalidity in domestic law on the basis of conflict with the primary legislation governing child support (paras 5-9), that it offended against the principle of legality (paras 10-14), and that it was irrational (paras 15-20). He went on to hold that sub-para (d) did not infringe Art 8 of the European Convention on Human Rights on its own or in conjunction with Art 14 (paras 21-29, discussed further in the commentary to the Human Rights Act 1998 – see p136). The Court of Appeal rejected the claimant's appeal, essentially adopting the same approach as the judge.

Paragraph (1)(e): Liability to connected company or trustee

This sub-para seeks to exclude a number of devices that in the DWP's view have been adopted in the past to circumvent the definition of "owner" in reg 2(1) and an older version of reg 7(1)(a)(i) and (ii) HB Regs 1987. These schemes have typically used the separate legal personality of a company or a trust as a vehicle to hold the freehold or leasehold interest in the home. The sub-para attacks agreements with a landlord that is a trust or a company where there is some connection between the landlord and the claimant or someone close to her/him. For convenience, in the following discussion the landlord is referred to as a "connected" company or trust, A is the claimant and B is the claimant's partner.

Who Must Have the Connection? There are three categories of people that can have a relationship with the connected company or trust that brings the claim within the scope of sub-para (e) (collectively referred to below as "a relevant person"):

(1)   A or B;

(2)   C, who is a "close relative" of A or B who "resides with" A. See reg 2(1) for the definition of "close relative", and reg 3(4) for the issue of whether C "resides with" A. Note that the use of that phrase excludes the argument discussed under sub-paras (b) and (c) above – there is no reference to the sharing of a dwelling in sub-para (e). So if A and B occupy a ground floor flat and C, B's elderly mother, occupies the basement flat, and they share only a kitchen, C may be a relevant person for the purposes of sub-para (e);

(3)   D, who is A or B's former partner. See the discussion in the Analysis to sub-para (c) above, though note that there is no requirement here that the home be the same as the one that D formerly occupied.

Connection With a Company. The legal and everyday uses of the word "company" are different. Many people use the word loosely to denote any arrangement under which people trade in company with other people. In this context, a "company" is a limited company registered under the Companies Act 1985. It is to be distinguished from a trading name or a partnership or firm.

The agreement falls within sub-para (e) if a connected person is a director or an employee of the company. A company is required by ss10(2) and 288 of the 1985 Act to register the names of its directors and any changes therein. The information required includes any other directorships held. Details of a company's directors may be obtained by carrying out a company search. These are held at the relevant Companies House for England and Wales or for Scotland. Company searches are also carried out by many independent organisations providing business services. The registration requirements, however, are frequently flouted and a person may still be treated as being a director of a company even when s/he is not registered as such. A director "includes any person occupying the position of director by whatever name called": s741(1) of the 1985 Act. This may not extend to include a "shadow director". A shadow director is "a person in accordance with whose directions or instructions the directors of a company are accustomed to act": s741(2). However, in *CH 4733/2003*, Commissioner Howell said that it was "for consideration whether the term "director" in reg 7(1)(e) HB Regs 1987 (now reg 9(1)(e) HB Regs) may need extending to include the concept of "shadow director" which it does not ordinarily do": para 37. Apart from those provisions, the term is not defined and the closest that case law has come to a definition is probably the following definition in *Re Forest of Dean Coal Mining Co* [1879] 10 Ch D 451 at 453: "commercial men managing a trading concern for the benefit of themselves and all the other shareholders in it".

A person is not necessarily an "employee" of a company simply because s/he does work for it. It may be that s/he is correctly to be seen as an independent contractor. The principal indicia of a contract of employment are an undertaking to provide work *personally* in exchange for remuneration and a sufficient degree of control by the employer over the employee: *Ready-Mixed Concrete (South East) Ltd v Minister of Pensions and National Insurance* [1968] 2 QB 497, CA. Authorities may find examination of the treatment of the claimant by the tax authorities helpful, but must be careful to reach their own conclusions. In *CH 4733/2003* the commissioner said that the term "employee" has to be understood in the absence of any more extended definition as a person with some form of contract of service or an office holder: para 37.

Connection With a Trust. This is likely to be a much more troublesome concept for authorities to apply, and so a short summary of the nature of trusts will be attempted here. A trust may be defined as a relationship in which property is held by a person or persons (the trustees) for the benefit of a person or persons (known as beneficiaries). The law imposes strict obligations on trustees as to their dealings with the property that is the subject-matter of the trust and requires them to act absolutely in the interest of the beneficiaries. One person may be both a trustee and a beneficiary.

The trust is a flexible concept and trusts range from small trusts of family property right up to huge corporate trusts such as pension funds and charities. Under reg 9(1), it will be mainly the former category of trust with which authorities will be concerned. In England and Wales, where there is a trust of real property, there must be at least two trustees unless the trustee is a trust company.

Trusts may be express or implied. In the case of an express trust, there will be a document setting out the terms of the trust and usually spelling out who the trustees and beneficiaries are, though informal documents may suffice to create an express trust if sufficiently certain. In certain circumstances, the courts may substitute trustees or alter the terms of a trust, including who is to benefit thereunder. Placing property in a trust constitutes a "disposition" of property, and the express trust is therefore only valid if evidenced in writing: see s53(1) Law of Property Act 1925 and s2(1) Law of Property (Miscellaneous Provisions) Act 1989 in relation to trusts created before and after 1989. If there is no document complying with the statutory requirements, then an implied trust may exist. There is nothing in sub-para (e) to prevent it applying to implied trusts. Broadly speaking, implied trusts are of two types. A resulting trust is imposed by the law when Z purchases property, or contributes towards the purchase of property, and it is agreed or understood between the trustees and Z that Z will be entitled to the property or, in the latter case, a proportional interest in it. A constructive trust arises in the absence of an agreement wherever it is unconscionable for the trustees to ignore Z's interests in the property.

This is only the briefest sketch of the law in England and Wales and reference should be made to standard works on equity for a full treatment of the law of trusts. Scottish trusts law has many similarities but also many fundamental differences: see *The Laws of Scotland* (1992) vol 14 para 1 and the full discussion in that volume.

Under sub-para (e), the liability must be to "a trustee". The normal rule in s6(c) of the Interpretation Act 1978 will apply here, so liability to more than one trustee will fall within the scope of the provision. However, it is suggested that the liability must be to a trustee *as such*, otherwise the landlord is not properly described as a "trustee". Where the home is not trust property, the provision does not apply. This is best illustrated with an example. A, X and Y are the joint trustees of a charity assisting the blind. X makes his living by buying, selling and renting property and rents one of his properties to A. Although A's liability to X is to a trustee of a trust of which he is also a trustee, X is not acting as a trustee when he rents the property to A and the agreement does not fall foul of sub-para (e).

The exception. Para (3) applies to cases falling within sub-para (e). See the Analysis to that provision below.

Paragraph (1)(f): Liability to child's trustee
Sub-para (f) excludes liabilities to a trustee, where "his or his partner's child" is a beneficiary under the trust. For an explanation of the trust concept see the Analysis to sub-para (e) above. Again it is suggested that the provision only applies where the liability is to a trustee as such.

"His or his partner's child" is not to be equated with a child for whom either is responsible under Pt 4. It is wider than that. It would appear that it should be interpreted in the same way as the phrase "a child of the person" in sub-para (d): see the Analysis to that sub-paragraph.

Paragraph (1)(g): Liability of former non-dependent
This excludes any claimant (A) who was formerly a non-dependant of someone (B) who continues to live in the dwelling. For the definition of "non-dependant" see reg 3 and the commentary thereto. It appears that A could fall within this provision even if B has never claimed HB. B must, however, reside in "the dwelling": see the Analysis to sub-paras (b) and (c) for the suggested significance of this phrase.

Para (3) applies to sub-para (e): see the discussion below.

Paragraph (1)(h): Former owners
This sub-paragraph applies in any case in which the claimant or her/his partner previously owned the dwelling. Again the phrase "the dwelling" is used: see the Analysis to sub-paras (b) and (c), although the

distinction discussed there is less likely to be of significance in this context. As originally enacted in the HB Regs 1987, sub-para (h) had no application where the claimant has lived elsewhere before returning to the property in question: *CH 716/2002* para 11; *CH 5302/2002* para 14. From 21 May 2001, the harsh effect of the provision was mitigated by applying it only to cases where less than five years have elapsed since the relevant person ceased to own the property. The provision does not have retrospective effect in relation to claims made prior to 21 May 2001, but the five years can start to run prior to that date. A person ceases to own property, in England and Wales in any event, when a sale is completed and not when a contract of sale is entered into. In *CH 3616/2003* para 12, the commissioner decided that there was no longer any reason to hold that the provision should be limited in its effect. This conclusion sits uneasily with the commissioner's view in the earlier decisions that the word "continued" supported a view that the occupation of the property had to be continuous in order for the provision to apply: *CH 716/2002* paras 8-9. Since the regulation had not been amended save as to impose the five-year limit of its operation, it does not seem logical or in accordance with the normal rule of interpretation (that phrases used in previous versions of legislation and retained for present versions should be given the same interpretation as was adopted under the previous version) to give a more restricted meaning to "continued" under the new form. However, in *CH 4733/2003* Commissioner Howell was of the view, albeit *obiter*, that the interpretation placed on the wording of the amended form of reg 7(1)(h) HB Regs 1987 (now reg 9(1)(h) HB Regs) in *CH 3616/2003* was the correct interpretation of the wording both of the amended and the unamended form of regulation 7(1)(h).

Sub-para (h) may apply even if a property has been divided into two separate properties or extended since the claimant owned it: *CH 3616/2003* paras 14-16. So if a claimant continues to occupy only part of the dwelling that was sold then s/he still falls within the scope of this provision because the new dwelling was part of the old dwelling.

Unless the claimant or partner fell within the definition of "owner" in reg 2(1), s/he cannot fall within the provision. Note that there is no requirement that the ownership of the claimant or partner immediately preceded that of the landlord, though it might be possible to make a similar argument as was adopted by the commissioner in *CH 716/2002* para 11 to support a conclusion that an intervening owner or owners would make sub-para (h) inapplicable.

There is an exception for anyone "who satisfies the appropriate authority that he or his partner could not have continued to occupy that dwelling without relinquishing ownership". GM A3.282 suggests that this exception is principally aimed at those who sell their home when a mortgage lender is "on the point of seeking possession". It is arguable that this is too strict an interpretation of the wording of the provision. A claimant who is in substantial mortgage arrears which are mounting (perhaps because IS housing costs do not meet the full mortgage) and who has no realistic prospect of stopping the increase in the arrears could be said to fall within the provision, even if the mortgage lender has not yet got around to taking proceedings. It would not be sound policy to require a claimant to run up a large amount of debt where s/he has a ready solution to the problem.

In *CH 3853/2001*, the claimant had inherited a house from his mother. He felt under a moral obligation to share the property with his sisters. He sold it and divided the proceeds of sale between them, and then agreed with the purchaser that he could continue to live in the property. The commissioner adopted a test (para 16) of whether the claimant was under a "practical compulsion" to sell the property. He held that the claimant was not, since it would have been possible for the claimant to take out a mortgage in order to meet the moral obligation. This will include consideration of both the reasonableness of the sale as well surrounding matters which could have acted to remove the need to relinquish ownership (eg, finding a new or alternative employment or sub-letting part of the property): *CH 1586/2004* (para 12).

The motive of the claimant in disposing of the property is irrelevant in determining the applicability of sub-para (h): *CH 396/2002* para 7. It is also important to note that the "practical compulsion" in *CH 3853/ 2001* does not require some *legal* compulsion to dispose of the property: *CH 396/2002* para 15. However, although the claimant's perceptions may be relevant as evidence of what is actually possible – so that in an exceptional case a claimant may be under so much stress that it is the interests of her/his own mental health to dispose of ownership as quickly as possible without investigating other possibilities short of sale – it has to be borne in mind that the statutory test to be applied is "could not" and not "believes s/he could not": *R(H) 6/07*.

A further important limitation of sub-para (h) is demonstrated by *CH 296/2004*, in which the former owner was the claimant's husband who had left the country at the time that the property was let by the new owner to the claimant. The commissioner held that in order for sub-para (h) to bite, the former owner had to be the claimant's *current* partner: para 31. There was evidence in the case that the husband might no longer be living in the same household as the claimant, which would mean that he was no longer her partner.

Paragraph (1)(ha): Former tenants of long tenancies

This is a similar provision to that in subpara (h). It applies where the claimant or her/his partner was a tenant under a long tenancy of the dwelling, but only where less than five years have elapsed since the tenancy ceased. "Long tenancy" is defined in reg 2(1). There is an exception for anyone who satisfies the appropriate authority that he or his partner could not have continued to occupy that dwelling without relinquishing the tenancy. See above for commentary on the similar exception in subpara (h).

Paragraph (1)(i): Tied accommodation

Where the claimant or her/his partner is employed by the landlord, and it is a condition of the employment that the home be occupied, any liability for rent cannot attract HB. There must be a relationship of employment: see the Analysis to sub-para (e) above. Furthermore the occupancy must be a *condition* of the employment. That means that it must be compulsory and not merely a "perk of the job" or provided by the employer to assist resettlement. Where the claimant or partner has a written contract of employment, it will normally be apparent from the terms and conditions therein whether occupying the property is truly a "condition". Otherwise the best indicator will come from considering the nature of the job: is there something about it which makes residence on a premises necessary? The classic example is a pub landlord.

Sub-para (i) only applies during the period of employment. Once the employment ends, a liability to the former employer for rent may attract HB.

Paragraph (1)(j): Members of religious orders

The words in brackets preclude any argument that the liability for rent prevents the claimant from being "wholly" maintained by the order. However, the maintenance must be whole and not partial.

"Religious order" is not defined. GM A3.256 suggests that a religious order "consists of a group of people who have given up all material belongings and have offered their services free for the benefit of the order". GM A3.257 draws a contrast with religious communities, which "may do paid work or keep their own possessions".

Paragraphs (1)(k) and (4): People in residential care

"Residential accommodation" is defined in para (4). Note also the modifications made by para 9 Sch 3 HB&CTB(CP) Regs (see p1123).

In *CH 1326/2004* (which was dealing with the pre-October 2005 form of paras (1)(k) and (3) of reg 7 HB Regs 1987, but the reasoning may remain applicable) it was accepted that where a person is living in a home run by a person registered to run a care home but is not in fact receiving the care which is contemplated in the registration then para (1)(k) will not apply to that person, as it is the care provided to the person in such a home (and not just residence in such a home) which is key to whether they fall within the meaning of "residential accommodation".

Paragraph (1)(l): Contrived agreements

There is a reference to the HB scheme established under Part 7 of the SSCBA 1992. This would suggest that if the liability was created when one of the predecessor schemes was in force, the provision cannot apply: compare *R(IS) 14/93* para 15.

Authorities need to consider all the evidence and relevant factors in determining whether an agreement is contrived. Apart from the old rent restriction rules, the "contrived tenancy" rule under reg 9(1)(l) has probably given rise to more litigation than any other part of the scheme. The usual trap into which Tribunals fall is to identify one factor which they find particularly persuasive and rely solely on that matter without considering the entire background to the agreement and its contents.

I. GENERAL PRINCIPLES. Before setting out the factors which will usually fall to be taken into account in para 9(1)(l) cases, it is useful to set out some points of general application. First, the meaning of "to take advantage" in this context means "to abuse" and not, as in some other parts of social security legislation such as SSCBA s73(1)(d), to benefit from or to avail oneself of the scheme. If that were the case, no-one could qualify for HB.

In *R v Solihull MBC HBRB ex p Simpson* [1995] 1 FLR 140 at 148E-F, CA, Kennedy LJ in the Court of Appeal cited Sedley J at first instance (1993) 26 HLR 370 at 378 as describing the purpose of the former reg 7(1)(a), (b) and (c) HB Regs 1987 as being "to shut out certain arrangements which, in the Secretary of State's view, would amount to an abuse of the system" and added:

"I believe that to be a correct approach, provided that abuse is not equated with bad faith on the part of the applicant. Bad faith would, of course, be persuasive evidence of abuse, but the appropriate Authority might in some cases properly conclude that there was a breach of regulation 7[(1)(l)] without it. In other words, the use of the words "take advantage" shows that at least in the eye of the beholder there has to be conduct which appears to some extent improper."

In *R v Stratford-upon-Avon DC HBRB ex p White* [1997] 30 HLR 178, QBD, Dyson J criticised this test on a number of grounds. He asked who was to judge whether there was impropriety, by what criteria, and what the policy of reg 7 HB Regs 1987 (now reg 9 HB Regs) was. The decision was reversed on appeal (1998) 31 HLR 126, CA. Mr White was a member of a religious commune, the Jesus Fellowship Church, that required certain categories of members to live in a commune, maximise their income and pool it. The Review Board found that there was a legal liability between Mr White and the Trust set up by the commune for the purposes of reg 6 HB Regs 1987 (now reg 8 HB Regs) but found that the obligation to make payments was "inextricably bound up" with the obligation to pool income. The Court of Appeal, holding that Mr White did not fall foul of subpara (1)(l), endorsed the interpretation of the subparagraph in *Simpson*:

"In my judgement the precise language of subpara [(l)] indicates that there must have been some purposive conduct on the part of those seeking benefit, the liability must appear "to have been created to take advantage". This connotes that something has been contrived or devised for the purpose of taking advantage of or exploiting the scheme. There is no evidence to suggest that Mr White (and, I would add, the landlord) has behaved in such a manner or been motivated by dubious ingenuity to create the liability." (Otton LJ at 137)

"For my part I share the judge's unhappiness at attempts to graft onto the express language of regulation 7(1)[(l)] an additional requirement .... having said that, I have little difficulty in finding in the language of paragraph [(l)] the connotation of an abuse of the housing benefit scheme." (Peter Gibson LJ at 141)

The mere fact that the arrangements between landlord and tenant are unusual and involve the creation of a "device of some sort" does not necessarily lead to the conclusion that the agreement is contrived: *R(H) 7/05* paras 46-47, though obviously the use of such means will call for some sort of innocent explanation.

The second point that must be made is that what is being examined is the *creation* of the liability to make payments. It would follow that the importance of the factors must be judged as at that time and not in the light of events which only became known to the parties subsequently: *CSHB 718/2002* para 33. However, that decision also notes (para 34) that an intention to abuse the HB scheme in the future would suffice to bring sub-para (l) into play. In *CH 3008/2002,* the claimant took a tenancy from a landlord with whom she had no relationship. During the contractual term, the landlord transferred the property to the claimant's sister. The contractual term subsequently expired and a statutory tenancy came into force by virtue of the Housing Act 1988. The commissioner confirmed (para 14) that since the claimant was unrelated to her landlord at the time that the tenancy was created, sub-para (l) could not apply to the creation of the contractual agreement. However, as to whether the liability could be "created to take advantage" of the HB scheme thereafter, he said (para 14):

"But what about the statutory protected [this should probably be 'periodic'] tenancy? The claimant's liability for rent has arisen under that tenancy since 16th July 1995. That tenancy was created by operation of law. How can a tenancy that exists by operation of law have been created with the necessary purpose? One answer may be this. If the sisters allowed the tenancy to come into existence when it could have been prevented, then it may be possible to find that the liability arising under the tenancy was created to take advantage of the scheme."

It is suggested that this is contrary to the wording of sub-para (l). When a statutory periodic tenancy is created at the point that the contractual period elapses, it is created by the Housing Act 1988 and not by the parties. It is hard to see how the parties "create" anything when a statutory periodic tenancy is allowed to come into force; rather, they allow the legislation to extend the tenancy. Moreover, nothing which is said in *R(H) 10/05* about the correctness of parts of *CH 3008/2002* detracts from this argument.

Even if the commissioner is right, extreme caution will be required before it will be legitimate to make a finding along the lines that he indicates. If the tenancy is not an assured shorthold tenancy giving an absolute right to terminate it under s21 of the 1988 Act, the landlord may be powerless to act. As to the tenant, it will be a rare case in which they can be blamed for choosing to stay in existing accommodation rather than face a move into new accommodation.

It should be borne in mind in similar cases that it may be necessary to examine the motivation of the original agreement. Thus, if the relative agreed with the original landlord that the property would be purchased shortly after the original tenancy, it might be possible to find that the original agreement fell foul of sub-para (l) if all the other circumstances justified such a finding.

Finally, there is no presumption against the claimant that s/he is guilty of abusing the scheme: see Sedley J in *Simpson* at 378. Once it is established that the claimant is under a liability to make the payments, the burden of proof is on the authority to show some grounds for believing that abuse exists. The words "the appropriate authority is satisfied" allow the authority to reach its own conclusion on the point but, as elsewhere in administrative law, it cannot make a decision for which there is insufficient evidence or which is not properly reasoned. In *White*, Dyson J suggested that the concept of the onus of proof was unhelpful. However, it may well be useful in cases where evidence is sparse, since if there is not enough information before an authority or a tribunal to give rise to an inference of impropriety, reg 9(1)(l) cannot be applied. If there is enough evidence to allow the inference to be drawn, however, it may then be legitimate to examine whether the claimant has any explanation for the circumstances which do not relate to the obtaining of HB: see Kennedy LJ in *Simpson* at 148F.

A failure by a Review Board to apply the burden of proof under subpara (1)(l) properly was Richards J's primary reason for the quashing of the Board's decision in *R v Greenwich LBC ex p Dhadly* [1999] 32 HLR 829. It is worthy of note that this step was taken even though the Board specifically reminded itself at the start of its statement of reasons that the burden of proof to show the applicability of subpara (1)(l) rested on the local authority. Richards J examined the whole of the decision and considered that it showed that the Board might well not have applied the principle it stated at the outset.

II. OBLIGATIONS OF APPEAL TRIBUNALS. R v South Tyneside MBC ex p Tooley [1996] COD 143 at 144, QBD, Ognall J stated that a Review Board's decision letter relating to a decision that a claimant falls foul of reg 7(1)(l) HB regs 1987 (now reg 9(1)(l) HB Regs) must include the following matters. It is suggested that the same approach is applicable to an appeal tribunal:

(1)   A summary of the claimant's case as to why s/he does not come within subpara (1)(l) (though note there is no presumption against the claimant).

(2)   An account of the evidence, if any, given by the claimant in support of her/his case.

(3)   The conclusion of the Review Board.

(4)   A reasoned statement as to why the Review Board concluded that the tenancy was a contrived one. The facts will often be open to a number of possible interpretations and if a review board concludes that a tenancy is "contrived" its decision must contain a statement of reasons which is sufficiently detailed for the claimant to be able to understand why an adverse interpretation has been preferred to an unfavourable one: see Sedley J in *Simpson* at 378 and *Sier* (Latham J). In *ex p Dhadly*, Richards J also emphasised failures by the Board to deal with aspects of the evidence called and submissions made by the claimant as a reason for quashing its decision. The message is clear: a decision must show that all relevant evidence and factors have been considered or it will be vulnerable to challenge.

It is not essential that an appeal tribunal should consider the intentions of landlord, tenant and any other relevant party separately in every case. What is necessary depends on the facts: *Jones v City of Glasgow DC HBRB* [1997] unreported, 4 July, CSOH.

III. THE RELEVANT FACTORS. Again it must be emphasised that the whole of the circumstances of the case must be considered and that none of the following can be determinative in any one case.

The Means, Circumstances and Intention of the Tenant. A tenant will often have a number of motives or purposes in entering into an agreement to pay rent. The relevant question for the purposes of reg 9(1)(l) is which of these purposes was the tenant's dominant purpose. In *Simpson*, Kennedy LJ observed, at 149A-C:

"Of course [attracting HB] was one of the aims. That is why the applicant properly made inquiries to try to establish if Housing Benefit would be payable before he made the agreement, but it is at least arguable that his dominant purpose when he entered into the tenancy agreement was not to obtain Housing Benefit but to provide accommodation for his family .... In my judgment, the Board had to reject that conclusion if it was to find that the applicant created his liability to make payments to take advantage of the Housing Benefit Scheme ...."

It follows that, subject to what is said below about the circumstances and intentions of the landlord, reg 9(1)(l) cannot apply where the claimant's dominant purpose is to provide a home for her/himself and her/his family. In cases where it is accepted that the claimant and her/his family are actually living in the accommodation, it will often be difficult for the authority to show that this was not the dominant purpose of the tenancy, even when the circumstances surrounding the creation of the tenancy seem to be unusual. Tenants who are reliant on income-related benefits do not have much bargaining power in the housing market and will often have to take whatever is available. This will often be the explanation for cases where relatives have purchased a house and rented it to the claimant. *Simpson* was one such case, where the applicant and his partner had a severely handicapped daughter and lived in unsatisfactory council accommodation. The council were unable to move the family, and the partner's father purchased the home so as to facilitate proximity to schools and the hospital. Other cases of this type are *R v Milton Keynes BC HBRB ex p Macklen* [1996] unreported, 30 April, QBD and *R v Gloucestershire CC ex p Dadds* [1996] 29 HLR 700, QBD.

In particular, it is not sufficient to establish abuse for the authority to show that one or both of the parties knew at the time the agreement was made that the claimant would be unable to pay the rent without recourse to HB. This may be taken into account: Sedley J in *Simpson* at 376; *R v Sutton LBC HBRB ex p Keegan* [1992] 27 HLR 92 at 99-100, QBD; *R v Poole Borough Council ex p Ross* [1995] 28 HLR 351, QBD; *CH 2516/2003* para 4. However, it will rarely be a factor of great weight. Many recipients of HB will be in this position and, as Sedley J stated in *Simpson* at 379:

"To use this fact to deny an applicant benefit is to undermine the whole purpose of the Scheme by making the claimant's need count against instead of for him."

This point was re-emphasised by Peter Gibson LJ in *White* at 142.

However, the converse to this, namely that the claimant did not anticipate having to claim HB when s/he took on the rent liability or has met the liability her/himself from time to time, may often be a very good indication that there was no attempt to take advantage of the HB scheme: Kennedy LJ in *Simpson* at 149E and Otton LJ in *White* at 137.

Whether or not the claimant has sought other accommodation on the open housing market before entering into the tenancy may be relevant in some circumstances but equally it may be entirely reasonable for someone who is offered a tenancy on beneficial terms by a friend or relative to take up that offer without bothering to search elsewhere. The absence of a prior search for accommodation elsewhere does not necessarily mean that the tenant's dominant purpose in entering into the agreement was other than to provide her/himself and any family with a roof over their heads.

In some cases it may be appropriate to consider the conduct of someone other than the tenant: *CH 1419/2005*, para 15. In that case the claimant was a young man who was severely mentally impaired and had severe learning difficulties. His mother worked in the HB section of the local authority and helped her son enter into a joint tenancy agreement with herself and her husband in respect of a flat the claimant had previously lived in with his grandmother. On these facts Commissioner Jacobs accepted that the mother's conduct could in principle be relevant to the question of whether the tenancy had been created to take advantage of the HB scheme. In his view, in a case where a tenant is unable to act wholly independently it is relevant to take account of the motives and purposes of those who help in setting up the tenancy.

The Means, Circumstances and Intention of the Landlord. In many cases the best pointers as to whether an agreement falls foul of reg 7(1)(l) will be found in analysing the landlord's motives. As Peter Gibson LJ said in *White*:

"A liability cannot be created unilaterally, but the reality, as Sir Christopher Slade pointed out in the course of argument, is that the purpose of the landlord is likely to be more significant than that of the tenant who will usually be incurring the liability for the proper purpose of providing himself with accommodation."

The fact that the landlord will make a profit from the rent charged is not conclusive evidence of abuse, as profit is the usual purpose and effect of any commercial letting. However, it is clear from *White* and the decision in *R v Manchester CC ex p Baragrove Properties Ltd* [1991] 23 HLR 337, QBD, that the landlord's intentions and circumstances can give rise to a finding of abuse even in the absence of any complicity or impropriety on the part of the tenant.

In *Baragrove Properties*, the applicant was a property management company managing about 340 houses on behalf of 140 landlords. They applied for judicial review of a policy adopted by the council on October 22, 1990 to the effect that where the rent payable exceeded the "market rent" fixed by the rent officer by 50 per cent plus £20, they would treat tenancies granted to persons covered by an older version of reg 11(3) HB Regs 1987 as having been "created to take advantage of the housing benefit scheme" pursuant to reg 7(1)(l) HB Regs 1987 (now reg 9(1)(l) HB Regs) and therefore no HB would be payable. Where such claimants renegotiated their rents after such a refusal, the council would continue to refuse benefit under reg 7(1)(l) HB Regs 1987 where the new rent exceeded the "market rent" by 50 per cent plus £20 "save in the most exceptional circumstances".

It was not disputed by the applicants that they were deliberately "targeting" these so-called "exempt groups" in terms of offering tenancies by advertising for such tenants and that they were not willing to let the properties concerned to HB claimants outside these groups. Nor would they have been able to levy the sort of rents involved, between twice and five times the "market rent", from non-HB tenants. Further, it was again not disputed that the sole and specific purpose of letting these properties at these rents to "exempt groups" was in order to "charge very high rents which they could not otherwise command". The case must be viewed against these rather remarkable circumstances.

The applicants argued that restrictions on excessive rents were governed by regs 11 and 12 HB Regs 1987 (provisions now found in Sch 3 para 5 of the HB&CTB(CP) Regs – see p1101) and could not therefore be used as the foundation for a refusal under reg 7(1)(l) HB Regs 1987 (now reg 9(1)(l) HB Regs). The respondents argued that these tenancies at these rents simply would not have been created but for the so-called "exemption" provisions of reg 11(3) and that they therefore came within reg 7(1)(l). It was part of the applicant's case that the rent officer set the market rent too low. This was rejected. Stuart-Smith LJ held (at 345-6) that "given that the applicants have been deliberately targeting the exempt groups .... for the purpose of charging very high rents" the creation of such tenancies could fall within reg 7(1)(l).

The tenancies in *Baragrove Properties* were found to be "contrived" even though the tenants did not benefit from the abuse and were unlikely to have been motivated to enter into the agreements by the prospect of extra profits which would accrue to their landlord. It seems to follow that an abusive intention on the part of the landlord can, in an appropriate case, bring the tenancy within reg 9(1)(l) even though the tenant's dominant purpose in entering the tenancy was to provide a home for her/himself and her/his family. In the more conventional case where the focus is on the tenant, it will be important for the authority to investigate what the consequences will be for the landlord if HB is not payable. If the landlord will be forced, or will wish to evict the claimant if rent is not paid and is unable to maintain the property without the receipt of rent, those factors will be suggestive of the agreement not being contrived: *R v Sutton LBC HBRB ex p Keegan* [1992] 27 HLR 92 at 99-100, QBD. However, if the evidence is that the landlord will take a commercial view and will not chase a tenant for rent where it would be uneconomical to do so, that will not justify a finding of contrivance: *R v Stratford-upon-Avon DC HBRB ex p White* [1998] 31 HLR 126.

Prior Relationship of Landlord and Tenant. The fact that the landlord and tenant knew each other or were friends before the tenancy was created, while it may be relevant, is far from being conclusive evidence of abuse. It may be a reasonable and commercial decision for a landlord to let to someone s/he knows, as s/he will be more certain of having a good tenant. Likewise, a tenant may feel more secure with a landlord who is known to her/him. If friends can reach a mutually acceptable agreement, then nothing in reg 9 compels them to go into the market, as long as the tenant's dominant purpose is to provide her/himself and her/his family with a home and the landlord's dominant purpose is to provide accommodation for a reasonable return: see *R v Poole Borough Council ex p Ross* [1995] 28 HLR 351, QBD.

Similarly, it is of little relevance that the parties are related, unless they reside together in which case see sub-para (b). Contrary to what seems to be popular belief, there is no legal rule which prevents members of the same family entering into binding legal agreements with each other, as long as all the parties intend to create legal relations. Again the question is what the dominant purpose of the agreement was at the time it was entered into.

Whether or not the Agreement is Commercial. This is itself a ground for exclusion under sub-para (a), but an agreement which is commercial, but less commercial than is normal may be some indication of contrivance.

The Rent Charged. If the rent payable under the agreement is high in comparison with the market rates prevailing in the area or if the accommodation is larger than is needed by the claimant and any family, then that may be evidence (taken together with other relevant factors) that the liability was created to take advantage of the scheme: see *Dadds* at 705 and *R v Barrow BC ex p Catnach* [1997] unreported, 3 September, QBD. If these are the only factors which suggest abuse, the authority does not need to rely on reg 9 and can instead restrict the claimant's eligible rent under reg 13. Reg 13 (which aims to ensure that rents paid through HB are in the bottom half of the property market) make it difficult to "take advantage" of the scheme by charging an excessive rent.

Where the rent officer has made a valuation which is not much lower than the contractual rent, it will be irrational for the authority to conclude that the agreement is contrived without other factors being present: *Dadds* at 705, where the contractual rent was £95 and the rent officer's assessment was £78.

Paragraph (3): The exception

This sets out an important escape route from sub-paras (e) and (g) (but not the others). The critical concept is again whether the liability "takes advantage" of the HB scheme: see sub-para (l). However, there are critical differences between sub-para (l) and this provision.

The first point is that the burden of proof is on the claimant. However, where there is adequate evidence relating to the issue, this is unlikely to be of great significance: see the discussion under paragraph (l) above.

Secondly, the question for consideration is whether "the liability was intended to be a means" of abusing the HB scheme. It is suggested that this involves the authority in carrying out an inquiry into two matters:

(1)   Is the existence of the liability an abuse of the HB scheme? It is inherent in the language of para (3) that the agreement is actually contrived, as well as that there was the requisite intention.

(2)   Was there an intention to abuse the scheme? In considering this question, particularly close attention must be had to the knowledge of the claimant and the landlord of the HB scheme and its operation. The paradigm case of an intention to abuse the HB scheme is *Baragrove Properties*, discussed above. It does not appear that it is necessary for *both* landlord and tenant to have the requisite intention. It will be sufficient if one of them does. But it is entirely possible that an agreement could be contrived, without landlord or tenant necessarily having intended to produce that result. A bald assertion by the claimant or landlord that there was no intention to abuse the scheme need not be accepted if their actions give the lie to that assertion. Clearly, however, in such a case careful findings of fact and reasons will have to be given by authorities and tribunals.

Persons from abroad

10.–(1)   A person from abroad who is liable to make payments in respect of a dwelling shall be treated as if he were not so liable but this paragraph shall not have effect in respect of a person to whom and for a period to which regulation 10A (entitlement of a refugee to housing benefit) and Schedule A1 (treatment of claims for housing benefit by refugees) apply.

[¹ (2)   In paragraph (1), "person from abroad" means, subject to the following provisions of this regulation, a person who is not habitually resident in the United Kingdom, the Channel Islands, the Isle of Man or the Republic of Ireland.

(3)   No person shall be treated as habitually resident in the United Kingdom, the Channel Islands, the Isle of Man or the Republic of Ireland unless he has a right to reside in (as the case may be) the United Kingdom, the Channel Islands, the Isle of Man or the Republic of Ireland other than a right to reside which falls within paragraph (3A).

(3A)   A right to reside falls within this paragraph if it is one which exists by virtue of, or in accordance with, one or more of the following–

(a)   regulation 13 of the Immigration (European Economic Area) Regulations 2006;

(b)   regulation 14 of those Regulations, but only in a case where the right exists under that regulation because the person is–

    (i)   a jobseeker for the purpose of the definition of "qualified person" in regulation 6(1) of those Regulations, or

    (ii)   a family member (within the meaning of regulation 7 of those Regulations) of such a jobseeker;

(c)   Article 6 of Council Directive No. 2004/38/EC; or

(d)   Article 39 of the Treaty establishing the European Community (in a case where the person is seeking work in the United Kingdom, the Channel Islands, the Isle of Man or the Republic of Ireland).

(3B)   A person is not a person from abroad if he is–

(a)   a worker for the purposes of Council Directive No. 2004/38/EC;

(b)   a self-employed person for the purposes of that Directive;

(c)   a person who retains a status referred to in sub-paragraph (a) or (b) pursuant to Article 7(3) of that Directive;

(d)   a person who is a family member of a person referred to in sub-paragraph (a), (b) or (c) within the meaning of Article 2 of that Directive;

(e)   a person who has a right to reside permanently in the United Kingdom by virtue of Article 17 of that Directive;

[⁵ (f)   a person who is treated as a worker for the purpose of the definition of "qualified person" in regulation 6(1) of the Immigration (European Economic Area) Regulations 2006 pursuant to–

    (i)   regulation 5 of the Accession (Immigration and Worker Registration) Regulations 2004 (application of the 2006 Regulations in relation to a national of the Czech Republic, Estonia, Latvia, Lithuania, Hungary, Poland, Slovenia or the Slovak Republic who is an "accession State worker requiring registration"), or

    (ii)   regulation 6 of the Accession (Immigration and Worker Authorisation) Regulations 2006 (right of residence of a Bulgarian or Romanian who is an "accession State national subject to worker authorisation");]

(g)   refugee;

[⁴ (h)   a person who has exceptional leave to enter or remain in the United Kingdom granted outside the rules made under section 3(2) of the Immigration Act 1971;

(hh)   a person who has humanitarian protection granted under those rules;]

(i)   a person who is not a person subject to immigration control within the meaning of section 115(9) of the Immigration and Asylum Act and who is in the United Kingdom as a result of his deportation, expulsion or other removal by compulsion of law from another country to the United Kingdom;

(j)   a person in Great Britain who left the territory of Montserrat after 1st November 1995 because of the effect on that territory of a volcanic eruption; [³]

[³ (jj) a person in Great Britain who left Lebanon on or after 12th July 2006 because of the armed conflict there; or]

(k)   in receipt of income support or on an income-based jobseeker's allowance.]

(4)   Paragraph 1 of Part 1 of the Schedule to, and regulation 2 as it applies to that paragraph of, the Social Security (Immigration and Asylum) Consequential Amendments Regulations 2000 shall not apply to a person who has been temporarily without funds for any period, or the aggregate of any periods, exceeding 42 days during any one period of limited leave (including any such period as extended).

[²]

(6)   In this regulation–

[²]

''refugee'' means a person recorded by the Secretary of State as a refugee within the definition in Article 1 of the Convention relating to the Status of Refugees.

Modifications

Reg 10(3B)(a) to (e) applies in relation to a national of Norway, Iceland, Liechtenstein or Switzerland or a member of her/his family (within the meaning of Art 2 Council Directive 2004/38/EC) as if such a national were a national of a member state. See reg 10 of SI 2006 No 1026 (p1134).

The amendments made by SI 2006 No 1026 do not affect the continued operation of the transitional and savings provided for in reg 12 Social Security (Persons From Abroad) Miscellaneous Amendments Regulations 1996 (see p1054), reg 6 Social Security (Habitual Residence) Amendment Regulations 2004 (see p1094) or Sch 3 para 6 HB&CTB(CP) Regs (see p1116). See reg 11 of SI 2006 No 1026 (p1134).

Amendments

1.   Substituted by reg 4(2)(a) of SI 2006 No 1026 as from 30.4.06.
2.   Omitted by reg 4(2)(b) and (c) of SI 2006 No 1026 as from 30.4.06.
3.   Amended by reg 5 of SI 2006 No 1981 from 25.7.06 until 31.1. 07 only.
4.   Amended by reg 5 of SI 2006 No 2528 as from 9.10.06.
5.   Substituted by reg 5 of SI 2006 No 3341 as from 1.1.07.

General Note
The scheme of the regulation

This reg has the effect of excluding certain categories of "persons from abroad" from entitlement to HB by deeming them not to be liable to make payments in respect of their home.

Before dealing with this question, however, a prior question may need to be addressed, namely whether the claimant is excluded from benefit altogether under s115 Immigration and Asylum Act 1999 and the Social Security (Immigration and Asylum) Consequential Provisions Regulations 2000 (see pp1026 and 1072) as a "person subject to immigration control". A person falling within s115 of the 1999 Act is barred from HB/CTB unless s/he can take advantage of the provisions in reg 2 of the 2000 Regs. However, even if s/he is not excluded under s115, the second question to address is whether s/he is caught by reg 10, which excludes those defined as "persons from abroad" from HB by deeming them not to be liable for rent. To add to the difficulties, para (4) limits the effect of certain provisions in the 2000 Regs, and modified versions of reg 10 in Sch 3 para 6 of the HB&CTB(CP) Regs (see p1116) limits the effect of reg 10.

To avoid confusion it is thus important to confine the label of "person from abroad" to those falling foul of reg 10. The regulation is a classic example of obscure social security drafting, but once unpicked its meaning is relatively plain. The starting point is para (2), which sets out that a "person from abroad" is a person who is not habitually resident in the UK, the Channel Islands, the Isle of Man or the Republic of Ireland (referred to collectively as the Common Travel Area or "CTA"). Under para (3), however, a person cannot be habitually resident in the CTA unless s/he has a right to reside in the CTA, but a right to reside which falls within paragraph (3A) will not count for these purposes. What paragaph (3A) covers is non-UK EU nationals, for example, for the first three months of their residence in the CTA (para (3A)(a)), or who have never previously worked in the CTA and are here "signing on" and looking for work (para (3A)(b)(i)), but not getting income-based JSA (because if that was the case they would not be a "person from abroad" in any event under para (3B)(k)). But if a person has a right to reside in the CTA which does not fall within para (3A) s/he may still have to show that s/he is habitually resident in the UK as a matter of fact (see further below). This may most obviously apply to UK nationals returning to the UK from abroad. If, however, the person falls within para (3B) then s/he cannot be a "person from abroad", and is exempted for the habitual residence test altogether. Paragraph 3B covers:

(1)   Those with relevant rights of residence under EU law: para (3B)(a)-(f).

(2) Those who have been adjudicated as being refugees under asylum law: para (3B)(g). Note that, perhaps confusingly and unnecessarily, such people are *also* said not to be "persons from abroad" at all under para (1) (see reg 10A and Sch A1 in Sch 4 HB&CTB(CP) Regs – on p1125 – and the special rules for retrospectively dealing with HB claims by refugees).

(3) Those granted exceptional leave to enter or remain: para (3B)(h).

(4) Those who have been deported or removed *to* the UK from another country: para (3B)(i).

(5) Those in receipt of IS or income-based JSA: para (3B)(k).

(6) Certain claimants from Montserrat and (until 31.01.07) the Lebanon: para (3B)(j) and (jj).

(7) Claimants to whom the modified versions of reg 10 in Sch 3 para 6 of the HB&CTB(CP) Regs (see p1116) apply.

(8) Claimants granted humanitarian protection under the immigration rules: para (3B)(hh).

Analysis

Paragraph (2): "Habitually resident in fact"

Along with the restrictions on availability of benefit to certain asylum seekers, the introduction of the habitual residence test in October 1994 has proved to be the most controversial of the restrictions imposed by reg 7A HB Regs 1987 (now reg 10 HB Regs). The test was introduced on the basis of a belief that the UK was suffering from an influx of "benefit tourists" taking advantage of generous welfare provision to fund excursions to the UK, despite the lack of any systematic study to suggest that there was such widespread abuse. A critical report by the Social Security Advisory Committee (Cm 2609) was not accepted by the Government.

The phrase "habitual residence" has been frequently used in international Conventions, many of which have been incorporated into English law by statute. As "habitual residence" does not have a special meaning for HB and CTB purposes (see below), caselaw on the meaning of the phrase in other contexts may be examined to determine the meaning in this context. In particular, there is a large amount of case law on the phrase as used in the Hague Convention on the Civil Aspects of Child Abduction 1980 Art 3 and the Child Abduction and Custody Act 1985. In addition, an identical test was introduced for IS claimants along with the amendments adding the HB and CTB test. There are now many decisions in relation to IS which must be regarded as highly persuasive authority.

Basic principles. The basic principles established by this large body of caselaw are now enumerated below. For a helpful review of the law on habitual residence see *CIS 4474/2003*. The quotations constituting the first two principles are taken from the speech of Lord Brandon in In *re J (a minor) (Abduction: Custody Rights)* [1990] 2 AC 562.

(1) "... the expression "habitually resident", as used in Art 3 of the Convention, is nowhere defined. It follows, I think, that the expression is not to be treated as a term of art with special meaning, but is rather to be understood according to the ordinary and natural meaning of the two words which it contains." This statement was approved and followed in *R(IS) 6/96* paras 17, 20 and *CIS 2326/1995* para 17.

(2) "... the question whether a person is or is not habitually resident in a specified country is a question of fact to be decided by reference to all the circumstances of any particular case". So it has been held that it is not possible to draw up a comprehensive list of factors to be considered: *R(IS) 6/96* paras 17, 20; *CIS 13498/1996* para 9. All the facts of the case must be considered.

(3) It is possible for a claimant to be habitually resident in more than one state at once: *CIS 2326/1995* para 27.

(4) In deciding whether a claimant is habitually resident, authorities and tribunals must examine the whole period down to the date that the decision is made, because the time period between the claim and the decision being made may be sufficient to allow the "appreciable period of time" to have accrued: *CIS 2326/1995* para 29; *CIS 11481/1995* paras 10-12.

(5) It is for the authority to justify a decision that the claimant is not habitually resident. It follows that if no evidence is available to support such a decision, the authority must accept the claimant as habitually resident: *R(IS) 6/96* para 15.

(6) A person cannot be habitually resident unless s/he is resident. If s/he is not resident, there is no need to consider the quality of the claimant's existence here. A future intention to reside here is insufficient: *CIS 15927/1996* paras 6, 9. Residence may be in the Republic of Ireland, the Channel Islands or the Isle of Man (the Common Travel Area or CTA). The residence must be lawful: *R v Brent LBC ex p Shah* [1983] 2 AC 309 at 343H-344B, HL. Residence is not the same as physical presence. One may be resident without being present: see the discussion of loss of habitual residence below. It is possible for a claimant to be resident in more than one country: *CIS 16410/1996* para 10. Likewise, one may be present without being resident. In *R(IS) 6/96* para 19 the following was said:

"Residence to my mind involves a more settled state than mere physical presence in a country, so that a person who is a short stay visitor, or has come here for an operation or to receive medical treatment other than long-term care, is neither resident nor habitually resident. To count as resident, a person must be seen to be making a home here; even though it need not be his or her home, nor need it be intended to be a permanent one, provided that it is genuinely home for the time being."

In many cases, the claimant will not previously have spent any substantial period of time in the CTA. The sole question will then be whether the claimant has acquired habitual residence status. However, there will also be cases in which the claimant was present in the CTA for a substantial period or periods of time before going away to another country. In such cases, the claimant may have been habitually resident in the CTA before s/he left and before considering the present period of residence, it will be necessary to decide whether the status of habitual residence was ever lost: *R(IS) 6/96* paras 31-2; *CIS 8111/1995* para 11. If it was not lost, it will not be necessary for the claimant to show that they have acquired the status during the present period of residence. It is therefore necessary to consider both how the status is acquired and how it is lost.

Acquisition of habitual residence. The starting point is the third point made by Lord Brandon in *re J (a minor) (Abduction: Custody Rights)* [1990] 2 AC 562 at 578G-H:

"... there is a significant difference between a person ceasing to be habitually resident in country A, and his subsequently becoming resident in country B instead. A person may cease to be habitually resident in country A in a single day if he or she leaves it with a settled intention not to return to it but to take up long-term residence in country B instead. Such a person cannot, however, become habitually resident in country B in a single day. An appreciable period of time and a settled intention will be necessary to enable him or her to become so. During that appreciable period of time the person will have ceased to be habitually resident in country A but not yet have become resident in country B."

In essence, therefore, two basic requirements need to be fulfilled: an appreciable period of time must elapse and the claimant must have a settled intention to reside in the UK.

"An Appreciable Period of Time". The need for an "appreciable period of time" to elapse before a person can become habitually resident has been a reasonably constant feature of the caselaw: see *R(IS) 6/96* para 21 and again in *CIS 2326/1995* paras 20-1, despite strenuous argument in the latter case that Lord Brandon's statement was *obiter* and of no assistance in the benefits context. This was confirmed by the majority in *Nessa v Chief Adjudication Officer* [1998] 2 All ER 728 at 733d-g, 743a-e-f, CA, which was an appeal from the latter decision, despite a powerful dissent from Thorpe LJ. *The House of Lords* [1999] 1 WLR 1937, [1999] 4 All ER 677 subsequently upheld the commissioner's decision unanimously. However, it is arguably noteworthy that Lord Slynn, in giving the only substantial judgment of the House of Lords in *Nessa* did not use the word "appreciable". Instead, he stated that it was "plain as a matter of ordinary language [that] a person is not habitually resident in any country unless he has taken up residence and lived there for a period". Although there would be some types of legislation which could not work if there could be a gap between leaving country A and establishing habitual residence in country B, the IS legislation (and hence the HB and CTB legislation) did not fall into that category. He then went on to give some general guidance:

"I do not consider that, when he spoke of residence for an appreciable period, Lord Brandon meant more than this. It is a question of fact to be determined on the date where the determination has to be made on the circumstances of each case whether and when that habitual residence had been established. Bringing possessions, doing everything necessary to establish residence before coming, having a right of abode, seeking to bring family, 'durable ties' with the country of residence or intended residence, and many other factors have to be taken into account.

The requisite period is not a fixed period. It may be longer where there are doubts. It may be short . . . . There may indeed be special cases where the person concerned is not coming here from the first time, but is resuming an habitual residence previously had . . . . On such facts, the adjudication officer may or of course may not be satisfied that the previous habitual residence has been resumed. This position is quite different from that of someone coming to the United Kingdom for the first time." (see *The House of Lords* [1999] 1 WLR 1937, [1999] 4 All ER 677 at 682f-683d)

The decision in *Nessa* therefore settles a number of points. First, unless the claimant falls within the scope of Regulation 1408/71 and can take advantage of the ruling in *Swaddling v Chief Adjudication Officer* (case C-90/97) [1999] 2 CMLR 679, ECJ (see below), the claimant must demonstrate that s/he has resided in the CTA for some period of time.

Secondly, it is confirmed that what the period of time is may vary and depends on the facts of the individual case.

In *R(IS) 6/96* para 28, the commissioner gave examples of periods of time which would normally be necessary for residence to have been for an appreciable period. This approach has been rejected in *CIS 2326/1995* para 24 and *CIS 8111/1995* para 17 as likely to lead to the suggested periods being treated as rules of thumb. In *Cameron v Cameron* [1996] SLT 306 at 313F, CS(IH) it was said that there was no minimum period of residence that could be described as "habitual". This approach was followed in *CIS 2326/1995* para 24. In paras 25-7, the commissioner pointed out that Lord Brandon's statement that habitual residence could not be acquired in a single day had to be seen in the child abduction context, where a child was removed and where intention or preparation for her/him taking up residence in the country where s/he was taken by the abductor have to be ignored. If there is a "sharp-edged" change of residence, where the claimant unequivocally abandons the former state of residence and commits to the CTA, the period may be quite short. In *CIS 4474/2003* the commissioner confirms that what constitutes the required period will depend on the circumstances of the particular case. However, he added that in the general run of cases the period will lie between one and three months, and that cogent reasons would need to be given by a tribunal supporting a decision in which a significantly longer period had been required. However, note that this approach was subsequently doubted by the Tribunal of Commissioners in *CIS 2559/2005* (para 17).

The "length, continuity and nature" of the residence will be relevant to whether it has been for a sufficient period: *R(IS) 6/96* para 21. However, in *CIS 2326/1995* para 26, the commissioner suggested that the period need not be continuous and preparatory acts in other states or preparatory visits to the CTA may be relevant if they are evidence of the claimant's settled intention (see below). It seems to follow from this that a strongly settled intention will tend to reduce the necessary period: *Re B (Minors) (Abduction)* [1993] 1 FLR 993 at 995C-D, FD (Waite J).

The provisions of the United Nations Convention on the Rights of the Child have no direct application here as it does not form part of domestic UK law. However, it can be taken into account in deciding what on the facts of a particular case may amount to a sufficient period: *CIS 1972/2003* para 17.

A "Settled Intention". The claimant must also have a "settled intention" to reside in the CTA. The intention need not be to reside permanently in the CTA: *Shah* at 344C-D, *Cameron* at 313G-I, *CIS 13498/1996* para 12.

Evidence of the claimant having a settled intention will usually come from their actions before entering the CTA and between that time and claiming benefit. However, the actions between the claim and a tribunal hearing may be relied on to show that the intention was always there: *CIS 2326/1995* para 28. In addition, the claimant's behaviour during a previous period of residence in the CTA may assist: *CIS 8111/1995* para 15.

Some factors which may be relevant in assessing whether the claimant has a "settled intention" are:

(1)   The claimant's employment or prospects of employment. The claimant's education and qualifications may be highly significant: *CIS 5136/1995* para 4. A higher proportion of time spent working and a stable job are good evidence for intention to stay. The work done by the claimant's partner may also be relevant, as an imminent offer of work will also be good evidence.

(2)   The claimant's reasons for coming to the CTA. A clear reason for presence will be more likely to demonstrate a settled intention. 1997 GM C13 Annex 3 para 18 gave retirement, studying, medical treatment, visiting relatives or domestic political unrest as examples.

(3)   The claimant's intentions as to where their future lies, which can be shown by an intention to move family and property here.

(4)   Where the claimant's "centre of interest" lies: *CIS 2326/1995* para 22. By this is meant the strength of ties to this country. Is the claimant's immediate family in this country? What about extended family? Are they members of clubs or associations? Where do they hold real or personal property? Have they registered with a doctor? Are they seeking work? Has money been spent in this country with a view to establishing residence?

(5)   The viability of continued residence in the CTA: see below.

(6)   In *CIS 2326/1995* para 17 and the child support case *R(CS) 5/96* para 9 it was stated that while habitual residence has a common meaning in all the statutory contexts in which it occurs, different factors may have different weight in different contexts. In the case of HB, it is suggested that the agreement pursuant to which HB is claimed will be of particular significance. Thus lodgers who can leave at will are less likely to have a settled intention to remain than tenants with statutory protection. The length of any lease or licence may also be relevant.

A Requirement of Viability? In *R(IS) 6/96* paras 28-9, it was suggested that there was an additional requirement, namely that the claimant should be able to demonstrate that they can maintain themselves during the appreciable period without reliance on state benefits. The supposed requirement of viability has been heavily criticised. As was pointed out in *CIS 5136/1995* para 4, it produces an "absurd circularity". A claimant cannot attain an appreciable period and hence be entitled to benefit unless they have had a viable existence, but many claimants cannot have a viable existence unless they receive benefit. This supposed requirement could result in the sick or retired never being habitually resident. It is now reasonably clear that the viability of residence without benefits is not a separate requirement, but is merely another factor giving evidence of settled intention: *CIS 2326/1995* para 28; *CIS 12703/1996* para 10; *CIS 8111/1995* para 20 (where it was said to be of "considerable relevance").

Loss of habitual residence. In *re J*, Lord Brandon stated that habitual residence may be lost in a day, but this will only happen where there is clear, unequivocal evidence of complete abandonment of the state by the claimant: see the comments in *CIS 2326/1995* referred to above. A "temporary absence" from the CTA will not prevent a claimant remaining habitually resident in the CTA: *R(IS) 6/96* para 21; *Shah* at 342D-E. This is so whether the absence is short or long, provided that the absence can be described as "temporary". Holidays will usually be regarded as "temporary": *CIS 5136/1995* para 5 (three weeks); 1997 GM C13 Annex 3 para 29(i) (three months). *CIS 12703/1996* para 7 suggests that an absence was not "temporary" where the return date was uncertain and habitual residence was lost, though this suggestion may be in conflict with *Chief Adjudication Officer v Ahmed* [1994] *The Times* 6 April, CA. A five-year absence lost the claimant her habitual residence status in *CIS 13498/1996* para 16. On the other side of the dividing line was *CIS 14591/1996* in which the claimant and his wife were resident in the UK for 15 months before leaving in October 1994 to be with their daughter-in-law pending her entry clearance. That process took 13 months. The family then returned and the claimant's IS claim was refused. It was held that as the absence abroad had always been intended to be temporary, the claimant had not lost his habitual residence status.

A further point emphasised by Lord Slynn in *Nessa,* in the final section of the passage quoted from above, is the need, when considering a person previously resident in the CTA, to decide whether a previous habitual residence was lost as well as whether a current habitual residence has been gained. It does not follow from Lord Slynn's words that a person who has previously been habitually resident in the UK must *necessarily* be found to be habitually resident here. If habitual residence was established in the state where the claimant lived during her/his absence from the UK, then the claimant will have to again demonstrate an appreciable period of residence to qualify for benefit on her/his return. The proper approach as to whether habitual residence was lost, and if so whether an "appreciable period" was required on a return to the UK, was considered in *CIS 1304/1997*. The commissioner suggested (para 34) that a tribunal should consider three matters:

(1)   Whether the claimant lost her/his earlier habitual residence and, if so, in what circumstances. It was reiterated that a temporary, albeit long-term absence need not lead to the claimant losing habitual residence in the UK. Similarly, if the continuation of a stay abroad is conditional, this may indicate that habitual residence was not lost.

(2)   The links between the claimant and the UK while s/he was abroad. If habitual residence was only lost because of events occurring after the claimant left the UK, that may indicate that no or only a short period is required.

(3)   The circumstances of the claimant's return to the UK.

In *CIS 376/2002* the claimant was a Bengali who had worked for many years in Britain before suffering ill-health. Over the five years prior to his claim, he had spent increasingly long periods abroad and less and less time in the UK. Commissioner Howell held (para 10) that it was appropriate to have regard to the whole of the claimant's history in determining when it could be said that a person with a long-established pattern of residence had been in the UK for a sufficient period. He decided that the claimant had not re-established habitual residence within three days of his return (para 13) but that he had done so less than three months after his return (para 14).

In *re A (Minors) (Abduction: Habitual Residence)* [1996] 1 WLR 25 at 33G, [1996] 1 All ER 24 at 32h-j, FD (Cazelet J), a suggestion that a British expatriate who goes abroad, lives in a community of expatriates and behaves as though he were in Britain remained habitually resident in the UK was rejected.

Persons from abroad, right to reside and EU law. In *Abdirahman and another v Secretary of State for Work and Pensions and another* [2007] EWCA Civ 657, the Court of Appeal rejected appeals by two claimants whose appeals had been dismissed by a Tribunal of Commissioners in *CIS 3573/2005* and others. The claimants were born in Somalia and were nationals of Sweden and Norway respectively and had entered the UK lawfully as EEA nationals. Neither claimant was at the relevant time a worker or economically self-sufficient. One claimed IS, HB and CTB, the other claimed PC. All claims were refused on the basis that the claimants did not have a right to reside in the UK.

The Court of Appeal held, firstly, that being lawfully present in the UK (as the claimants were) was not to be equated with a "right to reside", as UK law made a distinction between a right to reside and any lesser status (including, and here particularly, an EEA national who was in this country having entered lawfully and had committed no breach of immigration law, but who was not a 'qualified person' under the Immigration (EEA) Regs 2000). Following the logic of the Court of Appeal's decision in *Barnet LBC v Abdi* [2006] EWCA Civ 383 – in which the court held that if a person ceases to be a qualified person he no longer has an entitlement to reside in the UK – the claimants in this case, although lawfully present, did not have a right to reside, under UK law, at the time relevant to the appeals, because they were not qualified persons. Moreover, nothing in the ECSMA Treaty of 1953 conclusively militated against this conclusion, even when read in isolation. But the provisions of the EU Treaty were of more direct relevance. Having considered Art 18 of that Treaty, Directive 90/364/EEC, and ECJ caselaw thereunder (especially *Trojani* (Case C-456/02)

– the Court of Appeal noting with approval the view of the Advocate General in that case that "the basic principle of Community law is that persons who depend on social assistance will be taken care of in their own Member State"), the Court of Appeal concluded that Art 18 does not create a right of residence for an EU citizen in another member state, in a case in which the limitations imposed under Directive 90/364 are not satisfied, and where those limitations are proportionate to the legitimate objective in protecting the public finances of the host member state. Seen form this perspective, ECSMA could not properly be read as imposing obligations on states more onerous than those imposed by Art 18 as regards rights of residence.

This then left the claimants' second argument, based on Art 12 of the EC Treaty and that article's prohibition on discrimination. The Tribunal of Commissioners had found that the claimants' cases fell within Art 12 and thus called for the discrimination in not awarding them benefit on the grounds of nationality to be justified, but had found such justification. However, in the Court of Appeal's view the appeals did even get that far as the claims did not come "[w]ithin the scope of application of this Treaty", which are the opening words of Art 12. The benefits themselves were not within the scope of the Treaty. Furthermore, nor was the right to reside test within scope. The Court of Appeal recognised that the EC Treaty does speak of a right of residence, in Art 18, so such a right could be within the scope of application of the Treaty. However, Art 18 is qualified in its ambit, and did not here give the appellants any direct EU law right of residence. That was clear from consideration of the caselaw referred to above. The only case in which a person had been found to have a right of residence based on EU law, rather than under national law, was *Baumbast (Case C-413/ 99)*, but there Mr Baumbast was economically self-sufficient. However, *Trojani* showed that an EU citizen, lawfully present in another member state, but not economically self-sufficient, does not, merely by virtue of lawful presence in that state, acquire a Treaty-based right of residence. In the present cases, as the Court of Appeal had already held, neither appellant had a right of residence based directly on EU law. The 'scope of application of the Treaty', for the purposes of Art 12, will include both cases where a right of residence arises directly under the EC Treaty and those where it arises separately under the domestic law of the member state, but it does not extend to cases where no right of residence exists under either the EC Treaty or the relevant domestic law. It followed from this that the right claimed by the appellants did not fall within the scope of application of the Treaty, and so Art 12 had no application. Even if it did, however, the discrimination was justified.

What *Abdirahman* shows is that unless an EU national has a positive right to reside in the UK under EC Directive Directive 2004/38 which falls within paragraph (3B) then they be excluded form HB and CTB.

EC Directive 2004/38

EC Directive 2004/38 came into effect on 30 April 2006. It is a codifying measure which seeks to bring together the many previously disparate provisions of EU law concerning residence rights within the EU. It repeals and replaces many previous Directives (eg, Directive 68/360/EEC) and amends EC Regulation 1612/ 68. It is now the key starting point for determining the residence status of non-UK EU nationals in the UK; and thus their entitlement to HB and CTB.

Parags (3), (3A) and (3B) of reg 10 HB Regs seek to bring Directive 2004/38 into effect in Great Britain for the purposes of HB entitlement. The effect of these three paras is that it is only if the non-UK EU national can bring her/himself within para (3B) that s/he has a right to reside which will exempt them from the habitaul residence test altogether.

Given that the breadth of learning on EU residence law and benefits cannot properly be captured here, the commentary below seeks to focus on the the main qualifying routes to having a right to reside under paragraph (3B).

Paragraph (3B)(a): Workers

Workers: most of the caselaw under EC Regulation 1612/68 will remain relevant here.

The word "worker" is a label rather than a description and can include many categories of claimants who are not working at the time they claim benefit. Freedom of movement for workers and their families is one of the fundamental principles of EU law. As such, a liberal interpretation must be given to the phrase: *Levin v Staatssecretaris van Justitie* (Case 53/81) [1982] ECR 1035 at 1049, para 13, ECJ.

The word is not defined. The word is to be construed in accordance with EU law rather than domestic law: *Unger v BBDA* (Case 75/63) [1964] ECR 177 at 184, ECJ; *Levin* at 1049, paras 11-12. The leading case on this is now *Collins v Secretary of State for Work and Pensions* Case C-138/02, *The Times* 30 March 2004, ECJ, reported as *R(JSA) 3/06*. The key point it makes on Regulation 1612/68 is that the claimant must be a worker, not merely a person seeking work. The latter do not acquire rights under Regulation 1612/68 Art 7(2) (a point now given added force by the terms of para (3A)(b)(i) of reg 10): see also *Centre Public d'Aide Sociale, Courcelles v Lebon* (Case 316/87) [1987] ECR 2811 at 2839, para 27, ECJ; *R v Secretary of State for Social Security ex p Sarwar, Getachew, Urbanek and Urbanek* [1995] 7 Admin LR 781 (see below), QBD. As to the sort of work that makes someone a "worker", see *Lawrie-Blum v Land Baden-Wurtternberg* (Case 66/85) [1986] ECR 2121 at 2144, paras 17-21, ECJ discussed below. However, in *Collins* a careful distinction was made between what may be termed "pure" work-seekers (ie, those coming to work in the UK for the first time or after a very long break from any previous work in the UK), who are not workers under Regulation 1612/68 Art 7(2) (but may be for other parts of Regulation 1612/68), and those who have worked in the UK before, are temporarily out of work and are seeking work, who may be workers under Regulation 1612/68 Art 7(2): a distinction which quite significantly qualifies *Lebon*. Two questions thus arise: what sort of work may make someone a "worker", and what requirements are there for the acquisition or loss of the status?

(1)   The work must be "genuine and effective" rather than "marginal or ancillary": *Levin* at 1050, para 17. This will be a question of fact in each case. GM C13 Annex 4 para 4 suggests five factors which need to be weighed in deciding whether the work is "genuine and effective". To the extent indicated below, these provide a useful guide but it must be stressed that *all* the relevant factors must be taken into account. None will be decisive of itself.

(a)   The period of employment. The shorter the period of employment, the less likely it is that the status of "worker" is acquired, but it will not require a long period of employment to acquire the status. The minimum period should generally be no longer than a few months and may be substantially shorter.

(b)   The number of hours worked. A person may be a "worker" even if they only work part-time but there will be a point at which the length of time spent working is so short that the work can be described as a "marginal" part of the claimant's life. In *Rinner-Kuhn v FVW Spezial-Gebanderingung GmbH* (Case 127/88) [1989] ECR 2743, ECJ, a claimant working 10 hours per week was a worker and in *Kits van Heijerungen v Staatssecretaris van Justitie* (Case C-125/89) [1990] ECR I-1753, ECJ, a man working four hours per week was not. In *R(IS) 12/98* para 15, an au pair who had worked for 13 hours a week for a modest wage plus board and lodging was held to be a worker.

(c)   The level of earnings. If there is no remuneration, a person cannot be a worker: see below. However, the fact that the level of earnings is not sufficient to maintain the worker without recourse to benefit is not relevant to whether the work is "genuine and effective": *Kempf v Staatssecretaris van Justitie* (Case 139/85) [1986] ECR 1741 at 1751, para 15, ECJ. The same should arguably be true where the claimant is earning less than a subsidence wage: *URSSAF v Hostellerie Le Manoir SARL* (Case C-3/90) [1991] ECR I-5531 at 5541, para 8, ECJ. However, recently in *CH 3314/2005* Commissioner Rowland has separated out the question of whether the search for work is "genuine" from whether it is "effective", and in respect of the latter held that reference can be had to whether a person will continue to need to have recourse to social assistance even if he or she finds the work they are looking for in order to decide if the work is "effective". The commissioner was not, however, referred to case C-3/90, and it is therefore suggested that his conclusion on this (arguably *obiter*) point may need to be be treated with some caution. Remuneration may also be in kind: *Steymann v Staatssecretaris van Justitie* (Case 197/87) [1988] ECR 6159.

(d)   Whether the work was regular or erratic. Periods of work and unemployment will not prevent the acquisition of worker status: *Monteil v Secretary of State for the Home Department* [1983] Imm AR 149 at 152, IAT. However, some types of job where the worker is only given work at the whim of the employer may be too ancillary. For example, in *Raulin v Minister van Ondervijsen Wetenschappen* (Case C-357/89) [1992] I-ECR 1027, ECJ, the claimant was a waitress who made herself available, and was to be paid only when her employer required her services.

(e)   Whether the person has become voluntarily unemployed. The reasons for such unemployment should be carefully examined, but if there is no valid explanation other than a desire to gain benefit, this will generally be a strong factor indicating that the status of worker has not been acquired, particularly where the period of the work was very short and it is clear that the claimant is attempting to abuse her/his EU rights: *Lair v Universitat Hannover* (Case 39/86) [1988] ECR 3161 at 3191, para 43, ECJ. Involuntary unemployment will not mean that a claimant loses worker status, and voluntary unemployment may not have this effect if it is clear that the claimant is actively seeking further employment: *R(IS) 12/98* paras 22-3. The question is "whether the circumstances of the leaving, and in particular the person's intentions and actions at the time, indicate that the person was still in the labour market or not": *R(IS) 12/98* para 21; *CIS 16410/1996* para 14.

Generally, the claimant's intentions as to the effect of their work are irrelevant: *Levin* at 1052, para 11, except possibly where there is "objective evidence" of such abuse as was referred to in *Lair*. There may be some primary motive for the work other than the gaining of remuneration. All depends on whether the work actually done is genuine and effective. Thus a trainee may be a "worker" if the practical duties they perform are of "some economic value": *Lawrie-Blum* at 2144, para 18. A member of a religious community carrying out the duties prescribed by the community, including DIY and helping with the community's activities, may be a worker: *Steymann* at 6173, para 13. However, sheltered employment, where the sole objective is to rehabilitate the employee following disability, may not be sufficient: *Bettray v Straatssecretaris van Justitie* (Case 344/87) [1989] ECR 1621 at 1637, para 10, ECJ.

(2)   There must be an employment relationship where the worker accepts directions from an employer. Thus the self-employed are not workers: *Middleburgh v Chief Adjudication Officer* (Case C-15/90) [1991] ECR I-4655 at 4682, para 13, ECJ, though note that such claimants may have rights of residence under Directive 2004/38 (see below). Although whether someone is a worker must be determined according to EU law, this test is the same as that provided for by English law and domestic authority may be of some assistance.

(3)   There must be remuneration in return for the work done. But see the comments above for whether this needs to be sufficient to avoid recourse to subsistence benefits. Further, the remuneration need not be paid by the employer: *Bettray* at 1637, para 12 (sheltered employment paid for in part by government).

As to other requirements, it is clear that one can only be a worker if one is a national of a member state of the EU: Regulation 1612/68 Arts 1, 7. Whether a person is a national of a certain state is governed principally by the domestic law of that state.

The status of a worker under EU law arises as a result of the principle of freedom of movement for workers and a person does not acquire the status until the rights are exercised. Thus a UK national who has worked in the UK but nowhere else is not a worker: *Koua Pourrez v CAF* (Case C-206/91) [1992] ECR I-6685 at 6706, paras 10-13, ECJ. The same is true of a UK national who has worked in the UK and other non-EU states. It is not enough if those rights might hypothetically be exercised at some time: *Moser v Land Baden-Wurttenberg* (Case 180/83) [1984] ECR 2539 at 2547, para 18, ECJ. Furthermore, a person is only a worker if work has been carried out in the host state where the right is sought to be enforced: *Raulin* paras 17, 19. Thus a UK national who has never worked in the UK but only in France cannot enforce rights as a worker as against the UK authorities. This principal was applied in *R(IS) 3/97* paras 14-15, where the claimant was an Irish national who had worked in France prior to coming to the UK. He was not a worker as far as entitlement to IS was concerned. The commissioner described the decision in *Raulin* as "surprising" (para 15) but it is binding on authorities and tribunals. On the other hand, all periods of work carried out in the host state may be relied upon to show worker status and not just the most recent: *Raulin* para 19.

When does a person cease to be a worker? Periods of sickness or unemployment do not mean that the worker loses that status, provided that the worker can prove that s/he is still part of the labour market or will be when s/he recovers: *Giangregorio v Secretary of State for the Home Department* [1983] Imm AR 104 at 110-1, IAT; *R(IS) 3/97* para 13. This is clarified and added to by Directive 2004/38/EC Art 7(3). A person will remain a worker (or a self-employed person – see below):

(1)   while s/he is temporarily incapable of work as a result of an illness or accident. Curiously, pregnancy is not separately included, which may give rise to an Art 14 challenge under the Human Rights Act. The incapacity must relate to the claimant and not an ill child the claimant is caring for: *CIS 3182/2005*;

(2)   if s/he has worked for more than a year, is involuntarily unemployed and is registered as a jobseeker with the relevant employment office; or

(3)   for the first six months of involuntary employment after completign a fixed-term contract of less than 12 months or having become involuntarily unemployed within the first 12 months, as long as s/he has registered as a jobseeker with the relevant employment office.

Likewise, a year's imprisonment will not have the effect of removing worker status: *Monteil.*

On the other hand, those who become students (without continuing part-time employment) can only retain their status as workers if there is some link between their studies and work previously carried out, unless the person was involuntarily unemployed before taking up the vocational training (Directive 2004/38 Art 7(3)(d)). Provided this link exists, the study and work need not be in the same state: *Bernini v Minister van Ouderings en Wetenschappen* (case C-3/90) [1992] ECR I-1071 at 1106, para 21, ECJ.

Paragraph (3B)(e): Former workers

Former Workers: Regulation 1251/70 and Article 17 of Directive /2004/38/EC. These provisions give certain former workers the right to remain permanently in the territory of the host state. Three categories of former workers enjoy the rights:

(1)   A worker who has reached pensionable age, who has been employed in that state for the last 12 months and has resided there continuously for more than three years. Only work in the host state counts: *R(IS) 3/97* para 16.

(2)   A worker who ceases to work as a result of permanent (as opposed to merely temporary) incapacity. In addition, the worker must have *either* resided continuously for two years in the host state *or* be entitled to a pension for which an institution of the state is at least partly responsible. The latter condition could be fulfilled by receipt of incapacity benefit, industrial disablement benefit or severe disablement allowance in the UK, or if the employer is a public employer an occupational ill-health pension would appear to suffice.

(3)   A worker who has worked and resided for three years in the host state before working in another member state, while retaining her/his residence in the host state and returning there at least once per week.

Paragraph (3B)(d): Family members of workers or the self-employed

If a person has a right to reside either as a worker (see above) or a self-employed person (see below) the following relatives of the person also have a right to reside with a "right to install themselves" with workers, regardless of their nationality and gain a right to reside:

(1)   Spouses and registered civil partners, and descendants who are *either* under 21 *or* are dependants: Directive 2004/38 Art 2(2). A cohabitee is not a spouse: *Netherlands v Reed* (Case 59/85) [1986] ECR 1283 at 1300, para 14, ECJ. Whether someone is a "dependent" is a question of fact: *Lebon* at 2839, para 24. The dependency must pre-date arrival in the UK: *R v Secretary of State for the Home Department ex p Yennin* [1995] Imm AR 93 at 96, QBD (Harrison J).

(2)   Dependent parents or grandparents of the worker or her/his spouse or partner: Art 2(2)(d) .

The right of residence is derived from EU law and not from a residence permit itself, so a claimant need not have a residence permit: *Procureur du Roi v Royer* (Case 48/75) [1976] ECR 497 at 514, para 31, ECJ

A relative of the spouse of an EC national is "dependent" on the latter if s/he is not in a position to support her/himself and has a need for material support in her/his state of origin at the time when applying to join the EC national. A host member state may require proof of this, but a mere undertaking by the EC national or her/his spouse to support the relative will not suffice to establish the existence of real dependence: *Jia v Migrationsverket* (Case C-1/05), 9 January 2007, unreported (ECJ).

The permit may be revoked on public policy, security or health grounds and also where the holder of the permit is no longer a qualified person or family member of a qualified person: para 15(2). It is not necessary for the spouse or dependent to be living with the national with the right of residence and there may be complete alienation (though a spouse will lose her/his right on divorce): *Diatta v Land Berlin* (Case 267/83) [1985] ECR 567 at 589-590, paras 8-11, ECJ. The validity of the permit is not affected by absence of up to six months or military service: Directive 2004/38/EC Art 11(2).

Paragraph (3B)(b): The self-employed

Rights of Residence: Article 7(1)(a) of Directive 2004/38/EC

This takes the place of Directive 73/148. The self-employed or those seeking to provide services have a right to reside. This will not apply to those who are merely seeking opportunities to become self-employed: see the Northern Ireland Commissioner's decision in *CIS 10/1995*. In *R(IS) 6/2000* Commissioner Mesher considered the case of a French national who returned to the UK while she was pregnant. She placed an advert in a newspaper advertising French tuition. It was argued that she had a right of residence under Directive 73/148. The commissioner held that the conclusions and reasoning in *CIS 10/1995* could not be accepted in their entirety. He stated (paras 29-31) that there had to be a right of residence before a self-employed person actually began to trade in order to give effect to the community objective of freedom of movement. Thus a person taking preparatory steps to setting up her/his business would acquire a right of residence under Directive 73/148. He then considered whether a claimant with an intention to trade, but who had not yet taken any steps towards doing so, could qualify.

"The difficult question is whether the right extends not merely to those who are taking steps towards offering their services to the public (or whatever final step is appropriate to the nature of the business) in a Member State, but also to those who wish to do that, but have not yet taken any steps beyond arriving in the Member State concerned. In my judgment, it does not. It would be going further than justified by the purposes of the Directive to extend a right of residence, rather than the mere right of entry to the Member State under Article 3, to such persons. It also seems to me that the crucial factor is not so much whether the person's intentions are for the present or for the future or are conditional in some way, but whether the person is taking steps towards offering services to the public, or otherwise setting up as a self-employed person." (para 31)

Their permits are valid for five years and are automatically renewable. They are not affected by absence for less than six months or on military service.

For the position of spouses, civil partners and dependent of the self-employed person, see above.

EU nationals wishing to be recipients of services in other member states were previously covered by Art 1(1)(b) of Directive 73/148, but Directive 2004/38/EC is silent about recipients as is reg 10 HB Regs. This probably does not matter as recipients of services have a right to reside under EC Treaty Arts 49 and 50. "Services" are normally provided for remuneration: EC Treaty Art 60; *R v Westminster CC ex p Castelli and Tristan-Garcia* [1995] 8 Admin LR 73 at 92E-F, QBD (R Henderson QC) (EU national cannot seek to be recipient of NHS services to show right of residence). Examples of services which may be sought are tourism, business, education and medical treatment: *Luisi v Ministero del Tesoro* (Cases 286/82, 26/83) [1984] ECR 377 at 403, para 16, ECJ. Their permits are valid for the duration of the provision of the services: Art 4(2).

The limitations of the derivative residence rights under Arts 49 and 50 for those seeking to claim benefits were revealed in *CIS 3875/2005*. The Commissioner accepted that the provision of accommodation, social services and medical services are all capable of falling within the scope of Art 50. However, two important limiting factors then have to be considered. Firstly, the services must normally provided for remuneration. Secondly, Art 50 does not apply where a national of a member state goes to the territory of another member state and establishes her/his principal residence there in order to provide or receive services there for an *indefinite* period: *Steymann v Staatssecretaris van Justitie (Case 197/87) [1988] ECR 6159* and *Sodemare SA v Regione Lombardia* (Case C-70/95) [1997] ECR 3395. The residence right conferred by Arts 49 and 50 only arises if the services are being sought for a temporary period. However, from a practical perspective, establishing that fact would itself undermine any claim (for the habitual residence test) that the claimant had a settled intention to remain in the UK. In addition, the right to reside for recipients of services can only arise if the claimant came to the UK in order to receive services here, and not simply whether the claimant travelled to the UK in circumstances where it was likely that he or she would receive services even if that was not the purpose of the journey.

Paragraph (3B)(f)(i) and(ii): registered and authorised workers

Rights of residence: A8 Nationals registered as workers and A2 Nationals in authorised work.
Unless they have worked legally in the UK for a continuous 12-month period or in registered employment in the UK for 12 months or more, under this rule nationals of the Czech Republic, Poland, Hungary, Estonia, Latvia, Lithuania, Slovakia and Slovenia will only not be a person from abroad (and thus not excluded from HB and CTB) while in registered employment. A similar rule applies to Bulgarian and Romanian nationals in specified (limited) types of authorised employment.

All challenges to these special rules for A8 and A2 nationals have to date failed. Most notably in *Zalewska v Department for Social Development* [2007], unreported, 9 May where the Court of Appeal in Northern Ireland rejected an argument that an A8 national who had claimed IS after she had ceased working in registered employment for less than 12 months was protected by Art 7(2) of EC Regulation 1612/68. The court ruled that the effect of the Annexes to the Accession Treaty was to modify the impact of the rights of migrant workers under Art 39 of the EC Treaty and Arts 1-6 of Regulation 1612/68 so as to enable national rules to be applied to regulate A8 nationals access to the state's employment markets (following the Court of Appeal's refusal of leave decision in *D* [2004] EWCA Civ 1468). Of their very nature, these differential rules were intended to be, and were allowed to be, discriminatory. Once an A8 national had been admitted to the labour market in the UK (by taking up registered employment) then s/he would be a "worker" and fall under the protection of Art 7(2) of Regulation 1612/68 (now a worker covered by para (3B)(a)). However, the central question in the appeal was whether Ms Zalewska remained as a "worker" and so protected when she made her claim for IS. It was clear that the status of A8 nationals was intended to be different from that of other EU nationals and it was clearly not the intention of the Act of Accession to tie the hands of national authorities as to how they regulated their national labour markets. As the relevant Annexes to the Accession Treaty made plain, an A8 national properly admitted to the UK's labour market for 12 months would acquire full EU "worker" rights. But as the UK had been left to determine the conditions in which an A8 national has been properly admitted to the labour market for 12 months, whether Ms Zaleskwa had or had not had to be determined by considering UK law. That law showed that in order to be properly admitted to the labour market Ms Zaleskwa would need to have been in registered employment for 12 months before her claim for IS, which she had not. Following *D*, the registration scheme was a reasonable and proportionate concomitant of the permitted derogation. Further following *D*, if, during the 12-month period, an A8 national worker ceases to qualify as a worker (by ceasing registered work) s/he falls within the derogation from Art 39 of the Treaty and Art 7(2) of Regulation 1612/68 and so ceases to be protected by either.

Note that although *Zalewska* is a decision of the Court of Appeal in Northern Ireland and so is not binding on tribunals or commissioners in Great Britain, it should generally be followed as a matter of comity by those bodies in GB unless there are exceptional reasons for not doing so (*R(SB) 1/90* and *R(IB) 4/04*).

Rights under EU agreements. Certain claimants have sought to rely on association agreements made by the EU with non-member states which confer rights of residence on the nationals of the non-member states in certain situations. In *CJSA 4705/1999* paras 15-20, an attempt was made to rely upon the EU-Turkey Association Agreement but that failed because the claimant was not "lawfully resident" in this country. That decision was followed in *CJSA 3702/2002* para 7.

Paragraph (3B)(g): Refugees

Prior to 15 October 1996, a "refugee" was defined as being a person who came within the meaning of that term under the Convention Relating to the Status of Refugees. In *CIS 564/1994* paras 23-4 it was confirmed that a person who fulfilled the criteria under the Convention for being a refugee was a refugee even if the immigration authorities had yet to decide so. The suggestion to the contrary was described as "callous, unprincipled nonsense". Had that definition remained in place, it would therefore have been necessary for authorities and tribunals to decide for themselves whether a claimant was a refugee.

From that date, the definition in para (6) took effect, so that a person is only a "refugee" when the Secretary of State has recorded him as such. When this is done, the claimant is sent form GEN 22. There is special provision for the often lengthy period while refugees had their claims for asylum determined: see reg 10A and Sch A1 in Sch 4 of the HB&CTB(CP) Regs on p1125.

Paragraph (3B)(h): Persons granted exceptional leave to remain or enter

Exceptional leave to remain (ELR) is usually granted by the Secretary of State to claimants for asylum whose claims fail, but who can show compelling humanitarian reasons why they should not be deported. ELR is typically granted for a year initially and may then be extended for three years at a time. Those granted ELR are issued with form GEN 19 by the Home Office which shows when the leave expires.

A person with ELR who applies for an extension before the expiry of their leave is deemed to have ELR until the Secretary of State determines the application, but if they fail to apply in time they become overstayers.

Paragraph (3B)(k): Claimants in receipt of IS or income-based JSA(IB)

Note that a person "on income support and income-based jobseeker's allowance" includes those who are entitled but not being it due to a sanction, or on her/his "waiting days" or because of the "loss of benefit" provisions: reg 2(3).

Similar, though not identical, tests for "persons from abroad" appear in the Income Support (General) Regulations 1987 reg 21(3), Sch 7 para 17 and the Jobseeker's Allowance Regulations 1996 reg 85(4), Sch 5 para 14. The view expressed in previous editions of this book that if the claimant is receiving either of these benefits then the authority is not entitled to refuse benefit on the ground that s/he is a person from abroad following *R v Penwith DC ex p Menear* [1991] 24 HLR 115, QBD, was expressly rejected by the Deputy Commissioner in *R(H) 9/04* . In the Deputy Commissioner's view *Menear* is only authority for the proposition that an authority is bound by the DWP decision on income and capital: para 24. However, he went on to stress (para 39) that although the authority is not precluded from disagreeing with the DWP's decision on whether the claimant is a person from abroad, it is not obliged to decide the issue from scratch in every case and may follow the DWP decision in the absence of anything to compel them taking a contrary view.

Equally, if the DWP finds that a claimant is a person from abroad and refuses IS or JSA(IB), then the authority is still under a duty to determine the HB claim. Moreover, if the information is not complete, the authority ought to ask the claimant to supply it and not blindly follow the decision-maker's decision. Notwithstanding these qualifications, or the fact that the decision has been reported, it is respectfully suggested that *R(H) 9/04* is wrong in saying that an authority can come to to its own view about whether a claimant is a person from abroad even if that person is in receipt of IS. To start with, the views expressed by the Deputy Commissioner on this point are plainly *obiter*, as no question arose in that case of whether the claimant was a person from abroad. More importantly, however, the terms of reg 10(2) and (3) when read together, it is suggested, show that if a person is in receipt of IS, and so falls within para (3), s/he cannot by the terms of para (2) fall within para (2), and so s/he cannot be a person from abroad. However inapt the analogy with *ex parte Menear* may have been in previous editions of this book (as it is only authority, as *R(H) 9/04* rightly holds, for the proposition that the means tests cannot be applied by a HB authority if the claimant is already in receipt of IS), it is suggested that the view in those previous editions, that a person in receipt of IS cannot be refused HB (or CTB) on the basis that s/he is a person from abroad, was and remains sound. The only exception to this may be where the IS award was obtained by fraud: *R v South Ribble DC HBRB ex p Hamilton* [2000] 33 HLR 102, CA.

Paragraph (3B)(j): Claimants from Montserrat

So long as the claimant left Montserrat after 1 November 1995, and it was due to the catastrophic volcanic activity on that island, they cannot be a "person from abroad". There is no requirement that the claimant came straight into the UK from Montserrat.

Claimants to whom the modified versions of reg 10 apply (exemption 6)

See p1116 for the commentary to those provisions in Sch 3 para 6 HB&CTB(CP) Regs.

Entitlement of a refugee to Housing Benefit
[¹ 10A]

Modification

Reg 10A was inserted by Sch 4 para 2(1) of the HB&CTB(CP) Regs (see p1126). It only applied to claims for HB by some refugees. See also Sch A1 inserted by Sch 4 para 2(2) of the HB&CTB(CP) Regs.

Amendment

1. Lapsed by s12(2)(e) of the Asylum and Immigration (Treatment of Claimants, etc.) Act 2004 (for those recorded as refugees after 14.6.07).

PART 3
Payments in respect of a dwelling

General Note on Part 3

This Part of the regulations deals with the type of payments (and the amount of these) in respect of which HB may be paid. The power to make such regulations is granted by SSCBA s130(2).

The starting point in deciding whether a particular payment will attract HB is reg 11(1), which confirms that HB is to be paid in respect of all those payments set out in reg 12(1). Categories of payments which HB will not meet are set out in regs 11(2) and 12(2). Note also SSCBA s130(2) which confirms that there is no power to make regulations extending HB coverage to council tax payments (which, of course, are met by CTB), or payments under mortgages or heritable securities in Scotland (which can be met as housing costs under the IS, JSA(IB) or PC schemes).

Regs 13 and 14 deal with the schemes for restricting "eligible rent". It is important to note carefully the extensive transitional protection that exists in relation to these regulations and the local housing allowance provisions being piloted in Pathfinder areas (for which see reg 13A).

Note that the local housing allowance (LHA) provisions are to be introduced nationwide from April 2008 with the current form of the rules continuing to apply until a specific event occurs or until April 2009 if that is later. The new LHA provisions will be slightly different from those being operated in the Pathfinder areas. At the time of writing, the amended rules were only available in draft form.

Eligible housing costs

11.–(1)   Subject to the following provisions of this regulation, housing benefit shall be payable in respect of the payments specified in regulation 12(1) (rent) and a claimant's maximum housing benefit shall be calculated under Part 8 (amount of benefit) by reference to the amount of his eligible rent determined in accordance with regulations 12(3) and (7) and 13 (rent and maximum rent).

(2)   Subject to paragraph (4), housing benefit shall not be payable in respect of payments made by a person on income support or an income-based jobseeker's allowance whose applicable amount for that benefit includes an amount in respect of those payments.

(3)   Where any payment for which a person is liable in respect of a dwelling and which is specified in regulation 12(1) (payments of rent for which housing benefit is payable), is increased on account of–

(a)   outstanding arrears of any payment or charge; or

(b)   any other unpaid payment or charge,

to which paragraphs (1) to (3) of that regulation or Schedule 1(ineligible service charges) refer and which is or was formerly owed by him in respect of that or another dwelling, a rent rebate or, as the case may be, a rent allowance shall not be payable in respect of that increase.

(4)   Where a person who has been awarded housing benefit in respect of a dwelling becomes entitled to income support or an income-based jobseeker's allowance and his applicable amount for the purpose of calculating his entitlement to that benefit includes an amount in respect of a payment made by him in respect of that dwelling, the payments made by him in respect of that dwelling shall continue to be eligible for housing benefit for a period of 4 benefit weeks beginning with the benefit week after the date on which he becomes entitled to income support or an income-based jobseeker's allowance.

Modifications

Modification of reg 11 is provided in Sch 10 para 3 in relation to Pathfinder Authorities who are administering the pilot housing allowance scheme, as from the date specified in relation to each authority as specified in Sch 10 Part 1 (see p511).

Definitions

"applicable amount" – see s135 SSCBA.
"benefit week" – see reg 2(1).
"dwelling" – see reg 2(4) and s137(1) SSCBA.

"eligible rent" – see reg 12.
"rent allowance" – see s134(1A) SSAA.
"rent rebate" – see s134(1B) SSAA.
"payment" – see reg 2(1).
"person on an income-based jobseeker's allowance" – see reg 2(3).
"person on income support" – see reg 2(1).

General Note
Even if payment is covered by para (1), no HB may be paid in respect of it if paras (2) or (3) apply.

Analysis
Paragraph (1): The general rule
The general rule is that HB is payable in respect of all those categories of payment set out in reg 12(1). As will be seen from the commentary on that regulation, a wide variety of payments can be met by HB. Reg 12(3) sets out the payments which together comprise the claimant's eligible rent for HB purposes.
Paragraphs (2) and (4): Exclusion for payments met by IS or JSA(IB)
This sub-para excludes payment of HB in respect of payments which are already covered by IS or income-based JSA. Para (4) provides an exception to this rule for persons already receiving HB for a dwelling who become entitled to IS or income-based JSA with an applicable amount that includes amounts in respect of payments made for that dwelling, eg where they buy a home that they formerly rented. In that situation, HB may continue to be paid for an overlap period of four benefit weeks. The extra HB paid can be deducted from the IS due for that period.
Paragraph (3): Exclusion for increased rent to cover arrears
In the financial year 1991/92 a number of local housing authorities introduced rent setting arrangements for their dwellings that increased a tenant's weekly rent to include an amount in respect of her/his outstanding arrears from the existing or former tenancy. Para (3) provides that where a claimant's liability in respect of a dwelling is increased on account of outstanding arrears or unpaid sums which are owed or formerly owed by the claimant in respect of the current or former dwelling, then HB is not payable in respect of that increase. Nevertheless as a result of the rules relating to the housing authority's housing revenue account contained in Part VI of and the Schedule to the Local Government and Housing Act 1989, an authority has to increase the general level of rents for all tenants as the result of its need to provide for, or write off, bad debts and rent arrears. The general increase in rents due to such provision remains eligible for HB.

Cases where maximum housing benefit expires
11A

Modification
Reg 11A is inserted by Sch 10 para 4. It only applies to Pathfinder Authorities who are administering the pilot local housing allowance scheme, as from the date specified in relation to each authority as specified in Sch 10 Part 1 (see p511).

Rent
12.–(1) Subject to the following provisions of this regulation, the payments in respect of which housing benefit is payable in the form of a rent rebate or allowance are the following periodical payments which a person is liable to make in respect of the dwelling which he occupies as his home–

(a) payments of, or by way of, rent;
(b) payments in respect of a licence or permission to occupy the dwelling;
(c) payments by way of mesne profits or, in Scotland, violent profits;
(d) payments in respect of, or in consequence of, use and occupation of the dwelling;
(e) payments of, or by way of, service charges payment of which is a condition on which the right to occupy the dwelling depends;
(f) mooring charges payable for a houseboat;
(g) where the home is a caravan or a mobile home, payments in respect of the site on which it stands;
(h) any contribution payable by a person resident in an almshouse provided by a housing association which is either a charity of which particulars are

entered in the register of charities established under section 3 of the Charities Act 1993 (register of charities) or an exempt charity within the meaning of that Act, which is a contribution towards the cost of maintaining that association's almshouses and essential services in them;

(i) payments under a rental purchase agreement, that is to say an agreement for the purchase of a dwelling which is a building or part of one under which the whole or part of the purchase price is to be paid in more than one instalment and the completion of the purchase is deferred until the whole or a specified part of the purchase price has been paid; and

(j) where, in Scotland, the dwelling is situated on or pertains to a croft within the meaning of section 3(1) of the Crofters (Scotland) Act 1993, the payment in respect of the croft land.

(2) A rent rebate or, as the case may be, a rent allowance shall not be payable in respect of the following periodical payments–

(a) payments under a long tenancy except a shared ownership tenancy [¹];

(b) payments under a co-ownership scheme;

(c) payments by an owner;

(d) payments under a hire purchase, credit sale or conditional sale agreement except to the extent the conditional sale agreement is in respect of land; and

(e) payments by a Crown tenant.

[¹ (f)   payments by a person in respect of a dwelling where his partner is an owner of that dwelling.]

(3) Subject to paragraphs (4), (5) and (7), the amount of a person's eligible rent shall be–

(a) the maximum rent where a maximum rent has been, or falls to be, determined in accordance with regulations 13 (maximum rent); or

(b) except where sub-paragraph (a) applies, the aggregate of such payments specified in paragraph (1) as that person is liable to pay less–

　(i) except where he is separately liable for charges for water, sewerage or allied environmental services, an amount determined in accordance with paragraph (6);

　(ii) where payments include service charges which are wholly or partly ineligible, an amount in respect of the ineligible charges determined in accordance with Schedule 1; and

　(iii) where he is liable to make payments in respect of any service charges to which paragraph (1)(e) does not apply, but to which paragraph 3 (2) of Part 1 of Schedule 1 (unreasonably low service charges) applies in the particular circumstances, an amount in respect of such charges determined in accordance with paragraph 3(2) of Part 1 of Schedule 1.

(4) Where the payments specified in paragraph (1) are payable in respect of accommodation which consists partly of residential accommodation and partly of other accommodation, only such proportion thereof as is referable to the residential accommodation shall count as eligible rent for the purposes of these Regulations.

(5) Where more than one person is liable to make payments in respect of a dwelling, the payments specified in paragraph (1) shall be apportioned for the purpose of calculating the eligible rent for each such person having regard to all the circumstances, in particular, the number of such persons and the proportion of rent paid by each such person.

(6) The amount of the deduction referred to in paragraph (3) shall be–

(a) except in a case to which sub-paragraph (c) applies, if the dwelling occupied by the claimant is a self-contained unit, the amount of the charges;

(b) in any other case except one to which sub-paragraph (c) applies, the proportion of those charges in respect of the self-contained unit which is obtained by dividing the area of the dwelling occupied by the claimant by the area of the self-contained unit of which it forms part;

(c)   where the charges vary in accordance with the amount of water actually used, the amount which the appropriate authority considers to be fairly attributable to water, and sewerage services, having regard to the actual or estimated consumption of the claimant.

(7)   In any case where it appears to the authority that in the particular circumstances of that case the eligible rent as determined in accordance with the preceding paragraphs of this regulation is greater than it is reasonable to meet by way of housing benefit, the eligible rent shall be such lesser sum as seems to that authority to be an appropriate rent in that particular case.

(8)   In this regulation and Schedule 1 (ineligible service charges)–

''service charges'' means periodical payments for services, whether or not under the same agreement as that under which the dwelling is occupied, or whether or not such a charge is specified as separate from or separately identified within other payments made by the occupier in respect of the dwelling; and

''services'' means services performed or facilities (including the use of furniture) provided for, or rights made available to, the occupier of a dwelling.

Modifications

Modification of reg 12 is provided in Sch 10 para 5 in relation to Pathfinder Authorities who are administering the pilot local housing allowance scheme, as from the date specified in relation to each authority as specified in Sch 10 Part 1.

A different version of reg 12 is substituted and used to determine eligible rent for some claimants entitled to HB on 1 January 1996. See Sch 3 paras 4 and 5(1) HB&CTB(CP) Regs (p1101).

Definitions

"claimant" – see reg 2(1).
"co-ownership scheme" – see reg 2(1).
"dwelling" – see reg 2(4) and s137(1) SSCBA.
"housing association" – see reg 2(1).
"croft" – see "owner", reg 2.
"long tenancy" – see reg 2(1).
"maximum rent" – see reg 2(1).
"owner" – see reg 2(1).
"payment" – see reg 2(1).
"rent rebate", "rent allowance" – see ss134(1A) and (1B) and 191 SSAA.
"shared ownership tenancy" – see reg 2(1).

Amendment

1.   Amended by reg 2(4) of SI 2007 No 1356 as from 1.10.07.

General Note

This reg deals with the payments that may be met by HB and how much may be met. The structure of the regulation is as follows:

Paras (1) and (2) define those payments which qualify as rent, and therefore in respect of which HB, by way of rent rebate or allowance, may be paid. Paras (3) to (7), together with reg 13 and Sch 1, deal with the question of how much of the "rent" is to be "eligible" for the calculation of HB. Para (8) defines the terms "services" and "service charges" for the purposes of this reg and Sch 1.

The provisions as now found in reg 13 were introduced with effect from 2 January 1996. Certain claimants continue to have transitional protection and must have their eligible rent determined in accordance with the pre-1996 rules. See the commentary to Sch 3 paras 4 and 5 of the HB&CTB(CP) Regs on p1101.

Analysis

Paragraph (1): The Payments that Qualify for HB

In the same way that many people use "rent" as a portmanteau term for most types of payments that they make in return for occupying their home, the HB Regs use it as a convenient shorthand for various categories of payments. Some claimants may make payments falling into more than one of these categories, all of which will be eligible.

In order to attract HB, however, the payments must be "periodical". Thus in *CH 2329/2003*, the claimant and his wife were paying all the outgoings on their daughter's property while she was abroad. It was held that there was a commercial agreement: see the commentary to reg 9(1)(a) above. The payments made to the mortgagees on behalf of the daughter, therefore, could be met by HB, but the commissioner held that one-off payments for repairs fell outside the scope of the scheme (para 9). Discussing reg 10 HB Regs 1987 the commissioner said:

"For the occupier's payments to or on behalf of the landlord to come within the scope of regulation 10 they must, therefore, be made at regular intervals and be of an ascertainable amount so that the weekly rental figure can be calculated in accordance with regulation 69 of the regulations." Regs 10 and 69 HB regs 1987 are now regs 12 and 80 HB Regs.

For the issue of whether payments are those a person is "liable to make", see reg 8. For the question of whether a dwelling is occupied as the home, see reg 7.

Subpara (a). "Rent" in this sub-para, of course, refers to rent properly so-called and not merely some payment that the claimant refers to as rent and which does not fall into one of the other categories. It refers, therefore, to payments made to a landlord under a tenancy. Subject to the provisions for excluding certain categories of payment from eligible rent, it will include all payments described as or deemed to be rent in the tenancy agreement.

Subpara (b). The main indicators of a tenancy are that exclusive occupation is granted to the tenant or tenants for a certain period in return for periodic payments of rent. However, many claimants such as lodgers will not have tenancies because they have not been granted exclusive occupation of the premises. This is most obviously the case with lodgers, but may occur in cases where the landlord is not obviously resident. Although this can create headaches in other areas of law, such claimants occupy under a licence and so qualify for HB under subpara (b). The use of the word "permission" is probably aimed at cases of tolerated trespassers, where no formal licence is granted but the landlord agrees to refrain from seeking possession for a period.

Reg 10 HB Regs 1987 (now reg 12 HB Regs) was the battle-ground between authorities and the Jesus Fellowship Church, following the leading cases on liability for rent and contrived tenancies (see the commentary to regs 8 and 9). In *R v Milton Keynes CC HBRB ex p Saxby* [2000] unreported, 11 August, QBD; [2001] 33 HLR 82, CA, the courts were concerned with a claim by an Elder of the church. In broad terms, condition 4 required both "style 3" members (who are the rank and file members of the communities) and Elders (who are the heads of the communities and licensees of the trust property) to pay £55 to the common purse. Condition 6 required Elders to ensure that the payment due to the church's central trust fund from the common purse of £30 per resident, including themselves, was made.

The Board held that the Elder's liability for rent was that payable under condition 4 and not that under condition 6. Hidden J held that to be a wrong approach; the payments under condition 6 were sufficiently connected with the licence held by the Elders to enable it to be a payment "in respect of" that licence. The Court of Appeal upheld his decision. Hale LJ said:

"15. The argument is therefore about whether 'payments in respect of a dwelling which he occupies as his home' means 'payments in respect of his own (or his own and his family's) occupation of a dwelling as his home'. This would be to rewrite both section 123(1) of the Act and regulation 10(1). The non-dependant deduction provisions make it quite clear that the payments may relate to a dwelling in which other people also live. It would be strange indeed, and most unfair, if an Elder could only make a claim based upon his own contribution to the common purse, but then suffer fixed non-dependant deductions for all the adult residents (indeed that was what the local authority had earlier decided in this case).

16. It is also quite clear that the clause 6 payments made by the Elders are the rent paid by them, as licensees, in respect of their licence to occupy the house. They have to make those payments irrespective of whether or not the residents make their clause 4 payments: it is not therefore the simple transmission of payments made by others."

It should, however, be noted that it would appear that the full amount of each condition 6 payment has to be made by the Elder. If that is so, the amount of HB payable may fall to be restricted under the rent restrictions provisions.

Subparas (c) and (d). "Mesne profits" in England and Wales are the damages for which a former tenant whose lease is forfeit may be liable to pay as compensation for depriving the landlord of the use or occupation of her/his land. They are usually assessed according to the ordinary letting value of the land. These categories of payment cannot include any interest which a claimant has been ordered to pay a landlord by a court: *R v Kensington and Chelsea RBC ex p Brandt* [1995] 28 HLR 528, QBD.

In Scotland, "violent profits" are damages which a possessor of land in bad faith is liable to pay to the true occupier. They are assessed according to the profit the latter could have made from letting the land during the period s/he was dispossessed, plus compensation for any damage caused.

Payments for "use and occupation" is another phrase borrowed from the law of real property. Such payments are assessed by a court in the same way as mesne profits except that they are paid by a trespasser for use of the land rather than a former tenant. Sub-para (d) is to be interpreted as referring to payments for use and occupation in that sense rather than according to the normal meaning of those words which might include payments that must be made as an incidence of the occupation. In *R v Bristol CC ex p Jacobs* [1999] 32 HLR 841, QBD (Owen J), the claimant was liable to pay water rates as a consequence of her tenancy and argued that the rates fell within sub-para (d). The argument was rejected but leave to appeal was granted.

In *CH 844/2002*, for which see the notes to sub-para (f) below, the commissioner thought that a boat licence fee giving permission to use the boat on waterways fell within sub-para (d): para 13. That decision does not refer to the analysis in *ex p Jacobs* and it is suggested that it is erroneous.

Subpara (e). "Service charges" are defined by para (8). The payments must be made in return for "services", also defined in para (8). Under this sub-para only those charges paid as a condition of occupying the premises are treated as rent. Thus if it is something the landlord provides at the tenant's request, it is not a service charge. The payments must be periodical, which means that they must relate to a specified period. The periods need not be even, however, and they need not correlate to the periods over which rent is paid.

Para (3)(b) further restricts the category of charges which may be so treated by reference to Sch 1. The schedule renders certain charges ineligible even if paid as a condition of occupying the premises. Pt 2 deals with charges for fuel, which are generally ineligible, and Pt 1 with other charges. See the commentary of Sch 1 for full details.

Subpara (f). "Houseboat" is not defined in the HB legislation but the following definitions from tax law may be of assistance in any case of doubt:

". . . . a boat or similar structure designed or adapted for use as a place of permanent habitation." (s367(1) of the Income and Corporation Taxes Act 1988)

".... a boat or other floating decked structure designed or adapted for use solely as a place of permanent habitation and not having means of, or capable of being readily adapted for, self-propulsion." (Sch A1 para 3(4) of the Value Added Tax Act 1994)

This provision was considered by Commissioner Williams in *CH 844/2002*, which concerned the question of whether the claimant could claim HB in respect of the cost of a mooring permit and a boat licence fee payable to British Waterways. The commissioner held (para 8) that a houseboat did not necessarily have no engine and could be capable of movement. The commissioner also held (para 13) that "mooring charges" could cover both a houseboat certificate granted by the British Waterways Board as well as a mooring fee.

Subpara (g). Again, "caravan" and "mobile home" are not defined. This sub-para will cover all payments, not just for the space occupied by the caravan or mobile home. It will cover things like charges for electricity supply, toilet and shower facilities etc. Payments by mobile home owners are regulated by the Mobile Homes Act 1983. *CH 3110/2003* makes the valuable point that if the claimant's home does not count as a caravan or a mobile home (in this case it was a prefabricated chalet type structure resting on the land), s/he should nevertheless be entitled under regulation 12(1)(a) to housing benefit to meet the rent paid in respect of the land on which the home stands because it will count as "rent" for which s/he is "liable to make [periodical payments] in respect of the dwelling which he occupies as his home": per regulation 12(1). The fact that the rent was called "ground rent" was irrelevant, since the tenancy of the land was not a "long tenancy" falling within reg 12(2)(a) (the rent under such a tenancy ordinarily being called "ground rent").

Subpara (h). The "register of charities" is kept by the Charity Commissioners. "Exempt" charities are those listed in Sch 2 to the 1993 Act. This includes certain universities and colleges, the Church Commissioners, societies registered under the Industrial and Provident Societies Act 1893, and the Friendly Societies Act 1896. A registrar maintains a list of those bodies registered under each of those Acts.

Subpara (i). This is self-explanatory.

Subpara (j). This relates to agricultural land in Scotland. See the commentary to reg 2(4)(d).

Paragraph (2): Payments that do not Qualify

Para (2) sets out further categories of ineligible payments. "Long tenancy", "co-ownership scheme" and "owner" are all defined in reg 2 and reference should be made to the commentary to that regulation for a detailed discussion, particularly in relation to ownership which is an issue that arises very frequently. Note that since 1 October 2007, the exception for shared ownership tenancies applies to all such tenancies (ie, private sector shared ownership leases as well as shared ownership tenancies granted by a housing association or a housing authority).

Apart from that the categories are largely self-explanatory. Crown tenants have their own scheme to assist with rent: see the commentary to reg 2.

Paragraphs (3) to (6): Calculation of eligible rent

These paras, in combination with reg 13, set out the complex system of determining the claimant's "eligible rent" upon which a claimant's maximum HB is based (subject to discretionary increases for where there is hardship): reg 70. The following stages need to be followed in making the calculation:

(1)   Under para (4), where the accommodation occupied by the claimant is not solely residential accommodation, only that portion of the payments referable to the residential element can form part of the "eligible rent". This will typically arise in the case of accommodation that has both residential and commercial parts.

(2)   Under para (5), where the claimant is jointly liable to make certain of the payments set out in para (1), an apportionment must be made: see the separate commentary to this provision below.

(3)   Where a maximum rent has been determined (or falls to be determined) under reg 13, then this is the eligible rent: para (3)(a). The deductions set out in para (3)(b), which are steps (5) to (7), are *not* to be applied. Note, however, that the rent officer in making her/his determinations in respect of a property will have already dealt with eg ineligible service charges. See the commentary to reg 13 and the Rent Officers (Housing Benefit Functions) Order 1987.

(4)   If para (3)(a) does *not* apply, then eligible rent is the aggregate of the payments under para (1) that a person is liable to pay, less the deductions set out in para (3)(b)(i)-(iii). The first is a deduction for water, sewerage and allied environmental services, which is not made if (as is usually the case) a claimant is liable for such services separately from her/his tenancy. If the deduction is to be made, the rules are set out in para (6). If the claimant lives in a self-contained unit, the whole of the charges are disallowed under para (6)(a). If the dwelling is not self-contained, a share of the charges is paid. This is calculated by dividing the total area of the unit in which the dwelling is contained (such as a block of flats) by the area of the dwelling: para (6)(b). It seems that common parts are included in the total area of the unit for the purposes of this calculation. If in either case, the amount of the charges varies, then the authority may deduct a sum that is fairly attributable to charges: para (6)(c).

(5)   The second deduction is in respect of ineligible service charges. This is determined under Sch 1 para 1: see the commentary to that provision.

(6)   Finally, under para (3)(b)(iii), a deduction must be made in respect of certain service charges. They must be charges not falling within sub-para (e) because occupation of the property is not conditional on payment. They must also be charges in respect of which the local authority has decided that the amounts levied are unreasonably low. See the commentary to Sch 1 para 3(2). The amount identified under that provision must be deducted.

Paragraph (5): Apportionment of joint liabilities

This is only to be carried out if there is a joint liability, as where all three tenants in a property have signed the tenancy agreement. If each of the tenants had a separate tenancy agreement with the landlord, no apportionment is appropriate. The local authority has a discretion to decide the proportions to be attributed to each person. It may not be appropriate to divide the amounts equally. This will be the case, for example, where one person occupies a much larger room than another. Particular regard must be paid to the number of such persons and to the amounts paid by each, but the weight given to the latter could be reduced, for example, where it was clear that the division of the amounts had been arranged deliberately to maximise benefit entitlement.

A problem that has arisen is whether a person who is deemed not to be liable for rent by virtue of regs 9, 10 or 56 must be excluded from the apportionment exercise under para (5). In *R (Naghshbandi) v Camden LBC* [2001] EWHC Admin 813; [2003] HLR 280, CA, Rafferty J decided that the apportionment must be between the people who are actually liable to pay the rent and any deemed non-liability should be ignored for the purposes of reg 10(5) HB Regs 1987 (now reg 12(5) HB Regs). Rafferty J's decision was upheld by the Court of Appeal [2003] HLR 280.

In *CH 3776/2002*, the elderly claimant was a joint tenant of a property with his son, who had moved out some considerable time previously. He was no longer in contact with the son. He was in poor health. The local authority assessed his HB on the basis that he was liable for half the rent and he appealed.

Commissioner Jacobs first dealt with an argument for the claimant that he could be treated as liable for the son's share of the rent under reg 6(1)(c) HB Regs 1987 (now reg 8(1)(c) HB Regs) as well as his own share under reg 6(1)(a) (now reg 8(1)(a) HB Regs) and that no apportionment could therefore be made. He held that reg 10(5) HB Regs 1987 (now reg 12(5) HB Regs) required apportionment only of actual liabilities rather than liabilities which were deemed to exist under reg 6(1) HB Regs 1987: para 37 of the decision.

He then went on to consider the discretion as to apportionment and concluded that the whole of the rent should be apportioned to the claimant: para 60. He gave useful general guidance on the exercise of the discretion:

(1)   The proportion of the rent that had been paid by each joint tenant might be an important factor, but was not an overriding or even the predominant factor in every case: para 45.

(2)   The right to respect for the home under Art 8 of the European Convention on Human Rights was a relevant consideration: para 53. It was not determinative. Unless a failure to pay full HB would be a breach of Art 8.1, it is hard to see what the relevance of the Convention would be.

(3)   The paragraph specifies the number of tenants and the total rent paid as relevant: para 54.

(4)   The ability of the tenants to pay was relevant, but did not of itself justify placing a disproportionate responsibility on the claimant for HB: para 55.

(5)   The views of the landlord as to whom is expected to pay in practice are relevant, but the fact that a landlord has foreborn to enforce the full rent pending the outcome of a dispute about HB should not be held against the claimant: para 56.

(6)   Whether the claimant could be expected to move might be relevant. This would involve consideration of issues such as the claimant's age, state of health, connections with the local area and the availability of property in the locality: para 58.

The commissioner pointed out that it was possible for the local authority to make a different apportionment for a limited period only to give the claimant a fair chance to move or to find another co-tenant: para 57. However, caution needs to be exercised over the latter course because most tenancies strictly control the right of the tenant to get another person into the property.

The commissioner also stated that it was possible for an apportionment to be changed if a change of circumstances occurred: para 63. On present authority (see the commentary to Sch 7 para 11 CSPSSA), an authority can of course make its decision afresh on every new claim, with the claimant having a right of appeal to a tribunal if dissatisfied.

Paragraph (7): Restriction of eligible rent

Para (7) contains a general discretion to reduce the eligible rent still further. The power to reduce the eligible rent under para (7) is additional to any deductions made under reg 13 or the foregoing provisions of this regulation. Save for those claimants with transitional protection, the generality of the power enables authorities to ensure that HB should not be paid on any rent above a level which the authority considers to be reasonable in any particular case – even where the rent has already been restricted, or the claimant would otherwise be protected, under reg 13. In the case of council tenants, this provision could be used where the claimant is occupying a property larger than reasonably required, even though the rent is reasonable for that particular property. However, caution will be required where a rent officer's assessment has already restricted the claimant's rent. After all, that process should mean that the claimant's rent has been reduced to a reasonable level already.

Para (7) raises a number of questions of judgment that must be considered rationally. If the authority or tribunal reaches a decision that no sensible decision maker could reach then it may be held to be vulnerable to attack on appeal. There is no restriction in the paragraph as to which factors may be taken into account and so all facts relevant to the making of a deduction may be considered. No fixed rules or policies may be adopted. It is clear from the wording of the provision that each case must be considered individually. Decision makers should be prepared to give coherent reasons for imposing a further reduction.

In *R v Macclesfield BC HBRB ex p Temsamani* [1999] unreported, February 24, QBD, the High Court confirmed that an authority may properly reduce the eligible rent even where the Rent Officer has not given a significantly high rent determination provided that it has sufficient evidential basis to do so.

It was confirmed in *R (Laali) v Westminster CC HBRB* [2002] HLR 179, QBD, that when deciding whether or not to make a reduction under reg 10(6B) HB Regs 1987 (now reg 12(7) HB Regs), the claimant's personal circumstances were relevant. The Review Board had therefore been in error to disregard the claimant's need to live in St John's Wood because his daughter lived nearby, because of the length of time he had lived in the area, because the accommodation was all on one floor and hence more suitable for him (he was disabled) and that he was unable to pay a deposit or rent in advance on another property. The authority's contention that those matters fell to be considered on an application for an exceptional hardship payment pursuant to a former version of reg 61 HB Regs 1987 (since substituted) was rejected, though permission to appeal was granted.

Eligible rent and the maximum rent (standard local rate) 12A

Modification

Reg 12A is inserted by Sch 10 para 6. It only applies to Pathfinder Authorities who are administering the pilot local housing allowance scheme, as from the date specified in relation to each authority as specified in Sch 10 Part 1 (see p511).

Maximum rent

13.–(1)   Where an authority has applied to the rent officer for a determination in accordance with regulation 14 (requirement to refer to rent officers) and a rent officer has made a determination or redetermination in exercise of the Housing Act functions, the maximum rent shall be determined in accordance with paragraphs (2) to (17).

(2) In a case where the rent officer has determined a claim-related rent, but is not required to notify the authority of a local reference rent or a single room rent, the maximum rent shall be that claim-related rent.

(3) In a case where the rent officer has determined and is required to notify the authority of a local reference rent, the maximum rent shall not exceed twice that local reference rent.

(4) Subject to paragraph (5), in the case of a young individual–

(a) except where sub-paragraph (b) applies, where the rent officer has determined a single room rent and is required to notify the authority of it, the maximum rent shall not exceed that single room rent;

(b) where–

    (i) the rent officer has determined a single room rent and a claim-related rent and is required to notify the authority of them;

    (ii) the claim-related rent includes payment in respect of meals; and

    (iii) the single room rent is greater than the claim-related rent less an amount in respect of meals determined in accordance with paragraph 2 of Part 1 of Schedule 1 (ineligible service charges),

the maximum rent shall not exceed the claim-related rent less that amount in respect of meals.

(5) Paragraph (4) shall not apply in the case of a claimant–

(a) to whom paragraph 4 of Schedule 3 to the Consequential Provisions Regulations (saving provision) applies;

(b) to whom paragraph 14 of Schedule 3 (severe disability premium) applies; or

(c) who has a non-dependant residing with him.

(6) Subject to the limits specified in paragraphs (3) and (4), in a case where the rent officer has determined both a local reference rent of which he is required to notify the authority and a claim-related rent, and–

(a) the claim-related rent is higher than the local reference rent, the maximum rent shall be the local reference rent;

(b) the local reference rent is higher than the claim-related rent, the maximum rent shall be the claim-related rent.

(7) Subject to the limits specified in paragraphs (3) and (4), in a case where the rent officer has determined a local reference rent of which he is required to notify the authority, but has not determined a claim-related rent and the reckonable rent is more than the local reference rent, the maximum rent shall be the local reference rent.

(8) In a case where–

(a) the authority has determined a maximum rent in respect of a dwelling; and

(b) during the award of housing benefit the reckonable rent in respect of that dwelling is reduced to a sum which is less than the reckonable rent at the time that maximum rent was determined,

then–

    (i) the maximum rent shall not be reduced, where the sum is not less than the maximum rent, during a period ending on the effective date of a decision adopting a determination of a rent officer where that determination was made in exercise of the Housing Act functions pursuant to an application by the authority under regulation 14(1)(c), (d), (e), (f) or (g); and

    (ii) the maximum rent shall be reduced to an amount equal to that sum, where that sum is less than the maximum rent during a period ending on the effective date of a decision adopting a determination of a rent officer where that determination was made in exercise of the Housing

Act functions pursuant to an application by the authority under regulation 14(1)(c), (d), (e), (f) or (g).

(9) Subject to paragraph (10), in a case where–

(a) a rent officer has made a determination in exercise of the Housing Act functions pursuant to an application by an authority under regulation 14(1)(e); and

(b) subsequent to that determination the reckonable rent for that dwelling is changed,

then in determining a maximum rent in relation to a claim for benefit of a claimant who has a liability to make payments in respect of that dwelling, the authority shall treat the claim-related rent or, as the case may be, reckonable rent to be that determined in or, as the case may be, applicable to, that determination by the rent officer.

(10) Paragraph (9) shall not apply in a case where the reckonable rent is reduced to a figure below the figure that would have been the maximum rent if that reckonable rent had not changed; and where this paragraph applies, the maximum rent shall be the reckonable rent, as so reduced.

(11) In a case where the claimant occupies a dwelling which is the same as that occupied by him at the date of death of any person to whom paragraph (16)(b) to (d) applied or, had a claim been made, would have applied, the maximum rent shall be either–

(a) the maximum rent which applied before the death occurred; or

(b) in a case where there was no maximum rent, the reckonable rent due before the death occurred,

for a period of 12 months from the date of such a death.

(12) For the purposes of paragraph (11), a claimant shall be treated as occupying the dwelling if paragraph (13) of regulation 7 (circumstances in which a person is or is not to be treated as occupying a dwelling as his home) is satisfied and for that purpose sub-paragraph (b) of that paragraph of that regulation shall be treated as if it were omitted.

(13) In a case where a charge for meals is ineligible to be met by housing benefit under regulation 12(3) and paragraph 1 of Schedule 1, there shall be deducted an amount determined in accordance with paragraph 2 of Schedule 1 in respect of meals in the calculation of a person's maximum rent, except where the maximum rent is derived from a rent officer determination under–

(a) paragraph 3 (exceptional high rents) of Schedule 1 to the Rent Officers Order and the notice of claim-related rent states pursuant to paragraph 9(1)(c) of that Schedule that an ineligible payment has not been included in it; or

(b) paragraph 5 (single room rents) of that Schedule.

(14) Subject to paragraph (15), where the relevant authority is satisfied that a person to whom paragraph (16) applies was able to meet the financial commitments for his dwelling when they were entered into, there shall be no maximum rent during the first 13 weeks of the claimant's award of housing benefit.

(15) Paragraph (14) shall not apply where a claimant [¹ , or the claimant's partner,] was previously entitled to benefit in respect of an award of housing benefit which fell wholly or partly less than 52 weeks before the commencement of [¹ the claimant's] current award of housing benefit.

(16) This paragraph applies to the following persons–

(a) the claimant;

(b) any member of his family;

(c) if the claimant is a member of a polygamous marriage, any partners of his and any child or young person for whom he or a partner is responsible and who is a member of the same household;

(d)   subject to paragraph (17), any relative of the claimant or his partner who occupies the same dwelling as the claimant, whether or not they reside with him.

(17)   Paragraph (16)(d) shall only apply to a relative who has no separate right of occupation of the dwelling which would enable him to continue to occupy it even if the claimant ceased his occupation of it.

(18)   In this regulation–

"claim related rent" means the rent notified by the rent officer under paragraph 9(1) of Schedule 1 to the Rent Officers Order;

"deduction for meals" means any amount of a person's otherwise eligible rent which is an ineligible service charge by reason of and within the meaning of paragraph 1(a)(i) of Schedule 1;

"local reference rent" means the rent determined by a rent officer under paragraph 4 of Schedule 1 to the Rent Officers Order;

"reckonable rent" means those payments, which a person is liable to make in respect of the dwelling which he occupies as his home, and which are eligible, or would, but for this regulation, be eligible for housing benefit plus the amount of any deduction for fuel, deduction for meals or water charges, as the case may be, which that person is liable to pay;

"single room rent" means the rent determined by a rent officer under paragraph 5 of Schedule 1 to the Rent Officers Order.

Modifications

A different version of reg 13 is substituted for some claimants entitled to HB on 1 January 1996. See Sch 3 paras 4 and 5(2) HB&CTB(CP) Regs on p1101.

Reg 13 applies as modified by Sch 3 para 8 HB&CTB(CP) Regs (see p1106) for some claimants entitled to HB on or before 5 October 1997.

Definitions

"child" – see reg 2(1).
"claimant" – see reg 2(1).
"dwelling" – see reg 2(4) and s137(1) SSCBA.
"eligible rent" – see reg 2(1).
"non-dependants" – see reg 3.
"partner" – see reg 2(1).
"polygamous marriage" – see reg 2(1).
"relative" – see reg 2(1).
"rent" – see reg 2(1).
"young individual" – see reg 2(1).
"young person" – see reg 2(1).

Amendment

1.   Amended by reg 2(5) of SI 2007 No 1356 as from 1.10.07.

General Note

Reg 13 deals with the calculation of the claimant's maximum rent for HB purposes. The significance of the maximum rent is that the claimant's eligible rent cannot exceed it: reg 12(3)(a). "Eligible rent" is the figure upon which a claimant's maximum HB is based: reg 70.

The authority also has the power under reg 12(7) to reduce the maximum rent figure to such lesser amount as seems appropriate in the particular case.

Reg 13 could justifiably be described as being the most difficult provision to apply correctly of all the legislation in this book. There are two principal sources of this difficulty. The first is the cryptic jargon used in reg 13 to describe various figures produced by the rent officer and others extrapolated from those figures. While computer software used by rent officers and authorities undoubtedly makes their unenviable task somewhat easier, it is very hard for claimants or their advisers to check whether errors have been made.

The second problem is the multiple levels of transitional protection that are applicable to different categories of claimant. Indeed, although this form of the rules came into force on 2 January 1996, a number of claimants must still have the old form of reg 11 HB Regs 1987 (now an alternative version of reg 13 HB

Regs in Sch 3 para 5(2) of the HB&CTB(CP) Regs) and other regulations in Part 3 applied to them because they retain their transitional protection.

The maximum rent is determined by a mathematical process from the rent officer's determinations. The rent officer's determinations are extremely difficult to attack in judicial review proceedings and cannot, by virtue of Sch 7 para 6(2)(c) CSPSSA 2000, be appealed to an appeal tribunal. (For further discussion of challenges to rent officer's decisions and of the possible human rights issues involved, see the Rent Officers (Housing Benefit Functions) Order 1997 on p520.)

Summary of the maximum rent calculation

One of the most difficult aspects of reg 13 is the terminology applied to the various figures used for the calculation process. The terms are summarised here, with cross-reference to other commentary. Not all the various terms will be relevant in a particular case.

Where an authority has applied to the rent officer for a determination under reg 14 and this has been provided, maximum rent is calculated as follows:

(1)   The eligible rent (ER) is calculated by the authority in accordance with reg 12 above. The "reckonable rent" (RR) is then the sum of the claimant's ER plus any deductions imposed by the definition in para (18).

(2)   The following rent determinations are made by the rent officer:

(a)   A significantly high rent (SHR) determination is made if the rent is significantly higher than a reasonable rent: Sch 1 para 1 of the Rent Officer (Housing Benefit Functions) Order 1997 or its Scottish equivalent, which are referred to collectively as the RO Orders in this commentary.

(b)   A size-related rent determination is made (SizeRR) under Sch 1 para 2 of the RO Orders if it is decided that the property exceeds the size criteria set out in Sch 2.

(c)   An exceptionally high rent determination is made (EHR) if the rent officer decides under Sch 1 para 3 of the RO Orders that it needs to be given.

(d)   The local reference rent (LRR) is calculated under Sch 1 para 4 of the RO Orders. The LRR is broadly the mid-point of reasonable market rents for comparable assured tenancies in the locality.

(e)   The single room rent (SRR) is calculated under Sch 1 para 5 of the RO Orders. It is used in the calculation of the maximum rent of "young individuals" (broadly, single people under 25 but see the full definition in reg. 2(1) and the Commentary thereto). Since 2 July 2001, it has been assessed on the basis of the mid-point of reasonable rents for comparable assured tenancies in the locality comprising a single room occupied exclusively, with a shared, toilet, bathroom, kitchen and living room and which does not include payments for board and attendance.

(3)   The lowest of the determinations in (2)(a)-(c) above, or if none of them are determined, the rent payable under the tenancy is the claim-related rent (CRR): Sch 1 para 6 of the RO Orders. The rent officer notifies the authority of the CRR and if lower, the LRR or SRR.

(4)   The authority decides whether the claimant has transitional protection as an exempt claimant or because s/he is in "exempt accommodation": Sch 3 para 4 HB&CTB(CP) Regs. In this case, the alternative version of regs 12 and 13 HB Regs as well as the inserted reg 13ZA HB Regs (in sch 3 para 5 of the HB&CTB(CP) Regs) are used to determine HB entitlement.

(5)   If the claimant is not exempt or in "exempt accommodation", maximum rent is calculated by the authority using the determinations notifed in (3) above: reg 13(2)-(7). Maximum rent is the lowest of the CRR, the LRR, or if relevant the SRR unless the claimant has transitional protection, for which, see Sch 3 para 8 HB&CTB(CP) Regs (in Part 7) and the commentary to para (6).

(6)   The authority decides whether the use of the maximum rent in calculating HB entitlement can be delayed: reg 13(11), (12), (14) and (15).

Note that certain tenancies (some hostels and "excluded" tenancies) do not have to be referred for a determination by a rent officer: reg 14(4). In these cases, the rent restriction rules do not apply, although the authority can use its general powers under reg 12(7) to decrease eligible rent for HB purposes.

Analysis

Reg 13 applies, broadly, to those who do not live in certain types of supported accommodation and who make a claim for HB for the first time or in respect of a new dwelling after 1 January 1996. Careful consideration needs to be given in all cases to the possible applicability of the transitional protection contained in paras 4 and 5 Sch 3 HB&CTB(CP) Regs (see p1101) because the old rent restriction rules are considerably more generous than those applicable under the current reg 13, especially where the claimant is "vulnerable" for the purposes of the old provisions.

Note also that reg 13 does not apply to those in Pathfinder authority areas to whom the local housing allowance pilot scheme instead applies.

Paragraph (1): The general rule

This confirms that the reg 13 comes into force whenever an authority has applied to the rent officer for a determination under reg 14. See the commentary to that regulation for when the authority does this. The maximum rent is then to be determined as set out in the paras that follow.

Paragraphs (2) to (7): Calculation of maximum rent

These paras set out the bases on which the maximum rent is calculated. Generally, the maximum rent is the lowest of the CRR, the LRR, or in the case of a "young individual", the SRR.

Para (2) applies where the CRR is notified but not the SRR or LRR. In this case, the maximum rent is the CRR.

Paras (3), (6) and (7) Unless para (4) applies, maximum rent is the lower of the CRR and the LRR: para (6). There is transitional protection for some claimants. A "50 per cent taper" is preserved in relation to certain categories of claimants (broadly, those continuously entitled to, and in receipt of, HB for the same property since 5 October 1997): see para 8 Sch 3 HB&CTB(CP) Regs on p1122. For protected claimants, para (6)(a) as modified provides that the maximum rent is the LRR plus half the difference between the "relevant rent" (defined in para (18)) and the LRR. In this case, the maximum rent cannot be more than twice the LRR: para (3).

For example, if the rent officer's CRR for the dwelling is £150 and the rent officer's LRR figure is £40, the maximum rent is £95 if the claimant has the transitional protection but only £40 if s/he does not have it.

Subject to the limits set by paras (3) and (4), para (7) applies where a LRR has been notified that is lower than the "reckonable rent" (defined in para (18), but not a CRR. This is a little puzzling because it appears that a CRR will be notified in all cases referred to the rent officer (see para 9(1)(a) of Sch 1 to the RO Orders), so it may be that this paragraph has been left in by mistake. In any cases to which the paragraph may remain applicable, maximum rent is the LRR. The taper is again preserved for those who have the transitional protection, as set out in the previous paragraph.

Para (4) applies where the claimant is a young individual as defined in reg 2(1) and the rent officer has notified a SRR, the maximum rent is restricted to the SRR which will usually be much lower than the other determinations made by the rent officer. However, the effect of this provision is softened by para (5), which provides that para (4) is not applicable where the claimant either has transitional protection, qualifies for a severe disability premium or "has a non-dependent residing with him". See reg 3 for the question of whether someone has a non-dependant residing with her/him.

Paragraphs (8) to (10): Changes in rent

These paras deal with the effect on the maximum rent of changes in the claimant's RR during an award of HB. Generally the maximum rent is not changed, but under para (8), where the claimant's RR reduces during the award to a figure below the maximum rent figure determined by the authority, the maximum rent is set to an amount equal to the new lower RR figure.

Para (9) deals with the situation where a claimant has sought a pre-tenancy determination under reg 14(1)(e) and the RR is subsequently changed. In such a case the authority must determine the claim on the basis that the CRR or RR is that determined by, and the CRR or RR that referred to, the rent officer in the application for the pre-tenancy determination. By para (10) this does not apply where the RR goes below the maximum rent figure, in which case again maximum rent becomes equal to the RR.

Paragraphs (11), (12), (14) and (15): Delay in application of the maximum rent

A variety of different transitional protection available to different categories of claimants has been discussed above. Reg 13 itself provides for more limited protection for two further classes of claimants.

Para (11) provides a degree of protection for the recently bereaved. If a claimant is continuing to occupy a home which s/he occupied at the time a relevant person died, the maximum rent continues in force for 12 months from the date of death. In cases where there was no maximum rent in force, the maximum rent is the RR. Again, this protection lasts for 12 months from the date of death. A "relevant person" for these purposes is a member of the claimant's family (defined in s137(1) SSCBA), a partner in a polygamous marriage or a child or young person for whom he or a partner is responsible in such a relationship, or a relative of the claimant or her/his partner who occupies the same dwelling: para (16)(b) to (d).

As to the last of these categories, "relative" is defined in reg 2(1).

It is also explicitly provided that the deceased person need not have been residing with the claimant, provided only that they occupied the same dwelling. In this context, this arguably means someone living within the same building, provided that the living units of the claimant and the deceased are not completely self-contained. It might cover those who were sharing only a toilet, or some similar part of the accommodation. Para (17) requires that the relative should not have had a separate right of occupation. If the relative had her/his own tenancy from a landlord, the claimant cannot therefore take advantage of this provision. However, if the claimant and the relative were joint tenants, it could be argued that the relative's right of occupation was not "separate" because it was held jointly with the claimant.

By para (12), "occupation" of a home for the purposes of para (11) can include deemed occupation under reg 7(13), that is, where someone is treated as occupying a dwelling for up to 13 weeks while temporarily absent from it. The claimant need not, however, comply with sub-para (b) of that regulation, so it does not matter if the home was let or sublet.

Para (14) postpones the application of the maximum rent for 13 weeks if any of the people set out in para (16) could have met the financial commitments the dwelling (which will include things like bills besides the rent) at the time they were taken on. Para (16) applies to the claimant and to the three additional categories of persons analysed in the previous three paragraphs.

By para (15), the protection in para (14) does not apply where the claimant or her/his partner has been entitled to HB at some time within the 52 weeks prior to the commencement of the claimant's current HB award.

Paragraph (13): Deductions

This paragraph sets out the rules for deducting amounts from the maximum rent that relate to services provided to the claimant. Where eligible rent is reduced by amounts for meals, equivalent deductions are to be made to the maximum rent except where this is determined under para (4) above as being equivalent to the SRR. In *Shepherd v Dundee CC* [2002] SLT 1427, CS(IH), the claimant asserted that where eligible rent had already been restricted to a sum less than the contractual rent, it was not open to the local authority to make a further deduction in respect of the cost of board. Unsurprisingly, the court rejected that submission (paras 14-15). The cost of services is deducted after the restriction of eligible rent.

Restrictions on rent increases
13ZA

Modification

Reg 13ZA is inserted for some claimants entitled to HB on 1 January 1996. See Sch 3 paras 4 and 5(3) of the HB&CTB(CP) Regs on p1100.

Maximum rent (standard local rate)
13A

Modification

Reg 13A is inserted by Sch 10 para 7. It only applies to Pathfinder Authorities who are administering the pilot local housing allowance scheme, as from the date specified in relation to each authority as specified in Sch 10 Part 1 (see p511).

Publication of local housing allowances
13B

Modification

Reg 13B is inserted by Sch 10 para 7. It only applies to Pathfinder Authorities who are administering the pilot local housing allowance scheme, as from the date specified in relation to each authority as specified in Sch 10 Part 1 (see p511).

Requirement to refer to rent officers

14.–(1) Subject to the following provisions of this regulation, a relevant authority shall apply to a rent officer for a determination to be made in pursuance of the Housing Act functions where–

(a)   it has received a claim on which rent allowance may be awarded; or

(b)   it has received relevant information regarding a claim on which rent allowance may be awarded; or

(c)   it has received a notification of a change relating to a rent allowance; or

(d)   it has received a notification of a change of dwelling; or

(e)   it has received, except in the case where any liability to make payments in respect of a dwelling would be to a housing authority, a request from a person ("the prospective occupier"), on a properly completed form approved for the purpose by the relevant authority, signifying that he is contemplating occupying a dwelling as his home and that if he does so, he is likely to claim housing benefit, but only where that form–

    (i)   is signed by the prospective occupier;

    (ii)   is countersigned by the person to whom the prospective occupier would incur liability to make such payments; and

    (iii)   indicates that the person countersigning agrees to the application being made for that determination; or

(f)   52 weeks have elapsed since it last made an application under sub-paragraph (a), (b), (c), (d) or (e) above in relation to the claim or award in question; or

(g)   52 weeks have elapsed since–

    (i)   an application was made under sub-paragraph (f) above; or

    (ii)   an application was made under this sub-paragraph,

whichever last occurred.

(2)   When applying to the rent officer pursuant to paragraph (1) the relevant authority shall state the total amount of those payments referred to in regulation 12(1) (rent) which that claimant is liable to make in respect of the dwelling which he occupies as his home and shall provide the following information in respect of those payments–

(a)   whether they include any charges for water, sewerage or allied environmental services or charges in respect of meals or fuel which are ineligible by virtue of paragraph 2 and Part 2 of Schedule 1 (ineligible service charges); and

(b)   where they include any charges that are ineligible for housing benefit by reason of paragraph 1(a)(iv) and (c) to (f) of Schedule 1 (ineligible service charges)–

    (i)   that such charges are included; and

    (ii)   the value of those charges as determined by that authority pursuant to regulation 12(3) and that Schedule.

(3)   When applying to the rent officer pursuant to paragraph (1), the relevant authority shall state whether, in their opinion, the claimant is or may be a young individual.

(4)   An application shall not be required under paragraph (1) where a claim, relevant information regarding a claim, notification or request relates to either–

(a)   a dwelling in a hostel if, during the period of 12 months which ends on the day on which that claim, relevant information regarding a claim, notification or request is received by the relevant authority–

    (i)   a rent officer has already made a determination in the exercise of the Housing Act functions in respect of a dwelling in that hostel which is a similar dwelling to the dwelling to which the claim, relevant information regarding a claim, notification or request relates; and

    (ii)   there has been no change relating to a rent allowance that has affected the dwelling in respect of which that determination was made; or

(b)   an "excluded tenancy" within the meaning of Schedule 2 (excluded tenancies).

(5)   Where a relevant authority receives a request pursuant to paragraph (1)(e) and it is a case where, by reason of paragraph (4), an application to a rent officer is not required, the authority shall–

(a)   return it to the prospective occupier, indicating why no such application is required; and

(b)   where it is not required by reason of either paragraph (4)(a) of this regulation or paragraph 2 of Schedule 2 (cases where the rent officer has already made a determination), shall also send him a copy of that determination within 4 days of the receipt of that request by the authority.

(6)   Where an application to a rent officer is required by paragraph (1) it shall be made within 3 days, or as soon as practicable thereafter, of–

    (a)   the relevant authority receiving a claim on which rent allowance may be awarded; or

(b) the relevant authority receiving relevant information regarding a claim on which rent allowance may be awarded; or

(c) the relevant authority receiving a notification of a change relating to a rent allowance; or

(d) relevant authority receiving a notification of a change of dwelling; or

(e) the day on which the period mentioned in paragraph (1)(f) or (g) elapsed,

except that, in the case of a request to which paragraph (1)(e) applies, the application shall be made within 2 days of the receipt of that request by the authority.

(7) For the purpose of calculating any period of days mentioned in paragraphs (5) or (6), no regard shall be had to a day on which the offices of the relevant authority are closed for the purposes of receiving or determining claims.

(8) For the purpose of this regulation a dwelling in a hostel shall be regarded as similar to another dwelling in that hostel if each provides sleeping accommodation for the same number of persons.

(9) Where the relevant authority has identified charges to which paragraph (2)(b) applies, it shall–

(a) deduct those charges from the total amount of those payments which, in accordance with paragraph (2), it has stated that the claimant is liable to make in respect of the dwelling which he occupies as his home; and

(b) notify that total so reduced to the rent officer in its application under paragraph (1) for his use in making determinations under Schedule 1 (determinations) to the Rent Officers Order.

(10) In this regulation–

"change of dwelling" means a change of dwelling occupied by a claimant as his home during the award where the dwelling to which the claimant has moved is one in respect of which the authority may make a rent allowance;

"change relating to a rent allowance" means a change or increase to which paragraph 2(3)(a), (b), (c) or (d) of Schedule 2 applies;

"prospective occupier" shall include a person currently in receipt of housing benefit in respect of a dwelling which he occupies as his home and who is contemplating entering into a new agreement to occupy that dwelling, but not in a case where his current agreement commenced less than 11 months before such a request;

"registered housing association" means a housing association which–

(a) is registered in a register maintained by the Corporation or the National Assembly for Wales under chapter 1 of Part 1 of the Housing Act 1996 or,

(b) in Scotland, is registered by Scottish Ministers by virtue of section 57(3)(b) of the Housing (Scotland) Act 2001;

"relevant information" means information or evidence forwarded to the relevant authority by an appropriate DWP office regarding a claim on which rent allowance may be awarded, which completes the transfer of all information or evidence held by the appropriate DWP office relating to that claim;

"tenancy" includes–

(a) in Scotland, any other right of occupancy; and

(b) in any other case, a licence to occupy premises,

and reference to a tenant, landlord or any other expression appropriate to a tenancy shall be construed accordingly;

"the Corporation" has the same meaning as in section 56 of the Housing Act 1996.

Modifications

Modification of reg 14 is provided in Sch 10 para 8 in relation to Pathfinder Authorities who are administering the pilot local housing allowance scheme, as from the date specified in relation to each authority as specified in Sch 10 Part 1 (see p511).

Definitions

"Housing Act functions" – see reg 2(1).

General Note

Maximum rent is calculated under reg 13 where an authority has applied to the rent officer for a determination under reg 14. Reg 14, together with Sch 2 prescribes the circumstances in which the authority must ask the rent officer for a determination to be made, the information which must be given to the rent officer and the time limits which must be observed. For the rent officer's functions under the Housing Act see the Rent Officers (Housing Benefit Functions) Order 1997 and the Rent Officers (Housing Benefit Functions) (Scotland) Order 1997.

Note that reg 13 does not apply in all cases, ie where a claimant has transitional protection, an alternative version of reg 13 is applicable. See the commentary to reg 13.

Although there is no right of appeal against rent officer determinations, authorities may ask for redeterminations on a claimant's behalf under reg 16. Other provisions for redeterminations and substitute determinations are found in regs 15, 17 and 18.

Analysis

Paragraph (1): When referrals are to be made

Pursuant to para (1), there are seven circumstances in which a local authority is usually obliged to apply to a rent officer for a determination. These are subject to para (4), which provides for circumstances in which no reference is required.

A referral must only be made in cases concerning rent allowance and not rent rebate. This may cause difficulties in cases where claimants have been placed in accommodation by local housing authorities: see *CH 1208/2003* referred to in the commentary to reg 8 for an example. The situations when HB takes the form of rent allowance and rent rebate are in s134(1A) and (1B) SSAA 1992. Generally speaking, HB takes the form of a rent allowance in cases other than where rent is paid to the authority administering the HB scheme, eg where a claimant is a private or housing association tenant.

Sub-paras (a) and (b): Claims. These sub-paras apply where a claim for HB is received or an authority has received "relevant information" regarding a claim. Relevant information is defined in para (10).

Sub-paras (c) and (d): Changes. These sub-paras apply where the authority has received a notification of a change relating to a rent allowance or of a change of dwelling. By para (10), a "change relating to a rent allowance" is defined by reference to various parts of Sch 2. See the commentary to those provisions for details. "Change of dwelling" is also defined in para (10).

Sub-para (e): Pre-tenancy determinations. This establishes a scheme of pre-tenancy determinations. The policy aim is to prevent a tenant taking on a tenancy and then finding that her/his rent is restricted. The determinations inform prospective tenants, current tenants and landlords of the likely amount of rent that HB will meet. The determination is not dependent on an actual HB claim being made at the time of application for the pre-tenancy determination.

Pre-tenancy determinations are available to "prospective occupiers". By para (10), this term does not just include those considering taking on a tenancy but also includes claimants who are already living in their property and who are considering entering into a new agreement. In the latter case, however, any existing agreement must have started not less than eleven months prior to the request being made.

The prospective occupier must submit her/his request to the authority on a "properly completed form approved ... by the relevant authority". The form must be signed both by the prospective occupier and by the landlord or letting agent.

The pre-tenancy determinations are rent officer determinations for the purpose of reg 13 and are binding on the authority in the event of an HB claim in respect of that accommodation, either from the prospective tenant who made the original application or another tenant. However, in the latter case, the conditions under which the pre-tenancy determination was given by the rent officer must remain the same. For example, the size criteria should accord with the composition of the household.

Sub-paras (f) and (g): 52 weeks since previous application. These sub-paras apply where 52 weeks have elapsed since a previous application to the rent officer was made in relation to the claim or award in question.

Paragraphs (4), (5) and (8): The exceptions

Para (4) sets out the two exceptions to the requirement to refer a case to a rent officer. Under para (a), no dwelling within a hostel need be referred if a determination has been made within the previous 12 months in respect of a similar dwelling in that hostel and there has been no change of circumstances in relation to the similar dwelling. "Similar dwelling" means one sleeping the same number of people: para (8). Under para (b), no "excluded tenancy" as set out in Sch 2 need be referred. See the commentary to that Schedule.

Under para (5), where a request for a pre-tenancy determination would relate to a case where application to the rent officer is not required by reason of para (4), the local authority must return the request indicating why a referral is not necessary and, where the reason is that a determination has already been made, enclose a copy of that determination.

Paragraphs (2), (3), (6), (7) and (9): Making the referral

Paras (2), (3) and (9) set out the information which the local authority must give to the rent officer in order to enable her/him to make a correct determination. The information required by para (2) relates to whether the rent paid (or proposed to be paid) includes payments in respect of certain items that are ineligible to be met by HB. The authority must state the total amounts eligible to be met by HB under reg 12(1) and then set out information about charges relating to the following:

(1)   Water, sewerage and allied environmental services: sub-para (a).

(2)   Charges for meals and fuel rendered ineligible by Sch 1 (see the commentary for details): sub-para (a).

(3)   The cleaning of rooms and windows except the exterior of windows which cannot be cleaned by anyone in the household or communal areas: sub-para (b).

(4)   The provision of an emergency alarm system: sub-para (b).

(5)   Medical expenses: sub-para (b).

(6)   Nursing or personal care: sub-para (b).

(7)   General counselling or support services: sub-para (b).

Where charges in relation to categories (3) to (7) are present, the local authority must specify the charges that are included in the rent and give the amounts which it has decided are eligible and ineligible. Under para (9), the net rent after the deduction of ineligible charges must also be notified to the rent officer.

Under para (3), if it believes the claimant is or may be either a "young individual" (see reg 2(1) for the definition of this phrase) or someone who is exempt from the "single room" rent restrictions for those aged under 25, the authority must say so.

Paras (6) and (7) set out the time limits with which the authority must comply. Applications for pre-tenancy determinations must be referred to the rent officer within two working days. In other cases, the referral to the rent officer must be made within three working days from the authority receiving the claim or notification or "as soon as is practicable thereafter". Note that the two working day limit for pre-tenancy determinations is absolute and not subject to the "as soon as is practicable thereafter" qualification. By para (7), days on which the local authority's offices are closed do not count.

Applications to the rent officer for redeterminations

15.–(1)   Subject to paragraph (2) and regulation 16, where a relevant authority has obtained from a rent officer either or both of the following–

(a)   a determination on a reference made under regulation 14 (requirement to refer to rent officers);

(b)   a redetermination on a reference made under regulation 16(2)(application for redetermination by rent officer),

the authority may apply to the rent officer for a redetermination of any determination or redetermination he has made which has effect at the date of the application.

(2) No application shall be made for a further redetermination of a redetermination made in response to an application under paragraph (1).

Modifications

Modification of reg 15 is provided in Sch 10 para 9 in relation to Pathfinder Authorities who are administering the pilot local housing allowance scheme, as from the date specified in relation to each authority as specified in Sch 10 Part 1 (see p511).

General Note

Regs 15, 16, 17 and 18 allow for applications for redeterminations and substitute determinations. Under reg 15, an authority may apply for a redetermination of a determination, or for a second redetermination following one made at the person affected's request under reg 16(2). It may apply only once: see reg 15(2).

Application for redetermination by rent officer

16.–(1)   This paragraph applies where–

(a)   a person affected makes written representations which are signed by him, to a relevant authority concerning a decision which it makes in relation to him;

(b)   those representations relate, in whole or in part, to a rent officer's determination or redetermination in exercise of the Housing Act functions; and

(c)   those representations are made no later than [¹ one month] after the day on which the person affected was notified of the decision by the relevant authority.

(2)   Subject to paragraphs (3) and (4), where paragraph (1) applies, the relevant authority shall, within 7 days of receiving the representations, apply to the rent officer for a redetermination or, as the case may be, a further redetermination in exercise of the Housing Act functions and a copy of those representations shall accompany the local authority's application.

(3)   Except where paragraph (4) applies, a relevant authority, in relation to any determination by a rent officer of an application under regulation 14(1) (requirement to refer to rent officers), shall not apply for a redetermination under paragraph (2) more than once in respect of an individual claimant's dwelling to which that determination relates.

(4)   Paragraph (2) shall operate so as to require a relevant authority to make a second application where the following conditions are met in addition to those imposed by that paragraph–

(a)   the written representations made under paragraph (1) relate to a redetermination by a rent officer made in response to an application by the relevant authority under regulation 15 (application to the rent officer for redetermination);

(b)   by the time of that application, the rent officer has already provided a redetermination under this regulation of a determination made in response to an application under regulation 14(1); and

(c)   both the application under this regulation referred to in sub-paragraph (b) and the second application for which this paragraph provides relate to the same claimant.

(5)   Where a decision has been revised in consequence of a redetermination, substitute determination or substitute redetermination by a rent officer in exercise of the Housing Act functions and that redetermination, substitute determination or substitute redetermination has led to–

(a)   a reduction in the maximum rent, the redetermination, substitute determination or substitute redetermination shall be a change of circumstances;

(b)   an increase in the maximum rent, the redetermination, substitute determination or substitute redetermination shall have effect in place of the original determination.

Modifications

Modification of reg 16 is provided in Sch 10 para 10 in relation to Pathfinder Authorities who are administering the pilot local housing allowance scheme, as from the date specified in relation to each authority as specified in Sch 10 Part 1 (see p511).

Amendment

1.   Amended by reg 2(6) of SI 2007 No 1356 as from 1.10.07. By reg 2(8) of SI 2007 No1356, the amendment only applies to decisions notified by the relevant authority to the person affected on or after 1/10/07.

General Note

Under para 6(2)(c) CSPSSA, "so much of any decision of a relevant authority as adopts a decision of a rent officer under any order made by virtue of section 122 of the Housing Act 1996" does not carry a right of appeal to an appeal tribunal. Reg 16 provides a limited opportunity for a "person affected" to challenge such a decision. "Person affected" is defined in reg 2(1) by reference to reg 3 D&A Regs and so can include, as well as a claimant, a landlord or her/his agent.

The procedure is for the "person affected" to make signed written representations to the authority about a decision, which relate to the rent officer's determination. These must be made no later than one month after the day on which s/he was notified of the authority's decision. Note that the time limit is six weeks for decisions notified by the relevant authority to the "person affected" before 1 October 2007. The authority must then apply within seven days to the rent officer for a redetermination.

Claimants and those advising them should note that such representations may lead to a *decrease* in the maximum rent as well as an increase. If that occurs, it is treated by para (5)(a) as a change of circumstances and will lead to the supersession of the earlier award. By contrast an increase in the maximum rent takes effect as a revision of the original award: para (5)(b). It therefore leads to a payment of back-dated benefit: see also regs 4(3), 7(2)(c) and 8(6) D&A Regs. Paras (3) and (4) make it clear that only one redetermination can be required for each original rent officer determination except where, in relation to the same claimant, there has been a first redetermination at the claimant's request, then a further redetermination at the authority's request, and the claimant then makes further representations about the second redetermination.

Substitute determinations or substitute redeterminations

17.–(1) In a case where either–

(a) the appropriate authority discovers that an application it has made to the rent officer contained an error in respect of any of the following–

(i) the size of the dwelling;

(ii) the number of occupiers;

(iii) the composition of the household;

(iv) the terms of the tenancy; or

(b) the rent officer has, in accordance with article 7A of the Rent Officers Order, notified an appropriate authority of an error he has made (other than in the application of his professional judgement),

the authority shall apply to the rent officer for a substitute determination or substitute redetermination, as the case may be.

(2) In its application to the rent officer the relevant authority shall state the nature of the error and withdraw any previous application relating to the same case for a redetermination or substitute determination or substitute redetermination, which it has made but to which the rent officer has not yet responded.

Modifications

Modification of reg 17 is provided in Sch 10 para 11 in relation to Pathfinder Authorities who are administering the pilot local housing allowance scheme, as from the date specified in relation to each authority as specified in Sch 10 Part 1 (see p511).

General Note

Reg 17 requires an authority to apply for a substitute determination where any of the errors listed in para (1) comes to light. It appears that the error may be one of law as well as fact, but it would seem that if the local authority reaches a conclusion from primary facts, for example as to the composition of a household, it cannot describe that conclusion as an "error" merely because another officer later takes a different view.

There is no mechanism for a claimant to apply for a substitute determination, but an authority could be invited to exercise its duty under reg 17 and could be vulnerable to judicial review if it refuses to do so.

The references to "the appropriate authority" in paras (1)(a) and (b) appear to have been overlooked by the draftsman of SI 2001 No 1605 which amended reg 12C HB Regs 1987 (now reg 17 HB Regs).

Application of provisions to substitute determinations or substitute redeterminations

18. Regulations 15, 16 and 17 apply to a substitute determination or substitute redetermination as they apply to the determination or redetermination it replaces.

General Note

Reg 18 confirms that substitute determinations may themselves be the subject of applications for redeterminations.

Amended determinations
18A

Modification

Reg 18A is inserted by Sch 10 para 12. It only applies to Pathfinder Authorities who are administering the pilot local housing allowance scheme, as from the date specified in relation to each authority as specified in Sch 10 Part 1 (see p511).

PART 4
Membership of a family

Persons of prescribed description

19.–(1)   Subject to paragraph (2), a person of a prescribed description for the purposes of section 137(1) of the Act as it applies to housing benefit (definition of family) is a person [¹ who falls within the definition of qualifying young person in section 142 of the Act (child and qualifying young person)], and in these Regulations such a person is referred to as a ''young person''.

(2)   Paragraph (1) shall not apply to a person who is–

(a)   on income support or an income-based jobseeker's allowance; [¹ or]

[² (b)]

(c)   a person to whom section 6 of the Children (Leaving Care) Act 2000 (exclusion from benefits) applies.

(3)   A person of a prescribed description for the purposes of section 137(1) of the Act as it applies to housing benefit (definition of the family) includes a child or young person in respect of whom section 145A of that Act applies for the purposes of entitlement to child benefit but only for the period prescribed under section 145A(1) of that Act.

Definitions

"person on income support" – see reg 2(1).

"person on an income-based jobseeker's allowance" – see reg 2(3).

Amendments

1.   Amended by reg 4(2)(a) and (b) of SI 2006 No 718 as from 10.4.06.

2.   Omitted by reg 4(2)(c) of SI 2006 No 718 as from 10.4.06.

General Note

Section 137(1) SSCBA refers to "children" and "persons of prescribed description" in the definition of "family" for HB purposes. The section and reg 2 define "child" and this reg deals with those covered by the latter term, and provides that they shall be referred to as "young person" elsewhere in these regs.

Analysis

Para (1). "Young person" is defined by reference to the definition of a "qualifying young person" for child benefit purposes. s142 SSCBA and the Child Benefit (General) Regulations 2006 SI No 223 (the CB Regs) prescribe who may be treated as a "qualifying young person" for these purposes.

First, the young person must be 16 or over and under 20 and on a course of "full-time non-advanced education" (or having undertaken such a course be enrolled to undertake a further such course) or in "approved training". S/he must have started the first course or the training before reaching aged 19, and if 19 must have reached that age on or after 10 April 2006: regs 2(5) and 3 CB Regs.

The course of education must be at a school, college or similar institution (or elsewhere, eg, at home, if the Commissioners for for Her Majesty's Revenue and Customs (HMRC) agree and the young person was receiving the education before reaching aged 16). "Full time" for these purposes means over 12 hours per week excluding meal breaks and unsupervised study: reg 1(3) CB Regs. "Non-advanced" means not above 'A' level or 'Higher' standard, but it is the nature of the course that matters, not where the student is studying, provided the Commissioners for the HMRC have approved the studies if s/he is not at a recognised educational establishment.

"Approved training" means arrangements made by the Government: in England known as "Entry to Employment" or "Programme Led Pathways"; in Wales known as "Skillbuild", "Skillbuild+" or "Foundation Modern Apprenticeships" and in Scotland, known as "Get Ready for Work", "Skillseekers" or "Modern Apprenticeships": reg 1(3) CB Regs. The training cannot be provided under a contract of service: reg 3(2)(c) CB Regs.

If a young person leaves education or approved training before reaching age 20, s/he is still treated as a qualifying young person, if the rest of this Part applies:

(1)   If s/he is 16, until the 31 August following her/his 16th birthday: reg 4 CB Regs.

(2)   If s/he is 16 or 17, is registered for work, education or training, is not in remunerative work (here defined as 24 hours or more per week), until the end of her/his "extension period" – ie, from the Monday after the course of education or training ends and ending 20 weeks later: reg 1(3) and 5 CB Regs.

(3)   If s/he is at least 16 but under 20, and has not yet passed her/his "terminal date", until the first Sunday after her/his "terminal date" or if s/he reaches 20 before that date, the Sunday on or after her/his 20th birthday (unless that birthday is on a Monday in which case it is the Sunday before that birthday): reg 7 CB Regs. The "terminal date" is whichever of the following dates first follows the date s/he leaves the education or training: the last day in February, May, August or November: reg 7 CB Regs. A young person who is to return to take an external exam in connection with the education is treated as still being in the education until the date of the last exam. In Scotland, a young person who has taken the Higher or Advanced Higher Certificate can be treated as still being in education until the date a comparable course in England would end if this is later.

Some interruptions in satisfying the conditions for being a "qualifying young person" can be ignored: reg 6 CB Regs.

Para (2). A young person is not part of the claimant's family if s/he is her/himself on IS or income-based JSA. For when a young person may receive income-based JSA see the current edition of CPAG's *Welfare Benefits and Tax Credits Handbook*. Neither can a person excluded from entitlement to benefits under s6 Children (Leaving Care) Act 2000 – see p1031.

Para (3). s145A SSCBA, inserted by s55 TCA 2002, provides for entitlement to child benefit to continue for a prescribed period after the death of a child or qualifying young person. The prescribed period is eight weeks for a child under 16. For a "qualifying young person" it is also eight weeks unless s/he would have attained the age of 20 during that period. In this case, if it is shorter, it is the period commencing the week in which the death occurred and finishing on the Monday in the week following the week in which the qualifying young person would have attained the age of 20: reg 20 CB Regs. The effect of reg 19(3) is that the deceased child will continue to be treated as part of the claimant's family for HB purposes during that prescribed period.

Circumstances in which a person is to be treated as responsible or not responsible for another

20.–(1)   Subject to the following provisions of this regulation a person shall be treated as responsible for a child or young person who is normally living with him and this includes a child or young person to whom paragraph (3) of regulation 19 applies.

(2) Where a child or young person spends equal amounts of time in different households, or where there is a question as to which household he is living in, the child or young person shall be treated for the purposes of paragraph (1) as normally living with–

(a)   the person who is receiving child benefit in respect of him; or

(b)   if there is no such person–

(i)   where only one claim for child benefit has been made in respect of him, the person who made that claim, or

(ii)   in any other case the person who has the primary responsibility for him.

(3)   For the purposes of these Regulations a child or young person shall be the responsibility of only one person in any benefit week and any person other than the one treated as responsible for the child or young person under this regulation shall be treated as not so responsible.

Definitions

"benefit week" – see reg 2(1).

"child" – see s137(1) SSCBA and reg 2(1).

"household" – see note on s137 SSCBA.

"young person" – see reg 19.

General Note

For a child or young person to count as a member of a claimant's family for HB purposes, s/he must be a member of the claimant's household (for which see reg 21) and the claimant or her/his partner must be "responsible" for her/him: s137(1) SSCBA. A child or young person being a member of a claimant's family is important for a number of reasons, the main one being that the claimant's applicable amount will include allowances and premiums for her/him and hence the claimant's rate of HB is potentially higher.

Reg 20 sets out the situations in which a person is treated as responsible. By para (3) only one person can be treated as responsible for a particular child or young person in any benefit week. Paras (1) and (2) set out the rules for deciding who that person is, if there should be doubt or dispute. Para (1) sets out the general rule that a person is responsible for a child or young person "normally living" with her/him and para (2) provides a test for deciding where the child or young person "normally" lives.

Reg 20(1) HB Regs deems a person to be responsible for a person who is normally living with him. That includes a deceased child or young person falling within reg 19(3) inserted above.

Analysis

Para (1). The primary rule is that a person is responsible for a child who is "normally living with him". This means that s/he is spending more time with that person than with anyone else: *CFC 1537/1995*.

Para (2) contains deeming provisions to resolve doubtful cases. It will apply in two sets of circumstances. First, it applies where the amount of time spent in different households is equal. It need not be exactly equal in order to trigger the operation of para (2): *CFC 1537/1995*. Authorities should therefore consider the position in the round rather than carrying out an exact calculation. Secondly, para (2) applies "where there is a question" as to which household a child is living in. It is suggested that there must be a "question" of some difficulty, otherwise para (1) would be deprived of all effect.

Where para (2) applies, the test is determined in three stages. The child is treated as "normally living with:

(1)   The person who is in receipt of child benefit in respect of the child: sub-para (a). A person is not "receiving child benefit" where it is being paid to her/him, or eg into her/his bank account, by the person entitled to the child benefit: *CIS 2317/2006*.

(2)   If no one is receiving child benefit, the person who has claimed it in respect of the child: sub-para (b)(i).

(3)   In any other case (including where more than one person has claimed child benefit for the child), the person who has "primary responsibility" for the child: sub-para (b)(ii). This will require consideration of all the circumstances, financial and pastoral.

Circumstances in which a person is to be treated as being or not being a member of the household

21.–(1)   Subject to paragraphs (2) to (4), the claimant and any partner and, where the claimant or his partner is treated as responsible by virtue of regulation 20 (circumstances in which a person is to be treated as responsible or not responsible for another) for a child or young person, that child or young person and any child of that child or young person, shall be treated as members of the same household notwithstanding that any of them is temporarily living away from the other members of his family.

(2)   Paragraph (1) shall not apply to a person who is living away from the other members of his family where–

(a)   that person does not intend to resume living with the other members of his family; or

(b)   his absence from the other members of his family is likely to exceed 52 weeks, unless there are exceptional circumstances (for example where the person is in hospital or otherwise has no control over the length of his absence) and the absence is unlikely to be substantially more than 52 weeks.

(3)   A child or young person shall not be treated as a member of the claimant's household where he is–

(a)   placed with the claimant or his partner by a local authority under section 23(2)(a) of the Children Act 1989 or by a voluntary organisation under section 59(1)(a) of that Act, or in Scotland boarded out with the claimant or his partner under a relevant enactment; or

(b) placed, or in Scotland boarded out, with the claimant or his partner prior to adoption; or

(c) placed for adoption with the claimant or his partner in accordance with the Adoption and Children Act 2002 or the Adoption Agencies (Scotland) Regulations 1996.

(4) Subject to paragraph (5), paragraph (1) shall not apply to a child or young person who is not living with the claimant and he–

(a) is being looked after by, or in Scotland is in the care of, a local authority under a relevant enactment; or

(b) has been placed, or in Scotland boarded out, with a person other than the claimant prior to adoption; or

(c) has been placed for adoption in accordance with the Adoption and Children Act 2002 or the Adoption Agencies (Scotland) Regulations 1996.

(5) An authority shall treat a child or young person to whom paragraph (4)(a) applies as being a member of the claimants' household in any benefit week where–

(a) that child or young person lives with the claimant for part or all of that benefit week; and

(b) the authority considers that it is reasonable to do so taking into account the nature and frequency of that child's or young person's visits.

(6) In this regulation "relevant enactment" means the Army Act 1955, the Air Force Act 1955, the Naval Discipline Act 1957, the Matrimonial Proceedings Children Act 1958, the Social Work (Scotland) Act 1968, the Family Law Reform Act 1969, the Children and Young Persons Act 1969, the Matrimonial Causes Act 1973, the Children Act 1975, the Domestic Proceedings and Magistrates' Courts Act 1978, the Adoption (Scotland) Act 1978, the Child Care Act 1980, the Family Law Act 1986, the Children Act 1989 and the Children (Scotland) Act 1995.

Definitions

"benefit week" – see reg 2(1).
"child" – see reg 2(1) and s137(1) SSCBA.
"claimant" – see reg 2(1).
"household" – see note to s137 SSCBA.
"partner" – see reg 2(1).
"relevant enactment" – see para (6).
"young person" – see reg 19.

General Note

Reg 20 deals with the situations in which a claimant's family for HB purposes (that is her/his partner and children or young people) are treated as being members of the same houseold. Note that for a child or young person to count as a member of a claimant's family at all, s/he *must* be a member of the claimant's household and the claimant or her/his partner must be "responsible" for her/him (for which see reg 20): s137(1) SSCBA.

The first thing to notice is that this regulation does not define "household". See the Analysis to s137 SSCBA on p23. It does, however, set out the situations in which a person will continue to be treated as a member of a household despite physical absence from it.

Para (1) sets out the general rule.

Paras (2) to (5) immediately qualify this by setting out circumstances in which such persons shall not be treated as sharing the claimant's household.

Para (6) simply defines the term "relevant enactment".

Analysis

Para (1). The general rule is that claimants, their partner(s), any child or young person for whom they are responsible, and any child of such a child or young person shall be treated as members of the same household even where one of them is temporarily living away from the other members of the family. The definition of "partner" in reg 2(1) means that this regulation applies equally to polygamous and non-polygamous relationships. Exceptions to the rule are found in paras (2) to (5).

Para (2) treats a person who is living away from the other members of the family (eg, a partner working abroad, or in another part of the country) as not being a member of the household, if s/he does not intend to resume living with the family or s/he is likely to be absent for more than 52 weeks (unless there are exceptional circumstances). Examples of exceptional circumstances are given in sub-para (b). If such a person is the claimant's partner, her/his income will no longer fall to be treated as the claimant's under reg 25 and any money actually received from her/him should be treated as maintenance under Section 5 of Part 6.

Para (3) provides that certain children or young people placed with a claimant (or her/his partner) under child protection legislation are not to be treated as members of the claimant's household, and and hence as part of her/his family. Under sub-para (a), s23(1)(a) Children Act 1989 places a duty upon the local authority to provide accommodation for a child when s/he is in care. By s23(2)(a) of the Act, the authority is to provide that accommodation by placing the child with a family, a relative of hers/his, or any other suitable person. Where a voluntary organisation provides accommodation for a child under s59(1)(a) of the Children Act 1989 it must do so by placing the child with the same persons identified above. For the definition of "relevant enactment", see para (6).

Under sub-paras (b) and (c), a child placed with the claimant (boarded out in Scotland) as part of the adoption process is not to be treated as being a member of the claimant's family. The regulations referred to regulate adoption agencies and how they are to reach decisions.

Paras (4) and (5) Para (4) treats a child or young person who is being "looked after" (in care in Scotland) or is being prepared for adoption, as not being a member of the household (and hence part of the claimant's benefit family). However, if the child or young person is being "looked after" (or is in care) but lives with the claimant for part or all of any benefit week, then para (5) allows them to be treated as a member of the claimant's household, in that week. Para (5), however, only applies if the authority considers this reasonable taking into account the nature and frequency of the visits. The "nature" of the visits might refer to length of stay, and whether the child is treated as a member of the family during the stay, etc.

Reading paras (4) and (5) together, the phrase "living with" seems to have the narrow meaning of physical presence, because if a child or young person is physically present in any particular week, if para (5) applies it may be used to override the effect of para (4).

PART 5
Applicable amounts

General Note on Part 5

This Part is made under SSCBA s135 and together with Sch 3 prescribes the rules for ascertaining a claimant's applicable amount. The "applicable amount" is an essential component in the calculation of HB: see SSCBA s135 (p16) and Part 8 (p356).

Sch 3 sets out the different elements that can make up an applicable amount. The "allowances" depend on whether a claimant is single, a lone parent, part of a couple or polygamously married, and whether s/he is responsible for a child or young person. In addition to these basic amounts, the claimant may qualify to have one or more of the premiums set out in Parts 3 and 4 of Sch 3 included in her/his applicable amount (see pp454 and 464).

Applicable amounts

22. Subject to regulations 23, 24, 80 and 81 and Schedule A1 (polygamous marriages, patients, calculation of weekly amounts, rent free periods and treatment of claims for housing benefit by refugees), a claimant's weekly applicable amount shall be the aggregate of such of the following amounts as may apply in his case–

(a) an amount in respect of himself or, if he is a member of a couple, an amount in respect of both of them, determined in accordance with paragraph 1(1), (2) or (3), as the case may be, of Schedule 3;

(b) an amount determined in accordance with paragraph 2 of Schedule 3 in respect of any child or young person who is a member of his family;

(c) if he is a member of a family of which at least one member is a child or young person, an amount determined in accordance with Part 2 of Schedule 3 (family premium);

(d) the amount of any premiums which may be applicable to him, determined in accordance with Parts 3 and 4 of Schedule 3 (premiums).

Definitions

"applicable amount" – see s135 SSCBA.
"child" – reg 2(1).

"claimant" – see reg 2(1).
"couple" – see reg 2(1).
"family" – see s137(1) SSCBA.
"polygamous marriage" – see reg 2(1).
"young person" – regs 2(1) and 19(1).

General Note

This regulation sets out the basic rules for ascertaining the applicable amounts for any claimant who is not polygamously married. The basic rules are subject to regs 23, 80 and 81 and Sch A1. A claimant's notional financial needs for the purpose of working out her/his HB entitlement are the total amounts due to her/him under paras (a)-(d). Reg 24 was revoked in April 2006.

Analysis

Para (a). The amounts due under para (a) vary as set out in the General Note above and also according to age. For single people, the rate varies according to whether the claimant is aged under 25 or not. For lone parents and members of couples, the rates depend on whether the claimant or her/his partner is under 18 or not.

Para (b). For membership of a "family" see p22 and Part 4 of these regulations. Sch 3 para 2 provides allowances for children and qualifying young people. Although there are two bands depending on the age of the child or young person, the amounts for both age-band are currently the same.

Para (c). See note on para (b) and the analysis on the family premium in Sch 3 para 3.

Para (d). See the notes to Sch 3 for the details of the premiums. They are designed to meet the additional specific needs of some claimants. Note Sch 3 paras 5 and 6 limits the awards of more than one of certain premiums at the same time.

Polygamous marriages

23. Subject to regulations 24, 80 and 81 and Schedule A1 (patients, calculation of weekly amounts, rent free periods and treatment of claims for housing benefit by refugees), where a claimant is a member of a polygamous marriage, his weekly applicable amount shall be the aggregate of such of the following amounts as may apply in his case–

(a) the highest amount applicable to him and one of his partners determined in accordance with paragraph 1(3) of Schedule 3 as if he and that partner were a couple;

(b) an amount equal to the difference between the amounts specified in sub-paragraphs (3)(b) and (1)(b) of paragraph 1 of Schedule 3 in respect of each of his other partners;

(c) an amount determined in accordance with paragraph 2 of Schedule 3 (applicable amounts) in respect of any child or young person for whom he or a partner of his is responsible and who is a member of the same household;

(d) if he or another partner of the polygamous marriage is responsible for a child or young person who is a member of the same household, the amount specified in Part 2 of Schedule 3 (family premium);

(e) the amount of any premiums which may be applicable to him determined in accordance with Parts 3 and 4 of Schedule 3 (premiums).

Definitions

"applicable amount" – see s135 SSCBA.
"child" – see reg 2(1).
"claimant" – see reg 2(1).
"partner" – see reg 2(1).
"polygamous marriage" – see reg 2(1).
"young person" – see reg 19.

General Note

These rules apply solely to claimants who are polygamously married: see reg 2(1) for the definition. Because of the definition of "partner" in reg 2(1), an increased applicable amount can only be obtained under this regulation in respect of partners to a polygamous marriage who share the same household. The rules are subject to regs 80 and 81 and Sch A1. Reg 24 was revoked in April 2006. Paras (c) to (e) of this regulation have the same effect as paras (b) to (d) of reg 22: see notes on that regulation. The applicable amount is the total due under paras (a) to (e).

Analysis
Paras (a) and (b). The basic personal allowance awarded in respect of polygamously married couples is calculated by taking the highest amount awarded under Sch 3 para 1(3) in respect of any of the couples (depending on age). An additional personal allowance is then awarded for the other partner(s): the amount is the difference between the allowance for a single claimant aged not less than 25 and a couple aged not less than 18. So if a male claimant, A, aged 17 has three wives, B aged 17, C aged 16 and D aged 19, the couple allowance is calculated as between A and D and is for couples where at least one member is more than 18. A further amount is then awarded for B and C as stated above.
Paras (c) to (e) are identical to the premiums awarded under reg 22(b) to (d), save that in relation to family and child premiums the claimant is entitled if any of her/his partners is responsible for the children.

Patients
[¹**24.**]

Amendment
1.	Omitted by reg 2(4) of SI 2005 No 2502 as amended by Sch 2 para 27 of SI 2006 No 217 as from 1.4.06 (3.4.06 where rent payable weekly or at intervals of a week).

General Note
Until omitted, reg 24 varied the applicable amounts due under reg 22 or reg 23 as appropriate, in relation to claimants who had been patients for more than 52 weeks. Whether someone is a patient is still of relevance in the treatment of childcare costs (under reg 28) and to entitlement to the disability and enchanced disability premiums (paras 13 and 15 of Sch 3). The definition of "patient" for these purposes is in reg 28(11)(e).

Long-term hospital patients may still be caught by the requirement that they be occupying the home in reg 7, but see reg 7(16)(c)(ii). The definition of "patient" for these purposes is in reg 7(18). The definition there also applies in determining whether a non-dependant deduction is applicable under reg 74(7)(f).

PART 6
Income and capital

General Note on Part 6
The claimant's income and capital and that of her/his partner, together with her/his applicable amount (see Part 5) and her/his eligible rent (see Part 3) are the basic components of the HB calculation: see s130(1)(c) SSCBA (p4).

The rules are very detailed and are largely in line with the rules for IS and income-based JSA. Caselaw in relation to those benefits and that decided under the old supplementary benefit scheme will often be highly persuasive. There are a number of court judgments, and a vast volume of commissioner's decisions. Only the most significant are examined in the commentary to Part 6. See the current volume of *Social Security Legislation Vol 2* for a more comprehensive treatment.

There is provision for assessment of capital, and a capital limit on entitlement of £16,000.

Income and capital: the distinction
No attempt has been made at any sort of definition of the difference between income and capital. What is very clear is that a resource must be either one or the other; there is nothing in between. However, although a resource at any one time must be income or capital, it does not follow that such status is immutable as a sum of money can alter in status, particularly over time: *CH 1561/2005* paras 17 and 18.

In order to decide whether a particular resource is income or capital, careful note should be taken of the provisions for treatment of income as capital and *vice versa*: see regs 41 and 46 respectively. Further indications as to the nature of a resource may be found in Schs 5 and 6, which set out the categories of income and capital that are to be disregarded in the assessment process. If a resource is required to be partially disregarded as income or as capital, that is a good indication that the resource (or those of a similar nature) is intended by the regulations to be treated as such. For example, Sch 6 para 10(a) requires insurance payments relating to damage to the home to be ignored for up to 26 weeks. It follows that such payments will be treated as capital, and it can be deduced from that that most insurance pay-outs will fall to be treated as capital rather than income.

However, *CH 1561/2005* warns against assuming that the provisions of the legislation can determine the classification of whether a sum of money is income or capital. Indeed the decision goes further than this and holds that the regulations do not provide any definition of income or capital (either expressly – which is true – or by implication) but instead are predicated on the classification already having been made. Even if this approach is correct, it is suggested that the provisions of the regulations may provide helpful guidance as to whether an initial classification of a sum of money into income or capital is correct (which the commissioner in *CH 1561/2005* himself would seem to have done when deciding in that case that arrears of working families' tax credit were to be treated as income).

Where the legislation does not specifically or implicitly define how a payment should be treated, resort must be had to the caselaw. A useful starting point is the decision of Bridge J in *R v Supplementary Benefit Commission ex p Singer* [1973] 1 WLR 713. He stated that the "essential feature of receipts by way of income is that they display an element of periodic recurrence. Income cannot include ad hoc receipts." This is a useful rule of thumb but it does not provide a complete answer, because periodic payments may constitute capital in certain circumstances. It is also necessary to consider the nature of the obligation under which the payments are made. In *Lillystone v Supplementary Benefits Commission* [1982] 3 FLR 52, CA, the claimant was receiving £70 a month for 10 years towards the purchase price of his house. Because the payments went towards the sale price of a capital asset, it was held that the payments constituted capital.

Two cases decided under a former version of the HB Regs 1987 may also be of assistance. In *R v Oxford CC ex p Jack* [1984] 17 HLR 419, QBD, the High Court considered the meaning of "income other than earnings" and quashed a decision of a review board to base its assessment of the claimant's income on withdrawals from his current account. This was because "the Board failed to enquire where the various sums paid into the account had come from". It might have been reasonable to base the claimant's income on his current account if no other evidence was available, but there was in this case. The judge referred to the definition of income in the Shorter Oxford English Dictionary. The current definitions of income and capital are

"that which comes in as the periodical produce of one's work, business, lands or investment (commonly expressed in terms of money) annual or periodical receipts; revenue."

On the basis of the definition of "income", the judge made the following general remarks about the nature of income:

"income, in my view, is what would in the colloquial sense, be regarded as a person's income, including not merely periodical payments received as of legal right, but periodical payments received, not necessarily at regular intervals, as a result of parental or family feeling or as a result of an agreement not enforceable by law."

"[if] regular payments are made . . . it is much more likely that it will appear to be income than if it is an irregular amount which is paid at less regular intervals [although] the precise period for which payment is made is not critical".

Therefore, a lump sum paid at the start of a year with the expectation that it should gradually be drawn on for living expenses "would properly fall to be considered as income".

In *R v West Dorset DC ex p Poupard* [1988] 28 RVR 40, CA, Balcombe LJ considered the point and stated (at p43):

"if and insofar as what Glidewell J was saying was that it was a question of fact in any case, within the discretion of the review board, whether withdrawals from a bank account could be taken into account in estimating income, I respectfully agree [but] if he was intending to accept the concession 'prima facie that a withdrawal is not income', then in my judgment . . . his remarks were obiter and I do not accept them as laying down any general principle . . ."

In *Poupard,* the claimant's business was shown to have made a loss, but the claimant had made drawings both from the business receipts and from a bank overdraft facility in order to pay for living expenses, and those drawings were treated as income. Balcombe LJ's conclusions were as follows (at p43):

"(1)   Income is that which comes in to the applicant;

(2)   It may, depending on the facts of the case, be appropriate to take into account cash withdrawals from the gross receipts of an applicant's business, or withdrawals from an applicant's business, or withdrawals from an applicant's bank account or other moneys received by way of loan, notwithstanding that these may not be classified as income on accounting principles and notwithstanding that the loan may eventually be repaid out of capital.

(3)   Capital which is in no way utilised cannot be deemed to constitute or create income.

(4)   However, again depending on the facts of the particular case, the utilisation of capital, whether directly so as to pay for living expenses, or indirectly as security for a loan which is used to pay for living expenses, may thereby 'convert' the capital so used into 'income'."

Some care is required in using these cases, however, for two reasons. First, specific provision is now made to meet some of the points made: see, for example, reg 52(1) which *does* deem capital to create income.

Secondly, the old HB scheme did not contain any capital limit. In *ex p Jack*, Glidewell J had referred extensively to Bridge J's views as to the nature of "income" in *Singer* (see above). In *Poupard*, Balcombe LJ found this case "of no help" because the supplementary benefit legislation had separate provision for the assessment of income and capital in the same way that the current HB Regs do. Consequently the comments in *Singer* are more relevant now than when they were considered in *Poupard*. Despite the fact that *Poupard* is a decision of the Court of Appeal, it is submitted that this case is of little assistance given the current HB scheme's distinction between capital and income.

Because income and capital are treated separately under these regulations, as they were in *Singer*, the relevance of *Poupard* to the current regulations must be debatable where, say, only sporadic withdrawals of differing amounts are made. The Court of Appeal held in *Poupard* that borrowings by way of a bank overdraft secured by capital and used for day-to-day living expenses constitute "income" for HB purposes. This decision is not necessarily inconsistent with *ex p Jack* as the Court did have regard to the source of the money and the fact that the loan was secured by capital. Certainly, the more general comments in *ex p Jack* regarding the nature of income payments have not been interfered with.

However, in *R(H) 5/05* Commissioner Mesher reached the opposite conclusion, in holding that "the resources provided by the use of the overdraft facility do not amount to income" (para: 47); though it would appear that the contrary was not argued before him nor was *Poupard* cited to him. His reasoning, in paragraphs 44 to 47, was as follows:

"It is just possible that it could have been argued that the claimant's use of the overdraft facility with his bank produced income in his hands. Nowhere in his comprehensive written and oral submissions did Mr Stagg make that specific argument, and it does not specifically appear anywhere else in the papers. In those circumstances I have not sought any further submissions and explain only briefly why I conclude that that argument would not work.

"The argument could have run as follows. On the statements before me, the first cheque paid by the bank without funds in the account to cover it was paid on 28 March 2001. By 18 April 2001 the overdraft stood at £2,799.55. The overdraft seems initially not to have been agreed, although it probably was by 18 April 2001. But it is established that the drawing of a cheque in excess of the amount standing to a customer's credit is a request for a loan and if the cheque is honoured the customer has borrowed money (see paragraph 11 of *R(IS) 22/98*). Money drawn down under an agreed limit is also borrowing, as is the honouring of cheques taking an overdraft over an agreed limit. The first two payments from Ms LB reduced the amount by which the claimant was overdrawn. The payments on 17 July 2001 and 7 November 2001 took him into credit, but the effect did not last for more than a few weeks in either case. The payment on 14 January 2002 did enable the claimant to stay in credit until 2 April 2002. It might have been argued that the approach endorsed by the Court of Appeal in *Morrell, R(IS) 6/03*, applied to the loans made to the claimant by his bank by way of overdraft. That would have been on the basis that a purpose must have been to allow the claimant to meet the recurrent expenses ordinarily met out of his current account. Chief among these was the monthly rent of £1,785.33, and there were other regular payments for items like home and contents insurance and water rates, as well as payments for cable services and credit card bills. It could have been argued that the provision of resources for such regularly recurring items resulted in the receipt of income.

"That on its face is a powerful argument. But it seems to me that it is undermined by the principles laid down in *Leeves v Chief Adjudication Officer*, R(IS) 5/99, as followed in *Morrell*). In that case, a student abandoned his course on 27 April 1995 having received the summer term's instalment of grant from his local education authority on 24 April 1995 (and spent it all on paying off mortgage arrears and debts). He had undertaken, in accordance with the legislation then in force on student grants, to repay such sum as might be determined by the authority if he ceased to attend the course before its normal termination date. On 24 May 1995 the authority wrote to the student terminating his grant with effect from 27 April 1995 and requiring repayment of a particular amount. Under the income support rules the payment of grant on 24 April 1995 would be attributed as income to the whole of the summer term. The Court of Appeal held that as from 24 May 1995 the grant monies were not income. The court agreed with counsel for the student that "income" should be given its natural and ordinary meaning and that moneys accruing or to be treated as accruing "under a certain obligation of immediate payment (ie, an equivalent debt) do not amount to income". From 27 April 1995 to 23 May 1995, although there was no reason to think that the discretion to call for repayment would not be exercised, it was not clear when the student would be required to repay or what the precise sum would be. So there was no "crystallised" obligation. But there was from 24 May 1995.

"Although I have no evidence in the present case of the precise terms on which the overdraft was granted to the claimant, I can take judicial notice of the fact that the standard terms are that bank overdrafts are repayable on demand, although the demand may be not be made while the amount stays within an agreed limit. Those terms bring the claimant's repayment obligation within the *Leeves* principles. The obligation is certain, as the amount overdrawn can be identified day by day, and is immediate, even though the bank chooses not to enforce the immediate obligation. Accordingly, the resources provided by the use of the overdraft facility do not amount to income. In my judgment, that result is also in accord with the ordinary and natural meaning of "income". One would not naturally speak of a person having an income from incurring expenditure and running up an overdraft".

Another important point is the effect of retention of income. The most common example of a capital asset is, perhaps, a bank account which contains the accumulated earnings of the account-holder, minus their outgoings. Thus there comes a point at which income metamorphoses into capital. The general rule is that a payment is treated as income for a period equal to that to which it is attributable, whereon it becomes part of the claimant's capital: see *R(IS) 3/93* para 22.

Decision-making on income and capital issues

The rules in this Part only apply, effectively, to claimants who are not in receipt of IS or income-based JSA. Recipients of those benefits have already had their income and capital taken into account for the purposes of assessing entitlement to that benefit. By definition, IS and income-based JSA claimants have capital worth less than £16,000 and income less than their applicable amounts, and whatever income or capital as such claimants *do* possess is disregarded under Schs 4, 5 and 6. They are therefore entitled to HB under s130(1)(c)(i) SSCBA, and there is no need for local authorities to assess income and capital under this Part to determine entitlement: see *R v Penwith DC ex p Menear* [1990] 24 HLR 120, QBD. This means that the authority can, and usually must, consider itself bound by a DWP decision to award IS or income-based JSA.

There are two exceptions to this cardinal rule. The first arises where an authority has evidence which has not already been considered by the DWP and which raises a reasonable doubt as to whether the DWP decision on the means test was correct. The authority may notify the DWP of its views under the information-sharing powers in Part VII SSAA and may suspend payment of HB pending consideration by the DWP as to whether the award of benefit should be revised or superseded: see reg 11 D&A Regs.

The second exception is a product of the decision of the Court of Appeal in *R v South Ribble DC HBRB ex p Hamilton* [2000] 33 HLR 102, CA. In that case, the Review Board upheld the council's determinations that HB should be refused to the claimant on the basis that he was fraudulently concealing income and capital resources from the then DSS and the local authority. There was, indeed, strong evidence before the Board to this effect, but the authority did not refer the matter to the DSS for investigation. The Court of Appeal approved the decision in *ex p Menear*, but said that the decision did not require a council to pay HB (or even to award it and then withhold benefit pending examination of the issue). If the authority is able to conclude that the claimant is fraudulently concealing resources from the DWP, it may lawfully refuse to award benefit.

On its facts, the decision is justifiable as a matter of public policy. However, caution will be required in its application. In *Hamilton* there was apparently no evidence that the DWP had ever considered whether it shared the local authority's view that the claimant was acting fraudulently. However, there may be cases where the DWP has examined a claim and has concluded that there is no basis for taking away the claimant's IS or JSA, or where a decision by a decision maker that a claimant has been acting fraudulently is reversed on appeal to an appeal tribunal. In that event, *Hamilton* should not be read as giving the local authority an entitlement to take a different view. The structure of the legislation, as emphasised in *Menear*, is that it is for the DWP (and subsequently the appeal tribunal) to make decisions on income and capital. It will only be if the DWP has not had an adequate opportunity to decide whether the claimant is concealing resources that the local authority will be justified in refusing benefit on the basis of the decision in *Hamilton*. This will apply both to cases where the DWP has been unaware of any basis for questioning the decision to award benefit and also to cases where the DWP (or an appeal tribunal) has decided that benefit should not be withdrawn but the authority has fresh evidence at its disposal.

It should also be noted that if the DWP *refuses* IS or income-based JSA (or, for that matter, any other means-tested benefit) on the basis of excess income or capital, there is nothing in the legislation that requires or entitles the authority to follow suit. It must carry out its own assessment of income and capital and is entitled to come to a different conclusion, though it is entitled to inquire of the DWP under Pt VII of the SSAA as to the basis for its refusal of benefit.

Structure of the Part

Section 1 contains general rules about when another person's income/capital may be treated as belonging to the claimant, and when the HB calculation may be based on a non-dependant's income and capital rather than the claimant's own. The provisions of Sections 2 to 5 apply to the claimant's income as defined by Section 1 (thus including that of her/his partner or partners falling within reg 25).

Section 2 contains general rules about the calculation of income on a weekly basis and what counts as "income" for these purposes. Regs 27 to 31 provide a definition of the different categories of income which are subject to the specific rules in Sections 3 to 5. Reg 33 applies generally to convert payments of assessable income into weekly amounts where they are paid for periods other than a week, as HB is calculated on a weekly basis. Reg 34 deals with the effect of changes in certain statutory deductions from income and is really a provision to help authorities administer the scheme more efficiently. The total amount of weekly income to be taken into account under this Part is the claimant's weekly income assessed under regs 29 to 32, plus any "tariff income" and capital treated as income.

Section 3 contains specific rules about the assessment of earnings from "employed earners" employment.

Section 4 contains specific rules about earnings from employment as a "self-employed" earner.

Section 5 sets out specific rules about the assessment of income which is not earnings.

Section 6 contains the rules about the assessment of capital.

SECTION 1
General

General Note on Section 1

This Section deals with two matters pursuant to s136 SSCBA in relation to the calculation of a claimant's income and capital:

(1)   Reg 25, by authority of s136(1) SSCBA, prescribes the circumstances in which the income and capital of members of the claimant's family will be treated as the claimant's own. It also sets out the circumstances in which a claimant who is polygamously married will be treated as possessing the income and capital of her/his partners.

(2)   Reg 26, in pursuance of s136(5)(a) and (b) SSCBA, enables the authority assessing benefit to treat the claimant as possessing the income and capital of a non-dependant and members of the non-dependant's family rather than her/his own resources, which are then disregarded. This is an anti-abuse provision.

Calculation of income and capital of members of claimant's family and of a polygamous marriage

25.–(1)   The income and capital of a claimant's partner which by virtue of section 136(1) of the Act is to be treated as income and capital of the claimant, shall be calculated or estimated in accordance with the following provisions of this Part in like manner as for the claimant; and any reference to the "claimant" shall, except where the context otherwise requires, be construed for the purposes of this Part as if it were a reference to his partner.

(2)   Where a claimant or the partner of a claimant is married polygamously to two or more members of his household–

(a)   the claimant shall be treated as possessing capital and income belonging to each such member; and

(b)   the income and capital of that member shall be calculated in accordance with the following provisions of this Part in like manner as for the claimant.

(3)   The income and capital of a child or young person shall not be treated as the income and capital of the claimant.

Definitions

"child" – see reg 2(1).
"claimant" – see reg 2(1).
"family" – see s137(1) SSCBA.
"household" – see "family".
"married polygamously" – see reg 2(1).
"partner" – see reg 2(1).
"young person" – see reg 19.

General Note

According to s136(1) SSCBA, a claimant is to be treated as possessing the income and capital of members of her/his "family" "except in prescribed circumstances". Under s136(5)(a) SSCBA, regulations may prescribe circumstances in which a claimant may be treated as possessing income which s/he does not in fact possess. This regulation, together with the other provisions of this Part prescribes that a child or young person's income and capital are not to be treated as the claimants. Using the powers in s136(5)(a), it also provides that claimants who are polygamously married are to be treated as possessing the income/capital of their partners who share their household.

Analysis

Para (1). The effect of para (1) is that whenever a reference to the claimant's capital or income is made it is to be treated as including the capital/income of her/his partner.

Para (2) provides that where the claimant is polygamously married s/he is to be treated as possessing the income and capital of all partners to the marriage with whom s/he shares a household (see p23).

Para (3) states that the income and capital of a child or young person is not treated as that of the claimant.

Circumstances in which income of non-dependant is to be treated as claimant's

26.–(1)   Where it appears to the relevant authority that a non-dependant and the claimant have entered into arrangements in order to take advantage of the housing benefit scheme and the non-dependant has more capital and income than the claimant, that authority shall, except where the claimant is on income support or an income-based jobseeker's allowance, treat the claimant as possessing capital and income belonging to that non-dependant and, in such a case, shall disregard any capital and income which the claimant does possess.

(2)   Where a claimant is treated as possessing capital and income belonging to a non-dependant under paragraph (1) the capital and income of that non-dependant shall be calculated in accordance with the following provisions of this Part in like manner as for the claimant and any reference to the ''claimant'' shall, except where the context otherwise requires, be construed for the purposes of this Part as if it were a reference to that non-dependant.

Definitions

"claimant" – see reg 2(1).
"non-dependant" – see reg 3.

General Note

Made under s136(5)(a) and (b) SSCBA, this regulation gives an authority the power to assess entitlement to HB on the basis of a non-dependant's capital and income, rather than on the basis of the claimant's own, where the circumstances suggest to the authority that the claimant and non-dependant have made arrangements so as to take advantage of the HB scheme and the non-dependant has more income and capital than the claimant.

Analysis

Para (1). The language used in para (1), in particular the phrase "take advantage of the housing benefit scheme" are similar to that used in reg 9(1)(l) and so it is suggested that similar considerations arise and the caselaw will assist in resolving disputes on the application of this provision. Reference should be made to the Analysis to that provision, but some modification will be necessary.

The first step will be to identify some "arrangements" that the claimant and non-dependant have entered into. Some evidence of collusion will usually be required. Thus where A is a tenant whose uncle B lives with him and A becomes unemployed and claims HB to meet his rent liability, there is no basis for fixing him with B's resources. It is clear that the power cannot be used just because the non-dependant is wealthier than the claimant, and it is suggested that it should be used only where good reason exists.

If challenged, the onus will be on the authority to show grounds for its belief that arrangements have been made so as to take advantage of the HB scheme. The words "appears to the authority" do not absolve the authority from determining the question on proper principles and if it fails to do so, its decision will be vulnerable to challenge.

Note that this power may be used only where the non-dependant's income and capital *both* exceed that of the claimant and that it cannot be used where the claimant is on IS or income-based JSA.

Para (2). If the authority does decide to use this power, it must base the HB calculation on the non-dependant's income and capital. Previous editions have suggested that this will include resources belonging to the non-dependant's family, but it is suggested that is incorrect. Para (2) requires the non-dependant's resources to be calculated under the "following provisions" of this Part and it would appear that phrase excludes consideration of reg 25 which deals with the treatment of the resources of family members and of reg 26 itself.

If the power is exercised, the claimant's income and capital is to be disregarded under para (1).

Every reference to claimant in this part should be read as referring to the "non-dependant" unless the context of the regulation in question makes it clear that this is not intended. See particularly the note on Sch 4 para 3.

SECTION 2
Income

General Note on Section 2

This Section deals with the assessment of various types of income for HB purposes.

Reg 27 deals with the question of how total weekly income is calculated.

Reg 28 deals with childcare charges.

Reg 29, together with Section 3 and Sch 4, deals with the assessment of earnings from employed earner's employment.

Reg 30, together with Section 4 and Sch 4, deals with the assessment of earnings from self-employed earner's employment.

Reg 31, together with Section 5 and Sch 5, deals with the assessment of income from other sources than employment.

Reg 32 deals with the period over which income from tax credits is to be taken into account.

Reg 33 provides a mechanism for converting payments of income made other than on a weekly basis into weekly amounts.

Reg 34 gives authorities some discretion over when they take changes in tax and other statutory deductions from income into account for HB purposes.

Calculation of income on a weekly basis

27.–(1) Subject to regulations 34 (disregard of changes in tax, contributions etc), and 80 and 81 (calculation of weekly amounts and rent free periods) for the purposes of section 130(1)(c) of the Act (conditions of entitlement to housing benefit) the income of a claimant shall be calculated on a weekly basis–

(a)   by estimating the amount which is likely to be his average weekly income in accordance with this Section and Sections 3 to 5 of this Part and Sections 1 and 3 of Part 7;

(b)   by adding to that amount the weekly income calculated under regulation 52 (calculation of tariff income from capital); and

(c)   by then deducting any relevant child care charges to which regulation 28 (treatment of child care charges) applies from any earnings which form part of the average weekly income or, in a case where the conditions in paragraph (2) are met, from those earnings plus whichever credit specified in sub-paragraph (b) of that paragraph is appropriate, up to a maximum deduction in respect of the claimant's family of whichever of the sums specified in paragraph (3) applies in his case.

(2)   The conditions of this paragraph are that–

(a)   the claimant's earnings which form part of his average weekly income are less than the lower of either his relevant child care charges or whichever of the deductions specified in paragraph (3) otherwise applies in his case; and

(b)   that claimant or, if he is a member of a couple either the claimant or his partner, is in receipt of either working tax credit or child tax credit.

(3)   The maximum deduction to which paragraph (1)(c) above refers shall be–

(a)   where the claimant's family includes only one child in respect of whom relevant child care charges are paid, [2 £175.00] per week;

(b)   where the claimant's family includes more than one child in respect of whom relevant child care charges are paid, [2 £300] per week.

(4)   For the purposes of paragraph (1) "income" includes capital treated as income under regulation 41 (capital treated as income) and income which a claimant is treated as possessing under regulation 42 (notional income).

Amendments

1.   Confirmed by Art 19(2) of SI 2006 No 645 and reg 8 of SI 2006 No 217 as from 1.4.06 (3.4.06 where rent payable weekly or at intervals of a week).

2.   Confirmed by Art 19(2) of SI 2007 No 688 as from 1.4.07 (2.4.07 where rent payable weekly or at intervals of a week).

Definition
"claimant" – see reg 2(1).

General Note
Reg 27 sets out the basic formula for the calculation of income. It is the total income assessed under Sections 1 to 5 of this Part (and the special provisions for students in Part 7) plus any tariff income deemed to be generated by capital under reg 52, minus deductible child care charges up to the maximum figures stated in para (3). "Income" in this context includes notional income and capital deemed to be income as well as actual income: see para (4).

Analysis
> *Para (1)(b).* Under reg 52, a claimant is treated as receiving income from her/his capital if the latter is worth more than £6,000 but less than £16,000 as assessed under Section 6 of this Part and Sch 6. Any actual income from capital is generally treated as capital under reg 46(4).
>
> *Paras (1)(c), (2) and (3)* provide for childcare charges (as defined by reg 28 below) to be deducted from earnings subject to weekly maxima of a set amount where those charges are incurred in respect of one child and a higher amount where they are incurred in respect of more than one child. Where the claimant's earnings are lower than the childcare charges or the amounts specified in para (3), any tax credit to which the claimant is entitled will be added to the earnings for the purpose of calculating the deduction.
>
> *Para (4).* This confirms that notional income (reg 42) and capital treated as income (reg 41) should be included in the calculation of income on a weekly basis.

Treatment of child care charges

28.–(1)   This regulation applies where a claimant is incurring relevant child care charges and–

(a)   is a lone parent and is engaged in remunerative work;

(b)   is a member of a couple both of whom are engaged in remunerative work; or

(c)   is a member of a couple where one member is engaged in remunerative work and the other–

(i)   is incapacitated;

(ii)   is an in-patient in hospital; or

(iii)   is in prison (whether serving a custodial sentence or remanded in custody awaiting trial or sentence).

(2)   For the purposes of paragraph (1) and subject to paragraph (4), a person to whom paragraph (3) applies shall be treated as engaged in remunerative work for a period not exceeding 28 weeks during which he–

(a)   is paid statutory sick pay;

(b)   is paid short-term incapacity benefit at the lower rate under sections 30A to 30E of the Act;

(c)   is paid income support on the grounds of incapacity for work under regulation 4ZA of, and paragraph 7 or 14 of Schedule 1B to, the Income Support Regulations; or

(d)   is credited with earnings on the grounds of incapacity for work under regulation 8B of the Social Security (Credits) Regulations 1975.

(3)   This paragraph applies to a person who was engaged in remunerative work immediately before–

(a)   the first day of the period in respect of which he was first paid statutory sick pay, short-term incapacity benefit or income support on the grounds of incapacity for work; or

(b)   the first day of the period in respect of which earnings are credited,
as the case may be.

(4)   In a case to which paragraph (2)(c) or (d) applies, the period of 28 weeks begins on the day on which the person is first paid income support or on the first day of the period in respect of which earnings are credited, as the case may be.

(5)   Relevant child care charges are those charges for care to which paragraphs (6) and (7) apply, and shall be calculated on a weekly basis in accordance with paragraph (10).

(6)   The charges are paid by the claimant for care which is provided–

(a)   in the case of any child of the claimant's family who is not disabled, in respect of the period beginning on that child's date of birth and ending on the day preceding the first Monday in September following that child's fifteenth birthday; or

(b)   in the case of any child of the claimant's family who is disabled, in respect of the period beginning on that person's date of birth and ending on the day preceding the first Monday in September following that person's sixteenth birthday.

(7)   The charges are paid for care which is provided by one or more of the care providers listed in paragraph (8) and are not paid–

(a)   in respect of the child's compulsory education;

(b)   by a claimant to a partner or by a partner to a claimant in respect of any child for whom either or any of them is responsible in accordance with regulation 20 (circumstances in which a person is treated as responsible or not responsible for another); or

(c)   in respect of care provided by a relative of a child wholly or mainly in the child's home.

(8)   The care to which paragraph (7) refers may be provided–

(a)   out of school hours, by a school on school premises or by a local authority–

(i)   for children who are not disabled in respect of the period beginning on their eighth birthday and ending on the day preceding the first Monday in September following their fifteenth birthday; or

(ii)   for children who are disabled in respect of the period beginning on their eighth birthday and ending on the day preceding the first Monday in September following their sixteenth birthday;

(b)   by a child care provider approved in accordance with the Tax Credit (New Category of Child Care Provider) Regulations 1999;

(c)   by persons registered under Part 10A of the Children Act 1989; or

(d)   in schools or establishments which are exempted from registration under Part 10A of the Children Act 1989 by virtue of paragraph 1 or 2 of Schedule 9A to that Act; or

(e)   by–

(i)   persons registered under section 7(1) of the Regulation of Care (Scotland) Act 2001; or

(ii)   local authorities registered under section 33(1) of that Act,

where the care provided is child minding or daycare of children within the meaning of that Act; or

(f)   by a person prescribed in regulations made pursuant to section 12(4) of the Tax Credits Act.

(9)   In paragraphs (6) and (8)(a), "the first Monday in September" means the Monday which first occurs in the month of September in any year.

(10)   Relevant child care charges shall be estimated over such period, not exceeding a year, as is appropriate in order that the average weekly charge may be estimated accurately having regard to information as to the amount of that charge provided by the child minder or person providing the care.

(11)   For the purposes of paragraph (1)(c) the other member of a couple is incapacitated where–

(a)   the claimant's applicable amount includes–

(i)   a disability premium; or

(ii)   a higher pensioner premium by virtue of the satisfaction of paragraph 11(2)(b) of Schedule 3,

on account of the other member's incapacity;
- (b) the claimant's applicable amount would include a disability premium or a higher pensioner premium on account of the other member's incapacity but for that other member being treated as capable of work by virtue of a determination made in accordance with regulations made under section 171E of the Act;
- (c) the claimant (within the meaning of regulation 2) is, or is treated as, incapable of work and has been so incapable, or has been so treated as incapable, of work in accordance with the provisions of, and regulations made under, Part 12A of the Act (incapacity for work) for a continuous period of not less than 196 days; and for this purpose any two or more separate periods separated by a break of not more than 56 days shall be treated as one continuous period;
- (d) there is payable in respect of him one or more of the following pensions or allowances–
    - (i) long-term incapacity benefit or short-term incapacity benefit at the higher rate under Schedule 4 to the Act;
    - (ii) attendance allowance under section 64 of the Act;
    - (iii) severe disablement allowance under section 68 of the Act;
    - (iv) disability living allowance under section 71 of the Act;
    - (v) increase of disablement pension under section 104 of the Act;
    - (vi) a pension increase under a war pension scheme or an industrial injuries scheme which is analogous to an allowance or increase of disablement pension under head (ii), (iv) or (v) above;
- (e) a pension or allowance to which head (ii), (iv), (v) or (vi) of sub-paragraph (d) above refers was payable on account of his incapacity but has ceased to be payable in consequence of his becoming a patient [¹ , which in this regulation shall mean a person (other than a person who is serving a sentence of imprisonment or detention in a youth custody institution) who is regarded as receiving free in-patient treatment within the meaning of [² regulation 2(4) and (5) of the Social Security (Hospital In-Patients) Regulations 2005].];
- (f) sub-paragraph (d) or (e) would apply to him if the legislative provisions referred to in those sub-paragraphs were provisions under any corresponding enactment having effect in Northern Ireland; or
- (g) he has an invalid carriage or other vehicle provided to him by the Secretary of State under section 5(2)(a) of and Schedule 2 to the National Health Service Act 1977 or by Scottish Ministers under section 46 of the National Health Service (Scotland) Act 1978 or provided by the Department of Health and Social Services for Northern Ireland under Article 30(1) of the Health and Personal Social Services (Northern Ireland) Order 1972.

(12) For the purposes of paragraph (11), once paragraph (11)(c) applies to the claimant, if he then ceases, for a period of 56 days or less, to be incapable, or to be treated as incapable, of work, that paragraph shall, on his again becoming so incapable, or so treated as incapable, of work at the end of that period, immediately thereafter apply to him for so long as he remains incapable, or is treated as remaining incapable, of work.

(13) For the purposes of paragraphs (6) and (8)(a), a person is disabled if he is a person–
- (a) in respect of whom disability living allowance is payable, or has ceased to be payable solely because he is a patient;
- (b) who is registered as blind in a register compiled under section 29 of the National Assistance Act 1948 (welfare services) or, in Scotland, has been certified as blind and in consequence he is registered as blind in a register

maintained by or on behalf of a council constituted under section 2 of the Local Government (Scotland) Act 1994; or

(c) who ceased to be registered as blind in such a register within the period beginning 28 weeks before the first Monday in September following that person's fifteenth birthday and ending on the day preceding the first Monday in September following that person's sixteenth birthday.

(14) For the purposes of–

(a) paragraph (1) a person on maternity leave, paternity leave or adoption leave shall be treated as if she is engaged in remunerative work for the period specified in sub-paragraph (b) ("the relevant period") provided that–

   (i) in the week before the period of maternity leave, paternity leave or adoption leave began she was in remunerative work;

   (ii) the claimant is incurring relevant child care charges within the meaning of paragraph (5); and

   (iii) she is entitled to statutory maternity pay under section 164 of the Act, statutory paternity pay by virtue of section 171ZA or 171ZB of the Act, statutory adoption pay by virtue of section 171ZL of the Act, maternity allowance under section 35 of the Act or qualifying support;

(b) sub-paragraph (a) the relevant period shall begin on the day on which the person's maternity leave, paternity leave or adoption leave commences and shall end on–

   (i) the date that leave ends;

   (ii) if no child care element of working tax credit is in payment on the date that entitlement to maternity allowance, qualifying support, statutory maternity pay, statutory paternity pay or statutory adoption pay ends, the date that entitlement ends; or

   (iii) if a child care element of working tax credit is in payment on the date that entitlement to maternity allowance, qualifying support, statutory maternity pay, statutory paternity pay or statutory adoption pay ends, the date that entitlement to that award of the child care element of working tax credit ends,

whichever shall occur first.

(15) In paragraph (14)–

(a) "qualifying support" means income support to which that person is entitled by virtue of paragraph 14B of Schedule 1B to the Income Support Regulations; and

(b) "child care element" of working tax credit means the element of working tax credit prescribed under section 12 of the Tax Credits Act (child care element).

Amendments

1. Amended by reg 2(5) of SI 2005 No 2502 as amended by Sch 2 para 27 of SI 2006 No 217 as from 1.4.06 (3.4.06 where rent payable weekly or at intervals of a week).

2. Amended by reg 5(2) of SI 2005 No 3360 as subsituted by Sch 2 para 30 of SI 2006 No 217 as from 10.4.06.

General Note

This regulation defines the circumstances in which childcare charges may be deducted (subject to the weekly maxima in reg 27(3)) from a claimant's earnings (and in some cases, WTC or CTC) under reg 27(1)(c).

Analysis

Para (1) lists the categories of people who are entitled to have child care charges deducted from their earnings (and in some cases WTC or CTC). The relevant categories are lone parents who are in "remunerative work" (for which see reg 6 and paras (2) to (4) , (14) and (15)), and couples with children where either both partners are in remunerative work or one partner is and the other is "incapacitated" as defined by paras (11) and (12), an in-patient in hospital as defined in para (11)(e) or in prison (on remand or serving a sentence).

Paras (2) to (4). A person who is absent from work because s/he is ill cannot be treated as in remunerative work under reg 6. However, for the purposes of the childcare charges disregard, paras (2) to (4) *can* treat someone as in remunerative work for the first 28 weeks of a period of sickness, so long as s/he was in such work immediately before getting one of the benefits specified in para (2)(a) to (c) or NI credits for incapacity. Note that after the 28 week period, lone parents are no longer entitled to have a deduction made for childcare charges. However, couples will, if one of the couple is in remunerative work and the other is "incapacitated" as defined in paras (11) and (12).

Paras (5) to (9) define the type of childcare charges which are eligible to be deducted. There are four basic rules:

(1)   The charges must be paid by the claimant, or possibly by the claimant's partner. The definition is ambiguous: see below.

(2)   The child must be a member of the claimant's family: see s137 SSCBA (p22) and Part 4.

(3)   The care must be provided by a registered child minder or through certain types of official scheme, listed in para (8).

(4)   The charges must relate to a period before the first Monday in September following the child's 15th birthday or, if the child is disabled within the definition in para (13), following her/his 16th birthday.

The charges cannot be payments for the child's compulsory education or made by the claimant to her/his partner or made in respect of care provided by a relative of the child in the child's home: para (7). Para (7) also says that payments made to the claimant by her/his partner are also ineligible but, given that the earlier part of the regulation suggests that payments can only be eligible in the first place if they are made "by the claimant" the effect of this part of the para is unclear. It seems to imply that payments made by a claimant's partner to, say, a registered child minder would be eligible and that the reference to "the claimant" rather than to "the claimant or the claimant's partner" is an oversight

Para (10) tells the authority to estimate the childcare charges over an appropriate period of no more than one year so as to reduce them accurately to a weekly amount for inclusion in the means test calculation.

Paras (11) to (13) define who is incapacitated and a patient for the purposes of para (1) and who is disabled for the purposes of para (8). For a discussion on the definition of "patient" see below.

Paras (14) and (15). People who are absent from work on maternity, paternity or adoption leave cannot be treated as in remunerative work under reg 6. However, for the purposes of the childcare charge deduction, paras (14) and (15) *can* treat someone who is on such leave as in remunerative work. The person must have been in remunerative work immediately before the leave began, must be paying relevant childcare charges and must be entitled to statutory maternity, paternity or adoption pay or maternity allowance, or "qualifying support" (defined in para (15) as IS because of being on paternity leave). Para 14(b) provides that this special treatment ends when the leave ends (in which case it is no longer necessary) or, if earlier, when the claimant ceases to be entitled to statutory maternity, paternity or adoption pay or maternity allowance or "qualifying support" unless she was being paid a childcare element of WTC at that date. In the latter case, the special treatment continues until the end of entitlement to the childcare element.

Who is a patient?

Reg 2(4) and (5) of the Social Security (Hospital In-Patients) Regulations 2005 provide as follows:

"(4)   For the purposes of this regulation, a person shall be regarded as receiving or having received free in-patient treatment for any period for which he is or has been maintained free of charge while undergoing medical or other treatment as an in-patient–

(a) in a hospital or similar institution under the National Health Service Act 1977, the National Health Service (Scotland) Act 1978 or the National Health Service and Community Care Act 1990, or

(b) in a hospital or similar institution maintained or administered by the Defence Council,

and such a person shall for the purposes of sub-paragraph (a) be regarded as being maintained free of charge in a hospital or similar institution unless his accommodation and services are provided under section 65 of the National Health Service Act 1977, section 57 of the National Health Service (Scotland) Act 1978 or paragraph 14 of Schedule 2 to the National Health Service and Community Care Act 1990.

(5)   For the purposes of paragraph (4), a period during which a person is regarded as receiving or having received free in-patient treatment shall be deemed to begin on the day after the day on which he enters a hospital or similar institution referred to in that paragraph and to end on the day on which he leaves such a hospital or similar institution."

If a person is a prisoner or in youth custody they do not fall within the definition of "patient" for HB purposes. Other than that, however, a person is a "patient" if s/he falls within the scope of this definition. Four questions need to be posed.

Is the person an "in-patient"? A period of in-patient treatment begins on the day after the day of admission and ends on the day on which the person leaves. This affirms the commissioner's reasoning in *R(IS) 8/ 96*. There is an area of doubt in respect of the "day" on which a person enters hospital. The commissioner proceeded on the basis that a "day" for these purposes was the 24 hours between midnight and midnight. This interpretation does have the benefit of certainty, but is not necessarily inherent in the use of the word "day": *Halsbury's Laws of England* (1984 4th edn) vol 45 para 1113. The powerful arguments in favour of requiring a 24 hour stay in *R(S) 4/84* do not appear to be explicitly overridden by para (5).

Is the person receiving relevant treatment? The scope of the regulation is not confined to medical treatment. In *Botchett v Chief Adjudication Officer* [1996] 2 CCLR 121, CA the claimant had severe learning difficulties, although not a patient within the meaning of the Mental Health Act 1983, and required a high degree of care and supervision. She lived in a nursing home administered by a trust, which would take any amount of IS to which she was entitled over and above the standard nursing home rates. It was argued that the claimant was receiving care and not treatment in the home. However, the Court of Appeal ruled that the attention she received constituted "medical or other treatment".

Is the person in a "hospital or similar institution"? The definitions in s128 of the National Health Service Act 1977 must be applied: *White v Chief Adjudication Officer* [1993] *The Times* 2 August, CA. "Hospital" is "(a) any institution for the reception and treatment of persons suffering from illness; (b) any maternity home; and (c) any institution for the reception and treatment of persons during convalescence or persons requiring medical rehabilitation." "Illness" includes "mental disorder within the meaning of the Mental Health Act 1983 and any injury or disability requiring medical or dental treatment or nursing". It does not appear to cover those with disabilities if such disabilities do not of themselves require medical treatment – eg, blindness: *Jewish Blind Society Trustees v Henning* [1961] 1 WLR 24 at 30, 34, CA. In *Botchett*, it was held that the definition of "mental disorder" in the 1983 Act was wide enough to cover the claimant in that case. The home was therefore a "similar institution". In order to be an "institution" however, it would have to be a "building used by .... a society or organisation": see the *Shorter Oxford English Dictionary*. It might be possible to argue that very small, privately-run nursing homes are not therefore within the scope of the definition.

This suggestion is supported by *CDLA 7980/1995*, a decision on reg 8 Social Security (Disability Living Allowance) Regulations 1991, which is in similar terms to reg 2(4). In that case, the claimant had a learning disability and was epileptic. She lived in a privately rented house along with six people in a similar position. 24-hour care was provided by specialist carers from the local authority. Medication was provided by the claimant's GP. The tribunal decided that the house was not a "similar institution" and the commissioner upheld its ruling. He said (para 9):

> "In my judgement, when those words are used in connection with the word 'hospital', they connote some sort of formal body or structure which controls all aspects of the treatment or care that is provided including the premises in which that treatment or care is carried out. They mean more than just a building in which care or treatment takes place. In this appeal, the treatment or care takes place in a private house which is let to the six occupants. They are the persons responsible for the payment of rent and other outgoings and for the purchase of their food. The appeal tribunal so found as they were bound to find on the evidence presented to them. .... On the appeal tribunal's findings there is simply no institution in the sense in which I consider the words must be construed. Further, no-one would suggest that the arrangements at No 167 could be described as 'a hospital' in any popular sense even though treatment and care is carried out there."

The authority of the decision is undermined slightly by the fact that *Botchett* was not apparently cited. However, it is suggested that it is correct. Note also that the treatment must be provided under one of the Acts mentioned in sub-para (a) or by the institutions mentioned in sub-para (b). If it is provided under the National Assistance Act 1948 or otherwise, the claimant will not be a "patient". Another authority supporting this interpretation of reg 2(4) is *CS 2647/1997* in which a resident at a hostel was held to fall outside its scope.

Is the person maintained free of charge? The effect of the closing words of para (4) is that a person is deemed to satisfy this condition unless they are privately paying patients under the legislation mentioned there. Thus in *CS 249/1989* a claimant whose wife brought him meals every day because the hospital could not satisfy his dietary requirements it was held that as he was not a private patient, he was deemed to be maintained free of charge even though it was costing the family money to feed him: para 11.

Average weekly earnings of employed earners

29.–(1) Where a claimant's income consists of earnings from employment as an employed earner his average weekly earnings shall be estimated by reference to his earnings from that employment–

(a)   over a period immediately preceding the benefit week in which the claim is made or treated as made and being a period of–

    (i)   5 weeks, if he is paid weekly; or

    (ii)   2 months, if he is paid monthly; or

(b)   whether or not sub-paragraph (a)(i) or (ii) applies, where a claimant's earnings fluctuate, over such other period preceding the benefit week in which the claim is made or treated as made as may, in any particular case, enable his average weekly earnings to be estimated more accurately.

(2)   Where the claimant has been in his employment for less than the period specified in paragraph (1)(a)(i) or (ii)–

(a)   if he has received any earnings for the period that he has been in that employment and those earnings are likely to represent his average weekly earnings from that employment his average weekly earnings shall be estimated by reference to those earnings;

(b)   in any other case, the relevant authority shall require the claimant's employer to furnish an estimate of the claimant's likely weekly earnings over such period as the relevant authority may require and the claimant's average weekly earnings shall be estimated by reference to that estimate.

(3)   Where the amount of a claimant's earnings changes during an award the relevant authority shall estimate his average weekly earnings by reference to his likely earnings from the employment over such period as is appropriate in order that his average weekly earnings may be estimated accurately but the length of the period shall not in any case exceed 52 weeks.

(4)   For the purposes of this regulation the claimant's earnings shall be calculated in accordance with Section 3 of this Part.

Definitions

"benefit week" – see reg 2(1).

"claimant" – see reg 2(1).

"earnings" – see regs 2(1) and 35(1).

"employment as an employed earner" – see reg 2(1).

"income" – see General Note on this section.

"relevant authority" – reg 2(1).

General Note

This regulation deals with the earnings of an employed, as opposed to a self-employed, claimant. Para (4) refers to Section 3 for the assessment of earnings in this respect. Para (1) specifies the period over which a claimant's weekly earnings are to be averaged and reg 33 provides a mechanism for calculating weekly amounts of earnings where payment has been made for a period other than a week.

Para (2) modifies the rules in para (1) for persons who have recently started work and para (3) deals with the situation where a claimant's earnings change during an award.

Remember that the earnings of a partner or partners of a claimant are included.

Earnings are usually verified from pay slips or a certificate of earnings. GM BW2.248 reminds authorities that because of the Government's overall policy of reducing the burden on business, they should avoid asking employers about a claimant's earnings unless no other source of information is available or there is doubt about the authenticity of the evidence provided by the claimant.

Analysis

Para (1). The wording of this regulation is unfortunate. The use of the word "consists" suggests that it only applies to claimants whose sole income is earnings from employment, although this surely cannot be the intention. For "benefit week in which the claim is made or treated as made", see reg 83.

If the claimant's weekly earnings fluctuate, the authority must use sub-paragraph (b) to calculate her/his weekly average rather than sub-para (a). The wording suggests that where sub-para (b) applies, the periods mentioned in sub-para (a) cannot be used even if they do accurately reflect the claimant's weekly average. Note that the period chosen under sub-para (a) or sub-para (b) must precede the week in which the claim is made or treated as made, rather than be based on estimated future earnings.

See reg 33 if the claimant is paid in respect of a period other than a week, in order to work out the weekly amount due.

Para (2) deals with the situation where the claimant has not yet been in employment for the appropriate period under para (1)(a)(i) or (ii).

Sub-para (a) deals with claimants who have already been paid amounts which reflect their likely future earnings; for "earnings", see para (4). See also reg 33 where the amount paid relates to a period other than a week.

Sub-para (b) deals with claimants who have not yet been paid any earnings, or who have been paid but the amount received is not representative of what they will receive in the future.

For the treatment of advance earnings, see reg 46(5).

Para (3) deals with changes in a claimant's "earnings" during an award. Such changes are relevant "changes of circumstance". Claimants are under a duty to report such changes: see reg 88. Reg 79 specifies the date on which the changes will take effect. This paragraph obliges the authority to amend the claimant's entitlement to HB when such a change becomes effective. The averaging process is not bound by para (1), which applies only to the determination of entitlement on a claim, but the authority must choose an appropriate period in order to estimate earnings accurately. The length of the period can in no case exceed 52 weeks. Reg 33 applies to help ascertain the weekly value of earnings for these purposes.

Para (4). See section 3 and Sch 4, for the assessment of earnings.

Average weekly earnings of self-employed earners

30.–(1)   Where a claimant's income consists of earnings from employment as a self-employed earner his average weekly earnings shall be estimated by reference to his earnings from that employment over such period as is appropriate in order that his average weekly earnings may be estimated accurately but the length of the period shall not in any case exceed a year.

(2)   For the purposes of this regulation the claimant's earnings shall be calculated in accordance with Section 4 of this Part.

Definitions

"claimant" – see reg 2(1).
"income" – see General Note on this Section.
"self-employed earner" – see reg 2(1).

General Note

This regulation deals with the earnings from self-employment of claimants and their partners. Reg 33 applies to ascertain the weekly amounts of such earnings if payment is made for a period other than a week. Para (2) provides that earnings are to be assessed for these purposes under s4 and Sch 4.

Analysis

Unlike the provisions in respect of *employed* earners, there is no mechanism for dealing with unforeseen changes in the claimant's income over the period of an award. Also there is no prescribed period over which income should be averaged. The authority must simply choose a period it thinks appropriate that will enable it to estimate the claimant's income from this source accurately. The averaging period must not exceed a year.

It was emphasised in *CH 329/2003* that it may not always be appropriate to use the last year's accounts.

Average weekly income other than earnings

31.–(1)   A claimant's income which does not consist of earnings shall, except where paragraph (2) applies, be estimated over such period as is appropriate in order that his average weekly income may be estimated accurately but the length of the period shall not in any case exceed 52 weeks; and nothing in this paragraph shall authorise an authority to disregard any such income other than that specified in Schedule 5.

(2)   The period over which any benefit under the benefit Acts is to be taken into account shall be the period in respect of which that benefit is payable.

(3)   For the purposes of this regulation income other than earnings shall be calculated in accordance with Section 5 of this Part.

Definitions

"benefit Acts" – see s123 SSCBA.

"claimant" – see reg 2(1).

"income" – see General Note on this Section.

General Note

This deals with income which is not "earnings" under Regs 29 and 30. Para (3) provides that such income is to be taken into account as specified by s5 and Sch 5. Under reg 27(1)(a), this "other income" is to be assessed on the basis of what a claimant is likely to receive on an average weekly basis. See reg 33 for the conversion of payments made in respect of periods other than a week into weekly amounts.

Analysis

As with regs 29 and 30, the authority must estimate such income over an appropriate period in order to estimate earnings accurately. Here the length of the period can in no case exceed 52 weeks. The authority can only disregard such amounts as are authorised by Sch 5. See also reg 25 for income which is treated as the claimant's for these purposes.

The effect of para (2) is that benefits paid under the benefit Acts (as defined in reg 2(1)) should only be taken into account during period in respect of which they are payable (eg, the two weeks before actual payment if made two-weekly in arrears); and if not paid for every week, they should only be taken into account in respect of the number of weeks for which they actually are paid.

Calculation of average weekly income from tax credits

32.–(1)   This regulation applies where a claimant receives a tax credit.

(2)   Where this regulation applies, the period over which a tax credit is to be taken into account shall be the period set out in paragraph (3).

(3)   Where the instalment in respect of which payment of a tax credit is made is–

(a)   a daily instalment, the period is 1 day, being the day in respect of which the instalment is paid;

(b)   a weekly instalment, the period is 7 days, ending on the day on which the instalment is due to be paid;

(c)   a two weekly instalment, the period is 14 days, commencing 6 days before the day on which the instalment is due to be paid;

(d)   a four weekly instalment, the period is 28 days, ending on the day on which the instalment is due to be paid.

(4)   For the purposes of this regulation "tax credit" means child tax credit or working tax credit.

General note

This provides the mechanism for taking tax credits income into account. "Tax credits" are child tax credit (CTC) and working tax credit (WTC): para (4). See reg 33 for the conversion of payments made in respect of periods other than a week into weekly amounts. Note that Reg 34(e) allows a local authority to ignore legislative changes in the maximum rate of tax credits (ie, the annual uprating) for up to 30 weeks.

It is the amount of a tax credit "instalment" which is "due to be paid" that is taken into account. The instalments should be set out in the claimant's tax credit award notice. There are some important implications:

(1)   Where an overpayment that occurred during the current year's award of tax credits is being recovered by the Revenue, it is the reduced amount of tax credits (the "instalment") that should be taken into account for HB purposes. Note that where an overpayment of tax credits from a previous year is being recovered from the current year's award, the amount of tax credits that is taken into account is similarly, the amount actually being paid: reg 40(6).

(2)   Where the amount of an award of tax credits changes during the year, the local authority takes this into account when the instalment reflecting this is "due to be paid", not when the change occurs.

(3)   Where a payment is not a regular instalment, but a payment of arrears of of tax credits (eg, at the beginning of an award or after a change in circumstances has been taken into account), it should be not be treated as income, but as capital and disregarded for up to 52 weeks: Sch 6 para 9(e).

(4)   Tax credit "additional payments" or "top-up payments" (discretionary payments made by the Revenue where a reduced tax credits awards causes hardship) are effected by increasing the tax

credit award for the relevant year and hence the instalments due to be paid for the remainder of that year.

Calculation of weekly income

33.–(1) For the purposes of regulations 29 (average weekly earnings of employed earners), 31 (average weekly income other than earnings) and 32 (calculation of average weekly income from tax credits), where the period in respect of which a payment is made–

(a) does not exceed a week, the weekly amount shall be the amount of that payment;

(b) exceeds a week, the weekly amount shall be determined–

    (i) in a case where that period is a month, by multiplying the amount of the payment by 12 and dividing the product by 52;

    (ii) in any other case, by dividing the amount of the payment by the number equal to the number of days in the period to which it relates and multiplying the quotient by 7.

(2) For the purposes of regulation 30 (average weekly earnings of self-employed earners) the weekly amount of earnings of a claimant shall be determined by dividing his earnings over the assessment period by the number equal to the number of days in that period and multiplying the quotient by 7.

General Note

This regulation provides the means for converting the sums to be taken into account under regs 29 to 32 into weekly amounts.

Analysis

Para (1)(a). Under this sub-para, where a payment is made for a period of up to a week, the weekly amount is the amount of the payment.

Para (1)(b). Under this sub-para, payments in respect of a month are to be converted by multiplying by 12 to give the annual figure then dividing by 52 to produce a weekly figure. Sub-para (b)(ii) converts payments in respect of periods not covered by para (a) or sub-para (b)(i) by dividing by the number of days in the period to which the payment relates and multiplying by seven. Note that days during weekends must also be counted as days for this purpose.

Para (2) deals with the earnings of a self-employed earner. These are based on the estimated average of earnings received over the assessment period (up to one year – see reg 30). The average weekly amount of earnings is obtained by dividing those earnings by the number of days in the assessment period and multiplying the result by seven.

Disregard of changes in tax, contributions etc

34. In calculating the claimant's income the appropriate authority may disregard any legislative change–

(a) in the basic or other rates of income tax;

(b) in the amount of any personal tax relief;

(c) in the rates of social security contributions payable under the Act or in the lower earnings limit or upper earnings limit for Class 1 contributions under the Act, the lower or upper limits applicable to Class 4 contributions under the Act or the amount specified in section 11(4) of the Act (small earnings exception in relation to Class 2 contributions);

(d) in the amount of tax payable as a result of an increase in the weekly rate of Category A, B, C or D retirement pension or any addition thereto or any graduated pension payable under the Act;

(e) in the maximum rate of child tax credit or working tax credit,

for a period not exceeding 30 benefit weeks beginning with the benefit week immediately following the date from which the change is effective.

Definitions

"benefit weeks" – see reg 2(1).

"income" – see General Note on this Section.

General Note

This regulation is intended to assist the authority in administering the HB scheme by modifying the other provisions of this Part and reg 79 so that the effect of certain changes in the claimant's income are ignored for up to 30 benefit weeks after they take effect, giving an authority time to gather information and re-calculate an affected claimant's HB. The changes listed could reduce or increase a claimant's entitlement to HB. GM BW2.34 warns authorities that exercising their discretion under this paragraph does not mean that the claimant will have been over or under-paid, so when the authority does take the change into account there is no adjustment to be made to HB paid in the intervening period. This is because during that period "entitlement has been correctly assessed according to the treatment of income rules".

See also reg 42(8), about changes in the amount of certain benefits.

Analysis

Note that the "changes" which may be ignored as set out in sub-paras (a) to (e) are only those arising from changes in the legislation, not extra-statutory concessions.

Para (b) covers changes in personal tax relief by which is meant the tax thresholds.

Para (d). Pensioners will only pay tax on these amounts if their total income is sufficient to use up their tax allowances. Therefore the change in the amount of tax payable may not change some pensioners' HB entitlement in any case. Note that most pensioner claimants have their HB assessed under the HB(SPC) Regs, so this provision will generally only have application where a claimant under 60 has a partner over that age who is receiving one of the pensions listed.

SECTION 3
Employed earners

General Note on Section 3

See also regs 27 and 29 and the General Note to Section 2.

Reg 29(4) provides that for the purposes of that reg (ie, quantification of the employee's weekly earnings (together with the earnings of any partner)), this Section is to govern the amounts which are to be taken into account as earnings, and how they are to be assessed.

Reg 35 defines earnings for the purposes of this Chapter.

Reg 36 provides that for the purposes of reg 29 it is net earnings that are to be taken into account, minus the amounts which may be deducted under Sch 4, and sets out how "net" earnings are to be ascertained.

Earnings of employed earners

35.–(1) Subject to paragraph (2), ''earnings'' means in the case of employment as an employed earner, any remuneration or profit derived from that employment and includes–

(a) any bonus or commission;

(b) any payment in lieu of remuneration except any periodic sum paid to a claimant on account of the termination of his employment by reason of redundancy;

(c) any payment in lieu of notice or any lump sum payment intended as compensation for the loss of employment but only in so far as it represents loss of income;

(d) any holiday pay except any payable more than 4 weeks after termination or interruption of the employment;

(e) any payment by way of a retainer;

(f) any payment made by the claimant's employer in respect of expenses not wholly, exclusively and necessarily incurred in the performance of the duties of the employment, including any payment made by the claimant's employer in respect of–

   (i) travelling expenses incurred by the claimant between his home and place of employment;

   (ii) expenses incurred by the claimant under arrangements made for the care of a member of his family owing to the claimant's absence from home;

(g)   any award of compensation made under section 112(4) or 117(3)(a) of the Employment Rights Act 1996 (remedies and compensation for unfair dismissal);

[¹ (gg) any payment or remuneration made under section 28, 34, 64, 68 or 70 of the Employment Rights Act 1996 (right to guarantee payments, remuneration on suspension on medical or maternity grounds, complaints to employment tribunals);]

(h)   any such sum as is referred to in section 112 of the Act (certain sums to be earnings for social security purposes);

(i)   any statutory sick pay, statutory maternity pay, statutory paternity pay or statutory adoption pay, or a corresponding payment under any enactment having effect in Northern Ireland;

(j)   any remuneration paid by or on behalf of an employer to the claimant who for the time being is on maternity leave, paternity leave or adoption leave or is absent from work because he is ill;

(k)   the amount of any payment by way of a non-cash voucher which has been taken into account in the computation of a person's earnings in accordance with Part 5 of Schedule 3 to the Social Security (Contributions) Regulations 2001.

(2)   Earnings shall not include–

(a)   subject to paragraph (3), any payment in kind;

(b)   any payment in respect of expenses wholly, exclusively and necessarily incurred in the performance of the duties of the employment;

(c)   any occupational pension.

(3)   Paragraph (2)(a) shall not apply in respect of any non-cash voucher referred to in paragraph (1)(k).

Definitions
"employed earner" – see reg 2(1).
"occupational pension" – see reg 2(1).

Amendment
1.   Inserted by reg 11(4) of SI 2007 No 2618 as from 1.10.07.

General Note
This important regulation defines "earnings" for the purposes of this part. It includes all those payments listed in para (1) but excludes those listed in para (2).

Analysis
Paragraph (1): General
"Remuneration or profit derived from ... employment". Sub-paras (a) to (k) of this paragraph do not exclusively define earnings; they are simply a list of items which are deemed to be earnings for these purposes. The true test of which other payments are "earnings" is the phrase "remuneration or profit derived from . . . employment".

The phrase is well known to tax lawyers as defining the payments which may become liable to tax as employment income under the Income Tax (Earnings and Pensions) Act 2003. In *CFC 25/1989* para 30 the commissioner held that the similarity of wording under Revenue and Social Security legislation "cannot be accidental" and that income tax cases were "a useful guide". "Remuneration or profit" would seem to exclude payments of expenses but see paras (1)(f) and (2)(b) for a detailed look at the treatment of expenses. The issue of whether a payment is "derived from" employment is constantly before the courts regarding the question of liability to tax. A number of tests have evolved to decide whether a payment is so derived.

Generally, the phrase has been widely interpreted in relation to tax so that it is unusual for a payment passing between employer and employee not to be treated as "derived from" employment. A payment made to an employee by a third party is less likely to be so regarded. See – eg, *Moore v Griffiths* [1972] 1 WLR 1024, Ch D, where a payment made to Bobby Moore after the 1966 World Cup by a company seeking publicity from the prize-giving was not "derived from" employment despite the "work" relationship.

Where the payment has been made by an employer, the case of *Hochstrasser v Mayes* [1959] Ch 22, CA, is often quoted. In that case, the test of derivation was held to be whether the payment was made in return for services "past, present or future". This case also established that, in relation to tax at least, the employment relationship need only be one reason for the payment before it will be treated as "derived from" employment. Other important factors in deciding whether a payment is "derived from" employment have been held to be:

(1)   Whether the employee has a contractual right to payment: *Moorhouse v Dooland* [1955] Ch 284, CA.

(2)   Whether the employer's purpose in making the payment was to provide an incentive to the employee to work harder: *Tyrer v Smart* [1979] 1 WLR 113, HL.

(3)   The fact that the payment relates to terms and conditions of employment: *Hamblett v Godfrey* [1987] 1 WLR 357, CA. In that case, payments of £1,000 made to GCHQ employees to give up trade union rights were held to be derived from employment on this basis.

(4)   Whether the payment was of a recurrent nature; if so, it is more likely to be treated as derived from employment: *Blakiston v Cooper* [1909] AC 104, HL.

In *CH 2387/2002* Commissioner Fellner considered a case in which a company director had put forward accounts showing payment of directors' emoluments of £6,400. In fact, the claimant had only drawn just under £3,000 and the balance had been added to a loan account showing monies owed by the company to the claimant. This approach had been suggested by the company's accountants as a means of saving tax. The commissioner held (para 11) that it was not permissible to put forward one set of earnings figures for tax purposes and another set for benefits purposes. In *CTC 626/2001*, Commissioner Williams upheld a refusal of tax credit to a husband and wife who had adopted an artificial means of payment to themselves from their partnership to save tax, and then argued that for tax credits purposes the true position had to be taken into account. Commissioner Fellner applied that decision and held that the claimant's income for CTC purposes had to be calculated in accordance with the figure given in the accounts.

Payments made in respect of offices. "Employed earner" is defined in s2(1)(Ac) SSCBA: see reg 2(1) above. The definition provides as follows:

"a person who is gainfully employed in Great Britain either under a contract of service, or in an office (including elective office) with general earnings".

Thus it can be seen that the definition of "employed earner" does not solely relate to employment but also to office-holders, provided that they have "general earnings". "General earnings" are defined in s7(3) Income Tax (Earnings and Pensions) Act 2003. The reference to elective office means that councillors' allowances will be treated as "earnings" for the purposes of Part 6: see *R(IS) 6/92* para 5. There is important caselaw on the treatment of allowances: see the commentary to para (1)(f) below.

Paragraph (1): Categories of earnings

"Earnings" includes the payments listed in paragraphs (a) to (k) of para (1).

Sub-para (b). Payments "in lieu of remuneration" include awards made by employment tribunals and courts to compensate for loss of earnings. It will not, however, apply to redundancy payments.

A compensatory award made by an employment tribunal will fall under this sub-para, in so far as it consists of compensation for loss of earnings: *R(SB) 21/86* para 12. Similarly, where an applicant is awarded any compensation in a claim for discrimination which relate to lost earnings, they will fall under sub-para (b): *CIS 590/1993* para 7. It was also decided in that case, however, that awards covering injury to feelings and the loss of a tax rebate did not fall within sub-para (b).

It would appear that this provision would also extend to awards of damages for personal injury which contained some clearly demarked amount referable to loss of earnings.

Sub-para (c). This will apply, for example, to basic awards for unfair dismissal, payments explicitly made in lieu of notice, or payments made by the Secretary of State for Education and Employment under s167 of the Employment Rights Act 1996 to employees whose employer goes into liquidation before they can work their notice.

Sub-para (d). Note that holiday pay payable more than four weeks after employment terminates is treated as capital under reg 46(3).

Sub-para (e). GM BW2.70 defines "retainer" as "a payment made for a period when no actual work is carried out, such as payment made to employees of the school meals service during school holidays". Payments made during a period of "garden leave" would probably also fall under this provision.

Sub-para (f). The wording "wholly exclusively and necessarily" is the same test as is applied to ascertain deductible expenditure from earnings in relation to income tax. For a discussion of the meaning of the phrase, see note on para (2)(b) below, which provides that earnings which are so incurred are not to count as earnings for these purposes. That means that under this paragraph, all expenses not so incurred are to be seen as "earnings".

Heads (i) and (ii) deem that the items there specified are *not* to be treated as "wholly exclusively and necessarily" incurred for the purposes of the employment. So travelling expenses to work (but not those incurred whilst *at* work) are to be treated as earnings, and so are childminding and other care expenses necessitated when the carer goes to work. For the treatment of such expenses, see reg 28 above.

There is important caselaw on the treatment of councillor's allowances, concerning arguments that the allowances are supposed to cover expenses of councillors. The allowances are paid under s18 Local Government and Housing Act 1989 and the Local Authorities (Members Allowances) Regulations 1991. None of that legislation gives a clue as to how the allowances are to be treated. In *R(IS) 6/92* para 8 a commissioner concluded that the attendance allowance payable to councillors was "not a payment to meet expenses, but a payment to recompense a councillor for his attendance at authorised meetings". In *CIS 77/1993* para 8, however, the same commissioner pointed out that Department of the Environment Circular 2/91, which was issued following the introduction of the system of allowances in the 1991 Regulations, suggested that the purpose of the basic allowance was *both* to recompense a councillor for her/his efforts and for her/his expenses. He therefore concluded that if the councillor could show that s/he had incurred expenses which satisfied the stringent test set out in sub-para (f), the payment of the allowance could be regarded as falling within the provision.

It is therefore suggested that what is important is not the purpose for which any allowance is paid but rather whether the evidence shows that the councillor has incurred expenses "wholly exclusively and necessarily" as a consequence of her/his work as a councillor. Councillors claiming HB but not IS or JSA will therefore be well advised to keep full records of their expenses. It should also be noted that they have the right under reg 57 Income Tax (Employments) Regulations 1995 to have income tax deducted from an attendance allowance at the basic rate and then to ask the Revenue to direct the council to deduct expenses from the tax.

Sub-para (g) covers compensation awards made under s112(4) and 117(3)(b) Employment Rights Act 1996. The former provision refers to compensatory awards made by industrial tribunals where the complainant has established unfair dismissal but the tribunal does not recommend reinstatement or re-engagement. The latter provision refers to the higher rate awards made where reinstatement or re-engagement has been recommended but the employer has failed to comply.

Sub-para (gg) covers the payments or remuneration made under the sections of the Employment Rights Act 1996 listed. They are guarantee payments (ss28 and 34), remuneration to an employee who is suspended from work by his employer on medical grounds (ss64 and 70) or on maternity grounds (ss68 and 70).

Sub-para (h). The payments covered are:

(1)   Amounts representing arrears of pay paid in pursuance of an order for reinstatement or re-engagement under the Employment Rights Act 1996).

(2)   Amounts payable by way of pay in pursuance of an order for continuation of a contract of employment under the Employment Rights Act 1996 or the Trade Union and Labour Relations (Consolidation) Act 1992.

(3)   "Protective awards" made to employees where the employer has failed to comply with the consultation procedure for redundancies under the Trade Union and Labour Relations (Consolidation) Act 1992.

Sub-paras (i) and (j) confirm that sick pay and maternity, paternity and adoption pay, whether made under statute or as additional payments under contract, will count as earnings.

Sub-para (k). The principle is that if a "non-cash voucher" counts as earnings when calculating liability to pay NI contributions under the regulations cited, it also counts as earnings for HB. Note that the contributions legislation is changed very frequently, so in any case of doubt reference should be made to the current version of the regulations set out in The Law of Social Security published by the DWP (available at www.dwp.gov.uk) or current tax handbooks.

Paragraphs (2) and (3): Exclusions from the definition

Sub-paras (a) to (c) exclude certain types of payment from the definition of "earnings" in para (1). Such payments therefore count as "income other than earnings" to be assessed under Section 5, but under Sch 5 payments in kind and expenses "wholly exclusively and necessarily incurred" for the purposes set out are to be disregarded completely: see paras 23 and 3 respectively.

Sub-para (a) excludes any payment in kind, with the exception of vouchers that fall to be taken into account under para (1)(k) above: see para (3).

Sub-para (b). The phrase "wholly exclusively and necessarily incurred in performing the duties of the employment" has been rigidly interpreted in relation to tax law. Before a payment may fall into this category it must display all three attributes referred to:

(1)   "Wholly" means that all of the payment in question must be dedicated to this purpose, not just part. However, if a lump sum is paid in respect of some expenses which qualify and others which do not, there would seem to be no reason why an apportionment cannot be made: see the authorities on councillors' allowances referred to under para (1)(f).

(2)   "Exclusively" means that the payment must be for no other purpose than the duties of the employment – eg, expenditure on an item which is to be used partly for domestic use would not qualify.

(3)   Finally, before expenditure may be excluded from the definition of earnings on this basis, it must be "necessary" for the performance of the duties of employment. In relation to tax, the case of *Brown v Bullock* [1961] 1 WLR 1095, CA, decided that only expenditure necessitated by the duties themselves, and not simply the employer's policies, would qualify. For example, if the job is such that protective clothing is necessary, expenditure on that clothing which is reimbursed will not be "earnings", but if an employer insists that employees wear suits, when the job could be done adequately without the wearing of a suit, expenses in that respect will not be "necessarily" incurred for the purpose of performing the duties and so *will* count as earnings.

There is a vast amount of caselaw concerned with the phrase in relation to tax and reference should be made to textbooks on tax law in any case of doubt.

Note that expenses deemed not to be earnings by sub-bara (b) are disregarded as "income other than earnings" by Sch 5 para 3.

Sub-para (c). See reg 2(1) for the definition of "occupational pension".

Calculation of net earnings of employed earners

36.–(1)   For the purposes of regulation 29 (average weekly earnings of employed earners), the earnings of a claimant derived or likely to be derived from employment as an employed earner to be taken into account shall, subject to paragraph (2), be his net earnings.

(2)   There shall be disregarded from a claimant's net earnings, any sum, where applicable, specified in paragraphs 1 to 14 of Schedule 4.

(3)   For the purposes of paragraph (1) net earnings shall, except where paragraph (6) applies, be calculated by taking into account the gross earnings of the claimant from that employment over the assessment period, less–

(a)   any amount deducted from those earnings by way of–

(i)   income tax;

(ii)   primary Class 1 contributions under the Act;

(b)   one-half of any sum paid by the claimant by way of a contribution towards an occupational pension scheme;

(c)   one-half of the amount calculated in accordance with paragraph (5) in respect of any qualifying contribution payable by the claimant; and

(d)   where those earnings include a payment which is payable under any enactment having effect in Northern Ireland and which corresponds to statutory sick pay, statutory maternity pay, statutory paternity pay or statutory adoption pay, any amount deducted from those earnings by way of any contributions which are payable under any enactment having effect in Northern Ireland and which correspond to primary Class 1 contributions under the Act.

(4)   In this regulation "qualifying contribution" means any sum which is payable periodically as a contribution towards a personal pension scheme.

(5)   The amount in respect of any qualifying contribution shall be calculated by multiplying the daily amount of the qualifying contribution by the number equal to the number of days in the assessment period; and for the purposes of this regulation the daily amount of the qualifying contribution shall be determined–

(a)   where the qualifying contribution is payable monthly, by multiplying the amount of the qualifying contribution by 12 and dividing the product by 365;

(b)   in any other case, by dividing the amount of the qualifying contribution by the number equal to the number of days in the period to which the qualifying contribution relates.

(6)   Where the earnings of a claimant are estimated under sub-paragraph (b) of paragraph (2) of regulation 29 (average weekly earnings of employed earners), his net earnings shall be calculated by taking into account those earnings over the assessment period, less–

(a)   an amount in respect of income tax equivalent to an amount calculated by applying to those earnings the [¹ starting rate] or, as the case may be, the [¹ starting rate]and the basic rate of tax applicable to the assessment period less only the personal relief to which the claimant is entitled under sections 257(1) of the Income and Corporation Taxes Act 1988 (personal allowances) as is appropriate to his circumstances but, if the assessment period is less than a year, the earnings to which the [¹ starting rate] of tax is to be applied and the amount of the personal relief deductible under this sub-paragraph shall be calculated on a pro rata basis;

(b)   an amount equivalent to the amount of the primary Class 1 contributions that would be payable by him under the Act in respect of those earnings if such contributions were payable; and

(c)   one-half of any sum which would be payable by the claimant by way of a contribution towards an occupational or personal pension scheme, if the earnings so estimated were actual earnings.

Definitions
"claimant" – see reg 2(1).
"earnings" – see reg 35.
"employed earner" – see reg 2(1).

Amendment
1.   Amended by reg 11(5) of SI 2007 No 2618 as from 1.10.07.

General Note
Para (1) sets out the general rule that "earnings" to be taken into account under reg 29 are "net" earnings minus the deductions authorised by Sch 4: see para (2).

Paras (3) and (6) define "net" for these purposes. Para (3) relates to claimants whose earnings are to be averaged under reg 29(1). Their net earnings are to be ascertained by deducting income tax, NI contributions and half of occupational/personal pension contributions made by the employee from the gross figure. Para (6) deals with those whose earnings are estimated under reg 29(2).

Analysis
Para (2). In considering the scope of any disregard, decisions on similarly-worded disregards in other means-tested benefit schemes must be taken into account: *CH 2321/2002* para 8.

Paras (3) to (5) set out amounts which are to be deducted to generate a net earnings figure. See also reg 34 where the amounts of statutory deductions change during an award. The deductions are:

(1)   Amounts deducted by way of income tax and Class 1 NI contributions: para (3)(a).

(2)   Half of any contributions made by a claimant towards an occupational pension scheme: para (3)(b).

(3)   Half of any "qualifying contributions": para (3)(c). These are those made to a personal pension scheme: see para (4). Para (5) sets out the method of calculation.

(4)   Sums deducted from statutory sick and maternity pay in Northern Ireland which correspond to Class 1 contributions: para (3)(d).

Para (6)(a). The wording of para (6)(a) is odd, but the effect is that the appropriate personal allowance for tax purposes is deducted from gross earnings and the starting rate (or starting and basic rate) applied to what remains. A useful publication which sets out tax rates and national insurance contributions on a year-by-year basis is *Facts & Figures* published annually by Sweet & Maxwell.

"pro-rata" requires, for example, that if the assessment period is six months, one half of the appropriate personal reliefs should be deducted. Notice that if the HB is being assessed outside the year of assessment in which the claim was made, the basic rate of tax due in that year is used, but the personal relief applying in the current tax year will be applied.

SECTION 4
Self-employed earners

General Note on Section 4
This deals with the assessment of earnings from self-employment for the purposes of regs 27 and 30.
Reg 37 defines "earnings" so far as self-employed earners are concerned.

Reg 38 provides the rules under which such a person's "net profit" is to be calculated and reg 39 provides the details necessary in relation to reg 38 to enable deductions in respect of tax and NI contributions to be made.

The main disputes in relation to this Section are likely to be about the quantification of "profit". In particular it may be difficult for the claimant or those whose income is aggregated with the claimant's to provide adequate evidence of net profit.

The case of *R v West Dorset DC ex p Poupard* [1988] 28 RVR 40, CA, referred to in the General Note to Section 2 complicated matters in relation to the assessment of income in the case of self-employed claimants. In that case, a claimant was treated as having an income even though his business made a loss, because he made drawings from his business receipts and bank account to pay for living expenses. The drawings were treated as income. Useful guidance to estimating earnings from self-employment is given in *CH 329/2003* (paras 7-13).

GM BW2.390 to BW2.396 gives guidance on how to deal with drawings, whether or not proper accounts are kept and whether the business is being run at a loss or a profit. It says at para GM W2.394 that when accounts are kept but there is a loss and drawings have still been taken, authorities should ignore any drawings taken from capital or from loan or overdraft facilities and add back into the gross profit figure any drawings deducted from the gross profit figure declared. It points out that in some cases this may still result in a nil net profit. GM BW2.395 says that when no proper accounts are kept but there is some indication of potential earnings, authorities should make an assessment of average weekly income based on the best evidence to hand, such as sales ledgers, notebooks, bank statements, receipted invoices, chequebook stubs, etc. and to include tips, gratuities, royalties, etc in the earnings figure.

Earnings of self-employed earners

37.–(1) Subject to paragraph (2), "earnings", in the case of employment as a self-employed earner, means the gross income of the employment and shall include any allowance paid under section 2 of the 1973 Act or section 2 of the Enterprise and New Towns (Scotland) Act 1990 to the claimant for the purpose of assisting him in carrying on his business unless at the date of claim the allowance has been terminated.

(2) "Earnings" shall not include any payment to which paragraph 26 or 27 of Schedule 5 refers (payments in respect of a person accommodated with the claimant under arrangements made by a local authority or voluntary organisation and payments made to the claimant by a health authority, local authority or voluntary organisation in respect of persons temporarily in the claimant's care) nor shall it include any sports award.

Definitions
"claimant" – reg 2(1).
"self-employed earner" – see reg 2(1).

General Note
This regulation provides a general definition of the term "earnings" in relation to self-employed earners. Para (2) clarifies that local authority payments to foster parents should not be treated as self-employed earnings. Foster payments in fact are considered to be income other than earnings and are disregarded under Sch 5 para 26, as are certain payments made to those providing respite care (Sch 5 para 27).

The reference is to *gross* income and the other regulations in this Section provide for deductions from earnings to arrive at "net profit" for the purposes of reg 30.

Analysis
Section 2 of the Employment and Training Act 1973 enables the Training Agency to "make such arrangements as it considers appropriate for the purposes of assisting persons to select, train for, obtain and retain employment".

Calculation of net profit of self-employed earners

38.–(1) For the purposes of regulation 30 (average weekly earnings of self-employed earners) the earnings of a claimant to be taken into account shall be–

(a)   in the case of a self-employed earner who is engaged in employment on his own account, the net profit derived from that employment;

(b) in the case of a self-employed earner whose employment is carried on in partnership or is that of a share fisherman within the meaning of the Social Security (Mariners' Benefits) Regulations 1975, his share of the net profit derived from that employment, less–

  (i) an amount in respect of income tax and of social security contributions payable under the Act calculated in accordance with regulation 39 (deduction of tax and contributions for self-employed earners); and

  (ii) one-half of the amount calculated in accordance with paragraph (11) in respect of any qualifying premium.

(2) There shall be disregarded from a claimant's net profit, any sum, where applicable, specified in paragraphs 1 to 14 of Schedule 4.

(3) For the purposes of paragraph (1)(a) the net profit of the employment shall, except where paragraph (9) applies, be calculated by taking into account the earnings of the employment over the assessment period less–

(a) subject to paragraphs (5) to (7), any expenses wholly and exclusively incurred in that period for the purposes of that employment;

(b) an amount in respect of–

  (i) income tax; and

  (ii) social security contributions payable under the Act,

calculated in accordance with regulation 39 (deduction of tax and contributions for self-employed earners); and

(c) one-half of the amount calculated in accordance with paragraph (11) in respect of any qualifying premium.

(4) For the purposes of paragraph (1)(b) the net profit of the employment shall be calculated by taking into account the earnings of the employment over the assessment period less, subject to paragraphs (5) to (7), any expenses wholly and exclusively incurred in that period for the purposes of the employment.

(5) Subject to paragraph (6), no deduction shall be made under paragraph (3)(a) or (4), in respect of–

(a) any capital expenditure;

(b) the depreciation of any capital asset;

(c) any sum employed or intended to be employed in the setting up or expansion of the employment;

(d) any loss incurred before the beginning of the assessment period;

(e) the repayment of capital on any loan taken out for the purposes of the employment;

(f) any expenses incurred in providing business entertainment; and

(g) any debts, except bad debts proved to be such, but this sub-paragraph shall not apply to any expenses incurred in the recovery of a debt.

(6) A deduction shall be made under paragraph (3)(a) or (4) in respect of the repayment of capital on any loan used for–

(a) the replacement in the course of business of equipment or machinery; and

(b) the repair of an existing business asset except to the extent that any sum is payable under an insurance policy for its repair.

(7) The relevant authority shall refuse to make a deduction in respect of any expenses under paragraph (3)(a) or (4) where it is not satisfied given the nature and the amount of the expense that it has been reasonably incurred.

(8) For the avoidance of doubt–

(a) a deduction shall not be made under paragraph (3)(a) or (4) in respect of any sum unless it has been expended for the purposes of the business;

(b) a deduction shall be made thereunder in respect of–

  (i) the excess of any value added tax paid over value added tax received in the assessment period;

(ii)   any income expended in the repair of an existing business asset except to the extent that any sum is payable under an insurance policy for its repair;

(iii)   any payment of interest on a loan taken out for the purposes of the employment.

(9)   Where a claimant is engaged in employment as a child minder the net profit of the employment shall be one-third of the earnings of that employment, less–

(a)   an amount in respect of–

    (i)   income tax; and

    (ii)   social security contributions payable under the Act,

calculated in accordance with regulation 39 (deduction of tax and contributions for self-employed earners); and

(b)   one-half of the amount calculated in accordance with paragraph (11) in respect of any qualifying premium.

(10)   For the avoidance of doubt where a claimant is engaged in employment as a self-employed earner and he is also engaged in one or more other employments as a self-employed or employed earner any loss incurred in any one of his employments shall not be offset against his earnings in any other of his employments.

(11)   The amount in respect of any qualifying premium shall be calculated by multiplying the daily amount of the qualifying premium by the number equal to the number of days in the assessment period; and for the purposes of this regulation the daily amount of the qualifying premium shall be determined–

(a)   where the qualifying premium is payable monthly, by multiplying the amount of the qualifying premium by 12 and dividing the product by 365;

(b)   in any other case, by dividing the amount of the qualifying premium by the number equal to the number of days in the period to which the qualifying premium relates.

(12)   In this regulation, "qualifying premium" means any premium which is payable periodically in respect of [1] a personal pension scheme and is so payable on or after the date of claim.

Definitions

"assessment period" – see reg 30.
"capital" – see General Note on Section 6.
"claimant" – see reg 2(1).
"date of claim" – reg 2(1).
"earnings" – see reg 37.
"employed earner" – see reg 2(1).
"partner" – reg 2(1).
"qualifying premium" – see para (11).
"relevant authority" – see reg 2(1).
"self-employed earner" – reg 2(1).

Amendment

1.   Omitted by reg 4(3) of SI 2007 No 1749 as from 16.7.07.

General Note

This regulation deals with the assessment of "net profit" for the purposes of reg 30. It produces detailed rules as to what expenditure may be deducted from gross "earnings" (see reg 37) to arrive at the net figure. The wording follows the income tax law quite closely in relation to allowable deductions from chargeable income.

Analysis

Paragraphs (1) and (2): The basic calculation

Para (1) sets out the basic rule for what is to be taken into account as earnings for the self-employed under reg 30. See the Analysis to reg 35(1) for the meaning of "derived from". There are two categories of self-employed:

(1)   Those who are in self-employment in their own account. Their net profit is calculated under para (3). See commentary to para 5(d) below.

(2)   Those who are in partnerships or who are share fishermen. Their net profit will be calculated under para (4).

Note that childminders are dealt with separately. Their net profit is calculated under para (9).

Para (2) requires the deduction of the disregarded amounts set out in paras 1 to 14 of Sch 4. Para 14 of Sch 4 ensures that where a self-employed claimant's earnings are paid in a currency other than sterling then any banking or commission charges made on converting those earnings into sterling are deducted from the value of the earnings to be taken into account. In considering the scope of any disregard, decisions on similarly-worded disregards in other means-tested benefit schemes must be taken into account: *CH 2321/2002* para 8.

Paragraph (3): Those who are self-employed on their own account

Note that this paragraph does not apply to childminders, who are dealt with under para (9). For discussion of the method of assessment of "earnings of the employment", see the General Note to this Part. The total of the amounts available under sub-paras (a) to (c) must be deducted to arrive at the net profit.

Sub-para (a) must be read together with paras (5) to (8) to ascertain exactly which expenses are deductible.

The expenses set out in para (5) cannot be deducted, whereas those in para (6) must be deducted. There is a general requirement under para (7) that the expenses must be "reasonably incurred". Para (8) then sets out further deeming provisions.

In *R(H) 5/07* the commissioner followed *R(FC) 1/91* in holding that the part of the interest on the car loan apportionable to business use could be allowed as an expense "wholly and exclusively incurred . . . for the purposes of [the] employment".

Note that here there is no requirement that the expenses be necessary. Instead, the test of reasonableness is used.

Only expenses incurred during the period over which the profit is averaged out under reg 30 may be considered.

Sub-para (b) requires deduction of income tax and NI contributions. See reg 39, which supplements this.

Sub-para (c) requires the deduction of half of a "qualifying premium", which is defined in paras (11) and (12) below.

Paragraph (4): Partners and share fishermen

Where someone is a partner or a share fisherman, this paragraph with para (1)(b)(i) and (ii) above, is used to calculate earnings. Under para (1)(b)(i) and (ii), from the claimant's share of the net profit, deductions are made corresponding to para (3)(b) and (c). Para (4) enables business expenses to be deducted on a similar basis to that provided by para (3)(a) in relation to all other self-employed people except child minders.

See also the note to para (10) below.

Paragraph (5): Items which are not expenses

This paragraph lists items which are deemed not to satisfy para (3)(a) or para (4), except to the extent that para (6) provides otherwise.

Sub-para (a). Where para (6) applies, the expenditure to which it relates will be deductible under para (3)(a) or para (4), despite this provision.

Sub-para (b). There can be no deduction in this respect as tax relief and other allowances are already available.

Sub-para (d). Although losses incurred during the assessment period may be deducted as allowable expenses this can only ever take the net "profit" (per para (1)(a)) to a figure of nil; it cannot reduce the profit to a negative figure to be set off against any other income which the claimant may have: *CH 1009/ 2007* (paras 26-28).

Sub-para (e) must be read subject to para (8)(iii), which states that interest on such a loan may be an allowable expense. See also para (6).

Sub-para (g) prevents debts owed to the business being taken into account when calculating net profit. "Bad debts", however, may be taken into account. Bad debts are those that are irrecoverable in accounting terms, for example because the debtor is insolvent. The requirement that bad debts be "proven to be such" indicates that the claimant must prove that a debt is a bad debt. Expenses incurred in recovering a business debt are deductible in assessing "net profit" if para (3)(a), or paras (4) and (7) are satisfied.

Paragraph (6): Items deemed to be expenses

This paragraph qualifies para (5) by providing that capital used to repay loans for the items listed shall be deducted under para (3)(a) or para (4) when calculating net profit.

Sub-para (a). Note that the replacement must be in the "course of business" and not for personal use.

However, in *R(H) 5/07* the commissioner held that capital repayments in respect of a replacement car are deductible as a car is perfectly capable of amounting to "business equipment or machinery", regardless of how good accounting practice may view it.

Sub-para (b). If a sum is "payable" (whether or not actually paid) under an insurance policy for the repair in question, para (5)(e) operates to prevent deduction of capital repayments in this respect, to the extent that the insurance payment would cover them. See also para (8)(b)(iii).

Paragraph (7): Reasonableness of expenses

In deciding whether a business expense has been "reasonably" incurred, the authority has to take account of the nature as well as the amount of the expense, given the character of the claimant's business. The question is whether expenditure of this kind is reasonable. If para (6) or para (8)(b) deems expenses to be deductible, they need to also satisfy the "reasonableness" test under para (7).

Paragraph (8): Deeming provisions

Para (8) contains a number of deeming provisions confirming the effect of paras (3) to (6). Any amounts referred to here which are deductible must still be subjected to the reasonableness test in para (7).

Sub-para (a) simply reinforces the use of the word "wholly" in para (3)(a), confirming that any expenditure of which any part is not for business purposes is not deductible.

Sub-para (b) confirms that net payments of VAT, repair expenditure (except sums paid under insurance policies) and interest payments on loan may be deducted when calculating net profit.

Paragraph (9): Childminders

Para (9) provides special rules for the assessment of the net profit of child minders. "Child minder" is not defined but as "child" is defined as any person under the age of 16, it is suggested that any person looking after a "child" at any period of the day by way of a business will fall within that provision.

Paras (3) to (7) do not apply. Instead, child minders are deemed to have net profit of one-third of their earnings. Para (2) still applies and so the sums listed in Sch 4 paras 1 to 14 are deductible from a child minder's net profit for the purposes of reg 30.

As to deductions under sub-para (a), see reg 39. "Qualifying premiums" in sub-para (b) are defined in para (11). Half a qualifying premium may be deducted.

Paragraph (10): Offsetting

This paragraph provides that if a claimant has more than one employment, losses made in one during the averaging period cannot be offset against gains made in respect of another.

Paragraphs (11) and (12): "Qualifying premiums"

Para (11) deals with calculation of qualifying premiums.

Para (12) clarifies that the amount initially to be deducted should be based on the amounts payable on or after the date of claim.

Deduction of tax and contributions of self-employed earners

39.–(1)   The amount to be deducted in respect of income tax under regulation 38(1)(b)(i), (3)(b)(i) or (9)(a)(i) (calculation of net profit of self-employed earners) shall be calculated on the basis of the amount of chargeable income and as if that income were assessable to income tax at the [¹ starting rate] or, as the case may be, the [¹ starting rate] and the basic rate of tax applicable to the assessment period less only the personal relief to which the claimant is entitled under sections 257(1) of the Income and Corporation Taxes Act 1988 (personal allowances) as is appropriate to his circumstances; but, if the assessment period is less than a year, the earnings to which the [¹ starting rate] of tax is to be applied and the amount of the personal relief deductible under this paragraph shall be calculated on a pro rata basis.

(2)   The amount to be deducted in respect of social security contributions under regulation 38(1)(b)(i), (3)(b)(ii) or (9)(a)(ii) shall be the total of–

(a)   the amount of Class 2 contributions payable under section 11(1) or, as the case may be, 11(3) of the Act at the rate applicable to the assessment period except where the claimant's chargeable income is less than the amount specified in section 11(4) of the Act (small earnings exception) for the tax year applicable to the assessment period; but if the assessment period is less than a year, the amount specified for that tax year shall be reduced pro rata; and

(b)   the amount of Class 4 contributions (if any) which would be payable under section 15 of the Act (Class 4 contributions recoverable under the Income Tax Acts) at the percentage rate applicable to the assessment period on so much of the chargeable income as exceeds the lower limit but does not exceed the upper limit of profits and gains applicable for the tax year applicable to the assessment period; but if the assessment period is less than a year, those limits shall be reduced pro rata.

(3) In this regulation''chargeable income'' means–

(a) except where sub-paragraph (b) applies, the earnings derived from the employment less any expenses deducted under paragraph (3)(a) or, as the case may be, (4) of regulation 38;

(b) in the case of employment as a child minder, one third of the earnings of that employment.

Definitions
"self-employed earner" – see reg 2(1).

Amendment
1. Amended by reg 11(6) of SI 2007 No 2618 as from 1.10.07.

General Note
This relates to the calculation of "net profit" under reg 38 and in particular to deductions made under paras (1)(b), (3)(b) and (9)(a) of that regulation. Para (1) deals with the quantification of income tax to be deducted from "earnings" as defined in reg 37 under paras (1)(b)(i), (3)(b)(i) or (9)(a)(i) as appropriate.

Para (2) deals with the amount of NI contributions to be deducted from earnings; and para (3) defines the term "chargeable income" as used in this regulation.

Analysis
Para (1). "Chargeable income" is defined in para (3).

Para (2). A self-employed person may be liable to both class 2 and class 4 contributions depending on the level of her/his profits. The amount due is to be calculated on the basis of "chargeable income": see para (3). Deductions for NI should be based on the rates applicable to the assessment period (for which see reg 2(1)).

Para (3) defines "chargeable income" as the amount remaining after the deductions in paras (3)(a) and (4) of reg 38, as appropriate, have been made from gross earnings. In the case of a child minder, it is one-third of her/his income. See the Analysis to reg 38(9).

SECTION 5
Other income

General Note on Section 5
This Section provides the rules under which income which is not "earnings" under Sections 3 or 4 is to be assessed. Note, however, that student income is dealt with in Part 7.

Reg 40 sets out the general rules as to which income should be taken into account under reg 31 above.

Reg 41 deems capital to be treated as income in certain circumstances.

Reg 42 sets out various circumstances in which a claimant will be treated as possessing income which s/he does not actually possess.

Calculation of income other than earnings

40.–(1) For the purposes of regulation 31 (average weekly income other than earnings), the income of a claimant which does not consist of earnings to be taken into account shall, subject to paragraphs (2) to (7) be his gross income and any capital treated as income under regulation 41 (capital treated as income).

(2) There shall be disregarded from the calculation of a claimant's gross income under paragraph (1), any sum, where applicable, specified in Schedule 5.

[² (3)]

[²

(4)]

[² (4A)]

(5) Where the payment of any benefit under the benefit Acts is subject to any deduction by way of recovery the amount to be taken into account under paragraph (1) shall be the gross amount payable.

(6)   Where an award of any working tax credit or child tax credit under the Tax Credits Act is subject to a deduction by way of recovery of an overpayment of working tax credit or child tax credit which arose in a previous tax year the amount to be taken into account under paragraph (1) shall be the amount of working tax credit or child tax credit awarded less the amount of that deduction.

(7)   Paragraph (8) applies where–

(a)   a relevant payment has been made to a person in an academic year; and

(b)   that person abandons, or is dismissed from, his course of study before the payment to him of the final instalment of the relevant payment.

(8)   The amount of a relevant payment to be taken into account for the assessment period for the purposes of paragraph (1) in respect of a person to whom paragraph (7) applies, shall be calculated by applying the formula–

$$\frac{A - (B \times C)}{D}$$

where–

A= the total amount of the relevant payment which that person would have received had he remained a student until the last day of the academic term in which he abandoned, or was dismissed from, his course, less any deduction under regulation 64(5);

B= the number of benefit weeks from the benefit week immediately following that which includes the first day of that academic year to the benefit week which includes the day on which the person abandoned, or was dismissed from, his course;

C= the weekly amount of the relevant payment, before the application of the £10 disregard, which would have been taken into account as income under regulation 64(2) had the person not abandoned or been dismissed from, his course and, in the case of a person who was not entitled to housing benefit immediately before he abandoned or was dismissed from his course, had that person, at that time, been entitled to housing benefit;

D= the number of benefit weeks in the assessment period.

(9)   In paragraphs (7) and (8)–

"academic year" and "student loan" shall have the same meanings as for the purposes of Part 7;

"assessment period" means the period beginning with the benefit week immediately following that which includes the day on which the person abandoned, or was dismissed from, his course and ending with the benefit week which includes the last day of the last quarter for which an instalment of the relevant payment was payable to that person and for the purposes of this definition, "quarter" shall have the same meaning as for the purposes of the Education (Student Support) Regulations 2005;

"relevant payment" means either a student loan or an amount intended for the maintenance of dependants referred to in regulation 59(7) or both.

(10)   For the avoidance of doubt there shall be included as income to be taken into account under paragraph (1)–

(a)   any payment to which regulation 35(2) (payments not earnings) applies; or

(b)   in the case of a claimant who is receiving support under section 95 or 98 of the Immigration and Asylum Act including support provided by virtue of regulations made under Schedule 9 to that Act, the amount of such support provided in respect of essential living needs of the claimant and his dependants (if any) as is specified in regulations made under paragraph 3 of Schedule 8 to the Immigration and Asylum Act.

Amendments

1.   Inserted by reg 2 of SI 2006 No 2813 as from 20.11.06.

2.   Omitted by reg 4(b) of SI 2007 No 1619 as from 3.7.07.

Definitions

"capital" – see General Note on Section 6.

"claimant" – see reg 2(1).

"earnings" – see regs 35 and 37.

"income" – see General Note on Section 2.

General Note

Unlike ss3 and 4 the general rule is that gross, rather than net, income is to be taken into account together with any capital treated as income under reg 41.

Analysis

Para (1) confirms that gross income is taken into account. Note, however, that tax paid on the income is to be disregarded under Sch 5 para 1. For general comments about the nature of income, see the General Note to this Part.

Para (2) permits the disregards in Sch 5. In considering the scope of any disregard, decisions on similarly-worded disregards in other means-tested benefit schemes must be taken into account: *CH 2321/2002* (para 8).

Paras (3) to (4A) permitted a local authority to modify the scheme so as to disregard war widow's and widower's pensions and certain payments made under the Armed Forces and Reserve Forces (Compensation Scheme) Order 2005. The Housing Benefit and Council Tax Benefit (War Pension Disregards) Regulations 2007 (see p1137) now prescribe the pensions that can be disregarded. See s134(8)(a) SSAA for a discussion of the authority's powers to modify the HB scheme.

Para (5) refers only to the situation where a deduction is made from gross benefit paid under the benefit Acts (as defined in reg 2(1)) to recoup an overpayment, not to the situation where benefit is reduced for some other reason such as a trade dispute or for a JSA sanction. Tax credits are not dealt with under this paragraph, but under para (6) instead.

Para (6) makes it plain that where an award of WTC or CTC for the current year is subject of a deduction in order to recover an overpayment of tax credit(s) from the previous year (pursuant to s28(1) Tax Credits Act 2002), the amount of CTC or WTC to be taken into account in calculating the weekly level of income for HB purposes is the current year award of tax credit(s) less the deduction for the overpayment: generally, the amount being paid. This is confirmed in *CH 1450/2005*, where the commissioner rejected an argument that as the claimant was putting the overpaid sums of tax credits aside pending recovery, she was holding the sums on trust for the Revenue, had no beneficial interest in the sums, and so they should have been ignored as income in the year in which they were actually paid. The sums were clearly received by the claimant and were her income, and any different result would mean that the overpaid sums stood to be disregarded both in the year in which they were received and the following year, which would amount to a double disregard.

Paras (7) to (9) deal with students who leave their courses prematurely. Where the student has received a "relevant payment" (as defined in para (9)), that payment is apportioned according to the formula in para (8). The effect is that the former student is treated as having the same weekly income from the relevant payment as if s/he had completed the course but only for the period during which s/he was actually on the course.

In *CJSA 549/2003* (para 6), the commissioner confirmed that this formula has to be applied even in a case where the student had repaid a student loan that she had taken out in full. He was critical of the unfairness of this rule.

Para (10)(a) makes it clear that payments which are disregarded under reg 35(2) in the calculation of earnings are to be taken into account as "other income" under para (1). See, however, Sch 5 paras 3 and 23 for when these can be disregarded.

Capital treated as income

41.–(1)   Any capital payable by instalments which are outstanding at the date on which the claim is made or treated as made, or, at the date of any subsequent revision or supersession, shall, if the aggregate of the instalments outstanding and the amount of the claimant's capital otherwise calculated in accordance with Section 6 exceeds £16,000, be treated as income.

(2)   Any payment received under an annuity shall be treated as income.

(3)   Any earnings to the extent that they are not a payment of income shall be treated as income.

(4)   Any Career Development Loan paid pursuant to section 2 of the 1973 Act shall be treated as income.

(5)   Where an agreement or court order provides that payments shall be made to the claimant in consequence of any personal injury to the claimant and that such payments are to be made, wholly or partly, by way of periodic payments, any such periodic payments received by the claimant (but not a payment which is treated as capital by virtue of this Part), shall be treated as income.

Definitions

"capital" – see General Note on Section 6.
"claimant" – see reg 2(1).
"earnings" – see regs 35 and 37.
"income" – see General Note on Section 2.

General Note

Reg 41 provides for the treatment as income of payments which would normally be regarded as capital. They are disregarded as capital under para 22 of Sch 6.

Analysis

Para (1) aims to give a benevolent treatment of outstanding instalments of capital owed to a claimant. If the sum of the claimant's capital and the instalments outstanding is worth more than the £16,000 capital limit (and hence would normally disqualify the claimant from benefit), the value of the right to receive the instalments is disregarded as a capital asset under Sch 6 para 18 and the outstanding instalments are treated as income. This question is decided both on the date of claim (see reg 83) and on any subsequent revision or supersession.

Para (2) deems payments under an annuity to be income but see para 18 of Sch 5.

Para (3) requires that earnings be treated as income in all cases.

Para (4) deems career development loans to be income rather than capital.

Para (5) deals with income from structured settlements in personal injury cases. It is frequently a term of settlement in cases involving very serious injuries that the defendant purchases an annuity which will yield a regular income for the claimant.

Notional income

42.–(1)   A claimant shall be treated as possessing income of which he has deprived himself for the purpose of securing entitlement to housing benefit or increasing the amount of that benefit.

(2)   Except in the case of–

(a)   a discretionary trust;

(b)   a trust derived from a payment made in consequence of a personal injury;

(c)   a personal pension scheme [¹ , occupational pension scheme] [² [⁵] or a payment made by the Board of the Pension Protection Fund] where the claimant is aged under 60;

[⁴ (d)   any sum to which paragraph 45(2)(a) of Schedule 6 (capital to be disregarded) applies which is administered in the way referred to in paragraph 45(1)(a);

(da)   any sum to which paragraph 46(a) of Schedule 6 refers;]

(e)   rehabilitation allowance made under section 2 of the 1973 Act;

(f)   child tax credit; or

(g)   working tax credit,

any income which would become available to the claimant upon application being made, but which has not been acquired by him, shall be treated as possessed by the claimant but only from the date on which it could be expected to be acquired were an application made.

[⁵ (3)   This paragraph applies where a person aged not less than 60–

(a)   is a member of, or a person deriving entitlement to a pension under, a personal pension scheme;

(b)   fails to purchase an annuity with the funds available in that scheme; and

(c)   either–

(i) defers in whole or in part the payment of any income which would have been payable to him by his pension fund holder, or

(ii) fails to take any necessary action to secure that the whole of any income which would be payable to him by his pension fund holder upon his applying for it, is so paid, or

(iii) income withdrawal is not available to him under that scheme.

(3A) Where paragraph (3) applies, the amount of any income foregone shall be treated as possessed by that person, but only from the date on which it could be expected to be acquired were an application for it to be made.]

(4) The amount of any income foregone in a case [⁵ where paragraph (3)(c)(i) or (ii)] applies shall be the maximum amount of income which may be withdrawn from the fund and shall be determined by the relevant authority which shall take account of information provided by the pension fund holder in accordance with regulation 86(6) (evidence and information).

(5) The amount of any income foregone in a case [⁵ where paragraph (3)(c)(iii)] applies shall be the income that the claimant could have received without purchasing an annuity had the funds held under the relevant personal pension scheme [⁵] been held under a personal pension scheme where income withdrawal was available and shall be determined in the manner specified in paragraph (4).

(6) Any payment of income, other than a payment of income specified in paragraph (7), made–

(a) to a third party in respect of a single claimant or a member of the family (but not a member of the third party's family) shall, where that payment is a payment of an occupational pension [² , a pension or other periodical payment made under a personal pension scheme or a payment made by the Board of the Pension Protection Fund], be treated as possessed by that single claimant or, as the case may be, by that member;

(b) to a third party in respect of a single claimant or in respect of a member of the family (but not a member of the third party's family) shall, where it is not a payment referred to in sub-paragraph (a), be treated as possessed by that single claimant or by that member to the extent that it is used for the food, household fuel or, subject to paragraph (13), rent or ordinary clothing or footwear, of that single claimant or, as the case may be, of any member of that family or is used for any council tax or water charges for which that claimant or member is liable;

(c) to a single claimant or a member of the family in respect of a third party (but not in respect of another member of that family) shall be treated as possessed by that single claimant or, as the case may be, that member of the family to the extent that it is kept or used by him or used by or on behalf of any member of the family.

(7) Paragraph (6) shall not apply in respect of a payment of income made–

(a) under the Macfarlane Trust, the Macfarlane (Special Payments) Trust, the Macfarlane (Special Payments) (No. 2) Trust, the Fund, the Eileen Trust or the Independent Living Funds;

(b) pursuant to section 19(1)(a) of the Coal Industry Act 1994 (concessionary coal);

(c) pursuant to section 2 of the 1973 Act in respect of a person's participation–

(i) in an employment programme specified in regulation 75(1)(a)(ii) of the Jobseeker's Allowance Regulations;

(ii) in a training scheme specified in regulation 75(1)(b)(ii) of those Regulations;

(iii) in the Intensive Activity Period specified in regulation 75(1)(a)(iv) of those Regulations or in the Intensive Activity Period for 50 plus; or

(iv) in a qualifying course within the meaning specified in regulation 17A(7) of those Regulations;

(d)   under an occupational pension scheme [² , in respect of a pension or other periodical payment made under a personal pension scheme or a payment made by the Board of the Pension Protection Fund] where–
    (i)   a bankruptcy order has been made in respect of the person in respect of whom the payment has been made or, in Scotland, the estate of that person is subject to sequestration or a judicial factor has been appointed on that person's estate under section 41 of the Solicitors (Scotland) Act 1980;
    (ii)   the payment is made to the trustee in bankruptcy or any other person acting on behalf of the creditors; and
    (iii)   the person referred to in (i) and any member of his family does not possess, or is not treated as possessing, any other income apart from that payment.

(8)   Where a claimant is in receipt of any benefit (other than housing benefit) under the benefit Acts and the rate of that benefit is altered with effect from a date on or after 1st April in any year but not more than 14 days thereafter, the relevant authority shall treat the claimant as possessing such benefit at the altered rate–
(a)   in a case in which the claimant's weekly amount of eligible rent falls to be calculated in accordance with regulation 80(2)(b) [³ or (c)] (calculation of weekly amounts), from 1st April in that year;
(b)   in any other case, from the first Monday in April in that year,
to the date on which the altered rate is to take effect.

(9)   Subject to paragraph (10), where–
(a)   a claimant performs a service for another person; and
(b)   that person makes no payment of earnings or pays less than that paid for a comparable employment in the area,
the relevant authority shall treat the claimant as possessing such earnings (if any) as is reasonable for that employment unless the claimant satisfies the authority that the means of that person are insufficient for him to pay or to pay more for the service.

(10)   Paragraph (9) shall not apply–
(a)   to a claimant who is engaged by a charitable or voluntary organisation or who is a volunteer if the relevant authority is satisfied in any of those cases that it is reasonable for him to provide those services free of charge; or
(b)   in a case where the service is performed in connection with–
    (i)   the claimant's participation in an employment or training programme in accordance with regulation 19(1)(q) of the Jobseeker's Allowance Regulations, other than where the service is performed in connection with the claimant's participation in the Intense Activity Period specified in regulation 75(1)(a)(iv) of those Regulations or in the Intensive Activity Period for 50 plus; or
    (ii)   the claimant's or the claimant's partner's participation in an employment or training programme as defined in regulation 19(3) of those Regulations for which a training allowance is not payable or, where such an allowance is payable, it is payable for the sole purpose of reimbursement of travelling or meal expenses to the person participating in that programme. [⁶ ; or
(c)   to a claimant who is participating in a work placement approved by the Secretary of State (or a person providing services to the Secretary of State) before the placement starts.

(10A)   In paragraph (10)(c) "work placement" means practical work experience which is not undertaken in expectation of payment.]

(11)   Where a claimant is treated as possessing any income under any of paragraphs (1) to (8), the foregoing provisions of this Part shall apply for the purposes of calculating the amount of that income as if a payment had actually been made and as if it were actual income which he does possess.

(12)   Where a claimant is treated as possessing any earnings under paragraph (9) the foregoing provisions of this Part shall apply for the purposes of calculating the amount of those earnings as if a payment had actually been made and as if they were actual earnings which he does possess except that paragraph (3) of regulation 36 (calculation of net earnings of employed earners) shall not apply and his net earnings shall be calculated by taking into account those earnings which he is treated as possessing, less–

(a)   an amount in respect of income tax equivalent to an amount calculated by applying to those earnings the [⁶ starting rate] or, as the case may be, the [⁶ starting rate] and the basic rate of tax applicable to the assessment period less only the personal relief to which the claimant is entitled under sections 257(1) of the Income and Corporation Taxes Act 1988 (personal allowances) as is appropriate to his circumstances; but, if the assessment period is less than a year, the earnings to which the [⁶ starting rate] of tax is to be applied and the amount of the personal relief deductible under this sub-paragraph shall be calculated on a pro rata basis;

(b)   an amount equivalent to the amount of the primary Class 1 contributions that would be payable by him under the Act in respect of those earnings if such contributions were payable; and

(c)   one-half of any sum payable by the claimant by way of a contribution towards an occupational or personal pension scheme.

(13)   In paragraph (6) "rent" means eligible rent less any deductions in respect of non-dependants which fall to be made under regulation 74 (non-dependant deductions).

Amendments

1.   Amended by reg 5A(2) of SI 2005 No 2465 as inserted by Sch 2 para 28(5) of SI 2006 No 217 as from 6.4.06.
2.   Amended by reg 8(2)(a)-(c) of SI 2006 No 588 as from 6.4.06.
3.   Amended by reg 8(2)(d) of SI 2006 No 588 as from 1.4.06.
4.   Substituted by reg 6(2) of SI 2007 No 719 as from 2.4.07.
5.   Amended by reg 4(4) of SI 2007 No 1749 as from 16.7.07.
5.   Amended by reg 11(7) of SI 2007 No 2618 as from 1.10.07.

Definitions

"benefit Acts" – see SSCBA.
"benefit week" – see reg 2(1).
"claimant" – see reg 2(1).
"earnings" – see regs 35 and 37.
"eligible rent" – see reg 12.
"family" – see s137(1) SSCBA.
"income" – see General Note on Section 2.
"occupational/personal pension scheme" – see reg 2(1).
"relevant authority" – see reg 2(1).
"the Fund", "the Macfarlane Trust", "the Independent Living Fund", "the Macfarlane (Special Payments) Trust" – see reg 2(1).

General Note

This highly complex regulation deals with the situations in which a claimant may be treated as possessing income that s/he does not in fact possess. It covers a variety of situations.

Para (1) deals with income of which a claimant has deprived her/himself.

Paras (2) and (3) deal with income which a claimant has a right to receive.

Paras (3) to (5) deal with income from retirement schemes.

Paras (6) and (7) deal with payments involving third parties. Para (6)(b) requires an equivalent amount of payments made to third parties on behalf of a claimant to cover basic living expenses to be taken into account as income.

Para (6)(c) requires income paid to a claimant or a member of the family in respect of someone else who is not a member of the family to be taken into account if it is retained or used by the claimant or the member of the family.

Para (8) deals with the effect of changes in benefit rates.

Para (9) requires a claimant to be treated as possessing any earnings which would be reasonable if s/he is not paid or is paid too little.

Analysis

Paragraph (1): Income of which the claimant has deprived himself

The wording of this provision dates back to the old supplementary benefits scheme, though there is no discretion as there then was as to whether the consequences of the provision should apply. Caselaw decided by the commissioners will be highly relevant to deciding whether or not the terms of para (1) are met. That caselaw is summarised in the Analysis to reg 49(1).

The effect of the provision is that the claimant is deemed to possess income which s/he has got rid of in order to qualify for, or increase entitlement to, HB. That apparently simple question involves a fairly complex analysis and so careful reference needs to be made to the case law.

A child support commissioner has decided, in relation to the equivalent child support provision, that a refusal to take up an offer of employment does not amount to deprivation of income: *CCS 7967/1995*. In relation to claimants who do carry out work for which they are not paid or are paid too little, see para (9).

Paragraph (2): Income available on application

This makes it clear that, unless excepted by sub-paras (a) to (g), income a claimant could obtain on application being made is treated as possessed by the claimant, even if it is has not actually been acquired by her/him. Certain payments from trusts falling within the sub-paras are excluded. In relation to potential payments from other types of trust, s31 Trustee Act 1925 must be borne in mind. In most cases trustees are under a duty to pay the income produced by property held in trust for a beneficiary who is aged 18 or more to that beneficiary, unless the terms of the trust itself exclude such payments. Accordingly, in such a case, a beneficiary *would* be entitled to the income on application and therefore it must be taken into account under this paragraph. *Actual* payments of this kind should be assessed under reg 40 instead. The section only gives trustees a *power* to pay income where the potential beneficiary is aged under 18 so there is no guarantee that a beneficiary *would* be entitled to income on application in such a case, and therefore the potential income will not be assessable under this paragraph.

Para (2) may apply to entitlement to social security benefits, but the authority would have to be certain not merely that application for the benefit would result in entitlement, but also as to the amount of any entitlement. Where a social security benefit is concerned, entitlement decisions are for decision makers within the social security system. If there is any uncertainty, it is suggested that the wording of para (2) is not met because it is necessary for the authority to satisfy itself that income *would* be available on application.

Another point that needs to be borne in mind is that payments of benefits are often ignored in whole or in part as income for the purposes of assessing HB and CTB. If a benefit is disregarded under Sch 5, it cannot be taken into account as notional income under para (2).

With income from some sources, the problem will be in deciding what the claimant really could be paid if s/he applied. But if the authority decides that money would become available on application it must treat the claimant as possessing it, unless the source of the funds is set out in sub-paras (a) to (g).

Sub-para (a): Exclusion of discretionary trusts. This is because, by definition, a potential beneficiary has no right to payment. A discretionary trust is one in relation to which the trustees have a choice as to the beneficiary they should pay, or how much they pay. But if a claimant actually receives such a payment it is assessable under reg 40.

Sub-para (b): "Trust derived from a payment made in consequence of personal injury". This would cover a trust of funds from a vaccine damage payment, as well as an out-of-court settlement or actual damages under court order which are placed in a trust following a court order. The regulation does not apply to potential payments from such a source but reg 40 will apply to any actual payments of income: see *CIS 114/1999* para 21, upheld in *Beattie v Secretary of State for Social Security* [2001] 1 WLR 1404, CA, and both reported as *R(IS) 10/01*.

In *R(SB) 2/89* para 15 it was held that "personal injury" included injury suffered as a result of a disease (as well as accidental injury).

Sub-para (c) requires income to which a claimant would be entitled from a personal pension scheme or occupational pension scheme or a payment by the Board of the Pension Protection Fund if it was applied for not to be taken into account, so long as he is under the age of 60. See paras (3) to (5) for the rules after s/he attains that age.

Sub-paras (d) and (da) refer to funds derived from awards of damages for personal injury, administered either by a relevant court or by the Court of Protection on behalf of a claimant. See the Analysis to Sch 6 paras 45 and 46.

Sub-para (e). Rehabilitation allowance is paid to those on full-time rehabilitation courses. They are designed to help those who have been incapable of work for long periods to return to work.

Sub-paras (f) and (g). A claimant cannot be treated as in possession of CTC or WTC if s/he does not claim them.

Paragraphs (3) to (5): Income from retirement schemes

These complex-looking provisions aim to ensure that a claimant aged over 60 does not deprive her/himself of income available from a pension scheme. The claimant or other relevant person is expected to purchase an annuity with the funds available in a personal pension scheme. If s/he does not do so, s/he will be treated as possessing the maximum amount that can be withdrawn from the scheme, as assessed under para (4) or (5) as appropriate.

The provision is only triggered if one of the conditions in heads (3)(c)(i) to (iii) is also met.

Paragraphs (6), (7) and (13): Payments involving third parties

Para (6) deals with a number of different circumstances in which third parties are involved in relevant funds. The authority here is obliged to treat the family member as possessing income if one of the sub-paras applies. There is no discretion. However, if a payment to a third party is a voluntary payment (ie, one where the payer does not receive anything in return) this income or part of it may be disregarded under Sch 5 para 14. If the payment is made from one of the sources specified in para (7), it is ignored.

Para (6)(a) prevents a person depriving her/himself of income to which s/he is entitled from the pension schemes listed by assigning it to a third party. The amounts of any payments to third parties will be taken into account as the income of that person, but see para (7)(d).

Para (6)(b) deals with the situation where income for the benefit of a single claimant or a member of the family is paid direct to a third party. The aim is to prevent third parties paying for basic items which are usually covered by means-tested benefits. But if the payment is for a purpose other than those listed (eg, for a leisure item or educational purposes), the payment should be disregarded. The relevant items are:

(1)   Food.

(2)   Household fuel. This will cover coal (though note the effect of para (7)(b) in relation to concessionary coal), gas and electricity but will not cover, for example, petrol for a car purchased by someone outside the claimant's family.

(3)   Rent. This is defined in para (13) as being eligible rent less deductions made for non-dependants. For the determination of eligible rent see reg 12. The consequence of the wording of para (13) is that if the claimant's HB is reduced because certain payments of rent are not eligible or is restricted under the rent restrictions provisions in reg 13, the shortfall may be paid by a third party direct to the landlord without it being taken into account as the income of the claimant or other person liable for the rent.

(4)   Ordinary clothing or footwear. This is defined in reg 2(1). What "normal daily use" means will be a question of fact. Payments for school uniform and for clothing or footwear used only for sporting activities are explicitly made exempt. Whether, for example, a suit would fall under this sub-para might depend on the person's circumstances. For example, if s/he is in low paid work and wears the suit every day, it is probably an item for "normal daily use". If a suit is purchased for a single event such as a wedding or a funeral, that is arguably not "normal daily use". The provision therefore has the perverse effect that the price of luxuries will often not be taken into account as income but the cost of basic items bought for someone will be.

Para (6)(c) is more restrictive in its terms than sub-para (b). It applies to payments made to a claimant or a member of her/his family in respect of a third party, eg which actually belong to someone else, or are to be used for someone else's benefit. If the payee keeps the money or uses it for the benefit of her/himself or the member of the family, or any other member of her/his family so uses it, s/he will be treated as possessing it to the extent that it was so kept or used. This is the case no matter the purpose to which the money is put.

Para (7). Under para (7), any payments made from the Macfarlane Trust, Macfarlane (Special Payments) Trust, the Macfarlane (Special Payments) (No 2) Trust, the Fund, the Eileen Trust or the Independent Living Funds are exempt from the treatment in para (6) as are payments in lieu of concessionary coal and certain payments under s2 of the Employment and Training Act 1973 and the New Deal.

Para (7)(d) constitutes an exception to the treatment of assigned pension entitlements under para (6)(a) above. If the person entitled to the payments has been made bankrupt or sequestrated and the payments are being made to her/his trustee in bankruptcy or other person administering her/his affairs, and no member of the family has any other income, the payments will not be taken into account.

There were further modifications made to the definition under regulations implementing pilot schemes associated with the New Deal between November 1998 and November 2001. See the 14th edition for details.

Paragraph (8): Treatment of benefits

Para (8) provides that where a claimant receives a benefit other than HB and it is due to be altered between April 1 and 15 in any given year, the authority is obliged to treat the claimant as receiving the altered amount up to two benefit weeks before that week in which the different amount is paid to him. This rule is for the authority's administrative convenience to enable it to alter amounts so as to coincide with changes in rent, rather than cope with changes of circumstances later on.

Paragraphs (9), (10) and (10A): Notional earnings

Para (9), is sometimes known as the 'notional earnings' rule. The effect is to treat the claimant as having an income from unpaid or low paid work which s/he does, with the limited exceptions in para (10). The exceptions are work for charitable or voluntary bodies or other voluntary work (sub-para (a)), services performed in connection with certain employment or training schemes for which a training allowance is not payable or where the allowance is only for travel or meal expenses (sub-para (b) and certain approved work placements (sub-para (c)). "Work placement" is defined in para (10A). See also Sch 5 para 2.

The provision is directed at employers who pay too little and aims to prevent low-paid work being subsidised by the public purse. It is not directed at claimants who declare less than they earn, yet the effect is to penalise the claimant.

In applying the paragraph, however, the authority has many value judgments to make:

(1)   If the claimant is working for a charitable or voluntary body or is a volunteer, the authority must decide if it is "reasonable" for her/him to work free of charge. A "volunteer" is a person who without any obligation performs a service for someone else without expecting payment: *R(IS) 12/92* para 6. It might be reasonable for such work to be done where the worker is trying to obtain work experience. Other relevant factors are the closeness of the relationship between the provider and beneficiary of the service, the expectations of family members if there is a family relationship, the housing arrangements of the parties and why, if s/he did, the service provider gave up employment: see *CIS 93/1991* para 4.

(2)   Does the person for whom the work is performed pay less than the amount paid for "comparable employment" in the area? If there is no "comparable employment" and something is paid, it is arguable that the paragraph cannot apply: see sub-para (b). A particular difficulty that has arisen concerns employees who are being paid less than the national minimum wage. Some authorities have been proceeding on the basis that since it is generally unlawful to pay less than the minimum wage, employees working for less than the minimum wage have to be treated as being in receipt of notional earnings. This seems particularly harsh and wholly out of touch with the reality of work in tight labour markets in areas of high unemployment, where workers may have little option but to accept low-paid work to keep themselves in the job market. Thus unless the authority has evidence of comparable jobs paying higher wages, authorities ought readily to find that it is not reasonable to treat the relevant person as receiving more money.

(3)   What is a "reasonable" amount to treat the claimant as possessing from the employment? In certain circumstances it may be "reasonable" to treat the claimant as possessing *no* income from this source.

Even if the authority considers the terms of sub-paras (a) and (b) to be satisfied, the claimant can still avoid the effect of the paragraph by satisfying the authority that the person for whom the work is done cannot afford to pay, or to pay more. It may be difficult to provide evidence of the other person's means.

Paragraphs (11) and (12): Quantification of notional income

Para (11) deals with the quantification of income which a claimant is treated as possessing under paras (1) to (8). Basically, the notional income is quantified as if it were real.

Para (12) quantifies notional earnings which a claimant is deemed to receive under para (9). The deductions made under sub-paras (a) to (c) are the same as those in reg 36(6). See the Analysis to that paragraph.

SECTION 6
Capital

General Note on Section 6

This Section deals with the quantification of a claimant's "capital" for HB purposes. There is a bar on entitlement for anyone with capital exceeding £16,000 as assessed under this Section: see p15 and reg 43. If a claimant has capital worth between £6,000 and £16,000, s/he will be treated as receiving "tariff income" from that capital: see reg 52. *Actual* income produced by capital which is taken into account is itself treated as capital and disregarded as income: see reg 46(4) and Sch 5 para 17. Income produced by some *disregarded* capital is taken into account under Section 5: Sch 5 para 17.

There is a total disregard of capital belonging to IS or income-based JSA claimants as their capital has already been taken into account in the assessment of that benefit, though note the potential effect of the decision in *R v South Ribble DC HBRB ex p Hamilton* [2000] 33 HLR 102, CA: see the General Note to this Part on p278.

The term "capital" itself is not defined by the regulations. For the capital/income distinction, see the General Note to Section 2 of this Part on p284.

It is important to remember that a capital resource which appears to belong to the claimant, for example property in her/his name, may in fact legally belong to someone else because it is held subject to a trust or pursuant to some other form of equity. For example, a house in the claimant's name but purchased with someone else's money, not as a gift for the claimant, was held not to belong to the claimant, but to be held on "resulting trust" for the person advancing the money: *R(SB) 1/85* para 9. Likewise, if a claimant is paid money for a particular purpose in circumstances which make her/him a trustee for the carrying out of that purpose, and for some reason that purpose is not, or cannot, be carried out, s/he would normally not own the money but would hold it on trust for the person it originally belonged to. In *R(IS) 1/90*, the claimant tried to argue that he had transferred over £6,000 from a redundancy payment to his son, to pay for his education. It was held in a high interest account in the claimant's name as he feared his son might misuse the money. It was held that although the money was clearly earmarked for his son's education, he had done nothing to renounce ownership and control. A person should not be treated as voluntarily giving up an interest in property unless there is a very clear indication that this is his/her intention. There was no express or implied declaration of trust in this case. See the discussion in the commentary to reg 46 Income Support (General) Regulations 1987 in the current edition of vol II of *Social Security Legislation* for a more extensive analysis of the caselaw on beneficial ownership of capital.

In *Thomas v Chief Adjudication Officer* reported as an appendix to *R(SB) 17/87*, CA, it was held that money held by a solicitor for a client was an actual, not a notional resource, and that the solicitor should be looked at in the same way as a bank.

Sch 6 provides a long list of disregards for a claimant's capital. Reg 41 provides that certain capital is treated as income.

The structure of the Section is as follows.

Reg 43 prescribes the maximum level of capital a claimant may have and still potentially be entitled to HB. This figure may be updated every year if the Secretary of State thinks fit: see s150 SSAA.

Reg 44, together with the rest of this Part and Sch 6, sets out the general rules as to how a claimant's capital is to be assessed for HB purposes.

Reg 45 provides a total disregard of capital belonging to dependant children or young people in assessing the claimant's capital.

Reg 46 provides for certain types of *income* belonging to a claimant or her/his partner to be treated as the claimant's capital.

Regs 47 and 48 provide the rules for quantifying those parts of a claimant's capital which *are* to be taken into account; reg 47 deals with capital in the UK, reg 48 with capital elsewhere.

Reg 49 provides for certain situations in which a claimant will be *treated* as possessing capital which s/he does not in fact possess.

Reg 50 sets out the rules for diminishing capital where a claimant is treated as possessing notional capital under reg 49.

Reg 51 sets out the rules for assessing capital the claimant is entitled to jointly with someone else. See also para 17 of Sch 5 in respect of income derived from this capital.

Reg 52 sets out the rules under which "tariff income" is to be treated as produced by capital of certain levels and how that income is to be quantified. Actual income (other than from certain types of disregarded capital) is treated as capital itself from the date it is "normally due to be" credited to the claimant's account (reg 46(4)). See also para 17 Sch 5 (income from disregarded capital taken into account).

Capital limit

43. For the purposes of section 134(1) of the Act as it applies to housing benefit (no entitlement to benefit if capital exceeds prescribed amount), the prescribed amount is £16,000.

General Note

The "prescribed amount" has been £16,000 since April 1990.

Calculation of capital

44.–(1) For the purposes of Part 7 of the Act (income-related benefits) as it applies to housing benefit, the capital of a claimant to be taken into account shall, subject to paragraph (2), be the whole of his capital calculated in accordance with this Part and any income treated as capital under regulation 46 (income treated as capital).

(2) There shall be disregarded from the calculation of a claimant's capital under paragraph (1), any capital, where applicable, specified in Schedule 6.

Definitions
"capital" – see General Note.
"claimant" – see reg 2(1).

General Note
This regulation provides the general authority for assessing capital according to the rules set out in the rest of this Part, not just this Section, so income treated as capital under reg 46 is specifically included. But para (2), together with Sch 6, provides for the disregard of certain items of capital. In considering the scope of any disregard, decisions on similarly-worded disregards in other means-tested benefit schemes must be taken into account: *CH 2321/2002* para 8.

Disregard of capital of child and young person

45. The capital of a child or young person who is a member of the claimant's family shall not be treated as capital of the claimant.

Definitions
"child" – see reg 2(1).
"family" – see s137(1) SSCBA.
"membership of a family" – see Part 4.
"young person" – see reg 19.

General Note
The effect of this regulation is that the capital of a child or young person of the claimant or her/his partner is *not* to be treated as the claimant's.

Income treated as capital

46.–(1) Any bounty derived from employment to which paragraph 8 of Schedule 4 applies and paid at intervals of at least one year shall be treated as capital.

(2) Any amount by way of a refund of income tax deducted from profits or emoluments chargeable to income tax under Schedule D or E shall be treated as capital.

(3) Any holiday pay which is not earnings under regulation 35(1)(d) (earnings of employed earners) shall be treated as capital.

(4) Except any income derived from capital disregarded under paragraphs 1, 2, 4, 8, 14 [¹, 25 to 28, 45 or 46] of Schedule 6, any income derived from capital shall be treated as capital but only from the date it is normally due to be credited to the claimant's account.

(5) In the case of employment as an employed earner, any advance of earnings or any loan made by the claimant's employer shall be treated as capital.

(6) Any charitable or voluntary payment which is not made or due to be made at regular intervals, other than a payment which is made under the Macfarlane Trust, the Macfarlane (Special Payments) Trust, the Macfarlane (Special Payments) (No. 2) Trust, the Fund, the Eileen Trust or the Independent Living Funds, shall be treated as capital.

(7) There shall be treated as capital the gross receipts of any commercial activity carried on by a person in respect of which assistance is received under the self-employment route, but only in so far as those receipts were payable into a special account (as defined for the purposes of Chapter 4A of Part 8 of the Jobseeker's Allowance Regulations) during the period in which that person was receiving such assistance.

(8) Any arrears of subsistence allowance which are paid to a claimant as a lump sum shall be treated as capital.

(9) Any arrears of working tax credit or child tax credit shall be treated as capital.

Definitions
"claimant" – see reg 2(1).
"derived from" – see Analysis of reg 35.

"earnings" – see regs 35 and 36.
"employed earner" – reg 2(1).
"the fund" – see reg 2(1).
"self-employment route" – see reg 2(1).
"subsistence allowance" – see reg 2(1).

Amendment
1.　　Amended by reg 15(2) of SI 2006 No 2378 from the first day of the first benefit week to commence on or after 2.10.06.

General Note
This regulation deems certain types of income to be treated as capital and para 30 of Sch 5 provides that these are to be *ignored* for the purposes of assessing a claimant's income, to avoid double counting.

Analysis
Para (1). The relevant employments are part-time firefighters, part-time coastguards or those involved in launching lifeboats, and reservists.
Para (2) deals with income tax refunded on earnings from employed earners or self-employment.
Para (3). Under regulation 35(1)(d), holiday pay payable more than four weeks after termination or interruption of employment is not treated as earnings. However, it will be treated as capital under para (3).
Para (4). See the General Note to reg 52. The word "normally" is used so that occasional deviations from this date may be ignored. But see Sch 5 para 17 and Sch 6 para 15.
Para (5) is self-explanatory.
Para (6). For "charitable or voluntary payment" see the Analysis to Sch 5 para 14. Regular charitable or voluntary payments are income and may be disregarded in whole or in part under that paragraph.

Para (6) treats *irregular* charitable or voluntary payments (other than those specified) as capital. They will not affect entitlement to benefit at all if the claimant's total capital after receipt is less than £6,000. If total capital after receipt is between £6,000 and £16,000 the tariff income rule in reg 52 will apply. Note that irregular payments from the Macfarlane Trusts and etc are disregarded by Sch 6 para 24.
Para (7). "Self-employment route" is defined in reg 2(1). The definition of the special account referred to is in in reg 101A of the Jobseeker's Allowance Regulations 1996. See also Sch 5 para 58 for payments to those following this route that can be disregarded as income.

There were modifications to this regulation between November 1999 and November 2001 for New Deal participants. See the commentary in the 14th edn for details.
Para (8). Arrears of subsistence allowance paid as a lump sum are treated as capital. "Subsistence allowance" means that which an employment zone contractor has agreed to pay someone who is participating in an employment zone programme. "Employment zone" and "employment zone contractor" are defined in reg 2(1).
Para (9). Arrears of WTC and CTC are treated as capital. This will be an important provision when the Revenue is experiencing delays in deciding claims for tax credits. It provides that "any arrears" of tax credits are to be treated as capital. Note also the effect of Sch 6 para 9(1)(e) which provides for such arrears to be disregarded as capital for a period of 52 weeks from the date of receipt.

Where the Revenue pays tax credits, it will pay them by direct credit transfer either one week or four-weekly in arrears. It is clear that this provision is not intended to apply to such four-weekly payments (payments in arrears) as distinct from payments made in respect of a period prior to the current period(payments of arrears). However, it may be open to argument that payments in arrears, at least in so far as they relate to the three weeks previous to the week in which the payments are made, are "arrears" and should be treated as capital rather than income.

Calculation of capital in the United Kingdom

[¹**47.** Capital which a claimant possesses in the United Kingdom shall be calculated at its current market or surrender value less–
　　(a)　where there would be expenses attributable to the sale, 10 per cent; and
　　(b)　the amount of any encumbrance secured on it.]

Definitions
"capital" – see General Note on this Section.
"claimant" – see reg 2(1).

Amendment

1.   Substituted by reg 11(8) of SI 2007 No 2618 as from 1.10.07.

General Note

This deals with the quantification of capital which is taken into account for HB purposes and which is situated in the UK (a term which includes Northern Ireland). Until 1 October 2007, there was different rule for the valuation of National Savings Certificates. See p307 of the 19th edition of this book for the former version of the rule.

Analysis

Para (a). The authority has to decide what the current market or surrender value is. Authorities should avoid asking for evidence which would cause the claimant inordinate expenditure – eg, surveyor's reports. GM BW1.513 suggests:

"[where capital consists of stocks and shares] valuation should relate to the value on the date the claim for benefit is made, or treated as made, and be based on relevant information, such as the Stock Market pages in a national newspaper. . . "

GM BW1.470 suggests that as regards valuation of property (eg, a second home or business premises), authorities should obtain a current market valuation unless one is already available. GM BW1.484 advises authorities who receive invoices from the District Valuers Services that they should be directed to the DWP Benefit Delivery Specialist Operations Team for payment.

Where there is a conflict of valuation evidence, a tribunal is not obliged to give more weight to the lower valuation so as to grant rather than deny benefit. Valuation is "an art rather than a science" and, in an appropriate case, a tribunal is entitled to resolve the conflict by taking an average of the competing figures. The tribunal does not err by accepting valuation assumptions which were reasonable at the time the value of the capital has to be assessed, even if subsequent evidence has shown those assumptions to be incorrect: see *R v Doncaster MBC ex p Nortrop* [1998] unreported, 31 July, QBD.

From the current market/surrender value should be deducted the amounts referred to in sub-paras (a) and (b). In sub-para (b), the words "incumbrance secured on it" would include any debts secured on the capital eg, a mortgage on a house. In *R(IS) 21/93* para 19(7)(a), the commissioner concluded that a mere unsecured loan could not be an "incumbrance". The word should therefore be read as it applies in the law of real property.

R(IS) 2/90 concerned the valuation of shares in a private company. The articles of association of a private company provided that the shares must be offered first to the other shareholders at a "fair" value, determined by the company's auditors. Commissioner Rice held that the DWP could not just come to their own, higher valuation and the value of the shares could not be more than that set by the auditor. The value could have been lower as IS presupposed a quick sale.

Calculation of capital outside the United Kingdom

48.   Capital which a claimant possesses in a country outside the United Kingdom shall be calculated–

(a)   in a case where there is no prohibition in that country against the transfer to the United Kingdom of an amount equal to its current market or surrender value in that country, at that value;

(b)   in a case where there is such a prohibition, at the price which it would realise if sold in the United Kingdom to a willing buyer,

less, where there would be expenses attributable to sale, 10 per cent. and the amount of any encumbrances secured on it.

Definitions

"capital" – see General Note on this Section.
"claimant" – see reg 2(1).

General Note

This regulation provides for the quantification of capital owned by the claimant outside the UK, with different rules depending on whether or not capital equivalent to the value of that asset in the country in which it is situated may be transferred to the UK. There will undoubtedly be problems in quantifying the market value of such assets overseas and in converting the amount in question to sterling. GM BW1.400-407 gives some guidance.

If the value of the asset *can* be transferred to the UK from the country, para (a) applies and the claimant is treated as possessing an amount equal to the market or surrender value in that country, minus the deductions as available under reg 47(a) above. It is the "current market or surrender value *in that country*" which is relevant. Thus in *CH 4972/2002* (para 9) the commissioner stated that the market value of a property in France had to be assessed for a sale in France rather than the UK.

If the value of the asset in the country in which it is situated cannot be transferred to the UK, para (b) applies. The claimant is treated as possessing the amount, if any, which a "willing buyer" in the UK would pay to purchase the asset from the claimant, bearing in mind that such a buyer would not her/himself be able to liquidate the assets and transfer them here either. As with para (a), the deductions as available under reg 47(a) must be made. The amounts a claimant can be treated as possessing on this basis will usually be much smaller than the actual value of the asset if sold in the country in which it is situated.

Notional capital

49.–(1) A claimant shall be treated as possessing capital of which he has deprived himself for the purpose of securing entitlement to housing benefit or increasing the amount of that benefit except to the extent that that capital is reduced in accordance with regulation 50 (diminishing notional capital rule).

(2)   Except in the case of–

(a)   a discretionary trust; or

(b)   a trust derived from a payment made in consequence of a personal injury; or

(c)   any loan which would be obtained only if secured against capital disregarded under Schedule 6; or

(d)   a personal pension scheme [¹ , occupational pension scheme] [² [⁴] or a payment made by the Board of the Pension Protection Fund]; or

[³ (e) any sum to which paragraph 45(2)(a) of Schedule 6 (capital to be disregarded) applies which is administered in the way referred to in paragraph 45(1)(a); or

(ea)   any sum to which paragraph 46(a) of Schedule 6 refers; or]

(f)   child tax credit; or

(g)   working tax credit,

any capital which would become available to the claimant upon application being made, but which has not been acquired by him, shall be treated as possessed by him but only from the date on which it could be expected to be acquired were an application made.

(3)   Any payment of capital, other than a payment of capital specified in paragraph (4), made–

(a)   to a third party in respect of a single claimant or a member of the family (but not a member of the third party's family) shall, where that payment is a payment of an occupational pension [² , a pension or other periodical payment made under a personal pension scheme or a payment made by the Board of the Pension Protection Fund], be treated as possessed by that single claimant or, as the case may be, by that member;

(b)   to a third party in respect of a single claimant or in respect of a member of the family (but not a member of the third party's family) shall, where it is not a payment referred to in sub-paragraph (a), be treated as possessed by that single claimant or by that member to the extent that it is used for the food, household fuel or, subject to paragraph (8), rent or ordinary clothing or footwear, of that single claimant or, as the case may be, of any member of that family or is used for any council tax or water charges for which that claimant or member is liable;

(c)   to a single claimant or a member of the family in respect of a third party (but not in respect of another member of the family) shall be treated as possessed by that single claimant or, as the case may be, that member of the family to the extent that it is kept or used by him or used by or on behalf of any member of the family.

(4)   Paragraph (3) shall not apply in respect of a payment of capital made–

(a)   under the Macfarlane Trust, the Macfarlane (Special Payments) Trust, the Macfarlane (Special Payments) (No. 2) Trust, the Fund, the Eileen Trust, the Independent Living Funds, the Skipton Fund or the London Bombings Relief Charitable Fund;

(b)   pursuant to section 2 of the 1973 Act in respect of a person's participation–

    (i)   in an employment programme specified in regulation 75(1)(a)(ii) of the Jobseeker's Allowance Regulations;

    (ii)   in a training scheme specified in regulation 75(1)(b)(ii) of those Regulations;

    (iii)   in the Intense Activity Period specified in regulation 75(1)(a)(iv) of those Regulations or in the Intensive Activity Period for 50 plus; or

    (iv)   in a qualifying course within the meaning specified in regulation 17A(7) of those Regulations;

(c)   under an occupational pension scheme [2 , in respect of a pension or other periodical payment made under a personal pension scheme or a payment made by the Board of the Pension Protection Fund] where–

    (i)   a bankruptcy order has been made in respect of the person in respect of whom the payment has been made or, in Scotland, the estate of that person is subject to sequestration or a judicial factor has been appointed on that person's estate under section 41 of the Solicitors (Scotland) Act 1980;

    (ii)   the payment is made to the trustee in bankruptcy or any other person acting on behalf of the creditors; and

    (iii)   the person referred to in (i) and any member of his family does not possess, or is not treated as possessing, any other income apart from that payment.

(5)   Where a claimant stands in relation to a company in a position analogous to that of a sole owner or partner in the business of that company, he may be treated as if he were such sole owner or partner and in such a case–

(a)   the value of his holding in that company shall, notwithstanding regulation 44 (calculation of capital) be disregarded; and

(b)   he shall, subject to paragraph (6), be treated as possessing an amount of capital equal to the value or, as the case may be, his share of the value of the capital of that company and the foregoing provisions of this Section shall apply for the purposes of calculating that amount as if it were actual capital which he does possess.

(6)   For so long as the claimant undertakes activities in the course of the business of the company, the amount which he is treated as possessing under paragraph (5) shall be disregarded.

(7)   Where a claimant is treated as possessing capital under any of paragraphs (1) to (3) the foregoing provisions of this Section shall apply for the purposes of calculating its amount as if it were actual capital which he does possess.

(8)   In paragraph (3) "rent" means eligible rent less any deductions in respect of non-dependants which fall to be made under regulation 74 (non-dependant deductions).

Amendments

1.   Amended by reg 5A(3) of SI 2005 No 2465 as inserted by Sch 2 para 28(5) of SI 2006 No 217 as from 6.4.06.

2.   Amended by reg 8(3) of SI 2006 No 588 as from 6.4.06.

3.   Substituted by reg 6(3) of SI 2007 No 719 as from 2.4.07.

4.   Amended by reg 4(5) of SI 2007 No 1749 as from 16.7.07.

Definitions

"capital" – see General Note on this section.

"claimant" – see reg 2(1).

"family" – see s137(1) SSCBA.
"Macfarlane (Special Payments) Trust, the Fund, the Eileen Trust, the Independent Living Funds" – see reg 2(1).
"membership of family" – see Part 4.
"ordinary clothing or footware" – see reg 2(1).

General Note

This regulation sets out the situations in which a claimant must or may be treated as possessing capital even when s/he does not actually possess it. This regulation corresponds to reg 42 in respect of income.

Paras (1) to (5) set out these situations, para (6) qualifies para (5), and para (7) provides how capital that a claimant is deemed to possess under this regulation is to be quantified. Para (8) defines the term "rent" as it is used in para (3).

Note that para (4) is modified in its application to certain New Deal participants.

Analysis

Paragraph (1): Capital of which a claimant has deprived her/himself

Para (1) is similar to reg 42(1) in its effect. The notes below on the wording of this paragraph will be equally applicable to reg 42(1).

Guidance. Much of the relevant DWP guidance is useful but care must be taken to give precedence to the wording of the regulation and the caselaw.

The key factors in reaching a decision that deprivation has occurred are (1) that the resource had actually belonged to the claimant and (2) that the dates and period over which disposal occurred indicate at least a partial motive for the decision.

GM BW1.714, lists certain circumstances where the DWP suggests deprivation may have occurred:

(1)   A lump sum payment made to someone else – eg, as a gift or to repay a debt.
(2)   Substantial expenditure incurred – eg, on an expensive holiday.
(3)   Title deeds of property which is not, or will soon cease to be, the claimant's home transferred into someone else's name.
(4)   Money put into an irrevocable trust.
(5)   Money converted into a form (eg, personal possessions) which would fall to be disregarded.
(6)   Money reduced by extravagant living.

However, while the guidance provides a useful indication of the types of situation in which a claimant is likely to be subject to an inquiry as to the circumstances of the deprivation, the wording of the legislation and the relevant caselaw must always be followed. Note, therefore, some of the criticisms of the guidance set out below.

"A claimant shall be treated as possessing capital . . . ". The first point that needs to be made is that the capital of which the claimant is said to have deprived her/himself must be capital which would normally fall to be taken into account. Thus if the capital does not belong to the claimant in the first case (perhaps because it is subject to a trust: see the General Note on this Section) or if it falls to be disregarded under Sch 6, para (1) can have no application.

" . . . of which he has deprived himself . . . ". The word "deprived" is an ordinary English word and does not have any special meaning: *R(SB) 38/85* para 21. It is sufficient if a claimant ceases to possess the relevant asset, even if s/he receives something in exchange for the asset: *R(SB) 40/85* para 8.

It appears that a person can have "deprived himself" of an asset of which s/he was never in possession. So a deliberate failure to cash a cheque may amount to a "deprivation": *CSB 598/1987*, as may a release of a debtor: *CIS 1586/1997*.

" . . . for the purpose of securing entitlement to housing benefit or increasing the amount of that benefit . . . ". Three different issues arise from this part of the paragraph. First, there is the question of establishing the relevant "purpose". In deciding whether a person has deprived her/himself of capital to obtain HB or CTB, the authority must consider whether the obtaining of benefit was a "significant operative purpose" behind the decision to divest her/himself of the asset: *R(SB) 40/85* para 10. It is insufficient that the claimant knows that the obtaining of benefit is a natural consequence of the transaction: *R(SB) 9/91*. There must be a positive finding that the claimant actually knew of the capital limit in the light of all the facts, and it will not necessarily be sufficient for the authority to show that the information was available to the claimant in literature supplied by it: *CIS 124/1990* para 11; *CIS 30/ 1993*. These principles have recently been restated with force in *R(H) 1/06,* a case concerning a claimant who had a severe and enduring mental illness. Commissioner Howell in considering reg 43 HB Regs 1987 (now reg 49 HB Regs) at para 13 stated:

"there is no doubt that the test of whether a claimant is shown to have deprived himself of capital "for the purpose of" securing entitlement to housing benefit so as to fall within the notional capital provisions of regulation 43 Housing Benefit (General) Regulations 1987 SI No 1971 is a subjective one, depending on the evidence about the particular claimant in question. It does not in my view adequately address or answer the point to say as the chairman did that because a person is not completely incapable of managing his affairs or of realising he was spending his money imprudently, it follows as a matter of course and without further analysis that all such spending is done for the purpose of securing entitlement to benefit. Such a jump is impermissible as it omits any real consideration of the actual purpose of the particular person involved".

This decision was endorsed and followed by Commissioner Bano in *CIS 218/2005* (para 7), where the commissioner said that "the issue requires a determination of the actual, or subjective, intention of the claimant".

Commissioner Howell returned to this point later in *R(H) 1/06*, where he said (para 22):

"Whether the securing of entitlement to benefit was, in this sense, among the purposes which led any particular claimant to act as he did is a question that must be determined by the tribunal of fact in the circumstances of each individual case, the test as already noted being one of subjective purpose: see in the housing benefit context *R (Beeson) v Dorset County Council* [2001] EWHC Admin 986, 30 November 2001, *per* Richards J at paragraphs 9, 37 (not challenged on this point in the Court of Appeal). In the great majority of cases this must be a matter of drawing such inferences as the tribunal of fact thinks fit from the surrounding circumstances, such as the claimant's state of knowledge of the rules, the nature and timing of the disposals he makes and the timing and manner of his claims for benefit; since direct evidence to show such a purpose is in the nature of things unlikely. Such a task is however a perfectly normal one for a tribunal of fact to have to undertake, and this is of course by no means the only instance in the law when the purpose for which a thing is done may not be express, and has to be ascertained "as a matter of substance and of fact": *re South African Supply and Cold Storage Company* [1904] 2 Ch 268, per Buckley J at p282. In using the word "significant" Mr Monroe may perhaps have had in mind what was said by Lord Morris of Borth-y-Gest in *Sweet v Parsley* [1970] AC 132, 155A:

"In my opinion, the words 'premises . . . used for the purposes of . . . ' denote a purpose which is other than quite incidental or casual or fortuitous: they denote a purpose which is or has become either a significant one or a recognised one though certainly not necessarily an only one."

The mere fact that an asset has been disposed of at a substantial undervalue is insufficient, of itself, for an authority to conclude that a claimant should be treated as having notional capital. The claimant's explanation for the disposition needs to be properly considered: *R v South Tyneside MBC ex p Tooley* [1996] COD 143 at 144, QBD.

The caselaw on the correct approach to be taken to "purpose" where the deprivation is constituted in paying off a commercial debt (in this case credit cards) was reviewed in *CJSA 1425/2004*. Commissioner Rowland stressed that the approach of the Court of Appeal in *Jones v Secretary of State for Work and Pensions* [2003] EWCA 964, unreported, does not undermine the point in *R(SB) 12/91* that, if the debtor has no practical choice but to pay his debt, the repayment of the debt cannot reasonably be regarded as having been for the purpose of obtaining benefit and that, normally, if a debt is immediately repayable, the debtor has no practical choice. Moreover, *Jones* is not authority for the proposition that if the debtor thought that the debt would not be called in for some time, payment of the debt would be for the purpose of obtaining benefit. Commissioner Rowland commented (at para 38) that he found it:

"difficult to envisage a case where it would be unreasonable for a claimant to pay a debt that had become due, merely because the creditor had decided not to enforce it for the time being, unless, perhaps, the decision not to enforce the debt was entirely unconnected to the claimant's lack of means and amounted, in effect, to a variation of the terms upon which the debt became repayable".

He went on (para 40) to conclude:

"The effect of all these decisions is therefore that, if a claimant realised that one consequence of depriving himself of capital was that he might become entitled to jobseeker's allowance or income support and he nonetheless deprived himself of that capital, there arises the question whether obtaining benefit was a significant operative purpose of the deprivation. Because there will almost always be some other purpose as well, that question is determined by deciding whether, given his knowledge, it was reasonable in all the circumstances for him to act as he did, bearing in mind not only his obligation to tax payers to support himself, but also his obligations to other people. Moreover, insofar as his obligation to support himself is concerned, it is necessary to have regard to the long term as well as the short term."

In approaching the facts of the case before him, Commissioner Rowland made a number of useful observations.

(a)   If a claimant has mixed motives, the question whether the purpose of obtaining benefits is a significant operative purpose is to be determined by deciding whether it was reasonable for the claimant to act in the way that he did (*CJSA 1425/2004* para 46).

(b) The true significance of the timing of the deprivation is that the closer the deprivation was to the date of claim, the stronger the inference will be that the deprivation was made in the expectation that there would be a claim and with the knowledge that the deprivation would affect the claimant's entitlement to benefit (para 48).

(c) Even if the appellant's forthcoming application for "review" of his benefit claim may have prompted him into paying his credit card debts when he did, that merely suggested that obtaining benefit was one purpose behind the payments; leaving the question whether it was a significant operative purpose still to be answered (and that was to be determined by considering whether making the payments was reasonable. In other words, although a claimant's desire to obtain benefit may explain the timing of the payments, it is not necessarily to be taken to have been a significant operative purpose behind the making of the payments (para 49).

(d) The threat of having to make high interest payments is just as capable of making it reasonable to pay a debt as the threat of enforcement of a liability to repay (para 50).

The second point is that the intention must be to secure, or increase the amount of "housing benefit". The regulation does not operate where the claimant has deprived her/himself of capital in order to get other means-tested benefits. If, for example, it could be shown that a claimant had deprived himself of capital but that her/his purpose in doing so was to secure entitlement to IS or income-based JSA rather than HB then s/he might be entitled to continue to receive HB even though the other benefit was stopped or reduced.

In practice, this would probably be difficult to establish but it might be possible to show in some cases that the claimant had no knowledge of the existence of HB (perhaps because s/he had never previously rented property). This principle also applies when one benefit is abolished and replaced by another: in *R(IS) 14/93* paras 16-17 it was held that a claimant who had deprived himself of substantial amounts of capital in 1987 in order to secure entitlement to supplementary benefit was nevertheless entitled to IS because, at the date of the deprivation, that benefit did not exist and therefore the deprivation could not have had the purpose of securing entitlement to it. It is not unknown for similar cases to emerge even now and it is suggested that the reference to "housing benefit" in reg 49(1) must be read as a reference to "housing benefit" under the HB Regs and not under the previous schemes: compare *R v Middlesborough BC ex p Graville* [1993] unreported, 26 March, QBD and *Andrew v City of Glasgow DC* [1996] SLT 814 at 817H-L.

Third, notional capital may exist where the claimant's intention was to increase entitlement as well as to create entitlement where none existed as long as the capital was held.

However, in some circumstances a claimant may be fixed with notional capital even though the deprivation was by her/his partner *before* they became a couple: *CH 1822 2006*, a decision refusing leave to appeal to a commissioner (decided with *CIS 1757 2006*). This is because the focus of regulation 49 is at the time when entitlement is in issue but in respect of a past disposal of capital. In this situation the notional capital rule will only apply to a future partner when there has been conduct that is related to future entitlement to benefit either for the person alone or as a member of a family, and then only when there has been a deprivation of capital with the necessary intention. Note that the claimant failed in his application for a judicial review of the commissioner's decision: *R (Hook) v The Social Security Commissioner* [2007] EWHC 1705 (Admin), 3 July.

Paragraph (2): Capital available on application

This is similar to reg 42(2): see the commentary on that provision. The authority is obliged to treat the claimant as possessing any capital which would become available to her/him on application, unless it comes within the exceptions in sub-paras (a) to (g). If a claimant is a potential beneficiary under a discretionary trust or a trust derived from a payment made in consequence of personal injury (see reg 42), or could raise money on a loan, but only if the loan was secured by capital disregarded under Sch 6, s/he is not to be treated as possessing capital under this regulation. See also Sch 6 para 14 in respect of entitlement under a trust of funds paid in consequence of personal injury.

Actual payments made to the claimant under a discretionary or other type of trust will be dealt with under the rest of this Section and not this regulation.

If the trust or other source from which a claimant could obtain capital is not excluded from this regulation, it must still be established by the authority that s/he actually could get payment if s/he asked. This will cause problems. In relation to trusts, under s32 of the Trustee Act 1925, trustees have a restricted power to advance up to half a claimant's potential share of capital under a trust, whether or not the claimant's right to such capital is vested or subject to her/him satisfying a contingency. But the trustees cannot be *obliged* to exercise this power, so it is by no means certain that if a claimant is a potential beneficiary under a trust s/he *would* be paid on application. Further information will be necessary.

If the claimant is absolutely entitled to trust funds under the rule in *Saunders v Vautier* [1841] 4 Bear 115 s/he is treated as the legal owner of the funds so that it is arguable that the trust funds will be treated as *actual* capital and not be subject to this regulation. However, in *R(SB) 2/89*, which concerned a trust of personal injury compensation, the beneficiary of the trust was the sole beneficiary and therefore, under the law, absolutely entitled to the money in the trust fund, but this did not stop it being disregarded under the analogous provision. This makes sense, because otherwise sub-para (e) would be deprived of any effect.

Paragraphs (3), (4) and (8): Payments involving third parties
This is identical in effect to paras (6) and (7) of reg 42. See the Analysis to those provisions.

Paragraph (5) and (6): Business assets
The application of this paragraph by an authority is discretionary. Sub-paras (a) and (b) and para (6) quantify how much capital a claimant is to be treated as possessing in this respect, if the authority decides to exercise its discretion.

If this paragraph applies whilst the claimant is actually working for the company, the capital value of her/his share of it is to be totally ignored in assessing the claimant's assets; if para (6) does *not* apply, under para (5)(a) and (b) s/he is treated as possessing the capital value of the company or her/his share of that value, rather than the actual value of her/his *holding*, which is ignored.

The valuation is made according to the rules in the rest of this Section – ie, at market value, minus allowable deductions: see reg 47. If the claimant is the sole owner, see Sch 6 para 8, which allows its value to be ignored for a "reasonable" period after s/he stops work to allow the company to be sold.

Paragraph (7): Valuation
If a claimant is treated as possessing capital under paras (1) to (5), it is to be quantified according to the rules which pertain to *actual* capital assets under this Section.

Diminishing notional capital rule

50.–(1) Where a claimant is treated as possessing capital under regulation 49(1) (notional capital), the amount which he is treated as possessing–
  (a) in the case of a week that is subsequent to–
      (i) the relevant week in respect of which the conditions set out in paragraph (2) are satisfied; or
      (ii) a week which follows that relevant week and which satisfies those conditions,
  shall be reduced by an amount determined under paragraph (3);
  (b) in the case of a week in respect of which paragraph (1)(a) does not apply but where–
      (i) that week is a week subsequent to the relevant week; and
      (ii) that relevant week is a week in which the condition in paragraph (4) is satisfied,
  shall be reduced by the amount determined under paragraph (4).
  (2) This paragraph applies to a benefit week where the claimant satisfies the conditions that–
  (a) he is in receipt of housing benefit; and
  (b) but for regulation 49(1), he would have received an additional amount of housing benefit in that week.
  (3) In a case to which paragraph (2) applies, the amount of the reduction for the purposes of paragraph (1)(a) shall be equal to the aggregate of–
  (a) the additional amount to which sub-paragraph (2)(b) refers;
  (b) where the claimant has also claimed council tax benefit, the amount of any council tax benefit or any additional amount of council tax benefit to which he would have been entitled in respect of the benefit week to which paragraph (2) refers but for the application of regulation 39(1) of the Council Tax Benefit Regulations 2006 (notional capital);
  (c) where the claimant has also claimed income support, the amount of income support to which he would have been entitled in respect of the benefit week to which paragraph (2) refers but for the application of regulation 51(1) of the Income Support Regulations (notional capital); and
  (d) where the claimant has also claimed a jobseeker's allowance, the amount of an income-based jobseeker's allowance to which he would have been entitled in respect of the benefit week to which paragraph (2) refers but for the application of regulation 113 of the Jobseeker's Allowance Regulations (notional capital).

(4)   Subject to paragraph (5), for the purposes of paragraph (1)(b) the condition is that the claimant would have been entitled to housing benefit in the relevant week but for regulation 49(1), and in such a case the amount of the reduction shall be equal to the aggregate of–

(a)   the amount of housing benefit to which the claimant would have been entitled in the relevant week but for regulation 49(1) and, for the purposes of this sub-paragraph, if the relevant week is a week to which regulation 80(4)(a) refers (calculation of weekly amounts), that amount shall be determined by dividing the amount of housing benefit to which he would have been so entitled by the number of days in that week for which he was liable to make payments in respect of the dwelling he occupies as his home and multiplying the quotient so obtained by 7;

(b)   if the claimant would, but for regulation 39(1) of the Council Tax Benefit Regulations 2006, have been entitled to council tax benefit or to an additional amount of council tax benefit in respect of the benefit week which includes the last day of the relevant week, the amount which is equal to–

(i)   in a case where no council tax benefit is payable, the amount to which he would have been entitled; or

(ii)   in any other case, the amount equal to the additional amount of council tax benefit to which he would have been entitled;

and, for the purposes of this sub-paragraph, if the amount is in respect of a part-week, that amount shall be determined by dividing the amount of the council tax benefit to which he would have been so entitled by the number equal to the number of days in the part-week and multiplying the quotient so obtained by 7;

(c)   if the claimant would, but for regulation 51(1) of the Income Support Regulations, have been entitled to income support in respect of the benefit week, within the meaning of regulation 2(1) of those Regulations (interpretation), which includes the last day of the relevant week, the amount to which he would have been entitled and, for the purposes of this sub-paragraph, if the amount is in respect of a part-week, that amount shall be determined by dividing the amount of the income support to which he would have been so entitled by the number equal to the number of days in the part-week and multiplying the quotient so obtained by 7;

(d)   if the claimant would, but for regulation 113 of the Jobseeker's Allowance Regulations, have been entitled to an income-based jobseeker's allowance in respect of the benefit week, within the meaning of regulation 1(3) of those Regulations (interpretation), which includes the last day of the relevant week, the amount to which he would have been entitled and, for the purposes of this sub-paragraph, if the amount is in respect of a part-week, that amount shall be determined by dividing the amount of the income-based jobseeker's allowance to which he would have been so entitled by the number equal to the number of days in the part-week and multiplying the quotient so obtained by 7.

(5)   The amount determined under paragraph (4) shall be re-determined under that paragraph if the claimant makes a further claim for housing benefit and the conditions in paragraph (6) are satisfied, and in such a case–

(a)   sub-paragraphs (a) to (d) of paragraph (4) shall apply as if for the words "relevant week" there were substituted the words "relevant subsequent week"; and

(b)   subject to paragraph (7), the amount as re-determined shall have effect from the first week following the relevant subsequent week in question.

(6)   The conditions are that–

(a)   a further claim is made 26 or more weeks after–

(i)   the date on which the claimant made a claim for housing benefit in respect of which he was first treated as possessing the capital in question under regulation 49(1);

(ii)   in a case where there has been at least one redetermination in accordance with paragraph (5), the date on which he last made a claim for housing benefit which resulted in the weekly amount being re-determined; or

(iii)   the date on which he last ceased to be entitled to housing benefit,

whichever last occurred; and

(b)   the claimant would have been entitled to housing benefit but for regulation 49(1).

(7)   The amount as re-determined pursuant to paragraph (5) shall not have effect if it is less than the amount which applied in that case immediately before the redetermination and in such a case the higher amount shall continue to have effect.

(8)   For the purposes of this regulation–

(a)   ''part-week'' in paragraph (4)(b) means a period of less than a week for which council tax benefit is allowed;

(b)   ''part-week'' in paragraph (4)(c) and (d) means–

(i)   a period of less than a week which is the whole period for which income support, or, as the case may be, an income-based jobseeker's allowance, is payable; and

(ii)   any other period of less than a week for which it is payable;

(c)   ''relevant week'' means the benefit week in which the capital in question of which the claimant has deprived himself within the meaning of regulation 49(1)–

(i)   was first taken into account for the purpose of determining his entitlement to housing benefit; or

(ii)   was taken into account on a subsequent occasion for the purpose of determining or re-determining his entitlement to housing benefit on that subsequent occasion and that determination or redetermination resulted in his beginning to receive, or ceasing to receive, housing benefit;

and where more than one benefit week is identified by reference to heads (i) and (ii) of this sub-paragraph the later or latest such benefit week;

(d)   ''relevant subsequent week'' means the benefit week which includes the day on which the further claim or, if more than one further claim has been made, the last such claim was made.

General Note

Although this regulation is lengthy, the principle is simple enough. Reg 49(1), if applied, could result in unfairness. Without a mechanism for reducing "notional capital", a claimant's HB entitlement could be affected permanently. In other words, had the claimant not disposed of capital, s/he would be able to use her/his capital resources and would eventually regain entitlement (or the increased rate of) HB. Reg 50 therefore provides the mechanism whereby the amount of notional capital which the claimant has as a result of the operation of reg 49(1) is reduced by the weekly amount of benefits lost as a result of the application of the rule.

Analysis

Paragraphs (1) to (4): The basic calculation

Para (1) provides the source of the reductions. The calculation starts at the "relevant week" which is defined in para (8)(c) and hence can apply retrospectively. The "relevant week" will ordinarily be the first week in which the notional capital was taken into account for the purposes of determining entitlement to HB. If, however, there is one or more subsequent determinations and benefit is actually awarded under that determination, the "relevant week" will be the week of the most recent determination.

First, under sub-para (a), in relation to any subsequent week where the conditions in para (2) are met, a reduction is made according to the calculation in para (3). In relation to any other week in which the condition in para (4) is met, a reduction is made under that paragraph.

Paras (2) and (3). Para (2) sets out two relevant conditions: that a person is in receipt of HB and that the effect of reg 49(1) has been to reduce her/his entitlement in that week. This would apply where the claimant's capital (notional and actual) is below the upper, but above the lower, capital limit and hence tariff income calculated under reg 52 reduces the amount to which s/he is entitled.

If para (2) applies, para (3) requires the amount of the notional capital in that week to be reduced by the additional amount of HB to which the claimant would have been entitled in the absence of reg 49(1) plus any CTB, IS or income-based JSA to which s/he would have been entitled in the absence of operation of the equivalent provisions for those benefits. The claimant will need to show that a valid claim had been made, subject to the rules for deeming claims. See the current volume II of *Social Security Legislation* for the rules relating to claims for those benefits.

Para (4) imposes the condition for para (1)(b), which is that there would have been entitlement to HB but for the operation of reg 49(1). This would apply where there is no current entitlement to HB – ie, because the claimant's capital (notional and actual) is above the capital limit, or is below the upper, but above the lower, capital limit and hence tariff income calculated under reg 52 reduces the amount to which s/he is entitled to nil. The amount of notional capital is reduced in a similar way to para (3). Part-weeks are dealt with on a pro rata basis.

Paragraphs (5) to (7): Redeterminations

Under para (5), if the claimant then reclaims HB 26 or more weeks after the latest date set out in para (6), and is still not entitled due to the "notional capital" rule in reg 49(1), the rate of diminution is recalculated at that point. Any changes which would reduce the rate of diminution are ignored under para (7), although factors which would increase that rate (eg, annual uprating) are taken into account.

It follows that claimants excluded from benefit by this rule should re-claim at 26-week intervals to ensure that the "notional capital" reduces at the maximum rate. If the "diminishing capital" rule results in a claimant becoming entitled again at some later date any remaining "notional capital" reduces according to the rules in paras (1)(a), (2), (3) and (8)(b)(ii).

Capital jointly held

51. Except where a claimant possesses capital which is disregarded under regulation 49(5) (notional capital) where a claimant and one or more persons are beneficially entitled in possession to any capital asset they shall be treated as if each of them were entitled in possession to the whole beneficial interest therein in an equal share and the foregoing provisions of this Section shall apply for the purposes of calculating the amount of capital which the claimant is treated as possessing as if it were actual capital which the claimant does possess.

General Note

The legal owner of an asset may be, but is not always, the same as the beneficial owner – eg, if one person buys a house in his name, but part of the purchase price is paid by someone else, and that person does not intend to make the nominal purchaser an outright gift, or only intends to lend the nominal purchaser the money, that other person has a "beneficial interest" in the house, despite the fact that the legal ownership is in the person whose name is on the title deeds. The term "in possession" means that ownership can be enjoyed at present and is not postponed to some other legal interest, for example a life interest, or dependent on the satisfaction of some contingency. As the law on quantification of beneficial interests is complex, this paragraph simply deems each of those who have such an interest in a particular capital asset to have an equal share in it.

See also Sch 5 para 17 in respect of income produced by such an asset.

Analysis

Reg 51 has what is probably the most chequered legislative history of any regulation in this book. Before 2 October 1995, the wording of reg 44 HB Regs 1987 (now reg 51 HB Regs) was exactly the same as it is now. Then, as part of a series of changes to the rules for all the income-related benefits, it was amended. Those amendments were designed to reverse the decision of the Court of Appeal in *Chief Adjudication Officer v Palfrey*, [1995] *The Times*, 8 February, reported as *R(IS) 5/98*, CA. Then, in May 1998 the equivalent amendment to the IS Regs was then held to be *ultra vires* by a social security commissioner in *CIS 3283/1997*. The then DSS did not appeal that decision and accepted the commissioner's reasoning by returning the regulation to its original wording.

The regulation deals with the common situation where property (eg, a house) is owned by more than one person. Rather than become embroiled in difficult disputes as to the relative shares actually owned by each co-owner, the policy of the DWP has long been to calculate benefit entitlement as if the asset were owned in equal shares. However, whether or not reg 51 successfully carries that policy into effect is open to question. Two problems arise. The first is whether the wording of the regulation is apt to include all forms of co-ownership and the second is the basis on which the claimant's deemed equal share is to be valued.

Under English law, there are two forms of co-ownership, namely joint tenancy and tenancy in common. The word "tenancy" might seem to suggest leasehold ownership or entitlement under a tenancy agreement but in this context applies to freehold ownership as well. Under a joint tenancy, all co-owners own the whole property (and hence if one dies, his or her interest is simply subsumed in the interest(s) of the other(s) by a process known as "survivorship" rather than passing under the Will of the deceased owner). By contrast each owner under a tenancy in common owns an undivided share in the property. There was disagreement between commissioners as to whether reg 44 HB Regs 1987 (now reg 51 HB Regs) applied to both forms of co-ownership or merely to joint tenancies. It was confirmed by the Court of Appeal in *Secretary of State for Work and Pensions v Hourigan* [2003] 1 WLR 608 (reported as *R(IS) 4/03*), paras 17-21, 30, 32 that reg 51 has no application to tenants in common.

In *CIS 2575/1997* the commissioner held that the regulation also applied to foreign property and covered all forms of co-ownership whether existing under English law or not. Whether or not the latter finding can stand with *Hourigan* remains to be seen. Logically, if a form of foreign co-holding is akin to tenancy in common, the regulation should be inapplicable. If that is correct, evidence from a local lawyer in the country where the property was held would be required to ascertain the nature of the co-ownership.

If the regulation does apply, there are two possible approaches to the valuation of the deemed share. These may be illustrated by the example of a house which is owned jointly by two people. The first approach values the house as a whole and then, after deductions for the costs of sale and any mortgages or other charges, divides that figure by two and values each co-owner's deemed share at an amount equal to the dividend. The second approach looks at the value which would be obtained on the open market if, rather than sell the house as a whole, the claimant's deemed equal share was sold but the deemed equal share of the co-owner was not. In other words the second approach values the claimant's share on the basis that any purchaser would have to continue to share the property with the co-owner). The difference between the approaches can be summed up as being between "half the value" and the "value of half".

The Court of Appeal in *Palfrey* favoured the "value of half" approach, the 1995 amendments purported to replace it with the "half the value" rule and, as a result of *CIS 3283/1997* and amendments in October 1998, the "value of half" rule has now regained supremacy.

The "value of half" approach has, for the claimant, the advantage of consistently returning a lower valuation. In the case of a jointly-owned house, common sense suggests that the value of half (or a third or any other part-share) will quite often be nil simply because there will be no evidence of an actual market in part shares of houses and because it would not be possible for the buyer of a part-share to take out a mortgage on it. The correctness of this view is reinforced by the decision in *CH 1953/2003* which concerned the former matrimonial home occupied by the claimant's wife. The tribunal had simply found that the claimant had to be treated as entitled to half the property which would take him over the capital limit. Following *Hourigan*, that approach was incorrect as the form of co-ownership had to be investigated (para 11). The tribunal was not entitled to assume that the claimant's wife would buy him out of the property on his request (para 14). In valuing the property, account had to be taken of the potential difficulties with sale in the light of the rights of the claimant's wife (para 15). The commissioner observed that "I would need evidence of the existence of a real market for the claimant's interest in his former home" (para 16).

Arrangements for authorities to obtain valuations of jointly owned property from the are described in GM W1.491-492 but it will often be advisable for claimants involved in disputes to obtain their own valuation evidence. Although District Valuers can usually claim special expertise because details of every property purchase need to be produced to the Revenue as part of the conveyancing process, it is doubtful whether any such claim can be made in relation to sales of part shares. This is because there are unlikely to be many such sales. It will therefore always be worth asking for the number of real-life examples on which the official valuation is based.

In *CIS 2661/2006*, Commissioner Williams sets out that the approach to be taken in assessing the capital value of a claimant's share in a former joint home. The question of the value of a former joint home is only to be considered if none of the relevant capital disregards apply on the facts of the case (for which see Sch 6). If none of the disregards apply then one next has to consider whether the claimant's interest in the former home is as a tenant in common or a joint tenant. A joint tenancy should not be assumed (because nowadays it is far more common, for tax planning reasons for example, for couples to be advised to buy as tenants in common). However, this factual issue can be resolved easily by payment of a small fee and searching the land registry (at www.landregisteronline.gov.uk). If the the interest is as a joint tenant, it is the current market value of the claimant's half of the house that is relevant (ie, with the former partner still living in it and perhaps unwilling or unable to move out or buy out the claimant's half share), not half the value of the sale of proceeds of the whole house: *R(IS) 4/03*, *CH 3197/2003* and *R(JSA) 1/02* considered.

Calculation of tariff income from capital

52.–(1)   Except where the circumstances prescribed in paragraph [¹] (4) apply to the claimant, where the claimant's capital calculated in accordance with this Part exceeds [¹ £6,000] it shall be treated as equivalent to a weekly tariff income of £1 for each complete £250 in excess of [¹ £6,000] but not exceeding £16,000.

[¹ (2)]

(3)   Where the circumstances prescribed in paragraph (4) apply to a claimant and that claimant's capital calculated in accordance with this Part exceeds £10,000, it shall be treated as equivalent to a weekly tariff income of £1 for each complete £250 in excess of £10,000 but not exceeding £16,000.

(4)   For the purposes of paragraph (3), the prescribed circumstances are that the claimant–

    (a)   occupies residential accommodation as his home; or

    (b)   is a person–

        (i)   to whom on 3rd October 2005 paragraph (2) of regulation 7 of the former regulations as in force on that date applied; or

        (ii)   to whom on 3rd October 2005, paragraph (5) or paragraph (7) of regulation 7 of those Regulations as in force on that date applied and continues to apply;

(5)   For the purposes of paragraph (4), the claimant shall be treated as–

    (a)   occupying residential accommodation as his home; or

    (b)   a person to whom regulation 9(1A) as inserted by paragraph 9(3)(a) of Schedule 3 to the Consequential Provisions Regulations, applies; or

    (c)   a person to whom regulation 9(6) as inserted by paragraph 9(5)(a) of Schedule 3 to the Consequential Provisions Regulations, applies; or

    (d)   a person to whom regulation 9(6) as inserted by paragraph 9(7)(a) of Schedule 3 to the Consequential Provisions Regulations, applies,

in any period during which he is treated as occupying the accommodation as his home pursuant to regulation 7(12), (13) or (17).

(6)   Notwithstanding paragraphs (1) [¹] and (3) where any part of the excess is not a complete £250 that part shall be treated as equivalent to a weekly tariff income of £1.

(7)   For the purposes of paragraphs (1) [¹] and (3), capital includes any income treated as capital under regulation 46 (income treated as capital).

(8)   For the purposes of this regulation and subject to paragraph (9), "residential accommodation" means accommodation which is provided by an establishment–

    (a)   under sections 21 to 24 of the National Assistance Act 1948 (provision of accommodation) or under section 59 of the Social Work (Scotland) Act 1968 (provision of residential and other establishments) where board is not available to the claimant and the home in which the accommodation is provided is either owned or managed or owned and managed by a local authority;

    (b)   which is managed or provided by a body incorporated by Royal Charter or constituted by Act of Parliament (other than a social services authority) and provides both board and personal care for the claimant; and in this sub-paragraph, "personal care" means care which includes assistance with bodily functions where such assistance is required;

    (c)   which is an Abbeyfield Home,

and in this definition, "board" refers to the availability to the claimant in the home in which his accommodation is provided of cooked or prepared food, where the food is made available to him in consequence solely of his paying the charge for the accommodation or any other charge which he is required to pay as a condition of occupying the accommodation, or both those charges and is made available for his consumption without any further charge to him.

(9)   Paragraph (8) shall not apply to residential accommodation of the type referred to in sub-paragraphs (a) to (c) of paragraph (8) where such accommodation is residential accommodation for the purpose of regulation 9 unless the claimant is a person to whom paragraphs 10, 11 or 12 of Schedule 3 to the Social Security (Care Homes and Independent Hospitals) Regulations 2005 apply.

Modifications

Reg 52 applies as modified by Sch 3 para 9(3)(b) HB&CTB(CP) Regs (see p1123) to a claimant who on 3 October 2005 was someone to whom reg 7(2) of the HB Regs 1987 as then in force applied.

Reg 52 applies as modified by Sch 3 para 9(5)(b) HB&CTB(CP) Regs (see p1124) to a claimant who on 3 October 2005 was someone to whom reg 7(5) of the HB Regs 1987 as then in force applied.

Reg 52 applies as modified by Sch 3 para 9(7)(b) HB&CTB(CP) Regs (see p1125) to a claimant who on 3 October 2005 was someone to whom reg 7(7) of the HB Regs 1987 as then in force applied.

Amendment

1.   Amended by reg 5A(4) of SI 2005 No 2465 as inserted by Sch 2 para 28(5) of SI 2006 No 217 as from 1.4.06.

Definitions

"capital" – see General Note on this Part.

"claimant" – see reg 2(1).

General Note

This regulation applies to create "tariff income" which is deemed to be generated by capital held by a claimant which is nonetheless insufficient to take her/him over the capital limit. Actual income from assessable capital is usually treated as capital itself under reg 46. For income from disregarded capital, see para 17 of Sch 5 and reg 46(4).

Analysis

Paras (1), (6) and (7) set out the normal rule. Where para (4) does not apply to a claimant, and the total capital falling to be assessed under this Section is between £6,000 and £16,000, the claimant is treated as having income of £1 per week from each £250 or part of £250 in excess of £6,000. For example, a claimant has £7,765 assessed under this Part. S/he is treated as receiving 1,750 divided by 250 = 7. £15 left over gives rise to another £1 and so s/he is deemed to have £8 a week income from that capital.

Paras (3) to (5), (8) and (9) set out a special rule for certain claimants in "residential accommodation" as defined in paras (8) and (9). By para (5), those who are deemed to be in occupation by relevant provisions in reg 7 also qualify. For these claimants the lower capital limit is increased from £6,000 to £10,000, and they are treated as having weekly tariff income of £1 for each £250, or part thereof, of capital in excess of £10,000.

PART 7
Students

General Note on Part 6

Since 1 September 1990, government policy has been to exclude most, but not all, full-time students from entitlement to HB by treating them (under reg 56) as not liable to make payments in respect of their dwelling. These changes were part of a more general change in the structure of student finance, the aim of which was to provide for students' financial needs wholly through the system of grants and student loans. Educational establishments have been provided with further "access funds" to assist students suffering from financial hardship. Full-time students are not generally eligible for IS or JSA (except for limited categories similar to those who remain entitled to HB). For further information about other types of financial support available to students see CPAG's *Student Support and Benefits Handbook: England, Wales and Northern Ireland* and *Benefits for Students in Scotland Handbook* (the latter can be accessed online for free at http://scottishhandbooks.cpag.org.uk).

There are no comparable rules for students in the HB(SPC) Regs so claimants covered by those regulatations are not excluded from entitlement to HB for being students. In addition, student loan and grant income is ignored; it does not come within the definition of "income" in reg 29 HB(SPC) Regs and reg 19 CTB(SPC) Regs.

The excluded students

Reg 56(1) excludes anyone who is a "full-time student" from entitlement to HB subject to certain exceptions listed in reg 56(2).

The definition of "full-time student" is to be found in reg 53.

It must be borne in mind that a claimant may fall within the definition of "full-time student" from the date on which her/his course starts until the day it ends or the s/he abandons it or is dismissed from it: reg 53(2)-(4). This means that the special rules for full-time students can apply even if the claimant is not studying at the material time – eg, during the summer vacation or absences from a course due to ill health or pregnancy. For the difficult questions arising for students who have taken time off in the middle of their courses, see the Analysis to reg 56 below.

The treatment of student claims

Even if a student is not excluded from entitlement to HB by reg 56, s/he must still satisfy the other rules set out in this Part before qualifying. The general rule is that claims by students will, subject to the special rules in this Part, be decided in the same way as claims by non-students. The special rules can be summarised as follows:

(1)   If a full-time student is absent from her/his home where s/he lives to study outside a period of study, then s/he is deemed not to occupy the dwelling, unless the absence is due to hospitalisation: reg 55.

(2)   Unless a full-time student is someone entitled to HB by virtue of the exceptions in reg 56(2), HB is not payable during a period of study in respect of payments made to the student's educational institution, except in limited circumstances: reg 57.

(3)   There are detailed rules for the treatment of the sources of income for students – eg, grants, covenant income, student loans and access funds: regs 59 to 69. Note that education maintenance allowances (and similar payments) paid to young people on certain non-advanced courses are dealt with separately. They are disregarded as income under para 11 of Sch 5 and as capital under para 51 of Sch 6. Career development loans paid under s2 of the Employment and Training Act 1973 are taken into account as income (reg 41(4)) with provision for some or all of it to be disregarded (Sch 5 para 13).

Claimants with a student partner

The general exclusion of full-time students from HB does not prevent a claimant whose partner is a student from claiming HB. However, the provisions of reg 57 concerning claimants who pay rent to educational institutions will apply to such claimants: reg 58.

SECTION 1
General

Interpretation

53.–(1)   In this Part–

"academic year" means the period of twelve months beginning on 1st January, 1st April, 1st July or 1st September according to whether the course in question begins in the winter, the spring, the summer or the autumn respectively but if students are required to begin attending the course during August or September and to continue attending through the autumn, the academic year of the course shall be considered to begin in the autumn rather than the summer;

"access funds" means–

(a)   grants made under section 68 of the Further and Higher Education Act 1992 for the purpose of providing funds on a discretionary basis to be paid to students;

(b)   grants made under sections 73(a) and (c) and 74(1) of the Education (Scotland) Act 1980; or

(c)   grants made under Article 30 of the Education and Libraries (Northern Ireland) Order 1993 or grants, loans or other payments made under Article 5 of the Further Education (Northern Ireland) Order 1997 in each case being grants, or grants, loans or other payments as the case may be, for the purpose of assisting students in financial difficulties;

(d)   discretionary payments, known as "learner support funds", which are made available to students in further education by institutions out of funds provided by the Learning and Skills Council for England under sections 5, 6 and 9 of the Learning and Skills Act 2000; or

(e) Financial Contingency Funds made available by the National Assembly for Wales;

"college of further education" means a college of further education within the meaning of Part I of the Further and Higher Education (Scotland) Act 1992;

"contribution" means any contribution in respect of the income of a student or of any other person which the Secretary of State, the Scottish Ministers or an education authority takes into account in ascertaining the amount of the student's grant or student loan; or any sums, which in determining the amount of a student's allowance or bursary in Scotland under the Further and Higher Education (Scotland) Act 1992, the Scottish Ministers or the education authority takes into account being sums which the Scottish Ministers or the education authority consider that the holder of the allowance or bursary, the holder's parents and the holder's spouse or civil partner can reasonably be expected to contribute towards the holder's expenses;

"course of study" means any course of study, whether or not it is a sandwich course and whether or not a grant is made for undertaking or attending it;

"covenant income" means the gross income payable to a full-time student under a Deed of Covenant by his parent;

"education authority" means a government department, a local education authority specified in section 12 of the Education Act 1996 (local education authorities and their areas), a local education authority as defined in section 123 of the Local Government (Scotland) Act 1973, an education and library board established under Article 3 of the Education and Libraries (Northern Ireland) Order 1986, any body which is a research council for the purposes of the Science and Technology Act 1965 or any analogous government department, authority, board or body, of the Channel Islands, Isle of Man or any other country outside Great Britain;

"full-time course of study" means a full-time course of study which–

(a) is not funded in whole or in part by the Learning and Skills Council for England or by the [¹ National Assembly for Wales] or a full-time course of study which is not funded in whole or in part by the Scottish Ministers at a college of further education or a full-time course of study which is a course of higher education and is funded in whole or in part by the Scottish Ministers;

(b) is funded in whole or in part by the Learning and Skills Council for England or by the [¹ National Assembly for Wales] if it involves more than 16 guided learning hours per week for the student in question, according to the number of guided learning hours per week for that student set out–

(i) in the case of a course funded by the Learning and Skills Council for England, in his learning agreement signed on behalf of the establishment which is funded by that Council for the delivery of that course; or

(ii) in the case of a course funded by the [¹ National Assembly for Wales], in a document signed on behalf of the establishment which is funded by that Council for the delivery of that course; or

(c) is not higher education and is funded in whole or in part by the Scottish Ministers at a college of further education and involves–

(i) more than 16 hours per week of classroom-based or workshop-based programmed learning under the direct guidance of teaching staff according to the number of hours set out in a document signed on behalf of the college; or

(ii) 16 hours or less per week of classroom-based or workshop-based programmed learning under the direct guidance of teaching staff and it involves additional hours using structured learning packages supported by the teaching staff where the combined total of hours exceeds 21 hours per week, according to the number of hours set out in a document signed on behalf of the college;

"full-time student" means a person attending or undertaking a full-time course of study and includes a student on a sandwich course;

"grant" (except in the definition of "access funds") means any kind of educational grant or award and includes any scholarship, studentship, exhibition, allowance or bursary but does not include a payment from access funds or any payment to which paragraph 11 of Schedule 5 or paragraph 54 of Schedule 6 applies;

"grant income" means–

   (a)   any income by way of a grant;

   (b)   any contribution whether or not it is paid;

"higher education" means higher education within the meaning of Part 2 of the Further and Higher Education (Scotland) Act 1992;

"last day of the course" means–

   (a)   in the case of a qualifying course, the date on which the last day of that course falls or the date on which the final examination relating to that course is completed, whichever is the later;

   (b)   in any other case, the date on which the last day of the final academic term falls in respect of the course in which the student is enrolled;

"period of study" means–

   (a)   in the case of a course of study for one year or less, the period beginning with the start of the course and ending with the last day of the course;

   (b)   in the case of a course of study for more than one year, in the first or, as the case may be, any subsequent year of the course, other than the final year of the course, the period beginning with the start of the course or, as the case may be, that year's start and ending with either–

      (i)   in a case where the student's grant or loan is assessed at a rate appropriate to his studying throughout the year, or, if he does not have a grant or loan, where a loan would have been assessed at such a rate had he had one, the day before the start of the next year of the course; or

      (ii)   in any other case, the day before the start of the recognised summer vacation appropriate to his course;

   (c)   in the final year of a course of study of more than one year, the period beginning with that year's start and ending with the last day of the course;

"periods of experience" means periods of work experience which form part of a sandwich course;

"qualifying course" means a qualifying course as defined for the purposes of Parts 2 and 4 of the Jobseeker's Allowance Regulations;

"sandwich course" has the meaning prescribed in regulation 2(6) of the Education (Student Support) Regulations 2005, regulation 5(2) of the Education (Student Loans)(Scotland) Regulations 2000 or regulation 5(2) of the Education (Student Support) Regulations (Northern Ireland) 2001, as the case may be;

"standard maintenance grant" means–

   (a)   except where paragraph (b) or (c) applies, in the case of a student attending or undertaking a course of study at the University of London or an establishment within the area comprising the City of London and the Metropolitan Police District, the amount specified for the time being in paragraph 2(2)(a) of Schedule 2 to the Education (Mandatory Awards) Regulations 2003 ("the 2003 Regulations") for such a student;

   (b)   except where paragraph (c) applies, in the case of a student residing at his parent's home, the amount specified in paragraph 3 thereof;

(c)   in the case of a student receiving an allowance or bursary under the Education (Scotland) Act 1980, the amount of money specified as "standard maintenance allowance" for the relevant year appropriate for the student set out in the Student Support in Scotland Guide issued by the Student Awards Agency for Scotland, or its nearest equivalent in the case of a bursary provided by a college of further education or a local education authority and paid under the Further and Higher Education (Scotland) Act 1992;

(d)   in any other case, the amount specified in paragraph 2(2) of Schedule 2 to the 2000 Regulations other than in sub-paragraph (a) or (b) thereof;

"student" means a person, other than a person in receipt of a training allowance, who is attending or undertaking–

(a)   a course of study at an educational establishment; or

(b)   a qualifying course;

"student loan" means a loan towards a student's maintenance pursuant to any regulations made under section 22 of the Teaching and Higher Education Act 1998, section 73 of the Education (Scotland) Act 1980 or Article 3 of the Education (Student Support) (Northern Ireland) Order 1998 and shall include, in Scotland, a young student's bursary paid under regulation 4(1)(c) of the Students' Allowances (Scotland) Regulations 1999.

(2)   For the purposes of the definition of "full-time student" in paragraph (1), a person shall be regarded as attending or, as the case may be, undertaking a full-time course of study or as being on a sandwich course–

(a)   subject to paragraph (3), in the case of a person attending or undertaking a part of a modular course which would be a full-time course of study for the purposes of this Part, for the period beginning on the day on which that part of the course starts and ending–

    (i)   on the last day on which he is registered with the educational establishment as attending or undertaking that part as a full-time course of study; or

    (ii)   on such earlier date (if any) as he finally abandons the course or is dismissed from it;

(b)   in any other case, throughout the period beginning on the date on which he starts attending or undertaking the course and ending on the last day of the course or on such earlier date (if any) as he finally abandons it or is dismissed from it.

(3)   For the purposes of sub-paragraph (a) of paragraph (2), the period referred to in that sub-paragraph shall include–

(a)   where a person has failed examinations or has failed to successfully complete a module relating to a period when he was attending or undertaking a part of the course as a full-time course of study, any period in respect of which he attends or undertakes the course for the purpose of retaking those examinations or that module;

(b)   any period of vacation within the period specified in that paragraph or immediately following that period except where the person has registered with the educational establishment to attend or undertake the final module in the course and the vacation immediately follows the last day on which he is required to attend or undertake the course.

(4)   In paragraph (2), "modular course" means a course of study which consists of two or more modules, the successful completion of a specified number of which is required before a person is considered by the educational establishment to have completed the course.

Amendment

1.   Amended by reg 2 of SI 2005 No 3238 as amended by Sch 2 para 31 of SI 2006 No 217 as from 1.4.06.

Analysis

"academic year". This definition is relevant to the treatment of student loans. See reg 64(2) below.

"access funds". See reg 65 for the treatment of certain access funds. The definition includes the "learner support funds" paid under the Learning and Skills Act 2000 and Financial Contingency Funds made available by the National Assembly for Wales.

"contribution". The definition includes any contribution in respect of the income of the student or any other person taken into account in the assessment of a student's grant or loan or in Scotland, allowance or bursary, including amounts which the student, student's spouse, civil partner or parents could reasonably be expected to contribute. Note that this allows the reduction in the student's grant or loan on the basis of her/his own income to be treated as a "contribution".

"course of study". A course counts as a course of study whether or not it is a sandwich course and whether or not a grant is made for it. For the meaning of a "sandwich course", see below. It must be a course of study, and purely vocational work may not qualify: see for example *R(SB) 25/87* which decides that a pupil barrister is not studying; s/he is attending a barrister to assimilate vocational skills. However, where there is active tuition, the fact that the skills are vocational will not prevent the course being a course of study. Many such "courses" may be excluded by the requirement that no training allowance is being received (see the definition of "student" below). So in *R(IS) 19/98* para 11 it was held that a nurse on the Project 2000 scheme who was paid a bursary by the Department of Health during her training was on a course of study. For when a full-time student is treated as attending a course of study, see para (2).

"covenant income". Notice that this covers only income covenanted by a parent, not grandparent, etc. and that the beneficiary must be a full-time, not part-time, student. This definition refers to the gross amount of the payment.

"education authority". See GM C2 Annex A C2.03 for a list of the bodies falling under this heading.

"full-time course of study". See the Analysis to reg 56 below.

"full-time student". See the Analysis to reg 56 below.

"grant" means any kind of educational grant or award other than a payment from access funds or an education maintenance allowance which can be disregarded as income under para 11 of Sch 5. The definition in reg 46 HB Regs 1987 excluded education maintenance allowance which could be disregarded as capital. It is understood that an error occured when the consolidation of the regulations took place in 2006 and that the reference here to para 54 Sch 6 HB Regs should have been to para 51. The definition is to be amended. GM Annex A C2.11 advises local authorities not to include payments derived from funds made available by the Secretary of State to assist students in financial difficulties under s100 Education Act 1944, s65 Further and Higher Education Act 1992, s73 Education (Scotland) Act 1980 or s40 Further and Higher Education (Scotland) Act 1992.

There are conflicting decisions of the commissioners in relation to whether "award" can include loans made to students by educational authorities. In *R(SB) 20/83* para 10(3), it was held that it could, but in *R(IS) 16/95* para 10 it was pointed out that the word usually connoted an absolute gift when used in an educational context. It is suggested that this is plainly right in view of the examples of sources of income such as scholarships, which are almost invariably in the nature of gifts rather than loans. Likewise, it cannot apply to bank loans or overdrafts obtained by students. Note the special provisions for assessing income from student loans in reg 64.

"grant income". A contribution is deemed to have been received by the student whether paid or not.

Note that when a student abandons a course, s/he falls under an obligation to repay any grant made by the local education authority. The amount of the grant which is repayable cannot be treated as income from that date: *R(IS) 5/99* para 12. Changes were made to the IS scheme to provide for such treatment, but no corresponding amendments were made to the HB and CTB regulations. The commissioner's decision was upheld on a different basis by the Court of Appeal in *Chief Adjudication Officer v Leeves* [1999] ELR 90, CA (reported as *R(IS) 5/99*). Potter LJ held that once the LEA demanded repayment of an ascertained sum, the amount of the grant could not be treated as income from that date.

"last day of the course". This definition clarifies the treatment of those cases where, eg, the student is able to leave the course a few weeks early after having taken final exams. For "qualifying courses" (see below), since these are not organised along the lines of terms, the last day of the course is the later of the date of the final exam or the last day of the course. In other cases "the last day of the course" always means the date on which the last day of the final academic term is scheduled to fall and not the earlier date on which the student actually left.

Note that GM C2.352-354 says that full-time postgraduate students cease to be treated as full-time students when their course is completed. The guidance goes on to say that whether such a student who is doing further research or writing a thesis after this should be regarded as a full-time student depends on the amount of work being undertaken, not on the fact that the course was full-time.

"period of study". In a "course of study" (above) of more than one year, the date on which a "period of study" ends depends on whether grants or loans for that course are assessed on the basis of a full year's study, or whether no grant or loan is assessed for the summer vacation. In the latter case, which will be the norm, it ends at the beginning of that vacation and starts again when the vacation ends. This is the case whether or not the student in question receives a grant or loan. During the final year of a course, the "period of study" always ends on "the last day of the course" (above). See further the Analysis to reg 56.

"periods of experience". "Periods of work experience", the definition of which is, for example, found in reg 2 Education (Student Support) Regulations 2007 SI No 176, means–

"(a)   periods of industrial, professional or commercial experience associated with full-time study at an institution but at a place outside the institution,

(b)   periods during which a student is employed and residing in a country whose language is one that he is studying for his course (provided that the period of residence in that country is a requirement of his course and the study of one or more modern languages accounts for not less than one half of the total time spent studying on the course)."

"qualifying course". These courses form part of the elaborate package aimed at assisting the long-term unemployed. The definition of such a course is to be found in reg 17A(7) of the Jobseeker's Allowance Regulations 1996. Certain claimants on such courses may continue to receive JSA throughout the period of study. Three conditions must be fulfilled:

(1)   It must be an "employment-related course". By reg 1(3) of the 1996 Regulations, this is defined as "a course the purpose of which is to assist persons to acquire or enhance skills required for employment, for seeking employment or for a particular occupation".

(2)   It must last for no more than 12 consecutive months.

(3)   It must be a course of an appropriate level. The definition of what is an appropriate level is different in England and Wales on one hand and Scotland on the other. In England and Wales, Sch 2 to the Further and Higher Education Act 1992 provides the definition. It covers vocational courses approved by the Secretary of State, GCSE and A-Level courses, preparation for further education, preparatory courses for the foregoing, English and Welsh classes, basic mathematics courses, and courses teaching independent living and communication skills. In Scotland, s6 of the Further and Higher Education (Scotland) Act 1992 lists courses that: prepare people for vocational qualifications, prepare for SEB or GCE exams, assist those with learning difficulties, assist access to higher education, assist with English for those for whom it is not their first language, and preparatory courses covering the above. Note that there are wide powers to add categories of course. Not all such courses, of course, will be capable of fulfilling the first condition above. Note also that by reg 17A(8) of the 1996 Regulations, any courses of a higher standard may nonetheless be determined to be qualifying courses even if they do not fall within the scope of the definition above.

"sandwich course". Reg 2(6) of the Education (Student Support) Regulations 2005 SI No 52, for example says that a course is a sandwich course if it is not a course for the initial training of teachers, including such a course leading to a first degree, it consists of alternate periods of full-time study in an institution and periods of work experience, and taking the course as a whole, the student attends the periods of full-time study for an average of not less than 18 weeks in each year. For the purposes of calculating the student's attendance, the course is treated as beginning with the first period of full-time study and ending with the last such period.

"student". A person in receipt of a training allowance does not come within the definition of student. For "training allowance" see reg 2(1). The definition of student includes those on "qualifying courses": see above. For "course of study", as defined in this regulation, see above. By para (2), the student is treated as attending the course throughout all vacations as well as during the term, but the effect of this is partly offset by the use of the phrase "period of study" in various regulations: see above. See also the analysis of "course of study" above.

Treatment of students

54.   The provisions of Parts 2, 3 and 4 (entitlement to housing benefit, payments in respect of a dwelling, membership of a family) shall have effect in relation to students subject to the following provisions of this Part.

General Note

See General Note to Part 7. These regulations also affect Part 6.

Analysis

In *R (Naghshbandi) v Camden LBC* [2001] EWHC Admin 813; [2003] HLR 280, CA, the court was considering the interrelationship between Pts II and VII of the HB Regs 1987 (now Pts 2 and 7 HB Regs). The claimant had an adult son living in his household who was a student. There were a total of five members of the family who shared the rent liability and the issue was whether reg 48A(1) HB Regs 1987 (now reg 56(1) HB Regs) operated to deem the son not to be liable for rent and so to exclude him from the apportionment of the rent between those liable under reg 10(5) HB Regs 1987 (now reg 12(5) HB Regs). The council and Rafferty J decided that the deemed non-liability did not apply to reg 10(5).

On appeal, the Secretary of State for Work and Pensions intervened to support the council's position. Counsel for the Secretary of State argued that the rule had to be read as if it said "shall have effect in relation to students who are claimants for housing benefit". The court accepted that argument and dismissed the claimant's appeal. But reading reg 54 in this way produces some potentially odd results. See the commentary to regs 7(6)(b) and 55.

SECTION 2
Entitlement and payments in respect of a dwelling

General Note on Section 2

See General Note on this Part. The rules in Parts 2, 3 and 4 apply to students, but they are modified as set out below.

This Part should be read together with regs 7(3) and 7(6)(b) (see p206), which also make provision for students.

Occupying a dwelling as a person's home

55.–(1)   Subject to paragraph (2), a full-time student shall not be treated as occupying a dwelling as his home during any benefit week outside the period of study if he is absent from it for the whole of that week and if the main purpose of his occupation during the period of study would be to facilitate attendance on his course.

(2)   The provisions of paragraph (1) shall not apply to any absence occasioned by the need to enter hospital for treatment.

Definitions

"benefit week" – see reg 2(1).
"dwelling" – see reg 2(4).
"full-time student" – see reg 53.
"period of study" – see reg 53.
"student" – see reg 53.

General Note

Even if a full-time student is able to claim HB, this regulation prevents her/him claiming in respect of accommodation occupied to enable her/him to attend the course, for any whole week s/he is absent from it outside her/his period of study (defined in reg 53 above).

This regulation does not apply where the student is in hospital for treatment: para (2).

It is suggested that where the student is not the claimant, reg 55 can have no application because the application of this Part is limited to cases where the student is the claimant: *R (Naghshbandi) v Camden LBC* [2001] EWHC Admin 813; [2003] HLR 280, CA. Accordingly where a student's partner claims HB both in respect of the normal home and the student accommodation under reg 7(6)(b), HB will remain payable during the vacations.

Analysis

Para (1). For the meaning of "occupying a dwelling as his home", see reg 7 and particularly paras (3) and (6)(b) for special rules relating to students.

The student is only deemed not to be occupying the accommodation if the "main purpose" of her/his occupation during the "period of study" is to facilitate her/his attendance on the course. So the provision cannot apply to a student who would stay in her/his term-time residence even if not attending a course, or who has other, equally important, reasons for staying at that place. Examples would be where s/he is fully independent of, does not have, or is estranged from her/his parents, or where the claimant was already settled in the accommodation prior to study. GM C2.73 states that authorities may "readily accept" that the claimant's main purpose of residence is not study where the student's dependent children are living with her/him or where the student has no other accommodation which could be regarded as her/his home.

Where the student is under 25, whether or not the student has parents is also relevant. Authorities should "look carefully" at other categories of case: GM C2.74.

GM C2.71 suggests that the authority may generally assume that the main purpose of occupation is to facilitate study if the student returns to another home, where s/he would normally be living were not for the course.

Para (2). "Hospital" is not defined. It is suggested that it can cover a wider range of residential treatment than that offered by the NHS. It may cover private treatment and clinics where alternative medicine is practised, provided that there is a respectable medical basis for the treatment being given.

Full-time students to be treated as not liable to make payments in respect of a dwelling

56.–(1)   A full-time student shall be treated as if he were not liable to make payments in respect of a dwelling.

(2)   Paragraph (1) shall not apply to a full-time student–

(a)   who is a person on income support or an income-based jobseeker's allowance;

(b)   who is a lone parent;

(c)   whose applicable amount would, but for paragraph (1), include the pensioner premium for persons under 75 or, as the case may be, persons 75 or over, higher pensioner premium, disability premium or severe disability premium;

(d)   whose applicable amount would include the disability premium but for his being treated as capable of work by virtue of a determination made in accordance with regulations made under section 171E of the Act;

(e)   who is, or is treated as, incapable of work and has been so incapable, or has been so treated as incapable, of work in accordance with the provisions of, and regulations made under, Part 12A of the Act (incapacity for work) for a continuous period of not less than 196 days; and for this purpose any two or more separate periods separated by a break of not more than 56 days shall be treated as one continuous period;

(f)   who has a partner who is also a full-time student, if he or that partner is treated as responsible for a child or young person;

(g)   who is a single claimant with whom a child is–

(i)   placed by a local authority or voluntary organisation under section 23(2)(a) or section 59(1)(a) of the Children Act 1989 (provision of accommodation and maintenance); or

(ii)   in Scotland, boarded out by a local authority or voluntary organisation within the meaning of the Social Work (Scotland) Act 1968;

[¹ (h)   who is–

(i)   aged under 19 and whose course of study is not a course of higher education, or

(ii)   a qualifying young person or child within the meaning of section 142 of the Act (child and qualifying young person);] or

(i)   in respect of whom–

(i)   a supplementary requirement has been determined under paragraph 9 of Part 2 of Schedule 2 to the Education (Mandatory Awards) Regulations 2003; or

(ii)   an allowance or, as the case may be, bursary has been granted which includes a sum under paragraph (1)(d) of regulation 4 of the Students' Allowances (Scotland) Regulations 1999 or, as the case may be, under paragraph (1)(d) of regulation 4 of the Education Authority (Bursaries) (Scotland) Regulations 1995, in respect of expenses incurred; or

(iii)   a payment has been made under section 2 of the Education Act 1962 or under, or by virtue of regulations made under, the Teaching and Higher Education Act 1998; or

(iv) a grant has been made under regulation 13 of the Education (Student Support) Regulations 2005 or under regulation 13 of the Education (Student Support) Regulations (Northern Ireland) 2000; or

(v) a supplementary requirement has been determined under paragraph 9 of Schedule 6 to the Students Awards Regulations (Northern Ireland) 1999 or a payment has been made under Article 50(3) of the Education and Libraries (Northern Ireland) Order 1986,

on account of his disability by reason of deafness; or

(j) who–

(i) immediately before 1st September 1990 was in receipt of income support by virtue of paragraph 7 of Schedule 1 to the Income Support (General) Regulations 1987 as then in force; or

(ii) on or after that date makes a claim for income support or housing benefit (or both) and at any time during the period of 18 months immediately preceding the date of that claim was in receipt of income support either by virtue of that paragraph or regulation 13(2)(b) of those Regulations,

but this sub-paragraph shall cease to apply where the person has ceased to be in receipt of income support for a continuous period of 18 months or more.

(3) For the purposes of paragraph (2), once paragraph (2)(e) applies to a full-time student, if he then ceases, for a period of 56 days or less, to be incapable, or to be treated as incapable, of work, that paragraph shall, on his again becoming so incapable, or so treated as incapable, of work at the end of that period, immediately thereafter apply to him for so long as he remains incapable, or is treated as remaining incapable, of work.

(4) In paragraph (2)(h) reference to a course of higher education is a reference to a course of any description mentioned in Schedule 6 to the Education Reform Act 1988 refers.

(5) A full-time student to whom sub-paragraph (i) of paragraph (2) applies shall be treated as satisfying that sub-paragraph from the date on which he made a request for the supplementary requirement, allowance, bursary or payment, as the case may be.

(6) Paragraph (1) shall not apply to a full-time student for the period specified in paragraph (7) if–

(a) at any time during an academic year, with the consent of the relevant education establishment, he ceases to attend or undertake a course because he is–

(i) engaged in caring for another person; or

(ii) ill;

(b) he has subsequently ceased to be engaged in caring for that person or, as the case may be, he has subsequently recovered from that illness; and

(c) he is not eligible for a grant or a student loan in respect of the period specified in paragraph (7).

(7) The period specified for the purposes of paragraph (6) is the period not exceeding one year beginning on the day on which he ceased to be engaged in caring for that other person or, as the case may be, the day on which he recovered from that illness and ending on the day before–

(a) the day on which he resumes attending or undertaking the course; or

(b) the day from which the relevant educational establishment has agreed that he may resume attending or undertaking the course,

whichever shall first occur.

Amendment

1.   Inserted by reg 4(3) of SI 2006 No 718 as from 10.4.06.

Definitions

"disability premium" – see para 12 Sch 3.

"full-time student" – see reg 53.

"higher pensioner premium" – see para 11 Sch 3.

"partner" – see reg 2(1).

"pensioner premium" – see paras 9 and 10 Sch 3.

"person on income support" – see reg 2(1).

"person on an income-based jobseeker's allowance" – see reg 2(3).

"responsible for a child or young person" – see reg 20.

"severe disability premium" – see para 14 Sch 3.

"single claimant" – see reg 2(1).

"student" – see reg 53.

General Note

To qualify for HB, a claimant must be liable or treated as liable to make payments in respect of her/his dwelling (see s130(1)(a) SSCBA 1992 and reg 8 on pp10 and 217). Para (1) seeks to exclude most full-time students from entitlement to HB by treating them as not liable to make payments in respect of their dwelling. See the Analysis below for the difficult question of what a full-time student is. Paras (2) to (7) define the exceptions to the general rule.

If someone comes within the definition of full-time student, s/he is then treated as attending or undertaking a full-time course of study for the duration of the course or until s/he abandons the course or is dismissed from it: reg 53(2). In limited circumstances, claims for HB can be made during breaks from study.

Analysis

The general exclusion

This analysis deals with a number of points as to which students come within the definition of "full-time student". Note also that even if the student falls within the exclusion, her/his partner can be treated as liable to make payments in respect of the dwelling unless s/he is also a student: see reg 8(1)(e) above.

Do all full-time students come within the definition? Under the definition in reg 53, a full-time student "means a person attending or undertaking a full-time course of study", including a sandwich course. As to the question of precisely what constitutes a "course of study", see the Analysis to reg 53. If the claimant is not on a "course of study", then s/he cannot be affected by the general exclusion.

Unlike with IS and JSA, there are no special rules for those in "relevant education" (essentially full-time non-advanced education for those under 20 – eg, see s124(1)(d) SSCBA 1992 and reg 12 of the Income Support (General) Regulations 1987 SI No 1967). For this reason, a young person might be able to claim HB while in "relevant education" even if s/he cannot claim IS or JSA.

The phrase "full-time course of study" is defined in reg 53 as comprising three categories of student:

(1)   Sub-para (b) covers students whose courses at colleges of further education (CFEs) are funded in whole or in part by the Further Education Funding Council (FEFC) for England or the National Assembly for Wales as appropriate. For such students, the categorisation of the course depends on the number of guided learning hours (GLHs) a week. A course of more than 16 GLHs a week is full-time; one of 16 GLHs or less is part-time. The FEFC defines GLHs as the times when a member of staff is present to guide students' learning on a programme which includes lectures, tutorials and supervised study in – eg, a library, open learning centre or learning workshop. It also includes time spent assessing a student's achievements, for example, in the assessment of competence for National Vocational Qualifications. The definition excludes time spent in unsupervised study, homework and meal breaks. Unsupervised study includes time spent in libraries where a member of staff is present but is not in a position to assist a particular student with their particular study programme. CFEs provide a document, called a learning agreement in England, which will make it clear how many GLHs a course entails.

(2)   Sub-para (c) covers Scottish students on courses at a college of further education that are not higher education and are funded in whole or in part by the Scottish Ministers. For such students, the categorisation of a course depends on the number of hours of classroom-based or workshop-based "programmed learning" under the direct guidance of a teacher. A course of more than 16 hours per week is full-time. Also full-time is a course of more than 21 hours a week, 16 or less of which involve classroom-based or workshop-based "programmed learning" and the rest of which involve structured learning supported by a teacher. As in England and Wales, the CFE provides a document stating the number of hours of "learning" per week.

(3)   Sub-para (a) covers students on full-time courses of study at CFEs *not* funded in whole or in part by the FEFC for England or the National Assemby for Wales as appropriate. It also covers Scottish students on full-time courses of study:

(a) at a college of further education that are not higher education and *not* funded in whole or in part by the Scottish ministers; or

(b) which are courses of higher education funded in whole or in part by the Scottish ministers.

This category was potentially troublesome in its meaning prior to amendments made in August 2001. For an argument that most Scottish higher education students did not then come within the definition of "full time student" at all, see pp311-312 of the 13th edition of this work. That argument was not, as far as is known, tested in the courts. The definition now makes it clear that higher education courses will bring students within its scope provided that they are funded by the Scottish ministers.

In the first two categories, whether someone counts as a full- or part-time student depends on her/his personal pattern of attendance on the course. In the third category, this depends on the course as a whole.

The question as to how an authority is to judge whether a higher education course is full or part-time arises frequently in courses coming under the third category (sub-para (a)). In the absence of any definition, local authorities seek the advice of the institution where the student is studying: GM C2 Annex A C2.08. It is suggested that the view of the institution as to whether the course is full-time or part-time is not conclusive, but it may require weighty evidence to rebut it. The assessment is based on the amount of time that is normally expected of a student on the course, not the time that the individual claimant devotes to her/his studies: *R(SB) 41/83* paras 11-12. A good indicator of whether a course is full-time, in relation to higher education courses, will be whether or not the student is in receipt of a loan, since these are generally only available to full-time students: GM C2 Annex A C2.08. All the points in this paragraph were confirmed by the Court of Appeal in dismissing an application for leave to appeal in *Denton v Chief Adjudication Officer* [1999] ELR 86 at 87G-H.

Flexible (modular) courses. The August 2000 reforms aimed to cope with the problems with modular courses posed by *Chief Adjudication Officer v Webber* [1998] 1 WLR 625 at 633E, CA (reported as *R(IS) 15/98*), and *R(IS) 1/00* paras 14-17. Paras (2) to (4) of reg 53 deal with full-time students on modular courses. "Modular course" is defined in reg 53(4) as a course of study of two or more modules, a specified number of which the student must complete successfully before the educational establishment considers her/him to have completed the course.

If the part of the modular course the student is attending "would be a full-time course of study" (for which see above), reg 53(2)(a) deems her/him to be a full-time student from the day on which that part of the course began until the last day s/he is registered with the educational establishment as attending or undertaking that part as a full-time course or until s/he abandons the course or is dismissed from it. Included are periods of attendance to retake examinations or the module (where the student failed the examinations or failed to complete the module successfully): reg 53(3)(a). Also included are periods of vacation within the module as well as vacation that immediately follows it, unless this is the last day on which the student is required to attend or undertake the course: reg 53(3)(b).

The effect of the rules is that a claimant should not come within the definition of "full-time student" while studying part-time on a modular course or where s/he has changed from full-time to part-time attendance or has taken time out from the course.

The exceptions

Para (2) exempts the following categories of student from the general exclusion from HB provided for by para (1):

(1)   Those on IS or income-based JSA: sub-para (a). Once the claimant shows that s/he is on IS or income-based JSA, the authority is not entitled to treat the claimant as a full-time student not liable to make payments in respect of a dwelling. It is not entitled to look into the position for itself: compare the income and capital case of *R v Penwith DC ex p Menear* [1991] 24 HLR 115, QBD. However, in *R v South Ribble DC HBRB ex p Hamilton* [2000] 33 HLR 102, CA, the Court of Appeal confirmed that the definition of "person on income support" must be read as a person lawfully in receipt of income support. If the authority suspects that the claimant should not be receiving IS or income-based JSA, it ought to award HB, but could then suspend payment under reg 11 D&A Regs pending a query with the relevant DWP office.

(2)   Lone parents (defined in reg 2) and lone foster parents where the child has been formally boarded out with them by a local authority or voluntary agency: sub-paras (b) and (g).

(3)   Full-time students who would be entitled to one of the pensioner premiums: sub-para (c). Note that if a claimant or her/his partner has reached the qualifying age for PC (currently age 60) and if neither is on IS or income-based JSA the claim would be assessed under the HB(SPC) Regs under which there are no comparable rules for students. Sub-para (b) assists students whose partners are on IS or income-based JSA.

(4)   Full-time students who would be entitled to the disability or severe disability premium: sub-para (c). Claimants who are not terminally ill do not normally qualify for disability premium on the basis of

incapacity for work until they have been incapable of work for 364 days: see Sch 3 para 13(1)(b)(ii). So a student who has been incapacitated for between 196 days and 364 days cannot fall within this exception unless s/he qualifies for a disability premium for another reason, eg receipt of a qualifying benefit such as disability living allowance. S/he can, however, qualify under sub-para (e) below.

(5)   Full-time students who would be entitled to a disability premium but for being treated as capable of work under SSCBA 1992 s171: sub-para (d). This means that in situations where a DWP decision maker has made a determination under reg 18 Social Security (Incapacity for Work) Regulations 1995 (ie, where the claimant is disqualified from receiving benefit due to misconduct or failure to accept treatment), if the student is *actually* incapable of work, the determination is to be ignored.

(6)   Students who have been or have been treated as incapable of work for a period of not less than 196 days: sub-para (e). In determining whether there has been incapacity for 196 days, a number of periods may be added together if there are not more than 56 days between them. Furthermore, once the 196 day period has been attained, if the claimant becomes capable of work and then becomes incapable again within 56 days, the claimant falls within sub-para (e) without having to build up a further period of 196 days first: para (3). The starting date for calculating the period will be the date a claimant became incapable of work, shown on the first medical certificate furnished by her/him. Such certificates can be granted retrospectively. The decision as to whether a claimant is incapable or is treated as incapable of work is one for the DWP, but note that under reg 28 Social Security (Incapacity for Work) Regulations 1995, unless the decision maker applies the "personal capability assessment" to the claimant, it is deemed to be satisfied by virtue of the fact that medical certificates are being supplied. Note also the transitional protection in Sch 3 paras 2 and 3 of the HB&CTB(CP) Regs (see pp1099 and 1100).

(7)   A full-time student claimant with a full-time student partner if either is "treated as responsible for a child or young person", as to which see reg 20: sub-para (f). Unlike with IS and income-based JSA, this exception applies throughout the year.

(8)   Claimants under the age of 19 who are not on a course of higher education and claimants who are qualifying young people or children within the meaning of s142 SSCBA 1992: sub-para (h).

"Higher education" is defined in para (4) by reference to Sch 6 Education Reform Act 1988. This includes the following types of course: teacher and youth worker training, first and postgraduate degree courses, HND and HNC courses as well as courses at a higher level in preparation for a professional qualification. See GM C2 Annex A C2.12-14 for a list of the types of courses regarded as providing higher education.

"Qualifying young person" is defined by regs 2 to 7 of the Child Benefit (General) Regulations 2006 SI No 223. It includes certain young people aged at least 16 but under 20 on full-time courses of non-advanced education or in approved training and some who have left courses or training. They must have begun their course or training before reaching the age of 19. 19 year olds must have reached that age on or after 10 April 2006. For further information, see CPAG's *Welfare Benefits and Tax Credits Handbook.*

(9)   Certain categories of students entitled to disabled students allowance (DSA) or a payment under the discretionary awards scheme on the same basis and the equivalents available in Scotland and Northern Ireland, because they are deaf: sub-para (i). This includes cases where the underlying conditions for the DSA are satisfied but no actual payment is made as a result of means-testing parental income, since what is required is that an additional requirement has been determined by the LEA, not that it has been paid. Note that this exception takes effect from the date of application for the payment. GM C2.30 suggests that the authority should check with the education authority or claimant if it is not clear whether the grant was awarded as a consequence of the claimant's deafness.

(10)   Certain disabled students who fulfill either of two criteria in relation to receipt of IS: sub-para (j). This exception ensures that those disabled students who were entitled to IS under the rules as they were prior to 1 September 1990 continued to qualify for HB. It is therefore unlikely that there are many (if any) students to whom this exception would still apply. For details see p374 of the 13th edition of this work.

Breaks from study. A question which has caused acute controversy in relation to IS entitlement is whether students who take time out in the middle of their courses, for whatever reason, are deemed to retain the status of a full-time student for the period until they return to their courses. August 2000 reforms softened the harshest aspects of the treatment of such students, which had generated particularly sharp judicial criticism. See pp277-79 of the 12th edition of this work for the case law in relation to the old provisions.

Note that if a student abandons her/his course or is dismissed from it, s/he can claim HB straight away (see reg 53(2)).

Paras (6) and (7) of reg 56 provide most welcome relief for those full-time students who have to temporarily leave their courses with the consent of the educational establishment, due to illness or through having to care for another person. Such students cannot generally claim HB while caring or ill (however note the exceptions under paras (2)(c) and (e)), but can when the illness or caring responsibilities come to an end. The relief is available for a period of up to one year, so long as the student is not eligible for a grant or loan in respect of the period. The period starts on the day the illness or caring ceased and ends on the earlier of the day the student resumes the course or the day from which the educational establishment has agreed s/he could do so: para (7). "Caring for another person" in sub-para (6)(a)(i) is not further defined. It is suggested that it is not necessary, for example, for the carer to fulfil the conditions of entitlement to carer's allowance or to be caring for a person in any specific circumstances. Nor does the sub-para set out the number of hours a person would have to be caring for another.

What, however, of other students such as those who fail their exams? The starting point is to reproduce the definitions of "student" and "course of study" from reg 53.

"student" means a person, other than a person in receipt of a training allowance, who is attending or undertaking—

(a)   a course of study at an educational establishment; or

(b)   a qualifying course".

"course of study" means any course of study, whether or not it is a sandwich course and whether or not a grant is made for undertaking or attending it.

If a student fails exams, or hits financial trouble and is forced to take a year out, it would not appear possible to revive the analysis of Commissioner Howell in *CIS 13986/1996* paras 10-14, which was disapproved by *O'Connor v Chief Adjudication Officer* [1999] ELR 209, CA (*R(IS) 7/99*). The reasoning of the majority in that case proceeded on the basis that a student taking time out would return to the same "course".

O'Connor does, however, leave open the position of students who have failed exams or otherwise broken off their studies and who know that they will be invited back (if at all) to follow what is undoubtedly a different course from, the one they originally commenced (eg, because it is in a different subject or leads to a pass degree rather than an honours degree). It is suggested that such students must be treated as following a different course when they return and hence as not being full-time students when they are away from their studies.

In *R(IS) 1/96* the claimant was studying to be an architect. He had completed his university degree course, but then was to undertake a work placement prior to a further period of postgraduate study. Commissioner Howell said that as a matter of ordinary language "a course" is "a unified sequence of study, tuition and/or practical training, undertaken at or by arrangement with the education or training establishment, and intended to lead to one or more qualifications obtained on its completion," including modular courses leading to a single degree. He said that "a person who aspires to practice in a profession that requires more than one separately obtained qualification for which educational establishments do not provide a single sequence of tuition and/or experience, starts and completes one "course" and then moves on to another, rather than being engaged on one continuous "course" gaining intermediate qualifications and experience along the way": para 17. Thus if such a claimant has completed one course, s/he is not a full-time student in the period until s/he starts the next course. Note, however, the special rules for "sandwich courses".

R(JSA) 2/02 dealt with a claimant who had been attending a course at an educational establishment that provided training and education to enable her/him to take examinations that were set and marked by another, unconnected body. He failed the examinations and intended to re-sit them. Commissioner Williams said that it was possible to abandon, or be dismissed from, a course of training without abandoning or being dismissed from a course of examinations: para 11. This means that someone could cease to be a full-time student when a course is abandoned, even if s/he intends to re-sit the examinations at a later date.

If someone is taking time-out from study because of pregnancy, the rules do not provide relief until the baby is born. The JSA rules were challenged on the grounds that they directly discriminated against women. However, the Court of Appeal in *Secretary of State for Social Security v Walter* [2002] ICR 540 (reported as *R(JSA) 3/02*) rejected the arguments for the claimant. It is important to note that the Court did not consider, or decide on, whether the rules were *indirectly* discriminatory (ie, whether they had a disproportionate impact on women) nor if such discrimination was proved, whether it could be objectively justified. It also did not consider whether the rules are incompatible with the Human Rights Act.

Student's eligible housing costs

57.–(1)   Subject to paragraphs (2) and (4), housing benefit shall not be payable during the period of study in respect of payments made by a student to an educational establishment which the student is attending.

(2)   Subject to paragraph (4), where the educational establishment itself pays rent for the dwelling occupied by the student as his home to a third party (other than

to another educational establishment) the provisions of paragraph (1) shall only apply if rent is payable under the terms of a long tenancy or to an education authority which has provided the dwelling in exercise of its functions as an education authority.

(3)   Where it appears to the relevant authority that an educational establishment has arranged for accommodation to be provided by a person or body other than itself in order to take advantage of the housing benefit scheme, housing benefit shall not be payable during the period of study in respect of payments made to that person or body by a student.

(4)   Housing benefit shall be payable during the period of study in respect of payments made by a student to an educational establishment which the student is attending where the student–

(a)   is one who falls within a category specified in regulation 56(2); or

(b)   would fall within a category specified in regulation 56(2)(b) to (j) if he were a full-time student.

Definitions

"education authority" – see reg 53.
"dwelling" – see reg 2(4) and s137(1) SSCBA.
"long tenancy" – see reg 2(1).
"payments" – see reg 2(1).
"period of study" – see reg 53.
"rent" – see Part 3.
"student" – see reg 53.

General Note

The object of this regulation is to prevent students who pay rent to the educational establishment which they are attending, other than those to whom para (4) applies, from claiming HB, at least during their "period of study" (for which see reg 53(1)), whether they are full-time students or not. The rule also applies if a claimant's *partner* is a student but the claimant is not: see reg 58. In this case, the claimant is treated as if s/he were a student.

Para (2) provides an exception where the educational establishment is effectively acting as a letting agency for a third party, provided that third party is not another educational establishment, and that the establishment which is being paid does not have the property in question on a long tenancy from the third party.

Para (3) is an "anti-avoidance" device designed to stop bogus arrangements where the student pays a third party but the money ends up with the educational establishment.

Analysis

Para (1). The provision only has effect during the period of study, so students who rent from their institution during the summer vacation will not fall within its scope if the summer vacation is not part of their "period of study". Moreover, the institution from which the claimant rents must be the same one that the claimant is attending. However, such students may fall foul of para (3). An argument that para (1) is *ultra vires* was rejected by the High Court in *R (Bierman) v Secretary of State for Work and Pensions* [2004] EWHC 1024 (Admin), 23 April, unreported. Mr Justice Davis rejected the argument that ss130 and 137(2) SSCBA 1992 only empower the making of regulations which state that a person is not liable to pay rent and do not allow for regulations which speak of HB not being "payable". In the Court's view, the precise form of language used in reg 50(1) HB Regs 1987 (now reg 57(1) HB Regs) was not important; the intent was clearly to exclude entitlement for students who pay rent to the educational establishment which they are attending, and that intent is within the broad powers conferred by s130(2) SSCBA 1992. Moreover, the power to prescribe in s130(2) is not limited by the terms of section 137(2) to regulations which speak about treating persons as not being 'liable' to make payments in respect of a dwelling.

Para (2). As to the meaning of "dwelling occupied by the student as his home", see reg 7(3) and (6)(b), and reg 55. If the other establishment is not providing the accommodation in question "in the exercise of its functions", as where the institution has purchased property as an investment, the student should be able to claim HB if the rest of this paragraph is satisfied.

Para (3). It is suggested that the question of whether the institution has sought to "take advantage" of the HB scheme must be determined in the same way as a question as to whether a tenancy has been created for that purpose. See the Analysis to reg 9(1)(l) above. A student refused HB under this provision will have the normal rights to challenge a decision. GM C2.94 states that the exclusion will not apply when rent is paid to a housing association. There is no statutory basis for this statement, but it is unlikely that an arrangement at arms' length will fall foul of this paragraph.

Para (4). The Government recognised that living away from campus was preventing some students (in particular disabled students and lone parents) from having easy access to all the facilities that an educational establishment provides and to mix easily with other students. It also recognised that those who needed to live in accommodation provided by the educational establishment in order to attend a course, who could not afford such accommodation, might be prevented from taking up places on courses. Para (4) enables certain students to claim HB in respect of accommodation which they rent from their educational establishment. There are two categories:

(1)   full-time students who are exempt from the general exclusion from HB by reg 56(2): sub-para (a);

(2)   part-time students who would be exempt from the general exclusion from HB by reg 56(2) if they were full-time students, unless they would only be exempt because they are on income support or income-based JSA: sub-para (b).

Note that students who are only exempt from the general exclusion from HB under reg 56(6) (ie, while waiting to return to a course following a period of incapacity or caring) do not come within either category. Presumably few of these students would be living in accommodation rented from the educational establishment during a "period of study" in any case, in which case reg 57 would not apply (see para(1)).

Student partners

58.   Where a claimant is not, but his partner is, a student, the provisions of regulation 57 (student's eligible housing costs) shall apply as if the claimant were a student.

Definitions
"claimant" – see reg 2(1).
"partner" – see reg 2(1).
"student" – see reg 53.

General Note
See commentary to reg 57.

SECTION 3
Income

General Note on Section 3
See "General Note" on this Part. This Section sets out the special rules for treatment of student income, namely grant and loan income (regs 59, 64 and 69) as well as covenant income (regs 60 and 61) and payments from access funds and fee loans (regs 64A and 65). It supplements, and to some extent modifies, the provisions of Pt 6 of these regulations. Regs 63, 66 and 67 provide for additional disregards from a student's income which is other than grants, loans or covenant income. Reg 68 sets out situations when certain student income is to be treated as capital.

Other types of income received by students will be dealt with under the ordinary income and capital rules found in Part 6. Note that education maintenance allowances (and similar payments) paid to young people on certain non-advanced courses are excluded from the definition of "grant" and are dealt with separately. They are disregarded as income under Sch 5 para 11 and as capital under Sch 6 para 51. Career development loans paid under s2 of the Employment and Training Act 1973 are taken into account as income (reg 41(4)) with provision for some or all of such loans to be disregarded (Sch 5 para 13).

The effect of the apportionment rules on entitlement to HB

Grant income is in general spread over the weeks in a student's "period of study" (see reg 53(1)). A period of study can be a period of less than a calendar year (eg, it can exclude the summer vacation). Loan income is in general spread over the weeks in a student's "academic year" (see reg 53(1)). An academic year is a period of up to 12 months. Covenant income is spread over both the period of study and the academic year. For this reason, grant, loan and covenant income can be taken into account over different periods. This means that a student may be entitled to HB (or have increased entitlement to HB) outside her/his period of study. A fresh claim or a supersession request will be required in these circumstances.

Calculation of grant income

59.–(1)   The amount of a student's grant income to be taken into account shall, subject to paragraphs (2) and (3), be the whole of his grant income.

(2)   There shall be excluded from a student's grant income any payment–
(a)   intended to meet tuition fees or examination fees;
(b)   in respect of the student's disability;
(c)   intended to meet additional expenditure connected with term time residential study away from the student's educational establishment;
(d)   on account of the student maintaining a home at a place other than that at which he resides during his course;
(e)   on account of any other person but only if that person is residing outside of the United Kingdom and there is no applicable amount in respect of him;
(f)   intended to meet the cost of books and equipment;
(g)   intended to meet travel expenses incurred as a result of his attendance on the course;
(h)   intended for the child care costs of a child dependant.
(3)   Where a student does not have a student loan and is not treated as possessing such a loan, there shall be excluded from the student's grant income–
(a)   the sum of [² £290] in respect of travel costs; and
(b)   the sum of [² £370] towards the costs of books and equipment,
whether or not any such costs are incurred.
[¹ (4)   There shall also be excluded from a student's grant income the grant for dependants known as the parents' learning allowance paid pursuant to regulations made under Article 3 of the Education (Student Support) (Northern Ireland) Order 1998 or section 22 of the Teaching and Higher Education Act 1998.]
(5)   Subject to paragraphs (6) and (7), a student's grant income shall be apportioned–
(a)   subject to paragraph (8), in a case where it is attributable to the period of study, equally between the weeks in the period beginning with the benefit week, the first day of which coincides with, or immediately follows, the first day of the period of study and ending with the benefit week, the last day of which coincides with, or immediately precedes, the last day of the period of study;
(b)   in any other case, equally between the weeks in the period beginning with the benefit week, the first day of which coincides with, or immediately follows, the first day of the period for which it is payable and ending with the benefit week, the last day of which coincides with, or immediately precedes, the last day of the period for which it is payable.
(6)   Any grant in respect of dependants paid under section 63(6) of the Health Services and Public Health Act 1968 (grants in respect of the provision of instruction to officers of hospital authorities) and any amount intended for the maintenance of dependants under Part 3 of Schedule 2 to the Education (Mandatory Awards) Regulations 2003 shall be apportioned equally over the period of 52 weeks or, if there are 53 benefit weeks (including part-weeks) in the year, 53.
(7)   In a case where a student is in receipt of a student loan or where he could have acquired a student loan by taking reasonable steps but had not done so, any amount intended for the maintenance of dependants to which neither paragraph (6) nor regulation 63(2) (other amounts to be disregarded) apply, shall be apportioned over the same period as the student's loan is apportioned or, as the case may be, would have been apportioned.
(8)   In the case of a student on a sandwich course, any periods of experience within the period of study shall be excluded and the student's grant income shall be apportioned equally between the weeks in the period beginning with the benefit week, the first day of which immediately follows the last day of the period of experience and ending with the benefit week, the last day of which coincides with, or immediately precedes, the last day of the period of study.

Definitions

"applicable amount" – see Part 5.
"benefit week" – see reg 2(1).
"child" – see reg 2(1).
"full-time student" – see reg 53.
"grant income" – see reg 53.
"periods of experience" – see reg 53.
"period of study" – see reg 53.
"sandwich course" – see reg 53.
"student" – see reg 53.
"UK" – includes Northern Ireland.

Amendments

1.   Substituted by reg 3(2) and (3) of SI 2006 No 1752 as from, for students whose period of study begins on or after 1.8.06 but before 1.9.06, on the day the period of study begins; in any other case 1.9.06.
2.   Substituted by reg 4(2) of SI 2007 No 1632 as from, in the case of a person whose period of study begins on or after 1.8.07 but before 1.9.07, on the day the period of study begins; in any other case, 1.9.07.

General Note

Para (1) provides the general rule that a student's grant income is to be taken into account in full, whether or not s/he is in full-time education (see the definition of "student" in reg 53). Paras (2) to (4) list parts of the student's grant income which must be ignored.

Paras (5) to (7) set out the period over which grant income as calculated in paras (1) to (4) is to be taken into account, and how weekly amounts are to be calculated.

Reg 69 provides for treatment of changes in the amount of standard maintenance grant that occur in the recognised summer vacation. If that summer vacation does not form part of the student's period of study, the change is ignored from the date it occurs to the end of the vacation.

Note that if a student is eligible for a student loan in addition to the Higher Education grant, the general disregard is applied to the loan rather than the grant income. For students who have both grant and loan income, the effect is that in general, the grant will be taken into account.

Analysis

Para (1). For the meaning of "grant income", see the Analysis to reg 53.

Paras (2) and (4). The total of any amounts listed under these paragraphs which apply to a claimant are to be disregarded. The categories are:

(1)   Payments of tuition and exam fees: para (2)(a).
(2)   Payments in respect of the student's disability, eg where extra costs are incurred as a result of attending the course: para (2)(b). For example GM C2.322 tells local authorities to disregard Disabled Students Allowances (DSAs) as they are paid to provide help towards the costs of:
  (a)   a non-medical helper
  (b)   major items of equipment
  (c)   travel costs
  (d)   other items
(3)   Payments towards additional expenditure connected to term-time residential study away from the institution: para (2)(c).
(4)   Payments towards the maintenance of a home by the student while away studying: para (2)(d).
(5)   Payments "on account of any other person" outside the UK who is not residing with the claimant (eg, a partner or child) and for whom there is no HB applicable amount: para (2)(e).
(6)   Payments intended to meet the costs of books and equipment: para (2)(f).
(7)   Payments intended to meet travel expenses incurred as a result of attendance on the course: para (2)(g).
(8)   Payments intended for the child care costs of a child dependant: para (2)(h). A "child" is a person under the age of 16 (see reg 2(1)).
(9)   "Parents learning allowance" paid towards the maintenance of a dependent child under the provisions specified: para (4).

Note that the payments disregarded under para (2) are those "intended" for or paid "on account of" the types of expenditure mentioned or in respect of a student's disability, so there is no requirement that the student uses the payments for items listed.

See also regs 62, 63 and 67.

Para (3) permits deductions from grant income where a student does not have a loan and cannot be treated as having one. These are flat-rate deductions in respect of books, equipment and travel, whether or not the costs are incurred. If the student does have a loan, see reg 64(5).

Apportionment of grant income

Para (5)(a). Except in the case of a sandwich course, as to which see para (8), where a grant is said to be in respect of the "period of study" (see reg 53) it is divided equally between the weeks which that period covers.

Para (5)(b). In any other case (ie, where a grant is not said to be in respect of the "period of study"), grant income will be divided equally between the weeks in the period for which it is payable.

Para (6) deals with apportionment of grants for dependants paid under specific provisions. These are divided equally over 52 (or 53) benefit weeks.

Para (7) deals with grants for dependants not covered by para (6) or reg 63(2), paid to students in receipt of student loans or students who could receive a loan by taking reasonable steps. In this case, the grant is apportioned over the same period as the loan (see reg 64). Note that where a claimant could have obtained a student loan but did not in fact do so, s/he will be treated as being in receipt of one: reg 64(3)(b). If a student abandons or is dismissed from a course, the rules in reg 40(7), (8) and (9) specify how payments referred to in para (7) must be treated.

Para (8). If the student is on a "sandwich course" and the grant is said to be in respect of the "period of study", it should be divided equally over the weeks in that period during which the student is not on a "period of experience".

Calculation of covenant income where a contribution is assessed

60.–(1)   Where a student is in receipt of income by way of a grant during a period of study and a contribution has been assessed, the amount of his covenant income to be taken into account for that period and any summer vacation immediately following shall be the whole amount of the covenant income less, subject to paragraph (3), the amount of the contribution.

(2)   The weekly amount of the student's covenant income shall be determined–

(a)   by dividing the amount of income which falls to be taken into account under paragraph (1) by 52 or 53, whichever is reasonable in the circumstances; and

(b)   by disregarding from the resulting amount, £5.

(3)   For the purposes of paragraph (1), the contribution shall be treated as increased by the amount (if any) by which the amount excluded under regulation 59(2)(g) (calculation of grant income) falls short of the amount specified in paragraph 7(2) of Schedule 2 to the Education (Mandatory Awards) Regulations 2003 (travel expenditure).

Definitions

"covenant income" – see reg 53.
"contribution" – see reg 53.
"grant" – see reg 53.
"income" – see Part 6 also.
"period of study" – see reg 53.
"student" – see reg 53.

General Note

Prior to 1988, there was a provision for students to be paid under a deed of covenant whereby the payer could deduct the appropriate rate of tax from the gross amount of the payment and pay the student the net amount. The student could then claim a refund of the tax deducted, the refund being treated as capital under reg 68(1). Such tax relief has not been available since April 1988.

It is understood that it is now unlikely that there are any students still receiving covenant income. For general notes on, and an analysis of the rules for covenant income, see earlier editions of this work.

Covenant income where no grant income or no contribution is assessed

61.–(1)   Where a student is not in receipt of income by way of a grant the amount of his covenant income shall be calculated as follows–

    (a)   any sums intended for any expenditure specified in regulation 59(2)(a) to (e) (calculation of grant income) necessary as a result of his attendance on the course shall be disregarded;

    (b)   any covenant income, up to the amount of the standard maintenance grant, which is not so disregarded, shall be apportioned equally between the weeks of the period of study;

    (c)   there shall be disregarded from the amount so apportioned the amount which would have been disregarded under regulation 59(2)(f) and (3) (calculation of grant income) had the student been in receipt of the standard maintenance grant; and

    (d)   the balance, if any, shall be divided by 52 or 53 whichever is reasonable in the circumstances and treated as weekly income of which £5 shall be disregarded.

    (2)   Where a student is in receipt of income by way of a grant and no contribution has been assessed, the amount of his covenanted income shall be calculated in accordance with sub-paragraphs (a) to (d) of paragraph (1), except that–

    (a)   the value of the standard maintenance grant shall be abated by the amount of such grant income less an amount equal to the amount of any sums disregarded under regulation 59(2)(a) to (e); and

    (b)   the amount to be disregarded under paragraph (1)(c) shall be abated by an amount equal to the amount of any sums disregarded under regulation 59(2)(f) and (g) and (3).

Definitions
    "covenant income" – see reg 53.
    "grant" – see reg 53.
    "grant income" – see reg 53.
    "period of study" – see reg 53.
    "student" – see reg 53.

General Note
    See General Note to reg 60.

Relationship with amounts to be disregarded under Schedule 5

    62.   No part of a student's covenant income or grant income shall be disregarded under [1 paragraph 14] of Schedule 5 [2].

Definitions
    "covenant income" – see reg 53.
    "grant income" – see reg 53.
    "student" – see reg 53.

Amendments
    1.   Substituted by reg 3(4) of SI 2006 No 1752 as from, for students whose period of study begins on or after 1.8.06 but before 1.9.06, on the day the period of study begins; in any other case 1.9.06.
    2.   Amended by reg 15(3) of SI 2006 No 2378 from the 1st day of the 1st benefit week to commence on or after 2.10.06.

General Note
    This provides that the disregard of, for example, charitable or voluntary payments under para 14 of Sch 5 cannot apply to a claimant's covenant or grant income at all.

Other amounts to be disregarded

    63.–(1)   For the purposes of ascertaining income other than grant income, covenant income and loans treated as income in accordance with regulation 64 (treatment of student loans), any amounts intended for any expenditure specified in regulation 59(2) (calculation of grant income), necessary as a result of his attendance on the course shall be disregarded but only if, and to the extent that, the necessary expenditure exceeds or is likely to exceed the amount of the sums disregarded under regulation 59(2) or (3), 60(3), 61 (1)(a) or (c) or 64(5) (calculation of grant income, covenant income and treatment of student loans) on like expenditure.

(2)   Where a grant for school meals for dependant children or a grant for meals for dependant children aged 3 or 4 is paid pursuant to any regulations made under section 22 of the Teaching and Higher Education Act 1998 or under the Students' Allowance (Scotland) Regulations 1999 that payment shall be disregarded as income.

Definitions
"covenant income" – see reg 53.
"grant income" – see reg 53.

General Note
This regulation deals with income other than grant income, covenant income and student loans treated as income under reg 64 – eg, gifts, etc. Any amounts intended for some or all of the items listed in reg 59(2) which are necessary for attendance on the student's course are disregarded, but only to the extent that the total necessary expenditure on these items exceeds (or is likely to exceed) the amounts actually disregarded (from grant, covenant and loan income) by the regulations listed: para (1).

It is unclear whether sums covered by this regulation, and which are not to be disregarded, are to be taken into account over a full year or just over the "period of study". It is submitted that how the money is intended to be used is relevant (eg, if a grandparent makes a gift for the student's maintenance during the period of study) it should only be taken into account over that period.

Under para (2), amounts paid under the provisions specified for school meals for dependant children are disregarded. This includes grants for children aged 3 or 4.

Treatment of student loans
64.–(1)   A student loan shall be treated as income.

(2)   In calculating the weekly amount of the loan to be taken into account as income–
  (a)   in respect of a course that is of a single academic year's duration or less, a loan which is payable in respect of that period shall be apportioned equally between the weeks in the period beginning with–
    (i)   except in a case where head (ii) applies, the benefit week, the first day of which coincides with, or immediately follows, the first day of the single academic year;
    (ii)   where the student is required to start attending the course in August or where the course is less than an academic year's duration, the benefit week, the first day of which coincides with, or immediately follows, the first day of the course,
  and ending with the benefit week, the last day of which coincides with, or immediately precedes, the last day of the course;
  (b)   in respect of an academic year of a course which starts other than on 1st September, a loan which is payable in respect of that academic year shall be apportioned equally between the weeks in the period beginning with the benefit week the first day of which coincides with or immediately follows, the first day of that academic year and ending with the benefit week, the last day of which coincides with or immediately precedes, the last day of that academic year but excluding any benefit weeks falling entirely within the quarter during which, in the opinion of the Secretary of State, the longest of any vacation is taken and for the purposes of this sub-paragraph, "quarter" shall have the same meaning as for the purposes of the Education (Student Support) Regulations 2005;
  (c)   in respect of the final academic year of a course (not being a course of a single year's duration), a loan which is payable in respect of that final academic year shall be apportioned equally between the weeks in the period beginning with–

    (i)   except in a case where head (ii) applies, the benefit week, the first day of which coincides with, or immediately follows, the first day of that academic year;

    (ii)   where the final academic year starts on 1st September, the benefit week, the first day of which coincides with, or immediately follows, the earlier of 1st September or the first day of the autumn term,

and ending with the benefit week, the last day of which coincides with, or immediately precedes, the last day of the course;

  (d)   in any other case, the loan shall be apportioned equally between the weeks in the period beginning with the earlier of–

    (i)   the first day of the first benefit week in September; or

    (ii)   the benefit week, the first day of which coincides with, or immediately follows the first day of the autumn term,

and ending with the benefit week, the last day of which coincides with, or immediately precedes, the last day of June,

and, in all cases, from the weekly amount so apportioned there shall be disregarded £10.

(3)   A student shall be treated as possessing a student loan in respect of an academic year where–

  (a)   a student loan has been made to him in respect of that year; or

  (b)   he could acquire such a loan in respect of that year by taking reasonable steps to do so.

(4)   Where a student is treated as possessing a student loan under paragraph (3), the amount of the student loan to be taken into account as income shall be, subject to paragraph (5)–

  (a)   in the case of a student to whom a student loan is made in respect of an academic year, a sum equal to–

    (i)   the maximum student loan he is able to acquire in respect of that year by taking reasonable steps to do so; and

    (ii)   any contribution whether or not it has been paid;

  (b)   in the case of a student to whom a student loan is not made in respect of an academic year, the maximum student loan that would be made to the student if–

    (i)   he took all reasonable steps to obtain the maximum student loan he is able to acquire in respect of that year; and

    (ii)   no deduction in that loan was made by virtue of the application of a means test.

(5)   There shall be deducted from the amount of a student's loan income–

  (a)   the sum of [² £290] in respect of travel costs; and

  (b)   the sum of [² £370] towards the cost of books and equipment,

whether or not any such costs are incurred.

Definitions

"academic year" – see reg 53.
"benefit week" – see reg 2(1).
"last day of course" – see reg 53.
"student loan" – see reg 53.
"year" – see reg 53.

Amendments

1.   Substituted by reg 3(2) of SI 2006 No 1752 as from, for students whose period of study begins on or after 1.8.06 but before 1.9.06, on the day the period of study begins; in any other case 1.9.06.

2.   Substituted by reg 4(3) of SI 2007 No 1632 as from, in the case of a person whose period of study begins on or after 1.8.07 but before 1.9.07, on the day the period of study begins; in any other case, 1.9.07.

General Note

Under para (1) a "student loan" (defined in reg 53) is treated as income. It is disregarded as capital under para 22 of Sch 6.

Prior to 6 March 2006, a distinction was drawn between hardship loans and other loans – hardship loans were disregarded: reg 57A(1A) HB Regs 1987. It is understood that hardship loans are no longer available so the equivalent to reg 57A(1A) was not included in the HB Regs. Note that career development loans paid pursuant to s2 Employment and Training Act 1973 are dealt with under reg 41(4) and Sch 5 para 13.

Under para (2), the loan is apportioned on a weekly basis over the length of the course or the academic year, whichever is shorter. Sub-para (b) deals with courses where the academic year starts other than on 1 September. Note that the definition of "academic year" (reg 53(1)) specifies that where a course begins during August or September, the academic year of the course is considered to start on 1 September.

Under para (3), a student is treated as having a loan even where s/he has not applied for one, provided that s/he could obtain one. S/he is deemed to have the maximum loan available: para (4).

Under para (5), set deductions are made from loan income in respect of travel, books and equipment, whether or not the costs are incurred.

Note that if a student abandons or is dismissed from a course, the rules in reg 40(7) to (9) specify how a loan must be treated.

Loans paid to part-time students towards books and travel are technically dealt with under this regulation. However, it is understood that they are paid at a lower rate than the combination of disregards available for books and equipment and travel costs and so are disregarded in full: GM C2.230.

Analysis

Para (2). How a student loan is to be apportioned, in general depends on whether the course lasts for one year or for a longer period. There are four possibilities.

(1)   Courses that last for a single academic year or less: sub-para (a). The loan is to be divided equally between the weeks in the period beginning with the start of the academic year (or for courses lasting less than a year, the first day of the course) and ending on the last day of the course.

(2)   Courses that start other than on 1 September: sub-para (b). If the academic year of a course starts other than on 1 September, the loan is to be divided equally between the weeks in the period from the first to the last days of the academic year. Any benefit weeks falling entirely within the quarter during which, in the opinion of the Secretary of State for Work and Pensions, the longest vacation is taken, must be disregarded. "Quarter" in relation to an academic year, means a period in that year from 1 January to 31 March, 1 April to 30 June, 1 July to 31 August, or 1 September to 31 December. If it is the final year of the course, see below.

(3)   The final academic year of a course: sub-para (c). Unless the course is for a single year (for which see above), the loan payable in respect of the final academic year of a student's course is to be apportioned as follows. If the academic year starts on 1 September, the loan is to be divided equally between the weeks in the period beginning with the earliest of the 1 September or the first day of autumn term and ending with the benefit week the last day of which coincides with or immediately precedes the last day of the course. In other cases, the loan is to be divided equally between the weeks in the period from the first day of the academic year to the benefit week the last day of which coincides with or immediately precedes the last day of the course.

(4)   Any other case: sub-para (d). Unless it is the final year of the course (for which see above), sub-para (d) will apply to courses of more than an academic year's duration where the academic year starts on 1 September. The loan is to be divided equally between the weeks in the period beginning with the earlier of the first benefit week in September or in the autumn term and ending on the benefit week the last day of which coincides with or immediately precedes the last day of June.

In all four cases, a £10 weekly disregard must be applied. Note, however, that this disregard can overlap with disregards from covenant income and access funds as well as disregards from certain types of war pension income. A combined maximum of £20 is allowed: Sch 5 para 34.

Paras (3) and (4). A student is treated as possessing a student loan where one has been made to her/him, as well as where s/he could acquire a loan by taking reasonable steps to do so: para (3). GM C2.120 points out that student loans are available to most eligible full-time British students in higher education, whether or not a grant is payable, except for some students aged 50 to 55 and those over 55 when their course started. They are also available to postgraduate students studying for a Postgraduate Certificate of Education (PGCE). The amount of loan then taken into account is the maximum amount of loan available, even if less than this amount (or no loan) is actually borrowed: para (4). In the case of a student who has taken out a loan, any contribution assessed is also taken into account, even if it has not been paid (para (4)(a)(ii)). In the case of a student who has not taken out a loan, no account is taken of any deduction in that loan that could have been made as a result of the means-test.

[¹ Treatment of fee loans

64A. A loan for fees, known as a fee loan or a fee contribution loan, made pursuant to regulations made under Article 3 of the Education (Student Support) (Northern Ireland) Order 1998, section 22 of the Teaching and Higher Education Act 1998 or section 73(f) of the Education (Scotland) Act 1980, shall be disregarded as income.]

Amendment

1.   Inserted by reg 3(5) of SI 2006 No 1752 as from, for students whose period of study begins on or after 1.8.06 but before 1.9.06, on the day the period of study begins; in any other case 1.9.06.

General Note

From September 2006, eligible full-time higher education students can take out student loans to pay their fee contribution to the college or university. Reg 64A allows for these loans to be disregarded in full. Note that some students will be eligible for means-tested fee grants. It is understood that these are paid direct to the college or university so would not count as the notional income or capital of the student (payments to a third party in respect of a claimant) under regs 42(6)(b) and 49(3)(a) HB Regs. See also reg 59(2)(a).

Treatment of payments from access funds

65.–(1)   This regulation applies to payments from access funds that are not payments to which regulation 68(2) or (3) (income treated as capital) applies.

(2)   A payment from access funds, other than a payment to which paragraph (3) applies, shall be disregarded as income.

(3)   Subject to paragraph (5) of this regulation and paragraph 34 of Schedule 5, any payments from access funds which are intended and used for food, household fuel or rent or ordinary clothing or footwear, of a single claimant or any other member of his family, and any payments from access funds which are used for any council tax or water charges for which that claimant or member is liable shall be disregarded as income to the extent of £20 per week.

(4)   For the purposes of paragraph (3), "rent" means eligible rent less any deductions in respect of non-dependants which fall to be made under regulation 74 (non-dependant deductions).

(5)   Where a payment from access funds is made–

(a)   on or after 1st September or the first day of the course, whichever first occurs, but before receipt of any student loan in respect of that year and that payment is intended for the purpose of bridging the period until receipt of the student loan; or

(b)   before the first day of the course to a person in anticipation of that person becoming a student,

that payment shall be disregarded as income.

Definitions

"access funds" – see reg 53.
"ordinary clothing or footwear" – see reg 2(1).

General Note

Access funds are discretionary funds administered by colleges and universities who may call these funds by other names (eg, access bursary, mature students' bursary, child care support). DfES press notice 2002/0226 suggests that these will be called "access to learning funds" in English higher education institutions from September 2004.

Most payments from access funds which do not fall to be treated as capital under reg 68 (ie, which are not single lump sums) are disregarded: para (2). However, those intended for and used for specified basic necessities will be taken into account with a £20 disregard: para (3). Note, however, that this disregard can overlap with disregards from covenant income and student loan income as well as disregards from certain types of war pension income. A combined maximum of £20 is allowed: Sch 5 para 34. "Rent" is defined in para (4) and "ordinary clothing or footwear" in reg 2(1). Under para (5), an access fund payment used effectively as a bridging loan until a loan can be obtained is ignored, as is a payment made before the student commences study.

Disregard of contribution and rent

66. Where the claimant or his partner is a student and, for the purposes of assessing a contribution to the student's grant or student loan, the other partner's income has been taken into account, an amount equal to that contribution shall be disregarded for the purposes of assessing that other partner's income.

Definitions
"claimant" – see reg 2(1).
"contribution" – see reg 53.
"income" – see Part 6 and the rest of this Section.
"partner" – see reg 2(1).
"student" – see reg 53.

General Note
This regulation provides for an income disregard where a student's partner has been assessed for a contribution to her/his grant or loan. That contribution is taken into account as income and so, to avoid double counting, an equal amount of the contributing partner's income is disregarded.

Further disregard of student's income

67. Where any part of a student's income has already been taken into account for the purposes of assessing his entitlement to a grant or student loan, the amount taken into account shall be disregarded in assessing that student's income.

General Note
The regulation only applies where a student has been assessed as liable to make a contribution towards his or her *own* grant or loan by the LEA. In this case, the amount of income taken into account is disregarded under this regulation.

Amounts treated as capital

68.–(1) Any amount by way of a refund of tax deducted from a student's covenant income shall be treated as capital.

(2) An amount paid from access funds as a single lump sum shall be treated as capital.

(3) An amount paid from access funds as a single lump sum which is intended and used for an item other than food, household fuel, rent, ordinary clothing or footwear of a single claimant or, as the case may be, of the claimant or any other member of his family, or which is used for any council tax or water charges for which that claimant or member is liable, shall be disregarded as capital but only for a period of 52 weeks from the date of the payment.

(4) In paragraph (3), ''rent'' means eligible rent less any deductions in respect of non-dependants which fall to be made under regulation 74 (non-dependant deductions).

Definitions
"access funds" – see reg 53.
"capital" – see Part 6.
"covenant income" – see Part 6.
"ordinary clothing or footwear" – see reg 2(1).
"student" – see reg 53.

General Note
See the General Note to reg 60 on covenant income. Refunds of income tax deducted from a student's covenant income are treated as capital as are single payment access fund payments. An amount paid from access funds intended for and used for items other than specified basic necessities must be disregarded for 52 weeks from payment. "Rent" is defined in para (4) and "ordinary clothing and footware" in reg 2(1).

Disregard of changes occurring during summer vacation

69. In calculating a student's income the relevant authority shall disregard any change in the standard maintenance grant, occurring in the recognised summer vacation appropriate to the student's course, if that vacation does not form part of his period of study from the date on which the change occurred to the end of that vacation.

Definitions
"period of study" – see reg 53.
"student" – see reg 53.

General Note
See the commentary to reg 59.

PART 8
Amount of benefit

General Note on Part 8
This Part provides the rules under which the amount of HB to which a person is entitled is calculated.

Reg 70 sets out the rules for ascertaining the appropriate maximum HB to which a particular claimant may be entitled.

Reg 71 prescribes the percentage of the claimant's excess income which is to be deducted from this figure.

Regs 72 and 73 together with reg 80(7) and Schs 7 and 8 make provisions for extended payments of benefit, where HB was payable, in the circumstances prescribed – ie, where entitlement to IS, income-based JSA. Incapacity benefit or severe disablement allowance ceases on account of the commencement of employment or self-employment or an increase in the hours or earnings from such.

Reg 74 is ancillary to reg 70 in that a person's maximum HB is arrived at by deducting certain amounts in respect of "non-dependants" from the "eligible rent" figure calculated under reg 12; reg 74 sets out the appropriate amounts to be deducted in respect of different categories of non-dependant as well as the situations when no deduction can be made.

Reg 75 is made under s134(4) SSCBA and prescribes the minimum weekly amount of HB to which a claimant may be entitled and actually paid.

Note that if sanctions apply, a lower amount of HB than as calculated in this Part might be payable in the following circumstances:

(1)   A reduction can be applied for 13 weeks where the claimant or a member of her/his family is convicted of one or more benefit offences in two separate sets of proceedings (20 or 40 per cent of the appropriate personal allowance for a single person of the claimant's age): ss7 and 9 SSFA 2001 (see p1033) and the Social Security (Loss of Benefit) Regulations 2001 (see p1087).

(2)   From 1 November 2007, in Pilot areas only, a reduction can be applied following eviction on the grounds of anti-social behaviour, where (in England or Wales) the claimant fails to comply with a notice from a local authority to improve behaviour, or (in Scotland) fails to comply without good cause with a requirement by a local authority to take specified action having been warned that such a failure would affect the amount of HB payable (10 per cent for the first four weeks, 20 per cent for the next four weeks, then 100 per cent until the local authority considers the sanction should no longer apply or a period of five years has expired (30 percent if former occupier is a "person in hardship")): ss130B SSCBA 1992 (see p6) and the Housing Benefit (Loss of Benefit) (Pilot Scheme) Regulations 2007 (see p1139).

Maximum housing benefit

70. The amount of a person's appropriate maximum housing benefit in any week shall be 100 per cent. of his eligible rent calculated on a weekly basis in accordance with regulation 80 and 81 (calculation of weekly amount and rent free periods) less any deductions in respect of non-dependants which fall to be made under regulation 74 (non-dependant deductions).

Definitions
"eligible rent" – see reg 12.
"non-dependants" – see reg 3.

General Note

Where a claimant is entitled to HB under s130(1)(c)(i) SSCBA (where s/he has no income or her/his income does not exceed her/his applicable amount) the maximum HB is what s/he will actually receive. Where s/he is entitled under s130(1)(c)(ii) of SSCBA (ie, where her/his income exceeds her/his applicable amount) the HB due is to be calculated by deducting prescribed percentages of the claimant's "excess income" from the maximum HB to which s/he is potentially entitled. "Excess income" is the amount by which a claimant's income assessed under Pt 6 exceeds her/his "applicable amount" under Part 5.

Note that authorities have powers to top up HB with discretionary housing payments under the Discretionary Financial Assistance Regulations 2001 (see p1079). Former powers to pay increased HB are discussed on pp397-399 of the 14th edn of this book. There may be a few outstanding appeals on those issues and regard should be had to the discussion in *CH 1175/2002* in any such cases. See also *CH 5299/2002*, where Commissioner Jacobs gave detailed guidance as to the meaning of "exceptional hardship" in the former provisions.

Analysis

This regulation (together with reg 74) is determinative of the maximum HB which can be paid in any week (though note the situation where there is entitlement to "extended payments" of HB under reg 72 or 73).

A person's maximum HB is calculated by reference to her/his weekly eligible rent. "Eligible rent" is calculated under reg 12 (or reg 12A as inserted by Sch 10 in Pathfinder areas). Regs 80 and 81 set out how eligible rent is to be calculated on a weekly basis. Any of the non-dependant deductions listed in reg 74 which apply must be deducted from the eligible rent to produce the appropriate maximum HB in any case. Note that any actual payments made to the claimant by the non-dependant are disregarded under para 21 of Sch 5.

Where the claimant has for any reason to pay interest on the eligible rent, that interest cannot form part of the HB: *R v Kensington and Chelsea RBC ex p Brandt* [1995] 28 HLR 528, QBD.

Housing benefit tapers

71. The prescribed percentages for the purpose of sub-section (3)(b) of section 130 of the Act (percentage of excess of income over applicable amount which is deducted from maximum housing benefit) shall be 65 per cent.

Analysis

Reg 71 provides the percentage with which to calculate HB entitlement where the claimant is covered by s130(1)(c)(ii) SSCBA. HB in such a case is calculated as follows:

(1)   Work out "eligible rent" under reg 12 (or reg 12A). Work out weekly maximum HB under reg 70, deducting non-dependant deductions under reg 74 (if applicable) from "eligible rent".

(2)   Work out by how much the claimant's income exceeds her/his applicable amount.

(3)   To calculate HB due, deduct 65 per cent of the excess income so calculated from maximum HB.

Extended payments

72.–(1) Subject to paragraphs (7) and (8), paragraph (2) shall apply where–

(a)   a person ceases to be entitled to housing benefit–

(i) in accordance with regulation 77 (date on which housing benefit is to end); and

(ii) the conditions referred to in paragraphs 1 and 2 of Schedule 7 (extended payments of housing benefit) are satisfied in his case; or

(b)   a person ceases to be entitled to housing benefit because he has vacated the dwelling which he occupied as his home and the day on which he did so was either in the week in which he took up employment as an employed or self-employed earner, or in the preceding week, and–

(i)   he ceased to be entitled to income support or an income-based jobseeker's allowance by reason of taking up employment as an employed or self-employed earner; and

(ii)   the conditions referred to in paragraphs 1 and 2 of Schedule 7 are satisfied in his case.

(2)   A person to whom paragraph (1) applies shall be treated as having made a claim under this regulation and his housing benefit shall be determined in accordance

with Part 2 of Schedule 7 and any award so determined shall be referred to in these Regulations as an "extended payment".

(3)   For the purposes of any payment pursuant to this regulation–

(a)   except in a case to which paragraph 7(b) of Schedule 7 applies, the maximum housing benefit of any person mentioned in paragraph (1) shall be that which was applicable to him in the last benefit week of the award of housing benefit which has ceased as mentioned in paragraph (1);

(b)   the maximum housing benefit of any person to whom paragraph 7(b) of Schedule 7 applies shall be determined in accordance with paragraph 8 of that Schedule; and

(c)   any person who meets the requirements of paragraph (1) shall be treated as possessing no income or capital.

(4)   Regulations 82, 83 and 86 (claims, evidence and information) shall not apply to a claim pursuant to this regulation and, subject to regulation 80(7) and Part 9 (calculation of weekly amounts and changes of circumstances) shall not apply to any payment under it.

(5)   In paragraph (1)(a) and (b), references to a "person" include references to a person's partner.

(6)   In a case where a payment has been made under this regulation–

(a)   the beneficiary shall be treated for the purposes of these Regulations or, in a case to which regulation 4(2) applies, of as the Housing Benefit (Persons who have attained the qualifying age for state pension credit) Regulations 2006 as though he were entitled to and in receipt of housing benefit–

(i)   during the 4 weeks immediately following the last day of his entitlement to housing benefit; or

(ii)   until the date on which his liability for rent ends, whichever occurs first; and

(b)   any claim for housing benefit made by the beneficiary within the period which under sub-paragraph (a) applies in his case or the 4 weeks thereafter shall be treated as having been made in respect of a period beginning immediately after the end of his previous award of housing benefit.

(7)   This regulation shall not apply to a claimant where, on the day before his entitlement to income support ceased, regulation 6(5) of the Income Support Regulations (remunerative work: housing costs) applied to him.

(8)   In paragraph (6), "these Regulations" includes the Regulations as modified by paragraphs 4 and 5 of Schedule 3 to the Consequential Provisions Regulations.

General Note

Reg 72, together with Sch 7, establishes a scheme for "extended payments" of HB to be made to certain people who have been on IS or income-based JSA for at least 26 weeks, who come off that benefit because they or their partners commence remunerative work or increase hours or earnings (and hence by reg 77, cease to be entitled to HB). Note that by reg 5(2) this regulation and Sch 7 can apply to a person even if s/he or her/his partner has reached the qualifying age for state pension credit.

Extended payments of HB can be made for up to four weeks. See also the commentary to Sch 7.

See regs 73 and 78 and Sch 8 for a similar scheme where entitlement to severe disablement allowance or incapacity benefit ceases for employment reasons. See reg 80(7) for where HB entitlement can be adjusted if a claimant has received an extended payment under either reg 72 or reg 73.

Analysis

Para (1) sets out the basic conditions of entitlement to extended payments. By para (5) these apply to the claimant or her/his partner. The conditions are that either the claimant or her/his partner:

(1)   has ceased to be entitled to HB under reg 77, broadly, because entitlement to IS or income-based JSA ceased because of the commencement of employment or self-employment, or an increase in earnings from, or hours in, the employment: para (1)(a); or

(2)   has ceased to be entitled to HB because s/he moved home either in the week s/he took up employment or self-employment, or the week before that, and s/he ceased to be entitled to IS or income-based JSA because of the employment: para (1)(b).

In both cases, the conditions in paras 1 and 2 of Sch 7 must also be satisfied. Para 1 of Sch 7 sets out matters that must be certified by the DWP. Para 2 of Sch 7 sets out what a claimant or her/his partner must notify the local authority or the DWP and the strict time limit for doing so.

Note that this regulation does not apply to a person who, on the day before IS ceased, was being treated as not in remunerative work under reg 6(5) of the Income Support (General) Regulations 1987: para (7). Reg 6(5) provides a similar scheme for extended payments of IS for home ownership costs (known as "mortgage interest run-on").

For the importance of meeting the precise timing in para (1)(b) see *CH 1762/2004*, where the claimant failed to qualify for an extended payment because, although he had moved from his previous accommodation to take up employment, he did not do so either in the week in which he started his new job or in the previous week.

Paras (2) and (4). Para (2) treats someone to whom para (1) applies as having made a claim for extended payments, so no actual claim for these is necessary. However there is a strict time limit for notifying the matters set out in para 2 of Sch 7; if the claimant fails to notify within the time limit s/he would not satisfy the conditions of para 2 of Sch 7 (see para (1)) and would thus not be entitled to extended payments.

Given that for reg 72 to apply, entitlement to HB has ended under reg 77, a claim for HB *is* needed for entitlement to HB to continue after the extended payments end. Such claims can be given priority under reg 89(3). See paras (6) and (8) for the continuity of such a claim and Sch 7 para 10 where entitlement to HB under the claim is higher than the extended payments.

Para (3). Sub-paras (a) and (b) set out how maximum HB is to be calculated. The effect of these, when combined with the provisions in Sch 7, is as follows:

(1)   Unless the claimant has moved home, the weekly amount of the extended payments is the HB payable in the last full week of the IS or income-based JSA claim (ignoring rent-free weeks): sub-para (a) and Sch 7 para 3.

(2)   Where the claimant has moved (other than to local authority accommodation), the weekly amount of the extended payments is the HB payable in respect of the former home: sub-para (a) and Sch 7 paras 3, 5 and 7(a).

(3)   Where the claimant moves to local authority accommodation, the weekly amount of the extended payments is the eligible rent in the new home minus the non-dependant deductions that applied at the former home: sub-para (b) and Sch 7 paras 3, 6, 7(b) and 8.

Note that where a claim for HB is made (eg, on the basis of income from work) and entitlement under the claim is higher than the extended payments, the extended payments can be topped up under Sch 7 para 10.

Under sub-para (c), the claimant is treated as having no income or capital.

Para (6). Sub-para (a) and Sch 7 para 3 allow for extended payments to be made for four weeks or until liability for rent ends if this is sooner. Note also that by Sch 7 para 3(5) no extended payment can be made for a rent-free period as defined. Where a claim for actual HB is made within the period in sub-para (a) that applies, or in the four weeks after, HB entitlement is deemed to be continuous by sub-para (b). This means that if, for example, someone has a form of transitional protection that demands continuous entitlement, this protection can continue.

Extended payments (severe disablement allowance and incapacity benefit)

73.–(1) Paragraph (2) shall apply where–

(a)   a person ceases to be entitled to housing benefit–

    (i)   in accordance with regulation 78 (date on which entitlement to housing benefit is to end where entitlement to severe disablement allowance or incapacity benefit ceases); and

    (ii)   the condition referred to in paragraph 1 of Schedule 8 (extended payments (severe disablement allowance and incapacity benefit) of housing benefit) is satisfied in his case; or

(b)   a person ceases to be entitled to housing benefit because he has vacated the dwelling which he occupied as his home and the day on which he did so was either in the week in which he took up employment as an employed or self-employed earner, or in the preceding week, and–

    (i)   he ceased to be entitled to severe disablement allowance or incapacity benefit by reason of taking up employment as an employed or self-employed earner;

     (ii)   he had been entitled to and in receipt of severe disablement allowance, incapacity benefit or a combination of severe disablement allowance and incapacity benefit for a continuous period of at least 26 weeks;

     (iii)   he was not entitled to and in receipt of income support; and

     (iv)   the condition referred to in paragraph 1 of Schedule 8 is satisfied in his case.

(2) A person to whom paragraph (1) applies shall be treated as having made a claim under this regulation and his housing benefit shall be determined in accordance with Schedule 8 and any award so determined shall be referred to in these regulations as an ''extended payment (severe disablement allowance and incapacity benefit)''.

(3) For the purposes of any payment pursuant to this regulation–

(a) except in a case to which paragraph (b) applies the maximum housing benefit of any person mentioned in paragraph (1) shall be that which was applicable to him in the last week of the award of housing benefit which has ceased as mentioned in paragraph (1);

(b) the maximum housing benefit of any person the amount of whose extended payment (severe disablement allowance and incapacity benefit) is calculated in accordance with paragraph 6(b)(i) of Schedule 8 shall be determined in accordance with paragraph 7 of that Schedule;

(c) except in a case to which paragraph (d) applies, any person who meets the requirements of paragraph (1) shall be treated as possessing the same amounts of income and capital as they possessed in the last week of the award of housing benefit which has ceased as mentioned in paragraph (1); and

(d) any person whose maximum housing benefit is determined in accordance with paragraph 7 of Schedule 8 shall be treated as possessing no income or capital.

(4) Regulations 82, 83 and 86 (claims, evidence and information) shall not apply to a claim pursuant to this regulation and, subject to regulation 80(7) and Part 9 (calculation of weekly amounts and changes of circumstances) shall not apply to any payment under it.

(5) In paragraph (1), references to a ''person'' include references to a person's partner and references to taking up employment include receiving remuneration for employment or an increased amount of remuneration for employment or engaging in employment for an increased number of hours.

(6) In a case where payment has been made under this regulation–

(a) the beneficiary shall be treated for the purpose of these Regulations as though he were entitled to and in receipt of housing benefit–

     (i)   during the 4 weeks immediately following the last day of his entitlement to housing benefit; or

     (ii)   until the date on which his liability for rent ends,

whichever occurs first; and

(b) any claim for housing benefit made by the beneficiary within the period which under sub-paragraph (a) applies in his case or the 4 weeks thereafter shall be treated as having been made in respect of a period beginning immediately after the end of his previous award of housing benefit.

(7) In paragraph (6), ''these Regulations'' includes the Regulations as modified by paragraphs 4 and 5 of Schedule 3 to the Consequential Provisions Regulations.

General Note

Extended payments of HB and CTB are available to those who were not entitled to and in receipt of IS, whose entitlement to incapacity benefit or severe disablement allowance ended because they started employment as an employed or self-employed earner, or increased earnings from, or hours of, the employment. See also reg 78 and Sch 8.

The qualifying rules are broadly the same as the extended payment rules for those coming off IS or income-based JSA (see reg 72 above and Sch 7).

Non-dependant deductions

74.–(1) Subject to the following provisions of this regulation, the deductions referred to in regulation 70 (maximum housing benefit) shall be–

(a) in respect of a non-dependant aged 18 or over in remunerative work, [⁴ £47.75] per week;

(b) in respect of a non-dependant aged 18 or over to whom sub-paragraph (a) does not apply, [⁴ £7.40] per week.

(2) In the case of a non-dependant aged 18 or over to whom paragraph (1)(a) applies because he is in remunerative work, where it is shown to the appropriate authority that his normal weekly gross income is–

(a) less than [⁵ £111.00], the deduction to be made under this regulation shall be that specified in paragraph 1(b);

(b) not less than [⁵ £111.00] but less than [⁵ £164.00], the deduction to be made under this regulation shall be [⁴ £17.00];

(c) not less than [⁵ £164.00] but less than [⁵ £213.00], the deduction to be made under this regulation shall be [⁴ £23.35];

(d) not less than [⁵ £213.00] but less than [⁵ £283.00], the deduction to be made under this regulation shall be [⁴ £38.20];

(e) not less than [⁵ £283.00] but less than [⁵ £353.00], the deduction to be made under this regulation shall be [⁴ £43.50].

(3) Only one deduction shall be made under this regulation in respect of a couple or, as the case may be, members of a polygamous marriage and, where, but for this paragraph, the amount that would fall to be deducted in respect of one member of a couple or polygamous marriage is higher than the amount (if any) that would fall to be deducted in respect of the other, or any other, member, the higher amount shall be deducted.

(4) In applying the provisions of paragraph (2) in the case of a couple or, as the case may be, a polygamous marriage, regard shall be had, for the purpose of paragraph (2) to the couple's or, as the case may be, all members of the polygamous marriage's joint weekly gross income.

(5) Where a person is a non-dependant in respect of more than one joint occupier of a dwelling (except where the joint occupiers are a couple or members of a polygamous marriage), the deduction in respect of that non-dependant shall be apportioned between the joint occupiers (the amount so apportioned being rounded to the nearest penny) having regard to the number of joint occupiers and the proportion of the payments in respect of the dwelling payable by each of them.

(6) No deduction shall be made in respect of any non-dependants occupying a claimant's dwelling if the claimant or his partner is–

(a) blind or treated as blind by virtue of paragraph 13 of Schedule 3 (additional condition of the higher pensioner and disability premiums); or

(b) receiving in respect of himself either–
 (i) attendance allowance; or
 (ii) the care component of the disability living allowance.

(7) No deduction shall be made in respect of a non-dependant if–

(a) although he resides with the claimant, it appears to the appropriate authority that his normal home is elsewhere; or

(b) he is in receipt of a training allowance paid in connection with a Youth Training Scheme established under section 2 of the 1973 Act or section 2 of the Enterprise and New Towns (Scotland) Act 1990; or

(c) he is a full-time student during a period of study within the meaning of Part 7 (Students); or

(d) he is a full time student and during a recognised summer vacation appropriate to his course he is not in remunerative work; or

(e) he is a full-time student and the claimant or his partner has attained the age of 65; or

(f)   he is not residing with the claimant because he has been a patient for a period in excess of 52 weeks, or a prisoner, and for these purposes–

[¹ (i)   "patient" has the meaning given in paragraph (18) of regulation 7 (circumstances in which a person is or is not to be treated as occupying a dwelling as his home),

(ii)   where a person has been a patient for two or more distinct periods separated by one or more intervals each not exceeding 28 days, he shall be treated as having been a patient continuously for a period equal in duration to the total of those distinct periods, and]

(iii)   "prisoner" means a person who is detained in custody pending trial or sentence upon conviction or under a sentence imposed by a court other than a person who is detained in hospital under the provisions of the Mental Health Act 1983, or, in Scotland, under the provisions of the Mental Health (Care and Treatment) (Scotland) Act 2003 or the Criminal Procedure (Scotland) Act 1995.

(8)   No deduction shall be made in calculating the amount of a rent rebate or allowance in respect of a non-dependant aged less than 25 who is on income support or an income-based jobseeker's allowance.

(9)   In the case of a non-dependant to whom paragraph (2) applies because he is in remunerative work, there shall be disregarded from his weekly gross income–

(a)   any attendance allowance or disability living allowance received by him;

(b)   any payment made under the Macfarlane Trust, the Macfarlane (Special Payments) Trust, the Macfarlane (Special Payments) (No. 2) Trust, the Fund, the Eileen Trust or the Independent Living Funds which had his income fallen to be calculated under regulation 40 (calculation of income other than earnings) would have been disregarded under paragraph 23 of Schedule 5 (income in kind); and

(c)   any payment which had his income fallen to be calculated under regulation 40 would have been disregarded under paragraph 35 of Schedule 5 (payments made under certain trusts and certain other payments).

(10) No deduction shall be made in respect of a non-dependant who is on state pension credit.

Amendments

1.   Amended by reg 2(8) of SI 2005 No 2502 as amended by Sch 2 para 27 of SI 2006 No 217 as from 1.4.06 (3.4.06 where rent payable weekly or at intervals of a week).

2.   Confirmed by Art 19(3) of SI 2006 No 645 and reg 8 of SI 2006 No 217 as from 1.4.06 (3.4.06 where rent payable weekly or at intervals of a week).

3.   Amended by Art 19(3) of SI 2006 No 645 and reg 8 of SI 2006 No 217 as from 1.4.06 (3.4.06 where rent payable weekly or at intervals of a week).

4.   Confirmed by Art 19(3) of SI 2007 No 688 as from 1.4.07 (2.4.07 where rent payable weekly or at intervals of a week).

5.   Amended by Art 19(3) of SI 2007 No 688 as from 1.4.07 (2.4.07 where rent payable weekly or at intervals of a week).

Definitions

"claimant" – see reg 2(1).

"couple" – see reg 2(1).

"disability living allowance" – see reg 2(1).

"dwelling" – see s137(1) of SSCBA and reg 2(4).

"the Macfarlane Trust", "the Macfarlane (Special Payments) Trust", "the Macfarlane (Special Payments)(No 2) Trust", "the Fund", "the Eileen Trust" and "the Independent Living Funds" – see reg 2(1).

"non-dependant" – see reg 3.

"partner"– see reg 2(1).

"period of study" – see reg 53.

"person on an income-based jobseeker's allowance" – see reg 2(3).

"person on income support" – see reg 2(1).

"polygamous marriage" – see reg 2(1).
"rent rebate/allowance" – see ss134(1A) and (1B) and 191 SSAA.
"remunerative work" – see reg 6.
"student" – see reg 53.

General Note

This regulation sets out the situations in which non-dependant deductions must be made from a claimant's "eligible rent" to arrive at maximum HB, and the amounts of the relevant deductions. It is suggested that the appropriate procedure for determining whether a non-dependant deduction is to be made, and if so the amount of the deduction, is as follows:

(1)   The authority should first determine whether the claimant has any "non-dependants" normally residing with her/him. Reg 3 sets out who counts as a non-dependant and who does not. No deduction is applicable at *all* in respect of a person who does not come within the definition of "non-dependant".

(2)   If someone *is* a non-dependant, her/his age is relevant; it is only if s/he is aged 18 or over that a deduction is to be applied: paras (1) and (2).

(3)   If someone is a non-dependant aged 18 or over, it is perhaps easiest to begin by looking at paras (6) to (8) and (10), as they set out the situations in which *no* deductions are to be made in respect of a non-dependant.

(4)   If someone is a non-dependant aged 18 or over and paras (6) to (8) or (10) do *not* apply, paras (1) and (2) set out the relevant amounts of the deductions for different categories of non-dependants. These depend on whether or not the non-dependant is in "remunerative work". If not in remunerative work, the lowest rate deduction is made: para (1)(b). If in remunerative work, the amount of the deduction depends on the income of the non-dependant: paras (1)(a) and (2).

Paras (3) and (4) deal with non-dependants who are couples or partners to a polygamous marriage.

Para (5) deals with the apportionment of non-dependant deductions s where more than one person is liable for the rent on the dwelling in which the non-dependant is living.

Note that any actual payments made to the claimant by the non-dependant are disregarded under para 21 of Sch 5.

Analysis

Paragraphs (1) to (4) and (9): Amounts of deductions

Para (1) sets out the general rule. The deductions provided by this paragraph shall only be made if the non-dependant is 18 or over, and if paras (6) to (8) and (10) do not apply. The lowest rate deduction is made where the non-dependant is not in remunerative work, whatever her/his income: para (1)(b). The highest rate deduction is made where the non-dependant is in remunerative work: (1)(a). This is qualified by para (2) where the non-dependant has income below set levels. Both sub-paras (a) and (b) are qualified by paras (3) to (5).

Higher rates of non-dependant deductions are specified in respect of people who are in "remunerative work" as defined in reg 6. It is suggested that it is for the authority to prove that a person is a non-dependant, and also that such a non-dependant is (or is to be treated as) in remunerative work.

A person is treated as not in remunerative work in various circumstances, under reg 6(5) to (8). These include where s/he has good cause for her/his absence from it, and where s/he is on, for example, sick leave or maternity leave. Likewise, a person on IS or income-based JSA for more than three days in a benefit week is treated as not in remunerative work in that week. In such circumstances, para (1)(a) and (2) will not apply. It would be wrong to assume that only "extended" absences should qualify as "good cause", although of course the absence will have to last at least one benefit week (Monday to Sunday) to be of significance.

Para (2) enables lower rate deductions than that provided by para (1)(a) to be made where the non-dependant is aged 18 or over and is in remunerative work with normal weekly gross income below the levels shown in sub-paras (a) to (e). It is suggested that the burden of proof is on the claimant to show that the non-dependant has a low income. This follows from the words "where it is shown to". However, authorities should bear in mind that non-dependants will often be reluctant to disclose personal financial details and should not just sit back and expect the claimant to obtain the information unassisted.

In *CH 48/2006* the local authority assumed, in the absence of any actual evidence as to what the non-dependant was earning, that the highest rate of non-dependent deduction was to be made from the claimant's maximum CTB. Both the local authority and the tribunal had proceeded on the basis that because no positive evidence from the non-dependant or the claimant had been produced, the very worst had to be assumed. The commissioner recognised that a local authority is entitled to require evidence from claimants under reg 63 CTB Regs 1992 (now reg 72 CTB Regs; the equivalent for HB is reg 86 HB Regs) and that, in the absence of such evidence, it may make adverse inferences. However, any such adverse inferences have to be based in some sense of reality. Authorities have the duty to assess what the likely level of a non-dependant's earnings are, on the evidence available and on the balance of probabilities, and estimate a non-dependent's income, with reasonable adverse assumptions being made where inferences have to be drawn because no evidence is available.

All the non-dependant's income under Part 6 and not just her/his wages must be taken into account.

It is income before the various deductions allowable for tax and other factors under Part 6 have been made, but para (9) provides that income from attendance allowance or disability living allowance and certain other payments should be disregarded in calculating a non-dependant's gross weekly income.

Para (3) provides that there is to be only one non-dependant deduction made per couple or polygamous marriage. The deduction to be made is the highest amount that would apply to any of the individual partners under reg 74(1) or (2).

Para (4) must be read together with para (3). In deciding whether para (2) applies, the gross income of both/all partners is to be taken into account.

Para (9) provides that in calculating the gross weekly income of a non-dependant in remunerative work (para (2)) income from AA or DLA is disregarded. Also disregarded are payments from any of the Macfarlane Trusts, the Fund, the Eileen Trust or the Independent Living Funds.

Paragraph (5): Apportionment

The authority must first decide on the appropriate non-dependant deduction, then apportion it, not simply according to the number of joint occupiers, but also according to the share of the rent each of them pays. Note that this para does not apply where joint occupiers are members of a couple or polygamous marriage as only one of them will be eligible for HB in any case. This para does not apply in respect of boarders who are not non-dependants: see reg 3(2)(e).

"Joint occupier" refers to a person with a joint legal right to occupy the property rather than a person who merely happens to live in the same building: see *R v Chesterfield BC ex p Fullwood* (1993) 26 HLR 126 at 129, CA cited in the Analysis to reg 3((2)(d).

Paragraphs (6) to (8) and (10): Exclusions

Taken together, these paras set out circumstances in which non-dependant deductions are not to be made:

(1)   The claimant or his partner is blind, or is treated as blind: para (6)(a). See Sch 3 para 13 for the circumstances in which a person may be treated as blind. However, it is debatable whether the words "by virtue of" attach to "blind" as well as "treated as blind". If that is so, the claimant would have to show that s/he satisfies Sch 3 para 13(1)(a)(v). The better view is that registration need not be shown and so the sole question is whether on a common-sense view of the state of her/his eyesight, the relevant person can be said to be blind.

(2)   The claimant or her/his partner is receiving AA or DLA care component: para (6)(b).

(3)   The non-dependant's normal home is not with the claimant: para (7)(a). See the Analysis to reg 7(1) for discussion of "normal home".

(4)   Where the non-dependant is in receipt of a training allowance in connection with a youth training scheme under the provisions listed, irrespective of her/his age: para (7)(b).

(5)   Where the non-dependant is a "full-time student" during a "period of study" or where the claimant or her/his partner is 65 or over only, the non-dependant is a "full-time student", whether or not during a period of study: paras (7)(c) and (e). See reg 53 for the definition of those terms.

(6)   Where the non-dependant is a "full-time student", it is the summer vacation and s/he is not in remunerative work: para (7)(d).

(7)   Where the non-dependant has been a patient as defined in reg 7(18) for more than 52 weeks: para (7)(f). See reg 7(18) for a discussion of the term "patient". Note the linking rule in subpara (f)(ii). This allows those who are continuously in and out of hospital to be treated as "patients" in due course. The effect of this is that separate periods spent as a patient which are not more than 28 days apart are added together when calculating the 52 weeks.

(8)   Where the non-dependant is a prisoner: para 7(f). A "prisoner" includes those who are remanded in custody pending trial or sentence as well as those actually serving sentences. It does not, however, include those detained under the mental health legislation, nor those resident in bail hostels: *R(IS) 17/93* para 6.

(9)   Where the non-dependant is aged under 25 and is on IS or incom-based JSA: para (8). For the situations when a person is deemed to be "on" IS or income-based JSA, see reg 2(1) and (3) respectively. This bar to non-dependant deductions only applies where the non-dependant is less than 25. Note that someone is considered to be "on" income-based JSA not only on days when it is payable to her/him, but also on other days, eg when sanctioned for losing a job through misconduct. See the note on reg 2(3).

(10)   Where the non-dependant is on state pension credit: para (10).

Minimum housing benefit

75. Where housing benefit is payable in the form of a rent rebate or allowance, it shall not be payable where the amount to which a person would otherwise be entitled is less than 50 pence per benefit week.

Definitions

"benefit week" – see reg 2(1).

"rent rebate"/"rent allowance" – see ss134(1A) and (1B) and 191 SSAA.

General Note

This prescribes the minimum weekly amount that may be paid to a claimant in respect of the various forms of HB. If the claimant is entitled to less than 50p in respect of a particular category of rebate or allowance, that rebate or allowance shall not be paid.

PART 9

Calculation of weekly amounts and changes of circumstances

General Note on Part 9

Reg 76 provides the rules for deciding in which benefit week the claimant first becomes entitled to HB.

Regs 77 and 78 provide circumstances in which entitlement to HB ends.

Reg 79 sets out the dates on which changes of circumstance are to take effect for the purposes of calculating HB entitlement.

Reg 80 deals with how eligible rent is to be worked out on a weekly basis.

Reg 81 deals with the effect of "rent-free periods" on the calculation of weekly amounts of HB.

Date on which entitlement is to commence

76.–(1) Subject to [¹ paragraphs (2) and (3)], a person who makes a claim and is otherwise entitled to housing benefit shall be entitled to that benefit from the benefit week following the date on which his claim is or is treated as made.

(2) Where a claimant is otherwise entitled to housing benefit and becomes liable, for the first time, to make payments in respect of the dwelling which he occupies as his home in the benefit week in which his claim is or is treated as made, he shall be so entitled from that benefit week.

[¹ (3) A claimant shall become entitled to housing benefit from the benefit week in which the first day in respect of which his claim is made falls, where–

(a)   he is otherwise entitled to housing benefit;

(b)   paragraph (2) does not apply to him; and

[² (c) he becomes liable in that benefit week to make payments, which fall due on a daily basis, in respect of the accommodation listed in paragraph (4) which he occupies as his home.]]

[³ (4) The accommodation referred to in paragraph (3)(c) is–

(a)   a hostel;

(b)   board and lodging accommodation where the payments are to an authority under section 206(2) of the Housing Act 1996 or section 35(2)(b) of the Housing (Scotland) Act 1987;

(c)   accommodation which the authority holds on a licence agreement where the payments are to an authority under section 206(2) of the Housing Act 1996 or section 35(2)(b) of the Housing (Scotland) Act 1987; or

(d)   accommodation outside that authority's Housing Revenue Account which the authority holds on a lease granted for a term not exceeding 10 years.

(5)   In this regulation–

"board and lodging accommodation" means–

(a)   accommodation provided to a person or, if he is a member of a family, to him or any other member of his family, for a charge which is inclusive of the provision of that accommodation and at least some cooked or prepared meals which both are cooked or prepared (by a person other than a person to whom the accommodation is provided or by a member of his family) and are consumed in that accommodation or associated premises; or

(b)   accommodation provided to a person in a hotel, guest house, lodging house or some similar establishment,

but it does not include accommodation in a care home, an Abbeyfield Home, an independent hospital or a hostel; and

"Housing Revenue Account" has the same meaning as for the purposes of Part VIII of the Social Security Administration Act 1992.]

Amendments

1.   Amended by reg 8(4) of SI 2006 No 588 as from 1.4.06.
2.   Substituted by reg 2(2)(a) of SI 2007 No 294 as from 1.4.07.
3.   Inserted by reg 2(2)(b) of SI 2007 No 294 as from 1.4.07.

Definitions

"benefit week" – see reg 2(1).
"dwelling" – see s137(1) SSCBA and reg 2(4).

General Note

Reg 76 deals with when entitlement to HB commences and therefore from when it can be paid. Para (1) sets out the general rule and paras (2) and (3) provide exceptions where people who become liable for rent on their home claim (or are treated as claiming) HB during the same benefit week.

Analysis

Para (1). The general rule is that unless paras (2) or (3) apply, a person's right to payment of the HB to which s/he is entitled usually begins from the "benefit week" (running from Monday to Sunday) following the week in which the claim is made (or treated as made). Reg 83 deals with the dates on which a claim is to be treated as made.

Para (2). There are two conditions which must be satisfied before a claimant's entitlement to HB commences in the benefit week in which s/he claims rather than the one which follows:

(1)   S/he must become liable for rent on the dwelling she occupies as her/his home (see reg 7) for the *first time* during that benefit week (eg, s/he moves into a new home).

(2)   S/he must make her/his claim or be treated as doing so under reg 83 during that week.

The practical effect of this is that if para (2) applies, payment of HB starts from the same day the liability for rent began: see reg 80(2), (4)(a), (5) and (9).

In *Secretary of State for Work and Pensions v Robinson* [2004], 11 February, CA (reported as *R(H) 4/ 04*), the Court of Appeal allowed the Secretary of State's appeal in a case where a claim had been made on 11 March, the same day on which the claimant became liable for rent, but had not moved into the property until 20 March. The commissioner had awarded benefit under para (2) from the benefit week in which 11 March fell. However, the Court of Appeal held that para (2) could not apply on the facts of Ms Robinson's case as, although in the week in which 11 March fell the claimant was liable for the rent on the new dwelling, she was not occupying it as her home, and reg 65(2) HB Regs 1987 (now reg 76(2) HB Regs) – by its use of the phrase "becomes liable for the first time" – only applies where the liability to make payments in respect of the property for the first time coincides with the benefit week in which the claimant meets the other conditions of entitlement to HB. In Ms Robinson's case that did not arise as her liability arose for the first time in the week before she met the other conditions of entitlement for HB (ie, occupying the dwelling as her home) and so the general rule in reg 65(1) HB Regs 1987 applied. However, see reg 7 which allows for some claimants who are moving (or have moved home) to be treated as occupying the new home although they are not actually doing so.

In *R(H) 9/07* the claimant had made a claim for HB in advance of satisfying the rules of entitlement. A few weeks later he moved into his new home. This was in the benefit week following the week his liability for rent began. Applying *Robinson* the local authority awarded HB from the Monday following the date the claimant had moved into his new home. Commissioner Williams agreed this was the date on which this claimant's entitlement commenced. He gave detailed consideration to the interaction between an authorities discretion to treat a claim in advance of entitlement as made in the benefit week preceding the first week of entitlement under reg 76(11) HB Regs 1987 (now reg 83(10) HB Regs), and the rules on commencement of entitlement to HB in reg 65(1) and (2) HB Regs 1987 (now reg 76(1) and (2) HB Regs). The rules in reg 76(1) and (2) apply both to the actual date of claim and to the date treated as the date of claim. He therefore concluded that where a claim in advance is made, and reg 83(10) has been found to be relevant, it must be applied to both. The commissioner set out a helpful step-by-step approach authorities should take in reaching decisions in such cases. An authority should:

(1)   Identify the actual date of claim.

(2)   If the claim is made in the same week as that in which the claimant first becomes liable to make payments for her/his home, apply reg 76(2).

(3)   If on the facts reg 76(2) does not apply, apply reg 76(1).

(4)   Consider if reg 83(10) applies on the facts.

(5)   If reg 83(10) does not apply, the answer is that at step (3).

(6)   If reg 83(10) does apply, apply the date on which the claim is to be treated as made by reg 83(10) to reg 76(2).

(7)   If on the assumption in step (6), reg 76(2) is relevant to the claim, consider, as a matter of discretion, if reg 83(10) is to be applied.

(8)   If regulation 76(2) is not relevant on the assumption in step (6), apply the assumption to reg 76(1). If the answer is different to that given at step (3) consider if that answer should, as a matter of discretion, be applied instead of the answer at step (3).

Note that para (3) was inserted into reg 76 in April 2006. Reg 76(1) is now subject to reg 76(2) *and* (3).

Para (3) provides assistance to those living in the types of accommodation listed in para (4), who become liable for daily payments in respect of that accommodation which they occupy as a home. Unless para (2) applies, entitlement to HB commences in the benefit week in which the first day in respect of which the claim is made falls, which could include where a claim is made for a past period: reg 83.

Date on which housing benefit is to end

77.   A claimant's entitlement to housing benefit shall cease at the end of the benefit week in which entitlement to income support or income-based jobseeker's allowance ceases where–

(a)   the claimant or his partner was entitled to and in receipt of income support or an income-based jobseeker's allowance or that claimant and his partner were entitled to and in receipt of a joint-claim jobseeker's allowance and that entitlement has ceased;

(b)   that entitlement to income support or income-based jobseeker's allowance has ceased by reason of the claimant or his partner–

(i)   commencing employment as an employed or self-employed earner; or

(ii)   increasing their earnings from such employment; or

(iii)   increasing the number of hours worked in such employment;

(c)   the claimant had been entitled to and in receipt of income support or jobseeker's allowance for a continuous period of at least 26 weeks before the day on which his entitlement to income support or income-based jobseeker's allowance ceased, and for the purposes of this sub-paragraph–

(i)   a claimant satisfies the conditions of this sub-paragraph if he has been entitled to and in receipt of a combination of income support and a jobseeker's allowance for at least 26 weeks;

(ii)   the claimant shall be treated as having been entitled to and in receipt of income support or a jobseeker's allowance during any period of less than 5 weeks in respect of which he was not entitled to either of those because, as a consequence of his participation in an employment zone program, he was engaged in remunerative work;

(iii)   references to the claimant include references to his partner;

(iv)   a reference to the claimant being entitled to and in receipt of a jobseeker's allowance shall include a reference to the claimant and his partner being entitled to and in receipt of a joint-claim jobseeker's allowance; and

(d)   that work, increase in earnings or, as the case may be, increase in hours is expected to last at least 5 weeks or more.

General Note

Reg 77 provides a change of circumstances which terminates entitlement to HB, even where there would otherwise be continued entitlement. This is that entitlement to IS or income-based (or joint-claim) JSA has ceased, but *only* in the circumstances described in sub-paras (a) to (d). A fresh claim for HB will be required in these circumstances. Note that where someone ceases to be entitled to HB under reg 77, s/he may qualify for extended payments of HB under reg 72. A fresh claim for HB can be given priority under reg 89(3) where someone is treated as having claimed extended payments of HB under reg 72(2).

It is important to note that it is only in the circumstances described in reg 77 that entitlement to IS or income-based JSA ending has the effect of also ending entitlement to HB. If IS or income-based JSA entitlement ends for other reasons, HB entitlement does not end automatically, although there could be grounds for revision or supersession of the HB award – eg, where income has changed. This has been confirmed in *CH 3736/2006*. The Deputy Commissioner reminded authorities that after the abolition of "benefit periods" in October 2003 (for claimants 60 or over) and in April 2004 (for other claimants), except in the circumstances contemplated by reg 77, the cessation of IS or income-based JSA is an ordinary change of circumstances that must be assessed like any other and it does not have the effect of automatically ending entitlement to HB. It cannot even be assumed that the cessation of IS or income-based JSA will reduce entitlement to HB. Until the authority knows why entitlement has ended, it cannot conclude that it ended in circumstances that will provide grounds upon which to supersede the claimant's entitlement to HB. In cases where it is unclear why benefit has stopped, the correct approach is for the authority to suspend payment of benefit and make further enquiries to establish whether there are grounds for superseding the HB award.

Analysis

There are three conditions that must be satisfied before entitlement to HB ends under this regulation:

(1)   The claimant or her/his partner must have been entitled to IS or income-based JSA (or joint-claim JSA) which has ceased because s/he commenced employment (or self-employment) or increased her/his earnings from, or hours worked in, such employment: sub-paras (a) and (b).

(2)   There must have been continuous entitlement to, and receipt of, the IS or JSA (or a combination of these) for at least 26 weeks: sub-para (c). The 26-week period includes periods of less than five weeks when there was no entitlement because the person participated in an employment zone programme and hence counted as engaged in remunerative work. Remunerative work is defined in reg 6 for HB purposes, but here this must be a reference to such work as defined in the relevant IS and JSA regulations.

(3)   The work or increase in hours or earnings must be expected to last at least five weeks: sub-para (d).

HB entitlement ends at the end of the benefit week in which the entitlement to IS or JSA ceases.

Date on which housing benefit is to end where entitlement to severe disablement allowance or incapacity benefit ceases

78.–(1) A claimant's entitlement to housing benefit shall cease at the end of the benefit week in which entitlement to severe disablement allowance or incapacity benefit ceases where–

(a)   the claimant or his partner was not entitled to and in receipt of income support but was entitled to and in receipt of severe disablement allowance or incapacity benefit and that entitlement has ceased;

(b)   that entitlement to severe disablement allowance or incapacity benefit has ceased by reason of the claimant or his partner–

  (i)   commencing employment as an employed or self-employed earner; or

  (ii)   increasing their earnings from such employment; or

  (iii)   increasing the number of hours worked in such employment;

(c)   the claimant had been entitled to and in receipt of severe disablement allowance or incapacity benefit for a continuous period of at least 26 weeks before the day on which his entitlement to severe disablement allowance or incapacity benefit ceased, and for the purposes of this sub-paragraph–

  (i)   a claimant satisfies the conditions of this sub-paragraph if he has been entitled to and in receipt of a combination of severe disablement allowance and incapacity benefit for at least 26 weeks;

  (ii)   references to the claimant include references to his partner; and

(d)   that work, increase in earnings, or as the case may be, increase in hours is expected to last at least 5 weeks or more.

General Note

Entitlement to HB ends, even where there would otherwise be continued entitlement, where entitlement to severe disablement allowance or incapacity benefit has ceased because of earnings or employment in the circumstances described in this regulation. Note, however, that this only applies if the claimant or her/his partner was not in entitled to, and in receipt of, IS.

The rules are broadly the same as those in reg 77 above. See in particular the General Note to that regulation. See also reg 73 and Sch 8 for the scheme for extended payments in such a situation.

Date on which change of circumstances is to take effect

79.–(1)   Except in cases where [⁵ regulation 34 (disregard of changes in tax, contributions, etc) applies, and subject to regulation 8(3) of the Decisions and Appeals Regulations and] the following provisions of this regulation, and to regulation 80(6), a change of circumstances which affects entitlement to, or the amount of, housing benefit ("change of circumstances") shall take effect from the first day of the benefit week following the date on which the change of circumstances actually occurs, and where that change is cessation of entitlement to any benefit under the benefit Acts, the date on which the change actually occurs shall be the day immediately following the last day of entitlement to that benefit.

[¹ (2)   Subject to paragraph (8) [⁵ and regulation 8(3) of the Decisions and Appeals Regulations] where the change of circumstances is a change in the amount of rent payable in respect of a dwelling, that change shall take effect from the day on which it actually occurs.]

[² (2A)   Subject to paragraphs (8) [⁶ to (10)], except in a case where regulation 8(3) of the Decisions and Appeals Regulations applies, where the change of circumstances is–

(a)   that a person moves into a new dwelling occupied as the home, or

(b)   any other event which–
   (i)   entitles a person to be treated as occupying two dwellings as his home under regulation 7(6), or
   (ii)   brings to an end a person's right to be treated as occupying two dwellings as his home under that regulation, in a case where he has, immediately prior to the event, been treated as occupying two dwellings as his home,

that change of circumstances shall take effect on the day on which it actually occurs.

(2B)   Subject to paragraph (8), where the change of circumstances is the expiry of a maximum period of time, referred to in regulation 7(6), for which a person can be treated as occupying two dwellings as his home, that change shall take effect on the day after the last day of that period]

(3)   Subject to paragraphs (8) [³], where the change of circumstances is an amendment to these Regulations that change, subject to regulation 80(6), shall take effect as follows–

(a)   where the amendment is made by an order under section 150 of the Administration Act (annual up-rating of benefits)–
   (i)   in a case in which the claimant's weekly amount of eligible rent falls to be calculated in accordance with regulation 80(2)(b) [³ or (c)] (calculation of weekly amounts), from 1st April;
   (ii)   in any other case, from the first Monday in April,
in the year in which that order comes into force;

(b)   in respect of any other amendment, from the date on which the amendment of these Regulations comes into force in the particular case.

[¹ (4)   Subject to paragraph (8), if two or more changes of circumstances occurring in the same benefit week would, but for this paragraph, take effect in different benefit weeks in accordance with this regulation, they shall all take effect on the first day of the benefit week in which they occur, unless a change taking effect under paragraphs (2), (2A) or (2B) takes effect in that week, in which case the changes shall all take effect on the day on which that change takes effect.]

(5) Where, during a benefit week commencing on the first Monday in April–

(a) a change of circumstances takes effect in accordance with paragraph (3)(a)(ii);

(b) one or more changes of circumstances occur to which paragraph (1) applies; and

(c) no other change of circumstances occurs to which this regulation applies,

any change of circumstances to which paragraph (1) applies and which occurs in that benefit week shall take effect from the first day of that benefit week.

(6) Where the change of circumstances is that income, or an increase in the amount of income, other than a benefit or an increase in the amount of a benefit under the Act, is paid in respect of a past period and there was no entitlement to income of that amount during that period, the change of circumstances shall take effect from the first day on which such income, had it been paid in that period at intervals appropriate to that income, would have fallen to be taken into account for the purposes of these Regulations.

(7) Without prejudice to paragraph (6), where the change of circumstances is the payment of income, or arrears of income, in respect of a past period, the change of circumstances shall take effect from the first day on which such income, had it been timeously paid in that period at intervals appropriate to that income, would have fallen to be taken into account for the purposes of these Regulations.

[¹ (8) Subject to paragraph (9), where a change of circumstances occurs which has the effect of bringing entitlement to an end it shall take effect on the first day of the benefit week following the benefit week in which that change actually occurs except in a case where a person is liable to make payments, which fall due on a daily basis, [⁴] in which case that change shall take effect on the day on which it actually occurs.

(9) Where the change of circumstances is that a person moves to a new dwelling and immediately after the move he is treated as occupying his former dwelling as his home in accordance with regulation 7(7) or (10) then that change of circumstances shall take effect on the day after the last day for which he is treated as liable to make payments in respect of the former dwelling in accordance with whichever of those regulations applies in his case.]

[⁶ (10) Where the change of circumstances is that the person moves to a new dwelling and immediately before the move that person is treated as occupying the new dwelling in accordance with regulation 7(8) then that change of circumstances shall take effect on the first day on which the person is treated as occupying the new dwelling as the home under that regulation.]

Modifications

Reg 79 applies as if para (7) was omitted where a change of circumstances occurs as a result of the payment of arrears of any income which affects a determination or decision in respect of entitlement to, or the amount of, HB or CTB before 6 March 1995. See Sch 3 para 1 HB&CTB(CP) Regs on p1099.

Amendments

1. Substituted by reg 2(10)(b), (e) and (f) of SI 2005 No 2502 as amended by Sch 2 para 27 of SI 2006 No 217 as from 1.4.06 (3.4.06 where rent payable weekly or at intervals of a week).

2. Inserted by reg 2(10)(c) of SI 2005 No 2502 as amended by Sch 2 para 27 of SI 2006 No 217 as from 1.4.06 (3.4.06 where rent payable weekly or at intervals of a week).

3. Amended by reg 2(10)(d) of SI 2005 No 2502 as amended by Sch 2 para 27 of SI 2006 No 217 as from 1.4.06 (3.4.06 where rent payable weekly or at intervals of a week).

4. Amended by reg 2(3) of SI 2007 No 294 as from 1.4.07.

5. Substituted by reg 4 of SI 2007 No 2470 as from 24.9.07.

6. Amended by reg 11(9) of SI 2007 No 2618 as from 1.10.07.

Definitions

"benefit Acts" – see reg 2(1).

"benefit week" – see reg 2(1).

"rent" – see Part 3.

General Note

Para (1) lays down the general rule as to the date on which changes take effect. Paras (2) to (5) and (8) to (10) set out some exceptional circumstances in which the change affects benefit from the benefit week in which the change actually occurs. But see also regs 34 and 42(8).

This regulation is to be read together with regs 80 and 81 which deal with the ascertainment of weekly amounts of HB.

Analysis

Para (1) contains the general rule that changes in the claimant's circumstances, or those of anyone else whose circumstances affect the claimant's entitlement to HB or how much benefit s/he is due, are to take effect on the first day of the benefit week following the week in which the change takes place, that is, the Monday following the change. The changes referred to in this paragraph need not only be in the claimant's own circumstances. It is the effect of such a change on the claimant's entitlement to HB which is important, rather than who suffers the change.

The general rule does not apply where reg 34 applies. Reg 34 enables certain changes in a claimant's income to be ignored for up to 30 benefit weeks after the week in which they actually take effect.

There are two exceptions referred to:

(1)   By reg 8(3) D&A Regs, where a change is one that is required to be notified and it is advantageous to the claimant, it must be notified within one month of the change (or a longer period in limited circumstances). If the change is notified outside this period, the date of notification is treated as if it is the date the change occurred.

(2)   Reg 80(6) sets the effective date for changes in applicable amounts, income or non-dependant deductions which occur in the same benefit week that a claimant has moved or her/his eligible rent has altered (in specified circumstances).

Paras (2) to (5) and (8) to (10) set out the exceptions to the general rule specified in para (1). They are as follows:

(1)   Changes in rent payable usually take effect from the day the change occurs: para (2). As with para (1) this is subject to reg 8(3) D&A Regs.

(2)   If the change is that the claimant has moved to a new home, or can be (or can no longer be) treated as occupying more than one home under reg 7(6), the change usually takes effect from the day the change occurs: para (2A). As with para (1) there is an exception where reg 8(3) D&A Regs applies.

(3)   If the change is that the maximum period of time for which the claimant can be treated as occupying two homes under reg 7(6) has ended, the change usually takes effect on the day after the last day of the period: para (2B).

(4)   Changes consequent on benefit uprating usually take effect from the first Monday in April. However, where rent is payable monthly or daily, the change usually takes effect from 1 April: para (3)(a). Any other amendments to the regulations usually take effect on the date they come into force: para (3)(b).

(5)   Where more than one change of circumstances occurs in the same benefit week but would take effect in different weeks, they all take effect on the first day of the benefit week in which they occur: para (4). However, where a change referred to in either para (2), (2A) or (2B) takes effect that week, all the changes take effect on the day that change takes effect.

(6)   Where a change consequent on benefit uprating takes effect from the first Monday in April under para (3)(a) and there are changes falling under para (1) in the same week, all changes will take effect on the same date if there are no others: para (5). The purpose of these complex rules is to minimise the need to issue multiple notices of determination each covering just a few days.

(7)   Where a change ends entitlement to HB, it usually takes effect from the first day of the benefit week following the benefit week in which the change occurred: para (8). However, where the claimant is liable for daily payments, the change takes effect on the day it occurs.

(8)   If the change is that the claimant has moved to a new home and immediately after this is treated as occupying a former home under regs 7(7) or (10) (ie where liability for rent there continues and could not be avoided or where there was a fear of violence), the change takes effect on the day after the last day for which s/he is treated as liable to make payments in respect of the former home: para (9).

(9)   If the change is that the claimant has moved to a new home and immediately before the move is treated as occupying the new home under reg 7(8) (ie, where a there was a delay in moving for

specified reasons) the change takes effect on the day on which s/he is treated as occupying the new home.

Para (6) provides that arrears of non-benefit income should be taken into account over the period that it would have been taken into account if it had have been paid on time. For example, if the claimant should have received a pay increase at the end of May but it isn't actually received until the end of August the arrears should be treated as if received at the end of May.

Para (7) deals with difficulties posed by payment of benefit in arrears. Reg 31(2) provides that "The period over which any benefit . . . is to be taken into account shall be the period in respect of which that benefit is payable." Where claimants have received delayed awards of a social security benefit for past periods during the period of their HB or CTB claims authorities may be able to retrospectively alter benefit entitlement under the above rule and reg 4(2)(b) of the HB & CTB (Decisions and Appeals) Regs 2001 (and see also *CH 1561/2005*), thus creating overpayments which they can then seek to recover. But note the possible official error arguments which may arise in these situations: see *CH 943/2003* and commentary to reg 100(2) below. Note also that arrears of some benefits as well as working tax credit, child tax credit and discretionary housing payments count as capital, not income and can be disregarded for a period after they are paid (see Sch 6 para 9).

Calculation of weekly amounts

80.–(1) A person's entitlement to housing benefit in any benefit week shall be calculated in accordance with the following provisions of this regulation.

(2)   The weekly amount of a claimant's eligible rent shall be–

(a)   subject to [¹ paragraph (4)], where rent is payable at intervals of one week or a multiple thereof, the amount of eligible rent payable weekly or, where it is payable at intervals of a multiple of a week, the amount determined by dividing the amount of eligible rent payable by the number equal to the number of weeks in respect of which it is payable; or

[¹ (b) subject to paragraph (4), where the rent is payable at intervals of a calendar month or multiples thereof, the amount determined by dividing the amount payable by the number equal to the number of calendar months in respect of which it is payable, multiplying by 12 and dividing by 52;

(c)   subject to paragraph (4), where the rent is payable at intervals of a day or multiples thereof, the amount determined by dividing the amount payable by the number equal to the number of days in respect of which it is payable and multiplying by 7.]

[² (3)]

[¹ (4)   In a case–

(a)   to which regulation [⁴ 76(2) or (3)] (date on which entitlement is to commence) applies, his eligible rent for the benefit week in which he becomes liable to make payments in respect of a dwelling which he occupies as his home shall be calculated by multiplying his daily rent by the number equal to the number of days in that benefit week for which he is liable to make such payments;

(b)   where a change of circumstances takes effect in a benefit week under regulation 79(2A), (but is not a change described in sub-paragraph (c)(ii) of this regulation), (2B), (8) or (9) other than on the Monday of a benefit week then the claimant's eligible rent for that benefit week shall be calculated by multiplying his daily rent by the appropriate number of days in that benefit week;

(c)   where–

(i)   the amount of eligible rent which the claimant is liable to pay in respect of a dwelling is altered and that change of circumstances takes effect under regulation 79(2), or

(ii)   the claimant–

(aa)   moves to a new dwelling occupied as the home,

(bb)   he is not entitled to be treated, immediately after that move, as occupying two dwellings as his home or as occupying his former dwelling as his home, and (cc) that change of circumstances takes effect under regulation 79(2A),

other than on the Monday of a benefit week, then the claimant's eligible rent for that benefit week shall be calculated by multiplying his old and new daily rent by the number equal to the number of days in that week which relate respectively to the old and new amounts which he is liable to pay.]

(5) In the case of a claimant whose weekly eligible rent falls to be calculated in accordance with paragraph [¹ (4)(a) or (b)] by reference to the daily rent in his case, his weekly applicable amount, weekly income, the weekly amount of any non-dependant deductions and the minimum amount payable in his case shall be calculated in the same manner as his weekly eligible rent by reference to the amounts determined in his case in accordance with Parts 5 to 8 (applicable amounts, income and capital, students and amount of benefit).

(6) Where a change in the amount of a claimant's applicable amount, income or non-dependant deductions falls to be taken into account in the same benefit week as a change in his eligible rent to which paragraph [¹ (4)(c)] applies, it shall be taken into account in that week on a daily basis in the same manner and as if it had occurred on the same day as that change in his eligible rent.

(7) In any case where a claimant has received an extended payment or an extended payment (severe disablement allowance and incapacity benefit), his entitlement shall be adjusted in such circumstances and by such amount as are prescribed in Part 3 of Schedule 7 or paragraph 9 of Schedule 8, as the case may be.

(8) Any amount determined under these Regulations may, if it is appropriate, be rounded to the nearest whole penny by disregarding any amount less than half a penny and treating any amount of half a penny or more as a whole penny.

[³ (9) In this regulation "daily rent" shall mean the amount determined by dividing by 7 the amount determined under whichever sub-paragraph of paragraph (2) is appropriate in each case.

(10) Where a claimant is entitled to benefit in respect of two (but not more than two) dwellings in accordance with regulation 7(6) his eligible rent shall be calculated in respect of each dwelling in accordance with this regulation.]

Definitions

"applicable amount" – see Part 5 and s135 SSCBA.
"benefit week" – see reg 2(1).
"claimant" – see reg 2(1).
"dwelling" – see reg 2(4) and s137(1) SSCBA.
"eligible rent" – see reg 12.
"non-dependant deductions" – see regs 3 and 74.

Amendments

1. Substituted by reg 2(12)(a), (c), (d) and (e) of SI 2005 No 2502 as amended by Sch 2 para 27 of SI 2006 No 217 as from 1.4.06 (3.4.06 where rent payable weekly or at intervals of a week).
2. Omitted by reg 2(12)(b) of SI 2005 No 2502 as amended by Sch 2 para 27 of SI 2006 No 217 as from 1.4.06 (3.4.06 where rent payable weekly or at intervals of a week).
3. Inserted by reg 2(12)(f) of SI 2005 No 2502 as amended by Sch 2 para 27 of SI 2006 No 217 as from 1.4.06 (3.4.06 where rent payable weekly or at intervals of a week).
4. Amended by reg 15(4) of SI 2006 No 2378 as from 2.10.06.

General Note

The calculation of HB is based on weekly amounts. This regulation deals with how a claimant's "eligible rent" (for which see reg 12) is to be calculated on a weekly basis for the purpose of the HB calculation. Note also reg 81 where a claimant has a "rent free period".

The other components in the calculation, namely applicable amounts (Part 5), income (Part 6) and amount of benefit (Part 8), are converted into weekly figures by the Parts which specifically deal with them, and are only affected by this regulation so far as paras (5) and (6) allow.

Para (1) gives effect to the rest of this regulation.

Para (2) is the general rule. A distinction is drawn between claimants who pay rent on a weekly basis or for a period equivalent to a number of weeks (para (2)(a)) and those who pay rent at intervals of a month or a day or multiples of these (paras (2)(b) and (c)).

Para (4) deals with situations where eligible rent must be calculated for part-weeks (ie, where a claimant is not liable for rent for a full week), certain changes of circumstance affect rent due in a week or the amount of rent changes during a week.

Paras (5) and (6) are consequential on para (4) and refer to the quantification of the other components in the HB calculation where a change covered by para (4) has occurred.

Para (7), together with reg 72 and 73 and Schs 7 and 8, makes provisions for adjusting ongoing HB entitlement where extended payments of benefit are paid.

Para (8) allows for the rounding of figures determined under the regulations.

Para (9) defines "daily rent" for the purpose of para (4).

Para (10) makes it clear that where a claimant is entitled to HB for two homes, the eligible rent for each dwelling is calculated separately under this regulation.

The interaction between reg 79 and reg 80(4) to (6) is that reg 79 operates to fix the benefit week in which changes of circumstances are to take effect, and paras (4) to (6) of reg 80 provide how such a change is to affect the weekly amount of benefit due for the benefit week in question.

Analysis

Para (2) sets out the general rules for determining weekly amounts of eligible rent in circumstances where para (4) is not applicable.

Para (2)(a) provides that where rent is payable weekly, the weekly, eligible rent is the amount actually paid. Where rent is paid for a multiple of weeks, weekly eligible rent is the total payable for that period divided by the number of weeks in it (eg, where rent is paid fortnightly, the rent payable is divided by 2).

Para (2)(b) provides that the where rent is payable at intervals of (or in multiples of) a calendar month, weekly eligible rent is the total payable for the period divided by the number of months for that period, then multiplied by 12 and divided by 52.

Para (2)(c) provides that where rent is payable at intervals of (or in multiples of) a day, weekly eligible rent is the amount payable divided by the number of days in the period, then multiplied by 7.

Para (4) sets out the circumstances in which the normal rules in para (2) do not apply. The effect of para (4) combined with paras (5) and (6) is that for the week affected, eligible rent is calculated for a part-week on a daily basis. There are three situations:

(1) Where a claimant's entitlement to HB commences in her/his week of claim (rather than the week after) – ie, s/he both claims (or is treated as claiming) HB and first becomes liable to pay rent on her/his dwelling in the same week or becomes liable for daily payments in specified types of accommodation which s/he occupies as a home (see reg 76(2) and (3): sub-para (a). In such cases, eligible rent for the week in which s/he becomes liable (ie the first week of claim) is calculated by multiplying "daily rent" by the number of days in the week for which the claimant is liable to make payments.

(2) Where a change of circumstances takes effect other than on a Monday under reg 79(2A) (other than where para (c)(ii) of this reg applies, for which see below), (2B), (8) or (9) (all situations where the change takes effect during the week the change occurred rather than from the start of the next benefit week): sub-para (b). In such cases, eligible rent for the week in which the change takes effect is calculated by multiplying "daily rent" by the appropriate number of days in the benefit week.

(3) Where a change in the rent payable takes effect on the day it occurs under reg 79(2) or a claimant moves, cannot be treated as occupying the former home for HB purposes and the change takes effect on the day it occurs under reg 79(2A) and in both cases, this is other than on the Monday of a benefit week: sub-para (c). In such cases, eligible rent for the week in which the change takes effect is calculated by multiplying the old and the new "daily rent" by the number of days in the week for which the claimant is liable to pay each of these.

"Daily rent" for all three purposes is defined in para (9).

Para (5). In the first two situations (where para (4)(a) or (b) applies), HB entitlement is calculated for the part-week only. The other components which determine the amount of HB to which the claimant is entitled in that week are adjusted in the same manner as her/his eligible rent so that they, too, only relate to the number of days for which the claimant is liable to rent.

Para (6). In the third situation (where para (4)(c) applies), and in the same benefit week as her/his eligible rent alters, a change in one of the other components which affect her/his entitlement to HB takes effect, the weekly amount of that other component is calculated in the same way as the eligible rent, that is by apportioning the old and new amounts according to the number of days to which they relate.

Example: A claimant moves into a new home and claims HB in the same week (on a Friday). Her rent is £325 a calendar month. Applying reg 80(2)(b), her normal weekly eligible rent is £325 times 12 divided by 52 = £75. Applying reg 80(4)(a), her eligible rent for the first benefit week of entitlement is £75 divided by 7 times 3 days = £32.14. The other components determining the amount of HB are also apportioned for that week, applying reg 80(6).

Rent free periods

81.–(1) This regulation applies to a claimant for any period (referred to in this regulation as a rent free period) in, or in respect of, which he is not liable to pay rent except for any period to which regulation 8(1)(d) (waiver of rent by landlord in return for work done) applies.

[¹ (2)   In the case of the beginning or ending of a claimant's rent-free period, his eligible rent for the benefit week in which the rent free period begins and ends shall be calculated on a daily basis as if those benefit weeks were weeks to which regulation 80(4) applies.]

(3)   For the purpose of determining the weekly applicable amount and income of a claimant to whom this regulation applies, the weekly amount of any non-dependant deductions and the minimum amount payable in his case–

(a)   in a case to which regulation 80(2)(a) applies, the amounts determined in his case in accordance with Parts 5 to 8 (applicable amounts, income and capital, students and amount of benefit) shall be multiplied by 52 or 53, whichever is appropriate, and divided by the number equal to the number of weeks in that 52 or 53 week period in respect of which he is liable to pay rent;

(b)   subject to paragraph (4), in a case to which regulation 80(2)(b) [² or (c)] applies, the amounts determined in his case in accordance with Parts 5 to 8 shall be multiplied by 365 or 366, whichever is appropriate and divided by the number of days in that 365 or 366 day period in respect of which he is liable to pay rent.

(4)   In a case to which paragraph (3)(b) applies, where either regulation 80(5) or (6) also applies or it is the beginning or end of a rent-free period, the weekly amounts referred to in paragraph (3) shall first be calculated in accordance with sub-paragraph (b) of that paragraph and then determined on a daily basis in the same manner as the claimant's eligible rent.

Amendments
1.   Substituted by reg 2(13)(a) of SI 2005 No 2502 as amended by Sch 2 para 27 of SI 2006 No 217 as from 1.4.06 (3.4.06 where rent payable weekly or at intervals of a week).
2.   Amended by reg 2(13)(b) of SI 2005 No 2502 as amended by Sch 2 para 27 of SI 2006 No 217 as from 1.4.06 (3.4.06 where rent payable weekly or at intervals of a week).

Definitions
"applicable amount" – see reg 22 and s135 SSCBA.
"benefit week" – see reg 2(1).
"claimant" – see reg 2(1).
"eligible rent" – see reg 12.
"non-dependant deductions" – see regs 3 and 74.
"rent" – see Part 3.

General Note
Para (1) applies this regulation to a claimant in a "rent-free period". Those are periods in which (or in respect of which) a claimant who is normally liable to pay rent is not liable – eg, where a tenant pays rent over 48 weeks and has a rent-free period for the Christmas holidays. Reg 81 does not apply where the claimant is treated as liable for rent under reg 8(1)(d), ie where her/his rent has been waived temporarilly to compensate for work done.

Para (2) deals with eligible rent for the weeks in which the rent free period begins and ends.

Paras (3) and (4) deal with adjustments to the other components in the HB calculation. Because the claimant will not be entitled to HB during a rent-free period because s/he is not then *liable* for rent as required by s130(1)(a) SSCBA and or treated as liable by reg 8, this regulation provides that the various other components in the calculation of HB are adjusted to ensure that s/he does not receive more HB than s/he otherwise would during a year on account of having rent-free weeks. It works by ensuring that *all* of her/his assessable income for that year including that paid in respect of rent-free weeks, is taken into account during the weeks in which s/he actually pays rent, and correspondingly that the non-dependant deductions and applicable amounts which would normally be taken into account over a whole year are taken into account during those same weeks.

Analysis

Para (2). In all cases, eligible rent in the benefit weeks in which the rent free period begins and ends is calculated on a daily basis as if reg 80(4) applies. See the note on that provision. Sch 1 para 7(2) also affects the calculation of weekly fixed rate ineligible service charges where there are rent free periods.

Para (3). A distinction is drawn between situations where rent is payable weekly (sub-para (a)) or monthly or daily (sub-para (b)) or in multiples of those periods. Where rent is payable weekly, weekly income, applicable amounts and non-dependant deductions are multiplied by 52 (or 53 as appropriate) to give annual amounts. These are then divided by the number of weeks in that 52 (or 53) week period in respect of which there is a liability to pay rent. Where rent is payable monthly or daily the figures are multiplied by 365 (or 366 as appropriate) and the result then divided by the number of days in that 365 (or 366) day period in respect of which there is a liability to pay rent. So for example, where rent is payable monthly other than in December (31 days), all the figures are multiplied by 365 and divided by 334 (365 − 31).

Para (4) qualifies the process under para (3)(b) where reg 80(5) or (6) apply or it is the beginning or end of the rent free period. Amounts produced under para (3)(b) are calculated first, then the daily rate is worked out in the same way as eligible rent under reg 80.

PART 10

Claims

General Note on Part 10

This Part regulates how, and by whom, claims for HB are to be made, the fixing of the date on which the claim is treated as having been made, the authority's rights to require supporting evidence and the duty of the claimant (and certain other people) to notify the authority of changes in circumstances.

Who may claim

82.–(1)   In the case of a couple or members of a polygamous marriage a claim shall be made by whichever one of them they agree should so claim or, in default of agreement, by such one of them as the relevant authority shall determine.

(2)   Where a person who is liable to make payments in respect of a dwelling is unable for the time being to act, and–

(a)   a [¹ deputy] has been appointed by the Court of Protection with power to claim, or as the case may be, receive benefit on his behalf; or

(b)   in Scotland, his estate is being administered by a judicial factor or any guardian acting or appointed under the Adults with Incapacity (Scotland) Act 2000 who has power to claim or, as the case may be, receive benefit on his behalf; or

(c)   an attorney with a general power or a power to claim or as the case may be, receive benefit, has been appointed by that person under [¹ the Powers of Attorney Act 1971, the Enduring Powers of Attorney Act 1985 or the Mental Capacity Act 2005 or otherwise],

that [¹ deputy], judicial factor, guardian or attorney, as the case may be, may make a claim on behalf of that person.

(3)   Where a person who is liable to make payments in respect of a dwelling is unable for the time being to act and paragraph (2) does not apply to him, the relevant authority may, upon written application made to them by a person who, if a natural person, is over the age of 18, appoint that person to exercise on behalf of the person who is unable to act, any right to which that person might be entitled under the Act and to receive and deal on his behalf with any sums payable to him.

(4)   Where the relevant authority has made an appointment under paragraph (3) or treated a person as an appointee under paragraph (5)–

(a)   it may at any time revoke the appointment;

(b)   the person appointed may resign his office after having given 4 weeks notice in writing to the relevant authority of his intention to do so;

(c)   any such appointment shall terminate when the relevant authority is notified that a receiver or other person to whom paragraph (2)(b) or (c) applies has been appointed.

(5)   Where a person who is liable to make payments in respect of a dwelling is for the time being unable to act and the Secretary of State has appointed a person to act on his behalf for the purposes of the Act the relevant authority may, if that person agrees, treat him as if he had been appointed by them under paragraph (3).

(6)   Anything required by these Regulations to be done by or to any person who is for the time being unable to act may be done by or to the [¹ deputy], judicial factor, guardian or attorney, if any, or by or to the person appointed or treated as appointed under this regulation and the receipt of any such person so appointed shall be a good discharge to the relevant authority for any sum paid.

(7)   Where a claim is made at an office displaying the ONE logo, references in this regulation to a "relevant authority" shall be read as including a reference to the "designated authority".

Definitions

"claim" – see reg 2(1).
"designated authority" – see reg 2(1).
"dwelling" – see reg 2(4) and s137(1) SSCBA.
"liable to make payments" – see regs 8 and 9.
"polygamous marriage" – see reg 2(1).

Amendment

1.   Substituted by reg 11(10) of SI 2007 No 2618 as from 1.10.07.

General Note

The general rule (which is not expressly spelled out in the regulations) is that it is the person who "is liable to make payments in respect of a dwelling . . . which he occupies as his home" (see s130 SSCBA) who must make the claim for benefit required by s1 SSAA. Problems can however arise if that person is unable to manage her/his own affairs or if more than one member of the household is potentially eligible to claim by virtue of reg 8(1). This regulation makes provision for such cases.

In ONE areas, para (7) requires decisions as to who can claim to be made by a designated authority. It is understood that since autumn 2006 there have no longer been any ONE offices.

Analysis

Paragraph (1): The general rule

The effect of this paragraph is that only one partner in a couple or a polygamous marriage may claim HB in respect of the same dwelling. There is, therefore, no such thing as a joint claim for HB: *CH 3817/2004* (para 8). If the parties to the relationship cannot agree who is to claim, the authority must decide.

Paragraphs (2) to (5): Claims on behalf of claimants

Paras (2) to (5) are made under powers given to the Secretary of State by s5(1)(g) and (2)(e) of SSAA and cover the situation where the person who is liable to pay the rent is "unable for the time being to act". This will usually be because that person is mentally or physically incapable of managing her/his affairs permanently, but it would also cover a temporary incapacity – eg, following an accident. The quoted phrase is apt to cover inability to act, however caused, and the regulation is not restricted either to medical incapacities or to mental illness or handicap. It could, for example, apply to those with language difficulties.

Para (2) states that the representative of a person unable to act will be an attorney with powers to claim and receive benefit; or a deputy appointed by the Court of Protection in England and Wales with such powers; or a judicial factor or guardian in Scotland. The attorney, deputy, or judicial factor etc. may claim and receive HB on the liable person's behalf. Note that if the conditions of para (2) are satisfied, the authority has no choice but to accept a claim from a person who comes within sub-paras (a) to (c).

Paras (3) to (5) permit the authority to appoint someone to act on the claimant's behalf if s/he is unable to act. An appointee must, if s/he is a natural person as opposed to a corporate body, be aged over

18 and must apply for the appointment in writing: para (3). The authority may revoke the appointment under para (4)(a) or the appointee may resign on four weeks' notice under para (4)(b). This is so even if there is no other person who is prepared to claim on behalf of the liable person. If a person falling within para (2) is appointed, any appointment made under para (3) ceases: para (4)(c). If an appointment has been made by the DWP, the appointee may also act in relation to HB: para (5). A person who is unable to act but is otherwise eligible for HB will probably also be entitled to other benefits under SSCBA. This will usually be the most convenient course, but the authority is not under an absolute duty to accede to the request. Again, the only legal obligation is to exercise the discretion reasonably having regard to all the relevant circumstances of each individual case and directing itself properly as to the applicable law.

In most cases the identity of the most suitable appointee will be readily apparent. If, however, there are competing candidates, or if the most obvious person is thought to be unsuitable (perhaps because s/he is felt to be taking advantage of the liable person's vulnerability or has criminal convictions for offences of dishonesty in connection with social security benefits), the authority must exercise the discretion to appoint in accordance with the general principles of administrative law, having regard to all the relevant circumstances of each individual case. Although the paragraph is silent, it is doubted that an authority could lawfully stop a person who is unable to act from claiming HB by refusing everyone who applies to be appointed. If it is felt desirable to do so in order to protect the interests of the person who is unable to act, the authority could, in an appropriate case, appoint one of its own officers or an officer of the local social services authority to claim and receive HB (which would then usually be paid direct to the landlord). Any local government officer so appointed should always bear in mind her/his personal obligations under para (6) and possible liability to repay any benefit which may be overpaid.

Claims by agents. It may be that a liable person who is mentally competent is able to appoint an agent to claim benefit on her/his behalf whether or not s/he is "unable for the time being to act" and without formally granting the agent a power of attorney. It is a general principle of the common law that a person who may lawfully do an act her/himself may appoint another to do it for her/him as agent and in *R v Stoke-on-Trent CC ex p Highgate Projects* [1993] 26 HLR 551, QBD it was said in the context of an application for review that, as the claimants were legally competent, they could authorise their landlords to act for them as agent.

As a matter of the law of agency there is no reason why the appointment of an agent should even be in writing but, in practical terms, an authority is unlikely to accept on a balance of probabilities that an agency has been created unless the agent can produce some written evidence of her/his authority.

Para (6) empowers anyone appointed under paras (2) or (3) (or treated as appointed under para (5)) to do anything the regulations require a claimant to do and allows the authority to act towards the appointee as if s/he were a claimant. A receipt for HB received by the appointee discharges the authority from any obligation under the regulations to pay that HB to the claimant.

Time and manner in which claims are to be made

83.–(1)　[¹ Subject to paragraph (4A),] Every claim shall be in writing and made on a properly completed form approved for the purpose by the relevant authority or in such written form as the relevant authority may accept as sufficient in the circumstances of any particular case or class of cases having regard to the sufficiency of the written information and evidence.

(2)　The forms approved for the purpose of claiming shall be provided free of charge by the relevant authority or such persons as they may authorise or appoint for the purpose.

(3)　Each relevant authority shall notify the Secretary of State of the address to which claims delivered or sent to the appropriate DWP office are to be forwarded.

(4)　A claim [¹ in writing]–

(a)　may be sent or delivered to the appropriate DWP office where the claimant or his partner is also claiming income support, incapacity benefit, state pension credit or a jobseeker's allowance;

(b)　where it has not been sent or delivered to the appropriate DWP office, shall be sent or delivered to the designated office;

(c)　sent or delivered to the appropriate DWP office, other than one sent on the same form as a claim being made to income support, incapacity benefit or a jobseeker's allowance and as approved by the Secretary of State for the purpose of the benefits being claimed, shall be forwarded to the relevant authority within two working days of the date of the receipt of the claim at the appropriate DWP office, or as soon as practicable thereafter;

(d)   may, in the case of a claimant who has attained the age of 16 but not the age of 60 and is not engaged in remunerative work, be sent or delivered to a gateway office;

(e)   may be sent or delivered where the claimant has attained the age of 16 but not the age of 60 to an office or designated authority displaying the ONE logo;

(f)   where the claimant has attained the qualifying age for state pension credit, may be sent or delivered to an authorised office.

[³ (g)   may be sent or delivered to the offices of a county council in England if the council has arranged with the relevant authority for claims to be received at their offices (''county offices'').]

[¹ (4A)   the relevant authority has published a telephone number for the purpose of receiving claims for housing benefit, a claim may be made by telephone to that telephone number.

(4B)   The relevant authority may determine, in any particular case, that a claim made by telephone is not a valid claim unless the person making the claim approves a written statement of his circumstances, provided for the purpose by the relevant authority.

(4C)   A claim made by telephone in accordance with paragraph (4A) is defective unless the relevant authority is provided during that telephone call with all the information it requires to determine the claim.

(4D)   Where a claim made by telephone in accordance with paragraph (4A) is defective, the relevant authority is to provide the person making it with an opportunity to correct the defect.

(4E)   If the person corrects the defect within one month, or such longer period as the relevant authority considers reasonable, of the date it last drew attention to it, the relevant authority shall treat the claim as if it had been duly made in the first instance.]

(5)   Subject to paragraph (10), and to regulation 84 (date of claim where claim sent or delivered to a gateway office) the date on which a claim is made shall be–

(a)   in a case where an award of income support or an income-based jobseeker's allowance has been made to the claimant or his partner and the claim for housing benefit is made within one month of the date on which the claim for that income support or jobseeker's allowance was received at the appropriate DWP office, the first day of entitlement to income support or an income-based jobseeker's allowance arising from that claim; and for the purposes of this sub-paragraph a person who has an award entitling him to an income-based jobseeker's allowance shall be treated as also entitled to an income-based jobseeker's allowance for any days which immediately precede the first day in that award and on which in accordance with paragraph 4 of Schedule 1 to the Jobseekers Act (waiting days) he would not be entitled to that allowance;

(b)   in a case where the claimant or his partner is a person on income support or an income-based jobseeker's allowance and he becomes liable for the first time to make payments in respect of the dwelling which he occupies as his home, where the claim is received at the designated office or appropriate DWP office within one month of the claimant first becoming liable for such payments, the date he became liable for those payments;

(c)   in a case where the claimant is the former partner of a person who was, at the date of his death or their separation, entitled to housing benefit and the claimant makes a claim within one month of the date of the death or the separation, that date;

(d)   except where sub-paragraph (a), (b) or (c) is satisfied, in a case where a properly completed claim is received in a designated office, an authorised office [³ , county offices] or an appropriate DWP office within one month, or such longer period as the relevant authority considers reasonable, of the date on which the claim form was issued following the claimant first notifying, by whatever means, a designated office, an authorised office [³ , county offices] or an appropriate DWP office of his intention of making a claim, the date of first notification; and

(e)   in any other case, the date on which the claim is received at the designated office, authorised office [³ , county offices] or appropriate DWP office.

(6)   Where a claim received at the designated office has not been made in the manner prescribed in paragraph (1), that claim is for the purposes of these Regulations defective.

(7)   Where a claim is defective because–

(a)   it was made on the form approved for the purpose but that form is not accepted by the relevant authority as being properly completed; or

(b)   it was made in writing but not on the form approved for the purpose and the relevant authority does not accept the claim as being in a written form which is sufficient in the circumstances of the case having regard to the sufficiency of the written information and evidence,

the relevant authority may, in a case to which sub-paragraph (a) applies, request the claimant to complete the defective claim or, in the case to which sub-paragraph (b) applies, supply the claimant with the approved form or request further information or evidence.

(8)   The relevant authority shall treat a defective claim as if it had been validly made in the first instance if–

(a)   where paragraph (7)(a) applies, the authority receives at the designated office the properly completed claim or the information requested to complete it or the evidence within one month of the request, or such longer period as the relevant authority may consider reasonable; or

(b)   where paragraph (7)(b) applies–

(i)   the approved form sent to the claimant is received at the designated office properly completed within one month of it having been sent to him; or, as the case may be,

(ii)   the claimant supplies whatever information or evidence was requested under paragraph (7) within one month of the request,

or within such longer period as the relevant authority may consider reasonable.

(9)   A claim which is made on an approved form for the time being is, for the purposes of this regulation, properly completed if completed in accordance with the instructions on the form, including any instructions to provide information and evidence in connection with the claim.

[² (10)   Except in the case of a claim made by a person from abroad, where the claimant is not entitled to housing benefit in the benefit week immediately following the date of his claim but the relevant authority is of the opinion that unless there is a change of circumstances he will be entitled to housing benefit for a period beginning not later than the thirteenth benefit week following the date on which the claim is made, the relevant authority may treat the claim as made on a date in the benefit week immediately preceding the first benefit week of that period of entitlement and award benefit accordingly.]

(11)   In the case of a person who has attained, or whose partner has attained, the age of 59 years and 35 weeks, paragraph (10) shall apply as if for the reference to the thirteenth benefit week, there was substituted a reference to the seventeenth benefit week.

(12)   Where the claimant makes a claim in respect of a past period (a ''claim for backdating'') and, from a day in that period up to the date of the claim for backdating,

he had continuous good cause for his failure to make a claim, his claim in respect of that period shall be treated as made on–

(a)   the first day from which he had continuous good cause; or

(b)   the day 52 weeks before the date of the claim for backdating,

whichever fell later.

(13)   In this regulation ''authorised office'' means an office which is nominated by the Secretary of State and authorised by the relevant authority for receiving claims for decision by the relevant authority.

Definitions

"appropriate DWP office" – see reg 2(1).

"benefit week" – see reg 2(1).

"claimant" – see reg 2(1).

"claim" – see reg 2(1).

"gateway office" – see reg 2(1).

"partner" – see reg 2(1).

"person from abroad" – see reg 10.

"remunerative work" – see reg 6.

Amendments

1.   Inserted by reg 2(2) of SI 2006 No 2967 as from 20.12.06.

2.   Substituted by reg 3 of SI 2007 No 1331 as from 23.5.07.

3.   Amended by reg 7(2) of SI 2007 No 2911 as from 31.10.07.

General Note

Paras (1) to (4A) and (9) deal with how written and telephone claims are to be made. Para (5) provides for the date on which the claim is to be treated as made. Paras (4E), (8), (10) and (12) effectively qualify para (5) as they affect the date the claim is treated as made.

Paras (4B) to (4E) and (6) to (8) deal with rectification of claims not made in the proper manner. Para (10) deals with claims made in advance of entitlement and para (12) with backdating.

See also reg 86 for the evidence and information that can be required by an authority to support a claim and reg 87 for when a claim may be amended or withdrawn.

Analysis

Paragraphs (1) to (3): General requirements in relation to claims

Para (1), together with para (2),deals with the form a claim must take. Unless a telephone claim can be made, for which see para (4A), claims must be in writing, and normally made on a form, approved by the local authority for this purpose, which has been "properly completed": see para (9). However, the authority has a discretion to accept a claim in some other written form, if it considers the written information and evidence to be "sufficient in the circumstances". Note also that a claim can be made by means of an electronic communication if the conditions in sch 11 are satisfied: reg 83A.

Local authorities may have their own approved forms. These may be (or be based on) the model form HCTB1 (HCTB1(LHA) in the "local housing allowance" pathfinder areas; HCTB1(PCA) or HCTB1(PC) if the claimant or partner is 60 or over and not claiming IS or income-based JSA) available on the DWP website at www.dwp.gov.uk/housingbenefit/model.

A "rapid reclaim" form (HBRR1) can be accepted where a claimant is reclaiming IS, JSA or incapacity benefit (IB) at the same time as HB and this is within 12 weeks of a previous entitlement ending. This will only apply if s/he is entitled to IS, JSA or IB and her/his circumstances have not changed since s/he was last claiming HB: GM 2.560-565. The form is issued by JobCentre Plus offices to claimants who may be eligible.

Para (2) enables the authority to provide the approved forms referred to in para (1) itself, or to authorise or appoint someone else to provide them. In either case, the forms must be provided free of charge to claimants.

Para (3) is linked with para (4) and deals with the situation in which an HB claim is sent by an IS, IB, state pension credit or JSA claimant to a DWP office. The authority must tell the Secretary of State where it wishes the DWP to forward such claims.

Paragraph (4): Place of claim

Para (4) deals with the place to which a written HB claim may be sent or delivered. There are a number of possibilities according to the circumstances of the claimant.

(1) If the claimant (or her/his partner) is also claiming IS, JSA or IB, the HB claim can be sent or delivered to either the "appropriate DWP office" or the authority's "designated office" (both defined in reg 2(1)): sub-paras (a) and (b). The standard practice is to issue IS and JSA claimants with a standard housing benefit claim form HCTB1, together with their IS or JSA claim form. If claims for IS or JSA are made in JobCentre Plus offices, the HB claim is completed at the same time (and is referred to as an "input document"). Authorities may then send a claimant its own form to fill in, but the date of claim remains that set by para (5) below.

Sub-para (c) then provides that where a claim has been sent or delivered to the "appropriate DWP office", that office should send the claim to the authority within two working days of the date on which the HB claim is actually received. If this is not achieved, the claim must be sent on "as soon as practicable" after that. This requirement does not apply if the HB claim is made on the same form as that for IS, JSA or IB. The regulation does not set a time limit in such a situation.

Note that sub-paras (a) and (b) also make reference to those claiming state pension credit. As the HB Regs were a consolidation exercise, some regulations (and parts of regulations) had to be kept in, although they were otiose. This is one such provision. The time and manner in which HB claims are to be made by those of at least the qualifying age for state pension credit, not on IS or income-based JSA are now dealt with by reg 64 HB(SPC) Regs.

(2) Other HB claimants *must* send or deliver their claims to the authority's "designated office" (defined in reg 2(1): sub-para (b).

Sub-paras (d) to (g) allow claims to be sent or delivered to a "gateway office", a "ONE" office, an "authorised office" or the offices of a county council in the circumstances set out. In the cases of sub-paras (d) and (e), the date of claim will be ascertained under reg 84 or 85 rather than para (5). It is understood that since autumn 2006 there have no longer been any ONE offices.

Paragraphs (4A) and (4B): Telephone claims

Under para (4A), a claim for HB can be made by telephone where the local authority has published a telephone number for this purpose and the claim is made to that telephone number. The local authority might then provide a written statement of the claimant's circumstances for her/him to approve. The telephone claim might not be accepted as valid if the statement is not then approved: para (4B).

Note that even where a telephone claim is not permitted, a claimant can notify her/his intention to claim by telephone (or other means). If a written claim is then submitted within one month, the claim can be backdated to the date of notification: see para (5)(d) below.

Paragraphs (4C)-(4E): Validity of telephone claims

These mirror the rules in paras (6) to (9) which allow a claimant to remedy a defective written claim. A claim made by telephone is defective unless the claimant provides the local authority with all the information it requires during the telephone call: para (4C). However, if a claim is defective, the local authority must provide the claimant with an opportunity to correct the defect: para (4D). If the defect is corrected within one month of it being drawn to the claimant's attention, or within a longer period considered "reasonable" by the authority, the claim must be treated as if it was properly made in the first instance: para (4E).

Paragraph (5): Date that a claim is treated as made

This deals with the date on which a claim made in the proper manner (be it in writing, by telephone or by electronic communication) must be treated as being made. It is qualified by paras (4E), (8), (10) and (12).

Sub-paras (d) and (e): The general rules. The date on which a claim is treated as made is usually the earliest of the following:

(1) The date the claimant first notified a "designated office", an "authorised office" (see para (13)), "county offices" (see para (4)(g)) or an "appropriate DWP office", by whatever means, of her/his intention to claim, if a properly completed claim form is received in one of those offices within one month of the form being issued (or a longer period if the authority considers this reasonable): sub-para (d).

"By whatever means" could include by telephone or in person, or where someone notifies the claimant's intention on her/his behalf.

However, claimants and those advising them should note that in the event of a subsequent dispute, the absence of a written notification may cause evidential difficulties. Claimants should keep careful contemporaneous notes of any oral notification. Note that the one month (or longer) time limit for returning the claim form runs from the date it was issued, but if that time limit is met then the claim can be fixed as having been made on an earlier date than this even if there is a gap between the claimant contacting one of the offices saying they want to claim HB and the claim form then being issued to them, thus insulating the claimant from any administrative delays on the part of the authority in issuing the claim form.

(2) The date the claim is received at the "designated office", "authorised office", "county offices" or "appropriate DWP office": sub-para (e).

Sub-paras (a) to (c): The exceptions. There are three exceptions to the general rule.

(1)   If a claimant (or her/his partner) has been awarded IS or income-based JSA, and the HB claim is made within one month of the date on which the claim for IS or JSA was received at the "appropriate DWP", s/he will be treated as claiming HB on the first day on which s/he (or her/his partner) became entitled to IS/income-based JSA: sub-para (a). On new claims for income-based JSA the claimant normally has to serve three waiting days before being entitled to that benefit. However, for the purposes of para (5)(a) claimants are to be treated as if they are entitled to income-based JSA for any waiting days (which can be three or fewer if the claimant has interrupted the claim), if the waiting days immediately precede payment of income-based JSA. This means that they will be entitled to maximum HB (and CTB) from the outset. Liaison between the DWP and authorities in this respect will undoubtedly give rise to problems: both will have to be careful about recording the dates on which forms are received.

(2)   If a claimant (or her/his partner) is on IS or income-based JSA when s/he becomes liable for rent in a dwelling occupied as a home for the first time (eg, where s/he moves), s/he will be treated as claiming HB on the date s/he first became liable if the HB claim is received at a "designated office" or "appropriate DWP office" within one month of becoming liable: sub-para (b).

(3)   Sub-para (c) gives some relief from immediately having to claim when a couple relationship comes to an end either due to separation or the death of one of the couple. Where the claimant's former partner was entitled to HB at the time of her/his death or separation from the claimant, then if the claim is made within one month of the death or separation it will be treated as having been made on the date of the death or separation.

Paragraphs (6) to (9): Validity of written claims

Para (6). By para (6), claims which do not comply with para (1) are to be termed "defective" for the purposes of these regulations, but see para (8).

Para (7) goes on to say that if a claim is defective, for either of the reasons listed in sub-paras (a) (approved form but not properly completed) or (b) (not on approved form and not sufficient), the authority may give the claimant a chance to remedy things. It can return the form for completion, if sub-para (a) applies, or supply her/him with an approved form or request further information and evidence, if sub-para (b) applies. However, see also para (9).

Para (8). When an authority uses its powers under para (7) and the properly completed form or the information or evidence requested is returned within one month (or within a longer period considered "reasonable" by the authority), the claim must be treated as if it was properly made in the beginning. So para (5) will apply eg to the date on which the claim was first sent or delivered, rather than the date on which the remedied form (or information or evidence), is returned.

Para (9) provides that in paras (1) and (8), a form will be treated as "properly completed" if the claimant has followed the instructions as to its completion, including those as to provide information and evidence. So s/he will not be penalised if the instructions are inadequate. See also reg 86 for situations when additional evidence and information must be provided when requested.

Paragraphs (10) and (11): Advance claims

Other than where the claimant is a "person from abroad" (for which see reg 10), this paragraph gives an authority the discretion to treat an advance claim as made in the benefit week before the first week of entitlement. This applies where a claimant is not entitled to HB in the benefit week after the actual date of claim, but the authority considers s/he will become entitled in the next 13 weeks (17 weeks if the claimant or her/his partner is aged 59 years and 35 weeks) unless there is a change in circumstances. See reg 76(1) and (2) for the effect of this and in particular the note on *R(H) 9/07*. Excluding persons from abroad from this advance claim rule reverses the effect of the Court of Appeal's decision in *Secretary of State for Work and Pensions v Bhakta* [2006] EWCA Civ 65, (*R(IS) 7/06*). See also reg 7(8) for claimants becoming entitled for the first time when they move to a new home.

Paragraph (12): Backdating

For this paragraph to apply the claimant must have made a claim for a past period; secondly, from a date in that past period up to the date of the claim *for backdating* the claimant must have had continuous "good cause" for her/his failure to make the claim. If these two conditions are met then the claim for the past period is treated as made on the later of either the first day from which the claimant had continuous good cause, or the day 52 weeks before the date of the claim for backdating is treated as made. *CH 3402/2005* decides that the requirement that the claim is made for a past period should be covered by submission of a renewal claim form, as asking for renewal of benefit, where expiry of the previous award was set out on the renewal claim form, without further qualification meant that the claimant was making a claim in respect of the whole period from the expiry of the previous award.

Absent a person having been appointed under reg 82(3) to act on behalf of the claimant, the test of "good cause" applies to the claimant her/himself and not his or her landlord, even where the claimant is in supported housing and the landlord may, in fact, have been assisting the claimant with his or her claims for benefit: *CH 1791/2004* para 25. However, this decision emphasises that in the latter situation the actions or errors of the landlord will not be irrelevant , but have to be viewed from the perspective of whether the claimant acted reasonably in all the circumstances, in particular in allowing his or her landlord to act for him or her.

In the case of a couple (see reg 82(1) above), it is for the member of the couple who makes the claim for backdating to show that he or she has "good cause" and it is irrelevant whether the other member of the couple can show good cause or not: *CH 3817/2004* para 8.

The period over which the backdating occurs is a past period of up to 52 weeks prior to the claim for backdating, not from the original claim for ongoing benefit. The Court of Appeal in *R v Aylesbury Vale DC ex p England* [1996] 29 HLR 303 held that ordinarily a claim for HB is to be treated as prospective only so an express request must be included if backdating is required. For the position where a request for backdating was made before 1 April 1996 see p236 of the 9th edition and p7 of the supplement to that edition.

CH 996/2004 states that the issue of backdating does not arise (and so need not be considered) if the other conditions of entitlement are not satisfied in any event. Although perhaps this will be an issue of little practical importance, it is respectfully suggested that *CH 996/2004* is wrong on this point and is putting the proverbial horse before the cart. Axiomatically, the other conditions of entitlement cannot arise unless and until a claim has been made (including for a backdated period), and so establishing if a claim has been made for a backdated period must be logically prior to deciding whether the other conditions of entitlement are met.

The phrase "good cause" has frequently been considered by social security commissioners and in *R(S) 2/63(T)* was defined by a Tribunal of Commissioners as:

". . . some fact which, having regard to all the circumstances (including the claimant's state of health and the information which he had received and that which he might have obtained) would probably have caused a reasonable person of his age and experience to act (or fail to act) as the claimant did."

However, it is clear from *Chief Adjudication Officer v Upton* [1997] 2 CLY 4668, CA that, as long as the authority have regard to this legal test, the question of whether "good cause" exists is one of fact. The commissioner approved this view of *Upton* in *CH 2659/2002* para 24.

The burden of proof to establish "good cause" rests on the claimant: *CH 5135/2001* para 1.4. That case involved a claimant who relied on an illness from which he was suffering during the relevant period. The tribunal decided that an illness must be severe for a claimant to succeed in asserting "good cause", but the commissioner decided that was incorrect: para 6. The question was "whether the nature of the illness is sufficient to constitute or lead to good cause".

Where a claimant suffers from mental illness, the reasonableness of their actions must be judged by their mental age or capacity rather than their chronological age, though medical evidence would be required: *CH 393/2003* para 5-6; *CH 474/2002* para 9. An illness is not rendered irrelevant just because a claimant does not have an appointee: *CH393/2003* para 7.

In *CH 2191/2002*, the claimant failed to disclose to the DWP that her husband had started work. When the change of circumstances was discovered, her JSA was terminated retrospectively which led to a disallowance of HB during the same period. The commissioner held that the only conclusion that the tribunal could come to was that backdating should be refused, because she had failed to disclose the change of circumstances. This is to ask entirely the wrong question. The question is why the claimant did not make a claim earlier, not why she did not disclose a change of circumstances earlier. In any event, it is hard to see why she was not entitled to have her notional entitlement to HB offset under reg 104(1) HB Regs 1987 (now reg 104(1) HB Regs).

Before the abolition of "benefit periods", claimants were invited to make a renewal claim towards the end of their benefit period. In *CSHC 352/2002* a claimant complained of problems with her post and stated that she had never received a renewal claim form. This was then a common factual scenario. Deputy Commissioner Agnew stated that the tribunal had to make findings of fact as to the alleged problems and whether, on the balance of probabilities, the renewal form was received: para 21. He also stated that receipt of a council tax demand would not of itself mean that the claimant did not have continuous good cause for failing to make a claim, "unless the evidence shows that a reasonable person would have understood that there was a problem about . . . benefit, which required to be addressed": para 23.

Where there is a dispute as to whether a claimant received an invitation to make a renewal claim, the tribunal cannot simply apply the legal presumption that where a document is posted, it is received. The local authority must first prove that it would have been posted. Even then, the claimant may still succeed in proving that s/he did not receive the document and if s/he does so, will be entitled to have her/his claim considered on that basis: *CH 3009/2002* paras 9-14.

A tribunal may, when hearing an appeal against refusal of the backdating of a second claim, treat that claim as an application for revision of refusal of benefit on an earlier claim: *CH 3009/2002* para 21.

Note that if it is decided that "good cause" exists, the authority does not have a discretion whether or not to backdate. The relevant word here is "shall". Subject only to the 52 week limit, it *must* treat the claim "as made on the first day from which [the claimant has] continuous good cause".

[¹Electronic claims for benefit

83A. A claim for housing benefit may be made by means of an electronic communication in accordance with Schedule 11.]

Amendment

1.　　Inserted by Art 2(3) of SI 2006 No 2968 as from 20.12.06.

General Note

If authorisation given by means of a direction of the Chief Executive of the authority, a claim for HB can be made by electronic communication and such a claim is effectively dealt with as a written claim. The authorisation requirements and conditions for claims by electronic communication are found in Sch 11. By para 4 of Sch 11, any claim, certificate, notice, information or evidence which is delivered by means of an electronic communication must generally be treated as having been delivered in the manner or form required by any provision of the HB Regs, on the day the conditions imposed are satisfied.

　　The DWP reminds authorities in HB/CTB General Information Bulletin G11/2007, that claims made electronically where an authority has *not* obtained a Chief Executive's direction are not valid claims and that any benefit paid or credited as a result will not attract any subsidy.

Date of claim where claim sent or delivered to a gateway office

84.–(1)　Subject to paragraph (10) of regulation 83 (time and manner in which claims are to be made), and with the exception of those claims to which paragraph (3) of this regulation refers, where a claim for housing benefit has been sent or delivered to a gateway office in accordance with sub-paragraph (d) of paragraph (4) of regulation 83, the date on which that claim is made shall be–

(a)　in a case where a claimant or his partner–

(i)　is a person who has been awarded income support or an income-based jobseeker's allowance; and

(ii)　first notifies his intention to claim housing benefit within one month of the date on which his claim for that income support or jobseeker's allowance was received at an appropriate DWP office,

the first day of entitlement to income support or an income-based jobseeker's allowance, but if the first notification is by any means other than a claim which meets the requirements of regulation 83(1) such a claim must be received at a gateway office within one month of that notification; and for the purposes only of this sub-paragraph a person who has been awarded an income-based jobseeker's allowance shall be treated as also entitled to that allowance for any days which immediately precede the first day in that award and on which he would, but for regulations made under paragraph 4 of Schedule 1 to the Jobseekers Act (waiting days) have been entitled to that allowance;

(b)　in a case where the claimant or his partner–

(i)　claimed income support or a jobseeker's allowance; but

(ii)　has no entitlement to income support or an income-based jobseeker's allowance,

the first date on which notification is deemed to be given in accordance with paragraph (2), but if that notification is by any means other than a claim which meets the requirements of regulation 83(1) such a claim must be received at a gateway office within one month of that notification;

(c)　in a case where a claimant or his partner–

(i)　is a person on income support or entitled to an income-based jobseeker's allowance;

(ii)　has become liable for the first time to make payments in respect of the dwelling which he occupies as his home; and

> > (iii) first notifies his intention to make a claim for housing benefit within one month of the commencement of the rental liability,
> > the date on which the liability to make those payments arises, but if the first notification is by any means other than a claim which meets the requirements of regulation 83(1) such a claim must be received at the gateway office within one month of that notification;
> >
> > (d) in a case where neither the claimant nor his partner is a person on income support or entitled to an income-based jobseeker's allowance, the first date on which notification is deemed to be made in accordance with paragraph (2), but if that notification is by any means other than a claim which meets the requirements of regulation 83(1) such a claim must be received at the gateway office within one month of that notification; or
> >
> > (e) in any other case, the date on which the claim for housing benefit is received at the gateway office.
>
> (2) A notification of intention to make a claim is deemed to be given on the date on which notification from the claimant of his intention to claim housing benefit in whatever form is received at a gateway office.
>
> (3) This regulation does not apply to claims which are made at an office of a designated authority in accordance with regulation 83(4)(e).

General Note

This regulation sets out the rules for ascertaining the date of a claim where a claimant delivers the claim to a "gateway office" under reg 83(4)(d) or otherwise notifies the gateway office of his or her intention to claim HB. "Gateway office" is defined in reg 2(1).

Essentially the rules follow those in reg 83(5). It is only necessary to notify an *intention* to make a claim within one month of claiming IS or income-based JSA rather than actually to make the claim within that period. If the notification of intention does not take the form of a properly completed claim form, such a claim form must follow within a month after that.

By para (2) notification of intention to make a claim is treated as being given on the day it is received at the gateway office. Notification can be "in whatever form" so such a notification need not be in writing. See the note to reg 83(5)(d) for a discussion.

None of the rules in para (1) applies to claims which, because there is no current entitlement, are treated as made in advance of an anticipated future entitlement, for which see reg 83(10).

Date of claim where claim sent or delivered to an office of a designated authority

85.–(1) Where a claim for housing benefit has been sent or delivered to an office of a designated authority in accordance with regulation 83(4)(e), the date on which the claim is made shall be–

> (a) except where paragraph (b) applies, the date the claim is received at the office of the designated authority; or
>
> (b) where in the one month before the claim is received in an office of a designated authority, the person making the claim or a person acting on his behalf had notified an office of a designated authority of his intention to make such a claim, the date the notification was given.

(2) A notification of intention to make a claim is deemed to be given on the date on which notification of the intention to claim housing benefit is received, in whatever form, from the claimant, or the person acting on his behalf, at an office of a designated authority.

(3) Paragraph (2) applies where neither income support nor a jobseeker's allowance is claimed in conjunction with housing benefit.

(4) Where the person claiming housing benefit in accordance with regulation 83(4)(e), or the partner of that person–

> (a) has an award of income support or income-based jobseeker's allowance; or

(b)   has claimed such a benefit but no award has been made,

the date on which the claim for housing benefit is made shall be determined as if sub-paragraphs (a), (b), (c) and (e) of paragraph (1) of regulation 84 applied to that claim as they apply to claims under regulation 83(4)(d).

General Note

Reg 85 makes provision for claims to designated authorities operating the ONE scheme. It is understood that since autumn 2006 there have no longer been any ONE offices. For commentary on this provision, see page 371 of the 19th edn of this work.

Evidence and information

86.–(1)   Subject to paragraph (2) and to paragraph 5 of Schedule A1 (treatment of claims for housing benefit by refugees), a person who makes a claim, or a person to whom housing benefit has been awarded, shall furnish such certificates, documents, information and evidence in connection with the claim or the award, or any question arising out of the claim or the award, as may reasonably be required by the relevant authority in order to determine that person's entitlement to, or continuing entitlement to, housing benefit and shall do so within one month of being required to do so or such longer period as the relevant authority may consider reasonable.

(2)   Nothing in this regulation shall require a person to furnish any certificates, documents, information or evidence relating to a payment to which paragraph (4) applies.

(3)   Where a request is made under paragraph (1), the relevant authority shall–

(a)   inform the claimant or the person to whom housing benefit has been awarded of his duty under regulation 88 (duty to notify change of circumstances) to notify the designated office of any change of circumstances; and

(b)   without prejudice to the extent of the duty owed under regulation 88, indicate to him either orally or by notice or by reference to some other document available to him on application and without charge, the kind of change or circumstances which is to be notified.

(4)   This paragraph applies to any of the following payments–

(a)   a payment which is–

(i)   disregarded under paragraph 23 of Schedule 5 (income in kind) or paragraph 34 of Schedule 6 (certain payments in kind); and

(ii)   made under the Macfarlane Trust, the Macfarlane (Special Payments) Trust, the Macfarlane (Special Payments) (No 2) Trust, the Fund, the Eileen Trust, the Skipton Fund or the London Bombings Relief Charitable Fund;

(b)   a payment which is disregarded under paragraph 35 of Schedule 5 or paragraph 24 of Schedule 6 (payments made under certain trusts and certain other payments), other than a payment made under the Independent Living Funds;

(c)   a payment which is disregarded under regulation 74(9)(b) or (c) (income of non-dependant) other than a payment made under the Independent Living Funds.

(5)   Where a claimant or a person to whom housing benefit has been awarded or any partner is aged not less than 60 and is a member of, or a person deriving entitlement to a pension under, a personal pension scheme, [¹] he shall where the relevant authority so requires furnish the following information–

(a)   the name and address of the pension fund holder;

(b)   such other information including any reference or policy number as is needed to enable the personal pension scheme [¹] to be identified.

(6)   Where the pension fund holder receives from a relevant authority a request for details concerning a personal pension scheme [¹] relating to a person or any

partner to whom paragraph (5) refers, the pension fund holder shall provide the relevant authority with any information to which paragraph (7) refers.

(7)   The information to which this paragraph refers is–

(a) where the purchase of an annuity under a personal pension scheme has been deferred, the amount of any income which is being withdrawn from the personal pension scheme;

(b) in the case of–

(i)   a personal pension scheme where income withdrawal is available, the maximum amount of income which may be withdrawn from the scheme; or

(ii)   a personal pension scheme where income withdrawal is not available, [¹] the maximum amount of income which might be withdrawn from the fund if the fund were held under a personal pension scheme where income withdrawal was available,

calculated by or on behalf of the pension fund holder by means of tables prepared from time to time by the Government Actuary which are appropriate for this purpose.

Definitions

"claim" – see reg 2(1).
"claimant" – see reg 2(1).
"designated office" – see reg 2(1).
"the Fund",
"the Eileen Trust",
"the Macfarlane Trust",
"the Macfarlane (Special Payments) Trust",
"the Macfarlane (Special Payments) (No 2) Trust",
"the Independent Living Funds",
"the Skipton Fund" and
"the London Bombings Charitable Fund" – see reg 2(1).

Amendment

1.   Amended by reg 4(6) of SI 2007 No 1749 as from 16.7.07.

General Note

This regulation obliges the claimant to provide evidence to support her/his claim if requested to do so by the authority (either on the claim form or subsequently) within one month of the request, or such longer period as the authority considers reasonable.

The authority must inform the claimant of her/his obligation (under reg 88) to report certain changes of circumstance. See also reg 83 for the information and evidence requirements for valid claims.

Analysis

Paragraphs (1), (2) and (4): Power to require information

The time at which information may be demanded is the whole period during which HB is being claimed. The claimant or person to whom HB is awarded must provide "certificates, documents, information and evidence" (not further defined) as may be reasonably required. This will depend upon the personal circumstances of each individual claimant and on whether the authority has reasonable cause to doubt any previous statements made, or information given by, the claimant. However, the information must be required for the purpose of determining entitlement to HB and not for any other purpose.

There is no duty to disclose details of certain specific payments which are wholly disregarded: para (2). These are listed in para (4), namely:

(1)   Income or payments in kind disregarded under Sch 5 para 23 or Sch 6 para 34.

(2)   Payments from any of the Macfarlane Trusts (which were established by the Secretary of State for Social Security for the benefit of haemophiliacs), from the Fund, from the Eileen Trust, from the Skipton Fund and from the London Bombings Relief Charitable Fund.

(3)   Payments which are disregarded under Sch 5 para 34 or Sch 6 para 24 (except for payments from the Independent Living Funds). All such payments derive from payments made under the Macfarlane Trusts.

(4)   Payments to a non-dependant which are disregarded under reg 74(9)(b) or (c) (other than payments from the Independent Living Funds). Again these are payments under the Macfarlane Trusts, the Fund or the Eileen Fund.

The power is to require information from "a person who makes a claim or a person to whom housing benefit has been awarded". This will include anyone claiming on behalf of a claimant as appointee under reg 82 or as a duly appointed agent. The fact that specific mention is made of such payments indicates that claimants are potentially under an obligation to disclose all other income and capital (even where it falls to be disregarded in its entirety), at least when requested to do so. It might be argued that the existence of the disregard means that the authority does not need to know the amount of such income or capital to determine the claim but the reality is otherwise: the authority needs to know the amount and nature of all such payments in order to be satisfied that the disregard applies in the first place. It is perfectly reasonable for a local authority to require information or evidence not only at the time the claim form is completed but also "from time to time in the form of a signed statement given in response to direct questions from a council officer at a home visit": *CH 4390/2003* para 11. Moreover, a local authority is entitled (and, indeed, required) to demand information under reg 86(1) notwithstanding the fact that entitlement had ceased in order to correctly calculate the amount of an overpayment: *CH 4943/2001* paras 65-70. The decision in *Secretary of State for Work and Pensions v Chiltern DC* [2003] HLR 1019, CA (reported as *R(H) 2/03*) (also reported as *R(H) 2/03*), which reversed Commissioner Jacobs' decision on two points, does not affect this conclusion. The Court of Appeal did not endorse the submission for the local authority before the commissioner to the effect that the only way in which it could obtain information in order to operate reg 104 HB Regs 1987 (now reg 104 HB Regs) was by inviting a fresh claim and that it could only operate reg 104 if backdating for "good cause" is granted. The Court of Appeal says "can use that fresh claim" and does not say "can only use that fresh claim" or that the local authority is precluded from obtaining information by other means. Morover, such an approach would be inconsistent with the Court of Appeal's decision in *Adan* (*R(H) 5/04*): see commentary to reg 104.

In *R v Liverpool CC ex p Johnson* (*No 2*) [1995] COD 200, QBD it was held that reg 73(1) HB Regs 1987 (now reg 86(1) HB Regs) did not empower an authority to insist that a claimant attend for an interview or to decline to determine the claim if s/he did not do so. However, in the absence of such an interview, the authority may decide that it is not satisfied that the claimant has established her/his entitlement to HB, in which case the claim will be refused and the claimant left to her/his remedies of revision or appeal.

The authority may extend the one month time limit within which the claimant must supply the evidence requested for as long as it considers reasonable. An authority's practice of never extending the time limit, however reasonable the request, would be liable to be overturned on judicial review as imposing a fetter on the authority's discretion. An individual refusal could also be challenged if it could be shown that the authority had failed to have regard to a relevant factor (eg, the claimant's state of health or the difficulty of obtaining the information) or was *Wednesbury* unreasonable.

Where there is a failure to comply with the requirements in reg 86(1), note the possibility of payment of HB being suspended under regs 11 or 13 D&A Regs (see pp971 and 973). Entitlement to HB might then be terminated under reg 14 of those regulations.

Note that claims under Sch 4 of the HB&CTB(CP) Regs by people granted refugee status (see p1125) are subject to the rules in para 5 of Sch A1 (as inserted by para 2(2) of Sch 4 HB&CTB(CP) regs) rather than reg 86.

Extensive guidance is given to local authorities by the DWP's Verification Framework as to the type of evidence they should require of claimants when a claim is made. However, the Verification Framework has no status in law other than that of general guidance. In particular, it cannot override the prohibition in para (2) to seek information of the types set out in para (4) and nor can it override the requirement in para (1) that information must be "*reasonably* required". In *CH 999/2002* paras 13-15, the commissioner upheld the reasonableness of a requirement to provide utility bills as proof of residence. However, the commissioner made it clear that the reasonableness of any requirement would depend on the circumstances of the individual case: para 14. In short, it is reg 86(1) with which the claimant must comply, not the Verification Framework.

Paragraph (3): The authority's obligations

Para (3) obliges the authority to inform the claimant of her/his duty to report changes of circumstances to the authority: sub-para (a), and also tell her/him what *kind* of change s/he should report: sub-para (b). The latter duty may be discharged by word of mouth but it is good practice to provide a written guide in every case and to get the claimant to sign to say that s/he has received and read it. A document is of more use to the claimant because s/he can refer to it in the future and if the duty is discharged by telling the claimant orally of the kinds of changes which should be reported, disputes may arise subsequently as to what was said and indeed whether such a conversation ever took place at all. Needless to say, the authority should be as explicit as possible so that the claimant is not misled in any way.

The duty under this paragraph is stated to arise "where a request is made under paragraph (1)" but taken on its own this is apt to cause confusion. In practice, a request under para (1) is made in every case because information, documents and evidence, etc. are always requested by the questions in the authority's printed claim-form and there is no power other than reg 86(1) to require such information. It follows that the para (3) information should be given to the claimant at the time of the claim in every case and *again* if a supplementary request for further information or evidence is made.

The wording of para (3) (a) does not mean that a claimant is under a duty to provide information to an authority only where a prior request for information has been made by the authority: *CH 2794/2004* para 18. This is clearly correct. While the duty to provide evidence or information will only arise under reg 86(1) where that evidence or information has been requested, nothing in para (3) qualifies the claimant focused duty in reg 88(1).

Paragraphs (5) to (7): Pension funds

Para (5) entitles the authority to require a claimant or person to whom HB has been awarded (or any partner) who is aged 60 or over to supply information about pension fund holders and suppliers of pension schemes. Paras (6) and (7) require the provision of information by those administering the schemes. Such information may give rise to a finding of notional income under reg 42(3) if a claimant is failing to exercise her/his rights under the scheme.

Prior to 16 July 2007, reference was also made to "retirement annuity contracts". These were a method of saving for retirement. However, from April 2007 they were subsumed into "personal pension schemes" so it was no longer necessary to draw a distinction between retirement annuity contracts and personal pension schemes.

[²Amendment and withdrawal of claim

87.–(1)

A person who has made a claim may amend it at any time before a decision has been made on it, by a notice in writing delivered or sent to the designated office, except where the claim was made by telephone in accordance with regulation 83(4A) where the amendment may be made by telephone, and any claim so amended shall be treated as if it had been amended in the first instance.

(2)   A person who has made a claim may withdraw it at any time before a decision has been made on it, by notice to the designated office, and any such notice of withdrawal shall have effect when it is received.]

Definitions

"claim" – see reg 2(1).
"designated office" – see reg 2(1).

Amendments

1.   Inserted by reg 2(3) of SI 2006 No 2967 as from 20.12.06.
2.   Substituted by reg 6(4) of SI 2007 No 719 as from 2.4.07.

Analysis

Para (1). Before a decision has been made the claimant needs no permission to amend her/his claim provided s/he does so in writing and the claim is then treated as if first sent in or delivered as amended. Note that where the claim was made by telephone in accordance with reg 83(4A), the amendment can be made by telephone.

Para (2). There is no requirement as to the form of "notice" required to withdraw a claim; according to this paragraph it need not even be in writing. But notice must be received before any decision is made. Once properly withdrawn the claim ceases to exist and no decision or award can be made on it, nor can the claim then be reinstated: *R(H) 2/06* (para 9). It may be possible to show that the decision to withdraw was not freely made – thus depriving the withdrawal of legal effect – but this will only arise in an exceptional case where, for example, the claimant was acting under duress (*CJSA 3979/1999* para 26). However, even in a case of alleged duress, where a claimant is ordinarily able to understand the consequences of his or her actions, what will need to be shown is threatening or overbearing behaviour, or deception, leading to the claim being withdrawn: the fact that withdrawing the claim was not, with the benefit of hindsight, in the claimant's best interests will not be enough (*R(H) 2/06* para 11).

Duty to notify changes of circumstances

88.–(1) Subject to paragraphs (3) and (5), if at any time between the making of a claim and a decision being made on it, or during the award of housing benefit, there is a change of circumstances which the claimant, or any person by whom or on whose behalf sums payable by way of housing benefit are receivable, might reasonably be expected to know might affect the claimant's right to, the amount of or the receipt of housing benefit, that person shall be under a duty to notify that change of circumstances by giving notice [¹] to the designated office

[¹ (a) in writing or, where the relevant authority has published a telephone number for the purposes of regulation 83 (time and manner in which claims are to be made), by telephone unless the authority determines, in any particular case, that notice must be in writing or may be given otherwise than in writing or by telephone; or

(b) in writing if in any class of case the relevant authority requires written notice unless the authority determines, in any particular case, that notice may be given otherwise than in writing.]

(2) In the case of a claimant who sent or delivered his claim to a gateway office in accordance with regulation 84 (date of claim where claim sent or delivered to a gateway office), a change of circumstances may be reported in writing to that office, or to any other gateway office of which he was notified on or with his claim form.

(3) The duty imposed on a person by paragraph (1) does not extend to changes in–

(a) the amount of rent payable to a housing authority;

(b) the age of the claimant or that of any member of his family or of any non-dependants;

(c) these Regulations;

(d) in the case of a claimant on income support, any circumstances which affect the amount of income support or an income-based jobseeker's allowance but not the amount of housing benefit to which he is entitled, other than the cessation of that entitlement to income support or an income-based jobseeker's allowance.

(4) Notwithstanding paragraph (3)(b) or (d) a claimant shall be required by paragraph (1) to notify the designated office of any change in the composition of his family arising from the fact that a person who was a member of his family is now no longer such a person because he ceases to be a child or young person.

(5) Where a person resides in a postcode district identified in Part 1 or 2 of Schedule 2 to the Social Security (Claims and Information) Regulations 1999, he may notify the change of circumstances by giving notice in writing to any office of a designated authority displaying the ONE logo.

Definitions

"claimant" – reg 2(1).
"designated office" – see reg 2(1).
"designated authority" – see reg 2(1).
"family" – see s137(1) SSCBA and Part 4.
"gateway office" – see reg 2(1).
"housing authority" – see s191 SSAA.
"non-dependant" – see reg 3.
"rent" – see Part 3.

Amendment

1.   Amended by reg 2(4) of SI 2006 No 2967 as from 20.12.06.

General Note

This regulation imposes a general duty on the claimant and anyone by whom, or on whose behalf, HB may be receivable to report to the authority any change of circumstances which might affect the claimant's right to, the amount of, or the payment of benefit.

The regulation links to the rules on overpayments: see Part 13. Authorities should act promptly when notified of changes in circumstance as any subsequent overpayment may be irrecoverable as having been caused by official error.

Note also the possible offences where someone dishonestly fails to give a prompt notification of a change of circumstances: ss111A and 112 SSAA (on pp57 and 61). For these purposes, notification must be in writing: reg 4 Social Security (Notification of Change of Circumstances) Regulations 2001 (on p1086).

Analysis

Paragraph (1): The duty to report changes

The duty to report changes in circumstances is placed not merely on the claimant but on appointees and landlords who are in receipt of direct payment of HB: see regs 95 and 96. It is not contingent on a prior request being made by the authority: *CH 2794/2004* (para 18).

Notification must be in writing, or where the relevant authority has published a telephone number for the purposes of telephone claims, by telephone. However, in some cases, the authority can require written notice, or can accept notification in a form other than in writing or by telephone. Note that notice may also be given by means of an electronic communication in accordance with Sch 11 (if authorised): reg 88A.

Telephoning the authority with the information would, in many cases, be bad practice as it does not provide a permanent record. It is always best to ensure receipt of notifications by the authority by sending letters by recorded delivery post. Some authorities adopt a helpful practice of giving a receipt for documents handed over in person, and such documents should always be kept in a safe place.

The changes which must be reported are those which might effect the claimant's right to HB (eg, if s/he moves address or her/his capital increases above the capital limit), the amount of HB s/he is entitled to (eg, if her/his income increases, or s/he inherits capital which will increase her/his "tariff income" under reg 52); and his right to receive HB (eg, rent arrears which might justify payment to a landlord).

There are back up arrangements between authorities and DWP local offices where the claimant is also in receipt of IS or income-based JSA. The DWP should notify the authority of any changes which are reported to them and, if the claimant ceases to be entitled to IS or income-based JSA. There is often delay in this happening so this should *not* be relied on. The primary duty is imposed on the claimant (and/or appointee or landlord as the case may be) to report all relevant changes to the correct office irrespective of whether the DWP also does so. A breakdown in the back-up procedure will not mean that a resulting overpayment is unrecoverable as being the result of an official error: see the Analysis to reg 100.

Paragraphs (3) and (4): Exceptions to the general rule

Para (3) lists four types of change of circumstance which do not have to be reported to the authority by someone under the general duty in para (1).

(1)   Changes in the rent charged by the authority to its own tenants: sub-para (a).

(2)   Changes in the ages of the claimant and her/his family or of any non-dependants: sub-para (b). This is subject to the qualification in para (4).

(3)   Changes in the regulations themselves: sub-para (c).

(4)   Changes which affect the amount of IS or income-based JSA but not HB, other than the cessation of entitlement to one of those benefits: sub-para (d). This is subject to the qualification in para (4). Note that sub-para (d) only applies currently in the case of a claimaint on IS. This appears to have been an error when the regulations were consolidated in March 2006. Reg 75(2)(e) HB Regs 1987 also applied in the case of a claimant on income-based JSA (inserted by SI 1996 No 1510 as from 7 October 1996). It is understood that this is to be amended.

The changes in sub-paras (a), (b) and (c) are included because, although they do potentially affect entitlement, the authority will already be aware of them from other sources, as with those changes in sub-paras (a) and (c) or from the dates of birth supplied at the time of the claim.

The change set out in sub-para (d) would include, eg a change in income or capital that reduces (but does not end) entitlement to IS or income-based JSA. HB claimants who are also entitled to IS or income-based JSA receive maximum HB whatever the amount of their IS or income-based JSA (see s130(3)(a) of SSCBA, HB Regs Sch 4 para 12, Sch 5 para 4 and Sch 6 para 5 and the discussion on *R v Penwith DC ex p Menear* [1991] 24 HLR 115, QBD in the General Note to Pt 6). Apart from the change set out in para (4) (to which this sub-paragraph is subject), changes in the amount of IS payable to the claimant have no effect on her/his entitlement to, nor the amount of, HB.

Para (4). Although the general rule in para (2)(b) is that changes in the age of members of the family do not need to be reported, this paragraph requires disclosure when someone ceases to be a "child" or a "young person" for HB purposes (for which see commentary to reg 19). This is because the effect of such a change is usually that the person concerned ceases to be a member of the "family" and instead becomes a non-dependant (see reg 3 and s137(1) SSCBA).

The change from family member to non-dependant will affect the level of HB payable even if the claimant continues to receive IS or income-based JSA, because maximum HB is defined as eligible rent less non-dependant deductions: see reg 70. It must therefore be reported notwithstanding sub-para (3)(d).

Paragraphs (2) and (5): Disclosure to gateway and One offices

Paras (2) and (5) confirm when disclosure may be made to a gateway or ONE office. It is understood that since autumn 2006 there have no longer been any ONE offices.

[¹Notice of changes of circumstances given electronically

88A.   A person may give notice of a change of circumstances required to be notified under regulation 88 by means of an electronic communication in accordance with Schedule 11.

Amendment

1.   Inserted by Art 2(4) of SI 2006 No 2968 as from 20.12.06.

General Note

If a local authority authorises it, notifications can be made by electronic communication. The authorisation requirements and conditions are found in Sch 11. By para 4 of Sch 11, any claim, certificate, notice, information or evidence which is delivered by means of an electronic communication must generally be treated as having been delivered in the manner or form required by any provision of the HB Regs, on the day the conditions imposed are satisfied.

PART 11
Decisions on questions

General Note on Part 11

This Part deals with decisions and their notification to those affected by them.

Reg 89 provides that initial decisions are generally to be taken by the "relevant authority", sets out situations in which no decision need be taken and provides a flexible time limit for reaching decisions.

Reg 90 prescribes how and when authorities are to notify any person affected by a decision (this is not just claimants) of their decisions and requires every notification to include a statement as to the matters set out in Sch 9.

Decisions by a relevant authority

89.–(1)   Unless provided otherwise by these Regulations, any matter required to be determined under these Regulations shall be determined in the first instance by the relevant authority.

(2)   The relevant authority shall make a decision on each claim within 14 days of the provisions of regulations 83 and 86 being satisfied or as soon as reasonably practicable thereafter.

(3)   Without prejudice to the generality of the foregoing provisions of this regulation, in a case where a person–

   (a)   made the notification specified in paragraph 2 of Schedule 7 within 14 days from the day immediately after the day on which his entitlement to income support or an income-based jobseeker's allowance ceased (''the appropriate day'') and is treated as having claimed an extended payment under regulation 72(2); and

   (b)   has made a claim, which meets the requirements of regulation 83(1), (6) and (9), within 14 days of the appropriate day,

the relevant authority shall give priority to that claim over other claims which do not fall within the provisions of this paragraph.

General Note

This regulation reinforces s34 SSA 1998 by providing that the relevant authority is to have primary responsibility for taking decisions under these regulations: para (1). Para (2) sets out a flexible time limit for taking determinations and para (3) provides for certain claims for HB to be given priority over other claims in the prescribed circumstances.

Analysis

Paragraph (1)

This rule is subject to other bodies being given decision-making powers by individual regulations: the Rent Officer's involvement in determining the claimant's maximum rent under reg 13 is an example. See also s134(5) SSAA.

Paragraph (2)

The relevant authority must make a decision on each claim. This includes where a claim is defective. The previous version of this paragraph in the HB Regs 1987 – which stated that an authority was under no duty to make a decision on a claim which had not been properly made or where the claimant had failed to provide evidence or information in connection with the claim – was ruled *ultra vires* and of no effect by a Tribunal of Commissioners in *R(H) 3/05*. The essence of the commissioners' decision was that there was no power given by primary legislation to local authorities to decide not to determine a claim. See *CH 532/ 2006* for the retrospective application of this decision.

The effect of the decision and the subsequent amendments to reg 76 HB Regs 1987 (now consolidated in reg 88 HB Regs) is that a local authority must decide a defective claim at the point in time when the alleged defect will not or cannot reasonably be remedied, and when such a decision is made the claimant has a right of appeal to an appeal tribunal against the entitlement decision then arrived at. The decisions made by local authorities in these situations are simply decisions on claims, made on the evidence available, which in most cases will be negative decisions given the lack of evidence.

If any support for this is needed it can be gained from what was said in Committee by the Parliamentary Under-Secretary of State (Maria Eagle) when reg 4(3) of (the then draft) SI 2004 No.3368 (which amended reg 76 HB Regs 1987) was being considered, where she made it plain that the intent of the amendment was to implement in full the Tribunal of Commissioners' decision and that the terms of reg 76(1) HB regs 1987 required an authority to make a decision on every claim, defective or otherwise.

The time limit for making a decision. Where the authority is under a duty to make a decision on the claim, the general rule is that it must be done within 14 days. However, the time limit is qualified by the phrase "or as soon as reasonably practicable thereafter".

If the authority has made a decision on a claim but is delaying actual payment, see reg 91(3) and the Analysis thereto. Note also the obligation to make a payment on account under reg 93 if the claim is not decided within 14 days. This does not require the claimant to make a further application for such payment: *R v Haringey LBC ex p Ayub* [1992] 25 HLR 566, QBD. See the Analysis to reg 93.

Delays in making a decision can cause severe difficulties for private tenants.

A threat to apply for judicial review may have a salutary effect on an authority failing to make a decision on a claim. In *R v Liverpool CC ex p Johnson (No 1)* [1994] unreported, 23 June, QBD, it was said that it was "of the essence" that claims for HB should be determined speedily and an order of mandamus was granted to compel the authority to determine the claims. Of the corresponding provision for the adjudication of general benefits in SSAA s21(1), Commissioner Goodman stated that the word "imposes a fairly strict requirement .... and every effort should be made to secure compliance with the statutory provision ....": *R(SB) 2/88* (para 14).

Many authorities have sought to justify delays by staffing and financial constraints. In *R v Secretary of State for Social Services ex p CPAG* [1990] 2 QB 540 at 554C-555B, CA, a submission that the Secretary of State was under a duty to appoint enough adjudication officers (the term then used for decision makers) to enable every claim to be determined within 14 days was rejected. It was said, however, that s/he could not simply ignore the requirement and would be obliged to take it into account when determining how many officers to appoint. That discretion had to be exercised reasonably: at 555B-D. This suggests that a complete failure to have regard to the statutory duty under reg 89(2) will result in grounds for judicial review.

An alternative method of dealing with delays in assessment is to complain to a commissioner for Local Administration (local government ombudsman). If s/he considers the delay constitutes maladministration s/he may order compensation to be paid. As to when judicial review proceedings will be appropriate, note the suggestion in *R v Lambeth LBC ex p Crookes* [1995] 29 HLR 28 at 35, QBD that the ombudsman should normally be the first port of call in cases of delay. However, if the allegation is one of complete failure to make a decision rather than delay, the same analysis ought not to apply.

Paragraph (3)

A claim for HB is given priority if the claimant is also treated as having claimed extended payments of HB under reg 72(2) and given the authority or the DWP the specified notice within 14 days from the day after entitlement to IS or income-based JSA ceases. The claim must be made within 14 days of the IS or income-based JSA ceasing.

Notification of decisions

90.–(1)   An authority shall notify in writing any person affected by a decision made by it under these Regulations–

(a) in the case of a decision on a claim, forthwith or as soon as reasonably practicable thereafter;

(b) in any other case, within 14 days of that decision or as soon as reasonably practicable thereafter,

and every notification shall include a statement as to the matters set out in Schedule 9.

(2) A person affected to whom an authority sends or delivers a notification of decision may, by notice in writing signed by him, request the authority to provide a written statement setting out the reasons for its decision on any matter set out in the notice.

(3) For the purposes of paragraph (2), where a person affected who requests a written statement is not a natural person, the notice in writing referred to in that paragraph shall be signed by a person over the age of 18 who is authorised to act on that person's behalf.

(4) The written statement referred to in paragraph (2) shall be sent to the person requesting it within 14 days or as soon as is reasonably practical thereafter.

Definition

"person affected" – see reg 2(1).

General Note

Once an authority has made a decision, reg 90 sets out the rules which it must observe when notifying any person affected by its decision (see also reg 93 in respect of payments on account of rent allowance).

Every notification must include a statement as to the matters set out in Sch 9. While Sch 9 obliges an authority to provide information in its notification in specified circumstances, paras (2) and (4) enable a person affected to ask for a statement of the *reasons* a decision on any matter set out in the notice. Note also the additonal requirements for a notice of a decision against which there is a right of appeal in reg 10 D&A Regs (see p970).

There are no specifications as to the form or content of the decision but authorities should be encouraged to give full details rather than just quoting regulation numbers.

Analysis

Paragraph (1): General

"Person affected" is defined in reg 2(1) by reference to reg 3 of the D&A regs: see the Analysis thereof for a discussion of its meaning. See also the General Note to reg 95.

By reg 82(6) a notification to a receiver, judicial factor, guardian, attorney or appointee for a claimant who is unable to act is validly given even if (as will be usual) it is not also given to the claimant. A written notification can be validly given to a claimant who cannot read English, at least where such a claimant has assistance from friends, relatives or advisers available: *R v Newham LBC ex p Kaur* [1997] 29 HLR 776 at 784, QBD.

Sub-paras (a) and (b) give the time limits for making notifications in respect of claims and decisions on other matters.

Although the time limit for deciding on a claim is given by reg 89(2), once it is made the decision must be sent out "forthwith": sub-para (a). In any other case, the decision must be sent out within 14 days: sub-para (b). However, where this is not possible, both sub-paragraphs qualify the time periods. In this case, and authority must provide the notice "as soon as reasonably practicable thereafter". In respect of delays, see the Analysis to reg 89(2).

Paragraph (1): Validity of notifications

The duty in para (1) to provide a notification and the duty to ensure that the notification contains the matters prescribed by Sch 9 is mandatory. The question of whether a notification is valid has particular significance in the context of overpayments, but may also arise in other contexts. For example, a claimant may have missed the time limit for appealing and it may be necessary to decide upon the validity of a document purporting to be a decision, since if the decision has not been validly notified to the claimant, the authority can be compelled by judicial review proceedings to issue a proper notification which then attracts rights of appeal.

It must be borne in mind that a local authority is not precluded from issuing a valid decision by a tribunal's ruling that a previous purported decision is invalid and of no effect: *CH 5217/2001* para 12.

The form of the decision. The general approach of the High Court has been to look at the substance rather than the form of a communication to the claimant. Even if a communication to a claimant is not described as a "decision", the High Court has indicated that the communication will be examined to see whether it does in fact amount to a decision: *R v Islington LBC ex p Ewing* [1992] unreported, 5 February, QBD. In that case, letters from the authority refusing increases of benefit under what was reg 61(2) HB Regs 1987 (now revoked) were held arguably to be "decisions".

The Court of Appeal held that if a defect in a notice does not cause prejudice to a person affected, its validity should be upheld: *Haringey LBC v Awaritefe* [1999] 32 HLR 517. In that case the notice failed to refer to the defendant's right to seek a statement of reasons under reg 77(4) HB regs 1987 (now reg 90(2) HB Regs), referred to the right to seek a review as a right of "appeal" and did not refer to a right to seek a further hearing before a Review Board. The Court held that as there was no evidence that these failures had prevented the defendant from challenging the decision that the overpayment was recoverable, she had not suffered any prejudice and so the non-compliance with the requirements of Sch 6 HB Regs 1987 (now Sch 9 HB Regs) did not invalidate the determination and the overpayment was recoverable.

However, both *Awaritefe* and the *R v Thanet DC ex p Warren Court Hotels Ltd* [2000] 33 HLR 339, CA cases may now need to be treated with a little caution as they were decided when the ultimate challenge to a decision was by way of judicial review, where the substantive factual basis of the overpayment decision could not be considered, whereas on an appeal, an appeal tribunal can consider the factual basis of the decision and, if necessary, adjourn the hearing of the appeal so as to give the appellant sufficient opportunity to address points which may not have been addressed in the initial decision notice. Accordingly, the better starting point for considering alleged deficiencies in the decision notice may be the commissioners' decisions referred to below, in particular *R(H) 3/04*.

Awaritefe was applied by a commissioner in *R(H) 1/02* para 10. Since there was no prejudice to the claimant in not having detailed calculations of an overpayment, if there had been a duty to state those details (which the commissioner had held there was not) then the omission would not have rendered the overpayment irrecoverable: para 10.

Commissioner Jacobs applied *Awaritefe* in *CH 4943/2001* and held that although the constituent parts of the decision had emerged in dribs and drabs leading up to the appeal hearing, the landlord had sufficient information to be able to appeal and then argue its case before the tribunal (para 21). Accordingly the decision was not invalidated by the failure to provide all the required information at the outset. The same commissioner reached a consistent conclusion in *CH 5217/2001*, where the claimant complained that she had never been provided with a calculation of excess CTB alleged to have been paid to her. The commissioner held that the deprivation of a possible ground of appeal amounted to significant prejudice: paras 7, 9. Had the claimant been provided with a calculation before the tribunal, it would have been possible for her to address the point, with an adjournment if necessary, and the decision would not have been invalid. But it was too late to provide a calculation before the commissioner: para 13.

The terms of a decision may be proved by extraneous evidence even if the actual decision cannot be provided: *CH 4099/2002* paras 9-11; *CH 4943/2001* paras 10-11; *CH 216/2003* paras 12-16, though note para 20 where the commissioner is critical of the shortcomings of authorities' computer systems.

What impact deficiencies in the decision notice may have on any subsequent appeal were most recently considered by a Tribunal of Commissioners in *R(H) 3/04*. They concluded in respect of reg 77 HB Regs 1987 (now reg 90 HB Regs), at paras 74-76, as follows:

"74.   . . .the question of the effect of any procedural defect in the steps taken by the authority will only fall to be considered by an appeal tribunal on a properly constituted appeal, by a particular appellant against a recoverable overpayment determination for a particular amount made against him pursuant to section 75. Here the introduction of a full statutory right of appeal to a judicial tribunal having full jurisdiction to rehear and redetermine for itself the factual basis of the determination as to its recoverability as well as its legality, coupled with the requirement to give a full statement of reasons for its decision if requested, means that many of the arguments which formerly occupied the courts on judicial review applications concerning procedural defects on the part of an authority will cease to have so much practical effect.

75.   Failures for example by a local authority to provide particulars of the facts, grounds, amount and period of the overpayment as required by regulation 77, or to notify the appellant of the existence of his rights of appeal, will for practical purposes in the normal case have ceased to cause any significant injustice to an appellant by the time a properly constituted appeal does get before the tribunal. This is because the appeal process affords him the opportunity to adduce evidence and have a full rehearing before a judicial body able to go into the factual basis of the claim that the money is legally recoverable from him, as well as any maintainable challenge to the lawfulness of the whole process. It may still be necessary, in an extreme case where the Council's attempt at operation of the procedure has been so far defective or non-existent that the tribunal is satisfied there has never been a valid basis for a determination against the appellant at all, for the whole process to be held abortive and the appeal summarily allowed on that ground; but such cases of total rejection where the authority will have to

abandon its attempt at recovery or start again will now be rarer than in the days when the only judicial control was by way of review.

76.   Thus if the tribunal is satisfied on the facts before it that the case for a recoverable overpayment determination against the appellant is made out, incidental procedural defects in the local authority's determination that no longer have any continuing practical effect and have not caused any injustice still unremedied by the tribunal itself will not in our judgment prevent it confirming the authority's determination, or if necessary making its own findings and substituting its own decision as to the amount legally recoverable. Consequently we accept the arguments of the authorities and the Secretary of State summarised in paragraph 31 above, with the test of "significant prejudice" or "substantial compliance" explained in *Haringey LBC v Awaritefe* [1999] 32 HLR 517 applied as indicated above to take into account what happens in the tribunal appeal process itself. By the same token we reject the arguments for the landlords that any past failure of procedure must be fatal to recovery, or that past administrative cost and delay is a sufficient prejudice in this context to deprive a tribunal of the ability to confirm a determination or substitute its own, even where the original failures of notification, etc., have ceased to be of any practical effect".

Defective attempt at revision or supersession. The decision of the Tribunal of Commissioners in *R(IB) 2/04* has settled the law on defective attempts to make a decision to revise or supersede. It is suggested that these parts of the Tribunal's decision will apply to the HB scheme. After detailed consideration of the statutory scheme under the SSA 1998, the Tribunal concluded (para 55) that it was open to an Appeal Tribunal to substitute a revising decision for a superseding decision. It was also decided that defects in a revising or superseding decision would not generally render the decision invalid (para 72). It was said that:

". . . a decision should generally be regarded as having been made under Section 10, regardless of the form in which it may be expressed, if it has the effect of terminating an existing entitlement from the date of the decision (or from some later date than the effective date of the original decision). That is simply because there is no other general power which enables an existing entitlement to be terminated in that manner" (para 76).

The Tribunal of Commissioners' decision is not particularly helpful about the circumstances in which a revising or superseding decision would be invalid. They stated that:

"there may be some decisions made by the Secretary of State which have so little coherence or connection to legal powers that they do not amount to decisions under Section 10 at all. In the absence of specific facts, we do not consider it would be helpful here to seek to identify the characteristics which might lead to that conclusion in a particular case, but deal with the general principles below" (para 72).

Some assistance may be found in the decision of Commissioner Jacobs in *CDLA 4977/2001* para 28, in which he suggested cases where the officer took a decision without authority, where a similar decision had already been made by another officer, and where there had not been some step taken that was necessary to give the officer authority: para 28.

Paragraphs (2) to (4): Written statement of reasons

*Para (2).*The request for reasons must be in writing, although no time limit is specified. The right to reasons extends to "any matter set out in the notice". Sch 9 deals with what should be included in the notice. Note that the requirement that the request is "signed by him" means that the person affected must sign it personally. It is insufficient for it to be signed by a duly authorised agent such as a solicitor: *R v Lambeth LBC ex p Crookes* [1998] 31 HLR 59, QBD.

Although there is no time limit for requesting a written statement of reasons, there *are* strict time limits for seeking an "any grounds" revision of, and for appealing against, a decision (in regs 4 and 18 D&A Regs respectively). A "person affected" should keep within these time limits, though nothing prevents her/him from requesting a written statement of reasons later. Note that if a written statement is requested under reg 10 D&A Regs (where one has not already been provided) days between the date the authority receives the request and the date on which it is provided are ignored when calculating the time limits for seekign a revision or appealing: regs 4(4) and 18(2) D&A Regs.

Para (3) requires that where a person affected is not a "natural person" (eg, a corporate body, such as a landlord that is a company), the notice seeking a written statement of reasons must be signed by an authorised person who is over aged 18.

Para (5). The authority does have a time limit for providing a written statement. This is 14 days or as soon as "reasonably practicable" after. See notes on reg 89(2) in respect of delays.

PART 12
Payments

General Note on Part 12

This Part governs when (reg 91(3)), how (regs 91(1) and 91A), how frequently (regs 91 and 92) and to whom (regs 94 to 96) HB shall be paid, and makes provision for payment on account of rent allowance if an authority is slow in calculating actual entitlement (reg 93).

Reg 97 deals with payment where the person entitled has died.

Reg 98 provides for the offsetting of benefit already paid when the amount to which the claimant is entitled is revised.

Time and manner of payment

91.–(1)   Subject to paragraphs (2) and (3) and regulations 92 to 98 (frequency of payment of a rent allowance, and payment on account of a rent allowance, payment provisions, offsetting) the relevant authority shall pay housing benefit to which a person is entitled under these Regulations at such time and in such manner as is appropriate, having regard to–

(a)   the times at which and the frequency with which a person's liability to make payment of rent arises; and

(b)   the reasonable needs and convenience of the person entitled thereto.

(2)   Where a person's entitlement to housing benefit is less than £1 weekly the relevant authority may pay that benefit at 6 monthly intervals.

(3)   Subject to regulations 92 to 97 (frequency of payment of and payment on account of a rent allowance, payment provisions), every authority shall make the first payment of any housing benefit awarded by it within 14 days of the receipt of the claim at the designated office or, if that is not reasonably practical, as soon as possible thereafter.

Modifications

Reg 91(3) has effect as modified by Sch 3 para 7 of the HB&CTB(CP) Regs (see p1121) for some claimants entitled to and in receipt of HB in respect of their current home on 6 October 1996 and continuously since that date.

Definitions

"payment" – see reg 2(1).
"rent" – see Part 3.

General Note

Although the language in which this regulation is expressed is mandatory, it merely sets out the boundaries within which the authority's discretion may be exercised.

Para (1) lists certain factors which the authority must consider in deciding how and when to pay HB; para (2) provides a discretion to pay at six monthly intervals where only a small amount of benefit is involved.

Para (3) gives the time limit within which payment should be made after a successful claim.

Analysis

Para (1) is expressly subject to regs 92 to 98. The implication is that, if the authority's choice of time and method of payment is not "appropriate", it may be challenged.

The factors in sub-paras (a) and (b) must be considered in deciding what is appropriate. As to (b), an example is that crossed cheques should not be paid to claimants who have no bank account. Authorities who delay in paying rent rebates or allowances yet expect claimants to continue paying full rent in the meantime cannot be said to be taking account of a claimant's reasonable needs and convenience. In the case of private tenants, there will be no option but to pay in full despite outstanding HB entitlement. Such practices should be avoided.

Para (2) merely gives the authority a choice of paying at six monthly intervals when the claimant is entitled to less than £1 per week.

Para (3). The 14-day time limit for payment following a successful claim is qualified by the phrase "or if this is not reasonably practical . . . thereafter", and also by regs 92 to 97. For "reasonably practical" see reg 89(2) but note that payment must in any event be made "as soon as possible" after the 14-day limit expires, which may be an even more stringent test than that in reg 89(2). If it is impracticable for the authority to make a decision on a claim within 14 days, see reg 93 for when payments on account ("interim payments") must be made.

If a particular authority is persistently late in paying, legal action may be possible. See note on reg 89(2) in respect of dealing with delays. In an individual case, once entitlement to HB has been notified, that entitlement may be classed as a debt owed to the claimant, and if the authority delays unreasonably in paying thereafter, some success has been achieved in the past by suing in the county court for the HB owed.

It is now clear from two decisions of the Court of Appeal that if an authority determines that a claimant is entitled to HB (or a landlord is entitled to direct payments) but then fails to make payment, the person entitled to receive the payment may bring an action in the County Court in England and Wales or the Sheriff Court in Scotland (see p352 of the 12th edition for details to two cases at first instance that suggested that this was correct).

First, the Court of Appeal has stated that where a public body has decided that sums should be payable to an individual pursuant to statute but then fails to do so, it may be sued in debt: *Trustees of the Dennis Rye Pension Fund v Sheffield CC* [1998] 1 WLR 840 at 849F-M, 850A, CA. This principle was applied in the HB context in *Jones v Waveney DC* [1999] 33 HLR 3, CA. The claimant, Mr Jones, was a landlord of a number of properties with tenants in receipt of HB from the defendant council. He was paid by regular cheques for the HB due to him from his tenants. The council took the view that one of his tenants was overpaid just over £1,000. No determination to that effect was issued and the sum was deducted from one of the regular cheques. Mr Jones brought proceedings in the County Court for the balance of the HB due to him. The County Court judge found in Mr Jones' favour and the council appealed. Pill LJ, dismissing the appeal, set out the position as follows:

"A claimant who seeks to obtain relief must normally follow the procedures set out in the Regulations, as this Court held in *Cotter*. Where, however, as in this case, the Council have not themselves followed the procedures which they are obliged to follow under the regulations, and have thereby deprived the claimant of the protection and opportunities offered him by the regulations, he is entitled to bring a County Court action. In substance, by their defence the Council were seeking to "recover", under the regulations, what they had determined to be an overpayment under the regulations.

It is conceded that if a Council purported to make a payment by cheque of housing benefit they had determined to be due, but declined to sign the cheque, the sum determined to be due would be recoverable in the County Court. That would be a mere debt collecting exercise for which an ordinary action is appropriate."

The position can therefore be summarised as follows. Proceedings in the County Court or Sheriff Court may be brought by a claimant if benefit has been awarded to her/him but not paid. Proceedings may also be brought by a landlord where the benefit has been awarded and the council has also decided that direct payments should be made to her/him. Proceedings may be brought if a cheque has been issued but has been lost or, as Pill LJ suggested, not properly filled out with the result that it cannot be cashed by the intended recipient. However, proceedings may *never* be brought unless the council has actually awarded HB. If there is any dispute as to whether HB should have been awarded, the appeal process must be used to determine that issue.

[¹Cases in which payments to a housing authority are to take the form of a rent allowance

91A.–(1) Where the occupier of a dwelling is liable to make payments in respect of that dwelling to a housing authority as a result of the making of an order specified in paragraph (2), housing benefit in respect of those payments shall take the form of a rent allowance.

(2) The orders specified for the purposes of paragraph (1) are–

(a) a management control order made in accordance with section 74 of the Antisocial Behaviour etc. (Scotland) Act 2004;

(b) an interim management order made in accordance with section 102 of the Housing Act 2004;

(c) a final management order made in accordance with section 113 of that Act;

(d) an interim empty dwelling management order made in accordance with section 133 of that Act; and

(e) a final empty dwelling management order made in accordance with section 136 of that Act.]

Amendment

    1.   Inserted by reg 2 of SI 2006 No 644 as from 3.4.06.

General Note

    HB takes the form of a rent rebate where rent is paid to the authority paying the HB and otherwise takes the form of a rent allowance: s134(1A) and (1B) SSAA 1992. Various provisions within the HB Regs apply only where a rent allowance is payable. Where an occupier become liable to pay rent to an authority as a result of any of the orders specified in para (2) being made, rather than to her/his landlord, a rent rebate would ordinarily become payable. Reg 91A was inserted into the HB Regs to ensure that rent allowances continue to be paid so that claimants in this situation do not unfairly gain (eg, because their rent is not referred to the rent officer under reg 14) or lose (eg, if they live in a Pathfinder area and get HB at a higher rate than their rent under Sch 10).

Frequency of payment of a rent allowance

92.–(1)   Subject to the following provisions of this regulation any rent allowance other than a payment made in accordance with regulation 91(2) or (3) or 93 (time and manner of payment, payment on account of rent allowance) shall be paid at intervals of 2 or 4 weeks or one month or, with the consent of the person entitled, at intervals greater than one month.

    (2)   Except in a case to which paragraph (3) applies, any payment of a rent allowance shall be made, in so far as it is practicable to do so, at the end of the period in respect of which it is made.

    (3)   Except in a case to which regulation 96(2) applies and subject to paragraph (4), this paragraph applies where payment of a rent allowance is being made to a landlord (which for these purposes has the same meaning as in regulations 95 and 96 (payments to a landlord)), when that payment shall be made–

    (a)   at intervals of 4 weeks; and

    (b)   at the end of the period in respect of which it is made.

    (4)   Where paragraph (3) applies–

    (a)   in a case where the liability in respect of which the rent allowance is paid is monthly, the authority may make payment at intervals of 1 month;

    (b)   in a case where the authority is paying a rent allowance to a landlord in respect of more than one claimant, then the first such payment in respect of any claimant may be made to that landlord at such lesser interval as that authority considers is in the best interest of the efficient administration of housing benefit.

    (5)   Except in a case to which paragraph (3) applies, where a person's weekly entitlement to a rent allowance is more than £2 he may require payment at two weekly intervals and the relevant authority shall pay at two weekly intervals in such a case.

    (6)   Except in a case to which paragraph (3) applies, the relevant authority may pay a rent allowance at weekly intervals where either–

    (a)   it considers that unless the rent allowance is paid at weekly intervals an overpayment is likely to occur; or

    (b)   the person entitled is liable to pay his rent weekly and it considers that it is in his interest that his allowance be paid weekly.

    (7)   Subject to paragraphs (2), (3) and (5), the relevant authority may pay a rent allowance to a student once a term.

Modifications

    Reg 92 has effect as modified by Sch 3 para 7 of the HB&CTB(CP) Regs (see p1121) for some claimants entitled to and in receipt of HB in respect of their current home on 6 October 1996 and continuously since that date.

Definitions

    "payment" – see reg 2(1).

    "overpayment" – see reg 99.

"rent" – see Part 3.
"rent allowance" – see s134(1A) and (1B) SSAA.
"student" – see Part 7.

General Note

This regulation deals solely with rent allowances (eg, HB paid to private and housing association tenants). It effectively limits the authority's choice in deciding how frequently to pay this form of HB. The regulation only applies where a claim is made or treated as made on or after 7 October 1996 and the claimant is not exempt from these payment rules. See Sch 3 para 7 of the HB&CTB(CP) Regs (p1121) for the saving provision.

Para (1) sets out general rules, that is that HB is generally paid at intervals of 2 or four weeks or monthly. Para (2) provides that a rent allowance (in a case that is not exempt – see the analysis) should be paid at the end of the period to which it relates.

Para (3) provides that where direct payments are being made to a landlord, payment is to be made at intervals of four weeks and at the end of that period, subject to certain exceptions in para (4).

Para (6) gives a discretion to pay weekly.

Para (7), subject to paras (2), (3) and (5), gives a further option regarding the frequency of HB payments to students, where para (1) would otherwise apply.

Where the authority has a choice about how frequently to pay HB it must take into account the factors in reg 91(1).

Analysis

Paragraphs (1) and (2): Payments to claimants

Para (1). Under para (1), except where the claimant is entitled to less than £1 a week and the authority has used its powers in reg 91(2) or where an initial payment is made following a claim under reg 91(3), or where payment on account is made under reg 93, the authority may choose between the following periods in relation to frequency of payment: every two weeks, four weeks or monthly. Payment may only be made at longer intervals if the claimant agrees. If para (6) is satisfied, the authority can choose to pay weekly instead.

This para is specifically qualified by paras (5) to (7). Where reg 91(2), 91(3), or 93 applies, this regulation is irrelevant. Where the "person entitled" is unable to consent see reg 82(3) and (6).

Para (2). The authority should make any payment of a rent allowance at the end of the period to which it relates ("in so far as it is practicable"), that is, in arrears.

Paragraphs (3) and (4): Payments to landlords

Para (3). Where a HB takes the form of a rent allowance and payment is to be made to a landlord (excluding those cases where the authority is only making a first payment of benefit to the claimant by way of an instrument of payment payable to the landlord) payment must be made at intervals of four weeks under sub-para (a); and at the end of the period in respect of which it is made under sub-para (b).

Para (4) sets out two exceptions to the rule set out in para (3). First, where there is a calendar monthly rent liability, the authority has the discretion to make payment at calendar monthly intervals: sub-para (a). Second, where the authority is paying a rent allowance to a landlord in respect of more than one claimant, the first payment for any claimant may be made to that landlord at such shorter interval as the authority considers is in the best interest of the efficient administration of HB: sub-para (b). The latter might be appropriate where the authority has adopted a fixed cycle for a landlord with a number of properties – eg, agreeing to pay all monies due in respect of the tenants of that particular landlord on, say, every fourth Monday. The first direct payment in respect of any individual claimant could then be made in respect of a period of less than four weeks to bring it into cycle. Thereafter, payments should be made four-weekly in arrears on the pay-day agreed with the landlord.

Paragraphs (5) to (7): Special cases

Para (5). If this para applies, the authority must pay a rent allowance at two-weekly intervals if requested to do so. For "weekly entitlement", see regs 80 and 81 and Pt 8.

Para (6). The authority has a discretion to pay a rent allowance weekly if either of the sub-paras apply. Under sub-para (a), see Pt 13 for the rules about overpayments. This sub-para might apply where an authority is uncertain about a claimant's circumstances. Payment under sub-para (b) would be in a claimant's interest, for example, if rent is due weekly, to help her/him avoid getting into arrears.

Para (7) is expressly subject to paras (2), (3) and (5) above: eg, if this para is used, payment should be made on the date ascertained under para (2), and the claimant's right to request fortnightly payment under para (5) is protected. Even if para (5) does not apply, the authority is not obliged to use its powers under para (7) and may choose to pay a student at one of the intervals listed in para (1), or, impliedly, weekly under para (6).

Payment on account of a rent allowance

93.–(1)   Where it is impracticable for the relevant authority to make a decision on a claim for a rent allowance within 14 days of the claim for it having been made and that impracticability does not arise out of the failure of the claimant, without good cause, to furnish such information, certificates, documents or evidence as the authority reasonably requires and has requested or which has been requested by the Secretary of State, the authority shall make a payment on account of any entitlement to a rent allowance of such amount as it considers reasonable having regard to–

(a)   such information which may at the time be available to it concerning the claimant's circumstances; and

(b)   any relevant determination made by a rent officer in exercise of the Housing Act functions.

(2)   The notice of award of any payment on account of a rent allowance made under paragraph (1) shall contain a notice to the effect that if on the subsequent decision of the claim the person is not entitled to a rent allowance, or is entitled to an amount of rent allowance less than the amount of the payment on account, the whole of the amount paid on account or the excess of that amount over the entitlement to an allowance, as the case may be, will be recoverable from the person to whom the payment on account was made.

(3)   Where on the basis of the subsequent decision the amount of rent allowance payable differs from the amount paid on account under paragraph (1), future payments of rent allowance shall be increased or reduced to take account of any underpayment or, as the case may be, overpayment.

Definitions

"claimant" – see reg 2(1).
"overpayment" – see Part 13.
"payment" – see reg 2(1).
"rent allowance" – see ss134(1A) and (1B) SSAA.

General Note

This regulation only applies to claimants entitled to rent allowance (eg, HB paid to private and housing association tenants). Under it, the authority is obliged to make payments on account of HB to the claimant (interim payments) where the authority has been unable to make a formal decision on the claim under reg 89 and where the reason for the delay is not the claimant's failure to provide information or evidence, or, if it is, the claimant can show good cause for failing to do so.

The object of the provision is to ensure that private tenants do not lose accommodation due to delays in benefit administration, particularly now that it is a mandatory ground for possession in respect of assured tenancies that there are rent arrears of eight weeks or the equivalent: see Ground 8 in Sch 2 to the Housing Act 1988.

Subject only to the claimant not having failed to produce information or evidence without good cause when he has been required to do so, there is no exception of "reasonable practicability" in relation to this provision (see notes on regs 89 and 91). Payments are mandatory.

Under paras (2) and (3), if a claimant is paid more or less than he or she is entitled to under this provision, future payments of rent allowance will be altered accordingly.

Analysis

Para (1). The authority's duty to make payment on account arises at the latest on the fourteenth day after the claim is made: that is, if no request for further information, etc. has been made by that date or a request has been made, but the claimant has good cause for failing to supply the material requested the authority must make a payment on account, although the amount of the payment is, to a certain extent, at the authority's discretion. In *R v Haringey LBC ex p Ayub* [1990] 25 HLR 566, QBD it was held that there is no need for a separate claim for a payment on account.

Reg 95(1)(b) can require an authority to pay HB to a landlord where the tenant is eight weeks or more in arrears of rent. Schiemann J went on to find that if the tenant is eight weeks or more in arrears of rent and the conditions in reg 91 HB regs 1987 (now reg 93 HB Regs) are satisfied, *then* the authority is under a duty to make payment on account to the *claimant's landlord*. But that duty only arises if the landlord or someone else informs the authority that there are eight weeks or more arrears – ie, it is not up to the authority to find this out for itself. He stated that if the tenant disputes that there are eight weeks arrears, the landlord can ask the council to make a determination on the issue. If it goes against the landlord the council's duty to pay the landlord direct would not arise unless and until the dispute was resolved in her/his favour.

The judge confirmed that there was no duty to pay rent allowance under reg 88 HB Regs 1987 (now reg 91 HB Regs), as opposed to making a payment on account, until a decision is made (but the claimant might be entitled to an order of mandamus requiring the council to make a decision if prejudiced by the amount or frequency of payments on account).

For the date on which a claim is treated as made, see reg 83. For the authority's powers to request information, see reg 86. Examples of "good cause" might be illness or difficulty in contacting someone who can supply the relevant information.

The amount of a payment under this regulation depends on what the authority considers "reasonable" having regard to:

(1)   Such information which may at the time be available to it concerning the claimant's circumstances.
(2)   Any relevant determination made by a rent officer in exercise of the Housing Act functions – eg, the determination the authority must apply for under reg 14 (see that reg and the relevant Rent Officers (Housing Benefit Functions) Order).

Para (2) supplements reg 90 and Sch 9 by providing that the notice issued is to warn the claimant that if any excess payment to which he is not entitled is made under para (1), it can be recovered from the person to whom it was paid.

Para (3) supplements para (2) by providing that where a claimant is underpaid or overpaid under para (1), the overpayment shall be recovered or the under-payment made good by increasing or decreasing future payments of HB. There is no time limit specified in the regulation during which this must be done so that if a claimant is not actually entitled to HB when the para (1) payment is made, it may be recovered if he becomes entitled in the future.

If, on the "subsequent decision" referred to, it does transpire that the claimant is not entitled at all, however, the mere fact that he has been notified under para (2) that the payment made is a payment on account which may or may not be accurate does not of itself entitle the authority to recover the overpayment under reg 100: see *R v Liverpool CC ex p Griffiths* [1990] 22 HLR 312, QBD, and the note on reg 100.

Payment to be made to a person entitled

94.–(1)   Subject to regulations 95 to 97 (payment to landlords, payment on death) and the following provisions of this regulation, payment of any rent allowance to which a person is entitled shall be made to that person.

(2)   Where a person other than a person who is entitled to a rent allowance made the claim and that first person is a person referred to in regulation 82(2), (3) or (5) (persons appointed to act for a person unable to act), payment may be made to that person.

(3)   A person entitled to a rent allowance, although able to act on his own behalf, may request in writing that the appropriate authority make payments to a person, who if a natural person must be aged 18 or more, nominated by him, and the authority may make payments to that person.

Definitions

"payment" – see reg 2(1).
"rent allowance" – see s134(1A) and (1B) SSAA.

General Note

This regulation lays down the general rule, that a rent allowance must be paid to a person entitled to it under para (1) or, if he is unable to act, may be paid to the person who claimed on her/his behalf under para (2). This is qualified by regs 95 and 96 (which set out when payments can or must be made to a landlord) and reg 97 (which deals with payment where the person entitled has died). A further exception is provided by para (3): an authority may agree to pay the rent allowance to someone else, aged 18 or over, nominated by the person entitled.

Analysis

Once a payment of HB has in fact been made to a claimant under this provision then a second payment may not be made to a landlord covering the same period, even though had the local authority been made aware of the true state of affairs at the time of the payment to the claimant (more than eight weeks' arrears of rent) it would have made the payment instead to the landlord under reg 95(1)(b): *CH 3629 2006* para 39, relying on reg 98 below. However, in most cases this problem should be avoided if local authorities properly notify both parties (ie, landlord and claimant) of the decision changing who is to be paid: see *CH 2986/ 2005*.

Para (2). Payment to the appointee is discretionary so payment could still be made to the person entitled although this would be at the authority's risk as that person may not have mental capacity to give a valid receipt.

Para (3). For this paragraph to apply, the person entitled must be able to act for her/himself at the time the request is made. The reference to a "natural person" is to make a distinction between human beings and legal personalities such as companies. The authority has discretion whether or not to pay the nominee but the general principles of administrative law which govern the exercise of such discretions (see introduction) will mean that the authority must have a valid reason if it decides to depart from the claimant's wishes.

GM A6.181 refers to this procedure as nominating an "agent" and also misleadingly says that this power is to be used where the claimant is unable to collect money for her/himself, for example when s/he is away from home or disabled. There is nothing in the regulation to restrict it in this way.

Circumstances in which payment is to be made to a landlord

95.–(1) Subject to paragraph (2) and paragraph 8(4) of Schedule A1 (treatment of claims for housing benefit by refugees), a payment of rent allowance shall be made to a landlord (and in this regulation the "landlord" includes a person to whom rent is payable by the person entitled to that allowance)–

(a)   where under Regulations made under the Administration Act an amount of income support or a jobseeker's allowance payable to the claimant or his partner is being paid direct to the landlord; or

(b)   where sub-paragraph (a) does not apply and the person is in arrears of an amount equivalent to 8 weeks or more of the amount he is liable to pay his landlord as rent, except where it is in the overriding interest of the claimant not to make direct payments to the landlord.

(2)   Any payment of rent allowance made to a landlord pursuant to this regulation or to regulation 96 (circumstances in which payment may be made to a landlord) shall be to discharge, in whole or in part, the liability of the claimant to pay rent to that landlord in respect of the dwelling concerned, except in so far as–

(a)   the claimant had no entitlement to the whole or part of that rent allowance so paid to his landlord; and

(b)   the overpayment of rent allowance resulting was recovered in whole or in part from that landlord.

(3)   Where the relevant authority is not satisfied that the landlord is a fit and proper person to be the recipient of a payment of rent allowance no such payment shall be made direct to him under paragraph (1).

Modifications
Modification of reg 95 is provided in Sch 10 para 13 in relation to Pathfinder Authorities who are administering the pilot local housing allowance scheme, as from the date specified in relation to each authority as specified in Sch 10 Part 1.

Definitions
"claimant" – see reg 2(1).
"rent" – see Part 3.
"rent allowance" – see s134(1A) and (1B) SSAA.

General Note
Reg 95 is a further exception to reg 94(1) which requires payment to be made to the "person entitled".

Under this regulation payment *must* be made to the landlord (as defined by the reg itself) rather than the person entitled.

Once an authority has made a decision, reg 90(1) requires it to notify any "person affected" by the decision. A landlord is a "person affected" where a decision is made under reg 95 whether or not to pay HB direct to her/him: *CH 180/2006*.

Decisions made under reg 95 may be appealed to an appeal tribunal by either the claimant or the landlord, and it will be an error of law not to invite the claimant or landlord to the hearing of the other party's appeal as both are person's affected by such a decision: *CH 4108 2005.*

By contrast, reg 96 provides instances in which payment *may* be made to the landlord.

Like regs 92 to 94 this regulation only applies to payment of rent allowances.

Following a decision under reg 89(2), there is no duty to pay the landlord direct under reg 95 unless the DWP is paying part of the claimant's or her/his partner's income support or jobseeker's allowance direct to the landlord for rent arrears (para (1)(a)) or until the authority is told that eight or more weeks' arrears exist (para (1)(b)). Even then the duty does not arise until any dispute as to the amount of arrears has been resolved if necessary.

Major changes were made in the rules on the payment of HB, introduced with effect from 3 November 1997, in the context of a number of other regulations implementing the SSA(F)A 1997. These were described in guidance as measures to combat fraud. The regulations were, however, made under provisions of SSAA, principally ss5 and 6, which existed before the Fraud Act was passed.

The principal provisions are:

(1)   Authorities have discretion not to pay rent allowance to a landlord or agent who is not a "fit and proper person" to receive it: regs 95(3) and 96(3).

(2)   Landlords to whom direct payments are made are notified of their duty to report changes in the tenant's circumstances: Sch 9 part 4.

Analysis
Paragraph (1): The duty to pay to the landlord

There are two circumstances in which the authority is obliged to make direct payments to the landlord (this includes a person to whom rent is payable), provided there has been no finding that the landlord is not a "fit and proper" person under para (3).

(1)   Where direct payments of IS or JSA are being made to the claimant's landlord by the DWP: sub-para (a). There is a power in Sch 9 Social Security (Claims and Payments) Regulations 1987 to make deductions from a claimant's IS or JSA to pay small amounts towards arrears of rent.

(2)   Even if no IS or JSA is paid direct to the landlord, payment must be made to her/him where the person entitled is in arrears equivalent to eight weeks' rent or more: sub-para (b). However, the authority can still decide *not* to do so where this would not be in the claimant's "overriding interest". An example would be where he is withholding rent to try to get a landlord to do "essential repairs". Once the arrears have been reduced to less than eight weeks, compulsory payments to the landlord can no longer be made under this paragraph. However, the authority can continue to make such payments under para (a) or on a discretionary basis under reg 96. Note that what reg 95(1)(b) is concerned with is the tenant being eight weeks or more in arrears of liability for rent; it is not concerned with any set-off from that figure: *CH 4108 2005*. However, the view in that decision that the decision of a local authority as to whether it is in the overriding interest of the claimant not to make direct payments to a landlord may only be interfered with on appeal on judicial review error of law grounds (ie, that it is not for the appeal tribunal to decide for itself whether payment direct is not in the overriding interest of the claimant) has, rightly it is suggested, not been followed in *CH 1821 2006*. That later decision makes it plain that on an appeal it is for the appeal tribunal to exercise its normal decision making powers (per *R(IB) 2/04* para 25) on the evidence available and form its own judgment as to whether payment direct is not in the overriding interest of the claimant. *CH 1821/2006* also decides that it is permissible to suspend payment of housing benefit (under regulation 11(2)(a)(ii) of the D&A Regs) while enquiries are made as to which person the benefit should be paid to, as a change in payee requires the award to be revised or superseded.

Paragraph (2): Effect of recovery of an overpayment on rent liability

This paragraph purports to reverse the effect of *R v Haringey LBC ex p Ayub* [1992] 25 HLR 566, QBD by providing that where an overpayment is recovered from the landlord, rent arrears of the amount of the overpayment are created. It therefore purports to affect the substantive obligations and rights, under the general law of landlord and tenant, of the claimant and landlord *inter se*. It is strongly arguable that, in doing so, the paragraph is *ultra vires*. The regulation was made under s5(1)(p) of the SSAA which empowers the Secretary of State for Social Security to make regulations which provide:

". . .for the circumstances and manner in which payments of such a benefit may be made to another person on behalf of the beneficiary for any purpose, which may be to discharge in whole or in part, an obligation of the beneficiary or any other person."

The enabling power therefore only provides for "the circumstances and manner" of payments to persons other than the claimant. Discharging an obligation is only a *purpose* for which payments can be made. Section 5(1)(p) does not give any power to prescribe *whether* an obligation is in fact discharged by the payment or, *a fortiori*, that an obligation which would under the general law be regarded as discharged should in the future revive upon the recovery of an overpayment from the landlord. See the Analysis to reg 102 for the changes brought in by the Social Security Administration (Fraud) Act 1997.

Paragraph (3): Landlord not a "fit and proper person"

Para (3) does not allow authorities to make direct payments to landlords under this regulation where they are not satisfied that the landlord is "a fit and proper person to be the recipient of a payment of rent allowance'. This applies even if direct payments would otherwise be compulsory (eg, where the rent is more than eight weeks in arrears). A similar para is also in reg 96 where its effect is to allow authorities not to make direct payments to landlords who are not "fit and proper" even when the criteria for a discretionary direct payment would otherwise be met.

Guidance as to the meaning of the words "fit and proper person" in the context of HB is given in GM A6.195-212 which identifies four basic principles:

(1)   The test only applies where the landlord's honesty is in doubt. It should not be applied in every case where a request for direct payments has been made.

(2)   The test must be applied on an individual basis. So, for example, an authority could not decide that all landlords of a particular class (eg, those who let houses in multiple occupation) are *ipso facto* not fit and proper persons.

(3)   Each case has to be decided on its own individual facts. The circumstances in which a landlord is not a fit and proper person cannot be listed exhaustively in advance and the examples in the Guidance are illustrative only.

(4)   Before a landlord can be said not to be a fit and proper person s/he must have engaged in undesirable activity in relation to HB. It is suggested that an authority cannot take non-HB-related behaviour into account (even, it would seem, where the behaviour is housing-related, for example, failure to comply with a Housing Act notice).

The Guidance's insistence that the undesirable activity should be HB-related is probably over-cautious. It is suggested that any serious dishonesty or criminality should suffice to make a landlord not "fit and proper" at least where such criminality or dishonesty is social security related. If a landlord has, for example, been convicted of a multiple-claim IS fraud or of a sophisticated order-book forgery, it is difficult to see an authority's decision that s/he is not a fit and proper person being overturned merely because benefits other than HB were involved.

On the other hand, some convictions may not suffice even when they are HB-related. The offences introduced by the Fraud Act have the effect, in some cases, of criminalising what would in other contexts amount to no more than a negligent omission. It is difficult to see how a single failure, by oversight, to report a change in a tenant's circumstances, which is now *prima facie* criminal under s112(1A) SSAA calls a landlord's honesty into sufficient question to make her/him not "fit and proper" (although the position would be different if there were habitual failures).

It is suggested that a failure or refusal to comply with a notice requiring information under s126A of the Administration Act would also be a factor which would legitimately be taken into account in reaching a decision. Such a failure or refusal is a criminal offence: see reg 121 and s113 SSAA.

It is unclear whether an agreement to pay an administrative penalty under s115A SSAA is a matter which can be taken into account in deciding whether or not a landlord is a fit and proper person. Such an agreement is not the same as accepting a caution for a criminal offence as it does not amount to an admission of guilt, and the local authority only needs grounds for commencing criminal proceedings before serving a penalty notice rather than proof beyond a reasonable doubt. In some cases a landlord might agree to pay a penalty on the strictly commercial basis that to do so would be cheaper than to pay for legal representation to defend him/herself against a criminal prosecution. On the other hand, the regulations clearly do not regard an agreement to pay a penalty as morally neutral. For example, reg 107 prevents a landlord who has agreed to pay an administrative penalty in respect of an overpayment from suing the tenant for any money which the authority has recovered under s75(5)(b) SSAA. It is therefore suggested that an agreement to pay a penalty is a factor which the authority can take into account but that it does not carry as much weight as a criminal conviction. One administrative penalty would probably not usually (depending on the precise circumstances) be sufficient on its own to prevent a landlord from being "fit and proper", but payment of a series of administrative penalties would almost certainly justify such a decision against a landlord.

Some behaviour which falls short of criminality may also justify a decision that a landlord is not a fit and proper person. The Guidance suggests that a habitual failure to repay an overpayment which the authority has decided is recoverable from him/her would be sufficient. However, before a decision is based on this ground, the authority should ensure that the notifications relating to the overpayments comply fully with the requirements of Sch 9 as otherwise the landlord would be within his/her rights not to have paid: see the decision of the Court of Appeal in *Warwick DC v Freeman* [1994] 27 HLR 616, CA.

It seems likely that there is an overlap between the "fit and proper test" and other anti-abuse provisions, in particular the contrived tenancy rules in HB Regs, reg 9(1)(l). The Court of Appeal has held in *R v*

Stratford-upon-Avon DC HBRB ex p White [1998] 31 HLR 126 that the words "take advantage" in regulation 7 HB Regs 1987 (now reg 9 HB Regs) bear their "common meaning of avail oneself unfairly or improperly". In the circumstances, it would seem to be open to an authority to decide that a landlord who habitually created or was a party to contrived tenancies was not a fit and proper person. For example, although it would not today be possible to repeat the scheme devised by the landlords in *R v Manchester CC ex p Baragrove Properties Ltd* [1991] 23 HLR 337, QBD, a landlord who habitually targeted a particular class of claimant for no reason other than to exploit the favourable treatment afforded to that class by the HB scheme might be acting in a way which would justify a conclusion that s/he was not a fit and proper person.

The Guidance refers to circumstances in which a landlord has otherwise acted to obtain HB to which he is or was not entitled. One possible example of this would be the use of limited companies to avoid repayment of overpayments. Where one company had been closed down owing money to the authority and another set up with similar directors and/or shareholders, it might be possible for the authority to conclude that the second company was not a fit and proper person to receive direct payments even though it was the first company, which is a separate person from a legal point of view, which was responsible for the impropriety.

Whether or not a landlord is a fit and proper person to receive payments of rent allowance is a decision which can be made at the beginning of the claim and also during the period of an award if there are grounds for revision or supersession – eg, if there has been a change of circumstances or if the original decision was based on a mistake of fact or law.

Paradoxically, it does not follow automatically from a finding that a landlord is not a fit and proper person to receive payments of rent allowance, that rent allowance will not be paid to her/him. There is, of course, no question of payment to the landlord being mandatory in such circumstances but there is still a discretion to pay the landlord direct under reg 96. GM A6.192 states that an authority might decide that the claimant's overriding interests require that direct payments be made to the landlord, but that the landlord is not 'fit and proper' to receive them. In this unusual situation the authority would need to balance the risks and could decide to make direct payments. An authority could instead find alternative methods of payment. If direct payments are made, regular and frequent checks should be made on the claim.

Circumstances in which payment may be made to a landlord

96.–(1) Subject to paragraph 8(4) of Schedule A1 (treatment of claims for housing benefit by refugees), where regulation 95 (circumstances in which payment is to be made to a landlord) does not apply but subject to paragraph (3) of this regulation, a payment of a rent allowance may nevertheless be made to a person's landlord where–

(a)   the person has requested or consented to such payment;

(b)   payment to the landlord is in the interest of the claimant and his family;

(c)   the person has ceased to reside in the dwelling in respect of which the allowance was payable and there are outstanding payments of rent but any payment under this sub-paragraph shall be limited to an amount equal to the amount of rent outstanding.

(2)   Without prejudice to the power in paragraph (1), in any case where in the opinion of the authority–

(a)   the claimant has not already discharged his liability to pay his landlord for the period in respect of which any payment is to be made; and

(b)   it would be in the interests of the efficient administration of housing benefit,

a first payment of a rent allowance following the making of a decision on a claim or a supersession under paragraph 4 of Schedule 7 to the Child Support, Pensions and Social Security Act 2000 may be made, in whole or in part, by sending to the claimant an instrument of payment payable to that landlord.

(3)   In a case where the relevant authority is not satisfied that the landlord is a fit and proper person to be the recipient of a claimant's rent allowance, the authority may either–

(a)   not make direct payments to the landlord in accordance with paragraph (1); or

(b)   make such payments to the landlord where the authority is satisfied that it is nonetheless in the best interests of the claimant and his family that the payments be made.

(4) In this regulation "landlord" has the same meaning as in regulation 95 and paragraph (2) of that regulation shall have effect for the purposes of this regulation.

Modifications

Modification of reg 96 is provided in Sch 10 para 13 in relation to Pathfinder Authorities who are administering the pilot housing allowance scheme, as from the date specified in relation to each authority as specified in Sch 10 Part 1.

Definitions

"dwelling" – see reg 2(4) and s137(1) SSCBA.
"landlord" – see para (4) and reg 95.
"payment" – see reg 2(1).
"rent allowance" – see s134(1A) and (1B) SSAA.

General Note

Para (1) sets out three situations in which the authority has the discretion to pay rent allowance direct to the landlord, even though not obliged to do so under reg 95.

Para (2) enables the authority to make the first payment of a rent allowance to the claimant by way of an instrument of payment in favour of the "landlord".

Para (3) sets out the options available to an authority which would otherwise be prepared to make discretionary direct payments but which is not satisfied that a landlord is a "fit and proper person to receive payments of rent allowance".

Para (4) defines "landlord" by reference to reg 95 and purports to apply the rule in reg 95(2) to cases where discretionary direct payments have been made and then recovered as overpayments.

See also the General Note to reg 95. Note that once an authority has made a decision, reg 90(1) requires it to notify any "person affected" by the decision. A landlord is a "person affected" where a decision is made under reg 96 whether or not to pay HB direct to her/him: *CH 180/2006.*

Analysis

Para (1) gives a discretion to the authority to make direct payments to the landlord (this includes a person to whom rent is payable) in three instances.

(1)   Where the claimant requests or consents to such payments: sub-para (a). Even if such a request is made, payment to the landlord is at the authority's discretion.

(2)   Where the authority considers it to be in the interest of the claimant and her/his family, if any: sub-para (b). Payment can be made under this sub-para without the consent of the claimant.

(3)   Sub-para (c) covers the situation where the claimant has moved, leaving arrears of rent. The authority can only pay HB due in respect of the *former* home to the landlord and then only to the extent necessary to clear the arrears. Payment can be made under this sub-para without the consent of the claimant.

Para (2) enables the authority to make the first payment of a rent allowance following the determination of a claim or a supersession of an award, in whole or in part, by sending to the claimant an "instrument of payment" (usually a cheque) payable to the landlord. This rule only applies however, if, in the authority's opinion the following conditions are met:

(1)   The claimant has not already discharged her/his liability to pay the landlord for the period in respect of which any payment is to be made.

(2)   It would be in the interests of the "efficient administration" of HB.

The DWP described this power as tackling "an existing abuse when tenants abscond with the benefit without paying their rent", (*Social Security Departmental Report: The Government's Expenditure Plans, 1996-97 to 1998-99*, HMSO, March 1996, page 40).

The authority's "opinion" should be based on information held at the time the claim (or supersession) is dealt with. The authority is not required to make special enquiries for example, to establish from the landlord or specifically of the claimant whether the rental liability for the period in question has been discharged.

GM A6.163-166 advises authorities that they have a duty to safeguard the public purse by minimising the opportunities for fraud or abuse and that this duty would meet the criterion of the "efficient administration" of the benefit scheme. It suggests that an authority may wish to consider the amount of benefit payable and if there is evidence that the claimant has paid some or all of the rent for the period in question – the rent outstanding. If either the benefit due or the rent debt is small it may be inappropriate to invoke this power. Equally, it would be inappropriate to pay to the landlord more than the outstanding eligible rent. The Guidance suggests that the authority should consider paying the first payment to the landlord where, for example: the amount due is £100 or more, or the authority has reason to think that the claimant might default (perhaps because a previous landlord has reported non-payment), or there is a rent debt but the case is not appropriate for longer-term direct payment arrangements. The authority does not need to invoke this power where the claimant's circumstances warrant a permanent direct payment from the outset.

Para (3) applies the "fit and proper person" test to reg 96. See Analysis to reg 95(3).

Para (4). If, as is argued above, reg 95(2) is ultra vires, it will be equally ineffective in the context of reg 96.

Payment on death of the person entitled

97.–(1) Subject to paragraphs (3) and (5) where the person entitled to an allowance has died the relevant authority shall make payment either to his personal representative or, where there is none, his next of kin if aged 16 or over.

(2) For the purposes of paragraph (1) "next of kin" means in England and Wales the persons who would take beneficially on an intestacy and in Scotland the persons entitled to the moveable estate on intestacy.

(3) A payment under paragraph (1) or (5) shall not be made unless the landlord, the personal representative or the next of kin, as the case may be, makes written application for the payment of any sum of benefit to which the deceased was entitled, and such written application is sent to or delivered to the relevant authority at its designated office within 12 months of the deceased's death or such longer period as the authority may allow in any particular case.

(4) The authority may dispense with strict proof of title of any person claiming under paragraph (3) and the receipt of such a person shall be a good discharge to the authority for any sum so paid.

(5) Subject to paragraph (3), where the relevant authority determines, before the death of the person first mentioned in paragraph (1), that a rent allowance was payable to his landlord in accordance with regulation 95 or 96, that authority shall pay to that landlord so much of that allowance as does not exceed the amount of rent outstanding at the date of the person's death.

Definition

"designated office" – see reg 2(1).

General Note

This regulation deals with the situation where a claimant has died before receiving HB to which s/he was entitled. Para (1) sets out to whom such benefit should be paid, para (3) how those persons may apply for payment and paras (2) and (4) define those persons and enables such a payee to give the authority a good receipt for payments made under this regulation. Para (5) deals with situations where HB was payable direct to a landlord before the claimant's death.

Analysis

Para (1) just talks about "an allowance" (presumably "rent allowance"). Subject to paras (3) and (5), payment to the personal representative (or next of kin) is mandatory.

Para (2) defines "next of kin". In England and Wales the persons who take beneficially on intestacy are set out in the Administration of Estates Act 1925, the Intestates Act 1952, the Family Provision Act 1966 and the Family Law Reform Act 1969.

In Scotland, the Succession (Scotland) Act 1964 provides the rules.

A "personal representative" is someone appointed by a will (eg, an executor or executrix) to carry out the provisions of that will. Under para (4) the authority is not required to demand strict proof of whether the payee is a personal representative or next-of-kin.

Para (3). Before payment can be made to a landlord, personal representative or next-of-kin, s/he must apply in writing to the authority at its designated office, within 12 months of the deceased's death, or a longer period if the authority agrees.

Para (4). See also para (2) and the "General Note".

Para (5) makes clear that where the authority has decided to make HB payments direct to the landlord under regs 95 or 96, before the time of the claimant's death, any outstanding benefit, limited to the amount of rent outstanding at the time of the claimant's death, must be paid to the landlord if the landlord has made a written application for it: para (3).

Offsetting

98.–(1)   Where a person has been paid a sum of housing benefit under a decision which is subsequently revised or further revised, any sum paid in respect of a period covered by a subsequent decision shall be offset against arrears of entitlement under the subsequent decision except to the extent that the sum exceeds the arrears and shall be treated as properly paid on account of them.

(2)   Where an amount has been deducted under regulation 104(1) (sums to be deducted in calculating recoverable overpayments) an equivalent sum shall be offset against any arrears of entitlement under the subsequent decision except to the extent that the sum exceeds the arrears and shall be treated as properly paid on account of them.

(3)   No amount may be offset under paragraph (1) which has been determined to be an overpayment within the meaning of regulation 99 (meaning of overpayment).

General Note

This is an extremely tortuous piece of legislation designed, it seems, to cover the situation where a claimant has been underpaid for a period.

Analysis

Paras (1) and (2). If someone has been paid a sum of HB under a decision which is later revised (or further revised), and it is decided to pay her/him more for a particular period, what s/he will get under para (1) is the difference between what s/he has already been paid and what s/he was actually entitled to. Where, in calculating the amount of a recoverable overpayment, a sum of HB has been deducted under reg 104(1) which should have been determined to be payable, the same sum is offset against the arrears of entitlement under the revised decision under para (2).

The phrase "except to the extent . . . arrears" means that this regulation cannot be used with the result that the claimant owes the authority money. HB can only be recovered from a claimant under reg 100. For example, if the claimant has been paid £100 for a period and on revision s/he should have got £95, s/he will not owe the authority anything. £95 of what s/he has been paid is offset against revised entitlement, but the extra £5 will be ignored unless reg 100 makes it recoverable.

Para (3). But under para (1), in computing what s/he has already been paid, anything which has been determined to be an overpayment (see reg 99) paid during the same period is to be left out of account. Under reg 102, however, such a recoverable overpayment may be deducted from arrears of HB paid so that in the end the claimant is no better off.

PART 13
Overpayments

General Note on 13

This part of the regulations deals with the calculation and recovery of overpayments of HB. Incentives to detect fraud, recover overpayments and avoid official errors are given by the percentages of subsidy which are payable in respect of different categories of overpayment: see the Housing Benefit and Council Tax Benefit (Subsidy) Order 1998 and 1997 GM A7.56-58.

In considering overpayment issues, a systematic approach is helpful for advisers and authorities alike.

(1)   Has there been an overpayment? The definition is set out in reg 99.

(2)   What is the amount of the overpayment? This involves a complex process of calculation which is set out in the commentary to reg 103. Regs 103 and 104 set out deductions to be made from the gross amount of HB paid.

(3)   Is the overpayment recoverable, and if so from whom? The test is different from that applicable to DWP benefits. The criteria for recoverability are set out in reg 100 and the persons from whom it is recoverable are listed in reg 101.

(4)   Should the overpayment be recovered, and if so from whom? SSAA s75(2) and (3) give the authority the power to recover.

(5)   How should the overpayment be recovered? SSAA s75 and regs 101(2), 102 and 105 provide for various means of recovery. A full guide is in the Analysis to reg 102.

Meaning of overpayment

99.   In this Part, "overpayment" means any amount which has been paid by way of housing benefit and to which there was no entitlement under these Regulations (whether on the initial decision [¹ or as subsequently revised or superseded or further revised or superseded]) and includes any amount paid on account under regulation 93 (payment on account of a rent allowance) which is in excess of the entitlement to housing benefit as subsequently decided.

Amendment

1. Amended by reg 2 of SI 2005 No 2904 as amended by Sch 2 para 29 of SI 2006 No 217 as from 10.4.06.

General Note

This regulation defines an "overpayment" for the purposes of Part 13. It must be borne in mind that just because an amount comes within the above definition it does not follow that it can be recovered. That question is dealt with by reg 100.

Analysis

"... any amount which has been paid by way of housing benefit ... ". The provisions apply equally to rent allowance and rent rebate, though there are differences in the rules as to recoverability.

"... and to which there was no entitlement ... whether on the initial decision as subsequently revised or further revised ... ". This phrase has odd grammar. As it currently appears, it is far from clear that it applies, on the face of it, to cases where the decision awarding benefit was correct but the wrong amount was paid (since the decision has not had to be revised). In *R(H) 6/04* paras 9-11, the commissioner confirmed that "revised" in this context had to be read as "revised or superseded".

If an overpayment arises, as the vast majority do, from an incorrect award of benefit, the authority must revise or supersede the decisions awarding benefit before it can make a valid decision that there has been an overpayment. Whether the absence of a revision or supersession decision is fatal to any overpayment decision is now open to argument. One body of caselaw has held that the absence of a proper revision or supersession decision cannot be corrected by a tribunal or commissioner and a tribunal would have to decide that the decision was of no force or effect: *CH 4943/2001* para 8; *CH 2302/2002* para 5. See further the commentary to reg 90. On this line of argument, the authority must show the existence of the ground for revision or supersession and if it cannot do so, its decision cannot stand: *CH 2302/2002* para 13. However, it is doubtful if this line of caselaw remains correct given the recent decision of the Tribunal of Commissioners in *R(IB) 2/04*, where the commissioners concluded (para 55) that it was open to an appeal tribunal to substitute a revising decision for a superseding decision and also decided that defects in a revising and superseding decision would not generally render the decision invalid (para 72). *R(IB) 2/04* was applied to the revision (and supersession) requirement in regulation 98 HB Regs 1987 (now reg 99 HB Regs) by the commissioner in *CH 4354/2003*.

In overpayment cases, it is also important to determine any question of whether the claimant was actually entitled to benefit according to the legislation as it stood at the time: *R(H) 3/03* para 8. Account must also be taken of any transitional protection conferred by subsequent amending legislation.

It must be borne in mind that when determining whether a claimant has been overpaid, it is the legislation in force at the date of the payment that determines her/his eligibility and not the version effective at the time that the authority comes to consider whether s/he has been overpaid. The only exception to this is where amending legislation is expressed to have retrospective effect.

"... any amount paid on account ... in excess of the entitlement ... as subsequently decided". The third broad category is excessive estimated payments. So if the local authority estimates the claimant's entitlement at £100 a week and it is subsequently found to be £80, the £20 a week excess constitutes an overpayment.

Recoverable overpayments

100.–(1)   Any overpayment, except one to which paragraph (2) applies, shall be recoverable.

(2)   Subject to paragraph (4) this paragraph applies to an overpayment [¹ which arose in consequence of] an official error where the claimant or a person acting on his behalf or any other person to whom the payment is made could not, at the time of receipt of the payment or of any notice relating to that payment, reasonably have been expected to realise that it was an overpayment.

(3)   In paragraph (2), ''overpayment which arose [¹ in consequence of an official error]'' means an overpayment caused by a mistake made whether in the form of an act or omission by–

(a)   the relevant authority;

(b)   an officer or person acting for that authority;

(c)   an officer of–

       (i)   the Department for Work and Pensions; or

      (ii)   Revenue and Customs,

acting as such; or

(d)   a person providing services to the Department for Work and Pensions or to the Commissioners for Her Majesty's Revenue and Customs,

where the claimant, a person acting on his behalf or any other person to whom the payment is made, did not cause or materially contribute to that mistake, act or omission.

(4)   Where in consequence of an official error, a person has been awarded rent rebate to which he was not entitled or which exceeded the benefit to which he was entitled, upon the award being revised [¹ or superseded]any overpayment of benefit, which remains credited to him by the relevant authority in respect of a period after the date on which the revision [¹ or supersession] took place, shall be recoverable.

Amendment

1.   Amended by reg 4 of SI 2005 No 2904 as amended by Sch 2 para 29 of SI 2006 No 217 as from 10.4.06.

Definitions

"claimant" – see reg 2(1).

"overpayment" – see reg 99.

General Note

The rules governing the recoverability of HB and CTB overpayments are *considerably* more robust than the rules set out in Administration Act s71 for recovery of benefits paid by the DWP. Under that provision, the DWP must show that the claimant misled them through making a false statement or failing to disclose some material matter. Under reg 100, all overpayments are recoverable except where three criteria are fulfilled: *Warwick DC v Freeman* [1994] 27 HLR 616, CA. The three criteria are that:

(1)   The overpayment was caused by a relevant mistake.

(2)   No relevant person (that is, the claimant, a person acting on behalf of the claimant, or a person to whom the payment was made) caused or contributed to the official error.

(3)   No relevant person could reasonably have been expected to realise that there was an overpayment either at the time it was made or when they were notified of the payment.

It should also be noted that there are certain types of overpayment which are always recoverable whether or not the three criteria are fulfilled.

The recovery of overpayments does not therefore depend on fraudulent or negligent action on the part of the person from whom recovery is sought. An overpayment may be recoverable even where the person is wholly innocent and even unaware that there was an overpayment. The claimant's moral culpability is irrelevant: *West Somerset DC v Sykes* (1997) unreported 14 March, CA (Ward LJ refusing leave to appeal).

It should be noted that just because an overpayment is recoverable does not mean that it will be recovered: see the Analysis to reg 101.

Analysis

Paragraph (1)

This paragraph states the general rule that unless the criteria in para (2) apply, the overpayment is recoverable. Note that s68 Welfare Reform and Pensions Act 1999 renders certain overpayments irrecoverable even where the criteria specified in para (2) do not apply.

In *CH 4065/2001* para 1.3, the commissioner stated that the local authority (the decision contains an erroneous reference to the Secretary of State) must show that the overpayment is recoverable. However, where a claimant asserted facts which gave rise to an argument that the overpayment was irrecoverable, she had to prove those facts.

Paragraphs (2) and (3)

These paragraphs together set out the three criteria which have to be shown for the overpayment to be irrecoverable. Note that overpayments falling within para (4) will always be recoverable, regardless of whether the criteria are fulfilled. CTB Regs reg 83(4) and (5) specify further categories of overpayments of CTB to which the criteria do not apply.

The three-stage analysis above was approved by Commissioner Jacobs in *CH 3302/2002* paras 7-17, where he described reg 99 HB Regs 1987 (now reg 100 HB regs) as "particularly indigestible". The question as to whether these criteria are met must be considered during the whole period of the overpayment not merely at the beginning. Thus an official error that occurs during the period of the overpayment may render part of an overpayment irrecoverable: *CH 1296/2002* para 4. The commissioner in *CH 858/2006* left open whether a recoverable overpayment may be split between differing causes of the overpayment which exist over the same period of time (in that case an overpayment which in part arose because of an increase in the claimant's earnings and in part because of a wrong award of tax credits), but the tenor of his reasoning suggests that it should be possible to do so.

The first criterion: A relevant mistake

The overpayment must be caused by a relevant mistake made by the authority or a relevant person acting as such. Unless the person from whom recovery is sought can show a relevant mistake, the overpayment will always be recoverable regardless of the merits of the case: *Sykes*. See also *CH 2201/2002* para 9, where it was confirmed that an overpayment was recoverable where a claimant moved out without informing either the landlord or the local authority (provided, of course, that the local authority acts timeously once this information is passed to it). Note also the landlord's possible escape route under reg 101(1).

*"... **caused by...**".* It is suggested that the relevant mistake need not be the sole cause of the overpayment. It is sufficient if it is a significant contributory factor.

In *R (Sier) v Cambridge CC HBRB* [2001] EWHC Admin 160, QBD; [2001] EWCA Civ 1523, CA, dealing with reg 99 HB Regs 1987 (now reg 100 HB Regs) the claimant lived in Cambridge and claimed HB for a long period while he was recovering from a long illness. On his recovery, he decided to seek accommodation in London and live there during the week to assist his search for work. He gave evidence to the Review Board that he had sought advice from two London authorities where he was proposing to live as to whether he would be entitled to claim HB on two homes and that he received (erroneous) advice that he would be able to do so. The Board accepted that evidence. As a result of the advice he received, he did not inform Cambridge City Council when he took a tenancy in London and it became his normal home. The council did not ask any questions directed to the location of the claimant's normal home on its claim form. The claimant also moved his IS claim to a London Employment Service office, but no form NHB 8 was sent to Cambridge City Council in accordance with the normal procedure. An overpayment resulted.

Richards J accepted that the failure to send the NHB 8 form was a relevant mistake but held that it did not cause the overpayment. The judge accepted that an overpayment could have more than one cause but as a matter of common sense, the cause of the overpayment was the claimant's failure to notify Cambridge City Council. The common sense approach was required by *Environmental Agency v Empress Cars (Abertillery) Ltd* [1999] 2 AC 22, HL. The Court of Appeal upheld the judge's approach.

"In the present case, one has to have regard to the general legislative purpose, which seems to me to be clear. Parliament has laid down in the Regulations that a person is to be relieved of the obligation to repay an overpayment when that has been occasioned by an administrative mistake and not by any fault on the part of the recipient. That seems to me to be the basic thrust of the Regulation and one should approach the meaning of the word 'cause' and its application to the facts on that basis." (Latham LJ, para 25)

"Such a result . . . seems to me so entirely surprising and unsatisfactory that it requires one to approach regulation 99(3) rather differently. In my judgment a single composite question falls to be asked under regulation 99(3). One must ask: 'was the overpayment the result of a wholly uninduced official error, or was it rather the result of the claimant's own failings, here his failure in breach of duty to report a change of circumstance?' The answer to that question on the facts of this case is, of course, self-evident . . . It would be remarkable indeed if the claimant was liable to make repayment in a case where he merely contributed to what might be a fundamental error on the part of the department, and yet wholly escapes such liability even when himself primarily responsible for the overpayment." (Simon Brown LJ, paras 30-31)

Sier was followed by Commissioner Turnbull in *R(H) 1/04*. In that case, the claimant had informed the local authority that he was in receipt of occupational pensions, but had failed to disclose that information on his claim forms for IS. IS was duly awarded and CTB was awarded as a result of the award of IS. The commissioner decided that even had there been an official error (as to which see the discussion below), the substantial cause of the overpayment was the claimant's failure to notify the DWP of the award of IS: para 26. No attempt was made by the claimant to argue that there was an error on the part of the DWP, and the commissioner held that the fact that he had not challenged the decision disallowing IS was some evidence that there was no such error: para 24.

A similar conclusion was reached by Commissioner Howell in *R(H) 2/04* para 14. The true cause was the claimant's failure to disclose her new working families' tax credit (WFTC) award rather than the council's failure to await the level of the award before adjudicating her renewal claim for HB.

CH 2794/2004 sums up the position by saying that, despite the wording of reg 99(3) HB Regs 1987 (now reg 100(3) HB Regs), the question to be asked following the Court of Appeal's decision in *Sier* is the broader one of whether the claimant's act or omission caused (in the sense of contributed to) the overpayment being made. This analysis is taken a little further in *CH 3083/2005* (para 38) and *CH 3761/2005*, where Commissioner Turnbull states that the broad commonsense question to be asked is what was the substantial cause of the overpayment. In the latter case, at least for part of the period, the commissioner found that the substantial cause of the overpayment was the Jobcentre's mistakes in (i) telling the claimant that it would notify the local authority of his JSA stopping and he therefore did not need to do so, and (ii) its failure to then notify the local authority of that information.

"... a mistake made, whether in the form of an act or omission ...". No fault is required for the act or omission to amount to a "mistake". All that is necessary is that, with the benefit of hindsight, something is done which should not have been done or something is not done which should have been. An example of this point, although it did not arise for decision in the case, is *R v Liverpool CC ex p Griffiths* [1990] 22 HLR 312, QBD, in which the authority's housing benefit department was unable to implement changes to the HB scheme which had been brought in at very short notice. Estimated awards were made on review and reviewed again when the authority were able to work out claimants' exact entitlement. Some of the estimated awards were too high and the authority sought to recover the difference. Even though the authority could not have avoided making the error, it still amounted to a relevant mistake.

It has been suggested that mere delay cannot amount to an "omission" so as to amount to an official error: *R v Liverpool CC ex p Griffiths* [1990] 22 HLR 312, QBD.

This broad statement needs clarification in one respect. If there is no duty on the authority or relevant official to take a step, and it is not reasonable to expect them to do it by way of investigating the claim, there is no "omission" if it is not done. Thus the authority is under no duty to demand a particular piece of information on its standard claim form and there is no official error if it does not do so: *R v Islington LBC HBRB ex p de Grey* [1992] unreported 11 February, QBD, where the form did not ask the claimant if he was a co-ownership tenant; *de Grey* was followed in *Sier*. In that case, the claim form failed to ask any questions designed to elicit information about where the claimant's normal home was. It was argued that as this was a basic issue under the HB scheme, it was a relevant mistake not to ask the relevant question. Richards J rejected the submission, holding that the very complexity of reg 5 HB rRegs 1987 (now reg 7 HB Regs) and the rarity of claimants with two homes meant that it could not be said to be unreasonable not to ask any questions directed towards that point. That argument was not pursued before the Court of Appeal. However, note *CH 3679/2002*, where an overpayment occurred when a claimant continued to claim HB in respect of a liability to his ex-wife. The local authority's claim forms were not changed after January 1999 to seek information relevant to the then new form of reg 7 HB Regs 1987 (now reg 9 HB Regs). The commissioner held, accepting a concession by the local authority, that there was an "official error" in not changing the forms: paras 2, 7.

However, where a tribunal on an appeal finds a decision on benefits or tax credits entitlement to have been wrongly made by the DWP or the Revenue, this, in effect, is binding authority that the benefits or tax credits decision was made in "error" or was a "mistake" for the purposes of reg 100(3), and it is not open to the HB authority to go behind the tribunal's decision to try and identify the exact basis on which it set aside the DWP's or Revenue's decision: *CH 943/2003*. The commissioner did, however, point out that the claimant might have contributed to the error if s/he failed to put evidence before the Revenue decision maker which led the tribunal to allow her appeal, or might be taken to be aware that she was being overpaid if the decision maker's decision was clearly wrong: para 39. It is suggested that only the most brazen of mistakes could possibly come into the latter category.

If an officer of the DWP undertakes to forward information to the local authority and fails to do so, s/he will be guilty of an official error even if the undertaking is given outside normal procedures: *CH 939/2004* para 11. Equally, a failure to operate the verification framework properly or at all is capable of amounting to a 'mistake or omission': *CH 2794/2004* para 22; but this does not override the claimant's responsibility to answer the questions on claim forms accurately and completely.

When will there be an official error in a local authority failing to identify and query an apparent discrepancy in information before it? It is suggested that the problem will have to be clear and obvious before an official error will be made. In *R(H) 1/04* (see above), it was contended that the local authority should have queried the award of IS and it was an official error for them not to do so. Commissioner Turnbull rejected that contention (para 22), since the claimant might have been getting mortgage interest payments which would have entitled him to IS and "the information before the Council did not demonstrate that the income support award had been wrongly made".

This analysis will not, of course, be capable of application to a case involving an HB overpayment because the claimant ought not to be getting mortgage interest as part of an IS or JSA claim as well as HB.

It is suggested that a failure to follow up a glaring discrepancy may involve an official error. See, however, the discussion on causation above.

To similar effect is the decision in *R(H) 2/04*, where a claimant was awarded HB on a renewal claim when her award of WFTC was about to expire. It was argued that the local authority should have realised that the new award of WFTC might be different and that benefit should not have been paid until the new award was made. Commissioner Howell rejected that submission, holding that it was the claimant's fault that the local authority had not been made aware of the new award: para 12. There had to be a "clear and obvious" error of fact as to the facts disclosed: para 13. A further illustration of the difficulty in demonstrating official error in cases of this nature is *CH 69/2003*, where the local authority was held to be under no duty to analyse the payments going into a bank account from statements before them (para 9). Nor can it be argued that there was an official error in not suspending payment on the basis of a suspicion: *CSHB 718/2002* para 42. *CH 687/2006* holds that nothing said by the House of Lords in *Kerr* [2004] 1 WLR 1374 cuts down on the "clear and obvious discrepancy" analysis in *R(H) 1/04* and *R(H) 2/04*.

Before 1 April 1997, this phrase was worded "a mistake made or something done or omitted to be done". It is arguable that this wording did not require a "mistake" at all and rendered it unnecessary for this criterion to be met, because there was always "something done" which caused the overpayment, namely the act of authorising the payment. There was nothing in the amending regulations (SI 1997 No 65) to suggest that the phrase applied to payments made before April 1997 and so this argument can still be used in relation to periods prior to that date.

Who must make the mistake? The overpayment must have been caused by a mistake made by the authority or a relevant official. The relevant official could be any of the following:

(1) An officer of the local authority. It need not be an officer working in the HB section: *CH 2321/2002* para 37. For example, if a claimant is visited by an officer from the social services department, who then promises to notify the HB section of a change in the claimant's circumstances and fails to do so, that will be a relevant mistake.

(2) A person acting for that authority. This would cover employees of bodies carrying out HB functions which have been privatised or put out to tender under an enforcement determination issued by the Secretary of State (see SSAA s139G).

(3) An officer of the DWP. The typical situation here will be where there has been a failure to follow the standard procedures for passing information between the departments and the authority in relation to claimants claiming IS or JSA(IB). In *Freeman* at 621, Hale J said that it was "quite plain" that there was an official error, and the only possible mistake was the omission by the DSS to inform the authority of the cessation of the claimant's IS, and this was confirmed in *Sier* (in the High Court). Note here *CH 943/2003* (above), which holds that an error here will include where the DWP (or Revenue – see para (4) below) officer's decision is overturned by an appeal tribunal. But note also the comment of the commissioner in *CH 3761/2005* that the failure of an automatic computer notification system, without more, may not amount to an error on the part of an official of the DWP.

(4) An officer of the Revenue.

(5) A person providing services to any of the above Departments. Again, this covers the possibility of privatisation of functions of the DWP and the Revenue.

"... acting as such ...". The official must be acting in her/his official capacity. Thus the claimant whose neighbour works for the council and gives her/him erroneous advice as to entitlement to HB cannot rely on this advice as the relevant mistake. This is not, perhaps, as "fanciful" as Moses J thought in *Ash*.

Second criterion: No contribution by a relevant person to the mistake

By para (3), the person from whom recovery is sought cannot rely on the mistake if a relevant person has contributed to it.

Who is a relevant person? Para (3) provides that the mistake may be made by three categories of person:

(1) The claimant.

(2) A person acting on her/his behalf. People appointed under reg 82 to look after an incapacitated claimant's interests fall under this heading but it probably also includes those who are dealing with the authority on her/his behalf on an informal basis.

(3) Any other person to whom the payment is made. This includes appointees who made the original claim paid under reg 94(2), landlords paid under regs 95 and 96, or personal representatives or next of kin of deceased claimants paid under reg 97. Where the person is the landlord and that landlord is a company or a housing association, the tests in reg 100(2) focus on, say, what the housing association as a whole could reasonably have been expected to realise and not what any particular employee of the association may reasonably have been expected top realise: *CH 4918/2003* (para 18).

The same as the person from whom recovery is sought? In *Freeman*, the circuit judge had held that the overpayment was not recoverable from the defendant landlord, since he had not contributed to the official error. However, the claimant had done so by not disclosing her departure from the property to the authority. The authority argued that it was not necessary to show that the landlord was the relevant person. It was sufficient if one person falling into the categories set out above contributed to the error. Hale J (at 621) accepted this submission. Thus, had the authority issued a proper determination, it could have recovered from the landlord.

It is suggested that this conclusion may lead to highly undesirable results. Landlords in direct receipt of HB are placed in the position where they can only prevent themselves being liable for overpayments by making regular checks on their tenants. That is liable to lead to tensions in relations between landlord and tenant and possibly even to yet more landlords declining to accept tenants claiming HB.

Hale J accepted the argument that if the authority's submission were wrong "it would be difficult to determine that the overpayment was recoverable at all". That conclusion is unwarranted. The authority could have proceeded against the claimant instead, who was guilty of the contribution to the error. Authorities would still be able to recover from landlords where they knew of a change of circumstances and continued to receive the same amount of HB.

In view of the above factors, it is suggested that, contrary to *Freeman*, if it is the claimant who contributed to the omission, it must also be the claimant who should have realised that there was an overpayment. If a person acting on the claimant's behalf contributed to the omission, the same person must be the one who should have realised there was an overpayment and so on. The wording in reg 101(1) is not identical, but it does make the overpayment recoverable from those three categories of persons (though only from those acting on the claimant's behalf in special circumstances). It would follow that the person guilty of contribution and realising there was an overpayment should be the same one from whom recovery is sought.

Until the matter receives further consideration, however, *Freeman* remains the only authority on the point. It is arguable that this part of the decision was only *obiter*, since the case was decided on the absence of a proper determination. It is also noteworthy that the defendant landlord appeared in person in the Court of Appeal, and so it is unlikely that the argument against the authority's construction was put with great force.

In *CH 4465/2002* para 10, the commissioner noted the existence of the argument set out above but did not need to decide whether it was correct, since on the facts the tenant did not have knowledge that there was an overpayment and so there was no knowledge that an overpayment had occurred during a particular period.

"... did not cause or materially contribute ...". The relevant person need not be solely to blame. For the contribution to be "material", it must be shown that for the relevant person to act differently might have prevented the overpayment: *Saker v Secretary of State for Social Security* [1988] 16 January *The Times*, CA (reported as *R(I) 2/88)*. A claimant will not automatically have caused or materially contributed to the mistake if he or she notifies the authority of information other than in writing as required by reg 88(1): *CH 2409/2005* (para 22). In that case the claimant had not caused or materially contributed to the mistake, despite his breach of regulation 88(1), because he had given the authority the information by telephone, which it accepted, and had never been told by the authority that information had to be provided in writing.

"... to that mistake, act or omission...". The relevant person must induce the mistake in question. However, note the view of the Court of Appeal in *Sier* (as explained in para 13 of *CH 2794/2004*), that the broad question to be asked is whether the claimant's act or omission caused or contributed to the overpayment being made; and so a more focused enquiry on whether the claimant contributed to the 'official error' is unlikely , in most cases, to lead to any different conclusion.

Third criterion: Knowledge of the overpayment

It must be shown that a relevant person could not reasonably have known that there was an overpayment. It is for the person seeking to rely on reg 100(2) to prove that s/he could not reasonably have been expected to realise that an overpayment was being made and not for the authority to prove that she or he could reasonably have been expected to realise that an overpayment was being made: *CH 4918/2003* (para 16) and *CH 3439/2004* (para 22 – applying ratio of *Kerr v Department for Social Development* [2004] UKHL 23 (reported as *R 1/04 (SF)*)). For what is meant by a relevant person see the discussion above. In *Freeman*, Hale J ruled (at 621) that the person who should have known about the overpayment need not be the same person who contributed to the mistake or the person from whom recovery is sought. For the reasons given above, it is respectfully submitted that this part of the judgment is erroneous.

It must be borne in mind that where it can only be shown that the relevant person could have realised that there was an overpayment at some point after the commencement of the overpayment, the overpayment will only be recoverable from that time if the other two criteria are satisfied: 1997 GM A7.27.i.

"... could not ... reasonably have been expected to realise ...". It is not clear whether the test is objective or subjective. Is it whether the average person with average knowledge could reasonably be expected to know, or whether the particular person with their experience and education could have done? Because para (2) considers the knowledge of different specified categories of people, the latter test is probably correct. This has now been partially confirmed by Commissioner Jacobs in *CH 2554/2002*, in

which he was critical of a statement by a Tribunal that it did not impute "any more knowledge about the HB scheme than an ordinary reasonable person might have". He said (para 13):

"The question of imputation of knowledge to the claimant did not arise. The issue for the Tribunal was what could reasonably be expected of *the claimant*. There may be exceptional cases in which it is reasonable to expect a claimant to find out more about the housing benefit scheme, probably from the local authority or (possibly) elsewhere. If those cases exist in reality rather than theory, they will involve claimants with a special knowledge of the scheme, such as former housing benefit officers. They will, in any event, be rare. This case is not one of them. In the overwhelming majority of cases, there is no scope for imputing any knowledge to the claimant. The issue will be what could reasonably be deduced from the information available to the claimant. What a claimant could reasonably have been expected to realise is a question of fact. It depends on the information available to the person and on an analysis of what that information could have revealed." (para 13). See also *CH 609/2004* at para 8.

This statement of principle is a useful rebuttal to the arguments put forward by some local authorities in overpayment cases as to what can be reasonably expected of claimants. Some authorities appear to believe that any HB claimant should know the legislation inside out and should know instinctively when s/he is being overpaid. Plainly, such an approach is preposterous. As the commissioner goes on to state, in most cases the claimant's only sources of knowledge are past experience with the scheme and the documents provided by the local authority: para 15.

The commissioner declined to decide whether it was permissible to have regard to the individual claimant's ability to analyse the documentation: para 18. It is suggested that it follows from his approach to the case as a whole that the claimant's personal characteristics may be taken into account.

On the facts of the case, which concerned a failure to report income, the commissioner did not regard as conclusive the warnings given in the HB award letter to report changes of income: paras 20-22. However, he decided that since it was clear from the award letter that tax credits reduced the HB entitlement, the claimant ought to have realised that her income from employment should also do so: para 23.

A number of decisions now illustrate how critical close attention to the facts of an individual case will be. In *CH 2888/2002* para 15, the commissioner held that where a claimant had disclosed an increase in income and his wife had repeatedly inquired as to when his HB was to be reduced, the only permissible conclusion was that he should have known that he was being overpaid. This conclusion requires caution, since it is possible for such a claimant eventually to form the view, reasonably, that the local authority does not regard the increased income as relevant to her/his HB entitlement.

Where a landlord was clearly informed that she should report the departure of a tenant from a property, her belief that she was entitled to receive HB during the claimant's notice period did not preclude a finding that she could reasonably be expected to know that she was being overpaid: *CH 1172/2002* para 8. Rather more obviously, in *CH 4465/2002* para 9 a landlord's argument that it could not reasonably be expected to know that it was being overpaid when it was aware of the claimant's departure from the premises and had indeed placed another tenant therein was rejected.

A less rigorous view was taken in *CH 3629/2002* where the claimant started low-paid work. She knew that her HB would decrease, but did not know when or by how much. The commissioner held that for a few weeks at least she could not reasonably have been expected to know that she was being overpaid.

If a claimant receives clear advice from a local authority that a certain income resource is disregarded, then he cannot reasonably be expected to know that he is being overpaid: *CH 4383/2002* para 8. However, the effect of any contradictory advice in the documentation made available to a claimant should be taken into account in determining what is reasonable.

In *CH 4065/2001* a claimant had been overpaid because the local authority had incorrectly calculated her income from incapacity benefit. The authority alleged that she ought to have known that she was being overpaid and her response was that she had telephoned the local authority to query the award and had been told that it was correct. The authority's retort that there was no record of the call as should have been the case on the office system was held not to be a complete answer by Commissioner Jacobs. He said that "it is not my experience of life that administrative systems work perfectly in every case" (para 13). See also similar comments by the same commissioner in *CH 609/2004* (para 24). It is implicit from the directions given to the tribunal in *CH 4065/2001,* that the commissioner took the view that if the claimant's evidence was accepted, the claimant could not reasonably have been expected to know that she was being overpaid. The directions (para 21) are a very useful summary of the correct approach to this very common type of case.

"... at the time of receipt of the payment or of any notice relating to that payment ...". It seems that the person whom it is alleged ought to have known should be the person receiving the payment or the notice. For example, a person should probably realise at the time of receipt of a duplicate payment that they have been overpaid: *R v Liverpool CC ex p Griffiths* [1990] 22 HLR 312, QBD (Nolan J).

The purpose of this part of reg 99(2) HB Regs 1987 (now reg 100(2) HB Regs), and the basis for its interpretation, was explained clearly by Commissioner Jacobs in *CH 1176/2003* para 8 in the following terms:

"The context in which regulation 99(2) will operate is relevant. It only applies to cases in which the claimant was on low income at the time of the payment. And the payment involved will have been made to help the claimant pay rent on a dwelling. In those circumstances, it is likely that the money will be spent fairly quickly. That, I believe, accounts for the emphasis on the time of payment or notice relating to payment. If the claimant could not reasonably have been expected to realise that an overpayment had been made, it is likely that the money will have been spent and spent in reliance on the claimant being properly entitled to it. In other words, regulation 99(2) contains an element of protection for a claimant who has relied on being entitled to the payment. The provision is not worded in those terms or limited to cases where there has been reliance. But that rationale provides a context in which the terms of the legislation must be interpreted."

The phrase relating to notices causes difficulty. The amendment was apparently made to deal with rent rebate cases where the claimant never actually receives any rent: Circular HB/CCB 90/23, and see *CH 1675/2005*. The wording is not restricted to such cases: *CH 1176/2003* para 9. In the same case, the commissioner suggested that if a notice containing notice of an erroneous payment is sent out but promptly corrected by a telephone call to the claimant, it might be possible to see the whole process as one transaction: para 32-33. This seems to be an unwarranted gloss on the legislation and adds an additional complication to a tribunal's task.

In *R(H) 1/02*, the commissioner was concerned with a case where a claimant had omitted to inform the local authority of an increase in her wages until she signed a review form some six weeks later. However, the authority recalculated her benefit on the basis of an incorrect figure being entered into its computer for the benefit calculations. That recalculation was carried out at a later stage, with a result that a lump sum was payable to the claimant. The claimant was sent notifications which set out the calculation with the incorrect figure used for the amount of her wages.

The commissioner held, at para 6(2)(a) of the decision, that where a claimant both receives a notice relating to a payment and receives it, knowledge or presumed knowledge on the date of either event will suffice to make the overpayment recoverable. He also held that "notice relating to that payment" requires that the notice in question be sufficiently closely related to the payment: para 6(2)(b).

This point was also addressed in *CH 1176/2003*, where the commissioner held (para 31) that, although the notice need not be the notice *of* payment, and so is wider than the actual decision notice, it must relate to the *payment* and not the overpayment, otherwise para (2) would provide no protection as, by definition, at the time of the overpayment notice the claimant must have been able to realise that it was an overpayment (see also *CH 1675/2005*). In *CH 1176/2003* a cheque for HB was mistakenly issued to the claimant's bank on 18 February and credited to her account on the following day. The claimant made a series of withdrawals from her bank account before being informed by the local authority on 26 February of the mistake. Commissioner Jacobs held that a payment made by cheque is only received when it is credited to the claimant's bank account and not when the cheque is received by the claimant or presented at the bank: paras 20-23. He also held, remitting the case to the tribunal for reconsideration, that the "time" of receipt should not be judged according to the split-second at which the cheque was credited: para 26. It was a question of fact for the Tribunal but one possible approach was to examine the claimant's knowledge over the day of receipt: para 27.

"... that it was an overpayment...". It must be shown that the relevant person should have known that there was an overpayment, not that there might have been an overpayment. In *Griffiths* (above), the authority had sent out letters warning claimants that they might receive the wrong amount of benefit under the estimated award. It was argued that it was sufficient that Mrs Griffiths knew that she might be being overpaid. Nolan J held (at 317) that this was not enough. It was not reasonable to expect her to work out her entitlement herself to decide whether she was getting too much HB. This approach was confirmed in *CH 2554/2002* para 9. The corollary of this, as pointed out by Commissioner Jacobs in that case, is that the claimant need not be aware of the amount by which s/he is being overpaid. All that is necessary is that that the claimant "could reasonably have been expected to realise that the amount she was receiving definitely contained some element of overpayment".

Paragraph (4)

This paragraph provides that certain overpayments of rent rebate are always recoverable. There are four conditions for its operation:

(1)   There has been a revision of the award. It does not appear to apply if the award is correct but, for example, the claimant is credited twice on her/his account due to a clerical error.

(2)   It also appears that the claimant's rent account must be in credit for the paragraph to come into effect. So, if a claimant is wrongly awarded £100 rather than £50 rent rebate for four weeks, but

incurs an annual service charge on the rent account of £500, the account will be £300 in the red and so the paragraph does not apply.

(3) The credit is in respect of a period after the date of the revision. In respect of past periods, the exception does not apply and the three criteria can be considered.

(4) Even if there is a credit after the date of the revision, that credit must be the overpayment and not subsequent payments of rent rebate or made by the claimant. If the latter is the case, then the surplus ought to be presumed to relate to the latest of the payments made into the rent account: *Clayton's case* [1861] 1 Mer 572. For example, a claimant wrongly awarded £100 rather than £80 for four weeks then has her/his rent rebate suspended for two weeks. After one week, the £80 credit has gone; after two, the claimant is £80 in the red. However, at the end of the two weeks, before a revision is carried out, the claimant pays £160 into the rent account. There is an £80 credit on the account when the review is carried out, but that represents the claimant's voluntary payment rather than the overpayment.

Person from whom recovery may be sought

101.–(1) For the purposes of section 75(3)(a) of the Administration Act (prescribed circumstances in which an amount recoverable shall not be recovered from the person to whom it was paid), the prescribed circumstance is–

(a) housing benefit has been paid in accordance with regulation 95 (circumstances in which payment is to be made to the landlord) or regulation 96 (circumstances in which payment may be made to a landlord);

(b) the landlord has notified the relevant authority or the Secretary of State in writing that he suspects that there has been an overpayment;

[¹ (bb) the relevant authority is satisfied that the overpayment did not occur as a result of any change of dwelling occupied by the claimant as his home;]

(c) it appears to the relevant authority that, on the assumption that there has been an overpayment–

    (i) there are grounds for instituting proceedings against any person for an offence under section 111A or 112(1) of the Administration Act (dishonest or false representations for obtaining benefit); or

    (ii) there has been a deliberate failure to report a relevant change of circumstances contrary to the requirement of regulation 88 (duty to notify a change of circumstances) and the overpayment occurred as a result of that deliberate failure; and

(d) the relevant authority is satisfied that the landlord–

    (i) has not colluded with the claimant so as to cause the overpayment;

    (ii) has not acted, or neglected to act, in such a way so as to contribute to the period, or the amount, of the overpayment.

[² (2) For the purposes of section 75(3)(b) of the Administration Act (recovery from such other person, as well as or instead of the person to whom the overpayment was made), where recovery of an overpayment is sought by a relevant authority–

(a) the prescribed person from whom it is sought shall be–

    (i) in a case where an overpayment arose in consequence of a misrepresentation of or a failure to disclose a material fact (in either case, whether fraudulently or otherwise) by or on behalf of the claimant or any other person to whom housing benefit has been paid, the person who misrepresented or failed to disclose that material fact instead of, if different, the person to whom the payment was made;

    (ii) in a case where an overpayment arose in consequence of an official error where the claimant or a person acting on his behalf or any other person to whom the payment has been made could reasonably have been expected, at the time of receipt of the payment or of any notice relating to that payment, to realise that it was an overpayment, that person instead of, if different, the person to whom the payment was made; or

(b)   where sub-paragraphs (a)(i) and (ii) do not apply, the prescribed person from whom it is sought is–
    (i)   the claimant;
    (ii)   in a case where a recoverable overpayment is made to a claimant who has one or more partners, the claimant's partner or any of his partners.]

(3)   For the purposes of paragraph (1), "landlord" shall have the same meaning as it has for the purposes of regulation 95.

[¹ (3A)   For the purposes of paragraph (2)(a)(ii), "overpayment arose in consequence of an official error" shall have the same meaning as in regulation 100(3) above.]

(4)   For the purposes of [² paragraph (2)(b)(ii)], recovery of the overpayment may be by deduction from any housing benefit payable to a partner provided that the claimant and that partner were members of the same household both at the time of the overpayment and when the deduction is made.

Amendments

1.   Inserted by reg 6(2) and (4) of SI 2005 No 2904 as amended by Sch 2 para 29 of SI 2006 No 217 as from 10.4.06.
2.   Substituted by reg 6(3) of SI 2005 No 2904 as amended by Sch 2 para 29 of SI 2006 No 217 as from 10.4.06.

Definitions

"claimant" – see reg 2(1).
"membership of household" – see Part 4 and note on s20(11).
"partner" – see reg 2(1).
"overpayment" – see reg 99.
"recoverable" – see reg 100.

General Note

SSAA s75(3) provides that a recoverable overpayment is recoverable from the person to whom it was paid unless regulations provide otherwise, and also gives a power to make regulations allowing recovery to be made from other persons in certain circumstances. This regulation exercises those powers. See commentary to s75 SSAA 1992 above and the Tribunal of Commissioner's decision in *R(H) 6/06*.

In *R(H) 6/06* the commissioners also commented on the new version of reg 101 HB Regs in force from 10 April 2006. Reg 101(2)(a)(i) and (ii) expressly provides that recovery of an overpayment will be sought from the specified person *instead of* the person to whom the overpayment was made. However, reg 101(2)(b)(i) and (ii) does not make clear whether the overpayment is to be sought from the claimant or a partner of the claimant as well as, or instead of, the person to whom the overpayment was made. In the commissioners' view, however, the clear intention of the legislation is that recovery may be sought from the claimant and any partner of the claimant *as well as* the person to whom the overpayment was made. They also commented that, despite the title of the new reg 101, it was clear that it was dealing with the recoverability stage rather than (the later) enforcement of recovery. Although *R(H) 6/06* was not dealing with the post-9 April 2006 version of reg 101, it is clear from the decision that the commissioners considered that the same considerations as to the split between the recoverability and recovery stages of an overpayment, and appeal rights in respect of reg 101 decisions, should apply equally to the post-9 April 2006 regime.

Two issues which may still arise in respect of the post-9 April 2006 version of reg 101, however, are which overpayments it applies to and when a landlord may be said to have breached a legal duty to disclose so that he or she can be said to have failed to disclose (following *B v Secretary of State for Work and Pensions* [2005] EWCA Civ 929, [2005] 1 WLR 3796 (reported as *R(IS) 9/06*)). As to the former, it is arguable that as the 10 April 2006 version of reg 101 changes (in some respects at least) the substantive rights of the parties, it only applies in cases where the overpayment was made on or after 10 April 2006: applying, by analogy, *Plewa v Chief Adjudication Officer* [1995] 1 AC 248, HL. As to the latter, regns 86(1) and 88(1) (and the equivalent regulations in the HB(SPC) Regs – regs 67(1) and 69(1)) would seem to only impose a legal duty on a landlord to disclose if there is a subsequent change in circumstances after the claim has been awarded, and then only if he or she knows about the change and "might reasonably be expected to know" that it "might affect" the claimant's HB.

Note finally the commissioners' recommendation in *R(H) 6/06* that in every case where reg 101 provides for joint liability, the local authority should make a single decision referring to all of those from whom the overpayment is recoverable, rather than separate decisions addressed to each of them. Moreover, where a local authority decides that an overpayment is not recoverable from the person to whom it was made, a proper decision to that effect should be made and included in the decision about the person from whom the overpayment is recoverable, and that decision issued to both parties.

Para (1) deals with the case where a person receiving HB will not be liable to repay benefit, namely a blameless landlord in certain limited cases. Para (4) deals with recovery from partners of claimants.

There will be many cases in which an overpayment is recoverable from more than one person. By far the most common case is recoverability both from claimant and landlord. In every such case, the authority has a discretion to decide from whom recovery should be sought. As with the discretion to recover an overpayment, an authority must carefully consider all relevant factors when deciding on its target. Factors which will often be relevant include the relative prosperity of the different persons from whom recovery may be made; their moral culpability; the degree of financial benefit obtained by each person from the overpayment of benefit; the cost, difficulty and time span of recovery from them; and, in the case of corporate entities, whether they are profit-making organisations or not.

Again, over-rigid policies such as always recovering from landlords rather than claimants will be unlawful.

Analysis

Paragraph (1): Cases where an overpayment is not recoverable from a landlord

The origin of para (1) is probably the increasingly loud complaints of social landlords who were finding that overpayment recovery jeopardised their financial stability. Local authorities habitually recovered very large overpayments from social landlords as a matter of course, without exercising any real discretion and without regard to the circumstances of the case, in particular to cases where a claimant had acted fraudulently.

R(H) 6/06 provides a limited exception to the entitlement to recover from landlords in such a situation. Para (1) sets out four conditions that must all be satisfied if the landlord is to escape liability. Some of the drafting is rather loose and there will be plenty of scope for argument about the interpretation of the various limbs of the paragraph.

It is important to emphasise that if the four conditions in para (1) are satisfied, the overpayment is *irrecoverable:* see *CH 2791/2003,* which also emphasises that the conditions in para (1)(a) to (1)(d) are cumulative.

Sub-para (a). Direct payments made to landlord. A landlord cannot take advantage of para (1) unless direct payments were made under reg 95 or 96. Thus in the unlikely scenario of a landlord to whom direct payments were not being made being guilty of a misrepresentation or failure to disclose but still fulfilling the four conditions, the overpayment will still be recoverable.

The HB that has been paid direct must be the same as the HB of which recovery is sought. This is made clear by the scope of the enabling power in s75(3). So if a landlord received direct payments prior to the overpayment period but not during that period, then again the overpayment will not be recoverable.

Direct payments to a landlord's agent will satisfy this condition, since reg 101(3) imports the definition in reg 95: "a person to whom rent is payable". If a landlord appoints an agent to receive the rent, then for the purposes of reg 101 the agent will be treated as if s/he is the landlord.

Sub-para (b): Notification of overpayment. There must be a written notification. "Writing" will certainly extend to communication by fax and also ought to extend to correspondence by email. It is also suggested that it will be sufficient if a landlord makes an oral statement to an officer which is recorded by that officer, particularly if it is then signed by the landlord.

A notice given by an agent or company director will be sufficient for the purposes of sub-para (b), certainly if it is explicitly made on behalf of the landlord.

Another obvious question arising under sub-para (b) is what sort of information will satisfy the provision. On a narrow and literal reading, it would appear that the landlord must explicitly state a belief that an overpayment has occurred. It is suggested that would be an unduly restrictive interpretation. What is required is that the document should clearly impart information that suggests that an overpayment may have occurred. For example, it will suffice if a landlord writes to the local authority to state that it has discovered that one of its claimant tenants has apparently left the tenanted property. The policy intention behind para (1) is to reward landlords for being diligent in reporting suspicious circumstances. One thing is clear. The landlord need not be certain that an overpayment is occurring; a suspicion will suffice.

Sub-para (c): Offence committed or deliberate failure to disclose. The opening words "it appears to the relevant authority" do not restrict the scope of a challenge to an authority's decision that this sub-paragraph is not fulfilled. It is suggested that an appeal tribunal must decide for itself whether it appears that the condition is satisfied.

The two limbs of sub-para (c) are alternatives and while both will often be fulfilled, only one need be proved. Moreover, under head (i), it is not necessary to prove that the relevant person is guilty of the offence, merely that there is a case for her/him to answer. See the commentary to ss111A and 112(1) for the question of whether an offence is committed, and note that an offence of knowing non-disclosure under s112(1A) will not satisfy head (i), though it will usually satisfy head (ii).

Under head (ii), a breach of the duty in reg 88(1) must be shown. The duty only binds a claimant, a recipient of HB or an agent of a recipient. The breach must be deliberate. The *Shorter Oxford English Dictionary* defines "deliberate" as "carefully thought out, studied; intentional, done on purpose". A breach that is inadvertent or even negligent will not suffice. The breach must also have caused the overpayment. It need not be the sole cause. It will suffice if it is one of joint causes: *R (Sier) v Cambridge CC HBRB* [2001] EWHC Admin 160, QBD; [2001] EWCA Civ 1523, CA, Richards J, discussed in the commentary to reg 99 above.

Sub-para (d): No fault of landlord. This is the trickiest of the four conditions of which to unravel the meaning. It appears that both limbs under sub-para (d) must be satisfied. Again the wording "the relevant authority is satisfied" does not confine the appeal tribunal to a review of the authority's decision; it must decide the question for itself afresh.

In head (i), "colluded" is not defined. The *Shorter Oxford English Dictionary* gives "conspire, plot, connive, act in secret concert . . . . stir up or bring about by collusion". Effectively, there must be an agreement to act in such a way that an overpayment occurs, but it may be that a specific intention to commit fraud is not required.

Under head (ii), it must be shown that the landlord "has not acted, or neglected to act" in a way that caused the claimant to be overpaid. One of two things must be shown: a positive action of the landlord (or, it would seem, the landlord's agent) or some degree of inaction. The latter must involve "neglect". So if the landlord did not know of the relevant facts or if a reasonable person in the landlord's position would not have informed the local authority of the position, then the overpayment does not become recoverable.

The action or inaction must then have had an effect "so as to contribute to the period, or the amount, of the overpayment". It is difficult to avoid the conclusion from these words that if there is any increase in the amount or period of the overpayment, the *whole* of the overpayment will be recoverable, not just that portion occurring after the action or inaction of the landlord contributed to it. There are likely to be many cases where a local authority claims that the landlord should have notified it of a suspected change of circumstances earlier than it did, and so head (ii) is not satisfied. Landlords in such situations may well be able to argue that there was no "neglect" because it was not reasonable to expect it to form the view that it was necessary to report something any earlier than it did.

Note that head (ii) does not necessarily require a landlord to report a suspicion immediately. Provided a report was made prior to the next payment of HB being made, that would be sufficient to fulfil head (ii).

Applicability of para (1) to pre-October 2001 cases. SI 2001 No 1190, which introduced a new version of reg 101 HB Regs 1987 (now reg 101 HB Regs), is yet another example of the frequent failure of the DSS, as it then was, to include transitional provisions to enable easy determination of which cases fall to be judged under the new version of reg 101. It is therefore necessary to decide the effect on existing cases by reference to existing caselaw. Caselaw establishes, broadly, that legislation that affects existing rights is presumed not to be retrospective, whereas legislation that affects existing procedure will have effect in relation to existing cases. In the specific context of overpayments, three propositions may be stated:

(1)   Any alteration in the criteria for recoverability of an overpayment is a substantive, rather than a procedural amendment. Accordingly there is a presumption that the amendments do not have retrospective effect in such a case: *Plewa v Chief Adjudication Officer* [1995] 1 AC 248, HL.

(2)   Any change in the method by which overpayments are recovered is a procedural amendment and accordingly the presumption does not apply: *R v Secretary of State for Social Security ex p Britnell* [1989] *The Times* 27 January, QBD.

(3)   If there is a change in the law during the review process, the officer carrying out a first-stage review and a Review Board (or tribunal) must apply the law as it stood at the point of the decision under review: *R (Nicholson) v Leeds CC HBRB* [2000] unreported, 2 November, QBD.

(4)   The claimant's partner. See the commentary to reg 102 for a discussion of when there can be recovery from such a person.

The current reg 101 affects the substantive rights of the landlords falling within its scope and the local authority, since it will have the effect of preventing recovery from such landlords where such recovery could have been made previously. That would normally suggest that it cannot apply in respect of overpayments occurring prior to 1 October 2001. However, reg 101 provides that an overpayment "shall not be recovered" from such a landlord. It does not affect the right to recover from a claimant or any other responsible person. Because the language of the regulation looks forward rather than backward in its effect, it is highly arguable that it does apply to overpayments that were made but not adjudicated as being recoverable overpayments prior to 1 October 2001. It will not affect decisions made prior to that date, even if there is a pending review or appeal on 1 October 2001.

In *CH 3679/2002*, the commissioner stated, apparently without the benefit of argument, that the old form of reg 101 had to be considered in relation to appeals against decisions made prior to October 2001.

Paragraph (2): Targets for recovery

Para (2) sets out the categories of persons from whom an overpayment may be recovered. There are three categories:

(1)   The claimant, in every case.

(2)   The person to whom the payment was made. This includes appointees who made the original claim paid under reg 94(2) (but see below), people acting informally on behalf of claimants, landlords paid under regs 95 and 96 (provided that they do not escape liability under para (1), or personal representatives or next of kin of deceased claimants paid under reg 97.

(3)   A relevant person making a misrepresentation or failure to disclose.

Recovery can be made automatically from either of the first two categories in any case, but for other persons, it must be shown that the conditions in sub-para (a) are met. These conditions are identical to those for the recovery of benefits paid by the DWP: see Administration Act s71. There is a vast body of caselaw on s71 which must be treated as highly persuasive in relation to HB. Only a summary is given below: see the commentary to s71 in vol III of *Social Security Legislation.*

"... in consequence of ...". There must be a clear link between the misrepresentation or failure to disclose and the making of the overpayment. However, the misleading of the authority need not be the sole cause of the overpayment. It is sufficient if it is a significant contributing factor. So, where there has been a failure to disclose by a relevant person, it is no answer that the authority could have discovered the true situation by contacting the DWP or some other person: *Duggan v Chief Adjudication Officer* [1988] The Times 18 December, CA; *CSB 64/1986* para 11.

On the other hand, where the authority knows of the true situation, the misleading may not be sufficiently significant. The "clear link" will not be established where it can be shown that the authority has actually been informed of the true situation by the DWP or some other third person: *CIS 159/1990* para 4; *CS 12770/1996* para 9. When the relevant person has previously informed the authority of the true facts but later inadvertently misleads the authority, provided it is reasonable for them to assume the previous information has been acted on, the later misrepresentation may not be an effective cause of the overpayment: *CS 130/1992* paras 15-16. Furthermore, where the information before the authority clearly makes it clear that there is a need for further inquiries, and those inquiries are not made, then the sole cause of the overpayment may be the authority's error: *CIS 222/1991* paras 4-5.

Where there has been criminal activity by a third person, such as the theft of a cheque, that activity may be found to be the true cause of a resulting overpayment: *CIS 395/1992* para 10.

"... a misrepresentation ...". A misrepresentation is an actual statement which is untrue or misleading: *CSB 1006/1985* para 5. It may be made in writing, orally or even by conduct if sufficiently unambiguous: *R(SB) 18/85* para 10.

Claim forms provided by authorities often require a person claiming on behalf of the claimant to sign a declaration at the end of the form. If the declaration is false then that may amount to a misrepresentation even if none of the details given on the form are untrue of themselves. However, the courts have tended to give a narrow reading to such declarations: see *Jones v Chief Adjudication Officer* [1994] 1 WLR 62 at 71H, 72F, CA; *Franklin v Chief Adjudication Officer* [1995] *The Times* 29 December, CA; *CIS 393/1993* para 7; *CIS 372/1994* para 6.

"... or failure to disclose ...". Following the case of *B v Secretary of State for Work and Pensions* (see below for details) the authority must now establish only two matters; the additional test of whether disclosure was "reasonably to be expected" having been held to be unnecessary in *B*:

(1)   That the relevant person was under a duty to disclose. See HB Regs reg 86 for the duty to provide information to the authority and reg 88 for the statutory duty to notify a change of circumstances. In *CH 2443/2002* para 14 the commissioner held that an employer could not be under a duty to disclose because reg 75 HB regs 1987 (now reg 88 HB Regs) had no application to an employer. More recently the Court of Appeal in *B v Secretary of State for Work and Pensions* [2005] EWCA Civ 929, [2005] 1 WLR 3796 (reported as *R(IS) 9/06*) – affirming the decision of the Tribunal of Commissioners in *CIS 4348/2003* – has held that a failure to disclose can only arise if the person was under a legal duty which s/he has breached: *R(SB) 21/82*. However, there can be no duty to disclose information which is not known: *Franklin*; *R(SB) 54/83* para 13(2); *R(SB) 9/85* para 7.

(2)   That the relevant person did not disclose the relevant information. Disclosure means informing the authority in such a way that the information can be expected to come to the attention of a person with responsibility for handling the claim: *R(SB) 15/87* paras 25, 28 and *Hinchy v Secretary of State for Work and Pensions* [2005] UKHL 16 (*R(IS) 7/05*). Although HB Regs reg 88 and CTB Regs reg 74 require changes of circumstances to be notified "in writing to the designated office" oral disclosure has always been treated as sufficient in relation to DWP benefits, even before the Social Security (Claims and Payments) Regulations 1987 reg 32 was amended to permit oral disclosure to be accepted: see *R(SB) 40/84* para 5; *R(SB) 15/87* para 13. Once disclosure has been made, there is no duty to disclose the same information again: *R(SB) 15/87* para 28.

"... a material fact ...". This is one that the relevant person ought reasonably to realise might affect benefit: HB Regs reg 75(1) and *Saker v Secretary of State for Social Security* [1988] 16 January *The Times*, CA (reported as *R(I) 2/88*).

"... in either case whether fraudulently or otherwise ...". No moral culpability need be shown on the part of the relevant person. The misleading of authority may have been entirely innocent: *Page v Chief Adjudication Officer* [1991] The Times 4 July, CA.

"... by or on behalf of the claimant or any other person to whom a payment of housing benefit may be made ...". The misleading of the authority must fall into one of the following categories:

(1)   Misleading by the claimant, who is caught under para (c) anyway.

(2)   Misleading by any other person to whom a payment of benefit may be made. This category causes a difficulty. Logically, it might not be restricted to those to whom payment was actually made, since again those persons come under para (b) in any case. It appears highly arguable that it extends to other persons who come within category (ii) of the persons from whom recovery can be made (see the beginning of this Analysis) but who were not actually being paid. If that is right, where an authority makes an overpayment of benefit following a misrepresentation by a landlord who was not being paid directly under HB Regs reg 95 or 96, there can be recovery from that landlord.

(3)   Misleading on behalf of the claimant. This could cover persons who have not been appointed to deal with the claimant's affairs but who assist on an informal basis.

(4)   Misleading on behalf of any other person to whom a payment of benefit may be made. For the meaning of the latter phrase, see category (ii) above. This category may include parties such as landlord's agents.

"... the person who misrepresented or failed to disclose that material fact ...". In all cases, this includes the individual responsible who misled the authority. It probably also includes corporate entities for whom the individual works: see Interpretation Act 1978 Sch 1.

Recovery from appointees. The mechanism in HB Reg 82(3) for appointment of a person to act on behalf of another is similar to the procedure for appointment by the DWP under reg 33 of the Social Security (Claims and Payments) Regulations 1987. The question of whether appointees can be personally liable to repay an overpayment has caused controversy in relation to DWP benefits. This has now been settled by the decision of a Tribunal of Commissioners in *R(IS) 5/03*, in which it was held that such personal liability would ordinarily exist: para 57. Recovery will normally be available against both claimant and appointee: para 58. However, it was said that if the benefit was not paid over to the claimant, recovery could only be made from the appointee: para 59. It was also said that the appointee would have a right under general principles of agency law to be indemnified by her/his principal except in cases where s/he was guilty of negligence or a breach of duty: para 61. The principal is the local authority, because the local authority appoints the appointee to act. Accordingly, in cases where it is alleged that there is strict liability for a misrepresentation made by an appointee but the appointee acted with due diligence, the appointee will be able to counterclaim to proceedings brought by the local authority for an indemnity, and the claim for the amount of the overpayment and the counterclaim for the indemnity will cancel each other out.

Paragraph (4)

This paragraph deals with the circumstances in which there can be recovery of HB paid to the claimant's partner as a method of recovery from the claimant. Like all other methods of recovery, it is analysed in depth in the Analysis to reg 102.

Method of recovery

102.–(1)   Without prejudice to any other method of recovery, [² a relevant authority] may recover a recoverable overpayment from any person referred to in regulation 101 (persons from whom recovery may be sought) by deduction from any housing benefit to which that person is entitled (including arrears of entitlement after offsetting under regulation 98 (offsetting)) or, where it is unable to do so, may request the Secretary of State to recover any recoverable overpayment from the benefits prescribed in regulation 105 (recovery of overpayments from prescribed benefits).

[² (1A)   Where–

(a)   a claimant has moved into a dwelling which he occupies as his home;

(b)   a recoverable overpayment of housing benefit is thereafter made direct to him in connection with the dwelling he occupied as his home immediately preceding the date he moved to that dwelling; and

(c)   the same relevant authority which made the recoverable overpayment is paying housing benefit to that claimant in respect of that new dwelling,

the relevant authority may at its discretion deduct from the housing benefit it is paying to the claimant in respect of a benefit week an amount equal to the claimant's weekly entitlement to housing benefit at his new dwelling, and may do so for the number of benefit weeks equal to the number of weeks during which the claimant was overpaid housing benefit.]

(2)   Subject to paragraphs [² (1A),] (4) and (5), where [¹ a relevant authority] makes deductions permitted by paragraph (1) from the housing benefit it is paying to a claimant (other than deductions from arrears of entitlement), the deduction in respect of a benefit week shall be–

(a)   in a case to which paragraph (3) applies, not more than the amount there specified; and

(b)   in any other case, not more than three times five per cent. of the personal allowance for a single claimant aged not less than 25, that five per cent. being, where it is not a multiple of five pence, rounded to the next higher such multiple.

(3)   Where [¹ a relevant authority] makes deductions from housing benefit it is paying to a claimant who has, in respect of the whole or part of the recoverable overpayment–

(a)   been found guilty of an offence whether under a statute or otherwise;

(b)   made an admission after caution of deception or fraud for the purpose of obtaining relevant benefit; or

(c)   agreed to pay a penalty under section 115A of the Administration Act (penalty as an alternative to prosecution) and the agreement has not been withdrawn,

the amount deducted under paragraph (2) shall be not more than four times five per cent. of the personal allowance for a single claimant aged not less than 25, but where that five per cent. is not a multiple of 10 pence, it shall be rounded to the nearest 10 pence or, if it is a multiple of 5 pence but not of 10 pence, the next higher multiple of 10 pence.

(4)   Where, in the calculation of housing benefit, the amount of earnings or other income falling to be taken into account is reduced by reason of paragraphs 3 to 10 of Schedule 4 (sums to be disregarded in the calculation of earnings) or paragraph 14 or 15 of Schedule 5 (sums to be disregarded in the calculation of income other than earnings), the deduction under paragraph (2) may be increased by not more than half the amount of the reduction.

(5)   No deduction made under this regulation [² , except as made under paragraph (1A),] shall be applied so as to reduce the housing benefit in respect of a benefit week to less than 50 pence.

(6)   In this regulation–

''admission after caution'' means–

(i)   in England and Wales, an admission after a caution has been administered in accordance with a Code issued under the Police and Criminal Evidence Act 1984;

(ii)   in Scotland, admission after a caution has been administered, such admission being duly witnessed by two persons; and

''personal allowance for a single claimant aged not less than 25'' means the amount specified in paragraph 1(1)(b) of column 2 of Schedule 3 (applicable amounts).

(7)   This regulation shall not apply in respect of an offence committed or an admission after caution or an agreement to pay a penalty made before 2nd October 2000.

Amendments

1.   Substituted by reg 7(2) of SI 2005 No 2904 as amended by Sch 2 para 29 of SI 2006 No 217 as from 10.4.06.

2.   Inserted by reg 7(3)-(5) of SI 2005 No 2904 as amended by Sch 2 para 29 of SI 2006 No 217 as from 10.4.06.

Definitions

"authority" – see reg 2(2) and s134(4) SSAA.

"overpayment" – see reg 99.

"recoverable" – see reg 100.

General Note

A new version of reg 102 was introduced from 2 October 2000. Where an authority wishes to recover an overpayment and the claimant has an ongoing entitlement, many authorities habitually withheld the full amount of the ongoing benefit, despite being urged by guidance not to do this. This had often resulted in possession proceedings against the claimant which could have been avoided if recovery had been made at a more realistic level. Now paras (2) and (3) restrict the amount of HB which may be withheld in any benefit week.

Analysis

In the detailed consideration of the various methods of recovery available that follows, the person from whom recovery is sought will be referred to as "D". Note that the options available to the local authority are significantly expanded by the Social Security Administration (Fraud) Act 1997. It seems fairly clear that it will be possible to use these powers to recover overpayments arising before the provisions granting the new powers came into force. In *R v Secretary of State for Social Services ex p Britnell* [1989] COD 487, DC it was held that since a similar expansion in the power of the then DSS to recover overpayments merely changed the procedure as to recovery and not the claimant's substantive rights, the presumption against retrospectively did not apply to prevent recovery of the claimant's unemployment benefit. This point was not pursued in the Court of Appeal or House of Lords.

The fact that D has been declared bankrupt will not prevent recovery from benefits payable to her/him, since the specific statutory provisions dealing with recovery from benefit entitlement override the general law of bankruptcy in England and Wales: *R v Secretary of State for Social Security ex p Taylor and Chapman* [1996] *The Times* 5 February, QBD (Keene J), and the law of sequestration in Scotland: *Mulvey v Secretary of State for Social Security* [1997] SLT 753 at 756, HL. However, if an overpayment decision is made before a person is adjudged bankrupt, it will amount to a "contingent liability" under the Insolvency Act 1986 and a claimant should then be discharged from liability to repay that overpayment under s281 of the Insolvency Act 1986 if and when s/he is discharged from bankruptcy: *R(Balding) v Secretary of State for Work and Pensions* [2007] EWHC 759, 3 April 2007, (Admin) (but note that the decision is under appeal to the Court of Appeal).

The authority may not add interest to the overpayment: *R v Kensington and Chelsea RBC ex p Brandt* [1995] 28 HLR 528, QBD (Dyson J).

Recovery from HB payable to D

Under reg 102, there may be recovery from any HB owing to D to which D is entitled. This can be arrears owed to D (even if the arrears are referable to dates outside the period of the overpayment) or future payments. The effect of reg 102 is duplicated by SSAA s75(5)(a) and reg 106(2).

Where D is a claimant in receipt of rent allowance, this should not cause any difficulties. When determining the appropriate rate of recovery, the authority will wish to balance the need for enforcement against the need to avoid making the tenant homeless and possibly liable to be housed by the authority. The authority may deduct from payments made to D's landlord. Since the landlord has never been paid, this will create rent arrears as between landlord and claimant.

Reg 102 only authorises deduction from HB where D is not a claimant, if it is HB paid to D in his role as claimant. In particular, where D is a landlord, reg 102 does not authorise recovery from HB paid to D in respect of tenants other than the overpaid claimant. The recovery is only from HB "to which that person [ie the person from whom recovery is sought] is entitled". D is not entitled to HB; his tenants are.

In *R v Haringey LBC ex p Ayub* [1992] 25 HLR 566, QBD, the applicant was a landlord owning a large stock of housing in the authority's area. Many of his tenants received HB. When overpayments were made, the authority sought to withhold payment of HB payable in respect of other tenants. On judicial review, the authority admitted that this course of action was not sanctioned by reg 102. Instead, it was said that this was a convenient method of recovery. Furthermore, as the other tenants were debtors of the landlord, the authority could "garnish" their debts (that is, seize payments made to a debtor by his debtors). Schiemann J held that there was no right to garnish a debt until a court order was obtained, and then stated:

"When a council is making a payment to a landlord under regulations 93 or 94 *[now regs 95 and 96 HB Regs]* of rent allowance to which tenants B-Z are entitled it is in effect acting as the agent of those tenants and paying their rent for them. Upon such a payment being made the tenant's liability to the landlord is *pro tanto* extinguished and the latter cannot thereafter sue the former for more payment of that rent or repossess the property on the basis of non-payment of that rent. The authority is not allowed to use a tenant's rent allowance in order to extinguish any liability of the landlord to the authority. That is not a purpose for which Parliament has authorised the payment of rent allowance. The general right of set-off for which the authority contends would leave it totally unclear as to which unfortunate tenant's rent allowance is to be used for this purpose and indeed whether the choice of the unlucky tenant is to be in the hands of the landlord or in those of the authority."

However, the Administration Act s75(5)(b) and (c) (inserted by s16 Social Security (Administration) Fraud Act 1997) gives the authority the right to recover from "prescribed benefits" paid to D in respect of an obligation owed to him by another person. See reg 106(3) and note the effect of reg 107 on tenants' liabilities.

Paras (2) and (3) impose maximum weekly amounts that may be recovered from ongoing HB. This applies only to ongoing entitlement and not to arrears, as is clear from the words in parentheses in para (2). The maximum amount is subject to a needlessly complicated calculation. First, one takes the personal allowance for a single claimant aged over 25, take 5 per cent of that. That figure is then multiplied by three to give the maximum deduction.

A higher maximum applies wherever the claimant is convicted of an offence, admits the offence under caution or agrees to pay a penalty. However, that only applies where the offence, admission or agreement occurs after 2 October 2000: see para (7). An admission under caution must comply with Code C issued under the Police and Criminal Evidence Act 1984 in England and Wales. Some guidance is given on this in para 19 of Circular HB/CTB A42/2000, but careful reference should be made to the Code.

In either case, where the claimant has earnings which are being partially disregarded, a further amount of half of the disregard may be added to the amount being recovered.

It is to be noted, however, that these amounts remain the maxima and so authorities should give careful consideration to any hardship that may result in deciding whether to deduct the full amount: see para 20 of the Circular.

Recovery from HB payable to D's partner

Recovery from D's partner (S) is authorised by reg 101(2), provided the following conditions are met:

(1)   D is the claimant. The power cannot be used to recover, for example, from the partner of D who is an executor of the claimant's will and who has received benefit after the claimant's death.

(2)   D was receiving the HB. It does not apply where payment was made to the landlord under reg 93 or 94 or to any other payee.

(3)   D and S were living in the same household *both* at the time of the overpayment *and* at the time the deduction is made. It is suggested that the authority cannot make recovery of a proportion of the overpayment where S was only in the same household for a some of the weeks of the period of the overpayment. The "overpayment" is the full amount found to be recoverable. S must have been living in the same household for the full period before the provision can be used.

1997 GM A7.55 makes the obvious point that there can be no recovery from S where D has died, since they are not living in the same household after D's death.

Recovery from D's partner

There is some uncertainty as to whether, and if so in what circumstances, there may be recovery from D's partner other than by deduction from their HB entitlement. It is suggested that it is tolerably clear that there may be such recovery. Reg 101(4) is clearly only designed to make it clear that there may be deduction from benefit rather than prescribing this as the only method of recovery. The general rule is that specifically stated methods are without prejudice to other methods of recovery: reg 102(1).

On the other hand, it is suggested that reg 101(2)(b) restricts recovery to cases where the partner was the claimant's partner during the period of the overpayment. This appears to be clear from the present tense of the words "is" and "has" in the sub-paragraph. A counter-argument might be that reg 101(4) would then be superfluous, but it is suggested that it is the concomitant of reg 102(1) and merely makes it clear beyond doubt that there may be recovery by withholding HB due to a claimant. The restrictions on the amount so withheld under reg 102(2) will apply to a claimant's partner as well as a claimant.

Recovery from other benefits

The procedure for recovery from other benefits is specified by reg 105. It applies to benefits payable by the DWP and recovery is carried out by the Secretary of State on the authority's behalf.

There can be no recovery of overpaid HB from CTB or vice versa: 1997 GM A7.38. Neither can recovery be made of benefits payable to D's partner: 1997 GM A7.37iv.

Conditions for recovery from other benefits. The authority may only make a request to the Secretary of State to recover from other benefits payable to D when it is "unable" to recover by deduction from D's

HB. It is suggested that this requires that there is no HB in payment which the authority can withhold, not merely that the authority consider that the amount is insufficient.

The Secretary of State may not recover the overpayment unless requested to by the authority, and must be satisfied of three conditions before making recovery. However, once the three conditions are present, the minister has no discretion to decline to recover.

(1)   That there is a recoverable overpayment of HB. The Secretary of State will invariably follow the authority's final determination, but ought to refuse recovery where D is still exercising statutory rights of review or is seeking judicial review. Where an application is made by the authority under reg 102 in this situation, D is well advised to inform the local office in writing of the fact that recoverability is in dispute.

(2)   The overpayment is due to the misleading of the authority. For the meaning of the wording in the phrase in para (3)(a), see the Analysis of reg 101 above. It appears that it is for the Secretary of State to decide whether this condition is met, even if the authority has already concluded that it has been misled.

(3)   D is receiving a "sufficient" amount of a relevant benefit to enable recovery. What is a "sufficient" amount will depend on the facts of individual cases.

The relevant benefits. The following categories of benefit are prescribed by reg 105 as being candidates for recovery.

(1)   Any benefits except guardian's allowance: para (a). These are maternity allowance, widow's benefits, retirement pension, child's special allowance, carer's allowance, severe disablement allowance, industrial injuries benefits, disability living allowance and attendance allowance. It would also include arrears of defunct benefits such as mobility allowance and sickness, invalidity or unemployment benefit.

(2)   IS: para (b).

(3)   Benefits payable to D from other EU Member States under Regulation (EEC) No 1408/71, which provides for certain categories of benefit to be payable in other Member States when a claimant moves abroad. Benefits payable from overseas are administered by the DWP Overseas Benefit Directorate at Fylde: para (c).

(4)   JSA, whether income-based or contribution-based: para (d).

(5)   State pension credit: para (e)

Debit from D's rent account

Where D is in receipt of rent rebate, the authority may add the overpayment as a debit to the rent account. Caution is required, however. The debit must be carefully distinguished from any rent arrears that exist at the point of the debit and any that subsequently arise: 1997 GM A7.37.

The reason for this is that recovery of an overpayment of benefit from a landlord did not allow the landlord to recover the overpayment from the tenant as rent arrears. Once HB was paid to the landlord, the claimant's liability for rent is discharged to the extent of that HB payment: see the quotation from *Ayub* above. At most, the claimant owes the landlord a debt once there is recovery from the latter. But the debt is not rent arrears and the landlord cannot use the debt as the basis of a claim for possession for non-payment of rent.

This rule *may* have been abrogated in relation to rent allowance from April 1997 (see the Analysis to HB Regs reg 95(2) above), but the same principle applies to debits from the claimant's rent account. SSAA s134(2)(b) makes it clear that the effect of rent rebate is to reduce the claimant's liability to pay rent by the amount of the rebate. If the claimant fails to pay any balance, that will create rent arrears. However, once the rebate is credited to the rent account, the claimant's liability to pay the amount of the rebate is discharged, and it is not resurrected by a decision that the rebate should not have been paid. If an authority fails to distinguish between the overpayment and the rent arrears, it will be difficult to tell whether there is a valid claim for possession.

A further complication is the treatment of payments by the claimant after the overpayment is debited from the rent account. The general rule is that a debtor owing more than one debt to a creditor may elect to attribute a payment to any of the debts and in such proportions as she/he chooses. If, as will usually be the case, D does not indicate whether s/he is seeking to pay off the rent arrears or the overpayment, and the authority does not indicate to which debt it wishes to apply the payment, the debt is applied to the debt that first arose in time: *Clayton's case* [1861] 1 Mer 572. Two examples help clarify how this rule works:

(1)   In week 1, D is in rent arrears of £100. In week 2, a £500 overpayment is debited from the rent account, putting D £600 in the red. In week 3, D pays £200 into the rent account. Even though the account is in arrears in the sum of £400, the authority cannot seek possession on the basis of non-payment of rent, since the whole of that sum is attributable to the debited overpayment.

(2)   D's rent is £100 per week. In week 1, D's account is £200 in credit. In week 2, the day before the rent becomes due, a £500 overpayment is debited, making arrears of £300. D does not pay rent in either week 2 or week 3, but then pays £200 into the account in week 4. The account is £300 in the

red. If D specifically states that he is paying off the rent arrears, then the £300 would represent part of the overpayment. If he does not, then the £200 he paid is treated as paying off the overpayment, since that preceded the rent arrears in time. Claimants in such situations are therefore well advised to specifically state that they are paying off their rent arrears rather than the overpayment.

Court proceedings

Once a determination has been made that an overpayment is recoverable, a debt is created between the authority and D for which the authority may sue in the County Court. The claim must be brought within the relevant time limit, which is six years in England and Wales: Limitation Act 1980 s2. In Scotland, it is five years: Prescription and Limitation (Scotland) Act 1973 s6, Sch 1 para 1.

A number of recent cases have considered the extent to which D can raise a defence or counterclaim to such proceedings.

Defence alleging invalid determination. It is an essential pre-condition of recovery that a valid determination be issued by the authority complying with the requirements of HB Regs Sch 9 para 15. If no such determination is issued, no debt is created and the authority may not sue for the amount: *Warwick DC v Freeman* [1994] 27 HLR 616, CA (see Analysis to reg 100(1) above). In *Plymouth CC v Gigg* [1997] 30 HLR 284, CA, *Freeman* was distinguished and it is submitted that it remains good law on this point. The Court of Appeal so confirmed in *Haringey LBC v Awaritefe* [1999] 32 HLR 517.

Registration as a recoverable debt at court

SSAA s75(7) will permit the authority to avoid the need to bring proceedings by registering the overpayment at the relevant local court. Once registration is carried out, the authority may utilise the court's powers of enforcement such as the use of bailiffs and Attachment of Earnings orders.

In England and Wales, the relevant procedure is prescribed by Order 25 rule 12 of the County Court Rules 1981, now found in Sch 2 of the Civil Procedure Rules 1998. The authority must complete Form N322 certifying the amount due and attach a "copy of the award" which presumably means a copy of the final determination that the overpayment is recoverable and is to be recovered. This must be done within six years of the final determination: s7 Limitation Act 1980. The court order will be made by a court officer. If D wishes to challenge the validity of the determination, an application should be made to the District Judge to set aside the officer's order as one given in the absence of D.

There are equivalent procedures available in relation to the "extract registered decree arbitral" in the Sheriff Court in Scotland.

Compensation order

Where D is convicted of an offence in relation to the overpayment, the authority can ask the court to make a compensation order under s35 Powers of Criminal Courts Act 1973. This option is rarely used. Any authority with a compensation order in its favour must deduct the amount of the order from the amount it seeks to recovery, otherwise there will be double recovery: *CIS 683/1994* para 5.

Diminution of capital

103.–(1)   Where in the case of a recoverable overpayment, in consequence of a misrepresentation or failure to disclose a material fact (in either case whether fraudulent or otherwise) as to a person's capital, or an error, other than one to which regulation 100(2) (effect of official error) refers, as to the amount of a person's capital, the overpayment was in respect of a period ("the overpayment period") of more than 13 benefit weeks, the relevant authority shall, for the purpose only of calculating the amount of that overpayment–

  (a)   at the end of the first 13 benefit weeks of the overpayment period, treat the amount of that capital as having been reduced by the amount of housing benefit overpaid during those 13 weeks;

  (b)   at the end of each subsequent period of 13 benefit weeks, if any, of the overpayment period, treat the amount of that capital as having been further reduced by the amount of housing benefit overpaid during the immediately preceding 13 benefit weeks.

  (2)   Capital shall not be treated as reduced over any period other than 13 benefit weeks or in any circumstances other than those for which paragraph (1) provides.

Definitions

  "capital" – see Part 6, Section 6.
  "overpayment" – see reg 99.

General Note

Regs 103 and 104 deal with three categories of deduction that may be made in calculating the amount of the recoverable overpayment. Calculation of amounts can be a complex process and a systematic approach is required. The following method should ensure that mistakes are minimised.

(1)   Determine the dates between which the claimant has been paid too much benefit.

(2)   Check that the criteria for recovery are met for the whole of that period. This will often not be the case. For example, A is overpaid for 10 weeks due to the authority failing to adjust her/his benefit after she/he told them about an award of incapacity benefit. On the facts of the case, it was not reasonable for A to realise that she/he was being overpaid until the fourth week. The first three weeks of benefit will not be recoverable and should be disregarded for the purposes of calculating the amount. The period that is left is the relevant period.

(3)   Calculate the full amount of benefit paid during the relevant period.

(4)   Determine whether the claimant should have been receiving any lesser amount during the relevant period. If so, this should be deducted from the amount of benefit obtained under step (3): reg 104(1).

(5)   In a rent rebate case, determine whether the claimant has paid too much rent for the period. If so, deduct the excess: reg 104(3).

(6)   Where the claimant has had too much capital, consider the application of the diminishing capital rule under reg 103.

The claimant is not entitled to have other amounts deducted, such as housing costs which ought to have been met under IS or JSA(IB) where the claimant mistakenly claimed HB instead. However, the authority can be asked to consider exercising its discretion not to recover an appropriate portion of the overpayment in such circumstances.

Analysis

The injustice that reg 103 seeks to address concerns cases where overpayments arise through excess capital. Had HB been refused or reduced because of excess capital, the claimant would presumably have spent part of the capital on rent and eventually the level of capital would have reduced below the statutory limits. Without this provision, a claimant who would have fallen below one of the limits through such expenditure had the capital been properly taken into account would never qualify for the correct level of HB, since she/he did not in fact spend any of the capital.

Paragraph (1)

When the regulation applies. The rule comes into operation only where the relevant period (see above) is at least 13 weeks and then only in the following two cases:

(1)   Where the authority is misled as to an amount of the capital. For the meaning of "misrepresentation" and the other words and phrases in the first part of reg 103(1), see the Analysis to reg 101 above. It does not have to be the claimant who misled the authority about the amount of capital. Moreover, it does not have to be the claimant's capital.

(2)   Where there is an error as to the amount of the claimant's capital. It does not matter who makes the error. The reference to reg 100(2) means that if the error is an official error and the overpayment is irrecoverable because the other two criteria are met (see the Analysis to reg 100 above), the regulation has no application. If, however, there is more than one official error and the three criteria are met in relation to only one of them, then reg 103 will apply to such overpayment as has been made in consequence of the other error.

"... for the purpose only of calculating the amount of that overpayment ...". This makes it clear that reg 100 has no application in other cases. It cannot, for example, assist a claimant seeking to backdate a claim who had capital of just over one of the relevant limits. More importantly, it does not apply in respect of the claimant's future entitlement to HB after the end of the overpayment period. Until the actual capital goes below the relevant limit, the claimant's actual capital will affect his or her entitlement.

The operation of the rule. At the end of each successive period of 13 weeks, the claimant's capital is treated as if reduced by the amount of the overpayment during that 13 weeks. However, in calculating the correct amount of HB which should have been payable (so as to calculate the amount actually overpaid), note the possible effect of the 65 per cent taper under s130(3)(b) SSCBA 1992 and reg 71 of these regulations if the tarrif income from the capital gave the claimant an income figure in excess of his or her applicable amount.

It is not clear whether expenditure by the claimant during the same period should be taken into account, assuming that such expenditure is not caught by the diminishing capital rule. Para (2) probably does not mean that such expenditure should be ignored. It is suggested that it should be taken into account, since the regulation refers to "that capital" which is the capital that was not disclosed. As the claimant's capital, which was not disclosed, varied from time to time, logic would suggest that the reference to "that capital" must be read as being the capital (notional and actual) which the claimant actually had at the beginning of each 13 week period. If that is right, at the beginning of each 13 week period, any capital spent should be deducted and any capital acquired should be added. If this is not done, the diminishing capital rule would not work in such cases, because a claimant who reasonably purchased a car and reduced her/his capital from £7,000 to £3,500 would not get the benefit of the rule, whereas a claimant who received a legacy of £10,000 during the overpayment period could effectively insist that it was ignored. This interpretation is in accordance with the decision of the commissioner in *CIS 5825/1999* para 15.

Paragraph (2)

This makes it clear that no reduction can be applied where the overpayment period is less than 13 weeks or for any residue of less than that length of time. There is therefore no room to argue that the principle should be applied weekly.

Sums to be deducted in calculating recoverable overpayments

104.–(1)   Subject to paragraph (2), in calculating the amount of a recoverable overpayment, the relevant authority shall deduct any amount of housing benefit which should have been determined to be payable in respect of the whole or part of the overpayment period–

(a)   on the basis of the claim as presented to the authority;

(b)   on the basis of the claim as it would have appeared had any misrepresentation or non-disclosure been remedied before the decision; or

(c)   on the basis of the claim as it would have appeared if any change of circumstances [¹ , except a change of the dwelling which the claimant occupies as his home,] had been notified at the time that change occurred.

(2)   In the case of rent rebate only, in calculating the amount of a recoverable overpayment the relevant authority may deduct so much of any payment by way of rent in respect of the overpayment period which exceeds the amount, if any, which the claimant was liable to pay for that period under the original erroneous decision.

Amendment

1.   Amended by reg 8 of SI 2005 No 2904 as amended by Sch 2 para 29 of SI 2006 No 217 as from 10.4.06.

Definitions

"payment" – see reg 2(1).
"rent" – see Part 3.
"rent rebate" – see ss134(1) and (2) and 191 SSAA.

General Note

This regulation deals with two other deductions from the amount of an overpayment. See the General Note to reg 103 above. The rule was amended from 2 October 2000 to reverse the effect of the decision in *R v Wyre BC ex p Lord* [1997] unreported, 24 October, QBD, which was criticised on p433-5 of the 13th edition. That decision held that where a claimant's IS entitlement was retrospectively terminated and an HB overpayment was created, it was not possible to offset any HB which would have been due on the basis of the claimant's true financial circumstances against the amount of the overpayment. The broad purpose of the new provisions is to ensure that an overpayment is "calculated with regard to the claimant's correct circumstances and any underlying entitlement deducted" (Circular HB/CTB A42/2000). In any case of doubt, regard should be had to that policy intent. However, *R(H) 1/05* holds (para 16) that it is for the claimant to prove the correct amount that s/he is entitled to for the overpayment period.

In *CH 4817/2002*, the commissioner was considering an appeal from a decision made prior to October 2000 and to which the former version of reg 104 was applicable. He held that the criticism of *ex p Lord* was not valid, because it was open to a local authority to decide not to recover an overpayment and that discretion removed any unfairness: paras 16-26. The commissioner's decision failed to deal with the real issue of the construction of the old version of reg 104 HB Regs 1987 (now reg 104 HB Regs) in the context of the HB Regs as a whole, and it was reversed (and *ex p Lord* overruled) by the Court of Appeal in *R(H) 5/ 04*. The Court held that the local authority will be determining the amount of HB to which a claimant is entitled in revising or superseding the existing decisions to award benefit, thus generating an overpayment under reg 99. The former version of reg 104(a) would have been otiose had it not been intended to permit HB which would have been payable on the claimant's true circumstances to be offset against the amount of an overpayment. Accordingly, in any outstanding appeals relating to decisions made prior to October 2000 (a few of which are known still to exist) tribunals will have to ensure that any underlying entitlement on the basis of the claimant's true circumstances is set off.

Whether it is possible to take any action to take advantage of the Court of Appeal's ruling in cases in which existing appeal rights were exhausted remains to be seen. It seems to follow from the decision in *R(H) 3/04* that no application for revision or supersession can be made in respect of determinations as to the recoverability of an overpayment or the amount thereof: see the commentary to Sch 7 paras 1, 2, 3 and 6 CSPSSA on pp148–154. Note, however, that a local authority may have a common law power to revisit a determination in these circumstances: see the commentary to Sch 7 para 6(6) CSPSSA on p154. It might be possible to argue that in these circumstances no reasonable authority could refuse to revisit an old determination where the amount of an overpayment should have been nil or substantially reduced: compare *R (Sibley) v West Dorset DC* [2001] EWHC Admin 365.

Analysis

Para (1) deals with the basic entitlement to an offset. The wording "which should have been determined to be payable" emphasises that the exercise is looking into the past with the benefit of hindsight to see what the true circumstances are and to award benefit on that basis. Para (1) bears some resemblance to reg 13(b) of the Social Security (Payments on Account, Overpayments and Recovery) Regulations 1988 and so the Commissioners' decisions on that provision may provide some assistance. There are important differences, however. There is no equivalent of sub-para (c) in reg 13(b) of the 1988 Regulations. Moreover, an amount may only be deducted if it was payable "in respect of the whole or any part of the overpayment period", which words do not appear in reg 13(b). The ruling in *R(IS) 5/92* para 6 that it was permissible to offset an amount which should have been payable in a period before the overpayment period cannot therefore be applied here.

Bearing in mind those differences in the provisions and the having regard to the policy intention, the three considerations set out in sub-paras (a) to (c) need to be examined as follows:

(1)   Any additional amount that should have been awarded "on the basis of the claim as presented to the authority" must be deducted. This may include additional amounts that have nothing to do with the overpayment. If, for example, a claimant can show that an additional premium should have been awarded on the basis of assertions in the initial claim, it is open to her/him to present further evidence to support those assertions: *CIS 522/1992* para 10. Furthermore, "the claim as presented" includes any information that would have been elicited on a reasonable enquiry by the local authority: *R(IS) 5/92* para 8. However, since there is no appeal against the Secretary of State's decision as to whether to issue a certificate under Sch 7 para 1, it will not be possible to offset an alleged entitlement to extended payments against an overpayment: *CH 5553/2002* paras 15-18.

(2)   Any additional amount that should have been awarded if any misrepresentation or non-disclosure had been remedied before determination. This obviously means, for example, that if a claimant has been claiming as a single person while living together as husband and wife with a partner, any entitlement on the basis of a claim as a couple should be awarded: *CSIS 62/1991* para 10. However, sub-para (b) potentially has a wider application. The word "any" is of importance. If there are other erroneous statements or omissions on the form besides the statement or statements that led to the overpayment, they can also be corrected. It might be arguable that if a claimant failed to state matters that might have led to a higher award of benefit, that could be said to be a non-disclosure which should allow the true facts to be brought into account.

(3)   Sub-para (c), as already said, is not to be found in reg 13 of the 1988 Regulations and is at first sight worded a little strangely. When "change of circumstances" is being talked about, it is usually in the context of a change that occurs in the benefit period after the claim is made and so it seems odd to talk of how a claim would have appeared had a change been notified. The point, however, is that sub-para (c) applies both to the claim that was extant at the beginning of the overpayment period and to any renewal claims within the overpayment period.

The local authority is not entitled to absolve itself from applying reg 104 by the non-return of a fresh claim form sent to the claimant after HB had ceased. It was entitled to demand information under reg 86(1) of the HB Regs notwithstanding the fact that the claim had ceased: *CH 4943/2001* paras 65-70. It is suggested that there is nothing in the Court of Appeal's reasoning in *Secretary of State for Work and Pensions v Chiltern DC* [2003] HLR 1019, CA (reported as *R(H) 2/03*) (also reported as *R(H) 2/03*), which allowed an appeal from some aspects of the commissioner's decision, which detracts from his reasoning on this point. See further the commentary to reg 87 HB Regs on p390.

It appears from *CH 2349/2002* para 11 that in considering non-disclosed income and the effect of it on the claimant's notional HB entitlement under reg 104, the claimant's income may be assessed on a week-by-week basis and need not be averaged out under reg 27(1)(a) HB Regs.

Applicability of para (1) to pre-October 2000 cases. Reference should be made to the Analysis to reg 101 under the heading "Applicability of para (1) to pre-October 2001 cases" for discussion on the application of the presumption against retrospectively to the current overpayments provisions.

Reg 104 can make a substantial difference to the amount recoverable and accordingly affects substantive rights. However, the wording focuses upon actions taking place in the present "in calculating the amount of a recoverable overpayment". Accordingly, it is arguable that it does apply to overpayments occurring prior to 2 October 2000 but in respect of which no decision has been issued. As with reg 101(1), appeals from decisions made prior to 2 October 2000 must be decided under the old law.

Para (2) will principally deal with errors in handling local authority rent accounts. If the overpayment has been wholly or partly caused by the claimant being asked to pay too much rent, as a result of which too much HB is credited to the rent account, then the extra rent is deductible from the amount. The authority will already have received the excess rent.

Recovery of overpayments from prescribed benefits

105.–(1)   For the purposes of section 75(4) of the Administration Act (recovery of overpaid housing benefit by deduction from other benefits), the benefits prescribed by this regulation are–

(a)   any benefit except guardian's allowance;

(b)   income support under Part 7 of the Act;

(c)   any benefit payable under the legislation of any member State other than the United Kingdom concerning the branches of social security mentioned in Article 4(1) of Regulation (EEC) No 1408/71 on the application of social security schemes to employed persons, to self-employed persons and to members of their families moving within the Community, whether or not the benefit has been acquired by virtue of the provisions of that Regulation;

(d)   a jobseeker's allowance;

(e)   state pension credit.

[¹ (1A)   For the purposes of paragraph (1)(c) the term ''member State'' shall be understood to include Switzerland in accordance with and subject to the provisions of Annex II of the Agreement between the European Community and its Member States and the Swiss Confederation on the free movement of persons, signed at Brussels on 21st June 1999.]

(2)   Where the Secretary of State is satisfied that–

(a)   a recoverable overpayment of housing benefit has been made, in consequence of a misrepresentation of or failure to disclose a material fact (in either case whether fraudulently or otherwise), by or on behalf of a claimant or any other person to whom a payment of housing benefit has been made; and

(b)   the person who misrepresented that fact or failed to disclose it is receiving a sufficient amount of one or more of the benefits prescribed in paragraph (1) to enable deductions to be made for the recovery of the overpayment,

he shall, if requested to do so by an authority under regulation 102 (method of recovery), recover the overpayment by deduction from any of those benefits.

(3)   In paragraph (1)(a), ''benefit'' has the meaning it has in section 122(1) of the Act.

Amendment

1.   Inserted by reg 9 of SI 2005 No 2904 as amended by Sch 2 para 29 of SI 2006 No 217 as from 10.4.06.

Definitions

"attendance allowance" – see reg 2(1).
"claimant" – see reg 2(1).
"disability working allowance" – see reg 2(1).
"member State" of the EEC – see para (1)(c).
"recoverable overpayment" – see reg 100.

General Note

This regulation specifies the categories of benefit from which the Secretary of State may make reductions to recover an overpayment of HB. See the Analysis to reg 102 for full details. See also reg 106 below.

Prescribed benefits

106.–(1)   The benefits prescribed for the purposes of section 75(5) and (7) of the Administration Act (recovery of overpayments) are those set out in the following paragraphs.

(2)   Prescribed benefits within section 75(5) of the Administration Act (benefits to which a landlord or agent is entitled) are–
(a)   housing benefit; and
(b)   those benefits prescribed from time to time in regulation 105(1) (recovery of overpayments from prescribed benefits), but only in cases where–
    (i)   an authority has, pursuant to regulation 102 (method of recovery), requested the Secretary of State to recover an overpayment of housing benefit from such benefits; and
    (ii)   the Secretary of State is satisfied as to the matters prescribed in paragraph (3)(a) and (b) of regulation 105.
(3)   Housing benefit is prescribed for the purposes of section 75(5)(b) or (c) of the Administration Act (benefits paid to a landlord or agent to discharge an obligation owed by another person).
(4)   Prescribed benefits within section 75(7) of the Administration Act (benefits recoverable from the county court or the sheriff court) are housing benefit and those benefits prescribed from time to time in regulation 105(1).

General Note
This regulation specifies the benefits from which recovery may be made under SSAA s75(5). There is a certain amount of duplication of the powers which already exist under other regs in Part 13.

Analysis
Para (2). SSAA s75(5)(a) authorises recovery from benefits to which the landlord or agent is entitled personally. HB is prescribed, along with benefits falling within reg 105(1) HB Regs, provided the normal procedure prescribed by regs 102 and 105 is followed. This provision does not appear to add to the powers that authorities already had.
Para (3). SSAA s75(5)(b) authorises recovery from benefits which the landlord or agent is paid on behalf of claimant A, when claimant A was overpaid. SSAA s75(5)(c) authorises recovery from benefits paid on behalf of claimant A, when claimant B was overpaid. For the effect on rent obligations in the former case, see reg 107 below, and in the latter case see s75(6) which provides that B's obligation is discharged. Note also Sch 9 para 15(2) HB Regs that requires both landlord and claimant B to be informed of this fact.
Para (4). SSAA s75(7) provides that prescribed benefits may be recovered simply by registering the debt as recoverable under the respective procedures in the County Court and Sheriff Court. Para (4) provides that these powers apply to recovery of HB.

Restrictions on recovery of rent and consequent notifications

107.–(1)   Where, pursuant to section 75(5)(b) of the Administration Act, an amount has been recovered by deduction from housing benefit paid to a person (referred to as "the landlord" in this regulation) to discharge (in whole or in part) an obligation owed to him by the person on whose behalf the recoverable amount was paid (referred to as "the tenant" in this regulation) that obligation shall, in a case to which paragraph (2) applies, be taken to be discharged by the amount of the deduction.
(2)   This paragraph applies in a case where the amount recoverable from the landlord relates to an overpayment of housing benefit in relation to which the landlord has–
(a)   agreed to pay a penalty pursuant to section 115A of the Administration Act (penalty as an alternative to prosecution); or
(b)   been convicted of an offence arising under the Act or any other enactment.
(3)   In any case to which paragraph (2) applies or will apply when recovery is made the authority that has determined that there is an overpayment and that it is recoverable from the landlord shall notify both the landlord and the tenant that–
(a)   the overpayment that it has recovered or that it has determined to recover ("that sum") is or will be one to which paragraph (2) applies; and

(b)   the landlord has no right in relation to that sum against the tenant, and that his obligation to the landlord shall be taken to be discharged by the amount so recovered.

General Note

This regulation provides for the effects of recovery from a landlord by deductions from future payments of HB in respect of a claimant, where the same claimant was the one overpaid. By s75(6), where recovery is made from a different claimant's HB, her/his obligation to pay rent is always discharged.

Analysis

The effect of recovery of an overpayment from a landlord on the extent of the overpaid tenant's rent arrears has always been a cause of controversy. See the Analysis to regs 95(2) and 105. Reg 95(2) is in conflict with the provisions in reg 107. Even if reg 95(2) is validly made (as to which see the Analysis to that regulation) it is suggested that reg 107, made as it is under a specific rather than a general enabling power, must take precedence in relation to overpayments made after 3 November 1997.

Para (1) confirms the effect of the regulation. If the case falls within para (2), then the tenant's obligation is to be treated as discharged by the amount of the deduction. Presumably, the time of deemed payment of rent is the time when the deduction is made. This may be significant in possession proceedings, for example where the landlord is seeking a compulsory order under Ground 2 in Sch 2 of the Housing Act 1988. See further the Introductory Notes under the heading "Court Proceedings".

Curiously, the regulation does not state what happens in cases that do not fall within para (2). If reg 95(2) is valid, then the tenant is in rent arrears. If it is not, then the analysis in *R v Haringey LBC ex p Ayub* [1992] 25 HLR 566, QBD suggests that the tenant's obligation will be discharged. If reg 95(2) is invalid, the question is whether s75(6) and reg 107 change the position by implication. Certainly it can be argued that by saying that the obligation is discharged in prescribed cases, s75(6) is saying that it is not discharged in other cases. However, s75(6) does not say that the obligation is discharged *only* in prescribed cases and so there would be a powerful contrary argument that Parliament cannot be deemed to have changed the existing law as between landlord and tenant without explicitly saying so.

Para (2). The requirement is that the landlord has been required to pay a penalty under SSAA s115A or convicted of an offence "in relation to" that overpayment. It is suggested that this would cover, for example, a conviction under SSAA s113 for failing to supply information under the Housing Benefit (Information from Landlords and Agents) Regulations 1997 that is connected with the making of the overpayment.

It would appear that the landlord itself must be convicted of the offence. So if a company officer is convicted of an offence, that is insufficient to bring para (2) into effect because the company has a separate legal existence. On the other hand, as the singular must include the plural, conviction of one of joint landlords will bring para (2) into force, as will conviction of one of the partners in a partnership that holds property.

Para (3) provides that both landlord and tenant must be informed of the applicability of para (2) and that the landlord has no right to recover it from the tenant. It should logically have been an amendment to Sch 9 HB Regs.

PART 14
Information
SECTION 1
Claims and information

General Note on Section 1

The regulations in this Section, made principally under s7A SSAA, confirm the powers of local authorities in relation to the obtaining, retention and transmission of information in relation to claims for HB and CTB. This will prevent any allegation of a breach of the Data Protection Act 1998 where any dealing with information in the ways specified below takes place.

For powers to compel the provision of information, see Part 7 of the SSAA as amended by the SSFA (see p73). Reg 112 enables the Secretary of State or parties acting under his direction to demand information from a local authority.

Interpretation
108.   In this Section–

[¹ "county council" means a county council in England, but only if the council has made an arrangement in accordance with regulation 83(4)(g) or 109(3);]

"local authority" means an authority administering housing benefit;
"relevant authority" means–
  (a)   the Secretary of State; or
  (b)   a person providing services to the Secretary of State; [¹ or
  (c)   a county council;]
"relevant information" means information or evidence relating to the administration
    of claims to or awards of housing benefit.

Amendment
  1.   Amended by reg 7(3) of SI 2007 No 2911 as from 31.10.07.

[¹Collection of information
  109.–(1)   The Secretary of State, or a person providing services to him, may
receive or obtain relevant information from–
  (a)   persons making, or who have made, claims for housing benefit; or
  (b)   other persons in connection with such claims.
  (2)   In paragraph (1) references to persons who have made claims for housing
benefit include persons to whom awards of benefit have been made on those claims.
  (3)   Where a county council has made an arrangement with a local authority, or
a person authorised to exercise any function of a local authority relating to housing
benefit or council tax benefit, to receive and obtain information or evidence relating
to claims for housing benefit, the council may receive or obtain the information or
evidence from–
  (a)   persons making claims for housing benefit; or
  (b)   other persons in connection with such claims.
  (4)   A county council may receive information or evidence relating to an award
of housing benefit which is supplied by–
  (a)   the person to whom the award has been made; or
  (b)   other persons in connection with the award.]

Amendment
  1.   Substituted by reg 7(4) of SI 2007 No 2911 as from 31.10.07.

[¹Verifying information
  109A.   A relevant authority may verify relevant information supplied to, or
obtained by, the authority in accordance with regulation 109.]

Amendment
  1.   Inserted by reg 7(5) of SI 2007 No 2911 as from 31.10.07.

[¹Recording and holding information
  110.   A relevant authority which obtains relevant information or to whom such
information is supplied–
  (a)   shall make a record of such information; and
  (b)   may hold that information, whether as supplied or obtained or recorded, for
        the purpose of forwarding it to the person or authority for the time being
        administering housing benefit.]

Amendment
  1.   Substituted by reg 7(6) of SI 2007 No 2911 as from 31.10.07.

Forwarding of information
  111.   A relevant authority which holds relevant information–
  (a)   shall forward it to the person or authority for the time being administering
        claims to or awards of housing benefit to which the relevant information
        relates, being–
        (i)   a local authority;

    (ii)   a person providing services to a local authority; or

    (iii)   a person authorised to exercise any function of a local authority relating to housing benefit; and

[¹ (b) may, if the relevant authority is the Secretary of State or a person providing services to the Secretary of State, continue to hold a record of such information, whether as supplied or obtained or recorded, for such period as he considers appropriate.]

Amendment

1.   Substituted by reg 7(7) of SI 2007 No 2911 as from 31.10.07.

Request for information

112.   A relevant authority which holds information or evidence relating to social security matters shall forward such information or evidence as may be requested to the person or authority making that request, provided that–

(a)   the request is made by–

    (i)   a local authority;

    (ii)   a person providing services to a local authority; or

    (iii)   a person authorised to exercise any function of a local authority relating to housing benefit; and

(b)   the information or evidence requested includes relevant information;

(c)   the relevant authority is able to provide the information or evidence requested in the form in which it was originally supplied or obtained; and

(d)   provision of the information or evidence requested is considered necessary by the relevant authority to the proper performance by a local authority of its functions relating to housing benefit.

SECTION 2

Information from landlords and agents and between authorities etc.

General Note on Section 2

The Housing Benefit (Information from Landlords and Agents) Regulations 1997 SI No 2436 implemented s126A SSAA. These provisions are now in reg 113 (in part) and regs 117 to 121 HB Regs and reg 94 (in part) and regs 98 to 102 HB(SPC) Regs. These set out the circumstances in which local authorities may require information from landlords and agents, the information which must be supplied, the time limit for supplying it and the manner in which the information must be provided. Failure to comply with a notice requiring information under s126A is a criminal offence and would be a factor which a local authority could take into account when considering whether a landlord is a "fit and proper person" to receive payments of HB under regs 95 and 96 HB Regs (or regs 76 and 77 HB(SPC) Regs).

Interpretation

113.   In this Section–

"the notice" means the notice prescribed in regulation 118(1)(b) (circumstances for requiring information);

"relevant information" means such information as is prescribed in regulation 119 (relevant information);

"the requirer" means a person within regulation 117 (requiring information from landlords and agents), who requires information pursuant to that regulation;

"the supplier" means an appropriate person who is required, pursuant to regulations 117 and 118, to supply relevant information and any person who is not so required is not, for the purpose of supplying information pursuant to section 126A of the Administration Act and these Regulations, an appropriate person.

Evidence and information required by rent officers

114.   The relevant authority shall furnish as soon as is reasonably practicable such information or evidence relating to a claimant and his accommodation obtained by it in exercise of its functions relating to housing benefit as may be required by a rent officer for the purpose of a function conferred on him by an order under section 122 of the Housing Act 1996.

General Note

Note that the authority may only supply information obtained in the manner specified, and only in relation to the rent officer's functions as set out on in the appropriate Rent Officer (Housing Benefit Functions) Order.

Information to be supplied by an authority to another authority

115.–(1)   For the purposes of section 128A of the Administration Act (duty of an authority to disclose information to another authority) the circumstances in which information is to be disclosed are prescribed in paragraph (2) and the prescribed information is described in paragraph (3).

(2)   The circumstances prescribed in this paragraph are, where–

(a)   there is a mover who is or was in receipt of housing benefit from local authority "A";

(b)   either his second dwelling is within the area of another authority "B" or he is liable or treated as liable to make payments in respect of his second dwelling to housing authority B; and

(c)   either–

  (i)   the extended payment is claimed from authority A; or

  (ii)   the extended payment is claimed from authority B, who then requests the prescribed information from authority A,

authority A shall disclose to authority B the information prescribed in paragraph (3).

(3)   The information to be disclosed is–

(a)   in a case where that extended payment was claimed from authority A, details relevant to that claim of–

  (i)   the matters certified pursuant to regulation 72 and paragraph 1 of Schedule 7;

  (ii)   the matters notified pursuant to regulation 72 and paragraph 2 of that Schedule;

  (iii)   the date it was so claimed;

(b)   in the case of a person to whom regulation 6(5) of the Income Support Regulations (persons not treated as engaged in remunerative work) applies–

  (i)   the date on which he was first engaged in the work referred to in sub-paragraph (a) of regulation 6(5) of those Regulations; and

  (ii)   the date on which his entitlement to income support ceased or was expected to cease; and

(c)   in any case–

  (i)   the weekly rate of housing benefit awarded to the mover by authority A;

  (ii)   if any deduction was being made from that benefit in respect of non-dependants, pursuant to regulations 70 and 74, the amount of those deductions;

  (iii)   if any deduction was being made from that benefit in respect of a recoverable overpayment pursuant to regulation 102 (method of recovery), the amount of those deductions;

  (iv)   the date on which his entitlement to housing benefit ceased;

  (v)   if an extended payment was made to the mover, the amount and date of any such payment; and

  (vi)   if no extended payment was made, why none was made.

(4)   In this regulation, "the relevant day" has the meaning assigned to it in paragraph 11 of Schedule 7.

General Note

This facilitates the passing of information where extended payments of HB are claimed under reg 72 HB Regs and the claimant moves from the area of the authority where s/he had previously been in receipt of HB to another. See Sch 7 paras 5 to 7 and 9 for details of the application of the extended payments scheme to these so-called "movers". See also s128A SSAA on p80, which is still in force. See reg 116 where an extended payment is claimed under reg 73.

Supply of information: extended payments (severe disablement allowance and incapacity benefit)

116.–(1)   For the purposes of section 122E(3) of the Administration Act (duty of an authority to supply information to another authority) the circumstances in which information is to be supplied are prescribed in paragraph (2) and the prescribed information is described in paragraph (3).

(2)   The circumstances prescribed in this paragraph are, where–

(a)   there is a mover who is or was in receipt of housing benefit from a local authority "A";

(b)   either his second dwelling is within the area of another local authority "B" or he is liable or treated as liable to make payments in respect of his second dwelling to housing authority B; and

(c)   either–

(i)   the extended payment (severe disablement allowance and incapacity benefit) is claimed from authority A; or

(ii)   the extended payment (severe disablement allowance and incapacity benefit) is claimed from authority B, who then requests the information described in paragraph (3) from authority A,

authority A shall supply to authority B that information.

(3)   The information to be supplied is–

(a)   in a case where that extended payment (severe disablement allowance and incapacity benefit) was claimed from authority A, details relevant to that claim of–

(i)   the matters set out in regulation 78 or regulation 73(1)(b)(i) to (iii), as the case may be; and

(ii)   the matters notified pursuant to regulation 73(1)(a)(ii) or (b)(iv), as the case may be; and

(iii)   the date it was so claimed; and

(b)   in any case–

(i)   the weekly rate of housing benefit awarded to the mover by authority A;

(ii)   if any deduction was being made from that benefit in respect of non-dependants, pursuant to regulations 70 (maximum housing benefit) and 74 (non-dependant deductions), the amount of those deductions;

(iii)   if any deduction was being made from that benefit in respect of a recoverable overpayment pursuant to regulation 102 (method of recovery), the amount of those deductions;

(iv)   the date on which his entitlement to housing benefit ceased;

(v)   if an extended payment (severe disablement allowance and incapacity benefit) was made to the mover, the amount and date of any such payment; and

(vi)   if no extended payment (severe disablement allowance and incapacity benefit) was made, why none was made.

General Note

This facilitates the passing of information where extended payments of HB are claimed under reg 73 HB Regs and the claimant moves from the area of the authority where s/he had previously been in receipt of HB to another. See reg 115 where extended payments are claimed under reg 72.

Requiring information from landlords and agents

117. Pursuant to section 126A of the Administration Act (information from landlords and agents), where a claim is made to an authority, on which a rent allowance may be awarded, then, in the circumstances prescribed in regulation 118 (circumstances for requiring information), that authority, or any person authorised to exercise any functions of the authority relating to housing benefit, may require an appropriate person to supply to that authority or person relevant information, in the manner prescribed in regulation 120 (manner of supply of information).

General Note

This regulation confirms that the circumstances in which information may be sought are set out in reg 118 and the manner of the supply of information is set out in reg 120. Note that information may also be demanded by any body administering HB on behalf of an authority. Note also that it is not necessary that rent allowance has been awarded before the information may be required. The authority is probably entitled to delay determination of a claim pending the supply of the information by the landlord, but the delay must be reasonable in all the circumstances.

Circumstances for requiring information

118.–(1) A person is required to supply information in the following circumstances–

(a) he is an appropriate person in relation to any dwelling in respect of which–

    (i) housing benefit is being paid to an appropriate person pursuant to regulation 95 or 96 (circumstances in which payment is to be or may be made to a landlord); or

    (ii) a request has been made by an appropriate person or by the claimant for housing benefit to be so paid; and

(b) the requirer serves upon that appropriate person, whether by post or otherwise, a written notice stating that the requirer–

    (i) suspects that there is or may be an impropriety in relation to a claim in respect of any dwelling wherever situate in relation to which he is an appropriate person; or

    (ii) is already investigating an allegation of impropriety in relation to that person.

(2) In formation required to be supplied under paragraph (1) shall be supplied to the requirer at the address specified in the notice.

General Note

This sets out the circumstances in which information must be supplied by an "appropriate person".

Analysis

Para (1). A number of conditions must be fulfilled before the "appropriate person" comes under an obligation to supply the information requested.

(1) S/he must be an "appropriate person" in relation to a relevant dwelling. "Appropriate person" is defined in SSAA s126A(2): see the Analysis to that section. It includes landlords and their agents.

(2) HB is being paid direct to the "appropriate person" under reg 95 or reg 96, or a request has been made for such payment by her/him or a claimant.

(3) A written notice is served in relation to the authority's grounds for making the request. This must be either that an impropriety in relation to a claim is suspected in respect of a dwelling where the "appropriate person" is involved, or that there is an investigation of impropriety in relation to the "appropriate person": sub-para (b). Under sub-para (b)(i), the impropriety need not relate to the same property, it need not be the same claimant and s/he need not be the "appropriate person" in respect of the same capacity. The authority are not obliged to inform the person of the reasons for its suspicion, nor is it restricted in seeking information that relates only to that suspicion. However, it is clear that the authority must have formed a suspicion, which provided it is held in good faith is probably immune from challenge. The only basis for a challenge would be judicial review.

Para (2). The notice must specify an address and the information must be supplied at that address.

Relevant information

119.–(1) The information the supplier is to supply to the requirer is that prescribed in paragraphs (2) and (3) (referred to in this Part as "the relevant information").

(2) For a supplier who falls within paragraph (4) or section 126A(2)(b) of the Administration Act ("the landlord"), the information is–

- (a) where the landlord is a natural person–
    - (i) his appropriate details;
    - (ii) the relevant particulars of any residential property in which he has an interest; and
    - (iii) the appropriate details of any body corporate, in which he is a major shareholder or of which he is a director and which has an interest in residential property;
- (b) where the landlord is a trustee, except a trustee of a charity, in addition to any information that he is required to supply in accordance with sub-paragraph (a) or (c), as the case may be, the relevant particulars of any residential property held by the trust of which he is a trustee and the name and address of any beneficiary under the trust or the objects of that trust, as the case may be;
- (c) where the landlord is a body corporate or otherwise not a natural person, other than a charity–
    - (i) its appropriate details;
    - (ii) the relevant particulars of any residential property in which it has an interest;
    - (iii) the names and addresses of any directors of it;
    - (iv) the appropriate details of any person–
        - (aa) who owns 20 per cent. or more of it; or
        - (bb) of whom it owns 20 per cent. or more; and
    - (v) the names and addresses of its major shareholders;
- (d) where the landlord is a charity or is a recognised body, the appropriate details relating to the landlord and particulars of the landlord's registration as a charity.

(3) For a supplier who falls within section 126A(2)(c) of the Administration Act or paragraph (5)("the agent"), the information is–

- (a) the name and address of any person ("his principal")–
    - (i) to whom the agent has agreed to make payments in consequence of being entitled to receive relevant payments: or
    - (ii) for whom the agent is acting on behalf of or in connection with any aspect of the management of a dwelling,

    as the case may be;
- (b) the relevant particulars of any residential property in respect of which the agent–
    - (i) has agreed to make payments in consequence of being entitled to receive relevant payments; or
    - (ii) is acting on behalf of his principal in connection with any aspect of its management;
- (c) where the agent is a natural person–
    - (i) the relevant particulars of any residential property in which he has an interest;
    - (ii) the appropriate details of any body corporate or any person not a natural person, in which he is a major shareholder or of which he is a director and which has any interest in residential property; or
- (d) where the agent is a body corporate or other than a natural person–
    - (i) the relevant particulars of any residential property in which it has an interest;

      (ii)   the names and addresses of any directors of or major shareholders in the agent; and

      (iii) the appropriate details of any person–

          (aa) who owns 20 per cent. or more of the agent; or

          (bb) of whom the agent owns 20 per cent. or more.

(4)   A supplier falls within this paragraph (landlord receiving rent), if he falls within section 126A(2)(a) of the Administration Act, but does not fall within paragraph (5).

(5)   A supplier falls within this paragraph (agent receiving the rent), if he falls within subsection (2)(a) of section 126A of the Administration Act and has agreed to make payments, in consequence of being entitled to receive relevant payments, to a person falling within subsection (2)(b) of that section.

(6)   For the purposes of this regulation–

''appropriate details'' means the name of the person and (in the case of a company) its registered office and, in any case, the full postal address, including post code, of the principal place of business of that person and the telephone and facsimile number (if any) of that place;

''charity'' means a charity which is registered under section 3 of the Charities Act 1993 and is not an exempt charity within the meaning of that Act;

''major shareholder'' means, where a body corporate is a company limited by shares, any person holding one tenth or more of the issued shares in that company and, in any other case, all the owners of that body;

''recognised body'' has the same meaning as in section 1(7) of the Law Reform (Miscellaneous Provisions) (Scotland) Act 1990;

''relevant particulars'' means the full postal address, including post code, and number of current lettings of or within that residential property and, if that property includes two or more dwellings, that address and the number of such lettings for each such dwelling;

''residential property'' includes any premises, situate within the United Kingdom–

(a)   used or which has, within the last six months, been used; or

(b)   which may be used or is adapted for use,

as residential accommodation,

and other expressions used in this regulation and also in the Companies Act 1985 shall have the same meaning in this regulation as they have in that Act.

General Note

This regulation sets out the type of information that is to be supplied. It is worthy of note that all the information is to be supplied and there is no obligation on the authority to make a specific request for any of the information. However, it could presumably request only certain categories of information and if the rest was not supplied, a criminal prosecution might be regarded as an abuse of process. It would be useful for authorities to draw up questionnaires for different categories of suppliers of information to use.

A large amount of information may be supplied under this regulation about parties who will not be mixed up in the authority's investigation. It may be arguable that the low threshold in reg 118 for the requiring of the information is insufficient justification for the invasion of privacy that the supply of the information involves. There may well be grounds for challenge under the Human Rights Act 1998.

Analysis

Paragraph (2)

Paragraph (2) sets out the information to be supplied by landlords. That expression is defined as covering both landlords directly receiving the rent and tenants that sublet. The former are under the obligation provided that they do not fulfil para (5) as being agents: see para (4). The latter fall within SSAA s126A(2)(b).

The information to be provided depends on the status of the landlord. Four cases are dealt with:

(1)   A "natural person" must supply her/his "appropriate details". S/he must also supply the "relevant particulars" of any residential property in which s/he has an interest. Those expressions are defined in para (6). The property must be residential, but it is suggested that information in relation to properties with both business and residential elements must be supplied. The word "interest" must relate to a property interest, but could be legal or equitable (ie, as a beneficiary under a trust). The

"appropriate details" of any body corporate must be supplied provided that s/he is a "major shareholder" or a director, and the body corporate holds an interest in residential property. See para (6) for the meaning of "major shareholder".

(2) Trustees must supply further information *in addition* to any other information supplied under one of the other heads. Details of residential property held by the trust, its beneficiaries and the objects of the trust must be supplied. The latter can be satisfied by supplying the requirer with a copy of the trust deed.

(3) Bodies corporate (which will include partnerships in Scotland but not in England and Wales) must give its appropriate details, particulars of residential property, names and addresses of directors, the details of any person (which could be a natural or legal person) that owns 20 per cent or more of the body corporate or of which the body corporate owns 20 per cent or more, and the details of its major shareholders.

(4) Charities must give their appropriate details and matters relating to their registration.

Paragraph (3)

This paragraph deals with the agent falling within SSAA s126A(2)(c). Under sub-para (a), details of the principal must be given (ie, the person on whose behalf the agent is acting), along with particulars of any property in respect of which the agent is receiving HB or is acting on behalf of his principal: sub-para (b). This must be the same principal as the one whose name and address is disclosed under sub-para (a).

Where the agent is a natural person, details of any residential property in which he has an interest must be given. Again, "interest" can only refer to a legal or equitable interest in land and not merely a property that the agent is dealing with in the course of her/his business. S/he must also give details of interests in body corporate or "any person otherwise not a natural person" in which a major shareholding or directorship is held and which holds an interest in residential property. The latter expression would cover a partnership.

An agent that is a body corporate must give details of all residential property in which it is interested, the names and addresses of major shareholders and directors, and details of major ownership (see the Analysis to para (2) relating to bodies corporate).

Manner of supply of information

120.–(1) Subject to paragraph (2), the relevant information shall be supplied–

(a) in typewritten or printed form; or

(b) with the written agreement of the requirer, in electronic or handwritten form,

within a period of 4 weeks commencing on the date on which the notice was sent or given.

(2) Where–

(a) within a period of 4 weeks commencing on the date on which the notice was sent or given, the supplier requests that the time for the supply of the relevant information be extended; and

(b) the requirer provides written agreement to that request,

the time for the supply of the relevant information shall be extended to a period of 8 weeks commencing on the date on which the notice was sent or given.

General Note

The time limit for supplying the information is four weeks, which may be extended to eight weeks with the written agreement of the authority. It must normally be delivered in printed form but may, with the written agreement of the authority, be delivered in handwritten or electronic form.

Criminal offence

121. Any failure by the supplier to supply relevant information to the requirer as, when and how required under regulations 117 to 120 shall be an offence under section 113 of the Administration Act and there may be recovered from the supplier, on summary conviction for this offence, penalties not exceeding–

(a) for any one offence, level 3 on the standard scale; or

(b) for an offence of continuing any such failure after conviction, £40 for each day on which it is so continued.

General Note

See the commentary to s113 SSAA on p63.

PART 15
Pathfinder authorities

Modifications in respect of pathfinder authorities

122.–(1)   In this regulation and Schedule 10, ''pathfinder authority'' means a relevant authority specified in Part 1 of that Schedule.

(2)   The provisions of Part 2 of Schedule 10 apply in relation to the area of a pathfinder authority on and after the date specified in Part 1 in relation to that authority.

[¹ SCHEDULE A1]
Treatment of claims for housing benefit by refugees

Modification

Sch A1 was inserted by Sch 4 para 2(2) HB&CTB(CP) Regs in respect of claims for HB by some refugees (see p1126). Sch A1 was further modifed by Sch 4 para 4(2) for some HB claimants who were refugees who claimed asylum on or before 2 April 2000 (see p1132). See also reg 10A inserted by Sch 4 para 2(1) HB&CTB(CP) Regs (see p1126).

Amendment

1.   Lapsed by s12(2)(e) of the Asylum and Immigration (Treatment of Claimants, etc.) Act 2004 (for those recorded as refugees after 14.6.07).

SCHEDULE 1
REGULATION 11
Ineligible service charges

General Note

The general rule in reg 12(1)(e) is that services charges are "rent" for HB purposes and hence eligible to be met by HB under reg 11(1). This Schedule lists the exceptions to that rule. If a service charge is listed in the Schedule (and hence ineligible) a deduction must be made under reg 12(3)(b), unless the deduction has already been made when computing the maximum rent under reg 13.

The scope of the concepts in the Schedule in the past caused variance in the approach to certain charges for assistance given by bodies to vulnerable tenants. Prompt action by the government allowed an interim scheme to be brought in by the Housing Benefit (General) Amendment (No 2) Regulations 1997, which was subsequently replaced by Supporting People: see the commentary to para 1(f).

PART 1
Service charges other than for fuel

Ineligible service charges

1.   The following service charges shall not be eligible to be met by housing benefit–

(a)   charges in respect of day-to-day living expenses including, in particular, all provision of–

    (i)   subject to paragraph 2 meals (including the preparation of meals or provision of unprepared food);

    (ii)   laundry (other than the provision of premises or equipment to enable a person to do his own laundry);

    [¹ (iii)   leisure items such as either sports facilities (except a children's play area), or television rental, licence and subscription fees (except radio relay charges and charges made in respect of the conveyance and installation and maintenance of equipment for the conveyance of a television broadcasting service);]

    (iv)   cleaning of rooms and windows except cleaning of–

        (aa)   communal areas; or

        (bb)   the exterior of any windows where neither the claimant nor any member of his household is able to clean them himself,

where a payment is not made in respect of such cleaning by a local authority (including, in relation to England, a county council) or the National Assembly for Wales to the claimant or his partner, or to another person on their behalf; and

    (v)   transport;

(b)   charges in respect of–

(i)   the acquisition of furniture or household equipment; and

(ii)   the use of such furniture or equipment where that furniture or household equipment will become the property of the claimant by virtue of an agreement with the landlord;

(c)   charges in respect of the provision of an emergency alarm system;

(d)   charges in respect of medical expenses (including the cost of treatment or counselling related to mental disorder, mental handicap, physical disablement or past or present alcohol or drug dependence);

(e)   charges in respect of the provision of nursing care or personal care (including assistance at meal-times or with personal appearance or hygiene);

(f)   charges in respect of general counselling or of any other support services, whoever provides those services;

(g)   charges in respect of any services not specified in sub-paragraphs (a) to (f) which are not connected with the provision of adequate accommodation.

Amendment

1.   Substituted by reg 6(5) of SI 2007 No 719 as from 2.4.07.

Analysis

This para lists the ineligible services, including a catch-all para 1(g) which refers to charges in respect of services "which are not connected with the provision of adequate accommodation". GM A4.730 gives a non-exhaustive list of the items which are *not* covered by Pt 1 of the Schedule and are therefore still "eligible". These are: wardens and caretakers (in so far as they provide eligible services); removal of refuse; lifts; radio and TV relay (including ordinary UK channels and those where a satellite dish feeds the system); portering; communal telephone charges; entry-phones; cleaning of common areas; gardens; children's play areas.

It is for the claimant to satisfy the authority that a service charge is not ineligible: *R v Stoke-on-Trent CC ex p Highgate Projects* [1996] 29 HLR 271 at 278, CA.

Most of the categories of ineligible charge are self-explanatory, but the scope of sub-paras (e), (f) and (g) has caused considerable difficulty.

It is suggested that a service only falls under sub-para (e) if it involves a degree of physical proximity in the assistance that is given, and consists of doing something for the claimant rather than reminding or persuading the claimant to do it for her/himself. The distinction is perhaps easier to recognise than to state. A valid analogy might be the difference between "attention" and "supervision" in the context of awards of disability living allowance. Some assistance in drawing this distinction may also be obtained from the decision in *R v Allerdale DC HBRB ex p Doughty* [2000] COD 462, QBD, Elias J. In that case, the Applicant lived in a religious home. An application for registration of the home as a small residential home was rejected by the Registered Homes Tribunal. The Review Board found that because the home was not registered under the Registered Homes Act 1984, it could not therefore be said to be providing "personal care" under the scope of the previous definition and so the home was not "supported accommodation".

The judge held this approach to be wrong. The effect of the rejection of registration was that the landlord could not provide "personal care" as defined in s20(1) of the 1984 Act: "care which includes assistance with bodily functions where such assistance is required".

"[Counsel for the applicant] accepts that the concept will also embrace other forms of care, such as psychiatric and certain physical care, but submits that it clearly does not extend to general counselling and support services such as fall within the scope of para 1(f)(iii). This is, in my view, plainly correct, and, as I have already indicated, in the schedule itself the concept of personal care is found in para (e) and the concept of 'general counselling' or 'any other support services' are found in para (f). In my view, the concept of 'personal care' in para (e) is the same as that found in the Registered Homes Act, but in any event, even if that were not so, it would be, in substance, a similar concept."

The scope of para 1(f) has been considered by the courts on a number of occasions and the paragraph was usually amended in consequence. Following the introduction of the Supporting People scheme for supported accommodation, the complex former provisions have now been repealed and the question is now much simpler. For the old law, see pp397-398 of the 12th edition.

In order to fall foul of para 1(f), general counselling or any other support services must be provided. It does not matter who provides the services.

CIS 1460/1995 provides valuable guidance on the scope of para 1(g). Although it excludes services which relate purely to meeting the personal needs of residents, this does not mean that in deciding whether a service is related to the provision of adequate accommodation the question of suitability for the personal needs of the residents is not relevant (as the cleaning of the outside of windows – per para 1(a)(iv) – is connected both with adequate accommodation and the personal needs of the claimant), and therefore the Schedule itself contemplates that some personal needs may be relevant to assessing what are eligible service charges. What constitutes "adequate accommodation" will be a question of fact in each case. The terms of GM A4.730 set out above would suggest that the approach in *CIS 1460/1995* is accepted by the DWP as being correct.

Amount ineligible for meals

2.–(1)   Where a charge for meals is ineligible to be met by housing benefit under paragraph 1, the amount ineligible in respect of each week shall be the amount specified in the following provisions of this paragraph.

(2)   Subject to sub-paragraph (4), where the charge includes provision for at least three meals a day, the amount shall be–
   (a)   for a single claimant, [² £21.10];
   (b)   if the claimant is a member of a family–
      (i)   for the claimant and for each member of his family aged 16 or over, [² £21.10];
      (ii)   for each member of his family under age 16, [² £10.65].

(3)   Except where sub-paragraph (5) applies and subject to sub-paragraph (4), where the charge includes provision for less than three meals a day, the amount shall be–
   (a)   for a single claimant, [² £14.05];
   (b)   if the claimant is a member of a family–
      (i)   for the claimant and for each member of his family aged 16 or over, [² £14.05];
      (ii)   for each member of his family under age 16, [² £7.05].

(4)   For the purposes of sub-paragraphs (2)(b) and (3)(b), a person attains the age of 16 on the first Monday in September following his 16th birthday.

(5)   Where the charge for meals includes the provision of breakfast only, the amount for the claimant and, if he is a member of a family, for the claimant and for each member of his family, shall be [² £2.60].

(6)   Where a charge for meals includes provision for meals for a person who is not a member of the claimant's family sub-paragraphs (2) to (5) shall apply as if that person were a member of the claimant's family.

(7)   For the avoidance of doubt where the charge does not include provision for meals for a claimant or, as the case may be, a member of his family, sub-paragraphs (2) to (5) shall not apply in respect of that person.

Amendments

1.   Amended by Art 19(4) of SI 2006 No 645 and reg 8 of SI 2006 No 217 as from 1.4.06 (3.4.06 where rent payable weekly or at intervals of a week).
2.   Amended by Art 19(4) of SI 2007 No 688 as from 1.4.07 (2.4.07 where rent payable weekly or at intervals of a week).

Analysis

This paragraph makes it clear that when a service charge is paid for meals, only the appropriate amounts shown in that paragraph are to be treated as ineligible, whatever the actual charge for meals. The leeway afforded by paras 3 and 4 in relation to other types of service charge does not apply here. Only the amounts shown may be deducted from the eligible rent in this respect and the amount of the deduction varies according to the number of meals per day included in the charge and the age of the members of the claimant's "family", defined in s137(1) SSCBA (see p22). However, where the charge does not include meals for the claimant or a member of her/his family, no deduction is made for that person: sub-para (7).

Where the charge for meals included in the claimant's charge includes meals not only for members of a claimant's family but for someone else, the appropriate deduction is to be made in respect of that person as though s/he was a member of the claimant's family: sub-para (6).

Amount of ineligible charges

3.–(1)   Subject to paragraph 2 where an ineligible service charge is not separated from or separately identified within other payments made by the occupier in respect of the dwelling, the appropriate authority shall apportion such charge as is fairly attributable to the provision of that service, having regard to the cost of comparable services and such portion of those payments shall be ineligible to be met by housing benefit.

(2)   Subject to paragraph 2, where the relevant authority considers that the amount of any ineligible service charge which is separately identified within other payments made by the occupier in respect of the dwelling is unreasonably low having regard to the service provided, it shall substitute a sum for the charge in question which it considers represents the value of the services concerned and the amount so substituted shall be ineligible to be met by housing benefit.

(3)   In sub-paragraph (2) the expression "ineligible service charge" includes any service charge which does not qualify as a periodical payment under regulation 12(1)(e) (rent).

(4)   In any other case, the whole amount of the ineligible service charge shall be ineligible to be met by housing benefit.

Analysis
The general rule, as set out in para 3(4), is that the whole amount of an ineligible charge is deducted from eligible rent. However, this is subject to two qualifications. First, in many cases, the amount of such a charge will not be identifiable and in such a case para 3(1) gives power to deduct an amount "fairly attributable" to it, having regard to the actual cost of comparable services.

Secondly, para 3(2) gives authorities the power to substitute their own valuation for ineligible service charges in a case where the amounts are considered to be unreasonably low for the services provided. See para 4 where *eligible* charges are thought to be excessive.

Excessive service costs
4.   Subject to paragraph 2, where the relevant authority considers that the amount of a service charge to which regulation 12(1)(e) (rent) applies is excessive in relation to the service provided for the claimant or his family, having regard to the cost of comparable services, it shall make a deduction from that charge of the excess and the amount so deducted shall be ineligible to be met by housing benefit.

Analysis
Where eligible charges are thought to be excessive, the excess is deducted and treated as ineligible.

PART 2
Payments in respect of fuel charges
5.   A service charge for fuel except a charge in respect of services for communal areas shall be ineligible to be met by housing benefit.

Analysis
The general rule, as set out in para 5, is that service charges relating to fuel are ineligible unless they relate to communal areas, as defined in para 8.

6.–(1)   Where a charge is ineligible to be met by housing benefit under paragraph 5–
(a)   in the calculation of entitlement to a rent rebate; or
(b)   in the calculation of entitlement to a rent allowance if the amount of the charge is specified or is otherwise readily identifiable (except where the amount of the charge is unrealistically low in relation to the fuel provided or the charge cannot readily be distinguished from a charge for a communal area),
the amount ineligible to be met by housing benefit shall be the full amount of the service charge.
(2)   In any other case, subject to sub-paragraphs (3) and (4) and paragraph 7, the amount ineligible to be met by housing benefit shall be the following amounts in respect of each week–
(a)   for heating (other than hot water) [² £15.45];
(b)   for hot water [² £1.80];
(c)   for lighting [² £1.25];
(d)   for cooking [² £1.80].
(3)   Where the accommodation occupied by the claimant or, if he is a member of a family, by the claimant and the members of his family, consists of one room only, the amount ineligible to be met by housing benefit in respect of each week where heating only is, or heating and either hot water or lighting (or both) are, provided, shall be one-half of the aggregate of the amounts specified in sub-paragraphs (2)(a), (b) and (c).
(4)   In a case to which sub-paragraph (2) or (3) applies, if a claimant provides evidence on which the actual or approximate amount of the service charge for fuel may be estimated, the amount ineligible to be met by housing benefit under this paragraph shall be that estimated amount.

Amendments
1.   Amended by Art 19(5) of SI 2006 No 645 and reg 8 of SI 2006 No 217 as from 1.4.06 (3.4.06 where rent payable weekly or at intervals of a week).
2.   Amended by Art 19(5) of SI 2007 No 688 as from 1.4.07 (2.4.07 where rent payable weekly or at intervals of a week).

Analysis
Under para 6(1), the full amount of the service charge for fuel is deducted in all cases where the claimant has a rent rebate, and in rent allowance cases where the charge is specified or can otherwise be readily

identified. In the latter case, this does not apply if the charge is unrealistically low or if the charge cannot be distinguished from a portion relating to communal areas.

If para 6(1) does not apply, regard must be had to sub-paras (2), (3) and (4) to work out the deduction. Specified amounts are usually deducted under sub-para (2). If, however, the claimant provides evidence to allow the actual amounts to be estimated, those amounts are to be taken instead: sub-para (4).

Under sub-para (3), where the claimant and her/his family (if applicable) occupy a single room, lower deductions apply. GM A4.912-913 suggests that this applies where the claimant occupies one room only, including cases where the room or other communal areas are shared and that the reference to "one room only" is not a reference to the number of rooms occupied solely by the claimant, that is that if a claimant has her/his own room and shared occupation of other rooms the higher rate of deduction applies.

The scope of the provision is somewhat uncertain in two respects. First, this calculation only applies where "heating only is, or heating and either hot water or lighting (or both) are, provided". The intention of this tortuous wording appears to be that any case in which there is a charge for cooking is excluded from sub-para (3), as is any case in which there is no charge for heating but there are charges for water, lighting or both. However, it would appear arguable that where charges for cooking are made along with charges for heating and charges for hot water and/or lighting, the claimant falls within the second limb of the phraseology.

Secondly, there are difficulties in determining how much is to be deducted. The sub-paragraph provides that the ineligible amount is to be half the aggregate of the amounts set out in sub-para (2) for heating, hot water and lighting. What about, however, the case where a charge is only made for heating, or only for heating and one of the latter two categories of claimant? On a literal reading of sub-para (3), it would appear that all the amounts are to be aggregated, yet this seems illogical in view of the fact that charges for hot water, lighting or both are not actually being made.

7.–(1)   Where rent is payable other than weekly, any amount ineligible to be met by housing benefit which is specified in this Schedule as a weekly amount shall–

    (a)   where rent is payable in multiples of a week, be multiplied by the number equal to the number of weeks in respect of which it is payable; or

    (b)   in any other case, be divided by 7 and multiplied by the number of days in the period to be used by the relevant authority for the purpose of calculating the claimant's weekly eligible rent under regulation 80 (calculation of weekly amounts).

    (2)   In a case to which regulation 81 applies (rent free periods), any amount ineligible to be met by housing benefit which is specified in this Schedule as a weekly amount shall, where appropriate, be converted in accordance with sub-paragraph (1) and shall–

    (a)   where rent is payable weekly, or in multiples of a week, be multiplied by 52 or 53, whichever is appropriate, and divided by the number equal to the number of weeks in that 52 or 53 week period in respect of which he is liable to pay rent; or

    (b)   in any other case, be multiplied by 365 or 366, whichever is appropriate, and divided by the number of days in that 365 or 366 day period in respect of which he is liable to pay rent.

Analysis

Para 7 deals with the arithmetic of calculating ineligible charges where rent is paid other than weekly or where there are rent-free periods. Under para 7(1), the charges are converted to weekly amounts. Under para 7(2), where there are rent-free periods (see reg 81) the amount of ineligible charges is adjusted. Suppose, for example, the claimant has eligible rent of £50 per week and ineligible charges of £10 a week. She has a rent-free period of four weeks during a 52 week year. The £10 is multiplied by 52 and divided by 48, giving £10.84 as the ineligible amount during each week.

---

8.   In this Schedule–

"communal areas" mean areas (other than rooms) of common access (including halls and passageways) and rooms of common use in sheltered accommodation;

"fuel" includes gas and electricity and a reference to a charge for fuel includes a charge for fuel which includes an amount in respect of the facility of providing it other than a specified amount for the provision of a heating system.

SCHEDULE 2
REGULATION 14
Excluded tenancies

General Note

This Schedule lists circumstances in which the general obligation in reg 14 requiring local authorities to refer claims for a rent allowance to the Rent Officer does not apply. Although under para 1, these are referred to as "excluded tenancies", this is a misleading term because not all the agreements referred to in the Schedule relate to tenancies as distinct from licences and so on, and also because many of the exclusions relate not so much to the tenancy but to the person claiming. A tenancy may gain and lose its status as an "excluded tenancy" during its existence.

These rules can be quite complex and careful analysis will often be required to ascertain whether a decision to refer can be challenged. Even where that has been done, it may be to the claimant's advantage to allow a referral in certain circumstances, particularly if rents have increased since the determination was made. The outcome of the referral may well be a higher eligible rent.

---

1. An excluded tenancy is any tenancy to which any of the following paragraphs applies.

2.–(1) Subject to the following sub-paragraphs, where a rent officer has made a determination, which relates to the tenancy in question or any other tenancy of the same dwelling this paragraph applies to–

(a) the tenancy in respect of which that determination was made; and

(b) any other tenancy of the same dwelling on terms which are substantially the same, other than the term relating to the amount of rent, as those terms were at the time of that determination or, if earlier, at the end of the tenancy.

(2) For the purposes of any claim, notification, request or application under regulation 14(1) ("the later application"), a tenancy shall not be an excluded tenancy by virtue of sub-paragraph (1) by reference to a rent officer's determination made in consequence of an earlier claim, notification, request or application ("the earlier application") where–

(a) the earlier and later applications were made in respect of the same claimant or different claimants; and

(b) the earlier application was made more than 52 weeks before the later application was made.

(3) Sub-paragraph (1) shall not apply where subsequent to the making of the determination mentioned in that sub-paragraph–

(a) the number of occupiers of the dwelling has changed and that dwelling is not in a hostel;

(b) there has been a substantial change in the condition of the dwelling (including the making of improvements) or the terms of the tenancy other than a term relating to rent;

(c) there has been a rent increase under a term of the tenancy and the term under which that increase was made was either included in the tenancy at the time when the application for that determination was made (or was a term substantially the same as such a term) and that determination was not made under paragraph 1(2), 2(2) or 3(3) of Schedule 1 to the Rent Officers Order;

(d) in a case where the rent officer has made a determination under paragraph 2(2) of Schedule 1 to the Rent Officers Order (size and rent determinations), but since the date of the application for that determination–

(i) a child, who is a member of the household occupying the dwelling, has attained the age of 10 years; or

(ii) a young person, who is a member of the household occupying that dwelling, has attained the age of 16 years; or

(iii) there is a change in the composition of the household occupying the dwelling;

(e) the claimant is a young individual, except in a case where the determination mentioned in sub-paragraph (1) was, or was made in conjunction with, a determination of a single room rent pursuant to paragraph 5 of Schedule 1 to the Rent Officers Order on or after 2nd July 2001.

Analysis

This is by far the most common type of "excluded tenancy" and is designed to avoid the need for constant referrals to be made for properties where there are continual changes of tenant.

The general rule, as set out in sub-para (1), is that once a rent officer has made a determination in relation to accommodation, it remains valid during the term of the existing tenancy (which, it is suggested, will include any period during which the claimant becomes a statutory tenant by virtue of the operation of the Housing Act 1988 or similar legislation). It also remains valid in relation to subsequent tenancies, provided that they are on substantially the same terms as the tenancy in existence when the referral was made, except in relation to the amount of rent payable. It is to be noted that it does not matter if the claimant changes.

However, the effect of this exclusion is limited. It applies only for 52 weeks in any event. Furthermore, sub-para (3) disapplies it in a case where any of the following changes of circumstance apply:

(1) Where the number of occupiers of the dwelling, whether or not they are members of the claimant's family, changes: sub-para (3)(a). This does not apply to hostel accommodation.

(2) Where there is a substantial change in the condition of the dwelling or the terms of the tenancy except in so far as they relate to rent: sub-para (3)(b).

(3)   Where there has been a rent increase under a term of the tenancy: sub-para (3)(c). This only applies where the term, or one like it, was in the tenancy when the previous referral was made. It also only applies where the rent officer did not made a significantly high rent determination, an exceptionally high rent determination, or a size-related rent determination following the previous referral. That will be clear from the terms of the previous officer's determination.

(4)   Where the previous determination contained a size-related rent determination and there has been a relevant change in circumstances: sub-para (3)(d). Relevant changes are a change in the composition of the household occupying the dwelling, or a child becoming 10 or 16 which changes the rules about the number of bedrooms required: see Sch 2 para 1 Rent Officers (Housing Benefit Functions) Order 1997 and its Scottish equivalent.

(5)   Where the claimant is a "young individual" (defined in reg 2(1) as most claimants under the age of 25) and the previous determination did not include a single room rent: sub-para (3)(e). This would be the case if the previous tenant was not a young individual.

3.–(1)   This paragraph applies where the landlord is a registered housing association, except in a case where the local authority consider that–

(a)   the claimant occupies a dwelling larger than is reasonably required by him and any others who occupy that dwelling (including any non-dependants of his and any person paying rent to him); or

(b)   the rent payable for that dwelling is unreasonably high.

(2) Where the circumstances set out in head (a) or (b) of sub-paragraph (1) above exist, the authority shall so state in their application for a determination.

Analysis

"Housing association" is defined in reg 2(1). A "registered housing association" is one that is on the register of social landlords kept by the Housing Corporation or the Housing Corporation for Wales, as appropriate: Pt I Housing Act 1996. Tenancies of registered housing associations are excluded unless unless the authority considers the claimant's home to be unreasonably large or the rent to be unreasonably high. The wording mirrors the wording in the version of reg 13(3)(a) and (b) HB Regs as in Sch 3 para 5(2) HB&CTB(CP) Regs, except that no specific comparison with suitable alternative accommodation is called for. However, it would be hard for a local authority to reach a conclusion that the home was unreasonably large or expensive without carrying out such a comparison. See the commentary to substituted reg 13 on p1105 for the extensive caselaw relating to these concepts.

---

4.   This paragraph applies to a tenancy entered into before–

(a)   in Scotland, 2nd January 1989; and

(b)   in any other case, 15th January 1989.

5.   This paragraph applies to a regulated tenancy within the meaning of–

(a)   in Scotland, the Rent (Scotland) Act 1984; and

(b)   in any other case, the Rent Act 1977.

6.   This paragraph applies to a housing association tenancy which–

(a)   in Scotland, is a tenancy to which Part 6 of the Rent (Scotland) Act 1984 applies; and

(b)   in any other case, is a housing association tenancy to which Part 6 of the Rent Act 1977 applies.

7.   This paragraph applies to a protected occupancy or statutory tenancy within the meaning of the Rent (Agriculture) Act 1976.

8.   This paragraph applies to a tenancy at a low rent within the meaning of Part 1 of the Landlord and Tenant Act 1954 or Schedule 10 to the Local Government and Housing Act 1989.

9.   This paragraph applies to a tenancy of any dwelling which is a bail hostel or probation hostel approved by the Secretary of State under section 9(1) of the Criminal Justice and Court Services Act 2000.

10.   This paragraph applies to a tenancy of a housing action trust established under Part 3 of the Housing Act 1988.

11.–(1)   Subject to sub-paragraphs (2) and (3) this paragraph applies to a tenancy–

(a)   in respect of a dwelling comprised in land which has been disposed of under section 32 of the Housing Act 1985 or section 12 of the Housing (Scotland) Act 1987;

(b)   in respect of a dwelling comprised in land which has been disposed of with the consent required by section 43 of the Housing Act 1985 or section 12 of the Housing (Scotland) Act 1987;

(c)   in respect of which the fee simple estate has been acquired, under the right conferred by Chapter 2 of Part 1 of the Housing Act 1996, otherwise than from a housing action trust within the meaning of Part 3 of the Housing Act 1988, or in respect of which the house has been acquired under the right conferred by Part 3 of the Housing (Scotland) Act 1988; or

(d)   in respect of a dwelling disposed of under the New Towns (Transfer of Housing Stock) Regulations 1990 to a person who is an approved person for the purposes of disposal under those Regulations or in respect of a dwelling disposed of pursuant to powers contained in the New Towns (Scotland) Act 1968 to a housing association.

(2)   This paragraph shall not apply to a tenancy to which sub-paragraph (1) refers if—

(a)   there has been an increase in rent since the disposal or acquisition, as the case may be, occurred; and

(b)   the local authority stated in the application for determination that—

    (i)   the claimant occupies a dwelling larger than is reasonably required by him and any others who occupy that dwelling (including any non-dependant of his and any person paying rent to him); or

    (ii)   the rent payable for that dwelling is unreasonably high.

(3)   Where the disposal or acquisition, as the case may be, took place on or after 7th October 2002, sub-paragraph (2)(b) shall apply to a tenancy to which sub-paragraph (1) refers as if head (i) were omitted.

[1 **11A.**   This paragraph applies to a shared ownership tenancy.]

Amendment

1.   Inserted by reg 2(7) of SI 2007 No 1356 as from 1.10.07.

Analysis

Paras 4 to 11A exclude a number of tenancies, most of which arose under old legislation. The common theme with tenancies under the old legislation is that the rent will usually be very low in any event. Reference should be made to the legislation mentioned in the paragraphs in any case of doubt.

Para 9 excludes a tenancy of a dwelling which is a bail hostel or probation hostel approved by the Secretary of State under section 9(1) of the Criminal Justice and Court Services Act 2000. Note that those required to live in such accommodation are treated as not occupying the dwelling as a hom and so cannot qualify for HB in any case: reg 7(5).

Para 10 applies to a tenancy of a housing action trust established under Part 3 of the Housing Act 1988.

Para 11 excludes council dwellings transferred to some other landlord (eg, a housing association) under the powers cited. It also excludes properties the authority has a duty to sell to "approved landlords" under the "Tenants' Choice" provisions of Pt IV Housing Act 1988. The exclusion does not apply, however, once there has been an increase in rent and the authority thinks that the accommodation is unreasonably large or expensive. The former only applies if the transfer took place before 7 October 2002: para 11(3). See the commentary to para 3 and to the version of reg 13 mentioned there.

From 1 October 2007, para 11A excludes shared ownership tenancies (defined in reg 2(1)).

---

12.   In this Schedule, "rent" shall be construed in accordance with paragraph (10) of regulation 14 (interpretation of "tenancy" and other expressions appropriate to a tenancy) and, subject to that paragraph, has the same meaning—

(a)   in Scotland, as in section 25 of the Housing (Scotland) Act 1988, except that the reference to the house in subsection (3) shall be construed as a reference to the dwelling;

(b)   in any other case, as in section 14 of the Housing Act 1988, except that the reference to the dwelling-house in subsection (4) shall be construed as a reference to the dwelling,

and—

    (i)   other expressions have the same meanings as in regulation 14(10);

    (ii)   in the case of a determination by a rent officer pursuant to a request for such a determination under regulation 14(1)(e), any reference to a "tenancy" shall be taken as a reference to a prospective tenancy and any reference to an "occupier" or any person "occupying" a dwelling shall, in the case of such a determination, be taken to be a reference to a potential occupier or potential occupation of that dwelling.

SCHEDULE 3
REGULATION 22
Applicable amounts

Definitions

"claimant" – see reg 2(1).

"disability living allowance" – see reg 2(1).

"family" – see s137(1) SSCBA and Part 4.

"lone parent" – see reg 2(1).

"member of household" – see s137(1) SSCBA and reg 21.

"non-dependant" – see reg 3.

"partner" – see reg 2(1).
"person in receipt of benefit" – see para 19.
"polygamous marriage" – see reg 2(1).
"responsibility for child" – see Part 4.
"single claimant" – see reg 2(1).
"training allowance" – see reg 2(1).

General Note on Schedule 3

This Schedule sets out the amounts of the various components to be added together under regs 22 and 23 to arrive at a claimant's "applicable amount" on which the calculation of HB is based. The amounts are uprated each April. Part 1 sets out the personal allowances and Parts 2 and 3 the rules of entitlement for various additional components ("premiums") which can be added to these. Part 4 gives the values of various premiums. For the calculation of HB, see Part 8.

PART 1

Analysis

This Part sets out the amounts of the personal allowances which form the primary part of the applicable amount. For details of which personal allowances are appropriate, see the General Notes and Analyses to regs 22 and 23.

The different personal allowances for single people under and over the age of 25 do not infringe Arts 8, 14 or Prot 1 Art 1 of the European Convention on Human Rights: *R (Reynolds) v Secretary of State for Work and Pensions* [2002] EWHC Admin 426.

Personal allowances

1. The amounts specified in column (2) below in respect of each person or couple specified in column (1) shall be the amounts specified for the purposes of regulations 22(a) and 23(a) and (b)–

Column (1)	Column (2)
Person or couple	Amount
(1) Single claimant aged–	(1)
(a) less than 25;	(a) [² £46.85];
(b) not less than 25	(b) [² £59.15].
(2) Lone parent aged–	(2)
(a) less than 18;	(a) [² £46.85];
(b) not less than 18	(b) [² £59.15].
(3) Couple–	(3)
(a) where both members are aged less than 18;	(a) [² £70.70];
(b) where at least one member is aged not less than 18.	(b) [² £92.80].

Amendments

1. Amended by Art 19(6) and Sch 6 para 1 of SI 2006 No 645 and reg 8 of SI 2006 No 217 as from 1.4.06 (3.4.06 where rent payable weekly or at intervals of a week).
2. Amended by Art 19(6) and Sch 6 para 1 of SI 2007 No 688 as from 1.4.07 (2.4.07 where rent payable weekly or at intervals of a week).

2.–(1) The amount specified in column (2) below in respect of each person specified in column (1) shall, for the relevant period specified in column (1), be the amounts specified for the purposes of regulations 22(b) and 23(c)

Column (1)	*Column (2)*
Child or young person	Amount
Persons in respect of the period–	
(a) beginning on that person's date of birth and ending on the day preceding the first Monday in September following that person's sixteenth birthday;	(a) [³ £47.45];
(b) beginning on the first Monday in September following that person's sixteenth birthday and ending on the day preceding that person's [² twentieth] birthday.	(b) [³ £47.45].

(2) In column (1) of the table in paragraph (1), "the first Monday in September" means the Monday which first occurs in the month of September in any year.

Amendments

1. Amended by Art 19(6) and Sch 6 para 2 of SI 2006 No 645 and reg 8 of SI 2006 No 217 as from 1.4.06 (3.4.06 where rent payable weekly or at intervals of a week).
2. Amended by reg 4(4) of SI 2006 No 718 as from 10.4.06.
3. Amended by Art 19(6) and Sch 6 para 2 of SI 2007 No 688 as from 1.4.07 (2.4.07 where rent payable weekly or at intervals of a week).

PART 2
Family premium

3.–(1) Subject to sub-paragraph (2), the amount for the purposes of regulations 22(c) and 23(d) in respect of a family of which at least one member is a child or young person shall be–

    (a)   where the claimant is a lone parent to whom sub-paragraph (3) applies, [³ £22.20];

    (b)   in any other case, [⁴ £16.43].

    (2) The amounts specified in sub-paragraph (1)(a) and (b) shall be increased by [³ £10.50] where at least one child is under the age of one year and for the purposes of this paragraph where the child's first birthday does not fall on a Monday he shall be treated as under the age of one year until the first Monday after his first birthday.

    (3) The amount in sub-paragraph (1)(a) shall be applicable to a lone parent–

    (a)   who was entitled to housing benefit on 5th April 1998 and whose applicable amount on that date included the amount applicable under sub-paragraph (a) of this paragraph as in force on that date; or

    (b)   who was not entitled to housing benefit on 5th April 1998 because that date fell during a rent free period as defined in regulation 81(1) (rent free periods) and his applicable amount on that date would have included the amount applicable under sub-paragraph (a) of this paragraph as in force on that date; or

    (c)   on becoming entitled to housing benefit where that lone parent–
        (i) had been treated as entitled to that benefit in accordance with sub-paragraph (5)(a) as at the day before the date of claim for that benefit; and
        (ii) was entitled to council tax benefit as at the date of claim for housing benefit,

and in respect of whom, all of the conditions specified in sub-paragraph (4) have continued to apply.

    (4) The conditions specified for the purposes of sub-paragraph (3) are that, in respect of the period commencing on 6th April 1998–

    (a)   the claimant has not ceased to be entitled, or has not ceased to be treated as entitled, to housing benefit;

    (b)   the claimant has not ceased to be a lone parent;

    (c)   where the claimant was entitled to income support or to an income-based jobseeker's allowance on 5th April 1998, he has continued to be entitled to one or other of those benefits;

    (d)   where the claimant was not entitled to income support or to an income-based jobseeker's allowance on 5th April 1998, he has not become entitled to either of those benefits; and

    (e)   a premium under paragraph 9, 10, 11 or 12 has not become applicable to the claimant.

    (5) For the purposes of sub-paragraphs (3)(c)(i) and (4)(a), a claimant shall be treated as entitled to housing benefit–

    (a)   during any period where he was not, or had ceased to be, so entitled and throughout that period, he had been awarded council tax benefit and his applicable amount included the amount applicable under paragraph 3(1)(a) of Schedule 1 to the Council Tax Benefit Regulations 2006 (lone parent rate of family premium); or

    (b)   during any rent free period as defined for the purposes of regulation 81(1).

Amendments

1. Confirmed by Art 19(7) of SI 2006 No 645 and reg 8 of SI 2006 No 217 as from 1.4.06 (3.4.06 where rent payable weekly or at intervals of a week).
2. Amended by Art 19(7) of SI 2006 No 645 and reg 8 of SI 2006 No 217 as from 1.4.06 (3.4.06 where rent payable weekly or at intervals of a week).
3. Confirmed by Art 19(7) of SI 2007 No 688 as from 1.4.07 (2.4.07 where rent payable weekly or at intervals of a week).
4. Amended by Art 19(7) of SI 2007 No 688 as from 1.4.07 (2.4.07 where rent payable weekly or at intervals of a week).

Analysis

A family premium is included in a claimant's applicable amount if at least one child or young person is a member of the family: see regs 22(c) and 23(d). It is additional to any other premiums that may be included. Only one family premium may be included, not one for each child.

The higher rate family premium for lone parents found in sub-para (1)(a) was abolished for most claimants in April 1998. Sub-paras (3) to (5) gives transitional protection to certain groups of claimants. Claimants who do not fall within the scope of those provisions will receive the lower rate under sub-para (1)(b).

Paras (3) to (5). There are three categories of claimants that are entitled to the transitional protection and so to the higher rate of premium under sub-para (1)(a):

(1)   Claimants entitled to HB on 5 April 1998 and who had the higher rate of the family premium on that date: para (3)(a).

(2)   Claimants who were not entitled on that date, but only because they were in a rent-free period (see reg 81), and would otherwise have had the higher rate of premium at that time: para (3)(b).

(3)   Claimants who were not entitled on that date, but who were treated as if they were entitled on the day prior to their claim and who were entitled to CTB on the day of the claim: para (3)(c).

For these purposes a person is treated as being entitled to HB for any period in which s/he was entitled to CTB and was getting the higher rate of family premium for that benefit: sub-para (5)(a). That is the only way in which the first requirement can be fulfilled.

Sub-para (4) requires that from 6 April 1998, the claimant must also *continuously* fulfil the following five conditions:

(1)   The claimant has not ceased to be entitled or ceased to be *treated as* entitled to HB. For the purposes of deciding whether a person ceases to be treated as being entitled to HB, s/he can qualify under either limb of sub-para (5). So s/he will be treated as entitled if s/he is entitled to CTB including the higher rate of family premium for the whole of that period *and* during any rent-free period (see reg 81).

(2)   The claimant has not ceased to be a lone parent (see reg 2(1) for the definition).

(3)   The claimant has continued to be entitled to IS or JSA when s/he was entitled to one of those benefits on 5 April 1998. Note that if the claimant switches from one benefit to another during that period (as may happen, eg, when someone comes out of a period of sickness and signs on) the condition is still fulfilled.

(4)   The claimant has not become entitled to IS or JSA if not so entitled on 5 April 1998.

(5)   The claimant has not become entitled to pensioner premium, higher pensioner premium or disability premium.

PART 3
Premiums

General Note to Part 3

This Part sets out the rules under which a claimant may qualify to have one or more "premiums" included in her/his applicable amount: see regs 22(d) and 23(e). The aim is to allow those claimants that have particular financial burdens or responsibilities arising out of their family circumstances to qualify for higher rates of benefit.

Paras 4 to 7, 18 and 19 set out some general rules governing entitlement to premiums, including the rules when a claimant qualifies for more than one premium: see paras 5 and 6. Paras 8 to 17 set out the specific rules relating to entitlement to individual premiums. The premiums that are available, and their abbreviations in the commentary that follows, are:

(1)   Bereavement premium (BP): para 8

(2)   Pensioner premium (PP): para 9.

(3)   Pensioner premium for those aged 75 or over: para 10.

(4)   Higher pensioner premium (HPP): paras 11 and 13.

(5)   Disability premium (DP): paras 12 and 13.

(5)   Severe disability premium (SDP): para 14.

(6)   Enhanced disability premium (EDP): para 15

(7)   Disabled child premium (DCP): para 16.

(8)   Carer premium (CP): para 17.

In the commentary below, personal allowances will be referred to as PA and family premium as FP.

The rules of entitlement for some of the premiums are made more complicated by inconsistencies in the terminology used, specifically where a premium is affected by entitlement to, and/or receipt of, and/or payment of, another benefit – a "qualifying benefit". As a result, a number of issues arise, including:

(1)   A carer needs to consider how her/his claim for carer's allowance (CA) will affect the SDP entitlement of the person s/he cares for, or of that person's partner (under para 14), particularly where the only financial advantage for the carer is the value of the CP (under para 17). For example, a single claimant will lose the SDP if her/his carer is entitled to *and* receiving CA in

respect of caring for her/him. However, a carer can qualify for the CP, and a severely disabled person can at the same time qualify for the SDP, if if the carer is entitled to, but *not* receiving, CA.

(2)   Severely disabled couples may qualify for two CPs, and at the same time the SDP at the couple rate (under paras 14 and 17). This could be the case, for example, where both members of the couple are receiving AA or the highest or middle rate of DLA and both members are entitled to (but not receiving) CA –eg, because it overlaps with state retirement pension.

Note that where there is an award of HB and a "qualifying benefit" is later awarded (or reinstated), regs 4(7B) and (7C), 7(2)(i) and 8(14) D&A Regs effectively allow for backdating of entitlement to premiums which depend on entitlement to (or receipt of) that qualifying benefit, for the period for which arrears of that benefit are paid. See the commentary to those provisions.

---

4.   Except as provided in paragraph 5, the premiums specified in Part 4 of this Schedule shall, for the purposes of regulations 22(d) and 23(e), be applicable to a claimant who satisfies the condition specified in paragraphs 8 to 17 in respect of that premium.

Analysis

Para 4 gives effect to the rates of the various premiums which are set out in Part 4 of the Schedule.

---

5.   Subject to paragraph 6, where a claimant satisfies the conditions in respect of more than one premium in this Part of this Schedule, only one premium shall be applicable to him and, if they are different amounts, the higher or highest amount shall apply.

Analysis

Para 5 states the general rule that where a claimant is entitled to more than one of the premiums in Part 3 only the highest is included in her/his applicable amount. Note however that as the FP is included under Part 2 of the schedule, if applicable, it may therefore be added in addition to the highest premium from Part 3. Note also that a claimant's changing circumstances may shift the most beneficial combination of premiums available.

The general rule in para 5 is subject to the exceptions in para 6, namely that the SDP, the DCP and the CP may all be paid in addition to any other premium, including each other, and the EDP may be paid in addition to any other premium except the PP (under either para 9 or 10) and the HPP.

6.–(1)   Subject to sub-paragraph (2), the following premiums, namely–
(a)   a severe disability premium to which paragraph 14 applies;
(b)   an enhanced disability premium to which paragraph 15 applies;
(c)   a disabled child premium to which paragraph 16 applies; and
(d)   a carer premium to which paragraph 17 applies,
may be applicable in addition to any other premium which may apply under this Schedule.
(2)   An enhanced disability premium in respect of a person shall not be applicable in addition to–
(a)   a pensioner premium under paragraph 9 or 10; or
(b)   a higher pensioner premium under paragraph 11.

7.–(1)   Subject to sub-paragraph (2), for the purposes of this Part of this Schedule, once a premium is applicable to a claimant under this Part, a person shall be treated as being in receipt of any benefit for–
(a)   in the case of a benefit to which the Social Security (Overlapping Benefits) Regulations 1979 applies, any period during which, apart from the provisions of those Regulations, he would be in receipt of that benefit; and
(b)   any period spent by a person in undertaking a course of training or instruction provided or approved by the Secretary of State under section 2 of the 1973 Act, or by Scottish Enterprise or Highlands and Islands Enterprise under section 2 of the Enterprise and New Towns (Scotland) Act 1990 or for any period during which he is in receipt of a training allowance.
(2)   For the purposes of the carer premium under paragraph 17, a person shall be treated as being in receipt of carer's allowance by virtue of sub-paragraph (1)(a) only if and for so long as the person in respect of whose care the allowance has been claimed remains in receipt of attendance allowance, or the care component of disability living allowance at the highest or middle rate prescribed in accordance with section 72(3) of the Act.

Analysis

Para 7 deals with the situation where entitlement to one of the premiums depends on the claimant being entitled to some other benefit. The effect of para 7(1)(a) is that where a claimant is not receiving a benefit because the Social Security (Overlapping Benefits) Regulations 1979 apply, s/he will nevertheless be treated as being in receipt of that benefit. Under para 7(1)(b), if a claimant moves off benefit because s/he is participating in training, s/he is treated as being in receipt of benefit for the purposes of Part 3.

Para 7(2) was effectively made irrelevant by amendments to the carer premium rules (in April 2000 and October 2003). The issue for a carer premium under para 17 is whether the claimant or her/his partner is *entitled* to CA. The claimant or the partner are not required to be "in receipt" of that benefit. See the commentary to para 17. Note however that entitlement to CA will in any event end when the person being cared for is no longer in receipt of AA or the highest or middle rate of the care component of DLA.

[¹ Bereavement premium]
[¹ **8.**]

Amendment
1.   Revoked by reg 2 and the Sch of SI 2007 No 2618 as from 1.10.07.

Analysis
The BP was payable to widows and widowers who were, on 9 April 2001, aged between 55 and 60 and who were formerly entitled to bereavement allowance. From 9 April 2006, no claimants qualified for the bereavement premium. All such claimants were at least 60 and instead qualified for a pensioner premium (paid at a higher rate) under para 9. Para 8 was therefore revoked with effect from 1 October 2007.
    See the 18th edition of this book for commentary.

Pensioner Premium for persons under 75
9.   The condition is that the claimant–
(a)   is a single claimant or lone parent aged not less than 60 but less than 75; or
(b)   has a partner and is, or his partner is, aged not less than 60 but less than 75.

Analysis
Paras 9 and 10 provide two types of premiums for pensioners, both now paid at the same rate. The basic PP, is included under para 9 if the claimant or her/his partner is aged between 60 and 75. Where the claimant or her/his partner is aged between 75 and 80 a PP is instead included under para 10. Only one PP is received if both are within either age range: para 5.
    Note that claims by those who are (or whose partner is) of at least the qualifying age for state pension credit (currently aged 60) are assessed under the HB(SPC) Regs unless the claimant (or partner) is on IS or income-based JSA, or is claiming extended payments under reg 72: reg 5. In both cases, the amount of entitlement will be assessed without the need for an applicable amount (or income or capital) to be calculated.

Pensioner Premium for persons 75 and over
10.   The condition is that the claimant–
(a)   is a single claimant or lone parent aged not less than 75 but less than 80; or
(b)   has a partner and is, or his partner is, aged not less than 75 but less than 80.

Higher Pensioner Premium
11.–(1)   Where the claimant is a single claimant or a lone parent, the condition is that–
(a)   he is aged not less than 80; or
(b)   he is aged less than 80 but not less than 60, and–
          (i)   the additional condition specified in paragraph 13(1)(a) is satisfied; or
          (ii)   the claimant was in receipt of, or was treated as being in receipt of, housing benefit and the disability premium was or, as the case may be, would have been, applicable to him in respect of a benefit week within 8 weeks of his 60th birthday and he has, subject to sub-paragraph (3), remained continuously in receipt of housing benefit since attaining that age.
(2)   Where the claimant has a partner, the condition is that–
(a)   he or his partner is aged not less than 80; or
(b)   he or his partner is aged less than 80 but not less than 60 and either–
          (i)   the additional condition specified in paragraph 13(1)(a) is satisfied; or
          (ii)   the claimant was in receipt of, or was treated as being in receipt of, housing benefit and the disability premium was or, as the case may be, would have been, applicable to him in respect of a benefit week within 8 weeks of his 60th birthday and he has, subject to sub-paragraph (3), remained continuously in receipt of housing benefit since attaining that age.
(3)   For the purposes of this paragraph and paragraph 13–
(a)   once the higher pensioner premium is applicable to a claimant, if he then ceases, for a period of 8 weeks or less, to be entitled to or treated as entitled to housing benefit, he shall, on

becoming re-entitled to housing benefit, thereafter be treated as having been continuously entitled to that benefit;
(b)   where sub-paragraphs (1)(b)(ii) and (2)(b)(ii) apply, if a claimant ceases to be entitled to or treated as entitled to housing benefit for a period not exceeding 8 weeks which includes his 60th birthday, he shall, on becoming re-entitled to housing benefit, thereafter be treated as having been continuously entitled to that benefit.
(c)   where the claimant or his partner–
    (i)   was entitled to council tax benefit or, as the case may be, community charge benefit at any time in the period of 8 weeks before becoming entitled or re-entitled to housing benefit; and
    (ii)   satisfied the conditions in respect of the higher pensioner premium under paragraphs 11 and 13 of Schedule 1 to the Council Tax Benefit Regulations 2006 or, as the case may be, paragraphs 11 and 13 of Schedule 1 to the Community Charge Benefits (General) Regulations 1989,
for the purpose of establishing entitlement or re-entitlement to housing benefit, he or his partner shall be treated as satisfying the equivalent conditions for higher pensioner premium under this paragraph and paragraph 13.
(4)   In the case of a claimant who is a welfare to work beneficiary, references in sub-paragraphs (1)(b)(ii), (2)(b)(ii), (3)(b) and (3)(c)(i) to a period of 8 weeks shall be treated as references to a period of [¹ 104 weeks].
(5)   A person is a welfare to work beneficiary if he is a person–
(a)   to whom regulation 13A(1) of the Social Security (Incapacity for Work) (General) Regulations 1995 applies; and
(b)   who again becomes incapable of work for the purposes of Part 12A of the Act.
(6)   For the purposes of this paragraph, a claimant shall be treated as having been entitled to and in receipt of housing benefit throughout any period which comprises only days on which he was participating in an employment zone programme and was not entitled to that benefit because, as a consequence of his participation in that programme, he failed to satisfy the condition in section 130(1)(c) of the Act.

Amendment

1.   Amended by reg 15(5) of SI 2006 No 2378 as from 9.10.06.

Analysis

The HPP is now paid at the same rate as the pensioner premiums in paras 9 and 10. Note that claims by those who are (or whose partner is) of at least the qualifying age for state pension credit (currently aged 60) are assessed under the HB(SPC) Regs unless the claimant (or partner) is on IS or income-based JSA, or is claiming extended payments under reg 72: reg 5. In both cases, the amount of entitlement will be assessed without the need for an applicable amount (or income or capital) to be calculated. Entitlement to the HPP may still be relevant, however, for example, in determining whether a person is "incapacitated" for the purpose of entitlement to a childcare costs disregard under reg 28 HB Regs (and the equivalents in the HB(SPC), CTB and CTB(SPC) Regs) or because in claims for working tax credit (WTC), entitlement to the HPP enables the claimant to qualify for the disability element, itself a route into entitlement to WTC.

The HPP effectively maintains the link with the claimant's (or her/his partner's) incapacity for work once retirement age is reached and a disability premium is no longer available under para 12.

A claimant may qualify for HPP in two ways. First, there is entitlement if the claimant or her/his partner is at least 80 years old: sub-paras (1)(a), (2)(a).

The second route applies to a claimant who is aged between 60 and 80 or whose partner is within that age range and in respect of whom two conditions are fulfilled: sub-paras (1)(b) and (2)(b):
(1)   The claimant must have been in receipt of HB with the DP "applicable" within eight weeks prior to her/his 60th birthday, and must have remained in receipt of HB continuously since that time. Note the effect of the deeming provisions in sub-para (3). It is not possible to argue that a person entitled to HB but not actually in receipt of it should fulfil the requirement of receipt under this condition: para 19 below, reversing the effect of *R(SB) 12/87* para 7. Note also *CIS 11293/1996*, which decides that IS housing costs can be "applicable" if they are potentially applicable if the claimant had been getting IS. If this decision was applied to para 11, it would follow that a claimant not actually getting DP (perhaps because s/he failed to supply medical evidence) would remain entitled to HPP.
(2)   The claimant or his partner, as relevant, fulfils the condition set out in para 13(1)(a).
Sub-para (3) creates deeming provisions which have effect both in relation to para 11 and para 13. First, a claimant entitled to HPP who then has a break in entitlement to HB of eight weeks or less is deemed to be continuously entitled over that period: sub-para (3)(a). Secondly, if a claimant has a break in entitlement of eight weeks or less around her/his 60th birthday, again such a break is ignored: sub-para (3)(b). It is

possible that these provisions could have a wider effect. If a claimant has a later break in her/his claim which exceeds eight weeks, it might be possible to argue that such a break in claim would have to be ignored, since the closing words do not refer to continuous entitlement "during that period".

Thirdly, where a claimant was entitled to CTB or CCB during the period of eight weeks prior to HB entitlement commencing and got HPP as part of that benefit, the claimant or her/his partner shall be treated as fulfilling the conditions of entitlement for HPP under the HB scheme.

Sub-para (4) relaxes the eight week rules in respect of claimants who are "welfare to work beneficiaries" by expanding the linking period to 104 weeks. See para 13 for further information about welfare to work beneficiaries.

Sub-para (6) deems a person to be entitled to and in receipt of HB who is participating in an employment zone programme and hence has too much income to be in receipt of HB during the period of that training.

Disability Premium

12. The condition is that–
(a) where the claimant is a single claimant or a lone parent, he is aged less than 60 and the additional condition specified in paragraph 13 is satisfied; or
(b) where the claimant has a partner, either–
   (i) the claimant is aged less than 60 and the additional condition specified in paragraph 13(1)(a) or (b) is satisfied by him; or
   (ii) his partner is aged less than 60 and the additional condition specified in paragraph 13(1)(a) is satisfied by his partner.

Analysis

There are two conditions for entitlement to a DP. If the claimant is single or a lone parent, s/he must be under 60 and satisfy the condition in para 13. If s/he has a partner, there are two ways to qualify. Either the claimant must be under 60 and satisfy a condition in para 13(1), or the partner must be under 60 and satisfy the condition in para 13(1)(a). Note that satisfying para 13(1)(b) will not suffice in the case of a partner.

Additional Condition for the Higher Pensioner and Disability Premiums

13.–(1) Subject to sub-paragraph (2) and paragraph 7, the additional condition referred to in paragraphs 11 and 12 is that either–
(a) the claimant or, as the case may be, his partner–
   (i) is in receipt of one or more of the following benefits: attendance allowance, disability living allowance, the disability element or the severe disability element of working tax credit as specified in regulation 20(1)(b) and (f) of the Working Tax Credit Regulations, mobility supplement, long-term incapacity benefit under Part 2 of the Act or severe disablement allowance under Part 3 of the Act but, in the case of long-term incapacity benefit or severe disablement allowance only where it is paid in respect of him; or
   (ii) was in receipt of long-term incapacity benefit under Part 2 of the Act when entitlement to that benefit ceased on account of the payment of a retirement pension under that Act and the claimant has since remained continuously entitled to housing benefit and, if the long-term incapacity benefit was payable to his partner, the partner is still a member of the family; or
   (iii) [¹] was in receipt of attendance allowance or disability living allowance but payment of benefit has been suspended in accordance with regulations made under section 113(2) of the Act or otherwise abated as a consequence of the claimant or his partner becoming a patient within the meaning of [¹ regulation 28(11)(e) (treatment of child care charges)]; or
   (iv) is provided by the Secretary of State with an invalid carriage or other vehicle under section 5(2) of the National Health Service Act 1977 (other services) or, in Scotland by the Scottish Ministers, under section 46 of the National Health Service (Scotland) Act 1978 (provision of services) or receives payments by way of grant from the Secretary of State under paragraph 2 of Schedule 2 to the Act of 1977 (additional provisions as to vehicles) or, in Scotland by the Scottish Ministers, under section 46 of the Act of 1978; or
   (v) is blind and in consequence registered in a register compiled by a local authority under section 29 of the National Assistance Act 1948 (welfare services) or, in Scotland, has been certified as blind and in consequence he is registered in a register maintained by or on behalf of a council constituted under section 2 of the Local Government (Scotland) Act 1994; or

(b)   the claimant–

    (i)   is, or is treated as, incapable of work in accordance with the provisions of, and regulations made under, Part 12A of the Act (incapacity for work); and

    (ii)   has been incapable, or has been treated as incapable, of work for a continuous period of not less than–

        (aa)   in the case of a claimant who is terminally ill within the meaning of section 30B(4) of the Act, 196 days;

        (bb)   in any other case, 364 days.

(2)   For the purposes of sub-paragraph (1)(a)(v), a person who has ceased to be registered as blind on regaining his eyesight shall nevertheless be treated as blind and as satisfying the additional condition set out in that sub-paragraph for a period of 28 weeks following the date on which he ceased to be so registered.

(3)   For the purposes of sub-paragraph (1)(b), once the higher pensioner premium or the disability premium is applicable to a claimant by virtue of his satisfying the additional condition specified in that provision, if he then ceases, for a period of 8 weeks or less, to be treated as incapable of work or to be incapable of work he shall, on again becoming so incapable of work, immediately thereafter be treated as satisfying the condition in sub-paragraph (1)(b).

(4)   For the purpose of sub-paragraph (1)(a)(ii) and (iii), once the higher pensioner premium is applicable to the claimant by virtue of his satisfying the condition specified in that provision, if he then ceases, for a period of 8 weeks or less, to be entitled to housing benefit, he shall on again becoming so entitled to housing benefit, immediately thereafter be treated as satisfying the condition in sub-paragraph (1)(a)(ii) and (iii).

(5)   For the purposes of sub-paragraph (1)(b), once the disability premium is applicable to a claimant by virtue of his satisfying the additional condition specified in that provision, he shall continue to be treated as satisfying that condition for any period spent by him in undertaking a course of training provided under section 2 of the 1973 Act or for any period during which he is in receipt of a training allowance.

(6)   For the purposes of sub-paragraph (1)(b), where any two or more periods of incapacity are separated by a break of not more than 56 days, those periods shall be treated as one continuous period.

(7)   For the purposes of this paragraph, a reference to a person who is or was in receipt of long-term incapacity benefit includes a person who is or was in receipt of short-term incapacity benefit at a rate equal to the long-term rate by virtue of section 30B(4)(a) of the Act (short-term incapacity benefit for a person who is terminally ill), or who would be or would have been in receipt of short-term incapacity benefit at such a rate but for the fact that the rate of short-term incapacity benefit already payable to him is or was equal to or greater than the long-term rate.

(8)   In the case of a claimant who is a welfare to work beneficiary within the meaning of paragraph 11(5)–

(a)   the reference to a period of 8 weeks in sub-paragraph (3); and

(b)   the reference to a period of 56 days in sub-paragraph (6),

shall in each case be treated as a reference to a period of [² 104 weeks].

Amendments

1.   Amended by reg 2(15)(b) of SI 2005 No 2502 as amended by Sch 2 para 27 of SI 2006 No 217 as from 1.4.06 (3.4.06 where rent payable weekly or at intervals of a week).

2.   Amended by reg 15(5) of SI 2006 No 2378 as from 9.10.06.

Analysis

This highly complex piece of legislation sets out the additional conditions common to the premiums specified in paragraphs 11 and 12 (the HPP and the DP). To satisfy sub-para (1)(a), the claimant or her/his partner must fulfil any one of the five heads. To satisfy sub-para (1)(b), the claimant must fulfill all the criteria set out there. Note the deeming provisions in paras 7, 18 and 19 relating to receipt and payment of benefit.

Sub-Para (1)(a)(i). The claimant or her/his partner must be receiving one of the benefits or elements of WTC listed. Note that the relevant person must be receiving incapacity benefit or severe disablement allowance for themselves and not on behalf of some other person. This prevents arguments such as those raised in *Rider v Chief Adjudication Officer* [1996] Times 30 January, CA. See also para 19.

In the case of incapacity benefit (IB), only long-term IB normally suffices but if a claimant is getting short-term IB as a terminally ill person or would qualify as such were s/he not already getting a higher rate than that applicable to the terminally ill, s/he is deemed to be getting long-term IB for this purpose: sub-para (7).

Sub-Para (1)(a)(ii). The claimant or her/his partner must have been receiving long-term IB and subsequently retirement pension. If the IB was payable to the claimant's partner, the partner must still be a member of the family. Note the transitional protection in Sch 3 para 3 HB&CTB(CP) Regs (see p1100).

Once the HPP is applicable, if there is a gap of eight weeks or less in HB entitlement, this provision is deemed to operate immediately when entitlement is revived: sub-para (4).

Sub-Para (1)(a)(iii). This applies where the claimant or her/his partner are "patients". See the commentary to reg 28 for the meaning of patient. Either the claimant or his partner must have been in receipt of attendance allowance or disability living allowance. Payment must then have been suspended under the Social Security (Attendance Allowance) Regulations 1991 or the Social Security (Disability Living Allowance) Regulations 1991 due to her/him being a "patient". Both sets of regs do not speak in terms of suspension of benefit but rather as it being a "condition of receipt" of AA or DLA that the relevant person does not become a patient. Loss of benefit under the relevant provisions should be seen as a suspension of benefit for the purposes of this sub-paragraph.

Once the HPP is applicable, if there is a gap of eight weeks or less in HB entitlement, this provision is deemed to operate immediately when entitlement is revived: sub-para (4).

Sub-Para (1)(a)(iv). Under the 1977 Act, the Secretary of State may provide persons "suffering from a severe physical disability or defect" with such vehicles. Grants are also payable for "adapting, maintaining, repairing or insuring, paying road tax or providing a structure for a vehicle, or reimbursing duty paid in purchasing fuel for such a vehicle for a person suffering from a severe physical disability or defect".

The Secretary of State may also pay for driving lessons for a person suffering from a severe physical disability or defect in order that he may drive the vehicle in question. The Scottish legislation is of the same effect as the English. Receipt of any assistance of this kind will mean that head (iv) is satisfied.

Sub-Para (1)(a)(v). This covers those who are blind (certified blind in Scotland) and as a conseqwuence, registered in register as specified. Under sub-para (2), a person coming off the register is treated as fulfilling this condition for a period of 28 weeks after her/his name is removed from the register.

Sub-Para (1)(b). The requirement here is that the claimant is incapable of work for the purposes of the incapacity benefit legislation. Pursuant to Part 12A SSCBA, the question as to whether a claimant is, or is treated as, incapable for work is conclusively determined by the DWP decision maker. Therefore if there is any dispute as to whether a claimant is incapable of work, it must be referred to the DWP even if the claimant is not claiming DWP benefits.

A claimant who does not receive DWP benefits should make a claim for incapacity credits in order to obtain a determination that s/he is incapable of work which the local authority must then act upon.

The claimant must be incapable or so treated for 365 days. The period is reduced to 196 days in the case of a claimant who is terminally ill. It would seem that the question of whether someone is terminally ill must be resolved by the local authority and not by the DWP decision maker. By SSCBA s30B(4), "a person is terminally ill if he suffers from a progressive disease and his death in consequence of that disease can reasonably be expected within 6 months."

A prisoner may remain incapable of work, since serving as a prisoner prevents receipt of incapacity benefit but does not deem her/him to be capable of work: *CIS 15611/1996.*

Once a claimant has qualified for HPP or DP under sub-para (1)(b), there are deeming provisions that will protect entitlement to the premium:

(1)   For HPP and DP, a period where the claimant is capable of work for eight weeks or less will not prevent the claimant satisfying this provision: sub-para (3). In the case of a "welfare to work beneficiary" (see below), this period is extended to 104 weeks: sub-para (8).

(2)   For DP, a period during which the claimant is undertaking training under the Employment and Training Act 1973 or in receipt of a training allowance (see reg 2(1) for a definition): sub-para (5).

(3)   For HPP and DP a break in a period of incapacity of not more than 56 days will be ignored: sub-para (6). In the case of a "welfare to work beneficiary" (see below), this period is extended to 104 weeks: sub-para (8).

Note the transitional protection in Sch 3 para 2 of the HB&CTB(CP) (see p1099).

Welfare to work beneficiaries Under para 11(5) a welfare to work beneficiary is someone falling within the scope of reg 13A(1) of the Social Security (Incapacity for Work) (General) Regulations 1995, which prescribes four conditions. First, the claimant must have been incapable of work for more than 196 days. Secondly, s/he must have stopped receiving the benefit s/he was receiving as a result of the incapacity (eg, incapacity benefit or income support) on or after 5 October 1998. Thirdly, s/he must have commenced remunerative work or a training course for which training allowance is received within a month of benefit ceasing. Once a claimant then becomes incapable of work again, s/he is a welfare to work beneficiary for the purposes of this Schedule. For further information about the scheme, see CPAG's *Welfare Benefits and Tax Credits Handbook.*

In cases of doubt, clarification should be obtained from the DWP as to whether a claimant has acquired this status. However, it would appear that it is for the local authority and not the DWP to decide whether this condition is met for HB and CTB purposes (although the decision as to whether a claimant is incapable of work is made by the DWP: see below).

Severe Disability Premium

14.–(1)   The condition is that the claimant is a severely disabled person.

(2)   For the purposes of sub-paragraph (1), a claimant shall be treated as being a severely disabled person if, and only if–

(a)   in the case of a single claimant, a lone parent or a claimant who is treated as having no partner in consequence of sub-paragraph (3)–

   (i)   he is in receipt of attendance allowance, or the care component of disability living allowance at the highest or middle rate prescribed in accordance with section 72(3) of the Act; and

   (ii)   subject to sub-paragraph (4), he has no non-dependants aged 18 or over normally residing with him or with whom he is normally residing; and

   (iii)   no person is entitled to, and in receipt of, a carer's allowance under section 70 of the Act in respect of caring for him;

(b)   in the case of a claimant who has a partner–

   (i)   the claimant is in receipt of attendance allowance, or the care component of disability living allowance at the highest or middle rate prescribed in accordance with section 72(3) of the Act; and

   (ii)   his partner is also in receipt of such an allowance or, if he is a member of a polygamous marriage, all the partners of that marriage are in receipt of such an allowance; and

   (iii)   subject to sub-paragraph (4), the claimant has no non-dependants aged 18 or over normally residing with him or with whom he is normally residing,

and either a person is entitled to or in receipt of a carer's allowance in respect of caring for only one of a couple or, in the case of a polygamous marriage, for one or more but not all the partners of the marriage, or as the case may be, no person is entitled to and in receipt of such an allowance in respect of caring for either member of a couple or any partner of a polygamous marriage.

(3)   Where a claimant has a partner who does not satisfy the condition in sub-paragraph (2)(b)(ii), and that partner is blind or is treated as blind within the meaning of paragraph 13(1)(a)(v) and (2), that partner shall be treated for the purposes of sub-paragraph (2) as if he were not a partner of the claimant.

(4)   For the purposes of sub-paragraph (2)(a)(ii) and (2)(b)(iii) no account shall be taken of–

(a)   a person receiving attendance allowance, or the care component of disability living allowance at the highest or middle rate prescribed in accordance with section 72(3) of the Act; or

(b)   a person who is blind or is treated as blind within the meaning of paragraph 13(1)(a)(v) and (2).

(5)   For the purposes of sub-paragraph (2)(b) a person shall be treated–

(a)   as being in receipt of attendance allowance, or the care component of disability living allowance at the highest or middle rate prescribed in accordance with section 72(3) of the Act, if he would, but for his being a patient for a period exceeding 28 days, be so in receipt;

(b)   as being entitled to and in receipt of a carer's allowance if he would, but for the person for whom he was caring being a patient in hospital for a period exceeding 28 days, be so entitled and in receipt.

(6)   For the purposes of sub-paragraph (2)(a)(iii) and (2)(b), no account shall be taken of an award of carer's allowance to the extent that payment of such an award is backdated for a period before [¹ the date on which the award is first paid].

(7)   In sub-paragraph (2)(a)(iii) and (b), references to a person being in receipt of a carer's allowance shall include references to a person who would have been in receipt of that allowance but for the application of a restriction under section 7 of the Social Security Fraud Act 2001 (loss of benefit provisions).

Amendment

1.   Amended by reg 6(6) of SI 2007 No 719 as from 2.4.07.

Analysis

To qualify for SDP, the claimant must be a "severely disabled person": sub-para (1). The claimant may only be treated as such only in accordance with the terms of sub-para (2). See also the General Note to Part 3 of this schedule.

Sub-Para (2)(a) applies to single claimants and lone parents. It also applies to a claimant who is treated as having no partner under sub-para (3).

There are three criteria, all of which must be fulfilled:

(1)   The claimant must be in receipt of AA or the care component of DLA at the highest or middle rate. Note the deeming provisions in paras 18 and 19 relating to receipt and payment of benefit. AA is defined in reg 2(1) and includes constant attendance allowance and exceptionally severe disablement allowance (or equivalent war pension).

(2)   There are no non-dependants living with her/him. For the meaning of "non-dependant" and "normally resides" see reg 3. Note that if such people are themselves receiving AA or highest or

middle rate DLA care component or are blind or treated as blind for the purposes of para 13(1)(a)(v) and (2) then they are ignored: sub-para (4).

(3)   No one is entitled to and in receipt of carer's allowance (CA) in respect of caring for him/her. As with criterion (2), certain disabled people are ignored under sub-para (4). Backdated CA will not count: sub-para (6).

Sub-Para (2)(b) applies to claimants with partners. There are four criteria which must be fulfilled. The claimant must satisfy the first two of the criteria listed under sub-para (2)(a) above: sub-paras (2)(b)(i) and (iii). In addition:

(1)   The partner, or all the parties to a polygamous marriage, must also be in receipt of AA or highest or middle rate DLA care component. Again, note the deeming provisions in paras 18 and 19 relating to receipt and payment of benefit.

(2)   Either someone is entitled to and in receipt of CA in respect of caring for only one member of the couple (or one but not all the members of a polygamous marriage) or no one is entitled to and in receipt of CA for either (or any) partner.

For these purposes, but not, strangely, for the purposes of sub-para (2)(a)(i), suspension of payment of attendance allowance or disability living allowance due to the disabled person becoming a "patient" will be ignored: sub-para (5).

Again, backdated CA is ignored: sub-para (6).

Note that if someone is in receipt of CA for only one member of a couple (or polygamous marriage) or a claimant satisfies the conditions in sub-para (2)(b) only because of sub-para (5), an SDP is included in the claimant's applicable amount at the single person's rate: para 20(6)(b)(i).

For the purposes of sub-paras (2)(a)(iii) and (b), a claimant's entitlement to the SDP will only be affected if a person is both entitled to *and* in receipt of CA, although, note that under sub-para (7), someone is treated as in receipt of CA if s/he would have been in receipt but for the "loss of benefit" provisions cited. So where the person is *not* receiving CA because s/he receives another "overlapping benefit" (sometimes known as an "underlying entitlement"), entitlement to the SDP will not be affected. For the overlapping benefit rules, see the Social Security (Overlapping Benefits) Regulations 1979 SI No 597 (as amended). The benefits which overlap with CA are contribution-based JSA, MA, IB, retirement pension, widow's or bereavement benefits, severe disablement allowance and training allowances.

Sub-para (3). Under this, where a claimant's partner is not in receipt of AA or highest or middle rate DLA care component, but is blind for the purposes of para 13(1)(a)(v) and (2) (see commentary above), s/he is treated as not the claimant's partner for the purpose of sub-para (2)(a). Note that in practical terms, in order to qualify for an SDP where one member of a couple is in receipt of a relevant benefit and the other is blind, the one who is in receipt of the benefit should be the HB claimant.

Enhanced disability premium

15.–(1)   Subject to sub-paragraph (2), the condition is that the care component of disability living allowance is, or would, but for a suspension of benefit in accordance with regulations under section 113(2) of the Act or but for an abatement as a consequence of hospitalisation, be payable at the highest rate prescribed under section 72(3) of the Act in respect of–

(a)   the claimant; or

(b)   a member of the claimant's family,

who is aged less than 60.

(2)   An enhanced disability premium shall not be applicable in respect of–

(a)   a claimant who–

(i)   is not a member of a couple or a polygamous marriage; and

(ii)   is a patient within the meaning of [[1] regulation 28(11)(e)] and has been for a period of more than 52 weeks; or

(b)   a member of a couple or a polygamous marriage where each member is a patient within the meaning of regulation 24(2) and has been for a period of more than 52 weeks.

Amendment

1.   Amended by reg 2(15)(c) of SI 2005 No 2502 as amended by Sch 2 para 27 of SI 2006 No 217 as from 1.4.06 (3.4.06 where rent payable weekly or at intervals of a week).

Analysis

The EDP is payable where the highest rate of the care component of DLA is "payable" to the claimant or a member of her/his family (or would be but for a stay in hospital). It is suggested that "payable" here must mean entitled to (or entitled to be paid) DLA, but does not necessarily mean that is is actually in payment. Note also the deeming provisions in paras 18 and 19 relating to receipt and payment of benefit.

The person to whom the highest rate of the care component is payable must also be under 60. If the person entitled to the highest rate of the care component is the claimant and is single, the EDP is not applicable where s/he is a hospital in-patient and has been for more than 52 weeks. See the commentary to reg 28 for a discussion on the meaning of "patient". If the claimant is a member of a couple or of a polygamous marriage, the EDP remains payable unless both members of the couple or every member of the polygamous marriage are patients and have been so for more than 52 weeks. Note that here, the reference for the meaning of patient is to reg 24(2) which was revoked in April 2006.

Disabled child premium

16. The condition is that a child or young person for whom the claimant or a partner of his is responsible and who is a member of the claimant's household–

(a) is in receipt of disability living allowance or is no longer in receipt of such allowance because he is a patient, provided that the child or young person continues to be a member of the family; or

(b) is blind or treated as blind within the meaning of paragraph 13; or

(c) is a child or young person in respect of whom section 145A of the Act (entitlement to child benefit after death of child) applies for the purposes of entitlement to child benefit but only for the period prescribed under section 145A(1) of the Act and in respect of whom a disabled child premium was included in the claimant's applicable amount immediately before the death of that child.

Analysis

To get DCP, the claimant or her/his partner must be responsible for a child or young person who is a part of the claimant's household (for which see Part 4 above). One of three critera must be satisfied:

(1) The child or young person must be in receipt of DLA, or no longer be in receipt because s/he is a patient. In the latter case, s/he must still be a member of the family (see p22).

(2) The child or young person is blind (or treated as blind) for the purposes of para 13.

(3) The child or young person has died, the claimant was getting the DCP immediately before the death and child benefit is paid for the child following the death. This only applies for a period of eight weeks.

Carer premium

17.–(1) The condition is that the claimant or his partner is, or both of them are, entitled to a carer's allowance under section 70 of the Act.

(2) Where a carer premium is awarded but–

(a) the person in respect of whose care the carer's allowance has been awarded dies; or

(b) in any other case the person in respect of whom a carer premium has been awarded ceases to be entitled to a carer's allowance,

the condition for the award of the premium shall be treated as satisfied for a period of eight weeks from the relevant date specified in sub-paragraph (3).

(3) The relevant date for the purposes of sub-paragraph (2) shall be–

(a) where sub-paragraph (2)(a) applies, the Sunday following the death of the person in respect of whose care a carer's allowance has been awarded or the date of death if the death occurred on a Sunday;

(b) in any other case, the date on which the person who has been entitled to a carer's allowance ceases to be entitled to that allowance.

(4) Where a person who has been entitled to a carer's allowance ceases to be entitled to that allowance and makes a claim for housing benefit, the condition for the award of the carer premium shall be treated as satisfied for a period of eight weeks from the date on which–

(a) the person in respect of whose care the carer's allowance has been awarded dies;

(b) in any other case, the person who has been entitled to a carer's allowance ceased to be entitled to that allowance.

Analysis

To qualify for the carer premium the claimant or her/his partner must be entitled to carer's allowance (CA). See also the General Note to Part 3 of this Schedule and the Analysis of para 7(2).

A carer premium is applicable even if the claimant or her/his partner is not actually receiving CA – ie, s/he already receives another "overlapping' benefit". This is sometimes referred to as "underlying entitlement" to carer's allowance. For the overlapping benefit rules, see the Social Security (Overlapping Benefits) Regulations 1979 SI No 597 (as amended). The benefits which overlap with CA are contribution-based JSA, MA, IB, retirement pension, widow's or bereavement benefits, severe disablement allowance and training allowances. It is important to note that for someone to be entitled to carer's allowance, a claim must be made: s1 SSAA. GM W3.271 points out that claimants with an underlying entitlement to CA are notified by the DWP's CA Unit of that fact.

The premium is payable for each person who satisfies the condition, so both the claimant and her/his partner may qualify: para 20(8).

Where a carer is paid CA, the person being cared for might not be able to qualify for an SDP. Careful benefit advice is therefore needed before a claim for CA is made.

Sub-paras (2), (3) and (4) allow entitlement to the premium to continue for eight weeks after caring or entitlement to CA ceases. This also applies where the person being cared for has died. The eight weeks runs from the same day if the death occurs on a Sunday and from the following Sunday if occurring on another day.

Persons in receipt of concessionary payments

18. For the purpose of determining whether a premium is applicable to a person under paragraphs 13 to 17, any concessionary payment made to compensate that person for the non-payment of any benefit mentioned in those paragraphs shall be treated as if it were a payment of that benefit.

Analysis

Under para 18, a concessionary payment to compensate for non-payment of a benefit must be treated as a payment of that benefit. It has been suggested in previous editions that payment from non-governmental sources would suffice but that is not correct: see the definition of "concessionary payment" in reg 2(1).

Where a concessionary payment is "treated as if it were a payment of that benefit" under para 18, the benefit would be "payable" for the purpose of para 15 and a person would be "in receipt" of the benefit for the purposes of paras 13, 14 and 16. However, in para 17 the issue is whether someone is "entitled to" a benefit. However, it is suggested that where a payment is made in the circumstances set out in para 18, there has been a concession that there was an entitlement to the benefit concerned.

Person in receipt of benefit

19. For the purposes of this Part of this Schedule, a person shall be regarded as being in receipt of any benefit if, and only if, it is paid in respect of him and shall be so regarded only for any period in respect of which that benefit is paid.

Analysis

This paragraph clarifies what it means to be "in receipt of" benefit, a concept that occurs in several places in Part 3 (eg, paras 13 to 16). It was added to reverse *R(SB) 12/87*.

Under para 19, a person is "in receipt" of benefit only if it is actually paid in respect of her/him. The words "in respect of" mean that it does not have to be paid *to* her/him: it might be paid to an appointee. However, the person "in receipt" is the one who is entitled to the benefit. So for example where a claimant is entitled to attendance allowance but it is being paid to another person on her/his behalf, it is the claimant who is "in receipt" of the attendance allowance, not the other person.

PART 4
Amounts of premiums specified in Part 3

Premium	Amount
20.–[[4] (1)]	[[4] (1)].
(2) Pensioner Premium for persons aged under 75–	(2)
(a) where the claimant satisfied the condition in paragraph 9(a);	(a) [[3] £59.90];
(b) where the claimant satisfies the condition in paragraph 9(b).	(b) [[3] £88.90].
(3) Pensioner Premium for persons aged 75 and over–	(3)
(a) where the claimant satisfied the condition in paragraph 10(a);	(a) [[3] £59.90];
(b) where the claimant satisfies the condition in paragraph 10(b).	(b) [[3] £88.90].
(4) Higher Pensioner Premium–	(4)
(a) where the claimant satisfies the condition in paragraph 11(1)(a) or (b);	(a) [[3] £59.90];
(b) where the claimant satisfies the condition in paragraph 11(2)(a) or (b).	(b) [[3] £88.90].

Premium	Amount
(5) Disability Premium–	(5)
(a) where the claimant satisfies the condition in paragraph 12(a);	(a) [³ £25.25];
(b) where the claimant satisfies the condition in paragraph 12(b).	(b) [³ £36.00].
(6) Severe Disability Premium–	(6)
(a) where the claimant satisfies the condition in paragraph 14(2)(a);	(a) [³ £48.45];
(b) where the claimant satisfies the condition in paragraph 14(2)(b)–	
(i) in a case where there is someone in receipt of carer's allowance or if he or any partner satisfies that condition only by virtue of paragraph 14(5);	(b) (i) [³ £48.45];
	(ii) [³ £96.90].
(7) Disabled Child Premium.	(7) [³ £46.69] in respect of each child or young person in respect of whom the condition specified in paragraph 16 of Part 3 of this Schedule is satisfied.
(8) Carer Premium.	(8) [³ £27.15] in respect of each person who satisfies the condition specified in paragraph 17.
(9) Enhanced Disability Premium where the conditions in paragraph 15 are satisfied.	(9)
	(a) [³ £18.76] in respect of each child or young person in respect of whom the conditions specified in paragraph 15 are satisfied;

	(b) [³ £12.30] in respect of each person who is neither–
	    a child or young person; nor
	    (ii) a member of a couple or a polygamous marriage,
	    in respect of whom the conditions specified in paragraph 15 are satisfied;

	(c) [³ £17.75] where the claimant is a member of a couple or a polygamous marriage and the conditions specified in paragraph 15 are satisfied in respect of a member of that couple or polygamous marriage.

Amendments

1.   Amended by Art 19(8) and Sch 7 of SI 2006 No 645 and reg 8 of SI 2006 No 217 as from 1.4.06 (3.4.06 where rent payable weekly or at intervals of a week).
2.   Confirmed by Art 19(8) and Sch 7 of SI 2007 No 688 as from 1.4.07 (2.4.07 where rent payable weekly or at intervals of a week).
3.   Amended by Art 19(8) and Sch 7 of SI 2007 No 688 as from 1.4.07 (2.4.07 where rent payable weekly or at intervals of a week).
4.   Revoked by reg 2 and the Sch of SI 2007 No 2618 as from 1.10.07.

Analysis

This simply quantifies the appropriate amounts for the premiums set out in Part 3.

SCHEDULE 4
REGULATIONS 36(2) AND 38(2)

Sums to be disregarded in the calculation of earnings

General Note on Schedule 4

Paras 1–14 set out the types of and amounts of earnings which are to be ignored in the assessment of a claimant's or his partner's earnings or net profit in keeping with regs 36 and 38 respectively.

Paras 1 and 2 deal with earnings where employment terminates or is interrupted.

Paras 3 to 10 provide for disregards of £25, £20, £10 or £5 if specific conditions are satisifed.

Under para 11 some earnings can be disregarded where the claimant is making a parental contirbution to a student's grant or loan or contributes to a student's maintenance.

Under para 12 the earnings of those on IS or income-based JSA are fully disregarded.

Paras 13 and 14 deal with earnings payable in a country outside the UK and earnings in currencies other than Sterling.

Para 15 deals with the earnings of children and young people.

Para 16 defines "part-time employment" for the purposes of Sch 4.

Para 17 provides an additional earnings disregard for some claimants who are in, or whose partners are in, remunerative work.

Except where otherwise indicated, the disregards are cumulative.

Definitions

"applicable amount" – see Part 5.
"child" – see reg 2(1).
"claimant" – see reg 2(1).
"couple" – see s137(1) SSCBA.
"earnings" – see regs 35 and 37.
"employed earner" – see reg 2(1).
"family" – see s137(1) SSCBA.
"Great Britain" – excludes Northern Ireland.
"partner" – see reg 2(1).
"part-time employment" – see para 16.
"polygamous marriage" – see reg 2(1).
"remunerative work" – see reg 6.
"United Kingdom" – includes Northern Ireland.
"young person" – see reg 19.

---

1.   In the case of a claimant who has been engaged in remunerative work as an employed earner or, had the employment been in Great Britain, would have been so engaged–

(a)   where–

    (i)   the employment has been terminated because of retirement; and

    (ii)   on retirement he is entitled to a retirement pension under the Act, or is not so entitled solely because of his failure to satisfy the contribution conditions,

any earnings [¹ paid or due to be paid] in respect of that employment, but only for a period commencing on the day immediately after the date on which the employment was terminated;

[¹ (b)   where before the first day of entitlement to housing benefit the employment has been terminated otherwise than because of retirement, any earnings paid or due to be paid in respect of that employment except–

    (i)   any payment of the nature described in regulation 35(1)(e), or

    (ii)   any award, sum or payment of the nature described in–

        (aa)   regulation 35(1)(g) or (h), or

        (bb)   section 34 or 70 of the Employment Rights Act 1996 (guarantee payments and suspension from work: complaints to employment tribunals),

including any payment made following the settlement of a complaint to an employment tribunal or of court proceedings;

(c)   where before the first day of entitlement to housing benefit–

    (i)   the employment has not been terminated, but

    (ii)   the claimant is not engaged in remunerative work,

any earnings paid or due to be paid in respect of that employment except any payment or remuneration of the nature described in regulation 35(1)(e), (i) or (j).]

Amendment

1.   Amended by reg 11(11)(a) of SI 2007 No 2618 as from 1.10.07.

Analysis

This paragraph applies only to claimants who have been in "remunerative work" as employed earners (see above for definitions), or who would have been had their employment been in Great Britain. Sub-paras (a) and (b) deals with situations where the employment terminates. Para (c) deals with situations where employment has *not* been terminated, but the person is no longer in "remunerative work" – eg, where s/he is no longer doing sufficient hours or is on sick leave. By reg 25, this para also applies to claimants' partners. It provides a complete disregard of earnings paid on retirement and a more restricted disregard for earnings received where employment has ceased or has been interrupted as at the first day of entitlement to HB. If a claimant receives wages or is due to receive wages on the termination or interruption of part-time work, see para 2.

Sub-para (a) deals with the treatment of earnings on termination of employment because of retirement. Where a person's employment is terminated because of retirement, and s/he is entitled to retirement pension when s/he retires (or would be but for failing to satisfy the contribution conditions), earnings (paid or due to be paid) from that employment are disregarded, but only for the period starting on the day after the day the employment ended. It is the date on which the employment terminated which is important, not the date on which the claimant last worked, which may be earlier. So where HB entitlement commences *after* the employment has terminated, all earnings from that employment should be disregarded. Note that by reg 5, this para is effectively redundant as the HB Regs (other than reg 72 and Sch 7) do not apply to a claimant if s/he or her/his partner has reached the qualifying age for state pension credit (currently aged 60) unless either is on IS or income-based JSA. Claims by such claimants are instead dealt with under the HB(SPC) Regs. Note that if a claimant is on IS or income-based JSA, earnings are disregarded under para 12.

Sub-para (b) deals with the treatment of earnings on termination of employment before the first day of entitlement to HB, otherwise than on retirement. In this case, any earnings (paid or due to be paid) in respect of that employment should be disregarded, except those earnings shown in reg 35(1)(e), (g) and (h) (ie, retainers, compensation for unfair dismissal and payments deemed to be earnings by regulations made under s112 of the SSCBA) and guarantee payments and remuneration on suspension from work on medical or maternity grounds following a complaint to an employment tribunal under ss34 or 70 of the Employment Rights Act 1996. So where the employment terminates *after* the first day of entitlement to HB, earnings from that employment should be taken into account, subject only to the appropriate earnings disregard.

Sub-para (c) deals with earnings that are disregarded on "remunerative work" ending but where the person's employment has not been terminated – eg, where working hours have decreased to less than 16, or the person is ill, or is on maternity leave. Where that person was not engaged in remunerative work at the first day of entitlement to HB, any earnings (paid or due to be paid) in respect of that employment are disregarded except those earnings shown in regs 35(1)(e), (i) and (j) (ie, retainers, any statutory sick pay, statutory maternity, paternity or adoption pay and any employer's sick pay or maternity, paternity or adoption pay). So where the remunerative work ceases *after* the first day of entitlement to HB, earnings from that employment should be taken into account, subject only to the appropriate earnings disregard.

---

2.   In the case of a claimant who, before the [¹ first day of entitlement to housing benefit]–

(a)   has been engaged in part-time employment as an employed earner or, where the employment has been outside Great Britain, would have been so engaged had the employment been in Great Britain; and

(b)   has ceased to be engaged in that employment, whether or not that employment has been terminated,

any earnings [¹ paid or due to be paid] in respect of that employment except–

(i)   where that employment has been terminated, [¹ any payment of the nature described in regulation 35(1)(e)];

(ii)   where that employment has not been terminated, [¹ any payment or remuneration of the nature described in regulation 35(1)(e), (i) or (j)].

Amendment

1.   Amended by reg 11(11)(b) of SI 2007 No 2618 as from 1.10.07.

Analysis

This para deals with earnings disregarded on termination or interruption of part-time employment (less than 16 hours a week – see para 16). It clarifies that where a person has been in such employment (or would have been had her/his employment been in Great Britain) but this ceased before the first day of entitlement to HB (irrespective of whether or not that employment has terminated), then any earnings (paid or due to be paid) from that employment should be disregarded, except for:

(1)   Where the employment terminated, any payment of the nature of a retainer.

(2)   Where, although that employment has not been terminated, that person has ceased to be engaged in that employment because, for example, they are ill, payments of the nature of those in reg 35(1)(e), (i) and (j) of the HB Regs (ie, a retainer, statutory sick pay, statutory maternity, paternity or adoption pay and any employer's sick pay or maternity, paternity or adoption pay).

So where the employment was terminated or interrupted *after* the first day of entitlement to HB, earnings from that employment should be taken into account, subject only to the appropriate earnings disregard.

3.–(1) In a case to which this paragraph applies and paragraph 4 does not apply, £20; but notwithstanding regulation 25 (calculation of income and capital of members of a claimant's family and of a polygamous marriage) if this paragraph applies to a claimant it shall not apply to his partner except where, and to the extent that, the earnings of the claimant which are to be disregarded under this paragraph are less than £20.

(2)   This paragraph applies where the claimant's applicable amount includes an amount by way of the disability premium or severe disability premium under Schedule 3 (applicable amounts).

(3)   This paragraph applies where–

(a)   the claimant is a member of a couple and his applicable amount would, but for the higher pensioner premium under Schedule 3 being applicable include an amount by way of the disability premium under that Schedule; and

(b)   he or his partner is under the age of 60 and at least one is engaged in employment.

(4)   This paragraph applies where–

(a)   the claimant's applicable amount includes an amount by way of the higher pensioner premium under Schedule 3; and

(b)   the claimant or, if he is a member of a couple, either he or his partner has attained the age of 60; and

(c)   immediately before attaining that age he or, as the case may be, he or his partner was engaged in employment and the claimant was entitled by virtue of sub-paragraph (2) or (3) to a disregard of £20; and

(d)   he or, if he is a member of couple, he or his partner has continued in employment.

(5)   For the purposes of this paragraph, no account shall be taken of any period not exceeding eight consecutive weeks occurring on or after the date on which the claimant or, if he is a member of a couple, he or his partner attained the age of 60 during which either or both ceased to be engaged in employment or the claimant ceased to be entitled to any or all of the following benefits namely housing benefit, community charge benefit or council tax benefit.

Analysis

This provides a flat-rate £20 disregard of the earnings of the claimant and/or his partner if any of the conditions in sub-paras (2) to (4) apply. It does not apply if the claimant qualifies for a lone parent disregard under para 4.

There is a maximum £20 deduction, not a disregard of £20 of the earnings of each partner who has earnings. The disregard is first applied to the earnings of the claimant, then anything left over may be applied to the earnings, if any, of the partner(s). For example, if the claimant earns £10 a week and her/his partner earns £23, the claimant's earnings will be totally disregarded, but only £10 (balance of the disregard) of her/his partner's. If a non-dependant's earnings are used (see reg 26) it is still the *claimant* who must satisfy these conditions as they relate to applicable amount, not resources.

This paragraph seems very complex but its main object is to ensure that the £20 disregard applies where the claimant or, if s/he has a partner, her/his partner, either satisfies the rules for the disability or severe disability premium (see paras 12, 13 and 14 of Sch 3) or would satisfy the tests for the disability premium but for the fact that the higher pensioner premium now applies, or that the claimant or her/his partner previously satisfied the test for the disability premium but is now disqualified on age grounds.

Sub-para (5) provides a linking rule such that if the claimant or any partner is 60 or over and both cease work or the claimant ceases to be entitled to HB or CTB for up to eight weeks the £20 earnings disregard applies automatically on the restarting of work or reclaiming of HB as appropriate.

4.   In a case where the claimant is a lone parent, £25.

Analysis

This provides a flat-rate disregard of £25 where the claimant is a lone parent (as defined in reg 2(1)).

5.–(1)   In a case to which neither paragraph 3 nor paragraph 4 applies to the claimant, and subject to sub-paragraph (2), where the claimant's applicable amount includes an amount by way of the carer premium under Schedule 3 (applicable amounts), £20 of the earnings of the person who is, or at any time in the preceding eight weeks was, in receipt of carer's allowance or treated in accordance with paragraph 17(2) of that Schedule as being in receipt of carer's allowance.

(2)   Where the carer premium is awarded in respect of the claimant and of any partner of his, their earnings shall for the purposes of this paragraph be aggregated, but the amount to be disregarded in accordance with sub-paragraph (1) shall not exceed £20 of the aggregated amount.

Analysis

Paras 5 and 6 provide a £20 earnings disregard for claimants whose applicable amounts include the carer premium: see para 17, Sch 3. Para 5 applies to the earnings of the carer: sub-para (1). Where both the claimant and her/his partner qualifiy for the carer premium, £20 is disregarded from their combined earnings: sub-para (2).

6. Where the carer premium is awarded in respect of a claimant who is a member of a couple and whose earnings are less than £20, but is not awarded in respect of the other member of the couple, and that other member is engaged in an employment—
- (a) specified in paragraph 8(1), so much of the other member's earnings as would not when aggregated with the amount disregarded under paragraph 5 exceed £20;
- (b) other than one specified in paragraph 8(1), so much of the other member's earnings from such other employment up to £10 as would not when aggregated with the amount disregarded under paragraph 5 exceed £20.

Analysis

Paras 5 and 6 provide a £20 earnings disregard for claimants whose applicable amounts include the carer premium: see para 17, Sch 3. Where the claimant is the carer, has earnings less than £20 and is a member of a couple whose partner is engaged in any of the employments specified in para 8(1) (eg, part-time fire fighter or auxiliary coastguard), the remainder of the disregard can be applied to the partner's earnings: sub-para (a). If the partner is engaged in any other employment, up to £10 of her/his earnings can be disregarded: sub-para (b). The total can never exceed £20.

7. In a case where paragraphs 3, 5, 6 and 8 do not apply to the claimant and he is one of a couple and a member of that couple is in employment, £10; but, notwithstanding regulation 25 (calculation of income and capital of members of claimant's family and of a polygamous marriage), if this paragraph applies to a claimant it shall not apply to his partner except where, and to the extent that, the earnings of the claimant which are to be disregarded under this paragraph are less than £10.

Analysis

This deals with the earnings of claimants who are members of a couple and who do not satisfy the provisions of paras 3, 5, 6 and 8. It is not clear how this provision affects partners to polygamous marriages; presumably the claimant and one other partner would count as a "couple" for these purposes. A flat-rate disregard of £10 is available, irrespective of whether the earnings are from full-time or part-time work. Despite reg 25, the context requires that "partner" should not be substituted for "claimant" where the partner has earnings, as specific provision is made for the earnings of partners by the regulation. The effect is that there is only one disregard per couple, rather than a disregard of £10 of *each* of their earnings if each or some earn. See para 3 for an example of how this works. If reg 26 has been used, the rules apply to the earnings of the non-dependant and his partner as only the assessment of resources is involved. See para 8 if the claimant or her/his partner is engaged in any of the employments specified in para 8(1) (eg, part-time fire fighter or auxiliary coastguard). See para 9 applies if a claimant himself has earnings which would normally be covered by this paragraph as well as by para 8.

8.–(1) In a case where paragraphs 3, 4, 5 and 6 do not apply to the claimant, £20 of earnings derived from one or more employments as—
- (a) a part-time fire-fighter employed by a fire and rescue authority constituted by a scheme under section 2 of the Fire and Rescue Services Act 2004 or a scheme to which section 4 of that Act applies;
- (b) a part-time fire-fighter employed by a fire and rescue authority (as defined in section 1 of the Fire (Scotland) Act 2005 or a joint fire and rescue board constituted by an amalgamation scheme made under section 2(1) of that Act;
- (c) an auxiliary coastguard in respect of coast rescue activities;
- (d) a person engaged part-time in the manning or launching of a life boat;
- (e) a member of any territorial or reserve force prescribed in Part 1 of Schedule 6 to the Social Security (Contributions) Regulations 2001;

but, notwithstanding regulation 25 (calculation of income and capital of members of claimant's family and of a polygamous marriage), if this paragraph applies to a claimant it shall not apply to his partner except to the extent specified in sub-paragraph (2).
- (2) If the claimant's partner is engaged in employment—
- (a) specified in sub-paragraph (1), so much of his earnings as would not in aggregate with the amount of the claimant's earnings disregarded under this paragraph exceed £20;
- (b) other than one specified in sub-paragraph (1), so much of his earnings from that employment up to £10 as would not in aggregate with the claimant's earnings disregarded under this paragraph exceed £20.

Analysis

This paragraph provides a £20 disregard in respect of the employments listed in para (1) if the claimant is not covered by paras 3, 4, 5 or 6 above. See also reg 46(1) in respect of payments of annual bounty in relation to these employments. If the claimant has a partner and s/he or her/his partner has earnings from any other source of employment, see sub-para (2) of this paragraph if it is the partner who has such earnings, and para 9 if the claimant has earnings from other work. Because of para 9 it does not seem to be the intent that the claimant should be able to use the disregards in both paras 7 and 8, as paras 8 and 9 together provide a complete code where the claimant or his partner has earnings which would normally be covered by para 7 as well as by para 8(1) employment.

Sub-para (1) sets out the employments covered; under sub-para (1)(e), the forces listed are: retired and emergency lists of officers of the Royal Navy; Royal Naval reserves; Royal Marines reserves; Army reserves; Territorial Army and Volunteer reserves; RAF reserves; Royal Auxiliary Air Force; Royal Irish Regiment.

Sub-para (2) deals with the situation where the claimant is in any of the employments specified in sub-para (1) and a partner of the claimant also has earnings from a listed employment (sub-para (2)(a)), or from other work (sub-para (2)(b)).

The partner's earnings will only be disregarded if the claimant's sub-para (1) earnings do not exhaust the disregard available under that sub-paragraph, and even then only up to the maximum amount specified.

Sub-para (2)(a). If the claimant's earnings from an employment listed in sub-para (1) is less than £20, the unused part of the disregard may be set against his partner's earnings.

Sub-para (2)(b). If the claimants earnings from listed employment do not exhaust the £20 disregard under sub-para (1), up to £10 of what remains of the disregard may be set against his partner's earnings from other work.

---

9.   Where the claimant is engaged in one of more employments specified in paragraph 8(1), but his earnings derived from such employments are less than £20 in any week and he is also engaged in any other employment so much of his earnings from that other employment, up to £5 if he is a single claimant, or up to £10 if he has a partner, as would not in aggregate with the amount of his earnings disregarded under paragraph 6 exceed £20.

Analysis

This appears to substitute for para 7 where the claimant has employment covered by para 8(1) and also does other work. Where such a claimant has not exhausted his £20 disregard under para 8(1) if s/he is single, s/he can offset up to £5 of what is left against earnings covered by this paragraph, or if s/he has a partner s/he can offset up to £10 against such earnings, subject to a total disregard of £20 of the claimant's earnings as assessed under this paragraph and para 8. The relationship between this para and para 8(2) is not clear. It could be argued that this provision is in addition to, rather than in substitution for para 8(2) on the basis that the claimant's earnings here cannot be intended also to refer to her/his partner's earnings as specific provision has been made for the partner's earnings under para 8(2) so that, if both have earnings, the claimant's earnings covered by this para and those of her/his partner under para 8(2), disregards under both para 8(2) and this para may be available. However, the "aggregate disregard" of the claimant's earnings covered by this paragraph and para 8 must not exceed £20, which implies that sums due to a partner and covered by para 8(2) are to be treated as the "claimant's" for these purposes, so no duplication occurs.

---

10.   In a case to which none of the paragraphs 3 to 9 applies, £5.

Analysis

This provides a £5 earnings disregard where none of paras 3 to 9 apply, that is, where a claimant is single, is not a lone parent and does not qualify for a £20 earnings disregard. See para 9 where the claimant also has earnings from any of the employments specified in para 8(1).

---

11.   Any amount or the balance of any amount which would fall to be disregarded under paragraph 19 or 20 of Schedule 5 had the claimant's income which does not consist of earnings been sufficient to entitle him to the full disregarded thereunder.

Analysis

This paragraph applies where the claimant insufficient income, to use up the disregards under Sch 5 paras 19 and 20. Those paras deal with situations where the claimant is making a parental contirbution to a student's grant or loan or contributes to a student's maintenance. In such a case, the unused part of the disregards may be applied to the claimant's earnings. This provision is available in addition to any other disregard available under this Schedule.

12. Where a claimant is on income support or an income-based jobseeker's allowance, his earnings.

Analysis

This paragraph is necessary as claimants on IS or income-based JSA have already had their income taken into account for those purposes. "Person on income support" is defined by reg 2(1) and "person on an income-based jobseeker's allowance" by reg 2(3).

13. Any earnings derived from employment which are payable in a country outside the United Kingdom for such period during which there is a prohibition against the transfer to the United Kingdom of those earnings.

14. Where a payment of earnings is made in a currency other than Sterling, any banking charge or commission payable in converting that payment into Sterling.

15. Any earnings of a child or young person.

16. In this Schedule "part-time employment" means employment in which the person is engaged on average for less than 16 hours a week.

Analysis

This paragraph simply defines "part-time employment". See para 2 above.

17.–(1) In a case where the claimant is a person who satisfies at least one of the conditions set out in sub-paragraph (2), and his net earnings equal or exceed the total of the amounts set out in sub-paragraph (3), the amount of his earnings that falls to be disregarded under paragraphs 3 to 10 of this Schedule shall be increased by [² £15.45].

(2) The conditions of this sub-paragraph are that–

(a) the claimant, or if he is a member of a couple, either the claimant or his partner, is a person to whom regulation 20(1)(c) of the Working Tax Credit Regulations applies; or

(b) the claimant–

   (i) is, or if he is a member of a couple, at least one member of that couple is aged at least 25 and is engaged in remunerative work for on average not less than 30 hours per week; or

   (ii) is a member of a couple and–

   (aa) at least one member of that couple, is engaged in remunerative work for on average not less than 16 hours per week; and

   (bb) his applicable amount includes a family premium under paragraph 3 of Schedule 3; or

   (iii) is a lone parent who is engaged in remunerative work for on average not less than 16 hours per week; or

   (iv) is, or if he is a member of a couple, at least one member of that couple is engaged in remunerative work for on average not less than 16 hours per week; and–

      (aa) the claimant's applicable amount includes a higher pensioner premium or a disability premium under paragraph 11 or 12 of Schedule 3 respectively; and

      (bb) where he is a member of a couple, at least one member of that couple satisfies the qualifying conditions for the higher pensioner premium or disability premium referred to in sub-head (aa) above and is engaged in remunerative work for on average not less than 16 hours per week; or

(c) the claimant is, or, if he has a partner, one of them is, a person to whom regulation 18(3) of the Working Tax Credit Regulations (eligibility for 50 plus element) applies, or would apply if an application for working tax credit were to be made in his case.

(3) The following are the amounts referred to in sub-paragraph (1)–

(a) the amount to be disregarded from the claimant's earnings under paragraphs 3 to 10 of this Schedule;

(b) the amount of child care charges calculated as deductible under regulation 28(1)(c); and

(c) [² £15.45].

(4) The provisions of regulation 6 shall apply in determining whether or not a person works for on average not less than 30 hours per week, but as if the reference to 16 hours in paragraph (1) of that regulation were a reference to 30 hours.

Amendments

1. Amended by Art 19(9) of SI 2006 No 645 and reg 8 of SI 2006 No 217 as from 1.4.06 (3.4.06 where rent payable weekly or at intervals of a week).

2. Amended by Art 19(9) of SI 2007 No 688 as from 1.4.07 (2.4.07 where rent payable weekly or at intervals of a week).

Analysis

Para 17 provides an additional earnings disregard for some working claimants, broadly, those who qualify for a 30-hour element in the calculation of their working tax credit (or would do were they to claim). It lessens the impact of earnings on HB entitlement for those in low paid work. The categories of claimant who qualify are set out below.

The amount of the additional disregard is set out in para (1). It is generally uprated annually, in April. If the claimant's net earnings equal or exceed the sum of the additional disregard, the disregards allowed under Sch 4 paras 3 to 10 and her/his deductible child care charges under reg 28(1)(c), then the additional disregard is added to the other disregards: para (3). See para 56 Sch 5 if net earnings are less than the sum. In this case, the equivalent of the additional earnings disregard is deducted from any WTC awarded.

Six categories of claimant qualify for an additional disregard:

(1)   Claimants to whom (or to whose partners) reg 20(1)(c) Working Tax Credit (Entitlement and Maximum Rate) Regulations 2002 applies: para (2)(a). These are those who qualify for a 30-hour element with WTC, that is those who work 30 hours or more a week, or in the case of a couple with chidren, those who between them work 30 hours or more a week. The latter only applies if at least one of the couple is working 16 hours or more a week.

(2)   A claimant who is aged at least 25 and who works for at least 30 hours a week, or who has a partner who fulfils that description: para (2)(b)(i).

(3)   A claimant who is a member of a couple, one of whom is working 16 hours or more a week, and who is entitled to a family premium: para (2)(b)(ii).

(4)   A claimant who is a lone parent working 16 hours or more per week: para (2)(b)(iii).

(5)   A claimant who works, or whose partner (if any) works, 16 hours or more a week and whose applicable amount includes a higher pensioner premium or disability premium. In the case of couples, the one of them that satisfies the conditions for higher pensioner premium or disability premium must be working at least 16 hours per week: para (2)(b)(iv).

(6)   A claimant who, or whose partner (if any) is a person to whom regulation 18(3) of the Working Tax Credit Regulations applies, or would apply if an application for WTC were to be made. These are those who qualify for a WTC 50 plus element, or who would qualify if an application for WTC were to be made: para (2)(c).

In deciding how many hours a week are worked, the averaging rules in reg 6 HB Regs apply: sub-para (4).

SCHEDULE 5
REGULATION 40

Sums to be disregarded in the calculation of income other than earnings

Modifications

Para 51 is substituted by Sch 4 para 2(4) and paras 55A and 55B inserted by Sch 4 para 2(5) HB&CTB(CP) Regs in respect of claims for HB by some refugees (see p1126).

A different version of para 55B was substituted for para 56 by Sch 4 para 4(2)(b) HB&CTB(CP) Regs for some HB claimants who were refugees who claimed asylum on or before 2 April 2000 (see p1132).

See also reg 10A and Sch A1 inserted by Sch 4 para 2 HB&CTB(CP) Regs on p1126).

Note that paras 55A and 55B lapsed by s12(2)(e) of the Asylum and Immigration (Treatment of Claimants, etc.) Act 2004 (for those recorded as refugees after 14 June 2007).

Definitions

"boarder" – see reg 2(1).
"capital" – see reg 2(1).
"child" – see reg 2(1).
"claimant" – see reg 2(1).
"dwelling" – see s137(1) SSCBA.
"earnings" – see regs 35 and 37.
"employment zone contractor" – see reg 2(1).
"employment zone programme" – see reg 2(1).
"family" – see reg 2(1).
"income"–see Part 6.
"Independent Living Fund" – see reg 2(1).
"Local Authority" – see s191 SSAA.
"Macfarlane Trust"–see reg 2(1).
"non-dependant" – reg 3.

"partner" – see reg 2(1).
"payment" – see reg 2(1).
"occupies as a home" – see reg 7.
"ordinary clothing or footwear – see reg 2(1).
"student contribution" – see Part 7.
"subsistence allowance" – see reg 2(1).
"young person" – see reg 19.

---

1. Any amount paid by way of tax on income which is to be taken into account under regulation 40 (calculation of income other than earnings).

Analysis

This paragraph requires the deduction of any income tax *actually* paid on income other than earnings covered by reg 40.

---

2. Any payment in respect of any expenses incurred or to be incurred by a claimant who is–
(a)   engaged by a charitable or voluntary organisation; or
(b)   a volunteer,
if he otherwise derives no remuneration or profit from the employment and is not to be treated as possessing any earnings under regulation 42(9) (notional income).

Analysis

Notice that the types of expenses to be disregarded are unrestricted, unlike under reg 35(2)(b) or reg 38, but that the requirement that no "remuneration or profit" be made excludes any element of *gain* from the disregard. See reg 42(9) for where someone can be treated as having "notional" earnings.

---

3. In the case of employment as an employed earner, any payment in respect of expenses wholly, exclusively and necessarily incurred in the performance of the duties of the employment.

Analysis

The purpose is to avoid expenses which are deemed not to be "earnings" by reg 35(2)(b) being taken into account under any other regulation.

---

4. Where a claimant is on income support or an income-based jobseeker's allowance the whole of his income.

Analysis

This paragraph and para 5 are necessary as IS and income-based JSA claimants have already had their income fully considered in relation to that benefit – see General Note on Pt 6.

---

5. Where the claimant is a member of a joint-claim couple for the purposes of the Jobseekers Act and his partner is on an income-based jobseeker's allowance, the whole of the claimant's income.
6. Any disability living allowance.

Analysis

See para 7 for the treatment of concessionary payments of disability living allowance. See also Sch 6 para 9 where the concessionary payments are capital payments for arrears, or to compensate for arrears due.

---

7. Any concessionary payment made to compensate for the non-payment of–
(a)   any payment specified in paragraph 6 or 9;
(b)   income support;
(c)   an income-based jobseeker's allowance.

Analysis

See also Sch 6 para 9 where the concessionary payments are capital payments for arrears, or to compensate for arrears due.

---

8. Any mobility supplement under article 26A of the Naval, Military and Air Forces etc (Disablement and Death) Service Pensions Order 1983 (including such a supplement by virtue of any other scheme or order) or under article 25A of the Personal Injuries (Civilians) Scheme 1983 or any payment intended to compensate for the non-payment of such a supplement.

Analysis

Art 26A of the Order referred to relates to mobility supplement paid to members of the armed forces who are in receipt of retired pay or a pension due to injury which renders them unable to work or virtually unable to do so.

Art 25A refers to similar payments made to civilians and former civil defence volunteers due to "war/war service injuries sustained during the period September 3, 1939 to March 19, 1946". Notice that the paragraph also covers sums paid as compensation for non-payment of the benefits referred to.

---

9. Any attendance allowance.

Analysis

See para 7 for the treatment of concessionary payments of attendance allowance. See also Sch 6 para 9 where the concessionary payments are capital payments for arrears, or to compensate for arrears due.

---

10. Any payment to the claimant as holder of the Victoria Cross or of the George Cross or any analogous payment.

11.–(1) Any payment–
(a)   by way of an education maintenance allowance made pursuant to–
   (i)   regulations made under section 518 of the Education Act 1996 (payment of school expenses; grant of scholarships etc.);
   (ii)   regulations made under section 49 or 73(f) of the Education (Scotland) Act 1980 (power to assist persons to take advantage of educational facilities);
   (iii)   directions made under sections 12(2)(c) and 21 of the Further and Higher Education (Scotland) Act 1992 (provision of financial assistance to students); or
(b)   corresponding to such an education maintenance allowance, made pursuant to–
   (i)   section 14 or section 181 of the Education Act 2002 (power of Secretary of State and National Assembly for Wales to give financial assistance for purposes related to education or childcare, and allowances in respect of education or training); or
   (ii)   regulations made under section 181 of that Act.
(2)   Any payment, other than a payment to which sub-paragraph (1) applies, made pursuant to–
(a)   regulations made under section 518 of the Education Act 1996;
(b)   regulations made under section 49 of the Education (Scotland) Act 1980; or
(c)   directions made under sections 12(2)(c) and 21 of the Further and Higher Education (Scotland) Act 1992,
in respect of a course of study attended by a child or a young person or a person who is in receipt of an education maintenance allowance made pursuant to any provision specified in sub-paragraph (1).

Analysis

This provides for a disregard of education maintenance allowance (in Wales payments corresponding to such an allowance) and payments made to persons aged above compulsory school leaving age, whether or not that education is in, or equivalent to, secondary education. Also disregarded are payments paid to children below school leaving age to enable them to take part in activities at state schools, or, where appropriate, help pay fees for fee-paying schools, to avoid hardship to children or their parents. Note that the payments are also disregarded as capital under para 51 of Sch 6.

---

12. Any payment made to the claimant by way of a repayment under regulation 11(2) of the Education (Teacher Student Loans) (Repayment etc) Regulations 2002.

13.–(1) Any payment made pursuant to section 2 of the 1973 Act or section 2 of the Enterprise and New Towns (Scotland) Act 1990 except–
(a)   a payment made as a substitute for income support, a jobseeker's allowance, incapacity benefit or severe disablement allowance;
(b)   a payment of an allowance referred to in section 2(3) of the 1973 Act or section 2(5) of the Enterprise and New Towns (Scotland) Act 1990;
(c)   a payment intended to meet the cost of living expenses which relate to any one or more of the items specified in sub-paragraph (2) whilst a claimant is participating in an education, training or other scheme to help him enhance his employment prospects unless the payment is a Career Development Loan paid pursuant to section 2 of the 1973 Act and the period of education or training or the scheme, which is supported by that loan, has been completed; or
(d)   for the purpose only of assessing entitlement to housing benefit in respect of a dwelling other than the one which the claimant normally occupies as his home, a payment made to a person to whom regulation 7(5)(b) (circumstances in which a person is or is not to be treated as occupying a dwelling as his home) applies to the extent that the payment is made in respect of the cost of living away from home.

(2)   The items specified in this sub-paragraph for the purposes of sub-paragraph (1)(c) are food, ordinary clothing or footwear, household fuel or rent of the claimant or, where the claimant is a member of a family, any other member of his family, or any council tax or water charges for which that claimant or member is liable.

(3)   For the purposes of this paragraph, ''rent'' means eligible rent less any deductions in respect of non-dependants which fall to be made under regulation 74 (non-dependant deductions).

Analysis

This para relates to any arrangements for training made under s2 of the Acts referred to. For an explanation of s2(1) of the Employment and Training Act 1973, see the note on reg 37. Only the payments referred to in sub-paras (a) to (d) are to be taken into account.

14.–(1)   Subject to sub-paragraph (2), any of the following payments–
(a)   a charitable payment;
(b)   a voluntary payment;
(c)   a payment (not falling within sub-paragraph (a) or (b) above) from a trust whose funds are derived from a payment made in consequence of any personal injury to the claimant;
(d)   a payment under an annuity purchased–
    (i)   pursuant to any agreement or court order to make payments to the claimant; or
    (ii)   from funds derived from a payment made,
in consequence of any personal injury to the claimant; or
(e)   a payment (not falling within sub-paragraphs (a) to (d)) received by virtue of any agreement or court order to make payments to the claimant in consequence of any personal injury to the claimant.
(2)   Sub-paragraph (1) shall not apply to a payment which is made or due to be made by–
(a)   a former partner of the claimant, or a former partner of any member of the claimant's family; or
(b)   the parent of a child or young person where that child or young person is a member of the claimant's family.

Analysis

Note, first that para 35 below provides a complete disregard of certain charitable payments, such as those made from the Macfarlane Trust, the Macfarlane (Special Payments) Trust, the Macfarlane (Special Payments) (No 2) Trust and the Independent Living Fund. Note, second, that unlike previous versions of this para, if the income payment falls within para (1) – this includes payments made in consequence of personal injury suffered by a claimant – and is not caught by para (2), all of the payment is ignored. There is no £20 limit under this para (as there was under previous versions of this paragraph) nor does para 34 below apply to limit the total amount of income that may be ignored.

Sub-para (c) covers payments from trusts whose funds are derived from payments made in consequence of personal injury to the claimant. The value of the trust itself is disregarded under para 14 of Sch 6, as is the value of the right to receive payments under it. See also para 14A of Sch 6 for capital payments made from such a trust and paras 45 and 46 where damages paid to children or young people are administered by the Court.

The nature of charitable and voluntary payments was examined in detail in *R v Doncaster BC ex p Boulton* [1992] 25 HLR 195, QBD. Laws J held that:

"[t]he effect of specifying both charitable and voluntary payments is to enable payments which are not made for the payer's own benefit to be brought within the scope of the disregard without the need to engage with fine distinctions between charitable and non-charitable payments."

In addition it was found that the reference to charitable payments "must be to payments made under a charitable trust" – ie, those made by a registered charity. As with charitable payments, the Court decided that a payment is voluntary if it is made without anything being obtained by the payer in return.

The case itself dealt with the question of whether or not payments of cash in lieu of concessionary coal made to the widow of a miner by British Coal were voluntary payments which qualified for the disregard. This was found not to be the case on the basis that the agreement between British Coal and the Unions under which they are paid was entered into in the interests of good labour relations and for the efficient running of the coal industry. Laws J concluded that:

"This legitimate and proper purpose is, however, far away from the purpose and benevolence behind voluntary payments in the regulations . . . and that as a matter of the law the payments made to the applicant were not voluntary within the meaning of the relevant regulations."

Consequently authorities should take payments of cash in lieu of concessionary coal made by British Coal to ex-miners and their widows into account as "remuneration or profit derived from that employment" and should treat them as earnings. See now reg 42(6) and (7).

In *R(H) 5/05* Commissioner Mesher concluded that the phrase "voluntary payment" should have the same meaning here as it did in reg 40(6) HB Regs 1987 (now reg 46(6) HB Regs), even though the contexts are somewhat different, and that *Boulton* was correctly decided and applied as much to reg 40(6) HB regs 1987 as it did to this para. However, on the facts of the case before him, where an "informal loan" had been made to the claimant, the commissioner concluded that there had been no intention to create legal relations and therefore no legally enforceable rights or obligations were created by the payments to the claimant. This was a crucial point which distinguished the case from *Boulton*, because here the person making the "loan" payments to the claimant got nothing in return, tangible or otherwise, whereas in *Boulton* the Coal Board did at least benefit from the payments of cash in lieu of concessionary coal in the sense of fostering good labour relations. The maintenance of a relationship of personal affection or of familial duty on the part of the payer, in Commissioner Mesher's view, did not constitute an intangible benefit for the payer sufficient to disqualify the payments as voluntary payments: para 42.

---

15.   Subject to paragraph 34, £10 of any of the following, namely–

(a)   a war disablement pension (except insofar as such a pension falls to be disregarded under paragraph 8 or 9);

(b)   a war widow's pension or war widower's pension;

(c)   a pension payable to a person as a widow, widower or surviving civil partner under the Naval, Military and Air Forces Etc (Disablement and Death) Service Pensions Order 1983 insofar as that Order is made under the Naval and Marine Pay and Pensions Act 1865 or the Pensions and Yeomanry Pay Act 1884, or is made only under section 12(1) of the Social Security (Miscellaneous Provisions) Act 1977 and any power of Her Majesty otherwise than under an enactment to make provision about pensions for or in respect of persons who have been disabled or have died in consequence of service as members of the armed forces of the Crown;

(d)   a guaranteed income payment;

(e)   a payment made to compensate for the non-payment of such a pension or payment as is mentioned in any of the preceding sub-paragraphs;

(f)   a pension paid by the government of a country outside Great Britain which is analogous to any of the pensions or payments mentioned in sub-paragraphs (a) to (d) above;

(g)   pension paid to victims of National Socialist persecution under any special provision made by the law of the Federal Republic of Germany, or any part of it, or of the Republic of Austria.

Analysis

Great Britain does *not* include Northern Ireland. Para 15(f) extends the £10 statutory disregard to analogous payments made by the governments of other countries. Note that s134(8) SSAA allows an authority to resolve to disregard more than £10 (or all of) prescribed war pensions. This disregard can overlap with disregards from student covenant income and access funds as well as the disregard in para 16. A combined maximum of £20 is allowed: Sch 5 para 34.

---

16.   Subject to paragraph 34, £15 of any–

(a)   widowed mother's allowance paid pursuant to section 37 of the Act;

(b)   widowed parent's allowance paid pursuant to section 39A of the Act.

Analysis

This disregard can overlap with disregards from student covenant income and access funds as well as the disregard in para 15. A combined maximum of £20 is allowed: Sch 5 para 34.

17.–(1)   Any income derived from capital to which the claimant is or is treated under regulation 51 (capital jointly held) as beneficially entitled but, subject to sub-paragraph (2), not income derived from capital disregarded under paragraphs 1, 2, 4, 8, 14 or 25 to 28 of Schedule 6.

(2)   Income derived from capital disregarded under paragraphs 2, 4 or 25 to 28 of Schedule 6 but only to the extent of–

(a)   any mortgage repayments made in respect of the dwelling or premises in the period during which that income accrued; or

(b)   any council tax or water charges which the claimant is liable to pay in respect of the dwelling or premises and which are paid in the period during which that income accrued.

(3)   The definition of "water charges" in regulation 2(1) shall apply to sub-paragraph (2) of this paragraph with the omission of the words "in so far as such charges are in respect of the dwelling which a person occupies as his home".

Analysis

The effect of this para is that unless the *capital* to which the person is entitled is disregarded, under the provisions listed, the income produced by that capital is to be disregarded. Income from capital disregarded under the provisions listed is to be taken into account, however, except so far as sub-para (2) provides otherwise. See also reg 51. Note that reg 52 provides a formula for calculating "tariff" (deemed) income from capital that is not disregarded.

Sub-para (2). Where income is produced from capital disregarded under paras 2, 4, or 25 to 28 of Sch 6, it can be disregarded to the extent that mortgage repayments (of capital as well as interest) were made in respect of the premises in question during the period to which the income relates. Deductions can also be made for any payments of council tax or water charges for which the claimant is liable during the period to which the income relates.

18.–(1)   Where a claimant receives income under an annuity purchased with a loan which satisfies the following conditions–

(a)   that the loan was made as part of a scheme under which not less than 90 per cent. of the proceeds of the loan were applied to the purchase by the person to whom it was made of an annuity ending with his life or with the life of the survivor of two or more persons (in this paragraph referred to as ''the annuitants'') who include the person to whom the loan was made;

(b)   that the interest on the loan is payable by the person to whom it was made or by one of the annuitants;

(c)   that at the time the loan was made the person to whom it was made or each of the annuitants had attained the age of 65;

(d)   that the loan was secured on a dwelling in Great Britain and the person to whom the loan was made or one of the annuitants owns an estate or interest in that dwelling; and

(e)   that the person to whom the loan was made or one of the annuitants occupies the dwelling on which it was secured as his home at the time the interest is paid,

the amount, calculated on a weekly basis, equal to–

(i)   where, or insofar as, section 369 of the Income and Corporation Taxes Act 1988 (mortgage interest payable under deduction of tax) applies to the payments of interest on the loan, the interest which is payable after deduction of a sum equal to income tax on such payments at the applicable percentage of income tax within the meaning of section 369(1A) of that Act;

(ii)   in any other case the interest which is payable on the loan without deduction of such a sum.

Analysis

See also reg 41(2).

The basic effect of this paragraph is to provide a disregard from the income produced by an annuity under a "Home Income Plan", of an amount equal to the interest payments (net of tax) on the loan used to purchase the annuity.

Sub-paras (a) to (e). These set out the conditions which must be satisfied before the disregard can apply and sub-paras (i) and (ii) deal with how much of the annuity may be ignored.

(1)   The person to whom the loan was made (payee) must have used 90 per cent of it at least to purchase the annuity which must last for the life of the payee or another person (annuitant).

(2)   The interest on the loan must be payable by the payee or annuitant(s).

(3)   The payee and any annuitant(s) must have been aged 65 at the time the loan in question was made.

(4)   The loan must be secured on a dwelling which the payee or annuitant(s) owns (or owns an interest in).

(5)   The payee or annuitant(s) must actually occupy the dwelling.

Sub-paras (i) and (ii) s369 Income and Corporation Taxes Act 1988 allows basic rate tax relief on certain interest payments; where the section applies, the interest paid net of tax should be disregarded. Otherwise, all of the interest may be disregarded.

---

19.   Where the claimant makes a parental contribution in respect of a student attending a course at an establishment in the United Kingdom or undergoing education in the United Kingdom, which contribution has been assessed for the purposes of calculating–

(a)   under, or pursuant to regulations made under powers conferred by, sections 1 or 2 of the Education Act 1962 or section 22 of the Teaching and Higher Education Act 1998, that student's award;

(b)   under regulations made in exercise of the powers conferred by section 49 of the Education (Scotland) Act 1980, that student's bursary, scholarship, or other allowance under that section or under regulations made in exercise of the powers conferred by section 73 of that Act of 1980, any payment to that student under that section; or

(c)   the student's student loan,

an amount equal to the weekly amount of that parental contribution, but only in respect of the period for which that contribution is assessed as being payable.

Analysis

Under this para, a parental contribution taken into account in computing a student's grant or loan under the provisions listed is disregarded in computing the payer's "other" income during the period for which the contribution is payable. If "other" income is insufficient to use up the disregard, the unused part can be disregarded from earnings: see para 11 of Sch 4.

Sub-para (a). Section 1 of the 1962 Act deals with full time courses designated as first degree courses or comparable to these, at universities, colleges or other institutions in the UK.

Sub-para (b). Under s73 of the 1980 Act, the Secretary of State may award grants to assist the carrying out of educational research (Subs (1)(e)) or payments of allowances to persons attending "courses of education" (Subs (1)(f)).

Sub-para (c) refers to student loans. See reg 53 for the definition.

20.–(1)   Where the claimant is the parent of a student aged under 25 in advanced education who either–
  (a)   is not in receipt of any award, grant or student loan in respect of that education; or
  (b)   is in receipt of an award under section 2 of the Education Act 1962 or an award bestowed by virtue of the Teaching and Higher Education Act 1998, or regulations made thereunder, or a bursary, scholarship or other allowance under section 49(1) of the Education (Scotland) Act 1980, or a payment under section 73 of that Act of 1980,

and the claimant makes payments by way of a contribution towards the student's maintenance, other than a parental contribution falling within paragraph 19, an amount specified in sub-paragraph (2) in respect of each week during the student's term.
  (2)   For the purposes of sub-paragraph (1), the amount shall be equal to–
  (a)   the weekly amount of the payments; or
  (b)   the amount by way of a personal allowance for a single claimant under 25 less the weekly amount of any award, bursary, scholarship, allowance or payment referred to in sub-paragraph (1)(b),

whichever is less.

Analysis

This provides a partial disregard in computing the payer's "other income" for payments made by a parent to a student in advanced education who is aged under 25 who is not receiving a grant or loan (or who gets one of the awards listed). If "other" income is insufficient to use up the disregard, the unused part can be disregarded from earnings: see para 11 of Sch 4.

Note the, albeit very obiter, view in *CH 2517/2004* that the word "parent" in para 18 Sch 4 HB Regs 1987 (now para 20 Sch 5 HB Regs) should arguably not be restricted to a natural or adoptive parent.

Sub-para (2). This quantifies how much of the parent's income may be disregarded in this respect. The limit is set out in sub-para (2)(b).

---

21.   Any payment made to the claimant by a child or young person or a non-dependant.

Analysis

This paragraph provides a disregard of payments received by the claimant from a child, young person or non-dependant – but see reg 74 for the deductions that can be made from "eligible rent" in respect of non-dependants. See also paras 22 and 42 if payments are being made by someone residing in the claimant's home who is other than a child, young person or non-dependant.

---

22.   Where the claimant occupies a dwelling as his home and the dwelling is also occupied by a person other than one to whom paragraph 21 or 42 refers and there is a contractual liability to make payments to the claimant in respect of the occupation of the dwelling by that person or a member of his family–
  (a)   £4 of the aggregate of any payments made in respect of any one week in respect of the occupation of the dwelling by that person or a member of his family, or by that person and a member of his family; and
  (b)   a further [² £15.45], where the aggregate of any such payments is inclusive of an amount for heating.

Amendments

1. Amended by Art 19(10)(a) of SI 2006 No 645 and reg 8 of SI 2006 No 217 as from 1.4.06 (3.4.06 where rent payable weekly or at intervals of a week).
2. Amended by Art 19(10)(a) of SI 2007 No 688 as from 1.4.07 (2.4.07 where rent payable weekly or at intervals of a week).

Analysis

This paragraph deals with payments from persons other than a child, young person or non-dependant (for which see para 21) or someone to whom the claimant is providing "board and lodging accommodation" (for which see para 42). There must be a contractually liability (ie, as a licensee or tenant) to pay the claimant in return for living in her/his home. Such income is *not* treated as "earnings" and the only disregards are those set out here. Note that from 1 April 2008 (7 April 2008 where rent at intervals of a whole number of weeks), paras (a) and (b) are to be substituted and up to £20 weekly will be disregarded, whether heating is provided or not.

23.–(1) Any income in kind, except where regulation 40(10)(b) (provision of support under section 95 or 98 of the Immigration and Asylum Act in the calculation of income other than earnings) applies.

(2) The reference in sub-paragraph (1) to "income in kind" does not include a payment to a third party made in respect of the claimant which is used by the third party to provide benefits in kind to the claimant.

Analysis

Income in kind is excluded from the calculation of HB, as long as it is not caught by sub-para (2) or income to be taken into account under reg 40(10(b).

---

24. Any income which is payable in a country outside the United Kingdom for such period during which there is a prohibition against the transfer to the United Kingdom of that income.

25.–(1) Any payment made to the claimant in respect of a person who is a member of his family–

(a) pursuant to regulations under section 2(6)(b), 3 or 4 of the Adoption and Children Act 2002 or with a scheme approved by the Scottish Ministers under section 51 of the Adoption (Scotland) Act 1978 (schemes for payments of allowances to adopters);

(b) which is a payment made by a local authority in pursuance of section 15(1) of, and paragraph 15 of Schedule 1 to, the Children Act 1989 (local authority contribution to a child's maintenance where the child is living with a person as a result of a residence order) or, as the case may be, section 50 of the Children Act 1975 (payment towards maintenance of children);

(c) which is a payment made by an authority, as defined in Article 2 of the Children Order, in pursuance of Article 15 of, and paragraph 17 of Schedule 1 to, that Order (contribution by an authority to child's maintenance);

(d) in accordance with regulations made pursuant to section 14F of the Children Act 1989 (special guardianship support services);

to the extent specified in sub-paragraph (3).

(2) Any payment, other than a payment to which sub-paragraph (1)(a) applies, made pursuant to regulations under section 2(6)(b), 3 or 4 of the Adoption and Children Act 2002.

(3) In the case of a child or young person, so much of the weekly amount of the payment as exceeds the amount included under Schedule 3 in the calculation of the claimant's applicable amount for that child or young person by way of the personal allowance and disabled child premium, if any.

Analysis

The amount of the disregard allowed by para 25 is the amount by which the payments specified in paras (1) and (2) *exceeds* the personal allowance and disabled child premium (if any), applicable under Sch 3, to the child or young person in question (ie, such payments are to be taken into account *up to* that level): para (3).

Para (1)(b). Where a child lives, or is to live, with someone as a result of a residence order, s15(1) and para 15 of Sch 1 of the Children Act 1989 allow a local authority to make contributions to that person towards the cost of the accommodation and maintenance of the child.

---

26. Any payment made by a local authority to the claimant with whom a person is accommodated by virtue of arrangements made under section 23(2)(a) of the Children Act 1989 or, as the case may be, section 26 of the Children (Scotland) Act 1995 or by a voluntary organisation under section 59(1)(a) of the Children Act 1989 or by a [¹ local authority under regulation 9 of the Fostering of Children (Scotland) Regulations 1996 (payment of allowances)].

Amendment

1.   Amended by reg 15(6) of SI 2006 No 2378 as from 2.10.06.

Analysis

This paragraph provides a total disregard for the payments referred to in computing "other income".

Sections 23 and 59 of the Children Act 1989 refer to the local authority powers to provide accommodation and maintenance for a child they are looking after and for the provision of accommodation by voluntary organisations. Section 26 of the Scottish Act gives authorities wide powers to make provision for children aged less than 18 where such arrangements would be: "likely to diminish the need to receive children into or keep them in care or the need to refer them to a children's hearing under Pt III of the Act."

The regulations provide the same in respect of children already in care.

---

27.   Any payment made to the claimant or his partner for a person (''the person concerned''), who is not normally a member of the claimant's household but is temporarily in his care, by–

(a)   a health authority;

(b)   a local authority but excluding payments of housing benefit made in respect of the person concerned;

(c)   a voluntary organisation;

(d)   the person concerned pursuant to section 26(3A) of the National Assistance Act 1948; or

(e)   a primary care trust established under section 16A of the National Health Service Act 1977.

Analysis

For "membership of household", see p23, and Part 4 of these regulations.

GM BW2 Annex B para 16 interprets this paragraph as covering expenses plus any inducement element paid to enable a claimant to provide temporary respite care for an elderly or disabled person so that a principal family carer can go for a holiday.

There is a total disregard of such payments.

Para 25 of Sch 4 HB Regs 1987 (now para 27 of Sch 5 HB Regs) was considered by Commissioner Williams in *CH 2321/2002*. He decided it was part of a set of disregards designed to enable landlords to receive income in return for caring for vulnerable people without their benefit being affected (para 21). The provisions were, between them, designed to apply to all such payments (para 23). Guidance was also given on the meaning of "temporarily in his care" (para 32).

---

28.   Any payment made by a local authority in accordance with section 17, 23C or 24 of the Children Act 1989 or, as the case may be, section 12 of the Social Work (Scotland) Act 1968 or section 29 or 30 of the Children (Scotland) Act 1995 (provision of services for children and their families and advice and assistance to certain children).

Analysis

See Analysis of para 19 of Sch 6.

29.–(1)   Subject to sub-paragraph (2), any payment received under an insurance policy taken out to insure against the risk of being unable to maintain repayments–

(a)   on a loan which is secured on the dwelling which the claimant occupies as his home; or

(b)   under a regulated agreement as defined for the purposes of the Consumer Credit Act 1974 or under a hire-purchase agreement or a conditional sale agreement as defined for the purposes of Part 3 of the Hire-Purchase Act 1964.

(2)   A payment referred to in sub-paragraph (1) shall only be disregarded to the extent that the payment received under that policy does not exceed the amounts, calculated on a weekly basis, which are used to–

(a)   maintain the repayments referred to in sub-paragraph (1)(a) or, as the case may be, (b); and

(b)   meet any amount due by way of premiums on–

    (i)   that policy; or

    (ii)   in a case to which sub-paragraph (1)(a) applies, an insurance policy taken out to insure against loss or damage to any building or part of a building which is occupied by the claimant as his home and which is required as a condition of the loan referred to in sub-paragraph (1)(a).

Analysis

Payments received under an insurance policy taken out to insure against the risk of being unable to maintain certain loan repayments are disregarded. The loan insured must be: (1) secured on the home or

(2) an agreement of the types specified in sub-para (1)(b). The maximum disregarded is the total of the amounts in sub-paras (a) and (b).

---

30. Any payment of income which by virtue of regulation 46 (income treated as capital) is to be treated as capital.

Analysis

This paragraph is necessary to aviod double counting.

---

31. Any social fund payment made pursuant to Part 8 of the Act (the Social Fund).

32. Any payment under Part 10 of the Act (Christmas bonus for pensioners).

33. Where a payment of income is made in a currency other than sterling, any banking charge or commission payable in converting that payment into sterling.

34. The total of a claimant's income or, if he is a member of a family, the family's income and the income of any person which he is treated as possessing under regulation 25(2) (calculation of income and capital of members of claimant's family and of a polygamous marriage) to be disregarded under regulation 60(2)(b) and regulation 61(1)(d) (calculation of covenant income where a contribution assessed), covenant income where no grant income or no contribution is assessed regulation 64(2) (treatment of student loans), regulation 65(3) (treatment of payments from access funds) and paragraphs 15 and 16 shall in no case exceed £20 per week.

Analysis

Under this paragraph, the combined maximum disregard for the types of income listed is £20.

35.–(1) Any payment made under the Macfarlane Trust, the Macfarlane (Special Payments) Trust, the Macfarlane (Special Payments) (No. 2) Trust ("the Trusts"), the Fund, the Eileen Trust or the Independent Living Funds.

(2) Any payment by or on behalf of a person who is suffering or who suffered from haemophilia or who is or was a qualifying person, which derives from a payment made under any of the Trusts to which sub-paragraph (1) refers and which is made to or for the benefit of–

(a) that person's partner or former partner from whom he is not, or where that person has died was not, estranged or divorced or with whom he has formed a civil partnership that has not been dissolved or, where that person has died, had not been dissolved at the time of that person's death;

(b) any child who is a member of that person's family or who was such a member and who is a member of the claimant's family; or

(c) any young person who is a member of that person's family or who was such a member and who is a member of the claimant's family.

(3) Any payment by or on behalf of the partner or former partner of a person who is suffering or who suffered from haemophilia or who is or was a qualifying person provided that the partner or former partner and that person are not, or if either of them has died were not, estranged or divorced or, where the partner or former partner and that person have formed a civil partnership, the civil partnership has not been dissolved or, if either of them has died, had not been dissolved at the time of the death, which derives from a payment made under any of the Trusts to which sub-paragraph (1) refers and which is made to or for the benefit of–

(a) the person who is suffering from haemophilia or who is a qualifying person;

(b) any child who is a member of that person's family or who was such a member and who is a member of the claimant's family; or

(c) any young person who is a member of that person's family or who was such a member and who is a member of the claimant's family.

(4) Any payment by a person who is suffering from haemophilia or who is a qualifying person, which derives from a payment under any of the Trusts to which sub-paragraph (1) refers, where–

(a) that person has no partner or former partner from whom he is not estranged or divorced or with whom he has formed a civil partnership that has not been dissolved, nor any child or young person who is or had been a member of that person's family; and

(b) the payment is made either–

(i) to that person's parent or step-parent; or

(ii) where that person at the date of the payment is a child, a young person or a student who has not completed his full-time education and has no parent or step-parent, to his guardian,

but only for a period from the date of the payment until the end of two years from that person's death.

(5) Any payment out of the estate of a person who suffered from haemophilia or who was a qualifying person, which derives from a payment under any of the Trusts to which sub-paragraph (1) refers, where–

(a) that person at the date of his death (the relevant date) had no partner or former partner from whom he was not estranged or divorced or with whom he had formed a civil partnership that had not been dissolved, nor any child or young person who was or had been a member of his family; and

(b) the payment is made either–

    (i) to that person's parent or step-parent; or

    (ii) where that person at the relevant date was a child, a young person or a student who had not completed his full-time education and had no parent or step-parent, to his guardian,

but only for a period of two years from the relevant date.

(6) In the case of a person to whom or for whose benefit a payment referred to in this paragraph is made, any income which derives from any payment of income or capital made under or deriving from any of the Trusts.

(7) For the purposes of sub-paragraphs (2) to (6), any reference to the Trusts shall be construed as including a reference to the Fund, the Eileen Trust, the Skipton Fund or the London Bombing Relief Charitable Fund.

Modifications

References to "step-parent" in sub-paras (4)(b)(i) and (ii) and (5)(b)(i) and (ii) are modified by s246 Civil Partnership Act 2004 (see p1046) and art 3 and para 25 of the Schedule to SI 2005 No 3137 (see p1097).

Analysis

Sub-paras (1): This sub-paragraph provides an absolute disregard of payments from the Macfarlane Trust, the Macfarlane (Special Payments) Trust, the Macfarlane (Special Payments) (No 2) Trust, the Fund, the Eileen Trust or the Independent Living Funds.

Sub-paras (2)-(6) extend this disregard to certain situations where a payment made to someone who has (or had) haemophbilia or who is (or was) a "qualifying person" (defined in reg 2(1)) from the Trusts referred to in sub-para (1) or included by sub-para (7), is passed on to someone else by the person who originally received it. They are relevant where the claimant or her/his partner is the person to whom the money has been passed.

---

36. Any payment made by the Secretary of State to compensate for the loss (in whole or in part) of entitlement to housing benefit.

37. Any payment made by the Secretary of State to compensate for the loss of housing benefit supplement under regulation 19 of the Supplementary Benefit (Requirements) Regulations 1983.

38. Any resettlement benefit which is paid to the claimant by virtue of regulation 3 of the Social Security (Hospital In-Patients) Amendment (No. 2) Regulations 1987.

39. Any payment to a juror or witness in respect of attendance at a court other than compensation for loss of earnings or for the loss of a benefit payable under the benefit Acts.

Analysis

This would cover, for example, payments for travel, subsistence or accommodation.

---

40. Any community charge benefit.

41. Any payment in consequence of a reduction of council tax under section 13 or, as the case may be, section 80 of the Local Government Finance Act 1992 (reduction of liability for council tax).

42.–(1) Where the claimant occupies a dwelling as his home and he provides in that dwelling board and lodging accommodation, an amount, in respect of each person for whom such accommodation is provided for the whole or any part of a week, equal to–

(a) where the aggregate of any payments made in respect of any one week in respect of such accommodation provided to such person does not exceed £20.00, 100 per cent. of such payments; or

(b) where the aggregate of any such payments exceeds £20.00, £20.00 and 50 per cent. of the excess over £20.00.

(2) In this paragraph "board and lodging accommodation" means accommodation provided to a person or, if he is a member of a family, to him or any other member of his family, for a charge which is inclusive of the provision of that accommodation and at least some cooked or prepared meals which both are cooked or prepared (by a person other than the person to whom the accommodation is provided or a member of his family) and are consumed in that accommodation or associated premises.

Analysis

This provides a disregard of a portion of the payments made to a claimant, by people to whom s/he provides "board and lodging accommodation" (as defined in sub-para (2)) in the dwelling s/he occupies as her/his home. The first £20 of each boarder's payment is ignored plus half of the amount in excess of £20. Where the claimant has a business partner, the paragraph does not say to apportion the disregard, even if the claimant's income includes just her/his share of the weekly charge to the boarders. The full disregard for each boarder as set out in this para should be made: *CIS 521/2002.*

There is no requirement that the board and lodgings be provided on a commercial basis, and no bar on this para applying if, for example the lodger is a close relative of the claimant. However, if the arrangement is not commercial, the lodger could come within the definition of a "non-dependant" in reg 3. If so, the payments made by her/him would instead be disregarded in full under para 21 above, but a non-dependant deduction would be made under reg 74.

---

43. Any special war widows payment made under–
(a) the Naval and Marine Pay and Pensions (Special War Widows Payment) Order 1990 made under section 3 of the Naval and Marine Pay and Pensions Act 1865;
(b) the Royal Warrant dated 19th February 1990 amending the Schedule to the Army Pensions Warrant 1977;
(c) the Queen's Order dated 26th February 1990 made under section 2 of the Air Force (Constitution) Act 1917;
(d) the Home Guard War Widows Special Payments Regulations 1990 made under section 151 of the Reserve Forces Act 1980;
(e) the Orders dated 19th February 1990 amending Orders made on 12th December 1980 concerning the Ulster Defence Regiment made in each case under section 140 of the Reserve Forces Act 1980;

and any analogous payment made by the Secretary of State for Defence to any person who is not a person entitled under the provisions mentioned in sub-paragraphs (a) to (e) of this paragraph.

44.–(1) Any payment or repayment made–
(a) as respects England, under regulation 5, 6 or 12 of the National Health Service (Travel Expenses and Remission of Charges) Regulations (travelling expenses and health service supplies);
(b) as respects Wales, under regulations 3, 5 or 8 of the National Health Service (Travelling Expenses and Remission of Charges) Regulations 1988 (travelling expenses and health service supplies);
(c) as respects Scotland, under regulation 3, 5 or 8 of the National Health Service (Travelling Expenses and Remission of Charges) (Scotland) Regulations 2003 (travelling expenses and health service supplies).

(2) Any payment or repayment made by the Secretary of State for Health, Scottish Ministers or the National Assembly for Wales, which is analogous to a payment or repayment mentioned in sub-paragraph (1).

Analysis

Para 44 provides a disregard of payments made in respect of certain NHS charges (eg, dental and optical treatment).

---

45. Any payment made under regulation 6, 8, 12 or 14(2) of the Welfare Food Regulations 1996 (payments made in place of milk tokens or the supply of vitamins).

46. Any payment made by either the Secretary of State for [¹ Justice] or by Scottish Ministers under a scheme established to assist relatives and other persons to visit persons in custody.

Amendments

1. Amended by Art 8 and the Sch para 23 of SI 2007 No 2128 as from 22.8.07.

47.–(1) Where a claimant's applicable amount includes an amount by way of a family premium, £15 of any payment of maintenance, whether under a court order or not, which is made or due to be made by–
(a) the claimant's former partner, or the claimant's partner's former partner; or
(b) the parent of a child or young person where that child or young person is a member of the claimant's family except where that parent is the claimant or the claimant's partner.

(2) For the purposes of sub-paragraph (1), where more than one maintenance payment falls to be taken into account in any week, all such payments shall be aggregated and treated as if they were a single payment.

(3) A payment made by the Secretary of State in lieu of maintenance shall, for the purposes of sub-paragraph (1), be treated as a payment of maintenance made by a person specified in head (a) or (b) of that sub-paragraph.

Analysis

This provides a £15 disregard of maintenance payments where the claimant's applicable amount includes a family premium. In other words it only applies where the claimant is treated as responsible for a child or young person. To qualify for the disregard the maintenance payment must be made by: the claimant's former partner; the claimant's partner's former partner; or the parent of a child or young person where that child or young person is a member of the claimant's family but not where the person making the payments is the claimant or her/his partner. For example, the disregard will not apply where the claimant's former partner returns to the claimant's home but has a court order to pay maintenance.

---

48. Any payment made by the Secretary of State to compensate a person who was entitled to supplementary benefit in respect of a period ending immediately before 11th April 1988 but who did not become entitled to income support in respect of a period beginning with that day.

49. Any payment (other than a training allowance) made, whether by the Secretary of State or any other person, under the Disabled Persons (Employment) Act 1944 to assist disabled persons to obtain or retain employment despite their disability.

50. Any guardian's allowance.

51. Any council tax benefit.

52.–(1) Where the claimant is in receipt of any benefit under Parts 2, 3 or 5 of the Act or pension under the Naval, Military and Air Forces etc. (Disablement and Death) Service Pensions Order 1983, any increase in the rate of that benefit arising under Part 4 (increases for dependants) or section 106(a) (unemployability supplement) of the Act or the rate of that pension under that Order where the dependant in respect of whom the increase is paid is not a member of the claimant's family.

(2) For the purposes of sub-paragraph (1), an addition to a contribution-based jobseeker's allowance under regulation 10(4) of the Jobseeker's Allowance (Transitional Provisions) Regulations 1996 shall be treated as an increase of a benefit under the Act arising under Part 4 of the Act.

53. Any supplementary pension under article 29(1A) of the Naval, Military and Air Forces etc. (Disablement and Death) Service Pensions Order 1983 (pensions to widows, widowers or surviving civil partners).

54. In the case of a pension awarded at the supplementary rate under article 27(3) of the Personal Injuries (Civilians) Scheme 1983 (pensions to widows, widowers or surviving civil partners), the sum specified in paragraph 1(c) of Schedule 4 to that Scheme.

55.–(1) Any payment which is–

(a) made under any of the Dispensing Instruments to a widow, widower or surviving civil partner of a person–
    (i) whose death was attributable to service in a capacity analogous to service as a member of the armed forces of the Crown; and
    (ii) whose service in such capacity terminated before 31st March 1973; and

(b) equal to the amount specified in article 29(1A) of the Naval, Military and Air Forces etc. (Disablement and Death) Service Pensions Order 1983 (pensions to widows, widowers or surviving civil partners).

(2) In this paragraph "the Dispensing Instruments" means the Order in Council of 19th December 1881, the Royal Warrant of 27th October 1884 and the Order by His Majesty of 14th January 1922 (exceptional grants of pay, non-effective pay and allowances).

56. Except in a case which falls under sub-paragraph (1) of paragraph 17 of Schedule 4, where the claimant is a person who satisfies any of the conditions of sub-paragraph (2) of that paragraph, any amount of working tax credit up to [² £15.45].

Amendments

1.   Amended by Art 19(10)(b) of SI 2006 No 645 and reg 8 of SI 2006 No 217 as from 1.4.06 (3.4.06 where rent payable weekly or at intervals of a week).
2.   Amended by Art 19(10)(b) of SI 2007 No 688 as from 1.4.07 (2.4.07 where rent payable weekly or at intervals of a week).

Analysis

This paragraph allows for a disregard of WTC up to the amount specified where earnings are too low to use the whole of the disregard allowed by para 17 of Sch 4.

---

57. Any payment made under the Community Care (Direct Payments) Act 1996 or under section 12B of the Social Work (Scotland) Act 1968 or under regulations made under section 57 of the Health and Social Care Act 2001 (direct payments).

Analysis

Rather than provide services to disabled people directly, local authorities can pay community care "direct payments" to them to buy their own services. Under this paragraph, the direct payments are disregarded. Note that they are also disregarded as capital under Sch 6 para 58.

Note that "direct payments" could count as "earnings" if the disabled person is a member of a couple and "employs" her/his partner as the carer. In *CIS 1068/2006* the claimant was caring for his severely disabled wife, and claiming income support. "Direct payments" were made by the local authority to the claimant's wife. She used these to employ the claimant as her carer. The issue was whether the direct payments should be fully disregarded under para 58 of Schedule 9 of the Income Support (General) Regulations 1987 (the equivalent of this paragraph) or taken into account as the claimant's earnings (making an appropriate earnings disregard). Allowing the Secretary of State's appeal, Commissioner Turnbull held that it was not open to the tribunal to hold on the evidence before it that the claimant was not in receipt of earnings from his wife in the form of the payment made to him. In determining the claimant's wife's income the "direct payments" to her had to be disregarded under para 58 Sch 9. However, the claimant's wife then used those payments to "employ" him as her carer. It did not matter whether she formally employed him or he was engaged as a self-employed earner to provide services for her: in either case the sums paid to the claimant were earnings and so fell to be taken into account in calculating the amount of income support to which he was entitled. Nothing in s136(1) Social Security Contributions and Benefits Act 1992 altered this conclusion, or meant that the claimant had to be treated as receiving the payments as "direct payments" rather than earnings. Note that leave to appeal to the Court of Appeal has been granted: *Casewell v Secretary of State for Work and Pensions*.

58.–(1)   Subject to sub-paragraph (2), in respect of a person who is receiving, or who has received, assistance under the self-employment route, any payment to that person–

(a)   to meet expenses wholly and necessarily incurred whilst carrying on the commercial activity;

(b)   which is used or intended to be used to maintain repayments on a loan taken out by that person for the purpose of establishing or carrying on the commercial activity,

in respect of which such assistance is or was received.

(2)   Sub-paragraph (1) shall apply only in respect of payments which are paid to that person from the special account as defined for the purposes of Chapter 4A of Part 8 of the Jobseeker's Allowance Regulations.

Analysis

The payments set out in sub-para (1) to those following the "self-employment route" (defined in reg 2(1)) to meet expenses or to service loans are ignored, but only where paid a special account referred to in sub-para (2). See also reg 46(7) for receipts paid to those following this routed which are treated as capital.

59.–(1)   Any payment of a sports award except to the extent that it has been made in respect of any one or more of the items specified in sub-paragraph (2).

(2)   The items specified for the purposes of sub-paragraph (1) are food, ordinary clothing or footwear, household fuel or rent of the claimant or where the claimant is a member of a family, any other member of his family, or any council tax or water charges for which that claimant or member is liable.

(3)   For the purposes of sub-paragraph (2)–

''food'' does not include vitamins, minerals or other special dietary supplements intended to enhance the performance of the person in the sport in respect of which the award was made;

''rent'' means eligible rent less any deductions in respect of non-dependants which fall to be made under regulation 74 (non-dependant deductions).

Analysis

Sports awards (defined in reg 2(1) are ignored as income except in so far as they provide for basic needs. On the wording of para (2), see the Analysis to reg 42(6).

---

60.   Where the amount of subsistence allowance paid to a person in a benefit week exceeds the amount of income-based jobseeker's allowance that person would have received in that benefit week had it been payable to him, less 50p, that excess amount.

61.   In the case of a claimant participating in an employment zone programme, any discretionary payment made by an employment zone contractor to the claimant, being a fee, grant, loan or otherwise.

62.   Any discretionary housing payment paid pursuant to regulation 2(1) of the Discretionary Financial Assistance Regulations 2001.

63.–(1)   Any payment made by a local authority or by the National Assembly for Wales, to or on behalf of the claimant or his partner relating to a service which is provided to develop or sustain the capacity of the claimant or his partner to live independently in his accommodation.

(2)   For the purposes of sub-paragraph (1) "local authority" includes, in England, a county council.

Analysis
Under this para, payments made by a local authority or the National Assembly for Wales for support services to help the claimant or her/his partner live independantly (ie, under the Supporting People programme) are ignored as the claimant's income. This disregard does not apply to landlords receiving such payments for providing the services, although other paragraphs in this Schedule might apply.

<hr>

SCHEDULE 6
REGULATION 44
Capital to be disregarded

Modifications
Paras 48A and 48B are inserted by para 2(6) of the HB&CTB(CP) Regs in respect of claims for HB by some refugees.

A different version of para 48B is substituted for para 55B by Sch 4 para 4(2)(c) of the HB&CTB(CP) Regs for some HB claimants who are refugees who claimed asylum on or before 2 April 2000. See also reg 10A and Sch A1 inserted by Sch 4 para 2 of the HB&CTB(CP) Regs on p1126.

Note that paras 48A and 48B lapsed by s12(2)(e) of the Asylum and Immigration (Treatment of Claimants, etc.) Act 2004 (for those recorded as refugees after 14.6.07).

Definitions
"claimant" – see reg 2(1).
"croft land" – see note on reg 2(4).
"dwelling" – see reg 2(4) and s137(1) SSCBA.
"family" – see s137(1) SSCBA.
"income related benefit" – see s123(1) SSCBA.
"Independent Living Fund" – see reg 2(1).
"Macfarlane Trust" – see reg 2(1).
"partner" – see reg 2(1).
"polygamous marriage" – see reg 2(1).
"relative" – see reg 2(1).
"self-employed earner" – see reg 2(1).
"young person" – see reg 19.

General Note on Schedule 6
This Schedule sets out the items of a claimant's and her/his partner's capital which must be ignored for the purposes of calculating HB. See reg 44(2) and, generally, Section 6 of Pt 6. The disregards under the following paragraphs are cumulative unless specified otherwise. The effect is a mandatory disregard, but sometimes the *period* of the disregard is at the authority's discretion.

<hr>

1.   The dwelling together with any garage, garden and outbuildings, normally occupied by the claimant as his home including any premises not so occupied which it is impracticable or unreasonable to sell separately, in particular, in Scotland, any croft land on which the dwelling is situated; but, notwithstanding regulation 25 (calculation of income and capital of members of claimant's family and of a polygamous marriage), only one dwelling shall be disregarded under this paragraph.

Analysis
For the dwelling "normally occupied" by the claimant as her/his home, see reg 7. To be included as the home, provided they are part of the same "dwelling", are any premises it is "impractical or unreasonable" to sell separately.

This is in addition to land already treated as a dwelling under reg 2(4). This wording was used in respect of the meaning of the word "home" in reg 2(1) of the SB (Resources) Regs 1987. In *R(SB) 13/84* and *R(SB) 27/84* it was said that whether it is "impractical or unreasonable" to sell is a subjective question – ie, to be looked at from the claimant's point of view and circumstances. A dwelling could include an extension built to accommodate a relative, but not where this is separately rated or self contained. Only one "dwelling" may be ignored under this paragraph.

Note that para 1 would cease to apply to if the claimant no longer occupies home (eg, s/he moves home) but other paras below might apply to the now former home so that its value can continue to be disregarded (see eg, paras 4, 25, 26 and 28) or the proceeds of sale might be disregarded (see para 3).

2.   Any premises acquired for occupation by the claimant which he intends to occupy as his home within 26 weeks of the date of acquisition or such longer period as is reasonable in the circumstances to enable the claimant to obtain possession and commence occupation of the premises.

Analysis

Under this para, a claimant may have premises acquired for occupation as a home ignored for the purpose of calculating her/his entitlement to HB. The claimant must intend to occupy the premises as her/his home. The words "as his home" show that only potential residential premises are covered. Once the claimant moves into the premises, para 2 would no longer apply, but para 1 would if they are "normally occupied" by the claimant.

The period of disregard is 26 weeks from the date of acquisition which can be extended where "reasonable" to enable the claimant to obtain possession and occupy the home.

3.   Any sum directly attributable to the proceeds of sale of any premises formerly occupied by the claimant as his home which is to be used for the purchase of other premises intended for such occupation within 26 weeks of the date of sale or such longer period as is reasonable in the circumstances to enable the claimant to complete the purchase.

Analysis

This covers the situation where the claimant has sold her/his former home, but has not yet purchased a new one. It applies where the proceeds of the sale are to be used to purchase premises which the claimant intends to occupy as a home, within 26 weeks of that sale. A longer period can be allowed if this is "reasonable", and an extension is necessary to allow the claimant to complete the purchase. Once the new home is actually purchased, paras 1 or 2 could apply to the acquired premises, depending on whether the claimant moves in immediately or not. For the meaning of "occupied as home", see reg 7.

4.   Any premises occupied in whole or in part–
(a)   by a partner or relative of a single claimant or any member of the family as his home where that person is either aged 60 or over or incapacitated;
(b)   by the former partner of the claimant as his home; but this provision shall not apply where the former partner is a person from whom the claimant is estranged or divorced or with whom he had formed a civil partnership that has been dissolved.

Analysis

This allows the disregard of any dwelling owned by the claimant occupied by the people set out in sub-paras (a) or (b). This para is not restricted to the disregard of *one* dwelling only. It allows the whole premises to be ignored whether the partner/former partner/relative occupies all or part of them.

Sub-para (a). The partner or relative in question must be either aged 60 or over or "incapacitated". "Incapacitated" is not defined here but would appear to have a broader meaning than those who would qualify for disability premium (see Sch 3).

Sub-para (b) provides a disregard where the claimant's former partner occupies the premises as a home, so long as s/he and the claimant are not estranged or divorced nor their civil partnership dissolved. This would include situations where a couple continue to see themselves as a couple, but for HB purposes, are not treated as such – eg, because they are no longer members of the same household: regs 2(1), definitions of "partner" and "couple" and 21.

The meaning of "estranged" is not supplied by the regulation. In *R(IS) 5/05*, Commissioner Rowland said that it has a connotation of emotional disharmony. The question will be whether the parties have ceased to consider themselves to be a couple and not whether, despite that, they continue to maintain friendly relations. In *CPC 683/2007*, there was no emotional disharmony between the claimant and the former partner as adults, but there was emotional disharmony between them as partners. Commissioner Jacobs said that was a key distinction because the language used in the legislation is attempting to identify those cases in which the relationship between the parties is such that it is appropriate for their finances to be treated separately for the purposes of benefit entitlement.

See para 25 below when the claimant *is* "estranged" or divorced from the former partner or where a civil partnership has been dissolved.

5.   Where a claimant is on income support or an income-based jobseeker's allowance, the whole of his capital.

Analysis

This paragraph and paragraph 6 are necessary to avoid double counting – see General Notes on Pt 6 and para 12 of Sch 4 and paras 4 and 5 of Sch 5.

6.   Where the claimant is a member of a joint-claim couple for the purposes of the Jobseekers Act and his partner is on income-based jobseeker's allowance, the whole of the claimant's capital.

7.   Any future interest in property of any kind, other than land or premises in respect of which the claimant has granted a subsisting lease or tenancy, including sub-leases or sub-tenancies.

Analysis

A "future interest", or "reversionary interest" covers the situation where the claimant or her/his partner (see reg 25) will become entitled to possession of the asset at some future date, but someone else has that right at present – eg, where property has been left to another person for life, then to the claimant on that other person's death. The value of any such interest must be totally disregarded.

8.–(1)   The assets of any business owned in whole or in part by the claimant and for the purposes of which he is engaged as a self-employed earner, or if he has ceased to be so engaged, for such period as may be reasonable in the circumstances to allow for disposal of any such asset.

(2)   The assets of any business owned in whole or in part by the claimant where–

(a)   he is not engaged as a self-employed earner in that business by reason of some disease or bodily or mental disablement; but

(b)   he intends to become engaged or, as the case may be, re-engaged as a self-employed earner in that business as soon as he recovers or is able to become engaged or re-engaged in that business,

for a period of 26 weeks from the date on which the claim for housing benefit is made, or is treated as made, or, if it is unreasonable to expect him to become engaged or re-engaged in that business within that period, for such longer period as is reasonable in the circumstances to enable him to become so engaged or re-engaged.

(3)   In the case of a person who is receiving assistance under the self-employment route, the assets acquired by that person for the purpose of establishing or carrying on the commercial activity in respect of which such assistance is being received.

(4)   In the case of a person who has ceased carrying on the commercial activity in respect of which assistance was received as specified in sub-paragraph (3), the assets relating to that activity for such period as may be reasonable in the circumstances to allow for disposal of any such asset.

Analysis

This allows the disregard of business assets owned by the claimant while s/he is working for the business and also for a "reasonable" period after s/he ceases working for the business to allow time to sell or otherwise dispose of the assets. What is a "reasonable" period will depend on the type of business as well as the current economic situation. See also reg 49(5). Sub-para (2) ensures the disregard is also applicable during any period a self-employed claimant is temporarily unable to work due to an illness or injury for a period of up to 26 weeks from the date the claim is, or is treated as, made. The initial 26 week period should be extended where it is considered unreasonable to expect the claimant to become (re-)engaged in that period.

There were modifications to this provision between November 1999 and November 2001 for New Deal participants. See the commentary in the 14th edition for details.

9.–(1)   Subject to sub-paragraph (2), any arrears of, or any concessionary payment made to compensate for arrears due to the non-payment of–

(a)   any payment specified in paragraphs 6, 8 or 9 of Schedule 5;

(b)   an income-related benefit or supplementary benefit, family income supplement under the Family Income Supplement Act 1970, working families' tax credit under section 128 of the Act, disabled person's tax credit under section 129 of the Act, or housing benefit under Part 1 of the Social Security and Housing Benefits Act 1982;

(c)   an income-based jobseeker's allowance;

(d)   any discretionary housing payment paid pursuant to regulation 2(1) of the Discretionary Financial Assistance Regulations 2001;

(e)   working tax credit and child tax credit [¹],

but only for a period of 52 weeks from the date of the receipt of arrears or of the concessionary payment.

(2)   In a case where the total of any arrears and, if appropriate, any concessionary payment referred to in sub-paragraph (1) relating to one of the specified payments, benefits or allowances amounts to £5,000 or more (referred to in this sub-paragraph and in sub-paragraph (3) as ''the relevant sum'') and is–

(a)   paid in order to rectify or to compensate for, an official error as defined in regulation 1(2) of the Decisions and Appeals Regulations; and

(b)   received by the claimant in full on or after 14th October 2001,
sub-paragraph (1) shall have effect in relation to such arrears or concessionary payment either for a period of 52 weeks from the date of receipt, or, if the relevant sum is received in its entirety during the award of housing benefit, for the remainder of that award if that is a longer period.

(3)   For the purposes of sub-paragraph (2), ''the award of housing benefit'' means–

(a)   the award in which the relevant sum is first received (or the first part thereof where it is paid in more than one instalment); and

(b)   where that award is followed by one or more further awards which, or each of which, begins immediately after the end of the previous award, such further award provided that for that further award the claimant–

(i)   is the person who received the relevant sum; or

(ii)   is the partner of the person who received the relevant sum, or was that person's partner at the date of his death.

Amendment

1.   Amended by reg 2(16) of SI 2005 No 2502 as amended by Sch 2 para 27 of SI 2006 No 217 as from 1.4.06 (3.4.06 where rent payable weekly or at intervals of a week).

Analysis

This paragraph allows payments of arrears of, or compensation in respect of, the benefits listed to be ignored for a period of up to 52 weeks after they are received. If anything is left of such a payment after the 52 weeks, the payment will be taken into account as normal. WTC and CTC also receive the same treatment.

In *CIS 2448/2006* the local authority had paid the claimant compensation because it had wrongly charged him for after-care services pursuant to s117 Mental Health Act 1983: per *R v Manchester City Council ex parte Stennett* [2002] UKHL 34. The claimant argued that that the payment should be treated as arrears of compensation for non-payment of IS and so should be disregarded under para 7(1) Sch 10 IS Regs 1987 (the equivalent to para 9(1))because, had the local authority not in fact charged the claimant under the MHA for the costs of his residential accommodation, he would have received the full amount for IS and not just the sum for "personal expenses". The argument was rejected on the facts of the case. As the claimant had been paid full IS at all relevant times and then paid the residential fees element onto the care home, no arrears of IS were due. Even assuming that some of the IS was paid direct to the care home by the DWP, the argument was still ill-founded because whatever may have later been held in *Stennett*, at the time the IS would properly have been paid to the care home and so there could be no question of the claimant establishing that any sum of IS had been wrongfully withheld from him. Even if that was wrong, the payment here was not a payment of "arrears" of IS as that refers to a sum paid by the Secretary of State in satisfaction of an award of IS.

See also Sch 5 para 7 where the concessionary payments are income payments.

---

10.   Any sum–

(a)   paid to the claimant in consequence of damage to, or loss of the home or any personal possession and intended for its repair or replacement; or

(b)   acquired by the claimant (whether as a loan or otherwise) on the express condition that it is to be used for effecting essential repairs or improvement to the home,
which is to be used for the intended purpose, for a period of 26 weeks from the date on which it was so paid or acquired or such longer period as is reasonable in the circumstances to effect the repairs, replacement or improvement.

Analysis

This paragraph provides that certain sums for repairs to, or replacement of, personal possessions, or repairs or improvements to the home are to be ignored for a limited period. The initial 26-week period may be extended where this is considered reasonable where the claimant needs the extra time to get the repairs, etc done.

Sub-para (a) covers sums paid as a result of damage to, or the loss of, the claimants home or personal possessions, intended for their repair or replacement. "Personal possession" is not defined but would cover, for example, a car.

Sub-para (b). This might even cover a payment from a relative – it is the terms of the payment which are important, not the source. "Essential" work was distinguished in *R(SB) 10/81* from that which is a luxury, but it need not be so vital as to be indispensable for life to be maintained (that case was about a single payment for "essential redecoration").

An "improvement" may be distinguished from a repair in that it connotes the adding of something new other than remedying a damaged, pre-existing feature.

11. Any sum–

(a) deposited with a housing association as defined in section 1(1) of the Housing Associations Act 1985 or section 338(1) of the Housing (Scotland) Act 1987 as a condition of occupying the home;

(b) which was so deposited and which is to be used for the purchase of another home, for the period of 26 weeks or such longer period as may be reasonable in the circumstances to enable the claimant to complete the purchase.

Analysis

Sub-paragraph (a) provides a disregard for deposits held by a housing association, sub-para (b) for deposits which *were* so held until the claimant decided to purchase a home.

Sub-para (a). "Housing Association". s1 Housing Act 1985 refers to s5 of that Act. The definition in s338(1) of the Scottish Act is precisely the same. The payment of the deposit must be a condition of occupying the home for the paragraph to apply.

Sub-para (b). Here the disregard is a limited one. The initial 26-week period may be extended where this is considered reasonable in view of the fact that the claimant needs the extra time to complete purchase.

12. Any personal possessions except those which have been acquired by the claimant with the intention of reducing his capital in order to secure entitlement to housing benefit or to increase the amount of that benefit.

Analysis

"Personal possessions" is not defined but could cover everything from clothing to paintings, furniture, cars, etc. The only such items which cannot be ignored are those bought for the purposes of securing or increasing HB entitlement. See also notes on reg 49(1). See para 10 where a sum has been paid to the claimant for damage to, loss of, personal possessions.

13. The value of the right to receive any income under an annuity or the surrender value (if any) of such an annuity.

Analysis

This provides a total disregard of the surrender value of annuities or the right to receive income under them. For the treatment of income *actually* received under an annuity, see reg 41(2) and Sch 5 para 18.

14. Where the funds of a trust are derived from a payment made in consequence of any personal injury to the claimant [¹ or the claimant's partner], the value of the trust fund and the value of the right to receive any payment under that trust.

Amendment

1. Amended by reg 15(7)(a) of SI 2006 No 2378 from the first day of the first benefit week to commence on or after 2.10.06.

Analysis

"Payments made in consequence" of personal injury covers out of court settlements and insurance payments as well as damages under court order. The paragraph provides a disregard or the value of the trust fund, and the right to receive payments, for an indefinite period in all cases. See reg 42(2) in respect of income from such trusts. Payments of income are disregarded under para 14 Sch 5. See para 14A of this Schedule for capital payments and paras 45 and 46 where damages paid to children or young people are administered by the Court.

[¹**14A.** –(1) Any payment made to the claimant or the claimant's partner in consequence of any personal injury to the claimant or, as the case may be, the claimant's partner.

(2) But sub-paragraph (1)–

(a) applies only for the period of 52 weeks beginning with the day on which the claimant first receives any payment in consequence of that personal injury;

(b) does not apply to any subsequent payment made to him in consequence of that injury (whether it is made by the same person or another);

(c) ceases to apply to the payment or any part of the payment from the day on which the claimant no longer possesses it;

(d) does not apply to any payment from a trust where the funds of the trust are derived from a payment made in consequence of any personal injury to the claimant.

(3)   For the purposes of sub-paragraph (2)(c), the circumstances in which a claimant no longer possesses a payment or a part of it include where the claimant has used a payment or part of it to purchase an asset.

(4)   References in sub-paragraphs (2) and (3) to the claimant are to be construed as including references to his partner (where applicable).]

Amendment

1.   Inserted by reg 15(7)(b) of SI 2006 No 2378 from the first day of the first benefit week to commence on or after 2.10.06.

Analysis

A payment made in consequence of a personal injury to the claimant or her/his partner is disregarded for 52 weeks from the day is is received, though the amount of the disregard decreases as the payment is disposed of (eg as the claimant spends it): sub-paras (1), (2)(a) and (c) and (3). This gives the claimant time to spend all or part of the payment, or to put it into a trust which can itself be disregarded under para 14. However, the paragraph does not apply to:

(1)   subsequent payments made in consequence of the same injury: sub-para (2)(b). However, it is suggested that the amount could be disregarded if put into a trust (see reg 49(2)(b) and para 14).

(2)   payments of capital made from a trust derived from payments made in consequence of of a personal injury to the claimant or her/his partner: sub-para (2)(d). Note that payments of income from such a trust are disregarded under para 14 Sch 5.

Sub-para (4) confirms that in sub-paras (2) and (3) the references to "claimant" should also be read as "partner" where relevant.

---

15.   The value of the right to receive any income under a life interest or from a life rent.

Analysis

The terms "life interest" or "life rent" (in Scots Law) cover the situation where a beneficiary under a trust gets the right to enjoy an asset during her/his lifetime, but that asset will pass on her/his death to someone else. Such a right can be bought and sold and is therefore given a capital value, but that value is to be ignored for the purpose of assessing HB. If, however, a claimant receives actual payments (eg, of income, under such a life interest or life rent) that income will be assessable under Section 5 of Pt 6.

---

16.   The value of the right to receive any income which is disregarded under paragraph 11 of Schedule 4 or paragraph 24 of Schedule 5.

Analysis

The right to receive income can be bought and sold and so has a capital value, but that value is ignored for these purposes. Here actual income received can also be ignored under the paragraphs and Schedules mentioned.

---

17.   The surrender value of any policy of life insurance.

18.   Where any payment of capital falls to be made by instalments, the value of the right to receive any outstanding instalments.

Analysis

Reg 41 deems capital payable by instalments which are outstanding as at the date of claim to be treated income in certain circumstances. Under this paragraph, the value of the right to receive the outstanding instalments is ignored in the assessment of capital.

---

19.   Any payment made by a local authority in accordance with section 17, 23C or 24A of the Children Act 1989 or, as the case may be, section 12 of the Social Work (Scotland) Act 1968 or sections 28 or 30 of the Children (Scotland) Act 1995 (provision of services for children and their families and advice and assistance to certain children).

Analysis

Section 17 of the Children Act enables the local authority to give children in need, their families and others cash payments "in exceptional circumstances". Section 12 of the Scottish legislation is to the same effect. Sections 23 C and 24A enable the local authority to give individuals under 21 who at any time after reaching the age of 16 but while still a child had been looked after, accommodated or fostered by the local authority, cash payments "in exceptional circumstances". Sections 28 and 30 of the Scottish legislation foes also. For income payments, see para 28 Sch 5.

---

20. Any social fund payment made pursuant to Part 8 of the Act.

21. Any refund of tax which falls to be deducted under section 369 of the Income and Corporation Taxes Act 1988 (deduction of tax from certain loan interest) on a payment of relevant loan interest for the purpose of acquiring an interest in the home or carrying out repairs or improvements to the home.

22. Any capital which by virtue of regulation 41 or 64 (capital treated as income and treatment of student loans) is to be treated as income.

Analysis

As capital under reg 41 and student loans under reg 64 are to be treated as part of the claimant's income, this paragraph is necessary to avoid double counting. See also para 18, above.

---

23. Where any payment of capital is made in a currency other than Sterling, any banking charge or commission payable in converting that payment into Sterling.

24.–(1) Any payment made under the Macfarlane Trust, the Macfarlane (Special Payments) Trust, the Macfarlane (Special Payments) (No. 2) Trust ("the Trusts"), the Fund, the Eileen Trust, the Independent Living Funds, the Skipton Funds or the London Bombings Relief Charitable Fund.

(2) Any payment by or on behalf of a person who is suffering or who suffered from haemophilia or who is or was a qualifying person, which derives from a payment made under any of the Trusts to which sub-paragraph (1) refers and which is made to or for the benefit of–

(a) that person's partner or former partner from whom he is not, or where that person has died was not, estranged or divorced or with whom he has formed a civil partnership that has not been dissolved or, where that person has died, had not been dissolved at the time of that person's death;

(b) any child who is a member of that person's family or who was such a member and who is a member of the claimant's family; or

(c) any young person who is a member of that person's family or who was such a member and who is a member of the claimant's family.

(3) Any payment by or on behalf of the partner or former partner of a person who is suffering or who suffered from haemophilia or who is or was a qualifying person provided that the partner or former partner and that person are not, or if either of them has died were not, estranged or divorced or, where the partner or former partner and that person have formed a civil partnership, the civil partnership has not been dissolved or, if either of them has died, had not been dissolved at the time of the death, which derives from a payment made under any of the Trusts to which sub-paragraph (1) refers and which is made to or for the benefit of–

(a) the person who is suffering from haemophilia or who is a qualifying person;

(b) any child who is a member of that person's family or who was such a member and who is a member of the claimant's family; or

(c) any young person who is a member of that person's family or who was such a member and who is a member of the claimant's family.

(4) Any payment by a person who is suffering from haemophilia or who is a qualifying person, which derives from a payment under any of the Trusts to which sub-paragraph (1) refers, where–

(a) that person has no partner or former partner from whom he is not estranged or divorced or with whom he has formed a civil partnership that has not been dissolved, nor any child or young person who is or had been a member of that person's family; and

(b) the payment is made either–

(i) to that person's parent or step-parent; or

(ii) where that person at the date of the payment is a child, a young person or a student who has not completed his full-time education and has no parent or step-parent, to his guardian,

but only for a period from the date of the payment until the end of two years from that person's death.

(5) Any payment out of the estate of a person who suffered from haemophilia or who was a qualifying person, which derives from a payment under any of the Trusts to which sub-paragraph (1) refers, where–

(a) that person at the date of his death (the relevant date) had no partner or former partner from whom he was not estranged or divorced or with whom he had formed a civil partnership that had not been dissolved, nor any child or young person who was or had been a member of his family; and

(b) the payment is made either–

(i) to that person's parent or step-parent; or

    (ii)   where that person at the relevant date was a child, a young person or a student who had not completed his full-time education and had no parent or step-parent, to his guardian,

but only for a period of two years from the relevant date.

(6)   In the case of a person to whom or for whose benefit a payment referred to in this paragraph is made, any capital resource which derives from any payment of income or capital made under or deriving from any of the Trusts.

(7)   For the purposes of sub-paragraphs (2) to (6), any reference to the Trusts shall be construed as including a reference to the Fund, the Eileen Trust, the Skipton Fund or the London Bombings Relief Charitable Fund.

Modifications

References to "step-parent" in sub-paras (4)(b)(i) and (ii) and (5)(b)(i) and (ii) are modified by s246 Civil Partnership Act 2004 (see p1046) and art 3 and para 26 of the Schedule to SI 2005 No 3137 (see p1097).

Analysis

See analysis of Sch 5 para 35.

25.–(1)   Where a claimant has ceased to occupy what was formerly the dwelling occupied as the home following his estrangement or divorce from, or dissolution of his civil partnership with, his former partner, that dwelling for a period of 26 weeks from the date on which he ceased to occupy that dwelling or, where the dwelling is occupied as the home by the former partner who is a lone parent, for so long as it is so occupied.

(2)   In this paragraph ''dwelling'' includes any garage, garden and outbuildings, which were formerly occupied by the claimant as his home and any premises not so occupied which it is impracticable or unreasonable to sell separately, in particular, in Scotland, any croft land on which the dwelling is situated.

Analysis

Sub-para (1) allows the disregard of a claimant's former home s/he left following estrangement or divorce from her/his partner or where her/his civil partnership with the partner has been dissolved. The home must be occupied by the former partner. For "occupied as the home": see the note to reg 7. See para 4 above for a discussion of the term "estranged" and where the claimant and the former partner are not estranged or divorced from the former partner or where a civil partnership has not been dissolved.

(1)   If the former partner is a lone parent, the dwelling can be disregarded indefinitely, so long as s/he continues to occupy it as a home. "Lone parent" is defined in reg 2(1).

(2)   In all other cases, the dwelling can be disregarded for 26 weeks from the date the claimant ceased to occupy it. There is no discretion to extend (although a claimant subject to this para may also be covered by other paras below – eg, paras 26 or 27). It may be difficult to ascertain on which date the claimant finally ceased to occupy the dwelling for these purposes.

This provision is likely to give rise to a number of practical difficulties where there are no children or the former partner leaves the home (eg, for it to be sold) not least because the short time during which the disregard is available will frequently be inadequate to enable a couple's financial affairs to be sorted out in the case of a divorce. At the end of the 26-week period, even if financial arrangements have been made following the breakdown of a relationship, matters may not be clear-cut as the divorce courts sometimes make what are known as "Mesher" orders which order that the former matrimonial home be held on trust for the former partners in their respective shares, but that it should not be sold until the occurrence of a particular event – eg, the death or remarriage of the partner who remains in residence. In such a case, the partner who has left will continue to have an interest in the home which, after the initial 26-week period, will not be disregarded unless the other partner is a lone parent and continues to live in the home, or one of the other paragraphs of Sch 6 applies. A practical solution lies in the method of valuation of such capital – see regs 47 and 51. The asset (here the claimant's share) is to be valued at its current market value less 10 per cent and the value of any incumbrance secured on it. If what a claimant possesses is an interest in a house which s/he is unable to sell because her/his partner is still living in it and/or because a court order forbids the sale, the market value of that asset is likely to be very low. Authorities should be careful to take a realistic and humane approach to this problem.

Sub-para (2) is the same definition of a "dwelling" as appears in para 1 above.

---

26.   Any premises where the claimant is taking reasonable steps to dispose of those premises, for a period of 26 weeks from the date on which he first took such steps, or such longer period as is reasonable in the circumstances to enable him to dispose of those premises.

Analysis

The question of what are "reasonable steps" initially rests with the authority. Here the 26-week disregard may be extended where it appears "reasonable" to do so in the circumstances. Once the property has been disposed of, para 3 above may apply to the proceeds.

27. Any premises which the claimant intends to occupy as his home, and in respect of which he is taking steps to obtain possession and has sought legal advice, or has commenced legal proceedings, with a view to obtaining possession, for a period of 26 weeks from the date on which he first sought such advice or first commenced such proceedings whichever is the earlier, or such longer period as is reasonable in the circumstances to enable him to obtain possession and commence occupation of those premises.

Analysis

The starting date for the period of disregard under this paragraph is the date on which the claimant first sought legal advice if this is earlier (as it usually will be by several weeks if not months) than the date on which s/he commenced legal proceedings. There could be overlap between this paragraph and para 25 above, in which case this paragraph may operate to extend any period of disregard available under para 25: eg, if a claimant leaves the matrimonial home and 10 weeks later seeks advice on commencing divorce proceedings in which there is an application for the other partner, who is childless, to leave the premises and for the claimant to be permitted to re-enter, para 25 applies initially and then the full period in para 27 applies after advice is sought. In many cases, for reasons beyond the claimant's control, it is possible that possession proceedings will not be completed within six months of their commencement, and this should be reflected by the use of the discretion to extend the period of the disregard where necessary.

28. Any premises which the claimant intends to occupy as his home to which essential repairs or alterations are required in order to render them fit for such occupation, for a period of 26 weeks from the date on which the claimant first takes steps to effect those repairs or alterations, or such longer period as is necessary to enable those repairs or alterations to be carried out.

Analysis

"Essential" repairs or alterations are not defined but they must be such as are necessary to make the premises fit for the claimant's occupation. It is possible that cases will arise where this paragraph overlaps with para 2 of Sch 6, and the scheme should be operated with the claimant's interests in mind.

The scope of this paragraph was considered in *R v Tower Hamlets LBC HBRB ex p Kapur* [2000] *The Times* 28 June, QBD. The applicant owned a derelict house valued at £240,000 which was unfit for habitation. He wished to renovate the property and move back into it and made extensive efforts to obtain funding for the necessary works from lenders, relatives and public authorities in the form of various types of renovation grant. It took a great deal of time to assemble the funds. The Review Board held that "the date on which the claimant first takes steps to effect those repairs" could not be earlier than the date on which works actually commenced. Scott Baker J quashed the Board's decision, holding that to be a wrong approach. The judge had regard to the *Adjudication Officer's Guide*, which stated, in relation to the similar Sch 10 para 28 Income Support (General) Regulations 1987, that the relevant "steps" could include getting a grant or loan to pay for repairs or alterations, employing an architect, getting planning permission or finding someone to do the work, and that the relevant "date" could be the first date on which inquiries about those matters were made. It was a question of fact for the authority as to when the first steps were taken, but the Board's approach was clearly too restrictive and its decision was therefore quashed.

29. Any payment made by the Secretary of State to compensate for the loss of housing benefit supplement under regulation 19 of the Supplementary Benefit (Requirements) Regulations 1983.

30. Any payment made by the Secretary of State to compensate for the loss (in whole or in part) of entitlement to housing benefit.

31. The value of the right to receive an occupational or personal pension.

32. The value of any funds held under a personal pension scheme [¹].

Amendment

1. Amended by reg 4(7) of SI 2007 No 1749 as from 16.7.07.

33. The value of the right to receive any rent except where the claimant has a reversionary interest in the property in respect of which rent is due.

34. Any payment in kind made by a charity or under the Macfarlane (Special Payments) Trust, the Macfarlane (Special Payments) (No. 2) Trust, [¹ the Fund, the Independent Living (1993) Fund or the Independent Living Fund (2006)].

Amendments

1.   Amended by Art 8(3) of SI 2007 No 2538 as from 1.10.07.

Analysis

The implication of this para is that (except where the claimant is "on income support or an income-based jobseeker's allowance" see Sch 4 para 12, Sch 5 paras 4 and 5 and Sch 6 paras 5 and 6) other, non-charitable capital payments in kind are to be taken into account. The regulations provide no mechanism for quantifying the value of other payments in kind.

---

35.   Any payment made pursuant to section 2 of the 1973 Act or section 2 of the Enterprise and New Towns (Scotland) Act 1990, but only for the period of 52 weeks beginning on the date of receipt of the payment.

36.   Any community charge benefit.

37.   Any payment in consequence of a reduction of council tax under section 13 or, as the case may be, section 80 of the Local Government Finance Act 1992 (reduction of liability for council tax), but only for a period of 52 weeks from the date of the receipt of the payment.

38.   Any grant made to the claimant in accordance with a scheme made under section 129 of the Housing Act 1988 or section 66 of the Housing (Scotland) Act 1988 (schemes for payments to assist local housing authority and local authority tenants to obtain other accommodation) which is to be used–

(a)   to purchase premises intended for occupation as his home; or

(b)   to carry out repairs or alterations which are required to render premises fit for occupation as his home,

for a period of 26 weeks from the date on which he received such a grant or such longer period as is reasonable in the circumstances to enable the purchase, repairs or alterations to be completed and the claimant to commence occupation of those premises as his home.

39.   Any arrears of special war widows payment which is disregarded under paragraph 43 of Schedule 5 (sums to be disregarded in the calculation of income other than earnings) or of any amount which is disregarded under paragraph 53, 54 or 55 of that Schedule, but only for a period of 52 weeks from the date of the receipt of the arrears.

Analysis

This provides for a disregard of Ministry of Defence special payments to pre-1973 war widows for 52 weeks from the date of receipt.

40.–(1)   Any payment or repayment made–

(a)   as respects England, under regulation 5, 6 or 12 of the National Health Service (Travel Expenses and Remission of Charges) Regulations (travelling expenses and health service supplies);

(b)   as respect Wales, under regulation 3, 5 or 8 of the National Health Service (Travelling Expenses and Remission of Charges) Regulations 1988 (travelling expenses and health service supplies);

(c)   as respects Scotland, under regulation 3, 5 or 8 of the National Health Service (Travelling Expenses and Remission of Charges) (Scotland) Regulations 2003 (travelling expenses and health service supplies),

but only for a period of 52 weeks from the date of the receipt of the payment or repayment.

(2)   Any payment or repayment made by the Secretary of State for Health, Scottish Ministers or the National Assembly for Wales, which is analogous to a payment or repayment mentioned in sub-paragraph (1); but only for a period of 52 weeks from the date of the receipt of the payment or repayment.

Analysis

Paras 40-42 provide a disregard on payments made in respect of certain NHS charges (eg, dental and optical treatment), hospital travel costs, payments in lieu of milk tokens or the supply of vitamins, and for assisted prison visits. In all cases the disregard is only for 52 weeks.

---

41.   Any payment made under regulation 6, 8, 12 or 14(2) of the Welfare Food Regulations 1996 (payments made in place of milk tokens or the supply of vitamins) but only for a period of 52 weeks from the date of the receipt of the payment.

42.   Any payment made either by the Secretary of State for [¹ Justice] or Scottish Ministers under a scheme established to assist relatives and other persons to visit persons in custody, but only for a period of 52 weeks from the date of the receipt of the payment.

Amendment

1.   Amended by Art 8 and the Sch para 23 of SI 2007 No 2128 as from 22.8.07.

43. Any payment (other than a training allowance) made, whether by the Secretary of State or any other person, under the Disabled Persons (Employment) Act 1944 or to assist disabled persons to obtain or retain employment despite their disability.

44. Any payment made by a local authority under section 3 of the Disabled Persons (Employment) Act 1958 to homeworkers assisted under the Blind Homeworkers' Scheme.

[¹ **45.** (1) Any sum of capital to which sub-paragraph (2) applies and–

(a) which is administered on behalf of a person by the High Court or the County Court under Rule 21.11(1) of the Civil Procedure Rules 1998 or by the Court of Protection;

(b) which can only be disposed of by order or direction of any such court; or

(c) where the person concerned is under the age of 18, which can only be disposed of by order or direction prior to that person attaining age 18.

(2) This sub-paragraph applies to a sum of capital which is derived from–

(a) an award of damages for a personal injury to that person; or

(b) compensation for the death of one or both parents where the person concerned is under the age of 18.]

Amendment

1. Substituted by reg 15(7)(c) of SI 2006 No 2378 from the 1st day of the 1st benefit week to commence on or after 2.10.06.

Analysis

An adult who receives compensation for personal injuries can prevent it from reducing his entitlement to HB by putting it in a Trust (see para 14). However, where children and young people under 18 are awarded such compensation that is not possible as the money is not paid to them but retained in court until their 18th birthday. Paras 45 and 46 make it clear that compensation paid to children and young people for personal injury or the death of a parent is also disregarded while it is held by the court. At least as far as personal injury compensation is concerned they are probably unnecessary given the unreported decision of a commissioner in *CIS 368/1994*.

---

46. Any sum of capital administered on behalf of a person in accordance with an order made under section 13 of the Children (Scotland) Act 1995 or under Rule 36.14 of the Ordinary Cause Rules 1993 or under Rule 128 of those Rules, where such sum derives from–

(a) award of damages for a personal injury to that person; or

(b) compensation for the death of one or both parents where the person concerned is under the age of 18.

47. Any payment to the claimant as holder of the Victoria Cross or George Cross.

48. The amount of any child maintenance bonus payable by way of jobseeker's allowance or income support in accordance with section 10 of the Child Support Act 1995, or a corresponding payment under Article 4 of the Child Support (Northern Ireland) Order 1995, but only for a period of 52 weeks from the date of receipt.

49. In the case of a person who is receiving, or who has received, assistance under the self-employment route, any sum of capital which is acquired by that person for the purpose of establishing or carrying on the commercial activity in respect of which such assistance is or was received but only for a period of 52 weeks from the date on which that sum was acquired.

Analysis

There were modifications to this provision between November 1999 and November 2001 for New Deal participants. See the commentary in the 14th edition of this book for details.

50.–(1) Any payment of a sports award for a period of 26 weeks from the date of receipt of that payment except to the extent that it has been made in respect of any one or more of the items specified in sub-paragraph (2).

(2) The items specified for the purposes of sub-paragraph (1) are food, ordinary clothing or footwear, household fuel or rent of the claimant or, where the claimant is a member of a family, any other member of his family, or any council tax or water charges for which that claimant or member is liable.

(3) For the purposes of sub-paragraph (2)–

"food" does not include vitamins, minerals or other special dietary supplements intended to enhance the performance of the person in the sport in respect of which the award was made;

"rent" means eligible rent less any deductions in respect of non-dependants which fall to be made under regulation 74 (non-dependant deductions).

Analysis

See Sch 5 para 59.

51.–(1)   Any payment–
(a)   by way of an education maintenance allowance made pursuant to–
    (i)   regulations made under section 518 of the Education Act 1996 (payment of school expenses; grant of scholarships etc);
    (ii)   regulations made under section 49 or 73(f) of the Education (Scotland) Act 1980 (power to assist persons to take advantage of educational facilities);
    (iii)   directions made under sections 12(2)(c) and 21 of the Further and Higher Education (Scotland) Act 1992 (provision of financial assistance to students); or
(b)   corresponding to such an education maintenance allowance, made pursuant to–
    (i)   section 14 or section 181 of the Education Act 2002 (power of Secretary of State and National Assembly for Wales to give financial assistance for purposes related to education or childcare, and allowances in respect of education or training); or
    (ii)   regulations made under section 181 of that Act.
(2)   Any payment, other than a payment to which sub-paragraph (1) applies, made pursuant to–
(a)   regulations made under section 518 of the Education Act 1996;
(b)   regulations made under section 49 of the Education (Scotland) Act 1980; or
(c)   directions made under sections 12(2)(c) and 21 of the Further and Higher Education (Scotland) Act 1992,
in respect of a course of study attended by a child or a young person or a person who is in receipt of an education maintenance allowance made pursuant to any provision specified in sub-paragraph (1).

Analysis
See Sch 5 para 11.

52.   In the case of a claimant participating in an employment zone programme, any discretionary payment made by an employment zone contractor to the claimant, being a fee, grant, loan or otherwise, but only for the period of 52 weeks from the date of receipt of the payment.

Analysis
Under paras 52 and 53, discretionary payments made to claimants who are participating in an employment zone programme, by an employment zone contractor (as defined in reg 2(1)) are disregarded for 52 weeks from the date of the payment, as is subsistence allowance (again, as defined in reg 2(1)).

53.   Any arrears of subsistence allowance paid as a lump sum but only for the period of 52 weeks from the date of receipt of the payment.
54.   Where an ex-gratia payment of £10,000 has been made by the Secretary of State on or after 1st February 2001 in consequence of the imprisonment or interment of–
(a)   the claimant;
(b)   the claimant's partner;
(c)   the claimant's deceased spouse or deceased civil partner; or
(d)   the claimant's partner's deceased spouse or deceased civil partner,
by the Japanese during the Second World War, £10,000.

Analysis
The ex gratia payment of £10,000 made to former Japanese prisoners of war is disregarded in full and indefinitely.

55.–(1)   Subject to sub-paragraph (2), the amount of any trust payment made to a claimant or a member of a claimant's family who is–
(a)   a diagnosed person;
(b)   the diagnosed person's partner or the person who was the diagnosed person's partner at the time of the diagnosed person's death;
(c)   a parent of a diagnosed person, a person acting in place of the diagnosed person's parents or a person who was so acting at the date of the diagnosed person's death; or
(d)   a member of the diagnosed person's family (other than his partner) or a person who was a member of the diagnosed person's family (other than his partner) at the date of the diagnosed person's death.
(2)   Where a trust payment is made to–
(a)   a person referred to in sub-paragraph (1)(a) or (b), that sub-paragraph shall apply for the period beginning on the date on which the trust payment is made and ending on the date on which that person dies;
(b)   a person referred to in sub-paragraph (1)(c), that sub-paragraph shall apply for the period beginning on the date on which the trust payment is made and ending two years after that date;

(c) a person referred to in sub-paragraph (1)(d), that sub-paragraph shall apply for the period beginning on the date on which the trust payment is made and ending–
  (i) two years after that date; or
  (ii) on the day before the day on which that person–
    (aa) ceases receiving full-time education; or
    (bb) attains the age of [¹ 20],
whichever is the latest.

(3) Subject to sub-paragraph (4), the amount of any payment by a person to whom a trust payment has been made or of any payment out of the estate of a person to whom a trust payment has been made, which is made to a claimant or a member of a claimant's family who is–

(a) the diagnosed person's partner or the person who was the diagnosed person's partner at the date of the diagnosed person's death;

(b) a parent of a diagnosed person, a person acting in place of the diagnosed person's parents or a person who was so acting at the date of the diagnosed person's death; or

(c) a member of the diagnosed person's family (other than his partner) or a person who was a member of the diagnosed person's family (other than his partner) at the date of the diagnosed person's death,

but only to the extent that such payments do not exceed the total amount of any trust payments made to that person.

(4) Where a payment as referred to in sub-paragraph (3) is made to–

(a) a person referred to in sub-paragraph (3)(a), that sub-paragraph shall apply for the period beginning on the date on which that payment is made and ending on the date on which that person dies;

(b) a person referred to in sub-paragraph (3)(b), that sub-paragraph shall apply for the period beginning on the date on which that payment is made and ending two years after that date; or

(c) a person referred to in sub-paragraph (3)(c), that sub-paragraph shall apply for the period beginning on the date on which that payment is made and ending–
  (i) two years after that date; or
  (ii) on the day before the day on which that person–
    (aa) ceases receiving full-time education; or
    (bb) attains the age of [¹ 20],
whichever is the latest.

(5) In this paragraph, a reference to a person–

(a) being the diagnosed person's partner;

(b) being a member of a diagnosed person's family;

(c) acting in place of the diagnosed person's parents,

at the date of the diagnosed person's death shall include a person who would have been such a person or a person who would have been so acting, but for the diagnosed person residing in a care home, an Abbeyfield Home or an independent hospital on that date.

(6) In this paragraph–

"diagnosed person" means a person who has been diagnosed as suffering from, or who, after his death, has been diagnosed as having suffered from, variant Creutzfeld-Jakob disease;

"relevant trust" means a trust established out of funds provided by the Secretary of State in respect of persons who suffered, or who are suffering, from variant Creutzfeld-Jakob disease for the benefit of persons eligible for payments in accordance with its provisions;

"trust payment" means a payment under a relevant trust.

Amendment

1.   Amended by reg 4(5) of SI 2006 No 718 as from 10.4.06.

Analysis

These provisions provide a complex disregard covering payments from trusts (referred to as "relevant trusts") set up by the Secretary of State to compensate those suffering from variant Creutzfeldt-Jakob disease. Part of the reason for the complexity is that some people may only be diagnosed as suffering from that disease after they are dead and payments from such trusts may therefore need to be made to other family members.

Where a payment is made to someone who has the disease her/himself ("the diagnosed person") or to that person's partner or to a person who was the partner of a diagnosed person when the latter died, the disregard lasts for the life of the payee. In other cases, the disregard lasts for two years unless the payee is a child or young person for whom the diagnosed person is (or was at the date of her/his death) responsible: in the latter case, the period of the disregard ends on the day before the child or young person's 20th birthday, or the day before s/he leaves full-time education or two years from the date of payment, whichever is the latest. See para (5) for an extension of the definitions of "partner", member of the "family" and person acting in place of parents for these purposes.

Sub-para (3) establishes a similar disregard for payments made *by* a diagnosed person who has received money from a relevant trust to any of the people listed in heads (a) to (c). This includes payments made from the diagnosed person's estate after her/his death. The maximum amount which can be disregarded under subpara (3) is the total sum received by the diagnosed person from any relevant trust.

56. The amount of any payment, other than a war pension within the meaning of section 25 of the Social Security Act 1989, to compensate for the fact that the claimant, the claimant's partner, the claimant's deceased spouse or deceased civil partner or the claimant's partner's deceased spouse or deceased civil partner–

(a)   was a slave labourer or a forced labourer;

(b)   had suffered property loss or had suffered personal injury; or

(c)   was a parent of a child who had died,

during the Second World War.

Analysis

This paragraph provides a capital disregard of the amount of payments made to people who were slaves or forced labourers, suffered property loss or personal injury, or who were parents of a child who died during the Second World War. The disregard lasts for an unlimited time and even if there is a break in the claimant's benefit entitlement. It is additional to any other disregard, including the disregard for pensions for victims of persecution under Sch 5 para 15(g).

57.–(1)   Any payment made by a local authority, or by the National Assembly for Wales, to or on behalf of the claimant or his partner relating to a service which is provided to develop or sustain the capacity of the claimant or his partner to live independently in his accommodation.

(2)   For the purposes of sub-paragraph (1) "local authority" includes in England a county council.

Analysis

See Sch 5 para 63.

58. Any payment made under the Community Care (Direct Payments) Act 1996, or regulations made under section 57 of the Health and Social Care Act 2001 or under section 12B of the Social Work (Scotland) Act 1968.

Analysis

See Sch 5 para 57.

59. Any payment made to the claimant pursuant to regulations under section 2(6)(b), 3 or 4 of the Adoption and Children Act 2002.

60. Any payment made to the claimant in accordance with regulations made pursuant to section 14F of the Children Act 1989 (special guardianship support services).

SCHEDULE 7
REGULATION 72 AND 80(7)
Extended payments of housing benefit

General Note

This Schedule, together with reg 72, sets out the rules for "extended payments" of HB. Certain people can get an extra four weeks of HB when entitlement to IS or income-based JSA ceases when they return to work or increase earnings from, or hours of, work. An extended payment can be made where:

(1)   The claimant ceases to be entitled to housing benefit in accordance with reg 77 (or because s/he moved home in specific circumstances).

(2)   All the requirements of paras 1 and 2 of Sch 7 are met.

See also reg 73 and Sch 8 for extended payments where severe disablement allowance or incapacity benefit entitlement ceases on a return to work.

Note that by reg 5(2) this regulation and Sch 7 can apply to a person even if s/he or her/his partner has reached the qualifying age for PC.

PART 1
Conditions for an extended payment

1. The conditions prescribed in this paragraph are that the Secretary of State has certified to the relevant authority–

   (a)   that the claimant or his partner was entitled to and in receipt of income support or an income-based jobseeker's allowance or that the claimant and his partner were entitled to and in receipt of a joint-claim jobseeker's allowance and that entitlement has ceased;

   (b)   the relevant day in his case;

   (c)   that entitlement to income support or an income-based jobseeker's allowance had ceased by reason of the claimant or his partner–

       (i)   commencing employment as an employed or self-employed earner; or

       (ii)   increasing their earnings from such employment; or

       (iii) increasing the number of hours worked in such employment; and

   (d)   that the claimant had been entitled to and in receipt of income support or a jobseeker's allowance for a continuous period of at least 26 weeks until the relevant day, and for the purpose of this head–

       (i)   a claimant satisfies the conditions of this sub-paragraph if he has been entitled to and in receipt of a combination of income support and a jobseeker's allowance for at least 26 weeks and for the purposes of this sub-paragraph, a reference to the claimant being entitled to and in receipt of a jobseeker's allowance shall include a reference to the claimant and his partner being entitled to and in receipt of a joint-claim jobseeker's allowance;

       (ii)   the claimant shall be treated as having been entitled to and in receipt of income support or a jobseeker's allowance during any period of less than 5 weeks in respect of which he was not entitled to either of those benefits because, as a consequence of his participation in an employment zone programme, he was engaged in remunerative work; and

       (iii) references to the claimant include references to his partner.

Analysis

Para 1 sets out four matters which must be certified by the Secretary of State. There is no appeal against a failure by the Secretary of State to certify these matters and hence a Tribunal cannot offset a supposed entitlement to extended payments against an overpayment of benefit: *CH 5553/2002* paras 15-18. The matters that must be certified are:

   (1)   That the claimant or her/his partner was, but is no longer, entitled to IS, income-based JSA or joint claim JSA: sub-para (a).

   (2)   The "relevant day" in the claimant's case, defined in para 11 as the day on which entitlement to IS or income-based JSA ceased: sub-para (b).

   (3)   That IS or income-based JSA stopped because the claimant (or her/his partner) started employment or, if s/he was already in part-time work, because her/his hours or earnings increased: sub-para (c).

   (4)   That the claimant or her/his partner had been continuously entitled to IS or income-based JSA for at least 26 weeks, subject to the linking rules set out: sub-para (d).

---

   2.   The conditions prescribed in this paragraph are that the claimant or the claimant's partner–

   (a)   notifies either the designated office or an appropriate DWP office that he or his partner–

       (i)   has commenced , or is about to commence, remunerative work;

       (ii)   has commenced, or is about to commence, receiving remuneration for work or an increased amount of remuneration for work; or

       (iii) has commenced, or is about to commence, an increased number of hours of work,

so that entitlement to income support or to an income-based jobseeker's allowance ceases and that work or, as the case may be, remuneration, is expected to last 5 weeks or more; and

   (b)   makes that notification no later than 4 weeks after the day on which the claimant or his partner first undertakes the remunerative work referred to in sub-paragraph (a)(i) or first receives remuneration for the work or an increased amount of remuneration for the work referred to in sub-paragraph (a)(ii), or first commences the increased number of hours of work referred to in sub-paragraph (a)(iii).

Analysis

Under para 2, the claimant or her/his partner must notify the local authority or the DWP that s/he has started work or increased her/his remuneration or hours (or that this is about to happen) within four weeks and that the work or increased remuneration is expected to last five weeks or more. So, although there is no requirement to make a claim for extended payments, where someone fails to make the notifications required by para 2 in the time allowed s/he will not meet all the conditions of entitlement to extended payments (see reg 72(1)).

PART 2
Calculation and payment of an extended payment

3.–(1)   Subject to the following provisions of this paragraph and except in the case of a mover, the amount of the extended payment shall be equal to the amount of housing benefit which was payable to the claimant for the last benefit week before he ceased to be entitled to housing benefit.

(2)   In a case where the last benefit week referred to in sub-paragraph (1) fell, in whole or in part, within a rent free period, the last benefit week for the purposes of that sub-paragraph shall be taken to be the last benefit week that did not fall within a rent free period.

(3)   Where the last benefit week before he ceased to be entitled to housing benefit was a week in which the claimant's eligible rent was calculated in accordance with regulation 80(4)(c) (claimant ceases to occupy the dwelling as his home), sub-paragraph (1) shall have effect as if the reference to the last benefit week before he ceased to be entitled to housing benefit was a reference to the week before that week.

(4)   Subject to sub-paragraph (5) the extended payment shall be payable for each of the weeks in the period specified in regulation 72(6) and shall be paid at such time and in such manner as is appropriate, having regard to–

(a)   the times at which and the frequency with which a person's liability to make payment of rent arises; and

(b)   the reasonable needs and convenience of the person entitled thereto.

(5)   No extended payment shall be payable for a week which is a rent free period for the purposes of regulation 81(1).

Analysis

Para 3 provides that extended payments are to be made for the period specified in reg 72(6) at the same weekly rate which was payable for the last benefit week before entitlement to HB ceased. If the entitlement in the last week was reduced because it fell in a rent-free period or because the claimant moved during a benefit week and reg 80(4)(c) applies, then that week (and any other rent-free weeks) are ignored. Extended payments cannot be paid during a rent-free period: sub-para(5).

See also the analysis to reg 72(3).

Movers

4.   Paragraphs 5 to 7 below apply to movers from–

(a)   the day the move takes place where that day is a Monday; or

(b)   from the Monday following the day the move takes place where that day is not a Monday.

Analysis

Paras 4 to 9 deal with the entitlement to extended payments of "movers" as defined by para 11.

If the claimant moves to privately-rented property, the extended payment is calculated as if s/he had not moved. If the move was from other than local authority accommodation the payment is made by the authority which used to pay HB; if from a council property the payment is made by the authority for the area in which the new home is situated.

If the claimant moves to local authority accommodation, the extended payment is always made by the authority which is responsible for the new property. The amount of the extended payment is calculated using the rent for the new home but the non-dependent deductions which were applied when calculating the *old* HB claim.

See also the analysis to reg 72(3)

Movers and rent allowances

5.–(1)   Subject to sub-paragraph (2), in the case of a mover whose housing benefit was in the form of a rent allowance, the authority which, prior to the mover ceasing to be entitled to housing benefit, was paying that allowance, shall make an extended payment to that mover calculated on the same basis as in paragraph 3 and, for these purposes, the mover shall be treated as continuing to occupy and be liable to make payments in respect of the dwelling he was occupying as his home immediately before he ceased to be entitled to housing benefit.

(2)   Notwithstanding sub-paragraph (1), in a case where that mover's liability to make payments in respect of the second dwelling would be to a housing authority, any extended payment shall be made by that housing authority and shall be determined as provided in paragraph 7(b).

Movers and rent rebates

6.   Where, in a case of a mover–

(a)   his housing benefit was in the form of a rent rebate; and

(b)   he claims an extended payment,

the authority in which the second dwelling is situated or, as the case may be, where the mover's liability to make payments in respect of the second dwelling is to a housing authority, that housing authority, shall upon receiving the mover's claim for an extended payment, which meets the requirements of regulation 72(1), make an extended payment, calculated in accordance with paragraph 7, to that mover.

Movers and extended payments

7.   In a case to which paragraph 5(2) or 6 applies and a mover's liability referred to in that paragraph is–

(a)   other than to a housing authority, the extended payment shall be a payment by way of rent allowance calculated in accordance with paragraph 3;

(b)   to a housing authority, the extended payment shall be by way of a rent rebate to the value of such part of the rent in respect of the period specified in regulation 72(6) as is eligible for housing benefit, calculated in accordance with regulations 11 to 13, less, in a case where the rebate to which paragraph 6 refers, or the rent allowance to which paragraph 5 refers, as the case may be, was subject to any deductions in respect of non-dependants pursuant to regulations 70 (maximum housing benefit) and 74 (non-dependant deductions), the amount of those deductions.

Maximum housing benefit

8.   In a case to which sub-paragraph 7(b) applies the maximum housing benefit of a mover shall be calculated in accordance with regulation 70, save that no deduction shall be made in respect of non-dependants, other than any that fall to be taken into account pursuant to that sub-paragraph.

Movers with two homes

9.   Subject to Part 3 of this Schedule, any extended payment under this Part shall be without prejudice to any entitlement the claimant may have pursuant to regulation 7(6) (liability to make payments in respect of two homes).

Analysis

A claimant may be entitled to both an extended payment and to HB where s/he would have been entitled to HB for two homes under reg 7(6). Para 9 ensures that both can be paid in this situation. Note that the heading of para 9 is misleading: the rule in reg 7(6) is not restricted to "movers".

PART 3
Adjustment of entitlement in respect of an extended payment

10.   Where for any week–

(a)   a person is entitled to an extended payment; and

(b)   he also claims and is awarded housing benefit,

then the amount of the housing benefit payable in respect of that week shall be reduced by a sum equal to the amount of the extended payment and only the balance (if any) shall be payable to him for that week.

Analysis

A claimant might claim (and be awarded) HB for the same period in which s/he is entitled to an extended payment. Reg 80(7) requires adjustment of HB entitlement where a claimant has received an extended payment. Para 10 ensures that where an award of HB is made, the amount of the extended payment is offset against the amount of HB payable and only the balance is payable. Note that there are situations where a claimant might be entitled to a higher rate of HB on their "in work" claim, than the rate of her/his extended payment – eg, where a non-dependant moves out, or rent increases. The net effect in this case, is that the extended payment is topped up to the level of the new HB entitlement.

PART 4
Interpretation

11.   In this Schedule–

"claimant" means a person claiming an extended payment;

"mover" means a claimant who changes the dwelling which he occupies as his home in respect of which he is liable or treated as liable to make payments;

"the relevant day" means the day on which the claimant's entitlement to income support or an income-based jobseeker's allowance ceased; and

"second dwelling" means the dwelling to which a person has moved or is about to move which he is or will be occupying as his new home, and where the liability to make payments of rent in respect of his dwelling follows on immediately from the liability to make payments in respect of rent of his previous dwelling.

SCHEDULE 8
REGULATION 73
Extended Payments (severe disablement allowance and incapacity benefit) of housing benefit

Condition for an extended payment (severe disablement allowance and incapacity benefit)

1. The condition prescribed in this paragraph is that the claimant or the claimant's partner–

(a) notifies either the designated office or an appropriate DWP office that he or his partner–
- (i) has commenced, or is about to commence, remunerative work;
- (ii) has commenced, or is about to commence, receiving remuneration for work or an increased amount of remuneration for work; or
- (iii) has commenced, or is about to commence, an increased number of hours of work,

so that entitlement to severe disablement allowance or incapacity benefit ceases and that work, or as the case may be, remuneration, is expected to last 5 weeks or more; and

(b) the notification is made no later than 4 weeks after the day on which the claimant or his partner first undertakes the remunerative work referred to in sub-paragraph (a)(i), first receives remuneration for the work or an increased amount of remuneration for the work referred to in sub-paragraph (a)(ii), or first commences the increased number of hours of work referred to in sub-paragraph (a)(iii).

Calculation and payment of an extended payment (severe disablement allowance and incapacity benefit)

2.–(1) Subject to the following provisions of this paragraph and except in the case of a mover, the amount of the extended payment (severe disablement allowance and incapacity benefit) shall be equal to the amount of housing benefit which was payable to the claimant for the last benefit week before he ceased to be entitled to housing benefit.

(2) In a case where the last benefit week referred to in sub-paragraph (1) fell, in whole or in part, within a rent free period, the last benefit week for the purposes of that sub-paragraph shall be taken to be the last benefit week that did not fall within a rent free period.

(3) Where the last benefit week before he ceased to be entitled to housing benefit was a week in which the claimant's eligible rent was calculated in accordance with regulation 80(4)(c) (claimant ceases to occupy the dwelling as his home), sub-paragraph (1) shall have effect as if the reference to the last benefit week before he ceased to be entitled to housing benefit was a reference to the week before that week.

(4) Subject to sub-paragraph (5), the extended payment (severe disablement allowance and incapacity benefit) shall be payable for each of the weeks in the period specified in regulation 73(6)(a), and shall be paid at such time and in such manner as is appropriate, having regard to–

(a) the times at which and the frequency with which a person's liability to make payment of rent arises; and

(b) the reasonable needs and convenience of the person entitled thereto.

(5) No extended payment (severe disablement allowance and incapacity benefit) shall be payable for a week which is a rent free period for the purposes of regulation 81(1).

Movers

3. Paragraphs 4 to 6 below apply to movers from–

(a) the day the move takes place where that day is a Monday; or

(b) the Monday following the day the move takes place where that day is not a Monday.

Movers and rent allowances

4.–(1) Subject to sub-paragraph (2), in the case of a mover whose housing benefit was in the form of a rent allowance, the authority which, prior to the mover ceasing to be entitled to housing benefit, was paying that allowance, shall make an extended payment (severe disablement allowance and incapacity benefit) to that mover calculated on the same basis as in paragraph 2, and, for these purposes, the mover shall be treated as continuing to occupy and be liable to make payments in respect of the dwelling he was occupying as his home immediately before he ceased to be entitled to housing benefit.

(2) Notwithstanding sub-paragraph (1), in a case where that mover's liability to make payments in respect of the second dwelling would be to a housing authority, any extended payment (severe disablement allowance and incapacity benefit) shall be made by that housing authority and shall be determined as provided in paragraph 6(b).

Movers and rent rebates

5. Where, in the case of a mover–

(a)   his housing benefit was in the form of a rent rebate; and

(b)   he claims an extended payment (severe disablement allowance and incapacity benefit),

the authority in which the second dwelling is situated, or as the case may be, where the mover's liability to make payments in respect of the second dwelling is to a housing authority, that housing authority, shall upon receiving the mover's claim for an extended payment (severe disablement allowance and incapacity benefit), which meets the requirements of regulation 73(1), make an extended payment (severe disablement allowance and incapacity benefit), calculated in accordance with paragraph 6, to that mover.

Movers and extended payments (severe disablement allowance and incapacity benefit)

6.   In a case to which paragraph 4(2) or 5 applies and where a mover's liability referred to in that paragraph is–

(a)   other than to a housing authority, the extended payment (severe disablement allowance and incapacity benefit) shall be a payment by way of rent allowance calculated in accordance with paragraph 2;

(b)   to a housing authority, the extended payment (severe disablement allowance and incapacity benefit) shall be by way of a rent rebate to the value of the lesser of–

(i)   such part of the rent in respect of the period specified in regulation 73(6)(a) as is eligible for housing benefit, calculated in accordance with regulations 11 to 13, less, in a case where the rebate to which paragraph 5 refers, or the rent allowance to which paragraph 4 refers, as the case may be, was subject to any deductions in respect of non-dependants pursuant to regulations 70 and 74, the amount of those deductions; or

(ii)   the amount of extended payment (severe disablement allowance and incapacity benefit) calculated in accordance with paragraph 2.

Maximum housing benefit

7.   The maximum housing benefit of a mover the amount of whose extended payment (severe disablement allowance and incapacity benefit) is calculated in accordance with paragraph 6(b)(i) shall be calculated in accordance with regulation 70, save that no deduction shall be made in respect of non-dependants, other than any that fall to be taken into account pursuant to paragraph 6(b)(i).

Movers with two homes

8.   Subject to paragraph 9, any extended payment (severe disablement allowance and incapacity benefit) shall be without prejudice to any entitlement the claimant may have pursuant to regulation 7(6) (liability to make payments in respect of two homes).

Adjustment of entitlement in respect of an extended payment (severe disablement allowance and incapacity benefit)

9.   Where for any week–

(a)   a person is entitled to an extended payment (severe disablement allowance and incapacity benefit); and

(b)   he also claims and is awarded housing benefit,

then the amount of the housing benefit payable in respect of that week shall be reduced by a sum equal to the amount of the extended payment (severe disablement allowance and incapacity benefit) and only the balance, if any, shall be payable to him for that week.

Interpretation

10.   In this Schedule–

"claimant" means a person claiming an extended payment (severe disablement allowance and incapacity benefit);

"mover" means a claimant who changes the dwelling which he occupies as his home in respect of which he is liable or treated as liable to make payments;

"second dwelling" means the dwelling to which a person has moved, or is about to move, which he is or will be occupying as his new home, and where the liability to make payments of rent in respect of his dwelling follows on immediately from the liability to make payments of rent in respect of his previous dwelling.

SCHEDULE 9
REGULATION 90
Matters to be included in decision notice

Definitions

"applicable amount" – see Part 5.

"claimant" – see reg 2(1).

"earnings" – see regs 35 and 37.
"eligible rent" – see Part 3.
"income" – see General Note on Section 2 of Part 6.
"non-dependant" – see reg 3.
"rent allowance" "rent rebate" – see s134(1A) and (1B) SSAA.

General Note on Schedule 9

This lists matters to be included in written notices of decision issued to "persons affected" following decisions of a relevant authority: see reg 90. Many authorities fail to provide all the information required by the various Parts of the Schedule. See the Analysis to reg 90 above for the effects of a failure to provide the necessary information. Note that reg 10(1) D&A Regs may require the inclusion of additional information where a decision carries a right of appeal.

There are seven parts specifying information to be included in a notice in different circumstances:

(1)   Part 1 lists general matters which *always* need to appear within the terms of a notice of decision.

(2)   Part 2 applies only to notifications of a successful claim made by an IS or income-based JSA recipient. See Part 6 below where no HB award is made.

(3)   Part 3 applies only to notifications on a successful claim, this time when the claimant does not receive IS or income-based JSA. See Part 6 below where no HB award is made.

(4)   Part 4 applies where the authority has used its powers under regs 95 and 96 to pay HB direct to a landlord, whether or not on the decision of a claim.

(5)   Part 5 applies when the authority uses its powers to treat a non-dependant's income as if it was the claimant's under reg 26.

(6)   Part 6 only applies to notices informing a claimant that a claim for HB has been unsuccessful.

(7)   Part 7 applies to notifications informing a person affected that s/he has been overpaid where the overpayment is recoverable under reg 100.

PART 1
General

1.   The statement of matters to be included in any decision notice issued by a relevant authority to a person, and referred to in regulation 90 (notification of decisions) and in regulation 10 of the Decisions and Appeals Regulations are those matters set out in the following provisions of this Schedule.

Analysis

Para 1 makes it clear that the requirements of the Schedule are mandatory. They are not optional and they are not to be seen by authorities as a piece of unnecessary bureaucracy. Clear notices will assist claimants in understanding how a decision has been reached and will reduce confusion and dispute. On the question of validity of notifications, see the Analysis to reg 90(1).

The requirements apply to decision notices issued under reg 90 and also under reg 10 D&A Regs. They apply both to initial decisions and decisions following revision or supersession, except as otherwise stated.

2.   Every decision notice shall include a statement as to the right of any person affected by that decision to request a written statement under regulation 90(2) (requests for statement of reasons) and the manner and time in which to do so.

Analysis

Para 2 requires every notice to state that persons affected have the right to request a statement of reasons under reg 90(2), and the time limit within, and manner in which, this must be done. This applies to initial and decisions following a revision or supersession. For the meaning of "person affected" see reg 2(1).

3.   Every decision notice shall include a statement as to the right of any person affected by that decision to make an application for a revision in accordance with regulation 4(1)(a) of the Decisions and Appeals Regulations and, where appropriate, to appeal against that decision and the manner and time in which to do so.

Analysis

Para 3 requires every notice to set out the right to seek a revision under reg 4 of the D&A Regs. Note also reg 10 D&A Regs which specifies when a "person affected" must be notified of her/his right of appeal.

4.   Every decision notice following an application for a revision in accordance with regulation 4(1)(a) of the Decisions and Appeals Regulations shall include a statement as to whether the original decision in respect of which the person made his representations has been confirmed or revised and where the relevant authority has not revised the decision the reasons why not.

Analysis
If a claimant has requested a revision of an authority's decision under reg 4(1)(a) (an "any grounds" revision), this paragraph specifies the matters which must be included in the notice informing the person affected of the authority's decision on revision. Reasons need be given only where the authority decides not to revise its original decision, but note the separate right to request reasons for a decision under reg 10 D&A Regs where there is a right of appeal against a decision.

5.   Every decision notice following an application for a revision in accordance with regulation 4(1)(a) of the Decisions and Appeals Regulations shall, if the original decision has been revised, include a statement as to the right of any person affected by that decision to apply for a revision in accordance with regulation 4(1)(a) of those Regulations and the manner and time in which to do so.

Analysis
Para 5 specifies that the notice sent out following an application for a revision shall mention the right of any other person affected to apply for a further revision.

6.   An authority may include in the decision notice any other matters not prescribed by this Schedule which it sees fit, whether expressly or by reference to some other document available without charge to the person.

Analysis
The authority is not restricted to giving the information set out in the Schedule and there will be cases in which further information is appropriate.

7.   Parts 2, 3 and 6 of this Schedule shall apply only to the decision notice given on a claim.
8.   Where a decision notice is given following a revision of an earlier decision–
(a)   made of the authority's own motion which results in a revision of that earlier decision; or
(b)   made following an application for a revision in accordance with regulation 4(1)(a) of the Decisions and Appeals Regulations, whether or not resulting in a revision of that earlier decision,
that notice shall, subject to paragraph 6, contain a statement only as to all the matters revised.

Analysis
Para 8 refers to the notices covered by paras 4 and 5, whether or not the authority's decision is to revise. It also covers, by sub-para (a), notices which are issued following an authority's own decision to revise a decision.
The interaction of this paragraph with paras 4 and 5 is not totally clear, but the net effect seems to be that, apart from the factors listed in these paragraphs, the authority should not put information about matters which were not involved in the revision in the notice. The exception is those matters that it sees fit to include under para 6, to which para 8 is expressly subject. Para 6 is sufficiently wide, however, to completely negate para 8.

PART 2
Awards where income support or an income-based jobseeker's allowance is payable
9.   Where a person on income support or an income-based jobseeker's allowance is awarded housing benefit, the decision notice shall include a statement as to–
(a)   his weekly eligible rent, if any; and
(b)   the amount and an explanation of any deduction made under paragraph 6(2) or (3) of Schedule 1 (fuel deductions), if any, and that the deduction may be varied if he provides to the authority evidence on which it may estimate the actual or approximate amount of that service charge; and
(c)   the amount of and the category of non-dependant deductions made under regulation 74, if any; and
(d)   the normal weekly amount of rent allowance, or rent rebate as the case may be, to which he is entitled; and
(e)   in the case of a rent allowance or a rent rebate paid as if it were a rent allowance, the day of payment, and the period in respect of which payment of that allowance is to be made; and
(f)   the first day of entitlement to an allowance or rebate; and
(g)   his duty to notify any change of circumstances which might affect his entitlement to, or the amount of, housing benefit and (without prejudice to the extent of the duty owed under

regulation 88 (duty to notify changes of circumstances)) the kind of change of circumstances which is to be notified, either upon the notice or by reference to some other document available to him on application and without charge.

Analysis

IS and JSA claimants may claim HB via a local DWP office or Jobcentre Plus office. Where one of those benefits is claimed, much of the authority's decision-making is simplified because it has no need to consider the question of the claimant's resources. However, the relevant authority is still responsible for taking all decisions on the HB claim (except those expressly reserved to someone else under these regulations or the primary legislation) and, by virtue of reg 90 and the D&A Regs, for issuing notices of those decisions.

The requirements of Pt 2 only apply to initial decisions following a claim: see para 7. Moreover, they only apply to notices sent when the claimant is on IS or income-based JSA and *successfully* claims HB. If HB is refused, see Part 6. Paras 2, 3 and 6 of Pt 1 of this Schedule also apply.

The following sub-paras specify the necessary information:

(a)   The weekly eligible rent: see Part 3 HB Regs.

(b)   The amount of any deductions made under Sch 1 para 6 in respect of fuel charges and the fact that the deductions may be varied if material is provided to allow the authority to estimate the service charge.

(c)   The amount and type of non-dependant deductions under reg 74. See reg 3 for the question of who is a non-dependant.

(d)   The weekly amount of rent allowance or rent rebate: see Part 8 HB regs.

(e)   In the case of rent allowance, or a rent rebate that is paid to the claimant as if it were, the day of payment and period in respect of which payment is made: see Part 12 HB Regs.

(f)   The first day of entitlement: see reg 76.

(g)   Notification of the duty to notify changes of circumstances: see reg 88. The authority is obliged to give examples of the kinds of changes that must be notified. It would appear that it is also obliged to make it clear that the obligation under reg 88 is a general one and that the examples are just that. A failure to make such a statement could well constitute an "official error" for the purposes of overpayment recoverability: see reg 100. It may also affect the question of whether the claimant could reasonably be expected to know that s/he was being overpaid.

PART 3
Awards where no income support or an income-based jobseeker's allowance is payable

10.   Where a person is not on income support or on an income-based jobseeker's allowance but is awarded housing benefit, the decision notice shall include a statement as to–

(a)   the matters set out in paragraph 9; and

(b)   his applicable amount and how it is calculated; and

(c)   his weekly earnings; and

(d)   his weekly income other than earnings.

Analysis

In addition to the information set out in para 9 above, additional information must be given where the claimant gets HB but is not on IS or income-based JSA, since the authority is required to carry out its own assessment of the claimant's resources. The following information is required, in addition to the matters in paras 2, 3, 6 and 9:

(1)   The applicable amount and "how it is calculated": sub-para (a). This means that the applicable amount itself must be stated, but a full breakdown should also be given of to which personal allowances and premiums the claimant is entitled.

(2)   The claimant's weekly earnings: see regs 29, 30, 35 and 37.

(3)   The claimant's weekly income other than earnings: see regs 31 and 40.

It is curious that there is no requirement to state the amount of the capital that the claimant has. If there is capital between the lower limit and £16,000 and tariff income is calculated, without showing the source of the income, the claimant may well be left mystified.

PART 4
Awards where direct payments made to landlords

11.   Where a decision has been made under regulation 95 or 96 (circumstances in which payment is to be made, or may be made, direct to a landlord), the decision notice shall include a statement–

(a)   as to the amount of housing benefit which is to be paid direct to the landlord and the date from which it is to be paid; and

(b)   informing the landlord of the duty imposed upon him to notify the local authority of–

(i)   any change in circumstances which might affect the claimant's entitlement to housing benefit, or the amount of housing benefit payable in his case; and

(ii)   the kind of change of circumstances which is to be notified;

(c)   informing both landlords and claimants that where a payment of housing benefit is recoverable from a landlord and the recovery is made from housing benefit payable to the landlord to discharge (in whole or in part) an obligation owed to him by a claimant, then, in a case where that claimant is not the person on whose behalf the recoverable amount was paid, that obligation shall nonetheless be taken to be discharged by the amount so recovered,

and the notice shall be sent both to the claimant and to the landlord.

Analysis

The requirements as to content were substantially increased following the changes made by the Social Security Administration (Fraud) Act 1997 and the secondary legislation made thereunder.

"Landlord" in this paragraph has the same meaning as in reg 95: see para 12 below. The notice must be sent to both the landlord and the claimant and must contain the following information, in addition to the matters in paras 2, 3 and 6:

(1)   The amount of HB to be paid direct and the date from which it is to be paid: para 11(a).

(2)   A notification of the landlord's duty to notify changes of circumstances and the kind of changes that are to be notified: para 11(b). See the Analysis to para 9(g) above for commentary on this provision.

(3)   A warning to both landlord and tenant A that if payments in respect of tenant A's HB are withheld to recover an overpayment made to tenant B and recovered from the landlord, then tenant A's obligation is taken to be discharged: para 11(c). This is a consequence of SSAA s75(6). Note also the obligation in reg 107(3) when there is a decision that an overpayment is recoverable from the landlord.

Note that as a decision under reg 95 or reg 96 attracts a right of appeal (see para 1 of the Sch to the D&A Regs), notice of this right and the right to a written statement of reasons for the decision where not already provided) will also be required under reg 10 D&A Regs.

---

12.   In this Schedule, ''landlord'' has the same meaning as in regulation 95.

PART 5
Notice where income of non-dependant is treated as claimant's

13.   Where an authority makes a decision under regulation 26 (circumstances in which income and capital of a non-dependant is to be treated as claimant's) the decision notice shall contain a statement as to—

(a)   the fact that a decision has been made by reference to the income and capital of the claimant's non-dependant; and

(b)   the relevant authority's reasons for making that decision.

Analysis

Reg 26(1) permits an authority to treat a claimant as having a non-dependant's income and capital where it appears that they have entered into an arrangement to take advantage of the HB scheme. See the Analysis to reg 26.

Where such a decision is made, in addition to the matters in paras 2, 3 and 6, the decision notice must state the fact that reg 26(1) has been utilised and the reasons for making that decision, an unhelpfully vague phrase. It is suggested that authorities should give the following information:

(1)   The fact that it appears that the claimant and the non-dependant (who should be identified) have entered into an arrangement falling within reg 26 and a summary of the reasons why that view is taken. See the Analysis to reg 9(1)(l) for the meaning of "take advantage" in this context.

(2)   The assessment made by the authority of the income and capital of both the claimant and the non-dependant and details of the calculation made under the non-dependant's resources (which is probably required anyway by virtue of para 10).

It would appear that since a non-dependant is not a "person affected" within the meaning of reg 2(1), s/he is not entitled to receive notification of the decision or to challenge it.

PART 6
Notice where no award is made

14.   Where a person is not awarded housing benefit—

(a)   either on grounds of income or because the amount of any housing benefit is less than the minimum housing benefit prescribed by regulation 75, the decision notice shall include a statement as to—

      (i)   the matters set out in paragraphs 9(a) to (c), and in a case where the amount of entitlement is less than the minimum amount of housing benefit prescribed, paragraph 9(d) also; and

      (ii)   the matters set out in paragraphs 10(b) to (d) where the person is not on income support or an income-based jobseeker's allowance; and

      (iii)   where the amount of entitlement is less than the minimum amount of housing benefit prescribed, that fact and that such entitlement is not payable;

  (b)   for any reason other than one mentioned in sub-paragraph (a), the decision notice shall include a statement as to the reason why no award has been made.

Analysis

The requirements where HB is refused are set out in para 14. Two categories of notices are set out. If the refusal is on income grounds, the information prescribed by paras 9(a) to (c) must be given, and where the claimant is not on IS or income-based JSA, the information in paras 10(b) to (d). If HB is refused because the entitlement is less than the minimum HB payable under reg 75, the fact must be stated and the information in para 9(d).

If refusal is not for a reason specified in para (a), only the reason for the refusal need be given. It would be good practice for more information to be given under para 6, particularly where there has been a finding of no liability or of a contrived tenancy.

Paras 2, 3 and 6 apply to notices under para 14.

PART 7
Notice where recoverable overpayment

15.–(1)   Where the appropriate authority makes a decision that there is a recoverable overpayment within the meaning of regulation 100 (recoverable overpayments), the decision notice shall include a statement as to–

  (a)   the fact that there is a recoverable overpayment; and

  (b)   the reason why there is a recoverable overpayment; and

  (c)   the amount of the recoverable overpayment; and

  (d)   how the amount of the recoverable overpayment was calculated; and

  (e)   the benefit weeks to which the recoverable overpayment relates; and

  (f)   where recovery of the recoverable overpayment is to be made by deduction from a rent allowance or rebate, as the case may be, that fact and the amount of the deduction.

  (2)   In a case where it is–

  (a)   determined that there is a recoverable overpayment;

  (b)   determined that that overpayment is recoverable from a landlord; and

  (c)   decided that recovery of that overpayment is to be made by deduction from a rent allowance paid to that landlord to discharge (in whole or in part) an obligation owed to him by a claimant (''claimant A''), not being the claimant on whose behalf the recoverable amount was paid,

the decision notice sent to that landlord shall identify both–

      (i)   the person on whose behalf the recoverable amount was paid to that landlord; and

      (ii)   claimant A.

Analysis

Paras 2, 3 and 6 also apply to notices under para 15. The requirements of the notices were expanded following changes made by the Social Security Administration (Fraud) Act 1997 and the secondary legislation made thereunder. The following content is required:

(1)   The fact that there is a recoverable overpayment and the reason why there is one: sub-paras (1)(a) and (b). It is suggested that authorities should go systematically through each of the issues in reg 100 to determine the answer to this question. In *R v Thanet DC ex p Warren Court Hotels Ltd* [2000] 33 HLR 339, CA, the notifications of overpayment contained a statement that there had been a change in the claimant's circumstances, as a result of which an overpayment had occurred because the local authority was unaware of the change in circumstances. The council argued that for the purposes of para 14(1)(b) in Sch 6 HB Regs 1987 (now para 15(1)(b) of Sch 9 HB Regs), "the reason why there is a recoverable overpayment", it was sufficient to state that there had been a change in circumstances. Jackson J disagreed, holding that it was necessary to spell out what the change of circumstances was (see the Analyses to s75(2) of the SSAA and reg 90 for the effect of this defect and the other issues in the case).

"The phrase 'change of circumstances' in that letter could cover a multitude of events. To take one example, it could mean that Mr H was in paid employment from 12 October onwards. To take another example, it could mean that although Mr H was unemployed, there was a three-week break in his entitlement to housing benefit." (para 36 of the judgment).

The requirement to identify how an overpayment has occurred does not require detailed calculations of the revised amounts of benefit: *CH 3776/2001* para 10. All that is required is the old and new figures and the difference.

(2) The amount of the overpayment and how it is calculated: sub-paras (1)(c) and (d). Enough detail should be given to enable the claimant to follow the calculation through. That should include a complete breakdown of how much benefit is recoverable in each week it was paid, and details of a diminishing capital calculation if necessary. See regs 103 and 104.

(3) The benefit weeks to which the overpayment relates: sub-para (1)(e).

(4) Where recovery is to be made by deduction from ongoing payments of rent allowance or rent rebate, that fact and the amount of the deduction: sub-para (1)(f).

(5) Where the overpayment is recoverable from the landlord and recovery is to be made from claimant A's benefit where claimant B was overpaid, the landlord must be told the identities of claimants A and B: sub-para (2). Under SSAA s75(6), claimant A's obligation is deemed to be discharged by the amount of the deduction.

In *Godwin v Rossendale BC* [2002] *The Times* 24 May, [2002] EWCA Civ 726, para 51, the court stated that a notice under para 14(2) of Sch 6 HB Regs 1987 (now para 15(2) of Sch 9 HB Regs) should be given before recovery is made. However, the court rejected the suggestion that a failure to do so rendered the recovery unlawful, since there was no prejudice to the landlord by the omission.

Note the additional information that has to be provided under reg 107(3) in certain cases.

SCHEDULE 10
REGULATION 122
Pathfinder authorities

General note

Sch 10 contains the modified rules for determining the maximum rent (standard local rate) , and hence the maximum HB, for tenants in the deregulated private sector in the Pathfinder areas shown in Part 1 of Sch 10. This is known as the "local housing allowance" scheme. Maximum HB is determined by reg 70.

The DWP guidance to local authorities, the *Housing Benefit Local Housing Allowance Guidance Manual*, is available at www.dwp.gov.uk/housingbenefit/lha/. The guidance suggests that "local housing allowance" is a new or different form of HB. This is not the case; strictly speaking, it is a determination made by the rent officer upon which HB for relevant claimants is based. As Commissioner Williams points out in *CH 2986/2005*, save for the modifications, the HB Regulations apply in full, and the administrative provisions applying to decision making and appeals are the same as those applying to HB generally.

The pilot scheme rules apply from the date specified in relation to each authority. In outline:

(1) Regs 11, 12, 14-17, 95 and 96 HB Regs are amended: paras 3, 5, 8-11 and 13.

(2) Regs 11A, 12A, 13A and 13B, 18A HB Regs are inserted: paras 4, 6, 7 and 12.

Reg 13A(2) sets out the situations in which the scheme does not apply, namely, where the landlord is a registered social landlord (defined in reg 13A(9)), where the claimant lives in "exempt accommodation" (Sch 3 para 4(1)(b) HB&CTB(CP) Regs) or has an "excluded tenancy" (Sch 2 paras 4-10 HB Regs) or pays rent for a hostel, a houseboat, a caravan or a mobile home or for board and attendance. Transitional protection is provided for those who were already claiming HB when the "local housing allowance" scheme began in their area: reg 12A(2), (3) and (9)(a)-(c).

Information about the rules in practice can be found in CPAG's *Welfare Rights Bulletins* 179 and 194. The scheme will begin to be introduced nationwide from April 2008. The rules will be slightly different from those being operated in the Pathfinder areas, but there will be transitional protection for those to whom the Pathfinder rules applied before 7 April 2008. At the time of writing, the amended rules were only available in draft form.

Summary of the scheme

The pilot scheme includes the following:

(1) In Pathfinder areas, "eligible rent" for HB purposes is the maximum rent (standard local rate). This is the "local housing allowance" determined by the rent officer: regs 12A(1)(a) and 13A(3).

(2) The "local housing allowance" is set by the rent officer and is based on a mid-range local market rent for a property of the appropriate size in the area where the claimant lives. It must be made public: regs 13A(3) and 13B HB Regs and Sch 3A of the Rent Officers (Housing Benefit Functions) Order 1997 and the Rent Officers (Housing Benefit Functions) (Scotland) Order (referred to here as the RO Orders).

(3) The size criteria are broadly the same as those in Art 2 of the RO Orders: reg 13A(9).

(4) "Local housing allowances" are changed by the rent officer from time to time, if s/he considers it appropriate having regard to the rules: Art 4B of the RO Orders.

(5)　For a "young individual" (defined in reg 2(1), broadly single claimants under 25), the local housing allowance is based on accommodation in which the tenant has exclusive use of one bedroom only and all or some of the other facilities are shared. This does not apply if the young individual qualifies for a severe disability premium or has a non-dependant living with her/him: reg 13A(3)(b) HB Regs; Sch 3A para 1(1)(a) of the RO Orders.

(6)　Maximum rent (standard local rate) is based on the "local housing allowance" that is appropriate when the claim is assessed, and this lasts for a year even if the allowance changes. The local authority reassesses claims annually, using the allowance that is then appropriate for the property. However, claims can be reassessed earlier if there are certain changes in circumstances and this means a different allowance is appropriate (eg, a change in the size of the household, a rent increase under a term of the tenancy or where a single claimant turns 25); regs 12A(1) and 13A(1)(b)(iv).

(7)　If the appropriate "local housing allowance" for a claimant should be reduced, because of the death of a member of the claimant's family or a relative of the claimant or her/his partner who occupies the same dwelling, the decrease can be delayed for 12 months: reg 12A(4), (5), (8) and (9)(d). See the commentary to reg 13 HB Regs for the meaning of the terms.

(8)　A rent restriction can be delayed for 13 weeks if the claimant or a member of her/his family or a relative of the claimant or her/his partner who occupies the same dwelling could meet the costs of the dwelling when these were taken on: reg 12A(6)-(8) and (9)(e). See the commentary to reg 13 HB Regs for the meaning of the terms.

(9)　If the amount of rent the claimant is liable to pay to her/his landlord is lower than the "local housing allowance" (and therefore HB entitlement is higher than the rent liability) the claimant can keep the difference: reg 13A(8). Note that the Government has indicated that there may be a "cap" on the excess HB paid to claimants when the scheme is introduced nationwide.

(10)　In most cases, HB is paid to the claimant, not to the landlord (or agent). However, direct payments to landlords are still possible in some situations: regs 96 and 97 as modified. Note that in order to transfer payment of HB to a tenant from a landlord, a supersession decision is needed. The landlord has a right of appeal against the decision and the tenant is a party to any such appeal as a "person affected": *CH 2986/2005.*

PART 1
Commencement date in relation to each pathfinder authority

Pathfinder authority	Commencement date
Argyll and Bute	30th May 2005
Blackpool	17th November 2003
Brighton and Hove	2nd February 2004
Conwy	9th February 2004
Coventry	12th January 2004
East Riding of Yorkshire	18th April 2005
Edinburgh	9th February 2004
Guildford	4th July 2005
Leeds	9th February 2004
Lewisham	1st December 2003
North East Lincolnshire	9th February 2004
Norwich	13th June 2005
Pembrokeshire	20th June 2005
St Helens	23rd May 2005
Salford	25th July 2005
South Norfolk	6th June 2005
Teignbridge	12th January 2004
Wandsworth	11th April 2005

PART 2
Application of the Regulations

1.　These Regulations shall apply to pathfinder authorities subject to the provisions of this Part of this Schedule.

2.　In regulation 2(1) (interpretation), at the appropriate places, insert–

''amended determination'' means a determination made in accordance with article 7A of the Rent Officers Order;

''broad rental market area'' has the meaning specified in paragraph 4 of Part 1 of Schedule 3A to the Rent Officers Order;

"broad rental market area determination'' means a determination made in accordance with article 4B(1) of the Rent Officers Order;

"commencement date'' means in relation to a pathfinder authority specified in Part 1 of Schedule 10, the date specified in that Part in relation to that authority;

"local housing allowance'' means an allowance determined in accordance with paragraph 2 or 3 of Part 1 of Schedule 3A to the Rent Officers Order;

"local housing allowance determination'' means a determination made in accordance with article 4B(2) of the Rent Officers Order;

"maximum rent (standard local rate)'' means the amount determined in accordance with regulation 13A;

"pathfinder authority'' means a relevant authority specified in Part 1 of Schedule 10;

"relevant date'' means, as the case may require–

- (a) the commencement date in relation to a pathfinder authority specified in Part 1 of Schedule 10;
- (b) the date of the claim to which the claim or relevant information relates;
- (c) the date of the change relating to a rent allowance, or the change which affects the category of dwelling, date of death or rent increase, to which a notification referred to in regulation 13A(1)(b)(iii) or (iv) relate; or
- (d) the date on which the period mentioned in regulation 14 (1)(f) or (g) has elapsed;''.

Amendment of regulation 11

3. In regulation 11(1) (eligible housing costs), for the words "regulations 12(3),'' to the end of the paragraph substitute "regulations 12 and 13 or regulations 12 and 13A, whichever is applicable in his case''.

Insertion of regulation 11A

4. After regulation 11(eligible housing costs), insert the following regulation–

"Cases where maximum housing benefit expires

11A. A maximum housing benefit shall not have effect for any benefit week which begins on or after the day which is the first anniversary of the day by reference to which the local housing allowance most recently applicable for the purpose of determining that maximum housing benefit in accordance with regulation 12A(1) to (9) was identified.''.

Amendment of regulation 12

5. In regulation 12(3)(b), after the words "except where sub-paragraph (a)'', insert "or regulation 12A(1), (3) or (4)''.

Insert regulation 12A

6. After regulation 12 (rent), insert the following regulation–

" Eligible rent and the maximum rent (standard local rate)

12A.–(1) Where, by virtue of paragraph (1) of regulation 13A, a maximum rent (standard local rate) has been, or falls to be, determined in accordance with that regulation, then, except where paragraph (3)(a)(ii), (b)(ii) or (c)(ii), (4)(a) or (6)(a) applies–

- (a) the amount of a person's eligible rent shall be the maximum rent (standard local rate); and
- (b) it shall apply until the earlier of–
  - (i) the determination of a maximum rent (standard local rate) by virtue of regulation 13A(1)(b)(iv); or
  - (ii) the determination of a maximum rent (standard local rate) which relates to the local housing allowance applicable to the case on the first anniversary of the day by reference to which the local housing allowance which was applicable for the purpose of determining the eligible rent in sub-paragraph (a), was identified.

(2) This paragraph applies where a pathfinder authority is required to determine a maximum rent (standard local rate) by virtue of regulation 13A(1)(a) or (b)(i), (ii) or (iii)(aa) or (c) and the claimant has been continuously entitled to and in receipt of housing benefit in respect of the dwelling he occupies as his home for a period which includes the commencement date.

(3) Where paragraph (2) applies, subject to paragraph (9)–

- (a) except where sub-paragraph (b) or (c) applies, the amount of a person's eligible rent shall be–
  - (i) the eligible rent determined in accordance with paragraph (1) where that is not less than the eligible rent which applied on the day before the relevant date; or
  - (ii) the eligible rent which applied on the day before the relevant date;
- (b) where the eligible rent to which the person was entitled on the day before the relevant date was determined by reference to a maximum rent determined in accordance with regulation 13(11)(b), the person's eligible rent shall be–

   (i) the eligible rent determined in accordance with paragraph (1), where that is not less than the eligible rent which applied on the day before the relevant date; or

   (ii) the eligible rent which applied on the day before the relevant date; or

 (c) where the eligible rent to which the person was entitled on the day before the relevant date was, by virtue of regulation 13(14), determined in accordance with regulation 12(3)(b), the person's eligible rent shall be–

   (i) the eligible rent determined in accordance with paragraph (1), where that is not less than the eligible rent which applied on the day before the relevant date; or

   (ii) the eligible rent which applied on the day before the relevant date.

 (4) Subject to paragraph (9), where the pathfinder authority is required to determine a maximum rent (standard local rate) by virtue of regulation 13A(1)(b)(i), (ii) or (iv)(aa) to (cc) and the claimant occupies a dwelling which is the same as that occupied by him at the date of death of any person to whom any of sub-paragraphs (b) to (d) of paragraph (8) applied or, had a claim been made, would have applied, the eligible rent shall be–

 (a) either–

   (i) the eligible rent which applied on the day before the death occurred; or

   (ii) in a case where there was no eligible rent, subject to regulation 12(4) and (7), the reckonable rent due on that day; or

 (b) the eligible rent determined in accordance with paragraph (1), where it is not less than the eligible rent determined in accordance with sub-paragraph (a).

 (5) For the purpose of paragraph (4), a claimant shall be treated as occupying the dwelling if paragraph (13) of regulation 7 (circumstances in which a person is or is not to be treated as occupying a dwelling as his home) is satisfied and for that purpose that paragraph (13) shall have effect as if sub-paragraph (b) of that paragraph were omitted.

 (6) Subject to paragraphs (7) and (9), where a pathfinder authority is required to determine a maximum rent (standard local rate) by virtue of regulation 13A(1)(b)(i) or (ii) and the pathfinder authority is satisfied that a person to whom paragraph (8) applies was able to meet the financial commitments for his dwelling when they were entered into, the eligible rent shall be–

 (a) an eligible rent determined in accordance with regulation 12(3)(b); or

 (b) the eligible rent determined in accordance with paragraph (1), where it is not less than the eligible rent referred to in sub-paragraph (a).

 (7) Paragraph (6) shall not apply in the case of any claim for housing benefit where the claimant was previously entitled to housing benefit in respect of any period which ended less than 52 weeks before the commencement of the period to which the claim relates.

 (8) This paragraph applies to the following persons–

 (a) the claimant;

 (b) any member of his family;

 (c) if the claimant is a member of a polygamous marriage, any partners of his and any child or young person for whom he or a partner is responsible and who is a member of the same household;

 (d) any relative of the claimant or his partner who occupies the same dwelling as the claimant, whether or not they reside with him, except for a relative who has a separate right of occupation of the dwelling which would enable them to continue to occupy it even if the claimant ceased his occupation of it.

 (9) Where a person's eligible rent has been determined in accordance with–

 (a) paragraph (3)(a)(ii), it shall continue to apply until such time as the pathfinder authority determines an eligible rent–

   (i) in accordance with paragraph (1) which is equal to or exceeds it or is based on a maximum rent (standard local rate) determined by virtue of regulation 13A(1)(b)(iv)(dd); or

   (ii) where the maximum rent (standard local rate) on which it is based relates to the local housing allowance applicable to the case on the anniversary of the day by reference to which the local housing allowance which was applicable for the purpose of determining the eligible rent in paragraph (3)(a)(i) was identified, which is equal to or exceeds it,

whichever first occurs;

 (b) paragraph (3)(b)(ii), and–

   (i) the pathfinder authority determined a maximum rent (standard local rate) following receipt of a notification of change relating to a rent allowance that falls within paragraph 2(3)(a) of Schedule 2 as a result of the death of one of the occupiers to whom any of sub-paragraphs (b) to (d) of regulation 13(11) applied, it shall continue to apply until–

    (aa) the period of 12 months from the date of death has expired; or

    (bb) the pathfinder authority determines an eligible rent in accordance with paragraph (1) which is equal to or exceeds it or is based on a maximum rent (standard local rate) determined by virtue of regulation 13A(1)(b)(iv)(dd),

whichever first occurs; or
- (ii)   in any other case, it shall continue to apply until–
  - (aa)   the date on which the eligible rent which applied on the day before the relevant date would have ceased to apply; or
  - (bb)   the pathfinder authority determines an eligible rent in accordance with paragraph (1) which is equal to or exceeds it or is based on a maximum rent (standard local rate) determined by virtue of regulation 13A(1)(b)(iv)(dd),

    whichever first occurs;

- (c)   paragraph (3)(c)(ii), it shall continue to apply until–
  - (i)   the date on which the eligible rent which applied on the day before the relevant date would have ceased to apply; or
  - (ii)   the pathfinder authority determines an eligible rent in accordance with paragraph (1) which is equal to or exceeds it or is based on a maximum rent (standard local rate) determined by virtue of regulation 13A(1)(b)(iv)(dd),

    whichever first occurs;

- (d)   paragraph (4)(a), it shall continue to apply until–
  - (i)   the period of 12 months from the date of death has expired; or
  - (ii)   the pathfinder authority determines an eligible rent in accordance with paragraph (1) which is equal to or exceeds it or is based on a maximum rent (standard local rate) determined by virtue of regulation 13A(1)(b)(iv)(dd),

    whichever first occurs;

- (e)   paragraph (6)(a), it shall continue to apply until–
  - (i)   the first 13 weeks of the claimant's award of housing benefit have expired; or
  - (ii)   the pathfinder authority determines an eligible rent in accordance with paragraph (1) which is equal to or exceeds it or is based on a maximum rent (standard local rate) determined by virtue of regulation 13A(1)(b)(iv)(dd),

    whichever first occurs; and

- (f)   paragraph (1)(b)(ii), or sub-paragraph (a)(ii) or this sub-paragraph, that eligible rent ("the earlier eligible rent") shall continue to apply until–
  - (i)   the determination of a maximum rent (standard local rate) by virtue of regulation 13A(1)(b)(iv); or
  - (ii)   the determination of an eligible rent where the maximum rent (standard local rate) on which it is based relates to the local housing allowance applicable to the case on the first anniversary of the day by reference to which the local housing allowance which was applicable for the purpose of determining the earlier eligible rent was identified,

whichever first occurs.

(10)   Where an eligible rent ceases to apply by virtue of sub-paragraph (b)(i)(aa), (b)(ii)(aa), (c)(i), (d)(i) or (e)(i) of paragraph (9), the eligible rent that shall apply instead shall be the one which would have applied but for paragraphs (3)(b)(ii), (3)(c)(ii), (4)(a) and (6)(a).

(11)   In paragraph (4) "reckonable rent" has the same meaning as in regulation 13."

Insertion of regulations 13A and 13B

7. After regulation 13 (maximum rent) insert the following regulations–

" **Maximum rent (standard local rate)**

13A.–(1)   Subject to paragraph (2), where–

- (a)   the relevant authority is a pathfinder authority specified in Part I of Schedule 10 and it is the commencement date for that pathfinder authority; or
- (b)   a pathfinder authority has received–
  - (i)   a claim on which a rent allowance may be awarded, where the date of claim falls on or after the commencement date;
  - (ii)   relevant information regarding a claim on which a rent allowance may be awarded, where the date of claim falls on or after the commencement date;
  - (iii)   in relation to an award of housing benefit where the maximum rent was determined in accordance with regulation 13–
    - (aa)   a notification of a change relating to a rent allowance where the change occurs on or after the commencement date; or
    - (bb)   a notification of a change of dwelling where the change occurs on or after 9th April 2004; or
  - (iv)   in relation to an award of housing benefit where a maximum rent (standard local rate) was determined in accordance with this regulation–
    - (aa)   notification of a change of a kind which affects the category of dwelling applicable to the claim;

	(bb)	notification of the death of an occupier of the dwelling to whom any of sub-paragraphs (b) to (d) of regulation 12A(8) applies, where the notification does not fall within sub-head (aa);

       (cc)   notification that there has been a rent increase under a term of the tenancy to which the claim relates and the term under which that increase was made was either included in the tenancy at the date of the claim or is a term substantially the same as such a term; or

       (dd)   notification of a change of dwelling;

(c)   a pathfinder authority is required to apply to a rent officer for a determination in accordance with regulation 14(1)(f) or (g),

the pathfinder authority shall determine a maximum rent (standard local rate) in accordance with paragraphs (3) to (8).

(2)   Paragraph (1) shall not apply in a case where–

(a)   the landlord is a registered social landlord;

(b)   paragraph 4(1)(b) of Schedule 3 to the Consequential Provisions Regulations applies;

(c)   the tenancy is an excluded tenancy of a type falling within any of paragraphs 4 to 10 of Schedule 2;

(d)   the claim or award relates to–

       (i)   periodical payments of a kind falling within regulation 12(1) which a person is liable to make in relation to a houseboat, caravan or mobile home which he occupies as his home; or

       (ii)   rent payable in relation to a hostel; or

(e)   rent under the tenancy is attributable to board and attendance, and–

       (i)   the pathfinder authority has made an application to the rent officer in accordance with paragraph (6), regulation 15 or 17; and

       (ii)   the rent officer has determined that a substantial part of the rent under the tenancy is fairly attributable to board and attendance and has notified the pathfinder authority of this in accordance with article 4C, 4D or 4E of the Rent Officers Order.

(3)   The maximum rent (standard local rate) shall be the local housing allowance determined by the rent officer which is applicable to–

(a)   the broad rental market area in which the dwelling to which the claim or award of housing benefit relates is situated at the relevant date; and

(b)   the category of dwelling–

       (i)   specified in paragraph 1(1)(a) of Part 1 of Schedule 3A to the Rent Officers Order where–

          (aa)   the claimant is a young individual who has no non-dependant residing with him and to whom paragraph 14 of Schedule 3 (severe disability premium) does not apply; or

          (bb)   the category of dwelling specified in paragraph 1(1)(b) of Part 1 of Schedule 3A to the Rent Officers Order would apply in the claimant's case but neither requirement in head (ii)(aa) or (bb) is satisfied in his case;

       (ii)   specified in paragraph 1(1)(b) of Part 1 of Schedule 3A to the Rent Officers Order where that applies in the claimant's case at the relevant date in accordance with the size criteria and he is not a person to whom head (i)(aa) applies and where–

          (aa)   the claimant (together with his partner where he has one) has the exclusive use of two or more rooms; or

          (bb)   the claimant (together with his partner where he has one) has the exclusive use of one room, a bathroom and toilet and a kitchen or facilities for cooking;

       (iii) in any other case, which applies in the claimant's case at the relevant date in accordance with the size criteria.

(4)   Where no local housing allowance applicable to a claim or award of housing benefit falling within paragraph (3)(b)(iii) has been determined, the pathfinder authority shall–

(a)   apply to the rent officer for local housing allowance determinations for the category of dwelling applicable to the claim or award of housing benefit for each broad rental market area falling within its area, in whole or in part, at the relevant date, which shall be specified in the application; and

(b)   apply the local housing allowance so determined for the broad rental market area in which the dwelling to which the claim or award of housing benefit relates is situated at the relevant date.

(5)   Where–

(a)   a pathfinder authority receives a request on a properly completed form approved for the purpose by the pathfinder authority from a person stating that he is contemplating occupying as his home a dwelling containing a specified number of rooms, exceeding six, within the area of the pathfinder authority and that, if he does so, he is likely to claim housing benefit; and

(b) no local housing allowance determination is in effect for a broad rental market area, falling within, in whole or in part, the area of the pathfinder authority for the category of dwelling containing the number of rooms specified in the form,

the pathfinder authority shall apply to the rent officer for local housing allowance determinations for each broad rental market area for the category of dwelling containing the number of rooms specified in the form.

(6) In a case where–

(a) the pathfinder authority is required to determine a maximum rent (standard local rate) by virtue of paragraph (1); and

(b) part of the rent under the tenancy appears to the pathfinder authority to be likely to be attributable to board and attendance,

the pathfinder authority shall apply to the rent officer for a board and attendance determination to be made in accordance with article 4C of the Rent Officers Order.

(7) Where an application to a rent officer is required in accordance with paragraph (6)–

(a) it shall contain–

(i) a statement that the application is made in accordance with paragraph (6); and

(ii) such other statements, information and notifications as would be required were the application to be made in accordance with regulation 14(1); and

(b) it shall be made within the same period following the day on which the pathfinder authority becomes obliged to determine a maximum rent (standard local rate) by virtue of paragraph (1) as would be required if it were to be made under regulation 14(1).

(8) Where the maximum rent (standard local rate) exceeds the rent, the claimant shall be treated as liable to make payments in respect of the dwelling of an amount equal to the amount by which the maximum rent (standard local rate) exceeds the rent, except for the purposes of calculating any amount by which a rent allowance exceeds the amount which a claimant is liable to pay his landlord as rent, or rent and any arrears of rent, in accordance with regulation 95(2A).

(9) In this regulation–

"change of dwelling" has the same meaning as in regulation 14;

"change relating to a rent allowance" has the same meaning as in regulation 14;

"occupiers" means the persons whom the pathfinder authority is satisfied occupy as their home the dwelling to which the claim or award relates except for any joint tenant who is not a member of the claimant's household;

"registered social landlord" has the same meaning as in Part 1 of the Housing Act 1996 and, in Scotland, sections 57 and 59 of the Housing (Scotland) Act 2001;

"room" has the meaning specified in paragraph 1(2) of Part 1 of Schedule 3A to the Rent Officers Order;

"size criteria" has the meaning specified in article 2 of the Rent Officers Order except that the word "occupier" is to be construed in accordance with the definition of "occupiers" in this paragraph.

Publication of local housing allowances

13B. A pathfinder authority shall take such steps as appear to it to be appropriate for the purpose of securing that information in relation to broad rental market areas falling in whole or in part within its area, and local housing allowances applicable to such broad rental market areas, is brought to the attention of persons who may be entitled to housing benefit from the authority.".

Amendment of regulation 14

8. In regulation 14 (requirement to refer to rent officers) after paragraph (5), insert the following paragraph–

" (5A) An application shall not be required under paragraph (1)(a), (b), (c) (d) or (e) where the claim, relevant information, notification or request is received by a pathfinder authority, unless it is–

(a) a claim, relevant information or notification to which any of the circumstances specified in regulation 13A(2)(a) to (e)apply; or

(b) a request, and any of the circumstances in regulation 13A(2)(a) to (d) would apply were a claim to be made by the prospective occupier in relation to the dwelling which is the subject of the request,

and a referral would fall to be made were the claim, relevant information, notification or request made to a relevant authority which is not a pathfinder authority.

(5B) An application shall not be required in accordance with paragraph (1)(f) or (g) unless–

(a) it is a case to which regulation 13A(2) applies; and

(b) a referral would fall to be made were the relevant authority not a pathfinder authority.".

Amendment of regulation 15

9. In regulation 15(1)(a) (applications to the rent officers for redeterminations) after the words "reference made under" insert "regulation 13A(6) or".

Amendment of regulation 16

10. In regulation 16 (application for redetermination by rent officer)–

(a) in paragraph (1)(b) after the words "the Housing Act functions" insert the words "except for functions relating to broad rental market area determinations and local housing allowance determinations or amended determinations";

(b) in paragraphs (3) and (4)(b) after the words "application under regulation" insert the words "13A(6) or";

(c) in paragraph (5) after the words "the Housing Act functions" insert the words "(except for those relating to broad rental market area determinations and local housing allowance determinations or amended determinations)".

Amendment of regulation 17

11. In regulation 17 (substitute determinations or substitute redeterminations)–

(a) in paragraph (1)(b)–

    (i) for the words "article 7A" substitute the words "article 7A(1) or (2)"; and

    (ii) for the words "or substitute redetermination" substitute ", substitute redetermination, substitute board and attendance determination or substitute board and attendance redetermination"; and

(b) in paragraph (2) for the words "or substitute redetermination" substitute ", substitute redetermination, board and attendance redetermination, substitute board and attendance determination or substitute board and attendance redetermination".

Insertion of regulation 18A

12. After regulation 18 (application of provisions to substitute determinations or substitute redeterminations) insert the following regulation–

" Amended determinations

18A. Where a decision has been revised in consequence of an amended broad rental market area determination or amended local housing allowance determination by a rent officer and that amended determination has led to–

(a) a reduction in the maximum rent (standard local rate) applicable to a claimant, the amended determination shall be a change of circumstances in relation to that claimant; and

(b) an increase in the maximum rent (standard local rate) applicable to a claimant, the amended determination shall have effect in place of the original determination.".

Amendment of regulations 95 and 96

13.–(1) In regulation 95 (circumstances in which payment is to be made to a landlord) after paragraph (2) insert the following paragraph–

" (2A) In a case where–

(a) a pathfinder authority has determined a maximum rent (standard local rate) in accordance with regulation 13A(1); and

(b) the rent allowance exceeds the amount which the claimant is liable to pay his landlord by way of rent,

any payment of rent allowance made to a landlord pursuant to this regulation or to regulation 96 may include all or part of any amount by which the rent allowance exceeds the amount which the claimant is liable to pay his landlord as rent but shall not include any amount by which the rent allowance exceeds the amount which the claimant is liable to pay his landlord as rent and arrears of rent."

(2) In regulation 96 (circumstances in which payment may be made to a landlord)–

(a) in paragraph (1) for the words "paragraph (3)" substitute the words "paragraphs (3) and (3A)";

(b) in sub-paragraph (a) of paragraph (3) after the words "paragraph (1)" insert the words "or (3A)";

(c) after paragraph (3) insert the following paragraph–

" (3A) In a case where a pathfinder authority has determined a maximum rent (standard local rate) in accordance with regulation 13A–

(a) sub-paragraphs (a) and (b) of paragraph (1) shall not apply; and

(b) payment of a rent allowance to a person's landlord may be made where–

    (i) the eligible rent was determined by reference to a maximum rent (standard local rate) which was determined by virtue of regulation 13A(1)(a) and–

        (aa) the maximum rent (standard local rate) was determined less than six months previously;

        (bb) no subsequent maximum rent (standard local rate) has been determined in accordance with regulation 13A(1); and

        (cc) the claimant has, since the date the maximum rent (standard local rate) was determined, been continuously entitled to, and in receipt of, housing benefit in relation to the dwelling he occupied as his home at that date;

    (ii)   the pathfinder authority considers that the claimant is likely to have difficulty in managing his affairs;

    (iii)   the pathfinder authority considers that it is improbable that the claimant will pay his rent; or

    (iv)   a direct payment has previously been made by the pathfinder authority to the landlord in accordance with regulation 95 in respect of the current award of housing benefit.''.

[¹SCHEDULE 11
ELECTRONIC COMMUNICATION

Amendment

1.   Inserted by Art 2(5) of SI 2006 No 2968 as from 20.12.06.

General Note to Schedule 11

Reg 83A allows claims for HB to be made by electronic communication. The authorisation requirements and conditions for such claims are found in Sch 11. See the General Note to reg 83A.

PART 1
Introduction

Interpretation

1. In this Schedule ''official computer system'' means a computer system maintained by or on behalf of the relevant authority or of the Secretary of State for sending, receiving, processing or storing of any claim, certificate, notice, information or evidence.

PART 2
Electronic Communication – General Provisions

Conditions for the use of electronic communication

2.–(1)   The relevant authority may use an electronic communication in connection with claims for, and awards of, benefit under these Regulations.

    (2)   A person other than the relevant authority may use an electronic communication in connection with the matters referred to in sub-paragraph (1) if the conditions specified in sub-paragraphs (3) to (6) are satisfied.

    (3)   The first condition is that the person is for the time being permitted to use an electronic communication by an authorisation given by means of a direction of the Chief Executive of the relevant authority.

    (4)   The second condition is that the person uses an approved method of–

    (a)   authenticating the identity of the sender of the communication;

    (b)   electronic communication;

    (c)   authenticating any claim or notice delivered by means of an electronic communication; and

    (d)   subject to sub-paragraph (7), submitting to the relevant authority any claim, certificate, notice, information or evidence.

    (5)   The third condition is that any claim, certificate, notice, information or evidence sent by means of an electronic communication is in a form approved for the purposes of this Schedule.

    (6)   The fourth condition is that the person maintains such records in written or electronic form as may be specified in a direction given by the Chief Executive of the relevant authority.

    (7)   Where the person uses any method other than the method approved of submitting any claim, certificate, notice, information or evidence, that claim, certificate, notice, information or evidence shall be treated as not having been submitted.

    (8)   In this paragraph ''approved'' means approved by means of a direction given by the Chief Executive of the relevant authority for the purposes of this Schedule.

Use of intermediaries

3.   The relevant authority may use intermediaries in connection with–

    (a)   the delivery of any claim, certificate, notice, information or evidence by means of an electronic communication; and

    (b)   the authentication or security of anything transmitted by such means,

and may require other persons to use intermediaries in connection with those matters.

PART 3
Electronic Communication – Evidential Provisions

Effect of delivering information by means of electronic communication

4.–(1)   Any claim, certificate, notice, information or evidence which is delivered by means of an electronic communication shall be treated as having been delivered in the manner or form required by any provision of these Regulations, on the day the conditions imposed–

(a)   by this Schedule; and

(b)   by or under an enactment,

are satisfied.

(2)   The relevant authority may, by a direction, determine that any claim, certificate, notice, information or evidence is to be treated as delivered on a different day (whether earlier or later) from the day provided for in sub-paragraph (1).

(3)   Information shall not be taken to have been delivered to an official computer system by means of an electronic communication unless it is accepted by the system to which it is delivered.

Proof of identity of sender or recipient of information

5.   If it is necessary to prove, for the purpose of any legal proceedings, the identity of–

(a)   the sender of any claim, certificate, notice, information or evidence delivered by means of an electronic communication to an official computer system; or

(b)   the recipient of any such claim, certificate, notice, information or evidence delivered by means of an electronic communication from an official computer system,

the sender or recipient, as the case may be, shall be presumed to be the person whose name is recorded as such on that official computer system.

Proof of delivery of information

6.–(1)   If it is necessary to prove, for the purpose of any legal proceedings, that the use of an electronic communication has resulted in the delivery of any claim, certificate, notice, information or evidence this shall be presumed to have been the case where–

(a)   any such claim, certificate, notice, information or evidence has been delivered to the relevant authority, if the delivery of that claim, certificate, notice, information or evidence has been recorded on an official computer system; or

(b)   any such claim, certificate, notice, information or evidence has been delivered by the relevant authority, if the delivery of that certificate, notice, information or evidence has been recorded on an official computer system.

(2)   If it is necessary to prove, for the purpose of any legal proceedings, that the use of an electronic communication has resulted in the delivery of any such claim, certificate, notice, information or evidence, this shall be presumed not to be the case, if that claim, certificate, notice, information or evidence delivered to the relevant authority has not been recorded on an official computer system.

(3)   If it is necessary to prove, for the purpose of any legal proceedings, when any such claim, certificate, notice, information or evidence sent by means of an electronic communication has been received, the time and date of receipt shall be presumed to be that recorded on an official computer system.

Proof of content of information

7.   If it is necessary to prove, for the purpose of any legal proceedings, the content of any claim, certificate, notice, information or evidence sent by means of an electronic communication, the content shall be presumed to be that recorded on an official computer system.]

The Rent Officers (Housing Benefit Functions) Order 1997

(SI 1997 No.1984)

General Note

This order sets out the determinations to be made by rent officers when a tenancy is referred to them under reg 14 of both the HB and the HB(SPC) Regs by an authority in England and Wales. The equivalent Order for Scotland is SI 1997 No 1995 (see p540).

The determinations made by rent officers under this order are relevant in two ways. The first concerns the calculation of a claimant's "maximum housing benefit" (or the reduction of the "eligible rent") and the second the amount of subsidy received by an authority. As to the first, for most private sector tenants whose tenancies commenced after 1 January 1996, the rent officers' figures are the basis on which a "maximum rent" is calculated under reg 13 of both the HB and the HB(SPC) Regs. See the commentary to reg 13 HB Regs for a summary of how maximum rent is calculated.

For those tenants who have the benefit of the transitional protection set out in Sch 3 paras 4 and 5 HB&CTB(CP) Regs (see pp1101 and 1104), a rent officer's determination is not determinative of maximum rent. It is a factor to which an authority may have regard when considering whether the dwelling occupied by the claimant is larger than reasonably required or that the rent is unreasonably high by comparison with the rent payable in respect of suitable alternative accommodation elsewhere: see paras (3)(a) and (b) of the version of reg 13 of both the HB and the HB(SPC) Regs in Sch 3 para 5 HB&CTB(CP) Regs and the Analysis thereto.

Under the pilot local housing allowance scheme introduced from November 2003 in the "Pathfinder authorities" areas which are listed in Sch 1 to the Rent Officers (Housing Benefit Functions) (Pilot Housing Allowance) Order 2003 SI No 2398, "maximum rent" will instead be restricted to figures given by the rent officer under Arts 4B and 4C of this Order, as inserted by the 2003 Order.

The role of rent officers in rent allowance subsidy is governed by Art 16 of, and Sch 4 to the Income-Related Beneffits (Subsidy) Order 1998 (SI 1998 No 562). There are financial incentives resting on local authorities to apply the rent restrictions scheme correctly.

Citation and commencement

1.–(1)   This Order may be cited as the Rent Officers (Housing Benefit Functions) Order 1997.

(2)   This article and articles 8 and 10(1) shall come into force on 18th August 1997 and all the other articles shall come into force on 3rd September 1997.

Interpretation

2.–(1)   In this Order, unless the context otherwise requires–

"assured tenancy" has the same meaning as in Part I of the Housing Act 1988, except that it includes a tenancy which would be an assured tenancy but for paragraph 2 [³ , 8] or 10 of Schedule 1 to that Act and a licence which would be an assured tenancy (within the extended meaning given in this definition) were it a tenancy;

[² "board and attendance determination" means a determination made in accordance with article 4C;]

[² "broad rental market area" has the meaning specified in paragraph 4 of Part I of Schedule 3A to this Order;]

[² "broad rental market area determination" means a determination made in accordance with article 4B(1);]

"child" means a person under the age of 16;

"determination" means a determination made in accordance with Part I or IV of Schedule 1 to this Order;

"dwelling" means any residential accommodation whether or not consisting of the whole or part of a building and whether or not comprising separate and self-contained premises;

[⁴ "hostel" has the same meaning as in regulation 2(1) of the Housing Benefit Regulations or, as the case may be, regulation 2(1) of the Housing Benefit (State Pension Credit) Regulations;]

[⁵ "the Housing Benefit Regulations" mean the Housing Benefit Regulations 2006;

"the Housing Benefit (State Pension Credit) Regulations" means the Housing Benefit (Persons who have attained the qualifying age for state pension credit) Regulations 2006;]

"local authority" has the same meaning as in the Social Security Administration Act 1992 in relation to England and in relation to Wales;

[² "local housing allowance determination" means a determination made in accordance with article 4B(2);]

"occupier" means a person (whether or not identified by name) who is stated, in the application for the determination, to occupy the dwelling as his home;

[² "pathfinder authority" means a local authority specified in column (1) of the table in Part II of Schedule 3A, on and after the date specified in column (2) of that table in relation to that authority;]

"redetermination" means a redetermination made in accordance with article 4;

[⁴ "relevant date" means the date specified by a pathfinder authority in an application for a local housing allowance determination made in accordance with regulation 13A(4)(a) of the Housing Benefit Regulations or, as the case may be, regulation 13A(4)(a) of the Housing Benefit (State Pension Credit) Regulations;]

[¹ "relevant period" means–
   (a)   in relation to a determination, the period of five working days (or, where the determination does not relate to a prospective tenancy and the rent officer intends to inspect the dwelling before making the determination, 25 working days) beginning with-
      (i)   where the rent officer requests further information under article 5, the date on which he receives the information; and
      (ii)   in any other case, the date on which he receives the application for the determination; and
   (b)   in relation to a redetermination, the period of 20 working days beginning with-
      (i)   where the rent officer requests further information under article 5, the date on which he receives the information; and
      (ii)   in any other case, the date on which he receives the application for that redetermination;]

"relevant time" means the time the application for the determination [² or board and attendance determination] is made or, if earlier, the tenancy ends;

[⁴ "rent" means any of the periodical payments referred to in regulation 12(1) of the Housing Benefit Regulations or, as the case may be, regulation 12(1) of the Housing Benefit (State Pension Credit) Regulations;]

"size criteria" means the standards relating to bedrooms and rooms suitable for living in specified in Schedule 2 to this Order;

"tenancy" includes–
   (a)   a licence; and
   (b)   a prospective tenancy or licence; and
      references to a tenant, a landlord or any other expression appropriate to a tenancy shall be construed accordingly; and

[⁶]

(2)   In this Order any reference to a notice or application is to a notice or application in writing, except in a case where the recipient consents (whether generally or specifically) to the notice or application being transmitted by electronic means.

Amendments
1.   Substituted by art 3 of SI 2000 No 1 as from 3.4.00.
2.   Insertions made by Art 2 of SI 2003 No 2398 as from a date specified in Sch 1 to that SI in relation to each individual authority.

3.   Inserted by Art 2(1) of SI 2004 No 2101 as from 31.8.04.
4.   Substituted by Sch 1 para 11(2)(a), (c) and (d) of SI 2006 No 217 as from 6.3.06.
5.   Inserted by Sch 1 para 11(2)(b) of SI 2006 No 217 as from 6.3.06.
6.   Omitted by Sch 1 para 11(2)(e) of SI 2006 No 217 as from 6.3.06.

Analysis
"Assured tenancy". By s1 of the Housing Act 1988 an "assured tenancy" is a tenancy of a dwelling house
let to an individual or individuals as their "only or principal home". It has an extended definition in this
section. Sch 1 para 2 of the 1988 Act excludes houses with an annual rent of more than a set amount
from the Act, but tenancies of such properties fall within the definition for the purposes of this Order.
Sch 1 para 10, broadly speaking, excludes properties where the landlord is resident. The very complex
provisions of that paragraph and those accompanying it do not arise here either. Licenses also fall
within the definition of "assured tenancy", so there will be no issue as to whether or not exclusive
possession of the premises has been granted.
    Note that an assured shorthold tenancy is just a particular type of assured tenancy: see ss19A and 20
of the 1988 Act. Such tenancies therefore also fall within this definition.
*"Occupier".*The definition of "occupier" was discussed in *R v Swale BC HBRB ex p Marchant* [1999] 1
FLR 1087, QBD; [2000] 1 FLR 246, CA. The claimant was separated from his wife. Their children spent
alternate weeks with the claimant and his wife. She received child benefit for them. The rent officer was
instructed by the local authority to assess the claimant's rent on the basis that the children were not
"occupiers" of his property. Kay J [1999] 1 FLR 1087 upheld that decision on the basis that as the wife
was "responsible" for the children pursuant to reg 14 HB Regs 1987 (now reg 20 of both the HB and
the HB(SPC) Regs), they were members of her family. Consequently reg 5(1) HB regs 1987 (now reg
7(1) of both the HB and the HB(SPC) Regs) proceeded on the basis that they were normally occupying
the wife's home and that was the proper definition of "occupier" in Art 2.
    The Court of Appeal heard and dismissed an appeal from that decision. Potter LJ stated that it was
clear that resolution of the questions of with which parent a child normally lived and of whose household
the child was a member should also be regarded as determinative of the question of which dwelling a child
occupied for the purposes of the Rent Officers (Additional Functions) Order 1995 (which was in identical
terms to the 1997 Order). To permit the children to be taken into account in examining the sizes of both
households would lead to an "element of double provision" in the scheme.
    It was also confirmed in the judgment of Potter LJ that the decision as to whether or not a person is an
"occupier" is one for the local authority. This is made in the "application" to the Rent Officer pursuant to reg
14(1) of both the HB and the HB(SPC) Regs.
*"Relevant period".*The rent officer must provide a determination within five working days and a
redetermination within 20 working days of the relevant date. The relevant date is the date of receipt of
the request for the determination or, if the rent officer has to seek further information, the date on which
that information is received.
    In the case of a determination, the "relevant period" is lengthened to 25 days where the determination
sought is not a pre-tenancy determination under reg 14(1)(e) of both the HB and the HB(SPC) Regs and
where the rent officer wishes to inspect the home first.

Determinations

3.–(1)   Subject to [² articles 3A and 6], where a local authority, in accordance
with regulations made under section 136(2) or (3) of the Social Security
Administration Act 1992, [¹ or section 122(5) of the Housing Act 1996,] applies to a
rent officer for determinations in respect of a tenancy of a dwelling, a rent officer
shall–

(a)   make the determinations in accordance with Part I of Schedule 1
       (determinations);

(b)   comply with Part II of Schedule 1 when making the determinations
       (assumptions etc.); and

(c)   give notice in accordance with Part III of Schedule 1 (notifications) [¹ within
       the relevant period or as soon as is practicable after that period].

(2)   A rent officer for each registration area (within the meaning of section 62
of the Rent Act 1977), on the first working day of each month, shall–

(a)   make determinations in accordance with Part IV of Schedule 1 (indicative
       rent levels) in relation to the area of each local authority [³ , except for a
       local authority which is a pathfinder authority,] within the registration area;

(b)   comply with paragraph 8(2) of Part II of Schedule 1 (assumptions etc.) when making the determinations; and

(c)   give to the local authority notice of the determinations relating to its area when they have been made.

Amendments

1.   Amended by art 4 of SI 2000 No 1 as from 3.4.00.
2.   Amended by reg 3 of SI 2001 No 1325 as from 2.7.01.
3.   Insertion made by Art 2 of SI 2003 No 2398 as from a date specified in Sch 1 to that SI in relation to each individual authority.

Transitional arrangements for determination of Single Room Rents with effect from 2nd July 2001

3A.   In a case where the rent officer has made and notified an authority of a determination of a single room rent pursuant to paragraph 5 of Schedule 1 in the period of 12 months before 2nd July 2001 that determination shall cease to have effect on [² . . .] 2nd July 2001 and a rent officer shall–

(a)   make a new determination of that single room rent in accordance with Part I of Schedule 1;

(b)   comply with Part II of Schedule 1; and

(c)   give notice in accordance with Part III of Schedule 1 within the relevant period or as soon as is practicable after that period;

without an application for a determination under [³ regulation 14 of the Housing Benefit Regulations or, as the case may be, regulation 14 of the Housing Benefit (State Pension Credit) Regulations] having been made.]

Amendments

1.   Inserted by reg 3 of SI 2001 No 1325 as from 2.7.01.
2.   Amended by reg 2(2) of SI 2001 No 2317 as from 2.7.01.
3.   Amended by reg 5 and Sch 2 para 11(3) of SI 2006 No 217 as from 6.3.06.

General Note

The definition of the 'single room rent' was amended on 2 July 2001 so as to be more generous to the claimants who were subject to it. Art 3A aimed to ensure that those who were affected by this change benefited from it immediately. For further information, see the commentary in the 18th edn of this work at page 570.

Redeterminations

[¹**4.**–(1)   Subject to article 6, where the local authority applies to a rent officer for a redetermination of any determination or redetermination in respect of a tenancy of a dwelling the rent officer shall, in accordance with Schedule 3–

(a)   make redeterminations of any effective determinations and any effective redeterminations in respect of that tenancy; and

(b)   give notice within the relevant period or as soon as is practicable after that period.

(2)   For the purposes of paragraph (1)–

(a)   ''effective determinations'' means any determinations made in accordance with Part I of Schedule 1 which have effect at the date of the application for a redetermination of a determination or redetermination; and

(b)   ''effective redeterminations'' means any redeterminations made in accordance with Schedule 3 which have effect at that date.

(3)   A rent officer whose advice is sought as provided for in Schedule 3 shall give that advice.

Amendment

1.   Substituted by Art 5 of SI 2000 No 1 as from 3.4.00.

General Note
Art 4 makes it clear that only "effective" determinations or redeterminations need to be redetermined – that is those that have effect at the time that the local authority applies for a redetermination.

Substitute determinations and substitute redeterminations

[¹**4A.**–(1)   Where a local authority applies to a rent officer for a substitute determination, in accordance with [² regulation 17 of the Housing Benefit Regulations or, as the case may be, regulation 17 of the Housing Benefit (State Pension Credit) Regulations], the provisions of this Order shall apply to that substitute determination as they apply to a determination, but as if references to the relevant time were references to the date the application for the original determination was made or, if earlier, the date the tenancy ended.

(2)   Where a local authority applies to a rent officer for a substitute redetermination, in accordance with that regulation, the provisions of this Order shall apply to that substitute redetermination as they apply to a redetermination.]

Amendments
1.   Inserted by Art 5 of SI 2000 No 1 as from 3.4.00.
2.   Amended by reg 5 and Sch 2 para 11(4) of SI 2006 No 217 as from 6.3.06.

General Note
Art 4A(1) allows for determinations to be substituted on an application under reg 17 of both the HB and the HB(SPC) Regs. Reg 17 permits substitute determinations where either the local authority or the rent officer has made an error. See the commentary to reg 17 HB Regs.

[¹Broad rental market area determinations and local housing allowance determinations

4B.–(1) On the day on which this article comes into force in relation to a local authority and so often thereafter as a rent officer, having regard to the definition of "broad rental market area" in paragraph (1) of article 2, considers appropriate, a rent officer shall–
  (a)   determine one or more broad rental market areas which will (during the month which next begins after the determination is made) fall, in whole or in part, within the area of that local authority so that every part of the area of that authority falls within a broad rental market area and no part of the area of that authority falls within more than one broad rental market area; and
  (b)   give to that authority a notice which–
         (i)   specifies the area contained within each broad rental market area as falls, in whole or in part, within the area of that authority, by reference to the postcodes for each such broad rental market area; and
         (ii)   identifies such of those postcodes as fall within the area of that authority.
  (2)   No more than 5 and not less than 3 working days before the end of each month a rent officer shall–
  (a)   determine, in accordance with the provisions of Part I of Schedule 3A–
         (i)   a local housing allowance for each of the categories of dwelling set out in paragraph 1 of that Part; and
         (ii)   local housing allowances for such other categories of dwelling of more than six rooms as a rent officer believes are likely to be required for the purpose of calculating housing benefit,
for each broad rental market area falling within, in whole or in part, the area of any local authority which is (or will be) a pathfinder authority during the month which follows; and

(b)   give to each such authority notice of the local housing allowance determinations made in accordance with paragraph (a) for each broad rental market area falling within, in whole or in part, the area of that authority.

(3)   Any broad rental market area determination made in accordance with paragraph (1), or local housing allowance determination made in accordance with paragraph (2), shall take effect on the first working day of the month which begins after the day on which the determination is made.

(4)   Where a pathfinder authority–

(a)   makes an application in accordance with [² regulation 13A(4)(a) of the Housing Benefit Regulations or, as the case may be, regulation 13A(4)(a) of the Housing Benefit (State Pension Credit) Regulations, a rent officer shall determine, in accordance with the provisions of Part I of Schedule 3A and as soon as is reasonably practicable, the local housing allowance for that category of dwelling at the relevant date, for each broad rental market area falling within, in whole or in part, the area of the pathfinder authority that made the application, at the relevant date; or

(b)   makes an application in accordance with [² regulation 13A(5) of the Housing Benefit Regulations or, as the case may be, regulation 13A(5) of the Housing Benefit (State Pension Credit) Regulations, a rent officer shall determine, in accordance with the provisions of Part I of Schedule 3A and as soon as is reasonably practicable, the local housing allowance for that category of dwelling for each broad rental market area falling within, in whole or in part, the area of the pathfinder authority.

(5)   Where a rent officer has made a local housing allowance determination in accordance with paragraph (4)–

(a)   he shall give notice of the determination to the pathfinder authority that made the application;

(b)   any local housing allowance determination made in accordance with sub-paragraph (4)(a) shall take effect for the month in which the relevant date falls; and

(c)   any local housing allowance determination made in accordance with sub-paragraph (4)(b) shall take effect for the month in which notice is given in accordance with sub-paragraph (a).]

Amendments

1.   Inserted by Art 2(5) of SI 2003 No 2398 as from a date specified in Sch 1 to that SI in relation to each individual authority.

2.   Amended by reg 5 and Sch 2 para 11(5) of SI 2006 No 217 as from 6.3.06.

[¹Board and attendance determinations and notifications

4C.–(1) Where a pathfinder authority makes an application to a rent officer in accordance with [² regulation 17(6) of the Housing Benefit Regulations or, as the case may be, regulation 13A(6) of the Housing Benefit (State Pension Credit) Regulations], a rent officer shall determine whether or not a substantial part of the rent under the tenancy at the relevant time is fairly attributable to board and attendance.

(2)   Where a rent officer determines that a substantial part of the rent under the tenancy at the relevant time is fairly attributable to board and attendance, he shall–

(a)   notify the pathfinder authority accordingly; and

(b)   treat the application as if it has been made in accordance with [² regulation 14(1) of the Housing Benefit Regulations or, as the case may be, regulation 14(1) of the Housing Benefit (State Pension Credit) Regulations].

(3)   Where a rent officer determines that a substantial part of the rent under the tenancy at the relevant time is not fairly attributable to board and attendance, he shall notify the pathfinder authority accordingly.

(4)   Where an application for a board and attendance determination is treated as if it has been made in accordance with [² regulation 14(1) of the Housing Benefit Regulations or, as the case may be, regulation 14(1) of the Housing Benefit (State Pension Credit) Regulations], then, for the purposes of paragraph (a)(ii) of the definition of "relevant period" in article 2(1), it shall be treated as having been received on the day on which the determination referred to in paragraph (2) is made.]

Amendments

1.   Inserted by Art 2(5) of SI 2003 No 2398 as from a date specified in Sch 1 to that SI in relation to each individual authority.

2.   Amended by reg 5 and Sch 2 para 11(6) of SI 2006 No 217 as from 6.3.06.

[¹Board and attendance redeterminations

4D.–(1) Subject to article 6, where a pathfinder authority applies to a rent officer for a redetermination of a board and attendance determination or board and attendance redetermination, the rent officer shall, in accordance with paragraph (2)–

    (a)   make a redetermination of–

        (i)   the board and attendance determination, provided it was made in accordance with article 4C and had effect at the date of the application for it to be redetermined; or

        (ii)   the board and attendance redetermination provided it was made in accordance with head (i), and had effect at the date of the application for it to be redetermined; and

    (b)   notify the pathfinder authority of the redetermination.

(2)   When making a board and attendance redetermination under this article, the rent officer shall seek, and have regard to, the advice of one or two other rent officers in relation to the redetermination.

(3)   A rent officer whose advice is sought in accordance with paragraph (2) shall give that advice.

(4)   Article 4C shall apply in relation to a board and attendance redetermination but as if the references to the relevant time were references to the date on which the original application for a board and attendance determination was made, or if earlier, to the date on which the tenancy ended.]

Amendment

1.   Inserted by Art 2(5) of SI 2003 No 2398 as from a date specified in Sch 1 to that SI in relation to each individual authority.

[¹Substitute board and attendance determinations and substitute board and attendance redeterminations

4E.–(1)   Where a pathfinder authority applies to a rent officer for a substitute board and attendance determination in accordance with [² regulation 17 of the Housing Benefit Regulations or, as the case may be, regulation 17 of the Housing Benefit (State Pension Credit) Regulations], the provisions of this Order shall apply to that substitute board and attendance determination as they apply to a board and attendance determination but as if references to the relevant time were references to the date on which the original application for a board and attendance determination was made or, if earlier, the date on which the tenancy ended.

(2)   Where a pathfinder authority applies to a rent officer for a substitute board and attendance redetermination in accordance with [2 regulation 17 of the Housing Benefit Regulations or, as the case may be, regulation 17 of the Housing Benefit (State Pension Credit) Regulations], the provisions of this Order shall apply to that substitute board and attendance redetermination as they apply to a board and attendance redetermination.]

Amendments

1. Inserted by Art 2(5) of SI 2003 No 2398 as from a date specified in Sch 1 to that SI in relation to each individual authority.
2. Amended by reg 5 and Sch 2 para 11(7) of SI 2006 No 217 as from 6.3.06.

Insufficient information

5. If a rent officer needs further information in order to make a determination under article 3(1) [², a redetermination under article 4, a board and attendance determination under article 4C or a board and attendance redetermination under article 4D], he shall serve notice on the local authority requesting that information [¹ ...].

Amendments

1. Deleted by Art 6 of SI 2000 No 1 as from 3.4.00.
2. Substituted by Art 2(6) SI 2003 No 2398 as from a date specified in Sch 1 to that SI in relation to each individual authority.

Exceptions

6.–(1) No determination [¹, redetermination, board and attendance determination or board and attendance redetermination] shall be made if the application for it is withdrawn.

(2) No determination shall be made under paragraph 3, 4 or 5 of Part I of Schedule 1 if the tenancy is of residential accommodation, within the meaning of [² regulation 9(4) of the Housing Benefit Regulations or, as the case may be, regulation 9(4) of the Housing Benefit (State Pension Credit) Regulations] (registered homes etc.), or in a hostel.

(3) No determination shall be made under paragraph 5 of Part I of Schedule 1 unless the local authority states in the application that the claimant is, or may be, a young individual (which has the same meaning as in [² the Housing Benefit Regulations and the Housing Benefit (State Pension Credit) Regulations]).

(4) If the rent officer becomes aware that an application is not one which gives rise to a duty to make a determination [¹, redetermination, board and attendance determination or a board and attendance redetermination], the rent officer shall give the local authority notice to that effect.

Amendments

1. Substituted by Art 2(7) of SI 2003 No 2398 as from a date specified in Sch 1 to that SI in relation to each individual authority.
2. Amended by reg 5 and Sch 2 para 11(8) of SI 2006 No 217 as from 6.3.06.

Special cases

7.–(1) This Order shall apply as specified in Schedule 4 in relation to–

(a) mooring charges payable for a houseboat;

(b) payments in respect of the site on which a caravan or mobile home stands; or

(c) payments under a rental purchase agreement.

(2) Terms used in paragraph (1) have the same meaning in this article and in Schedule 4 as they have in [² regulation 12(1) of the Housing Benefit Regulations or, as the case may be, regulation 12(1) of the Housing Benefit (State Pension Credit) Regulations] (rents).[¹ ...]

Amendments

1. Omitted by Art 7 of SI 2000 No 1 as from 3.4.00.
2. Amended by reg 5 and Sch 2 para 11(9) of SI 2006 No 217 as from 6.3.06.

[¹Errors

7A.–[² (1)] If a rent officer is of the opinion that he has made an error (other than in the application of his professional judgement) in relation to a determination or redetermination, he shall notify the local authority which made the application for that determination or redetermination of the error as soon as practicable after he becomes aware of it.]

[² (2)   If a rent officer is of the opinion that he has made an error (other than in the application of his professional judgement) in relation to a board and attendance determination or board and attendance redetermination, he shall notify the pathfinder authority which made the application for that board and attendance determination or board and attendance redetermination of the error as soon as practicable after he becomes aware of it.

(3)   If a rent officer is of the opinion that he has made an error (other than in the application of his professional judgement) in relation to a broad rental market area determination or a local housing allowance determination, he shall notify any pathfinder authority to which notification of that determination was sent of the error, and the amended determination, as soon as practicable after he becomes aware of it.]

Amendments

1.   Inserted by Art 8 of SI 2000 No 1 as from 3.4.00.
2.   Inserted by Art 2(8) of SI 2003 No 2398 as from a date specified in Sch 1 to that SI in relation to each individual authority.

General Note

Art 7A requires a rent officer to notify the local authority of an error, which will then require the local authority to apply under reg 17 of both the HB and the HB(SPC) Regs for a substitute determination under Art 4A. The words in brackets, "other than in the application of his professional judgement", are important. A rent officer may not notify a local authority where s/he has second thoughts about a figure that s/he has assessed for a property. There must be some basic error of fact or law that vitiates the decision.

Amendment to 1995 Order

8.   The Rent Officers (Additional Functions) Order 1995 shall be amended by the insertion at the end of article 6 (special cases) of the following–

"(3) In a case where the local authority states in the application that the rent includes charges for general counselling or any other support services which are eligible for housing benefit solely by virtue of paragraph 1(f)(iii) of Schedule 1 to the 1987 Regulations (landlord's support services: supported accommodation) or solely by virtue of that provision and paragraph 1(f)(ii) of that Schedule, the rent officer shall assume when making a determination on a redetermination that–

(a)   the services were not to be provided or made available; and

(b)   the rent payable under the tenancy at the relevant time is such amount as is specified in the application as the rent which would have been payable under the tenancy at that time if those items were not to be provided or made available.

(4)   In a case where the local authority states in the application that the rent includes charges for general counselling or any other support services and the charges–

(a)   are eligible for housing benefit by virtue of paragraph 1(f)(iii) of Schedule 1 to the 1987 Regulations (landlord's support services: supported accommodation) or that provision and paragraph 1(f)(ii) of that Schedule; and

(b)   are also eligible for housing benefit by virtue of paragraph 1(f)(i) of that Schedule (support services: other exceptions);

the rent officer shall include in the notice to the local authority, required under article 3(1)(c), a statement of the amount of the rent payable for the tenancy (which has the same meaning as in paragraph 3(1) of Schedule 1 to this Order) which relates to those charges.''.

Revocations

9.   The Rent Officers (Additional Functions) Order 1995, the Rent Officers (Additional Functions) (Amendment) Order 1995, the Rent Officers (Additional

Functions) (Amendment No. 2) Order 1995, the Rent Officers (Additional Functions) (Amendment) Order 1996 and the Rent Officers (Additional Functions) (Amendment) Order 1997 are hereby revoked.

Application

10.–(1)   The amendment made by article 8 does not have effect in a case where an application for a determination is made before the date that article comes into force.

(2)   The remaining articles of the Order (other than paragraph (1)) do not have effect in a case where an application is made for a determination before the date those articles come into force

SCHEDULE 1

Analysis
"Vicinity", "Neighbourhood" and "Locality"

Significantly high rent (SHR) and size related rent (SizeRR) figures are determined on the basis of rents in the "vicinity". Para 1(4) defines "vicinity" in fairly restrictive terms. "Immediately surrounding" must, on any view, connote a limited geographical area. It cannot of course be taken literally so as to preclude any comparators other than immediately neighbouring dwellings, but it cannot sensibly be extended to a zone extending further than, say, a few streets away. Only if there are no homes of a comparable size in that area may the "vicinity" be extended, but then only to an area where such homes exist: para 1(4)(b). It is not clear whether the "vicinity" is then expanded for the purpose of calculating the SHR as well as the SizeRR. It would appear from the wording of para 1(4)(b) that it is to be expanded for both purposes.

"Neighbourhood" is used for the purposes of an exceptionally high rent determination. Para 3(5)(a) defines "neighbourhood" in a town or city as the part of that town or city where the home is located that is a "distinct area of residential accommodation". This is an even more vague definition than that of "vicinity" and could cause much dispute, particularly in densely populated inner city areas where affluent areas and deprived areas are mixed freely and closely. And what is a "town or city"? Outside a town or city, the "neighbourhood" is expanded by para 3(5)(b) to as much as is required to incorporate comparator dwellings.

"Locality" is the zone of comparison for generating a local reference rent and the single room rent. Para 4(6) defines a "locality" as an area of more than one neighbourhood, including that where the relevant dwelling is situated, within which a claimant could be expected to live in the light of the available amenities. "Neighbourhood" has the same meaning as in para 3(5). The test under para 4(6)(b) is centred upon the reasonable expectations of the tenant judged objectively: *The Rent Service v R(Heffernan) [2007] EWCA Civ 544, 13 June, CA*. So the fact that the tenant may be disabled, for example, may be relevant to fixing the locality, and accessible facilities within it, within which s/he may reasonably be expected to live. However, a locality is not to be constrained to an area where the relevant services and facilites are of the same quality after a detailed analysis: all that is required is that the services and facilities are of a similar standard, and all 'standard' means in this context is services which meet the requirments of law and the appropriate public authorities (*Heffernan* (paras 35(f) and 36).   Again, a considerable degree of local knowledge and judgement is called for. No maximum area is laid down and in *Heffernan* the Court of Appeal saw no error of law in the rent officer's choice of the City of Sheffield as one "locality", although the court accepted that Greater Manchester would be too large an area for properly assessing a local reference rent.

Quite clearly, there is considerable room for judgement here, both as to what the "vicinity", "locality" and "neighbourhood" are and the area to which they should be expanded if applicable. It is therefore unsatisfactory that there is no provision for disclosure to claimants of the area which has been taken into account.

Significant amendments were made to Sch 1 from 6 November 2001. For commentary on the former provisions, see pp 576-77 of the 18th edition of this book.

Part I
Determinations

Significantly high rents

1.–(1)   The rent officer shall determine whether, in his opinion, the rent payable under the tenancy of the dwelling at the relevant time is significantly higher than the rent which the landlord might reasonably have been expected to obtain under the tenancy at that time.

(2)   If the rent officer determines under sub-paragraph (1) that the rent is significantly higher, the rent officer shall also determine the rent which the landlord might reasonably have been expected to obtain under the tenancy at the relevant time.

(3)   When making a determination under this paragraph, the rent officer shall have regard to the level of rent under similar tenancies of similar dwellings in the [¹ vicinity] (or as similar as regards tenancy, dwelling and [¹ vicinity] as is reasonably practicable) and shall assume that no one who would have been entitled to housing benefit had sought or is seeking the tenancy.

[²(4)   For the purposes of this paragraph and paragraph 2 ''vicinity'' means-

(a)   the area immediately surrounding the dwelling; or

(b)   where, for the purposes of sub-paragraph (2)(c) of paragraph 2, there is no dwelling in the area immediately surrounding the dwelling which satisfies the description in heads (i), (ii) and (iii) of that sub-paragraph, the area nearest to the dwelling where there is such a dwelling.]

Amendments

1.   Amended by art 2(2) of SI 2001 No 3561 as from 6.11.01.

2.   Inserted by art 2(2) of SI 2001 No 3561 as from 6.11.01.

Size and rent

2.–(1)   The rent officer shall determine whether the dwelling, at the relevant time, exceeds the size criteria for the occupiers.

(2)   If the rent officer determines that the dwelling exceeds the size criteria, the rent officer shall also determine the rent which a landlord might reasonably have been expected to obtain, at the relevant time, for a tenancy which is–

(a)   similar to the tenancy of the dwelling;

(b)   on the same terms other than the term relating to the amount of rent; and

(c)   of a dwelling which is in the same [¹ vicinity] as the dwelling, but which–

    (i)   accords with the size criteria for the occupiers;

    (ii)   is in a reasonable state of repair; and

    (iii)   corresponds in other respects, in the rent officer's opinion, as closely as is reasonably practicable to the dwelling.

(3)   When making a determination under sub-paragraph (2), the rent officer shall have regard to the same matter and make the same assumption as specified in paragraph 1(3), except that in judging the similarity of other tenancies and dwellings the comparison shall be with the tenancy of the second dwelling referred to in sub-paragraph (2) and shall assume that no one who would have been entitled to housing benefit had sought or is seeking that tenancy.

Amendment

1.   Amended by art 2(3) of SI 2001 No 3561 as from 6.11.01.

Exceptionally high rents

3.–(1)   The rent officer shall determine whether, in his opinion, the rent payable for the tenancy of the dwelling at the relevant time is exceptionally high.

(2)   In sub-paragraph (1) ''rent payable for the tenancy'' means–

(a)   where a determination is made under sub-paragraph (2) of paragraph 2, the rent determined under that sub-paragraph;

(b)   where no determination is so made and a determination is made under sub-paragraph (2) of paragraph 1, the rent determined under that sub-paragraph; and

(c)   in any other case, the rent payable under the tenancy [¹ at the relevant time].

(3)   If the rent officer determines under sub-paragraph (1) that the rent is exceptionally high, the rent officer shall also determine the highest rent, which is not an exceptionally high rent and which a landlord might reasonably have been expected to obtain at the relevant time (on the assumption that no one who would have been entitled to housing benefit had sought or is seeking the tenancy) for an assured tenancy of a dwelling which–

(a)   is in the same [² neighbourhood] as the dwelling;

(b)   has the same number of bedrooms and rooms suitable for living in as the dwelling (or, where the dwelling exceeds the size criteria for the occupiers, accords with the size criteria); and

(c)   is in a reasonable state of repair.

(4)   For the purpose of determining whether a rent is an exceptionally high rent under this paragraph, the rent officer shall have regard to the levels of rent under assured tenancies of dwellings which–

(a)   are in the same [² neighbourhood] as the dwelling (or in as similar a locality as is reasonably practicable); and

(b) have the same number of bedrooms and rooms suitable for living in as the dwelling (or, in a case where the dwelling exceeds the size criteria for the occupiers, accord with the size criteria).

[³ (5) For the purposes of this paragraph and paragraph 4(6) ''neighbourhood'' means-

(a) where the dwelling is in a town or city, the part of that town or city where the dwelling is located which is a distinct area of residential accommodation; or

(b) where the dwelling is not in a town or city, the area surrounding the dwelling which is a distinct area of residential accommodation and where there are dwellings satisfying the description in sub-paragraph (4)(b).]

Amendments

1. Inserted by arts 9 and 10 of SI 2000 No 1 as from 3.4.00.
2. Amended by art 2(4) of SI 2001 No 3561 as from 6.11.01.
3. Inserted by art 2(4) of SI 2001 No 3561 as from 6.11.01.

Local reference rents

4.–(1) The rent officer shall make a determination of a local reference rent in accordance with the formula–

$$R = \frac{H+L}{2}$$

where–

R is the local reference rent;

H is the highest rent, in the rent officer's opinion–

(a) which a landlord might reasonably have been expected to obtain, at the relevant time, for an assured tenancy of a dwelling which meets the criteria in sub-paragraph (2); and

(b) which is not an exceptionally high rent; and

L is the lowest rent, in the rent officer's opinion,–

(a) which a landlord might reasonably have been expected to obtain, at the relevant time, for an assured tenancy of a dwelling which meets the criteria in sub-paragraph (2); and

(b) which is not an exceptionally low rent; and

(2) The criteria are–

(a) that the dwelling under the assured tenancy–

    (i) is in the same locality as the dwelling;

    (ii) is in a reasonable state of repair; and

    (iii) has the same number of bedrooms and rooms suitable for living in as the dwelling (or, in a case where the dwelling exceeds the size criteria for the occupiers, accords with the size criteria); and

(b) if the tenant does not have the use under the tenancy of the dwelling[¹ at the relevant time] of more than one bedroom or room suitable for living in–

    (i) that under the assured tenancy the tenant does not have the use of more than one bedroom or room suitable for living in;

    (ii) if the rent under the tenancy [¹ at the relevant time] includes payments for board and attendance and the rent officer considers the amount fairly attributable to board and attendance is a substantial part of the rent, that a substantial part of the rent under the assured tenancy is fairly attributable to board and attendance;

    (iii) if sub-paragraph (ii) does not apply and the tenant shares a [² kitchen, toilet, bathroom and room suitable for living in] with a person other than a member of his household, a non-dependant or a person who pays rent to the tenant, that the assured tenancy provides for the tenant to share a [² kitchen, toilet, bathroom and room suitable for living in]; and

    (iv) if sub-paragraphs (ii) and (iii) do not apply, that the circumstances described in sub-paragraphs (ii) and (iii) do not apply in relation to the assured tenancy.

(3) Where ascertaining H and L under sub-paragraph (1), the rent officer:

(a) shall assume that no one who would have been entitled to housing benefit had sought or is seeking the tenancy; and

(b) shall exclude the amount of any rent which, in the rent officer's opinion, is fairly attributable to the provision of services which are ineligible to be met by housing benefit

[⁴ . . .]

(4) In sub-paragraph (2)(b)–

''bedroom or room suitable for living in'' does not include a room which the tenant shares with any person other than–

(a) a member of his household;

(b) a non-dependant (as defined in this sub-paragraph); or

(c)   a person who pays rent to the tenant; and

[[5] "non-dependant" means a non-dependant of the tenant within the meaning of regulation 3 of the Housing Benefit Regulations or, as the case may be, regulation 3 of the Housing Benefit (State Pension Credit) Regulations;]

(5)   In sub-paragraph (3), "services" means services performed or facilities (including the use of furniture) provided for, or rights made available to, the tenant, but not [[1], in the case of a tenancy where a substantial part of the rent under the tenancy is fairly attributable to board and attendance, the provision of meals (including the preparation of meals or provision of unprepared food).]

[[3] (6)   For the purposes of this paragraph and paragraph 5 "locality" means an area-

(a)   comprising two or more neighbourhoods, including the neighbourhood where the dwelling is situated, each neighbourhood adjoining at least one other in the area;

(b)   within which a tenant of the dwelling could reasonably be expected to live having regard to facilities and services for the purposes of health, education, recreation, personal banking and shopping which are in or accessible from the neighbourhood of the dwelling, taking account of the distance of travel, by public and private transport, to and from facilities and services of the same type and similar standard; and

(c)   containing residential premises of a variety of types, and including such premises held on a variety of tenancies.]

Amendments

1.   Inserted by arts 9 and 10 of SI 2000 No 1 as from 3.4.00.
2.   Amended by reg 2(3) of SI 2001 No 2317 as from 2.7.01.
3.   Amended by art 2(5) of SI 2001 No 3561 as from 6.11.01.
4.   Deleted by art 2 of SI 2003 No 478 as from 1.4.03 (7.4.03 where rent payable weekly or in multiples of a week).
5.   Substituted by reg 5 and Sch 2 para 11(10)(a) of SI 2006 No 217 as from 6.3.06.

Single room rents

5.–(1)   The rent officer shall determine a single room rent in accordance with the following formula–

$$S = \frac{H+L}{2}$$

where–

S is the single room rent;

H is the highest rent, in the rent officer's opinion,–

(a)   which a landlord might reasonably have been expected to obtain, at the relevant time, for an assured tenancy of a dwelling which meets the criteria in sub-paragraph (2); and

(b)   which is not an exceptionally high rent.

L is the lowest rent, in the rent officer's opinion,–

(a)   which a landlord might reasonably have been expected to obtain, at the relevant time, for an assured tenancy of a dwelling which meets the criteria in sub-paragraph (2); and

(b)   which is not an exceptionally low rent.

(2)   The criteria are–

(a)   that the dwelling under the assured tenancy is in the same locality as the dwelling and is in a reasonable state of repair;

(b)   that, under the assured tenancy, the tenant–

    (i)   has the exclusive use of one bedroom;

    (ii)   does not have the use of any other bedroom [[1]...];

    [[1](iia)   shares the use of a room suitable for living in;]

    (iii)   shares the use of a toilet [[1] and bathroom]; and

    (iv)   shares the use of a kitchen and does not have the exclusive use of facilities for cooking food; and

(c)   that the rent does not include any payment for board and attendance.

(3)   Sub-paragraphs [[3] (3) and (5)] of paragraph 4 apply when ascertaining H and L under this sub-paragraph as if the reference in those sub-paragraphs to H and L were to H and L under [[3] this paragraph].

Amendments

1.   Amended by reg 4 of SI 2001 No 1325 as from 2.7.01.
2.   Substituted by Art 2(9) of SI 2003 No 2398 as from a date specified in Sch 1 to that SI in relation to each individual authority.
3.   Amended by Arts 2(1) and 3 of SI 2005 No 236 as from 13.3.05.

Analysis

The single room rent (SRR) applies where the claimant is a "young individual" (see definition in reg 2(1) of both the HB and the HB(SPC) Regs and the Commentary to reg 13 HB Regs) which, in broad terms, means a single person under the age of 25. The policy is that HB should not pay for such people to live in self-contained accommodation but only in a single bed-room with shared facilities. Until 2 July 2001, sub-para (2) provided for the determination to be made on the basis of "bed-sitting" accommodation (ie, a single room with shared kitchen and toilet). The definition was extended from that date to include accommodation with a shared bathroom (surely an omission by oversight from the previous definition) and a shared living room.

Although the amendments made by SI 2003 No 2398 only strictly apply to pathfinder authorities, they are incorporated here because they do not appear to alter the meaning of sub-para (3).

Claim-related rent

[¹**6.**–(1)   In this paragraph, and in paragraph 9 below, "claim-related rent" means–
(a)   where the rent officer makes a determination under sub-paragraph (2) of paragraph 1, sub-paragraph (2) of paragraph 2 and sub-paragraph (3) of paragraph 3, the lowest of the three rents determined under those sub-paragraphs;
(b)   where the rent officer makes a determination under only two of the sub-paragraphs referred to in paragraph (a) above, the lower of the two rents determined under those sub-paragraphs;
(c)   where the rent officer makes a determination under only one of the sub-paragraphs referred to in paragraph (a) above, the rent determined under that sub-paragraph;
(d)   where the rent officer does not make a determination under any of the sub-paragraphs referred to in paragraph (a) above, the rent payable under the tenancy of the dwelling at the relevant time.
(2)   Where a rent officer makes any determinations under paragraphs 1, 2 or 3, he shall also determine which rent is the claim-related rent.
(3)   Where the dwelling is not in a hostel, the rent officer shall also determine the total amount of ineligible charges, as defined in paragraph 7, which he has not included in the claim-related rent because of the assumptions made in accordance with that paragraph.]

Amendment
1.   Substituted by arts 11 and 12 of SI 2000 No 1 as from 3.4.00.

Analysis
The "claim-related rent" (CRR) is the lowest of the rent officer determinations, or if there are none, the rent payable under the tenancy. It is the lowest of the CRR , the local reference rent and, if relevant, the single room rent which determines maximum rent under reg 13.

There is a potential drawback in that claimants do not usually get an opportunity to examine the notifications given by the rent officer to the authority, still less the basis on which the rent officer has reached those calculations. This may make it questionable whether the procedure before the rent officer may infringe Art 6 of the European Convention on Human Rights, because the claimant has no effective means of challenging the determination.

The prevous concepts of relevant rent, size-related rent and property-specific rent were removed from the HB Regs 1987 as from 3 April 2000. See earlier editions of this book for details.

Part II
Assumptions

Ineligible charges and support charges

[¹**7.**–(1)   For the purposes of this paragraph–
(a)   [³ "ineligible charges" means service charges which are ineligible to be met by housing benefit by virtue of regulation 12(3) (rent) of and Schedule 1 (ineligible service charges) to the Housing Benefit Regulations or, as the case may be, the Housing Benefit (State Pension Credit) Regulations except in the case of a tenancy where the rent includes payments for board and attendance, and the rent officer considers that a substantial part of the rent under the tenancy is fairly attributable to board and attendance, charges specified in paragraph 1(a)(i) of Schedule 1 to the Housing Benefit Regulations or, as the case may be, in paragraph 1(a)(i) of Schedule 1 to the Housing Benefit (State Pension Credit) Regulations (charges for meals).]
[².. .]
(2)   When making a determination under paragraph 1, 2 or 3 of this Schedule, the rent officer shall assume that–
(a)   the items to which the ineligible charges relate;
[². . .]
were not to be provided or made available.
(3)   For the purposes of paragraphs 1, 2, 3 and 6 of this Schedule, the rent officer shall assume that the rent payable under the tenancy at the relevant time is–

(a) where an amount is notified to the rent officer under [³ regulation 14(9)(b) of the Housing Benefit Regulations or, as the case may be, regulation 14(8)(b) of the Housing Benefit (State Pension Credit) Regulations] in respect of that tenancy, that notified amount less the total of any ineligible charges included in that amount; or

(b) in any other case, the total amount stated under regulation [³ 14(2) of the Housing Benefit Regulations or, as the case may be, regulation 14(2) of the Housing Benefit (State Pension Credit) Regulations] less the total of any ineligible charges included in that stated amount.

(4) The total of any ineligible charges, referred to in sub-paragraph (3), shall be the total of the amounts (excluding any amount which he considers is negligible) of any charges included in the notified amount or the stated amount, as the case may be, which, in the rent officer's opinion, are at the relevant time fairly attributable to any items to which ineligible charges relate.]

Amendments

1. Substituted by arts 11 and 12 of SI 2000 No 1 as from 3.4.00.
2. Deleted by art 2 of SI 2003 No 478 as from 1.4.03 (7.4.03 where rent payable weekly or in multiples of a week).
3. Amended by reg 5 and Sch 2 para 11(10)(b) of SI 2006 No 217 as from 6.3.03.

Analysis

Para 7 specifies how ineligible service charges are dealt with. It is a fairly complex provision and requires close examination.

"Ineligible charges" are those which are ineligible under Sch 1 of both the HB and the HB(SPC) Regs, with the exception of charges for meals in certain cases. These are where board and attendance are included in the rent and a "substantial" part of the rent is attributable to those elements.

"Substantial" will be taken to mean "more than minimal". "Attendance", however, is not defined and it is not precisely clear what it refers to. In context, it is suggested that it must be intended to refer to the cooking and serving of meals, rather than the provision of some sort of physical attendance by way of nursing care or similar.

Para (2) requires the rent officer to leave out of account ineligible and support charges in determining what the various appropriate rents would be.

Para (3) sets out what the rent officer is to assume the rent payable by the claimant is. The normal rule, set out in sub-para (b), is that the rent is treated as being the amount stated by the local authority minus any ineligible charges. Sub-para (a) applies where the local authority states an amount under reg 14(9)(b) HB Regs (or reg 14(8)(b) HB(SPC) Regs).

Para (4) specifies that "ineligible" charges for the purpose of para (3)(b) are those which the rent officer considers to be ineligible under the HB or HB(SPC) Regs.

Housing associations etc.

8.–(1) In a case where the local authority states in the application that the landlord is a housing association or a charity, the rent officer shall assume that the landlord is not such a body.

(2) The rent officer shall not take into account the rent under any tenancy where the landlord is a housing association or where the landlord is a charity and the dwelling is provided by the landlord in the pursuit of its charitable purposes.

(3) In this paragraph–

"charity" has the same meaning as in the Charities Act 1993, except that it includes a Scottish charity (which has the same meaning as in section 1(7) of the Law Reform (Miscellaneous Provisions) (Scotland) Act 1990); and

"housing association" has the same meaning as in the Housing Associations Act 1985.

PART III
Notifications of Part I determinations

Notifications

9.–[¹ (1) Subject to sub-paragraph (2), the rent officer shall give notice to the local authority of–

(a) the claim-related rent determined under Part I;

(b) where the dwelling is not in a hostel, the total amount of ineligible charges determined under paragraph 6(3) in relation to that claim-related rent;

(c) whether that claim-related rent includes an amount which would be ineligible for housing benefit under [² paragraph 1(a)(i) of Schedule 1 to the Housing Benefit Regulations or, as the case may be, paragraph 1(a)(i) of Schedule 1 to the Housing Benefit (State Pension Credit) Regulations] (charges for meals);

(d) any rent determined by the rent officer under paragraph 4 (local reference rents); and

(e)   any rent determined by the rent officer under paragraph 5 (single room rents).]
(2)   If the rent officer determines a rent under–
(a)   paragraph 4 (local reference rents); or
(b)   paragraph 5 (single room rents);
which is equal to or more than the [¹ claim-related rent], the rent officer shall give notice to the local authority of this in place of giving notice of the determination made under paragraph 4 or, as the case may be, paragraph 5.

Amendments
1.   Amended by art 13 of SI 2000 No 1 as from 3.4.00.
2.   Amended by reg 5 and Sch 2 para 11(10)(c) of SI 2006 No 217 as from 6.3.06.

Part IV
Indicative Rent Levels
11.–(1)   The rent officer shall determine the indicative rent level for each category described in sub-paragraph (3) in accordance with the following formula–

$$I = \frac{H+3L}{4}$$

where–
I is the indicative rent level;
H is the highest rent, in the rent officer's opinion,–
(a)   which a landlord might reasonably be expected to obtain at the time the determination is being made for an assured tenancy of a dwelling meeting the criteria in sub-paragraph (2); and
(b)   which is not an exceptionally high rent; and
L is the lowest rent, in the rent officer's opinion,–
(a)   which a landlord might reasonably be expected to obtain at the time the determination is being made for an assured tenancy of a dwelling meeting the criteria in sub-paragraph (2); and
(b)   which is not an exceptionally low rent.
(2)   The criteria are that–
(a)   the dwelling is in the area of the local authority;
(b)   the dwelling is in a reasonable state of repair; and
(c)   the dwelling and tenancy accord with the category to which the determination relates.
(3)   The categories for the purposes of this paragraph are–
(a)   a dwelling where the tenant does not have use of more than one room where a substantial part of the rent under the tenancy is fairly attributable to board and attendance;
(b)   a dwelling where the tenant does not have use of more than one room, the tenancy provides for him to share a kitchen or toilet and paragraph (a) does not apply;
(c)   a dwelling where the tenant does not have use of more than one room and where paragraphs (a) and (b) do not apply;
(d)   a dwelling where the tenant does not have use of more than two rooms and where none of paragraphs (a) to (c) applies;
(e)   a dwelling where the tenant does not have use of more than three rooms and where none of paragraphs (a) to (d) applies;
(f)   a dwelling where the tenant does not have use of more than four rooms and where none of paragraphs (a) to (e) applies;
(g)   a dwelling where the tenant does not have use of more than five rooms and where none of paragraphs (a) to (f) applies; and
(h)   a dwelling where the tenant does not have use of more than six rooms and where none of paragraphs (a) to (g) applies.
(4)   When ascertaining H and L under sub-paragraph (1), the rent officer:
(a)   shall assume that no one who would have been entitled to housing benefit had sought or is seeking the tenancy; and
(b)   shall exclude the amount of any rent which, in the rent officer's opinion, is fairly attributable to the provision of services which are ineligible to be met by housing benefit
[¹ . . .].]
(5)   In this paragraph–
''room'' means a bedroom or room suitable for living in and in paragraphs (a), (b) and (c) of sub-paragraph (3) does not include a room which the tenant shares with any person other than–
(a)   a member of his household;
(b)   a non-dependant of the tenant (within the meaning of [² regulation 3 of the Housing Benefit Regulations or, as the case may be, regulation 3 of the Housing Benefit (State Pension Credit) Regulations]); or

(c)   a person who pays rent to the tenant; and "services" has the meaning given by paragraph 4(5).

Amendments

1.   Deleted by art 2 of SI 2003 No 478 as from 1.4.03 (7.4.03 where rent payable weekly or in multiples of a week).

2.   Amended by reg 5 and Sch 2 para 11(10)(d) of SI 2006 No 217 as from 6.3.06.

SCHEDULE 2
ARTICLE 2
Size Criteria

1.   One bedroom or room suitable for living in shall be allowed for each of the following categories of occupier (and each occupier shall come within only the first category for which he is eligible)–

(a)   [¹ a couple] (within the meaning of Part VII of the Social Security Contributions and Benefits Act 1992);

(b)   a person who is not a child;

(c)   two children of the same sex;

(d)   two children who are less than ten years old;

(e)   a child.

2.   The number of rooms (excluding any allowed under paragraph 1) suitable for living in allowed are–

(a)   if there are less than four occupiers, one;

(b)   if there are more than three and less than seven occupiers, two; and

(c)   in any other case, three.

Amendment

1.   Substituted by art 29 of SI 2005 No 2877 as from 5.12.05.

SCHEDULE 3
REDETERMINATIONS

[¹**1.**   Schedules 1 and 2 shall apply in relation to a redetermination as they apply to a determination, but as if references in those Schedules to the relevant time were references to the date the application for the original determination was made or, if earlier, the date the tenancy ended.]

Amendment

1.   Substituted by SI 2000 No 1 from 3.4.00.

---

2.   The rent officer making the redetermination shall seek and have regard to the advice of one or two other rent officers in relation to the redetermination.

[¹ SCHEDULE 3A

Amendment

1.   Schedule inserted by Art 2(10) of SI 2003 No 2398 as from a date specified in Sch 1 to that SI in relation to each individual authority.

PART I
Categories of dwelling

1.–(1) The categories of dwelling for which a rent officer is required to determine a local housing allowance in accordance with article 4B(2)(a)(i) are–

(a)   a dwelling where the tenant has the exclusive use of only one bedroom and where the tenancy provides for him to–

(i)   share the use of a kitchen, a bathroom and toilet and a room suitable for living in;

(ii)   have the exclusive use of a kitchen or facilities for cooking and share the use of a bathroom and toilet and a room suitable for living in; or

(iii)   have the exclusive use of a bathroom and toilet and share the use of a kitchen and a room suitable for living in;

(b)   a dwelling where the tenant has the use of only two rooms;

(c)   a dwelling where the tenant has the use of only three rooms;

(d)   a dwelling where the tenant has the use of only four rooms;

(e)   a dwelling where the tenant has the use of only five rooms;

(f)   a dwelling where the tenant has the use of only six rooms.

(2)   In sub-paragraph (1)(b) to (f) of this paragraph and in paragraph 3 ''room'' means a bedroom or room suitable for living in, except for a room which the tenant shares with any person other than–

(a)   a member of his household;

(b)   a non-dependant of the tenant (within the meaning of [¹ regulation 3 of the Housing Benefit Regulations or, as the case may be, regulation 3 of the Housing Benefit (State Pension Credit) Regulations]); or

(c)   a person who pays rent to the tenant.

Amendment

1.   Amended by reg 5 and sch 2 para 11(11) of SI 2006 No 217 as from 6.3.06.

Formula for local housing allowance for category of dwelling in paragraph 1(1)(a)

2.–(1)   The rent officer shall determine a local housing allowance for the category of dwelling in paragraph 1(1)(a) in accordance with the following formula–

$$A = \frac{H+L}{2}$$

where–

A is the local housing allowance;

H is the highest rent which, in the rent officer's opinion–

(a)   a landlord might reasonably have been expected to obtain, at the date of the determination, for an assured tenancy of a dwelling which meets the criteria specified in sub-paragraph (2); and

(b)   is not an exceptionally high rent;

L is the lowest rent which, in the rent officer's opinion–

(a)   a landlord might reasonably have been expected to obtain, at the date of the determination, for an assured tenancy of a dwelling which meets the criteria specified in sub-paragraph (2); and

(b)   is not an exceptionally low rent.

(2)   The criteria are–

(a)   that the dwelling under the assured tenancy–

    (i)   is in the broad rental market area for which the local housing allowance is being determined; and

    (ii)   is in a reasonable state of repair;

(b)   that under the assured tenancy, the tenant has the exclusive use of only one bedroom and the tenancy provides for him to–

    (i)   share the use of a kitchen, a bathroom and toilet and a room suitable for living in;

    (ii)   have the exclusive use of a kitchen or facilities for cooking and share the use of a bathroom and toilet and a room suitable for living in; or

    (iii)   have the exclusive use of a bathroom and toilet and share the use of a kitchen and a room suitable for living in; and

(c)   that the rent does not include any payment for board and attendance.

(3)   When ascertaining H and L under sub-paragraph (1) the rent officer shall–

(a)   assume that no one who would have been entitled to housing benefit had sought or is seeking the tenancy; and

(b)   exclude the amount of any rent which, in the rent officer's opinion, is fairly attributable to the provision of services performed for, or facilities (including the use of furniture) provided for, or rights made available to, the tenant which are ineligible to be met by housing benefit.

(4)   When ascertaining H and L under sub-paragraph (1) the rent officer may, where he is not satisfied that–

(a)   the broad rental market area contains a sufficient number of dwellings that accord with the category of dwelling set out in paragraph 1(1)(a) to enable him to make a local housing allowance determination; or

(b)   he has sufficient other information about the market in the broad rental market area to enable him to make a local housing allowance determination,

take account of rents in other similar areas in which he believes a comparable market exists.

Formula for local housing allowance for other categories of dwelling

3.–(1)   For categories of dwelling other than the category of dwelling in paragraph 1(1)(a), the rent officer shall determine a local housing allowance in accordance with the formula-

$$B = \frac{H+L}{2}$$

where–

B is the local housing allowance;

H is the highest rent which, in the rent officer's opinion–

(a)   a landlord might reasonably have been expected to obtain, at the date of the determination, for an assured tenancy of a dwelling which meets the criteria specified in sub-paragraph (2); and

(b)   is not an exceptionally high rent; and

L is the lowest rent which, in the rent officer's opinion–

(a)   a landlord might reasonably have been expected to obtain, at the date of the determination, for an assured tenancy of a dwelling which meets the criteria specified in sub-paragraph (2); and

(b)   is not an exceptionally low rent.

(2)   The criteria are that the dwelling under the assured tenancy–

(a)   is in the broad rental market area for which the local housing allowance is being determined;

(b)   is in a reasonable state of repair; and

(c)   has the same number of rooms as the category of dwelling in respect of which the local housing allowance is being determined.

(3)   Sub-paragraphs (3) and (4) of paragraph 2 apply when ascertaining H and L under this paragraph as if the reference in those sub-paragraphs to H and L were to H and L under this paragraph, except that "in respect of which the local housing allowance is being determined" shall be substituted for "set out in paragraph 1(1)(a)".

Broad rental market area

4.   In this Schedule "broad rental market area" means an area–

(a)   comprising two or more distinct areas of residential accommodation, each distinct area of residential accommodation adjoining at least one other in the area;

(b)   within which a person could reasonably be expected to live having regard to facilities and services for the purposes of health, education, recreation, personal banking and shopping, taking account of the distance of travel, by public and private transport, to and from facilities and services of the same type and similar standard; and

(c)   containing residential premises of a variety of types, and including such premises held on a variety of tenancies.

PART II

Column (1)Local authority	*Column (2)Date*
[¹ Blackpool	17th November 2003
Brighton and Hove	2nd February 2004
Conwy	9th February 2004
Coventry	12th January 2004
East Riding of Yorkshire	18th April 2005
Guildford	4th July 2005
Leeds	9th February 2004
Lewisham	1st December 2003
North East Lincolnshire	9th February 2004
Norwich	13th June 2005
Pembrokeshire	20th June 2005
St Helens	23rd May 2005
Salford	25th July 2005
South Norfolk	6th June 2005
Teignbridge	12th January 2004
Wandsworth	11th April 2005.]]

Amendment

1.   Amended by art 2(2) of SI 2005 No 236 as from 13.3.05.

SCHEDULE 4
SPECIAL CASES
Houseboats

1.   Where an application for a determination or a redetermination relates in whole or in part to mooring charges for a houseboat, this Order applies in relation to that application (or, as the case may be, to that part which relates to those charges) with the following modifications–

(a)   references to a tenancy, a tenancy of a dwelling or an assured tenancy are references to an agreement under which those charges are payable (and references to a landlord and a tenant shall be construed accordingly); and

(b)   no determination shall be made under paragraph 2 of Part I of Schedule 1 (size criteria) and references to the dwelling exceeding the size criteria shall not apply.

Mobile homes

2.   Where an application for a determination or redetermination relates in whole or in part to payments in respect of the site on which a caravan or a mobile home stands, this Order applies in relation to that application (or, as the case may be, that part which relates to those payments) with the following modifications–

(a)   references to a tenancy, a tenancy of a dwelling or an assured tenancy are references to an agreement under which those payments are payable (and references to a landlord and a tenant shall be construed accordingly); and

(b)   no determination shall be made under paragraph 2 of Part I of Schedule 1 (size criteria) and references to the dwelling exceeding the size criteria shall not apply.

Rental purchase agreements

3.   Where an application for a determination or a redetermination relates to a rental purchase agreement, the agreement is to be treated as if it were a tenancy.

The Rent Officers (Housing Benefit Functions) (Scotland) Order 1997

(SI 1997 No.1995 (S.144))

General Note

This Order is the Scottish equivalent of SI 1997 No.1984 and sets out the determinations to be made by rent officers when a tenancy is referred to them under reg 14 of both the HB and the HB(SPC) Regs by an authority in Scotland. See the commentary to SI 1997 No 1984.

Citation and commencement

1.–(1)   This Order may be cited as the Rent Officers (Housing Benefit Functions) (Scotland) Order 1997.

(2)   This Order shall come into force for the purposes of article 8 on 18th August 1997 and for all other purposes on 3rd September 1997.

Interpretation

2.–(1)   In this Order, unless the context otherwise requires–

"assured tenancy" has the same meaning as in Part II of the Housing (Scotland) Act 1988, except that it includes a tenancy which would be an assured tenancy but for paragraph [³ 7 or] 9 of Schedule 4 to that Act;

[² "board and attendance determination" means a determination made in accordance with article 4C;]

[² "broad rental market area" has the meaning specified in paragraph 4 of Part I of Schedule 3A to this Order;]

[² "broad rental market area determination" means a determination made in accordance with article 4B(1);]

"child" means a person under the age of 16;

"determination" means a determination made in accordance with Part I or IV of Schedule 1 to this Order;

"dwelling" means any residential accommodation whether or not consisting of the whole or part of a building and whether or not comprising separate and self-contained premises;

[⁴ "hostel" has the same meaning as in regulation 2(1) of the Housing Benefit Regulations or, as the case may be, regulation 2(1) of the Housing Benefit (State Pension Credit) Regulations;]

[⁵ "the Housing Benefit Regulations" mean the Housing Benefit Regulations 2006; "the Housing Benefit (State Pension Credit) Regulations" means the Housing Benefit (Persons who have attained the qualifying age for state pension credit) Regulations 2006;]

"local authority" has the same meaning as in the Social Security Administration Act 1992 in relation to England and in relation to Wales;

[² "local housing allowance determination" means a determination made in accordance with article 4B(2);]

"occupier" means a person (whether or not identified by name) who is stated, in the application for the determination, to occupy the dwelling as his home;

[² "pathfinder authority" means a local authority specified in column (1) of the table in Part II of Schedule 3A, on and after the date specified in column (2) of that table in relation to that authority;]

"redetermination" means a redetermination made in accordance with article 4;

[⁴ "relevant date" means the date specified by a pathfinder authority in an application for a local housing allowance determination made in accordance with regulation 13A(4)(a) of the Housing Benefit Regulations or, as the case may be, regulation 13A(4)(a) of the Housing Benefit (State Pension Credit) Regulations;]

[¹ ''relevant period'' means–
   (a)   in relation to a determination, the period of five working days (or, where the determination does not relate to a prospective tenancy and the rent officer intends to inspect the dwelling before making the determination, 25 working days) beginning with-
       (i)   where the rent officer requests further information under article 5, the date on which he receives the information; and
      (ii)   in any other case, the date on which he receives the application for the determination; and
   (b)   in relation to a redetermination, the period of 20 working days beginning with-
       (i)   where the rent officer requests further information under article 5, the date on which he receives the information; and
      (ii)   in any other case, the date on which he receives the application for that redetermination;]

''relevant time'' means the time the application for the determination [² or board and attendance determination] is made or, if earlier, the tenancy ends;

[⁴ ''rent'' means any of the periodical payments referred to in regulation 12(1) of the Housing Benefit Regulations or, as the case may be, regulation 12(1) of the Housing Benefit (State Pension Credit) Regulations;]

''size criteria'' means the standards relating to bedrooms and rooms suitable for living in specified in Schedule 2 to this Order;

''tenancy'' includes any other right of occupancy and a prospective tenancy or right of occupancy and references to a tenant, a landlord or any other expression appropriate to a tenancy shall be construed accordingly; and

[⁶]

   (2)   In this Order any reference to a notice or application is to a notice or application in writing, except in a case where the recipient consents (whether generally or specifically) to the notice or application being transmitted by electronic means.

Amendments

1.   Inserted by Art 3 of SI 2000 No 3 as from 3.4.00.
2.   Insertions made by Art 3 of SI 2003 No 2398 as from a date specified in Sch 1 to that SI in relation to each individual authority.
3.   Inserted by Art 2(2) of SI 2004 No 2101 as from 31.8.04.
4.   Substituted by reg 5 and Sch 2 para 12(2)(a), (c) and (d) of SI 2006 No 217 as from 6.3.06.
5.   Inserted by reg 5 and Sch 2 para 12(2)(b) of SI 2006 No 217 as from 6.3.06.
6.   Omitted by reg 5 and Sch 2 para 12(2)(e) of SI 2006 No 217 as from 6.3.06.

Determinations

   3.–(1)   Subject to [² articles 3A and 6], where a local authority, in accordance with regulations made under section 136(2) or (3) of the Social Security Administration Act 1992 [¹ or section 122(5) of the Housing Act 1996], applies to a rent officer for determinations in respect of a tenancy of a dwelling, a rent officer shall–
   (a)   make the determinations in accordance with Part I of Schedule 1 (determinations);
   (b)   comply with Part II of Schedule 1 when making the determinations (assumptions etc.); and
   (c)   give notice in accordance with Part III of Schedule 1 (notifications) [¹ within the relevant period or as soon as is practicable after that period].

   (2)   A rent officer for each registration area (within the meaning of section 43 of the Rent (Scotland) Act 1984) on the first working day of each month shall–

(a) make determinations in accordance with Part IV of Schedule 1 (indicative rent levels) in the registration area [⁴ except in relation to the area of a local authority which is a pathfinder authority];

(b) comply with paragraph 8(2) of Part II of Schedule 1 (assumptions etc.) when making the determinations; and

(c) give to the local authority notice of the determinations relating to its area when they have been made.

Amendments

1. Amended by Art 4 of SI 2000 No 3 as from 3.4.00.
2. Amended by Art 3(1) of SI 2001 No 1326 as from 2.7.01.
3. Substitution made by Art 3 of SI 2003 No 2398 as from a date specified in Sch 1 to that SI in relation to each individual authority.
4. Amended by art 5(2)(a) of SI 2005 No 236 as from 13.3.05.

[¹Transitional arrangements for determination of Single Room Rents with effect from 2nd July 2001

3A. In a case where the rent officer has made and notified an authority of a determination of a single room rent pursuant to paragraph 5 of Schedule 1 in the period of 12 months before 2nd July 2001 that determination shall cease to have effect on [² . . .] 2nd July 2001 and a rent officer shall–

(a) make a new determination of that single room rent in accordance with Part I of Schedule 1;

(b) comply with Part II of Schedule 1; and

(c) give notice in accordance with Part III of Schedule 1 within the relevant period or as soon as is practicable after that period;

without an application for a determination under [³ regulation 14 of the Housing Benefit Regulations or, as the case may be, regulation 14 of the Housing Benefit (State Pension Credit) Regulations] having been made.]

Amendments

1. Inserted by Art 3(2) of SI 2001 No 1326 as from 2.7.01.
2. Amended by Art 2(2) of SI 2001 No 2318 as from 2.7.01.
3. Amended by reg 5 and Sch 2 para 12(3) of SI 2006 No 217 as from 6.3.06.

Redeterminations

[⁴4.–(1) Subject to article 6, where the local authority applies to a rent officer for a redetermination of any determination or redetermination in respect of a tenancy of a dwelling the rent officer shall, in accordance with Schedule 3–

(a) make redeterminations of any effective determinations and any effective redeterminations in respect of that tenancy; and

(b) give notice within the relevant period or as soon as is practicable after that period.

(2) For the purposes of paragraph (1)–

"effective determinations" means any determinations made in accordance with Part I of Schedule 1 which have effect at the date of the application for a redetermination of a determination or redetermination; and

"effective redeterminations" means any redeterminations made in accordance with Schedule 3 which have effect at that date.

(3) A rent officer whose advice is sought as provided for in Schedule 3 shall give that advice.]

Amendment

1. Substituted by Art 5 of SI 2000 No 3 as from 3.4.00.

Substitute determinations and substitute redeterminations

[¹4A.–(1)   Where a local authority applies to a rent officer for a substitute determination, in accordance with [² regulation 17 of the Housing Benefit Regulations or, as the case may be, regulation 17 of the Housing Benefit (State Pension Credit) Regulations], the provisions of this Order shall apply to that substitute determination as they apply to a determination, but as if references to the relevant time were references to the date the application for the original determination was made or, if earlier, the date the tenancy ended.

(2)   Where a local authority applies to a rent officer for a substitute redetermination, in accordance with that regulation, the provisions of this Order shall apply to that substitute redetermination as they apply to a redetermination.]

Amendment

1.   Inserted by Art 5 of SI 2000 No 3 as from 3.4.00.
2.   Amended by reg 5 and Sch 2 para 12(4) of SI 2006 No 217 as from 6.3.06.

[¹Broad rental market area determinations and local housing allowance determinations

4B.–(1) On the day on which this article comes into force in relation to a local authority and so often thereafter as a rent officer, having regard to the definition of ''broad rental market area'' in paragraph (1) of article 2, considers appropriate, a rent officer shall–

(a)   determine one or more broad rental market areas which will (during the month which next begins after the determination is made) fall, in whole or in part, within the area of that local authority so that every part of the area of that authority falls within a broad rental market area and no part of the area of that authority falls within more than one broad rental market area; and

(b)   give to that authority a notice which–
(i)   specifies the area contained within each broad rental market area as falls, in whole or in part, within the area of that authority, by reference to the postcodes for each such broad rental market area; and
(ii)   identifies such of those postcodes as fall within the area of that authority.

(2)   No more than 5 and not less than 3 working days before the end of each month a rent officer shall–

(a)   determine, in accordance with the provisions of Part I of Schedule 3A–
(i)   a local housing allowance for each of the categories of dwelling set out in paragraph 1 of that Part; and
(ii)   local housing allowances for such other categories of dwelling of more than six rooms as a rent officer believes are likely to be required for the purpose of calculating housing benefit,

for each broad rental market area falling within, in whole or in part, the area of any local authority which is (or will be) a pathfinder authority during the month which follows; and

(b)   give to each such authority notice of the local housing allowance determinations made in accordance with paragraph (a) for each broad rental market area falling within, in whole or in part, the area of that authority.

(3)   Any broad rental market area determination made in accordance with paragraph (1), or local housing allowance determination made in accordance with paragraph (2), shall take effect on the first working day of the month which begins after the day on which the determination is made.

(4)   Where a pathfinder authority–

(a)   makes an application in accordance with [² regulation 13A(4)(a) of the Housing Benefit Regulations or, as the case may be, regulation 13A(4)(a) of the Housing Benefit (State Pension Credit) Regulations], a rent officer shall determine, in accordance with the provisions of Part I of Schedule 3A and as soon as is reasonably practicable, the local housing allowance for that category of dwelling at the relevant date, for each broad rental market area falling within, in whole or in part, the area of the pathfinder authority that made the application, at the relevant date; or

(b) makes an application in accordance with [² regulation 13A(5) of the Housing Benefit Regulations or, as the case may be, regulation 13A(5) of the Housing Benefit (State Pension Credit) Regulations], a rent officer shall determine, in accordance with the provisions of Part I of Schedule 3A and as soon as is reasonably practicable, the local housing allowance for that category of dwelling for each broad rental market area falling within, in whole or in part, the area of the pathfinder authority.

(5) Where a rent officer has made a local housing allowance determination in accordance with paragraph (4)–

(a) he shall give notice of the determination to the pathfinder authority that made the application;

(b) any local housing allowance determination made in accordance with sub-paragraph (4)(a) shall take effect for the month in which the relevant date falls; and

(c) any local housing allowance determination made in accordance with sub-paragraph (4)(b) shall take effect for the month in which notice is given in accordance with sub-paragraph (a).]

Amendments

1. Inserted by Art 3(5) of SI 2003 No 2398 as from a date specified in Sch 1 to that SI in relation to each individual authority.
2. Amended by reg 5 and Sch 2 para 12(5) of SI 2006 No 217 as from 6.3.06.

[¹Board and attendance determinations and notifications

4C.–(1) Where a pathfinder authority makes an application to a rent officer in accordance with [² regulation 17(6) of the Housing Benefit Regulations or, as the case may be, regulation 13A(6) of the Housing Benefit (State Pension Credit) Regulations], a rent officer shall determine whether or not a substantial part of the rent under the tenancy at the relevant time is fairly attributable to board and attendance.

(2) Where a rent officer determines that a substantial part of the rent under the tenancy at the relevant time is fairly attributable to board and attendance, he shall–

(a) notify the pathfinder authority accordingly; and

(b) treat the application as if it has been made in accordance with [² regulation 14(1) of the Housing Benefit Regulations or, as the case may be, regulation 14(1) of the Housing Benefit (State Pension Credit) Regulations].

(3) Where a rent officer determines that a substantial part of the rent under the tenancy at the relevant time is not fairly attributable to board and attendance, he shall notify the pathfinder authority accordingly.

(4) Where an application for a board and attendance determination is treated as if it has been made in accordance with [² regulation 14(1) of the Housing Benefit Regulations or, as the case may be, regulation 14(1) of the Housing Benefit (State Pension Credit) Regulations], then, for the purposes of paragraph (a)(ii) of the definition of ''relevant period'' in article 2(1), it shall be treated as having been received on the day on which the determination referred to in paragraph (2) is made.]

Amendments

1. Inserted by Art 3(5) of SI 2003 No 2398 as from a date specified in Sch 1 to that SI in relation to each individual authority.
2. Amended by reg 5 and Sch 2 para 12(6) of SI 2006 No 217 as from 6.3.06.

[¹Board and attendance redeterminations

4D.–(1)   Subject to article 6, where a pathfinder authority applies to a rent officer for a redetermination of a board and attendance determination or board and attendance redetermination, the rent officer shall, in accordance with paragraph (2)–

(a)   make a redetermination of–
  (i)   the board and attendance determination, provided it was made in accordance with article 4C and had effect at the date of the application for it to be redetermined; or
  (ii)   the board and attendance redetermination provided it was made in accordance with head (i), and had effect at the date of the application for it to be redetermined; and

(b)   notify the pathfinder authority of the redetermination.

(2)   When making a board and attendance redetermination under this article, the rent officer shall seek, and have regard to, the advice of one or two other rent officers in relation to the redetermination.

(3)   A rent officer whose advice is sought in accordance with paragraph (2) shall give that advice.

(4)   Article 4C shall apply in relation to a board and attendance redetermination but as if the references to the relevant time were references to the date on which the original application for a board and attendance determination was made, or if earlier, to the date on which the tenancy ended.]

Amendment

1.   Inserted by Art 3(5) of SI 2003 No 2398 as from a date specified in Sch 1 to that SI in relation to each individual authority.

[¹Substitute board and attendance determinations and substitute board and attendance redeterminations

4E.–(1)   Where a pathfinder authority applies to a rent officer for a substitute board and attendance determination in accordance with [² regulation 17 of the Housing Benefit Regulations or, as the case may be, regulation 17 of the Housing Benefit (State Pension Credit) Regulations, the provisions of this Order shall apply to that substitute board and attendance determination as they apply to a board and attendance determination but as if references to the relevant time were references to the date on which the original application for a board and attendance determination was made or, if earlier, the date on which the tenancy ended.

(2)   Where a pathfinder authority applies to a rent officer for a substitute board and attendance redetermination in accordance with [² regulation 17 of the Housing Benefit Regulations or, as the case may be, regulation 17 of the Housing Benefit (State Pension Credit) Regulations], the provisions of this Order shall apply to that substitute board and attendance redetermination as they apply to a board and attendance redetermination.]

Amendments

1.   Inserted by Art 3(5) of SI 2003 No 2398 as from a date specified in Sch 1 to that SI in relation to each individual authority.
2.   Amended by reg 5 and Sch 2 para 12(7) of SI 2006 No 217 as from 6.3.06.

Insufficient information

5.   If a rent officer needs further information in order to make a determination under article 3(1) or a [² redetermination under article 4, a board and attendance determination under article 4C or a board and attendance redetermination under article 4D], he shall serve notice on the local authority requesting that information. [¹ ...]

Amendments

1.   Deleted by Art 6 of SI 2000 No 1 as from 3.4.00.

2.   Substituted by Art 3(6) of SI 2003 No 2398 as from a date specified in Sch 1 to that SI in relation to each individual authority.

Exceptions

6.–(1)   No determination [¹, redetermination, board and attendance determination or board and attendance redetermination] shall be made if the application for it is withdrawn.

(2)   No determination shall be made under paragraph 3, 4 or 5 of Part I of Schedule 1 if the tenancy is of residential accommodation, within the meaning of [² regulation 9(4) of the Housing Benefit Regulations or, as the case may be, regulation 9(4) of the Housing Benefit (State Pension Credit) Regulations], or in a hostel.

(3)   No determination shall be made under paragraph 5 of Part I of Schedule 1 unless the local authority states in the application that the claimant is, or may be, a young individual (which has the same meaning as in [² the Housing Benefit Regulations and the Housing Benefit (State Pension Credit) Regulations]).

(4)   If the rent officer becomes aware that an application is not one which gives rise to a duty to make a determination [¹, redetermination, board and attendance determination or a board and attendance redetermination] , the rent officer shall give the local authority notice to that effect.

Amendments
1.   Substituted by Art 3(7) of SI 2003 No 2398 as from a date specified in Sch 1 to that SI in relation to each individual authority.
2.   Amended by reg 5 and Sch 2 para 12(8) of SI 2006 No 217 as from 6.3.06.

Special cases

7.–(1)   This Order shall apply as specified in Schedule 4 in relation to–
(a)   mooring charges payable for a houseboat;
(b)   payments in respect of the site on which a caravan or a mobile home stands; or
(c)   payments under a rental purchase agreement.

(2)   Terms used in paragraph (1) have the same meaning in this article and in Schedule 4 as they have in [² regulation 12(1) of the Housing Benefit Regulations or, as the case may be, regulation 12(1) of the Housing Benefit (State Pension Credit) Regulations].
[¹ ...]

Amendments
1.   Deleted by Art 7 of SI 2000 No 3 as from 3.4.00.
2.   Amended by reg 5 and Sch 2 para 12(9) of SI 2006 No 217 as from 6.3.06.

[¹Errors

7A.–[² (1)]   If a rent officer is of the opinion that he has made an error (other than in the application of his professional judgement) in relation to a determination or redetermination, he shall notify the local authority which made the application for that determination or redetermination of the error as soon as practicable after he becomes aware of it.]

[² (2)   If a rent officer is of the opinion that he has made an error (other than in the application of his professional judgement) in relation to a board and attendance determination or board and attendance redetermination, he shall notify the pathfinder authority which made the application for that board and attendance determination or board and attendance redetermination of the error as soon as practicable after he becomes aware of it.

(3)   If a rent officer is of the opinion that he has made an error (other than in the application of his professional judgement) in relation to a broad rental market area determination or a local housing allowance determination, he shall notify any

pathfinder authority to which notification of that determination was sent of the error, and the amended determination, as soon as practicable after he becomes aware of it.]

Amendments

1.   Inserted by Art 8 of SI 2000 No 3 as from 3.4.00.

2.   Inserted by Art 2(8) of SI 2003 No 2398 as from a date specified in Sch 1 to that SI in relation to each individual authority.

Amendment to 1995 Order

8.–(1)   The Rent Officers (Additional Functions) (Scotland) Order 1995 shall be amended by the insertion at the end of article 6 (special cases) of the following:–

"(3)   In a case where the local authority states in the application that the rent includes charges for general counselling or any other support services which are eligible for housing benefit solely by virtue of paragraph 1(f)(iii) of Schedule 1 to the 1987 Regulations (landlord's support services: supported accommodation) or solely by virtue of that provision and paragraph 1(f)(ii) of that Schedule, the rent officer shall assume when making a determination or a redetermination that–

(a)   the services were not to be provided or made available; and

(b)   the rent payable under the tenancy at the relevant time is such amount as is specified in the application as the rent which would have been payable under the tenancy at that time if those items were not to be provided or made available.

(4)   In a case where the local authority states in the application that the rent includes charges for general counselling or any other support services and the charges–

(a)   are eligible for housing benefit by virtue of paragraph 1(f)(iii) of Schedule 1 to the 1987 Regulations, or that provision and paragraph 1(f)(ii) of that Schedule; and

(b)   are also eligible for housing benefit by virtue of paragraph 1(f)(i) of that Schedule (support services: other exceptions), the rent officer shall include in the notice to the local authority, required under article 3(1)(c), a statement of the amount of the rent payable for the tenancy (which has the same meaning as in paragraph 3(1) of Schedule 1 to this Order) which relates to those charges.".

(2)   The amendment made by paragraph (1) above does not have effect in a case where an application for a determination is made before 18th August 1997.

Revocations and application

9.–(1)   Subject to paragraph (2), article 8 of this Order and the Orders specified in Schedule 5 are hereby revoked.

(2)   Nothing in articles 2 to 7 has effect in a case where an application for a determination is made before 3rd September 1997 and, in such a case, the Rent Officers (Additional Functions) (Scotland) Order 1995 shall continue to have effect.

SCHEDULE 1

PART I

Determinations

Significantly high rents

1.–(1)   The rent officer shall determine whether, in his opinion, the rent payable under the tenancy of the dwelling at the relevant time is significantly higher than the rent which the landlord might reasonably have been expected to obtain under the tenancy at that time.

(2)   If the rent officer determines under sub-paragraph (1) that the rent is significantly higher, the rent officer shall also determine the rent which the landlord might reasonably have been expected to obtain under the tenancy at the relevant time.

(3)   When making a determination under this paragraph, the rent officer shall have regard to the level of rent under similar tenancies of similar dwellings in the [¹ vicinity] (or as similar as regards

tenancy, dwelling and [¹ vicinity] as is reasonably practicable) and shall assume that no one who would have been entitled to housing benefit had sought or is seeking the tenancy.

[²(4)   For the purposes of this paragraph and paragraph 2 ''vicinity'' means–
(a)   the area immediately surrounding the dwelling; or
(b)   where, for the purposes of sub-paragraph (2)(c) of paragraph 2, there is no dwelling in the area immediately surrounding the dwelling which satisfies the description in heads (i), (ii) and (iii) of that sub-paragraph, the area nearest to the dwelling where there is such a dwelling.]

Amendments
1.   Amended by art 3(2) of SI 2001 No 3561 as from 6.11.01.
2.   Inserted by art 3(2) of SI 2001 No 3561 as from 6.11.01.

Size and rent

2.–(1)   The rent officer shall determine whether the dwelling, at the relevant time, exceeds the size criteria for the occupiers.

(2)   If the rent officer determines that the dwelling exceeds the size criteria, the rent officer shall also determine the rent which a landlord might reasonably have been expected to obtain, at the relevant time, for a tenancy which is–
(a)   similar to the tenancy of the dwelling;
(b)   on the same terms other than the term relating to the amount of rent; and
(c)   of a dwelling which is in the same [¹ vicinity] as the dwelling, but which–
    (i)   accords with the size criteria for the occupiers;
    (ii)   is in a reasonable state of repair; and
    (iii)   corresponds in other respects, in the rent officer's opinion, as closely as is reasonably practicable to the dwelling.

(3)   When making a determination under sub-paragraph (2), the rent officer shall have regard to the same matter and make the same assumption as specified in paragraph 1(3), except that in judging the similarity of other tenancies and dwellings the comparison shall be with the tenancy of the second dwelling referred to in sub-paragraph (2), and shall assume that no one who would have been entitled to housing benefit had sought or is seeking that tenancy.

Amendment
1.   Amended by art 3(3) of SI 2001 No 3561 as from 6.11.01.

Exceptionally high rents

3.–(1)   The rent officer shall determine whether, in his opinion, the rent payable for the tenancy of the dwelling at the relevant time is exceptionally high.

(2)   In sub-paragraph (1), ''rent payable for the tenancy'' means–
(a)   where a determination is made under sub-paragraph (2) of paragraph 2, the rent determined under that sub-paragraph;
(b)   where no determination is so made and a determination is made under sub-paragraph (2) of paragraph 1, the rent determined under that sub-paragraph; and
(c)   in any other case, the rent payable under the tenancy [¹ at the relevant time].

(3)   If the rent officer determines under sub-paragraph (1) that the rent is exceptionally high, the rent officer shall also determine the highest rent, which is not an exceptionally high rent and which a landlord might reasonably have been expected to obtain at the relevant time (on the assumption that no one who would have been entitled to housing benefit had sought or is seeking the tenancy) for an assured tenancy of a dwelling which–
(a)   is in the same [² neighbourhood] as the dwelling;
(b)   has the same number of bedrooms and rooms suitable for living in as the dwelling (or, where the dwelling exceeds the size criteria for the occupiers, accords with the size criteria); and
(c)   is in a reasonable state of repair.

(4)   For the purpose of determining whether a rent is an exceptionally high rent under this paragraph, the rent officer shall have regard to the levels of rent under assured tenancies of dwellings which–
(a)   are in the same [² neighbourhood] as the dwelling (or in as similar a locality as is reasonably practicable); and
(b)   have the same number of bedrooms and rooms suitable for living in as the dwelling (or, in a case where the dwelling exceeds the size criteria for the occupiers, accord with the size of criteria).

[³ (5)   For the purposes of this paragraph and paragraph 4(6) ''neighbourhood'' means-
(a)   where the dwelling is in a town or city, the part of that town or city where the dwelling is located which is a distinct area of residential accommodation; or

(b) where the dwelling is not in a town or city, the area surrounding the dwelling which is a distinct area of residential accommodation and where there are dwellings satisfying the description in sub-paragraph (4)(b).]

Amendments
1. Amended by Art 9 of SI 2000 No 3 as from 3.4.00.
2. Amended by art 3(4) of SI 2001 No 3561 as from 6.11.01.
3. Inserted by art 3(4) of SI 2001 No 3561 as from 6.11.01.

Local reference rents

4.–(1) The rent officer shall make a determination of a local rent in accordance with the formula–

$$R = \frac{H+L}{2}$$

where–
R is the local reference rent;
H is the hughest rent, in the rent officer's opinion–
(a) which a landlord might reasonably have been expected to obtain, at the relevant time, for an assured tenancy of a dwelling which meets the criteria in sub-paragraph (2); and
(b) which is not an exceptionally high rent; and
L is the lowest rent, in the rent officer's opinion–
(a) which a landlord might reasonably have been expected to obtain, at the relevant time, for an assured tenancy of a dwelling which meets the criteria in sub-paragraph (2); and
(b) which is not an exceptionally low rent.
(2) The criteria are–
(a) that the dwelling under the assured tenancy–
   (i) is in the same locality as the dwelling;
   (ii) is in a reasonable state of repair; and
   (iii) has the same number of bedrooms and rooms suitable for living in as the dwelling (or, in a case where the dwelling exceeds the size criteria for the occupiers, accords with the size criteria); and
(b) if the tenant does not have the use under the tenancy of the dwelling [¹ at the relevant time] of more than one bedroom or room suitable for living in–
   (i) that under the assured tenancy the tenant does not have the use of more than one bedroom or room suitable for living in;
   (ii) if the rent under the tenancy [¹ at the relevant time] includes payments for board and attendance and the rent officer considers that the amount fairly attributable to board and attendance is a substantial part of the rent, that a substantial part of the rent under the assured tenancy is fairly attributable to board and attendance;
   (iii) if sub-paragraph (ii) does not apply and the tenant shares a [⁴ kitchen, toilet, bathroom and room suitable for living in] with a person other than a member of his household, a non-dependant or a person who pays rent to the tenant, that the assured tenancy provides for the tenant to share a [⁴ kitchen, toilet, bathroom and room suitable for living in]; and
   (iv) if sub-paragraphs (ii) and (iii) do not apply, that the circumstances described in sub-paragraphs (ii) and (iii) do not apply in relation to the assured tenancy.
(3) When ascertaining H and L under sub-paragraph (1), the rent officer–
(a) shall assume that no one who would have been entitled to housing benefit had sought or is seeking the tenancy; and
(b) shall exclude the amount of any rent which, in the rent officer's opinion, is fairly attributable to the provision of services which are ineligible to be met by housing benefit; [⁵. . .]
(4) In sub-paragraph (2)(b)–
''bedroom or room suitable for living in'' does not include a room which the tenant shares with any person other than–
(a) a member of his household;
(b) a non-dependant (as defined in this sub-paragraph); or
(c) a person who pays rent to the tenant; and
[⁶ ''non-dependant'' means a non-dependant of the tenant within the meaning of regulation 3 of the Housing Benefit Regulations or, as the case may be, regulation 3 of the Housing Benefit (State Pension Credit) Regulations;].
(5) In sub-paragraph (3), ''services'' means services performed or facilities (including the use of furniture) provided for, or rights made available to, the tenant, but not [², in the case of a tenancy where a substantial part of the rent under the tenancy is fairly attributable to board and attendance, the provision of meals (including the preparation of meals or provision of unprepared food).]

[³(6)   For the purposes of this paragraph and paragraph 5 "locality" means an area–

(a)   comprising two or more neighbourhoods, including the neighbourhood where the dwelling is situated, each neighbourhood adjoining at least one other in the area;

(b)   within which a tenant of the dwelling could reasonably be expected to live having regard to facilities and services for the purposes of health, education, recreation, personal banking and shopping which are in or accessible from the neighbourhood of the dwelling, taking account of the distance of travel, by public and private transport, to and from facilities and services of the same type and similar standard; and

(c)   containing residential premises of a variety of types, and including such premises held on a variety of tenancies.]

Amendments

1.   Amended by Art 9 of SI 2000 No 3 as from 3.4.00.
2.   Substituted by Art 10 of SI 2000 No 3 as from 3.4.00.
3.   Inserted by art 3(5) of SI 2001 No 3561 as from 6.11.01.
4.   Amended by Art 2(3) of SI 2001 No2318 as from 2.7.01.
5.   Deleted by art 3 of SI 2003 No 478 as from 1.4.03 (7.4.03 where rent payable weekly or in multiples of a week).
6.   Amended by reg 5 and Sch 2 para 12(10)(a) of SI 2006 No 217 as from 6.3.06.

Single room rents

5.–(1)   The rent officer shall determine a single room rent in accordance with the following formula–

$$S = \frac{H+L}{2}$$

where–

S is the single room rent;

H is the highest rent, in the rent officer's opinion–

(a)   which a landlord might reasonable have been expected to obtain, at the relevant time, for an assured tenancy of a dwelling which meets the criteria in sub-paragraph (2); and

(b)   which is not an exceptionally high rent; and

L is the lowest rent, in the rent officer's opinion–

(a)   which a landlord might reasonably have been expected to obtain, at the relevant time, for an assured tenancy of a dwelling which meets the criteria in sub-paragraph (2); and

(b)   which is not an exceptionally low rent.

(2)   The criteria are–

(a)   that the dwelling under the assured tenancy is in the same locality as the dwelling and is in a reasonable state of repair;

(b)   that, under the assured tenancy, the tenant–

(i)   has the exclusive use of one bedroom;

(ii)   does not have the use of any other bedroom [¹ . . .] or room suitable for living in;

[² (iia)   shares the use of a room suitable for living in]

(iii)   shares the use of a toilet [¹ and bathroom]; and

(iv)   shares the use of a kitchen and does not have the exclusive use of facilities for cooking food; and

(c)   that the rent does not include any payment for board and attendance.

(3)   Sub-paragraphs [³ (3) and (5)] of paragraph 4 apply when ascertaining H and L under this sub-paragraph as if the reference in those sub-paragraphs to H and L were to H and L under [³ this paragraph].

Amendments

1.   Amended by reg 4 of SI 2001 No 1326 as from 2.7.01.
2.   Substituted by Art 2(9) of SI 2003 No 2398 as from a date specified in Sch 1 to that SI in relation to each individual authority.
3.   Amended by arts 5(1) and 6 of SI 2005 No 236 as from 13.3.05.

Claim-related rent

[¹**6.**–(1)   In this paragraph, and in paragraph 9 below, "claim-related rent" means–

(a)   where the rent officer makes a determination under sub-paragraph (2) of paragraph 1, sub-paragraph (2) of paragraph 2 and sub-paragraph (3) of paragraph 3, the lowest of the three rents determined under those sub-paragraphs;

(b)   where the rent officer makes a determination under only two of the sub-paragraphs referred to in paragraph (a) above, the lower of the two rents determined under those sub-paragraphs;

(c)   where the rent officer makes a determination under only one of the sub-paragraphs referred to in paragraph (a) above, the rent determined under that sub-paragraph;

(d)   where the rent officer does not make a determination under any of the sub-paragraphs referred to in paragraph (a) above, the rent payable under the tenancy of the dwelling at the relevant time.

(2)   Where a rent officer makes any determinations under paragraphs 1, 2 or 3, he shall also determine which rent is the claim-related rent.

(3)   Where the dwelling is not in a hostel, the rent officer shall also determine the total amount of ineligible charges, as defined in paragraph 7, which he has not included in the claim-related rent because of the assumptions made in accordance with that paragraph.]

Amendment
1.   Substituted by Art 11 of SI 2000 No 3 as from 3.4.00.

Part II
Assumptions

Ineligible charges and support charges

[¹**7.**–(1)   For the purposes of this paragraph–
(a)   [³ "ineligible charges" means service charges which are ineligible to be met by housing benefit by virtue of regulation 12(3) (rent) of and Schedule 1 (ineligible service charges) to the Housing Benefit Regulations or, as the case may be, the Housing Benefit (State Pension Credit) Regulations except in the case of a tenancy where the rent includes payments for board and attendance, and the rent officer considers that a substantial part of the rent under the tenancy is fairly attributable to board and attendance, charges specified in paragraph 1(a)(i) of Schedule 1 to the Housing Benefit Regulations or, as the case may be, in paragraph 1(a)(i) of Schedule 1 to the Housing Benefit (State Pension Credit) Regulations (charges for meals).]
[².. .].

(2)   When making a determination under paragraph 1, 2 or 3 of this Schedule, the rent officer shall assume that–
(a)   the items to which the ineligible charges relate; [² . . .],
were not to be provided or made available.

(3)   For the purposes of paragraphs 1, 2, 3 and 6 of this Schedule, the rent officer shall assume that the rent payable under the tenancy at the relevant time is–
(a)   where an amount is notified to the rent officer under [³ regulation 14(9)(b) of the Housing Benefit Regulations or, as the case may be, regulation 14(8)(b) of the Housing Benefit (State Pension Credit) Regulations] in respect of that tenancy, that notified amount less the total of any ineligible charges included in that amount; or
(b)   in any other case, the total amount stated under [³14(2) of the Housing Benefit Regulations or, as the case may be, regulation 14(2) of the Housing Benefit (State Pension Credit) Regulations] less the total of any ineligible charges included in that stated amount.

(4)   The total of any ineligible charges, referred to in sub-paragraph (3), shall be the total of the amounts (excluding any amount which he considers is negligible) of any charges included in the notified amount or the stated amount, as the case may be, which, in the rent officer's opinion, are at the relevant time fairly attributable to any items to which ineligible charges relate.]

Amendments
1.   Amended by Art 9 of SI 2000 No 3 as from 3.4.00.
2.   Deleted by art 3 of SI 2003 No 478 as from 1.4.03 (7.4.03 where rent payable weekly or in multiples of a week).
3.   Amended by reg 5 and Sch 2 para 12(10)(b) of SI 2006 No 217 as from 6.3.06.

Housing associations etc.

8.–(1)   In a case where the local authority states in the application that the landlord is a housing association or a charity, the rent officer shall assume that the landlord is not such a body.

(2)   The rent officer shall not take into account the rent under any tenancy where the landlord is a housing association or where the landlord is a charity and the dwelling is provided by the landlord in the pursuit of its charitable purposes.

(3)   In this paragraph–
"charity" has the same meaning as in the Charities Act 1993, except that it includes a Scottish charity (which has the same meaning as in section 1(7) of the Law Reform (Miscellaneous Provisions) (Scotland) Act 1990); and
"housing association" has the same meaning as in the Housing Associations Act 1985.

Part III
Notifications of Part I Determinations

Notifications

9.–[¹(1)   Subject to sub-paragraph (2), the rent officer shall give notice to the local authority of–

(a)   the claim-related rent determined under Part I;

(b)   where the dwelling is not in a hostel, the total amount of ineligible charges determined under paragraph 6(3) in relation to that claim-related rent;

(c)   whether that claim-related rent includes an amount which would be ineligible for housing benefit under [² paragraph 1(a)(i) of Schedule 1 to the Housing Benefit Regulations or, as the case may be, paragraph 1(a)(i) of Schedule 1 to the Housing Benefit (State Pension Credit) Regulations] (charges for meals);

(d)   any rent determined by the rent officer under paragraph 4 (local reference rents); and

(e)   any rent determined by the rent officer under paragraph 5 (single room rents).]

(2)   If the rent officer determines a rent under–

(a)   paragraph 4 (local reference rents); or

(b)   paragraph 5 (single room rents),

which is equal to or more than the [¹ claim-related rent], the rent officer shall give notice to the local authority of this in place of giving notice of the determination made under paragraph 4 or, as the case may be, paragraph 5.

Amendments

1.   Amended by Art 9 of SI 2000 No 3 as from 3.4.00.

2.   Amended by reg 5 and Sch 2 para 12(10)(c) of SI 2006 No 217 as from 6.3.06.

Part IV
Indicative Rent Levels

11.–(1)   The rent officer shall determine the indicative rent level for each category described in sub-paragraph (3) in accordance with the following formula–

$$I = \frac{H+3L}{4}$$

where–

I is the indicative rent level;

H is the highest rent, in the rent officer's opinion–

(a)   which a landlord might reasonably be expected to obtain at the time the determination is being made for an assured tenancy of a dwelling meeting the criteria in sub-paragraph (2); and

(b)   which is not an exceptionally high rent; and

L is the lowest rent, in the rent officer's opinion–

(a)   which a landlord might reasonably be expected to obtain at the time the determination is being made for an assured tenancy of a dwelling meeting the criteria in sub-paragraph (2); and

(b)   which is not an exceptionally low rent.

(2)   The criteria are that–

(a)   the dwelling is in the area of the local authority;

(b)   the dwelling is in a reasonable state of repair; and

(c)   the dwelling and tenancy accord with the category to which the determination relates.

(3)   The categories for the purposes of this paragraph are–

(a)   a dwelling where the tenant does not have use of more than one room where a substantial part of the rent under the tenancy is fairly attributable to board and attendance;

(b)   a dwelling where the tenant does not have use of more than one room, the tenancy provides for him to share a kitchen or toilet and paragraph (a) does not apply;

(c)   a dwelling where the tenant does not have use of more than one room and where paragraphs (a) and (b) do not apply;

(d)   a dwelling where the tenant does not have use of more than two rooms and where none of paragraphs (a) to (c) applies;

(e)   a dwelling where the tenant does not have use of more than three rooms and where none of paragraphs (a) to (d) applies;

(f)   a dwelling where the tenant does not have use of more than four rooms and where none of paragraphs (a) to (e) applies;

(g)   a dwelling where the tenant does not have use of more than five rooms and where none of paragraphs (a) to (f) applies; and

(h)   a dwelling where the tenant does not have use of more than six rooms and where none of paragraphs (a) to (g) applies.

(4)   When ascertaining H and L under sub-paragraph (1), the rent officer–

(a)   shall assume that no one who would have been entitled to housing benefit had sought or is seeking the tenancy; and

(b)   shall exclude the amount of any rent which, in the rent officer's opinion, is fairly attributable to the provision of services which are ineligible to be met by housing benefit; [¹ . . .]

(5)   In this paragraph–

"room" means a bedroom or room suitable for living in and in paragraphs (a), (b) and (c) of sub-paragraph (3) does not include a room which the tenant shares with any person other than–

(a)   a member of his household;

(b)   a non-dependant of the tenant (within the meaning of [² regulation 3 of the Housing Benefit Regulations or, as the case may be, regulation 3 of the Housing Benefit (State Pension Credit) Regulations]); or

(c)   a person who pays rent to the tenant;

"services" has the meaning given by paragraph 4(5).

Amendments

1.   Deleted by art 3 of SI 2003 No 478 as from 1.4.03 (7.4.03 where rent payable weekly or in multiples of a week).

2.   Amended by reg 5 and Sch 2 para 12(10)(d) of SI 2006 No 217 as from 6.3.06.

SCHEDULE 2
SIZE CRITERIA

1.   One bedroom or room suitable for living in shall be allowed for each of the following categories of occupier (and each occupier shall come within only the first category for which he is eligible)–

(a)   [¹ a couple] (within the meaning of Part VII of the Social Security Contributions and Benefits Act 1992);

(b)   a person who is not a child;

(c)   two children of the same sex;

(d)   two children who are less than ten years old;

(e)   a child.

2.   The number of rooms (excluding any allowed under paragraph 1) suitable for living in allowed are–

(a)   if there are less than four occupiers, one;

(b)   if there are more than three and less than seven occupiers, two; and

(c)   in any other case, three.

Amendment

1.   Substituted by art 30 of SI 2005 No 2877 as from 5.12.05.

SCHEDULE 3
REDETERMINATIONS

[¹**1.**   Schedules 1 and 2 shall apply in relation to a redetermination as they apply to a determination, but as if references in those Schedules to the relevant time were references to the date the application for the original determination was made or, if earlier, the date the tenancy ended.]

Amendment

1.   Substituted by Art 12 of SI 2000 No 3 as from 3.4.00.

2.   The rent officer making the redetermination shall seek and have regard to the advice of one or two other rent officers in relation to the redetermination.

[¹ SCHEDULE 3A

Amendment

1.   Schedule inserted by Art 2(10) of SI 2003 No 2398 as from a date specified in Sch 1 to that SI in relation to each individual authority.

PART I
Categories of dwelling

1.–(1) The categories of dwelling for which a rent officer is required to determine a local housing allowance in accordance with article 4B(2)(a)(i) are–

(a)   a dwelling where the tenant has the exclusive use of only one bedroom and where the tenancy provides for him to–
  (i)   share the use of a kitchen, a bathroom and toilet and a room suitable for living in;
  (ii)   have the exclusive use of a kitchen or facilities for cooking and share the use of a bathroom and toilet and a room suitable for living in; or
  (iii)   have the exclusive use of a bathroom and toilet and share the use of a kitchen and a room suitable for living in;

(b)   a dwelling where the tenant has the use of only two rooms;
(c)   a dwelling where the tenant has the use of only three rooms;
(d)   a dwelling where the tenant has the use of only four rooms;
(e)   a dwelling where the tenant has the use of only five rooms;
(f)   a dwelling where the tenant has the use of only six rooms.

(2)   In sub-paragraph (1)(b) to (f) of this paragraph and in paragraph 3 ''room'' means a bedroom or room suitable for living in, except for a room which the tenant shares with any person other than–

(a)   a member of his household;
(b)   a non-dependant of the tenant (within the meaning of [¹ regulation 3 of the Housing Benefit Regulations or, as the case may be, regulation 3 of the Housing Benefit (State Pension Credit) Regulations]); or
(c)   a person who pays rent to the tenant.

Amendment
1.   Amended by reg 5 and Sch 2 para 12(11) of SI 2006 No 217 as from 6.3.06.

Formula for local housing allowance for category of dwelling in paragraph 1(1)(a)
2.–(1)   The rent officer shall determine a local housing allowance for the category of dwelling in paragraph 1(1)(a) in accordance with the following formula–

$$A = \frac{H+L}{2}$$

where–
A is the local housing allowance;
H is the highest rent which, in the rent officer's opinion–
(a)   a landlord might reasonably have been expected to obtain, at the date of the determination, for an assured tenancy of a dwelling which meets the criteria specified in sub-paragraph (2); and
(b)   is not an exceptionally high rent;
L is the lowest rent which, in the rent officer's opinion–
(a)   a landlord might reasonably have been expected to obtain, at the date of the determination, for an assured tenancy of a dwelling which meets the criteria specified in sub-paragraph (2); and
(b)   is not an exceptionally low rent.

(2)   The criteria are–
(a)   that the dwelling under the assured tenancy–
  (i)   is in the broad rental market area for which the local housing allowance is being determined; and
  (ii)   is in a reasonable state of repair;
(b)   that under the assured tenancy, the tenant has the exclusive use of only one bedroom and the tenancy provides for him to–
  (i)   share the use of a kitchen, a bathroom and toilet and a room suitable for living in;
  (ii)   have the exclusive use of a kitchen or facilities for cooking and share the use of a bathroom and toilet and a room suitable for living in; or
  (iii)   have the exclusive use of a bathroom and toilet and share the use of a kitchen and a room suitable for living in; and
(c)   that the rent does not include any payment for board and attendance.

(3)   When ascertaining H and L under sub-paragraph (1) the rent officer shall–
(a)   assume that no one who would have been entitled to housing benefit had sought or is seeking the tenancy; and
(b)   exclude the amount of any rent which, in the rent officer's opinion, is fairly attributable to the provision of services performed for, or facilities (including the use of furniture) provided for, or rights made available to, the tenant which are ineligible to be met by housing benefit.

(4)   When ascertaining H and L under sub-paragraph (1) the rent officer may, where he is not satisfied that–
(a)   the broad rental market area contains a sufficient number of dwellings that accord with the category of dwelling set out in paragraph 1(1)(a) to enable him to make a local housing allowance determination; or

(b)   he has sufficient other information about the market in the broad rental market area to enable him to make a local housing allowance determination,

take account of rents in other similar areas in which he believes a comparable market exists.

Formula for local housing allowance for other categories of dwelling

3.–(1) For categories of dwelling other than the category of dwelling in paragraph 1(1)(a), the rent officer shall determine a local housing allowance in accordance with the formula-

$$B = \frac{H+L}{2}$$

where–

B is the local housing allowance;

H is the highest rent which, in the rent officer's opinion–

(a)   a landlord might reasonably have been expected to obtain, at the date of the determination, for an assured tenancy of a dwelling which meets the criteria specified in sub-paragraph (2); and

(b)   is not an exceptionally high rent; and

L is the lowest rent which, in the rent officer's opinion–

(a)   a landlord might reasonably have been expected to obtain, at the date of the determination, for an assured tenancy of a dwelling which meets the criteria specified in sub-paragraph (2); and

(b)   is not an exceptionally low rent.

(2)   The criteria are that the dwelling under the assured tenancy–

(a)   is in the broad rental market area for which the local housing allowance is being determined;

(b)   is in a reasonable state of repair; and

(c)   has the same number of rooms as the category of dwelling in respect of which the local housing allowance is being determined.

(3)   Sub-paragraphs (3) and (4) of paragraph 2 apply when ascertaining H and L under this paragraph as if the reference in those sub-paragraphs to H and L were to H and L under this paragraph, except that ''in respect of which the local housing allowance is being determined'' shall be substituted for ''set out in paragraph 1(1)(a)''.

Broad rental market area

4.   In this Schedule ''broad rental market area'' means an area–

(a)   comprising two or more distinct areas of residential accommodation, each distinct area of residential accommodation adjoining at least one other in the area;

(b)   within which a person could reasonably be expected to live having regard to facilities and services for the purposes of health, education, recreation, personal banking and shopping, taking account of the distance of travel, by public and private transport, to and from facilities and services of the same type and similar standard; and

(c)   containing residential premises of a variety of types, and including such premises held on a variety of tenancies.

PART II

Column (1) Local authority	*Column (2) Date*
[¹ Argyll and Bute	30th May 2005
Edinburgh	9th February 2004]

Amendment

1.   Amended by art 5(1)(b) of SI 2005 No 236 as from 13.3.05.

SCHEDULE 4
SPECIAL CASES
Houseboats

1.   Where an application for a determination or a redetermination relates in whole or in part to mooring charges for a houseboat, this Order applies in relation to that application (or, as the case may be, to that part which relates to those charges) with the following modifications–

(a)   references to a tenancy, a tenancy of a dwelling or an assured tenancy are references to an agreement under which those charges are payable (and references to a landlord and a tenant shall be construed accordingly); and

(b)   no determination shall be made under paragraph 2 of Part I of Schedule 1 (size criteria) and references to the dwelling exceeding the size criteria shall not apply.

Mobile homes

2.   Where an application for a determination or redetermination relates in whole or in part to payments in respect of the site on which a caravan or a mobile home stands, this Order applies in relation to that application (or, as the case may be, that part which relates to those payments) with the following modifications–

(a)   references to a tenancy, a tenancy of a dwelling or an assured tenancy are references to an agreement under which those payments are payable (and references to a landlord and a tenant shall be construed accordingly); and

(b)   no determination shall be made under paragraph 2 of Part I of Schedule 1 (size criteria) and references to the dwelling exceeding the size criteria shall not apply.

Rental purchase agreements

3.   Where an application for a determination or a redetermination relates to a rental purchase agreement, the agreement is to be treated as if it were a tenancy.

The Rent Officers (Housing Benefit Functions) (Local Housing Allowance) Amendment Order 2003

SI 2003 No.2398

General Note

This Order modifies the Rent Officers (Housing Benefit Functions) Orders in respect of the implementation of the pilot housing allowance scheme in Pathfinder Authorities. Only the commencement dates are reproduced here.

Citation, commencement and interpretation

1.–(1)   This Order may be cited as the Rent Officers (Housing Benefit Functions) (Local Housing Allowance) Amendment Order 2003 and shall come into force in relation to the area of a local authority specified in Schedule 1 to this Order on the date specified in that Schedule in relation to that local authority.

(2)   *[omitted]*

SCHEDULE 1
DATE ON WHICH ORDER COMES INTO FORCE FOR LOCAL AUTHORITY AREAS

Local authority	Date
Blackpool	17th October 2003
Brighton and Hove	19th January 2004
Conwy	19th January 2004
Coventry	15th December 2003
Edinburgh	19th January 2004
Leeds	19th January 2004
Lewisham	17th November 2003
North East Lincolnshire	19th January 2004
Teignbridge	15th December 2003

The Rent Officers (Housing Benefit Functions) (Local Housing Allowance) Amendment Order 2005

(SI 2005 No.236)

Citation, commencement and interpretation

1.–(1)   This order may be cited as the Rent Officers (Housing Benefit Functions) (Local Housing Allowance) Amendment Order 2005.

(2)   This article and articles 2, 3, 5 and 6 shall come into force on 13th March 2005.

(3)   Articles 4 and 7 shall come into force in relation to the area of a local authority specified in the Schedule to this Order on the date specified in that Schedule in relation to that local authority.

(4)   In this Order–

(a)   "local authority" has the same meaning as in the Social Security Administration Act 1992; and

(b)   "the 2003 Order" means the Rent Officers (Housing Benefit Functions) (Local Housing Allowance) Amendment Order 2003.

The Rent Officers (Housing Benefit Functions) Order 1997: additional pathfinder authorities

4.   The Rent Officers (Housing Benefit Functions) Order 1997 shall apply in relation to the area of a local authority in England and Wales specified in the Schedule to this Order as it applies in relation to the area of a local authority in England and Wales specified in Schedule 1 to the 2003 Order.

The Rent Officers (Housing Benefit Functions) (Scotland) Order 1997: additional pathfinder authorities

7.   The Rent Officers (Housing Benefit Functions) (Scotland) Order 1997 shall apply in relation to the area of a local authority in Scotland specified in the Schedule to this Order as it applies in relation to the area of a local authority in Scotland specified in Schedule 1 to the 2003 Order.

SCHEDULE
ARTICLE 1(5)
DATE ON WHICH ARTICLES 4 AND 7 COME INTO FORCE FOR LOCAL AUTHORITY AREAS

Relevant authority	*Date*
Argyll and Bute	25th April 2005
East Riding of Yorkshire	21st March 2005
Guildford	6th June 2005
Norwich	16th May 2005
Pembrokeshire	23rd May 2005
St Helens	25th April 2005
Salford	20th June 2005
South Norfolk	9th May 2005
Wandsworth	14th March 2005.

Part 3

Main secondary legislation
Council tax benefit

The Council Tax Benefit Regulations 2006
(SI 2006 NO.215)

Arrangement of Regulations
PART 1
General

1.   Citation and commencement
2.   Interpretation
3.   Definition of non-dependant
4.   Disapplication of section 1(1A) of the Administration Act
5.   Persons who have attained the qualifying age for state pension credit
6.   Remunerative work
7.   Persons from abroad
7A.   Entitlement of a refugee to council tax benefit
8.   Prescribed persons for the purposes of section 131(3)(b) of the Act

PART 2
Membership of a family

9.   Persons of prescribed description for the definition of family in section 137(1) of the Act
10.   Circumstances in which a person is to be treated as responsible or not responsible for another
11.   Circumstances in which a person is to be treated as being or not being a member of the household

PART 3
Applicable amounts

12.   Applicable amounts
13.   Polygamous marriages
14.   Patients

PART 4
Income and capital
SECTION 1
General

15.   Calculation of income and capital of members of claimant's family and of a polygamous marriage
16.   Circumstances in which capital and income of non-dependant is to be treated as claimant's

SECTION 2
Income

17.   Calculation of income on a weekly basis
18.   Treatment of child care charges
19.   Average weekly earnings of employed earners
20.   Average weekly earnings of self-employed earners
21.   Average weekly income other than earnings
22.   Calculation of average weekly income from tax credits
23.   Calculation of weekly income
24.   Disregard of changes in tax, contributions etc

SECTION 3
Employed earners

25.   Earnings of employed earners
26.   Calculation of net earnings of employed earners

SECTION 4
Self-employed earners

27.   Earnings of self-employed earners
28.   Calculation of net profit of self-employed earners
29.   Deduction of tax and contributions of self-employed earners

SECTION 5
Other income

30.   Calculation of income other than earnings
31.   Capital treated as income
32.   Notional income

SECTION 6
Capital

33.   Capital limit
34.   Calculation of capital
35.   Disregard of capital of child and young person
36.   Income treated as capital
37.   Calculation of capital in the United Kingdom
38.   Calculation of capital outside the United Kingdom
39.   Notional capital
40.   Diminishing notional capital rule
41.   Capital jointly held
42.   Calculation of tariff income from capital

PART 5
Students
SECTION 1
General

43.   Interpretation
44.   Treatment of students
45.   Students who are excluded from entitlement to council tax benefit

SECTION 2
Income

46.   Calculation of grant income
47.   Calculation of covenant income where a contribution is assessed
48.   Covenant income where no grant income or no contribution is assessed
49.   Relationship with amounts to be disregarded under Schedule 4
50.   Other amounts to be disregarded
51.   Treatment of student loans
52.   Treatment of payments from access funds
53.   Disregard of contribution
54.   Further disregard of student's income
55.   Income treated as capital
56.   Disregard of changes occurring during summer vacation

PART 6
Amount of benefit

57.   Maximum council tax benefit
58.   Non-dependant deductions
59.   Council tax benefit taper
60.   Extended payments
61.   Extended payments (severe disablement allowance and incapacity benefit)

62. Alternative maximum council tax benefit
63. Residents of a dwelling to whom section 131(6) of the Act does not apply

PART 7
Changes of circumstances and increases for exceptional circumstances
64. Date on which entitlement is to begin
65. Date on which council tax benefit is to end
66. Date on which council tax benefit is to end where entitlement to severe disablement allowance or incapacity benefit ceases
67. Date on which change of circumstances is to take effect

PART 8
Claims
68. Who may claim
69. Time and manner in which claims are to be made
69A. Electronic claims for benefit
70. Date of claim where claim sent or delivered to a gateway office
71. Date of claim where claim sent or delivered to an office of a designated authority
72. Evidence and information
73. Amendment and withdrawal of claim
74. Duty to notify changes of circumstances
74A. Notice of change of circunstances given electrinically

PART 9
Decisions on questions
75. Decisions by a relevant authority
76. Notification of decision

PART 10
Awards or payments of benefit
77. Time and manner of granting council tax benefit
78. Persons to whom benefit is to be paid
79. Shortfall in benefit
80. Payment on the death of the person entitled
81. Offsetting

PART 11
Excess benefit
82. Meaning of excess benefit
83. Recoverable excess benefit
84. Authority by which recovery may be made
85. Persons from whom recovery may be sought
86. Methods of recovery
87. Further provision as to recovery of excess benefit
88. Diminution of capital
89. Sums to be deducted in calculating recoverable excess benefit
90. Recovery of excess benefit from prescribed benefits

PART 12
Information
SECTION 1
Claims and information
91. Interpretation
92. Collection of information

93.   Recording and holding information
94.   Forwarding of information
95.   Request for information

SECTION 2
Information between authorities etc.
96.   Information to be supplied by an authority to another authority
97.   Supply of information: extended payments (severe disablement allowance and incapacity benefit)

SCHEDULES
A1.   Treatment of claims for council tax benefit by refugees
1.   Applicable amounts
2.   Amount of alternative maximum council tax benefit
3.   Sums to be disregarded in the calculation of earnings
4.   Sums to be disregarded in the calculation of income other than earnings
5.   Capital to be disregarded
6.   Extended payments of council tax benefit
7.   Extended payments (severe disablement allowance and incapacity benefit) of council tax benefit
8.   Matters to be included in decision notice
9.   Electronic communication

General Note

These regulations are largely similar to the Housing Benefit Regulations 2006 (SI 2006 No.213, referred to below as "the HB Regs"). Where a regulation is substantially the same as a corresponding regulation in the HB Regs, no commentary appears below and reference should be made to the table on pxxxi to ascertain the comparable HB regulation.

PART 1
General

Citation and commencement

1.–(1)   These Regulations may be cited as the Council Tax Benefit Regulations 2006.

(2)   These Regulations are to be read, where appropriate, with the Consequential Provisions Regulations.

(3)   Except as provided in Schedule 4 to the Consequential Provisions Regulations, these Regulations shall come into force on 6th March 2006.

(4)   The regulations consolidated by these Regulations are revoked, in consequence of the consolidation, by the Consequential Provisions Regulations.

Interpretation

2.–(1)   In these Regulations–

"the Act" means the Social Security Contributions and Benefits Act 1992;

"the Administration Act" means the Social Security Administration Act 1992;

"the 1973 Act" means the Employment and Training Act 1973;

"the 1992 Act" means the Local Government Finance Act 1992;

[¹ "the 2000 Act" means the Electronic Communications Act 2000;]

"Abbeyfield Home" means an establishment run by the Abbeyfield Society including all bodies corporate or incorporate which are affiliated to that Society;

"adoption leave" means a period of absence from work on ordinary or additional adoption leave by virtue of section 75A or 75B of the Employment Rights Act 1996;

"alternative maximum council tax benefit" means the amount determined in accordance with regulation 62 and Schedule 2;

"appropriate DWP office" means an office of the Department for Work and Pensions dealing with state pension credit or claim office which is normally open to the public for the receipt of claims for income support or a jobseeker's allowance;

"assessment period" means such period as is prescribed in regulations 19 to 21 over which income falls to be calculated;

"attendance allowance" means–

(a)   an attendance allowance under Part 3 of the Act;

(b)   an increase of disablement pension under section 104 or 105 of the Act;

(c)   a payment under regulations made in exercise of the power conferred by paragraph 7(2)(b) of Part 2 of Schedule 8 to the Act;

(d)   an increase of an allowance which is payable in respect of constant attendance under paragraph 4 of Part 1 of Schedule 8 to the Act;

(e)   a payment by virtue of article 14, 15, 16, 43 or 44 of the Personal Injuries (Civilians) Scheme 1983 or any analogous payment; or

(f)   any payment based on need for attendance which is paid as part of a war disablement pension;

"the benefit Acts" means the Act and the Jobseekers Act;

"benefit week" means a period of 7 consecutive days commencing upon a Monday and ending on a Sunday;

"care home" in England and Wales has the meaning assigned to it by section 3 of the Care Standards Act 2000 and in Scotland means a care home service within the meaning assigned to it by section 2(3) of the Regulation of Care (Scotland) Act 2001;

"child" means a person under the age of 16;

"child tax credit" means a child tax credit under section 8 of the Tax Credits Act;

"the Children Order" means the Children (Northern Ireland) Order 1995;

"claim" means a claim for council tax benefit;

"claimant" means a person claiming council tax benefit;

"close relative" means a parent, parent-in-law, son, son-in-law, daughter, daughter-in-law, step-parent, step-son, step-daughter, brother, sister, or if any of the preceding persons is one member of a couple, the other member of that couple;

"community charge benefit" means community charge benefits under Part 7 of the Act as originally enacted;

"concessionary payment" means a payment made under arrangements made by the Secretary of State with the consent of the Treasury which is charged either to the National Insurance Fund or to a Departmental Expenditure Vote to which payments of benefit under the Act are charged;

"the Consequential Provisions Regulations" means the Housing Benefit and Council Tax Benefit (Consequential Provisions) Regulations 2006;

"council tax benefit" means council tax benefit under Part 7 of the Act;

"couple" means–

(a)   a man and a woman who are married to each other and are members of the same household;

(b)   a man and a woman who are not married to each other but are living together as husband and wife;

(c)   two people of the same sex who are civil partners of each other and are members of the same household; or

(d)   two people of the same sex who are not civil partners of each other but are living together as if they were civil partners,

and for the purposes of sub-paragraph (d), two people of the same sex are to be regarded as living together as if they were civil partners if, but only if, they would be regarded as living together as husband and wife were they instead two people of the opposite sex;

"date of claim" means the date on which the claim is made, or treated as made, for the purposes of regulation 69 (time and manner in which claims are to be made);

"the Decisions and Appeals Regulations" means the Housing Benefit and Council Tax Benefit (Decisions and Appeals) Regulations 2001;

"designated authority" means any of the following–

(a)   the Secretary of State;

(b)   a person providing services to the Secretary of State;

(c)   a local authority;

(d)   a person providing services to, or authorised to exercise any function of, any such authority;

"designated office" means the office designated by the relevant authority for the receipt of claims to council tax benefit–

(a)   by notice upon or with a form approved by it for the purpose of claiming council tax benefit; or

(b)   by reference upon or with such a form to some other document available from it and sent by electronic means or otherwise on application and without charge; or

(c)   by any combination of the provisions set out in sub-paragraphs (a) and (b) above;

"disability living allowance" means a disability living allowance under section 71 of the Act;

"dwelling" has the same meaning in section 3 or 72 of the 1992 Act;

"earnings" has the meaning prescribed in regulation 25 or, as the case may be, 27;

"the Eileen Trust" means the charitable trust of that name established on 29th March 1993 out of funds provided by the Secretary of State for the benefit of persons eligible for payment in accordance with its provisions;

[¹ "electronic communication" has the same meaning as in section 15(1) of the 2000 Act;]

"employed earner" is to be construed in accordance with section 2(1)(a) of the Act and also includes a person who is in receipt of a payment which is payable under any enactment having effect in Northern Ireland and which corresponds to statutory sick pay or statutory maternity pay;

"employment zone" means an area within Great Britain designated for the purposes of section 60 of the Welfare Reform and Pensions Act 1999 and an "employment zone programme" means a programme established for such an area or areas designed to assist claimants for a jobseeker's allowance to obtain sustainable employment;

"employment zone contractor" means a person who is undertaking the provision of facilities in respect of an employment zone programme on behalf of the Secretary of State for Work and Pensions;

"extended payment" means council tax benefit allowed pursuant to regulation 60;

"extended payment (severe disablement allowance and incapacity benefit)" means council tax benefit allowed pursuant to regulation 61;

"family" has the meaning assigned to it by section 137(1) of the Act;

"the Fund" means moneys made available from time to time by the Secretary of State for the benefit of persons eligible for payment in accordance with the provisions of a scheme established by him on 24th April 1992 or, in Scotland, on 10th April 1992;

"gateway office" means an appropriate DWP office or an office designated by the appropriate authority which is nominated by the Secretary of State as a gateway office and referred to in a notice upon or attached to a form approved by the appropriate authority for the purpose of claiming council tax benefit;

"a guaranteed income payment" means a payment made under article 14(1)(b) or article 21(1)(a) of the Armed Forces and Reserve Forces (Compensation Scheme) Order 2005;

"housing benefit" means housing benefit under Part 7 of the Act;

"the Housing Benefit Regulations" means the Housing Benefit Regulations 2006;

"Immigration and Asylum Act" means the Immigration and Asylum Act 1999;

"an income-based jobseeker's allowance" and "a joint-claim jobseeker's allowance" have the same meaning as they have in the Jobseekers Act by virtue of section 1(4) of that Act;

"Income Support Regulations" means the Income Support (General) Regulations 1987;

"independent hospital" in England and Wales has the meaning assigned to it by section 2 of the Care Standards Act 2000 and in Scotland means an independent healthcare service as defined in section 2(5)(a) and (b) of the Regulation of Care (Scotland) Act 2001;

"the Independent Living Fund" means the charitable trust established out of funds provided by the Secretary of State for the purpose of providing financial assistance to those persons incapacitated by or otherwise suffering from very severe disablement who are in need of such assistance to enable them to live independently;

[⁴ "the Independent Living Fund (2006)" means the Trust of that name established by a deed dated 10th April 2006 and made between the Secretary of State for Work and Pensions of the one part and Margaret Rosemary Cooper, Michael Beresford Boyall and Marie Theresa Martin of the other part;]

"the Independent Living Funds" means the Independent Living Fund, [⁴ the Independent Living (Extension) Fund, the Independent Living (1993) Fund and the Independent Living Fund (2006)];

"the Independent Living (Extension) Fund" means the Trust of that name established by a deed dated 25th February 1993 and made between the Secretary of State for Social Security of the one part and Robin Glover Wendt and John Fletcher Shepherd of the other part;

"the Independent Living (1993) Fund" means the Trust of that name established by a deed dated 25th February 1993 and made between the Secretary of State for Social Security of the one part and Robin Glover Wendt and John Fletcher Shepherd of the other part;

"Intensive Activity Period for 50 plus" means the programme known by that name and provided in pursuance of arrangements made by or on behalf of the Secretary of State under section 2 of the 1973 Act, being a programme lasting for up to 52 weeks for any one individual aged 50 years or over on the day that he first joined any such programme, and consisting for that individual of any one or more of the following elements, namely assistance in pursuing self-employed earner's employment, education and training, work experience, assistance with job search, motivation and skills training;

"invalid carriage or other vehicle" means a vehicle propelled by a petrol engine or by electric power supplied for use on the road and to be controlled by the occupant;

"Jobseekers Act" means the Jobseekers Act 1995;

"Jobseeker's Allowance Regulations" means the Jobseeker's Allowance Regulations 1996;

"the London Bombings Relief Charitable Fund" means the company limited by guarantee (number 5505072), and registered charity of that name established on 11th July 2005 for the purpose of (amongst other things) relieving sickness, disability or financial need of victims (including families or dependants of victims) of the terrorist attacks carried out in London on 7th July 2005;

"lone parent" means a person who has no partner and who is responsible for and a member of the same household as a child or young person;

[⁶]

"the Macfarlane (Special Payments) Trust" means the trust of that name, established on 29th January 1990 partly out of funds provided by the Secretary of State, for the benefit of certain persons suffering from haemophilia;

"the Macfarlane (Special Payments) (No. 2) Trust" means the trust of that name, established on 3rd May 1991 partly out of funds provided by the Secretary of State, for the benefit of certain persons suffering from haemophilia and other beneficiaries;

"the Macfarlane Trust" means the charitable trust, established partly out of funds provided by the Secretary of State to the Haemophilia Society, for the relief of poverty or distress among those suffering from haemophilia;

"maternity leave" means a period during which a woman is absent from work because she is pregnant or has given birth to a child, and at the end of which she has a right to return to work either under the terms of her contract of employment or under Part 8 of the Employment Rights Act 1996;

"member of a couple" means a member of a married or unmarried couple;

"mobility supplement" means a supplement to which paragraph 9 of Schedule 4 refers;

"net earnings" means such earnings as are calculated in accordance with regulation 26;

"net profit" means such profit as is calculated in accordance with regulation 28;

"the New Deal options" means the employment programmes specified in regulation 75(1)(a)(ii) of the Jobseeker's Allowance Regulations and the training scheme specified in regulation 75(1)(b)(ii) of those Regulations;

"non-dependant" has the meaning prescribed in regulation 3;

"non-dependant deduction" means a deduction that is to be made under regulation 58;

"occupational pension" means any pension or other periodical payment under an occupational pension scheme but does not include any discretionary payment out of a fund established for relieving hardship in particular cases;

"ordinary clothing or footwear" means clothing or footwear for normal daily use, but does not include school uniforms, or clothing or footwear used solely for sporting activities;

"partner" means–
   (a)   where a claimant is a member of a couple, the other member of that couple; or
   (b)   where a claimant is polygamously married to two or more members of his household, any such member to whom he is married;

"paternity leave" means a period of absence from work on leave by virtue of section 80A or 80B of the Employment Rights Act 1996;

"payment" includes part of a payment;

"pension fund holder" means with respect to a personal pension scheme or [³ an occupational pension scheme], the trustees, managers or scheme administrators, as the case may be, of the scheme [³] concerned;

"person affected" shall be construed in accordance with regulation 3 of the Decisions and Appeals Regulations;

"person on income support" means a person in receipt of income support;

"person on state pension credit" means a person in receipt of state pension credit;

[³ "personal pension scheme" means–
   (a)   a personal pension scheme as defined by section 1 of the Pension Schemes Act 1993;

(b) an annuity contract or trust scheme approved under section 620 or 621 of the Income and Corporation Taxes Act 1988 or a substituted contract within the meaning of section 622(3) of that Act which is treated as having become a registered pension scheme by virtue of paragraph 1(1)(f) of Schedule 36 to the Finance Act 2004;

(c) a personal pension scheme approved under Chapter 4 of Part 14 of the Income and Corporation Taxes Act 1988 which is treated as having become a registered pension scheme by virtue of paragraph 1(1)(g) of Schedule 36 to the Finance Act 2004;]

"policy of life insurance" means any instrument by which the payment of money is assured on death (except death by accident only) or the happening of any contingency dependent on human life, or any instrument evidencing a contract which is subject to payment of premiums for a term dependent on human life;

"polygamous marriage" means a marriage to which section 133(1) of the Act refers;

"qualifying age for state pension credit" means (in accordance with section 1(2)(b) and (6) of the State Pension Credit Act)–

(a) in the case of a woman, pensionable age; or

(b) in the case of a man, the age which is pensionable age in the case of a woman born on the same day as the man;

"qualifying person" means a person in respect of whom payment has been made from the Fund, the Eileen Trust, the Skipton Fund or the London Bombings Relief Charitable Fund;

"relative" means a close relative, grandparent, grandchild, uncle, aunt, nephew or niece;

"relevant authority" means an authority administering council tax benefit;

"remunerative work" has the meaning prescribed in regulation 6;

"rent" means "eligible rent" to which regulation 12 of the Housing Benefit Regulations refers less any deductions in respect of non-dependants which fall to be made under regulation 74 (non-dependant deductions) of those Regulations;

"resident" has the meaning it has in Part 1 or 2 of the 1992 Act;

[³]

"second adult" has the meaning given to it in Schedule 2;

"self-employed earner" is to be construed in accordance with section 2(1)(b) of the Act;

"self-employment route" means assistance in pursuing self-employed earner's employment whilst participating in–

(a) an employment zone programme; or

(b) a programme provided or other arrangements made pursuant to section 2 of the 1973 Act (functions of the Secretary of State) or section 2 of the Enterprise and New Towns (Scotland) Act 1990 (functions in relation to training for employment, etc.);

"single claimant" means a claimant who neither has a partner nor is a lone parent;

"the Skipton Fund" means the ex-gratia payment scheme administered by the Skipton Fund Limited, incorporated on 25th March 2004, for the benefit of certain persons suffering from hepatitis C and other persons eligible for payment in accordance with the scheme's provisions;

"sports award" means an award made by one of the Sports Councils named in section 23(2) of the National Lottery etc Act 1993 out of sums allocated to it for distribution under that section;

[⁵ "starting rate", where it relates to the rate of tax, has the same meaning as in the Income Tax Act 2007 (see section 989 of that Act);]

"State Pension Credit Act" means the State Pension Credit Act 2002;

"student" has the meaning prescribed in regulation 43;

"subsistence allowance" means an allowance which an employment zone contractor has agreed to pay to a person who is participating in an employment zone programme;

"supplementary benefit" means a supplementary pension or allowance under section 1 or 4 of the Supplementary Benefit Act 1976;

"the Tax Credits Act" means the Tax Credits Act 2002;

"training allowance" means an allowance (whether by way of periodical grants or otherwise) payable–

(a) out of public funds by a Government department or by or on behalf of the Secretary of State, Scottish Enterprise or Highlands and Islands Enterprise, the Learning and Skills Council for England or the National Assembly for Wales;

(b) to a person for his maintenance or in respect of a member of his family; and

(c) for the period, or part of the period, during which he is following a course of training or instruction provided by, or in pursuance of arrangements made with, that department or approved by that department in relation to him or so provided or approved by or on behalf of the Secretary of State, Scottish Enterprise or Highlands and Islands Enterprise or the National Assembly for Wales,

but it does not include an allowance paid by any Government department to or in respect of a person by reason of the fact that he is following a course of full-time education, other than under arrangements made under section 2 of the 1973 Act or is training as a teacher;

"the Trusts" means the Macfarlane Trust, the Macfarlane (Special Payments) Trust and the Macfarlane (Special Payments) (No. 2) Trust;

"voluntary organisation" means a body, other than a public or local authority, the activities of which are carried on otherwise than for profit;

[²]

"water charges" means–

(a) as respects England and Wales, any water and sewerage charges under Chapter 1 of Part 5 of the Water Industry Act 1991,

(b) as respects Scotland, any water and sewerage charges established by Scottish Water under a charges scheme made under section 29A of the Water Industry (Scotland) Act 2002,

in so far as such charges are in respect of the dwelling which a person occupies as his home;

"working tax credit" means a working tax credit under section 10 of the Tax Credits Act;

"Working Tax Credit Regulations" means the Working Tax Credit (Entitlement and Maximum Rate) Regulations 2002; and

"young person" has the meaning prescribed in regulation 9(1).

(2) In these Regulations, references to a claimant occupying a dwelling or premises as his home shall be construed in accordance with regulation 7 of the Housing Benefit Regulations.

(3) In these Regulations, where an amount is to be rounded to the nearest penny, a fraction of a penny shall be disregarded if it is less than half a penny and shall otherwise be treated as a whole penny.

(4) For the purpose of these Regulations, a person is on an income-based jobseeker's allowance on any day in respect of which an income-based jobseeker's allowance is payable to him and on any day–

(a) in respect of which he satisfies the conditions for entitlement to an income-based jobseeker's allowance but where the allowance is not paid in accordance with section 19 or 20A of the Jobseekers Act (circumstances in which a jobseeker's allowance is not payable); or

(b) which is a waiting day for the purposes of paragraph 4 of Schedule 1 to that Act and which falls immediately before a day in respect of which an income-based jobseeker's allowance is payable to him or would be payable to him but for section 19 or 20A of that Act;

(c) in respect of which he is a member of a joint-claim couple for the purposes of the Jobseekers Act and no joint-claim jobseeker's allowance is payable in respect of that couple as a consequence of either member of that couple being subject to sanctions for the purposes of section 20A of that Act;

(d) in respect of which an income-based jobseeker's allowance or a joint-claim jobseeker's allowance would be payable but for a restriction imposed pursuant to section 62 or 63 of the Child Support, Pensions and Social Security Act 2000 or section 7, 8 or 9 of the Social Security Fraud Act 2001 (loss of benefit provisions).

(5) For the purposes of these Regulations, two persons shall be taken to be estranged only if their estrangement constitutes a breakdown of the relationship between them.

(6) In these Regulations, references to any person in receipt of state pension credit includes a person who would be in receipt of state pension credit but for regulation 13 of the State Pension Credit Regulations 2002 (small amounts of state pension credit).

Modifications

References to "step-parent", step-children and the various in-laws in the definition of "close relative" are modified by s246 of the Civil Partnership Act 2004 and Article 3 and para 44 of the Schedule to SI 2005 No.3137 (see pp1046 and 1097).

Amendments

1. Inserted by Art 4(2) of SI 2006 No 2968 as from 20.12.06.
2. Omitted by Reg 5(a) of SI 2007 No 1619 as from 3.7.07.
3. Amended by reg 6(2) of SI 2007 No 1749 as from 16.7.07.
4. Amended by Art 9(2) of SI 2007 No 2538 as from 16.7.07.
5. Inserted by reg 13(2) of SI 2007 No 2618 as from 1.10.07.
6. Revoked by reg 2 and the Sch of SI 2007 No 2618 as from 1.10.07.

Analysis

Paragraph (1)

Many of the definitions in para (1) are shared with those for HB. Commentary is only given below on those that are unique to CTB. Reference should be made to the commentary to reg 2(1) of the HB Regs for analysis of definitions that are common to HB and CTB.

"dwelling" – England and Wales definition. Section 3 Local Government Finance Act 1992 (the 1992 Act) provides that a dwelling for council tax and hence CTB purposes is any property which fulfils the following criteria:

(1) It would have been a hereditament (ie, a unit of accommodation) for the purposes of the General Rate Act 1967.

(2) It is not shown or required to be shown in local or a central non-domestic rating list.

(3) It is not exempt from local non-domestic rating.

A building is also a "dwelling" if it is a "composite hereditament" which means that only part is used wholly for the purpose of living accommodation. Houses, flats, bungalows, cottages and maisonettes all normally count as dwellings. The pitch occupied by a caravan or a mooring occupied by a boat may also count as a dwelling, though holiday caravans and the like used for non-domestic purposes are subject to non-domestic rates.

"dwelling" – Scottish definition. In Scotland, by s72 of the 1992 Act a "dwelling" means any lands and heritages which fulfil the following criteria:

(1) It consists of one or more dwelling-houses with any garden, yard, garage, outhouse or pertinent belonging to and occupied with such dwelling-house or dwelling-houses.

(2) It would, but for the fact that it is a dwelling, be entered separately in the valuation roll. The valuation roll now only records the details of non-domestic and part residential subjects.

The Scottish dwelling includes the residential part of part residential subjects and that part of any premises which has been apportioned, as at 1 April 1989, as a dwelling house. It includes caravans but only if they are someone's sole or main residence. Certain types of property are explicitly included in or excluded from the Scottish definition of a dwelling by statutory instruments. Among the properties excluded from the Scottish definition of a dwelling are women's refuges: see SI 1992 No 2955.

"person on state pension credit". A person is on PC if in receipt of it. Note that this includes those who would be in receipt of PC but for the amount payable being less than 10 pence per week: reg 2(6).

"resident". See ss6(5) (on p1003) and 99(1) of the 1992 Act. "Resident" is defined in both the subsections as "an individual who has attained the age of 18 years and has his sole or main residence in the dwelling".

The critical part of the definition is the term "sole or main residence". This is not defined in the legislation, but there is a body of caselaw in relation to council tax and the community charge, which uses the same expression. In *Stevenson v Rogers* [1992] SLT 558, IH, it was said that the principal consideration in identifying a person's "main residence" was the length of time s/he spent in each place. This now has to be read with the Court of Appeal decision in *Williams v Horsham District Council* [2004] EWCA Civ 39, 21 January, CA, which, drawing on *Frost v Feltham* [1981] 1 WLR 455 (and the latter's apparent acceptance that "main" means "principal" or "most important"), concludes that "sole or main residence" refers to premises in which a person actually resides rather than the dwelling of itself. The Court of Appeal went on to state that it is probably impossible to produce a definition of "main residence" that will provide the appropriate test in all circumstances. However, the Court of Appeal said that usually a person's main residence will be the dwelling that a reasonable onlooker, with knowledge of the material facts, would regard as the person's home at the material time. Arguably, the factors identified in the cases below may now be seen as material facts which the hypothetical reasonable onlooker would be expected to have regard to under the *Williams* test.

Ownership of a dwelling is not equivalent to residence, and an owner of a dwelling is not, without more, resident in it: *Parry v Derbyshire Dales District Council* [2006] EWHC 988 (Admin), 5 May, unreported.

That case also decides (a) (see immediately following paragraph) that security of tenure may be relevant to the question whether the property is the person's main residence but is not relevant to whether he in fact resides there and (b) (see last paragraph on "resident" below) that Mr Parry ceased to reside in the property in question when he went abroad for a protracted period and let the property for two years.

The question of whether different accommodation was rented or owned was said in *Stevenson* to be irrelevant, though a comparison of security of tenure at two competing properties may be: *Ward v Kingston upon Hull CC* [1993] RA 71, QBD.

However, the authority is also entitled to take into account where the claimant's family live and where her/his children go to school: *Codner v Wiltshire Valuation and Community Charge Tribunal* [1994] 34 RVR 169, QBD; *Cox v London (South West) Valuation and Community Charge Tribunal* [1994] 34 RVR 171, QBD. A person who owns a property and continues a relationship with a person living in another may be found to be mainly resident in the latter: *Mullaney v Watford BC* [1997] RA 225, QBD.

There is conflicting authority on the position where a person maintains a home in this country and works for long periods outside the jurisdiction. In *Ward*, the fact that the charge payer worked for most of the year in Saudi Arabia did not prevent him being mainly resident here. Merchant seamen have also given rise to litigation: in *Bradford MBC v Anderton* [1991] RA 45, QBD it was said that the home had to be the main residence because a ship could not be a residence. In *Cameron v Henry* [1992] SLT 586, IH, the Court of Session reached the opposite conclusion and held that when the charge payer was at sea, he was not mainly resident on the mainland. Some of the "habitual residence" caselaw may also be helpful: see the Analysis to reg 10 HB Regs on p242.

Because a "resident" is defined in the same terms for CTB as for council tax, it ought never to be an issue for CTB purposes. If someone is not a "resident", s/he is not liable for council tax and has no need to claim CTB. If someone is a "resident", and hence liable for council tax, s/he ought also to be treated as a "resident" for the purposes of CTB. This has been confirmed in *CH 3933/2006*. The claimant and his family occupied two properties as a home. He was liable for council tax on both dwellings, but the authority only awarded CTB in respect of one of them. The issue was whether a person could be a "resident", in terms of section 6(5) of the 1992 Act, in two properties being occupied and used together as one combined residence, when they were listed separately on the valuation list as two hereditaments and were taxed as two chargeable dwellings rather than a single one. The commissioner said that although the question of what is a person's "sole or main residence" is always a question of fact and degree for the tribunal of first instance to determine on the evidence, there is a material difference between the kind of case (such as *Mullaney*) where a person is dividing his or her time between two distinct homes and a decision has to be made on which is the "main" one, and cases such as this, where a person is occupying contiguous premises as a single combined home. Whereas it is true that a person can only have one "sole or main" residence, it did not follow that this always had to be identified with one single "chargeable dwelling".

Paragraph (2)
See reg 7 HB Regs (on p206) for the definition of when a claimant is occupying a dwelling and the Analysis
to reg 8 (on p578) where the claimant is temporarilly absent from home.
Paragraph (4)
This is identical to reg 2(3) HB Regs: see the Analysis on p198.
Paragraph (5)
This definition rather begs the question of when such a breakdown occurs.

Definition of non-dependant

3.–(1)   In these Regulations, "non-dependant" means any person, except
someone to whom paragraph (2) applies, who normally resides with a claimant or
with whom a claimant normally resides.

(2)   This paragraph applies to–

(a)   any member of the claimant's family;

(b)   if the claimant is polygamously married, any partner of his and any child or
young person who is a member of his household and for whom he or one
of his partners is responsible;

(c)   a child or young person who is living with the claimant but who is not a
member of his household by virtue of regulation 11 (membership of the
same household);

(d)   subject to paragraph (3), any person who, with the claimant, is jointly and
severally liable to pay council tax in respect of a dwelling for any day under
sections 6, 7 or 75 of the 1992 Act (persons liable to pay council tax);

(e)   subject to paragraph (3), any person who is liable to make payments on a
commercial basis to the claimant or the claimant's partner in respect of the
occupation of the dwelling;

(f)   a person who lives with the claimant in order to care for him or a partner of
his and who is engaged by a charitable or voluntary organisation which
makes a charge to the claimant or his partner for the services provided by
that person.

(3)   Excepting persons to whom paragraph (2)(a) to (c) and (f) refer, a person to
whom any of the following sub-paragraphs applies shall be a non-dependant–

(a)   a person who resides with the person to whom he is liable to make payments
in respect of the dwelling and either–

(i)   that person is a close relative of his or his partner; or

(ii)   the tenancy or other agreement between them is other than on a
commercial basis;

(b)   a person whose liability to make payments in respect of the dwelling
appears to the relevant authority to have been created to take advantage of
the council tax benefit scheme except someone who was, for any period
within the eight weeks prior to the creation of the agreement giving rise to
the liability to make such payments, otherwise liable to make payments of
rent in respect of the same dwelling;

(c)   a person who becomes jointly and severally liable with the claimant for
council tax in respect of a dwelling and who was, at any time during the
period of eight weeks prior to his becoming so liable, a non-dependant of
one or more of the other residents in that dwelling who are so liable for the
tax, unless the relevant authority is satisfied that the change giving rise to
the new liability was not made to take advantage of the council tax benefit
scheme.

Analysis

This regulation is similar to reg 3 HB Regs, but there are a number of important differences:

(1)   Sub-para (2)(d) is different in that it exempts those who are jointly and severally liable to pay the
council tax with the claimant instead of those who have a legal joint right of occupation: see Analysis
to reg 3(2)(d) HB Regs on p201. In reality, these will usually be the same people.

(2) There is no equivalent of reg 3(4) HB Regs. It appears that the intention is that it cannot be said that a person "resides with" someone unless s/he is a "resident" within the meaning of that phrase in reg 2.

(3) There is no equivalent of reg 3(2)(e)(ii) and (iii) HB Regs. It follows that resident landlords and their families may be treated as non-dependants.

(4) The deeming provision in para (3) is similar, but again not identical. A person whose liability to pay rent to the claimant would fall foul of reg 9(1)(a) HB Regs if s/he claimed HB would count as a non-dependant for CTB purposes, just as s/he is for HB purposes: sub-para (a). However, sub-paras (b) and (c) refer to a liability created to take advantage of the CTB scheme rather than the HB scheme. It does not follow that an arrangement that falls foul of reg 9(1)(l) HB Regs will also have been created to take advantage of the CTB scheme. In most cases, the parties will probably not even have considered the council tax implications of the agreement. It is suggested that unless it can be shown that the dominant purpose of the parties was to secure CTB, as opposed to HB, the deeming provision in sub-para (b) cannot be satisfied: see the Analysis on p225.

Disapplication of section 1(1A) of the Administration Act

4. Section 1(1A) of the Administration Act (requirement to state national insurance number) shall not apply in the case of a child or young person in respect of whom council tax benefit is claimed.

Persons who have attained the qualifying age for state pension credit

5.–(1) These Regulations apply to a person who–

(a) has not attained the qualifying age for state pension credit; or

(b) has attained the qualifying age for state pension credit if he, or if he has a partner, his partner, is a person on income support or on an income-based jobseeker's allowance.

(2) Regulations 60 (extended payments) and Schedule 6 apply to a person if he, or if he has a partner, his partner, has attained the qualifying age for state pension credit.

(3) Except as provided in paragraphs (1)(b) and (2), these Regulations shall not apply in relation to any person if he, or if he has a partner, his partner, has attained the qualifying age for state pension credit.

General Note

The CTB Regs apply where neither the claimant nor her/his partner has reached the qualifying age for state pension credit (currently aged 60) or if either have reached that age, where one of them is in receipt of IS or JSA(IB). This is qualified in para (2) for the purposes of reg 60 and Sch 6. Where the claimant or her/his partner has reached the qualifying age for state pension credit and neither are in receipt of IS or JSA(IB) the CTB(SPC) Regs instead apply (see p812).

Remunerative work

6.–(1) Subject to the following provisions of this regulation, a person shall be treated for the purposes of these Regulations as engaged in remunerative work if he is engaged, or, where his hours of work fluctuate, he is engaged on average, for not less than 16 hours a week, in work for which payment is made or which is done in expectation of payment.

(2) Subject to paragraph (3), in determining the number of hours for which a person is engaged in work where his hours of work fluctuate, regard shall be had to the average of hours worked over–

(a) if there is a recognisable cycle of work, the period of one complete cycle (including, where the cycle involves periods in which the person does no work, those periods but disregarding any other absences);

(b) in any other case, the period of 5 weeks immediately prior to the date of claim, or such other length of time as may, in the particular case, enable the person's weekly average hours of work to be determined more accurately.

(3) Where, for the purposes of paragraph (2)(a), a person's recognisable cycle of work at a school, other educational establishment or other place of employment is

one year and includes periods of school holidays or similar vacations during which he does not work, those periods and any other periods not forming part of such holidays or vacations during which he is not required to work shall be disregarded in establishing the average hours for which he is engaged in work.

(4)   Where no recognisable cycle has been established in respect of a person's work, regard shall be had to the number of hours or, where those hours will fluctuate, the average of the hours, which he is expected to work in a week.

(5)   A person shall be treated as engaged in remunerative work during any period for which he is absent from work referred to in paragraph (1) if the absence is either without good cause or by reason of a recognised, customary or other holiday.

(6)   A person on income support or an income-based jobseeker's allowance for more than 3 days in any benefit week shall be treated as not being in remunerative work in that week.

(7)   A person shall not be treated as engaged in remunerative work on any day on which the person is on maternity leave, paternity leave or adoption leave, or is absent from work because he is ill.

(8)   A person shall not be treated as engaged in remunerative work on any day on which he is engaged in an activity in respect of which–

(a)   a sports award has been made, or is to be made, to him; and

(b)   no other payment is made or is expected to be made to him.

Persons from abroad

7.–(1)   A person from abroad is a person of a prescribed class for the purposes of section 131(3)(b) of the Act but this paragraph shall not have effect in respect of a person to whom and for a period to which regulation 7A and Schedule A1 apply.

[¹ (2)   In paragraph (1), ''person from abroad'' means, subject to the following provisions of this regulation, a person who is not habitually resident in the United Kingdom, the Channel Islands, the Isle of Man or the Republic of Ireland.

(3)   No person shall be treated as habitually resident in the United Kingdom, the Channel Islands, the Isle of Man or the Republic of Ireland unless he has a right to reside in (as the case may be) the United Kingdom, the Channel Islands, the Isle of Man or the Republic of Ireland other than a right to reside which falls within paragraph (4).

(4)   A right to reside falls within this paragraph if it is one which exists by virtue of, or in accordance with, one or more of the following–

(a)   regulation 13 of the Immigration (European Economic Area) Regulations 2006;

(b)   regulation 14 of those Regulations, but only in a case where the right exists under that regulation because the person is–

(i)   a jobseeker for the purpose of the definition of ''qualified person'' in regulation 6(1) of those Regulations, or

(ii)   a family member (within the meaning of regulation 7 of those Regulations) of such a jobseeker;

(c)   Article 6 of Council Directive No. 2004/38/EC; or

(d)   Article 39 of the Treaty establishing the European Community (in a case where the person is seeking work in the United Kingdom, the Channel Islands, the Isle of Man or the Republic of Ireland).

(4A)   A person is not a person from abroad if he is–

(a)   a worker for the purposes of Council Directive No. 2004/38/EC;

(b)   a self-employed person for the purposes of that Directive;

(c)   a person who retains a status referred to in sub-paragraph (a) or (b) pursuant to Article 7(3) of that Directive;

(d)   a person who is a family member of a person referred to in sub-paragraph (a), (b) or (c) within the meaning of Article 2 of that Directive;

(e)   a person who has a right to reside permanently in the United Kingdom by virtue of Article 17 of that Directive;

[⁵ (f) a person who is treated as a worker for the purpose of the definition of "qualified person" in regulation 6(1) of the Immigration (European Economic Area) Regulations 2006 pursuant to–

    (i)   regulation 5 of the Accession (Immigration and Worker Registration) Regulations 2004 (application of the 2006 Regulations in relation to a national of the Czech Republic, Estonia, Latvia, Lithuania, Hungary, Poland, Slovenia or the Slovak Republic who is an "accession State worker requiring registration"), or

    (ii)   regulation 6 of the Accession (Immigration and Worker Authorisation) Regulations 2006 (right of residence of a Bulgarian or Romanian who is an "accession State national subject to worker authorisation");]

(g)   a refugee;

[⁴ (h) a person who has exceptional leave to enter or remain in the United Kingdom granted outside the rules made under section 3(2) of the Immigration Act 1971;

(hh) a person who has humanitarian protection granted under those rules;]

(i)   a person who is not a person subject to immigration control within the meaning of section 115(9) of the Immigration and Asylum Act and who is in the United Kingdom as a result of his deportation, expulsion or other removal by compulsion of law from another country to the United Kingdom;

(j)   a person in Great Britain who left the territory of Montserrat after 1st November 1995 because of the effect on that territory of a volcanic eruption; [³]

[³ (jj) a person in Great Britain who left Lebanon on or after 12th July 2006 because of the armed conflict there; or]

(k)   in receipt of income support or on an income-based jobseeker's allowance.]

(5)   Paragraph 1 of Part 1 of the Schedule to, and regulation 2 as it applies to that paragraph of, the Social Security (Immigration and Asylum) Consequential Amendments Regulations 2000 shall not apply to a person who has been temporarily without funds for any period, or the aggregate of any periods, exceeding 42 days during any one period of limited leave (including any such period as extended).

(6)   In this regulation–

[²]

"refugee" in this regulation, regulation 7A (entitlement of a refugee to council tax benefit) and Schedule A1 (treatment of claims for council tax benefit by refugees), means a person recorded by the Secretary of State as a refugee within the definition in Article 1 of the Convention relating to the Status of Refugees.

Modifications

Reg 7(4A)(a) to (e) applies in relation to a national of Norway, Iceland, Liechtenstein or Switzerland or a member of her/his family (within the meaning of Art 2 of Council Directive No. 2004/38/EC) as if such a national were a national of a member State. See reg 10 of SI 2006 No 1026 on p1134.

The amendments made by SI 2006 No 1026 do not affect the continued operation of the transitional and savings provided for in reg 12 of the Social Security (Persons From Abroad) Miscellaneous Amendments Regulations 1996 (see p1134), reg 6 of the Social Security (Habitual Residence) Amendment Regulations 2004 (see p1094) or para 6 of Sch 3 of the HB&CTB(CP) Regs (see p1099). See reg 11 of SI 2006 No 1026 on p1134.

Amendments

1.   Substituted by reg 2(2)(a) of SI 2006 No 1026 as from 30.4.06.
2.   Omitted by reg 2(2)(b) of SI 2006 No 1026 as from 30.4.06.
3.   Amended by reg 7 of SI 2006 No 1981 from 25.7.06 until 31.1.07 only.
4.   Amended by reg 7 of SI 2006 No 2528 as from 9.10.06.
5.   Substituted by reg 7 of SI 2006 No 3341 as from 1.1.07.

Entitlement of a refugee to council tax benefit
[¹ 7A]

Modification

Reg 7A was inserted by Sch 4 para 3(1) of the HB&CTB(CP) Regs (see p1129). It only applied to claims for CTB by some refugees. See also Sch A1 inserted by Sch 4 para 3(2) of the HB&CTB(CP) Regs (see p1130).

Amendment

1.   Lapsed by s12(2)(g) of the Asylum and Immigration (Treatment of Claimants, etc.) Act 2004 (for those recorded as refugees after 14.6.07).

Prescribed persons for the purposes of section 131(3)(b) of the Act

8.–(1) Subject to paragraph (2), a person who is throughout any day referred to in section 131(3)(a) of the Act absent from the dwelling referred to in that section, shall be a prescribed person for the purposes of section 131(3)(b) of the Act in relation to that day.

(2) A person shall not, in relation to any day which falls within a period of temporary absence from that dwelling, be a prescribed person under paragraph (1).

(3) In paragraph (2), a "period of temporary absence" means–
(a)   a period of absence not exceeding 13 weeks, beginning with the first whole day on which a person resides in residential accommodation where and for so long as–
    (i)   the person resides in that accommodation;
    (ii)   the part of the dwelling in which he usually resided is not let or sub-let; and
    (iii)   that period of absence does not form part of a longer period of absence from the dwelling of more than 52 weeks,
where he has entered the accommodation for the purpose of ascertaining whether it suits his needs and with the intention of returning to the dwelling if it proves not to suit his needs;
(b)   a period of absence not exceeding 13 weeks, beginning with the first whole day of absence from the dwelling, where and for so long as–
    (i)   the person intends to return to the dwelling;
    (ii)   the part of the dwelling in which he usually resided is not let or sub-let; and
    (iii)   that period is unlikely to exceed 13 weeks; and
(c)   a period of absence not exceeding 52 weeks, beginning with the first whole day of that absence, where and for so long as–
    (i)   the person intends to return to the dwelling;
    (ii)   the part of the dwelling in which he usually resided is not let or sub-let;
    (iii)   the person is a person to whom paragraph (4) applies; and
    (iv)   the period of absence is unlikely to exceed 52 weeks or, in exceptional circumstances, is unlikely substantially to exceed that period.
(4)   This paragraph applies to a person who is–
(a) detained in custody on remand pending trial or required, as a condition of bail, to reside–
    (i)   in a dwelling, other than the dwelling referred to in paragraph (1), or
    (ii)   in premises approved under section 9 of the Criminal Justice and Court Services Act 2000,
or, detained in custody pending sentence upon conviction;
(b)   resident in a hospital or similar institution as a patient;

(c)   undergoing, or his partner or his dependent child is undergoing, in the United Kingdom or elsewhere, medical treatment, or medically approved convalescence, in accommodation other than residential accommodation;

(d)   following, in the United Kingdom or elsewhere, a training course;

(e)   undertaking medically approved care of a person residing in the United Kingdom or elsewhere;

(f)   undertaking the care of a child whose parent or guardian is temporarily absent from the dwelling normally occupied by that parent or guardian for the purpose of receiving medically approved care or medical treatment;

(g)   a person who is, in the United Kingdom or elsewhere, receiving medically approved care provided in accommodation other than residential accommodation;

(h)   a student;

(i)   a person who is receiving care provided in residential accommodation other than a person to whom paragraph (3)(a) applies; or

(j)   a person who has left the dwelling he resides in through fear of violence, in that dwelling, or by a person who was formerly a member of the family of the person first mentioned.

(5)   This paragraph applies to a person who is–

(a)   detained in custody pending sentence upon conviction or under a sentence imposed by a court (other than a person who is detained in hospital under the provisions of the Mental Health Act 1983, or, in Scotland, under the provisions of the Mental Health (Care and Treatment) (Scotland) Act 2003 or the Criminal Procedure (Scotland) Act 1995); and

(b)   on temporary release from detention in accordance with Rules made under the provisions of the Prison Act 1952 or the Prisons (Scotland) Act 1989.

(6)   Where paragraph (5) applies to a person, then, for any day when he is on temporary release–

(a)   if such temporary release was immediately preceded by a period of temporary absence under paragraph (3)(b) or (c), he shall be treated, for the purposes of paragraph (1), as if he continues to be absent from the dwelling, despite any return to the dwelling;

(b)   for the purposes of paragraph (4)(a), he shall be treated as if he remains in detention;

(c)   if he does not fall within sub-paragraph (a), he shall be a prescribed person for the purposes of section 131(3)(b) of the Act.

(7)   In this regulation–

''medically approved'' means certified by a medical practitioner;

''patient'' means a person who is undergoing medical or other treatment as an in-patient in any hospital or similar institution;

''residential accommodation'' means accommodation which is provided–

(a)   in a care home;

(b)   in an independent hospital;

(c)   in an Abbeyfield Home; or

(d)   in an establishment managed or provided by a body incorporated by Royal Charter or constituted by Act of Parliament other than a local social services authority;

''training course'' means a course of training or instruction provided wholly or partly by or on behalf of or in pursuance of arrangements made with, or approved by or on behalf of, Scottish Enterprise, Highlands and Islands Enterprise, a government department or the Secretary of State.

Analysis

This provision was extensively modified in April 2005 in order to get round the difficulties created by the previous drafting of regs 4B and 4C CTB Regs 1992 (now reg 8 CTB Regs – see p577), and more particularly the decision of Commissioner Fellner in *R(H) 4/05* that reg 4C(3) Regs 1992 in its pre-April 2005 was *ultra vires* and of no effect. For a discussion of those difficulties and the decision in *R(H) 4/05*, see the commentary to the 17th edition of this work.

Reg 8 seeks to overcome *R(H) 4/05* by treating a person who is absent from the dwelling and not temporarily absent as being a prescribed person for the purposes of s131(3)(b) SSCBA 1992, and so not entitled to CTB under s131(10) of the same Act. Whether the prescription exercise is lawful may be open to some argument, but a similar (but stronger) type of argument was not successful in the case of *Foster v Chief Adjudication Officer* [1993] AC 754, HL.

Assuming it is lawful, then reg 8 is broadly similar in effect to regulation 7(13), (16) and (17) HB Regs (ie, enabling entitlement to be retained if temporarily absent from the dwelling for up to 13 or 52 weeks in certain specified circumstances), to which reference should be made for the principles to be applied.

PART 2
Membership of a family

Persons of prescribed description for the definition of family in section 137(1) of the Act

9.–(1) Subject to paragraph (2), a person of a prescribed description for the purposes of section 137(1) of the Act (definition of family) as it applies to council tax benefit is a person [¹ who falls within the definition of qualifying young person in section 142 of the Act (child and qualifying young person)], and in these Regulations such a person is referred to as a ''young person''.

(2) Paragraph (1) shall not apply to a person who is–

(a) on income support or an income-based jobseeker's allowance; [² or]

[³ (b)]

(c) a person to whom section 6 of the Children (Leaving Care) Act 2000 (exclusion from benefits) applies.

(3) A person of a prescribed description for the purposes of section 137(1) of the Act as it applies to council tax benefit (definition of the family) includes a child or young person in respect of whom section 145A of the Act applies for the purposes of entitlement to child benefit but only for the period prescribed under section 145A(1) of the Act.

Amendments
1. Amended by reg 5(2)(a) of SI 2006 No 718 as from 10.4.06.
2. Inserted by reg 5(2)(b) of SI 2006 No 718 as from 10.4.06.
3. Omitted by reg 5(2)(c) of SI 2006 No 718 as from 10.4.06.

Circumstances in which a person is to be treated as responsible or not responsible for another

10.–(1) Subject to the following provisions of this regulation a person shall be treated as responsible for a child or young person who is normally living with him and this includes a child or young person to whom paragraph (3) of regulation 9 applies.

(2) Where a child or young person spends equal amounts of time in different households, or where there is a question as to which household he is living in, the child or young person shall be treated for the purposes of paragraph (1) as normally living with–

(a) the person who is receiving child benefit in respect of him; or

(b) if there is no such person–

(i) where only one claim for child benefit has been made in respect of him, the person who made that claim; or

(ii) in any other case the person who has the primary responsibility for him.

(3) For the purposes of these Regulations a child or young person shall be the responsibility of only one person in any benefit week and any person other than the

one treated as responsible for the child or young person under this regulation shall be treated as not so responsible.

Circumstances in which a person is to be treated as being or not being a member of the household

11.–(1)   Subject to paragraphs (2) and (3), the claimant and any partner and, where the claimant or his partner is treated as responsible by virtue of regulation 10 (circumstances in which a person is to be treated as responsible or not responsible for another) for a child or young person, that child or young person and any child of that child or young person, shall be treated as members of the same household notwithstanding that any of them is temporarily absent from that household.

(2)   A child or young person shall not be treated as a member of the claimant's household where he is–

(a)   placed with the claimant or his partner by a local authority under section 23(2)(a) of the Children Act 1989 or by a voluntary organisation under section 59(1)(a) of that Act, or in Scotland boarded out with the claimant or his partner under a relevant enactment; or

(b)   placed, or in Scotland boarded out, with the claimant or his partner prior to adoption; or

(c)   placed for adoption with the claimant or his partner in accordance with the Adoption and Children Act 2002 or the Adoption Agencies (Scotland) Regulations 1996.

(3)   Subject to paragraph (4), paragraph (1) shall not apply to a child or young person who is not living with the claimant and he–

(a)   is being looked after by, or in Scotland is in the care of, a local authority under a relevant enactment; or

(b)   has been placed, or in Scotland boarded out, with a person other than the claimant prior to adoption; or

(c)   has been placed for adoption in accordance with the Adoption and Children Act 2002 or the Adoption Agencies (Scotland) Regulations 1996.

(4)   An authority shall treat a child or young person to whom paragraph (3)(a) applies as being a member of the claimant's household in any benefit week where–

(a)   that child or young person lives with the claimant for part or all of that benefit week; and

(b)   the authority considers that it is reasonable to do so taking into account the nature and frequency of that child's or young person's visits.

(5)   In this regulation "relevant enactment" means the Army Act 1955, the Air Force Act 1955, the Naval Discipline Act 1957, the Matrimonial Proceedings (Children) Act 1958, the Social Work (Scotland) Act 1968, the Family Law Reform Act 1969, the Children and Young Persons Act 1969, the Matrimonial Causes Act 1973, the Children Act 1975, the Domestic Proceedings and Magistrates' Courts Act 1978, the Adoption (Scotland) Act 1978, the Family Law Act 1986, the Children Act 1989 and the Children (Scotland) Act 1995.

General Note

This regulation is similar to reg 21 HB Regs (see p274), except that reg 21(1) and (2) are effectively combined in reg 11(1). The difference is that in relation to reg 21, "temporary living away" is defined, whereas no such definition is given here.

As noted in reg 21, this regulation does not define household – see note on "family" on p22 – but sets out the situations in which a member of a household will continue to be treated as such, despite physical absence from it.

Para (1) sets out the general rule that claimants, their partner(s), any child or young person for whom they are responsible, and any child of such a child or young person, shall continue to be treated as members of the same household even when one or more of them is "temporarily absent" from the household.

Para (2) excludes certain children and young people from the claimant's household even when they actually live there.

Para (3) excludes certain children and young people who are absent from the household and living in the circumstances set out in para (3)(a) to (c), but para (4) itself provides an exception to para (3)(a). That means that children or young people to whom both paras (3)(a) and (4) apply *are* to be treated as members of the claimant's household, that is certain children or young people who are being "looked after" (in care in Scotland) but are living with the claimant for part or all of certain benefit weeks.

Para (5) defines "relevant enactment" for these purposes.

Analysis

Para (1)

As noted above, there is no definition of "temporary absence", although reg 21(2) HB Regs gives some indication of what is meant. The lack of definition means that authorities will have more discretion in relation to CTB than they do in relation to HB in this respect.

Paras (2) to (5)

See "Analysis" on p275.

PART 3
Applicable amounts

Applicable amounts

12.   Subject to regulations 13 and 14 and Schedule A1 (polygamous marriages, patients and treatment of claims for council tax benefit by refugees), a claimant's weekly applicable amount shall be the aggregate of such of the following amounts as may apply in his case–

(a)   an amount in respect of himself or, if he is a member of a couple, an amount in respect of both of them, determined in accordance with paragraph 1(1), (2) or (3), as the case may be, of Schedule 1;

(b)   an amount determined in accordance with paragraph 2 of Schedule 1 in respect of any child or young person who is a member of his family;

(c)   if he is a member of a family of which at least one member is a child or young person, an amount determined in accordance with Part 2 of Schedule 1 (family premium);

(d)   the amount of any premiums which may be applicable to him, determined in accordance with Parts 3 and 4 of Schedule 1 (premiums).

Polygamous marriages

13. Subject to regulation 14 and Schedule A1 (patients and treatment of claims for council tax benefit by refugees), where a claimant is a member of a polygamous marriage, his weekly applicable amount shall be the aggregate of such of the following amounts as may apply in his case–

(a)   the amount applicable to him and one of his partners determined in accordance with paragraph 1(3) of Schedule 1 as if he and that partner were a couple;

(b)   an amount equal to the difference between the amounts specified in sub-paragraphs (3) and (1)(b) of paragraph 1 of Schedule 1 in respect of each of his other partners;

(c)   an amount determined in accordance with paragraph 2 of Schedule 1 (applicable amounts) in respect of any child or young person for whom he or a partner of his is responsible and who is a member of the same household;

(d)   if he or another partner of the polygamous marriage is responsible for a child or young person who is a member of the same household, the amount specified in Part 2 of Schedule 1 (family premium);

(e)   the amount of any premiums which may be applicable to him determined in accordance with Parts 3 and 4 of Schedule 1 (premiums).

Patients

[¹**14.**]

Amendment
1.   Omitted by reg 3(4) of SI 2005 No 2502 as amended by Sch 2 para 27 of SI 2006 No 217 as from 1.4.06.

PART 4
Income and capital
SECTION 1
General

Calculation of income and capital of members of claimant's family and of a polygamous marriage

15.–(1)   The income and capital of a claimant's partner which by virtue of section 136(1) of the Act is to be treated as income and capital of the claimant, shall be calculated or estimated in accordance with the following provisions of this Part in like manner as for the claimant; and any reference to the "claimant" shall, except where the context otherwise requires, be construed for the purposes of this Part as if it were a reference to his partner.

(2)   Where a claimant or the partner of a claimant is married polygamously to two or more members of his household–

(a)   the claimant shall be treated as possessing capital and income belonging to each such member; and

(b)   the income and capital of that member shall be calculated in accordance with the following provisions of this Part in like manner as for the claimant.

(3)   The income and capital of a child or young person shall not be treated as the income and capital of the claimant.

Circumstances in which capital and income of non-dependant is to be treated as claimant's

16.–(1)   Where it appears to the relevant authority that a non-dependant and the claimant have entered into arrangements in order to take advantage of the council tax benefit scheme and the non-dependant has more capital and income than the claimant, that authority shall, except where the claimant is on income support or an income-based jobseeker's allowance, treat the claimant as possessing capital and income belonging to that non-dependant and, in such a case, shall disregard any capital and income which the claimant does possess.

(2)   Where a claimant is treated as possessing capital and income belonging to a non-dependant under paragraph (1) the capital and income of that non-dependant shall be calculated in accordance with the following provisions of this Part in like manner as for the claimant and any reference to the "claimant" shall, except where the context otherwise requires, be construed for the purposes of this Part as if it were a reference to that non-dependant.

SECTION 2
Income

Calculation of income on a weekly basis

17.–(1)   Subject to regulation 24 (disregard of changes in tax, contributions etc.), for the purposes of section 131(5) of the Act (conditions of entitlement to council tax benefit) the income of a claimant shall be calculated on a weekly basis–

(a)   by estimating the amount which is likely to be his average weekly income in accordance with this Section and Sections 3 to 5 of this Part and Part 5;

(b)   by adding to that amount the weekly income calculated under regulation 42 (calculation of tariff income from capital); and

(c)   by then deducting any relevant child care charges to which regulation 18 (treatment of child care charges) applies from any earnings which form part of the average weekly income or, in a case where the conditions in paragraph (2) are met, from those earnings plus whichever credit specified in sub-paragraph (b) of that paragraph is appropriate, up to a maximum deduction in respect of the claimant's family of whichever of the sums specified in paragraph (3) applies in his case.

(2)   The conditions of this paragraph are that–

(a)   the claimant's earnings which form part of his average weekly income are less than the lower of either his relevant child care charges or whichever of the deductions specified in paragraph (3) otherwise applies in his case; and

(b)   that claimant or, if he is a member of a couple either the claimant or his partner, is in receipt of either working tax credit or child tax credit.

(3)   The maximum deduction to which paragraph (1)(c) above refers shall be–

(a)   where the claimant's family includes only one child in respect of whom relevant child care charges are paid, [² £175.00] per week;

(b)   where the claimant's family includes more than one child in respect of whom relevant child care charges are paid, [² £300] per week.

(4)   For the purposes of paragraph (1) "income" includes capital treated as income under regulation 31 (capital treated as income) and income which a claimant is treated as possessing under regulation 32 (notional income).

Amendments

1.   Confirmed by Art 21(2) of SI 2006 No 645 and reg 8 of SI 2006 No 217 as from 1.4.06.

2.   Confirmed by Art 21(2) of SI 2007 No 688 as from 1.4.07.

Treatment of child care charges

18.–(1)   This regulation applies where a claimant is incurring relevant child care charges and–

(a)   is a lone parent and is engaged in remunerative work;

(b)   is a member of a couple both of whom are engaged in remunerative work; or

(c)   is a member of a couple where one member is engaged in remunerative work and the other–

    (i)   is incapacitated;

    (ii)   is an in-patient in hospital; or

    (iii)   is in prison (whether serving a custodial sentence or remanded in custody awaiting trial or sentence).

(2)   For the purposes of paragraph (1) and subject to paragraph (4), a person to whom paragraph (3) applies shall be treated as engaged in remunerative work for a period not exceeding 28 weeks during which he–

(a)   is paid statutory sick pay;

(b)   is paid short-term incapacity benefit at the lower rate under sections 30A to 30E of the Act;

(c)   is paid income support on the grounds of incapacity for work under regulation 4ZA of, and paragraph 7 or 14 of Schedule 1B to, the Income Support Regulations; or

(d)   is credited with earnings on the grounds of incapacity for work under regulation 8B of the Social Security (Credits) Regulations 1975.

(3)   This paragraph applies to a person who was engaged in remunerative work immediately before–

(a)   the first day of the period in respect of which he was first paid statutory sick pay, short-term incapacity benefit or income support on the grounds of incapacity for work; or

(b)   the first day of the period in respect of which earnings are credited, as the case may be.

(4)   In a case to which paragraph (2)(c) or (d) applies, the period of 28 weeks begins on the day on which the person is first paid income support or on the first day of the period in respect of which earnings are credited, as the case may be.

(5)   Relevant child care charges are those charges for care to which paragraphs (6) and (7) apply, and shall be calculated on a weekly basis in accordance with paragraph (10).

(6)   The charges are paid by the claimant for care which is provided–

(a)   in the case of any child of the claimant's family who is not disabled, in respect of the period beginning on that child's date of birth and ending on the day preceding the first Monday in September following that child's fifteenth birthday; or

(b)   in the case of any child of the claimant's family who is disabled, in respect of the period beginning on that person's date of birth and ending on the day preceding the first Monday in September following that person's sixteenth birthday.

(7)   The charges are paid for care which is provided by one or more of the care providers listed in paragraph (8) and are not paid–

(a)   in respect of the child's compulsory education;

(b)   by a claimant to a partner or by a partner to a claimant in respect of any child for whom either or any of them is responsible in accordance with regulation 10 (circumstances in which a person is treated as responsible or not responsible for another); or

(c)   in respect of care provided by a relative of the child wholly or mainly in the child's home.

(8)   The care to which paragraph (7) refers may be provided–

(a)   out of school hours, by a school on school premises or by a local authority–

(i)   for children who are not disabled in respect of the period beginning on their eighth birthday and ending on the day preceding the first Monday in September following their fifteenth birthday; or

(ii)   for children who are disabled in respect of the period beginning on their eighth birthday and ending on the day preceding the first Monday in September following their sixteenth birthday; or

(b)   by a child care provider approved in accordance with by the Tax Credit (New Category of Child Care Provider) Regulations 1999;

(c)   by persons registered under Part 10A of the Children Act 1989; or

(d)   in schools or establishments which are exempted from registration under Part 10A of the Children Act 1989 by virtue of paragraph 1 or 2 of Schedule 9A to that Act; or

(e)   by–

(i)   persons registered under section 7(1) of the Regulation of Care (Scotland) Act 2001, or

(ii)   local authorities registered under section 33(1) of that Act,

where the care provided is child minding or daycare within the meaning of that Act; or

(f)   by a person prescribed in regulations made pursuant to section 12(4) of the Tax Credits Act.

(9)   In paragraphs (6) and (8)(a), "the first Monday in September" means the Monday which first occurs in the month of September in any year.

(10)   Relevant child care charges shall be estimated over such period, not exceeding a year, as is appropriate in order that the average weekly charge may be estimated accurately having regard to information as to the amount of that charge provided by the child minder or person providing the care.

(11)   For the purposes of paragraph (1)(c) the other member of a couple is incapacitated where–

(a)   the claimant's applicable amount includes–

      (i)   a disability premium

      (ii)   a higher pensioner premium by virtue of the satisfaction of paragraph 11(2)(b) of Schedule 1,

on account of the other member's incapacity;

   (b)   the claimant's applicable amount would include a disability premium or a higher pensioner premium on account of the other member's incapacity but for that other member being treated as capable of work by virtue of a determination made in accordance with regulations made under section 171E of the Act;

   (c)   the claimant (within the meaning of regulation 2) is, or is treated as, incapable of work and has been so incapable, or has been so treated as incapable, of work in accordance with the provisions of, and regulations made under, Part 12A of the Act (incapacity for work) for a continuous period of not less than 196 days; and for this purpose any two or more separate periods separated by a break of not more than 56 days shall be treated as one continuous period;

   (d)   there is payable in respect of him one or more of the following pensions or allowances–

      (i)   long-term incapacity benefit or short-term incapacity benefit at the higher rate under Schedule 4 to the Act;

      (ii)   attendance allowance under section 64 of the Act;

      (iii)   severe disablement allowance under section 68 of the Act;

      (iv)   disability living allowance under section 71 of the Act;

      (v)   increase of disablement pension under section 104 of the Act;

      (vi)   a pension increase under a war pension scheme or an industrial injuries scheme which is analogous to an allowance or increase of disablement pension under head (ii), (iv) or (v) above;

   (e)   a pension or allowance to which head (ii), (iv), (v) or (vi) of sub-paragraph (d) above refers was payable on account of his incapacity but has ceased to be payable in consequence of his becoming a patient, [¹ , which in this regulation shall mean a person (other than a person who is serving a sentence of imprisonment or detention in a youth custody institution) who is regarded as receiving free in-patient treatment within the meaning of [² regulation 2(4) and (5) of the Social Security (Hospital In-Patients) Regulations 2005].];

   (f)   sub-paragraph (d) or (e) would apply to him if the legislative provisions referred to in those sub-paragraphs were provisions under any corresponding enactment having effect in Northern Ireland; or

   (g)   he has an invalid carriage or other vehicle provided to him by the Secretary of State under section 5(2)(a) of and Schedule 2 to the National Health Service Act 1977 or under section 46 of the National Health Service (Scotland) Act 1978 or provided by the Department of Health and Social Services for Northern Ireland under Article 30(1) of the Health and Personal Social Services (Northern Ireland) Order 1972.

  (12) For the purposes of paragraph (11), once paragraph (11)(c) applies to the claimant, if he then ceases, for a period of 56 days or less, to be incapable, or to be treated as incapable, of work, that paragraph shall, on his again becoming so incapable, or so treated as incapable, of work at the end of that period, immediately thereafter apply to him for so long as he remains incapable, or is treated as remaining incapable, of work.

  (13) For the purposes of paragraphs (6) and (8)(a), a person is disabled if he is a person–

   (a)   in respect of whom disability living allowance is payable, or has ceased to be payable solely because he is a patient;

(b)   who is registered as blind in a register compiled under section 29 of the National Assistance Act 1948 (welfare services) or, in Scotland, has been certified as blind and in consequence he is registered as blind in a register maintained by or on behalf of a council constituted under section 2 of the Local Government (Scotland) Act 1994; or

(c)   who ceased to be registered as blind in such a register within the period beginning 28 weeks before the first Monday in September following that person's fifteenth birthday and ending on the day preceding that person's sixteenth birthday.

(14)   For the purposes of paragraph (1) a woman on maternity leave, paternity leave or adoption leave shall be treated as if she is engaged in remunerative work for the period specified in paragraph (15) ("the relevant period") provided that–

(a)   in the week before the period of maternity leave, paternity leave or adoption leave began she was in remunerative work;

(b)   the claimant is incurring relevant child care charges within the meaning of paragraph (5); and

(c)   she is entitled to either statutory maternity pay under section 164 of the Act, statutory paternity pay by virtue of section 171ZA or 171ZB of the Act, statutory adoption pay by of section 171ZL of the Act, maternity allowance under section 35 of the Act or qualifying support.

(15)   For the purposes of paragraph (14) the relevant period shall begin on the day on which the person's maternity, paternity leave or adoption leave commences and shall end on–

(a)   the date that leave ends;

(b)   if no child care element of working tax credit is in payment on the date that entitlement to maternity allowance, qualifying support, statutory maternity pay, statutory paternity pay or statutory adoption pay ends, the date that entitlement ends; or

(c)   if a child care element of working tax credit is in payment on the date that entitlement to maternity allowance or qualifying support, statutory maternity pay or statutory adoption pay ends, the date that entitlement to that award of the child care element of the working tax credit ends,

whichever shall occur first.

(16)   In paragraphs (14) and (15)–

(a)   "qualifying support" means income support to which that person is entitled by virtue of paragraph 14B of Schedule 1B to the Income Support Regulations; and

(b)   "child care element" of working tax credit means the element of working tax credit prescribed under section 12 of the Tax Credits Act (child care element).

Amendments

1.   Substituted by reg 3(5) of SI 2005 No 2502 as amended by Sch 2 para 27 of SI 2006 No 217 as from 1.4.06.

2.   Amended by reg 5(2) of SI 2005 No 3360 as amended by Sch 2 para 30 of SI 2006 No 217 as from 10.4.06.

Average weekly earnings of employed earners

19.–(1)   Where a claimant's income consists of earnings from employment as an employed earner his average weekly earnings shall be estimated by reference to his earnings from that employment–

(a)   over a period immediately preceding the benefit week in which the claim is made or treated as made and being a period of–

(i)   5 weeks, if he is paid weekly; or

(ii)   2 months, if he is paid monthly; or

(b) whether or not sub-paragraph (a)(i) or (ii) applies, where a claimant's earnings fluctuate, over such other period preceding the benefit week in which the claim is made or treated as made as may, in any particular case, enable his average weekly earnings to be estimated more accurately.

(2) Where the claimant has been in his employment for less than the period specified in paragraph (1)(a)(i) or (ii)–

(a) if he has received any earnings for the period that he has been in that employment and those earnings are likely to represent his average weekly earnings from that employment his average weekly earnings shall be estimated by reference to those earnings;

(b) in any other case, the relevant authority shall require the claimant's employer to furnish an estimate of the claimant's likely weekly earnings over such period as the relevant authority may require and the claimant's average weekly earnings shall be estimated by reference to that estimate.

(3) Where the amount of a claimant's earnings changes during an award the relevant authority shall estimate his average weekly earnings by reference to his likely earnings from the employment over such period as is appropriate in order that his average weekly earnings may be estimated accurately but the length of the period shall not in any case exceed 52 weeks.

(4) For the purposes of this regulation the claimant's earnings shall be calculated in accordance with Section 3 of this Part.

Average weekly earnings of self-employed earners

20.–(1) Where a claimant's income consists of earnings from employment as a self-employed earner his average weekly earnings shall be estimated by reference to his earnings from that employment over such period as is appropriate in order that his average weekly earnings may be estimated accurately but the length of the period shall not in any case exceed a year.

(2) For the purposes of this regulation the claimant's earnings shall be calculated in accordance with Section 4 of this Part.

Average weekly income other than earnings

21.–(1) A claimant's income which does not consist of earnings shall, except where paragraph (2) applies, be estimated over such period as is appropriate in order that his average weekly income may be estimated accurately but the length of the period shall not in any case exceed 52 weeks; and nothing in this paragraph shall authorise an authority to disregard any such income other than that specified in Schedule 4.

(2) The period over which any benefit under the benefit Acts is to be taken into account shall be the period in respect of which that benefit is payable.

(3) For the purposes of this regulation income other than earnings shall be calculated in accordance with Section 5 of this Part.

Calculation of average weekly income from tax credits

22.–(1) This regulation applies where a claimant receives a tax credit.

(2) Where this regulation applies, the period over which a tax credit is to be taken into account shall be the period set out in paragraph (3).

(3) Where the instalment in respect of which payment of a tax credit is made is–

(a) a daily instalment, the period is 1 day, being the day in respect of which the instalment is paid;

(b) a weekly instalment, the period is 7 days, ending on the day on which the instalment is due to be paid;

(c) a two weekly instalment, the period is 14 days, commencing 6 days before the day on which the instalment is due to be paid;

(d)   a four weekly instalment, the period is 28 days, ending on the day on which the instalment is due to be paid.

(4)   For the purposes of this regulation "tax credit" means child tax credit or working tax credit.

Calculation of weekly income

23.–(1)   For the purposes of regulations 19 (average weekly earnings of employed earners), 21 (average weekly income other than earnings) and 22 (calculation of average weekly income from tax credits), where the period in respect of which a payment is made–

(a)   does not exceed a week, the weekly amount shall be the amount of that payment;

(b)   exceeds a week, the weekly amount shall be determined–

(i)   in a case where that period is a month, by multiplying the amount of the payment by 12 and dividing the product by 52;

(ii)   in any other case, by dividing the amount of the payment by the number equal to the number of days in the period to which it relates and multiplying the quotient by 7.

(2)   For the purposes of regulation 20 (average weekly earnings of self-employed earners) the weekly amount of earnings of a claimant shall be determined by dividing his earnings over the assessment period by the number equal to the number of days in that period and multiplying the quotient by 7.

Disregard of changes in tax, contributions etc

24.   In calculating the claimant's income the appropriate authority may disregard any legislative change–

(a)   in the basic or other rates of income tax;

(b)   in the amount of any personal tax relief;

(c)   in the rates of social security contributions payable under the Act or in the lower earnings limit or upper earnings limit for Class 1 contributions under the Act, the lower or upper limits applicable to Class 4 contributions under the Act or the amount specified in section 11(4) of the Act (small earnings exception in relation to Class 2 contributions);

(d)   in the amount of tax payable as a result of an increase in the weekly rate of Category A, B, C or D retirement pension or any addition thereto or any graduated pension payable under the Act;

(e)   in the maximum rate of child tax credit or working tax credit,

for a period not exceeding 30 benefit weeks beginning with the benefit week immediately following the date from which the change is effective.

SECTION 3
Employed earners

Earnings of employed earners

25.–(1)   Subject to paragraph (2), "earnings" means in the case of employment as an employed earner, any remuneration or profit derived from that employment and includes–

(a)   any bonus or commission;

(b)   any payment in lieu of remuneration except any periodic sum paid to a claimant on account of the termination of his employment by reason of redundancy;

(c)   any payment in lieu of notice or any lump sum payment intended as compensation for the loss of employment but only in so far as it represents loss of income;

(d)   any holiday pay except any payable more than 4 weeks after termination or interruption of the employment;

(e)   any payment by way of a retainer;

(f)   any payment made by the claimant's employer in respect of expenses not wholly, exclusively and necessarily incurred in the performance of the duties of the employment, including any payment made by the claimant's employer in respect of–

    (i)   travelling expenses incurred by the claimant between his home and place of employment;

    (ii)   expenses incurred by the claimant under arrangements made for the care of a member of his family owing to the claimant's absence from home;

(g)   any award of compensation made under section 112(4) or 117(3)(a) of the Employment Rights Act 1996 (remedies and compensation for unfair dismissal);

[¹ (gg) any payment or remuneration made under section 28, 34, 64, 68 or 70 of the Employment Rights Act 1996 (right to guarantee payments, remuneration on suspension on medical or maternity grounds, complaints to employment tribunals);]

(h)   any such sum as is referred to in section 112 of the Act (certain sums to be earnings for social security purposes);

(i)   any statutory sick pay, statutory maternity pay, statutory paternity pay or statutory adoption pay, or a corresponding payment under any enactment having effect in Northern Ireland;

(j)   any remuneration paid by or on behalf of an employer to the claimant who for the time being is on maternity leave, paternity leave or adoption leave or is absent from work because he is ill;

(k)   the amount of any payment by way of a non-cash voucher which has been taken into account in the computation of a person's earnings in accordance with Part 5 of Schedule 3 to the Social Security (Contributions) Regulations 2001.

(2)   Earnings shall not include–

(a)   subject to paragraph (3), any payment in kind;

(b)   any payment in respect of expenses wholly, exclusively and necessarily incurred in the performance of the duties of the employment;

(c)   any occupational pension.

(3)   Paragraph (2)(a) shall not apply in respect of any non-cash voucher referred to in paragraph (1)(k).

Amendment

1.   Amended by reg 13(3) of SI 2007 No 2618 as from 1.10.07.

Calculation of net earnings of employed earners

26.–(1)   For the purposes of regulation 19 (average weekly earnings of employed earners), the earnings of a claimant derived or likely to be derived from employment as an employed earner to be taken into account shall, subject to paragraph (2), be his net earnings.

(2)   There shall be disregarded from a claimant's net earnings, any sum, where applicable, specified in paragraphs 1 to 14 of Schedule 3.

(3)   For the purposes of paragraph (1) net earnings shall, except where paragraph (6) applies, be calculated by taking into account the gross earnings of the claimant from that employment over the assessment period, less–

(a)   any amount deducted from those earnings by way of–

    (i)   income tax;

    (ii)   primary Class 1 contributions under the Act;

(b) one-half of any sum paid by the claimant by way of a contribution towards an occupational pension scheme;

(c) one-half of the amount calculated in accordance with paragraph (5) in respect of any qualifying contribution payable by the claimant; and

(d) where those earnings include a payment which is payable under any enactment having effect in Northern Ireland and which corresponds to statutory sick pay, statutory maternity pay, statutory paternity pay or statutory adoption pay, any amount deducted from those earnings by way of any contributions which are payable under any enactment having effect in Northern Ireland and which correspond to primary Class 1 contributions under the Act.

(4) In this regulation "qualifying contribution" means any sum which is payable periodically as a contribution towards a personal pension scheme.

(5) The amount in respect of any qualifying contribution shall be calculated by multiplying the daily amount of the qualifying contribution by the number equal to the number of days in the assessment period; and for the purposes of this regulation the daily amount of the qualifying contribution shall be determined–

(a) where the qualifying contribution is payable monthly, by multiplying the amount of the qualifying contribution by 12 and dividing the product by 365;

(b) in any other case, by dividing the amount of the qualifying contribution by the number equal to the number of days in the period to which the qualifying contribution relates.

(6) Where the earnings of a claimant are estimated under sub-paragraph (b) of paragraph (2) of regulation 19 (average weekly earnings of employed earners), his net earnings shall be calculated by taking into account those earnings over the assessment period, less–

(a) an amount in respect of income tax equivalent to an amount calculated by applying to those earnings the [¹ starting rate] or, as the case may be, the [¹ starting rate] and the basic rate of tax applicable to the assessment period less only the personal relief to which the claimant is entitled under sections 257(1) of the Income and Corporation Taxes Act 1988 (personal allowances) as is appropriate to his circumstances but, if the assessment period is less than a year, the earnings to which the [¹ starting rate] of tax is to be applied and the amount of the personal relief deductible under this sub-paragraph shall be calculated on a pro rata basis;

(b) an amount equivalent to the amount of the primary Class 1 contributions that would be payable by him under the Act in respect of those earnings if such contributions were payable; and

(c) one-half of any sum which would be payable by the claimant by way of a contribution towards an occupational or personal pension scheme, if the earnings so estimated were actual earnings.

Amendment

1.   Amended by reg 13(4) of SI 2007 No 2618 as from 1.10.07.

SECTION 4
Self-employed earners

Earnings of self-employed earners

27.–(1) Subject to paragraph (2), "earnings", in the case of employment as a self-employed earner, means the gross income of the employment and shall include any allowance paid under section 2 of the 1973 Act or section 2 of the Enterprise and New Towns (Scotland) Act 1990 to the claimant for the purpose of assisting him in carrying on his business unless at the date of claim the allowance has been terminated.

(2)   ''Earnings'' shall not include any payment to which paragraph 27 or 28 of Schedule 4 refers (payments in respect of a person accommodated with the claimant under arrangements made by a local authority or voluntary organisation and payments made to the claimant by a health authority, local authority or voluntary organisation in respect of persons temporarily in the claimant's care) nor shall it include any sports award.

Calculation of net profit of self-employed earners

28.–(1)   For the purposes of regulation 20 (average weekly earnings of self-employed earners) the earnings of a claimant to be taken into account shall be–

    (a)   in the case of a self-employed earner who is engaged in employment on his own account, the net profit derived from that employment;

    (b)   in the case of a self-employed earner whose employment is carried on in partnership or is that of a share fisherman within the meaning of the Social Security (Mariners' Benefits) Regulations 1975, his share of the net profit derived from that employment, less–

        (i)   an amount in respect of income tax and of social security contributions payable under the Act calculated in accordance with regulation 29 (deduction of tax and contributions for self-employed earners); and

        (ii)   one-half of the amount calculated in accordance with paragraph (11) in respect of any qualifying premium.

(2)   There shall be disregarded from a claimant's net profit, any sum, where applicable, specified in paragraphs 1 to 14 of Schedule 3.

(3)   For the purposes of paragraph (1)(a) the net profit of the employment shall, except where paragraph (9) applies, be calculated by taking into account the earnings of the employment over the assessment period less–

    (a)   subject to paragraphs (5) to (7), any expenses wholly and exclusively incurred in that period for the purposes of that employment;

    (b)   an amount in respect of–

        (i)   income tax; and

        (ii)   social security contributions payable under the Act,

calculated in accordance with regulation 29 (deduction of tax and contributions for self-employed earners); and

    (c)   one-half of the amount calculated in accordance with paragraph (11) in respect of any qualifying premium.

(4)   For the purposes of paragraph (1)(b) the net profit of the employment shall be calculated by taking into account the earnings of the employment over the assessment period less, subject to paragraphs (5) to (7), any expenses wholly and exclusively incurred in that period for the purposes of the employment.

(5)   Subject to paragraph (6), no deduction shall be made under paragraph (3)(a) or (4), in respect of–

    (a)   any capital expenditure;

    (b)   the depreciation of any capital asset;

    (c)   any sum employed or intended to be employed in the setting up or expansion of the employment;

    (d)   any loss incurred before the beginning of the assessment period;

    (e)   the repayment of capital on any loan taken out for the purposes of the employment;

    (f)   any expenses incurred in providing business entertainment; and

    (g)   any debts, except bad debts proved to be such, but this sub-paragraph shall not apply to any expenses incurred in the recovery of a debt.

(6)   A deduction shall be made under paragraph (3)(a) or (4) in respect of the repayment of capital on any loan used for–

(a) the replacement in the course of business of equipment or machinery; and

(b) the repair of an existing business asset except to the extent that any sum is payable under an insurance policy for its repair.

(7) The relevant authority shall refuse to make a deduction in respect of any expenses under paragraph (3)(a) or (4) where it is not satisfied given the nature and the amount of the expense that it has been reasonably incurred.

(8) For the avoidance of doubt–

(a) a deduction shall not be made under paragraph (3)(a) or (4) in respect of any sum unless it has been expended for the purposes of the business;

(b) a deduction shall be made thereunder in respect of–

    (i) the excess of any value added tax paid over value added tax received in the assessment period;

    (ii) any income expended in the repair of an existing business asset except to the extent that any sum is payable under an insurance policy for its repair;

    (iii) any payment of interest on a loan taken out for the purposes of the employment.

(9) Where a claimant is engaged in employment as a child minder the net profit of the employment shall be one-third of the earnings of that employment, less–

(a) an amount in respect of–

    (i) income tax; and

    (ii) social security contributions payable under the Act,

calculated in accordance with regulation 29 (deduction of tax and contributions for self-employed earners); and

(b) one-half of the amount calculated in accordance with paragraph (11) in respect of any qualifying premium.

(10) For the avoidance of doubt where a claimant is engaged in employment as a self-employed earner and he is also engaged in one or more other employments as a self-employed or employed earner any loss incurred in any one of his employments shall not be offset against his earnings in any other of his employments.

(11) The amount in respect of any qualifying premium shall be calculated by multiplying the daily amount of the qualifying premium by the number equal to the number of days in the assessment period; and for the purposes of this regulation the daily amount of the qualifying premium shall be determined–

(a) where the qualifying premium is payable monthly, by multiplying the amount of the qualifying premium by 12 and dividing the product by 365;

(b) in any other case, by dividing the amount of the qualifying premium by the number equal to the number of days in the period to which the qualifying premium relates.

(12) In this regulation, "qualifying premium" means any premium which is payable periodically in respect of [¹] a personal pension scheme and is so payable on or after the date of claim.

Amendment

1.   Amended by reg 6(3) of SI 2007 No 1749 as from 16.7.07.

Deduction of tax and contributions of self-employed earners

29.–(1) The amount to be deducted in respect of income tax under regulation 28(1)(b)(i), (3)(b)(i) or (9)(a)(i) (calculation of net profit of self-employed earners) shall be calculated on the basis of the amount of chargeable income and as if that income were assessable to income tax at the [¹ starting rate] or, as the case may be, the [¹ starting rate] and the basic rate of tax applicable to the assessment period less only the personal relief to which the claimant is entitled under sections 257(1) of the Income and Corporation Taxes Act 1988 (personal allowances) as is appropriate to his circumstances; but, if the assessment period is less than a year, the earnings to which the [¹ starting rate] of tax is to be applied and the amount of the personal reliefs deductible under this paragraph shall be calculated on a pro rata basis.

(2)   The amount to be deducted in respect of social security contributions under regulation 28(1)(b)(i), (3)(b)(ii) or (9)(a)(ii) shall be the total of–

(a)   the amount of Class 2 contributions payable under section 11(1) or, as the case may be, 11(3) of the Act at the rate applicable to the assessment period except where the claimant's chargeable income is less than the amount specified in section 11(4) of the Act (small earnings exception) for the tax year applicable to the assessment period; but if the assessment period is less than a year, the amount specified for that tax year shall be reduced pro rata; and

(b)   the amount of Class 4 contributions (if any) which would be payable under section 15 of the Act (Class 4 contributions recoverable under the Income Tax Acts) at the percentage rate applicable to the assessment period on so much of the chargeable income as exceeds the lower limit but does not exceed the upper limit of profits and gains applicable for the tax year applicable to the assessment period; but if the assessment period is less than a year, those limits shall be reduced pro rata.

(3)   In this regulation "chargeable income" means–

(a)   except where sub-paragraph (b) applies, the earnings derived from the employment less any expenses deducted under paragraph (3)(a) or, as the case may be, (4) of regulation 28;

(b)   in the case of employment as a child minder, one-third of the earnings of that employment.

Amendment

1.   Amended by reg 13(5) of SI 2007 No 2618 as from 1.10.07.

SECTION 5
Other income

Calculation of income other than earnings

30.–(1)   For the purposes of regulation 21 (average weekly income other than earnings), the income of a claimant which does not consist of earnings to be taken into account shall, subject to paragraphs (2) to (8), be his gross income and any capital treated as income under regulation 31 (capital treated as income).

(2)   There shall be disregarded from the calculation of a claimant's gross income under paragraph (1), any sum, where applicable, specified in Schedule 4.

[² (3)]

[² (4)]

[² (4A)]

(5)   Where the payment of any benefit under the benefit Acts is subject to any deduction by way of recovery the amount to be taken into account under paragraph (1) shall be the gross amount payable.

(6)   Where an award of any working tax credit or child tax credit under the Tax Credits Act is subject to a deduction by way of recovery of an overpayment of working tax credit or child tax credit which arose in a previous tax year the amount to be taken into account under paragraph (1) shall be the amount of working tax credit or child tax credit awarded less the amount of that deduction.

(7)   In paragraph (6), "tax year" means a period beginning with 6th April in one year and ending with 5th April in the next.

(8)   Paragraph (9) applies where–

(a)   a relevant payment has been made to a person in an academic year; and

(b)   that person abandons, or is dismissed from, his course of study before the payment to him of the final instalment of the relevant payment.

(9)   The amount of a relevant payment to be taken into account for the assessment period for the purposes of paragraph (1) in respect of a person to whom paragraph (8) applies, shall be calculated by applying the formula—

$$\frac{A - (B \times C)}{D}$$

where—

A = the total amount of the relevant payment which that person would have received had he remained a student until the last day of the academic term in which he abandoned, or was dismissed from, his course, less any deduction under regulation 51(5);

B = the number of benefit weeks from the benefit week immediately following that which includes the first day of that academic year to the benefit week which includes the day on which the person abandoned, or was dismissed from, his course;

C = the weekly amount of the relevant payment, before the application of the £10 disregard, which would have been taken into account as income under regulation 51(2) had the person not abandoned or been dismissed from, his course and, in the case of a person who was not entitled to council tax benefit immediately before he abandoned or was dismissed from his course, had that person, at that time, been entitled to housing benefit;

D = the number of benefit weeks in the assessment period.

(10)   In paragraphs (8) and (9)—

"academic year" and "student loan" shall have the same meanings as for the purposes of Part 5;

"assessment period" means the period beginning with the benefit week immediately following that which includes the day on which the person abandoned, or was dismissed from, his course and ending with the benefit week which includes the last day of the last quarter for which an instalment of the relevant payment was payable to that person and for the purposes of this definition, "quarter" shall have the same meaning as for the purposes of the Education (Student Support) Regulations 2005;

"relevant payment" means either a student loan or an amount intended for the maintenance of dependants referred to in regulation 46(7) or both.

(11)   For the avoidance of doubt there shall be included as income to be taken into account under paragraph (1)—

(a)   any payment to which regulation 25(2) (payments not earnings) applies; or

(b)   in the case of a claimant who is receiving support under section 95 or 98 of the Immigration and Asylum Act including support provided by virtue of regulations made under Schedule 9 to that Act, the amount of such support provided in respect of essential living needs of the claimant and his dependants (if any) as is specified in regulations made under paragraph 3 of Schedule 8 to the Immigration and Asylum Act.

Amendments

1.   Inserted by reg 4 of SI 2006 No 2813 as from 20.11.06.
2.   Omitted by reg 5(b) of SI 2007 No 1619 as from 3.7.07.

Capital treated as income

31.–(1)   Any capital payable by instalments which are outstanding at the date on which the claim is made or treated as made, or, at the date of any subsequent revision or supersession, shall, if the aggregate of the instalments outstanding and the amount of the claimant's capital otherwise calculated in accordance with Section 6 exceeds £16,000, be treated as income.

(2)   Any payment received under an annuity shall be treated as income.

(3)   Any earnings to the extent that they are not a payment of income shall be treated as income.

(4)   Any Career Development Loan paid pursuant to section 2 of the 1973 Act shall be treated as income.

(5)   Where an agreement or court order provides that payments shall be made to the claimant in consequence of any personal injury to the claimant and that such payments are to be made, wholly or partly, by way of periodic payments, any such periodic payments received by the claimant (but not a payment which is treated as capital by virtue of this Part), shall be treated as income.

Notional income

32.–(1)   A claimant shall be treated as possessing income of which he has deprived himself for the purpose of securing entitlement to housing benefit or increasing the amount of that benefit.

(2)   Except in the case of–

(a)   a discretionary trust;

(b)   a trust derived from a payment made in consequence of a personal injury;

(c)   a personal pension scheme [¹ , occupational pension scheme] [² [⁴] or a payment made by the Board of the Pension Protection Fund] where the claimant is aged under 60;

[³ (d)   any sum to which paragraph 47(2)(a) of Schedule 5 (capital to be disregarded) applies which is administered in the way referred to in paragraph 47(1)(a);

(da)   any sum to which paragraph 48(a) of Schedule 5 refers;]

(e)   rehabilitation allowance made under section 2 of the 1973 Act;

(f)   child tax credit; or

(g)   working tax credit,

any income which would become available to the claimant upon application being made, but which has not been acquired by him, shall be treated as possessed by the claimant but only from the date on which it could be expected to be acquired were an application made.

[⁴ (3)   This paragraph applies where a person aged not less than 60–

(a)   is a member of, or a person deriving entitlement to a pension under, a personal pension scheme;

(b)   fails to purchase an annuity with the funds available in that scheme; and

(c)   either–

    (i)   defers in whole or in part the payment of any income which would have been payable to him by his pension fund holder, or

    (ii)   fails to take any necessary action to secure that the whole of any income which would be payable to him by his pension fund holder upon his applying for it, is so paid, or

    (iii)   income withdrawal is not available to him under that scheme.

(3A)   Where paragraph (3) applies, the amount of any income foregone shall be treated as possessed by that person, but only from the date on which it could be expected to be acquired were an application for it to be made.]

(4)   The amount of any income foregone in a case [⁴ where paragraph (3)(c)(i) or (ii)] applies shall be the maximum amount of income which may be withdrawn from he fund and shall be determined by the relevant authority which shall take account of information provided by the pension fund holder in accordance with regulation 72(6) (evidence and information).

(5)   The amount of any income foregone in a case [⁴ where paragraph (3)(c)(iii)] applies shall be the income that the claimant could have received without purchasing an annuity had the funds held under the relevant personal pension scheme [⁴] been held under a personal pension scheme where income withdrawal was available and shall be determined in the manner specified in paragraph (4).

(6)　Any payment of income, other than a payment of income specified in paragraph (7), made–

(a)　to a third party in respect of a single claimant or a member of the family (but not a member of the third party's family) shall, where that payment is a payment of an occupational pension [² , a pension or other periodical payment made under a personal pension scheme or a payment made by the Board of the Pension Protection Fund], be treated as possessed by that single claimant or, as the case may be, by that member;

(b)　to a third party in respect of a single claimant or in respect of a member of the family (but not a member of the third party's family) shall, where it is not a payment referred to in sub-paragraph (a), be treated as possessed by that single claimant or by that member to the extent that it is used for the food, ordinary clothing or footwear, household fuel or rent of that single claimant or, as the case may be, of any member of that family or is used for any council tax or water charges for which that claimant or member is liable;

(c)　to a single claimant or a member of the family in respect of a third party (but not in respect of another member of that family) shall be treated as possessed by that single claimant or, as the case may be, that member of the family to the extent that it is kept or used by him or used by or on behalf of any member of the family.

(7)　Paragraph (6) shall not apply in respect of a payment of income made–

(a)　under the Macfarlane Trust, the Macfarlane (Special Payments) Trust, the Macfarlane (Special Payments) (No. 2) Trust, the Fund, the Eileen Trust or the Independent Living Funds;

(b)　pursuant to section 19(1)(a) of the Coal Industry Act 1994 (concessionary coal);

(c)　pursuant to section 2 of the 1973 Act in respect of a person's participation–

(i)　in an employment programme specified in regulation 75(1)(a)(ii) of the Jobseeker's Allowance Regulations;

(ii)　in a training scheme specified in regulation 75(1)(b)(ii) of those Regulations;

(iii)　in the Intense Activity Period specified in regulation 75(1)(a)(iv) of those Regulations or in the Intense Activity Period for 50 plus; or

(iv)　in a qualifying course within the meaning specified in regulation 17A(7) of those Regulations;

(d)　under an occupational pension scheme [² , in respect of a pension or other periodical payment made under a personal pension scheme or a payment made by the Board of the Pension Protection Fund] where–

(i)　a bankruptcy order has been made in respect of the person in respect of whom the payment has been made or, in Scotland, the estate of that person is subject to sequestration or a judicial factor has been appointed on that person's estate under section 41 of the Solicitors (Scotland) Act 1980;

(ii)　the payment is made to the trustee in bankruptcy or any other person acting on behalf of the creditors; and

(iii)　the person referred to in (i) and any member of his family does not possess, or is not treated as possessing, any other income apart from that payment.

(8)　Where a claimant is in receipt of any benefit (other than council tax benefit) under the benefit Acts and the rate of that benefit is altered with effect from a date on or after 1st April in any year but not more than 14 days thereafter, the relevant authority shall treat the claimant as possessing such benefit at the altered rate from either 1st April or the first Monday in April in that year, whichever date the relevant authority shall select to apply in its area, to the date on which the altered rate is to take effect.

(9)   Subject to paragraph (10), where–

(a)   a claimant performs a service for another person; and

(b)   that person makes no payment of earnings or pays less than that paid for a comparable employment in the area,

the relevant authority shall treat the claimant as possessing such earnings (if any) as is reasonable for that employment unless the claimant satisfies the authority that the means of that person are insufficient for him to pay or to pay more for the service.

(10)   Paragraph (9) shall not apply–

(a)   to a claimant who is engaged by a charitable or voluntary organisation or who is a volunteer if the relevant authority is satisfied in any of those cases that it is reasonable for him to provide those services free of charge; or

(b)   in a case where the service is performed in connection with–

(i)   the claimant's participation in an employment or training programme in accordance with regulation 19(1)(q) of the Jobseeker's Allowance Regulations, other than where the service is performed in connection with the claimant's participation in the Intense Activity Period specified in regulation 75(1)(a)(iv) of those Regulations or in the Intense Activity Period for 50 plus; or

(ii)   the claimant's or the claimant's partner's participation in an employment or training programme as defined in regulation 19(3) of those Regulations for which a training allowance is not payable or, where such an allowance is payable, it is payable for the sole purpose of reimbursement of travelling or meal expenses to the person participating in that programme. [⁵ or

(c)   to a claimant who is participating in a work placement approved by the Secretary of State (or a person providing services to the Secretary of State) before the placement starts.

(10A)   In paragraph (10)(c) ''work placement'' means practical work experience which is not undertaken in expectation of payment.]

(11)   Where a claimant is treated as possessing any income under any of paragraphs (1) to (8), the foregoing provisions of this Part shall apply for the purposes of calculating the amount of that income as if a payment had actually been made and as if it were actual income which he does possess.

(12)   Where a claimant is treated as possessing any earnings under paragraph (9) the foregoing provisions of this Part shall apply for the purposes of calculating the amount of those earnings as if a payment had actually been made and as if they were actual earnings which he does possess except that paragraph (3) of regulation 26 (calculation of net earnings of employed earners) shall not apply and his net earnings shall be calculated by taking into account those earnings which he is treated as possessing, less–

(a)   an amount in respect of income tax equivalent to an amount calculated by applying to those earnings the [⁵ starting rate] or, as the case may be, the [⁵ starting rate] and the basic rate of tax applicable to the assessment period less only the personal relief to which the claimant is entitled under sections 257(1) of the Income and Corporation Taxes Act 1988 (personal allowances) as is appropriate to his circumstances; but, if the assessment period is less than a year, the earnings to which the [⁵ starting rate] of tax is to be applied and the amount of the personal relief deductible under this sub-paragraph shall be calculated on a pro rata basis;

(b)   an amount equivalent to the amount of the primary Class 1 contributions that would be payable by him under the Act in respect of those earnings if such contributions were payable; and

    (c)   one-half of any sum payable by the claimant by way of a contribution towards an occupational or personal pension scheme.

Amendments

1.   Amended by reg 4A(2) of SI 2005 No 2465 as inserted by Sch 2 para 28(3) of SI 2006 No 217 as from 6.4.06.

2.   Substituted by reg 9(2) of SI 2006 No 588 as from 6.4.06.

3.   Substituted by reg 8(2) of SI 2007 No 719 as from 2.4.07.

4.   Amended by reg 6(4) of SI 2007 No 1749 as from 16.7.07.

5.   Amended by reg 13(6) of SI 2007 No 2618 as from 1.10.07.

SECTION 6
Capital

Capital limit

33.   For the purposes of section 134(1) of the Act as it applies to council tax benefit (no entitlement to benefit if capital exceeds prescribed amount), the prescribed amount is £16,000.

Calculation of capital

34.–(1)   For the purposes of Part 7 of the Act as it applies to council tax benefit, the capital of a claimant to be taken into account shall, subject to paragraph (2), be the whole of his capital calculated in accordance with this Part and any income treated as capital under regulation 36 (income treated as capital).

(2)   There shall be disregarded from the calculation of a claimant's capital under paragraph (1), any capital, where applicable, specified in Schedule 5.

Disregard of capital of child and young person

35.   The capital of a child or young person who is a member of the claimant's family shall not be treated as capital of the claimant.

Income treated as capital

36.–(1)   Any bounty derived from employment to which paragraph 8 of Schedule 3 applies and paid at intervals of at least one year shall be treated as capital.

(2)   Any amount by way of a refund of income tax deducted from profits or emoluments chargeable to income tax under Schedule D or E shall be treated as capital.

(3)   Any holiday pay which is not earnings under regulation 25(1)(d) (earnings of employed earners) shall be treated as capital.

(4)   Except any income derived from capital disregarded under paragraphs 1, 2, 4, 8, 14 [¹ , 25 to 28, 47 or 48] of Schedule 5, any income derived from capital shall be treated as capital but only from the date it is normally due to be credited to the claimant's account.

(5)   In the case of employment as an employed earner, any advance of earnings or any loan made by the claimant's employer shall be treated as capital.

(6)   Any charitable or voluntary payment which is not made or due to be made at regular intervals, other than a payment which is made under the Trusts, the Fund, the Eileen Trust, the Independent Living Funds or the London Bombings Charitable Relief Fund, shall be treated as capital.

(7)   There shall be treated as capital the gross receipts of any commercial activity carried on by a person in respect of which assistance is received under the self-employment route, but only in so far as those receipts were payable into a special account (as defined for the purposes of Chapter 4A of Part 8 of the Jobseeker's Allowance Regulations) during the period in which that person was receiving such assistance.

(8)   Any arrears of subsistence allowance which are paid to a claimant as a lump sum shall be treated as capital.

(9)   Any arrears of working tax credit or child tax credit shall be treated as capital.

Amendment

1.   Amended by reg 17(2) of SI 2006 No 2378 from the first day of the first benefit week to commence on or after 2.10.06.

[¹Calculation of capital in the United Kingdom

37.   Capital which a claimant possesses in the United Kingdom shall be calculated at its current market or surrender value less–

(a)   where there would be expenses attributable to the sale, 10 per cent.; and

(b)   the amount of any encumbrance secured on it.]

Amendment

1.   Substituted by reg 13(7) of SI 2007 No 2618 as from 1.10.07.

Calculation of capital outside the United Kingdom

38.   Capital which a claimant possesses in a country outside the United Kingdom shall be calculated–

(a)   in a case where there is no prohibition in that country against the transfer to the United Kingdom of an amount equal to its current market or surrender value in that country, at that value;

(b)   in a case where there is such a prohibition, at the price which it would realise if sold in the United Kingdom to a willing buyer,

less, where there would be expenses attributable to sale, 10 per cent. and the amount of any encumbrances secured on it.

Notional capital

39.–(1)   A claimant shall be treated as possessing capital of which he has deprived himself for the purpose of securing entitlement to council tax benefit or increasing the amount of that benefit except to the extent that that capital is reduced in accordance with regulation 40 (diminishing notional capital rule).

(2)   Except in the case of–

(a)   a discretionary trust; or

(b)   a trust derived from a payment made in consequence of a personal injury; or

(c)   any loan which would be obtained only if secured against capital disregarded under Schedule 5; or

(d)   a personal pension scheme [¹ , occupational pension scheme] [² [⁴] or a payment made by the Board of the Pension Protection Fund]; or

[³ (e)   any sum to which paragraph 47(2)(a) of Schedule 5 (capital to be disregarded) applies which is administered in the way referred to in paragraph 47(1)(a); or

(ea)   any sum to which paragraph 48(a) of Schedule 5 refers; or]

(f)   child tax credit; or

(g)   working tax credit,

any capital which would become available to the claimant upon application being made, but which has not been acquired by him, shall be treated as possessed by him but only from the date on which it could be expected to be acquired were an application made.

(3)   Any payment of capital, other than a payment of capital specified in paragraph (4), made–

(a)   to a third party in respect of a single claimant or a member of the family (but not a member of the third party's family) shall, where that payment is a payment of an occupational pension [² , a pension or other periodical payment made under a personal pension scheme or a payment made by the Board of the Pension Protection Fund], be treated as possessed by that single claimant or, as the case may be, by that member;

(b) to a third party in respect of a single claimant or in respect of a member of the family (but not a member of the third party's family) shall, where it is not a payment referred to in sub-paragraph (a), be treated as possessed by that single claimant or by that member to the extent that it is used for the food, ordinary clothing or footwear, household fuel or rent of that single claimant or, as the case may be, of any member of that family or is used for any council tax or water charges for which that claimant or member is liable;

(c) to a single claimant or a member of the family in respect of a third party (but not in respect of another member of the family) shall be treated as possessed by that single claimant or, as the case may be, that member of the family to the extent that it is kept or used by him or used by or on behalf of any member of the family.

(4) Paragraph (3) shall not apply in respect of a payment of capital made–

(a) under any of the Trusts, the Fund, the Eileen Trust, the Independent Living Funds, the Skipton Fund, or the London Bombings Relief Charitable Fund;

(b) pursuant to section 2 of the 1973 Act in respect of a person's participation–
   (i) in an employment programme specified in regulation 75(1)(a)(ii) of the Jobseeker's Allowance Regulations;
   (ii) in a training scheme specified in regulation 75(1)(b)(ii) of those Regulations;
   (iii) in the Intense Activity Period specified in regulation 75(1)(a)(iv) of those Regulations or in the Intensive Activity Period for 50 plus; or
   (iv) in a qualifying course within the meaning specified in regulation 17A(7) of those Regulations;

(c) under an occupational pension scheme [² , in respect of a pension or other periodical payment made under a personal pension scheme or a payment made by the Board of the Pension Protection Fund] where–
   (i) a bankruptcy order has been made in respect of the person in respect of whom the payment has been made or, in Scotland, the estate of that person is subject to sequestration or a judicial factor has been appointed on that person's estate under section 41 of the Solicitors (Scotland) Act 1980;
   (ii) the payment is made to the trustee in bankruptcy or any other person acting on behalf of the creditors; and
   (iii) the person referred to in (i) and any member of his family does not possess, or is not treated as possessing, any other income apart from that payment.

(5) Where a claimant stands in relation to a company in a position analogous to that of a sole owner or partner in the business of that company, he may be treated as if he were such sole owner or partner and in such a case–

(a) the value of his holding in that company shall, notwithstanding regulation 34 (calculation of capital) be disregarded; and

(b) he shall, subject to paragraph (6), be treated as possessing an amount of capital equal to the value or, as the case may be, his share of the value of the capital of that company and the foregoing provisions of this Section shall apply for the purposes of calculating that amount as if it were actual capital which he does possess.

(6) For so long as the claimant undertakes activities in the course of the business of the company, the amount which he is treated as possessing under paragraph (5) shall be disregarded.

(7)   Where a claimant is treated as possessing capital under any of paragraphs (1) to (3) the foregoing provisions of this Section shall apply for the purposes of calculating its amount as if it were actual capital which he does possess.

Amendments

1.	Amended by reg 4A(3) of SI 2005 No 2465 as inserted by Sch 2 para 28(3) of SI 2006 No 217 as from 6.4.06.
2.	Amended by reg 9(3) of SI 2006 No 588 as from 6.4.06.
3.	Substituted by reg 8(3) of SI 2007 No 719 as from 2.4.07.
4.	Amended by reg 6(5) of SI 2007 No 1749 as from 16.7.07.

Diminishing notional capital rule

40.–(1)   Where a claimant is treated as possessing capital under regulation 39(1) (notional capital), the amount which he is treated as possessing–

(a)   in the case of a week that is subsequent to–

    (i)   the relevant week in respect of which the conditions set out in paragraph (2) are satisfied; or

    (ii)   a week which follows that relevant week and which satisfies those conditions,

shall be reduced by an amount determined under paragraph (3);

(b)   in the case of a week in respect of which paragraph (1)(a) does not apply but where–

    (i)   that week is a week subsequent to the relevant week; and

    (ii)   that relevant week is a week in which the condition in paragraph (4) is satisfied,

shall be reduced by the amount determined under paragraph (4).

(2)   This paragraph applies to a benefit week or part-week where the claimant satisfies the conditions that–

(a)   he is in receipt of council tax benefit; and

(b)   but for regulation 39(1), he would have received an additional amount of council tax benefit in that week.

(3)   In a case to which paragraph (2) applies, the amount of the reduction for the purposes of paragraph (1)(a) shall be equal to the aggregate of–

(a)   the additional amount to which sub-paragraph (2)(b) refers;

(b)   where the claimant has also claimed housing benefit, the amount of any housing benefit or any additional amount of that benefit to which he would have been entitled in respect of the whole or part of the benefit week to which paragraph (2) refers but for the application of regulation 49(1) of the Housing Benefit Regulations (notional capital);

(c)   where the claimant has also claimed income support, the amount of income support to which he would have been entitled in respect of the whole or part of the benefit week to which paragraph (2) refers but for the application of regulation 51(1) of the Income Support Regulations (notional capital); and

(d)   where the claimant has also claimed a jobseeker's allowance, the amount of an income-based jobseeker's allowance to which he would have been entitled in respect of the whole or part of the benefit week to which paragraph (2) refers but for the application of regulation 113 of the Jobseeker's Allowance Regulations (notional capital).

(4)   Subject to paragraph (5), for the purposes of paragraph (1)(b) the condition is that the claimant would have been entitled to council tax benefit in the relevant week but for regulation 39(1), and in such a case the amount of the reduction shall be equal to the aggregate of–

(a)   the amount of council tax benefit to which the claimant would have been entitled in the relevant week but for regulation 39(1); and for the purposes of this sub-paragraph if the amount is in respect of a part-week, that amount shall be determined by dividing the amount of council tax benefit to which he would have been so entitled by the number equal to the number of days in the part-week and multiplying the quotient so obtained by 7;

(b)　if the claimant would, but for regulation 49(1) of the Housing Benefit Regulations, have been entitled to housing benefit or to an additional amount of housing benefit in respect of the benefit week which includes the last day of the relevant week, the amount which is equal to–

　　(i)　in a case where no housing benefit is payable, the amount to which he would have been entitled; or

　　(ii)　in any other case, the amount equal to the additional amount of housing benefit to which he would have been entitled,

and, for the purposes of this sub-paragraph, if the amount is in respect of a part-week, that amount shall be determined by dividing the amount of housing benefit to which he would have been so entitled by the number equal to the number of days in the part-week and multiplying the quotient so obtained by 7;

(c)　if the claimant would, but for regulation 51(1) of the Income Support Regulations, have been entitled to income support in respect of the benefit week, within the meaning of regulation 2(1) of those Regulations (interpretation), which includes the last day of the relevant week, the amount to which he would have been entitled and, for the purposes of this sub-paragraph, if the amount is in respect of a part-week, that amount shall be determined by dividing the amount of the income support to which he would have been so entitled by the number equal to the number of days in the part-week and multiplying the quotient so obtained by 7; and

(d)　if the claimant would, but for regulation 113 of the Jobseeker's Allowance Regulations, have been entitled to an income-based jobseeker's allowance in respect of the benefit week, within the meaning of regulation 1(3) of those Regulations (interpretation), which includes the last day of the relevant week, the amount to which he would have been entitled and, for the purposes of this sub-paragraph, if the amount is in respect of a part-week, that amount shall be determined by dividing the amount of the income-based jobseeker's allowance to which he would have been so entitled by the number equal to the number of days in the part-week and multiplying the quotient so obtained by 7.

(5)　The amount determined under paragraph (4) shall be re-determined under that paragraph if the claimant makes a further claim for council tax benefit and the conditions in paragraph (6) are satisfied, and in such a case–

(a)　sub-paragraphs (a) to (d) of paragraph (4) shall apply as if for the words "relevant week" there were substituted the words "relevant subsequent week"; and

(b)　subject to paragraph (7), the amount as re-determined shall have effect from the first week following the relevant subsequent week in question.

(6)　The conditions are that–

(a)　a further claim is made 26 or more weeks after–

　　(i)　the date on which the claimant made a claim for council tax benefit in respect of which he was first treated as possessing the capital in question under regulation 39(1);

　　(ii)　in a case where there has been at least one re-determination in accordance with paragraph (5), the date on which he last made a claim for council tax benefit which resulted in the weekly amount being re-determined, or

　　(iii)　the date on which he last ceased to be entitled to council tax benefit, whichever last occurred; and

(b)　the claimant would have been entitled to council tax benefit but for regulation 39(1).

(7)   The amount as re-determined pursuant to paragraph (5) shall not have effect if it is less than the amount which applied in that case immediately before the re-determination and in such a case the higher amount shall continue to have effect.

(8)   For the purposes of this regulation–

(a)   ''part-week''–

 (i)   in paragraph (4)(a) means a period of less than a week for which council tax benefit is allowed;

 (ii)   in paragraph (4)(b) means a period of less than a week for which housing benefit is payable;

 (iii)   in paragraph (4)(c) and (d) means–

  (aa)   a period of less than a week which is the whole period for which income support or, as the case may be, an income-based jobseeker's allowance is payable; and

  (bb)   any other period of less than a week for which it is payable;

(b)   ''relevant week'' means the benefit week or part-week in which the capital in question of which the claimant has deprived himself within the meaning of regulation 39(1)–

 (i)   was first taken into account for the purpose of determining his entitlement to council tax benefit; or

 (ii)   was taken into account on a subsequent occasion for the purpose of determining or re-determining his entitlement to council tax benefit on that subsequent occasion and that determination or re-determination resulted in his beginning to receive, or ceasing to receive, council tax benefit;

and where more than one benefit week is identified by reference to heads (i) and (ii) of this sub-paragraph the later or latest such benefit week or, as the case may be, the later or latest such part-week;

(c)   ''relevant subsequent week'' means the benefit week or part-week which includes the day on which the further claim or, if more than one further claim has been made, the last such claim was made.

Capital jointly held

41.   Except where a claimant possesses capital which is disregarded under regulation 39(5) (notional capital) where a claimant and one or more persons are beneficially entitled in possession to any capital asset they shall be treated as if each of them were entitled in possession to the whole beneficial interest therein in an equal share and the foregoing provisions of this Section shall apply for the purposes of calculating the amount of capital which the claimant is treated as possessing as if it were actual capital which the claimant does possess.

Calculation of tariff income from capital

42.–[¹ (1)   Where the claimant's capital calculated in accordance with this Part exceeds £6,000, it shall be treated as equivalent to a weekly income of £1 for each complete £250 in excess of £6,000 but not exceeding £16,000.]

(2)   Notwithstanding paragraph (1) where any part of the excess is not a complete £250 that part shall be treated as equivalent to a weekly tariff income of £1.

(3)   For the purposes of paragraph (1), capital includes any income treated as capital under regulation 36 (income treated as capital).

Amendment

 1.   Substituted by reg 4A(4) of SI 2005 No 2465 as inserted by Sch 2 para 28(3) of SI 2006 No 217 as from 6.4.06.

PART 5
Students
SECTION 1
General

General Note

Most full-time students are excluded from entitlement to CTB, as are students who are "persons from abroad" defined in reg 7: reg 45. Exceptions to the rule are found in reg 45(3). Full-time students are not precluded from claiming the alternative maximum CTB (second adult rebate): reg 45(1).

Even if a student is not excluded from entitlement to CTB, s/he must still satisfy the other rules set out in this Part before qualifying. The general rule is that claims by students are decided in the same way as claims by non-students, subject to the special income and capital rules found in regs 46–56.

The general exclusion of full-time students from CTB does not prevent a claimant whose partner is a student from claiming CTB.

There are no comparable rules for students in the CTB(SPC) Regs so claimants covered by those regulations are not excluded from entitlement to CTB for being students. In addition, student loan and grant income is ignored; it does not come within the definition of "income" in reg 19 CTB(SPC) Regs.

Interpretation

43.–(1)   In this Part–

"academic year" means the period of twelve months beginning on 1st January, 1st April, 1st July or 1st September according to whether the course in question begins in the winter, the spring, the summer or the autumn respectively but if students are required to begin attending the course during August or September and to continue attending through the autumn, the academic year of the course shall be considered to begin in the autumn rather than the summer;

"access funds" means–

(a) grants made under section 68 of the Further and Higher Education Act 1992 for the purpose of providing funds on a discretionary basis to be paid to students;

(b) grants made under sections 73(a) and (c) and 74(1) of the Education (Scotland) Act 1980;

(c) grants made under Article 30 of the Education and Libraries (Northern Ireland) Order 1993 or grants, loans or other payments made under Article 5 of the Further Education (Northern Ireland) Order 1997 in each case being grants, or grants, loans or other payments as the case may be, for the purpose of assisting students in financial difficulties;

(d) discretionary payments, known as "learner support funds", which are made available to students in further education by institutions out of funds provided by the Learning and Skills Council for England under sections 5, 6 and 9 of the Learning and Skills Act 2000; or

(e) Financial Contingency Funds made available by the National Assembly for Wales;

"college of further education" means a college of further education within the meaning of Part 1 of the Further and Higher Education (Scotland) Act 1992;

"contribution" means any contribution in respect of the income of a student or of any other person which the Secretary of State, the Scottish Ministers or an education authority takes into account in ascertaining the amount of the student's grant or student loan; or any sums, which in determining the amount of a student's allowance or bursary in Scotland under the Further and Higher Education (Scotland) Act 1992 Scottish Ministers or the education authority takes into account being sums which Scottish Ministers or the education authority consider that the holder of the allowance or bursary, the holder's parents and the holder's spouse or civil partner can reasonably be expected to contribute towards the holder's expenses;

"course of study" means any course of study, whether or not it is a sandwich course and whether or not a grant is made for attending or undertaking it;

"covenant income" means the gross income payable to a full-time student under a Deed of Covenant by his parent;

"education authority" means a government department, a local education authority as defined in section 12 of the Education Act 1996 (interpretation), a local education authority as defined in section 123 of the Local Government (Scotland) Act 1973, an education and library board established under Article 3 of the Education and Libraries (Northern Ireland) Order 1986, any body which is a research council for the purposes of the Science and Technology Act 1965 or any analogous government department, authority, board or body, of the Channel Islands, Isle of Man or any other country outside Great Britain;

"full-time course of study" means a full-time course of study which–

(a) is not funded in whole or in part by the Learning and Skills Council for England or by the [¹ National Assembly for Wales] or a full-time course of study which is not funded in whole or in part by the Scottish Ministers at a college of further education or a full-time course of study which is a course of higher education and is funded in whole or in part by the Scottish Ministers;

(b) is funded in whole or in part by the Learning and Skills Council for England or by the [¹ National Assembly for Wales] if it involves more than 16 guided learning hours per week for the student in question, according to the number of guided learning hours per week for that student set out–

(i) in the case of a course funded by the Learning and Skills Council for England, in his learning agreement signed on behalf of the establishment which is funded by that Council for the delivery of that course; or

(ii) in the case of a course funded by the [¹ National Assembly for Wales], in a document signed on behalf of the establishment which is funded by that Council for the delivery of that course; or

(c) is not higher education and is funded in whole or in part by the Scottish Ministers at a college of further education and involves–

(i) more than 16 hours per week of classroom-based or workshop-based programmed learning under the direct guidance of teaching staff according to the number of hours set out in a document signed on behalf of the college; or

(ii) 16 hours or less per week of classroom-based or workshop-based programmed learning under the direct guidance of teaching staff and it involves additional hours using structured learning packages supported by the teaching staff where the combined total of hours exceeds 21 hours per week, according to the number of hours set out in a document signed on behalf of the college;

"full-time student" means a person attending or undertaking a full-time course of study and includes a student on a sandwich course;

"grant" (except in the definition of "access funds") means any kind of educational grant or award and includes any scholarship, studentship, exhibition, allowance or bursary but does not include a payment from access funds or any payment to which paragraph 12 of Schedule 4 or paragraph 53 of Schedule 5 applies;

"grant income" means–

(a) any income by way of a grant;

    (b)   any contribution whether or not it is paid;

"higher education" means higher education within the meaning of Part 2 of the Further and Higher Education (Scotland) Act 1992;

"last day of the course" means–

    (a)   in the case of a qualifying course, the date on which the last day of that course falls or the date on which the final examination relating to that course is completed, whichever is the later;

    (b)   in any other case, the date on which the last day of the final academic term falls in respect of the course in which the student is enrolled;

"period of study" means–

    (a)   in the case of a course of study for one year or less, the period beginning with the start of the course and ending with the last day of the course;

    (b)   in the case of a course of study for more than one year, in the first or, as the case may be, any subsequent year of the course, other than the final year of the course, the period beginning with the start of the course or, as the case may be, that year's start and ending with either–

        (i)   in a case where the student's grant or loan is assessed at a rate appropriate to his studying throughout the year, or, if he does not have a grant or loan, where a loan would have been assessed at such a rate had he had one, the day before the start of the next year of the course; or

        (ii)   in any other case, the day before the start of the recognised summer vacation appropriate to his course;

    (c)   in the final year of a course of study of more than one year, the period beginning with that year's start and ending with the last day of the course;

"periods of experience" means periods of work experience which form part of a sandwich course;

"qualifying course" means a qualifying course as defined for the purposes of Parts 2 and 4 of the Jobseeker's Allowance Regulations;

"sandwich course" has the meaning prescribed in regulation 2(6) of the Education (Student Support) Regulations 2005, regulation 5(2) of the Education (Student Loans)(Scotland) Regulations 2000 or regulation 5(2) of the Education (Student Support) Regulations (Northern Ireland)2001, as the case may be;

"standard maintenance grant" means–

    (a)   except where paragraph (b) or (c) applies, in the case of a student attending or undertaking a course of study at the University of London or an establishment within the area comprising the City of London and the Metropolitan Police District, the amount specified for the time being in paragraph 2(2)(a) of Schedule 2 to the Education (Mandatory Awards) Regulations 2003 ("the 2003 Regulations") for such a student;

    (b)   except where paragraph (c) applies, in the case of a student residing at his parent's home, the amount specified in paragraph 3 thereof;

    (c)   in the case of a student receiving an allowance or bursary under the Education (Scotland) Act 1980, the amount of money specified as "standard maintenance allowance" for the relevant year appropriate for the student set out in the Student Support in Scotland Guide issued by the Student Awards Agency for Scotland, or its nearest equivalent in the case of a bursary provided by a college of further education or a local education authority and paid under the Further and Higher Education (Scotland) Act 1992;

    (d)   in any other case, the amount specified in paragraph 2(2) of Schedule 2 to the 2003 Regulations other than in sub-paragraph (a) or (b) thereof;

"student" means a person, other than a person in receipt of a training allowance, who is attending or undertaking–

(a)   a course of study at an educational establishment; or

(b)   a qualifying course;

''student loan'' means a loan towards a student's maintenance pursuant to any regulations made under section 22 of the Teaching and Higher Education Act 1998, section 73 of the Education (Scotland) Act 1980 or Article 3 of the Education (Student Support) (Northern Ireland) Order 1998 and shall include, in Scotland, a young student's bursary paid under regulation 4(1)(c) of the Students' Allowances (Scotland) Regulations 1999.

(2)   For the purposes of the definition of ''full-time student'' in paragraph (1), a person shall be regarded as attending or, as the case may be, undertaking a full-time course of study or as being on a sandwich course–

(a)   subject to paragraph (3), in the case of a person attending or undertaking a part of a modular course which would be a full-time course of study for the purposes of this Part, for the period beginning on the day on which that part of the course starts and ending–

(i)   on the last day on which he is registered with the educational establishment as attending or undertaking that part as a full-time course of study; or

(ii)   on such earlier date (if any) as he finally abandons the course or is dismissed from it;

(b)   in any other case, throughout the period beginning on the date on which he starts attending or undertaking the course and ending on the last day of the course or on such earlier date (if any) as he finally abandons it or is dismissed from it.

(3)   For the purposes of sub-paragraph (a) of paragraph (2), the period referred to in that sub-paragraph shall include–

(a)   where a person has failed examinations or has failed to successfully complete a module relating to a period when he was attending or undertaking a part of the course as a full-time course of study, any period in respect of which he attends or undertakes the course for the purpose of retaking those examinations or that module;

(b)   any period of vacation within the period specified in that paragraph or immediately following that period except where the person has registered with the educational establishment to attend or undertake the final module in the course and the vacation immediately follows the last day on which he is required to attend or undertake the course.

(4)   In paragraph (2), ''modular course'' means a course of study which consists of two or more modules, the successful completion of a specified number of which is required before a person is considered by the educational establishment to have completed the course.

Amendment

1.   Substituted by reg 3 of SI 2005 No 3238 as amended by Sch 2 para 31 of SI 2006 No 217 as from 1.4.06.

General Note

See the commentary to reg 53 HB Regs (on p332) for the definitions of "academic year", "access funds", "contribution", "course of study", "covenant income", "education authority", "full-time course of study", "full-time student", "grant", "grant income", "last day of the course", "period of study", "periods of experience", "qualifying course", "sandwich course" and "student". The definitions for HB purposes are the same as for CTB.

Treatment of students

44.   These Regulations shall have effect in relation to students subject to the following provisions of this Part.

Students who are excluded from entitlement to council tax benefit

45.–(1)   Except to the extent that a student may be entitled to an alternative maximum council tax benefit by virtue of section 131(3) and (6) of the Act, a student to whom paragraph (2) applies is a person of a prescribed class for the purposes of section 131(3)(b) of the Act (persons excluded from entitlement to council tax benefit).

(2)   Subject to paragraph (3) and (7), this paragraph applies to a full-time student and students who are persons from abroad within the meaning of regulation 7 (persons from abroad).

(3)   Paragraph (2) shall not apply to a student–

(a)   who is a person on income supportor an income-based jobseeker's allowance;

(b)   who is a lone parent;

(c)   whose applicable amount would, but for this regulation, include the disability premium or severe disability premium;

(d)   whose applicable amount would include the disability premium but for his being treated as capable of work by virtue of a determination made in accordance with regulations made under section 171E of the Act;

(e)   who is, or is treated as, incapable of work and has been so incapable, or has been so treated as incapable, of work in accordance with the provisions of, and regulations made under, Part 12A of the Act (incapacity for work) for a continuous period of not less than 196 days; and for this purpose any two or more separate periods separated by a break of not more than 56 days shall be treated as one continuous period;

(f)   who has a partner who is also a full-time student, if he or that partner is treated as responsible for a child or young person;

(g)   who is a single claimant with whom a child is placed by a local authority or voluntary organisation within the meaning of the Children Act 1989 or, in Scotland, boarded out within the meaning of the Social Work (Scotland) Act 1968;

[¹ (h)   who is–

  (i)   aged under 19 and whose course of study is not a course of higher education, or

  (ii)   a qualifying young person or child within the meaning of section 142 of the Act (child and qualifying young person);]

(i)   in respect of whom–

  (i)   a supplementary requirement has been determined under paragraph 9 of Part 2 of Schedule 2 to the Education (Mandatory Awards) Regulations 2003;

  (ii)   an allowance, or as the case may be, bursary has been granted which includes a sum under paragraph (1)(d) or regulation 4 of the Students' Allowances (Scotland) Regulations 1999 or, as the case may be, under paragraph (1)(d) of regulation 4 of the Education Authority (Bursaries) (Scotland) Regulations 1995, in respect of expenses incurred;

  (iii)   a payment has been made under section 2 of the Education Act 1962 or under or by virtue of regulations made under the Teaching and Higher Education Act 1998;

  (iv)   a grant has been made under regulation 13 of the Education (Student Support) Regulations 2005 or under regulation 13 of the Education (Student Support) Regulations (Northern Ireland) 2000; or

  (v)   a supplementary requirement has been determined under paragraph 9 of Schedule 6 to the Students Awards Regulations (Northern Ireland) 1999 or a payment has been made under Article 50(3) of the Education and Libraries (Northern Ireland) Order 1986,

on account of his disability by reason of deafness.

(4)　For the purposes of paragraph (3), once paragraph (3)(e) applies to a full-time student, if he then ceases, for a period of 56 days or less, to be incapable, or to be treated as incapable, of work, that paragraph shall, on his again becoming so incapable, or so treated as incapable, of work at the end of that period, immediately thereafter apply to him for so long as he remains incapable or is treated as remaining incapable, of work.

(5)　In paragraph (3)(h) the reference to a course of higher education is a reference to a course of any description mentioned in Schedule 6 to the Education Reform Act 1988.

(6)　A full-time student to whom sub-paragraph (i) of paragraph (3) applies, shall be treated as satisfying that sub-paragraph from the date on which he made a request for the supplementary requirement, allowance, bursary or payment as the case may be.

(7)　Paragraph (2) shall not apply to a full-time student for the period specified in paragraph (8) if–

(a)　at any time during an academic year, with the consent of the relevant educational establishment, he ceases to attend or undertake a course because he is–

(i)　engaged in caring for another person; or

(ii)　ill;

(b)　he has subsequently ceased to be engaged in caring for that person or, as the case may be, he has subsequently recovered from that illness; and

(c)　he is not eligible for a grant or a student loan in respect of the period specified in paragraph (8).

(8)　The period specified for the purposes of paragraph (7) is the period, not exceeding one year, beginning on the day on which he ceased to be engaged in caring for that person or, as the case may be, the day on which he recovered from that illness and ending on the day before–

(a)　the day on which he resumes attending or undertaking the course; or

(b)　the day from which the relevant educational establishment has agreed that he may resume attending or undertaking the course,

whichever shall first occur.

Amendment

1.　Substituted by reg 5(3) of SI 2006 No 718 as from 10.4.06.

General Note

This regulation is similar to reg 56 HB Regs (see p339) in that it operates to exclude those students specified in para (2) from entitlement to CTB, though this is done simply by exclusion from benefit rather than treating them as not liable to make payments on their homes. Full-time students are *not* precluded from entitlement to an alternative maximum CTB – known as "second adult rebate": reg 45(1). This should be assessed in the normal way. The general exclusion of full-time students from CTB does not prevent a claimant whose partner is a student from claiming CTB.

Excluded from entitlement to CTB are full-time students (defined in reg 43) and students who are "persons from abroad" within the meaning of reg 7. The latter has no equivalent in reg 56 HB Regs, which merely bars full-time students. Para (2) confirms that even a part-time student is excluded from benefit if s/he is a "person from abroad". The end result is the same, since reg 7 excludes a student who is a "person from abroad" in any case.

The categories of students entitled to CTB are specified in para (3). These are the same as those entitled to HB in reg 56(2), save that there is no equivalent of reg 56(2)(j) here, which is spent in any case. See the commentary to reg 56.

In some cases, it does not matter that a student cannot claim CTB. This is because some dwellings occupied by students are exempt from council tax (eg, dwellings where all of the residents are students and unoccupied dwellings owned by students): the Council Tax (Exempt Dwellings) Order 1993 as amended (for England and Wales); the Council Tax (Exempt Dwellings)(Scotland) Order 1997 (for Scotland). Where a dwelling is not exempt from council tax, students who share with non-students are not jointly and severally liable for council tax with the non-students: ss6(4) and 9(2) Local Government Finance Act 1992 as amended by s74 Local Government Act 2003 (for England and Wales); ss75 and 77 Local Government Finance Act 1992 as amended by s4 Education (Graduate Endowment and Student Support)(Scotland) Act 2001 (for Scotland). Note that the definition of student is different for these purposes than for CTB: Sch 1 para 4(2) Local Government Finance Act 1992.

SECTION 2
Income

Calculation of grant income

46.–(1)   The amount of a student's grant income to be taken into account shall, subject to paragraphs (2) and (3), be the whole of his grant income.

(2)   There shall be excluded from a student's grant income any payment–

(a)   intended to meet tuition fees or examination fees;

(b)   in respect of the student's disability;

(c)   intended to meet additional expenditure connected with term time residential study away from the student's educational establishment;

(d)   on account of the student maintaining a home at a place other than that at which he resides during his course;

(e)   on account of any other person but only if that person is residing outside of the United Kingdom and there is no applicable amount in respect of him;

(f)   intended to meet the cost of books and equipment;

(g)   intended to meet travel expenses incurred as a result of his attendance on the course;

(h)   intended for the child care costs of a child dependant.

(3)   Where a student does not have a student loan and is not treated as possessing such a loan, there shall be excluded from the student's grant income–

(a)   the sum of [² £290] in respect of travel costs; and

(b)   the sum of [² £370] towards the costs of books and equipment,

whether or not any such costs are incurred.

[¹ (4)   There shall also be excluded from a student's grant income the grant for dependants known as the parents' learning allowance paid pursuant to regulations made under Article 3 of the Education (Student Support) (Northern Ireland) Order 1998 or section 22 of the Teaching and Higher Education Act 1998.]

(5)   Subject to paragraphs (6) and (7), a student's grant income shall be apportioned–

(a)   subject to paragraph (8), in a case where it is attributable to the period of study, equally between the weeks in that period beginning with the benefit week, the first day of which coincides with, or immediately follows, the first day of the period of study and ending with the benefit week, the last day of which coincides with, or immediately precedes, the last day of the period of study;

(b)   in any other case, equally between the weeks in the period beginning with the benefit week, the first day of which coincides with, or immediately follows, the first day of the period for which it is payable and ending with the benefit week, the last day of which coincides with, or immediately precedes, the last day of the period for which it is payable.

(6)   Any grant in respect of dependants paid under section 63(6) of the Health Services and Public Health Act 1968 (grants in respect of the provision of instruction to officers of hospital authorities) and any amount intended for the maintenance of dependants under Part 3 of Schedule 2 to the Education (Mandatory Awards) Regulations 2003 shall be apportioned equally over the period of 52 weeks or, if there are 53 benefit weeks (including part-weeks) in the year, 53.

(7)   In a case where a student is in receipt of a student loan or where he could have acquired a student loan by taking reasonable steps but had not done so, any amount intended for the maintenance of dependants to which neither paragraph (6)

nor regulation 50(2) (other amounts to be disregarded) apply, shall be apportioned over the same period as the student's loan is apportioned or, as the case may be, would have been apportioned.

(8)   In the case of a student on a sandwich course, any periods of experience within the period of study shall be excluded and the student's grant income shall be apportioned equally between the weeks in the period beginning with the benefit week, the first day of which immediately follows the last day of the period of experience and ending with the benefit week, the last day of which coincides with, or immediately precedes, the last day of the period of study.

Amendments
1.   Substituted by reg 2(2) and (3) of SI 2006 No 1752 as from, for students whose period of study begins on or after 1.8.06 but before 1.9.06, on the day the period of study begins; in any other case 1.9.06.
2.   Substituted by reg 5(2) of SI 2007 No 1632 as from, in the case of a person whose period of study begins on or after 1.8.07 but before 1.9.07, on the day the period of study begins; in any other case, 1.9.07.

Calculation of covenant income where a contribution is assessed

47.–(1)   Where a student is in receipt of income by way of a grant during a period of study and a contribution has been assessed, the amount of his covenant income to be taken into account for that period and any summer vacation immediately following shall be the whole amount of the covenant income less, subject to paragraph (3), the amount of the contribution.

(2)   The weekly amount of the student's covenant shall be determined–
(a)   by dividing the amount of income which falls to be taken into account under paragraph (1) by 52 or 53, whichever is reasonable in the circumstances; and
(b)   by disregarding from the resulting amount, £5.

(3)   For the purposes of paragraph (1), the contribution shall be treated as increased by the amount (if any) by which the amount excluded under regulation 46(2)(g) (calculation of grant income) falls short of the amount specified in paragraph 7(2) of Schedule 2 to the Education (Mandatory Awards) Regulations 2003 (travel expenditure).

Covenant income where no grant income or no contribution is assessed

48.–(1)   Where a student is not in receipt of income by way of a grant the amount of his covenant income shall be calculated as follows–
(a)   any sums intended for any expenditure specified in regulation 46(2)(a) to (e) (calculation of grant income) necessary as a result of his attendance on the course shall be disregarded;
(b)   any covenant income, up to the amount of the standard maintenance grant, which is not so disregarded, shall be apportioned equally between the weeks of the period of study;
(c)   there shall be disregarded from the amount so apportioned the amount which would have been disregarded under regulation 46(2)(f) and (3) (calculation of grant income) had the student been in receipt of the standard maintenance grant; and
(d)   the balance, if any, shall be divided by 52 or 53 whichever is reasonable in the circumstances and treated as weekly income of which £5 shall be disregarded.

(2)   Where a student is in receipt of income by way of a grant and no contribution has been assessed, the amount of his covenanted income shall be calculated in accordance with sub-paragraphs (a) to (d) of paragraph (1), except that–

(a)   the value of the standard maintenance grant shall be abated by the amount of such grant income less an amount equal to the amount of any sums disregarded under regulation 46(2)(a) to (e); and

(b)   the amount to be disregarded under paragraph (1)(c) shall be abated by an amount equal to the amount of any sums disregarded under regulation 46(2)(f) and (g) and (3).

Relationship with amounts to be disregarded under Schedule 4

49.   No part of a student's covenant income or grant income shall be disregarded under paragraph 15 of Schedule 4 [¹].

Amendment

1.   Amended by reg 17(3) of SI 2006 No 2378 from the first day of the first benefit week to commence on or after 2.10.06.

Other amounts to be disregarded

50.–(1)   For the purposes of ascertaining income other than grant income, covenant income and loans treated as income in accordance with regulation 51, any amounts intended for any expenditure specified in regulation 46(2) (calculation of grant income), necessary as a result of his attendance on the course shall be disregarded but only if, and to the extent that, the necessary expenditure exceeds or is likely to exceed the amount of the sums disregarded under regulation 46(2) or (3), 47(3), 48(1)(a) or (c) or 51(5) (calculation of grant income, covenant income and treatment of student loans) on like expenditure.

(2)   Where a grant for school meals for dependant children or a grant for meals for dependent children aged 3 or 4 is paid pursuant to any regulations made under section 22 of the Teaching and Higher Education Act 1998 or under the Students' Allowance (Scotland) Regulations 1999 that payment shall be disregarded as income.

Treatment of student loans

51.–(1)   A student loan shall be treated as income.

(2)   In calculating the weekly amount of the loan to be taken into account as income–

(a)   in respect of a course that is of a single academic year's duration or less, a loan which is payable in respect of that period shall be apportioned equally between the weeks in the period beginning with–

(i)   except in a case where head (ii) applies, the benefit week, the first day of which coincides with, or immediately follows, the first day of the single academic year;

(ii)   where the student is required to start attending the course in August or where the course is less than an academic year's duration, the benefit week, the first day of which coincides with, or immediately follows, the first day of the course,

and ending with the benefit week, the last day of which coincides with, or immediately precedes, the last day of the course;

(b)   in respect of an academic year of a course which starts other than on 1st September, a loan which is payable in respect of that academic year shall be apportioned equally between the weeks in the period beginning with the benefit week, the first day of which coincides with or immediately follows, the first day of that academic year and ending with the benefit week, the last day of which coincides with or immediately precedes, the last day of that academic year but excluding any benefit weeks falling entirely within the quarter during which, in the opinion of the Secretary of State, the longest of any vacation is taken and for the purposes of this sub-paragraph, ''quarter'' shall have the same meaning as for the purposes of the Education (Student Support) Regulations 2005;

(c)   in respect of the final academic year of a course (not being a course of a single year's duration), a loan which is payable in respect of that final academic year shall be apportioned equally between the weeks in the period beginning with–

    (i)   except in a case where head (ii) applies, the benefit week, the first day of which coincides with, or immediately follows, the first day of that academic year;

    (ii)   where the final academic year starts on 1st September, the benefit week, the first day of which coincides with, or immediately follows, the earlier of 1st September or the first day of the autumn term,

and ending with the benefit week, the last day of which coincides with, or immediately precedes, the last day of the course;

(d)   in any other case, the loan shall be apportioned equally between the weeks in the period beginning with the earlier of–

    (i)   the first day of the first benefit week in September; or

    (ii)   the benefit week, the first day of which coincides with, or immediately follows the first day of the autumn term,

and ending with the benefit week, the last day of which coincides with, or immediately precedes, the last day of June,

and, in all cases, from the weekly amount so apportioned there shall be disregarded £10.

(3)   A student shall be treated as possessing a student loan in respect of an academic year where–

(a)   a student loan has been made to him in respect of that year; or

(b)   he could acquire such a loan in respect of that year by taking reasonable steps to do so.

(4)   Where a student is treated as possessing a student loan under paragraph (3), the amount of the student loan to be taken into account as income shall be, subject to paragraph (5)–

(a)   in the case of a student to whom a student loan is made in respect of an academic year, a sum equal to–

    (i)   the maximum student loan he is able to acquire in respect of that year by taking reasonable steps to do so; and

    (ii)   any contribution whether or not it has been paid to him;

(b)   in the case of a student to whom a student loan is not made in respect of an academic year, the maximum student loan that would be made to the student if–

    (i)   he took all reasonable steps to obtain the maximum student loan he is able to acquire in respect of that year; and

    (ii)   no deduction in that loan was made by virtue of the application of a means test.

(5)   There shall be deducted from the amount of income taken into account under paragraph (4)–

(a)   the sum of [² £290] in respect of travel costs; and

(b)   the sum of [² £370] towards the cost of books and equipment,

whether or not any such costs are incurred.

Amendment

1.   Substituted by reg 2(2) of SI 2006 No 1752 as from, for students whose period of study begins on or after 1.8.06 but before 1.9.06, on the day the period of study begins; in any other case 1.9.06.

2.   Substituted by reg 5(3) of SI 2007 No 1632 as from, in the case of a person whose period of study begins on or after 1.8.07 but before 1.9.07, on the day the period of study begins; in any other case, 1.9.07.

[¹ Treatment of fee loans

51A.   A loan for fees, known as a fee loan or a fee contribution loan, made pursuant to regulations made under Article 3 of the Education (Student Support) (Northern Ireland) Order 1998, section 22 of the Teaching and Higher Education Act 1998 or section 73(f) of the Education (Scotland) Act 1980, shall be disregarded as income.]

Amendment
1.   Inserted by reg 2(4) of SI 2006 No 1752 as from, for students whose period of study begins on or after 1.8.06 but before 1.9.06, on the day the period of study begins; in any other case 1.9.06.

Treatment of payments from access funds

52.–(1)   This regulation applies to payments from access funds that are not payments to which regulation 55 (2) or (3) (income treated as capital) applies.

(2)   A payment from access funds, other than a payment to which paragraph (3) applies, shall be disregarded as income.

(3)   Subject to paragraph (4) of this regulation and paragraph 35 of Schedule 4, any payments from access funds which are intended and used for an item of food, ordinary clothing or footwear, household fuel, or rent of a single claimant or, as the case may be, of the claimant or any other member of his family and any payments from access funds which are used for any council tax or water charges for which that claimant or member is liable, shall be disregarded as income to the extent of £20 per week.

(4)   Where a payment from access funds is made–

(a)   on or after 1st September or the first day of the course, whichever first occurs, but before receipt of any student loan in respect of that year and that payment is intended for the purpose of bridging the period until receipt of the student loan; or

(b)   before the first day of the course to a person in anticipation of that person becoming a student,

that payment shall be disregarded as income.

Disregard of contribution

53.   Where the claimant or his partner is a student and, for the purposes of assessing a contribution to the student's grant or student loan, the other partner's income has been taken into account, an amount equal to that contribution shall be disregarded for the purposes of assessing that other partner's income.

Further disregard of student's income

54.   Where any part of a student's income has already been taken into account for the purposes of assessing his entitlement to a grant or student loan, the amount taken into account shall be disregarded in assessing that student's income.

Income treated as capital

55.–(1)   Any amount by way of a refund of tax deducted from a student's covenant income shall be treated as capital.

(2)   An amount paid from access funds as a single lump sum shall be treated as capital.

(3)   An amount paid from access funds as a single lump sum which is intended and used for an item other than food, ordinary clothing or footwear, household fuel or rent, or which is used for an item other than any council tax or water charges for which that claimant or member is liable, shall be disregarded as capital but only for a period of 52 weeks from the date of the payment.

General Note

The CTB rule is the same as that for HB save that "ordinary clothing or footwear" and "rent" are defined in reg 2(1). See the commentary to reg 68 HB Regs on p355.

Disregard of changes occurring during summer vacation

56. In calculating a student's income the relevant authority shall disregard any change in the standard maintenance grant, occurring in the recognised summer vacation appropriate to the student's course, if that vacation does not form part of his period of study from the date on which the change occurred to the end of that vacation.

PART 6
Amount of benefit

Maximum council tax benefit

57.–(1) Subject to paragraphs (2) to (5), the amount of a person's maximum council tax benefit in respect of a day for which he is liable to pay council tax, shall be 100 per cent. of the amount A/B where–

(a) A is the amount set by the appropriate authority as the council tax for the relevant financial year in respect of the dwelling in which he is a resident and for which he is liable, subject to any discount which may be appropriate to that dwelling under the 1992 Act; and

(b) B is the number of days in that financial year,

less any deductions in respect of non-dependants which fall to be made under regulation 58 (non-dependant deductions).

(2) In calculating a person's maximum council tax benefit any reduction in the amount that person is liable to pay in respect of council tax, which is made in consequence of any enactment in, or made under, the 1992 Act, shall be taken into account.

(3) Subject to paragraph (4), where a claimant is jointly and severally liable for council tax in respect of a dwelling in which he is resident with one or more other persons but excepting any person so residing with the claimant who is a student to whom regulation 45(2) (students who are excluded from entitlement to council tax benefit) applies, in determining the maximum council tax benefit in his case in accordance with paragraph (1), the amount A shall be divided by the number of persons who are jointly and severally liable for that tax.

(4) Where a claimant is jointly and severally liable for council tax in respect of a dwelling with only his partner, paragraph (3) shall not apply in his case.

(5) In any case where an extended payment or an extended payment (severe disablement allowance and incapacity benefit) has been allowed to a claimant, his entitlement shall be adjusted in such circumstances and by such amount as are prescribed in Part 3 of Schedule 6 or paragraph 6 of Schedule 7, as the case may be.

Analysis

Reg 57 provides the basis for establishing a claimant's maximum CTB. The starting point is the net liability for council tax after deductions and discounts have been applied, less non-dependant deductions applicable under reg 58: paras (1) and (2).

Where the claimant is jointly and severally liable for council tax with one or more other persons (excluding any liable person residing with the claimant who is a student not entitled to CTB), such person not being her/his partner, her/his benefit will be calculated only in respect of the appropriate proportion of the maximum: paras (3) and (4). This gives rise, potentially, to hardship in that, under the 1992 Act, a person who is jointly and severally liable can be pursued for the full amount of the tax due on the property while receiving benefit only on her/his "share".

Note that prior to 1 April 2004, the level of CTB allowable was restricted to those who were liable to pay council tax in respect of dwellings in valuation bands F, G and H. See reg 51 CTB Regs 1992 in the 16th edition of this book for the text of the former version of this reg and commentary on it.

Non-dependant deductions

58.–(1) Subject to the following provisions of this regulation, the non-dependant deductions in respect of a day referred to in regulation 57 (maximum council tax benefit) shall be–

    (a) in respect of a non-dependant aged 18 or over in remunerative work, [⁴ £6.95] × 1/7;

    (b) in respect of a non-dependant aged 18 or over to whom sub-paragraph (a) does not apply, [⁴ £2.30] × 1/7.

    (2) In the case of a non-dependant aged 18 or over to whom paragraph (1)(a) applies, where it is shown to the appropriate authority that his normal gross weekly income is–

    (a) less than [⁵ £164.00], the deduction to be made under this regulation shall be that specified in paragraph (1)(b);

    (b) not less than [⁵ £164.00] but less than [⁵ £283.00], the deduction to be made under this regulation shall be [⁴ £4.60];

    (c) not less than [⁵ £283.00] but less than [⁵ £353.00], the deduction to be made under this regulation shall be [⁴ £5.80].

    (3) Only one deduction shall be made under this regulation in respect of a couple or, as the case may be, members of a polygamous marriage and, where, but for this paragraph, the amount that would fall to be deducted in respect of one member of a couple or polygamous marriage is higher than the amount (if any) that would fall to be deducted in respect of the other, or any other, member, the higher amount shall be deducted.

    (4) In applying the provisions of paragraph (2) in the case of a couple or, as the case may be, a polygamous marriage, regard shall be had, for the purpose of that paragraph, to the couple's or, as the case may be, all members of the polygamous marriage's joint weekly gross income.

    (5) Where in respect of a day–

    (a) a person is a resident in a dwelling but is not himself liable for council tax in respect of that dwelling and that day;

    (b) other residents in that dwelling (the liable persons) have joint and several liability for council tax in respect of that dwelling and that day otherwise than by virtue of section 9 or 77 or 77A of the 1992 Act (liability of spouses and civil partners); and

    (c) the person to whom sub-paragraph (a) refers is a non-dependant of two or more of the liable persons,

the deduction in respect of that non-dependant shall be apportioned equally between those liable persons.

    (6) No deduction shall be made in respect of any non-dependants occupying a claimant's dwelling if the claimant or his partner is–

    (a) blind or treated as blind by virtue of paragraph 13 of Schedule 1 (additional condition of the higher pensioner and disability premiums); or

    (b) receiving in respect of himself either–

        (i) attendance allowance; or

        (ii) the care component of the disability living allowance.

    (7) No deduction shall be made in respect of a non-dependant if–

    (a) although he resides with the claimant, it appears to the relevant authority that his normal home is elsewhere; or

    (b) he is in receipt of a training allowance paid in connection with a Youth Training Scheme established under section 2 of the 1973 Act or section 2 of the Enterprise and New Towns (Scotland) Act 1990; or

    (c) he is a full-time student within the meaning of Part 5 (Students); or

    (d) he is not residing with the claimant because he has been a patient for a period in excess of 52 weeks, and for these purposes–

[¹ (i)   "patient" has the meaning given in paragraph (7) of regulation 8, and

(ii)   where a person has been a patient for two or more distinct periods separated by one or more intervals each not exceeding 28 days, he shall be treated as having been a patient continuously for a period equal in duration to the total of those distinct periods.]

(8)   No deduction shall be made in respect of a non-dependant–

(a)   who is on income support, state pension credit or an income-based jobseeker's allowance; or

(b)   to whom Schedule 1 of the 1992 Act applies (persons disregarded for purposes of discount) but this sub-paragraph shall not apply to a non-dependant who is a student to whom paragraph 4 of that Schedule refers.

(9)   In the application of paragraph (2) there shall be disregarded from his weekly gross income–

(a)   any attendance allowance or disability living allowance received by him;

(b)   any payment made under the Trusts, the Fund, the Eileen Trust or the Independent Living Funds which had his income fallen to be calculated under regulation 30 (calculation of income other than earnings) would have been disregarded under paragraph 24 of Schedule 4 (income in kind); and

(c)   any payment which had his income fallen to be calculated under regulation 30 would have been disregarded under paragraph 36 of Schedule 4 (payments made under certain trusts and certain other payments).

Amendments

1.   Substituted by reg 3(7) of SI 2005 No 2502 as amended by Sch 2 para 27 of SI 2006 No 217 as from 1.4.06.

2.   Confirmed by Art 21(3) of SI 2006 No 645 and reg 8 of SI 2006 No 217 as from 1.4.06.

3.   Amended by Art 21(3) of SI 2006 No 645 and reg 8 of SI 2006 No 217 as from 1.4.06.

4.   Confirmed by Art 21(3) of SI 2007 No 688 as from 1.4.07.

5.   Amended by Art 21(3) of SI 2007 No 688 as from 1.4.07.

Council tax benefit taper

59.   The prescribed percentage for the purpose of sub-section (5)(c)(ii) of section 131 of the Act as it applies to council tax benefit, (percentage of excess of income over the applicable amount which is deducted from maximum council tax benefit), shall be 2 6/7 per cent.

General Note

Maximum CTB is calculated under reg 57 on a daily basis. The weekly equivalent of the taper is 2 and 6/7 times 7, which is 20 per cent.

Extended payments

60.–(1)   Subject to paragraphs (7), paragraph (2) shall apply where–

(a)   a person ceases to be entitled to council tax benefit–

(i)   in accordance with regulation 65 (date on which council tax benefit is to end); and

(ii)   the conditions in paragraphs 1 and 2 of Schedule 6 are satisfied in his case; or

(b)   a person ceases to be entitled to council tax benefit because he has vacated the dwelling of which he was a resident and the day on which he did so was either in the week in which he took up employment as an employed or self-employed earner, or in the preceding week, and–

(i)   he ceased to be entitled to income support or an income-based jobseeker's allowance by reason of taking up employment as an employed or self-employed earner; and

    (ii)   the conditions in paragraphs 1 and 2 of Schedule 6 are satisfied in his case.

(2)   A person to whom paragraph (1) applies shall be treated as having made a claim under this regulation and his council tax benefit shall be determined in accordance with Part 2 of Schedule 6 and any award so determined shall be referred to in these Regulations as an ''extended payment''.

(3)   For the purposes of any payment pursuant to this regulation–

(a)   except in a case to which paragraph 4 of Schedule 6 applies, the maximum council tax benefit of any person mentioned in paragraph (1) shall be determined in accordance with paragraph 3 of Schedule 6;

(b)   the maximum council tax benefit of any person to whom paragraph 4 of Schedule 6 applies shall be determined in accordance with paragraph 5(a) of Schedule 6; and

(c)   any person who meets the requirements of paragraph (1) shall be treated as possessing no income and no capital.

(4)   Regulations 68, 69 and 72 (claims, evidence and information) shall not apply to a claim pursuant to this regulation and, subject to regulation 57(5) (maximum council tax benefit), Part 7 (changes of circumstances and increases for exceptional circumstances) shall not apply to any payment under it.

(5)   In paragraph (1)(a) and (b), references to a ''person'' include references to a person's partner.

(6)   In a case where a payment has been made under this regulation–

(a)   the beneficiary shall be treated for the purposes of these Regulations as though he were entitled to and in receipt of council tax benefit–

    (i)   during the 4 weeks immediately following the last day of his entitlement to council tax benefit; or

    (ii)   until the date on which his liability for council tax ends, whichever occurs first; and

(b)   any claim for council tax benefit made by the beneficiary within the period which under sub-paragraph (a) applies in his case or the 4 weeks thereafter shall be treated as having been made in respect of a period beginning immediately after the end of his previous award of council tax benefit.

(7)   This regulation shall not apply to a claimant where, on the day before his entitlement to income support ceased, regulation 6(5) of the Income Support Regulations (remunerative work: housing costs) applied to him.

Extended payments (severe disablement allowance and incapacity benefit)

61.–(1)   Paragraph (2) shall apply where–

(a)   a person ceases to be entitled to council tax benefit–

    (i)   in accordance with regulation 66 (date on which entitlement to council tax benefit is to end where entitlement to severe disablement allowance or incapacity benefit ceases); and

    (ii)   the condition referred to in paragraph 1 of Schedule 7 is satisfied in his case; or

(b)   a person ceases to be entitled to council tax benefit because he has vacated the dwelling of which he was a resident and the day on which he did so was either in the week in which he took up employment as an employed or self-employed earner, or in the preceding week, and–

    (i)   he ceased to be entitled to severe disablement allowance or incapacity benefit by reason of taking up employment as an employed or self-employed earner;

    (ii)   he had been entitled to and in receipt of severe disablement allowance, incapacity benefit or a combination of severe disablement allowance and incapacity benefit for a continuous period of at least 26 weeks;

    (iii)   he was not entitled to and in receipt of income support; and

(iv)   the condition referred to in paragraph 1 of Schedule 7 is satisfied in his case.

(2)   A person to whom paragraph (1) applies shall be treated as having made a claim under this regulation and his council tax benefit shall be determined in accordance with Schedule 7 and any award so determined shall be referred to in these Regulations as an "extended payment (severe disablement allowance and incapacity benefit)".

(3)   For the purposes of any payment pursuant to this regulation–

(a)   except in a case to which paragraph 4(a) of Schedule 7 applies, the maximum council tax benefit of any person mentioned in paragraph (1) shall be determined in accordance with paragraph 3 of Schedule 7;

(b)   the maximum council tax benefit of any person to whom paragraph 4(a) of Schedule 7 applies shall be determined in accordance with paragraph 5 of that Schedule;

(c)   except in a case to which paragraph (d) applies, any person who meets the requirements of paragraph (1) shall be treated as possessing the amount of income and the amount of capital that they possessed in the last week of the award of council tax benefit which has ceased as mentioned in paragraph (1); and

(d)   any person whose maximum council tax benefit is determined in accordance with paragraph 5 of Schedule 7 shall be treated as possessing no income or capital.

(4)   Regulations 68, 69 and 72 (claims, evidence and information) shall not apply to a claim pursuant to this regulation and, subject to regulation 57(5) (maximum council tax benefit), Part 7 (changes of circumstances and increases for exceptional circumstances) shall not apply to any payment under it.

(5)   In paragraph (1), references to a "person" include references to a person's partner and references to taking up employment include receiving remuneration for employment or an increased amount of remuneration for employment or engaging in employment for an increased number of hours.

(6)   In a case where payment has been made under this regulation–

(a)   the beneficiary shall be treated for the purpose of these Regulations as though he were entitled to and in receipt of council tax benefit–

(i)   during the 4 weeks immediately following the last day of his entitlement to council tax benefit; or

(ii)   until the date on which his liability for council tax ends,

whichever occurs first; and

(b)   any claim for council tax benefit made by the beneficiary within the period which under sub-paragraph (a) applies in his case or the 4 weeks thereafter shall be treated as having been made in respect of a period beginning immediately after the end of his previous award of council tax benefit.

Alternative maximum council tax benefit

62.–(1)   Subject to paragraphs (2) and (3), the alternative maximum council tax benefit where the conditions set out in section 131(3) and (6) of the Act are fulfilled, shall be the amount determined in accordance with Schedule 2.

(2)   Subject to paragraph (3), where a claimant is jointly and severally liable for council tax in respect of a dwelling in which he is resident with one or more other persons, in determining the alternative maximum council tax benefit in his case, the amount determined in accordance with Schedule 2 shall be divided by the number of persons who are jointly and severally liable for that tax.

(3)   Where a claimant is jointly and severally liable for council tax in respect of a dwelling with only his partner, solely by virtue of section 9, 77 or 77A of the 1992 Act (liability of spouses and civil partners), paragraph (2) shall not apply in his case.

General Note

If the claimant does not qualify for CTB under s131(4) and (5) SSCBA (eg, because s/he has too much income or capital) in restricted circumstances s/he can claim benefit based on the income of second adult(s) residing with her/him under s131(3) and (6) SSCBA. Alternative maximum CTB is sometimes referred to as "second adult rebate". If the claimant would be entitled to CTB under s131(4) and (5) *and* using the "alternative maximum", s/he will get whichever is the higher amount (s131(9) SSCBA).

Where a claimant satisfies the s131(3) and (6) conditions, the whole of her/his capital is disregarded under Sch 5 para 46. This means that even where a claimant has capital in excess of the limit provided by s134 SSCBA and reg 33, s/he is treated as having capital below that limit. The claimant's income makes no difference to entitlement to the alternative maximum CTB as the amount of this is calculated under Sch 2 CTB Regs by reference only to the income of the second adult(s).

Reference should also be made to s131(3) and (6) SSCBA and reg 63 and Sch 2 below.

Analysis

Para (1)

A claimant can qualify for alternative maximum CTB where a second adult is resident in the dwelling and none of the other residents are liable to pay the claimant rent: s131(6)(a) SSCBA. The other resident(s) whose income the claimant wishes to use as a basis for her/his benefit assessment must not be persons covered by Sch 1 to the 1992 Act (residents disregarded for the purposes of discounts) or under reg 63. Reg 63 further restricts the categories of persons whose income can be used for these purposes (see Analysis to that regulation on p621).

Perhaps the most common example of when there is potential entitlement to alternative maximum CTB is where the claimant is a single person and has a non-dependant young person or an elderly relative on a low income, living rent-free with her/him. If there is more than one other person residing with the claimant to whom s131(6) applies, their income may be aggregated (see Sch 2). The combined effect of s131 and this regulation is that non-dependant deductions do not apply where the "alternative maximum" applies.

Paras (2) and (3)

Where there is a joint liability for council tax, every liable person must make her/his own claim for a share of the alternative maximum CTB: para (2). This potentially raises the same difficulty as reg 57(3) (see Analysis on p615). However, where the joint liability is only with a partner, the claimant will receive the full alternative maximum CTB: para (3). On ss9, 77 or 77A, see Anaylsis on p621.

Residents of a dwelling to whom section 131(6) of the Act does not apply

63. Subsection (6) of section 131 of the Act (residents of a dwelling in respect of whom entitlement to an alternative maximum council tax benefit may arise) shall not apply in respect of any person referred to in the following paragraphs namely–

(a) a person who is liable for council tax solely in consequence of the provisions of sections 9, 77 or 77A of the 1992 Act (spouse's or civil partner's joint and several liability for tax);

(b) a person who is residing with a couple or with the members of a polygamous marriage where the claimant for council tax benefit is a member of that couple or of that marriage and–

(i) in the case of a couple, neither member of that couple is a person who, in accordance with Schedule 1 to the 1992 Act, falls to be disregarded for the purposes of discount; or

(ii) in the case of a polygamous marriage, two or more members of that marriage are not persons who, in accordance with Schedule 1 to the 1992 Act, fall to be disregarded for the purposes of discount;

(c) a person who jointly with the claimant for benefit falls within the same paragraph of sections 6(2)(a) to (e) or 75(2)(a) to (e) of the 1992 Act (persons liable to pay council tax) as applies in the case of the claimant;

(d) a person who is residing with two or more persons both or all of whom fall within the same paragraph of sections 6(2)(a) to (e) or 75(2)(a) to (e) of the 1992 Act and two or more of those persons are not persons who, in accordance with Schedule 1 to the 1992 Act, fall to be disregarded for the purposes of discount.

Analysis

Reg 63 should be read together with reg 62 and the Analysis on p620. s131(7) restricts the categories of people who count as "second adults" and hence whose income can be used as a basis for the alternative maximum CTB. Reg 63 provides further restrictions.

Para (a)

A spouse or civil partner who is jointly and severally liable for council tax under s9 (England and Wales) or s77 or 77A (Scotland) of the Local Government Finance Act 1992 cannot count as a "second adult". Sections 9, 77 and 77A do not apply to persons referred to in para 2 of Sch 1 to the 1992 Act.

Para (b)

This excludes any person residing with a couple or partners in a polygamous marriage, where the claimant is a member of the couple or the marriage, save in the fairly unusual circumstances where the couple are both, or two or more members of the polygamous marriage, are disregarded under Sch 1 Local Government Finance Act 1992 (discounts). The effect of this is that the claimant cannot qualify for the alternative maximum CTB.

Para (c)

Para (c) excludes people who are joint owners or joint tenants, or otherwise share the same status as the claimant under s6(2) (England and Wales) or s75(2) (Scotland) of the Act. Note that although such a person would not count as a second adult, s/he might her/him qualify for ordinary CTB for her share of the council tax bill under s131(4) and (5).

Para (d)

Para (d) excludes any person residing with two or more people who are not married or cohabiting but who share the same status under ss6 or 75 (that is, they are jointly liable for the council tax) and at least two of those liable are not disregarded under Sch 1 to the Local Government Finance Act 1992 (discounts). The effect of this is that the claimant cannot qualify for the alternative maximum CTB.

PART 7
Changes of circumstances and increases for exceptional circumstances

Date on which entitlement is to begin

64.–(1) Subject to paragraph (2), any person to whom or in respect of whom a claim for council tax benefit is made and who is otherwise entitled to that benefit shall be so entitled from the benefit week following the date on which that claim is made or is treated as made.

(2) Where a person is otherwise entitled to council tax benefit and becomes liable for the first time for a relevant authority's council tax in respect of a dwelling of which he is a resident in the benefit week in which his claim is made or is treated as made, he shall be so entitled from that benefit week.

Date on which council tax benefit is to end

65. A claimant's entitlement to council tax benefit shall cease at the end of the benefit week in which entitlement to income support or income-based jobseeker's allowance ceases where–

(a) the claimant or his partner was entitled to and in receipt of income support or an income-based jobseeker's allowance or that claimant and his partner were entitled to and in receipt of a joint-claim jobseeker's allowance and that entitlement has ceased;

(b) that entitlement to income support or income-based jobseeker's allowance has ceased by reason of the claimant or his partner–

(i) commencing employment as an employed or self-employed earner; or

(ii) increasing their earnings from such employment; or

(iii) increasing the number of hours worked in such employment;

(c) the claimant had been entitled to and in receipt of income support or jobseeker's allowance for a continuous period of at least 26 weeks before the day on which his entitlement to income support or income-based jobseeker's allowance ceased and for the purposes of this sub-paragraph–

(i)   a claimant satisfies the conditions of this sub-paragraph if he has been entitled to and in receipt of a combination of income support and a jobseeker's allowance for at least 26 weeks;

(ii)   the claimant shall be treated as having been entitled to and in receipt of income support or a jobseeker's allowance during any period of less than 5 weeks in respect of which he was not entitled to either of those because, as a consequence of his participation in an employment zone programme, he was engaged in remunerative work;

(iii)   references to the claimant include references to his partner;

(iv)   a reference to the claimant being entitled to and in receipt of a jobseeker's allowance shall include a reference to the claimant and his partner being entitled to and in receipt of a joint-claim jobseeker's allowance; and

(d)   that work, increase in earnings or, as the case may be, increase in hours is expected to last at least 5 weeks or more.

Date on which council tax benefit is to end where entitlement to severe disablement allowance or incapacity benefit ceases

66.   A claimant's entitlement to council tax benefit shall cease at the end of the benefit week in which entitlement to severe disablement allowance or incapacity benefit ceases where–

(a)   the claimant or his partner was not entitled to and in receipt of income support but was entitled to and in receipt of severe disablement allowance or incapacity benefit and that entitlement has ceased;

(b)   that entitlement to severe disablement allowance or incapacity benefit has ceased by reason of the claimant or his partner–

(i)   commencing employment as an employed or self-employed earner; or

(ii)   increasing their earnings from such employment; or

(iii)   increasing the number of hours worked in such employment;

(c)   the claimant had been entitled to and in receipt of severe disablement allowance or incapacity benefit for a continuous period of at least 26 weeks before the day on which his entitlement to severe disablement allowance or incapacity benefit ceased, and for the purposes of this sub-paragraph–

(i)   a claimant satisfies the conditions of this sub-paragraph if he has been entitled to and in receipt of a combination of severe disablement allowance and incapacity benefit for at least 26 weeks;

(ii)   references to the claimant include references to his partner; and

(d)   that work, increase in earnings, or as the case may be, increase in hours is expected to last at least 5 weeks or more.

Date on which change of circumstances is to take effect

67.–(1)   Except in cases where regulation 24 (disregard of changes in tax, contributions, etc) [¹ applies, and subject to regulation 8(3) of the Decisions and Appeals Regulations, and] the following provisions of this regulation, a change of circumstances which affects entitlement to, or the amount of, council tax benefit (''change of circumstances''), shall take effect from the first day of the benefit week following the date on which the change actually occurs, and where that change is cessation of entitlement to any benefit under the benefit Acts, the date on which the change actually occurs shall be the day immediately following the last day of entitlement to that benefit.

(2)   Subject to paragraph (3), where the change of circumstances is a change in the amount of council tax payable, it shall take effect from the day on which it actually occurs.

(3)   Where the change of circumstances is a change in the amount a person is liable to pay in respect of council tax in consequence of regulations under section 13 or 80 of the 1992 Act (reduced amounts of council tax) or changes in the discount to which a dwelling may be subject under sections 11, 12 or 79 of that Act, it shall take effect from the day on which the change in amount has effect.

(4)   Where the change of circumstances is an amendment to these Regulations, it shall take effect from the date on which the amendment to these Regulations comes into force.

(5)   Where the change of circumstances is the claimant's acquisition of a partner, the change shall have effect on the day on which the acquisition takes place.

(6)   Where the change of circumstances is the death of a claimant's partner or their separation, it shall have effect on the day the death or separation occurs.

(7)   If two or more changes of circumstances occurring in the same benefit week would, but for this paragraph, take effect in different benefit weeks in accordance with paragraphs (1) to (6) they shall take effect from the day to which the appropriate paragraph from (2) to (6) above refers, or, where more than one day is concerned, from the earlier day.

(8)   Where the change of circumstances is that income, or an increase in the amount of income, other than a benefit or an increase in the amount of a benefit under the Act, is paid in respect of a past period and there was no entitlement to income of that amount during that period, the change of circumstances shall take effect from the first day on which such income, had it been paid in that period at intervals appropriate to that income, would have fallen to be taken into account for the purposes of these Regulations.

(9)   Without prejudice to paragraph (8), where the change of circumstances is the payment of income, or arrears of income, in respect of a past period, the change of circumstances shall take effect from the first day on which such income, had it been timeously paid in that period at intervals appropriate to that income, would have fallen to be taken into account for the purposes of these Regulations.

Modifications

Reg 67 applies as if para (9) was omitted where a change of circumstances occurs as a result of the payment of arrears of any income which affects a determination or decision in respect of entitlement to, or the amount of, HB or CTB before 6 March 1995. See Sch 3 para 1 HB&CTB(CP) Regs on p1099.

Amendment

1.   Substituted by reg 6 of SI 2007 No 2470 as from 24.9.07.

PART 8
Claims

Who may claim

68.–(1)   In the case of a couple or members of a polygamous marriage a claim shall be made by whichever one of them they agree should so claim or, in default of agreement, by such one of them as the relevant authority shall determine.

(2)   Where a person who is liable to pay council tax in respect of a dwelling is unable for the time being to act, and–

(a)   a [¹ deputy] has been appointed by the Court of Protection with power to claim, or as the case may be, receive benefit on his behalf; or

(b)   in Scotland, his estate is being administered by a judicial factor or any guardian acting or appointed under the Adults with Incapacity (Scotland) Act 2000 who has power to claim or, as the case may be, receive benefit on his behalf; or

(c)   an attorney with a general power or a power to claim or as the case may be, receive benefit, has been appointed by that person under [¹ the Powers of

Attorney Act 1971, the Enduring Powers of Attorney Act 1985 or the Mental Capacity Act 2005] or otherwise,
that [¹ deputy], judicial factor, guardian or attorney, as the case may be, may make a claim on behalf of that person.

(3)   Where a person who is liable to pay council tax in respect of a dwelling is unable for the time being to act and paragraph (2) does not apply to him, the relevant authority may, upon written application made to them by a person who, if a natural person, is over the age of 18, appoint that person to exercise on behalf of the person who is unable to act, any right to which that person might be entitled under the Act and to receive and deal on his behalf with any sums payable to him.

(4)   Where the relevant authority has made an appointment under paragraph (3) or treated a person as an appointee under paragraph (5)–
(a)   it may at any time revoke the appointment;
(b)   the person appointed may resign his office after having given 4 weeks notice in writing to the relevant authority of his intention to do so;
(c)   any such appointment shall terminate when the relevant authority is notified of the appointment of a person mentioned in paragraph (2).

(5)   Where a person who is liable to pay council tax in respect of a dwelling is for the time being unable to act and the Secretary of State has appointed a person to act on his behalf under regulation 33 of the Social Security (Claims and Payments) Regulations 1987 (persons unable to act), the relevant authority may if that person agrees, treat him as if he had been appointed by them under paragraph (3).

(6)   Anything required by these Regulations to be done by or to any person who is for the time being unable to act may be done by or to the persons mentioned in paragraph (2) above or by or to the person appointed or treated as appointed under this regulation and the receipt of any such person so appointed shall be a good discharge to the relevant authority for any sum paid.

(7)   In its application to regulation 71, references in this regulation to an "relevant authority" shall be read as including a reference to the "designated authority".

Amendment
1.   Amended by reg 13(8) of SI 2007 No 2618 as from 1.10.07.

Time and manner in which claims are to be made

69.–(1)   [¹ Subject to paragraph (4A),] Every claim shall be in writing and made on a properly completed form approved for the purpose by the relevant authority or in such written form as the relevant authority may accept as sufficient in the circumstances of any particular case or class of cases having regard to the sufficiency of the written information and evidence.

(2)   The forms approved for the purpose of claiming shall be provided free of charge by the relevant authority or such persons as they may authorise or appoint for the purpose.

(3)   Each relevant authority shall notify the Secretary of State of the address to which claims delivered or sent to the appropriate DWP office are to be forwarded.

(4)   A claim [¹ in writing]–
(a)   may be sent or delivered to the appropriate DWP office where the claimant or his partner is also claiming income support, incapacity benefit, state pension credit or a jobseeker's allowance;
(b)   where it has not been sent or delivered to the appropriate DWP office, shall be sent or delivered to the designated office;
(c)   sent or delivered to the appropriate DWP office, other than one sent on the same form as a claim made to income support, incapacity benefit or a jobseeker's allowance and as approved by the Secretary of State for the purpose of the benefits being claimed, shall be forwarded to the relevant

authority within two working days of the date of the receipt of the claim at the appropriate DWP office, or as soon as practicable thereafter;

(d)   may, in the case of a claimant who has attained the age of 16 but not the age of 60 and is not engaged in remunerative work, be sent or delivered to a gateway office;

(e)   may be sent or delivered where the claimant has attained the age of 16 but not the age of 60 to an office or designated authority displaying the ONE logo; and

(f)   where the claimant has attained the qualifying age for state pension credit, may be sent or delivered to an authorised office.

[³ (g)   may be sent or delivered to the offices of a county council in England if the council has arranged with the relevant authority for claims to be received at their offices (''county offices'').]

[¹ (4A)   Where the relevant authority has published a telephone number for the purpose of receiving claims for council tax benefit, a claim may be made by telephone to that telephone number.

(4B)   The relevant authority may determine, in any particular case, that a claim made by telephone is not a valid claim unless the person making the claim approves a written statement of his circumstances, provided for the purpose by the relevant authority.

(4C)   A claim made by telephone in accordance with paragraph (4A) is defective unless the relevant authority is provided during that telephone call with all the information it requires to determine the claim.

(4D)   Where a claim made by telephone in accordance with paragraph (4A) is defective, the relevant authority is to provide the person making it with an opportunity to correct the defect.

(4E)   If the person corrects the defect within one month, or such longer period as the relevant authority considers reasonable, of the date it last drew attention to it, the relevant authority shall treat the claim as if it had been duly made in the first instance.]

(5)   Subject to paragraph (12), and to regulation 70 (date of claim where claim sent or delivered to a gateway office) the date on which a claim is made shall be–

(a)   in a case where an award of income support or an income-based jobseeker's allowance has been made to the claimant or his partner and the claim for council tax benefit is made within one month of the date on which the claim for that income support or jobseeker's allowance was received at the appropriate DWP office, the first day of entitlement to income support or an income-based jobseeker's allowance arising from that claim; and for the purposes of this sub-paragraph a person who has an award entitling him to an income-based jobseeker's allowance shall be treated as also entitled to an income-based jobseeker's allowance for any days which immediately precede the first day in that award and on which in accordance with paragraph 4 of Schedule 1 to the Jobseekers Act (waiting days) he would not be entitled to that allowance;

(b)   in a case where a claimant or his partner is a person on income support or on an income-based jobseeker's allowance and he becomes liable for the first time to pay council tax in respect of the dwelling which he occupies as his home, where the claim to the authority is received at the designated office or appropriate DWP office within one month of the date of the change, the date on which the change takes place;

(c)   in a case where the claimant is the former partner of a person who was, at the date of his death or their separation, entitled to council tax benefit and where the claimant makes a claim for council tax benefit within one month of the date of the death or the separation, that date;

    (d)   except where sub-paragraph (a), (b) or (c) is satisfied, in a case where a properly completed claim is received in a designated office, an authorised office [³ , county offices] or an appropriate DWP office within one month of the date on which a claim form was issued following the claimant first notifying, by whatever means, a designated office, an authorised office [³ , county offices] or an appropriate DWP office of his intention of making a claim, the date of first notification;

    (e)   in any other case, the date on which the claim is received at the designated office, authorised office [³ , county offices] or appropriate DWP office.

    (6)   Where a claim received at the designated office has not been made in the manner prescribed in paragraph (1), that claim is for the purposes of these Regulations defective.

    (7)   Where a claim is defective because–

    (a)   it was made on the form approved for the purpose but that form is not accepted by the relevant authority as being properly completed; or

    (b)   it was made in writing but not on the form approved for the purpose and the relevant authority does not accept the claim as being in a written form which is sufficient in the circumstances of the case, having regard to the sufficiency of the written information and evidence,

the relevant authority may, in a case to which sub-paragraph (a) applies, request the claimant to complete the defective claim or, in a case to which sub-paragraph (b) applies, supply the claimant with the approved form or request further information or evidence.

    (8)   The relevant authority shall treat a defective claim as if it had been made in the first instance if–

    (a)   where paragraph (7)(a) applies, the authority receives at the designated office the properly completed claim or the information requested to complete it or the evidence within one month of the request, or such longer period as the relevant authority may consider reasonable; or

    (b)   where paragraph (7)(b) applies–

        (i)   the approved form sent to the claimant is received at the designated office properly completed within one month of it having been sent to him; or, as the case may be;

        (ii)   the claimant supplies whatever information or evidence was requested under paragraph (7) within one month of the request,

or within such longer period as the relevant authority may consider reasonable.

    (9)   A claim which is made on an approved form for the time being is, for the purposes of this regulation, properly completed if completed in accordance with the instructions on the form, including any instructions to provide information and evidence in connection with the claim.

    [² (10)   Except in the case of a claim made by a person from abroad, where a person has not become liable for council tax to a relevant authority but it is anticipated that he will become so liable within the period of 8 weeks (the relevant period), he may claim council tax benefit at any time in that period in respect of that tax and, provided that liability arises within the relevant period, the authority shall treat the claim as having been made on the day on which the liability for the tax arises.]

    (11)   Where, exceptionally, a relevant authority, has not set or imposed its council tax by the beginning of the financial year, if a claim for council tax benefit is properly made or treated as properly made and–

    (a)   the date on which the claim is made or treated as made is in the period from the 1st April of the current year and ending one month after the date on which the authority sets or imposes the tax; and

    (b)   if the tax had been determined, the claimant would have been entitled to council tax benefit either from–

(i)   the benefit week in which the 1st April of the current year fell; or

(ii)   a benefit week falling after the date specified in head (i) but before the claim was made,

the relevant authority shall treat the claim as made in the benefit week immediately preceding the benefit week in which such entitlement would have commenced.

[² (12)   Except in the case of a claim made by a person from abroad, where the claimant is not entitled to council tax benefit in the benefit week immediately following the date of his claim but the relevant authority is of the opinion that unless there is a change of circumstances he will be entitled to council tax benefit for a period beginning not later than the thirteenth benefit week following the date on which the claim is made, the relevant authority may treat the claim as made on a date in the benefit week immediately preceding the first benefit week of that period of entitlement and award benefit accordingly.]

(13)   In the case of a person who has attained, or whose partner has attained, the age of 59 years and 35 weeks, paragraph (12) shall apply as if for the reference to the thirteenth benefit week, there was substituted a reference to the seventeenth benefit week.

(14)   Where the claimant makes a claim in respect of a past period (a "claim for backdating") and, from a day in that period up to the date of the claim for backdating, he had continuous good cause for his failure to make a claim, his claim in respect of that period shall be treated as made on–

(a)   the first day from which he had continuous good cause; or

(b)   the day 52 weeks before the date of the claim for backdating,

whichever fell later.

(15)   In this regulation "authorised office" means an office which is nominated by the Secretary of State and authorised by the relevant authority for receiving claims for decision by the relevant authority.

Amendments

1.   Inserted by reg 4(2) of SI 2006 No 2967 as from 20.12.06.
2.   Substituted by reg 5 of SI 2007 No 1331 as from 23.5.07.
3.   Amended by reg 9(2) of SI 2007 No 2911 as from 31.10.07

[¹Electronic claims for benefit

69A.   A claim for council tax benefit may be made by means of an electronic communication in accordance with Schedule 9.]

Amendment

1.   Inserted by Art 4(3) of SI 2006 No 2968 as from 20.12.06.

Date of claim where claim sent or delivered to a gateway office

70.–(1)   Subject to paragraphs (10), (11) and (12) of regulation 69 (time and manner in which claims are to be made), and with the exception of those claims to which paragraph (3) of this regulation refers, where a claim for council tax benefit has been sent or delivered to a gateway office in accordance with sub-paragraph (d) of paragraph (4) of regulation 69, the date on which that claim is made shall be–

(a)   in a case where a claimant or his partner–

(i)   is a person who has been awarded income support or an income-based jobseeker's allowance; and

(ii)   first notifies his intention to claim council tax benefit within 4 weeks of the date on which his claim for that income support or jobseeker's allowance was received at an appropriate DWP office,

the first day of entitlement to income support or an income-based jobseeker's allowance, but if the first notification is by any means other than a claim which meets the requirements of regulation 69(1) such a claim must be received at a gateway office within one month of that notification; and for the purposes only of this sub-paragraph a person who has been awarded an income-based jobseeker's allowance shall be treated as also entitled to that allowance for any days which immediately precede the first day in that award and on which he would, but for regulations made under paragraph 4 of Schedule 1 to the Jobseekers Act (waiting days) have been entitled to that allowance;

(b) in a case where the claimant or his partner–
  (i) claimed income support or a jobseeker's allowance; but
  (ii) has no entitlement to income support or an income-based jobseeker's allowance,

the first date on which notification is deemed to be given in accordance with paragraph (2), but if that notification is by any means other than a claim which meets the requirements of regulation 69(1) such a claim must be received at a gateway office within one month of that notification;

(c) in a case where a claimant or his partner–
  (i) is a person on income support or entitled to an income-based jobseeker's allowance;
  (ii) has become liable for the first time to pay council tax in respect of the dwelling which he occupies as his home; and
  (iii) first notifies his intention to make a claim for council tax benefit within 4 weeks of the change,

the date on which that change takes place, but if the first notification is by any means other than a claim which meets the requirements of regulation 69(1) such a claim must be received at the gateway office within one month of that notification;

(d) in a case where neither the claimant nor his partner is a person on income support or entitled to an income-based jobseeker's allowance, the first date on which notification is deemed to be made in accordance with paragraph (2), but if that notification is by any means other than a claim which meets the requirements of regulation 69(1) such a claim must be received at the gateway office within one month of that notification; or

(e) in any other case, the date on which the claim for council tax benefit is received at the gateway office.

(2) A notification of intention to make a claim is deemed to be given on the date on which notification from the claimant of his intention to claim council tax benefit is received in whatever form at a gateway office.

(3) This regulation does not apply to claims which are made at an office of a designated authority in accordance with regulation 69(4)(e).

Date of claim where claim sent or delivered to an office of a designated authority

71.–(1) Where a claim for council tax benefit has been sent or delivered to an office of a designated authority in accordance with regulation 69(4)(e), the date on which the claim is made shall be–

(a) except where paragraph (b) applies, the date the claim is received at an office of the designated authority; or

(b) where in the 4 weeks before the claim is received in an office of a designated authority, the person making the claim or a person acting on his behalf had notified an office of a designated authority of his intention to make such a claim, the date the notification was given.

(2) A notification of intention to make a claim is deemed to be given on the date on which notification of the intention to claim council tax benefit is received, in whatever form, from the claimant, or the person acting on his behalf, at an office of a designated authority.

(3) Paragraph (2) applies where neither income support nor a jobseeker's allowance is claimed in conjunction with council tax benefit.

(4)   Where the person claiming council tax benefit in accordance with regulation 69(4)(e), or the partner of that person,–

    (a)   has an award of income support or income-based jobseeker's allowance; or

    (b)   has claimed such a benefit but no award has been made,

the date on which the claim for council tax benefit is made shall be determined as if sub-paragraphs (a), (b), (c) and (e) of paragraph (1) of regulation 70 applied to that claim as they apply to claims under regulation 69(4)(d).

General Note

Like reg 85 HB Regs, reg 71 makes provision for claims to designated authorities. Note, however, that here for the date of claim to be the date the claimant notifies her/his intention to claim, the notification must have been made within the four weeks before the claim is received, rather than one month: para (1)(b). It is understood that this was a drafting error at the time the regulations were consolidated and that para (1)(b) is to be amended. Note that the time limit in reg 62B CTB Regs 1992 (now reg 71) was amended by reg 3(15) of SI 2005 No 2894 as from 10 November 2005.

Evidence and information

72.–(1)   Subject to paragraph (2) and to paragraph 4 of Schedule A1 (treatment of claims for council tax benefit by refugees), a person who makes a claim, or a person to whom council tax benefit has been awarded, shall furnish such certificates, documents, information and evidence in connection with the claim or the award, or any question arising out of the claim or the award, as may reasonably be required by the relevant authority in order to determine that person's entitlement to, or continuing entitlement to council tax benefit and shall do so within 4 weeks of being required to do so or such longer period as the relevant authority may consider reasonable.

(2)   Nothing in this regulation shall require a person to furnish any certificates, documents, information or evidence relating to a payment to which paragraph (4) applies.

(3)   Where a request is made under paragraph (1), the relevant authority shall–

    (a)   inform the claimant or the person to whom council tax benefit has been awarded of his duty under regulation 74 (duty to notify change of circumstances) to notify the designated office of any change of circumstances; and

    (b)   without prejudice to the extent of the duty owed under regulation 74, indicate to him either orally or by notice or by reference to some other document available to him on application and without charge, the kind of change of circumstances which are to be notified.

(4)   This paragraph applies to any of the following payments–

    (a)   a payment which is–

        (i)   disregarded under paragraph 24 of Schedule 4 (income in kind) or paragraph 34 of Schedule 5 (certain payments in kind); and

        (ii)   made under the Trusts, the Fund, the Eileen Trust, the Skipton Fund, or the London Bombings Relief Charitable Fund;

    (b)   a payment which is disregarded under paragraph 36 of Schedule 4 or under paragraph 24 of Schedule 5 (payments made under certain trusts and certain other payments), other than a payment under the Independent Living Funds;

    (c)   a payment which is disregarded under regulation 58(9)(b) or (c) (non-dependant deductions) or paragraph 2(b) or (c) of Schedule 2 (second adult's gross income) other than a payment under the Independent Living Funds.

(5)   Where a claimant or a person to whom council tax benefit has been awarded or any partner is aged not less than 60 and is a member of, or a person deriving entitlement to a pension under, a personal pension scheme, [¹] he shall where the relevant authority so requires furnish the following information–

    (a)   the name and address of the pension fund holder;

(b)   such other information including any reference or policy number as is needed to enable the personal pension scheme [¹] to be identified.

(6)   Where the pension fund holder receives from a relevant authority a request for details concerning a personal pension scheme [¹] relating to a person or any partner to whom paragraph (5) refers, the pension fund holder shall provide the relevant authority with any information to which paragraph (7) refers.

(7)   The information to which this paragraph refers is–

(a)   where the purchase of an annuity under a personal pension scheme has been deferred, the amount of any income which is being withdrawn from the personal pension scheme;

(b)   in the case of–

    (i)   a personal pension scheme where income withdrawal is available, the maximum amount of income which may be withdrawn from the scheme; or

    (ii)   a personal pension scheme where income withdrawal is not available, [¹] the maximum amount of income which might be withdrawn from the fund if the fund were held under a personal pension scheme where income withdrawal was available,

calculated by or on behalf of the pension fund holder by means of tables prepared from time to time by the Government Actuary which are appropriate for this purpose.

Amendment

1.   Amended by reg 6(6) of SI 2007 No 1749 as from 16.7.07.

General Note

Like reg 86 HB Regs, reg 72 obliges the claimant to provide evidence to support her/his claim if requested to do so by the authority. Note, however, that here the time limit for providing the evidence is four weeks rather than one month: para (1). It is understood that this was a drafting error at the time the regulations were consolidated and that para (1) is to be amended. Note that the time limit in reg 63 CTB Regs 1992 (now reg 72) was amended by reg 3(15) of SI 2005 No 2894 as from 10 November 2005.

[²Amendment and withdrawal of claim

73.–(1)   A person who has made a claim may amend it at any time before a decision has been made on it, by a notice in writing delivered or sent to the designated office, except where the claim was made by telephone in accordance with regulation 69(4A) where the amendment may be made by telephone, and any claim so amended shall be treated as if it had been amended in the first instance.

(2)   A person who has made a claim may withdraw it at any time before a decision has been made on it, by notice to the designated office, and any such notice of withdrawal shall have effect when it is received.]

Amendments

1.   Inserted by reg 4(3) of SI 2006 No 2967 as from 20.12.06.
2.   Substituted by reg 8(4) of SI 2007 No 719 as from 2.4.07.

Duty to notify changes of circumstances

74.–(1)   Subject to paragraphs (3), (5) and (6), if at any time between the making of a claim and a decision being made on it, or during the award of council tax benefit there is a change of circumstances which the claimant, or any person by whom or on whose behalf sums payable by way of council tax benefit are receivable, might reasonably be expected to know might affect the claimant's right to, the amount of or the receipt of council tax benefit, that person shall be under a duty to notify that change of circumstances by giving notice [¹] to the designated office

[¹ (a) in writing or, where the relevant authority has published a telephone number for the purposes of regulation 69 (time and manner in which claims are to be made), by telephone unless the authority determines, in any particular case, that notice must be in writing or may be given otherwise than in writing or by telephone; or

(b)   in writing if in any class of case the relevant authority requires written notice unless the authority determines, in any particular case, that notice may be given otherwise than in writing.]

(2)   In the case of a claimant who sent or delivered his claim to a gateway office in accordance with regulation 70 (date of claim where claim sent or delivered to a gateway office), a change of circumstances may be reported in writing to that office, or to any other gateway office of which he was notified to him on or with his claim form.

(3)   The duty imposed on a person by paragraph (1) does not extend to notifying changes–

(a)   in the amount of council tax payable to the relevant authority;

(b)   in the age of the claimant or that of any member of his family;

(c)   in these Regulations;

(d)   in the case of a claimant on income support or an income-based jobseeker's allowance, in circumstances which affect the amount of income support or an income-based jobseeker's allowance but not the amount of council tax benefit to which he is entitled, other than the cessation of that entitlement to income support or an income-based jobseeker's allowance.

(4)   Notwithstanding paragraph (3)(b) or (d) a claimant shall be required by paragraph (1) to notify the designated office of any change in the composition of his family arising from the fact that a person who was a member of his family is now no longer such a person because he ceases to be a child or young person.

(5)   Where the amount of a claimant's council tax benefit is the alternative maximum council tax benefit in his case, the claimant shall be under a duty to give written notice to the designated office of changes which occur in the number of adults in the dwelling or in their total gross incomes which might reasonably be expected to change his entitlement to that council tax benefit and where any such adult ceases to be in receipt of income support or an income-based jobseeker's allowance the date when this occurs.

(6)   Where a person resides in a postcode district identified in Part 1 or 2 of Schedule 2 to the Social Security (Claims and Information) Regulations 1999, he may notify the change of circumstances by giving notice in writing to any office of a designated authority displaying the ONE logo.

Amendment

1.   Amended by reg 4(4) of SI 2006 No 2967 as from 20.12.06.

General Note

For the alternatve maximum council tax referred to in para (5), see reg 62 on p619.

Reg 74 equates to reg 88 HB Regs, but there is no equivalent to reg 74(5) in those Regs.

[¹Notice of changes of circumstances given electronically

74A.   A person may give notice of a change of circumstances required to be notified under regulation 74 by means of an electronic communication in accordance with Schedule 9.]

Amendment

1.   Inserted by Art 4(4) of SI 2006 No 2968 as from 20.12.06.

PART 9
Decisions on questions

General Note on Part 9

As with Part 11 of the HB Regs, the introduction of the adjudication system under Sch 7 CSPSSA resulted in the revocation of large parts of Part 9 of the CTB Regs 1992. For the final text of the repealed provisions, see the 14th edition of this book.

Decisions by a relevant authority

75.–(1)   Unless provided otherwise by these Regulations, any matter required to be determined under these Regulations shall be determined in the first instance by the relevant authority.

(2)   The relevant authority shall make a decision on each claim within 14 days of the provisions of regulations 69 and 72 (time and manner for making claims and evidence and information required) being satisfied or as soon as reasonably practicable thereafter.

(3)   Without prejudice to the generality of the foregoing provisions of this regulation in a case where a person–

   (a)   made the notification specified in paragraph 2 of Schedule 6 within 14 days from the day immediately after the day on which his entitlement to income support or an income-based jobseeker's allowance ceased ("the appropriate day") and is treated as having claimed an extended payment under regulation 60(2) (extended payments); and

   (b)   has made a claim, which meets the requirements of regulation 69(1), (6) and (9), within 14 days of the appropriate day,

the relevant authority shall give priority to that claim over other claims which do not fall within the provisions of this paragraph.

Notification of decision

76.–(1)   Except in cases to which paragraphs (a) and (b) of regulation 82 (excess benefit in consequence of a reduction of a relevant authority's council tax) refer, an Authority shall notify in writing any person affected by a decision made by it under these Regulations–

   (a)   in the case of a decision on a claim, forthwith or as soon as reasonably practicable thereafter;

   (b)   in any other case, within 14 days of that decision or as soon as reasonably practicable thereafter,

and every notification shall include a statement as to the matters set out in Schedule 8.

(2)   A person affected to whom an authority sends or delivers a notification of decision may request in writing the authority to provide a written statement setting out the reasons for its decision on any matter set out in the notice.

(3)   The written statement referred to in paragraph (2) shall be sent to the person requesting it within 14 days or as soon as is reasonably practical thereafter.

PART 10
Awards or payments of benefit

Time and manner of granting council tax benefit

77.–(1)   Subject to regulations 80 and 81 (payments on death and offsetting), where a person is entitled to council tax benefit in respect of his liability for a relevant authority's council tax as it has effect in respect of the relevant or any subsequent chargeable financial year, the relevant authority shall discharge his entitlement–

   (a)   by reducing, so far as possible, the amount of his liability to which regulation 20(2) of the Council Tax (Administration and Enforcement) Regulations

1992 (the English and Welsh Regulations) or regulation 20(2) of the Council Tax (Administration and Enforcement) (Scotland) Regulations 1992 (the Scottish Regulations) refers; or

(b)   where–
  (i)   such a reduction is not possible; or
  (ii)   such a reduction would be insufficient to discharge the entitlement to council tax benefit; or
  (iii)   the person entitled to council tax benefit is jointly and severally liable for the tax and the relevant authority determines that such a reduction would be inappropriate,

by making payments to him of the benefit to which he is entitled, rounded where necessary to the nearest penny.

(2)   The relevant authority shall notify the person entitled to council tax benefit of the amount of that benefit and how his entitlement is to be discharged in pursuance of paragraph (1).

(3)   In a case to which paragraph (1)(b) refers–

(a)   if the amount of the council tax for which he remains liable in respect of the relevant chargeable financial year, after any reduction to which paragraph (1)(a) refers has been made, is insufficient to enable his entitlement to council tax benefit in respect thereof to be discharged in that year, upon the final instalment of that tax becoming due any outstanding benefit–
  (i)   shall be paid to that person if he so requires; or
  (ii)   in any other case shall (as the relevant authority determines) either be repaid or credited against any subsequent liability of the person to make a payment in respect of the authority's council tax as it has effect for any subsequent year;

(b)   if that person has ceased to be liable for the relevant authority's council tax and has discharged the liability for that tax, the outstanding balance (if any) of the council tax benefit in respect thereof shall be paid within 14 days or, if that is not reasonably practicable, as soon as practicable thereafter;

(c)   in any other case, the council tax benefit shall be paid within 14 days of the receipt of the claim at the designated office or, if that is not reasonably practicable, as soon as practicable thereafter.

(4)   For the purposes of this regulation "instalment" means any instalment of a relevant authority's council tax to which regulation 19 of either the English and Welsh Regulations or as the case may be the Scottish Regulations refers (council tax payments).

Persons to whom benefit is to be paid

78.–(1)   Subject to regulation 80 (payment on death) and paragraph (2), any payment of council tax benefit under regulation 77(1)(b) shall be made to that person.

(2)   Where a person other than a person who is entitled to council tax benefit made the claim and that first person is a person acting pursuant to an appointment under regulation 68(3) (persons appointed to act for a person unable to act) or is treated as having been so appointed by virtue of regulation 68(5), benefit may be paid to that person.

General Note

Para (1) provides that, unless a person entitled to CTB has died or someone has been appointed to act for her/him (for which see para (2)), if CTB is not paid under reg 77(1)(a) by reducing the claimant's council tax bill CTB must be paid direct to that person.

Shortfall in benefit

79.–(1)   Except in cases to which paragraph (2) refers, where, on the revision of a decision allowing council tax benefit to a person, it is determined that the amount allowed was less than the amount to which that person was entitled, the relevant authority shall either–

(a) make good any shortfall in benefit which is due to that person, by reducing so far as possible the next and any subsequent payments he is liable to make in respect of the council tax of the authority concerned as it has effect for the relevant chargeable financial year until that shortfall is made good; or

(b) where this is not possible or the person concerned so requests, pay any shortfall in benefit due to that person within 14 days of the revision of the decision being made or if that is not reasonably practicable, as soon as possible afterwards.

(2) A shortfall in benefit need not be paid in any case to the extent that there is due from the person concerned to the relevant authority any recoverable excess benefit to which regulation 83(1) refers.

General Note

This regulation deals with the situation when an authority has underpaid a claimant. By para (1), unless para (2) applies and a recoverable overpayment under reg 83 is owed by the claimant, when it is decided that a claimant has been underpaid, the authority has a choice. If the claimant requests payment, the shortfall must be paid to her/him within 14 days or as soon as "reasonably practicable": see note on reg 89(2) HB Regs on p393. Otherwise, the amount outstanding should be deducted from the claimant's remaining liability for that chargeable financial year. If this is not possible – eg, because the remaining liability is less than the amount due to the claimant, again payment should be made to the claimant within the timescale set out in sub-paragraph (b).

Payment on the death of the person entitled

80.–(1) Where the person entitled to any council tax benefit has died and it is not possible to award any council tax benefit which is due in the form of a reduction of the council tax for which he was liable, the relevant authority shall make payment either to his personal representative or, where there is none, his next of kin aged 16 or over.

(2) For the purposes of paragraph (1), "next of kin" means in England and Wales the persons who would take beneficially on an intestacy and in Scotland the person entitled to the moveable estate on intestacy.

(3) A payment under paragraph (1) may not be made unless the personal representative or the next of kin, as the case may be, makes written application for the payment of any sum of benefit to which the deceased was entitled, and such written application is sent to or delivered to the relevant authority at its designated office within 12 months of the deceased's death or such longer period as the authority may allow in any particular case.

(4) The authority may dispense with strict proof of title of any person claiming under paragraph (3) and the receipt of such a person shall be a good discharge to the authority for any sum so paid.

Offsetting

81.–(1) Where a person has been allowed or paid a sum of council tax benefit under a decision which is subsequently revised or further revised, any sum allowed or paid in respect of a period covered by the subsequent decision shall be offset against arrears of entitlement under the subsequent decision except to the extent that the sum exceeds the arrears and shall be treated as properly awarded or paid on account of them.

(2) Where an amount has been deducted under regulation 89(1) an equivalent sum shall be offset against any arrears of entitlement under the subsequent determination.

(3) No amount may be offset under paragraph (1) which has been determined to be excess benefit within the meaning of regulation 82 (meaning of excess benefit).

PART 11

Excess benefit

General Note on Part 11

Many of the provisions in this Part are equivalent to those in Part 13 of the HB Regs. See the General Note on that Part on p410. Overpayments of CTB are termed "excess benefit", but there is no particular significance about this. The rules on recovery are slightly different.

Meaning of excess benefit

82. In this Part "excess benefit" means any amount which has been allowed by way of council tax benefit and to which there was no entitlement under these Regulations (whether on the initial decision [¹ or as subsequently revised or superseded or further revised or superseded]) and includes any excess which arises by reason of–

(a) a reduction in the amount a person is liable to pay in respect of council tax in consequence of–

    (i) regulations made under section 13 of the 1992 Act (reduction in the amount of a person's council tax); or

    (ii) any discount to which that tax is subject by virtue of section 11 or 79 of that Act;

(b) a substitution under sections 31 or, in Scotland, section 94 of the 1992 Act (substituted amounts) of a lesser amount for an amount of council tax previously set by the relevant authority under section 30 or, in Scotland section 93 of that Act (amount set for council tax).

Amendment

1. Amended by reg 3 of SI 2005 No 2904 as amended by Sch 2 para 29 of SI 2006 No 217 as from 10.4.06.

General Note

See reg 99 HB Regs on p410. There is no equivalent to reg 93 HB Regs. For "overpayment" read "excess benefits".

Sub-paras (a) and (b) have no equivalent in the HB Regs. Sub-para (a) refers to cases where a claimant's liability for CTB is subsequently reduced due to a disability reduction, discount, transitional relief or charge-capping. Sub-para (b) deals with cases where an authority subsequently substitutes a lower council tax for the year. Any excess benefit falling within either of these sub-paras is always recoverable, whether or not there is an official error: reg 83(4).

Recoverable excess benefit

83.–(1) Any excess benefit, except benefit to which paragraph (2) applies, shall be recoverable.

(2) Subject to paragraph (4) and (5) and excepting any excess benefit arising in consequence of a reduction in tax or substitution to which regulation 82 refers, this paragraph applies to excess benefit allowed in consequence of an official error, where the claimant or a person acting on his behalf or any other person to whom the excess benefit is allowed could not, at the time the benefit was allowed or upon the receipt of any notice relating to the allowance of that benefit, reasonably have been expected to realise that it was excess benefit.

(3) In paragraph (2), "excess benefit allowed in consequence of an official error" means an overpayment caused by a mistake made whether in the form of an act or omission by–

(a) the relevant authority;

(b) an officer or person acting for that authority;

(c) an officer of–

    (i) the Department for Work and Pensions; or

    (ii) the Commissioners for Her Majesty's Revenue and Customs,

acting as such; or

(d)   a person providing services to the Department or to the Commissioners referred to in (c),

where the claimant, a person acting on his behalf or any other person to whom the payment is made, did not cause or materially contribute to that mistake, act or omission.

(4)   Paragraph (2) shall not apply with respect to excess benefit to which regulation 82(a) and (b) refers.

(5)   Where in consequence of an official error a person has been awarded excess benefit, upon the award being revised [¹ or superseded] any excess benefit which remains credited to him by the relevant authority in respect of a period after the date of the revision [¹ or supersession], shall be recoverable.

Amendment
1.   Amended by reg 5 of SI 2005 No 2904 as amended by Sch 2 para 29 of SI 2006 No 217 as from 10.4.06.

General Note
It is submitted that the use of the phrase "in consequence of" in para (3) as opposed to "caused by" in reg 100(2) HB Regs is not significant.

Para (4) has no equivalent in reg 100 HB Regs and means that all of the excess payments referred to in paras (a) and (b) of reg 82 are by definition recoverable. Para (5) is generally the equivalent of reg 100(4), but see *CH 1384/2007* (paras 12 and 13) for for the different operational effect of the rule in the CTB context, where benefit is awarded/credited to the claimant's council tax account for the period up to the end of the council tax year.

Authority by which recovery may be made
84.   The relevant authority which allowed the recoverable excess benefit may recover it.

General Note
This reg confirms the discretion to recover excess CTB by the authority that allowed it. See the Analysis to s75(2) SSAA on p42 for consideration of the discretion in the HB context.

Persons from whom recovery may be sought
85.–(1)   Subject to paragraph (2), recoverable excess benefit shall be due from the claimant or the person to whom the excess benefit was allowed.

(2)   Where recoverable excess benefit is allowed to a claimant who has one or more partners, recovery of the excess may be made by deduction from any council tax benefit allowed to a partner, provided the claimant and that partner were members of the same household both at the time the excess benefit is allowed and when the deduction is made.

General Note
This regulation is narrower than reg 101 HB Regs in that recovery cannot be made from a person who misrepresented or failed to disclose a material fact if that person is not otherwise covered by paras (1) or (2).

Methods of recovery
86.–(1)   Without prejudice to any other method of recovery a relevant authority may recover any recoverable excess benefit due from any person referred to in regulation 85 (person from whom recovery may be sought) by any of the methods specified in paragraph (2) and (3) or any combination of those methods.

(2)   Excess benefit may be recovered either–

(a)   by payment by or on behalf of the person to whom regulation 85(1) refers; or

(b)   by an addition being made by the relevant authority to any amount payable in respect of the council tax concerned.

(3)   Where recoverable excess benefit due from any person cannot be recovered by either of the methods specified in paragraph (2), the relevant authority may request the Secretary of State to recover the outstanding excess from the benefits prescribed in regulation 90 in accordance with the provisions of that regulation.

General Note

Like reg 102 HB Regs, this reg does not purport to be an exhaustive list of the methods of recovery. It simply sets out some permissible methods. Reg 87 sets out another. See the Analysis to reg 102 HB Regs on p426 for a complete guide to the methods of recovery, though see the General Note to reg 87 on p637.

Analysis

Para 2. Recovery of excess CTB may be effected by payment from the claimant or other person to whom the benefit was allowed or by an addition to the claimant's council tax bill. It is not possible to recover, as is the case with HB, by demand for payment from any other person whose misrepresentation or failure to disclose led to the overpayment.

Para 3 provides a further means of recovery, but only if para (2) cannot be used.

Further provision as to recovery of excess benefit

87.   In addition to the methods for recovery of excess benefit which are specified in regulation 86, any sum or part of a sum which is due from the person concerned and which is not paid within 21 days of his being notified of the amount that is due, shall be recoverable in a court of competent jurisdiction by the authority to which the excess benefit is due.

General Note

This power is additional to any other methods of recovery adopted. Although HB overpayments can be recovered in a similar manner there is no such express power in the HB Regs.

Note that this regulation does not give the power to recover the excess benefit by registration as a recoverable debt at court, as to which see the Analysis to reg 102 HB Regs on p426. This is because the wording of reg 87 does not conform with that specified in Sch 2 CCR Ord 25 in the procedure of the Sheriff Court in Scotland, to enable recovery under that rule.

Therefore all reg 87 does is confirm the right to sue for the debt in the appropriate court. Note that proceedings cannot be taken until 21 days after the notification of the amount due. This time period is a minimum and is less than the one-month period for seeking a revision or supersession of the decision. Authorities should consider the possibility of the claimant seeking such a revision or supersession when deciding whether to issue a demand notice for payment. In any event, is is arguable that a final decision is not made until any revision or supersession of, or appeal against, the decsion has been resolved, or the time limits for enabling such challenges to be made have expired (see *R(SB) 5/91*), and so the 21 day time limit can only begin to run from one month after the date of the decision that the excess benefit is recoverable.

Diminution of capital

88.–(1)   Where in the case of recoverable excess benefit, in consequence of a misrepresentation or failure to disclose a material fact (in either case whether fraudulent or otherwise) as to a person's capital, or an error, other than one to which regulation 83(2) (effect of official error) refers, as to the amount of a person's capital, the excess benefit was in respect of a period (''the excess benefit period'') of more than 13 benefit weeks, the relevant authority shall, for the purpose only of calculating the amount of excess–

(a)   at the end of the first 13 benefit weeks of the excess benefit period, treat the amount of the capital as having been reduced by the amount of excess council tax benefit allowed during those 13 weeks;

(b)   at the end of each subsequent period of 13 benefit weeks, if any, of the excess benefit period, treat the amount of that capital as having been further reduced by the amount of excess council tax benefit allowed during the immediately preceding 13 benefit weeks.

(2)   Capital shall not be treated as reduced over any period other than 13 benefit weeks or in any circumstances other than those, for which paragraph (1) provides.

Sums to be deducted in calculating recoverable excess benefit

89.–(1) In calculating the amount of recoverable excess benefit, the relevant authority shall deduct any amount of council tax benefit which should have been determined to be payable in respect of the whole or part of the overpayment period–

  (a) on the basis of the claim as presented to the authority;

  (b) on the basis of the claim as it would have appeared had any misrepresentation or non-disclosure been remedied before the decision; or

  (c) on the basis of the claim as it would have appeared if any change of circumstances had been notified at the time that change occurred.

(2) In calculating the amount of recoverable excess benefit, the relevant authority may deduct so much of any payment of council tax in respect of the excess benefit period which exceeds the amount, if any, which the claimant was liable to pay for that period under the original erroneous decision.

Recovery of excess benefit from prescribed benefits

90.–(1) For the purposes of section 76(3)(c) of the Administration Act (deduction of excess council tax benefit from prescribed benefits), the benefits prescribed by this regulation are–

  (a) any benefit payable under the Act, except guardian's allowance or housing benefit;

  (b) any benefit payable under the legislation of any member State, other than the United Kingdom, concerning the branches of social security mentioned in article 4(1) of Regulation (EEC) No. 1408/71 on the application of social security schemes to employed persons, to self-employed persons and to members of their families moving within the Community, whether or not the benefit has been acquired by virtue of the provisions of that Regulation;

  (c) a jobseeker's allowance;

  (d) state pension credit.

[¹ (1A) For the purposes of paragraph (1)(b) the term "member State" shall be understood to include Switzerland in accordance with and subject to the provisions of Annex II of the Agreement between the European Community and its Member States and the Swiss Confederation on the free movement of persons, signed at Brussels on 21st June 1999.]

(2) Where the Secretary of State is satisfied that–

  (a) recoverable excess benefit has been allowed in consequence of a misrepresentation of or failure to disclose a material fact (in either case whether fraudulent or otherwise), by a claimant or any other person to whom council tax benefit has been allowed; and

  (b) the person who misrepresented that fact or failed to disclose it is receiving a sufficient amount of one or more of the benefits prescribed in paragraph (1) to enable deductions to be made for the recovery of the excess,

he shall if requested to do so by a relevant authority under regulation 86 (methods of recovery) recover the excess by deduction from any of those benefits.

Amendment

  1. Inserted by reg 10 of SI 2005 No 2904 as amended by Sch 2 para 29 of SI 2006 No 217 as from 10.4.06.

PART 12
Information
SECTION 1
Claims and information

Interpretation

91. In this Section–

[¹ "county council" means a county council in England, but only if the council has made an arrangement in accordance with regulation 69(4)(g) or 92(3);]

"local authority" means an authority administering council tax benefit;

"relevant authority" means–

    (a)   the Secretary of State;

    (b)   a person providing services to the Secretary of State; [¹ or

    (c)   a county council;]

"relevant information" means information or evidence relating to the administration of claims to or awards of council tax benefit.

Amendment

    1.   Amended by reg 9(3) of SI 2007 No 2911 as from 31.10.07.

[¹Collection of information

92.–(1) The Secretary of State, or a person providing services to him, may receive or obtain relevant information from–

    (a)   persons making, or who have made, claims for council tax benefit; or

    (b)   other persons in connection with such claims.

(2) In paragraph (1) references to persons who have made claims for council tax benefit include persons to whom awards of benefit have been made on those claims.

(3) Where a county council has made an arrangement with a local authority, or a person authorised to exercise any function of a local authority relating to housing benefit or council tax benefit, to receive and obtain information and evidence relating to claims for council tax benefit, the council may receive or obtain the information or evidence from–

    (a)   persons making claims for council tax benefit; or

    (b)   other persons in connection with such claims.

(4) A county council may receive information relating to an award of council tax benefit which is supplied by–

    (a)   the person to whom an award has been made; or

    (b)   other persons in connection with the award.]

Amendment

    1.   Substituted by reg 9(4) of SI 2007 No 2911 as from 31.10.07.

[¹Verifying information

92A. A relevant authority may verify relevant information supplied to, or obtained by, the authority in accordance with regulation 92.]

Amendment

    1.   Inserted by reg 9(5) of SI 2007 No 2911 as from 31.10.07.

[¹Recording and holding information

93. A relevant authority which obtains relevant information or to whom such information is supplied–

    (a)   shall make a record of such information; and

(b)   may hold that information, whether as supplied or obtained or recorded, for the purpose of forwarding it to the person or authority for the time being administering council tax benefit.]

Amendment

1.   Substituted by reg 9(6) of SI 2007 No 2911 as from 31.10.07.

Forwarding of information

94.   A relevant authority which holds relevant information–

(a)   shall forward it to the person or authority for the time being administering claims to or awards of council tax benefit to which the relevant information relates, being–

    (i)   a local authority;

    (ii)   a person providing services to a local authority; or

    (iii)   a person authorised to exercise any function of a local authority relating to council tax benefit; and

[¹ (b)   may, if the relevant authority is the Secretary of State or a person providing services to the Secretary of State, continue to hold a record of such information, whether as supplied or obtained or recorded, for such period as he considers appropriate.]

Amendment

1.   Substituted by reg 9(7) of SI 2007 No 2911 as from 31.10.07.

Request for information

95.   A relevant authority which holds information or evidence relating to social security matters shall forward such information or evidence as may be requested to the person or authority making that request, provided that–

(a)   the request is made by–

    (i)   a local authority;

    (ii)   a person providing services to a local authority; or

    (iii)   a person authorised to exercise any function of a local authority relating to council tax benefit; and

(b)   the information or evidence requested includes relevant information;

(c)   the relevant authority is able to provide the information or evidence requested in the form in which it was originally supplied or obtained; and

(d)   provision of the information or evidence requested is considered necessary by the relevant authority to the proper performance by a local authority of its functions relating to council tax benefit.

SECTION 2

Information between authorities etc.

Information to be supplied by an authority to another authority

96.–(1)   For the purposes of section 128A of the Administration Act (duty of an authority to disclose information to another authority) the circumstances in which information is to be disclosed are prescribed in paragraph (2) and the information prescribed by this regulation is described in paragraph (3).

(2)   The circumstances prescribed in this paragraph are, where–

(a)   there is a mover who is or was allowed council tax benefit by appropriate authority ''A'';

(b)   who is liable to pay council tax in respect of his second dwelling to authority ''B''; and

(c)   either–

    (i)   the extended payment is claimed from authority A; or

(ii)   the extended payment is claimed from authority B, who then requests the prescribed information from authority A,

authority A shall disclose to authority B the information prescribed in paragraph (3).

(3)   The information to be disclosed is–

(a)   in a case where that extended payment was claimed from authority A, details relevant to that claim of–

(i)   the matters certified pursuant to regulation 60 and paragraph 1 of Schedule 6; and

(ii)   the matters notified pursuant to regulation 60 and paragraph 2 of Schedule 6; and

(iii)   the date it was claimed;

(b)   in the case of a person to whom regulation 6(5) of the Income Support Regulations (persons not treated as engaged in remunerative work) applies–

(i)   the date on which he was first engaged in the work referred to in sub-paragraph (a) of regulation 6(5) of those Regulations; and

(ii)   the date on which his entitlement to income support ceased or is expected to cease; and

(c)   in any case–

(i)   the weekly rate of council tax benefit allowed to the mover by authority A;

(ii)   if any deduction was being made from that benefit in respect of non-dependants, pursuant to regulations 57(1) and 58, the amount of those deductions;

(iii)   if any addition was being made to any amount payable in respect of council tax to recover recoverable excess benefit pursuant to regulation 86(2)(b), the amount of those additions;

(iv)   the date on which his entitlement to council tax benefit ceased;

(v)   if an extended payment was allowed to the mover, the amount and date of any such payment;

(vi)   if no extended payment was allowed, why none was allowed.

(4)   In this regulation "mover" and "second dwelling" have the meanings assigned to them in paragraph 7 of Schedule 6.

General Note

This regulation is made under s128A. Although s128A was to be repealed by the SSA(F)A (see General Note to the section) the repeal has not yet been brought into force. It is the equivalent of reg 115 HB Regs (see the General Note on that regulation on p439), except that the equivalent of reg 72 HB Regs is reg 60 of these regulations and the reference to "movers" is to be found in Sch 6 paras 4 and 5.

Supply of information: extended payments (severe disablement allowance and incapacity benefit)

97.–(1)   For the purposes of section 122E(3) of the Administration Act (duty of an authority to supply information to another authority) the circumstances in which information is to be supplied are prescribed in paragraph (2) and the information prescribed by this regulation is described in paragraph (3).

(2)   The circumstances prescribed in this paragraph are, where–

(a)   there is a mover who is or was allowed council tax benefit by appropriate authority "A";

(b)   who is liable to pay council tax in respect of his second dwelling to authority "B"; and

(c)   either–

(i)   the extended payment (severe disablement allowance and incapacity benefit) is claimed from authority A; or

    (ii)   the extended payment (severe disablement allowance and incapacity benefit) is claimed from authority B, who then requests the information described in paragraph (3) from authority A,

authority A shall supply to authority B that information.

(3)   The information to be supplied is–

(a)   in a case where that extended payment (severe disablement allowance and incapacity benefit) was claimed from authority A, details relevant to that claim of–

    (i)   the matters set out in regulation 66 or regulation 61(1)(b)(i) to (iii), as the case may be; and

    (ii)   the matters notified pursuant to regulation 61(1)(a)(ii) or (b)(iv), as the case may be; and

    (iii)   the date it was so claimed; and

(b)   in any case–

    (i)   the weekly rate of council tax benefit allowed to the mover by authority A;

    (ii)   if any deduction was being made from that benefit in respect of non-dependants, pursuant to regulations 57(1) and 58, the amount of those deductions;

    (iii)   if any addition was being made to any amount payable in respect of council tax to recover recoverable excess benefit pursuant to regulation 86(2)(b), the amount of those additions;

    (iv)   the date on which his entitlement to council tax benefit ceased;

    (v)   if an extended payment (severe disablement allowance and incapacity benefit) was allowed to the mover, the amount and date of any such payment; and

    (vi)   if no extended payment (severe disablement allowance and incapacity benefit) was allowed, why none was allowed.

(4)   In this regulation ''mover'' and ''second dwelling'' shall have the meanings assigned to them in paragraph 7 of Schedule 7.

[¹ SCHEDULE A1]
Treatment of claims for council tax benefit by refugees

Modification
Sch A1 was inserted by Sch 4 para 3(2) of the HB&CTB(CP) Regs (see p1129) in respect of claims for CTB by some refugees. Sch A1 was further modifed by Sch 4 para 4(4) for some CTB claimants who were refugees who claimed asylum on or before 2 April 2000.

See also reg 7A inserted by Sch 4 para 3(1) of the HB&CTB(CP) Regs on p1129.

Amendment
1.   Lapsed by s12(2)(g) of the Asylum and Immigration (Treatment of Claimants, etc.) Act 2004 (for those recorded as refugees after 14.6.07).

SCHEDULE 1
REGULATION 12
Applicable amounts

General Note
This Schedule is broadly equivalent to Sch 3 to the HB Regs. One difference of substance is to be found in the transitional protection for those who were entitled to the lone parent premium prior to the enactment of the Social Security (Lone Parents) Regulations 1998, in para 3(3). In the CTB Regulations, a person is deemed to be in receipt of CTB for a period during which s/he was getting HB or would have been but for the fact that s/he was then in a rent-free period for the purposes of reg 81 HB Regs.

PART 1
Personal Allowances
1.   The amounts specified in column (2) below in respect of each person or couple specified in column (1) shall be the amounts specified for the purposes of regulations 12(a) and 13(a) and (b)–

Column (1); *Person or couple*	*Column (2);* *Amount;*
(1) Single claimant aged–	(1)
(a) Not less than 18 but less than 25;	(a) [² £46.85];
(b) Not less than 25.	(b) [² £59.15].
(2) Lone parent.	(2) [² £59.15].
(3) Couple.	(3) [² £92.80].

Amendments
1.   Amended by Art 21(4) and Sch 10 of SI 2006 No 645 and reg 8 of SI 2006 No 217 as from 1.4.06.
2.   Amended by Art 21(4) and Sch 10 of SI 2007 No 688 as from 1.4.07.

2.–(1)   The amount specified in column (2) below in respect of each person specified in column (1) shall, for the relevant period specified in column (1), be the amounts specified for the purposes of regulations 12(b) and 13(c)–

Column (1); *Child or young person*	*Column (2);* *Amount;*
Persons in respect of the period–	
(a) beginning on that person's date of birth and ending on the day preceding the first Monday in September following that person's sixteenth birthday;	(a) [³ £47.45];
(b) beginning on the first Monday in September following that person's sixteenth birthday and ending on the day preceding that person's [² twentieth] birthday.	(b) [³ £47.45].

(2)   In column (1) of the table in paragraph (1), "the first Monday in September" means the Monday which first occurs in the month of September in any year.

Amendments
1.   Amended by Art 21(4) and Sch 10 of SI 2006 No 645 and reg 8 of SI 2006 No 217 as from 1.4.06.
2.   Amended by reg 5(4) of SI 2006 No 718 as from 10.4.06.
3.   Amended by Art 21(4) and Sch 10 of SI 2007 No 688 as from 1.4.07.

PART 2
Family Premium
3.–(1)   Subject to sub-paragraph (2), the amount for the purposes of regulations 12(c) and 13(d) in respect of a family of which at least one member is a child or young person shall be–
(a)   where the claimant is a lone parent to whom sub-paragraph (3) applies, [³ £22.20];
(b)   in any other case, [⁴ £16.43].
(2)   The amounts specified in sub-paragraph (1)(a) and (b) shall be increased by [³ £10.50] where at least one child is under the age of one year and for the purposes of this paragraph where the child's first birthday does not fall on a Monday he shall be treated as under the age of one year until the first Monday after his first birthday.
(3)   The amount in sub-paragraph (1)(a) shall be applicable to a lone parent–
(a)   who was entitled to council tax benefit on 5th April 1998 and whose applicable amount on that date included the amount applicable under sub-paragraph (a) of this paragraph as in force on that date; or
(b)   on becoming entitled to council tax benefit where that lone parent–
(i) had been treated as entitled to that benefit in accordance with sub-paragraph (4) as at the day before the date of claim for that benefit; and
(ii) was entitled to housing benefit as at the date of claim for council tax benefit or would have been entitled to housing benefit as at that date had that day not fallen during a rent free period as defined in regulation 81 of the Housing Benefit Regulations,
and in respect of whom, all of the conditions specified in sub-paragraph (4) have continued to apply.
(4)   The conditions specified for the purposes of sub-paragraph (3) are that, in respect of the period commencing on 6th April 1998–

(a)   the claimant has not ceased to be entitled, or has not ceased to be treated as entitled, to council tax benefit;

(b)   the claimant has not ceased to be a lone parent;

(c)   where the claimant was entitled to income support or to an income-based jobseeker's allowance on 5th April 1998, he has continued to be entitled to one or other of those benefits;

(d)   where the claimant was not entitled to income support or to an income-based jobseeker's allowance on 5th April 1998, he has not become entitled to either of those benefits; and

(e)   a premium under paragraph 9, 10, 11 or 12 has not become applicable to the claimant.

(5)   For the purposes of sub-paragraphs (3)(b)(i) and (4)(a), a claimant shall be treated as entitled to council tax benefit during any period where he was not, or had ceased to be, so entitled and–

(a)   throughout that period, he had been awarded housing benefit and his applicable amount included the amount applicable under paragraph 3(1)(a) of Schedule 3 to the Housing Benefit Regulations (lone parent rate of family premium); or

(b)   he would have been awarded housing benefit during that period had that period not been a rent free period as defined in regulation 81 of the Housing Benefit Regulations and his applicable amount throughout that period would have included the amount applicable under paragraph 3(1)(a) of Schedule 3 to those Regulations.

Amendments

1.   Confirmed by Art 21(5)(a) and (c) of SI 2006 No 645 and reg 8 of SI 2006 No 217 as from 1.4.06.
2.   Amended by Art 21(5)(b) and Sch 10 of SI 2006 No 645 and reg 8 of SI 2006 No 217 as from 1.4.06.
3.   Confirmed by Art 21(5)(a) and (c) of SI 2007 No 688 as from 1.4.07.
4.   Amended by Art 21(5)(b) of SI 2007 No 688 as from 1.4.07.

PART 3
Premiums

4.   Except as provided in paragraph 5, the premiums specified in Part 4 of this Schedule shall, for the purposes of regulations 12(d) and 13(e), be applicable to a claimant who satisfies the condition specified in paragraphs 8 to 17 in respect of that premium.

5.   Subject to paragraph 6, where a claimant satisfies the conditions in respect of more than one premium in this Part of this Schedule, only one premium shall be applicable to him and, if they are different amounts, the higher or highest amount shall apply.

6.–(1)   Subject to sub-paragraph (2), the following premiums, namely–

(a)   a severe disability premium to which paragraph 14 applies;

(b)   an enhanced disability premium to which paragraph 15 applies;

(c)   a disabled child premium to which paragraph 16 applies; and

(d)   a carer premium to which paragraph 17 applies,

may be applicable in addition to any other premium which may apply under this Schedule.

(2)   An enhanced disability premium in respect of a person shall not be applicable in addition to–

(a)   a pensioner premium under paragraph 9 or 10; or

(b)   a higher pensioner premium under paragraph 11.

7.–(1)   Subject to sub-paragraph (2), for the purposes of this Part of this Schedule, once a premium is applicable to a claimant under this Part, a person shall be treated as being in receipt of any benefit for–

(a)   in the case of a benefit to which the Social Security (Overlapping Benefits) Regulations 1979 applies, any period during which, apart from the provisions of those Regulations, he would be in receipt of that benefit; and

(b)   any period spent by a person in undertaking a course of training or instruction provided or approved under section 2 of the 1973 Act or section 2 of the Enterprise and New Town (Scotland) Act 1990 for any period during which he is in receipt of a training allowance.

(2)   For the purposes of the carer premium under paragraph 17, a person shall be treated as being in receipt of carer's allowance by virtue of sub-paragraph (1)(a) only if and for so long as the person in respect of whose care the allowance has been claimed remains in receipt of attendance allowance, or the care component of disability living allowance at the highest or middle rate prescribed in accordance with section 72(3) of the Act.

[¹ Bereavement premium]

[¹8.]

Amendment

1.   Revoked by reg 2 and the Sch of SI 2007 No 2618 as from 1.10.07.

Pensioner Premium for persons under 75

9.   The condition is that the claimant–

(a)   is a single claimant or lone parent aged not less than 60 but less than 75; or
(b)   has a partner and is, or his partner is, aged not less than 60 but less than 75.

Pensioner Premium for persons 75 and over
10.   The condition is that the claimant–
(a)   is a single claimant or lone parent aged not less than 75 but less than 80; or
(b)   has a partner and is, or his partner is, aged not less than 75 but less than 80.

Higher Pensioner Premium
11.–(1)   Where the claimant is a single claimant or a lone parent, the condition is that–
(a)   he is aged not less than 80; or
(b)   he is aged less than 80 but not less than 60, and–
    (i)   the additional condition specified in paragraph 13(1)(a) is satisfied; or
    (ii)   the claimant was in receipt of, or was treated as being in receipt of, council tax benefit and the disability premium was or, as the case may be, would have been, applicable to him in respect of a benefit week within 8 weeks of his 60th birthday and he has, subject to sub-paragraph (3), remained continuously in receipt of council tax benefit since attaining that age.
(2)   Where the claimant has a partner, the condition is that–
(a)   he or his partner is aged not less than 80; or
(b)   he or his partner is aged less than 80 but not less than 60 and either–
    (i)   the additional condition specified in paragraph 13(1)(a) is satisfied, or
    (ii)   the claimant was in receipt of, or was treated as being in receipt of, council tax benefit and the disability premium was or, as the case may be, would have been, applicable to him in respect of a benefit week within 8 weeks of his 60th birthday and he has, subject to sub-paragraph (3), remained continuously in receipt of council tax benefit since attaining that age.
(3)   For the purposes of this paragraph and paragraph 13–
(a)   once the higher pensioner premium is applicable to a claimant, if he then ceases, for a period of 8 weeks or less, to be entitled to or treated as entitled to council tax benefit, he shall, on becoming re-entitled to council tax benefit, thereafter be treated as having been continuously entitled to that benefit;
(b)   where sub-paragraphs (1)(b)(ii) and (2)(b)(ii) apply, if a claimant ceases to be entitled to or treated as entitled to council tax benefit for a period not exceeding 8 weeks which includes his 60th birthday, he shall, on becoming re-entitled to council tax benefit, thereafter be treated as having been continuously entitled to that benefit; or
(c)   where the claimant or his partner–
    (i)   was entitled to housing benefit or, as the case may be, community charge benefit at any time in the period of 8 weeks before becoming entitled or re-entitled to council tax benefit; and
    (ii)   satisfied the conditions in respect of the higher pensioner premium under paragraphs 11 and 13 of Schedule 3 to the Housing Benefit Regulations or, as the case may be, paragraphs 11 and 13 of Schedule 1 to the Community Charge Benefits (General) Regulations 1989,
for the purpose of establishing entitlement or re-entitlement to council tax benefit, he or his partner shall be treated as satisfying the equivalent conditions for higher pensioner premium under this paragraph and paragraph 13.
(4)   In the case of a claimant who is a welfare to work beneficiary, references in sub-paragraphs (1)(b)(ii), (2)(b)(ii), (3)(b) and (3)(c)(i) to a period of 8 weeks shall be treated as references to a period of [¹ 104 weeks].
(5)   A person is a welfare to work beneficiary if he is a person–
(a)   to whom regulation 13A(1) of the Social Security (Incapacity for Work) (General) Regulations 1995 applies; and
(b)   who again becomes incapable of work for the purposes of Part 12A of the Act.
(6)   For the purposes of this paragraph, a claimant shall be treated as having been entitled to and in receipt of council tax benefit throughout any period which comprises only days on which he was participating in an employment zone programme and was not entitled to that benefit because, as a consequence of his participation in that programme, he failed to satisfy the condition in section 130(1)(c) of the Act.

Amendment
1.   Amended by reg 17(4) of SI 2006 No 2378 as from 9.10.06.

Disability Premium

12. The condition is that–

(a) where the claimant is a single claimant or a lone parent, he is aged less than 60 and the additional condition specified in paragraph 13 is satisfied; or

(b) where the claimant has a partner, either–
(i) the claimant is aged less than 60 and the additional condition specified in paragraph 13 (1)(a) or (b) is satisfied by him; or
(ii) his partner is aged less than 60 and the additional condition specified in paragraph 13(1)(a) is satisfied by his partner.

Additional Condition for the Higher Pensioner and Disability Premiums

13.–(1) Subject to sub-paragraph (2) and paragraph 7, the additional condition referred to in paragraphs 11 and 12 is that either–

(a) the claimant or, as the case may be, his partner–
(i) is in receipt of one or more of the following benefits: attendance allowance, disability living allowance, the disability element or the severe disability element of working tax credit as specified in regulation 20(1)(b) and (f) of the Working Tax Credit Regulations, mobility supplement, long-term incapacity benefit under Part 2 of the Act or severe disablement allowance under Part 3 of the Act but, in the case of long-term incapacity benefit or severe disablement allowance, only where it is paid in respect of him; or
(ii) was in receipt of long-term incapacity benefit under Part 2 of the Act when entitlement to that benefit ceased on account of the payment of a retirement pension under that Act and the claimant has since remained continuously entitled to community charge benefit or, as the case may be, council tax benefit and, if the long-term incapacity benefit was payable to his partner, the partner is still a member of the family; or
(iii) [¹] was in receipt of attendance allowance or disability living allowance but payment of benefit has been suspended in accordance with regulations made under section 113(2) of the Act or otherwise abated as a consequence of the claimant or his partner becoming a patient within the meaning of [² regulation 18(11)(e) (treatment of child care charges)]; or
(iv) is provided by the Secretary of State with an invalid carriage or other vehicle under section 5(2) of the National Health Service Act 1977 (other services) or, in Scotland, under section 46 of the National Health Service (Scotland) Act 1978 (provision of services by Scottish Ministers) or receives payments by way of grant from the Secretary of State under paragraph 2 of Schedule 2 to the Act of 1977 (additional provisions as to vehicles) or, in Scotland, by Scottish Ministers under section 46 of the Act of 1978; or
(v) is blind and in consequence registered in a register compiled by a local authority under section 29 of the National Assistance Act 1948 (welfare services) or, in Scotland, has been certified as blind and in consequence he is registered in a register maintained by or on behalf of a council constituted under section 2 of the Local Government (Scotland) Act 1994; or

(b) the claimant–
(i) is, or is treated as, incapable of work in accordance with the provisions of, and regulations made under, Part 12A of the Act (incapacity for work); and
(ii) has been incapable, or has been treated as incapable, of work for a continuous period of not less than–
(aa) in the case of a claimant who is terminally ill within the meaning of section 30B(4) of the Act, 196 days;
(bb) in any other case, 364 days.

(2) For the purposes of sub-paragraph (1)(a)(v), a person who has ceased to be registered as blind on regaining his eyesight shall nevertheless be treated as blind and as satisfying the additional condition set out in that sub-paragraph for a period of 28 weeks following the date on which he ceased to be so registered.

(3) For the purposes of sub-paragraph (1)(b), once the higher pensioner premium or the disability premium is applicable to a claimant by virtue of his satisfying the additional condition specified in that provision, if he then ceases, for a period of 8 weeks or less, to be treated as incapable of work or to be incapable of work he shall, on again becoming so incapable of work, immediately thereafter be treated as satisfying the condition in sub-paragraph (1)(b).

(4) For the purpose of sub-paragraph (1)(a)(ii) and (iii), once the higher pensioner premium is applicable to the claimant by virtue of his satisfying the condition specified in that provision, if he then ceases, for a period of 8 weeks or less, to be entitled to council tax benefit, he shall on again becoming so entitled to council tax benefit, immediately thereafter be treated as satisfying the condition in sub-paragraph (1)(a)(ii) and (iii).

(5)   For the purposes of sub-paragraph (1)(b), once the disability premium is applicable to a claimant by virtue of his satisfying the additional condition specified in that provision, he shall continue to be treated as satisfying that condition for any period spent by him in undertaking a course of training provided under section 2 of the 1973 Act or section 2 of the Enterprise and New Towns (Scotland) Act 1990 or for any period during which he is in receipt of a training allowance.

(6)   For the purposes of sub-paragraph (1)(b), where any two or more periods of incapacity are separated by a break of not more than 56 days, those periods shall be treated as one continuous period.

(7)   For the purposes of this paragraph, a reference to a person who is or was in receipt of long-term incapacity benefit includes a person who is or was in receipt of short-term incapacity benefit at a rate equal to the long-term rate by virtue of section 30B(4)(a) of the Act (short-term incapacity benefit for a person who is terminally ill), or who would be or would have been in receipt of short-term incapacity benefit at such a rate but for the fact that the rate of short-term incapacity benefit already payable to him is or was equal to or greater than the long-term rate.

(8)   For the purposes of sub-paragraph (1)(b), once the disability premium is applicable to a claimant by virtue of his satisfying the additional condition specified in that provision, he shall continue to be treated as satisfying that condition for any period spent by him in undertaking a course of training provided under section 2 of the 1973 Act or section 2 of the Enterprise and New Towns (Scotland) Act 1990.

(9)   In the case of a claimant who is a welfare to work beneficiary within the meaning of paragraph 11(5)–

(a)   the reference to a period of 8 weeks in sub-paragraph (3); and

(b)   the reference to a period of 56 days in sub-paragraph (6),

shall in each case be treated as a reference to a period of [³ 104 weeks].

Amendments

1.   Omitted by reg 3(11)(a)(i) of SI 2005 No 2502 as amended by Sch 2 para 27 of SI 2006 No 217 as from 1.4.06.

2.   Amended by reg 3(11)(a)(ii) of SI 2005 No 2502 as amended by Sch 2 para 27 of SI 2006 No 217 as from 1.4.06.

3.   Amended by reg 17(4) of SI 2006 No 2378 as from 9.10.06.

Severe Disability Premium

14.–(1)   The condition is that the claimant is a severely disabled person.

(2)   For the purposes of sub-paragraph (1), a claimant shall be treated as being a severely disabled person if, and only if–

(a)   in the case of a single claimant, a lone parent or a claimant who is treated as having no partner in consequence of sub-paragraph (3)–

    (i)   he is in receipt of attendance allowance, or the care component of disability living allowance at the highest or middle rate prescribed in accordance with section 72(3) of the Act; and

    (ii)   subject to sub-paragraph (4), he has no non-dependants aged 18 or over normally residing with him or with whom he is normally residing; and

    (iii)   no person is entitled to, and in receipt of, a carer's allowance under section 70 of the Act in respect of caring for him;

(b)   in the case of a claimant who has a partner–

    (i)   the claimant is in receipt of attendance allowance, or the care component of disability living allowance at the highest or middle rate prescribed in accordance with section 72(3) of the Act; and

    (ii)   his partner is also in receipt of such an allowance or, if he is a member of a polygamous marriage, all the partners of that marriage are in receipt of such an allowance; and

    (iii)   subject to sub-paragraph (4), the claimant has no non-dependants aged 18 or over normally residing with him or with whom he is normally residing,

and either a person is entitled to or in receipt of a carer's allowance in respect of caring for only one of a couple or, in the case of a polygamous marriage, for one or more but not all the partners of the marriage, or as the case may be, no person is entitled to and in receipt of such an allowance in respect of caring for either member of a couple or any partner of a polygamous marriage.

(3)   Where a claimant has a partner who does not satisfy the condition in sub-paragraph (2)(b)(ii), and that partner is blind or is treated as blind within the meaning of paragraph 13(1)(a)(v) and (2), that partner shall be treated for the purposes of sub-paragraph (2)(b)(ii) as if he were not a partner of the claimant.

(4)   For the purposes of sub-paragraph (2)(a)(ii) and (2)(b)(iii) no account shall be taken of–

(a)   a person receiving attendance allowance, or disability living allowance by virtue of the care component at the highest or middle rate prescribed in accordance with section 72(3) of the Act; or

(b)   a person who is blind or is treated as blind within the meaning of paragraph 13(1)(a)(v) and (2).

(5)   For the purposes of sub-paragraph (2)(b) a person shall be treated–

(a)   as being in receipt of attendance allowance, or the care component of disability living allowance at the highest or middle rate prescribed in accordance with section 72(3) of the Act, if he would, but for his being a patient for a period exceeding 28 days, be so in receipt;

(b)   as being entitled to and in receipt of a carer's allowance if he would, but for the person for whom he was caring being a patient in hospital for a period exceeding 28 days, be so entitled and in receipt.

(6)   For the purposes of sub-paragraph (2)(a)(iii) and (2)(b), no account shall be taken of an award of carer's allowance to the extent that payment of such an award is back-dated for a period before [¹ the date on which the award is first paid].

(7)   In sub-paragraph (2)(a)(iii) and (b), references to a person being in receipt of a carer's allowance shall include references to a person who would have been in receipt of that allowance but for the application of a restriction under section 7 of the Social Security Fraud Act 2001 (loss of benefit provisions).

Amendment

1.   Amended by reg 8(5) of SI 2007 No 719 as from 2.4.07.

Enhanced disability premium

15.–(1)   Subject to sub-paragraph (2), the condition is that the care component of disability living allowance is, or would, but for a suspension of benefit in accordance with regulations under section 113(2) of the Act or but for an abatement as a consequence of hospitalisation, be payable at the highest rate prescribed under section 72(3) of the Act in respect of–

(a)   the claimant; or

(b)   a member of the claimant's family,

who is aged less than 60.

(2)   An enhanced disability premium shall not be applicable in respect of–

(a)   a claimant who–

    (i)   is not a member of a couple or a polygamous marriage; and

    (ii)   is a patient within the meaning of [¹ regulation 18(11)(e)] (patients) and has been for a period of more than 52 weeks; or

(b)   a member of a couple or a polygamous marriage where each member is a patient within the meaning of [¹ regulation 18(11)(e)] and has been for a period of more than 52 weeks.

Amendment

1.   Amended by reg 3(11)(b) of SI 2005 No 2502 as amended by Sch 2 para 27 of SI 2006 No 217 as from 1.4.06.

Disabled Child Premium

16.   The condition is that a child or young person for whom the claimant or a partner of his is responsible and who is a member of the claimant's household–

(a)   is in receipt of disability living allowance or is no longer in receipt of such allowance because he is a patient, provided that the child or young person continues to be a member of the family; or

(b)   is blind or treated as blind within the meaning of paragraph 13; or

(c)   is a child or young person in respect of whom section 145A of the Act applies for the purposes of entitlement to child benefit but only for the period prescribed under section 145A(1) of the Act and in respect of whom a disabled child premium was included in the claimant's applicable amount immediately before the death of that child.

Carer Premium

17.–(1)   The condition is that the claimant or his partner is, or both of them are, entitled to a carer's allowance under section 70 of the Act.

(2)   Where a carer premium is awarded but–

(a)   the person in respect of whose care the carer's allowance has been awarded dies; or

(b)   in any other case the person in respect of whom a carer premium has been awarded ceases to be entitled to a carer's allowance,

the condition for the award of the premium shall be treated as satisfied for a period of eight weeks from the relevant date specified in sub-paragraph (3).

(3)   The relevant date for the purposes of sub-paragraph (2) shall be–

(a) where sub-paragraph (2)(a) applies, the Sunday following the death of the person in respect of whose care a carer's allowance has been awarded or the date of death if the death occurred on a Sunday;

(b) in any other case, the date on which the person who has been entitled to a carer's allowance ceases to be entitled to that allowance.

(4) Where a person who has been entitled to a carer's allowance ceases to be entitled to that allowance and makes a claim for council tax benefit, the condition for the award of the carer premium shall be treated as satisfied for a period of eight weeks from the date on which–

(a) the person in respect of whose care the carer's allowance has been awarded dies;

(b) in any other case, the person who has been entitled to a carer's allowance ceased to be entitled to that allowance.

Persons in receipt of concessionary payments

18. For the purpose of determining whether a premium is applicable to a person under paragraphs 13 to 17, any concessionary payment made to compensate that person for the non-payment of any benefit mentioned in those paragraphs shall be treated as if it were a payment of that benefit.

Persons in receipt of benefit for another

19. For the purposes of this Part of this Schedule, a person shall be regarded as being in receipt of any benefit if, and only if, it is paid in respect of him and shall be so regarded only for any period in respect of which that benefit is paid.

PART 4
Amounts of premiums specified in Part 3

Premium	*Amount*
20.–[⁴ (1)]	[⁴ (1)].
(2) Pensioner Premium for Persons aged under 75–	(2)
(a) where the claimant satisfies the condition in paragraph 9(a);	(a) [³ £59.90];
(b) where the claimant satisfies the condition in paragraph 9(b).	(b) [³ £88.90].
(3) Pensioner premium for persons aged 75 and over–	(3)
(a) where the claimant satisfies the condition in paragraph 10(a);	(a) [³ £59.90];
(b) where the claimant satisfies the condition in paragraph 10(b).	(b) [³ £88.90].
(4) Higher Pensioner Premium–	(4)
(a) where the claimant satisfies the condition in paragraph 11(1)(a) or (b);	(a) [³ £59.90];
(b) where the claimant satisfies the condition in paragraph 11(2)(a) or (b).	(b) [³ £88.90].
(5) Disability Premium–	(5)
(a) where the claimant satisfies the condition in paragraph 12(a) or (b);	(a) [³ £25.25];
(b) where the claimant satisfies the condition in paragraph 12(b).	(b) [³ £36.00].
(6) Severe Disability Premium–	(6)
(a) where the claimant satisfies the condition in paragraph 14(2)(a);	(a) [³ £48.45];
(b) where the claimant satisfies the condition in paragraph 14(2)(b)–	
(i) in a case where there is someone in receipt of carer's allowance or if he or any partner satisfies that condition only by virtue of paragraph 14(5);	(b) (i) [³ £48.45];
(ii) in a case where there is no one in receipt of such an allowance.	(b) (ii) [³ £96.90].
(7) Disabled Child Premium.	(7) [³ £46.69] in respect of each child or young person in respect of whom the condition specified in paragraph 16 of Part 3 of this Schedule is satisfied.

(8) Carer Premium.

(9) Enhanced Disability Premium where the conditions in paragraph 15 are satisfied.

(8) [³ £27.15] in respect of each person who satisfies the condition specified in paragraph 17.

(9)
    (a) [³ £18.76] in respect of each child or young person in respect of whom the conditions specified in paragraph 15 are satisfied;
    (b) [³ £12.30] in respect of each person who is neither–
       (i) a child or young person; nor
      (ii) a member of a couple or a polygamous marriage,
    in respect of whom the conditions specified in paragraph 15 are satisfied;
    (c) [³ £17.75] where the claimant is a member of a couple or a polygamous marriage and the conditions specified in paragraph 15 are satisfied in respect of a member of that couple or polygamous marriage.

Amendments

1.   Amended by Art 21(6) and Sch 11 of SI 2006 No 645 and reg 8 of SI 2006 No 217 as from 1.4.06.
2.   Confirmed by Art 21(6) and Sch 11 of SI 2007 No 688 as from 1.4.07.
3.   Amended by Art 21(6) and Sch 11 of SI 2007 No 688 as from 1.4.07.
4.   Revoked by reg 2 and the Sch of SI 2007 No 2618 as from 1.10.07.

SCHEDULE 2
REGULATION 62
Amount of alternative maximum council tax benefit

General Note

For ss13 and 80 and Sch 1 Local Government Finance Act 1992 see Part 6 of this book. See also the commentary to reg 62 on p620.

1.–(1) Subject to paragraphs 2 and 3, the alternative maximum council tax benefit in respect of a day for the purpose of regulation 62 shall be determined in accordance with the following Table and in this Table [¹ –

    (a)   ''second adult'' means any person or persons residing with the claimant to whom section 131(6) of the Act applies; and

    (b)   ''persons to whom regulation 45(2) applies'' includes any person to whom that regulation would apply were they, and their partner if they had one, below the qualifying age for state pension credit.]

(2) In this Schedule ''council tax due in respect of that day'' means the council tax payable under section 10 or 78 of the 1992 Act less [¹ –

    (a)   any reductions made in consequence of any enactment in, or under, the 1992 Act; and

    (b)   in a case to which sub-paragraph (c) in column (1) of the table below applies, the amount of any discount which may be appropriate to the dwelling under the 1992 Act.]

(1) *Second adult*	(2) *Alternative maximum council tax benefit*
(a) Where the second adult or all second adults are in receipt of income support or state pension credit or are persons on an income-based jobseeker's allowance;	(a) 25 per cent. of the council tax due in respect of that day;
(b) where the gross income of the second adult or, where there is more than one second adult, their aggregate gross income disregarding any income of persons on income support, state pension credit or an income-based jobseeker's allowance–	(b)
(i) is less than [⁴ £162.00] per week;	(i) 15 per cent. of the council tax due in respect of that day;

(ii) is not less than [⁴ £162.00] per week but less than [⁴ £210.00] per week.

(ii) 7.5 per cent. of the council tax due in respect of that day.

[² (c) Where the dwelling would be wholly occupied by one or more persons to whom regulation 45(2) applies but for the presence of one or more second adults who are in receipt of income support, state pension credit or are persons on an income-based jobseeker's allowance.

[² (c) 100 per cent. of the council tax due in respect of that day.

Amendments

1. Amended by reg 9(4)(a) and (b) of SI 2006 No 588 as from 1.4.06.
2. Inserted by reg 9(4)(c) of SI 2006 No 588 as from 1.4.06.
3. Amended by Art 21(7) of SI 2006 No 645 and reg 8 of SI 2006 No 217 as from 1.4.06.
4. Amended by Art 21(7) of SI 2007 No 688 as from 1.4.07.

General Note

The amount of the alternative maximum CTB is the relevant percentage (as set out in the table) of gross council tax liability minus the reductions and discounts listed in para 1(2). Note that this is not the same figure used for main CTB.

Para (a) of the table is self explanatory.

Under para (b) of the table, the combined gross income of all the second adults not on IS, income-based JSA or pension credit is used. Paras 2 and 3 provide for some gross income to be disregarded.

Para (c) of the table applies to dwellings which would be occupied wholly by students excluded from entitlement to main CTB but for the presence of one or more second adults on IS, income-based JSA or pension credit. Such a dwelling would not be exempt from council tax (as dwellings occupied wholly by students are), but the CTB claimant(s) will be entitled to 100 per cent alternative maximum CTB. For these purposes, someone counts as a student excluded from entitlement to main CTB if s/he would be so excluded were s/he (or her partner) under the qualifying age for pension credit (currently aged 60): para 1(1)(b). See the General Note to reg 45 where the non-student is liable for council tax on a dwelling shared with students.

---

2. In determining a second adult's gross income for the purposes of this Schedule, there shall be disregarded from that income–
    (a) any attendance allowance, or any disability living allowance under section 71 of the Act;
    (b) any payment made under the Trusts, the Fund, the Eileen Trust or the Independent Living Funds which had his income fallen to be calculated under regulation 30 (calculation of income other than earnings) would have been disregarded under paragraph 24 of Schedule 4 (income in kind); and
    (c) any payment which had his income fallen to be calculated under regulation 30 would have been disregarded under paragraph 36 of Schedule 4 (payments made under certain trusts and certain other payments).

3. Where there are two or more second adults residing with the claimant for benefit and any such second adult falls to be disregarded for the purposes of discount in accordance with Schedule 1 of the 1992 Act, his income shall be disregarded in determining the amount of any alternative maximum council tax benefit, unless that second adult is a member of a couple and his partner does not fall to be disregarded for the purposes of discount.

SCHEDULE 3
REGULATION 26(2) AND 28(2)
Sums to be disregarded in the calculation of earnings

1. In the case of a claimant who has been engaged in remunerative work as an employed earner or, had the employment been in Great Britain, would have been so engaged–
    (a) where–
        (i) the employment has been terminated because of retirement; and
        (ii) on retirement he is entitled to a retirement pension under the Act, or is not so entitled solely because of his failure to satisfy the contribution conditions,
    any earnings [¹ paid or due to be paid] in respect of that employment, but only for a period commencing on the day immediately after the date on which the employment was terminated;
    [¹ (b) where before the first day of entitlement to council tax benefit the employment has been terminated otherwise than because of retirement, any earnings paid or due to be paid in respect of that employment except–

       (i)   any payment of the nature described in regulation 25(1)(e), or

      (ii)   any award, sum or payment of the nature described in–

          (aa)   regulation 25(1)(g) or (h), or

          (bb)   section 34 or 70 of the Employment Rights Act 1996 (guarantee payments and suspension from work: complaints to employment tribunals),

including any payment made following the settlement of a complaint to an employment tribunal or of court proceedings;

(c)   where before the first day of entitlement to council tax benefit–

      (i)   the employment has not been terminated, but

      (ii)   the claimant is not engaged in remunerative work,

any earnings paid or due to be paid in respect of that employment except any payment or remuneration of the nature described in regulation 25(1)(e), (i) or (j).]

Amendment

1.   Amended by reg 13(9)(a) of SI 2618 No2 007 as from 1.10.07.

---

2.   In the case of a claimant who, before the [¹ first day of entitlement to council tax benefit] –

(a)   has been engaged in part-time employment as an employed earner or, where the employment has been outside Great Britain, would have been so engaged had the employment been in Great Britain; and

(b)   has ceased to be engaged in that employment, whether or not that employment has been terminated,

any earnings [¹ paid or due to be paid] in respect of that employment except–

      (i)   where that employment has been terminated, [¹ any payment of the nature described in regulation 25(1)(e)];

      (ii)   where that employment has not been terminated, [¹ any payment or remuneration of the nature described in regulation 25(1)(e), (i) or (j)].

Amendment

1.   Amended by reg 13(9)(b) of SI 2618 No2 007 as from 1.10.07.

3.–(1)   In a case to which this paragraph applies and paragraph 4 does not apply, £20; but notwithstanding regulation 15 (calculation of income and capital of members of a claimant's family and of a polygamous marriage) if this paragraph applies to a claimant it shall not apply to his partner except where, and to the extent that, the earnings of the claimant which are to be disregarded under this paragraph are less than £20.

(2)   This paragraph applies where the claimant's applicable amount includes an amount by way of the disability premium or severe disability premium under Schedule 1 (applicable amounts).

(3)   This paragraph applies where–

(a)   the claimant is a member of a couple and his applicable amount would, but for the higher pensioner premium under Schedule 1 being applicable include an amount by way of the disability premium under that Schedule; and

(b)   he or his partner is under the age of 60 and at least one is engaged in employment.

(4)   This paragraph applies where–

(a)   the claimant's applicable amount includes an amount by way of the higher pensioner premium under Schedule 1; and

(b)   the claimant or, if he is a member of a couple, either he or his partner has attained the age of 60; and

(c)   immediately before attaining that age he or, as the case may be, he or his partner was engaged in employment and the claimant was entitled by virtue of sub-paragraph (2) or (3) to a disregard of £20; and

(d)   he or, if he is a member of couple, he or his partner has continued in employment.

(5)   For the purposes of this paragraph, no account shall be taken of any period not exceeding eight consecutive weeks occurring on or after the date on which the claimant or, if he is a member of a couple, he or his partner attained the age of 60 during which either or both ceased to be engaged in employment or the claimant ceased to be entitled to any or all of the following benefits namely community charge benefit, council tax benefit or housing benefit.

4.   In a case where the claimant is a lone parent, £25.

5.–(1)   In a case to which neither paragraph 3 nor paragraph 4 applies to the claimant and, subject to sub-paragraph (2), where the claimant's applicable amount includes an amount by way of the carer premium under Schedule 1 (applicable amounts), £20 of the earnings of the person who is, or at any time in the preceding eight weeks was, in receipt of carer's allowance or treated in accordance with paragraph 17(2) of that Schedule as being in receipt of carer's allowance.

(2)   Where the carer premium is awarded in respect of the claimant and of any partner of his, their earnings shall for the purposes of this paragraph be aggregated, but the amount to be disregarded in accordance with sub-paragraph (1) shall not exceed £20 of the aggregated amount.

6.   Where the carer premium is awarded in respect of a claimant who is a member of a couple and whose earnings are less than £20, but is not awarded in respect of the other member of the couple, and that other member is engaged in an employment–

(a)   specified in paragraph 8(1), so much of the other member's earnings as would not when aggregated with the amount disregarded under paragraph 5 exceed £20;

(b)   other than one specified in paragraph 8(1), so much of the other member's earnings from such other employment up to £10 as would not when aggregated with the amount disregarded under paragraph 5 exceed £20.

7.   In a case where paragraphs 3, 5, 6 and 8 do not apply to the claimant and he is one of a couple and a member of that couple is in employment, £10; but, notwithstanding regulation 15 (calculation of income and capital of members of claimant's family and of a polygamous marriage), if this paragraph applies to a claimant it shall not apply to his partner except where, and to the extent that, the earnings of the claimant which are to be disregarded under this paragraph are less than £10.

8.–(1)   In a case where paragraphs 3, 4, 5 and 6 do not apply to the claimant, £20 of earnings derived from one or more employments as–

(a)   as a part-time fire-fighter employed by a fire and rescue authority constituted by a scheme under section 2 of the Fire and Rescue Services Act 2004 or a scheme to which section 4 of that Act applies;

(b)   a part-time fire-fighter employed by a fire and rescue authority (as defined in section 1 of the Fire (Scotland) Act 2005) or a joint fire and rescue board constituted by an amalgamation scheme made under section 2(1) of that Act;

(c)   an auxiliary coastguard in respect of coast rescue activities;

(d)   a person engaged part-time in the manning or launching of a life boat;

(e)   a member of any territorial or reserve force prescribed in Part I of Schedule 6 to the Social Security (Contributions) Regulations 2001;

but, notwithstanding regulation 15 (calculation of income and capital of members of claimant's family and of a polygamous marriage), if this paragraph applies to a claimant it shall not apply to his partner except to the extent specified in sub-paragraph (2).

(2)   If the claimant's partner is engaged in employment–

(a)   specified in sub-paragraph (1), so much of his earnings as would not in aggregate with the amount of the claimant's earnings disregarded under this paragraph exceed £20;

(b)   other than one specified in sub-paragraph (1), so much of his earnings from that employment up to £10 as would not in aggregate with the claimant's earnings disregarded under this paragraph exceed £20.

9.   Where the claimant is engaged in one of more employments specified in paragraph 8(1), but his earnings derived from such employments are less than £20 in any week and he is also engaged in any other employment so much of his earnings from that other employment, up to £5 if he is a single claimant, or up to £10 if he has a partner, as would not in aggregate with the amount of his earnings disregarded under paragraph 8 exceed £20.

10.   In a case to which none of the paragraphs 3 to 9 applies, £5.

11.   Any amount or the balance of any amount which would fall to be disregarded under paragraph 19 or 20 of Schedule 4 had the claimant's income which does not consist of earnings been sufficient to entitle him to the full disregard thereunder.

12.   Where a claimant is on income support or an income-based jobseeker's allowance, his earnings.

13.   Any earnings derived from employment which are payable in a country outside the United Kingdom for such period during which there is a prohibition against the transfer to the United Kingdom of those earnings.

14.   Where a payment of earnings is made in a currency other than Sterling, any banking charge or commission payable in converting that payment into Sterling.

15.   Any earnings of a child or young person.

16.–(1)   In a case where the claimant is a person who satisfies at least one of the conditions set out in sub-paragraph (2), and his net earnings equal or exceed the total of the amounts set out in sub-paragraph (3), the amount of his earnings that falls to be disregarded under paragraphs 3 to 10 of this Schedule shall be increased by [² £15.45].

(2)   The conditions of this sub-paragraph are that–

(a)   the claimant, or if he is a member of a couple, either the claimant or his partner, is a person to whom regulation 20(1)(c) of the Working Tax Credit Regulations applies; or

(b)   the claimant–

	(i)	is, or if he is a member of a couple, at least one member of that couple is aged at least 25 and is engaged in remunerative work for on average not less than 30 hours per week; or
	(ii)	is a member of a couple and–
	(aa)	at least one member of that couple, is engaged in remunerative work for on average not less than 16 hours per week; and
	(bb)	his applicable amount includes a family premium under paragraph 3 of Schedule 1; or
	(iii)	is a lone parent who is engaged in remunerative work for on average not less than 16 hours per week; or
	(iv)	is, or if he is a member of a couple, at least one member of that couple is engaged in remunerative work for on average not less than 16 hours per week; and–

		(aa)	the claimant's applicable amount includes a higher pensioner premium or a disability premium under paragraph 11 or 12 of Schedule 1 respectively; and
		(bb)	where he is a member of a couple, at least one member of that couple satisfies the qualifying conditions for the higher pensioner premium or disability premium referred to in sub-head (aa) above and is engaged in remunerative work for on average not less than 16 hours per week; or

(c) the claimant is, or if he has a partner, one of them is, a person to whom regulation 18(3) of the Working Tax Credit Regulations (eligibility for 50 plus element) applies, or would apply if an application for working tax credit were to be made in his case.

(3) The following are the amounts referred to in sub-paragraph (1)–

(a) the amount calculated as disregardable from the claimant's earnings under paragraphs 3 to 10 of this Schedule;

(b) the amount of child care charges calculated as deductible under regulation 17(1)(c); and

(c) [² £15.45].

(4) The provisions of regulation 6 shall apply in determining whether or not a person works for on average not less than 30 hours per week, but as if the reference to 16 hours in paragraph (1) of that regulation were a reference to 30 hours.

Amendments

1. Amended by Art 21(8) of SI 2006 No 645 and reg 8 of SI 2006 No 217 as from 1.4.06.
2. Amended by Art 21(8) of SI 2007 No 688 as from 1.4.07.

---

17. In this Schedule "part-time employment" means employment in which the person is engaged on average for less than 16 hours a week.

SCHEDULE 4
REGULATION 30(2)
Sums to be disregarded in the calculation of income other than earnings

Modifications

Para 37 is substituted by Sch 4 para 3(4) and paras 56A and 56B inserted by para 3(5) of the HB&CTB(CP) Regs in respect of claims for CTB by some refugees (see p1129).

A different version of para 56B is substituted for para 56B by Sch 4 para 4(4)(b) of the HB&CTB(CP) Regs for some CTB claimants who are refugees who claimed asylum on or before 2 April 2000 (see p1132). See also reg 7A and Sch A1 inserted by Sch 4 para 3 of the HB&CTB(CP) Regs.

Note that paras 56A and 56B lapsed by s12(2)(g) of the Asylum and Immigration (Treatment of Claimants, etc.) Act 2004 (for those recorded as refugees after 14.6.07).

---

1. Any amount paid by way of tax on income which is to be taken into account under regulation 30 (calculation of income other than earnings).

2. Any payment in respect of any expenses incurred or to be incurred by a claimant who is–

(a) engaged by a charitable or voluntary organisation, or

(b) volunteer,

if he otherwise derives no remuneration or profit from the employment and is not to be treated as possessing any earnings under regulation 32(8) (notional income).

3. In the case of employment as an employed earner, any payment in respect of expenses wholly, exclusively and necessarily incurred in the performance of the duties of the employment.

4. Where a claimant is on income support or an income-based jobseeker's allowance the whole of his income.

5. Where the claimant is a member of a joint-claim couple for the purposes of the Jobseekers Act and his partner is on an income-based jobseeker's allowance, the whole of the claimant's income.

6. Where the claimant, or the person who was the partner of the claimant on 31st March 2003, was entitled on that date to income support or an income-based jobseeker's allowance but ceased to be so entitled on or before 5th April 2003 by virtue only of regulation 13 of the Housing Benefit (General) Amendment (No. 3) Regulations 1999 as in force at that date, the whole of his income.

7. Any disability living allowance.

8. Any concessionary payment made to compensate for the non-payment of–

(a) any payment specified in paragraph 7 or 10;

(b) income support;

(c) an income-based jobseeker's allowance.

9. Any mobility supplement under article 26A of the Naval, Military and Air Forces etc (Disablement and Death) Service Pensions Order 1983 (including such a supplement by virtue of any other scheme or order) or under article 25A of the Personal Injuries (Civilians) Scheme 1983 or any payment intended to compensate for the non-payment of such a supplement.

10. Any attendance allowance.

11. Any payment to the claimant as holder of the Victoria Cross or of the George Cross or any analogous payment.

12.–(1) Any payment–

(a) by way of an education maintenance allowance made pursuant to–

    (i) regulations made under section 518 of the Education Act 1996 (payment of school expenses; grant of scholarships etc);

    (ii) regulations made under section 49 or 73(f) of the Education (Scotland) Act 1980 (power to assist persons to take advantage of educational facilities);

    (iii) directions made under sections 12(2)(c) and 21 of the Further and Higher Education (Scotland) Act 1992 (provision of financial assistance to students); or

(b) corresponding to such an education maintenance allowance, made pursuant to–

    (i) section 14 or section 181 of the Education Act 2002 (power of Secretary of State and National Assembly for Wales to give financial assistance for purposes related to education or childcare, and allowances in respect of education or training); or

    (ii) regulations made under section 181 of that Act.

(2) Any payment, other than a payment to which sub-paragraph (1) applies, made pursuant to–

(a) regulations made under section 518 of the Education Act 1996;

(b) regulations made under section 49 of the Education (Scotland) Act 1980; or

(c) directions made under sections 12(2)(c) and 21 of the Further and Higher Education (Scotland) Act 1992,

in respect of a course of study attended by a child or a young person or a person who is in receipt of an education maintenance allowance made pursuant to any provision specified in sub-paragraph (1).

13. Any payment made to the claimant by way of a repayment under regulation 11(2) of the Education (Teacher Student Loans) (Repayment etc) Regulations 2002.

14.–(1) Any payment made pursuant to section 2 of the 1973 Act or section 2 of the Enterprise and New Towns (Scotland) Act 1990 except a payment–

(a) made as a substitute for income support, a jobseeker's allowance, incapacity benefit or severe disablement allowance;

(b) of an allowance referred to in section 2(3) of the 1973 Act or section 2(5) of the Enterprise and New Towns (Scotland) Act 1990; or

(c) intended to meet the cost of living expenses which relate to any one or more of the items specified in sub-paragraph (2) whilst a claimant is participating in an education, training or other scheme to help him enhance his employment prospects unless the payment is a Career Development Loan paid pursuant to section 2 of the 1973 Act and the period of education or training or the scheme, which is supported by that loan, has been completed.

(2) The items specified in this sub-paragraph for the purposes of sub-paragraph (1)(c) are food, ordinary clothing or footwear, household fuel or rent of the claimant or, where the claimant is a member of a family, any other member of his family, or any council tax or water charges for which that claimant or member is liable.

15.–(1) Subject to sub-paragraph (2), any of the following payments–

(a) a charitable payment;

(b) a voluntary payment;

(c) a payment (not falling within sub-paragraph (a) or (b) above) from a trust whose funds are derived from a payment made in consequence of any personal injury to the claimant;

(d) a payment under an annuity purchased–

    (i) pursuant to any agreement or court order to make payments to the claimant; or

    (ii) from funds derived from a payment made,

in consequence of any personal injury to the claimant; or

(e) a payment (not falling within sub-paragraphs (a) to (d) received by virtue of any agreement or court order to make payments to the claimant in consequence of any personal injury to the claimant.

(2) Sub-paragraph (1) shall not apply to a payment which is made or due to be made by–

(a) a former partner of the claimant, or a former partner of any member of the claimant's family; or

(b) the parent of a child or young person where that child or young person is a member of the claimant's family.

16. Subject to paragraph 35, £10 of any of the following, namely–

(a) a war disablement pension (except insofar as such a pension falls to be disregarded under paragraph 9 or 10);

(b) a war widow's pension or war widower's pension;

(c) a pension payable to a person as a widow, widower or surviving civil partner under the Naval, Military and Air Forces etc. (Disablement and Death) Service Pensions Order 1983 insofar as that Order is made under the Naval and Marine Pay and Pensions Act 1865 or the Pensions and Yeomanry Pay Act 1884, or is made only under section 12(1) of the Social Security (Miscellaneous Provisions) Act 1977 and any power of Her Majesty otherwise than under an enactment to make provision about pensions for or in respect of persons who have been disabled or have died in consequence of service as members of the armed forces of the Crown;

(d) a guaranteed income payment;

(e) a payment made to compensate for the non-payment of such a pension or payment as is mentioned in any of the preceding sub-paragraphs;

(f) a pension paid by the government of a country outside Great Britain which is analogous to any of the pensions or payments mentioned in sub-paragraphs (a) to (d) above;

(g) pension paid to victims of National Socialist persecution under any special provision made by the law of the Federal Republic of Germany, or any part of it, or of the Republic of Austria.

17. Subject to paragraph 35, £15 of any–

(a) widowed mother's allowance paid pursuant to section 37 of the Act;

(b) widowed parent's allowance paid pursuant to section 39A of the Act.

18.–(1) Any income derived from capital to which the claimant is or is treated under regulation 41 (capital jointly held) as beneficially entitled but, subject to sub-paragraph (2), not income derived from capital disregarded under paragraphs 1, 2, 4, 8, 14 or 25 to 28 of Schedule 5.

(2) Income derived from capital disregarded under paragraphs 2, 4 or 25 to 28 of Schedule 5 but only to the extent of–

(a) any mortgage repayments made in respect of the dwelling or premises in the period during which that income accrued; or

(b) any council tax or water charges which the claimant is liable to pay in respect of the dwelling or premises and which are paid in the period during which that income accrued.

(3) The definition of ''water charges'' in regulation 2(1) shall apply to sub-paragraph (2) of this paragraph with the omission of the words ''in so far as such charges are in respect of the dwelling which a person occupies as his home''.

19. Where the claimant makes a parental contribution in respect of a student attending a course at an establishment in the United Kingdom or undergoing education in the United Kingdom, which contribution has been assessed for the purposes of calculating–

(a) under, or pursuant to regulations made under powers conferred by, sections 1 or 2 of the Education Act 1962 or section 22 of the Teaching and Higher Education Act 1998, that student's award;

(b) under regulations made in exercise of the powers conferred by section 49 of the Education (Scotland) Act 1980, that student's bursary, scholarship, or other allowance under that section or under regulations made in exercise of the powers conferred by section 73 of that Act of 1980, any payment to that student under that section; or

(c) the student's student loan,

an amount equal to the weekly amount of that parental contribution, but only in respect of the period for which that contribution is assessed as being payable.

20.–(1) Where the claimant is the parent of a student aged under 25 in advanced education who either–

(a) is not in receipt of any award, grant or student loan in respect of that education; or

(b) is in receipt of an award under section 2 of the Education Act 1962 (discretionary awards) or an award bestowed by virtue of the Teaching and Higher Education Act 1998, or regulations made thereunder, or a bursary, scholarship or other allowance under section 49(1) of the Education (Scotland) Act 1980, or a payment under section 73 of that Act of 1980,

and the claimant makes payments by way of a contribution towards the student's maintenance, other than a parental contribution falling within paragraph 19, an amount specified in sub-paragraph (2) in respect of each week during the student's term.

(2) For the purposes of sub-paragraph (1), the amount shall be equal to–

(a) the weekly amount of the payments; or

(b) the amount by way of a personal allowance for a single claimant under 25 less the weekly amount of any award, bursary, scholarship, allowance or payment referred to in sub-paragraph (1)(b),

whichever is less.

21. Any payment made to the claimant by a child or young person or a non-dependant.

22. Where the claimant occupies a dwelling as his home and the dwelling is also occupied by a person other than one to whom paragraph 21 or 23 refers and there is a contractual liability to make payments to the claimant in respect of the occupation of the dwelling by that person or a member of his family–

(a) £4 of the aggregate of any payments made in respect of any one week in respect of the occupation of the dwelling by that person or a member of his family, or by that person and a member of his family; and

(b) a further [² £15.45], where the aggregate of any such payments is inclusive of an amount for heating.

Amendments

1. Amended by Art 21(9)(a) of SI 2006 No 645 and reg 8 of SI 2006 No 217 as from 1.4.06.
2. Amended by Art 21(9)(a) of SI 2007 No 688 as from 1.4.07.

23.–(1) Where the claimant occupies a dwelling as his home and he provides in that dwelling board and lodging accommodation, an amount, in respect of each person for which such accommodation is provided for the whole or any part of a week, equal to–

(a) where the aggregate of any payments made in respect of any one week in respect of such accommodation provided to such person does not exceed £20.00, 100 per cent. of such payments;

(b) where the aggregate of any such payments exceeds £20.00, £20.00 and 50 per cent. of the excess over £20.00.

(2) In this paragraph, "board and lodging accommodation" means accommodation provided to a person or, if he is a member of a family, to him or any other member of his family, for a charge which is inclusive of the provision of that accommodation and at least some cooked or prepared meals which both are cooked or prepared (by a person other than the person to whom the accommodation is provided or a member of his family) and are consumed in that accommodation or associated premises.

24.–(1) Any income in kind, except where regulation 30(11)(b) (provision of support under section 95 or 98 of the Immigration and Asylum Act in the calculation of income other than earnings) applies.

(2) The reference in sub-paragraph (1) to "income in kind" does not include a payment to a third party made in respect of the claimant which is used by the third party to provide benefits in kind to the claimant.

25. Any income which is payable in a country outside the United Kingdom for such period during which there is a prohibition against the transfer to the United Kingdom of that income.

26.–(1) Any payment made to the claimant in respect of a person who is a member of his family–

(a) pursuant to regulations under section 2(6)(b), 3 or 4 of the Adoption and Children Act 2002 or in accordance or with a scheme approved by the Scottish Ministers under section 51 of the Adoption (Scotland) Act 1978 (schemes for payments of allowances to adopters);

(b) which is a payment made by a local authority in pursuance of section 15(1) of, and paragraph 15 of Schedule 1 to, the Children Act 1989 (local authority contribution to a child's maintenance where the child is living with a person as a result of a residence order) or, as the case may be, section 50 of the Children Act 1975 (payment towards maintenance of children);

(c) which is a payment made by an authority, as defined in Article 2 of the Children Order, in pursuance of Article 15 of, and paragraph 17 of Schedule 1 to, that Order (contribution by an authority to child's maintenance);

(d) in accordance with regulations made pursuant to section 14F of the Children Act 1989 (special guardianship support services);

to the extent specified in sub-paragraph (3).

(2) Any payment, other than a payment to which sub-paragraph (1)(a) applies, made to the claimant pursuant to regulations under section 2(6)(b), 3 or 4 of the Adoption and Children Act 2002.

(3) In the case of a child or young person, so much of the weekly amount of the payment as exceeds the amount included under Schedule 1 in the calculation of the claimant's applicable amount for that child or young person by way of the personal allowance and disabled child premium, if any.

27. Any payment made by a local authority to the claimant with whom a person is accommodated by virtue of arrangements made under section 23(2)(a) of the Children Act 1989 or, as the case may be, section 26 of the Children (Scotland) Act 1995 or by a voluntary organisation under section 59(1)(a) of the Children Act 1989 or by a [¹ local authority under regulation 9 of the Fostering of Children (Scotland) Regulations 1996 (payment of allowances)].

Amendment

1.   Amended by reg 17(5) of SI 2006 No 2378 as from 2.10.06.

---

28.   Any payment made to the claimant or his partner for a person (''the person concerned''), who is not normally a member of the claimant's household but is temporarily in his care, by–

(a)   a health authority;

(b)   a local authority but excluding payments of housing benefit made in respect of the person concerned;

(c)   a voluntary organisation;

(d)   the person concerned pursuant to section 26(3A) of the National Assistance Act 1948; or

(e)   a primary care trust established under section 16A of the National Health Service Act 1977.

29.   Any payment made by a local authority in accordance with section 17, 23C or 24A of the Children Act 1989 or, as the case may be, section 12 of the Social Work (Scotland) Act 1968 or section 29 or 30 of the Children (Scotland) Act 1995 (provision of services for children and their families and advice and assistance to certain children).

30.–(1)   Subject to sub-paragraph (2), any payment received under an insurance policy taken out to insure against the risk of being unable to maintain repayments–

(a)   on a loan which is secured on the dwelling which the claimant occupies as his home; or

(b)   under a regulated agreement as defined for the purposes of the Consumer Credit Act 1974 or under a hire-purchase agreement or a conditional sale agreement as defined for the purposes of Part 3 of the Hire-Purchase Act 1964.

(2)   A payment referred to in sub-paragraph (1) shall only be disregarded to the extent that the payment received under that policy does not exceed the amounts, calculated on a weekly basis, which are used to–

(a)   maintain the repayments referred to in sub-paragraph (1)(a) or, as the case may be, (b); and

(b)   meet any amount due by way of premiums on–

(i)   that policy; or

(ii)   in a case to which sub-paragraph (1)(a) applies, an insurance policy taken out to insure against loss or damage to any building or part of a building which is occupied by the claimant as his home and which is required as a condition of the loan referred to in sub-paragraph (1)(a).

31.   Any payment of income which by virtue of regulation 36 (income treated as capital) is to be treated as capital.

32.   Any social fund payment made pursuant to Part 8 of the Act (the Social Fund).

33.   Any payment under section 148 of the Act (Christmas bonus for pensioners).

34.   Where a payment of income is made in a currency other than sterling, any banking charge or commission payable in converting that payment into sterling.

35.   The total of a claimant's income or, if he is a member of a family, the family's income and the income of any person which he is treated as possessing under regulation 15(2) (calculation of income and capital of members of claimant's family and of a polygamous marriage) to be disregarded under regulation 47(2)(b) and regulation 48(1)(d) (calculation of covenant income where a contribution assessed, covenant income where no grant income or no contribution is assessed), regulation 51(2) (treatment of student loans), regulation 52(3) (treatment of payments from access funds) and paragraphs 16 and 17 shall in no case exceed £20 per week.

36.–(1)   Any payment made under any of the Trusts, the Fund, the Eileen Trust or the Independent Living Funds.

(2)   Any payment by or on behalf of a person who is suffering or who suffered from haemophilia or who is or was a qualifying person, which derives from a payment made under any of the Trusts to which sub-paragraph (1) refers and which is made to or for the benefit of–

(a)   that person's partner or former partner from whom he is not, or where that person has died was not, estranged or divorced or with whom he has formed a civil partnership that has not been dissolved or, where that person has died, had not been dissolved at the time of that person's death;

(b)   any child who is a member of that person's family or who was such a member and who is a member of the claimant's family; or

(c)   any young person who is a member of that person's family or who was such a member and who is a member of the claimant's family.

(3)   Any payment by or on behalf of the partner or former partner of a person who is suffering or who suffered from haemophilia or who is or was a qualifying person provided that the partner or former partner and that person are not, or if either of them has died were not, estranged or divorced or, where the partner or former partner and that person have formed a civil partnership, the civil partnership has not

been dissolved or, if either of them has died, had not been dissolved at the time of the death, which derives from a payment made under any of the Trusts to which sub-paragraph (1) refers and which is made to or for the benefit of–

(a)   the person who is suffering from haemophilia or who is a qualifying person;

(b)   any child who is a member of that person's family or who was such a member and who is a member of the claimant's family; or

(c)   any young person who is a member of that person's family or who was such a member and who is a member of the claimant's family.

(4)   Any payment by a person who is suffering from haemophilia or who is a qualifying person, which derives from a payment under any of the Trusts to which sub-paragraph (1) refers, where–

(a)   that person has no partner or former partner from whom he is not estranged or divorced or with whom he has formed a civil partnership that has not been dissolved, nor any child or young person who is or had been a member of that person's family; and

(b)   the payment is made either–

(i)   to that person's parent or step-parent, or

(ii)   where that person at the date of the payment is a child, a young person or a student who has not completed his full-time education and has no parent or step-parent, to his guardian,

but only for a period from the date of the payment until the end of two years from that person's death.

(5)   Any payment out of the estate of a person who suffered from haemophilia or who was a qualifying person, which derives from a payment under any of the Trusts to which sub-paragraph (1) refers, where–

(a)   that person at the date of his death (the relevant date) had no partner or former partner from whom he was not estranged or divorced or with whom he has formed a civil partnership that has not been dissolved, nor any child or young person who was or had been a member of his family; and

(b)   the payment is made either–

(i)   to that person's parent or step-parent, or

(ii)   where that person at the relevant date was a child, a young person or a student who had not completed his full-time education and had no parent or step-parent, to his guardian,

but only for a period of two years from the relevant date.

(6)   In the case of a person to whom or for whose benefit a payment referred to in this paragraph is made, any income which derives from any payment of income or capital made under or deriving from any of the Trusts.

(7)   For the purposes of sub-paragraphs (2) to (6), any reference to the Trusts shall be construed as including a reference to the Fund, the Eileen Trust, the Skipton Fund and the London Bombings Relief Charitable Fund.

Modifications

References to "step-parent" in sub-paras (4)(b)(i) and (ii) and (5)(b)(i) and (ii) are modified by s246 of the Civil Partnership Act 2004 (see p1046) and art 3 and para 45 of the Schedule to SI 2005 No 3137 (see p1097).

---

37.   Any housing benefit.

38.   Any payment made by the Secretary of State to compensate for the loss (in whole or in part) of entitlement to housing benefit.

39.   Any payment made by the Secretary of State to compensate for the loss of housing benefit supplement under regulation 19 of the Supplementary Benefit (Requirements) Regulations 1983.

40.   Any resettlement benefit which is paid to the claimant by virtue of regulation 3 of the Social Security (Hospital In-Patients) Amendment (No. 2) Regulations 1987.

41.   Any payment to a juror or witness in respect of attendance at a court other than compensation for loss of earnings or for the loss of a benefit payable under the benefit Acts.

42.   Any community charge benefit.

43.   Any payment in consequence of a reduction of council tax under section 13 or, as the case may be, section 80 of the 1992 Act (reduction of liability for council tax).

44.   Any special war widows payment made under–

(a)   the Naval and Marine Pay and Pensions (Special War Widows Payment) Order 1990 made under section 3 of the Naval and Marine Pay and Pensions Act 1865;

(b)   the Royal Warrant dated 19th February 1990 amending the Schedule to the Army Pensions Warrant 1977;

(c)   the Queen's Order dated 26th February 1990 made under section 2 of the Air Force (Constitution) Act 1917;

(d)   the Home Guard War Widows Special Payments Regulations 1990 made under section 151 of the Reserve Forces Act 1980;

(e)   the Orders dated 19th February 1990 amending Orders made on 12th December 1980 concerning the Ulster Defence Regiment made in each case under section 140 of the Reserve Forces Act 1980;

and any analogous payment made by the Secretary of State for Defence to any person who is not a person entitled under the provisions mentioned in sub-paragraphs (a) to (e) of this paragraph.

45.–(1)   Any payment or repayment made–

(a)   as respects England and Wales, under regulation 3, 5 or 8 of the National Health Service (Travelling Expenses and Remission of Charges) Regulations 1988 (travelling expenses and health service supplies);

(b)   as respects Scotland, under regulation 3, 5 or 8 of the National Health Service (Travelling Expenses and Remission of Charges) (Scotland) Regulations 1988 (travelling expenses and health service supplies).

(2)   Any payment or repayment made by the Secretary of State for Health, Scottish Ministers or the National Assembly for Wales, which is analogous to a payment or repayment mentioned in sub-paragraph (1).

46.   Any payment made under regulation 6, 8, 12 or 14(2) of the Welfare Food Regulations 1988 (payments made in place of milk tokens or the supply of vitamins).

47.   Any payment made by either the Secretary of State for [¹ Justice] or by the Secretary of State for Scotland under a scheme established to assist relatives and other persons to visit persons in custody.

Amendment

1.   Amended by Art 8 and the Sch para 24 of SI 2007 No 2128 as from 22.8.07.

48.–(1)   Where a claimant's applicable amount includes an amount by way of a family premium, £15 of any payment of maintenance, whether under a court order or not, which is made or due to be made by–

(a)   the claimant's former partner, or the claimant's partner's former partner; or

(b)   the parent of a child or young person where that child or young person is a member of the claimant's family except where that parent is the claimant or the claimant's partner.

(2)   For the purposes of sub-paragraph (1), where more than one maintenance payment falls to be taken into account in any week, all such payments shall be aggregated and treated as if they were a single payment.

(3)   A payment made by the Secretary of State in lieu of maintenance shall, for the purposes of sub-paragraph (1), be treated as a payment of maintenance made by a person specified in head (a) or (b) of that sub-paragraph.

49.   Any payment made by the Secretary of State to compensate a person who was entitled to supplementary benefit in respect of a period ending immediately before 11th April 1988 but who did not become entitled to income support in respect of a period beginning with that day.

50.   Any payment (other than a training allowance) made, whether by the Secretary of State or any other person, under the Disabled Persons (Employment) Act 1944 to assist disabled persons to obtain or retain employment despite their disability.

51.   Any guardian's allowance.

52.–(1)   Where the claimant is in receipt of any benefit under Parts 2, 3 or 5 of the Act or pension under the Naval, Military and Air Forces etc. (Disablement and Death) Service Pensions Order 1983, any increase in the rate of that benefit arising under Part 4 (increases for dependants) or section 106(a) (unemployability supplement) of the Act or the rate of that pension under that Order where the dependant in respect of whom the increase is paid is not a member of the claimant's family.

(2) For the purposes of sub-paragraph (1), an addition to a contribution-based jobseeker's allowance under regulation 10(4) of the Jobseeker's Allowance (Transitional Provisions) Regulations 1996 shall be treated as an increase of a benefit under the Act arising under Part 4 of the Act.

53.   Any supplementary pension under article 29(1A) of the Naval, Military and Air Forces etc. (Disablement and Death) Service Pensions Order 1983 (pensions to widows, widowers or surviving civil partners).

54.   In the case of a pension awarded at the supplementary rate under article 27(3) of the Personal Injuries (Civilians) Scheme 1983 (pensions to widows, widowers or surviving civil partners), the sum specified in paragraph 1(c) of Schedule 4 to that Scheme.

55.–(1)   Any payment which is–

(a)   made under any of the Dispensing Instruments to a widow, widower or surviving civil partner of a person–

    (i)   whose death was attributable to service in a capacity analogous to service as a member of the armed forces of the Crown; and

    (ii)   whose service in such capacity terminated before 31st March 1973; and

(b)   equal to the amount specified in article 29(1A) of the Naval, Military and Air Forces etc. (Disablement and Death) Service Pensions Order 1983 (pensions to widows, widowers or surviving civil partners).

(2)   In this paragraph "the Dispensing Instruments" means the Order in Council of 19th December 1881, the Royal Warrant of 27th October 1884 and the Order by His Majesty of 14th January 1922 (exceptional grants of pay, non-effective pay and allowances).

56.   Except in a case which falls under sub-paragraph (1) of paragraph 16 of Schedule 3, where the claimant is a person who satisfies any of the conditions of sub-paragraph (2) of that paragraph, any amount of working tax credit up to [² £15.45].

Amendments
1.   Amended by Art 21(9)(b) of SI 2006 No 645 and reg 8 of SI 2006 No 217 as from 1.4.06.
2.   Amended by Art 21(9)(b) of SI 2007 No 688 as from 1.4.07.

---

57.   Any payment made under the Community Care (Direct Payments) Act 1996 or under section 12B of the Social Work (Scotland) Act 1968 or under regulations made under section 57 of the Health and Social Care Act 2001 (direct payments).

58.–(1)   Subject to sub-paragraph (2), in respect of a person who is receiving, or who has received, assistance under the self-employment route, any payment to that person–
   (a)   to meet expenses wholly and necessarily incurred whilst carrying on the commercial activity;
   (b)   which is used or intended to be used to maintain repayments on a loan taken out by that person for the purpose of establishing or carrying on the commercial activity,
in respect of which such assistance is or was received.

(2)   Sub-paragraph (1) shall apply only in respect of payments which are paid to that person from the special account as defined for the purposes of Chapter 4A of Part 8 of the Jobseeker's Allowance Regulations.

59.–(1)   Any payment of a sports award except to the extent that it has been made in respect of any one or more of the items specified in sub-paragraph (2).

(2)   The items specified for the purposes of sub-paragraph (1) are food, ordinary clothing or footwear, household fuel or rent of the claimant or where the claimant is a member of a family, any other member of his family, or any council tax or water charges for which that claimant or member is liable.

(3)   For the purposes of sub-paragraph (2) "food" does not include vitamins, minerals or other special dietary supplements intended to enhance the performance of the person in the sport in respect of which the award was made.

60.   Where the amount of subsistence allowance paid to a person in a benefit week exceeds the amount of income-based jobseeker's allowance that person would have received in that benefit week had it been payable to him, less 50p, that excess amount.

61.   In the case of a claimant participating in an employment zone programme, any discretionary payment made by an employment zone contractor to the claimant, being a fee, grant, loan or otherwise.

62.   Any discretionary housing payment paid pursuant to regulation 2(1) of the Discretionary Financial Assistance Regulations 2001.

63.–(1)   Any payment made by a local authority or by the National Assembly for Wales, to or on behalf of the claimant or his partner relating to a service which is provided to develop or sustain the capacity of the claimant or his partner to live independently in his accommodation.

(2)   For the purposes of sub-paragraph (1) "local authority" includes, in England, a county council.

64.   Where a claimant receives income under an annuity purchased with a loan which satisfies the following conditions–
   (a)   that the loan was made as part of a scheme under which not less than 90 per cent. of the proceeds of the loan were applied to the purchase by the person to whom it was made of an annuity ending with his life or with the life of the survivor of two or more persons (in this paragraph referred to as "the annuitants") who include the person to whom the loan was made;
   (b)   that the interest on the loan is payable by the person to whom it was made or by one of the annuitants;
   (c)   that at the time the loan was made the person to whom it was made or each of the annuitants had attained the age of 65;
   (d)   that the loan was secured on a dwelling in Great Britain and the person to whom the loan was made or one of the annuitants owns an estate or interest in that dwelling; and
   (e)   that the person to whom the loan was made or one of the annuitants occupies the dwelling on which it was secured as his home at the time the interest is paid,
the amount, calculated on a weekly basis, equal to–
      (i)   where, or insofar as, section 369 of the Income and Corporation Taxes Act 1988 (mortgage interest payable under deduction of tax) applies to the payments of interest on the loan, the interest which is payable after deduction of a sum equal to income tax on such payments at the applicable percentage of income tax within the meaning of section 369(1A) of that Act;

(ii) in any other case the interest which is payable on the loan without deduction of such a sum.

SCHEDULE 5
REGULATION 34(2)
Capital to be disregarded

Modifications

Paras 53A and 53B are inserted by Sch 4 para 3(6)of the HB&CTB(CP) Regs in respect of claims for CTB by some refugees (see p1129).

A different version of para 53B is substituted for para 53B by Sch 4 para 4(4)(c) of the HB&CTB(CP) Regs for some CTB claimants who are refugees who claimed asylum on or before 2 April 2000 (see p1132). See also reg 7A and Sch A1 inserted by Sch 4 para 3 of the HB&CTB(CP) Regs (p1132).

Note that paras 53A and 53B lapsed by s12(2)(g) of the Asylum and Immigration (Treatment of Claimants, etc.) Act 2004 (for those recorded as refugees after 14.6.07).

1.   The dwelling together with any garage, garden and outbuildings, normally occupied by the claimant as his home including any premises not so occupied which it is impracticable or unreasonable to sell separately, in particular any croft land on which the dwelling is situated; but, notwithstanding regulation 15 (calculation of income and capital of members of claimant's family and of a polygamous marriage), only one dwelling shall be disregarded under this paragraph.

2.   Any premises acquired for occupation by the claimant which he intends to occupy as his home within 26 weeks of the date of acquisition or such longer period as is reasonable in the circumstances to enable the claimant to obtain possession and commence occupation of the premises.

3.   Any sum directly attributable to the proceeds of sale of any premises formerly occupied by the claimant as his home which is to be used for the purchase of other premises intended for such occupation within 26 weeks of the date of sale or such longer period as is reasonable in the circumstances to enable the claimant to complete the purchase.

4.   Any premises occupied in whole or in part–

(a)   by a partner or relative of a single claimant or any member of the family as his home where that person is either aged 60 or over or incapacitated;

(b)   by the former partner of the claimant as his home; but this provision shall not apply where the former partner is a person from whom the claimant is estranged or divorced or with whom he had formed a civil partnership that has been dissolved.

5.   Where a claimant is on income support or an income-based jobseeker's allowance, the whole of his capital.

6.   Where the claimant is a member of a joint-claim couple for the purposes of the Jobseekers Act 1995 and his partner is on income-based jobseeker's allowance, the whole of the claimant's capital.

7.   Any future interest in property of any kind, other than land or premises in respect of which the claimant has granted a subsisting lease or tenancy, including sub-leases or sub-tenancies.

8.–(1)   The assets of any business owned in whole or in part by the claimant and for the purposes of which he is engaged as a self-employed earner, or if he has ceased to be so engaged, for such period as may be reasonable in the circumstances to allow for disposal of any such asset.

(2)   The assets of any business owned in whole or in part by the claimant where–

(a)   he is not engaged as a self-employed earner in that business by reason of some disease or bodily or mental disablement; but

(b)   he intends to become engaged or, as the case may be, re-engaged as a self-employed earner in that business as soon as he recovers or is able to become engaged or re-engaged in that business;

for a period of 26 weeks from the date on which the claim for council tax benefit is made, or is treated as made, or, if it is unreasonable to expect him to become engaged or re-engaged in that business within that period, for such longer period as is reasonable in the circumstances to enable him to become so engaged or re-engaged.

(3)   In the case of a person who is receiving assistance under the self-employment route, the assets acquired by that person for the purpose of establishing or carrying on the commercial activity in respect of which such assistance is being received.

(4)   In the case of a person who has ceased carrying on the commercial activity in respect of which assistance was received as specified in sub-paragraph (3), the assets relating to that activity for such period as may be reasonable in the circumstances to allow for disposal of any such asset.

9.–(1)   Subject to sub-paragraph (2), any arrears of, or any concessionary payment made to compensate for arrears due to the non-payment of–

(a)   any payment specified in paragraphs 7, 9 or 10 of Schedule 4;

(b)   an income-related benefit or supplementary benefit, family income supplement under the Family Income Supplement Act 1970, working families' tax credit under section 128 of the Act, disabled person's tax credit under section 129 of the Act, or housing benefit under Part 2 of the Social Security and Housing Benefits Act 1982;

(c)   an income-based jobseeker's allowance;

(d)   any discretionary housing payment paid pursuant to regulation 2(1) of the Discretionary Financial Assistance Regulations 2001;

(e)   working tax credit and child tax credit [¹],

but only for a period of 52 weeks from the date of the receipt of arrears or of the concessionary payment.

(2)   In a case where the total of any arrears and, if appropriate, any concessionary payment referred to in sub-paragraph (1) relating to one of the specified payments, benefits or allowances amounts to £5,000 or more (referred to in this sub-paragraph and in sub-paragraph (3) as "the relevant sum") and is–

(a)   paid in order to rectify or to compensate for, an official error as defined in regulation 1(2) of the Decisions and Appeals Regulations; and

(b)   received by the claimant in full on or after 14th October 2001,

sub-paragraph (1) shall have effect in relation to such arrears or concessionary payment either for a period of 52 weeks from the date of receipt, or, if the relevant sum is received in its entirety during the award of council tax benefit, for the remainder of that award if that is a longer period.

(3)   For the purposes of sub-paragraph (2), "the award of council tax benefit" means–

(a)   the award in which the relevant sum is first received (or the first part thereof where it is paid in more than one instalment); and

(b)   where that award is followed by one or more further awards which, or each of which, begins immediately after the end of the previous award, such further award provided that for that further award the claimant–

(i)   is the person who received the relevant sum; or

(ii)   is the partner of the person who received the relevant sum, or was that person's partner at the date of his death.

Amendment

1.   Amended by reg 3(13) of SI 2005 No 2502 as amended by Sch 2 para 27 of SI 2006 No 217 as from 1.4.06.

---

10.   Any sum–

(a)   paid to the claimant in consequence of damage to, or loss of the home or any personal possession and intended for its repair or replacement; or

(b)   acquired by the claimant (whether as a loan or otherwise) on the express condition that it is to be used for effecting essential repairs or improvement to the home,

which is to be used for the intended purpose, for a period of 26 weeks from the date on which it was so paid or acquired or such longer period as is reasonable in the circumstances to effect the repairs, replacement or improvement.

11.   Any sum–

(a)   deposited with a housing association as defined in section 1(1) of the Housing Associations Act 1985 or section 338(1) of the Housing (Scotland) Act 1987 as a condition of occupying the home;

(b)   which was so deposited and which is to be used for the purchase of another home, for the period of 26 weeks or such longer period as may be reasonable in the circumstances to enable the claimant to complete the purchase.

12.   Any personal possessions except those which have been acquired by the claimant with the intention of reducing his capital in order to secure entitlement to council tax benefit or to increase the amount of that benefit.

13.   The value of the right to receive any income under an annuity or the surrender value (if any) of such an annuity.

14.   Where the funds of a trust are derived from a payment made in consequence of any personal injury to the claimant [¹ or claimant's partner], the value of the trust fund and the value of the right to receive any payment under that trust.

Amendment

1.   Amended by reg 17(6)(a) of SI 2006 No 2378 from the first day of the first benefit week to commence on or after 2.10.06.

[¹**14A.**–(1)   Any payment made to the claimant or the claimant's partner in consequence of any personal injury to the claimant or, as the case may be, the claimant's partner.

(2)   But sub-paragraph (1)–

    (a)   applies only for the period of 52 weeks beginning with the day on which the claimant first receives any payment in consequence of that personal injury;

    (b)   does not apply to any subsequent payment made to him in consequence of that injury (whether it is made by the same person or another);

    (c)   ceases to apply to the payment or any part of the payment from the day on which the claimant no longer possesses it;

    (d)   does not apply to any payment from a trust where the funds of the trust are derived from a payment made in consequence of any personal injury to the claimant.

    (3)   For the purposes of sub-paragraph (2)(c), the circumstances in which a claimant no longer possesses a payment or a part of it include where the claimant has used a payment or part of it to purchase an asset.

    (4)   References in sub-paragraphs (2) and (3) to the claimant are to be construed as including references to his partner (where applicable).]

Amendment

    1.   Inserted by reg 17(6)(b) of SI 2006 No 2378 from the first day of the first benefit week to commence on or after 2.10.06.

---

    15.   The value of the right to receive any income under a life interest or from a life rent.

    16.   The value of the right to receive any income which is disregarded under paragraph 13 of Schedule 3 or paragraph 25 of Schedule 4.

    17.   The surrender value of any policy of life insurance.

    18.   Where any payment of capital falls to be made by instalments, the value of the right to receive any outstanding instalments.

    19.   Any payment made by a local authority in accordance with section 17, 23C or 24A of the Children Act 1989 or, as the case may be, section 12 of the Social Work (Scotland) Act 1968 or sections 28 or 30 of the Children (Scotland) Act 1995 (provision of services for children and their families and advice and assistance to certain children).

    20.   Any social fund payment made pursuant to Part 8 of the Act.

    21.   Any refund of tax which falls to be deducted under section 369 of the Income and Corporation Taxes Act 1988 (deduction of tax from certain loan interest) on a payment of relevant loan interest for the purpose of acquiring an interest in the home or carrying out repairs or improvements to the home.

    22.   Any capital which by virtue of regulation 31 or 51 (capital treated as income, treatment of student loans) is to be treated as income.

    23.   Where any payment of capital is made in a currency other than sterling, any banking charge or commission payable in converting that payment into sterling.

    24.–(1)   Any payment made under the Trusts, the Fund, the Eileen Trust, the Independent Living Funds, the Skipton Funds or the London Bombings Relief Fund.

    (2)   Any payment by or on behalf of a person who is suffering or who suffered from haemophilia or who is or was a qualifying person, which derives from a payment made under any of the Trusts to which sub-paragraph (1) refers and which is made to or for the benefit of–

    (a)   that person's partner or former partner from whom he is not, or where that person has died was not, estranged or divorced or with whom he has formed a civil partnership that has not been dissolved or, where that person has died, had not been dissolved at the time of that person's death;

    (b)   any child who is a member of that person's family or who was such a member and who is a member of the claimant's family; or

    (c)   any young person who is a member of that person's family or who was such a member and who is a member of the claimant's family.

    (3)   Any payment by or on behalf of the partner or former partner of a person who is suffering or who suffered from haemophilia or who is or was a qualifying person provided that the partner or former partner and that person are not, or if either of them has died were not, estranged or divorced or, where the partner or former partner and that person have formed a civil partnership, the civil partnership has not been dissolved or, if either of them has died, had not been dissolved at the time of the death, which derives from a payment made under any of the Trusts to which sub-paragraph (1) refers and which is made to or for the benefit of–

    (a)   the person who is suffering from haemophilia or who is a qualifying person;

    (b)   any child who is a member of that person's family or who was such a member and who is a member of the claimant's family; or

    (c)   any young person who is a member of that person's family or who was such a member and who is a member of the claimant's family.

    (4)   Any payment by a person who is suffering from haemophilia or who is a qualifying person, which derives from a payment under any of the Trusts to which sub-paragraph (1) refers, where–

(a)   that person has no partner or former partner from whom he is not estranged or divorced or with whom he has formed a civil partnership that has not been dissolved, nor any child or young person who is or had been a member of that person's family; and

(b)   the payment is made either–

     (i)   to that person's parent or step-parent; or

     (ii)   where that person at the date of the payment is a child, a young person or a student who has not completed his full-time education and has no parent or step-parent, to his guardian,

but only for a period from the date of the payment until the end of two years from that person's death.

(5)   Any payment out of the estate of a person who suffered from haemophilia or who was a qualifying person, which derives from a payment under any of the Trusts to which sub-paragraph (1) refers, where–

(a)   that person at the date of his death (the relevant date) had no partner or former partner from whom he was not estranged or divorced or with whom he had formed a civil partnership that had not been dissolved, nor any child or young person who was or had been a member of his family; and

(b)   the payment is made either–

     (i)   to that person's parent or step-parent; or

     (ii)   where that person at the relevant date was a child, a young person or a student who had not completed his full-time education and had no parent or step-parent, to his guardian,

but only for a period of two years from the relevant date.

(6)   In the case of a person to whom or for whose benefit a payment referred to in this paragraph is made, any capital resource which derives from any payment of income or capital made under or deriving from any of the Trusts.

(7)   For the purposes of sub-paragraphs (2) to (6), any reference to the Trusts shall be construed as including a reference to the Fund, the Eileen Trust, the Skipton Fund, and the London Bombings Relief Charitable Fund.

Modifications

References to "step-parent" in sub-paras (4)(b)(i) and (ii) and (5)(b)(i) and (ii) are modified by s246 of the Civil Partnership Act 2004 (see p1046) and art 3 and para 46 of the Schedule to SI 2005 No 3137 (see p1097).

25.–(1)   Where a claimant has ceased to occupy what was formerly the dwelling occupied as the home following his estrangement or divorce from, or dissolution of his civil partnership with, his former partner, that dwelling for a period of 26 weeks from the date on which he ceased to occupy that dwelling or, where the dwelling is occupied as the home by the former partner who is a lone parent, for so long as it is so occupied.

(2)   In this paragraph "dwelling" includes any garage, garden and outbuildings, which were formerly occupied by the claimant as his home and any premises not so occupied which it is impracticable or unreasonable to sell separately, in particular, in Scotland, any croft land on which the dwelling is situated.

26.   Any premises where the claimant is taking reasonable steps to dispose of those premises, for a period of 26 weeks from the date on which he first took such steps, or such longer period as is reasonable in the circumstances to enable him to dispose of those premises.

27.   Any premises which the claimant intends to occupy as his home, and in respect of which he is taking steps to obtain possession and has sought legal advice, or has commenced legal proceedings, with a view to obtaining possession, for a period of 26 weeks from the date on which he first sought such advice or first commenced such proceedings whichever is the earlier, or such longer period as is reasonable in the circumstances to enable him to obtain possession and commence occupation of those premises.

28.   Any premises which the claimant intends to occupy as his home to which essential repairs or alterations are required in order to render them fit for such occupation, for a period of 26 weeks from the date on which the claimant first takes steps to effect those repairs or alterations, or such longer period as is necessary to enable those repairs or alterations to be carried out.

29.   Any payment made by the Secretary of State to compensate for the loss (in whole or in part) of entitlement to housing benefit.

30.   Any payment made by the Secretary of State to compensate for the loss of housing benefit supplement under regulation 19 of the Supplementary Benefit (Requirements) Regulations 1983.

31.   The value of the right to receive an occupational or personal pension.

32.   The value of any funds held under a personal pension scheme [¹].

Amendment

1.   Amended by reg 6(7) of SI 2007 No 1749 as from 16.7.07.

33. The value of the right to receive any rent except where the claimant has a reversionary interest in the property in respect of which rent is due.

34. Any payment in kind made by a charity or under the Trusts, [¹ the Fund, the Independent Living (1993) Fund or the Independent Living Fund (2006)].

Amendment

1.   Amended by Art 9(3) of SI 2007 No 2538 as from 1.10.07.

---

35. Any payment made pursuant to section 2 of the 1973 Act or section 2 of the Enterprise and New Towns (Scotland) Act 1990, but only for the period of 52 weeks beginning on the date of receipt of the payment.

36. Any community charge benefit.

37. Any payment in consequence of a reduction of council tax under section 13 or, as the case may be, section 80 of the Local Government Finance Act 1992 (reduction of liability for council tax), but only for a period of 52 weeks from the date of the receipt of the payment.

38. Any grant made in accordance with a scheme made under section 129 of the Housing Act 1988 or section 66 of the Housing (Scotland) Act 1988 (schemes for payments to assist local housing authority and local authority tenants to obtain other accommodation) which is to be used–

   (a)   to purchase premises intended for occupation as his home; or

   (b)   to carry out repairs or alterations which are required to render premises fit for occupation as his home,

for a period of 26 weeks from the date on which he received such a grant or such longer period as is reasonable in the circumstances to enable the purchase, repairs or alterations to be completed and the claimant to commence occupation of those premises as his home.

39. Any arrears of special war widows payment which is disregarded under paragraph 44 of Schedule 4 (sums to be disregarded in the calculation of income other than earnings) or of any amount which is disregarded under paragraph 53, 54 or 55 of that Schedule, but only for a period of 52 weeks from the date of the receipt of the arrears.

40.–(1)   Any payment or repayment made–

   (a)   as respects England, under regulation 5, 6 or 12 of the National Health Service (Travel Expenses and Remission of Charges) Regulations (travelling expenses and health service supplies);

   (b)   as respects Wales, under regulation 3, 5 or 8 of the National Health Service (Travelling Expenses and Remission of Charges) Regulations 1988 (travelling expenses and health service supplies);

   (c)   as respects Scotland, under regulation 3, 5 or 8 of the National Health Service (Travelling Expenses and Remission of Charges) (Scotland) Regulations 2003 (travelling expenses and health service supplies),

but only for a period of 52 weeks from the date of the receipt of the payment or repayment.

   (2)   Any payment or repayment by the Secretary of State for Health, Scottish Ministers or the National Assembly for Wales which is analogous to a payment or repayment mentioned in sub-paragraph (1); but only for a period of 52 weeks from the date of the receipt of the payment or repayment.

41. Any payment made under regulation 6, 8, 12 or 14(2) of the Welfare Food Regulations 1996 (payments made in place of milk tokens or the supply of vitamins) but only for a period of 52 weeks from the date of the receipt of the payment.

42. Any payment made either by the Secretary of State for [¹ the Justice] or by Scottish Ministers under a scheme established to assist relatives and other persons to visit persons in custody, but only for a period of 52 weeks from the date of the receipt of the payment.

Amendment

1.   Amended by Art 8 and the Sch para 24 of SI 2007 No 2128 as from 22.8.07.

---

43. Any payment (other than a training allowance) made, whether by the Secretary of State or any other person, under the Disabled Persons (Employment) Act 1944 or to assist disabled persons to obtain or retain employment despite their disability.

44. Any payment made by the Secretary of State to compensate a person who was entitled to supplementary benefit in respect of a period ending immediately before 11th April 1988 but who did not become entitled to income support in respect of a period beginning with that day.

45. Any payment made by a local authority under section 3 of the Disabled Persons (Employment) Act 1958 to homeworkers assisted under the Blind Homeworkers' Scheme.

46.–(1)   Subject to sub-paragraph (2), where a claimant satisfies the conditions in section 131(3) and (6) of the Act (entitlement to alternative maximum council tax benefit), the whole of his capital.

(2)   Where in addition to satisfying the conditions in section 131(3) and (6) of the Act the claimant also satisfies the conditions in section 131(4) and (5) of the Act (entitlement to the maximum council tax benefit), sub-paragraph (1) shall not have effect.

[¹**47.** (1) Any sum of capital to which sub-paragraph (2) applies and–
(a)   which is administered on behalf of a person by the High Court or the County Court under Rule 21.11(1) of the Civil Procedure Rules 1998 or by the Court of Protection;
(b)   which can only be disposed of by order or direction of any such court; or
(c)   where the person concerned is under the age of 18, which can only be disposed of by order or direction prior to that person attaining age 18.
(2)   This sub-paragraph applies to a sum of capital which is derived from–
(a)   an award of damages for a personal injury to that person; or
(b)   compensation for the death of one or both parents where the person concerned is under the age of 18.]

Amendment
1.   Substituted by reg 17(6)(c) of SI 2006 No 2378 from the first day of the first benefit week to commence on or after 2.10.06.

---

48.   Any sum of capital administered on behalf of a person in accordance with an order made under section 13 of the Children (Scotland) Act 1995, or under Rule 36.14 of the Ordinary Cause Rules 1993 or under Rule 128 of those Rules, where such sum derives from–
(a)   award of damages for a personal injury to that person; or
(b)   compensation for the death of one or both parents where the person concerned is under the age of 18.
49.   Any payment to the claimant as holder of the Victoria Cross or George Cross.
50.   The amount of any child maintenance bonus payable by way of jobseeker's allowance or income support in accordance with section 10 of the Child Support Act 1995, or a corresponding payment under Article 4 of the Child Support (Northern Ireland) Order 1995, but only for a period of 52 weeks from the date of receipt.
51.   In the case of a person who is receiving, or who has received, assistance under the self-employment route, any sum of capital which is acquired by that person for the purpose of establishing or carrying on the commercial activity in respect of which such assistance is or was received but only for a period of 52 weeks from the date on which that sum was acquired.
52.–(1)   Any payment of a sports award for a period of 26 weeks from the date of receipt of that payment except to the extent that it has been made in respect of any one or more of the items specified in sub-paragraph (2).
(2)   The items specified for the purposes of sub-paragraph (1) are food, ordinary clothing or footwear, household fuel or rent of the claimant or, where the claimant is a member of a family, any other member of his family, or any council tax or water charges for which that claimant or member is liable.
(3)   For the purposes of sub-paragraph (2) ''food'' does not include vitamins, minerals or other special dietary supplements intended to enhance the performance of the person in the sport in respect of which the award was made.
53.–(1)   Any payment–
(a)   by way of an education maintenance allowance made pursuant to–
         (i)   regulations made under section 518 of the Education Act 1996;
         (ii)   regulations made under section 49 or 73(f) of the Education (Scotland) Act 1980;
         (iii)   directions made under sections 12(2)(c) and 21 of the Further and Higher Education (Scotland) Act 1992; or
(b)   corresponding to such an education maintenance allowance, made pursuant to–
         (i)   section 14 or section 181 of the Education Act 2002 (power of Secretary of State and National Assembly for Wales to give financial assistance for purposes related to education or childcare, and allowances in respect of education or training); or
         (ii)   regulations made under section 181 of that Act.
(2)   Any payment, other than a payment to which sub-paragraph (1) applies, made pursuant to–
(a)   regulations made under section 518 of the Education Act 1996;
(b)   regulations made under section 49 of the Education (Scotland) Act 1980; or
(c)   directions made under sections 12(2)(c) and 21 of the Further and Higher Education (Scotland) Act 1992,
in respect of a course of study attended by a child or a young person or a person who is in receipt of an education maintenance allowance made pursuant to any provision specified in sub-paragraph (1).
54.   In the case of a claimant participating in an employment zone programme, any discretionary payment made by an employment zone contractor to the claimant, being a fee, grant, loan or otherwise, but only for the period of 52 weeks from the date of receipt of the payment.

55. Any arrears of subsistence allowance paid as a lump sum but only for the period of 52 weeks from the date of receipt of the payment.

56. Where an ex-gratia payment of £10,000 has been made by the Secretary of State on or after 1st February 2001 in consequence of the imprisonment or interment of–

(a)   the claimant;

(b)   the claimant's partner;

(c)   the claimant's deceased spouse or deceased civil partner; or

(d)   the claimant's partner's deceased spouse or deceased civil partner,

by the Japanese during the Second World War, £10,000.

57.–(1)   Subject to sub-paragraph (2), the amount of any trust payment made to a claimant or a member of a claimant's family who is–

(a)   a diagnosed person;

(b)   the diagnosed person's partner or the person who was the diagnosed person's partner at the time of the diagnosed person's death;

(c)   a parent of a diagnosed person, a person acting in place of the diagnosed person's parents or a person who was so acting at the date of the diagnosed person's death; or

(d)   a member of the diagnosed person's family (other than his partner) or a person who was a member of the diagnosed person's family (other than his partner) at the date of the diagnosed person's death.

(2)   Where a trust payment is made to–

(a)   a person referred to in sub-paragraph (1)(a) or (b), that sub-paragraph shall apply for the period beginning on the date on which the trust is made and ending on the date on which that person dies;

(b)   a person referred to in sub-paragraph (1)(c), that sub-paragraph shall apply for the period beginning on the date on which the trust payment is made and ending two years after that date;

(c)   a person referred to in sub-paragraph (1)(d), that sub-paragraph shall apply for the period beginning on the date on which the trust payment is made and ending–

(i)   two years after that date; or

(ii)   on the day before the day on which that person–

(aa)   ceases receiving full-time education; or

(bb)   attains the age of [¹ 20],

whichever is the latest.

(3)   Subject to sub-paragraph (4), the amount of any payment by a person to whom a trust payment has been made or of any payment out of the estate of a person to whom a trust payment has been made, which is made to a claimant or a member of a claimant's family who is–

(a)   the diagnosed person's partner or the person who was the diagnosed person's partner at the date of the diagnosed person's death;

(b)   a parent of a diagnosed person, a person acting in place of the diagnosed person's parents or a person who was so acting at the date of the diagnosed person's death; or

(c)   a member of the diagnosed person's family (other than his partner) or a person who was a member of the diagnosed person's family (other than his partner) at the date of the diagnosed person's death,

but only to the extent that such payments do not exceed the total amount of any trust payments made to that person.

(4)   Where a payment as referred to in sub-paragraph (3) is made to–

(a)   a person referred to in sub-paragraph (3)(a), that sub-paragraph shall apply for the period beginning on the date on which that payment is made and ending on the date on which that person dies;

(b)   a person referred to in sub-paragraph (3)(b), that sub-paragraph shall apply for the period beginning on the date on which that payment is made and ending two years after that date; or

(c)   person referred to in sub-paragraph (3)(c), that sub-paragraph shall apply for the period beginning on the date on which that payment is made and ending–

(i)   two years after that date; or

(ii)   on the day before the day on which that person–

(aa)   ceases receiving full-time education; or

(bb)   attains the age of [¹ 20],

whichever is the latest.

(5)   In this paragraph, a reference to a person–

(a)   being the diagnosed person's partner;

(b)   being a member of a diagnosed person's family;

(c)   acting in place of the diagnosed person's parents,

at the date of the diagnosed person's death shall include a person who would have been such a person or a person who would have been so acting, but for the diagnosed person residing in a care home, an Abbeyfield Home or an independent hospital on that date.

(6)   In this paragraph–

"diagnosed person" means a person who has been diagnosed as suffering from, or who, after his death, has been diagnosed as having suffered from, variant Creutzfeld-Jakob disease;

"relevant trust" means a trust established out of funds provided by the Secretary of State in respect of persons who suffered, or who are suffering, from variant Creutzfeld-Jakob disease for the benefit of persons eligible for payments in accordance with its provisions;

"trust payment" means a payment under a relevant trust.

Amendment

1.   Amended by reg 5(5) of SI 2006 No 718 as from 10.4.06.

---

58.   The amount of any payment, other than a war pension within the meaning of section 25 of the Social Security Act 1989, to compensate for the fact that the claimant, the claimant's partner, the claimant's deceased spouse or deceased civil partner or the claimant's partner's deceased spouse or deceased civil partner–

(a)   was a slave labourer or a forced labourer;

(b)   had suffered property loss or had suffered personal injury; or

(c)   was a parent of a child who had died,

during the Second World War.

59.–(1)   Any payment made by a local authority, or by the National Assembly for Wales, to or on behalf of the claimant or his partner relating to a service which is provided to develop or sustain the capacity of the claimant or his partner to live independently in his accommodation.

(2)   For the purposes of sub-paragraph (1) "local authority" includes in England a county council.

60.   Any payment made under the Community Care (Direct Payments) Act 1996, or regulations made under section 57 of the Health and Social Care Act 2001 or under section 12B of the Social Work (Scotland) Act 1968.

61.   Any payment made to the claimant pursuant to regulations under section 2(6)(b), 3 or 4 of the Adoption and Children Act 2002.

62.   Any payment made to the claimant in accordance with regulations made pursuant to section 14F of the Children Act 1989 (special guardianship support services).

SCHEDULE 6

REGULATION 60

Extended payments of council tax benefit

PART 1

Conditions for an extended payment

1.   The conditions prescribed in this paragraph are that the Secretary of State has certified to the relevant authority–

(a)   that the claimant or his partner was entitled to and in receipt of income support or an income-based jobseeker's allowance or that the claimant and his partner were entitled to and in receipt of a joint-claim jobseeker's allowance and that entitlement has ceased;

(b)   the relevant day in his case;

(c)   that entitlement to income support or an income-based jobseeker's allowance had ceased by reason of the claimant or his partner–

(i)   commencing employment as an employed or self-employed earner; or

(ii)   increasing their earnings from such employment; or

(iii)   increasing the number of hours worked in such employment; and

(d)   that the claimant had been entitled to and in receipt of income support or a jobseeker's allowance for a continuous period of at least 26 weeks until the relevant day, and for the purpose of this sub-paragraph–

(i)   a claimant satisfies the conditions of this sub-paragraph if he has been entitled to and in receipt of a combination of income support and a jobseeker's allowance for at least 26 weeks and for the purposes of this sub-paragraph, a reference to the claimant being entitled to and in receipt of a jobseeker's allowance shall include a reference to the claimant and his partner being entitled to and in receipt of a joint-claim jobseeker's allowance;

(ii)   the claimant shall be treated as having been entitled to and in receipt of income support or a jobseeker's allowance during any period of less than 5 weeks in respect of which he was not entitled to either of those benefits because, as a consequence of his participation in an employment zone programme, he was engaged in remunerative work; and

(iii)   references to the claimant include references to his partner.

2.   The conditions prescribed in this paragraph are that the claimant or the claimant's partner–

(a)   notifies either the designated office or an appropriate DWP office that he or his partner–

    (i)   has commenced, or is about to commence, remunerative work;

    (ii)   has commenced, or is about to commence, receiving remuneration for work or an increased amount of remuneration for work; or

    (iii)   has commenced, or is about to commence, an increased number of hours of work,

so that entitlement to income support or to an income-based jobseeker's allowance ceases and that work or, as the case may be, remuneration, is expected to last 5 weeks or more; and

(b)   makes that notification no later than 4 weeks after the day on which the claimant or his partner first undertakes the remunerative work referred to in sub-paragraph (a)(i) or first receives remuneration for the work or an increased amount of remuneration for the work referred to in sub-paragraph (a)(ii), or first commences the increased number of hours of work referred to in sub-paragraph (a)(iii).

PART 2

Calculation and payment of an extended payment

3.   Except in the case of a mover, the amount of the extended payment shall be equal to the amount of council tax benefit allowed to the claimant for the last benefit week before he ceased to be entitled to council tax benefit.

Movers

4.   In the case of a mover who claims an extended payment the relevant authority to whom the mover is liable to pay council tax in respect of the second dwelling shall, upon receiving the mover's claim for an extended payment which meets the requirements of regulation 60, allow an extended payment, calculated in accordance with paragraph 5, to the mover.

Movers and extended payments

5.   In a case to which paragraph 4 applies–

(a)   the maximum council tax benefit of the mover shall be the amount of the council tax calculated in accordance with regulation 57, save that no deduction shall be made in respect of non-dependants, other than any that fall to be taken into account pursuant to sub-paragraph (b);

(b)   the extended payment shall be by way of a discharge to the value of such part of the liability to council tax for the period specified in regulation 60(6) less, in a case where the rebate to which paragraph 4 refers was subject to any deductions in respect of non-dependants pursuant to regulations 57(1) and 58, the amount of those deductions.

PART 3

Adjustment of entitlement in respect of an extended payment

6.   Where an extended payment has been allowed and the person to whom it was made has also claimed council tax benefit for a period that includes any part of the period specified in regulation 60(6), the entitlement to council tax benefit, if any, of that claimant for council tax benefit, in respect of any or each of those weeks, shall be reduced by the amount that that extended payment has discharged his council tax liability, in respect of any such week.

PART 4

Interpretation

7.   In this Schedule, except where the context otherwise requires–

"claimant" means a person claiming an extended payment;

"mover" means a claimant who changes the dwelling in which he is resident and in respect of which he is liable to pay council tax;

"the relevant day" means the day on which the claimant's entitlement to income support or an income-based jobseeker's allowance ceased; and

"second dwelling" means the dwelling to which a person has moved or is about to move, in which he is or will be resident, and where the liability to pay council tax in respect of his dwelling follows on immediately from the liability to pay council tax in respect of his previous dwelling.

SCHEDULE 7
REGULATION 61
Extended payments (severe disablement allowance and incapacity benefit) of council tax benefit

Condition for an extended payment (severe disablement allowance and incapacity benefit)

1. The condition prescribed in this paragraph is that the claimant or the claimant's partner–

(a) notifies either the designated office or an appropriate DWP office that he or his partner–

    (i) has commenced, or is about to commence, remunerative work;

    (ii) has commenced, or is about to commence, receiving remuneration for work or an increased amount of remuneration for work; or

    (iii) has commenced, or is about to commence, an increased number of hours of work,

so that entitlement to severe disablement allowance or incapacity benefit ceases and that work, or as the case may be, remuneration, is expected to last 5 weeks or more; and

(b) the notification is made no later than 4 weeks after the day on which the claimant or his partner first undertakes the remunerative work referred to in sub-paragraph (a)(i), first receives remuneration for the work or an increased amount of remuneration for the work referred to in sub-paragraph (a)(ii), or first commences the increased number of hours of work referred to in sub-paragraph (a)(iii).

Calculation and payment of an extended payment (severe disablement allowance and incapacity benefit)

2. Except in the case of a mover, the amount of the extended payment (severe disablement allowance and incapacity benefit) shall be equal to the amount of council tax benefit allowed to the claimant for the last benefit week before he ceased to be entitled to council tax benefit.

Movers

3. In the case of a mover who claims an extended payment (severe disablement allowance and incapacity benefit) the relevant authority to whom the mover is liable to pay council tax in respect of the second dwelling shall, upon receiving the mover's claim for an extended payment (severe disablement allowance and incapacity benefit) which meets the requirements of regulation 61(1), allow an extended payment (severe disablement allowance and incapacity benefit) calculated in accordance with paragraph 4 to the mover.

Movers and extended payments

4. In a case to which paragraph 3 applies the amount of the extended payment (severe disablement allowance and incapacity benefit) shall be the lesser of–

(a) the amount required to discharge such part of the liability for council tax for the period specified in regulation 61(6)(a), less, in a case where the rebate to which paragraph 2 refers was subject to any deductions in relation to non-dependants pursuant to regulations 57(1) and 58, the amount of those deductions; or

(b) the amount of extended payment (severe disablement allowance and incapacity benefit) calculated in accordance with paragraph 2.

5. The maximum council tax benefit of a mover the amount of whose extended payment (severe disablement allowance and incapacity benefit) is calculated in accordance with paragraph 4(a) shall be calculated in accordance with regulation 57(1), save that no deduction shall be made in respect of non-dependants, other than any that fall to be taken into account pursuant to paragraph 4(a).

Adjustment of entitlement in respect of an extended payment (severe disablement allowance and incapacity benefit)

6. Where an extended payment (severe disablement allowance and incapacity benefit) has been allowed and the person to whom it was made has also claimed council tax benefit for a period that includes any part of the period specified in regulation 61(6)(a), the entitlement to council tax benefit, if any, of that claimant, in respect of each or any of those weeks, shall be reduced by the amount that that extended payment (severe disablement allowance and incapacity benefit) has discharged his council tax liability, in respect of any such week.

Interpretation

7. In this Schedule–

"claimant" means a person claiming an extended payment (severe disablement allowance and incapacity benefit);

"mover" means a claimant who changes the dwelling in which he is resident and in respect of which he is liable to pay council tax;

"second dwelling" means the dwelling to which a person has moved, or is about to move, in which he is or will be resident, and where the liability to pay council tax in respect of his dwelling follows on immediately from the liability to pay council tax in respect of his previous dwelling.

SCHEDULE 8
REGULATION 76(1)
Matters to be included in decision notice

PART 1
General

1.   The statement of matters to be included in any decision notice issued by a relevant authority to a person, and referred to in regulation 76 (notification of decisions) and in regulation 10 of the Decisions and Appeals Regulations are those matters set out in the following provisions of this Schedule.

2.   Every decision notice shall include a statement as to the right of any person affected by that decision to request a written statement under regulation 76(2) (requests for statement of reasons) and the manner and time in which to do so.

3.   Every decision notice shall include a statement as to the right of any person affected by that decision to make an application for a revision in accordance with regulation 4(1)(a) of the Decisions and Appeals Regulations and, where appropriate, to appeal against that decision and the manner and time in which to do so.

4.   Every decision notice following an application for a revision in accordance with regulation 4(1)(a) of the Decisions and Appeals Regulations shall include a statement as to whether the original decision in respect of which the person made his representations has been confirmed or revised and where the relevant authority has not revised the decision the reasons why not.

5.   Every decision notice following an application for a revision in accordance with regulation 4(1)(a) of the Decisions and Appeals Regulations shall, if the original decision has been revised, include a statement as to the right of any person affected by that decision to apply for a revision in accordance with regulation 4(1)(a) of those Regulations and the manner and time in which to do so.

6.   An authority may include in the decision notice any other matters not prescribed by this Schedule which it sees fit, whether expressly or by reference to some other document available without charge to the person.

7.   Parts 2, 3 and 4 of this Schedule shall apply only to the decision notice given on a claim.

8.   Where a decision notice is given following a revision of an earlier decision–

(a)   made of the authority's own motion which results in a revision of that earlier decision; or

(b)   made following an application for a revision in accordance with regulation 4(1)(a) of the Decisions and Appeals Regulations, whether or not resulting in a revision of that earlier decision,

that notice shall, subject to paragraph 6, contain a statement only as to all the matters revised.

PART 2
Awards where income support or an income-based jobseeker's allowance is payable

9.   Where a person on income support or an income-based jobseeker's allowance is awarded council tax benefit, the decision notice shall include a statement as to–

(a)   his normal weekly amount of council tax which may be rounded to the nearest penny;

(b)   the normal weekly amount of the council tax benefit, which amount may be rounded to the nearest penny;

(c)   the amount of and the category of non-dependant deductions made under regulation 58, if any;

(d)   the first day of entitlement to the council tax benefit;

(e)   his duty to notify any change of circumstances which might affect his entitlement to, or the amount of council tax benefit and, without prejudice to the extent of the duty owed under regulation 74 (duty to notify changes of circumstances) the kind of change of circumstances which is to be notified, either upon the notice or by reference to some other document available to him on application and without charge,

and in any case where the amount to which sub-paragraph (a) or (b) refers disregards fractions of a penny, the notice shall include a statement to that effect.

PART 3
Awards where no income support or an income-based jobseeker's allowance is payable

10.   Where a person is not on income support or on an income-based jobseeker's allowance but is awarded council tax benefit, the decision notice shall include a statement as to–

(a)   the matters set out in paragraph 9;

(b)   his applicable amount and how it is calculated;

(c)   his weekly earnings; and
(d)   his weekly income other than earnings.

PART 4
Notice where income of non-dependant is treated as claimant's income
11.   Where an authority makes a decision under regulation 16 (circumstances in which income and capital of a non-dependant is to be treated as claimant's) the decision notice shall contain a statement as to–
(a)   the fact that a decision has been made by reference to the income and capital of the claimant's non-dependant; and
(b)   the relevant authority's reasons for making that decision.

PART 5
Notice where no award is made
12.   Where a person is not awarded council tax benefit under regulation 57 (maximum council tax benefit)–
(a)   on grounds of income, the decision notice shall include a statement as to–
    (i)   the matters set out in paragraphs 9(a); and
    (ii)   the matters set out in paragraphs 10(b) to (d) where the person is not on income support or an income-based jobseeker's allowance;
(b)   on the grounds that the amount of the alternative maximum council tax benefit exceeds the appropriate maximum council tax benefit, the matters set our in paragraph 15;
(c)   for any reason other than one mentioned in sub-paragraphs (a) and (b), the decision notice shall include a statement as to the reason why no award has been made.

PART 6
Awards where alternative maximum council tax benefit is payable in respect of a day
13.   Where a person is awarded council tax benefit determined in accordance with regulation 62 and Schedule 2 (alternative maximum council tax benefit) the decision notice shall include a statement as to–
(a)   the normal weekly amount of council tax, which amount may be rounded to the nearest penny;
(b)   the normal weekly amount of the alternative maximum council tax benefit, which amount may be rounded to the nearest penny;
(c)   the gross income or incomes and the rate of benefit which apply under Schedule 2;
(d)   the first day of entitlement to benefit;
(e)   the gross income of any second adult used to determine the rate of the alternative maximum council tax benefit or if any such adult is on income support, state pension credit or an income-based jobseeker's allowance;
(f)   the claimant's duty to notify any change of circumstances which might affect his entitlement to, or the amount of the alternative maximum council tax benefit and, without prejudice to the extent of the duty owed under regulation 74 (duty to notify changes of circumstances) the kind of change of circumstances which are to be notified, either upon the notice or by reference to some other document available to the claimant free of charge on application,
and in any case where the amount to which sub-paragraph (a) or (b) refers disregards fractions of a penny, the notice shall include a statement to that effect.

Notice where no award of alternative maximum council tax benefit is made
14.   Where a person is not awarded council tax benefit in accordance with regulation 62 and Schedule 2 (alternative maximum council tax benefit)–
(a)   on the grounds that the gross income or as the case may be the aggregate gross incomes, of any second adult or adults in the claimant's dwelling is too high, the decision notice shall include a statement as to the matters set out in paragraphs 13(a), (c) and (e);
(b)   on the grounds that the appropriate maximum council tax benefit is higher than the alternative maximum council tax benefit, the decision notice shall include a statement as to the matters set out in paragraph 15 below;
(c)   for any reason not referred to in sub-paragraphs (a) and (b), the decision notice shall include a statement as to why no award has been made.

Notice where council tax benefit is awarded and section 131(9) of the Act applies
15.   Where the amount of a claimant's council tax benefit in respect of a day is the greater of the appropriate maximum council tax benefit and the alternative maximum council tax benefit in his case the notice shall in addition to the matters set out in paragraphs 9, 10 or 13, as the case may be, include a statement as to–

(a)   the amount of whichever is the lesser of the appropriate maximum council tax benefit or the alternative maximum council tax benefit in his case, which amount may be rounded to the nearest penny; and

(b)   that this amount has not been awarded in consequence of the award of council tax benefit at a higher rate,

and in any case where the amount to which sub-paragraph (a) refers disregards fractions of a penny, the notice shall include a statement to that effect.

PART 7
Notice where there is recoverable excess benefit

16.–(1)   Except in cases to which paragraphs (a) and (b) of regulation 82 (excess benefit in consequence of a reduction in a relevant authority's council tax) refers, where the relevant authority makes a decision that there is recoverable excess benefit within the meaning of regulation 83 (recoverable excess benefits), the decision notice shall include a statement as to–

(a)   the fact that there is recoverable excess benefit;

(b)   the reason why there is recoverable excess benefit;

(c)   the amount of recoverable excess benefit;

(d)   how the amount of recoverable excess benefit was calculated;

(e)   the benefit weeks to which the recoverable excess benefit relates; and

(f)   the method or combination of methods by which the authority intends to recover the recoverable excess benefit, including–

　　(i)   payment by or on behalf of the person concerned of the amount due by the specified date;

　　(ii)   addition of the amount due to any amount in respect of the tax concerned for payment whether by instalments or otherwise by the specified date or dates; or

　　(iii)   if recovery cannot be effected in accordance with heads (i) or (ii), requesting the Secretary of State to recover the excess benefits by deduction from the benefit prescribed in regulation 90 (recovery of excess benefits from prescribed benefits).

[¹SCHEDULE 9
ELECTRONIC COMMUNICATION

Amendment

1.   Inserted by Art 4(5) of SI 2006 No 2968 as from 20.12.06.

PART 1
Introduction

Interpretation

1.   In this Schedule "official computer system" means a computer system maintained by or on behalf of the relevant authority or of the Secretary of State for sending, receiving, processing or storing of any claim, certificate, notice, information or evidence.

PART 2
Electronic Communication – General Provisions

Conditions for the use of electronic communication

2.–(1)   The relevant authority may use an electronic communication in connection with claims for, and awards of, benefit under these Regulations.

(2)   A person other than the relevant authority may use an electronic communication in connection with the matters referred to in sub-paragraph (1) if the conditions specified in sub-paragraphs (3) to (6) are satisfied.

(3)   The first condition is that the person is for the time being permitted to use an electronic communication by an authorisation given by means of a direction of the Chief Executive of the relevant authority.

(4)   The second condition is that the person uses an approved method of–

(a)   authenticating the identity of the sender of the communication;

(b)   electronic communication;

(c)   authenticating any claim or notice delivered by means of an electronic communication; and

(d)   subject to sub-paragraph (7), submitting to the relevant authority any claim, certificate, notice, information or evidence.

(5)   The third condition is that any claim, certificate, notice, information or evidence sent by means of an electronic communication is in a form approved for the purposes of this Schedule.

(6)   The fourth condition is that the person maintains such records in written or electronic form as may be specified in a direction given by the Chief Executive of the relevant authority.

(7)   Where the person uses any method other than the method approved of submitting any claim, certificate, notice, information or evidence, that claim, certificate, notice, information or evidence shall be treated as not having been submitted.

(8)   In this paragraph ''approved'' means approved by means of a direction given by the Chief Executive of the relevant authority for the purposes of this Schedule.

Use of intermediaries
3.   The relevant authority may use intermediaries in connection with–

(a)   the delivery of any claim, certificate, notice, information or evidence by means of an electronic communication; and

(b)   the authentication or security of anything transmitted by such means,

and may require other persons to use intermediaries in connection with those matters.

PART 3
Electronic Communication – Evidential Provisions

Effect of delivering information by means of electronic communication
4.–(1)   Any claim, certificate, notice, information or evidence which is delivered by means of an electronic communication shall be treated as having been delivered in the manner or form required by any provision of these Regulations, on the day the conditions imposed–

(a)   by this Schedule; and

(b)   by or under an enactment,

are satisfied.

(2)   The relevant authority may, by a direction, determine that any claim, certificate, notice, information or evidence is to be treated as delivered on a different day (whether earlier or later) from the day provided for in sub-paragraph (1).

(3)   Information shall not be taken to have been delivered to an official computer system by means of an electronic communication unless it is accepted by the system to which it is delivered.

Proof of identity of sender or recipient of information
5.   If it is necessary to prove, for the purpose of any legal proceedings, the identity of–

(a)   the sender of any claim, certificate, notice, information or evidence delivered by means of an electronic communication to an official computer system; or

(b)   the recipient of any such claim, certificate, notice, information or evidence delivered by means of an electronic communication from an official computer system,

the sender or recipient, as the case may be, shall be presumed to be the person whose name is recorded as such on that official computer system.

Proof of delivery of information
6.–(1)   If it is necessary to prove, for the purpose of any legal proceedings, that the use of an electronic communication has resulted in the delivery of any claim, certificate, notice, information or evidence this shall be presumed to have been the case where–

(a)   any such claim, certificate, notice, information or evidence has been delivered to the relevant authority, if the delivery of that claim, certificate, notice, information or evidence has been recorded on an official computer system; or

(b)   any such claim, certificate, notice, information or evidence has been delivered by the relevant authority, if the delivery of that certificate, notice, information or evidence has been recorded on an official computer system.

(2)   If it is necessary to prove, for the purpose of any legal proceedings, that the use of an electronic communication has resulted in the delivery of any such claim, certificate, notice, information or evidence, this shall be presumed not to be the case, if that claim, certificate, notice, information or evidence delivered to the relevant authority has not been recorded on an official computer system.

(3)   If it is necessary to prove, for the purpose of any legal proceedings, when any such claim, certificate, notice, information or evidence sent by means of an electronic communication has been received, the time and date of receipt shall be presumed to be that recorded on an official computer system.

Proof of content of information

7.   If it is necessary to prove, for the purpose of any legal proceedings, the content of any claim, certificate, notice, information or evidence sent by means of an electronic communication, the content shall be presumed to be that recorded on an official computer system.]

Part 4

Main secondary legislation

The Housing Benefit (Persons who have attained the qualifying age for state pension credit) Regulations 2006

(2006 No. 214)

ARRANGEMENT OF REGULATIONS

PART 1
GENERAL

1. Citation and commencement
2. Interpretation
3. Definition of non-dependant
4. Cases in which section 1(1A) of the Administration Act is disapplied
5. Persons who have attained the qualifying age for state pension credit
6. Remunerative work

PART 2
PROVISIONS AFFECTING ENTITLEMENT TO HOUSING BENEFIT

7. Circumstances in which a person is or is not to be treated as occupying a dwelling as his home
8. Circumstances in which a person is to be treated as liable to make payments in respect of a dwelling
9. Circumstances in which a person is to be treated as not liable to make payments in respect of a dwelling
10. Persons from abroad
10A. Entitlement of a refugee to Housing Benefit

PART 3
PAYMENTS IN RESPECT OF A DWELLING

11. Eligible housing costs
11A. Cases where maximum housing benefit expires
12. Rent
12A. Eligible rent and the maximum rent (standard local rate)
13. Maximum rent
13ZA. Restrictions on rent increases
13A. Maximum rent (standard local rate)
13B. Publication of local housing alowances
14. Requirement to refer to rent officers
15. Applications to the rent officer for redeterminations
16. Application for redermination by rent officer
17. Substitute determinations or substitute redeterminations
18. Application of provisions to substitute determinations or substitute redeterminations
18A. Amended determinations

PART 4
MEMBERSHIP OF A FAMILY

19. Persons of prescribed description
20. Circumstances in which a person is to be treated as responsible or not responsible for another
21. Circumstances in which a person is to be treated as being or not being a member of the household

PART 5
APPLICABLE AMOUNTS

22. Applicable amounts

PART 6

ASSESSMENT OF INCOME AND CAPITAL

SECTION 1

General

23. Calculation of income and capital of members of claimant's family and of a polygamous marriage
24. Circumstances in which income of non-dependant is to be treated as claimant's

SECTION 2

Income

25. Calculation of income and capital
26. Claimant in receipt of guarantee credit
27. Calculation of claimant's income and capital in savings credit only cases
28. Calculation of income and capital where state pension credit is not payable
29. Meaning of "income"
30. Calculation of income on a weekly basis
31. Treatment of child care charges
32. Calculation of average weekly income from tax credits
33. Calculation of weekly income
34. Disregard of changes in tax, contributions etc

SECTION 3

Employed earners

35. Earnings of employed earners
36. Calculation of net earnings of employed earners

SECTION 4

Self-employed earners

37. Calculation of earnings of self-employed earners
38. Earnings of self-employed earners
39. Calculation of net profit of self-employed earners
40. Deduction of tax and contributions of self-employed earners

SECTION 5

Other income

41. Notional income
42. Income paid to third parties

SECTION 6

Capital

43. Capital limit
44. Calculation of capital
45. Calculation of capital in the United Kingdom
46. Calculation of capital outside the United Kingdom
47. Notional capital
48. Diminishing notional capital rule
49. Capital jointly held

PART 7

Amount of benefit

50. Maximum housing benefit
51. Housing benefit tapers
52. Reduction where amount payable under regulation 72 of the Housing Benefit Regulations

53.   Extended payments (severe disablement allowance and incapacity benefit)
54.   Continuing payments where state pension credit claimed
55.   Non-dependant deductions
56.   Minimum housing benefit

PART 8
Calculation of weekly amounts and changes of circumstances
57.   Date on which entitlement is to commence
58.   Date on which housing benefit is to end where entitlement to severe disablement allowance or incapacity benefit ceases
59.   Date on which change of circumstances is to take effect
60.   Change of circumstances where state pension credit payable
61.   Calculation of weekly amounts
62.   Rent free periods

PART 9
Claims
63.   Who may claim
64.   Time and manner in which claims are to be made
64A.   Electronic claims for benefit
65.   Date of claim where claim sent or delivered to a gateway office
66.   Date of claim where claim sent or delivered to an office of a designated authority
67.   Evidence and information
68.   Amendment and withdrawal of claim
69.   Duty to notify changes of circumstances
69A.   Notice of changes of circumstances given electronically

PART 10
Decisions on questions
70.   Decisions by a relevant authority
71.   Notification of decision

PART 11
Payments
72.   Time and manner of payment
72A.   Cases in which payments to a housing authority are to take the form of a rent allowance
73.   Frequency of payment of a rent allowance
74.   Payment on account of a rent allowance
75.   Payment to be made to a person entitled
76.   Circumstances in which payment is to be made to a landlord
77.   Circumstances in which payment may be made to a landlord
78.   Payment on death of the person entitled
79.   Offsetting

PART 12
Overpayments
80.   Meaning of overpayment
81.   Recoverable overpayments
82.   Person from whom recovery may be sought
83.   Method of recovery
84.   Diminution of capital
85.   Sums to be deducted in calculating recoverable overpayments
86.   Recovery of overpayments from prescribed benefits

87.   Prescribed benefits
88.   Restrictions on recovery of rent and consequent notifications

PART 13
Information
SECTION 1
Claims and information
89.   Interpretation
90.   Collection of information
91.   Recording and holding information
92.   Forwarding of information
93.   Request for information

SECTION 2
Evidence and Information
94.   Interpretation
95.   Evidence and information required by rent officers
96.   Information to be supplied by an authority to another authority
97.   Supply of information: extended payments (severe disablement allowance and incapacity benefit)
98.   Requiring information from landlords and agents
99.   Circumstances for requiring information
100.   Relevant information
101.   Manner of supply of information
102.   Criminal offence

PART 14
Pathfinder authorities
103.   Modifications in respect of pathfinder authorities

SCHEDULES
A1.   Treatment of claims for housing benefit by refugees
1.   Ineligible service charges
2.   Excluded Tenancies
3.   Applicable amounts
4.   Sums disregarded from claimant's earnings
5.   Amounts to be disregarded in the calculation of income other than earnings
6.   Capital to be disregarded
7.   Extended payments (severe disablement allowance and incapacity benefit) of housing benefit
8.   Matters to be included in decision notice
9.   Pathfinder authorities
10.   Electronic communication

PART 1
General

General Note to the HB(SPC) Regs

These regulations, rather than the HB Regs, apply where the claimant has attained the qualifying age for PC, as defined in reg 2. However, they do not apply in relation to any claimant who remains (or whose partner remains) in receipt of IS or income-based JSA: reg 5. It is vital to note that receipt of PC by an HB claimant is not a requirement for these regulations to apply to her/him.

Citation and commencement

1.–(1)   These Regulations may be cited as the Housing Benefit (Persons who have attained the qualifying age for state pension credit) Regulations 2006.

(2)   These Regulations are to be read, where appropriate, with the Consequential Provisions Regulations.

(3)   Except as provided in Schedule 4 to the Consequential Provisions Regulations, these Regulations shall come into force on 6th March 2006.

(4)   The regulations consolidated by these Regulations are revoked, in consequence of the consolidation, by the Consequential Provisions Regulations.

Interpretation

2.–(1)   In these Regulations–

"the Act" means the Social Security Contributions and Benefits Act 1992;

"the 1973 Act" means the Employment and Training Act 1973;

[² "the 2000 Act" means the Electronic Communications Act 2000;]

"Abbeyfield Home" means an establishment run by the Abbeyfield Society including all bodies corporate or incorporate which are affiliated to that Society;

"adoption leave" means a period of absence from work on ordinary or additional adoption leave by virtue of section 75A or 75B of the Employment Rights Act 1996;

"the Administration Act" means the Social Security Administration Act 1992;

"appropriate DWP office" means an office of the Department for Work and Pensions dealing with state pension credit or an office which is normally open to the public for the receipt of claims for income support or a jobseeker's allowance;

"assessment period" means the period determined–

(a)   in relation to the earnings of a self-employed earner, in accordance with regulation 37 (calculation of earnings of self-employed earners) for the purpose of calculating the weekly earnings of the claimant; or

(b)   in relation to any other income, in accordance with regulation 33 (calculation of weekly income) for the purpose of calculating the weekly income of the claimant;

"attendance allowance" means–

(a)   an attendance allowance under Part 3 of the Act;

(b)   an increase of disablement pension under section 104 or 105 of the Act;

(c)   a payment under regulations made in exercise of the power conferred by paragraph 7(2)(b) of Part 2 of Schedule 8 to the Act;

(d)   an increase of an allowance which is payable in respect of constant attendance under paragraph 4 of Part 1 of Schedule 8 to the Act;

(e)   a payment by virtue of article 14, 15, 16, 43 or 44 of the Personal Injuries (Civilians) Scheme 1983 or any analogous payment; or

(f)   any payment based on need for attendance which is paid as part of a war disablement pension;

"the benefit Acts" means the Act, the Jobseekers Act and the State Pension Credit Act;

"benefit week" means a period of 7 consecutive days commencing upon a Monday and ending on a Sunday;

"board and lodging accommodation" means accommodation provided to a person or, if he is a member of a family, to him or any other member of his family, for a charge which is inclusive of the provision of that accommodation and at least some cooked or prepared meals which both are cooked or prepared (by a person other than the person to whom the accommodation is provided or a member of his family) and are consumed in that accommodation or associated premises;

"care home" in England and Wales has the meaning assigned to it by section 3 of the Care Standards Act 2000 and in Scotland means a care home service within the meaning assigned to it by section 2(3) of the Regulation of Care (Scotland) Act 2001;

"child" means a person under the age of 16;

"child tax credit" means a child tax credit under section 8 of the Tax Credits Act;

"the Children Order" means the Children (Northern Ireland) Order 1995;

"claim" means a claim for housing benefit;

"claimant" means a person claiming housing benefit;

"close relative" means a parent, parent-in-law, son, son-in-law, daughter, daughter-in-law, step-parent, step-son, step-daughter, brother, sister, or if any of the preceding persons is one member of a couple, the other member of that couple;

"concessionary payment" means a payment made under arrangements made by the Secretary of State with the consent of the Treasury which is charged either to the National Insurance Fund or to a Departmental Expenditure Vote to which payments of benefit under the Act or the Social Security Act 1975;

"the Consequential Provisions Regulations" means the Housing Benefit and Council Tax Benefit (Consequential Provisions) Regulations 2006;

"co-ownership scheme" meansa scheme under which the dwelling is let by a housing association and the tenant, or his personal representative, will, under the terms of the tenancy agreement or of the agreement under which he became a member of the association, be entitled, on his ceasing to be a member and subject to any conditions stated in either agreement, to a sum calculated by reference directly or indirectly to the value of the dwelling;

"couple" means–
  (a) a man and a woman who are married to each other and are members of the same household;
  (b) a man and a woman who are not married to each other but are living together as husband and wife;
  (c) two people of the same sex who are civil partners of each other and are members of the same household; or
  (d) two people of the same sex who are not civil partners of each other but are living together as if they were civil partners,
  and for the purposes of sub-paragraph (d), two people of the same sex are to be regarded as living together as if they were civil partners if, but only if, they would be regarded as living together as husband and wife were they instead two people of the opposite sex;

"course of study" means any course of study, whether or not it is a sandwich course and whether or not a grant is made for undertaking or attending it;

"Crown tenant" means a person who occupies a dwelling under a tenancy or licence where the interest of the landlord belongs to Her Majesty in right of the Crown or to a government department or is held in trust for Her Majesty for the purposes of a government department, except (in the case of an interest belonging to Her Majesty in right of the Crown) where the interest is under the management of the Crown Estate Commissioners;

"date of claim" means the date on which the claim is made, or treated as made, for the purposes of regulation 64 (time and manner in which claims are to be made);

"the Decisions and Appeals Regulations" means the Housing Benefit and Council Tax Benefit (Decisions and Appeals) Regulations 2001;

"the designated authority" means any of the following–
  (a) the Secretary of State;
  (b) a person providing services to the Secretary of State;
  (c) a local authority;
  (d) a person providing services to, or authorised to exercise any function of, any such local authority;

"designated office" means the office designated by the relevant authority for the receipt of claims to housing benefit–

(a) by notice upon or with a form approved by it for the purpose of claiming housing benefit; or

(b) by reference upon or with such a form to some other document available from it and sent by electronic means or otherwise on application and without charge; or

(c) by any combination of the provisions set out in sub-paragraphs (a) and (b) above;

"disability living allowance" means a disability living allowance under section 71 of the Act;

"dwelling occupied as the home" means the dwelling, together with any garage, garden and outbuildings, normally occupied by the claimant as his home, including any premises not so occupied which it is impracticable or unreasonable to sell separately, in particular, in Scotland, any croft land on which the dwelling is situated;

"earnings" has the meaning prescribed in regulation 35 (earnings of employed earners) or, as the case may be, 38 (earnings of self-employed earners);

"the Eileen Trust" means the charitable trust of that name established on 29th March 1993 out of funds provided by the Secretary of State for the benefit of persons eligible for payment in accordance with its provisions;

[² "electronic communication" has the same meaning as in section 15(1) of the 2000 Act;]

"eligible rent" is to be construed in accordance with regulation 12 (rent);

"employed earner" is to be construed in accordance with section 2(1)(a) of the Act and also includes a person who is in receipt of a payment which is payable under any enactment having effect in Northern Ireland and which corresponds to statutory sick pay or statutory maternity pay;

"extended payment (severe disablement allowance and incapacity benefit)" means a payment of housing benefit pursuant to regulation 53;

"family" has the meaning assigned to it by section 137(1) of the Act;

"the former Regulations" means the Housing Benefit (General) Regulations 1987;

"the Fund" means moneys made available from time to time by the Secretary of State for the benefit of persons eligible for payment in accordance with the provisions of a scheme established by him on 24th April 1992 or, in Scotland, on 10th April 1992;

"gateway office" means an appropriate DWP office or an office designated by the appropriate authority which is nominated by the Secretary of State as a gateway office and referred to in a notice upon or attached to a form approved by the appropriate authority for the purpose of claiming housing benefit;

[¹ "the Graduated Retirement Benefit Regulations" means the Social Security (Graduated Retirement Benefit) Regulations 2005;]

"guarantee credit" is to be construed in accordance with sections 1 and 2 of the State Pension Credit Act;

"a guaranteed income payment" means a payment made under article 14(1)(b) or article 21(1)(a) of the Armed Forces and Reserve Forces (Compensation Scheme) Order 2005;

"hostel" means a building–

(a) in which there is provided for persons generally or for a class of persons, domestic accommodation, otherwise than in separate and self-contained premises, and either board or facilities for the preparation of food adequate to the needs of those persons, or both; and

(b) which is–

(i) managed or owned by a registered housing association; or

        (ii)   operated other than on a commercial basis and in respect of which funds are provided wholly or in part by a government department or agency or a local authority; or

        (iii)   managed by a voluntary organisation or charity and provides care, support or supervision with a view to assisting those persons to be rehabilitated or resettled within the community; and

   (c)   which is not–

        (i)   a care home;

        (ii)   an independent hospital; or

        (iii)   an Abbeyfield Home;

"Housing Act functions" has the same meaning as in section 136(1) of the Administration Act;

"housing association" has the meaning assigned to it by section 1(1) of the Housing Associations Act 1985;

"an income-based jobseeker's allowance" and "a joint-claim jobseeker's allowance" have the same meaning as they have in the Jobseekers Act by virtue of section 1(4) of that Act;

"Income Support Regulations" means the Income Support (General) Regulations 1987;

"independent hospital" in England and Wales has the meaning assigned to it by section 2 of the Care Standards Act 2000 and in Scotland means an independent healthcare service as defined in section 2(5)(a) and (b) of the Regulation of Care (Scotland) Act 2001;

"the Independent Living Fund" means the charitable trust established out of funds provided by the Secretary of State for the purpose of providing financial assistance to those persons incapacitated by or otherwise suffering from very severe disablement who are in need of such assistance to enable them to live independently;

[⁶ "the Independent Living Fund (2006)" means the Trust of that name established by a deed dated 10th April 2006 and made between the Secretary of State for Work and Pensions of the one part and Margaret Rosemary Cooper, Michael Beresford Boyall and Marie Theresa Martin of the other part;]

"the Independent Living Funds" means the Independent Living Fund, [⁶ the Independent Living (Extension) Fund, the Independent Living (1993) Fund and the Independent Living Fund (2006)];

"the Independent Living (Extension) Fund" means the Trust of that name established by a deed dated 25th February 1993 and made between the Secretary of State for Social Security of the one part and Robin Glover Wendt and John Fletcher Shepherd of the other part;

"the Independent Living (1993) Fund" means the Trust of that name established by a deed dated 25th February 1993 and made between the Secretary of State for Social Security of the one part and Robin Glover Wendt and John Fletcher Shepherd of the other part;

"invalid carriage or other vehicle" means a vehicle propelled by petrol engine or by electric power supplied for use on the road and to be controlled by the occupant;

"Jobseekers Act" means the Jobseekers Act 1995;

"Jobseeker's Allowance Regulations" means the Jobseeker's Allowance Regulations 1996;

"the London Bombings Relief Charitable fund" means the company limited by guarantee (number 5505072) and registered charity of that name established on 11th July 2005 for the purpose of (amongst other things) relieving sickness, disability or financial need of victims (including families or dependants of victims) of the terrorist attacks carried out in London on 7th July 2005;

"lone parent" means a person who has no partner and who is responsible for and a member of the same household as a child or young person;

"long tenancy" means a tenancy granted for a term of years certain exceeding twenty one years, whether or not the tenancy is, or may become, terminable before the end of that term by notice given by or to the tenant or by re-entry, forfeiture (or, in Scotland, irritancy) or otherwise and includes a lease for a term fixed by law under a grant with a covenant or obligation for perpetual renewal unless it is a lease by sub-demise from one which is not a long tenancy;

[⁸]

"the Macfarlane (Special Payments) Trust" means the trust of that name, established on 29th January 1990 partly out of funds provided by the Secretary of State, for the benefit of certain persons suffering from haemophilia;

"the Macfarlane (Special Payments) (No. 2) Trust" means the trust of that name, established on 3rd May 1991 partly out of funds provided by the Secretary of State, for the benefit of certain persons suffering from haemophilia and other beneficiaries;

"the Macfarlane Trust" means the charitable trust, established partly out of funds provided by the Secretary of State to the Haemophilia Society, for the relief of poverty or distress among those suffering from haemophilia;

"maternity leave" means a period during which a woman is absent from work because she is pregnant or has given birth to a child, and at the end of which she has a right to return to work either under the terms of her contract of employment or under Part 8 of the Employment Rights Act 1996;

"maximum rent" means the amount to which the eligible rent is restricted in a case where regulation 13 applies;

"net earnings" means such earnings as are calculated in accordance with regulation 36 (calculation of net earnings of employed earners);

"net profit" means such profit as is calculated in accordance with regulation 39 (calculation of net profit of self-employed earners);

"non-dependant" has the meaning prescribed in regulation 3;

"non-dependant deduction" means a deduction that is to be made under regulation 55 (non-dependant deductions);

"occupational pension" means any pension or other periodical payment under an occupational pension scheme but does not include any discretionary payment out of a fund established for relieving hardship in particular cases;

"owner" means–

    (a)   in relation to a dwelling in England and Wales, the person who, otherwise than as a mortgagee in possession, is for the time being entitled to dispose of the fee simple, whether or not with the consent of other joint owners;

    (b)   in relation to a dwelling in Scotland, the proprietor under udal tenure or the proprietor of the dominion utile or the tenant's or the lessee's interest in a long tenancy, a kindly tenancy, a lease registered or registerable under the Registration of Leases (Scotland) Act 1857 or the Land Registration (Scotland) Act 1979 or a tenant-at-will as defined in section 20(8) of that Act of 1979;

"partner" means–

    (a)   where a claimant is a member of a couple, the other member of that couple; or

    (b)   where a claimant is polygamously married to two or more members of his household, any such member;

"paternity leave" means a period of absence from work on leave by virtue of section 80A or 80B of the Employment Rights Act 1996;

"payment" includes part of a payment;

"pension fund holder" means with respect to a personal pension scheme or [⁴ an occupational pension scheme], the trustees, managers or scheme administrators, as the case may be, of the scheme [⁴] concerned;

"person affected" shall be construed in accordance with regulation 3 of the Decisions and Appeals Regulations;

"person on income support" means a person in receipt of income support;

"person on state pension credit" means a person in receipt of state pension credit;

[⁴ "personal pension scheme" means–

    (a)   a personal pension scheme as defined by section 1 of the Pension Schemes Act 1993;

    (b)   an annuity contract or trust scheme approved under section 620 or 621 of the Income and Corporation Taxes Act 1988 or a substituted contract within the meaning of section 622(3) of that Act which is treated as having become a registered pension scheme by virtue of paragraph 1(1)(f) of Schedule 36 to the Finance Act 2004;

    (c)   a personal pension scheme approved under Chapter 4 of Part 14 of the Income and Corporation Taxes Act 1988 which is treated as having become a registered pension scheme by virtue of paragraph 1(1)(g) of Schedule 36 to the Finance Act 2004;]

"policy of life insurance" means any instrument by which the payment of money is assured on death (except death by accident only) or the happening of any contingency dependent on human life, or any instrument evidencing a contract which is subject to payment of premiums for a term dependent on human life;

"polygamous marriage" means any marriage during the subsistence of which a party to it is married to more than one person and the ceremony of marriage took place under the law of a country which permits polygamy;

"qualifying age for state pension credit" means (in accordance with section 1(2)(b) and (6) of the State Pension Credit Act)–

    (a)   in the case of a woman, pensionable age; or

    (b)   in the case of a man, the age which is pensionable age in the case of a woman born on the same day as the man;

"qualifying course" means a qualifying course as defined for the purposes of Parts 2 and 4 of the Jobseeker's Allowance Regulations;

"qualifying person" means a person in respect of whom payment has been made from the Fund, the Eileen Trust, the Skipton Fund or the London Bombings Relief Charitable Fund;

"relative" means a close relative, grandparent, grandchild, uncle, aunt, nephew or niece;

"relevant authority" means an authority administering housing benefit;

"remunerative work" has the meaning prescribed in regulation 6 (remunerative work);

"rent" includes all those payments in respect of a dwelling specified in regulation 12(1);

"the Rent Officers Order" means the Rent Officers (Housing Benefit Functions) Order 1997 or, as the case may be, the Rent Officers (Housing Benefit Functions) (Scotland) Order 1997;

[⁴]

"sandwich course" has the meaning given in regulation 5(2) of the Education (Student Support) Regulations 2002, regulation 5(2) of the Education (Student Loans)(Scotland) Regulations 2000 or regulation 5(2) of the Education (Student Support) Regulations (Northern Ireland)2002, as the case may be;

"savings credit" shall be construed in accordance with sections 1 and 3 of the State Pension Credit Act;

"self-employed earner" is to be construed in accordance with section 2(1)(b) of the
Act;
"shared ownership tenancy" means–
  (a) in relation to England and Wales, a [⁵ lease] granted on payment of a
       premium calculated by reference to a percentage of the value of the dwelling
       or the cost of providing it;
  (b) in relation to Scotland, an agreement by virtue of which the tenant of a
       dwelling of which he and the landlord are joint owners is the tenant in
       respect of the landlord's interest in the dwelling or by virtue of which the
       tenant has the right to purchase the dwelling or the whole or part of the
       landlord's interest therein;
"single claimant" means a claimant who neither has a partner nor is a lone parent;
"the Skipton Fund" means the ex-gratia payment scheme administered by the
       Skipton Fund Limited, incorporated on 25th March 2004, for the benefit of
       certain persons suffering from hepatitis C and other persons eligible for
       payment in accordance with the scheme's provisions;
"sports award" means an award made by one of the Sports Councils named in
       section 23(2) of the National Lottery etc Act 1993 out of sums allocated to
       it for distribution under that section;
[⁷ "starting rate", where it relates to the rate of tax, has the same meaning as in the
       Income Tax Act 2007 (see section 989 of that Act);]
"State Pension Credit Act" means the State Pension Credit Act 2002;
"student" means a person, other than a person in receipt of a training allowance,
       who is attending or undertaking–
  (a) a course of study at an educational establishment; or
  (b) a qualifying course;
"the Tax Credits Act" means the Tax Credits Act 2002;
"tax year" means a period beginning with 6th April in one year and ending with 5th
       April in the next;
"training allowance" means an allowance (whether by way of periodical grants or
       otherwise) payable–
  (a) out of public funds by a Government department or by or on behalf of the
       Secretary of State, Scottish Enterprise or Highlands and Islands Enterprise,
       the Learning and Skills Council for England or the National Assembly for
       Wales;
  (b) to a person for his maintenance or in respect of a member of his family; and
  (c) for the period, or part of the period, during which he is following a course
       of training or instruction provided by, or in pursuance of arrangements
       made with, that department or approved by that department in relation to
       him or so provided or approved by or on behalf of the Secretary of State,
       Scottish Enterprise or Highlands and Islands Enterprise or the National
       Assembly for Wales,
       but it does not include an allowance paid by any Government department to or in
       respect of a person by reason of the fact that he is following a course of full-time
       education, other than under arrangements made under section 2 of the 1973 Act
       or is training as a teacher;
"voluntary organisation" means a body, other than a public or local authority, the
       activities of which are carried on otherwise than for profit;
[³]
"water charges" means–
  (a) as respects England and Wales, any water and sewerage charges under
       Chapter 1 of Part 5 of the Water Industry Act 1991;
  (b) as respects Scotland, any water and sewerage charges established by
       Scottish Water under a charges scheme made under section 29A of the
       Water Industry (Scotland) Act 2002,

in so far as such charges are in respect of the dwelling which a person occupies as his home;

"working tax credit" means a working tax credit under section 10 of the Tax Credits Act;

"Working Tax Credit Regulations" means the Working Tax Credit (Entitlement and Maximum Rate) Regulations 2002;

"young individual" means a single claimant who has not attained the age of 25 years, but does not include such a claimant–

(a) whose landlord is a registered housing association;

(b) who has not attained the age of 22 years and has ceased to be the subject of a care order made pursuant to section 31(1)(a) of the Children Act 1989 which had previously been made in respect to him either–

　(i) after he attained the age of 16 years; or

　(ii) before he attained the age of 16 years, but had continued after he attained that age;

(c) who has not attained the age of 22 years and was formerly provided with accommodation under section 20 of the Children Act 1989;

(d) who has not attained the age of 22 years and has ceased to be subject to a supervision requirement by a children's hearing under section 70 of the Children (Scotland) Act 1995 ("the 1995 Act") made in respect of him which had continued after he attained the age of 16 years, other than a case where–

　(i) the ground of referral was based on the sole condition as to the need for compulsory measures of care specified in section 52(2)(g) of the 1995 Act (commission of offences by child); or

　(ii) he was required by virtue of the supervision requirement to reside with a parent or guardian of his within the meaning of the 1995 Act, or with a friend or relative of his or of his parent or guardian;

(e) who has not attained the age of 22 years and has ceased to be a child in relation to whom the parental rights and responsibilities were transferred to a local authority under a parental responsibilities order made in accordance with section 86 of the 1995 Act or treated as so vested in accordance with paragraph 3 of Schedule 3 to that Act, either–

　(i) after he attained the age of 16 years; or

　(ii) before he attained the age of 16 years, but had continued after he attained that age; or

(f) who has not attained the age of 22 years and has ceased to be provided with accommodation by a local authority under section 25 of the 1995 Act where he has previously been provided with accommodation by the authority under that provision either–

　(i) after he attained the age of 16 years; or

　(ii) before he attained the age of 16 years, but had continued to be in such accommodation after he attained that age; and

"young person" has the meaning prescribed in regulation 19(1).

(2) References in these Regulations to a person who is liable to make payments shall include references to a person who is treated as so liable under regulation 8 (circumstances in which a person is to be treated as liable to make payments in respect of a dwelling).

(3) For the purposes of these Regulations, a person is on an income-based jobseeker's allowance on any day in respect of which an income-based jobseeker's allowance is payable to him and on any day–

(a) in respect of which he satisfies the conditions for entitlement to an income-based jobseeker's allowance but where the allowance is not paid in accordance with section 19 or 20A of the Jobseekers Act (circumstances in which a jobseeker's allowance is not payable); or

(b)   which is a waiting day for the purposes of paragraph 4 of Schedule 1 to that Act and which falls immediately before a day in respect of which an income-based jobseeker's allowance is payable to him or would be payable to him but for section 19 or 20A of that Act; or

(c)   in respect of which he is a member of a joint-claim couple for the purposes of the Jobseekers Act and no joint-claim jobseeker's allowance is payable in respect of that couple as a consequence of either member of that couple being subject to sanctions for the purpose of section 20A of that Act; or

(d)   in respect of which an income-based jobseeker's allowance or a joint-claim jobseeker's allowance would be payable but for a restriction imposed pursuant to section 62 or 63 of the Child Support, Pensions and Social Security Act 2000 or section 7, 8 or 9 of the Social Security Fraud Act 2001 (loss of benefit provisions).

(4)   For the purposes of these Regulations, the following shall be treated as included in a dwelling–

(a)   subject to sub-paragraphs (b) to (d) any land (whether or not occupied by a structure) which is used for the purposes of occupying a dwelling as a home where either–

    (i)   the occupier of the dwelling acquired simultaneously the right to use the land and the right to occupy the dwelling, and, in the case of a person liable to pay rent for his dwelling, he could not have occupied that dwelling without also acquiring the right to use the land; or

    (ii)   the occupier of the dwelling has made or is making all reasonable efforts to terminate his liability to make payments in respect of the land;

(b)   where the dwelling is a caravan or mobile home, such of the land on which it stands as is used for the purposes of the dwelling;

(c)   where the dwelling is a houseboat, the land used for the purposes of mooring it;

(d)   where in Scotland, the dwelling is situated on or pertains to a croft within the meaning of section 3(1) of the Crofters (Scotland) Act 1993, the croft land on which it is situated or to which it pertains.

(5)   In these Regulations references to any person in receipt of a guarantee credit, a savings credit or state pension credit includes a reference to a person who would be in receipt thereof but for regulation 13 of the State Pension Credit Regulations 2002 (small amounts of state pension credit).

Modifications

Some definitions are inserted by Sch 9 para 2. These apply only to Pathfinder Authorities who are administering the pilot local housing allowance scheme, as from the date specified in relation to each authority as specified in Sch 9 Part 1.

References to "step-parent", step-children and the various in-laws in the definition of "close relative" are modified by s246 Civil Partnership Act 2004 (see p1046) and article 3 and para 24 of the Schedule to SI 2005 No.3137 (see pp1097 and 1097).

Amendments

1.   Inserted by reg 11(2) of SI 2005 No 2677 and reg 2 of SI 2006 No 217 as from 6.4.06.
2.   Inserted by Art 3(2) of SI 2006 No 2968 as from 20.12.06.
3.   Omitted by Reg 6(a) of SI 2007 No 1619 as from 3.7.07.
4.   Amended by reg 5(2) of SI 2007 No 1749 as from 16.7.07.
5.   Amended by reg 3(2) of SI 2007 No 1356 as from 1.10.07.
6.   Amended by Art 9 of SI 2007 No 2538 as from 1.10.07.
7.   Inserted by reg 12(2) of SI 2007 No 2618 as from 1.10.07.
8.   Revoked by reg 2 and the Sch of SI 2007 No 2618 as from 1.10.07.

Analysis

"board and lodging accommodation" is defined as accommodation in which "cooked or prepared meals are provided and consumed". This definition is identical to that found in reg 2(1) of the Income Support

(General) Regulations 1987. Preparation, in the context of this definition, requires something more than merely leaving the ingredients out for the lodger: *CSB 950/1987*.

"guarantee credit". See the General Note to the SPCA on p1042.

"qualifying age for state pension credit" "Pensionable age" for a woman is currently 60, but will rise gradually to 65 between 2010 and 2020 by virtue of s126 of and Sch 4 to the Pensions Act 1995.

"savings credit". See the General Note to the SPCA on p1042.

Definition of non-dependant

3.–(1) In these Regulations, "non-dependant" means any person, except someone to whom paragraph (2) applies, who normally resides with a claimant or with whom a claimant normally resides.

(2) This paragraph applies to–

(a) any member of the claimant's family;

(b) if the claimant is polygamously married, any partner of his and any child or young person who is a member of his household and for whom he or one of his partners is responsible;

(c) a child or young person who is living with the claimant but who is not a member of his household by virtue of regulation 21 (circumstances in which a person is to be treated as being or not being a member of the same household);

(d) subject to paragraph (3), a person who jointly occupies the claimant's dwelling and is either a co-owner of that dwelling with the claimant or his partner (whether or not there are other co-owners) or is liable with the claimant or his partner to make payments in respect of his occupation of the dwelling;

(e) subject to paragraph (3)–

(i) any person who is liable to make payments on a commercial basis to the claimant or the claimant's partner in respect of the occupation of the dwelling;

(ii) any person to whom or to whose partner the claimant or the claimant's partner is liable to make payments on a commercial basis in respect of the occupation of the dwelling; or

(iii) any other member of the household of the person to whom or to whose partner the claimant or the claimant's partner is liable to make payments on a commercial basis in respect of the occupation of the dwelling;

(f) a person who lives with the claimant in order to care for him or a partner of his and who is engaged by a charitable or voluntary organisation which makes a charge to the claimant or his partner for the services provided by that person.

(3) Sub-paragraphs (d) and (e) of paragraph (2) shall not apply to any person who is treated as if he were not liable to make payments in respect of a dwelling under paragraph (1) of regulation 9 (circumstances in which a person is to be treated as not liable to make payments in respect of a dwelling).

(4) For the purposes of this regulation and regulation 9 a person resides with another only if they share any accommodation except a bathroom, a lavatory or a communal area within the meaning prescribed in paragraph 8 of Schedule 1 but not if each person is separately liable to make payments in respect of his occupation of the dwelling to the landlord.

Cases in which section 1(1A) of the Administration Act is disapplied

4. Section 1(1A) of the Administration Act (requirement to state national insurance number) shall not apply–

(a) to a claim for housing benefit where the person making the claim, or in respect of whom the claim is made, is liable to make payments in respect of a dwelling which is a hostel;

(b)   to any child or young person in respect of whom housing benefit is claimed.

Persons who have attained the qualifying age for state pension credit

5.–(1)   Except as provided in paragraph (2), these Regulations apply to a person who has attained the qualifying age for state pension credit.

(2)   These Regulations shall not apply in relation to any person if he, or if he has a partner, his partner, is a person on income support or on an income-based jobseeker's allowance.

Definitions

"person on an income-based jobseeker's allowance" – see reg 2(3).
"person on income support" – see reg 2(3).
"qualifying age for state pension credit" – see reg 2(1).

General Note

The HB(SPC) Regs apply where a person has reached the qualifying age for PC (currently 60). However, they do not apply if either the claimant or her/his partner is on IS or income-based JSA. In this case, the HB Regs instead apply. Note that the HB Regs also apply to a person for the purpose of reg 72 and Sch 7 of the HB Regs (extended payments of HB) even if s/he or her/his partner has reached the qualifying age for PC: reg 5(2) HB Regs.

Remunerative work

6.–(1)   Subject to the following provisions of this regulation, a person shall be treated for the purposes of these Regulations as engaged in remunerative work if he is engaged, or, where his hours of work fluctuate, he is engaged on average, for not less than 16 hours a week, in work for which payment is made or which is done in expectation of payment.

(2)   Subject to paragraph (3), in determining the number of hours for which a person is engaged in work where his hours of work fluctuate, regard shall be had to the average of hours worked over–

(a)   if there is a recognisable cycle of work, the period of one complete cycle (including, where the cycle involves periods in which the person does no work, those periods but disregarding any other absences);

(b)   in any other case, the period of 5 weeks immediately prior to the date of claim, or such other length of time as may, in the particular case, enable the person's weekly average hours of work to be determined more accurately.

(3)   Where, for the purposes of paragraph (2)(a), a person's recognisable cycle of work at a school, other educational establishment or other place of employment is one year and includes periods of school holidays or similar vacations during which he does not work, those periods and any other periods not forming part of such holidays or vacations during which he is not required to work shall be disregarded in establishing the average hours for which he is engaged in work.

(4)   Where no recognisable cycle has been established in respect of a person's work, regard shall be had to the number of hours or, where those hours will fluctuate, the average of the hours, which he is expected to work in a week.

(5)   A person shall be treated as engaged in remunerative work during any period for which he is absent from work referred to in paragraph (1) if the absence is either without good cause or by reason of a recognised, customary or other holiday.

(6)   A person on income support or an income-based jobseeker's allowance for more than 3 days in any benefit week shall be treated as not being in remunerative work in that week.

(7)   A person shall not be treated as engaged in remunerative work on any day on which the person is on maternity leave, paternity leave or adoption leave, or is absent from work because he is ill.

(8)   A person shall not be treated as engaged in remunerative work on any day on which he is engaged in an activity in respect of which–

(a) a sports award has been made, or is to be made, to him; and

(b) no other payment is made or is expected to be made to him.

PART 2
Provisions affecting entitlement to housing benefit

Circumstances in which a person is or is not to be treated as occupying a dwelling as his home

7.–(1) Subject to the following provisions of this regulation, a person shall be treated as occupying as his home the dwelling normally occupied as his home–

(a) by himself or, if he is a member of a family, by himself and his family; or

(b) if he is polygamously married, by himself, his partners and any child or young person for whom he or any partner of his is responsible and who is a member of that same household,

and shall not be treated as occupying any other dwelling as his home.

(2) In determining whether a dwelling is the dwelling normally occupied as a person's home for the purpose of paragraph (1) regard shall be had to any other dwelling occupied by that person or any other person referred to in paragraph (1) whether or not that dwelling is in Great Britain.

(3) Where a single claimant or a lone parent is a student, other than one to whom regulation 56(1) of the Housing Benefit Regulations 2006 applies (circumstances in which certain students are treated as not liable to make payments in respect of a dwelling), or is on a training course and is liable to make payments (including payments of mortgage interest or, in Scotland, payments under heritable securities or, in either case, analogous payments) in respect of either (but not both) the dwelling which he occupies for the purpose of attending his course of study or, his training course, or as the case may be, the dwelling which he occupies when not attending his course, he shall be treated as occupying as his home the dwelling in respect of which he is liable to make such payments.

(4) Where a claimant has been required to move into temporary accommodation by reason of essential repairs being carried out to the dwelling normally occupied as his home, and is liable to make payments (including payments of mortgage interest or, in Scotland, payments under heritable securities or, in either case, analogous payments) in respect of either (but not both) the dwelling which he normally occupied as his home or the temporary accommodation, he shall be treated as occupying as his home the dwelling in respect of which he is liable to make payments.

(5) Where a person is required to reside in a dwelling which is a bail hostel or probation hostel approved by the Secretary of State under section 9(1) of the Criminal Justice and Court Services Act 2000, he shall not be treated as occupying that dwelling as his home.

(6) Where a person is liable to make payments in respect of two(but not more than two) dwellings, he shall be treated as occupying both dwellings as his home only–

(a) for a period not exceeding 52 weeks in the case where he has left and remains absent from the former dwelling occupied as his home through fear of violence in that dwelling or by a former member of his family and–

(i) it is reasonable that housing benefit should be paid in respect of both his former dwelling and his present dwelling occupied as the home; and

(ii) he intends to return to occupy the former dwelling as his home; or

(b) in the case of a couple or a member of a polygamous marriage, where he or one partner is a student, other than one to whom regulation 56(1) of the Housing Benefit Regulations 2006 applies (circumstances in which certain students are treated as not liable to make payments in respect of a dwelling), or is on a training course and it is unavoidable that the partners should occupy two separate dwellings and reasonable that housing benefit should be paid in respect of both dwellings; or

(c) in the case where, because of the number of persons referred to in paragraph (1), they have been housed by a housing authority in two separate dwellings; or

(d) in the case where a person has moved into a newdwelling occupied as the home, except where paragraph (4) applies, for a period not exceeding four benefit weeks [¹ from the date on which he moved] if he could not reasonably have avoided liability in respect of two dwellings; or

(e) in the case where a person–
  (i) is treated by virtue of paragraph (8) as occupying a dwelling as his home (''the new dwelling'') and sub-paragraph (c)(i) of that paragraph applies; and
  (ii) he has occupied another dwelling as his home on any day within the period of 4 weeks immediately preceding the date he moved to the new dwelling, for a period not exceeding 4 benefit weeks immediately preceding the date on which he moved.

(7) Where–
(a) a person has moved into a dwelling for which he is not liable to make payments (''the new dwelling''); and
(b) immediately before that move, he was liable to make payments for the dwelling he previously occupied as his home (''the former dwelling''); and
(c) that liability continues after he has moved into the new dwelling,
he shall be treated as occupying the former dwelling as his home for a period not exceeding four benefit weeks if he could not reasonably have avoided liability in respect of that former dwelling.

(8) [² Where]–
(a) [² a person] has moved into a dwelling and was liable to make payments in respect of that dwelling before moving in; and
[² (b) either–
  (i) that person had claimed housing benefit before moving in and either no decision has yet been made on that claim or it has been refused but a further claim has been made or treated as made within 4 weeks of the date on which the claimant moved into the new dwelling occupied as the home; or
  (ii) that person notified the move to the new dwelling as a change of circumstances under regulation 69 (duty to notify changes of circumstances) before the move, or the move to the new dwelling was otherwise notified before the move under that regulation; and]
(c) the delay in moving into the dwelling in respect of which there was liability to make payments before moving in was reasonable and–
  (i) that delay was necessary in order to adapt the dwelling to meet the disablement needs of that person or any member of his family; or
  (ii) the move was delayed pending the outcome of an application under Part 3 of the Act for a social fund payment to meet a need arising out of the move or in connection with setting up the home in the dwelling and either a member of the claimant's family is aged 5 or under or the claimant is a person who has attained or whose partner has attained the qualifying age for state pension credit; or
  (iii) the claimant became liable to make payments in respect of the dwelling while he was a patient or in residential accommodation,
[² the person shall be treated] as occupying the dwelling as his home for any period not exceeding 4 weeks immediately prior to the date on which he moved into the dwelling and in respect of which he was liable to make payments.

(9)   Where a person is treated by virtue of paragraph (8) as occupying a dwelling as his home in respect of the period before moving in, his claim for housing benefit in respect of that dwelling shall be treated as having been made on–

(a)   in the case of a claim in respect of which a decision has not yet been made the date that claim was or was treated as made in accordance with regulation 64 (time and manner in which claims are to be made); or

(b)   in the case of a claim for housing benefit in respect of that dwelling which has been refused and a further claim was or was treated as made in accordance with Part 9 (claims) within 4 weeks of the date on which he moved into the dwelling, the date on which the claim was refused or was treated as made; or

(c)   the date from which he is treated by virtue of paragraph (8) as occupying the dwelling as his home,

whichever of those dates is the later.

(10)   Where a person to whom neither paragraph (6)(a) nor (16)(c)(x) applies–

(a)   formerly occupied a dwelling but has left and remains absent from it through fear of violence–

(i)   in the dwelling; or

(ii)   by a person who was formerly a member of the family of the person first mentioned; and

(b)   has a liability to make payments in respect of that dwelling which is unavoidable,

he shall be treated as occupying the dwelling as his home for a period not exceeding 4 benefit weeks.

(11)   This paragraph shall apply to a person who enters residential accommodation–

(a)   for the purpose of ascertaining whether the accommodation suits his needs; and

(b)   with the intention of returning to the dwelling which is normally occupied by him as his home should, in the event, the residential accommodation prove not to suit his needs; and

(c)   while the part of the dwelling which is normally occupied by him as his home is not let, or as the case may be, sublet.

(12)   A person to whom paragraph (11) applies shall be treated as if he is occupying the dwelling he normally occupies as his home for a period not exceeding, subject to an overall limit of 52 weeks on the absence from that home, 13 weeks beginning from the first day he enters a residential accommodation.

(13)   Subject to paragraph (17) a person shall be treated as occupying a dwelling as his home while he is temporarily absent therefrom for a period not exceeding 13 weeks beginning from the first day of that absence from the home only if–

(a)   he intends to return to occupy the dwelling as his home; and

(b)   the part of the dwelling normally occupied by him has not been let or, as the case may be, sub-let; and

(c)   the period of absence is unlikely to exceed 13 weeks.

(14)   This paragraph applies to a person who is–

(a)   detained in custody pending sentence upon conviction or under a sentence imposed by a court (other than a person who is detained in hospital under the provisions of the Mental Health Act 1983, or, in Scotland, under the provisions of the Mental Health (Care and Treatment) (Scotland) Act 2003 or the Criminal Procedure (Scotland) Act 1995); and

(b)   on temporary release from detention in accordance with Rules made under the provisions of the Prison Act 1952 or the Prisons (Scotland) Act 1989.

(15)   Where paragraph (14) applies to a person, then, for any day when he is on temporary release–

(a)   if such temporary release was immediately preceded by a period of temporary absence under paragraph (13) or (16), he shall be treated as if he continues to be absent from the dwelling, despite any occupation of the dwelling;

(b)   for the purposes of paragraph (16)(c)(i), he shall be treated as if he remains in detention; and

(c)   if he does not fall within sub-paragraph (a), he shall be treated as if he does not occupy his dwelling as his home despite any such occupation of the dwelling.

(16)   This paragraph shall apply to a person who is temporarily absent from the dwelling he normally occupies as his home (''absence''), if–

(a)   he intends to return to occupy the dwelling as his home; and

(b)   while the part of the dwelling which is normally occupied by him has not been let, or as the case may be, sublet; and

(c)   he is–

    (i)   detained in custody on remand pending trial or, as a condition of bail, required to reside–

        (aa)   in a dwelling, other than the dwelling he occupies as his home; or

        (bb)   in premises approved under section 9 of the Criminal Justice and Court Services Act 2000,

    or, as the case may be, detained pending sentence upon conviction; or

    (ii)   resident in a hospital or similar institution as a patient; or

    (iii)   undergoing, or as the case may be, his partner or his dependant child is undergoing, in the United Kingdom or elsewhere, medical treatment, or medically approved convalescence, in accommodation other than residential accommodation; or

    (iv)   following, in the United Kingdom or elsewhere, a training course; or

    (v)   undertaking medically approved care of a person residing in the United Kingdom or elsewhere; or

    (vi)   undertaking the care of a child whose parent or guardian is temporarily absent from the dwelling normally occupied by that parent or guardian for the purpose of receiving medically approved care or medical treatment; or

    (vii)   a person who is, in the United Kingdom or elsewhere, receiving medically approved care provided in accommodation other than residential accommodation; or

    (viii)   a student to whom paragraph (3) or (6)(b) does not apply; or

    (ix)   a person who is receiving care provided in residential accommodation other than a person to whom paragraph (11) applies; or

    (x)   a person who has left the dwelling he occupies as his home through fear of violence, in that dwelling, or by a person who was formerly a member of the family of the person first mentioned, and to whom paragraph (6)(a) does not apply; and

(d)   the period of his absence is unlikely to exceed 52 weeks or, in exceptional circumstances, is unlikely substantially to exceed that period.

(17)   A person to whom paragraph (16) applies shall be treated as occupying the dwelling he normally occupies at his home during any period of absence not exceeding 52 weeks beginning from the first day of that absence.

(18)   In this regulation–

''medically approved'' means certified by a medical practitioner;

''patient'' means a person who is undergoing medical or other treatment as an in-patient in any hospital or similar institution;

''residential accommodation'' means accommodation which is provided in–

(a)   a care home;

(b)   an independent hospital;
(c)   an Abbeyfield Home; or
(d)   an establishment managed or provided by a body incorporated by Royal Charter or constituted by Act of Parliament other than a local social services authority;

"training course" means a course of training or instruction provided wholly or partly by or on behalf of or in pursuance of arrangements made with, or approved by or on behalf of, Scottish Enterprise, Highlands and Islands Enterprise, a government department or the Secretary of State.

Amendments
1.   Amended by reg 6 of SI 2006 No 3274 as from 8.1.07.
2.   Amended by reg 12(3) of SI 2007 No 2618 as from 1.10.07.

General Note
Reg 7 is nearly identical to reg 7 HB Regs (see p211). The only difference is in para (8)(c)(ii). Here, among the other conditions, rather than making it a requirement that the claimant's applicable amount includes one of specific premiums, the claimant or her/his partner need only have reached the qualifying age for PC (currently 60).

Circumstances in which a person is to be treated as liable to make payments in respect of a dwelling
8.–(1)   Subject to regulation 9 (circumstances in which a person is to be treated as not liable to make payments in respect of a dwelling), the following persons shall be treated as if they were liable to make payments in respect of a dwelling–
(a)   the person who is liable to make those payments;
(b)   a person who is a partner of the person to whom sub-paragraph (a) applies;
(c)   a person who has to make the payments if he is to continue to live in the home because the person liable to make them is not doing so and either–
　　(i)   he was formerly a partner of the person who is so liable; or
　　(ii)   he is some other person whom it is reasonable to treat as liable to make the payments;
(d)   a person whose liability to make such payments is waived by his landlord as reasonable compensation in return for works actually carried out by the tenant in carrying out reasonable repairs or redecoration which the landlord would otherwise have carried out or be required to carry out but this sub-paragraph shall apply only for a maximum of 8 benefit weeks in respect of any one waiver of liability;
(e)   a person who is a partner of a student to whom regulation 56(1) of the Housing Benefit Regulations 2006 (circumstances in which certain students are treated as not liable to make payments in respect of a dwelling) applies.

(2)   A person shall be treated as liable to make a payment in respect of a dwelling for the whole of the period in, or in respect of, which the payment is to be made notwithstanding that the liability is discharged in whole or in part either before or during that period and, where the amount which a person is liable to pay in respect of a period is varied either during or after that period, he shall, subject to regulations 59 to 62 (dates of relevant changes of circumstances, weekly amounts and housing benefit for rent free periods), be treated as liable to pay the amount as so varied during the whole of that period.

Circumstances in which a person is to be treated as not liable to make payments in respect of a dwelling
9.–(1)   A person who is liable to make payments in respect of a dwelling shall be treated as if he were not so liable where–
(a)   the tenancy or other agreement pursuant to which he occupies the dwelling is not on a commercial basis;

(b)   his liability under the agreement is to a person who also resides in the dwelling and who is a close relative of his or of his partner;

(c)   his liability under the agreement is–
    (i)   to his former partner and is in respect of a dwelling which he and his former partner occupied before they ceased to be partners; or
    (ii)   to his partner's former partner and is in respect of a dwelling which his partner and his partner's former partner occupied before they ceased to be partners;

(d)   he is responsible, or his partner is responsible, for a child of the person to whom he is liable under the agreement;

(e)   subject to paragraph (3), his liability under the agreement is to a company or a trustee of a trust of which–
    (i)   he or his partner;
    (ii)   his or his partner's close relative who resides with him; or
    (iii)   his or his partner's former partner,

is, in the case of a company, a director or an employee, or, in the case of a trust, a trustee or a beneficiary;

(f)   is liability under the agreement is to a trustee of a trust of which his or his partner's child is a beneficiary;

(g)   subject to paragraph (3), before the liability was created, he was a non-dependant of someone who resided, and continues to reside, in the dwelling;

(h)   he previously owned, or his partner previously owned, the dwelling in respect of which the liability arises and less than five years have elapsed since he or, as the case may be, his partner, ceased to own the property, save that this sub-paragraph shall not apply where he satisfies the appropriate authority that he or his partner could not have continued to occupy that dwelling without relinquishing ownership;

[¹ (ha) he or his partner–
    (i)   was a tenant under a long tenancy in respect of the dwelling; and
    (ii)   less than five years have elapsed since that tenancy ceased,
except where he satisfies the appropriate authority that he or his partner could not have continued to occupy that dwelling without relinquishing the tenancy;]

(i)   his occupation, or his partner's occupation, of the dwelling is a condition of his or his partner's employment by the landlord;

(j)   he is a member of, and is wholly maintained (disregarding any liability he may have to make payments in respect of the dwelling he occupies as his home) by, a religious order;

(k)   he is in residential accommodation;

(l)   in a case to which the preceding sub-paragraphs do not apply, the appropriate authority is satisfied that the liability was created to take advantage of the housing benefit scheme established under Part 7 of the Act.

(2)   In determining whether a tenancy or other agreement pursuant to which a person occupies a dwelling is not on a commercial basis regard shall be had inter alia to whether the terms upon which the person occupies the dwelling include terms which are not enforceable at law.

(3)   Sub-paragraphs (e) and (g) of paragraph (1) shall not apply in a case where the person satisfies the appropriate authority that the liability was not intended to be a means of taking advantage of the housing benefit scheme.

(4)   In this regulation ''residential accommodation'' means accommodation which is provided in–

(a)   a care home; or

(b)   an independent hospital.

Modifications

Reg 9 applies as modified by Sch 3 para 9(3)(a) HB&CTB(CP) Regs (see p1123) to a claimant who on 3 October 2005 was someone to whom reg 7(2) of the HB Regs 1987 as then in force applied.

Reg 9 applies as modified by Sch 3 para 9(5)(a) HB&CTB(CP) Regs (see p1124) to a claimant who on 3 October 2005 was someone to whom reg 7(5) of the HB Regs 1987 as then in force applied.

Reg 9 applies as modified by Sch 3 para 9(7)(a) HB&CTB(CP) Regs (see p1124) to a claimant who on 3 October 2005 was someone to whom reg 7(7) of the HB Regs 1987 as then in force applied.

Amendment

1.　　Inserted by reg 3(3) of SI 2007 No 1356 as from 1.10.07.

Persons from abroad

10.–(1)　A person from abroad who is liable to make payments in respect of a dwelling shall be treated as if he were not so liable but this paragraph shall not have effect in respect of a person to whom and for a period to which regulation 10A (entitlement of a refugee to housing benefit) and Schedule A1 (treatment of claims for housing benefit by refugees) apply.

[¹ (2)　In paragraph (1), "person from abroad" means, subject to the following provisions of this regulation, a person who is not habitually resident in the United Kingdom, the Channel Islands, the Isle of Man or the Republic of Ireland.

(3)　No person shall be treated as habitually resident in the United Kingdom, the Channel Islands, the Isle of Man or the Republic of Ireland unless he has a right to reside in (as the case may be) the United Kingdom, the Channel Islands, the Isle of Man or the Republic of Ireland other than a right to reside which falls within paragraph (4).

(4)　A right to reside falls within this paragraph if it is one which exists by virtue of, or in accordance with, one or more of the following–

(a)　regulation 13 of the Immigration (European Economic Area) Regulations 2006;

(b)　regulation 14 of those Regulations, but only in a case where the right exists under that regulation because the person is–

(i)　a jobseeker for the purpose of the definition of "qualified person" in regulation 6(1) of those Regulations, or

(ii)　a family member (within the meaning of regulation 7 of those Regulations) of such a jobseeker;

(c)　Article 6 of Council Directive No. 2004/38/EC; or

(d)　Article 39 of the Treaty establishing the European Community (in a case where the person is seeking work in the United Kingdom, the Channel Islands, the Isle of Man or the Republic of Ireland).

(4A)　A person is not a person from abroad if he is–

(a)　a worker for the purposes of Council Directive No. 2004/38/EC;

(b)　a self-employed person for the purposes of that Directive;

(c)　a person who retains a status referred to in sub-paragraph (a) or (b) pursuant to Article 7(3) of that Directive;

(d)　a person who is a family member of a person referred to in sub-paragraph (a), (b) or (c) within the meaning of Article 2 of that Directive;

(e)　a person who has a right to reside permanently in the United Kingdom by virtue of Article 17 of that Directive;

[⁵ (f)　a person who is treated as a worker for the purpose of the definition of "qualified person" in regulation 6(1) of the Immigration (European Economic Area) Regulations 2006 pursuant to–

(i)　regulation 5 of the Accession (Immigration and Worker Registration) Regulations 2004 (application of the 2006 Regulations in relation to a national of the Czech Republic, Estonia, Latvia, Lithuania, Hungary, Poland, Slovenia or the Slovak Republic who is an "accession State worker requiring registration"), or

(ii)   regulation 6 of the Accession (Immigration and Worker Authorisation) Regulations 2006 (right of residence of a Bulgarian or Romanian who is an ''accession State national subject to worker authorisation'');]

(g)   a refugee;

[⁴ (h) a person who has exceptional leave to enter or remain in the United Kingdom granted outside the rules made under section 3(2) of the Immigration Act 1971;

(hh)   a person who has humanitarian protection granted under those rules;]

(i)   a person who is not a person subject to immigration control within the meaning of section 115(9) of the Immigration and Asylum Act 1999[26] and who is in the United Kingdom as a result of his deportation, expulsion or other removal by compulsion of law from another country to the United Kingdom;

(j)   a person in Great Britain who left the territory of Montserrat after 1st November 1995 because of the effect on that territory of a volcanic eruption; [³]

[³ (jj) a person in Great Britain who left Lebanon on or after 12th July 2006 because of the armed conflict there; or]

(k)   on state pension credit.]

(5)   Paragraph (1) of Part 1 of the Schedule to, and regulation 2 as it applies to that paragraph of, the Social Security (Immigration and Asylum) Consequential Amendments Regulations 2000 shall not apply to a person who has been temporarily without funds for any period, or the aggregate of any periods, exceeding 42 days during any one period of limited leave (including any such period as extended).

(6)   In this regulation–

[²]

''refugee'' in this regulation means a person recorded by the Secretary of State as a refugee within the definition in Article 1 of the Convention relating to the Status of Refugees.

Modifications

Reg 10(4A)(a) to (e) applies in relation to a national of Norway, Iceland, Liechtenstein or Switzerland or a member of her/his family (within the meaning of Article 2 of Council Directive No.2004/38/EC) as if such a national were a national of a member state. See reg 10 of SI 2006 No.1026 on p1134.

The amendments made by SI 2006 No.1026 do not affect the continued operation of the transitional and savings provided for in reg 12 of the Social Security (Persons From Abroad) Miscellaneous Amendments Regulations 1996 (see p1054), reg 6 of the Social Security (Habitual Residence) Amendment Regulations 2004 (see p1094) or Sch 3 para 6 HB&CTB(CP) Regs (see p1116). See reg 11 of SI 2006 No.1026 on p1134.

Definition

"person on state pension credit" – see reg 2(1).

Amendments

1.   Substituted by reg 5(2)(a) of SI 2006 No 1026 as from 30.4.06.
2.   Omitted by reg 5(2)(b) of SI 2006 No 1026 as from 30.4.06.
3.   Amended by reg 6 of SI 2006 No 1981 from 25.7.06 until 31.1.07 only.
4.   Amended by reg 6 of SI 2006 No 2528 as from 9.10.06.
5.   Substituted by reg 6 of SI 2006 No 3341 as from 1.1.07.

Analysis

Claimants in receipt of PC are exempt from having the habitual residence test applied to them for HB purposes: para (4A)(k).

Entitlement of a refugee to Housing Benefit
[¹ **10A.**]

Modification

Reg 10A was inserted by Sch 4 para 2(1) HB&CTB(CP) Regs (see p1126). It only applied to claims for HB by some refugees. See also Sch A1 inserted by Sch 4 para 2(2) HB&CTB(CP) Regs on p1127.

Amendment

1.   Lapsed by s12(2)(e) of the Asylum and Immigration (Treatment of Claimants, etc.) Act 2004 (for those recorded as refugees after 14.6.07).

PART 3
Payments in respect of a dwelling

Eligible housing costs

11.–(1)   Subject to the following provisions of this regulation, housing benefit shall be payable in respect of the payments specified in regulation 12(1) (rent) and a claimant's maximum housing benefit shall be calculated under Part 7 (amount of benefit) by reference to the amount of his eligible rent determined in accordance with regulations 12(3) and (7) and 13 (rent and maximum rent).

(2)   Where any payment for which a person is liable in respect of a dwelling and which is specified in regulation 12(1) (payments of rent for which housing benefit is payable), is increased on account of–

(a)   outstanding arrears of any payment or charge; or

(b)   any other unpaid payment or charge,

to which paragraphs (1) to (3) of that regulation or Schedule 1 (ineligible service charges) refer and which is or was formerly owed by him in respect of that or another dwelling, a rent rebate or, as the case may be, a rent allowance shall not be payable in respect of that increase.

Modification

Modification of reg 11 is provided in Sch 9 para 3 (see p802) in relation to Pathfinder Authorities who are administering the pilot local housing allowance scheme, as from the date specified in relation to each authority in Sch 9 Part 1 (see p801).

Cases where maximum housing benefit expires
11A.

Modification

Reg 11A is inserted by Sch 9 para 4 (see p802). It only applies to Pathfinder Authorities who are administering the pilot local housing allowance scheme, as from the date specified in relation to each authority in Sch 9 Part 1 (see p801).

Rent

12.–(1)   Subject to the following provisions of this regulation, the payments in respect of which housing benefit is payable in the form of a rent rebate or allowance are the following periodical payments which a person is liable to make in respect of the dwelling which he occupies as his home–

(a)   payments of, or by way of, rent;

(b)   payments in respect of a licence or permission to occupy the dwelling;

(c)   payments by way of mesne profits or, in Scotland, violent profits;

(d)   payments in respect of, or in consequence of, use and occupation of the dwelling;

(e)   payments of, or by way of, service charges payment of which is a condition on which the right to occupy the dwelling depends;

(f)   mooring charges payable for a houseboat;

(g)   where the home is a caravan or a mobile home, payments in respect of the site on which it stands;

(h)   any contribution payable by a person resident in an almshouse provided by a housing association which is either a charity of which particulars are entered in the register of charities established under section 3 of the Charities Act 1993 (register of charities) or an exempt charity within the meaning of that Act, which is a contribution towards the cost of maintaining that association's almshouses and essential services in them;

(i) payments under a rental purchase agreement, that is to say an agreement for the purchase of a dwelling which is a building or part of one under which the whole or part of the purchase price is to be paid in more than one instalment and the completion of the purchase is deferred until the whole or a specified part of the purchase price has been paid; and

(j) where, in Scotland, the dwelling is situated on or pertains to a croft within the meaning of section 3(1) of the Crofters (Scotland) Act 1993, the payment in respect of the croft land.

(2) A rent rebate or, as the case may be, a rent allowance shall not be payable in respect of the following periodical payments–

(a) payments under a long tenancy except a shared ownership tenancy [¹];

(b) payments under a co-ownership scheme;

(c) payments by an owner;

(d) payments under a hire purchase, credit sale or conditional sale agreement except to the extent the conditional sale agreement is in respect of land; and

(e) payments by a Crown tenant.

[¹ (f) payments by a person in respect of a dwelling where his partner is an owner of that dwelling.]

(3) Subject to paragraphs (4), (5) and (7), the amount of a person's eligible rent shall be–

(a) the maximum rent where a maximum rent has been, or falls to be, determined in accordance with regulation 13 (maximum rent); or

(b) except where sub-paragraph (a) applies, the aggregate of such payments specified in paragraph (1) as that person is liable to pay less–

　(i) except where he is separately liable for charges for water, sewerage or allied environmental services, an amount determined in accordance with paragraph (6);

　(ii) where payments include service charges which are wholly or partly ineligible, an amount in respect of the ineligible charges determined in accordance with Schedule 1; and

　(iii) where he is liable to make payments in respect of any service charges to which paragraph (1)(e) does not apply, but to which paragraph 3(2) of Part 1 of Schedule 1 (unreasonably low service charges) applies in the particular circumstances, an amount in respect of such charges determined in accordance with paragraph 3(2) of Part 1 of Schedule 1.

(4) Where the payments specified in paragraph (1) are payable in respect of accommodation which consists partly of residential accommodation and partly of other accommodation, only such proportion thereof as is referable to the residential accommodation shall count as eligible rent for the purposes of these Regulations.

(5) Where more than one person is liable to make payments in respect of a dwelling, the payments specified in paragraph (1) shall be apportioned for the purpose of calculating the eligible rent for each such person having regard to all the circumstances, in particular, the number of such persons and the proportion of rent paid by each such person.

(6) The amount of the deduction referred to in paragraph (3) shall be–

(a) except in a case to which sub-paragraph (c) applies, if the dwelling occupied by the claimant is a self-contained unit, the amount of the charges;

(b) in any other case except one to which sub-paragraph (c) applies, the proportion of those charges in respect of the self-contained unit which is obtained by dividing the area of the dwelling occupied by the claimant by the area of the self-contained unit of which it forms part;

(c)   where the charges vary in accordance with the amount of water actually used, the amount which the appropriate authority considers to be fairly attributable to water, and sewerage services, having regard to the actual or estimated consumption of the claimant.

(7)   In any case where it appears to the authority that in the particular circumstances of that case the eligible rent as determined in accordance with the preceding paragraphs of this regulation is greater than it is reasonable to meet by way of housing benefit, the eligible rent shall be such lesser sum as seems to that authority to be an appropriate rent in that particular case.

(8)   In this regulation and Schedule 1 (ineligible service charges)–

"service charges" means periodical payments for services, whether or not under the same agreement as that under which the dwelling is occupied, or whether or not such a charge is specified as separate from or separately identified within other payments made by the occupier in respect of the dwelling; and

"services" means services performed or facilities (including the use of furniture) provided for, or rights made available to, the occupier of a dwelling.

Modifications

Modification of reg 12 is provided in Sch 9 para 5 (see p802) in relation to Pathfinder Authorities who are administering the pilot local housing allowance scheme, as from the date specified in relation to each authority as specified in Sch 9 Part 1 (see p801).

A different version of reg 12 is substituted and used to determine eligible rent for some claimants entitled to HB on 1 January 1996. See Sch 3 paras 4 and 5 (1) of the HB&CTB(CP) Regs on p1101.

Amendment

1.   Inserted by reg 3(4) of SI 2007 No 1356 as from 1.10.07.

Eligible rent and the maximum rent (standard local rate)
12A.

Modification

Reg 12A is inserted by Sch 9 para 6 (see p802). It only applies to Pathfinder Authorities who are administering the pilot local housing allowance scheme, as from the date specified in relation to each authority as specified in Sch 9 Part 1 (see p801).

Maximum rent

13.–(1)   Where an authority has applied to the rent officer for a determination in accordance with regulation 14 (requirement to refer to rent officers) and a rent officer has made a determination or redetermination in exercise of the Housing Act functions, the maximum rent shall be determined in accordance with paragraphs (2) to (17).

(2)   In a case where the rent officer has determined a claim-related rent, but is not required to notify the authority of a local reference rent or a single room rent, the maximum rent shall be that claim-related rent.

(3)   In a case where the rent officer has determined and is required to notify the authority of a local reference rent, the maximum rent shall not exceed twice that local reference rent.

(4)   Subject to paragraph (5), in the case of a young individual–

(a)   except where sub-paragraph (b) applies, where the rent officer has determined a single room rent and is required to notify the authority of it, the maximum rent shall not exceed that single room rent;

(b)   where–

    (i)   the rent officer has determined a single room rent and a claim-related rent and is required to notify the authority of them;

(ii)   the claim-related rent includes payment in respect of meals; and

(iii)   the single room rent is greater than the claim-related rent less an amount in respect of meals determined in accordance with paragraph 2 of Part 1 of Schedule 1 (ineligible service charges),

the maximum rent shall not exceed the claim-related rent less that amount in respect of meals.

(5)   Paragraph (4) shall not apply in the case of a claimant–

(a)   to whom paragraph 4 of Schedule 3 to the Housing Benefit and Council Tax Benefit (Consequential Provisions) Regulations 2006 (saving provision) applies;

(b)   to whom paragraph 6 of Schedule 3 (severe disability premium) applies; or

(c)   who has a non-dependant residing with him.

(6)   Subject to the limits specified in paragraphs (3) and (4), in a case where the rent officer has determined both a local reference rent of which he is required to notify the authority and a claim-related rent, and–

(a)   the claim-related rent is higher than the local reference rent, the maximum rent shall be the local reference rent;

(b)   the local reference rent is higher than the claim-related rent, the maximum rent shall be the claim-related rent.

(7)   Subject to the limits specified in paragraphs (3) and (4), in a case where the rent officer has determined a local reference rent of which he is required to notify the authority, but has not determined a claim-related rent and the reckonable rent is more than the local reference rent, the maximum rent shall be the local reference rent.

(8)   In a case where–

(a)   the authority has determined a maximum rent in respect of a dwelling; and

(b)   during the award of housing benefit the reckonable rent in respect of that dwelling is reduced to a sum which is less than the reckonable rent at the time that maximum rent was determined,

then–

(i)   the maximum rent shall not be reduced, where the sum is not less than the maximum rent, during a period ending on the effective date of a decision adopting a determination of a rent officer where that determination was made in exercise of the Housing Act functions pursuant to an application by the authority under regulation 14(1)(c), (d), (e), (f) or (g); and

(ii)   the maximum rent shall be reduced to an amount equal to that sum, where that sum is less than the maximum rent during a period ending on the effective date of a decision adopting a determination of a rent officer where that determination was made in exercise of the Housing Act functions pursuant to an application by the authority under regulation 14(1)(c), (d), (e), (f) or (g).

(9)   Subject to paragraph (10), in a case where–

(a)   a rent officer has made a determination in exercise of the Housing Act functions pursuant to an application by an authority under regulation 14(1)(e); and

(b)   subsequent to that determination the reckonable rent for that dwelling is changed,

then in determining a maximum rent in relation to a claim for benefit of a claimant who has a liability to make payments in respect of that dwelling, the authority shall treat the claim-related or, as the case may be, reckonable rent to be that determined in or, as the case may be, applicable to, that determination by the rent officer.

(10)   Paragraph (9) shall not apply in a case where the reckonable rent is reduced to a figure below the figure that would have been the maximum rent if that reckonable rent had not changed; and where this paragraph applies, the maximum rent shall be the reckonable rent, as so reduced.

(11)   In a case where the claimant occupies a dwelling which is the same as that occupied by him at the date of death of any person to whom paragraph (16)(b) to (d) applied or, had a claim been made, would have applied, the maximum rent shall be either–

(a)   the maximum rent which applied before the death occurred; or

(b)   in a case where there was no maximum rent, the reckonable rent due before the death occurred,

for a period of 12 months from the date of such a death.

(12)   For the purposes of paragraph (11), a claimant shall be treated as occupying the dwelling if paragraph (13) of regulation 7 (circumstances in which a person is or is not to be treated as occupying a dwelling as his home) is satisfied and for that purpose sub-paragraph (b) of that paragraph of that regulation shall be treated as if it were omitted.

(13)   In a case where a charge for meals is ineligible to be met by housing benefit under regulation 12(3) and paragraph 1 of Schedule 1, there shall be deducted an amount determined in accordance with paragraph 2 of Schedule 1 in respect of meals in the calculation of a person's maximum rent, except where the maximum rent is derived from a rent officer determination under–

(a)   paragraph 3 (exceptional high rents) of Schedule 1 to the Rent Officers Order and the notice of claim-related rent states pursuant to paragraph 9(1)(c) of that Schedule that an ineligible payment has not been included in it; or

(b)   paragraph 5 (single room rents) of that Schedule.

(14)   Subject to paragraph (15), where the relevant authority is satisfied that a person to whom paragraph (16) applies was able to meet the financial commitments for his dwelling when they were entered into, there shall be no maximum rent during the first 13 weeks of the claimant's award of housing benefit.

(15)   Paragraph (14) shall not apply where a claimant [¹ , or the claimant's partner,] was previously entitled to benefit in respect of a award of housing benefit which fell wholly or partly less than 52 weeks before the commencement of the [¹ claimant's] current award of housing benefit.

(16)   This paragraph applies to the following persons–

(a)   the claimant;

(b)   any member of his family;

(c)   if the claimant is a member of a polygamous marriage, any partners of his and any child or young person for whom he or a partner is responsible and who is a member of the same household;

(d)   subject to paragraph (17), any relative of the claimant or his partner who occupies the same dwelling as the claimant, whether or not they reside with him.

(17)   Paragraph (16)(d) shall only apply to a relative who has no separate right of occupation of the dwelling which would enable him to continue to occupy it even if the claimant ceased his occupation of it.

(18)   In this regulation–

"claim-related rent" means the rent notified by the rent officer under paragraph 9(1) of Schedule 1 to the Rent Officers Order;

"deduction for meals" means any amount of a person's otherwise eligible rent which is an ineligible service charge by reason of and within the meaning of paragraph 1(a)(i) of Schedule 1;

"local reference rent" means the rent determined by a rent officer under paragraph 4 of Schedule 1 to the Rent Officers Order;

"reckonable rent" means those payments, which a person is liable to make in respect of the dwelling which he occupies as his home, and which are eligible, or would, but for this regulation, be eligible for housing benefit plus the amount of any deduction for fuel, deduction for meals or water charges, as the case may be, which that person is liable to pay;

"single room rent" means the rent determined by a rent officer under paragraph 5 of Schedule 1 to the Rent Officers Order.

Modifications

A different version of reg 13 is substituted for some claimants entitled to HB on 1 January 1996. See Sch 3 paras 4 and 5 (2) HB&CTB(CP) Regs on p1101.

Reg 13 applies as modified by Sch 3 para 8 HB&CTB(CP) Regs (see p1122) for some claimants entitled to HB on or before 5 October 1997.

Amendment

1. Amended by reg 3(5) of SI 2007 No 1356 as from 1.10.07.

Restrictions on rent increases
13ZA.

Modification

Reg 13ZA is inserted for some claimants entitled to HB on 1 January 1996. See Sch 3 paras 4 and 5(3) HB&CTB(CP) Regs on p1101.

Maximum rent (standard local rate)
13A.

Modification

Reg 13A is inserted by Sch 9 para 7 (see p805). It only applies to Pathfinder Authorities who are administering the pilot local housing allowance scheme, as from the date specified in relation to each authority in Sch 9 Part 1 (see p801).

Publication of local housing allowances
13B.

Modification

Reg 13B is inserted by Sch 9 para 7 (see p805). It only applies to Pathfinder Authorities who are administering the pilot local housing allowance scheme, as from the date specified in relation to each authority in Sch 9 Part 1 (see p801).

Requirement to refer to rent officers

14.–(1) Subject to the following provisions of this regulation, a relevant authority shall apply to a rent officer for a determination to be made in pursuance of the Housing Act functions where–

(a) it has received a claim on which rent allowance may be awarded; or

(b) it has received relevant information regarding a claim on which rent allowance may be awarded; or

(c) it has received a notification of a change relating to a rent allowance; or

(d) it has received a notification of a change of dwelling; or

(e) it has received, except in the case where any liability to make payments in respect of a dwelling would be to a housing authority, a request from a person ("the prospective occupier"), on a properly completed form approved for the purpose by the relevant authority, signifying that he is contemplating occupying a dwelling as his home and that if he does so, he is likely to claim housing benefit, but only where that form–

    (i) is signed by the prospective occupier;

    (ii) is countersigned by the person to whom the prospective occupier would incur liability to make such payments; and

    (iii) indicates that the person countersigning agrees to the application being made for that determination; or

(f)   52 weeks have elapsed since it last made an application under sub-paragraph (a), (b), (c), (d) or (e) above in relation to the claim or award in question; or

(g)   52 weeks have elapsed since–

(i)   an application was made under sub-paragraph (f) above; or

(ii)   an application was made under this sub-paragraph,

whichever last occurred.

(2)   When applying to the rent officer pursuant to paragraph (1) the relevant authority shall state the total amount of those payments referred to in regulation 12(1) (rent) which that claimant is liable to make in respect of the dwelling which he occupies as his home and shall provide the following information in respect of those payments–

(a)   whether they include any charges for water, sewerage or allied environmental services or charges in respect of meals or fuel which are ineligible by virtue of paragraph 2 and Part 2 of Schedule 1 (ineligible service charges); and

(b)   where they include any charges that are ineligible for housing benefit by reason of paragraph 1(a)(iv) and (c) to (f) of Schedule 1 (ineligible service charges)–

(i)   that such charges are included; and

(ii)   the value of those charges as determined by that authority pursuant to regulation 13(3) and that Schedule.

(3)   When applying to the rent officer pursuant to paragraph (1), the relevant authority shall state whether, in their opinion, the claimant is or may be a young individual.

(4)   An application shall not be required under paragraph (1) where a claim, relevant information regarding a claim, notification or request relates to either–

(a)   a dwelling in a hostel if, during the period of 12 months which ends on the day on which that claim, relevant information regarding a claim, notification or request is received by the relevant authority–

(i)   a rent officer has already made a determination in the exercise of the Housing Act functions in respect of a dwelling in that hostel which is a similar dwelling to the dwelling to which the claim, relevant information, notification or request relates; and

(ii)   there has been no change relating to a rent allowance that has affected the dwelling in respect of which that determination was made; or

(b)   an ''excluded tenancy'' within the meaning of Schedule 2 (excluded tenancies).

(5)   Where a relevant authority receives a request pursuant to paragraph (1)(e) and it is a case where, by reason of paragraph (4), an application to a rent officer is not required, the authority shall–

(a)   return it to the prospective occupier, indicating why no such application is required; and

(b)   where it is not required by reason of either paragraph (4)(a) of this regulation or paragraph 2 of Schedule 2 (cases where the rent officer has already made a determination), shall also send him a copy of that determination within 4 days of the receipt of that request by the authority.

(6)   Where an application to a rent officer is required by paragraph (1) it shall be made within 3 days, or as soon as practicable thereafter, of–

(a)   the relevant authority receiving a claim on which rent allowance may be awarded; or

(b)   the relevant authority receiving relevant information regarding a claim on which rent allowance may be awarded; or

(c)   the relevant authority receiving a notification of a change relating to a rent allowance; or

(d)   the relevant authority receiving a notification of a change of dwelling; or

(e)   the day on which the period mentioned in paragraph (1)(f) or (g) elapsed,
except that, in the case of a request to which paragraph (1)(e) applies, the application
shall be made within 2 days of the receipt of that request by the authority.

(7)   For the purpose of calculating any period of days mentioned in paragraphs
(5) or (6), no regard shall be had to a day on which the offices of the relevant
authority are closed for the purposes of receiving or determining claims.

(8)   Where the relevant authority has identified charges to which paragraph
(2)(b) applies, it shall–

(a)   deduct those charges from the total amount of those payments which, in
accordance with paragraph (2), it has stated that the claimant is liable to
make in respect of the dwelling which he occupies as his home; and

(b)   notify that total so reduced to the rent officer in its application under
paragraph (1) for his use in making determinations under Schedule 1
(determinations) to the Rent Officers Order.

(9)   For the purposes of this regulation a dwelling in a hostel shall be regarded
as similar to another dwelling in that hostel if each provides sleeping accommodation
for the same number of persons.

(10)   In this regulation–

"change of dwelling" means a change of dwelling occupied by a claimant as his
home during the award where the dwelling to which the claimant has moved
is one in respect of which the authority may make a rent allowance;

"change relating to a rent allowance" means a change or increase to which paragraph
2(3)(a), (b), (c) or (d) of Schedule 2 applies;

"prospective occupier" shall include a person currently in receipt of housing benefit
in respect of a dwelling which he occupies as his home and who is
contemplating entering into a new agreement to occupy that dwelling, but
not in a case where his current agreement commenced less than 11 months
before such a request;

"registered housing association" means a housing association which–

(a)   is registered in a register maintained by the Corporation or the National
Assembly for Wales under chapter 1 of Part 1 of the Housing Act 1996; or

(b)   in Scotland, is registered by Scottish Ministers by virtue of section 57(3)(b)
of the Housing (Scotland) Act 2001;

"relevant information" means information or evidence forwarded to the relevant
authority by an appropriate DWP office regarding a claim on which rent
allowance may be awarded, which completes the transfer of all information
or evidence held by the appropriate DWP office relating to that claim;

"tenancy" includes–

(i)   in Scotland, any other right of occupancy; and

(ii)   in any other case, a licence to occupy premises,

and reference to a tenant, landlord or any other expression appropriate to a tenancy
shall be construed accordingly;

"the Corporation" has the same meaning as in section 56 of the Housing Act 1996.

Modifications

Modification of reg 14 is provided in Sch 9 para 8 (see p808) in relation to Pathfinder Authorities who are
administering the pilot local housing allowance scheme, as from the date specified in relation to each
authority in Sch 9 Part 1 (see p801).

Applications to the rent officer for redeterminations

15.–(1)   Subject to paragraph (2) and regulation 17 (substitute determinations or
substitute redeterminations), where a relevant authority has obtained from a rent
officer either or both of the following–

(a)   a determination on a reference made under regulation 14 (requirement to
refer to rent officers);

(b)   a redetermination on a reference made under regulation 16(2) (application for redetermination by rent officer),

the authority may apply to the rent officer for a redetermination of any determination or redetermination he has made which has effect at the date of the application.

(2)   No application shall be made for a further redetermination of a redetermination made in response to an application under paragraph (1).

Modifications

Modification of reg 15 is provided in Sch 9 para 9 (see p808) in relation to Pathfinder Authorities who are administering the pilot local housing allowance scheme, as from the date specified in relation to each authority in Sch 9 Part 1 (see p801).

Application for redermination by rent officer

16.–(1)   This paragraph applies where–

(a)   a person affected makes written representations which are signed by him, to a relevant authority concerning a decision which it makes in relation to him;

(b)   those representations relate, in whole or in part, to a rent officer's determination or redermination in exercise of the Housing Act functions; and

(c)   those representations are made no later than [¹ one month] after the day on which the person affected was notified of the decision by the relevant authority.

(2)   Subject to paragraphs (3) and (4), where paragraph (1) applies, the relevant authority shall, within 7 days of receiving the representations, apply to the rent officer for a redetermination or, as the case may be, a further redetermination in exercise of the Housing Act functions and a copy of those representations shall accompany the local authority's application.

(3)   Except where paragraph (4) applies, a relevant authority, in relation to any determination by a rent officer of an application under regulation 14(1) (requirement to refer to rent officers), shall not apply for a redetermination under paragraph (2) more than once in respect of an individual claimant's dwelling to which that determination relates.

(4)   Paragraph (2) shall operate so as to require a relevant authority to make a second application where the following conditions are met in addition to those imposed by that paragraph–

(a)   the written representations made under paragraph (1) related to a determination by a rent officer made in response to an application by the relevant authority under regulation 15 (application to the rent officer for redetermination);

(b)   by the time of that application, the rent officer has already provided a redetermination under this regulation of a determination made in response to an application under regulation 14(1); and

(c)   both the application under this regulation referred to in sub-paragraph (b) and the second application for which this paragraph provides relate to the same claimant.

(5)   Where a decision has been revised in consequence of a redetermination, substitute determination or substitute redetermination by a rent officer in exercise of the Housing Act functions and that redetermination, substitute determination or substitute redetermination has led to–

(a)   a reduction in the maximum rent, the redetermination, substitute determination or substitute redetermination shall be a change of circumstances;

(b)   an increase in the maximum rent, the redetermination, substitute determination or substitute redetermination shall have effect in place of the original determination.

Modifications

Modification of reg 16 is provided in Sch 9 para 10 (see p801) in relation to Pathfinder Authorities who are administering the pilot local housing allowance scheme, as from the date specified in relation to each authority in Sch 9 Part 1 (see p808).

Amendment

1.　　Amended by reg 3(6) of SI 2007 No 1356 as from 1.10.07. By reg 3(8) of SI 2007 No1356, the amendment only applies to decisions notified by the relevant authority to the person affected on or after 1.10.07.

General Note

When the regulations were consolidated in March 2006, an error was made in the heading to, and para 1(b) of, reg 16. The term "redermination" was used rather than "redetermination". It is understood that the regulation is to be amended.

Substitute determinations or substitute redeterminations

17.–(1)　　In a case where either–

(a)　　the appropriate authority discovers that an application it has made to the rent officer contained an error in respect of any of the following–

(i)　　the size of the dwelling;

(ii)　　the number of occupiers;

(iii)　　the composition of the household;

(iv)　　the terms of the tenancy; or

(b)　　the rent officer has, in accordance with article 7A of the Rent Officers Order, notified an appropriate authority of an error he has made (other than in the application of his professional judgement),

the authority shall apply to the rent officer for a substitute determination or substitute redetermination as the case may be.

(2)　　In its application to the rent officer the relevant authority shall state the nature of the error and withdraw any previous application relating to the same case for a redetermination or substitute determination or substitute redetermination, which it has made but to which the rent officer has not yet responded.

Modifications

Modification of reg 17 is provided in Sch 9 para 11 (see p808) in relation to Pathfinder Authorities who are administering the pilot local housing allowance scheme, as from the date specified in relation to each authority in Sch 9 Part 1 (see p801).

Application of provisions to substitute determinations or substitute redeterminations

18.　　Regulations 15, 16 and 17 apply to a substitute determination or substitute redetermination as they apply to the determination or redetermination it replaces.

Amended determinations

18A.

Modification

Reg 18A is inserted by Sch 9 para 12 (see p809). It only applies to Pathfinder Authorities who are administering the pilot local housing allowance scheme, as from the date specified in relation to each authority in Sch 9 Part 1 (see p801).

PART 4
Membership of a family

Persons of prescribed description

19.–(1)　　Subject to paragraph (2), a person of a prescribed description for the purposes of section 137(1) of the Act as it applies to housing benefit (definition of family) is a person [¹ who falls within the definition of qualifying young person in section 142 of the Act (child and qualifying young person)], and in these Regulations such a person is referred to as a "young person".

(2)   Paragraph (1) shall not apply to a person who is–

(a)   on income support or an income-based jobseeker's allowance; [² or]

[³ (b)]

(c)   a person to whom section 6 of the Children (Leaving Care) Act 2000 (exclusion from benefits) applies.

(3)   A person of a prescribed description for the purposes of section 137(1) of the Act as it applies to housing benefit (definition of the family) includes a child or young person in respect of whom section 145A of that Act applies for the purposes of entitlement to child benefit but only for the period prescribed under section 145A(1) of that Act.

Amendments

1.   Substituted by reg 4(2)(a) of SI 2006 No 718 as from 10.4.06.
2.   Inserted by reg 4(2)(b) of SI 2006 No 718 as from 10.4.06.
3.   Omitted by reg 4(2)(c) of SI 2006 No 718 as from 10.4.06.

Circumstances in which a person is to be treated as responsible or not responsible for another

20.–(1)   Subject to the following provisions of this regulation a person shall be treated as responsible for a child or young person who is normally living with him and this includes a child or young person to whom paragraph (3) of regulation 19 applies.

(2)   Where a child or young person spends equal amounts of time in different households, or where there is a question as to which household he is living in, the child or young person shall be treated for the purposes of paragraph (1) as normally living with–

(a)   the person who is receiving child benefit in respect of him; or

(b)   if there is no such person–

(i)   where only one claim for child benefit has been made in respect of him, the person who made that claim; or

(ii)   in any other case the person who has the primary responsibility for him.

(3)   For the purposes of these Regulations a child or young person shall be the responsibility of only one person in any benefit week and any person other than the one treated as responsible for the child or young person under this regulation shall be treated as not so responsible.

Circumstances in which a person is to be treated as being or not being a member of the household

21.–(1)   Subject to paragraphs (2) to (4), the claimant and any partner and, where the claimant or his partner is treated as responsible by virtue of regulation 20 (circumstances in which a person is to be treated as responsible or not responsible for another) for a child or young person, that child or young person and any child of that child or young person, shall be treated as members of the same household notwithstanding that any of them is temporarily living away from the other members of his family.

(2)   Paragraph (1) shall not apply to a person who is living away from the other members of his family where–

(a)   that person does not intend to resume living with the other members of his family; or

(b)   his absence from the other members of his family is likely to exceed 52 weeks, unless there are exceptional circumstances (for example where the person is in hospital or otherwise has no control over the length of his absence) and the absence is unlikely to be substantially more than 52 weeks.

(3)   A child or young person shall not be treated as a member of the claimant's household where he is–

(a)   placed with the claimant or his partner by a local authority under section 23(2)(a) of the Children Act 1989 or by a voluntary organisation under section 59(1)(a) of that Act, or in Scotland boarded out with the claimant or his partner under a relevant enactment; or

(b)   placed, or in Scotland boarded out, with the claimant or his partner prior to adoption; or

(c)   placed for adoption with the claimant or his partner in accordance with the Adoption and Children Act 2002 or the Adoption Agencies (Scotland) Regulations 1996.

(4)   Subject to paragraph (5), paragraph (1) shall not apply to a child or young person who is not living with the claimant and he–

(a)   is being looked after by, or in Scotland is in the care of, a local authority under a relevant enactment; or

(b)   has been placed, or in Scotland boarded out, with a person other than the claimant prior to adoption; or

(c)   has been placed for adoption in accordance with the Adoption and Children Act 2002 or the Adoption Agencies (Scotland) Regulations 1996.

(5)   An authority shall treat a child or young person to whom paragraph (4)(a) applies as being a member of the claimants' household in any benefit week where–

(a)   that child or young person lives with the claimant for part or all of that benefit week; and

(b)   the authority considers that it is reasonable to do so taking into account the nature and frequency of that child's or young person's visits.

(6)   In this regulation "relevant enactment" means the Army Act 1955, the Air Force Act 1955, the Naval Discipline Act 1957, the Matrimonial Proceedings Children Act 1958,the Social Work (Scotland) Act 1968, the Family Law Reform Act 1969, the Children and Young Persons Act 1969, the Matrimonial Causes Act 1973, the Children Act 1975, the Domestic Proceedings and Magistrates' Courts Act 1978, the Adoption (Scotland) Act 1978, the Child Care Act 1980, the Family Law Act 1986, the Children Act 1989 and the Children (Scotland) Act 1995.

PART 5
Applicable amounts

Applicable amounts

22.–(1)   Subject to regulations 61 and 62 and Schedule A1 (calculation of weekly amounts, rent free periods and treatment of claims for housing benefit by refugees), the applicable amount of a claimant shall be the aggregate of such of the following amounts as apply in his case–

(a)   an amount in respect of his personal allowance, determined in accordance with paragraph 1 of Schedule 3;

(b)   an amount in respect of any child or young person who is a member of his family, determined in accordance with paragraph 2 of that Schedule;

(c)   if he is a member of a family of which at least one member is a child or young person, an amount determined in accordance with paragraph 3(1) of Part 2 of that Schedule (family premium);

(d)   if he is a member of a family of which one member is a child under the age of one year, an additional amount determined in accordance with paragraph 3(2) of Part 2 of that Schedule;

(e)   the amount of any premiums which may be applicable to him, determined in accordance with Parts 3 and 4 of that Schedule (premiums).

[¹ (2)]
[¹ (3)]
[¹ (4)]
[² (5)   In Schedule 2A–

"additional spouse" means a spouse of either party to the marriage who is additional to the other party to the marriage;

"patient" means a person (other than a person who is serving a sentence of imprisonment or detention in a youth custody institution) who is regarded as receiving free in-patient treatment within the meaning of [³ regulation 2(4) and (5) of the Social Security (Hospital In-Patients) Regulations 2005].]

[¹ (6)]
[¹ (7)]

Amendments

1.   Omitted by reg 2(3)(a) of SI 2005 No 2502 as amended by Sch 2 para 27 of SI 2006 No 217 as from 1.4.06 (3.4.06 where rent payable weekly or at intervals of a week).
2.   Substituted by reg 2(3)(b) of SI 2005 No 2502 as amended by Sch 2 para 27 of SI 2006 No 217 as from 1.4.06 (3.4.06 where rent payable weekly or at intervals of a week).
3.   Amended by reg 5(1) of SI 2005 No 3360 as amended by Sch 2 para 30 of SI 2006 No 217 as from 10.4.06.

Analysis

Para (1). The same technique for calculating applicable amounts is used as under regs 22 and 23 HB Regs, save that the amounts and conditions of the premiums are as stated in Sch 3.

Paras (2) to (7). Until omitted, these varied the applicable amounts due in relation to claimants who had been patients for more than 52 weeks. See pp776-778 of the 18th edition of this book for the text and commentary of the substituted version of reg 16 HB Regs 1987 (now reg 22 HB(SPC) Regs).

It is presumed that the reference to Sch 2A in para (5) should be taken, because of Art 2(4) HB&CTB(CP) Regs, as a reference to Sch 3.

Long-term hospital patients may still be caught by the requirement that they be occupying the home in reg 7, but see reg 7(16)(c)(ii). After 52 weeks or an extension thereof for exceptional circumstances, the patient can no longer be treated as occupying the home by virtue of reg 7(16) and (17) in any event. See p289 for a discussion of the meaning of "patient".

PART 6
Assessment of income and capital
SECTION 1
General

Calculation of income and capital of members of claimant's family and of a polygamous marriage

23.–(1)   The income and capital of a claimant's partner which by virtue of section 136(1) of the Act is to be treated as income and capital of the claimant, shall be calculated or estimated in accordance with the following provisions of this Part in like manner as for the claimant; and any reference to the "claimant" shall, except where the context otherwise requires, be construed for the purposes of this Part as if it were a reference to his partner.

(2)   Where a claimant or the partner of a claimant is married polygamously to two or more members of his household–

(a)   the claimant shall be treated as possessing capital and income belonging to each such member; and

(b)   the income and capital of that member shall be calculated in accordance with the following provisions of this Part in like manner as for the claimant.

(3)   The income and capital of a child or young person shall not be treated as the income and capital of the claimant.

Circumstances in which income of non-dependant is to be treated as claimant's

24.–(1)   Where it appears to the relevant authority that a non-dependant and the claimant have entered into arrangements in order to take advantage of the housing benefit scheme and the non-dependant has more capital and income than the claimant, that authority shall, except where the claimant is on income support or an income-based jobseeker's allowance, treat the claimant as possessing capital and income belonging to that non-dependant and, in such a case, shall disregard any capital and income which the claimant does possess.

(2)   Where a claimant is treated as possessing capital and income belonging to a non-dependant under paragraph (1) the capital and income of that non-dependant shall be calculated in accordance with the following provisions of this Part in like manner as for the claimant and any reference to the "claimant" shall, except where the context otherwise requires, be construed for the purposes of this Part as if it were a reference to that non-dependant.

SECTION 2
Income

General Note to Section 2

Note that although the heading for Section 2 is "Income", the capital of some claimants is also dealt with in this section. Section 2 requires the treatment of resources in three ways:

(1)   If a claimant (or her/his partner) is in receipt of the guarantee credit of PC all her/his income and capital are disregarded: reg 26. There is effectively no capital limit for such claimants. See p281 for the question of how far the decisions of the DWP are binding on the local authority.

(2)   If a claimant (or her/his partner) is in receipt of the savings credit of PC only, the special rules in reg 27 apply.

(3)   If a claimant (or her/his partner) is not receiving either the guarantee credit or savings credit of PC, the rules in regs 29 to 49 apply: reg 28.

Calculation of income and capital

25.   The income and capital of–

(a)   the claimant; and

(b)   any partner of the claimant,

shall be calculated in accordance with the rules set out in this Part; and any reference in this Part to the claimant shall apply equally to any partner of the claimant.

Claimant in receipt of guarantee credit

26.   In the case of a claimant who is in receipt, or whose partner is in receipt, of a guarantee credit, the whole of his capital and income shall be disregarded.

Analysis

For an explanation of 'guarantee credit' see reg 2(1) and p1042.

Calculation of claimant's income and capital in savings credit only cases

27.–(1)   In determining the income and capital of a claimant who has, or whose partner has, an award of state pension credit comprising only the savings credit, the relevant authority shall, subject to the following provisions of this regulation, use the calculation or estimate of the claimant's or, as the case may be, the claimant's partner's income and capital made by the Secretary of State for the purpose of determining that award.

(2)   The Secretary of State shall provide the relevant authority with details of the calculation or estimate–

(a) if the claimant is on housing benefit or has claimed housing benefit, within the two working days following the day the calculation or estimate was determined, or as soon as reasonably practicable thereafter; or

(b) if sub-paragraph (a) does not apply, within the two working days following the day he receives information from the relevant authority that the claimant or his partner has claimed housing benefit, or as soon as reasonably practicable thereafter.

(3) The details provided by the Secretary of State shall include the amount taken into account in that determination in respect of the net income of the person claiming state pension credit.

(4) The relevant authority shall modify the amount of the net income provided by the Secretary of State only in so far as necessary to take into account–

(a) the amount of the savings credit payable;

(b) in respect of any dependent children of the claimant, childcare charges taken into account under regulation 30(1)(c) (calculation of income on a weekly basis);

(c) the higher amount disregarded under these Regulations in respect of–

   (i) lone parent's earnings;

   (ii) payments of maintenance, whether under a court order or not, which is made or due to be made by–

      (aa) the claimant's former partner, or the claimant's partner's former partner; or

      (bb) the parent of a child or young person where that child or young person is a member of the claimant's family except where that parent is the claimant or the claimant's partner;

(d) any amount to be disregarded by virtue of paragraph 9(1) of Schedule 4;

(e) the income and capital of any partner of the claimant who is treated as a member of the claimant's household under regulation 21 (circumstances in which a person is to be treated as being or not being a member of the household) to the extent that it is not taken into account in determining the net income of the person claiming state pension credit;

(f) regulation 24 (circumstances in which income of a non-dependent is to be treated as claimant's), if the relevant authority determines that this provision applies in the claimant's case;

(g) any modification under section 134(8) of the Administration Act (modifications by resolution of an authority) which is applicable in the claimant's case.

(5) Regulations 29 to 49 shall not apply to the amount of the net income to be taken into account by the local authority under paragraph (1), but shall apply (so far as relevant) for the purpose of determining any modifications which fall to be made to that amount under paragraph (4).

(6) The relevant authority shall for the purpose of determining the claimant's entitlement of housing benefit use, except where paragraphs (7) and (8) apply, the calculation of the claimant's capital made by the Secretary of State, and shall in particular apply the provisions of regulation 43 if the claimant's capital is calculated as being in excess of £16,000.

(7) If paragraph (8) applies, the relevant authority shall calculate the claimant's capital in accordance with regulations 43 to 49 below.

(8) This paragraph applies if–

(a) the Secretary of State notifies the relevant authority that the claimant's capital has been determined as being £16,000 or less;

(b) subsequent to that determination the claimant's capital rises to more than £16,000; and

(c) the increase occurs whilst there is in force an assessed income period within the meaning of sections 6 and 9 of the State Pension Credit Act.

General Note

Reg 27 sets out the capital and income rules if the claimant or her/his partner has been awarded the savings credit of PC, but not the guarantee credit. Income and capital for HB purposes are the income and capital figure used by the DWP to work out PC, as modified by paras (4) to (8). The figure is sometimes referred to as the "assessed income figure" or AIF.

Analysis

Paras (1) to (3). The general rule is that for the purpose of working out HB and CTB entitlement, authorities must use the calculation or estimate of income and capital made by the DWP in determining entitlement to the savings credit of PC. It is suggested that the mandatory wording of para (1) means that the reasoning of the Court of Appeal in *R v South Ribble DC HBRB ex p Hamilton* [2000] 33 HLR 102, CA cannot apply to such claimants. See p281 for a full discussion of the *Hamilton* decision, but it is suggested that the local authority is not entitled to disregard the DWP's assessment merely because it believes that there has been a failure by the claimant to disclose resources to the DWP. It must refer its evidence to the DWP with a view to revision or supersession of the award of savings credit, suspending HB entitlement if necessary.

Para (2) imposes strict time limits for the provision of the information to the authority by the DWP on behalf of the Secretary of State.

Paras (4) and (5) deal with modifications an authority must make to the income figure provided by the DWP. By para (5), the rules in the remainder of Section 2 are used to determine the modifications – eg, reg 31 forms the basis for the calculation of childcare charges under para (4)(b). The following modifications must be made (if relevant):

(1)   The authority must add the savings credit that is payable: para (4)(a).

(2)   Childcare charges must be deducted from earnings under reg 30(1)(c): para (4)(b).

(3)   The more generous HB disregards for the lone parents' earnings and mainteance must be applied: para (4)(c). For example, lone parents have only £20 of earnings disregarded for PC purposes but £25 is ignored for HB purposes, so such claimants will have an additional £5 disregard applied to the assessment of income for HB purposes.

(4)   The additional earnings disregard under para 9(1) of Sch 4 for some claimants in work must be applied: para (4)(d).

(5)   The income and capital of the claimant's partner must be added, if it was not taken into account for PC purposes (eg, where the claimant is treated as a single claimant for PC purposes) but under reg 21 is treated as having a partner: para (4)(e).

(6)   The income of a non-dependant must be added, but only if the authority decides the income of that non-dependant is to be treated as the claimant's under reg 24: para (4)(f). Note that in this case, the income and the capital of the claimant are disregarded under reg 24(1).

(7)   Any disregard of war pensions adopted by the authority must be applied: para (4)(g).

Paras (6) to (8) deal with the calculation of capital. The DWP's assessment must be used and the capital limit of £16,000 applies. The only time when the authority does its own capital assessment is where capital rises above £16,000 after entitlement to PC has been assessed and during an "assessed income period" – broadly, a set period during which the PC claimant is not required to report changes in retirement provision to the DWP, including the amount of her/his capital. Note that a mere increase in capital does not justify a departure from the DWP's figure unless it has the effect of disqualifying the claimant from HB.

Calculation of income and capital where state pension credit is not payable

28.   The income and capital of a person to whom neither regulation 26 nor regulation 27 applies shall be calculated or estimated by the relevant authority in accordance with regulations 29 to 49.

Meaning of ''income''

29.–(1)   For the purposes of these Regulations, ''income'' means income of any of the following descriptions–

(a)   earnings;

(b)   working tax credit;

(c)   retirement pension income within the meaning of the State Pension Credit Act;

(d)   income from annuity contracts (other than retirement pension income);

(e)   a war disablement pension or war widow's or widower's pension;

(f)   a foreign war disablement pension or war widow's or widower's pension;

(g)   a guaranteed income payment;

(h)   a payment made under article 21(1)(c) of the Armed Forces and Reserve Forces (Compensation Scheme) Order 2005 but only where the condition referred to in article 23(2)(c) is met;

(i)   income from capital, other than capital disregarded under Part 1 of Schedule 6;

(j)   social security benefits, other than retirement pension income or any of the following benefits–

    (i)   disability living allowance;

    (ii)   attendance allowance payable under section 64 of the Act;

    (iii)   an increase of disablement pension under section 104 or 105 of the Act;

    (iv)   a payment under regulations made in exercise of the power conferred by paragraph 7(2)(b) of Part 2 of Schedule 8 to the Act;

    (v)   an increase of an allowance payable in respect of constant attendance under paragraph 4 of Part 1 of Schedule 8 to the Act;

    (vi)   child benefit;

    (vii)   any guardian's allowance payable under section 77 of the Act;

    (viii)   any increase for a dependant, other than the claimant's partner, payable in accordance with Part 4 of the Act;

    (ix)   any social fund payment made under Part 8 of the Act;

    (x)   Christmas bonus payable under Part 10 of the Act;

    (xi)   housing benefit;

    (xii)   council tax benefit;

    (xiii)   bereavement payment;

    (xiv)   statutory sick pay;

    (xv)   statutory maternity pay;

    (xvi)   statutory paternity pay payable under Part 12ZA of the Act;

    (xvii)   statutory adoption pay payable under Part 12ZB of the Act;

    (xviii)   any benefit similar to those mentioned in the preceding provisions of this paragraph payable under legislation having effect in Northern Ireland;

(k)   all foreign social security benefits which are similar to the social security benefits prescribed above;

(l)   any payment made under article 37 of the Naval, Military and Air Forces etc. (Disablement and Death) Service Pensions Order 1983;

(m)   a pension paid to victims of National Socialist persecution under any special provision made by the law of the Federal Republic of Germany, or any part of it, or of the Republic of Austria;

(n)   payments under a scheme made under the Pneumoconiosis etc. (Worker's Compensation) Act 1979;

(o)   payments made towards the maintenance of the claimant by his spouse, civil partner, former spouse or former civil partner or towards the maintenance of the claimant's partner by his spouse, civil partner, former spouse or former civil partner, including payments made–

    (i)   under a court order;

    (ii)   under an agreement for maintenance; or

    (iii)   voluntarily;

(p)   payments due from any person in respect of board and lodging accommodation provided by the claimant;

(q)   payments consisting of royalties or other sums received as a consideration for the use of, or the right to use, any copyright, patent or trade mark;

(r)   any payment made to the claimant in respect of any book registered under the Public Lending Right Scheme 1982;

(s)   any payment, other than a payment ordered by a court or made in settlement of a claim, made by or on behalf of a former employer of a person on account of the early retirement of that person on grounds of ill-health or disability;

(t)   any sum payable by way of pension out of money provided under the Civil List Act 1837, the Civil List Act 1937, the Civil List Act 1952, the Civil List Act 1972 or the Civil List Act 1975;

(u)   any income in lieu of that specified in sub-paragraphs (a) to (r);

(v)   any payment of rent made to a claimant who–
  (i)   owns the freehold or leasehold interest in any property or is a tenant of any property;
  (ii)   occupies part of the property; and
  (iii)   has an agreement with another person allowing that person to occupy that property on payment of rent; [¹]

(w)   any payment made at regular intervals under an equity release scheme.

[² (x) PPF periodic payments within the meaning of section 17(1) of the State Pension Credit Act.]

(2)   For the purposes of these Regulations, a claimant's capital, other than capital disregarded under Schedule 6, shall be treated as if it were a weekly income–

(a)   in the case of a claimant residing permanently in accommodation to which paragraph (6) applies, of £1 for each £500 in excess of £10,000 and £1 for any excess which is not a complete £500;

(b)   in any other case, of £1 for each £500 in excess of £6,000 and £1 for any excess which is not a complete £500.

(3)   Where the payment of any social security benefit prescribed under paragraph (1) is subject to any deduction (other than an adjustment specified in paragraph (4)) the amount to be taken into account under paragraph (1) shall be the amount before the deduction is made.

(4)   The adjustments specified in this paragraph are those made in accordance with–

(a)   the Social Security (Overlapping Benefits) Regulations 1979;

(b)   the Social Security (Hospital In-Patients) Regulations 1975;

(c)   section 30DD or section 30E of the Act (reductions in incapacity benefit in respect of pensions and councillor's allowances).

(5)   Where an award of any working tax credit or child tax credit under the Tax Credits Act 2002 is subject to a deduction by way of recovery of an overpayment of working tax credit or child tax credit which arose in a previous tax year the amount to be taken into account under paragraph (1) shall be the amount of working tax credit or child tax credit awarded less the amount of that deduction.

(6)   This paragraph applies to accommodation provided–

(a)   in a care home;

(b)   in an Abbeyfield Home;

(c)   under section 3 of, and Part 2 of the Schedule to, the Polish Resettlement Act 1947 (provision of accommodation) where the claimant requires personal care;

(d)   in an independent hospital.

(7)   For the purposes of paragraph (6), a person shall be treated as residing permanently in the accommodation–

(a)   except where sub-paragraph (b) applies, notwithstanding that he is absent from it for a period not exceeding 52 weeks;

(b)   if it is accommodation to which paragraph (6)(c) applies–
  (i)   notwithstanding that he is absent from it for a period not exceeding 13 weeks; and
  (ii)   if he, with the agreement of the manager of the home, intends to return to it in due course.

(8)   In paragraph (1)(w), "equity release scheme" means a loan–
(a)   made between a person ("the lender") and the claimant;
(b)   by means of which a sum of money is advanced by the lender to the claimant by way of payments at regular intervals; and
(c)   which is secured on a dwelling in which the claimant owns an estate or interest and which he occupies as his home.

Amendments

1.   Amended by reg 10(2)(a) of SI 2006 No 588 as from 6.4.06.
2.   Inserted by reg 10(2)(b) of SI 2006 No 588 as from 6.4.06.

Analysis

Paragraph (1): The definition of "income"

Unlike under the HB Regs, "income" is defined by reg 29(1). Therefore, any category of income that does not fall within any of the categories listed does not count as income and is not taken into account at all. Note that there are earnings disregards in Sch 4 (see p785) and amounts to be disregarded from income other than earnings in Sch 5 (see p788).

Most of the categories are self-explanatory but some require explanation.

"Retirement pension income" under sub-para (c) is defined in s16 SPCA. It includes Category A, B, C and D state retirement pension, occupational and personal pension schemes and other private arrangements. Under sub-para (j), social security benefits, other than retirement pension (which instead counts as income under sub-para (c)) and the benefits listed in sub-subparas (i) to (xviii), count as income. Sub-para (s) seems to be directed at income from private health insurance schemes provided by an employer. Note that "equity release scheme" in sub-para (w) is defined in para (8).

Paragraphs (2) to (7): Miscellaneous rules about income

Para (2) deals with deemed income from capital, sometimes referred to as "tariff income". The tariff is lower than under the HB Regs: under the HB(SPC) Regs, a claimant is to be treates as having is £1 weekly income for every £500 of capital over the lower capital limit. The rules for qualification for the £10,000 lower capital limit are also different than under the HB Regs. The claimant must be residing permanently in the relevant accommodation, although s/he will be deemed to be doing so under para (7) for all types of accommodation for an absence of up to 52 weeks and Polish Resettlement homes where the limit is 13 weeks.

Under paras (3) and (4), where there are adjustments in the amount of a social security benefit other than under the overlapping benefits provisions or the other circumstances listed in para (4), the unadjusted amount of income is taken into account.

Para (5) makes it plain that where an award of WTC or CTC for the current tax year is subject to a deduction in order to recover an overpayment of tax credit(s) from the previous year (pursuant to s28(1) Tax Credits Act 2002), the amount of WTC or CTC to be taken into account in calculating the weekly level of income for HB/CTB purposes is the current year award of tax credit(s) less the deduction for the overpayment.

Calculation of income on a weekly basis

30.–(1)   Subject to regulation 34 (disregard of changes in tax, contributions etc.) and 61 and 62 (calculation of weekly amounts and rent free periods), for the purposes of section 130(1)(c) of the Act (conditions for entitlement to housing benefit) the income of a claimant who has reached the qualifying age for state pension credit shall be calculated on a weekly basis–
(a)   by calculating or estimating the amount which is likely to be his average weekly income in accordance with this Part;
(b)   by adding to that amount the weekly income calculated under regulation 29(2);
(c)   by then deducting any relevant child care charges to which regulation 31 (treatment of child care charges) applies from any earnings which form part of the average weekly income or, in a case where the conditions in paragraph (2) are met, from those earnings plus whichever credit specified in sub-paragraph (b) of that paragraph is appropriate, up to a maximum deduction in respect of the claimant's family of whichever of the sums specified in paragraph (3) applies in his case.

(2) The conditions of this paragraph are that–
(a) the claimant's earnings which form part of his average weekly income are less than the lower of either his relevant child care charges or whichever of the deductions specified in paragraph (3) otherwise applies in his case; and
(b) that claimant or, if he is a member of a couple either the claimant or his partner, is in receipt of working tax credit or child tax credit.
(3) The maximum deduction to which paragraph (1)(c) above refers shall be–
(a) where the claimant's family includes only one child in respect of whom relevant child care charges are paid, [² £175.00] per week;
(b) where the claimant's family includes more than one child in respect of whom relevant child care charges are paid, [² £300] per week.

Amendments

1. Confirmed by Art 20(3) of SI 2006 No 645 and reg 8 of SI 2006 No 217 as from 1.4.06 (3.4.06 where rent payable weekly or at intervals of a week).
2. Confirmed by Art 20(2) of SI 2007 No 688 as from 1.4.07 (2.4.07 where rent payable weekly or at intervals of a week).

Analysis

This is, for practical purposes, identical to reg 27 HB Regs (see p284).

Treatment of child care charges

31.–(1) This regulation applies where a claimant is incurring relevant child care charges and–
(a) is a lone parent and is engaged in remunerative work;
(b) is a member of a couple both of whom are engaged in remunerative work; or
(c) is a member of a couple where one member is engaged in remunerative work and the other–
(i) is incapacitated;
(ii) is an in-patient in hospital; or
(iii) is in prison (whether serving a custodial sentence or remanded in custody awaiting trial or sentence).
(2) For the purposes of paragraph (1) and subject to paragraph (4), a person to whom paragraph (3) applies shall be treated as engaged in remunerative work for a period not exceeding 28 weeks during which he–
(a) is paid statutory sick pay;
(b) is paid short-term incapacity benefit at the lower rate under sections 30A to 30E of the Act;
(c) is paid income support on the grounds of incapacity for work under regulation 4ZA of, and paragraph 7 or 14 of Schedule 1B to, the Income Support Regulations; or
(d) is credited with earnings on the grounds of incapacity for work under regulation 8B of the Social Security (Credits) Regulations 1975.
(3) This paragraph applies to a person who was engaged in remunerative work immediately before–
(a) the first day of the period in respect of which he was first paid statutory sick pay, short-term incapacity benefit or income support on the grounds of incapacity for work; or
(b) the first day of the period in respect of which earnings are credited, as the case may be.
(4) In a case to which paragraph (2)(c) or (d) applies, the period of 28 weeks begins on the day on which the person is first paid income support or on the first day of the period in respect of which earnings are credited, as the case may be.

(5)   Relevant child care charges are those charges for care to which paragraphs (6) and (7) apply, and shall be estimated on a weekly basis in accordance with paragraph (10).

(6)   The charges are paid by the claimant for care which is provided–

(a)   in the case of any child of the claimant's family who is not disabled, in respect of the period beginning on that child's date of birth and ending on the day preceding the first Monday in September following that child's fifteenth birthday; or

(b)   in the case of any child of the claimant's family who is disabled, in respect of the period beginning on that person's date of birth and ending on the day preceding the first Monday in September following that person's sixteenth birthday.

(7)   The charges are paid for care which is provided by one or more of the care providers listed in paragraph (8) and are not paid–

(a)   in respect of the child's compulsory education;

(b)   by a claimant to a partner or by a partner to a claimant in respect of any child for whom either or any of them is responsible in accordance with regulation 20 (circumstances in which a person is treated as responsible or not responsible for another); or

(c)   in respect of care provided by a relative of a child wholly or mainly in the child's home.

(8)   The care to which paragraph (7) refers may be provided–

(a)   out of school hours, by a school on school premises or by a local authority–

(i)   for children who are not disabled in respect of the period beginning on their eighth birthday and ending on the day preceding the first Monday in September following their fifteenth birthday; or

(ii)   for children who are disabled in respect of the period beginning on their eighth birthday and ending on the day preceding the first Monday in September following their sixteenth birthday;

(b)   by a child care provider approved by an organisation accredited by the Secretary of State under the scheme established by the Tax Credit (New Category of Child Care Provider) Regulations 1999;

(c)   by persons registered under Part 10A of the Children Act 1989;

(d)   in schools or establishments which are exempted from registration under Part 10A of the Children Act 1989 by virtue of paragraph 1 or 2 of Schedule 9A to that Act;

(e)   by–

(i)   persons registered under section 7(1) of the Regulation of Care (Scotland) Act 2001; or

(ii)   local authorities registered under section 33(1) of that Act,

where the care provided is childminding or day care of children within the meaning of that Act; or

(f)   by a person prescribed in regulations made pursuant to section 12(4) of the Tax Credits Act.

(9)   In paragraphs (6) and (8)(a), "the first Monday in September" means the Monday which first occurs in the month of September in any year.

(10)   Relevant child care charges shall be estimated over such period, not exceeding a year, as is appropriate in order that the average weekly charge may be estimated accurately having regard to information as to the amount of that charge provided by the child minder or person providing the care.

(11)   For the purposes of paragraph (1)(c) the other member of a couple is to be treated as incapacitated where–

(a)   he is aged not less than 80;

(b)   he is aged less than 80 and–

    (i)   the additional conditions specified in paragraph 13 of Schedule 3 to the Housing Benefit Regulations 2006 are treated as applying in his case; and

    (ii)   he satisfies those conditions or would satisfy them but for his being treated as capable of work by virtue of a determination made in accordance with regulations made under section 171E of the Act;

(c)   the claimant is, or is treated as, incapable of work and has been so incapable, or has been so treated as incapable, of work in accordance with the provisions of, and regulations made under, Part 12A of the Act (incapacity for work) for a continuous period of not less than 196 days; and for this purpose any two or more separate periods separated by a break of not more than 56 days shall be treated as one continuous period;

(d)   there is payable in respect of him one or more of the following–

    (i)   long-term incapacity benefit or short-term incapacity benefit at the higher rate specified in paragraph 2 of Part 1 of Schedule 4 to the Act;

    (ii)   attendance allowance under section 64 of the Act;

    (iii)   severe disablement allowance under section 68 of the Act;

    (iv)   disability living allowance under section 71 of the Act;

    (v)   increase of disablement pension under section 104 of the Act;

    (vi)   a pension increase under a war pension scheme or an industrial injuries scheme which is analogous to an allowance or increase of disablement pension under head (ii), (iv) or (v) above;

(e)   a pension or allowance to which head (ii), (iv), (v) or (vi) of sub-paragraph (d) above refers was payable on account of his incapacity but has ceased to be payable in consequence of his becoming a patient within the meaning of regulation 22(5) (applicable amounts);

(f)   sub-paragraph (c) or (d) would apply to him if the legislative provisions referred to in those sub-paragraphs were provisions under any corresponding enactment having effect in Northern Ireland; or

(g)   he has an invalid carriage or other vehicle provided to him by the Secretary of State under section 5(2)(a) of and Schedule 2 to the National Health Service Act 1977 or by Scottish Ministers under section 46 of the National Health Service (Scotland) Act 1978 or provided by the Department of Health and Social Services for Northern Ireland under Article 30(1) of the Health and Personal Social Services (Northern Ireland) Order 1972.

(12)   For the purposes of paragraph (11), once paragraph (11)(c) applies to the claimant, if he then ceases, for a period of 56 days or less, to be incapable, or to be treated as incapable, of work, that paragraph shall, on his again becoming so incapable, or so treated as incapable, of work at the end of that period, immediately thereafter apply to him for so long as he remains incapable, or is treated as remaining incapable, of work.

(13)   For the purposes of paragraphs (6) and (8)(a), a person is disabled if he is a person–

(a)   in respect of whom disability living allowance is payable, or has ceased to be payable solely because he is a patient;

(b)   who is registered as blind in a register compiled under section 29 of the National Assistance Act 1948 (welfare services) or, in Scotland, has been certified as blind and in consequence he is registered as blind in a register maintained by or on behalf of a council constituted under section 2 of the Local Government (Scotland) Act 1994; or

(c)   who ceased to be registered as blind in such a register within the period beginning 28 weeks before the first Monday in September following that person's fifteenth birthday and ending on the day preceding the first Monday in September following that person's sixteenth birthday.

(14)   For the purposes of paragraph (1) a person on maternity leave, paternity leave or adoption leave shall be treated as if he is engaged in remunerative work for the period specified in paragraph (15) ("the relevant period") provided that–

    (a)   in the week before the period of maternity leave, paternity leave or adoption leave began he was in remunerative work;

    (b)   the claimant is incurring relevant child care charges within the meaning of paragraph (5); and

    (c)   he is entitled to statutory maternity pay under section 164 of the Act, statutory paternity pay by virtue of section 171ZA or 171ZB of the Act, statutory adoption pay by virtue of section 171ZL of the Act or maternity allowance under section 35 of the Act.

(15)   The relevant period shall begin on the day on which the person's maternity leave, paternity leave or adoption leave commences and shall end on–

    (a)   the date that leave ends;

    (b)   if no child care element of working tax credit is in payment on the date that entitlement to maternity allowance, statutory maternity pay, statutory paternity pay or statutory adoption pay ends, the date that entitlement ends; or

    (c)   if a child care element of working tax credit is in payment on the date that entitlement to maternity allowance, statutory maternity pay, statutory paternity pay or statutory adoption pay ends, the date that entitlement to that award of the child care element of working tax credit ends,

whichever shall occur first.

(16)   In paragraph (15), "child care element" of working tax credit means the element of working tax credit prescribed under section 12 of the Tax Credits Act (child care element).

Analysis
This is, for practical purposes, identical to reg 28 HB Regs (see p285).

Calculation of average weekly income from tax credits
32.–(1)   This regulation applies where a claimant receives a tax credit.

(2)   Where this regulation applies, the period over which a tax credit is to be taken into account shall be the period set out in paragraph (3).

(3)   Where the instalment in respect of which payment of a tax credit is made is–

    (a)   a daily instalment, the period is 1 day, being the day in respect of which the instalment is paid;

    (b)   a weekly instalment, the period is 7 days, ending on the day on which the instalment is due to be paid;

    (c)   a two weekly instalment, the period is 14 days, commencing 6 days before the day on which the instalment is due to be paid;

    (d)   a four weekly instalment, the period is 28 days, ending on the day on which the instalment is due to be paid.

(4)   For the purposes of this regulation "tax credit" means working tax credit.

Analysis
This is, for practical resons, identical to reg 32 HB Regs (see p293).

Calculation of weekly income
33.–(1)   Except where paragraphs (2) and (4) apply, for the purposes of calculating the weekly income of the claimant, where the period in respect of which a payment is made–

    (a)   does not exceed a week, the whole of that payment shall be included in the claimant's weekly income;

    (b)   exceeds a week, the amount to be included in the claimant's weekly income shall be determined–

        (i)   in a case where that period is a month, by multiplying the amount of the payment by 12 and dividing the product by 52;

        (ii)   in a case where that period is three months, by multiplying the amount of the payment by 4 and dividing the product by 52;

        (iii)   in a case where that period is a year, by dividing the amount of the payment by 52;

        (iv)   in any other case, by multiplying the amount of the payment by 7 and dividing the product by the number of days in the period in respect of which it is made.

(2)   Where–

(a)   the claimant's regular pattern of work is such that he does not work the same hours every week; or

(b)   the amount of the claimant's income fluctuates and has changed more than once,

the weekly amount of that claimant's income shall be determined–

        (i)   if, in a case to which sub-paragraph (a) applies, there is a recognised cycle of work, by reference to his average weekly income over the period of the complete cycle (including, where the cycle involves periods in which the claimant does no work, those periods but disregarding any other absences); or

        (ii)   in any other case, on the basis of–

            (aa)   the last two payments if those payments are one month or more apart;

            (bb)   the last four payments if the last two payments are less than one month apart; or

            (cc)   calculating or estimating such other payments as may, in the particular circumstances of the case, enable the claimant's average weekly income to be determined more accurately.

(3)   For the purposes of paragraph (2)(b) the last payments are the last payments before the date the claim was made or treated as made or, if there is a subsequent supersession under paragraph 4 of Schedule 7 to the Child Support, Pensions and Social Security Act 2000, the last payments before the date of the supersession.

(4)   If a claimant is entitled to receive a payment to which paragraph (5) applies, the amount of that payment shall be treated as if made in respect of a period of a year.

(5)   This paragraph applies to–

(a)   royalties or other sums payable as a consideration for the use of, or the right to use, any copyright, patent or trade mark;

(b)   any payment made to the claimant in respect of any book registered under the Public Lending Right Scheme 1982; and

(c)   any payment which is made on an occasional basis.

(6)   The period under which any benefit under the benefit Acts is to be taken into account shall be the period in respect of which that benefit is payable.

(7)   Where payments are made in a currency other than Sterling, the value of the payment shall be determined by taking the Sterling equivalent on the date the payment is made.

(8)   The sums specified in Schedule 4 shall be disregarded in calculating–

(a)   the claimant's earnings; and

(b)   any amount to which paragraph (5) applies if the claimant or his partner is the first owner of the copyright, patent or trade mark, or the author of the book registered under the Public Lending Right Scheme 1982.

(9)   Income specified in Schedule 5 is to be disregarded in the calculation of a claimant's income.

[² (10)]

(11)   Schedule 6 shall have effect so that–

(a)   the capital specified in Part 1 shall be disregarded for the purpose of determining a claimant's income; and

(b)   the capital specified in Part 2 shall be disregarded for the purpose of determining a claimant's income under regulation 29(2) (weekly income from capital).

(12)   In the case of any income taken into account for the purpose of calculating a person's income, there shall be disregarded any amount payable by way of tax.

[² (13)]

[² (14)]

Amendments

1.   Inserted by reg 3 of SI 2006 No 2813 as from 20.11.06.

2.   Omitted by reg 6(b) of SI 2007 No 1619 as from 3.7.07.

Analysis

Reg 33 contains a number of rules to facilitate the calculation of income on a weekly basis.

Para (1) contains the general rule and is similar in effect to reg 33 HB Regs. It is subject to the specific circumstances set out in paras (2) and (4) (and also para (6), though para (1) does not specifically state so).

Paras (2) and (3) deal with fluctuating income from work, whether employed or self-employed. Where the hours of work change, the first step is to look for a pattern of work under sub-para (b)(i). The wording is similar to that of reg 6(2)(a) HB Regs and caselaw under that and the equivalent IS and income-based JSA provisions are relevant to the question of whether a cycle exists and, if so, what it is.

In the absence of a cycle, either the last two or four payments may be taken according to their time period. There is also the option of using other means of estimating weekly income under (b)(ii)(cc). It appears that (b)(ii)(cc) is an alternative to (b)(ii)(aa) or (bb).

Paras (4) and (5) require royalty payments and analogous income, along with any payments made on an "occasional" basis, to be taken into account as referable to a year. It is inherent in the word "occasional" that the payments must be infrequent and irregular.

Para (6) requires payments of benefit to be taken into account over a period equivalent to that in respect of which it is payable. Note that reg 44(3) provides for certain arrears of PC to be treated as capital.

Para (7) requires foreign payments to be converted into Sterling for the purpose of assessment of income. The exchange rate at the date of payment is to be used.

Paras (8), (9) and (11) bring in the schedules for disregards of income and capital. Note that Sch 6 Part 2 contains capital disregarded for the purposes of generating deemed income under reg 29(2).

Para (12) requires tax liabilities to be ignored when calculating income. "Tax" covers income tax and presumably also national insurance contributions, which are a form of taxation, as well as any other forms of tax that might apply to the particular type of income.

Paras (10), (13) and (14) contained a power to modify the HB scheme so as to disregard war widow's and widower's pensions and certain payments made under the Armed Forces and Reserve Forces (Compensation Scheme) Order 2005. s134(8) SSAA 1992 sets out the circumstances in which modifications can be made. The prescribed pensions are now found in the Schedule to the Housing Benefit and Council Tax Benefit (War Pension Disregards) Regulations 2007 SI No. 1619 (on p1137). See the commentary to s134(8) for a discussion of an authority's powers.

Disregard of changes in tax, contributions etc

34.   In calculating the claimant's income the appropriate authority may disregard any legislative change–

(a)   in the basic or other rates of income tax;

(b)   in the amount of any personal tax relief;

(c)   in the rates of social security contributions payable under the Act or in the lower earnings limit or upper earnings limit for Class 1 contributions under that Act, the lower or upper limits applicable to Class 4 contributions under that Act or the amount specified in section 11(4) of the Act (small earnings exception in relation to Class 2 contributions);

(d)   in the amount of tax payable as a result of an increase in the weekly rate of Category A, B, C or D retirement pension or any addition thereto or any graduated pension payable under the Act; and

(e)   in the maximum rate of child tax credit or working tax credit,

for a period not exceeding 30 benefit weeks beginning with the benefit week immediately following the date from which the change is effective.

Analysis

This is the equivalent of reg 34 HB Regs (see p294).

SECTION 3
Employed earners

Earnings of employed earners

35.–(1)   Subject to paragraph (2), "earnings" means in the case of employment as an employed earner, any remuneration or profit derived from that employment and includes–

(a)   any bonus or commission;

(b)   any payment in lieu of remuneration except any periodic sum paid to a claimant on account of the termination of his employment by reason of redundancy;

(c)   any payment in lieu of notice;

(d)   any holiday pay;

(e)   any payment by way of a retainer;

(f)   any payment made by the claimant's employer in respect of expenses not wholly, exclusively and necessarily incurred in the performance of the duties of the employment, including any payment made by the claimant's employer in respect of–

(i)   travelling expenses incurred by the claimant between his home and place of employment;

(ii)   expenses incurred by the claimant under arrangements made for the care of a member of his family owing to the claimant's absence from home;

(g)   the amount of any payment by way of a non-cash voucher which has been taken into account in the computation of a person's earnings in accordance with Part 5 of Schedule 3 to the Social Security (Contributions) Regulations 2001;

(h)   statutory sick pay and statutory maternity pay payable by the employer under the Act;

(i)   statutory paternity pay payable under Part 12ZA of the Act;

(j)   statutory adoption pay payable under Part 12ZB of the Act;

(k)   any sums payable under a contract of service–

(i)   for incapacity for work due to sickness or injury; or

(ii)   by reason of pregnancy or confinement.

(2)   Earnings shall not include–

(a)   subject to paragraph (3), any payment in kind;

(b)   any payment in respect of expenses wholly, exclusively and necessarily incurred in the performance of the duties of the employment;

(c)   any occupational pension;

(d)   any lump sum payment made under the Iron and Steel Re-adaptation Benefits Scheme;

(e)   any payment of compensation made pursuant to an award by an employment tribunal established under the Employment Tribunals Act 1996 in respect of unfair dismissal or unlawful discrimination.

(3)   Paragraph (2)(a) shall not apply in respect of any non-cash voucher referred to in paragraph (1)(g).

Analysis

This is equivalent to reg 35 HB Regs (see p295), save that the payments listed in para (2)(d) and (e) are additional categories of income which are not treated as earnings.

Calculation of net earnings of employed earners

36.–(1)   For the purposes of regulation 30 (calculation of income on a weekly basis), the earnings of a claimant derived or likely to be derived from employment as an employed earner to be taken into account shall, subject to regulation 33(5) and Schedule 4, be his net earnings.

(2)   For the purposes of paragraph (1) net earnings shall, except in relation to any payment to which regulation 33(5) refers, be calculated by taking into account the gross earnings of the claimant from that employment over the assessment period, less–

(a)   any amount deducted from those earnings by way of–
  (i)   income tax;
  (ii)   primary Class 1 contributions under the Act;

(b)   one-half of any sum paid by the claimant by way of a contribution towards an occupational pension scheme;

(c)   one-half of the amount calculated in accordance with paragraph (4) in respect of any qualifying contribution payable by the claimant; and

(d)   where those earnings include a payment which is payable under any enactment having effect in Northern Ireland and which corresponds to statutory sick pay, statutory maternity pay, statutory paternity pay or statutory adoption pay, any amount deducted from those earnings by way of any contributions which are payable under any enactment having effect in Northern Ireland and which correspond to primary Class 1 contributions under the Act.

(3)   In this regulation "qualifying contribution" means any sum which is payable periodically as a contribution towards a personal pension scheme.

(4)   The amount in respect of any qualifying contribution shall be calculated by multiplying the daily amount of the qualifying contribution by the number equal to the number of days in the assessment period; and for the purposes of this regulation the daily amount of the qualifying contribution shall be determined–

(a)   where the qualifying contribution is payable monthly, by multiplying the amount of the qualifying contribution by 12 and dividing the product by 365;

(b)   in any other case, by dividing the amount of the qualifying contribution by the number equal to the number of days in the period to which the qualifying contribution relates.

(5)   Where the earnings of a claimant are determined under sub-paragraph (b) of paragraph (2) of regulation 33 (calculation of weekly income), his net earnings shall be calculated by taking into account those earnings over the assessment period, less–

(a)   an amount in respect of income tax equivalent to an amount calculated by applying to those earnings the [¹ starting rate] or, as the case may be, the [¹ starting rate] and the basic rate of tax applicable to the assessment period less only the personal relief to which the claimant is entitled under section 257(1) of the Income and Corporation Taxes Act 1988 (personal allowances) as is appropriate to his circumstances but, if the assessment period is less than a year, the earnings to which the [¹ starting rate] of tax is to be applied and the amount of the personal relief deductible under this sub-paragraph shall be calculated on a pro rata basis;

(b) an amount equivalent to the amount of the primary Class 1 contributions that would be payable by him under the Act in respect of those earnings if such contributions were payable; and

(c) one-half of any sum which would be payable by the claimant by way of a contribution towards an occupational or personal pension scheme, if the earnings so estimated were actual earnings.

Amendment

1.   Amended by reg 12(4) of SI 2007 No 2618 as from 1.10.07.

General Note

This is equivalent to reg 36 HB Regs (see p299).

SECTION 4

Self-employed earners

Calculation of earnings of self-employed earners

37.–(1) Where a claimant's earnings consist of earnings from employment as a self-employed earner, the weekly amount of his earnings shall be determined by reference to his average weekly earnings from that employment–

(a) over a period of one year; or

(b) where the claimant has recently become engaged in that employment or there has been a change which is likely to affect the normal pattern of business, over such other period (''computation period'') as may, in the particular case, enable the weekly amount of his earnings to be determined more accurately.

(2)   For the purposes of determining the weekly amount of earnings of a claimant to whom paragraph (1)(b) applies, his earnings over the computation period shall be divided by the number equal to the number of days in that period and multiplying the quotient by 7.

(3)   The period over which the weekly amount of a claimant's earnings is calculated in accordance with this regulation shall be his assessment period.

Analysis

This has no equivalent in the HB Regs. It simply states that self-employed earners have their weekly earnings calculated from average earnings over a year or where the business has recently started or there has been a change in the pattern of the business, such other period that enables the earnings to be determined more accurately.

Earnings of self-employed earners

38.–(1)   Subject to paragraph (2), ''earnings'', in the case of employment as a self-employed earner, means the gross receipts of the employment and shall include any allowance paid under section 2 of the 1973 Act or section 2 of the Enterprise and New Towns (Scotland) Act 1990 to the claimant for the purpose of assisting him in carrying on his business unless at the date of claim the allowance has been terminated.

(2)   ''Earnings'' in the case of employment as a self-employed earner does not include–

(a) where a claimant occupies a dwelling as his home and he provides in that dwelling board and lodging accommodation for which payment is made, those payments;

(b) any payment made by a local authority to a claimant–

(i) with whom a person is accommodated by virtue of arrangements made under section 23(2)(a) of the Children Act 1989(provision of accommodation and maintenance for a child whom they are looking after) or, as the case may be, section 26(1) of the Children (Scotland) Act 1995; or

(ii)   with whom a local authority foster a child under the Fostering of Children (Scotland) Regulations 1996;

(c)   any payment made by a voluntary organisation in accordance with section 59(1)(a) of the Children Act 1989 (provision of accommodation by voluntary organisations);

(d)   any payment made to the claimant or his partner for a person (''the person concerned'') who is not normally a member of the claimant's household but is temporarily in his care, by–

(i)   a health authority;

(ii)   a local authority, but excluding payments of housing benefit made in respect of the person concerned;

(iii)   a voluntary organisation;

(iv)   the person concerned pursuant to section 26(3A) of the National Assistance Act 1948; or

(v)   a primary care trust established under section 16A of the National Health Service Act 1977;

(e)   any sports award.

Analysis

Para (1) is equivalent to reg 37(1) HB Regs. On para (2)(c) to (d), see Sch 5 paras 26 and 27 HB Regs on p479.

Calculation of net profit of self-employed earners

39.–(1)   For the purposes of regulation 30 (calculation of income on a weekly basis) the earnings of a claimant to be taken into account shall be–

(a)   in the case of a self-employed earner who is engaged in employment on his own account, the net profit derived from that employment;

(b)   in the case of a self-employed earner whose employment is carried on in partnership, his share of the net profit derived from that employment, less–

(i)   an amount in respect of income tax and of social security contributions payable under the Act calculated in accordance with regulation 40 (deduction of tax and contributions for self-employed earners); and

(ii)   one-half of the amount calculated in accordance with paragraph (10) in respect of any qualifying premium.

(2)   For the purposes of paragraph (1)(a) the net profit of the employment shall, except where paragraph (8) applies, be calculated by taking into account the earnings of the employment over the assessment period less–

(a)   subject to paragraphs (4) to (7), any expenses wholly and exclusively incurred in that period for the purposes of that employment;

(b)   an amount in respect of–

(i)   income tax; and

(ii)   social security contributions payable under the Act,

calculated in accordance with regulation 40 (deduction of tax and contributions for self-employed earners); and

(c)   one-half of the amount calculated in accordance with paragraph (10) in respect of any qualifying premium.

(3)   For the purposes of paragraph (1)(b) the net profit of the employment shall be calculated by taking into account the earnings of the employment over the assessment period less, subject to paragraphs (4) to (7), any expenses wholly and exclusively incurred in that period for the purposes of the employment.

(4)   Subject to paragraph (5), no deduction shall be made under paragraph (2)(a) or (3), in respect of–

(a)   any capital expenditure;

(b)   the depreciation of any capital asset;

(c)   any sum employed or intended to be employed in the setting up or expansion of the employment;

(d)   any loss incurred before the beginning of the assessment period;

(e)   the repayment of capital on any loan taken out for the purposes of the employment; and

(f)   any expenses incurred in providing business entertainment.

(5)   A deduction shall be made under paragraph (2)(a) or (3) in respect of the repayment of capital on any loan used for–

(a)   the replacement in the course of business of equipment or machinery; and

(b)   the repair of an existing business asset except to the extent that any sum is payable under an insurance policy for its repair.

(6)   The relevant authority shall refuse to make a deduction in respect of any expenses under paragraph (2)(a) or (3) where it is not satisfied given the nature and the amount of the expense that it has been reasonably incurred.

(7)   For the avoidance of doubt–

(a)   a deduction shall not be made under paragraph (2)(a) or (3) in respect of any sum unless it has been expended for the purposes of the business;

(b)   a deduction shall be made thereunder in respect of–

(i)   the excess of any value added tax paid over value added tax received in the assessment period;

(ii)   any income expended in the repair of an existing business asset except to the extent that any sum is payable under an insurance policy for its repair;

(iii)   any payment of interest on a loan taken out for the purposes of the employment.

(8)   Where a claimant is engaged in employment as a child minder the net profit of the employment shall be one-third of the earnings of that employment, less–

(a)   an amount in respect of–

(i)   income tax; and

(ii)   social security contributions payable under the Act,

calculated in accordance with regulation 40 (deduction of tax and contributions for self-employed earners); and

(b)   one-half of the amount calculated in accordance with paragraph (10) in respect of any qualifying premium.

(9)   For the avoidance of doubt where a claimant is engaged in employment as a self-employed earner and he is also engaged in one or more other employments as a self-employed or employed earner any loss incurred in any one of his employments shall not be offset against his earnings in any other of his employments.

(10)   The amount in respect of any qualifying premium shall be calculated by multiplying the daily amount of the qualifying premium by the number equal to the number of days in the assessment period; and for the purposes of this regulation the daily amount of the qualifying premium shall be determined–

(a)   where the qualifying premium is payable monthly, by multiplying the amount of the qualifying premium by 12 and dividing the product by 365;

(b)   in any other case, by dividing the amount of the qualifying premium by the number equal to the number of days in the period to which the qualifying premium relates.

(11)   In this regulation, "qualifying premium" means any premium which is payable periodically in respect of [¹] a personal pension scheme and is so payable on or after the date of claim.

Amendment

1.   Omitted by reg 5(3) of SI 2007 No 1749 as from 16.7.07.

Analysis
This is equivalent to reg 38 HB Regs (see p301), save that the disregards provided by reg 38(2) HB Regs are dealt with in reg 38(2) HB(SPC) Regs.

Deduction of tax and contributions of self-employed earners

40.–(1)   The amount to be deducted in respect of income tax under regulation 39(1)(b)(i), (2)(b)(i) or (8)(a)(i) (calculation of net profit of self-employed earners) shall be calculated on the basis of the amount of chargeable income and as if that income were assessable to income tax at the [¹ starting rate] or, as the case may be, the [¹ starting rate] and the basic rate of tax applicable to the assessment period less only the personal relief to which the claimant is entitled under sections 257(1) of the Income and Corporation Taxes Act 1988 (personal allowance) as is appropriate to his circumstances; but, if the assessment period is less than a year, the earnings to which the [¹ starting rate] of tax is to be applied and the amount of the personal reliefs deductible under this paragraph shall be calculated on a pro rata basis.

(2)   The amount to be deducted in respect of social security contributions under regulation 39(1)(b)(i), (2)(b)(ii) or (8)(a)(ii) shall be the total of–

(a)   the amount of Class 2 contributions payable under section 11(1) or, as the case may be, 11(3) of the Act at the rate applicable to the assessment period except where the claimant's chargeable income is less than the amount specified in section 11(4) of the Act (small earnings exception) for the tax year applicable to the assessment period; but if the assessment period is less than a year, the amount specified for that tax year shall be reduced pro rata; and

(b)   the amount of Class 4 contributions (if any) which would be payable under section 15 of the Act (Class 4 contributions recoverable under the Income Tax Acts) at the percentage rate applicable to the assessment period on so much of the chargeable income as exceeds the lower limit but does not exceed the upper limit of profits and gains applicable for the tax year applicable to the assessment period; but if the assessment period is less than a year, those limits shall be reduced pro rata.

(3)   In this regulation "chargeable income" means–

(a)   except where sub-paragraph (b) applies, the earnings derived from the employment less any expenses deducted under paragraph (2)(a) or, as the case may be, (3) of regulation 39;

(b)   in the case of employment as a child minder, one-third of the earnings of that employment.

Amendment
1.   Amended by reg 12(5) of SI 2007 No 2618 as from 1.10.07.

General Note
This is equivalent to reg 39 HB Regs (see p305).

SECTION 5
Other income

Notional income

41.–(1)   A claimant shall be treated as possessing–

(a)   subject to paragraph (2), the amount of any retirement pension income–

(i)   for which no claim has been made; and

(ii)   to which he might expect to be entitled if a claim for it were made;

(b)   income from an occupational pension scheme which the claimant elected to defer.

(2)   Paragraph (1)(a) shall not apply to the following where entitlement has been deferred–

(a) Category A or Category B retirement pension payable under sections 43 to 55 of the Act;
(b) a shared additional pension payable under section 55A of the Act; and
(c) graduated retirement benefit payable under sections 36 or 37 of the National Insurance Act 1965.
(3) For the purposes of paragraph (2), entitlement has been deferred–
(a) in the case of a Category A or Category B pension, in the circumstances specified in section 55(3) of the Act;
(b) in the case of a shared additional pension, in the circumstances specified in section 55C(3) of the Act;
(c) in the case of graduated retirement benefit, in the circumstances specified in section 36(4) and (4A) of the National Insurance Act 1965.
[⁴ (4) This paragraph applies where a person aged not less than 60–
(a) is entitled to money purchase benefits under an occupational pension scheme or a personal pension scheme;
(b) fails to purchase an annuity with the funds available in that scheme; and
(c) either–
  (i) defers in whole or in part the payment of any income which would have been payable to him by his pension fund holder, or
  (ii) fails to take any necessary action to secure that the whole of any income which would be payable to him by his pension fund holder upon his applying for it, is so paid, or
  (iii) income withdrawal is not available to him under that scheme.
(4A) Where paragraph (4) applies, the amount of any income foregone shall be treated as possessed by that person, but only from the date on which it could be expected to be acquired were an application for it to be made.]
(5) The amount of any income foregone in a case [⁴ where paragraph (4)(c)(i) or (ii)] applies shall be the maximum amount of income which may be withdrawn from the fund and shall be determined by the relevant authority which shall take account of information provided by the pension fund holder in accordance with regulation 67(6) (evidence and information).
(6) The amount of any income foregone in a case [⁴ where paragraph (4)(c)(iii)] applies shall be the income that the claimant could have received without purchasing an annuity had the funds held under the relevant scheme [⁴] been held under a personal pension scheme or occupational pension scheme where income withdrawal was available and shall be determined in the manner specified in paragraph (5).
(7) In paragraph (4), "money purchase benefits" has the meaning it has in the Pension Schemes Act 1993.
(8) [² Subject to paragraph (8A),] A person shall be treated as possessing income of which he has deprived himself for the purpose of securing entitlement to housing benefit or increasing the amount of that benefit.
[² (8A) Paragraph (8) shall not apply in respect of the amount of an increase of pension or benefit where a person, having made an election in favour of that increase of pension or benefit under Schedule 5 or 5A to the Contributions and Benefits Act or under Schedule 1 to the Graduated Retirement Benefit Regulations, changes that election in accordance with regulations made under Schedule 5 or 5A to that Act in favour of a lump sum.
(8B) In paragraph (8A), "lump sum" means a lump sum under Schedule 5 or 5A to the Contributions and Benefits Act or under Schedule 1 to the Graduated Retirement Benefit Regulations.]
(9) Where a claimant is in receipt of any benefit (other than housing benefit) under the benefit Acts and the rate of that benefit is altered with effect from a date on or after 1st April in any year but not more than 14 days thereafter, the relevant authority shall treat the claimant as possessing such benefit at the altered rate–

(a)   in a case in which the claimant's weekly amount of eligible rent falls to be calculated in accordance with regulation 61(2)(b) [¹ or (c)] (calculation of weekly amounts), from 1st April in that year;

(b)   in any other case, from the first Monday in April in that year,

to the date on which the altered rate is to take effect.

(10)   In the case of a claimant who has, or whose partner has, an award of state pension credit comprising only the savings credit, where a relevant authority treats the claimant as possessing any benefit (other than housing benefit) at the altered rate in accordance with paragraph (9), that authority shall–

(a)   determine the income and capital of that claimant in accordance with regulation 27(1) (calculation of claimant's income in savings credit only cases) where the calculation or estimate of that income and capital is altered with effect from a date on or after 1st April in any year but not more than 14 days thereafter; and

(b)   treat that claimant as possessing such income and capital at the altered rate by reference to the period referred to in paragraph (9)(a) or (b), as the case may be.

[³ (11)   For the purposes of paragraph (8), a person is not to be regarded as depriving himself of income where–

(a)   his rights to benefits under a registered pension scheme are extinguished and in consequence of this he receives a payment from the scheme, and

(b)   that payment is a trivial commutation lump sum within the meaning given by paragraph 7 of Schedule 29 to the Finance Act 2004.

(12)   In paragraph (11), "registered pension scheme" has the meaning given in section 150(2) of the Finance Act 2004.]

Amendments

1.   Amended by reg 2(7) of SI 2005 No 2502 as amended by Sch 2 para 27 of SI 2006 No 217 as from 1.4.06 (3.4.06 where rent payable weekly or at intervals of a week).

2.   Inserted by reg 11(3) of SI 2005 No 2677 and reg 2 of SI 2006 No 217 as from 6.4.06.

3.   Amended by reg 16(2) of SI 2006 No 2378 as from 2.10.06.

4.   Amended by reg 5(4) of SI 2007 No 1749 as from 16.7.07.

Analysis

This, together with reg 42, is largely a simplified and re-ordered version of reg 42 HB Regs (see p309).

Paras (1) to (3) have no equivalent in reg 42 HB Regs. They deal with "retirement pension income" as defined in s16 SPCA (see reg 29(c)) or income from an occupational pension scheme. If a claimant or her/his partner fails to take up income from one of those sources, s/he will be treated as having income of that amount. Note the phrase "might expect to be entitled if a claim for it were made" in para (1)(a)(ii) which sets a lower burden of proof of availability. Para (1)(a) does not apply where entitlement to the types of pension listed in para (2) has been deferred in the circumstances set out in para (3).

Paras (4) to (6) are equivalent to paras (3) to (5) of reg 42 HB Regs.

Paras (8) to (8B). Para (8) is the equivalent of reg 42(1) HB Regs, but here it is subject to paras (8A), (8B) and (11). Under para (8A), where someone defers claiming a pension or benefit opting for an increase in it, then opts to take a lump sum instead, the deprivation rules does not apply to the increase. "Lump sum" is defined in para (8B). Para (11) concerns trivial lump sum payments made to a claimant in consequence of the ending of her/his right to receive benefits under a registered pension scheme (defined in para (12)). The effect of para (11) is that the person cannot be treated as still receiving as income the benefits s/he used to receive under the registered pension scheme. The lump sum payment itself should be treated as capital.

Paras (9) and (10). Para (9) is designed to ease administration connected with the uprating of benefits. The increased amount of benefit is treated as possessed from 1 April each year unless rent is not payable weekly in which case it will apply from the first Monday in April. Where para (9) applies and a claimant or her/his partner has an award of the savings credit of PC only, para (10) tells an authority to redetermine such a claimant's income and capital and to treat the altered rate as the claimant's by reference to the relevant period in para (9).

Income paid to third parties

42.–(1) Any payment of income, other than a payment specified in paragraph (2), to a third party in respect of the claimant shall be treated as possessed by the claimant.

(2)　Paragraph (1) shall not apply in respect of a payment of income made under an occupational pension scheme [¹ , in respect of a pension or other periodical payment made under a personal pension scheme or a payment made by the Board of the Pension Protection Fund] where–

(a)　a bankruptcy order has been made in respect of the person in respect of whom the payment has been made or, in Scotland, the estate of that person is subject to sequestration or a judicial factor has been appointed on that person's estate under section 41 of the Solicitors (Scotland) Act 1980;

(b)　the payment is made to the trustee in bankruptcy or any other person acting on behalf of the creditors; and

(c)　the person referred to in sub-paragraph (a) and his partner does not possess, or is not treated as possessing, any other income apart from that payment.

Amendment

1.　　Substituted by reg 10(3) of SI 2006 No 588 as from 6.4.06.

Analysis

This is significantly different in effect to the more complex reg 42(6) HB Regs (see p309). Under para (1), any payment of income (as defined in reg 29(1) above) to a third party in respect of the claimant is treated as possessed by the claimant. Para (2) contains the only exception and is equivalent to the standard reg 42(7)(d) HB Regs.

SECTION 6

Capital

Capital limit

43.　For the purposes of section 134(1) of the Act as it applies to housing benefit (no entitlement to benefit if capital exceeds a prescribed amount), the prescribed amount is £16,000.

Analysis

This is equivalent to reg 43 HB Regs (see p316). Note, however, that if a claimant or her/his partner is in receipt of the guarantee credit of PC, income and capital are ignored under reg 26; effectively, such claimants have no capital limit.

Calculation of capital

44.–(1)　For the purposes of Part 7 of the Act as it applies to housing benefit, the capital of a claimant to be taken into account shall, subject to paragraph (2), be the whole of his capital calculated in accordance with this Part.

(2)　There shall be disregarded from the calculation of the claimant's capital under paragraph (1) any capital, where applicable, specified in Schedule 6.

(3)　A claimant's capital shall be treated as including any payment made to him by way of arrears of–

(a)　child tax credit;

(b)　working tax credit;

(c)　state pension credit,

if the payment was made in respect of a period for the whole or part of which housing benefit was paid before those arrears were paid.

Analysis

Paras (1) and (2) are equivalent to reg 44 HB Regs (see p316). Para (3) requires arrears of CTC, WTC and PC to be treated as capital if HB was paid to the claimant in respect of the period to which the credit is attributable. This is to avoid the creation of overpayments.

Note that where a claimant or her/his partner is awarded the savings credit of PC but not the guarantee credit, the authority must use the assessment of income and capital the DWP used for PC purposes to calculate HB: reg 27(1) to (6). It is only where such a claimant's capital increases to more than £16,000 during an assessed income period that the authority is required to calculate capital for itself under regs 43 to 49: reg 27(7) and (8).

[¹Calculation of capital in the United Kingdom

45. Capital which a claimant possesses in the United Kingdom shall be calculated at its current market or surrender value less–

(a) where there would be expenses attributable to the sale, 10 per cent.; and

(b) the amount of any encumbrance secured on it.

Amendment

1. Substituted by reg 12(6) of SI 2007 No 2618 as from 1.10.07.

General Note

This is equivalent to reg 47 HB Regs (see p318).

Calculation of capital outside the United Kingdom

46. Capital which a claimant possesses in a country outside the United Kingdom shall be calculated–

(a) in a case where there is no prohibition in that country against the transfer to the United Kingdom of an amount equal to its current market or surrender value in that country, at that value;

(b) in a case where there is such a prohibition, at the price which it would realise if sold in the United Kingdom to a willing buyer,

less, where there would be expenses attributable to sale, 10 per cent. and the amount of any encumbrance secured on it.

Analysis

This is equivalent to the standard reg 48 HB Regs (see p319).

Notional capital

47.–(1) A claimant shall be treated as possessing capital of which he has deprived himself for the purpose of securing entitlement to housing benefit or increasing the amount of that benefit except to the extent that the capital which he is treated as possessing is reduced in accordance with regulation 48 (diminishing notional capital rule).

(2) A person who disposes of capital for the purpose of–

(a) reducing or paying a debt owed by the claimant; or

(b) purchasing goods or services if the expenditure was reasonable in the circumstances of the claimant's case,

shall be regarded as not depriving himself of it.

(3) Where a claimant stands in relation to a company in a position analogous to that of a sole owner or partner in the business of that company, he shall be treated as if he were such sole owner or partner and in such a case–

(a) the value of his holding in that company shall, notwithstanding regulation 44 (calculation of capital), be disregarded; and

(b) he shall, subject to paragraph (4), be treated as possessing an amount of capital equal to the value or, as the case may be, his share of the value of the capital of that company and the foregoing provisions of this Part shall apply for the purposes of calculating that amount as if it were actual capital which he does possess.

(4) For so long as a claimant undertakes activities in the course of the business of the company, the amount which he is treated as possessing under paragraph (3) shall be disregarded.

(5)   Where under this regulation a person is treated as possessing capital, the amount of that capital shall be calculated in accordance with the provisions of this Part as if it were actual capital which he does possess.

Analysis
> ***Para (1)*** is equivalent to reg 49(1) HB Regs (see p320) and paras (3) to (5) are equivalent to paras (5) to (7) of that regulation.
>
> ***Para (2)*** confirms the existing caselaw. There is no deprivation if the claimant is reducing or paying a debt or buying goods or services. The latter are subject to a test of reasonableness, the former is not.

Diminishing notional capital rule

48.–(1)   Where a claimant is treated as possessing capital under regulation 47(1) (notional capital), the amount which he is treated as possessing–

(a)   in the case of a week that is subsequent to–

(i)   the relevant week in respect of which the conditions set out in paragraph (2) are satisfied; or

(ii)   a week which follows that relevant week and which satisfies those conditions,

shall be reduced by an amount determined under paragraph (3);

(b)   in the case of a week in respect of which paragraph (1)(a) does not apply but where–

(i)   that week is a week subsequent to the relevant week; and

(ii)   that relevant week is a week in which the condition in paragraph (4) is satisfied,

shall be reduced by the amount determined under paragraph (4).

(2)   This paragraph applies to a benefit week where the claimant satisfies the conditions that–

(a)   he is in receipt of housing benefit; and

(b)   but for regulation 47(1), he would have received an additional amount of housing benefit in that week.

(3)   In a case to which paragraph (2) applies, the amount of the reduction for the purposes of paragraph (1)(a) shall be equal to the aggregate of–

(a)   the additional amount to which paragraph (2)(b) refers;

(b)   where the claimant has also claimed state pension credit, the amount of any state pension credit or any additional amount of state pension credit to which he would have been entitled in respect of the benefit week to which paragraph (2) refers but for the application of regulation 21(1) of the State Pension Credit Regulations 2002 (notional capital);

(c)   where the claimant has also claimed council tax benefit, the amount of any council tax benefit or any additional amount of council tax benefit to which he would have been entitled in respect of the benefit week to which paragraph (2) refers but for the application of regulation 39(1) of the Council Tax Benefit Regulations 2006 or regulation 37(1) (notional capital)of the Council Tax Benefit (Persons who have obtained the qualifying age for state pensions credit) Regulations 2006;

(d)   where the claimant has also claimed a jobseeker's allowance, the amount of an income-based jobseeker's allowance to which he would have been entitled in respect of the benefit week to which paragraph (2) refers but for the application of regulation 113 of the Jobseeker's Allowance Regulations (notional capital).

(4)   Subject to paragraph (5), for the purposes of paragraph (1)(b) the condition is that the claimant would have been entitled to housing benefit in the relevant week but for regulation 47(1), and in such a case the amount of the reduction shall be equal to the aggregate of–

(a)   the amount of housing benefit to which the claimant would have been entitled in the relevant week but for regulation 47(1) and, for the purposes of this sub-paragraph, if the relevant week is a week to which regulation 61(4)(a) refers (calculation of weekly amounts), that amount shall be determined by dividing the amount of housing benefit to which he would have been so entitled by the number of days in that week for which he was liable to make payments in respect of the dwelling he occupies as his home and multiplying the quotient so obtained by 7;

(b)   if the claimant would, but for regulation 21 of the State Pension Credit Regulations 2002, have been entitled to state pension credit in respect of the benefit week, within the meaning of regulation 1(2) of those Regulations (interpretation), which includes the last day of the relevant week, the amount to which he would have been entitled and, for the purposes of this sub-paragraph, if the amount is in respect of a part-week, that amount shall be determined by dividing the amount of the state pension credit to which he would have been so entitled by the number equal to the number of days in the part-week and multiplying the quotient so obtained by 7;

(c)   if the claimant would, but for regulation 37(1) of the Council Tax Benefit (Persons who have attained the qualifying age for state pension credit) Regulations 2006, have been entitled to council tax benefit or to an additional amount of council tax benefit in respect of the benefit week which includes the last day of the relevant week, the amount which is equal to–

    (i)   in a case where no council tax benefit is payable, the amount to which he would have been entitled; or

    (ii)   in any other case, the amount equal to the additional amount of council tax benefit to which he would have been entitled;

and, for the purposes of this sub-paragraph, if the amount is in respect of a part-week, that amount shall be determined by dividing the amount of the council tax benefit to which he would have been so entitled by the number equal to the number of days in the part-week and multiplying the quotient so obtained by 7;

(d)   if the claimant would, but for regulation 113 of the Jobseeker's Allowance Regulations, have been entitled to an income-based jobseeker's allowance in respect of the benefit week, within the meaning of regulation 1(3) of those Regulations (interpretation), which includes the last day of the relevant week, the amount to which he would have been entitled and, for the purposes of this sub-paragraph, if the amount is in respect of a part-week, that amount shall be determined by dividing the amount of the income-based jobseeker's allowance to which he would have been so entitled by the number equal to the number of days in the part-week and multiplying the quotient so obtained by 7.

(5)   The amount determined under paragraph (4) shall be redetermined under that paragraph if the claimant makes a further claim for housing benefit and the conditions in paragraph (6) are satisfied, and in such a case–

(a)   sub-paragraphs (a) to (d) of paragraph (4) shall apply as if for the words "relevant week" there were substituted the words "relevant subsequent week"; and

(b)   subject to paragraph (7), the amount as redetermined shall have effect from the first week following the relevant subsequent week in question.

(6)   The conditions are that–

(a)   a further claim is made 26 or more weeks after–

    (i)   the date on which the claimant made a claim for housing benefit in respect of which he was first treated as possessing the capital in question under regulation 47(1);

    (ii)   in a case where there has been at least one redetermination in accordance with paragraph (5), the date on which he last made a claim for housing benefit which resulted in the weekly amount being redetermined; or

(iii)   the date on which he last ceased to be entitled to housing benefit,

whichever last occurred; and

(b)   the claimant would have been entitled to housing benefit but for regulation 47(1) of these Regulations or regulation 49(1) of the Housing Benefit Regulations 2006.

(7)   The amount as re-determined pursuant to paragraph (5) shall not have effect if it is less than the amount which applied in that case immediately before the redetermination and in such a case the higher amount shall continue to have effect.

(8)   For the purposes of this regulation–

(a)   ''part-week'' in paragraph (4)(b) and (d) means–

   (i)   a period of less than a week which is the whole period for which state pension credit, or, as the case may be, an income-based jobseeker's allowance, is payable; and

   (ii)   any other period of less than a week for which either of those benefits is payable;

(b)   ''part-week'' in paragraph (4)(c) means a period of less than a week for which council tax benefit is allowed;

(c)   ''relevant week'' means the benefit week in which the capital in question of which the claimant has deprived himself within the meaning of regulation 47(1)–

   (i)   was first taken into account for the purpose of determining his entitlement to housing benefit; or

   (ii)   was taken into account on a subsequent occasion for the purpose of determining or redetermining his entitlement to housing benefit on that subsequent occasion and that determination or redetermination resulted in his beginning to receive, or ceasing to receive, housing benefit,

and where more than one benefit week is identified by reference to heads (i) and (ii) of this sub-paragraph, means the later or latest such benefit week;

(d)   ''relevant subsequent week'' means the benefit week which includes the day on which the further claim or, if more than one further claim has been made, the last such claim was made.

Analysis

This is, for the most part, equivalent to reg 50 HB Regs (see p325). Paras (3) and (4) are different. Only notional entitlements to PC, CTB and income-based JSA will be taken into account in calculating diminished notional capital.

Capital jointly held

49.   Where a claimant and one or more other persons are beneficially entitled in possession to any capital asset, other than a capital asset disregarded under regulation 47(3), they shall be treated as if each of them were entitled in possession to the whole beneficial interest therein in an equal share and the foregoing provisions of this Part shall apply for the purposes of calculating the amount of capital which the claimant is treated as possessing as if it were actual capital which the claimant does possess.

Analysis

This is equivalent to reg 51 HB Regs (see p328).

PART 7
Amount of benefit

Maximum housing benefit

50.   The amount of a person's appropriate maximum housing benefit in any week shall be 100 per cent. of his eligible rent calculated on a weekly basis in accordance with regulation 61 and 62 (calculation of weekly amount and rent free periods) less any deductions in respect of non-dependants which fall to be made under regulation 55 (non-dependant deductions).

Housing benefit tapers

51. The prescribed percentages for the purpose of sub-section (3)(b) of section 130 of the Act (percentage of excess of income over applicable amount which is deducted from maximum housing benefit) shall be 65 per cent.

Reduction where amount payable under regulation 72 of the Housing Benefit Regulations

52. Where for any week–

(a) a person is entitled to a payment in accordance with regulation 72 of the Housing Benefit Regulations 2006 (an "extended payment"); and

(b) he also claims and is awarded housing benefit,

then the amount of the housing benefit payable in respect of that week shall be reduced by a sum equal to the amount of the extended payment and only the balance (if any) shall be payable to him for that week.

Analysis

A claimant might claim (and be awarded) HB under these regs for the same period in which s/he is entitled to an extended payment under reg 72 HB Regs (see p357). See also reg 5 HB Regs on p202. Reg 52 ensures that where an award of HB is made, the amount of the extended payment is offset against the amount of HB payable and only the balance is payable. Note that there are situations where a claimant might be entitled to a higher rate of HB on her/his "in work" claim, than the rate of her/his extended payment – eg, where a non-dependant moves out or rent increases. The net effect in this case, is that the extended payment is topped up to the level of the new HB entitlement.

Extended payments (severe disablement allowance and incapacity benefit)

53.–(1) Except in a case in which a person is in receipt of state pension credit, paragraph (2) shall apply where–

(a) a person ceases to be entitled to housing benefit–

    (i) in accordance with regulation 58 (date on which entitlement to housing benefit is to end where entitlement to severe disablement allowance or incapacity benefit ceases); and

    (ii) the condition referred to in paragraph 1 of Schedule 7 is satisfied in his case; or

(b) a person ceases to be entitled to housing benefit because he has vacated the dwelling which he occupied as his home and the day on which he did so was either in the week in which he took up employment as an employed or self-employed earner, or in the preceding week, and–

    (i) he ceased to be entitled to severe disablement allowance or incapacity benefit by reason of taking up employment as an employed or self-employed earner;

    (ii) he had been entitled to and in receipt of severe disablement allowance, incapacity benefit or a combination of severe disablement allowance and incapacity benefit for a continuous period of at least 26 weeks;

    (iii) he was not entitled to and in receipt of income support; and

    (iv) the condition referred to in paragraph 1 of Schedule 7 is satisfied in his case.

(2) A person to whom paragraph (1) applies shall be treated as having made a claim under this regulation and his housing benefit shall be determined in accordance with Schedule 7 and any award so determined shall be referred to in these regulations as an "extended payment (severe disablement allowance and incapacity benefit)".

(3)   For the purposes of any payment pursuant to this regulation–

(a)   except in a case to which paragraph (b) applies the maximum housing benefit of any person mentioned in paragraph (1) shall be that which was applicable to him in the last week of the award of housing benefit which has ceased as mentioned in paragraph (1);

(b)   the maximum housing benefit of any person the amount of whose extended payment (severe disablement allowance and incapacity benefit) is calculated in accordance with paragraph 6(b)(i) of Schedule 7 shall be determined in accordance with paragraph 7 of that Schedule;

(c)   except in a case to which paragraph (d) applies, any person who meets the requirements of paragraph (1) shall be treated as possessing the same amounts of income and capital as they possessed in the last week of the award of housing benefit which has ceased as mentioned in paragraph (1); and

(d)   any person whose maximum housing benefit is determined in accordance with paragraph 7 of Schedule 7 shall be treated as possessing no income or capital.

(4)   Regulations 63, 64 and 67 (claims, evidence and information) shall not apply to a claim pursuant to this regulation and, subject to regulation 61(8) and Part 8 (calculation of weekly amounts and changes of circumstances) shall not apply to any payment under it.

(5)   In paragraph (1), references to a ''person'' include references to a person's partner and references to taking up employment include receiving remuneration for employment or an increased amount of remuneration for employment or engaging in employment for an increased number of hours.

(6)   In a case where payment has been made under this regulation–

(a)   the beneficiary shall be treated for the purpose of these Regulations as though he were entitled to and in receipt of housing benefit–

(i)   during the 4 weeks immediately following the last day of his entitlement to housing benefit; or

(ii)   until the date on which his liability for rent ends,

whichever occurs first; and

(b)   any claim for housing benefit made by the beneficiary within the period which under sub-paragraph (a) applies in his case or the 4 weeks thereafter shall be treated as having been made in respect of a period beginning immediately after the end of his previous award of housing benefit.

(7)   In paragraph (6), ''these Regulations'' includes the Regulations as modified by paragraphs 4 and 5 of Schedule 3 to the Consequential Provisions Regulations.

Continuing payments where state pension credit claimed

54.–(1)   This regulation applies where–

(a)   the claimant is entitled to housing benefit;

(b)   paragraph (2) is satisfied; and

(c)   either–

(i)   the claimant has attained the qualifying age for state pension credit or, if his entitlement to income-based jobseeker's allowance continued beyond that age, has attained the age of 65; or

(ii)   the claimant's partner has actually claimed state pension credit.

(2)   This regulation is only satisfied if the Secretary of State has certified to the relevant authority that the claimant's partner has actually claimed state pension credit or that–

(a)   the claimant's award of–

(i)   income support has terminated because the claimant has attained the qualifying age for state pension credit; or

       (ii)   income-based jobseeker's allowance has terminated because the claimant has attained the qualifying age for state pension credit or the age of 65; and

    (b)   the claimant has claimed or is treated as having claimed or is required to make a claim for state pension credit.

(3)   Subject to paragraph (4), in a case to which this regulation applies housing benefit shall continue to be paid for the period of 4 weeks beginning on the day following the day the claimant's entitlement to income support or, as the case may be, income-based jobseeker's allowance, ceased, if and for so long as the claimant otherwise satisfies the conditions for entitlement to housing benefit.

(4)   Where housing benefit is paid for the period of 4 weeks in accordance with paragraph (3) above, and the last day of that period falls on a day other than the last day of a benefit week, then housing benefit shall continue to be paid until the end of the benefit week in which the last day of that period falls.

(5)   Throughout the period of 4 weeks specified in paragraph (3) and any further period specified in paragraph (4)–

    (a)   the whole of the income and capital of the claimant shall be disregarded;

    (b)   subject to paragraph (6) the appropriate maximum housing benefit of the claimant shall be that which was applicable in his case immediately before that period commenced.

(6)   The appropriate maximum housing benefit shall be calculated in accordance with regulation 50 if, since the date it was last calculated–

    (a)   the claimant's rent has increased; or

    (b)   a change in the deduction under regulation 55 falls to be made.

Analysis

Reg 54 provides a further scheme of extended payments to that in reg 53, but are here called "continuing payments". In this case, they are designed to ease the transition into retirement. To qualify for continuing payments, two conditions must be fulfilled:

(1)   Either the claimant has attained the qualifying age for PC (currently 60) or has attained the age of 65 if he continued claiming income-based JSA beyond that date, or the claimant's partner has claimed PC: para (1).

(2)   The Secretary of State certifies two matters: that an award of IS has ceased because the claimant has attained the qualifying age for PC or an award of income-based JSA has ceased because the claimant has attained the qualifying age for PC or the age of 65; *and* that the claimant has claimed (or has been treated as having claimed) PC or is required to make such a claim: para (2).

Continuing payments last for four weeks from the day after the day IS or income-based JSA ceases or if the four-week period ends before the end of a benefit week, until the end of the benefit week in which the end of the four-week period falls: paras (3) and (4). They are paid at the rate of maximum HB applicable immediately preceding the start of the continuing payments: para (5). They may be adjusted, however, for rent increases or a change in applicable non-dependant deductions: para (6).

Non-dependant deductions

55.–(1)   Subject to the following provisions of this regulation, the deductions referred to in regulation 50 (maximum housing benefit) shall be–

    (a)   in respect of a non-dependant aged 18 or over who is engaged in remunerative work, [4 £47.75];

    (b)   in respect of a non-dependant aged 18 or over to whom sub-paragraph (a) does not apply, [4 £7.40] per week.

(2)   In the case of a non-dependant aged 18 or over to whom paragraph (1)(a) applies because he is in remunerative work, where it is shown to the appropriate authority that his normal weekly gross income is–

    (a)   less than [5 £111.00], the deduction to be made under this regulation shall be that specified in paragraph 1(b);

    (b)   not less than [5 £111.00] but less than [5 £164.00 , the deduction to be made under this regulation shall be [4 £17.00];

(c)   not less than [⁵ £164.00] but less than [⁵ £213.00], the deduction to be made under this regulation shall be [⁴ £23.35];

(d)   not less than [⁵ £213.00] but less than [⁵ £283.00], the deduction to be made under this regulation shall be [⁴ £38.20];

(e)   not less than [⁵ £283.00] but less than [⁵ £353.00], the deduction to be made under this regulation shall be [⁴ £43.50].

(3)   Only one deduction shall be made under this regulation in respect of a couple or, as the case may be, members of a polygamous marriage and, where, but for this paragraph, the amount that would fall to be deducted in respect of one member of a couple or polygamous marriage is higher than the amount (if any) that would fall to be deducted in respect of the other, or any other, member, the higher amount shall be deducted.

(4)   In applying the provisions of paragraph (2) in the case of a couple or, as the case may be, a polygamous marriage, regard shall be had, for the purpose of paragraph (2) to the couple's or, as the case may be, all members of the polygamous marriage's joint weekly gross income.

(5)   Where a person is a non-dependant in respect of more than one joint occupier of a dwelling (except where the joint occupiers are a couple or members of a polygamous marriage), the deduction in respect of that non-dependant shall be apportioned between the joint occupiers (the amount so apportioned being rounded to the nearest penny) having regard to the number of joint occupiers and the proportion of the payments in respect of the dwelling payable by each of them.

(6)   No deduction shall be made in respect of any non-dependants occupying a claimant's dwelling if the claimant or his partner is–

(a)   blind or treated as blind by virtue of paragraph 6(5) of Schedule 3 (severe disability premiums); or

(b)   receiving in respect of himself either–

(i)   attendance allowance; or

(ii)   the care component of the disability living allowance.

(7)   No deduction shall be made in respect of a non-dependant if–

(a)   although he resides with the claimant, it appears to the appropriate authority that his normal home is elsewhere; or

(b)   he is in receipt of a training allowance paid in connection with a Youth Training Scheme established under section 2 of the 1973 Act or section 2 of the Enterprise and New Towns (Scotland) Act 1990; or

(c)   he is a full-time student during a period of study within the meaning of regulation 53(1) of the Housing Benefit Regulations 2006 (Students); or

(d)   he is a full time student and during a recognised summer vacation appropriate to his course he is not in remunerative work; or

(e)   he is a full-time student and the claimant or his partner has attained the age of 65; or

(f)   he is not residing with the claimant because he has been a patient for a period in excess of 52 weeks, or a prisoner, and for these purposes–

[¹ (i)   "patient" has the meaning given in paragraph (18) of regulation 7 (circumstances in which a person is or is not to be treated as occupying a dwelling as his home),

(ii)   where a person has been a patient for two or more distinct periods separated by one or more intervals each not exceeding 28 days, he shall be treated as having been a patient continuously for a period equal in duration to the total of those distinct periods, and]

(iii)   "prisoner" means a person who is detained in custody pending trial or sentence upon conviction or under a sentence imposed by a court other than a person who is detained in hospital under the provisions of the Mental Health Act 1983, or, in Scotland, under the provisions of the Mental Health (Care and Treatment) (Scotland) Act 2003 or the Criminal Procedure (Scotland) Act 1995.

(8)   No deduction shall be made in calculating the amount of a rent rebate or allowance in respect of a non-dependant aged less than 25 who is on income support or an income-based jobseeker's allowance.

(9)   No deduction shall be made in respect of a non-dependant who is on state pension credit.

(10)   In the case of a non-dependant to whom paragraph (2) applies because he is in remunerative work, there shall be disregarded from his weekly gross income–

(a)   any attendance allowance or disability living allowance received by him;

(b)   any payment made under the Macfarlane Trust, the Macfarlane (Special Payments) Trust, the Macfarlane (Special Payments) (No. 2) Trust, the Fund, the Eileen Trust or the Independent Living Funds which had his income fallen to be calculated under regulation 40 (calculation of income other than earnings) of the Housing Benefit Regulations 2006 would have been disregarded under paragraph 23 of Schedule 5 (income in kind) to those Regulations; and

(c)   any payment which had his income fallen to be calculated under regulation 40 of the Housing Benefit Regulations 2006 would have been disregarded under paragraph 35 of Schedule 5 to those Regulations (payments made under certain trusts and certain other payments).

Amendments

1.   Substituted by reg 2(8) of SI 2005 No 2502 as amended by Sch 2 para 27 of SI 2006 No 217 as from 1.4.06 (3.4.06 where rent payable weekly or at intervals of a week).

2.   Confirmed by Art 19(3) of SI 2006 No 645 and reg 8 of SI 2006 No 217 as from 1.4.06 (3.4.06 where rent payable weekly or at intervals of a week).

3.   Amended by Art 19(3) of SI 2006 No 645 and reg 8 of SI 2006 No 217 as from 1.4.06 (3.4.06 where rent payable weekly or at intervals of a week).

4.   Confirmed by Art 20(3) of SI 2007 No 688 as from 1.4.07 (2.4.07 where rent payable weekly or at intervals of a week).

5.   Amended by Art 20(3) of SI 2007 No 688 as from 1.4.07 (2.4.07 where rent payable weekly or at intervals of a week).

Minimum housing benefit

56.   Where housing benefit is payable in the form of a rent rebate or allowance, it shall not be payable where the amount to which a person would otherwise be entitled is less than 50 pence per benefit week.

PART 8
Calculation of weekly amounts and changes of circumstances

Date on which entitlement is to commence

57.–(1)   Subject to paragraph (2), a person who makes a claim for, and is otherwise entitled to, housing benefit shall be entitled to that benefit from the benefit week following the first day in respect of which that claim is made.

[¹ (2)   A claimant shall become entitled to housing benefit from the benefit week in which the first day in respect of which his claim is made falls, where he is otherwise entitled to housing benefit and–

(a)   he becomes liable in that benefit week, for the first time, to make payments in respect of a dwelling which he occupies as his home; or,

[² (b)   he becomes liable in that benefit week to make payments, which fall due on a daily basis, in respect of the accommodation listed in paragraph (3) which he occupies as his home.]]

(3)   The accommodation referred to in paragraph (2)(b) is–

(a)   a hostel;

(b) board and lodging accommodation where the payments are to an authority under section 206(2) of the Housing Act 1996 or section 35(2)(b) of the Housing (Scotland) Act 1987;

(c) accommodation which the authority holds on a licence agreement where the payments are to an authority under section 206(2) of the Housing Act 1996 or section 35(2)(b) of the Housing (Scotland) Act 1987; or

(d) accommodation outside that authority's Housing Revenue Account which the authority holds on a lease granted for a term not exceeding 10 years.

[³ (4) In this regulation–

"board and lodging accommodation" means–

(a) accommodation provided to a person or, if he is a member of a family, to him or any other member of his family, for a charge which is inclusive of the provision of that accommodation and at least some cooked or prepared meals which both are cooked or prepared (by a person other than a person to whom the accommodation is provided or by a member of his family) and are consumed in that accommodation or associated premises; or

(b) accommodation provided to a person in a hotel, guest house, lodging house or some similar establishment,

but it does not include accommodation in a care home, an Abbeyfield Home, an independent hospital or a hostel; and

"Housing Revenue Account" has the same meaning as for the purposes of Part VIII of the Social Security Administration Act 1992.]

Amendments

1. Substituted by reg 2(9) of SI 2005 No 2502 as amended by Sch 2 para 27 of SI 2006 No 217 as from 1.4.06 (3.4.06 where rent payable weekly or at intervals of a week).
2. Substituted by reg 3(2)(a) SI 2007 No. 294 as from 1.4.07.
3. Inserted by reg 3(2)(b) SI 2007 No. 294 as from 1.4.07.

Analysis

Reg 57 has the same effect as reg 76 HB Regs (see p365).

Date on which housing benefit is to end where entitlement to severe disablement allowance or incapacity benefit ceases

58. Except in a case in which the claimant or his partner is in receipt of state pension credit, a claimant's entitlement to housing benefit shall cease at the end of the benefit week in which entitlement to severe disablement allowance or incapacity benefit ceases where–

(a) the claimant or his partner was not entitled to and in receipt of income support but was entitled to and in receipt of severe disablement allowance or incapacity benefit and that entitlement has ceased;

(b) that entitlement to severe disablement allowance or incapacity benefit has ceased by reason of the claimant or his partner–

    (i) commencing employment as an employed or self-employed earner; or

    (ii) increasing their earnings from such employment; or

    (iii) increasing the number of hours worked in such employment;

(c) the claimant had been entitled to and in receipt of severe disablement allowance or incapacity benefit for a continuous period of at least 26 weeks before the day on which his entitlement to severe disablement allowance or incapacity benefit ceased, and for the purposes of this sub-paragraph–

    (i) a claimant satisfies the conditions of this sub-paragraph if he has been entitled to and in receipt of a combination of severe disablement allowance and incapacity benefit for at least 26 weeks;

    (ii) references to the claimant include references to his partner; and

(d)   that work, increase in earnings, or as the case may be, increase in hours is expected to last at least 5 weeks or more.

Date on which change of circumstances is to take effect

59.–(1)   Except in cases where regulation 34 (disregard of changes in tax, contributions, etc) [⁶ applies, and subject to regulation 8(3) of the Decisions and Appeals Regulations and] the following provisions of this regulation and to regulations 60 and 61(6), a change of circumstances which affects entitlement to, or the amount of, housing benefit (''change of circumstances'') shall take effect from the first day of the benefit week following the date on which the change of circumstances actually occurs, and where that change is cessation of entitlement to any benefit under the benefit Acts, the date on which the change actually occurs shall be the day immediately following the last day of entitlement to that benefit.

[¹ (2)   Subject to paragraph (8) [⁶ and regulation 8(3) of the Decisions and Appeals Regulations] where the change of circumstances is a change in the amount of rent payable in respect of a dwelling, that change shall take effect from the day on which it actually occurs.]

[² (2A)   Subject to paragraphs (8) [⁷ to (9A), except in a case where regulation 8(3) of the Decisions and Appeals Regulations applies, where the change of circumstances is–
(a)   that a person moves into a new dwelling occupied as the home, or
(b)   any other event which–
    (i)   entitles a person to be treated as occupying two dwellings as his home under regulation 7(6), or
    (ii)   brings to an end a person's right to be treated as occupying two dwellings as his home under that regulation, in a case where he has, immediately prior to the event, been treated as occupying two dwellings as his home,
that change of circumstances shall take effect on the day on which it actually occurs.

(2B)   Subject to paragraph (8), where the change of circumstances is the expiry of a maximum period of time, referred to in regulation 7(6), for which a person can be treated as occupying two dwellings as his home, that change shall take effect on the day after the last day of that period]

(3)   Subject to paragraphs (8) [³], where the change of circumstances is an amendment to these Regulations that change, subject to regulation 61(6), shall take effect as follows–
(a)   where the amendment is made by an order under section 150 of the Administration Act (annual up-rating of benefits)–
    (i)   in a case in which the claimant's weekly amount of eligible rent falls to be calculated in accordance with regulation 61(2)(b) [³ or (c)](calculation of weekly amounts), from 1st April;
    (ii)   in any other case, from the first Monday in April,
in the year in which that order comes into force;
(b)   in respect of any other amendment, from the date on which the amendment of these Regulations comes into force in the particular case.

[¹ (4)   Subject to paragraph (8), if two or more changes of circumstances occurring in the same benefit week would, but for this paragraph, take effect in different benefit weeks in accordance with this regulation, they shall all take effect on the first day of the benefit week in which they occur, unless a change taking effect under paragraphs (2), (2A) or (2B) takes effect in that week, in which case the changes shall all take effect on the day on which that change takes effect.]

(5)   Where, during a benefit week commencing on the first Monday in April–
(a)   a change of circumstances takes effect in accordance with paragraph (3)(a)(ii);

(b)   one or more changes of circumstances occur to which paragraph (1) applies; and

(c)   no other change of circumstances occurs to which this regulation applies, any change of circumstances to which paragraph (1) applies and which occurs in that benefit week shall take effect from the first day of that benefit week.

(6)   Where the change of circumstances is that income, or an increase in the amount of income, other than a benefit or an increase in the amount of a benefit under the Act, is paid in respect of a past period and there was no entitlement to income of that amount during that period, the change of circumstances shall take effect from the first day on which such income, had it been paid in that period at intervals appropriate to that income, would have fallen to be taken into account for the purposes of these Regulations.

(7)   Without prejudice to paragraph (6), where the change of circumstances is the payment of income, or arrears of income, in respect of a past period, the change of circumstances shall take effect from the first day on which such income, had it been timeously paid in that period at intervals appropriate to that income, would have fallen to be taken into account for the purposes of these Regulations.

[¹ (8)   Subject to paragraph (9), where a change of circumstances occurs which has the effect of bringing entitlement to an end it shall take effect on the first day of the benefit week following the benefit week in which that change actually occurs except in a case where a person is liable to make payments, which fall due on a daily basis, [⁵] in which case that change shall take effect on the day on which it actually occurs.

(9)   Where the change of circumstances is that a person moves to a new dwelling and immediately after the move he is treated as occupying his former dwelling as his home in accordance with regulation 7(7) or (10) then that change of circumstances shall take effect on the day after the last day for which he is treated as liable to make payments in respect of the former dwelling in accordance with whichever of those regulations applies in his case.]

[⁷ (9A)   Where the change of circumstances is that the person moves to a new dwelling and immediately before the move that person is treated as occupying the new dwelling in accordance with regulation 7(8) then that change of circumstances shall take effect on the first day on which the person is treated as occupying the new dwelling as the home under that regulation.]

(10)   Paragraph (11) applies if–

(a)   the claimant or his partner has attained the age of 65; and

(b)   either–

    (i)   a non-dependant took up residence in the claimant's dwelling; or

    (ii)   there has been a change of circumstances in respect of a non-dependant so that the amount of the deduction which falls to be made under regulation 55 (non-dependant deductions) increased.

(11)   Where this paragraph applies, the change of circumstances [⁴ referred to in paragraph (10)(b)] shall take effect from the effective date.

(12)   In paragraph (11) but subject to paragraph (13), "the effective date" means–

(a)   where more than one change of a kind referred to in paragraph (10)(b) relating to the same non-dependant has occurred since–

    (i)   the date on which the claimant's entitlement to housing benefit first began; or

    (ii)   the date which was the last effective date in respect of such a change; whichever is the later, the date which falls 26 weeks after the date on which the first such change occurred;

(b)   where sub-paragraph (a) does not apply, the date which falls 26 weeks after the date on which the change referred to in paragraph (10)(b) occurred.

(13)   If in any particular case the date determined under paragraph (12) is not the first day of the benefit week, the effective date in that case shall be the first day of the next benefit week to commence after the date determined under that paragraph.

Modifications

Reg 59 applies as if para (7) was omitted where a change of circumstances occurs as a result of the payment of arrears of any income which affects a determination or decision in respect of entitlement to, or the amount of, HB or CTB before 6 March 1995. See Sch 3 para 1 HB&CTB(CP) Regs on p1099.

Amendments

1.   Substituted by reg 2(10)(b), (e) and, (f) of SI 2005 No 2502 as amended by Sch 2 para 27 of SI 2006 No 217 as from 1.4.06 (3.4.06 where rent payable weekly or at intervals of a week).
2.   Inserted by reg 2(10)(c) of SI 2005 No 2502 as amended by Sch 2 para 27 of SI 2006 No 217 as from 1.4.06 (3.4.06 where rent payable weekly or at intervals of a week).
3.   Amended by reg 2(10)(d) of SI 2005 No 2502 as amended by Sch 2 para 27 of SI 2006 No 217 as from 1.4.06 (3.4.06 where rent payable weekly or at intervals of a week).
4.   Amended by reg 16(3) of SI 2006 No 2378 as from 2.10.06.
5.   Amended by reg 3(3) SI 2007 No. 294 as from 1.4.07.
6.   Substituted by reg 5 of SI 2007 No 2470 as from 24.9.07.
7.   Amended by reg 12(7) of SI 2007 No 2618 as from 1.10.07.

General Note

Note the exceptions to the normal rules for determining the effective date of changes in circumstance in reg 59 set out in reg 60 immediately below.

Change of circumstances where state pension credit payable

60.–(1)   Paragraphs (2) to (4) apply where–
  (a)   the claimant is also on state pension credit;
  (b)   the amount of state pension credit awarded to him is changed in consequence of a change in the claimant's circumstances or the correction of an official error; and
  (c)   the change in the amount of state pension credit payable to the claimant results in a change in the rate of housing benefit payable to the claimant.
  (2)   Where the change of circumstance is that an increase in the amount of state pension credit payable to the claimant results in–
  (a)   an increase in the rate at which housing benefit is payable to him, the change shall take effect from the first day of the benefit week in which state pension credit becomes payable at the increased rate; or
  (b)   a decrease in the rate at which housing benefit is payable to him, the change shall take effect from the first day of the benefit week next following the date on which–
    (i)   the local authority receives notification from the Secretary of State of the increase in the amount of state pension credit; or
    (ii)   state pension credit is increased,
  whichever is the later.
  (3)   Where the change of circumstance is that the claimant's state pension credit is reduced and in consequence the rate of housing benefit payable to the claimant reduces–
  (a)   in a case where the claimant's state pension credit is reduced because the claimant failed to notify the Secretary of State timeously of the change of circumstances, the change shall take effect from the first day of the benefit week from which state pension credit was reduced; or
  (b)   in any other case the change shall take effect from the first day of the benefit week next following the date on which–
    (i)   the local authority receives notification from the Secretary of State of the reduction in the amount of state pension credit; or

(ii)   state pension credit is reduced,

whichever is the later.

(4)   Where the change of circumstance is that–

(a)   state pension credit is reduced; and

(b)   in consequence of the change the rate of housing benefit payable to the claimant is increased,

the change shall take effect from the first day of the benefit week in which state pension credit becomes payable at the reduced rate.

(5)   Where a change of circumstances occurs in that an award of state pension credit has been made to the claimant or his partner and this would result in a decrease in the rate of housing benefit payable to the claimant, the change shall take effect from the first day of the benefit week next following the date on which–

(a)   the local authority receives notification from the Secretary of State of the award; or

(b)   entitlement to state pension credit begins,

whichever is the later.

(6)   Where, in the case of a claimant who, or whose partner, is or has been awarded state pension credit comprising only the savings credit, there is–

(a)   a change of circumstances of a kind described in any of paragraphs (2) to (5) which results from a relevant calculation or estimate; and

(b)   a change of circumstances which is a relevant determination,

each of which results in a change in the rate of housing benefit payable to the claimant, the change of circumstances referred to in sub-paragraph (b) shall take effect from the day specified in paragraphs (2), (3), (4) or (5) as the case may be, in relation to the change referred to in sub-paragraph (a).

(7)   Where a change of circumstance occurs in that a guarantee credit has been awarded to the claimant or his partner and this would result in an increase in the rate of housing benefit payable to the claimant, the change shall take effect from the first day of the benefit week next following the date in respect of which the guarantee credit is first payable.

(8)   Where a change of circumstances would but for this paragraph take effect under the preceding provisions of this regulation within the 4 week period specified in regulation 54 (continuing payments where state pension credit claimed), that change shall take effect on the first day of the first benefit week to commence after the expiry of the 4 week period.

(9)   Where the change of circumstances is an amendment of these Regulations, that change, subject to regulation 61(6) (calculation of weekly amounts), shall take effect as follows–

(a)   where the amendment is made by an order under section 150 of the Administration Act (annual uprating of benefits)–

(i)   in a case in which the claimant's weekly amount of eligible rent falls to be calculated in accordance with regulation 61(2)(b) [¹ or (c)], from 1st April;

(ii)   in any other case, from the first Monday in April, in the year in which that order comes into force;

(b)   in respect of any other amendment, from the date on which the amendment of these Regulations comes into force in the particular case.

(10)   In this regulation–

"official error" has the meaning it has in the Decisions and Appeals Regulations by virtue of regulation 1(2) of those Regulations;

"relevant calculation or estimate" means the calculation or estimate made by the Secretary of State of the claimant's or, as the case may be, the claimant's partner's income and capital for the purposes of the award of state pension credit;

"relevant determination" means a change in the determination by the relevant authority of the claimant's income and capital using the relevant calculation or estimate, in accordance with regulation 27(1) (calculation of claimant's income and capital in savings credit only cases).

Amendment

1.　　Amended by reg 2(11) of SI 2005 No 2502 as amended by Sch 2 para 27 of SI 2006 No 217 as from 1.4.06 (3.4.06 where rent payable weekly or at intervals of a week).

General Note

Reg 60 provides exceptions to the normal rules for determining the effective date of changes in circumstance in reg 59. The effect of reg 60 is that overpayments are not created where there has been a delay in the DWP passing information to authorities about a claimant's (or her/his partner's) PC. It applies when PC is awarded or a PC award is changed which in turn requires an HB award to be modified. Generally speaking, where HB increases as a result of the change in entitlement to PC, the change generally takes effect from the week the PC entitlement alters. However, where HB decreases, the change takes effect from the week the authority is notified of the change in entitlement to PC, or the date the PC changes if this is later. Exceptions are found in paras (8) and (9) where continuing payments are being made and where the change is an amendment to the HB(SPC) Regs.

Analysis

Paragraphs (1) to (5) and (7): The general rules

Where HB payable increases or decreases due to a change in circumstances or the correction of an official error, the change generally takes effect from the first day of the benefit week in which the rate of PC is altered: paras (2)(a) and (4). However, where HB increases because an award of guarantee credit of PC is made to the claimant or her/his partner, the change takes effect from the first day of the benefit week after the date the guarantee credit is payable: para (7).

　　Where HB payable decreases there are three possibilities. Where:

(1)　　a claimant's PC increases due to a change in circumstances or the correction of an official error, the change takes effect from the first day in the benefit week following the later of the date the authority receives notification of the increase from the DWP or the date the PC increases: para (2)(b);

(2)　　a claimant's PC decreases, the change takes effect from the first day in the benefit week following the later of the date the authority receives notification of the decreased PC from the DWP or the PC decreases, unless the reduction was due to a failure by the claimant to notify a change to the DWP "timeously". In this case it takes effect from the first day of the benefit week in which the PC decreased: para (3);

(3)　　an award of PC is made to the claimant or her/his partner, the change takes effect from the first day of the benefit week following the later of the date the authority receives notification of the award of PC from the DWP or the date entitlement to PC begins: para (5).

Paragraph (6): Savings credit only cases

Where a claimant or her/his partner is getting the savings credit of PC only and the HB payable changes as a result of a change in the DWP assessment of income and capital and a change in the assessment of income and capital by the authority, the change in the authority's assessment takes effect under whichever of paras (2) to (5) applies in relation to the change in PC as a result of the DWP assessment. The definitions of "relevant calculation or estimate" and "relevant determination" are in para (10).

Paragraph (8): Where continuing payments are made

By virtue of para (8), a change taking place while continuing payments are being made under reg 54 above takes effect on the first day of the benefit week after continuing payments end.

Paragraph (9): Amendments to regulations

Where the change is an amendment to the HB(SPC) Regs, it takes effect from the date on which the amendment comes into force unless it is an amendment in respect iof the annual uprating of benefits. In this case, if rent is payable monthly or daily, the change takes effect from 1 April or in any other case, from the first Monday in April.

Calculation of weekly amounts

　　61.–(1)　　A person's entitlement to housing benefit in any benefit week shall be calculated in accordance with the following provisions of this regulation.

　　(2)　　The weekly amount of a claimant's eligible rent shall be–

(a) subject to [¹ paragraph (4)], where rent is payable at intervals of one week or a multiple thereof, the amount of eligible rent payable weekly or, where it is payable at intervals of a multiple of a week, the amount determined by dividing the amount of eligible rent payable by the number equal to the number of weeks in respect of which it is payable;

[¹ (b) subject to paragraph (4), where the rent is payable at intervals of a calendar month or multiples thereof, the amount determined by dividing the amount payable by the number equal to the number of calendar months in respect of which it is payable, multiplying by 12 and dividing by 52;

(c) subject to paragraph (4), where the rent is payable at intervals of a day or multiples thereof, the amount determined by dividing the amount payable by the number equal to the number of days in respect of which it is payable and multiplying by 7.]

[² (3)]

[¹ (4) In a case–

(a) to which regulation 57(2) (date on which entitlement is to commence) applies, his eligible rent for the benefit week in which he becomes liable to make payments in respect of a dwelling which he occupies as his home shall be calculated by multiplying his daily rent by the number equal to the number of days in that benefit week for which he is liable to make such payments;

(b) where a change of circumstances takes effect in a benefit week under regulation 59(2A), (but is not a change described in sub-paragraph (c)(ii) of this regulation), (2B), (8) or (9) other than on the Monday of a benefit week then the claimant's eligible rent for that benefit week shall be calculated by multiplying his daily rent by the appropriate number of days in that benefit week;

(c) where–

    (i) the amount of eligible rent which the claimant is liable to pay in respect of a dwelling is altered and that change of circumstances takes effect under regulation 59(2), or

    (ii) the claimant–

        (aa) moves to a new dwelling occupied as the home,

        (bb) he is not entitled to be treated, immediately after that move, as occupying two dwellings as his home or as occupying his former dwelling as his home, and

        (cc) that change of circumstances takes effect under regulation 59(2A),

other than on the Monday of a benefit week, then the claimant's eligible rent for that benefit week shall be calculated by multiplying his old and new daily rent by the number equal to the number of days in that week which relate respectively to the old and new amounts which he is liable to pay.]

(5) In the case of a claimant whose weekly eligible rent falls to be calculated in accordance with paragraph [¹ (4)(a) or (b)] by reference to the daily rent in his case, his weekly applicable amount, weekly income, the weekly amount of any non-dependant deductions and the minimum amount payable in his case shall be calculated in the same manner as his weekly eligible rent by reference to the amounts determined in his case in accordance with Parts 5 to 7 (applicable amounts, income and capital and amount of benefit).

(6) Where a change in the amount of a claimant's applicable amount, income or non-dependant deductions falls to be taken into account in the same benefit week as a change in his eligible rent to which paragraph [¹ (4)(c)] applies, it shall be taken into account in that week on a daily basis in the same manner and as if it had occurred on the same day as that change in his eligible rent.

(7)   Any amount determined under these Regulations may, if it is appropriate, be rounded to the nearest whole penny by disregarding any amount less than half a penny and treating any amount of half a penny or more as a whole penny.

(8)   In any case where a claimant has received–

(a)   an extended payment under regulation 72 of the Housing Benefit Regulations 2006, his entitlement shall be adjusted in such circumstances and by such amount as are prescribed in Part 3 of Schedule 7 to those Regulations; or

(b)   an extended payment (severe disablement allowance and incapacity benefit), his entitlement shall be adjusted in such circumstances and by such amount as are prescribed in paragraph 9 of Schedule 7 to these Regulations.

[³ (9)   In this regulation "daily rent" shall mean the amount determined by dividing by 7 the amount determined under whichever sub-paragraph of paragraph (2) is appropriate in each case.

(10)   Where a claimant is entitled to benefit in respect of two (but not more than two) dwellings in accordance with regulation 7(6) his eligible rent shall be calculated in respect of each dwelling in accordance with this regulation.]

Amendments

1.   Substituted by reg 2(12)(a), (c), (d) and (e) of SI 2005 No 2502 as amended by Sch 2 para 27 of SI 2006 No 217 as from 1.4.06 (3.4.06 where rent payable weekly or at intervals of a week).

2.   Omitted by reg 2(12)(b) of SI 2005 No 2502 as amended by Sch 2 para 27 of SI 2006 No 217 as from 1.4.06 (3.4.06 where rent payable weekly or at intervals of a week).

3.   Inserted by reg 2(12)(f) of SI 2005 No 2502 as amended by Sch 2 para 27 of SI 2006 No 217 as from 1.4.06 (3.4.06 where rent payable weekly or at intervals of a week).

Rent free periods

62.–(1)   This regulation applies to a claimant for any period (referred to in this regulation as a rent free period) in, or in respect of, which he is not liable to pay rent except for any period to which regulation 8(1)(d) (waiver of rent by landlord in return for work done) applies.

[¹ (2) In the case of the beginning or ending of a claimant's rent-free period, his eligible rent for the benefit week in which the rent free period begins and ends shall be calculated on a daily basis as if those benefit weeks were weeks to which regulation 61(4) applies.]

(3)   For the purpose of determining the weekly applicable amount and income of a claimant to whom this regulation applies, the weekly amount of any non-dependant deductions and the minimum amount payable in his case–

(a)   in a case to which regulation 61(2)(a) applies, the amounts determined in his case in accordance with Parts 5 to 7 (applicable amounts, income and capital and amount of benefit) shall be multiplied by 52 or 53, whichever is appropriate, and divided by the number equal to the number of weeks in that 52 or 53 week period in respect of which he is liable to pay rent;

(b)   subject to paragraph (4), in a case to which regulation 61(2)(b) [² or (c)] applies, the amounts determined in his case in accordance with Parts 5 to 7 shall be multiplied by 365 or 366, whichever is appropriate and divided by the number of days in that 365 or 366 day period in respect of which he is liable to pay rent.

(4)   In a case to which paragraph (3)(b) applies, where either regulation 61(5) or (6) also applies or it is the beginning or end of a rent-free period, the weekly amounts referred to in paragraph (3) shall first be calculated in accordance with sub-paragraph (b) of that paragraph and then determined on a daily basis in the same manner as the claimant's eligible rent.

Amendments

1.   Substituted by reg 2(13)(a) of SI 2005 No 2502 as amended by Sch 2 para 27 of SI 2006 No 217 as from 1.4.06 (3.4.06 where rent payable weekly or at intervals of a week).

2. Amended by reg 2(13)(b) of SI 2005 No 2502 as amended by Sch 2 para 27 of SI 2006 No 217 as from 1.4.06 (3.4.06 where rent payable weekly or at intervals of a week).

PART 9
Claims

Who may claim

63.–(1) In the case of a couple or members of a polygamous marriage a claim shall be made by whichever one of them they agree should so claim or, in default of agreement, by such one of them as the relevant authority shall determine.

(2) Where a person who is liable to make payments in respect of a dwelling is unable for the time being to act, and–

  (a) a [¹ deputy] has been appointed by the Court of Protection with power to claim, or as the case may be, receive benefit on his behalf; or

  (b) in Scotland, his estate is being administered by a judicial factor or any guardian acting or appointed under the Adults with Incapacity (Scotland) Act 2000 who has power to claim or, as the case may be, receive benefit on his behalf; or

  (c) an attorney with a general power or a power to claim or as the case may be, receive benefit, has been appointed by that person under [¹ the Powers of Attorney Act 1971, the Enduring Powers of Attorney Act 1985 or the Mental Capacity Act 2005 or otherwise],

that [¹ deputy], judicial factor, guardian or attorney, as the case may be, may make a claim on behalf of that person.

(3) Where a person who is liable to make payments in respect of a dwelling is unable for the time being to act and paragraph (2) does not apply to him, the relevant authority may, upon written application made to them by a person who, if a natural person, is over the age of 18, appoint that person to exercise on behalf of the person who is unable to act, any right to which that person might be entitled under the Act and to receive and deal on his behalf with any sums payable to him.

(4) Where the relevant authority has made an appointment under paragraph (3) or treated a person as an appointee under paragraph (5)–

  (a) it may at any time revoke the appointment;

  (b) the person appointed may resign his office after having given four week's notice in writing to the relevant authority of his intention to do so;

  (c) any such appointment shall terminate when the relevant authority is notified that a receiver or other person to whom paragraph (2)(b) or (c) applies has been appointed.

(5) Where a person who is liable to make payments in respect of a dwelling is for the time being unable to act and the Secretary of State has appointed a person to act on his behalf for the purposes of the Act the relevant authority may if that person agrees treat him as if he had been appointed by them under paragraph (3).

(6) Anything required by these Regulations to be done by or to any person who is for the time being unable to act may be done by or to the [¹ deputy], judicial factor, guardian or attorney, if any, or by or to the person appointed or treated as appointed under this regulation and the receipt of any such person so appointed shall be a good discharge to the relevant authority for any sum paid.

(7) Where a claim is made at an office displaying the ONE logo, references in this regulation to a "relevant authority" shall be read as including a reference to the "designated authority".

Amendment

1. Amended by reg 12(8) of SI 2007 No 2618 as from 1.10.07.

Time and manner in which claims are to be made

64.–(1)   The prescribed time for claiming housing benefit is as regards any day on which, apart from satisfying the condition of making a claim, the claimant is entitled to housing benefit, that day and the period of twelve months immediately following it.

(2)   [¹ Subject to paragraph (5A) and (5B),] Every claim shall be in writing and made on a properly completed form approved for the purpose by the relevant authority or in such written form as the relevant authority may accept as sufficient in the circumstances of any particular case or class of cases having regard to the sufficiency of the written information and evidence.

(3)   The forms approved for the purpose of claiming shall be provided free of charge by the relevant authority or such persons as they may authorise or appoint for the purpose.

(4)   Each relevant authority shall notify the Secretary of State of the address to which claims delivered or sent to the appropriate DWP office are to be forwarded.

(5)   A claim [¹ in writing]–

(a)   may be sent or delivered to the appropriate DWP office where the claimant or his partner is also claiming income support, incapacity benefit, state pension credit or a jobseeker's allowance;

(b)   where it has not been sent or delivered to the appropriate DWP office, shall be sent or delivered to the designated office;

(c)   sent or delivered to the appropriate DWP office, other than one sent on the same form as a claim made to income support, incapacity benefit or a jobseeker's allowance and as approved by the Secretary of State for the purpose of the benefits being claimed, shall be forwarded to the relevant authority within two working days of the date of the receipt of the claim at the appropriate DWP office, or as soon as practicable thereafter;

(d)   may, in the case of a claimant who has attained the age of 16 but not the age of 60 and is not engaged in remunerative work, be sent or delivered to a gateway office;

(e)   may be sent or delivered where the claimant has attained the age of 16 but not the age of 60 to an office or designated authority displaying the ONE logo;

(f)   where the claimant has attained the qualifying age for entitlement to state pension credit may be sent or delivered to an authorised office.

[³ (g) may be sent or delivered to the offices of a county council in England if the council has arranged with the relevant authority for claims to be received at their offices (''county offices'').]

[¹ (5A)   Where the relevant authority has published a telephone number for the purpose of receiving claims for housing benefit a claim may be made by telephone to that telephone number.

(5B)   A person who is making a claim for state pension credit in accordance with regulation 4D(6A) of the Social Security (Claims and Payments) Regulations 1987[4] may make his claim for housing benefit to the Secretary of State.

(5C)   The relevant authority may determine, in any particular case, that a claim made by telephone is not a valid claim unless the person making the claim approves a written statement of his circumstances, provided for the purpose by the relevant authority or the Secretary of State.

(5D)   A claim made by telephone in accordance with paragraph (5A) or (5B) is defective unless the relevant authority or the Secretary of State, as the case may be, is provided during that telephone call with all the information the relevant authority requires to determine the claim.

(5E)   Where a claim made by telephone in accordance with paragraph (5A) or (5B) is defective, the relevant authority is to provide the person making it with an opportunity to correct the defect.

(5F) If the person corrects the defect within one month, or such longer period as the relevant authority considers reasonable, of the date the relevant authority last drew attention to it, the relevant authority shall treat the claim as if it had been duly made in the first instance.]

(6) Subject to paragraph (11) and to regulation 65 (date of claim where claim sent or delivered to a gateway office) the date on which a claim is made shall be–

(a) in a case where an award of state pension credit which comprises a guarantee credit has been made to the claimant or his partner and the claim for housing benefit is made within one month of the date on which the claim for state pension credit was received at the appropriate DWP office, the first day of entitlement to state pension credit arising from that claim;

(b) in a case where a claimant or his partner is a person in receipt of a guarantee credit and he becomes liable for the first time to make payments in respect of the dwelling which he occupies as his home, where the claim is received at the designated office or appropriate DWP office within one month of the claimant first becoming liable for such payments, the date he became liable for those payments;

(c) in a case where the claimant is the former partner of a person who was, at the date of his death or their separation, entitled to housing benefit and the claimant makes a claim within one month of the date of the death or the separation, that date;

(d) except where sub-paragraph (a), (b) or (c) is satisfied, in a case where a properly completed claim is received in a designated office, an authorised office [³ , county offices] or an appropriate DWP office within one month, or such longer period as the relevant authority considers reasonable, of the date on which the claim form was issued following the claimant first notifying, by whatever means, a designated office, an authorised office [³ , county offices] or an appropriate DWP office of his intention of making a claim, the date of first notification; and

(e) in any other case, the date on which the claim is received at the designated office, authorised office [³ , county offices] or appropriate DWP office.

(7) Where a claim received at the designated office has not been made in the manner prescribed in paragraph (2), that claim is for the purposes of these Regulations defective.

(8) Where a claim is defective because–

(a) it was made on the form approved for the purpose but that form is not accepted by the relevant authority as being properly completed; or

(b) it was made in writing but not on the form approved for the purpose and the relevant authority does not accept the claim as being in a written form which is sufficient in the circumstances of the case having regard to the sufficiency of the written information and evidence,

the relevant authority may, in a case to which sub-paragraph (a) applies, request the claimant to complete the defective claim or, in the case to which sub-paragraph (b) applies, supply the claimant with the approved form or request further information or evidence.

(9) The relevant authority shall treat a defective claim as if it had been validly made in the first instance if–

(a) where paragraph (8)(a) applies, the authority receives at the designated office the properly completed claim or the information requested to complete it or the evidence within one month of the request, or such longer period as the relevant authority may consider reasonable; or

(b) where paragraph (8)(b) applies–

(i) the approved form sent to the claimant is received at the designated office properly completed within one month of it having been sent to him; or, as the case may be,

(ii)   the claimant supplies whatever information or evidence was requested under paragraph (8) within one month of the request,
or within such longer period as the relevant authority may consider reasonable.

(10)   A claim which is made on an approved form for the time being is, for the purposes of this regulation, properly completed if completed in accordance with the instructions on the form, including any instructions to provide information and evidence in connection with the claim.

[² (11)   Except in the case of a claim made by a person from abroad, where the claimant is not entitled to housing benefit in the benefit week immediately following the date of his claim but the relevant authority is of the opinion that unless there is a change of circumstances he will be entitled to housing benefit for a period beginning not later than the seventeenth benefit week following the date on which the claim is made, the relevant authority may treat the claim as made on a date in the benefit week immediately preceding the first benefit week of that period of entitlement and award benefit accordingly.]

(12)   Paragraph (11) applies in the case of a person who has attained, or whose partner has attained, the age of 59 years and 35 weeks.

(13)   Where the claimant makes a claim in respect of a past period (a "claim for backdating") and, from a day in that period up to the date of the claim for backdating, he had continuous good cause for his failure to make a claim, his claim in respect of that period shall be treated as made on–
(a)   the first day from which he had continuous good cause; or
(b)   the day 52 weeks before the date of the claim for backdating,
whichever fell later.

(14)   In this regulation "authorised office" means an office which is nominated by the Secretary of State and authorised by the relevant authority for receiving claims for decision by the relevant authority.

Amendments
1.   Inserted by reg 3(2) of SI 2006 No 2967 as from 20.12.06.
2.   Substituted by reg 4 of SI 2007 No 1331 as from 23.5.07.
3.   Amended by reg 8(2) of SI 2007 No 2911 as from 31.10.07.

Analysis
This is the equivalent of reg 83 HB Regs (see p378). There are some differences.
Para (1) This is not a backdating provision as such, but rather acts to fix the first day of the claim. Accordingly, all the claimant has to show is that s/he was entitled to HB throughout the relevant 12-month period; unlike under the HB Regs, there is no test of good cause, and so judgements as to why the claimant did not claim previously are irrelevant. If the claimant only qualified under the HB(SPC) Regs for part of the 12-month period before the actual claim or was not entitled to HB for all of the 12-month period, s/he should still benefit from this rule for that part of the 12-month period that s/he was entitled, as long as that period runs continuously up to the date of the actual claim, applying, by analogy, *R(IS) 3/01* and *R(IS) 16/04*.
Para (13) is not needed for those making backdated claims under these regulations. These can be backdated automatically for 12 months under para (1). As the HB(SPC) Regs were a consolidation exercise, some regulations (and parts of regulations) had to be kept in, although they were otiose. This is one such provision.

[¹Electronic claims for benefit

64A.   A claim for housing benefit may be made by means of an electronic communication in accordance with Schedule 10.]

Amendment
1.   Inserted by Art 3(3) of SI 2006 No 2968 as from 20.12.06.

Date of claim where claim sent or delivered to a gateway office

65.–(1)   Subject to paragraph (11) of regulation 64, and with the exception of those claims to which paragraph (3) of this regulation refers, where a claim for housing benefit has been sent or delivered to a gateway office in accordance with sub-paragraph (d) of paragraph (5) of regulation 64, the date on which that claim is made shall be–

(a) in a case where the claimant or his partner–
 (i) claimed income support or a jobseeker's allowance; but
 (ii) has no entitlement to income support or an income-based jobseeker's allowance,

the first date on which notification is deemed to be given in accordance with paragraph (2), but if that notification is by any means other than a claim which meets the requirements of regulation 64(2) such a claim must be received at a gateway office within one month of that notification;

(b) in a case where neither the claimant nor his partner is a person on income support or entitled to an income-based jobseeker's allowance, the first date on which notification is deemed to be made in accordance with paragraph (2), but if that notification is by any means other than a claim which meets the requirements of regulation 64(2) such a claim must be received at the gateway office within one month of that notification; or

(c) in any other case, the date on which the claim for housing benefit is received at the gateway office.

(2) A notification of intention to make a claim is deemed to be given on the date on which notification from the claimant of his intention to claim housing benefit in whatever form is received at a gateway office.

(3) This regulation does not apply to claims which are made at an office of a designated authority in accordance with regulation 64(5)(c).

Date of claim where claim sent or delivered to an office of a designated authority

66.–(1) Where a claim for housing benefit has been sent or delivered to an office of a designated authority in accordance with regulation 64(5)(e), the date on which the claim is made shall be–

(a) except where paragraph (b) applies, the date the claim is received at the office of the designated authority; or

(b) where in the one month before the claim is received in an office of a designated authority, the person making the claim or a person acting on his behalf had notified an office of a designated authority of his intention to make such a claim, the date the notification was given.

(2) A notification of intention to make a claim is deemed to be given on the date on which notification of the intention to claim housing benefit is received, in whatever form, from the claimant, or the person acting on his behalf, at an office of a designated authority.

(3) Paragraph (2) applies where neither income support nor a jobseeker's allowance is claimed in conjunction with housing benefit.

(4) Where the person claiming housing benefit in accordance with regulation 64(5)(e), or the partner of that person, has claimed income support or income-based jobseeker's allowance but no award has been made, the date on which the claim for housing benefit is made shall be determined as is sub-paragraphs (a), and (c) of paragraph (1) of regulation 65 applied to that claim as they apply to claims under regulation 64(5)(d).

Evidence and information

67.–(1) Subject to paragraph (2) and to paragraph 5 of Schedule A1 (treatment of claims for housing benefit by refugees), a person who makes a claim, or a person to whom housing benefit has been awarded, shall furnish such certificates, documents, information and evidence in connection with the claim or the award, or any question arising out of the claim or the award, as may reasonably be required by the relevant authority in order to determine that person's entitlement to, or continuing entitlement to, housing benefit and shall do so within one month of being required to do so or such longer period as the relevant authority may consider reasonable.

(2)   Nothing in this regulation shall require a person to furnish any certificates, documents, information or evidence relating to a payment to which paragraph (4) applies.

(3)   Where a request is made under paragraph (1), the relevant authority shall–

(a)   inform the claimant or the person to whom housing benefit has been awarded of his duty under regulation 69 (duty to notify change of circumstances) to notify the designated office of any change of circumstances; and

(b)   without prejudice to the extent of the duty owed under regulation 69, indicate to him either orally or by notice or by reference to some other document available to him on application and without charge, the kind of change or circumstances which is to be notified.

(4)   This paragraph applies to any of the following payments–

(a)   a payment which is–

    (i)   disregarded under paragraph 23 of Schedule 5 to the Housing Benefit Regulations 2006 (income in kind) or paragraph 34 of Schedule 6 to those Regulations (certain payments in kind); and

    (ii)   made under the Macfarlane Trust, the Macfarlane (Special Payments) Trust, the Macfarlane (Special Payments) (No 2) Trust, the Fund, the Eileen Trust, the Skipton Fund or the London Bombings Charitable Relief Fund;

(b)   a payment which is disregarded under paragraph 35 of Schedule 5 to the Housing Benefit Regulations 2006 or paragraph 24 of Schedule 6 to those Regulations (payments made under certain trusts and certain other payments), other than a payment made under the Independent Living Funds;

(c)   a payment which is disregarded under regulation 55(10)(b) or (c) (income of non-dependant) other than a payment made under the Independent Living Funds.

(5)   Where a claimant or a person to whom housing benefit has been awarded or any partner is aged not less than 60 and is a member of, or a person deriving entitlement to a pension under, a personal pension scheme, [¹] he shall where the relevant authority so requires furnish the following information–

(a)   the name and address of the pension fund holder;

(b)   such other information including any reference or policy number as is needed to enable the personal pension scheme [¹] to be identified.

(6)   Where the pension fund holder receives from a relevant authority a request for details concerning a personal pension scheme [¹] relating to a person or any partner to whom paragraph (5) refers, the pension fund holder shall provide the relevant authority with any information to which paragraph (7) refers.

(7)   The information to which this paragraph refers is–

(a)   where the purchase of an annuity under a personal pension scheme has been deferred, the amount of any income which is being withdrawn from the personal pension scheme;

(b)   in the case of–

    (i)   a personal pension scheme where income withdrawal is available, the maximum amount of income which may be withdrawn from the scheme; or

    (ii)   a personal pension scheme where income withdrawal is not available, [¹] the maximum amount of income which might be withdrawn from the fund if the fund were held under a personal pension scheme where income withdrawal was available, calculated by or on behalf of the pension fund holder by means of tables prepared from time to time by the Government Actuary which are appropriate for this purpose.

Amendment

1.   Amended by reg 5(5) of SI 2007 No 1749 as from 16.7.07.

[²Amendment and withdrawal of claim

68.–(1)   A person who has made a claim may amend it at any time before a decision has been made on it, by a notice in writing delivered or sent to the designated office, except where the claim was made by telephone in accordance with regulation 64(5A) where the amendment may be made by telephone, and any claim so amended shall be treated as if it had been amended in the first instance.

(2)   A person who has made a claim may withdraw it at any time before a decision has been made on it, by notice to the designated office, and any such notice of withdrawal shall have effect when it is received.]

Amendments

1.   Inserted by reg 3(3) of SI 2006 No 2967 as from 20.12.06.
2.   Substituted by reg 7(2) of SI 2007 No 719 as from 2.4.07.

Duty to notify changes of circumstances

69.–(1)   Subject to paragraphs (3) and (5) to (7), if at any time between the making of a claim and a decision being made on it, or during the award of housing benefit, there is a change of circumstances which the claimant, or any person by whom or on whose behalf sums payable by way of housing benefit are receivable, might reasonably be expected to know might affect the claimant's right to, the amount of or the receipt of housing benefit, that person shall be under a duty to notify that change of circumstances by giving notice [²] to the designated office–

[² (a)   in writing or, where the relevant authority has published a telephone number for the purposes of regulation 64 (time and manner in which claims are to be made), by telephone unless the authority determines, in any particular case, that notice must be in writing or may be given otherwise than in writing or by telephone; or

(b)   in writing if in any class of case the relevant authority requires written notice unless the authority determines, in any particular case, that notice may be given otherwise than in writing.]

(2)   In the case of a claimant who sent or delivered his claim to a gateway office in accordance with regulation 65, a change of circumstances may be reported in writing to that office, or to any other gateway office of which he was notified on or with his claim form.

(3)   The duty imposed on a person by paragraph (1) does not extend to changes–

(a)   in the amount of rent payable to a housing authority;

(b)   in the age of the claimant or that of any member of his family or of any non-dependants;

(c)   in these Regulations.

(4)   Notwithstanding paragraph (3)(b) a claimant shall be required by paragraph (1) to notify the designated office of any change in the composition of his family arising from the fact that a person who was a member of his family is now no longer such a person because he ceases to be a child or young person.

(5)   Where a person resides in a postcode district identified in Part 1 or 2 of Schedule 2 to the Social Security (Claims and Information) Regulations 1999, he may notify the change of circumstances by giving notice in writing to any office of a designated authority displaying the ONE logo.

(6)   A person on housing benefit who is also on state pension credit must report–

(a) changes to his tenancy, but not changes in the amount of rent payable to a housing authority;

(b) changes affecting the residence or income of any non-dependant normally residing with the claimant or with whom the claimant normally resides;

(c) any absence from the dwelling which exceeds or is likely to exceed 13 weeks.

(7) In addition to the changes required to be reported under paragraph (6) a person whose state pension credit comprises only a savings credit must also report–

(a) changes affecting a child living with him which may result in a change in the amount of housing benefit payable in his case, but not changes in the age of the child;

[¹ (b)]

(c) any change in the amount of the claimant's capital to be taken into account which does or may take the amount of his capital to more than £16,000;

(d) any change in the income or capital of–

 (i) a non-dependant whose income and capital are treated as belonging to the claimant in accordance with regulation 24 (circumstances in which income of a non-dependant is to be treated as claimant's); or

 (ii) a person to whom regulation 27(4)(e) refers,

and whether such a person or, as the case may be, non-dependant stops living or begins or resumes living with the claimant.

(8) A person who is on housing benefit and on state pension credit need only report to the designated office the changes specified in paragraphs (6) and (7).

Amendments

1. Omitted by reg 2(14) of SI 2005 No 2502 as amended by Sch 2 para 27 of SI 2006 No 217 as from 1.4.06 (3.4.06 where rent payable weekly or at intervals of a week).

2. Inserted by reg 3(3) of SI 2006 No 2967 as from 20.12.06.

Analysis

Paras (1) to (5) are identical to reg 88 HB Regs (see p390).

Paras (6) and (7) set out the types of change that PC recipients need to report to the local authority. All PC recipients must report changes relating to the residence or income of non-dependants, absences which exceed (or are likely to exceed) 13 weeks and "changes to his tenancy": para (6). This presumably includes changes to the demise, rent-free periods and so on, as well as increases or decreases in rent, other than the rent payable to a housing authority which is specifically excluded.

Para (7) lists further changes to be reported by PC recipients who are only getting savings credit. They must report changes in respect of dependant children (other than age), changes in the income and capital of the non-dependants and partners specified, and changes which may take capital over £16,000.

[¹Notice of changes of circumstances given electronically

69A. A person may give notice of a change of circumstances required to be notified under regulation 69 by means of an electronic communication in accordance with Schedule 10.]

Amendment

1. Inserted by Art 3(4) of SI 2006 No 2968 as from 20.12.06.

PART 10
Decisions on questions

Decisions by a relevant authority

70.–(1) Unless provided otherwise by these Regulations, any matter required to be determined under these Regulations shall be determined in the first instance by the relevant authority.

(2) The relevant authority shall make a decision on each claim within 14 days of the provisions of regulations 64 and 67 (time and manner in which claims are to

be made and evidence and information) being satisfied or as soon as reasonably practicable thereafter.

(3)　Without prejudice to the generality of the foregoing provisions of this regulation, in a case where a person–

    (a)　made the notification specified in paragraph 2 of Schedule 7 to the Housing Benefit Regulations 2006 within 14 days from the day immediately after the day on which his entitlement to income support or an income-based jobseeker's allowance ceased ("the appropriate day") and is treated as having claimed an extended payment under regulation 72(2) of those Regulations; and

    (b)　has made a claim, which meets the requirements of regulation 64(2), (7) and (10), within 14 days of the appropriate day,

the relevant authority shall give priority to that claim over other claims which do not fall within the provisions of this paragraph.

Notification of decision

71.–(1)　An authority shall notify in writing any person affected by a decision made by it under these Regulations–

    (a)　in the case of a decision on a claim, forthwith or as soon as reasonably practicable thereafter;

    (b)　in any other case, within 14 days of that decision or as soon as reasonably practicable thereafter,

and every notification shall include a statement as to the matters set out in Schedule 8.

(2)　A person affected to whom an authority sends or delivers a notification of decision may, by notice in writing signed by him, request the authority to provide a written statement setting out the reasons for its decision on any matter set out in the notice.

(3)　For the purposes of paragraph (2), where a person affected who requests a written statement is not a natural person, the notice in writing referred to in that paragraph shall be signed by a person over the age of 18 who is authorised to act on that person's behalf.

(4)　The written statement referred to in paragraph (2) shall be sent to the person requesting it within 14 days or as soon as is reasonably practical thereafter.

PART 11

Payments

Time and manner of payment

72.–(1)　Subject to paragraphs (2) and (3) and regulations 73 to 79 (frequency of payment of rent allowance, payment on account of a rent allowance, payment provisions, offsetting) the relevant authority shall pay housing benefit to which a person is entitled under these Regulations at such time and in such manner as is appropriate, having regard to–

    (a)　the times at which and the frequency with which a person's liability to make payment of rent arises; and

    (b)　the reasonable needs and convenience of the person entitled thereto.

(2)　Where a person's entitlement to housing benefit is less than £1 weekly the relevant authority may pay that benefit at 6 monthly intervals.

(3)　Subject to regulations 73 to 78 (frequency of payment of and payment on account of rent allowance, payment provisions), every authority shall make the first payment of any housing benefit awarded by it within 14 days of the receipt of the claim at the designated office or, if that is not reasonably practical, as soon as possible thereafter.

[¹Cases in which payments to a housing authority are to take the form of a rent allowance

72A.–(1)   Where the occupier of a dwelling is liable to make payments in respect of that dwelling to a housing authority as a result of the making of an order specified in paragraph (2), housing benefit in respect of those payments shall take the form of a rent allowance.

(2)   The orders specified for the purposes of paragraph (1) are–

(a)   a management control order made in accordance with section 74 of the Antisocial Behaviour etc. (Scotland) Act 2004;

(b)   an interim management order made in accordance with section 102 of the Housing Act 2004;

(c)   a final management order made in accordance with section 113 of that Act;

(d)   an interim empty dwelling management order made in accordance with section 133 of that Act; and

(e)   a final empty dwelling management order made in accordance with section 136 of that Act.]

Amendment
1.   Inserted by reg 3 of SI 2006 No 644 as from 3.4.06.

Frequency of payment of a rent allowance

73.–(1)   Subject to the following provisions of this regulation any rent allowance other than a payment made in accordance with regulation 72(2) or (3) or 74 (time and manner of payment, payment on account of rent allowance) shall be paid at intervals of 2 or 4 weeks or one month or, with the consent of the person entitled, at intervals greater than one month.

(2)   Except in a case to which paragraph (3) applies, any payment of a rent allowance shall be made, in so far as it is practicable to do so, at the end of the period in respect of which it is made.

(3)   Except in a case to which regulation 77(2) applies and subject to paragraph (4), this paragraph applies where payment of a rent allowance is being made to a landlord (which for these purposes has the same meaning as in regulations 76 and 77 (payments to a landlord)), when that payment shall be made–

(a)   at intervals of 4 weeks; and

(b)   at the end of the period in respect of which it is made.

(4)   Where paragraph (3) applies–

(a)   in a case where the liability in respect of which the rent allowance is paid is monthly, the authority may make payment at intervals of 1 month;

(b)   in a case where the authority is paying a rent allowance to a landlord in respect of more than one claimant, then the first such payment in respect of any claimant may be made to that landlord at such lesser interval as that authority considers is in the best interest of the efficient administration of housing benefit.

(5)   Except in a case to which paragraph (3) applies, where a person's weekly entitlement to a rent allowance is more than £2 he may require payment at two weekly intervals and the relevant authority shall pay at two weekly intervals in such a case.

(6)   Except in a case to which paragraph (3) applies, the relevant authority may pay a rent allowance at weekly intervals where either–

(a)   it considers that unless the rent allowance is paid at weekly intervals an overpayment is likely to occur; or

(b)   the person entitled is liable to pay his rent weekly and it considers that it is in his interest that his allowance be paid weekly.

(7)   Subject to paragraphs (2), (3) and (5), the relevant authority may pay a rent allowance to a student once a term.

Modifications

Reg 73 has effect as modified by Sch 3 para 7 HB&CTB(CP) Regs (see p1121) for some claimants entitled to and in receipt of HB in respect of their current home on 6 October 1996 and continuously since that date.

Payment on account of a rent allowance

74.–(1)   Where it is impracticable for the relevant authority to make a decision on a claim for a rent allowance within 14 days of the claim for it having been made and that impracticability does not arise out of the failure of the claimant, without good cause, to furnish such information, certificates, documents or evidence as the authority reasonably requires and has requested or which has been requested by the Secretary of State, the authority shall make a payment on account of any entitlement to a rent allowance of such amount as it considers reasonable having regard to–
(a)   such information which may at the time be available to it concerning the claimant's circumstances; and
(b)   any relevant determination made by a rent officer in exercise of the Housing Act functions.

(2)   The notice of award of any payment on account of a rent allowance made under paragraph (1) shall contain a notice to the effect that if on subsequent decision of the claim the person is not entitled to a rent allowance, or is entitled to an amount of rent allowance less than the amount of the payment on account, the whole of the amount paid on account or the excess of that amount over the entitlement to an allowance, as the case may be, will be recoverable from the person to whom the payment on account was made.

(3)   Where on the basis of the subsequent decision the amount of rent allowance payable differs from the amount paid on account under paragraph (1), future payments of rent allowance shall be increased or reduced to take account of any underpayment or, as the case may be, overpayment.

Payment to be made to a person entitled

75.–(1)   Subject to regulations 76 to 78 (payment to landlords, payment on death) and the following provisions of this regulation, payment of any rent allowance to which a person is entitled shall be made to that person.

(2)   Where a person other than a person who is entitled to a rent allowance made the claim and that first person is a person referred to in regulation 63(2), (3) or (5) (persons appointed to act for a person unable to act), payment may be made to that person.

(3)   A person entitled to a rent allowance, although able to act on his own behalf, may request in writing that the appropriate authority make payments to a person, who if a natural person must be aged 18 or more, nominated by him, and the authority may make payments to that person.

Circumstances in which payment is to be made to a landlord

76.–(1)   Subject to paragraph (2) and paragraph 8(4) of Schedule A1 (treatment of claims for housing benefit by refugees), a payment of rent allowance shall be made to a landlord (and in this regulation the "landlord" includes a person to whom rent is payable by the person entitled to that allowance)–
(a)   where under Regulations made under the Administration Act an amount of state pension credit payable to the claimant or his partner is being paid direct to the landlord; or

(b)   where sub-paragraph (a) does not apply and the person is in arrears of an amount equivalent to 8 weeks or more of the amount he is liable to pay his landlord as rent, except where it is in the overriding interest of the claimant not to make direct payments to the landlord.

(2)   Any payment of rent allowance made to a landlord pursuant to this regulation or to regulation 77 (circumstances in which payment may be made to a landlord) shall be to discharge, in whole or in part, the liability of the claimant to pay rent to that landlord in respect of the dwelling concerned, except in so far as–

(a)   the claimant had no entitlement to the whole or part of that rent allowance so paid to his landlord; and

(b)   the overpayment of rent allowance resulting was recovered in whole or in part from that landlord.

(3)   Where the relevant authority is not satisfied that the landlord is a fit and proper person to be the recipient of a payment of rent allowance no such payment shall be made direct to him under paragraph (1).

Modifications

Modification of reg 76 is provided in Sch 9 para 13 (see p809) in relation to Pathfinder Authorities who are administering the pilot local housing allowance scheme, as from the date specified in relation to each authority in Sch 9 Part 1 (see p801).

Circumstances in which payment may be made to a landlord

77.–(1)   Subject to paragraph 8(4) of Schedule A1 (treatment of claims for housing benefit by refugees), where regulation 76 (circumstances in which payment is to be made to a landlord) does not apply but subject to paragraph (3), a payment of a rent allowance may nevertheless be made to a person's landlord where–

(a)   the person has requested or consented to such payment;

(b)   payment to the landlord is in the interest of the claimant and his family;

(c)   the person has ceased to reside in the dwelling in respect of which the allowance was payable and there are outstanding payments of rent but any payment under this sub-paragraph shall be limited to an amount equal to the amount of rent outstanding.

(2)   Without prejudice to the power in paragraph (1), in any case where in the opinion of the authority–

(a)   the claimant has not already discharged his liability to pay his landlord for the period in respect of which any payment is to be made; and

(b)   it would be in the interests of the efficient administration of housing benefit, a first payment of a rent allowance following the making of a decision on a claim, or a supersession under paragraph 4 of Schedule 7 to the Child Support, Pensions and Social Security Act 2000 may be made, in whole or in part, by sending to the claimant an instrument of payment payable to that landlord.

(3)   In a case where the relevant authority is not satisfied that the landlord is a fit and proper person to be the recipient of a claimant's rent allowance, the authority may either–

(a)   not make direct payments to the landlord in accordance with paragraph (1); or

(b)   make such payments to the landlord where the authority is satisfied that it is nonetheless in the best interests of the claimant and his family that the payments be made.

(4)   In this regulation "landlord" has the same meaning as in regulation 76 and paragraph (2) of that regulation shall have effect for the purposes of this regulation.

Modifications

Modification of reg 77 is provided in Sch 9 para 13 (see p809) in relation to Pathfinder Authorities who are administering the pilot local housing allowance scheme, as from the date specified in relation to each authority in Sch 9 Part 1 (see p801).

Payment on death of the person entitled

78.–(1)   Subject to paragraphs (3) and (5) where the person entitled to an allowance has died the relevant authority shall make payment either to his personal representative or, where there is none, his next of kin if aged 16 or over.

(2)   For the purposes of paragraph (1) "next of kin" means in England and Wales the persons who would take beneficially on an intestacy and in Scotland the persons entitled to the moveable estate on intestacy.

(3)   A payment under paragraph (1) or (5) shall not be made unless the landlord, the personal representative or the next of kin, as the case may be, makes written application for the payment of any sum of benefit to which the deceased was entitled, and such written application is sent to or delivered to the relevant authority at its designated office within 12 months of the deceased's death or such longer period as the authority may allow in any particular case.

(4)   The authority may dispense with strict proof of title of any person claiming under paragraph (3) and the receipt of such a person shall be a good discharge to the authority for any sum so paid.

(5)   Subject to paragraph (3), where the relevant authority determines, before the death of the person first mentioned in paragraph (1), that a rent allowance was payable to his landlord in accordance with regulation 76 or 77, that authority shall pay to that landlord so much of that allowance as does not exceed the amount of rent outstanding at the date of the person's death.

Offsetting

79.–(1)   Where a person has been paid a sum of housing benefit under a decision which is subsequently revised or further revised, any sum paid in respect of a period covered by a subsequent decision shall be offset against arrears of entitlement under the subsequent decision except to the extent that the sum exceeds the arrears and shall be treated as properly paid on account of them.

(2)   Where an amount has been deducted under regulation 85(1) (sums to be deducted in calculating recoverable overpayments) an equivalent sum shall be offset against any arrears of entitlement under the subsequent decision except to the extent that the sum exceeds the arrears and shall be treated as properly paid on account of them.

(3)   No amount may be offset under paragraph (1) which has been determined to be an overpayment within the meaning of regulation 80 (meaning of overpayment).

PART 12

Overpayments

Meaning of overpayment

80.   In this Part, "overpayment" means any amount which has been paid by way of housing benefit and to which there was no entitlement under these Regulations (whether on the initial decision [¹ or as subsequently revised or superseded or further revised or superseded]) and includes any amount paid on account under regulation 74 (payment on account of a rent allowance) which is in excess of the entitlement to housing benefit as subsequently decided.

Amendment

1.   Amended by reg 2 of SI 2005 No 2904 as amended by Sch 2 para 29 of SI 2006 No 217 as from 10.4.06.

Recoverable overpayments

81.–(1)   Any overpayment, except one to which paragraph (2) applies, shall be recoverable.

(2)   Subject to paragraph (4) this paragraph applies to an overpayment caused by an official error where the claimant or a person acting on his behalf or any other

person to whom the payment is made could not, at the time of receipt of the payment or of any notice relating to that payment, reasonably have been expected to realise that it was an overpayment.

(3)   In paragraph (2), "overpayment caused by official error" means an overpayment caused by a mistake made whether in the form of an act or omission by–

(a)   the relevant authority;

(b)   an officer or person acting for that authority;

(c)   an officer of–

(i)   the Department for Work and Pensions;

(ii)   Revenue and Customs,

acting as such; or

(d)   a person providing services to the Department for Work and Pensions or to the Commissioners for Her Majesty's Revenue and Customs,

where the claimant, a person acting on his behalf or any other person to whom the payment is made, did not cause or materially contribute to that mistake, act or omission.

(4)   Where in consequence of an official error, a person has been awarded a rent rebate to which he was not entitled or which exceeded the benefit to which he was entitled, upon the award being revised any overpayment of benefit, which remains credited to him by the relevant authority in respect of a period after the date on which the revision took place, shall be recoverable.

Amendment

1.   Amended by reg 2 of SI 2005 No 2904 as amended by Sch 2 para 29 of SI 2006 No 217 as from 10.4.06.

Person from whom recovery may be sought

82.–(1)   For the purposes of section 75(3)(a) of the Administration Act (prescribed circumstances in which an amount recoverable shall not be recovered from the person to whom it was paid), the prescribed circumstance is–

(a)   housing benefit has been paid in accordance with regulation 76 (circumstances in which payment is to be made to the landlord) or regulation 77 (circumstances in which payment may be made to a landlord);

(b)   the landlord has notified the relevant authority or the Secretary of State in writing that he suspects that there has been an overpayment;

[¹ (bb)   the relevant authority is satisfied that the overpayment did not occur as a result of any change of dwelling occupied by the claimant as his home;]

(c)   it appears to the relevant authority that, on the assumption that there has been an overpayment–

(i)   there are grounds for instituting proceedings against any person for an offence under section 111A or 112(1) of the Administration (dishonest or false representations for obtaining benefit); or

(ii)   there has been a deliberate failure to report a relevant change of circumstances contrary to the requirement of regulation 69 (duty to notify a change of circumstances) and the overpayment occurred as a result of that deliberate failure; and

(d)   the relevant authority is satisfied that the landlord–

(i)   has not colluded with the claimant so as to cause the overpayment;

(ii)   has not acted, or neglected to act, in such a way so as contribute to the period, or the amount, of the overpayment.

[² (2)   For the purposes of section 75(3)(b) of the Administration Act (recovery from such other person, as well as or instead of the person to whom the overpayment was made), where recovery of an overpayment is sought by a relevant authority–

(a)   the prescribed person from whom it is sought shall be–

(i)   in a case where an overpayment arose in consequence of a misrepresentation of or a failure to disclose a material fact (in either case, whether fraudulently or otherwise) by or on behalf of the claimant or any other person to whom housing benefit has been paid, the person who misrepresented or failed to disclose that material fact instead of, if different, the person to whom the payment was made;

(ii)   in a case where an overpayment arose in consequence of an official error where the claimant or a person acting on his behalf or any other person to whom the payment has been made could reasonably have been expected, at the time of receipt of the payment or of any notice relating to that payment, to realise that it was an overpayment, that person instead of, if different, the person to whom the payment was made; or

(b)   where sub-paragraphs (a)(i) and (ii) do not apply, the prescribed person from whom it is sought is–

(i)   the claimant;

(ii)   in a case where a recoverable overpayment is made to a claimant who has one or more partners, the claimant's partner or any of his partners.]

(3)   For the purposes of paragraph (1), "landlord" shall have the same meaning as it has for the purposes of regulation 76.

(4)   For the purposes of paragraph (2)(b), recovery of the overpayment may be by deduction from any housing benefit payable to a partner provided that the claimant and that partner were members of the same household both at the time of the overpayment and when the deduction is made.

Amendments

1.   Inserted by reg 6(2) and (4A) of SI 2005 No 2904 as amended by Sch 2 para 29 of SI 2006 No 217 as from 10.4.06.

2.   Substituted by reg 6(3) and (5) of SI 2005 No 2904 as amended by Sch 2 para 29 of SI 2006 No 217 as from 10.4.06.

Method of recovery

83.–(1)   Without prejudice to any other method of recovery, [1 a relevant authority] may recover a recoverable overpayment from any person referred to in regulation 82 (persons from whom recovery may be sought) by deduction from any housing benefit to which that person is entitled (including arrears of entitlement after offsetting under regulation 79 (offsetting)) or, where it is unable to do so, may request the Secretary of State to recover any recoverable overpayment from the benefits prescribed in regulation 86 (recovery of overpayments from prescribed benefits).

[2 (1A)   Where–

(a)   a claimant has moved into a dwelling which he occupies as his home;

(b)   a recoverable overpayment of housing benefit is thereafter made direct to him in connection with the dwelling he occupied as his home immediately preceding the date he moved to that dwelling; and

(c)   the same relevant authority which made the recoverable overpayment is paying housing benefit to that claimant in respect of that new dwelling,

the relevant authority may at its discretion deduct from the housing benefit it is paying to the claimant in respect of a benefit week an amount equal to the claimant's weekly entitlement to housing benefit at his new dwelling, and may do so for the number of benefit weeks equal to the number of weeks during which the claimant was overpaid housing benefit.]

(2)   Subject to paragraphs [2 (1A),] (4) and (5), where [1 a relevant authority] makes deductions permitted by paragraph (1) from the housing benefit it is paying to a claimant (other than deductions from arrears of entitlement), the deduction in respect of a benefit week shall be–

(a)　in a case to which paragraph (3) applies, not more than the amount there specified; and

(b)　in any other case, not more than 3 times five per cent. of the personal allowance for a single claimant aged not less than 25, that five per cent. being, where it is not a multiple of five pence, rounded to the next higher such multiple.

(3)　Where [¹ a relevant authority] makes deductions from housing benefit it is paying to a claimant who has, in respect of the whole or part of the recoverable overpayment–

(a)　been found guilty of an offence whether under a statute or otherwise;

(b)　made an admission after caution of deception or fraud for the purpose of obtaining relevant benefit; or

(c)　agreed to pay a penalty under section 115A of the Administration Act and the agreement has not been withdrawn,

the amount deducted under paragraph (2) shall be not more than four times five per cent. of the personal allowance for a single claimant aged not less than 25, but where that five per cent. is not a multiple of 10 pence, it shall be rounded to the nearest 10 pence or, if it is a multiple of 5 pence but not of 10 pence, the next higher multiple of 10 pence.

(4)　Where, in the calculation of housing benefit, the amount of earnings or other income falling to be taken into account is reduced by reason of paragraphs 3 to 8 of Schedule 4 (sums to be disregarded in the calculation of earnings) or paragraph 1 of Schedule 5 (sums to be disregarded in the calculation of income other than earnings), the deduction under paragraph (2) may be increased by not more than half the amount of the reduction.

(5)　No deduction made under this regulation [², except as made under paragraph (1A),] shall be applied so as to reduce the housing benefit in respect of a benefit week to less than 50 pence.

(6)　In this regulation–

"admission after caution" means–

(i)　in England and Wales, an admission after a caution has been administered in accordance with a Code issued under the Police and Criminal Evidence Act 1984;

(ii)　in Scotland, admission after a caution has been administered, such admission being duly witnessed by two persons; and

"personal allowance for a single claimant aged not less than 25" means the amount specified in paragraph 1(1)(b) of column 2 of Schedule 3 to the Housing Benefit Regulations 2006 (applicable amounts).

(7)　This regulation shall not apply in respect of an offence committed or an admission after caution or an agreement to pay a penalty made before 2nd October 2000.

Amendments

1.　Substituted by reg 7(2) of SI 2005 No 2904 as amended by Sch 2 para 29 of SI 2006 No 217 as from 10.4.06.

2.　Inserted by reg 7(3), (4) and (5) of SI 2005 No 2904 as amended by Sch 2 para 29 of SI 2006 No 217 as from 10.4.06.

Diminution of capital

84.–(1)　Where, in the case of a recoverable overpayment, in consequence of a misrepresentation or failure to disclose a material fact (in either case whether fraudulent or otherwise) as to a person's capital, or an error, other than one to which regulation 81(2) (effect of official error) refers, as to the amount of a person's capital, the overpayment was in respect of a period ("the overpayment period") of more than 13 benefit weeks, the relevant authority shall, for the purposes only of calculating the amount of that overpayment–

(a) at the end of the first 13 benefit weeks of the overpayment period, treat the amount of that capital as having been reduced by the amount of housing benefit overpaid during those 13 weeks;

(b) at the end of each subsequent period of 13 benefit weeks, if any, of the overpayment period, treat the amount of that capital as having been further reduced by the amount of housing benefit overpaid during the immediately preceding 13 benefit weeks.

(2) Capital shall not be treated as reduced over any period other than 13 benefit weeks or in any circumstances other than those for which paragraph (1) provides.

Sums to be deducted in calculating recoverable overpayments

85.–(1) Subject to paragraph (2), in calculating the amount of a recoverable overpayment, the relevant authority shall deduct any amount of housing benefit which should have been determined to be payable in respect of the whole or part of the overpayment period–

(a) on the basis of the claim as presented to the authority;

(b) on the basis of the claim as it would have appeared had any misrepresentation or non-disclosure been remedied before the decision; or

(c) on the basis of the claim as it would have appeared if any change of circumstances [¹ , except a change of the dwelling which the claimant occupies as his home,] had been notified at the time that change occurred.

(2) In the case of rent rebate only, in calculating the amount of a recoverable overpayment the relevant authority may deduct so much of any payment by way of rent in respect of the overpayment period which exceeds the amount, if any, which the claimant was liable to pay for that period under the original erroneous determination.

Amendment

1. Inserted by reg 8 of SI 2005 No 2904 as amended by Sch 2 para 29 of SI 2006 No 217 as from 10.4.06.

Recovery of overpayments from prescribed benefits

86.–(1) For the purposes of section 75(4) of the Administration Act (recovery of overpaid housing benefit by deduction from other benefits), the benefits prescribed by this regulation are–

(a) any benefit except guardian's allowance;

(b) income support under Part 7 of the Act;

(c) any benefit payable under the legislation of any member State other than the United Kingdom concerning the branches of social security mentioned in Article 4(1) of Regulation (EEC) No 1408/71 on the application of social security schemes to employed persons, to self-employed persons and to members of their families moving within the Community, whether or not the benefit has been acquired by virtue of the provisions of that Regulation;

(d) a jobseeker's allowance;

(e) state pension credit.

[¹ (1A) For the purposes of paragraph (1)(c) the term "member State" shall be understood to include Switzerland in accordance with and subject to the provisions of Annex II of the Agreement between the European Community and its Member States and the Swiss Confederation on the free movement of persons, signed at Brussels on 21st June 1999.]

(2) Where the Secretary of State is satisfied that–

(a) a recoverable overpayment of housing benefit has been made, in consequence of a misrepresentation of or failure to disclose a material fact (in either case whether fraudulently or otherwise), by or on behalf of a claimant or any other person to whom a payment of housing benefit has been made; and

(b)   the person who misrepresented that fact or failed to disclose it is receiving a sufficient amount of one or more of the benefits prescribed in paragraph (1) to enable deductions to be made for the recovery of the overpayment,

he shall, if requested to do so by an authority under regulation 83 (method of recovery), recover the overpayment by deduction from any of those benefits.

(3)   In paragraph (1)(a), ''benefit'' has the meaning it has in section 122(1) of the Act.

Amendment

1.   Inserted by reg 9 of SI 2005 No 2904 as amended by Sch 2 para 29 of SI 2006 No 217 as from 10.4.06.

Prescribed benefits

87.–(1)   The benefits prescribed for the purposes of section 75(5) and (7) of the Administration Act (recovery of overpayments) are those set out in the following paragraphs.

(2)   Prescribed benefits within section 75(5)(a) of the Administration Act (benefits to which a landlord or agent is entitled) are–
  (a)   housing benefit; and
  (b)   those benefits prescribed from time to time in regulation 86(1) (recovery of overpayments from prescribed benefits), but only in cases where–
    (i)   an authority has, pursuant to regulation 83 (method of recovery), requested the Secretary of State to recover an overpayment of housing benefit from such benefits; and
    (ii)   the Secretary of State is satisfied as to the matters prescribed in paragraph (2)(a) and (b) of regulation 86.

(3)   Housing benefit is prescribed for the purposes of section 75(5)(b) or (c) of the Administration Act (benefits paid to a landlord or agent to discharge an obligation owed by another person).

(4)   Prescribed benefits within section 75(7) of the Administration Act (benefits recoverable from the county court or the sheriff court) are housing benefit and those benefits prescribed from time to time in regulation 86(1).

Restrictions on recovery of rent and consequent notifications

88.–(1)   Where, pursuant to section 75(5)(b) of the Administration Act, an amount has been recoveredby deduction from housing benefit paid to a person (referred to as ''the landlord'' in this regulation) to discharge (in whole or in part) an obligation owed to him by the person on whose behalf the recoverable amount was paid (referred to as ''the tenant'' in this regulation) that obligation shall, in a case to which paragraph (2) applies, be taken to be discharged by the amount of the deduction.

(2)   This paragraph applies in a case where the amount recoverable from the landlord relates to an overpayment of housing benefit in relation to which the landlord has–
  (a)   agreed to pay a penalty pursuant to section 115A of the Administration Act (penalty as an alternative to prosecution); or
  (b)   been convicted of an offence arising under the Act or any other enactment.

(3)   In any case to which paragraph (2) applies or will apply when recovery is made the authority that has determined that there is an overpayment and that it is recoverable from the landlord shall notify both the landlord and the tenant that–
  (a)   the overpayment that it has recovered or that it has determined to recover (''the sum'') is or will be one to which paragraph (2) applies; and
  (b)   the landlord has no right in relation to that sum against the tenant, and that his obligation to the landlord shall be taken to be discharged by the amount so recovered.

PART 13
Information
SECTION 1
Claims and information

Interpretation
89. In this Section–
[¹ "county council" means a county council in England, but only if the council has made an arrangement in accordance with regulation 64(5)(g) or 90(3);]
"local authority" means an authority administering housing benefit;
"relevant authority" means–
    (a)   the Secretary of State;
    (b)   a person providing services to the Secretary of State; [¹ or
    (c)   a county council;]
"relevant information" means information or evidence relating to the administration of claims to or awards of housing benefit.

Amendment
1.   Amended by reg 8(3) of SI 2007 No 2911 as from 31.10.07.

[¹Collection of information
90.–(1)   The Secretary of State, or a person providing services to him, may receive or obtain relevant information from–
    (a)   persons making, or who have made, claims for housing benefit; or
    (b)   other persons in connection with such claims.
    (2)   In paragraph (1) references to persons who have made claims for housing benefit include persons to whom awards of benefit have been made on those claims.
    (3)   Where a county council has made an arrangement with a local authority, or a person authorised to exercise any function of a local authority relating to housing benefit or council tax benefit, to receive and obtain information and evidence relating to claims for housing benefit, the council may receive or obtain the information or evidence from–
    (a)   persons making claims for housing benefit; or
    (b)   other persons in connection with such claims.
    (4)   A county council may receive information or evidence relating to an award of housing benefit which is supplied by–
    (a)   the person to whom the award has been made; or
    (b)   other persons in connection with the award.]

Amendment
1.   Substituted by reg 8(4) of SI 2007 No 2911 as from 31.10.07.

[¹Verifying information
90A.   A relevant authority may verify relevant information supplied to, or obtained by, the authority in accordance with regulation 90.]

Amendment
1.   Inserted by reg 8(5) of SI 2007 No 2911 as from 31.10.07.

[¹Recording and holding information
91. A relevant authority which obtains relevant information or to whom such information is supplied–
    (a)   shall make a record of such information; and
    (b)   may hold that information, whether as supplied or obtained or recorded, for the purpose of forwarding it to the person or authority for the time being administering housing benefit.]

Amendment

1.   Substituted by reg 8(6) of SI 2007 No 2911 as from 31.10.07.

Forwarding of information

92.   relevant authority which holds relevant information–

(a)   shall forward it to the person or authority for the time being administering claims to or awards of housing benefit to which the relevant information relates, being either–

(i)   a local authority;

(ii)   a person providing services to a local authority; or

(iii)   a person authorised to exercise any function of a local authority relating to housing benefit; and

[¹ (b) may, if the relevant authority is the Secretary of State or a person providing services to the Secretary of State, continue to hold a record of such information, whether as supplied or obtained or recorded, for such period as he considers appropriate.]

Amendment

1.   Substituted by reg 8(7) of SI 2007 No 2911 as from 31.10.07.

Request for information

93.   relevant authority which holds information or evidence relating to social security matters shall forward such information or evidence as may be requested to the person or authority making that request, provided that–

(a)   the request is made by–

(i)   a local authority;

(ii)   a person providing services to a local authority; or

(iii)   a person authorised to exercise any function of a local authority relating to housing benefit; and

(b)   the information or evidence requested includes relevant information;

(c)   the relevant authority is able to provide the information or evidence requested in the form in which it was originally supplied or obtained; and

(d)   provision of the information or evidence requested is considered necessary by the relevant authority to the proper performance by a local authority of its functions relating to housing benefit.

SECTION 2
Evidence and Information

Interpretation

94.   In this Section–

"the notice" means the notice prescribed in regulation 99(1)(b) (circumstances for requiring information);

"relevant information" means such information as is prescribed in regulation 100 (relevant information);

"the requirer" means a person within regulation 98 (requiring information from landlords and agents), who requires information pursuant to that regulation;

"the supplier" means an appropriate person who is required, pursuant to regulations 98 and 99, to supply relevant information and any person who is not so required is not, for the purpose of supplying information pursuant to section 126A of the Administration Act and these Regulations, an appropriate person.

Evidence and information required by rent officers

95.   The relevant authority shall furnish as soon as is reasonably practicable such information or evidence relating to a claimant and his accommodation obtained by it in exercise of its functions relating to housing benefit as may be required by a rent officer for the purpose of a function conferred on him by an order under section 122 of the Housing Act 1996.

Information to be supplied by an authority to another authority

96.–(1)   For the purposes of section 128A of the Administration Act (duty of an authority to disclose information to another authority) the circumstances in which information is to be disclosed are prescribed in paragraph (2) and the information prescribed by this regulation is described in paragraph (3).

(2)   The circumstances prescribed in this paragraph are, where–

(a)   there is a mover who is or was in receipt of housing benefit from local authority "A";

(b)   either his second dwelling is within the area of another authority "B" or he is liable or treated as liable to make payments in respect of his second dwelling to housing authority B; and

(c)   either–

   (i)   a payment under regulation 72 of the Housing Benefit Regulations 2006 is claimed from authority A; or

   (ii)   such a payment is claimed from authority B, who then requests the prescribed information from authority A,

authority A shall disclose to authority B the information prescribed in paragraph (3).

(3)   The information to be disclosed is–

(a)   in a case where the payment under regulation 72 of the Housing Benefit Regulations 2006 was claimed from authority A, details relevant to that claim of–

   (i)   the matters certified pursuant to regulation 72 of and paragraph 1 of Schedule 7 to the Housing Benefit Regulations 2006;

   (ii)   the matters notified pursuant to regulation 72 of and paragraph 2 of that Schedule;

   (iii)   the date it was so claimed;

(b)   in the case of a person to whom regulation 6(5) of the Income Support Regulations (persons not treated as engaged in remunerative work) applies–

   (i)   the date on which he was first engaged in the work referred to in sub-paragraph (a) of regulation 6(5) of those Regulations; and

   (ii)   the date on which his entitlement to income support ceased or was expected to cease; and

(c)   in any case–

   (i)   the weekly rate of housing benefit awarded to the mover by authority A;

   (ii)   if any deduction was being made from that benefit in respect of non-dependants, pursuant to regulations 50 (maximum housing benefit) and 55 (non-dependant deductions), the amount of those deductions;

   (iii)   if any deduction was being made from that benefit in respect of a recoverable overpayment pursuant to regulation 83 (method of recovery), the amount of those deductions;

   (iv)   the date on which his entitlement to housing benefit ceased;

   (v)   if a payment under regulation 72 of the Housing Benefit Regulations 2006 was made to the mover, the amount and date of any such payment; and

   (vi)   if no such payment was made, why none was made.

(4)   In this regulation, "mover", "the relevant day" and "second-dwelling" have the meanings assigned to them in paragraph 11 of Schedule 7 to the Housing Benefit Regulations 2006.

Supply of information: extended payments (severe disablement allowance and incapacity benefit)

97.–(1) For the purposes of section 122E(3) of the Administration Act (duty of an authority to supply information to another authority) the circumstances in which information is to be supplied are prescribed in paragraph (2) and the information prescribed by this regulation is described in paragraph (3).

(2) The circumstances prescribed in this paragraph are, where–

(a) there is a mover who is or was in receipt of housing benefit from a local authority ''A'';

(b) either his second dwelling is within the area of another local authority ''B'' or he is liable or treated as liable to make payments in respect of his second dwelling to housing authority B; and

(c) either–

   (i) the extended payment (severe disablement allowance and incapacity benefit) is claimed from authority A; or

   (ii) the extended payment (severe disablement allowance and incapacity benefit) is claimed from authority B, who then requests the information described in paragraph (3) from authority A,

authority A shall supply to authority B that information.

(3) The information to be supplied is–

(a) in a case where that extended payment (severe disablement allowance and incapacity benefit) was claimed from authority A, details relevant to that claim of–

   (i) the matters set out in regulation 58 or regulation 53(1)(b)(i) to (iii), as the case may be; and

   (ii) the matters notified pursuant to regulation 53(1)(a)(ii) or (b)(iv), as the case may be; and

   (iii) the date it was so claimed; and

(b) in any case–

   (i) the weekly rate of housing benefit awarded to the mover by authority A;

   (ii) if any deduction was being made from that benefit in respect of non-dependants, pursuant to regulations 50 and 55, the amount of those deductions;

   (iii) if any deduction was being made from that benefit in respect of a recoverable overpayment pursuant to regulation 83, the amount of those deductions;

   (iv) the date on which his entitlement to housing benefit ceased;

   (v) if an extended payment (severe disablement allowance and incapacity benefit) was made to the mover, the amount and date of any such payment; and

   (vi) if no extended payment (severe disablement allowance and incapacity benefit) was made, why none was made.

(4) In this regulation ''mover'' and ''second dwelling'' shall have the meanings assigned to them in paragraph 10 of Schedule 7.

Requiring information from landlords and agents

98. Pursuant to section 126A of the Administration Act, where a claim is made to an authority, on which a rent allowance may be awarded, then, in the circumstances prescribed in regulation 99 (circumstances for requiring information), that authority, or any person authorised to exercise any function of the authority relating to housing benefit, may require an appropriate person to supply to that authority or person relevant information, in the manner prescribed in regulation 101 (manner of supply of information).

Circumstances for requiring information

99.–(1)   A person is required to supply information in the following circumstances–

(a)   he is an appropriate person in relation to any dwelling in respect of which–

    (i)   housing benefit is being paid to an appropriate person pursuant to regulation 76 or 77 (circumstances in which payment is to be or may be made to a landlord); or

    (ii)   a request has been made by an appropriate person or by the claimant for housing benefit to be so paid; and

(b)   the requirer serves upon that appropriate person, whether by post or otherwise, a written notice stating that the requirer–

    (i)   suspects that there is or may be an impropriety in relation to a claim in respect of any dwelling wherever situated in relation to which he is an appropriate person; or

    (ii)   is already investigating an allegation of impropriety in relation to that person.

(2)   Information required to be supplied under paragraph (1) shall be supplied to the requirer at the address specified in the notice.

Relevant information

100.–(1)   The information the supplier is to supply to the requirer is that prescribed in paragraphs (2) and (3) (referred to in this Part as "the relevant information").

(2)   For a supplier who falls within paragraph (4) or section 126A(2)(b) of the Administration Act ("the landlord"), the information is–

(a)   where the landlord is a natural person–

    (i)   his appropriate details;

    (ii)   the relevant particulars of any residential property in which he has an interest; and

    (iii)   the appropriate details of any body corporate, in which he is a major shareholder or of which he is a director and which has an interest in residential property;

(b)   where the landlord is a trustee, except a trustee of a charity, in addition to any information that he is required to supply in accordance with sub-paragraph (a) or (c), as the case may be, the relevant particulars of any residential property held by the trust of which he is a trustee and the name and address of any beneficiary under the trust or the objects of that trust, as the case may be;

(c)   where the landlord is a body corporate or otherwise not a natural person, other than a charity–

    (i)   its appropriate details;

    (ii)   the relevant particulars of any residential property in which it has an interest;

    (iii)   the names and addresses of any directors of it;

    (iv)   the appropriate details of any person–

        (aa)   who owns 20 per cent. or more of it; or

        (bb)   of whom it owns 20 per cent. or more; and

    (v)   the names and addresses of its major shareholders;

(d)   where the landlord is a charity or is a recognised body the appropriate details relating to the landlord and particulars of the landlord's registration as a charity.

(3)   For a supplier who falls within section 126A(2)(c) of the Administration Act or paragraph (5) ("the agent"), the information is–

(a)   the name and address of any person ("his principal")–

      (i)   to whom the agent has agreed to make payments in consequence of being entitled to receive relevant payments; or

      (ii)   for whom the agent is acting on behalf of or in connection with any aspect of the management of a dwelling,

as the case may be;

(b)   the relevant particulars of any residential property in respect of which the agent–

      (i)   has agreed to make payments in consequence of being entitled to receive relevant payments; or

      (ii)   is acting on behalf of his principal in connection with any aspect of its management;

(c)   where the agent is a natural person–

      (i)   the relevant particulars of any residential property in which he has an interest;

      (ii)   the appropriate details of any body corporate or any person not a natural person, in which he is a major shareholder or of which he is a director and which has any interest in residential property; or

(d)   where the agent is a body corporate or other than a natural person–

      (i)   the relevant particulars of any residential property in which it has an interest;

      (ii)   the names and addresses of any directors of or major shareholders in the agent; and

      (iii) the appropriate details of any person–

          (aa) who owns 20 per cent. or more of the agent; or

          (bb) of whom the agent owns 20 per cent. or more.

(4)   A supplier falls within this paragraph (landlord receiving rent), if he falls within section 126A(2)(a) of the Administration Act, but does not fall within paragraph (5).

(5)   A supplier falls within this paragraph (agent receiving the rent), if he falls within subsection (2)(a) of section 126A of the Administration Act and has agreed to make payments, in consequence of being entitled to receive relevant payments, to a person falling within subsection (2)(b) of that section.

(6)   For the purposes of this regulation–

"appropriate details" means the name of the person and (in the case of a company) its registered office and, in any case, the full postal address, including post code, of the principal place of business of that person and the telephone and facsimile number (if any) of that place;

"charity" means a charity which is registered under section 3 of the Charities Act 1993 and is not an exempt charity within the meaning of that Act;

"major shareholder" means, where a body corporate is a company limited by shares, any person holding one tenth or more of the issued shares in that company and, in any other case, all the owners of that body;

"recognised body" has the same meaning as in section 1(7) of the Law Reform (Miscellaneous Provisions) (Scotland) Act 1990;

"relevant particulars" means the full postal address, including post code, and number of current lettings of or within that residential property and, if that property includes two or more dwellings, that address and the number of such lettings for each such dwelling;

"residential property" includes any premises, situated within the United Kingdom–

      (i)   used or which has, within the last six months, been used; or

      (ii)   which may be used or is adapted for use,

as residential accommodation,

and other expressions used in this regulation and also in the Companies Act 1985 shall have the same meaning in this regulation as they have in that Act.

Manner of supply of information
101.–(1) Subject to paragraph (2), the relevant information shall be supplied–
(a)   in typewritten or printed form; or
(b)   with the written agreement of the inquirer, in electronic or handwritten form,
within a period of 4 weeks commencing on the date on which the notice was sent or given.
(2)   Where–
(a)   within a period of 4 weeks commencing on the date on which the notice was sent or given, the supplier requests that the time for the supply of the relevant information be extended; and
(b)   the requirer provides written agreement to that request,
the time for the supply of the relevant information shall be extended to a period of 8 weeks commencing on the date on which the notice was sent or given.

Criminal offence
102.   Any failure by the supplier to supply relevant information to the requirer as, when and how required under regulations 98 to 101 shall be an offence under section 113 of the Administration Act and there may be recovered from the supplier, on summary conviction for this offence, penalties not exceeding–
(a)   for any one offence, level 3 on the standard scale; or
(b)   for an offence of continuing any such failure after conviction, £40 for each day on which it is so continued.

PART 14
Pathfinder authorities

Modifications in respect of pathfinder authorities
103.–(1)   In this regulation and Schedule 9, ''pathfinder authority'' means a relevant authority specified in Part 1 of that Schedule.
(2)   The provisions of Part 2 of Schedule 9 apply in relation to the area of a pathfinder authority on and after the date specified in Part 1 in relation to that authority.

[¹ SCHEDULE A1]
Treatment of claims for housing benefit by refugees

Modifications

Sch A1 was inserted by Sch 4 para 2(2) as modified by Sch 4 para 2(3) HB&CTB(CP) Regs (see p1127) in respect of claims for HB by some refugees. Sch A1 was further modifed by Sch 4 para 4(2) and (3) for some HB claimants who were refugees who claimed asylum on or before 2 April 2000. See also reg 10A inserted by Sch 4 para 2(1) HB&CTB(CP) Regs on p1126.

Amendment

1.   Lapsed by s12(2)(e) of the Asylum and Immigration (Treatment of Claimants, etc.) Act 2004 (for those recorded as refugees after 14.6.07).

SCHEDULE 1
REGULATION 11
Ineligible service charges

PART 1
Service charges other than for fuel

Ineligible service charges
1.   The following service charges shall not be eligible to be met by housing benefit–

(a) charges in respect of day-to-day living expenses including, in particular, all provision of–
    (i) subject to paragraph 2 meals (including the preparation of meals or provision of unprepared food);
    (ii) laundry (other than the provision of premises or equipment to enable a person to do his own laundry);
    [¹ (iii) leisure items such as either sports facilities (except a children's play area), or television rental, licence and subscription fees (except radio relay charges and charges made in respect of the conveyance and installation and maintenance of equipment for the conveyance of a television broadcasting service);]
    (iv) cleaning of rooms and windows except cleaning of–
        (aa) communal areas; or
        (bb) the exterior of any windows where neither the claimant nor any member of his household is able to clean them himself,
where a payment is not made in respect of such cleaning by a local authority (including, in relation to England, a county council) or the National Assembly for Wales to the claimant or his partner, or to another person on their behalf; and
    (v) transport;
(b) charges in respect of–
    (i) the acquisition of furniture or household equipment; and
    (ii) the use of such furniture or equipment where that furniture or household equipment will become the property of the claimant by virtue of an agreement with the landlord;
(c) charges in respect of the provision of an emergency alarm system;
(d) charges in respect of medical expenses (including the cost of treatment or counselling related to mental disorder, mental handicap, physical disablement or past or present alcohol or drug dependence);
(e) charges in respect of the provision of nursing care or personal care (including assistance at meal-times or with personal appearance or hygiene);
(f) charges in respect of general counselling or of any other support services, whoever provides those services;
(g) charges in respect of any services not specified in sub-paragraphs (a) to (f) which are not connected with the provision of adequate accommodation.

Amendment
1.   Substituted by reg 7(3) of SI 2007 No 719 as from 2.4.07.

Amount ineligible for meals
    2.–(1)   Where a charge for meals is ineligible to be met by housing benefit under paragraph 1, the amount ineligible in respect of each week shall be the amount specified in the following provisions of this paragraph.
    (2)   Subject to sub-paragraph (4), where the charge includes provision for at least three meals a day, the amount shall be–
    (a) for a single claimant, [² £21.10];
    (b) if the claimant is a member of a family–
        (i) for the claimant and for each member of his family aged 16 or over, [² £21.10];
        (ii) for each member of his family under age 16, [² £10.65].
    (3)   Except where sub-paragraph (5) applies and subject to sub-paragraph (4), where the charge includes provision for less than three meals a day, the amount shall be–
    (a) for a single claimant, [² £14.05];
    (b) if the claimant is a member of a family–
        (i) for the claimant and for each member of his family aged 16 or over, [² £14.05];
        (ii) for each member of his family under age 16, [² £7.05].
    (4)   For the purposes of sub-paragraphs (2)(b) and (3)(b), a person attains the age of 16 on the first Monday in September following his 16th birthday.
    (5)   Where the charge for meals includes the provision of breakfast only, the amount for the claimant and, if he is a member of a family, for the claimant and for each member of his family, shall be [² £2.60].
    (6)   Where a charge for meals includes provision for meals for a person who is not a member of the claimant's family sub-paragraphs (2) to (5) shall apply as if that person were a member of the claimant's family.
    (7)   For the avoidance of doubt where the charge does not include provision for meals for a claimant or, as the case may be, a member of his family, sub-paragraphs (2) to (5) shall not apply in respect of that person.

Amendments

1.   Amended by Art 19(4) of SI 2006 No 645 and reg 8 of SI 2006 No 217 as from 1.4.06 (3.4.06 where rent payable weekly or at intervals of a week).
2.   Amended by Art 20(4) of SI 2007 No 688 as from 1.4.07 (2.4.07 where rent payable weekly or at intervals of a week).

Amount of ineligible charges

3.–(1)   Subject to paragraph 2 where an ineligible service charge is not separated from or separately identified within other payments made by the occupier in respect of the dwelling, the appropriate authority shall apportion such charge as is fairly attributable to the provision of that service, having regard to the cost of comparable services and such portion of those payments shall be ineligible to be met by housing benefit.

(2)   Subject to paragraph 2, where the relevant authority considers that the amount of any ineligible service charge which is separately identified within other payments made by the occupier in respect of the dwelling is unreasonably low having regard to the service provided, it shall substitute a sum for the charge in question which it considers represents the value of the services concerned and the amount so substituted shall be ineligible to be met by housing benefit.

(3)   In sub-paragraph (2) the expression "ineligible service charge" includes any service charge which does not qualify as a periodical payment under regulation 12(1)(e) (rent).

(4)   In any other case, the whole amount of the ineligible service charge shall be ineligible to be met by housing benefit.

Excessive service costs

4.   Subject to paragraph 2, where the relevant authority considers that the amount of a service charge to which regulation 12(1)(e) (rent) applies is excessive in relation to the service provided for the claimant or his family, having regard to the cost of comparable services, it shall make a deduction from that charge of the excess and the amount so deducted shall be ineligible to be met by housing benefit.

PART 2
Payments in respect of fuel charges

5.   A service charge for fuel except a charge in respect of services for communal areas shall be ineligible to be met by housing benefit.

6.–(1)   Where a charge is ineligible to be met by housing benefit under paragraph 5–

(a)   in the calculation of entitlement to a rent rebate; or

(b)   in the calculation of entitlement to a rent allowance if the amount of the charge is specified or is otherwise readily identifiable (except where the amount of the charge is unrealistically low in relation to the fuel provided or the charge cannot readily be distinguished from a charge for a communal area),

the amount ineligible to be met by housing benefit shall be the full amount of the service charge.

(2)   In any other case, subject to sub-paragraphs (3) and (4) and paragraph 7, the amount ineligible to be met by housing benefit shall be the following amounts in respect of each week–

(a)   for heating (other than hot water) [² £15.45];

(b)   for hot water [² £1.80];

(c)   for lighting [² £1.25];

(d)   for cooking [² £1.80].

(3)   Where the accommodation occupied by the claimant or, if he is a member of a family, by the claimant and the members of his family, consists of one room only, the amount ineligible to be met by housing benefit in respect of each week where heating only is, or heating and either hot water or lighting (or both) are, provided, shall be one-half of the aggregate of the amounts specified in sub-paragraphs (2)(a), (b) and (c).

(4)   In a case to which sub-paragraph (2) or (3) applies, if a claimant provides evidence on which the actual or approximate amount of the service charge for fuel may be estimated, the amount ineligible to be met by housing benefit under this paragraph shall be that estimated amount.

Amendments

1.   Amended by Art 19(5) of SI 2006 No 645 and reg 8 of SI 2006 No 217 as from 1.4.06 (3.4.06 where rent payable weekly or at intervals of a week).
2.   Amended by Art 20(5) of SI 2007 No 688 as from 1.4.07 (2.4.07 where rent payable weekly or at intervals of a week).

7.–(1)   Where rent is payable other than weekly, any amount ineligible to be met by housing benefit which is specified in this Schedule as a weekly amount shall–

(a)   where rent is payable in multiples of a week, be multiplied by the number equal to the number of weeks in respect of which it is payable; or

(b)   in any other case, be divided by 7 and multiplied by the number of days in the period to be used by the relevant authority for the purpose of calculating the claimant's weekly eligible rent under regulation 61 (calculation of weekly amounts).

(2)   In a case to which regulation 62 applies (rent free periods), any amount ineligible to be met by housing benefit which is specified in this Schedule as a weekly amount shall, where appropriate, be converted in accordance with sub-paragraph (1) and shall–

(a)   where rent is payable weekly, or in multiples of a week, be multiplied by 52 or 53, whichever is appropriate, and divided by the number equal to the number of weeks in that 52 or 53 week period in respect of which he is liable to pay rent; or

(b)   in any other case, be multiplied by 365 or 366, whichever is appropriate, and divided by the number of days in that 365 or 366 day period in respect of which he is liable to pay rent.

8.   In this Schedule–

"communal areas" mean areas (other than rooms) of common access (including halls and passageways) and rooms of common use in sheltered accommodation;

"fuel" includes gas and electricity and a reference to a charge for fuel includes a charge for fuel which includes an amount in respect of the facility of providing it other than a specified amount for the provision of a heating system.

SCHEDULE 2
REGULATION 14
Excluded tenancies

1.   An excluded tenancy is any tenancy to which any of the following paragraphs applies.

2.–(1)   Subject to sub-paragraphs (2) to (3), where a rent officer has made a determination, which relates to the tenancy in question or any other tenancy of the same dwelling this paragraph applies to–

(a)   the tenancy in respect of which that determination was made; and

(b)   any other tenancy of the same dwelling on terms which are substantially the same, other than the term relating to the amount of rent, as those terms were at the time of that determination or, if earlier, at the end of the tenancy.

(2)   For the purposes of any claim, notification, request or application under regulation 14(1) ("the later application"), a tenancy shall not be an excluded tenancy by virtue of sub-paragraph (1) by reference to a rent officer's determination made in consequence of an earlier claim, notification, request or application ("the earlier application") where–

(a)   the earlier and later applications were made in respect of the same claimant or different claimants; and

(b)   the earlier application was made more than 52 weeks before the later application was made.

(3)   Sub-paragraph (1) shall not apply where subsequent to the making of the determination mentioned in that sub-paragraph–

(a)   the number of occupiers of the dwelling has changed and that dwelling is not in a hostel;

(b)   there has been a substantial change in the condition of the dwelling (including the making of improvements) or the terms of the tenancy other than a term relating to rent;

(c)   there has been a rent increase under a term of the tenancy and the term under which that increase was made was either included in the tenancy at the time when the application for that determination was made (or was a term substantially the same as such a term) and that determination was not made under paragraph 1(2), 2(2) or 3(3) of Schedule 1 to the Rent Officers Order;

(d)   in a case where the rent officer has made a determination under paragraph 2(2) of Schedule 1 to the Rent Officers Order (size and rent determinations), but since the date of the application for that determination–

(i)   a child, who is a member of the household occupying the dwelling, has attained the age of 10 years; or

(ii)   a young person, who is a member of the household occupying that dwelling, has attained the age of 16 years; or

(iii)   there is a change in the composition of the household occupying the dwelling;

(e)   the claimant is a young individual, except in a case where the determination mentioned in sub-paragraph (1) was, or was made in conjunction with, a determination of a single room rent pursuant to paragraph 5 of Schedule 1 to the Rent Officers Order on or after 2nd July 2001.

3.–(1)   This paragraph applies where the landlord is a registered housing association, except in a case where the local authority consider that–

(a)   the claimant occupies a dwelling larger than is reasonably required by him and any others who occupy that dwelling (including any non-dependants of his and any person paying rent to him); or

(b)   the rent payable for that dwelling is unreasonably high.

(2)   Where the circumstances set out in head (a) or (b) of sub-paragraph (1) above exist, the authority shall so state in their application for a determination.

4.   This paragraph applies to a tenancy entered into before–
(a)   in Scotland, 2nd January 1989; and
(b)   in any other case, 15th January 1989.

5.   This paragraph applies to a regulated tenancy within the meaning of–
(a)   in Scotland, the Rent (Scotland) Act 1984; and
(b)   in any other case, the Rent Act 1977.

6.   This paragraph applies to a housing association tenancy which–
(a)   in Scotland, is a tenancy to which Part 6 of the Rent (Scotland) Act 1984 applies; and
(b)   in any other case, is a housing association tenancy to which Part 6 of the Rent Act 1977 applies.

7.   This paragraph applies to a protected occupancy or statutory tenancy within the meaning of the Rent (Agriculture) Act 1976.

8.   This paragraph applies to a tenancy at a low rent within the meaning of Part 1 of the Landlord and Tenant Act 1954 or Schedule 10 to the Local Government and Housing Act 1989.

9.   This paragraph applies to a tenancy of any dwelling which is a bail hostel or probation hostel approved by the Secretary of State under section 9(1) of the Criminal Justice and Court Services Act 2000.

10.   This paragraph applies to a tenancy of a housing action trust established under Part 3 of the Housing Act 1988.

11.–(1)   Subject to sub-paragraphs (2) and (3) this paragraph applies to a tenancy–
(a)   in respect of a dwelling comprised in land which has been disposed of under section 32 of the Housing Act 1985 or section 12 of the Housing (Scotland) Act 1987;
(b)   in respect of a dwelling comprised in land which has been disposed of with the consent required by section 43 of the Housing Act 1985 or section 12 of the Housing (Scotland) Act 1987;
(c)   in respect of which the fee simple estate has been acquired, under the right conferred by Chapter 2 of Part 1 of the Housing Act 1996, otherwise than from a housing action trust within the meaning of Part 3 of that Act or in respect of which the house has been acquired under the right conferred by Part 3 of the Housing (Scotland) Act 1988; or
(d)   in respect of a dwelling disposed of under the New Towns (Transfer of Housing Stock) Regulations 1990 to a person who is an approved person for the purposes of disposal under those Regulations or in respect of a dwelling disposed of pursuant to powers contained in the New Towns (Scotland) Act 1968 to a housing association.

(2)   This paragraph shall not apply to a tenancy to which sub-paragraph (1) refers if–
(a)   there has been an increase in rent since the disposal or acquisition, as the case may be, occurred; and
(b)   the local authority stated in the application for determination that–
(i)   the claimant occupies a dwelling larger than is reasonably required by him and any others who occupy that dwelling (including any non-dependant of his and any person paying rent to him); or
(ii)   the rent payable for that dwelling is unreasonably high.

(3)   Where the disposal or acquisition, as the case may be, took place on or after 7th October 2002, sub-paragraph (2)(b) shall apply to a tenancy to which sub-paragraph (1) refers as if head (i) were omitted.

[¹**11A.**   This paragraph applies to a shared ownership tenancy.]

Amendment
1.   Inserted by reg 3(7) of SI 2007 No 1356 as from 1.10.07.

---

12.   In this Schedule, "rent" shall be construed in accordance with paragraph (10) of regulation 14 (interpretation of "tenancy" and other expressions appropriate to a tenancy) and, subject to that sub-paragraph, has the same meaning–
(a)   in Scotland, as in section 25 of the Housing (Scotland) Act 1988, except that the reference to the house in subsection (3) shall be construed as a reference to the dwelling;
(b)   in any other case, as in section 14 of the Housing Act 1988, except that the reference to the dwelling-house in subsection (4) shall be construed as a reference to the dwelling,
(c)   and–
(i)   other expressions have the same meaning as in regulation 14(10);
(ii)   in the case of a determination by a rent officer pursuant to a request for such a determination under regulation 14(1)(e), any reference to a "tenancy" shall be taken as a reference to a prospective tenancy and any reference to an "occupier" or any person "occupying" a dwelling shall, in the case of such a determination, be taken to be a reference to a potential occupier or potential occupation of that dwelling.

SCHEDULE 3

REGULATION 22

Applicable amounts

General Note to Schedule 3

The amounts of the personal allowances and premiums are different than for those to whom the HB Regs apply. Of the premiums, only family premium (FP), severe disability premium (SDP), enhanced disability premium (EDP), disabled child premium (DCP) and carer premium (CP) are available. However, although the pensioner premiums are not available, an equivalent amount is included within the adult personal allowances.

The rules for SDP are identical to those in the HB Regs: see p461. EDP is only available in relation to children or young persons for whom the highest rate of the care component of DLA is payable (or would be payable in specified circumstances).

For commentary on paras 6 to 11, see the equivalent provisions in the HB Regs on pp461-464.

PART 1
Personal allowances

1. The amount specified in column (2) below in respect of each person or couple specified in column (1) shall be the amount specified for the purposes of regulation 22–

Column (1); *Person, couple or polygamous marriage*	*Column (2)*; *Amount*;
(1) Single claimant or lone parent–	(1) –
(a) aged under 65;	(a) [² £119.05];
(b) aged 65 or over.	(b) [² £138.10].
(2) Couple–	(2) –
(a) both members aged under 65;	(a) [² £181.70];
(b) one member or both members aged 65 or over.	(b) [² £207.00].
(3) If the claimant is a member of a polygamous marriage and none of the members of the marriage have attained the age of 65–	(3) –
(a) for the claimant and the other party to the marriage;	(a) [² £181.70];
(b) for each additional spouse who is a member of the same household as the claimant.	(b) [² £62.65].
(4) If the claimant is a member of a polygamous marriage and one or more members of the marriage are aged 65 or over–	(4) –
(a) for the claimant and the other party to the marriage;	(a) [² £207.00];
(b) for each additional spouse who is a member of the same household as the claimant.	(b) [² £68.90].

Amendments

1. Amended by Art 20(4) and Sch 8 para 1 of SI 2006 No 645 and reg 8 of SI 2006 No 217 as from 1.4.06 (3.4.06 where rent payable weekly or at intervals of a week).
2. Amended by Art 20(6) and Sch 8 of SI 2007 No 688 as from 1.4.07 (2.4.07 where rent payable weekly or at intervals of a week).

2.–(1) The amounts specified in column (2) below in respect of each person specified in column (1) shall, for the relevant period specified in column (1), be the amounts specified for the purposes of regulation 22–

Column (1); *Child or young person*	*Column (2)*; *Amount*;
Person in respect of the period–	
(a) beginning on that person's date of birth and ending on the day preceding the first Monday in September following that person's sixteenth birthday;	[³ £47.45];;
(b) beginning on the first Monday in September following that persons 16th birthday and ending on the day preceding that person's [² twentieth] birthday.	[³ £47.45].;

(2) In column (1) of the Table above, "the first Monday in September" means the Monday which first occurs in the month of September in any year.

Amendments

1. Amended by Art 20(4) and Sch 8 para 2 of SI 2006 No 645 and reg 8 of SI 2006 No 217 as from 1.4.06 (3.4.06 where rent payable weekly or at intervals of a week).
2. Amended by reg 4(4) of SI 2006 No 718 as from 10.4.06.
3. Amended by Art 20(6) and Sch 8 of SI 2007 No 688 as from 1.4.07 (2.4.07 where rent payable weekly or at intervals of a week).

PART 2
Family premium

3.–(1)   The amount for the purposes of regulations 22(1)(c) and (d) in respect of a family of which at least one member is a child or young person shall be [³ £16.43].

(2)   The amount specified in sub-paragraph (1) shall be increased by [⁴ £10.50] where at least one child is under the age of one year and for the purposes of this sub-paragraph where that child's first birthday does not fall on a Monday he shall be treated as under the age of one year until the first Monday after his first birthday.

Amendments

1. Amended by Art 20(5)(a) of SI 2006 No 645 and reg 8 of SI 2006 No 217 as from 1.4.06 (3.4.06 where rent payable weekly or at intervals of a week).
2. Confirmed by Art 20(5)(b) of SI 2006 No 645 and reg 8 of SI 2006 No 217 as from 1.4.06 (3.4.06 where rent payable weekly or at intervals of a week).
3. Amended by Art 20(7)(a) of SI 2007 No 688 as from 1.4.07 (2.4.07 where rent payable weekly or at intervals of a week).
4. Confirmed by Art 20(7)(b) of SI 2007 No 688 as from 1.4.07 (2.4.07 where rent payable weekly or at intervals of a week).

PART 3
Premiums

4.   The premiums specified in Part 4 shall, for the purposes of regulation 22(1)(e), be applicable to a claimant who satisfies the condition specified in this Part in respect of that premium.

5.–(1)   Subject to sub-paragraph (2), for the purposes of this Part of this Schedule, once a premium is applicable to a claimant under this Part, a person shall be treated as being in receipt of any benefit for–

(a)   in the case of a benefit to which the Social Security (Overlapping Benefits) Regulations 1979 applies, any period during which, apart from the provisions of those Regulations, he would be in receipt of that benefit; and

(b)   any period spent by a person in undertaking a course of training or instruction provided or approved by the Secretary of State under section 2 of the 1973 Act, or by Scottish Enterprise or Highlands and Islands Enterprise under section 2 of the Enterprise and New Towns (Scotland) Act 1990 or for any period during which he is in receipt of a training allowance.

(2)   For the purposes of the carer premium under paragraph 9, a person shall be treated as being in receipt of a carer's allowance under section 70 of the Act by virtue of sub-paragraph (1)(a) only if and for so long as the person in respect of whose care the allowance has been claimed remains in receipt of attendance allowance, or the care component of disability living allowance at the highest or middle rate prescribed in accordance with section 72(3) of the Act.

Severe disability premium

6.–(1)   The condition is that the claimant is a severely disabled person.

(2)   For the purposes of sub-paragraph (1), a claimant shall be treated as being a severely disabled person if, and only if–

(a)   in the case of a single claimant, lone parent or a claimant who is treated as having no partner in consequence of sub-paragraph (3)–

    (i)   he is in receipt of attendance allowance, or the care component of disability living allowance at the highest or middle rate prescribed in accordance with section 72(3) of the Act; and

    (ii)   subject to sub-paragraph (6), he has no non-dependants aged 18 or over normally residing with him or with whom he is normally residing; and

    (iii)   no person is entitled to, and in receipt of, a carer's allowance in respect of caring for him;

(b)   in the case of a claimant who has a partner–

    (i)   the claimant is in receipt of attendance allowance, or the care component of disability living allowance at the highest or middle rate prescribed in accordance with section 72(3) of the Act; and

(ii)   his partner is also in receipt of such an allowance or, if the claimant is a member of a polygamous marriage, each other member of that marriage is in receipt of such an allowance; and

(iii)   subject to sub-paragraph (6), the claimant has no non-dependants aged 18 or over normally residing with him or with whom he is normally residing,

and either a person is entitled to and in receipt of a carer's allowance in respect of caring for only one of the couple or, if he is a member of a polygamous marriage, for one or more but not all the members of the marriage, or as the case may be, no person is entitled to and in receipt of such an allowance in respect of caring for either member of a couple or any of the members of the marriage.

(3)   Where a claimant has a partner who does not satisfy the condition in sub-paragraph (2)(b)(ii), and that partner is blind or is treated as blind within the meaning of sub-paragraph (4), that partner shall be treated for the purposes of sub-paragraph (2) as if he were not a partner of the claimant.

(4)   For the purposes of sub-paragraph (3), a person is blind if he is registered in a register compiled by a local authority under section 29 of the National Assistance Act 1948 (welfare services) or, in Scotland, has been certified as blind and in consequence he is registered in a register maintained by or on behalf of a council constituted under section 2 of the Local Government (Scotland) Act 1994.

(5)   For the purposes of sub-paragraph (4), a person who has ceased to be registered as blind on regaining his eyesight shall nevertheless be treated as blind and as satisfying the additional condition set out in that sub-paragraph for a period of 28 weeks following the date on which he ceased to be so registered.

(6)   For the purposes of sub-paragraph (2)(a)(ii) and (2)(b)(iii) no account shall be taken of–

(a)   a person receiving attendance allowance, or the care component of disability living allowance at the highest or middle rate prescribed in accordance with section 72(3) of the Act; or

(b)   a person who is blind or is treated as blind within the meaning of sub-paragraphs (4) and (5).

(7)   For the purposes of sub-paragraph (2)(b) a person shall be treated–

(a)   as being in receipt of attendance allowance, or the care component of disability living allowance at the highest or middle rate prescribed in accordance with section 72(3) of the Act, if he would, but for his being a patient for a period exceeding 28 days, be so in receipt;

(b)   as being entitled to and in receipt of a carer's allowance if he would, but for the person for whom he was caring being a patient in hospital for a period exceeding 28 days, be so entitled and in receipt.

(8)   For the purposes of sub-paragraph (2)(a)(iii) and (2)(b)–

(a)   no account shall be taken of an award of a carer's allowance to the extent that payment of such an award is backdated for a period before [¹ the date on which the award is first paid]; and

(b)   references to a person being in receipt of a carer's allowance shall include references to a person who would have been in receipt of that allowance but for the application of a restriction under section 7 of the Social Security Fraud Act 2001 (loss of benefit).

Amendment

1.   Amended by reg 7(4) of SI 2007 No 719 as from 2.4.07.

Enhanced disability premium

7.   The condition is that the care component of disability living allowance is, or would, but for a suspension of benefit in accordance with regulations under section 113(2) of the Act or but for an abatement as a consequence of hospitalisation, be payable at the highest rate prescribed under section 72(3) of the Act in respect of a child or young person who is a member of the claimant's family.

Disabled child premium

8.   The condition is that a child or young person for whom the claimant or a partner of his is responsible and who is a member of the claimant's household–

(a)   is in receipt of disability living allowance or is no longer in receipt of such allowance because he is a patient, provided that the child or young person continues to be a member of the family; or

(b)   is blind within the meaning of paragraph 6(4) or is treated as blind in accordance with paragraph 6(5);

(c)   is a child or a young person in respect of whom section 145A of the Act (entitlement to child benefit after death of child) applies for the purposes of entitlement to child benefit, but only for the period prescribed under that section, and in respect of whom a disabled child premium was included in the claimant's applicable amount immediately before the death of that child.

Carer premium

9.–(1)   The condition is that the claimant or his partner is, or both of them are, entitled to a carer's allowance.

(2)   Where a carer premium has been awarded but–

(a)   the person in respect of whose care the carer's allowance has been awarded dies; or

(b)   the person in respect of whom the premium was awarded ceases to be entitled, or ceases to be treated as entitled, to a carer's allowance.

this paragraph shall be treated as satisfied for a period of eight weeks from the relevant date specified in sub-paragraph (3).

(3)   The relevant date for the purposes of sub-paragraph (2) is–

(a)   the Sunday following the death of the person in respect of whose care the carer's allowance has been awarded (or beginning with the date of death if the date occurred on a Sunday);

(b)   where head (a) above does not apply, the date on which that person who was entitled to a carer's allowance ceases to be entitled to it.

(4)   For the purposes of this paragraph, a person shall be treated as being entitled to and in receipt of a carer's allowance for any period not covered by an award but in respect of which a payment is made in lieu of an award.

Persons in receipt of concessionary payments

10.   For the purpose of determining whether a premium is applicable to a person under paragraphs 6 to 9, any concessionary payment made to compensate that person for the non-payment of any benefit mentioned in those paragraphs shall be treated as if it were a payment of that benefit.

Person in receipt of benefit

11.   For the purposes of this Part of this Schedule, a person shall be regarded as being in receipt of any benefit if, and only if, it is paid in respect of him and shall be so regarded only for any period in respect of which that benefit is paid.

PART 4
Amounts of premiums specified in Part 3

Premium	*Amount*;
12.–(1) Severe Disability Premium	(1)
(a) where the claimant satisfies the condition in paragraph 6(2)(a);	(a) [² £48.45];
(b) where the claimant satisfies the condition in paragraph 6(2)(b)–	(b)
(i) in a case where there is someone in receipt of a carer's allowance or if he or any partner satisfies that condition only by virtue of paragraph 6(7);	(i) [² £48.45];
(b)	(b)
(ii) in a case where there is no-one in receipt of such an allowance	(ii) [² £96.90].
(2) Enhanced disability premium.	(2) [² £18.76] in respect of each child or young person in respect of whom the conditions specified in paragraph 7 are satisfied.
(3) Disabled child premium.	(3) [² £46.69] in respect of each child or young person in respect of whom the condition specified in paragraph 8 is satisfied.
(4) Carer premium.	(4) [² £27.15] in respect of each person who satisfies the condition specified in paragraph 9.

Amendments

1.   Amended by Art 20(5) and Sch 9 of SI 2006 No 645 and reg 8 of SI 2006 No 217 as from 1.4.06 (3.4.06 where rent payable weekly or at intervals of a week).

2.   Amended by Art 20(8) and Sch 9 of SI 2007 No 688 as from 1.4.07 (2.4.07 where rent payable weekly or at intervals of a week).

SCHEDULE 4
REGULATION 36(1)
Sums disregarded from claimant's earnings

General Note to Schedule 4

The earnings disregard is a maximum of £25 for lone parents and £20 for everyone else. The categories of people qualifying for a disregard of £20 are the following:

(1)   Claimants working for the rescue services and reserve armed forces: para 3. If the claimant is earning less than £20, any earnings of her/his partner will be disregarded up to that amount.

(2)   Carers who are in employment: para 4. Again, the earnings of both partners may be added together for the purposes of the disregard.

(3)   Certain disabled claimants: para 5(1). Much of para 5(1) is similar to Sch 3 para 13(1) HB Regs, to which reference should be made.

(4)   Claimants who had a £20 disregard in an award of HB or CTB in the 8 weeks before attaining the qualifying age for PC and where employment continues after the termination of that award: para 5(2). That disregard continues as long as HB entitlement continues: para 5(3).

Other claimants qualify for disregards of £10 (couples) and £5 (single claimants): para 7. There are then a number of other disregards. Para 6 requires the disregarding of any balance of parental contributions made to a student which are not disregarded under Sch 5 paras 18 and 19. Para 8 requires earnings derived from employment pre-dating the claim to be ignored, save for royalties and analogous payments. Para 9 is equivalent to Sch 4 para 17 HB Regs.

---

1.   Where two or more of paragraphs 2 to 5 apply in any particular case the overall maximum sum which falls to be disregarded in that case under those paragraphs is restricted to–

(a)   £25 in the case of a lone parent;

(b)   £20 in any other case.

2.   In a case where a claimant is a lone parent, £25 of earnings.

3.–(1)   In a case of earnings from any employment or employments to which sub-paragraph (2) applies, £20.

(2)   This paragraph applies to employment–

(a)   as a part-time fire-fighter employed by a fire and rescue authority constituted by a scheme under section 2 of the Fire and Rescue Services Act 2004 or a scheme to which section 4 of that Act applies;

(b)   as a part-time fire-fighter employed by a fire and rescue authority (as defined in section 1 of the Fire (Scotland) Act 2005) or a joint fire and rescue board constituted by an amalgamation scheme made under section 2(1) of that Act;

(c)   as an auxiliary coastguard in respect of coast rescue activities;

(d)   in the manning or launching of a lifeboat if the employment is part-time;

(e)   as a member of any territorial or reserve force prescribed in Part 1 of Schedule 6 to Social Security (Contributions) Regulations 2001.

(3)   If–

(a)   any of the earnings of the claimant or, if he has a partner, his partner, or both of them, are disregarded under sub-paragraph (1); and

(b)   either of them has, or they both have, other earnings,

so much of those other earnings as would not, in aggregate with the earnings disregarded under that sub-paragraph, exceed £20.

4.–(1)   If the claimant or, if he has a partner, his partner is a carer, or both are carers, £20 of any earnings received from his or their employment.

(2)   Where the carer premium is awarded in respect of the claimant and of any partner of his, their earnings shall for the purposes of this paragraph be aggregated, but the amount to be disregarded in accordance with sub-paragraph (1) shall not exceed £20 of the aggregated amount.

(3)   In this paragraph the claimant or his partner is a carer if paragraph 9 of Part 3 of Schedule 3 (amount applicable for carers) is satisfied in respect of him.

5.–(1)   £20 is disregarded if the claimant or, if he has a partner, his partner–

(a)   is in receipt of–

    (i)   long-term incapacity benefit under Section 30A of the Act;

    (ii)   severe disablement allowance under section 68 of the Act;

    (iii)   attendance allowance;

    (iv)   disability living allowance under sections 71 to 76 of the Act;

    (v)   any mobility supplement under article 26A of the Naval, Military and Air Forces etc. (Disablement and Death) Service Pensions Order 1983 (including such a supplement by virtue of any other scheme or order) or under article 25A of the Personal Injuries (Civilians) Scheme 1983; or

    (vi)   the disability element or the severe disability element of working tax credit under Schedule 2 to the Working Tax Credit Regulations; or

(b)   is or are registered as blind in a register compiled by a local authority under section 29 of the National Assistance Act 1948 (welfare services) or, in Scotland, has been certified as blind and in consequence is registered as blind in a register maintained by or on behalf of a council constituted under section 2 of the Local Government (Scotland) Act 1994; or

(c)   is, or is treated as, incapable of work in accordance with the provisions of, and regulations made under, Part 12A of the Act (incapacity for work), and has been incapable, or has been treated as incapable, of work for a continuous period of not less than—
      (i)   in the case of a claimant who is terminally ill within the meaning of section 30B(4) of that Act, 196 days;
      (ii)   in any other case, 364 days.

(2)   Subject to sub-paragraph (3), £20 is disregarded if the claimant or, if he has a partner, his partner has, within a period of 8 weeks ending on the day in respect of which the claimant or his partner attains the qualifying age for state pension credit, had an award of housing benefit or council tax benefit and–
      (a)   £20 was disregarded in respect of earnings taken into account in that award;
      (b)   the person whose earnings qualified for the disregard continues in employment after the termination of that award.

(3)   The disregard of £20 specified in sub-paragraph (2) applies so long as there is no break, other than a break which does not exceed 8 weeks, in a person's entitlement to housing benefit or council tax benefit or in employment following the first day in respect of which that benefit is awarded.

(4)   £20 is the maximum amount which may be disregarded under this paragraph, notwithstanding that, where the claimant has a partner, both the claimant and his partner satisfy the requirements of this paragraph.

6.   Any amount or the balance of any amount which would fall to be disregarded under paragraph 18 or 19 of Schedule 5 had the claimant's income which does not consist of earnings been sufficient to entitle him to the full disregard thereunder.

7.   Except where the claimant or his partner qualifies for a £20 disregard under the preceding provisions of this Schedule–
      (a)   £5 shall be disregarded if a claimant who has no partner has earnings;
      (b)   £10 shall be disregarded if a claimant who has a partner has earnings.

8.   Any earnings, other than earnings referred to in regulation 33(8)(b) (copyright, patent or trade mark), derived from employment which ended before the day in respect of which the claimant first satisfies the conditions for entitlement to housing benefit.

9.–(1)   In a case where the claimant is a person who satisfies at least one of the conditions set out in sub-paragraph (2), and his net earnings equal or exceed the total of the amounts set out in sub-paragraph (3), the amount of his earnings that falls to be disregarded under this Schedule shall be increased by [² £15.45].

(2)   The conditions of this sub-paragraph are that–
      (a)   the claimant, or if he has a partner, either the claimant or his partner, is a person to whom regulation 20(1)(c) of the Working Tax Credit Regulations applies; or
      (b)   the claimant–
          (i)   is, or any partner of his is, aged at least 25 and is engaged in remunerative work for on average not less than 30 hours per week; or
          (ii)   if he is a member of a couple–
              (aa)   at least one member of that couple is engaged in remunerative work for on average not less than 16 hours per week; and
              (bb)   his applicable amount includes a family premium under paragraph 3 of Schedule 3; or
          (iii)   is a lone parent who is engaged in remunerative work for on average not less than 16 hours per week; or
          (iv)   is, or if he has a partner, one of them is, engaged in remunerative work for on average not less than 16 hours per week, and paragraph 5(1) above is satisfied in respect of that person; or
      (c)   the claimant is, or, if he has a partner, one of them is, a person to whom regulation 18(3) of the Working Tax Credit Regulations (eligibility for 50 plus element) applies, or would apply if an application for working tax credit were to be made in his case.

(3)   The following are the amounts referred to in sub-paragraph (1)–
      (a)   any amount disregarded under this Schedule;
      (b)   the amount of child care charges calculated as deductible under regulation 31(1)(c) (treatment of child care charges); and
      (c)   [² £15.45].

(4)   The provisions of regulation 6 (remunerative work) shall apply in determining whether or not a person works for on average not less than 30 hours per week, but as if the reference to 16 hours in paragraph (1) of that regulation was a reference to 30 hours.

Amendments

1.   Amended by Art 20(7) of SI 2006 No 645 and reg 8 of SI 2006 No 217 as from 1.4.06 (3.4.06 where rent payable weekly or at intervals of a week).

2.   Amended by Art 20(9) of SI 2007 No 688 as from 1.4.07 (2.4.07 where rent payable weekly or at intervals of a week).

---

10.   Where a payment of earnings is made in a currency other than Sterling any banking charge or commission payable in converting that payment into Sterling.

SCHEDULE 5
REGULATION 33(9)
Amounts to be disregarded in the calculation of income other than earnings

1.   In addition to any sum which falls to bedisregarded in accordance with paragraphs 2 to 6, £10 of any of the following, namely–

(a)   a war disablement pension (except insofar as such a pension falls to be disregarded under paragraph 2 or 3);

(b)   a war widow's or war widower's pension;

(c)   a pension payable to a person as a widow, widower or surviving civil partner under the Naval, Military and Air Forces etc. (Disablement and Death) Service Pensions Order 1983 insofar as that Order is made under the Naval and Marine Pay and Pensions Act 1865 or the Pensions and Yeomanry Pay Act 1884 or is made only under section 12(1) of the Social Security (Miscellaneous Provisions) Act 1977 and any power of Her Majesty otherwise than under an enactment to make provision about pensions for or in respect of persons who have been disabled or have died in consequence of service as members of the armed forces of the Crown;

(d)   a guaranteed income payment;

(e)   a payment made to compensate for the non-payment of such a pension or payment as is mentioned in any of the preceding sub-paragraphs;

(f)   a pension paid by the government of a country outside Great Britain which is analogous to any of the pensions or payments mentioned in sub-paragraphs (a) to (d) above;

(g)   a pension paid to victims of National Socialist persecution under any special provision made by the law of the Federal Republic of Germany, or any part of it, or of the Republic of Austria.

Analysis

See Sch 5 para 15 HB Regs (see p476), but note para 2 below, which is not to be found in Sch 4.

---

2.   The whole of any amount included in a pension to which paragraph 1 relates in respect of–

(a)   the claimant's need for constant attendance;

(b)   the claimant's exceptionally severe disablement.

Analysis

These are supplements payable in respect of various war pensions for the exceptional needs of a recipient. The whole of such supplements are disregarded.

---

3.   Any mobility supplement under article 26A of the Naval, Military and Air Forces etc. (Disablement and Death) Service Pensions Order 1983 (including such a supplement by virtue of any other scheme or order) or under article 25A of the Personal Injuries (Civilians) Scheme 1983 or any payment intended to compensate for the non-payment of such a supplement.

Analysis

This is equivalent to Sch 5 para 8 HB Regs (see p473).

---

4.   Any supplementary pension under article 29(1A) of the Naval, Military and Air Forces etc. (Disablement and Death) Service Pensions Order 1983 (pensions to widows, widowers or surviving civil partners).

5.   In the case of a pension awarded at the supplementary rate under article 27(3) of the Personal Injuries (Civilians) Scheme 1983 (pensions to widows, widowers or surviving civil partners), the sum specified in paragraph 1(c) of Schedule 4 to that Scheme.

6.–(1)   Any payment which is–

(a)   made under any of the Dispensing Instruments to a widow, widower or surviving civil partner of a person–

    (i)   whose death was attributable to service in a capacity analogous to service as a member of the armed forces of the Crown; and

    (ii)   whose service in such capacity terminated before 31st March 1973; and

(b)   equal to the amount specified in article 29(1A) of the Naval, Military and Air Forces etc. (Disablement and Death) Service Pensions Order 1983 (pensions to widows, widowers or surviving civil partners).

(2)   In this paragraph ''the Dispensing Instruments'' means the Order in Council of 19th December 1881, the Royal Warrant of 27th October 1884 and the Order by His Majesty of 14th January 1922 (exceptional grants of pay, non-effective pay and allowances).

7.   £15 of any widowed parent's allowance to which the claimant is entitled under section 39A of the Act.

8.   £15 of any widowed mother's allowance to which the claimant is entitled under section 37 of the Act.

9.   Where the claimant occupies a dwelling as his home and he provides in that dwelling board and lodging accommodation, an amount, in respect of each person for whom such accommodation is provided for the whole or any part of a week, equal to–

(a)   where the aggregate of any payments made in respect of any one week in respect of such accommodation provided to such person does not exceed £20, 100 per cent. of such payments; or

(b)   where the aggregate of any such payments exceeds £20, £20 and 50 per cent. of the excess over £20.

10.   If the claimant–

(a)   owns the freehold or leasehold interest in any property or is a tenant of any property; and

(b)   occupies a part of that property; and

(c)   has an agreement with another person allowing that person to occupy another part of that property on payment of rent and–

(i)   the amount paid by that person is less than £20 per week, the whole of that amount; or

(ii)   the amount paid is £20 or more per week, £20.

Analysis
This has no equivalent in Sch 5 HB Regs. Up to £20 of rent payable by a lodger may be disregarded even if board is not also provided.

---

11.   Where a claimant receives income under an annuity purchased with a loan, which satisfies the following conditions–

(a)   that the loan was made as part of a scheme under which not less than 90 per cent. of the proceeds of the loan were applied to the purchase by the person to whom it was made of an annuity ending with his life or with the life of the survivor of two or more persons (in this paragraph referred to as ''the annuitants'') who include the person to whom the loan was made;

(b)   that at the time the loan was made the person to whom it was made or each of the annuitants had attained the age of 65;

(c)   that the loan was secured on a dwelling in Great Britain and the person to whom the loan was made or one of the annuitants owns an estate or interest in that dwelling;

(d)   that the person to whom the loan was made or one of the annuitants occupies the dwelling on which it was secured as his home at the time the interest is paid; and

(e)   that the interest payable on the loan is paid by the person to whom the loan was made or by one of the annuitants,

the amount, calculated on a weekly basis, equal to–

(i)   where, or insofar as, section 369 of the Income and Corporation Taxes Act 1988 (mortgage interest payable under deduction of tax) applies to the payments of interest on the loan, the interest which is payable after deduction of a sum equal to income tax on such payments at the applicable percentage of income tax within the meaning of section 369(1A) of that Act;

(ii)   in any other case, the interest which is payable on the loan without deduction of such a sum.

Analysis
This is equivalent to Sch 5 para 18 HB Regs (see p477).

12.–(1)   Any payment, other than a payment to which sub-paragraph (2) applies, made to the claimant by Trustees in exercise of a discretion exercisable by them.

(2)   This sub-paragraph applies to payments made to the claimant by Trustees in exercise of a discretion exercisable by them for the purpose of–

(a)   obtaining food, ordinary clothing or footwear or household fuel;

(b)   the payment of rent, council tax or water charges for which that claimant or his partner is liable;

(c)   meeting housing costs of a kind specified in Schedule 2 to the State Pension Credit Regulations 2002.

(3)   In a case to which sub-paragraph (2) applies, £20 or–

(a)   if the payment is less than £20, the whole payment;

(b)   if, in the claimant's case, £10 is disregarded in accordance with paragraph 1(a) to (g), £10 or the whole payment if it is less than £10; or

(c)   if, in the claimant's case, £15 is disregarded under paragraph 7 or paragraph 8 and–

  (i)   he has no disregard under paragraph 1(a) to (g), £5 or the whole payment if it is less than £5;

  (ii)   he has a disregard under paragraph 1(a) to (g), nil.

(4)   For the purposes of this paragraph–

"ordinary clothing and footwear" means clothing or footwear for normal daily use, but does not include school uniforms, or clothing and footwear used solely for sporting activities; and

"rent" means eligible rent for the purposes of these Regulations less any deductions in respect of non-dependants which fall to be made under regulation 55 (non-dependant deductions).

Analysis

This paragraph has no equivalent in Sch 5 HB Regs. All payments under a discretionary trust are ignored, except for those which are used for the essentials set out in para (2), which receive only a limited disregard calculated according to the amounts of other disregards.

---

13.   Any increase in pension under Part 4 of the Naval, Military and Air Forces etc. (Disablement and Death) Service Pensions Order 1983 paid in respect of a dependent other than the pensioner's spouse or civil partner.

Analysis

This paragraph has no equivalent in Sch 5 HB Regs. It deals with increases in war pensions for dependants, which are to be ignored completely.

---

14.   Any payment ordered by a court to be made to the claimant or the claimant's partner in consequence of any accident, injury or disease suffered by the person or a child of the person to or in respect of whom the payments are made.

15.   Periodic payments made to the claimant or the claimant's partner under an agreement entered into in settlement of a claim made by the claimant or, as the case may be, the claimant's partner for an injury suffered by him.

Analysis to paras 14 and 15

The phrase "any accident, injury or disease" used in para 14 is probably wider than the phrase used in reg 42(2)(b) HB Regs "a personal injury". It might, for example, cover wrongful birth claims which can be said to arise from an "accident" such as a negligently carried out sterilisation.

Para 15 does not appear to include payments from an annuity purchased by a defendant's insurer, since those are payments made under the annuity contract rather than under the settlement agreement.

---

16.   Any income which is payable outside the United Kingdom for such period during which there is a prohibition against the transfer to the United Kingdom of that income.

17.   Any banking charges or commission payable in converting to Sterling payments of income made in a currency other than Sterling.

18.   Where the claimant makes a parental contribution in respect of a student attending a course at an establishment in the United Kingdom or undergoing education in the United Kingdom, which contribution has been assessed for the purposes of calculating–

(a)   under, or pursuant to regulations made under powers conferred, by section 1 or 2 of the Education Act 1962, or section 22 of the Teaching and Higher Education Act 1998, that student's award;

(b)   under regulations made in exercise of the powers conferred by section 49 of the Education (Scotland) Act 1980, that student's bursary, scholarship, or other allowance under that section or under regulations made in exercise of the powers conferred by section 73 of that Act of 1980, any payment to that student under that section; or

(c)   the student's student loan,

an amount equal to the weekly amount of that parental contribution, but only in respect of the period for which that contribution is assessed as being payable.

Analysis

This is equivalent to Sch 5 para 19 HB Regs (see p477).

19.–(1)   Where the claimant is the parent of a student aged under 25 in advanced education who either–

(a) is not in receipt of any award, grant or student loan in respect of that education; or

(b) is in receipt of an award under section 2 of the Education Act 1962 (discretionary awards) or an award bestowed by virtue of the Teaching and Higher Education Act 1998, or regulations made thereunder, or a bursary, scholarship or other allowance under section 49(1) of the Education (Scotland) Act 1980, or a payment under section 73 of that Act of 1980,

and the claimant makes payments by way of a contribution towards the student's maintenance, other than a parental contribution falling within paragraph 18, an amount specified in sub-paragraph (2) in respect of each week during the student's term.

(2) For the purposes of sub-paragraph (1), the amount shall be equal to–

(a) the weekly amount of the payments; or

(b) the amount by way of a personal allowance for a single claimant under 25 less the weekly amount of any award, bursary, scholarship, allowance or payment referred to in sub-paragraph (1)(b),

whichever is less.

Analysis
This is equivalent to Sch 5 para 20 HB Regs (see p478).

20.–(1) Where a claimant's applicable amount includes an amount by way of a family premium, £15 of any payment of maintenance, whether under a court order or not, which is made or due to be made by the claimant's spouse, civil partner, former spouse or former civil partner or the claimant's partner's spouse, civil partner, former spouse, or former civil partner.

(2) For the purposes of sub-paragraph (1), where more than one maintenance payment falls to be taken into account in any week, all such payments shall be aggregated and treated as if they were a single payment.

Analysis
This is equivalent to Sch 5 para 47 HB Regs (see p483).

---

21. Except in a case which falls under paragraph 9 of Schedule 4, where the claimant is a person who satisfies the conditions of sub-paragraph (2) of that paragraph, any amount of working tax credit up to [² £15.45].

Amendment
1. Amended by Art 20(8) of SI 2006 No 645 and reg 8 of SI 2006 No 217 as from 1.4.06 (3.4.06 where rent payable weekly or at intervals of a week).
2. Amended by Art 20(10) of SI 2007 No 688 as from 1.4.07 (2.4.07 where rent payable weekly or at intervals of a week).

Analysis
See the commentary to Sch 4 para 17 HB Regs on p476.

---

22. Except in the case of income from capital specified in Part 2 of Schedule 6, any actual income from capital.

23. Any special war widows payment made under–

(a) the Naval and Marine Pay and Pensions (Special War Widows Payment) Order 1990 made under section 3 of the Naval and Marine Pay and Pensions Act 1865;

(b) the Royal Warrant dated 19th February 1990 amending the Schedule to the Army Pensions Warrant 1977;

(c) the Queen's Order dated 26th February 1990 made under section 2 of the Air Force (Constitution) Act 1917;

(d) the Home Guard War Widows Special Payments Regulations 1990 made under section 151 of the Reserve Forces Act 1980;

(e) the Orders dated 19th February 1990 amending Orders made on 12th December 1980 concerning the Ulster Defence Regiment made in each case under section 140 of the Reserve Forces Act 1980;

and any analogous payment made by the Secretary of State for Defence to any person who is not a person entitled under the provisions mentioned in sub-paragraphs (a) to (e) of this paragraph.

24. Where the total value of any capital specified in Part 2 of Schedule 6 does not exceed–

(a) in the case of a claimant residing permanently in accommodation to which regulation 29(6) applies, £10,000; or

(b) in any other case, £6,000,

any income actually derived from such capital.

SCHEDULE 6
REGULATION 44(2)
Capital to be disregarded

PART 1
Capital to be disregarded generally

1.　　　Any premises acquired for occupation by the claimant which he intends to occupy as his home within 26 weeks of the date of acquisition or such longer period as is reasonable in the circumstances to enable the claimant to obtain possession and commence occupation of the premises.

2.　　　Any premises which the claimant intends to occupy as his home, and in respect of which he is taking steps to obtain possession and has sought legal advice, or has commenced legal proceedings, with a view to obtaining possession, for a period of 26 weeks from the date on which he first sought such advice or first commenced such proceedings whichever is the earlier, or such longer period as is reasonable in the circumstances to enable him to obtain possession and commence occupation of those premises.

3.　　　Any premises which the claimant intends to occupy as his home to which essential repairs or alterations are required in order to render them fit for such occupation, for a period of 26 weeks from the date on which the claimant first takes steps to effect those repairs or alterations, or such longer period as is necessary to enable those repairs or alterations to be carried out.

4.　　　Any premises occupied in whole or in part–

(a)　　　by a person who is a relative of the claimant or of his partner as his home where that person is either aged 60 or over or incapacitated;

(b)　　　by the former partner of the claimant as his home; but this provision shall not apply where the former partner is a person from whom the claimant is estranged or divorced or with whom he had formed a civil partnership that has been dissolved.

5.　　　Any future interest in property of any kind, other than land or premises in respect of which the claimant has granted a subsisting lease or tenancy, including sub-leases or sub-tenancies.

6.　　　Where a claimant has ceased to occupy what was formerly the dwelling occupied as the home following his estrangement or divorce from his former partner or the dissolution of a civil partnership with his former partner, that dwelling for a period of 26 weeks from the date on which he ceased to occupy that dwelling or, where the dwelling is occupied as the home by the former partner who is a lone parent, for so long as it is so occupied.

7.　　　Any premises where the claimant is taking reasonable steps to dispose of the whole of his interest in those premises, for a period of 26 weeks from the date on which he first took such steps, or such longer period as is reasonable in the circumstances to enable him to dispose of those premises.

Analysis to paras 1 to 7

These are equivalent to HB Regs Sch 6 paras 2, 27, 28, 4, 7, 25 and 26 respectively (see p486).

8.　　　All personal possessions.

Analysis

This is different to Sch 6 para 12 HB Regs because it contains no exception for possessions purchased in order to reduce capital and increase benefit. Unless the notional capital provision in reg 47 applies, the value of such possessions must be completely ignored.

9.　　　The assets of any business owned in whole or in part by the claimant and for the purposes of which he is engaged as a self-employed earner or, if he has ceased to be engaged, for such period as may be reasonable in the circumstances to allow for disposal of those assets.

10.　　　The assets of any business owned in whole or in part by the claimant if—

(a)　　　he is not engaged as a self-employed earner in that business by reason of some disease or bodily or mental disablement; but

(b)　　　he intends to become engaged (or, as the case may be, re-engaged) as a self-employed earner in that business as soon as he recovers or is able to become engaged, or re-engaged, in that business,

for a period of 26 weeks from the date on which the claim for housing benefit is made or, if it is unreasonable to expect him to become engaged or re-engaged in that business within that period, for such longer period as is reasonable in the circumstances to enable him to become so engaged or re-engaged.

Analysis to paras 9 and 10

These are equivalent to Sch 6 para 8 HB Regs (see p488).

11.　　　The surrender value of any policy of life insurance.

12. The value of any funeral plan contract; and for this purpose, "funeral plan contract" means a contract under which–

(a) the claimant makes one or more payments to another person ("the provider");

(b) the provider undertakes to provide, or secure the provision of, a funeral in the United Kingdom for the claimant on his death; and

(c) the sole purpose of the plan is to provide or secure the provision of a funeral for the claimant on his death.

Analysis

This has no equivalent in Sch 6 HB Regs but is self-explanatory.

---

13. Where an ex-gratia payment has been made by the Secretary of State on or after 1st February 2001 in consequence of the imprisonment or internment of–

(a) the claimant;

(b) the claimant's partner;

(c) the claimant's deceased spouse or deceased civil partner; or

(d) the claimant's partner's deceased spouse or deceased civil partner,

by the Japanese during the Second World War, an amount equal to that payment.

14.–(1) Subject to sub-paragraph (2), the amount of any trust payment made to a claimant or a claimant's partner who is–

(a) a diagnosed person;

(b) a diagnosed person's partner or was a diagnosed person's partner at the time of the diagnosed person's death;

(c) a parent of a diagnosed person, a person acting in place of the diagnosed person's parents or a person who was so acting at the date of the diagnosed person's death.

(2) Where a trust payment is made to–

(a) a person referred to in sub-paragraph (1)(a) or (b), that sub-paragraph shall apply for the period beginning on the date on which the trust payment is made and ending on the date on which that person dies;

(b) a person referred to in sub-paragraph (1)(c), that sub-paragraph shall apply for the period beginning on the date on which the trust payment is made and ending two years after that date.

(3) Subject to sub-paragraph (4), the amount of any payment by a person to whom a trust payment has been made or of any payment out of the estate of a person to whom a trust payment has been made, which is made to a claimant or a claimant's partner who is–

(a) the diagnosed person;

(b) a diagnosed person's partner or was a diagnosed person's partner at the date of the diagnosed person's death; or

(c) a parent of a diagnosed person, a person acting in place of the diagnosed person's parents or a person who was so acting at the date of the diagnosed person's death.

(4) Where a payment such as referred to in sub-paragraph (3) is made to–

(a) a person referred to in sub-paragraph (3)(a) or (b), that sub-paragraph shall apply for the period beginning on the date on which the payment is made and ending on the date on which that person dies;

(b) a person referred to in sub-paragraph (3)(c), that sub-paragraph shall apply for the period beginning on the date on which the payment is made and ending two years after that date.

(5) In this paragraph, a reference to a person–

(a) being the diagnosed person's partner;

(b) acting in place of the diagnosed person's parents,

at the date of the diagnosed person's death shall include a person who would have been such a person or a person who would have been so acting, but for the diagnosed person residing in a care home or an independent hospital.

(6) In this paragraph–

"diagnosed person" means a person who has been diagnosed as suffering from, or who, after his death, has been diagnosed as having suffered from, variant Creutzfeldt-Jakob disease;

"relevant trust" means a trust established out of funds provided by the Secretary of State in respect of persons who suffered, or who are suffering, from variant Creutzfeldt-Jakob disease for the benefit of persons eligible for payments in accordance with its provisions;

"trust payment" means a payment under a relevant trust.

15. The amount of any payment, other than a war disablement pension or a war widow's or widower's pension, to compensate for the fact that the claimant, the claimant's partner, the claimant's deceased spouse or civil partner or the claimant's partner's deceased spouse or civil partner–

(a) was a slave labourer or a forced labourer;

(b) had suffered property loss or had suffered personal injury; or

(c)   was a parent of a child who had died,

during the Second World War.

16.–(1)   Any payment made under–

(a)   the Macfarlane Trust, the Macfarlane (Special Payments) Trust, the Macfarlane (Special Payments) (No. 2) Trust, the Fund, the Eileen Trust, the Skipton Fund or the London Bombings Relief Charitable Fund (collectively referred to in this paragraph as ''the Trusts''); or

(b)   the Independent Living Funds.

(2)   Any payment by or on behalf of a person who is suffering or who suffered from haemophilia or who is or was a qualifying person, which derives from a payment made under any of the Trusts and which is made to or for the benefit of that person's partner or former partner from whom he is not, or where that person has died was not, estranged or divorced or with whom he has formed a civil partnership that has not been dissolved or, where that person has died, had not been dissolved at the time of that person's death.

(3)   Any payment by or on behalf of the partner or former partner of a person who is suffering or who suffered from haemophilia or who is or was a qualifying person provided that the partner or former partner and that person are not, or if either of them has died were not, estranged or divorced or, where the partner or former partner and that person have formed a civil partnership, the civil partnership has not been dissolved or, if either of them has died, had not been dissolved at the time of the death, which derives from a payment made under any of the Trusts and which is made to or for the benefit of the person who is suffering from haemophilia or who is a qualifying person.

(4)   Any payment by a person who is suffering from haemophilia or who is a qualifying person, which derives from a payment under any of the Trusts, where–

(a)   that person has no partner or former partner from whom he is not estranged or divorced or with whom he has formed a civil partnership that has not been dissolved nor any child who is or had been a member of that person's household; and

(b)   the payment is made either–

     (i)   to that person's parent or step-parent; or

     (ii)   where that person at the date of the payment is a child or a student who has not completed his full-time education and has no parent or step-parent, to any person standing in the place of his parent,

but only for a period from the date of the payment until the end of two years from that person's death.

(5)   Any payment out of the estate of a person who suffered from haemophilia or who was a qualifying person, which derives from a payment under any of the Trusts, where–

(a)   that person at the date of his death (''the relevant date'') had no partner or former partner from whom he was not estranged or divorced or with whom he had formed a civil partnership that had not been dissolved, nor any child who was or had been a member of his household; and

(b)   the payment is made either–

     (i)   to that person's parent or step-parent; or

     (ii)   where that person at the relevant date was a child or a student who had not completed his full-time education and had no parent or step-parent, to any person standing in place of his parent,

but only for a period of two years from the relevant date.

(6)   In the case of a person to whom or for whose benefit a payment referred to in this paragraph is made, any capital resource which derives from any payment of income or capital made under or deriving from any of the Trusts.

Modifications

References to "step-parent" in sub-paras (4)(b)(i) and (ii) and (5)(b)(i) and (ii) are modified by s246 Civil Partnership Act 2004 (see p1046) and Article 3 and para 27 of the Schedule to SI 2005 No 3137 (see pp1097 and 1097).

Analysis to paras 13 to 16

These are equivalent to HB Regs Sch 6 paras 54 (although there is no reference to the amount of the payment being £10,000), 55, 56 and 24 respectively (see p486).

17.–(1)   An amount equal to the amount of any payment made in consequence of any personal injury to the claimant or, if the claimant has a partner, to the partner.

(2)   Where the whole or part of the payment is administered–

[¹ (a)   by the High Court or the County Court under Rule 21.11(1) of the Civil Procedure Rules 1998, or the Court of Protection, or on behalf of a person where the payment can only be disposed of by order or direction of any such court;]

(b)   in accordance with an order under Rule 36.14 of the Ordinary Cause Rules 1993 or under Rule 128 of those Rules; or

(c)   in accordance with the terms of a trust established for the benefit of the claimant or his partner, the whole of the amount so administered.

Amendment

1.   Substituted by reg 16(4) of SI 2006 No 2378 from the first day of the first benefit week to commence on or after 2.10.06.

Analysis

On sub-para (2), see Sch 6 paras 45 and 46 HB Regs on p496. For the words "in consequence of any personal injury" see reg 42(2) HB Regs on p309.

---

18.   Any amount specified in paragraphs 19, 20 or 21 for a period of one year beginning with the date of receipt.

19.   Amounts paid under a policy of insurance in connection with the loss of or damage to the property occupied by the claimant as his home and to his personal possessions.

20.   So much of any amounts paid to the claimant or deposited in the claimant's name for the sole purpose of–

(a)   purchasing premises which the claimant intends to occupy as his home; or

(b)   effecting essential repairs or alterations to the premises occupied or intended to be occupied by the claimant as his home.

21.–(1)   Subject to paragraph 22 any amount paid–

(a)   by way of arrears of benefit;

(b)   by way of compensation for the late payment of benefit;

(c)   in lieu of the payment of benefit;

(d)   to rectify, or compensate for, an official error, as defined for the purposes of paragraph 22, being an amount to which that paragraph does not apply;

(e)   by a local authority (including, in relation to England, a county council), or by the National Assembly for Wales, to or on behalf of the claimant or his partner relating to a service which is provided to develop or sustain the capacity of the claimant or his partner to live independently in his accommodation.

(2)   In sub-paragraph (1), "benefit" means–

(a)   attendance allowance under section 64 of the Act;

(b)   disability living allowance;

(c)   income support;

(d)   income-based jobseeker's allowance;

(e)   state pension credit;

(f)   housing benefit;

(g)   council tax benefit;

(h)   child tax credit;

(i)   an increase of a disablement pension under section 104 of the Act (increase where constant attendance is needed), and any further increase of such a pension under section 105 of the Act (increase for exceptionally severe disablement);

(j)   any amount included on account of the claimant's exceptionally severe disablement or need for constant attendance in a war disablement pension or a war widow's or widower's pension.

[¹ (k)   any discretionary housing payment paid pursuant to regulation 2(1) of the Discretionary Financial Assistance Regulations 2001; or

(l)   working tax credit.]

Amendment

1.   Inserted by reg 2(17) of SI 2005 No 2502 as amended by Sch 2 para 27 of SI 2006 No 217 as from 1.4.06 (3.4.06 where rent payable weekly or at intervals of a week).

Analysis to Paras 18 to 21

The categories of capital in paras 19 to 21 are disregarded for one year from the date of receipt: para 18. They are payments under insurance policies following damage to home or contents, arrears of benefit or compensatory payments and payments under the Supporting People scheme.

See also para 22 below where arrears of benefit are paid to compensate for "official error".

22.–(1)   Subject to sub-paragraph (3), any payment of £5,000 or more which has been made to rectify, or to compensate for, an official error relating to a relevant benefit and has been received by the claimant in full on or after the day on which he became entitled to benefit under these Regulations or the Housing Benefit Regulations 2006.

(2)   Subject to sub-paragraph (3), the total amount of any payments disregarded under–

(a)   paragraph 7(2) of Schedule 10 to the Income Support Regulations;
(b)   paragraph 12(2) of Schedule 8 to the Jobseeker's Allowance Regulations;
(c)   paragraph 9(2) of Schedule 5 to the Housing Benefit Regulations 2006;
(d)   paragraph 20A of Schedule 5 to the State Pension Credit Regulations 2002,
where the award in respect of which the payments last fell to be disregarded under those Regulations either terminated immediately before the relevant date or is still in existence at that date.

(3)   Any disregard which applies under sub-paragraph (1) or (2) shall have effect until the award comes to an end.

(4)   In this paragraph–
"the award", except in sub-paragraph (2), means–
(a)   the award of benefit under these Regulations during which the relevant sum or, where it is paid in more than one instalment, the first instalment of that sum is received; and
(b)   where that award is followed by one or more further awards which, or each of which, begins immediately after the previous award ends, such further awards until the end of the last such award, provided that, for such further awards, the claimant–
      (i)   is the person who received the relevant sum;
      (ii)   is the partner of that person; or
      (iii)   was the partner of that person at the date of his death;
"official error"–
(a)   where the error relates to housing benefit or council tax benefit, has the meaning given by regulation 1(2) of the Decisions and Appeals Regulations;
(b)   where the error relates to any other relevant benefit, has the meaning given by regulation 1(3) of the Social Security and Child Support (Decisions and Appeals) Regulations 1999;
"the relevant date" means–
(a)   in the case of an existing award of benefit under these Regulations or the Housing Benefit Regulations 2006, 6th October 2003; and
(b)   in any other case, the date on which the claim for benefit under these Regulations or the Housing Benefit Regulations 2006 was made;
"relevant benefit" means any benefit specified in paragraph 21(2); and
"the relevant sum" means the payment referred to in sub-paragraph (1) or the total amount referred to in sub-paragraph (2).

23.   Where a capital asset is held in a currency other than Sterling, any banking charge or commission payable in converting that capital into Sterling.

24.   The value of the right to receive income from an occupational pension scheme or a personal pension scheme.

[¹**25.**]

Amendment
1.   Omitted by reg 5(6) of SI 2007 No 1749 as from 16.7.07.

---

26.   The dwelling occupied as the home; but only one dwelling shall be disregarded under this paragraph.

[¹**26A.**   Where a person elects to be entitled to a lump sum under Schedule 5 or 5A to the Contributions and Benefits Act or under Schedule 1 to the Graduated Retirement Benefit Regulations, or is treated as having made such an election, and a payment has been made pursuant to that election, an amount equal to–
(a)   except where sub-paragraph (b) applies, the amount of any payment or payments made on account of that lump sum;
(b)   the amount of that lump sum,
but only for so long as that person does not change that election in favour of an increase of pension or benefit.]

Amendment
1.   Inserted by reg 11(4) of SI 2005 No 2677 and reg 2 of SI 2006 No 217 as from 6.4.06.

PART 2
Capital disregarded only for the purposes of determining deemed income
27.   The value of the right to receive any income under a life interest or from a life rent.

Analysis
This is the equivalent, save for the fact that the disregard only operates for the calculation of tariff income, of HB Regs Sch 6 para 15 (see p491).

28. The value of the right to receive any rent except where the claimant has a reversionary interest in the property in respect of which rent is due.

29. The value of the right to receive any income under an annuity or the surrender value (if any) of such an annuity.

Analysis

This is the equivalent, save for the fact that the disregard only operates for the calculation of tariff income, of HB Regs Sch 6 para 13 (see p490).

30. Where property is held under a trust, other than–

(a) a charitable trust within the meaning of the Charities Act 1993; or

(b) a trust set up with any payment to which paragraph 16 of this Schedule applies,

and under the terms of the trust, payments fall to be made, or the trustees have a discretion to make payments, to or for the benefit of the claimant or the claimant's partner, or both, that property.

Analysis

Para 30 requires beneficial interests under a trust to be ignored.

SCHEDULE 7
REGULATION 53
Extended payments (severe disablement allowance and incapacity benefit) of housing benefit

Condition for an extended payment (severe disablement allowance and incapacity benefit)

1. The condition prescribed in this paragraph is that the claimant or the claimant's partner–

(a) notifies either the designated office or an appropriate DWP office that he or his partner–

    (i) has commenced, or is about to commence, remunerative work;

    (ii) has commenced, or is about to commence, receiving remuneration for work or an increased amount of remuneration for work; or

    (iii) has commenced, or is about to commence, an increased number of hours of work,

so that entitlement to severe disablement allowance or incapacity benefit ceases and that work, or as the case may be, remuneration, is expected to last 5 weeks or more; and

(b) the notification is made no later than 4 weeks after the day on which the claimant or his partner first undertakes the remunerative work referred to in sub-paragraph (a)(i), first receives remuneration for the work or an increased amount of remuneration for the work referred to in sub-paragraph (a)(ii), or first commences the increased number of hours of work referred to in sub-paragraph (a)(iii).

Calculation and payment of an extended payment (severe disablement allowance and incapacity benefit)

2.–(1) Subject to the following provisions of this paragraph and except in the case of a mover, the amount of the extended payment (severe disablement allowance and incapacity benefit) shall be equal to the amount of housing benefit which was payable to the claimant for the last benefit week before he ceased to be entitled to housing benefit.

(2) In a case where the last benefit week referred to in sub-paragraph (1) fell, in whole or in part, within a rent free period, the last benefit week for the purposes of that sub-paragraph shall be taken to be the last benefit week that did not fall within a rent free period.

(3) Where the last benefit week before he ceased to be entitled to housing benefit was a week in which the claimant's eligible rent was calculated in accordance with regulation 61(4)(c) (claimant ceases to occupy the dwelling as his home), sub-paragraph (1) shall have effect as if the reference to the last benefit week before he ceased to be entitled to housing benefit was a reference to the week before that week.

(4) Subject to paragraph (5), the extended payment (severe disablement allowance and incapacity benefit) shall be payable for each of the weeks in the period specified in regulation 53(6)(a), and shall be paid at such time and in such manner as is appropriate, having regard to–

(a) the times at which and the frequency with which a person's liability to make payment of rent arises; and

(b) the reasonable needs and convenience of the person entitled thereto.

(5) No extended payment (severe disablement allowance and incapacity benefit) shall be payable for a week which is a rent free period for the purposes of regulation 62(1) (rent free periods).

Movers

3. Paragraphs 4 to 6 below apply to movers from–

(a) the day the move takes place where that day is a Monday; or

(b)   from the Monday following the day the move takes place where that day is not a Monday.

Movers and rent allowances

4.–(1)   Subject to sub-paragraph (2), in the case of a mover whose housing benefit was in the form of a rent allowance, the authority which, prior to the mover ceasing to be entitled to housing benefit, was paying that allowance, shall make an extended payment (severe disablement allowance and incapacity benefit) to that mover calculated on the same basis as in paragraph 2, and, for these purposes, the mover shall be treated as continuing to occupy and be liable to make payments in respect of the dwelling he was occupying as his home immediately before he ceased to be entitled to housing benefit.

(2)   Notwithstanding sub-paragraph (1), in a case where that mover's liability to make payments in respect of the second dwelling would be to a housing authority, any extended payment (severe disablement allowance and incapacity benefit) shall be made by that housing authority and shall be determined as provided in paragraph 6(b).

Movers and rent rebates

5.   Where, in the case of a mover–

(a)   his housing benefit was in the form of a rent rebate; and

(b)   he claims an extended payment (severe disablement allowance and incapacity benefit),

the authority in which the second dwelling is situated, or as the case may be, where the mover's liability to make payments in respect of the second dwelling is to a housing authority, that housing authority, shall upon receiving the mover's claim for an extended payment (severe disablement allowance and incapacity benefit), which meets the requirements of regulation 53(1), make an extended payment (severe disablement allowance and incapacity benefit), calculated in accordance with paragraph 6, to that mover.

Movers and extended payments (severe disablement allowance and incapacity benefit)

6.   In a case to which paragraph 4(2) or 5 applies and where a mover's liability referred to in that paragraph is–

(a)   other than to a housing authority, the extended payment (severe disablement allowance and incapacity benefit) shall be a payment by way of rent allowance calculated in accordance with paragraph 2;

(b)   to a housing authority, the extended payment (severe disablement allowance and incapacity benefit) shall be by way of a rent rebate to the value of the lesser of–

(i)   such part of the rent in respect of the period specified in regulation 53(6)(a) as is eligible for housing benefit, calculated in accordance with regulations 11 to 13, less, in a case where the rebate to which paragraph 5 refers, or the rent allowance to which paragraph 4 refers, as the case may be, was subject to any deductions in respect of non-dependants pursuant to regulations 50 and 55, the amount of those deductions; or

(ii)   the amount of extended payment (severe disablement allowance and incapacity benefit) calculated in accordance with paragraph 2.

Maximum housing benefit

7.   The maximum housing benefit of a mover the amount of whose extended payment (severe disablement allowance and incapacity benefit) is calculated in accordance with paragraph 6(b)(i) shall be calculated in accordance with regulation 50, save that no deduction shall be made in respect of non-dependants, other than any that fall to be taken into account pursuant to paragraph 6(b)(i).

Movers with two homes

8.   Subject to paragraph 9, any extended payment (severe disablement allowance and incapacity benefit) shall be without prejudice to any entitlement the claimant may have pursuant to regulation 7(6) (liability to make payments in respect of two homes).

Adjustment of entitlement in respect of an extended payment (severe disablement allowance and incapacity benefit)

9.   Where for any week–

(a)   a person is entitled to an extended payment (severe disablement allowance and incapacity benefit); and

(b)   he also claims and is awarded housing benefit,

then the amount of the housing benefit payable in respect of that week shall be reduced by a sum equal to the amount of the extended payment (severe disablement allowance and incapacity benefit) and only the balance, if any, shall be payable to him for that week.

Interpretation

10. In this Schedule–

''claimant'' means a person claiming an extended payment (severe disablement allowance and incapacity benefit);

''mover'' means a claimant who changes the dwelling which he occupies as his home in respect of which he is liable or treated as liable to make payments;

''second dwelling'' means the dwelling to which a person has moved, or is about to move, which he is or will be occupying as his new home, and where the liability to make payments of rent in respect of his dwelling follows on immediately from the liability to make payments of rent in respect of his previous dwelling.

SCHEDULE 8

REGULATION 71

Matters to be included in decision notice

PART 1

General

1. The statement of matters to be included in any decision notice issued by a relevant authority to a person, and referred to in regulation 71 (notification of decisions) and in regulation 10 of the Decisions and Appeals Regulations are those matters set out in the following provisions of this Schedule.

2. Every decision notice shall include a statement as to the right of any person affected by that decision to request a written statement under regulation 71(2) (requests for statement of reasons) and the manner and time in which to do so.

3. Every decision notice shall include a statement as to the right of any person affected by that decision to make an application for a revision in accordance with regulation 4(1)(a) of the Decisions and Appeals Regulations and, where appropriate, to appeal against that decision and the manner and time in which to do so.

4. Every decision notice following an application for a revision in accordance with regulation 4(1)(a) of the Decisions and Appeals Regulations shall include a statement as to whether the original decision in respect of which the person made his representations has been confirmed or revised and where the relevant authority has not revised the decision the reasons why not.

5. Every decision notice following an application for a revision in accordance with regulation 4(1)(a) of the Decisions and Appeals Regulations shall, if the original decision has been revised, include a statement as to the right of any person affected by that decision to apply for a revision in accordance with regulation 4(1)(a) of those Regulations and the manner and time in which to do so.

6. An authority may include in the decision notice any other matters not prescribed by this Schedule which it sees fit, whether expressly or by reference to some other document available without charge to the person.

7. Parts 2, 3 and 6 of this Schedule shall apply only to the decision notice given on a claim.

8. Where a decision notice is given following a revision of an earlier decision–

(a) made of the authority's own motion which results in a revision of that earlier decision; or

(b) made following an application for a revision in accordance with regulation 4(1)(a) of the Decisions and Appeals Regulations, whether or not resulting in a revision of that earlier decision,

that notice shall, subject to paragraph 6, contain a statement only as to all the matters revised.

PART 2

Awards where state pension credit is payable

9.–(1) Where a person on state pension credit is awarded housing benefit, the decision notice shall include a statement as to–

(a) his weekly eligible rent, if any; and

(b) the amount and an explanation of any deduction made under paragraph 6(2) or (3) of Schedule 1 (fuel deductions), if any, and that the deduction may be varied if he provides to the authority evidence on which it may estimate the actual or approximate amount of that service charge; and

(c) the amount of and the category of non-dependant deductions made under regulation 55 (non-dependant deductions), if any; and

(d) the normal weekly amount of rent allowance, or rent rebate as the case may be, to which he is entitled; and

(e) in the case of a rent allowance and a rate rebate paid as if it were a rent allowance, the day of payment, and the period in respect of which payment of that allowance is to be made; and

(f) the first day of entitlement to an allowance or rebate; and

(g)   his duty to notify any change of circumstances which might affect his entitlement to, or the amount of, housing benefit and (without prejudice to the extent of the duty owed under regulation 69 (duty to notify changes of circumstances)) the kind of change of circumstances which is to be notified, either upon the notice or by reference to some other document available to him on application and without charge.

(2)   In a case where a person on state pension credit has entitlement only to the savings credit, the following additional matters shall also be set out–

(a)   the applicable amount and the basis of calculation;

(b)   the amount of the savings credit [¹] taken into account;

(c)   the amount of the person's income and capital as notified to the local authority by the Secretary of State and taken into account for the purposes of the housing benefit assessment;

(d)   any modification of the claimant's income or capital made in accordance with regulation 27 (calculation of claimant's income in savings credit only cases); and

(e)   the amount of the claimant's capital if paragraph (7) of regulation 27 applies in his case.

Amendment

1.   Amended by reg 2(18) of SI 2005 No 2502 as amended by Sch 2 para 27 of SI 2006 No 217 as from 1.4.06 (3.4.06 where rent payable weekly or at intervals of a week).

PART 3
Awards where no state pension credit is payable

10.   Where a person is not on state pension credit but is awarded housing benefit, the decision notice shall include a statement as to–

(a)   the matters set out in paragraph 9; and

(b)   his applicable amount and how it is calculated; and

(c)   his weekly earnings; and

(d)   his weekly income other than earnings.

PART 4
Awards where direct payments made to landlords

11.   Where a decision has been made under regulation 76 or 77 (circumstances in which payment is to be made, or may be made, direct to a landlord), the decision notice shall include a statement–

(a)   as to the amount of housing benefit which is to be paid direct to the landlord and the date from which it is to be paid; and

(b)   informing the landlord of the duty imposed upon him to notify the local authority of–

    (i)   any change in circumstances which might affect the claimant's entitlement to housing benefit, or the amount of housing benefit payable in his case; and

    (ii)   the kind of change of circumstances which is to be notified,

and the notice shall be sent both to the claimant and to the landlord; and

(c)   informing both landlords and claimants that where a payment of housing benefit is recoverable from a landlord and the recovery is made from housing benefit payable to the landlord to discharge (in whole or in part) an obligation owed to him by a claimant, then, in a case where that claimant is not the person on whose behalf the recoverable amount was paid, that obligation shall nonetheless be taken to be discharged by the amount so recovered.

12.   In this Schedule, ''landlord'' has the same meaning as in regulation 76.

PART 5
Notice where income of non-dependant is treated as claimant's

13.   Where an authority makes a decision under regulation 24 (circumstances in which income of non-dependant is to be treated as claimant's) the decision notice shall contain a statement as to–

(a)   the fact that a decision has been made by reference to the income and capital of the claimant's non-dependant; and

(b)   the relevant authority's reasons for making that decision.

PART 6
Notice where no award is made

14.   Where a person is not awarded housing benefit–

(a)   either on grounds of income or because the amount of any housing benefit is less than the minimum housing benefit prescribed by regulation 56, the decision notice shall include a statement as to–

    (i)   the matters set out in paragraphs 9(1)(a) to (c), and in a case where the amount of entitlement is less than the minimum amount of housing benefit prescribed, paragraph 9(1)(d) also; and

(ii)   the matters set out in paragraphs 10(b) to (d) where the person is not on income support or an income-based jobseeker's allowance; and

(iii)   where the amount of entitlement is less than the minimum amount of housing benefit prescribed, that fact and that such entitlement is not payable;

(b)   for any reason other than one mentioned in sub-paragraph (a), the decision notice shall include a statement as to the reason why no award has been made.

PART 7
Notice where recoverable overpayment

15.–(1)   Where the appropriate authority makes a decision that there is a recoverable overpayment within the meaning of regulation 81 (recoverable overpayments), the decision notice shall include a statement as to–

(a)   the fact that there is a recoverable overpayment; and

(b)   the reason why there is a recoverable overpayment; and

(c)   the amount of the recoverable overpayment; and

(d)   how the amount of the recoverable overpayment was calculated; and

(e)   the benefit weeks to which the recoverable overpayment relates; and

(f)   where recovery of the recoverable overpayment is to be made by deduction from a rent allowance or rebate, as the case may be, that fact and the amount of the deduction.

(2)   In a case where it is–

(a)   determined that there is a recoverable overpayment;

(b)   determined that that overpayment is recoverable from a landlord; and

(c)   decided that recovery of that overpayment is to be made by deduction from a rent allowance paid to that landlord to discharge (in whole or in part) an obligation owed to him by a claimant ("claimant A"), not being the claimant on whose behalf the recoverable amount was paid,

the decision notice sent to that landlord shall identify both–

(i)   the person on whose behalf the recoverable amount was paid to that landlord; and

(ii)   claimant A.

SCHEDULE 9
REGULATION 103
Pathfinder authorities

PART 1
Commencement date in relation to each pathfinder authority

Pathfinder authority	Commencement date
Argyll and Bute	30th May 2005
Blackpool;	17th November 2003
Brighton and Hove	2nd February 2004
Conwy;	9th February 2004
Coventry;	12th January 2004
East Riding of Yorkshire	18th April 2005
Edinburgh;	9th February 2004
Guildford;	4th July 2005
Leeds;	9th February 2004
Lewisham;	1st December 2003
North East Lincolnshire	9th February 2004
Norwich;	13th June 2005
Pembrokeshire;	20th June 2005
St Helens;	23rd May 2005
Salford;	25th July 2005
South Norfolk	6th June 2005
Teignbridge;	12th January 2004
Wandsworth;	11th April 2005

PART 2
Application of the Regulations

1.   These Regulations shall apply to pathfinder authorities subject to the provisions of this Part of this Schedule.

2.   In regulation 2(1) (interpretation), at the appropriate places, insert–

""'amended determination'' means a determination made in accordance with article 7A of the Rent Officers Order;

"broad rental market area" has the meaning specified in paragraph 4 of Part 1 of Schedule 3A to the Rent Officers Order;

"broad rental market area determination" means a determination made in accordance with article 4B(1) of the Rent Officers Order;

"commencement date" means in relation to a pathfinder authority specified in Part 1 of Schedule 9, the date specified in that Part in relation to that authority;

"local housing allowance" means an allowance determined in accordance with paragraph 2 or 3 of Part 1 of Schedule 3A to the Rent Officers Order;

"local housing allowance determination" means a determination made in accordance with article 4B(2) of the Rent Officers Order;

"maximum rent (standard local rate)" means the amount determined in accordance with regulation 13A;

"pathfinder authority" means a relevant authority specified in Part 1 of Schedule 9;

"relevant date" means, as the case may require–

(a) the commencement date in relation to a pathfinder authority specified in Part 1 of Schedule 9;

(b) the date of the claim to which the claim or relevant information relates;

(c) the date of the change relating to a rent allowance, or the change which affects the category of dwelling, date of death or rent increase, to which a notification referred to in regulation 13A(1)(b)(iii) or (iv) relate; or

(d) the date on which the period mentioned in regulation 14(1)(f) or (g) has elapsed;".

Amendment of regulation 11

3.   In regulation 11(1) (eligible housing costs), for the words "regulations 12(3)," to the end of the paragraph substitute "regulations 12 and 13 or regulations 12 and 13A, whichever is applicable in his case.".

Insertion of regulation 11A

4.   After regulation 11 (eligible housing costs), insert the following regulation–

"Cases where maximum housing benefit expires

11A. A maximum housing benefit shall not have effect for any benefit week which begins on or after the day which is the first anniversary of the day by reference to which the local housing allowance most recently applicable for the purpose of determining that maximum housing benefit in accordance with regulation 12A(1) to (9) was identified.".

Amendment of regulation 12

5.   In regulation 12(3)(b), after the words "except where sub-paragraph (a)"", insert "or regulation 12A(1), (3) or (4)".

Insert regulation 12A

6.   After regulation 12 (rent), insert the following regulation–

"Eligible rent and the maximum rent (standard local rate)

12A.–(1)   Where, by virtue of paragraph (1) of regulation 13A, a maximum rent (standard local rate) has been, or falls to be, determined in accordance with that regulation, then, except where paragraph (3)(a)(ii), (b)(ii) or (c)(ii), (4)(a) or (6)(a) applies–

(a)   the amount of a person's eligible rent shall be the maximum rent (standard local rate); and

(b)   it shall apply until the earlier of–

(i)   the determination of a maximum rent (standard local rate) by virtue of regulation 13A(1)(b)(iv); or

(ii)   the determination of a maximum rent (standard local rate) which relates to the local housing allowance applicable to the case on the first anniversary of the day by reference to which the local housing allowance which was applicable for the purpose of determining the eligible rent in sub-paragraph (a), was identified.

(2)   This paragraph applies where a pathfinder authority is required to determine a maximum rent (standard local rate) by virtue of regulation 13A(1)(a) or (b)(i), (ii) or (iii)(aa) or (c) and the claimant has been continuously entitled to and in receipt of housing benefit in respect of the dwelling he occupies as his home for a period which includes the commencement date.

(3)   Where paragraph (2) applies, subject to paragraph (9)–

(a)   except where sub-paragraph (b) or (c) applies, the amount of a person's eligible rent shall be–

    (i)   the eligible rent determined in accordance with paragraph (1) where that is not less than the eligible rent which applied on the day before the relevant date; or

    (ii)   the eligible rent which applied on the day before the relevant date;

(b)   where the eligible rent to which the person was entitled on the day before the relevant date was determined by reference to a maximum rent determined in accordance with regulation 13(11)(b), the person's eligible rent shall be–

    (i)   the eligible rent determined in accordance with paragraph (1), where that is not less than the eligible rent which applied on the day before the relevant date; or

    (ii)   the eligible rent which applied on the day before the relevant date; or

(c)   where the eligible rent to which the person was entitled on the day before the relevant date was, by virtue of regulation 13(14), determined in accordance with regulation 12(3)(b), the person's eligible rent shall be–

    (i)   the eligible rent determined in accordance with paragraph (1), where that is not less than the eligible rent which applied on the day before the relevant date; or

    (ii)   the eligible rent which applied on the day before the relevant date.

(4)   Subject to paragraph (9), where the pathfinder authority is required to determine a maximum rent (standard local rate) by virtue of regulation 13A(1)(b)(i), (ii) or (iv)(aa) to (cc) and the claimant occupies a dwelling which is the same as that occupied by him at the date of death of any person to whom any of sub-paragraphs (b) to (d) of paragraph (8) applied or, had a claim been made, would have applied, the eligible rent shall be–

(a)   either–

    (i)   the eligible rent which applied on the day before the death occurred; or

    (ii)   in a case where there was no eligible rent, subject to regulation 12(4) and (7), the reckonable rent due on that day; or

(b)   the eligible rent determined in accordance with paragraph (1), where it is not less than the eligible rent determined in accordance with sub-paragraph (a).

(5)   For the purpose of paragraph (4), a claimant shall be treated as occupying the dwelling if paragraph (13) of regulation 7 (circumstances in which a person is or is not to be treated as occupying a dwelling as his home) is satisfied and for that purpose that paragraph (13) shall have effect as if sub-paragraph (b) of that paragraph were omitted.

(6)   Subject to paragraphs (7) and (9), where a pathfinder authority is required to determine a maximum rent (standard local rate) by virtue of regulation 13A(1)(b)(i) or (ii) and the pathfinder authority is satisfied that a person to whom paragraph (8) applies was able to meet the financial commitments for his dwelling when they were entered into, the eligible rent shall be–

(a)   an eligible rent determined in accordance with regulation 12(3)(b); or

(b)   the eligible rent determined in accordance with paragraph (1), where it is not less than the eligible rent referred to in sub-paragraph (a).

(7)   Paragraph (6) shall not apply in the case of any claim for housing benefit where the claimant was previously entitled to housing benefit in respect of any period which ended less than 52 weeks before the commencement of the period to which the claim relates.

(8)   This paragraph applies to the following persons–

(a)   the claimant;

(b)   any member of his family;

(c)   if the claimant is a member of a polygamous marriage, any partners of his and any child or young person for whom he or a partner is responsible and who is a member of the same household;

(d)   any relative of the claimant or his partner who occupies the same dwelling as the claimant, whether or not they reside with him, except for a relative who has a separate right of occupation of the dwelling which would enable them to continue to occupy it even if the claimant ceased his occupation of it.

(9)   Where a person's eligible rent has been determined in accordance with–

(a)   paragraph (3)(a)(ii), it shall continue to apply until such time as the pathfinder authority determines an eligible rent–

    (i)   in accordance with paragraph (1) which is equal to or exceeds it or is based on a maximum rent (standard local rate) determined by virtue of regulation 13A(1)(b)(iv)(dd); or

    (ii)   where the maximum rent (standard local rate) on which it is based relates to the local housing allowance applicable to the case on the anniversary of the day by reference to which the local housing allowance which was applicable for the purpose of determining the eligible rent in paragraph (3)(a)(i) was identified, which is equal to or exceeds it,

whichever first occurs;

(b)   paragraph (3)(b)(ii), and–

    (i)   the pathfinder authority determined a maximum rent (standard local rate) following receipt of a notification of change relating to a rent allowance that falls within paragraph 2(3)(a) of Schedule 2 as a result of the death of one of the occupiers to whom any of sub-paragraphs (b) to (d) of regulation 13(16) applied, it shall continue to apply until–

        (aa)   the period of 12 months from the date of death has expired; or

        (bb)   the pathfinder authority determines an eligible rent in accordance with paragraph (1) which is equal to or exceeds it or is based on a maximum rent (standard local rate) determined by virtue of regulation 13A(1)(b)(iv)(dd),

whichever first occurs; or

    (ii)   in any other case, it shall continue to apply until–

        (aa)   the date on which the eligible rent which applied on the day before the relevant date would have ceased to apply; or

        (bb)   the pathfinder authority determines an eligible rent in accordance with paragraph (1) which is equal to or exceeds it or is based on a maximum rent (standard local rate) determined by virtue of regulation 13A(1)(b)(iv)(dd),

whichever first occurs;

(c)   paragraph (3)(c)(ii), it shall continue to apply until–

    (i)   the date on which the eligible rent which applied on the day before the relevant date would have ceased to apply; or

    (ii)   the pathfinder authority determines an eligible rent in accordance with paragraph (1) which is equal to or exceeds it or is based on a maximum rent (standard local rate) determined by virtue of regulation 13A(1)(b)(iv)(dd),

whichever first occurs;

(d)   paragraph (4)(a), it shall continue to apply until–

    (i)   the period of 12 months from the date of death has expired; or

    (ii)   the pathfinder authority determines an eligible rent in accordance with paragraph (1) which is equal to or exceeds it or is based on a maximum rent (standard local rate) determined by virtue of regulation 13A(1)(b)(iv)(dd),

whichever first occurs;
(e) paragraph (6)(a), it shall continue to apply until–
    (i) the first 13 weeks of the claimant's award of housing benefit have expired; or
    (ii) the pathfinder authority determines an eligible rent in accordance with paragraph (1) which is equal to or exceeds it or is based on a maximum rent (standard local rate) determined by virtue of regulation 13A(1)(b)(iv)(dd),
whichever first occurs; and
(f) paragraph (1)(b)(ii), or sub-paragraph (a)(ii) or this sub-paragraph, that eligible rent (''the earlier eligible rent'') shall continue to apply until–
    (i) the determination of a maximum rent (standard local rate) by virtue of regulation 13A(1)(b)(iv); or
    (ii) the determination of an eligible rent where the maximum rent (standard local rate) on which it is based relates to the local housing allowance applicable to the case on the first anniversary of the day by reference to which the local housing allowance which was applicable for the purpose of determining the earlier eligible rent was identified,
whichever first occurs.

(10) Where an eligible rent ceases to apply by virtue of sub-paragraph (b)(i)(aa), (b)(ii)(aa), (c)(i), (d)(i) or (e)(i) of paragraph (9), the eligible rent that shall apply instead shall be the one which would have applied but for paragraphs (3)(b)(ii), (3)(c)(ii), (4)(a) and (6)(a).

(11) In paragraph (4) ''reckonable rent'' has the same meaning as in regulation 13.''.

Insertion of regulation 13A and 13B
    7. After regulation 13 (maximum rent) insert the following regulations–

''Maximum rent (standard local rate)

13A.–(1) Subject to paragraph (2), where–
(a) the relevant authority is a pathfinder authority specified in Part 1 of Schedule 9 and it is the commencement date for that pathfinder authority; or
(b) a pathfinder authority has received–
    (i) a claim on which a rent allowance may be awarded, where the date of claim falls on or after the commencement date;
    (ii) relevant information regarding a claim on which a rent allowance may be awarded, where the date of claim falls on or after the commencement date;
    (iii) in relation to an award of housing benefit where the maximum rent was determined in accordance with regulation 13–
        (aa) a notification of a change relating to a rent allowance where the change occurs on or after the commencement date; or
        (bb) a notification of a change of dwelling where the change occurs on or after 9th April 2004; or
    (iv) in relation to an award of housing benefit where a maximum rent (standard local rate) was determined in accordance with this regulation–
        (aa) notification of a change of a kind which affects the category of dwelling applicable to the claim;
        (bb) notification of the death of an occupier of the dwelling to whom any of sub-paragraphs (b) to (d) of regulation 12A(8) applies, where the notification does not fall within sub-head (aa);
        (cc) notification that there has been a rent increase under a term of the tenancy to which the claim relates and the term under which that increase was made was either included in the tenancy at the

date of the claim or is a term substantially the same as such a term; or

    (dd) notification of a change of dwelling; or

(c)   a pathfinder authority is required to apply to a rent officer for a determination in accordance with regulation 14(1)(f) or (g),

the pathfinder authority shall determine a maximum rent (standard local rate) in accordance with paragraphs (3) to (8).

(2)   Paragraph (1) shall not apply in a case where–

(a)   the landlord is a registered social landlord;

(b)   paragraph 4(1)(b) of Schedule 3 to the Consequential Provisions Regulations applies;

(c)   the tenancy is an excluded tenancy of a type falling within any of paragraphs 4 to 10 of Schedule 2;

(d)   the claim or award relates to–

    (i)   periodical payments of a kind falling within regulation 12(1) which a person is liable to make in relation to a houseboat, caravan or mobile home which he occupies as his home; or

    (ii)   rent payable in relation to a hostel; or

(e)   rent under the tenancy is attributable to board and attendance, and–

    (i)   the pathfinder authority has made an application to the rent officer in accordance with paragraph (6), regulation 15 or 17; and

    (ii)   the rent officer has determined that a substantial part of the rent under the tenancy is fairly attributable to board and attendance and has notified the pathfinder authority of this in accordance with article 4C, 4D or 4E of the Rent Officers Order.

(3)   The maximum rent (standard local rate) shall be the local housing allowance determined by the rent officer which is applicable to–

(a)   the broad rental market area in which the dwelling to which the claim or award of housing benefit relates is situated at the relevant date; and

(b)   the category of dwelling–

    (i)   specified in paragraph 1(1)(a) of Part 1 of Schedule 3A to the Rent Officers Order where–

        (aa) the claimant is a young individual who has no non-dependant residing with him and to whom paragraph 6 of Schedule 3 (severe disability premium) does not apply; or

        (bb) the category of dwelling specified in paragraph 1(1)(b) of Part 1 of Schedule 3A to the Rent Officers Order would apply in the claimant's case but neither requirement in head (ii)(aa) or (bb) is satisfied in his case;

    (ii)   specified in paragraph 1(1)(b) of Part 1 of Schedule 3A to the Rent Officers Order where that applies in the claimant's case at the relevant date in accordance with the size criteria and he is not a person to whom head (i)(aa) applies and where–

        (aa) the claimant (together with his partner where he has one) has the exclusive use of two or more rooms; or

        (bb) the claimant (together with his partner where he has one) has the exclusive use of one room, a bathroom and toilet and a kitchen or facilities for cooking;

    (iii) in any other case, which applies in the claimant's case at the relevant date in accordance with the size criteria.

(4)   Where no local housing allowance applicable to a claim or award of housing benefit falling within paragraph (3)(b)(iii) has been determined, the pathfinder authority shall–

(a)   apply to the rent officer for local housing allowance determinations for the category of dwelling applicable to the claim or award of housing benefit for each broad rental market area falling within its area, in whole or in part, at the relevant date, which shall be specified in the application; and

(b) apply the local housing allowance so determined for the broad rental market area in which the dwelling to which the claim or award of housing benefit relates is situated at the relevant date.

(5) Where–

(a) a pathfinder authority receives a request on a properly completed form approved for the purpose by the pathfinder authority from a person stating that he is contemplating occupying as his home a dwelling containing a specified number of rooms, exceeding six, within the area of the pathfinder authority and that, if he does so, he is likely to claim housing benefit; and

(b) no local housing allowance determination is in effect for a broad rental market area, falling within, in whole or in part, the area of the pathfinder authority for the category of dwelling containing the number of rooms specified in the form,

the pathfinder authority shall apply to the rent officer for local housing allowance determinations for each broad rental market area for the category of dwelling containing the number of rooms specified in the form.

(6) In a case where–

(a) the pathfinder authority is required to determine a maximum rent (standard local rate) by virtue of paragraph (1); and

(b) part of the rent under the tenancy appears to the pathfinder authority to be likely to be attributable to board and attendance,

the pathfinder authority shall apply to the rent officer for a board and attendance determination to be made in accordance with article 4C of the Rent Officers Order.

(7) Where an application to a rent officer is required in accordance with paragraph (6)–

(a) it shall contain–

   (i) a statement that the application is made in accordance with paragraph (6); and

   (ii) such other statements, information and notifications as would be required were the application to be made in accordance with regulation 14(1); and

(b) it shall be made within the same period following the day on which the pathfinder authority becomes obliged to determine a maximum rent (standard local rate) by virtue of paragraph (1) as would be required if it were to be made under regulation 14(1).

(8) Where the maximum rent (standard local rate) exceeds the rent, the claimant shall be treated as liable to make payments in respect of the dwelling of an amount equal to the amount by which the maximum rent (standard local rate) exceeds the rent, except for the purposes of calculating any amount by which a rent allowance exceeds the amount which a claimant is liable to pay his landlord as rent, or rent and any arrears of rent, in accordance with regulation 76(2A).

(9) In this regulation–

"change of dwelling" has the same meaning as in regulation 14;

"change relating to a rent allowance" has the same meaning as in regulation 14;

"occupiers" means the persons whom the pathfinder authority is satisfied occupy as their home the dwelling to which the claim or award relates except for any joint tenant who is not a member of the claimant's household;

"registered social landlord" has the same meaning as in Part 1 of the Housing Act 1996 and, in Scotland, sections 57 and 59 of the Housing (Scotland) Act 2001;

"room" has the meaning specified in paragraph 1(2) of Part 1 of Schedule 3A to the Rent Officers Order;

"size criteria" has the meaning specified in article 2 of the Rent Officers Order except that the word "occupier" is to be construed in accordance with the definition of "occupiers" in this paragraph.

Publication of local housing allowances
13B. A pathfinder authority shall take such steps as appear to it to be appropriate for the purpose of securing that information in relation to broad rental market areas falling in whole or in part within its area, and local housing allowances applicable to such broad rental market areas, is brought to the attention of persons who may be entitled to housing benefit from the authority.''.

Amendment of regulation 14
8. In regulation 14 (requirement to refer to rent officers) after paragraph (5), insert the following paragraphs–

"(5A) An application shall not be required under paragraph (1)(a), (b), (c), (d) or (e) where the claim, relevant information, notification or request is received by a pathfinder authority, unless it is–
(a) a claim, relevant information or notification to which any of the circumstances specified in regulation 13A(2)(a) to (e) apply; or
(b) a request, and any of the circumstances in regulation 13A(2)(a) to (d) would apply were a claim to be made by the prospective occupier in relation to the dwelling which is the subject of the request,
and a referral would fall to be made were the claim, relevant information, notification or request made to a relevant authority which is not a pathfinder authority.
(5B) An application shall not be required in accordance with paragraph (1)(f) or (g) unless–
(a) it is a case to which regulation 13A(2) applies; and
(b) a referral would fall to be made were the relevant authority not a pathfinder authority.''.

Amendment of regulation 15
9. In regulation 15(1)(a) (applications to the rent officers for redeterminations) after the words ''reference made under'' insert ''regulation 13A(6) or''.

Amendment of regulation 16
10. In regulation 16 (application for redetermination by rent officer)–
(a) in paragraph (1)(b) after the words ''the Housing Act functions'' insert the words ''except for functions relating to broad rental market area determinations and local housing allowance determinations or amended determinations'';
(b) in paragraphs (3) and (4)(b) after the words ''application under regulation'' insert the words ''13A(6) or'';
(c) in paragraph (5) after the words ''the Housing Act functions'' insert the words ''(except for those relating to broad rental market area determinations and local housing allowance determinations or amended determinations)''.

Amendment of regulation 17
11. In regulation 17 (substitute determinations or substitute redeterminations)–
(a) in paragraph (1)(b)–
(i) for the words ''article 7A'' substitute the words ''article 7A(1) or (2)''; and
(ii) for the words ''or substitute redetermination'' substitute '', substitute redetermination, substitute board and attendance determination or substitute board and attendance redetermination''; and
(b) in paragraph (2) for the words ''or substitute redetermination'' substitute '', substitute redetermination, board and attendance redetermination, substitute board and attendance determination or substitute board and attendance redetermination''.

Insertion of regulation 18A

12. After regulation 18 (application of provisions to substitute determinations or substitute redeterminations) insert the following regulation–

'' Amended determinations

18A. Where a decision has been revised in consequence of an amended broad rental market area determination or amended local housing allowance determination by a rent officer and that amended determination has led to–

    (a)   a reduction in the maximum rent (standard local rate) applicable to a claimant, the amended determination shall be a change of circumstances in relation to that claimant; and

    (b)   an increase in the maximum rent (standard local rate) applicable to a claimant, the amended determination shall have effect in place of the original determination.''.

Amendment of regulations 76 and 77

13.–(1) In regulation 76 (circumstances in which payment is to be made to a landlord) after paragraph (2) insert the following paragraph–

'' (2A)   In a case where–

    (a)   a pathfinder authority has determined a maximum rent (standard local rate) in accordance with regulation 13A(1); and

    (b)   the rent allowance exceeds the amount which the claimant is liable to pay his landlord by way of rent,

any payment of rent allowance made to a landlord pursuant to this regulation or to regulation 77 may include all or part of any amount by which the rent allowance exceeds the amount which the claimant is liable to pay his landlord as rent but shall not include any amount by which the rent allowance exceeds the amount which the claimant is liable to pay his landlord as rent and arrears of rent.''.

    (2)   In regulation 77 (circumstances in which payment may be made to a landlord)–

    (a)   in paragraph (1) for the words ''paragraph (3)'' substitute the words ''paragraphs (3) and (3A)'';

    (b)   in sub-paragraph (a) of paragraph (3) after the words ''paragraph (1)'' insert the words ''or (3A)'';

    (c)   after paragraph (3) insert the following paragraph–

'' (3A)   In a case where a pathfinder authority has determined a maximum rent (standard local rate) in accordance with regulation 13A–

    (a)   sub-paragraphs (a) and (b) of paragraph (1) shall not apply; and

    (b)   payment of a rent allowance to a person's landlord may be made where–

        (i)   the eligible rent was determined by reference to a maximum rent (standard local rate) which was determined by virtue of regulation 13A(1)(a) and–

            (aa)   the maximum rent (standard local rate) was determined less than six months previously;

            (bb)   no subsequent maximum rent (standard local rate) has been determined in accordance with regulation 13A(1); and

            (cc)   the claimant has, since the date the maximum rent (standard local rate) was determined, been continuously entitled to, and in receipt of, housing benefit in relation to the dwelling he occupied as his home at that date;

        (ii)   the pathfinder authority considers that the claimant is likely to have difficulty in managing his affairs;

        (iii)   the pathfinder authority considers that it is improbable that the claimant will pay his rent; or

(iv)   a direct payment has previously been made by the pathfinder authority to the landlord in accordance with regulation 76 in respect of the current award of housing benefit.''.

[¹SCHEDULE 10
ELECTRONIC COMMUNICATION

Amendment
1.   Inserted by Art 3(5) of SI 2006 No 2968 as from 20.12.06.

PART 1
Introduction

Interpretation
    1.   In this Schedule ''official computer system'' means a computer system maintained by or on behalf of the relevant authority or of the Secretary of State for sending, receiving, processing or storing of any claim, certificate, notice, information or evidence.

PART 2
Electronic Communication – General Provisions

Conditions for the use of electronic communication
    2.–(1)   The relevant authority may use an electronic communication in connection with claims for, and awards of, benefit under these Regulations.
    (2)   A person other than the relevant authority may use an electronic communication in connection with the matters referred to in sub-paragraph (1) if the conditions specified in sub-paragraphs (3) to (6) are satisfied.
    (3)   The first condition is that the person is for the time being permitted to use an electronic communication by an authorisation given by means of a direction of the Chief Executive of the relevant authority.
    (4)   The second condition is that the person uses an approved method of–
    (a)   authenticating the identity of the sender of the communication;
    (b)   electronic communication;
    (c)   authenticating any claim or notice delivered by means of an electronic communication; and
    (d)   subject to sub-paragraph (7), submitting to the relevant authority any claim, certificate, notice, information or evidence.
    (5)   The third condition is that any claim, certificate, notice, information or evidence sent by means of an electronic communication is in a form approved for the purposes of this Schedule.
    (6)   The fourth condition is that the person maintains such records in written or electronic form as may be specified in a direction given by the Chief Executive of the relevant authority.
    (7)   Where the person uses any method other than the method approved of submitting any claim, certificate, notice, information or evidence, that claim, certificate, notice, information or evidence shall be treated as not having been submitted.
    (8)   In this paragraph ''approved'' means approved by means of a direction given by the Chief Executive of the relevant authority for the purposes of this Schedule.

Use of intermediaries
    3.   The relevant authority may use intermediaries in connection with–
    (a)   the delivery of any claim, certificate, notice, information or evidence by means of an electronic communication; and
    (b)   the authentication or security of anything transmitted by such means,
    and may require other persons to use intermediaries in connection with those matters.

PART 3
Electronic Communication – Evidential Provisions

Effect of delivering information by means of electronic communication
    4.–(1)   Any claim, certificate, notice, information or evidence which is delivered by means of an electronic communication shall be treated as having been delivered in the manner or form required by any provision of these Regulations, on the day the conditions imposed–
    (a)   by this Schedule; and

(b)   by or under an enactment,

are satisfied.

(2)   The relevant authority may, by a direction, determine that any claim, certificate, notice, information or evidence is to be treated as delivered on a different day (whether earlier or later) from the day provided for in sub-paragraph (1).

(3)   Information shall not be taken to have been delivered to an official computer system by means of an electronic communication unless it is accepted by the system to which it is delivered.

Proof of identity of sender or recipient of information

5.   If it is necessary to prove, for the purpose of any legal proceedings, the identity of–

(a)   the sender of any claim, certificate, notice, information or evidence delivered by means of an electronic communication to an official computer system; or

(b)   the recipient of any such claim, certificate, notice, information or evidence delivered by means of an electronic communication from an official computer system,

the sender or recipient, as the case may be, shall be presumed to be the person whose name is recorded as such on that official computer system.

Proof of delivery of information

6.–(1)   If it is necessary to prove, for the purpose of any legal proceedings, that the use of an electronic communication has resulted in the delivery of any claim, certificate, notice, information or evidence this shall be presumed to have been the case where–

(a)   any such claim, certificate, notice, information or evidence has been delivered to the relevant authority, if the delivery of that claim, certificate, notice, information or evidence has been recorded on an official computer system; or

(b)   any such claim, certificate, notice, information or evidence has been delivered by the relevant authority, if the delivery of that certificate, notice, information or evidence has been recorded on an official computer system.

(2)   If it is necessary to prove, for the purpose of any legal proceedings, that the use of an electronic communication has resulted in the delivery of any such claim, certificate, notice, information or evidence, this shall be presumed not to be the case, if that claim, certificate, notice, information or evidence delivered to the relevant authority has not been recorded on an official computer system.

(3)   If it is necessary to prove, for the purpose of any legal proceedings, when any such claim, certificate, notice, information or evidence sent by means of an electronic communication has been received, the time and date of receipt shall be presumed to be that recorded on an official computer system.

Proof of content of information

7.   If it is necessary to prove, for the purpose of any legal proceedings, the content of any claim, certificate, notice, information or evidence sent by means of an electronic communication, the content shall be presumed to be that recorded on an official computer system.]

The Council Tax Benefit (Persons who have attained the qualifying age for state pension credit) Regulations 2006
2006 No. 216

ARRANGEMENT OF REGULATIONS
PART 1
General

1. Citation and commencement
2. Interpretation
3. Definition of non-dependant
4. Section 1(1A) of the Administration Act disapplied
5. Application of Regulations
6. Remunerative work
7. Persons from abroad
7A. Entitlement of a refugee to council tax benefit
8. Prescribed persons for the purposes of section 131(3)(b) of the Act

PART 2
Membership of a family

9. Persons of prescribed description for the definition of family in section 137(1) of the Act
10. Circumstances in which a person is to be treated as responsible or not responsible for another
11. Circumstances in which a person is to be treated as being or not being a member of the household

PART 3
Applicable amounts

12. Applicable amounts

PART 4
Income and capital

SECTION 1
General

13. Calculation of income and capital of members of claimant's family and of a polygamous marriage
14. Circumstances in which income of non-dependant is to be treated as claimant's

SECTION 2
Income and capital

15. Calculation of income and capital
16. Claimant in receipt of guarantee credit
17. Calculation of claimant's income in savings credit only cases
18. Calculation of income and capital where state pension credit is not payable
19. Meaning of "income"
20. Calculation of income on a weekly basis
21. Treatment of child care charges
22. Calculation of average weekly income from tax credits
23. Calculation of weekly income
24. Disregard of changes in tax, contributions etc

SECTION 3
Employed earners
25. Earnings of employed earners
26. Calculation of net earnings of employed earners

SECTION 4
Self-employed earners
27. Calculation of earnings of self-employed earners
28. Earnings of self-employed earners
29. Calculation of net profit of self-employed earners
30. Deduction of tax and contributions for self-employed earners

SECTION 5
Other income
31. Notional income
32. Income paid to third parties

SECTION 6
Capital
33. Capital limit
34. Calculation of capital
35. Calculation of capital in the United Kingdom
36. Calculation of capital outside the United Kingdom
37. Notional capital
38. Diminishing notional capital rule
39. Capital jointly held

PART 5
Amount of benefit
40. Maximum council tax benefit
41. Reduction where amount payable under regulation 60 of the Council Tax Regulations 2006
42. Non-dependant deductions
43. Council tax benefit taper
44. Extended payments (severe disablement allowance and incapacity benefit)
45. Continuing payments where state pension credit claimed
46. Alternative maximum council tax benefit
47. Residents of a dwelling to whom section 131(6) of the Act does not apply

PART 6
Period of entitlement, changes of circumstances and increases for exceptional circumstances
48. Date on which entitlement is to begin
49. Date on which council tax benefit is to end where entitlement to severe disablement allowance or incapacity benefit ceases
50. Date on which change of circumstances is to take effect
51. Change of circumstances where state pension credit in payment

PART 7
Claims
52. Who may claim
53. Time and manner in which claims are to be made
53A. Electronic claims for benefit
54. Date of claim where claim sent or delivered to a gateway office

55.   Date of claim where claim sent or delivered to an office of a designated authority
56.   Time for claiming council tax benefit
57.   Evidence and information
58.   Amendment and withdrawal of claim
59.   Duty to notify changes of circumstances
59A.   Notice of change of circumstances given electronically

PART 8
Decisions on questions
60.   Decisions by a relevant authority
61.   Notification of decision

PART 9
Awards or payments of benefit
62.   Time and manner of granting council tax benefit
63.   Person to whom benefit is to be paid
64.   Shortfall in benefit
65.   Payment on the death of the person entitled
66.   Offsetting

PART 10
Excess benefit
67.   Meaning of excess benefit
68.   Recoverable excess benefit
69.   Authority by which recovery may be made
70.   Persons from whom recovery may be sought
71.   Methods of recovery
72.   Further provision as to recovery of excess benefit
73.   Diminution of capital
74.   Sums to be deducted in calculating recoverable excess benefit
75.   Recovery of excess benefit from prescribed benefits

PART 11
Information
SECTION 1
Claims and information
76.   Interpretation
77.   Collection of information
78.   Recording and holding information
79.   Forwarding of information
80.   Request for information

SECTION 2
Information between authorities etc.
81.   Information to be supplied by an authority to another authority
82.   Supply of information: extended payments (severe disablement allowance and incapacity benefit)

SCHEDULES
A1.   Schedule A1
1.   Applicable amounts
2.   Sums disregarded from claimant's earnings
3.   Amounts to be disregarded in the calculation of income other than earnings
4.   Capital disregards

5. Extended payments (severe disablement allowance and incapacity benefit) of council tax benefit
6. Amount of alternative maximum council tax benefit
7. Matters to be included in the decision notice
8. Electronic communication

PART 1
General

Citation and commencement

1.–(1) These Regulations may be cited as the Council Tax Benefit (Persons who have attained the qualifying age for state pension credit) Regulations 2006.

(2) These Regulations are to be read, where appropriate, with the Consequential Provisions Regulations.

(3) Except as provided in Schedule 4 to the Consequential Provisions Regulations, these Regulations shall come into force on 6th March 2006.

(4) The regulations consolidated by these Regulations are revoked, in consequence of the consolidation, by the Consequential Provisions Regulations.

Interpretation

2.–(1) In these Regulations–

"the Act" means the Social Security Contributions and Benefits Act 1992;

"the Administration Act" means the Social Security Administration Act 1992;

"the 1973 Act" means the Employment and Training Act 1973;

"the 1992 Act" means the Local Government Finance Act 1992;

[² "the 2000 Act" means the Electronic Communications Act 2000;]

"Abbeyfield Home" means an establishment run by the Abbeyfield Society including all bodies corporate or incorporate which are affiliated to that Society;

"adoption leave" means   a period of absence from work on ordinary or additional adoption leave by virtue of section 75A or 75B of the Employment Rights Act 1996;

"alternative maximum council tax benefit" means the amount determined in accordance with regulation 46 and Schedule 6;

"appropriate DWP office" means an office of the Department for Work and Pensions dealing with state pension credit or an office which is normally open to the public for the receipt of claims for income support or a jobseeker's allowance;

"assessment period" means the period determined–

(a) in relation to the earnings of a self-employed earner, in accordance with regulation 27 for the purpose of calculating the weekly earnings of the claimant; or

(b) in relation to any other income, in accordance with regulation 23 for the purpose of calculating the weekly income of the claimant;

"attendance allowance" means–

(a) an attendance allowance under Part 3 of the Act;

(b) an increase of disablement pension under section 104 or 105 of the Act;

(c) a payment under regulations made in exercise of the power conferred by paragraph 7(2)(b) of Part 2 of Schedule 8 to the Act;

(d) an increase of an allowance which is payable in respect of constant attendance under paragraph 4 of Part 1 of Schedule 8 to the Act;

(e) a payment by virtue of article 14, 15, 16, 43 or 44 of the Personal Injuries (Civilians) Scheme 1983 or any analogous payment; or

(f) any payment based on need for attendance which is paid as part of a war disablement pension;

"the benefit Acts" means the Act, the Jobseekers Act and the State Pension Credit Act;

"benefit week" means a period of 7 consecutive days commencing upon a Monday and ending on a Sunday;

"board and lodging accommodation" means accommodation provided to a person or, if he is a member of a family, to him or any other member of his family, for a charge which is inclusive of the provision of that accommodation and at least some cooked or prepared meals which both are cooked or prepared (by a person other than the person to whom the accommodation is provided or a member of his family) and are consumed in that accommodation or associated premises;

"care home" in England and Wales has the meaning assigned to it by section 3 of the Care Standards Act 2000 and in Scotland means a care home service within the meaning assigned to it by section 2(3) of the Regulation of Care (Scotland) Act 2001;

"carer's allowance" means carer's allowance under section 70 of the Act;

"child" means a person under the age of 16;

"child tax credit" means a child tax credit under section 8 of the Tax Credits Act;

"the Children Order" means the Children (Northern Ireland) Order 1995;

"claim" means a claim for council tax benefit;

"claimant" means a person claiming council tax benefit;

"close relative" means a parent, parent-in-law, son, son-in-law, daughter, daughter-in-law, step-parent, step-son, step-daughter, brother, sister, or if any of the preceding persons is one member of a couple, the other member of that couple;

"concessionary payment" means a payment made under arrangements made by the Secretary of State with the consent of the Treasury which is charged either to the National Insurance Fund or to a Departmental Expenditure Vote to which payments of benefit under the Act are charged;

"the Consequential Provisions Regulations" means the Housing Benefit and Council Tax Benefit (Consequential Provisions) Regulations 2006;

"council tax benefit" means council tax benefit under Part 7 of the Act;

"couple" means–
  (a) a man and a woman who are married to each other and are members of the same household;
  (b) a man and a woman who are not married to each other but are living together as husband and wife;
  (c) two people of the same sex who are civil partners of each other and are members of the same household; or
  (d) two people of the same sex who are not civil partners of each other but are living together as if they were civil partners,

and for the purposes of sub-paragraph (d), two people of the same sex are to be regarded as living together as if they were civil partners if, but only if, they would be regarded as living together as husband and wife were they instead two people of the opposite sex;

"course of study" means any course of study, whether or not it is a sandwich course and whether or not a grant is made for undertaking or attending it;

"date of claim" means the date on which the claim is made, or treated as made, for the purposes of regulation 53 (time and manner in which claims are to be made);

"the Decisions and Appeals Regulations" means the Housing Benefit and Council Tax Benefit (Decisions and Appeals) Regulations 2001;

"designated authority" means any of the following–
  (a) the Secretary of State;
  (b) a person providing services to the Secretary of State;

(c)   a local authority;

(d)   a person providing services to, or authorised to exercise any functions of, any such authority;

"designated office" means the office designated by the relevant authority for the receipt of claims to council tax benefit–

(a)   by notice upon or with a form approved by it for the purpose of claiming council tax benefit; or

(b)   by reference upon or with such a form to some other document available from it and sent by electronic means or otherwise on application and without charge; or

(c)   by any combination of the provisions set out in sub-paragraphs (a) and (b) above;

"disability living allowance" means a disability living allowance under section 71 of the Act;

"dwelling" has the same meaning in section 3 or 72 of the 1992 Act;

"earnings" has the meaning prescribed in regulation 25 or, as the case may be, 28;

"the Eileen Trust" means the charitable trust of that name established on 29th March 1993 out of funds provided by the Secretary of State for the benefit of persons eligible for payment in accordance with its provisions;

[² "electronic communication" has the same meaning as in section 15(1) of the 2000 Act;]

"employed earner" is to be construed in accordance with section 2(1)(a) of the Act and also includes a person who is in receipt of a payment which is payable under any enactment having effect in Northern Ireland and which corresponds to statutory sick pay or statutory maternity pay;

"extended payment (severe disablement allowance and incapacity benefit)" means council tax benefit allowed pursuant to regulation 44;

"family" has the meaning assigned to it by section 137(1) of the Act;

"the Fund" means moneys made available from time to time by the Secretary of State for the benefit of persons eligible for payment in accordance with the provisions of a scheme established by him on 24th April 1992 or, in Scotland, on 10th April 1992;

"gateway office" means an appropriate DWP office or an office designated by the appropriate authority which is nominated by the Secretary of State as a gateway office and referred to in a notice upon or attached to a form approved by the appropriate authority for the purpose of claiming council tax benefit;

[¹ "the Graduated Retirement Benefit Regulations" means the Social Security (Graduated Retirement Benefit) Regulations 2005;]

"guarantee credit" is to be construed in accordance with sections 1 and 2 of the State Pension Credit Act;

"a guaranteed income payment" means a payment made under article 14(1)(b) or article 21(1)(a) of the Armed Forces and Reserve Forces (Compensation Scheme) Order 2005;

"housing benefit" means housing benefit under Part 7 of the Act;

"the Housing Benefit Regulations" means the Housing Benefit Regulations 2006;

"Immigration and Asylum Act" means the Immigration and Asylum Act 1999;

"an income-based jobseeker's allowance" and "a joint-claim jobseeker's allowance" have the same meaning as they have in the Jobseekers Act by virtue of section 1(4) of that Act;

"Income Support Regulations" means the Income Support (General) Regulations 1987;

"independent hospital" in England and Wales has the meaning assigned to it by section 2 of the Care Standards Act 2000 and in Scotland means an independent healthcare service as defined in section 2(5)(a) and (b) of the Regulation of Care (Scotland) Act 2001;

"the Independent Living Fund" means the charitable trust established out of funds provided by the Secretary of State for the purpose of providing financial assistance to those persons incapacitated by or otherwise suffering from very severe disablement who are in need of such assistance to enable them to live independently;

[5 "the Independent Living Fund (2006)" means the Trust of that name established by a deed dated 10th April 2006 and made between the Secretary of State for Work and Pensions of the one part and Margaret Rosemary Cooper, Michael Beresford Boyall and Marie Theresa Martin of the other part;]

"the Independent Living Funds" means the Independent Living Fund, [5 the Independent Living (Extension) Fund, the Independent Living (1993) Fund and the Independent Living Fund (2006)];

"the Independent Living (Extension) Fund" means the Trust of that name established by a deed dated 25th February 1993 and made between the Secretary of State for Social Security of the one part and Robin Glover Wendt and John Fletcher Shepherd of the other part;

"the Independent Living (1993) Fund" means the Trust of that name established by a deed dated 25th February 1993 and made between the Secretary of State for Social Security of the one part and Robin Glover Wendt and John Fletcher Shepherd of the other part;

"invalid carriage or other vehicle" means a vehicle propelled by petrol engine or by electric power supplied for use on the road and to be controlled by the occupant;

"Jobseekers Act" means the Jobseekers Act 1995;

"Jobseeker's Allowance Regulations" means the Jobseeker's Allowance Regulations 1996;

"The London Bombing Relief Charitable Fund" means the company limited by guarantee (number 5505072) and registered charity of that name established on 11th July 2005 for the purpose of (amongst other things) relieving sickness, disability or financial need of victims (including families or dependants of victims) of the terrorist attacks carried out in London on 7th July 2005;

"lone parent" means a person who has no partner and who is responsible for and a member of the same household as a child or young person;

[7]

"the Macfarlane (Special Payments) Trust" means the trust of that name, established on 29th January 1990 partly out of funds provided by the Secretary of State, for the benefit of certain persons suffering from haemophilia;

"the Macfarlane (Special Payments) (No. 2) Trust" means the trust of that name, established on 3rd May 1991 partly out of funds provided by the Secretary of State, for the benefit of certain persons suffering from haemophilia and other beneficiaries;

"the Macfarlane Trust" means the charitable trust, established partly out of funds provided by the Secretary of State to the Haemophilia Society, for the relief of poverty or distress among those suffering from haemophilia;

"maternity leave" means a period during which a woman is absent from work because she is pregnant or has given birth to a child, and at the end of which she has a right to return to work either under the terms of her contract of employment or under Part 8 of the Employment Rights Act 1996;

"member of a couple" means a member of a married or unmarried couple;

"mobility supplement" means a supplement to which paragraph 5(1)(a)(v) of Schedule 2 refers;

"net earnings" means such earnings as are calculated in accordance with regulation 26;

"net profit" means such profit as is calculated in accordance with regulation 29;

"non-dependant" has the meaning prescribed in regulation 3;

"non-dependant deduction" means a deduction that is to be made under regulation 42;

"occupational pension" means any pension or other periodical payment under an occupational pension scheme but does not include any discretionary payment out of a fund established for relieving hardship in particular cases;

"partner" means–

(a)   where a claimant is a member of a couple, the other member of that couple; or

(b)   where a claimant is polygamously married to two or more members of his household, any such member to whom he is married;

"paternity leave" means a period of absence from work on leave by virtue of section 80A or 80B of the Employment Rights Act 1996;

"payment" includes part of a payment;

"pension fund holder" means with respect to a personal pension scheme or [4 an occupational pension scheme], the trustees, managers or scheme administrators, as the case may be, of the scheme [4] concerned;

"person affected" shall be construed in accordance with regulation 3 of the Decisions and Appeals Regulations;

"person on income support" means a person in receipt of income support;

"person on state pension credit" means a person in receipt of state pension credit;

[4 "personal pension scheme" means–

(a)   a personal pension scheme as defined by section 1 of the Pension Schemes Act 1993;

(b)   an annuity contract or trust scheme approved under section 620 or 621 of the Income and Corporation Taxes Act 1988 or a substituted contract within the meaning of section 622(3) of that Act which is treated as having become a registered pension scheme by virtue of paragraph 1(1)(f) of Schedule 36 to the Finance Act 2004;

(c)   a personal pension scheme approved under Chapter 4 of Part 14 of the Income and Corporation Taxes Act 1988 which is treated as having become a registered pension scheme by virtue of paragraph 1(1)(g) of Schedule 36 to the Finance Act 2004;]

"policy of life insurance" means any instrument by which the payment of money is assured on death (except death by accident only) or by the happening of any contingency dependent on human life, or any instrument evidencing a contract which is subject to payment of premiums for a term dependent on human life;

"polygamous marriage" means any marriage to which section 133(1) of the Act refers;

"qualifying age for state pension credit" means (in accordance with section 1(2)(b) and (6) of the State Pension Credit Act)–

(a)   in the case of a woman, pensionable age; or

(b)   in the case of a man, the age which is pensionable age in the case of a woman born on the same day as the man;

"qualifying course" means a qualifying course as defined for the purposes of Parts 2 and 4 of the Jobseeker's Allowance Regulations;

"qualifying person" means a person in respect of whom payment has been made from the Fund, the Eileen Trust; the Skipton Fund or the London Bombings Relief Charitable Fund;

"relative" means a close relative, grandparent, grandchild, uncle, aunt, nephew or niece;

"relevant authority" means an authority administering council tax benefit;

"remunerative work" has the meaning prescribed in regulation 6;

"rent" means "eligible rent" to which regulation 12 of the Housing Benefit (Persons who have attained the qualifying age for state pension credit) Regulations 2006 refers, less any deductions in respect of non-dependants which fall to be made under regulation 55 (non-dependant deductions) of those Regulations;

"resident" has the meaning it has in Part 1 or 2 of the 1992 Act;

[⁴]

"sandwich course" has the meaning given in regulation 5(2) of the Education (Student Support) Regulations 2002, regulation 5(2) of the Education (Student Loans)(Scotland) Regulations 2000 or regulation 5(2) of the Education (Student Support) Regulations (Northern Ireland)2001, as the case may be;

"savings credit" shall be construed in accordance with sections 1 and 3 of the State Pension Credit Act;

"second adult" has the meaning given to it in Schedule 6;

"self-employed earner" is to be construed in accordance with section 2(1)(b) of the Act;

"single claimant" means a claimant who neither has a partner nor is a lone parent;

"the Skipton Fund" means the ex-gratia payment scheme administered by the Skipton Fund Limited, incorporated on 25th March 2004, for the benefit of certain persons suffering from hepatitis C and other persons eligible for payment in accordance with the scheme's provisions;

"sports award" means an award made by one of the Sports Councils named in section 23(2) of the National Lottery etc Act 1993 out of sums allocated to it for distribution under that section;

[⁶ "starting rate", where it relates to the rate of tax, has the same meaning as in the Income Tax Act 2007 (see section 989 of that Act);]

"State Pension Credit Act" means the State Pension Credit Act 2002;

"student" means a person, other than a person in receipt of a training allowance, who is attending or undertaking–

    (a)   a course of study at an educational establishment; or

    (b)   a qualifying course;

"tax year" means a period beginning with 6th April in one year and ending with 5th April in the next;

"the Tax Credits Act" means the Tax Credits Act 2002;

"training allowance" means an allowance (whether by way of periodical grants or otherwise) payable–

    (a)   out of public funds by a Government department or by or on behalf of the Secretary of State, Scottish Enterprise or Highlands and Islands Enterprise, the Learning and Skills Council for England or the National Assembly for Wales;

    (b)   to a person for his maintenance or in respect of a member of his family; and

    (c)   for the period, or part of the period, during which he is following a course of training or instruction provided by, or in pursuance of arrangements made with, that department or approved by that department in relation to him or so provided or approved by or on behalf of the Secretary of State, Scottish Enterprise or Highlands and Islands Enterprise or the National Assembly for Wales,

but it does not include an allowance paid by any Government department to or in respect of a person by reason of the fact that he is following a course of full-time education, other than under arrangements made under section 2 of the 1973 Act or is training as a teacher;

"the Trusts" means the Macfarlane Trust, the Macfarlane (Special Payments) Trust and the Macfarlane (Special Payments) (No. 2) Trust;

"voluntary organisation" means a body, other than a public or local authority, the activities of which are carried on otherwise than for profit;

[³]

"water charges" means–

(a) as respects England and Wales, any water and sewerage charges under Chapter 1 of Part 5 of the Water Industry Act 1991;

(b) as respects Scotland, any water and sewerage charges established by Scottish Water under a charges scheme made under section 29A of the Water Industry (Scotland) Act 2002,

in so far as such charges are in respect of the dwelling which a person occupies as his home;

"working tax credit" means a working tax credit under section 10 of the Tax Credits Act;

"Working Tax Credit Regulations" means the Working Tax Credit (Entitlement and Maximum Rate) Regulations 2002;

"young person" has the meaning prescribed in regulation 9(1).

(2) In these Regulations, references to a claimant occupying a dwelling or premises as his home shall be construed in accordance with regulation 7 of the Housing Benefit Regulations.

(3) In these Regulations, where an amount is to be rounded to the nearest penny, a fraction of a penny shall be disregarded if it is less than half a penny and shall otherwise be treated as a whole penny.

(4) For the purpose of these Regulations, a person is on an income-based jobseeker's allowance on any day in respect of which an income-based jobseeker's allowance is payable to him and on any day–

(a) in respect of which he satisfies the conditions for entitlement to an income-based jobseeker's allowance but where the allowance is not paid in accordance with section 19 or 20A of the Jobseekers Act (circumstances in which a jobseeker's allowance is not payable); or

(b) which is a waiting day for the purposes of paragraph 4 of Schedule 1 to that Act and which falls immediately before a day in respect of which an income-based jobseeker's allowance is payable to him or would be payable to him but for section 19 or 20A of that Act;

(c) in respect of which he is a member of a joint-claim couple for the purposes of the Jobseekers Act and no joint-claim jobseeker's allowance is payable in respect of that couple as a consequence of either member of that couple being subject to sanctions for the purposes of section 20A of that Act;

(d) in respect of which an income-based jobseeker's allowance or a joint-claim jobseeker's allowance would be payable but for a restriction imposed pursuant to section 62 or 63 of the Child Support, Pensions and Social Security Act 2000 or section 7, 8 or 9 of the Social Security Fraud Act 2001 (loss of benefit provisions).

(5) For the purposes of these Regulations, two persons shall be taken to be estranged only if their estrangement constitutes a breakdown of the relationship between them.

(6) In these Regulations references to any person in receipt of a guarantee credit, a savings credit or state pension credit includes a reference to a person who would be in receipt thereof but for regulation 13 of the State Pension Credit Regulations 2002 (small amounts of state pension credit).

Amendments

1.   Inserted by reg 12(2) of SI 2005 No 2677 and reg 2 of SI 2006 No 217 as from 6.4.06.

2.   Inserted by Art 5(2) of SI 2006 No 2968 as from 20.12.06.

3.   Omitted by Reg 7(a) of SI 2007 No 1619 as from 3.7.07.
4.   Amended by reg 7(2) of SI 2007 No 1749 as from 16.7.07.
5.   Amended by Art 10 of SI 2007 No 2538 as from 1.10.07.
6.   Inserted by reg 14(2) of SI 2007 No 2618 as from 1.10.07.
7.   Revoked by reg 2 and the Sch of SI 2007 No 2618 as from 1.10.07.

Definition of non-dependant

3.–(1)   In these Regulations, "non-dependant" means any person, except someone to whom paragraph (2) applies, who normally resides with a claimant or with whom a claimant normally resides.

(2)   This paragraph applies to–

(a)   any member of the claimant's family;

(b)   if the claimant is polygamously married, any partner of his and any child or young person who is a member of his household and for whom he or one of his partners is responsible;

(c)   a child or young person who is living with the claimant but who is not a member of his household by virtue of regulation 11 (membership of the same household);

(d)   subject to paragraph (3), any person who, with the claimant, is jointly and severally liable to pay council tax in respect of a dwelling for any day under sections 6, 7 or 75 of the 1992 Act (persons liable to pay council tax);

(e)   subject to paragraph (3), any person who is liable to make payments on a commercial basis to the claimant or the claimant's partner in respect of the occupation of the dwelling;

(f)   a person who lives with the claimant in order to care for him or a partner of his and who is engaged by a charitable or voluntary organisation which makes a charge to the claimant or his partner for the services provided by that person.

(3)   Excepting persons to whom paragraph (2)(a) to (c) and (f) refer, a person to whom any of the following sub-paragraphs applies shall be a non-dependant–

(a)   a person who resides with the person to whom he is liable to make payments in respect of the dwelling and either–

(i)   that person is a close relative of his or his partner; or

(ii)   the tenancy or other agreement between them is other than on a commercial basis;

(b)   a person whose liability to make payments in respect of the dwelling appears to the relevant authority to have been created to take advantage of the council tax benefit scheme except someone who was, for any period within the eight weeks prior to the creation of the agreement giving rise to the liability to make such payments, otherwise liable to make payments of rent in respect of the same dwelling;

(c)   a person who becomes jointly and severally liable with the claimant for council tax in respect of a dwelling and who was, at any time during the period of eight weeks prior to his becoming so liable, a non-dependant of one or more of the other residents in that dwelling who are so liable for the tax, unless the relevant authority is satisfied that the change giving rise to the new liability was not made to take advantage of the council tax benefit scheme.

Section 1(1A) of the Administration Act disapplied

4.   Section 1(1A) of the Administration Act (requirement to state national insurance number) shall not apply in the case of a child or young person in respect of whom council tax benefit is claimed.

Application of Regulations

5.–(1)   Except as provided in paragraph (2), these Regulations apply in relation to a person who has attained the qualifying age for state pension credit.

(2)   These Regulations shall not apply in relation to any person if he or, if he has a partner, his partner, is a person on income support or on an income-based jobseeker's allowance.

Remunerative work

6.–(1)   Subject to the following provisions of this regulation, a person shall be treated for the purposes of these Regulations as engaged in remunerative work if he is engaged, or, where his hours of work fluctuate, he is engaged on average, for not less than 16 hours a week, in work for which payment is made or which is done in expectation of payment.

(2)   Subject to paragraph (3), in determining the number of hours for which a person is engaged in work where his hours of work fluctuate, regard shall be had to the average of hours worked over–

  (a) if there is a recognisable cycle of work, the period of one complete cycle (including, where the cycle involves periods in which the person does no work, those periods but disregarding any other absences);

  (b) in any other case, the period of 5 weeks immediately prior to the date of claim, or such other length of time as may, in the particular case, enable the person's weekly average hours of work to be determined more accurately.

(3)   Where, for the purposes of paragraph (2)(a), a person's recognisable cycle of work at a school, other educational establishment or other place of employment is one year and includes periods of school holidays or similar vacations during which he does not work, those periods and any other periods not forming part of such holidays or vacations during which he is not required to work shall be disregarded in establishing the average hours for which he is engaged in work.

(4)   Where no recognisable cycle has been established in respect of a person's work, regard shall be had to the number of hours or, where those hours will fluctuate, the average of the hours, which he is expected to work in a week.

(5)   A person shall be treated as engaged in remunerative work during any period for which he is absent from work referred to in paragraph (1) if the absence is either without good cause or by reason of a recognised, customary or other holiday.

(6)   A person on income support or an income-based jobseeker's allowance for more than 3 days in any benefit week shall be treated as not being engaged in remunerative work in that week.

(7)   A person shall not be treated as engaged in remunerative work on any day on which the person is on maternity leave, paternity leave or adoption leave, or is absent from work because he is ill.

(8)   A person shall not be treated as engaged in remunerative work on any day on which he is engaged in an activity in respect of which—

  (a) a sports award has been made, or is to be made, to him; and

  (b) no other payment is made or is expected to be made to him.

Persons from abroad

7.–(1)   A person from abroad is a person of a prescribed class for the purposes of section 131(3)(b) of the Act but this paragraph shall not have effect in respect of a person to whom and for a period to which regulation 7A and Schedule A1 apply.

[¹ (2)   In paragraph (1), "person from abroad" means, subject to the following provisions of this regulation, a person who is not habitually resident in the United Kingdom, the Channel Islands, the Isle of Man or the Republic of Ireland.

(3)   No person shall be treated as habitually resident in the United Kingdom, the Channel Islands, the Isle of Man or the Republic of Ireland unless he has a right to reside in (as the case may be) the United Kingdom, the Channel Islands, the Isle

of Man or the Republic of Ireland other than a right to reside which falls within paragraph (4).

(4)   A right to reside falls within this paragraph if it is one which exists by virtue of, or in accordance with, one or more of the following–

(a)   regulation 13 of the Immigration (European Economic Area) Regulations 2006;

(b)   regulation 14 of those Regulations, but only in a case where the right exists under that regulation because the person is–

(i)   a jobseeker for the purpose of the definition of "qualified person" in regulation 6(1) of those Regulations, or

(ii)   a family member (within the meaning of regulation 7 of those Regulations) of such a jobseeker;

(c)   Article 6 of Council Directive No. 2004/38/EC; or

(d)   Article 39 of the Treaty establishing the European Community (in a case where the person is seeking work in the United Kingdom, the Channel Islands, the Isle of Man or the Republic of Ireland).

(4A)   A person is not a person from abroad if he is–

(a)   a worker for the purposes of Council Directive No. 2004/38/EC;

(b)   a self-employed person for the purposes of that Directive;

(c)   a person who retains a status referred to in sub-paragraph (a) or (b) pursuant to Article 7(3) of that Directive;

(d)   a person who is a family member of a person referred to in sub-paragraph (a), (b) or (c) within the meaning of Article 2 of that Directive;

(e)   a person who has a right to reside permanently in the United Kingdom by virtue of Article 17 of that Directive;

[⁵ (f)   a person who is treated as a worker for the purpose of the definition of "qualified person" in regulation 6(1) of the Immigration (European Economic Area) Regulations 2006 pursuant to–

(i)   regulation 5 of the Accession (Immigration and Worker Registration) Regulations 2004 (application of the 2006 Regulations in relation to a national of the Czech Republic, Estonia, Latvia, Lithuania, Hungary, Poland, Slovenia or the Slovak Republic who is an "accession State worker requiring registration"), or

(ii)   regulation 6 of the Accession (Immigration and Worker Authorisation) Regulations 2006 (right of residence of a Bulgarian or Romanian who is an "accession State national subject to worker authorisation");]

(g)   a refugee;

[⁴ (h)   a person who has exceptional leave to enter or remain in the United Kingdom granted outside the rules made under section 3(2) of the Immigration Act 1971;

(hh)   a person who has humanitarian protection granted under those rules;]

(i)   a person who is not a person subject to immigration control within the meaning of section 115(9) of the Immigration and Asylum Act and who is in the United Kingdom as a result of his deportation, expulsion or other removal by compulsion of law from another country to the United Kingdom;

(j)   a person in Great Britain who left the territory of Montserrat after 1st November 1995 because of the effect on that territory of a volcanic eruption; [³]

[³ (jj)   a person in Great Britain who left Lebanon on or after 12th July 2006 because of the armed conflict there; or]

(k)   on state pension credit.]

(5)   Paragraph 1 of Part 1 of the Schedule to, and regulation 2 as it applies to that paragraph of, the Social Security (Immigration and Asylum) Consequential Amendments Regulations 2000 shall not apply to a person who has been temporarily

without funds for any period, or the aggregate of any periods, exceeding 42 days during any one period of limited leave (including any such period as extended).

(6)　In this regulation–

[²]

"refugee" in this regulation, regulation 7A (entitlement of a refugee to council tax benefit) and Schedule A1 (treatment of claims for council tax benefit by refugees), means a person recorded by the Secretary of State as a refugee within the definition in Article 1 of the Convention relating to the Status of Refugees.

Modifications

Reg 7(4A)(a) to (e) applies in relation to a national of Norway, Iceland, Liechtenstein or Switzerland or a member of her/his family (within the meaning of Article 2 of Council Directive No. 2004/38/EC) as if such a national were a national of a member state. See reg 10 of SI 2006 No 1026 on p1134.

The amendments made by SI 2006 No 1026 do not affect the continued operation of the transitional and savings provided for in reg 12 Social Security (Persons From Abroad) Miscellaneous Amendments Regulations 1996 (see p1054), reg 6 of the Social Security (Habitual Residence) Amendment Regulations 2004 (see p1094) or para 6 of Sch 3 of the HB&CTB(CP) Regs (see p1116). See reg 11 of SI 2006 No 1026 on p1134.

Amendments

1.	Substituted by reg 3(2)(a) of SI 2006 No 1026 as from 30.4.06.
2.	Omitted by reg 3(2)(b) of SI 2006 No 1026 as from 30.4.06.
3.	Amended by reg 8 of SI 2006 No 1981 from 25.7.06 until 31.1.07 only.
4.	Amended by reg 8 of SI 2006 No 2528 as from 9.10.06.
5.	Substituted by reg 8 of SI 2006 No 3341 as from 1.1.07.

Entitlement of a refugee to council tax benefit
7A.

Modification

Reg 7A was inserted by Sch 4 para 3(1) HB&CTB(CP) Regs (see p1129). It only applied to claims for CTB by some refugees. See also Sch A1 inserted by Sch 4 para 3(2) HB&CTB(CP) Regs (p1129).

Amendment

1.	Lapsed by s12(2)(g) of the Asylum and Immigration (Treatment of Claimants, etc.) Act 2004 (for those recorded as refugees after 14.6.07).

Prescribed persons for the purposes of section 131(3)(b) of the Act

8.–(1)　Subject to paragraph (2), a person who is throughout any day referred to in section 131(3)(a) of the Act absent from the dwelling referred to in that section, shall be a prescribed person for the purposes of section 131(3)(b) of the Act in relation to that day.

(2)　A person shall not, in relation to any day which falls within a period of temporary absence from that dwelling, be a prescribed person under paragraph (1).

(3)　In paragraph (2), a "period of temporary absence" means–

(a)　a period of absence not exceeding 13 weeks, beginning with the first whole day on which a person resides inresidential accommodation where and for so long as–

(i)　the person resides in that accommodation;

(ii)　the part of the dwelling in which he usually resided is not let or sub-let; and

(iii)　that period of absence does not form part of a longer period of absence from the dwelling of more than 52 weeks,

where he has entered the accommodation for the purpose of ascertaining whether it suits his needs and with the intention of returning to the dwelling if it proves not to suit his needs;

    (b)   a period of absence not exceeding 13 weeks, beginning with the first whole day of absence from the dwelling, where and for so long as–

        (i)   the person intends to return to the dwelling;

        (ii)   the part of the dwelling in which he usually resided is not let or sub-let; and

        (iii)   that period is unlikely to exceed 13 weeks; and

    (c)   a period of absence not exceeding 52 weeks, beginning with the first whole day of that absence, where and for so long as–

        (i)   the person intends to return to the dwelling;

        (ii)   the part of the dwelling in which he usually resided is not let or sub-let;

        (iii)   the person is a person to whom paragraph (4) applies; and

        (iv)   the period of absence is unlikely to exceed 52 weeks or, in exceptional circumstances, is unlikely substantially to exceed that period.

(4)   This paragraph applies to a person who–

    (a)   is detained incustody on remand pending trial or required, as a condition of bail, to reside–

        (i)   in a dwelling, other than the dwelling referred to in paragraph (1); or

        (ii)   in premises approved under section 9 of the Criminal Justice and Court Services Act 2000;

or, is detained in custody pending sentence upon conviction;

    (b)   is resident in a hospital or similar institution as a patient;

    (c)   is undergoing, or his partner or his dependent child is undergoing, in the United Kingdom or elsewhere, medical treatment, or medically approved convalescence, in accommodation other than residential accommodation;

    (d)   is following, in the United Kingdom or elsewhere, a training course;

    (e)   is undertaking medically approved care of a person residing in the United Kingdom or elsewhere;

    (f)   is undertaking the care of a child whose parent or guardian is temporarily absent from the dwelling normally occupied by that parent or guardian for the purpose of receiving medically approved care or medical treatment;

    (g)   is, in the United Kingdom or elsewhere, receiving medically approved care provided in accommodation other than residential accommodation;

    (h)   is a student;

    (i)   is receiving care provided in residential accommodation other than a person to whom paragraph (3)(a) applies; or

    (j)   has left the dwelling he resides in through fear of violence, in that dwelling, or by a person who was formerly a member of the family of the person first mentioned.

(5)   This paragraph applies to a person who is–

    (a)   detained in custody pending sentence upon conviction or under a sentence imposed by a court (other than a person who is detained in hospital under the provisions of the Mental Health Act 1983, or, in Scotland, under the provisions of the Mental Health (Care and Treatment) (Scotland) Act 2003 or the Criminal Procedure (Scotland) Act 1995); and

    (b)   on temporary release from detention in accordance with Rules made under the provisions of the Prison Act 1952 or the Prisons (Scotland) Act 1989.

(6)   Where paragraph (5) applies to a person, then, for any day when he is on temporary release–

    (a)   if such temporary release was immediately preceded by a period of temporary absence under paragraph (3)(b) or (c), he shall be treated, for the purposes of paragraph (1), as if he continues to be absent from the dwelling, despite any return to the dwelling;

    (b)   for the purposes of paragraph (4)(a), he shall be treated as if he remains in detention;

(c)   if he does not fall within sub-paragraph (a), he shall be a prescribed person for the purposes of section 131(3)(b) of the Act.

(7)   In this regulation–

"medically approved" means certified by a medical practitioner;

"patient" means a person who is undergoing medical or other treatment as an in-patient in any hospital or similar institution;

"residential accommodation" means accommodation which is provided–

(a)   in a care home;

(b)   in an independent hospital;

(c)   in an Abbeyfield Home; or

(d)   in an establishment managed or provided by a body incorporated by Royal Charter or constituted by Act of Parliament other than a local social services authority;

"training course" means a course of training or instruction provided wholly or partly by or on behalf of or in pursuance of arrangements made with, or approved by or on behalf of, Scottish Enterprise, Highlands and Islands Enterprise, a government department or the Secretary of State.

PART 2

Membership of a family

Persons of prescribed description for the definition of family in section 137(1) of the Act

9.–(1)   Subject to paragraph (2), a person of a prescribed description for the purposes of section 137(1) of the Act (definition of family) as it applies to council tax benefit is a person [¹ who falls within the definition of qualifying young person in section 142 of the Act (child and qualifying young person)], and in these Regulations such a person is referred to as a "young person".

(2)   Paragraph (1) shall not apply to a person who is–

(a)   on income support or an income-based jobseeker's allowance; [² or]

[³ (b)]

(c)   a person to whom section 6 of the Children (Leaving Care) Act 2000 (exclusion from benefits) applies.

(3)   A person of a prescribed description for the purposes of section 137(1) of the Act as it applies to council tax benefit (definition of the family) includes a child or young person in respect of whom section 145A of the Act applies for the purposes of entitlement to child benefit but only for the period prescribed under section 145A(1) of the Act.

Amendments

1.   Amended by reg 5(2)(a) of SI 2006 No 718 as from 10.4.06.

2.   Inserted by reg 5(2)(b) of SI 2006 No 718 as from 10.4.06.

3.   Omitted by reg 5(2)(c) of SI 2006 No 718 as from 10.4.06.

Circumstances in which a person is to be treated as responsible or not responsible for another

10.–(1)   Subject to the following provisions of this regulation a person shall be treated as responsible for a child or young person who is normally living with him this includes a child or young person to whom paragraph (3) of regulation 9 applies.

(2)   Where a child or young person spends equal amounts of time in different households, or where there is a question as to which household he is living in, the child or young person shall be treated for the purposes of paragraph (1) as normally living with–

(a)   the person who is receiving child benefit in respect of him; or

(b)   if there is no such person–

(i)   where only one claim for child benefit has been made in respect of him, the person who made that claim, or

(ii)   in any other case the person who has the primary responsibility for him.

(3)   For the purposes of these Regulations a child or young person shall be the responsibility of only one person in any benefit week and any person other than the one treated as responsible for the child or young person under this regulation shall be treated as not so responsible.

Circumstances in which a person is to be treated as being or not being a member of the household

11.–(1)   Subject to paragraphs (2) and (3), the claimant and any partner and, where the claimant or his partner is treated as responsible by virtue of regulation 10 (circumstances in which a person is to be treated as responsible or not responsible for another) for a child or young person, that child or young person and any child of that child or young person, shall be treated as members of the same household notwithstanding that any of them is temporarily absent from that household.

(2)   A child or young person shall not be treated as a member of the claimant's household where he is–

(a)   placed with the claimant or his partner by a local authority under section 23(2)(a) of the Children Act 1989 or by a voluntary organisation under section 59(1)(a) of that Act, or in Scotland boarded out with the claimant or his partner under a relevant enactment; or

(b)   placed, or in Scotland boarded out, with the claimant or his partner prior to adoption; or

(c)   placed for adoption with the claimant or his partner in accordance with the Adoption and Children Act 2002 or the Adoption Agencies (Scotland) Regulations 1996.

(3)   Subject to paragraph (4), paragraph (1) shall not apply to a child or young person who is not living with the claimant and he–

(a)   is being looked after by, or in Scotland is in the care of, a local authority under a relevant enactment; or

(b)   has been placed, or in Scotland boarded out, with a person other than the claimant prior to adoption; or

(c)   has been placed for adoption pursuant to a decision under the Adoption Agencies Regulations 1983 or the Adoption Agencies (Scotland) Regulations 1996.

(4)   An authority shall treat a child or young person to whom paragraph (3)(a) applies as being a member of the claimants' household in any benefit week where–

(a)   that child or young person lives with the claimant for part or all of that benefit week; and

(b)   the authority considers that it is reasonable to do so taking into account the nature and frequency of that child's or young person's visits.

(5)   In this regulation "relevant enactment" means the Army Act 1955, the Air Force Act 1955, the Naval Discipline Act 1957, the Matrimonial Proceedings (Children) Act 1958, the Social Work (Scotland) Act 1968, the Family Law Reform Act 1969, the Children and Young Persons Act 1969, the Matrimonial Causes Act 1973, the Children Act 1975, the Domestic Proceedings and Magistrates' Courts Act 1978, the Adoption (Scotland) Act 1978, the Family Law Act 1986, the Children Act 1989 and the Children (Scotland) Act 1995.

PART 3
Applicable amounts

Applicable amounts

12.–(1)   Subject to Schedule A1 (treatment of claims for council tax benefit by refugees), the applicable amount of a person shall be the aggregate of such of the following amounts as apply in his case–

(a)   an amount in respect of his personal allowance, determined in accordance with paragraph 1 of Schedule 1;

(b)   an amount in respect of any child or young person who is a member of his family, determined in accordance with paragraph 2 of that Schedule;

(c)   if he is a member of a family of which at least one member is a child or young person, an amount determined in accordance with paragraph 3(1) of Part 2 of that Schedule (family premium);

(d)   if he is a member of a family of which one member is a child under the age of one year, an additional amount determined in accordance with paragraph 3(2) of Part 2 of that Schedule;

(e)   the amount of any premiums which may be applicable to him, determined in accordance with Parts 3 and 4 of that Schedule (premiums).

[¹ (2)]
[¹ (3)]
[¹ (4)]

[² (5)   In Schedule 1–

"additional spouse" means a spouse by the party to the marriage who is additional to the party to the marriage;

"patient" means a person (other than a person who is serving a sentence of imprisonment or detention in a youth custody institution) who is regarded as receiving free in-patient treatment within the meaning of [³ regulation 2(4) and (5) of the Social Security (Hospital In-Patients) Regulations 2005].]

[¹ (6)]
[¹ (7)]

Amendments

1.   Omitted by reg 3(3)(a) and (c) of SI 2005 No 2502 as amended by Sch 2 para 27 of SI 2006 No 217 as from 1.4.06.

2.   Inserted by reg 3(3)(b) of SI 2005 No 2502 as amended by Sch 2 para 27 of SI 2006 No 217 as from 1.4.06.

3.   Amended by reg 5(1) of SI 2005 No 3360 as amended by Sch 2 para 30 of SI 2006 No 217 as from 10.4.06.

PART 4
Income and capital
SECTION 1
General

Calculation of income and capital of members of claimant's family and of a polygamous marriage

13.–(1)   The income and capital of a claimant's partner which by virtue of section 136(1) of the Act is to be treated as income and capital of the claimant, shall be calculated or estimated in accordance with the following provisions of this Part in like manner as for the claimant; and any reference to the "claimant" shall, except where the context otherwise requires, be construed for the purposes of this Part as if it were a reference to his partner.

(2)   Where a claimant or the partner of a claimant is married polygamously to two or more members of his household–

    (a)   the claimant shall be treated as possessing capital and income belonging to each such member; and

    (b)   the income and capital of that member shall be calculated in accordance with the following provisions of this Part in like manner as for the claimant.

    (3)   The income and capital of a child or young person shall not be treated as the income and capital of the claimant.

Circumstances in which income of non-dependant is to be treated as claimant's

14.–(1)   Where it appears to the relevant authority that a non-dependant and the claimant have entered into arrangements in order to take advantage of the council tax benefit scheme and the non-dependant has more capital and income than the claimant, that authority shall treat the claimant as possessing capital and income belonging to that non-dependant and, in such a case, shall disregard any capital and income which the claimant does possess.

    (2)   Where a claimant is treated as possessing capital and income belonging to a non-dependant under paragraph (1) the capital and income of that non-dependant shall be calculated in accordance with the following provisions of this Part in like manner as for the claimant and any reference to the "claimant" shall, except where the context otherwise requires, be construed for the purposes of this Part as if it were a reference to that non-dependant.

SECTION 2
Income and capital

Calculation of income and capital

15.   The income and capital of–

    (a)   the claimant; and

    (b)   any partner of the claimant,

shall be calculated in accordance with the rules set out in this Section; and any reference in this Part to the claimant shall apply equally to any partner of the claimant.

Claimant in receipt of guarantee credit

16.   In the case of a claimant who is in receipt, or whose partner is in receipt, of a guarantee credit, the whole of his capital and income shall be disregarded.

Calculation of claimant's income in savings credit only cases

17.–(1)   In determining the income and capital of a claimant who has, or whose partner has, an award of state pension credit comprising only the savings credit, the relevant authority shall, subject to the following provisions of this regulation, use the calculation or estimate of the claimant's or as the case may be, the claimant's partner's income and capital made by the Secretary of State for the purpose of determining that award.

    (2)   The Secretary of State shall provide the relevant authority with details of the calculation or estimate–

    (a)   if the claimant is allowed council tax benefit or claimed council tax benefit, within the two working days following the day the calculation or estimate was determined, or as soon as reasonably practicable thereafter; or

    (b)   if sub-paragraph (a) does not apply, within the two working days following the day he receives information from the relevant authority that the claimant or his partner has claimed council tax benefit, or as soon as reasonably practicable thereafter.

    (3)   The details provided by the Secretary of State shall include the amount taken into account in that determination in respect of the net income of the person claiming state pension credit.

(4)   The relevant authority shall modify the amount of the net income provided by the Secretary of State only in so far as necessary to take into account–
(a)   the amount of any savings credit payable;
(b)   in respect of any dependent children of the claimant, child care charges taken into account under regulation 20(1)(c);
(c)   the higher amount disregarded under these Regulations in respect of–
    (i)   lone parent's earnings; or
    (ii)   payments of maintenance, whether under a court order or not, which is made or due to be made by–
        (aa)   the claimant's former partner, or the claimant's partner's former partner; or
        (bb)   the parent of a child or young person where that child or young person is a member of the claimant's family except where that parent is the claimant or the claimant's partner;
(d)   any amount to be disregarded by virtue of paragraph 9(1) of Schedule 2;
(e)   the income and capital of any partner of the claimant who is treated as a member of the claimant's household under regulation 11, to the extent that it is not taken into account in determining the net income of the person claiming state pension credit;
(f)   regulation 14 (circumstances in which income of a non-dependant is to be treated as claimant's), if the relevant authority determines that this provision applies in the claimant's case;
(g)   any modification under section 139(6) of the Administration Act (modifications by resolution of an authority) which is applicable in the claimant's case.
(5)   Regulations 19 to 39 shall not apply to the amount of the net income to be taken into account by the local authority under paragraph (1), but shall apply (so far as relevant) for the purpose of determining any modifications which fall to be made to that amount under paragraph (4).
(6)   The relevant authority shall for the purpose of determining the claimant's entitlement to council tax benefit use, except where paragraphs (7) and (8) apply, the calculation of the claimant's capital made by the Secretary of State, and shall in particular apply the provisions of regulation 33 if the claimant's capital is calculated as being in excess of £16,000.
(7)   If paragraph (8) applies, the relevant authority shall calculate the claimant's capital in accordance with regulations 33 to 39 below.
(8)   This paragraph applies if–
(a)   the Secretary of State notifies the relevant authority that the claimant's capital has been determined as being £16,000 or less;
(b)   subsequent to that determination the claimant's capital rises to more than £16,000; and
(c)   the increase occurs whilst there is in force an assessed income period within the meaning of sections 6 and 9 of the State Pension Credit Act.

Calculation of income and capital where state pension credit is not payable
    18.   Where neither regulation 16 nor 17 applies in the claimant's case, his income and capital shall be calculated or estimated by the relevant authority in accordance with regulations 19 to 39 below.

Meaning of "income"
    19.–(1)   For the purposes of these Regulations, "income" means income of any of the following descriptions–
(a)   earnings;
(b)   working tax credit;

(c)   retirement pension income within the meaning of the State Pension Credit Act;

(d)   income from annuity contracts (other than retirement pension income);

(e)   a war disablement pension or war widow's or widower'' pension;

(f)   a foreign war disablement pension or war widow's or widower's pension;

(g)   a guaranteed income payment;

(h)   a payment made under article 21(1)(c) of the Armed Forces and Reserve Forces (Compensation Scheme) Order 2005 but only where the condition referred to in article 23(2)(c) is met;

(i)   income from capital other than capital disregarded under Part 1 of Schedule 4;

(j)   social security benefits, other than retirement pension income or any of the following benefits–

  (i)   disability living allowance;
  (ii)   attendance allowance payable under section 64 of the Act;
  (iii) an increase of disablement pension under section 104 or 105 of the Act;
  (iv)   a payment under regulations made in exercise of the power conferred by paragraph 7(2)(b) of Part 2 of Schedule 8 to the Act;
  (v)   an increase of an allowance payable in respect of constant attendance under paragraph 4 of Part 1 of Schedule 8 to the Act;
  (vi)   child benefit;
  (vii) any guardian's allowance payable under section 77 of the Act;
  (viii) any increase for a dependant, other than the claimant's partner, payable in accordance with Part 4 of the Act;
  (ix)   any social fund payment made under Part 8 of the Act;
  (x)   Christmas bonus payable under Part 10 of the Act;
  (xi)   housing benefit;
  (xii) council tax benefit;
  (xiii) bereavement payment;
  (xiv) statutory sick pay;
  (xv)   statutory maternity pay;
  (xvi) statutory paternity pay payable under Part 12ZA of the Act;
  (xvii) statutory adoption pay payable under Part 12ZB of the Act;
  (xviii) any benefit similar to those mentioned in the preceding provisions of this paragraph payable under legislation having effect in Northern Ireland;

(k)   all foreign social security benefits which are similar to the social security benefits prescribed above;

(l)   any payment made under article 37 of the Naval, Military and Air Forces etc. (Disablement and Death) Service Pensions Order 1983;

(m)   a pension paid to victims of National Socialist persecution under any special provision made by the law of the Federal Republic of Germany, or any part of it, or of the Republic of Austria;

(n)   payments under a scheme made under the Pneumoconiosis etc. (Worker's Compensation) Act 1979;

(o)   payments made towards the maintenance of the claimant by his spouse, civil partner, former spouse or former civil partner or towards the maintenance of the claimant's partner by his spouse, civil partner, former spouse or former civil partner, including payments made–

  (i)   under a court order;
  (ii)   under an agreement for maintenance; or
  (iii) voluntarily;

(p)   payments due from any person in respect of board and lodging accommodation provided by the claimant;

(q) payments consisting of royalties or other sums received as a consideration for the use of, or the right to use, any copyright, patent or trade mark;

(r) any payment made to the claimant in respect of any book registered under the Public Lending Right Scheme 1982;

(s) any payment, other than a payment ordered by a court or made in settlement of a claim, made by or on behalf of a former employer of a person on account of the early retirement of that person on grounds of ill-health or disability;

(t) any sum payable by way of pension out of money provided under the Civil List Act 1837, the Civil List Act 1937, the Civil List Act 1952, the Civil List Act 1972 or the Civil List Act 1975;

(u) any income in lieu of that specified in sub-paragraphs (a) to (r);

(v) any payment of rent made to a claimant who–

    (i) owns the freehold or leasehold interest in any property or is a tenant of any property;

    (ii) occupies part of the property; and

    (iii) has an agreement with another person allowing that person to occupy that property on payment of rent; [1]

(w) any payment made at regular intervals under an equity release scheme.

[² (x) PPF periodic payments within the meaning of section 17(1) of the State Pension Credit Act.]

(2) For the purposes of these Regulations, a claimant'scapital, other than capital disregarded under Schedule 4, shall be treated as if it were a weekly income–

(a) in the case of a claimant residing permanently in accommodation to which paragraph (6) applies, of £1 for each £500 in excess of £10,000 and £1 for any excess which is not a complete £500;

(b) in any other case, of £1 for each £500 in excess of £6,000 and £1 for any excess which is not a complete £500.

(3) Where the payment of any social security benefit prescribed under paragraph (1) is subject to any deduction (other than an adjustment specified in paragraph (5)) the amount to be taken into account under paragraph (1) shall be the amount before the deduction is made.

(4) Where an award of any working tax credit or child tax credit is subject to a deduction by way of recovery of an overpayment of working tax credit or child tax credit which arose in a previous tax year the amount to be taken into account under paragraph (1) shall be the amount of working tax credit or child tax credit awarded less the amount of that deduction.

(5) The adjustments specified in this paragraph are those made in accordance with–

(a) the Social Security (Overlapping Benefits) Regulations 1979;

(b) the Social Security (Hospital In-Patients) Regulations 1975;

(c) section 30DD or section 30E of the Act (reductions in incapacity benefit in respect of pensions and councillor's allowances).

(6) This paragraph applies to accommodation provided–

(a) in a care home;

(b) in an Abbeyfield home;

(c) under section 3 of, and Part 2 of the Schedule to, the Polish Resettlement Act 1947 (provision of accommodation) where the claimant requires personal care;

(d) in an independent hospital.

(7) For the purposes of paragraph (6), a person shall be treated as residing permanently in the accommodation–

(a) except where sub-paragraph (b) applies, notwithstanding that he is absent from it for a period not exceeding 52 weeks;

(b) if it is accommodation to which paragraph (6)(c) applies–

(i) notwithstanding that he is absent from it for a period not exceeding 13 weeks; and

(ii) if he, with the agreement of the manager of the home, intends to return to it in due course.

(8) In paragraph (1)(w), "equity release scheme" means a loan–

(a) made between a person ("the lender") and the claimant;

(b) by means of which a sum of money is advanced by the lender to the claimant by way of payments at regular intervals; and

(c) which is secured on a dwelling in which the claimant owns an estate or interest and which he occupies as his home.

Amendments

1.   Omitted by reg 11(2)(a) of SI 2006 No 518 as from 6.4.04.

2.   Inserted by reg 11(2)(b) of SI 2006 No 518 as from 6.4.04.

Calculation of income on a weekly basis

20.–(1) Subject to regulation 24 (disregard of changes in tax, contributions etc.), for the purposes of section 131(5) of the Act (conditions for entitlement to council tax benefit) the claimant's income shall be calculated on a weekly basis–

(a) by calculating or estimating the amount which is likely to be his average weekly income in accordance with this Part;

(b) by adding to that amount the weekly income calculated under regulation 19(2);

(c) by then deducting any relevant child care charges to which regulation 21 (treatment of child care charges) applies from any earnings which form part of the average weekly income or, in a case where the conditions in paragraph (2) are met, from those earnings plus whichever credit specified in sub-paragraph (b) of that paragraph is appropriate, up to a maximum deduction in respect of the claimant's family of whichever of the sums specified in paragraph (3) applies in his case.

(2) The conditions of this paragraph are that–

(a) the claimant's earnings which form part of his average weekly income are less than the lower of either his relevant child care charges or whichever of the deductions specified in paragraph (3) otherwise applies in his case; and

(b) that claimant or, if he is a member of a couple either the claimant or his partner, is in receipt of working tax credit or child tax credit.

(3) The maximum deduction to which paragraph (1)(c) above refers shall be–

(a) where the claimant's family includes only one child in respect of whom relevant child care charges are paid, [² £175.00] per week;

(b) where the claimant's family includes more than one child in respect of whom relevant child care charges are paid, [² £300] per week.

Amendments

1.   Confirmed by Art 22(3) of SI 2006 No 645 and reg 8 of SI 2006 No 217 as from 1.4.06.

2.   Confirmed by Art 22(2) of SI 2007 No 688 as from 1.4.07.

Treatment of child care charges

21.–(1) This regulation applies where a claimant is incurring relevant child care charges and–

(a) is a lone parent and is engaged in remunerative work;

(b) is a member of a couple both of whom are engaged in remunerative work; or

(c) is a member of a couple where one member is engaged in remunerative work and the other–

(i) is incapacitated;

(ii) is an in-patient in hospital; or

      (iii)   is in prison (whether serving a custodial sentence or remanded in custody awaiting trial or sentence).

(2)   For the purposes of paragraph (1) and subject to paragraph (4), a person to whom paragraph (3) applies shall be treated as engaged in remunerative work for a period not exceeding 28 weeks during which he–

(a)   is paid statutory sick pay;

(b)   is paid short-term incapacity benefit at the lower rate under sections 30A to 30E of the Act;

(c)   is paid income support on the grounds of incapacity for work under regulation 4ZA of, and paragraph 7 or 14 of Schedule 1B to, the Income Support (General) Regulations 1987; or

(d)   is credited with earnings on the grounds of incapacity for work under regulation 8B of the Social Security (Credits) Regulations 1975.

(3)   This paragraph applies to a person who was engaged in remunerative work immediately before–

(a)   the first day of the period in respect of which he was first paid statutory sick pay, short-term incapacity benefit or income support on the grounds of incapacity for work; or

(b)   the first day of the period in respect of which earnings are credited, as the case may be.

(4)   In a case to which paragraph (2)(c) or (d) applies, the period of 28 weeks begins on the day on which the person is first paid income support or on the first day of the period in respect of which earnings are credited, as the case may be.

(5)   Relevant child care charges are those charges for care to which paragraphs (6) and (7) apply, and shall be estimated on a weekly basis in accordance with paragraph (10).

(6)   The charges are paid by the claimant for care which is provided–

(a)   in the case of any child of the claimant's family who is not disabled, in respect of the period beginning on that child's date of birth and ending on the day preceding the first Monday in September following that child's fifteenth birthday; or

(b)   in the case of any child of the claimant's family who is disabled, in respect of the period beginning on that person's date of birth and ending on the day preceding the first Monday in September following that person's sixteenth birthday.

(7)   The charges are paid for care which is provided by one or more of the care providers listed in paragraph (8) and are not paid–

(a)   in respect of the child's compulsory education;

(b)   by a claimant to a partner or by a partner to a claimant in respect of any child for whom either or any of them is responsible in accordance with regulation 10 (circumstances in which a person is treated as responsible or not responsible for another); or

(c)   in respect of care provided by a relative of a child wholly or mainly in the child's home.

(8)   The care to which paragraph (7) refers may be provided–

(a)   out of school hours, by a school on school premises or by a local authority–

      (i)   for children who are not disabled in respect of the period beginning on their eighth birthday and ending on the day preceding the first Monday in September following their fifteenth birthday; or

      (ii) for children who are disabled in respect of the period beginning on their eighth birthday and ending on the day preceding the first Monday in September following their sixteenth birthday;

(b)   by a child care provider approved in accordance with the Tax Credit (New Category of Child Care Provider) Regulations 1999;

(c)   by persons registered under Part 10A of the Children Act 1989;

(d) in schools or establishments which are exempted from registration under Part 10A of the Children Act 1989 by virtue of paragraph 1 or 2 of Schedule 9A to that Act;

(e) by–
    (i) persons registered under section 7(1) of the Regulation of Care (Scotland) Act 2001; or
    (ii) local authorities registered under section 33(1) of that Act,
where the care provided is childminding or day care of children within the meaning of that Act; or

(f) by a person prescribed in regulations made pursuant to section 12(4) of the Tax Credits Act.

(9) In paragraphs (6) and (8)(a), ''the first Monday in September'' means the Monday which first occurs in the month of September in any year.

(10) Relevant child care charges shall be estimated over such period, not exceeding a year, as is appropriate in order that the average weekly charge may be estimated accurately having regard to information as to the amount of that charge provided by the child minder or person providing the care.

(11) For the purposes of paragraph (1)(c) the other member of a couple is to be treated as incapacitated where–

(a) he is aged not less than 80;

(b) he is aged less than 80; and–
    (i) the additional conditions specified in paragraph 13 of Schedule 1 of the Council Tax Benefit Regulations are treated as applying in his case; and
    (ii) he satisfies those conditions or would satisfy them but for his being treated as capable of work by virtue of a determination made in accordance with regulations made under section 171E of the Act;

(c) the claimant (within the meaning of regulation 2(1)) is, or is treated as, incapable of work and has been so incapable, or has been so treated as incapable, of work in accordance with the provisions of, and regulations made under, Part 12A of the Act (incapacity for work) for a continuous period of not less than 196 days; and for this purpose any two or more separate periods separated by a break of not more than 56 days shall be treated as one continuous period;

(d) there is payable in respect of him one or more of the following–
    (i) long-term incapacity benefit or short-term incapacity benefit at the higher rate specified in Schedule 4 to Act;
    (ii) attendance allowance under section 64 of the Act;
    (iii) severe disablement allowance under section 68 of the Act;
    (iv) disability living allowance under section 71 of the Act;
    (v) increase of disablement pension under section 104 of the Act;
    (vi) a pension increase under a war pension scheme or an industrial injuries scheme which is analogous to an allowance or increase of disablement pension under head (ii), (iv) or (v) above;

(e) a pension or allowance to which head (ii), (iv), (v) or (vi) of sub-paragraph (d) above refers was payable on account of his incapacity but has ceased to be payable in consequence of his becoming a patient within the meaning of regulation 12(5) (applicable amounts);

(f) sub-paragraph (c) or (d) would apply to him if the legislative provisions referred to in those sub-paragraphs were provisions under any corresponding enactment having effect in Northern Ireland; or

(g) he has an invalid carriage or other vehicle provided to him by the Secretary of State under section 5(2)(a) of and Schedule 2 to the National Health Service Act 1977 or by Scottish Ministers under section 46 of the National Health Service (Scotland) Act 1978 or provided by the Department of

Health and Social Services for Northern Ireland under Article 30(1) of the
Health and Personal Social Services (Northern Ireland) Order 1972.

(12) For the purposes of paragraph (11), once paragraph (11)(c) applies to the
claimant, if he then ceases, for a period of 56 days or less, to be incapable, or to be
treated as incapable, of work, that paragraph shall, on his again becoming so
incapable, or so treated as incapable, of work at the end of that period, immediately
thereafter apply to him for so long as he remains incapable, or is treated as remaining
incapable, of work.

(13) For the purposes of paragraphs (6) and (8)(a), a person is disabled if he is
a person–

(a) in respect of whom disability living allowance is payable, or has ceased to
be payable solely because he is a patient;

(b) who is registered as blind in a register compiled under section 29 of the
National Assistance Act 1948 (welfare services) or, in Scotland, has been
certified as blind and in consequence he is registered as blind in a register
maintained by or on behalf of a council constituted under section 2 of the
Local Government (Scotland) Act 1999; or

(c) who ceased to be registered as blind in such a register within the period
beginning 28 weeks before the first Monday in September following that
person's fifteenth birthday and ending on the day preceding the first Monday
in September following that person's sixteenth birthday.

(14) For the purposes of paragraph (1) a person on maternity leave, paternity
leave or adoption leave shall be treated as if she is engaged in remunerative work for
the period specified in paragraph (15) ("the relevant period") provided that–

(a) in the week before the period of maternity, paternity leave or adoption leave
began she was in remunerative work;

(b) the claimant is incurring relevant child care charges within the meaning of
paragraph (5); and

(c) she is entitled to statutory maternity pay under section 164 of the Act,
statutory paternity pay by virtue of section 171ZA or 171ZB of the Act,
statutory adoption pay by virtue of section 171ZL of the Act or maternity
allowance under section 35 of the Act.

(15) The relevant period shall begin on the day on which the person's maternity
leave, paternity leave or adoption leave commences and shall end on–

(a) the date that leave ends;

(b) if no child care element of working tax credit is in payment on the date that
entitlement to maternity allowance, statutory maternity pay, statutory
paternity pay or statutory adoption pay ends, the date that entitlement ends;
or

(c) if a child care element of working tax credit is in payment on the date that
entitlement to maternity allowance, statutory maternity pay, statutory
paternity pay or statutory adoption pay ends, the date that entitlement to
that award of the child care element of working tax credit ends,
whichever shall occur first.

(16) In paragraph (15), "child care element" of working tax credit means the
element of working tax credit prescribed under section 12 of the Tax Credits Act
(child care element).

Calculation of average weekly income from tax credits

22.–(1) This regulation applies where a claimant receives a tax credit.

(2) Where this regulation applies, the period over which a tax credit is to be
taken into account shall be the period set out in paragraph (3).

(3) Where the instalment in respect of which payment of a tax credit is made
is–

(a)   a daily instalment, the period is 1 day, being the day in respect of which the instalment is paid;

(b)   a weekly instalment, the period is 7 days, ending on the day on which the instalment is due to be paid;

(c)   a two weekly instalment, the period is 14 days, commencing 6 days before the day on which the instalment is due to be paid;

(d)   a four weekly instalment, the period is 28 days, ending on the day on which the instalment is due to be paid.

(4)   For the purposes of this regulation "tax credit" means working tax credit.

Calculation of weekly income

23.–(1)   Except where paragraphs (2) and (4) apply, for the purposes of calculating the weekly income of the claimant, where the period in respect of which a payment is made–

(a)   does not exceed a week, the whole of that payment shall be included in the claimant's weekly income;

(b)   exceeds a week, the amount to be included in the claimant's weekly income shall be determined–

(i)   in a case where that period is a month, by multiplying the amount of the payment by 12 and dividing the product by 52;

(ii)   in a case where that period is three months, by multiplying the amount of the payment by 4 and dividing the product by 52;

(iii)   in a case where that period is a year, by dividing the amount of the payment by 52;

(iv)   in any other case, by multiplying the amount of the payment by 7 and dividing the product by the number of days in the period in respect of which it is made.

(2)   Where–

(a)   the claimant's regular pattern of work is such that he does not work the same hours every week; or

(b)   the amount of the claimant's income fluctuates and has changed more than once,

the weekly amount of that claimant's income shall be determined–

(i)   if, in a case to which sub-paragraph (a) applies, there is a recognised cycle of work, by reference to his average weekly income over the period of the complete cycle (including, where the cycle involves periods in which the claimant does no work, those periods but disregarding any other absences); or

(ii)   in any other case, on the basis of–

(aa)   the last two payments if those payments are one month or more apart;

(bb)   the last four payments if the last two payments are less than one month apart; or

(cc)   calculating or estimating such other payments as may, in the particular circumstances of the case, enable the claimant's average weekly income to be determined more accurately.

(3)   For the purposes of paragraph (2)(b) the last payments are the last payments before the date the claim was made or treated as made or, if there is a subsequent supersession under paragraph 4 of Schedule 7 to the Child Support, Pensions and Social Security Act 2000, the last payments before the date of the supersession.

(4)   If a claimant is entitled to receive a payment to which paragraph (5) applies, the amount of that payment shall be treated as if made in respect of a period of a year.

(5)   This paragraph applies to–

(a) royalties or other sums payable as a consideration for the use of, or the right to use, any copyright, patent or trade mark;

(b) any payment made to the claimant in respect of any book registered under the Public Lending Right Scheme 1982; and

(c) any payment which is made on an occasional basis.

(6) The period under which any benefit under the benefit Acts is to be taken into account shall be the period in respect of which that benefit is payable.

(7) Where payments are made in a currency other than Sterling, the value of the payment shall be determined by taking the Sterling equivalent on the date the payment is made.

(8) The sums specified in Schedule 2 shall be disregarded in calculating–

(a) the claimant's earnings; and

(b) any amount to which paragraph (5) applies if the claimant or his partner is the first owner of the copyright, patent or trade mark, or the author of the book registered under the Public Lending Right Scheme 1982.

(9) Income specified in Schedule 3 is to be disregarded in the calculation of a claimant's income.

[² (10)]

(11) Schedule 4 shall have effect so that–

(a) the capital specified in Part 1 shall be disregarded for the purpose of determining a claimant's income; and

(b) the capital specified in Part 2 shall be disregarded for the purpose of determining a claimant's income under regulation 19(2).

(12) In the case of any income taken into account for the purpose of calculating a person's income, there shall be disregarded any amount payable by way of tax.

[² (13)]

[² (14)]

Amendments

1. Inserted by reg 5 of SI 2006 No 2813 as from 20.11.06.
2. Omitted by Reg 7(b) of SI 2007 No 1619 as from 3.7.07.

Disregard of changes in tax, contributions etc

24. In calculating the claimant's income the appropriate authority may disregard any legislative change–

(a) in the basic or other rates of income tax;

(b) in the amount of any personal tax relief;

(c) in the rates of social security contributions payable under the Act or in the lower earnings limit or upper earnings limit for Class 1 contributions under that Act, the lower or upper limits applicable to Class 4 contributions under that Act or the amount specified in section 11(4) of that Act (small earnings exception in relation to Class 2 contributions);

(d) in the amount of tax payable as a result of an increase in the weekly rate of Category A, B, C or D retirement pension or any addition thereto or any graduated pension payable under the Act; and

(e) in the maximum rate of child tax credit or working tax credit,

for a period not exceeding 30 benefit weeks beginning with the benefit week immediately following the date from which the change is effective.

SECTION 3
Employed earners

Earnings of employed earners

25.–(1) Subject to paragraph (2), "earnings" means in the case of employment as an employed earner, any remuneration or profit derived from that employment and includes–

(a)   any bonus or commission;

(b)   any payment in lieu of remuneration except any periodic sum paid to a claimant on account of the termination of his employment by reason of redundancy;

(c)   any payment in lieu of notice;

(d)   any holiday pay;

(e)   any payment by way of a retainer;

(f)   any payment made by the claimant's employer in respect of expenses not wholly, exclusively and necessarily incurred in the performance of the duties of the employment, including any payment made by the claimant's employer in respect of–

    (i)   travelling expenses incurred by the claimant between his home and place of employment;

    (ii)   expenses incurred by the claimant under arrangements made for the care of a member of his family owing to the claimant's absence from home;

(g)   the amount of any payment by way of a non-cash voucher which has been taken into account in the computation of a person's earnings in accordance with Part 5 of Schedule 3 to the Social Security (Contributions) Regulations 2001;

(h)   statutory sick pay and statutory maternity pay payable by the employer under the Act;

(i)   statutory paternity pay payable under Part 12ZA of the Act;

(j)   statutory adoption pay payable under Part 12ZB of the Act;

(k)   any sums payable under a contract of service–

    (i)   for incapacity for work due to sickness or injury; or

    (ii)   by reason of pregnancy or confinement.

(2)   Earnings shall not include–

(a)   subject to paragraph (3), any payment in kind;

(b)   any payment in respect of expenses wholly, exclusively and necessarily incurred in the performance of the duties of the employment;

(c)   any occupational pension;

(d)   any lump sum payment made under the Iron and Steel Re-adaptation Benefits Scheme;

(e)   any payment of compensation made pursuant to an award by an employment tribunal established under the Employment Tribunals Act 1996 in respect of unfair dismissal or unlawful discrimination.

(3)   Paragraph (2)(a) shall not apply in respect of any non-cash voucher referred to in paragraph (1)(g).

Calculation of net earnings of employed earners

26.–(1)   For the purposes of regulation 20 (calculation of income on a weekly basis), the earnings of a claimant derived or likely to be derived from employment as an employed earner to be taken into account shall, subject to regulation 23(4) and Schedule 2, be his net earnings.

(2)   For the purposes of paragraph (1) net earnings shall, except where paragraph (5) applies, be calculated by taking into account the gross earnings of the claimant from that employment over the assessment period, less–

(a)   any amount deducted from those earnings by way of–

    (i)   income tax;

    (ii)   primary Class 1 contributions under the Act;

(b)   one-half of any sum paid by the claimant by way of a contribution towards an occupational pension scheme;

(c)   one-half of the amount calculated in accordance with paragraph (4) in respect of any qualifying contribution payable by the claimant; and

(d)   where those earnings include a payment which is payable under any enactment having effect in Northern Ireland and which corresponds to statutory sick pay, statutory maternity pay, statutory paternity pay or statutory adoption pay, any amount deducted from those earnings by way of any contributions which are payable under any enactment having effect in Northern Ireland and which correspond to primary Class 1 contributions under the Act.

(3)   In this regulation ''qualifying contribution'' means any sum which is payable periodically as a contribution towards a personal pension scheme.

(4)   The amount in respect of any qualifying contribution shall be calculated by multiplying the daily amount of the qualifying contribution by the number equal to the number of days in the assessment period; and for the purposes of this regulation the daily amount of the qualifying contribution shall be determined–

(a)   where the qualifying contribution is payable monthly, by multiplying the amount of the qualifying contribution by 12 and dividing the product by 365;

(b)   in any other case, by dividing the amount of the qualifying contribution by the number equal to the number of days in the period to which the qualifying contribution relates.

(5)   Where the earnings of a claimant are determined under sub-paragraph (b) of paragraph (2) of regulation 23 (calculation of weekly income), his net earnings shall be calculated by taking into account those earnings over the assessment period, less–

(a)   an amount in respect of income tax equivalent to an amount calculated by applying to those earnings the [¹ starting rate] or, as the case may be, the [¹ starting rate] and the basic rate of tax applicable to the assessment period less only the personal relief to which the claimant is entitled under sections 257(1) of the Income and Corporation Taxes Act 1988 (personal allowances) as is appropriate to his circumstances but, if the assessment period is less than a year, the earnings to which the [¹ starting rate] of tax is to be applied and the amount of the personal relief deductible under this sub-paragraph shall be calculated on a pro rata basis;

(b)   an amount equivalent to the amount of the primary Class 1 contributions that would be payable by him under the Act in respect of those earnings if such contributions were payable; and

(c)   one-half of any sum which would be payable by the claimant by way of a contribution towards an occupational or personal pension scheme, if the earnings so estimated were actual earnings.

Amendment
1.   Amended by reg 13(3) of SI 2007 No 2618 as from 1.10.07.

SECTION 4
Self-employed earners

Calculation of earnings of self-employed earners

27.–(1)   Where a claimant's earnings consist of earnings from employment as a self-employed earner, the weekly amount of his earnings shall be determined by reference to his average weekly earnings from that employment–

(a)   over a period of one year; or

(b)   where the claimant has recently become engaged in that employment or there has been a change which is likely to affect the normal pattern of business, over such other period (''computation period'') as may, in the particular case, enable the weekly amount of his earnings to be determined more accurately.

(2)   For the purposes determining the weekly amount of earnings of a claimant to whom paragraph (1)(b) applies, his earnings over the computation period shall be divided by the number equal to the number of days in that period and multiplying the quotient by 7.

(3)   The period over which the weekly amount of a claimant's earnings is calculated in accordance with this regulation shall be his assessment period.

Earnings of self-employed earners

28.–(1)   Subject to paragraph (2), "earnings", in the case of employment as a self-employed earner, means the gross receipts of the employment and shall include any allowance paid under section 2 of the 1973 Act or section 2 of the Enterprise and New Towns (Scotland) Act 1990 to the claimant for the purpose of assisting him in carrying on his business unless at the date of claim the allowance has been terminated.

(2)   "Earnings" in the case of employment as a self-employed earner does not include–

(a)   where a claimant occupies a dwelling as his home and he provides in that dwelling board and lodging accommodation for which payment is made, those payments;

(b)   any payment made by a local authority to a claimant–
    (i)   with whom a person is accommodated by virtue of arrangements made under section 23(2)(a) of the Children Act 1989 (provision of accommodation and maintenance for a child whom they are looking after) or, as the case may be, section 26(1) of the Children (Scotland) Act 1995; or
    (ii)   with whom a local authority foster a child under the Fostering of Children (Scotland) Regulations 1996;

(c)   any payment made by a voluntary organisation in accordance with section 59(1)(a) of the Children Act 1989 (provision of accommodation by voluntary organisations);

(d)   any payment made to the claimant or his partner for a person ("the person concerned") who is not normally a member of the claimant's household but is temporarily in his care, by–
    (i)   a health authority;
    (ii)   a local authority but excluding payments of housing benefit made in respect of the person concerned;
    (iii)   a voluntary organisation;
    (iv)   the person concerned pursuant to section 26(3A) of the National Assistance Act 1948; or
    (v)   a primary care trust established under section 16A of the National Health Service Act 1977;

(e)   any sports award.

Calculation of net profit of self-employed earners

29.–(1)   For the purposes of regulation 20 (calculation of income on a weekly basis) the earnings of a claimant to be taken into account shall be–

(a)   in the case of a self-employed earner who is engaged in employment on his own account, the net profit derived from that employment;

(b)   in the case of a self-employed earner whose employment is carried on in partnership, his share of the net profit derived from that employment, less–
    (i)   an amount in respect of income tax and of social security contributions payable under the Act calculated in accordance with regulation 30 (deduction of tax and contributions of self-employed earners); and
    (ii)   one-half of the amount calculated in accordance with paragraph (10) in respect of any qualifying premium.

(2)   For the purposes of paragraph (1)(a) the net profit of the employment shall, except where paragraph (8) applies, be calculated by taking into account the earnings of the employment over the assessment period less–

(a)   subject to paragraphs (4) to (7), any expenses wholly and exclusively incurred in that period for the purposes of that employment;

(b)   an amount in respect of–

  (i)   income tax; and

  (ii)   social security contributions payable under the Act,

calculated in accordance with regulation 30 (deduction of tax and contributions of self-employed earners); and

(c)   one-half of the amount calculated in accordance with paragraph (10) in respect of any qualifying premium.

(3)   For the purposes of paragraph (1)(b), the net profit of the employment shall be calculated by taking into account the earnings of the employment over the assessment period less, subject to paragraphs (4) to (7), any expenses wholly and exclusively incurred in that period for the purposes of the employment.

(4)   Subject to paragraph (5), no deduction shall be made under paragraph (2)(a) or (3), in respect of–

(a)   any capital expenditure;

(b)   the depreciation of any capital asset;

(c)   any sum employed or intended to be employed in the setting up or expansion of the employment;

(d)   any loss incurred before the beginning of the assessment period;

(e)   the repayment of capital on any loan taken out for the purposes of the employment; and

(f)   any expenses incurred in providing business entertainment.

(5)   A deduction shall be made under paragraph (2)(a) or (3) in respect of the repayment of capital on any loan used for–

(a)   the replacement in the course of business of equipment or machinery; and

(b)   the repair of an existing business asset except to the extent that any sum is payable under an insurance policy for its repair.

(6)   The relevant authority shall refuse to make a deduction in respect of any expenses under paragraph (2)(a) or (3) where it is not satisfied given the nature and the amount of the expense that it has been reasonably incurred.

(7)   For the avoidance of doubt–

(a)   a deduction shall not be made under paragraph (2)(a) or (3) in respect of any sum unless it has been expended for the purposes of the business;

(b)   a deduction shall be made thereunder in respect of–

  (i)   the excess of any value added tax paid over value added tax received in the assessment period;

  (ii)   any income expended in the repair of an existing business asset except to the extent that any sum is payable under an insurance policy for its repair;

  (iii)   any payment of interest on a loan taken out for the purposes of the employment.

(8)   Where a claimant is engaged in employment as a child minder the net profit of the employment shall be one-third of the earnings of that employment, less–

(a)   an amount in respect of–

  (i)   income tax; and

  (ii)   social security contributions payable under the Act,

calculated in accordance with regulation 30 (deduction of tax and contributions of self-employed earners); and

(b)   one-half of the amount calculated in accordance with paragraph (10) in respect of any qualifying premium.

(9)   For the avoidance of doubt where a claimant is engaged in employment as a self-employed earner and he is also engaged in one or more other employments as a self-employed or employed earner any loss incurred in any one of his employments shall not be offset against his earnings in any other of his employments.

(10)   The amount in respect of any qualifying premium shall be calculated by multiplying the daily amount of the qualifying premium by the number equal to the number of days in the assessment period; and for the purposes of this regulation the daily amount of the qualifying premium shall be determined–

(a)   where the qualifying premium is payable monthly, by multiplying the amount of the qualifying premium by 12 and dividing the product by 365;

(b)   in any other case, by dividing the amount of the qualifying premium by the number equal to the number of days in the period to which the qualifying premium relates.

(11)   In this regulation, "qualifying premium" means any premium which is payable periodically in respect of [¹] a personal pension scheme and is so payable on or after the date of claim.

Amendment

1.   Amended by reg 7(3) of SI 2007 No 1749 as from 16.7.07.

Deduction of tax and contributions for self-employed earners

30.–(1)   The amount to be deducted in respect of income tax under regulation 29(1)(b)(i), (2)(b)(i) or (8)(a)(i) (calculation of net profit of self-employed earners) shall be calculated on the basis of the amount of chargeable income and as if that income were assessable to income tax at the [¹ starting rate] or, as the case may be, the [¹ starting rate] and the basic rate of tax applicable to the assessment period less only the personal relief to which the claimant is entitled under sections 257(1) of the Income and Corporation Taxes Act 1988 (personal allowances) as is appropriate to his circumstances; but, if the assessment period is less than a year, the earnings to which the [¹ starting rate] of tax is to be applied and the amount of the personal reliefs deductible under this paragraph shall be calculated on a pro rata basis.

(2)   The amount to be deducted in respect of social security contributions under regulation 29(1)(b)(i), (2)(b)(ii) or (8)(a)(ii) shall be the total of–

(a)   the amount of Class 2 contributions payable under section 11(1) or, as the case may be, 11(3) of the Act at the rate applicable to the assessment period except where the claimant's chargeable income is less than the amount specified in section 11(4) of that Act (small earnings exception) for the tax year applicable to the assessment period; but if the assessment period is less than a year, the amount specified for that tax year shall be reduced pro rata; and

(b)   the amount of Class 4 contributions (if any) which would be payable under section 15 of the Act (Class 4 contributions recoverable under the Income Tax Acts) at the percentage rate applicable to the assessment period on so much of the chargeable income as exceeds the lower limit but does not exceed the upper limit of profits and gains applicable for the tax year applicable to the assessment period; but if the assessment period is less than a year, those limits shall be reduced pro rata.

(3)   In this regulation "chargeable income" means–

(a)   except where sub-paragraph (b) applies, the earnings derived from the employment less any expenses deducted under paragraph (2)(a) or, as the case may be, (3) of regulation 29;

(b)   in the case of employment as a child minder, one third of the earnings of that employment.

Amendment

1.   Amended by reg 13(4) of SI 2007 No 2618 as from 1.10.07.

SECTION 5
Other income

Notional income
    31.–(1)   A claimant shall be treated as possessing–
   (a)   subject to paragraph (2), the amount of any retirement pension income–
       (i)   for which no claim has been made; and
       (ii)   to which he might expect to be entitled if a claim for it were made;
   (b)   income from an occupational pension scheme which the claimant elected to defer.
    (2)   Paragraph (1)(a) shall not apply to the following where entitlement has been deferred–
   (a)   a Category A or Category B retirement pension payable under sections 43 to 55 of the Act;
   (b)   a shared additional pension payable under section 55A of the Act;
   (c)   graduated retirement benefit payable under sections 36 and 37 of the National Insurance Act 1965.
    (3)   For the purposes of paragraph (2), entitlement has been deferred–
   (a)   in the case of a Category A or Category B pension, in the circumstances specified in section 55(3) of the Act;
   (b)   in the case of a shared additional pension, in the circumstances specified in section 55C(3) of the Act; and
   (c)   in the case of graduated retirement benefit, in the circumstances specified in section 36(4) and (4A) of the National Insurance Act 1965.
   [³ (4)   This paragraph applies where a person aged not less than 60–
   (a)   is entitled to money purchase benefits under an occupational pension scheme or a personal pension scheme;
   (b)   fails to purchase an annuity with the funds available in that scheme; and
   (c)   either–
       (i)   defers in whole or in part the payment of any income which would have been payable to him by his pension fund holder, or
       (ii)   fails to take any necessary action to secure that the whole of any income which would be payable to him by his pension fund holder upon his applying for it, is so paid, or
       (iii)   income withdrawal is not available to him under that scheme.
    (4A)   Where paragraph (4) applies, the amount of any income foregone shall be treated as possessed by that person, but only from the date on which it could be expected to be acquired were an application for it to be made.]
    (5)   The amount of any income foregone in a case [³ where paragraph (4)(c)(i) or (ii)] applies shall be the maximum amount of income which may be withdrawn from the fund and shall be determined by the relevant authority which shall take account of information provided by the pension fund holder in accordance with regulation 57(6) (evidence and information).
    (6)   The amount of any income foregone in a case [³ either paragraph (4)(c)(iii)] applies shall be the income that the claimant could have received without purchasing an annuity had the funds held under the relevant scheme [³] been held under a personal pension scheme or occupational pension scheme where income withdrawal was available and shall be determined in the manner specified in paragraph (5).
    (7)   In paragraph (4), ''money purchase benefits'' has the meaning it has in the Pensions Scheme Act 1993.
    (8)   [¹ Subject to paragraph (8A),] A person shall be treated as possessing income of which he has deprived himself for the purpose of securing entitlement to council tax benefit or increasing the amount of that benefit.
   [¹ (8A)   Paragraph (8) shall not apply in respect of the amount of an increase of pension or benefit where a person, having made an election in favour of that increase

of pension or benefit under Schedule 5 or 5A to the Contributions and Benefits Act 1992 or under Schedule 1 to the Graduated Retirement Benefit Regulations, changes that election in accordance with regulations made under Schedule 5 or 5A to that Act in favour of a lump sum.

(8B)   In paragraph (8A), "lump sum" means a lump sum under Schedule 5 or 5A to the Contributions and Benefits Act 1992 or under Schedule 1 to the Graduated Retirement Benefit Regulations.]

(9)   Where a claimant is in receipt of any benefit (other than council tax benefit) under the benefit Acts and the rate of that benefit is altered with effect from a date on or after 1st April in any year but not more than 14 days thereafter, the relevant authority shall treat the claimant as possessing such benefit at the altered rate from either 1st April or the first Monday in April in that year, whichever date the relevant authority shall select to apply in its area, to the date on which the altered rate is to take effect.

(10)   In the case of a claimant who has, or whose partner has, an award of state pension credit comprising only the savings credit, where a relevant authority treats the claimant as possessing any benefit (other than council tax benefit) at the altered rate in accordance with paragraph (9), that authority shall–

(a)   determine the income and capital of that claimant in accordance with regulation 17(1) (calculation of claimant's income in savings credit only cases) where the calculation or estimate of that income and capital is altered with effect from a date on or after 1st April in any year but not more than 14 days thereafter; and

(b)   treat that claimant as possessing such income and capital at the altered rate by reference to the date selected by the relevant authority to apply in its area, for the purposes of establishing the period referred to in paragraph (9).

[² (11)   For the purposes of paragraph (8), a person is not to be regarded as depriving himself of income where–

(a)   his rights to benefits under a registered pension scheme are extinguished and in consequence of this he receives a payment from the scheme, and

(b)   that payment is a trivial commutation lump sum within the meaning given by paragraph 7 of Schedule 29 to the Finance Act 2004.

(12)   In paragraph (11), "registered pension scheme" has the meaning given in section 150(2) of the Finance Act 2004.]

Amendments

1.   Inserted by reg 12(3) of SI 2005 No 2677 and reg 2 of SI 2006 No 217 as from 6.4.06.
2.   Inserted by reg 18(2) of SI 2006 No 2378 as from 2.10.06.
3.   Amended by reg 7(4) of SI 2007 No 1749 as from 16.7.07.

Income paid to third parties

32.–(1)   Any payment of income, other than a payment specified in paragraph (2), to a third party in respect of the claimant shall be treated as possessed by the claimant.

(2)   Paragraph (1) shall not apply in respect of a payment of income made under an occupational pension scheme [¹ , in respect of a pension or other periodical payment made under a personal pension scheme or a payment made by the Board of the Pension Protection Fund] where–

(a)   a bankruptcy order has been made in respect of the person in respect of whom the payment has been made or, in Scotland, the estate of that person is subject to sequestration or a judicial factor has been appointed on that person's estate under section 41 of the Solicitors (Scotland) Act 1980;

(b)   the payment is made to the trustee in bankruptcy or any other person acting on behalf of the creditors; and

(c)   the person referred to in sub-paragraph (a) and his partner does not possess, or is not treated as possessing, any other income apart from that payment.

Amendment

1.   Amended by reg 11(3) of SI 2006 No 518 as from 6.4.04.

SECTION 6
Capital

Capital limit

33.   For the purposes of section 134(1) of the Act as it applies to council tax benefit (no entitlement to benefit if capital exceeds a prescribed amount), the prescribed amount is £16,000.

Calculation of capital

34.–(1)   For the purposes of Part 7 of the Act as it applies to council tax benefit, the capital of a claimant to be taken into account shall, subject to paragraph (2), be the whole of his capital calculated in accordance with this Part.

(2)   There shall be disregarded from the calculation of the claimant's capital under paragraph (1) any capital, where applicable, specified in Schedule 4.

(3)   A claimant's capital shall be treated as including any payment made to him by way of arrears of–

(a)   child tax credit;

(b)   working tax credit;

(c)   state pension credit,

if the payment was made in respect of a period for the whole or part of which council tax benefit was allowed before those arrears were paid.

[¹Calculation of capital in the United Kingdom

35.   Capital which a claimant possesses in the United Kingdom shall be calculated at its current market or surrender value less–

(a)   where there would be expenses attributable to the sale, 10 per cent.; and

(b)   the amount of any encumbrance secured on it.]

Amendment

1.   Substituted by reg 13(5) of SI 2007 No 2618 as from 1.10.07.

Calculation of capital outside the United Kingdom

36.   Capital which a claimant possesses in a country outside the United Kingdom shall be calculated–

(a)   in a case where there is no prohibition in that country against the transfer to the United Kingdom of an amount equal to its current market or surrender value in that country, at that value;

(b)   in a case where there is such a prohibition, at the price which it would realise if sold in the United Kingdom to a willing buyer,

less, where there would be expenses attributable to sale, 10 per cent. and the amount of any encumbrance secured on it.

Notional capital

37.–(1)   A claimant shall be treated as possessing capital of which he has deprived himself for the purpose of securing entitlement to council tax benefit or increasing the amount of that benefit except to the extent that the capital which he is treated as possessing is reduced in accordance with regulation 38 (diminishing notional capital rule).

(2)   A person who disposes of capital for the purpose of–

(a)   reducing or paying a debt owed by the claimant; or

(b)   purchasing goods or services if the expenditure was reasonable in the circumstances of the claimant's case, shall be regarded as not depriving himself of it.

(3) Where a claimant stands in relation to a company in a position analogous to that of a sole owner or partner in the business of that company, he shall be treated as if he were such sole owner or partner and in such a case–

    (a) the value of his holding in that company shall, notwithstanding regulation 34 (calculation of capital), be disregarded; and

    (b) he shall, subject to paragraph (4), be treated as possessing an amount of capital equal to the value or, as the case may be, his share of the value of the capital of that company and the foregoing provisions of this Section shall apply for the purposes of calculating that amount as if it were actual capital which he does possess.

(4) For so long as a claimant undertakes activities in the course of the business of the company, the amount which he is treated as possessing under paragraph (3) shall be disregarded.

(5) Where under this regulation a person is treated as possessing capital, the amount of that capital shall be calculated in accordance with the provisions of this Part as if it were actual capital which he does possess.

Diminishing notional capital rule

38.–(1) Where a claimant is treated as possessing capital under regulation 37(1) (notional capital), the amount which he is treated as possessing–

    (a) in the case of a week that is subsequent to–

        (i) the relevant week in respect of which the conditions set out in paragraph (2) are satisfied; or

        (ii) a week which follows that relevant week and which satisfies those conditions,

    shall be reduced by an amount determined under paragraph (3);

    (b) in the case of a week in respect of which paragraph (1)(a) does not apply but where–

        (i) that week is a week subsequent to the relevant week; and

        (ii) that relevant week is a week in which the condition in paragraph (4) is satisfied,

    shall be reduced by the amount determined under paragraph (4).

(2) This paragraph applies to a benefit week where the claimant satisfies the conditions that–

    (a) he is in receipt of council tax benefit; and

    (b) but for regulation 37(1), he would have received an additional amount of council tax benefit in that week.

(3) In a case to which paragraph (2) applies, the amount of the reduction for the purposes of paragraph (1)(a) shall be equal to the aggregate of–

    (a) the additional amount to which paragraph (2)(b) refers;

    (b) where the claimant has also claimed state pension credit, the amount of any state pension credit or any additional amount of state pension credit to which he would have been entitled in respect of the benefit week to which paragraph (2) refers but for the application of regulation 21(1) of the State Pension Credit Regulations 2002 (notional capital);

    (c) where the claimant has also claimed housing benefit, the amount of any housing benefit or any additional amount of housing benefit to which he would have been entitled in respect of the whole or part of that benefit week to which paragraph (2) refers but for the application of regulation 47(1) of the Housing Benefit (Persons who have attained the qualifying age for state pension credit) Regulations 2006 (notional capital);

    (d) where the claimant has also claimed a jobseeker's allowance, the amount of an income-based jobseeker's allowance to which he would have been entitled in respect of the benefit week to which paragraph (2) refers but for the application of regulation 113 of the Jobseeker's Allowance Regulations (notional capital).

(4) Subject to paragraph (5), for the purposes of paragraph (1)(b), the condition is that the claimant would have been entitled to council tax benefit in the relevant week but for regulation 37(1), and in such a case the amount of the reduction shall be equal to the aggregate of–

(a) the amount of council tax benefit to which the claimant would have been entitled in the relevant week but for regulation 37(1); and for the purposes of this sub-paragraph if the amount is in respect of a part-week that amount shall be determined by dividing the amount of council tax benefit to which he would have been so entitled by the number equal to the number of days in the part-week and multiplying the quotient so obtained by 7;

(b) if the claimant would, but for regulation 21 of the State Pension Credit Regulations 2002, have been entitled to state pension credit in respect of the benefit week, within the meaning of regulation 1(2) of those Regulations (interpretation), which includes the last day of the relevant week, the amount to which he would have been entitled and, for the purposes of this sub-paragraph, if the amount is in respect of a part-week, that amount shall be determined by dividing the amount of the state pension credit to which he would have been so entitled by the number equal to the number of days in the part-week and multiplying the quotient so obtained by 7;

(c) if the claimant would, but for regulation 47(1) of the Housing Benefit (Persons who have attained the qualifying age for state pension credit) Regulations 2006, have been entitled to housing benefit or to an additional amount of housing benefit in respect of the benefit week which includes the last day of the relevant week, the amount which is equal to–

(i) in a case where no housing benefit is payable, the amount to which he would have been entitled; or

(ii) in any other case, the amount equal to the additional amount of housing benefit to which he would have been entitled,

and, for the purposes of this sub-paragraph, if the amount is in respect of a part-week, that amount shall be determined by dividing the amount of the housing benefit to which he would have been so entitled by the number equal to the number of days in the part-week and multiplying the quotient so obtained by 7;

(d) if the claimant would, but for regulation 113 of the Jobseeker's Allowance Regulations, have been entitled to an income-based jobseeker's allowance in respect of the benefit week, within the meaning of regulation 1(3) of those Regulations (interpretation), which includes the last day of the relevant week, the amount to which he would have been entitled and, for the purposes of this sub-paragraph, if the amount is in respect of a part-week, that amount shall be determined by dividing the amount of the income-based jobseeker's allowance to which he would have been so entitled by the number equal to the number of days in the part-week and multiplying the quotient so obtained by 7.

(5) The amount determined under paragraph (4) shall be redetermined under that paragraph if the claimant makes a further claim for council tax benefit and the conditions in paragraph (6) are satisfied, and in such a case–

(a) sub-paragraphs (a) to (d) of paragraph (4) shall apply as if for the words "relevant week" there were substituted the words "relevant subsequent week"; and

(b) subject to paragraph (7), the amount as redetermined shall have effect from the first week following the relevant subsequent week in question.

(6) The conditions are that–

(a) a further claim is made 26 or more weeks after–

    (i)   the date on which the claimant made a claim for council tax benefit in respect of which he was first treated as possessing the capital in question under regulation 37(1);

    (ii)   in a case where there has been at least one redetermination in accordance with paragraph (5), the date on which he last made a claim for council tax benefit which resulted in the weekly amount being redetermined; or

    (iii) the date on which he last ceased to be entitled to council tax benefit,

whichever last occurred; and

(b)   the claimant would have been entitled to council tax benefit but for regulation 37(1).

(7)   The amount as redetermined pursuant to paragraph (5) shall not have effect if it is less than the amount which applied in that case immediately before the redetermination and in such a case the higher amount shall continue to have effect.

(8)   For the purposes of this regulation–

(a)   ''part-week'' in paragraph (4)(a) means a period of less than a week for which council tax benefit is allowed;

(b)   ''part-week'' in paragraph (4)(b) and (d) means–

    (i)   a period of less than a week which is the whole period for which state pension credit, or, as the case may be, an income-based jobseeker's allowance, is payable; and

    (ii)   any other period of less than a week for which either of those benefits is payable;

(c)   ''part-week'' in paragraph (4)(c) means a period of less than a week for which housing benefit is payable;

(d)   ''relevant week'' means the benefit week or part-week in which the capital in question of which the claimant has deprived himself within the meaning of regulation 37(1)–

    (i)   was first taken into account for the purpose of determining his entitlement to council tax benefit; or

    (ii)   was taken into account on a subsequent occasion for the purpose of determining or re-determining his entitlement to council tax benefit on that subsequent occasion and that determination or redetermination resulted in his beginning to receive, or ceasing to receive, council tax benefit,

and where more than one benefit week or part week is identified by reference to heads (i) and (ii) of this sub-paragraph the later or latest such benefit week or, as the case may be, the later or latest such part-week;

(e)   ''relevant subsequent week'' means the benefit week or part-week which includes the day on which the further claim or, if more than one further claim has been made, the last such claim was made.

Capital jointly held

39.   Where a claimant and one or more other persons are beneficially entitled in possession to any capital asset, other than a capital asset disregarded under regulation 37(4), they shall be treated as if each of them were entitled in possession to the whole beneficial interest therein in an equal share and the foregoing provisions of this Section shall apply for the purposes of calculating the amount of capital which the claimant is treated as possessing as if it were actual capital which the claimant does possess.

PART 5
Amount of benefit

Maximum council tax benefit

40.–(1) Subject to paragraphs (2) to (5), the amount of a person's maximum council tax benefit in respect of a day for which he is liable to pay council tax, shall be 100 per cent. of the amount A/B where–

(a) A is the amount set by the appropriate authority as the council tax for the relevant financial year in respect of the dwelling in which he is a resident and for which he is liable, subject to any discount which may be appropriate to that dwelling under the 1992 Act; and

(b) B is the number of days in that financial year,

less any deductions in respect of non-dependants which fall to be made under regulation 42 (non-dependant deductions).

(2) In calculating a person's maximum council tax benefit any reduction in the amount that a person is liable to pay in respect of council tax, which is made in consequence of any enactment in, or made under, the 1992 Act, shall be taken into account.

(3) Subject to paragraph (4), where a claimant is jointly and severally liable for council tax in respect of a dwelling in which he is resident with one or more other persons but excepting any person so residing with the claimant who is a student to whom regulation 45(2) of the Council Tax Benefit Regulations 2006 (students who are excluded from entitlement to council tax benefit) applies, in determining the maximum council tax benefit in his case in accordance with paragraph (1), the amount A shall be divided by the number of persons who are jointly and severally liable for that tax.

(4) Where a claimant is jointly and severally liable for council tax in respect of a dwelling with only his partner, paragraph (3) shall not apply in his case.

(5) In any case where an extended payment under regulation 60 of the Council Tax Benefit Regulations 2006 or an extended payment (severe disablement allowance and incapacity benefit) under regulation 44 of these Regulations has been allowed to a claimant, his entitlement shall be adjusted in such circumstances and by such amount as are prescribed in regulation 41 or paragraph 6 of Schedule 5, as the case may be.

Reduction where amount payable under regulation 60 of the Council Tax Regulations 2006

41. Where–

(a) a payment in accordance with regulation 60 of the Council Tax Benefit Regulations 2006 (an ''extended payment'') has been allowed, and

(b) the person to whom it was made has also claimed council tax benefit for a period that includes any part of the period specified in regulation 60(6) of those Regulations,

then the entitlement to council tax benefit, if any, of that claimant for council tax benefit, in respect of any or each of those weeks, shall be reduced by the amount that that extended payment has discharged his council tax liability, in respect of any such week.

Non-dependant deductions

42.–(1) Subject to the following provisions of this regulation, the non-dependant deductions in respect of a day referred to in regulation 40 (maximum council tax benefit) shall be–

(a) in respect of a non-dependant aged 18 or over in remunerative work, [^{4} £6.95] × 1/7;

 (b) in respect of a non-dependant aged 18 or over to whom sub-paragraph (a) does not apply, [⁴ £2.30] × 1/7.

 (2) In the case of a non-dependant aged 18 or over to whom paragraph (1)(a) applies, where it is shown to the appropriate authority that his normal gross weekly income is–

 (a) less than [⁵ £164.00], the deduction to be made under this regulation shall be that specified in paragraph (1)(b);

 (b) not less than [⁵ £164.00] but less than [⁵ £283.00], the deduction to be made under this regulation shall be [⁴ £4.60];

 (c) not less than [⁵ £283.00] but less than [⁵ £353.00], the deduction to be made under this regulation shall be [⁴ £5.80].

 (3) Only one deduction shall be made under this regulation in respect of a couple or, as the case may be, members of a polygamous marriage and, where, but for this paragraph, the amount that would fall to be deducted in respect of one member of a couple or polygamous marriage is higher than the amount (if any) that would fall to be deducted in respect of the other, or any other, member, the higher amount shall be deducted.

 (4) In applying the provisions of paragraph (2) in the case of a couple or, as the case may be, a polygamous marriage, regard shall be had, for the purpose of that paragraph, to the couple's or, as the case may be, all members of the polygamous marriage's joint weekly gross income.

 (5) Where in respect of a day–

 (a) a person is a resident in a dwelling but is not himself liable for council tax in respect of that dwelling and that day;

 (b) other residents in that dwelling (the liable persons) have joint and several liability for council tax in respect of that dwelling and that day otherwise than by virtue of section 9, 77 or 77A of the 1992 Act (liability of spouses and civil partners); and

 (c) the person to whom sub-paragraph (a) refers is a non-dependant of two or more of the liable persons,

the deduction in respect of that non-dependant shall be apportioned equally between those liable persons.

 (6) No deduction shall be made in respect of any non-dependants occupying a claimant's dwelling if the claimant or his partner is–

 (a) blind or treated as blind by virtue of paragraph 13 of Schedule 1 (additional condition of the higher pensioner and disability premiums) to the Council Tax Benefit Regulations 2006; or

 (b) receiving in respect of himself either–

  (i) attendance allowance; or

  (ii) the care component of the disability living allowance.

 (7) No deduction shall be made in respect of a non-dependant if–

 (a) although he resides with the claimant, it appears to the relevant authority that his normal home is elsewhere; or

 (b) he is in receipt of a training allowance paid in connection with a Youth Training Scheme established under section 2 of the 1973 Act or section 2 of the Enterprise and New Towns (Scotland) Act 1990; or

 (c) he is a full-time student within the meaning of Part 5 (Students) of the Council Tax Benefit Regulations 2006; or

 (d) he is not residing with the claimant because he has been a patient for a period in excess of 52 weeks, and for these purposes–

  [¹ (i) "patient" has the meaning given in paragraph (7) of regulation 8, and

  (ii) where a person has been a patient for two or more distinct periods separated by one or more intervals each not exceeding 28 days, he shall be treated as having been a patient continuously for a period equal in duration to the total of those distinct periods.]

(8) No deduction shall be made in respect of a non-dependant–

(a) who is on income support, on state pension credit or an income-based jobseeker's allowance; or

(b) to whom Schedule 1 of the 1992 Act applies (persons disregarded for purposes of discount) but this sub-paragraph shall not apply to a non-dependant who is a student to whom paragraph 4 of that Schedule refers.

(9) In the application of paragraph (2) there shall be disregarded from his weekly gross income–

(a) any attendance allowance or disability living allowance received by him;

(b) any payment made under the Trusts, the Fund, the Eileen Trust or the Independent Living Funds which had his income fallen to be calculated under regulation 30 of the Council Tax Benefit Regulations 2006 (calculation of income other than earnings) would have been disregarded under paragraph 24 of Schedule 4 to those Regulations (income in kind); and

(c) any payment which had his income fallen to be calculated under regulation 30 of those Regulations would have been disregarded under paragraph 36 of Schedule 4 to those Regulations (payments made under certain trusts and certain other payments).

Amendments

1. Substituted by reg 3(7) of SI 2005 No 2502 as amended by Sch 2 para 27 of SI 2006 No 217 as from 1.4.06.
2. Confirmed by Art 21(3) of SI 2006 No 645 and reg 8 of SI 2006 No 217 as from 1.4.06.
3. Amended by Art 21(3) of SI 2006 No 645 and reg 8 of SI 2006 No 217 as from 1.4.06
4. Confirmed by Art 22(3) of SI 2007 No 688 as from 1.4.07.
5. Amended by Art 22(3) of SI 2007 No 688 as from 1.4.07.

Council tax benefit taper

43. The prescribed percentage for the purpose of sub-section (5)(c)(ii) of section 131 of the Act as it applies to council tax benefit, (percentage of excess of income over the applicable amount which is deducted from maximum council tax benefit)(a), shall be 2 6/7 per cent.

Extended payments (severe disablement allowance and incapacity benefit)

44.–(1) Except in a case in which a person is in receipt of state pension credit, paragraph (2) shall apply where–

(a) a person ceases to be entitled to council tax benefit–

(i) in accordance with regulation 49 (date on which council tax benefit is to end where entitlement to severe disablement allowance or incapacity benefit ceases); and

(ii) the condition referred to in paragraph 1 of Schedule 5 is satisfied in his case; or

(b) a person ceases to be entitled to council tax benefit because he has vacated the dwelling of which he was a resident and the day on which he did so was either in the week in which he took up employment as an employed or self-employed earner, or in the preceding week, and–

(i) he ceased to be entitled to severe disablement allowance or incapacity benefit by reason of taking up employment as an employed or self-employed earner;

(ii) he had been entitled to and in receipt of severe disablement allowance, incapacity benefit or a combination of severe disablement allowance and incapacity benefit for a continuous period of at least 26 weeks;

(iii) he was not entitled to and in receipt of income support; and

(iv)   the condition referred to in paragraph 1 of Schedule 5 is satisfied in his case.

(2)   A person to whom paragraph (1) applies shall be treated as having made a claim under this regulation and his council tax benefit shall be determined in accordance with Schedule 5 and any award so determined shall be referred to in these Regulations as an "extended payment (severe disablement allowance and incapacity benefit)".

(3)   For the purposes of any payment pursuant to this regulation–

(a)   except in a case to which paragraph 4(a) of Schedule 5 applies, the maximum council tax benefit of any person mentioned in paragraph (1) shall be determined in accordance with paragraph 2 of Schedule 5;

(b)   the maximum council tax benefit of any person to whom paragraph 4(a) of Schedule 5 applies shall be determined in accordance with paragraph 5 of that Schedule;

(c)   except in a case to which paragraph (d) applies, any person who meets the requirements of paragraph (1) shall be treated as possessing the amount of income and the amount of capital that they possessed in the last week of the award of council tax benefit which has ceased as mentioned in paragraph (1); and

(d)   any person whose maximum council tax benefit is determined in accordance with paragraph 5 of Schedule 5 shall be treated as possessing no income or capital.

(4)   Regulations 52, 53 and 57 (claims, evidence and information) shall not apply to a claim pursuant to this regulation and, subject to regulation 40(5) (maximum council tax benefit), Part 6 (period of entitlement, changes of circumstances and increases for exceptional circumstances) shall not apply to any payment under it.

(5)   In paragraph (1), references to a "person" include references to a person's partner and references to taking up employment include receiving remuneration for employment or an increased amount of remuneration for employment or engaging in employment for an increased number of hours.

(6)   In a case where payment has been made under this regulation–

(a)   the beneficiary shall be treated for the purpose of these Regulations as though he were entitled to and in receipt of council tax benefit–

(i)   during the 4 weeks immediately following the last day of his entitlement to council tax benefit; or

(ii)   until the date on which his liability for council tax ends,

whichever occurs first; and

(b)   any claim for council tax benefit made by the beneficiary within the period which under sub-paragraph (a) applies in his case or the 4 weeks thereafter shall be treated as having been made in respect of a period beginning immediately after the end of his previous award of council tax benefit.

Continuing payments where state pension credit claimed

45.–(1)   This regulation applies where–

(a)   the claimant is entitled to council tax benefit;

(b)   paragraph (2) is satisfied; and

(c)   either–

(i)   the claimant has attained the qualifying age for state pension credit or, if his entitlement to income-based jobseeker's allowance continued beyond that age, has attained the age of 65; or

(ii)   the claimant's partner has actually claimed state pension credit.

(2)   This regulation is only satisfied if the Secretary of State has certified to the relevant authority that the claimant's partner has actually claimed state pension credit or that–

(a)   the claimant's award of–

(i)   income support has terminated because the claimant has attained the qualifying age for state pension credit; or

(ii)   income-based jobseeker's allowance has terminated because the claimant has attained the qualifying age for state pension credit or the age of 65; and

(b)   the claimant has claimed or is treated as having claimed or is required to make a claim for state pension credit.

(3)   Subject to paragraph (4), in a case to which this regulation applies, council tax benefit shall continue to be paid for the period of 4 weeks beginning on the day following the day the claimant's entitlement to income support or, as the case may be, income-based jobseeker's allowance, ceased, if and for so long as the claimant otherwise satisfies the conditions for entitlement to council tax benefit.

(4)   Where council tax benefit is paid for the period of 4 weeks in accordance with paragraph (3) above, and the last day of that period falls on a day other than the last day of a benefit week, then council tax benefit shall continue to be paid until the end of the benefit week in which the last day of that period falls.

(5)   Throughout the period of 4 weeks specified in paragraph (3) and any further period specified in paragraph (4)–

(a)   the whole of the income and capital of the claimant shall be disregarded;

(b)   the appropriate maximum council tax benefit of the claimant shall be that which was applicable in his case immediately before that period commenced.

(6)   The appropriate maximum council tax benefit shall be calculated in accordance with regulation 40(1) if, since the date it was last calculated–

(a)   the claimant's council tax liability has increased; or

(b)   a change in the deduction under regulation 42 falls to be made.

Alternative maximum council tax benefit

46.–(1)   Subject to paragraphs (2) and (3), the alternative maximum council tax benefit where the conditions set out in section 131(3) and (6) of the Act are fulfilled, shall be the amount determined in accordance with Schedule 6.

(2)   Subject to paragraph (3), where a claimant is jointly and severally liable for council tax in respect of a dwelling in which he is resident with one or more other persons, in determining the alternative maximum council tax benefit in his case, the amount determined in accordance with Schedule 6 shall be divided by the number of persons who are jointly and severally liable for that tax.

(3)   Where a claimant is jointly and severally liable for council tax in respect of a dwelling with only his partner, solely by virtue of section 9, 77 or 77A of the 1992 Act (liability of spouses and civil partners), paragraph (2) shall not apply in his case.

General Note

See the commentary to reg 62 and Sch 2 CTB Regs on pp619 and 650. However, note there is no equivalent in the CTB(SPC) Regs to Sch 5 para 46 CTB Regs. This means that unless the claimant or her/his partner is in receipt of the guarantee credit of pension credit (in which case the whole of her/his capital is ignored under reg 16) the capital limit provided by s134 SSCBA and reg 33 will apply. It is not clear whether this was an error, or the intention.

Residents of a dwelling to whom section 131(6) of the Act does not apply

47.   Subsection (6) of section 131 of the Act (residents of a dwelling in respect of whom entitlement to an alternative maximum council tax benefit may arise) shall not apply in respect of any person referred to in the following paragraphs namely–

(a)   a person who is liable for council tax solely in consequence of the provisions of sections 9, 77 or 77A of the 1992 Act (spouse's or civil partner's joint and several liability for tax);

(b)   a person who is residing with a couple or with the members of a polygamous marriage where the claimant for council tax benefit is a member of that couple or of that marriage and–

      (i)   in the case of a couple, neither member of that couple is a person who, in accordance with Schedule 1 to the 1992 Act, falls to be disregarded for the purposes of discount; or

      (ii)   in the case of a polygamous marriage, two or more members of that marriage are not persons who, in accordance with Schedule 1 to the 1992 Act, fall to be disregarded for the purposes of discount;

  (c)   a person who jointly with the claimant for benefit falls within the same paragraph of sections 6(2)(a) to (e) or 75(2)(a) to (e) of the 1992 Act (persons liable to pay council tax) as applies in the case of the claimant;

  (d)   a person who is residing with two or more persons both or all of whom fall within the same paragraph of sections 6(2)(a) to (e) or 75(2)(a) to (e) of the 1992 Act and two or more of those persons are not persons who, in accordance with Schedule 1 to the 1992 Act, fall to be disregarded for the purposes of discount.

PART 6
Period of entitlement, changes of circumstances and increases for exceptional circumstances

Date on which entitlement is to begin

48.–(1)   Subject to paragraph (2), any person by whom or in respect of whom a claim for council tax benefit is made and is otherwise entitled to that benefit shall be entitled from the benefit week following the first day in respect of which that claim is made.

(2)   A claimant who is otherwise entitled to council tax benefit and becomes liable, for the first time, for a relevant authority's council tax in respect the dwelling of which he is a resident in the benefit week in which the first day in respect of which his claim was made falls, shall be so entitled from that benefit week.

Date on which council tax benefit is to end where entitlement to severe disablement allowance or incapacity benefit ceases

49.   Except in a case in which the claimant or his partner is in receipt of state pension credit, a claimant's entitlement to council tax benefit shall cease at the end of the benefit week in which entitlement to severe disablement allowance or incapacity benefit ceases where–

  (a)   the claimant or his partner was not entitled to and in receipt of income support but was entitled to and in receipt of severe disablement allowance or incapacity benefit and that entitlement has ceased;

  (b)   that entitlement to severe disablement allowance or incapacity benefit has ceased by reason of the claimant or his partner–

      (i)   commencing employment as an employed or self-employed earner; or

      (ii)   increasing their earnings from such employment; or

      (iii) increasing the number of hours worked in such employment;

  (c)   the claimant had been entitled to and in receipt of severe disablement allowance or incapacity benefit for a continuous period of at least 26 weeks before the day on which his entitlement to severe disablement allowance or incapacity benefit ceased, and for the purposes of this sub-paragraph–

      (i)   a claimant satisfies the conditions of this sub-paragraph if he has been entitled to and in receipt of a combination of severe disablement allowance and incapacity benefit for at least 26 weeks;

      (ii)   references to the claimant include references to his partner; and

  (d)   that work, increase in earnings, or as the case may be, increase in hours is expected to last at least 5 weeks or more.

Date on which change of circumstances is to take effect

50.–(1)   Except in cases where regulation 24 (disregard of changes in tax, contributions, etc) [² applies, and subject to regulation 8(3) of the Decisions and Appeals Regulations, and] the following provisions of this regulation and regulation 51, a change of circumstances which affects entitlement to, or the amount of, council tax benefit (''change of circumstances''), shall take effect from the first day of the benefit week following the date on which the change actually occurs, and where that change is cessation of entitlement to any benefit under the benefit Acts, the date on which the change actually occurs shall be the day immediately following the last day of entitlement to that benefit.

(2)   Subject to paragraph (3), where the change of circumstances is a change in the amount of council tax payable, it shall take effect from the day on which it actually occurs.

(3)   Where the change of circumstances is a change in the amount a person is liable to pay in respect of council tax in consequence of regulations under section 13 or 80 of the 1992 Act (reduced amounts of council tax) or changes in the discount to which a dwelling may be subject under sections 11, 12 or 79 of that Act, it shall take effect from the day on which the change in amount has effect.

(4)   Where the change of circumstances is an amendment to these Regulations, it shall take effect from the date on which the amendment to these Regulations comes into force.

(5)   Where the change of circumstances is the claimant's acquisition of a partner, the change shall have effect on the day on which the acquisition takes place.

(6)   Where the change of circumstances is the death of a claimant's partner or their separation, it shall have effect on the day the death or separation occurs.

(7)   If two or more changes of circumstances occurring in the same benefit week would, but for this paragraph, take effect in different benefit weeks in accordance with paragraphs (1) to (6) they shall take effect from the day to which the appropriate paragraph from (2) to (6) above refers, or, where more than one day is concerned, from the earlier day.

(8)   Where the change of circumstances is that income, or an increase in the amount of income, other than a benefit or an increase in the amount of a benefit under the Act, is paid in respect of a past period and there was no entitlement to income of that amount during that period, the change of circumstances shall take effect from the first day on which such income, had it been paid in that period at intervals appropriate to that income, would have fallen to be taken into account for the purposes of these Regulations.

(9)   Without prejudice to paragraph (8), where the change of circumstances is the payment of income, or arrears of income, in respect of a past period, the change of circumstances shall take effect from the first day on which such income, had it been timeously paid in that period at intervals appropriate to that income, would have fallen to be taken into account for the purposes of these Regulations.

(10)   Paragraph (11) applies if–
(a)   the claimant or his partner has attained the age of 65; and
(b)   either–
   (i)   a non-dependant took up residence in the claimant's dwelling; or
   (ii)   there has been a change of circumstances in respect of a non-dependant so that the amount of the deduction which falls to be made under regulation 42 increased.

(11)   Where this paragraph applies, the change of circumstances [¹ referred to in paragraph (10)(b)] shall take effect from the effective date.

(12)   In paragraph (11) but subject to paragraph (13), ''the effective date'' means–
(a)   where more than one change of a kind referred to in paragraph (10)(b) relating to the same non-dependant has occurred since–

(i)   the date on which the claimant's entitlement to council tax benefit first began; or

(ii)   the date which was the last effective date in respect of such a change, whichever is the later, the date which falls 26 weeks after the date on which the first such change occurred;

(b)   where sub-paragraph (a) does not apply, the date which falls 26 weeks after the date on which the change referred to in paragraph (10)(b) occurred.

(13)   If in any particular case the date determined under paragraph (12) is not the first day of a benefit week, the effective date in that case shall be the first day of the next benefit week to commence after the date determined under that paragraph.

Modifications

Reg 50 applies as if para (9) was omitted where a change of circumstances occurs as a result of the payment of arrears of any income which affects a determination or decision in respect of entitlement to, or the amount of, housing benefit or council tax benefit before 6 March 1995. See Sch 3 para 1 to the HB&CTB(CP) Regs on p1099.

Amendments

1.   Amended by reg 18(3) of SI 2006 No 2378 as from 2.10.06.
2.   Substituted by reg 7 of SI 2007 No 2470 as from 24.9.07.

Change of circumstances where state pension credit in payment

51.–(1)   Paragraphs (2) to (4) apply where–

(a)   the claimant is also on state pension credit;

(b)   the amount of state pension credit awarded to him is changed in consequence of a change in the claimant's circumstances or the correction of an official error; and

(c)   the change in the amount of state pension credit payable to the claimant results in a change in the rate at which council tax benefit is allowed to him.

(2)   Where the change of circumstance is that an increase in the amount of state pension credit payable to the claimant results in–

(a)   an increase in the rate at which council tax benefit is allowed to him, the change shall take effect from the first day of the benefit week in which state pension credit becomes payable at the increased rate; or

(b)   a decrease in the rate at which council tax benefit is payable to him, the change shall take effect from the first day of the benefit week next following the date on which–

(i)   the local authority receives notification from the Secretary of State of the increase in the amount of state pension credit; or

(ii)   state pension credit is increased,

whichever is the later.

(3)   Where the change of circumstance is that the claimant's state pension credit has been reduced and in consequence the rate of council tax benefit allowed to the claimant reduces–

(a)   in a case where the claimant's state pension credit is reduced because the claimant failed to notify the Secretary of State timeously of the change of circumstances, the change shall take effect from the first day of the benefit week from which state pension credit was reduced; or

(b)   in any other case the change shall take effect from the first day of the benefit week next following the date on which–

(i)   the local authority receives notification from the Secretary of State of the reduction in the amount of state pension credit; or

(ii)   state pension credit is reduced,

whichever is the later.

(4)   Where the change of circumstance is that state pension credit is reduced and in consequence of the change, the rate of council tax benefit allowed to the

claimant is increased, the change shall take effect from the first day of the benefit week in which state pension credit becomes payable at the reduced rate.

(5)   Where a change of circumstance occurs in that an award of state pension credit has been made to the claimant or his partner and this would result in a decrease in the rate of council tax benefit payable to the claimant, the change shall take effect from the first day of the benefit week next following the date on which–

(a)   the local authority receives notification from the Secretary of State of the award of state pension credit; or

(b)   entitlement to state pension credit begins,

whichever is the later.

(6)   Where, in the case of a claimant who, or whose partner, is or has been awarded state pension credit comprising only the savings credit, there is–

(a)   a change of circumstances of a kind described in any of paragraphs (2) to (5) which results from a relevant calculation or estimate; and

(b)   a change of circumstances which is a relevant determination,

each of which results in a change in the rate of council tax benefit payable to the claimant, the change of circumstances referred to in sub-paragraph (b) shall take effect from the day specified in paragraphs (2), (3), (4) or (5) as the case may be, in relation to the change referred to in sub-paragraph (a).

(7)   Where a change of circumstance occurs in that a guarantee credit has been awarded to the claimant or his partner and this would result in an increase in the rate of council tax benefit payable to the claimant, the change shall take effect from the first day of the benefit week next following the date in respect of which the guarantee credit is first payable.

(8)   Where a change of circumstances would, but for this paragraph, take effect under the preceding provisions of this regulation within the 4 week period specified in regulation 45 (continuing payments where state pension credit claimed), that change shall take effect on the first day of the first benefit week to commence after the expiry of the 4 week period.

(9)   Where the change of circumstances is an amendment of these Regulations that change shall take effect from the date on which the amendment to these Regulations, comes into force.

(10)   In paragraph (1) "official error" has the meaning it has in the Decisions and Appeals Regulations by virtue of regulation 1(2) of those Regulations.

(11)   In this regulation–

"relevant calculation or estimate" means the calculation or estimate made by the Secretary of State of the claimant's or, as the case may be, the claimant's partner's income and capital for the purposes of the award of state pension credit;

"relevant determination" means a change in the determination by the relevant authority of the claimant's income and capital using the relevant calculation or estimate, in accordance with regulation 17(1).

PART 7

Claims

Who may claim

52.–(1)   In the case of a couple or members of a polygamous marriage a claim shall be made by whichever one of them they agree should so claim or, in default of agreement, by such one of them as the relevant authority shall determine.

(2)   Where a person who is liable to pay council tax in respect of a dwelling is unable for the time being to act, and–

(a)   a [¹ deputy] has been appointed by the Court of Protection with power to claim, or as the case may be, receive benefit on his behalf; or

   (b)   in Scotland, his estate is being administered by a judicial factor or any guardian acting or appointed under the Adults with Incapacity (Scotland) Act 2000 who has power to claim or, as the case may be, receive benefit on his behalf; or

   (c)   an attorney with a general power or a power to claim or, as the case may be, receive benefit, has been appointed by that person under [¹ the Powers of Attorney Act 1971, the Enduring Powers of Attorney Act 1985 or the Mental Capacity Act 2005] or otherwise,

that [¹ deputy], judicial factor, guardian or attorney, as the case may be, may make a claim on behalf of that person.

   (3)   Where a person who is liable to pay council tax in respect of a dwelling is unable for the time being to act and paragraph (2) does not apply to him, the relevant authority may, upon written application made to them by a person who, if a natural person, is over the age of 18, appoint that person to exercise on behalf of the person who is unable to act, any right to which that person might be entitled under the Act and to receive and deal on his behalf with any sums payable to him.

   (4)   Where the relevant authority has made an appointment under paragraph (3) or treated a person as an appointee under paragraph (5)–

   (a)   it may at any time revoke the appointment;

   (b)   the person appointed may resign his office after having given 4 weeks notice in writing to the relevant authority of his intention to do so;

   (c)   any such appointment shall terminate when the relevant authority is notified of the appointment of a person mentioned in paragraph (2).

   (5)   Where a person who is liable to pay council tax in respect of a dwelling is for the time being unable to act and the Secretary of State has appointed a person to act on his behalf under regulation 33 of the Social Security (Claims and Payments) Regulations 1987 (persons unable to act), the relevant authority may if that person agrees, treat him as if he had been appointed by them under paragraph (3).

   (6)   Anything required by these Regulations to be done by or to any person who is for the time being unable to act may be done by or to the persons mentioned in paragraph (2) above or by or to the person appointed or treated as appointed under this regulation and the receipt of any such person so appointed shall be a good discharge to the relevant authority for any sum paid.

   (7)   In its application to regulation 55, references in this regulation to a "relevant authority" shall be read as including a reference to the "designated authority".

Amendment

1.   Amended by reg 13(6) of SI 2007 No 2618 as from 1.10.07.

Time and manner in which claims are to be made

53.–[¹ (1ZA)   The prescribed time for claiming council tax benefit is as regards any day on which, apart from satisfying the condition of making a claim, the claimant is entitled to council tax benefit, that day and the period of twelve months immediately following it .]

   (1)   [¹ Subject to paragraph (4A) and (4B),] Every claim shall be in writing and made on a properly completed form approved for the purpose by the relevant authority or in such written form as the relevant authority may accept as sufficient in the circumstances of any particular case or class of cases having regard to the sufficiency of the written information and evidence.

   (2)   The forms approved for the purpose of claiming shall be provided free of charge by the relevant authority or such persons as they may authorise or appoint for the purpose.

   (3)   Each relevant authority shall notify the Secretary of State of the address to which claims delivered or sent to the appropriate DWP office are to be forwarded.

   (4)   A claim [¹ in writing]–

(a)   may be sent or delivered to the appropriate DWP office where the claimant or his partner is also claiming income support, incapacity benefit, state pension credit or a jobseeker's allowance;

(b)   where it has not been sent or delivered to the appropriate DWP office, shall be sent or delivered to the designated office;

(c)   sent or delivered to the appropriate DWP office, other than one sent on the same form as a claim being made to income support, incapacity benefit or a jobseeker's allowance and as approved by the Secretary of State for the purpose of the benefits being claimed, shall be forwarded to the relevant authority within two working days of the date of the receipt of the claim at the appropriate DWP office, or as soon as practicable thereafter;

(d)   may, in the case of a claimant who has attained the age of 16 but not the age of 60 and is not engaged in remunerative work, be sent or delivered to a gateway office;

(e)   may be sent or delivered where the claimant has attained the age of 16 but not the age of 60 to an office or designated authority displaying the ONE logo;

(f)   where the claimant has attained the qualifying age for state pension credit, may be sent or delivered to an office which is an authorised office.

[³ (g) may be sent or delivered to the offices of a county council in England if the council has arranged with the relevant authority for claims to be received at their offices (''county offices'').]

[¹ (4A)   Where the relevant authority has published a telephone number for the purpose of receiving claims for council tax benefit, a claim may be made by telephone to that telephone number.

(4B)   A person who is making a claim for state pension credit in accordance with regulation 4D(6A) of the Social Security (Claims and Payments) Regulations 1987 may make his claim for council tax benefit to the Secretary of State.

(4C)   The relevant authority may determine, in any particular case, that a claim made by telephone is not a valid claim unless the person making the claim approves a written statement of his circumstances, provided for the purpose by the relevant authority or the Secretary of State.

(4D)   A claim made by telephone in accordance with paragraph (4A) or (4B) is defective unless the relevant authority or the Secretary of State, as the case may be, is provided during that telephone call with all the information the relevant authority requires to determine the claim.

(4E)   Where a claim made by telephone in accordance with paragraph (4A) or (4B) is defective, the relevant authority is to provide the person making it with an opportunity to correct the defect.

(4F)   If the person corrects the defect within one month, or such longer period as the relevant authority considers reasonable, of the date it last drew attention to it, the relevant authority shall treat the claim as if it had been duly made in the first instance.]

(5)   Subject to paragraph (12), and to regulation 54 (date of claim where claim sent or delivered to a gateway office) the date on which a claim is made shall be–

(a)   in a case where an award of state pension credit which comprises a guarantee credit has been made to the claimant or his partner and the claim for council tax benefit is made within one month of the date on which the claim for that state pension credit which comprises a guarantee credit was received at the appropriate DWP office, the first day of entitlement to, state pension credit which comprises a guarantee credit arising from that claim;

(b)   in a case where a claimant or his partner is a person in receipt of a guarantee credit and he becomes liable for the first time to pay council tax in respect of the dwelling he occupies as his home, where the claim to the authority is received at the designated office or appropriate social security office within one month of the date of the change, the date on which the change takes place;

(c) in a case where the claimant is the former partner of a person who was, at the date of his death or their separation, entitled to council tax benefit and where the claimant makes a claim for council tax benefit within one month of the date of the death or the separation, that date;

(d) except where sub-paragraph (a), (b) or (c) is satisfied, in a case where a properly completed claim is received in a designated office, an authorised office [³ , county offices] or an appropriate DWP office within one month of the date on which a claim form was issued following the claimant first notifying, by whatever means, a designated office, an authorised office [³ , county offices] or an appropriate DWP office of his intention of making a claim, the date of first notification; and

(e) in any other case, the date on which the claim is received at the designated office [¹ or authorised office [³ , county offices] or appropriate DWP office].

(6) Where a claim received at the designated office has not been made in the manner prescribed in paragraph (1), that claim is for the purposes of these Regulations defective.

(7) Where a claim is defective because—

(a) it was made on the form approved for the purpose but that form is not accepted by the relevant authority as being properly completed; or

(b) it was made in writing but not on the form approved for the purpose and the relevant authority does not accept the claim as being in a written form which is sufficient in the circumstances of the case having regard to the sufficiency of the written information and evidence,

the relevant authority may, in a case to which sub-paragraph (a) applies, request the claimant to complete the defective claim or, in the case to which sub-paragraph (b) applies, supply the claimant with the approved form or request further information and evidence.

(8) The relevant authority shall treat a defective claim as if it had been validly made in the first instance if—

(a) where paragraph (7)(a) applies, the authority receives at the designated office the properly completed claim or the information requested to complete it or the evidence within one month of the request, or such longer period as the relevant authority may consider reasonable; or

(b) where paragraph (7)(b) applies—

(i) the approved form sent to the claimant is received at the designated office properly completed within one month of it having been sent to him; or, as the case may be,

(ii) the claimant supplies whatever information or evidence was requested under paragraph (7) within one month of the request,

or within such longer period as the relevant authority may consider reasonable.

(9) A claim which is made on an approved form for the time being is, for the purposes of this regulation, properly completed if completed in accordance with the instructions on the form, including any instructions to provide information and evidence in connection with the claim.

[² (10) Except in the case of a claim made by a person from abroad, where a person has not become liable for council tax to a relevant authority but it is anticipated that he will become so liable within the period of 8 weeks (the relevant period), he may claim council tax benefit at any time in that period in respect of that tax and, provided that liability arises within the relevant period, the authority shall treat the claim as having been made on the day on which the liability for the tax arises.]

(11)   Where, exceptionally, a relevant authority, has not set or imposed its council tax by the beginning of the financial year, if a claim for council tax benefit is properly made or treated as properly made and–
  (a)   the date on which the claim is made or treated as made is in the period from the 1st April of the current year and ending one month after the date on which the authority sets or imposes the tax; and
  (b)   if the tax had been determined, the claimant would have been entitled to council tax benefit either from–
      (i)   the benefit week in which the 1st April of the current year fell; or
      (ii)   a benefit week falling after the date specified in head (i) but before the claim was made,
the relevant authority shall treat the claim as made in the benefit week immediately preceding the benefit week in which such entitlement would have commenced.

[² (12)   Except in the case of a claim made by a person from abroad, where the claimant is not entitled to council tax benefit in the benefit week immediately following the date of his claim but the relevant authority is of the opinion that unless there is a change of circumstances he will be entitled to council tax benefit for a period beginning not later than the seventeenth benefit week following the date on which the claim is made, the relevant authority may treat the claim as made on a date in the benefit week immediately preceding the first benefit week of that period of entitlement and award benefit accordingly.]

(13)   Where the claimant makes a claim in respect of a past period (a "claim for backdating") and, from a day in that period up to the date of the claim for backdating, he had continuous good cause for his failure to make a claim, his claim in respect of that period shall be treated as made on–
  (a)   the first day from which he had continuous good cause; or
  (b)   the day 52 weeks before the date of the claim for backdating,
whichever fell later.

(14)   In this regulation "authorised office" means an office which is nominated by the Secretary of State and authorised by relevant authority for receiving claims for decision by the relevant authority.

Amendments

  1.   Inserted by reg 5(2) of SI 2006 No 2967 as from 20.12.06.
  2.   Substituted by reg 6 of SI 2007 No 1331 as from 23.5.07.
  3.   Amended by reg 10(2) of SI 2007 No 2911 as from 31.10.07.

General Note

  Para (13) will not be needed for those making backdated claims under these regulations. These can be backdated automatically for 12 months under para (1ZA) and reg 56. As the HB(CTB) Regs were a consolidation exercise, some regulations (and parts of regulations) had to be kept in, although they were *otiose*. This is one such provision. Note that the para (1ZA) and reg 56 are effectively the same.

[¹Electronic claims for benefit

53A.   A claim for council tax benefit may be made by means of an electronic communication in accordance with Schedule 8.]

Amendment

  1.   Inserted by Art 5(3) of SI 2006 No 2968 as from 20.12.06.

Date of claim where claim sent or delivered to a gateway office

54.–(1)   Subject to paragraphs (10), (11) and (12) of regulation 53 (time and manner in which claims are to be made), and with the exception of those claims to which paragraph (3) of this regulation refers, where a claim for council tax benefit has been sent or delivered to a gateway office in accordance with sub-paragraph (d) of paragraph (4) of regulation 53, the date on which that claim is made shall be–

(a)   in a case where the claimant or his partner–
  (i)   claimed income support or a jobseeker's allowance; but
  (ii)   has no entitlement to income support or an income-based jobseeker's allowance,
the first date on which notification is deemed to be given in accordance with paragraph (2), but if that notification is by any means other than a claim which meets the requirements of regulation 53(1) such a claim must be received at a gateway office within one month of that notification;
(b)   in a case where neither the claimant nor his partner is a person on income support or entitled to an income-based jobseeker's allowance, the first date on which notification is deemed to be given in accordance with paragraph (2), but if that notification is by any means other than a claim which meets the requirements of regulation 53(1) such a claim must be received at the gateway office within one month of that notification; or
(c)   in any other case, the date on which the claim for council tax benefit is received at the gateway office.

(2)   A notification of intention to make a claim is deemed to be given on the date on which notification from the claimant of his intention to claim council tax benefit is received in whatever form at a gateway office.

(3)   This regulation does not apply to claims which are made at an office of a designated authority in accordance with regulation 53(4)(e).

Date of claim where claim sent or delivered to an office of a designated authority

55.–(1)   Where a claim for council tax benefit has been sent or delivered to an office of a designated authority in accordance with regulation 53(4)(e), the date on which the claim is made shall be–
(a)   except where paragraph (b) applies, the date the claim is received at an office of the designated authority; or
(b)   where in the one month before the claim is received in an office of a designated authority, the person making the claim or a person acting on his behalf had notified an office of a designated authority of his intention to make such a claim, the date the notification was given.

(2)   A notification of intention to make a claim is deemed to be given on the date on which notification of the intention to claim council tax benefit is received, in whatever form, from the claimant, or the person acting on his behalf, at an office of a designated authority.

(3)   Paragraph (2) applies where neither income support nor a jobseeker's allowance is claimed in conjunction with council tax benefit.

(4)   Where the person claiming council tax benefit in accordance with regulation 53(4)(e), or the partner of that person has claimed income support or income-based jobseeker's allowance but no award of that benefit has been made, the date on which the claim for council tax benefit is made shall be determined as if sub-paragraphs (a) and (c) of paragraph (1) of regulation 54 applied to that claim as they apply to claims under regulation 53(4)(d).

Time for claiming council tax benefit

56.   The prescribed time for claiming council tax benefit is as regards any day on which, apart from satisfying the condition for making the claim, the claimant is entitled to council tax benefit, that day and the period of 12 months immediately following it.

Evidence and information

57.–(1)   Subject to paragraph (2) and to paragraph 4 of Schedule A1 (treatment of claims for council tax benefit by refugees), a person who makes a claim, or a person to whom council tax benefit has been awarded, shall furnish such certificates, documents, information and evidence in connection with the claim or the award, or any question arising out of the claim or the award, as may reasonably be required by the relevant authority in order to determine that person's entitlement to, or continuing entitlement to council tax benefit and shall do so within one month of being required to do so or such longer period as the relevant authority may consider reasonable.

(2)   Nothing in this regulation shall require a person to furnish any certificates, documents, information or evidence relating to a payment to which paragraph (4) applies.

(3)   Where a request is made under paragraph (1), the relevant authority shall–

(a)   inform the claimant or the person to whom council tax benefit has been awarded of his duty under regulation 59 (duty to notify change of circumstances) to notify the designated office of any change of circumstances; and

(b)   without prejudice to the extent of the duty owed under regulation 59, indicate to him either orally or by notice or by reference to some other document available to him on application and without charge, the kind of change of circumstances which is to be notified.

(4)   This paragraph applies to any of the following payments–

(a)   a payment which is made under the Trusts, the Fund, the Eileen Trust, the Skipton Fund or the London Bombings Relief Charitable Fund;

(b)   a payment which is disregarded under paragraph 16 of Schedule 4 (payments made under certain trusts and certain other payments), other than a payment under the Independent Living Funds;

(c)   a payment which is disregarded under regulation 42(9)(b) or (c) (non-dependant deductions) or paragraph 2(b) or (c) of Schedule 6 (second adult's gross income) other than a payment under the Independent Living Funds.

(5)   Where a claimant or a person to whom council tax benefit has been awarded or any partner is aged not less than 60 and is a member of, or a person deriving entitlement to a pension under, a personal pension scheme, [¹] he shall where the relevant authority so requires furnish the following information–

(a)   the name and address of the pension fund holder;

(b)   such other information including any reference or policy number as is needed to enable the personal pension scheme [¹] to be identified.

(6)   Where the pension fund holder receives from a relevant authority a request for details concerning a personal pension scheme [¹] relating to a person or any partner to whom paragraph (5) refers, the pension fund holder shall provide the relevant authority with any information to which paragraph (7) refers.

(7)   The information to which this paragraph refers is–

(a)   where the purchase of an annuity under a personal pension scheme has been deferred, the amount of any income which is being withdrawn from the personal pension scheme;

(b)   in the case of–

(i)   a personal pension scheme where income withdrawal is available, the maximum amount of income which may be withdrawn from the scheme; or

(ii)   a personal pension scheme where income withdrawal is not available, [¹] the maximum amount of income which might be withdrawn from the fund if the fund were held under a personal pension scheme where income withdrawal was available,

calculated by or on behalf of the pension fund holder by means of tables prepared from time to time by the Government Actuary which are appropriate for this purpose.

Amendment

1.   Amended by reg 7(5) of SI 2007 No 1749 as from 16.7.07.

[²Amendment and withdrawal of claim

58.–(1)   A person who has made a claim may amend it at any time before a decision has been made on it, by a notice in writing delivered or sent to the designated office, except where the claim was made by telephone in accordance with regulation 53(4A) where the amendment may be made by telephone, and any claim so amended shall be treated as if it had been amended in the first instance.

(2)   A person who has made a claim may withdraw it at any time before a decision has been made on it, by notice to the designated office, and any such notice of withdrawal shall have effect when it is received.]

Amendments

1.   Inserted by reg 5(3) of SI 2006 No 2967 as from 20.12.06.
2.   Substituted by reg 9(2) of SI 2007 No 719 as from 2.4.07.

Duty to notify changes of circumstances

59.–(1)   Subject to paragraphs (3), (5) to (8), if at any time between the making of a claim and a decision being made on it, or during the award of council tax benefit, there is a change of circumstances which the claimant or any person by whom or on whose behalf sums payable by way of council tax benefit are receivable might reasonably be expected to know might affect the claimant's right to, the amount of, or the receipt of council tax benefit, that person shall be under a duty to notify that change of circumstances by giving notice [²] to the designated office

[² (a) in writing or, where the relevant authority has published a telephone number for the purposes of regulation 53 (time and manner in which claims are to be made), by telephone unless the authority determines, in any particular case, that notice must be in writing or may be given otherwise than in writing or by telephone; or

(b)   in writing if in any class of case the relevant authority requires written notice unless the authority determines, in any particular case, that notice may be given otherwise than in writing.]

(2)   In the case of a claimant who sent or delivered his claim to a gateway office in accordance with regulation 54 (date of claim where claim sent or delivered to a gateway office), a change of circumstances may be reported in writing to that office, or to any other gateway office that was notified to him on or with his claim form.

(3)   The duty imposed on a person by paragraph (1) does not extend to notifying changes in–

(a)   the amount of a council tax payable to the relevant authority;

(b)   the age of the claimant or that of any member of his family;

(c)   in these Regulations.

(4)   Notwithstanding paragraph (3)(b) a claimant shall be required by paragraph (1) to notify the designated office of any change in the composition of his family arising from the fact that a person who was a member of his family is now no longer such a person because he ceases to be a child or young person.

(5)   Where the amount of a claimant's council tax benefit is the alternative maximum council tax benefit in his case, the claimant shall be under a duty to give written notice to the designated office of changes which occur in the number of adults in the dwelling or in their total gross incomes which might reasonably be expected to change his entitlement to that council tax benefit and where any such adult ceases to be in receipt of income support or an income-based jobseeker's allowance the date when this occurs.

(6)   Where a person resides in a postcode district identified in Part 1 or 2 of Schedule 2 to the Social Security (Claims and Information) Regulations 1999, he

may notify the change of circumstances to any office of a designated authority displaying the ONE logo.

(7)   A person entitled to council tax benefit who is also on state pension credit must report–

(a)   changes affecting the residence or income of any non-dependant normally residing with the claimant or with whom the claimant normally resides;

(b)   any absence from the dwelling which exceeds or is likely to exceed 13 weeks.

(8)   In addition to the changes required to be reported under paragraph (7), a person whose state pension credit comprises only a savings credit must also report–

(a)   changes affecting a child living with him which may result in a change in the amount of council tax benefit allowed in his case, but not changes in the age of the child;

[¹ (b)]

(c)   any change in the amount of the claimant's capital to be taken into account which does or may take the amount of his capital to more than £16,000;

(d)   any change in the income or capital of–

(i)   a non-dependant whose income and capital are treated as belonging to the claimant in accordance with regulation 14 (circumstances in which income of a non-dependant is to be treated as claimant's); or

(ii)   a person to whom regulation 17(4)(e) refers,

and whether such a person or, as the case may be, non-dependant stops living or begins or resumes living with the claimant.

(9)   A person who is entitled to council tax benefit and on state pension credit need only report to the designated office the changes specified in paragraphs (7) and (8).

Amendments

1.   Omitted by reg 3(9) of SI 2005 No 2502 as amended by Sch 2 para 27 of SI 2006 No 217 as from 1.4.06.

2.   Amended by reg 5(4) of SI 2006 No 2967 as from 20.12.06.

[¹Notice of changes of circumstances given electronically

59A.   A person may give notice of a change of circumstances required to be notified under regulation 59 by means of an electronic communication in accordance with Schedule 8.]

Amendment

1.   Inserted by Art 5(4) of SI 2006 No 2968 as from 20.12.06.

PART 8
Decisions on questions

Decisions by a relevant authority

60.–(1)   Unless provided otherwise by these Regulations, any matter required to be determined under these Regulations shall be determined in the first instance by the relevant authority.

(2)   The relevant authority shall make a decision on each claim within 14 days of the provisions of regulations 53 and 57 (time and manner in which claims are to be made and evidence and information) being satisfied or as soon as reasonably practicable thereafter.

(3)   Without prejudice to the generality of the foregoing provisions of this regulation, in a case where a person–

(a)   made the notification specified in paragraph 2 of Schedule 6 to the Council Tax Benefit Regulations 2006 (extended payments of council tax) within

14 days from the day immediately after the day on which his entitlement to income support or an income-based jobseeker's allowance ceased ("the appropriate day") and is treated as having claimed an extended payment under regulation 60(2) of those Regulations; and

(b) has made a claim, which meets the requirements of regulation 53(1), (6) and (9), within 14 days of the appropriate day,

the relevant authority shall give priority to that claim over other claims which do not fall within the provisions of this paragraph.

Notification of decision

61.–(1) Except in cases to which paragraphs (a) and (b) of regulation 67 (excess benefit in consequence of a reduction of a relevant authority's council tax) refer, an Authority shall notify in writing any person affected by a decision made by it under these Regulations–

(a) in the case of a decision on a claim, forthwith or as soon as reasonably practicable thereafter;

(b) in any other case, within 14 days of that decision or as soon as reasonably practicable thereafter,

and every notification shall include a statement as to the matters set out in Schedule 7.

(2) A person affected to whom an authority sends or delivers a notification of decision may request in writing the authority to provide a written statement setting out the reasons for its decision on any matter set out in the notice.

(3) The written statement referred to in paragraph (2) shall be sent to the person requesting it within 14 days or as soon as is reasonably practical thereafter.

PART 9
Awards or payments of benefit

Time and manner of granting council tax benefit

62.–(1) Subject to regulations 65 and 66 (payments on death and offsetting), where a person is entitled to council tax benefit in respect of his liability for a relevant authority's council tax as it has effect in respect of the relevant or any subsequent chargeable financial year, the relevant authority shall discharge his entitlement–

(a) by reducing, so far as possible, the amount of his liability to which regulation 20(2) of the Council Tax (Administration and Enforcement) Regulations 1992 (the English and Welsh Regulations) or regulation 20(2) of the Council Tax (Administration and Enforcement) (Scotland) Regulations 1992 (the Scottish Regulations) refers; or

(b) where–
  (i) such a reduction is not possible; or
  (ii) such a reduction would be insufficient to discharge the entitlement to council tax benefit; or
  (iii) the person entitled to council tax benefit is jointly and severally liable for the tax and the relevant authority determines that such a reduction would be inappropriate,

by making payments to him of the benefit to which he is entitled, rounded where necessary to the nearest penny.

(2) The relevant authority shall notify the person entitled to council tax benefit of the amount of that benefit and how his entitlement is to be discharged in pursuance of paragraph (1).

(3) In a case to which paragraph (1)(b) refers–

(a) if the amount of the council tax for which he remains liable in respect of the relevant chargeable financial year, after any reduction to which paragraph (1)(a) refers has been made, is insufficient to enable his entitlement to council tax benefit in respect thereof to be discharged in that year, upon the final instalment of that tax becoming due any outstanding benefit–

(i) shall be paid to that person if he so requires; or

(ii) in any other case shall (as the relevant authority determines) either be repaid or credited against any subsequent liability of the person to make a payment in respect of the authority's council tax as it has effect for any subsequent year;

(b) if that person has ceased to be liable for the relevant authority's council tax and has discharged the liability for that tax, the outstanding balance (if any) of the council tax benefit in respect thereof shall be paid within 14 days or, if that is not reasonably practicable, as soon as practicable thereafter;

(c) in any other case, the council tax benefit shall be paid within 14 days of the receipt of the claim at the designated office or, if that is not reasonably practicable, as soon as practicable thereafter.

(4) For the purposes of this regulation "instalment" means any instalment of a relevant authority's council tax to which regulation 19 of either the English and Welsh Regulations or as the case may be the Scottish Regulations refers (council tax payments).

Person to whom benefit is to be paid

63.–(1) Subject to regulation 65 (payment on death) and paragraph (2), any payment of council tax benefit under regulation 62(1)(b) shall be made to that person.

(2) Where a person other than a person who is entitled to council tax benefit made the claim and that first person is a person acting pursuant to an appointment under regulation 52(3) (persons appointed to act for a person unable to act) or is treated as having been so appointed by virtue of regulation 52(5), benefit may be paid to that person.

Shortfall in benefit

64.–(1) Except in cases to which paragraph (2) refers, where, on the revision of a decision allowing council tax benefit to a person, it is determined that the amount allowed was less than the amount to which that person was entitled, the relevant authority shall either–

(a) make good any shortfall in benefit which is due to that person, by reducing so far as possible the next and any subsequent payments he is liable to make in respect of the council tax of the authority concerned as it has effect for the relevant chargeable financial year until that shortfall is made good; or

(b) where this is not possible or the person concerned so requests, pay any shortfall in benefit due to that person within 14 days of the revision of the decision being made or if that is not reasonable practicable, as soon as possible afterwards.

(2) A shortfall in benefit need not be paid in any case to the extent that there is due from the person concerned to the relevant authority any recoverable excess benefit to which regulation 68(1) refers.

Payment on the death of the person entitled

65.–(1) Where the person entitled to any council tax benefit has died and it is not possible to award any council tax benefit which is due in the form of a reduction of the council tax for which he was liable, the relevant authority shall make payment either to his personal representative or, where there is none, his next of kin aged 16 or over.

(2)   For the purposes of paragraph (1), "next of kin" means in England and Wales the persons who would take beneficially on an intestacy and in Scotland the person entitled to the moveable estate on intestacy.

(3)   A payment under paragraph (1) may not be made unless the personal representative or the next of kin, as the case may be, makes written application for the payment of any sum of benefit to which the deceased was entitled, and such written application is sent to or delivered to the relevant authority at its designated office within 12 months of the deceased's death or such longer period as the authority may allow in any particular case.

(4)   The authority may dispense with strict proof of title of any person claiming under paragraph (3) and the receipt of such a person shall be a good discharge to the authority for any sum so paid.

Offsetting

66.–(1)   Where a person has been allowed or paid a sum of council tax benefit under a decision which is subsequently revised or further revised, any sum allowed or paid in respect of a period covered by the subsequent decision shall be offset against arrears of entitlement under the subsequent decision except to the extent that the sum exceeds the arrears and shall be treated as properly awarded or paid on account of them.

(2)   Where an amount has been deducted under regulation 74(1) an equivalent sum shall be offset against any arrears of entitlement under the subsequent determination.

(3)   No amount may be offset under paragraph (1) which has been determined to be excess benefit within the meaning of regulation 67 (meaning of excess benefit).

PART 10
Excess benefit

Meaning of excess benefit

67.   In this Part "excess benefit" means any amount which as been allowed by way of council tax benefit and to which there was no entitlement under these Regulations (whether on the initial decision [1 or as subsequently revised or superseded or further revised or superseded]) and includes any excess which arises by reason of–

(a)   a reduction in the amount a person is liable to pay in respect of council tax in consequence of–
  (i)   regulations made under section 13 of the 1992 Act (reduction in the amount of a person's council tax); or
  (ii)   any discount to which that tax is subject by virtue of section 11 or 79 of that Act;

(b)   a substitution under sections 31 or 60 or, in Scotland, section 94 of the 1992 Act (substituted amounts) of a lesser amount for an amount of council tax previously set by the relevant authority under section 30 or, in Scotland section 93 of that Act (amount set for council tax).

Amendment

1.   Amended by reg 3 of SI 2005 No 2904 as amended by Sch 2 para 29 of SI 2006 No 217 as from 10.4.06.

Recoverable excess benefit

68.–(1)   Any excess benefit, except benefit to which paragraph (2) applies, shall be recoverable.

(2)   Subject to paragraph (4) and (5) and excepting any excess benefit arising in consequence of a reduction in tax or substitution to which regulation 67 refers, this

paragraph applies to excess benefit allowed in consequence of an official error, where the claimant or a person acting on his behalf or any other person to whom the excess benefit is allowed could not, at the time the benefit was allowed or upon the receipt of any notice relating to the allowance of that benefit, reasonably have been expected to realise that it was excess benefit.

(3) In paragraph (2), "excess benefit allowed in consequence of an official error" means an overpayment caused by a mistake made whether in the form of an act or omission by–

(a) the relevant authority;

(b) an officer or person acting for that authority;

(c) an officer of–

(i) the Department for Work and Pensions; or

(ii) the Commissioners for Her Majesty's Revenue and Customs,

acting as such; or

(d) a person providing services to the Department or to the Commissioners referred to in (c),

where the claimant, a person acting on his behalf or any other person to whom the payment is made, did not cause or materially contribute to that mistake, act or omission.

(4) Paragraph (2) shall not apply with respect to excess benefit to which regulation 67(a) and (b) refers.

(5) Where in consequence of an official error a person has been awarded excess benefit, upon the award being revised [¹ or superseded] any excess benefit which remains credited to him by the relevant authority in respect of a period after the date of the revision [¹ or supersession], shall be recoverable.

Amendment

1. Amended by reg 5 of SI 2005 No 2904 as amended by Sch 2 para 29 of SI 2006 No 217 as from 10.4.06.

Authority by which recovery may be made

69. The relevant authority which allowed the recoverable excess benefit may recover it.

Persons from whom recovery may be sought

70.–(1) Subject to paragraph (2), recoverable excess benefit shall be due from the claimant or the person to whom the excess benefit was allowed.

(2) Where recoverable excess benefit is allowed to a claimant who has one or more partners, recovery of the excess may be made by deduction from any council tax benefit allowed to a partner, provided the claimant and that partner were members of the same household both at the time the excess benefit is allowed and when the deduction is made.

Methods of recovery

71.–(1) Without prejudice to any other method of recovery a relevant authority may recover any recoverable excess benefit due from any person referred to in regulation 70 (person from whom recovery may be sought) by any of the methods specified in paragraph (2) and (3) or any combination of those methods.

(2) Excess benefit may be recovered either–

(a) by payment by or on behalf of the person to whom regulation 70(1) refers; or

(b) by an addition being made by the relevant authority to any amount payable in respect of the council tax concerned.

(3) Where recoverable excess benefit due from any person cannot be recovered by either of the methods specified in paragraph (2), the relevant authority may

request the Secretary of State to recover the outstanding excess from the benefits prescribed in regulation 75 in accordance with the provisions of that regulation.

Further provision as to recovery of excess benefit

72. In addition to the methods for recovery of excess benefit which are specified in regulation 71, any sum or part of a sum which is due from the person concerned and which is not paid within 21 days of his being notified of the amount that is due, shall be recoverable in a court of competent jurisdiction by the authority to which the excess benefit is due.

Diminution of capital

73.–(1) Where in the case of recoverable excess benefit, in consequence of a misrepresentation or failure to disclose a material fact (in either case whether fraudulent or otherwise) as to a person's capital, or an error, other than one to which regulation 68(2) (effect of official error) refers, as to the amount of a person's capital, the excess benefit was in respect of a period ("the excess benefit period") of more than 13 benefit weeks, the relevant authority shall, for the purpose only of calculating the amount of excess–

    (a)   at the end of the first 13 benefit weeks of the excess benefit period, treat the amount of the capital as having been reduced by the amount of excess council tax benefit allowed during those 13 weeks;

    (b)   at the end of each subsequent period of 13 benefit weeks, if any, of the excess benefit period, treat the amount of that capital as having been further reduced by the amount of excess council tax benefit allowed during the immediately preceding 13 benefit weeks.

    (2) Capital shall not be treated as reduced over any period other than 13 benefit weeks or in any circumstances other than those, for which paragraph (1) provides.

Sums to be deducted in calculating recoverable excess benefit

74.–(1) In calculating the amount of recoverable excess benefit, the relevant authority shall deduct any amount of council tax benefit which should have been determined to be payable in respect of the whole or part of the overpayment period–

    (a)   on the basis of the claim as presented to the authority;

    (b)   on the basis of the claim as it would have appeared had any misrepresentation or non-disclosure been remedied before the decision; or

    (c)   on the basis of the claim as it would have appeared if any change of circumstances had been notified at the time that change occurred.

    (2) In calculating the amount of recoverable excess benefit, the relevant authority may deduct so much of any payment of council tax in respect of the excess benefit period which exceeds the amount, if any, which the claimant was liable to pay for that period under the original erroneous decision.

Recovery of excess benefit from prescribed benefits

75.–(1) For the purposes of section 76(3)(c) of the Administration Act (deduction of excess council tax benefit from prescribed benefits), the benefits prescribed by this regulation are–

    (a)   any benefit payable under the Act, except guardian's allowance or housing benefit;

    (b)   any benefit payable under the legislation of any member State, other than the United Kingdom, concerning the branches of social security mentioned in article 4(1) of Regulation (EEC) No. 1408/71 on the application of social security schemes to employed persons, to self-employed persons and to members of their families moving within the Community, whether or not the benefit has been acquired by virtue of the provisions of that Regulation;

    (c)   a jobseeker's allowance;

(d)   state pension credit.

[¹ (1A)   For the purposes of paragraph (1)(b) the term ''member State'' shall be understood to include Switzerland in accordance with and subject to the provisions of Annex II of the Agreement between the European Community and its Member States and the Swiss Confederation on the free movement of persons, signed at Brussels on 21st June 1999.]

(2)   Where the Secretary of State is satisfied that–

(a)   recoverable excess benefit has been allowed in consequence of a misrepresentation of or failure to disclose a material fact (in either case whether fraudulent or otherwise), by a claimant or any other person to whom council tax benefit has been allowed; and

(b)   the person who misrepresented that fact or failed to disclose it is receiving a sufficient amount of one or more of the benefits prescribed in paragraph (1) to enable deductions to be made for the recovery of the excess,

he shall, if requested to do so by a relevant authority under regulation 71 (methods of recovery) recover the excess by deduction from any of those benefits.

Amendment

1.   Inserted by reg 10 of SI 2005 No 2904 as amended by Sch 2 para 29 of SI 2006 No 217 as from 10.4.06.

PART 11
Information
SECTION 1
Claims and information

Interpretation

76.   In this Section–

[¹ ''county council'' means a county council in England, but only if the council has made an arrangement in accordance with regulation 53(4)(g) or 77(3);]

''local authority'' means an authority administering council tax benefit;

''relevant authority'' means–

(a)   the Secretary of State;

(b)   a person providing services to the Secretary of State; [¹ or

(c)   a county council;]

''relevant information'' means information or evidence relating to the administration of claims to or awards of council tax benefit.

Amendment

1.   Amended by reg 10(3) of SI 2007 No 2911 as from 31.10.07.

[¹Collection of information

77.–(1)   The Secretary of State, or a person providing services to him, may receive or obtain relevant information from–

(a)   persons making, or who have made, claims for council tax benefit; or

(b)   other persons in connection with such claims.

(2)   In paragraph (1) references to persons who have made claims for council tax benefit include persons to whom awards of benefit have been made on those claims.

(3)   Where a county council has made an arrangement with a local authority, or a person authorised to exercise any function of a local authority relating to housing benefit or council tax benefit, to receive and obtain information and evidence relating to a claim for council tax benefit, the council may receive or obtain the information or evidence from–

(a)   persons making claims for council tax benefit; or

(b)   other persons in connection with such claims.

(4)   A county council may receive information relating to an award of council tax benefit which is supplied by–

(a)   the person to whom the award has been made; or

(b)   other persons in connection with the award.]

Amendment

1.   Substituted by reg 10(4) of SI 2007 No 2911 as from 31.10.07.

[¹Verifying information

77A.   A relevant authority may verify relevant information supplied to, or obtained by, the authority in accordance with regulation 77.]

Amendment

1.   Inserted by reg 10(5) of SI 2007 No 2911 as from 31.10.07.

[¹Recording and holding information

78.   A relevant authority which obtains relevant information or to whom such information is supplied–

(a)   shall make a record of such information; and

(b)   may hold that information, whether as supplied or obtained or recorded, for the purpose of forwarding it to the person or authority for the time being administering council tax benefit.]

Amendment

1.   Substituted by reg 10(6) of SI 2007 No 2911 as from 31.10.07.

Forwarding of information

79.   A relevant authority which holds relevant information–

(a)   shall forward it to the person or authority for the time being administering claims to or awards of council tax benefit to which the relevant information relates, being–

   (i)   a local authority;

   (ii)   a person providing services to a local authority; or

   (iii)   a person authorised to exercise any function of a local authority relating to council tax benefit; and

[¹ (b)   may, if the relevant authority is the Secretary of State or a person providing services to the Secretary of State, continue to hold a record of such information, whether as supplied or obtained or recorded, for such period as he considers appropriate.]

Amendment

1.   Substituted by reg 10(7) of SI 2007 No 2911 as from 31.10.07.

Request for information

80.   A relevant authority which holds information or evidence relating to social security matters shall forward such information or evidence as may be requested to the person or authority making that request, provided that–

(a)   the request is made by–

   (i)   a local authority;

   (ii)   a person providing services to a local authority; or

   (iii)   a person authorised to exercise any function of a local authority relating to council tax benefit; and

(b)   the information or evidence requested includes relevant information;

(c)   the relevant authority is able to provide the information or evidence requested in the form in which it was originally supplied or obtained; and

(d) provision of the information or evidence requested is considered necessary by the relevant authority to the proper performance by a local authority of its functions relating to council tax benefit.

SECTION 2
Information between authorities etc.

Information to be supplied by an authority to another authority

81.–(1) For the purposes of section 128A of the Administration Act (duty of an authority to disclose information to another authority) the circumstances in which information is to be disclosed are prescribed in paragraph (2) and the information prescribed by this regulation is described in paragraph (3).

(2) The circumstances prescribed in this paragraph are, where–

(a) there is a mover who is or was allowed council tax benefit by appropriate authority ''A'';

(b) who is liable to pay council tax in respect of his second dwelling to authority ''B''; and

(c) either–

    (i) the extended payment is claimed from authority A; or

    (ii) the extended payment is claimed from authority B, who then requests the prescribed information from authority A,

authority A shall disclose to authority B the information prescribed in paragraph (3).

(3) The information to be disclosed is–

(a) in a case where that extended payment was claimed from authority A, details relevant to that claim of–

    (i) the matters certified pursuant to regulation 60 of and paragraph 1 of Schedule 6 to the Council Tax Benefits Regulations 2006; and

    (ii) the matters notified pursuant to regulation 60 of and paragraph 2 of Schedule 6 to those Regulations; and

    (iii) the date it was so claimed;

(b) in the case of a person to whom regulation 6(5) of the Income Support (General) Regulations 1987 (persons not treated as engaged in remunerative work) applies–

    (i) the date on which he was first engaged in the work referred to in sub-paragraph (a) of regulation 6(5) of those Regulations; and

    (ii) the date on which his entitlement to income support ceased or was expected to cease; and

(c) in any case–

    (i) the weekly rate of council tax benefit allowed to the mover by authority A;

    (ii) if any deduction was being made from that benefit in respect of non-dependants, pursuant to regulations 40(1) and 42, the amount of those deductions;

    (iii) if any addition was being made to any amount payable in respect of council tax to recover recoverable excess benefit pursuant to regulation 71(2)(b), the amount of those additions;

    (iv) the date on which his entitlement to council tax benefit ceased;

    (v) if an extended payment was allowed to the mover, the amount and date of any such payment;

    (vi) if no extended payment was allowed, why none was allowed.

(4) In this regulation ''mover'' and ''second dwelling'' have the meanings assigned to them in paragraph 7 of Schedule 6 to the Council Tax Benefit Regulations 2006.

Supply of information: extended payments (severe disablement allowance and incapacity benefit)

82.–(1)   For the purposes of section 122E(3) of the Administration Act (duty of an authority to supply information to another authority) the circumstances in which information is to be supplied are prescribed in paragraph (2) and the information prescribed by this regulation is described in paragraph (3).

(2)   The circumstances prescribed in this paragraph are, where–

(a)   there is a mover who is or was allowed council tax benefit by appropriate authority "A";

(b)   who is liable to pay council tax in respect of his second dwelling to authority "B"; and

(c)   either–

   (i)   the extended payment (severe disablement allowance and incapacity benefit) is claimed from authority A; or

   (ii)   the extended payment (severe disablement allowance and incapacity benefit) is claimed from authority B, who then requests the information described in paragraph (3) from authority A,

authority A shall supply to authority B that information.

(3)   The information to be supplied is–

(a)   in a case where that extended payment (severe disablement allowance and incapacity benefit) was claimed from authority A, details relevant to that claim of–

   (i)   the matters set out in regulation 49 or regulation 44(1)(b)(i) to (iii), as the case may be; and

   (ii)   the matters notified pursuant to regulation 44(1)(a)(ii) or (b)(iv), as the case may be; and

   (iii)   the date it was so claimed; and

(b)   in any case–

   (i)   the weekly rate of council tax benefit allowed to the mover by authority A;

   (ii)   if any deduction was being made from that benefit in respect of non-dependants, pursuant to regulations 40(1) and 42, the amount of those deductions;

   (iii)   if any addition was being made to any amount payable in respect of council tax to recover recoverable excess benefit pursuant to regulation 71(2)(b), the amount of those additions;

   (iv)   the date on which his entitlement to council tax benefit ceased;

   (v)   if an extended payment (severe disablement allowance and incapacity benefit) was allowed to the mover, the amount and date of any such payment; and

   (vi)   if no extended payment (severe disablement allowance and incapacity benefit) was allowed, why none was allowed.

(4)   In this regulation "mover" and "second dwelling" shall have the meanings assigned to them in paragraph 7 of Schedule 5.

[¹ SCHEDULE A1]

Modification

Sch A1 was inserted by Sch 4 para 3(2) as modified by Sch 4 para 3(3) of the HB&CTB(CP) Regs in respect of claims for CTB by some refugees (see p1129). Sch A1 was further modifed by Sch 4 para 4(4) and (5) for some CTB claimants who were refugees who claimed asylum on or before 2 April 2000 (see p1132). See also reg 7A inserted by Sch 4 para 3(1) of the HB&CTB(CP) Regs (p1129).

Amendment

1.   Lapsed by s12(2)(g) of the Asylum and Immigration (Treatment of Claimants, etc.) Act 2004 (for those recorded as refugees after 14.6.07).

SCHEDULE 1
REGULATION 12
Applicable amounts

PART 1
Personal allowances
1. The amounts specified in column (2) below in respect of each person or couple specified in column (1) shall be the amount specified for the purposes of regulation 12–

Column (1)	*Column (2)*
Person, couple or polygamous marriage	*Amount*
(1) Single claimant or lone parent–	(1)
(a) aged under 65;	(a) [² £119.05];
(b) aged 65 or over.	(b) [² £138.10].
(2) Couple–	(2)
(a) both members aged under 65;	(a) [² £181.70];
(b) one member or both members aged 65 or over.	(b) [² £207.00].
(3) If the claimant is a member of a polygamous marriage and none of the members of the marriage have attained the age of 65–	(3)
(a) for the claimant and the other party to the marriage;	(a) [² £181.70];
(b) for each additional spouse who is a member of the same household as the claimant.	(b) [² £62.65].
(4) If the claimant is a member of a polygamous marriage and one or more members of the marriage are aged 65 or over–	(4)
(a) for the claimant and the other party to the marriage;	(a) [² £207.00];
(b) for each additional spouse who is a member of the same household as the claimant.	(b) [² £68.90].

Amendments
1. Amended by Art 22(4) and Sch 12 of SI 2006 No 645 and reg 8 of SI 2006 No 217 as from 1.4.06.
2. Amended by Art 22(4) and Sch 12 of SI 2007 No 688 as from 1.4.07.

2.–(1) The amount specified in column (2) below in respect of each person specified in column (1) shall, for the relevant period specified in column (1), be the amounts specified for the purposes of regulation 12(1)(b)–

Column (1)	*Column (2)*
Child or young person	*Amount*
Persons in respect of the period–	
(a) beginning on that person's date of birth and ending on the day preceding the first Monday in September following that person's sixteenth birthday;	(a) [³ £47.45];
(b) beginning on the first Monday in September following that person's sixteenth birthday and ending on the day preceding that person's [² twentieth] birthday.	(b) [³ £47.45].

(2) In column (1) of the table above, "the first Monday in September" means the Monday which first occurs in the month of September in any year.

Amendments
1. Amended by Art 22(4) and Sch 12 of SI 2006 No 645 and reg 8 of SI 2006 No 217 as from 1.4.06.
2. Amended by reg 5(4) of SI 2006 No 718 as from 10.4.06.
3. Amended by Art 22(4) and Sch 12 of SI 2007 No 688 as from 1.4.07.

PART 2
Family premium
3.–(1) The amount for the purposes of regulation 12(1)(c) and (d) in respect of a family of which at least one member is a child or young person shall be [³ £16.43].

(2) The amounts specified in sub-paragraph (1) shall be increased by [⁴ £10.50] where at least one child is under the age of one year and for the purposes of this sub-paragraph where that child's first birthday does not fall on a Monday he shall be treated as under the age of one year until the first Monday after his first birthday.

Amendments

1.   Amended by Art 22(4)(a) and Sch 12 of SI 2006 No 645 and reg 8 of SI 2006 No 217 as from 1.4.06.
2.   Confirmed by Art 22(4)(b) and Sch 12 of SI 2006 No 645 and reg 8 of SI 2006 No 217 as from 1.4.06.
3.   Amended by Art 22(5)(a) of SI 2007 No 688 as from 1.4.07.
4.   Confirmed by Art 22(5)(b) of SI 2007 No 688 as from 1.4.07.

PART 3
Premiums

4.   The premiums specified in Part 4 shall, for the purposes of regulation 12(1)(e), be applicable to a claimant who satisfies the condition specified in this Part in respect of that premium.

5.–(1)   Subject to sub-paragraph (2), for the purposes of this Part of this Schedule, once a premium is applicable to a claimant under this Part, a person shall be treated as being in receipt of any benefit for–

(a)   in the case of a benefit to which the Social Security (Overlapping Benefits) Regulations 1979 applies, any period during which, apart from the provisions of those Regulations, he would be in receipt of that benefit; and

(b)   any period spent by a person in undertaking a course of training or instruction provided or approved by the Secretary of State under section 2 of the 1973 Act, or by Scottish Enterprise or Highlands and Islands Enterprise under section 2 of the Enterprise and New Towns (Scotland) Act 1990 or for any period during which he is in receipt of a training allowance.

(2)   For the purposes of the carer premium under paragraph 9, a person shall be treated as being in receipt of a carer's allowance by virtue of sub-paragraph (1)(a) only if and for so long as the person in respect of whose care the allowance has been claimed remains in receipt of attendance allowance, or the care component of disability living allowance at the highest or middle rate prescribed in accordance with section 72(3) of the Act.

Severe Disability Premium

6.–(1)   The condition is that the claimant is a severely disabled person.

(2)   For the purposes of sub-paragraph (1), a claimant shall be treated as being a severely disabled person if, and only if–

(a)   in the case of a single claimant, lone parent or a claimant who is treated as having no partner in consequence of sub-paragraph (3)–

    (i)   he is in receipt of attendance allowance, or the care component of disability living allowance at the highest or middle rate prescribed in accordance with section 72(3) of the Act; and

    (ii)   subject to sub-paragraph (6), he has no non-dependants aged 18 or over normally residing with him or with whom he is normally residing; and

    (iii)   no person is entitled to, and in receipt of, a carer's allowance in respect of caring for him;

(b)   in the case of a claimant who has a partner–

    (i)   the claimant is in receipt of attendance allowance, or the care component of disability living allowance at the highest or middle rate prescribed in accordance with section 72(3) of the Act; and

    (ii)   his partner is also in receipt of such an allowance or, if he is a member of a polygamous marriage, each other member of that marriage is in receipt of such an allowance; and

    (iii)   subject to sub-paragraph (6), the claimant has no non-dependants aged 18 or over normally residing with him or with whom he is normally residing,

and either a person is entitled to or in receipt of a carer's allowance in respect of caring for only one of the couple or, if he is a member of a polygamous marriage, for one or more but not all the members of the marriage, or as the case may be, no person is entitled to and in receipt of such an allowance in respect of caring for either member of a couple or any of the members of the marriage.

(3)   Where a claimant has a partner who does not satisfy the condition in sub-paragraph (2)(b)(ii), and that partner is blind or is treated as blind within the meaning of sub-paragraph (4), that partner shall be treated for the purposes of sub-paragraph (2) as if he were not a partner of the claimant.

(4)   For the purposes of sub-paragraph (3), a person is blind if he is registered in a register compiled by a local authority under section 29 of the National Assistance Act 1948 (welfare services) or, in Scotland, has been certified as blind and in consequence he is registered in a register maintained by or on behalf of a council constituted under section 2 of the Local Government (Scotland) Act 1994.

(5)   For the purposes of sub-paragraph (4), a person who has ceased to be registered as blind on regaining his eyesight shall nevertheless be treated as blind and as satisfying the additional condition set out in that sub-paragraph for a period of 28 weeks following the date on which he ceased to be so registered.

(6)   For the purposes of sub-paragraph (2)(a)(ii) and (2)(b)(iii) no account shall be taken of–

(a)   a person receiving attendance allowance, or the care component of disability living allowance at the highest or middle rate prescribed in accordance with section 72(3) of the Act; or

(b)   a person who is blind or is treated as blind within the meaning of sub-paragraphs (4) and (5).

(7)   For the purposes of sub-paragraph (2)(b) a person shall be treated–

(a)   as being in receipt of attendance allowance, or the care component of disability living allowance at the highest or middle rate prescribed in accordance with section 72(3) of the Act, if he would, but for his being a patient for a period exceeding 28 days, be so in receipt;

(b)   as being entitled to and in receipt of a carer's allowance if he would, but for the person for whom he was caring being a patient in hospital for a period exceeding 28 days, be so entitled and in receipt.

(8)   For the purposes of sub-paragraph (2)(a)(iii) and (2)(b)–

(a)   no account shall be taken of an award of carer's allowance to the extent that payment of such an award is back-dated for a period before [¹ the date on which the award is first paid]; and

(b)   references to a person being in receipt of a carer's allowance shall include references to a person who would have been in receipt of that allowance but for the application of a restriction under section 7 of the Social Security Fraud Act 2001 (loss of benefit).

Amendment

1.   Amended by reg 9(3) of SI 2007 No 719 as from 2.4.07.

Enhanced disability premium

7.   The condition is that the care component of disability living allowance is, or would, but for a suspension of benefit in accordance with regulations under section 113(2) of the Act or but for an abatement as a consequence of hospitalisation, be payable at the highest rate prescribed under section 72(3) of the Act in respect of a child or young person who is a member of the claimant's family.

Disabled Child Premium

8.   The condition is that a child or young person for whom the claimant or a partner of his is responsible and who is a member of the claimant's household–

(a)   is in receipt of disability living allowance or is no longer in receipt of such allowance because he is a patient, provided that the child or young person continues to be a member of the family; or

(b)   is blind within the meaning of paragraph 6(4) or treated as blind in accordance with paragraph 6(5); or

(c)   is a child or a young person in respect of whom section 145A of the Act applies for the purposes of entitlement to child benefit, but only for the period prescribed under that section, and in respect of whom a disabled child premium was included in the claimant's applicable amount immediately before the death of that child.

Carer Premium

9.–(1)   The condition is that the claimant or his partner is, or both of them are, entitled to a carer's allowance.

(2)   Where a carer premium has been awarded but–

(a)   the person in respect of whose care the carer's allowance has been awarded dies; or

(b)   the person in respect of whom the premium was awarded ceases to be entitled, or ceases to be treated as entitled, to a carer's allowance,

this paragraph shall be treated as satisfied for a period of eight weeks from the relevant date specified in sub-paragraph (3).

(3)   The relevant date for the purposes of sub-paragraph (2) is–

(a)   the Sunday following the death of the person in respect of whose care the carer's allowance has been awarded (or beginning with the date of death if the date occurred on a Sunday);

(b)   where head (a) above does not apply, the date on which that person who was entitled to a carer's allowance ceases to be entitled to it.

(4)   For the purposes of this paragraph, a person shall be treated as being entitled to and in receipt of a carer's allowance for any period not covered by an award but in respect of which a payment is made in lieu of an award.

Persons in receipt of concessionary payments

10.   For the purpose of determining whether a premium is applicable to a person under paragraphs 6 to 9, any concessionary payment made to compensate that person for the non-payment of any benefit mentioned in those paragraphs shall be treated as if it were a payment of that benefit.

Person in receipt of benefit

11. For the purposes of this Part of this Schedule, a person shall be regarded as being in receipt of any benefit if, and only if, it is paid in respect of him and shall be so regarded only for any period in respect of which that benefit is paid.

PART 4
Amounts of premiums specified in Part 3

Premium	*Amount*
12.–(1) Severe Disability Premium–	(1)
(a) where the claimant satisfies the condition in paragraph 6(2)(a);	(a) [² £48.45];
(b) where the claimant satisfies the condition in paragraph 6(2)(b)–	(b)
(i) in a case where there is someone in receipt of carer's allowance or if he or any partner satisfies that condition only by virtue of paragraph 6(7);	(i) [² £48.45];
(ii) in a case where there is no one in receipt of such an allowance.	(ii) [² £96.90].
(2) Enhanced CTB aged 60 or overdisability premium	(2) [² £18.76] in respect of each child or young person in respect of whom the conditions specified in paragraph 7 are satisfied.
(3) Disabled Child Premium	(3) [² £46.69] in respect of each child or young person in respect of whom the condition specified in paragraph 8 is satisfied.
(4) Carer Premium	(4) [² £27.15] in respect of each person who satisfies the condition specified in paragraph 9.

Amendments

1. Amended by Art 22(6) and Sch 13 of SI 2006 No 645 and reg 8 of SI 2006 No 217 as from 1.4.06.
2. Amended by Art 22(6) and Sch 13 of SI 2007 No 688 as from 1.4.07.

SCHEDULE 2
REGULATION 23(8)
Sums disregarded from claimant's earnings

1. Where two or more of paragraphs 2 to 5 apply in any particular case the overall maximum sum which falls to be disregarded in that case under those paragraphs is restricted to–
(a) £25 in the case of a lone parent;
(b) £20 in any other case.
2. In a case where a claimant is a lone parent, £25 of earnings.
3.–(1) In a case of earnings from any employment or employments to which sub-paragraph (2) applies, £20.
(2) This paragraph applies to employment–
(a) as a part-time fire-fighter employed by a fire and rescue authority constituted by a scheme under section 2 of the Fire and Rescue Services Act 2004 or a scheme to which section 4 of that Act applies;
(b) a part-time fire-fighter employed by a fire and rescue authority (as defined in section 1 of the Fire (Scotland) Act 2005) or a joint fire and rescue board constituted by an amalgamation scheme made under section 2(1) of that Act;
(c) as an auxiliary coastguard in respect of coast rescue activities;
(d) in the manning or launching of a lifeboat if the employment is part-time;
(e) as a member of any territorial or reserve force prescribed in Part I of Schedule 6 to Social Security (Contributions) Regulations 2001.
(3) If–
(a) any of the earnings of the claimant or, if he has a partner, his partner, or both of them, are disregarded under sub-paragraph (1); and
(b) either of them has, or both of them have, other earnings,
so much of those other earnings as would not, in the aggregate with the earnings disregarded under that sub-paragraph, exceed £20.
4.–(1) If the claimant or, if he has a partner, his partner is a carer, or both are carers, £20 of any earnings received from his or their employment.

(2)   Where the carer premium is awarded in respect of the claimant and of any partner of his, their earnings shall for the purposes of this paragraph be aggregated, but the amount to be disregarded in accordance with sub-paragraph (1) shall not exceed £20 of the aggregated amount.

(3)   In this sub-paragraph the claimant or his partner is a carer if paragraph 9 of Part 3 of Schedule 1 (amount applicable for carers) is satisfied in respect of him.

5.–(1)   £20 is disregarded if the claimant or, if he has a partner, his partner–

(a)   is in receipt of–
    (i)   long-term incapacity benefit under section 30A of the Act;
    (ii)   severe disablement allowance under section 68 of the Act;
    (iii)   attendance allowance;
    (iv)   disability living allowance under section 71 to 76 of the Act;
    (v)   any mobility supplement under article 26A of the Naval, Military and Air Forces etc. (Disablement and Death) Service Pensions Order 1983 (including such a supplement by virtue of any other scheme or order) or under article 25A of the Personal Injuries (Civilians) Scheme 1983; or
    (vi)   the disability element or the severe disability element of working tax credit under Schedule 2 to the Working Tax Credit Regulations; or

(b)   is or are registered as blind in a register compiled by a local authority under section 29 of the National Assistance Act 1948 (welfare services) or, in Scotland, has been certified as blind and in consequence is registered in a register maintained by or on behalf of a council constituted under section 2 of the Local Government (Scotland) Act 1994; or

(c)   is, or is treated as, incapable of work in accordance with the provisions of, and regulations made under, Part 12A of the Act (incapacity for work), and has been incapable, or has been treated as incapable, of work for a continuous period of not less than—
    (i)   in the case of a claimant who is terminally ill within the meaning of section 30B(4) of the Act, 196 days;
    (ii)   in any other case, 364 days.

(2)   Subject to sub-paragraph (3), £20 is disregarded if the claimant or, if he has a partner, his partner has, within a period of 8 weeks ending on the day in respect of which the claimant or his partner attains the qualifying age for state pension credit, had an award of housing benefit or council tax benefit and–

(a)   £20 was disregarded in respect of earnings taken into account in that award;
(b)   the person whose earnings qualified for the disregard continues in employment after the termination of that award.

(3)   The disregard of £20 specified in sub-paragraph (2) applies so long as there is no break, other than a break which does not exceed 8 weeks, in a person's entitlement to housing benefit or council tax benefit or in employment following the first day in respect of which that benefit is awarded.

(4)   £20 is the maximum amount which may be disregarded under this paragraph, notwithstanding that, where the claimant has a partner, both the claimant and his partner satisfy the requirements of this paragraph.

6.   Any amount or the balance of any amount which would fall to be disregarded under paragraph 18 or 19 of Schedule 3 had the claimant's income which does not consist of earnings been sufficient to entitle him to the full disregarded thereunder.

7.   Except where the claimant or his partner qualifies for a £20 disregard under the preceding provisions of this Schedule–

(a)   £5 shall be disregarded if a claimant who has no partner has earnings;
(b)   £10 shall be disregarded if a claimant who has a partner has earnings.

8.   Any earnings, other than earnings referred to in regulation 23(8)(b), derived from employment which ended before the day in respect of which the claimant first satisfies the conditions for entitlement to council tax benefit.

9.–(1)   In a case where the claimant is a person who satisfies at least one of the conditions set out in sub-paragraph (2), and his net earnings equal or exceed the total of the amounts set out in sub-paragraph (3), the amount of his earnings that falls to be disregarded under this Schedule shall be increased by [² £15.45].

(2)   The conditions of this sub-paragraph are that–

(a)   the claimant, or if he has a partner, either the claimant or his partner, is a person to whom regulation 20(1)(c) of the Working Tax Credit Regulations applies; or

(b)   the claimant–
    (i)   is, or any partner of his is, aged at least 25 and is engaged in remunerative work for on average not less than 30 hours per week; or
    (ii)   if he is a member of a couple–
        (aa)   at least one member of that couple is engaged in remunerative work for on average not less than 16 hours per week; and

   (bb) his applicable amount includes a family premium under paragraph 3 of Schedule 1; or

  (iii) is a lone parent who is engaged in remunerative work for on average not less than 16 hours per week; or

  (iv) is, or if he has a partner, one of them is, engaged in remunerative work for on average not less than 16 hours per week and paragraph 5(1) above is satisfied in respect of that person; or

 (c) the claimant is, or, if he has a partner, one of them is, a person to whom regulation 18(3) of the Working Tax Credit Regulations (eligibility for 50 plus element) applies, or would apply if an application for working tax credit were to be made in his case.

 (3) The following are the amounts referred to in sub-paragraph (1)–

 (a) any amount disregarded under this Schedule;

 (b) the amount of child care charges calculated as deductible under regulation 20(1)(c); and

 (c) [² £15.45].

 (4) The provisions of regulation 6 shall apply in determining whether or not a person works for on average not less than 30 hours per week, but as if the reference to 16 hours in paragraph (1) of that regulation was a reference to 30 hours.

Amendments

 1. Amended by Art 22(7) of SI 2006 No 645 and reg 8 of SI 2006 No 217 as from 1.4.06.

 2. Amended by Art 22(7) of SI 2007 No 688 as from 1.4.07.

---

 10. Where a payment of earnings is made in a currency other than Sterling, any banking charge or commission payable in converting to that payment into Sterling.

SCHEDULE 3
REGULATION 23(9)
Amounts to be disregarded in the calculation of income other than earnings

 1. In addition to any sum which falls to be disregarded in accordance with paragraphs 2 to 6, £10 of any of the following, namely–

 (a) a war disablement pension (except insofar as such a pension falls to be disregarded under paragraph 2 or 3);

 (b) a warwidow's or war widower's pension;

 (c) a pension payable to a person as a widow, widower or surviving civil partner under the Naval, Military and Air Forces etc. (Disablement and Death) Service Pensions Order 1983 insofar as that Order is made under the Naval and Marine Pay and Pensions Act 1865 or the Pensions and Yeomanry Pay Act 1884, or is made only under section 12(1) of the Social Security (Miscellaneous Provisions) Act 1977 and any power of Her Majesty otherwise than under an enactment to make provision about pensions for or in respect of persons who have been disabled or have died in consequence of service as members of the armed forces of the Crown;

 (d) a guaranteed income payment;

 (e) a payment made to compensate for the non-payment of such a pension or payment as is mentioned in any of the preceding sub-paragraphs;

 (f) a pension paid by the government of a country outside Great Britain which is analogous to any of the pensions or payments mentioned in sub-paragraphs (a) to (d) above;

 (g) a pension paid to victims of National Socialist persecution under any special provision made by the law of the Federal Republic of Germany, or any part of it, or of the Republic of Austria.

 2. The whole of any amount included in a pension to which paragraph 1 relates in respect of–

 (a) the claimant's need for constant attendance;

 (b) the claimant's exceptionally severe disablement.

 3. Any mobility supplement under article 26A of the Naval, Military and Air Forces etc. (Disablement and Death) Service Pensions Order 1983 (including such a supplement by virtue of any other scheme or order) or under article 25A of the Personal Injuries (Civilians) Scheme 1983 or any payment intended to compensate for the non-payment of such a supplement.

 4. Any supplementary pension under article 29(1A) of the Naval, Military and Air Forces etc. (Disablement and Death) Service Pensions Order 1983 (pensions to widows, widowers or surviving civil partners).

 5. In the case of a pension awarded at the supplementary rate under article 27(3) of the Personal Injuries (Civilians) Scheme 1983 (pensions to widows, widowers or surviving civil partners), the sum specified in paragraph 1(c) of Schedule 4 to that Scheme.

 6.–(1) Any payment which is–

 (a) made under any of the Dispensing Instruments to a widow, widower or surviving civil partner of a person–

(i)   whose death was attributable to service in a capacity analogous to service as a member of the armed forces of the Crown; and

(ii)   whose service in such capacity terminated before 31st March 1973; and

(b)   equal to the amount specified in article 29(1A) of the Naval, Military and Air Forces etc. (Disablement and Death) Service Pensions Order 1983 (pensions to widows, widowers or surviving civil partners).

(2)   In this paragraph "the Dispensing Instruments" means the Order in Council of 19th December 1881, the Royal Warrant of 27th October 1884 and the Order by His Majesty of 14th January 1922 (exceptional grants of pay, non-effective pay and allowances).

7.   £15 of any widowed parent's allowance to which the claimant is entitled under section 39A of the Act.

8.   £15 of any widowed mother's allowance to which the claimant is entitled under section 37 of the Act.

9.   Where the claimant occupies a dwelling as his home and he provides in that dwelling board and lodging accommodation, an amount, in respect of each person for whom such accommodation is provided for the whole or any part of a week, equal to–

(a)   where the aggregate of any payments made in respect of any one week in respect of such accommodation provided to such person does not exceed £20.00, 100 per cent. of such payments; or

(b)   where the aggregate of any such payments exceeds £20.00, £20.00 and 50 per cent. of the excess over £20.00.

10.   If the claimant–

(a)   owns the freehold or leasehold interest in any property or is a tenant of any property; and

(b)   occupies a part of that property; and

(c)   has an agreement with another person allowing that person to occupy another part of that property on payment of rent and–

(i)   the amount paid by that person is less than £20 per week, the whole of that amount; or

(ii)   the amount paid is £20 or more per week, £20.

11.   Where a claimant receives income under an annuity purchased with a loan, which satisfies the following conditions–

(a)   that the loan was made as part of a scheme under which not less than 90 per cent. of the proceeds of the loan were applied to the purchase by the person to whom it was made of an annuity ending with his life or with the life of the survivor of two or more persons (in this paragraph referred to as "the annuitants") who include the person to whom the loan was made;

(b)   that at the time the loan was made the person to whom it was made or each of the annuitants had attained the age of 65;

(c)   that the loan was secured on a dwelling in Great Britain and the person to whom the loan was made or one of the annuitants owns an estate or interest in that dwelling;

(d)   that the person to whom the loan was made or one of the annuitants occupies the dwelling on which it was secured as his home at the time the interest is paid; and

(e)   that the interest payable on the loan is paid by the person to whom the loan was made or by one of the annuitants,

the amount, calculated on a weekly basis, equal to–

(i)   where, or insofar as, section 369 of the Income and Corporation Taxes Act 1988 (mortgage interest payable under deduction of tax) applies to the payments of interest on the loan, the interest which is payable after deduction of a sum equal to income tax on such payments at the applicable percentage of income tax within the meaning of section 369(1A) of that Act;

(ii)   in any other case, the interest which is payable on the loan without deduction of such a sum.

12.–(1)   Any payment, other than a payment to which sub-paragraph (2) applies, made to the claimant by Trustees in exercise of a discretion exercisable by them.

(2)   This sub-paragraph applies to payments made to the claimant by Trustees in exercise of a discretion exercisable by them for the purpose of–

(a)   obtaining food, ordinary clothing and footwear or household fuel;

(b)   the payment of rent, council tax or water charges for which that claimant or his partner is liable;

(c)   meeting housing costs of a kind specified in Schedule 2 to the State Pension Credit Regulations 2002.

(3)   In a case to which sub-paragraph (2) applies, £20 or–

(a)   if the payment is less than £20, the whole payment;

(b)   if, in the claimant's case, £10 is disregarded in accordance with paragraph 1 (a) to (g), £10 or the whole payment if it is less than £10; or

(c)   if, in the claimant's case, £15 is disregarded under paragraph 7 or paragraph 8 and–

    (i)   he has no disregard under paragraph 1(a) to (g), £5 or the whole payment if it is less than £5;

    (ii)   he has a disregard under paragraph 1(a) to (g), nil.

(4)   For the purposes of this paragraph, "ordinary clothing and footwear" means clothing or footwear for normal daily use, but does not include school uniforms, or clothing and footwear used solely for sporting activities.

13.   Any increase in pension under Part 4 of the Naval, Military and Air Forces etc. (Disablement and Death) Service Pensions Order 1983 paid in respect of a dependent other than the pensioner's spouse or civil partner.

14.   Any payment ordered by a court to be made to the claimant or the claimant's partner in consequence of any accident, injury or disease suffered by the person or a child of the person to or in respect of whom the payments are made.

15.   Periodic payments made to the claimant or the claimant's partner under an agreement entered into in settlement of a claim made by the claimant or, as the case may be, the claimant's partner for an injury suffered by him.

16.   Any income which is payable outside the United Kingdom for such period during which there is a prohibition against the transfer to the United Kingdom of that income.

17.   Any banking charges or commission payable in converting to Sterling payments of income made in a currency other than Sterling.

18.   Where the claimant makes a parental contribution in respect of a student attending a course at an establishment in the United Kingdom or undergoing education in the United Kingdom, which contribution has been assessed for the purposes of calculating–

(a)   under, or pursuant to regulations made under powers conferred by, sections 1 or 2 of the Education Act 1962 or section 22 of the Teaching and Higher Education Act 1998, that student's award;

(b)   under regulations made in exercise of the powers conferred by section 49 of the Education (Scotland) Act 1980, that student's bursary, scholarship, or other allowance under that section or under regulations made in exercise of the powers conferred by section 73 of that Act of 1980, any payment to that student under that section; or

(c)   the student's student loan,

an amount equal to the weekly amount of that parental contribution, but only in respect of the period for which that contribution is assessed as being payable.

19.–(1)   Where the claimant is the parent of a student aged under 25 in advanced education who either–

(a)   is not in receipt of any award, grant or student loan in respect of that education; or

(b)   is in receipt of an award under section 2 of the Education Act 1962 (discretionary awards) or an award bestowed by virtue of the Teaching and Higher Education Act 1998, or regulations made thereunder, or a bursary, scholarship or other allowance under section 49(1) of the Education (Scotland) Act 1980, or a payment under section 73 of that Act of 1980,

and the claimant makes payments by way of a contribution towards the student's maintenance, other than a parental contribution falling within paragraph 18, an amount specified in sub-paragraph (2) in respect of each week during the student's term.

(2)   For the purposes of sub-paragraph (1), the amount shall be equal to–

(a)   the weekly amount of the payments; or

(b)   the amount by way of a personal allowance for a single claimant under 25 less the weekly amount of any award, bursary, scholarship, allowance or payment referred to in sub-paragraph (1)(b),

whichever is less.

20.–(1)   Where a claimant's applicable amount includes an amount by way of a family premium, £15 of any payment of maintenance, whether under a court order or not, which is made or due to be made by the claimant's spouse, civil partner, former spouse or former civil partner or the claimant's partner's spouse, civil partner, former spouse, or former civil partner.

(2)   For the purposes of sub-paragraph (1), where more than one maintenance payment falls to be taken into account in any week, all such payments shall be aggregated and treated as if they were a single payment.

21.   Except in a case which falls under paragraph 9 of Schedule 2, where the claimant is a person who satisfies the conditions of sub-paragraph (2) of that paragraph, any amount of working tax credit up to [2 £15.45].

Amendments

1.   Amended by Art 22(8) of SI 2006 No 645 and reg 8 of SI 2006 No 217 as from 1.4.06.

2.   Amended by Art 22(8) of SI 2007 No 688 as from 1.4.07.

22.	Any special war widows payment made under–
(a)	the Naval and Marine Pay and Pensions (Special War Widows Payment) Order 1990 made under section 3 of the Naval and Marine Pay and Pensions Act 1865;
(b)	the Royal Warrant dated 19th February 1990 amending the Schedule to the Army Pensions Warrant 1977;
(c)	the Queen's Order dated 26th February 1990 made under section 2 of the Air Force (Constitution) Act 1917;
(d)	the Home Guard War Widows Special Payments Regulations 1990 made under section 151 of the Reserve Forces Act 1980;
(e)	the Orders dated 19th February 1990 amending Orders made on 12th December 1980 concerning the Ulster Defence Regiment made in each case under section 140 of the Reserve Forces Act 1980,

and any analogous payment made by the Secretary of State for Defence to any person who is not a person entitled under the provisions mentioned in sub-paragraphs (a) to (e) of this paragraph.

23.	Where the total value of any capital specified in Part 2 of Schedule 4 does not exceed–
(a)	in the case of a claimant residing permanently in accommodation to which regulation 19(6) applies, £10,000; or
(b)	in any other case, £6,000,

any income actually derived from such capital.

24.   Except in the case of income from capital specified in Part 2 of Schedule 4, any actual income from capital.

SCHEDULE 4
REGULATION 34(2)
Capital disregards

PART 1
Capital to be disregarded

1.   Any premises acquired for occupation by the claimant which he intends to occupy as his home within 26 weeks of the date of acquisition or such longer period as is reasonable in the circumstances to enable the claimant to obtain possession and commence occupation of the premises.

2.   Any premises which the claimant intends to occupy as his home, and in respect of which he is taking steps to obtain possession and has sought legal advice, or has commenced legal proceedings, with a view to obtaining possession, for a period of 26 weeks from the date on which he first sought such advice or first commenced such proceedings whichever is the earlier, or such longer period as is reasonable in the circumstances to enable him to obtain possession and commence occupation of those premises.

3.   Any premises which the claimant intends to occupy as his home to which essential repairs or alterations are required in order to render them fit for such occupation, for a period of 26 weeks from the date on which the claimant first takes steps to effect those repairs or alterations, or such longer period as is necessary to enable those repairs or alterations to be carried out.

4.	Any premises occupied in whole or in part–
(a)	by a person who is a relative of the claimant or his partner as his home where that person is either aged 60 or over or incapacitated;
(b)	by the former partner of the claimant as his home; but this provision shall not apply where the former partner is a person from whom the claimant is estranged or divorced or with whom he had formed a civil partnership that has been dissolved.

5.   Any future interest in property of any kind, other than land or premises in respect of which the claimant has granted a subsisting lease or tenancy, including sub-leases or sub-tenancies.

6.   Where a claimant has ceased to occupy what was formerly the dwelling occupied as the home following his estrangement or divorce from his former partner or the dissolution of a civil partnership with his former partner, that dwelling for a period of 26 weeks from the date on which he ceased to occupy that dwelling or, where the dwelling is occupied as the home by the former partner who is a lone parent, for so long as it is so occupied.

7.   Any premises where the claimant is taking reasonable steps to dispose of the whole of his interest in those premises, for a period of 26 weeks from the date on which he first took such steps, or such longer period as is reasonable in the circumstances to enable him to dispose of those premises.

8.   All personal possessions.

9.   The assets of any business owned in whole or in part by the claimant and for the purposes of which he is engaged as a self-employed earner or, if he has ceased to be so engaged, for such period as may be reasonable in the circumstances to allow for disposal of those assets.

10.	The assets of any business owned in whole or in part by the claimant if–
(a)	he is not engaged as a self-employed earner in that business by reason of some disease or bodily or mental disablement; but

    (b)   he intends to become engaged (or, as the case may be, re-engaged) as a self-employed earner in that business as soon as he recovers or is able to become engaged, or re-engaged, in that business,

for a period of 26 weeks from the date on which the claim for council tax benefit is made or, if it is unreasonable to expect him to become engaged or re-engaged in that business within that period, for such longer period as is reasonable in the circumstances to enable him to become so engaged or re-engaged.

    11.   The surrender value of any policy of life insurance.

    12.   The value of any funeral plan contract; and for this purpose, "funeral plan contract" means a contract under which–

    (a)   the claimant makes one or more payments to another person ("the provider");

    (b)   the provider undertakes to provide, or secure the provision of, a funeral in the United Kingdom for the claimant on his death; and

    (c)   the sole purpose of the plan is to provide or secure the provision of a funeral for the claimant on his death.

    13.   Where an ex-gratia payment has been made by the Secretary of State on or after 1st February 2001 in consequence of the imprisonment or internment of–

    (a)   the claimant;

    (b)   the claimant's partner;

    (c)   the claimant's deceased spouse or deceased civil partner; or

    (d)   the claimant's partner's deceased spouse or deceased civil partner,

by the Japanese during the Second World War, an amount equal to that payment.

    14.–(1)   Subject to sub-paragraph (2), the amount of any trust payment made to a claimant or a claimant's partner who is–

    (a)   a diagnosed person;

    (b)   a diagnosed person's partner or was a diagnosed person's partner at the time of the diagnosed person's death; or

    (c)   a parent of a diagnosed person, a person acting in place of the diagnosed person's parents or a person who was so acting at the date of the diagnosed person's death.

    (2)   Where a trust payment is made to–

    (a)   a person referred to in sub-paragraph (1)(a) or (b), that sub-paragraph shall apply for the period beginning on the date on which the trust payment is made and ending on the date on which that person dies;

    (b)   a person referred to in sub-paragraph (1)(c), that sub-paragraph shall apply for the period beginning on the date on which the trust payment is made and ending two years after that date.

    (3)   Subject to sub-paragraph (4), the amount of any payment by a person to whom a trust payment has been made or of any payment out of the estate of a person to whom a trust payment has been made, which is made to a claimant or a claimant's partner who is–

    (a)   the diagnosed person;

    (b)   a diagnosed person's partner or was a diagnosed person's partner at the date of the diagnosed person's death; or

    (c)   a parent of a diagnosed person, a person acting in place of the diagnosed person's parents or a person who was so acting at the date of the diagnosed person's death.

    (4)   Where a payment such as referred to in sub-paragraph (3) is made to–

    (a)   a person referred to in sub-paragraph (3)(a) or (b), that sub-paragraph shall apply for the period beginning on the date on which the payment is made and ending on the date on which that person dies;

    (b)   a person referred to in sub-paragraph (3)(c), that sub-paragraph shall apply for the period beginning on the date on which the payment is made and ending two years after that date.

    (5)   In this paragraph, a reference to a person–

    (a)   being the diagnosed person's partner;

    (b)   acting in place of the diagnosed person's parents,

at the date of the diagnosed person's death shall include a person who would have been such a person or a person who would have been so acting, but for the diagnosed person residing in a care home or an independent hospital.

    (6)   In this paragraph–

"diagnosed person" means a person who has been diagnosed as suffering from, or who, after his death, has been diagnosed as having suffered from, variant Creutzfeldt-Jakob disease;

"relevant trust" means a trust established out of funds provided by the Secretary of State in respect of persons who suffered, or who are suffering, from variant Creutzfeldt-Jakob disease for the benefit of persons eligible for payments in accordance with its provisions;

"trust payment" means a payment under a relevant trust.

    15.   The amount of any payment, other than a war disablement pension or a war widow's or widower's pension, to compensate for the fact that the claimant, the claimant's partner, the claimant's deceased spouse or civil partner or the claimant's partner's deceased spouse or civil partner–

(a)   was a slave labourer or a forced labourer;
(b)   had suffered property loss or had suffered personal injury; or
(c)   was a parent of a child who had died,
during the Second World War.

16.–(1)   Any payment made under–
(a)   the Macfarlane Trust, the Macfarlane (Special Payments) Trust, the Macfarlane (Special Payments) (No. 2) Trust, the Fund, the Eileen Trust, the Skipton Fund, or the London Bombings Relief Charitable Fund (collectively referred to in this paragraph as "the Trusts"); or
(b)   the Independent Living Funds.

(2)   Any payment by or on behalf of a person who is suffering or who suffered from haemophilia or who is or was a qualifying person, which derives from a payment made under any of the Trusts and which is made to or for the benefit of that person's partner or former partner from whom he is not, or where that person has died was not, estranged or divorced or with whom he has formed a civil partnership that has not been dissolved or, where that person has died, had not been dissolved at the time of that person's death.

(3)   Any payment by or on behalf of the partner or former partner of a person who is suffering or who suffered from haemophilia or who is or was a qualifying person provided that the partner or former partner and that person are not, or if either of them has died were not, estranged or divorced or, where the partner or former partner and that person have formed a civil partnership, the civil partnership has not been dissolved or, if either of them has died, had not been dissolved at the time of the death, which derives from a payment made under any of the Trusts and which is made to or for the benefit of the person who is suffering from haemophilia or who is a qualifying person.

(4)   Any payment by a person who is suffering from haemophilia or who is a qualifying person, which derives from a payment under any of the Trusts, where–
(a)   that person has no partner or former partner from whom he is not estranged or divorced or with whom he has formed a civil partnership that has not been dissolved, nor any child who is or had been a member of that person's household; and
(b)   the payment is made either–
     (i)   to that person's parent or step-parent; or
     (ii)   where that person at the date of the payment is a child or a student who has not completed his full-time education and has no parent or step-parent, to any person standing in the place of his parent,
but only for a period from the date of the payment until the end of two years from that person's death.

(5)   Any payment out of the estate of a person who suffered from haemophilia or who was a qualifying person, which derives from a payment under any of the Trusts, where–
(a)   that person at the date of his death ("the relevant date") had no partner or former partner from whom he was not estranged or divorced or with whom he had formed a civil partnership that had not been dissolved, nor any child who was or had been a member of his household; and
(b)   the payment is made either–
     (i)   to that person's parent or step-parent; or
     (ii)   where that person at the relevant date was a child or a student who had not completed his full-time education and had no parent or step-parent, to any person standing in place of his parent,
but only for a period of two years from the relevant date.

(6)   In the case of a person to whom or for whose benefit a payment referred to in this paragraph is made, any capital resource which derives from any payment of income or capital made under or deriving from any of the Trusts.

Modifications
References to "step-parent" in sub-paras (4)(b)(i) and (ii) and (5)(b)(i) and (ii) are modified by s246 Civil Partnership Act 2004 and article 3 and para 27 of the Schedule to SI 2005 No 3137 (in Parts 6 and 7 respectively).

17.–(1)   An amount equal to the amount of any payment made in consequence of any personal injury to the claimant or, if the claimant has a partner, to the partner.
(2)   Where the whole or part of the payment is administered–
[¹ (a)   by the High Court or the County Court under Rule 21.11(1) of the Civil Procedure Rules 1998, or the Court of Protection, or on behalf of a person where the payment can only be disposed of by order or direction of any such court;]
(b)   in accordance with an order made under Rule 36.14 of the Ordinary Cause Rules 1993 or under Rule 128 of those Rules; or
(c)   in accordance with the terms of a trust established for the benefit of the claimant or his partner, the whole of the amount so administered.

Amendment

1. Substituted by reg 18(4) of SI 2006 No 2378 from the 1st day of the 1st benefit week to commence on or after 2.10.06.

---

18.   Any amount specified in paragraph 19, 20 or 21 for a period of one year beginning with the date of receipt.

19.   Amounts paid under a policy of insurance in connection with the loss of or damage to the property occupied by the claimant as his home and to his personal possessions.

20.   So much of any amounts paid to the claimant or deposited in the claimant's name for the sole purpose of–

(a) purchasing premises which the claimant intends to occupy as his home; or

(b) effecting essential repairs or alterations to the premises occupied or intended to be occupied by the claimant as his home.

21.–(1)   Subject to paragraph 22 any amount paid–

(a) by way of arrears of benefit;

(b) by way of compensation for the late payment of benefit;

(c) in lieu of the payment of benefit;

(d) to rectify, or compensate for, an official error, as defined for the purposes of paragraph 22, being an amount to which that paragraph does not apply;

(e) by a local authority out of funds provided under either section 93 of the Local Government Act 2000 under a scheme known as "Supporting People" or section 91 of the Housing (Scotland) Act 2001.

(2)   In sub-paragraph (1), "benefit" means–

(a) attendance allowance under section 64 of the Act;

(b) disability living allowance;

(c) income support;

(d) income-based jobseeker's allowance;

(e) state pension credit;

(f) housing benefit;

(g) council tax benefit;

(h) child tax credit;

(i) an increase of a disablement pension under section 104 of the Act (increase where constant attendance is needed), and any further increase of such a pension under section 105 of the Act (increase for exceptionally severe disablement);

(j) any amount included on account of the claimant's exceptionally severe disablement or need for constant attendance in a war disablement pension or a war widow's or widower's pension.

[¹ (k) any discretionary housing payment paid pursuant to regulation 2(1) of the Discretionary Financial Assistance Regulations 2001; or

(l) working tax credit.]

Amendment

1. Inserted by reg 3(14) of SI 2005 No 2502 as amended by Sch 2 para 27 of SI 2006 No 217 as from 1.4.06.

22.–(1)   Subject to sub-paragraph (3), any payment of £5,000 or more which has been made to rectify, or to compensate for, an official error relating to a relevant benefit and has been received by the claimant in full on or after the day on which he became entitled to benefit under these Regulations or under the Council Tax Benefit Regulations 2006.

(2)   Subject to sub-paragraph (3), the total amount of any payments disregarded under–

(a) paragraph 7(2) of Schedule 10 to the Income Support (General) Regulations 1987;

(b) paragraph 12(2) of Schedule 8 to the Jobseeker's Allowance Regulations;

(c) paragraph 9(2) of Schedule 5 to the Council Tax Benefit Regulations 2006;

(d) paragraph 20A of Schedule 5 to the State Pension Credit Regulations 2002,

where the award in respect of which the payments last fell to be disregarded under those Regulations either terminated immediately before the relevant date or is still in existence at that date.

(3)   Any disregard which applies under sub-paragraph (1) or (2) shall have effect until the award comes to an end.

(4)   In this paragraph–

"the award", except in sub-paragraph (2), means–

(a) the award of benefit under these Regulations during which the relevant sum or, where it is paid in more than one instalment, the first instalment of that sum is received; and

(b) where that award is followed by one or more further awards which, or each of which, begins immediately after the previous award ends, such further awards until the end of the last such award, provided that, for such further awards, the claimant–

(i)	is the person who received the relevant sum;	
(ii)	is the partner of that person; or	
(iii)	was the partner of that person at the date of his death;	

"official error"–
- (a) where the error relates to housing benefit or council tax benefit, has the meaning given by regulation 1(2) of the Decisions and Appeals Regulations; and
- (b) where the error relates to any other relevant benefit, has the meaning given by regulation 1(3) of the Social Security and Child Support (Decisions and Appeals) Regulations 1999;

"the relevant date" means–
- (a) in the case of an existing award of benefit under these Regulations or the Council Tax Benefit Regulations 2006, 6th October 2003; and
- (b) in any other case, the date on which the claim for benefit under these Regulations or the Council Tax Benefit Regulations 2006 was made;

"relevant benefit" means any benefit specified in paragraph 21(2); and

"the relevant sum" means the payment referred to in sub-paragraph (1) or the total amount referred to in sub-paragraph (2).

23. Where a capital asset is held in a currency other than Sterling, any banking charge or commission payable in converting that capital into Sterling.

24. The value of the right to receive income from an occupational pension scheme or a personal pension scheme.

[¹**25.**]

Amendment

1.   Omitted by reg 7(6) of SI 2007 No 1749 as from 16.7.07.

---

26. The dwelling occupied as the home; but only one dwelling shall be disregarded under this paragraph.

[¹**26B.** Where a person elects to be entitled to a lump sum under Schedule 5 or 5A to the Contributions and Benefits Act 1992 or under Schedule 1 to the Graduated Retirement Benefit Regulations, or is treated as having made such an election, and a payment has been made pursuant to that election, an amount equal to–
- (a) except where sub-paragraph (b) applies, the amount of any payment or payments made on account of that lump sum;
- (b) the amount of that lump sum,

but only for so long as that person does not change that election in favour of an increase of pension or benefit.

Amendment

1.   Inserted by reg 12(4) of SI 2005 No 2677 and reg 2 of SI 2006 No 217 as from 6.4.06.

PART 2
Capital disregarded only for the purposes of determining deemed income

27. The value of the right to receive any income under a life interest or from a life rent.

28. The value of the right to receive any rent except where the claimant has a reversionary interest in the property in respect of which rent is due.

29. The value of the right to receive any income under an annuity or the surrender value (if any) of such an annuity.

30. Where property is held under a trust, other than–
- (a) a charitable trust within the meaning of the Charities Act 1993; or
- (b) a trust set up with any payment to which paragraph 16 of this Schedule applies,

and under the terms of the trust, payments fall to be made, or the trustees have a discretion to make payments, to or for the benefit of the claimant or the claimant's partner, or both, that property.

SCHEDULE 5
REGULATION 44
Extended payments (severe disablement allowance and incapacity benefit) of council tax benefit

---

Condition for an extended payment (severe disablement allowance and incapacity benefit)

1. The condition prescribed in this paragraph is that the claimant or the claimant's partner–
- (a) notifies either the designated office or an appropriate DWP office that he or his partner–
  - (i) has commenced, or is about to commence, remunerative work;
  - (ii) has commenced, or is about to commence, receiving remuneration for work or an increased amount of remuneration for work; or

        (iii)   has commenced, or is about to commence, an increased number of hours of work,

so that entitlement to severe disablement allowance or incapacity benefit ceases and that work, or as the case may be, remuneration, is expected to last 5 weeks or more; and

    (b)   the notification is made no later than 4 weeks after the day on which the claimant or his partner first undertakes the remunerative work referred to in sub-paragraph (a)(i), first receives remuneration for the work or an increased amount of remuneration for the work referred to in sub-paragraph (a)(ii), or first commences the increased number of hours of work referred to in sub-paragraph (a)(iii).

Calculation and payment of an extended payment (severe disablement allowance and incapacity benefit)

    2.   Except in the case of a mover, the amount of the extended payment (severe disablement allowance and incapacity benefit) shall be equal to the amount of council tax benefit allowed to the claimant for the last benefit week before he ceased to be entitled to council tax benefit.

Movers

    3.   In the case of a mover who claims an extended payment (severe disablement allowance and incapacity benefit) the relevant authority to whom the mover is liable to pay council tax in respect of the second dwelling shall, upon receiving the mover's claim for an extended payment (severe disablement allowance and incapacity benefit) which meets the requirements of regulation 44(1), allow an extended payment (severe disablement allowance and incapacity benefit) calculated in accordance with paragraph 4 to the mover.

    4.   In a case to which paragraph 3 applies the amount of the extended payment (severe disablement allowance and incapacity benefit) shall be the lesser of–

    (a)   the amount required to discharge such part of the liability for council tax for the period specified in regulation 44(6)(a), less, in a case where the rebate to which paragraph 2 refers was subject to any deductions in relation to non-dependants pursuant to regulations 40(1) and 42, the amount of those deductions; or

    (b)   the amount of extended payment (severe disablement allowance and incapacity benefit) calculated in accordance with paragraph 2.

    5.   The maximum council tax benefit of a mover the amount of whose extended payment (severe disablement allowance and incapacity benefit) is calculated in accordance with paragraph 4(a) shall be calculated in accordance with regulation 40(1), save that no deduction shall be made in respect of non-dependants, other than any that fall to be taken into account pursuant to paragraph 4(a).

Adjustment of entitlement in respect of an extended payment (severe disablement allowance and incapacity benefit)

    6.   Where an extended payment (severe disablement allowance and incapacity benefit) has been allowed and the person to whom it was made has also claimed council tax benefit for a period that includes any part of the period specified in regulation 44(6)(a), the entitlement to council tax benefit, if any, of that claimant, in respect of each or any of those weeks, shall be reduced by the amount that that extended payment (severe disablement allowance and incapacity benefit) has discharged his council tax liability, in respect of any such week.

Interpretation

    7.   In this Schedule–

''claimant'' means a person claiming an extended payment (severe disablement allowance and incapacity benefit);

''mover'' means a claimant who changes the dwelling in which he is resident and in respect of which he is liable to pay council tax;

''second dwelling'' means the dwelling to which a person has moved, or is about to move, in which he is or will be resident, and where the liability to pay council tax in respect of his dwelling follows on immediately from the liability to pay council tax in respect of his previous dwelling.

SCHEDULE 6
REGULATION 46
Amount of alternative maximum council tax benefit

    1.–(1)   Subject to paragraphs 2 and 3, the alternative maximum council tax benefit in respect of a day for the purpose of regulation 46 shall be determined in accordance with the following Table and in this Table [¹–

    (a)   ''second adult'' means any person or persons residing with the claimant to whom section 131(6) of the Act applies; and

(b) "persons to whom regulation 45(2) of the Council Tax Benefit Regulations 2006 applies" includes any person to whom that regulation would apply were they, and their partner if they had one, below the qualifying age for state pension credit.]

(2) In this Schedule "council tax due in respect of that day" means the council tax payable under section 10 or 78 of the 1992 Act less [¹–

(a) any reductions made in consequence of any enactment in, or under, the 1992 Act; and

(b) in a case to which sub-paragraph (c) in column (1) of the table below applies, the amount of any discount which may be appropriate to the dwelling under the 1992 Act.]

Table

(1)	*(2)*
Second adult	*Alternative maximum council tax benefit*
(a) Where the second adult or all second adults are in receipt of income support or state pension credit or are persons on an income based jobseeker's allowance;	(a) 25 per cent. of the council tax due in respect of that day;
(b) Where the gross income of the second adult or, where there is more than one second adult, their aggregate gross income disregarding any income of person on income support, state pension credit or an income based jobseeker's allowance–	(b)
(i) is less than [³ £162.00] per week;	(i) 15 per cent. of the council tax due in respect of that day;
(ii) is not less than [³ £162.00 per week but less than [² £210.00] per week.	(ii) 7.5 per cent. of the council tax due in respect of that day.
[² (c) Where the dwelling would be wholly occupied by one or more persons to whom regulation 45(2) of the Council Tax Benefit Regulations 2006 applies but for the presence of one or more second adults who are in receipt of income support, state pension credit or are persons on an income-based jobseeker's allowance.]	[² (c) 100 per cent. of the council tax due in respect of that day.]

Amendments

1. Amended by reg 11(4)(a) and (b) of SI 2006 No 588 as from 1.4.06.
2. Inserted by reg 11(4)(c) of SI 2006 No 588 as from 1.4.06.
3. Amended by Art 22(9) of SI 2007 No 688 as from 1.4.07.

2. In determining a second adult's gross income for the purposes of this Schedule, there shall be disregarded from that income–

(a) any attendance allowance, or any disability allowance under section 71 of the Act;

(b) any payment made under the Trusts, the Fund, the Eileen Trust or the Independent Living Funds which had his income fallen to be calculated under regulation 30 of the Council Tax Benefit Regulations 2006 (calculation of income other than earnings) would have been disregarded under paragraph 24 of Schedule 4 to those Regulations (income in kind); and

(c) any payment which had his income fallen to be calculated under regulation 30 of the Council Tax Benefit Regulations 2006 would have been disregarded under paragraph 36 of Schedule 4 to those Regulations (payments made under certain trusts and certain other payments).

3. Where there are two or more second adults residing with the claimant for benefit and any such second adult falls to be disregarded for the purposes of discount in accordance with Schedule 1 to the 1992 Act, his income shall be disregarded in determining the amount of any alternative maximum council tax benefit, unless that second adult is a member of a couple and his partner does not fall to be disregarded for the purposes of discount.

SCHEDULE 7
REGULATION 61(1)
Matters to be included in the decision notice

PART 1
General

1. The statement of matters to be included in any decision notice issued by a relevant authority to a person, and referred to in regulation 61 (notification of decision) and in regulation 10 of the Decisions and Appeals Regulations are those matters set out in the following provisions of this Schedule.

2.   Every decision notice shall include a statement as to the right of any person affected by that decision to request a written statement under regulation 61(2) (requests for statement of reasons) and the manner and time in which to do so.

3.   Every decision notice shall include a statement as to the right of any person affected by that decision to make an application for a revision in accordance with regulation 4(1)(a) of the Decisions and Appeals Regulations and, where appropriate, to appeal against that decision and the manner and time in which to do so.

4.   Every decision notice following an application for a revision in accordance with regulation 4(1)(a) of the Decisions and Appeals Regulations shall include a statement as to whether the original decision in respect of which the person made his representations has been confirmed or revised and where the relevant authority has not revised the decision the reasons why not.

5.   Every decision notice following an application for a revision in accordance with regulation 4(1)(a) of the Decisions and Appeals Regulations shall, if the original decision has been revised, include a statement as to the right of any person affected by that decision to apply for a revision in accordance with regulation 4(1)(a) of those Regulations and the manner and time in which to do so.

6.   An authority may include in the decision notice any other matters not prescribed by this Schedule which it sees fit, whether expressly or by reference to some other document available without charge to the person.

7.   Parts 2, 3 and 4 of this Schedule shall apply only to the decision notice given on a claim.

8.   Where a decision notice is given following a revision of an earlier decision–

(a)   made of the authority's own motion which results in a revision of that earlier decision; or

(b)   made following an application for a revision in accordance with regulation 4(1)(a) of the Decisions and Appeals Regulations, whether or not resulting in a revision of that earlier decision,

that notice shall, subject to paragraph 6, contain a statement only as to all the matters revised.

PART 2
Awards where state pension credit is payable

9.–(1)   Where a person on state pension credit is awarded council tax benefit, the decision notice shall include a statement as to–

(a)   the normal weekly amount of council tax which may be rounded to the nearest penny;

(b)   the normal weekly amount of the council tax benefit, which amount may be rounded to the nearest penny;

(c)   the amount of and the category of non-dependant deductions made under regulation 42, if any;

(d)   the first day of entitlement to the council tax benefit; and

(e)   his duty to notify any change of circumstances which might affect his entitlement to, or the amount of council tax benefit and, without prejudice to the extent of the duty owed under regulation 59 (duty to notify changes of circumstances), the kind of change of circumstances which is to be notified, either upon the notice or by reference to some other document available to him on application without charge,

and in any case where the amount to which sub-paragraph (a) or (b) refers disregards fractions of a penny, the notice shall include a statement to that effect.

(2)   In a case where a person on state pension credit has entitlement only to the savings credit, the following additional matters shall also be set out–

(a)   the applicable amount and the basis of calculation;

(b)   the amount of the savings credit [¹] taken into account;

(c)   the amount of the person's income and capital as notified to the local authority by the Secretary of State and taken into account for the purposes of the council tax benefit assessment;

(d)   any modification of the claimant's income or capital made in accordance with regulation 17 (calculation of claimant's income in savings credit only cases); and

(e)   the amount of the claimant's capital if paragraph (7) of regulation 17 applies in his case.

Amendment

1.   Omitted by reg 3(15) of SI 2005 No 2502 as amended by Sch 2 para 27 of SI 2006 No 217 as from 1.4.06.

PART 3
Awards of council tax benefit where state pension credit not in payment

10.   Where a person is not on state pension credit but is awarded council tax benefit, the decision notice shall include a statement as to–

(a)   the matters set out in paragraph 9;

(b)   his applicable amount and how it is calculated;

(c)   his weekly earnings; and

(d)   his weekly income other than earnings.

PART 4
Notice where income of non-dependant is treated as claimant's income

11.   Where an authority makes a decision under regulation 14 (circumstances in which income of non-dependant is to be treated as claimant's) the decision notice shall contain a statement as to–
    (a)   the fact that a decision has been made by reference to the income and capital of the claimant's non-dependant; and
    (b)   the relevant authority's reasons for making that decision.

PART 5
Notice where no award is made

12.   Where a person is not awarded council tax benefit under regulation 40 (maximum council tax benefit)–
    (a)   on grounds of income, the decision notice shall include a statement as to–
        (i)   the matters set out in paragraph 9(1)(a); and
        (ii)   the matters set out in paragraph 10(b) to (d) where the person is not on state pension credit;
    (b)   on the grounds that the amount of the alternative maximum council tax benefit exceeds the appropriate maximum council tax benefit, the matters set out in paragraph 15;
    (c)   for any reason other than one mentioned in sub-paragraph (a) or (b), the decision notice shall include a statement as to the reason why no award has been made.

PART 6
Awards where alternative maximum council tax benefit is payable in respect of a day

13.   Where a person is awarded council tax benefit determined in accordance with regulation 46 and Schedule 6 (alternative maximum council tax benefit) the decision notice shall include a statement as to–
    (a)   the normal weekly amount of council tax, which amount may be rounded to the nearest penny;
    (b)   the normal weekly amount of the alternative maximum council tax benefit, which amount may be rounded to the nearest penny;
    (c)   the gross income or incomes and the rate of benefit which apply under Schedule 6;
    (d)   the first day of entitlement to benefit;
    (e)   the gross income of any second adult used to determine the rate of the alternative maximum council tax benefit or if any such adult is on income support, state pension credit or an income-based jobseeker's allowance;
    (f)   the claimant's duty to notify any change of circumstances which might affect his entitlement to, or the amount of the alternative maximum council tax benefit and, without prejudice to the extent of the duty owed under regulation 59 (duty to notify changes of circumstances) the kind of change of circumstances which are to be notified, either upon the notice or by reference to some other document available to the claimant free of charge on application,
and in any case where the amount to which sub-paragraph (a) or (b) refers disregards fractions of a penny, the notice shall include a statement to that effect.

Notice where no award of alternative maximum council tax benefit is made

14.   Where a person is not awarded council tax benefit in accordance with regulation 46 and Schedule 6 (alternative maximum council tax benefit)–
    (a)   on the grounds that the gross income or as the case may be the aggregate gross incomes, of any second adult or adults in the claimant's dwelling is too high, the decision notice shall include a statement as to the matters set out in paragraphs 13(a), (c) and (e);
    (b)   on the grounds that the appropriate maximum council tax benefit is higher than the alternative maximum council tax benefit, the decision notice shall include a statement as to the matters set out in paragraph 15 below;
    (c)   for any reason not referred to in sub-paragraphs (a) and (b), the decision notice shall include a statement as to why no award has been made.

Notice where council tax benefit is awarded and section 131(9) of the Act applies

15.   Where the amount of a claimant's council tax benefit in respect of a day is the greater of the appropriate maximum council tax benefit and the alternative maximum council tax benefit in his case the notice shall in addition to the matters set out in paragraphs 9, 10 or 13, as the case may be, include a statement as to–

(a)   the amount of whichever is the lesser of the appropriate maximum council tax benefit or the alternative maximum council tax benefit in his case, which amount may be rounded to the nearest penny; and

(b)   that this amount has not been awarded in consequence of the award of council tax benefit at a higher rate,

and in any case where the amount to which sub-paragraph (a) refers disregards fractions of a penny, the notice shall include a statement to that effect.

PART 7
Notice where there is recoverable excess benefit

16.   Except in cases to which paragraphs (a) and (b) of regulation 67 (excess benefit in consequence of a reduction in a relevant authority's council tax) refers, where the relevant authority makes a decision that there is recoverable excess benefit within the meaning of regulation 68 (recoverable excess benefit), the decision notice shall include a statement as to–

(a)   the fact that there is recoverable excess benefit;

(b)   the reason why there is recoverable excess benefit;

(c)   the amount of recoverable excess benefit;

(d)   how the amount of recoverable excess benefit was calculated;

(e)   the benefit weeks to which the recoverable excess benefit relates; and

(f)   the method or combination of methods by which the authority intends to recover the recoverable excess benefit, including–

    (i)   payment by or on behalf of the person concerned of the amount due by the specified date;

    (ii)   addition of the amount due to any amount in respect of the tax concerned for payment whether by instalments or otherwise by the specified date or dates; or

    (iii)   if recovery cannot be effected in accordance with heads (i) or (ii), requesting the Secretary of State to recover the excess benefits by deduction from the benefit prescribed in regulation 75 (recovery of excess benefits from prescribed benefits).

[¹SCHEDULE 8
ELECTRONIC COMMUNICATION

Amendment

1.   Inserted by Art 5(5) of SI 2006 No 2968 as from 20.12.06.

PART 1
Introduction

Interpretation

1.   In this Schedule "official computer system" means a computer system maintained by or on behalf of the relevant authority or of the Secretary of State for sending, receiving, processing or storing of any claim, certificate, notice, information or evidence.

PART 2
Electronic Communication – General Provisions

Conditions for the use of electronic communication

2.–(1)   The relevant authority may use an electronic communication in connection with claims for, and awards of, benefit under these Regulations.

(2)   A person other than the relevant authority may use an electronic communication in connection with the matters referred to in sub-paragraph (1) if the conditions specified in sub-paragraphs (3) to (6) are satisfied.

(3)   The first condition is that the person is for the time being permitted to use an electronic communication by an authorisation given by means of a direction of the Chief Executive of the relevant authority.

(4)   The second condition is that the person uses an approved method of–

(a)   authenticating the identity of the sender of the communication;

(b)   electronic communication;

(c)   authenticating any claim or notice delivered by means of an electronic communication; and

(d)   subject to sub-paragraph (7), submitting to the relevant authority any claim, certificate, notice, information or evidence.

(5)   The third condition is that any claim, certificate, notice, information or evidence sent by means of an electronic communication is in a form approved for the purposes of this Schedule.

(6)   The fourth condition is that the person maintains such records in written or electronic form as may be specified in a direction given by the Chief Executive of the relevant authority.

(7)   Where the person uses any method other than the method approved of submitting any claim, certificate, notice, information or evidence, that claim, certificate, notice, information or evidence shall be treated as not having been submitted.

(8)   In this paragraph ''approved'' means approved by means of a direction given by the Chief Executive of the relevant authority for the purposes of this Schedule.

Use of intermediaries
3.   The relevant authority may use intermediaries in connection with–

(a)   the delivery of any claim, certificate, notice, information or evidence by means of an electronic communication; and

(b)   the authentication or security of anything transmitted by such means,

and may require other persons to use intermediaries in connection with those matters.

PART 3
Electronic Communication – Evidential Provisions

Effect of delivering information by means of electronic communication
4.–(1)   Any claim, certificate, notice, information or evidence which is delivered by means of an electronic communication shall be treated as having been delivered in the manner or form required by any provision of these Regulations, on the day the conditions imposed–

(a)   by this Schedule; and

(b)   by or under an enactment,

are satisfied.

(2)   The relevant authority may, by a direction, determine that any claim, certificate, notice, information or evidence is to be treated as delivered on a different day (whether earlier or later) from the day provided for in sub-paragraph (1).

(3)   Information shall not be taken to have been delivered to an official computer system by means of an electronic communication unless it is accepted by the system to which it is delivered.

Proof of identity of sender or recipient of information
5.   If it is necessary to prove, for the purpose of any legal proceedings, the identity of–

(a)   the sender of any claim, certificate, notice, information or evidence delivered by means of an electronic communication to an official computer system; or

(b)   the recipient of any such claim, certificate, notice, information or evidence delivered by means of an electronic communication from an official computer system,

the sender or recipient, as the case may be, shall be presumed to be the person whose name is recorded as such on that official computer system.

Proof of delivery of information
6.–(1)   If it is necessary to prove, for the purpose of any legal proceedings, that the use of an electronic communication has resulted in the delivery of any claim, certificate, notice, information or evidence this shall be presumed to have been the case where–

(a)   any such claim, certificate, notice, information or evidence has been delivered to the relevant authority, if the delivery of that claim, certificate, notice, information or evidence has been recorded on an official computer system; or

(b)   any such claim, certificate, notice, information or evidence has been delivered by the relevant authority, if the delivery of that certificate, notice, information or evidence has been recorded on an official computer system.

(2)   If it is necessary to prove, for the purpose of any legal proceedings, that the use of an electronic communication has resulted in the delivery of any such claim, certificate, notice, information or evidence, this shall be presumed not to be the case, if that claim, certificate, notice, information or evidence delivered to the relevant authority has not been recorded on an official computer system.

(3)   If it is necessary to prove, for the purpose of any legal proceedings, when any such claim, certificate, notice, information or evidence sent by means of an electronic communication has been received, the time and date of receipt shall be presumed to be that recorded on an official computer system.

Proof of content of information

7.   If it is necessary to prove, for the purpose of any legal proceedings, the content of any claim, certificate, notice, information or evidence sent by means of an electronic communication, the content shall be presumed to be that recorded on an official computer system.]

Part 5

Secondary legislation
Decision making and appeals

The Social Security Commissioners (Procedure) Regulations 1999
(SI 1999 No.1495)

ARRANGEMENT OF REGULATIONS
PART I
General Provisions

1. Citation and Commencement
4. Interpretation
5. General powers of a Commissioner
6. Transfer of proceedings between Commissioners
7. Delegation of functions to authorised officers
8. Manner of and time for service of notices, etc.
8A. Funding of legal services

PART II
Applications For Leave To Appeal, Appeals And References

9. Application to a Commissioner for leave to appeal
10. Notice of application to a Commissioner for leave to appeal
11. Determination of application
12. Notice of appeal
13. Time limit for appealing after leave obtained
16. Acknowledgement of a notice of appeal or a reference and notification to each respondent

PART III
Procedure

17. Representation
18. Respondent's written observations
19. Written observations in reply
20. Directions
22. Non-disclosure of medical evidence
23. Requests for hearings
24. Hearings
25. Summoning of witnesses
26. Withdrawal of applications for leave to appeal, appeals and references
27. Irregularities

PART IV
Decisions

28. Determinations and decisions of a Commissioner
30. Correction of accidental errors in decisions
31. Setting aside of decisions on certain grounds
32. Provisions common to regulations 30 and 31

PART V
Applications For Leave To Appeal To The Appellate Court

33. Application to a Commissioner for leave to appeal to the Appellate Court

---

PART I
General Provisions

General Note

An appeal from the decision of a tribunal lies to a commissioner under Sch 7 para 8 CSPSSA 2000 if the decision was erroneous in a point of law. For a discussion of the grounds for appeal, how appeals are made and the powers of commissioners, see p159.

These regulations deal with procedural matters, in particular:

(1) Determination of the date of service of applications and notices: reg 8.
(2) Funding of legal services: reg 8A.
(3) Applications to a commissioner for leave to appeal where an application has been refused or rejected by a tribunal chair: regs 9 and 10.
(4) The requirement to serve notice of appeal once leave to appeal has been granted and the time limit for doing so: regs 12 and 13.
(5) Applications for leave to appeal to the Court of Appeal (in Scotland the Court of Session): reg 33.

Citation and commencement

1. These Regulations may be cited as the Social Security Commissioners (Procedure) Regulations 1999 and shall come into force on 1st June 1999.

Interpretation

4.–(1) In these Regulations, unless the context otherwise requires–

[² "the 1998 Act"] means the Social Security Act 1998;

[⁴ "the 1943 Act" means the Pensions Appeal Tribunals Act 1943]

[² "the 2000 Act" means the Child Support, Pensions and Social Security Act 2000;]

[⁵ "appeal tribunal" means–
    (i) an appeal tribunal constituted under Chapter 1 of Part 1 of the 1998 Act; or
    (ii) a Pensions Appeal Tribunal;]

"authorised officer" means an officer authorised by the Lord Chancellor, or in Scotland by the Secretary of State, in accordance with paragraph 6 of Schedule 4 to [² the 1998 Act][⁶ or section 6D(2) of the 1943 Act];

[¹ "the Board" means the Commissioners of Inland Revenue;]

"the chairman" for the purposes of regulations 9 and 10 means–
    (i) the person who was the chairman or sole member of the appeal tribunal which gave the decision against which leave to appeal is being sought; or
    (ii) any other person authorised to deal with applications for leave to appeal to a Commissioner against that decision under [² section 14 of the 1998 Act [⁶ , section 6A of the 1943 Act]or paragraph 8 of Schedule 7 to the 2000 Act];

[³ "child benefit" means child benefit under Part 9 of the Social Security Contributions and Benefits Act 1992;]

[⁵ "Commissioner" means the Chief Social Security Commissioner or any other Social Security Commissioner appointed under the 1998 Act, and includes a tribunal of:
    (i) three or more Commissioners constituted under section 16(7) of the 1998 Act or paragraph 10(5) of Schedule 7 to the 2000 Act; and
    (ii) two or more Commissioners constituted under section 6D(5) of the 1943 Act or section 16(7) of the 1998 Act;]

[³ "funding notice" means the notice or letter from the Legal Services Commission confirming that legal services are to be funded;

"guardian's allowance" means guardian's allowance under section 77 of the Social Security Contributions and Benefits Act 1992;

"legal aid certificate" means the certificate issued by the Scottish Legal Aid Board confirming that legal services are to be funded;]

"legally qualified" means being a solicitor or barrister, or in Scotland, a solicitor or advocate;

[³ "Legal Services Commission" means the Legal Services Commission established under section 1 of the Access to Justice Act 1999;

"live television link" means a television link or other audio and video facilities which allow a person who is not physically present at an oral hearing to see and hear proceedings and be seen and heard by all others who are present (whether physically present or otherwise);]

"month" means a calendar month;

"office" means an Office of the Social Security Commissioners;

"party" means a party to the proceedings;

[² "person affected" means, subject to paragraph (2), a person who is a person affected under regulation 3 of the Housing Benefit and Council Tax Benefit (Decision and Appeals) Regulations 2001 provided that he is an appellant against the appeal tribunal's decision or was a party to the appeal tribunal proceedings;]

"proceedings" means any proceedings before a Commissioner, whether by way of an application for leave to appeal to, or from, a Commissioner, by way of an appeal or reference, or otherwise;

[² "relevant authority" has the same meaning as in paragraph 1(1) of Schedule 7 to the 2000 Act;]

[² "respondent" means–

(i) any person or organisation other than the applicant, appellant or person making the reference who is one of the principal parties as defined in section 13 of the 1998 Act,

(ii) any other person taking part in the proceedings in accordance with section 14 of the 1998 Act or as a person affected or as a relevant authority or at the direction or with the leave of the Commissioner,

(iii) the Secretary of State in any case where he is not otherwise a respondent and has given notice to the Commissioner of his wish to be joined as a party to the proceedings;

[⁴ (iv) in the case of an application or appeal under the 1943 Act, the person with a right to appeal under section 6A(2) of that Act other than the applicant or appellant]

[³ "Scottish Legal Aid Board" means the Scottish Legal Aid Board established under section 1 of the Legal Aid (Scotland) Act 1986;]

"summons", in relation to Scotland, corresponds to "citation" and regulation 25 shall be construed accordingly.

[¹ "tax credits" means working families' tax credit and disabled person's tax credit, construing those terms in accordance with section 1(1) of the Tax Credits Act 1999.]

[² (2) For the purpose of paragraph 8(2)(c) of Schedule 7 to the 2000 Act "person affected" shall be construed in accordance with regulation 3 of the Housing Benefit and Council Tax Benefit (Decision and Appeals) Regulations 2001 and for the purpose of paragraph 8(3) of Schedule 7 to the 2000 Act "person affected" shall have the meaning given in paragragh (1).]

[(3) *Omitted*]

Amendments

1. Inserted by reg 3 of SI 2000 No 2854 as from 10.11.00.
2. Amended by reg 3 of SI 2001 No 1095 as from 2.7.01.
3. Amended by reg 2(3) of SI 2005 No 207 as from 28.2.05.
4. Inserted by reg 2(a) and (f) of SI 2005 No 870 as from 6.04.05.
5. Substituted by reg 2(b) and (e) of SI 2005 No 870 as from 6.04.05.
6. Amended by reg 2(c) and (d) of SI 2005 No 870 as from 6.04.05.

Analysis

Note that for the purposes of these regulations "person affected" means a person affected by a decision as defined in reg 3 D&A Regs (see p951). However, subject to para (2) (which concerns people with a right of appeal to the commissioner under Sch 7 para 8(2)(c) CSPSSA), this is only if s/he was an appellant against the tribunal's decision or a party to the tribunal proceedings.

General powers of a Commissioner

5.–(1) Subject to the provisions of these Regulations, a Commissioner may adopt any procedure in relation to proceedings before him.

(2) A Commissioner may–

(a)   extend or abridge any time limit under these Regulations (including, subject to regulations 9(3) and 13(2), granting an extension where the time limit has expired);

(b)   expedite, postpone or adjourn any proceedings.

(3)   Subject to paragraph (4), a Commissioner may, on or without the application of a party, strike out any proceedings for want of prosecution or abuse of process.

(4)   Before making an order under paragraph (3), the Commissioner shall send notice to the party against whom it is proposed that it should be made giving him an opportunity to make representations why it should not be made.

(5)   A Commissioner may, on application by the party concerned, give leave to reinstate any proceedings which have been struck out in accordance with paragraph (3) and, on giving leave, he may give directions as to the conduct of the proceedings.

(6)   Nothing in these Regulations shall affect any power which is exercisable apart from these Regulations.

Analysis

Reg 5 allows commissioners to adopt any procedure in the proceedings before her/him. Importantly, it allows a commissioner to extend or abridge *any* time limit under the regulations subject to regs 9(3) (late applications for leave to appeal) and 13(2) (late notice of appeal): para (2)(a). Late applications for leave to appeal and late notices of appeal may be accepted "for special reasons".

Paras (3) and (4) allow a commissioner to strike out proceedings for 'want of prosecution' (see p925) or abuse of process. Notice must be sent to the person against whom an order to strike out is proposed, giving her/him the opportunity to make representations. Proceedings which have been struck out may be reinstated under para (5).

The functions of commissioners under this regulation may be delegated to legal officers under reg 7(1)(d) and (g).

Transfer of proceedings between Commissioners

6.   If it becomes impractical or inexpedient for a Commissioner to continue to deal with proceedings which are or have been before him, any other Commissioner may rehear or deal with those proceedings and any related matters.

Delegation of functions to authorised officers

7.–(1)   The following functions of Commissioners may be exercised by legally qualified authorised officers, to be known as legal officers to the Commissioners–

(a)   giving directions under regulations 8 and 20;

(b)   determining requests for or directing hearings under regulation 23;

(c)   summoning witnesses, and setting aside a summons made by a legal officer, under regulation 25;

(d)   postponing a hearing under regulation 5;

(e)   giving leave to withdraw or reinstate applications, appeals or references under regulation 26;

(f)   waiving irregularities under regulation 27 in connection with any matter being dealt with by a legal officer;

(g)   extending or abridging time, directing expedition, giving notices, striking out and reinstating proceedings under regulation 5.

(2)   Any party may, within 14 days of being sent notice of the direction or order of a legal officer, make a written request to a Commissioner asking him to reconsider the matter and confirm or replace the direction or order with his own, but, unless ordered by a Commissioner, a request shall not stop proceedings under the direction or order.

General Note

Legal officers perform an invaluable role in progressing appeals. They are appointed by the Lord Chancellor or, in Scotland, the Secretary of State, under Sch 4 para 6 SSA 1998. Most have extensive practical experience of social security law in legal practice or the advice sector or both. While many of the functions set out above seem to be of a mundane nature, they will often raise points of law for the consideration of the parties in directions under sub-para (a) which may not have been previously considered. Legal officers can also assist with managing cases – eg, by directing that a number of appeals be listed together.

Manner of and time for service of notices, etc.

8.–(1)   A notice to or other document for any party shall be deemed duly served if it is–

(a)   delivered to him personally; or

(b)   properly addressed and sent to him by prepaid post at the address last notified by him for this purpose, or to his ordinary address; or

[¹ (ba)   subject to paragraph (1A), sent by email; or]

(c)   served in any other manner a Commissioner may direct.

[¹ (1A)   A document may be served by email on any party if the recipient has informed the person sending the email in writing–

(a)   that he is willing to accept service by email;

(b)   of the email address to which the documents should be sent; and

(c)   if the recipient wishes to so specify, the electronic format in which documents must be sent.]

(2)   A notice to or other document for a Commissioner shall be–

[² (a) delivered to the office in person;

(b)   sent to the office by prepaid post;

(c)   sent to the office by fax; or

(d)   where the office has given written permission in advance, sent to the office by email].

(3)   For the purposes of any time limit, a properly addressed notice or other document sent by prepaid post, fax or email is effective from the date it is sent.

Definition

"office" – see reg 4.

Amendments

1.   Inserted by reg 2(4)(a) and (b) of SI 2005 No 207 as from 28.2.05.
2.   Amended by reg 2(4)(c) of SI 2005 No 207 as from 28.2.05.

General Note

Reg 8 deals with service and differs considerably from reg 2 SSCS D&A Regs and reg 2 D&A Regs. The important practical difference is that for the purposes of any time limit, documents sent by post, fax or email to one of the Offices of the Commissioners are deemed to be effective on the date they were sent, rather than on the day on which they are received: para (3).

So, for example, where a decision is sent to the parties on 16 March, an application for leave to appeal posted on 15 June but received on 17 June is made within the three month time limit in reg 33(1). Clearly, being able to prove the date of despatch will be important where there is a dispute. In *CSDLA 1207/2000* (para 11), the commissioner warned he might find it "difficult to accept" the word of a party as to the date on which a document was sent.

Notices and other documents for a commissioner are to be delivered in person or sent by pre-paid post, fax or email. Note, however, that service by email is only permissable where the office has given written permission in advance: para (2)(d).

The function of commissioners to give directions under this regulation may be delegated to legal officers under reg 7(1)(a).

[¹ Funding of legal services

8A.   If a party is granted funding of legal services at any time, he shall–

(a)   where funding is granted by the Legal Services Commission, send a copy of the funding notice to the office;

(b)   where funding is granted by the Scottish Legal Aid Board, send a copy of the legal aid certificate to the office; and

(c)   notify every other party that funding has been granted.]

Amendment

1.   Inserted by reg 2(5) of SI 2005 No 207 as from 28.2.05.

General Note

In *CSG 336/2003* the commissioner (at para 10) expressed concern that what he described as "responsible solicitors" had made a request for an oral hearing when they were unsure whether they would be able to appear at such a hearing due to funding considerations. He suggested that it would be good practice for solicitors appearing in appeals to the commissioners for claimants to indicate, when applying for oral hearings, whether they had applied for legal aid (or other funding) and the outcome of that funding application. Thereafter, it would also be good practice for such solicitors to keep the Commissioners' Office up to date with the progress of any such applications for funding, and inform that Office of any other reasons why they may not be able to appear at the oral hearing.

Now reg 8A sets out what an appellant must do if granted funding of legal services by the Legal Services Commission (the Legal Aid Board in Scotland). A copy of the funding notice (or legal aid certificate) must be sent to an Office of the Social Security Commissioners and notice that funding has been granted must be given to all other parties. The Chief Commissioner's Practice Memorandum No 5 "Notification of Public Funding" (1 March 2005) states that the sending of a copy of a funding notice (or legal aid certificate) to the Office of the Social Security Commissioners shall be regarded as adequate notification to every other party for the purposes of reg 8A because it will send a copy to all other parties.

PART II

Applications for leave to appeal, appeals and references

Application to a Commissioner for leave to appeal

9.–(1)   An application to a Commissioner for leave to appeal against the decision of an appeal tribunal may be made only where the applicant has sought to obtain leave from the chairman and leave has been refused or the application has been rejected.

(2)   Subject to paragraph (3) an application to a Commissioner shall be made within one month of notice of the refusal or rejection being sent to the applicant by the appeal tribunal.

(3)   A Commissioner may for special reasons accept a late application or an application where the applicant failed to seek leave from the chairman within the specified time, but did so on or before the final date.

(4)   In paragraph (3) the final date means the end of a period of 13 months from the date on which the decision of the appeal tribunal or, if later, any separate statement of the reasons for it, was sent to the applicant by the appeal tribunal.

Definitions

"the chairman" – see reg 4.
"month" – see reg 4.

General Note

Reg 9 deals with renewed applications for leave to appeal to the commissioner following a refusal by a tribunal chair to grant leave or the rejection of the application by her/him. For initial applications to the chair, see reg 58 SSCS D&A Regs.

Representatives making applications for leave to appeal to a commissioner on someone's behalf should ensure they discuss the question of whether to appeal and on what grounds with their clients, both at the stage of application to the chair and at the stage of applying direct to a commissioner. The general mandate for representation before tribunals terminates when the tribunal gives its decision. There must therefore be a clear and new mandate given by the claimant to her/his representative for the purpose of an appeal to the commissioner: *CSDLA 2/2001* (para 14).

A grant of leave to appeal by a commissioner which seeks to restrict the grounds of appeal does not prevent the commissioner hearing the appeal itself from permitting other grounds to be argued (whether or not they were put forward in the leave application); though if such other grounds are to be allowed then it may be necessary to adjourn the hearing of the appeal so as to enable the respondent to the appeal to properly address them: *CH 4354/2003*.

Analysis

Para (1) provides that the commissioner may only be asked to grant leave where an application for leave has previously been considered by a tribunal chair. Under the definition in reg 4(1), "chairman" means not just the sole member of the tribunal (or, in the very rare cases where more than one member sits, the chair – normally the legally qualified member) but also means a "person authorised to deal with applications". This refers to a person authorised under reg 58(6) SSCS D&A Regs to consider an application for leave (see pp944 and 159).

The paragraph refers to leave being refused or the application being rejected. That formulation covers cases not merely where an application has been considered but refused, but also where the chair has rejected an application – eg, because it was late or because there is no statement of reasons for the decision (under reg 53(4) SSCS D&A Regs): *CSDLA 536/1999*. The commissioner can waive irregularities in an application under reg 27. The grounds on which a commissioner will be prepared to consider an appeal in such cases, however, are limited. In particular, if there is no statement of reasons for the decision, it might not be possible to appeal on the basis of a failure to give adequate reasons, since that is the purpose of the statement of reasons: *R(IS) 11/99* (paras 6-7). See also p944.

Para (2) requires an application to be "made within one month" of notification of the refusal or rejection being sent to the applicant for leave to appeal. See p956 on the meaning of "within".

Paras (3) and (4) permit a late application made up to 13 months from the date the tribunal decision or the statement of reasons was sent to the applicant (if later) – the "final date". Late applications can be made even where an applicant sought the chairman's leave late, so long as this was on or before the "final date". The 13-month absolute time limit is meant to mirror the time period in regs 58(1)(a) and (5). However, in calculating the time limit for seeking leave to appeal to her/him, a chair must ignore certain days before an accidental error in a decision has been corrected or notice of a refusal to set aside a decision is sent or given: reg 58(1A) SSCS D&A Regs. No such provision is available to commissioners.

It was confirmed in *CCS 3175/2002* (paras 15-16) that the 13-month time limit was absolute and that if a party had not received the statement of reasons from the Appeals Service, the only course of action open to her/him was to apply for judicial review out of time.

The very restricted grounds for extending time for an appeal to a tribunal do not apply. This is almost certainly due to the fact that the Secretary of State as well as a person affected may have to seek the indulgence of the chairman or commissioner, and there have been a number of cases in which time limits have been missed by the Secretary of State's officers.

The criterion is "special reasons" which is a phrase that previously appeared in reg 78(3) HB Regs 1987. There is a substantial amount of caselaw on what may constitute special reasons. The following principles can be discerned:

(1) The scope of "special reasons" is not restricted. It is to be given a broad interpretation. In *R v Secretary of State for the Home Department ex p Mehta* [1975] 1 WLR 1087 at 1091F-G, CA, it was said that a similarly worded rule in immigration law "gives a discretion to do what is just and right. It should be liberally interpreted . . . so as not to let [a claimant] suffer unfairly".

(2) There is no limit on the length of such an extension and it may be granted before or after the original time limit has expired. There is no need for a specific application for an extension of time, so the commissioner must consider the question even when not raised by the applicant, provided that it appears that an explanation has been given so that reg 10(1)(c) has been complied with.

(3) The applicant must be able to show more than just the fact that the respondent or respondents will not be prejudiced by the delay: *CU 12/1994* (para 7).

(4) The length of the delay, and the applicant's health, personal circumstances and understanding of the HB scheme are all relevant: *R(I) 5/91*. However, the mere fact that the application is only out of time by one day will not mean that "special reasons" exist, although the explanation for the delay clearly need not be so compelling as where the delay is measured in months: *CSDLA 71/1999*.

(5) The reasons do not have to relate to the delay: *R v Newham LBC ex p Kaur* [1997] 29 HLR 776 at 784, QBD. So the merits of the case should be taken into account. The commissioner stated in *CCS 3175/2002* (para 18) that leave would generally be given out of time where a decision was "plainly erroneous in point of law".

(6) The fact that the understanding of the law has been changed as a result of a court decision or a change in regulations may be taken into account, though it is doubtful whether it constitutes a good reason of itself: *R(S) 8/85*; *CIS 147/1995* (para 6).

(7) The importance of the appeal to the claimant in financial terms is also relevant: *R(M) 1/87* (para 7).

(8) The fact that the claimant may have a cause of action against a lawyer or adviser for giving negligent advice should not result of itself in the rejection of an extension of time: *Mehta* at 1091B-C.

(9) If the delay will cause any difficulty in making findings of fact, perhaps because a witness is no longer available or documents have been lost, that will militate against the grant of an extension: *CCS 2064/1999*.

(10)   The respective contributions of the parties to the delay will be relevant: *CCS 2064/1999*. Thus, leave sought one day out of time ought to be more readily granted to a claimant where a local authority has taken months to issue initial decisions.

Where there is more than one party to an appeal, the legitimate expectation of a party that a tribunal decision is final will be highly relevant: *CCS 3175/2002* (paras 19-20). This might be of relevance – eg, in an appeal concerning the question of from whom recovery of an overpayment should be made.

The functions of commissioners to extend the time limit for applications for leave to appeal under this regulation may be delegated to legal officers under reg 7(1)(g).

Notice of application to a Commissioner for leave to appeal

10.–(1)   An application to a Commissioner for leave to appeal shall be made by notice in writing, and shall contain–
(a)   the name and address of the applicant;
(b)   the grounds on which the applicant intends to rely;
(c)   if the application is made late, the grounds for seeking late acceptance; and
(d)   an address for sending notices and other documents to the applicant.
(2)   The notice in paragraph (1) shall have with it copies of–
(a)   the decision against which leave to appeal is sought;
(b)   if separate, the written statement of the appeal tribunal's reasons for it; and
(c)   the notice of refusal or rejection sent to the applicant by the appeal tribunal.
(3)   Where an application for leave to appeal is made [¹ by the Secretary of State, the Board or a relevant authority], the applicant shall send each respondent a copy of the notice of application and any documents sent with it when they are sent to the Commissioner.

Definition
"relevant authority" – see reg 4.

Amendment
1.   Substituted by reg 4 of SI 2001 No 1095 as from 2.7.01.

General Note
Applications for leave to appeal must be made in writing and must contain the information set out in para (1). It is preferable to use the commissioners' own form (OSSC1 for "persons affected" and OSSC2 for local authorities), although there is no requirement to do so. The forms are available from the Office of the Social Security and Child Support Commissioners or at www.osscsc.gov.uk. Notice "in writing" includes a successfully delivered email: *CI 2000/2004*. Note, however, that service by email is only permissable where the Office has given permission in advance: reg 8(2)(d).

Copies of the documents set out in para (2) must accompany the application. See pp935 and 938 on written statements of a tribunal's reasons for its decision.

A failure to comply with the requirements specified in paras (1) and (2) may be waived as an irregularity under reg 27 (eg, where the applicant applied for but was refused a written statement of reasons for the tribunal's decision). However, in *CSDLA 300/2000* the commissioner refused to accept an application which failed to include a statement of reasons in a case where the complaint was of a failure to give adequate reasons. In *CSDLA 1207/2000* para 8 it was held that a faxed letter indicating an intention to appeal could not comply with reg 10(1), even if a letter was subsequently sent containing substantive grounds of appeal.

An application for leave to appeal may be withdrawn under reg 26(1) before it is determined without the leave of the commissioner.

Determination of application

11.–(1)   The office shall send written notice to the applicant and each respondent of the determination of an application for leave to appeal to a Commissioner.
(2)   Subject to a direction by a Commissioner, where a Commissioner grants leave to appeal under regulation 9–
(a)   notice of appeal shall be deemed to have been sent on the date when notice of the determination is sent to the applicant; and
(b)   the notice of application shall be deemed to be a notice of appeal sent under regulation 12.

(3)   If a Commissioner grants an application for leave to appeal he may, with the consent of the applicant and each respondent, treat and determine the application as an appeal.

Definitions
> "office" – see reg 4.
> "respondent" – see reg 4.

General Note
> Para (2) provides for the continuation of the long-standing practice of the Offices of the Commissioners to treat the application for leave as the notice of appeal once leave is granted.
>
> Para (3) gives the commissioner a power to finally determine an application as an appeal once leave is granted, provided that all parties consent.

Notice of appeal

12.–(1)   Subject to regulation 11(2), an appeal shall be made by notice in writing and shall contain–
- (a)   the name and address of the appellant;
- (b)   the date on which the appellant was notified that leave to appeal had been granted;
- (c)   the grounds on which the appellant intends to rely;
- (d)   if the appeal is made late, the grounds for seeking late acceptance; and
- (e)   an address for sending notices and other documents to the appellant.
- (2)   The notice in paragraph (1) shall have with it copies of–
- (a)   the notice informing the appellant that leave to appeal has been granted;
- (b)   the decision against which leave to appeal has been granted; and
- (c)   if separate, the written statement of the appeal tribunal's reasons for it.

General Note
> Reg 12 will generally only need to be complied with where a chairman grants leave to appeal (see reg 11(2)). "Notice in writing" includes a successfully delivered email: *CI 2000/2004*. Note, however, that service by email is only permissable where the Office has given permission in advance: reg 8(2)(d) above. In *CI 2000/2004* the commissioner also considers when a notice of appeal might or might not be invalid.
>
> The time limit for serving notice of appeal is found in reg 13. As with the requirements imposed by reg 10(2) above, the requirements can be waived in an appropriate case under reg 27.

Time limit for appealing after leave obtained

13.–(1)   Subject to paragraph (2), a notice of appeal shall not be valid unless it is sent to a Commissioner within one month of the date on which the appellant was sent written notice that leave to appeal had been granted.

(2)   A Commissioner may for special reasons accept a late notice of appeal.

Definition
> "month" – see reg 4.

General Note
> See p956 for the meaning of "within".
>
> Para (2) provides for acceptance of a late notice of appeal. For the meaning of "special reasons", see p905.
>
> The function of commissioners to extend the time limit for a notice of appeal under this regulation may be delegated to legal officers under reg 7(1)(g).

Acknowledgement of a notice of appeal or a reference and notification to each respondent

16.   The office shall send–
- (a)   to the appellant or person making the reference, an acknowledgement of the receipt of the notice of appeal or the reference;
- (b)   to each respondent, a copy of the notice of appeal or the reference.

Definitions
"office" – see reg 4.
"respondent" – see reg 4.

PART III
Procedure

Representation
17. A party may conduct his case himself (with assistance from any person if he wishes) or be represented by any person whom he may appoint for the purpose.

General Note
There is no requirement that a representative need have any legal or other qualifications, and the standard of representation of claimants by lay advisers is, for the most part, extremely high. For their part, officers may conduct appeals to the commissioners on behalf of their local authorities. Note, however, the question of validity of appeals made by officers on behalf of their authorities: see p164.

Respondent's written observations
18.–(1) A respondent may submit to a Commissioner written observations on an appeal or reference within one month of being sent written notice of it.

(2) Written observations shall include–

(a) the respondent's name and address and address for sending documents;

(b) in the case of observations on an appeal, a statement as to whether or not he opposes the appeal, and

(c) in any case, the grounds upon which the respondent proposes to rely.

(3) The office shall send a copy of any written observations from a respondent to every other party.

[¹(4) Where there is more than one respondent, the order of and time for written observations shall be as directed by a Commissioner under regulation 20.]

Definitions
"month" – see reg 4.
"respondent" – see reg 4.

Amendment
1.   Inserted by reg 7 of SI 2001 No 1095 as from 2.7.01.

General Note
Commissioner Howell reminds local authorities in *CH 3579/2003* that appeals to tribunals and commissioners are legal proceedings and that they should "make it their business to find out how to conduct a case properly and present submissions covering (and confined to) the points of fact and law that are relevant". In the case before him, the local authority had submitted material that included a number of observations veering into general assertions of fact and opinion, but nowhere set out a clear analysis of the issues or arguments on the law.

In *CDLA 487/2006*, Commissioner Rowland said that it would be helpful for respondents to indicate with a brief reason whether it still wished to stand by its original decision in every respect, in all cases where a claimant's appeal is supported and there is more evidence before the commissioner than was available to the local authority when it made its last submission to the tribunal. A commissioner cannot usually substitute her/his own decision without such a concession.

General guidance about the writing of respondent's observations was given in *CH 3853/2001* (paras 25-30). It was recommended that authorities should prepare their observations in a form similar to that used by the Secretary of State's representatives, namely in a separate document headed "Submission to the Commissioner" rather than in letter form. This was confirmed in a Practice Memorandum. The Memorandum has since been revoked but the guidance it contains is still correct.

PRACTICE MEMORANDUM

OBSERVATIONS BY LOCAL AUTHORITIES

(Housing benefit and council tax benefit cases)

1. This Memorandum is issued in order to ensure that observations made on appeals by Local Authorities are in an appropriate form.

2. Observations are formally made to the Commissioner, who is a judge appointed to determine applications and appeals. They must be sent to the Commissioners' Office, which provides the administrative support for the Commissioners, acting as the processing centre for applications and appeals.

3. Observations should not be on the Local Authority's headed paper, as this can cause confusion when the claimant's representative is a welfare rights officer from the same Authority.

4. The form used by the Secretary of State in social security and child support cases provides a useful model for Local Authorities to follow. It is headed **SUBMISSION TO THE COMMISSIONER**. It identifies the case by the claimant's name and the Commissioners' case reference number. It sets out the observations in numbered paragraphs, which is convenient for ease of reference. It records clearly whether or not the appeal is supported and whether an oral hearing before the Commissioner is requested. It is sent with a covering letter to the Commissioners' Office.

HH Judge Michael Harris
Chief Commissioner
13th February 2002

Written observations in reply

19.–(1)   Any party may submit to a Commissioner written observations in reply within one month of being sent written observations under regulation 18.

(2)   The office shall send a copy of any written observations in reply to every other party.

(3)   Where–

(a)   written observations have been received [¹ . . .] under regulation 18; and

(b)   each of the principal parties expresses the view that the decision appealed against was erroneous in point of law,

a Commissioner may make an order under [¹ section 14(7) of the 1998 Act [² , section 6A(3) of the 1943 Act] or paragraph 8(3) of Schedule 7 to the 2000 Act] setting aside the decision and may dispense with the procedure in paragraphs (1) and (2).

Definition
"month" – see reg 4.

Amendments
1.   Amended by reg 8 of SI 2001 No 1095 as from 2.7.01.
2.   Amended by reg 4 of SI 2005 No 870 as from 6.04.05.

General Note
When written observations are received, it will be apparent whether each of the principal parties is of the opinion that the decision appealed against was erroneous in law. See p166 on the power of the commissioner to set aside a decision in this situation.

Directions

20.–(1)   Where a Commissioner considers that an application, appeal or reference made to him gives insufficient particulars to enable the question at issue to be determined, he may direct the party making the application, appeal or reference, or any respondent, to furnish any further particulars which may be reasonably required.

(2)   In the case of an application for leave to appeal, or an appeal from an appeal tribunal, a Commissioner may, before determining the application or appeal, direct the tribunal to submit a statement of such facts or other matters as he considers necessary for the proper determination of that application or appeal.

(3)   At any stage of the proceedings, a Commissioner may, on or without an application, give any directions as he may consider necessary or desirable for the efficient despatch of the proceedings.

(4)   Without prejudice to regulations 18 and 19, or to paragraph (3), a Commissioner may direct any party before him to make any written observations as may seem to him necessary to enable the question at issue to be determined.

(5)   An application under paragraph (3) shall be made in writing to a Commissioner and shall set out the direction which the applicant seeks.

(6)   Unless a Commissioner shall otherwise determine, the office shall send a copy of an application under paragraph (3) to every other party.

General Note

Commissioners may issue directions in the circumstances described in paras (1) to (4). In *CH 2553/2005*, Commissioner Rowland had grave doubts as to the propriety of commissioners directing tribunals to provide statements of reasons under para (2), although these might be encompassed by the term "other matters".

Parties to an appeal can ask a commissioner to issue directions to other parties: see paras (3) and (5).

The commissioner might, for example, ask the parties to provide a summary of the arguments they are going to make, known as a "skeleton argument", in advance of the hearing. If the commissioner does so, one must be provided: *R(I) 1/03* (para 2).

The function of commissioners to give directions under this regulation may be delegated to legal officers under reg 7(1)(a).

Non-disclosure of medical evidence

22.–(1)   Where, in any proceedings, there is before a Commissioner medical evidence relating to a person which has not been disclosed to that person and in the opinion of the Commissioner the disclosure to that person of that evidence would be harmful to his health, such evidence shall not be disclosed to that person.

(2)   Evidence such as is mentioned in paragraph (1)–

(a)   shall not be disclosed to any person acting for or representing the person to whom it relates,

(b)   in a case where a claim for benefit is made by reference to the disability of a person other than the claimant and the evidence relates to that other person, shall not be disclosed to the claimant or any person acting for or representing the claimant,

unless the Commissioner considers that it is in the interests of the person to whom the evidence relates to disclose it.

(3)   Non-disclosure under paragraphs (1) or (2) does not preclude the Commissioner from taking the evidence concerned into account for the purpose of the proceedings.

General Note

Reg 22 will very rarely, if ever, be of relevance to HB and CTB appeals, particularly as discretionary housing payments are outside the scope of the appeal system.

Requests for hearings

23.–(1)   Subject to paragraphs (2), (3) and (4), a Commissioner may determine any proceedings without a hearing.

(2)   Where a request for a hearing is made by any party, a Commissioner shall grant the request unless he is satisfied that the proceedings can properly be determined without a hearing.

(3)   Where a Commissioner refuses a request for a hearing, he shall send written notice to the person making the request, either before or at the same time as making his determination or decision.

(4)   A Commissioner may, without an application and at any stage, direct a hearing.

Definition

"party" – see reg 4.

General Note

A commissioner decides whether an appeal should be determined at an oral hearing and generally holds an oral hearing if any of the parties requests one, unless s/he feels the appeal can be determined properly without one: para (2). Even without a request for an oral hearing, a commissioner may nevertheless hold one: para (4).

See reg 8A for what an appellant must do if granted funding of legal services by the Legal Services Commission (in England) or the Legal Aid Board (in Scotland).

The functions of commissioners to determine requests for or direct hearings under this regulation may be delegated to legal officers under reg 7(1)(b).

Hearings

24.–(1) This regulation applies to any hearing of an application, appeal or reference to which these Regulations apply.

(2) Subject to paragraph (3), the office shall give reasonable notice of the time and place of any hearing before a Commissioner.

(3) Unless all the parties concerned agree to a hearing at shorter notice, the period of notice specified under paragraph (2) shall be at least 14 days before the date of the hearing.

(4) If any party to whom notice of a hearing has been sent fails to appear at the hearing, the Commissioner may proceed with the case in that party's absence, or may give directions with a view to the determination of the case.

(5) Any hearing before a Commissioner shall be in public, unless the Commissioner for special reasons directs otherwise.

(6) Where a Commissioner holds a hearing the following persons or organisations shall be entitled to be present and be heard–

(a) the person or organisation making the application, appeal or reference;

(b) the claimant;

[⁵ (ba) in the case of an application or appeal under the 1943 Act, the respondent;]

(c) the Secretary of State [¹ or, in proceedings concerning tax credits, the Board];

(d) a trade union, employers' association or other association which would have had a right of appeal under [² the 1998 Act];

[³ (e)]

(f) a person from whom it is determined that any amount is recoverable under or by virtue of [²section 71, 74, 75 or 76 of the Social Security Administration Act 1992; [² . . .]

[²(ff) in cases concerning housing benefit or council tax benefit, the relevant authority and any person affected; and]

(g) with the leave of a Commissioner, any other person.

[⁴ (6A) Subject to the direction of a Commissioner–

(a) any person or organisation entitled to be present and be heard at a hearing; and

(b) any representatives of such a person or organisation,

may be present by means of a live television link.

(6B) Any provision in these Regulations which refers to a party or representative being present is satisfied if the party or representative is present by means of a live television link.]

(7) Any person entitled to be heard at a hearing may–

(a) address the Commissioner;

(b) with the leave of the Commissioner, give evidence, call witnesses and put questions directly to any other person called as a witness.

(8)   Nothing in these Regulations shall prevent a member of the Council on Tribunals or of the Scottish Committee of the Council in his capacity as such from being present at a hearing before a Commissioner which is not held in public.

Amendments

1.	Inserted by reg 7 of SI 2000 No 2854 as from 10.11.00.
2.	Amended by reg 10 of SI 2001 No 1095 as from 2.7.01.
3.	Omitted by reg 2(8) of SI 2005 No 207 as from 28.2.05.
4.	Inserted by reg 2(9) of SI 2005 No 207 as from 28.2.05.
5.	Amended by reg 5 of SI 2005 No 870 as from 6.04.05.

General Note

At least 14 days' notice must be given of a hearing unless all the parties concerned agree to a shorter notice period: paras (2) and (3). Hearings are usually held at the commissioners' offices in London, Edinburgh or Belfast or at the law courts in Cardiff, Doncaster or Plymouth. Exceptionally, hearings are held in other court centres if someone is unable to travel. People entitled to attend and be heard at hearings are listed in para (6). They and their representatives can be present at hearings by means of a live television link: paras (6A) and (6B). Video conferenced hearings are available in some locations, but not currently for child support, HB or CTB cases.

Summoning of witnesses

25.–(1)   Subject to paragraph (2), a Commissioner may summon any person to attend a hearing as a witness, at such time and place as may be specified in the summons, to answer any questions or produce any documents in his custody or under his control which relate to any matter in question in the proceedings.

(2)   A person shall not be required to attend in obedience to a summons under paragraph (1) unless he has been given at least 14 days' notice before the date of the hearing or, if less than 14 days, has informed the Commissioner that he accepts such notice as he has been given.

(3)   Upon the application of a person summoned under this regulation, a Commissioner may set the summons aside.

(4)   A Commissioner may require any witness to give evidence on oath and for this purpose an oath may be administered in due form.

Definition

"summons" – see reg 4.

General Note

Reg 25 is similar in form to reg 43 SSCS D&A Regs (see p924). Note that by virtue of the definition of "summons" in reg 4, "summons" includes "citation", the Scottish equivalent. There is no equivalent of reg 43(2) here, but as there is no power to punish for non-compliance, in the unlikely event of a commissioner requiring a witness to give non-compellable evidence, the witness could refuse to do so with impunity.

The reference to affirmations together with oaths in reg 43(5) is missing but a witness would have a right under s5(1) of the Oaths Act 1978 to affirm nonetheless.

The summoning witnesses under this regulation may be delegated to legal officers under reg 7(1)(c). Legal officers may also set aside summons made by them under that provision.

Withdrawal of applications for leave to appeal, appeals and references

26.–(1)   At any time before it is determined, an applicant may withdraw an application to a Commissioner for leave to appeal against a decision of an appeal tribunal by giving written notice to a Commissioner.

(2)   At any time before the decision is made, the appellant or person making a reference to a Commissioner may withdraw his appeal or reference with the leave of a Commissioner.

(3)   A Commissioner may, on application by the party concerned, give leave to reinstate any application, appeal or reference which has been withdrawn in accordance with paragraphs (1) and (2) and, on giving leave, he may make directions as to the conduct of the proceedings.

General Note
> The functions of commissioners of giving leave to withdraw or reinstate applications, appeals or references under this regulation may be delegated to legal officers under reg 7(1)(e).

Irregularities
27. Any irregularity resulting from failure to comply with the requirements of these Regulations shall not by itself invalidate any proceedings, and the Commissioner, before reaching his decision, may waive the irregularity or take steps to remedy it.

General Note
> Irregularities resulting from a failure to comply with the requirements of these regulations can be waived by a commissioner. This means, for example, that where an applicant for leave to appeal has not obtained a written statement of reasons for a decision from the tribunal required by reg 9(2), the application can still be considered. However, the applicant must still show that the tribunal possibly made an error of law without it. See p160 on what amounts to an error of law.
>
> The power to waive irregularities in connection with any matter being dealt with by a legal officer may be delegated to legal officers under reg 7(1)(f).

PART IV
Decisions

Determinations and decisions of a Commissioner
28.–(1) The determination of a Commissioner on an application for leave to appeal shall be in writing and signed by him.

(2) The decision of a Commissioner on an appeal or reference shall be in writing and signed by him and, unless it was a decision made with the consent of the parties or an order setting aside a tribunal's decision under [¹ section 14(7) of the 1998 Act [² , section 6A(3) of the 1943 Act] or paragraph 8(3) of Schedule 7 to the 2000 Act], he shall include the reasons.

(3) The office shall send a copy of the determination or decision and any reasons to each party.

(4) Without prejudice to paragraphs (2) and (3), a Commissioner may announce his determination or decision at the end of a hearing.

Definition
> "office" – see reg 4.

Amendments
> 1. Amended by reg 11 of SI 2001 No 1095 as from 2.7.01.
> 2. Amended by reg 6 of SI 2005 No 870 as from 6.04.05.

General Note
> There is no obligation to give reasons for a determination on an application for leave to appeal under para (1), but short reasons are now given as a matter of practice. Reasons are, of course, given for a decision on an appeal unless the summary procedure for setting aside a tribunal's decision by consent is used.
>
> Commissioners have frequently adopted a procedure by which more than one decision is issued during a case. These have traditionally been described as "interim" and "final" decisions. The interim decisions tend to deal with preliminary points which the parties needed to consider before other issues were dealt with. There is no specific statutory authorisation for this practice, but in the unlikely event of any challenge being made to it, it is likely that it would be concluded that the general power under reg 5(1) for a commissioner to determine the procedure to be followed would enable such a course to be adopted.

Correction of accidental errors in decisions
30.–(1) Subject to regulations 6 and 32, the Commissioner who gave the decision may at any time correct accidental errors in any decision or record of a decision.

(2)   A correction made to, or to the record of, a decision shall become part of the decision or record, and the office shall send a written notice of the correction to any party to whom notice of the decision has been sent.

Definition
"office" – see reg 4.

General Note
"Decision" here includes determinations of applications for leave to appeal, orders setting aside tribunal decisions under Sch 7 para 8(3) CSPSSA as well as decisions on appeals and references: see reg 32(1).
There is no right of appeal against a correction or a refusal to correct: see reg 32(2).

Setting aside decisions on certain grounds

31.–(1)   Subject to regulations 6 and 32, on an application made by any party, the Commissioner who gave the decision in proceedings may set it aside where it appears just to do so on the ground that–
(a)   a document relating to the proceedings was not sent to, or was not received at an appropriate time by, a party or his representative or was not received at an appropriate time by the Commissioner; or
(b)   a party or his representative was not present at a hearing before the Commissioner; [¹]
[¹ (c)]
(2)   An application under this regulation shall be made in writing to a Commissioner within one month from the date on which the office gave written notice of the decision to the party making the application.
(3)   Unless the Commissioner considers that it is unnecessary for the proper determination of an application made under paragraph (1), the office shall send a copy of it to each respondent, who shall be given a reasonable opportunity to make representations on it.
(4)   The office shall send each party written notice of a determination of an application to set aside a decision and the reasons for it.

Definitions
"month" – see reg 4.
"office" – see reg 4.
"party" – see reg 4.
"respondent" – see reg 4.

Amendment
1.   Omitted by reg 2(10) of SI 2005 No 207 as from 28.2.05.

General Note
"Decision" here includes determinations of applications for leave to appeal, orders setting aside tribunal decisions under Sch 7 para 8(3) CSPSSA as well as decisions on appeals and references: see reg 32(1).
Para (1) gives similar grounds for setting aside a decision as are found in reg 57(1) SSCS D&A Regs. Until 28 February 2005, a commissioner could also set aside a decision if there had been a "procedural irregularity or mishap". This had been widely interpreted to include a situation where a commissioner took the view that a refusal of leave to appeal was plainly wrong (*CCS 910/1999*) or where the justice of the case clearly so required: *CG 3657/2001*.
Perhaps controversially, sub-para (1)(c) was deleted by SI 2005 No 207 from 28 February 2005, so that a setting aside ground is now only available if a party or her/his representative was not present at a hearing or some document was not before the commissioner when s/he made her/his decision. It is strongly arguable that the narrow terms of s28(1)(b) SSA 1998 never authorised reg 31(1)(c), but it may also be argued that such a setting aside ground may be implied under s28(2) SSA 1998 on the facts of a particular case.
A refusal of leave will not be set aside simply because a claimant's representative asserts that there is an arguable point of law and there is no breach of Art 6 of the European Convention on Human Rights in doing so, or in the same commissioner determining the application: *CDLA 3432/2001* (paras 2-3). Nor will

a refusal of leave to appeal be set aside where the applicant produces evidence which was in existence at the time of the appeal tribunal's decision but was not produced to it; and such applications should not be advanced by responsible representatives: *CIB 805/2004*. The remedy in this situation is to ask for the appeal tribunal's decision to be superseded on the basis of mistake of, or ignorance of, a material fact or change of circumstances.

The time limit under para (2) of one month could be extended under reg 5(2)(a). For the meaning of "within one month from the date", see p907. Notice is given on the date on which it is sent to the applicant: reg 8(3).

There is no right of appeal against a determination of an application to set aside a decision: see reg 32(2).

Provisions common to regulations 30 and 31

32.–(1) In regulations 30 and 31, the word "decision" shall include determinations of applications for leave to appeal, orders setting aside tribunal decisions under [¹ section 14(7) of the 1998 Act [² , section 6A(3) of the 1943 Act] or paragraph 8(3) of Schedule 7 to the 2000 Act] and decisions on appeals and references.

(2) There shall be no appeal against a correction or a refusal to correct under regulation 30 or a determination given under regulation 31.

Amendments
1.   Substituted by reg 13 of SI 2001 No 1095 as from 2.7.01.
2.   Amended by reg 7 of SI 2005 No 870 as from 6.04.05.

PART V
Applications for leave to appeal to the appellate court

Application to a Commissioner for leave to appeal to the Appellate Court

33.–(1)   Subject to paragraph (2), an application to a Commissioner under [¹ section 15 of the 1998 Act [⁴ , section 6C of the 1943 Act] or paragraph 9 of Schedule 7 to the 2000 Act] for leave to appeal against a decision of a Commissioner shall be made in writing, stating the grounds of the application, within three months from the date on which the applicant was sent written notice of the decision.

[³ (2)   Where–
(a)   any decision or record of a decision is corrected under regulation 30; or
(b)   an application for a decision to be set aside under regulation 31 is refused for reasons other than that the application was made outside the period specified in regulation 31(2),

the period specified in paragraph (1) shall run from the date on which written notice of the correction or refusal of the application to set aside is sent to the applicant.]

(3)   Regulation 33 of the Social Security (Claims and Payments) Regulations 1987 (persons unable to act) [⁵ regulation 82(2) to (6) of the Housing Benefit Regulations 2006, regulation 63(2) to (6) of the Housing Benefit (Persons who have attained the qualifying age for state pension credit) Regulations 2006, regulation 68(2) to (6) of the Council Tax Benefit Regulations 2006 and regulation 52(2) to (6) of the Council Tax Benefit (Persons who have attained the qualifying age for state pension credit) Regulations 2006] shall apply to the right of appeal conferred by [¹section 15 of the 1998 Act and paragraph 9 of Schedule 7 to the 2000 Act] (appeal from Commissioner on point of law) [¹ as they apply] to rights arising under the Social Security Acts generally.

[² (4)   *[omitted]*]
(5)   Regulations 26(1) and 26(3) shall apply to an application to a Commissioner for leave to appeal from a Commissioner's decision as they apply to the proceedings in that regulation.

Definition
    "month" – see reg 4.

Amendments

1.   Amended by reg 14 of SI 2001 No 1095 as from 2.7.01.
2.   Inserted by reg 9 of SI 2000 No 2854 as from 10.11.00.
3.   Substituted by reg 2(11) of SI 2005 No 207 as from 28.2.05.
4.   Amended by reg 8 of SI 2005 No 870 as from 6.04.05.
5.   Substituted by reg 5 and Sch 2 para 15 of SI 2006 No 217 as from 6.3.06.

General Note

The time limit for applying for leave to appeal to the Court of Appeal is three months rather than the one month specified elsewhere: para (1). See p956 on the meaning of "within", but as the wording is "from the date" it is suggested that here the date on which the decision was sent is included rather than excluded. Note that where a decision is corrected under reg 30 or an application for a decision to be set aside under reg 31 is refused other than because it was made outside the time limit for this, the time limit runs from the date notice of the correction or refusal is sent to the applicant: para (2).

Para (3) permits appointees to appeal on behalf of a claimant. Para (5) permits withdrawal of applications for leave to appeal or subsequent reinstatement.

The Social Security and Child Support (Decisions and Appeals) Regulations 1999
(SI 1999 No.991)

General Note on the Regulations

Certain of these regulations, originally made to govern decision-making and appeals in relation to benefits administered by the DWP, are applied to HB and CTB appeals by virtue of reg 23 D&A Regs. They are printed here in their modified form following the modifications made by reg 23.

ARRANGEMENT OF REGULATIONS
PART I
General
1.   Citation, commencement and interpretation

PART V
Appeal Tribunals For Social Security Contracting Out Of Pensions Vaccine Damage And Child Support
CHAPTER II
Procedure In Connection With Determination And Referrals Of Appeals
38.   Consideration and determination of appeals and referrals
39.   Choice of hearing
40.   Withdrawal of appeal or referral
42.   Non-disclosure of medical advice or evidence
43.   Summoning of witnesses and administration of oaths

CHAPTER III
Striking Out Appeals
46.   Appeals which may be struck out
47.   Reinstatement of struck out appeals

CHAPTER IV
Oral Hearings
49.   Procedure at oral hearings
50.   Manner of providing expert assistance
51.   Postponement and adjournment

CHAPTER V
Decisions Of Appeal Tribunals And Related Matters

Appeal Tribunals Decisions
53.   Decisions of appeal tribunals
54.   Late applications for statement of reasons of tribunal decision
55.   Record of tribunal proceedings
56.   Correction of accidental errors
57.   Setting aside decisions on certain grounds
57A. Provisions common to regulations 56 and 57
57B. Interpretation of Chapter V

Applications For Leave To Appeal To Commissioner (Not Including Child Support)
58.   Application for leave to appeal to a Commissioner from an appeal tribunal

PART I

General

Citation, commencement and interpretation

1.–(1) These Regulations may be cited as the Social Security and Child Support (Decisions and Appeals) Regulations 1999.

(2) *[omitted]*

(3) In these Regulations, unless the context otherwise requires–

"appeal" means an appeal to an appeal tribunal;

"clerk to the appeal tribunal" means a clerk assigned to the appeal tribunal in accordance with regulation 37;

[⁹ "the Deferral of Retirement Pensions etc. Regulations" means the Social Security (Deferral of Retirement Pensions, Shared Additional Pension and Graduated Retirement Benefit) (Miscellaneous Provisions) Regulations 2005;]

[⁴ "designated authority" means–

(a) the Secretary of State;

(b) a person providing services to the Secretary of State;

(c) a local authority;

(d) a person providing services to, or authorised to exercise any functions of, any such authority;]

"financially qualified panel member" means a panel member who satisfies the requirements of paragraph 4 of Schedule 3;

"legally qualified panel member" means a panel member who satisfies the requirements of paragraph 1 of Schedule 3;

"medically qualified panel member" means a panel member who satisfies the requirements of paragraph 2 of Schedule 3;

[⁹ "the Graduated Retirement Benefit Regulations" means the Social Security (Graduated Retirement Benefit) Regulations 2005;]

[⁸]

[⁶ "out of jurisdiction appeal" means an appeal brought against a decision which is specified in–

(a) Schedule 2 to the Act or a decision prescribed in regulation 27 (decision against which no appeal lies); or

(b) paragraph 6(2) of Schedule 7 to the Child Support, Pensions and Social Security Act 2000 (appeal to appeal tribunal) or a decision prescribed in regulation 16 of the Housing Benefit and Council Tax Benefit (Decisions and Appeals) Regulations 2001 (decision against which no appeal lies);]

"panel" means the panel constituted under section 6;

"panel member" means a person appointed to the panel;

"panel member with a disability qualification" means a panel member who satisfies the requirements of paragraph 5 of Schedule 3;

[¹ "the Transfer Act" means the Social Security Contributions (Transfer of Functions, etc.) Act 1999.]

[⁷ "work-focused interview" means an interview in which a person is required to take part in accordance with regulations made under section 2A or 2AA of the Administration Act;]

[⁵ . . .]

[²(3A) *[omitted]*]

(4) *[omitted]*

Amendments

    1.   Inserted by reg 2(2) of SI 1999 No 1670 as from 5.7.99.

    2.   Inserted by Art 3(2) of SI 1999 No 1662 as from 5.7.99.

    3.   Inserted by reg 16(5) and Sch 6 para 2 of SI 2000 No 897 as from 3.4.00.

    4.   Substituted by Sch 2 para 6 of SI 2002 No 1703 as from 30.9.02.

    5.   Deleted by Sch 2 para 6 of SI 2002 No 1703 as from 30.9.02.

6.   Amended by reg 3(1) of SI 2003 No 1050 as from 5.5.03.
7.   Substituted by reg 24 of SI 2004 No 959 as from 26.4.04.
8.   Omitted by reg 2(2) of SI 2004 No 3368 as from 21.12.04.
9.   Inserted by Reg 9(2) of SI 2005 No 2677 as from 6.4.06.

General Note

For what constitutes a "legally qualifed panel member", see p109.

PART V
Appeal Tribunals for Social Security Contracting Out of Pensions, Vaccine Damage and Child Support
Procedure in Connection with Determination of Appeals and References

---

Consideration and determination of appeals and referrals

38.–(1)   The procedure in connection with the consideration and determination of an appeal or a referral shall, subject to the following provisions of these Regulations, be such as a legally qualified panel member shall determine.

(2)   A legally qualified panel member may give directions requiring a [¹ principal] party to the proceedings to comply with any provision of these Regulations and may at any stage of the proceedings, either of his own motion or on a written application made to the clerk to the appeal tribunal by any [¹ principal] party to the proceedings, give such directions as he may consider necessary or desirable for the just, effective and efficient conduct of the proceedings and may direct any [¹ principal] party to the proceedings to provide such particulars or to produce such documents as may be reasonably required.

(3)   Where a clerk to the appeal tribunal is authorised to take steps in relation to the procedure of the tribunal he may give directions requiring any [¹ principal] party to the proceedings to comply with any provision of these Regulations.

Modification

1.   Made by reg 23(3)(b) of SI 2001 No 1002.

General Note

Reg 38 contains extremely wide powers for dealing with appeals. Para (1) gives a general power to determine procedure and para (2) confirms that directions may be given for the conduct of the appeal. This can include the provision of information or documents. This is an underused power which claimants can use to considerable effect to extract documents and information from reticent authorities and vice versa. The scope of the powers in paras (1) and (2) is limited only by the requirements of fairness and reasonableness and other legislation. Reg 43(3) provides a useful guide to other instances where a tribunal must tread with caution before ordering disclosure of information or documents.

Para (3) confers a more limited power on a tribunal clerk to give directions. The directions must be for compliance with the provisions of the regulations. Note the power under reg 46(1)(c) to strike out an appeal where an appellant fails to comply with directions and is warned of the consequences of failure to do so.

The availability of sanctions for a failure to comply with directions is limited. Any sanctions imposed must be proportionate to the offence: *CDLA 4977/2001* (para 35). An appeal cannot be struck out unless the procedure specified by reg 46(1)(c) is followed. There is no specific power to impose other sanctions. Commissioner Jacobs considered the issues in *CIB 4253/2004*. The appellant's appeal hearing had been adjourned and he had been directed to produce documents he wished to rely upon to the then Appeals Service within 28 days. He failed to do so, but at the reconvened hearing of his appeal he referred to documents which he wished to produce. The tribunal refused to accept any further documents because he had not complied with the direction. The commissioner said the tribunal could and should have considered the evidence. By declining to do so it had denied the appellant a fair hearing. He said:

"9.   Directions may be appropriate for a variety of reasons. Some claimants do not prosecute their appeals. Others purport to want their day in tribunal, but connive to postpone it for as long as possible. But for most claimants whose cases come on for hearing, the purpose of directions is to provide guidance and assistance on what evidence is required and when and how it should be produced. Underlying this is a proper concern by tribunals that appeals should be handled efficiently and that tribunals should have the evidence to allow soundly-based decisions. This is an aspect of the enabling approach which forms part of the philosophy on which tribunals' procedure is based.

10. The appropriate response to a failure to comply with a direction depends on the circumstances of the case and the purposes for which the direction was given. If the case comes on for hearing, the response must be consistent with the principles of natural justice and the claimant's Convention right to a fair hearing. In some circumstances, the appropriate response is to strike out the appeal. In other circumstances, the appropriate response may be to draw inferences adverse to the party who has failed to comply with a direction. But the availability of a penalty is not an essential feature of a direction. Directions, like rules of procedure and law, ultimately and mainly depend for their effectiveness on consent and co-operation, not on enforcement or penalties.

15. All the parties are entitled to a fair hearing. But what is required may differ as between the parties. The Secretary of State and an unrepresented claimant are not equally informed. The equality of arms aspect of the Convention right to a fair hearing and the enabling approach to a tribunal's procedure overlap and combine to allow and require the tribunal to redress the imbalance between the parties. That imbalance includes the difference in understanding. The tribunal's response to a failure to comply with a direction has to take account of that imbalance."

In *CSDLA 866/2002*, Commissioner Parker considered the difficulties posed by a tribunal's decision to adjourn which was overruled by a District Chairman's direction that the appeal should be relisted. She gave guidance on the use of the powers conferred by reg 38(2) in such a situation.

"20. The regulatory power given to a legally qualified panel member (in practice, a DC) is a wide one, designed to ensure that the appeal process runs smoothly. This may involve overruling directions from a tribunal which cannot be followed in a practicable manner. An obvious example is where a tribunal adjourns for a report from a general practitioner or a consultant and such a report is not produced, despite the best efforts of the Appeals Service. Another example might be where a hearing is adjourned for attendance by a particular witness who then refuses to attend or is ill or goes abroad. A balance has to be drawn between carrying out the prior tribunal's directions and deciding the appeal within a reasonable time frame.

21. However, the rationale for allowing an independent tribunal to adjourn where it considers it is right to do so would be frustrated if the DC makes an inappropriate use of the power to give directions. . .

22. Adjournments cause delay for other appellants waiting in the queue . . . But I do not accept the Secretary of State's argument that unlimited powers are given by regulation 38(2). To ensure the independence of tribunals, even a poor adjournment direction has to be respected unless it frustrates the determination of the appeal within a reasonable time or is very difficult to fulfil."

[²Choice of hearing

39.–(1) Where an appeal or a referral is made to an appeal tribunal the appellant and any other party to the proceedings shall notify the clerk to the appeal tribunal, on a form approved by the Secretary of State, whether he wishes to have an oral hearing of the appeal or whether he is content for the appeal or referral to proceed without an oral hearing.

(2) Except in the case of a referral, the form shall include a statement informing the appellant that, if he does not notify the clerk to the appeal tribunal as required by paragraph (1) within the period specified in paragraph (3), the appeal may be struck out in accordance with regulation 46(1).

(3) Notification in accordance with paragraph (1)–

(a) if given by the appellant or a party to the proceedings other than the Secretary of State, must be sent or given to the clerk to the appeal tribunal within 14 days of the date on which the form is issued to him; or

(b) if given by the Secretary of State, must be sent or given to the clerk–

 (i) in the case of an appeal, within 14 days of the date on which the form is issued to the appellant; or

 (ii) in the case of a referral, on the date of referral,

or within such longer period as the clerk may direct.

(4) Where an oral hearing is requested in accordance with paragraphs (1) and (3) the appeal tribunal shall hold an oral hearing unless the appeal is struck out under regulation 46(1).]

(5)   The chairman, or in the case of an appeal tribunal which has only one member, that member, may of his own motion direct that an oral hearing of the appeal or referral be held if he is satisfied that such a hearing is necessary to enable the appeal tribunal to reach a decision.

Modification
1.   Made by reg 23(3)(b) of SI 2001 No 1002.

Amendment
2.   Substituted by reg 2(5) of SI 2004 No 3368 as from 21.12.04.

General Note
Once an appeal has been made, the authority should prepare a submission to the tribunal. That submission is then sent to the Tribunals Service and to every person affected (including, of course, the appellant). The appellant is also sent a standard questionnaire (Form TAS1) with a reply paid envelope. Among other things, the questionnaire asks whether the person affected wants an oral hearing or a hearing on the papers.

An oral hearing will normally take place at the local tribunal venue closest to the appellant's home and *not* at the regional office of the Tribunals Service to which the questionnaire must be returned.

It cannot be over-emphasised that an appellant should normally ask for an oral hearing. Statistical evidence shows that appeals in which an oral hearing is requested are substantially more likely to succeed. There are two reasons for this. The first concerns the burden of proof. The tribunal is obliged to decide the facts of the appeal "on a balance of probabilities". In other words, it must decide what is more likely than not to have happened. Where the written evidence does not make this clear, the appeal will normally be decided in favour of the authority because the burden of proof is usually – though not always – on the appellant. Secondly, the written evidence will almost always leave things unclear. An unrepresented claimant may not appreciate what factors are legally relevant and may therefore base her/his written evidence and submissions on points that cannot make any difference to the outcome of the appeal. If so, s/he will lose at a paper hearing. If, on the other hand, s/he requests and attends an oral hearing, the tribunal can exercise its enabling role by explaining what points it actually needs to know about and taking oral evidence on those points. And even if the appellant understands what the issues are, it is still unlikely that written evidence and submissions will deal with those issues as well as oral evidence. Most people, however highly educated, over-estimate the clarity of their written style: there will often be ambiguities and nuances of meaning that are not noticed by the writer (who knows what s/he is trying to say) but will affect how the writing is understood by the reader. Or they will assume that the tribunal already knows important facts about their backgrounds that the tribunal does not in fact know. Finally, tribunal members are human and may sometimes simply misunderstand what is written even though to other readers it would be perfectly clear. All those types of misunderstanding and imperfect communication can be corrected at an oral hearing. Tribunal members can ask supplementary questions about points on which they are unclear and the parties can explain their side of things in far more detail than is practicable in writing.

The second reason concerns the assessment of credibility. Tribunal members tend to feel that the best way to assess whether people are telling the truth is to hear them in person, question them and observe their demeanour. Some research suggests that this may not always be the case. Nevertheless, most tribunal members will have experience of appeals that seemed hopeless on the papers but which succeeded at an oral hearing because it was obvious once the appellant had given oral evidence that s/he was telling the truth. Improbable things sometimes happen and in such cases the fact that the appellant is a credible witness may sometimes outweigh what would otherwise be the improbability of her/his evidence. That cannot happen if the appeal is considered on the papers alone.

It should also be noted that it is much harder to have an unfavourable tribunal decision set aside on procedural grounds (ie, under reg 57 below) if it was considered without an oral hearing. Some appellants may think they can ask for a paper appeal first and then ask for an oral hearing if they do are unhappy with the result. That is not the case.

Many people are anxious about attending tribunals (and, although tribunals are very much less formal than courts, a tribunal hearing will often be the most formal event that a person ever attends). But, for the reasons given above, it is important that appellants should try not to let such anxieties prevent them from requesting an oral hearing and attending it. The tribunal will be pleased that the appellant has turned up to help it make a decision and although it may have to ask detailed questions, those questions should not be hostile and, in a HB or CTB appeal, it is unlikely that it will have to ask the sort of questions about intimate personal and medical matters that are sometimes necessary in disability living allowance and incapacity for work appeals. Appellants are entitled to be accompanied by a friend or relative at the hearing (see reg

49(8)) and it may also be possible to get free advice and representation from a Citizen's Advice Bureau, a local authority welfare rights unit, a law centre or from some firms of solicitors.

The Tribunals Service may be able to assist with any difficulty the parties may have in travelling to the hearing (and will certainly reimburse the appellant's reasonable travel expenses).

A problem with the operation of the reg 39(1) was revealed in *CIB 4193/2003*. In that case, the claimant had initially asked for his appeal to be dealt with on the papers and not at an oral hearing, and the resultant decision of the tribunal had then been set aside under s13 SSA 1998 (see also Sch 7 para 7 CSPSSA). At that time, the clerk to the tribunal was required to direct the parties to the appeal to notify her/him whether they wanted an oral hearing. However, no fresh direction had then been made by the clerk asking if the claimant wanted an oral hearing of the remitted appeal. In the commissioner's view, this was based on an unjustified assumption that the appellant's perspective about the need for an oral hearing would not have changed in the intervening period. However, a substantial proportion of those who initially opt for a paper hearing presumably do so on the basis that they have a reasonable prospect of succeeding on such an appeal and some of those would undoubtedly wish to reconsider their position in the light of having lost the appeal on the papers and having had to apply for leave to appeal. The commissioner therefore said that fairness dictated that, when a decision made at a paper hearing is set aside under s13, the claimant is at least offered the opportunity to ask for an oral hearing of the appeal when it is reheard. It is suggested that the same would apply under the current version of reg 39.

If any party to the proceedings (ie, appellant or local authority or, in appropriate cases, a landlord or agent) opts for an oral hearing, one must be held: para (4). Failure to do so is an error of law: *CDLA 3224/ 2001*.

Para (5) gives a power to a tribunal to require an oral hearing to be held even if the appellant wishes for a paper hearing, if it is "necessary" to enable a decision to be made. In *CDLA 1347/1999* the commissioner interpreted "necessary" to mean "reasonably necessary in the circumstances of the case", not "essential". In *CDLA 1347/1999* (para 10) it was said that if justice could not be done without such a hearing, the power should be exercised, but it would be rare that a claimant would be able to impugn a tribunal's decision for error of law if it elected to proceed with a paper hearing.

Withdrawal of appeal or referral

40.–(1) An appeal may be withdrawn by the appellant or an authorised representative of the appellant and a referral may be withdrawn by the Secretary of State, as the case may be, either–

(a)   at an oral hearing; or

(b)   at any other time before the appeal or referral is determined, by giving notice in writing of withdrawal to the clerk to the appeal tribunal.

(2)   If an appeal or a referral is withdrawn (as the case may be) in accordance with paragraph (1)(a), the clerk to the appeal tribunal shall send a notice in writing to any [1 principal] party to the proceedings who is not present when the appeal or referral is withdrawn, informing him that the appeal or referral (as the case may be) has been withdrawn.

(3)   If an appeal or a referral is withdrawn (as the case may be) in accordance with paragraph (1)(b), the clerk to the appeal tribunal shall send a notice in writing to every [1 principal] party to the proceedings informing them that the appeal or referral (as the case may be) has been withdrawn.

Modification

1.   Made by reg 23(3)(b) of SI 2001 No 1002.

General Note

An appeal may be withdrawn by an appellant or her/his authorised representative so long as this is done before the appeal is determined by the appeal tribunal: para (1). The Court of Appeal decided in *Rydqvist v Secretary of State for Work and Pensions* [2002] *The Times* 8 July, [2002] EWCA Civ 947 that once an appeal has been withdrawn validly it cannot be re-instated. The appeal concerned an earlier provision in respect of the withdrawal of appeals; however, the reasoning in *Rydqvist* should apply with equal force to the current rule. The only option for an appellant in this situation is to make a fresh appeal, with an application for an extension of time under reg 19 D&A Regs if relevant.

Non-disclosure of medical advice or evidence

42.–(1)   Where, in connection with [¹ ...] an appeal or referral there is [¹ ...] medical advice or medical evidence relating to a person which has not been disclosed to him and in the opinion of [¹ a legally qualified panel member], the disclosure to that person of that advice or evidence would be harmful to his health, such advice or evidence shall not be required to be disclosed to that person.

(2)   Advice or evidence such as is mentioned in paragraph (1) shall not be disclosed to any person acting for or representing the person to whom it relates or, in a case where a claim for benefit is made by reference to the disability of a person other than the claimant and the advice or evidence relates to that other person, shall not be disclosed to the claimant or any person acting for or representing him, unless [¹ a legally qualified panel member], is satisfied that it is in the interests of the person to whom the advice or evidence relates to do so.

(3)   A tribunal shall not be precluded from taking into account for the purposes of the determination advice or evidence which has not been disclosed to a person under the provisions of paragraph (1) or (2).

Amendment

1.   Substituted by reg 25 of SI 2000 No 1596 as from 19.6.00.

General Note

Reg 42 will very rarely, if ever, be of relevance to HB and CTB appeals, particularly as discretionary housing payments are outside the scope of the appeals system.

Summoning of witnesses and administration of oaths

43.–(1)   A chairman, or in the case of an appeal tribunal which has only one member, that member, may by summons, or in Scotland, by citation, require any person in Great Britain to attend as a witness at a hearing of an appeal, application or referral at such time and place as shall be specified in the summons or citation and, subject to paragraph (2), at the hearing to answer any question or produce any documents in his custody or under his control which relate to any matter in question in the appeal, application or referral but–

(a)   no person shall be required to attend in obedience to such summons or citation unless he has been given at least 14 days' notice of the hearing or, if less than 14 days' notice is given, he has informed the tribunal that the notice given is sufficient; and

(b)   no person shall be required to attend and give evidence or to produce any document in obedience to such summons or citation unless the necessary expenses of attendance are paid or tendered to him.

(2)   No person shall be compelled to give any evidence or produce any document or other material that he could not be compelled to give or produce on a trial of an action in a court of law in that part of Great Britain where the hearing takes place.

(3)   In exercising the powers conferred by this regulation, the chairman, or in the case of an appeal tribunal which has only one member, that member, shall take into account the need to protect any matter that relates to intimate personal or financial circumstances, is commercially sensitive, consists of information communicated or obtained in confidence or concerns national security.

(4)   Every summons or citation issued under this regulation shall contain a statement to the effect that the person in question may apply in writing to a chairman to vary or set aside the summons or citation.

(5)   A chairman, or in the case of an appeal tribunal which has only one member, that member, may require any witness, including a witness summoned under the powers conferred by this regulation, to give evidence on oath or affirmation and for that purpose there may be administered an oath or affirmation in due form.

General Note

The power set out in reg 43(1) looks impressive, but is without teeth because there is no sanction for disobedience. A person disregarding a witness summons would not be in contempt of court. In England and Wales, r34.4 of the Civil Procedure Rules 1998 confers a power on the High Court or County Court to issue a witness summons "in aid of . . . a tribunal" but this only applies to a tribunal "that does not have power to issue a witness summons in relation to proceedings before it". On the face of it, reg 43 excludes the exercise of the power under r34.4 unless it could be said that "witness summons" in the rule refers to a summons that carries sanctions for disobedience. There are a surprisingly large number of cases which will turn on the evidence of some third party and if that third party can disobey a tribunal's summons with impunity, serious injustice may occur.

In Scotland it is arguable that the Sheriff Court has jurisdiction, in respect of tribunals established by law with a power to cite witnesses, to use a procedure known as the granting of letters of second diligence to compel the attendance of a witness: *Presbytery of Lews v Fraser* [1874] 1 R 888. There is no modern authority on the use of the procedure which is provided for in the Sheriff Courts (Scotland) Act 1907, Sch 1 – Ordinary Causes Rules 1993, rule 29.9.

See *CJSA 5100/2001* for discussion of the application of Art 6 of the European Convention of Human Rights in respect of an appeal tribunal's failure to use this provision to obtain the attendance of a DWP investigating officer at the adjourned hearing. The commissioner ruled that the failure to require the officer to attend was a breach of the "equality of arms" principle and set aside the tribunal's decision: para 14.

In *CIS 3811/2005*, an appellant had asked the then named Appeals Service what help and assistance could be provided to enable two witnesses she wished to call to attend her appeal hearing. The Appeals Service only notified her that expenses could be met the day before the hearing; this was too late to arrange for the witnesses to attend. The commissioner noted that although it had been considered that the evidence of the witnesses was of sufficient importance to justify payment of their expenses, no witness summons was issued under reg 43. The commissioner decided that because, as a result of the failings of the Appeals Service, the appellant did not have the opportunity to adduce the evidence of her witnessess, the tribunal had erred in law in proceeding with the hearing.

Striking Out Appeals

Appeals which may be struck out

46.–(1)   Subject to paragraphs (2) and (3), an appeal may be struck out by the clerk to the appeal tribunal–

(a)   where it is an out of jurisdiction appeal and the appellant has been notified by [¹ a relevant authority] that an appeal brought against such a decision may be struck out;

(b)   for want of prosecution including an appeal not made within the time specified in [² the Housing Benefit and Council Tax Benefit (Decisions and Appeals) Regulations 2001]; [³]

(c)   [³] for failure of the appellant to comply with a direction given under these Regulations where the appellant has been notified that failure to comply with the direction could result in the appeal being struck out [³ ; or]

[⁴ (d)   for failure of the appellant to notify the clerk to the appeal tribunal, in accordance with regulation 39, whether or not he wishes to have an oral hearing of his appeal.]

(2)   Where the clerk to the appeal tribunal determines to strike out the appeal, he shall notify the appellant that his appeal has been struck out and of the procedure for reinstatement of the appeal as specified in regulation 47.

(3)   The clerk to the appeal tribunal may refer any matter for determination under this regulation to a legally qualified panel member for decision by the panel member rather than the clerk to the appeal tribunal.

[⁵ (4)]

Definition

"out of jurisdiction appeal" – see reg 1(3).

Modifications

1.   Made by reg 23(3)(a) of SI 2001 No 1002.

2.   Made by reg 23(3)(c) of SI 2001 No 1002.

Amendments
3.   Amended by reg 2(6)(a)(i) and (ii) of SI 2004 No 3368 as from 21.12.04.
4.   Inserted by reg 2(6)(a)(iii) of SI 2004 No 3368 as from 21.12.04.
5.   Omitted by reg 2(6)(b) of SI 2004 No 3368 as from 21.12.04.

General Note
An appeal may be struck out by a clerk, or on a reference under para (3) by a legally qualified tribunal panel member, where it is an "out of jurisdiction appeal", for "want of prosecution", for failure to comply with a direction or for failure by an appellant to notify the clerk as required by reg 39 whether or not s/he wishes an oral hearing: para (1).

"Out of jurisdiction appeal" is defined in reg 1(3) as an appeal against an unappealable decision (a decision under Sch 7 para 6(2) CSPSSA and decisions prescribed by reg 16 D&A Regs). Para (1)(a) requires the local authority to notify the appellant that an appeal brought against such a decision may be struck out.

"Want of prosecution" is an arcane phrase which formerly provided a ground for striking out court proceedings: see *Birkett v James* [1978] AC 297, HL. The equivalent term in Scotland is "want of insistence". The mass of caselaw in relation to striking out court proceedings generally required some form of prejudice to other parties in addition to serious delay, but in the context of appeals it is unlikely that such a requirement will be imposed, though the existence of such prejudice will no doubt make it more likely that an appeal will be struck out.

It may be thought to be unfortunate that such a draconian procedure can be exercised by a clerk rather than by a legally qualified panel member in all cases, but it is understood that in practice, the clerk to the tribunal will only strike out appeals under sub-para (1)(d) – failure by an appellant to notify the clerk whether or not s/he wishes an oral hearing. In all other cases, a legally qualified tribunal panel member exercises the procedure: House of Commons, *Hansard*, Ninth Standing Committee on Delegated Legilsation, 8 December 2004, col 5.

Note the power to reinstate a struck out appeal under reg 47.

Until 21 December 2004, under para (4), subject to reg 48 (both now omitted), a "misconceived appeal" could be struck out by a legally qualified panel member once certain requirements were satisfied. See the commentary to those provisions in the 17th edition of this work at pp886-89.

Reinstatement of struck out appeals

47.–[²(1)   The clerk to the appeal tribunal may reinstate an appeal which has been struck out in accordance with regulation [³ 46(1)(d)] where–
  (a)   the appellant has made representations to him or, as the case may be, further representations in support of his appeal with reasons why he considers that his appeal should not have been struck out;
  (b)   the representations are made in writing within one month of the order to strike out the appeal being issued; and
  (c)   the clerk is satisfied in the light of those representations that there are reasonable grounds for reinstating the appeal
but if the clerk is not satisfied that there are reasonable grounds for reinstatement a legally qualified panel member shall consider whether the appeal should be reinstated in accordance with paragraph (2).]

[²(2)]   A legally qualified panel member may reinstate an appeal which has been struck out in accordance with regulation 46 [⁴] where–
  (a)   the appellant has made representations, or as the case may be, further representations in support of his appeal with reasons why he considers that his appeal should not have been struck out, to the clerk to the appeal tribunal, in writing within one month of the order to strike out the appeal being issued, and the panel member is satisfied in the light of those representations that there are reasonable grounds for reinstating the appeal;
  [⁵ (b)]
  (c)   the panel member is satisfied that the appeal is not an appeal which may be struck out under regulation 46; or

(d)   the panel member is satisfied that notwithstanding that the appeal is one which may be struck out under regulation 46, it is not in the interests of justice for the appeal to be struck out.

Amendments

1.   Amended by reg 26 of SI 2000 No 1596 as from 19.6.00.
2.   Amended by reg 13 of SI 2002 No 1379 as from 20.5.02.
3.   Amended by reg 2(7)(a) of SI 2004 No 3368 as from 21.12.04.
4.   Amended by reg 2(7)(b)(i) of SI 2004 No 3368 as from 21.12.04.
5.   Omitted by reg 2(7)(b)(ii) of SI 2004 No 3368 as from 21.12.04.

General Note

This regulation gives the clerk to the tribunal (para (1)) and a legally qualified tribunal panel member (para (2)) powers to reinstate appeals that have been struck out. Applications under para (1) or (2)(a) must be made within one month of the order to strike out the appeal being issued.

Under para (1), a clerk to the tribunal can only reinstate an appeal if it has been struck out in accordance with reg 46(1)(d) (failure by an appellant to notify the clerk whether or not s/he wishes an oral hearing) – ie, where an appeal has been struck out because an appellant failed to return the Tribunals Service standard enquiry form within 14 days (see p921). The clerk must be satisfied that there are reasonable grounds for the appeal to be reinstated. However, if the clerk is not so satisfied, a legally qualified tribunal panel member must consider whether it can be reinstated under para (2).

Under para (2) a legally qualified tribunal panel member can reinstate an appeal struck out in accordance with reg 46 for any of the reasons listed in sub-paras (a)-(d).

If reinstatement of an appeal is refused an option would be for the appellant to make a fresh appeal, with an application for an extension of time under reg 19 D&A Regs if relevant.

Misconceived appeals

[¹**48.**]

Amendment

1.   Omitted by reg 2(8) of SI 2004 No 3368 as from 21.12.04.

General Note

Regulation 48 was revoked by reg 2(8) of the Social Security, Child Support and Tax Credits (Decisions and Appeals) Amendment Regulations 2004. For the text of the regulation and commentary on it, see the 17th edition of this work at pp888-89.

Oral Hearings

Procedure at oral hearings

49.–(1)   Subject to the following provisions of this Part, the procedure for an oral hearing shall be such as the chairman, or in the case of an appeal tribunal which has only one member, such as that member, shall determine.

(2)   Except where paragraph (3) applies, not less than 14 days notice (beginning with the day on which the notice is given and ending on the day before the hearing of the appeal is to take place) of the time and place of any oral hearing of an appeal shall be given to every [¹ principal] party to the proceedings, and if such notice has not been given to a person to whom it should have been given under the provisions of this paragraph the hearing may proceed only with the consent of that person.

(3)   Any [¹ principal] party to the proceedings may waive his right to receive not less than 14 days notice of the time and place of any oral hearing by giving notice to the clerk to the appeal tribunal.

(4)   If a [¹ principal] party to the proceedings to whom notice has been given under paragraph (2) fails to appear at the hearing the chairman, or in the case of an appeal tribunal which has only one member, that member, may, having regard to all the circumstances including any explanation offered for the absence, proceed with the hearing notwithstanding his absence, or give such directions with a view to the determination of the appeal as he may think proper.

(5)   If a [¹ principal] party to the proceedings has waived his right to be given notice under paragraph (2) the chairman, or in the case of an appeal tribunal which has only one member, that member, may proceed with the hearing notwithstanding his absence.

[³ (6)   An oral hearing shall be in public except where the chairman, or in the case of an appeal tribunal which has only one member, that member, is satisfied that it is necessary to hold the hearing, or part of the hearing, in private–
- (a)   in the interests of national security, morals, public order or children;
- (b)   for the protection of the private or family life of one or more parties to the proceedings; or
- (c)   in special circumstances, because publicity would prejudice the interests of justice.]

[⁴ (7)   At an oral hearing–
- (a)   any [¹ principal] party to the proceedings shall be entitled to be present and be heard; and
- (b)   the following persons may be present by means of a live television link–
  - (i)   a [¹ principal] party or his representative or both; or
  - (ii)   where an appeal tribunal consists of more than one member, a tribunal member other than the chairman,

provided that the person who constitutes or is the chairman of the tribunal gives permission [⁸]

(8)   A person who has the right to be heard at a hearing may be accompanied and may be represented by another person whether having professional qualifications or not and, for the purposes of the proceedings at the hearing, any such representative shall have all the rights and powers to which the person whom he represents is entitled.

(9)   The following persons shall also be entitled to be present at an oral hearing (whether or not it is otherwise in private) but shall take no part in the proceedings–
- (a)   the President;
- (b)   any person undergoing training as a chairman or [⁵ .....] member of an appeal tribunal or as a clerk to an appeal tribunal;
- (c)   any person acting on behalf of the President in the training or supervision of panel members or in the monitoring of standards of decision-making by panel members;
- (d)   with the leave of the chairman, or in the case of an appeal tribunal which has only one member, with the leave of that member, [⁵ .....] any other person; and
- (e)   a member of the Council on Tribunals or of the Scottish Committee of the Council on Tribunals.

[⁶ (10)   Nothing in paragraph (9) affects the rights of–
- (a)   any person mentioned in sub-paragraphs (a) and (b) of that paragraph where he is sitting as a member of a tribunal or acting as its clerk; or
- (b)   the clerk to the tribunal,

and nothing in this regulation prevents the presence at an oral hearing of any witness or of any person whom the chairman, or in the case of an appeal tribunal which has only one member, that member, permits to be present in order to assist the appeal tribunal or the clerk.]

(11)   Any person entitled to be heard at an oral hearing may address the tribunal, may give evidence, may call witnesses and may put questions directly to any other person called as a witness.

(12)   For the purpose of arriving at its decision an appeal tribunal shall, and for the purpose of discussing any question of procedure may, notwithstanding anything contained in these Regulations, order all persons not being members of the tribunal, other than the person acting as clerk to the appeal tribunal, to withdraw from the hearing except that–

    (a)   a member of the Council on Tribunals or of the Scottish Committee of the Council on Tribunals, the President or any person mentioned in paragraph (9)(c); and

    (b)   with the leave of the chairman, or in the case of an appeal tribunal which has only one member, with the leave of that member, any person mentioned in paragraph (9)(b) or (d),

may remain present at any such sitting.

[[7](13)   In this regulation "live television link" means a live television link or other facilities which allow a person who is not physically present at an oral hearing to see and hear proceedings and be seen and heard by those physically present.]

Modification

1.   Made by reg 23(3)(b) of SI 2001 No 1002.

Definition

"principal parties" – see reg 1(2) D&A Regs and Sch 7 para 7(4) CSPSSA 2000.

Amendments

2.   Inserted by reg 27 of SI 2000 No 1596 as from 19.6.00.
3.   Substituted by reg 14(a) of SI 2002 No 1379 as from 20.5.02.
4.   Substituted by reg 14(b) of SI 2002 No 1379 as from 20.5.02.
5.   Amended by reg 14(c) of SI 2002 No 1379 as from 20.5.02.
6.   Substituted by reg 14(d) of SI 2002 No 1379 as from 20.5.02.
7.   Inserted by reg 14(e) of SI 2002 No 1379 as from 20.5.02.
8.   Amended by reg 2(9) of SI 2005 No 337 as from 18.3.05.

General note

Reg 49 is largely self-explanatory.

An appeal is heard in public unless the chair thinks it should be in private for any of the reasons listed in para (6). Since 20 May 2002, it is no longer possible for an appellant to request a private hearing, although if one is requested, the chair can still consider whether any of sub-paras (a) to (c) apply.

Any of the principal parties to an appeal have a right to be present and heard at an oral hearing under para (7). By para (11), they are entitled to address the tribunal, give evidence, call witnesses and put questions to any other witnesses. Certain people can be present via video link, as defined in para (13), with the consent of the the person who constitutes or is the chair of the tribunal. To see if a video link can be arranged, contact should be made with the local Social Security and Child Support Appeal Tribunal office.

It is no part of the tribunal's judicial function to seek to bargain with an appellant or her/his representative as to which parts of the appeal the tribunal might accept if other parts are not pressed for at the hearing: *CSDLA 606/2003*. In this case the appeal tribunal's record of proceedings noted that an offer had been put to the appellant by the Chair of the tribunal just to reinstate her higher rate mobility component of DLA if she did not seek to argue for the care component, and the case was adjourned for 10 minutes for her to think about this. On reconvening the hearing the appellant, who at that point said she wished to proceed with her appeal, was then told that if she went ahead and sought to argue for the care component then she could risk losing everything, and she was told to think again about the matter. After a further short adjournment of five minutes the appellant "accepted the offer". Unsurprisingly, the commissioner concluded that this was not a fair and proper hearing. In her view, a "travesty of justice" had occurred in which the tribunal had pressurised the appellant into giving up her right to a hearing on the care component and had awarded the mobility component without any proper application of the relevant legal tests.

A person attending a hearing, representing a local authority against whose decision an appeal has been brought, is known as the presenting officer. Where a tribunal issues a direction requiring a presenting officer to attend a hearing, one should always be sent by the local authority. It is suggested that local authorities should also consider sending a presenting officer to all hearings where the issues are complex, the impact of the tribunal's decision on the appellant could be serious (eg, where a large amount of benefit is at stake) or there is likely to be a dispute about the evidence.

In *R(IS) 17/04*, a Tribunal of Commissioners considered whether the absence of a presenting officer from an appeal hearing made it unfair and what a tribunal should do when faced with a presenting officer's failure to attend. In this appeal, the written material submitted by the DWP had included a clear statement of the factual case it was seeking to make against the claimant and a number of pieces of documentary evidence in support of this. This established that there was a case which needed to be answered by the claimant. An earlier hearing had been specifically adjourned to enable the attendance of a presenting officer to argue the DWP's case. However, at the new hearing, no presenting officer attended. After efforts were made to establish whether a presenting officer would be able to attend and then a short adjournment, the chair allowed the claimant's appeal without hearing any further evidence. The Tribunal of Commissioner's had a great deal of sympathy for the chair. However, it decided that in deciding the appeal in the way it did, the tribunal had erred in law. A tribunal is inquisitorial and its function is to carry out a complete reconsideration and redetermination of the facts and merits of the decision under appeal: *R(IB) 2/ 04* and *Kerr v Department for Social Development (Northern Ireland)* [2004] UKHL 23 considered and applied. What a tribunal is not entitled to do is to decide an appeal on the burden of proof ground alone without carrying out its inquisitorial function and considering the evidence for itself. The Tribunal of Commissioners commended the view in *CI 1021/2001* that "a failure to discharge the burden of proof is [not] a substitute for a proper enquiry where there is evidence that there is something into which there needs to be an enquiry." In the absence of a presenting officer, it will not be impossible for a fair hearing to be conducted; this may involve the tribunal putting points made in any local authority written submissions to the appellant. Putting the decision maker's case to the claimant would not compromise the tribunal's independance or impartiality as the tribunal's duty to investigate the issues before it can legitimately involve putting probing questions to the claimant: *R(S) 4/82* applied. The alternative would be to adjourn the hearing under reg 51(4) and request a presenting officer to attend a hearing at another date.

A local authority should not approach an appeal as a litigant and be concerned only with winning the case. It is under a duty to assist the tribunal in its investigation of the case, and for that reason all relevant evidence in its possession must ordinarily be produced to the tribunal. Comments by Commissioner Jacobs in early HB and CTB decisions suggest that local authorities do not appear to appreciate the extent of that duty. Local authorities were first reminded of it in *CH 5221/2001* (para 3.1). In *CH 396/2002*, the commissioner stated:

"17.   There is a feature of this case which I mention because it is of concern to me and to my fellow Commissioners who are hearing housing benefit and council tax benefit appeals. In response to a point made by the claimant's son, the local authority has now produced a copy of a record of an interview with him. This is not the first time that relevant information has been provided by a local authority only when a case has come before a Commissioner. I make no judgment on the motives of the officers involved. What concerns me is what they do.

18.   On appeal against a local authority's decision, the appeal tribunal has to undertake a complete reconsideration of the issues that arise. In effect, the tribunal stands in the position of the decision maker in the local authority and makes the decision afresh. It can only fulfil its duty if it is provided by the local authority with all material from its files that is potentially relevant to the appeal. The Secretary of State in social security appeals takes that approach and local authorities must do the same. Without it, the appeal tribunals cannot provide good quality decision-making for both parties. Commissioners are primarily concerned with issues of law, not of fact. It is too late to produce evidence to a commissioner. The commissioner will determine whether the tribunal went wrong in law on the evidence before it.

19.   I direct the local authority in this case to provide to the tribunal and the claimant any other evidence from its files that is, or may be, relevant to the issues raised by this appeal. This is not just a requirement for this case. It is a duty that must be complied with in all cases at the time the local authority makes its submission to the appeal tribunal."

Where the appeal is against a decision that has been revised or superseded, it is essential for the local authority to explain the process that has been followed and to explain the relevant decisions, providing copies if possible: *CH 1085/2002* (paras 16-19). See the commentary to reg 90 HB Regs on p395 for the effect of a failure to do so.

In *CH 4943/2001* (paras 23-29 and 71), the commissioner confirmed that generally, all relevant evidence had to be disclosed. In particular, where recovery of an overpayment was being sought from a landlord, the local authority was obliged to disclose details of the claimant's income in order to determine whether an offset was applicable under reg 104 HB Regs 1987 (now reg 104 HB Regs and reg 85 HB(SPC) Regs). He thereby implicitly accepted the submission that neither the Data Protection Act 1998 (because s35(1) authorises disclosure of personal data for the purposes of legal proceedings), the law of confidence (because there is an exception for disclosure for public purposes) nor Art 8.1 of the European Convention on Human Rights (because disclosure was to protect the landlord's rights under Art 8.2) offered grounds for withholding disclosure. It is suggested that there is nothing in the Court of Appeal's reasoning in *Secretary of State for Work and Pensions v Chiltern DC* [2003] HLR 1019, CA (reported as *R(H) 2/03*), which allowed an appeal from some aspects of the commissioner's decision, which detracts from his reasoning on this point. See further the commentary to reg 86 HB Regs on p388.

There may, however, be cases in which relevant evidence has to be withheld, for example for reasons of privilege or under reg 42 SSCS D&A Regs. In such cases, authorities should normally inform the tribunal of the existence of such evidence so that the tribunal can consider the authority's reasons for withholding the evidence.

Apart from those restrictions, there are no limits as to the type of evidence that may be called or relied upon before a tribunal provided that it is relevant to the issues that are being considered. However, it is suggested that evidence which is subject to public interest immunity must be withheld from disclosure, although the tribunal should consider whether it should instead exercise its power in reg 49(6)(a) to hear a case in private. Similarly, if a party's right to legal professional privilege will be breached by reliance on evidence, the tribunal ought not generally to admit it. These issues will probably only arise very rarely and reference should be made to standard textbooks on the law of evidence to determine the scope of these and related principles. With these possible qualifications, the general approach to evidence which is obtained or used in breach of some obligation arising from statute (such as documents, the use of which is restricted under the Data Protection Act 1998) or common law (such as confidential information) is set out in *CH 4970/2002* para 19:

> "if evidence is relevant to an issue before an appeal tribunal and is of probative value, it must be taken into account even if it was obtained in breach of some domestic law or even something as fundamental as the European Convention on Human Rights, providing that the overall proceedings are fair."

The freedom as to use and type of evidence leads to a number of conclusions. There is no restriction whatever on the use of hearsay evidence (eg, evidence as to what a person said outside the tribunal hearing, or a document which is not produced to the tribunal). It is a matter for the common sense of the tribunal as to what weight should be given to such evidence, but it cannot be ignored. In *CIS 4901/2002*, the appellant had not attended the oral hearing of his appeal, but his representative had attended on his behalf. Evidence presented by the representative of various dates on which the appellant had made telephone calls about his benefit claim was rejected by the tribunal as hearsay as it did not appear in documents signed or otherwise tendered by the appellant. Commissioner Angus said that hearsay evidence was not automatically inadmissible. A tribunal must consider hearsay evidence along with other available evidence. The tribunal here had misdirected itself as to the law on evidence as it applies to tribunals. Further, it had erred in law in failing to ask the representative why she was satisfied as to the accuracy of what the appellant had told her.

Even more fundamentally, there is no rule that oral or written evidence given by a witness has to be corroborated by other evidence. Again, the weight of the evidence of a witness has to be assessed in the light of supporting or contradictory documentary evidence, but it cannot simply be shut out: *CH 4831/2002* (para 20).

The DWP's Verification Framework has no relevance to proceedings before tribunals. A tribunal may not reject evidence simply because it does not comply with the Framework: *CH 5088/2002* (paras 14-20); *CH 2323/2002* (para 1.3). It must examine the evidence and decide whether it accepts it, free of the DWP's administrative strait-jacket.

Tribunals are generally right to require an appellant to give her/his own evidence and to not allow a representative to give it on her/his behalf. However, in *CDLA 1138/2003*, the commissioner said that there was nothing inherently unsatisfactory about a representative giving her/his own evidence based on observations. The matter for the tribunal is the weight to be given to the evidence, not its admissibility. In another appeal, *CDLA 2462/2003*, Commissioner Jacobs said at para 8:

> "Tribunals operate less formally than courts. They do not operate rights of audience. They allow, of course, professional legal representation. But they also allow lay representation and assistance from anyone whom the claimant wishes to assist in presenting a case to a tribunal. Given that breadth of representation, it is inevitable that the roles of representative and witness cannot be separated in the way that they would be in a court. The same person may wish to put the claimant's case and give evidence in support of that case. The tribunal must take care to distinguish evidence from representation so that the former's provenance is known and can be the subject of questioning by the tribunal and other parties. But, subject to the practicalities of the way in which the taking of evidence is handled, there is no objection in principle to the same person acting in different capacities as a witness and as a representative. Nor is there any reason in principle why the probative value of evidence should depend upon whether or not it came from a representative."

In *CSIB 377/2003*, an appeal concerning the appellant's capacity for work, the appellant's experienced representative chose to argue the case only on the basis of mental health descriptors and not on the basis of physical descriptors. However, the appellant gave evidence of physical as well as mental disabilities both before and at the hearing. Commissioner Parker found nothing unfair in a tribunal considering that suggested a weakness in the reliability and credibility of the appellant's evidence. She decided that the tribunal had not erred in law by drawing an adverse inference from the fact that the appellant's case prior to the hearing was very different from that later presented by the representative.

For a more detailed discussion of the issues, see the article *Speak for yourself: reps, claimants and evidence* in CPAG's *Welfare Rights Bulletin176*, October 2003.

Analysis

Para (2): Notice of an oral hearing

Provision for 14 days' notice of an oral hearing is made in para (2). In *CH 3594/2002*, the appellant was given the local authority's submission at the oral hearing of her appeal and was not given sufficient time to consider it. The commissioner said that to ensure a fair hearing, the provision for notice must apply to provision of the submissions and evidence as well as the notice of the time and date of the hearing. He said that was so "unless the appeal tribunal is prepared to take the time during the oral hearing itself to redress the unfairness by ensuring that all the evidence and submissions are presented orally by both parties." In the absence of one of the parties, this could mean that the tribunal will find it necessary to adjourn the hearing.

Para (4): Failure to attend an oral hearing

It is suggested that the power to give directions for the determination of the appeal in para (4) does not extend to striking it out in the absence of the party, given the carefully circumscribed powers to strike out in reg 46. See also reg 51 for the powers of a tribunal to postpone and adjourn oral hearings.

Para (8): Right to representation

There is a right to representation under para (8). In *CIB 2058/2004*, Commissioner Jacobs outlined the functions of a representative of which he considered there were at least three: to act as a companion for the claimant; to assist the tribunal in gathering evidence from the claimant; to make submissions on the law and draw issues of evidence, fact and law to the attention of the tribunal. He said that the full functions of a representative must be taken into account by a tribunal in deciding whether to adjourn an appeal hearing to allow a representative to attend.

How far the right to representation extends, and more importantly by whom, was considered in *CIB 1009/2004*, where the named representative from a local authority welfare rights service was unable to attend a tribunal date at the last minute due to illness. The chair refused to adjourn the hearing because in her view the welfare rights service should have been able to provide another representative to attend at the hearing.

In allowing the appeal Commissioner Rowland made the following comments, which are of general application in this context.

> "9. It is axiomatic that whether or not a hearing should be postponed or adjourned [see reg 51] is a matter within the discretion of the chairman or the tribunal but that the discretion must be exercised judicially. Thus, provided a tribunal's decision to adjourn or not to adjourn is rational and relevant considerations have been taken into account and irrelevant considerations have not been taken into account, the decision cannot be successfully challenged either on judcial review or on an appeal against the tribunal's decision on the appeal.
>
> 12. If a claimant is accompanied by a representative, he is entitled to have that representative heard, by virtue of regulation 49(8) of the Social Security and Child Support (Decisions and Appeals) Regulations 1999. However, in *R v Social Security Commissioner ex parte Bibi* [2000] 23 May, unreported, HC, it was made plain that there is no absolute right to representation and therefore, if a person is not accompanied by a representative, a tribunal is not bound to adjourn to enable him to obtain one merely because he wishes to do so. Thus, regulation 49(8) does not prevent a tribunal from proceeding in the absence of a representative and, *a fortiori*, as was held in *CIB 24/1997*, the absence of a particular representative. On the other hand, it was also held in *Bibi* that there is an absolute right to be dealt with fairly and that not only must a desire to be represented be taken onto account in considering whether a case is to be adjourned but it is also not unreasonable to take account of a desire to be represented by a particular representative. In that case, the tribunal did not act fairly in hearing the claimant's appeal on a date on which the claimant's solicitor had given due warning he personally would not be available".

Commissioner Rowland then goes on to emphasise that it is usually the claimant her/himself who suffers the disadvantage of delay, and therefore if s/he judges that disadvantage to be less than that s/he would incur by proceeding without a representative then a tribunal should be slow to substitute a different view on the relative weight of these two factors. This will then leave the main consideration for the tribunal in such cases as being whether the adjournment can be justified in terms of the additional cost of a further hearing and the delay which there will be for another case whose place the adjourned case takes. However, if the claimant or her/his representative is to blame for the need to request an adjournment then less weight may be attached to their interests. But, even in the event of an error by the representative, Commissioner Rowland cautions against causing injustice to a claimant by "visiting upon him the sins of his representative". Any ruling by a tribunal in such a context "must be proportionate, having regard to the consequences for the claimant of possibly losing his appeal".

CIB 1009/2004 lastly addresses the issue of what a tribunal may reasonably expect of a local authority welfare rights unit where the named representative from that unit is unable to attend the hearing of the appeal. Disagreeing with *CSDLA 90/1998* – and its suggestion that the local authority in such a situation must arrange alternative representation, even by its legal department – Commissioner Rowland states that a local authority is under no statutory duty to provide representation before tribunals and is entitled to limit the resources available for representation. However, the unit cannot therefore expect a case to be adjourned merely because the representative whose case it is is ill. The unit can reasonably be expected to act responsibly, which implies that reasonable efforts will be made to secure alternative representation, even if that means another adviser changing her/his own appointments to accommodate the hearing. However, the commissioner stresses that "the competence of non-lawyer representatives varies and that it is not always reasonable to expect such a representative to pick up the details of the new case as quickly as a lawyer might". Moreover, some cases will require more preparation than others.

A further implication of a representative service's duty to act responsibly – as *CIB 1009/2004* recognises and is in any event common sense (but something which does not always prevail when adjournments are being requested) – is that some explanation is given in the adjournment request about why the named representative cannot attend and why no one else can represent in her/his place (eg, because of the complexity of the case or because everyone else in the welfare rights unit has other appointments at the relevant time which cannot be altered).

No explanation as to why no one other than the named representative could attend the hearing was given in *CIB 1009/2004*. However, the error the tribunal made in not adjourning was its failure to properly have regard to the value of representation, particularly in a complex case which was not obviously unwinnable.

A representative has the discretion to present the case on behalf of the appellant in any way considered appropriate. A representative need not present the entire case and may merely assist at certain stages, and a tribunal may not insist that the whole case is presented by a representative or none of it: *CS 1753/2000* (para 16). A failure to permit a party to be represented is an error of law: *CDLA 3965/2001* (para 12). In that case, the claimant's representative had been banned by a Regional Chair from appearing before tribunals following an incident at a previous hearing. No order had been made under reg 38(2) by the Regional Chair or under reg 49(1) by the tribunal excluding the representative in relation to that specific hearing, although the commissioner appears to envisage that such an order could be made in appropriate circumstances: para 11. There is no bar to a claimant being represented on an appeal by a welfare rights worker from the local authority which is the HB/CTB respondent authority on the appeal (*CSHC 729/2003* para 5), though it is undoubtedly good practice for welfare rights officers from the local authority, who may give rise to a perception of conflict of interest, to put this to the appellant at the earliest opportunity. The commissioner declined to rule on whether – like other courts (eg, *Geveran v Skjeveslan Trading Company Limited* [2003] 1 All ER 1) – the appeal tribunal or the commissioners have any inherent powers enabling them to intervene in respect of representation before them.

In *CDLA 1465/2005,* Commissioner Jacobs considered the relevance of the funding of representation when assessing evidence. The appellant's representative had in the past been known by the tribunal chairman to represent clients on the basis that a third of any backdated award of benefit was paid to her/his company.

In granting permission to appeal, the Chief Commissioner referred to the rule of public policy that an agreement to support a legal action in return for a share of anything recovered (a champterous agreement) is not enforceable. Commissioner Jacobs did not consider that the rule applied in proceedings before an appeal tribunal and that applying it would undermine and be inconsistent with the claimant's right to representation. In so far as the chair's comments about the appellant's representative in any way related to the assessment of the evidence, they were wrong in law. Further, if a tribunal takes account of the method of funding relied on by the representative, it is taking account of an irrelevant consideration.

Manner of providing expert assistance

50.–(1) Where an appeal tribunal require one or more experts to provide assistance to it in dealing with a question of fact of special difficulty under section 7(4), such an expert shall, if the chairman, or in the case of a tribunal with only one member, that member, so requests, attend at the hearing and give evidence and if the chairman or member sitting alone considers it appropriate, the expert shall enquire into and provide a written report on the question.

(2)   A copy of any written report received from an expert in accordance with paragraph (1) shall be supplied to every [¹ principal] party to the proceedings.

Modification

1.   Made by reg 23(3)(b) of SI 2001 No 1002.

General Note

Under s7(4) SSA 1998, a tribunal may require one or more experts to assist it where an appeal involves a question of fact of special difficulty. By s7(5) of the SSA 1998, the "expert" must be a member of the panel of members of appeal tribunals. However, the expert is not a member of the appeal tribunal seeking her/his assistance and so cannot take part in making the tribunal's decision.

Postponement and adjournment

51.–(1)   Where a person [¹ or relevant authority] to whom notice of an oral hearing is given wishes to request a postponement of that hearing he shall do so in writing to the clerk to the appeal tribunal stating his reasons for the request, and the clerk to the appeal tribunal may grant or refuse the request as he thinks fit or may pass the request to a legally qualified panel member who may grant or refuse the request as he thinks fit.

(2)   Where the clerk to the appeal tribunal or the panel member, as the case may be, refuses a request to postpone the hearing he shall–

(a)   notify in writing the person [¹ or relevant authority] making the request of the refusal; and

(b)   place before the appeal tribunal at the hearing both the request for the postponement and notification of its refusal.

(3)   A panel member or the clerk to the appeal tribunal may of his own motion at any time before the beginning of the hearing postpone the hearing.

(4)   An oral hearing may be adjourned by the appeal tribunal at any time on the application of any [¹ principal] party to the proceedings or of its own motion.

(5)   [² . . . .]

Modification

1.   Made by reg 23(3)(d) of SI 2001 No 1002.

Amendment

2.   Deleted by reg 15 of SI 2002 No 1379 as from 20.5.02.

General Note

Reg 51 requires a tribunal clerk who receives a request for a postponement to grant the request, refuse the request or to pass it to a legally qualified tribunal panel member. Where a request is refused by the clerk, para (2) requires the the clerk to notify the applicant in writing – this ensures that the applicant knows the outcome prior to the hearing – and to place the request and the notification of refusal before the tribunal. A failure to follow this procedure is an error of law: *CDLA 4389/2004.*

Postponements can be granted prior to an oral hearing and adjournments at the beginning of, or during, a hearing. If a postponement is refused, the tribunal hearing a case is not precluded from adjourning if it considers it appropriate. Parties or their representatives assume that a postponement or adjournment will be granted at their peril. This point is emphasised in *CDLA 1290/2004,* where the commissioner said, in the context of an appeal tribunal hearing where neither the claimant nor her representative had attended an appeal hearing, that he had great difficulty in understanding representatives:

"who appear not to take adequate steps to warn claimants that applications for postponements may not be successful and that they should be ready to attend a hearing if necessary, and who then devote great effort to pursuing the case on appeal. If there was any merit in the claimant's case – and on the papers it appears to have quite a lot – I cannot see how her interests could possibly have been served by her not attending the hearing if the postponement was not granted".

The discretion to grant a postponement or adjournment or to refuse it is a wide one, but a hearing should not be proceeded with if it is not possible to do justice to a party. In certain circumstances, a failure to postpone or adjourn may be a breach of natural justice which may lead to a successful appeal to the commissioner. One particularly striking example may be found in *CIS 6002/1997* (paras 9-11) where an illiterate claimant appealing against a decision that he had been overpaid over £6,000 asked for an adjournment to obtain representation. The commissioner said that it was impossible to be confident that justice could be done without giving such a claimant a chance to be represented and the tribunal erred in law by proceeding. Likewise, where an appellant was unable to attend a hearing because she was in prison, but her evidence could be expected to play an important part in the tribunal reaching its decision, the tribunal was wrong not to adjourn: *CIS 2292/2000* (para 11). That decision contains a useful discussion of the circumstances in which a tribunal will be found to have erred in law by refusing to adjourn. For the position when an adjournment is sought because a particular representative cannot attend the hearing date, see the discussion of *CIB 1009/2004* in the commentary to reg 49.

In *CH 3439/2004*, an appeal against a decision in a paper hearing, a local authority argued that it should have been allowed to produce further evidence. Commissioner Jacobs reminded local authorities that they must have their cases in order prior to the hearing and cannot rely on adjournments to allow them to make these good. He said:

"This point has been made abundantly clear by Commissioners over the period in which they have had this jurisdiction. No local authority had any excuse in 2004 for not realising that this was necessary. No local authority had any reason to expect a tribunal to adjourn to allow the local authority another chance to make its case. The local authority, like the claimant, was entitled to a fair hearing. But what is necessary for a fair hearing varies between the parties. Local authorities are in a more informed position than many claimants. They cannot expect the same assistance by way of adjournments in order to make their case."

Tribunals ought to give short reasons for a refusal in a statement of reasons. See commentary to reg 53.

An appeal can only be made against a decision to adjourn a hearing if it is a "final decision" – eg, there are no major issues to resolve or it is inevitable what the tribunal will eventually decide: *CDLA 557/2001*.

A decision refusing to adjourn an oral hearing is not, however, appealable: *Carpenter v Secretary of State for Work and Pensions* [2003] EWCA Civ 33 (reported as *R(IB) 6/03*); *CIS 1363/2005*. See the commentary to Sch 7 para 8(1) CSPSSA on p159.

Prior to 20 May 2002, if an appeal hearing was adjourned and it was not practicable or would have caused undue delay for it to be resumed before the same tribunal, the appeal was heard by a differently constituted tribunal and was by way of a complete rehearing. This is no longer a requirement: para (5) revoked. However, it is suggested that where one or more tribunal members at the new hearing were not present at the hearing that was postponed, there will still have to be a complete re-hearing. *CDLA 2429/2004* decides that the revocation of para (5) has not affected the right to a fair hearing conferred by Article 6 of the European Convention on Human Rights. Effectively, all the revocation of para (5) has removed is the necessity to consider in all such cases the practicability or delay associated with assembling the same members of the tribunal. Absent para (5), a differently constituted tribunal can now be assembled without considering these factors. However, in cases where the first tribunal has heard a not insignificant amount of evidence (either in terms of its duration or its nature) before adjourning, the effect of *CDLA 2429/2004* is that there should be a complete rehearing of the appeal. The only exception to this is where the new tribunal is constituted exactly the same as the first tribunal, where presumably it may start from where the evidence at the first hearing ended.

Appeal Tribunals Decisions

Decisions of appeal tribunals

53.–(1)   Every decision of an appeal tribunal shall be recorded in summary by the chairman, or in the case of an appeal tribunal which has only one member, by that member.

(2)   The decision notice specified in paragraph (1) shall be in such written form as shall have been approved by the President and shall be signed by the chairman, or in the case of an appeal tribunal which has only one member, by that member.

(3)   As soon as may be practicable after an appeal or referral has been decided by an appeal tribunal, a copy of the decision notice [5] shall be sent or given to every [1 principal] party to the proceedings who shall also be informed of–

(a)   his right under paragraph (4); and

[2(b)   except in the case of an appeal under the Vaccine Damage Payments Act, the conditions governing appeals to a Commissioner.]

[4 (4)   [5 Subject to paragraph (4A)] A [1 principal] party to the proceedings may apply in writing to the clerk to the appeal tribunal for a statement of the reasons for the tribunal's decision within one month of the sending or giving of the decision notice to every [1 principal] party to the proceedings or within such longer period as may be allowed in accordance with regulation 54 and following that application the chairman, or in the case of a tribunal with only one member, that member shall record a statement of the reasons and a copy of that statement shall be given to every [1 principal] party to the proceedings as soon as may be practicable.]

[6 (4A) Where–

(a)   the decision notice is corrected in accordance with regulation 56; or

(b)   an application under regulation 57 for the decision to be set aside is refused for reasons other than a refusal to extend the time for making the application,

the period specified in paragraph (4) shall run from the date on which notice of the correction or the refusal of the application for setting aside is sent to the applicant.]

(5)   If the decision is not unanimous, the decision notice specified in paragraph (1) shall record that one of the members dissented and the statement of reasons referred to in paragraph (4) shall include the reasons given by the dissenting member for dissenting.

Modification

1.   Made by reg 23(3)(b) of SI 2001 No 1002.

Amendments

2.   Amended by reg 10 of SI 1999 No 2677 from 18.10.99.

3.   Inserted by reg 28 of SI 2000 No 1596 as from 19.6.00.

4.   Substituted by reg 16 of SI 2002 No 1379 as from 20.5.02.

5.   Amended by reg 2(10)(a) and (b) of SI 2005 No 337 as from 18.3.05.

6.   Inserted by reg 2(10)(c) of SI 2005 No 337 as from 18.3.05.

General Note

Recording a decision is a three-stage process. First, under reg 55, the tribunal must make a record of the proceedings. Second, once the decision is made, under para (1) a decision notice is created which records the decision "in summary". The notice is in a form approved by the President of the appeal tribunals (see s5 SSA 1998). The decision notice simply sets out the decision. The current form does not contain a space for reasons to be given but a tribunal may give a summary if it is thought appropriate. The decision notice must be sent or given to every principal party to the proceedings as soon as practicable: para (3).

Third, a party then has the right to apply for a statement of the reasons for the decision within one month of being sent or given the decision notice: para (4). For these purposes, a properly addressed copy of a decision notice sent by electronic mail is effective from the date it is sent: reg 57AA. Where the decision notice is corrected under reg 56 or an application for the decision to be set aside under reg 57 is refused other than because it was outside the time limit for this, the time limit runs from the date notice of the correction or refusal is sent to the applicant: para (4A). An extension of time for seeking a statement can be sought under reg 54.

Analysis

Paras (1) to (3): Decision notices

The better view is that it is generally not open to a party to complain of a lack of reasons found within the decision notice itself on appeal. In *CIB 4497/1998* (paras 8-10) and *CSDLA 531/2000* it was said that the whole point of requiring a statement of reasons to be applied for was to obviate such complaints. However, in *CIS 2345/2001* (paras 17 and 18), the commissioner considered the effect of an unsatisfactory explanation of reasons in a decision notice on the validity of the tribunal's decision and set out general principles. There is no obligation to set out any reasons for a decision in a decision notice. If reasons are given and these are not inconsistent with an adequate explanation of the reasons contained in the statement of reasons given under para (4), the unsatisfactory nature of the explanation in the decision notice is unlikely to render the decision wrong in law. However, if a decision notice positively indicates that the tribunal did not apply the law correctly, that is likely to be a more reliable statement of the tribunal's reasons than a later conflicting explanation in a statement of reasons. A conflict between the reasons given in the decision notice and those given in the full statement is likely to amount to an error of law.

A decision is not treated as being final until a decision notice is completed under reg 53(3). Before a decision notice is given to a party at the conclusion of a hearing or sent to her/him at a later stage, the tribunal is entitled to alter its decision, though it may be that in such circumstances natural justice would then require that the case be re-heard: *CI 141/1987* para 5. It would therefore be unwise for a tribunal to inform the appellant of a decision orally without completing a decision notice at the same time.

Paras (4) and (4A): Statements of reasons

The tribunal is only obliged to give a statement of reasons for its "decision", rather than any procedural determination that it reaches. Thus it is not obliged to give a statement of reasons for a decision which amounts to a procedural determination such as a refusal to adjourn: *Carpenter v Secretary of State for Work and Pensions* [2003] EWCA Civ 33 (reported as *R(IB) 6/03*), para 16. However, since such a decision may give rise to a breach of natural justice and hence an error of law, it may be necessary for a tribunal to give short reasons in its decision notice or statement of reasons to explain the course it took. In *Carpenter* (para 23) the court cited with approval the views of Commissioner Jacobs in the decision under appeal as to the standard of reasoning required to avoid such a consequence:

"In some circumstances, the reason for a refusal may be obvious. The most obvious example is if no reason is given for the application. In most cases, a reason is needed. However, those reasons need not be elaborate. They must be read against the background of the terms of the application and the circumstances of the case. They need not set out every factor that the tribunal took into account. It will usually be sufficient to set out in a sentence the principal factor that the tribunal took into account. That reason need not be set out in the full statement of the tribunal's decision. It is sufficient if it appears from the record of proceedings or the decision notice."

Carpenter was applied in *CH 4483/2002* (paras 11-12) where a tribunal was held to have erred in law where no reasons for its refusal of an adjournment were given at all. Likewise, in *CSDLA 866/2002*, the commissioner said that while the Court of Appeal in *Carpenter* held that there was no duty to provide a statement of reasons on an adjournment, "good practice requires a brief reason for the benefit of the parties and the next tribunal": para 21.

The duty to prepare a statement of reasons rests on the chairman of the tribunal (or where only one member sits, the panel member) hearing the appeal. The failure of the chairman (or panel member) to provide a written statement of reasons where there is an obligation to do so is an error of law: *CCS 1664/2001* (paras 9-10). A statement of reasons may be prepared even after the termination of the appointment of the member and should not be prepared by another member in such circumstances: *CIS 2132/1998*.

The duty is triggered by an application by a party to the proceedings. It may be appropriate to treat an application for leave to appeal as a request for a statement where one has not yet been obtained: *CDLA 5793/1997* para 26. Para (4) was amended with effect from 20 May 2002. Now, an application for a statement of reasons must be made to the clerk to the tribunal. This means that the application must be received by (rather than sent to) the clerk within one month of the sending or giving of the decision notice: reg 2(a). The one-month time limit can be extended under reg 54.

It has been debated at times whether an appeal tribunal can supplement the reasons for a decision already given or can be asked by a commissioner or other parties to supplement their reasons. Support may have been lent to the view that tribunals can on occasions add to their reasons for decision by the Court of Appeal in an employment case, *Barke v SEETEC Business Technology Centre Limited* [2005] EWCA Civ 578, 16 May 2005, unreported. However, the commissioner in *CA 4297/2004* having considered the application of *Barke* in the context of social security appeal tribunals decided that there is no provision for a further or alternative statement of reasons to be issued by the chairman of the tribunal (or panel member) nor for any other chairman to require this to be done. The commissioner said that there were good policy reasons for this: there could be confusion as to from when the time limit for appealing would run; there would be a danger that the chairman or whoever had requested further reasons would be introducing issues never raised before the tribunal and this would be inconsistent with the duty to act fairly and in accordance with the rules of natural justice or in compliance with Article 6 of the European Convention on Human Rights.

There is no specific duty to record findings of fact relevant to the decision. However, it has been held that such a duty is implicit in the requirement to give reasons for the decision and a failure to state clearly the findings of fact where they are in dispute will be an error of law. In particular, where there are disputes of fact, it is not acceptable simply for the tribunal to state that the facts were as set out in the local authority's submission: *CSHC 352/2002* (para 10).

The extent of reasoning required in a statement of reasons will depend on the case before the tribunal. Caselaw on decision-making by Review Boards will still be relevant. The courts have repeatedly emphasised that the duty to give reasons is not mere bureaucracy but is essential to good decision-making: see the emphatic statement of Sedley J in these terms in *R v Solihull MBC HBRB ex p Simpson* [1993] 26 HLR 370 at 377, QBD. On the other hand, it has been equally often repeated that the members of a Review Board could not be expected to express their reasons with the clarity and precision to be expected of a court: *R v Sefton MBC ex p Cunningham* [1991] 23 HLR 534 at 538, QBD; *R v East Devon DC HBRB ex p Gibson* [1993] 25 HLR, CA. The same will be true of a tribunal, but given that a legally qualified member sits on every tribunal the commissioners will be less forgiving of sparse or defective reasoning.

The reasons for the decision must be adequate. In *CH 2659/2002* (para 20) the commissioner said "Adequacy has to be measured against the legitimate expectation of a losing party that a tribunal should explain its decision sufficiently to establish that it did apply the right legal test to a proper review of all relevant evidence. In other words it must make clear that it did not make any appealable errors." The minimum that can be expected is that the parties must be able to tell, from looking at the decision, why the tribunal has found in the way that it has: *R(A) 1/72* (para 5); *Cunningham* at 538; *R v Cardiff CC HBRB ex p Thomas* (1991) 25 HLR 1 at 5, QBD. Ideally, the tribunal should deal with all the arguments raised by the parties and state reasons for accepting or rejecting each. There must be a "proper evaluation" of the evidence: *R v South Tyneside MBC ex p Tooley* [1996] COD 143 at 144, QBD. If evidence is rejected, the tribunal must state its reasons for doing so. It will usually be necessary for the tribunal, as part of its explanation for its decision, to make findings on disputed issues of fact even though there is no longer a specific statutory requirement that it should do so: *CI 5880/1999*. Likewise, wherever there has been conflicting evidence, it must state why it has accepted the evidence which has been accepted: *R v Lambeth LBC HBRB ex p Harrington* [1996] unreported 22 November, QBD.

There will often be a breach of the requirement to give reasons if the tribunal cites more than one reason for a conclusion and at least one of those reasons discloses an error of law, even if the other reasons cannot be impugned. Elias J said, in *R v Allerdale DC HBRB ex p Doughty* [2000] COD 462, QBD:

"... where the two strands of reasoning lead to a particular conclusion (in this case relating to the need for general counselling and support), and only one of these is effective as a matter of law, then in order to rely on the lawful strand the court must be satisfied that it was not tainted by being interwoven with the other unlawful strand. So in this case if the factual finding . . . as to the services needed may itself have been influenced by the view the Board took as to the services lawfully offered, then it would not, in my view, be right to rely on that finding."

A copy of the statement of reasons must be given to the parties to the proceedings as soon as is practicable. Delay in providing the statement of reasons in itself is not automatically an error of law. However, in *CJSA 322/2001*, the commissioner said at para 9, "the issue is whether the delay in writing the reasons indicates that they are unreliable as an accurate statement of the tribunal's reasoning. If they are unreliable, the reasons are inadequate." In *R(IS) 5/04*, Commissioner Parker agreed that delay is relevant to the adequacy of the tribunal's reasoning. Even if an accurate record of reasons is given, if given late it can appear less credible and can therefore more easlily be attacked as inadequate. The commissioner said that delay by a chairman of a tribunal in producing a statement of reasons might be relevant in another way; it may also form part of an infringment of Article 6(1) of the Convention on Human Rights. However, the delay would have to be sufficiently serious.

An inconsistency between a decision notice and a statement of reasons will ordinarily result in the tribunal's decision being set aside for error of law if the inconsistency concerns an important part of the decision. However, where the decision notice stated a series of dates correctly but they were incorrectly set out in the statement of reasons, but it was clear from the case papers what the correct dates were, the decision was upheld: *CH 299/2003* (para 22).

Para (5): Dissent of a tribunal member

Under reg 22(1)(a) D&A Regs, some appeals involving financial matters are heard by a financially qualified member as well as a legally qualified member. The President may also appoint an additional member under reg 22(2). Where an appeal tribunal has more than one member, under s7(3) SSA 1998, decisions are taken by a majority of votes, the chair having any casting vote. If a decision is not unanimous, para (5) requires the reasons for a dissent to be recorded. The decision will be set aside for error of law if the tribunal fails to comply with para (5): *CDLA 572/2001* (para 3).

Late applications for a statement of reasons of tribunal decision

54.–(1)   The time for making an application for [²...] the statement of the reasons for a tribunal's decision may be extended where the conditions specified in paragraphs (2) to (8) are satisfied, but [² , subject to [⁵ regulation 53(4A)],] no application shall in any event be brought more than three months after the date of the sending or giving of the notice of the decision of the appeal tribunal.

(2)   An application for an extension of time under this regulation shall be made in writing and shall be determined by a legally qualified panel member.

(3)   An application under this regulation shall contain particulars of the grounds on which the extension of time is sought, including details of any relevant special circumstances for the purposes of paragraph (4).

(4)   The application for an extension of time shall not be granted unless the panel member is satisfied that it is in the interests of justice for the application to be granted.

(5)   For the purposes of paragraph (4) it is not in the interests of justice to grant the application unless the panel member is satisfied that–

(a)   the special circumstances specified in paragraph (6) are relevant to the application; or

(b)   some other special circumstances are relevant to the application,
and as a result of those special circumstances it was not practicable for the application to be made within the time limit specified in regulation 53(4).

(6)   For the purposes of paragraph (5)(a), the special circumstances are that–

(a)   the applicant or a [³ partner] or dependant of the applicant has died or suffered serious illness;

(b)   the applicant is not resident in the United Kingdom; or

(c)   normal postal services were adversely disrupted.

(7)   In determining whether it is in the interests of justice to grant the application, the panel member shall have regard to the principle that the greater the amount of time that has elapsed between the expiration of the time within which the application for a copy of the statement of reasons for a tribunal's decision is to be made and the making of the application for an extension of time, the more compelling should be the special circumstances on which the application is based.

(8)   In determining whether it is in the interests of justice to grant the application, no account shall be taken of the following–

(a)   that the person making the application or any person acting for him was unaware of, or misunderstood, the law applicable to his case (including ignorance or misunderstanding of the time limits imposed by these Regulations); or

(b)   that a Commissioner or a court has taken a different view of the law from that previously understood and applied.

(9)   An application under this regulation for an extension of time which has been refused may not be renewed.

(10)   The panel member who determines the application shall record a summary of his [³ determination] in such written form as has been approved by the President.

(11)   As soon as practicable after the [³ determination] is made [³ notice] of the [³ determination] shall be sent or given to every [¹ principal] party to the proceedings.

(12)   Any person who under paragraph (11) receives [³ notice] of the [³ determination] may, within one month of the [³ determination] being sent to him, apply in writing for a copy of the reasons for that [³ determination] and a copy shall be supplied to him.

[⁶ (13)]

Modification

1.   Made by reg 23(3)(b) of SI 2001 No 1002.

Amendments

2.   Amended by reg 29 of SI 2000 No 1596 as from 19.6.00.
3.   Amended by reg 17(a) to (d) of SI 2002 No 1379 as from 20.5.02.
4.   Substituted by reg 17(e) of SI 2002 No 1379 as from 20.5.02.
5.   Amended by reg 2(11)(a) of SI 2005 No 337 as from 18.3.05.
6.   Omitted by reg 2(11)(b) of SI 2005 No 337 as from 18.3.05.

General Note

The power to extend time for seeking a statement of reasons is very similar to that for admitting late appeals in reg 19 D&A Regs. Reference should be made to the commentary to reg 19 on p981, but some differences should be noted. The absolute time limit for an application for a statement is three months from the date the decision notice is sent or given: para (1). There is no duty to issue a statement of reasons following an application later than that, but such an application may amount to an invitation to the legally qualified panel member to exercise her/his power to provide a statement of reasons on an extra-statutory basis: *CH2553/2005*. However, Commissioner Rowland said that even if it were possible to show that a a legally qualified tribunal panel member had erred in law in declining to exercise that power, the most a commissioner could properly do would be to adjourn the proceedings and invite the panel member to reconsider.

For these purposes, a properly addressed copy of a decision notice sent by electronic mail is effective from the date it is sent: reg 57AA.

A legally qualified tribunal panel member need only be satisfied that it is in the interests of justice to grant the application: para (4). Para (5)(b) is watered down compared with reg 19(6)(b) D&A Regs, in that the "special circumstances" need not be "wholly exceptional". It is likely that "special circumstances" will be given much the same interpretation as "special reasons" in reg 9(3) SSCP Regs, save that the usual matters are purportedly excluded from consideration under para (8). See p982 for the question of the validity of this provision.

If there is any possibility that a party may wish to seek leave to appeal to a commissioner, it is always best to request a statement of the tribunal's reasons for its decision within the one month time limit specified in reg 53(4) even if s/he is first going to apply for the decision to be set aside. Note, however, that by reg 53(4A), where a decision notice is corrected under reg 56 or an application for the decision to be set aside under reg 57 is refused other than because it was outside the time limit for this, the one month time limit runs from the date notice of the correction or refusal is sent to the applicant.

In *CDLA 164/2002*, the commissioner found that the claimant had not received the copy of the decision notice that had been sent to him. The claimant did not therefore apply for a statement of reasons and, when the fact that the decision was adverse was discovered, was refused a statement out of time under reg 54. The commissioner held (para 19) that there were plainly "special reasons" under para (5) for the lateness of the application and accordingly, since a statement of reasons should have been given, the decision would be set aside for want of reasons (para 20).

Record of tribunal proceedings

55.–(1) A record of the proceedings at an oral hearing, which is sufficient to indicate the evidence taken, shall be made by the chairman, or in the case of an appeal tribunal which has only one member, by that member, in such medium as he may direct.

[² (2) The clerk to the appeal tribunal shall preserve–

(a) the record of proceedings;

(b) the decision notice; and

(c) any statement of the reasons for the tribunal's decision,

for the period specified in paragraph (3).

(3) That period is six months from the date of–

(a) the decision made by the appeal tribunal;

(b) any statement of reasons for the tribunal's decision;

(c) any correction of the decision in accordance with regulation 56;

(d) any refusal to set aside the decision in accordance with regulation 57; or

(e) any determination of an application under regulation 58 for leave to appeal against the decision,

or until the date on which those documents are sent to the office of the Social Security and Child Support Commissioners in connection with an appeal against the decision or an application to a Commissioner for leave to appeal, if that occurs within the six months.

(4) Any party to the proceedings may within the time specified in paragraph (3) apply in writing for a copy of the record of proceedings and a copy shall be supplied to him.]

Modification

1.   Made by reg 23(3)(b) of SI 2001 No 1002.

Amendment

2.   Substituted by reg 2(12) of SI 2005 No 337 as from 18.3.05.

General Note

A record of proceedings at an oral hearing must be made by the chair, or in the case of a tribunal with a single panel member, that panel member: para (1). It must be sufficient to indicate the evidence taken at the hearing. In practice, this can be difficult for a single panel member, responsible not only for the procedure at and conduct of the hearing, but for taking evidence and making observations.

The record of proceedings will be needed in any case where there is a dispute as to the evidence that was given or the submissions that were made. Those making applications for leave to appeal to a commissioner should ensure a record is obtained within the period allowed by paras (3) and (4). There is nothing to stop an appellant or her/his representative keeping her/his own record; having two records to compare can make the task of the commissioner easier: *CDLA 581/2004*.

A failure to make an accurate record of the proceedings may vitiate a tribunal's decision for error of law, but only if the inaccuracy is relevant to the decision: *CIS 1769/1999* (para 9); *CDLA 1389/1997* (paras 7-19). Given that there is a right to apply for a copy of the record, it must also be legible: *CIB 3013/ 1997*. *CSHC 352/2002* (para 12) confirms that a failure to produce a legible record of proceedings will render the tribunal's decision erroneous in point of law.

While tribunal members are provided with standard form pads to use, some members record proceedings on computers.

Correction of accidental errors

56.–(1)   The clerk to the appeal tribunal, [³ or a legally qualified panel member] may at any time correct accidental errors in [⁴ the notice of any decision] of an appeal tribunal made under [²Schedule 7 of the Act], the Child Support Act or the Vaccine Damage Payments Act.

[⁵ (2)   A correction made to a decision notice shall be deemed to be part of the decision notice and written notice of the correction shall be given as soon as practicable to every party to the proceedings.]

(3)   *[omitted]*

Modifications

1.   Made by reg 23(3)(b) of SI 2001 No 1002.
2.   Made by reg 23(3)(e) of SI 2001 No 1002.

Amendments

3.   Amended by reg 30 of SI 2000 No 1596 as from 19.6.00.
4.   Amended by reg 2(13)(a) of SI 2005 No 337 as from 18.3.05.
5.   Substituted by reg 2(13)(b) of SI 2005 No 337 as from 18.3.05.

General Note

Once the decision notice is given, the decision may not be altered in such a way as to alter the substantive effect of the decision: *CM 264/1993* (para 16) and *CI 3887/1999*. However, accidental errors in decision notices may be corrected under this provision. They must be genuine errors such as typing or spelling mistakes, not errors of law on an important issue in the appeal: *CI 3887/1999* (para 8).

Setting aside decisions on certain grounds

57.–(1)   On an application made by a [¹ principal] party to the proceedings, a decision of an appeal tribunal made under [² Schedule 7 of the Act], the Child Support Act or the Vaccine Damage Payments Act, may be set aside by a legally qualified panel member in a case where it appears just to set the decision aside on the ground that–

(a)   a document relating to the proceedings in which the decision was made was not sent to, or was not received at an appropriate time by, a [¹ principal] party to the proceedings or the party's representative or was not received at an appropriate time by the person who made the decision;

(b)   a [¹ principal] party to the proceedings in which the decision was made or the party's representative was not present at a hearing relating to the proceedings.

(2)   In determining whether it is just to set aside a decision on the ground set out in paragraph (1)(b), the panel member shall determine whether the party making the application gave notice that he wished to have an oral hearing, and if that party did not give such notice the decision shall not be set aside unless [⁴ . . . .] that member is satisfied that the interests of justice manifestly so require.

[⁵ (3)   An application under this regulation shall–

(a)   be made within one month of the date on which–

(i)   a copy of the decision notice is sent or given to the parties to the proceedings in accordance with regulation 53(3); or

(ii)   the statement of the reasons for the decision is given or sent in accordance with regulation 53(4),

whichever is later;
(b)   be in writing and signed by a [¹ principal] party to the proceedings or, where the party has provided written authority to a representative to act on his behalf, that representative;
(c)   contain particulars of the grounds on which it is made; and
(d)   be sent to the clerk to the appeal tribunal.]
(4)   Where an application to set aside a decision is entertained under paragraph (1), every [¹ principal] party to the proceedings shall be sent a copy of the application and shall be afforded a reasonable opportunity of making representations on it before the application is determined.
[⁷ (4A)   Where a legally qualified panel member refuses to set aside a decision he may treat the application to set aside the decision as an application under regulation 53(4) for a statement of the reasons for the tribunal's decision, subject to the time limits set out in regulation 53(4) and (4A).]
(5)   Notice in writing of a determination on an application to set aside a decision shall be sent or given to every [¹ principal] party to the proceedings as soon as may be practicable and the notice shall contain a statement giving the reasons for the determination.
[⁶(6)   The time within which an application under this regulation must be made may be extended by a period not exceeding one year where the conditions specified in paragraphs (7) to (11) are satisfied.
(7)   An application for an extension of time shall be made in accordance with paragraph (3)(b) to (d), shall include details of any relevant special circumstances for the purposes of paragraph (9) and shall be determined by a legally qualified panel member.
(8)   An application for an extension of time shall not be granted unless the panel member is satisfied that–
(a)   if the application is granted there are reasonable prospects that the application to set aside will be successful; and
(b)   it is in the interests of justice for the application for an extension of time to be granted.
(9)   For the purposes of paragraph (8) it is not in the interests of justice to grant an application for an extension of time unless the panel member is satisfied that–
(a)   the special circumstances specified in paragraph (10) are relevant to that application; or
(b)   some other special circumstances exist which are wholly exceptional and relevant to that application,
and as a result of those special circumstances, it was not practicable for the application to set aside to be made within the time limit specified in paragraph (3)(a).
(10)   For the purposes of paragraph (9)(a) the special circumstances are that–
(a)   the applicant or a partner or dependant of the applicant has died or suffered serious illness;
(b)   the applicant is not resident in the United Kingdom; or
(c)   normal postal services were disrupted.
(11)   In determining whether it is in the interests of justice to grant an application for an extension of time, the panel member shall have regard to the principle that the greater the amount of time that has elapsed between the expiry of the time within which the application to set aside is to be made and the making of the application for an extension of time, the more compelling should be the special circumstances on which the application for an extension is based.
(12)   An application under this regulation for an extension of time which has been refused may not be renewed.]

Modifications
1.   Made by reg 23(3)(b) of SI 2001 No 1002.

2.   Made by reg 23(3)(e) of SI 2001 No 1002.

Amendments
3.   Inserted by reg 31 of SI 2000 No 1596 as from 19.6.00.
4.   Amended by reg 18(a) of SI 2002 No 1379 as from 20.5.02.
5.   Amended by reg 18(a) of SI 2002 No 1379 as from 20.5.02.
6.   Substituted by reg 18(c) of SI 2002 No 1379 as from 20.5.02.
7.   Inserted by reg 2(14) of SI 2005 No 337 as from 18.3.05.

General Note
The setting aside procedure provides an expeditious alternative to appealing where there has been some procedural difficulty, but it is important to bear in mind that setting aside is not a substitute for an appeal in all cases and to consider carefully which course is appropriate. If a set aside is refused, an application for leave to appeal to the commissioner can still be made. By reg 58(1A) where, after a written statment of reasons has been sent to the parties to the proceedings, an application for a decision to be set aside under reg 57 is refused other than because it was outside the time limit for this, the time limit runs from the date notice of the refusal is sent to the applicant. If it is possible that an application for leave to appeal might be made, it is important to request a written statement of the reasons for the tribunal's decision under reg 53 while waiting to hear the result of the application for a set aside.

Note also the provision for a tribunal's decision to be set aside by a legally qualified tribunal panel member dealing with an application for permission to appeal to a commissioner where there is agreement that the tribunal made an error of law: Sch 7 para 7 CSPSSA.

Analysis
Paras (1) and (2): Grounds for setting aside.
Two grounds are given. The first relates to missing documents. This could be a notice of hearing that went astray or a piece of evidence that was missing. It could also be documents relevant to the production of a statement of reasons for a tribunal's decision (under reg 53(4)) going astray after the decision has been given: *CDLA 1685/2004*. The ground will be made out if the document was not received by the applicant, her/his representative or the tribunal.

Secondly, there is absence from a hearing by the applicant or her/his representative. This is immediately qualified by para (2) which precludes an application on this ground where the applicant failed to ask for an oral hearing, unless "the interests of justice manifestly so require". *CIS 6002/1997*, referred to in the commentary to reg 52, provides an example of circumstances which might fall within this provision.

Once the existence of one of the grounds is demonstrated, the legally qualified tribunal panel member considering the application must go on to consider whether it is "just to set the decision aside" on that ground. This will not always be so. For example, it may be possible for the member to conclude that the procedural mistake made no difference to the result. Furthermore, a party could not normally have a decision set aside on the ground of an absent document if the document was not before the tribunal due to her/his own fault.

The old third ground of setting aside "where the interests of justice so require", which caused so much trouble when used in an old version of reg 86(1)(c) HB Regs 1987, no longer exists. It may be possible to argue that a power to set aside a decision where a procedural problem causes unfairness should be implied: *Lloyd v McMahon* [1987] AC 625, HL. Sch 7 para 19(2) CSPSSA and reg 57A(3) appear to envisage the existence of such an implied power. Alternatively, it may be possible to appeal even where there is not a breach of natural justice in the strict sense, on the ground that the party has not had the fair hearing to which s/he is entitled under Art 6 of the European Convention on Human Rights. See *CDLA 5413/1999* for an example of this approach.

Paras (3) to (12): Procedure.
An application to set aside must normally be made within one month of the decision notice or, if later, the statement of reasons being given to the parties. For these purposes, a properly addressed copy of a decision notice sent by electronic mail is effective from the date it is sent: reg 57AA. Under para (4), other parties to the appeal must be given an opportunity to comment upon the application.

An application may be made out of time. The one-month time limit can be extended by up to one year: para (6). The criteria bear resemblance to those for late appeals under reg 19 D&A Regs. Special circumstances other than those in para (10) must be "wholly exceptional" but there is no equivalent of the obnoxious provision in reg 54(8) and reg 19(9) D&A Regs.

Where an application is refused, the legally qualified tribunal member can treat it as an application for a written statement of reasons under reg 53(4). Note that this is subject to the usual time limits: para (4A).

[³Provisions common to regulations 56 and 57

57A.– [⁴ (1)]

(2)   There shall be no appeal against a correction made under regulation 56 or a refusal to make such a correction or against a determination made under regulation 57.

(3)   Nothing in this Chapter shall be construed as derogating from any power to correct errors or set aside decisions which is exercisable apart from [¹ the Housing Benefit and Council Tax Benefit (Decisions and Appeals) Regulations 2001].

Modification

1.   Made by reg 23(3)(c) of SI 2001 No 1002.

Amendments

2.   Inserted by reg 32 of SI 2000 No 1596 as from 19.6.00.
3.   Substituted by reg 19 of SI 2002 No 1379 as from 20.5.02.
4.   Omitted by reg 2(15) of SI 2005 No 337 as from 18.3.05.

General Note

Para (1) required that periods during which a determination on an application for correction or setting-aside of a tribunal decision was awaited (except where the decision was not set aside because of a refusal to extend the time limit for applying) were not taken into account in calculating the time limit set out in reg 58(1)(a). A similar provision is now found in reg 58(1A). Para (2) confirms that there is no right of appeal against a correction, refusal to correct or a determination on setting-aside. The only remedy is judicial review.

[¹Service of decision notice by electronic mail

57AA.   For the purposes of the time limits in regulations 53 to 57, a properly addressed copy of a decision notice sent by electronic mail is effective from the date it is sent.]

Amendment

1.   Inserted by reg 2(16) of SI 2005 No 337 as from 18.3.05.

[¹Interpretation of Chapter V

[²**57B.**–(1)   In Chapter V, except in regulations 58 and 58A–
''Commissioner'' includes Child Support Commissioner;
''decision'' includes a determination on referral.

(2)   In Chapter V–
''decision notice'' has the meaning given in regulation 53(1) and (2).]

Amendments

1.   Inserted by reg 32 of SI 2000 No 1596 as from 19.6.00.
2.   Substituted by reg 2(17) of SI 2005 No 337 as from 18.3.05.

Applications for leave to appeal to Commissioner (not including Child Support)

Application for leave to appeal to a Commissioner from an appeal tribunal

58.–(1)   [⁹ Subject to paragraph (1A),] An application for leave to appeal to a Commissioner from a decision of an appeal tribunal under [⁵ section 13 of the 1997 Act or under [² paragraphs 6 and 7 of Schedule 7 of the Act] shall–

(a)   be [⁵ sent to the clerk to the appeal tribunal within the period of one month of the date of the applicant being sent] a written statement of the reasons for the decision against which leave to appeal is sought; and

[⁹ (b) be in writing and signed by the applicant or, where he has given written authority to a representative to make the application on his behalf, by that representative;

(c)   contain particulars of the grounds on which the applicant intends to rely;

(d)   contain sufficient particulars of the decision of the appeal tribunal to enable the decision to be identified; and

(e)   if the application is made late, contain the grounds for seeking late acceptance.]

[¹⁰ (1A)   Where after the written statement of the reasons for the decision has been sent to the parties to the proceedings–

(a)   the decision notice is corrected in accordance with regulation 56; or

(b)   an application under regulation 57 for the decision to be set aside is refused for reasons other than a refusal to extend the time for making the application,

the period specified in paragraph (1)(a) shall run from the date on which notice of the correction or the refusal of the application for setting aside is sent to the applicant.]

(2)   Where an application for leave to appeal to a Commissioner is made by the Secretary of State [³ or [² a relevant authority]], the clerk to an appeal tribunal shall, as soon as may be practicable, send a copy of the application to every other [¹ principal] party to the proceedings.

[⁶ 3 . . .]

[⁷(4)   A person determining an application for leave to appeal to a Commissioner shall record his determination in writing and send a copy to every [¹ principal] party to the proceedings.]

(5)   Where there has been a failure to apply for leave to appeal within the period of time specified in paragraph (1)(a) [¹¹ or (1A)] but an application is made within one year of the last date for making an application within that period, a legally qualified panel member may, if for special reasons he thinks fit, accept and proceed to consider and determine the application.

[⁸(6)   Where an application for leave to appeal against a decision of an appeal tribunal is made–

(a)   if the person who constituted, or was the chairman of, the appeal tribunal when the decision was given was a fee-paid legally qualified panel member, the application may be determined by a salaried legally qualified panel member; or

(b)   if it is impracticable, or it would be likely to cause undue delay, for the application to be determined by whoever constituted, or was the chairman of, the appeal tribunal when the decision was given, the application may be determined by another legally qualified panel member.]

Modifications

1.   Made by reg 23(3)(b) of SI 2001 No 1002.
2.   Made by reg 23(3)(f) of SI 2001 No 1002.

Amendments

3.   Amended by SI 1999 No 2570 from 5.10.99.
4.   Inserted by reg 33 of SI 2000 No 1596 as from 19.6.00.
5.   Amended by reg 20(a) of SI 2002 No 1379 as from 20.5.02.
6.   Deleted by reg 18(b) of SI 2002 No 1379 as from 20.5.02.
7.   Substituted by reg 18(c) of SI 2002 No 1379 as from 20.5.02.
8.   Substituted by reg 18(d) of SI 2002 No 1379 as from 20.5.02.
9.   Inserted by reg 2(18)(a) of SI 2005 No 337 as from 18.3.05.
10.   Inserted by reg 2(18)(b) of SI 2005 No 337 as from 18.3.05.
11.   Amended by reg 2(18)(c) of SI 2005 No 337 as from 18.3.05.

General Note

An appeal can be made against a tribunal's decision to a commissioner if the decision was erroneous in law. See Sch 7 para 8 CSPSSA. An application for leave to appeal to a commissioner must be made for determination by a legally qualified tribunal panel member in the first instance. If leave is refused or the application is rejected, an application can then be made to a commissioner. See reg 9 SSCP Regs. There is no right of appeal against the refusal of leave made by the legally qualified tribunal panel member. See the discussion on this point in the commentary to Sch 7 para 8(1) CSPSSA on p159.

The application to the panel member must be received by the clerk to the tribunal within one month of a statement of reasons being sent out. Note that where, after a written statment of reasons has been sent to the parties to the proceedings, a decision notice is corrected under reg 56 or an application for a decision to be set aside under reg 57 is refused other than because it was outside the time limit for this, the time limit runs from the date notice of the correction or refusal is sent to the applicant: para (1A). The time limit may be extended by up to a year for "special reasons", see the commentary to reg 9(3) SSCP Regs on p904: para (5).

Applications must be made in writing and signed by the applicant, or where written authority is given to a representative to make an application, signed by her/him: sub-para (1)(b). The application must contain details of the grounds for appeal and sufficient particulars of the tribunal's decision for it to be identified. If the application is made late, the grounds for seeking late acceptance must also be given: sub-paras (1)(c)-(e).

Applications to tribunal panel members do not need to be made on any particular form; an ordinary letter, containing what is required is sufficient.

Until 18 March 2005, an application had to have annexed to it a copy of the written statement of reasons for the tribunal's decision. This is no longer the case (sub-para (1)(b) amended by SI 2005 No 337). The explanatory memorandum to the amending regulations says this is because the person deciding the application will already have a copy. Note, however, that if the legally qualified panel member refuses or rejects an application, the statement of reasons does have to be attached to the application for leave made to the commissioner (reg 10 SSCP Regs) although commissioners have powers to waive irregularities in applications made to them.

Note that the rules are silent as to the time limit for making applications if the applicant is never sent a statement of reasons, either because s/he did not ask for one or did not ask in time or because the legally qualified panel member simply does not provide one. Commissioner Rowland dealt with this issue (in respect of an older form of the rules) in *R(IS) 11/99*. He decided that the absence of a statement of reasons did not prevent someone from appealing to a commissioner (although it could make it difficult to show that there had been an error of law). He did not consider that a chairman of a tribunal had any jurisdiction to entertain an application for leave to appeal to a commissioner in a case where no statement of the tribunal's decision had been given as the time limit never starts to run. Practically speaking this means that where an applicant has not obtained a statement of reasons for a tribunal's decision, the application for leave to appeal would have to be rejected by the legally qualified tribunal panel member. The application could then be renewed with a commissioner. See reg 9 SSCP Regs on p904 for the time limit and procedure.

It is understood that the DWP has made a standing request that local authorities alert it where they are appealing to a commissioner to enable the DWP to intervene. The DWP may wish to intervene, for example, to represent the views of the Secretary of State (who has overall responsibility for the HB and CTB schemes) or where an appeal raises an issue of general importance.

Representatives making applications for leave to appeal to a commissioner on someone's behalf should ensure they discuss the question of whether to appeal and on what grounds with their clients, both at the stage of application to the legally qualified tribunal panel member and at the stage of applying direct to a commissioner. The general mandate for representation before tribunals terminates when the tribunal gives its decision. There must therefore be a clear and new mandate given by the claimant to her/his representative for the purpose of an appeal to the commissioner: *CSDLA 2/2001* (para 14).

Since 20 May 2002, other parties do not have a right to make representations on an application for leave and if representations are made, the tribunal panel member no longer has to take these into account: since the deletion of para (3) and the substitution of para (4) by SI 2002 No 1379. It is therefore difficult to see how the occasion will arise for a tribunal's decision to be set aside under Sch 7 para 7(3) CSPSSA.

Para (6) is, in the context of HB and CTB, an exercise of the power under Sch 7 para 8(7)(c) CSPSSA to require applications for leave to appeal to be considered by some party other than the chairman of the tribunal which heard the case. See Sch 7 para 8 on p159 for discussion of the Tribunals Service's practice in this regard.

Where leave to appeal is granted by a legally qualified tribunal panel member, notice of appeal must then be lodged: reg 12 SSCP Regs. Forms OSSC1 ("persons affected") and OSSC2 (local authorities) can be used for this purpose. The forms are available from the Office of the Social Security and Child Support Commissioners and at www.osscsc.gov.uk.

The Housing Benefit and Council Tax Benefit (Decisions and Appeals) Regulations 2001

(SI 2001 No.1002)

Arrangement of Regulations

PART I
General

1. Citation, commencement and interpretation
2. Service of notices or documents
3. Person treated as a person affected by a decision

PART II
Revisions and supersessions

4. Revision of decisions
5. Late application for a revision
6. Date from which a revision takes effect
7. Decisions superseding earlier decisions
8. Date from which a decision superseding an earlier decision takes effect
9. Effective date for late notification of change of circumstances
10. Notice of a decision against which an appeal lies

PART III
Suspension and termination of benefit and other matters

11. Cases where a relevant authority may suspend
12. Making or restoring of payments or reductions suspended
13. Suspension for failure to furnish information etc.
14. Termination in cases of a failure to furnish information
15. Decisions involving issues that arise on appeal in other cases

PART IV
Rights of appeal and procedure for bringing appeals

16. Decisions against which no appeal lies
17. Appeal against a decision which has been revised
18. Time within which an appeal is to be brought
19. Late appeals
20. Making of appeals and applications
21. Death of a party to an appeal

PART V
Appeal Tribunals

22. Composition of appeal tribunals
23. Procedure in connection with appeals

SCHEDULE
Decisions against which no appeal lies

PART I
General

Citation, commencement and interpretation

1.–(1) These Regulations may be cited as the Housing Benefit and Council Tax Benefit (Decisions and Appeals) Regulations 2001 and shall come into force on 2nd July 2001.

(2)   In these Regulations, unless the context otherwise requires–

"the Act" means the Child Support, Pensions and Social Security Act 2000;

[³ "the 1998 Act" means the Social Security Act 1998;]

"the Administration Act" means the Social Security Administration Act 1992;

"appeal" means an appeal to an appeal tribunal;

"appropriate relevant authority" has the meaning it has in paragraph 4 of Schedule 7 to the Act;

"benefit week" means a period of seven consecutive days commencing on a Monday and ending on a Sunday;

"claimant" means a person claiming housing benefit or council tax benefit or both;

"clerk to an appeal tribunal" means a clerk assigned to an appeal tribunal in accordance with regulation 37 of the Decisions and Appeals Regulations 1999;

[⁷ *the Contributions and Benefits Act" means the Social Security Contributions and Benefits Act 1992;*]

[⁶ "Council Tax Benefit Regulations" means the Council Tax Benefit Regulations 2006;]

[⁶ "Council Tax Benefit (State Pension Credit) Regulations" means the Council Tax Benefit (Persons who have attained the qualifying age for state pension credit) Regulations 2006;]

[⁴ "couple" means–

    (a)   a man and woman who are married to each other and are members of the same household;

    (b)   a man and woman who are not married to each other but are living together as husband and wife;

    (c)   two people of the same sex who are civil partners of each other and are members of the same household; or

    (d)   two people of the same sex who are not civil partners of each other but are living together as if they were civil partners,

and for the purposes of paragraph (d), two people of the same sex are to be regarded as living together as if they were civil partners if, but only if, they would be regarded as living together as husband and wife were they instead two people of the opposite sex;]

"Decisions and Appeals Regulations 1999" means the Social Security and Child Support (Decisions and Appeals) Regulations 1999;

[² . . .]

[³ "family" has the same meaning as in section 137 of the Social Security Contributions and Benefits Act 1992;]

"financially qualified panel member" means a panel member who is an accountant and a member of–

    (a)   the Institute of Chartered Accountants in England and Wales;

    (b)   the Institute of Chartered Accountants in Scotland;

    (c)   the Institute of Chartered Accountants in Ireland;

    [¹(cc) the Institute of Certified Public Accountants in Ireland;]

    (d)   the Association of Chartered Certified Accountants;

    (e)   the Chartered Institute of Management Accountants; or

    (f)   the Chartered Institute of Public Finance and Accountancy;

[⁶ "Housing Benefit Regulations" means the Housing Benefit Regulations 2006;]

[⁶ "Housing Benefit (State Pension Credit) Regulations" means the Housing Benefit (Persons who have attained the qualifying age for state pension credit) Regulations 2006;]

"legally qualified panel member" means a panel member who–

    (a)   has a general qualification (construed in accordance with section 71 of the Courts and Legal Services Act 1990); or

    (b)   is an advocate or solicitor in Scotland;

"official error" means an error made by–

    (a)   a relevant authority or a person–

        (i)   authorised to carry out any function of a relevant authority relating to housing benefit or council tax benefit; or

        (ii)   providing services relating to housing benefit or council tax benefit directly or indirectly to a relevant authority;

    [¹ (b) an officer of–

        (i)   the Department for Work and Pensions; or

        (ii)   the Commissioners of Inland Revenue,

acting as such;]–

[²(c) . . .]

but excludes any error caused wholly or partly by any person or body not specified in sub-paragraphs (a) to (c)   of this definition and any error of law which is shown to have been an error only by virtue of a subsequent decision of a Commissioner (construed in accordance with paragraph 23(1) of Schedule 7 to the Act) or the court;

"panel member" means a person appointed to a panel constituted under section 6 of the Social Security Act 1998;

"partner" means–

    (a)   where a claimant is a member of [⁵ a couple], the other member of that couple; or

    (b)   where a claimant is polygamously married to two or more members of his household, any such member;

"person affected" shall be construed in accordance with regulation 3;

[⁷ the Pilot Scheme Regulations" means the Housing Benefit (Loss of Benefit) (Pilot Scheme) Regulations 2007;]

"President" means the President of appeal tribunals appointed under section 5 of the Social Security Act 1998;

"principal parties" has the same meaning as in paragraph 7(4) of Schedule 7 to the Act;

"relevant authority" has the same meaning as in paragraph 1(1) of Schedule 7 to the Act;

"relevant decision" has the same meaning as in paragraph 1(2) of Schedule 7 to the Act;

[² . . .]

[² . . .]

    (3)   In these Regulations, unless the context otherwise requires, a reference–

    (a)   to a numbered regulation is to the regulation in these Regulations bearing that number;

    (b)   in a regulation to a numbered paragraph is to the paragraph in that regulation bearing that number.

Modifications

Reg 1 is modified in respect of people to whom the Housing Benefit (Loss of Benefit) (Pilot Scheme) (Supplementary) Regulations 2007 SI No. 2474 apply. The modifications apply until 31 October 2009 unless revoked with effect from an earlier date. They are shown in italics above.

Amendments

    1.   Amended by reg 23 of SI 2002 No 1379 as from 20.5.02.

    2.   Deleted by Sch 2 para 8 (a) of SI 2002 No 1703 as from 30.9.02.

    3.   Inserted by reg 5(2)(a) of SI 2003 No 2275 as from 6.10.03.

    4.   Inserted by reg 9(2)(a) of SI 2005 No 2878 as from 5.12.05.

    5.   Substituted by reg 9(b) of SI 2005 No 2878 as from 5.12.05.

    6.   Amended by reg 5 and Sch 2 para 17(2) of SI 2006 No 217 as from 6.3.06.

    7.   Modified by reg 8(a) of SI 2007 No 2474 as from 1.11.07.

Analysis

For what constitutes a "legally qualifed panel member", see p109.

"official error" is a ground for revision under reg 4(2)(a). It is an error wholly caused by one of the named categories of people. Those falling into sub-paras (a) and (b) are equivalent to the categories in sub-paras (a) to (c) of reg 100(3) HB Regs and reference should be made to the commentary to that provision on p412. From 30 September 2002, "official error" no longer includes errors made by someone employed by an authority acting on behalf of the relevant HB and CTB authority for the area: sub-para (c) deleted.

The tailpiece excludes an error caused by a person not falling within the categories listed in the definition. That person may be wholly or only partly to blame for the error occurring.

Official errors include errors of law. However, an error of law is not an official error if it is "shown to have been" a mistake by a subsequent decision of a commissioner or a court. "Court" is not defined but will inevitably be interpreted to cover all superior courts in Scotland, England and Wales. If, however, as often occurs, there is a pre-existing commissioner's decision which gives a ruling on the point but the significance of which was not fully appreciated at the time, the failure to follow that decision will still be an official error.

It is suggested that official error also includes situations where there is specific evidence which the authority or person had, but which was not taken into account even though it was relevant and where there is documentary or other written evidence of entitlement which the authority had, but failed to give to the person making the decision at the time it was made.

Note that the difference in wording in sub-para (a) means that the restrictive reasoning in *R(I) 5/02* – error of law made by an adjudication officer on a decision made prior to the inception of the SSA 1998 does not fall within the definition at all and so that decision cannot ever be revised for "official error" – has no application to HB/CTB decisions. Note in any case that in *CG 2122/2001* Commissioner Mesher was reluctant to accept the tribunal's reasoning on this point in *R(I) 5/02* and in *R(CS) 3/04* Commissioner Turnbull decided that *R(I) 5/02* was wrongly decided on this point and he did not need to follow it.

Service of notices or documents

2.   Where, by, or in consequence of, any provision of these Regulations or Schedule 7 to the Act–

(a)   any notice or other document is required to be given or sent to the clerk to an appeal tribunal, the Secretary of State or the relevant authority, that notice or document shall be treated as having been so given or sent on the day that it is received by the clerk to the appeal tribunal, the Secretary of State or the relevant authority, as the case may be; and

(b)   any notice (including notification of a decision of a relevant authority) or other document is required to be given or sent to any person other than the clerk to an appeal tribunal, the Secretary of State or the relevant authority, as the case may be, that notice or document shall, if sent by post to that person's last known address, be treated as having been so given or sent on the day it was posted.

General Note

Reg 2 governs when notices and other documents are to be treated as having been served. It applies to all documents that are "required to be given or sent" by, or in consequence of, "any provision of these Regulations or Schedule 7" to CSPSSA. Note that this includes documents relating to HB and CTB that are "required to be given or sent" by Part V of the SSCS D&A Regs: Part V is applied to HB and CTB by reg 23 (below) and any such documents will therefore be required to be given or sent "in consequence of [a] provision of these Regulations".

There are two rules:

(1)   Under para (a), documents sent to the clerk to the tribunal or the local authority are served when they are received.

(2)   Under para (b), a document sent to other parties (eg, by a local authority or the Tribunals Service to a claimant) is deemed to be served on the day that it is posted.

Analysis

Para (a). The fact that a document sent to the tribunal or to a local authority is only treated as having been given or sent when it is actually received is a constant source of dispute and a trap for claimants who are often placed in the position of having to establish that it was more likely than not that a document was received by an authority when all the evidence relevant to that issue lies in the hands of the authority. The best advice for claimants is that they should either deliver all documents in person and obtain a receipt or send them by recorded delivery so that the Royal Mail can be approached for evidence of delivery if necessary. Unfortunately that advice will often be impracticable either in terms of time (the claimant may well be in full-time low-waged work) or money (as recorded delivery greatly increases the cost of posting a letter and many letters may be necessary during the course of a claim). A compromise may be to advise claimants to send letters by ordinary post but obtain a free certificate of posting from the Post Office counter: proof of posting may help persuade a tribunal that it is more likely than not that the authority received the letter and subsequently misplaced it. But even if it does not, a claimant who can prove that s/he committed a document to the post is in a much stronger position to argue for any necessary extension of time if that document subsequently goes astray.

Local authorities are under a duty to ensure that those who are entitled to benefit receive it as well as to ensure that those with no entitlement do not. As entitlement may depend upon when they receive a particular document, it is important that all authorities should have rigorous and documented procedures for the opening of post. It is not unusual for tribunals to question presenting officers in detail about such procedures.

Documents sent by fax can raise particular difficulties. Provided a fax is sent to the clerk to the tribunal prior to midnight and successfully transmitted, it will have been "received" on that day: *CDLA 4895/2001* (para 7). This issue was further considered in *R(DLA) 3/05*, in the context of a request for a statement of the appeal tribunal's reasons for its decision being faxed to a tribunal venue within the relevant time limit, but where that faxed request had not been picked up by the clerk to the tribunal – to whom such applications must be made, see reg 53(4) of the SSCS D&A Regs – until after that time limit had expired, because the venue was not used on a daily basis. Commissioner Jacobs decided that, in such circumstances, an application is made when it is received by a fax machine, and that this is the case regardless of when the clerk actually collects the fax from the machine, which may be hours or days later (para 18). However, the fax machine used must relate in some way to the case to which the application relates, and at the very least it must be a fax machine within the relevant Tribunals Service Region (para 19). Nor is it sufficient to send an application to a fax machine at a casual venue, such as a Town Hall, as the fax machine there will belong to the owner or occupier of the premises and not the clerk to the tribunal (para 20). In this case the application had been made to a dedicated appeals venue (albeit one that was not used for appeals each and every day), where the claimant's appeal had been heard and where the fax number for that venue had been made available to those with appeals at that venue. In these circumstances, and in the absence of any directions to the contrary, service on that fax machine was good service, and so the request for the statement of reasons had been made within time.

Para (b). The effect of this is that where on service of a document, a time limit begins to run, it runs from the date of posting, not date of receipt of the document. This presumes that if the document was sent to the correct address, it has been delivered. Extensions of time ought readily to be granted where a document is lost in the post or has been sent to an incorrect address. As Commissioner Williams pointed out in *CH 3009/2002*, there is no matching presumption that a document which it was intended to be posted was actually posted. He said that where, as in this case, an appellant challenges whether something has been posted for good reason, evidence of office practice is required to show that on the balance of probabilities, the document was posted: paras 12 and 13.

The divergent treatment of documents sent to local authorities and documents sent to other parties to the appeal, would seem to raise issues about the "equality of arms" (see the commentary to Article 6 of the European Convention on Human Rights on p132). The point is perhaps most clear when – as is often the case – a tribunal sends a notice of hearing to the local authority and the appellant at the same time: under para (a), the notice is only validly served on the authority when it is received whereas, under para (b), it is deemed to have been validly served on the appellant as soon as it is committed to the post even if it is not in fact delivered. More generally, reg 2 means that the risk of documents going astray in the post is always born by the claimant or appellant, never by the local authority, and that, in the event of a dispute, the claimant or appellant either has to prove that s/he did not receive the document (which involves proving a negative) or that the authority did receive the document (which involves proving a fact when all the potential evidence for that fact is in the possession of the other party). The harsh effects of reg 2 will often (but not always) be mitigated by the possibility of obtaining an extension of time or of a tribunal decision's being set aside under reg 57 SSCS D&A Regs if the appellant does not attend because of a failure of notice. Nevertheless, it is wrong in principle for the procedural rules of a judicial body overtly to favour one party over another. That is particularly so when the advantaged party is the more powerful (in this case the state) and the disadvantaged the citizen.

Person treated as a person affected by a decision

3.–(1)   For the purposes of Schedule 7 to the Act and subject to paragraph (2), a person is to be treated as a person affected by a relevant decision of a relevant authority where that person is–

(a)   a claimant;

(b)   in the case of a person who is liable to make payments in respect of a dwelling and is unable for the time being to act–

   (i)   a [² deputy] appointed by the Court of Protection with power to claim, or as the case may be, receive benefit on his behalf,

   (ii)   in Scotland, a tutor, curator, judicial factor or other guardian acting or appointed in terms of law administering that person's estate, or

   (iii)   an attorney with a general power or a power to receive benefit appointed by the person liable to make those payments under [² the Powers of Attorney Act 1971, the Enduring Powers of Attorney Act 1985 or the Mental Capacity Act 2005 or otherwise];

[¹ (c)   a person appointed by the relevant authority under regulation 82(3) of the Housing Benefit Regulations, regulation 63(3) of the Housing Benefit (State Pension Credit) Regulations, regulation 68(3) of the Council Tax Benefit Regulations or, as the case may be, regulation 52(3) of the Council Tax Benefit (State Pension Credit) Regulations (appointments for persons unable to act);

(d)   a person from whom the relevant authority determines that–

   (i)   an overpayment is recoverable in accordance with Part 13 of the Housing Benefit Regulations or Part 12 of the Housing Benefit (State Pension Credit) Regulations; or

   (ii)   excess benefit is recoverable in accordance with Part 11 of the Council Tax Benefit Regulations or Part 10 of the Council Tax Benefit (State Pension Credit) Regulations; or

(e)   a landlord or agent acting on behalf of that landlord and that decision is made under–

   (i)   regulation 95 (circumstances in which payment is to be made to the landlord) of the Housing Benefit Regulations;

   (ii)   regulation 96 (circumstances in which payment may be made to the landlord) of those Regulations;

   (iii)   regulation 76 (circumstances in which payment is to be made to the landlord) of the Housing Benefit (State Pension Credit) Regulations;

   (iv)   regulation 77 (circumstances in which payment may be made to the landlord) of those Regulations.]

(2)   Paragraph (1) only applies in relation to a person referred to in paragraph (1) where the rights, duties or obligations of that person are affected by a relevant decision.

Amendments
1.   Substituted by reg 5 and Sch 2 para 17(3) of SI 2006 No 217 as from 6.3.06.
2.   Amended by reg 9 of SI 2007 No 2618 as from 1.10.07.

Analysis
Para (1) sets out the categories of "person affected". This definition is of vital importance, since it is a "person affected" who has the right to challenge decisions and appeal under Sch 7 CSPSSA and these regulations. The categories are:

(1)   The claimant: sub-para (a).

(2)   A deputy or attorney in England and Wales, or the Scottish equivalents, who is acting on behalf of the person who is liable to make payments: sub-para (b). The deemed non-liability in regs 9(1) and 10(1) of both the HB and the HB(SPC) Regs and reg 56(1) HB Regs will not preclude such a person acting on an appeal against such a decision.

(3)   An appointee appointed by the relevant authority: sub-para (c).

(4) A person from whom it is decided that an overpayment is recoverable: sub-para (d). This could be a landlord. In *CH 3679/2002* (para 3) it was held that a landlord would be a "person affected" in relation to an appeal by a claimant against a decision that an overpayment was recoverable from a landlord. The failure to notify the landlord of the appeal rendered the decision erroneous in law.

(5) A landlord or her/his agent, where the decision relates to direct payments (including a decision that the landlord is not a "fit and proper person" – see commentary to regs 95 and 96 HB Regs on pp405 and 408: sub-para (e)).

In *CH 3817/2004*, Commissioner Mesher holds that the list in para (1) is not exhaustive. Para 23(2) Sch 7 CSPSSA allows regulations to specify who is to be treated as a person affected and who is not to be so treated and reg 3 only gives effect to the first part of that power. Para (1) does not say that those listed are the *only* persons affected and there is no list of persons who are *not* to be treated as persons affected. In those circumstances, the effect of para (1) is to put the status of the listed categories of person beyond argument. But it is still open to a person to argue that she is a person affected by a relevant decision for the purposes of para 6(3) Sch 7 CSPSSA in the ordinary meaning to be given to that term (para 14). In *CH 3817/2004* itself, a woman who was jointly and severally liable with her partner to pay rent and council tax was held to be a person affected by a decisions to refuse a claim for backdating that the local authority had treated as having been made by her partner.

Para (2) provides that a person will only be a "person affected" if her/his rights duties and obligations are affected by the decision in question. As far as the people listed in para (1) are concerned, this will always be the case. The rights of the claimant are affected by a decision to pay HB directly to a landlord or agent, or to recover an overpayment from such a person, because (in the former case) the entitlement to benefit is the claimant's and s/he is *prima facie* entitled to receive payment (see reg 94 HB Regs and reg 75 HB (SPC) Regs) and (in the latter) because recovery of an HB overpayment from the landlord or agent will create a debt from the claimant to the recoveree and (at least if reg 95(2)(b) HB Regs and reg 76(2)(b) of the HB (SPC) Regs are validly made: reg 95(2)(b)) will create arrears of rent that could lead to eviction (see p405). The rights of deputies (etc) and appointees (para (1)(b) and (c)) are affected because they are acting in the place of the claimant.

Para (2) will, however, be relevant in cases in which a person who is not on the list in para (1) seeks to argue that s/he is a person affected within the ordinary meaning of that phrase (see *CH 3817/2004* above). See also the commentary to reg 21 below in relation to who has a right of appeal where the claimant has died.

PART II
Revisions and Supersessions

General Note on Part II

Pt II contains the very detailed provisions for revisions and supersessions, which are two of the three means by which a decision can be altered. The third is for the decision to be reversed or varied on appeal.

Reference should be made to Sch 7 paras 3 and 4 for the enabling provisions governing revisions and supersessions. Regs 4 to 6 contain the detailed provisions for the operation of revisions under Sch 7 para 4 CSPSSA. Reg 4 deals with grounds on which a revision can be made and the procedure for doing so. Reg 5 deals with applications for revision made outside the time limit in reg 4(1), and reg 6 deals with the effective date of a decision which has been revised. Regs 7 and 8 deal with the grounds and procedure (reg 7) and the effective date (reg 8) of a supersession. Reg 9 deals with late notifications of changes of circumstances (which are under reg 7(2)(a) grounds for a supersession) and reg 10 deals with notifications of decisions generally.

See also the commentary to reg 90 HB Regs on p395 for consideration of the question of whether a decision is rendered invalid by virtue of a failure to revise or supersede or where there is a defective attempt at revision or supersession.

Revision of decisions

4.–(1) Subject to the provisions in this regulation, a relevant decision ("the original decision") may be revised or further revised by the relevant authority which made the decision where–

(a) [² subject to regulation 10A(3),] the person affected makes an application for a revision within–

  (i) one month of the date of notification of the original decision; or

  (ii) such extended time as the relevant authority may allow under regulation 5;

(b)   within one month of the date of notification of the original decision that authority has information which is sufficient to show that the original decision was made in ignorance of, or was based upon a mistake as to, some material fact; or

(c)   an appeal is made under paragraph 6 of Schedule 7 to the Act against the original decision within the time prescribed in regulation 18 or, in a case to which regulation 19 applies the time prescribed in that regulation, but the appeal has not been determined.

(2)   An original decision may be revised or further revised by the relevant authority which made the decision, at any time by that authority, where that decision–

(a)   arose from an official error; or

(b)   was made in ignorance of, or was based upon a mistake as to, some material fact and as a result of that ignorance of or mistake as to that fact, the decision was more advantageous to the person affected than it would otherwise have been but for that ignorance or mistake.

(3)   Notwithstanding the provisions in paragraph (1), a relevant decision which adopts a rent officer's determination [⁶ , board and attendance determination, broad rental market area determination or local housing allowance determination] may be revised or further revised by the relevant authority which made the decision at any time in consequence of a rent officer's redetermination, substitute determination [⁶substitute redetermination, board and attendance redetermination, substitute board and attendance determination, substitute board and attendance redetermination, amended broad rental market area determination or amended local housing allowance determination] made under the Rent Officers (Housing Benefit Functions) Order 1997 or the Rent Officers (Housing Benefit Functions) (Scotland) Order 1997 which resulted in an increase in the amount which represents the rent for the purposes of calculating entitlement to benefit.

(4)   For the purposes of calculating the period in paragraph (1)(a)(i), where a written statement is requested under regulation 10, no account shall be taken of any period beginning with the day on which the relevant authority received the request for a statement and ending with the day on which that statement was provided to that person.

(5)   Where the relevant authority requires further evidence or information in order to consider all the issues raised by an application under paragraph (1)(a) ("the original application"), that authority shall notify the applicant that further evidence or information is required and, if it does so, the decision may be revised–

(a)   where the evidence or information so requested is provided within one month of the date of the notification or such longer period as the relevant authority may allow; or

(b)   where such evidence or information is not provided within the period referred to in sub-paragraph (a), on the basis of the original application.

(6)   A relevant decision that is prescribed under paragraph 6(2)(e) or (4)(a) of Schedule 7 to the Act may be revised at any time.

(7)   A relevant decision made in respect of a claim or an award may be revised where–

(a)   a decision in respect of that claim or that award is given by an appeal tribunal, Commissioner or court on appeal against a decision ("decision A");

(b)   the relevant decision was made after decision A; and

(c)   the relevant decision would have been made differently had the relevant authority been aware of that appeal decision at the time it made the relevant decision.

[¹(7A)   Where a court convicts a person of an offence, that conviction results in a restriction being imposed under section 7, 8 or 9 of the Social Security Fraud Act 2001 (loss of benefit provisions) and that conviction is quashed or set aside by that or any other court, a decision of the relevant authority made in accordance with regulation 7(2)(g) or (h) may be revised at any time.]

[⁴ (7B)   Where–

(a)   the relevant authority makes an original decision awarding housing benefit or council tax benefit to a claimant; and

(b)   entitlement to a relevant benefit within the meaning of section 8(3) of the 1998 Act or to an increase in the rate of that relevant benefit is awarded to the claimant or a member of his family for a period which includes the date on which the original decision took effect,

the relevant authority may revise or further revise that original decision at any time.

(7C)   Where entitlement to housing benefit or council tax benefit has ceased (''decision A'') because entitlement to a relevant benefit within the meaning of section 8(3) of the 1998 Act has ceased (''decision B''), decision A may be revised at any time if the entitlement to the relevant benefit to which decision B applies has been reinstated in consequence of a decision made under [⁵ section 9 or 10 of the 1998 Act or on an appeal under section 12 of that Act.]]

[⁸ (7D)   Where–

(a)   a person elects for an increase of–

(i)   a Category A or Category B retirement pension in accordance with paragraph A1 or 3C of Schedule 5 to the Contributions and Benefits Act (pension increase or lump sum where entitlement to retirement pension is deferred);

(ii)   a shared additional pension in accordance with paragraph 1 of Schedule 5A to that Act (pension increase or lump sum where entitlement to shared additional pension is deferred); or, as the case may be,

(iii)   graduated retirement benefit in accordance with paragraph 12 or 17 of Schedule 1 to the Social Security (Graduated Retirement Benefit) Regulations 2005 (further provisions replacing section 36(4) of the National Insurance Act 1965: increases of graduated retirement benefit and lump sums);

(b)   the relevant authority decides that the person or his partner is entitled to housing benefit or council tax benefit and takes into account the increase of pension or benefit in making or superseding that decision; and

(c)   the person's election for an increase is changed so that he is entitled to a lump sum,

the relevant authority may revise the housing benefit or council tax benefit decision.]

[⁹ (7E)   Where a court makes an order under section 71 of the Antisocial Behaviour etc. (Scotland) Act 2004 and that order is set aside by the sheriff principal following an appeal under section 72(1) of that Act, a decision made in accordance with regulation 7(2)(a) may be revised at any time.

(7F)   Where a local authority has served a notice in accordance with section 94 of the Antisocial Behaviour etc. (Scotland) Act 2004 and that notice is set aside by a court following an appeal under section 97(1) of that Act, a decision made in accordance with regulation 7(2)(a) may be revised at any time.]

[¹⁰ *(7G)   Where the court makes a relevant order for possession, as defined in section 130C of the Contributions and Benefits Act (relevant orders for possession) and the order is set aside, a decision in accordance with regulation 7(2)(k) may be revised at any time.]*

(8)   An application for a revision shall be made in writing and delivered, by whatever means, to the relevant authority [³ . . .].

(9)   The relevant authority may treat an application for a supersession as an application for a revision.

(10)   Paragraph (1) shall not apply in respect of a change of circumstances which occurred since the decision [⁷ had effect] or where the relevant authority has evidence or information which indicates that a relevant change of circumstances will occur.

Modifications

Reg 4 is modified in respect of people to whom the Housing Benefit (Loss of Benefit) (Pilot Scheme) (Supplementary) Regulations 2007 SI No. 2474 apply (see p1144). The modifications apply until 31 October 2009 unless revoked with effect from an earlier date. They are shown in italics above.

Amendments

1.   Inserted by reg 9(a) of SI 2002 No 490 as from 1.4.02.
2.   Amended by reg 24 of SI 2002 No 1379 as from 20.5.02.
3.   Deleted by Sch 2 para 8(b) of SI 2002 No 1703 as from 30.9.02.
4.   Inserted by reg 5(3) of SI 2003 No 2275 as from 6.10.03.
5.   Amended by reg 2 of SI 2003 No 2526 as from 5.10.03.
6.   Inserted by reg 16 of SI 2003 No 2399 as from a date specified in Sch 8 in relation to each particular authority.
7.   Amended by reg 3(2) of SI 2005 No 337 as from 18.3.05.
8.   Inserted by Reg 10(2) of SI 2005 No 2677 as from 6.4.06.
9.   Inserted by Reg 4 of SI 2006 No 644 as from 3.4.06.
10.   Modified by reg 8(b) of SI 2007 No 2474 as from 1.11.07.

Definition

"family" – see reg 1(2) and s137(1) SSCBA 1992.

General Note

A decision can be revised by a relevant authority following an application made by a "person affected" (defined in reg 3) on any ground: para (1)(a).

A decision can also be revised by a relevant authority in specific circumstances. Under paras (1)(b) and (c), a revision is only possible within a specific time frame. Under paras (2), (3), (6), (7) and (7A)-(7F) a revision is only possible if specific grounds apply – referred to here as "any time revisions".

Authorities may treat an application for a supersession as one for revision: para (9).

Authorities cannot, in general, supersede a decision where it can be revised (see reg 7(4) – the exception is where there are grounds for revision and further grounds for supersession that are not also grounds for a revision (eg, a subsequent change of circumstances)). In receiving any application for revision or supersession, a local authority should therefore first consider whether a revision under para (1) is possible, including whether an extension of time for the application can be granted under reg 5. If this is not possible, a revision under any of the other grounds provided by reg 4 should be considered before consideration of any grounds for supersession under reg 7.

If the decision is one which carried a right of appeal, the authority must issue a new decision under reg 10. The time limit for appealing then runs as provided for in Sch 7 para 3(5) CSPSSA and reg 18(3).

Commissioner Williams, applying the decision in *R(IB) 2/04*, said that appeal tribunals have the power to take any decision that the initial decision maker could have taken. This includes "considering in appropriate cases whether a claim should be considered as a request for a revision or supersession of a decision on a previous claim, subject to time limits and other statutory provisions": *CH 3009/2002* (para 21). The general limit is that this must be raised by the appeal or be a matter that the tribunal acting in its investigatory role decides it should consider. Further, he said that if the point is in issue before the tribunal or if it identifies the point as significant, it must consider any revision necessary to correct an official error in a decision before it, where there has been no decision on this point: *CDLA 1821/2003*, per *R(IS) 15/04* (para 78).

See also the commentary to reg 90 HB Regs on p395 for consideration of the question of whether a decision is rendered invalid by virtue of a failure to revise or where there is a defective attempt at revision or supersession.

Analysis

In *CIS 6249/1999* (paras 21-25) – a case decided under the system of social security adjudication that was in place before SSA 1998 – the commissioner decided that if it would be so unfair to a claimant to "review" a decision that it would be an abuse of process to do so, the Secretary of State (and, on appeal, an appeal tribunal) could decline to do so. It is unclear whether this decision applies to the revision of decisions under SSA 1998 or Sch 7 CSPSSA. Certainly, it will be a rare case where it will be legitimate for an authority to refrain from revising an earlier decision on this ground. See also the commentary to paras (2), (3), (6), (7) and (7A)-(7F). The use of the word 'may' in paras (1) and (2) does not mean that a HB or CTB authority has a general discretion to refuse to revise a decision. Where the grounds of revision are made out, particularly where the ground is 'official error', the authority must revise: *R(IS) 15/04*.

Paragraphs (1)(a), (4) and (5): Applications for revision

Para (1)(a) sets out circumstances in which a person affected can apply for a revision on "any grounds". A person affected may apply for a revision within one month of the date of notification of the decision which is sought to be revised. If an accidental error in a decision has been corrected under reg 10A, any day falling before the day on which notice of the correction is given must be ignored in calculating the one-month period. For the date of notification, see reg 2. Where something must be done "within" a certain period of time, time runs from the day after notification: R(IB) 4/02 para 15. An act is done "within" a certain period of time if it is done at midnight on the last day of the period: *Manorlike Ltd v Le Vitas Travel Agency and Consultancy Services Ltd* [1986] 1 All ER 573 at 575e-h, 576b-d, CA.

Where a request is made for a written statement of reasons for a decision under reg 10, para (4) effectively stops the clock in respect of the one-month time limit for seeking a revision. The period from the date on which the request is received until the date on which the statement of reasons is provided to the person affected must be ignored in calculating whether an application was made within the one-month time limit. For the reasons given in the commentary to reg 18(3), it is suggested that the statement of reasons is not "provided" until it is received by the person affected. Although a person affected may believe a written statement of reasons has not been included with a decision or that what has been provided is inadequate, the local authority could disagree. If there is any doubt about the situation, it is advisable to presume the clock has not stopped and to apply for a revision within the time limit as if it has not done so.

The time limit can be extended in the restricted circumstances set out in reg 5.

It is important to note that where a decision carries a right of appeal, revision is only one of the two means of disputing the decision, the other being an appeal under Sch 7 para 6 CSPSSA. Revision is not a mandatory step that must be taken prior to an appeal as appears to be the presumption with some authorities. A "person affected" can exercise her/his right of appeal without having first sought a revision. Authorities can then revise a decision, if appropriate, pending determination of that appeal: see para (1)(c) below. However, an appeal should not be held up while this is done as appears to be the practice with some local authorities. The Local Government Ombudsman has made it clear in a report in Complaint No 01/C/13400 against Scarborough BC that authorities should aim to refer all appeals to the Tribunals Service within 28 days.

Para (5) gives an authority a power to require further evidence or information to be furnished within one month or a further period that may be allowed. If the evidence or information is not forthcoming, a decision as to whether to revise must be made on the existing material before the authority.

Paragraph (1)(b): Revision of decisions made on basis of incorrect facts

A local authority may revise a decision within one month of the date of notification of the original decision, where the information before it shows that the original decision was made on the wrong factual basis. There will some overlap between this provision and revision for official error under para (2)(a). Outside of the one-month period, a supersession under reg 7(2)(b) is appropriate instead.

In *Saker v Secretary of State for Social Security* [1988] 16 January *The Times*, CA (reported as *R(I) 2/88*) – decided under the old "review" regime in place prior to the SSA 1998 – it was held that a material fact is one which may affect the extent of entitlement. However, under the SSA 1998 and the CSPSSA 2000, as explained by the Court of Appeal in *Wood v Secretary of State for Work and Pensions* [2003] EWCA Civ 53, CA (reported as *R(DLA) 1/03*), for a revision or supersession to be made out the award must change. In the Tribunal of Commissioner's decision *R(IB) 2/04*, the commissioners further explained *Wood* by stating that: (i) there can be no revision or supersession unless one of the grounds for revision or supersession is actually found to exist, and (ii) that ground forms the basis of the revision or supersession decision, in the sense that the original decision can only be altered in a way which follows from that ground. For appeal rights on revision or supersession decisions, see the commentary to Sch 7 para 1 CSPSSA on p158. A distinction must be drawn between facts and the inference to be drawn from those facts. Again, if the authority simply changes its mind about how it sees the evidence, the original determination is not open to revision on the ground of a mistake of fact: *R(S) 4/86* (para 6).

A distinction also needs to be drawn between mistakes of fact and law, though the distinction is not always easy to make. In addition, if a fact did not exist at the time a decision was made, that decision cannot be said to have been taken in ignorance of that fact: *Chief Adjudication Officer v Combe* [1998] SLT 15 at 17D-F, IH (reported as *R(IS) 8/98*). Supersession will be appropriate instead in such a situation.

Paragraph (1)(c): Revision while appeal pending

An authority may revise a decision which has been appealed within the time limit, where the appeal is still pending. The process of deciding whether to revise pending an appeal has, confusingly, been termed "reconsideration" by the DWP and local authorities and is carried out as a matter of course whenever an appeal is made. An appeal will lapse if a revision is carried out and the new decision is more advantageous to the appellant: see Sch 7 para 3 CSPSSA and reg 17 below.

At least in the past, some local authorities have abused the possibility of "reconsideration" created by para (1)(c) to delay, sometimes virtually indefinitely, the submission of the appeal to the tribunal. The technique involves asking a large number of supplementary questions, often in tendentious terms, so that the "reconsideration" can be carried out. If the questions are not answered, or information is not supplied, the appellant is told – quite unlawfully – that the claim has been treated as withdrawn or that the award has been terminated. If the questions are answered, further questions are asked seeking to exploit supposed inconsistencies with information previously given. In extreme cases, the claimant is then told that a decision has been taken not to change the original decision and that as this is a "revision" (which it is not: see the commentary to para 3 Sch 7 CSPSSA on p158) the appeal has therefore lapsed (which is also wrong because there has not in fact been a revision and, anyway, the new decision is not more advantageous to the claimant than the old: see the commentary to reg 17 (below)). The hapless appellant then makes a fresh appeal and the whole sorry process starts all over again.

It cannot be over-emphasised, that the primary duty on a local authority that receives an appeal is to prepare a submission and send it to the Tribunals Service without delay. The Local Government Ombudsman requires that this should normally be done within 28 days. Where there is delay (which would, in practice, have to be considerably longer than 28 days), or wilful refusal, to submit an appeal the tribunal has a residual power to hear the appeal without such a submission – see *R(H) 1/07*.

If, in the course of preparing the submission, it becomes clear that the decision was wrong then the authority should, of course, revise it under para (1)(c). But if all that can be said is that there are unanswered questions that, if answered, might make a difference to the decision, then the best practice is for the authority to list those questions in the submission (so that the appellant will be aware of the type of further evidence that might be relevant) and, in an appropriate case, to apply for an interlocutory direction from the tribunal that the appellant should produce such evidence.

Paragraphs (2), (3), (6), (7) and (7A)-(7F): "Any time" revisions
There are several further grounds for revision which can be applied by the authority at any time. They apply in the following circumstances:

(1)   Where the decision "arose from an official error": para (2)(a). For the definition of "official error", see reg 1(2). The official error must have influenced the outcome of the decision in question.

(2)   The decision was made on the wrong factual basis and was more advantageous to a person affected as a result: para (2)(b). For the meaning of "material fact" see the commentary to para (1)(b). Reg 17(2) does not specifically apply to para (2)(b) but will no doubt give a good guide as to the types of case where a decision is more "advantageous". It will include situations where on the correct factual basis, the claimant was not entitled to as much benefit as originally determined. This ground will therefore often be used in overpayment situations. In other circumstances, revision is possible under para (1)(b) or supersession is possible under reg 7(2)(b).

(3)   Where a rent officer's redetermination or other subsequent decision has resulted in an *increase* in "the rent for the purposes of calculating entitlement to benefit": para (3). The latter phrase must refer to the maximum rent under reg 13 of both the HB and the HB(SPC) Regs. A reduction in the maximum rent is grounds for a supersession under reg 7(2)(c).

(4)   Where the decision revised is one against which there is no right of appeal: para (6). See the Schedule for details of the decisions against which an appeal does not lie to a tribunal.

(5)   Where an appeal is made against a decision to a tribunal, a commissioner or court and after its decision (decision A), a fresh claim is decided or the decision is changed, for example, by a supersession (decision B): para (7). However, a revision is only possible on this ground if decision B would have been made differently had the relevant authority been aware of decision A at the time it made its decision. It does not appear that this ground can apply where the decision maker was aware of the decision but did not appreciate its significance. However, such an approach would constitute an "official error" and a revision could be made under para (2)(a) instead.

(6)   Where a conviction resulted in benefit being restricted under ss7, 8 or 9 Social Security Fraud Act 2001 (loss of benefit provisions) and that conviction has since been quashed or set aside: para (7A). Only decisions made in accordance with regs 7(2)(g) or (h) below (grounds for supersession) can be revised on this ground.

(7)   Where a local authority awards HB or CTB and, for a period which includes the date that award took effect, the claimant or a member of her/his family is awarded a "relevant benefit" or an increase in its rate: para (7B). "Relevant benefit" is defined in s8(3) SSA 1998 as any benefit under Parts II to V SSCBA 1992, JSA, PC, IS, a social fund grant for maternity or funeral expenses, child benefit and other benefits which may be prescribed. This is a welcome addition of what is known as a "qualifying benefit" rule. It allows HB and CTB awards to be increased and arrears to be paid back to the date the awards took effect where a relevant benefit is awarded or its rate is increased for a

period including that date – eg, where an award of DLA (a relevant benefit) is made to a claimant and thus a disability premium should be included in her/his HB and CTB applicable amount. Where entitlement to a relevant benefit or an increase in its rate commences *after* the date the HB or CTB award took effect, the decision awarding HB or CTB can instead be superseded under reg 7(2)(i). This ground for revision is only available where there is an existing award of HB and/or CTB. Where there is no entitlement to HB or CTB until an award of a relevant benefit (or increase in its rate) is made, a claimant will be wise to make a claim for HB and/or CTB while the claim for the relevant benefit is being considered, asking the local authority to delay making a decision until the claim for the relevant benefit is determined – known as "stockpiling" a claim. If a decision maker fails to delay making a decision until the result of the claim for a relevant benefit is known, *CG 1479/ 1999* and *CIS 217/1999* suggest that this may be an error of law, giving rise to a ground for revision under para (2)(a) above. Alternatively, a claim for backdated HB and CTB will be required under reg 83(12) HB Regs, reg 64(1) HB(SPC) Regs, reg 69(14) CTB Regs or reg 56 CTB(SPC) Regs as the case may be. See also para (7C) below for the situation where HB or CTB ceases when entitlement to a relevant benefit ceases.

(8) Where entitlement to HB or CTB ceases because entitlement to a "relevant benefit" ceases, and the relevant benefit is re-instated in consequence of a revision or supersession decision or an appeal: para (7C). For the definition of "relevant benefit" see the commentary to para (7B) above. In some cases, a claimant is only entitled to HB or CTB because s/he or a member of her/his family is entitled to a relevant benefit – eg, where s/he would not be entitled to HB or CTB but for the fact that a carer premium should be included in her/his applicable amount because s/he is entitled to carer's allowance (a relevant benefit). In such a situation, if entitlement to the relevant benefit ceases, so does the entitlement to HB and CTB. However, where the relevant benefit is re-instated because of a revision, a supersession or an appeal, para (7C) allows the decision ceasing entitlement to HB and CTB to be revised. The effect of this is that HB and CTB can be reinstated and arrears paid back to the date from which entitlement ceased.

(9) Where the claimant or her/his partner deferred claiming Category A or B retirement pension, shared additional pension or graduated retirement benefit and originally opted for an increase in the pension, but then opts for a lump sum instead: para (7D). This only applies where the authority has made a decision on her/his entitlement to HB or CTB and takes the increase in pension or benefit into account in making or superseding that decision.

(10) Where a court makes an order under s71 Antisocial Behaviour etc. (Scotland) Act 2004 (or a local authority has served a notice in accordance with s94 of that Act) and that order is set aside by the sheriff principal (or that notice is set aside by a court) following an appeal: paras (7E) and (7F). Since 30 April 2006, in Scotland, where a local authority serves an anti-social behaviour notice on a landlord and s/he has failed to take reasonable management steps to deal with the behaviour, the local authority can ask a court to make a "no rent payable order" or a management control order (in the latter case rent then becomes payable to the local authority under reg 91A HB Regs or reg 72A HB(SPC) Regs). In addition, if a landlord fails to register with the local authority, it can serve a notice stating that no rent is payable on the property – known as a "no rent payable" notice. Where the order or notice is then set aside following an appeal, paras (7E) and (7D) enable a decision ending HB entitlement under reg 7(2)(a) below to be revised. In practice, this means that a claimant does not have to make a fresh claim for HB in these circumstnaces. A helpful explanation of the Antisocial Behaviour etc (Scotland) Act 2004 provisions and their impact on HB is available in Circular HB/CTB A10/2006.

Is an authority obliged to carry out an "any time" revision?

The above grounds all confer, on the face of it, a discretion on the local authority as to whether it in fact goes ahead and revises. However, a HB/CTB authority does not have a general discretion to refuse to revise a decision. Where the grounds of revision are made out, particularly where the ground is 'official error', the authority must revise: *R(IS) 15/04* (para 39). Sometimes the person affected will not want the revision to be made, because it will inevitably be less advantageous. However, sometimes it may benefit the person affected, but s/he will not be able to apply for a revision under para (1) and will wish the authority to exercise its power to carry out the revision.

If the application cannot be treated as made within the time limit under para (1), an authority may simply reject the application as being out of time under that provision or refuse to extend the time for applying under reg 5. That rejection or refusal would not be a decision giving rise to a right of appeal. The only remedy is judicial review. However, it is open to a person affected to invite an authority to exercise its power to carry out an "any time" revision. If the authority refuses to revise, reg 18(3) appears to envisage a notification of a decision that no revision is to be carried out and allow for an appeal to be made, within one month of the notification of the refusal to revise, against the original decision; that is, the decision being sought to be revised. However, the Tribunal of Commissioners in *R(IS) 15/04* has held that the extension of time for cases under reg 18(3)(b) only applies to applications for revision under paragraphs (1)(a), (4) and (5), and does not apply to 'any time' revision requests under paragraph (2). Accordingly, where a claimant has applied for an 'any time' revision on the ground of official error and the authority decides not to revise, the time for appealing against the original decision (which has not been revised) cannot be extended under regulation 18. The Court of Appeal in *Beltekian v Westminster City Council and Secretary of State for Work and Pensions* [2004] EWCA Civ 1784, 8 December 2004 (reported as *R(H) 8/05*) followed the reasoning in *R(IS) 15/04* and decided that the extension of time for appealing against the original decision by reg 18(3), where there has been a refusal to revise, only applies where the request for revision was made under reg 4(1) and not under reg 4(2).

Paragraphs (8), (9) and (10): Procedural matters

Applications for revision are to be made in writing to the authority "by whatever means", for the significance of which, see the commentary to reg 20(1).

Para (9) is a welcome power to treat an application for supersession as an application for revision. For the corresponding power, see reg 7(6).

A decision can only be revised under para (1) on the basis of the circumstances at the time the decision had effect: para (10). Where a change of circumstances occurs after the decision took effect or the authority has evidence or information that indicates a change is due to take place, supersession under reg 7(2)(a) is appropriate instead. An application for revision on such grounds should be treated as an application for supersession under reg 7(6).

Late application for a revision

5.–(1) The time limit for making an application for a revision specified in regulation 4 may be extended where the conditions specified in the following paragraphs of this regulation are satisfied.

(2) An application for an extension of time (''the application'') shall be made in writing by the person affected by a relevant decision.

(3) The application shall–

(a) contain particulars of the grounds on which the extension of time is sought and shall contain sufficient details of the decision which it is sought to have revised to enable that decision to be identified;

(b) [² subject to regulation 4(4)] be made within 13 months of the date of notification of the decision which it is sought to have revised; and

(c) be delivered, by whatever means, to the relevant authority [¹ . . .].

(4) The application shall not be granted unless the person affected satisfies the relevant authority that–

(a) it is reasonable to grant the application;

(b) the application for revision has merit; and

(c) special circumstances are relevant to the application and as a result of those special circumstances it was not practicable for the application to be made within the time limit specified in regulation 4.

(5) In determining whether it is reasonable to grant the application for an extension of time, no account shall be taken of the following–

(a) that the person affected was unaware of or misunderstood the law applicable to his case (including ignorance or misunderstanding of the time limits imposed by these Regulations); or

(b) that a Commissioner or a court has taken a different view of the law from that previously understood and applied.

(6) In determining whether it is reasonable to grant an application, the relevant authority shall have regard to the principle that the greater the amount of time that has elapsed between the expiration of the time specified in regulation 4 for applying for a revision and the making of the application for an extension of time, the more compelling should be the special circumstances on which the application is based.

(7) An application under this regulation for an extension of time which has been refused may not be renewed.

Amendments

1.   Deleted by Sch 2 para 8(c) of SI 2002 No 1703 as from 30.9.02.

2.   Amended by reg 3(3) of SI 2005 No 337 as from 18.3.05.

Analysis
Reg 5 deals with extensions of time for making an application for a revision under reg 4(1)(a).
    It refers to the authority "determining" the question of whether an extension of time should be granted. The ruling is not a "decision" and no appeal to a tribunal lies against it. In *R(TC) 1/05*, Commissioner Turnbull said that an appeal tribunal does not have any jurisdiction to determine whether a decision maker ought to have exercised the power to extend time for applying for a revision and that a refusal or failure to extend the time was not a decision capable of being appealed. If, by the time an extension has been refused, fewer than 13 months have passed since the original decision, the person affected should consider applying to the tribunal for an extension of time in which to appeal against that decision. In some circumstances, the rules for admitting late appeals under reg 19 are more favourable to persons affected than the rules for a late revision in para (4). In particular, under reg 19(5)(a) a late appeal should be admitted, irrespective of the reasons – or lack of reasons – for the delay if it can be shown that the appeal itself has reasonable prospects of success. Even if it is necessary to rely upon the less favourable provisions in reg 19(5)(b), it may still be to the advantage of the person affected to have the decision taken by an independent tribunal chairman rather than an officer of the local authority. If, on the other hand, more than 13 months have passed since the original decision then the only remedy is judicial review. That reasoning was in the context of reg 4 of the SSCS D&A Regs, but would seem to apply four square to the same rule that reg 5 here embodies. What is appealable is the original decision made under Sch 7 para 2 or 4 CSPSSA, as revised under para 3.
    Paras (2) and (3) set out the procedural requirements. An application must be made in writing with sufficient detail of the decision under attack to enable it to be identified and the grounds on which the late application is made. It must be made within 13 months of the date of notification of the decision (subject to reg 4(4) which extends the normal time limit where a written statement of reasons is requested). See p956 on the meaning of "within". It must be delivered to the authority "by whatever means": see the commentary to reg 20(1).
    Paras (4) to (6) set out the criteria under which a late revision may be carried out. Under para (4), there are four principle conditions that must be met:
(1)   It must be reasonable to grant the application. Paras (5) and (6) are similar to reg 19(8) and (9): see the commentary to those provisions.
(2)   There must be merit in the application for revision. It need not be certain to succeed, but it must be shown that a serious issue is raised for consideration.
(3)   There are "special circumstances" relevant to the application. "Special circumstances" is not defined, but is likely to be interpreted in a similar way to "special reasons" under the former reg 78(3) HB Regs 1987. See the commentary to reg 9 SSCP Regs on p905.
(4)   It was not practicable, as a result of the circumstances, to make the application within the time limit. See the commentary to reg 19(6) which contains similar wording.
Para (7) appears to prevent a second bite at the cherry of an extension of time for applying for a revision. However, *CIS 93/1992*, held (at para 16) that reg 3(4) of the Social Security Adjudication Regulations 1986, which was in similar terms, "does not . . . prohibit a reconsideration by the chairman. It merely provides that a chairman is not *obliged* to consider a renewed application for extension of time". Although that was necessary to prevent repeated applications. If the chairman did consider a further application for extension of time after an earlier refusal of such extension, then s/he was entitled to do so and to change her/his mind if s/he wished. It is nevertheless important that all relevant matters are placed before the authority on the initial application.

Date from which a revision takes effect
6.   Where, on a revision under paragraph 3 of Schedule 7 to the Act, the relevant authority decides that the date from which a relevant decision ("the original decision") took effect was erroneous, the decision under that paragraph shall take effect on the date the original decision would have taken effect had the error not been made.

Analysis
The general rule is that a revised decision has effect from the same date as the original decision took effect, regardless of how long ago the original decision was made: Sch 7 para 3(3) CSPSSA. Where on a revision it is decided that the effective date of the original decision was wrong, the correct date will be taken.

Decisions superseding earlier decisions

7.–(1)   Subject to the provisions in this regulation, the prescribed cases and circumstances in which a decision may be made under paragraph 4 of Schedule 7 to the Act (decisions superseding earlier decisions) are as set out in paragraph (2).

(2)   The appropriate relevant authority may make a decision under paragraph 4 of Schedule 7 to the Act upon its own initiative or on an application made for the purpose on the basis that the decision to be superseded is a decision–

(a)   in respect of which–
  (i)   there has been a change of circumstances [³ since the decision had effect]; or
  (ii)   it is anticipated that a change of circumstances will occur;

(b)   which is erroneous in point of law or made in ignorance of, or was based upon a mistake as to, some material fact provided that the decision–
  (i)   cannot be revised on the basis of that error, ignorance or mistake; and
  (ii)   is not a decision prescribed in regulations under paragraph 6(2)(e) or (4)(a) of Schedule 7 to the Act;

(c)   which adopts a rent officer's determination [⁶ , board and attendance determination, broad rental market area determination or local housing allowance determination] and in consequence of a rent officer's redetermination, substitute determination, [⁶ substitute redetermination, board and attendance redetermination, substitute board and attendance determination, substitute board and attendance redetermination, amended broad rental market area determination or amended local housing allowance determination] made under the Rent Officers (Housing Benefit Functions) Order 1997 or the Rent Officers (Housing Benefit Functions) (Scotland) Order 1997 the amount which represents the rent for the purposes of calculating entitlement to benefit is reduced;

[³ (d)   of an appeal tribunal or of a Commissioner–
  (i)   that was made in ignorance of, or was based upon a mistake as to, some material fact; or
  (ii)   that was made in accordance with paragraph 17(4)(b) of Schedule 7 to the Act, in a case where paragraph 17(5) of that Schedule to the Act applies;]

(e)   which is prescribed in regulations made under paragraph 6(2)(e) or (4)(a) of Schedule 7 to the Act;

[² (f) . . .]

[¹(g)   which is affected by a decision of the Secretary of State that a sanctionable benefit payable to a claimant ceases to be payable or falls to be reduced under section 7 or 9 of the Social Security Fraud Act 2001 and for this purpose "sanctionable benefit" has the same meaning as in section 7 of that Act; or

(h)   which is affected by a decision of the Secretary of State that a joint-claim jobseeker's allowance ceases to be payable or falls to be reduced under section 8 of the Social Security Fraud Act 2001.]

[⁵ (i)   where–
  (i)   the claimant has been awarded entitlement to housing benefit or council tax benefit; and
  (ii)   subsequent to the first day of the period to which that entitlement relates, the claimant or a member of his family becomes entitled to an award of a relevant benefit within the meaning of section 8(3) of the 1998 Act or an increase in the rate of that relevant benefit.]

[⁹ (j)   where–
  (i)   the claimant or his partner makes, or is treated as having made, an election for a lump sum in accordance with—

        (aa)   paragraph A1 or 3C of Schedule 5 to the Contributions and Benefits Act;

        (bb)   paragraph 1 of Schedule 5A to that Act; or, as the case may be,

        (cc)   paragraph 12 or 17 of Schedule 1 to the Social Security (Graduated Retirement Benefit) Regulations 2005; or

    (ii)   such a lump sum is repaid in consequence of an application to change an election for a lump sum in accordance with regulation 5 of the Social Security (Deferral of Retirement Pensions, Shared Additional Pension and Graduated Retirement Benefit) (Miscellaneous Provisions) Regulations 2005[38] or, as the case may be, paragraph 20D of Schedule 1 to the Social Security (Graduated Retirement Benefit) Regulations 2005.]

[¹² (k) that housing benefit is payable to a claimant where that benefit is reduced under regulation 4 of the Pilot Scheme Regulations (reduction of benefit);

(l)   made under sub-paragraph (k) and the claimant is a person in hardship under regulation 5 of the Pilot Scheme Regulations (meaning of "person in hardship");

(m)   made under sub-paragraph (k) or (l) where section 130B(6) of the Contributions and Benefits Act applies so that the restriction period under that section stops running;

(n)   made under sub-paragraph (m) where section 130B(6) of that Act applies so that the restriction period starts running again.]

[⁷ (2ZA) An appropriate relevant authority may, upon its own initiative, make a decision under paragraph 4 of Schedule 7 to the Act in any case to which [¹⁰ regulation 14(1)(f) or (g) of the Housing Benefit Regulations or regulation 14(1)(f) or (g) of the Housing Benefit (State Pension Credit) Regulations] (requirement to refer to rent officers) applies.]

[⁸ [¹¹ (2A)]]

[⁶ (2B) The appropriate relevant authority may make a decision under paragraph 4 of Schedule 7 to the Act upon its own initiative on the basis that the decision to be superseded is a decision in respect of which the maximum housing benefit would cease to have effect by virtue of [¹⁰ regulation 11A of the Housing Benefit Regulations or regulation 11A of the Housing Benefit (State Pension Credit) Regulations(cases where maximum housing benefit expires)], but for the decision made in accordance with this regulation.

(2C) For the purposes of paragraph (2B) and paragraph (15) of regulation 8 "maximum housing benefit" means the maximum housing benefit determined in accordance with regulations made under section 130(4) of the Social Security Contributions and Benefits Act 1992.]

(3) The reference to a change of circumstances in paragraph (2)(a) shall include changes of circumstances specified in [¹⁰ regulation 88(3) of the Housing Benefit Regulations, regulation 69(3) of the Housing Benefit (State Pension Credit) Regulations, regulation 74(3) of the Council Tax Benefit Regulations or regulation 59(3) of the Council Tax Benefit (State Pension Credit) Regulations (changes of circumstances which do not need to be notified)].

(4) A decision which may be revised under regulation 4 may not be superseded under this regulation except where–

    (a)   circumstances arise in which the appropriate relevant authority may revise that decision under regulation 4; and

    (b)   further circumstances arise in relation to that decision which are not specified in regulation 4 but are specified in paragraph (2) or (5).

(5) Where the appropriate relevant authority requires further evidence or information from the applicant in order to consider all the issues raised by an application under paragraph (2) ("the original application"), the authority shall

notify the applicant that further evidence or information is required and, if it does so, the decision may be superseded–

(a)   where the applicant provides further relevant evidence or information within one month of the date of notification or such longer period of time as the appropriate relevant authority may allow; or

(b)   where the applicant does not provide such evidence or information within the time allowed under sub-paragraph (a), on the basis of the original application.

(6)   The appropriate relevant authority may treat an application for a revision or a notification of a change of circumstances as an application for a supersession.

(7)   An application under this regulation shall be made in writing and delivered, by whatever means, to the relevant authority [² . . .].

Modifications

Reg 7 is modified in respect of people to whom the Housing Benefit (Loss of Benefit) (Pilot Scheme) (Supplementary) Regulations 2007 SI No. 2474 apply (see p1144). The modifications apply until 31 October 2009 unless revoked with effect from an earlier date. They are shown in italics above.

Amendments

1.   Inserted by reg 9(b) of SI 2002 No 490 as from 1.4.02.
2.   Deleted by Sch 2 para 8(d) of SI 2002 No 1703 as from 30.9.02.
3.   Amended by reg 4(1) of SI 2003 No 1050 as from 5.5.03.
4.   Amended by reg 24(1) of SI 2003 No 1338 as from 6.10.03.
5.   Amended by reg 5(4) of SI 2003 No 2275 as from 6.10.03.
6.   Inserted by reg 16 of SI 2003 No 2399 as from a date specified in Sch 8 in relation to each particular authority.
7.   Inserted by reg 34(1) of SI 2004 No 14 as from 5.4.04.
8.   Revoked by reg 33 of SI 2004 No 14 as from 5.4.04.
9.   Inserted by reg 10(3) of SI 2005 No 2677 as from 6.4.06.
10.   Amended by reg 5 and sch 2 para 17(3) of SI 2006 No 217 as from 6.3.06.
11.   Revoked by reg 8 of SI 2007 No 2470 as from 24.9.07.
12.   Modified by reg 8(c) of SI 2007 No 2474 as from 1.11.07.

Definition

"family" – see reg 1(2) and s137(1) SSCBA 1992.

General Note

A decision can be superseded by a relevant authority on its own initiative or following an application made by a "person affected" by it (defined in reg 3). There must be grounds for supersession: paras (2), (2ZA) and (2B). See *Wood v Secretary of State for Work and Pensions* [2003] EWCA Civ 53, CA (reported as *R(DLA) 1/03*) for an authoritative analysis of the supersession scheme. *Wood* was further explained by the Tribunal of Commissioners in *R(IB) 2/04*. The commissioners ruled that: (i) there can be no supersession unless one of the grounds for supersession is actually found to exist; and (ii) that ground forms the basis of the supersession decision, in the sense that the original decision can only be altered in a way which follows from that ground. See also the commentary to reg 90 HB Regs on p395 for consideration of the question of whether a decision is rendered invalid by virtue of a failure to revise or supersede or where there is a defective attempt at revision or supersession.

There is no time limit for applying for a supersession. However, where the ground for supersession is a change in circumstances (para (2)(a)) and the superseding decision is to the advantage of the claimant, the change must be reported within one month of it occurring (or any longer period allowed by the authority) for full arrears of benefit to be paid. See regs 8(3) and reg 9 below.

Authorities may treat an application for a revision as one for supersession: para (6).

By virtue of reg 7(4), there is no power to supersede a decision that could be revised except where there are grounds for revision and further grounds for supersession that are not also grounds for revision – eg, a subsequent change of circumstances. In those circumstances, local authorities that receive an application to supersede a decision should first consider whether a revision under reg 4(1) is possible, including whether an extension of time for the application can be granted under reg 5. If this is not possible, a revision under any of the other grounds provided by reg 4 should be considered before consideration of any grounds for supersession under reg 7.

Commissioner Williams, applying *R(IB) 2/04*, said that appeal tribunals have the power to take any decision that the initial decision maker could have taken. This includes "considering in appropriate cases whether a claim should be considered as a request for a revision or supersession of a decision on a previous claim, subject to time limits and other statutory provisions": *CH 3009/2002* (para 21). The general limit is that this must be raised by the appeal or be a matter that the tribunal acting in its investigatory role decides it should consider. Interestingly, however, the same commissioner took a different view on the facts in *CIS 1675/2004*, because the errors in the appeal were so extensive that the only safe course was to declare that none of the "decisions" were operative, and the matter (which was an overpayment "decision") was referred back to the Secretary of State for fresh consideration.

Analysis
Paragraphs (2), (2ZA), (2B) and (2C): Grounds for supersession
Para (2) sets out the various bases on which a supersession of a decision can be made.

(1) Where there has been a change of circumstances since the decision had effect, or where such a change is expected in the future: sub-para (a). The words added with effect from 5 May 2003 confirm that a supersession of a decision can be made not only where there has been a change of circumstances since the decision was made, but also after it took effect – eg, after a tribunal's decision.

The wording omits the word "relevant" that was formerly present in reg 79(1)(a) HB Regs 1987, but nothing turns on this. A change of circumstances will be relevant if it is one that would affect the claimant's entitlement to HB, the extent of entitlement or to whom it should be paid. A change in the law is a relevant change of circumstances, but a court decision that changes the authority's view of the law is not: *Chief Adjudication Officer v McKiernon* [1993], 3 July, CA (*R(I) 2/94*). Such issues are dealt with under sub-para (b) or by way of revision. Furthermore, the fact that an officer of the authority disagrees with the inferences to be drawn from the evidence is not a relevant change of circumstances, but if new evidence shows that there has been a change in the claimant's status, there can be a supersession: *R(S) 4/86* (para 5). A change of circumstances includes the types of changes which need not be disclosed: para (3).

(2) Where the decision is based on incorrect facts or a mistake as to the law: sub-para (b). For the meaning of "material fact", see the commentary to reg 4(1)(b) above. This ground is subject to two qualifications. Head (i) prohibits its use if a revision is possible on the same grounds (see reg 4(1)(b) and (2)(b)) and head (ii) renders it non-available where no appeal lies against the decision (see the Schedule). In the latter case, sub-para (e) can apply instead.

(3) Where a rent officer's redetermination or other further determination has resulted in a *reduction* in "the rent for the purposes of calculating entitlement to benefit": sub-para (c). The latter phrase must refer to the maximum rent under reg 13 of both the HB and the HB(SPC) Regs. An increase in the maximum rent is grounds for a revision: see reg 4(3).

(4) Where a decision of a tribunal or commissioner was based on incorrect facts or was made pending a "test case" under Sch 7 para 17(4)(b) CSPSSA where the "test case" has subsequently been decided: sub-para (d). However, the latter of these grounds for supersession is not currently relevant as Sch 7 para 17 is not yet in force. It is understood that the Government does not intend to bring it into force.

(5) Where the decision is one against which there is no right of appeal: sub-para (e). See the Schedule for details of the decisions against which an appeal does not lie to a tribunal.

(6) Where a decision is affected by a DWP decision stopping or restricting benefit under section 7 or 9 of the Social Security Fraud Act 2001 (loss of benefit provisions): sub-paras (g) and (h).

(7) Where a local authority awards HB or CTB and, after the first day of the period of that award, the claimant or a member of her/his family becomes entitled to a "relevant benefit" or an increase in its rate: sub-para (i). "Relevant benefit" is defined in s8(3) SSA 1998 as any benefit under Parts II to V SSCBA 1992, JSA, PC, IS, a social fund grant for maternity or funeral expenses, child benefit and other benefits which may be prescribed. This is a welcome addition of what is known as a "qualifying benefit" rule. It allows HB and CTB awards to be increased and arrears to be paid back to the date of entitlement to a relevant benefit or an increase in its rate – eg, where an award of DLA is made to a claimant and thus a disability premium should be included in her/his HB and CTB applicable amount. Where the claimant or family member is awarded a relevant benefit or an increase in its rate for a period which includes the date the HB or CTB award took effect, the decision awarding HB or CTB can instead be revised under reg 4(7B). See the commentary to reg 4(7B) for the situation when there is no entitlement to HB and/or CTB until an award of a relevant benefit (or an increase in its rate) is made.

(8) Where the claimant or her/his partner deferred claiming Category A or B retirement pension, shared additional pension or graduated retirement benefit and originally opted (or is treated as opting) for

and is paid a lump sum or repays a lump sum because she opts instead for an increase in the pension: sub-para (j).

Para (2ZA) was inserted consequent to the abolition of benefit periods on 5 April 2004. A local authority may supersede a decision on its own initiative in any case where it is required to make an application to a rent officer for a determination under reg 14(1)(f) or (g) of either the HB or the HB(SPC) Regs, that is, where 52 weeks have elapsed since it last made an application. Para (2A) (which made identical provision for claimants of the qualifying age for state pension credit) was therefore revoked.

Paras (2B) and (2C) are inserted by reg 16 of SI 2003 No 2399 only in relation to Pathfinder Authorities who are administering the pilot local housing allowance scheme. Under reg 11A of both the HB and the HB(SPC) Regs as inserted by Sch 10 and Sch 9 of those regulations respectively, maximum HB expires annually. Para (2B) provides a ground for supersession to prevent this happening.

Paragraph (4): Relationship between revision and supersession

Para (4) provides that if a revision is possible as well as supersession, a revision must be carried out unless there are grounds for supersession which are not covered by the revision rules in reg 4 above. On receiving an application for revision or supersession, an authority should therefore first consider whether a revision under reg 4 is possible. It may be necessary to carry out a supersession at the same time as a revision, if some of the matters raised can be the subject matter of a revision but not all of them.

Paragraphs (5) to (7): Procedure

Paras (5) and (7) are in similar terms to reg 4(5) and (8). See the commentary to those provisions. Para (6) entitles an authority to treat an application for revision or a notification of a change in circumstances as being an application for a supersession.

Date from which a decision superseding an earlier decision takes effect

8.–(1)   A decision made by virtue of paragraph 4 of Schedule 7 to the Act (''the superseding decision'') shall take effect on a date other than the date on which it is made or the date on which the application was made in the cases or circumstances prescribed in paragraphs (2) to (7).

(2)   Subject to paragraphs (3) and (6), where the superseding decision is made on the ground that there has been, or it is anticipated that there will be, a change of circumstances, the superseding decision shall take effect on the date on which the change of circumstances is to take effect [[10] in accordance with–

(a)   regulation 79 of the Housing Benefit Regulations;

(b)   regulation 59 or 60 of the Housing Benefit (State Pension Credit) Regulations;

(c)   regulation 67 of the Council Tax Benefit Regulations; or

(d)   regulation 50 or 51 of the Council Tax Benefit (State Pension Credit) Regulations

as the case may be.]

(3)   For the purposes of determining the date on which a superseding decision is to take effect in accordance with paragraph (2), in a case where–

(a)   the change of circumstances is a change of circumstances that is required by regulations to be notified, other than any change of circumstances to which regulation 68A [[2] or 68B] of the Housing Benefit Regulations or regulation 59A [[2] or 59B] of the Council Tax Benefit Regulations applies; and

(b)   that change of circumstances is notified more than one month after it occurs, or such longer period as may be allowed under regulation 9; and

(c)   the superseding decision is advantageous to the claimant,

the date of notification of the change of circumstances shall be treated as the date on which the change of circumstances occurred.

(4)   Where the superseding decision is advantageous to the claimant and is made on the ground that the superseded decision was made in ignorance of, or was based upon a mistake as to, some material fact, the superseding decision shall take effect from the first day of the benefit week in which–

(a)   except where sub-paragraph (b) applies, the appropriate relevant authority first has information which is sufficient to show that the superseded decision was made in ignorance of, or was based upon a mistake as to, some material fact;

(b) where the superseding decision was made pursuant to an application, that application was received by the appropriate relevant authority.

(5) For the purpose of paragraphs (3)(c) and (4), the reference to the decision which is advantageous to the claimant includes a decision specified in regulation 17(2).

(6) A superseding decision made in consequence of a rent officer's redetermination, substitute determination, [⁶ substitute redetermination, board and attendance redetermination, substitute board and attendance determination, substitute board and attendance redetermination, amended broad rental market area determination or amended local housing allowance determination] under the Rent Officers (Housing Benefit Functions) Order 1997 or the Rent Officers (Housing Benefit Functions) (Scotland) Order 1997 shall take effect on the date on which a change of circumstances is to take effect in accordance with regulation 68 of the Housing Benefit Regulations as if that determination or redetermination were the relevant change of circumstances.

[⁷ (6A) Except in a case where entitlement to housing benefit ceases, where a rent officer has made a determination in exercise of the Housing Act functions pursuant to an application by a relevant authority under [¹⁰ regulation 14(1)(f) or (g) of the Housing Benefit Regulations or, as the case may be, regulation 14(1)(f) or (g) of the Housing Benefit (State Pension Credit) Regulations, any decision to which regulation 7(2ZA) applies which adopts that determination shall take effect from–

(a) in a case where the amount of the rent officer's determination has increased or remains unchanged, and–

    (i) rent is payable weekly or in multiples of weeks, the first day of the benefit week in which the day following the last day of the period mentioned in [¹⁰ regulation 14(1)(f) or (g) of the Housing Benefit Regulations or, as the case may be, regulation 14(1)(f) or (g) of the Housing Benefit (State Pension Credit) Regulations] occurs;

    (ii) rent is payable other than in accordance with head (i), the first day following the last day of the period mentioned in [¹⁰ regulation 14(1)(f) or (g) of the Housing Benefit Regulations or, as the case may be, regulation 14(1)(f) or (g) of the Housing Benefit (State Pension Credit) Regulations];

(b) in a case where the amount of the rent officer's determination has decreased, the first day of the benefit week following the date on which that determination was received by a relevant authority;

(6B) For the purposes of paragraph (6A) "Housing Act functions" has the same meaning as in regulation 2(1) of the Housing Benefit Regulations [¹⁰ or, as the case may be, regulation 2(1) of the Housing Benefit (State Pension Credit) Regulations.].]

(7) Where a decision is made superseding a decision of an appeal tribunal or of a Commissioner ("the appeal decision") which–

(a) was made in ignorance of, or was based upon a mistake as to, some material fact; and

(b) was more advantageous to the claimant than it would otherwise have been but for that ignorance or mistake,

that superseding decision shall take effect on the date on which the appeal decision took or was to take effect.

(8) A superseding decision made as a consequence of a determination which is a relevant determination for the purposes of paragraph 18 of Schedule 7 to the Act (restrictions on entitlement to benefit in certain cases of error) shall take effect from the date of the relevant determination.

[¹(9)   A decision to which regulation 7(2)(g) or (h) applies shall take effect from the first day of the disqualification period prescribed for the purposes of section 7 of the Social Security Fraud Act 2001.]

[³ (10)   Where the decision is superseded in accordance with regulation 7(2)(a)(i) and the relevant circumstances are that there has been a change in the legislation in relation to housing benefit or council tax benefit, the superseding decision shall take effect from the date on which that change in the legislation had effect.

(11)   Where a superseding decision is made in a case to which regulation 7(2)(d)(ii) applies the superseding decision shall take effect from the date on which the appeal tribunal or the Commissioner's decision would have taken effect had it been decided in accordance with the determination of the Commissioner or the court in the appeal referred to in paragraph 17(1)(b) of Schedule 7 to the Act.]

[⁸ [¹¹ (12)]]

[⁸ [¹¹ (13)]]

[⁵ (14)   Where the decision is superseded in accordance with regulation 7(2)(i) the superseding decision shall take effect from the date on which entitlement arises to the relevant benefit referred to in regulation 7(2)(i)(ii) or to an increase in the rate of that relevant benefit.]

[⁹ (14A)   Where a decision is superseded in accordance with regulation 7(2)(j), the superseding decision shall take effect from the day on which a lump sum, or a payment on account of a lump sum, is paid or repaid if that day is the first day of the benefit week but, if it is not, from the next following such day.]

[¹² *(14B)   A decision to which regulation 7(2)(k) applies shall take effect in accordance with regulation 4 of the Pilot Scheme Regulations;*

(14C)   A decision to which regulation 7(2)(l) applies shall take effect on the day the claimant first represented himself to be a person in hardship in accordance with regulation 5 of the Pilot Scheme Regulations.]

[⁶ (15)   A decision to which regulation 7(2B) applies shall take effect from the day immediately following the day on which the maximum housing benefit would have ceased to have effect by virtue of [¹⁰ regulation 11A of the Housing Benefit Regulations or, as the case may be, regulation 11A of the Housing Benefit (State Pension Credit) Regulations], but for the decision made in accordance with regulation 7(2B).]

Modifications

Reg 8 is modified in respect of people to whom the Housing Benefit (Loss of Benefit) (Pilot Scheme) (Supplementary) Regulations 2007 SI No. 2474 apply (see p1144). The modifications apply until 31 October 2009 unless revoked with effect from an earlier date. They are shown in italics above.

Amendments

1.   Inserted by reg 9(c) of SI 2002 No 490 as from 1.4.02.
2.   Amended by reg 28(a) of SI 2003 No 325 as from 6.10.03.
3.   Inserted by reg 4(2) of SI 2003 No 1050 as from 5.5.03.
4.   Amended by reg 24(2) of SI 2003 No 1338 as from 6.10.03.
5.   Amended by reg 5(5) of SI 2003 No 2275 as from 6.10.03.
6.   Inserted by reg 16 of SI 2003 No 2399 as from a date specified in Sch 8 in relation to each particular authority.
7.   Inserted by reg 34(2) of SI 2004 No 14 as from 5.4.04.
8.   Revoked by reg 33 of SI 2004 No 14 as from 5.4.04.
9.   Inserted by Reg 10(4) of SI 2005 No 2677 as from 6.4.06.
10.   Amended by reg 5 and sch 2 para 17(3) of SI 2006 No 217 as from 6.3.06.
11.   Revoked by reg 8 of SI 2007 No 2470 as from 24.9.07.
12.   Modified by reg 8(d) of SI 2007 No 2474 as from 1.11.07.

Analysis

Paragraph (1): The general rule

Para (1) reflects the general rule as set out in Sch 7 para 4(5) CSPSSA, namely that a supersession takes effect on the date that the superseding decision was made or the date of the application, as the case may be. Exceptions to the general rule are found in paras (2) to (15).

Paragraphs (2), (3), (6) and (10): Changes of circumstances

Para (2) provides that superseding decisions made on the ground of change of circumstances generally take effect from the date on which the change falls to be taken into account under reg 79 HB Regs, regs 59 or 60 HB(SPC) Regs, reg 67 CTB Regs or regs 50 or 51 CTB(SPC) Regs. See the commentary to those provisions. Similarly, under para (6), where a rent officer has made a redetermination or other altering decision, that will be treated as a change of circumstances and will have similar effect. Note that article 3 of the Civil Partnership (Pensions, Social Security and Child Support) (Consequential, etc. Provisions) Order 2005 (see p1095) disapplies para (2) and provides transitional provisions for setting the effective date of a supersession for some claimants who are members of a couple who live together as if they are civil partners on or after 5 December 2005, and have an award of HB or CTB on 5 December 2005.

Where a change of circumstances is one which someone is required to report (other than one under the regulations listed), para (3) effectively sets a one-month time limit for reporting the change, if the resulting supersession decision is to the advantage of the claimant. Note that regs 68A HB Regs and reg 59A CTB Regs were revoked in September 2002 subject to savings and transitional protection. Note also that by reg 2(4) of the HB&CTB(CP) Regs, the references to reg 68B HB Regs and reg 59B CTB Regs should be read as reg 60 HB(SPC) Regs and reg 51 CTB(SPC) Regs.

If such a change is reported within one month, the decision takes effect in accordance with para (2). The day of the change will be excluded, so a change occurring on 25 May and notified on 25 June is notified within the time period. Where notification of a change is made more than a month after it occurs and the new decision is advantageous to the claimant, the date of notification is treated as the date the change occurred: para (3). In such a case, this will normally be less beneficial to the claimant. An "advantageous" decision includes where it falls within reg 17(2): see para (5). The one-month period can be extended under reg 9. Note also that it was held in *CIS 1277/2002* (paras 13-15) that "notified to an appropriate office" in reg 7(2)(a)(ii) of the SSCS D&A Regs could include a case where a different office of the DWP passed the information to the office dealing with the relevant claim as well as a case where the claimant made the notification. Since that provision is in different form to reg 8(2), it is open to argument as to whether that analysis can be applied here, although there is nothing explicit to prevent its application.

Para (10) provides that where the change of circumstances is that there has been a change in the legislation in relation to HB or CTB, the superseding decision takes effect from the date the change in legislation has effect. Note that article 3 of the Civil Partnership (Pensions, Social Security and Child Support) (Consequential, etc. Provisions) Order 2005 (see p1095) disapplies para (10) and provides transitional provisions for setting the effective date of a supersession for some claimants who are members of a couple who live together as if they are civil partners on or after 5 December 2005, and have an award of HB or CTB on 5 December 2005.

Paragraph (4): Decisions based on incorrect facts and supersession advantageous to the claimant

In such a case, the superseding decision has effect from the first day of the benefit week in which an application for a supersession was received *or* the authority had the relevant information justifying the supersession before it.

An "advantageous" decision includes where it falls within reg 17(2): see para (5).

Paragraphs (6A) and (6B): Supersession where rent officer determination required

Paras (6A) and (6B) deal with supersessions made under reg 7(2ZA) above. Except where entitlement to HB ceases, where a rent officer has made a determination following a local authority application under reg 14(1)(f) or (g) of either the HB or the HB(SPC) Regs, a supersession decision which adopts that determination takes effect as follows:

(1)   If the determination is the same or has increased and rent is payable weekly or in multiplies of weeks, it takes effect from the first day of the benefit week which includes the day after the end of the period covered by the previous determinations: sub-para (a)(i).

(2)   If the determination is the same or has increased and rent is payable at intervals of other than a week, it takes effect from the day after the end of the period covered by the previous determinations: sub-para (a)(ii).

(3)   If the determination has decreased, it takes effect from the first day of the week after the local authority receives it: sub-para (b).

Paragraph (7): Erroneous appeal decisions

If a Tribunal or Commissioner's decision was based on incorrect facts and was more advantageous to the claimant than it would otherwise have been, a decision superseding it takes effect from the date on which the appeal decision took (or was to take) effect.

Note that if an *authority's* decision was based on incorrect facts and was more advantageous to the claimant, it can be revised at any time under reg 4(2)(b), taking effect from the date of the original decision: reg 6.

Paragraph (8): Supersession following a "test case"

If a decision is being superseded because of a decision by a commissioner or a court in a "test case" (a relevant determination for the purposes of Sch 7 para 18 CSPSSA) the supersession is effective from the date of the commissioner's or court's decision.

Paragraph (9): Supersession where decision affected by "loss of benefit" provisions

Where a decision is affected by a DWP decision stopping or restricting benefit and is superseded under reg 7(2)(g) or (h), the supersession is effective from the first day of the disqualification period.

Paragraph (11): Supersession where decision made pending a "test case"

The ground for supersession in reg 7(2)(d)(ii) is not currently relevant for the reasons stated in the commentary to that regulation.

Paragraph 14: Supersession on entitlement to a "relevant benefit" or an increase in its rate

Where a decision is superseded under reg 7(2)(i), the superseding decision has effect from the date of entitlement to the relevant benefit or the increase in its rate.

Paragraph 14A: Supersession on opting for or repaying a lump sum on deferring claiming pension

Where a decision is superseded under reg 7(2)(j), the superseding decision has effect from the day on which a lump sum (or a payment on account of a lump sum) is paid or repaid if that day is the first day of the benefit week. If not, it takes effect from the first day of the following benefit week.

Effective date for late notification of change of circumstances

9.–(1)   For the purposes of making a decision under paragraph 4 of Schedule 7 to the Act a longer period of time may be allowed for the notification of a change of circumstances in so far as it affects the effective date of the change where the conditions specified in the following provisions of this regulation are satisfied.

(2)   An application for the purposes of paragraph (1) shall–

(a)   include particulars of the change of circumstances and the reasons for the failure to notify the change of circumstances on an earlier date; and

(b)   be made within 13 months of the date on which the change occurred.

(3)   An application for the purposes of paragraph (1) shall not be granted unless the appropriate relevant authority is satisfied that–

(a)   it is reasonable to grant the application;

(b)   the change of circumstances notified by the applicant is relevant to the decision which is to be superseded; and

(c)   special circumstances are relevant and as a result of those special circumstances it was not practicable for the applicant to notify the change of circumstances within one month of the change occurring.

(4)   In determining whether it is reasonable to grant the application, the appropriate relevant authority shall have regard to the principle that the greater the amount of time that has elapsed between the date one month after the change of circumstances occurred and the date the application for a superseding decision is made, the more compelling should be the special circumstances on which the application is based.

(5)   In determining whether it is reasonable to grant an application, no account shall be taken of the following–

(a)   that the applicant was unaware of, or misunderstood, the law applicable to his case (including ignorance or misunderstanding of the time limits imposed by these Regulations); or

(b)   that a Commissioner or a court has taken a different view of the law from that previously understood and applied.

(6)   An application under this regulation which has been refused may not be renewed.

Analysis

Reg 9 deals with the circumstances in which a notification of a change of circumstances made more than one month after it occurs may nonetheless be treated as if made in time. In this situation a superseding decision takes effect as set out in reg 8(2) rather than in reg 8(3), to the advantage of the claimant. The structure of reg 9 is similar to that of reg 5.

Para (2) deals with applications for an extension of time to report a change of circumstances and is similar to reg 5(3), save that the operative decision need not be identified and there is no provision for the place at which disclosure must be made (which is dealt with by reg 88 HB Regs, reg 69 HB(SPC) Regs, reg 74 CTB Regs and reg 59 CTB(SPC) Regs). An application must be made within 13 months of the date the change of circumstances occurred.

Para (3) is similar to reg 5(4), save that there is no need for the application to have merit – instead, the change of circumstances must be relevant. Practicability "involves a test of feasibility, not a test of desirability or convenience or anything of that sort": *CH 282/2006* applying *Singh v Post Office* [1973] ICR 437 at 440. Moreover, as the impracticability must result from the special circumstances, those circumstances must in some way relate to or affect the practicability of reporting the change of time within one month.

Paras (4), (5) and (6) are comparable to paras (6), (5) and (7) of reg 5 respectively.

Notice of a decision against which an appeal lies

10.–(1) A person affected who has a right of appeal against a relevant decision shall be given written notice–

(a) of the decision against which the appeal lies;

(b) in a case where that notice does not include a statement of reasons for the decision, that he may request the relevant authority to provide him with a written statement of the reasons for that decision; and

(c) of his right of appeal against that decision.

(2) Where a written statement of the reasons for the decision is not included in the written notice of the decision and is requested under paragraph (1)(b), the relevant authority shall, so far as practicable, provide that statement within 14 days.

Definition

"person affected" – see reg 3.

Analysis

If there is a right of appeal against a decision, written notice of it must be given of it to a person affected by the decision. It must contain information as specified in paras (b) and (c). "Person affected" is defined in reg 3. The obligation in reg 10(1) is additional to those set out in Sch 9 HB Regs, Sch 8 HB(SPC) Regs, Sch 8 CTB Regs and Sch 7 CTB(SPC) Regs.

If a request for a written statement of reasons is made (where not already provided), the local authority must provide one within 14 days if this is practicable. The onus to provide a statement of reasons within 14 days if "practicable" is a heavy one. Days between the date a request is received by the authority and the date on which it is provided are ignored when calculating the one-month time limits for seeking a revision and appealing: see commentary to regs 4(4) and 18(2).

[¹ Correction of accidental errors

10A.–(1) Accidental errors in a relevant decision, or a revised decision, or the record of such a decision, may be corrected by the relevant authority at any time.

(2) A correction made to a relevant decision, or a revised decision, or the record of such a decision, shall be deemed to be part of the decision, or of that record, and the relevant authority shall give a written notice of the correction as soon as practicable to the claimant.

(3) In calculating the time within which an application can be made under regulation 4(1)(a) for a relevant decision to be revised, or the time within which an appeal may be brought under regulation 18(1), there shall be disregarded any day falling before the day on which notice was given of a correction of the decision or to the revision or record thereof under paragraph (2).

Definition

"relevant decision" – see reg 1(2) above and Sch 7 para 19(2) CSPSSA.

Amendment

1. Inserted by reg 25 of SI 2002 No 1379 as from 20.5.02.

General Note

Accidental errors in decisions can be corrected under reg 10A. Written notice of the correction must be given to the claimant as soon as it is practicable. In calculating the time limit for seeking a revision under reg 4(1)(a) or appealing against the decision under reg 18(1), days before the day on which notice is given of the correction must be ignored.

PART III

Suspension and Termination of Benefit and Other Matters

Cases where a relevant authority may suspend

11.–(1)   A relevant authority may suspend, in whole or in part–

(a)   any payment of housing benefit or council tax benefit;

(b)   any reduction (by way of council tax benefit) in the amount that a person is or will become liable to pay in respect of council tax,

in the circumstances prescribed in paragraph (2).

(2)   The prescribed circumstances are where–

(a)   it appears to the relevant authority that an issue arises whether–

(i)   the conditions for entitlement to housing benefit or council tax benefit are or were fulfilled; or

(ii)   a decision as to an award of such a benefit should be revised under paragraph 3 of Schedule 7 to the Act or superseded under paragraph 4 of that Schedule;

(b)   an appeal is pending against–

(i)   a decision of an appeal tribunal, a Commissioner or a court; or

(ii)   a decision given by a Commissioner or a court in a different case,

and it appears to the relevant authority that if the appeal were to be determined in a particular way an issue would arise whether the award of housing benefit or council tax benefit in the case itself ought to be revised or superseded; or

(c)   an issue arises whether–

(i)   an amount of housing benefit is recoverable under section 75 (overpayments) of the Administration Act or regulations made under that section; or

(ii)   an excess payment of council tax benefit under section 76 of the Administration Act or regulations made under that section has occurred.

General Note

Reg 11 is made under Sch 7 para 13 CSPSSA (see p170). Reg 12 sets out the situations in which a suspension must be lifted.

Analysis

Para (1) specifies that the power to suspend may be exercised in the whole amount of the benefit payable or only part thereof. Payments of HB (whether or not made to the claimant) and CTB may be suspended. A reduction in council tax may also be suspended, but a claimant will only in this instance become liable to pay an increased amount of council tax where a fresh bill is sent to her/him: reg 18 Council Tax (Administration and Enforcement) Regulations 1992.

Suspension is discretionary, and the discretion must be exercised reasonably even if one of the specified circumstances exists. Thus if, for example, an issue arises as to whether a few hundred pounds of benefit was overpaid and the claimant has capital of that sum, it might not be reasonable for the authority to suspend ongoing entitlement to benefit under para (2)(c) if it could readily be recovered. However, as there is no right of appeal against a decision to suspend (see para 5 of the Schedule) the claimant's only remedy against an unreasonable suspension is judicial review. It is often quicker, easier and less expensive to seek to provide the authority with the information and evidence it needs to resolve the question that has arisen.

Para (2) specifies the circumstances in which a suspension can be made. There is a degree of overlap between the provisions.

(1)   There may be a suspension where current or past entitlement is in issue, or when a revision or supersession is being considered: sub-para (a). It need not be clear that an existing decision was

incorrect; all that is required is that "an issue arises" through a reasonable doubt existing as to the correctness of a decision. The power to suspend where an issue arises cannot be used merely to check the accuracy of an existing award where there are no particular grounds for doubting that it is correct. In *CH 2995/2006*, the commissioner stated:

"26. The second of the two situations I mentioned earlier as the ones that I presume were envisaged by Parliament is where a local authority has no particular doubt, or only a weak doubt, about the claimant's entitlement to . . . benefit but, as a matter of good administration, wishes the claimant to provide information and evidence in order, in effect, to update the information and evidence provided on the original claim and check its accuracy. Parliament seems to have expected that there would be no suspension of payment while that information was awaited but, if it was not forthcoming within the time allowed, there would be a suspension and, if the information was still not forthcoming, there would eventually be a termination of entitlement".

(2) Pending appeals may give rise to a suspension under sub-para (b).
The appeals referred to in head (i) must, by implication, apply to appeals involving the claimant whose benefit is suspended. Note that the appeal must be pending: see Sch 7 para 13(3) CSPSSA on p170 for the extended definition of "pending". It includes cases where an application for leave to appeal has been lodged or where the time limit for applying for leave or lodging an appeal has not expired. It does not, however, appear to extend to a situation where a statement of reasons has been requested under reg 53 SSCS D&A Regs, though it may be arguable that sub-para (a)(i) can apply in such a situation. It would not be reasonable to continue a suspension where a decision had been taken by an authority not to pursue an appeal.
Under head (ii), appeals in other cases may also result in a suspension. However, this power only applies to an appeal *from* a commissioner or a court. It does not, therefore, apply where an appeal is pending *to* the commissioner. For discussion of "different case", see Sch 7 para 13(4) CSPSSA and the commentary on p170.

(3) Suspected overpayments may also give rise to a right to suspend: sub-para (c). Again, "an issue arises" means it need not be clear that an overpayment has occurred. All that is necessary is reasonable grounds to suspect that too much benefit has been paid.

Making or restoring of payments or reductions suspended

12.–(1) Subject to paragraph (2), the prescribed circumstances for the purposes of paragraph 13(1)(c) of Schedule 7 to the Act (the subsequent making, or restoring, of any or all of the payments or reductions so suspended) are–

(a) in a case to which regulation 11(2)(a) applies, where the relevant authority is satisfied that the benefit so suspended is properly payable and no outstanding issues remain to be resolved;

(b) in a case to which regulation 11(2)(b) applies, an appeal is no longer pending and the benefit suspended remains payable following the determination of that appeal.

(2) Where any of the circumstances in paragraph (1) is satisfied, the relevant authority shall, so far as practicable, make the payment, or as the case may be, restore the reduction within 14 days of the decision to make or restore that payment or reduction.

Analysis

Reg 12 deals with the circumstances in which a suspension must be lifted under Sch 7 para 13(1)(c) CSPSSA. It is not well drafted.

Para (1) first, by sub-para (a), requires that accrued arrears be paid where any issues referred to in reg 11(2)(a) have been resolved. It should be noted that there must be "no outstanding issues" and so if an authority has been satisfied that its initial concerns had no basis but further issues have arisen as a result of its inquiries, the suspension can remain in force.

Sub-para (b) deals with suspension pending appeals. For the question of when an appeal is "pending", see Sch 7 para 13(3) CSPSSA on p170 and reg 11(2)(b) above. The phrase "determination of that appeal" is inapt in the context of a suspension having been imposed during the period when the time limit for applying for leave or appealing has yet to expire but no application or leave has actually been made. In that situation, it is suggested that the "determination" of the appeal occurs once a final decision is taken not to pursue an appeal.

Para (2) requires an authority to make good a suspension which is brought to an end under para (1). Curiously, there is no specific provision governing suspensions under reg 11(2)(c) for suspected overpayments. However, if a suspension is revoked, it is suggested that the ordinary provisions as to payment in the HB and HB(SPC) Regs and the CTB and CTB(SPC) Regs would then become enforceable by a claimant by way of a debt action or a claim for judicial review.

Suspension for failure to furnish information etc.

13.–(1) The relevant authority may suspend in whole or in part–

(a) any payment of housing benefit or council tax benefit;

(b) any reduction (by way of council tax benefit) in the amount that a person is or will become liable to pay in respect of council tax,

in relation to persons who fail to comply with the information requirements (as defined in paragraph 14 of Schedule 7 to the Act) as provided for in regulations made pursuant to section 5(1)(hh) and 6(1)(hh) of the Administration Act (person required to satisfy the information provisions).

(2) For the purposes of section 5(1)(hh) in so far as it applies to housing benefit and section 6(1)(hh) of the Administration Act the prescribed persons are–

(a) a person in respect of whom payment of benefit or a reduction has been suspended under regulation 11(2)(a);

(b) a person who has made an application for a decision of the relevant authority to be revised or superseded;

(c) a person in respect of whom a question has arisen in connection with his award of benefit and who fails to comply with the requirement in [¹ regulation 86 of the Housing Benefit Regulations, regulation 67 of the Housing Benefit (State Pension Credit) Regulations, regulation 72 of the Council Tax Benefit Regulations or regulation 57 of the Council Tax Benefit (State Pension Credit) Regulations] to furnish information or evidence needed for a determination whether a decision on an award should be revised under paragraph 3 or superseded under paragraph 4 of Schedule 7 to the Act.

(3) The relevant authority shall notify any person to whom paragraph (2) refers of the requirements of this regulation.

(4) A person to whom paragraph (2) refers must–

(a) furnish the information or evidence needed within a period of–

(i) one month beginning with the date on which the notification under paragraph (3) was sent to him; or

(ii) such longer period as the relevant authority considers necessary in order to enable him to comply with the requirement; or

(b) satisfy the relevant authority within the period provided for in paragraph (4)(a) that–

(i) the information or evidence so required does not exist; or

(ii) it is not possible for him to obtain the information or evidence so required.

(5) Where a person satisfies the requirements in paragraph (4), the relevant authority shall, so far as practicable, make, or as the case may be restore, the payment within 14 days of the decision to make or restore that payment.

Amendment

1.   Amended by reg 5 and Sch 2 para 17(3) of SI 2006 No 217 as from 6.3.06.

Analysis

Reg 13 provides a power to suspend which is additional to those set out in reg 11. It deals with cases in which a person is required to provide information to an authority. The relationship between regs 11 and 13 was explained by Commissioner Rowland in *CH 2995/2006* as follows:

"21.   The 2001 Regulations make adequate, albeit complicated, provision for the . . . [situation]. . . where a local authority considers that there may be a question as to the claimant's continued entitlement to benefit and perhaps also as to his or her entitlement in the past. In those circumstances, payments may be suspended under regulation 11(1) and (2)(a) while investigations are carried out. When the investigations have been concluded, the local authority must either restore the payments under regulation 12 or else revise or supersede the decision awarding benefit. If, as part of the investigation, the local authority asks the claimant for further information or evidence, the case falls within regulation 13(2)(a) and the claimant must be given the notice required by regulation 13(3) and in particular must be informed of the time within which the information must be provided under regulation 13(4)(a). If the claimant then fails to provide the information within the time allowed under regulation 13(4)(a), the local authority may, instead of restoring the payments or revising or superseding the award on any other ground, terminate the award under regulation 14 with effect from the date of the suspension under regulation 11(1) and (2)(a)."

The commissioner also notes (at para 24) that paras (2) to (4) "apply where there has been a suspension under reg 11(1) and (2)(a) just as much as where there has been a suspension under regulation 13(1)".

Paras (1) and (2) set out the situation in which the power to suspend may be exercised. The two provisions in the SSAA referred to give power to require information during the currency of a claim. The extended versions of reg 86(1) HB Regs, reg 67(1) HB(SPC) Regs, reg 72(1) CTB Regs and reg 57(1) CTB(SPC) Regs are made under ss5(1)(hh) and 6(1)(hh) SSAA respectively.

In order for a suspension to be lawful, the authority must show that the person of whom information is required falls into one of the categories in para (2).

The first two categories are self-explanatory. However, as noted by the commissioner in *CH 2995/2006* (at paras 25-27), the drafting of para (2)(c) is flawed. When para 2(c) is read together with the requirement in para (1) that the person should "fail to comply with the information requirements . . . *as provided for in regulations made pursuant to section 5(1)(hh) and 6(1)(hh) of the Administration Act*" (emphasis added) it is arguable that – at least prior to the consolidation of the HB and CTB Regs on 6 March 2006 – a person does not fall within para (2)(c) until s/he has failed to comply with *two* requests for information, the first under reg 86 HB Regs etc and the second under para (4)(a). This is because the predecessor regulations to reg 86 HB Regs etc were made under ss5(1)(h) and 6(1)(h) SSAA and not under ss5(1)(hh) and 6(1)(hh). Certainly, there cannot be any suspension under para (1) until there has been at least one failure to comply with a request for information (although suspension may still be possible under reg 11). Note that a refusal to allow a home visit does not amount to a failure to comply with an information requirement (see *CH 2995/2006* (para 35)) although in some circumstances, it might give rise to a question about entitlement that would justify suspension under reg 11. The same would, presumably, be true of a failure to attend an interview under caution. **Paras (3) to (5)** deal with the procedure for operating the regulation. The first step is for the authority to give the person notice under para (3) of "the requirements of this regulation". Those requirements are set out in para (4) and are as follows:

(1)   **The information or evidence that is needed**. It is suggested that the information or evidence required by the authority must be specified in sufficient detail for the person to know what is required and for it to be possible to demonstrate whether or not the requirement has been complied with for the purposes of reg 14. For example, telling the person to telephone the benefits office is not, without more, a request for information or evidence.

(2)   **The time limit for the provision of the evidence**. The clamant must be given a "firm deadline" for the provision of the information (*CH 2995/2006* para 43) and that deadline must be at least one month after the date on which the notification is sent (para (4)(a)). Despite the fact that the one-month time limit is explicitly set out in the regulations, many local authorities purport to impose shorter periods in practice. Time limits of 7 and 14 days that have no basis in law and appear to have been plucked from the air by optimistic benefit officers – or, more probably, by the companies responsible for their computer software – are particularly common. A failure to specify a time limit of at least one month will invalidate any subsequent termination of benefit under reg 14.

The notice should also advise the person of the possibility of applying for an extension of time under para (4)(a)(ii) if s/he needs longer than a month in which to comply with the requirement.

(3)   **Evidence that does not exist or cannot be obtained**. As an alternative to providing the information within the one-month (or longer) time limit, the person may instead seek to persuade the authority that that information does not exist or that it is not possible for her/him to obtain it. The standard-form notices issued by many authorities fail to mention this alternative and it is suggested that, at least in a case where the evidence actually does not exist or cannot be obtained, that failure would invalidate any subsequent termination. Alternatively, it could be argued that a person who does not provide information that does not exist or that s/he cannot obtain does not "fail" to comply with an information requirement for the purposes of reg 14(1) but merely omits to comply with that requirement. The word "failure" carries connotations of breach of duty (see, eg, *B v Secretary of*

State for Work and Pensions [2005] EWCA Civ 929, [2005] 1 WLR 3796 (reported as *R(IS) 9/06*) and tribunals should be slow to find that a person is under a duty to perform the impossible.

Unfortunately, it is not all that uncommon to find authorities purporting to impose information requirements with which claimants obviously cannot comply: an example is demanding that a claimant who has just started work and is paid monthly should produce her/his "three most recent pay slips" within a month.

Paras (3) and (4) do not require an authority to tell the person that her/his entitlement to benefit may be terminated under reg 14 if the information requirement is not satisfied. However, it is good practice to do so. By definition, the person's benefit has already been suspended (which a claimant is likely to see as "stopped"). S/he may therefore not understand the serious consequences of failing to comply unless these are explained. In those circumstances, it is in the authority's interests as well as the claimant's to give the explanation: a claimant who understands the nature to the penalty for non-compliance is more likely to comply.

In *CH 2995/2006*, the commissioner left open the possibility that some failures to comply with para (3) might not be fatal to a subsequent termination (para 43). However, it is suggested that that possibility ought not to be accepted. As the commissioner acknowledges, reg 14 imposes a procedural penalty for failing to provide information on a person who may well be otherwise entitled to benefit. In general terms, all para (3) requires is that, before such a penalty is imposed, the authority must tell the person in sufficient detail what s/he has to do and when s/he has to do it by. It is very difficult to imagine cases in which it would be just to impose a penalty where that information had not been given.

Paras (3) to (5) deal with the procedure for operating the regulation. The first step is notification of the requirement to provide information under para (3). Only if that warning is given is the duty in para (4) to supply the information within the period specified in sub-para (a) triggered. There is a welcome escape clause specifically provided in para (4)(b) for cases where the authority is asking the impossible. The authority must be persuaded within the period specified in para (4)(a) that the information required does not exist or cannot be obtained. The most common example of this is where a landlord refuses to supply a claimant with evidence such as proof of rent. Another concerns the income of non-dependants. Authorities should always be willing to consider other alternative means of proof where a claimant has difficulty obtaining the primary evidence required.

Under para (5), once the person has satisfied the requirements of para (4), the suspension imposed under reg 13 must be lifted.

Termination in cases of a failure to furnish information

14.–(1)   A person in respect of whom payment of benefit or a reduction has been suspended–

(a)   under regulation 11 and who subsequently fails to comply with an information requirement; or

(b)   under regulation 13 for failing to comply with such a requirement,

shall cease to be entitled to the benefit from the date on which the payments or reduction were so suspended, or such earlier date on which entitlement to benefit ceases.

(2)   Paragraph (1) does not apply–

[¹ (a)   subject to sub-paragraph (b), before the end of the period under regulation 13(4) for the provision of information;]

(b)   where payment of benefit or a reduction has been suspended in part under regulation 11 or regulation 13.

Amendment

1.   Substituted by reg 4 of SI 2005 No 2894 as from 10.11.05.

Analysis

Under reg 14, a claimant ceases to be entitled to benefit if, following suspension under regs 11 or 13, s/he fails to comply with a request for information.

Decisions made by virtue of reg 14 are "decisions superseding earlier decisions" within Sch 7 para 4 CSPSSA: *CH 402/2007*. It follows that they can be revised under Sch 7 para 3 CSPSSA and that they carry a right of appeal to a tribunal: *CH 402/2007* and *CH 2995/2006*. That right is expressly preserved by para 5 of the Sch to these regulations. Given the decision of the ECtHR in *Tsfayo v United Kingdom* (application no: 60860/00) [2006], 14 November, unreported, ECtHR, any other arrangement would be an infringement of the claimant's Convention Rights.

It also follows that any person affected by the decision to terminate must be properly notified of that decision and of her/his right to appeal against it. In the absence of such a notification, the time for bringing an appeal will not normally begin to run.

The view expressed in previous editions that termination is "a third mechanism for altering decisions to add to revision and supersession" is wrong: *CH 2995/2006*, para 22. So is the DWP advice in Circular HB/ CTB A2/2006 that "decisions given under Regulations 11-14 of the HB/CTB Decision and Appeals Regulations are made outside the normal revision/supersession rules" and instead are "administrative decisions" that do not carry a right of appeal: *CH 402/2007* (in particular para 24). The word "termination" (which only appears in the heading to reg 14, and not in the operative words) describes the *outcome* of the process established by regs 11, 13 and 14 and not the process itself.

The scope of the appeal against a decision under reg 14 is less clear. It is certainly open to the claimant to argue that s/he did not "cease to be entitled to benefit" because the original decision to suspend was invalid, or because mandatory procedural requirements (particularly in reg 13) have not been observed, or because s/he did not in fact fail to comply with an information requirement. It is suggested, however, that where a claimant accepts (or the tribunal finds) that that the procedure in regs 11-14 was validly operated, and that the claimant did not produce the necessary information and evidence at the time, the tribunal has no power to reinstate benefit on the basis that, by the time of the appeal hearing, the necessary information and evidence has been supplied. This is because, whatever might have been the case if the claimant had produced the information or evidence on time, the fact that s/he did not do so caused her/his entitlement to cease from the date on which payments were suspended. The position is therefore different from an appeal against a decision where the authority does not rely on the Part III procedure, but instead draws an adverse inference against the claimant and supersedes on the basis that entitlement has ended on substantive, rather than procedural, grounds: *CH 3736/2006* para 27.

It is suggested that the only remedy open to a claimant whose entitlement has been validly terminated under reg 14 but who is subsequently in a position to provide the information and evidence requested, is to ask the authority to extend time for the production of that information and evidence under reg 13(4)(a)(ii) and then to revise the termination decision. A refusal to revise the termination decision may, in some circumstances, give rise to a technical right of appeal against that decision but that right may be of little practical value because the tribunal has no jurisdiction to interfere with the authority's refusal to extend time under reg 13: see para 5 of the Schedule.

Para (1). Termination can take place in two circumstances. First, there are cases where there has been a suspension under reg 11 and then a failure to comply with a requirement to supply information: see the definition of "information requirement" in Sch 7 para 14(3) CSPSSA on p170. The latter must have taken place "subsequently". If a reg 11 suspension is imposed as a result of a failure to provide information (when reg 13 could have been used instead), then a further chance would have to be given to the claimant before reg 14 can operate.

Secondly, there are cases where a requirement imposed by reg 13 is not complied with.

It is important for authorities to ensure (and, on appeal, for tribunals to satisfy themselves) that all the procedural safeguards (particularly in reg 13(3)) have been complied with. A failure to give a valid notice under reg 13(3) will almost always be fatal to a termination under reg 14. In particular, the claimant must be given a "firm deadline" by which to provide the evidence and information: *CH 2995/2006*, paras 43 and 44. See further the commentary to reg 13.

CH 2995/2006 also confirms (para 41) that termination under reg 14 cannot be effective from any date before the date on which the decision to suspend was made. Para (1) appears to allow the possibility that termination might take effect from "such earlier date on which entitlement to benefit ceases" but those words are either meaningless or *ultra vires*. From a formal point of view, the provision is circular: stripped of irrelevant words it states that: "A person . . . shall cease to be entitled to the benefit . . . from such earlier date on which entitlement to benefit ceases". That proposition conveys no useful information whatsoever. Secondly, if entitlement to benefit ceases from some "earlier date" then that can only be because there are substantive grounds on which to revise or supersede the decision awarding benefit with effect from that earlier date. An authority that had such grounds would not need to rely upon reg 14 in the first place. Finally, reg 14 is made under para 15 Sch 7 CSPSSA, which only empowers the Secretary of State to make regulations that bring entitlement to HB to an end "not earlier than the date on which payments were suspended". It follows that, if reg 14 did permit a termination from an earlier date, it would be *ultra vires*: *CH 3736/2006* (para 27). At best, the words "or such earlier date on which entitlement to benefit ceases" should be interpreted as confirming that the possibility of a termination under reg 14 does not prevent an authority from making a substantive revision or supersession with effect from an earlier date where there are grounds upon which to do so.

An example demonstrates this. Benefit is awarded on 1 February, but on 1 June a question arises about the award, a reg 11 suspension is imposed and the claimant is required to supply information. By 1 September, the claimant has failed to comply with the information requirement. Entitlement can be terminated from 1 June, but in order to deprive the claimant of the award from any earlier, grounds for revision or supersession must be shown.

Para (2) prevents termination of an award in two situations: where the suspension was only partial: sub-para (b), and before the end of the period specified in reg 13(4) for the provision of information: sub-para (a). Although an authority is not obliged to accept information late, it is suggested that it will rarely, if ever, be appropriate for an authority to proceed to terminate entitlement in circumstances in which the information requirement is complied with a few days late. This will be a trap for many authorities which were prone to reject or 'cancel' claims automatically if a claimant was even one day late with supplying information.

Decisions involving issues that arise on appeal in other cases

15.–(1)   For the purposes of paragraph 16(3)(b) of Schedule 7 to the Act (prescribed cases and circumstances in which a decision may be made) the prescribed cases and circumstances are those in which the claimant would be entitled to benefit to which the decision which falls to be made relates, even if the appeal in the other case referred to in paragraph 16(1)(b) of that Schedule were decided in the way which is most unfavourable to him.

(2)   For the purposes of paragraph 16(3)(b) of Schedule 7 to the Act (prescribed basis) the prescribed basis on which the relevant authority may make a decision is as if–

(a)   the appeal in the other case referred to in paragraph 16(1)(b) of that Schedule 7 had already been determined; and

(b)   the appeal had been decided in the way which is most unfavourable to the claimant.

Analysis

Sch 7 para 16 CSPSSA generally excuses an authority from making a decision where there is an appeal pending in a test case. Sch 7 para 16(3) gives a discretion to issue a decision where regulations so prescribe. Reg 15 exercises that power. If it chooses to issue a decision, the authority must make its decision on the assumption that the appeal is decided in the way most unfavourable to the claimant: para (2)(b).

The discretion conferred by Sch 7 para 16(3) and reg 15 must be exercised reasonably. Where it is clear that the claimant is entitled to a substantial award of HB or CTB whatever the outcome of the appeal, it would not be reasonable to refuse to make a decision. Persons affected will, however, have to ensure that they then appeal against the authority's decision in order to protect their interests.

PART IV

Rights of Appeal and Procedure for Bringing Appeals

Decisions against which no appeal lies

16.–(1)   No appeal shall lie against a decision specified in the Schedule to these Regulations.

(2)   An appeal made against a decision specified in the Schedule to these Regulations may be struck out in accordance with the provisions in regulation 23 of these Regulations and regulation 46 of the Decisions and Appeals Regulations 1999.

(3)   In this regulation references to a decision include references to a determination embodied in or necessary to a decision.

Analysis

See the commentary to the Schedule for those decisions which are excluded from the appeal regime. All other decisions may be appealed, but note that an appeal may only lie against an "outcome decision" (see the commentary to Sch 7 para 6(1) CSPSSA). Reg 16(3) reflects the distinction between decisions and determinations referred to in that commentary. The effect of para (3) is to confirm that it is not possible to appeal against a determination embodied in a decision which falls within the Schedule.

Reg 16(2) confirms that appeals against decisions in the Schedule may be struck out. See also the commentary to regs 46 and 47 SSCS D&A Regs on pp925 and 926.

Appeal against a decision which has been revised

17.–(1)   An appeal against a decision of the relevant authority shall not lapse where the decision is revised under paragraph 3 of Schedule 7 to the Act before the appeal is determined and the decision as revised is not more advantageous to the appellant than the decision before it was so revised.

(2)   For the purposes of this regulation, a decision which is more advantageous includes any decision where–

(a)   any housing benefit or council tax benefit paid or any reduction in the amount that a person is liable to pay in respect of council tax is greater or is awarded for a longer period in consequence of a decision made under paragraph 3 of Schedule 7 to the Act;

(b)   the amount of housing benefit or council tax benefit in payment or reduction in the amount a person is liable to pay in respect of council tax would have been greater but for the operation of the Administration Act in suspending the payment of, or disqualifying a claimant from receiving, some or all of the benefit;

(c)   as a result of the decision, a denial of, or disqualification for the receiving of, housing benefit or council tax benefit is lifted, wholly or in part; or

(d)   in consequence of the revised decision, housing benefit or council tax benefit paid is not recoverable by virtue of or as a consequence of section 75 or 76 of the Administration Act, or an amount so recoverable is reduced.

(3)   Where a decision as revised under paragraph 3 of Schedule 7 to the Act is not more advantageous to the appellant than the decision before it was revised, the appeal shall be treated as though it had been brought against the decision as revised.

(4)   The appellant shall have a period of one month from the date of notification of the decision as revised to make further representations as to the appeal.

(5)   After the expiration of the period specified in paragraph (4), or within that period if the appellant consents in writing, the appeal to the appeal tribunal shall proceed except where, in the light of further representations from the appellant, the relevant authority further revises its decision and that decision is more advantageous to the appellant than the decision before it was revised.

Analysis

Sch 7 para 3(6) CSPSSA provides that if a decision is revised while an appeal against it is pending, the appeal lapses except in the circumstances prescribed by regulations. Reg 17 is made under that power.

Para (1) sets out the general rule, which is that an appeal will only lapse if the decision is "more advantageous" to the claimant than the appealed decision was. The claimant has a fresh right of appeal against the revised decision: see Sch 7 para 6(1) CSPSSA. However, it is inevitable that some claimants will find the procedures confusing and will assume that their appeal is still pending. Authorities ought to seek to emphasise that the appeal is no longer proceeding in their correspondence with a claimant in these circumstances. The time limit for appealing runs from the date of notification of the new decision: reg 18(3).

If the fresh appeal is late then, as long as 13 months have not passed since the revision, an extension of time is possible under reg 19(5). If the fresh appeal has reasonable prospects of success then the tribunal chairman (but not the local authority) can grant an extension under reg 19(5)(a) without going into why the appeal is late. In those cases where it is necessary to consider the appellant's reasons for lateness (ie, under reg 19(5)(b)) the fact (if it be) that the local authority had failed to advise the appellant that the previous appeal had lapsed and/or of the need to make a fresh appeal would probably amount to a "special circumstance" within reg19(6)(b). If, however, the local authority had correctly advised the appellant but the appellant failed to make the appeal on time because s/he misunderstood, or disbelieved, that advice, that would not be a circumstance that could be taken into account (see reg 19(9)(a)).

In some circumstances, particularly where an appeal has already been part-heard and adjourned and where the revision will not give the appellant everything s/he seeks from the appeal, it will often be preferable for the authority to make a supplementary submission to the tribunal, asking the tribunal to substitute the proposed new decision rather than to issue the revised decision itself so as to cause the appeal to lapse and force the appellant to re-start the process from the beginning.

Para (2) offers a partial definition of "more advantageous". It only "includes" the four comparisons set out in sub-paras (a) to (d) and so if other changes make a decision better for a claimant, they may also fall within para (1). Some revisions may amount to a curate's egg and result in changes both for the good and bad from the claimant's perspective. In such circumstances, the best approach is to look at the result in pure money terms: is the claimant entitled to and/or receiving more money as a result of the revised decision?

Sub-para (a) deals with the most common situation, which is an increase in the amount of benefit payable or period for which it is awarded. Sub-para (b) deals with the same situation where the claimant's right to receive benefit is suspended. Revisions which lift disqualifications and reduce or eliminate recoverable overpayments are also "more advantageous".

Para (3) confirms that where the appeal does not lapse, it continues as if it was against the original decision as revised.

Paras (4) to (5) provide that an appeal will proceed after the claimant has a period of one month to make further representations. It is suggested that it will be open to a claimant to raise new issues for consideration if s/he wishes. At the end of the one-month period (or earlier if the appellant agrees in writing), the appeal must proceed unless the decision is further revised and is then more advantageous.

Time within which an appeal is to be brought

18.–(1) Subject to the following paragraphs and [¹ regulations 10A(3) and] 19, an appeal which lies from a relevant decision must be brought within one month of the date of notification of that decision.

(2) For the purposes of calculating the period in paragraph (1), where a written statement is requested under regulation 10, no account shall be taken of any period beginning with the day on which the relevant authority received the request for a statement and ending with the day on which that statement was provided to that person.

(3) Where the relevant authority–

(a) revises a decision under paragraph 3 of Schedule 7 to the Act;

(b) following an application for a revision under regulation 4, does not revise; or

(c) supersedes a decision under paragraph 4 of Schedule 7 to the Act,

subject to paragraph (2), the period of one month shall begin to run from the date of notification of that revision or supersession, or following an application for a revision, the date the authority issues a notice that it is not revising the decision.

(4) Where a dispute arises as to whether an appeal was brought within the time limit specified in this regulation, the dispute shall be referred to, and be determined by, a legally qualified panel member.

(5) The time limit specified in this regulation for bringing an appeal may be extended in accordance with regulation 19.

Definition

"relevant decision" – see reg 1(2) above and Sch 7 para 19(2) CSPSSA.

Amendment

1. Amended by reg 26 of SI 2002 No 1379 as from 20.5.02.

Analysis

Para (1) specifies the general time limit within which an appeal must be made. For the scope of the right of appeal, see Sch 7 para 6 CSPSSA and reg 16 and the Schedule to these regulations.

An appeal must be made "within one month" of the date of notification, which is defined in reg 2(1) as being the date on which the notification of the decision was sent to the person affected (not the day on which it was received). See the commentary to reg 4(1)(b) on the meaning of "within". If an accidental error in a decision has been corrected under reg 10A, any day falling before the day on which notice of the correction is given must be ignored in calculating the one-month period.

If the notification of the decision is invalid because it fails to comply with the requirements of reg 90 and Sch 9 HB Regs, and the comparable provisions in the HB(SPC), CTB and CTB(SPC) Regs (as to which see the Analysis to reg 90) then the time for appealing does not start to run until a valid notification is issued: *CP 4479/2000* (paras 22-23).

Paras (2) and (3) modify the time limit in certain cases. First, under para (2), the clock in respect of the one-month time limit for appealing effectively stops where a written statement of reasons is requested under reg 10(2). The period from the date on which the request is received until the date on which the statement of reasons is "provided to" the person affected must be ignored in calculating whether an appeal is in time. This is potentially productive of uncertainty. For example, if a decision is issued on 10 April, and a statement of reasons is requested on 10 May, it is unclear whether the time limit expires 20 days after 10 May (because the statement of reasons was requested 20 days prior to the expiry of the time limit on 10 May) or 21 days after that date (because May has one more day than April). The former is probably correct, but the position is unclear. It is suggested that the phrase "provided to" requires that the statement should have actually been received by the recipient and that the one-month period will not start running until that date. Something is not "provided" to a person until it is actually in the possession of that person.

Although a person affected may believe a written statement of reasons has not been included with a decision or that what has been provided is inadequate, the local authority could disagree. If there is any doubt about the situation, it is advisable to presume the clock has not stopped and to appeal within the time limit as if it has not done so.

Note that the time limit is modified by reg 20(6).

A Tribunal of Commissioners ruled in *R(IS) 15/04* that the extension of time under regulation 18(3)(b) only applies to applications for revision under reg 4(1)(a), (4) and (5), and does not apply to 'any time' revision requests under regulation 4(2). The Court of Appeal in *Beltekian v Westminster City Council and Secretary of State for Work and Pensions* [2004] EWCA Civ 1784, 8 December 2004 (reported as *R(H) 8/05*) followed the reasoning in *R(IS) 15/04* and decided that the extension of time for appealing against the original decision by reg 18(3), where there has been a refusal to revise, only applies where the request for revision was made under reg 4(1) and not under reg 4(2). Accordingly, where a claimant has applied for an 'any time' revision on the ground of official error and the authority decides not to revise, the time for appealing against the original decision cannot be extended.

Para (4) provides that where there is a dispute about whether the appeal is in-time, the local authority must refer it to the tribunal for decision. Local authorities are occasionally reluctant to do this. It is unclear whether the principle in *R(H) 1/07* applies in such cases or whether the appellant's only remedy is judicial review.

In practice, a tribunal chairman who decides under para (4) that an appeal is out-of-time will immediately go on to consider whether an extension of time should nevertheless be granted under reg 19. For a discussion of whether there is a further appeal to the commissioner against either decision see the commentary to reg 19(10) below and to Sch 7 para 8(1) CSPSSA and, in particular, *Secretary of State for Work and Pensions v Morina and Borrowdale* [2007] EWCA Civ 749.

Para (5) permits an extension of the time limit under reg 19.

Late appeals

19.–(1) Subject to the following paragraphs, the time limit referred to in regulation 18 may be extended only if the conditions set out in this regulation are satisfied.

(2) No appeal shall be brought more than one year after the expiration of the last day for appealing under regulation 18.

(3) An application for an extension of time within which an appeal may be brought ("an application") shall be determined by a legally qualified panel member [¹, except that where the relevant authority considers that the conditions in paragraphs (5)(b) to (9) are satisfied the relevant authority may grant the application].

(4) An application shall contain particulars of the grounds on which the extension of time is sought, including details of any relevant special circumstances for the purposes of paragraph (7).

[² (5) An application for an extension of time shall not be granted unless–
(a) the panel member is satisfied that, if the application is granted, there are reasonable prospects that the appeal will be successful; or
(b) the panel member or the relevant authority, as the case may be, is satisfied that it is in the interests of justice for the application to be granted.]–

(6) For the purposes of paragraph (5)(b), it is not in the interests of justice to grant an application unless the panel member [³ or the relevant authority] is satisfied that–
(a) any of the special circumstances specified in paragraph (7) are relevant to the application; or
(b) some other special circumstances exist which are wholly exceptional and relevant to the application,

and as a result of those special circumstances, it was not practicable for the appeal to be made within the time limit referred to in regulation 18.

(7)   For the purposes of paragraph (6)(a), the special circumstances are–

(a)   the applicant or a partner or dependant of the applicant has died or suffered serious illness;

(b)   the applicant is not resident in the United Kingdom; or

(c)   normal postal services were disrupted.

(8)   In determining whether it is in the interests of justice to grant the application, [⁴ regard shall be had] to the principle that the greater the amount of time that has elapsed between the expiration of the time within which the appeal is to be brought under regulation 18 and the making of the application for an extension of time, the more compelling should be the special circumstances on which the application is based.

(9)   In determining whether it is in the interests of justice to grant an application, no account shall be taken of the following–

(a)   that the applicant was unaware of or misunderstood the law applicable to his case (including ignorance or misunderstanding of the time limits imposed by these Regulations); or

(b)   that a Commissioner or a court has taken a different view of the law from that previously understood and applied.

(10)   An application under this regulation which has been refused may not be renewed.

(11)   The panel member who determines an application shall record a summary of his decision in such written form as has been approved by the President.

(12)   As soon as practicable after the decision is made, a copy of the decision shall be sent or given to the principal parties to the proceedings.

Definition

"partner" – see reg 1(2).

Amendments

1.   Amended by reg 27(a) of SI 2002 No 1379 as from 20.5.02.
2.   Substituted by reg 27(b) of SI 2002 No 1379 as from 20.5.02.
3.   Amended by reg 27(c) of SI 2002 No 1379 as from 20.5.02.
4.   Amended by reg 27(d) of SI 2002 No 1379 as from 20.5.02.

Analysis

The scope for bringing late challenges to decisions is restricted by this regulation and by reg 5 above. Ensuring compliance with time limits is important.

Paragraph (2): The absolute time limit

Para (2) sets the absolute time limit for an appeal as one year after the expiry of the time limit in reg 18. No appeal may therefore be brought after that date in any circumstances.

Paragraphs (3) and (10) to (12): Decision-making on late appeals

Under para (3), the question of whether an extension of time should be granted must be determined by a legally qualified tribunal panel member unless the local authority considers that the conditions in paras (5)(b) to (9) are satisfied. In this case the authority can grant the application.

If the application is determined by a panel member, under paras (11) and (12), a summary of the decision must be prepared and sent to the "principal parties" as defined in reg 1 and Sch 7 para 7(4) CSPSSA. The rules are silent as to notification where an application is determined by a local authority.

Para (10). See the commentary to reg 5(7) above.

In *R(TC) 1/05*, Commissioner Turnbull held (at para 21) that there was no appeal to the commissioner against a refusal by a tribunal chairman to extend time for a late appeal under the equivalent provision of the SSCS D&A Regs. See, however, the commentary to Sch 7 para 8(1) CSPSSA and *Secretary of State for Work and Pensions v Morina and Borrowdale* [2007] EWCA Civ 749.

Paragraphs (5) to (9): Criteria for late appeals

Para (5) sets out the grounds for the admission of a late appeal. There are two possibilities:

(1)   A legally qualified tribunal panel member is satisfied that the appeal has reasonable prospects of success *or* it is in the "interests of justice" to grant an extension of time.

(2)   The local authority is satisfied that it is in the "interests of justice" to grant an extension of time.
It is clear from the word "or" following sub-para (a) that it is sufficient to satisfy one of the two criteria in para (5), although the standard form used by the Tribunals Service fails to make this clear.

As an application must be delivered to the local authority under reg 20, it follows that the local authority must first decide whether to grant an extension of time. If the authority does not grant an extension, it must pass the application to the Tribunals Service for a legally qualified panel member to decide. If the local authority grants an extension, section 4 of the authority's submission to the tribunal should include a statement to the effect that the time for appealing has been extended, and by whom (see Code of Appeals Procedure para 2060).

"reasonable prospects of success" is not a particularly high threshold. It need not be shown that the appeal is more likely than not to succeed, merely that there is a substantial chance. Thus a one-third chance of success might well be regarded as "reasonable". A useful rule of thumb might be whether a reasonable lay adviser would advise pursuing an appeal to a tribunal, given the fact that an appellant is not under any risk of having to pay legal costs.

"the interests of justice". The meaning of this phrase is extensively modified by paras (6) to (9). However, once any relevant modifications made by those rules have been taken into account, it will still be necessary for the local authority or panel member to stand back and consider the overall interests of justice. Given the highly deserving nature of the "special circumstances" that need to be shown under paras (6) and (7), however, it will be a rare case where such circumstances exist and yet an extension of time is refused.

Paras (6) and (7) set up an exclusionary rule. An appellant must bring her/himself within either sub-para (a) or (b) in para (6). Effectively, this means that one of the following must be shown:

(1)   The appellant, her/his partner or a dependant has died or suffered serious illness: paras (6)(a) and (7)(a). Whether an illness is "serious" is a question of fact and degree. "Partner" is defined in reg 1(2).

(2)   The appellant is not resident in the United Kingdom: paras (6)(a) and (7)(b). On first impression, this is an odd provision in regulations dealing with benefits where, to be entitled at all, the claimant must (for HB) occupy a dwelling in Great Britain as her/his home (s130(1)(a) SSCBA) or (for CTB) is "liable to pay council tax [a tax only levied on dwellings in the UK] for a dwelling of which he is a resident" (s131(3)(a) SSCBA). It is suggested that the provision might apply to landlords who are resident abroad but in receipt of direct payments of HB or where an appellant was resident in the UK at the time of the events that gave rise to the appeal but has since become resident elsewhere. The view expressed in previous editions of this book, that the provision applies whenever the appellant is not physically present in the UK at the relevant time, cannot be correct. If that was what was intended by the regulation, it is what it would have said. Absence from the country may nevertheless amount to a special circumstance within para (6)(b), as to which see below.

(3)   Normal postal services were disrupted: paras (6)(a) and (7)(c). Strike action need not be shown; it will be sufficient if there is some delay in a decision letter or a letter of appeal reaching its destination. The caselaw on reg 19(7)(c) SSCS D&A Regs, which is in similar terms, will also be relevant here. See, in particular, the decisions of Commissioner Angus in *CIS 4901/2002* and Deputy Commissioner Poynter in *CJSA 3960/2006*. For postal delays over the Christmas period see *R(IS) 16/04*.

(4)   There are some other special circumstances which are "wholly exceptional" and "relevant to the application": para (6)(b). "Wholly" emphasises the need for the circumstances to be unusual in nature, though not necessarily unique to the appellant. "Relevant" must simply mean that the circumstances are relevant to the question of whether it is in the interests of justice to admit the appeal. "Special circumstances" are not defined, but is likely to be interpreted in a similar way to "special reasons" under the former reg 78(3) HB Regs 1987. See the commentary to reg 9 SSCP Regs.

Once it is shown that the appellant can bring her/himself within one of the four situations above, s/he must also show that it was not practicable for the appeal to be made within the reg 18 time limit as a result of the circumstances. "Practicable" is a stiffer test than "reasonably practicable", but the phrase "as a result" does not require that the circumstances should be the sole cause of the delay, though it will have to be a substantial cause. Questions of reasonableness may well enter into consideration – eg, was it reasonable to expect an appellant to deal with an appeal even though her/his partner was in hospital? In considering such matters, it may be legitimate for the local authority or panel member to consider other deserving factors even where these do not fall within any of the categories set out above.

It is suggested that there is no rigid rule that every single day of delay after the one-month period must be explained, in the way that good cause for a late claim must be shown. All that is necessary is that the additional period of delay was broadly caused by the special circumstances on which reliance is placed. Some support for this approach can be seen in para (8).

Para (8) requires the common-sense approach that the later the appeal is, the more compelling the special circumstances must be for it to be regarded as being in the interests of justice to admit the appeal.

Para (9) requires two factors, which would otherwise be relevant, to be left out of account. First, under sub-para (a), ignorance of, or mistakes as to, the law on the part of the appellant (or, it is suggested, her/his adviser) cannot be taken into account. This includes ignorance of the time limit. The rule applies, on the face of it, irrespective of the reasonableness of the mistake. However, it is suggested that the view expressed in previous editions that it might prevent an extension of time even where the appellant's mistake arose from incorrect advice given by a local authority officer is itself mistaken. In such a case, the incorrect advice would be the cause of the delay, would amount to a special circumstance under para (6)(b) and would not be excluded from consideration under para (9).

Second, under sub-para (b), the fact that a court or commissioner has interpreted the law in a different way than previously "understood and applied" cannot be taken into account. This aims to prevent a torrent of late appeals relying on a favourable "test case" decision of a commissioner or a court. However, "understood and applied" will cause difficulties. Understood and applied by whom? It is likely that the phrase refers to the views of the local authorities and DWP practice, though this cannot be regarded as certain. And what about cases where a provision is not being applied consistently?

In view of the potential difficulties caused by para (9), it may be worth recalling that paras (6)(b) and (7)–(9) have no application where there are reasonable prospects of success under para 6(a). As local authorities cannot extend time under para (6)(a), an appellant who is refused an extension of time by the authority should always insist that the application be referred to the tribunal under para (3)

Making of appeals and applications

20.–(1)   An appeal or application for an extension of time must–

(a)   be in writing on a form approved for the purpose by the relevant authority or in such other format as the relevant authority may accept;

(b)   be signed by the person who has a right of appeal under paragraph 6(3) of Schedule 7 to the Act;

(c)   be delivered, by whatever means, to the relevant authority [¹ . . .];

(d)   contain particulars of the grounds on which it is made; and

(e)   contain sufficient particulars of the decision or subject of the application to enable that decision or subject of the application to be identified.

(2)   A form which is not completed in accordance with the instructions on the form, except where paragraph (3) applies, does not satisfy the requirements of paragraph (1), and may be returned by the relevant authority to the sender for completion in accordance with those instructions.

(3)   Where the relevant authority is satisfied that the form, although not completed in accordance with the instructions on it, includes sufficient information to enable the appeal or application to proceed, it may treat the form as satisfying the requirements of paragraph (1).

(4)   Where an appeal or application is made in writing otherwise than on the approved form (''the letter''), and the letter includes sufficient information to enable the appeal or application to proceed, the relevant authority may treat the letter as satisfying the requirements of paragraph (1).

(5)   Where the letter does not include sufficient information to enable the appeal or application to proceed, the relevant authority may request, in writing, further particulars.

(6)   Where a person to whom a form is returned or from whom further particulars are requested duly completes and returns the form or sends the further particulars and the form or particulars, as the case may be, are received by the relevant authority within–

(a)   14 days of the date on which the form was returned to him, the time for making the appeal shall be extended by 14 days from the date on which the form was returned;

(b)   14 days of the date on which the relevant authority's request was made, the time for making the appeal shall be extended by 14 days from the date of the request;

(c)   such longer period as the relevant authority may direct, the time for making the appeal shall be extended by a period equal to that longer period directed by the relevant authority.

(7)   Where a person to whom a form is returned or from whom further particulars are requested does not complete and return the form or send further particulars within the period of time specified in paragraph (6)–

(a)   the relevant authority shall forward a copy of the form, or as the case may be, the letter, together with any other relevant documents or evidence to a legally qualified panel member; and

(b)   the panel member shall determine whether the form or the letter satisfies the requirements of paragraph (1), and shall inform the relevant authority and appellant or applicant of his determination.

(8)   Where–

(a)   a form is duly completed and returned or further particulars are sent after the expiry of the period of time allowed in accordance with paragraph (6); and

(b)   no decision has been made under paragraph (7) at the time the form or the further particulars are received by the relevant authority,

the form or further particulars shall also be forwarded to the legally qualified panel member who shall take into account any further information or evidence set out in the form or further particulars.

(9)   The relevant authority may discontinue action on an appeal where the appeal has not been forwarded to the clerk to an appeal tribunal or to a legally qualified panel member and the appellant or an authorised representative of the appellant has given written notice that the appellant does not wish the appeal to continue.

Amendment

1.   Deleted by Sch 2 para 8(e) of SI 2002 No 1703 as from 30.9.02.

General Note

Reg 20 contains the rules for making appeals as well as applications for extensions of time under reg 19 above. For convenience, "appeal" will be taken to refer to such applications in these notes. The requirements for a valid appeal are found in para (1). Where an appeal does not meet the requirements or does not contain sufficient information, paras (2) to (8) allow an authority to give an appellant an opportunity to put things right. It is important to note that although a local authority can treat an appeal as validly made under paras (3) and (4), it is only a legally qualified tribunal panel member who can reject an appeal as invalidly made: para (7)(b).

There is no provision in the regulations for dealing with the process by which local authorities refer appeals to the Tribunals Service save where a tribunal member is required to rule on the validity of an appeal under paras (7) and (8). In particular, there is no time limit within which this is required to be done. However, the Local Government Ombudsman has made it clear in *Complaint No 01/C/13400 against Scarborough BC* that authorities should aim to refer all appeals to the Tribunals Service within 28 days. The power to revise a decision under reg 4(1)(c) is still available to authorities after an appeal has been referred to the Tribunals Service, until such time as the appeal has been determined.

In *CH 3497/2005*, there had been serious delay in the local authority's referral of a claimant's appeals to the Appeals Service (now the Tribunals Service). Deputy Commissioner Mark pointed out that under Article 6 of the European Convention on Human Rights, a claimant is entitled to have her/his appeal heard within a reasonable time by an appeal tribunal and that this could be particularly important in HB appeals, where delay could cost claimants their homes. Under s6(1) HRA 1998, it is unlawful for a public authority to act in a way which is incompatible with a Convention right. By s6(6), "an act" includes a failure to act – eg, a failure to refer an appeal to the Tribunals Service in a reasonable time. The Deputy Commissioner said at para 6 of his decision:

"In any event, it is wholly unacceptable to the proper operation of the system of appeals in housing benefit and council tax benefit appeals that delays of this sort should occur. If a local authority receives an appeal, it must be processed promptly and passed to the Appeals Service without delay. This applies also in cases where there is an issue which requires to be dealt with by a legally qualified panel member under regulation 20(7) or (8) of the 2001 Regulations."

What if a local authority does not refer an appeal to the Tribunals Service? In *R(H) 1/07* Commissioner Jacobs considered whether, in such a case, a tribunal has power to deal with the appeal until it is referred. The local authority argued that where an appeal is not referred to the Tribunals Service, the claimant had to apply for judicial review of the local authority's failure or refusal to refer. The commissioner disagreed. He said that the usual principle is exclusivity of jurisdiction; if an issue is allocated to a judicial body, only that body has jurisdiction over it. A tribunal has power to determine whether it has jurisdiction and any challenge should be by appeal to the commissioners and from them to the Court of Appeal. Reg 20 does not deal with a challenge by the local authority to the tribunal's jurisdiction. However, its structure is relevant to whether a tribunal can deal with an appeal when it has not been referred to it by the local authority. The commissioner said:

"31. . . .

    First, so long as regulation 20(1) is satisfied, the appeal tribunal has jurisdiction. Second, the only role of the local authority is to receive the appeal documents and to ensure, as far as it can, that they contain the necessary information. It has no power to decide whether the information provided is sufficient. That is for the legally qualified panel member and there is an express duty to refer the issue to that member. The local authority's function is essentially administrative.

33.   If the appeal were lodged with the tribunal, there would be no problem. However, as the appeal is lodged elsewhere, there has to be a procedure by which it comes to the notice of the clerk or the tribunal. It is possible for legislation expressly to provide for an appeal that is lodged with one body to be referred to the tribunal. In the case of housing benefit, there is no express provision. The referral is but one of the many necessary administrative steps that have to be taken to bring a case before a tribunal. Others include the notification of sittings to the members of a tribunal and the photocopying and sending of the papers to the members. Most of these tasks are not spelt out in the legislation. They are assumed as necessary to allow the statutory powers and duties of the tribunal to operate. In legal terms, that assumption takes effect by implication, either as a general duty and power or as a series of specific duties and powers. It is not rational to interpret the legislation as making the tribunal's jurisdiction depend on a particular exercise of these administrative tasks. That would be incompatible with their function, which is to ensure that the tribunal established by the legislation can discharge its statutory function and do so efficiently and effectively. They are supportive not jurisdictional.

34.   In other words, an administrative task need not be performed by a particular person or in a particular way. So long as there is an appeal that satisfies the conditions of regulation 20(1), the tribunal has jurisdiction to deal with any issues that arise in respect of it, regardless of how they are brought to the tribunal's attention. This does not mean that the parties are free to disregard the usual procedures at will. Claimants cannot simply bypass the local authority and lodge appeals with the tribunal. Likewise, they cannot usually expect the tribunal to deal with a case before the local authority has had a chance to prepare the submission and assemble the papers for the parties and the tribunal. But what the tribunal is free to do is to allow matters to be handled differently if circumstances require it. The circumstances of this case did require it for two reasons. First, the local authority was refusing to refer the cases to the tribunal on the basis of an issue which the tribunal had (perhaps exclusive) jurisdiction to decide. Second, the local authority was trying to force the claimant to embark on an expensive legal procedure, which was risky in that the Administrative Court might not accept jurisdiction."

Analysis

Paragraph (1): The requirements of a valid appeal

Para (1) sets out the requirements for a valid appeal. These are:

(1)   The appeal must be made in writing: sub-para (a). It must either be on an "approved" form which should be available on application from the local authority or may be made in some other format "as the relevant authority may accept". This refers to documents accepted under para (4) below. The discretion to accept appeals in a different form should normally be exercised where all the required details are provided: see the commentary to para (2) below.

(2)   The document is to be "signed by" the person who has a right of appeal: sub-para (b). A "person affected" by a decision has a right of appeal under Sch 7 para 6 CSPSSA. See the commentary to reg 3 above for who is a "person affected". The decision in *R v Lambeth LBC ex p Crookes* [1998] 31 HLR 59, QBD may suggest that sub-para (b) cannot be met by a signature of a solicitor. However, the correctness of *Crookes* on this point has arguably been seriously undermined by the recent decision of the Privy Council in *General Legal Council ex parte Basil Whitter v Barrington Earl Frankson* [2006] UKPC 42, 27 July, and its holding that in *re Prince Blucher [1931] 2 Ch D 70* (an authority on which *Crookes* strongly relied) was wrongly decided.

(3)   The document must be delivered to the authority: sub-para (c). The document may be delivered "by whatever means", which includes personal delivery (for which a receipt should be required), post of any kind, fax, or by email or completion of an electronic form on a website if such facilities exist.

(4)   Particulars of the grounds of appeal must be given: sub-para (d). It is unrealistic to expect persons affected, at least those that are unrepresented, to identify all the relevant points with precision. Simply to say "I want to appeal" is insufficient, but authorities should not adopt an unduly strict approach. For example, "I disagree with your decision that I have no liability for rent" is probably sufficient, since that is a question of fact, although authorities may well want to seek further details of the challenge on an informal basis in order to respond to the appeal. However, appellants and their representatives are advised to remember that under Sch 7 para 6(9(a) CSPSSA, the tribunal "need not consider any issue that is not raised by the appeal". See the commentary to that provision. It may therefore be important to raise all possible issues at this stage.

(5)   Details of the decision against which the appeal is made must be given: sub-para (e). These must be sufficient to enable the decision or subject of the application to be identified.

Paragraphs (2) and (3): Appeals made on a form

Para (2) gives an authority a power to return an appeal form to a person affected for completion where it is not completed in accordance with the instructions on the form. Alternatively, if the authority takes the view that sufficient information has been given, it may simply accept the appeal under para (3). Although both these provisions confer a power to take those steps rather than impose a duty to do so, an authority that does not give an appellant an opportunity to put an appeal in order will run the risk of breaching Art 6 of the European Convention on Human Rights by stifling the appeal.

It is suggested that the authority may exercise this power even after a tribunal member has given a ruling on the validity of the appeal under para (7) or (8) below, though it is more likely for it to be reasonable not to do so.

Paragraphs (4) and (5): Appeals made by other means

Para (4) allows an authority to treat an application made otherwise than on an approved form as satisfying the requirements of a valid appeal. Para (5) is the equivalent of para (2). The further particulars an authority requires should be clearly set out in a letter to the appellant.

Paragraphs (6) to (8): Provision of further particulars

Under para (6), if the form is returned for completion or the further particulars are sought, an extension of time for appealing of 14 days is automatically conferred if the completed form or further particulars are received back by the authority within 14 days. An authority may grant a longer period, which then allows an equivalent extension of time: sub-para (c). This need not be done at the same time that the form is returned or particulars sought and it is suggested that it may be done after the 14-day period has expired.

If the authority's request is not complied with, it is required under para (7) to send all relevant documentation to a legally qualified tribunal panel member who will then decide whether the appeal has been validly made. If the completed form or further particulars are received by the authority after the time limit has expired, they must be sent to the member under para (8) for consideration. Any further details provided must be taken into account. For the reasons given in the commentary to reg 18(4) above, it is suggested that there is no appeal to the commissioner from a ruling by a tribunal member and the only remedy is judicial review.

Paragraph (9): Withdrawal of an appeal

If an appeal has not yet been passed to the Tribunals Service, an authority is absolved from taking action on it where it is withdrawn by a notice in writing. An "authorised representative" can withdraw an appeal on behalf of an appellant. A representative is only "authorised" where there is a validly given authorisation to act on behalf of the person affected. If an appeal is withdrawn but subsequently a second appeal on the same or similar grounds is made within the time limit, there seems to be no reason why the withdrawal of the first appeal affects the validity of the second appeal.

An appeal that has been passed to the Tribunals Service can be withdrawn under reg 40 SSCS D&A Regs (p922).

Death of a party to an appeal

21.–(1)   In any proceedings, on the death of a party to those proceedings, the relevant authority may appoint such person as it thinks fit to proceed with the appeal in the place of the deceased.

(2)   A grant of probate, confirmation or letters of administration in respect of the deceased, whenever taken out, shall have no effect on an appointment made under paragraph (1).

(3)   Where a person appointed under paragraph (1) has, prior to the date of such appointment, taken any action in relation to the appeal on behalf of the deceased, the effective date of appointment shall be treated as the day immediately prior to the first day on which such action was taken.

Analysis

Reg 21 makes provision for the death of a party to an appeal. Where an appellant dies in the course of an appeal to a tribunal, the local authority has power to appoint another person to act in her/his place. If, following reasonable enquiries, no-one is available to be appointed then the appeal will abate (see below).

Unfortunately, reg 21 is unclear in parts and, where it is clear, it is less helpful than would be desirable. To understand the problems, it is necessary, to go back a stage to the claim for benefit and the authority's decision on that claim. It is not possible for a new claim for HB or CTB to be made on behalf of someone who is dead (see, by analogy, *R(IS) 3/04*: reg 30 of the Social Security (Claims and Payments) Regulations 1987, and in particular, reg 30(5), probably does not extend to HB or CTB). But if a claimant dies after having made a claim, it is possible for the authority to pay any benefit due to her/his personal representative or next of kin under reg 97 HB Regs, reg 78 HB (SPC) Regs, reg 80 CTB Regs and reg 65 CTB (SPC) Regs. Unfortunately, those regulations contain no provision equivalent to reg 30(1) of the Social Security (Claims and Payments) Regulations 1987, which allows the Secretary of State to appoint a person "to proceed with the claim" of someone who has died.

This probably does not matter too much in a case where the authority needs further information before it is able to reach a decision. The personal representative or next of kin cannot be compelled to produce the necessary information (because, at this stage s/he is neither a "person who makes a claim" or "a person to whom . . . benefit has been awarded" for the purposes of reg 86 HB Regs etc or a "person by whom . . . . sums payable by way of . . . benefit are receivable" for the purposes of reg 88 HB Regs etc). But if s/he does not do so, the authority will take a decision on the basis of the information it does have. That decision will inevitably be to refuse the claim on the basis that the claimant has not established entitlement.

It does, however, matter where the personal representative or next of kin wishes to appeal against the authority's decision. Reg 97 HB Regs etc does not expressly give them standing to appeal and reg 21 does not assist because the opening words "In any proceedings" and the phrase "*proceed* with the appeal" (emphasis added) show that an appeal must already exist before the power of appointment can be exercised. It might be possible for the personal representative or next of kin to make an appeal even though s/he had no standing to do so, seek appointment under para (1) and then rely on para (3) to validate the appeal retrospectively but such a solution would be unsatisfactory because of the circularity involved: the appeal would not become valid until the appointment was made and the appointment could not be made in the absence of a valid appeal.

It is suggested that the answer is for the personal representative or next of kin to make the appeal as a person affected *in her/his own right* rather than as representing the deceased. Although not listed as a person affected in reg 3(1), *CH 3817/2004* holds that that list is not exhaustive and that other people may show that they are a person affected in the ordinary meaning of that term. The personal representative or next of kin would appear to satisfy reg 3(2) by virtue of the fact that any benefit awarded would be payable to her/him under reg 97 HB Regs etc.

Even once that hurdle is surmounted, there are still problems with reg 21. As noted by Commissioner Levenson in *CH 3631/2007* (at para 13):

- it is unclear whether the authority's power to appoint "such person as it thinks fit" includes the power to appoint someone who does not consent to be appointed and may refuse to act under the appointment.
- it is also unclear whether a power to appoint a person "to proceed with the appeal" includes a power to appoint someone to act as respondent to an appeal brought by the local authority.

However, the previous question is academic because such a situation could only arise on an appeal to the commissioner (local authorities having no right of appeal to a tribunal against their own decisions) and *CH 3631/2007* holds that reg 21 does not apply to appeals to the commissioner because the word "appeal" in the phrase "proceed with the appeal" is defined by reg 1(2) as meaning "an appeal to an appeal tribunal".

In *CH 3631/2007* (a case concerning the recovery of an overpayment), the commissioner held, following *R(IS) 6/01*, that the estate of a deceased claimant is not itself a legal person and cannot be a party to an appeal. In the absence of a grant of probate or letters of administration, there was no one with power to represent the estate before the commissioner and the appeal to the commissioner therefore abated. Although the commissioner's reasoning about the status of the deceased's estate is uncontroversial, the conclusion that the appeal must therefore abate may require further consideration. The authorities relied on by the commissioner at paras 14 and 15 are all cases in which the appeal abated on the death of the *appellant* and *R(SB) 25/84* states expressly that abatement is not appropriate where the deceased is the respondent to the appeal and the appellant is not willing to withdraw it. However, as abatement does not bring the appeal permanently to an end but merely suspends it, leaving open the possibility that it will be revived in the future (eg, by a grant of probate or letters of administration – see *R(I) 7/62* and *R(I) 2/83*) it may be that nothing turns on what procedure is followed.

Local authorities who wish to recover overpayments from unrepresented estates may wish to consider applying for a grant of limited representation under s116 Supreme Court Act 1981 – see *R(IS) 6/01* (para 38).

PART V

Appeal Tribunals

Composition of appeal tribunals

22.–(1)   Subject to paragraph (2), for the purposes of Schedule 7 to the Act and Regulations made thereunder, an appeal tribunal shall consist of–

(a) a financially qualified panel member and a legally qualified panel member where the appeal may require consideration by members of the appeal tribunal of issues which are, in the opinion of the President, difficult and which relate to–

    (i) profit and loss accounts, revenue accounts or balance sheets relating to any enterprise;

    (ii) an income and expenditure account in the case of an enterprise not trading for profit; or

    (iii) the accounts of any trust fund; and

(b) in any other case, a legally qualified panel member.

(2)   The President may determine that an appeal tribunal constituted in accordance with paragraph (1) shall include an additional member drawn from the panel constituted under section 6 of the Social Security Act 1998 for the purposes of providing experience for that additional member or for assisting the President in the monitoring of standards of decision making by panel members.

[¹ (3)]

Amendment

1.   Omitted by reg 3(2) of SI 2004 No 3368 as from 21.12.04.

Analysis

In almost all cases, HB and CTB appeals are heard by a legally qualified tribunal panel member sitting alone: para (1)(b). It is only in the rare cases of appeals raising difficult financial questions as set out in para (1)(a) that a financially qualified panel member will sit with the legally qualified member. Any party who considers that an appeal requires, or would benefit from, a tribunal that includes a financially qualified panel member, should write to the Tribunals Service at the earliest opportunity and ask for the file to be referred to a regional or district chairman so that an appropriate direction can be given.

The only other circumstance in which an additional member will sit is set out in para (2). In those circumstances, the additional member will have equal status to the legally qualified panel member appointed under para (1). If they disagree, the chair, who will usually be the legally qualified panel member, has the casting vote: s7(3) SSA 1998.

Procedure in connection with appeals

23.–(1)   Subject to paragraphs (2) and (3), the provisions in Chapters II to V of Part V of the Decisions and Appeals Regulations 1999 as [¹ amended by [² the [³ [⁴ the Social Security (Civil Partnership) (Consequential Amendments) Regulations 2005]]]] shall apply in relation to the procedure to be followed in respect of appeals under Schedule 7 to the Act.

(2)   Regulations 38A, 41, 44, 45, 52 and 57B of the Decisions and Appeals Regulations 1999 shall not apply in relation to the procedure to be followed in respect of appeals under Schedule 7 to the Act.

(3)   The provisions of the Decisions and Appeals Regulations 1999 referred to in paragraph (1) shall have effect as if a reference to–

(a) the Secretary of State, except in regulations [² 39(1) (choice of hearing),] 40 (withdrawal of appeal or referral) and 58 (application for leave to appeal to a Commissioner from an appeal tribunal), were a reference to a relevant authority;

(b) party to the proceedings were a reference to principal parties;

(c) ''these Regulations'' in regulations 46(1)(b) (appeals which may be struck out) and 57A (provisions common to regulations 56 and 57) were a reference to the Housing Benefit and Council Tax Benefit (Decisions and Appeals) Regulations 2001;

(d) a person in regulation 51 (postponement and adjournment) included a reference to a relevant authority;

(e) a relevant enactment, in regulations 56 and 57 (correction of accidental errors and setting aside decisions) were a reference to Schedule 7 to the Act; and

(f) in regulation 58–

   (i) section 12 [¹ or] 13 were a reference to paragraphs 6 [¹ or] 7 of Schedule 7 to the Act; and

   (ii) the Board were a reference to a relevant authority.

Amendments

1. Amended by reg 28 of SI 2002 No 1379 as from 20.5.02.
2. Amended by reg 3(3) of SI 2004 No 3368 as from 21.12.04.
3. Amended by reg 3(4) of SI 2005 No 337 as from 18.3.05.
4. Substituted by reg 9(3) of SI 2005 No 2878 as from 5.12.05.

Analysis

The SSCS D&A Regs are printed, in the form modified by paras (2) and (3), from p917. They are applied to HB and CTB appeals "as amended by the Social Security (Civil Partnership) (Consequential Amendments) Regulations 2005". This is problematical because the relevant provisions of the SSCS D&A Regs have been amended many times both before and since 5 December 2005 when the Social Security (Civil Partnership) (Consequential Amendments) Regulations 2005 took effect. Under ss20(2) and 23 Interpretation Act 1978, the reference to the SSCS D&A Regs would normally be to those regulations as amended "unless the contrary intention appears". The issue therefore arises whether the inclusion of an express reference to the 2005 civil partnership amendments amounts to a contrary intention. If the intention was that all the amendments to the relevant parts of the SSCS D&A Regs (ie, including the 2005 civil partnership amendments) should automatically apply to HB and CTB, why single out the 2005 civil partnership amendments for special mention: they would have applied in any event. On the other hand, it does not seem likely that the draftsman should have intended that the SSCS D&A Regs should apply to HB and CTB in a form that included the 2005 civil partnership arrangements but otherwise as they stood on 2 July 2001 without any other amendment. The better view is therefore that the express reference to the Social Security (Civil Partnership) (Consequential Amendments) Regulations 2005 was included by oversight or out of an abundance of caution and was not intended to have the effect of disapplying all other amendments to the SSCS D&A Regs in HB and CTB appeals.

SCHEDULE

DECISIONS AGAINST WHICH NO APPEAL LIES

General Note

The Schedule, made under reg 16, sets out the categories of decisions which would otherwise fall within the right of appeal but which cannot be subject to an appeal to a tribunal. See the commentary to reg 16 and Sch 7 para 6(1) CSPSSA for discussion of the types of decisions that can be appealed.

Note that certain exclusions of the right of appeal may infringe Art 6 of the European Convention on Human Rights: see *R(IS) 6/04*, discussed in the commentary to Art 6 on p132.

1. No appeal shall lie against a decision made by virtue of, or as a consequence of, any of the provisions in Part X (claims), Part XII (payments) and Part XIII (overpayments) of the Housing Benefit Regulations except a decision under–

[² (a) regulations 83 (time and manner in which claims are to be made), 84(1) and 85(1) and (4) (date of claim);

(b) regulation 93(3) (adjustments to payments to take account of underpayment or overpayment on account of rent allowance);
(c) regulation 95 (circumstances in which payment is to be made to a landlord);
(d) regulation 96 (circumstances in which payment may be made to a landlord);
(e) regulation 100 (recoverable overpayments);
(f) regulation 101 (person from whom recovery may be sought);
(g) regulation 103 (diminution of capital); or
(h) regulation 104 (sums to be deducted in calculating recoverable overpayments).]

Amendments
1. Substituted by reg 3(4)(a) of SI 2004 No 3368 as from 21.12.04.
2. Substituted by reg 5 and para 17(3) of SI 2006 No 217 as from 6.3.06.

[¹**1A.** No appeal shall lie against a decision made by virtue of, or as a consequence of, any of the provisions in Part 9 (claims), Part 11 (payments) and Part 12 (overpayments) of the Housing Benefit (State Pension Credit) Regulations except a decision under–
(a) regulations 64 (time and manner in which claims are to be made), 65(1) and 66(1) and (4) (date of claim);
(b) regulation 74(3) (adjustments to payments to take account of underpayment or overpayment on account of rent allowance);
(c) regulation 76 (circumstances in which payment is to be made to a landlord);
(d) regulation 77 (circumstances in which payment may be made to a landlord);
(e) regulation 81 (recoverable overpayments);
(f) regulation 84 (diminution of capital); or
(g) regulation 85 (sums to be deducted in calculating recoverable overpayments).]

Amendment
1. Inserted by reg 5 and sch 2 para 17(3)(e)(ii) of SI 2006 No 217 as from 6.3.06.

2. No appeal shall lie against a decision made by virtue of, or as a consequence of, any of the provisions in Part VIII (claims), Part X (awards or payments of benefit) and Part XI (excess benefit) of the Council Tax Benefit Regulations except a decision under–
[² (a) regulations 69 (time and manner in which claims are to be made), 69(1) and 70(1) and (4) (date of claim);
(b) regulation 83 (recoverable excess benefit);
(c) regulation 85 (persons from whom recovery may be sought);
(d) regulation 88 (diminution of capital); or
(e) regulation 89 (sums to be deducted in calculating recoverable excess benefit).]

Amendments
1. Substituted by reg 3(4)(b) of SI 2004 No 3368 as from 21.12.04.
2. Substituted by reg 5 and Sch 2 para 17(3)(e) of SI 2006 No 217 as from 6.3.06

[¹**2A.** No appeal shall lie against a decision made by virtue of, or as a consequence of, any of the provisions in Part 7 (claims), Part 9 (awards or payments of benefit) and Part 10 (excess benefit) of the Council Tax Benefit (State Pension Credit) Regulations except a decision under–
(a) regulations 53 (time and manner in which claims are to be made), 54(1) and 55(1) and (4) (date of claim);
(b) regulation 68 (recoverable excess benefit);
(c) regulation 70 (persons from whom recovery may be sought);
(d) regulation 73 (diminution of capital); or
(e) regulation 74 (sums to be deducted in calculating recoverable excess benefit).]

Amendment
1. Inserted by reg 5 and Sch 2 para 17(3)(e)(iv) of SI 2006 No 217 as from 6.3.06.

Analysis
Paras 1, 1A, 2 and 2A effectively reverse the presumption that an appeal lies against any "decision" not within the scope of the Schedule and provide that in relation to decisions on claims, payments and overpayment, an appeal only lies against the decisions listed. They are:
(1) A decision as to the time and manner in which a claim was made and the date on which a claim was made.
(2) A decision as to whether a claim should be backdated for good cause.

(3) A decision to make, or not to make, adjustments to ongoing payments of HB to reflect underpayments or overpayments made where payments on account under reg 93(3) HB Regs or 74(3) HB(SPC) Regs are made.

(4) A decision as to whether direct payments of HB should be made to a landlord. This includes decisions on whether a landlord is a "fit and proper person" to receive direct payments.

(5) A decision as to whether an overpayment is recoverable, and if so how much is recoverable.

(6) A decision as to from whom an overpayment is recoverable. See also the commentary to para 3.

(7) A decision as to the amount of a recoverable overpayment taking into account the diminishing capital rule and the rules in reg 104 HB Regs, reg 85 HB(SPC) Regs, reg 89 CTB Regs or reg 74 CTB(SPC) Regs.

---

3. Subject to paragraphs 1(f) and 2(c), no appeal shall lie against a decision as to the exercise of discretion to recover an overpayment of housing benefit or, as the case may be, excess council tax benefit.

Analysis

Whatever the correctness of the Court of Appeal's decision in *Secretary of State for Work and Pensions v Chiltern District Council* [2003] EWCA Civ 508 (*R(H) 2/03*) and the Tribunal of Commissioner's decision in *R(H) 3/04* in respect of the regime in place prior to October 2001 (and the correctness of the Court of Appeal's decision is strongly doubted in *R(H) 6/06*), the Tribunal of Commissioner's decision in *R(H) 6/06* holds that rights of appeal only attach to decisions going to the recoverability of an overpayment and do not attach to decisions concerning the recovery (or enforcement) of such recoverable overpayment decisions. As the Tribunal of Commissioners said:

"under the legislation in force from 1 October 2001 to 9 April 2006, an overpayment of housing benefit is always recoverable from any person within the scope of reg 101(2) as well as, if different, the person to whom the overpayment was made, except where reg 101(1) applies in which case it is recoverable only from any person within the scope of reg 101(2). No non-justiciable issues fall within the scope of the right of appeal and so there is no longer any need to apply *R(H) 3/04* and construe that right as being limited to points of law."

So the only appealable point (apart from whether there has in fact been an overpayment and whether it is recoverable) under s75(3) of the SSAA 1992 and reg 101 HB Regs is whether the person does in fact fall within reg 101. Once that point has been finally decided, *R(H) 6/06* makes it clear that no appeal right attaches to the enforcement decision of the local authority as against whom the recoverable overpayment should actually be recovered from.

---

4. No appeal shall lie against a decision of a relevant authority under paragraph 16(3)(a) or (b) and (4) of Schedule 7 to the Act (decisions involving issues that arise on appeal in other cases).

Analysis

Sch 7 para 16(3) CSPSSA and reg 15 of these regulations permits an authority to postpone a decision pending a decision in a "test case", while giving it a discretion to issue a decision in certain cases. Para 4 confirms that there is no appeal against a decision to issue, or not to issue, a decision. The only remedy is judicial review.

---

5. No appeal shall lie against a decision under Part III of these Regulations of a relevant authority relating to—

(a) suspension of a payment of benefit or of a reduction; or

(b) restoration following a suspension of payment of benefit or of a reduction,

except a decision that entitlement to benefit is terminated under regulation 14.

Analysis

There is no appeal against a decision to suspend or restore benefit under Pt III of these regulations. There is, however, an appeal against a termination of benefit under reg 14: see *CH 402/2007*.

[¹**6** No appeal shall lie against the calculation or estimate of the claimant's, or the claimant's partner's, income or capital used by a relevant authority in accordance with [² regulation 27(1) of the Housing Benefit (State Pension Credit) Regulations or regulation 17(1) of the Council Tax Benefit (State Pension Credit) Regulations] (calculation of claimant's income in savings credit only cases), as modified, in both cases, by the Housing Benefit and Council Tax Benefit (State Pension Credit) Regulations 2003.]

Amendments

1. Inserted by reg 3 of SI 2003 No 1581 as from 18.6.03.
2. Amended by reg 5 and sch 2 para 17(3)(e) of SI 2006 No 217 as from 6.3.06.

Analysis

Reg 27(1) of the HB(SPC) Regs and 17(1) of the CTB(SPC) Regs provide for local authorities to use the calculation or estimate of a claimant's (or her/his partner's) income and capital provided by the DWP (known as the "assessed income figure") where there is entitlement to the "savings credit" of pension credit only. There is no appeal against the local authority use of the DWP calculation or estimate of income and capital. An appeal would need to be made against the DWP income/capital decision instead.

Note that if the local authority modifies the "assessed income figure" under reg 27(4) HB(SPC) Regs or reg 17(4) CTB(SPC) Regs as the case may be, there *is* a right of appeal against the modification. There is therefore a potential for appeals against both the income/capital decision made by the DWP and the modification decision made by the local authority. It is suggested that it would be good practice to deal with both appeals together and that the former appeal should be dealt with first.

If a claimant wrongly lodges an appeal against the DWP income/capital decision with the local authority, the DWP's *Housing Benefit and Council Tax Benefit Pension Credit Handbook* (at Part 1 para 1103) reminds a local authority what it should do. The local authority should advise the claimant that the correct thing to do is to lodge an appeal with the DWP. It should also advise the claimant that the appeal lodged with the local authority will be processed as "out of jurisdiction" (see regs 1(3) and 46 of the SSCS D&A Regs on pp918 and 924). The guidance rightly suggests that if the situation is ambiguous, claimants should be advised to consider lodging an appeal with the DWP as well as that with the local authority.

The Housing Benefit and Council Tax Benefit (Decisions and Appeals) (Transitional and Savings) Regulations 2001
(SI 2001 No.1264)

General Note to the Regulations

Before 2 July 2001, HB and CTB adjudication was governed by Part XI of the HB Regs 2007 and Part IX of the CTB Regs 1992 (see pp368-395 and 659-666 of the 13th edition). In summary:

(1) The initial decision on all matters arising out of a claim was made by the local authority (ie, by a local government officer) and was called a "determination". The authority had to give written notice of a determination to every person affected (regs 76-77 HB Regs 1987 and regs 66-67CTB Regs 1992).

(2) A person affected had six weeks from the date on which the notice was sent to her/him (or longer if the authority was prepared to extend time) in which to make written representations to the authority about the decision. The authority was then obliged to carry out a review (referred to colloquially as an "internal review") of its decision (regs 78-79 HB Regs 1987 and regs 68-69 CTB Regs 1992). It was good practice – and normal – for the internal review to be undertaken by an officer who was senior to the officer who made the original determination.

(3) If the person affected was dissatisfied with the outcome of the internal review, s/he then had four weeks in which to request a "further review". Further reviews were carried out at an oral hearing by a Review Board consisting of members (ie, councillors) of the authority concerned. Decisions made by Review Boards were described as "decisions" to distinguish them from the "determinations" made by officers (regs 81-84 HB Regs 1987 and regs 70-73 CTB Regs 1992).

(4) In certain circumstances, the decision of a Review Board could be set aside for procedural reasons (reg 86 HB Regs 1987 and reg 75 CTB Regs 1992). But there was no appeal against the decision either on fact or law. The only remedy open to an unsuccessful applicant for further review was to seek a judicial review of the Board's decision in the High Court. As the High Court had no power on judicial review to substitute its own view on a question of fact, that situation did not comply with Art 6 of the European Convention on Human Rights (see *Tsfayo v United Kingdom* (application no: 60860/00) [2006], 14 November, unreported, ECtHR). The system therefore had to be changed following the incorporation of the Convention into domestic UK law by the Human Rights Act 1998 so as to allow an appeal to an independent tribunal from a local authority's decision.

(5) Even if no written representations had been made, the authority had power to review its own determinations, and – in some cases – the decisions of a Review Board, at any time if there had been a relevant change of circumstances or if the original determination or decision had been made in ignorance of, or was based on a mistake as to, a material fact. The authority also had power to review its own determinations, but not the decisions of a Review Board, for most types of error of law (reg 79(1) HB Regs 1987 and reg 69(1) CTB Regs 1992).

These Regulations contain transitional provisions that govern what happens where that process for disputing an authority's determination commenced before 2 July 2001 but had not finished by that date. Reg 2 applies where the person affected had made written representations but no review determination had been made. Reg 3 applies to outstanding applications for a further review and reg 4 deals with the consequences of the abolition of Review Boards. Regs 5 and 6 deal with technical points about, respectively, the suspension and withholding of benefit and the effective date of a determination that should have been made before 2 July 2001 but is not actually made until after that date.

Given the length of time that has now passed since 2 July 2001, one could be forgiven for hoping that these Regulations had ceased to perform any practical function. In fact, the level of delay and maladministration at certain local authorities is such that tribunals need to consider them with depressing frequency: see, for example, *R(H) 1/07*.

Note that these Regulations do *not* deal with the situation where a determination was made before 2 July 2001 but the person affected did not apply to change it – or the authority did not exercise its powers of "any time" review – until after that date. In those circumstances, the determination is a "relevant decision" within para 1(2) of Sch 7 CSPSSA (*R(H) 6/04* and see further the commentary to para 1(2)).

Citation, commencement and interpretation

1.–(1)   These Regulations may be cited as the Housing Benefit and Council Tax Benefit (Decisions and Appeals) (Transitional and Savings) Regulations 2001 and shall come into force on 2nd July 2001.

(2)   In these Regulations, unless the context otherwise requires–

"the Act" means the Child Support, Pensions and Social Security Act 2000;

"the Council Tax Benefit Regulations" means the Council Tax Benefit (General) Regulations 1992;

"the Decisions and Appeals Regulations" means the Housing Benefit and Council Tax Benefit (Decisions and Appeals) Regulations 2001;

"the Housing Benefit Regulations" means the Housing Benefit (General) Regulations 1987;

"panel member" means a person appointed to a panel constituted under section 6 of the Social Security Act 1998;

"person affected" has the meaning as in regulation 3 (person treated as a person affected by a decision) of the Decisions and Appeals Regulations;

"relevant authority" has the meaning as in paragraph 1(1) of Schedule 7 to the Act;

"relevant date" means 2nd July 2001;

"Review Board" shall, notwithstanding the revocation of regulation 81(3) of the Housing Benefit Regulations or, as the case may be, regulation 70(3) of the Council Tax Benefit Regulations, be construed in accordance with those provisions; and

"the Work-focused Interviews Regulations" means the Social Security (Work-focused Interviews) Regulations 2000.

(3)   In these Regulations, unless the context otherwise requires, a reference–

(a)   to a numbered regulation is to a regulation in these Regulations bearing that number; and

(b)   in a regulation to a numbered paragraph or sub-paragraph is to the paragraph or sub-paragraph in that regulation bearing that number.

Provision in respect of reviews of determinations made by relevant authorities

2.–(1)   Subject to the following paragraphs and notwithstanding regulation 4(1)(a) of the Decisions and Appeals Regulations (revision of decisions), where a person affected makes written representations signed by him to a relevant authority concerning a determination made by that authority before the relevant date and–

(a)   such representations are made within six weeks of the date on which the person was notified of that determination or within such longer period as may be allowed under paragraph (5), those representations shall be treated as an application duly made for a revision under paragraph 3 of Schedule 7 to the Act (revision of decisions); or

(b)   such representations are not made within the period provided by virtue of sub-paragraph (a) or allowed under paragraph (5), those representations shall be treated as an application duly made for a supersession under paragraph 4 of Schedule 7 to the Act (decisions superseding earlier decisions).

(2)   Paragraph (1) shall–

(a)   apply only in a case to which regulation 79(2) of the Housing Benefit Regulations, or as the case may be, regulation 69(2) of the Council Tax Benefit Regulations could have applied had Schedule 7 to the Act and regulations made thereunder not come into force;

(b)   not apply in a case where a review of the determination was made under regulation 79(2) of the Housing Benefit Regulations, or as the case may be, regulation 69(2) of the Council Tax Benefit Regulations before the relevant date.

(3)   Where a person makes written representations signed by him to a relevant authority concerning a determination made by them before the relevant date and that authority–

(a)   accepted the late submission of those representations in accordance with regulation 78(3) of the Housing Benefit Regulations, or as the case may be, in accordance with regulation 68(3) of the Council Tax Benefit Regulations before the relevant date; and

(b)   made no determination in respect of those representations before the relevant date,

those representations shall be treated as an application duly made for a revision under paragraph 3 of Schedule 7 to the Act.

(4)   For the purposes of calculating the period of six weeks in paragraph (1)(a), no account shall be taken of any period beginning with the receipt by a relevant authority of a request for a statement under regulation 77(4) of the Housing Benefit Regulations, or as the case may be, under regulation 67(2) of the Council Tax Benefit Regulations (requests for statement of reasons) and ending with the provision to that person of that statement.

(5)   The period of six weeks specified in paragraph (1)(a) may be extended where an application for such an extension is made before 2nd August 2002 by a person affected and the application contains–

(a)   the grounds on which an extension of time is sought; and

(b)   sufficient details of the determination to enable it to be identified.

(6)   An application for an extension of time shall be made in writing by the person affected and delivered, by whatever means, to the relevant authority or, in a case to which the Work-focused Interviews Regulations apply, either to the relevant authority or to an office of a designated authority which displays the ONE logo.

(7)   An application for an extension of time shall not be granted unless the relevant authority which made the determination to which the representations relate is satisfied that–

(a)   it is reasonable to grant that application;

(b)   the representations have merit; and

(c)   special circumstances are relevant to the application for an extension of time as a result of which it was not practicable for the representations to be made within the six week period specified in paragraph (1)(a).

(8)   In deciding whether to grant an extension of time no account shall be taken of the following factors–

(a)   that the person affected was unaware of or misunderstood the law applicable to his case (including ignorance or misunderstanding of the time limits specified in paragraph (1)(a)); or

(b)   that a court has taken a different view of the law from that previously understood and applied by the relevant authority.

(9)   An application under this regulation for an extension of time which has been refused may not be renewed.

General Note

Reg 2 is concerned with applications for review made, but not determined, prior to 2 July 2001. The general rule is that such an application is to be treated as an application for a revision if it was made within six weeks of the original determination, or as an application for supersession if made later.

Analysis

Para (1) sets out the general rule as summarised in the General Note. Note that by para (4), time spent awaiting a statement of reasons is to be ignored in calculating the six week period.

There is no definition in the D&A Transitional Regs as to when representations are "made", but it is suggested that the definitions in the repealed reg 78 HB Regs 1987 have to be imported for the sake of consistency. In other words, a request for a review is only "made" when it is received by the authority: reg 78(1) HB Regs 1987. Similarly, "signed by him" requires that the person affected should have signed the representations personally. Since this is plainly not possible in the case of a legal person, it is suggested that the provisions of reg 79(2A) HB Regs 1987 should be regarded as imported into para (1) as well.

The distinction between treatment of the outstanding request for review as an application for revision or supersession is the date on which such applications take effect. See regs 4 to 9 D&A Regs.

Para (2) limits the effect of para (1) to situations where reg 79(2) HB Regs 1987 or reg 69(2) CTB Regs 1992 "could have applied" had the new adjudication provisions not been brought into force. What this means, it is suggested, is that the person affected is only entitled to challenge matters within the competence of the authority to decide. It is not, for example, possible to challenge a rent officer's decision by this route.

Reg 79(2) or reg 69(2) still "could have applied" even where the time limits for seeking a review under those regs had expired, otherwise the provisions for extending time would have no practical effect.

By sub-para (b), where a review has already been carried out, reg 2 has no application. The operation of reg 2 is excluded whenever a review has been carried out under reg 79(2) HB Regs 1987, and not just where the review considered a point now in dispute between a person affected and the authority.

Para (3) provides that where an extension of time for seeking a review under reg 79(2) HB Regs 1987 or 69(2) CTB Regs 1992 had already been granted but the review had not been determined, it was to be treated as an application for revision.

Paras (5) to (9) deal with extensions of the six week period specified in para (1)(a). The test is similar to that specified in regs 5 and 9 D&A Regs (refer to pp960 and 969 for discussion), but there are important differences. First, the application must have been made before 2 August 2002. Secondly, there is no equivalent of reg 5(6), but it is suggested that the principle that a greater delay requires a more compelling explanation must be applied as a matter of common sense in any event. Finally, there is no reference to a decision of the commissioner in para (8)(b). So a decision of a commissioner overturning what had formerly been the view of the law taken by a local authority may be a relevant matter in deciding whether to extend time.

Provision in respect of requests for further review of determinations

3.–(1)   Subject to the following paragraphs and notwithstanding regulation 23 of the Decisions and Appeals Regulations (procedure in connection with appeals), where a person affected gives or sends written notice signed by him to a relevant authority requesting a further review of a determination (''reviewed determination''), that notice shall be treated as an application duly made for an appeal to an appeal tribunal from a relevant decision.

(2)   Paragraph (1) shall–

(a)   apply only in a case to which regulation 81(3) of the Housing Benefit Regulations or, as the case may be, regulation 70(3) of the Council Tax Benefit Regulations could have applied had Schedule 7 to the Act and regulations made thereunder not come into force;

(b)   not apply in a case where a further review of the determination was made under regulation 81(3) of the Housing Benefit Regulations or, as the case may be, regulation 70(3) of the Council Tax Benefit Regulations before the relevant date.

(3)   For the purposes of paragraph (1), the written notice must be given or sent within–

(a)   four weeks of the date the person was notified of the reviewed determination; or

(b)   the period allowed for under paragraph (5).

(4)   Where written notice is given or sent–

(a)   before the relevant date and the provisions in regulation 81(1), (1A) and (2) of the Housing Benefit Regulations, or as the case may be, regulation 70(1) and (2) of the Council Tax Benefit Regulations were satisfied before that date; or

(b)   by the person affected more than four weeks after the date on which the person was notified of the reviewed determination and a Review Board extended the time before the relevant date for giving such notice under regulation 78(3) of the Housing Benefit Regulations, or as the case may be, regulation 68(3) of the Council Tax Benefit Regulations,

that notice shall be treated as an application duly made for an appeal from a relevant decision.

(5)   The period of four weeks referred to in paragraph (3)(a) may be extended where an application for such an extension is made before 2nd August 2002 by a person affected and the application contains–

(a)   the grounds on which an extension is sought; and

(b)   sufficient details of the decision to enable it to be identified.

(6)   An application for an extension of time shall be made in writing by the person affected and delivered, by whatever means, to the relevant authority or, in a

case to which the Work-focused Interviews Regulations apply, either to the relevant authority or to an office of a designated authority which displays the ONE logo.

(7)   An application for an extension of time within which written notice may be given or sent shall be determined by a legally qualified panel member.

(8)   An application for an extension of time shall not be granted unless the panel member is satisfied that the requirements imposed by regulation 19(5) to (9) of the Decisions and Appeals Regulations have been met.

(9)   An application for an extension of time that has been refused may not be renewed.

(10)   Regulation 16 of, and the Schedule to, the Decisions and Appeals Regulations, save for paragraph 3 of that Schedule, shall not apply in respect of a reviewed determination.

General Note

Reg 3 is concerned with outstanding applications for further review, which are treated as appeals to a tribunal under the new provisions. This is part of the 'big bang' approach of the D&A provisions, under which any outstanding application to a Review Board was to be considered by a tribunal instead. The only purposes for which Review Boards survived were those specified by Art 2(2)(c) CSPSSA 2000 (Commencement No.8) Order 2001 SI No 1252. These purposes were: to enable a Review Board to record its decision and send it out, to permit correction of accidental errors, to enable a Review Board to appear in judicial review proceedings and to enable effect to be given to a Review Board's decision. See also reg 4.

Analysis

Paras (1) and (2) specify the general rule. As with reg 2, the phrases "gives or sends" and "signed by him" fall to be interpreted as they were under the HB Regs 1987. "Could have applied" must also, it is suggested, be interpreted in the same way as in reg 2.

Para (2)(b) excludes a case where a Review Board gave a decision before 2 July 2001 from the operation of reg 3. However, if a Review Board's decision is quashed on judicial review, the effect will be as if it was never made and reg 3 will operate so as to require the decision to be reheard by a tribunal, even if the court's order is silent on the subject.

Para (3) specifies the normal time limit within which an application for further review by a Review Board must have been made for it to be considered as an appeal. This is four weeks or any longer period allowed under para (5).

Para (4) contains two more deeming provisions. Sub-para (a) treats an application for further review which is actually made prior to 2 July 2001 as being an application for an appeal. This is in contrast with para (1), which deals with situations where the application for further review is made after that date. Sub-para (b) deems an application for further review made out of time, but admitted for hearing by a Review Board prior to 2 July 2001, to be an application for an appeal.

Paras (5) to (9) contain provisions relating to late applications for further review. Applications must have been made before 2 August 2002. The provisions did not apply to cases in which a Review Board had already admitted a late application for further review prior to 2 July 2001, as to which see para (4)(b). However, although para (5) refers only to para (3)(a), it is also relevant to para (1) by virtue of para (3)(b). It is a legally qualified tribunal panel member who determines whether to grant an extension of time. The criteria in reg 19(5) to (9) D&A Regs are used (see p980).

Para (10) excludes the jurisdictional limits imposed by reg 16 D&A Regs (decisions against which no appeal lies). However, a tribunal is still prohibited from considering issues relating to recovery of overpayments, but see Sch para 3 D&A Regs on p989.

Provision in respect of the abolition of Review Boards

4.–(1) Where a Review Board has held an oral hearing in accordance with–

(a)   regulation 82 of the Housing Benefit Regulations (procedure on further review) before the relevant date–

(i)   regulation 83(4) and (5) (decisions upon further review),

(ii)   regulation 84 (effect of revising a decision), and

(iii)   regulation 85 (correction of accidental errors in determinations and decisions)

of those Regulations shall continue to have effect in relation to any decision of that Review Board as if section 68 of, and paragraph 22(1) of Schedule 7 to, the Act had not come into force; or

     (b)   regulation 71 of the Council Tax Benefit Regulations (procedure on further review) before the relevant date–

         (i)   regulation 72(4) and (5) (decisions upon further review),

         (ii)   regulation 73 (effect of revising a determination), and

         (iii) regulation 74 (correction of accidental errors in determinations and decisions)

of those Regulations shall continue to have effect in relation to any decision of that Review Board as if section 68 of, and paragraph 22(1) of Schedule 7 to, the Act had not come into force.

(2)   Where a part-heard hearing by a Review Board stands adjourned before the relevant date an appeal tribunal shall completely rehear the case as if it were an appeal under paragraph 6 of Schedule 7 to the Act.

(3)   Subject to paragraph (1), any decision that would, but for the coming into force of section 68 of, and paragraph 22(1) of Schedule 7 to, the Act, fall to be made by a Review Board shall be made by an appeal tribunal.

(4)   Subject to paragraph (5), a decision of a Review Board shall be treated for the purposes of paragraph 4 of Schedule 7 to the Act (decisions superseding earlier decisions) as if it were a decision of a tribunal made under paragraph 6 of Schedule 7 to the Act.

(5)   Notwithstanding the coming into force of section 68 of, and paragraph 22 of Schedule 7 to, the Act, regulations made in accordance with section 34(4) and (5) of the Social Security Act 1998, as in force immediately before the relevant date, shall continue to have effect for the purpose of any claim for judicial review of a decision made by a Review Board and any appeal from a decision on such a claim.

(6)   Subject to paragraph (7), where–

     (a)   an application to set aside a decision of a Review Board is made by a person affected by that decision within 13 weeks of the day on which notice of that decision was given; and

     (b)   the application is not determined before the relevant date,

the application to set aside shall be treated as if it were an application duly made to set aside a decision of an appeal tribunal made under regulation 23 of the Decisions and Appeals Regulations and regulation 57 of the Social Security and Child Support (Decisions and Appeals) Regulations 1999.

(7)   A legally qualified panel member may set aside the decision of a Review Board as if it were a decision of an appeal tribunal on the grounds–

     (a)   specified in regulation 57(1) of the Social Security and Child Support (Decisions and Appeals) Regulations 1999; or

     (b)   that the interests of justice so require.

General Note

Reg 4 deals with cases which have already come before a Review Board. For provisions relating to outstanding Review Board cases, see reg 3.

Analysis

Para (1) provides that where a Review Board hearing was completed before 2 July 2001, the regulations governing the issue of decisions and correction continue to apply. What that means, in conjunction with the commencement provisions (see the General Note to reg 3) is that such a Review Board must issue a decision. An application to set aside such a decision must be dealt with by a tribunal member under paras (6) and (7). An application for a correction must, it seems, be dealt with by a Review Board.

Para (2) requires that where a Review Board has adjourned part-heard, a rehearing of the case by a tribunal must take place. The tribunal will not be bound by any expression of opinion given by the Review Board.

Para (3) confirms the effect of reg 3, which is that all outstanding applications for further review are now dealt with as appeals except as specified in para (1).

It is unclear whether a tribunal considering an application for further review under paras (2) or (3) is bound by para 6(9)(b) Sch 7 CSPSSA not to consider changes in circumstances after the date of the authority's original determination. The better view is that it is not. Para (2) says that where the application was part-heard on 2 July 2001, the tribunal must rehear it "as if it were an appeal under paragraph 6 of Schedule 7". The implication is that the "down to the date of the decision" rule applies. By contrast, para (3) does not convert applications for further review into appeals. It merely states that decisions that were previously to be taken by a Review Board are now to be taken by an appeal tribunal. The implication is that if the Board was previously obliged to consider the application "down to the date of the hearing", then a tribunal stepping into the Board's shoes is also so obliged. However, it is unlikely that a distinction was intended between applications to a Review Board that were part-heard on 2 July 2001 and those that were unheard on that date. It is suggested that, if Review Boards were bound to apply the "down to the date of the hearing" rule then existing applicants had an accrued right to have their appeals decided on that basis within s16(1)(c) Interpretation Act 1978 (see *CIB 213/1999*).

Unfortunately, there is an unresolved conflict of authority as to which rule Review Boards had to apply. In *R v London Borough of Waltham Forest HBRB ex parte Iqbal* [1997] EWHC Admin 810 (16 September 1997), a deputy High Court Judge held that the Board was bound not to decide "down to the date of the decision" whereas, in *R v Westminster CC HBRB ex parte Mehanne* [1997] EWHC Admin 1117 (11 December 1997), another deputy High Court Judge took the opposite approach. For reasons that are discussed in more detail on p459 of the 14th edition, it is suggested that the approach in *Mehanne* is to be preferred and that the "down to the date of the hearing" rule that applied to all social security appeals until SSA 1998 came into force also applied to Review Boards before 2 July 2001.

Paras (4) and (5) contain further deeming provisions relating to Review Board decisions. Para (4) provides that a Review Board decision may be superseded (though not, interestingly, revised) and para (5) gives a Review Board decision continuing force for judicial review purposes. However, it is suggested that the provision does not give the court any power to direct a rehearing by a Review Board if the Board's decision is quashed. It should direct that a tribunal rehear the case instead.

Paras (6) and (7) deal with applications to set aside Review Board decisions. If an application was outstanding on 2 July 2001 but was not decided, it must be considered by a legally qualified tribunal panel member. Such an application must be considered as if it was an application to set aside under reg 57 SSCS D&A Regs. The only exception is the retention of the additional ground for setting aside formerly found in reg 86(1)(c) HB Regs 1987, namely that "the interests of justice so require": para (7)(b).

Suspension and withholding

5. Where, immediately before the relevant date–

(a)   a payment of housing benefit was withheld under regulation 95(4) or (4A) (withholding of benefit) or suspended by virtue of regulation 96A (suspension of benefit) of the Housing Benefit Regulations; or

(b)   in the case of a claim for council tax benefit–

  (i)   a payment of council tax benefit was withheld under regulation 80(1), (2) or (2A) of the Council Tax Benefit Regulations (withholding of benefit), or

  (ii)   a payment of that benefit or a reduction in the amount that a person is or will be liable to pay in respect of council tax was suspended by virtue of regulation 81A of the Council Tax Benefit Regulations (suspension of benefit),

the provisions of Part III of the Decisions and Appeals Regulations (suspension and termination of benefit) shall apply with respect to that suspension or withholding as if it were a suspension imposed by virtue of those provisions.

General Note

Reg 5 is straightforward. It simply provides for any withholding or suspension of HB or CTB pending a review under the old rules to be treated as a suspension under the new rules.

Decisions of relevant authorities outstanding at the relevant date

6. Subject to regulations 2 to 5, where a determination by a relevant authority–

(a)   fell to be made before the relevant date;

(b)   is made after the relevant date;

(c)   is to the advantage of the claimant, and

(d)   takes effect from a date later than the date ("the earlier date") from which benefit, or an increase in benefit, would have been payable had the decision been made immediately before the relevant date,

that decision shall take effect on the earlier date.

General Note

Reg 6 aimed to prevent prejudice to a claimant arising out of a delay in decision making which extends to a period after 2 July 2001.

Analysis

The basic effect of reg 6 is to deem a determination to have been made prior to 2 July 2001 if it is made after that date, and as a result of being made late, the claimant is prejudiced. Four conditions must be shown for reg 6 to take effect:

(1)   A determination "fell to be made" prior to 2 July 2001. It is suggested that, in the absence of evidence that it was not reasonably practicable to make a determination, a determination "fell to be made" on the expiry of the time limit specified for example in reg 77(1)(b) or 79(2) HB Regs 1987, as the case was. So an application for review made on 1 March 2001 but not determined until 1 August 2001 must be treated as if determined on 15 March 2001.

(2)   The determination was made after 2 July 2001.

(3)   The determination is to the advantage of the claimant. It need not give the claimant all that s/he is seeking. It is sufficient if there is entitlement to an amount, or a higher amount of benefit following the determination.

(4)   The determination takes effect later than it would have done under the old provisions. It will be necessary to compare the position under the old and new provisions. The main effect of reg 6 will be in relation to applications for review which have to be treated as applications for supersession under the new rules.

Note the loose usage of "determination" and "decision" in reg 6 which is some foundation for the argument that the old adjudication rules are preserved in so far as they are not specifically dealt with in the D&A Transitional Regs.

Part 6

Other primary legislation

Local Government Finance Act 1992
(1992 c14)

Arrangement Of Sections
PART I
COUNCIL TAX: ENGLAND AND WALES
Chapter I: Main Provisions
Liability to tax
6.   Persons liable to pay council tax

Amounts of tax payable
11.   Discounts
13.   Reduced amounts

Chapter III: Setting of Council Tax

Setting of amounts
31.   Substituted amounts

PART II
Council Tax: Scotland
Liability to tax
75.   Persons liable to pay council tax

Amounts of tax payable
79.   Discounts
80.   Reduced amounts

Setting of the tax
94.   Substituted and reduced settings

Schedules
1.   Persons disregarded for Purposes of Discount

General note to the Act

This Act introduced the council tax and CTB to replace the former community charge (or poll tax) and community charge benefit. The council tax itself is outside the scope of this work – see CPAG's *Council Tax Handbook*. The parts of the Act reproduced below are those which are most necessary for a full understanding of CTB, usually because they are referred to in the CTB and the CTB(SPC) Regulations.

Section 103 and Schedule 9 to the Act substantially amended the Social Security Contributions and Benefits Act 1992 and the Social Security Administration Act 1992 so as to introduce CTB. Those provisions are not reproduced here as their effects have been incorporated in the text of the amended Acts as Part 1.

PART I
Council Tax: England and Wales
Chapter I: Main ProvisionsLiability to tax

Persons liable to pay council tax

6.–(1)   The person who is liable to pay council tax in respect of any chargeable dwelling and any day is the person who falls within the first paragraph of subsection (2) below to apply, taking paragraph (a) of that subsection first, paragraph (b) next, and so on.

(2)   A person falls within this subsection in relation to any chargeable dwelling and any day if, on that day–

(a)   he is a resident of the dwelling and has a freehold interest in the whole or any part of it;

(b)   he is such a resident and has a leasehold interest in the whole or any part of the dwelling which is not inferior to another such interest held by another such resident;

(c)   he is both such a resident and a statutory [¹ ...secure or introductory tenant] of the whole or any part of the dwelling;

(d)   he is such a resident and has a contractual licence to occupy the whole or any part of the dwelling;

(e)   he is such a resident.

(3)   Where, in relation to any chargeable dwelling and any day, two or more persons fall within the first paragraph of subsection (2) above to apply, they shall be jointly and severally liable to pay the council tax payable in respect of that dwelling and that day.

(4)   Subsection (3) above shall not apply as respects any day on which one or more of the persons there mentioned fall to be disregarded for the purposes of discount by virtue of [³ paragraph 2 (severely mentally impaired) or 4 (students etc.) of Schedule 1 to this Act] and one or more of them do not; and liability to pay the council tax in respect of the dwelling and that day shall be determined as follows–

(a)   if only one of those persons does not fall to be so disregarded, he shall be solely liable;

(b)   if two or more of those persons do not fall to be so disregarded, they shall be jointly and severally liable.

(5)   In this Part, unless the context otherwise requires–

"owner", in relation to any dwelling, means the person as regards whom the following conditions are fulfilled–

(a)   he has a material interest in the whole or any part of the dwelling; and

(b)   at least part of the dwelling or, as the case may be, of the part concerned is not subject to a material interest inferior to his interest;

"resident", in relation to any dwelling, means an individual who has attained the age of 18 years and has his sole or main residence in the dwelling

(6)   In this section–

[² "introductory tenant" means a tenant under an introductory tenancy within the meaning of Chapter I of Part V of the Housing Act 1996]

"material interest" means a freehold interest or a leasehold interest which was granted for a term of six months or more;

"secure tenant" means a tenant under a secure tenancy within the meaning of Part IV of the Housing Act 1985;

"statutory tenant" means a statutory tenant within the meaning of the Rent Act 1977 or the Rent (Agriculture) Act 1976.

Amendments

1.   Substituted by SI 1997 No. 74, Art 2 and Sch para 8(a) (12.2.97).

2.   Substituted by SI 1997 No. 74, Art 2 and Sch para 8(b) (12.2.97).

3.   Amended by s74(1) of the Local Government Act 2003 (effective in relation to financial years beginning on or after 1.4.04).

Amounts of tax payable

Discounts

    11.–(1)   The amount of council tax payable in respect of any chargeable dwelling and any day shall be subject to a discount equal to the appropriate percentage of that amount if on that day–

(a)   there is only one resident of the dwelling and he does not fall to be disregarded for the purposes of discount; or

(b)   there are two or more residents of the dwelling and each of them except one falls to be disregarded for those purposes.

(2)   Subject to [¹ sections 11A and 12] below, the amount of council tax payable in respect of any chargeable dwelling and any day shall be subject to a discount equal to twice the appropriate percentage of that amount if on that day–

(a)   there is no resident of the dwelling; or

(b)   there are one or more residents of the dwelling and each of them falls to be disregarded for the purposes of discount.

(3)   In this section [²] ''the appropriate percentage'' means 25 per cent. or, if the Secretary of State by order so provides in relation to the financial year in which the day falls, such other percentage as may be specified in the order.

(4)   No order under subsection (3) above shall be made unless a draft of the order has been laid before and approved by resolution of the House of Commons.

(5)   Schedule 1 to this Act shall have effect for determining who shall be disregarded for the purposes of discount.

Amendments

1.   Amended by the Local Government Act 2003, s127(1) and Sch 7 para 41.

2.   Repealed by the Local Government Act 3002, s127(2) and Part 1 Sch 8 (18.11.03).

Reduced Amounts

13.–(1)   The Secretary of State may make regulations as regards any case where–

(a)   a person is liable to pay an amount to a billing authority in respect of council tax for any financial year which is prescribed; and

(b)   prescribed conditions are fulfilled.

(2)   The regulations may provide that the amount he is liable to pay shall be an amount which–

(a)   is less than the amount it would be apart from the regulations; and

(b)   is determined in accordance with prescribed rules.

(3)   This section applies whether the amount mentioned in subsection (1) above is determined under section 10 above or under that section read with section 11[¹, 11A] or 12 above.

(4)   The conditions mentioned in subsection (1) above may be prescribed by reference to such factors as the Secretary of State thinks fit; and in particular such factors may include the making of an application by the person concerned and all or any of–

(a)   the factors mentioned in subsection (5) below; or

(b)   the factors mentioned in subsection (6) below.

(5)   The factors referred to in subsection (4)(a) above are–

(a)   community charges for a period before 1st April 1993;

(b)   the circumstances of, or other matters relating to, the person concerned;

(c)   an amount relating to the authority concerned and specified, or to be specified, for the purposes of the regulations in a report laid, or to be laid, before the House of Commons;

(d)   such other amounts as may be prescribed or arrived at in a prescribed manner.

(6)   The factors referred to in subsection (4)(b) above are–

(a)   a disabled personhaving his sole or main residence in the dwelling concerned;

(b)   the circumstances of, or other matters relating to, that persons;

(c)   the physical characteristics of, or other matters relating to, that dwelling.

(7)   The rules mentioned in subsection (2) above may be prescribed by reference to such factors as the Secretary of State thinks fit; and in particular such factors may include all or any of the factors mentioned in subsection (5) or subsection (6)(b) or (c) above.

(8)   Without prejudice to the generality of section 113(2) below, regulations under this section may include–

(a)   provision requiring the Secretary of State to specify in a report, for the purposes of the regulations, an amount in relation to each billing authority;

(b)   provision requiring him to lay the report before the House of Commons;

(c)   provision for the review of any prescribed decision of a billing authority relating to the application or operation of the regulations;

(d)   provision that no appeal may be made to a valuation tribunal in respect of such a decision, notwithstanding section 16(1) below.

(9)   To the extent that he would not have power to do so apart from this subsection, the Secretary of State may–

(a)   include in regulations under this section such amendments of any social security instrument as he thinks expedient in consequence of the regulations under this section;

(b)   include in any social security instrument such provision as he thinks expedient in consequence of regulations under this section.

(10)   In subsection (9) above "social security instrument" means an order or regulations made, or falling to be made, by the Secretary of State under the Social Security Acts, that is to say, the Social Security Contributions and Benefits Act 1992 and the Social Security Administration Act 1992.

Amendment

1.   Amended by the Local Government Act 2003 s127(1) and Sch 7 para 42.

General Note

For the 1997, 1998 and 1999 financial years para (5) was modified by reg 4 Local Government Changes for England (Council Tax) (Transitional Reduction) Regulations for that particular year: see 1997 SI No 215, 1998 SI No.214 and 1999 SI No.259. The modification applies only to chargeable dwellings in England (ie, not Wales) and only during the years for which the Regulations apply. In such circumstances, para (5) is to be read as if it contained an additional subparagraph (e) as follows:

"(e) the location of the dwelling concerned in the area of a district or county council which is affected by a structural change, or a boundary change, made by or in consequence of an order under section 17 of the Local Government Act 1992; and for this purpose a "structural change" and a "boundary change" shall be construed in accordance with section 14 of that Act"

Chapter III: Setting of Council Tax

Substituted amount

31.–(1)   Where a billing authority has set amounts for a financial year under section 30 above and at any later time–

(a)   it makes substitute calculations under section 37 or 60 below; or

(b)   it is issued with a precept for the year (originally or by way of substitute) by a major precepting authority,

it shall as soon as reasonably practicable after that time set amounts in substitution so as to give effect to those calculations or that precept.

(2)   Any amount set in substitution under subsection (1) above must be set in accordance with section 30 above, but subsection (6) of that section shall be ignored for this purpose.

(3)   Where a billing authority sets any amount in substitution under subsection (1) above (a new amount), anything paid to it by reference to the amount from which it is substituted (the old amount) shall be treated as paid by reference to the new amount.

(4)   If the old amount exceeds the new amount, the following shall apply as regards anything paid if it would not have been paid had the old amount been the same as the new amount–

(a)   it shall be repaid if the person by whom it was paid so requires;

(b)   in any other case it shall (as the billing authority determines) either be repaid or be credited against any subsequent liability of the person to pay in respect of any council tax set by the authority in accordance with section 30 above.

(5)   Where an authority sets amounts in substitution under subsection (1)(b) above, it may recover from the major precepting authority administrative expenses incurred by it in, or in consequence of, so doing.

PART II

Council Tax: Scotland

Liability to tax

Persons liable to pay council tax

75.–(1)   The person who is liable to pay council tax in respect of any chargeable dwelling and any day is the person who falls within the first paragraph of subsection (2) below to apply, taking paragraph (a) of that subsection first, paragraph (b) next, and so on.

(2)   A person falls within this subsection in relation to any chargeable dwelling and any day if, on that day–

(a)   he is the resident owner of the whole or any part of the dwelling;

(b)   he is a resident tenant of the whole or any part of the dwelling;

(c)   he is a resident statutory tenant, resident statutory assured tenant or resident secure tenant of the whole or any part of the dwelling;

(d)   he is a resident sub-tenant of the whole or any part of the dwelling;

(e)   he is a resident of the dwelling.

(3)   Where, in relation to any chargeable dwelling and any day, two or more persons fall within the first paragraph of subsection (2) above to apply, they shall be jointly and severally liable to pay the council tax payable in respect of that dwelling and that day.

(4)   Subsection (3)above shall not apply as respects any day on which one or more of the persons there mentioned fall to be disregarded for the purposes of discount [1 either] by virtue of paragraph 2 of Schedule 1 to this Act (the severely mentally impaired) [1 or, being a student, by virtue of paragraph 4 of that Schedule] and one or more of them do not; and liability to pay the council tax in respect of the dwelling and that day shall be determined as follows–

(a)   if only one of those persons does not fall to be so disregarded, he shall be solely liable;

(b)   if two or more of those persons do not fall to be so disregarded, they shall be jointly and severally liable.

(5)   In this section–

[2 "Scottish secure tenant" means a tenant under a Scottish secure tenancy within the meaning of the Housing (Scotland) Act 2001 (asp 10)];

"statutory tenant" means a statutory tenant within the meaning of the Rent (Scotland) Act 1984;

"statutory assured tenant" means a statutory assured tenant within the meaning of the Housing (Scotland) Act 1988.

Amendments

1.   Amended by s4 of the Education (Graduate Endowment and Student Support) Act 2001 as from 1.6.01.

2.   Amended by Sch 10 para 19 of the Housing (Scotland) Act 2001.

Amounts of tax payable

Discounts

79.–(1)   The amount of council tax payable in respect of any chargeable dwelling and any day shall be subject to a discount equal to the appropriate percentage of that amount if on that day–

(a)   there is only one resident of the dwelling and he does not fall to be disregarded for the purposes of discount; or

(b)   there are two or more residents of the dwelling and each of them except one falls to be disregarded for those purposes.

(2)   The amount of council tax payable in respect of any chargeable dwelling and any day shall be subject to a discount equal to twice the appropriate percentage of that amount if on that day–

[¹ (a)]

(b)   there are one or more residents of the dwelling and each of them falls to be disregarded for the purposes of discount.

(3)   In this section ''the appropriate percentage'' means 25 per cent. or, if the Secretary of State by order so provides in relation to the financial year in which the day falls, such other percentage as may be specified in the order.

(4)   No order under subsection (3) above shall be made unless a draft of the order has been laid before and approved by resolution of the House of Commons.

(5)   Schedule 1 to this Act shall have effect for determining who shall be disregarded for the purposes of discount.

Amendment

1.   Repealed by reg 2 of SI 2005 No 51 as from 1.4.05.

Reduced amounts

80.–(1)   The Secretary of State may make regulations as regards any case where–

(a)   a person is liable to pay an amount to a [¹ ...local] authority in respect of council tax for any financial year which is prescribed; and

(b)   prescribed conditions are fulfilled.

(2)   The regulations may provide that the amount he is liable to pay shall be an amount which–

(a)   is less than the amount it would be apart from the regulations; and

(b)   is determined in accordance with prescribed rules.

(3)   This section applies whether the amount mentioned in subsection (1) above is determined under section 78 above or under that section read with section 79 above.

(4)   The conditions mentioned in subsection (1) above may be prescribed by reference to such factors as the Secretary of State thinks fit; and in particular such factors may include the making of an application by the person concerned and all or any or–

(a)   the factors mentioned in subsection (5) below; or

(b)   the factors mentioned in subsection (6) below.

(5)   The factors mentioned in subsection (4)(a) above are–

(a)   community charges for a period before 1st April 1993;

(b)   the circumstances of, or other matters relating to, the person concerned;

(c)   an amount–

[²(i)   relating to the local authority whose council tax constitutes the amount referred to in subsection (1) above;] and

(ii)   which is specified, or is to be specified, in a report laid, or to be laid, before the House of Commons;

(6)   The factors referred to in subsection (4)(b) above are

(a)   a disabled person having his sole or main residence in the dwelling concerned;

(b)   the circumstances of, or other matters relating to, that person;

(c)   the physical characteristics of, or other matters relating to, that dwelling.

(7)   The rules mentioned in subsection (2) above may be prescribed by reference to such factors as the Secretary of State thinks fit; and in particular such factors may include all or any of the factors mentioned in subsection (5) or subsection (6)(b) or (c) above.

(8)   Without prejudice to the generality of section 113(2) below, regulations under this section may include–

(a)   provision requiring the Secretary of State to specify in a report, for the purposes of the regulations, an amount in relation to each local authority;

(b)   provision requiring him to lay the report before the House of Commons;

(c)   provision for the review of any prescribed decision of a [¹ ...local] authority relating to the application or operation of the regulations;

(d)   provision that no appeal may be made to a valuation appeal committee in respect of such a decision, notwithstanding section 81(1) below.

(9)   To the extent that he would not have power to do so apart from this subsection, the Secretary of State may–

(a)   include in regulations under this section such amendments of any social security instrument as he thinks expedient in consequence of the regulations under this section;

(b)   include in any social security instrument such provision as he thinks expedient in consequence of regulations under this section.

(10)   In subsection (9) above ''social security instrument'' means an order or regulations made, or falling to be made, by the Secretary of State under the Social Security Acts.

Amendments

1.   Substituted by Local Government Etc. (Scotland) Act 1994 c.39 s180(1) and Sch 13 para 176(4)(a).
2.   Substituted by Local Government Etc. (Scotland) Act 1994 c.39 s180(1) and Sch 13 para 176(4)(b).

Setting of the tax

Substituted and reduced settings

94.–(1)   Subject to subsection (3) below, a local authority may set, in substitution for an amount of council tax already set or deemed to have been set, a lesser amount of council tax for the same financial year.

(2)   Schedule 7 to this Act has effect for the purpose of making provision as to the reduction of council tax where the Secretary of State is satisfied, in accordance with that Schedule, that the total estimated expenses mentioned in section 93(3) above of a local authority are excessive or that an increase in those expenses is excessive.

(3)   A local authority may not set a substitute amount of council tax during the period between the approval by the House of Commons of a report in respect of that authority made by the Secretary of State under paragraph 1 of that Schedule and the setting or deemed setting of a reduced amount of council tax under paragraph 3 of that Schedule.

(4)   Section 93(2) above shall not apply for the purposes of this section.

(5)   A local authority who, in respect of any financial year, set (or are deemed to have set) a substituted or reduced council tax shall neither wholly nor partially offset the difference between–

(a)   the amount produced by that substituted or reduced setting; and

(b)   the amount which would have been produced had they not substituted or reduced their setting, with sums advanced from their loans fund established under Schedule 3 to the 1975 Act:

Provided that such offsetting may nevertheless be permitted by the Secretary of State in any case on such terms and conditions as he considers appropriate.

(6)   If the Secretary of State is of the opinion that subsection (5) above, or any term or condition imposed under the proviso thereto, has been contravened, the local authority shall, on such opinion being intimated to them, reimburse their loans fund forthwith or within such time as the Secretary of State may allow.

(7)   Anything paid by reference to one setting of council tax shall be treated as paid by reference to a substitute setting by virtue of paragraph 3 of Schedule 7 to this Act.

(8)   Where a person has paid by reference to one setting of council tax more than is due under a substituted or reduced setting–

(a)   the balance shall be repaid to the person if s/he so requires;

(b)   in any other case the balance shall (as the [¹ ...local] authority determine) either be repaid to the person or be credited against any subsequent liability of the person to pay in respect of any council tax due to the authority.

(9)   Where–

(a)   a substitute amount of council tax has been set under subsection (1) above; or

(b)   a reduced amount of council tax has been set or been deemed to have been set under paragraph 3 of that Schedule,

the regional council shall levy and collect that substituted or reduced amount in place of the previous amount of council tax and may recover from the district council any administrative expenses incurred in so doing in relation to a substituted or reduced amount of district council tax.

Amendment

1.   Substituted by Local Government Etc. (Scotland) Act 1994 c.39 s180(1) and Sch 13 para 176(9).

SCHEDULE 1
PERSONS DISREGARDED FOR PURPOSES OF DISCOUNT
Persons in detention

1.–(1)   A person shall be disregarded for the purposes of discount on a particular day if on the day–

(a)   he is detained in a prison, a hospital or any other place by virtue of an order of a court to which sub-paragraph (2) below applies;

(b)   he is detained under paragraph 2 of Schedule 3 to the Immigration Act 1971 (deportation);

(c)   he is detained under Part II or section 46, 47, 48 or 136 of the Mental Health Act 1983; or

(d)   he is detained under Part V or section 69, 70, 71 or 118 of the Mental Health (Scotland) Act 1984.

(2)   This sub-paragraph applies to the following courts–

(a)   a court in the United Kingdom; and

(b)   a Standing Civilian Court established under the Armed Forces Act 1976.

(3)   If a person–

(a)   is temporarily discharged under section 28 of the Prison Act 1952, or temporarily released under rules under section 47(5) of that Act; or

(b)   is temporarily discharged under section 27 of the Prisons (Scotland) Act 1989, or temporarily released under rules under section 39(6) or that Act,

for the purposes of sub-paragraph (1) above he shall be treated as detained.

(4)   Sub-paragraph (1) above does not apply where the person–

(a)   is detained under regulations made under paragraph 8 of Schedule 4 to this Act;

(b)   is detained under section 76 of the Magistrates' Courts Act 1980, or section 9 of the Criminal Justice Act 1982, for default in payment of a fine; or

(c)   is detained only under section 407 of the Criminal Procedure (Scotland) Act 1975.

(5)   In sub-paragraph (1) above "order" includes a sentence, direction, warrant or other means of giving effect to the decision of the court concerned.

(6)   The Secretary of State may by order provide that a person shall be disregarded for the purposes of discount on a particular day if–

(a) on the day he is imprisoned, detained or in custody under the Army Act 1955, the Air Force Act 1955 or the Naval Discipline Act 1957; and

(b) such conditions as may be prescribed by the order are fulfilled.

The severely mentally impaired

2.–(1) A person shall be disregarded for the purposes of discount on a particular day if

(a) on the day he is severely mentally impaired;

(b) as regards any period which includes the day he is stated in a certificate of a registered medical practitioner to have been or to be likely to be severely mentally impaired; and

(c) as regards the day he fulfils such conditions as may be prescribed by order made by the Secretary of State.

(2) For the purposes of this paragraph a person is severely mentally impaired if he has a severe impairment of intelligence and social functioning (however caused) which appears to be permanent.

(3) The Secretary of State may by order substitute another definition for the definition in sub-paragraph (2) above as for the time being effective for the purposes of this paragraph.

Persons in respect of whom child benefit is payable

3.–(1) A person shall be disregarded for the purposes of discount on a particular day if on the day he–

(a) has attained the age of 18 years; but

(b) is a person in respect of whom another person is entitled to child benefit, or would be so entitled but for paragraph 1(c) of Schedule 9 to the Social Security Contributions and Benefits Act 1992.

(2) The Secretary of State may by order substitute another provision for sub-paragraph (1)(b) above as for the time being effective for the purposes of this paragraph.

Students etc

4.–(1) A person shall be disregarded for the purposes of discount on a particular day if–

(a) on the day he is a student, student nurse, apprentice or youth training trainee; and

(b) such conditions as may be prescribed by order made by the Secretary of State are fulfilled.

(2) In this paragraph ''apprentice'', ''student'', ''student nurse'' and ''youth training trainee'' have the meanings for the time being assigned to them by order made by the Secretary of State.

5.–(1) An institution shall, on request, supply a certificate under this paragraph to any person who is following or, subject to sub-paragraph (3) below, has followed a course of education at that institution as a student or student nurse.

(2) A certificate under this paragraph shall contain such information about the person to whom it refers as may be prescribed by order made by the Secretary of State.

(3) An institution may refuse to comply with a request made more than one year after the person making it has ceased to follow a course of education at that institution.

(4) In this paragraph–

''institution'' means any such educational establishment or other body as may be prescribed by order made by the Secretary of State; and

''student'' and ''student nurse'' have the same meanings as in paragraph 4 above.

Hospital patients

6.–(1) A person shall be disregarded for the purposes of discount on a particular day if on the day he is a patient who has his sole or main residence in a hospital.

(2) In this paragraph ''hospital'' means–

(a) a health service hospital within the meaning of the National Health Service Act 1977 or section 108(1) (interpretation) of the National Health Service (Scotland) Act 1978; and

(b) a military, air-force or naval unit or establishment at or in which medical or surgical treatment is provided for persons subject to military law, air-force law or the Naval Discipline Act 1957.

(3) The Secretary of State may by order substitute another definition for the definition in sub-paragraph (2) above as for the time being effective for the purposes of this paragraph.

Patients in homes in England and Wales

7.–(1) A person shall be disregarded for the purposes of discount on a particular day if on the day–

(a) he has his sole or main residence in a [¹ care home, independent hospital] or hostel in England and Wales; and

(b) he is receiving care or treatment (or both) in the home [¹ , hospital] or hostel.

[¹ (2) In this paragraph–

''care home'' means–

(a) a care home within the meaning of the Care Standards Act 2000; or

(b)   a building or part of a building in which residential accommodation is provided under section 21 of the National Assistance Act 1948;

"hostel" means anything which falls within any definition of hostel for the time being prescribed by order made by the Secretary of State under this sub-paragraph;

"independent hospital" has the same meaning as in the Care Standards Act 2000.]

(3)   The Secretary of State may by order substitute another definition for any definition of [¹ "care home" or "independent hospital"] for the time being effective for the purposes of this paragraph.

Amendment

1.   Amended by Sch 10 para 20 of the Care Standards Act 2000.

Patients in homes in Scotland

8.–(1)   A person shall be disregarded for the purposes of discount on a particular day if on the day–

[¹ (a)   either–

    (i)   he has as his sole or main residence a private hospital in Scotland; or

    (ii)   a care home service provides, in Scotland, accommodation which is his sole or main residence; and

(b)   he is receiving care or treatment (or both) in the hospital or in the accommodation so provided.]

(2)   In this paragraph–

[¹ "care home service" has the same meaning as in the Regulation of Care (Scotland) Act 2001 (asp 8); and]

[¹ . . .]

"private hospital" means a private hospital within the meaning of section 12 (registration of private hospitals) of the Mental Health (Scotland) Act 1984;

[¹ . . .]

(3)   [¹ . . .]

(4)   The Secretary of State may by order substitute another definition for any definition of [¹ . . .] "private hospital" or [¹ "care home service"] for the time being effective for the purposes of this paragraph.

Amendment

1.   Amended by Sch 3 para 18 of the Regulation of Care (Scotland) Act 2001.

Care workers

9.–(1)   A person shall be disregarded for the purposes of discount on a particular day if–

(a)   on the day he is engaged in providing care or support (or both) to another person or other persons; and

(b)   such conditions as may be prescribed are fulfilled.

(2)   Without prejudice to the generality of sub-paragraph (1)(b) above the conditions may–

(a)   require the care or support (or both) to be provided on behalf of a charity or a person fulfilling some other description;

(b)   relate to the period for which the person is engaged in providing care of support (or both);

(c)   require his income for a prescribed period (which contains the day concerned) not to exceed a prescribed amount;

(d)   require his capital not to exceed a prescribed amount;

(e)   require him to be resident in prescribed premises;

(f)   require him not to exceed a prescribed age;

(g)   require the other person or persons to fulfil a prescribed description (whether relating to age, disablement or otherwise).

Residents of certain dwellings

10.–(1)   A person shall be disregarded for the purposes of discount on a particular day if on the day he has his sole or main residence in a dwelling to which sub-paragraph (2) below applies.

(2)   This sub-paragraph applies to any dwelling if–

(a)   it is for the time being providing residential accommodation, whether as a hostel or night shelter or otherwise; and

(b)   the accommodation is predominantly provided–

    (i)   otherwise than in separate and self-contained sets of premises;

    (ii)   for persons of no fixed abode and no settled way of life; and

    (iii)   under licences to occupy which do not constitute tenancies.

Persons of other descriptions

11. A person shall be disregarded for the purposes of discount on a particular day if–

(a) on the day he falls within such descriptions as may be prescribed; and

(b) such conditions as may be prescribed are fulfilled.

Housing Act 1996

(1996 c52)

Functions of rent officers in connection with housing benefit and rent allowance subsidy

122.–(1)   The Secretary of State may by order require rent officers to carry out such functions as may be specified in the order in connection with housing benefit and council tax benefit.

(2)   Without prejudice to the generality of subsection (1), an order under this section may contain provision–

(a)   enabling a prospective landlord to apply for a determination for the purposes of any application for housing benefit which may be made by a tenant of a dwelling which he proposed to let;

(b)   as to the payment of a fee by the landlord for that determination;

(c)   requiring the landlord to give a copy of the determination to the appropriate local authority; and

(d)   enabling the appropriate local authority to seek a redetermination when a claim for housing benefit or rent allowance subsidy is made.

(3)   Regulations under section 130(4) of the Social Security Contributions and Benefits Act 1992 (housing benefit: manner of determining appropriate maximum benefit) may provide for benefit to be limited by reference to determinations made by rent officers in exercise of functions conferred under this section.

(4)   In relation to rent allowance subsidy, the Secretary of State may by order under section 140B of the Social Security Administration Act 1992–

(a)   provide for any calculation under subsection (2) of that section to be made,

(b)   specify any additions and deductions as are referred to in that subsection, and

(c)   exercise his discretion as to what is unreasonable for the purposes of subsection (4) of that section,

by reference to determinations made by rent officers in exercise of functions conferred on them under this section.

(5)   The Secretary of State may by any such regulations or order as are mentioned in subsection (3) or (4) require a local authority in any prescribed case–

(a)   to apply to a rent officer for a determination to be made in pursuance of the functions conferred on them under this section; and

(b)   to do so within such time as may be specified in the order or regulations.

(6)   An order under this section–

(a)   shall be made by statutory instrument which shall be subject to annulment in pursuance of a resolution of either House of Parliament;

(b)   may make different provision for different cases or classes of case and for different areas; and

(c)   may contain such transitional, incidental and supplementary provisions as appear to the Secretary of State to be desirable.

(7)   In this section "housing benefit" and "rent allowance subsidy" have the same meaning as in Part VIII of the Social Security Administration Act 1992.

Commencement

1.4.97.

General Note

This section allows the Secretary of State to further expand the role of rent officers in HB matters. See the Rent Officers (Housing Benefit Functions) Order 1997 (p520) and the Scottish equivalent (p540).

Subs (1) is a general power to give rent officers additional functions in relation to HB and rent allowance subsidy. The Secretary of State's powers are not restricted to those in Subs (2).

Subs (2) allows landlords and tenants to know, prior to the entry of a tenancy agreement, precisely what level of rent will be met by a rent allowance. It is the landlord's responsibility to obtain that assessment. Note, however, that provision may be made for a local authority to seek a fresh determination on a claim for HB. See reg 14(1)(e) of both the HB and the HB(SPC) Regs.

Subs (3) authorises the current form of reg 13(2) of both the HB and the HB(SPC) Regs.

Welfare Reform and Pensions Act 1999

(1999 c30)

Arrangement Of Sections

MISCELLANEOUS
68.   Certain overpayments of benefit not be recoverable
72.   Supply of information for certain purposes
79.   Measures to reduce under-occupation by housing benefit claimants

SUPPLEMENTARY
83.   Regulations and orders
84.   Consequential amendments etc
85.   Transitional provisions
86.   General financial provisions
87.   Corresponding provisions for Northern Ireland
88.   Repeals
89.   Commencement
90.   Extent
91.   Short title, general interpretation and Scottish devolution

SCHEDULES
8.   Administration of benefits

General Note to the Act

The principal innovation made by the Act, as far as this book is concerned, was a greatly expanded role for local authorities as providers of benefit services. The Act seeks to permit the implementation of the Single Work-Focused Gateway, or ONE as it was subsequently re-christened. The scheme set up a number of offices to handle claims and inquiries relating to all benefits and provided "work-focused interviews" to assist claimants in finding employment.

It is understood that there are no longer any ONE offices still in existence.

There are important provisions in s68 making certain overpayments irrecoverable and in s79, which enables the setting-up of a scheme of incentives to reduce the occupation by HB claimants of homes that are felt to be larger than those required by them.

Miscellaneous

Certain overpayments of benefit not to be recoverable

68.–(1)   An overpayment to which this section applies shall not be recoverable from the payee, whether by the Secretary of State or a local authority, under any provision made by or under Part III of the Administration Act (overpayments and adjustments of benefit).

(2)   This section applies to an overpayment if–

(a)   it is in respect of a qualifying benefit;

(b)   it is referable to a decision given on a review that there has been an alteration in the relevant person's condition, being a decision to which effect is required to be given as from a date earlier than that on which it was given;

(c)   the decision was given before 1st June 1999; and

(d)   the overpayment is not excluded by virtue of subsection (6).

(3)   In subsection (2)(b) the reference to a decision on a review that there has been an alteration in the relevant person's condition is a reference to a decision so given that that person's physical or mental condition either was at the time when the original decision was given, or has subsequently become, different from that on which that decision was based, with the result–

(a)   that he did not at that time, or (as the case may be) has subsequently ceased to, meet any of the conditions contained in the following provisions of the Contributions and Benefits Act, namely–

      (i)   section 64 (attendance allowance),

      (ii)   section 72(1) or (2) (care component of disability living allowance), and

      (iii)   section 73(1) or (2) (mobility component of that allowance); or

(b)   that he was at that time, or (as the case may be) has subsequently become, capable of work in accordance with regulations made under section 171C(2) of that Act (the all work test).

(4)   For the purposes of this section ''qualifying benefit'' means–

(a)   attendance allowance;

(b)   disability living allowance;

(c)   any benefit awarded wholly or partly by reason of a person being (or being treated as being) in receipt of a component (at any rate) of disability living allowance or in receipt of attendance allowance;

(d)   incapacity benefit;

(e)   any benefit (other than incapacity benefit) awarded wholly or partly by reason of a person being (or being treated as being) incapable of work; or

(f)   any benefit awarded wholly or partly by reason of a person being (or being treated as being) in receipt of any benefit falling within paragraph (c), (d) or (e).

(5)   For the purposes of this section–

(a)   ''review'' means a review taking place by virtue of section 25(1)(a) or (b), 30(2)(a) or (b) or 35(1)(a) or (b) of the Administration Act;

(b)   ''the relevant person'', in relation to a review, means the person to whose entitlement to a qualifying benefit or to whose incapacity for work the review related; and

(c)   ''the original decision'', in relation to a review, means the decision as to any such entitlement or incapacity to which the review related.

(6)   An overpayment is excluded by virtue of this subsection if (before or after the passing of this Act)–

(a)   the payee has agreed to pay a penalty in respect of the overpayment under section 115A of the Administration Act,

(b)   the payee has been convicted of any offence (under section 111A or 112(1) or (1A) of that Act or otherwise) in connection with the overpayment, or

(c)   proceedings have been instituted against the payee for such an offence and the proceedings have not been determined or abandoned.

(7)   Nothing in this section applies to an overpayment to the extent that it was recovered from the payee (by any means) before 26ᵗʰ February 1999.

(8)   In this section–

''benefit'' includes any amount included in–

(a)   the applicable amount in relation to an income-related benefit (as defined by section 135(1) of the Contributions and Benefits Act), or

(b)   the applicable amount in relation to a jobseeker's allowance (as defined by section 4(5) of the Jobseekers Act 1995);

''income-related benefit'' has the meaning given by section 123(1) of the Contributions and Benefits Act;

''overpayment'' means an amount of benefit paid in excess of entitlement;

''the payee'', in relation to an overpayment, means the person to whom that amount was paid.

Commencement

    11.11.99: see s89(4)(a).

General Note

    This provision was prompted by concern over the effect of the application of the Government's "Benefit Integrity Project" (BIP). The aim of the BIP was to identify those in receipt of benefits related to illness or disability whose conditions did not justify such an award. A number of claimants found that not only did entitlement to benefit cease, but that large overpayments were sought to be recovered from them. This provision aimed to alleviate the problems caused by the BIP. By sub-section (2)(c), it only applies to decisions given before 1 June 1999.

The section basically works by deeming certain overpayments caused by a change in the claimant's condition to be irrecoverable. Although HB and CTB are not themselves paid as a result of medical conditions, certain premiums are dependent on receipt of medical-related benefits and so the section may well have application to certain overpayments of HB and CTB. For a more detailed analysis, see the commentary to s68 in the 18th edition of this book.

Supply of information for certain purposes

72.–(1)   The Secretary of State may by regulations make such provision for or in connection with any of the following matters, namely–

(a)   the use by a person within subsection (2) of social security information held by that person,

(b)   the supply (whether to a person within subsection (2) or otherwise) of social security information held by a person within that subsection,

(c)   the relevant purposes for which a person to whom such information is supplied under the regulations may use it, and

(d)   the circumstances and extent (if any) in and to which a person to whom such information is supplied under the regulations may supply it to any other person (whether within subsection (2) or not), as the Secretary of State considers appropriate in connection with any provision to which subsection (3) applies or in connection with any scheme or arrangements to which subsection (4) applies.

(2)   The persons within this subsection are–

(a)   a Minister of the Crown;

(b)   a person providing services to, or designated for the purposes of this section by an order of, a Minister of the Crown;

(c)   a local authority (within the meaning of the Administration Act); and

(d)   a person providing services to, or authorised to exercise any function of, any such authority.

(3)   This subsection applies to any provision made by or under–

(a)   any of the sections of the Administration Act inserted by section 57, 58 or 71 of this Act,

(b)   section 60 of this Act, or

(c)   the Jobseekers Act 1995.

(4)   This subsection applies to–

(a)   any scheme designated by regulations under subsection (1), being a scheme operated by the Secretary of State (whether under arrangements with any other person or not) for any purposes connected with employment or training in the case of persons of a particular category or description;

(b)   any arrangements of a description specified in such regulations, being arrangements made by the Secretary of State for any such purposes.

(5)   Regulations under subsection (1) may, in particular, authorise information supplied to a person under the regulations–

(a)   to be used for the purpose of amending or supplementing other information held by that person; and

(b)   if it is so used, to be supplied to any other person, and used for any purpose, to whom or for which that other information could be supplied or used.

(6)   In this section–

''relevant purposes'' means purposes connected with–

(a)   social security, child support or war pensions, or

(b)   employment or training;

''social security information'' means information relating to social security, child support or war pensions; and in this subsection ''war pensions'' means war pensions within the meaning of section 25 of the Social Security Act 1989 (establishment and functions of war pensions committees).

(7)   Any reference in this section to purposes connected with employment or training includes purposes connected with the existing or future employment or training prospects or needs of persons, and (in particular) assisting or encouraging persons to enhance their employment prospects.

Commencement

11.11.99: see s89(4)(c).

General Note

This permits regulations governing the passing of information the people listed in s72(2), including between a local authority and other public officials.

Measures to reduce under-occupation by housing benefit claimants

79.–(1)   The Secretary of State may by regulations make a scheme providing for a housing benefit claimant, where he moves from an under-occupied dwelling in the public or social rented sector to a qualifying dwelling, to be entitled to be paid an amount calculated by reference to the difference between–

(a)   the prescribed payments he was liable to make in respect of his former dwelling, and

(b)   those he is liable to make in respect of his new dwelling.

(2)   In subsection (1) the reference to a qualifying dwelling is to a dwelling (whether in the public or social rented sector or not) which, in relation to the claimant, either–

(a)   is not under-occupied, or

(b)   is under-occupied to a lesser extent than the claimant's former dwelling.

(3)   Regulations under this section may, in particular, make provision–

(a)   as to the circumstances in which, in relation to a housing benefit claimant, a dwelling is or is not to be regarded for the purposes of the scheme as under-occupied or under-occupied to a lesser extent than another dwelling;

(b)   as to the manner in which an amount payable to such a claimant under the scheme is to be calculated;

(c)   for any such amount to be payable (subject to subsection (7))–

    (i)   in a case where the claimant's former and new dwellings are situated in the area of the same local authority, by that authority, or

    (ii)   in a case where they are situated in the areas of different local authorities, by whichever of those authorities is prescribed.

(4)   Regulations made in pursuance of subsection (3)(b) may provide for the amount payable to a housing benefit claimant under the scheme ("the relevant amount") to be reduced on account of–

(a)   any arrears of rent payable by him, or

(b)   any amount paid to him by way of housing benefit which constitutes an overpayment for housing benefit purposes; but regulations under this section shall not otherwise provide for the making of any reduction in the relevant amount on account of any sum due to or recoverable by any public or local authority.

(5)   A person aggrieved by a determination of any prescribed description made under regulations under this section may appeal to such court or tribunal as may be prescribed; and the regulations may make provision as to the procedure to be followed in connection with appeals under this subsection.

(6)   Regulations under this section may provide that the scheme is to apply only in relation to one or more prescribed areas; and, if they do so, they may also–

(a)   provide that (unless continued in force by subsequent regulations under this section) the scheme is to remain in force there only for a prescribed period;

(b)   include such transitional, consequential or saving provisions as the Secretary of State considers appropriate in connection with the scheme ceasing to be in force in relation to the area or areas at the end of that period.

(7)   Despite the fact that the scheme is in force in relation to the area of a local authority (whether by virtue of subsection (6) or otherwise), it shall not have effect in relation to the authority unless it has been adopted by resolution of the authority.

(8)   Where a local authority makes any payment under the scheme the authority shall be reimbursed by the Secretary of State in respect of that payment in such manner and subject to such conditions as to claims, records, certificates or other information or evidence as may be prescribed (any reduction made by virtue of subsection (4) being disregarded for the purposes of this subsection).

(9)   Subject to any prescribed exceptions or modifications, the provisions of the Administration Act shall have effect in relation to payments under the scheme as they have effect in relation to housing benefit.

(10)   For the purposes of this section a dwelling occupied by a housing benefit claimant is in the public or social rented sector if the payments which the claimant is liable to make in respect of the dwelling (and on account of which he is entitled to housing benefit) are to be made to–

(a)   a local authority,

(b)   a body eligible for registration as a social landlord under Part I of the Housing Act 1996 (whether so registered or not), or

(c)   in Scotland, a registered housing association within the meaning of the Housing Associations Act 1985.

(11)   In this section–

"dwelling" has the same meaning as in Part VII of the Contributions and Benefits Act (income-related benefits);

"housing benefit claimant", in relation to a dwelling, means a person entitled to housing benefit by virtue of being liable to make payments in respect of the dwelling;

"local authority" has the same meaning as in the Administration Act;

"prescribed" means specified in or determined in accordance with regulations under this section.

Commencement

11.11.99: see s89(4)(d).

General Note

This section permitted the introduction of a scheme giving incentives for claimants to move from "public or social rented" housing which is larger than they require to a smaller home. Public or social rented housing is defined in subs (10) as tenancies of local authorities or social landlords entitled to register under Part I of the Housing Act 1996 or registered under the Housing Associations Act 1985 in Scotland. The rent restrictions provisions in reg 13 of both the HB and the HB(SPC) Regs, of course, provide quite ample incentive to private tenants to avoid generously-sized accommodation. The Social Security (Payments to Reduce Under-occupation) Regulations 2000, SI No 637 brought the scheme into force in certain local authority areas. The regulations ceased to have effect on 31 March 2003. For more information, see the commentary to s79 in the 18th edition of this book.

Supplementary

Regulations and orders

83.–(1)   Any power under this Act to make regulations or orders (other than orders under section 72(2)) shall be exercisable by statutory instrument.

(2)   A statutory instrument–

(a)   which contains (whether alone or with other provisions) regulations made under this Act, and

(b)   which is not subject to any requirement that a draft of the instrument be laid before and approved by a resolution of each House of Parliament, shall be subject to annulment in pursuance of a resolution of either House of Parliament.

(3)   A statutory instrument containing an order under section 27(3) shall be subject to annulment in pursuance of a resolution of either House of Parliament.

(4)   Any power under this Act to make regulations or orders may be exercised–

(a)   either in relation to all cases to which the power extends, or in relation to those cases subject to specified exceptions, or in relation to any specified cases or classes of case;

(b)   so as to make, as respects the cases in relation to which it is exercised–

    (i)   the full provision to which the power extends or any less provision (whether by way of exception or otherwise);

    (ii)   the same provision for all cases in relation to which the power is exercised, or different provision for different cases or different classes of case or different provision as respects the same case or class of case for different purposes of this Act;

    (iii)   any such provision either unconditionally or subject to any specified condition.

(5)   Where any such power is expressed to be exercisable for alternative purposes it may be exercised in relation to the same case for any or all of those purposes.

(6)   Any such power includes power–

(a)   to make such incidental, supplementary, consequential, saving or transitional provision (including provision amending, repealing or revoking enactments) as appears to the authority making the regulations or order to be expedient; and

(b)   to provide for a person to exercise a discretion in dealing with any matter.

(7)   Any power to make regulations or an order for the purposes of any provision of this Act is without prejudice to any power to make regulations or an order for the purposes of any other provision of this or any other Act.

(8)   Any power conferred by this Act to make regulations or an order relating to–

(a)   housing benefit, or

(b)   council tax benefit, includes power to make different provision for different areas or different authorities; and regulations under section 60 or 79 may make different provision for different areas.

(9)   Without prejudice to the generality of any of the preceding provisions of this section, regulations under section 60 or 72 may provide for all or any of the provisions of the regulations to apply only in relation to any area or areas specified in the regulations.

(10)   Any power to make regulations under Part IV, except sections 28 and 48, shall, if the Treasury so direct, be exercisable only in conjunction with them.

(11)   Before exercising any power to make regulations under Part IV, the authority on whom the power is conferred, or, if the power is the subject of a direction under subsection (10), that authority and the Treasury acting jointly, shall consult such persons as the authority, or the authority and the Treasury, may consider appropriate.

Consequential amendments etc

84.–(1)   The consequential amendments specified in Schedule 12 shall have effect.

(2)   The Secretary of State may by regulations make such amendments or revocations of any instrument made under an Act as he thinks necessary or expedient

in consequence of the coming into force of any of the provisions specified in subsection (4).

(3)　The Secretary of State may, for the purposes of or in connection with the coming into force of any of the provisions specified in subsection (4), make by regulations any provision which could be made by an order bringing the provision into force.

(4)　The provisions mentioned in subsections (2) and (3) are–

(a)　Part IV;

(b)　subsection (1) above so far as relating to paragraphs 14 to 63 of Schedule 12; and

(c)　section 88 so far as relating to Part III of Schedule 13.

Transitional provisions

85.–(1)　The Secretary of State may, for the purposes of or in connection with the coming into force of any provisions of Parts I and II, by regulations make such transitional adaptations or modifications–

(a)　of those provisions, or

(b)　in connection with those provisions, of any provisions of–

(i)　this Act,

(ii)　the Pension Schemes Act 1993, or

(iii)　the Pensions Act 1995, then in force, as he considers necessary or expedient

(2) to (8) *[omitted]*.

General financial provisions

86.–(1)　There shall be paid out of money provided by Parliament–

(a)　any expenditure incurred by a Minister of the Crown or government department under this Act; and

(b)　any increase attributable to this Act in the sums which under any other Act are payable out of money so provided.

(2)　There shall be paid into the Consolidated Fund any increase attributable to this Act in the sums which under any other Act are payable into that Fund.

Corresponding provisions for Northern Ireland

87.　An Order in Council under paragraph 1(1)(b) of Schedule 1 to the Northern Ireland Act 1974 (legislation for Northern Ireland in the interim period) which contains a statement that it is made only for purposes corresponding to those of this Act–

(a)　shall not be subject to paragraph 1(4) and (5) of that Schedule (affirmative resolution of both Houses of Parliament), but

(b)　shall be subject to annulment in pursuance of a resolution of either House of Parliament.

Repeals

88.　The enactments specified in Schedule 13 (which include certain enactments no longer of practical utility) are hereby repealed to the extent specified in the third column of that Schedule.

Commencement

89.–(1)　Subject to the provisions of this section, the provisions of this Act shall not come into force until such day as the Secretary of State may by order appoint.

(2)　The following provisions shall not come into force until such day as the Lord Chancellor may by order appoint–

(a)   sections 19, 21 and 22;

(b)   section 84(1) so far as relating to paragraphs 1 to 4 and 64 to 66 of Schedule 12;

(c)   section 85(3) and (4); and

(d)   section 88 so far as relating to the entries in Part II of Schedule 13 in respect of the Matrimonial Causes Act 1973, the Matrimonial and Family Proceedings Act 1984 and sections 9(8) and 16 of the Family Law Act 1996.

(3)   The following provisions shall not come into force until such day as the Treasury may by order appoint–

(a)   sections 73 to 78;

(b)   section 84(1) so far as relating to paragraphs 74, 76 to 78 and 84 to 86 of Schedule 12; and

(c)   section 88 so far as relating to Parts VI and VII of Schedule 13.

(4)   The following provisions come into force on the day on which this Act is passed–

(a)   sections 52, 57, 58, 60, 68 and 71;

(b)   section 70 so far as relating to Part V of Schedule 8;

(c)   section 72;

(d)   sections 79 to 83;

(e)   section 84(1) so far as relating to paragraphs 13, 79 to 83 and 87 of Schedule 12;

(f)   section 84(2) to (4);

(g)   section 85(1), (2), (6) and (7); and

(h)   sections 86 and 87, this section and sections 90 and 91.

(5)   The following provisions come into force on the day on which this Act is passed, but for the purpose only of the exercise of any power to make regulations–

(a)   Parts I to IV;

(b)   sections 59 and 61; and

(c)   section 70 so far as relating to paragraph 23 of Schedule 8.

Without prejudice to section 83, an order under this section may appoint different days for different purposes or different areas.

Extent

90.–(1)   The following provisions extend to England and Wales only–

(a)   section 15;

(b)   paragraph 2 of Schedule 2, and section 18 so far as relating thereto;

(c)   sections 19, 21 and 22 and Schedules 3 and 4;

(d)   paragraphs 1 to 4, 64 to 66 and 70 to 72 of Schedule 12, and section 84(1) so far as relating thereto; and

(e)   section 85(3) and (4).

(2)   The following provisions extend to Scotland only–

(a)   sections 13 and 16;

(b)   paragraph 1 of Schedule 2, and section 18 so far as relating thereto;

(c)   section 20;

(d)   paragraphs 5 to 12 and 67 to 69 of Schedule 12, and section 84(1) so far as relating thereto; and

(e)   section 85(5).

(3)   The following provisions extend to England and Wales and Scotland only–

(a)   Part I;

(b)   sections 9 to 12, 14 and 17;

(c)   Schedule 2 (except for paragraphs 1, 2, 3(1), 7(2) and 16), and section 18 so far as relating thereto;

(d)   sections 23, 24 and 26;

(e)   Part IV except sections 42 to 44;

(f)   Chapter I of Part V (except paragraph 1 of Schedule 8, and section 70 so far as relating thereto);

(g)   sections 73, 75 and 77 and Schedule 9;

(h)   section 79;

(i)   paragraphs 1 to 8, 20 to 23, 32(b), 33, 35 and 37 of Schedule 11, and section 81 so far as relating thereto;

(j)   paragraphs 14 to 63, 66(17), 76 to 80, 82, 83 and 87 of Schedule 12, and section 84(1) so far as relating thereto; and

(k)   section 84(2) to (4).

(4)   The following provisions extend to England and Wales, Scotland and Northern Ireland–

(a)   paragraphs 3(1) and 16 of Schedule 2, and section 18 so far as relating thereto;

(b)   sections 42 to 44;

(c)   paragraph 1 of Schedule 8, and section 70 so far as relating thereto;

(d)   section 80;

(e)   paragraphs 29 to 31 and 32(a) of Schedule 11, and section 81 so far as relating thereto;

(f)   sections 82 and 83;

(g)   paragraphs 13, 73 to 75 and 81 of Schedule 12, and section 84(1) so far as relating thereto;

(h)   sections 85(1), (2), (6) and (7) and 86; and

(i)   section 89, this section and section 91.

(5)   The following provisions extend to Northern Ireland only–

(a)   paragraph 7(2) of Schedule 2, and section 18 so far as relating thereto;

(b)   sections 74, 76 and 78 and Schedule 10;

(c)   paragraphs 9 to 19, 24 to 28, 34, 36 and 38 of Schedule 11, and section 81 so far as relating thereto;

(d)   paragraphs 84 to 86 of Schedule 12, and section 84(1) so far as relating thereto; and

(e)   section 87.

(6)   Nothing in the preceding provisions of this section applies to any repeal made by this Act; and the extent of any such repeal is the same as that of the enactment repealed.

Short title, general interpretation and Scottish devolution

91.–(1)   This Act may be cited as the Welfare Reform and Pensions Act 1999.

(2)   In this Act–

"the Administration Act" means the Social Security Administration Act 1992;

"the Contributions and Benefits Act" means the Social Security Contributions and Benefits Act 1992.

(3)   In this Act, except sections 84(2) and (3), 85(1) and (6) and 89, and in any Act amended by this Act, references to the coming into force of any provision of this Act are to its coming into force otherwise than for the purpose of authorising the making of regulations.

(4)   For the purposes of the Scotland Act 1998, the following provisions shall be taken to be pre-commencement enactments within the meaning of that Act–

(a)   paragraphs 8(3) and (4) and 10 of Schedule 12; and

(b)   so far as relating to those provisions, sections 83, 84(1) and 89(1) and (5).

SCHEDULE 8
Part VIII
Administration of benefits

34.–(1) In each of the provisions of the Administration Act to which this paragraph applies–

(a) any reference to a person authorised to exercise any function of a relevant authority relating to housing benefit or council tax benefit shall include a reference to a person providing services to a relevant authority which relate to such a benefit; and

(b) any reference to the exercise of any function relating to such a benefit shall include a reference to the provision of any services so relating.

(2) This paragraph applies to the following provisions of the Administration Act–

(a) [¹ . . .];

(b) sections 122C, 122D and 122E (supply of information in connection with administration of housing benefit or council tax benefit);

(c) section 126A (power to require information from landlords etc. in connection with claims for housing benefit);

(d) section 182B (information about redirection of post); and

(e) Schedule 4 (persons covered by offence relating to unauthorised disclosures).

(3) In this paragraph "relevant authority" means an authority administering housing benefit or council tax benefit.

Commencement

6.4.03. See SI 2003 No 936.

Amendment

1. Repealed by the CSPSSA 2000 s85(1) and Sch 9 Pt VI (1.4.2001).

Immigration and Asylum Act 1999
(1999 c33)

Exclusion from benefits
115.–(1)   No person is entitled to income-based jobseeker's allowance under the Jobseekers Act 1995 or to–

[. . . .]

(j)   housing benefit, or

(k)   council tax benefit,

under the Social Security Contributions and Benefits Act 1992 while he is a person to whom this section applies.

(2)   No person in Northern Ireland is entitled to–

(a)   [. . . .]

(b)   any of the benefits mentioned in paragraphs (a) to (j) of subsection (1),

under the Social Security Contributions and Benefits (Northern Ireland) Act 1992 while he is a person to whom this section applies.

(3)   This section applies to a person subject to immigration control unless he falls within such category or description, or satisfies such conditions, as may be prescribed.

(4)   Regulations under subsection (3) may provide for a person to be treated for prescribed purposes only as not being a person to whom this section applies.

(5)   In relation to [¹ child benefit], "prescribed" means prescribed by regulations made by the Treasury.

(6)   In relation to the matters mentioned in subsection (2) (except so far as it relates to [¹ child benefit]), "prescribed" means prescribed by regulations made by the Department.

(7)   Section 175(3) to (5) of the Social Security Contributions and Benefits Act 1992 (supplemental power in relation to regulations) applies to regulations made by the Secretary of State or the Treasury under subsection (3) as it applies to regulations made under that Act.

(8)   Sections 133(2), 171(2) and 172(4) of the Social Security Contributions and Benefits (Northern Ireland) Act 1992 apply to regulations made by the Department under subsection (3) as they apply to regulations made by the Department under that Act.

(9)   "A person subject to immigration control" means a person who is not a national of an EEA State and who–

(a)   requires leave to enter or remain in the United Kingdom but does not have it;

(b)   has leave to enter or remain in the United Kingdom which is subject to a condition that he does not have recourse to public funds;

(c)   has leave to enter or remain in the United Kingdom given as a result of a maintenance undertaking; or

(d)   has leave to enter or remain in the United Kingdom only as a result of paragraph 17 of Schedule 4.

(10)   "Maintenance undertaking", in relation to any person, means a written undertaking given by another person in pursuance of the immigration rules to be responsible for that person's maintenance and accommodation.

Amendment

1.   Amended by the TCA 2002 Sch 4 para 21 (1.4.03).

Commencement

1.1.2000 for the purpose only of making regulations: Immigration and Asylum Act 1999 (Commencement No 1) Order 1999 SI No 3190.

3.4.2000 for all other purposes: Immigration and Asylum Act 1999 (Commencement No 3) Order 2000 SI No 464.

General Note

Although s115 appears in Part VI of the Act headed "Support for Asylum-Seekers", it has an impact on the entitlements of a wider range of claimants than asylum seekers. The scheme of the section is to introduce a general exclusion from HB and CTB in respect of "persons subject to immigration control" with exceptions to be set out in regulations. In order to work out whether a particular claimant is excluded from entitlement, it is necessary to consider two separate questions:

(1)   Is the claimant a "person subject to immigration control" within the meaning of s115? If so, s/he is excluded from entitlement to HB and CTB unless s/he can show that s/he falls within para (1), (4)(a) or (6) of reg 2 Social Security (Immigration and Asylum) Consequential Amendments Regulations 2000 SI No 636 (see p1072).

(2)   Is the claimant a "person from abroad" within the meaning of the post-April 2000 version of reg 10 of both the HB and the HB(SPC) Regs or reg 7 of both the CTB and the CTB(SPC) Regs. If so, s/he is excluded from benefit.

Analysis

Subsections (1) to (6): The general exclusion

Subs (1)(j) and (k) introduce a general exclusion from HB and CTB for persons to whom s115 applies in England, Wales and Scotland and subs (2) makes similar provision in relation to Northern Ireland in respect of the separate HB scheme there (council tax does not apply to Northern Ireland).

Subs (3) and (4) exclude "a person subject to immigration control" subject to wide powers to make regulations. That critical phrase is defined in subs (9) and is discussed below. It should be noted that those wide powers do *not* include powers to create further categories of people within the definition; the powers are to exclude people from the effect of s115 only.

Subsections (9) and (10): "Person subject to immigration control"

The first point is that for the purposes of s115, a national of a member state of the European Economic Area (EEA) is never subject to immigration control (whatever may be the effect of other immigration legislation in relation to them). The member states are: UK, Austria, Liechtenstein, Germany, France, Belgium, Luxembourg, Holland, Denmark, Norway, Sweden, Finland, Iceland, Ireland, Spain, Portugal and Italy.

Subject to that consideration, there are four categories of "person" listed in subs (9):

(1)   "A person who requires leave to enter or remain in the United Kingdom but does not have it". The *Statement of Changes in Immigration Rules* (HC 395) para 7 defines such a person as someone who is not a British citizen, an EEA national (excluded from s115 by virtue of subs (9) in any case), or a Commonwealth citizen with a right of abode. For those who fall into the latter category, see s2(1)(b) of the Immigration Act 1971 which requires that the person should have fallen within s2(1)(d) or (2) of the 1971 Act at the time that the British Nationality Act 1981 came into force on 30 October 1981. For the text of s2 of the 1971 Act at that time, see *Halsbury's Statutes* vol 31 pp63-4. Those that fall into this category of claimant will include illegal entrants, overstayers and those with temporary admission under Sch 2 para 21 Immigration Act 1971 (who had been entitled to HB and CTB under reg 7A HB Regs 1987 and reg 4A CTB Regs 1992 prior to April 2000).

(2)   "A person who has leave to enter or remain in the United Kingdom which is subject to a condition that he does not have recourse to public funds". It should be clear from the stamp on a claimant's passport whether or not there is such a condition. Most of the categories of limited leave granted under the *Immigration Rules* are subject to such a condition: see, eg, para 41(vi) (visitors), para 57(vi) (students), para 128(v) (holders of work permits).

(3)   "A person who has leave to enter or remain in the UK given as a result of a maintenance undertaking". See the definition in subs (10). Under para 35 of the *Immigration Rules* a person may be given leave to enter as a result of a sponsor giving an undertaking to be responsible for her/his maintenance and accommodation "for the period of any leave granted, including any further variation". Typically such an undertaking is given for five years (unless a shorter period of leave is granted). There are now a number of decisions on the meaning of the phrase. The undertaking need not be on the standard RON 112 form but may be, for example, in a letter. There must be a clear link between the giving of the undertaking and the granting of leave to enter or remain, which must be investigated by the tribunal if necessary. However, it need not be shown that the undertaking was the sole matter taken into account by the immigration officer as long as it was taken into

account: *Shah v Secretary of State for Social Security [2002] EWCA Civ 285, CA; CIS 3508/2001* paras 10, 24; *CIS 47/2002* para 27. Note, however, that in order for it to count as an undertaking it must amount to a promise, and not simply a general willingness, to maintain the person: *CIS 426/ 2003.*

(4)   "A person who has leave to enter or remain in the United Kingdom only as a result of paragraph 17 of Schedule 4". That provision deems leave to enter or remain to continue while an appeal is pending under s61 or 69(2) of the 1999 Act. These relate to appeals against variations or refusals to vary limited leave, and appeals to an adjudicator against a decision to require someone to leave following a refusal of asylum.

Back-dating of benefits where person recorded as refugee
[⁴**123.**]

Amendments

1.   Inserted by the TCA 2002, Sch 4 para 22(2) (1.4.03).
2.   Amended by the TCA 2002, Sch 4 para 22(3) (1.4.03).
3.   Amended by the SPCA 2002, Sch 2 para 42 (2.7.02 for the making of regulations). Commencement from October 2003.
4.   Repealed by s12(1) of the Asylum and Immigration (Treatment of Claimants, etc.) Act 2004 (for those recorded as refugees after 14.6.07).

Commencement

1.1.2000 for the purpose only of making regulations: Immigration and Asylum Act 1999 (Commencement No 1) Order 1999 SI No 3190.
3.4.2000 for all other purposes: Immigration and Asylum Act 1999 (Commencement No 3) Order 2000 SI No 464.

General Note

The section ceased to have effect from 14 June 2007 for those recorded as refugees after that date: s12(1) of the Asylum and Immigration (Treatment of Claimants, etc.) Act 2004, brought into effect by the Asylum and Immigration (Treatment of Claimants, etc.) Act 2004 (Commencement No. 7 and Transitional Provisions) Order 2007 SI No 1602. For these purposes, a person is 'recorded as a refugee' on the day on which the Secretary of State notifies her/him that s/he has been recognised as a refugee and granted asylum in the UK. For the full text of the section, see the 19th edn of this work, pp985-86.

The section authorised the making of regulations to permit backdated claims by asylum seekers who succeed in establishing refugee status for benefits for the whole of that period. The relevant provisions in relation to HB and CTB were reg 10A and Sch A1 of both the HB and the HB(SPC) Regs and reg 7A and Sch A1 of both the CTB and the CTB(SPC) Regs as inserted by Sch 4 of the HB&CTB(CP) Regs (see p1125). There were specific powers to provide for one authority to determine all the entitlement over the period during which a person's status was being determined: subs (6) and (7). See para 2 in Sch A1 to all the sets of Regulations. The power in subs (7) to deduct the value of any asylum support provided has not yet been exercised in relation to HB or CTB (compare reg 3(5) Social Security (Immigration and Asylum) Consequential Provisions Regulations 2000 which has provided for the value of support to be deducted from backdated IS).

Local Government Act 2000
(2000 c22)

General Note

This contains some of the most fundamental reforms made in local government constitutional and administrative law. Among other things, it contains very wide and sweeping powers for local authorities to act for the social, economic or environmental well-being of their areas, an option for local authorities to adopt an executive model of government, and new systems for regulating the conduct of those involved in local government.

The significance of the 2000 Act for HB purposes lies in the introduction, by s93, of a new system of grants to organisations providing welfare services such as counselling and support. This system replaced the provision made by Sch 1B of the HB Regs 1987.

Disclosure of information

94.–(1)   Subsection (3) applies to information which is held by, or by a person providing services to, the Secretary of State and which relates to income support [1, income-based jobseeker's allowance or state pension credit].

(2)   Subsection (3) also applies to information relating to housing benefit which is held by–
  (a)   an authority administering housing benefit, or
  (b)   a person authorised to exercise any function of such an authority relating to housing benefit.

(3)   Information to which this subsection applies may be supplied to–
  (a)   a local authority to which any grant is or will be paid under section 93, or
  (b)   a person authorised to exercise any function of that authority relating to that grant,
for purposes connected with the application of that grant towards expenditure falling within section 93(1) or (2) (as the case may be).

(4)   Information which is supplied to an authority or other person under subsection (3) may be supplied by the authority or person to a person who provides qualifying welfare services for purposes connected with the provision of those services.

(5)   For the purposes of this section a person is to be regarded as providing qualifying welfare services if–
  (a)   he provides welfare services,
  (b)   a local authority contribute or will contribute to the expenditure incurred by him in providing those services, and
  (c)   that contribution is or will be derived (in whole or in part) from any grant which is or will be paid to the authority under section 93.

(6)   In this section "local authority" and "welfare services" have the same meaning as in section 93.

(7)   The Secretary of State may by order make such modifications of this section as he considers necessary or expedient in consequence of any provision corresponding to section 93 which is enacted by the Scottish Parliament.

Commencement

1.8.01: Art 2 of SI 2001 No 2684.

Amendment

1.   Amended by SPCA 2002 Sch 2 para 43 (2.7.02 for the purpose of making regulations, 6.10.03 in full).

Unauthorised disclosure of information

95.–(1)   The persons to whom this section applies are–
  (a)   any person ("the recipient") to whom information is supplied by virtue of section 94,

(b)   any person who is or has been a director, member of the committee of management, manager, secretary or other similar officer of the recipient, and

(c)   any person who is or has been employed by the recipient.

(2)   A person to whom this section applies is guilty of an offence if he discloses without lawful authority any information which is supplied by virtue of section 94 and which relates to a particular person.

(3)   It is not an offence under this section–

(a)   to disclose information in the form of a summary or collection of information so framed as not to enable information relating to any particular person to be ascertained from it, or

(b)   to disclose information which has previously been disclosed to the public with lawful authority.

(4)   It is a defence for a person charged with an offence under this section to prove that at the time of the alleged offence–

(a)   he believed that he was making the disclosure in question with lawful authority and had no reasonable cause to believe otherwise, or

(b)   he believed that the information in question had previously been disclosed to the public with lawful authority and had no reasonable cause to believe otherwise.

(5)   A person guilty of an offence under this section is to be liable–

(a)   on conviction on indictment, to imprisonment for a term not exceeding two years or a fine or both, or

(b)   on summary conviction, to imprisonment for a term not exceeding six months or a fine not exceeding the statutory maximum or both.

(6)   For the purposes of this section a disclosure is to be regarded as made with lawful authority if, and only if, it is made–

(a)   in accordance with section 94(4) or any other enactment,

(b)   in accordance with an order of a court,

(c)   for the purpose of instituting, or otherwise for the purposes of, any proceedings before a court or tribunal, or

(d)   with the consent of the appropriate person (as defined in section 123(10) of the Social Security Administration Act 1992).

(7)   The Secretary of State may by order make such modifications of this section as he considers necessary or expedient in consequence of any provision corresponding to section 93 which is enacted by the Scottish Parliament.

Commencement

1.8.01: Art 2 of SI 2001 No 2684.

Children (Leaving Care) Act 2000
(2000 c35)

General Note to the Act

The Children (Leaving Care) Act 2000 makes provision for assistance by local authority social services departments to children who are leaving local authority care. The Act makes detailed provision for a package of assistance for children in such a position, both before and after they leave care and of a financial and practical nature. Such children are generally excluded from entitlement to IS, income-based JSA and HB to prevent duplication of provision. However, children will always be entitled either to assistance or to benefits and advisers should therefore be prepared to press authorities to act where there is a dispute between benefits and social services departments as to whether a child has a right to assistance.

The bulk of this Act only applies to England and Wales, but by s8(6), s6 also applies to Scotland.

Exclusion from benefits

6.–(1) No person is entitled to income-based jobseeker's allowance under the Jobseekers Act 1995, or to income support or housing benefit under the Social Security Contributions and Benefits Act 1992, while he is a person to whom this section applies.

(2) Subject to subsection (3), this section applies to–

(a) an eligible child for the purposes of paragraph 19B of Schedule 2 to the Children Act 1989;

(b) a relevant child for the purposes of section 23A of that Act; and

(c) any person of a description prescribed in regulations under subsection (4).

(3) The Secretary of State may by regulations provide that this section does not apply to a person who falls within subsection (2)(a) or (b) but who also falls within such category or description, or satisfies such conditions, as may be prescribed in the regulations.

(4) The Secretary of State may make regulations prescribing descriptions of person who do not fall within subsection (2)(a) or (b) but who–

(a) have been looked after by a local authority in Scotland (within the meaning of section 17(6) of the Children (Scotland) Act 1995); and

(b) otherwise correspond (whether or not exactly) to eligible or relevant children.

(5) The Secretary of State may in regulations make such transitional, consequential and saving provision as he considers necessary or expedient in connection with the coming into force of this section.

(6) Section 175(3) to (5) of the Social Security Contributions and Benefits Act 1992 (supplemental power in relation to regulations) applies to regulations made under this section as it applies to regulations made under that Act.

(7) Powers to make regulations under this section include power to make different provision for different areas.

(8) Powers to make regulations under this section are exercisable by statutory instrument.

(9) No statutory instrument containing regulations under subsection (4) is to be made unless a draft of the instrument has been laid before Parliament and approved by a resolution of each House of Parliament.

(10) A statutory instrument containing regulations under subsection (3) or (5) shall be subject to annulment in pursuance of a resolution of either House of Parliament.

Commencement

10.9.01 for making regulations and 1.10.01 for other purposes: Art 2 of SI 2001 No 3070.

General Note

This section excludes children who receive assistance under the 2000 Act from entitlement to IS, income-based JSA and HB. Subs (2) to (4) refer to regulation-making powers. The relevant regulations are the

Children (Leaving Care) Social Security Benefits Regulations 2001 SI No 3074, made under subs (3) and the Children (Leaving Care) Social Security Benefits (Scotland) Regulations 2004 No 747, made under subs (4).

The Children (Leaving Care) (Wales) Regulations 2001 SI No 2189 (amended by the Children (Leaving Care) (Wales) Amendment Regulations 2002 SI No 1855) and the Children (Leaving Care) (England) Regulations 2001 SI No 2874 deal with the definitions of "eligible child" and "relevant child". These are not identical and are referred to below as the "Wales Regulations" and "England Regulations".

Analysis

Subs (1) has the effect of excluding children to whom the arrangements apply from entitlement to HB, unless such a child is brought back into entitlement by regulations made under subss (3) or (4). The Children (Leaving Care) Social Security Benefits Regulations 2001 SI No 3074, made under subs (3), do not apply to HB. The Children (Leaving Care) Social Security Benefits (Scotland) Regulations 2004 No 747 bring certain children back into entitlement to IS and income-based JSA, but not to HB. So at present any child falling within subs (2) will be excluded from HB.

Subs (2) and (4) set out the categories of children to whom the exclusion applies. They are:

(1)   An "eligible child". Sch 2 para 19B Children Act 1989, inserted by s1 of the 2000 Act, defines such a child as being a child aged 16/17 who has spent some time in local authority care. The child must have been in care at some point since the age of 14 and must have spent a minimum of 13 weeks in care: reg 3(1) of both the Wales and the England Regulations. Both sets of regulations then exclude specified categories of child. Reg 3(2)(a) of the Wales Regulations and reg 3(3) of the England Regulations excludes a child who has had a series of short-term placements of less than four weeks' duration before returning to her/his parent or guardian. Reg 3(2)(b) of the Wales Regulations formerly excluded a child who had been living with a parent or guardian for more than six months. Reg 3(2)(b) was deleted by reg 2(a) of the 2002 Regulations with effect from 1 August 2002, but see the note on reg 4(4) below. The local authority social services department is required to prepare for the child to become independent by preparing a "pathway plan".

(2)   A "relevant child", which is defined by s23A(2) of the 1989 Act, as inserted by s2(4) of the 2000 Act, as being a child aged 16/17 who is not presently in local authority care but who was an "eligible child" when last looked after. By s23A(3)(a), there is power to prescribe additional categories of "relevant child", and by s23A(3)(b), there is a power to exclude people from the definition. Reg 4(2) of the Wales Regulations includes a child who was in detention or in hospital at the age of 16 and who has spent at least 13 weeks in care between the ages of 14 and 16. Reg 4(2) of the England Regulations has the same effect provided that there is no care order in force in respect of the child. Reg 4(4) of the Wales Regulations excludes a child who has had a family placement of at least six months' duration, except where the placement breaks down and it is more than six months since the placement began: reg 4(6). Reg 4(5) of the England Regulations also makes the same exclusion, save where the family placement "breaks down": see reg 4(7).

(3)   Those prescribed under subs (4). See the note to subs (1).

Social Security Fraud Act 2001

(2001 c11)

Contents

Obtaining and sharing information

3.   Code of practice about use of information powers
4.   Arrangements for payments in respect of information

Loss of benefit provisions

7.   Loss of benefit for commission of benefit offences
9.   Effect of offence on benefits for members of offender's family
10.   Power to supplement and mitigate loss of benefit provisions
11.   Loss of benefit regulations
13.   Interpretation of sections 7 to 12

Supplemental

18.   Meaning of ''the Administration Act''
20.   Commencement
21.   Short title and extent

General Note to the Act

This was the second Act of Parliament in four years, following the Social Security Administration (Fraud) Act 1997, to be explicitly dedicated in its short title to the prevention of social security fraud. It amended the provisions for obtaining information in Pt VI of the SSAA. In addition controversial provisions were put into place for reducing the entitlement of recidivist benefit fraud offenders. There is an expansion of the powers to offer the payment of a penalty rather than prosecution.

The next group of sections, ss7 to 13, provide "loss of benefit" provisions. See p1087 for the Social Security (Loss of Benefit) Regulations 2001, made under those sections.

Obtaining and sharing information

Code of practice about use of information powers

3.–(1)   The Secretary of State shall issue a code of practice relating to the exercise of–

   (a)   the powers that are exercisable by an authorised officer under section 109B of the Administration Act in relation to the persons mentioned in subsection (2A) of that section; and

   (b)   the powers conferred on an authorised officer by sections 109BA and 110AA of that Act.

   (2)   The Secretary of State may from time to time–

   (a)   revise the whole or any part of the code for the time being in force under this section; and

   (b)   issue a revised code.

   (3)   Before issuing or revising the code of practice under this section, the Secretary of State shall–

   (a)   prepare and publish a draft of the code, or of the revised code; and

   (b)   consider any representations made to him about the draft;

and the Secretary of State may incorporate in the code he issues any modifications made by him to his proposals after their publication.

   (4)   The Secretary of State shall lay before each House of Parliament the code of practice, and every revised code, issued by him under this section.

   (5)   The code of practice issued under this section and any revisions of the code shall come into force at the time at which the code or, as the case may be, the revised code is issued by the Secretary of State.

(6)   An authorised officer exercising any power in relation to which provision must be made by the code of practice under this section shall have regard, in doing so, to the provisions (so far as they are applicable) of the code for the time being in force under this section.

(7)   A failure on the part of any person to comply with any provision of the code of practice for the time being in force under this section shall not of itself render him liable to any civil or criminal proceedings.

(8)   The code of practice for the time being in force under this section shall be admissible in evidence in any civil or criminal proceedings.

(9)   In this section ''authorised officer'' has the same meaning as in Part 6 of the Administration Act.

Commencement
   28.1.02: SI 2002 No 117.

General Note
   This welcome provision, added during passage of the Act through Parliament as a result of concerns about the absence of any comprehensive guidance for investigators, requires a Code of Practice to be issued. The critical provision is subs (6), which only requires an officer to "have regard" to the provisions. It is therefore clear that a breach of the Code will not require evidence to be excluded in a criminal prosecution, although such a breach would no doubt be a ground on which to base a submission to exclude such evidence under s78 Police and Criminal Evidence Act 1984. Under subs (7), a failure to comply with the Code cannot give rise to civil or criminal proceedings and so could not give rise, for example, to a claim for misfeasance in a public office unless the elements of that tort were present in the absence of a breach of the Code.
   The first version of the Code was included in Circular HB/CTB F2/2002.

Arrangements for payments in respect of information
   4.–(1)   It shall be the duty of the Secretary of State to ensure that such arrangements (if any) are in force as he thinks appropriate for requiring or authorising, in such cases as he thinks fit, the making of such payments as he considers appropriate in respect of compliance with relevant obligations by any of the following–
   (a)   a credit reference agency (within the meaning given by section 145(8) of the Consumer Credit Act 1974 (c. 39)) or any servant or agent of such an agency;
   (b)   a person providing a telecommunications service (within the meaning of the Regulation of Investigatory Powers Act 2000 (c. 23)) or any servant or agent of such a person;
   (c)   a water undertaker or a water and sewerage authority constituted under section 62 of the Local Government etc. (Scotland) Act 1994 (c. 39) or any servant or agent of such an undertaker or authority,
   (d)   any person who (within the meaning the Gas Act 1986 (c. 44)) supplies gas conveyed through pipes, or any servant or agent of such a person;
   (e)   any person who (within the meaning of the Electricity Act 1989 (c. 29)) supplies electricity conveyed by distribution systems, or any servant or agent of such a person;
   (f)   any person added to the list of persons falling within subsection (2A) of section 109B of the Administration Act by an order under subsection (6) of that section, or any person's servant or agent who falls within that subsection by virtue of such an order.
   (2)   In subsection (1) ''relevant obligation''–
   (a)   in relation to a person falling within paragraph (a), (b) or (f) of that subsection, means–
       (i)   an obligation to provide information in pursuance of a requirement imposed on that person under section 109B of the Administration Act by virtue only of his falling within subsection (2A) of that section; or

(ii)   any obligation to comply, for the purpose of enabling an authorised officer to obtain information which might otherwise be obtained by the imposition of such a requirement, with any requirements imposed on that person under section 109BA or 110AA of that Act; and

(b)   in relation to a person falling within any of paragraphs (c) to (e) of that subsection, means any obligation to provide information in pursuance of a requirement imposed by such an exercise of the powers conferred by section 109B of that Act as is mentioned in subsection (2D) of that section.

(3)   For the purpose of complying with his duty under this section, the Secretary of State may make arrangements for payments to be made out of money provided by Parliament.

(4)   It shall be the duty of an authority administering housing benefit or council tax benefit to comply with such general or specific directions as to the making of payments as may be given by the Secretary of State in accordance with any arrangements for the time being in force for the purposes of subsection (1).

Commencement

1.4.02: SI 2002 No 1222.

General Note

Section 4 gives powers to pay for information. Not every body will be paid; only those bodies specified in subs (1) and then only to the extent that they have complied with "relevant obligations" as defined in subs (2).

The Secretary of State may issue directions under subs (4) to local authorities to make payments.

Loss of benefit provisions

Loss of benefit for commission of benefit offences

7.–(1)   If–

(a)   a person (''the offender'') is convicted of one or more benefit offences in each of two separate sets of proceedings,

(b)   the benefit offence, or one of the benefit offences, of which he is convicted in the later proceedings is one committed within the period of three years after the date, or any of the dates, on which he was convicted of a benefit offence in the earlier proceedings,

(c)   the later set of proceedings has not been taken into account for the purposes of any previous application of this section or section 8 or 9 in relation to the offender or any person who was then a member of his family,

(d)   the earlier set of proceedings has not been taken into account as the earlier set of proceedings for the purposes of any previous application of this section or either of those sections in relation to the offender or any person who was then a member of his family, and

(e)   the offender is a person with respect to whom the conditions for an entitlement to a sanctionable benefit are or become satisfied at any time within the disqualification period,

then, even though those conditions are satisfied, the following restrictions shall apply in relation to the payment of that benefit in the offender's case.

(2)   Subject to subsections (3) to (5), the sanctionable benefit shall not be payable in the offender's case for any period comprised in the disqualification period.

(3)   *[omitted]*

(4)   *[omitted]*

[² (4A)   The Secretary of State may by regulations provide that, where the sanctionable benefit is state pension credit, the benefit shall be payable in the offender's case for any period comprised in the disqualification period as if the rate of the benefit were reduced in such manner as may be prescribed.]

(5)   The Secretary of State may by regulations provide that, where the sanctionable benefit is housing benefit or council tax benefit, the benefit shall be payable, during the whole or a part of any period comprised in the disqualification period, as if one or both of the following applied–

(a)   the rate of the benefit were reduced in such manner as may be prescribed;

(b)   the benefit were payable only if the circumstances are such as may be prescribed.

(6)   For the purposes of this section the disqualification period, in relation to the conviction of a person of one or more benefit offences in each of two separate sets of proceedings, means the period of thirteen weeks beginning with such date, falling after the date of the conviction in the later set of proceedings, as may be determined by or in accordance with regulations made by the Secretary of State.

(7)   Where–

(a)   the conviction of any person of any offence is taken into account for the purposes of the application of this section in relation to that person, and

(b)   that conviction is subsequently quashed,

all such payments and other adjustments shall be made as would be necessary if no restriction had been imposed by or under this section that could not have been imposed if the conviction had not taken place.

(8)   In this section–

"benefit offence" means–

(a)   any post-commencement offence in connection with a claim for a disqualifying benefit;

(b)   any post-commencement offence in connection with the receipt or payment of any amount by way of such a benefit;

(c)   any post-commencement offence committed for the purpose of facilitating the commission (whether or not by the same person) of a benefit offence;

(d)   any post-commencement offence consisting in an attempt or conspiracy to commit a benefit offence;

"disqualifying benefit" means (subject to any regulations under section 10(1))–

(a)   any benefit under the Jobseekers Act 1995 or the Jobseekers (Northern Ireland) Order 1995;

[² (aa) any benefit under the State Pension Credit Act 2002 or under any provision having effect in Northern Ireland corresponding to that Act;]

(b)   any benefit under the Social Security Contributions and Benefits Act 1992 or the Social Security Contributions and Benefits (Northern Ireland) Act 1992 other than–

(i)   maternity allowance;

[¹ . . .]

[¹ . . .]

(iv)   statutory sick pay and statutory maternity pay;

(c)   any war pension

"sanctionable benefit" means (subject to subsection (11) and to any regulations under section 10(1)) any disqualifying benefit other than–

(a)   joint-claim jobseeker's allowance;

(b)   any retirement pension;

(c)   graduated retirement benefit;

(d)   disability living allowance;

(e)   attendance allowance;

(f)   child benefit;

(g)   guardian's allowance;

(h)   a payment out of the social fund in accordance with Part 8 of the Social Security Contributions and Benefits Act 1992;

(i)   a payment under Part X of that Act (Christmas bonuses).

(9)   For the purposes of this section–

(a)   the date of a person's conviction in any proceedings of a benefit offence shall be taken to be the date on which he was found guilty of that offence in those proceedings (whenever he was sentenced); and

(b)   references to a conviction include references to a conviction in relation to which the court makes an order for a conditional discharge or a court in Scotland makes a probation order and to a conviction in Northern Ireland.

(10)   In this section references to any previous application of this section or section 8 or 9–

(a)   include references to any previous application of a provision having an effect in Northern Ireland corresponding to provision made by this section, or either of those sections; but

(b)   do not include references to any previous application of this section, or of either of those sections, the effect of which was to impose a restriction for a period comprised in the same disqualification period.

(11)   In its application to Northern Ireland this section shall have effect as if references to a sanctionable benefit were references only to a war pension.

Amendments

1.   Repealed by the TCA 2002, Sch 6 (8.4.03).

2.   Amended by SPCA 2002 Sch 2 para 45 (2.7.02 for making regulations, 6.10.03 in full).

Commencement

17.11.01 for making regulations and 1.4.02 generally: SI 2001 No 3689.

General Note

This section sets up the controversial "two strikes" scheme for loss of benefit following commission of offences. The regulations made under this section are the Social Security (Loss of Benefit) Regulations 2001 (see p1087).

In essence, the scheme operates by providing for loss of benefit for a repeat offender (under s7) or a member of her/his family (under s9). HB and CTB are both "disqualifying benefits" (those which can trigger a sanction if an offence is committed) and "sanctionable benefits" (those which may be affected by a repeat offence), though they are not sanctionable under this Act in Northern Ireland, which has its own legislation: see subs (11). HB and CTB can be partly reduced, though only in circumstances where a claimant is not in receipt of IS or income-based JSA in which case the sanction applies to IS/income-based JSA alone.

An appeal lies to a tribunal against a decision made under s7 by virtue of Sch 3 para 3(f) SSA 1998, inserted by s12(2) of this Act.

Analysis

Subsection (1): The conditions for operation of the scheme

There are three conditions under s7(1) for the scheme to bite upon a particular claimant who has been guilty of repeated benefit fraud offences:

(1)   The claimant has been convicted of offences in "each of two separate sets of proceedings": para (a). Note the definition of conviction in subs (9). There are provisions in paras (c) and (d) and in subs (10)(b) to prevent a particular set of proceedings being taken into account more than once. Para (c) provides that the later conviction can only affect benefit entitlement of the claimant or a member of his family under s9 on one occasion. Para (d) prevents the earlier conviction triggering a loss of benefit in relation to a third conviction. Subs (10)(b) prevents double counting if, for example, both s7 and s9 can apply because both a claimant and a member of her/his family are convicted twice. However, it is clear that a fourth conviction would then trigger a second loss of benefit. By subs (10)(a), the previous offence may have been committed in Northern Ireland. One uncertainty relates to the meaning of "separate". Does it apply to a case where an indictment is severed or separate trials take place of different charges on a summons? It is suggested that the two trials remain part of the same set of proceedings and a further conviction on a separate indictment or summons would be required in order to allow a loss of benefit.

(2)   The offence giving rise to the later conviction was committed within three years of the earlier conviction: para (b). See subs (9)(a) for the date of a conviction. There may be some difficulties in determining when an offence was committed where it involves an omission to notify a change of circumstances. It is suggested that the wording of the charge will be critical. Thus if the claimant is charged in the later proceedings with a failure to notify, the date on which it is said in the charge

that notification should have occurred will be the relevant date for the purposes of para (b). If no date is specified in the charge, then it will have to be determined at what point the offence was committed.

(3) The claimant must be, or must become entitled to, a "sanctionable benefit" during the "disqualification period" which is defined in subs (6): para (e).

Subsections (2), (5) and (7): Imposition of the sanction

The general rule under subs (2) is that the "sanctionable benefit" shall not be payable in respect of any period during the "disqualification period". However, in the case of HB and CTB, subs (5) and reg 17 Social Security (Loss of Benefit) Regulations 2001 provide for a reduction of benefit instead.

Subs (7) provides that where a conviction is quashed and the sanction could not have been applied unless that conviction stood, payment of the sanctionable benefit should be made as normal. The words "could not have been imposed" are, however, of importance. If a claimant is convicted of two offences on the latter occasion and only one is quashed, then if the remaining conviction falls to be taken into account under subs (1) then the sanction will remain in place.

Subsection (6): The disqualification period

The period is 13 weeks from the date specified in reg 2 Social Security (Loss of Benefit) Regulations 2001.

Subsections (8) and (9): Definitions

"Benefit offence" is widely defined in subs (8) to cover offences relating to claims and receipt of benefit, as well as aiding and abetting or attempting or conspiring to commit such an offence. Critically, it does not include any offence committed prior to the commencement date: see the definition of "post-commencement offence" in s13 below.

"Disqualifying benefit" and *"sanctionable benefit"* both include HB and CTB within the definition, subject to subs (11).

Subs (9)(a) confirms that the date of conviction is the date on which a claimant was "found guilty" rather than the date of sentence. "Found guilty" will include cases where the defendant pleads guilty as well as those where s/he is convicted on a plea of not guilty. If a guilty plea is subsequently changed to a plea of not guilty, it is suggested that the relevant date will be the date on which either a subsequent plea of guilty is entered or on which the claimant is convicted.

Subs (9)(b) confirms that "conviction" includes convictions in Northern Ireland or convictions in respect of which probation is imposed in Scotland or a *conditional* discharge in England. South of the border, s14(1) Powers of Criminal Courts (Sentencing) Act 2000 provides that absolute and conditional discharges are not to be treated as convictions, and s14(3) prevents either type of discharge biting in relation to legislation which imposes a "disqualification or disability" on convicted persons. Quite clearly, this Act falls within that description. There is no specific exception to s14(3) for other legislation which specifically imposes a disqualification on those subjected to a conditional discharge, so there is a conflict between s14(3) of the 2000 Act and s7(9)(b) of this Act. It is likely that the courts will apply the rule of statutory construction that the general provision is overridden by the specific provision and that s7(9)(b) of this Act prevails over s14(3) of the 2000 Act, particularly since this Act was passed on a later date.

Effect of offence on benefits for members of offender's family

9.–(1)   This section applies to–

(a)   income support;

(b)   jobseeker's allowance;

[¹ (bb) state pension credit;]

(c)   housing benefit; and

(d)   council tax benefit.

(2)   The Secretary of State may by regulations make provision in accordance with the following provisions of this section in relation to any case in which–

(a)   the conditions for entitlement to any benefit to which this section applies are or become satisfied in the case of any person (''the offender's family member'');

(b)   that benefit falls to be paid in that person's case for the whole or any part of a period comprised in a period (''the relevant period'') which is the disqualification period in relation to restrictions imposed under section 7 in the case of a member of that person's family; or

(c)   that member of that family (''the offender'') is a person by reference to whom–

    (i)   the conditions for the entitlement of the offender's family member to the benefit in question are satisfied; or

    (ii)   the amount of benefit payable in the case of the offender's family member would fall (apart from any provision made under this section) to be determined.

(3)   *[omitted]*

(4)   *[omitted]*

[¹ (4A) In relation to cases in which the benefit is state pension credit, the provision that may be made by virtue of subsection (2) is provision that, in the case of the offender's family member, the benefit shall be payable for the whole or any part of any period comprised in the relevant period as if the rate of the benefit were reduced in such manner as may be prescribed.]

(5)   In relation to cases in which the benefit is housing benefit or council tax benefit, the provision that may be made by virtue of subsection (2) is provision that, in the case of the offender's family member, the benefit shall be payable, during the whole or a part of any period comprised in the relevant period, as if one or both of the following applied–

   (a)   the rate of the benefit were reduced in such manner as may be prescribed;

   (b)   the benefit were payable only if the circumstances are such as may be prescribed.

(6)   Where–

   (a)   the conviction of any member of a person's family for any offence is taken into account for the purposes of any restriction imposed by virtue of any regulations under this section, and

   (b)   that conviction is subsequently quashed,

all such payments and other adjustments shall be made in that person's case as would be necessary if no restriction had been imposed that could not have been imposed had the conviction not taken place.

Commencement

17.11.01 for making regulations and 1.4.02 generally: SI 2001 No 3689.

Amendment

1.   Inserted by SPCA 2002 Sch 2 para 46 (2.7.02 for making regulations, 6.10.03 in full).

General Note

This section deals with cases where the offender is not the person claiming benefit on behalf of the family. The effect is that equivalent reductions in HB or CTB are still imposed.

    The effect of s9 may in some cases be to impose a sanction on a blameless claimant. There is no requirement that the offender should have been part of the claimant's family at the time that the offence was committed. There may well be arguments that the imposition of a sanction in such a case infringes Art 8 of the European Convention on Human Rights (because it shows a lack of respect for the home which cannot be justified) or Art 14 (because there is discrimination in comparison with those who do not have a benefit offender in their households).

    An appeal lies to a Tribunal against a decision made under s7 by virtue of Sch 3 para 3(f) SSA 1998, inserted by s12(2) of this Act.

Analysis

Subsection (2): Cases where section 9 is applicable

The conditions for imposing a sanction under s9 are the following:

(1)   A person is claiming benefit to which s9 applies: subs (a).

(2)   The claimant will be paid that benefit for a period which forms part or the whole of the "disqualification period" under s7 in respect of a member of the claimant's family: subs (b). "Member of . . . . family" refers to a person falling to be treated as part of the claimant's family under s137(1) SSCBA and Pt 4 HB and HB(SPC) Regs or Pt 2 CTB and CTB(SPC) Regs: see the definition of "family" in s13 below.

(3)   The offender is a person in relation to whom the conditions of entitlement are satisfied (such as where HB is claimed by in respect of a partner's liability for rent) or who falls to be taken into

account in calculating benefit: subs (c). Although non-dependents would fall within the latter description, it is suggested that s9 cannot bite in such cases because they are not members of the claimant's family for the purposes of subs (b).

Subsections (5) and (6): Imposition of the sanction
Subs (5) imposes identical sanctions in s9 cases to those imposed by s7(5) above. Subs (6) is the equivalent of s7(7).

Power to supplement and mitigate loss of benefit provisions

10.–(1)   The Secretary of State may by regulations provide for any social security benefit to be treated for the purposes of sections 7 to 9–

(a)   as a disqualifying benefit but not a sanctionable benefit; or

(b)   as neither a sanctionable benefit nor a disqualifying benefit.

(2)   The Secretary of State may by regulations provide for any restriction in section 7, 8 or 9 not to apply in relation to payments of benefit to the extent of any deduction that (if any payment were made) would fall, in pursuance of provision made by or under any enactment, to be made from the payments and paid to a person other than the offender or, as the case may be, a member of his family.

(3)   In this section ''social security benefit'' means–

(a)   any benefit under the Social Security Contributions and Benefits Act 1992 or the Social Security Contributions and Benefits (Northern Ireland) Act 1992; [² . . .]

(b)   any benefit under the Jobseekers Act 1995 or the Jobseekers (Northern Ireland) Order 1995;

[¹ (bb) any benefit under the State Pension Credit Act 2002 or under any provision having effect in Northern Ireland corresponding to that Act; or]

(c)   any war pension.

Commencement
17.11.01 for making regulations and 1.4.02 generally: SI 2001 No 3689.

Amendments
1.   Inserted by SPCA 2002 Sch 2 para 47 (2.7.02 for making regulations). Commenced from October 2003.
2.   Amended by SPCA 2002 Sch 3 (2.7.02 for making regulations). Commenced from October 2003.

General Note
None of the powers conferred by subs (1) or (2) have been exercised in relation to HB or CTB.

Loss of benefit regulations

11.–(1)   In sections 7 to 10 ''prescribed'' means prescribed by or determined in accordance with regulations made by the Secretary of State.

(2)   Regulations under any of the provisions of sections 7 to 10 shall be made by statutory instrument which (except in the case of regulations to which subsection (3) applies) shall be subject to annulment in pursuance of a resolution of either House of Parliament.

(3)   A statutory instrument containing (whether alone or with other provisions)–

(a)   a provision by virtue of which anything is to be treated for the purposes of section 7 as a disqualifying benefit but not a sanctionable benefit,

(b)   a provision prescribing the manner in which the applicable amount is to be reduced for the purposes of section 7(3) or 9(3),

(c)   a provision the making of which is authorised by section 7(4) [¹ , (4A)] or (5), 8(4) or 9(4) [¹ , (4A)] or (5), or

(d)   a provision prescribing the manner in which the amount of joint-claim jobseeker's allowance is to be reduced for the purposes of section 8(3)(a),

shall not be made unless a draft of the instrument has been laid before, and approved by a resolution of, each House of Parliament.

(4)   Subsections (4) to (6) of section 189 of the Administration Act (supplemental and incidental powers etc.) shall apply in relation to a power to make regulations that is conferred by any of the provisions of sections 7 to 10 as they apply in relation to the powers to make regulations that are conferred by that Act.

(5)   The provision that may be made in exercise of the powers to make regulations that are conferred by sections 7 to 10 shall include different provision for different areas.

Commencement
17.11.01 for making regulations and 1.4.02 generally: SI 2001 No 3689.

Amendment
1.   Amended by SPCA 2002 Sch 2 para 48 (2.7.02 for making regulations, 6.10.03 in full).

Interpretation of sections 7 to 12

13. In this section and sections 7 to 12–

''benefit'' includes any allowance, payment, credit or loan;

''disqualification period'' has the meaning given by section 7(6);

''family'' has the same meaning as in Part VII of the Social Security Contributions and Benefits Act 1992;

''income-based jobseeker's allowance'', ''joint-claim jobseeker's allowance'' and ''joint-claim couple'' have the same meanings as in the Jobseekers Act 1995;

''post-commencement offence'' means any criminal offence committed after the commencement of section 7;

''sanctionable benefit'' has the meaning given by section 7(8);

[¹ ''state pension credit'' means state pension credit under the State Pension Credit Act 2002;]

''war pension'' has the same meaning as in section 25 of the Social Security Act 1989 (establishment and functions of war pensions committees).

Commencement
17.11.01 for making regulations and 1.4.02 generally: SI 2001 No 3689.

Amendment
1.   Amended by SPCA 2002 Sch 2 para 49 (2.7.02 for regulations, 6.10.03 in full).

Supplemental

Meaning of ''the Administration Act''

18.   In this Act ''the Administration Act'' means the Social Security Administration Act 1992 (c. 5).

Commencement

20.–(1)   The preceding provisions of this Act shall come into force on such day as the Secretary of State may by order made by statutory instrument appoint.

(2)   Subject to subsection (3), different days may be appointed under this section for different purposes.

(3)   The power under this section to appoint a day for the coming into force of the provisions of sections 1 and 2 shall not authorise the appointment for those purposes of any day before the issue of the code of practice that must be issued under section 3.

Short title and extent

21.–(1)   This Act may be cited as the Social Security Fraud Act 2001.

(2)   Sections 5(2), 7, 10, 11, 12(3), 13 and 20, and this section, extend to Northern Ireland; and the other provisions of this Act do not so extend.

State Pension Credit Act 2002
(2002 c16)

General Note to the Act

The State Pension Credit Act 2002 (SPCA 2000) created, from October 2003, a new social security benefit, the state pension credit (PC), available to claimants of at least the pensionable age for women (currently aged 60, an age which will rise with the increases in the state retirement age for women from 2010). It is administered by the Pensions Service on behalf of the DWP and is often called "pension credit".

PC has two elements. The guarantee credit (GC) replaced IS for this age-group of claimants. It works in a similar way to IS, with some differences in terminology. The first step in the calculation of GC is to work out the "appropriate minimum guarantee" which consists of a "standard minimum guarantee" plus "additional amounts" and "a transitional amount" where the GC would leave a claimant worse off than s/he was before PC was introduced. Secondly, resources must be calculated. There is no upper capital limit, but a claimant is treated as having £1 of income for each £500 over £6,000 (£10,000 if the claimant lives in a care home). The GC is the appropriate minimum guarantee minus income.

The second element of PC is savings credit (SC). This can be claimed by those who are (or whose partners are) 65 or over. The aim is to reward those who have made some provision for their retirement. SC may be awarded to those who have "qualifying income" (which is anything except certain benefits or tax credits) above the savings credit "threshold".

For full details of the rules for PC, see CPAG's *Welfare Benefits and Tax Credits Handbook*.

As far as HB and CTB are concerned, the HB(SPC) Regs and the CTB(SPC) Regs, to an extent, align the capital and income rules in the HB and CTB schemes with those for PC.

Transitional provisions

13.–(1) The Secretary of State may by regulations make such transitional provision, consequential provision or savings as he considers necessary or expedient for the purposes of, or in connection with,–

    (a)   the coming into force of any of the state pension credit provisions of this Act; or

    (b)   the operation of any enactment repealed or amended by any of those provisions during any period when the repeal or amendment is not wholly in force.

(2)   The provision that may be made by regulations under this section includes in particular–

    (a)   provision for a person who attains or has attained the qualifying age on or before the appointed day and who immediately before that day is entitled to income support–

        (i)   to be treated as having been awarded on, and with effect as from, that day state pension credit of an amount specified in or determined in accordance with the regulations; or

        (ii)   to be treated as having made a claim for state pension credit; and

    (b)   provision for an assessed income period under section 6 of such length as may be specified in or determined in accordance with the regulations (which may be longer than the maximum period provided for by section 9(1)) to have effect in the case of a person who attains or has attained the qualifying age on or before the appointed day.

(3)   In this section–

"the appointed day" means such day as the Secretary of State may by order appoint;

"the state pension credit provisions of this Act" means this Act other than section 18.

Minor and consequential amendments

14.   Schedule 2 (which makes minor and consequential amendments relating to state pension credit) shall have effect.

Tax Credits Act 2002
(2002 c21)

General Note to the Act

The Tax Credits Act 2002 replaced working families tax credit, disabled person's tax credit, amounts for children within the IS and JSA schemes, increases to non-means test benefits for children and other allowances with two tax credits, working tax credit (WTC) and child tax credit (CTC). Child benefit is paid in addition to CTC. HB and CTB continue to contain personal allowances for children who are members of the family.

WTC and CTC are administered by HM Revenue and Customs (referred to as the Revenue in this book).

WTC and CTC became available from April 2003. IS and income-based JSA no longer include amounts for children (allowances and premiums) unless the claimant was getting these on 5 April 2004 and has not yet become entitled to CTC. Such claimants will be transferred onto CTC (and hence lose the amounts for children) by the DWP. This will not take place until 2008 at the earliest.

CTC is payable in full to those who have income lower than the "income threshold figure". Any excess reduces the CTC by a percentage of the excess (currently 37 per cent). There is a family element which allows for a higher amount where there is a baby in the family as well as elements for disability and severe disability, where a child in the family is disabled.

WTC is payable to people in full-time remunerative work. The rules define this as 16 or 30 hours per week, depending on the circumstances. Maximum WTC is comprised of a number of elements, including those for disability, severe disability, lone parents, couples, those working more than 30 hours a week, those aged over 50 and those who incur childcare costs as a result of their work.

For full details of the rules for WTC and CTC, see CPAG's *Welfare Benefits and Tax Credits Handbook*.

For HB and CTB purposes, there were consequential amendments made by the Social Security (Working Tax Credit and Child Tax Credit) Consequential Amendments Regulations 2003 SI No.455. The only directly relevant parts of the Act are those concerning the sharing of information between local authorities and the Revenue.

SCHEDULE 5
USE AND DISCLOSURE OF INFORMATION

Exchange of information between Board and authorities administering certain benefits

7.–(1) This paragraph applies to information which is held for the purposes of functions relating to tax credits, child benefit or guardian's allowance–

    (a)   by the Board, or

    (b)   by a person providing services to the Board, in connection with the provision of those services.

    (2)   Information to which this paragraph applies may be supplied by or under the authority of the Board–

    (a)   to an authority administering housing benefit or council tax benefit, or

    (b)   to a person authorised to exercise any function of such an authority relating to such a benefit,

for use in the administration of such a benefit.

    (3)   Information supplied under this paragraph is not to be supplied by the recipient to any other person or body unless it is supplied–

    (a)   to a person to whom the information could be supplied directly by or under the authority of the Board,

    (b)   for the purposes of any civil or criminal proceedings relating to the Social Security Contributions and Benefits Act 1992 (c. 4), the Social Security Administration Act 1992 (c. 5) or the Jobseekers Act 1995 (c. 18) or to any provision of Northern Ireland legislation corresponding to any of them, or

    (c)   under paragraph 8 below.

8.–(1) The Board may require–

    (a)   an authority administering housing benefit or council tax benefit, or

    (b)   a person authorised to exercise any function of such an authority relating to such a benefit,

to supply benefit administration information held by the authority or other person to, or to a person providing services to, the Board for use for any purpose relating to tax credits, child benefit or guardian's allowance.

    (2)   In sub-paragraph (1) ''benefit administration information'', in relation to an authority or other person, means any information which is relevant to the exercise of any function relating to housing benefit or council tax benefit by the authority or other person.

Gender Recognition Act 2004

(2004 c7)

General Note

This Act came into force on 4 April 2005: see The Gender Recognition Act 2004 (Commencement) Order 2005 (SI 2005 No.54). It introduced a system of statutory recognition in respect of an adult's (18 or over) change of gender from male to female or female to male. It is unnecessary to set out the detail of how this is to be achieved, but the consequences for entitlement to HB/CTB arise from s9 in particular. For more detail on this see paragraphs 28 to 37 of the DWP's General Information Bulletin HB/CTB G3/2005 (16 March 2005).

Consequences of issue of gender recognition certificate etc.

9 General

(1)   Where a full gender recognition certificate is issued to a person, the person's gender becomes for all purposes the acquired gender (so that, if the acquired gender is the male gender, the person's sex becomes that of a man and, if it is the female gender, the person's sex becomes that of a woman).

(2)   Subsection (1) does not affect things done, or events occurring, before the certificate is issued; but it does operate for the interpretation of enactments passed, and instruments and other documents made, before the certificate is issued (as well as those passed or made afterwards).

(3)   Subsection (1) is subject to provision made by this Act or any other enactment or any subordinate legislation.

Age-Related Payments Act 2004
(2004 c10)

General Note

This short Act came into force in July 2004. It introduced under ss2 and 3 a one-off cash payment for older people. Publicity available at the time said these were to help with council tax bills, though there was no requirement that the payments be used for this purpose. The payments were for 2004 only, to those aged 70 or over and were either of £50 or £100. Section 6 provides in effect that those payments were to be disregarded in full (both as income and capital) for all means-tested benefits, including HB and CTB.

Section 7 authorises the Secretary of State to provide for similar 'age-related payments' in future years, which he did under the Age-Related Payments Regulations 2005 (SI No.1983). The payments for 2005 were £100 or £200 to those aged 65 or over and £50 to those age 70 or over. Note, however, that the disregard in s6 does not apply to such payments (as they arise under s7 of the Act and not ss2 or 3). However, reg 8 of SI 2005 No.1983 provided such a disregard. The text of that reg is:

"8. No account shall be taken of entitlement to a payment under any of regulations 2 to 5 in considering a person's–
   (a) liability to tax;
   (b) entitlement to benefit under an enactment relating to social security (irrespective of the name or nature of the benefit), or
   (c) entitlement to a tax credit."

---

6 Payment to be disregarded for tax and social security

No account shall be taken of entitlement to a payment under section 2 or 3 in considering a person's–

(a)   liability to tax,

(b)   entitlement to benefit under an enactment relating to social security (irrespective of the name or nature of the benefit), or

(c)   entitlement to a tax credit.

Civil Partnership Act 2004

(2004 Chapter 33)

General Note

The Civil Partnership Act 2004 (Relationships Arising Through Civil Partnership) Order 2005 SI No 3137 sets out the provisions to which s246 of this Act applies for HB and CTB purposes. The Order is on p1097.

246 Interpretation of statutory references to stepchildren etc.

(1)   In any provision to which this section applies, references to a stepchild or step-parent of a person (here, ''A''), and cognate expressions, are to be read as follows–

A's stepchild includes a person who is the child of A's civil partner (but is not A's child);

A's step-parent includes a person who is the civil partner of A's parent (but is not A's parent);

A's stepdaughter includes a person who is the daughter of A's civil partner (but is not A's daughter);

A's stepson includes a person who is the son of A's civil partner (but is not A's son);

A's stepfather includes a person who is the civil partner of A's father (but is not A's parent);

A's stepmother includes a person who is the civil partner of A's mother (but is not A's parent);

A's stepbrother includes a person who is the son of the civil partner of A's parent (but is not the son of either of A's parents);

A's stepsister includes a person who is the daughter of the civil partner of A's parent (but is not the daughter of either of A's parents).

(2)   For the purposes of any provision to which this section applies–

''brother-in-law'' includes civil partner's brother,

''daughter-in-law'' includes daughter's civil partner,

''father-in-law'' includes civil partner's father,

''mother-in-law'' includes civil partner's mother,

''parent-in-law'' includes civil partner's parent,

''sister-in-law'' includes civil partner's sister, and

''son-in-law'' includes son's civil partner.

247 Provisions to which section 246 applies: Acts of Parliament etc.

(1)   Section 246 applies to–

(a)   any provision listed in Schedule 21 (references to stepchildren, in-laws etc. in existing Acts),

(b)   except in so far as otherwise provided, any provision made by a future Act, and

(c)   except in so far as otherwise provided, any provision made by future subordinate legislation.

(2)   A Minister of the Crown may by order–

(a)   amend Schedule 21 by adding to it any provision of an existing Act;

(b)   provide for section 246 to apply to prescribed provisions of existing subordinate legislation.

(3)   The power conferred by subsection (2) is also exercisable–

(a)   by the Scottish Ministers, in relation to a relevant Scottish provision;

(b)   by a Northern Ireland department, in relation to a provision which deals with a transferred matter;

(c)   by the National Assembly for Wales, if the order is made by virtue of subsection (2)(b) and deals with matters with respect to which functions are exercisable by the Assembly.

(4)   Subject to subsection (5), the power to make an order under subsection (2) is exercisable by statutory instrument.

(5)   Any power of a Northern Ireland department to make an order under subsection (2) is exercisable by statutory rule for the purposes of the Statutory Rules (Northern Ireland) Order 1979 (S.I. 1979/1573 (N.I. 12)).

(6)   A statutory instrument containing an order under subsection (2) made by a Minister of the Crown is subject to annulment in pursuance of a resolution of either House of Parliament.

(7)   A statutory instrument containing an order under subsection (2) made by the Scottish Ministers is subject to annulment in pursuance of a resolution of the Scottish Parliament.

(8)   A statutory rule containing an order under subsection (2) made by a Northern Ireland department is subject to negative resolution (within the meaning of section 41(6) of the Interpretation Act (Northern Ireland) 1954 (c. 33 (N.I.))).

(9)   In this section–

"Act" includes an Act of the Scottish Parliament;

"existing Act" means an Act passed on or before the last day of the Session in which this Act is passed;

"existing subordinate legislation" means subordinate legislation made before the day on which this section comes into force;

"future Act" means an Act passed after the last day of the Session in which this Act is passed;

"future subordinate legislation" means subordinate legislation made on or after the day on which this section comes into force;

"Minister of the Crown" has the same meaning as in the Ministers of the Crown Act 1975 (c. 26);

"prescribed" means prescribed by the order;

"relevant Scottish provision" means a provision that would be within the legislative competence of the Scottish Parliament if it were included in an Act of that Parliament;

"subordinate legislation" has the same meaning as in the Interpretation Act 1978 (c. 30) except that it includes an instrument made under an Act of the Scottish Parliament;

"transferred matter" has the meaning given by section 4(1) of the Northern Ireland Act 1998 (c. 47) and "deals with" in relation to a transferred matter is to be construed in accordance with section 98(2) and (3) of the 1998 Act.

---

254 Social security, child support and tax credits

(1)   Schedule 24 contains amendments relating to social security, child support and tax credits.

(2)   Subsection (3) applies in relation to any provision of any Act, Northern Ireland legislation or subordinate legislation which–

(a)   relates to social security, child support or tax credits, and

(b)   contains references (however expressed) to persons who are living or have lived together as husband and wife.

(3)   The power under section 259 to make orders amending enactments, Northern Ireland legislation and subordinate legislation is to be treated as including power to amend the provision to refer to persons who are living or have lived together as if they were civil partners.

(4)   Subject to subsection (5), section 175(3), (5) and (6) of the Social Security Contributions and Benefits Act 1992 (c. 4) applies to the exercise of the power under section 259 in relation to social security, child support or tax credits as it applies to any power under that Act to make an order (there being disregarded for the purposes of this subsection the exceptions in section 175(3) and (5) of that Act).

(5)   Section 171(3), (5) and (6) of the Social Security Contributions and Benefits (Northern Ireland) Act 1992 (c. 7) applies to the exercise by a Northern Ireland department of the power under section 259 in relation to social security and child support as it applies to any power under that Act to make an order (there being disregarded for the purposes of this subsection the exceptions in section 171(3) and (5) of that Act).

(6)   The reference in subsection (2) to an Act or Northern Ireland legislation relating to social security is to be read as including a reference to–

(a)   the Pneumoconiosis etc. (Workers' Compensation) Act 1979 (c. 41), and

(b)   the Pneumoconiosis, etc., (Workers' Compensation) (Northern Ireland) Order 1979 (S.I. 1979/925 (N.I. 9));

and the references in subsections (4) and (5) to social security are to be construed accordingly.

SCHEDULE 21

SECTION 247

REFERENCES TO STEPCHILDREN ETC. IN EXISTING ACTS

24	Section 113(2) of the Housing Act 1985 (c. 68) (members of a person's family).
25	Section 186(2) of that Act (members of a person's family).
44	Section 62(2) of the Housing Act 1996 (c. 52) (members of a person's family: Part 1).
45	Section 140(2) of that Act (members of a person's family Chapter 1).
46	Section 143P(3) of that Act (members of a person's family: Chapter 1A).
47	The definition of ''relative'' in section 178(3) of that Act (meaning of associated person).

Part 7

Other secondary legislation
Common and transitional
provisions

The Social Security (Claims and Payments) Regulations 1987
(1987 No. 1968)

Making a claim for benefit

4.–(1)-(6)   *Omitted*

[¹(6A) [⁵   This paragraph applies to a person]–

(a)   who has attained the qualifying age and makes a claim for–
   (i)   an attendance allowance, a bereavement benefit, a carer's allowance, a disability living allowance or incapacity benefit; or
   (ii)   a retirement pension of any category [³ or a shared additional pension] for which a claim is required or a winter fuel payment for which a claim is required under regulation 3(1)(b) of the Social Fund Winter Fuel Payment Regulations 2000;

(b)   who has not yet attained the qualifying age and makes a claim for a retirement pension [³or a shared additional pension] in advance in accordance with regulation 15(1); [⁴...]

[⁵ (c) who makes a claim for income support; or

(d)   who has not attained the qualifying age and who makes a claim for a carer's allowance, disability living allowance or incapacity benefit.]

(6B)   A person to whom paragraph (6A) applies may make a claim by sending or delivering it to, or by making it in person at–

(a)   an office designated by the Secretary of State for accepting such claims; or

[⁵ (b) the offices of–
   (i)   a local authority administering housing benefit or council tax benefit,
   (ii)   a county council in England,
   (iii)   a person providing services to a person mentioned in head (i) or (ii),
   (iv)   a person authorised to exercise any function of a local authority relating to housing benefit or council tax benefit, or
   (v)   a person authorised to exercise any function a county council in England has under section 7A of the Social Security Administration Act 1992,

if the Secretary of State has arranged with the local authority, county council or other person for them to receive claims in accordance with this sub-paragraph,]

(6C)   Where a person to whom paragraph (6A) applies makes a claim in accordance with paragraph (6B)(b), on receipt of the claim the local authority or other person specified in that sub-paragraph–

(a)   shall forward the claim to the Secretary of State as soon as reasonably practicable;

(b)   may receive information or evidence relating to the claim supplied by–
   (i)   the person making, or who has made, the claim; or
   (ii)   other persons in connection with the claim,

and shall forward it to the Secretary of State as soon as reasonably practicable;

(c)   may obtain information or evidence relating to the claim from the person who has made the claim, but not any medical information or evidence except for that which the claimant must provide in accordance with instructions on the form, and shall forward the information or evidence to the Secretary of State as soon as reasonably practicable;

[⁵ (cc) may verify any non-medical information or evidence supplied or obtained in accordance with sub-paragraph (b) or (c) and shall forward it to the Secretary of State as soon as reasonably practicable;]

(d)   may record information or evidence relating to the claim supplied or obtained in accordance with sub-paragraphs (b) or (c) and may hold the information or evidence (whether as supplied or obtained or as recorded) for the purpose of forwarding it to the Secretary of State; and

(e) may give information and advice with respect to the claim to the person who makes, or who has made, the claim.

[²(6CC) Paragraphs (6C)(b) to (e) apply in respect of information, evidence and advice relating to any claim by a person to whom paragraph (6A) applies, whether the claim is made in accordance with paragraph (6B)(b) or otherwise.]

(6D) The benefits specified in paragraph (6A) are relevant benefits for the purposes of section 7A of the Social Security Administration Act 1992.]

(7)-(14) *Omitted*

Amendments

1. Inserted by reg 2(2) of SI 2003 No 1632 as from 7.21.03.
2. Inserted by reg 7(2) of SI 2005 No 337 as from 3.18.05.
3. Amended by reg 2(4) of SI 2005 No 1551 as from 7.6.05.
4. Amended by reg 2(3) of SI 2006 No 832 as from 4.10.06.
5. Amended by reg 6(2) of SI 2007No 2911 as from 31.10.07.

[¹Making a claim for state pension credit

4D.–(1)–(3A) *Omitted*

[³ (4) A claim made in writing may also be made at the offices of–
(a) a local authority administering housing benefit or council tax benefit;
(b) a county council in England;
(c) a person providing services to a person mentioned in sub-paragraph (a) or (b);
(d) a person authorised to exercise any functions of a local authority relating to housing benefit or council tax benefit; or
(e) a person authorised to exercise any function a county council in England has under section 7A of the Social Security Administration Act 1992,
if the Secretary of State has arranged with the local authority, county council or other person for them to receive claims in accordance with this paragraph.]

[²(5) Where a claim is made in accordance with paragraph (4), the local authority or other specified person–
(a) shall forward the claim to the Secretary of State as soon as reasonably practicable;
(b) may receive information or evidence relating to the claim supplied by the person making, or who has made, the claim or another person, and shall forward it to the Secretary of State as soon as reasonably practicable;
(c) may obtain information or evidence relating to the claim from the person who has made the claim and shall forward it to the Secretary of State as soon as reasonably practicable;
[³ (cc) may verify any non-medical information or evidence supplied or obtained in accordance with sub-paragraph (b) or (c) and shall forward it to the Secretary of State as soon as reasonably practicable;]
(d) may record information or evidence relating to the claim supplied or obtained in accordance with sub-paragraph (b) or (c) and may hold the information or evidence (whether as supplied or obtained or as recorded) for the purpose of forwarding it to the Secretary of State; and
(e) may give information and advice with respect to the claim to the person who makes, or has made, the claim.]

[²(5A) Paragraph (5)(b) to (e) applies in respect of information, evidence and advice relating to any claim for state pension credit, whether it is made in accordance with paragraph (4) or otherwise .]

(6)–(12) *Omitted*

(13) State pension credit is a relevant benefit for the purposes of section 7A of the Social Security Administration Act 1992.]

Amendments
1. Inserted by reg 4(3) of SI 2002 No 3019 as from 4.7.03.
2. Inserted by reg 7(3) of SI 2005 No 337 as from 3.18.05.
3. Amended by reg 6(3) of SI 2007 No 2911 as from 31.10.07.

[¹ Information relating to awards of benefit

32B.–(1) Where an authority or person to whom paragraph (2) applies has arranged with the Secretary of State for the authority or person to receive claims for a specified benefit or obtain information or evidence relating to claims for a specified benefit in accordance with regulation 4 or 4D, the authority or person may–
- (a) receive information or evidence which relates to an award of that benefit and which is supplied by–
  - (i) the person to whom the award has been made; or
  - (ii) other persons in connection with the award,

and shall forward it to the Secretary of State as soon as reasonably practicable;
- (b) verify any information or evidence supplied; and
- (c) record the information or evidence supplied and hold it (whether as supplied or recorded) for the purpose of forwarding it to the Secretary of State.

(2) This paragraph applies to–
- (a) a local authority administering housing benefit or council tax benefit;
- (b) a county council in England;
- (c) a person providing services to a person mentioned in sub-paragraph (a) or (b);
- (d) a person authorised to exercise any function of a local authority relating to housing benefit or council tax benefit;
- (e) a person authorised to exercise any function a county council in England has under section 7A of the Social Security Administration Act 1992.

(3) In paragraph (1), ''specified benefit'' means one or more of the following benefits–
- (a) attendance allowance;
- (b) bereavement allowance;
- (c) bereavement payment;
- (d) carer's allowance;
- (e) disability living allowance;
- (f) incapacity benefit;
- (g) income support;
- (h) jobseeker's allowance;
- (i) retirement pension;
- (j) state pension credit;
- (k) widowed parent's allowance;
- (l) winter fuel payment.]

Amendment
1. Inserted by reg 6(5) of SI 2007 No 2911 as from 31.10.07.

Social Security (Persons From Abroad) Miscellaneous Amendments Regulations 1996

(SI 1996 No.30)

Saving

12.–(1)   Where, before the coming into force of these Regulations, a person who becomes an asylum seeker under regulation 4A(5)(a)(i) of the Council Tax Benefit Regulations, regulation 7A(5)(a)(i) of the Housing Benefit Regulations or regulation 70(3A)(a) of the Income Support Regulations, as the case may be, is entitled to benefit under any of those Regulations, those provisions of those Regulations as then in force shall continue to have effect [¹ (both as regards him and as regards persons who are members of his family at the coming into force of these Regulations)] as if regulations 3(a) and (b), 7(a) and (b) or 8(2) and (3)(c), as the case may be, of these Regulations had not been made.

(2)   Where, before the coming into force of these Regulations, a person, in respect of whom an undertaking was given by another person or persons to be responsible for his maintenance and accommodation, claimed benefit to which he is entitled, or is receiving benefit, under the Council Tax Benefit Regulations, the Housing Benefit Regulations or the Income Support regulations, as the case may be, those Regulations as then in force shall have effect as if regulations 3, 7 or 8, as the case may be, of these Regulations had not been made.

Amendment

1.   Amended by the Asylum and Immigration Act 1996 Sch 1 para 5 from 24.7.96. The effect of this amendment is preserved by reg 12(11)(a) of SI 2000 No 636 from 3.4.00 following the repeal of Sch 1 of the 1996 Act on the same date.

Modifications

The amendments made by SI 2006 No 1026 to the HB Regs, HB(SPC) Regs, CTB Regs and CTB(SPC) Regs do not affect the continued operation of the transitional and savings provided for in reg 12 of the Social Security (Persons From Abroad) Miscellaneous Amendments Regulations 1996, reg 6 of the Social Security (Habitual Residence) Amendment Regulations 2004 or para 6 of Sch 3 of the HB&CTB(CP) Regs. See reg 11 of SI 2006 No 1026 (on p1134).

General Note

This important saving provision prevents retrospective effect of the draconian restrictions on the receipt of benefit by asylum seekers which were introduced by these Regulations. The belief of the Government that the UK was seen as an easy target for economic migrants masquerading as asylum seekers resulted in these Regulations being made. An asylum seeker, B, and the Joint Council for the Welfare of Immigrants commenced judicial review proceedings claiming that the removal of benefit conflicted with the right to have an asylum claim determined in accordance with the Asylum and Immigration Appeals Act 1993 and the Regulations were therefore *ultra vires*. It was pointed out that asylum seekers were forbidden from obtaining employment while their claims were determined. Many would arrive in this country without means to support themselves. If they could not rely on public funds, then they would be destitute and unable to maintain themselves. Ultimately, they would be unable to survive while their claims were being determined.

At first instance, the Divisional Court refused the application but the Court of Appeal in *R v Secretary of State for Social Security ex p B and JCWI* [1997] 1 WLR 275 held, by a majority, that the regulations were indeed *ultra vires*. In a judgment that is a high watermark of judicial activism, Simon Brown LJ said (at 292E-F, 293C):

".... the 1993 Act confers on asylum seekers fuller rights than they had ever previously enjoyed, the right of appeal in particular. And yet these regulations for some genuine asylum seekers at least, must now be regarded as rendering these rights nugatory. Either that, or the 1996 regulations necessarily contemplate for some a life so destitute that, to my mind, no civilised nation can tolerate it. .... Parliament cannot have intended a significant number of genuine asylum seekers to be impaled on the horns of so intolerable a dilemma: the need either to abandon their claims to refugee status or alternatively to maintain themselves as best they can but in a state of utter destitution. Primary legislation alone could in my judgement achieve that sorry state of affairs."

However, the Asylum and Immigration Act 1996 was making its way through Parliament at the time of the Court of Appeal's decision and the Government took the opportunity to legislate to ensure that the "sorry state of affairs" continued by introducing an amendment to enact s11 and Sch 1, which effectively resurrected the 1996 Regulations, with amendments. Suggestions that a better way of solving the alleged difficulties (the existence of which was unsupported by any reliable evidence) would be to employ more special adjudicators to reduce the lengthy delays in the determination of asylum claims, fell on deaf ears.

The enduring result of the striking down of these Regulations by the decision of the Court of Appeal in *ex p B* and their subsequent resurrection by the 1996 Act is that there has been considerable difficulty in determining which claimants are entitled to transitional protection.

Where someone is entitled to HB or CTB by virtue of reg 12(1) or (2) of SI 1996 No. 30 immediately before 6 March 2006, the modifications to the current CTB and CTB(SPC) Regs and the current HB Regs and HB(SPC) Regs are now to be found in Sch 3 para 6 of the HB&CTB(CP) Regs.

Under reg 12(11)(b) of the Social Security (Immigration and Asylum) Consequential Provisions Regulations 2000 SI No 636, the effect of the saving provisions of reg 12 of these Regulations remains the same, despite the repeal of much of the then reg 7A HB Regs 1987 and reg 4A CTB Regs 1992 by the 2000 Regulations.

Analysis
Paragraph (1)
".... before the coming into force of these Regulations ....". The unusual method chosen by the Government of re-activating the Regulations struck down in *ex p B and JCWI* rather than simply granting itself the powers to pass such Regulations and enacting a new set caused difficulties in determining the scope of the transitional protection.

Before the Court of Appeal's decision, the meaning of paras (1) and (2) in relation to the two categories of claimants was clear enough. Where the claim was made or treated as made before 5 February 1996, the Regulations had no effect on her/his entitlement. It appears that this would have applied to a claimant who had the date of her/his claim backdated under reg 72(15) HB Regs 1987 or reg 64(16) CTB Regs 1992 to before 5 February 1996 for good cause. Where the claim was made or treated as made after that date, the exclusions in the Regulations took effect.

The question that arose was as to the effect of the Court of Appeal's decision in *ex p B and JCWI* on reg 12. The order made by the court did not declare the Regulations as a whole to be *ultra vires*: merely those parts that purported to exclude asylum seekers from benefit. That being so, when was "the coming into force" of the Regulations? Was it on 5 February 1996, or was it on 24 July 1996, when the Regulations were revived by Sch 1 of the 1996 Act (with the amendment made by para 5 to reg 12(1))? The question arises in relation to "in country" asylum seekers whose claims were made or treated as made between 5 February and 23 July ("the window period").

In *ex p T*, it was held that the date referred to was the earlier date of 5 February. Because reg 12(1) had not been altered by the 1996 Act to refer to 24 July, it was reasonable to assume that the earlier commencement date represented Parliament's intention. Therefore asylum seekers who claimed benefits in the window period are not entitled to receive benefit. Potts J's ruling was upheld by the Court of Appeal [1997] 5 CL 619.

".... those provisions of those Regulations then in force ....". It is important to recall that prior to the enactment of these regulations, all asylum seekers were a group of "persons from abroad" who were exempted from the general exclusion from benefit. See reg 10(6)(a)(i) of both the HB and the HB(SPC) Regs and reg 7(6)(a)(i) of both the CTB and the CTB(SPC) Regs as provided by Sch 3 para 6(1)-(3) of the HB&CTB(CP) Regs.

After these Regulations were enacted, only "on arrival" applicants for asylum were exempt: see reg 10(1)of both the HB and the HB(SPC) Regs and 7(1) of both the CTB and the CTB(SPC) regs as modified by Sch 3 para 6(10)-(13) of the HB&CTB(CP) Regs. The question is therefore which "in country" applicants are protected by reg 12.

".... is entitled to benefit .... shall continue to have effect ....". The provisions can only have effect if the claimant is entitled to benefit on the date these Regulations came into force, which, following the decision in *ex p T* referred to above, is to be taken to be 5 February 1996. It is not sufficient that a claimant has been in receipt of benefit at some time prior to that date and then seeks to claim again after it: *R v Secretary of State for Social Security ex p Vijeikis* [1998] COD 49, QBD; *CIS 16992/1996* para 20. As Dyson J said in *Vijeikis* at 50, "for something to continue, it must exist; it cannot be something that once existed, but no longer exists."

This analysis applies even where the claimant has found work and later has to go back onto benefit, no matter how unfair that is. Parliament, by resurrecting the regulations, has clearly intended to produce that unfair result: *Vijeikis* at 50. The decision in that case was upheld by the Court of Appeal [1998] unreported, 5 March.

However, what happens where there is a break in claim for a period after 5 February 1996? Is the transitional protection lost? It was suggested in previous editions of this book that the transitional protection should not cease. A number of commissioners, however, issued decisions on the effect of para (1). All the cases were where there have been breaks in claims for income support (IS). In *CIS 3955/1997* the claimant went to India for 11 weeks and in *CIS 1115/1999* and *CIS 6258/1999* the claimant obtained employment for a period. The commissioners all ruled that the transitional protection was lost once the previous claim for IS ended. The commissioner in *CIS 6258/1999* expressed some doubt about the reasoning in the other two cases that preceded his decision but decided that he could not be satisfied that those decisions were wrongly decided so as to entitle him to decline to follow them.

In *Yildiz v Secretary of State for Social Security* [2001] *The Independent* 9 March, [2001] EWCA Civ 309, CA, the Court of Appeal allowed an appeal from the decision in *CIS 6258/1999*. The court held (para 15 of the judgment of Buxton LJ) that the only pre-condition for the application of the transitional protection in para (1) is that the claimant must have been in receipt of benefit on 5 February 1996. Once that is shown, the protection remains until the claimant's claim for asylum is determined, regardless of any intervening period of employment or other non-entitlement to benefit.

Authorities administering HB will be faced far more frequently with the question of whether the transitional protection is preserved on the making of a renewal claim. None of the commissioners dealt with this situation, because IS is normally awarded for an indefinite period, and neither was the Court of Appeal in *Yildiz* directly concerned with such a case. However, it is an inevitable consequence of the decision in *Yildiz* that entitlement to HB will not disappear on a renewal claim. If it is not lost on a break in claim, there is no basis for any suggestion that it is lost on a renewal claim.

".... both as regards him and as regards persons who are members of his family at the coming into force of these Regulations ....". The effect of this amendment is to confirm that the claimant's immigration status determines the entitlement to benefit for the rest of the family. Suppose an asylum seeker arrived in Britain and did not claim on her arrival, but claimed benefit on 1 February 1996, and her partner arrived in the UK on 1 March with their son. They remain members of her family (eg, by virtue of reg 21(1) HB Regs). The claimant is entitled to claim benefit in respect of both of them. If the claimant and her partner separate, the partner can claim in his own right, even though he arrived after the cut-off date. If the son reaches the age of 16, he can claim in his own right.

However, it must be remembered that this only applies where the claimant and partner are a couple on 5 February 1996. If the relationship breaks down before then, the partner will not be entitled to the benefit of the transitional protection if s/he claims after that date: *R v Department of Social Security ex p Okito* [1998] COD 48 at 49, QBD (this case was heard with *Vijeikis*).

Paragraph (2)

This paragraph provides transitional protection for sponsored immigrants, who were not "persons from abroad" until 5 February 1996. These parts of the 1996 Regulations were not challenged in *Okito*. Note that where someone is entitled to HB or CTB by virtue of reg 12(2) when the consolidating regulations came into force on 6 March 2006 the HB and CTB Regs will have effect subject to the modifications provided in Sch 3 para 6(2) and (3) HB&CTB(CP) Regs: Sch 3 para 6(4) HB&CTB(CP) Regs.

Claimants whose entitlement was terminated before 5 February 1996. In *CIS 16992/1996* para 7 it was said that the scope of the transitional protection was the same as for para (1) above, so that the claimant could not rely on a period of entitlement that terminated prior to 5 February 1996. This was also assumed by Dyson J in *Vijeikis*, although none of the three cases before him were concerned with sponsored immigrants. However, there is a significant difference in language between paras (1) and (2). Para (1) refers to a claimant who "is entitled to benefit" on 5 February, for whom the old rules "continue to have effect". The language there clearly refers to a claimant who is entitled on the commencement date. Nothing else will do.

Para (2), however, refers to a person who "*before* the coming into force of the Regulations . . . *claimed* benefit to which he *is* entitled, *or is* receiving benefit". Para (2) clearly contemplates two separate categories of claimant. The second category covers those who are receiving benefit on 5 February. The first category could be read in two ways. Either it covers those who made a claim prior to 5 February which was not adjudicated until after that date, or it covers all those who made a claim for some period prior to 5 February. Which construction is to be preferred?

The difficulty with adopting the first construction is that the first category is then otiose, since a claimant who claimed on 1 February and whose claim was adjudicated on 1 March "is receiving benefit" for the four weeks in February, including the critical date of 5 February. It can therefore be said that s/he falls within the second category. The first category must therefore mean something different. If it was not intended to do so, why include it?

The second, wider construction is not altogether satisfactory either. The past tense of the word "claimed" supports it. The difficulty lies with the word "is". That would suggest that the entitlement must be a current one, as Dyson J thought. However, it can be explained by the need to exclude from the provision those claimants who claimed, and were awarded, benefit on a false basis. Although it could be said that such a claimant *was* entitled to benefit following the award on the claim, if the award was subsequently reviewed before or after the 5 February threshold, it could not be said that the claimant *is* entitled to the award of benefit on that claim. It is therefore suggested that if the first category of claimants is to have any meaning, the second, wider construction is to be preferred.

Breaks in claim after 5 February 1996. It is suggested that the same analysis applies for para (2) as for para (1) (see above). In *CIS 1077/1999* and *CIS 6088/1999* para 120, Commissioner Jacobs suggested that once an award of IS ceases, the transitional protection is lost. Although this decision was issued prior to and without the benefit of the analysis in *Yildiz*, on a further appeal to the Court of Appeal (*Shah v Secretary of State for Social Security [2002] EWCA Civ 285, CA*, also reported as *R(IS) 2/02*), the argument based on paragraph (2) was abandoned in the light of the House of Lords' decision in *M (A Minor) v Secretary of State for Social Security* [2001] 1 WLR 1453 (*R(IS) 2/02*).

The Housing Benefit (Permitted Totals) Order 1996
(SI 1996 No.677)

General Note
This Order sets out the basis for calculating the permitted totals of rebates or allowances for the year 1996/1997 and subsequent years for authorities granting rebates or allowances under Part VIII of the Social Security Administration Act 1992. The Order limits the amount by which HB payments may be increased on the exercise of the discretions formerly provided by reg 61(2) and (3) HB Regs 1987, and to war widows through modified schemes.

Citation, commencement and interpretation

1.–(1)   This Order may be cited as the Housing Benefit (Permitted Totals) Order 1996 and shall come into force on 1st April 1996.

(2)   In this Order–

"the Act" means the Social Security Administration Act 1992;

"housing benefit" means either rent rebate or rent allowance as the circumstances may require;

"the Housing Benefit Regulations" means the Housing Benefit (General) Regulations 1987;

"increase in housing benefit" means the difference between–
- (a)   the amount of housing benefit granted in a case in which an authority makes a determination under regulation 61(2) of the Housing Benefit Regulations (increase in the appropriate maximum housing benefit)(e), and
- (b)   the amount of housing benefit which would have been granted in that case if the authority had not made a determination under regulation 61(2) of those Regulations; and

"increase above maximum rent" means the difference between–
- (a)   the amount of housing benefit granted in a case in which an authority makes a determination under regulation 61(3) of the Housing Benefit Regulations, and
- (b)   the amount of housing benefit which would have been granted in that case if the authority had not made a determination under regulation 61(3) of those Regulations.

Permitted total of benefit awarded in exercise of a discretion

2.   For the purpose of section 134(11) of the Act, the permitted total of housing benefit–
- [¹ (a)   for the year commencing on 1st April 1996 in relation to an authority shall be the total of the amounts obtained by the calculations set out in articles 3 and 4 below.
- (b)   for the year commencing on 1st April 1997 in relation to an authority shall be the total of the amounts obtained by the calculations set out in articles 3 and 4 below; and
- (c)   for any year commencing on or after 1st April 1998 in relation to an authority shall be the total of the amount obtained by the calculation in article 3 below and the amount specified in the Schedule to this Order.]

Amendment
1.   Amended by reg 2 of SI 1998 No 566 from 31.3.98.

Increase in housing benefit

3.   The calculation referred to in article 2 above shall be the amount obtained by deducting 100% of any increases in housing benefit in cases in which that authority has during that year made a determination under regulation 61(2) of the Housing Benefit Regulations from the total housing benefit granted by that authority during that year, after deduction of any increase above maximum rent, and multiplying the resulting figure by [¹100.025%].

Amendment

1.   Amended by reg 2 SI 2001 No 1129 as from 1.04.01.

Increase above maximum rent

4.–(1)   The calculation referred to in article 2 above shall be the amount obtained by deducting 100% of any increases above maximum rent in cases in which that authority has during that year made a determination under regulation 61(3) of the Housing Benefit Regulations from the total housing benefit granted by that authority during that year, less the deductions specified in paragraph (2) below, and multiplying the resulting figure by [¹ 101.08%]

(2)   The deductions referred to in paragraph (1) above are–

(a)   all rent rebates granted during that year;

(b)   subject to paragraph (3) below, all rent allowances granted during that year in cases where the local authority did not refer a claim for housing benefit, in relation to the dwelling in respect of which that allowance was granted, to the rent officer pursuant to regulation 12A of the Housing Benefit Regulations; and

(c)   any increase in housing benefit.

(3)   No rent allowance shall be deducted pursuant to paragraph (2) above, if that case was not referred to the rent officer by reason of paragraph (2) of regulation 12A of those Regulations.

Amendment

1.   101.08% substituted for 100.9% by art 2 of SI 1996 No 2326 as from 7.10.1996.

Permitted total of benefit in modified schemes

5.   For the purpose of section 134(9) of the Act (modifications other than war disablement pension or war widows pension within the Act), the permitted total of housing benefit for [¹ any year commencing on or after] 1st April 1996 in relation to an authority shall be the total of the amounts obtained by deducting 100% of any housing benefit awarded as a consequence of any determination to disregard made by that authority during that year pursuant to a modification adopted by them under section 134(8) of the Act (power to modify housing benefit schemes as prescribed) and regulation 7 of the Income Related Benefits Schemes Amendment (No. 2) Regulations 1995 (power to modify in respect of certain pensions to war widows) from the total housing benefit granted by that authority during that year and multiplying the resulting figure by 100.7%.

Amendment

1.   Amended by reg 3 of SI 1998 No 566 from 31.3.98.

Revocation

6.   The Housing Benefit (Permitted Totals) Order 1995 is hereby revoked.

SCHEDULE 1
[² TOTALS FOR INCREASES ABOVE MAXIMUM RENT

Authority	Permitted total £	Authority	Permitted total £
England		Chester	16,699
Adur	11,073	Chester le Street	5,524
Allerdale	14,001	Chesterfield	14,802
Alnwick	2,832	Chichester	15,367
Amber Valley	12,361	Chiltern	4,842
Arun	41,402	Chorley	9,480
Ashfield	12,423	Christchurch	6,318
Ashford	/12,112	City of London	1,439
Aylesbury Vale	13,412	Colchester	28,238
Babergh	10,044	Congleton	4,887
Barking	38,065	Copeland	12,193
Barnet	133,375	Corby	12,013
Barnsley	31,155	Cotswold	9,367
Barrow in Furness	23,278	Coventry	67,163
Basildon	21,576	Craven	6,118
Basingstoke and Deane	12,982	Crawley	7,786
Bassetlaw	14,013	Crewe and Nantwich	13,121
Bath and NE Somerset	31,322	Croydon	145,919
Bedford	25,697	Dacorum	13,429
Berwick upon Tweed	3,833	Darlington	19,355
Bexley	49,763	Dartford	15,715
Birmingham	198,165	Daventry	4,365
Blaby	4,376	Derby	48,483
Blackburn with Darwen	33,307	Derbyshire Dales	3,813
Blackpool	117,965	Derwentside	10,221
Blyth Valley	8,004	Doncaster	39,071
Bolsover	13,007	Dover	36,954
Bolton	46,138	Dudley	21,784
Boston	5,138	Durham	5,937
Bournemouth	95,696	Ealing	158,493
Bracknell Forest	13,822	Easington	10,063
Bradford	123,752	East Cambridgeshire	7,026
Braintree	14,434	East Devon	18,050
Breckland	12,774	East Dorset	6,974
Brent	193,395	East Hampshire	11,956
Brentwood	7,087	East Hertfordshire	10,036
Bridgnorth	4,120	East Lindsey	32,105
Brighton and Hove	180,857	East Northamptonshire	8,204
Bristol	96,138	East Riding of Yorkshire	57,413
Broadland	8,928	East Staffordshire	12,968
Bromley	50,991	Eastbourne	42,495
Bromsgrove	4,359	Eastleigh	12,311
Broxbourne	13,260	Eden	5,083
Broxtowe	11,299	Ellesmere Port and Neston	5,910
Burnley	25,828	Elmbridge	22,072
Bury	29,838	Enfield	109,407
Calderdale	28,108	Epping Forest	20,508
Cambridge	16,167	Epsom and Ewell	9,885
Camden	132,750	Erewash	13,294
Cannock Chase	6,657	Exeter	35,462
Canterbury	33,324	Fareham	9,844
Caradon	20,600	Fenland	17,307
Carlisle	13,889	Forest Heath	6,146
Carrick	24,764	Forest of Dean	10,316
Castle Morpeth	3,056	Fylde	17,760
Castle Point	21,278	Gateshead	27,463
Charnwood	17,868	Gedling	12,914
Chelmsford	14,838	Gloucester	38,822
Cheltenham	24,155	Gosport	11,207
Cherwell	23,520	Gravesham	21,343

Authority	Permitted total £	Authority	Permitted total £
Great Yarmouth	40,174	Middlesbrough	30,388
Greenwich	56,280	Milton Keynes	30,589
Guildford	17,990	Mole Valley	6,461
Hackney	159,737	New Forest	19,869
Halton	17,626	Newark and Sherwood	12,775
Hambleton	8,380	Newcastle under Lyme	8,317
Hammersmith and Fulham	92,023	Newcastle upon Tyne	75,679
Harborough	4,066	Newham	236,456
Haringey	254,022	North Cornwall	22,078
Harlow	10,481	North Devon	33,937
Harrogate	24,943	North Dorset	5,647
Harrow	74,970	North East Derby	5,846
Hart	6,633	North East Lincoln	42,198
Hartlepool	20,158	North Hertfordshire	15,823
Hastings	70,070	North Kesteven	6,418
Havant	15,981	North Lincolnshire	20,707
Havering	36,693	North Norfolk	19,096
Herefordshire	31,035	North Shropshire	6,383
Hertsmere	10,520	North Somerset	58,091
High Peak	11,583	North Tyneside	49,049
Hillingdon	48,018	North Warwickshire	3,801
Hinckley and Bosworth	6,864	North West Leicester	5,509
Horsham	11,381	North Wiltshire	9,457
Hounslow	81,898	Northampton	32,163
Huntingdonshire	12,412	Norwich	26,986
Hyndburn	23,110	Nottingham	59,030
Ipswich	23,448	Nuneaton and Bedworth	14,606
Isle of Wight	48,692	Oadby and Wigston	4,630
Isles of Scilly	112	Oldham	34,150
Islington	75,538	Oswestry	4,760
Kennet	6,553	Oxford	48,078
Kensington and Chelsea	95,011	Pendle	19,716
Kerrier	23,573	Penwith	23,242
Kettering	11,336	Peterborough	41,089
Kings Lynn & West Norfolk	19,448	Plymouth	95,680
Kingston upon Hull	61,181	Poole	29,167
Kingston upon Thames	23,020	Portsmouth	67,055
Kirklees	61,583	Preston	23,230
Knowsley	24,691	Purbeck	7,603
Lambeth	166,917	Reading	51,780
Lancaster	52,083	Redbridge	142,324
Leeds	161,079	Redcar and Cleveland	22,464
Leicester	51,758	Redditch	5,822
Lewes	24,395	Reigate and Banstead	13,661
Lewisham	118,483	Restormel	32,194
Lichfield	3,550	Ribble Valley	5,025
Lincoln	20,575	Richmond upon Thames	34,918
Liverpool	201,524	Richmondshire	4,019
Luton	63,742	Rochdale	43,229
Macclesfield	16,110	Rochford	10,624
Maidstone	17,903	Rossendale	11,986
Maldon	18,921	Rother	22,310
Malvern Hills	7,025	Rotherham	23,596
Manchester	195,674	Rugby	7,523
Mansfield	14,897	Runnymede	9,170
Medway	108,499	Rushcliffe	9,619
Melton	3,109	Rushmoor	11,126
Mendip	21,594	Rutland	1,986
Merton	57,194	Ryedale	5,138
Mid Bedfordshire	8,266	Salford	77,097
Mid Devon	12,064	Salisbury	19,512
Mid Suffolk	6,806	Sandwell	31,220
Mid Sussex	13,107	Scarborough	37,313

Authority	Permitted total £	Authority	Permitted total £
Sedgefield	7,215	Torridge	18,849
Sedgemoor	21,337	Tower Hamlets	45,003
Sefton	84,267	Trafford	35,417
Selby	6,559	Tunbridge Wells	14,206
Sevenoaks	10,096	Tynedale	3,800
Sheffield	52,222	Uttlesford	6,206
Shepway	51,579	Vale of White Horse	9,747
Shrewsbury and Atcham	12,479	Vale Royal	7,303
Slough	36,269	Wakefield	27,358
Solihull	11,316	Walsall	18,945
South Bedfordshire	10,573	Waltham Forest	158,176
South Bucks	3,586	Wandsworth	121,014
South Cambridgeshire	8,860	Wansbeck	6,844
South Derbyshire	11,106	Warrington	13,911
South Gloucestershire	20,227	Warwick	15,350
South Hams	19,260	Watford	16,358
South Holland	5,045	Waveney	51,698
South Kesteven	13,603	Waverley	13,121
South Lakeland	15,835	Wealdon	21,509
South Norfolk	9,469	Wear Valley	7,507
South Northants	5,306	Wellingborough	10,445
South Oxfordshire	19,106	Welwyn Hatfield	9,713
South Ribble	6,160	West Berkshire	10,976
South Shropshire	6,168	West Devon	12,775
South Somerset	22,317	West Dorset	11,805
South Staffordshire	4,463	West Lancashire	13,010
South Tyneside	32,453	West Lindsey	9,532
Southampton	73,593	West Oxfordshire	11,866
Southend on Sea	97,336	West Somerset	10,899
Southwark	90,007	West Wiltshire	20,797
Spelthorne	10,818	Westminster	189,131
St Albans	9,953	Weymouth and Portland	23,141
St Edmundsbury	8,585	Wigan	26,933
St Helens	23,507	Winchester	8,637
Stafford	7,452	Windsor and Maidenhead	17,452
Staffordshire Moorlands	7,006	Wirral	104,453
Stevenage	9,376	Woking	10,638
Stockport	51,884	Wokingham	11,843
Stockton on Tees	28,021	Wolverhampton	28,921
Stoke on Trent	34,205	Worcester	24,231
Stratford on Avon	11,053	Worthing	33,956
Stroud	14,432	Wychavon	6,710
Suffolk Coastal	17,852	Wycombe	12,804
Sunderland	53,243	Wyre	22,173
Surrey Heath	7,169	Wyre Forest	11,956
Sutton	34,929	York	29,336
Swale	41,749	**Scotland**	
Swindon	23,721	Aberdeen	17,118
Tameside	36,307	Aberdeenshire	15,810
Tamworth	9,172	Angus	10,333
Tandridge	7,092	Argyll and Bute	17,435
Taunton Deane	21,426	Comhairle Nan Eilean Sair	2,249
Teesdale	2,865	Clackmannanshire	3,067
Teignbridge	29,864	Dumfries and Galloway	19,846
Telford and Wrekin	18,049	Dundee	23,135
Tendring	44,271	East Ayrshire	8,128
Test Valley	6,818	East Dunbartonshire	5,812
Tewkesbury	8,100	East Lothian	12,140
Thanet	88,716	East Renfrewshire	5,656
Three Rivers	8,128	Edinburgh	116,558
Thurrock	24,684	Falkirk	8,674
Tonbridge and Malling	9,546	Fife	43,080
Torbay	85,563	Glasgow	122,279

Authority	Permitted total £	Authority	Permitted total £
Highland	18,909	Cardiff	60,004
Inverclyde	9,892	Carmarthenshire	32,572
Midlothian	5,423	Ceredigion	18,702
Moray	9,487	Conwy	37,048
North Ayrshire	17,642	Denbighshire	30,347
North Lanarkshire	12,042	Flintshire	16,400
Orkney	2,857	Gwynedd	31,422
Perth and Kinross	21,140	Isle of Anglesey	18,958
Renfrewshire	14,138	Merthyr Tydfil	9,430
Scottish Borders	7,350	Monmouthshire	9,465
Shetland	775	Neath and Port Talbot	20,810
South Ayrshire	22,019	Newport	22,985
South Lanarkshire	17,803	Pembrokeshire	26,943
Stirling	7,290	Powys	16,586
West Dunbartonshire	5,438	Rhondda Cynon Taff	38,661
West Lothian	12,617	Swansea	52,344
Wales		Torfaen	7,729
Blaenau Gwent	10,753	Vale of Glamorgan	30,658
Bridgend	25,789	Wrexham	14,500
Caerphilly	24,394		

Amendments

1.   Schedule added by reg 2 of SI 1998 No 566 from 31.3.98.
2.   Amended by reg 3 of SI 2001 No 1129 as from 1.04.01.

The Council Tax Benefit (Permitted Totals) Order 1996
(SI 1996 No.678)

General Note

This Order sets out the basis for calculating the permitted totals of council tax benefit for any year for authorities granting such benefit under Part VIII of the Social Security Administration Act 1992. The Order limits the amount by which CTB allowed by an authority may be increased in the case of claimants whose circumstances are exceptional or in the case of war widows where the authority's scheme has been modified.

Citation, commencement and interpretation

1.–(1)   This Order may be cited as the Council Tax Benefit (Permitted Totals) Order 1996 and shall come into force on 1st April 1996.

(2)   In this Order–

"the Act" means the Social Security Administration Act 1992;

"council tax benefit" means council tax benefit under Part VII of the Contributions and Benefits Act;

"the Council Tax Benefit Regulations" means the Council Tax Benefit (General) Regulations 1992;

"increase in council tax benefit" means the difference between–

   (a)   in a case in which an authority makes a determination under regulation 51(5) or 54(4) of the Council Tax Benefit Regulations (increase in the appropriate maximum council tax benefit or alternative maximum council tax benefit)(f), the amount of council tax benefit granted; and

   (b)   the amount of council tax benefit which would have been granted in that case if the authority had not made a determination under the said regulation 51(5) or 54(4).

Permitted total of benefit allowed in exercise of a discretion

2.   For the purpose of section 139(9) of the Act, the permitted total of council tax benefit for any year commencing on or after 1st April 1996 in relation to an authority shall be the amount obtained by deducting 100% of any increases in council tax benefit allowed by that authority during that year from the total council tax benefit granted by that authority during that year and multiplying the resulting figure by [¹ 100.025%].

Amendment

   1.   Amended by reg 2 of SI 2001 No 1130 as from 1.04.01.

Permitted total of benefit in modified schemes

3.   For the purpose of section 139(7) of the Act (modifications other than war disablement pension or war widows pension within the Act), the permitted total of council tax benefit for any year commencing on or after 1st April 1996 in relation to an authority shall be the total of the amounts obtained by deducting 100% of any council tax benefit awarded as a consequence of any determination to disregard made by that authority during that year pursuant to a modification adopted by them under section 139(6)(b) of the Act (power to modify council tax benefit schemes as prescribed) and regulation 8 of the Income-related Schemes Amendment (No. 2) Regulations 1995 (power to modify in respect of certain pensions to war widows) from the total council tax benefit granted by that authority during that year and multiplying the resulting figure by 100.7%.

Revocation

4.   The Council Tax Benefit (Permitted Total) Order 1994 and the Housing Benefit (Permitted Totals) and Council Tax Benefit (Permitted Total) (Pensions for War Widows) Amendment Order 1995 are hereby revoked.

The Housing Benefit (Information from Landlords and Agents) Regulations 1997

(SI 1997 No.2436)

General Note

These regulations implemented s126A SSAA by setting out the circumstances in which local authorities may require information from landlords and agents, the information which must be supplied, the time limit for supplying it and the manner in which the information must be provided. Failure to comply with a notice requiring information under s126A is a criminal offence and would be a factor which a local authority could take into account when considering whether a landlord is a "fit and proper person" to receive payments of HB under regs 95 and 96 HB Regs (or regs 76 and 77 HB(SPC) Regs).

These regs were not amended or revoked when the consolidating regulations came into force on 6 March 2006. However, the provisions are now also in the HB and the HB(SPC) Regs as follows:

Reg 1 is now, in part, reg 113 HB Regs (see p437) and reg 94 HB(SPC) Regs (see p772).

Reg 2 is now reg 117 HB Regs (see p440) and reg 98 HB(SPC) Regs (see p774).

Reg 3 is now reg 118 HB Regs (see p440) and reg 99 HB(SPC) Regs (see p775).

Reg 4 is now reg 119 HB Regs (see p441) and reg 100 HB(SPC) Regs (see p775).

Reg 5 is now reg 120 HB Regs (see p443) and reg 101 HB(SPC) Regs (see p777).

Reg 6 is now reg 121 HB Regs (see p443) and reg 102 HB(SPC) Regs (see p777).

See the commentary to regs 117-121 HB Regs (pp440-443).

Citation, commencement and interpretation

1.–(1) These Regulations, which may be cited as the Housing Benefit (Information from Landlords and Agents) Regulations 1997, shall come into force on 3rd November 1997.

(2) In these Regulations, unless the context otherwise requires–

''the Act'' means the Social Security Administration Act 1992;

''the Housing Benefit Regulations'' means the Housing Benefit (General) Regulations 1987;

''the notice'' means the notice prescribed in regulation 3(1)(b);

''relevant information'' means such information as is prescribed in regulation 4;

''the requirer'' means a person within regulation 2, who requires information pursuant to that regulation;

''the section'' means section 126A of the Act and references to a subsection are to a subsection of the section;

''the supplier'' means an appropriate person who is required, pursuant to regulations 2 and 3, to supply relevant information and any person who is not so required is not, for the purposes of supplying information pursuant to the section and these Regulations, an appropriate person,

and other expressions used both in these Regulations and in the Housing Benefit Regulations shall have the same meanings in these Regulations as they have in the Housing Benefit Regulations.

(3) In these Regulations a reference to a numbered regulation is to the regulation in these Regulations bearing that number and, unless the context otherwise requires, a reference in a regulation to a numbered or lettered paragraph is to the paragraph bearing that letter or number in that regulation and a reference in a paragraph to a lettered or numbered sub-paragraph is to the sub-paragraph in that paragraph bearing that letter or number.

Requiring information

2. Pursuant to the section, where a claim is made to an authority, on which a rent allowance may be awarded, then, in the circumstances prescribed in regulation 3, that authority, or any person authorised to exercise any function of the authority relating to housing benefit, may require an appropriate person to supply to that authority or person relevant information, in the manner prescribed in regulation 5.

Circumstances for requiring information

3.–(1)   A person is required to supply information in the following circumstances–

(a)   he is an appropriate person in relation to any dwelling in respect of which–

   (i)   housing benefit is being paid to an appropriate person pursuant to regulation 93 or 94 of the Housing Benefit Regulations (circumstances in which payment is to be or may be made to a landlord); or

   (ii)   a request has been made by an appropriate person or by the claimant for housing benefit to be so paid; and

(b)   the requirer serves upon that appropriate person, whether by post or otherwise, a written notice stating that the requirer–

   (i)   suspects that there is or may be an impropriety in relation to a claim in respect of any dwelling wherever situate in relation to which he is an appropriate person; or

   (ii)   is already investigating an allegation of impropriety in relation to that person.

(2)   Information required to be supplied under paragraph (1) shall be supplied to the requirer at the address specified in the notice.

Relevant information

4.–(1)   The information the supplier is to supply to the requirer is that prescribed in paragraphs (2) and (3) (referred to in these Regulations as "the relevant information").

(2)   For a supplier who falls within paragraph (4) or sub-section (2)(b) ("the landlord"), the information is–

(a)   where the landlord is a natural person–

   (i)   his appropriate details;

   (ii)   the relevant particulars of any residential property in which he has an interest; and

   (iii)   the appropriate details of any body corporate, in which he is a major shareholder or of which he is a director and which has an interest in residential property;

(b)   where the landlord is a trustee, except a trustee of a charity, in addition to any information that he is required to supply in accordance with sub-paragraph (a) or (c), as the case may be, the relevant particulars of any residential property held by the trust of which he is a trustee and the name and address of any beneficiary under the trust or the objects of that trust, as the case may be;

(c)   where the landlord is a body corporate or otherwise not a natural person, other than a charity–

   (i)   its appropriate details;

   (ii)   the relevant particulars of any residential property in which it has an interest;

   (iii)   the names and addresses of any directors of it;

   (iv)   the appropriate details of any person–

      (aa)   who owns 20 per cent. or more of it; or

      (bb)   of whom it owns 20 per cent. or more; and

   (v) the names and addresses of its major shareholders.

(d)   where the landlord is a charity or is a recognised body the appropriate details relating to the landlord and particulars of the landlord's registration as a charity.

(3)   For a supplier who falls within subsection (2)(c) or paragraph (5) ("the agent"), the information is–

(a)   the name and address of any person ("his principal")–

(i) to whom the agent has agreed to make payments in consequence of being entitled to receive relevant payments; or

(ii) for whom the agent is acting on behalf of or in connection with any aspect of the management of a dwelling,

as the case may be;

(b) the relevant particulars of any residential property in respect of which the agent–

    (i) has agreed to make payments in consequence of being entitled to receive relevant payments; or

    (ii) is acting on behalf of his principal in connection with any aspect of its management;

(c) where the agent is a natural person–

    (i) the relevant particulars of any residential property in which he has an interest;

    (ii) the appropriate details of any body corporate or any person otherwise not a natural person, in which he is a major shareholder or of which he is a director and which has any interest in residential property; or

(d) where the agent is a body corporate or other than a natural person–

    (i) the relevant particulars of any residential property in which it has an interest;

    (ii) the names and addresses of any directors of or major shareholders in the agent; and

    (iii) the appropriate details of any person–

        (aa) who owns 20 per cent. or more of the agent; or

        (bb) of whom the agent owns 20 per cent. or more.

(4) A supplier falls within this paragraph (landlord receiving the rent), if he falls within subsection (2)(a), but does not fall within paragraph (5).

(5) A supplier falls within this paragraph (agent receiving the rent), if he falls within subsection (2)(a) and has agreed to make payments, in consequence of being entitled to receive relevant payments, to a person falling within subsection (2)(b).

(6) For the purposes of this regulation, except where the context otherwise requires–

"appropriate details" means the name of the person and (in the case of a company) its registered office and, in any case, the full postal address, including post code, of the principal place of business of that person and the telephone and facsimile numbers (if any) of that place;

"charity" means a charity which is registered under section 3 of the Charities Act 1993 and is not an exempt charity within the meaning of that Act;

"major shareholder" means, where a body corporate is a company limited by shares, any person holding one tenth or more of the issued shares in that company and, in any other case, all the owners of that body;

"recognised body" has the same meaning as in section 1(7) of the Law Reform (Miscellaneous Provisions) (Scotland) Act 1990;

"relevant particulars" means the full postal address, including post code, and number of current lettings of or within that residential property and, if that property includes two or more dwellings, that address and the number of such lettings for each such dwelling;

"residential property" includes any premises, situated within the United Kingdom–

    (i) used or which has, within the last six months, been used; or

    (ii) which may be used or is adapted for use,

as residential accommodation,

and other expressions used in this regulation and also in the Companies Act 1985 shall have the same meaning in this regulation as they have in that Act.

Manner of supply of information

[¹**5.**–(1)   Subject to paragraph (2) the relevant information shall be supplied–
- (a)   in typewritten or printed form; or
- (b)   with the written agreement of the requirer, in electronic or handwritten form,

within a period of 4 weeks commencing on the date on which the notice was sent or given.
- (2)   Where–
- (a)   within a period of 4 weeks commencing on the date on which the notice was sent or given, the supplier requests that the time for supply of the relevant information be extended; and
- (b)   the requirer provides written agreement to that request,

the time for supply of the relevant information shall be extended to a period of 8 weeks commencing on the date on which the notice was sent or given.]

Amendment

1.   Substituted by reg 2 of SI 2000 No 4 as from 1.4.00 or 3.4.00.

Criminal offence

6.   Any failure by the supplier to supply relevant information to the requirer as, when and how required under these Regulations shall be an offence under section 113 of the Act and there may be recovered from the supplier, on summary conviction for this offence, penalties not exceeding–
- (a)   for any one offence, level 3 on the standard scale; or
- (b)   for an offence of continuing any such failure after conviction, £40 for each day on which it is so continued.

The Social Security (Penalty Notice) Regulations 1997
(SI 1997 No.2813)

General Note

These regulations implement the provisions of s115A SSAA 1992 which allows payment of an administrative penalty as an alternative to prosecution for an offence in relation to an overpayment of benefit. The regulations specify in detail the contents of the written notice referred to in s115A(2) in which a local authority may invite a claimant or landlord to pay such a penalty. For details of the penalty scheme, see p65.

The purpose of prescribing the content of a notice is to provide the recipient with the information that s/he needs to consider whether or not to accept the penalty. It is therefore suggested that a failure to supply the notice in the required form will render the penalty a nullity if the claimant is prejudiced by the omission: *Warwick DC v Freeman* [1994] 27 HLR 616, CA; *Haringey LBC v Awaritefe* [1999] 32 HLR 517.

Citation and commencement

1. These Regulations may be cited as the Social Security (Penalty Notice) Regulations 1997 and shall come into force on 18th December 1997.

Notice

2.–(1) Where the Secretary of State or authority gives to a person a written notice under section 115A(2) of the Social Security Administration Act 1992, the notice shall contain the information that–

(a) the penalty only applies to an overpayment which is recoverable under section 71, 71A, 75 or 76 of the Social Security Administration Act 1992;

(b) the penalty only applies where it appears to the Secretary of State or authority that the making of the overpayment was attributable to an act or omission by the person and that there are grounds for instituting proceedings for an offence relating to the overpayment;

(c) the penalty is 30 per cent. of the amount of the overpayment, is payable in addition to repayment of the overpayment and is recoverable by the same methods as those by which the overpayment is recoverable;

(d) a person who agrees to pay a penalty may withdraw the agreement within 28 days (including the date of the agreement) by notifying the Secretary of State or authority in the manner specified by the Secretary of State or authority; if the person withdraws the agreement, so much of the penalty as has already been recovered shall be repaid and he will no longer be immune from proceedings for an offence;

(e) if it is decided on review or appeal (or in accordance with regulations) that the overpayment is not recoverable or due, so much of the penalty as has already been recovered shall be repaid;

(f) if the amount of the overpayment is revised on review or appeal, except as covered by a new agreement to pay the revised penalty, so much of the penalty as has already been recovered shall be repaid and the person will no longer be immune from proceedings for an offence;

(g) the payment of a penalty does not give the person immunity from prosecution in relation to any other overpayment or any offence not relating to an overpayment.

(2) The notice shall set out–

(a) the manner specified by the Secretary of State or authority by which the person may agree to pay a penalty;

(b) the manner specified by the Secretary of State or authority by which the person may notify the withdrawal of his agreement to pay a penalty.

The New Deal (Miscellaneous Provisions) Order 1998
(SI 1998 No.217)

General Note

This Order specifies that participation in the training options of the "New Deal" specified is to be treated as training under s2 Employment and Training Act 1973 (rather than employment) and that in consequence any payment received by the trainee is to be treated as a training allowance for the purposes of HB and CTB.

Citation, commencement and interpretation

1.–(1) This Order may be cited as the New Deal (Miscellaneous Provisions) Order 1998 and shall come into force on 2nd March 1998.

(2) In this Order, unless the context otherwise requires–

[¹ "facilities" means facilities provided for the participant in pursuance of one or more of the New Deal Components;]

"the New Deal" means the arrangements known by that name and made under section 2 of the 1973 Act for which only persons who are aged 18 years or over and less than 26 years immediately prior to entry are eligible and which are designed to help New Deal Participants to obtain work or to improve their prospects of obtaining work;

"the New Deal Components" means any of the following, that is to say, the programmes of employment or employment-related training under the New Deal known individually as "the Full-time Education and Training Option", "the Voluntary Sector Option" [¹ , "the Employment Option"] and "the Environment Task Force Option";

[¹ "trading receipt" means, in relation to a New Deal Participant under the Employment Option, any payment made to him in consideration of goods or services supplied by him in the course of his participation under that option;]

"training allowance" means a payment made directly by the Secretary of State to a New Deal Participant in connection with his participation in one or more of the New Deal components;

and a person is, or, as the case may be, was, at any material time, a "New Deal Participant" if he is, or, as the case may be, was, at that time, using facilities. [¹ . . .]

Amendment

1. Amended by reg 2 of 1998 SI No 1425 as from 3.7.98.

Treatment of persons and payments for the purposes of the Social Security Contributions and Benefits Act 1992, the Jobseekers Act 1995 and specified subordinate legislation

[¹**2.**–(1) The provisions of this article apply for the purposes of–

(a) Part I of the Social Security Contributions and Benefits Act 1992,

(b) the Jobseekers Act 1995 and

(c) the subordinate legislation specified in the Schedule to this Order.

(2) If, for any period or periods commencing with or falling after the date on which this Order comes into force, during which a person is a New Deal Participant and is participating in either the Full-time Education and Training Option, the Voluntary Sector Option or the Environment Task Force Option, that person receives, or is eligible to receive, a training allowance, he is to be treated for that period or those periods and in respect of his participation as not being employed but as participating in arrangements for training under section 2 of the 1973 Act; and accordingly any payment made to such a person during that period or those periods in connection with his use of facilities shall be treated in the same manner as a payment of training allowance made in respect of such training.

(3)   If, for any period or periods commencing with or falling after the date on which this paragraph comes into force, during which a person is a New Deal Participant and is participating in the Employment Option in a capacity other than that of employee, that person receives, or is eligible to receive, a training allowance, he is to be treated for that period or those periods and in respect of his participation as not being employed but as participating in arrangements for training under section 2 of the 1973 Act; and accordingly any payment, other than a trading receipt, made to such a person during that period or those periods in connection with his use of facilities shall be treated in the same manner as a payment of training allowance made in respect of such training.

Amendment

1.   Substituted by reg 3 of 1998 SI No 1425 as from 3.7.98.

SCHEDULE ARTICLE 2
LIST OF SUBORDINATE LEGISLATION

[. . .]

[¹ The Housing Benefit Regulations 2006;]

[¹ The Housing Benefit (Persons who have attained the qualifying age for state pension credit) Regulations 2006;]

[¹ The Council Tax Benefit Regulations 2006;]

[¹ The Council Tax Benefit (Persons who have attained the qualifying age for state pension credit) Regulations 2006;]

Amendment

1.   Substituted by reg 5 and Sch 2 para 14 of SI 2006 No 217 as from 6.3.06.

The Social Security (Immigration and Asylum) Consequential Amendments Regulations 2000
(SI 2000 No.636)

General Note

Regs 2, 12 and the Schedule to these Regulations exclude certain categories of claimant from the effect of s115 of the Immigration and Asylum Act 1999, which precludes a "person subject to immigration control" from claiming HB. See p1027 for a summary of the way in which s115, reg 10 of both the HB and the HB(SPC) Regs and reg 7 of both the CTB and the CTB(SPC) Regs and these Regulations combine.

Citation, commencement and interpretation

1.–(1)   These Regulations may be cited as the Social Security (Immigration and Asylum) Consequential Amendments Regulations 2000.

(2)   These Regulations shall come into force on 3rd April 2000.

(3)   In these Regulations–

"the Act" means the Immigration and Asylum Act 1999;

"the Contributions and Benefits Act" means the Social Security Contributions and Benefits Act 1992;

[¹]

[¹]

"the Persons from Abroad Regulations" means the Social Security (Persons from Abroad) Miscellaneous Amendments Regulations 1996;

(4)   In these Regulations, unless the context otherwise requires, a reference–

(a)   to a numbered regulation or Schedule is to the regulation in, or the Schedule to, these Regulations bearing that number;

(b)   in a regulation or Schedule to a numbered paragraph is to the paragraph in that regulation or Schedule bearing that number.

Amendment

1.   Revoked by reg 3 and sch 1 of SI 2006 No 217 as from 6.3.06.

Persons not excluded from specified benefits under section 115 of the Immigration and Asylum Act 1999

2.–(1)   For the purposes of entitlement to income-based jobseeker's allowance, income support, a social fund payment, housing benefit or council tax benefit under the Contributions and Benefits Act, [¹or state pension credit under the State Pension Credit Act 2002] as the case may be, a person falling within a category or description of persons specified in Part I of the Schedule is a person to whom section 115 of the Act does not apply.

(2) and (3)   *[omitted]*

(4)   For the purposes of entitlement to–

(a)   income support, a social fund payment, housing benefit or council tax benefit under the Contributions and Benefits Act, as the case may be, a person who is entitled to or is receiving benefit by virtue of paragraph (1) or (2) of regulation 12 of the Persons from Abroad Regulations is a person to whom section 115 of the Act does not apply;

(b)   [. . .]

[¹(c)   state pension credit under the State Pension Credit Act 2002, a person to whom sub-paragraph (a) would have applied but for the fact that they have attained the qualifying age for the purposes of state pension credit, is a person to whom section 115 of the Act does not apply.]

(5)   *[omitted]*

(6)   For the purposes of entitlement to housing benefit, council tax benefit or a social fund payment under the Contributions and Benefits Act, as the case may be, a

person to whom regulation 12(6) applies is a person to whom section 115 of the Act does not apply.

(7)   For the purposes of entitlement to state pension credit under the State Pension Credit Act 2002, a person to whom paragraph (5) would have applied but for the fact that they have attained the qualifying age for the purposes of state pension credit, is a person to whom section 115 of the Act does not apply.

(8)   Where paragraph 1 of Part I of the Schedule to these Regulations applies in respect of entitlement to state pension credit, the period for which a claimant's state pension credit is to be calculated shall be any period, or the aggregate of any periods, not exceeding 42 days during any one period of leave to which paragraph 1 of Part I of the Schedule to these Regulations applies.]

Amendment

1.   Inserted by reg 6 of SI 2003 No 2274 as from 6.10.03.

General Note

Reg 2 is the primary provision which creates the six categories of claimant that are exempted from the effect of s115.

Analysis

Para (1) exempts the four categories listed in Part I of the Schedule.

Para (4) exempts those who retain their transitional protection under reg 12 Social Security (Persons from Abroad) Miscellaneous Amendments Regulations 1996 SI No 30 (see p1073). Broadly, it relates to those who did not claim asylum "on arrival".

Such claimants only retain their transitional protection if they were in receipt of HB on 5 February 1996 and their entitlements have continued since then. It will only apply to those who are still receiving benefit (or to those who are not receiving benefit but have an underlying entitlement) pursuant to those rules, not to those who once did so.

The effect of the saving provision in reg 12 of the 1996 Regulations is that the rules as now found in Sch 3 para 6(1)-(4) of the HB&CTB(CP) Regs apply. A person remains an asylum seeker while the Secretary of State has yet to record the claim as determined or, if the asylum claim was recorded as determined prior to 5 February 1996, while an appeal was pending. A person does not retain her/his status as an asylum seeker while a further appeal to the Asylum and Immigration Tribunal is pending from an adverse decision by a special adjudicator: *CIS 3418/1998* para 45. Note also the effect of reg 12(11)(b) below.

Para (6) exempts those falling within reg 12(6).

Transitional arrangements and savings

12.– [² (1)]

[² (2)]

(3), (4) and (5) *[omitted]*

[¹ (6)]

[¹

(7)]

[¹

(8)]

(9)   In paragraphs (4) and (7) "the Common Travel Area" means the United Kingdom, the Channel Islands, the Isle of Man and the Republic of Ireland collectively and "the Convention" means the Convention relating to the Status of Refugees done at Geneva on 28th July 1951 as extended by Article 2(1) of the Protocol relating to the Status of Refugees done at New York on 31st January 1967

(10)   *[omitted]*

(11)   In the Persons from Abroad Regulations–

(a)   *[omitted]*

(b)   notwithstanding the amendments and revocations in regulations 3, 6 and 7, regulations 12(1) and (2) of the Persons from Abroad Regulations shall continue to have effect as they had effect before those amendments and revocations came into force.

Amendments

1. Revoked by reg 3 and Sch 1 of SI 2006 No 217 as from 6.3.06.
2. Ceased to have effect by s12(1) of the Asylum and Immigration (Treatment of Claimants, etc.) Act 2004 (for those recorded as refugees after 14.6.07).

General Note

This regulation contained transitional arrangements and savings.

Analysis

Paragraphs (1) and (2): Amendments to backdated entitlements of refugees

Paras (1) and (2) ceased to have effect from 14 June 2007 for those recorded as refugees after that date: s12(3) of the Asylum and Immigration (Treatment of Claimants, etc.) Act 2004, brought into effect by the Asylum and Immigration (Treatment of Claimants, etc.) Act 2004 (Commencement No. 7 and Transitional Provisions) Order 2007 SI No 1602. For these purposes, a person is "recorded as a refugee" on the day the Secretary of State notifies her/him that s/he has been recognised as a refugee and granted asylum in the UK. For the full text, see the 19th edn of this work, p1030. Paras (1) and (2) prevented the amendments made to the entitlements of refugees to backdated HB and CTB from having effect where the claimant sought asylum prior to 2 April 2000. Reference should be made to the version of the provisions listed in para (2) that is reproduced in the 12th edition of this book for the provisions as they stood in relation to those claimants.

Paragraphs (6) to (9)

These paragraphs prevented certain asylum seekers either from falling foul of reg 7A HB Regs 1987 by being a person from abroad and also, by virtue of reg 2(3) above, from exclusion from HB under s115 of the 1999 Act. These savings rules are now to be found in Sch 3 para 6(10)-(11) of the HB&CTB(CP) Regs (see p1116). See the detailed commentary there.

Paragraph (11)(b): Preservation of the effect of the 1996 Regulations

The effect of this provision is to prevent the repeal of large parts of reg 7A HB Regs 1987 and reg 4A CTB 1992 Regs from affecting the scope of the transitional protection afforded by reg 12 of the Social Security (Persons from Abroad) Miscellaneous Amendments Regulations 1996 SI No 30 (see p1073) and hence the scope of reg 2(4)(a) above.

SCHEDULE

Persons not excluded under section 115 of the Immigration and Asylum Act 1995 from entitlement to income-based jobseeker's allowance, income support, a social fund payment, housing benefit or council tax benefit

General Note

These categories of claimant are exempted from the operation of s115 of the Immigration and Asylum Act 1999 by virtue of reg 2(1) above.

---

1. A person who–
(a) has limited leave (as defined in section 33(1) of the 1971 Act) to enter or remain in the United Kingdom which was given in accordance with the immigration rules (as defined in that section) relating to–
   (i) there being, or to there needing to be, no recourse to public funds, or
   (ii) there being no charge on public funds,
   during that limited leave; and
(b) having, during any one period of limited leave (including any such period as extended), supported himself without recourse to public funds, other than any such recourse by reason of the previous application of this sub-paragraph, is temporarily without funds during that period of leave because remittances to him from abroad have been disrupted, provided that there is a reasonable expectation that his supply of funds will be resumed.

Analysis

There are three requirements here: first that the claimant has a relevant "limited leave", secondly that the claimant should have supported her/himself without recourse to public funds and thirdly that there has been a disruption to her/his funds coming from abroad.

"Limited leave" means leave to enter the UK which is limited to duration: Immigration Act 1971 s33(1). It should be clear from the stamp on the claimant's passport whether s/he has limited leave or not.

Most of the categories of limited leave granted under the Immigration Rules (HC 395) make it a condition that there be no recourse to public funds: see eg, para 41(vi) (visitors), para 57(vi) (students), para 128(v) (holders of work permits). The words do not appear on the claimant's passport, but the claimant may have been sent a letter making it clear. Failing this, reference should be made to the Rules or to the Home Office. The definition of "public funds" in para 6 of the Rules includes HB and CTB.

GM C7/7.140 states that a spouse of a claimant with limited leave who lives with a claimant and causes the level of HB to be raised is relying on public funds, but that the authority is not required to inform the Home Office of this.

If the immigrant's money is disrupted, they may be treated as not being persons from abroad for a maximum of 42 days in any one period of leave to enter. A period which has been extended on application to the immigration authorities counts as a single period.

"*. . . having during any one period of limited leave . . . supported himself without recourse to public funds . . . .".* A period which has been extended on application to the immigration authorities counts as a single period. The protection is lost if, contrary to the condition attached to the limited leave, the claimant has made use of public funds. However, the words "any one period" seem to suggest that where a claimant has had a previous period of limited leave during which the condition was not broken but has broken it during the present period, s/he may still fulfil para 1.

A previous use of public funds due to a previous disruption of money from abroad does not prevent this condition being fulfilled. It might be arguable that the reference to "this sub-paragraph" might include a reference to a person who received HB under the old reg 7A(4A) and (6) HB Regs 1987 during a temporary disruption: see p166 of the 12th edition. Para 1(b) might be viewed as a re-enactment of reg 7A(4A) with amendments, so as to require the reference to "this sub-paragraph" to include a reference to the predecessor legislation under the Interpretation Act 1978.

"*. . . . is temporarily without funds . . . . because remittances to him from abroad have been disrupted . . . ."* It must be noted that only immigrants whose funds from abroad have been disrupted may benefit. An immigrant whose sponsor is failing to meet his obligations in the UK cannot benefit from its provisions. It is suggested that the disruption need not be to funds directly sent to the claimant. So if a sponsor is receiving money in the UK and that flow of funds has been disrupted, then provided that part of that money is designated for the immigrant, then the immigrant is entitled to the benefit of this provision.

Whether there is a reasonable expectation that the supply of funds will be resumed is a question of fact.

If the immigrant's money is disrupted, they may be treated as not being persons from abroad for a maximum of 42 days in any one period of leave to enter. A period which has been extended on application to the immigration authorities counts as a single period.

---

2.   A person who has been given leave to enter or remain in, the United Kingdom by the Secretary of State upon an undertaking given by another person or persons pursuant to the immigration rules within the meaning of the Immigration Act 1971, to be responsible for his maintenance and accommodation and who has not been resident in the United Kingdom for a period of at least five years beginning on the date of entry or the date on which the undertaking was given in respect of him, whichever date is the later and the person or persons who gave the undertaking to provide for his maintenance and accommodation has, or as the case may be, have died.

Analysis

Under the Immigration Rules (HC 395) para 35, a sponsor of a person seeking leave to enter may be required to give an undertaking to be responsible for that person's maintenance and accommodation. If the sponsor is dead, para 2 excludes the sponsored person from the effect of s115 of the 1999 Act. If there is more than one sponsor, all must be deceased.

The wording of the former reg 21(3)(i) of the Income Support (General) Regulations 1987, which was identical to the former reg 7A(4)(f) HB Regs 1987 (see p150 of the 12th edition of this book) and to para 2 save for the reference to the sponsor being deceased, was closely scrutinised in *R(IS) 2/02.* Commissioner Jacobs held where a claimant has been present with leave in the UK prior to the undertaking being given, the five year period runs from the date the undertaking is given. When the undertaking was given before leave, time runs from the time that leave was granted: paras 67 to 71. He also held that the five year period need not be continuous, but may be the sum of several different periods of residence: paras 72 to 75. Although this issue was discussed by one of the judges on a further appeal to the Court of Appeal – *Shah v Secretary of State for Social Security [2002] EWCA Civ 285, CA,* also reported as part of *R(IS) 2/02* – the court did not interfere with the commissioner's conclusion on this point. See also the commentary to reg 12 of the Social Security (Persons from Abroad) Miscellaneous Amendments Regulations 1996.

---

3.   A person who–

(a)   has been given leave to enter, or remain in, the United Kingdom by the Secretary of State upon an undertaking given by another person or persons in writing in pursuance of immigration rules within the meaning of the 1971 Act, to be responsible for his maintenance and accommodation; and

(b)   he has been resident in the United Kingdom for a period of at least five years beginning from the date of entry or the date on which the undertaking was given in respect of him, whichever date is the later.

Analysis

If a sponsored immigrant is resident for five years from the *later* of the date of entry or the date of the undertaking, para 3 excludes him/her from s115.

---

4.   A person who is a national of a state which has ratified the European Convention on Social and Medical Assistance (done in Paris on 11th December 1953) or a state which has ratified the Council of Europe Social Charter (signed in Turin on 18th October 1961) and who is lawfully present in the United Kingdom.

Analysis

The relevant states. This paragraph applies to nationals of states that have ratified the ECSMA or the European Social Charter. All ECSMA states are at present signatories of the European Social Charter. At the time of writing, all the EEA states had ratified the Social Charter, namely the UK, Austria, Liechtenstein, Germany, France, Belgium, Luxembourg, Holland, Denmark, Norway, Sweden, Finland, Iceland, Ireland, Spain, Portugal and Italy. In addition, the following states had ratified it: Bulgaria, Cyprus, the Czech Republic, Hungary, Malta, Poland, Romania, Slovakia, and Turkey. It is not sufficient if the state of nationality has signed the Social Charter and so nationals of Croatia, Latvia, Liechtenstein, Macedonia, Romania, Slovenia, Switzerland and the Ukraine cannot fall within para 4. Similarly, Estonian nationals cannot fall within para 4 since Estonia has signed but not ratified the ECSMA.

An up-to-date list of signatories and ratifications is available at http://conventions.coe.int.

"Lawfully present" is a phrase defined in Art 11 of ECSMA. Any person who has "a permit or such other permission as is required by the laws and regulations of the country concerned to reside therein" is lawfully present in the host state. It will encompass anyone who has leave to remain in the United Kingdom. It will include those with limited leave, including those who have their leave automatically extended under the immigration legislation pending the determination of an application for an extension of leave.

A person who is present in the UK by virtue of having been granted temporary admission is "lawfully present": *Szoma v Secretary of State for Work and Pensions* [2005] UKHL 64, [2006] 1 All ER 1 (reported as *R(IS) 2/06*).

Note, however, that most ECSMA country nationals entitlement to HB/CTB will now be governed by whether they can satisfy the "right to reside test" in regs 10 and 7 of the HB (and HB(SPC)) and CTB (and CTB(SPC)) Regs respectively, as most will be A8 and A2 nationals.

New Deal (Miscellaneous Provisions) Order 2001
(SI 2001 No.970)

General Note

This Order specifies that participation in the "Intensive Activity Period" options specified is to be treated as training under s2 Employment and Training Act 1973 (rather than employment) and that in consequence any payment received by the trainee is to be treated as a training allowance for the purposes of HB and CTB.

Citation, commencement and interpretation

1.–(1) This Order may be cited as the New Deal (Miscellaneous Provisions) Order 2001 and shall come into force on 9th April 2001.

(2) In this Order–

"facilities" means facilities provided for the participant in pursuance of the Intensive Activity Period or the Intensive Activity Period for 50 plus;

"the Intensive Activity Period" means the arrangements known by that name and made under section 2 of the 1973 Act for which only persons who are aged 25 years or over and less than 50 years on the day of entry are eligible and which are designed to help participants to obtain work or to improve their prospects of obtaining work;

"the Intensive Activity Period for 50 plus" means the arrangements known by that name and made under section 2 of the 1973 Act for which only persons who are aged 50 years or over on the day of entry are eligible and which are designed to help participants to obtain work or to improve their prospects of obtaining work;

"training allowance" means a payment made directly by the Secretary of State to a participant in the Intensive Activity Period or the Intensive Activity Period for 50 plus in connection with his participation.

Treatment of persons and payments for the purposes of the Social Security Contributions and Benefits Act 1992, the Jobseekers Act 1995 and specified subordinate legislation

2.–(1) The provisions of this article apply for the purposes of–

(a) Part I of the Social Security Contributions and Benefits Act 1992,

(b) The Jobseekers Act 1995, and

(c) The subordinate legislation specified in the Schedule to this Order.

(2) If, for any period or periods commencing with or falling after the date on which this Order comes into force, during which a person is participating in the Intensive Activity Period or the Intensive Activity Period for 50 plus, that person receives, or is eligible to receive, a training allowance, he is to be treated for that period or those periods and in respect of his participation as not being employed but as participating in arrangements for training under section 2 of the 1973 Act; and accordingly, subject to paragraph (3), any payment made to such a person during that period or these periods in connection with his use of facilities shall be treated in the same manner as a payment of training allowance made in respect of such training.

(3) Paragraph (2) shall not apply in respect of any trading payment made to a person receiving assistance in pursuing self-employed earner's employment whilst participating in the Intensive Activity Period or the Intensive Activity Period for 50 plus.

SCHEDULE
LIST OF SUBORDINATE LEGISLATION

[¹ The Housing Benefit Regulations 2006;]

[¹ The Housing Benefit (Persons who have attained the qualifying age for state pension credit) Regulations 2006;]

[¹ The Council Tax Benefit Regulations 2006;]
[¹ The Council Tax Benefit (Persons who have attained the qualifying age for state pension credit) Regulations 2006;]

Amendment

1.   Amended by reg 5 and Sch 2 para 14 of SI 2006 No 217 as from 6.3.06.

The Discretionary Financial Assistance Regulations 2001
(SI 2001 No.1167)

General Note to the Regulations

The DFA Regs, made under s69 CSPSSA, provide the detail of the discretionary housing payments ("DHPs") scheme, which replaced the provisions formerly found in reg 61 HB Regs 1987, for increases in HB on the grounds of exceptional circumstances of hardship.

The regulations are considerably more flexible than the repealed provisions as to the circumstances in which DHPs may be made. However, a downside of the scheme from the point of view of claimants is its exclusion from the right of appeal to an appeal tribunal. The government's reason for doing this was to keep the discretion firmly in the hands of the relevant local authority, and it is said that as the making of DHPs is discretionary, there is no breach of Art 6 of the European Convention of Human Rights in failing to provide for an appeal. See the commentary to Art 6 in the Human Rights Act 1998 on p132 for discussion of this point, and the commentary to Art 8 on p134 on the question of whether a refusal to make a DHP might interfere with the right to respect for the home.

The absence of an appeal will mean that there is some scope for judicial review proceedings in relation to DHPs.

Discretionary housing payments are disregarded as both income and capital for HB and CTB purposes: Sch 5 para 62 and Sch 6 para 9(1)(d) HB Regs; Sch 4 para 62 and Sch 5 para 9(1)(d) CTB Regs. They do not come within the definition of income under the HB(SPC) Regs or the CTB(SPC) Regs.

Citation, commencement and interpretation

1.–(1)   These Regulations may be cited as the Discretionary Financial Assistance Regulations 2001 and shall come into force on 2nd July 2001.

[¹ (2)   In these Regulations–

"the Housing Benefit Regulations" means the Housing Benefit Regulations 2006; and

"the Housing Benefit (State Pension Credit) Regulations" means the Housing Benefit (Persons who have attained the qualifying age for state pension credit) Regulations 2006.]

Amendment

1.   Amended by reg 5 and Sch 2 para 18(2) of SI 2006 No 217 as from 6.3.06.

Discretionary housing payments

2.–(1)   Subject to paragraphs (2) and (3) and the following regulations, a relevant authority may make payments by way of financial assistance ("discretionary housing payments") to persons who–

(a)   are entitled to housing benefit or council tax benefit or to both; and

(b)   appear to such an authority to require some further financial assistance (in addition to the benefit or benefits to which they are entitled) in order to meet housing costs.

(2)   Subject to paragraph (3) and regulations 4 and 5, a relevant authority has a discretion–

(a)   as to whether or not to make discretionary housing payments in a particular case; and

(b)   as to the amount of the payments and the period for, or in respect of which, they are made.

(3)   Paragraphs (1) and (2) shall not apply in respect of housing costs incurred in any period before 2nd July 2001–

(a)   in the case of a person entitled to council tax benefit who requires further financial assistance in order to meet his liability to pay council tax;

(b)   in the case of a person entitled to housing benefit who requires further financial assistance in order to meet housing costs (other than costs in respect of council tax) arising from his liability to make periodical payments in respect of the dwelling which he occupies as his home.

Analysis

Para (1) reproduces the basic conditions of entitlement found in s69(1) CSPSSA. A claimant need not be in receipt of both HB and CTB to qualify; entitlement to either benefit will suffice. "Housing costs" is not defined and so in principle could cover any expenditure that is related to the provision of accommodation for the claimant and her/his family. Reg 3 excludes certain categories of need but does not otherwise cut down the breadth of the phrase. It would appear that it could cover, for example, payments of capital to a mortgagee where a CTB claimant is in danger of losing her/his home. It could also cover payments in respect of a second home that are not met by HB.

The claimant must "require" financial assistance. While there is no need to show that the claimant's circumstances are exceptional, it is likely that authorities will impose a fairly high threshold. If, for example, a claimant has any savings or other realisable capital asset at all, it is unlikely that an application for a DHP would succeed unless it could be shown that there was a need to utilise those savings in some other way (eg, to discharge a different debt) or to retain the asset. However, it is suggested that a claimant need not show that her/his circumstances are desperate – eg, by showing that eviction is imminent. It would be sufficient to show that the household budget simply cannot be balanced and that debts will inevitably mount up unless a DHP is paid. An authority considering refusal of a DHP on the ground that the claimant could obtain a loan would have to be prepared to show how such a loan could be financed.

While a claimant is not "entitled" to benefits unless they are claimed, there seems to be no reason why an authority could not refuse a DHP on the basis that a claimant should be entitled to some other benefit if a claim is made. The same would apply where other forms of social assistance are available such as social fund payments, social services assistance and housing grants. However, as s73(14) SSCBA requires the mobility component of DLA to "be disregarded in applying any enactment or instrument under which regard is to be had to a person's means", it is suggested that any amount of that benefit must be ignored.

Para (2) gives a very broad discretion as to the amount of a DHP and the form that the payments take. Except as specified in reg 4, there is no restriction on the amount of a DHP and one-off payments may be made as well as weekly payments.

It is suggested that the amounts specified in the Discretionary Housing Payments (Grants) Order 2001 (see p1203) may provide some indication as to the annual expenditure that each authority should be making on DHPs. If an authority is spending considerably less, then it may be possible to challenge a decision by way of judicial review on the ground that it is adopting an approach to its discretion that is too restrictive, as its permitted expenditure is a relevant factor in the exercise of its discretion: *R v Gloucestershire CC ex p Barry* [1997] AC 584, HL. However, in *CH 1175/2002* para 10, Commissioner Fellner expressed scepticism about a similar suggestion made in this book in relation to the old exceptional hardship payments: see p399 of the 14th edn.

There is also a broad discretion as to the period for, or in respect of which, payments can be made, subject to reg 5.

Para (3) prevents a DHP being paid in respect of liabilities arising prior to 2 July 2001. Note, however, that it appears that a CTB claimant who is not receiving HB could claim a DHP in respect of arrears of rent or mortgage payments arising prior to that date.

Circumstances in which discretionary housing payments may be made

3. For the purposes of section 69(2)(a) of the Child Support, Pensions and Social Security Act 2000, the prescribed circumstance in which discretionary housing payments may be made is where a person has made a claim for a discretionary housing payment and the requirement for financial assistance does not arise as a consequence of–

(a)   a liability to meet any of the ineligible service charges specified in [³ Schedule 1 to the Housing Benefit Regulations or Schedule 1 to the Housing Benefit (State Pension Credit) Regulations] (ineligible service charges);

(b)   a liability to meet charges for water, sewerage or allied environmental services;

(c)   a liability to meet council tax payments in a case where the person is entitled to housing benefit but not council tax benefit;

(d)   a liability to make periodical payments in respect of such housing costs as are referred to in regulation 10 of the Housing Benefit Regulations in a case where the person is entitled to council tax benefit but not housing benefit;

(e)   a liability to meet council tax where the conditions in section 131(4) and (5) of the Social Security Contributions and Benefits Act 1992 are not satisfied and alternative maximum council tax benefit is payable;

(f)   a liability to meet the increase in such payment as is referred to in regulation 8(2A) of the Housing Benefit Regulations;

(g)   a reduction of an amount of benefit by virtue of section 46(11) of the Child Support Act 1991;

(h)   a reduction of a specified amount of benefit by virtue of section 2A of the Social Security Administration Act 1992;

(i)   a reduction in the amount of a jobseeker's allowance payable by virtue of section 17 of the Jobseekers Act 1995;

(j)   the non-payability of a jobseeker's allowance or a reduction in the amount of a jobseeker's allowance payable, pursuant to a decision made by virtue of section 19 or 20A of the Jobseekers Act 1995;

(k)   the suspension of payment of an amount of benefit by virtue of section 21, 22 or 24 of the Social Security Act 1998 or section 68 of, and paragraphs 13 and 14 of Schedule 7 to, the Child Support, Pensions and Social Security Act 2000.

[¹(l)   a restriction in relation to the payment of benefit imposed pursuant to section 62 or 63 of the Child Support, Pensions and Social Security Act 2000 [² or section 7, 8 or 9 of the Social Security Fraud Act 2001] (loss of benefit provisions).]

[⁴ (m)   a reduction of housing benefit imposed pursuant to section 130B of the Social Security Contributions and Benefits Act 1992 (loss of housing benefit following eviction on certain grounds).]

Modifications

Reg 3 is modified in respect of people to whom the Housing Benefit (Loss of Benefit) (Pilot Scheme) (Supplementary) Regulations 2007 SI No. 2474 apply. The modification applies until 31 October 2009 unless revoked with effect from an earlier date. It is shown in italics above.

Amendments

1.   Inserted by reg 2(6) of SI 2001 No 1711 as from 15.10.01.
2.   Amended by reg 10 of SI 2002 No 490 as from 1.4.02.
3.   Amended by reg 5 and sch 2 para 18(3) of SI 2006 No 217 as from 6.3.06.
4.   Modified by reg 9 of SI 2007 No 2474 as from 1.11.07.

Analysis

Reg 3 imposes a requirement that a claim be made for a DHP. In addition, a number of circumstances are set out in which DHPs cannot be paid as a result of some specific situation, that is, where the need for financial assistance arises as a consequence of:

(1)   a liability for ineligible service charges: para (a). See the commentary to Sch 1 of the HB Regs on p445;

(2)   a liability for water, sewerage or "allied environmental services": para (b). The latter phrase would cover, for example, charges for the emptying of a septic tank;

(3)   council tax liabilities where a person is entitled to HB but not to CTB, or liabilities for payments listed in reg 10 HB Regs where a person is entitled to CTB but not to HB: paras (c) and (d). Note that although the liabilities that can be met by HB are now found in reg 12 HB Regs, the reference to reg 10 was not amended as a consequence of the consolidation of the regulations in March 2006;

(4)   council tax liabilities where a person is not entitled to main CTB and "alternative maximum CTB" is payable: para (e). See the commentary to s131(6) SSCBA (see p13) and reg 62 CTB Regs (see p620);

(5)   increases in rent to cover arrears of rent or other charges, whether on the present or a previous claim: para (f). Note that although the increases referred to are now found in reg 11(3) HB Regs, the reference to reg 8(2A) was not amended as a consequence of the consolidation of the regulations in March 2006;

(6)   reductions in benefit for failure to co-operate with the Child Support Agency or for failing to participate in a work-focused interview: paras (g) and (h);

(7)   JSA being stopped or reduced because the claimant left her/his job voluntarily or lost a job because of misconduct: paras (i) and (j);

(8)   suspension of benefit under the provisions listed – eg, for non-provision of information: para (k);

(9) reductions in benefit under the provisions of ss62 or 63 CSPSSA (failure to comply with a community order) or ss7, 8 or 9 of the Social Security Fraud Act 2001 (loss of benefit for benefit offences): para (l);

(10) reductions in benefit under the provisions of s130B SSCBA (loss of housing benefit following eviction on certain grounds): para (m). This sub-para applies in pilot areas only. See the Housing Benefit (Loss of Benefit) (Pilot Scheme) (Supplementary) Regulations 2007 SI No. 2474 on p1144 and the Housing Benefit (Loss of Benefit) (Pilot Scheme) Regulations 2007 SI No. 2202 on p1139.

Limit on the amount of the discretionary housing payment that may be made

4. The amount of a discretionary housing payment (if calculated as a weekly sum) shall not exceed, in a case where the need for further financial assistance arises as a consequence of the liability to make–

[¹ (a) periodical payments in respect of the dwelling which a person occupies as his home, other than payments in respect of council tax, an amount equal to the amount of the aggregate of the payments specified in–

    (i) regulation 12(1) of the Housing Benefit Regulations less the aggregate of the amounts referred to in regulations 12(3)(b)(i) to (iii) of those Regulations, calculated on a weekly basis in accordance with regulations 80 and 81 of those Regulations; or

    (ii) regulation 12(1) of the Housing Benefit (State Pension Credit) Regulations less the aggregate of the amounts referred to in regulations 12(3)(b)(i) to (iii) of those Regulations, calculated on a weekly basis in accordance with regulations 61 and 62 of those Regulations; or]

  (b) payments in respect of council tax, an amount equal to the weekly amount of council tax liability of that person calculated on a weekly basis.

Amendment
1. Amended by reg 5 and sch 2 para 18(4) of SI 2006 No 217 as from 6.3.06.

Analysis
Reg 4 imposes a limit on DHPs paid weekly. Larger sums could, therefore, be paid by way of a lump sum.

In relation to periodical payments of rent or similar payments, the DHPs may not be more than the weekly amount of the payments which can be met by HB, less the amounts referred to in reg 12(3)(b) of both the HB and the HB(SPC) Regs. However, HB entitlement need not be deducted, and so in theory the total payment (of HB and DHPs) could be greater than the amount of the rent liability. Liabilities that do not fall within reg 12(1) HB Regs (reg 12(1) HB(SPC) Regs), such as those listed in reg 12(2), cannot be the subject of weekly payments, though that does not prevent a lump sum being awarded.

As far as liabilities for council tax are concerned, weekly DHPs may not exceed the weekly council tax liability.

Period for, or in respect of which, discretionary housing payments may be made

5. A relevant authority may restrict the period for or in respect of which discretionary housing payments may be made to such period as it considers appropriate in the particular circumstances of a case.

Analysis
Reg 5 is self-explanatory. It is important to note that claims can be made in respect of a past period as well as the future, without any need to explain a delay in seeking a DHP.

Form, manner and procedure for claims

6.–(1) A relevant authority may accept a claim for discretionary housing payments–

  (a) in such form and manner as it approves;

  (b) from–

    (i) a person entitled to either housing benefit or, as the case may be, council tax benefit; or

(ii)   where it appears reasonable in the circumstances of a particular case, a person acting on behalf of a person so entitled.

(2)   A relevant authority may pay discretionary housing payments to either the person entitled to housing benefit or council tax benefit, or where it appears reasonable in the circumstances of a particular case, such other person as the authority thinks appropriate.

(3)   A relevant authority shall give a person who has claimed discretionary housing payments or who has requested a review of a decision made in respect of his claim, written notice of its decision in respect of that claim or review and the reasons for that decision as soon as is reasonably practicable.

Analysis

Para (1) gives an authority a broad discretion as to the form that claims for DHPs take. An authority could accept an oral claim and interesting arguments could arise as to the circumstances in which an individual officer can bind the authority as to the validity of a claim. Claims may be accepted from agents where it appears reasonable to do so. Authorities ought to be ready, for example, to accept claims made by solicitors and social landlords on behalf of claimants.

Para (2) gives a power to make payments to a third party where it is reasonable to do so. Thus rent arrears can be directed to a landlord. However, it seems doubtful whether an authority can effectively pay itself where there are arrears of CTB, since it is not "such other person".

Para (3) is an important provision. First, it is suggested that it confers a right to a review of a decision on a DHP, even though reg 8(1) appears to make it discretionary as to whether a review is carried out. It is suggested that reg 8(1) is concerned with the situation where a local authority wishes to review a decision of its own motion rather than on a request. If that is right, there is no specific time limit for a request, although a substantial delay in applying for a review could possibly be relevant to the exercise of a discretion on the review. The review need not take any particular form, although good administrative practice would suggest that at minimum a different officer should reconsider the case.

Secondly, there must be a written decision for which adequate reasons must be given. It is likely that the courts would expect, as a minimum, a clear explanation for why an application had failed or only succeeded in part. See the commentary to reg 54 SSCS D&A Regs. A failure to comply with reg 6(3) would render a decision liable to be quashed on judicial review, although it is likely that a court would expect a claimant to seek a review first where one was available.

Provision of information

7.   A person claiming or receiving discretionary housing payments shall provide a relevant authority with the following information–

(a)   particulars of the grounds of claim or, as the case may be, particulars of the grounds for a review;

(b)   changes in circumstances which may be relevant to the continuance of discretionary housing payments,

and such other information as may be specified by the relevant authority within such time as that authority thinks appropriate.

Analysis

The requirement to specify particulars of the grounds for a review is a further indication that there is a right to a review rather than it purely being in the discretion of the authority. Changes of circumstances must be disclosed, but other information has to be demanded. Note that there is no prohibition on requiring information about payments such as those specified in reg 86(4) HB Regs (see p387).

Reviews

8.–(1)   A relevant authority may review any decision it has made with respect to the making, cancellation or recovery of discretionary housing payments in such circumstances as it thinks fit.

(2)   Without prejudice to the generality of paragraph (1) above, a relevant authority may, on any such review, cancel the making of further such payments and recover a payment already made where that authority has determined that–

(a) whether fraudulently or otherwise, any person has misrepresented, or failed to disclose, a material fact and, as a consequence of that misrepresentation or failure to disclose, a payment has been made; or

(b) an error has been made when determining the application for a payment, and as a consequence of that error, a payment had been made which would not have been made but for that error.

Analysis

Para (1) states that an authority "may" review a decision on whatever grounds it sees fit. However, it is suggested that reg 6(3) above has the effect of conferring a right to a review on application. If that is not right, then the discretion to review must still be exercised reasonably and the decisions in *R (Sibley) v West Dorset DC* [2001] EWHC Admin 365, Silber J and *R (Naghshbandi) v Camden LBC* [2001] EWHC Admin 813; [2003] HLR 280, CA, Rafferty J may assist as to the circumstances in which a refusal to review may be challenged.

Para (2) deals with the effect of a review. The making of further payments may be cancelled on any basis, but the circumstances in which there can be recovery of overpayments are limited.

A review of the decision awarding a DHP is a necessary precondition of recovery. Under sub-para (a), a DHP may be recovered on similar grounds to those in s71 SSAA and reg 101(2)(a) HB Regs (see the Analysis on p422). Sub-para (b) requires the error to take place during the course of the determination, but need not necessarily be that of the officer making the decision. It would be sufficient if an officer carrying out some inquiries made an error. "Error" must, however, mean a mistake as to law or fact. It cannot apply to a situation where a reviewing officer takes the view that s/he disagrees with the first officer's judgment or exercise of discretion.

The New Deal (Lone Parents) (Miscellaneous Provisions) Order 2001

(SI 2001 No.2915)

General Note

This Order specifies that payments received during participation in the self-employment route of the "New Deal for Lone Parents" are to be treated as a training premium for the purposes of HB and CTB.

Citation, commencement and interpretation

1.–(1)   This Order may be cited as the New Deal (Lone Parents) (Miscellaneous Provisions) Order 2001 and shall come into force on 13th September 2001.

(2) In this Order–

"the New Deal for Lone Parents" means the arrangements known by that name and made under section 2 of the 1973 Act for which only persons who are lone parents are eligible and which are designed to help participants to obtain work or to improve their prospects of obtaining work;

"lone parent" means a person who has no partner and who is responsible for, and a member of the same household as, a child or young person;

"the self-employment route" means receiving assistance in pursuing self-employed earner's employment whilst participating in the New Deal for Lone Parents.

Treatment of payments for the purposes of the Social Security Contributions and Benefits Act 1992, the Jobseekers Act 1995 and specified subordinate legislation

2.–(1)   The provisions of this article apply for the purposes of–

(a)   Part I of the Social Security Contributions and Benefits Act 1992;

(b)   the Jobseekers Act 1995; and

(c)   the subordinate legislation specified in the Schedule to this Order.

(2)   If during any period or periods commencing with or falling after the date on which this Order comes into force a person is participating in the New Deal for Lone Parents within the self-employment route and that person receives, or is eligible to receive, either a top-up payment or other payment made to him in order to assist with the expenses of participation, any such payments made to such a person during that period or those periods in connection with his use of those facilities shall be treated–

(a)   for the purposes of regulation 6(1)(d) of the Income Support (General) Regulations 1987, as a training allowance;

(b)   for all other purposes, as a training premium.

The Social Security (Notification of Change of Circumstances) Regulations 2001

(SI 2001 No.3252)

General Note to the Regulations

Possible offences under ss111A and 112 SSAA 1992 include where someone fails to give prompt notification of a change of circumstances. Reg 4 of these regulations prescribe to whom, and the manner in which, a change must be reported for these purposes. Note that although for the purposes of the general duty to report a change of circumstances in reg 88 HB Regs, reg 69 HB(SPC) Regs, reg 74 CTB Regs and reg 59 CTB(SPC) Regs, notice can be accepted in a form other than in writing, for the purposes of ss111A and 112, notice *must* be in writing.

Citation and commencement

1. These Regulations may be cited as the Social Security (Notification of Change of Circumstances) Regulations 2001 and shall come into force on 18th October 2001.

Notification for purposes of sections 111A and 112 of the Social Security Administration Act 1992

2. Regulations 3 to 5 below prescribe the person to whom, and manner in which, a change of circumstances must be notified for the purposes of sections 111A(1A) to (1G) and 112(1A) to (1F) of the Social Security Administration Act 1992 (offences relating to failure to notify a change of circumstances).

Change affecting housing benefit or council tax benefit

4.–(1) Where the benefit affected by the change of circumstances is housing benefit or council tax benefit, notice must be given or sent in writing to the relevant authority at–

(a) the designated office; or

(b) in a case where notification at another office is permitted under [¹ regulation 88 of the Housing Benefit Regulations 2006, regulation 69 of the Housing Benefit (Persons who have attained the qualifying age for state pension credit) Regulations 2006, regulation 74 of the Council Tax Benefit Regulations 2006 or regulation 59 of the Council Tax Benefit (Persons who have attained the qualifying age for state pension credit) Regulations 2006], that other office.

(2) In this regulation ''designated office'' and ''relevant authority'' have the same meaning as in the Housing Benefit (General) Regulations 1987 and the Council Tax Benefit (General) Regulations 1992.

Amendment

1. Amended by reg 5 and Sch 2 para 19 of SI 2006 No 217 as from 6.3.06.

The Social Security (Loss of Benefit) Regulations 2001
(SI 2001 No.4022)

General Note to the Regulations

ss7 to 13 of the Social Security Fraud Act 2001 (see p1035) provide "loss of benefit" provisions where a claimant or a member of her/his family is convicted of repeat benefit offences. These regulations deal with the commencement of the disqualification period and the amount by which HB and CTB can be reduced.

PART I
GENERAL

Citation, commencement and interpretation

1.–(1)   These Regulations may be cited as the Social Security (Loss of Benefit) Regulations 2001 and shall come into force on 1st April 2002.

(2)   In these Regulations, unless the context otherwise requires–

"the Act" means the Social Security Fraud Act 2001;

"the Benefits Act" means the Social Security Contributions and Benefits Act 1992;

[¹ "the Council Tax Benefit Regulations" means the Council Tax Benefit Regulations 2006;]

[¹ "the Council Tax Benefit (State Pension Credit) Regulations" means the Council Tax Benefit (Persons who have attained the qualifying age for state pension credit) Regulations 2006;]

[¹ "the Housing Benefit Regulations" means the Housing Benefit (General) Regulations 1987;]

[¹ "the Housing Benefit (State Pension Credit) Regulations" means the Housing Benefit (Persons who have attained the qualifying age for state pension credit) Regulations 2006;]

"the Income Support Regulations" means the Income Support (General) Regulations 1987;

"the Jobseekers Act" means the Jobseekers Act 1995;

"the Jobseeker's Allowance Regulations" means the Jobseeker's Allowance Regulations 1996;

"claimant" in a regulation means the person claiming the sanctionable benefit referred to in that regulation;

"disqualification period" means the period in respect of which the restrictions on payment of a relevant benefit apply in respect of an offender in accordance with section 7(6) of the Act and shall be interpreted in accordance with regulation 2; and

"offender" means the person who is subject to the restriction in the payment of his benefit in accordance with section 7 of the Act.

(3)   Expressions used in these Regulations which are defined either for the purposes of the Jobseekers Act or for the purposes of the Jobseeker's Allowance Regulations shall, except where the context otherwise requires, have the same meaning as for the purposes of that Act or, as the case may be, those Regulations.

(4)   In these Regulations, unless the context otherwise requires, a reference–

(a)   to a numbered regulation is to the regulation in these Regulations bearing that number;

(b)   in a regulation to a numbered paragraph is to the paragraph in that regulation bearing that number.

Amendment

1.   Amended by reg 5 and Sch 2 para 20(2) of SI 2006 No 217 as from 6.3.06.

Disqualification period

2.–(1)   Subject to paragraph (2), the first day of the disqualification period for the purpose of section 7(6) of the Act shall be–

(a) [¹subject to sub-paragraph (c)]where, on the determination day–
    (i) the offender is in receipt of a sanctionable benefit;
    (ii) the offender is a member of a joint-claim couple which is in receipt of a joint-claim jobseeker's allowance; or
    (iii) the offender's family member is in receipt of [¹ income support or jobseeker's allowance],
the day which is 28 days after the determination day;

(b) [omitted]

[²(c) where the only sanctionable benefits which the offender or, as the case may be, the offender's family member, is in receipt of are housing benefit or council tax benefit or both of them, the day which is 28 days after the first day after the determination day on which the Secretary of State is notified by the relevant authority that the offender or an offender's family member is in receipt of either or both of those benefits or, as the case may be, has been awarded either or both of those benefits and in this sub-paragraph, "relevant authority" means the relevant authority administering the offender's or the offender's family member's housing benefit or council tax benefit.]

(2) For the purposes of [¹paragraph (1)], the first day of the disqualification period shall be no later than 3 years and 28 days after the date of the conviction of the offender for the benefit offence in the later proceedings referred to in section 7(1) of the Act and section 7(9) of the Act (date of conviction and references to conviction) shall apply for the purposes of this paragraph as it applies for the purposes of section 7 of the Act.

(3) In this regulation, "the determination day" means the day on which the Secretary of State determines that a restriction under–

(a) section 7 of the Act would be applicable to the offender were he in receipt of a sanctionable benefit;

(b) section 8 of the Act would be applicable to the offender were he a member of a joint-claim couple which is in receipt of a joint-claim jobseeker's allowance; or

(c) section 9 of the Act would be applicable to the offender's family member were that member in receipt of income support, jobseeker's allowance, housing benefit or council tax benefit.

Amendments

1.   Amended by reg 2 of SI 2002 No 486 as from 1.4.02.
2.   Inserted by reg 2 of SI 2002 No 486 as from 1.4.02.

General Note

Made under s7(6) SSFA 2001, reg 2 defines the commencement of the "disqualification period" applicable in respect of repeat offenders. Where HB and CTB are reduced under reg 17 below, this can only be because they are the only sanctionable benefits: see reg 18. Therefore reg 2(1)(c) will always be the applicable date, and this provides for 28 days after the date on which the Secretary of State is notified by the local authority that an offender or member of her/his family is in receipt of, or has been awarded, HB or CTB. The date cannot be more than three years and 28 days after the conviction for the later offence: reg 2(2).

The scheme is that the Secretary of State determines whether a restriction is applicable and will then notify local authorities of the persons in relation to whom a restriction is imposed. The local authority will then notify the Secretary of State that an award of benefit has been made. The Secretary of State will then require a reduction in HB or CTB to be imposed.

PART V
HOUSING BENEFIT AND COUNCIL TAX BENEFIT

Circumstances where a reduced amount of housing benefit and council tax benefit is payable

17.–(1)   Subject to [² paragraph (4) and] regulation 18, any payment of housing benefit or, as the case may be, council tax benefit which falls to be made to an offender in respect of any week in the disqualification period or to an offender's family member in respect of any week in the relevant period shall be reduced–

(a)   where the claimant or a member of his family is pregnant or seriously ill, by a sum equivalent to 20 per cent.;

(b)   in any other case, by a sum equivalent to 40 per cent.,

of the amount which is or, where he is not the claimant or is not single, would be applicable to the offender in respect of a single claimant for those benefits on the first day of the disqualification period or, where the payment falls to be made to an offender's family member, on the first day of the relevant period and specified in [¹ paragraph 1 of Schedule 3 to the Housing Benefit Regulations or, as the case may be, in paragraph 1(1) of Schedule 3 of the Housing Benefit (State Pension Credit) Regulations, in paragraph 1(1) of Schedule 1 to the Council Tax Benefit Regulations, or in paragraph 1(1) of Schedule 1 of the Council Tax Benefit (State Pension Credit) Regulations.

(2)   A reduction under paragraph (1) shall, if it is not a multiple of 5p, be rounded to the nearest such multiple or, if it is a multiple of 2.5p but not of 5p, to the next lower multiple of 5p.

(3)   Where the rate of housing benefit or council tax benefit payable to a claimant changes, the rules set out above for a reduction in the benefit payable shall be applied to the new rates and any adjustment to the reduction shall take effect from the beginning of the first benefit week to commence for the claimant following the change and in this paragraph "benefit week" shall have the same meaning as in [¹ regulation 2(1) of the Housing Benefit Regulations or, as the case may be, regulation 2(1) of the Housing Benefit (State Pension Credit) Regulations, regulation 2(1) of the Council Tax Benefit Regulations, or regulation 2(1) of the Council Tax Benefit (State Pension Credit) Regulations.]

[² (4)   In any case where the housing benefit of an offender or an offender's family member is subject to both a reduction under this regulation and a reduction by virtue of section 130B of the Social Security Contributions and Benefits Act 1992 (loss of benefit following eviction on certain grounds), any payment of housing benefit which is to be made to the offender in respect of any week in the disqualification period, or to an offender's family member in respect of any week in the relevant period, shall be reduced in accordance with paragraph (5).

(5)   The amount of housing benefit payable in respect of any week in the disqualification period, or relevant period (in the case of an offender's family member) shall be reduced by the greater of either–

(a)   the amount by which it would be reduced under this regulation; or

(b)   the amount by which it would be reduced under regulation 4 of the Housing Benefit (Loss of Benefit) (Pilot Scheme) Regulations 2007.]

Amendment

1.   Amended by reg 5 and Sch 2 para 20(3) of SI 2006 No 217 as from 6.3.06.
2.   Amended by reg 7(2) of SI 2007 No 2202 as from 1.11.07. The amendment ceases to have effect on 31.10.09 unless revoked with effect from an earlier date.
3.   Inserted by reg 7(3) of SI 2007 No 2202 as from 1.11.07. The amendment ceases to have effect on 31.10.09 unless revoked with effect from an earlier date.

General Note

The amount of the reduction imposed is normally 40 per cent of the personal allowance for a single claimant of the offender's age as at the first day of the disqualification period or the relevant period. If, however, any member of the family is pregnant or seriously ill, the reduction is 20 per cent. Where both HB and CTB are being claimed, it appears that the reduction is applicable to both.

A reduction will be recalculated from the next benefit week where there is a change in the amount of entitlement: reg 17(3).

Note that where a reduction is being applied under both this regulation and s130B SSCBA 1992 (loss of benefit following eviction on certain grounds), the reduction is the greater of the amounts in para (5)(a) or (b). The Housing Benefit (Loss of Benefit) (Pilot Scheme) Regulations 2007 (on p1139) only apply in Pilot Areas and only until 21 October 2009, unless revoked from an earlier date.

Circumstances where housing benefit and council tax benefit is payable

18. Regulation 17 shall not apply and housing benefit or, as the case may be, council tax benefit shall be payable to an offender or to an offender's family member–

(a) where the offender is the claimant, he is entitled to either of those benefits during the disqualification period;

(b) where the offender's family member is the claimant, he is entitled to either of those benefits during the relevant period,

and the claimant is, at the same time, also entitled to income support or to an income-based jobseeker's allowance.

General Note

Reg 18 confirms that where the claimant is entitled to IS or income-based JSA, the reductions will be applied to those benefits and not to HB or CTB entitlement.

The Contracting Out (Functions of Local Authorities: Income-Related Benefits) Order 2002

(2002 No.1888)

General Note to the Order

The Deregulation and Contracting Out Act 1994 confers power on ministers to make orders permitting public bodies to contract out work to private contractors. Hitherto, powers of delegation and contracting out have been limited. This Order permits local authorities to contract out most of their benefit-related functions, with the limited exceptions set out in art 3(2). Authorities are not obliged to contract the functions out, and many authorities have experienced severe difficulties with contractors employed to carry out benefit functions, but many will do so in pursuit of the Best Value principles.

Local authorities are obliged to carry out random checks on decisions made by contractors: art 4. Art 5 prohibits any contractor or employee of a contractor making a decision on a claim made by them or in which they have a financial interest.

The Order was made on 18 July 2002 and so came into force, by virtue of art 1, on 25 July 2002.

Citation and commencement

1. This Order may be cited as the Contracting Out (Functions of Local Authorities: Income-Related Benefits) Order 2002 and shall come into force on the seventh day after the day on which it is made.

Interpretation

2. In this Order–

"the Administration Act" means the Social Security Administration Act 1992;

"the Benefits Act" means the Social Security Contributions and Benefits Act 1992;

"council tax benefit" means the benefit to which section 123(1)(e) of the Benefits Act refers;

"decisions on claims" means any decisions in relation to those benefits or payments referred to in article 3(1) that fall to be made under or by virtue of–

   (a)   the Administration Act;

   (b)   the Benefits Act;

   (c)   section 34 of the Social Security Act 1998; and

   (d)   the Child Support, Pensions and Social Security Act 2000

and any Regulations and Orders made under those provisions for the time being in force and, for the purposes of this Order, references to decisions include references to any determinations embodied in, or necessary to, a decision;

"discretionary housing payment" means any payment made by virtue of regulations under section 69 of the Child Support, Pensions and Social Security Act 2000;

"housing benefit" means the benefit to which section 123(1)(d) of the Benefits Act refers;

"local authority" means a billing authority, housing authority or local authority as they are defined in section 191 of the Administration Act;

"subsidy" means rent rebate subsidy, rent allowance subsidy or council tax benefit subsidy as referred to in section 140A(2) of the Administration Act or any grant made under section 70 of the Child Support, Pensions and Social Security Act 2000 (grants towards costs of discretionary housing payments).

Functions which may be contracted out

3.–(1) In so far as it is not already lawful for functions of a local authority in relation to council tax benefit, discretionary housing payments and housing benefit under the provisions of–

   (a)   the Benefits Act,

   (b)   the Administration Act,

   (c)   section 34 of the Social Security Act 1998, and

(d)   the Child Support, Pensions and Social Security Act 2000,

and any Regulations and Orders made under those provisions for the time being in force, to be exercised by, or by employees of, such a person (if any) authorised to do so by that authority, any such function of an authority under those provisions (not being a function excluded from section 70 of the Deregulation and Contracting Out Act 1994 by section 71(1) of that Act), other than a function specified in paragraph (2), may, if and in so far as that authority may authorise, be so exercised.

(2)   The functions referred to in paragraph (1) are–

(a)   any function relating to the claiming and receipt of subsidy;

(b)   the issue of a certificate under section 116(3)(b) of the Administration Act (as to the date on which evidence sufficient to justify prosecution came to the local authority's knowledge);

(c)   the grant or withdrawal of authorisations under section 110A(3) to (7) of the Administration Act (to exercise the powers of inspection);

(d)   the function of requiring a person to enter into arrangements under section 110AA of the Administration Act (to allow access to electronic records); and

(e)   any function under sections 139D to 139H of the Administration Act (directions by the Secretary of State).

Checking requirement attaching to the exercise of functions

4.–(1)   Subject to paragraph (5) an authorisation given under this Order in relation to any function involving decisions on claims shall include the checking requirement specified in paragraph (2), and the authorisation shall be subject to the inclusion of that requirement.

(2)   The checking requirement shall require the authorised person to–

(a)   provide a random sample of decisions on claims made on a day, of not less than 10 per cent. of those decisions, to the local authority for checking within two working days of that day;

(b)   take all reasonable steps to prevent errors identified by the local authority from recurring.

(3)   When providing a random sample for the purposes of paragraph (2)(a) above, the authorised person shall use such method of random selection as may be specified by the local authority in the authorisation or, where no such method has been specified, the authorised person shall notify the local authority of the method of random selection that has been used.

(4)   When taking reasonable steps to prevent identified errors from recurring for the purposes of paragraph (2)(b) above, the authorised person shall take such steps to prevent that error from recurring as may be required by the local authority.

(5)   An authorised person shall be subject to the checking requirement only if he employs at least one other person to carry out the work in relation to the exercise of any function involving decisions on claims.

(6)   For the purposes of this article "working day" means any day other than a Saturday, a Sunday, Christmas Day, Good Friday or a day which is a bank holiday under the Banking and Financial Dealings Act 1971 in any part of the United Kingdom.

Extent of an authorisation

5.–(1)   An authorisation given under this Order in relation to any function involving decisions on claims shall not extend to any decisions on any claims where the authorised person–

(a)   is a person to whom rent is payable for a dwelling in respect of which the claim is made; or

(b)   may otherwise be affected financially by reason of a payment of housing benefit under that claim.

(2)   An authorisation given under this Order in relation to any function involving decisions on claims shall not extend to a decision made by an employee of an authorised person on any claim where that employee–

(a)   is a person to whom rent is payable for a dwelling in respect of which that claim is made; or

(b)   may otherwise be affected financially by reason of a payment of housing benefit under that claim.

The Social Security (Habitual Residence) Amendment Regulations 2004

(SI 2004 No.1232)

Citation, commencement and interpretation

1.–(1) These Regulations shall be cited as the Social Security (Habitual Residence) Amendment Regulations 2004 and shall come into force on 1st May 2004.

(2) In these Regulations–

[¹]

[¹]

Amendment

1.   Revoked by reg 3 and Sch 1 of SI 2006 No 217 as from 6.3.06.

Transitional arrangements and savings

6.–(1) Paragraph (2) shall apply where a person–

(a)   is entitled to a specified benefit in respect of a period which includes 30th April 2004;

(b)   claims a specified benefit on or after 1st May 2004 and it is subsequently determined that he is entitled to that benefit in respect of a period which includes 30th April 2004;

(c)   claims a specified benefit on or after 1st May 2004 and it is subsequently determined that he is entitled to such a benefit in respect of a period which is continuous with a period of entitlement to the same or another specified benefit which includes 30th April 2004;

[(d) omitted]

(2)   Where this paragraph applies–

[¹ (a)]

[(b) omitted]

[(c) omitted]

[(d) omitted]

(3)   The provisions saved by paragraph (2) shall continue to have effect until the date on which entitlement to a specified benefit for the purposes of paragraph (1) ceases, and if there is more than one such specified benefit, until the last date on which such entitlement ceases.

(4)   In this regulation "specified benefit" means income support, housing benefit, council tax benefit, jobseeker's allowance and state pension credit.

Amendment

1.   Revoked by reg 3 and Sch 1 of SI 2006 No 217 as from 6.3.06.

General Note

The transitional protection provided by reg 6 is now replicated in Sch 3 para 6(5)-(7) of the HB&CTB(CP) Regs (see p1116). Reg 10 of both the HB and the HB(SPC) Regs and reg 7 of both the CTB and the CTB(SPC) Regs are modified for those with transitional protection by those paras.

Note that the amendments made by SI 2006 No 1026 to the HB Regs, HB(SPC) Regs, CTB Regs and CTB(SPC) Regs do not affect the continued operation of the transitional and savings provided for in reg 12 of the Social Security (Persons From Abroad) Miscellaneous Amendments Regulations 1996, reg 6 of the Social Security (Habitual Residence) Amendment Regulations 2004 or para 6 of Sch 3 of the HB&CTB(CP) Regs. See reg 11 of SI 2006 No 1026 (on p1134).

The Civil Partnership (Pensions, Social Security and Child Support) (Consequential, etc. Provisions) Order 2005

(SI 2005 No.2877)

Citation and commencement

1. This Order may be cited as the Civil Partnership (Pensions, Social Security and Child Support) (Consequential, etc. Provisions) Order 2005 and shall come into force on 5th December 2005.

Transitional provision relating to housing benefit and council tax benefit

3.–(1) Paragraph (2) applies in the case of a claimant who is a member of a couple who live together as if they were civil partners on or after 5th December 2005, in respect of whom there is an award of housing benefit or council tax benefit on 5th December 2005.

(2)   In such a case, subject to paragraphs (3) and (4)–

(a)   the provisions of regulation 8(2) and (10) of the Decisions and Appeals Regulations shall not apply; and

(b)   a superseding decision made in consequence of the amendments made by paragraph 15, 16, 21 or 22 of Schedule 3 to this Order shall take effect–

    (i)   from the date that the claimant reports to the relevant authority that the couple live together as if they were civil partners; or

    (ii)   from the date on which the relevant authority otherwise becomes aware that the couple are living together as if they were civil partners; or

    (iii)   where there exists an award of a relevant benefit on 5th December 2005, from the date the superseding decision is made in relation to the relevant benefit that is consequential on the amendments made by paragraph 13, 26 or 35 of Schedule 3 to this Order,

    whichever is the earliest date.

(3)   The relevant authority may, where the provisions of paragraph (2)(b)(i) or (ii) apply, determine such earlier effective date for the superseding decision as it considers appropriate if it is satisfied that the claimant could reasonably have been expected to report that he is a member of a couple who live together as if they were civil partners earlier than the date which would otherwise apply under that paragraph.

(4)   The provisions of regulation 8(2) and (10) of the Decisions and Appeals Regulations shall apply in a case falling within paragraph (1) where the application of those provisions is advantageous to the claimant.

(5)   In this article–

''couple'' has the same meaning as in regulation 2(1) of the Housing Benefit (General) Regulations 1987;

''the Decisions and Appeals Regulations'' means the Housing Benefit and Council Tax Benefit (Decisions and Appeals) Regulations 2001;

''relevant authority'' has the same meaning as in regulation 2(1) of the Housing Benefit (General) Regulations 1987;

''relevant benefit'' means income support, income-based jobseeker's allowance or a guarantee credit awarded under section 2(1) of the State Pension Credit Act 2002.

General Note

This transitional provision concerns the coming into force of the Civil Partnership Act 2004 on 5 December 2005 and when it may bite in respect of same sex couples claiming HB/CTB on or after that date. As with most social security transitional provisions, it is densely worded.

The first point to note is that the transitional rules in reg 3 apply only to same sex couples who are not civil partners but are living together as if they were civil partners, so the rule will have no application to same sex couples who have in fact entered into a contract of civil partnership. The logic for the transitional rules not applying to such couples would seem to be twofold. Firstly, on and shortly after 5 December 2005 there are likely to be few contracts of civil partnership which will have been entered into. Secondly, once such a contract has been entered into then, subject to those civil partners being members of the same household, the entering into the civil partnership contract will be a change of circumstances which the "ordinary" supersession rules will apply to (that is, the onus will fall on the civil partnership couple to notify the local authority of the change of circumstance).

The key starting point for same sex couples who are living together as if they were civil partners is that they will not be so treated, and therefore their claim(s) for HB/CTB not altered on acount of this, until they report to the relevant local authority that they are living together as if civil partners (unless – per subpara (3) – the claimant could reasonably have been expected to report that s/he was living together with someone as a civil partner from an earlier date).

On the face of the regulation the rule in subpara 2(b)(ii) is of equal importance. This allows the local authority to supersede from the date when, other than being told by the claimant, it first became aware that the claimant was living with someone as if civil partners. However, it is understood that the DWP is advising authorities to adopt a softly softly approach to the changes introduced by the Civil Partnership Act 2004 and not enter into proactive and intrusive investigations, and so (initially at least) most awards will only be superseded from the date one of the couple report that they are living together as if civil partners.

The only other way in which the HB/CTB awarding decision may be superseded is if there has been a supersession of the claimant's (or her/his partner's) award of income support (IS), income-based jobseeker's allowance (JSA) or the guarantee credit of pension credit (PC) on 'civil partnership' grounds. In such a situation the award of HB/CTB will stand to be superseded from the same date that the IS, income-based JSA or PC award was superseded.

The Civil Partnership Act 2004 (Relationships Arising Through Civil Partnership) Order 2005
(2005 No.3137)

Citation and commencement
1.   This Order may be cited as the Civil Partnership Act 2004 (Relationships Arising Through Civil Partnership) Order 2005 and comes into force on 5th December 2005.

References to stepchildren etc. in existing subordinate legislation
3.–(1)   Section 246 of the Civil Partnership Act 2004 (interpretation of statutory references to stepchildren etc.) applies to the provisions of existing subordinate legislation listed in the Schedule.

(2)   The application of section 246 of the Civil Partnership Act 2004 to the provisions in the Regulations set out in paragraphs 24 and 44 of the Schedule applies to those Regulations as modified in their application to persons to whom regulations 2(1) and 12(1) of the Housing Benefit and Council Tax Benefit (State Pension Credit) Regulations 2003 apply and to those Regulations as not so modified.

(3)   The application of section 246 of the Civil Partnership Act 2004 to the provisions in the Regulations set out in paragraphs 27 and 47 of the Schedule applies to those Regulations as modified in their application to persons to whom regulations 2(1) and 12(1) of the Housing Benefit and Council Tax Benefit (State Pension Credit) Regulations 2003 apply.

SCHEDULE

Article 3

REFERENCES TO STEPCHILDREN ETC. IN EXISTING SUBORDINATE LEGISLATION
24.   The definition of ''close relative'' in regulation 2(1) of the Housing Benefit (General) Regulations 1987 (interpretation).
25.   Paragraphs 34(4)(b)(i) and (ii) and 34(5)(b)(i) and (ii) of Schedule 4 to those Regulations (sums to be disregarded in the calculation of income other than earnings).
26.   Paragraphs 23(4)(b)(i) and (ii) and 23(5)(b)(i) and (ii) of Schedule 5 to those Regulations (capital to be disregarded).
27.   Paragraphs 16(4)(b)(i) and (ii) and 16(5)(b)(i) and (ii) of Schedule 5ZA to those Regulations (Part I: capital to be disregarded).
44.   The definition of ''close relative'' in regulation 2(1) of the Council Tax Benefit (General) Regulations 1992 (interpretation).
45.   Paragraphs 35(4)(b)(i) and (ii) and 35(5)(b)(i) and (ii) of Schedule 4 to those Regulations (sums to be disregarded in the calculation of income other than earnings).
46.   Paragraphs 23(4)(b)(i) and (ii) and 23(5)(b)(i) and (ii) of Schedule 5 to those Regulations (capital to be disregarded).
47.   Paragraphs 16(4)(b)(i) and (ii) and 16(5)(b)(i) and (ii) of Schedule 5ZA to those Regulations (Part I: capital to be disregarded).

The Housing Benefit and Council Tax Benefit (Consequential Provisions) Regulations 2006
(2006 No.217)

Citation, commencement and interpretation

1.–(1)   These Regulations may be cited as the Housing Benefit and Council Tax Benefit (Consequential Provisions) Regulations 2006 and shall come into force on 6th March 2006.

(2)   In these Regulations–

"the Act" means the Social Security Contributions and Benefits Act 1992;

"the 1987 Regulations" means the Housing Benefit (General) Regulations 1987;

"the 1992 Regulations" means the Council Tax Benefit (General) Regulations 1992;

"Council Tax Benefit Regulations" means the Council Tax Benefit Regulations 2006;

"the Council Tax Benefit (State Pension Credit) Regulations" means the Council Tax Benefit (Persons who have attained the qualifying age for state pension credit) Regulations 2006;

"the Housing Benefit Regulations" means the Housing Benefit Regulations 2006;

"the Housing Benefit (State Pension Credit) Regulations" means the Housing Benefit (Persons who have attained the qualifying age for state pension credit) Regulations 2006;

"the consolidating Regulations" means the Council Tax Benefit Regulations, the Council Tax Benefit (State Pension Credit) Regulations, the Housing Benefit Regulations and the Housing Benefit (State Pension Credit) Regulations.

Continuity of the law

2.–(1)   The coming into force of the consolidating Regulations does not affect the continuity of the law.

(2)   Anything done or having effect as if done under or for the purposes of a provision revoked by these Regulations has effect, if it could have been done under or for the purposes of the corresponding provision of the consolidating Regulations, as if done under or for the purposes of that provision.

(3)   Any reference, whether express or implied, in the consolidating Regulations or any other instrument or document to a provision of the consolidating Regulations shall, in so far as the context permits, be construed as including, in relation to the times, circumstances and purposes in relation to which the corresponding provision of any regulation revoked by these Regulations has effect, a reference to that corresponding provision.

(4)   Any reference, whether express or implied, in any instrument or document to a provision of a regulation revoked by these Regulations shall be construed, so far as is required for continuing effect, as including a reference to the corresponding provision of the consolidating Regulations.

Documents referring to revoked provisions

4.   Any document made, served or issued after the consolidating Regulations comes into force which contains a reference to any of the regulations revoked by these Regulations shall be construed, except so far as a contrary intention appears, as referring or, as the context may require, including a reference to the corresponding provision of the consolidating Regulations.

Transitional provisions and savings

6.–(1)   The provisions of Schedule 3 to these Regulations (which contains transitional provisions and savings) shall have effect.

(2)   The revocation by these Regulations of any provision previously repealed subject to savings does not affect the continued operation of those savings.

Transitory modifications
7.   The transitory modifications in Schedule 4 to these Regulations shall have effect.

Amending Orders
8.   An order which is made under section 150 of the Social Security Administration Act 1992 after the consolidating Regulations have been made and which amends any of the Regulations scheduled to be revoked by these Regulations shall have the effect also of making a corresponding amendment of the consolidating Regulations.

SCHEDULE 3
REGULATION 6(1)
TRANSITIONAL AND SAVINGS PROVISIONS
1.–(1)   Where a change of circumstances occurs as a result of the payment of arrears of any income (and for the avoidance of doubt income includes any benefit within the meaning of the Act) which affects a determination or decision in respect of entitlement to, or the amount of, housing benefit or council tax benefit before 6th March 1995, the provisions specified in paragraph (2) shall apply subject to the omissions specified in relation to that provision.

(2)   The provisions specified in this paragraph (which all relate to the date on which changes of circumstances are to take effect) are–
- (a)   regulations 79 of the Housing Benefit Regulations which shall apply as if paragraph (7) was omitted;
- (b)   regulation 59 of the Housing Benefit (State Pension Credit) Regulations which shall apply as if paragraph (7) was omitted;
- (c)   regulation 67 of the Council Tax Benefit Regulations which shall apply as if paragraph (9) was omitted;
- (d)   regulation 50 of the Council Tax Benefit (State Pension Credit) Regulations which shall apply as if paragraph (9) was omitted.

General Note

This is a saving provision. The Housing Benefit and Council Tax Benefit (Amendment) Regulations 1995 SI No 511 amended reg 68 HB Regs 1987 following the decision in *R v Middlesborough BC ex p Holmes* [1995] unreported, 15 February, QBD. The transitional protection provided in that SI is now in para 1. The sub-paras in the regulations cited in para 1(2) are not to have affect where arrears of income are to be taken into account for a period prior to 6 March 1995. See the Analysis to reg 79 HB Regs on p371 for more details. The amendment may be of continuing relevance in overpayment cases involving a failure to disclose receipt of income.

Persons incapable of work
2.–(1)   Where, on 12th April 1995, the disability premium was applicable to a claimant by virtue of paragraph 12(1)(b) of Schedule 2 to the 1987 Regulations or paragraph 13(1)(b) of Schedule 1 to the 1992 Regulations, as in force on that date, the disability premium shall continue to be applicable to that claimant from 13th April 1995 and for so long as he is incapable of work in accordance with the provisions of, and regulations made under, Part 12A of the Act (incapacity for work).

(2)   Where, on 12th April 1995, the disability premium was applicable to a claimant and in the period from 13th April 1995 to 1st October 1995 paragraph (1) either did not apply or ceased to apply in his case, if–
- (a)   for the period for which paragraph (1) did not apply or ceased to apply, the claimant was incapable of work or was treated as incapable of work in accordance with the provisions of, and regulations made under, Part 12A of the Act (the period of incapacity); and
- (b)   any break in the period of incapacity did not exceed a period of 56 continuous days,

with effect from 2nd October 1995 for so long as he is incapable of work or is treated as incapable of work, the disability premium shall be applicable in his case.

(3)   Paragraphs (1) and (2) shall not apply to a claimant who ceases to be incapable of work or ceases to be treated as incapable of work in accordance with the provisions of, and regulations made under, Part 12A of the Act (incapacity for work) for a period of more than 56 continuous days.

(4)   Where, in any period immediately preceding 13th April 1995, the circumstances mentioned in paragraph 12(6) of Schedule 2 to the 1987 Regulations, or paragraph 13(6) of Schedule 1 to the 1992 Regulations, as in force on 12th April 1995, applied to a claimant to whom the disability premium was not applicable, that claimant shall be treated for the purposes of–

(a)   regulations 28(8)(c) and 56(2)(e) of, and paragraph 13(1)(b) of Schedule 3 to, the Housing Benefit Regulations;

(b)   regulations 18(11)(e) and 45(3)(e) of, and paragraph 13(1)(b) of Schedule 1 to, the Council Tax Benefit Regulations; or as the case may be,

as if he had been incapable of work in accordance with the provisions of, and regulations made under, Part 12A of the Act (incapacity for work) throughout that period.

General Note

The Housing Benefit and Council Tax Benefit (Miscellaneous Amendments)(No. 2) Regulations 1995 SI No 626 introduced amendments to the conditions for qualifying for various premiums payable as part of HB and CTB. The transitional and savings provisions for those receiving the premiums on 12 April 1995 are now in paras 2 and 3.

Analysis

Para 2. The requirement under para 13 (1)(b) of Sch 3 HB Regs is that the claimant is incapable of work for the purposes of the incapacity benefit legislation. Under para 2, disability premium continues to be applicable to a claimant to whom it was applicable on 12 April 1995 so long as s/he is incapable of work. Gaps of up to 56 days in incapacity between 13 April and 1 October 1995 were ignored if the claimant was incapable of work on 2 October 1995. A subsequent gap of 56 days in incapacity will destroy the transitional protection. For the text of the old version of the para see the 1994-5 edition of this book.

Para 3. The requirement under para 13(1)(a)(ii) of Sch 3 HB Regs is the claimant or her/his partner must have been receiving long-term IB and subsequently retirement pension. Prior to April 1995, the rules referred to receipt of invalidity pension as the requirement. The transitional rules apply where the HPP was "applicable" (as to which see *CIS 11293/1996* referred to in the commentary to Sch 3 para 11 HB Regs) to a claimant on 12 April 1995 or during the 56 days preceding that day.

R v Secretary of State for Social Security ex p Smithson (case C-243/90) [1992] ECR I-467, ECJ dealt with the former version of Sch 3 para 11. It was an attempt to argue that the paragraph offended against EC Directive 79/7 in that it discriminated on the grounds of sex because women lost their right to opt for invalidity benefit at 65 and not 70. It was held that HB did not fall within the directive because it was a benefit calculated on the basis of the relationship between notional and actual income, even though the notional income was calculated by reference to a risk which was within the directive – ie, sickness or invalidity.

3.–(1)   Where the higher pensioner premium was applicable to a claimant on, or at any time during the 56 days immediately preceding, 12th April 1995 by virtue of paragraph 13(1)(a)(ii) of Schedule 2 to the 1987 Regulations, or paragraph 13(1)(a)(ii) of Schedule 1 to the 1992 Regulations, as in force on that date, paragraph 13 of each of the Schedules specified in sub-paragraph (2) shall, in so far as it applies to those claimants, apply subject to the amendments specified in sub-paragraph (3).

(2)   Those Schedules (which all relate to the applicable amount) are–

(a)   Schedule 3 to the Housing Benefit Regulations; and

(b)   Schedule 1 to the Council Tax Benefit Regulations.

(3)   The amendments specified in this sub-paragraph are–

(a)   in sub-paragraph (1)(a)(i), for the words "long-term incapacity benefit", substitute "an invalidity pension" and for the words "in the case of long-term incapacity benefit", substitute "in the case of invalidity pension";

(b)   in sub-paragraph (1)(a)(ii) for the words "long-term incapacity benefit" substitute "invalidity pension";

(c)   for head (b) of sub-paragraph (1), substitute–

"(b)   the circumstances of the claimant fall, and have fallen, in respect of a continuous period of not less than 28 weeks, within sub-paragraph (6) or, if he was in Northern Ireland for the whole or part of that period, within one or more comparable Northern Irish provisions.";

(d)   in sub-paragraph (3), for the words "or to be incapable of work", substitute "for the purposes of the provisions specified in that provision";

(e)   for sub-paragraphs (6) and (7), substitute–

"(6)   For the purposes of sub-paragraph (1)(b) the circumstances of a claimant fall within this sub-paragraph if–

(a)   he provides evidence of incapacity in accordance with regulation 2 of the Social Security (Medical Evidence) Regulations 1976 (evidence of incapacity for work) in support of a claim for sickness benefit, invalidity pension or severe disablement allowance within the meaning of sections 31, 33 or 68 of the Act, provided that an adjudication officer has not determined he is not incapable of work, or

(b)   he is in receipt of statutory sick pay within the meaning of Part 11 of the Act.''.

Eligible rent

4.–(1)   Subject to the following provisions of this paragraph, the eligible rent of a person–

(a)   who was entitled to housing benefit on both the first date and the second date; or

(b)   who is liable to make payments in respect of a dwelling occupied by him as his home, which is exempt accommodation,

shall be determined in accordance with–

    (i)   regulations 12 (rent) and 13 (maximum rent) of the Housing Benefit Regulations, or, as the case may be,

    (ii)   regulations 12 (rent) and 13 (maximum rent) of the Housing Benefit (State Pension Credit) Regulations,

as set out in paragraph 5.

(2)   Sub-paragraph (1)(a) shall not apply to–

(a)   any determination of a person's eligible rent in a case where a pathfinder authority is required to determine a maximum rent (standard local rate) by virtue of regulation 13A of the Housing Benefit Regulations or, as the case may be, regulation 13A of the Housing Benefit (State Pension Credit) Regulations; or

(b)   any subsequent determination of his eligible rent.

(3)   Sub-paragraph (1)(a) shall only apply in a case where–

(a)   either–

    (i)   the dwelling occupied as his home by a person to whom sub-paragraph (1)(a) refers is the same on both the first date and the second date; or

    (ii)   the dwelling so occupied was not the same by reason only that the change was caused by a fire, flood, explosion or natural catastrophe rendering the dwelling occupied as the home on the first date uninhabitable; and

(b)   the person–

    (i)   was continuously entitled to and in receipt of housing benefit between the first date and the second date in respect of the dwelling to which head (a) above applies; or

    (ii)   was not entitled to or receiving housing benefit for a period not exceeding 4 weeks, but was in continuous occupation of the dwelling to which head (a) above refers between the first date and the second date; or

    (iii)   is a person to whom sub-paragraph (4) applies.

(4)   This sub-paragraph applies in the case of a person (''the claimant'') who becomes, or whose partner becomes, a welfare to work beneficiary, and–

(a)   the claimant ceases to be entitled to housing benefit in respect of his residence in the dwelling he occupies as his home;

(b)   the claimant subsequently becomes re-entitled to housing benefit–

    (i)   in respect of the same dwelling, or

    (ii)   in respect of a different dwelling in a case to which sub-paragraph (3)(a)(ii) applies; and

(c)   the first day of that entitlement is within 52 weeks of the claimant or his partner becoming a welfare to work beneficiary.

(5)   A person shall be deemed to fulfil the requirements of sub-paragraphs (1)(a) and (3), where–

(a)   he occupies the dwelling which he occupied on the relevant date;

(b)   this paragraph applied to the previous beneficiary on the relevant date, and

(c)   the requirements of sub-paragraphs (6) and (7) are satisfied in his case.

(6)   The requirements of this sub-paragraph are that the person was, on the relevant date–

(a)   the partner of the previous beneficiary; or

(b)   in a case where the previous beneficiary died on the relevant date, was a person to whom paragraph (10)(b), (c) or (d) of regulation 13 (restrictions on unreasonable rents), as specified in paragraph 5, applied and for the purposes of this sub-paragraph ''claimant'' in that paragraph of that regulation shall be taken to be a reference to the previous beneficiary.

(7)   The requirements of this sub-paragraph are that a claim for housing benefit is made within 4 weeks of the relevant date and where such a claim is made it shall be treated as having been made on the relevant date.

(8)   The eligible rent of a person to whom–

(a)   regulation 10A of and Schedule A1 to the Housing Benefit Regulations (entitlement to housing benefit by refugees), or, as the case may be,

(b)   regulation 10A of and Schedule A1 to the Housing Benefit (State Pension Credit) Regulations (entitlement to housing benefit by refugees)

apply, shall be determined in accordance with–

      (i)   regulations 12 (rent) and 13 (maximum rent) of the Housing Benefit Regulations, or, as the case may be,

      (ii)   regulations 12 (rent) and 13 (maximum rent) of the Housing Benefit (State Pension Credit) Regulations,

as set out in paragraph 5.

(9)   Sub-paragraphs (1) to (8) above shall continue to have effect in the case of a claimant who has ceased to be a welfare to work beneficiary or whose partner has ceased to be such a beneficiary where the claimant is entitled to housing benefit at the end of the 52 week period to which sub-paragraph (4)(c) refers.

(10)   In this paragraph–

"the first date" means 1st January 1996, except in a case to which sub-paragraph (5) applies, when it shall be the relevant date;

"the second date" means any day after the first date for which a claimant's entitlement to housing benefit is to be determined;

"exempt accommodation" means accommodation which is–

      (a)   a resettlement place provided by persons to whom the Secretary of State has given assistance by way of grant pursuant to section 30 of the Jobseekers Act 1995 (grants for resettlement places); and for this purpose "resettlement place" shall have the same meaning as it has in that section; or

      (b)   provided by a non-metropolitan county council in England within the meaning of section 1 of the Local Government Act 1972, a housing association, a registered charity or voluntary organisation where that body or a person acting on its behalf also provides the claimant with care, support or supervision;

"imprisoned" means detained in custody pending sentence upon conviction or under a sentence imposed by a court;

"previous beneficiary" means a person–

      (a)   who died, left the dwelling or was imprisoned, as the case may be;

      (b)   who was on that date in receipt of housing benefit or was on that date within 52 weeks of having become a welfare to work beneficiary; and

      (c)   to whom this regulation applied on that date;

and, in this paragraph, a reference to a person occupying a dwelling as his home shall be taken to include a person who is treated as occupying a dwelling as his home by virtue of regulation 7 of the Housing Benefit Regulations or, as the case may be, regulation 7 of the Housing Benefit (State Pension Credit) Regulations;

"the qualifying age for state pension credit" means (in accordance with section 1(2)(b) and (6) of the State Pension Credit Act 2002–

      (a)   in the case of a woman, pensionable age; or

      (b)   in the case of a man, the age which is pensionable age in the case of a woman born on the same day as the man;

"the relevant date" means the date–

      (a)   of the death of a previous beneficiary;

      (b)   on which a previous beneficiary who was the claimant's partner left the dwelling so that he and the claimant ceased to be living together as husband and wife; or

      (c)   on which a previous beneficiary, other than a beneficiary to whom regulation 7(13) of the Housing Benefit Regulations or, as the case may be, regulation 7(13) of the Housing Benefit (State Pension Credit) Regulations applied, was imprisoned, but only where on that date he was the partner of the claimant,

as the case may be;

"state pension credit" means state pension credit under the State Pension Credit Act 2002;

"welfare to work beneficiary" means a person to whom regulation 13A(1) of the Social Security (Incapacity for Work) (General) Regulations 1995 applies.

General Note

Reg 10 of the Housing Benefit (General) Amendment Regulations 1995 SI No 1644 provided important protection for existing claimants and their families (and for the residents of certain types of accommodation) from the rules on rent restrictions which were introduced on 2 January 1996. For those categories of claimant, see reg 11 HB Regs 1987 applied in its old form. This protection is now in para 4. For the purposes of para 4(1), the regs 12 and 13 of both the HB Regs and the HB(SPC) Regs to be applied are as set out in para 5 below.

Note that paras 4 and 5 are to be amended as the local housing allowance provisions are introduced nationwide between April 2008 and April 2009. At the time of writing, the amended rules were only available in draft form.

Analysis
Sub-paragraphs (1) and (3): Standard protection
The general rule, as set out in sub-para (1), is that there are two categories of claimants who have the benefit of transitional protection.

(1)   Those who have been continuously entitled to HB since 1 January 1996, and who fulfil other conditions: subpara (1)(a). Breaks in claim of up to four weeks are ignored: sub-para (3)(b)(ii). This is extended to 52 weeks if the claimant or her/his partner is a "welfare to work beneficiary" (WtWB), as defined in subpara (10): sub-paras (3)(b)(ii)and (4). WtWBs are broadly those who have stopped receiving benefits claimed on the basis of their incapacity for work to try out paid work or training. The rules allow the WtWB to return to the same level of benefit that s/he was receiving before starting the work or training, so long as this was within a 104 week linking period. See CPAG's *Welfare Benefits and Tax Credits Handbook* for further details.

Further conditions are set out in sub-para (3). The claimant must be occupying the same dwelling throughout the whole period, save for any period in which the dwelling was uninhabitable as a result of one of the disasters mentioned in sub-para (3)(a)(ii). If the dwelling is permanently uninhabitable then the transitional protection is presumably retained at the claimant's new property. If the property is repaired, it appears that the transitional protection is lost unless the claimant moves back. Clearly, a certain period of time will have to be allowed to enable her/him to move back in. Note that by virtue of sub-para (10), the question of whether a person can be treated as occupying a dwelling must be resolved by reference to reg 7 of both the HB Regs and the HB(SPC) Regs.

(2)   Those living in "exempt accommodation": sub-para (1)(b). See sub-para (10) for the definition. It is the dwelling occupied by the claimant as his home which must come within the definition of exempt accommodation. If a building contains two or more dwellings, the definition of "exempt accommodation" must be applied in relation to each dwelling, and not in relation to the building as a whole: *CH 1289/2007*.

Sub-paragraphs (5) to (7): Inherited protection
Under these provisions, a claimant is deemed to fall within category (1) above if s/he fulfils four conditions. The common theme is that the claimant takes over the protection from a "previous beneficiary" who was claiming in respect of the same home. That person must have died, left the dwelling or been imprisoned.

(1)   The claimant occupies the same dwelling as was occupied on the relevant date: sub-para (5)(a). "Relevant date" is defined in sub-para (10)

(2)   The previous beneficiary had the benefit of the transitional protection: sub-para (5)(b). It would appear that the previous beneficiary need not have fallen within the above two categories himself – it is sufficient if s/he also inherited the transitional protection under these provisions. An example will show how this might work. A and B were living in a property on 31 December 1995. A claimed HB. A then left B on 1 April 1996. B claimed HB herself. On 1 November 1997 C moved in with B. B dies on 1 January 1999. C is entitled to the transitional protection if he satisfies all the other conditions.

(3)   Under sub-para (6), the claimant must either have been the partner of the previous beneficiary or a person to whom para (10)(b), (c) or (d) of reg 13 as set out in para 5(2) below applied in relation to the previous beneficiary. See the Analysis of reg 13(11) HB Regs above, which refers to the same categories of person.

(4)   The claimant claims HB within four weeks of the relevant date: sub-para (7). The claim is then treated as made on the relevant date.

Sub-paragraph (10): Exempt accommodation
In *R(H) 2/07* Commissioner Turnbull concluded – when dealing with the same definition of exempt accommodation in regulation 10(6) of the Housing Benefit (General) Amendment Regulations 1995 (SI 1995/1644), which sub-para 10(b) replaces – that the definition does not extend to a situation where the accommodation provider (ie, the landlord) neither provides nor has provided on its behalf the care, support or supervision. The landlord must either actually provide the care itself or have contracted for it to be provided on its behalf. Accordingly if the care provider is not the landlord and instead has a contract with the local authority Supporting People section to provide support, the accommodation will not normally be exempt. The same commissioner in *R(H) 7/07*, emphasises that if the landlord is providing the care, support or supervision s/he need not be the main provider, nor must s/he be providing it pursuant to some contractual or statutory obligation; but the care support or supervision provided by the landlord must be more than a token or minimal amount.

In his interim decision in *CH 779/2007*, Commissioner Turnbull considered to what extent it is permissible to take into account support which is available to tenants generally, but not taken advantage of by a particular tenant. "Care" and "supervision" must actually be provided by the landlord. It is not enough that they are available should the tenant wish to call for them. However, it may be that the making available of certain types of service itself amounts to the provision of "support", but the support provided must be more than minimal. He said that there were at least two factors to which regard must be had. The first is the extent of the support services which are in reality available, having regard to the resources devoted by the landlord to providing the support and the number of tenants among whom those resources are spread. The second factor is the extent to which there is in practice any real likelihood that the claimant would need the available support.

In another decision, *CH 1289/2007*, Commissioner Turner said that the definition of "exempt accommodation" turns on whether the landlord provides "the claimant" with care, support or supervision. A claimant's accommodation will not be exempt if no (or only minimal) care, support or supervision is provided to her/him by the landlord, however much care, support or supervision may be provided to other tenants of the landlord. He pointed out that this "does not of course mean that it will always, or perhaps even usually, be necessary, in a case where a landlord has a number of tenants in a building (or even several buildings) to obtain and present evidence directed to the provision of care, support or supervision to each occupant individually. The landlord may be able to present evidence showing that the level of support provided is broadly similar in relation to all of them. Or there may be evidence of an assessment process whereby only applicants with at least a particular level of need are accepted as tenants."

5.–(1)   For the purposes of paragraph 4(1), regulation 12 of both the Housing Benefit Regulations and the Housing Benefit (State Pension Credit) Regulations is as follows–

''**Rent**

12.–(1) Subject to the following provision of this regulation, the payments in respect of which housing benefit is payable in the form of a rent rebate or allowance are the following periodical payments which a person is liable to make in respect of the dwelling which he occupies as his home–

(a)   payments of, or by way of, rent;

(b)   payments in respect of a licence or permission to occupy the dwelling;

(c)   payments by way of mesne profits or, in Scotland, violent profits;

(d)   payments in respect of, or in consequence of, use and occupation of the dwelling;

(e)   payments of, or by way of, service charges payment of which is a condition on which the right to occupy the dwelling depends;

(f)   mooring charges payable for a houseboat;

(g)   where the home is a caravan or a mobile home, payments in respect of the site on which it stands;

(h)   any contribution payable by a person resident in an almshouse provided by a housing association which is either a charity of which particulars are entered in the register of charities established under section 3 of the Charities Act 1993 (register of charities) or an exempt charity within the meaning of that Act, which is a contribution towards the cost of maintaining that association's almshouses and essential services in them;

(i)   payments under a rental purchase agreement, that is to say an agreement for the purchase of a dwelling which is a building or part of one under which the whole or part of the purchase price is to be paid in more than one instalment and the completion of the purchase is deferred until the whole or a specified part of the purchase price has been paid; and

(j)   where, in Scotland, the dwelling is situated on or pertains to a croft within the meaning of section 3(1) of the Crofters (Scotland) Act 1993, the payment in respect of the croft land.

(2)   A rent rebate or, as the case may be, a rent allowance shall not be payable in respect of the following periodical payments–

(a)   payments under a long tenancy except a shared ownership tenancy granted by a housing association or a housing authority;

(b)   payments under a co-ownership scheme;

(c)   payments by an owner;

(d)   payments under a hire purchase, credit sale or conditional sale agreement except to the extent the conditional sale agreement is in respect of land; and

(e)   payments by a Crown tenant.

(3)   Subject to any apportionment in accordance with paragraphs (4) and (5) and to regulations 13 and 13ZA (restrictions on unreasonable payments and rent increases), the amount of a person's eligible rent shall be the aggregate of such payments specified in paragraph (1) as he is liable to pay less–

(a)   except where he is separately liable for charges for water, sewerage or allied environmental services, an amount determined in accordance with paragraph (6);

(b)   where payments include service charges which are wholly or partly ineligible, an amount in respect of the ineligible charges determined in accordance with Schedule 1; and

(c)   where he is liable to make payments in respect of any service charges to which paragraph (1)(e) does not apply, but to which paragraph 3(2) of Schedule 1 (unreasonably low service charges) applies in the particular circumstances, an amount in respect of such charges determined in accordance with paragraph 3(2) of Schedule 1.

(4)   Where the payments specified in paragraph (1) are payable in respect of accommodation which consists partly of residential accommodation and partly of other accommodation, only such proportion

thereof as is referable to the residential accommodation shall count as eligible rent for the purposes of these Regulations.

(5)　　Where more than one person is liable to make payments in respect of a dwelling, the payments specified in paragraph (1) shall be apportioned for the purpose of calculating the eligible rent for each such person having regard to all the circumstances, in particular, the number of such persons and the proportion of rent paid by each such person.

(6)　　The amount of the deduction referred to in paragraph (3) shall be–

(a)　　except in a case to which sub-paragraph (c) applies, if the dwelling occupied by the claimant is a self-contained unit, the amount of the charges;

(b)　　in any other case except one to which sub-paragraph (c) applies, the proportion of those charges in respect of the self-contained unit, which is obtained by dividing the area of the dwelling occupied by the claimant by the area of the self-contained unit of which it forms part; or

(c)　　where the charges vary in accordance with the amount of water actually used, the amount which the appropriate authority considers to be fairly attributable to water and sewerage services, having regard to the actual or estimated consumption of the claimant.

(7)　　In this regulation and Schedule 1–

"service charges" means periodical payments for services, whether or not under the same agreement as that under which the dwelling is occupied, or whether or not such a charge is specified as separate from or separately identified within other payments made by the occupier in respect of the dwelling; and

"services" means services performed or facilities (including the use of furniture) provided for, or rights made available to, the occupier of a dwelling."

General Note

As noted above, reg 10 of SI 1995 No 1644 provided important protection for existing claimants and their families (and for the residents of certain types of accommodation) from the rules on rent restrictions which were introduced on 2 January 1996. For those categories of claimant, see reg 10 HB Regs 1987 applied in its old form. The old form of reg 10 is now provided in the version of reg 12 of both the HB Regs and the HB(SPC) Regs as set out in para 5(1). The reg is largely the same as the current version of both the reg 12 HB Regs and the HB(SPC) Regs, so reference to the commentary to in the HB Regs can be made. For:

Paras (1), (2), (4) to (6) and (8), see reg 12(1), (2), (4) to (6) and (8) HB Regs;

Para (3)(a) to (c), see reg 12(3)(b)(i) to (iii) HB Regs.

Note that under this version of reg 12, eligible rent is, subject any apportionment under paras (4) and (5), and to reg 13 (as set out in para 5(2)) and reg 13ZA (as set out in para 5(3)), the aggregate of the payments specified in para (1), less the charges set out in para (3)(a)-(c).

---

(2)　　For the purposes of paragraph 4(1), regulation 13 of both the Housing Benefit Regulations and the Housing Benefit (State Pension Credit) Regulations is as follows–

"**Restrictions on unreasonable payments**

13.–(1)　　Where a rent is registered in respect of a dwelling under Part 4 or 5 of the Rent Act 1977 or Part 4 or 7 of the Rent (Scotland) Act 1984 and the rent recoverable from a claimant is limited to the rent so registered, his eligible rent determined in accordance with regulation 12 (rent) shall not exceed the rent so registered.

(2)　　Where a rent has been determined by a rent assessment committee in respect of a dwelling under Part 1 of the Housing Act 1988 or Part 2 of the Housing (Scotland) Act 1988, the claimant's eligible rent determined in accordance with regulation 12 shall not exceed the rent determined by the committee during the twelve months beginning with the first day on which that determination had effect.

(3)　　The relevant authority shall consider–

(a)　　whether by reference to a determination or re-determination made by a rent officer in exercise of a function conferred on him by an order under section 122 of the Housing Act 1996 or otherwise, whether a claimant occupies a dwelling larger than is reasonably required by him and others who also occupy that dwelling (including any non-dependants of his and any person paying rent to him) having regard in particular to suitable alternative accommodation occupied by a household of the same size; or

(b)　　whether by reference to a determination or re-determination made by a rent officer in exercise of a function conferred on him by an order under section 122 of the Housing Act 1996 or otherwise, whether the rent payable for his dwelling is unreasonably high by comparison with the rent payable in respect of suitable alternative accommodation elsewhere,

and, where it appears to the authority that the dwelling is larger than is reasonably required or that the rent is unreasonably high, the authority shall, subject to paragraphs (4) to (7), treat the claimant's eligible rent, as reduced by such amount as it considers appropriate having regard in particular to the cost of suitable alternative accommodation elsewhere and the claimant's maximum housing benefit shall be calculated by reference to the eligible rent as so reduced.

(4)   If any person to whom paragraph (10) applies–

(a)   is aged 60 or over; or

(b)   is incapable of work for the purposes of one or more of the provisions of the Social Security Act, or Part 2 of the Act; or

(c)   is treated as capable of work in accordance with regulations made under section 171E of the Act; or

(d)   is a member of the same household as a child or young person for whom he or his partner is responsible,

no deduction shall be made under paragraph (3) unless suitable cheaper alternative accommodation is available and the authority considers that, taking into account the relevant factors, it is reasonable to expect the claimant to move from his present accommodation.

(5)   No deduction shall be made under paragraph (3) for a period of 12 months from the date of death of any person to whom paragraph (10) applied or, had a claim been made, would have applied, if the dwelling which the claimant occupies is the same as that occupied by him at that date except where the deduction began before the death occurred.

(6)   For the purposes of paragraph (5), a claimant shall be treated as occupying the dwelling if paragraph (13) of regulation 7 (circumstances in which a person is to be treated as occupying a dwelling) is satisfied and for that purpose sub-paragraph (b) of that paragraph shall be treated as if it were omitted.

(7)   Without prejudice to the operation of paragraph (4), but subject to paragraph (8), where the relevant authority is satisfied that a person to whom paragraph (10) applies was able to meet the financial commitments for his dwelling when they were entered into, no deduction shall be made under paragraph (3) during the first 13 benefit weeks of the claimant's award of housing benefit.

(8)   Paragraph (7) shall not apply where a claimant was previously entitled to benefit in respect of an award of housing benefit which fell wholly or partly less than 52 weeks before the commencement of his current award of housing benefit.

(9)   For the purposes of this regulation–

(a)   in deciding what is suitable alternative accommodation, the relevant authority shall take account of the nature of the alternative accommodation and the facilities provided having regard to the age and state of health of all the persons to whom paragraph (10) applies and, in particular, where a claimant's present dwelling is occupied with security of tenure, accommodation shall not be treated as suitable alternative accommodation unless that accommodation will be occupied on terms which will afford security of tenure reasonably equivalent to that presently enjoyed by the claimant; and

(b)   the relevant factors in paragraph (4) are the effects of a move to alternative accommodation on–

(i)   the claimant's prospects of retaining his employment; and

(ii)   the education of any child or young person referred to in paragraph (4)(d) if such a move were to result in a change of school.

(10)   This paragraph applies to the following persons–

(a)   the claimant;

(b)   any member of his family;

(c)   if the claimant is a member of a polygamous marriage, any partners of his and any child or young person for whom he or a partner is responsible and who is a member of the same household;

(d)   subject to paragraph (11), any relative of the claimant or his partner who occupies the same dwelling as the claimant, whether or not they reside with him.

(11)   Paragraph (10)(d) shall only apply to a relative who has no separate right of occupation of the dwelling which would enable him to continue to occupy it even if the claimant ceased his occupation of it.''

General Note

As noted above, reg 10 of SI 1995 No 1644 provided important protection for existing claimants and their families (and for the residents of certain types of accommodation) from the rules on rent restrictions which were introduced on 2 January 1996. For those categories of claimant, see reg 11 HB Regs 1987 applied in its old form. The old form of reg 11 is now provided in the version of reg 13 of both the HB Regs and the HB(SPC) Regs as set out in para 5(2).

Analysis of reg 13 as set out in para 5(2)

Much of the large body of caselaw concerned with the old reg 11 HB Regs 1987 consists of cases decided on the facts and evidence before the court. However, many of these offer useful illustrations of the approach of the court.

Paragraphs (1) and (2): Set rents

Para (1) only affects tenancies created before 15 January 1989 or, in Scotland, 2 January 1989. The Rent Acts do not apply to any tenancies created after those dates. Where they do apply – and a rent has been registered – the tenant is not legally liable to pay the landlord more than the registered rent so the eligible rent could never exceed the registered rent in any event. This paragraph merely makes that explicit.

A register of the accommodation in respect of which a fair rent has been registered in any particular area is maintained by the local rent officer and is open to public inspection.

If a "fair rent" has been registered but the authority uses its powers under para (3) to restrict the eligible rent to a lower figure, the tenant remains liable to the landlord for the balance. This is unlikely to happen in practice unless the claimant's accommodation is unreasonably large under sub-para (3)(a).

Para (2). Rent Assessment Committees have the power to assess market rents for certain assured and assured shorthold tenancies under the Housing Act 1988. These will have been created on or after 15 January 1989 or, in Scotland, 2 January 1989. The restriction of eligible rent imposed by this paragraph lasts only for 12 months from the time when the Committee's determination first takes effect. Again, this requirement is in addition to the general power under para (3).

Paragraph (3): Introduction
The scope of this provision has been the main battleground in judicial review proceedings and it requires careful application by authorities. The duty imposed on authorities by this paragraph is to consider whether the circumstances of the tenancy are such as are set out in sub-paras (a) or (b) and, if so, to reduce the eligible rent by an amount which it "considers appropriate having regard in particular to the cost of suitable alternative accommodation elsewhere".

It is plain from the word "or" that appears at the end of sub-para (a) that the authority is obliged to reduce the claimant's eligible rent if either of the sub-paras is satisfied. It is not necessary that both should be satisfied: *R v Kensington and Chelsea RBC ex p Pirie* [1997] unreported, 26 March, QBD.

Once it is shown that one of the sub-paras is applicable, before reducing the eligible rent the authority should be sure that it has given proper consideration to the limiting provisions in paras (4) to (8). For a discussion as to what "suitable alternative accommodation" is and the evidence that must be produced by the authority, see the Analysis to para (9)(a) below.

Paragraph (3)(a): Size of the accommodation
The authority must consider whether that accommodation is "larger than is reasonably required" by the claimant's household. In reaching this decision, the authority must have regard to any suitable alternative accommodation occupied by a "household of the same size". The use of the phrases "or otherwise" and "in particular" make it clear that other factors may also be relevant. Some assistance may be obtained from the size criteria set out in Sch 2 of the Rent Officers (Housing Benefit Functions) Order 1997 and its Scottish equivalent, but the regulation requires a more general approach and the particular needs of any person in the house need close consideration. For the importance of the rent officer's determination generally, see the Analysis to para (3)(b) below.

In *Pirie* it was confirmed that the word "required" means "needed" and not, as the claimant suggested "demanded" (transcript at 2F-3B).

Although the regulation refers to the comparison being with alternative accommodation "occupied by a household of the same size", it is suggested that "household" in this context cannot be restricted to its normal meaning in social security law, which requires a degree of financial and social interdependence between the members of the household: see the Analysis to SSCBA s137. This is because the regulation provides that the requirements of others occupying the dwelling are to be taken into account, including non-dependants and lodgers, which need not be living in the same "household" as the claimant. The comparison must be with alternative accommodation which is suitable for that group, not with a narrower group comprised simply of the claimant and the members of her/his household within the dwelling.

Paragraph (3)(b): Cost of the accommodation
The authority is told to consider whether the claimant's rent "is unreasonably high by comparison with the rent payable in respect of suitable alternative accommodation elsewhere". "Rent" for these purposes includes all payments eligible under reg 12: *R v Beverley DC HBRB ex p Hare* [1995] 27 HLR 637, QBD.

In determining the application of para (3)(b), a number of principles can be derived from the authorities and are set out below.

The rent must be "unreasonably" higher. The question is not whether the restricted rent is reasonable but whether the full rent is unreasonably higher than rents for comparable properties. In any market for rented property there will be a range of rents which are being charged for similar properties. The fact that one such rent is higher than another does not per se make the former rent unreasonably high. That conclusion can only be justified if the rent is beyond the top end of the range of rents which a landlord might reasonably charge.

Authority for this approach may be found in the decision of Lord Clyde in *Malcolm v Tweeddale District HBRB* [1994] SLT 1212, CS(OH). Discussing the examples of alternative accommodation provided to the Board by the authority, Lord Clyde said at 1215E-G:

"Even if the examples given were of comparable accommodation and even if the rents quoted were reasonable, it does not follow that the petitioner's rent, although higher, was unreasonably high. There may well be a band of rentals within which all may be reasonable. That one is higher than the others does not necessarily mean that it is unreasonably higher."

On this point *Malcolm* followed the earlier decision of Lord Weir in *McLeod v HBRB for Banff and Buchan District HBRB* [1988] SLT 753, CS(OH). Although these were Scottish cases and the former was concerned with the meaning of a pre-1987 predecessor of the old reg 11 rather than this version of reg 13, they should be treated as highly persuasive authority in England and Wales. *McLeod*, in particular, has been cited with approval by Hutchison J in *R v Sefton MBC ex p Cunningham* [1991] 23 HLR 534 at 538, QBD and by the Court of Appeal in *R v East Devon DC HBRB ex p Gibson* [1993] 25 HLR, CA although in the latter case it was suggested that in some respects the test which *McLeod* imposes may be "higher than the statute strictly requires".

The comparison is with the range of rents charged for alternative accommodation. This is another point originating in the judgment of Lord Weir in *McLeod*. The Review Board in that case had decided that because the claimant's rent was higher than the lowest rents charged for suitable alternative accommodation, it was entitled to apply the regulation then being considered (under the pre-1988 HB scheme). Lord Weir made it clear, at 756C, that this approach was incorrect and that there had to be an "overall examination of the spectrum of rents".

It follows from this that where it is demonstrated that the claimant's rent falls into the "spectrum of rents" charged elsewhere, it will be impossible for the authority to conclude rationally that para (3)(b) is applicable. In one of the cases heard together in *R v Coventry CC ex p Waite* [1995] unreported, 7 July, QBD, the bracket of comparable rents was said to be £25 to £37. The claimant's rent was £37. A finding that the rent was unreasonably high was quashed. In *R v Kensington and Chelsea RBC ex p Abou-Jaoude* (1996) unreported, 10 May, QBD, the evidence before the Review Board was that two-thirds of comparable properties had rents of below £240 and the rest had higher rents. The claimant's rent was £275, but Turner J held that in the absence of more detail of the rents payable under the more expensive comparators, it was impossible to conclude that his rent was unreasonably high.

The combination of the first two principles produces the result that even if the claimant's rent is in excess of the top end of the spectrum of rents, a conclusion that the rent was unreasonably high will still not be justified where the difference is small: *Waite* (transcript at 31F-G).

The local authority's financial position is irrelevant. The use of concepts of "reasonableness" and "appropriateness" in para (3) mean that the decision to be made by the authority does contain elements of discretion and judgment. However, this discretion is a narrow one and the only factors which are relevant to its exercise are those which relate to the personal circumstances of the claimant and her/his household and the existence and state of the market in suitable alternative accommodation. Successive Subsidy Orders have contained strong incentives to authorities to restrict eligible rents to a "threshold" level or to the level specified in the rent officer's determination and authorities have often succumbed to the temptation to do so, some even adopting formal policies to this effect.

However tempting this may be for authorities, it is clear from the case of *R v Brent LBC HBRB ex p Connery* [1989] 22 HLR 40 at 44, QBD, that to take the amount of subsidy payable into consideration under sub-paras (a) or (b) is impermissible.

The role of the rent officer's determination. On one reading of sub-paras (a) and (b), the authority would seem to be entitled to make decisions under those sub-paragraphs solely "by reference to" a determination under s122 Housing Act 1996 (or its Scottish equivalent). However, such a conclusion cannot always be reconciled with the terms of the Rent Officers (Housing Benefit Functions) Orders made under those sections.

For example, Art 3 and Sch 1 para 1 obliges rent officers to make a "rent determination" as to whether the rent "is significantly higher than the rent which the landlord might reasonably have been expected to obtain from the tenancy at that time" having regard to "the level of rent under similar tenancies of similar dwellings in the vicinity" but on the assumption that no-one who would have been entitled to HB has sought or is seeking the tenancy. The following points need to be made:

(1)   A "significantly high" rent is not necessarily the same as an "unreasonably high" one.

(2)   "Similar" accommodation is not necessarily the same as "suitable" alternative accommodation: the former concept does not pay as much regard to the individual circumstances of the claimant and her/his household as the latter, and those circumstances are directly relevant to the decision to be made by the authority under para (3).

(3)   As the rent officer's determination is predominantly for subsidy purposes, it includes an artificial assumption as to the type of tenant who is seeking the tenancy which is not reflected in the real world. The result is that the rent officer's determination is unlikely ever to be the same as an actual market rent. Under reg 13(3) no such assumption is made and, as stated above, it is impermissible to take subsidy considerations into account when reaching decisions under sub-paras (a) and (b).

Although, the link between a rent officer determination and an unreasonably high rent may be stronger if the rent officer makes an exceptionally high rent determination (the assumptions underlying the determination are different and an "exceptionally" high rent is more likely to be unreasonably high than a "significantly" high one) the distinction between "suitable" and "similar" accommodation still remains. In these circumstances, it is inconceivable that an authority could in practice be satisfied of all matters which must be established before applying para (3) simply on the basis of a rent officer's significantly high rent determination.

It follows that, while an authority may have regard to such a determination in reaching its decision, the simple fact that the reasonable rent determined by the rent officer is lower than the contractual rent is not sufficient on its own to justify a reduction under sub-para (b).

This is supported by *R v Coventry CC ex p Waite* (1995) unreported, 7 October, QBD. However, it is clear that the rent officer's determination will often be a factor of great weight and may be conclusive in some cases: *Waite; R v East Devon DC HBRB ex p Gibson* [1993] 25 HLR, CA. In the absence of any evidence to the contrary, it is to be assumed that the rent officer is doing her/his job properly and the local authority may simply produce the determinations to a Review Board: *R v Manchester CC ex p Harcup* [1993] 26 HLR 402 at 408, QBD; *R v Kensington and Chelsea RBC ex p Pirie* [1997] unreported, 26 March, QBD.

In *R v Sandwell MBC ex p Wilkinson* [1998] 31 HLR 22, QBD, Laws J emphasised the separation of the functions of the Rent Officer and the Review Board in determining whether a claimant's rent should be restricted under the old reg 11. He robustly rejected criticisms of the way in which the rent officer had made his recommendations, both on the basis that his decision was not the subject-matter of the application for judicial review and because, as he correctly pointed out, the valuation was only "a starting point for the Board to consider". He further confirmed that in any case, authorities concerning the duties of Rent Officers and Rent Assessment Committees under the Rent Act 1977 and the Housing Act 1988 were of no assistance in examining whether the correct approach had been taken to a determination for HB purposes for the purposes of the old reg 11.

Suitable alternative accommodation. For the meaning of this phrase, see the Analysis to para (9)(a) below.

The approach of tribunals. Many of the cases brought against Review Boards under the old reg 11 have complained (often successfully) of failures on the part of the Boards to comply with their statutory obligations to make findings of fact and give full reasons under the former reg 83(4) HB Regs 1987. As with other areas of the Regulations which are particularly replete with pitfalls, a systematic approach will assist a tribunal considering a case under para (3)(b). One such approach was that put forward by Schiemann J in *R v Beverley DC HBRB ex p Hare* [1995] 27 HLR 637, QBD. It involves six stages.

(1)   Establish the rent, in the wide definition including all of the elements which are set out in reg 12(1), for the current dwelling: reg 12 as set out in para 5(1) above.

(2)   Indicate what type of accommodation is regarded as a suitable alternative (this involves expressing a view on what services are necessary for this particular claimant).

(3)   Indicate the rent (in the wide sense) which is considered to be payable in respect of such accommodation.

(4)   Find whether the rent (in the wide sense) is unreasonably high in comparison with the rent payable in respect of suitable alternative accommodation elsewhere.

(5)   If so, indicate the reduction found appropriate.

(6)   Indicate how the tribunal arrived at that amount.

Paragraph (3): Making the reduction

Once it has been established that either sub-para (a) or (b) is applicable, the question of the amount of the reduction needs to be considered. As originally enacted, the paragraph did not oblige authorities to reduce the claimant's eligible rent but merely gave them a discretion to do so where one of the sub-paras applied. However, that discretion was removed by SI 1991 No 235 with effect from 1 April 1991 and the authority must reduce the eligible rent. Previous editions have suggested that the authority could elect to impose a nil reduction. However, it does not appear that this is an option open to the authority in view of the removal of the discretion not to apply a reduction, though Collins J thought, without resolving the point, that this was a possible construction: *R v Coventry CC ex p Waite* [1995] unreported, 7 July, QBD (transcript at 28B-29B). However, substantially the same effect could be achieved in an appropriate case by imposing a nominal reduction, such as one penny.

In determining the appropriate reduction, the authority may have regard to its financial position: *R v Brent LBC HBRB ex p Connery* [1989] 22 HLR 40 at 44, QBD. However, *Connery* also makes it clear that the rent may not be reduced below the level paid for suitable alternative accommodation. Neither, it is suggested, will an authority normally be justified in reducing the eligible rent to a figure at the bottom of the rental brackets. A rough average ought to be the starting point.

The language of the closing words to reg 13(3) makes it clear that any relevant factors may be taken into account in determining the level to which the claimant's rent should be reduced. The "relevant factors" listed in para (9)(b) may also be relevant here, as may other factors which exist in individual cases. The fact that the authority must consider all relevant factors when deciding whether to reduce the claimant's eligible rent and if so, by how much, was confirmed in *R v Westminster CC HBRB ex p Mehanne* [1999] 2 All ER 319, CA. Although the cost of suitable accommodation elsewhere was "singled out for special mention and is thereby given the status of a mandatory consideration which carries the most weight", other factors could be taken into account. In particular, the pregnancy of the claimant's wife, his difficulty in obtaining other accommodation and the consequences of having to move from his present home were all matters relevant to the claimant's ability to pay his rent and so should have been considered by the Review Board. *The House of Lords* [2001] 1 WLR 539 unanimously dismissed the authority's appeal. Lord Bingham and Lord Hope, who gave the two substantial speeches, both emphasised the generality of the language in the then para (2) (now para (3)) and the breadth of the discretion thereby conferred, along with the purpose of the HB Regs as being to prevent homelessness: see paras 13 and 24-26 at 546B-C, 548E-549E.

A tribunal must consider the amount of the reduction to be made and give reasons for its decision, or it will err in law: *CH 4970/2002* para 14.

Paragraph (4): Vulnerable families

Para (4) modifies the application of para (3) so as to forbid any reduction unless certain factors are shown to be present. A local authority should consider three questions.

Is there a relevant vulnerable person? Anyone falling within those categories of person set out in para (10) needs to be considered. The categories are exactly the same as those provided for in 13(16) of both the HB Regs and the HB(SPC) Regs and reference should be made to the Analysis of reg 13(11) HB Regs for a discussion.

A relevant person is "vulnerable" if s/he falls into any of the categories of person set out in the four sub-paras in para (4). "Vulnerable" is not a term used by the regulations but is simply used here as a convenient label. The categories are as follows:

(1)   Those aged 60 or over: sub-para (a).
(2)   Those that are incapable of work: sub-para (b). The test for incapacity for work is that which arises under the current incapacity for work regime rather than the law which was in place to determine this question when reg 11(3)(b) HB Regs 1987 (now this version of reg 13(4(b) HB Regs) was originally enacted: *R(H) 3/06* (para 15). That decision also decides that, because of the terms of reg 11 of the Social Security and Child Support (Decisions and Appeals) Regulations 1999, it is for the Secretary of State (ie, the DWP) to determine whether the claimant is incapable of work (under Part XIIA of the SSCBA 1992); it is not a matter which the housing benefit decision maker can determine.
(3)   Those who are only to be treated as capable of work because they have been disqualified from receipt of incapacity benefit: sub-para (c). Disqualification can be made for up to six weeks under reg 18 of the Social Security (Incapacity for Work) (General) Regulations 1995 on the grounds set out in that provision. The effect of this sub-para is that such disqualification does not prevent the claimant falling within the scope of para (4).
(4)   Those that are responsible for a child or young person who is a member of the same houshold: sub-para (d). For the question of whether a relevant person is responsible for a child or young person, see reg 20 of both the HB and the HB(SPC) Regs.

Is suitable alternative accommodation available? This question is discussed in the Analysis to para (9)(a) below.

Is it reasonable to expect the claimant to move? This question must be considered separately by the authority, and if a tribunal fails to mention it in its decision, it will be presumed not to have applied its mind to it: *R v Sefton MBC ex p Cunningham* [1991] 23 HLR 534 at 538, QBD; *R v Allerdale DC HBRB ex p Doughty* [2000] COD 462, QBD. The question must be determined "taking into account the relevant factors". These are those set out in para (9)(b) and are the following:

(1)   The effect of a move on claimant's prospects of retaining her/his employment: sub-para (b)(i).
(2)   The effect on any child taken into account under the third category of relevant person in relation to her/his education. This factor appears only to be relevant if the move would force a change of school. In *R v Kensington and Chelsea RBC ex p Sheikh* [1997] unreported, 14 January, QBD a Review Board came to the conclusion that even if the applicant was forced to move to the other side of London, travel arrangements could be made to enable the applicant's child to remain at her school. Latham J described this conclusion as "not very sensible" but decided that enough consideration had been given to the effect of a move on the child.

Can other factors be taken into account?

In *R v Kensington and Chelsea RBC ex p Carney* [1997] COD 124 at 125, QBD, Carnwath J decided that only the two factors in the then para (6)(b) (now para (9)(b)) were relevant. The medical evidence produced by the applicant in that case to the effect that a move would have a detrimental effect on her health could not therefore be relied upon. The same conclusion was reached by Buxton J in *R v Oadby and Wigston DC ex p Dickman* [1995] 28 HLR 807 at 817. He pointed to the fact that the then para (3) (now para (4)) referred to "the relevant factors" and suggested that the intention was to determine what was relevant and what was not relevant.

In *R v Camden LBC HBRB ex p W* (unreported) 21 May 1999, QBD (Turner J), a case concerning an HIV-positive claimant, the judge, referring to the old reg 11 HB Regs 1987, decided that "reasonableness as to the expectation that the applicant should move finds no place in the authority's determination, unless reg 11(6)(b) is satisfied". In support of the decisions in these cases, a contrast can usefully be made with Sch 3 para 13(5) of the Income Support (General) Regulations 1987, which is cast in substantially wider terms than para (9)(b).

The decision in *ex p W* was upheld by the Court of Appeal (1999) 32 HLR 879. The Court held that only the two factors set out in the then para (6)(b) of old reg 11 (now para (9)(b)) may be considered by the authority in deciding whether it is reasonable for the claimant to move.

"As both of those counsel [for the authority and the Secretary of State] submit, credible reasons why a claimant cannot move can properly be considered under other aspects of regulation 11. That, as it seems to me, is a powerful argument. In my judgment, [counsel for the authority and the Secretary of State] are right in relation to this issue of construction. The authority can only properly conclude that it is reasonable to expect the claimant to move if it has regard to relevant factors and not to irrelevant ones. Paragraph 11(6)(b) sets out what, for the purposes of paragraph 11(3) are 'the relevant factors'. The use of the definite article in both paragraphs is important. It makes it clear that all other factors are irrelevant .... the closely confined wording of regulation 11(3) can be contrasted with the more open wording of regulation 11(2) where the authority makes its decision 'having regard in particular to ....'. Clearly the draftsman was well able to qualify an obligation when he chose to do so, but in the subsequent paragraph he deliberately chose precise words."

This decision must be treated as authoritatively resolving the question of whether other factors besides those set out in para (9)(b) can be taken into account. However, it is suggested that it is highly arguable that these cases were wrongly decided on this point. The use of the words "taking into account" would certainly suggest that other factors may be relevant. Schiemann J expressed doubts about the correctness of the position set out in the previous paragraph in *R v Canterbury CC ex p Woodhouse* [1994] unreported, 2 August, QBD. Moreover, the decisions are arguably inconsistent with the decision of the Court of Appeal in *R v Westminster CC HBRB ex p Mehanne* [1999] 2 All ER 319, CA (see the Analysis to para (3) above). The court's conclusion in *Mehanne* was that the words "having regard to" did not require only the factors set out in para (3) to be considered, merely that those factors were to be regarded as being particularly persuasive. There is, it is suggested, no difference between the wording used in the two sections. The fact that certain matters are to be considered to be relevant does not mean that other matters are necessarily irrelevant. In *R v Allerdale DC HBRB ex p Doughty* [2000] COD 462, QBD, Elias J gave powerful reasons why the analysis in *Carney* and *Dickman* should not be followed (paras 58 to 64). However, it appears that the decision of the Court of Appeal in *ex p W* was not cited and therefore his reasoning should not be adopted by authorities or tribunals, unless the House of Lords ever has occasion to pronounce on the matter.

However, there is comfort for claimants in the acknowledgment by the Court of Appeal, dealing with the old reg 11 in *ex p W*, that "credible reasons why a claimant cannot move can properly be considered under other aspects of regulation 11". It is suggested that the Court is here referring to the question of whether the alternative accommodation identified by the council is in truth suitable. If the claimant cannot move, alternative accommodation cannot be suitable for him. The Court is thereby effectively approving the approach taken in *R v Westminster CC HBRB ex p Pallas* (1997) unreported, 23 September, QBD discussed in the Analysis to para (9)(a) below. If correct, this allows the interpretation of para (6)(b) (now para (9)(b)) propounded in *Carney, Dickman* and *ex p W* to be avoided.

Paragraphs (5) to (8): Temporary disapplication

These provisions allow for the effect of para (3) to be temporarily postponed in two circumstances:

(1)   Where the claimant has been bereaved and occupies the same dwelling as s/he did before the relevant death: paras (5) and (6). These provisions are identical to those in the current reg 13(11) and (12) of both the HB Regs and the HB(SPC) Regs, save that the effect is to prevent a deduction under para (3), rather than altering the calculation of the maximum rent.

(2)   Where the financial expenditure in relation to the property could have been met by a relevant person when it was taken on: paras (7) and (8). This has a similar effect to the the current reg 13(14) and (15) of both the HB Regs and the HB(SPC) Regs.

See the Analysis to the current reg 13 HB Regs above for details of how these provisions operate.

Paragraph (9)(a): Suitable alternative accommodation

This phrase occurs at several places in the regulation. The wording used is not always consistent. The basic concepts that must be applied, however, remain the same throughout.

Para (9)(a) does not purport to provide an exclusive definition of "suitable alternative accommodation". Thus other factors may be taken into account, though if the factors mentioned give rise to a satisfactory result, the accommodation will *prima facie* be considered to be suitable: *R v Waltham Forest LBC ex p Holder* [1996] 29 HLR 71 at 78-9. In *R v Slough BC ex p Green* [1996] unreported, 15 November, QBD, Collins J referred to the phrase as "a composite phrase .... the Court in construing it must indeed give appropriate weight to each of the words that are used". The factors specifically mentioned in para (9)(a) relate mainly to the question of suitability. It is worth making the point, however, that the accommodation must be "alternative", that is accommodation other than the present accommodation: *R v East Devon DC HBRB ex p Gibson* [1993] 25 HLR, CA.

The question for consideration is whether alternative accommodation is suitable for the claimant. In *R v Canterbury CC ex p Woodhouse* [1994] unreported, 2 August, QBD, the applicants were a brother and sister who occupied a two-bedroom flat together. They had separate tenancy agreements under which both paid £299 per month rent. Both claimed HB to meet their rent. The only evidence of suitable alternative accommodation before the Review Board was that of one two-bedroom flat for rent at £380 per month. The Board's approach was to treat the applicants as paying a combined rent of nearly £600, and reduced their HB entitlement accordingly. Schiemann J held that this approach was erroneous (transcript at 13A-14A) and that each claimant had to be viewed as an individual, despite their close relationship. However, he pointed out that in view of this conclusion, the authority would have been entitled to compare the rent paid with comparable one-bedroom flats.

R(H) 2/05 concludes that the wording of old reg 11(6)(a) (now reg 13(9)(a)), and particularly the use of the word "shall", means that the authority must actually take each of the relevant factors below into account in every case and is not entitled to assume that they are met unless the claimant specifically raises them. That is, the onus of proof rests with the local authority. However, he went on:

"In the case of a claimant who is elderly, for example, it may be sufficient for the authority to show that there is a supply of accommodation to rent designed or adapted for elderly residents, and in such a case it will not be necessary for the authority to identify any specific properties actually available for occupation by the claimant": para 18.

Relevant Factors in Deciding Suitability. Bearing those general observations in mind, the factors in determining whether accommodation is suitable for the claimant include the following:

(1)   ".... the nature of the .... accommodation". This would encompass matters that do not relate so much to the facilities available, but have more to do with whether it comprises a flat, maisonette or house, the arrangement of the rooms, and the standard of repair it is in. For example, if a claimant was unable to walk, accommodation containing one toilet accessible only up a flight of stairs could not be said to be suitable.

(2)   ".... the facilities provided ....". Sufficient detail must be provided by the local authority to enable it to be demonstrated that the facilities are broadly comparable. In *R v Lambeth LBC HBRB ex p Harrington* [1996] unreported 22 November, QBD, the Board's decision was quashed because the comparable bed and breakfast accommodation was only specified to have heating, furnishings and a lounge available, which was insufficient (transcript at 17B-18D). See also *Malcolm v Tweeddale District HBRB* [1994] SLT 1212, CS(OH).

(3)   ".... the age and state of health of all the persons to whom paragraph (10) applies ....". For the identity of these people, see the Analysis to the current reg 13(16) HB Regs above.

(4)   ".... security of tenure reasonably equivalent ....". This is to be regarded as a particularly important factor. An assured shorthold tenancy is not to be regarded as "reasonably equivalent" to an assured tenancy: *R v Coventry CC ex p Waite* (1995) unreported, 7 October, QBD (transcript at 29B-G); *R v Kensington and Chelsea RBC ex p Pirie* [1997] unreported, 26 March, QBD (transcript at 4D-E). Nor should an assured tenancy be viewed as being equivalent to a protected tenancy under the Rent Acts: the rent control is much less strict and the grounds for seeking possession less onerous. There is a conflict of authorities on whether public sector tenancies can be taken into account when the claimant is a private sector tenant. In *McLeod v HBRB for Banff and Buchan District HBRB* [1988] SLT 753, CS(OH), it was suggested that this was possible but Collins J dissented from this view in *Waite* at 30E-G. However, in *R(H) 2/05* the commissioner rejected an argument that it is necessary for a local authority to show a mix of public and private sector tenancies in order to show an "active market" in houses of the appropriate type (para 15) in a case involving a private sector tenancy. Different durations of assured shorthold tenancies may be permissible: *R v Sefton MBC HBRB ex p Brennan* [1996] 29 HLR 735 at 741, QBD ("very difficult" to see how six to 12 month tenancy equivalent to five year tenancy, though decision not perverse); *R v Kensington and Chelsea RBC ex p Sheikh* [1997] unreported, 14 January, QBD (six month tenancy equivalent to three year

tenancy). Latham J in the latter case said (transcript at 14F-15B) that the words "security of tenure" were concerned not with the length of the tenancy but with the claimant's rights to resist possession. Such a narrow construction seems at odds with the general wording of the paragraph.

(5)   Size of the accommodation. In *Sheikh*, a claimant had been living with a friend in a three bedroom flat, and then moved to a two bedroom property to relieve financial difficulties. It was held that in the circumstances, the local authority should have considered some three bedroom flats in their comparison (transcript at 20A-22C). Some flexibility therefore needs to be shown.

(6)   Area covered by the comparators. In *Holder*, it was said that the alternative accommodation had to be reasonably local. That does not mean, however, that it has to be within the same borough, at any rate in London: *Sheikh* (transcript at 15C-16B). 1997 GM A4.1172 stated that alternative accommodation need not necessarily be "in the same immediate area as the current accommodation. You may, if you consider it appropriate, compare the current accommodation with the cost of similar accommodation outside your authority's area if that would be suitable for the claimant's needs. This might be appropriate when it is not possible to make valid comparisons with accommodation within your area. However, do not make comparisons with other parts of the country where accommodation costs differ widely from those which apply locally."

(7)   The effect of a move on the claimant. In *Pallas* there was evidence before the Board from the claimant's GP that moving house would cause grave risk to his health. The claimant suffered from chronic heart disease. George Bartlett QC, sitting as a deputy judge, held that "if there is evidence that moving to other accommodation would be likely to give rise to the risk of the claimant's death, that is a material consideration for the purposes of deciding whether suitable alternative accommodation exists".

One factor which the local authority may leave out of account is the fact that claimants will usually have taken on a liability for rent which, if their eligible rent is reduced, they will not be in a position to meet and that no other accommodation is therefore "available" or "suitable" for the claimant. That would deprive the this regulation of any real effect: *Woodhouse* (transcript at 15E-G)

Evidence of comparable accommodation. One of the most controversial issues is the type of evidence that has to be produced by the local authority relating to the alternative accommodation. It was argued that it was necessary to identify specific comparable properties. That was accepted, at least implicitly, in *Malcolm*. However, the argument was categorically rejected by the Court of Appeal in *Gibson*. Referring to the old reg 11, Lord Bingham MR stated at 494:

"It is not part of the local authority's function and no part of the Review Board's function to identify specific property available for a recipient's occupation . . . Neither the local authority nor the Review Board is an accommodation agency; neither of them can be expected to assume what would be an inappropriate role. A situation should never arise, therefore, where the local authority or the Review Board is in the position of saying: 'Number 3, Laburnum Avenue is the same size as the house you are now occupying, it is available for letting at a rent substantially below what you are now paying; why do you not move there?' That would, as I say, be an entirely inappropriate approach to this matter. Moreover, it must be borne in mind that details of payment of HB are confidential matters and it can therefore never be incumbent on local authorities to disclose the names or addresses of beneficiaries to whom the benefit is paid. It is, in my judgment, quite sufficient if an active market is shown to exist in houses of the appropriate type in an appropriate place at the level of rent to which rent is restricted. There must, however, be evidence at least of that in a case falling within paragraph 11(3); otherwise the recipient, if he had to move, would have nowhere to go. It is, however, sufficient, as I wish to stress, to point to a range of properties, or a block of property, which is available without specific identification of particular dwelling-houses."

In that case, the Review Board's decision on suitable alternative accommodation was based on the monitoring of HB claims over the previous month (and showed that there had been 400 new or renewed claims, some of which related to the type of accommodation required by the claimants and their family) and on the fact that local "surgeries" had not revealed any general difficulty in obtaining rented accommodation. The claimants, on the other hand, presented detailed evidence of the searches they had actually made for somewhere cheaper to live and the reasons why those attempts had been unsuccessful. The Court was not prepared to say that there was no evidence on which the Review Board could have based its decision that the actual rent was unreasonably high by comparison with that payable for suitable alternative accommodation but remitted the decision to the Board because it had failed to supply adequate reasons as to why it had reached its conclusion and rejected the claimants' evidence.

The possible inconsistency between *Gibson* and *Malcolm* would require a Scottish court to consider whether it considered itself bound by *Gibson*, but there is no doubt as to the position in England and Wales. In *R v Sandwell MBC ex p Wilkinson* [1998] 31 HLR 22, QBD, an extremely bold submission was made that *Gibson*, a decision of the Court of Appeal, was wrongly decided. Unsurprisingly, Laws J held that he was bound to apply the decision in *Gibson*.

The English courts have followed and applied *Gibson* reasonably consistently. The practice has developed of local authorities providing comparables showing properties on the market around the relevant time. These need not actually be available when the claimant, hypothetically, is looking on the market. In *Brennan*, evidence of 16 properties coming onto the market over a seven month period was held to be sufficient. Further, an appeal tribunal may be entitled to use its local knowledge to conclude that some of the properties on a list provided by the authority would be suitable for the claimant: *Abou-Jaoude*.

If local authorities choose to provide evidence based on claims made by other claimants, then any breach of the Data Protection Act 1998 in the provision of such information to the tribunal does not render the evidence inadmissible: *CH 4970/2002* para 19.

Availability of the accommodation. The question of the extent to which the local authority must prove the availability of the alternative accommodation has also been a vexed one. A contrast needs to be drawn between paras (3) and (4). In para (3), there is no express requirement to show that the accommodation "is available". Evans LJ stated in *Gibson* at 501-2 that it was implicit in the wording "suitable alternative" that there had to be "some degree of availability". However, this part of his judgment was obiter and later decisions have consistently declined to read a requirement of availability into the legislation: *Malcolm*; *R v Ipswich BC ex p Flowers* [1994] unreported, 1 March, QBD (transcript at 14E-15E); *Waite* (transcript at 26B-28A). So under para (3), it is not necessary to exclude properties which are not, in practice, available to a claimant because s/he cannot afford to pay a deposit: *Holder*; *Green*.

In *Wilkinson* at 31, it was confirmed that the words "or otherwise" now in para (3)(b) cannot require the local authority to take the personal or other circumstances of the applicant into account. All that they meant was that the Rent Officer's decision was not determinative of whether the claimant's eligible rent should be restricted.

By contrast, under para (4) the authority must prove that the accommodation is available, and the availability or otherwise of properties for which a deposit is required may then be considered: *Holder* at 79; *R v Oadby and Wigston DC ex p Dickman* [1995] 28 HLR 807 at 816. In the latter case, Buxton J referred at 816 to "material about the difficulty of new tenants in obtaining properties and difficulties about deposits" being relevant. It was reiterated that the test was whether the applicant was in fact able to obtain such accommodation and not whether it was, as had been found by the Review Board in that case, generally available. Buxton J explained the *Gibson* decision as being about the *evidence* required to prove availability, stating at 816:

"I quite accept that the starting point in realistic terms must be the availability of a pool or market of accommodation in general terms. It is then in accordance with the approach in *Gibson* for the applicant to put forward grounds which are unlikely to prove persuasive unless they are supported by evidence of some sort as to why that pool is either not available to her at all or only available in such a limited way or to such a limited extent that the Review Board feels that it cannot realistically say that suitable alternative accommodation is indeed available."

A tribunal considering whether suitable alternative accommodation "is available" must consider evidence that a claimant requires accommodation of the same type and with the same facilities. Where a vulnerable young single mother was staying in sheltered accommodation and there was evidence from her GP and from social services stating that she required the support that the accommodation provided, if the Review Board rejected that evidence it had to state explicitly that it was doing so and give reasons for that rejection. As it had failed to do so, its decision was quashed: *R v East Devon DC HBRB ex p Preston* [1998] 31 HLR 936, QBD.

The old form of reg 11 was applied to the context of sheltered accommodation in two joined cases, *CH 1992/2002* and *CH 1993/2002*. The claimants were two men with learning disabilities who had been placed in accommodation which had been adapted to their physical needs and which had room for a carer to sleep. The local authority restricted their rent on the ground that the "bricks and mortar" element of the rent was unreasonably high in relation to other suitable alternative accommodation. The commissioner emphasised that it was for the tribunal to decide the questions of fact on the evidence before it and that he was unable to overturn the decision: paras 25-26. In para 24, he concluded that the word "is" in the phrase "suitable alternative cheaper accommodation is available" in now para (4) did not require that the accommodation was available for occupation immediately, since the claimant's existing tenancy would first have to be terminated by notice. Thus alternative accommodation could be suitable if it was capable of being easily adapted. On the other hand, it would not be suitable if it could only be provided after a delay of 18 months while modifications were carried out.

---

(3)   For the purposes of regulation 12(3) of both the Housing Benefit Regulations and the Housing Benefit (State Pension Credit) Regulations, as inserted by paragraph (2) above, regulation 13ZA of both those Regulations is as follows–

"Restrictions on rent increases

13ZA.–(1) Subject to paragraph (2), where a claimant's eligible rent is increased during an award of housing benefit, the relevant authority shall, if it considers, whether by reference to a determination or re-determination made by a rent officer in exercise of a function conferred on him by an order under section 122 of the Housing Act 1996, or otherwise, either–

(a) that the increase is unreasonably high having regard in particular to the level of increases for suitable alternative accommodation, or

(b) in the case of an increase which takes place less than 12 months after the date of the previous increase, that the increase is unreasonable having regard to the length of time since that previous increase,

treat the eligible rent as reduced either by the full amount of the increase or, if it considers that a lesser increase was reasonable in all the circumstances, by the difference between the full amount of the increase and the increase that is reasonable having regard in particular to the level of increases for suitable alternative accommodation, and the claimant's maximum housing benefit shall be calculated by reference to the eligible rent as so reduced.

(2) No deduction shall be made under this regulation for a period of 12 months from the date of death of any person to whom paragraph (11) of regulation 13 (restrictions on unreasonable payments) applied or, had a claim been made, would have applied, if the dwelling which the claimant occupies is the same as that occupied by him at that date except where the deduction began before the death occurred.

(3) For the purposes of paragraph (2), a claimant shall be treated as occupying the dwelling if paragraph (13) of regulation 7 (circumstances in which a person is to be treated as occupying a dwelling) is satisfied and for that purpose sub-paragraph (b) of that paragraph shall be treated as if it were omitted."

General Note

Reg 12 of the HB Regs 1987 was repealed by reg 3(3) of the Housing Benefit and Council Tax Benefit (General) Amendment Regulations 1997, SI No 852 reg 3(3) as from 6 October 1997.

Before the repeal, reg 12 dealt with an authority's powers to restrict rent and applied to claimants who were already receiving HB and whose rent was increased while they were claiming. The reason for the repeal was that, given the introduction of the January 1996 changes to the old form of reg 11 HB Regs 1987 and the abolition, also on 6 October 1997, of the 50 per cent taper a change in contractual rent during the period when a rent officer's determination is in force has no effect on the level of HB actually payable. It is therefore no longer possible for landlords to abuse the scheme by imposing unreasonable rent increases.

This, however, is not the case where the January 1996 changes do not apply because the claimant or the accommodation is exempt (see para 4 above). Reg 4(3) of SI 1997 No 852 preserved reg 12 as it stood immediately before 6 October 1997. This is now in reg 13ZA as set out in para 5(3).

Analysis

Para (1). Prior to April 2000, there was a discretion as to whether the increase in rent was to be restricted. From that date, a restriction must be applied if para (1) is applicable, unless any of the following paragraphs apply. The terms on which eligible rent may be restricted are two-fold:

(1) Where the authority thinks the increase is "unreasonable" having regard to the level of increases for suitable alternative accommodation: para (a).

(2) Where the increase is considered unreasonable because it is less than a year since the last increase: para (b). In so deciding, as mentioned above, the authority may take a rent officer's determination into account but does not have to do so, and if the authority always simply follows the rent officer's determinations it has wrongfully fettered its discretion.

In deciding whether an increase is reasonable GM A4.1310 suggests that the authority take into account first the general level of rent increases locally, and second any improvements made to the accommodation that might justify an increase. This view can be criticised, however, in that the comparison under reg 13ZA(1)(a) is with the level of increase for *suitable alternative* accommodation, not accommodation in general. "Suitable alternative" is not defined here but arguably it has a similar meaning to the version of reg 13 in para 5(2) as it is part of the same "code" of restrictive measures. It is submitted that, in considering the "level of increase" it is better to consider and compare the end figures involved rather than the percentage increase. For example, if a very low rent is brought up to the named level for "suitable alternative" accommodation, HB should not be restricted under this provision simply because the *percentage* increase is relatively higher.

CH 2214/2003 emphasises that it is the *increase* in rent, rather than the level of the total rent itself, with which this regulation is concerned, and holds that any decision on this issue will need to be based on adequate evidence as to the level of increases in rents for suitable alternative accommodation. On the facts, it was decided that an increase in rent from £10,920 pa to £15,600 pa was not unreasonably high in London where there had been no previous rent increase for three years. The decision further holds that the level of increases for suitable alternative accommodation is not the only factor which can be taken into account (because of the words "in particular"), and that other factors which may be relevant are:

(1)   whether the claimant would have to move if the increase were not met;

(2)   the quality of the accommodation;

(3)   the effect on the claimant of having to move;

(4)   the length of time the claimant has lived in the accommodation;

(5)   the age, state of health and social mobility of the claimant;

(6)   the effects on job prospects of having to move; and

(7)   the effect on other members of the household of having to move.

If either paragraph of reg 13ZA is satisfied, and the authority does decide to use its powers, either the whole or part of the increase may be treated as "ineligible". Thus even though the discretion to apply para (1) has been removed, if an authority decided that an increase ought to be permitted it could achieve virtually the same effect by allowing virtually the whole of the increase, minus a penny.

Paras (2) and (3) provide the same restrictions on an authority's powers under this regulation as are now found in reg 13(11) and (12) of both the HB Regs and the HB(SPC) Regs and in reg 13(5) and (6) as set out in para 5(2). See the Analysis of reg 13 HB Regs.

Persons from abroad

6.–(1) Where, immediately before the coming into force of the Consolidating Regulations, a person is entitled to council tax benefit or, as the case may be, housing benefit, by virtue of regulation 12(1) of the Social Security (Persons From Abroad) Miscellaneous Amendments Regulations 1996 ("the 1996 Regulations"), the modifications specified in relation to council tax benefit in paragraph (2) or, as the case may be, in relation to housing benefit in paragraph (3), shall continue to have effect both as regards that person and as regards persons who are members of his family on 5th February 1996.

(2)   The modifications specified in this paragraph are that for regulation 7 of both the Council Tax Benefit Regulations and the Council Tax Benefit (State Pension Credit) Regulations there shall be substituted–

"**Persons from abroad**

7. –(1) A person from abroad is a person of a prescribed class for the purposes of section 131(3)(b) of the Act.

(2) In paragraph (1) a "person from abroad" means a person other than a person to whom paragraph (3) or (6) applies, who has limited leave (as defined in section 33(1) of the 1971 Act) to enter or remain in the United Kingdom which was given in accordance with any provision in the immigration rules (as defined in that section) relating to–

(a)   there being, or to there needing to be, no recourse to public funds, or

(b)   there being no charge on public funds,

during that limited leave.

(3)   Subject to paragraph (7) this paragraph applies to a person who–

(a)   is a national of a European Economic Area State, a state which is a signatory to the European Convention on Social and Medical Assistance (done in Paris on 11th December 1953), a state which is a signatory to the Council of Europe Social Charter (signed in Turin on 18th October 1961), the Channel Islands or the Isle of Man; or

(b)   having, during any one period of limited leave (including any such period as extended), supported himself without recourse to public funds other than any such recourse by reason of the previous application of this sub-paragraph, is temporarily without funds during that period of leave because remittances to him from abroad have been disrupted, provided that there is a reasonable expectation that his supply of funds will be resumed.

(4)   In paragraph (1) "person from abroad" also means any person other than a person to whom paragraph (6) applies who–

(a) having a limited leave (as defined in section 33(1) of the 1971 Act) to enter or remain in the United Kingdom, has remained without further leave under that Act beyond the time limited by the leave; or

(b)   is the subject of a deportation order being an order under section 5(1) of the 1971 Act (deportation) requiring him to leave and prohibiting him from entering the United Kingdom except where his removal from the United Kingdom has been deferred in writing by the Secretary of State; or

(c)   is adjudged by the immigration authorities to be an illegal entrant (as defined in section 33(1) of the 1971 Act) who has not subsequently been given leave under that Act to enter or remain in the United Kingdom except a person who has been allowed to remain in the United Kingdom with the consent in writing of the Secretary of State; or

(d)   is a national of a European Economic Area State and is required by the Secretary of State to leave the United Kingdom; or

(e) is not habitually resident in the United Kingdom, the Republic of Ireland, the Channel Islands or the Isle of Man, but for this purpose no person shall be treated as not habitually resident in the United Kingdom who is–

(i)   a worker for the purposes of Council Regulation (EEC) No. 1612/68 or (EEC) No. 1251/70 or a person with a right to reside in the United Kingdom pursuant to Council Directive No. 68/360/EEC or No. 73/148/EEC; or

(ii)   a refugee within the definition in Article 1 of the Convention relating to the Status of Refugees done at Geneva on 28th July 1951, as extended by Article 1(2) of the Protocol relating to the Status of Refugees done at New York on 31st January 1967; or

(iii)   a person who has been granted exceptional leave to remain in the United Kingdom by the Secretary of State; or

(iv)   person to whom paragraph (5) applies; or

(v)   the subject of a deportation order, being an order under section 5(1) of the 1971 Act (deportation) requiring him to leave and prohibiting him from entering the United Kingdom, and whose removal from the United Kingdom has been deferred in writing by the Secretary of State; or

(vi)   adjudged by the immigration authorities to be an illegal entrant (as defined in section 33(1) of the 1971 Act), has not subsequently been given leave under that Act to enter or remain in the United Kingdom but has been allowed to remain in the United Kingdom with the consent in writing of the Secretary of State.

(5)   Subject to paragraph (7) this paragraph applies to a person who, having, during any one period of limited leave (including any such period as extended), supported himself without recourse to public funds other than any such recourse by reason of the previous application of this sub-paragraph, is temporarily without funds during that period of leave because remittances to him from abroad have been disrupted, provided that there is a reasonable expectation that his supply of funds will be resumed.

(6)   This paragraph applies to a person who–

(a)   is an asylum seeker, and for this purpose a person–

(i)   becomes an asylum seeker when he has submitted a claim for asylum to the Secretary of State that it would be contrary to the United Kingdom's obligations under the Convention relating to the Status of Refugees done at Geneva on 28th July 1951, and the protocol to that convention, for him to be removed from, or required to leave, the United Kingdom and that claim is recorded by the Secretary of State as having been made; and

(ii)   ceases to be an asylum seeker when his claim is recorded by the Secretary of State as having been finally determined or abandoned; or

(b)   is awaiting the outcome of an appeal under Part 2 of the 1971 Act (including any period for which the appeal is treated as pending under section 33(4) of that Act); or

(c)   has no or no further right of appeal under the 1971 Act but has been allowed to remain in the United Kingdom while an application so to remain is, or representations on his behalf are, being considered by the Secretary of State; or

(d)   except where he is a person to whom paragraph (4)(b) applies, has been granted permission to remain in the United Kingdom pending the removal from the United Kingdom of a person who is the subject of a deportation order but whose deportation has been deferred in writing by the Secretary of State; or

(e)   is subject to a direction for his removal from the United Kingdom but whose removal has been deferred in writing by the Secretary of State; or

(f)   is in receipt of income support.

(7)   Paragraphs (3)(b) and (5) shall not apply to a person who has been temporarily without funds for any period, or the aggregate of any periods, exceeding 42 days during any one period of limited leave (including any such period as extended).

(8)   In this regulation–

"the 1971 Act" means the Immigration Act 1971; and

a "European Economic Area State" means a Member State, or Norway, Sweden, Iceland, Austria or Finland..".

(3)   The modifications specified in this paragraph are that for regulation 10 of both the Housing Benefit Regulations and the Housing Benefit (State Pension Credit) Regulations, there shall be substituted–

"Persons from abroad

10.–(1)   A person from abroad who is liable to make payments in respect of a dwelling shall be treated as if he were not so liable.

(2)   In paragraph (1) a "person from abroad" means a person, other than a person to whom paragraph (3) or (6) applies, who has limited leave (as defined in section 33(1) of the 1971 Act) to enter or remain in the United Kingdom which was given in accordance with any provision in the immigration rules (as defined in that section) relating to–

(a)   there being, or to there needing to be, no recourse to public funds, or

(b)   there being no charge on public funds,

during that limited leave.

(3)   Subject to paragraph (7) this paragraph applies to a person who–

(a)   is a national of a European Economic Area State, a state which is a signatory to the European Convention on Social and Medical Assistance (done in Paris on 11th December 1953), a state which is a signatory to the Council of Europe Social Charter (signed in Turin on 18th October 1961), the Channel Islands or the Isle of Man; or

(b)   having, during any one period of limited leave (including any such period as extended), supported himself without recourse to public funds other than any such recourse by reason of the previous application of this sub-paragraph, is temporarily without funds during that period of leave because remittances to him from abroad have been disrupted, provided that there is a reasonable expectation that his supply of funds will be resumed.

(4)   In paragraph (1) "person from abroad" also means any person other than a person to whom paragraph (6) applies who–

(a)   having a limited leave (as defined in section 33(1) of the 1971 Act) to enter or remain in the United Kingdom, has remained without further leave under that Act beyond the time limited by the leave; or

(b)   is the subject of a deportation order being an order under section 5(1) of the 1971 Act (deportation) requiring him to leave and prohibiting him from entering the United Kingdom except where his removal from the United Kingdom has been deferred in writing by the Secretary of State; or

(c)   is adjudged by the immigration authorities to be an illegal entrant (as defined in section 33(1) of the 1971 Act) who has not subsequently been given leave under that Act to enter or remain in the United Kingdom except a person who has been allowed to remain in the United Kingdom with the consent in writing of the Secretary of State.

(d)   is a national of a European Economic Area State and is required by the Secretary of State to leave the United Kingdom; or

(e)   is not habitually resident in the United Kingdom, the Republic of Ireland, the Channel Islands or the Isle of Man, but for this purpose no person shall be treated as not habitually resident in the United Kingdom who is–

(i)   a worker for the purposes of Council Regulation (EEC) No. 1612/68 or (EEC) No. 1251/70 or a person with a right to reside in the United Kingdom pursuant to Council Directive No. 68/360/EEC or No. 73/148/EEC; or

(ii)   a refugee within the definition in Article 1 of the Convention relating to the Status of Refugees done at Geneva on 28th July 1951, as extended by Article 1(2) of the Protocol relating to the Status of Refugees done at New York on 31st January 1967; or

(iii)   a person who has been granted exceptional leave to remain in the United Kingdom by the Secretary of State; or

(iv)   a person to whom paragraph (5) applies; or

(v)   the subject of a deportation order, being an order under section 5(1) of the 1971 Act (deportation) requiring him to leave and prohibiting him from entering the United Kingdom, and whose removal from the United Kingdom has been deferred in writing by the Secretary of State; or

(vi)   adjudged by the immigration authorities to be an illegal entrant (as defined in section 33(1) of the 1971 Act), has not subsequently been given leave under that Act to enter or remain in the United Kingdom but has been allowed to remain in the United Kingdom with the consent in writing of the Secretary of State.

(5)   Subject to paragraph (7) this paragraph applies to a person who, having, during any one period of limited leave (including any such period as extended), supported himself without recourse to public funds other than any such recourse by reason of the previous application of this sub-paragraph, is temporarily without funds during that period of leave because remittances to him from abroad have been disrupted, provided that there is a reasonable expectation that his supply of funds will be resumed.

(6)   This paragraph applies to a person who–

(a)   is an asylum seeker, and for this purpose a person–

(i)   becomes an asylum seeker when he has submitted a claim for asylum to the Secretary of State that it would be contrary to the United Kingdom's obligations under the Convention relating to the Status of Refugees done at Geneva on 28th July 1951, and the protocol to that convention, for him to be removed from, or required to leave, the United Kingdom and that claim is recorded by the Secretary of State as having been made; and

(ii)   ceases to be an asylum seeker when his claim is recorded by the Secretary of State as having been finally determined or abandoned; or

(b)   is awaiting the outcome of an appeal under Part 2 of the 1971 Act (including any period for which the appeal is treated as pending under section 33(4) of that Act); or

(c)   has no or no further right of appeal under the 1971 Act but has been allowed to remain in the United Kingdom while an application so to remain is, or representations on his behalf are, being considered by the Secretary of State; or

(d)   except where he is a person to whom paragraph (4)(b) applies, has been granted permission to remain in the United Kingdom pending the removal from the United Kingdom of a person who is the subject of a deportation order but whose deportation has been deferred in writing by the Secretary of State; or

(e)   is subject to a direction for his removal from the United Kingdom but whose removal has been deferred in writing by the Secretary of State; or

(f)   is in receipt of income support.

(7)   Paragraphs (3)(b) and (5) shall not apply to a person who has been temporarily without funds for any period, or the aggregate of any periods, exceeding 42 days during any one period of limited leave (including any such period as extended).

(8)   In this regulation–

"the 1971 Act" means the Immigration Act 1971;

a "European Economic Area State" means a Member State or Norway, Sweden, Iceland, Austria or Finland..".

(4)   Where, immediately before the coming into force of the Consolidating Regulations, a person is entitled to council tax benefit or, as the case may be, housing benefit, by virtue of regulation 12(2) of the Social Security (Persons From Abroad) Miscellaneous Amendments Regulations 1996–

(a)   the Council Tax Benefit Regulations shall have effect in relation to him subject to the modifications set out in paragraph (2);

(b)   the Housing Benefit Regulations shall have effect in relation to him subject to the modifications set out in paragraph (3).

(5)   Sub-paragraph (6) applies where a person–

(a)   is entitled to a specified benefit in respect of a period which includes 30th April 2004;

(b)   claims a specified benefit on or after 1st May 2004 and it is subsequently determined that he is entitled to that benefit in respect of a period which includes 30th April 2004;

(c)   claims a specified benefit on or after 1st May 2004 and it is subsequently determined that he is entitled to such a benefit in respect of a period which is continuous with a period of entitlement to the same or another specified benefit which includes 30th April 2004;

(d)   claims jobseeker's allowance on or after 1st May 2004 and it is subsequently determined that he is entitled to jobseeker's allowance in respect of a period of entitlement to that benefit which is linked to a previous period of entitlement which includes 30th April 2004 by virtue of regulations made under paragraph 3 of Schedule 1 to the Jobseekers Act 1995.

(6)   Where this sub-paragraph applies–

(a)   the Council Tax Benefit Regulations and the Council Tax Benefit (State Pension Credit) Regulations shall both have effect as if in regulation 7 (persons from abroad)–

    (i)   in paragraph (2)(a) the words "or a person who is an accession State worker requiring registration who is treated as a worker for the purpose of the definition of "qualified person" in regulation 5(1) of the Immigration (European Economic Area) Regulations 2000 pursuant to regulation 5 of the Accession (Immigration and Worker Registration) Regulations 2004" were omitted; and

    (ii)   paragraph (3) were omitted.

(b)   the Housing Benefit Regulations and the Housing Benefit (State Pension Credit) Regulations shall both have effect as if in regulation 10 (persons from abroad)–

    (i)   in paragraph (2)(a) the words "or a person who is an accession State worker requiring registration who is treated (i) as a worker for the purpose of the definition of "qualified person" in regulation 5(1) of the Immigration (European Economic Area) Regulations 2000 pursuant to regulation 5 of the Accession (Immigration and Worker Registration) Regulations 2004" were omitted; and

    (ii)   paragraph (3) were omitted.

(7)   The provisions saved by sub-paragraph (6) shall continue to have effect until the date on which entitlement to a specified benefit for the purposes of sub-paragraph (5) ceases, and if there is more than one such specified benefit, until the last date on which such entitlement ceases.

(8)   In sub-paragraphs (5) and (7), "specified benefit" means income support, housing benefit, council tax benefit, jobseeker's allowance and state pension credit.

(9)   In regulation 12 of the 1996 Regulations–

(a)   in paragraph (1), for the words "those provisions" to the end of the paragraph, substitute "the provisions of the Income Support Regulations as then in force shall continue to have effect as if regulation 8(2) and (3)(c) of these Regulations had not been made"; and

(b)   in paragraph (2), for the words "those Regulations as then in force" to the end of the paragraph, substitute "the Income Support Regulations as then in force shall have effect as if regulation 8 of these Regulations had not been made".

(10)   For the purposes of–

(a)   regulation 10(1) of the Housing Benefit Regulations;

(b)   regulation 10(1) of the Housing Benefit (State Pension Credit) Regulations;

(c)   regulation 7(1) of the Council Tax Benefit Regulations; and

(d)   regulation 7(1) of the Council Tax Benefit (State Pension Credit) Regulations,

a person who is an asylum seeker within the meaning of sub-paragraph (11) who has not ceased to be an asylum seeker by virtue of sub-paragraph (12), is not a person from abroad within the meaning of paragraph (1) of those regulations.

(11)   An asylum seeker within the meaning of this paragraph is a person who–

(a)   submits on his arrival (other than on his re-entry) in the United Kingdom from a country outside the Common Travel Area a claim for asylum on or before 2nd April 2000 to the Secretary of State that it would be contrary to the United Kingdom's obligations under the Convention for him to be removed or required to leave, the United Kingdom and that claim is recorded by the Secretary of State has having been made before that date; or

(b)   on or before 2nd April 2000 becomes, while present in Great Britain, an asylum seeker when–

    (i)   the Secretary of State makes a declaration to the effect that the country of which he is a national is subject to such a fundamental change of circumstances that he would not normally order the return of a person to that country; and

    (ii)   he submits, within a period of three months from the date that declaration was made, a claim for asylum to the Secretary of State under the Convention relating to the Status of Refugees; and

    (iii)   his claim for asylum under that Convention is recorded by the Secretary of State has having been made.

(12)   A person ceases to be an asylum seeker for the purposes of this paragraph when his claim for asylum is recorded by the Secretary of State as having been decided (other than on appeal) or abandoned.

(13)   In paragraph (11) "the Common Travel Area" means the United Kingdom, the Channel Islands, the Isle of Man and the Republic of Ireland collectively and "the Convention" means the Convention relating to the Status of Refugees done at Geneva on 28th July 1951 as extended by Article 2(1) of the Protocol relating to the Status of Refugees done at New York on 31st January 1967.

General Note

Paras (1)-(4) The Social Security (Persons from Abroad) Miscellaneous Amendments Regulations 1996 SI No 30 provided a savings provision for entitlement to HB and CTB by some asylum seekers. The modifications to the HB Regs, HB(SPC) Regs, CTB Regs and CTB(SPC) Regs to effect this are now in para 6(1)-(4). See the commentary to SI 1996 No 30 above.

Paras (5)-(8) The Social Security (Habitual Residence) Amendment Regulations 2004 SI No 1232 provided a savings provision for those entitled to HB and CTB when the "right to reside" test was intorduced from 1 May 2004. The modifications of the HB Regs, HB(SPC) Regs, CTB Regs and CTB(SPC) Regs to effect this are now in para 6(5)-(7). See the commentary on p1094.

Paras (10)-(13) See the Analysis below.

Note that the amendments made by SI 2006 No 1026 to the HB Regs, HB(SPC) Regs, CTB Regs and CTB(SPC) Regs do not affect the continued operation of the transitional and savings provided for in reg 12 of the Social Security (Persons From Abroad) Miscellaneous Amendments Regulations 1996, reg 6 of the Social Security (Habitual Residence) Amendment Regulations 2004 or para 6 of Sch 3 of the HB&CTB(CP) Regs. See reg 11 of SI 2006 No 102 on p1134.

Analysis

Paragraphs (10) to (13): Introduction

These paragraphs prevent certain asylum seekers either from falling foul of reg 10 of either the HB or the HB(SPC) Regs or reg 7 of either the CTB or CTB(SPC) Regs by being a person from abroad and also, by virtue of reg 2(3) of the Social Security (Immigration and Asylum) Consequential Amendments Regulations 2000 SI No 636, from exclusion from HB under s115 of the 1999 Act. In summary, they are those who claimed asylum on or before 2 April 2000, and either claimed asylum "on his arrival" in the UK or who were present in the UK and claimed asylum within three months of an 'upheaval declaration' having been made in relation to the country of her/his nationality.

The notes below discuss these two categories of asylum seeker in more detail and then go on to outline how a person loses her/his status as a relevant asylum seeker.

Paragraphs (11)(a) and (13): Those who claimed asylum "on . . . arrival"

"On his arrival". For the (now almost moribund) debate on whether these three words mean claiming asylum on the very moment of a person arriving in the UK (ie, before he or she passes immigration control) see pages 1073-1075 of the Nineteenth edition of this book.

However, a definitive answer may shortly be given to this debate by the House of Lords in *Kola and another v Secretary of State for Work and Pensions*, which was heard in October 2007.

". . . other than on his re-entry". This is presumably intended to prevent a person present in the UK who wishes to claim asylum but who wishes to avoid being found to be a person from abroad from simply leaving the UK and re-entering to claim asylum "on his arrival". It is suggested that it does not mean that a person cannot come within the exception if s/he has visited the UK before. It only makes sense if it is read as meaning "re-entry during the same period of limited leave". That prevents the possible evasion of the "on his arrival" requirement while ensuring that a person who has visited the UK 20 years previously is not prevented from fulfilling the criterion.

"... in the United Kingdom from a country outside the Common Travel Area". The common travel area (CTA) is the UK, Channel Islands, Isle of Man and the Republic of Ireland: para (13). The phrase does not prevent the claimant from having been in another part of the CTA before arrival in the UK. If that were so, an asylum seeker from Columbia who landed in Ireland before claiming asylum in the UK could not fulfil the "on his arrival" criterion. It is suggested that a period of travel through another part of the CTA must be ignored.

"... a claim for asylum". There is no set procedure for making a claim for asylum under the Immigration Rules, save that para 328 provides that an application made at a port or airport will be referred to the Secretary of State by the immigration officer. In particular, it does not need to be done in writing and it is probable that most applications are made orally. In *CIS 1137/1997*, the claimant asserted that he had tried to speak to an official at the airport and a policeman but had been unable to communicate with them. The fact that the Commissioner remitted the case for further consideration of these points (para 9) suggests that such attempts could amount for a claim for asylum. Note also *CIS 4341/1998*.

". . . and that claim is recorded by the Secretary of State as having been made before that date". In order for the claimant to fall within the scope of para (11)(a), or indeed para (6)(b), the claim for asylum must not merely have been made but must have been recorded by the Secretary of State prior to 3 April 2000. The date on the claimant's Standard Acknowledgment Letter will be the best available evidence of this.

Paragraph (11)(b): Asylum seekers claiming after declarations

In conditions of extreme turmoil in a state, the Home Secretary may make a declaration that there will normally be no return of people to that country. These vary according to the conditions of the moment and last for three months at a time.

Any national of such a state making a claim for asylum from within the UK within three months of the declaration falls within this category of asylum seekers. It only applies to nationals of that state and not to those of other states: *R v Secretary of State for Social Security ex p Grant* [1997] unreported, 31 July, QBD.

The relevant claimants will be nationals of the former Zaire who claimed asylum between 16 May 1997 and 16 August 1997 and those from Sierra Leone who claimed between 1 January 1997 and 1 October 1997.

Paragraph (12): Loss of asylum seeker status

By para (12), a person ceases to be an asylum seeker on the date on which her/his claim is "recorded as determined" by the Secretary of State. The question then arises as to when a claim is "recorded as determined". In *R (Anufrijeva) v Secretary of State for the Home Department* [2003] 3 WLR 353, HL, the House of Lords ruled that it was contrary to fundamental constitutional principles for an uncommunicated administrative decision to affect the rights of a person to whom that decision related. Accordingly, the claimant did not lose her entitlement to IS until the refusal of her asylum claim was communicated to her. The same will apply to HB entitlement.

Frequency of payment of rent allowance

7.–(1) The regulations specified in sub-paragraphs (3) to (5) shall apply in accordance with the amendments so specified where the claimant–

(a) was entitled to and in receipt of housing benefit on account of his liability to make payments in respect of a dwelling, which he occupied or was treated as occupying as his home, on 06 October 1996;

(b) regulation 11 of the Housing Benefit (General) Amendment Regulations 1996 applied in the case of payments made to the claimant immediately before the consolidating Regulations came into force; and

(c) continues to be entitled to and in receipt of housing benefit on account of such occupation of that dwelling.

(2)   In this regulation, "claimant" includes the deceased partner of a claimant in any case where a claim is made by the surviving partner within 4 weeks of the death, provided that this regulation or regulation 11 of the Housing Benefit (General) Amendment Regulations 1996 applied to that deceased on the day of his death.

(3)   Regulation 91 of the Housing Benefit Regulations shall have effect as if, in paragraph (3), for the words "Subject to regulations 92 to 97 (frequency of payment of and payment on account of rent allowance, payment provisions)," there are substituted the words "Subject to regulations 93 to 97 (payment on account of rent allowance, payment provisions)".

(4)   Regulation 72 of the Housing Benefit (State Pension Credit) Regulations shall have effect as if, in paragraph (3), for the words "Subject to regulations 73 to 78 (frequency of payment of and payment on account of rent allowance, payment provisions)," there are substituted the words "Subject to regulations 74 to 78 (payment on account of rent allowance, payment provisions)".

(5)   Regulation 92 of the Housing Benefit Regulations and regulation 73 of the Housing Benefit (State Pension Credit) Regulations (frequency of payment of a rent allowance) shall both have effect as if–

(a)   for paragraph (2), there is substituted–

"(2)   A payment of a rent allowance in accordance with paragraph (1) shall be made insofar as it is practicable to do so, 2 weeks before the end of the period in respect of which it is made unless the liability to pay rent of the person entitled is in respect of a past period, in which case payment of the rent allowance may be made at the end of that period.";

(b)   paragraphs (3) and (4) are omitted;

(c)   in paragraphs (5) and (6), the words "Except in a case to which paragraph (3) applies," are omitted; and

(d)   in paragraph (7) the words "Subject to paragraphs (2), (3) and (5)," are omitted.

General Note

The effect of this saving provision, formerly found in reg 11 of the Housing Benefit (General) Amendment Regulations 1996 SI No 965, is that the payment rules (either payment to the claimant or direct to the landlord – see the analysis to reg 92(2) HB Regs) do not apply to existing claimants who were entitled to and in receipt of HB in respect of dwellings which they occupied on 6 October 1996, and who continue to be entitled to and in receipt of HB on the same dwelling. New claimants are also protected if they were the partner of a former claimant who would have been entitled to the protection of the savings rule but who has died. Such new claimants must claim HB in their own name within four weeks from the date of death: sub-para (2).

If para 7 applies, HB in the form of a rent allowance is paid, if practicable, two weeks before the end of period in respect of which it is made. So payments for two weeks are made in advance and payments for four weeks or a month, mid-way through the period: reg 92(2) as substituted by sub-para (5)(a).

A dispute has arisen in at least one authority as to the meaning of "in receipt of" in reg 11(1)(a) of SI 1996 No 965 (now in para 7(1)(a)). The circumstances were that a number of former council tenants had their homes transferred into the ownership of a registered social landlord, which was then paid the HB entitlements of those tenants direct. The social landlord argued that the transitional protection continued to apply to claimants who had been in continuous receipt of HB since 1996. It is suggested that the wording "in receipt of" is loose enough to include a claimant whose HB is paid direct to her/his landlord, since it cannot have been intended that the mode of payment should make a difference. The words "in receipt of" are used in a number of other contexts in the HB Regs where the mode of payment cannot have been intended to affect their applicability: see eg, the definition of "prospective occupier" in reg 14(10), reg 50(2), reg 72(6)(a) and Sch 3 para 11(1) and (2) HB Regs. The matter may, however, be open to argument.

Local reference rent taper

8.–(1)   Regulation 13 of both the Housing Benefit Regulations and the Housing Benefit (State Pension Credit) Regulations (maximum rent) shall have effect in the case of a claimant to whom any of sub-paragraphs (3) to (6) applies subject to the amendments specified in sub-paragraph (2).

(2)   The amendments of regulation 13 are–

(a)   in paragraph (6) in sub-paragraph (a), at the end, add "plus 50 per cent. of the amount by which the relevant rent exceeds the local reference rent;";

(b)   in paragraph (7) at the end, add the words "plus 50 per cent. of the amount by which that reckonable rent exceeds the local reference rent."

(3)   This sub-paragraph applies to a claimant who has been continuously entitled to and in receipt of housing benefit–

(a)   in respect of the same dwelling for a period which includes 5th October 1997; and

(b)   which included an addition by virtue of paragraph (3) or (4) of regulation 11 of the 1987 Regulations as they had effect on 5th October 1997.

(4)   Sub-paragraph (3) above shall continue to have effect in the case of a person who has ceased to be a welfare to work beneficiary or whose partner has ceased to be such a beneficiary where the person is entitled to housing benefit at the end of the 52 week period to which sub-paragraph (5) refers.

(5)   This sub-paragraph applies in the case of a person–

(a)   who was entitled to housing benefit in respect of the dwelling he occupied as his home on or before 5th October 1997;

(b)   whose entitlement to housing benefit in respect of that dwelling was continuous from that date until it ceased because either the person or his partner became a welfare to work beneficiary;

(c)   who on the day before entitlement to housing benefit ceased, was in receipt of an addition to benefit by virtue of paragraph (4) or (5) of regulation 11 of the 1987 Regulations as they had effect on 5th October 1997; and

(d)   who subsequently becomes re-entitled to housing benefit in respect of that dwelling within 52 weeks of him or his partner becoming a welfare to work beneficiary.

(6)   In this paragraph, "welfare to work beneficiary" means a person to whom regulation 13A(1) of the Social Security (Incapacity for Work) (General) Regulations 1995 applies.

General Note

Para 8 preserves the old "50 per cent taper" (see p264 for an explanation) for three specified groups of claimants.

Analysis

Sub-paras (1) and (2) provide an amended version of reg 13 of both the HB Regs and the HB(SPC) Regs where any of sub-paras (3) to (6) apply.

Sub-para (3) provides transitional protection to a claimant if s/he was actually benefiting from the 50 per cent taper on 5 October 1997 and has been continuously entitled to, and in receipt of, HB in respect of the same dwelling since then. The transitional protection continues until the claimant ceases to be entitled to HB or moves home. It would seem that even a single day's non-entitlement to HB is sufficient to bring the protection of this sub-paragraph to an end.

Sub-para (4) The transitional protection under sub-para (3) is also retained even if the claimant or her/his partner ceases to be a welfare to work beneficiary as long as entitlement to HB is re-established by the end of the 52-week period.

Sub-para (5) applies to a welfare to work beneficiary (or her/his partner) who would, under sub-para (3), have been entitled to transitional protection but for the fact that s/he had returned to work. S/he can regain the protection if s/he has to re-claim HB within 52 weeks. "Welfare to work beneficiary" is defined in sub-para (6) by reference to reg 13A of the Social Security (Incapacity for Work) Regulations 1995 SI No 311. A "welfare to work beneficiary" is a claimant who has been incapable of work for at 196 days and comes off benefit after 5 October 1998 because s/he has voluntarily returned to work (ie, not because s/he has been found capable of work). Welfare to work beneficiaries enjoy a number of advantages in the social security system as an incentive to people to try to return to work where possible.

Care homes

9.–(1) In regulation 2(1) of both the Housing Benefit Regulations and the Housing Benefit (State Pension Credit) Regulations there shall be inserted in the appropriate place–

'' "the 1987 Regulations" means the Housing Benefit (General) Regulations 1987;''

(2)   Sub-paragraph (3) shall apply to a person who, on 3rd October 2005 was a person to whom paragraph (2) of regulation 7 of the 1987 Regulations as in force on that date applied.

(3)   Where this paragraph applies–

(a)   regulation 9 of both the Housing Benefit Regulations and the Housing Benefit (State Pension Credit) Regulations shall have effect as if–

(i)   in paragraph (1)(k), at the beginning there were inserted the words "except where paragraph (1A) applies";

(ii)   after paragraph (1) there were inserted–

"(1A)   This paragraph applies to a person who–

(a)   was or became entitled immediately before 30th October 1990 to housing benefit in respect of residential accommodation; or

(b)   became or becomes entitled to housing benefit in respect of such accommodation on or after that date but only if the claim was made or, as the case may be, the appropriate authority is satisfied that the claim was sent or delivered to the appropriate DWP office or designated office in accordance with regulation 83(4) (time and manner in which claims are made), before that date.'';

(iii)   for paragraph (4) there were substituted paragraph (3) of regulation 7 of the 1987 Regulations as in force on 23rd October 2005;

(b)   regulation 52 of the Housing Benefit Regulations shall have effect as if–

      (i)   paragraph (4) there were substituted–

"(4)   For the purposes of paragraph (3), the prescribed circumstances are that the claimant–

(a)   occupies residential accommodation as his home; or

(b)   is a person to whom paragraph (1A), as inserted by paragraph 9(3)(a)(ii) of Schedule 3 to the Consequential Provisions Regulations (exceptions to circumstances in which a person is to be treated as not liable to make payments in respect of a dwelling) applies.";

      (ii)   for paragraph (9), there were substituted–

"(9)   Paragraph (8) shall not apply to residential accommodation of the type referred to in sub-paragraph (b) or (c) of paragraph (8) where such accommodation is residential accommodation for the purposes of regulation 9 and paragraph (4)(b) does not apply to the claimant in respect of that accommodation.".

(4)   Sub-paragraph (5) shall apply to a person who, on 3rd October 2005, was a person to whom paragraph (5) of regulation 7 of the 1987 Regulations as in force on that date applied.

(5)   Where this paragraph applies–

(a)   regulation 9 of both the Housing Benefit Regulations and the Housing Benefit (State Pension Credit) Regulations shall have effect as if–

      (i)   for paragraph (4) there were substituted paragraph (3) of regulation 7 of the 1987 Regulations as in force on 23rd October 2005;

      (ii)   after paragraph (4), there was inserted–

"(5)   Subject to the following provisions of this regulation, paragraph (6) applies to a person who–

(a)   occupies or is treated by regulation 6(8) of the 1987 Regulations as occupying residential accommodation on 31st March 1993;

(b) is or was liable to pay rent in respect of that accommodation for that day;

(c)   is a person to whom sub-paragraph (a) or (b) of paragraph (2) of regulation 7 of the 1987 Regulations applies immediately before 1st April 1993; and

(d)   is or was entitled to housing benefit in respect of the liability mentioned in sub-paragraph (b).

(6)   In the case of a person to whom this paragraph applies, regulation 9 of these Regulations shall continue to apply to him as if the amendments to the 1987 Regulations specified in regulation 5(2) of the Social Security Benefits (Amendments Consequential Upon the Introduction of Community Care) Regulations 1992 had not been made.

(7)   Subject to paragraph (8), where on 1st April 1993 paragraph (6) applies to a person that paragraph shall cease to apply to him–

(a)   on the day on which he is first absent from the accommodation which he occupied or was treated under regulation 7(8) of the 1987 Regulations as occupying on 31st March 1993; and

(b)   on any day which falls after that day.

(8)   For the purposes of paragraph (7), any absence shall be disregarded during which the person is treated as occupying the accommodation as his home pursuant to regulation 7(12), (13) or (17) of these Regulations.

(9)   Where a person–

(a)   ceases to be entitled to housing benefit; and

(b)   was before he ceased to be entitled a person to whom paragraph (6) applied,

that paragraph shall not apply to him in the case of any subsequent claim for housing benefit.";

(b)   regulation 52 of the Housing Benefit Regulations shall have effect as if–

      (i)   for paragraph (4) there were substituted–

"(4)   For the purposes of paragraph (3), the prescribed circumstances are that the claimant–

(a)   occupies residential accommodation as his home; or

(b)   is a person to whom paragraph (6), as inserted by paragraph 9(5)(a)(ii) of Schedule 3 to the Consequential Provisions Regulations (exceptions to circumstances in which a person is to be treated as not liable to make payments in respect of a dwelling) applies.";

      (ii)   for paragraph (9), there were substituted–

"(9)   Paragraph (8) shall not apply to residential accommodation of the type referred to in sub-paragraph (b) or (c) of paragraph (8) where such accommodation is residential accommodation for the purposes of regulation 9 and paragraph (4)(b) does not apply to the claimant in respect of that accommodation.".

(6)   Sub-paragraph (7) shall apply to a person who, on 3rd October 2005, was a person to whom paragraph (7) of regulation 7 of the 1987 Regulations as in force on that date applied.

(7)   Where this paragraph applies–

(a)   regulation 9 of both the Housing Benefit Regulations and the Housing Benefit (State Pension Credit) Regulations shall have effect as if–

      (i)   for paragraph (4) there were substituted paragraph (3) of regulation 7 of the 1987 Regulations as in force on 23rd October 2005;

      (ii)   after paragraph (4), there was inserted–

"(5)   Subject to the following provisions of this regulation, paragraph (6) applies to a person who–

(a) occupies or is treated under regulation 5(7C), (8) or (8C) of the 1987 Regulations as occupying accommodation in an establishment which on 1st April 1993 is registered as a small home under Part I of the Registered Homes Act 1984 or is deemed to be so registered under section 2(3) of the Registered Homes (Amendment) Act 1991 (registration of small homes where application for registration not determined);

(b) was occupying, or was treated under regulation 7(8) of the 1987 Regulations as occupying, that accommodation on 31st March 1993;

(c) is or was liable to pay rent in respect of that accommodation for 31st March 1993; and

(d) is or was entitled to housing benefit in respect of that liability.

(6) In the case of a person to whom this paragraph applies, paragraph (4), as substituted by paragraph 9(7)(a)(i) of Schedule 3 to the Consequential Provisions Regulations, shall apply as if sub-paragraph (a) of the substituted paragraph was omitted.

(7) Subject to paragraph (8), where on 1st April 1993 paragraph (6) applies to a person that paragraph shall cease to apply to him—

(a) on the day on which he is first absent from the accommodation which he occupied or was treated under regulation 7(8) of the 1987 Regulations as occupying on 31st March 1993; and

(b) on any day which falls after that day.

(8) For the purposes of paragraph (7), any absence shall be disregarded during which the person is treated as occupying the accommodation as his home pursuant to regulation 7(12), (13) or (17) of these Regulations.

(9) Where a person—

(a) ceases to be entitled to housing benefit; and

(b) was before he ceased to be entitled a person to whom paragraph (6) applied,

that paragraph shall not apply to him in the case of any subsequent claim for housing benefit.

(10) Where on 31st March 1993 a person occupies or is treated as occupying an establishment mentioned in paragraph (5)(a) and on a day subsequent to that date the establishment—

(a) if it was registered under Part I of the Registered Homes Act 1984, ceases to be so registered; or

(b) if it was deemed to be so registered is neither registered nor deemed to be registered,

then on that day and on any day thereafter paragraph (9) shall not apply to that person.

(11) In this regulation, "small home" has the same meaning as it had in Part 1 of the Registered Homes Act 1984 by virtue of section 1(4A) of that Act.".

(b) regulation 52 of the Housing Benefit Regulations shall have effect as if—

(i) for paragraph (4) there were substituted—

"(4) For the purposes of paragraph (3), the prescribed circumstances are that the claimant—

(a) occupies residential accommodation as his home; or

(b) is a person to whom paragraph (6), as inserted by paragraph 9(7)(a)(ii) of Schedule 3 to the Consequential Provisions Regulations (exceptions to circumstances in which a person is to be treated as not liable to make payments in respect of a dwelling) applies.";

(ii) for paragraph (9), there were substituted—

"(9) Paragraph (8) shall not apply to residential accommodation of the type referred to in sub-paragraph (b) or (c) of paragraph (8) where such accommodation is residential accommodation for the purposes of regulation 9 and paragraph (4)(b) does not apply to the claimant in respect of that accommodation.".

SCHEDULE 4
REGULATION 7
TRANSITORY MODIFICATIONS
PROVISIONS NOT YET IN FORCE

1.–(1) If–

(a) no date has been appointed as the date on which a provision mentioned in column 1 of the following Table is to come into force before 24th February 2006; or

(b) a date has been appointed which is later than 24th February 2006,

then the paragraph of this Schedule mentioned in column 2 of the Table opposite that provision shall have effect until the appointed day.

TABLE

Provision	Paragraph of this Schedule
Section 12(2)(e) of the Asylum and Immigration (Treatment of Claimants, etc.) Act 2004.	*Paragraph 2*
Section 12(2)(g) of the Asylum and Immigration (Treatment of Claimants, etc.) Act 2004.	*Paragraph 3*
Section 12(3) of the Asylum and Immigration (Treatment of Claimants, etc.) Act 2004.	*Paragraph 4*

(2)   If a date has been appointed as the date on which a provision mentioned in column 1 of the Table above is to come into force for some purposes of that provision but not for others, then the paragraph of this Schedule mentioned in column 2 of the Table opposite that provision shall have effect for those other purposes of that provision (in so far as it is capable of doing so) until the provisions are brought into force for the remaining purposes.

General Note

Section 12 of the Asylum and Immigration (Treatment of Claimants, etc.) Act 2004 came into force on 14 June 2007 by the Asylum and Immigration (Treatment of Claimants, etc.) Act 2004 (Commencement No. 7 and Transitional Provisions) Order 2007 SI No 1602. The commencement does not apply to those recorded as refugees on or before 14 June 2007. For these purposes, a person is "recorded as a refugee" on the day the Secretary of State notifies her/him that s/he has been recognised as a refugee and granted asylum in the UK. For those to whom the commencement applies, the following provisions lapse:

(1)   Reg 10A and Sch A1 of both the HB Regs and the HB(SPC) Regs, as inserted by para 2(1) and (2).

(2)   Paras 55A and 55B of Sch 5 and paras 48A and 48B of Sch 6 of the HB Regs, as inserted by para 2(5) and (6).

(3)   Reg 7A and Sch A1 of both the CTB Regs and the CTB(SPC) Regs, as inserted by para 3(1) and (2).

(4)   Paras 56A and 56B of Sch 4 and paras 53A and 53B of Sch 5 of the CTB Regs, as inserted by para 3(5) and (6).

(5)   The modifications made to the above, as made by para 4 of this Schedule.

Refugees – Housing Benefit

2.–(1) After regulation 10 of both the Housing Benefit Regulations and the Housing Benefit (State Pension Credit) Regulations, insert–

"Entitlement of a refugee to Housing Benefit

10A.–(1)   Where a person, who has made a claim for asylum, is notified that he has been recorded by the Secretary of State as a refugee, these Regulations shall have effect with respect to his entitlement to housing benefit for the relevant period which applies in his case in accordance with Schedule A1(treatment of claims for housing benefit by refugees), but that entitlement is–

(a)   subject to the provisions of Schedule A1; and

(b)   with respect to regulations 12 (rent) and 13 (maximum rent), subject to paragraph 4(8) of Schedule 3 to the Housing Benefit and Council Tax Benefit (Consequential Provisions) Regulations 2006 (saving).

(2)   Any housing benefit which is payable in consequence of this regulation shall be in the form of a rent allowance.

(3)   In this regulation and in Schedule A1, "refugee" means a person recorded by the Secretary of State as a refugee within the definition in Article 1 of the Convention relating to the Status of Refugees.".

General Note

Regulation 10A lapsed from 14 June 2007 for those recorded as refugees after that date: see the General Note to para 1 above. This regulation provided for special rules for retrospective claims for HB by asylum seekers whose claims were accepted, whether by the Secretary of State or on appeal. Sch A1 (inserted by para 2(2) below) set out the scheme, which is summarised in the Analysis below. Note that by virtue of para (1)(b), the rent restriction rules applied to the refugee's backdated claim were the pre-January 1996 versions.

Note that Sch A1 in this form only applied to those claiming asylum after 2 April 2000. For those seeking asylum on or before that date, Sch A1 had effect as amended by para 4(2)(a) below. For the text as it stood prior to April 2000, see pp389-391 of the 12th edition of this work.

Analysis

The following rules apply for the determination of retrospective claims to HB under Sch A1. Apart from as set out below, the normal rules apply:

(1)   Under para 2, claims are made to the appropriate authority for the applicant's dwelling: para 2(1). A claim must be made within 28 days of the notification by the Secretary of State that s/he is recorded as a refugee: para 2(4). It is not possible to backdate for good cause: para 2(5).

(2)   The claim is to be made to the appropriate authority. Where the claimant has lived in the area of more than one authority, the claim is submitted to the authority for the dwelling "which he last occupied in that period" and that authority determines entitlement for the whole period in question: para 2(2) and (3). The determining authority may seek information from the other relevant authorities in the latter case: para 5(4).

(3) Under para 1(2), the claim is then treated as made on the date of the claim for asylum. Benefit is then determined for the period between that date and the date of notification, or any part of that period for which HB is claimed: para 1(3).

(4) For HB claims, the claim is to be assessed on the basis of the rent restrictions rules in force on 1 January 1996 (before the introduction of the provisions making the rent officer's determinations binding) and there is to be no reference to a rent officer: para 3. Part 8 HB Regs (or Part 7 HB(SPC) Regs) is to be applied as it was in force during the period of the claim, and the maximum rent provisions do not apply: para 7.

(5) As to payments, any benefit already paid to the claimant or her/his partner during the relevant period is to offset against the payment: para 9. For HB, regs 95 and 96 HB Regs (or regs 76 and 77 HB(SPC) Regs) concerning payment to landlords do not apply, but the authority may pay direct to the landlord where it is shown that for the whole or part of the relevant period, no rent has been paid: para 8(4). So if the claimant has paid part of her/his rent, the authority may not pay the landlord direct.

---

(2) Before Schedule 1 to both the Housing Benefit Regulations and the Housing Benefit (State Pension Credit) Regulations, insert, subject to sub-paragraph (3)–

"SCHEDULE A1
Treatment of claims for housing benefit by refugees

General Note
Schedule A1 lapsed from 14 June 2007 for those recorded as refugees after that date: see the General Note to para 1 above. The Schedule dealt with the administration of retrospective claims for HB by those subsequently granted refugee status. See the Analysis to reg 10A inserted by para 2(1) above for commentary on this issue.

Claim for housing benefit by a refugee
1.–(1) Where a person (in this Schedule called ''the claimant''), who has made a claim for asylum–
(a)   is subsequently notified by the Secretary of State that he has been recorded as a refugee; and
(b)   claims housing benefit–
    (i)   within the period specified in paragraph 2(4); and
    (ii)   in respect of one or more periods from the date of his claim for asylum to the date he is so notified,
his claim for housing benefit shall be treated as having been made on the date specified in sub-paragraph (2).
(2)   A claim for housing benefit to which sub-paragraph (1) refers shall be treated as made on the date on which his claim for asylum was recorded by the Secretary of State as having been made.
(3)   In this Schedule ''the relevant period'' means the period or any part of the period, from the date on which the claim for benefit is treated as made in accordance with sub-paragraph (2), to the date the claimant concerned is notified by the Secretary of State that he has been recorded as a refugee, for which housing benefit is claimed in accordance with this paragraph.

Relevant authority to whom a claim for housing benefit by a refugee shall be made and time for making a claim
2.–(1)   A claim for housing benefit made by a refugee on or after 3rd April 2000 for the relevant period may be made to the relevant authority for the area in which the dwelling which the claimant occupied as his home was situate and in respect of which he was liable to make payments.
(2)   Where the claimant has occupied more than one dwelling as his home in the relevant period, only one claim for housing benefit shall be made in respect of that period and such a claim shall be made to the authority for the area in which the dwelling occupied by the refugee is situate and in respect of which he was liable to make payments when, after he is notified that he has been recorded by the Secretary of State as a refugee, he makes a claim for housing benefit.
(3)   The relevant authority to which a claim for housing benefit is made in accordance with this paragraph, shall determine the claimant's entitlement to that benefit for the whole of the relevant period.
(4)   A claim for housing benefit to which this paragraph refers, shall be made within 28 days of a claimant receiving notification from the Secretary of State that he has been recorded as a refugee.
(5)   Regulation 83(12) of these Regulations (backdating of claims) shall not have effect with respect to claims to which this Schedule applies.

Eligible rent
3.–(1)   Subject to sub-paragraph (2), for the purpose of determining a claimant's eligible rent–

(a)   regulations 12 and 13 have effect as they were in force on 1st January 1996;

(b)   in paragraph (1) of regulation 12 of the former Regulations (restrictions on rent increases) as saved by paragraph 5 of Schedule 3 to the Housing Benefit and Council Tax Benefit (Consequential Provisions) Regulations 2006 the words from "whether by reference" to "or otherwise" shall be omitted; and

(c)   regulation 14 (requirement to refer to a rent officer) shall not have effect.

(2)   In determining a claimant's eligible rent for the relevant period, the relevant authority may have regard to information in their possession or which they may obtain, as to the level of rents which had effect in that period in respect of any area in which the claimant occupied a dwelling as his home and in respect of which his claim for housing benefit is made.

Applicable amounts

4.   With respect to a claim for housing benefit under this Schedule, the applicable amounts for the purposes of Part 5 shall be the aggregate of any personal allowance and premium which would have been applicable in the claimant's case in the relevant period at the rates for each tax year to which the claim relates set by an Order made under section 150 of the Administration Act (annual up-rating of benefits).

Evidence and information

5.–(1)   A claimant who makes a claim for housing benefit for the relevant period shall furnish such certificates, documents, information and evidence in connection with the claim, or evidence needed for the determination of the claim or any questions arising in connection with the claim, as may be reasonably required by the relevant authority in order to determine that person's entitlement to that benefit and which are in his possession or which he may reasonably be expected to obtain.

(2)   The relevant authority may require information to be provided by–

(a)   the landlord of any dwelling in respect of which a claim for housing benefit arises under this Schedule;

(b)   any other person to whom the rent for the dwelling was paid; and

(c)   any person who made payments of rent to a landlord on behalf of a claimant in the relevant period,

in particular as to the amount of any such rent and any service charges which were included in the rent.

(3)   Where the claimant is unable to furnish the necessary evidence to substantiate his claim the authority shall determine the claim on the basis of the evidence that is produced, including any statements made by the claimant himself, any information provided by a landlord under sub-paragraph (2) or by any other person.

(4)   Where the claimant has resided in the areas of two or more local authorities in Great Britain in the relevant period, the relevant authority to which the claim for housing benefit is made may require any such other authority in whose area the claimant has resided, to provide such information as the relevant authority may reasonably require in connection with the exercise of its functions under regulation 10A and this Schedule and such other authority shall provide the necessary information within 14 days of receiving the request for the information concerned or such longer period as is reasonable in that case.

Changes of circumstances

6.   With respect to claims for housing benefit to which paragraph 1 above applies, for paragraph (1) of regulation 88 (duty to notify changes of circumstances) there shall be substituted the following paragraph–

"(1)   Upon claiming housing benefit in accordance with Schedule A1 (treatment of claims for housing benefit by refugees) a claimant, or any person by whom or on whose behalf sums payable by way of housing benefit are receivable, shall provide the relevant authority with information concerning any change of circumstances which occurred during the period to which the claim relates which the claimant or that other person might reasonably expect to affect the claimant's right to and the amount of benefit."

Calculation of amount of benefit

7.   The appropriate maximum housing benefit to which a claimant is entitled under regulation 10A and this Schedule shall be calculated on a weekly basis in accordance with Part 8 as it had effect for the relevant period.

Payments

8.–(1)   Subject to sub-paragraph (5), where it is determined that the claimant is entitled to housing benefit in accordance with regulation 10A and this Schedule, payment of the amount due shall be made within 14 days of the date of that determination.

(2)   The relevant authority in respect of a claim to which this Schedule applies is made, shall be solely responsible for the payment of any housing benefit to which the claimant is entitled for the relevant period.

(3)   Regulation 93 (payment on account of a rent allowance) shall not have effect with respect to any payment to which a claimant is entitled under regulation 10.

(4)   Regulations 95 and 96 (circumstances in which payment of benefit will be made to a landlord) shall not have effect with respect to a payment to which this Schedule applies but where–

(a)   a landlord shows that, for the whole or any part of the relevant period for which housing benefit in the form of a rent allowance has been awarded, no payment of rent has been made;

(b)   information is provided to show the rent that remains due;

(c)   the claimant has been notified that a payment to the landlord may be made; and

(d)   the relevant authority, having taken account of any representations made by the claimant with respect to such a payment being made, consider that it is reasonable that the benefit or part of the benefit due should be paid to the landlord,

any benefit to which the claimant is entitled under regulation 10A and this Schedule up to the amount of the eligible rent that is due, may be paid direct to the landlord concerned in respect of that rent.

(5)   Where a claimant was the tenant of a housing or local authority for the whole or part of the relevant period, to the extent that any eligible rent remains due to the authority concerned in respect of the whole or part of that period, any housing benefit to which the claimant is entitled under regulation 10A and this Schedule shall–

(a)   where that authority is the authority to whom the claim under this Schedule is made, be reduced by the amount of the eligible rent remaining due to that authority; and

(b)   in any other case, be paid to the authority concerned,

and any balance of benefit remaining due in respect of that period shall be paid to the claimant.

Offsets

9.   Any housing benefit which has otherwise been paid to the claimant or any partner of his, in respect of any part of the relevant period, shall be offset against any award due to the claimant by virtue of regulation 10A and this Schedule, except to the extent that the benefit paid or allowed to that partner was due in respect of a period for which he was not a partner of the claimant.

Matters to be included in the decision notice

(10).   Parts 1 to 3, 5 and 6 of Schedule 9 (matters to be included in the decision notice) shall apply with respect to claims made in accordance with regulation 10A.''.

(3)   In its application to the Housing Benefit (State Pension Credit) Regulations, Schedule A1 shall have effect as if–

(a)   for the reference to ''Regulation 83(12)'' in paragraph 2(5), there were substituted a reference to ''Regulation 64(13)'';

(b)   for the reference to ''regulation 88'' in paragraph 6, there were substituted a reference to ''regulation 69'';

(c)   for the reference to ''Part 8'' in paragraph 7, there were substituted a reference to ''part 7'';

(d)   for the reference to ''regulation 93'' in paragraph 8(3), there were substituted a reference to ''regulation 74'';

(e)   for the reference to ''Regulations 95 and 96'' in paragraph 8(4), there were substituted a reference to ''Regulations 76 and 77'';

(f)   for the reference to ''Schedule 9'' in paragraph 10, there were substituted a reference to ''Schedule 8''.

(4)   For paragraph 51 of Schedule 5 to the Housing Benefit Regulations, substitute–

''**51.**   Any council tax benefit, including any amount of council tax benefit to which a person is entitled by virtue of regulation 7A of the Council Tax Benefit Regulations 2006.''.

(5)   After paragraph 55 of Schedule 5 to the Housing Benefit Regulations insert–

''**55A.**   Any amount of housing benefit to which a person is entitled by virtue of regulation 10A (entitlement of a refugee to housing benefit).

55B. Any amount of income support to which a person is entitled by virtue of regulation 21ZB of the Income Support Regulations (treatment of refugees).''.

(6)   After paragraph 48 of Schedule 6 to the Housing Benefit Regulations insert–

''**48A.**   Any amount of housing benefit to which a person is entitled by virtue of regulation 10A (entitlement of a refugee to housing benefit) but only for a period of 52 weeks from the date that such an amount is received pursuant to that regulation.

48B.   Any amount of income support to which a person is entitled by virtue of regulation 21ZB of the Income Support Regulations (treatment of refugees) but only for a period of 52 weeks from the date that such an amount is received pursuant to that regulation.''.

Refugees – council tax benefit

3.–(1)   After regulation 7 of both the Council Tax Benefit Regulations and the Council Tax Benefit (State Pension Credit) Regulations, insert–

"Entitlement of a refugee to council tax benefit

7A. Where a person, who has made a claim for asylum, is notified that he has been recorded by the Secretary of State as a refugee, these Regulations shall have effect with respect to his entitlement to council tax benefit for the relevant period which applies in his case in accordance with Schedule A1 (treatment of claims for council tax benefit by refugees) but subject to the provisions of that Schedule.".

(2)   Before Schedule 1 to both the Council Tax Benefit Regulations and the Council Tax Benefit (State Pension Credit) Regulations, insert, subject to sub-paragraph (3)–

General Note

Regulation 7A lapsed from 14 June 2007 for those recorded as refugees after that date: see the General Note to para 1 above.

"SCHEDULE A1
Regulation 7A
Treatment of claims for council tax benefit by refugees

General Note

Schedule A1 lapsed from 14 June 2007 for those recorded as refugees after that date: see the General Note to para 1 above. The Schedule deals with the administration of retrospective claims for CTB by those subsequently granted refugee status. See the analysis to reg 10A HB Regs inserted by para 2(1) for more detailed commentary on this issue.

Claim for council tax benefit by a refugee

1.–(1)   Where a person (in this Schedule called "the claimant"), who has made a claim for asylum–
(a)   is subsequently notified by the Secretary of State that he has been recorded as a refugee; and
(b)   claims council tax benefit–
    (i)   within the period specified in paragraph 2(4); and
    (ii)   in respect of one or more periods from the date of his claim for asylum to the date he is so notified,
his claim for council tax shall be treated as having been made on the dates specified in sub-paragraph (2).

(2)   A claim for council tax benefit to which sub-paragraph (1) refers shall be treated as made on the date on which his claim for asylum was recorded by the Secretary of State as having been made.

(3)   In this Schedule "the relevant period" means the period or any part of the period from the date on which the claim for benefit is treated as made, in accordance with subparagraph (2), to the date the claimant concerned is notified by the Secretary of State that he has been recorded as a refugee, for which council tax benefit is claimed in accordance with this paragraph.

Relevant authority to whom a claim for council tax benefit by a refugee shall be made and time for making a claim

2.–(1)   A claim for council tax benefit made by a refugee on or after 3rd April 2000 for the relevant period may be made to the relevant authority for the area where the dwelling in which the claimant occupied as his home was situate and in respect of which he was liable for council tax.

(2)   Where the claimant has occupied more than one dwelling as his home in the relevant period, only one claim for council tax benefit shall be made in respect of that period and such a claim shall be made to the authority for the area in which the dwelling occupied by the refugee is situate and in respect of which he was liable to make payment when, after he is notified that he has been recorded by the Secretary of State as a refugee, he makes a claim for council tax benefit.

(3)   The relevant authority to which a claim for council tax benefit is made in accordance with this paragraph, shall determine the claimant's entitlement to that benefit for the whole of the relevant period.

(4)   A claim for council tax benefit, to which his paragraph refers, shall be made within 28 days of a claimant receiving notification from the Secretary of State that he has been recorded as a refugee.

Applicable amounts

3.   With respect to a claim for council tax benefit under this Schedule, the applicable amounts for the purposes of Part 3 of these Regulations shall be the aggregate of any personal allowance and premium which would have been applicable in the claimant's case in the relevant period at the rates for each tax year to which the claim relates set by an Order made under section 150 of the Administration Act (annual up-rating of benefits).

Evidence and information

4–(1)   A claimant who makes a claim for council tax benefit for the relevant period shall furnish such certificates, documents, information and evidence in connection with the claim, or evidence needed for the determination of the claim or any questions arising in connection with the claim, as may be reasonably required by the relevant authority in order to determine that person's entitlement to that benefit and which are in his possession or which he may reasonably be expected to obtain.(2) The relevant authority may require information to be provided by the landlord of any dwelling in respect of which a claim for council tax benefit arises under this Schedule, in particular as to the period for which the claimant resided in the dwelling during the relevant period.

(2) Where the claimant is unable to furnish the necessary evidence to substantiate his claim, the authority shall determine the claim on the basis of the evidence that is produced including any statements made by the claimant himself and any information provided by a landlord of any dwelling in respect of which the claim under this Schedule arises or by any other person.

(3) Where the claimant has resided in the areas of two or more local authorities in Great Britain in the relevant period, the relevant authority to which the claim for council tax benefit is made may require such other authority in whose area the claimant has resided, to provide such information as the relevant authority may reasonably require in connection with the exercise of its functions under regulation 7A and this Schedule and that other authority shall provide the necessary information within 14 days of receiving the request for the information concerned or such longer period as is reasonable in that case.

Change of circumstances
5.   With respect to claims for council tax benefit to which paragraph 1 above applies, for paragraph (1) of regulation 74 (duty to notify changes of circumstances) there shall be substituted the following paragraph–

"(1)   Upon claiming council tax benefit in accordance with Schedule A1 (treatment of clams for council tax benefit by refugees) a claimant, or any person by whom or on whose behalf sums payable by way of council tax benefit are receivable, shall provide the relevant authority to whom the claim is made with information concerning any change of circumstances which occurred during the period to which the claim relates which the claimant or that other person might reasonably expect to affect the claimant's right to the amount of benefit.''.

Calculation of amount of council tax benefit
6.   The appropriate maximum council tax benefit, or alternative maximum council tax benefit to which a claimant is entitled under regulation 7A and this Schedule shall be calculated on a daily basis in accordance with Part 6 as it had effect for the relevant period.

Payments
7.–(1)   Where it is determined that the claimant is entitled to council tax benefit in accordance with regulation 7A and this Schedule, the amount due shall be paid or allowed within 14 days of the date of that determination in accordance with regulation 77 (time and manner of granting council tax benefit).

(2)   The relevant authority in respect of a claim to which this Schedule applies is made, shall be solely responsible for paying or allowing any council tax benefit to which the claimant is entitled for the relevant period.

(3)   Subject to paragraph (4), where council tax is outstanding from the claimant to the relevant authority referred to in sub-paragraph (2), in respect of any part of the relevant period, that council tax shall be offset against any council tax benefit to which the claimant is entitled under this Schedule and only the balance remaining, (if any), shall be paid to the claimant.

(4)   Where council tax is outstanding from the claimant to an authority other than the relevant authority referred to in sub-paragraph (2) in respect of any part of the relevant period, council tax benefit due under this Schedule in respect of any such a part shall be paid to the authority concerned for the discharge of the council tax due.

Offsets
8.   Any council tax benefit which has otherwise been paid or allowed to the claimant or any partner of his in respect of any part of the relevant period, shall be offset against any award due to the claimant by virtue of regulation 7A and this Schedule, except to the extent that the benefit paid or allowed to that partner was due in respect of a period for which he was not a partner of the claimant.

Matters to be included in the decision notice
9.   Parts 1 to 6 of Schedule 8 to these Regulations (matters to be included in the decision notice) shall apply with respect to claims made in accordance with regulation 8.''.

(3)   In its application to the Council Tax Benefit (State Pension Credit) Regulations, Schedule A1 shall have effect as if–
    (a)   for the reference to "regulation 74" in paragraph 5, there were substituted a reference to "regulation 59";
    (b)   for the reference to "Part 6" in paragraph 6, there were substituted a reference to "Part 5";

(c) for the reference to "regulation 77" in paragraph 7(1), there were substituted a reference to "regulation 62"; and

(d) for the reference to "Schedule 8" in paragraph 9, there were substituted a reference to "Schedule 7".

(4) For paragraph 37 of Schedule 4 to the Council Tax Benefit Regulations, substitute–

"**37.** Any housing benefit, including any amount of housing benefit to which a person is entitled by virtue of regulation 11A of the Housing Benefit Regulations 2006.".

(5) After paragraph 56 of Schedule 4 to the Council Tax Benefit Regulations, insert–

"**56A.** Any council tax benefit to which the claimant is entitled including any amount of council tax benefit to which a person is entitled by virtue of regulation 7A of the Council Tax Benefit Regulations (entitlement of a refugee to council tax benefit).

56B. Any amount of income support to which a person is entitled by virtue of regulation 21ZB of the Income Support Regulations (treatment of refugees).".

(6) After paragraph 53 of Schedule 5 to the Council Tax Benefit Regulations, insert–

"**53A.** Any amount of council tax benefit to which a person is entitled by virtue of regulation 7A (entitlement of a refugee to council tax benefit) but only for a period of 52 weeks from the date that such an amount is received pursuant to that regulation.

53B. Any amount of income support to which a person is entitled by virtue of regulation 21ZB of the Income Support Regulations (treatment of refugees) but only for a period of 52 weeks from the date that such an amount is received pursuant to that regulation.".

Persons from abroad

4.–(1) Sub-paragraphs (2) to (5) apply where, in relation to a claim for income support, a social fund payment, housing benefit or council tax benefit, as the case may be, a person has submitted a claim for asylum on or before 2nd April 2000 and is notified that he has been recorded by the Secretary of State as a refugee within the definition in Article 1 of the Convention relating to the Status of Refugees done at Geneva on 28th July 1951 as extended by Article 1(2) of the Protocol relating to the Status of Refugees done at New York on 31st January 1967.

General Note

Schedule A1 as inserted by para 2(2) above only applied to those claiming asylum after 2 April 2000. For those seeking asylum prior to on or before that date, Sch A1 had effect as amended by para 4(2)(a). For the text as it stood prior to April 2000, see pp389-391 of the 12th edition of this work. Note that Schedule A1 lapsed from 14 June 2007 for those recorded as refugees after that date: see the General Note to para 1 above.

(2) Where this paragraph applies, the Housing Benefit Regulations and the Housing Benefit (State Pension Credit) Regulations shall have effect, subject to sub-paragraph (3), as if–

(a) in Schedule A1 to both those Regulations–

   (i) in paragraph 1, in sub-paragraph (1), for the words "his claim for housing benefit" to the end of the sub-paragraph, substitute "his claim for housing benefit shall be treated as having been made on whichever of the dates specified in sub-paragraph (2) applies in his case";

   (ii) for sub-paragraph (2), substitute–

"(2) A claim for housing benefit to which sub-paragraph (1) refers shall be treated as made–

(a) in the case of a claimant who made a claim for asylum upon arrival in the United Kingdom, on the date on which his claim for asylum was first refused by the Secretary of State or 5th February 1996 if that is later; or

(b) in the case of a claimant whose claim for asylum was made other than on arrival in the United Kingdom, on the date of that claim for asylum or 5th February 1996 if that is later.";

   (iii) for paragraph 2, substitute–

"**2.**–(1) A claim for housing benefit for the relevant period may be made to the relevant authority for the area in which the dwelling which the claimant occupied as his home was situate and in respect of which he was liable to make payments.

(2) Where the claimant has occupied more than one dwelling as his home in the relevant period, only one claim for housing benefit shall be made in respect of that period and shall be made to the relevant authority for the area in which the dwelling which he last occupied in that period was situate.

(3) The relevant authority to which a claim for housing benefit is made in accordance with this paragraph, shall determine the claimant's entitlement to that benefit for the whole of the relevant period.

(4) A claim for housing benefit, to which this paragraph refers, shall be made–

(a) in the case of a claimant who was notified by the Secretary of State in the period from 24th July 1996 to 15th October 1996 that he had been recorded as a refugee, within 28 days of the later date;

(b)   in any other case, within 28 days of a claimant being notified by the Secretary of State that he has been recorded as a refugee.

(5)   Regulation 83(12) of these Regulations (backdating of claims) shall not have effect with respect to claims to which this Schedule applies.'';

(b)   in Schedule 5 to the Housing Benefit Regulations (sums to be disregarded in the calculation of income other than earnings), for paragraph 56, substitute–

"**55B.**   Any amount of income support to which a person is entitled by virtue of regulation 21ZA of the Income Support (General) Regulations 1987 (treatment of refugees), as in force on 2nd April 2000.'';

(c)   in Schedule 6 to the Housing Benefit Regulations (capital to be disregarded), for paragraph 55B, substitute–

"**48B.**   Any amount of income support to which a person is entitled by virtue of regulation 21ZA of the Income Support Regulations (treatment of refugees), as in force on 2nd April 2000.''.

(3)   In the Housing Benefit (State Pension Credit) Regulations, the reference to regulation 83(12) in paragraph 2(5) of Schedule 1A, as substituted by sub-paragraph (2) above, is a reference to regulation 64(13).

(4)   Where this paragraph applies, the Council Tax Benefit Regulations and the Council Tax Benefit (State Pension Credit) Regulations shall have effect, subject to sub-paragraph (5), as if–

(a)   in Schedule A1 to both those Regulations–

    (i)   in paragraph 1, in sub-paragraph (1), for the words ''his claim for council tax benefit'' to the end of the sub-paragraph, substitute ''his claim for council tax benefit shall be treated as having been made on whichever of the dates specified in sub-paragraph (2) applies in his case'';

    (ii)   for sub-paragraph (2), substitute–

"(2)   A claim for council tax benefit to which sub-paragraph (1) refers shall be treated as made–

(a)   in the case of a claimant who made a claim for asylum upon arrival in the United Kingdom, on the date on which his claim for asylum was first refused by the Secretary of State or 5th February 1996 if that is later; or

(b)   in the case of a claimant whose claim for asylum was made other than on arrival in the United Kingdom, on the date of that claim for asylum or 5th February 1996 if that is later.'';

    (iii)   for paragraph 2, substitute–

"**2.**–(1)   A claim for council tax benefit for the relevant period may be made to the relevant authority for the area where the dwelling in which the claimant resided was situate and in respect of which he was liable for council tax.

(2)   Where the claimant has resided in more than one such dwelling in the relevant period, only one claim for council tax benefit shall be made in respect of that period and shall be made to the relevant authority for the area in which the dwelling in which he last resided in that period was situate.

(3)   The relevant authority to which a claim for council tax benefit is made in accordance with this paragraph, shall determine the claimant's entitlement to that benefit for the whole of the relevant period.

(4)   A claim for council tax benefit, to which this paragraph refers, shall be made–

(a)   in the case of a claimant who was notified by the Secretary of State in the period from 24th July 1996 to 15th October 1996 that he had been recorded as a refugee, within 28 days of the later date;

(b)   in any other case, within 28 days of a claimant being notified by the Secretary of State that he has been recorded as a refugee.

(5)   Regulation 69(14) of these Regulations (backdating of claims) shall not have effect with respect to claims to which this Schedule applies.''

(b)   in Schedule 4 to the Council Tax Benefit Regulations (sums to be disregarded in the calculation of income other than earnings), for paragraph 56B, substitute–

"**56B.**   Any amount of income support to which a person is entitled by virtue of regulation 21ZA of the Income Support (General) Regulations 1987 (treatment of refugees), as in force on 2nd April 2000.''.

(c)   in Schedule 5 to the Council Tax Benefit Regulations (capital to be disregarded), for regulation 53B, substitute–

"**53B.**   Any amount of income support to which a person is entitled by virtue of regulation 21ZA of the Income Support Regulations (treatment of refugees), as in force on 2nd April 2000.''.

(5)   In the Council Tax Benefit (State Pension Credit) Regulations, the reference to regulation 69(14) in paragraph 2(5) of Schedule 1A, as substituted by sub-paragraph (4) above, is a reference to regulation 53(13).

The Social Security (Persons from Abroad) Amendment Regulations 2006
(SI 2006 No.1026)

Citation and commencement
1. These Regulations shall be cited as the Social Security (Persons from Abroad) Amendment Regulations 2006 and shall come into force on 30th April 2006.

Nationals of Norway, Iceland, Liechtenstein and Switzerland
10. The following provisions shall apply in relation to a national of Norway, Iceland, Liechtenstein or Switzerland or a member of his family (within the meaning of Article 2 of Council Directive No. 2004/38/EC) as if such a national were a national of a member State–
  (a) regulation 7(4A)(a) to (e) of the Council Tax Benefit Regulations 2006;
  (b) regulation 7(4A)(a) to (e) of the Council Tax Benefit (Persons who have attained the qualifying age for state pension credit) Regulations 2006;
  (c) regulation 10(3B)(a) to (e) of the Housing Benefit Regulations 2006;
  (d) regulation 10(4A)(a) to (e) of the Housing Benefit (Persons who have attained the qualifying age for state pension credit) Regulations 2006;
  (e)-(h) *Omitted*

Revocations and savings
11.–(1) *Omitted*
  (2) Nothing in these Regulations shall affect the continued operation of the transitional arrangements and savings provided for in–
  (a) regulation 12 of the Social Security (Persons From Abroad) Miscellaneous Amendments Regulations 1996;
  (b) regulation 6 of the Social Security (Habitual Residence) Amendment Regulations 2004; or
  (c) paragraph 6 of Schedule 3 to the Housing Benefit and Council Tax Benefit (Consequential Provisions) Regulations 2006.

The Rent Repayment Orders (Supplementary Provisions) (England) Regulations 2007
(SI 2007 No.572)

General Note on the Regulations

Parts 2 and 3 of the Housing Act 2004 give local authorities powers to apply to a residential property tribunal for a rent repayment order to be made in respect of a house, or a house in multiple occupation, required to be licensed, but which is not licensed. These Regulations enable a local housing authority to amend its application for an order where there may have been a payment of HB that was not "properly payable": reg 2. They also specify the purposes for which payments received under a rent repayment order may be applied and require any amount not applied for one of these purposes to be paid into the Consolidated Fund: regs 3 and 4.

Citation, commencement, application and interpretation

1.–(1) These Regulations may be cited as the Rent Repayment Orders (Supplementary Provisions) (England) Regulations 2007 and shall come into force on 6th April 2007.

(2) These Regulations apply in relation to England only.

(3) In these Regulations, ''the Act'' means the Housing Act 2004.

Overpayments of housing benefit

2.–(1) Paragraph (2) applies if, in the course of proceedings on an application under subsection (5) of section 73 of the Act (other consequences of operating unlicensed HMOs: rent repayment orders) or subsection (5) of section 96 of the Act (other consequences of operating unlicensed houses: rent repayment orders), it comes to the notice of the local housing authority that in respect of periodical payments payable in connection with occupation of the part or parts of the HMO or of the whole or part of the house to which the application applies there may have been a payment of housing benefit that was not properly payable.

(2) A local housing authority may apply to the residential property tribunal for leave to amend their application by substituting for the total amount of housing benefit paid, such part of that amount as they believe is properly payable.

(3) For the purposes of paragraphs (1) and (2)–

(a) an amount of housing benefit is properly payable if the person to whom, or in respect of whom, it is paid is entitled to it under the Housing Benefit Regulations 2006 or the Housing Benefit (Persons who have attained the qualifying age for state pension credit) Regulations 2006 (whether on the initial decision or as subsequently revised or superseded or further revised or superseded), and

(b) ''overpayment of housing benefit'' has the meaning given by regulation 99 of the Housing Benefit Regulations 2006 or, as the case may be, regulation 80 of the Housing Benefit (Persons who have obtained the qualifying age for state pension credit) Regulations 2006.

3.–(1) Subject to paragraph (3), a local housing authority may apply an amount recovered under a rent repayment order for any of the purposes mentioned in paragraph (2).

(2) The purposes are the reimbursement of the authority's costs and expenses (whether administrative or legal) incurred in, or associated with–

(a) the making of the application under section 73(5) of the Act or, as the case may be, section 96(5) of the Act;

(b) the registration and enforcement of any legal charge under section 74(9)(b) or 97(9)(b) of the Act on the relevant property;

(c) dealing with any application for the grant of a licence in respect of the relevant property under Part 2 of the Act (licensing of HMOs) or, as the case may be, Part 3 of the Act (selective licensing of other residential accommodation);

(d) the prosecution of the appropriate person for an offence under section 72(1) of the Act or, as the case may be, section 95(1) of the Act, in relation to the relevant property (whether proceedings are instituted before or after the making of the order);

(e) the making of an interim or final management order under Chapter 1 of Part 4 of the Act (interim and final management orders) in respect of the relevant property (whether the management order is made before or after the making of the rent repayment order);

(f) the management of the relevant property while an interim or final management order is in force;

(g) the execution of works undertaken in relation to the relevant property while an interim management order is in force; and

(h) the preparation of, or execution of works under, a management scheme under section 119 of the Act (management schemes and accounts) while a final management order is in force.

(3) Nothing in paragraph (1) authorises the application of an amount by way of reimbursement of an authority's costs or expenses where a court or residential property tribunal has made an order with respect to all or some of those costs or expenses.

(4) In paragraph (2), ''the relevant property'' means the HMO or house to which the rent repayment order relates.

Treatment of surpluses

4. An amount recovered under a rent repayment order which is not applied for a purpose mentioned in regulation 3(2), shall be paid into the Consolidated Fund.

The Housing Benefit and Council Tax Benefit (War Pension Disregards) Regulations 2007
(SI 2007 No.1619)

General Note on the Regulations

In the assessment of income for HB (and CTB) £10 of certain war pensions must be disregarded. ss134(8) and 139(6) SSAA allow an authority to resolve to disregard more of (or all of) prescribed war pensions as income for the purposes of its HB and CTB schemes. The prescribed pensions are in the Schedule to these regulations. Note that "war widow's pension" includes any corresponding pension payable to a widower or a surviving civil partner: see, for example, s134(14) SSAA on p81.

Citation and commencement
1. These Regulations may be cited as The Housing Benefit and Council Tax Benefit (War Pension Disregards) Regulations 2007 and shall come into force on 3rd July 2007.

War disablement pensions
2. The war disablement pensions that are prescribed for the purpose of sections 134(8)(a) and 139(6)(a) of the Social Security Administration Act 1992, are specified in Part 1 of the Schedule.

War widow's pensions
3. The war widow's pensions that are prescribed for the purpose of sections 134(8)(a) and 139(6)(a) of the Social Security Administration Act, are specified in Part 2 of the Schedule.

THE SCHEDULE

Regulations 2 and 3
War disablement and war widow's pensions
PART 1

War disablement pensions
1. The war disablement pensions prescribed are–
(a) any retirement pay, pension or allowance granted in respect of disablement under powers conferred by or under–
    (i) the Air Force (Constitution) Act 1917;
    (ii) the Personal Injuries (Emergency Provisions) Act 1939;
    (iii) the Pensions (Navy, Army, Air Force and Mercantile Marine) Act 1939;
    (iv) the Polish Resettlement Act 1947;
    (v) Part VII or section 151 of the Reserve Forces Act 1980;
(b) the following pay, pension or allowances, but only the part attributable to disablement or disability–
    (i) a wounds pension granted to a member of the armed forces of the Crown;
    (ii) retired pay of a disabled officer granted on account of medical unfitness attributable to or aggravated by service in the armed forces of the Crown;
    (iii) a disablement or disability pension granted to a member of the armed forces of the Crown, other than a commissioned officer, on account of medical unfitness attributable to or aggravated by service in the armed forces of the Crown;
    (iv) a disablement pension granted to a person who has been employed in the nursing services of any of the armed forces of the Crown on account of medical unfitness attributable to or aggravated by service in the armed forces of the Crown; and
(c) a payment made under article 14(1)(b) of the Armed Forces and Reserve Forces (Compensation Scheme) Order 2005.

PART 2

War widow's pensions
2. The war widow's pensions prescribed are–

(a)   pensions or allowances granted in respect of death due to service or war injury and payable to widows, widowers or surviving civil partners by virtue of–
    (i)   the Air Force (Constitution) Act 1917;
    (ii)   the Personal Injuries (Emergency Provisions) Act 1939;
    (iii) the Pensions (Navy, Army, Air Force and Mercantile Marine) Act 1939;
    (iv)   the Polish Resettlement Act 1947;
    (v)   Part VII or section 151 of the Reserve Forces Act 1980;
(b)   the whole or any part of a pension payable to a widow, widower or surviving civil partner–
    (i)   under the Naval, Military and Air Forces etc. (Disablement and Death) Service Pensions Order 2006 insofar as that Order is made under the Naval and Marine Pay and Pensions Act 1865; or
    (ii)   only under section 12(1) of the Social Security (Miscellaneous Provisions) Act 1977;
and under any power of Her Majesty otherwise than under an enactment to make provision about pensions for or in respect of persons who have been disabled or have died in consequence of service as members of the Armed Forces of the Crown;
(c)   a payment made under article 21(1)(a) of the Armed Forces and Reserve Forces (Compensation Scheme) Order 2005.

The Housing Benefit (Loss of Benefit) (Pilot Scheme) Regulations 2007
(SI 2007 No. 2202)

General Note to the Regulations

ss130B to 130G SSCBA provide for a scheme of loss of benefit following eviction for anti-social behaviour, under which HB is paid at a reduced rate (or not paid at all). Under s130B SSCBA, HB is paid at a reduced rate, or is non-payable, if a claimant is entitled to HB, but a "relevant order for possession" (defined in s130C SSCBA – see p7) of a dwelling the claimant formerly occupied as her/his home was made and in consequence of the order, s/he ceased to occupy that home. These regulations deal with the amount by which HB can be reduced during the restriction period. They can only apply to a former occupier where the conditions in reg 3 are met.

The rules are being piloted in the local authority areas listed in the Schedule to these regulations, all of which are in England. The regulations cease to have effect on 31 October 2009 unless revoked with effect from an earlier date. See also the Housing Benefit (Loss of Benefit) (Pilot Scheme) (Supplementary) Regulations 2007 on p1144.

Citation, commencement and duration

1.–(1)   These Regulations may be cited as the Housing Benefit (Loss of Benefit) (Pilot Scheme) Regulations 2007 and shall come into force on 1st November 2007.

(2)   These Regulations shall cease to have effect on 31st October 2009 unless revoked with effect from an earlier date.

Interpretation

2.–(1)   In these Regulations–

"the Fraud Act" means the Social Security Fraud Act 2001;

"attendance allowance" means–

(a)   an attendance allowance under section 64;

(b)   an increase of disablement pension under section 104 or 105 (increases where constant attendance needed and for exceptionally severe disablement);

(c)   a payment in respect of the need for constant attendance under regulations made in accordance with section 111 and paragraph 7(2) of Schedule 8 (payments for constant attendance in workmen's compensation cases);

(d)   an increase in allowance which is payable in respect of constant attendance under section 111 and paragraph 4 of Schedule 8 (industrial diseases benefit schemes);

(e)   a payment by virtue of article 14, 15, 16, 43 or 44 of the Personal Injuries (Civilians) Scheme 1983 or any analogous payment;

(f)   any payment based on the need for attendance which is paid as an addition to a war disablement pension;

"disability living allowance" means a disability living allowance under section 71;

"partner" means–

(a)   where a claimant is a member of a couple, the other member of that couple;

(b)   where a claimant is polygamously married to two or more members of his household, any such member;

"relevant authority" has the same meaning as in paragraph 1 of Schedule 7 to the Child Support, Pensions and Social Security Act 2000;

"war disablement pension" means–

(a)   any retirement pay, pension or allowance granted in respect of disablement under powers conferred by or under–

(i)   the Air Force (Constitution) Act 1917;

(ii)   the Personal Injuries (Emergency Provisions) Act 1939;

(iii)   the Pensions (Navy, Army, Air Force and Mercantile Marine) Act 1939;

(iv)   the Polish Resettlement Act 1947;

(v)   Part VII or section 151 of the Reserve Forces Act 1980;
(b) the following pay, pension or allowances, but only the part attributable to disablement or disability–

(i)   a wounds pension granted to a member of the armed forces of the Crown;

(ii)   retired pay of a disabled officer granted on account of medical unfitness attributable to or aggravated by service in the armed forces of the Crown;

(iii)   a disablement or disability pension granted to a member of the armed forces of the Crown, other than a commissioned officer, on account of medical unfitness attributable to or aggravated by service in the armed forces of the Crown;

(iv)   a disablement pension granted to a person who has been employed in the nursing services of any of the armed forces of the Crown on account of medical unfitness attributable to or aggravated by service in the armed forces of the Crown; and

(c)   a payment made under article 14(1)(b) of the Armed Forces and Reserve Forces (Compensation Scheme) Order 2005.

(2)   Unless the context otherwise requires, any reference in these Regulations to a numbered section or Schedule is a reference to the section of, or Schedule to, the Social Security Contributions and Benefits Act 1992 bearing that number.

Application of pilot scheme

3.   These Regulations apply in relation to a former occupier only where the following conditions are satisfied in his case–

(a)   the relevant order for possession relates to a dwelling which is within the area of a relevant authority specified in the Schedule and was made on or after the date there specified in relation to that authority;

(b)   the warning notice was served on him by a relevant local authority specified in the Schedule on or after the date there specified in relation to that authority; and

(c)   housing benefit is awarded in respect of a dwelling which is within the area of a relevant authority specified in the Schedule.

Reduction of benefit

4.–(1)   The housing benefit to which the former occupier would, apart from this regulation, be entitled in respect of any week in the restriction period is to be reduced as set out in this regulation.

(2)   In any case where the former occupier's housing benefit in respect of any week in the restriction period is also subject to a reduction due to the application of section 7 of the Fraud Act (loss of benefit for commission of benefit offences), this regulation shall be applied subject to regulation 6.

(3)   The restriction period is to contain three phases–

(a)   Phase A is a period of four weeks beginning on the first Monday of the restriction period;

(b)   Phase B is a period of four weeks beginning on the Monday following the last day of Phase A; and

(c)   Phase C is the remainder of the restriction period and begins on the Monday following the last day of Phase B.

(4)   Where the restriction period stops running under section 130B(6) and starts running again under that subsection, for the purposes of identifying the relevant phase, the restriction period is to start to run again from the point when it previously stopped running.

(5)   The former occupier's entitlement to housing benefit in respect of any week in–

(a)   Phase A is to be reduced by 10%.

(b)   Phase B is to be reduced by 20%.

(c)   Phase C is to be reduced by–

      (i)   100%; or

      (ii)   where the former occupier is a person in hardship under regulation 5 (meaning of "person in hardship"), 30%.

(6)   A reduction under sub-paragraphs (5)(a), (b) or (c)(ii) shall, if it is not a multiple of 5p, be rounded to the nearest such multiple or, if it is a multiple of 2.5p but not of 5p, to the next lower multiple of 5p.

Analysis

s130B(4) provides powers to prescribe the rate of HB and the circumstances when HB is payable where the conditions for sanction are met. The rates and circumstances are in reg 4. See reg 6 where s7 of the SSFA 2001 (loss of benefit for benefit offences) also applies: para (2).

Paras (3) and (5) The start and end of the "restriction period" are dealt with in s130B(5) to (8) SSCBA. The restriction period is divided into three phases: for the first four weeks, HB is reduced by 10 per cent; for the next four weeks, HB is reduced by 20 per cent; for the rest of the restriction period, no HB is paid unless the former occupier is a "person in hardship" (for which see reg 5), in which case, HB is reduced by 30 per cent.

Para (4) applies where a restriction period has stopped and then started again under s130B(6) SSCBA. In this case, the period runs on from where it previously stopped. For example, a claimant's HB is reduced by 10 per cent for four weeks, and then by 20 per cent for two weeks. The local authority then disappplies the restriction as the claimant's behaviour has improved. However, the claimant fails to comply with a further warning notice and the restriction period starts again. The claimant's HB is reduced by 20 per cent for a further two weeks and is then not payable.

Meaning of "person in hardship"

5.–(1)   A former occupier is a "person in hardship" if he–

(a)   has provided the relevant authority with a signed statement, on a form approved for the purpose by the Secretary of State, of the circumstances on which he relies to establish that he is a person in hardship; and

(b)   falls within paragraph (2), (3) or (5).

(2)   A former occupier falls within this paragraph if–

(a)   she is pregnant;

(b)   a member of his family is pregnant;

(c)   he is a single person aged less than 18; or

(d)   he is a member of a couple and both members are aged less than 18.

(3)   Subject to paragraph (4), a former occupier falls within this paragraph if he or his partner–

(a)   is responsible for a child or young person who is a member of the former occupier's household;

(b)   has been awarded an attendance allowance or the care component of disability living allowance at one of the two higher rates prescribed under section 72(4);

(c)   has claimed either attendance allowance or disability living allowance and the claim has not been determined;

(d)   devotes a considerable portion of each week to caring for another person who–

      (i)   has been awarded an attendance allowance or the care component of disability living allowance at one of the two higher rates prescribed under section 72(4); or

      (ii)   has claimed either attendance allowance or disability living allowance and the claim has not been determined; or

(e)   is aged 60 or more.

(4)   A former occupier to whom paragraph (3)(c) or (3)(d)(ii) applies is a person in hardship only for 26 weeks from the date of the claim unless he is a person in hardship under another provision of this regulation.

(5)   A former occupier falls within this paragraph where, after taking account of all the circumstances of the case including those set out in paragraph (6), the relevant authority is satisfied that, unless housing benefit is paid, he, or a member of his family, will suffer hardship.

(6)   The circumstances which the relevant authority is to take into account in determining whether the former occupier, or a member of his family, will suffer hardship include–

(a)   the resources which are likely to be available to his family and the length of time for which they might be available; and

(b)   whether there is a substantial risk that essential items, including food, clothing and heating, will cease to be available to him or a member of his family, or will be available at considerably reduced levels and the length of time for which this might be so.

(7)   For the purposes of this regulation "young person" has the meaning prescribed in regulation 19(1) of the Housing Benefit Regulations 2006 (persons of prescribed description).

Analysis

Under reg 4(5)(c), in the third phase of the restriction period, no HB is paid unless the former occupier is a "person in hardship", in which case, HB is reduced by 30 per cent. To be a person in hardship, the former occupier must provide a signed statement, on an approved form, setting out the circumstances and must fall within para (2), (3) or (5).

Paras (2), (3) and (5). A former occupier is a person in hardship if:

(1)   She is pregnant (or a member of her/his family is pregnant): para (2)(a) and (b).

(2)   She is a single person under 18, or a member of a couple both of whom are under 18: para (2)(c) and (d).

(3)   S/he or her/his partner is responsible for a child or young person who is a member of the former occupier's household: para (3)(a). Note that "young person" is defined for these purposes in reg 19(1) HB Regs: para (7).

(4)   S/he or her/his partner has been awarded attendance allowance (AA – see reg 2 for the extended definition) or the middle or higher rate of disability living allowance (DLA) care component, or has claimed AA or DLA and the claim has not yet been determined: para (3)(b) and (c). In the latter case, this only applies for 26 weeks from the date of the claim unless s/he is a person in hardship under another provision of reg 5: para (4).

(5)   S/he or her/his partner "devotes a considerable portion of each week" caring for someone who has been awarded AA or the middle or higher rate of DLA care component, or someone who has claimed AA or DLA and whose claim has not yet been determined: para (3)(d). In the latter case, this only applies for 26 weeks from the date of the claim unless s/he is a person in hardship under another provision of reg 5: para (4). Note that there is no requirement for the carer to have claimed, or to be entitled to, carer's allowance.

(6)   S/he or her/his partner is 60 or over: para (3)(e).

(7)   The local authority is satisfied that unless HB is paid, s/he or a member of her/his family will suffer hardship. The authority must take into account all the circumstances of the case, including those set out in para (6).

Reduction of benefit in cases where section 7 of the Fraud Act applies

6.–(1)   In any case where the former occupier's housing benefit is subject to both a reduction under these Regulations and a reduction due to the application of regulations made under section 7 of the Fraud Act (loss of benefit for commission of benefit offences), his housing benefit in any week in the restriction period is to be reduced by the greater of either–

(a)   the amount by which it would be reduced under regulation 4; or

(b)   the amount by which it would be reduced under regulation 17 of the Social Security (Loss of Benefit) Regulations 2001.

Analysis

Reg 4 deals with the circumstances when HB is payable where the conditions for sanction are met and the rate at which HB is payable. Reg 6 deals with situations where s7 of the SSFA 2001 (loss of benefit for benefit offences) also applies. In such a case, HB in any week in the restriction period is reduced by the greater of the amounts in sub-paras (a) or (b). Reg 17 of the Social Security (loss of Benefit) Regulations is on p1089.

SCHEDULE

REGULATION 3

PART 1

Relevant Authorities

Name of Authority	*relevant date*
Blackburn with Darwen Borough Council	1st November 2007
Blackpool Borough Council	1st November 2007
Dover District Council	1st November 2007
Manchester City Council	1st November 2007
New Forest District Council	1st November 2007
Newham London Borough Council	1st November 2007
South Gloucestershire Council	1st November 2007
Wirral Metropolitan Borough Council	1st November 2007

PART 2

Relevant Local Authorities

Name of Authority	*relevant date*
Blackburn with Darwen Borough Council	1st November 2007
Blackpool Borough Council	1st November 2007
Dover District Council	1st November 2007
Manchester City Council	1st November 2007
New Forest District Council	1st November 2007
Newham London Borough Council	1st November 2007
South Gloucestershire Council	1st November 2007
Wirral Metropolitan Borough Council	1st November 2007

The Housing Benefit (Loss of Benefit) (Pilot Scheme) (Supplementary) Regulations 2007
(SI 2007 No. 2474)

General Note to the Regulations
ss130B to 130G SSCBA provide for a scheme of loss of benefit following eviction for anti-social behaviour, under which HB is paid at a reduced rate (or not paid at all). The rules are being piloted in the local authority areas listed in the Schedule to the Housing Benefit (Loss of Benefit) (Pilot Scheme) Regulations 2007, all of which are in England. Under s130B SSCBA, HB is paid at a reduced rate, or is non-payable, if a claimant is entitled to HB, but a "relevant order for possession" (defined in s130C SSCBA) of a dwelling the claimant formerly occupied as her/his home was made and in consequence of the order, s/he ceased to occupy that home. In England, the former occupier must have failed without "good cause" (dealt with in regs 5 and 6 of these regulations) to comply with a warning notice to improve behaviour, served on her/him by the local authority. Under reg 4 of these regulations, the warning must be in writing. The regulations can only apply to a former occupier where the conditions in reg 3 are met.

Reg 7 provides the rules which must be observed when a local authority notifies a former occupier of a sanction, by reference to reg 90 HB regs and reg 71 HB(SPC) Regs.

Regs 10 to 13 deal with the provision of information by courts which make relevant possession orders, local authorities and relevant authorities (defined in reg 2).

The regulations cease to have effect on 31 October 2009 unless revoked with effect from an earlier date. See also the the Housing Benefit (Loss of Benefit) (Pilot Scheme) Regulations 2007 on p1139.

Citation, commencement and duration

1.–(1)   These Regulations may be cited as the Housing Benefit (Loss of Benefit) (Pilot Scheme) (Supplementary) Regulations 2007 and shall come into force on 1st November 2007.

(2)   These Regulations shall cease to have effect on 31st October 2009 unless revoked with effect from an earlier date.

Interpretation

2.–(1)   In these Regulations–

"the Pilot Scheme Regulations" means the Housing Benefit (Loss of Benefit) (Pilot Scheme) Regulations 2007;

"rehabilitation services" means the services referred to in section 130B(10), namely services provided by a relevant local authority to a former occupier with the aim of ending, or preventing repetition of, the conduct which may lead or has led to the making of a relevant order for possession;

"relevant authority" and "relevant decision" have the same meaning as in paragraph 1 of Schedule 7 to the Child Support, Pensions and Social Security Act 2000.

(2)   Unless the context otherwise requires, any reference in these Regulations to a numbered section or Schedule is a reference to the section of or Schedule to, the Social Security Contributions and Benefits Act 1992 bearing that number.

Application of pilot scheme

3.   These Regulations apply in relation to a former occupier only where the following conditions are satisfied in his case–

(a)   the relevant order for possession relates to a dwelling which is within the area of a relevant authority specified in the Schedule to the Pilot Scheme Regulations and was made on or after the date there specified in relation to that authority;

(b)   the warning notice was served on him by a relevant local authority specified in that Schedule on or after the date there specified in relation to that authority;

(c)   housing benefit is awarded in respect of a dwelling which is within the area of a relevant authority specified in that Schedule.

Warning notice
4.   The warning notice served under section 130B(2) must be in writing.

Matters which are to be taken into account in determining good cause
5.–(1)   In determining whether a person has, or does not have, good cause for failing to take action specified in a warning notice, the matters and circumstances which are to be taken into account include the following–
(a)   any condition or personal circumstance of that person which indicates that taking the action specified in the warning notice would be likely to or did–
   (i)   cause significant harm to his health; or
   (ii)   subject him to excessive physical or mental stress;
(b)   the person was suffering from some disease or bodily or mental disablement on account of which–
   (i)   he could not take the action specified in the warning notice;
   (ii)   taking the action specified in the warning notice would have put his health at risk; or
   (iii)   taking the action specified in the warning notice would have put at risk the health of other persons;
(c)   whether the person misunderstood the requirement on him because of that person's learning, language or literacy difficulties or because of any misleading information contained in the warning notice;
(d)   the fact that the failure to take the action in question resulted from a sincerely held religious or conscientious objection;
(e)   any caring responsibilities which would, or did, make it unreasonable for the person to take the action in question;
(f)   the fact that the person was attending court as a party to any proceedings, or as a witness or a juror;
(g)   the fact that the person was arranging or attending the funeral of–
   (i)   his partner;
   (ii)   a close friend; or
   (iii)   a parent, step-parent, grandparent, parent-in-law, son, step-son, son-in-law, daughter, step-daughter, daughter-in-law, brother, sister, grand-child or, if one member of the preceding is a member of a couple, the other member of that couple;
(h)   the fact that the person was engaged in–
   (i)   the manning or launching of a lifeboat; or
   (ii)   the performance of duty as a part-time fire-fighter employed by a fire and rescue authority;
(i)   the fact that the person was required to deal with some domestic emergency;
(j)   the fact that the person was engaged during an emergency in duties for the benefit of others;
(k)   subject to paragraph (2), the time it took, or would normally take, for the person to travel to and from the place mentioned in the warning notice where the action in question was to have been taken by a route and means appropriate to his circumstances and to the action which was to have been taken;
(l)   the expense which was, or would be, necessarily incurred by the person for the purposes of taking the action in question, together with the cost of travelling to and from the place mentioned in the warning notice where the action in question was to have been taken by a route and means appropriate to his circumstances and to the action which was to have been taken;
(m)   any difficulty with the person's normal mode of transport and whether there was any reasonable available alternative;
(n)   whether the person was attending a medical or dental appointment, or accompanying a person for whom the person has caring responsibilities to

such an appointment, and whether it would have been unreasonable, in the circumstances, to rearrange the appointment;

(o) whether the person was unable to take the action in question because of his employment responsibilities; and

(p) whether the person was searching for or moving to a suitable dwelling to occupy as his home.

(2) The time it took, or would normally take, for the person to travel to and from the place mentioned in the warning notice where the action in question was to have been taken may only be taken into account if the time is more than one hour and thirty minutes each way unless, in view of his health or caring responsibilities, that time was or is unreasonable.

(3) In this regulation–

(a) ''caring responsibilities'' means responsibility for caring for a child or for an elderly person or for a person whose physical or mental condition requires him to be cared for, who is either in the same household or a close relative;

(b) ''elderly person'' means a person of over pensionable age;

(c) ''employment responsibilities'' means–
    (i) attending an interview for employment;
    (ii) carrying out employed earner's employment; or
    (iii) carrying out self-employed earner's employment.

(d) ''partner'' means–
    (i) where a claimant is a member of a couple, the other member of that couple;
    (ii) where a claimant is polygamously married to two or more members of his household, any such member.

Circumstances in which a person is to be regarded as having good cause

6. A person is to be regarded as having good cause for failing to take any action specified in a warning notice if the time specified in the warning notice for taking the action is less than one week after the date the warning notice was issued.

Notification by relevant authority where sanction for anti-social behaviour applies

7.–(1) Except where paragraph (2) applies, regulation 90 of the Housing Benefit Regulations 2006 (notification of decisions) applies to a decision made under section 130B (loss of housing benefit following eviction on certain grounds) as if that decision had been made under those regulations.

(2) Where the claimant has attained the qualifying age for state pension credit, regulation 71 of the Housing Benefit (Persons who have attained the qualifying age for state pension credit) Regulations 2006 (notification of decisions) applies to decisions made under section 130B as if the decision had been made under those Regulations.

Provision of information by court to Secretary of State

10.–(1) Where, in respect of a dwelling situated in the area of an authority specified in the Schedule to the Pilot Scheme Regulations, a court–

(a) makes a relevant order for possession;

(b) suspends or stays the execution of a relevant order for possession or postpones the date for possession;

(c) varies the terms of a relevant order for possession; or

(d) sets aside a relevant order for possession

the court must notify the Secretary of State in writing within 4 weeks of doing so.

(2) When the court notifies the Secretary of State under paragraph (1), it must provide–

(a)   the name of the court which made the order which is the subject of the notification;
(b)   the date when the order for possession was made;
(c)   the date when any stay, suspension, postponement or variation was ordered;
(d)   the date when the order for possession was set aside;
(e)   the case or claim number of the order for possession and any subsequent orders to stay, suspend, vary or set it aside;
(f)   the name of the person against whom the order was made and, if known, the name of any members of that person's household;
(g)   the full postal address, including postcode, of the person against whom the order was made; and
(h)   details of any conditions attached to the order.
    (3)   The Secretary of State may request a court to provide, in relation to a relevant order for possession, any of the information listed in paragraphs (1) and (2).
    (4)   Where the Secretary of State requests information under paragraph (3), the court must send the information to the Secretary of State within the period of 4 weeks beginning on the date when the request for information was issued.
    (5)   In this regulation, "court" means a county court, the High Court, the Court of Appeal and the Judicial Committee of the House of Lords.

Supply of relevant information to Secretary of State for housing benefit purposes

    11.–(1)   The relevant local authority, or person authorised to exercise any function of such an authority relating to rehabilitation services, must notify the Secretary of State or any person providing services to him if any of the following occur–
(a)   the person against whom the relevant order for possession was made leaves the dwelling which is the subject of the order;
(b)   the former occupier has been awarded housing benefit;
(c)   the former occupier has been served with a warning notice;
(d)   the former occupier has failed to comply with that notice;
(e)   the former occupier's housing benefit has been reduced under section 130B(4)(a);
(f)   the restriction period has stopped running or starts running again under section 130B(6).
    (2)   Information supplied under paragraph (1) must be supplied in writing within 4 weeks of the event to which it relates.

Provision of relevant information for purposes relating to housing benefit administration

    12.–(1)   The following authorities and persons, namely–
(a)   a relevant authority;
(b)   a person authorised to exercise any function of a relevant authority relating to housing benefit;
(c)   a relevant local authority; or
(d)   a person authorised to exercise any function of a relevant local authority relating to rehabilitation services
must provide any information specified in paragraph (2) which is held by that authority or person to an authority or person mentioned in sub-paragraphs (a) or (b) if requested in writing by that authority or person.
    (2)   The information that must be provided is information which relates to a person who has been served with a warning notice; and–
(a)   is information about the relevant order for possession made against that person; or

(b)   relates to any action in relation to that person that may need to be taken by the authority in connection with sections 130B (loss of benefit following eviction on certain grounds), 130D (loss of housing benefit: supplementary) and 130E (couples).

(3)   Information received under paragraph (1) may be used only for any purpose relating to the administration of housing benefit.

(4)   The information must be provided within the period of 4 weeks beginning with the date when the authority or person receives the written request.

(5)   This regulation does not limit the circumstances in which information may be supplied apart from this regulation.

Provision of relevant information for use in the provision of rehabilitation services

13.–(1)   The following authorities and persons, namely–

(a)   a relevant authority;

(b)   a person authorised to exercise any function of a relevant authority relating to housing benefit;

(c)   a relevant local authority, or

(d)   a person authorised to exercise any function of a relevant local authority relating to the services mentioned in section 130B(10)

must provide any information specified in paragraph (2) held by that authority or person to an authority or person mentioned in sub-paragraphs (c) or (d) if requested in writing by that authority or person.

(2)   The information which must be provided is information which–

(a)   relates to a person who has been served with a warning notice; and

(b)   is relevant to the provision of rehabilitation services to that person by the authority to whom the information is provided.

(3)   Information received under paragraph (1) may be used only in the provision of rehabilitation services.

(4)   The information must be provided within the period of 4 weeks beginning with the date when the authority or person receives the written request.

(5)   This regulation does not limit the circumstances in which information may be supplied apart from this regulation.

The Social Security (Claims and Information) Regulations 2007
(SI 2007 No.2911)

Citation, commencement and interpretation

1.–(1)   These Regulations may be cited as the Social Security (Claims and Information) Regulations 2007 and shall come into force on 31st October 2007.

(2)   In regulations 4 and 5 "the Administration Act" means the Social Security Administration Act 1992.

(3)   In regulations 2 to 4–

"specified benefit" means one or more of the following benefits–

- (a)   attendance allowance;
- (b)   bereavement allowance;
- (c)   bereavement payment;
- (d)   carer's allowance;
- (e)   disability living allowance;
- (f)   incapacity benefit;
- (g)   income support;
- (h)   jobseeker's allowance;
- (i)   retirement pension;
- (j)   state pension credit;
- (k)   widowed parent's allowance;
- (l)   winter fuel payment;

"the Secretary of State" includes persons providing services to the Secretary of State;

"local authority" includes persons providing services to a local authority and persons authorised to exercise any function of a local authority relating to housing benefit or council tax benefit.

Use of social security information: local authorities

2.–(1)   This regulation applies where social security information held by a local authority was supplied by the Secretary of State to the local authority and this information–

- (a)   was used by the Secretary of State in connection with a person's claim for, or award of, a specified benefit; and
- (b)   is relevant to that person's claim for, or award of, council tax benefit or housing benefit.

(2)   The local authority must, for the purposes of the person's claim for, or award of, council tax benefit or housing benefit, use that information without verifying its accuracy.

(3)   Paragraph (2) does not apply where–

- (a)   the information is supplied more than twelve months after it was used by the Secretary of State in connection with a claim for, or an award of, a specified benefit; or
- (b)   the information is supplied within twelve months of its use by the Secretary of State but the local authority has reasonable grounds for believing the information has changed in the period between its use by the Secretary of State and its supply to the local authority; or
- (c)   the date on which the information was used by the Secretary of State cannot be determined.

Use of social security information: Secretary of State

3.–(1)   This regulation applies where social security information held by the Secretary of State was supplied by a local authority to the Secretary of State and this information–

(a)   was used by the local authority in connection with a person's claim for, or award of, council tax benefit or housing benefit; and

(b)   is relevant to that person's claim for, or award of, a specified benefit.

(2)   The Secretary of State must, for the purposes of the person's claim for, or award of, a specified benefit, use that information without verifying its accuracy.

(3)   Paragraph (2) does not apply where–

(a)   the information is supplied more than twelve months after it was used by a local authority in connection with a claim for, or an award of, council tax benefit or housing benefit; or

(b)   the information is supplied within twelve months of its use by the local authority but the Secretary of State has reasonable grounds for believing the information has changed in the period between its use by the local authority and its supply to the Secretary of State; or

(c)   the date on which the information was used by the local authority cannot be determined.

Social security information verified by local authorities

4.–(1)   This regulation applies where social security information is verified by a local authority by virtue of regulations made under section 7A(2)(e) of the Administration Act and forwarded by that local authority to the Secretary of State.

(2)   The Secretary of State must, for the purposes of a person's claim for, or award of, a specified benefit, use this information without verifying its accuracy.

(3)   Paragraph (2) does not apply where–

(a)   the Secretary of State has reasonable grounds for believing the social security information received from the local authority is inaccurate; or

(b)   the Secretary of State receives the information more than four weeks after it was verified by the local authority.

Specified benefits for the purpose of section 7B(3) of the Administration Act

5.   The benefits specified for the purpose of section 7B(3) of the Administration Act are–

(a)   a "specified benefit" within the meaning given in regulation 1(3);

(b)   housing benefit; and

(c)   council tax benefit.

Part 8

Secondary legislation
Subsidy

The Income-Related Benefits (Subsidy to Authorities) Order 1998

(SI 1998 No.562)

Arrangement of Articles

PART I

General

1.   Citation, commencement and interpretation

PART II

Claims for and payments of subsidy

2.   Interpretation of Parts II and IV
3.   Conditions for payment of subsidy
3A.   Electronic communications
4.   Requirement of claim
5.   Requirement to keep records and provide information
6.   Requirement of audit
7.   Final condition for the payment of subsidy
8.   In year payments of subsidy
8A.   Payment of subsidy before audit complete
9.   Payments of subsidy for the relevant year
9A.   Transitional Protection Adjustments
10.   Estimating subsidy

PART III

Calculation of subsidy

11.   Interpretation of Part III
12.   Amount of subsidy
13.   Relevant benefit
14.   Backdated benefit
15.   Disproportionate rent increase
15A.   Dispoportionate rent increases – Wales
16.   Treatment of high rents in rent allowance cases
17.   Subsidy in respect of homeless and short lease rebate cases
18.   Additions to subsidy
19.   Deductions to be made in calculating subsidy
20.   Deduction from subsidy
20A.   Deductions from subsidy for dwellings within the Housing Revenue Account
21.   Additions to subsidy in respect of security against fraud and error

PART IV

Transitional and savings

22.   Provisions for claims for 1997/98
23.   Transitional provisions in relation to rent officer determinations
24.   Modification of exemption from improvements rule

SCHEDULES

1.   Sums to be used in the calculation of subsidy
2.   Adjustment for prioritisation of claims
3.   Period overruns
4.   High rents and rent allowances
4A.   Rent rebate limitation deductions (Housing Revenue Account dwellings)
5.   Benefit savings

General Note

This Order sets out the arrangements for HB and CTB subsidy for the year commencing 1 April 1997 and subsequent years. The Order marked a change from the previous practice whereby new Housing Benefit and Council Tax Benefit (Subsidy) Orders (usually in very similar terms) were made each year and the previous year's order was revoked. Regular amendments are made each year to meet changing circumstances and policy.

The scheme of the Order is as follows:

Part I defines the terms used throughout the Order. In particular, the "relevant year" for subsidy purposes is the financial year used by all authorities (ie, 1 April to 31 March) and "relevant benefit" is defined by s140B(6) of SSAA 1992 as "housing benefit or council tax benefit as the case may be" (see p91).

Part II sets out in greater detail than before the conditions for the receipt of subsidy and states expressly (in art 3) that final subsidy cannot be paid unless all the conditions have been complied with.

Part III provides for the calculation of the subsidy due.

Part IV sets out transitional and savings provisions.

The rent rebate subsidy element of Housing Revenue Account Subsidy was abolished from 1 April 2004 (see the General Note on p1085 of the 17th edition of this work). Rent rebate subsidy is now governed by this Order, particularly arts 20A and Sch 4A.

PART I
General

Citation, commencement and interpretation

1.–(1)   This Order, which may be cited as the Income-related Benefits (Subsidy to Authorities) Order 1998, shall come into force on 31st March 1998 and shall have effect in relation to any relevant year.

(2)   In this Order, unless the context otherwise requires–

"the Act" means the Social Security Administration Act 1992;

"authority" means a billing, housing or, as the case may be, local authority;

"a 1997 authority" means a successor authority, whose reorganisation date was 1st April 1997;

"a 1998 authority" means a successor authority, whose reorganisation date was 1st April 1998;

"new authority" means

(i)   in England, a successor authority, whose reorganisation date was 1st April 1996;

(ii)   in Wales, an authority constituted under sections 20 and 21 of the Local Government Act 1972, and

(iii)   in Scotland, an authority constituted under section 2 of the Local Government etc. (Scotland) Act 1994;

"the English Regulations" means the Local Government Changes for England (Housing Benefit and Council Tax Benefit) Regulations 1995;

[²]

"the previous Orders" means the 1989 Order, the 1990 Order, the 1991 Order, the 1992 Order, the 1993 Order, the 1994 Order, the 1995 Order, the 1996 Order and the 1997 Order;

"relevant benefit" has the meaning ascribed to it in section 140B(6) of the Act;

"following year" means the year following the relevant year;

"relevant year" means the year, commencing on 1st April 1997 or on the 1st April in any year thereafter, in respect of which a claim for subsidy is made;

"the 1989 Order" means the Housing Benefit (Subsidy) Order 1989;

"the 1990 Order" means the Housing Benefit (Subsidy) Order 1990;

"the 1991 Order" means the Housing Benefit and Community Charge Benefit (Subsidy) Order 1991;

"the 1992 Order" means the Housing Benefit and Community Charge Benefit (Subsidy) Order 1992;

"the 1993 Order" means the Housing Benefit and Community Charge Benefit (Subsidy) (No. 2) Order 1993;

"the 1994 Order" means the Housing Benefit and Council Tax Benefit (Subsidy) Order 1994;

"the 1995 Order" means the Housing Benefit and Council Tax Benefit (Subsidy) Order 1995;

"the 1996 Order" means the Housing Benefit and Council Tax Benefit (Subsidy) Order 1996, and

"the 1997 Order" means the Housing Benefit and Council Tax Benefit (Subsidy) Order 1997.

(3) In paragraph (2), "successor authority" and "reorganisation date" have the same meanings as in regulation 2(1) of the English Regulations.

(4) In this Order, unless the context otherwise requires, a reference–

(a) to a numbered Part in this Order or a Schedule to this Order, is to the Part in this Order, or that Schedule, as the case may be, bearing that number;

(b) to a numbered article in or Schedule to this Order, is to the article in or Schedule to this Order, as the case may be, bearing that number;

(c) in an article or a Schedule to a lettered or numbered paragraph is to the paragraph bearing that letter or number in that article or that Schedule; and

(d) in a paragraph to a lettered or numbered sub-paragraph is to the sub-paragraph in that paragraph bearing that letter or number.

Amendments

1. Inserted by art 2(1) of SI 2002 No 3116 (retrospectively to 1.4.01).
2. Amended by art 2 of SI 2005 No 369 (retrospectively from 1.4.02).

PART II
Claims for and Payment of Subsidy

General Note on Part II

This Part sets out the conditions for entitlement to subsidy and the obligations of the DWP to pay it if those conditions are met.

The conditions are that:

(1) Subsidy must be claimed (art 4).

(2) The authority must keep adequate records to support the claim for subsidy and provide the DWP with the information required to verify the claim (art 5).

(3) The claim for subsidy must be audited no later than 31 December following the 31 March on which the subsidy year ends (art 6).

(4) The authority must satisfy the DWP that the claim for subsidy is "true and complete"; supported and/or supplemented by all the information reasonably required and fairly represents the expenditure incurred or likely to be incurred by the authority (art 7).

Claims are to be made on three occasions during the year:

(1) The "initial claim" under art 4(2)(a) must be made no later than 1 March in the preceding subsidy year (ie, at least one month before the year begins on 1 April) and is based on an estimate of the amount of "relevant benefit" which it will pay in the coming year.

(2) The "mid-year claim" under art 4(2)(b) must be made no later than 31 August in the year to which it relates and is based on an estimate of the amount of "relevant benefit" which the authority has paid up to that time and expects to pay by the following 31 May.

(3) The "final claim" under art 4(2)(c) must be made no later than 31 May following the end of the subsidy year and is based on the amount of "relevant benefit" which has actually been paid during the year (which, by that time, should be known precisely).

In addition to these claims, authorities must, under art 4(4), make quarterly returns on 15 July, 15 October, 15 January and 15 April giving details of "benefit savings" and "benefit related savings" (see para 1 of Sch 5).

As long as these above claims and returns are properly made, the DWP must:

(1) Under art 8, pay monthly instalments of subsidy to the authority (known as "interim subsidy"). The amount of each monthly payment is in the discretion of the DWP but the total payments during the year must not exceed the amount which is likely to be paid as final subsidy.

(2) Under art 9, pay final subsidy (or, more precisely the balance of final subsidy less interim subsidy) calculated in accordance with Part III.

Interpretation of Parts II and IV

2. In this Part and also in Part IV, unless the context otherwise requires–

[² "base data return" means a return pursuant to article 4(4A);]

[³]

"claim" means an initial claim, mid-year claim, final claim or a return pursuant to article 4(4), as the case may be;

"claim form" means the form supplied by the Secretary of State pursuant to article 4(2)(a), (b) or (c) or (4), as the case may be;

[⁵ "electronic communication" has the same meaning as in section 15(1) of the Electronic Communications Act 2000"]

[³]

"initial claim" means a claim for subsidy pursuant to article 4(2)(a);

"final claim" means a claim for subsidy pursuant to article 4(2)(c);

"mid-year claim" means a claim for subsidy pursuant to article 4(2)(b);

"final subsidy" means any subsidy which is not interim subsidy [⁴ or an amount paid, withheld or deducted pursuant to article 8A];

"interim subsidy" means subsidy pursuant to articles[¹ . . .], 8(1) or 9(4), as the case may be;

"the form" means a printed document or any other format upon which a claim may be set out, or any combination of such formats or alternative formats, as the Secretary of State determines; and

"the relevant office" means such office as may be designated by the Secretary of State.

Amendments
1. Inserted by art 2 of SI 2000 No 1091 (retrospectively to 1.4.99).
2. Inserted by art 1 of SI 2004 No 646 as from 1.4.04.
3. Amended by art 3(2) of SI 2005 No 369 (retrospectively from 1.4.03).
4. Amended by art 2(2) of SI 2006 No 54 (retrospectively from 1.4.04).
5. Amended by art 2(2) of SI 2007 No 26 as from 5.2.07.

Conditions for payment of subsidy

3. Subject to articles 9(3) and 10, no final subsidy shall be paid unless the conditions specified in the following provisions of this Part have been complied with.

[¹ Electronic communications

3A.–(1) The Secretary of State, an authority or auditor may use an electronic communication in connection with any claim, audit or payment of subsidy provided it is made in accordance with the provisions set out in Part 2 of Schedule 6.

(2) Any reference to an electronic communication in this Order means an electronic communication made in accordance with those provisions.

(3) Schedule 6 makes further provisions relating to electronic communications.]

Amendment
1. Inserted by art 2(3) of SI 2007 No 26 as from 5.2.07.

Requirement of claim

4.–(1) The first condition is that subsidy shall be claimed in accordance with the provisions of and in the manner specified by this article.

(2) There shall be submitted by an authority to the Secretary of State, at the relevant office, on the form supplied by him to that authority [⁹ or by means of an electronic communication], the following claims for subsidy, by reference to the amount of relevant benefit that that authority–

(a) estimates it will pay during the relevant year, by 1st March in the year preceding the relevant year;

(b)   estimates it has up to that time and will by the end of that relevant year have paid, by 31st August in the relevant year;

(c)   has paid in the relevant year, by [¹⁰ 31st May] in the following year.

(3)   [⁹ Except where an authority submits a claim by means of an electronic communication,] The final claim shall be copied to the authority's auditor, by [¹⁰ 31st May] in the following year.

(4)   In addition to the above claims, each authority shall submit to the Secretary of State at the relevant office, on the form supplied by him to that authority [⁹ or by means of an electronic communication], the following returns–

(a)   on the 15th day ("the return date") of each of July, October and January of the relevant year, details of the [⁵ qualifying activities]] in the relevant year that that authority has achieved by the end of the month immediately preceding the return date; and

(b)   on the 15th April in the following year, details of the [⁵ qualifying activities]] that that authority achieved in the relevant year.

[⁷ (4ZA)   In paragraph (4) above, "qualifying activities" means the activities referred to in article 21(1)(b).]

[⁹ (4A)]

(4B)   An authority in Wales shall–

(a)   if required to do so by the Secretary of State, submit to him, at the relevant office, in any of the above claims or returns, or

(b)   if required to do so by the Secretary of State or the National Assembly for Wales, submit to him or, as the case may be, to them, at the relevant office, by way of an additional return on such form as is supplied by him or them [⁹ or by means of an electronic communication] to that authority and not later than such date as he or they may require,

details in relation to subsidy in respect of rebates granted to tenants of dwellings within the authority's Housing Revenue Account.]

(5)   All claims and returns submitted by an authority consequent upon this article shall be signed [⁹ or submitted by means of an electronic communication]–

(a)   in the case of an authority in England or Wales, by [⁴ the authority's chief finance officer, as defined in section 5(8) of the Local Government and Housing Act 1989, or an officer to whom that officer has made a formal delegation];

(b)   in the case of an authority in Scotland, by the proper officer pursuant to section 95 of the Local Government (Scotland) Act 1973.

Amendments

1.   Inserted by art 3 of SI 2000 No 1091 (retrospectively to 1.4.99).
2.   Inserted by art 2 of SI 2003 No 3179 (retrospectively to 1.4.02).
3.   Inserted by art 2(a) od SI 2004 No 646 as from 1.4.04.
4.   Amended by art 2(b) of SI 2004 No 646 as from 1.4.04.
5.   Amended by art 3(3)(a) of SI 2005 No 369 (retrospectively from 1.4.03).
6.   Amended by art 3(3)(b) of SI 2005 No 369 (retrospectively from 1.4.02).
7.   Inserted by art 3(3)(c) of SI 2005 No 369 (retrospectively from 1.4.02).
8.   Amended by art 2(3) of SI 2006 No 54 (retrospectively from 1.4.04).
9.   Amended by art 2(4)(a) and (c)-(f) of SI 2007 No 26 as from 5.2.07.
10.   Amended by art 2(4)(b) of SI 2007 No 26 (retrospectively from 1.4.05).

[¹Requirement to keep records and provide information

5. –(1)   The second condition is that the authority submitting a claim shall–

(a)   provide to the Secretary of State the information referred to in paragraph (2) [² in written or electronic form]; and

(b)   keep and, where the Secretary of State required it or it is otherwise appropriate to do so, produce records [² in written or electronic form] with a bearing on that claim.

(2)   The information referred to in this paragraph is such information as the Secretary of State requires, or as may otherwise be necessary, to satisfy him that–

(a)   the claim is [² fairly stated and in accordance with the relevant articles of this Order]; and

(b)   any subsidy claimed or paid for the relevant year or for an earlier year has been properly claimed or paid in accordance with the provision of this Order or, as the case may be, the previous Orders.".]

Amendments

1.   Substituted by art 3 of SI 1998 No 2865 as from 14.12.98.

2.   Amended by art 2(5) of SI 2007 No 26 as from 5.2.07.

Requirement of audit

6.–(1)   Subject to article 9(4), the third condition is that the authority

[¹ (ia) shall, in the case of an authority in England, procure that their base data return is audited by the authority's auditor and that the audited return is submitted to the Secretary of State [² in written or electronic form] at the relevant office by 10th October in the year before the relevant year;]

(a)   shall procure that their final claim is audited by the authority's auditor by 31st December in the following year; and

(b)   shall comply with the following provisions of this article.

(2)   The authority shall–

(a)   provide such information [² in written or electronic form]; and

[² (b) keep, and where asked to do so, produce records in written or electronic form with a bearing on its claim,

as may be required by the auditor or as may be otherwise required to enable that authority to show and its auditor to check, that that claim is fairly stated and in accordance with the relevant articles of this Order.]

[² (3)   No final subsidy shall be paid until the authority's auditor has certified on the claim for or by means of an electronic communication that the final claim is fairly stated and in accordance with the relevant articles of this Order.]

Amendments

1.   Inserted by art 3 of SI 2004 No 646 as from 1.4.04.

2.   Amended by art 2(6) of SI 2007 No 26 as from 5.2.07.

Final condition for the payment of subsidy

7.   Subject to article 9(4), the fourth condition is that an authority shall satisfy the Secretary of State that its claim–

(a)   is true and complete;

(b)   is supported and, if appropriate, supplemented by all the information the Secretary of State requires; and

(c)   fairly represents the expenditure in relation to relevant benefit incurred or likely to be incurred, as the case may be, by the authority in the relevant year.

In year instalments of subsidy

8.–(1)   Where an authority has submitted, by the due date–

(a)   the initial claim, mid-year claim and the returns under article 4(4), as the case may be, in accordance with the requirements of this Part; and

(b)   the conditions of this Part in relation to such claims have been complied with,

the Secretary of State shall pay each month, to each such authority that has submitted such claims as are by that date due, instalments of subsidy, in accordance with paragraph (2).

(2)   The instalments payable by way of interim subsidy to an authority under paragraph (1) shall be such amounts as the Secretary of State considers appropriate in the circumstances of the case, but the total amount of such instalments paid in the relevant year shall not exceed the amount which, in his estimation, is likely to be payable by way of final subsidy, taking account of any withholding, reducing or deducting of subsidy by him, following the submission and audit of that authority's final claim.

[¹ Payment of subsidy before audit complete

8A. (1)   Where an authority has submitted the final claim by the due date in accordance with article 4(2)(c) but the claim has not yet been audited in accordance with article 6 and–

(a)   the Secretary of State estimates that the final subsidy will exceed the amount of interim subsidy that was paid to the authority in the relevant year, taking account of any withholding, reducing or deducting of subsidy by him, following the audit of that authority's final claim, he may pay subsidy in accordance with paragraph (2); or

(b)   the Secretary of State estimates that the interim subsidy that was paid to the authority in the relevant year will exceed the amount of final subsidy, taking account of any withholding, reducing or deducting of subsidy by him, following the audit of that authority's final claim, he may withhold or deduct subsidy in accordance with paragraph (2).

(2)   The amounts that may be paid to, withheld or deducted from an authority under paragraph (1) shall be equal to the amount which the Secretary of State estimates is likely to be payable by way of final subsidy, taking account of any withholding, reducing or deducting of subsidy by him, following the audit of that authority's final claim.]

Amendment
1.   Inserted by art 2(4) of SI 2006 No 54 (retrospectively from 1.4.04).

Payment of subsidy for the relevant year

9.–(1)   Subject to paragraphs (2) and (3) and to any subsidy withheld, reduced or deducted in accordance with sections 140B(4) or 140C(3), as the case may be, where he is satisfied that–

(a)   the authority has submitted its final claim;

(b)   the auditor has audited and certified that claim; and

(c)   the conditions of this Part have been complied with,

the Secretary of State shall pay to that authority final subsidy calculated in accordance with Part III.

[¹ (2)   Any payment pursuant to paragraph (1) shall only be in respect of the balance of subsidy due after the Secretary of State–

(a)   has deducted any interim subsidy paid during or in respect of the relevant year;

(b)   has added or deducted, as the case may be, any amount paid, recovered or withheld pursuant to article 8A in respect of the relevant year;

(c)   has added any amount pursuant to article 9A(3); and

(d)   has deducted any amount pursuant to article 9A(4).]

(3)   The Secretary of State may pay subsidy under paragraph (1) once that submission, audit or certification, as the case may be, has occurred, despite it occurring after the time required in this Part.

(4)   In a case where the third or fourth condition, as the case may be, are not met in relation to any authority, the Secretary of State may pay such amount of subsidy as he is satisfied will be due when that condition is met.

[² (5)   In paragraph (1), a reference to paying final subsidy calculated in accordance with Part III may also be a reference to deducting or withholding subsidy, as the case may be.]

Amendments
1.   Substituted by art 2(5)(a) of SI 2006 No 54 (retrospectively from 1.4.04).
2.   Inserted by art 2(5)(b) of SI 2006 No 54 (retrospectively from 1.4.04).

[¹ Transitional Protection Adjustments

9A.–(1)   After 1st September in the year after the following year the Secretary of State shall calculate an authority's final subsidy in accordance with Part III.

(2)   The Secretary of State shall compare the final subsidy in respect of a relevant year with the nominal subsidy calculated in accordance with paragraph (6).

(3)   Where, in accordance with paragraph (2), the final subsidy that an authority would receive is less than the nominal subsidy, the Secretary of State may add such amounts to any payment made pursuant to article 9(1) to ensure that the difference between the final subsidy and the nominal subsidy will be limited to–
  (a)   0.5 per cent in the year 2004/05;
  (b)   1 per cent in the year 2005/06, but only if sub-paragraph (a) applied to the authority; and
  (c)   2 per cent in the year 2006/07, but only if sub-paragraphs (a) and (b) applied to the authority.

(4)   Where, in accordance with paragraph (2), the final subsidy is greater than the nominal subsidy then the Secretary of State may deduct such amounts from any payment made pursuant to article 9(1) as he considers appropriate, taking into account–
  (a)   the circumstances of the case; and
  (b)   the amount of subsidy other authorities will receive pursuant to this article, but the amount deducted shall not result in a final subsidy which is less than the nominal subsidy.

(5)   If an authority has not complied with any condition specified in this Part by 1st September in the year after the following year the Secretary of State may estimate the amount of any subsidy, including any nominal subsidy and any additions or deductions which may be made as a result of paragraphs (3) and (4), payable to that authority and he may take into account for that purpose such information as he considers relevant.

(6)   For the purpose of this article the Secretary of State shall calculate the nominal subsidy by–
  (a)   calculating the authority's final subsidy as if that authority's final subsidy had been calculated at 31st March 2004; and
  (b)   adding an amount equivalent to that part of the revenue support grant that would have been paid to the Authority in relation to Housing Benefit and Council Tax Subsidy for the relevant year.

(7)   In paragraph (6)(b) above, "revenue support grant" means a grant that was paid under section 78 of the Local Government Finance Act 1988 or, for Scotland, section 191 of the Housing (Scotland) Act 1973.]

Amendment
1.   Inserted by art 2(6) of SI 2006 No 54 (retrospectively from 1.4.04).

Estimating subsidy

10.   If an authority has not, at the time specified in articles 4 or 6(1), as the case may be, complied with any condition specified in this Part, the Secretary of State may estimate the amount of any subsidy, including any interim subsidy, payable to that authority and he may employ for that purpose such criteria as he considers relevant.

Definitions
"authority" – see art 1(2).
"interim subsidy" – see reg 2.

General Note
If the authority fails to meet the time limits for submitting its claims and returns and for arranging for the final claim to be audited, the DWP may, under art 10, estimate the amount of subsidy due. In performing this task, the Secretary of State "may employ . . . such criteria as he considers relevant": subsidy estimated on this basis is unlikely to exceed the sum which would have been calculated as due had the forms been returned on time.

Amendments
1.   Deleted by reg(2) of SI 1998 No 2865 as from 14.12.98.
2.   Substituted by regs(5)(1) and (2) of SI 1998 No 2865 from 14.12.98.

PART III
Calculation of Subsidy

General Note on Part III
There are three components of subsidy:
1.   Under s140B(1) SSAA 1992 and arts 12(1)(a) and 13, the authority receives 100 per cent of its "qualifying expenditure" (see art 11(2), but essentially all the money it has properly spent by way of HB and CTB) less any adjustments made under arts 14-17 and deductions made under arts 20, 20A and 21(3) plus any additions under arts 18 and 21(2).
2.   Under s140B(4A) SSAA 1992 and art 12(1)(b), the authority receives a sum fixed by Sch 1 to cover its costs of administering the benefits.
3.   If the authority has modifed the HB or CTB scheme under ss134(8) or 139(6) SSAA (which allow for certain war pensions to be disregarded), the authority receives an additional amount calculated under art 12(4).

Interpretation of Part III

11.–(1)   In this Part, unless the context otherwise requires–
"allowance" means a rent allowance;
[² "appeal tribunal" has the meaning it bears in section 39(1) of the Social Security Act 1998;]
"board and lodging accommodation" means–
  (a)   accommodation provided for a charge which is inclusive of the provision of that accommodation and at least some cooked or prepared meals which are both cooked or prepared and consumed in that accommodation or associated premises; or
  (b)   accommodation provided in a hotel, guest house, lodging house or some similar establishment,
  but it does not include accommodation in a residential care home or nursing home within the meaning of regulation 19(3) of the Income Support (General) Regulations 1987 nor in a hostel within the meaning of [⁷ regulation 14 of the Housing Benefit Regulations or, as the case may be, regulation 14 of the Housing Benefit (State Pension Credit) Regulations];
[² "Commissioner" has the meaning it bears in section 39(1) of the Social Security Act 1998;]
"the Community Charge Benefits Regulations" means the Community Charge Benefits (General) Regulations 1989;
[⁷ "the Council Tax Benefit Regulations" means the Council Tax Benefit Regulations 2006;]
[⁷ "the Council Tax Benefit (State Pension Credit) Regulations" means the Council Tax Benefit (Persons who have attained the qualifying age for state pension credit) Regulations 2006;]
[⁷ "the Housing Benefit Regulations" means the Housing Benefit Regulations 2006;]

[⁷ "the Housing Benefit (State Pension Credit) Regulations" means the Housing Benefit (Persons who have attained the qualifying age for state pension credit) Regulations 2006;]

"overpayment" includes excess benefits under the Community Charge Benefits Regulations and excess benefit under the Council Tax Benefit Regulations as well as overpayments under the Housing Benefit Regulations and any reference in this Order to "overpayment" in relation to any of the previous Orders shall bear the meaning it has in this Order;

"period overrun" has the meaning assigned to it by paragraph 1 of Schedule 3;

"rebate" means a rent rebate [⁴];

"the Rent Officers Order" means the Rent Officers (Housing Benefits Functions) Order 1997 or the Rent Officers (Housing Benefits Functions) (Scotland) Order 1997, as the case may be;

"the Rent Officers Order 1995" means the Rent Officers (Additional Functions) Order 1995 or the Rent Officers (Additional Functions) (Scotland) Order 1995, as the case may be;

"scheme" means the housing benefit scheme or council tax benefit scheme, as the case may be, as prescribed under section 123(1) of the Social Security [¹ Contributions and Benefits Act 1992;

[⁶]

and other expressions used in this Part and in [⁷ the Housing Benefit Regulations, the Housing Benefit (State Pension Credit) Regulations, the Council Tax Benefit Regulations or the Council Tax Benefit (State Pension Credit)Regulations], as the case may be, shall have the same meanings in this Part as they have in those Regulations.

(2)   In this Part

"qualifying expenditure" means, in relation to an authority, the total of relevant benefit, including any payments under [⁷ regulation 93] of the Housing Benefit Regulations [⁷ and regulation 74 of the Housing Benefit (State Pension Credit) Regulations] (payments on account of a rent allowance) and any extended payments, lawfully paid [² or treated as lawfully paid under paragraph (3)] by the authority during the relevant year, less–

(a)   the deduction, if any, calculated for that authority in article 15 [⁶ or 15A];

(b)   any deductions specified in article 19 relevant to that authority, and

(c)   where, under sections 134(8) (arrangements for housing benefit) or 139(6) (arrangements for council tax benefit) of the Act, as the case may be, the authority has modified any part of a scheme it administers, any amount by which the total of relevant benefit paid under that scheme during the relevant year by it exceeds the total it would have paid if the scheme had not been so modified.

[² (3)   An amount of relevant benefit which–

(a)   would fall to be paid in the relevant year for a period in a preceding year; and

(b)   is not paid by virtue of [⁷ regulation 98 or 102 of the Housing Benefit Regulations or, as the case may be, regulation 79 or 83 of the Housing Benefit (State Pension Credit) Regulations] (offsetting and method of recovery) on the ground that an overpayment of benefit was made in that preceding year for that period,

shall be treated as lawfully paid in the relevant year for that period.]

Amendments

1.   Inserted by art 4(1) of SI 2000 No 1091 (retrospectively to 1.4.99).
2.   Inserted by reg 2(a) of SI 2000 No 2340 as from 25.09.00.
3.   Amended by art 3 of SI 2003 No 3179 (retrospectively to 1.4.02).
4.   Amended by art 4 of SI 2004 No 646 as from 1.4.04.
5.   Amended by art 4(2) of SI 2005 No 369 (retrospectively from 1.4.03).

6.   Amended by art 3(2) of SI 2006 No 54 (retrospectively from 1.4.04).
7.   Amended by reg 5 and Sch 2 para 13(2) of SI 2006 No 217 as from 6.3.06.

Amount of subsidy

12.–[¹(1)   Subject to paragraph (2),]the amount of an authority's subsidy for the relevant year, to be paid pursuant to article 9–

(a)   for the purposes of section 140B(1) of the Act (calculation of amount of subsidy), shall be the amount or total of the amounts calculated in accordance with article 13;

[² (b) for the purposes of section 140B(4A)(a) of the Act (subsidy in respect of costs of administering relevant benefits) shall include, for an authority identified in column (1) of Schedule 1, the sum specified in column (2) of the Schedule for that authority; and

(c)   shall include an additional amount calculated in accordance with paragraph (4), if the authority has modified any part of a scheme it administers in recognition of the operation of a local scheme under sections 134(8) (arrangements for housing benefit) or 139(6) (arrangements for council tax benefit) of the Act.]

[¹(2)   Subject to paragraph (3), any sum paid after 1st April 1997 by way of subsidy in respect of an overpayment of relevant benefit shall be deducted from any amount of subsidy which would otherwise fall to be paid in respect of any payment of benefit which is treated, in accordance with paragraph 11(3), as made for the same period as that overpayment.

(3)   A deduction shall not be made under paragraph (2) where the sum already paid by way of subsidy is greater than the amount which would fall to be paid.]

[³ (4)   For the purposes of sub-paragraph (1)(c), the additional amount will be 0.2 per cent of the amount or total of amounts calculated in accordance with article 13 but will not exceed 75 per cent of the cost of the total of relevant benefit paid under the scheme.''.]

Amendments
1.   Inserted by reg 2(b) of SI 2000 No 2340 as from 25.09.00.
2.   Substituted by art 3(3)(a) of SI 2006 No 54 (retrospectively from 1.4.04).
3.   Inserted by art 3(3)(b) of SI 2006 No 54 (retrospectively from 1.4.04).

Relevant benefit

13.–[¹(1)   Subject to any adjustment in accordance with paragraph (3), for the purposes of section 140A(4) of the Act, the subsidy to be paid to an authority shall [⁴] be–

(a)   in the case of any authority to which none of articles 14, 16 and 17 applies, an amount equal to the aggregate of–
    (i)   [⁷ 100 per cent] of its qualifying expenditure attributable to expenditure in respect of housing benefit; and
    (ii)   [⁷ 100 per cent] of its qualifying expenditure attributable to expenditure in respect of council tax benefit;

(b)   in the case of any authority to which at least one of those articles applies an amount equal to the aggregate of–
    (i)   [⁷ 100 per cent] of so much of its qualifying expenditure attributable to expenditure in respect of housing benefit as remains after deducting from that expenditure the amount of expenditure attributable to housing benefit to which each of those articles which is relevant applies;
    (ii)   [⁷ 100 per cent] of so much of its qualifying expenditure attributable to expenditure in respect of council tax benefit as remains after deducting from that expenditure the amount of expenditure attributable to council tax benefit to which article 14 applies; and

(iii)   the appropriate amount calculated in respect of the relevant benefit under each such article,

plus, in each case, the additions, where applicable, under [⁶ articles 18 and 21, but subject, in each case, to the deductions, where applicable, under articles 20 and 20A].]

[⁴]

[⁷]

Amendments

1.   Inserted by art 4(2) of SI 2000 No 1091 (retrospectively to 1.4.99).
2.   Amended by art 2 of SI 2001 No. 2350.
3.   Amended by art 2 of SI 2002 No 1859 (retrospectively to 1.4.01).
4.   Omitted by art 4 of SI 2003 No 3179 (retrospectively to 1.4.02).
5.   Amended by art 5 of SI 2004 No 646 as from 1.4.04.
6.   Amended by art 4(3) of SI 2005 No 369 (retrospectively from 1.4.02).
7.   Amended by art 3(4) of SI 2006 No 54 (retrospectively from 1.4.04).

Backdated benefit

14.–(1)   Subject to paragraph (2), where–

(a)   during the relevant year an authority has, under [⁷ regulation 83(12) of the Housing Benefit Regulations or, as the case may be, regulation 64(13) of the Housing Benefit (State Pension Credit) Regulations, regulation 69(13) of the Council Tax Benefit Regulations or regulation 53(13) of the Council Tax Benefit (State Pension Credit) Regulations] (time and manner of claiming), treated any claim as made on a day earlier than that on which it is made; and

(b)   any part of that authority's qualifying expenditure is attributable to such earlier period,

for the purposes of article 13(1)(b)[¹(iii)], the appropriate amount for the relevant year in respect of such part shall be [⁶ 100 per cent] of the qualifying expenditure so attributable.

(2)   This article shall not apply [⁵ in relation to expenditure to which article 17(2)(a)(i) or (b)(i) or (3)(b)(ii) or 18(1)(b)(iii)] or paragraph 6 of Schedule 4 applies.

Amendments

1.   Amended by art 3 of SI 2350 as from 25.07.01.
2.   Amended by art 2(c) of SI 2000 No 2340 as from 25.09.00.
3.   Amended by art 3 of SI 2002 No 3116 (retrospectively to 1.4.01).
4.   Amended by art 5 of SI 2003 No 3179 (retrospectively to 1.4.02).
5.   Amended by art 4(4) of SI 2005 No 369 (retrospectively from 1.4.03).
6.   Amended by art 3(5) of SI 2006 No 54 (retrospectively from 1.4.04).
7.   Amended by reg 5 and sch 2 para 13(3) of SI 2006 No 217 as from 6.3.06.

Disproportionate rent increase

15.–(1)   Except where paragraph (5), (6) or (7) applies, in the case of an authority in Scotland, whose average rent increase differential, as calculated in accordance with paragraph (2) (''the proportion''), has a value greater than zero, the deduction from qualifying expenditure specified in article 11(2)(a) shall be the proportion multiplied by the sum calculated for that authority in accordance with paragraph (4).

(2)   The average rent increase differential for each authority shall be calculated by applying the formula–

$$(1 + A) \times \left(\frac{B}{C} \times \frac{D}{E} \right) - 1$$

where

A, B, C, D and E each has the value determined in accordance with paragraph (3).

(3) For the purposes of paragraph (2)–

(a) the value of A shall be the proportion calculated for that authority pursuant to paragraphs (3) and (4) of–

    (i) in relation to the relevant year commencing on 1st April 1997, article 6 of the 1997 Order, or

    (ii) in relation to a relevant year commencing on or after 1st April 1998, this article of this Order for the year immediately preceding the relevant year;

(b) the value of B shall be the average rent charged by the authority in respect of Category 1 dwellings on the final date;

(c) the value of C shall be the average rent charged by the authority in respect of Category 1 dwellings on the initial date;

(d) the value of D shall be the average rent charged by the authority in respect of Category 2 dwellings on the initial date; and

(e) the value of E shall be the average rent charged by the authority in respect of Category 2 dwellings on the final date.

(4) The sum referred to in paragraph (1) shall be that part of qualifying expenditure attributable to rebates granted during the relevant year before any deduction by reason of this article, but less any part of such expenditure to which article 13(1)(b)(ii) applies.

(5) Subject to paragraph (6), this article shall not apply in the case of an authority–

(a) which has–

    (i) set the rent for the relevant year according to the type, condition, class or description of the dwellings and the services, facilities or rights provided to the tenants, where that rent is reasonable having regard to those matters;

    (ii) not taken account of whether a tenant was a beneficiary when setting rents for the relevant year, and

    (iii) not let dwellings, either in the relevant year or in either of the two previous years, to beneficiaries irrespective of their housing needs; or

(b) where–

    (i) any increases in rent between the initial date and 1st April in the following year were of the same percentage and applied on the same day to all tenants irrespective of whether they were beneficiaries, and

    (ii) the average rent increase differential calculated in accordance with–

        (aa) in relation to the relevant year commencing on 1st April 1997, article 6 of the 1997 Order; or

        (bb) in relation to a relevant year commencing on or after 1st April 1998, this article of this Order for the year immediately preceding the relevant year,

    for that authority had a value which was zero or less than zero.

(6) In the case of a new authority, sub-paragraph (a)(iii) of paragraph (5) shall be modified so that, in relation to the relevant year commencing on 1st April 1997, for the words ''or in either of the two previous years'' there shall be substituted the words ''or in the previous year''.

(7) This article shall not apply in a case to which article 17 (subsidy in respect of homeless and short lease rebate cases) applies.

(8) In this article (and, in the case of the meaning ascribed to the word ''beneficiary'', also in article 19(2))–

''average'' means the arithmetic mean;

''beneficiary'' means a person who is entitled or likely to become entitled to a rebate;

''Category 1 dwellings'' means dwellings rented out by the authority, on both the initial date and the final date, in respect of which, on the final date, the persons liable to pay such rent were in receipt of rebates;

"Category 2 dwellings" means dwellings rented out by the authority, on both the
    initial date and the final date, in respect of which, on the final date, the
    persons liable to pay such rent were not in receipt of rebates;

"final date" means the last day of the relevant year;

"initial date" means the day before the relevant year; and

"rent" means either–

(a)   the payments specified in [¹ sub-paragraphs (a) to (j) in paragraph (1) of
    regulation 12 of the Housing Benefit Regulations or, as the case may be,
    sub-paragraphs (a) to (j) in paragraph (1) of regulation 12 of the Housing
    Benefit (State Pension Credit) Regulations] (rent); or

(b)   the eligible rent,

as the authority may determine, provided that wherever the expression "rent" occurs
in paragraph (3) it has the same meaning throughout in relation to that authority.

Amendment

1.   Amended by reg 5 and Sch 2 para 13(4) of SI 2006 No 217 as from 6.3.06.

[¹Disproportionate rent increase – Wales

15A.–(1)   Subject to paragraphs (5) to (7), in the case of an authority in Wales
whose average rent increase differential, as calculated in accordance with paragraph
(2) ("the proportion"), has a value greater than zero, the deduction from qualifying
expenditure specified in article 11(2)(a) shall be the proportion multiplied by the
sum calculated for that authority in accordance with paragraph (4).

(2)   The average rent increase differential for each authority shall be calculated
by applying the formula–

$$(1 + A) \times \left(\frac{B}{C} \times \frac{D}{E} \right) - 1$$

where A, B, C, D and E each has the value determined in accordance with
paragraph (3).

(3)   For the purposes of paragraph (2)–

(a)   the value of A shall be the proportion calculated for that authority pursuant
    to that paragraph for the year immediately preceding the relevant year;

(b)   the value of B shall be the average rent charged by the authority in respect
    of Category 1 dwellings on the final date;

(c)   the value of C shall be the average rent charged by the authority in respect
    of Category 1 dwellings on the initial date;

(d)   the value of D shall be the average rent charged by the authority in respect
    of Category 2 dwellings on the initial date; and

(e)   the value of E shall be the average rent charged by the authority in respect
    of Category 2 dwellings on the final date.

(4)   The sum referred to in paragraph (1) shall be that part of qualifying
expenditure attributable to rebates granted during the relevant year before any
deduction by reason of this article, but less any part of such expenditure to which
article 13(1)(b)(iii) applies.

(5)   This article shall not apply in the case of an authority–

(a)   which has–

(i)   set the rent for the relevant year according to the type, condition, class
    or description of the dwellings and the services, facilities or rights
    provided to the tenants, where that rent is reasonable having regard to
    those matters,

(ii)   not taken account of whether a tenant was a beneficiary when setting
    rents for the relevant year, and

(iii)   not let dwellings, either in the relevant year or in either of the two
    previous years, to beneficiaries irrespective of their housing needs; or

(b)   where–
- (i)   any increases in rent between the initial date and 1st April in the following year were of the same percentage and applied on the same day to all tenants irrespective of whether they were beneficiaries, and
- (ii)   the average rent increase differential calculated in accordance with paragraph (2) for the year immediately preceding the relevant year, for that authority had a value which was zero or less than zero.

(6)   Where the relevant year is the year beginning on 1st April 2004–

(a)   paragraph (3)(a) shall have effect as if, for the words from "the proportion" to "the relevant year" there were substituted "equal to the value of G calculated for that authority for the purposes of paragraph 6.5.1 of the 2003-04 Determination;"; and

(b)   paragraph (5)(b)(ii) shall have effect as if, for the words from "average" to "relevant year" there were substituted "value of G calculated for the purposes of paragraph 6.5.1 of the 2003-04 Determination".

(7)   This article shall not apply in a case to which article 17 (subsidy in respect of homeless and short lease rebate cases) applies.

(8)   In this article–

"average" means the arithmetic mean;

"beneficiary" means a person who is entitled or likely to become entitled to a rebate;

"Category 1 dwellings" means dwellings rented out by the authority, on both the initial date and the final date, in respect of which, on the final date, the persons liable to pay such rent were in receipt of rebates;

"Category 2 dwellings" means dwellings rented out by the authority, on both the initial date and the final date, in respect of which, on the final date, the persons liable to pay such rent were not in receipt of rebates;

"2003-04 Determination" means the Housing Revenue Account Subsidy (Wales) Determination 2003-04;

"final date" means the last day of the relevant year;

"initial date" means the day before the first day of the relevant year; and

"rent" means either–

(a)   the payments specified in sub-paragraphs (a) to (i) in paragraph (1) of [² regulation 12 of the Housing Benefit Regulations or, as the case may be, regulation 12 of the Housing Benefit (State Pension Credit) Regulations] (rent); or

(b)   the eligible rent,

as the authority may determine, provided that wherever the expression "rent" occurs in paragraph (3) it has the same meaning throughout in relation to that authority.]

Amendments
1.   Inserted by art 4(5) of SI 2005 No 369 (retrospectively from 1.4.04).
2.   Amended by reg 5 and Sch 2 para 13(5) of SI 2006 No 217 as from 6.3.06.

Treatment of high rents in rent allowance cases

16.–(1)   Except in a case to which article 14 (backdated benefit) applies, and subject to paragraphs (2), [²] and (4) and to article 23 (transitional provisions in relation to rent officer determinations), this article applies in a rent allowance case and, where this article applies, the appropriate amount, for the purposes of article 13(1)(b)[¹(iii)], shall be calculated in accordance with Part II of Schedule 4.

(2)   This article shall not apply where a dwelling is an excluded tenancy by virtue of

[⁵(a)   paragraph 1 and any of paragraphs 3 to 11 of Schedule 2 to the Housing Benefit Regulations (excluded tenancies); or

(b)   paragraph 1 and any of paragraphs 3 to 11 of Schedule 2 to the Housing Benefit (State Pension Credit) Regulations (excluded tenancies)]

[³]
(4)   This article shall not apply in a case where a maximum rent has been determined, except where–

(a)   it was determined by reference to a reckonable rent and a local reference rent, when the appropriate amount shall be calculated in accordance with paragraph 14 of Schedule 4; or

(b)   prior to its determination, a payment was made pursuant to [⁴ regulation 93] (payment on account) of the Housing Benefit Regulations [⁴ or, as the case may be, regulation 74 of the Housing Benefit (State Pension Credit) Regulations], when the appropriate amount, in respect of that payment, shall be calculated in accordance with paragraph 11 of Schedule 4; or

(c)   [⁴ regulation 13(14) of the Housing Benefit Regulations or, as the case may be, regulation 13(14) of the Housing Benefit (State Pension Credit) Regulations] (no maximum rent for first 13 weeks) applies, when the appropriate amount shall be calculated in respect of the first 13 weeks in accordance with paragraph 15 of Schedule 4.

(5)   Expressions used in this article and in Schedule 4 have the same meanings in this article as they have in that Schedule.

Amendments

1.   Amended by art 3 of SI 2350 as from 25.07.01.
2.   Amended by art 3(6)(a) and (b) of SI 2006 No 54 (retrospectively from 1.4.04).
3.   Omitted by art 6(c) of SI 2006 No 54 (retrospectively from 1.4.04).
4.   Amended by reg 5 and Sch 2 para 13(6) of SI 2006 No 217 as from 6.3.06.

Subsidy in respect of homeless and short lease rebate cases

17.–(1)   [²] where paragraph (4) applies and any part of the qualifying expenditure of an authority identified in column (1) of Schedule 1 [²] is attributable to any rebate granted in respect of a person whose weekly eligible rent exceeds the threshold, then for the purposes of article 13(1)(b)[¹(iii)], where that weekly eligible rent–

(a)   does not exceed the cap, the appropriate amount in respect of that rebate shall be calculated in accordance with paragraph (2);

(b)   does exceed the cap, the appropriate amount in respect of that rebate shall be calculated in accordance with paragraph (3).

(2)   Subject to paragraph (7), where paragraph (1)(a) applies, and the rebate granted–

(a)   is the same as or is less than the amount by which the eligible rent exceeds the threshold, the appropriate amount [² shall be–
      (i)   where paragraph (4)(a) applies, [³ 10 per cent] of that part of the qualifying expenditure attributable to such rebates; or
      (ii)   where paragraph (4)(b) or (c) applies, [⁴ 100 per cent] of that part of the qualifying expenditure attributable to such rebates;]

(b)   is greater than the amount by which the eligible rent exceeds the threshold, the appropriate amount shall be [² [⁴ 100 per cent] of the qualifying expenditure attributable to the balance after deducting the excess plus -
      (i)   where paragraph (4)(a) applies, [³ 10 per cent] of that part of the qualifying expenditure attributable to such rebates which is equal to that excess; or
      (ii)   where paragraph (4)(b) or (c) applies, [⁴ 100 per cent] of that part of the qualifying expenditure attributable to such rebates which is equal to that excess.]

(3)   Subject to paragraph (7), where paragraph (1)(b) applies, and the rebate granted–

(a)　is the same as or is less than the amount by which the eligible rent exceeds the cap, the appropriate amount shall be nil per cent. of that part of the qualifying expenditure attributable to such rebates;

(b)　is greater than the amount by which the eligible rent exceeds the cap, the appropriate amount shall be the aggregate of–

　　(i)　nil per cent. of that part of the qualifying expenditure attributable to such rebates which is equal to the excess over the cap;

　　[² (ii)　where paragraph (4)(a) applies, [³ 10 per cent] of that part of the qualifying expenditure attributable to such rebates which is equal to the excess over the threshold, but not over the cap;

　　(iia)　where paragraph (4)(b) or (c) applies, [⁴ 100 per cent] of that part of the qualifying expenditure attributable to such rebates which is equal to the excess over the threshold, but not over the cap; and]

　　(iii)　[⁴ 100 per cent] of the qualifying expenditure attributable to the balance after deducting an amount equal to the excess over the threshold.

(4)　This paragraph applies where a rebate is payable by an authority in respect of rents which exceed the threshold and

(a)　a person is required to pay to an authority under section 69(2)(b) of the Housing Act 1985, section 206 of the Housing Act 1996 or section 35(2)(b) of the Housing (Scotland) Act 1987, as the case may be, for board and lodging accommodation made available to that person;

(b)　a person is required to pay to an authority under section 69(2)(b) of the Housing Act 1985, section 206 of the Housing Act 1996 or section 35(2)(b) of the Housing (Scotland) Act 1987, as the case may be, for accommodation, which the authority holds on a licence agreement from a landlord, and which it makes available to that person;

(c)　a person is required to pay to an authority for accommodation outside that authority's Housing Revenue Account, which the authority holds on a lease granted for a term not exceeding 10 years, and which it makes available to that person.

[²]

[⁵]

(8)　In this article, in relation to an authority falling within paragraph (1)–

''the cap'' means the sum specified in relation to that authority in column (4) of Schedule 1, and

''the threshold'' means the sum specified in relation to that authority in column (3) of Schedule 1.

Amendments

1.　Amended by art 3 of SI 2350 as from 25.07.01.
2.　Amended by art 6 of SI 2003 No 3179 (retrospectively to 1.4.02).
3.　Amended by art 4(6) of SI 2005 No 369 (retrospectively from 1.4.03).
4.　Amended by art 3(7)(a) of SI 2006 No 54 (retrospectively from 1.4.04).
5.　Omitted by art 3(7)(b) of SI 2006 No 54 (retrospectively from 1.4.04).

Additions to subsidy

18.–(1)　Subject to paragraphs (8), (9) and (10), the additions referred to in article 13(1) are–

(a)　where following the loss, destruction or non-receipt, or alleged loss, destruction or non-receipt of original instruments of payment of relevant benefit, an authority makes duplicate payments and the original instruments have been or are subsequently encashed, an amount equal to 25 per cent. of the amount of the duplicate payments;

(b)　[¹ subject to paragraphs (2) and (3), where, during the relevant year, it is discovered that an overpayment of community charge benefit or relevant benefit has been made and an amount is to be deducted under article 19 in relation to that overpayment, an amount equal to–

    (i)   in the case of a departmental error overpayment where the overpayment is overpayment of housing benefit, [¹⁴ 100 per cent] of so much of the overpayment as has not been recovered by the authority;

    (ii)   in the case of a departmental error overpayment where the overpayment is overpayment of community charge benefit or council tax benefit, [¹⁴ 100 per cent] of so much of the overpayment as has not been recovered by the authority;

    [¹⁰ ...]

    (iii)   [¹⁰ except where heads (i) or (ii) above apply, 40 per cent. of the overpayment;]

    [¹⁰ ...]

(c)   where, during the relevant year, it is discovered that an overpayment in respect of which a deduction was made under article 11 or 19 of the 1994 Order, the 1995 Order, the 1996 Order or the 1997 Order (other than a deduction under article 11(1)(g) or 19(1)(c) of the 1994 Order or 11(1)(f) or 19(1)(c) of the 1995, 1996 or 1997 Orders) or, in respect of a year earlier than the relevant year, under article 19 (other than a deduction under article 19(1)(f)), as the case may be, was a fraudulent overpayment, the amount, if any, by which [¹⁰] 40 per cent.] of any such overpayment exceeds the amount of any subsidy that has been paid in respect of that overpayment;

(d)   [¹⁰ where, during the relevant year, it is discovered that an overpayment in respect of which a deduction was made–

    (i)   under article 19 (other than a deduction under article 19(1)(ea)); and

    (ii)   in respect of a year which begins after 31st March 2001 and which is earlier than the relevant year,

was a claimant error overpayment, the amount, if any, by which 40 per cent. of any such overpayment exceeds the amount of any subsidy that has been paid in respect of that overpayment.]

[¹⁵ (e) where, during the relevant year, it is discovered that an overpayment in respect of which a deduction is to be made under article 19 is an authority error overpayment, where the proportion of total authority error overpayments as a percentage of the total specified subsidy is–

    (aa)   less than or equal to 0.48 per cent, the addition shall be 100 per cent of the total authority error overpayment;

    (bb)   greater than 0.48 per cent but less than or equal to 0.54 per cent, the addition shall be 40 per cent of the total authority error overpayment; and

    (cc)   greater than 0.54 per cent, the addition shall be nil.]

(2)   The amount under paragraph (1)(b) shall not include an amount in relation to–

(a)   an authority error overpayment;

(b)   any technical overpayment; or

(c)   any overpayment discovered in the relevant year, which arose as a result of a reduction in the amount of council tax a person is or was liable to pay.

(3)   In the case of a departmental error overpayment, where some or all of that overpayment is recovered by the authority, no addition shall be applicable to the authority in respect of the amount so recovered.

[⁷(4)   In paragraphs (1)(b)(i) and (3) and in article 19(1)(e), "departmental error overpayment" means [¹¹ an overpayment of a kind to which paragraph (4ZA) applies or] an overpayment caused by a mistake made, whether in the form of an act or omission–

[⁹ (a) by an officer of the Department for Work and Pensions [¹⁰ or of the Inland Revenue], acting as such, or a person providing services to that Department [¹⁰ or to the Inland Revenue];] or

(b) in a decision of an appeal tribunal or a Commissioner,

where the claimant, a person acting on his behalf or any other person to whom the payment is made did not cause or materially contribute to that mistake but excludes any mistake of law which is shown to have been an error only by virtue of a subsequent decision of a Commissioner or a court.]

[¹² (4ZA) This paragraph applies to an overpayment where–

(a) the overpayment was made during the period beginning with 5th April 2003 and ending with 13th June 2003 ("the specified period");

(b) the overpayment would, but for paragraph (4), fall to be regarded as an authority error overpayment on the ground that it was made as a result of a failure by the authority to take account of information about the amount of any tax credit payable to the claimant; and

(c) the Secretary of State is satisfied that the authority took reasonable steps to avoid making overpayments of the kind described in sub-paragraph (b) during the specified period.]

[⁸ (4A) In paragraph [¹⁰ (1)(d) and in article 19(1)(ea)], "claimant error overpayment" means an overpayment [¹³ which]–

(a) is caused by–
    (i) the claimant, or
    (ii) a person acting on the claimant's behalf under regulation 71 of the Housing Benefit Regulations (who may claim housing benefit)[9] or regulation 61 of the Council Tax Benefit Regulations (who may claim council tax benefit)[10],

    failing to provide information in accordance with regulation 72(1), 73 or 75 of, or paragraph 5 of Schedule A1 to, the Housing Benefit Regulations (duties on claimant to provide information)[11] or regulation 62(1), 63 or 65 of, or paragraph 5 of Schedule A1 to, the Council Tax Benefit Regulations (duties on claimant to provide information)[12]; and

(b) is not a fraudulent overpayment.]

(5) In [⁸ paragraphs [¹⁰ (1)(c) and (4A)], [¹⁴ and in article 19(1)(f)] "fraudulent overpayment" means an overpayment in respect of a period falling wholly or partly after 31st March 1993 and which–

[¹⁸ (a)]

(b) occurs as a result of the payment of relevant benefit or community charge benefit arising in consequence of–
    (i) a breach of section 111A or [¹⁴ 112] of the Act (dishonest or false representations for obtaining benefit); or
    (ii) a person knowingly failing to report a relevant change of circumstances, contrary to the requirements of [¹⁷ regulation 88 of the Housing Benefit Regulations, regulation 69 of the Housing Benefit (State Pension Credit) Regulations], regulation 63 of the Community Charge Benefits Regulations [¹⁷ , regulation 74 of the Council Tax Benefit Regulations or regulation 59 of the Council Tax Benefit (State Pension Credit) Regulations], as the case may be, (duty to notify change of circumstances), with intent to obtain or retain such relevant benefit or community charge benefit for himself or another.

[⁷(6) [¹⁴ In paragraphs (1)(e) and (2)(a)], "authority error overpayment" means an overpayment caused by a mistake made, whether in the form of an act or omission, by an authority where the claimant, a person acting on his behalf or any other person to whom the payment is made did not cause or materially contribute to that mistake but excludes any mistake of law which is shown to have been an error only by virtue of a subsequent decision of a court]

[15 (6A)   In paragraph (1)(e), "total specified subsidy" means the total amount of housing benefit and council tax benefit that attracts 100 per cent subsidy for the relevant year, including any subsidy paid pursuant to article 14.]

(7)   In paragraph (2)(b) "technical overpayment" means that part of an overpayment which occurs as a result of a rebate or council tax benefit being awarded in advance of the payment when–

(a)   a change of circumstances, which occurs subsequent to that award, reduces or eliminates entitlement to that rebate or benefit; or

(b)   the authority identifies, subsequent to that award, a recoverable overpayment which does not arise from a change in circumstances,

but shall not include any part of that overpayment occurring before the benefit week following the week in which the change is disclosed to the authority or it identifies that overpayment.

(8)   Except for [4 paragraphs (1)(b)(iii)], (1)(c) and (5), this article shall not apply to that part of any community charge benefit or relevant benefit in respect of a case to which [17 paragraph (12) of regulation 83 of the Housing Benefit Regulations, paragraph (13) of regulation 64 of the Housing Benefit (State Pension Credit) Regulations, paragraph (13) of regulation 69 of the Council Tax Benefit Regulations of paragraph (13) of regulation 53 of the Council Tax Benefit (State Pension Credit) Regulations] or paragraph (18) of regulation 60 of the Community Charge Benefits Regulations (time and manner in which claims are to be made), as the case may be, applies.

[16]

(10)   This article shall not apply to any expenditure in respect of which, had it been qualifying expenditure, the appropriate amount would have been nil.

[15 (11)   Where the addition payable under this article would be greater than a sum equivalent to the appropriate amount under article 17(2)(b)(i), (2)(b)(ii) and (3)(b)(ii) had the expenditure been qualifying expenditure, then the addition will be a sum equivalent to the appropriate amount.

(12)   Where, during the relevant year, an overpayment that has been classified as an overpayment under one of paragraphs (4), (4ZA) (4A), (5), (6) or (7) is reclassified, the addition referred to in article 13(1) shall be the amount payable under paragraph (1) for the final classification of the overpayment.]

Amendments

1.   Inserted by art 4(3) of SI 2000 No 1091 (retrospectively to 1.4.99).
2.   Inserted by art 4(4) of SI 2000 No 1091 (retrospectively to 1.4.99).
3.   Inserted by art 4(5) of SI 2000 No 1091 (retrospectively to 1.4.99).
4.   Inserted by art 4(6) of SI 2000 No 1091 (retrospectively to 1.4.99).
5.   Inserted by art 6 of SI 2000 No 1091 (retrospectively to 1.4.98).
6.   Inserted by art 7 of SI 2000 No 1091 (retrospectively to 1.4.99).
7.   Amended by art 2(d) of SI 2000 No 2340 as from 25.09.00.
8.   Amended by art 4 of SI 2002 No 3116 (retrospectively to 1.4.01).
9.   Amended by sch para 31 of SI 2002 No 1397 as from 27.6.02.
10.   Amended by art 7 of SI 2003 No 3179 (retrospectively to 1.4.02).
11.   Amended by art 4(7)(a) of SI 2005 No 369 (retrospectively from 1.4.03).
12.   Inserted by art 4(7)(b) of SI 2005 No 369 (retrospectively from 1.4.03).
12.   Amended by art 4(7)(c) of SI 2005 No 369 (retrospectively from 1.4.02).
13.   Amended by art 4(7)(d) of SI 2005 No 369 (retrospectively from 1.4.02).
14.   Amended by art 3(8)(a), (b), (d) and (e) of SI 2006 No 54 (retrospectively from 1.4.04).
15.   Inserted by art 3(8)(c), (f) and (h) of SI 2006 No 54 (retrospectively from 1.4.04).
16.   Omitted by art 3(8)(g) of SI 2006 No 54 (retrospectively from 1.4.04).
17.   Amended by reg 5 and Sch 2 para 13(7) of SI 2006 No 217 as from 6.3.06.
18.   Omitted by art 3(1) of SI 2007 No 26 as (retrospectively from 1.4.05).

Deductions to be made in calculating subsidy

19.–(1)   The deductions referred to in article 11(2)(b) are, subject to paragraph (4), to be of the following amounts where–

(a)   subject to paragraphs (2) and (3), a tenant of an authority, who is in receipt of a rebate while continuing to occupy, or when entering into occupation of a dwelling as his home, either under his existing tenancy agreement or by entering into a new tenancy agreement–

   (i)   is during, or was at any time prior to, the relevant year able to choose whether or not to be provided with any services, facilities or rights (''improvements'') and chooses or chose to be so provided;

   (ii)   is during, or was at any time prior to, the relevant year, able to choose either to be provided with any improvements or, whether or not in return for an award or grant from the authority, to provide such improvements for himself; or

   (iii)   would be able during, or would have been able at any time prior to, the relevant year to exercise the choice set out in head (i) or (ii) of this sub-paragraph if he were not or had not at that time been in receipt of a rebate,

the amounts attributed during the relevant year to such improvements whether they are or would be expressed as part of the sum fixed as rent, otherwise reserved as rent or expressed as an award or grant from the authority;

(b)   during the relevant year a person becomes entitled to a rent-free period which has not been, or does not fall to be, taken into account in calculating the amount of rebate to which he is entitled under the Housing Benefit Regulations, the amount of rebate which is or was payable to him in respect of such rent-free period;

(c)   during the relevant year an award in the form of a payment of money or monies worth, a credit to the person's rent account or in some other form is made by an authority to one of its tenants in receipt of a rebate, whether or not the person is immediately entitled to the award, the amount or value of the award, but no such deduction shall be made in respect of an award–

   (i)   made to a tenant for a reason unrelated to the fact that he is a tenant;

   (ii)   made under a statutory obligation;

   (iii)   made under section 137 of the Local Government Act 1972 or section 83 of the Local Government (Scotland) Act 1973 (power of local authorities to incur expenditure for certain purposes not otherwise authorised);

   (iv)   except where sub-paragraph (a)(ii) applies, made as reasonable compensation for reasonable repairs or redecoration the tenant has, or has caused to be, carried out whether for payment or not and which the authority would otherwise have carried out or have been required to carry out; or

   (v)   of a reasonable amount made as compensation for loss, damage or inconvenience of a kind which occurs only exceptionally and which was suffered by the tenant by virtue of his occupation of his home;

[²]

(e)   during the relevant year an amount is recovered in relation to a departmental error overpayment, within the meaning of article 18(4), the amount so recovered, in a case where the overpayment had occurred and been discovered in a year earlier than the relevant year;

[¹ (ea)   during the relevant year a claimant error overpayment, within the meaning of article 18(4A), is identified, the amount of the overpayment, but only to the extent that the amount of the overpayment or any part of it has not been deducted from qualifying expenditure under article 11(2);]

(f)   during the relevant year a fraudulent overpayment, within the meaning of article 18(5), is identified, the amount of the overpayment, but only to the extent that the amount of overpayment or any part of it has not been deducted from qualifying expenditure under article 4 or 19 of the 1994 Order, the 1995 Order, the 1996 Order or the 1997 Order or article 11(2), as the case may be;

(g)   subject to sub-paragraphs (e) [¹ ,(ea)] and (f), during the relevant year it is discovered that an overpayment of relevant benefit has been made, the amount of such overpayment, but only to the extent that–

    (i)   the amount of such overpayment or any part of it has not been deducted from qualifying expenditure under article 3 of the 1989 Order or the 1990 Order or under article 4 or 15 of the 1991 Order or articles 4 or 16 of the 1992 Order or the 1993 Order or articles 4 or 19 of respectively the 1994 Order, the 1995 Order, the 1996 Order or the 1997 Order, or article 11(2), as the case may be; and

    (ii)   the amount of the overpayment or any part of it does not include an amount to which paragraph (15) of regulation 72 of the [³ Housing Benefit (General) Regulations 1987, paragraph (7) of article 2 of the Community Charge Benefits (Transitional) Order 1989, paragraph (18) of regulation 59 of the Housing Benefit (Community Charge Rebates) (Scotland) Regulations 1988, paragraph (16) of regulation 62 of the [³ Council Tax Benefit (General) Regulations 1992] [³ paragraph (18) of regulation 60 of the Community Charge Benefits Regulations, paragraph (12) of regulation 83 of the Housing Benefit Regulations, paragraph (13) of regulation 64 of the Housing Benefit (State Pension Credit) Regulations, paragraph (13) of regulation 69 of the Council Tax Benefit Regulations or paragraph (13) of regulation 53 of the Council Tax Benefit (State Pension Credit) Regulations] (time and manner in which claims are to be made), as the case may be, applied;

(h)   during the relevant year any instrument of payment of relevant benefit issued by an authority during that year is returned to that authority without being presented for payment or is found by that authority to have passed its date of validity without being presented for payment, the amount of any such instrument;

(i)   during the relevant year an amount is recovered in respect of which subsidy was paid pursuant to paragraph 6(2) of Schedule 6 to the 1996 Order or the 1997 Order or paragraph 11(2) of Schedule 4 (subsidy on payments on account), the amount so recovered, where the payment on account was made in a year earlier than the relevant year.

(2)   Subject to paragraph (3), no deduction shall be made under sub-paragraph (1)(a) where the eligible rent for a tenant has been increased in a case to which that sub-paragraph would apply, but–

(a)   any such services, facilities or rights (''improvements'')–

    (i)   relate solely to the physical needs of the property in question or the needs of that tenant; and

    (ii)   the increased rent in relation to such improvements is reasonable;

(b)   the tenant was eligible whether or not he was a beneficiary; and

(c)   the authority has not let properties, to which they intend to make improvements, either in the relevant year or in the two years preceding that year, solely or largely to beneficiaries.

(3)   In paragraph (2)–

(a)   ''beneficiary'' has the meaning it is given by article 15(8); and

(b)   in a case to which article 24 applies, sub-paragraph (c) shall have effect as modified by article 24(2).

(4)   Where in relation to any amount of a rebate or allowance a deduction falls to be made under two or more of the sub-paragraphs of paragraph (1), as the case may be, only the higher or highest, or, where the amounts are equal, only one amount, shall be deducted.

Amendments
1.   Amended by art 8 of SI 2003 No 3179 (retrospectively to 1.4.02).
2.   Omitted by art 3(9) of SI 2006 No 54 (retrospectively from 1.4.04).
3.   Amended by reg 5 and Sch 2 para 13(8) of SI 2006 No 217 as from 6.3.06.

Deduction from subsidy
20.   Where, during the relevant year, it is found by an authority that any instrument of payment issued by it as payment of any relevant benefit or community charge benefit on or after 1st April 1988, but before the relevant year, has been returned to that authority without having been presented for payment or has passed its date of validity without having been presented for payment, the deduction referred to in article 13(1) shall be the amount of any subsidy that has been paid in respect of that instrument.

[¹ Deductions from subsidy for rebate for dwellings within the Housing Revenue Account

20A.–(1)   This article applies–
(a)   in the case of an authority in England, where paragraph 2 of Schedule 4A applies, and
(b)   in the case of an authority in Wales, where paragraph 4 of that Schedule applies.
(2)   Where this article applies the deduction from subsidy referred to in article 13(1) shall be calculated–
(a)   in the case of an authority in England, in accordance with paragraph 3 of Schedule 4A, and
(b)   in the case of an authority in Wales, in accordance with paragraph 5 of that Schedule.]

Amendment
1.   Inserted by art 6 of SI 2004 No 646 as from 1.4.04.

[²Additions to subsidy in respect of security against fraud and error
21.–(1)   The addition to subsidy referred to in article 13(1) is applicable in the case of an authority which–
(a)   is a participant in the scheme of arrangements for security against fraud and error ("SAFE") in the administration of housing benefit and council tax benefit described in the [³ Housing Benefit and Council Tax Benefit Security Manual and Circular HB/CTB F10/2004]; and
(b)   qualifies, by virtue of its performance of activities specified in [³ the Housing Benefit and Council Tax Benefit Security Manual and Circular HB/CTB F10/2004] with a view to the prevention or reduction of fraud and error for additional payments in accordance with the terms of [³ the Housing Benefit and Council Tax Benefit Security Manual and Circular HB/CTB F10/2004].
[⁴]]

Amendments
1.   Substituted by art 8 of SI 2000 No 1091 (retrospectively to 1.4.99).
2.   Substituted by art 4(8)(c) of SI 2005 No 369 (retrospectively from 1.4.02).
3.   Amended by art 3(10)(a) and (b) of SI 2006 No 54 (retrospectively from 1.4.04).
4.   Omitted by art 3(10)(c) of SI 2006 No 54 (retrospectively from 1.4.04).

PART IV
Transitional and Savings

Provisions for claims for 1997/98

22. In relation to the relevant year commencing on 1st April 1997 the–
(a) initial claim;
(b) mid-year claim; and
(c) returns pursuant to article 4(4) due on 15th April, 15th July and 15th October 1997 and 15th January 1998,

may be submitted not later than 7 days after the day on which this Order comes into force, but no duty to pay interim subsidy to an authority shall arise until that claim or return, as the case may be, is submitted by the authority.

Transitional provisions in relation to rent officer determinations

23.–(1) In the relevant year commencing on 1st April 1997, the expression "property-specific rent less ineligible amounts" in both paragraph 17(1) of Schedule 4 and paragraph 13(1) of Schedule 6 to the 1997 Order has effect as if after the words ''("ineligible payments")", there were inserted the words "or, in the case of a determination prior to 2nd October 1995, the authority is of the opinion that the exceptionally high rent did not include ineligible payments,''.

[² (2)]

Amendments

1. Amended by reg 5 and sch 2 para 13(9) of SI 2006 No 217 as from 6.3.06.
2. Omitted by Art 3(2) of SI 2007 No 26 as (retrospectively from 1.4.05).

Modifications of exemption from improvements rule

24.–(1) This article applies in the case of a new authority, a 1997 authority or a 1998 authority, as the case may be, and, in these cases, the modifications set out in paragraph (2) shall apply.
(2) In relation to the relevant year commencing on–
(a) 1st April 1997, in the case of a–
   (i) new authority, for the words "or in the two years preceding that year" in article 19(2)(c) there shall be substituted the words "or in the year preceding that year";
   (ii) 1997 authority, the words "or in the two years preceding that year" shall be omitted from article 19(2)(c);
(b) 1st April 1998, in the case of a–
   (i) 1997 authority, for the words "or in the two years preceding that year" in article 19(2)(c) there shall be substituted the words "or in the year preceding that year";
   (ii) 1998 authority, the words "or in the two years preceding that year" shall be omitted from article 19(2)(c);
(c) 1st April 1999, in the case of a 1998 authority, for the words "or in the two years preceding that year" in article 19(2)(c) there shall be substituted the words "or in the year preceding that year''.

[⁶ SCHEDULE 1 ARTICLES 12(1)(B) AND 17(1) AND (8)
SUMS TO BE USED IN THE CALCULATION OF SUBSIDY

	Administration subsidy Threshold	Non-HRA Rent Rebates Cap	
England	(£)	(£)	(£)
Adur	541,150	117.63	203.30
Allerdale	820,662	94.42	162.87
Alnwick	187,588	81.85	141.83

	Administration subsidy Threshold (£)	Non-HRA Rent Rebates Cap (£)	(£)
Amber Valley	2,177,537	94.89	163.87
Arun	801,040	123.12	212.38
Ashfield	694,574	89.10	153.87
Ashford	544,777	116.91	201.88
Aylesbury Vale	553,713	113.05	195.67
Babergh	391,953	108.20	186.83
Barking and Dagenham	3,467,516	223.51	346.99
Barnet	2,459,834	223.51	346.99
Barnsley	1,679,991	79.15	137.65
Barrow in Furness	576,998	98.76	170.54
Basildon	1,197,999	114.95	198.50
Basingstoke and Deane	719,350	117.07	201.95
Bassetlaw	630,003	99.33	171.53
Bath & North East Somerset	1,112,332	100.71	173.73
Bedford	962,281	93.24	161.42
Berwick upon Tweed	184,582	88.60	152.98
Bexley	1,362,860	223.51	346.99
Birmingham	10,721,429	95.47	165.32
Blaby	295,933	85.08	147.23
Blackburn with Darwen	1,550,729	108.94	187.92
Blackpool	2,142,732	90.73	160.83
Blyth Valley	604,122	75.02	129.88
Bolsover	639,470	77.36	136.39
Bolton	2,657,289	81.72	142.4
Boston	411,275	85.21	147.31
Bournemouth	1,474,200	102.41	187.95
Bracknell Forest	493,431	127.2	223.22
Bradford	4,201,293	86.20	158.19
Braintree	670,747	104.64	180.69
Breckland	960,122	107.01	185.25
Brent	3,652,904	223.51	366.97
Brentwood	388,832	118.62	204.84
Bridgnorth	304,791	96.45	167.79
Brighton and Hove	2,451,490	105.84	203.09
Bristol	3,016,186	93.23	180.00
Broadland	564,628	107.01	185.25
Bromley	1,833,635	223.51	346.99
Bromsgrove	599,819	99.45	179.46
Broxbourne	416,427	126.48	218.41
Broxtowe	1,083,155	81.36	141.69
Burnley	963,316	96.75	166.89
Bury	1,259,114	94.23	162.72
Calderdale	1,471,710	83.75	144.71
Cambridge	614,340	111.41	192.38
Camden	3,367,912	223.51	365.30
Cannock Chase	518,977	99.89	178.38
Canterbury	879,676	112.34	193.97
Caradon	455,141	94.69	163.51
Carlisle	908,624	92.14	159.10
Carrick	546,892	107.83	186.20
Castle Morpeth	202,845	88.89	153.50
Castle Point	673,294	122.30	211.18
Charnwood	584,764	85.61	147.85
Chelmsford	796,312	119.70	207.46
Cheltenham	601,259	121.58	209.93
Cherwell	633,201	117.87	203.82
Chester	847,625	89.00	153.52
Chester le Street	499,581	82.28	142.53
Chesterfield	794,632	81.69	141.06
Chichester	642,039	118.48	204.37
Chiltern	376,484	117.07	201.95

	Administration subsidy Threshold (£)	Non-HRA Rent Rebates Cap (£)	(£)
Chorley	481,619	83.82	145.54
Christchurch	264,923	100.71	184.64
City of London	102,295	223.51	346.99
Colchester	804,419	110.25	191.93
Congleton	387,214	94.42	162.87
Copeland	958,391	88.71	164.58
Corby	329,919	91.42	163.13
Cotswold	558,760	100.71	173.73
Coventry	2,977,295	81.21	155.64
Craven	250,835	100.12	172.89
Crawley	563,744	126.74	219.64
Crewe and Nantwich	715,779	99.90	179.69
Croydon	3,439,965	223.51	360.44
Dacorum	741,450	110.97	194.04
Darlington	787,433	86.96	150.16
Dartford	700,602	114.85	198.32
Daventry	242,633	91.32	157.69
Derby	1,907,939	90.19	155.76
Derbyshire Dales	309,095	91.57	158.47
Derwentside	1,047,550	89.71	154.91
Doncaster	2,029,010	82.28	144.48
Dover	870,579	116.94	201.93
Dudley	2,201,242	95.78	167.82
Durham	713,680	84.71	148.23
Ealing	2,370,849	223.51	351.19
Easington	952,559	87.21	150.59
East Cambridgeshire	363,667	107.01	185.25
East Devon	549,226	91.41	167.75
East Dorset	391,512	100.71	184.64
East Hampshire	500,372	117.07	201.95
East Hertfordshire	508,022	127.90	221.65
East Lindsey	957,002	87.82	151.81
East Northamptonshire	412,822	98.10	169.60
East Riding of Yorkshire	1,651,981	87.66	155.41
East Staffordshire	746,426	85.52	147.52
Eastbourne	929,671	105.32	193.31
Eastleigh	497,202	117.07	201.95
Eden	216,951	94.42	162.87
Ellesmere Port and Neston	681,717	73.57	145.96
Elmbridge	683,799	133.53	230.32
Enfield	2,962,511	223.51	346.99
Epping Forest	574,529	113.34	196.26
Epsom and Ewell	239,878	117.07	201.95
Erewash	606,111	83.97	145.31
Exeter	793,266	88.54	162.50
Fareham	315,483	110.95	195.45
Fenland	548,408	100.56	173.66
Forest Heath	213,305	99.04	171.03
Forest of Dean	705,851	96.52	166.67
Fylde	373,689	82.51	142.31
Gateshead	4,151,653	87.29	150.74
Gedling	550,834	83.14	144.18
Gloucester	720,049	105.41	182.02
Gosport	418,312	108.81	187.90
Gravesham	916,856	111.04	191.76
Great Yarmouth	1,267,467	83.55	153.34
Greenwich	3,455,031	223.51	346.99
Guildford	508,357	134.07	231.52
Hackney	4,098,097	223.51	347.48
Halton	1,405,420	86.83	155.33
Hambleton	535,304	83.08	152.54

	Administration subsidy Threshold (£)	Non-HRA Rent Rebates Cap (£)	(£)
Hammersmith and Fulham	2,405,655	223.51	346.99
Harborough	428,222	103.09	178.01
Haringey	2,767,088	223.51	346.99
Harlow	579,851	109.42	188.94
Harrogate	585,388	106.57	184.04
Harrow	1,307,876	223.51	381.29
Hart	513,841	117.07	201.95
Hartlepool	1,182,656	90.16	155.69
Hastings	1,018,078	117.07	201.95
Havant	642,013	117.07	201.95
Havering	1,249,238	223.51	346.99
Herefordshire	1,117,571	89.64	154.80
Hertsmere	530,671	107.01	185.25
High Peak	449,673	96.94	167.39
Hillingdon	1,591,178	223.51	383.39
Hinckley and Bosworth	356,258	93.60	161.64
Horsham	703,607	138.41	238.74
Hounslow	1,569,795	223.51	346.99
Huntingdonshire	725,955	115.92	200.68
Hyndburn	656,521	93.45	161.20
Ipswich	929,602	99.72	172.19
Isle of Wight	1,076,317	117.07	201.95
Isles of Scilly	7,951	104.08	179.73
Islington	3,485,205	223.51	359.52
Kennet	359,786	100.71	173.73
Kensington and Chelsea	2,158,521	223.51	396.15
Kerrier	810,317	100.71	173.73
Kettering	404,257	90.21	157.06
Kings Lynn and West Norfolk	1,024,778	87.62	159.42
Kingston upon Hull	3,087,282	90.63	162.38
Kingston upon Thames	695,047	223.51	372.60
Kirklees	2,566,641	91.86	158.64
Knowsley	2,069,706	102.02	176.17
Lambeth	4,509,682	223.51	346.99
Lancaster	902,217	90.85	156.87
Leeds	6,087,011	83.41	153.46
Leicester	3,156,743	92.52	159.61
Lewes	492,190	113.59	197.50
Lewisham	4,044,602	223.51	346.99
Lichfield	606,649	92.82	160.12
Lincoln	796,442	87.56	151.20
Liverpool	6,165,922	93.12	160.83
Luton	1,292,893	114.55	197.81
Macclesfield	645,726	103.10	193.20
Maidstone	762,416	116.30	200.82
Maldon	306,138	107.01	185.25
Malvern Hills	464,980	92.82	160.12
Manchester	5,994,281	109.17	188.51
Mansfield	739,362	93.71	161.65
Medway	1,576,395	114.85	198.32
Melton	159,782	84.14	149.23
Mendip	769,027	99.23	171.18
Merton	1,048,254	223.51	346.99
Mid Bedfordshire	665,055	106.32	184.26
Mid Devon	367,375	94.27	162.80
Mid Suffolk	307,758	100.56	173.66
Mid Sussex	1,442,432	117.07	201.95
Middlesbrough	1,540,524	98.66	170.37
Milton Keynes	1,229,471	114.35	198.30
Mole Valley	278,432	113.82	196.54
New Forest	726,720	126.10	217.76

	Administration subsidy Threshold (£)	Non-HRA Rent Rebates Cap (£)	(£)
Newark and Sherwood	555,099	87.56	151.19
Newcastle under Lyme	755,700	78.70	150.86
Newcastle upon Tyne	3,540,011	85.76	148.09
Newham	3,270,945	223.51	346.99
North Cornwall	785,134	95.06	164.14
North Devon	761,263	109.95	189.66
North Dorset	442,945	100.71	173.73
North East Derby	555,051	79.87	141.45
North East Lincoln	1,425,452	85.81	153.36
North Hertfordshire	804,148	115.06	204.65
North Kesteven	477,640	87.53	151.13
North Lincolnshire	1,017,814	83.07	143.97
North Norfolk	694,904	92.45	159.84
North Shropshire	279,310	86.90	151.02
North Somerset	1,113,123	115.92	200.17
North Tyneside	1,964,942	80.25	139.34
North Warwickshire	437,768	91.58	160.70
North West Leicestershire	372,649	86.63	149.59
North Wiltshire	623,597	100.71	173.73
Northampton	2,002,351	113.90	196.67
Norwich	1,147,991	90.26	156.40
Nottingham	2,783,167	83.96	144.99
Nuneaton and Bedworth	822,002	88.81	154.92
Oadby and Wigston	286,631	85.39	148.27
Oldham	1,908,799	83.75	153.13
Oswestry	187,813	89.56	154.65
Oxford	866,910	122.71	213.93
Pendle	753,190	87.23	150.64
Penwith	812,198	94.58	173.40
Peterborough	1,499,900	114.08	197.00
Plymouth	2,452,020	92.07	158.97
Poole	1,072,501	104.52	191.62
Portsmouth	1,561,051	111.09	191.81
Preston	984,115	94.99	164.01
Purbeck	216,233	116.19	200.62
Reading	1,238,833	135.67	234.27
Redbridge	1,493,193	223.51	352.76
Redcar and Cleveland	1,486,136	94.34	162.90
Redditch	571,209	100.51	173.57
Reigate and Banstead	513,075	131.92	227.79
Restormel	927,144	108.16	186.57
Ribble Valley	160,730	81.96	141.52
Richmond upon Thames	971,006	223.51	346.99
Richmondshire	179,836	97.21	167.85
Rochdale	3,608,972	87.10	150.41
Rochford	353,263	103.82	179.26
Rossendale	570,634	88.21	152.16
Rother	655,384	117.07	201.95
Rotherham	1,793,414	73.64	132.52
Rugby	542,118	94.15	163.62
Runnymede	312,692	138.57	239.29
Rushcliffe	364,891	96.48	168.17
Rushmoor	421,480	117.07	201.95
Rutland	101,833	102.90	177.70
Ryedale	364,478	83.08	152.54
Salford	2,769,586	96.36	166.39
Salisbury	481,187	121.97	216.09
Sandwell	2,939,378	103.71	180.64
Scarborough	1,061,827	98.94	170.84
Sedgefield	892,905	85.26	147.64
Sedgemoor	578,007	106.66	184.18

	Administration subsidy Threshold (£)	Non-HRA Rent Rebates Cap (£)	(£)
Sefton	2,523,338	98.01	169.49
Selby	550,697	92.79	160.24
Sevenoaks	684,206	117.07	201.95
Sheffield	4,342,187	83.75	144.74
Shepway	753,323	107.33	185.33
Shrewsbury and Atcham	655,452	95.11	164.24
Slough	869,970	122.26	213.37
Solihull	963,097	99.57	171.94
South Bedfordshire	489,805	119.67	207.86
South Bucks	715,344	117.07	201.95
South Cambridgeshire	408,947	119.89	207.03
South Derbyshire	353,337	94.21	162.67
South Gloucestershire	2,774,785	102.68	180.81
South Hams	786,066	100.71	173.73
South Holland	575,231	89.35	154.30
South Kesteven	514,260	92.28	161.34
South Lakeland	453,490	106.13	188.71
South Norfolk	573,411	97.21	167.85
South Northamptonshire	201,640	106.08	184.62
South Oxfordshire	535,396	117.07	201.95
South Ribble	655,774	94.42	162.87
South Shropshire	236,887	92.82	160.12
South Somerset	820,781	100.71	173.73
South Staffordshire	744,790	92.82	160.12
South Tyneside	1,868,061	78.12	136.67
Southampton	1,772,938	98.03	188.07
Southend on Sea	1,451,034	106.44	183.80
Southwark	5,314,651	223.51	346.99
Spelthorne	446,961	117.07	201.95
St Albans	537,738	118.06	205.35
St Edmundsbury	524,174	106.04	183.78
St Helens	1,706,323	100.64	173.78
Stafford	681,083	92.82	160.12
Staffordshire Moorlands	459,312	90.27	155.71
Stevenage	566,404	116.92	201.89
Stockport	1,508,996	85.47	164.34
Stockton on Tees	1,303,882	89.51	155.97
Stoke on Trent	2,999,929	89.33	154.24
Stratford on Avon	575,445	92.82	160.12
Stroud	617,771	107.03	184.81
Suffolk Coastal	593,364	97.13	168.14
Sunderland	4,104,354	97.04	167.40
Surrey Heath	246,977	117.07	201.95
Sutton	937,379	223.51	346.99
Swale	988,384	117.07	201.95
Swindon	891,670	95.38	166.55
Tameside	1,983,153	99.17	171.06
Tamworth	391,561	97.36	169.29
Tandridge	250,169	116.83	203.44
Taunton Deane	785,620	94.94	163.94
Teesdale	141,953	87.05	150.31
Teignbridge	904,466	112.26	193.86
Telford and Wrekin	1,252,063	92.82	160.12
Tendring	1,052,313	98.00	179.86
Test Valley	472,663	113.80	196.29
Tewkesbury	351,544	92.87	160.20
Thanet	1,560,632	106.35	183.64
Three Rivers	348,065	120.56	209.77
Thurrock	910,565	113.49	195.95
Tonbridge and Malling	605,472	117.07	201.95
Torbay	1,319,475	103.66	178.81

	Administration subsidy Threshold (£)	Non-HRA Rent Rebates Cap (£)	(£)
Torridge	463,075	102.57	177.11
Tower Hamlets	4,313,752	223.51	374.38
Trafford	1,304,835	95.94	165.66
Tunbridge Wells	655,838	117.07	201.95
Tynedale	356,005	93.57	161.41
Uttlesford	283,576	117.32	202.66
Vale of White Horse	446,705	117.07	201.95
Vale Royal	1,056,871	94.94	163.95
Wakefield	2,009,095	83.83	156.34
Walsall	2,722,971	95.48	164.89
Waltham Forest	2,188,169	223.51	367.87
Wandsworth	2,402,306	223.51	390.57
Wansbeck	490,155	74.07	127.90
Warrington	1,265,550	95.33	164.61
Warwick	659,071	101.13	176.96
Watford	480,458	117.41	202.72
Waveney	1,015,793	92.30	159.38
Waverley	429,795	127.22	219.45
Wealden	557,215	99.81	191.49
Wear Valley	629,981	86.22	148.87
Wellingborough	361,833	93.99	162.29
Welwyn Hatfield	535,731	110.25	193.38
West Berkshire	905,001	117.07	201.95
West Devon	265,001	100.71	173.73
West Dorset	546,291	100.71	173.73
West Lancashire	934,290	89.13	155.22
West Lindsey	491,595	86.71	149.91
West Oxfordshire	420,810	112.22	193.59
West Somerset	283,361	100.71	173.73
West Wiltshire	658,210	115.04	198.44
Westminster	2,260,565	223.51	428.82
Weymouth and Portland	613,230	104.29	179.90
Wigan	2,162,909	89.41	154.39
Winchester	399,158	117.53	202.95
Windsor and Maidenhead	768,568	117.07	201.95
Wirral	2,975,390	104.37	180.21
Woking	346,099	151.4	261.45
Wokingham	305,817	118.29	210.01
Wolverhampton	2,283,266	86.71	160.13
Worcester	592,374	89.41	156.05
Worthing	610,368	117.07	201.95
Wychavon	654,519	116.85	201.54
Wycombe	630,922	134.52	232.29
Wyre	785,444	94.80	163.52
Wyre Forest	798,083	96.56	166.56
York	802,154	98.23	169.61
Wales			
Blaenau Gwent	799,019	91.65	158.24
Bridgend	988,768	93.01	160.62
Caerphilly	1,250,336	98.31	169.76
Cardiff	2,228,733	103.42	179.59
Carmarthenshire	1,180,478	89.75	154.98
Ceredigion	379,744	98.37	169.86
Conwy	1,792,884	86.52	156.20
Denbighshire	630,626	84.15	146.72
Flintshire	797,706	89.49	154.73
Gwynedd	753,834	89.13	153.90
Isle of Anglesey	669,910	87.88	151.74
Merthyr Tydfil	817,642	89.17	153.98

	Administration subsidy Threshold (£)	Non-HRA Rent Rebates Cap (£)	(£)
Monmouthshire	475,585	103.25	179.51
Neath Port Talbot	1,124,438	90.39	156.09
Newport	1,012,024	97.89	171.18
Pembrokeshire	851,138	87.86	151.70
Powys	725,790	92.14	159.35
Rhondda Cynon Taff	1,987,547	87.70	151.44
Swansea	1,737,342	93.70	161.81
Torfaen	627,677	101.74	177.30
Vale of Glamorgan	807,675	105.59	182.34
Wrexham	891,479	83.92	145.37
Scotland			
Aberdeen	1,488,421	79.65	139.02
Aberdeenshire	1,162,226	75.09	133.40
Angus	932,799	70.27	126.75
Argyll and Bute	606,884	85.63	147.88
Clackmannanshire	419,879	75.46	139.24
Comhairle nan Eilean Siar	183,493	88.56	154.86
Dumfries and Galloway	1,315,712	80.33	141.23
Dundee	2,072,708	87.31	152.30
East Ayrshire	1,136,017	76.85	132.82
East Dunbartonshire	453,465	82.14	145.45
East Lothian	5,435,595	73.87	127.56
East Renfrewshire	354,131	78.82	144.59
Edinburgh	4,324,973	100.39	173.35
Falkirk	1,101,183	80.03	147.09
Fife	2,807,442	76.13	136.38
Glasgow	11,743,523	101.72	175.65
Highland	1,369,487	93.42	161.30
Inverclyde	922,614	95.55	170.47
Midlothian	762,226	66.98	115.67
Moray	449,823	67.74	116.96
North Ayrshire	1,390,101	71.99	127.46
North Lanarkshire	3,005,055	83.85	146.60
Orkney Islands	94,955	78.51	135.56
Perth & Kinross	734,348	71.28	123.09
Renfrewshire	1,918,068	87.13	158.90
Scottish Borders	828,671	75.83	130.93
Shetland	84,568	102.20	176.47
South Ayrshire	908,735	78.20	135.01
South Lanarkshire	2,633,563	85.82	148.19
Stirling	544,644	80.89	139.66
West Dunbartonshire	1,212,914	80.57	139.14
West Lothian	1,547,073	82.78	169.42]

Amendments

1. Substituted by art 4 of SI 2001 N0 2350 as from 25.07.01.
2. Substituted by art 3 of SI 2002 No 1859 (retrospectively from 1.4.01).
3. Substituted by art 9 of SI 2003 No 3179 (retrospectively from 1.4.02).
4. Substituted by art 5(1) of SI 2005 No 369 (retrospectively from 1.4.03).
5. Substituted by art 4(1) of SI 2006 No 54 (retrospectively from 1.4.04).
6. Substituted by art 4(1) of SI 2007 No 26 (retrospectively from 1.4.05).

[² SCHEDULE 2]

Amendments

1. Inserted by art 10 of SI 2000 No 1091 (retrospectively to 1.4.99).
2. Omitted by art 4(2) of SI 2006 No 54 (retrospectively from 1.4.04).

[² SCHEDULE 3]

Amendments

1.　Inserted by reg 5 SI 1999 No 550.
2.　Omitted by art 4(3) of SI 2006 No 54 (retrospectively from 1.4.04).

SCHEDULE 4
HIGH RENTS AND RENT ALLOWANCES
Part I
Regulated Tenancies

[¹]

Amendment

1.　Omitted by art 4(4)(a) of SI 2006 No 54 (retrospectively from 1.4.04).

Part II
Rent Officers' Determinations

Calculation of the appropriate amount

2.　The appropriate amount, in a case to which this Part applies, in respect of that part of the qualifying expenditure which is attributable to allowances granted for the period beginning on the relevant date and ending on the termination date, shall be calculated in accordance with paragraph 6, 7, 8, 9 or 11 as appropriate.

Rent officers' determinations

3.　Except in a case to which Part III applies, this Part applies where an authority applies to a rent officer for a determination to be made under the Rent Officers Order or the Rent Officers Order 1995 in relation to a dwelling and the officer makes such a determination.

4.　This Part also applies in a case where the dwelling A is in a hostel and, by virtue of [¹ regulation 14(4) of the Housing Benefit Regulations or, as the case may be, regulation 14(4) of the Housing Benefit (State Pension Credit) Regulations] (exemptions from requirement to refer to rent officers), an application for a determination in respect of that dwelling A is not required, because the dwelling is regarded as similar to dwelling B in that hostel in respect of which a determination has been made, and in such a case the determination made in respect of dwelling B shall, for the purposes of this Part, be treated as if it were a determination in respect of dwelling A.

Amendment

1.　Amended by reg 5 and Sch 2 para 13(10)(a) of SI 2006 No 217 as from 6.3.06.

5.　This Part also applies in a case where a rent officer has made a determination in respect of a tenancy of a dwelling and by virtue of [¹ paragraph 2 of Schedule 2 to the Housing Benefit Regulations or, as the case may be, paragraph 2 of Schedule 2 to the Housing Benefit (State Pension Credit) Regulations] (cases with existing determinations) a new determination is not required in respect of another tenancy of the dwelling and in such a case the determination made shall, for the purposes of this Part, be treated as if it were a determination made in respect of that tenancy.

Amendment

1.　Amended by reg 5 and Sch 2 para 13(10)(b) of SI 2006 No 217 as from 6.3.06.

[¹**6.**　Except where paragraph 5 applies, this Part also applies in a case where an authority is required under [² regulation 14 of the Housing Benefit Regulations or, as the case may be, regulation 14 of the Housing Benefit (State Pension Credit) Regulations] (requirement to refer to rent officer) to apply for a determination in relation to a dwelling, but the appropriate amount shall be nil if the authority fails to apply for that determination—

(a)　during the relevant year; or
(b)　as soon as possible thereafter but before the date of the due date for the submission of the final subsidy claim for the relevant year.]

Amendments

1.　Substituted by art 4(4)(b) of SI 2006 No 54 (retrospectively from 1.4.04).
2.　Amended by reg 5 and sch 2 para 13(10)(c) of SI 2006 No 217 as from 6.3.06.

Rent officers' property-specific rent [and claim related rent]

7.   [¹ Where the rent officer either–
(a)   determines a property-specific rent but not a size-related rent and the amount of eligible rent does not exceed the property-specific rent less ineligible amounts, or
(b)   determines a claim-related rent and the amount of eligible rent does not exceed the aggregate of the claim-related rent and those service charges which the authority has determined as eligible to be met by housing benefit [³ under sub-paragraphs (a)(iv)(c) and (f) of paragraph 1 of Schedule 1 to the Housing Benefit Regulations or, as the case may be, under sub-paragraphs (a)(iv)(c) and (f) of paragraph 1 of Schedule 1 to the Housing Benefit (State Pension Credit) Regulations (ineligible service charges)], less ineligible amounts,
the appropriate amount in respect of the period beginning with the relevant date and ending with the termination date shall be [³ 100 per cent] of that part of the qualifying expenditure attributable to the eligible rent.]

Amendments
1.   Amended by art 7(2) SI 2001 No 2350 as from 25.07.01.
2.   Amended by reg 5 and Sch 2 para 13(10)(d) of SI 2006 No 217 as from 6.3.06.
3.   Amended by art 4(2) of SI 2007 No 26 (retrospectively from 1.4.04).

8.–[¹(1)   Where the rent officer either–
(a)   determines a property-specific rent, but not a size-related rent and the amount of eligible rent exceeds the property-specific rent less ineligible amounts, or
(b)   determines a claim-related rent and the amount of eligible rent exceeds the aggregate of the claim-related rent and those service charges which the authority has determined as eligible to be met by housing benefit under [² under sub-paragraphs (a)(iv)(c) and (f) of paragraph 1 of Schedule 1 to the Housing Benefit Regulations or, as the case may be, under sub-paragraphs (a)(iv)(c) and (f) of paragraph 1 of Schedule 1 to the Housing Benefit (State Pension Credit) Regulations (ineligible service charges)], less ineligible amounts,
then, for the period beginning with the relevant date and ending with the termination date, the appropriate amount shall be determined in accordance with sub-paragraph (2) or (3), as the case may be]
(2)   Where the allowance granted is the same as or is less than the excess–
(a)   except in a case to which paragraph 10 applies, the appropriate amount shall be nil;
(b)   where paragraph 10 applies, the appropriate amount shall be 60 per cent. of the qualifying expenditure attributable to such allowance.
(3)   Where the allowance granted is greater than the excess the appropriate amount shall be
(a)   except where paragraph 10 applies, nil per cent. of the qualifying expenditure which is equal to the excess;
(b)   where paragraph 10 applies, 60 per cent. of the qualifying expenditure which is equal to the excess,
together with [³ 100 per cent] of the qualifying expenditure which remains after deducting the excess.

Amendments
1.   Amended by art 7(3) SI 2001 No 2350 as from 25.07.01.
2.   Amended by reg 5 and Sch 2 para 13(10)(d) of SI 2006 No 217 as from 6.3.06.
3.   Amended by art 4(2) of SI 2007 No 26 (retrospectively from 1.4.04).

Rent officers' property-specific and size-related rents

9.–(1)   Where the rent officer makes a determination that the dwelling exceeds the size criteria for its occupiers and determines both a property-specific rent and a size-related rent for that dwelling, the appropriate amount in respect of the period beginning on the relevant date and ending on the termination date shall be the appropriate amounts determined in accordance with the relevant sub-paragraphs of this paragraph.
(2)   Where the eligible rent does not exceed the designated rent, less ineligible amounts, the appropriate amount shall be [² 100 per cent]. of that part of the qualifying expenditure attributable to the eligible rent.
(3)   For the period of 13 weeks beginning on the relevant date or, if shorter, for the period beginning on that date and ending on the termination date, if the amount of the eligible rent does not exceed the property-specific rent less ineligible amounts, the appropriate amount shall be [² 100 per cent]. of that part of the qualifying expenditure attributable to the eligible rent.

(4)   For the period of 13 weeks beginning on the relevant date or, if shorter, for the period beginning on that date and ending on the termination date, if the amount of the eligible rent exceeds the property-specific rent less ineligible amounts–

(a)   where the allowance is the same as or is less than the excess–
    (i)   except in a case to which paragraph 10 applies, the appropriate amount shall be nil;
    (ii)   where paragraph 10 applies, the appropriate amount shall be 60 per cent of the qualifying expenditure attributable to such allowance;

(b)   where the allowance granted is greater than the excess the appropriate amount shall be–
    (i)   except where paragraph 10 applies, nil per cent. of the qualifying expenditure which is equal to the excess;
    (ii)   where paragraph 10 applies, 60 per cent. of the qualifying expenditure which is equal to the excess,

and in either case [² 100 per cent]. of the qualifying expenditure which remains after deducting the excess.

(5)   For the period after the end of that 13 week period, if the amount of the eligible rent exceeds the designated rent less ineligible amounts–

(a)   where the allowance is the same as or is less than the excess–
    (i)   except in a case to which paragraph 10 applies, the appropriate amount shall be nil;
    (ii)   where paragraph 10 applies, the appropriate amount shall be 60 per cent. of the qualifying expenditure attributable to such allowance;

(b)   where the allowance granted is greater than the excess the appropriate amount shall be–
    (i)   except where paragraph 10 applies, nil per cent. of the qualifying expenditure which is equal to the excess;
    (ii)   where paragraph 10 applies, 60 per cent. of the qualifying expenditure which is equal to the excess,

and in either case [² 100 per cent]. of the qualifying expenditure which remains after deducting the excess.

[¹(6)   This paragraph does not apply where a rent officer determines a claim-related rent.]

Amendments
1.   Amended by Art 7(4) SI 2001 No 2350 as from 25.07.01.
2.   Amended by Art 4(2) of SI 2007 No 26 (retrospectively from 1.4.04).

Restriction on unreasonable rents or on rent increases

10.   This paragraph applies where an authority has been unable to treat a person's eligible rent as reduced by reason of regulation 11(3), (3A), (4), as in force on 1st January 1996, or 12(2) of the [¹ Housing Benefit (General) Regulations 1987] (restrictions on unreasonable rents or rent increases), as in force on 5th October 1997.

Amendment
1.   Amended by reg 5 and Sch 2 para 13(10)(e) of SI 2006 No 217 as from 6.3.06.

Payments on account of rent allowance

11.–(1)   This paragraph applies in a case where–
(a)   an authority makes a payment on account pursuant to [¹ regulation 93 of the Housing Benefit Regulations or, as the case may be, regulation 74 of the Housing Benefit (State Pension Credit) Regulations] (payments on account); and
(b)   on the subsequent determination by that authority the amount of rent allowance payable is less than the amount of that payment.

(2)   In a case where this paragraph applies, the appropriate amount shall be [² 100 per cent]. of so much of any amount which–
(a)   is not in excess of the appropriate indicative rent level in relation to the dwelling, in respect of which the claim for rent allowance, pursuant to which the payment on account was paid, was made; and
(b)   has not been recovered pursuant to either [¹ regulation 93(3) or regulation 100 (recoverable overpayments) of the Housing Benefit Regulations or, as the case may be, regulation 74(3) or regulation 81 of the Housing Benefit (State Pension Credit) Regulations].

(3)   In any case to which this paragraph applies where any such payments on account were in excess of the appropriate indicative rent level, the appropriate amount shall be nil.

Amendments
1.   Amended by reg 5 and Sch 2 para 13(10)(f) of SI 2006 No 217 as from 6.3.06.
2.   Amended by art 4(2) of SI 2007 No 26 (retrospectively from 1.4.04).

Relevant date

12. For the purposes of this Part–

(a) in a case where a claim for rent allowance is made on or after 1st April in the relevant year, the relevant date is the date on which entitlement to benefit commences;

(b) in a case where, on 1st April in the relevant year, there is current on that date both a claim for an allowance in relation to the dwelling and a rent officer's determination in relation to that dwelling, the relevant date is that day and for this purpose a rent officer's determination includes a determination, further determination or re-determination made under the Rent Officers Order or the Rent Officers Order 1995, as the case may be, save that, where a determination had not taken effect by 31st March of the year immediately preceding the relevant year, the relevant date will be 13 weeks after the relevant date determined under the 1997 Order, or, in a relevant year commencing on or after 1st April 1998, the relevant date determined for the year immediately preceding that relevant year;

(c) in a case where, during the relevant year–
   (i) there has been a change relating to a rent allowance within the meaning of [² regulation 14(10) of the Housing Benefit Regulations or, as the case may be, regulation 14(10) of the Housing Benefit (State Pension Credit) Regulations]; and
   (ii) by virtue of [² regulation 14 of the Housing Benefit Regulations or, as the case may be, regulation 14 of the Housing Benefit (State Pension Credit) Regulations] (requirement to refer to rent officer) an application for a determination in respect of that dwelling is required,

the relevant date is the date on which the relevant change of circumstances takes effect for the purposes of [² regulation 79 of the Housing Benefit Regulations or, as the case may be, regulation 59 of the Housing Benefit (State Pension Credit) Regulations] (date on which change of circumstances is to take effect) or, if the relevant change of circumstances does not affect entitlement to an allowance, the Monday following the date on which the relevant change occurred;

(d) in a case where, prior to any rent officer determination being notified to the authority, the authority determines a rent allowance on a claim in respect of a dwelling, the relevant date is–
   (i) if the designated rent less ineligible amounts determined under the determination eventually notified by the rent officer is higher than or equal to the eligible rent determined by the authority in relation to that dwelling, the date determined under the foregoing sub-paragraphs of this paragraph as appropriate;
   (ii) if the designated rent less ineligible amounts is lower than the eligible rent determined by the authority but that eligible rent is equal to or more than the appropriate indicative rent level for that dwelling, the Monday following the date on which the determination is made by the rent officer;
   (iii) if the designated rent less ineligible amounts is lower than the eligible rent determined by the authority in relation to that dwelling, the Monday following the date on which the determination is made by the rent officer and, in so far as the eligible rent determined by the authority in relation to that dwelling was in excess of the appropriate indicative rent level for that dwelling, paragraph 7 shall apply to that excess;

(e) [¹ in a case where the rent officer has made a re-determination, substitute determination or substitute re-determination, the relevant date is
   (i) if the designated rent determination under the re-determination, substitute determination or substitute re-determination is higher than or equal to the amount determined under the original determination, the date determined under the foregoing sub-paragraphs of this paragraph as appropriate;
   (ii) if the designated rent determination under the re-determination, substitute determination or substitute re-determination is lower than the amount determined under the original determination, the Monday following the date on which the re-determination, substitute determination or substitute re-determination is made by the rent officer.]

Amendments
1. Amended by art 7(5) SI 2001 No 2350 as from 25.07.01.
2. Amended by reg 5 and Sch 2 para 13(10)(g) of SI 2006 No 217 as from 6.3.06.

Termination date

13. For the purposes of this Part "termination date" means–

(a) 31st March in the relevant year; or

(b) where the rent officer's determination replaces a determination made in relation to the same dwelling, the day before the relevant date of the new determination by the rent officer in relation to the same dwelling as defined by paragraph 12; or

(c)   the date on which the allowance ceases to be paid in respect of the tenancy,
whichever is the earlier date in the relevant year.

Part III: Reckonable Rent Cases

[¹]

Amendment
1.   Omitted by art 4(4)(c) of SI 2006 No 54 (retrospectively from 1.4.04).

---

15.   In a case where article 16(4)(c) applies, the appropriate amount shall be, for the period of 13
weeks prescribed in [¹ regulation 13(14) of the Housing Benefit Regulations or, as the case may be,
regulation 13(14) of the Housing Benefit (State Pension Credit) Regulations], [² 100 per cent]. of the
eligible rent less ineligible amounts.

Amendments
1.   Amended by reg 5 and Sch 2 para 13(10)(h) of SI 2006 No 217 as from 6.3.06.
2.   Amended by art 4(2) of SI 2007 No 26 (retrospectively from 1.4.04).

Part IV
General And Interpretation

Apportionment

16.   For the purposes of this Schedule, where more than one person is liable to make payments in
respect of a dwelling the designated rent shall be apportioned on the same basis as such payments are
apportioned under [¹ regulation 12(5) of the Housing Benefit Regulations or, as the case may be, regulation
12(5) of the Housing Benefit (State Pension Credit) Regulations] (rent).

Amendment
1.   Amended by reg 5 and Sch 2 para 13(10)(i) of SI 2006 No 217 as from 6.3.06.

Interpretation

17.–(1)   In this Schedule, unless the context otherwise requires–
''appropriate indicative rent level'' means the indicative rent level for the category of dwelling into which
            the dwelling in question falls, as described in paragraph 11 of Schedule 1 to the Rent Officers
            Order or paragraph 9 of Schedule 1 to the Rent Officers Order 1995, as the case may be,
            except that, where a payment on account is made to a young individual, the category of
            dwelling shall be that within head (b) of paragraph 9(3) of that Schedule, less, in the case of a
            dwelling falling within that head or head (a) of that paragraph, any amount ineligible to be
            met under [³ paragraph 2 of Part 1 of Schedule 1 to the Housing Benefit Regulations or, as the
            case may be, paragraph 2 of Part 1 of Schedule 1 to the Housing Benefit (State Pension Credit)
            Regulations] (meal charges);
[¹ ''claim-related rent'' means the rent notified by the rent officer under paragraph 9(1) of Schedule 1 to
            the Rent Officers (Housing Benefit Functions) Order 1997 or, as the case may be, the Rent
            Officers (Housing Benefit Functions) (Scotland) Order 1997;]
''designated rent'' means–
    (a)   in a case where a rent officer has determined both a property-specific rent and a size-related
            rent, whichever is the lower of the two;
    (b)   in a case where a rent officer has determined only a property-specific rent or a size-related
            rent, as the case may be, that rent;
    [²(c)   in a case where a rent officer has determined a claim-related rent, that rent;]
''ineligible amounts'' means–
    (a)   [¹ in a case where the rent officer has determined a claim-related rent
        (i)   any amount in respect of amounts ineligible to be met by housing benefit under [³
                paragraph 2 of Part 1 of Schedule 1 to the Housing Benefit Regulations or, as the case
                may be, paragraph 2 of Part 1 of Schedule 1 to the Housing Benefit (State Pension
                Credit) Regulations] (amounts ineligible for meals)
        [³ (ii) where the dwelling is a hostel as defined in regulation 2(1) of the Housing Benefit
                Regulations or, as the case may be, regulation 2(1) of the Housing Benefit (State
                Pension Credit) Regulations (interpretation), any amount ineligible to be met by
                housing benefit under (as the case may be)–
            (aa)   paragraph 1 of Schedule 1 to the Housing Benefit Regulations (ineligible
                    service charges), other than sub-paragraphs (d) to (f) of that paragraph; or

        (bb)   paragraph 1 of Schedule 1 to the Housing Benefit (State Pension Credit) Regulations (ineligible service charges), other than sub-paragraphs (d) to (f) of that paragraph;]

(b)   in any other case, except as provided in the definition of "property-specific rent less ineligible amounts" below,

        (i)   any amount which the rent officer determines is attributable to the provision of services ineligible to be met by housing benefit, plus the amount in respect of fuel charges ineligible to be met [³ under Part 2 of Schedule 1 to the Housing Benefit Regulations or, as the case may be, Part 2 of Schedule 1 to the Housing Benefit (State Pension Credit) Regulations] (payments in respect of fuel charges);

        (ii)   any amount in respect of amounts ineligible to be met by housing benefit under [³ paragraph 2 of Schedule 1 to the Housing Benefit Regulations or, as the case may be, paragraph 2 of Schedule 1 to the Housing Benefit (State Pension Credit) Regulations] (amounts ineligible for meals);

        (iii)   where the dwelling is in a hostel as defined in regulation 2 of the Housing Benefit Regulations (interpretation), any amount ineligible to be met by housing benefit under [³ paragraph 1 of Schedule 1 to those Regulations or, as the case may be, paragraph 1 of Schedule 1 to the Housing Benefit (State Pension Credit) Regulations (ineligible service charges), other than sub-paragraphs (d) to (f) of those paragraphs].]

(c)   where the dwelling is a hostel within the meaning of regulation 12A of the Housing Benefit Regulations (requirement to refer to rent officers), any amount ineligible to be met by housing benefit under paragraph 1 of Schedule 1 to the Housing Benefit (ineligible service charges), other than under sub-paragraphs (d) to (f) of that paragraph;

[¹(d)   any amount determined in accordance with regulation 10(6) of the Housing Benefit Regulations and deducted under regulation 10(3) of those Regulations]

"property-specific rent", except as provided in the definition of "property-specific rent less ineligible amounts" below, means the rent determined by a rent officer under paragraph 1(2) of Schedule 1 to the Rent Officers Order or to the Rent Officers Order 1995, as the case may be, except in a case where a rent officer has made a rent determination under paragraph 3 of that Schedule, when it means that rent;

"property-specific rent less ineligible amounts" has the meaning otherwise ascribed to those terms in this paragraph, except, subject to article 23(1), in a case where the property-specific rent is an exceptionally high rent and the rent officer has notified the authority that the exceptionally high rent determined by him does not include a payment ineligible for housing benefit under [³ paragraph 1(a)(i) or paragraph 5 of Schedule 1 to the Housing Benefit Regulations or, as the case may be, paragraph 1(a)(i) or paragraph 5 of Schedule 1 to the Housing Benefit (State Pension Credit) Regulations] (ineligible service charges for food and fuel), as the case may be ("ineligible payments"), when it means that exceptionally high rent less ineligible amounts other than ineligible payments;

"size-related rent" means the rent determined by a rent officer under paragraph 2(2) of Schedule 1 to the Rent Officers Order or the Rent Officers Order 1995, as the case may be,

and other expressions used both in this Schedule and in the Rent Officers Order or the Rent Officers Order 1995, as the case may be, or in both this Schedule [³ and (as the case may be) in regulation 13 of the Housing Benefit Regulations or regulation 13 of the Housing Benefit (State Pension Credit) Regulations] shall have the same meanings in this Schedule as they have in that Order or in that regulation, as the case may be.

    (2)   Except in a case to which sub-paragraph (3) applies, in this Schedule any reference to a rent officer's determination is, in any case where there has been more than one such determination, a reference to the last such determination.

    (3)   In a case where the last determination referred to in sub-paragraph (2) was made on the basis of–

(a)   the terms of the tenancy of a dwelling; or

(b)   the size or composition of the household occupying that dwelling,

which were not appropriate to the claim for a rent allowance in respect of which the allowance was granted, any reference to a rent officer's determination is to the last such determination which was appropriate to that claim.

Amendments

1.   Inserted by art 11 of SI 2000 No 1091 (retrospectively to 1.4.99).
2.   Amended by art 7(6) of SI 2001 No 2350 as from 25.07.01.
3.   Amended by reg 5 and Sch 2 para 13(10)(j) of SI 2006 No 217 as from 6.3.06.

[³ PART V

THRESHOLD ABOVE WHICH REDUCED SUBSIDY IS PAYABLE ON RENT ALLOWANCES

18. The Table referred to in paragraph 1 is–

(1) Threshold (weekly sum)	(2) Rent Registration Area (£)	(1) Threshold (weekly sum)	(2) Rent Registration Area (£)
ENGLAND		Merseyside	183.43
Avon	169.06	Merton	223.17
Barking & Dagenham	173.53	Newham	163.27
Barnet	228.90	Norfolk	85.12
Bedfordshire	93.92	North Yorkshire	120.36
Berkshire	176.00	Northamptonshire	134.38
Bexley	183.83	Northumberland	118.67
Brent	201.33	Nottinghamshire	132.56
Bromley	206.83	Oxfordshire	259.00
Buckinghamshire	214.25	Redbridge	164.61
Cambridgeshire	96.04	Richmond upon Thames	252.06
Camden	258.22	Shropshire	163.64
Cheshire	192.69	Somerset	151.91
City	257.93	South Yorkshire	90.46
Cleveland	123.96	Southwark	174.93
Cornwall	152.47	Staffordshire	153.70
Croydon	210.30	Suffolk	87.52
Cumbria	148.07	Surrey	285.52
Derbyshire	109.04	Sutton	191.01
Devon	159.42	Tower Hamlets	181.82
Dorset	161.43	Tyne & Wear	113.32
Durham	120.78	Waltham Forest	140.88
Ealing	201.31	Wandsworth	221.47
East Sussex	243.14	Warwickshire	164.56
Enfield	171.21	West Midlands	161.13
Essex	112.27	West Sussex	249.11
Gloucestershire	150.23	West Yorkshire	100.63
Greater Manchester	166.32	Westminster	257.93
Greenwich	184.28	Wiltshire	156.85
Hackney	168.29	**WALES**	
Hammersmith and Fulham	198.12	Clwyd	87.91
Hampshire	229.91	Dyfed	77.40
Haringey	190.26	Gwent	85.12
Harrow	212.68	Gwynedd	78.89
Havering	172.24	Mid Glamorgan	90.05
Hereford and Worcester	171.24	Powys	86.11
Hertfordshire	123.15	South Glamorgan	100.64
Hillingdon	182.32	West Glamorgan	86.67
Hounslow	204.37	**SCOTLAND**	
Humberside	100.85	Aberdeen	116.83
Isle of Wight	196.27	Aberdeenshire	126.66
Islington	196.67	Angus	116.83
Kensington and Chelsea	246.89	Argyll-Bute	107.61
Kent	236.29	Clackmannanshire	150.40
Kingston upon Thames	252.06	Comhairlie Nan Eilean Siar	172.53
Lambeth	162.14	Dumfries & Galloway	125.40
Lancashire	167.71	Dundee	116.83
Leicestershire	124.72	East Ayrshire	103.93
Lewisham	150.72	East Dunbartonshire	133.48
Lincolnshire	114.45	East Lothian	132.78

(1) *Threshold (weekly sum)*	(2) *Rent Registration Area (£)*	(1) *Threshold (weekly sum)*	(2) *Rent Registration Area (£)*
East Renfrewshire	180.26	Orkney	116.83
Edinburgh,City of	132.78	Perth & Kinross	124.08
Falkirk	117.91	Renfrewshire	103.93
Fife	116.83	Scottish Borders	132.78
Glasgow	103.93	Shetland	116.83
Highland	114.79	South Ayrshire	119.53
Inverclyde	103.93	South Lanarkshire	103.93
Midlothian	132.78	Stirling	121.19
Moray	116.83	West Dunbartonshire	103.93
North Ayrshire	103.93	West Lothian	132.78]
North Lanarkshire	103.93		

Amendments

1. Added by art 5 Sch 2 of SI 2001 No 2350 as from 25.07.01.
2. Substituted by art 4 of SI 2002 No 1859 (retrospectively from 1.4.01).
3. Substituted by art 11 of SI 2003 No 3179 (retrospectively from 1.4.02).

[¹ SCHEDULE 4A

Amendment

1. Inserted by art 7 of SI 2004 No 646 as from 1.4.04.

ARTICLE 20A
RENT REBATE LIMITATION DEDUCTIONS (HOUSING REVENUE
ACCOUNT DWELLINGS)
PART 1

INTERPRETATION

1. In this Schedule–

[¹ "dwelling" has the same meaning it bears in the determination made under section 80(1) of the Local Government and Housing Act 1989,]

"HRA" means the Housing Revenue Account of the authority the amount of whose subsidy is under consideration,

"new service" means–

(a) a service provided in the relevant year that was not provided in 2001-02,

[¹ (b) an extension to a service, where the service is provided in the relevant year to a greater extent than in 2001-02, or]

(c) a service provided in the relevant year for which a charge is imposed which is a service which was previously provided without charge because it was funded by a specific grant or subsidy (other than HRA subsidy),

"rent", in relation to a dwelling, means the total of the payments in respect of the dwelling specified in [² regulation 12(1) of the Housing Benefit Regulations or, as the case may be, regulation 12(1) of the Housing Benefit (State Pension Credit) Regulations], other than a payment specified in regulation 10(1)(e),

[³ "RPI figure" means the annual percentage change at September of the index of retail prices for the United Kingdom published by the Office for National Statistics,"]

"service charge", in relation to a dwelling, means a payment in respect of the dwelling specified in [² regulation 12(1)(e) of the Housing Benefit Regulations or, as the case may be, regulation 12(1)(e) of the Housing Benefit (State Pension Credit) Regulations] which–

(a) is eligible for housing benefit at the time it is paid, and

(b) is not of a type which was specified in paragraphs 2 to 4 of Schedule 1B to the [² Housing Benefit (General) Regulations 1987] while regulation 9 of the Housing Benefit (General) Amendment (No. 3) Regulations 1999[6] (which inserted that Schedule) had effect,

"void dwelling" means a dwelling that is unoccupied,

"2001-02" means the year beginning with 1st April 2001 (and any corresponding expression in which two years are similarly mentioned is to be read in the same way).

Amendments

1.   Amended by art 4(5) of SI 2006 No 54 (retrospectively from 1.4.04).
2.   Amended by reg 5 and Sch 2 para 13(11) of SI 2006 No 217 as from 6.3.06.
3.   Amended by art 2 and Sch para 1 of SI 2006 No 559 as from 1.4.06.

PART 2

ENGLAND

Liability to deduction

2.–(1)   This paragraph applies in the case of an authority in England in relation to the relevant year if the authority is specified in the Table in Part 3 of this Schedule for that year and the weekly rent limit for a dwelling that is so specified for the authority is less than the subsidy limitation rent.

The subsidy limitation rent for an authority is equal to

$$Q + (P \times R),$$

where–

Q is the average weekly rent for a dwelling for the authority for the relevant year (see sub-paragraph (3)),

P is the average weekly unpooled service charges for the authority for the relevant year (see sub-paragraph (4)), and

R is the annual factor (see sub-paragraph (7)).

[² (3)   or the purposes of sub-paragraph (2), the average weekly rent for a dwelling for the authority for the relevant year is calculated by dividing the total rent charged for all dwellings in the HRA in that year by the total number of weeks for which rent was charged for all dwellings in the HRA.]

(4)   For the purposes of sub-paragraph (2), the average weekly unpooled service charges for the authority are calculated as follows–

[²**Step 1**

Find the average weekly service charge for a dwelling for the authority for the relevant year by dividing the total service charges imposed in respect of all dwellings in the HRA in that year by the total number of weeks for which [³ rent was charged] for all dwellings in the HRA.]

[²**Step 2**

Find the average weekly service charge for a dwelling for the authority for the year 2001-02 by dividing the total service charges imposed in that year in respect of all dwellings that are both in the HRA in that year and in the relevant year by the total number of weeks for which [³ rent was charged] for all dwellings in the HRA in the relevant year.]

Step 3

Multiply the result of step 2 by the [² RPI figure] for the period beginning with the year 2001-02 and ending with the relevant year (see sub-paragraph (6)).

[²**Step 4**

Find the average weekly service charge for new services for a dwelling for the authority for the relevant year by dividing the total charges for new services imposed in that year by the total number of weeks in that year for which [³ rent was charged] for all dwellings in the HRA.]

Step 5

If the result of step 1 exceeds the sum of the results of steps 3 and 4, deduct the sum of those results from the result of step 1.

If the result of step 1 does not exceed the sum of the results of steps 3 and 4, the average weekly unpooled service charges for the authority are nil.

(5)   For the purposes of sub-paragraphs (3) and (4), void dwellings are disregarded.

[⁴ (6)

The RPI figure for the period beginning with September 2001 and ending with September of the year prior to the relevant year is 1.1663.

(7)   The annual factor for 2007-08 is 0.4.]

[³ (8)   For the purposes of calculating the total number of weeks for which rent is charged in sub-paragraphs (3) and (4) rent free periods shall be included.]

Amendments

1.	Substituted by art 2 and Sch of SI 2005 No 535 as from 1.4.05.
2.	Substituted by art 2 and Sch of SI 2006 No 559 as from 1.4.06.
3.	Amended by art 4(3) of SI 2007 No 26 (retrospectively from 1.4.06).
4.	Substituted by art 2 and Sch para 1 of SI 2007 No 731 as from 1.4.07.

Amount of deduction

3.–(1) The amount of the deduction from subsidy referred to in article 20A(2) shall be calculated as follows.

Step 1

Divide the amount of rebates paid by the authority in the relevant year in respect of dwellings in the HRA by the income of the authority for that year from rent and service charges (including rent and charges remitted by way of rebate) in respect of such dwellings.

Step 2

If the result of step 1 does not exceed the rebate proportion in England for the relevant year (see sub-paragraph (3))–

(a)   divide the weekly rent limit for a dwelling for the authority for the relevant year as specified in Part 3 of this Schedule by the subsidy limitation rent (see paragraph 2(2)),

(b)   subtract the result of paragraph (a) from the number 1, and

(c)   multiply the amount of the subsidy (apart from any deduction to be calculated under this Schedule) by the result of paragraph (b).

If the result of step 1 exceeds the rebate proportion in England for the relevant year–

(i)   multiply the amount by which the subsidy limitation rent exceeds the weekly rent limit for a dwelling for the authority for the relevant year as specified in Part 3 of this Schedule by the rebate proportion in England for the relevant year,

(ii)   multiply the subsidy limitation rent by the result of step 1,

(iii)   divide the result of paragraph (i) by the result of paragraph (ii), and

(iv)   multiply the amount of the subsidy (apart from any deduction to be calculated under this Schedule) by the result of paragraph (iii).

(2)   For the purposes of the calculation in sub-paragraph (1), void dwellings are to be disregarded.

[³ (3)   The rebate proportion for each year commencing with 2007-08 is 0.77.]

Amendments

1.	Substituted by art 2 and Sch of SI 2005 No 535 as from 1.4.05.
2.	Substituted by art 2 and Sch of SI 2006 No 559 as from 1.4.06.
3.	Substituted by art 2 and Sch para 2 of SI 2007 No 731 as from 1.4.07.

[⁴ PART 3
WEEKLY RENT LIMITS FOR PURPOSES OF PART 2: AUTHORITIES IN ENGLAND
RELEVANT YEAR 2007-08

Authority	Weekly rent limit	Authority	Weekly rent limit
Adur	66.34	Basildon	62.19
Alnwick	51.35	Bassetlaw	53.06
Arun	70.81	Berwick upon Tweed	49.72
Ashfield	48.78	Birmingham	59.44
Ashford	67.47	Blaby	53.99
Aylesbury Vale	71.81	Blackpool	51.07
Babergh	63.94	Blyth Valley	47.11
Barking and Dagenham	65.19	Bolsover	53.11
Barnet	77.23	Bolton	51.89
Barnsley	51.11	Bournemouth	61.45
Barrow in Furness	57.17	Bracknell Forest	70.86

Authority	Weekly rent limit	Authority	Weekly rent limit
Braintree	65.52	Harborough	59.59
Brent	82.88	Haringey	78.53
Brentwood	70.10	Harlow	65.55
Bridgnorth	62.20	Harrogate	61.25
Brighton and Hove	61.62	Harrow	85.50
Bristol	57.59	Havering	67.02
Broxtowe	62.82	High Peak	54.56
Bury	56.57	Hillingdon	85.18
Cambridge	69.60	Hinckley and Bosworth	54.98
Camden	86.42	Hounslow	75.89
Cannock Chase	56.54	Hyndburn	53.39
Canterbury	66.10	Ipswich	58.20
Caradon	54.03	Isles of Scilly	61.04
Carrick	52.16	Islington	83.34
Castle Morpeth	51.74	Kensington and Chelsea	92.15
Castle Point	68.93	Kettering	57.24
Charnwood	52.62	Kings Lynn and West Norfolk	56.71
Cheltenham	61.66	Kingston upon Hull	53.10
Chesterfield	54.17	Kingston upon Thames	84.77
Chester-le-Street	51.30	Kirklees	53.16
Chorley	51.49	Lambeth	76.96
City of London	79.30	Lancaster	55.86
City of York	58.47	Leeds	52.30
Colchester	63.33	Leicester	54.17
Corby	54.45	Lewes	65.54
Crawley	71.30	Lewisham	69.36
Croydon	81.52	Lincoln	48.63
Dacorum	71.95	Liverpool	56.95
Darlington	52.24	Luton	61.34
Dartford	65.86	Macclesfield	60.27
Daventry	61.09	Manchester	59.56
Derby	55.69	Mansfield	52.76
Derwentside	53.53	Medway Towns	60.29
Doncaster	51.02	Melton	53.97
Dover	65.26	Merton	76.86
Dudley	59.17	Mid Devon	60.23
Durham	52.36	Mid Suffolk	60.57
Ealing	80.92	Milton Keynes	60.05
Easington	50.28	Mole Valley	74.00
East Devon	57.42	New Forest	71.94
East Riding	54.95	Newark and Sherwood	55.05
Eastbourne	57.87	Newcastle upon Tyne	53.10
Ellesmere Port and Neston	53.76	Newham	68.72
Enfield	74.47	Northampton	59.01
Epping Forest	70.61	North Cornwall	55.35
Exeter	54.40	North East Derbyshire	53.83
Fareham	65.66	North Kesteven	55.36
Fenland	60.63	North Lincolnshire	52.59
Gateshead	53.74	North Norfolk	57.79
Gedling	52.64	North Shropshire	56.49
Gloucester	59.53	North Somerset	55.35
Gosport	63.20	North Tyneside	51.97
Gravesham	66.11	North Warwickshire	59.29
Great Yarmouth	52.75	North West Leicestershire	55.09
Greenwich	72.98	Norwich	56.32
Guildford	78.31	Nottingham	52.99
Hackney	76.25	Nuneaton and Bedworth	55.08
Hammersmith and Fulham	81.45	Oadby and Wigston	54.99

Authority	Weekly rent limit	Authority	Weekly rent limit
Oldham	52.00	Southwark	75.27
Oswestry	56.34	St Albans	76.45
Oxford	72.25	Stevenage	71.50
Pendle	51.98	Stockport	52.45
Plymouth	49.18	Stockton on Tees	55.76
Poole	62.61	Stoke-on-Trent	53.27
Portsmouth	61.30	Stroud	61.56
Reading	78.84	Sutton	73.84
Redbridge	81.65	Swindon	58.21
Redditch	56.76	Tamworth	58.67
Ribble Valley	52.40	Tandridge	69.79
Richmondshire	57.34	Taunton Deane	58.89
Rochdale	53.10	Teesdale	53.05
Rochford	64.37	Tendring	60.16
Rossendale	52.44	Thanet	61.82
Rotherham	50.42	Three Rivers	73.64
Rugby	57.37	Thurrock	62.03
Runnymede	79.37	Torridge	53.10
Rutland	59.33	Tower Hamlets	75.91
Salford	56.99	Uttlesford	71.92
Salisbury	68.31	Waltham Forest	71.25
Sandwell	61.31	Wandsworth	88.74
Sedgefield	50.92	Wansbeck	46.96
Sedgemoor	59.51	Warrington	55.08
Sefton	58.64	Warwick	65.14
Selby	57.27	Watford	72.72
Sheffield	50.50	Waveney	56.91
Shepway	62.57	Waverley	77.60
Slough	76.74	Wealden	61.49
Solihull	60.15	Wear Valley	52.16
South Bedfordshire	70.02	Wellingborough	56.04
South Cambridgeshire	70.87	Welwyn Hatfield	71.78
South Derbyshire	56.62	West Lancashire	54.13
South Gloucestershire	63.23	Westminster	91.55
South Holland	53.44	Wigan	53.79
South Kesteven	54.81	Winchester	74.09
South Lakeland	61.94	Woking	77.96
South Northants	67.67	Wokingham	76.94
South Tyneside	51.09	Wolverhampton	54.93
Southampton	60.64	Wycombe	77.77]
Southend-on-Sea	63.69		

Amendment

1.   Substituted by art 2 and Sch of SI 2005 No 535 as from 1.4.05.
2.   Substituted by art 2 and Sch of SI 2006 No 559 as from 1.4.06.
3.   Substituted by art 4(3)(c) of SI 2007 No 26 (retrospectively from 1.4.06).
4.   Substituted by art 2 and Sch para 3 of SI 2007 No 731 as from 1.4.07.

PART 4
WALES

Liability to deduction

4.   This paragraph applies in the case of an authority in Wales in relation to the relevant year if the authority is specified in the Table in Part 5 of this Schedule for that year and

O + P is less than Q,

where–

O is the amount specified in column 1 of that Table for the authority,

P is the guideline rent increase specified in column 2 of that Table for the authority, and

Q is the average weekly rent for a dwelling for the authority for the relevant year (see paragraph 2(3)).

Amount of deduction

5.–(1)   The amount of the deduction from subsidy referred to in article 20A(2) shall be calculated as follows.

Step 1

Divide the amount of rebates granted by the authority in the relevant year in respect of dwellings in the HRA by the income of the authority for that year from rent (including rent remitted by way of rebate) in respect of such dwellings.

Step 2

If the result of step 1 does not exceed the rebate proportion for the relevant year (see sub-paragraph (2))–

(a)   deduct (O + P) from Q (see paragraph 4),

(b)   divide the result of paragraph (a) by Q,

(c)   multiply the amount of the subsidy (apart from any deduction to be calculated under this Schedule) by the result of paragraph (b).

If the result of step 1 exceeds the rebate proportion for the relevant year–

(i)   deduct (O + P) from Q (see paragraph 4),

(ii)   divide the result of paragraph (i) by Q,

(iii)   divide the rebate proportion for Wales (see sub-paragraph (2)) by the result of step 1,

(iv)   multiply the result of paragraph (ii) by the result of paragraph (iii),

(v)   multiply the amount of the subsidy (apart from any deduction to be calculated under this Schedule) by the result of paragraph (iv).

[² (2)   The rebate proportion for Wales for each relevant year commencing with 2006-07 is 0.66.]

Amendments

1.   Substituted by art 2 and Sch of SI 2005 No 535 as from 1.4.05.

2.   Substituted by art 2 and Sch of SI 2006 No 559 as from 1.4.06.

[³ PART 5
AMOUNTS FOR PURPOSES OF PART 4, PARAGRAPH 4:
AUTHORITIES IN WALES
TABLE
RELEVANT YEAR 2007-08

Authority	(1) Specified amount "O"	(2) Guideline rent increase
Blaenau Gwent	48.43	1.74
Caerphilly	54.16	2.62
Cardiff	60.25	3.20
Carmarthenshire	50.60	3.03
Ceredigion	54.08	2.48
Conwy	53.01	3.52
Denbighshire	49.26	2.73
Flintshire	51.55	3.13
Gwynedd	51.27	3.07
Isle of Anglesey	49.74	2.48
Merthyr Tydfil	46.99	3.22
Monmouthshire	58.36	2.67
Neath Port Talbot	49.62	2.21
Newport	55.55	2.91
Pembrokeshire	50.72	3.12
Powys	53.96	2.51
Rhondda, Cynon, Taff	49.87	2.29
Swansea	52.07	2.67
Torfaen	56.45	2.79
Vale of Glamorgan	57.99	2.67
Wrexham	49.42	3.26]

Amendments

1.   Substituted by art 2 and Sch of SI 2005 No 535 as from 1.4.05.
2.   Substituted by art 2 and Sch of SI 2006 No 559 as from 1.4.06.
3.   Substituted by art 2 and Sch para 4 of SI 2007 No 731 as from 1.4.07.

[⁷ SCHEDULE 5
BENEFIT SAVINGS]

Amendments

1.   Substituted by art 13 of SI 2000 No 1091 (retrospectively to 1.4.99).
2.   Substituted by art 5(a) of SI 2002 No 1859 (retrospectively to 1.4.01).
3.   Inserted by art 5(b) of SI 2002 No 1859 (retrospectively to 1.4.01).
4.   Inserted by art 5(c) of SI 2002 No 1859 (retrospectively to 1.4.01).
5.   Deleted by art 2(2) of SI 2002 No 3116 (retrospectively to 1.4.01).
6.   Amended by art 12 of SI 2003 No 3179 (retrospectively to 1.4.02).
7.   Omitted by art 5(2) of SI 2005 No 369 (retrospectively from 1.4.02).

General Note

Schedule 5 was omitted by art 5(2) of the Income-related Beneffits (Subsidy to Authorities) Amendment Order 2005 SI No.369 with retrospective effect from 1 April 2002. For the text of the schedule and commentary on it see the 17th edition of this work.

[¹ SCHEDULE 6
ARTICLES 3A
ELECTRONIC COMMUNICATIONS
PART 1
INTERPRETATION

Interpretation
1.   In this Schedule ''official computer system'' means a computer system maintained by or on behalf of the Secretary of State for the sending, receipt, processing or storage of any claim or return.

PART 2
ELECTRONIC COMMUNICATIONS – GENERAL PROVISIONS

Conditions for the use of electronic communications
2.–(1)   An authority or auditor must use an approved method of–
(a)   electronic communication;
(b)   authenticating the identity of the sender of the communication;
(c)   authenticating any claim or return delivered by means of an electronic communication; and
(d)   submitting to the Secretary of State any claim or return.
(2)   An authority or auditor must submit any claim or return by means of an electronic communication in an approved form.
(3)   Where a claim or return is submitted electronically but not in accordance with the conditions specified in this paragraph, that claim or return shall be treated as not having been submitted.
(4)   In this paragraph ''approved'' means approved by means of a direction given by the Secretary of State.

Use of intermediaries
3.   The Secretary of State may–
(a)   use intermediaries in connection with the receipt, authentication or security of any claim or return delivered by means of an electronic communication; and
(b)   require authorities or auditors to use intermediaries in connection with those matters.

PART 3
ELECTRONIC COMMUNICATION – EVIDENTIAL PROVISIONS

Effect of delivering information by means of electronic communication
4.–(1)   Any claim or return which is delivered by means of an electronic communication shall be treated as having been delivered in the approved manner or form on the day the conditions imposed–

(a)   by or under this Schedule; and

(b)   by or under Part II of this Order

are satisfied.

(2)   The Secretary of State may, by a direction, determine that any claim or return is to be treated as delivered on a different day (whether earlier or later) from the day provided for in sub-paragraph (1).

(3)   A claim or return shall not be treated as delivered to an official computer system by means of an electronic communication unless it is accepted by the system to which it is delivered.

Proof of identify of sender or recipient of information

5.   For the purpose of any legal proceedings, it shall be presumed that the identity of the sender or recipient, as the case may be, of any claim or return delivered by means of an electronic communication to an official computer system is the same as is recorded on that official computer system.

Proof of delivery of information

6.–(1)   For the purpose of any legal proceedings, it shall be presumed that–

(a)   if the delivery of any claim or return has been recorded on an official computer system, the use of an electronic communication has resulted in the delivery of that claim or return to the Secretary of State;

(b)   if the delivery of any claim or return submitted by means of an electronic communication to the Secretary of State has not been recorded on an official computer system, no delivery has been made;

(c)   any claim or return submitted by means of an electronic communication has been received on the time and date recorded on an official computer system.

Proof of content of information

7.   For the purpose of any legal proceedings, the content of any claim or return submitted by means of an electronic communication shall be presumed to be that recorded on an official computer system.]

Amendment

1.   Inserted by Art 4(4) of SI 2007 No 26 as from 5.2.07.

The Housing Benefit and Council Tax Benefit (Subsidy) Regulations 1994
(SI 1994 No.781)

General Note

These Regulations specify the particulars which are required to be provided by an authority to the Secretary of State on the making of claims for HB subsidy and CTB subsidy, the time within which claims for subsidy are to be made, the conditions as to audit of claims and information and records to be produced to the Secretary of State and the authority's auditor in support of such claims. The Housing Benefit and Community Charge Benefit (Subsidy) Regulations 1991, as amended, were revoked, but saved in respect of any year prior to 1 April 1993.

Citation, commencement and interpretation

1.–(1)   These Regulations may be cited as the Housing Benefit and Council Tax Benefit (Subsidy) Regulations 1994 and shall come into force on 11 April 1994.

(2)   In these Regulations, unless the context otherwise requires–

"the Act" means the Social Security Administration Act 1992;

"the 1987 Regulations" means the Housing Benefit (General) Regulations 1987;

"the 1989 Regulations" means the Community Charge Benefits (General) Regulations 1989;

"the 1992 Regulations" means the Council Tax Benefit (General) Regulations 1992;

"authority"–

  (a)   with respect to claims for council tax benefit subsidy, means a billing authority or, as the case may be, a levying authority to which section 140(2) of the Act refers;

  (b)   with respect to claims for housing benefit subsidy, means a housing or local authority, as the case may be;

"community charge benefits" and "excess community charge benefits" shall have the same meanings as in the 1989 Regulations;

"excess awards" means overpayments of housing benefit, excess community charge benefits and excess council tax benefit, as the case may be;

"Subsidy Order" means an Order in respect of the relevant year made under section 135(2) (subsidy order with respect to housing benefit) or section 140(2) (subsidy order with respect to council tax benefit) of the Act;

[¹ "the Subsidy Order 1995" means the Housing Benefit and Council Tax Benefit (Subsidy) Order 1995;]

[² "the Subsidy Order 1996" means the Housing Benefit and Council Tax Benefit (Subsidy) Order 1996.]

"the relevant year" means the year in respect of which a claim for housing benefit subsidy of council tax benefit subsidy is made;

"rent rebate" and "rent allowance" shall be construed in accordance with section 134 of the Act but shall exclude, in the case of a local authority in England and Wales, any Housing Revenue Account rebates granted by them,

and other expressions used in these Regulations, the 1992 Regulations or the Housing Benefit and Council Tax Benefit (Subsidy) Order 1994, as the case may be, shall have the same meanings in these Regulations as they have in those Regulations or in that Order.

Amendments

1.   Inserted by reg 2 of SI 1995 No 874 as from 20.4.95.
2.   Inserted by reg 2 of SI 1996 No 1314 as from 11.6.96.

Particulars to be supplied by an authority to the Secretary of State in relation to a claim for housing benefit subsidy or council tax benefit subsidy

2.   For the purposes of sections 137(2) and 140(7) of the Act (power for the Secretary of State to withhold payments of housing benefit subsidy or council tax benefit subsidy) the prescribed particulars which are to be supplied to the Secretary of State by an authority in connection with its claim for housing benefit subsidy or council tax benefit subsidy for the relevant year are those specified in the Schedule to these Regulations.

Conditions to be complied with on making a claim for housing benefit subsidy or council tax benefit subsidy

3. A claim for housing benefit subsidy or for council tax benefit subsidy shall be certified by the authority"s auditor; and the authority making the claim shall in addition provide such information and produce such records as are required to satisfy the Secretary of State that the claim is properly calculated and shall keep all records with a bearing on its claim such a way as to enable them to show and the auditor to check that entitlement to subsidy has been correctly calculated.

Time within which claims for housing benefit subsidy and council tax benefit subsidy are to be made and prescribed particulars provided to the Secretary of State

4.–(1) An authority making a claim for housing benefit subsidy or council tax benefit subsidy shall submit it to the Secretary of State by the 30th September in the year immediately following the relevant year.

(2) Any particulars relating to a claim for subsidy to which regulation 2 of and the Schedule to these Regulations refer shall be supplied to the Secretary of State on the date the claim is made together with any certificates, records or other information required by the Secretary of State under regulation 3 above (conditions to be complied with on making a claim for subsidy).

Revocation and savings

5. The Housing Benefit and Community Charge Benefit (Subsidy) Regulations 1991, the Housing Benefit and Community Charge Benefit (Subsidy) Amendment Regulations 1992 and the Housing Benefit and Community Charge Benefit (Subsidy) Amendment (No. 2) Regulations 1993 are hereby revoked, except that they shall continue to apply to any claims for a subsidy, particulars to be supplied therewith and conditions and questions relating to the payment of subsidy under the Act for any relevant year before 1st April 1993, as if these Regulations had not been made.

SCHEDULE
PRESCRIBED PARTICULARS RELATING TO CLAIMS FOR HOUSING BENEFIT SUBSIDY
AND COUNCIL TAX BENEFIT SUBSIDY FOR THE RELEVANT YEAR

1. The total rent rebate and total rent allowance expenditure in the relevant year.

2. The total rent expenditure in the relevant year in cases to which paragraph 20 below refers, which is attributable to that part of the eligible rent which exceeds the relevant threshold specified in a Subsidy Order for the purpose of calculating subsidy on such rents.

3. The total rent rebate expenditure in the relevant year in respect of rents payable to an authority–

(a) under section 69(2)(b) of the Housing Act 1985 or section 35(2)(b) of the Housing (Scotland) Act 1987 for board and lodging accommodation or accommodation which the authority holds on a licence agreement, or

(b) for accommodation outside the Housing Revenue Account under Part VI of the Local Government and Housing Act 1989, which an authority in England or Wales holds on a lease granted for a term not exceeding 3 years, or

(c) for accommodation which an authority in Scotland holds on a lease granted for a term not exceeding 3 years.

4. The total rent rebate expenditure in the relevant year in cases to which paragraph 3 above refers which is attributable to that part of the eligible rent which exceeds the relevant threshold specified in a Subsidy Order for the purpose of calculating subsidy on such rents.

5. The total number of awards for each of rent rebates, rent allowances, community charge benefits and council tax benefit in the relevant year made in respect of periods before the date of a person's claim where there is good cause for the claim not having been made at an earlier date and the total amount awarded for those periods of each of such rebates, allowances and benefits.

6.–(1) Where any excess awards to which sub-paragraph (2) below applies have been made in the circumstances specified in sub-paragraph (3) below, the total number and the amounts of those awards and the circumstances on which they were made.

(2)   This paragraph applies to awards of–
(a)   housing benefit by way of rent rebates;
(b)   housing benefit by way of rent allowances;
(c)   housing benefit by way of community charge rebates;
(d)   community charge benefits; and
(e)   council tax benefit,
which are identified in the relevant year.

(3)   The circumstances specified in this sub-paragraph are–
(a)   departmental error;
(b)   error of the authority making the payment and claiming subsidy;
(c)   technical overpayments and technical excess benefits;
(d)   errors of claimants;
(e)   fraudulent overpayments and fraudulent excess benefits;
[. . .]
(g)   duplicate payments following non-receipt, loss or theft of benefit where the original instrument of payment has been encashed; and
(h)   any other excess awards.

(4)   In this paragraph "departmental error", "error of the authority making the payment and claiming subsidy", "technical overpayments", "technical excess benefits", "fraudulent overpayments" and "fraudulent excess benefits" have the meanings assigned to them by article 10 or article 18, as the case may be, of the Housing Benefit and Council Tax Benefit (Subsidy) Order 1994.

7.   [¹ . . .]

8.   The total amount of excess awards in the relevant year in consequence of departmental error which are recovered in the relevant year.

9.   The total number and total amount of awards of benefit backdated in the relevant year under each of regulation 72(15) of the 1987 Regulations, regulation 60(18) of the 1989 Regulations and regulation 62(16) of the 1992 Regulations (backdated awards of benefit), as the case may be, which are excess awards.

10.   The total rent allowance expenditure in the relevant year attributable to each of–
(a)   that part of any weekly eligible rents which exceeds any relevant threshold specified in a Subsidy Order for the purpose of calculating subsidy on such rents;
(b)   that part of any weekly eligible rents which were at or below any such threshold; and
(c)   that part of any weekly eligible rents to which any such threshold did not apply excluding cases which have been referred to a rent officer for determination under section 121 of the Housing Act 1988.

11.   The total rent allowance expenditure in the relevant year not attributable to any excess of eligible rent over the threshold in cases to which paragraph 10(a) above refers.

[⁵**12.**   The total rent allowance expenditure in the relevant year attributable to tenancies liable to determinations by the rent officer
(a)   under the Rent Officers (Additional Functions) Order 1995 or as the case may be the Rent Officers (Additional Functions) (Scotland) Order 1995; and
(b)   where the application for determination by the Rent Officer was made before 2nd January 1996, under the Rent Officer (Additional Functions) Order 1990 or as the case may be the Rent Officers (Additional Functions) (Scotland) Order 1990.]

[⁶**13.**   The total rent allowance expenditure in the relevant year as specified in each of the following paragraphs–
(a)   expenditure on eligible in respect of deregulated housing association tenancies not referred to a rent officer;
(b)   expenditure in cases subject to referral to a rent officer for determination, but where no such referral was made;
(c)   expenditure in cases referred to a rent officer before 2nd January 1996, and in cases to which regulation 10 of the Housing Benefit (General) Amendment Regulations 1995 applies, which falls under each of the following sub-paragraphs–
       (i)   weekly eligible rents which do not exceed any determination made under the Orders to which paragraph 12 above refers;
       (ii)   expenditure representing the difference between the property-specific rent for the accommodation and the size-related rent in cases where a rent officer has determined that accommodation is unreasonably large but has not determined a high rent under;
              (aa)   paragraph 2A (high rent determinations) of Schedule 1 to the Rent Officers (Additional Functions) Order 1995 or as the case may be the Rent Officers (Additional Functions) (Scotland) Order 1995; or

    (bb)   in a case where the application for a determination by the rent officer is made on or after 2nd January 1996, paragraph 3 of the Rent Officers (Additional Functions) Order 1995 or as the case may be the Rent Officers (Additional Functions) (Scotland) Order 1995,

incurred over a period of up to 13 calendar weeks;

    (iii)   that part of the weekly eligible rents which exceeded the relevant rent, in respect of a case to which paragraph 5 of Schedule 6 to the Subsidy Order 1996 (no restriction on unreasonable rents or on rent increases) applies other than expenditure to which sub-paragraph (ii) of this paragraph refers;

    (iv)   expenditure to which paragraph 7 of Schedule 6 to the Subsidy Order 1996 (deductions in respect of allowances) applies;

  (d)   expenditure in cases referred to a rent officer and determined in accordance with regulations 10 and 11 of the 1987 Regulations as in force on 2nd January 1996;

  (e)   expenditure incurred by an authority resulting from the authority placing on the ineligible amounts a value less than that placed by the rent officer.].

    (2)   In this paragraph "property-specific rent", "size-related rent" and "relevant rent" have the meanings assigned to them by paragraph 10 of Schedule 6 to the Subsidy Order 1995.]

    14.   The total council tax benefit expenditure in the relevant year.

    15.   The total expenditure in the relevant year in respect of discretionary increases of benefit where modifications of the 1987 Regulations have been made in accordance with section 134(8) of the Act or modifications of the 1989 or 1992 Regulations have been made in accordance with section 139(6) of the Act.

    [⁷**16.**   The total expenditure in the relevant year in respect of increases of benefit under each of regulation 61(2) or (3) of the 1987 Regulations and [³] regulation 51(5) or 54(4) of the 1992 Regulations (increases of weekly benefit for exceptional circumstances), as the case may be.]

    17.   The total amount of any instruments of payment in relation to housing benefit, community charge benefit or council tax benefit issued during the relevant year returned to the authority without having been presented for payment or found by the authority to have passed their date of validity without having been so presented.

    18.   The total amount of any housing benefit subsidy or community charge benefit subsidy paid for any year before the relevant year in respect of any instrument of payment either returned to the authority during the relevant year without having been presented for payment or found by the authority during the relevant year to have passed their date of validity without having been so presented.

    19.   The total number of benefit weeks and of overrun weeks, if any, in the relevant year, in the case of each of–

  (a)   rent rebates;

  (b)   rent allowances; and

  (c)   council tax benefit.

    [⁴**20.**–(1)   In respect of dwellings of an authority in Scotland or the Development Board for Rural Wales, the average rent payable in respect of Category 1 dwellings and Category 2 dwellings respectively on the specified date and the final date.

    (2)   In this paragraph "Category 1 dwellings", "Category 2 dwellings", "specified date" and "final date" have the meanings assigned to them by article 6(7) of the Subsidy Order 1995.

    21.–(1)   The total amount obtained in the relevant year in each of the following categories–

  (a)   housing benefit savings;

  (b)   council tax benefit savings;

  (c)   housing benefit related savings;

  (d)   council tax benefit related savings.

    (2)   In this paragraph "council tax benefit savings", "council tax benefit related savings", "housing benefit savings" and "housing benefit related savings" have the meanings assigned to them by paragraph 1(2) of Schedule 8 to the Subsidy Order 1995.]

Amendments

    1.   Deleted by reg 3(2) of SI 1995 No 874 as from 20.4.95.

    2.   Substituted by reg 3(3) of SI 1995 No 874 as from 20.4.95.

    3.   Substituted by reg 3(4) of SI 1995 No 874 as from 20.4.95.

    4.   Substituted by reg 3(5) and (6) of SI 1995 No 874 as from 20.4.95.

    5.   Substituted by reg 3(2) of SI 1996 No 1314 as from 11.6.96.

    6.   Substituted by reg 3(3) of SI 1996 No 1314 as from 11.6.96.

    7.   Substituted by reg 3(4) of SI 1996 No 1314 as from 11.6.96.

The Discretionary Housing Payments (Grants) Order 2001
(SI 2001 No.2340)

General Note

This order sets out the basis on which authorities may claim and be paid grants under s70 CSPSSA to reimburse the costs of making discretionary housing payments under s69 and the Discretionary Financial Assistance Regulations 2001. Art 1 defines terms used elsewhere in the order. Art 2 gives the Secretary of State for Work and Pensions a broad discretion as to the determination of the level of the grant. Art 3 provides for authorities to make regular claims, which must be signed by the authority's Chief Financial Officer. Arts 3 and 4 require authorities to keep records and to have the final claim in each financial year audited by 30 September in the following financial year unless that claim is for less than £50,000. Art 6 allows the Secretary of State to make interim payments, subject to art 6A, but the final claim cannot be paid until it has been audited and all outstanding requests for information in support of that claim resolved. Under art 7 (which is made under s70(3)(a) CSPSSA) an authority may not spend more on discretionary financial assistance than 2.5 times the amount of the grant determined by the Secretary of State for the financial year in question.

Citation, commencement and interpretation

1.–(1)   This Order may be cited as the Discretionary Housing Payments (Grants) Order 2001 and shall come into force on 2nd July 2001.

(2)   In this Order, unless the context otherwise requires–

"the Act" means the Child Support, Pensions and Social Security Act 2000;

"claim" means a claim by a relevant authority for payments towards the cost of making discretionary housing payments;

[¹ "final claim" means any claim which falls to be made in accordance with article 3(2)(g);]

[¹ "non-audit claim" means any claim made by a relevant authority [²] under article 3(2)(f) where the total amount of the claim in respect of the relevant year is less than £50,000;]

"relevant year" means any year commencing on or after 1st April 2002.

Amendments

1.   Inserted by art 2(2) of SI 2004 No 2329 as from 29.9.04.
2.   Amended by art 2(1) of SI 2005 No 2052 as from 1.4.04.

Determining the amount of grant

2.   The payments made to a relevant authority in accordance with section 70 of the Act (grants towards the cost of discretionary housing payments) shall be determined by the Secretary of State having regard to–

(a)   the most recent figures available in respect of the level of expenditure for housing benefit and council tax benefit by the authority; and

(b)   such other matters as he considers appropriate.

Claims

3.–(1)   Subject to the following paragraphs, a claim made under this Order shall be submitted in such manner and on such form, whether in a printed document or any other format, as may be approved or supplied by the Secretary of State.

(2)   A claim shall be submitted by the relevant authority–

(a)   estimating the amount of payments that the relevant authority believes it will make during the period from 2nd July 2001 to 31st March 2002, by 15th July 2001;

(b)   showing the amount of payments made during the year ending 31st March 2002, by 30th June 2002;

(c)   by 30th September 2002–

(i)   showing the amount of payments made during the year ending 31st March 2002, and

      (ii)   certified by the auditor of the relevant authority that the entries on the claim are fairly stated;

(d)   estimating the amount of payments it believes it will make during the relevant year, by 1st April in that relevant year;

(e)   by 1st September in a relevant year, estimating the amount of payments it has made from 1st April of that relevant year and estimating the amount it shall be making during the remaining part of that relevant year;

(f)   showing the amount of payments made during the relevant year, by [² 31st May] in the following relevant year; and

(g)   [¹ except where the claim is a non-audit claim,] by 30th September in a relevant year–

      (i)   showing the amount of payments made during the previous relevant year, and

      (ii)   certified by the auditor of the relevant authority that the entries on the claim are fairly stated.

(3)   Claims submitted by a relevant authority in accordance with paragraph (2) of this article shall be signed–

(a)   in the case of a relevant authority in England and Wales, by the officer who is responsible for finance pursuant to section 151 of the Local Government Act 1972;

(b)   in the case of a relevant authority in Scotland, by the proper officer pursuant to section 95 of the Local Government (Scotland) Act 1973.

Amendments

1.   Amended by art 2(3) of SI 2004 No 2329 as from 29.9.04.

2.   Amended by art 2(3) of SI 2005 No 2052 as from 1.4.05.

Records and information provisions

[¹**4.**–(1)   A relevant authority shall, in relation to any relevant year–

(a)   keep such records as are likely to be required for the purpose described in paragraph (2), should there be a final claim by that authority in respect of that year; and

(b)   where there is such a claim, on request–

      (i)   produce such of those records, and

      (ii)   provide such other information,

as the auditor may require for the purpose described in paragraph (2).

(2)   The purpose referred to in paragraph (1) is the purpose of satisfying the auditor that–

(a)   the entries on the claim form are correctly stated; and

(b)   expenditure on which the claim is based has been properly incurred,

so that a final claim may be made by the date specified in article 3(2)(g).

(3)   The relevant authority shall, in relation to any relevant year-

(a)   keep such records as are likely, in connection with any claim the authority may make in respect of that year, to be required for the purpose described in sub-paragraph (b); and

(b)   on request–

      (i)   produce in time such of those records, and

      (ii)   provide in time such other information,

as the Secretary of State may require for the purpose of satisfying himself that the claim is accurate and properly calculated.

(4)   In paragraph (3), ''in time'' means no later than the end of the period of six weeks beginning with the day on which the request referred to in that paragraph is sent to the relevant authority.]

Amendment
1.   Substituted by art 2(4) of SI 2004 No 2329 as from 29.9.04.

Audit provisions
5.   A relevant authority shall procure that the final claim is audited by its auditor by 30th September in the year following the year to which that claim relates.

Payment
[¹**6.**   Subject to article 6A, the Secretary of State may make payments by way of instalments by reference to claims submitted in accordance with article 3 but no final payment shall be made until–
   (a)   in the case of a non-audit claim, the Secretary of State is satisfied that no request for relevant information made in accordance with article 4(3) is outstanding; or
   (b)   in the case of a final claim–
     (i) the relevant authority's auditor has certified on the claim form that the entries on the claim referred to in article 3(2)(c) and (g) are fairly stated;
     (ii) the final claim is audited; and
     (iii) the Secretary of State is satisfied that no request for relevant information made in accordance with article 4 is outstanding.]

Amendment
1.   Substituted by art 2(5) of SI 2004 No 2329 as from 29.9.04.

[¹ Estimating amounts
6A.–(1)   Where, in relation to any relevant year, a relevant authority has not, before the time specified in article 3, 4 or 5, as the case may be, complied with any condition with which it is required under that article to comply, the Secretary of State may estimate the amount of any payment, including any payment by instalments, payable to that authority in accordance with section 70 of the Act in respect of that year, and may employ for that purpose such criteria as he considers relevant.]

Amendment
1.   Inserted by art 2(6) of SI 2004 No 2329 as from 29.9.04.

Limit on total expenditure
7.–(1)   Subject to paragraph (2), for the purposes of section 70(3)(a) of the Act (the limit on the total amount of expenditure in any year that may be incurred by a relevant authority in making discretionary housing payments) the limit in any year is the amount of grant the Secretary of State determines to make to the relevant authority at the beginning of that year multiplied by 2.5.
   (2)   In the case of the period commencing 2nd July 2001 and ending 31st March 2002, the limit is the amount the Secretary of State has determined to make to a relevant authority as at 2nd July 2001 multiplied by 2.5.

Index

Entries against the bold headings direct you to the general information on the subject, or where the subject is covered most fully. Sub-entries are listed alphabetically and direct you to specific aspects of the subject.

(CTB)   Council tax benefit

(HB)   Housing benefit

A

A8 nationals 250

abroad
  calculation of capital abroad
    CTB 599
    CTB aged 60 or over 847
    HB 319
    HB aged 60 or over 736
  dwelling outside GB
    HB 206
    HB aged 60 or over 694
  payment for employment abroad
    CTB 653
    HB 471
  payment in currencies other than sterling
    CTB 653, 658, 664
    CTB aged 60 or over 882
    HB 471, 481
    HB aged 60 or over 788
  see also: persons from abroad

absence from home
  CTB 577, 580
  CTB aged 60 or over 828
  detention in custody
    CTB 577
    CTB aged 60 or over 826
    HB 208
    HB aged 60 or over 696
  domestic violence
    HB 209
    HB aged 60 or over 697
  HB 208, 274
  HB aged 60 or over 696, 712
  repairs
    HB 206
    HB aged 60 or over 694
  students
    CTB 578
    HB 209, 338
    HB aged 60 or over 697
  temporary absence
    CTB 577
    CTB aged 60 or over 825
    HB 208, 215
    HB aged 60 or over 697
  trial stay in care home
    CTB 577
    CTB aged 60 or over 825
    HB 208
    HB aged 60 or over 696

absence from work
  CTB 575
  CTB aged 60 or over 823
  HB 203, 363
  HB aged 60 or over 693

academic year
  CTB 604
  HB 332

access funds
  definition 332
    CTB 604
  treatment as capital
    CTB 614
    HB 355
  treatment as income
    CTB 614
    HB 354

accommodation
  size criteria
    HB 536

adaptations to home
  claiming before moving home 695
    HB 207

administration of benefits
  benefits administration information 76
  contracting out benefit functions by local
    authorities 1091
  reports on local authorities 85

administrative costs
  subsidy 1163

adoption
  definition of adoption leave
    CTB 564
    CTB aged 60 or over 815
    HB 185, 564
  disregard of allowances
    CTB 657
    HB 479
  treatment as member of household
    CTB 580
    CTB aged 60 or over 828
    HB 275
    HB aged 60 or over 713

adoption leave
  in remunerative work
    CTB 586
    CTB aged 60 or over 837
    HB 288
    HB aged 60 or over 724

adoption pay
  see also: statutory adoption pay

advance claims
HB 207, 383
advance payment of rent
HB 217
HB aged 60 or over 698
advantage
taking advantage of benefit scheme
CTB 573
CTB aged 60 or over 822
HB 197, 235
age rules
HB 220
age-related payments
disregard of payments 1045
agents 79
aggregation
applicable amount 16
CTB 581
CTB aged 60 or over 829
HB 276
HB aged 60 or over 713
income and capital 16
CTB 14
treatment of child's income and capital
CTB 598
treatment of family's income and capital
CTB 582
CTB aged 60 or over 829
HB 282
HB aged 60 or over 714
almshouses
HB 253
HB aged 60 or over 702
alternative maximum council tax benefit 619,
631, 855
aggregation 14
amount 619, 650, 855
CTB aged 60 or over 890
duty to notify change of circumstances 631
entitlement 12, 620, 855
notification 673, 893
students 608
amending a claim
CTB 630
CTB aged 60 or over 866
HB 390
HB aged 60 or over 759
amount of benefit
alternative maximum CTB 619, 650, 855
couples
CTB 14
CTB 12
CTB aged 60 or over 890
HB 5
maximum amount
amount of benefit : maximum amount :
CTB aged 60 or over 851
CTB 615
HB 356
HB aged 60 or over 739
minimum
HB 365
HB aged 60 or over 744
non-dependant deductions

CTB 616
CTB aged 60 or over 851
tapers
CTB 617
CTB aged 60 or over 853
HB 330
weekly amount
HB 372
HB aged 60 or over 750
annuities
disregarded
CTB 663
CTB aged 60 or over 883
HB 477, 490
HB aged 60 or over 789
notional capital/income
HB 314
self-employed earners
CTB 591
CTB aged 60 or over 843, 844
HB 303
HB aged 60 or over 730
treatment as income
CTB 594
HB 308
anti-social behaviour
eviction
HB 7, 177, 1139, 1144
pilot scheme 10, 1139, 1143
anti-test case rule 173
appeal tribunals 108, 114
composition of tribunal
HB/CTB 988
decisions of tribunals 934
procedures 919
appeals 143, 147, 946
against decision of Commissioner 915
appeal tribunals 151
applying for an appeal
HB/CTB 983
before July 2001 993
death of person involved
HB/CTB 986
decisions of a Commissioner 913
decisions which can be appealed 151
decisions with no right of appeal 989, 1079
HB/CTB 977
effect of other appeal 172
from Commissioner 166
late appeals
HB/CTB 980
leave to appeal 906
legal aid 904
notice of appeal 907
notice of decision
HB/CTB 970
oral hearings – procedure 926, 928, 931
oral or paper hearing 920
procedure 900
HB/CTB 988
recovery of overpayments 154
reinstating struck out appeals 925
revised decision
HB/CTB 978

service of notices and documents 903
  HB/CTB 949
setting aside tribunal decisions 940
statement of reasons of tribunal decision
  937
struck out 924
summoning witnesses 923
test case pending
  HB/CTB 977
time limits
  HB/CTB 979
to Commissioner 159
to Commissioner against tribunal decision
  901, 904, 943
to Commissioner – procedure 908
transitional arrangements 993
who has right of appeal 152
withdrawal of appeal to Commissioner 912
withdrawing an appeal 922
applicable amounts 16
  CTB 581, 642
  CTB aged 60 or over 829, 877
  HB 276, 451
  HB aged 60 or over 713
  hospital patients
    CTB 581
    HB 278
  personal allowance
    CTB 643
    CTB aged 60 or over 877
    HB 451
  polygamous marriages
    CTB 581
    HB 277
applications
  appeals
    HB/CTB 983
appointees
  acting on behalf of the claimant
    HB 377
  person to receive benefit for claimant
    CTB 623, 633
    CTB aged 60 or over 859, 869
    HB 376, 403
    HB aged 60 or over 753, 763
  recovery of overpayments
    HB 424
apportionment
  alternative maximum CTB 619, 855
  council tax 615
  designated rent 1188
  non-dependants 743
    CTB 616
    CTB aged 60 or over 852
    HB 361
  student grant income
    CTB 610
    HB 347
  student loans
    CTB 612
    HB 351
appropriate indicative rent level 1188

appropriate social security office
  CTB 565
  CTB aged 60 or over 815
  HB 185
  HB for people aged 60 or over 683
armed services
  mobility supplement disregarded
    CTB 655
    HB 473
arrears
  disregard of benefit arrears
    CTB 662
    CTB aged 60 or over 888
    HB 488
    HB aged 60 or over 795
  offsetting against overpayments
    CTB 634
    CTB aged 60 or over 870
    HB 410
    HB aged 60 or over 765
  rent arrears
    HB 252
    HB aged 60 or over 702
  treatment of arrears of income
    CTB 623
    CTB aged 60 or over 857
    HB 370
    HB aged 60 or over 747
  treatment of benefit arrears
    CTB 623
    CTB aged 60 or over 857
    HB 372
assessment period
  definition
    CTB 565
    CTB aged 60 or over 815
    HB 186
    HB aged 60 or over 683
  employed earners
    CTB 586
    HB 290
  income other than earnings
    CTB 587
    HB 292
  self-employed earners
    CTB 587
    HB 292
assured tenancy
  definition
    HB 520, 522, 540
asylum seekers 1026, 1118
  calculation of income
    CTB 594
    HB 307
  exclusion from benefits 1026
  loss of status 1121
  on arrival claims 1121
  retrospective claim for benefit
    CTB 1073, 1130
    HB 1073, 1126
  transitional protection 1054, 1073
    HB/CTB 1054
  upheaval declarations 1121

attendance allowance
  disregarded
    CTB 655
    CTB aged 60 or over 832
    HB 474
    HB aged 60 or over 718
audit
  requirement for subsidy claims 1158

B
backdating
  CTB 627
  CTB aged 60 or over 863
  HB 365, 380, 383
  HB aged 60 or over 756
  refugees 1028, 1073
    CTB 577
    HB 444
  subsidy 1164
bankruptcy
  HB 426
  recovery of overpayments 101
  treatment of payments from pension
    schemes
    CTB 596, 600
    HB 311, 321
beneficial interest
  CTB 603, 656
  CTB aged 60 or over 850
  HB 197, 328, 476
benefit changes
  treatment as income
    HB 311, 314
    HB aged 60 or over 733
benefit offences
  definition 1036
  disqualification from benefit
    HB/CTB 1087
  effect on family's benefit 1038
  loss of benefit 1035
  reduction of benefit
    HB/CTB 1089
benefit savings 1175, 1176
benefit week
  CTB 565
  CTB aged 60 or over 816
  HB 186, 365
  HB aged 60 or over 683
bereavement benefits
  disregarded income
    CTB 656
    HB 476
bereavement premium
  CTB 644
  HB 456
billing authority
  administration
    CTB 84
  definition 19
blind
  non-dependant deductions
    CTB 616
    CTB aged 60 or over 852
    HB 361
    HB aged 60 or over 743

blind homeworkers' scheme
  CTB 666
  HB 496
board
  definition 1161
    HB aged 60 or over 683
boarders
  date entitlement begins
    HB 365
    HB aged 60 or over 745
  non-dependants
    HB 199, 364
    HB aged over 60 692
  payments disregarded
    CTB 657
    CTB aged 60 or over 883
    HB 482
    HB aged 60 or over 789
bonus of wages
  treatment as earnings
    CTB 588
    CTB aged 60 or over 840
    HB 295
    HB aged 60 or over 727
business
  assets disregarded as capital
    CTB 662
    CTB aged 60 or over 885
    HB 488
    HB aged 60 or over 792
  expenses/debts
    CTB 591
    CTB aged 60 or over 843
    HB 302
    HB aged 60 or over 730
  use of accommodation
    HB 199, 254
    HB aged 60 or over 703
business partners
  calculation of net profit
    HB 302
    HB aged 60 or over 730

C
calculations
  CTB 615
  CTB aged 60 or over 851
campsite fees
  HB 527, 539, 546, 555
  HB aged 60 or over 702
capital 16
  abroad
    CTB 599
    CTB aged 60 or over 847
    HB 319
    HB aged 60 or over 736
  arrears of benefit
    CTB 662
    HB 488
    HB aged 60 or over 735
  calculation
    CTB 598
    CTB aged 60 or over 830, 847
    HB 316
    HB aged 60 or over 715, 735

calculation of capital in UK
  CTB 599
  CTB aged 60 or over 847
  HB 318
  HB aged 60 or over 736
calculation of capital outside UK
  CTB 599
  CTB aged 60 or over 847
  HB 319
  HB aged 60 or over 736
capital limit 15
  CTB 598
  CTB aged 60 or over 847
  HB 316
  HB aged 60 or over 735
capital limit increase backdating a claim
  HB 365
charitable payments
  CTB 598
  HB 317
child/young person's
  CTB 598
  HB 282, 317
  HB aged 60 or over 714
CTB 598
deprivation of capital
  CTB 599
  CTB aged 60 or over 847
  HB 320
  HB aged 60 or over 736
difference between income and capital
  HB 278
diminishing notional capital rule
  CTB 601
  CTB aged 60 or over 848
  HB 325
  HB aged 60 or over 737
diminution of capital
  CTB 637
  CTB aged 60 or over 872
  HB 429
  HB aged 60 or over 768
disregards
  CTB 598, 662
  CTB aged 60 or over 847, 885
  HB 316, 486
  HB aged 60 or over 735, 792
family's capital 16
  CTB 14, 582
  CTB aged 60 or over 829
  HB 282
  HB aged 60 or over 714
HB 278, 315
income from capital 16
  CTB 582, 598, 603, 656
  CTB aged 60 or over 834
  HB 317, 330, 476
income treated as capital 17
  CTB 598, 658
  HB 317, 481, 492
instalments of capital
  CTB 594
  HB 308
jointly held capital

CTB 603
  CTB aged 60 or over 850
  HB 328
  HB aged 60 or over 739
non-dependant's
  CTB 582
  CTB aged 60 or over 830
  HB 283
  HB aged 60 or over 715
notional capital
  CTB 599
  CTB aged 60 or over 847
  HB 320
  HB aged 60 or over 736
partner's
  CTB 582
  CTB aged 60 or over 829
  HB 282
qualifying age for PC 18
tariff income 16
  CTB 582, 603
  CTB aged 60 or over 834
  HB 330
  HB aged over 60 720
third party payments
  CTB 599
  HB 320
treatment as income 17
  CTB 583, 594, 664
  CTB aged 60 or over 833
  HB 284, 306, 308
  HB aged 60 or over 719, 720
treatment of guarantee credit
  CTB aged 60 or over 830
  HB aged 60 or over 715
treatment of savings credit
  CTB aged 60 or over 830
  HB aged 60 or over 715
valuation of capital
  CTB 599
  CTB aged 60 or over 847
  HB 318
  HB aged 60 or over 736
care
  child/young person
    HB 274
    HB aged 60 or over 713
care homes
  absence from home
    CTB 577, 578
    CTB aged 60 or over 826
    HB 209
    HB aged 60 or over 697
  counselling and care charges 111
  definition
    CTB 578
    HB 210
    HB aged 60 or over 683, 697
  HB 1123
  not liable to make payments on a dwelling
    HB 223, 235
    HB aged 60 or over 699
  public bodies 123

residents disregarded for council tax
  discount 1011, 1012
tariff income
  HB 330
trial period
  CTB 577
  CTB aged 60 or over 825
  HB 208
  HB aged 60 or over 696
care leavers
  exclusion from benefits 1031
career development loans
  HB 308
carers
  cost of care paid by employer
    CTB 589
    CTB aged 60 or over 840
    HB 295
    HB aged 60 or over 727
  disregard of care payments
    CTB 657
    HB 479
  disregarded for council tax discount 1012
  earnings disregard
    CTB 653
    CTB aged 60 or over 880
    HB 469
    HB aged 60 or over 786
  non-dependants
    CTB 573
    CTB aged 60 or over 822
    HB 200
    HB aged 60 or over 692
  students entitled to benefit
    CTB 609
    HB 340
  treatment of care payments
    CTB 591
    HB 301
    HB aged 60 or over 730
carer's premium
  amount
    CTB 650
    CTB aged 60 or over 880
    HB aged 60 or over 785
  CTB 648
  CTB aged 60 or over 879
  earnings disregards
    CTB 652
    HB 468
  HB 463
  HB aged 60 or over 784
change of circumstances
  arrears of income 1099
  CTB 629
  CTB aged 60 or over 865
  date change takes effect
    CTB 622
    CTB aged 60 or over 857
    HB 369
    HB aged 60 or over 746
  duty to notify
    CTB 630
    CTB aged 60 or over 866

    HB 390
    HB aged 60 or over 759
  duty to report
    HB/CTB 1086
  HB 369, 387
  HB aged 60 or over 746, 758
  pension credit
    CTB aged 60 or over 858, 867
    HB aged 60 or over 748, 760
  supersessions 965
  supersessions – late application
    HB/CTB 969
charitable payments
  disregarded
    CTB 666
    HB 475, 494
  students
    CTB 612
    HB 350
  treatment as income and capital
    CTB 598
    HB 317
child benefit
  CTB 579, 1011
  CTB aged 60 or over 827, 832
  HB 272
  HB aged 60 or over 718
child tax credit 1043
  arrears treated as capital
    HB 317
  calculation of average weekly income 293
    HB 293
    HB aged over 60 724
  notional income/capital
    CTB 599
    HB 309
  treatment as income
    CTB 593
    CTB aged 60 or over 833
    HB 307
    HB aged 60 or over 719
childcare
  deduction of charges
    CTB 583
    HB 284, 285
    HB aged 60 or over 721
  eligible charges
    CTB 584
    CTB aged 60 or over 835
  estimating relevant charges
    CTB 584
    CTB aged 60 or over 836
    HB 286
    HB aged 60 or over 722
  maternity leave
    HB 288
  parental leave
    CTB 586
    CTB aged 60 or over 837
  relevant charges
    HB 286
    HB aged 60 or over 722
  student grant income – disregards
    CTB 610

treatment of charges
CTB 583
CTB aged 60 or over 834
childminders
calculation of net profit
CTB 592, 593
CTB aged 60 or over 843
HB 303, 306
HB aged 60 or over 731, 732
costs paid by employer
CTB 589
CTB aged 60 or over 840
HB aged 60 or over 727
children
applicable amount
CTB 581
CTB aged 60 or over 829
claiming for a child
HB 274
HB aged 60 or over 712
death of a child
HB 273
definition 19
CTB 565, 579
CTB aged 60 or over 827
HB 186
HB aged 60 or over 684
disregarded capital
CTB 598
HB 317
disregarded for council tax discount 1011
duty to notify changes in family
CTB 631
CTB aged 60 or over 866
HB 391
HB aged 60 or over 759
landlord's child – responsibility for
HB 223
HB aged 60 or over 699
leaving care 1031
member of household
CTB 580
CTB aged 60 or over 828
HB aged 60 or over 712
non-dependants
CTB 573
CTB aged 60 or over 822
HB 199
HB aged over 60 692
payments from child disregarded
CTB 657
HB 478
responsibility for child
CTB 579, 608
CTB aged 60 or over 827
HB 273, 339
HB aged 60 or over 712
treatment of income and capital
CTB 598, 653
HB 282, 471
HB aged 60 or over 714
children in care
disregard of care payments
CTB 591, 657

HB 301, 479
HB aged 60 or over 730
leaving care 1031
treatment as member of household
CTB 580
CTB aged 60 or over 828
HB 274
HB aged 60 or over 713
children in need
payments disregarded
CTB 664
HB 480, 491
civil partners 21
close relatives 1046
definition of couple 19, 947
stepchildren 1097
transitional arrangements 1095
claim forms
CTB 624
CTB aged 60 or over 860
HB 378
HB aged 60 or over 754
claim-related rent 1185, 1188
HB 260, 263, 533, 550
claims 29
advance claims
HB 383
amending a claim
CTB 630
CTB aged 60 or over 866
HB 390
HB aged 60 or over 759
backdating
CTB aged 60 or over 863
HB 365, 380, 383
HB aged 60 or over 756
claim forms
CTB 624
HB 378
claiming procedure
CTB 624
CTB aged 60 or over 860
HB 378
HB aged 60 or over 754
date entitlement begins
CTB 621
CTB aged 60 or over 856
HB 365
HB aged 60 or over 744
date of claim
CTB 566, 625, 627
CTB aged 60 or over 816, 861, 863
HB 187, 379, 385
HB aged 60 or over 684, 755, 756
defective claims
CTB 626
CTB aged 60 or over 862
HB 380
HB aged 60 or over 755
discretionary housing payments 1082
electronic claims
CTB 627
CTB aged 60 or over 863
HB 385

HB aged 60 or over 756
end of claim
  CTB 621, 622
  CTB aged 60 or over 856
  HB 367, 368
  HB aged 60 or over 745
evidence to support claim 29
  CTB 629
  CTB aged 60 or over 864
  HB 387
  HB aged 60 or over 757
information required by local authority
  CTB 639
  CTB aged 60 or over 873
  HB 435
  HB aged 60 or over 771
late claims
  CTB aged 60 or over 863
  HB 380, 383
  HB aged 60 or over 756
national insurance number requirement 29
  CTB 574
power to make regulations about
  administration of claims 35
  CTB 37
retrospective effect of requirement for
  claim 30
subsidy claims by local authority 1155,
  1199
telephone claims
  CTB 625
  CTB aged 60 or over 861
  HB 379
  HB aged 60 or over 754
where to claim
  CTB 624
  HB 378, 381
  HB aged 60 or over 754
who can claim
  CTB 623
  CTB aged 60 or over 859
  HB 376
  HB aged 60 or over 753
withdrawing a claim
  CTB 630
  HB 390
  HB aged 60 or over 759
written claims
  CTB 624
  CTB aged 60 or over 860
  HB 378
  HB aged 60 or over 754
close relatives
civil partners 1046
definition
  CTB 565
  CTB aged 60 or over 816
  HB 186
  HB aged 60 or over 684
landlord
  HB 223, 230
  HB aged 60 or over 699

co-ownership scheme
definition
  HB aged 60 or over 684
  HB 254
  HB aged 60 or over 703
coastguard
earnings disregard
  CTB 653
  CTB aged 60 or over 880
  HB 469
  HB aged 60 or over 786
  HB 469
commencement
Council Tax Benefit (Persons who have
  attained the qualifying age for stated
  pension credit) Regulations 2006 815
Council Tax Benefit Regulations 2006 564
Housing Benefit (Persons who have
  attained the qualifying age for state
  pension credit) Regulations 2006 682
Housing Benefit Regulations 2006 185
Social Security Act 1998 113
Social Security Administration Act 105
Social Security Contributions and Benefits
  Act 26
commercial basis
CTB 573
CTB aged 60 or over 822
HB 197, 199, 223
HB aged 60 or over 692, 698, 699
non-commercial agreements
  HB 226
commission
treatment as earnings
  CTB 588
  CTB aged 60 or over 840
  HB 295
  HB aged 60 or over 727
Commissioners See Social Security
Commissioners 116
communal areas
definition
  HB 448
  HB aged 60 or over 780
fuel charges
  HB 447
  HB aged 60 or over 779
community care payments
HB 484
compensation
for unfair dismissal
  CTB 588
  HB 295
income/capital disregards
  CTB 663, 667
  HB 488, 490, 496
  HB aged 60 or over 795
concessionary payment
CTB 662
definition
  CTB 565
  CTB aged 60 or over 816
  HB 186
  HB aged 60 or over 684

disregards
    CTB 655
    HB 473
HB 488
conditional sale agreement
HB 254
HB aged 60 or over 703
contrived tenancy
CTB 573
CTB aged 60 or over 822
HB 197, 223
taking advantage of benefit scheme
    CTB 582
    CTB aged 60 or over 830
    HB 223, 235, 283
    HB aged 60 or over 699, 715
council tax
age-related payments 1045
discounts 635, 1004, 1008
disregards for discount 1010
joint liability 615, 619, 855
liability 1003, 1007
reduction 1005
reduction of liability 635, 870
reductions 1008
setting amounts 1006, 1009
council tax benefit 3
administration 84
claiming other benefits 39
disregarded income
    HB 484
entitlement 11
permitted totals 1064
power to modify scheme 84
councillors' allowances
HB 298
counselling services
grants to organisations to provide services
    1029
service charges 111
couples
alternative maximum CTB 619, 855
applicable amount
    CTB 581
    CTB aged 60 or over 829
    HB 276
capital of partner
    HB 282
    HB aged 60 or over 714
change of circumstances
    CTB 623
    CTB aged 60 or over 857
claiming
    CTB 623
    CTB aged 60 or over 859
    HB 217, 376
    HB aged 60 or over 698, 753
definition
    HB aged 60 or over 684, 687
entitlement to CTB 14
estrangement
    CTB 571
    CTB aged 60 or over 821
eviction

HB 9
former partner is landlord
    HB 223
    HB aged 60 or over 699
income of partner 16
    CTB 14, 582
    CTB aged 60 or over 829
    HB 282
maximum CTB 615
member of household
    CTB 580
    CTB aged 60 or over 828
    HB 274
    HB aged 60 or over 712
non-dependant deductions
    CTB 616
    CTB aged 60 or over 852
    HB 361
    HB aged 60 or over 743
partner
    CTB 568
    CTB aged 60 or over 819
    HB 190
partner absent from home
    HB 274
recovery of overpayments
    CTB 636
    CTB aged 60 or over 871
    HB 427
same sex couples 19
student partners
    CTB 608, 614
    HB 217, 339, 346, 355
    HB aged 60 or over 698
course of study
definition
    CTB 605
    HB 333
court action
delays in payment
    HB 399
recovery of overpayments
    CTB 46, 637
    CTB aged 60 or over 872
    HB 43, 429
Court of Appeal
appealing against decision of
    Commissioner 915
Court of Protection
CTB 623
CTB aged 60 or over 859
HB 376
HB aged 60 or over 753
covenants
CTB 605, 611
HB 333, 349, 355
credit sale
HB 254
HB aged 60 or over 703
Creutzfeldt-Jakob disease
payments from trusts
    CTB 668
    CTB aged 60 or over 886
    HB aged 60 or over 793

criminal proceedings
dishonesty 57
false representations 61
obstructing inspector 56
penalty alternatives 64, 1069
time limits 70
unauthorised disclosure of information 76
croft land
disregarded as capital
CTB 662
HB 486
HB 254
HB aged 60 or over 691, 703
Crown tenants
HB 254
definition
HB 187
HB aged 60 or over 684
HB aged 60 or over 703

D
date of claim
CTB 621, 627
CTB aged 60 or over 856, 861, 863
HB 365, 379, 385
HB aged 60 or over 744, 755, 756
refugee claims
HB 1127
deafness
students
HB 340
death
appeals
HB/CTB 986
change of circumstances
CTB 623
CTB aged 60 or over 857
disregard of compensation
CTB 667
HB 496
effect on carer premium
HB 464
payments on death
CTB 634
CTB aged 60 or over 869
HB 409
HB aged 60 or over 765
recovery of overpayments
HB 427
decisions
appeal tribunals 147, 934
delayed – appeal pending 171
no right of appeal 989
HB/CTB 977
notice of decisions which can be appealed
HB/CTB 970
of Commissioner in appeals process 913
relevant 148
revision of decisions
HB/CTB 952
setting aside appeal tribunal decisions 940
time limits for appeals
HB/CTB 979
transitional arrangements 993

decisions by local authority 110
CTB 632
duty to determine claim
CTB 632
CTB aged 60 or over 867
notification to claimant 110
CTB 632, 672
CTB aged 60 or over 868, 891
HB 394, 504
HB aged 60 or over 761, 799
statement of reasons
CTB 632
CTB aged 60 or over 868
HB 395
HB aged 60 or over 761
validation of decisions 111
deductions from benefits
non-dependant
CTB 616
CTB aged 60 or over 851
prescribed benefits
HB 433
HB aged 60 or over 769
recovery of overpayments
CTB 593, 637, 638
CTB aged 60 or over 872
HB 424, 426, 427, 433
HB aged 60 or over 767, 769
recovery of overpayments from other
benefits
CTB 46
HB 42, 306
deductions from eligible rent
HB 444
HB aged 60 or over 777
defective claims
CTB 626
CTB aged 60 or over 862
HB 380
HB aged 60 or over 755
delays
in making payments
CTB 633
CTB aged 60 or over 869
HB 398
HB aged 60 or over 761
moving home
HB 207
HB aged 60 or over 695
deprivation of resources
CTB 599
CTB aged 60 or over 847
diminishing notional capital rule
CTB 601
CTB aged 60 or over 848
HB 325
HB aged 60 or over 737
HB 313, 320
HB aged 60 or over 736
income
CTB 595
CTB aged 60 or over 845

designated authority
definition
CTB aged 60 or over 816
HB 187
HB aged 60 or over 684
designated office
definition
CTB 566
CTB aged 60 or over 817
HB 187
designated rent 1188
detention
disregarded for council tax discount 1010
determinations by local authority
board and attendance
HB 525, 544
broad rental market area
HB 524, 543
categories of dwelling
HB 536, 553
deemed to be made prior to July 2001 999
definition
HB 520, 540
definition of relevant period
HB 521, 522, 541
definition of relevant time
HB 521
errors
HB 527, 546
HB 529, 541
indicative rent calculation
HB 535, 552
local housing allowance 543
HB 524
notifications
HB 534, 552
redeterminations
HB 269
HB aged 60 or over 709
significantly high rent
HB 529
substitute determinations
HB 271
HB aged 60 or over 711
diminishing notional capital rule
calculating the reduction
HB 327
CTB 601
CTB aged 60 or over 848
HB 325
HB aged 60 or over 737
tariff income
HB 330
direct payments to landlord
claims by refugees
HB 1127
death of claimant
HB 409
HB aged 60 or over 765
frequency of payment
HB 400, 404
HB aged 60 or over 762
HB 407
HB aged 60 or over 763, 764

information requirements
HB 1065
notification
HB 395, 507
HB aged 60 or over 800
obligation to make direct payments
HB 405
payments on account
HB 402
person affected
HB 395
disability
childcare costs 583, 834
CTB 584
HB 285
HB aged 60 or over 721, 836
council tax reductions 1005, 1009
disability living allowance
disregarded
CTB 655
CTB aged 60 or over 832
HB 473
HB aged 60 or over 718
disability premium
amount
CTB 649
CTB 646
earnings disregard
HB 468
HB 458
incapable of work 1100
disability reduction 635, 870, 1005, 1008
disabled child premium
amount
CTB 649
CTB aged 60 or over 880
HB aged 60 or over 785
CTB 648
CTB aged 60 or over 879
HB 463
HB aged 60 or over 784
disabled students
CTB 608
disabled students' allowance
CTB 608
HB 339
discount
council tax 635, 870, 1004, 1008
disregarded for discount 1010
discretionary housing payments 143, 1079, 1203
circumstances in which payments may be made 1080
claims 1081, 1082
disregard of payments 485
excluded from right to appeal 1079
grants to local authority 144
HB 357
information 1083
maximum weekly payments 1082
reviews 1083
discretionary powers
CTB 84
HB 81

recovery of overpayments
HB 42
dishonesty 57
disqualification from benefit
benefit offences 1035
effect on offender's family 1038
period of disqualification
HB/CTB 1087
disqualifying benefits
definition 1036
disregards
age-related payments 1045
benefits
CTB 654
CTB aged 60 or over 832
HB 472
HB aged 60 or over 718
capital
CTB 598, 662
CTB aged 60 or over 847, 885
HB 316, 486
HB aged 60 or over 735, 792
changes in tax and contributions
CTB 588
CTB aged 60 or over 839
HB 294
HB aged 60 or over 726
child's capital
CTB 598
HB 317
child's earnings
CTB 653
employee's earnings
CTB 589, 651, 653
CTB aged 60 or over 880
HB 299, 466
HB aged 60 or over 785
income other than earnings
CTB 587, 593, 654
CTB aged 60 or over 882
HB 306, 472
HB aged 60 or over 788
non-dependant's income
CTB 617
CTB aged 60 or over 853
HB 362
HB aged 60 or over 744
second adult's income
CTB 651
self-employed earnings
CTB 591, 592, 653
CTB aged 60 or over 842, 843, 844
HB 301, 302, 305
HB aged 60 or over 729, 732
student loans
CTB 612
HB 352
student's income
CTB 610, 612, 614, 615
HB 347, 350, 355
war pensions
CTB 84
CTB aged 60 or over 882

HB 82
HB aged 60 or over 788
divorce
former partner pays the mortgage
HB 223
HB aged 60 or over 699
dwelling
definition 19, 104
CTB 566
CTB aged 60 or over 817
HB 193, 520, 540
HB aged 60 or over 685, 691
disregarded as capital
CTB 662, 665
HB 486, 493
larger than reasonably required
HB 530, 548, 1107
liability to make payments
aged 60 or over 698
HB 217
not liable to make payments
aged 60 or over 698
HB 223
occupation of home
CTB 570, 577
CTB aged 60 or over 821
HB 206, 338
HB aged 60 or over 694
rent officer categories
HB 536, 553

E
earnings
child/young person's earnings
CTB 653
HB 471
deduction of childcare costs
CTB 583
CTB aged 60 or over 834
definition
CTB aged 60 or over 839
HB aged 60 or over 727
disregards from employed earnings
CTB 589, 651, 653
CTB aged 60 or over 880
HB 299, 305, 465
HB aged 60 or over 785
disregards from self-employed earnings
CTB 591, 592, 653
CTB aged 60 or over 842, 843, 844
HB 301
HB aged 60 or over 729, 732
employed earner
CTB 588
CTB aged 60 or over 839
employed earner average weekly earnings
CTB 586
HB 290, 294
HB aged 60 or over 724
employed earner calculation of net
earnings
CTB 589
CTB aged 60 or over 840
HB 299
HB aged 60 or over 728

fluctuating earnings of employed earner
CTB 587
HB 291
low earnings-notional income
CTB 597
HB 311
self-employed assessment period
HB 292
self-employed average weekly earnings
CTB 587
HB 292
self-employed calculation of net profit
CTB 591
CTB aged 60 or over 842
HB 301
HB aged 60 or over 730
self-employed earner
CTB 590
CTB aged 60 or over 842
HB 301
HB aged 60 or over 729
education authority
CTB 605
education maintenance allowance
CTB 655
HB 474
EEA nationals
A8 nationals 250
former worker 248
right of residence
HB 249
workers
CTB 576
CTB aged 60 or over 824
HB 240, 246
HB aged 60 or over 700
Eileen Trust
definition
CTB 566
HB 187
disregarded as capital
CTB 598, 664
CTB aged 60 or over 887
HB 317, 492
HB aged 60 or over 794
disregarded as income
CTB 658
HB 481
disregarded from second adult's income
CTB 651
third party payments
CTB 596, 600
HB 310, 321
electronic communications
claims
CTB 627, 675
HB 385, 518, 519
HB aged 60 or over 756, 810
CTB 566
CTB aged 60 or over 817, 863, 894
decisions sent by email 943
HB 187
HB aged 60 or over 685
use by local authorities 1156, 1197

CTB 674
CTB aged 60 or over 894
HB 518
HB aged 60 or over 810
eligible housing costs
calculation
HB 372
HB aged 60 or over 750
eligible rent
HB 252, 253
HB aged 60 or over 702
HB 252
rent-free periods
HB 375
HB aged 60 or over 752
students
HB 344
eligible rent
calculation
HB 372
HB aged 60 or over 750
transitional protection 1101
employed earners
average weekly earnings
CTB 586
HB 290, 294
HB aged 60 or over 724
calculation of net earnings
CTB 589
CTB aged 60 or over 840
HB 299
HB aged 60 or over 728
definition
CTB 566
CTB aged 60 or over 817
HB 187
HB aged 60 or over 685
disregards
CTB 589, 651
CTB aged 60 or over 880
HB 299
HB aged 60 or over 785
earnings
CTB 586, 588
CTB aged 60 or over 839
HB 295
HB aged 60 or over 727
fluctuating earnings
CTB 587
HB 291
loans and advances from employer
CTB 598
HB 317
employers
colluding in fraud 67
employment zone programme
definition
CTB 566
HB 187
disregard of payments
CTB 661, 667
HB 485, 497

end of claim
date entitlement ends
CTB 621, 622
CTB aged 60 or over 856
HB 367, 368
HB aged 60 or over 745
enduring power of attorney
CTB aged 60 or over 860
HB 376
enforcement notices 88
enhanced disability premium
amount
HB aged 60 or over 785
CTB 648
CTB aged 60 or over 879
HB aged 60 or over 880
HB 462
HB aged 60 or over 784
entitlement
conditions of entitlement
CTB 11, 14
HB 4
date entitlement begins
CTB 621
CTB aged 60 or over 856
HB 365
HB aged 60 or over 744
end of entitlement
CTB 621, 622
CTB aged 60 or over 856
HB 367, 368
HB aged 60 or over 745
exclusions 15
extended payments
CTB 669, 671
CTB aged 60 or over 889
HB 499, 503
HB aged 60 or over 797
occupation of dwelling
CTB 570, 577
CTB aged 60 or over 821
persons from abroad
CTB 575
CTB aged 60 or over 823
HB 239
restriction in cases of error 173
work-focused interview 31
entry
inspectors' powers of entry 53
equity release schemes
treatment as income
CTB aged 60 or over 833
HB aged 60 or over 719
equity sharing schemes
HB 194
errors
correction 175, 913, 940, 970
official error – definition
HB/CTB 948, 949
overpayment caused by official error
CTB 635, 637
CTB aged 60 or over 871, 872
HB 411, 429
HB aged 60 or over 765, 768

rent officer
HB 527
rent officer application
HB 271
HB aged 60 or over 711
rent officers
HB 546
restriction on benefit entitlement 173
estrangement
CTB 571
CTB aged 60 or over 821
European Commission on Human Rights 119
European Convention on Human Rights 118
Articles 131
declaration of incompatibility 121
impact on UK law 120
judicial remedies 125
legal proceedings 124
European Court of Human Rights 119
eviction
loss of HB 6, 177, 1139, 1144
pilot scheme 10, 1139, 1143
evidence
experts at appeal tribunals 932
in support of claims 29
CTB 629
CTB aged 60 or over 864
HB 387
HB aged 60 or over 757
of liability for rent
HB 219
required by rent officer
HB 437
HB aged 60 or over 772
exceptional leave to remain
HB 251
exceptionally high rent
HB 530, 548
excluded tenancies 1168
HB aged 60 or over 780
referrals to rent officers
HB 266
HB aged 60 or over 708
expectation of payment for work
HB 204
expenses
disregarded income
CTB 654
HB 473
paid work
CTB 654
HB 473
self-employed
CTB 591
CTB aged 60 or over 843
treatment as earnings
CTB 589
CTB aged 60 or over 840
HB 295
HB aged 60 or over 727
voluntary/charity work
CTB 654
HB 473

extended payments
calculation
CTB 670, 671
CTB aged 60 or over 890
HB 501, 503
HB aged 60 or over 797
CTB 566, 615, 617, 618, 669, 671
CTB aged 60 or over 817, 853, 854, 889
entitlement due to PC
CTB 854
HB 741
HB 187, 357, 359, 373, 503
HB aged 60 or over 685, 740, 741, 752, 797
information to be supplied
CTB 641
CTB aged 60 or over 876
HB 439
HB aged 60 or over 774
moving home
CTB 618, 670, 671
CTB aged 60 or over 853, 890
HB 359, 438, 501
HB aged 60 or over 740
reduction in benefit
CTB 670, 671
CTB aged 60 or over 851, 890
HB 502, 504
HB aged 60 or over 740, 798
two homes
CTB 671
CTB aged 60 or over 890
HB 502, 504
HB aged 60 or over 798

F
failure to
disclose a material fact
CTB 636, 637
CTB aged 60 or over 872
disclose overpayments
HB 419, 423, 429
HB aged 60 or over 767, 768
supply information
HB 443
HB aged 60 or over 777
fair rent
HB 1107
families
aggregation
CTB 14
aggregation of applicable amounts
CTB 581
CTB aged 60 or over 829
HB 276
HB aged 60 or over 713
death of a child
HB 273
definition 19
CTB 566, 579
CTB aged 60 or over 827
duty to notify changes in family
CTB 631
CTB aged 60 or over 866
HB 391
HB aged 60 or over 759

membership of family
HB 272
HB aged 60 or over 711
non-dependants
CTB 573
CTB aged 60 or over 822
HB 199
HB aged over 60 692
responsibility for a child
HB 273
HB aged 60 or over 712
treatment of income and capital 16
CTB 14, 582, 598, 653
CTB aged 60 or over 829
HB 282, 317, 469
HB aged 60 or over 714
family premium
amount
HB 453
HB aged 60 or over 783
CTB 643
CTB aged 60 or over 877
HB 453
HB aged 60 or over 783
firefighters
earnings disregard
CTB 653
CTB aged 60 or over 880
HB 469
HB aged 60 or over 786
HB 469
fluctuating earnings
CTB 587
CTB aged 60 or over 838
HB 291
HB aged 60 or over 725, 726
fluctuating hours of work
CTB 574, 575
CTB aged 60 or over 823, 838
HB 202, 203
HB aged 60 or over 693
fostering
allowances
HB 301, 479
HB aged 60 or over 730
disregard of allowances
CTB 658
HB 479
treatment as member of household
CTB 580
CTB aged 60 or over 828
HB 274
HB aged 60 or over 713
fraud
authorisation of inspectors 47
employers colluding 67
landlords
HB 406
local authorities requirement to prevent fraud 86
loss of benefit 1033
penalties 57, 61
penalty as alternative to prosecution 64
powers of entry 53

powers to require information 49
prevention affecting subsidy 91
prosecution of offences 70
recovery of overpayments
    CTB 637
    CTB aged 60 or over 872
    HB 419, 429
    HB aged 60 or over 767, 768
redirected mail 99
reports on local authorities administration
    87
fuel
definition
    HB 448
    HB aged 60 or over 780
fuel costs
communal areas
    HB 447
    HB aged 60 or over 779
deductions from eligible rent
    HB 447
    HB aged 60 or over 779
service charges
    HB 447
    HB aged 60 or over 779
full-time course of study
definition
    CTB 605
    HB 333
sandwich course
    CTB 607
    HB 335
full-time education
definition
    HB 333
Fund, The
definition
    CTB 566
    HB 188
disregarded as capital
    CTB 598, 664
    HB 317, 492
disregarded as income
    CTB 658
    HB 481
disregarded from second adult's income
    CTB 651
notional income
    CTB 596
third party payments
    CTB 600
    HB 310, 321
further review
transitional arrangements 996

G
gateway office
    CTB 566, 627
    CTB aged 60 or over 817, 863
    HB 188, 385
    HB aged 60 or over 685, 756
gay couples 21
    see also: civil partners

gender recognition certificates 1044
George Cross payments
    CTB 655, 667
    HB 474, 496
good cause
absence from work 575
    CTB 575
    CTB aged 60 or over 823
    HB 203
    HB aged 60 or over 693
for late claim
    CTB aged 60 or over 863
    HB aged 60 or over 756
for not complying with notice to improve
    behaviour 1145
grants
student
    CTB 605, 610
    HB 334, 346
guarantee payments
treatment as earnings
    CTB 589
    HB 296
guardian's allowance
    CTB 660
    CTB aged 60 or over 832
    HB 484
    HB aged 60 or over 718

H
habitual residence 1118
    CTB 575
    CTB aged 60 or over 823
    HB 240, 242
    HB aged 60 or over 700, 701
haemophilia
    CTB 658
    CTB aged 60 or over 887
    HB 481, 492
    HB aged 60 or over 794
health benefits
    CTB 660, 666
    HB 483
heritable securities 5
    HB 252
higher education
    CTB 606
higher pensioner premium
amount
    CTB 649
    CTB 645, 646
earnings disregards
    CTB 652
    HB 468
    HB 456, 458
hire purchase agreement
    HB 254
    HB aged 60 or over 703
holiday pay
    CTB 589, 598
    CTB aged 60 or over 840
    HB 295, 317
    HB aged 60 or over 727
treatment as earnings

CTB 589
CTB aged 60 or over 840
holidays
treatment of hours of work
CTB 575
CTB aged 60 or over 823
HB aged 60 or over 693
home
disregarded as capital
CTB 662, 665
CTB aged 60 or over 885
HB 486, 493
HB aged 60 or over 792
occupation of home
CTB 577
CTB aged 60 or over 821
HB 338
HB aged 60 or over 694
two homes
HB 206
HB aged 60 or over 694
homeless
disregarded for council tax discount 1012
subsidy 1168, 1176
homeowner
definition
HB 190
HB aged 60 or over 687
hospital
absence from home
CTB 577
CTB aged 60 or over 826
HB 209
HB aged 60 or over 697
applicable amount
CTB 581
HB aged 60 or over 714
definition of patient
HB 210
HB aged 60 or over 697
disregarded for council tax discount 1011
HB 278
non-dependant deductions
CTB 616
CTB aged 60 or over 852
HB 362
HB aged 60 or over 743
students
HB 338
hostels
accommodation payments met by benefit
HB 253
date entitlement begins
HB 365
HB aged 60 or over 744
NINO requirement
HB 201
HB aged 60 or over 692
referrals to rent officer
HB 266, 527, 546
HB aged 60 or over 708
residents disregarded for council tax
discount 1012

hours of work
CTB 574
CTB aged 60 or over 823
HB 202
HB aged 60 or over 693
increased hours
extended CTB 669, 671, 889
extended HB 500, 503
HB aged 60 or over 797
house sale
CTB 662, 665
HB 487, 493
two homes
HB 207
HB aged 60 or over 695
houseboats
CTB 571
HB 194, 253, 527, 538, 546, 555
HB aged 60 or over 691, 702
household
definition 23
duty to notify changes in family
CTB 631
CTB aged 60 or over 866
HB 391
HB aged 60 or over 759
treated as member of
CTB 580
CTB aged 60 or over 828
HB 274
HB aged 60 or over 712
housing association
co-ownership scheme
HB 186
HB aged 60 or over 684
CTB 663
definition
HB 188
HB aged 60 or over 686
HB 490, 534, 551
housing authority
definition 82
housing benefit 3
absence from home 209, 697
administration 81
entitlement 4
power to modify scheme 81
housing costs
calculation
HB 372
HB aged 60 or over 750
eligible rent
HB 252, 253
HB aged 60 or over 702
HB 252
HB aged 60 or over 702
ineligible housing costs 4
rent-free periods
HB 375
HB aged 60 or over 752
students
HB 344

housing revenue account 81
human rights
    benefits treated as possessions 139
    freedom of thought, conscience and
        religion 135
    limitation on use of restrictions on rights
        139
    prohibition of abuse of rights 139
    prohibition of discrimination 136
    prohibition of torture 131
    protection of property 139
    public bodies – definition 122
    remedies through the courts 125
    right to a fair trial 132
    right to education 141
    right to respect for private and family life
        134
    taking legal action 124
Human Rights Act
    commencement 130

I
Iceland 1134
immigration authority
    CTB 567
incapacity benefit
    incapacity for work 1100
incapacity for work 1099
    students able to claim benefit
        CTB 608
        HB 339
income 16
    arrears of income
        CTB 623
        CTB aged 60 or over 857
        HB 370
        HB aged 60 or over 747
    assessment period
        CTB 586
        CTB aged 60 or over 815
        HB 186, 292
    average weekly income other than
        earnings
        CTB 587
        HB 292
    calculation of income
        CTB 582, 588
        CTB aged 60 or over 830, 834, 838
        HB 282, 284, 294, 306
        HB aged 60 or over 714, 715, 720, 724
    calculation of income other than earnings
        CTB 593
        HB 292
    capital treated as income 17
        CTB 583, 594, 664
        CTB aged 60 or over 833
        HB 284, 306, 308, 492
        HB aged 60 or over 719
    change in income
        CTB 623
        CTB aged 60 or over 857
        HB 370
        HB aged 60 or over 747
    chargeable income
        HB 306

child/young person's income
    HB 282
    HB aged 60 or over 714
    CTB 582, 593
    CTB aged 60 or over 834
definition
    CTB aged 60 or over 831
    HB aged 60 or over 717, 720
deprivation of income
    CTB 595
    CTB aged 60 or over 845
    HB 309
    HB aged 60 or over 732
difference between capital and income
    HB 278
disregards
    CTB 588, 593, 654
    CTB aged 60 or over 839, 882
    HB 292, 306, 472
    HB aged 60 or over 788
effect of PC on calculation
    CTB aged 60 or over 830
    HB aged 60 or over 715
family's income 16
    CTB 14, 582
    CTB aged 60 or over 829
    HB 282
    HB aged 60 or over 714
    HB 278
income from capital 16
    CTB 582, 598, 603, 656
    CTB aged 60 or over 834
    HB 284, 317, 330, 476
income other than earnings
    CTB 654
    CTB aged 60 or over 882
    HB 472
    HB aged 60 or over 788
income treated as capital 17
    CTB 598, 658
    HB 317, 481
non-dependant's income
    CTB 582, 616
    CTB aged 60 or over 830, 852
    HB 283, 361
    HB aged 60 or over 715, 742
notional income
    CTB 583, 595
    CTB aged 60 or over 845
    HB 284, 309
    HB aged 60 or over 732
partner's income
    HB 282
    HB aged 60 or over 714
qualifying age for PC 18
second adult's income
    CTB 650
    CTB aged 60 or over 891
student grants
    CTB 610
    HB 346
student loans
    CTB 612
    HB 351

tariff income 16
CTB 582, 603
HB 284, 317, 330
HB aged 60 or over 720
third party payments
CTB 596
HB 310
treatment of guarantee credit
CTB aged 60 or over 830
HB aged 60 or over 715
treatment of savings credit
CTB aged 60 or over 830
HB aged 60 or over 715
weekly income
CTB 582, 588
CTB aged 60 or over 834, 838
HB 284
HB aged 60 or over 720
income related benefits 3
definition 104
income support
change of circumstances
CTB 631
HB 391
disregarded income
CTB 653
HB 473
information passed between authorities 80
non-dependant deductions
CTB 617
CTB aged 60 or over 853
HB 362
HB aged 60 or over 744
persons from abroad
HB 251
students on IS
CTB 608
HB 339
income tax
calculating net profit
CTB 592
deducted from earnings
CTB 589
CTB aged 60 or over 840
HB 299
HB aged 60 or over 728
deducted from notional earnings
CTB 597
HB 312
deducted from self-employed net profit
CTB 592
CTB aged 60 or over 843, 844
HB 302, 303, 305
HB aged 60 or over 730, 731, 732
disregard of changes
CTB 588
CTB aged 60 or over 839
HB 294
HB aged 60 or over 726
disregarded from income other than
earnings
CTB 654
HB 473
refund of tax

CTB 614, 664
HB 317, 355, 492
Independent Living Funds
definition
CTB 567
CTB aged 60 or over 818
HB 188
HB aged 60 or over 686
disregarded as capital
CTB 598, 664
CTB aged 60 or over 794, 887
HB 317, 492
disregarded as income
CTB 658
HB 481
disregarded from second adult's income
CTB 651
third party payments
CTB 596, 600
HB 310, 321
indicative rent levels 1188
HB 535, 552
information 73
benefits administration information 76
claiming subsidy 1157, 1199, 1200
collection of information
CTB 639
CTB aged 60 or over 873
HB 436
HB aged 60 or over 771
disclosure by authorities 80
HB 1029
discretionary housing payments 1083
electronic information 55
forwarding information
CTB 640
CTB aged 60 or over 874
HB 436
HB aged 60 or over 772
fraud investigations 49
holding information
CTB 639
CTB age 60 or over 874
HB 436
HB aged 60 or over 771
in support of claim
CTB 629
CTB aged 60 or over 864
HB 387
HB aged 60 or over 757
included in notification of decision
CTB 672
CTB aged 60 or over 891
HB 505
HB aged 60 or over 799
insufficient information for rent officer
HB 527, 545
passed between benefit authorities
CTB 640, 641
passed between local authorities
CTB aged 60 or over 875
HB 438
HB aged 60 or over 773
passed on by ONE offices 1018

payments on account
  HB 402
  HB aged 60 or over 763
penalty notices 1069
possessions 9
requesting information
  CTB 640
  CTB aged 60 or over 874
  HB 437
  HB aged 60 or over 772
required by rent officers
  HB 266, 437
  HB aged 60 or over 708, 772
required from landlords and agents 79
  HB 440, 1065
  HB aged 60 or over 774
social security information 41, 1149
suspension of benefit 170
  HB/CTB 973
to/from Secretary of State 1149, 1156
verifying information
  CTB 639
  CTB aged 60 or over 874
  HB 436
  HB aged 60 or over 771
wrongful disclosure 73, 76, 1029
inspection
  administration of benefits 85
  authorisation of inspectors 47
  directions for improvement 87
  enforcement determinations 89
  enforcement notices 88
  obstruction of inspectors 56
  power to require information 49
  powers 54
  powers of entry 53
instalments
  capital
    CTB 594, 664
    HB 308, 491
  subsidy payments 1158
Intensive Activity Period for 50 plus
  definition
    CTB 567
interim payments
  HB 44, 402
  HB aged 60 or over 763
invalid vehicles
  definition
    CTB 567
    CTB aged 60 or over 818
    HB 189
    HB aged 60 or over 686
invalidity pension
  incapacity for work 1100
investigators
  administration of benefits 85
  authorisation 47
  code of practice 1033
  powers of investigators 54
investments
  valuation of capital
    CTB 599
    HB aged 60 or over 736

J
jobseeker's allowance
  change of circumstances
    CTB 631
  CTB 570
  CTB aged 60 or over 821
  disregarded income
    CTB 653
    HB 473
  HB 193, 391
  information passed between authorities 80
  non-dependant deductions
    CTB 617
    CTB aged 60 or over 853
    HB 362
    HB aged 60 or over 744
  persons from abroad
    HB 251
  students on JSA
    CTB 608
    HB 339
joint beneficial interest
  CTB 603
  CTB aged 60 or over 850
  HB 328
joint capital
  CTB 603
  CTB aged 60 or over 850
  HB 328
  HB aged 60 or over 739
joint liability for council tax
  alternative maximum CTB 619, 855
  amount of CTB 615
  non-dependants 573, 616, 822, 852
joint occupiers
  liability for rent
    HB 223
    HB aged 60 or over 699
  non-dependants
    CTB 616
    CTB aged 60 or over 852
    HB 199, 361
    HB aged 60 or over 692, 743
joint owner
  CTB 603
  CTB aged 60 or over 850
  HB 197
  HB aged 60 or over 739
joint tenants
  HB 201, 329
jury service
  allowances
    CTB 659
    HB 482

L
landlords
  assessment of rent level 1014
  close relative
    HB 223
    HB aged 60 or over 699
  connected trust or company
    HB 223, 232
    HB aged 60 or over 699
  direct payments

HB 404, 407
  HB aged 60 or over 763, 764
duty to notify change of circumstances
  HB 391
  HB aged 60 or over 759
fit and proper person
  HB 406
former partner
  HB 230
  HB aged 60 or over 699
information required by local authority
  HB 440, 1065
  HB aged 60 or over 774
notification of decision
  HB 507
  HB aged 60 or over 800
overpayments which are not recoverable
  HB 419
  HB aged 60 or over 766
payments on account
  HB 402
recovery of overpayments
  HB 434
  HB aged 60 or over 770
resident landlord
  HB 223
  HB aged 60 or over 699
responsibility for landlord's child
  HB 223, 231
  HB aged 60 or over 699
late claims
  CTB aged 60 or over 863
  HB 380, 383
  HB aged 60 or over 756
learner support funds
  CTB 604
  HB 332
Lebanon
  not treated as person from abroad
    CTB 576
    CTB aged 60 or over 824
    HB 241
    HB aged 60 or over 701
legal aid
  funding for appeals 904
lesbian couples 21
  see also: civil partners
liability to make payments for a home
  evidence of liability
    HB 219
  HB 217
  liability defined
    HB 218
  persons from abroad
    HB 239
  persons treated as not liable
    HB 223
  who can be treated as liable
    HB 222
licence
  HB 253, 702
Liechtenstein 1134

life insurance policy
  definition
    CTB 569
    CTB aged 60 or over 819
    HB 191
    HB aged 60 or over 688
  payments disregarded
    CTB 658
    HB 480
  surrender value disregarded
    CTB 664
    CTB aged 60 or over 886
    HB 491
    HB aged 60 or over 792
lifeboat crew
  earnings disregard
    CTB 653
    CTB aged 60 or over 880
    HB 469
    HB aged 60 or over 786
  HB 469
limited leave to enter or remain 1074
loans
  business loans disregarded
    CTB 591
    CTB aged 60 or over 843
    HB 302
    HB aged 60 or over 731
  from employer
    CTB 598
    HB 317
  student
    CTB 612
    HB 351
local authorities
  acting on behalf of another authority 81
  benefit administration information 75
  children leaving care 1031
  claiming costs of discretionary housing
    payments 1203
  collection of information
    CTB 639
    CTB aged 60 or over 873
    HB 436
    HB aged 60 or over 771
  contracting out benefit functions 1091
  directions for improvement 87
  disclosure of information
    CTB 640, 641
  duty to publicise benefit schemes 4
  enforcement notices 88
  forwarding information
    CTB 640
    CTB aged 60 or over 874
    HB 436
    HB aged 60 or over 772
  holding information
    CTB 639
    CTB aged 60 or over 874
    HB 436
    HB aged 60 or over 771
  information between authorities
    CTB 640
    CTB aged 60 or over 875

HB 438
HB aged 60 or over 773
information from landlords
HB 440, 1065
information required by rent officers
HB 266
HB aged 60 or over 708
information to/from Secretary of State
1149
inspection of benefits administration 85
joint arrangements 94
permitted spending totals
CTB 1064
HB 1058
power to appoint inspectors 54
relevant decisions 148
requesting information
CTB 640
CTB aged 60 or over 874
HB 437
HB aged 60 or over 772
standards of service 88
local housing allowance
definition 510
introduction 252
local authority pilot areas 557
local reference rent
definition
HB 262
HB aged 60 or over 706
HB 260, 263, 531, 549
HB aged 60 or over 704
taper 1122
locality
rent officer determinations
HB 529
London Bombings Relief Charitable Fund
definition
CTB 567
CTB aged 60 or over 818
HB 189
disregarded as capital
CTB 664
CTB aged 60 or over 887
HB 492
HB aged 60 or over 794
third party payments
CTB 600
HB 321
lone parents
childcare costs
CTB 583
CTB aged 60 or over 834
HB 285
HB aged 60 or over 721
definition
CTB 568
CTB aged 60 or over 818
HB 189
HB aged 60 or over 687
earnings disregards
CTB 652
CTB aged 60 or over 880
HB 468

HB aged 60 or over 786
family premium
CTB 643
CTB aged 60 or over 877
HB 453
students able to claim benefit
CTB 608
HB 339
students – occupation of home
HB 206
HB aged 60 or over 694
long tenancy
HB 254
definition
HB 189
HB aged 60 or over 687
HB aged 60 or over 703
low paid work
earnings and notional income
CTB 597
HB 311

M
Macfarlane Trusts
definition
CTB 570
CTB aged 60 or over 818
HB 189
HB aged 60 or over 687
disregarded as capital
CTB aged 60 or over 887
HB 317, 492
HB aged 60 or over 794
disregarded as income
CTB 658
HB 481
third party payments
CTB 596
HB 310, 321
mail
Post Office requirement to report
redirected mail 100
return of redirected mail 99
maintenance
disregard of payments
CTB 660
HB 483
maintenance undertaking
definition for asylum seekers 1026
maternity leave
definition
CTB 568
CTB aged 60 or over 818
earnings disregards
HB 296, 467
in remunerative work
CTB 586
CTB aged 60 or over 837
HB 288
HB aged 60 or over 724
not in remunerative work
CTB 575
CTB aged 60 or over 823
HB 203
HB aged 60 or over 693

maternity pay
see: *statutory maternity pay*
maximum benefit
CTB 11, 615
CTB aged 60 or over 851
expiry
HB 512
HB aged 60 or over 702, 802
HB 4, 356
HB aged 60 or over 739
moving home
HB 502, 504
HB aged 60 or over 798
maximum rent 259, 510, 704
calculation
HB 264
definition
HB 190
HB aged 60 or over 687
increases above
HB 1059
transitional arrangements
HB 264
meals
excluded from HB 446, 778
service charges
HB 444, 446, 549
HB aged 60 or over 778
medical evidence
disclosure in appeals to Commissioner 910
disclosure to appeals tribunal 923
medical treatment 111
absence from home
CTB 578
CTB aged 60 or over 826
HB 209
HB aged 60 or over 697
mental illness
charges for counselling/support 111
liability to pay rent
HB 221
mesne profits
HB 253
HB aged 60 or over 702
minimum benefit 16
HB 365
HB aged 60 or over 744
misrepresentation
criminal offences 61
overpayment
CTB 636, 637
CTB aged 60 or over 872
HB 419, 423, 429
HB aged 60 or over 767, 768
mistakes
leading to overpayment
HB 411, 413
HB aged 60 or over 766
mobile homes
campsite fees
HB 253
HB aged 60 or over 702
CTB 571

HB 194, 527, 539, 546, 555
HB aged 60 or over 691
mobility supplement
disregarded
CTB aged 60 or over 882
HB 473
HB aged 60 or over 788
Montserrat volcanic eruption
CTB aged 60 or over 824
HB 240, 251
HB aged 60 or over 701
mooring charges
HB 253, 527, 538, 546, 555
HB aged 60 or over 702
mortgage payments 5
disregard of mortgage protection
payments
CTB 658
HB 480
HB 196, 252, 254
HB aged 60 or over 703
moving home
date entitlement begins
HB 365
HB aged 60 or over 744
entitlement to extended payments due to
PC
HB 741
extended payments
CTB 617, 618, 670, 671
CTB aged 60 or over 853, 854, 890
HB 357, 359, 501
HB aged 60 or over 740, 741
liaison between local authorities
CTB 640, 641
HB 438
maximum benefit
HB 502, 504
HB aged 60 or over 798
rent allowance
HB 501, 503
HB aged 60 or over 798
rent rebate
HB 501, 503
HB aged 60 or over 798
two homes
HB 207
HB aged 60 or over 695

N
national insurance contributions
deducted from earnings
CTB 589
CTB aged 60 or over 840
HB 299
HB aged 60 or over 728
deducted from notional income
CTB 597
HB 312
deducted from self-employed net profit
CTB 591, 592
CTB aged 60 or over 844
HB 302, 305
HB aged 60 or over 730, 731, 732
disregard of changes

CTB 588
HB 294
HB aged 60 or over 726
national insurance number 29
CTB 574
NINO requirement
CTB 574
CTB aged 60 or over 822
HB 201
HB aged over 60 692
neighbourhood
rent officer determinations
HB 529
net earnings
CTB 568
definition
CTB aged 60 or over 819
HB 190
HB aged 60 or over 687
net profit
CTB 568, 591
deductions of tax and national insurance
CTB 592
definition
CTB aged 60 or over 819
HB 190
HB aged 60 or over 687
HB 301
HB aged 60 or over 730
self-employed earners
CTB 591
CTB aged 60 or over 842
new authority 1154
New Deal 1070
definition
CTB 568
lone parents 1085
notional income
CTB 597
HB 311
payments to trainees 1070
payments treated as capital
CTB 598
people aged 50+ 1077
self-employed earnings
HB 317
third party payments
CTB 596, 600
HB 321
next of kin
definition 409
CTB 634
CTB aged 60 or over 870
HB aged 60 or over 765
nil award 149
no fixed abode
disregarded for council tax discount 1012
non-dependants 673
calculation of non-dependant's income
CTB 616
CTB aged 60 or over 852
HB 361
HB aged 60 or over 742
deductions

CTB 616
CTB aged 60 or over 851
HB 361
HB aged 60 or over 742
definition
CTB 573
CTB aged 60 or over 822
HB 199
HB aged 60 or over 692
disregard of payments
CTB 657
HB 478
exceptions 573
CTB aged 60 or over 822
HB 199
HB aged 60 or over 692
exclusions from non-dependant
deductions
HB 361
HB aged 60 or over 743
income/capital
CTB 582
CTB aged 60 or over 830
HB 283
HB aged 60 or over 715
notification of decisions
HB 508
HB aged 60 or over 800
taking advantage of benefit scheme
CTB 573, 582
CTB aged 60 or over 822, 830
HB 283
HB aged 60 or over 715
Norway 1134
notice
payments in lieu
CTB 588
CTB aged 60 or over 840
HB 295, 467
HB aged 60 or over 727
notification
board and attendance
HB 525, 544
decisions 110
CTB 632, 672
CTB aged 60 or over 868, 891
HB 394, 504
HB aged 60 or over 761, 799
rent officer determinations
HB 534, 552
notional capital
CTB 599
CTB aged 60 or over 847
diminishing notional capital rule
CTB 601
CTB aged 60 or over 848
HB 325
HB aged 60 or over 737
HB 320
HB aged 60 or over 736
notional income
CTB 583
CTB aged 60 or over 845

HB 284, 309, 315
HB aged 60 or over 732
nursing care 111

O
obstruction of inspector 56
occupation
normally occupied
HB 211
of home
CTB 570, 577
CTB aged 60 or over 821
HB 206, 338
occupational pensions
contributions deducted from earnings
CTB 590
CTB aged 60 or over 840
HB 299
HB aged 60 or over 728
contributions deducted from notional
earnings
CTB 598
HB 312
definition
CTB 568
CTB aged 60 or over 819
HB 190
HB aged 60 or over 687
disregarded
CTB 665
HB 494
notional capital/income
CTB aged 60 or over 845
HB 309, 320
HB aged 60 or over 732
third party payments
CTB 596, 600
HB 310, 320
treatment as earnings
CTB aged 60 or over 840
HB 296
HB aged 60 or over 727
treatment as income
CTB 589
occupier
definition
HB 521, 522, 540
official error
causing overpayment
CTB 635
CTB aged 60 or over 871
HB 411
HB aged 60 or over 765
older people
age-related payments 1045
ombudsman
HB 394
ONE
additional functions for local authorities
33, 40
date of claim
CTB 628
CTB aged 60 or over 864
HB 386
HB aged 60 or over 757

enabling legislation 1016
notifying change of circumstances
HB 391
HB aged 60 or over 759
pilot schemes 34
supplying information 1018
oral hearing
paper or oral hearing 920
postponement and adjournement 933
procedure 926, 928, 931
record of tribunal proceedings 939
overlapping benefits
CTB 644
CTB aged 60 or over 878
HB 455
overpayments
appeals 154
arising from arrears
HB 372
calculation
CTB 637
CTB aged 60 or over 872
HB 429
HB aged 60 or over 768
challenging a decision 155
challenging a decision on recovery 155
challenging method of recovery 155
court action
CTB 46, 637
CTB aged 60 or over 872
HB 43, 429
CTB 45
deductions from recoverable
overpayments
CTB 638
CTB aged 60 or over 872
HB 431
HB aged 60 or over 769
definition
HB 410
HB aged 60 or over 765
diminution of capital
CTB 637
CTB aged 60 or over 872
HB 429
HB aged 60 or over 768
discretion to recover
CTB 45
HB 42
HB 42
involvement of relevant person
HB 415
irrecoverable overpayments 1016
knowledge of overpayment 416
landlord, payments direct 42
method of recovery
CTB 636
CTB aged 60 or over 871
HB 424
HB aged 60 or over 767
mistakes
HB 413
notification of recoverable overpayments
CTB 674

CTB aged 60 or over 894
HB 509
HB aged 60 or over 801
official error
 CTB 635
 CTB aged 60 or over 871
 HB 411
 HB aged 60 or over 765
offsetting against arrears
 CTB 634
 CTB aged 60 or over 870
 HB 410
 HB aged 60 or over 765
payments on account
 HB 402, 411
person from whom recovery may be
 sought
 CTB 45
 HB 42
prescribed benefits
 HB 433
 HB aged 60 or over 769
recoverable overpayments
 CTB 635, 636
 CTB aged 60 or over 870, 871
 HB 411, 419
 HB aged 60 or over 765
recovery by court action
 CTB 637
 CTB aged 60 or over 872
recovery from benefits
 CTB 46, 637, 638
 CTB aged 60 or over 872
 HB 42, 424, 433
 HB aged 60 or over 766, 767, 769
recovery from landlord
 HB 434
 HB aged 60 or over 770
reduced council tax liability
 CTB 635
 CTB aged 60 or over 870
rent repayment orders 1135
time limit for recovery
 HB 429
treatment as rent arrears
 HB 405
two homes
 HB 212
overseas assets
 CTB 599
 CTB aged 60 or over 847
 HB 319
 HB aged 60 or over 736
owner
 beneficial interest
 CTB 603
 CTB aged 60 or over 850
 HB 197, 328
 definition
 HB 190
 HB aged 60 or over 687

P
parental contribution
 covenant income
 CTB 611
 HB 349
 definition
 CTB 604
 HB 333
 disregarded
 CTB 656
 CTB aged 60 or over 884
 HB 477
 HB aged 60 or over 790
part-time work
 earnings disregards
 HB 467
 HB 471
partner
 definition
 CTB 568
 CTB aged 60 or over 819
 HB 190
 HB aged 60 or over 687
paternity leave
 definition
 CTB 568
 CTB aged 60 or over 819
 HB 190
 HB aged 60 or over 687
 in remunerative work
 CTB 586
 CTB aged 60 or over 837
 HB aged 60 or over 724
paternity pay
 see also: statutory paternity pay
pathfinder authority
 definition
 HB 444, 521, 540
 HB aged 60 or over 777
 list of authorities 510, 801
pay in lieu of notice
 treatment as earnings
 CTB 588
 HB 295
 HB aged 60 or over 727
payment in kind
 CTB 589
 CTB aged 60 or over 840
 treatment as earnings
 HB 296
 HB aged 60 or over 727
payment of benefit
 death of person entitled
 CTB 634
 CTB aged 60 or over 869
 HB 409
 HB aged 60 or over 765
 extended payments
 CTB 670, 671
 CTB aged 60 or over 890
 HB 501, 503
 HB aged 60 or over 797
 frequency of payment
 HB 398, 1121

HB aged 60 or over 761
landlord direct
  HB 404
  HB aged 60 or over 763
late payment
  CTB 633
  CTB aged 60 or over 869
  HB 398
  HB aged 60 or over 761
method
  CTB 83, 632
  CTB aged 60 or over 868
  HB 81
power to make regulations about
  administration of payments 35
  CTB 37
rent allowance
  HB 400
  HB aged 60 or over 762
underpayment 633
  CTB 46
  CTB aged 60 or over 869
who is paid
  CTB 633
  CTB aged 60 or over 869
  HB 403
  HB aged 60 or over 763
payments on account 44, 1186
  HB 402, 411
  HB aged 60 or over 763
penalties 64, 1069
pension age
definition 19, 692
pension credit 1042
pension credit 1042
change of circumstances
  CTB aged 60 or over 858
  HB aged 60 or over 748
extended payments of CTB 854
extended payments of HB 741
guarantee credit
  CTB aged 60 or over 830
  HB aged 60 or over 715
non-dependant deductions
  CTB aged 60 or over 853
notifying change of circumstances
  CTB aged 60 or over 867
  HB aged 60 or over 760
persons from abroad 1072
  HB aged over 60 701
qualifying age 18, 19
  CTB 574
  HB 191, 688, 693
savings credit
  CTB aged 60 or over 830
  HB aged 60 or over 715
transitional provisions 1042
pension fund holder
CTB 568
definition
  CTB aged 60 or over 819
  HB 190
  HB aged 60 or over 688

pensionable age
PC 692
pensioner premium
amount
  CTB 649
  CTB 644, 645
  HB 456
period of experience
definition
  CTB 606
  HB 334
period of study
definition
  CTB 606
  HB 334
permitted totals
CTB 85, 1064
HB 82, 1058
person affected
CTB 632
CTB aged 60 or over 868
definition
  CTB aged 60 or over 819
  HB 190
  HB aged 60 or over 688
  HB 395
  HB/CTB 951
person in hardship
benefit reduction following eviction 1141
person subject to immigration control
definition 1026
entitlement to claim benefits 1072, 1074
personal allowances
CTB 643
CTB aged 60 or over 877
HB aged 60 or over 782
rates
  CTB 643
  CTB aged 60 or over 877
  HB 451
  HB aged 60 or over 782
personal injuries
disregard of compensation
  CTB 595
  CTB aged 60 or over 887
  HB 309, 320, 490
  HB aged 60 or over 794
periodical payments
  CTB 595
personal pensions
contributions deducted from earnings
  CTB 590, 592
  CTB aged 60 or over 841, 844
  HB 299, 303
  HB aged 60 or over 728, 731
contributions deducted from notional
  earnings
  CTB 598
  HB 312
definition
  CTB 568
  CTB aged 60 or over 819
  HB 190
  HB aged 60 or over 688

disregarded
  CTB 665
  HB 494
information to be provided
  CTB 629
  CTB aged 60 or over 865
  HB 387
  HB aged 60 or over 758
notional income/capital
  CTB 599
  CTB aged 60 or over 845
  HB 309, 314, 320
  HB aged 60 or over 733
third party payments
  CTB 596, 600
  HB 310, 320
persons from abroad 1116
definition
  CTB 575
  CTB aged 60 or over 823
  HB 239
  HB aged 60 or over 700
entitlement to claim benefits 1072, 1074
  CTB 575
  CTB aged 60 or over 823
  HB 239
  HB aged 60 or over 700
students
  CTB 608
transitional protection 1054
polygamous marriages
alternative maximum CTB 620, 855
applicable amounts
  CTB 581
  HB 277
claims
  CTB 623
  CTB aged 60 or over 859
  HB 376
  HB aged 60 or over 753
CTB 15
definition
  CTB 569
  CTB aged 60 or over 819
  HB 191
  HB aged 60 or over 688
earnings disregards
  CTB 652
  HB 468
non-dependants
  CTB 573, 616
  CTB aged 60 or over 822, 852
  HB 199, 361
  HB aged 60 or over 743
occupation of home
  HB 206
  HB aged 60 or over 694
recovery of overpayments
  CTB 636
  CTB aged 60 or over 871
treatment of income and capital
  CTB 582
  CTB aged 60 or over 829

HB 282
  HB aged 60 or over 714
possession orders
loss ofHB 7, 1144
post
return of redirected post 99
Post Office
reporting redirected mail 100
power of attorney
  CTB aged 60 or over 860
  HB 376, 377
  HB aged 60 or over 753
premiums
amounts
  CTB 649
  CTB aged 60 or over 880
  HB 464
HB 454
  HB aged 60 or over 783
prescribed benefits
  CTB 638
  CTB aged 60 or over 872
  HB 433
  HB aged 60 or over 770
prisoners
absence from home
  CTB 577
  CTB aged 60 or over 826
  HB 208
  HB aged 60 or over 696
disregard of payments for visits
  CTB 660, 666
  HB 483
disregarded for council tax discount 1010
non-dependant deductions
  HB 362
  HB aged 60 or over 743
temporary release
  CTB 578
  HB 209
  HB aged 60 or over 697
property
benefits treated as possessions 139
valuation of capital
  HB 318
  HB aged 60 or over 736
property specific rent 1185, 1189
public bodies
definition 123
human rights 122

Q
qualifying contribution
  CTB 590
  CTB aged 60 or over 841
definition
  HB 299
  HB aged 60 or over 728
qualifying course
definition
  CTB 606
  HB 334

qualifying expenditure 1162
qualifying person
  definition
    CTB 569
    CTB aged 60 or over 819
qualifying premium
  CTB 591
  CTB aged 60 or over 842
  HB 302
  HB aged 60 or over 730

R
reckonable rent 1188
  definition
    HB 262
    HB aged 60 or over 706
  HB 260, 263
  HB aged 60 or over 705
recovery of benefits
  appeals relating to overpayments 154
  court action
    CTB 46, 637
    CTB aged 60 or over 872
    HB 43, 429
  deduction from benefits
    CTB 46, 593, 637, 638
    CTB aged 60 or over 872
    HB 42, 306, 433
    HB aged 60 or over 767, 769
  discretion to recover
    CTB 45
    HB 42
  from landlord
    HB 434
    HB aged 60 or over 770
  methods of recovery
    CTB 636
    CTB aged 60 or over 871
    HB 424
    HB aged 60 or over 767
  notification to claimant
    CTB 674
    CTB aged 60 or over 894
    HB 509
    HB aged 60 or over 801
  overpayments which are not recoverable
    1016
  payments on account
    HB 402
    HB aged 60 or over 763
  person from whom recovery made
    CTB 45, 636
    CTB aged 60 or over 871
    HB 42, 419
    HB aged 60 or over 766
  recoverable overpayments
    CTB 635
    CTB aged 60 or over 870
    HB 411
    HB aged 60 or over 765
redeterminations
  appeals by tribunal 158
  board and attendance
    HB 526, 545
  challenging decision of rent officer

    HB 269
    HB aged 60 or over 710
  definition
    HB 521, 540
  errors
    HB 527, 546
  HB 269
  HB aged 60 or over 709
  rent officer
    HB 523, 542
  substitute redeterminations
    HB 271
    HB aged 60 or over 711
reduction of benefit 170
  benefit offences
    HB/CTB 1089
  eviction 1089, 1139
  failure to provide information
    HB/CTB 973
  HB/CTB 971
  reduction lifted
    HB/CTB 972
reductions for council tax 1005, 1008
redundancy
  CTB 588
  CTB aged 60 or over 840
  HB aged 60 or over 727
  treatment as earnings
    CTB 588
    CTB aged 60 or over 840
    HB 295
refugees
  CTB 577, 642, 1129
  CTB aged 60 or over 825, 876, 1129
  definition
    CTB aged 60 or over 825
    HB 241
    HB aged 60 or over 701
  evidence to support a claim
    HB 387
    HB aged 60 or over 757
  habitual residence
    CTB aged 60 or over 824
    HB 240, 250
    HB aged 60 or over 701
  HB 251, 444, 1126
  HB aged 60 or over 701, 777, 1126
  retrospective claim for benefit 1028
    CTB 1073, 1130
    HB 1073, 1126
  transitional protection 1073
regulations
  parliamentary control 103, 112
  power to make 24, 101, 112
rehabilitation allowance
  CTB 595
  HB 309
relative
  definition
    CTB 569
    CTB aged 60 or over 819
    HB 191
    HB aged 60 or over 688

relevant authority
decisions 148
CTB 632
CTB aged 60 or over 867
HB 393
HB aged 60 or over 760
definition
CTB aged 60 or over 820
HB 191
HB aged 60 or over 688
relevant education
definition
HB 272
relevant year 1154
religious orders
HB 223, 235
HB aged 60 or over 699
remunerative work
definition
CTB 574
CTB aged 60 or over 823
HB 202, 203
HB aged 60 or over 693
rent
advance payments
HB 217
claim-related rent
HB 260, 263, 533, 550
definition
CTB 569
CTB aged 60 or over 820
HB 191, 253, 255
HB aged 60 or over 688, 702
designated rent 1188
disregards
CTB 657
HB 478
eligible rent
HB 252, 253, 255
HB aged 60 or over 702
exceptionally high rent
HB 530, 548
excluded tenancies 1168
high rents 1184
increases in rent 1164, 1186
increases to cover arrears
HB aged 60 or over 702
indicative rent levels 1188
HB 535, 552
liability to pay
HB 217
local reference rent
HB 260, 263, 531, 549
HB aged 60 or over 704
maximum rent
HB 190
property specific 1185, 1189
reckonable rent 1188
HB 260, 262, 263
HB aged 60 or over 705, 706
rent increase
HB aged 60 or over 780
rent officer determinations
HB 529, 547

rent-free periods 1173
HB 217, 356, 375, 448
HB aged 60 or over 698, 752, 780
significantly high rent
HB 263, 529, 547
single room rent
HB 260, 262, 263, 532, 550
HB aged 60 or over 704, 707
size-related rent 1185
HB 262, 263, 530, 536, 548
HB aged 60 or over 707
thresholds 1168
unreasonable rent restriction 1186
unreasonably high
HB 1107
weekly rent
HB 372
HB aged 60 or over 750
rent allowance
definition 81
frequency of payment
HB 400
HB aged 60 or over 762
high rents 1184
moving home
HB 501, 503
HB aged 60 or over 798
payments on account
HB 402
subsidy 1167
rent arrears
overpayments of benefit to landlord
HB 405
payment direct to landlord
HB 404, 407
HB aged 60 or over 764
payment on account to landlord
HB 402
rent increases to cover arrears
HB 252
HB aged 60 or over 702
rent assessment committee determinations
HB 1107
rent officer
categories of dwelling
HB 536, 553
challenging decision of rent officer
HB 269
HB aged 60 or over 710
claim-related rent
HB 533, 550
determinations 259, 1184
HB 522, 529, 541, 547
HB aged 60 or over 704
errors
HB 527, 546
evidence/information required
HB 437
HB aged 06 or over 772
excluded tenancies
HB aged 60 or over 780
functions 1014
HB 265
HB aged 60 or over 707

indicative rent calculation
HB 535, 552
information from local authority
HB 437
local housing allowance 510
notifications
HB 534, 552
pre-tenancy determination
HB 265
HB aged 60 or over 707
property specific 1185
redeterminations 259, 269
HB 523, 542
HB aged 60 or over 704, 709
rent increases
HB aged 60 or over 780
substitute determinations
HB 271
HB aged 60 or over 711
time limit for referrals
HB 266
HB aged 60 or over 708
rent rebate
definition 81
moving home
HB 501, 503
HB aged 60 or over 798
recovery of overpayment
HB 428
subsidy 93
rent repayment orders 1135
rent restrictions
increases of rent 1115
transitional protection
HB 1101
rent thresholds 1168
rent-free period 1173
HB 217, 356, 375, 448
HB aged 60 or over 698, 740, 752, 780
rental purchase agreements
HB 254, 527, 539, 546, 556
HB aged 60 or over 703
repairs
disregard of dwelling awaiting repairs
CTB 665
HB 494
set-off against rent
HB 217, 375
HB aged 60 or over 698
temporary accommodation
HB 206
HB aged 60 or over 694
withholding direct payments of benefit
HB 405
resettlement benefit
CTB 659
HB 482
resident
definition
CTB 12
residential care
see: care homes

retainer fee
treatment as earnings
CTB 589
CTB aged 60 or over 840
HB 295
HB aged 60 or over 727
retirement
annuity contracts
HB 314
earnings disregards
CTB 651
HB 466
retirement pensions
notional income
HB aged 60 or over 732
treatment as income
HB aged 60 or over 720
Review Board
outstanding cases 997
reviews
discretionary housing payments 1083
replacement of reviews 147
transitional arrangements 994
revision 143, 147
any time revisions 957
appealing a revised decision
HB/CTB 978
difference between revision and
supersessionew Index term 150
late application
HB/CTB 959
refusal to revise 148
revision of decisions 150
HB/CTB 952
rounding up of benefit
CTB 570, 633
CTB aged 60 or over 821, 868
HB 373
HB aged 60 or over 752

S
same sex couples
definition 19, 947
transitional arrangements 1095
sanctionable benefits
definition 1036
sanctions
anti-social behaviour
HB 7, 1142
benefit offences 1035
disqualification from benefit
HB/CTB 1087
effect on offender's family 1038
sandwich courses
CTB 606, 611
HB 334, 335, 347
school holidays
treatment of hours of work
CTB 575
CTB aged 60 or over 823
HB 202
HB aged 60 or over 693
second adult
alternative maximum CTB 619, 855
duty to notify change of circumstances

CTB 631
    CTB aged 60 or over 866
  income
    CTB 650
    CTB aged 60 or over 891
Second World War
  ex-gratia payments
    CTB 668
    HB 497
self-employed earner
  average weekly earnings
    CTB 587
    HB 292
  calculation of net profit
    CTB 591
    CTB aged 60 or over 842
    HB 301
    HB aged 60 or over 730
  chargeable income
    HB 306
  definition
    CTB 569
    CTB aged 60 or over 820
    HB 191
    HB aged 60 or over 689
  disregards from earnings
    CTB 591, 592
    CTB aged 60 or over 842, 844
    HB 301, 302, 305
    HB aged 60 or over 729, 732
  earnings
    CTB 590
    CTB aged 60 or over 842
    HB aged 60 or over 729
  earnings defined
    CTB aged 60 or over 842
    HB 301
    HB aged 60 or over 729
  expectation of payment
    HB 204
  notional capital
    CTB 600
    HB 321
self-employment route
  definition
    CTB 569
    HB 191
separation
  date change of circumstances takes effect
    CTB 623
    CTB aged 60 or over 857
  disregard of home
    CTB 665
    HB 493
  estrangement
    CTB 571
    CTB aged 60 or over 821
  former partner
    HB 217
    HB aged 60 or over 698
  former partner is landlord
    HB 223, 230
    HB aged 60 or over 699

service charges
  counselling and support 111
  definition
    HB 255
    HB aged 60 or over 704
  excessive
    HB 447
    HB aged 60 or over 779
  fuel
    HB 447
    HB aged 60 or over 779
    HB 253
    HB aged 60 or over 702
  ineligible service charges 1188
    HB 444, 531, 533, 549, 551
    HB aged 60 or over 777
  meals
    HB 444
    HB aged 60 or over 778
  rent officer referrals
    HB 266, 531, 549
    HB aged 60 or over 708
  validated charges 111
service of notices for appeals 903
  email 907
  HB/CTB 949
services
  definition
    HB 255
    HB aged 60 or over 704
setting aside decision 175, 914, 940
severe disability premium
  amount
    CTB 649
    CTB aged 60 or over 880
    HB aged 60 or over 785
  CTB 647
  CTB aged 60 or over 878
  earnings disregards
    CTB 652
    HB 468
  HB 461
  HB aged 60 or over 783
severe mental impairment
  disregarded for council tax discount 1011
share fishermen
  CTB 591
  HB 302
shared accommodation
  HB 200
shared ownership tenancy
  definition
    HB 191
    HB aged 60 or over 689
  HB 254
shares
  valuation of capital
    CTB 599
    CTB aged 60 or over 847
    HB 318
    HB aged 60 or over 736
sickness
  earnings disregards
    HB 467

not in remunerative work
CTB 575
CTB aged 60 or over 823
HB 203
HB aged 60 or over 693
students entitled to benefit
CTB 609
HB 340
significant rent
HB 550
significantly high rent
HB 263, 529, 547
single room rent
definition
HB 262
HB aged 60 or over 707
HB 260, 263, 532, 550
HB aged 60 or over 704
transitional arrangements
HB 523, 542
site fees
HB 253, 539, 555
size criteria
definition
HB 521, 541
HB 530, 536, 548
size-related rent 1185
definition
HB 262
HB aged 60 or over 707
HB 263, 530, 536, 548
Skipton Fund
definition
CTB 569
CTB aged 60 or over 820
HB 191
HB aged 60 or over 689
disregarded as capital
CTB 664
CTB aged 60 or over 887
HB 492
HB aged 60 or over 794
third party payments
HB 321
Social Security Advisory Committee 95
Social Security Commissioners 115, 159
appealing against appeal tribunal
decisions 904
appealing against decision 915
appeals from appeals tribunals 943
decisions on leave to appeal 913
delegating to authorised officers 902
powers 901
sponsorship of people from abroad
transitional protection 1054
sports award
definition
CTB aged 60 or over 820
HB 192
HB aged 60 or over 689
disregard of payments
CTB 661, 667
HB 301, 485
HB aged 60 or over 730

not in remunerative work
CTB 574
CTB aged 60 or over 823
HB 203
HB aged 60 or over 694
standard maintenance allowance
CTB 606
HB 335
statement of reasons
CTB 632
CTB aged 60 or over 868
decision of appeal tribunals 937
decisions which can be appealed
HB/CTB 970
HB 395
HB aged 60 or over 761
statutory adoption pay
HB 296
treatment as earnings
CTB 589
CTB aged 60 or over 840
HB aged 60 or over 727
statutory instruments
parliamentary control 103, 112
power to make 24, 101, 112
statutory maternity pay
treatment as earnings
CTB 589
CTB aged 60 or over 840
HB 296
HB aged 60 or over 727
statutory paternity pay
HB 296
treatment as earnings
CTB 589
CTB aged 60 or over 840
HB aged 60 or over 727
statutory sick pay
treatment as earnings
CTB 589
CTB aged 60 or over 840
HB 296
HB aged 60 or over 727
student loans
defnition
CTB 607
fee loans
CTB 614
HB 354
giving up course
CTB 594
HB 307
treatment as income
HB 307
students
absence from home
CTB 578
CTB aged 60 or over 826
HB 209
HB aged 60 or over 697
academic year
CTB 604
HB 332
accommodation during vacations

HB 338
accommodation owned by institution
  HB 344
alternative maximum CTB 608
breaks from study
  HB 343
course of study
  CTB 605
  HB 333, 341
covenants
  CTB 611
  HB 349
deaf students
  CTB 608
  HB 340
definition
  CTB 606
  HB 335, 341
disabled students
  CTB 608
disregarded for council tax discount 1011
disregards
  CTB 610
  HB 347, 350
eligible housing costs
  HB 344
entitlement to benefit
  CTB 608
  HB 339
excluded from benefit
  CTB 608
exemptions from exclusion from benefits
  CTB 608
  HB 339
failing exams
  HB 344
frequency of payment
  HB 400
  HB aged 60 or over 763
full-time course
  CTB 605
  HB 333
giving up course
  CTB 594
  HB 307
grant income
  CTB 605, 610
  HB 334, 346
income treated as capital
  CTB 614
  HB 355
last day of course
  CTB 606
  HB 334
loans
  CTB 612
  HB 351
lone parents
  CTB 608
  HB 339
modular courses
  HB 342
non-dependant deductions
  CTB 616

CTB aged 60 or over 852
  HB 361
  HB aged 60 or over 743
occupation of home
  HB 206, 338
  HB aged 60 or over 694
overseas students
  CTB 608
pension age
  HB 339
period of study
  CTB 606
  HB 334
receiving IS/JSA
  CTB 608
  HB 339
student partners
  CTB 608
  HB 217, 339, 355
  HB aged 60 or over 698
summer vacations
  CTB 615
  HB 356
two homes
  HB 207
  HB aged 60 or over 695
subordinate legislation
  power to make regulations 24, 101
subsidiary limit
  CTB 85
  HB 82
subsidy 91, 1156
  additions 1169, 1176
  amount 1163
  backdated benefit 1164
  benefit savings 1175
  calculation 91, 1161, 1176
  claims from local authority 1155, 1199
  conditions 1200
  deductions 1173
  discretionary housing payments 144, 1203
  estimated subsidy 1160
  fraud prevention 91
  high rents 1167
  information required 1157
  payment 92, 1159
  payment in instalments 1158
  rent increases 1164
  rent officer determinations 1176, 1184
  rent rebate 93
  rent-free periods 1173
    HB 356
    HB aged 60 or over 740
  thresholds 1176
  time limits for claims 1200
  transitional provisions 1176
  unreasonable size/rent 1186
suitable alternative accommodation
  HB 1107, 1112
supersession 147, 151, 961
  change of circumstances after decision 149
  date of taking effect 965
  difference between supersession and
    revision 150

grounds for 963
refusal to supersede 148
support charges
ineligible charges
HB 533, 551
surrender value
valuation of investments
CTB 599
CTB aged 60 or over 847
suspension of benefit 170
failure to provide information
HB/CTB 973
HB/CTB 971
lifting of suspension
HB/CTB 972
old rules 999
suspension leading to termination
HB/CTB 975
Switzerland 1134

T
tapers
CTB 617
CTB aged 60 or over 853
HB 264, 330, 357, 1115
HB aged 60 or over 740
tariff income 16
CTB 603
CTB aged 60 or over 833, 834
HB 284, 330
HB aged 60 or over 719, 720
tax year
definition
CTB aged 60 or over 820
HB 192
HB aged 60 or over 689
teachers
student loans disregarded
CTB 655
television link 900
temporary accommodation
HB on two homes 206, 694
tenancy
definition
HB 521, 541
tenancy in common
HB 329
termination date 1187
termination of benefit
HB/CTB 975
Territorial Army
earnings disregard
CTB 653
CTB aged 60 or over 880
HB 469
HB aged 60 or over 786
test case pending
HB/CTB 964, 977
third party payments
capital
CTB 599
HB 320
income
CTB 596
notional capital

CTB 599
HB 320
notional income
CTB 596
CTB aged 60 or over 846
HB 310, 314
HB aged 60 or over 735
tied accommodation
HB 223, 235
HB aged 60 or over 699
time limits 395, 761
appealing against decision of
Commissioner 915
appeals
HB/CTB 979
appeals to Commissioner 907, 943
applying for revision of decision
HB/CTB 952
challenging decision of rent officer
HB 270
HB aged 60 or over 710
criminal proceedings 70
first payment of benefit
CTB 633
CTB aged 60 or over 869
HB 398
HB aged 60 or over 761
landlord to supply information
HB 1068
notice of decisions which can be appealed
HB/CTB 970
notification of decision
CTB 632
CTB aged 60 or over 868
notification of rent officer determinations
HB 534
recovery of overpayment
HB 429
referrals to rent officers
HB 266
HB aged 60 or over 708
statement of reasons
CTB 632
CTB aged 60 or over 868
HB 395
HB aged 60 or over 761
subsidy claims 1200
supplying information to support a claim
HB 387
HB aged 60 or over 758
training
definition of training course
CTB 578
disregard of payments
CTB 655
HB 474, 495
New Deal payments 1070
non-dependant deductions
CTB 616
CTB aged 60 or over 852
training allowance
definition
CTB 570
CTB aged 60 or over 820

HB 192
  HB aged 60 or over 689
disregarded
  CTB 655
  HB 474
New Deal payments
  HB/CTB 1070
non-dependant deductions
  HB 361
  HB aged 60 or over 743
training course
definition
  HB 210
  HB aged 60 or over 698
transitional arrangements
appeals 993
asylum seekers 1054, 1073
pension credit 1042
persons from abroad
  HB/CTB 1054
rent restrictions 1101
reviews 994
subsidy 1176
transsexual people
gender recognition certificates 1044
travel expenses
treated as earnings
  CTB 589, 654
  CTB aged 60 or over 840
  HB 295, 473
  HB aged 60 or over 727
voluntary/charity work
  CTB 654
treatment as member of household
  HB 274
trusts
  CTB 595, 599
  HB 309, 320
landlord is a connected trust
  HB 223, 232
  HB aged 60 or over 699
two homes
extended payments
  CTB 671
  CTB aged 60 or over 890
  HB 502, 504
  HB aged 60 or over 798
  HB 206
  HB aged 60 or over 694
students
  HB 206
  HB aged 60 or over 694

U
udal tenure
definition
  HB 197
under-occupancy payments
  HB 1019
underpayments 633
  CTB 46
  CTB aged 60 or over 869
offsetting against overpayments
  CTB 634
  CTB aged 60 or over 870

HB 410
  HB aged 60 or over 765
payments on account
  HB 402
  HB aged 60 or over 763
unfair dismissal
  CTB 589
  HB 295, 467
unmarried couple 21
unreasonable rent restriction
  HB aged 60 or over 780
rent increases 1186
transitional protection 1105
unreasonably large accommodation
  HB 530, 548, 1107
  HB aged 60 or over 780
size criteria
  HB 536

V
vacations
summer vacations for students
  CTB 615
  HB 356
treatment of hours of work
  CTB 575
  CTB aged 60 or over 823
  HB 202
  HB aged 60 or over 693
vaccine damage payment
  HB 313
validated charges 111
valuation of capital
  CTB 599
  CTB aged 60 or over 847
  HB 318, 319
  HB aged 60 or over 736
vicinity
rent officer determinations
  HB 529
Victoria Cross payments
  CTB 655, 667
  HB 474, 496
violence
absence from home
  HB 209
  HB aged 60 or over 697
housing costs for two homes
  HB 206, 208
  HB aged 60 or over 694, 696
treated as occupying former home
  HB 208
  HB aged 60 or over 696
violent profits
  HB 253
  HB aged 60 or over 702
voluntary payments
disregards
  HB 475
students
  CTB 612
  HB 350
treatment as income/capital
  CTB 598
  HB 317